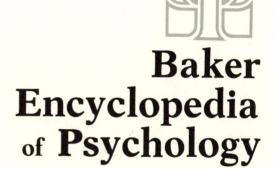

Baker
Encyclopedia
of Psychology

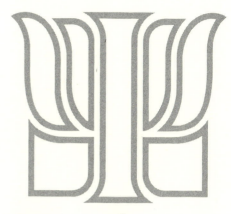

Baker
Encyclopedia
of Psychology

Edited by
David G. Benner

BAKER BOOK HOUSE
Grand Rapids, Michigan 49506

ISBN: 0-8010-0865-4

Second printing, September 1987

Library of Congress Catalog Card Number: 85-70713

Printed in the United States of America

Preface

This book was born out of an awareness of the need for a comprehensive treatment of psychology from a Christian point of view. The rapidly expanding body of knowledge in psychology has led to the publication of a number of encyclopedias in recent years, each written from one viewpoint or more usually from several. None of these, however, has been written from a Christian perspective, identifying the issues and applications of particular importance from that perspective and suggesting ways of evaluating the concepts, theories, and research findings in light of biblical teachings. This volume fills that void.

First and foremost this is an encyclopedia, factually presenting the major current findings and theories in the field. Thus it presents psychology in its own terms. Second, many articles also contain an explicit biblical or theological perspective. This is broadly evangelical, though it is much less monolithic and narrowly defined than it would be if all articles had been written by one author. I made no effort to force my viewpoint on the articles, preferring instead to allow contributors the liberty to speak for themselves. This work derives its strength from numerous authors writing on their areas of expertise and from their individual Christian perspectives.

Although providing representative coverage of important aspects of the entire field, this volume focuses on the areas of personality, psychopathology (psychological problems), psychotherapy and other treatment approaches, major systems and theories of psychology, and the psychology of religion. These areas interest Christians the most and are often crucial in efforts to relate psychology and Christianity. Approximately 80% of the 1,050 articles in this volume fall in these areas,

the remaining ones being divided among social psychology, developmental psychology, and general experimental psychology. The goal for all articles has been to be both readily understandable to nonpsychologists and useful to psychologists and other mental health professionals.

The encyclopedia was designed around the topics identified in the category index on pages xiii–xxiii. For example, articles in the category "Psychopathology" include 184 disorders found in the third edition of the *Diagnostic and Statistical Manual of Mental Disorders*, 99 symptoms and reactions, and 25 general topics. The category "Treatment Approaches and Issues" contains 149 articles on different approaches to counseling or psychotherapy, 75 on specific techniques used in these approaches, and 34 on general issues involved in treating psychological problems.

Although planned topically, articles appear in alphabetical order. The topical index, which includes all articles, helps the reader find articles of interest. Cross references within and at the end of articles also lead the reader to related articles. These references are identified by capital letters (for an example, see the cross references on page 8 following the first article). Bibliographies identify books and articles for further reading. These may include References (sources cited in the article) and Additional Readings (sources not cited but recommended).

An encyclopedia is only as good as its contributors. I have been extremely fortunate to enlist most of the major scholars involved in current discussions of the relationship between psychology and Christianity. Drawn from the ranks of both academicians and practitioners, they are mostly psychologists. Some, however,

Preface

specialize in psychiatry, social work, and pastoral care. Authors are identified at the end of each article. Short definitional articles lacking an author's name are mine. Contributors are listed on pages vii–xii with brief biographical data.

Considerable help in preparing this volume has come from a wide circle of friends and colleagues. I wish to acknowledge the invaluable help of my secretary and editorial assistant, Marcy Bump, who worked with me from the earliest stages to the book's completion. Thanks go to my graduate assistants, Toby Drew, Tom Gill, David Dunkerton, John Robertson, and Melody Patterson, for technical and research support. Special thanks also go to Walter Elwell, who provided the initial idea for the project; Allan Fisher, the Baker Book House editor whose experience with similar projects enabled him to provide much guidance and assistance; and Jean Hager of the Word Works, who provided invaluable help as the copyeditor. Finally, I most appreciate the love and support of Juliet and Sean, who shared a husband and a father with this project.

Contributors

Ihsan Al-Issa, Ph.D.
Professor of Psychology
University of Calgary

Elizabeth M. Altmaier, Ph.D.
Associate Professor
Division of Counselor Education
University of Iowa

David E. Anderson, Ph.D.
Chairperson and Associate Professor of
    Psychology
Bethel College, St. Paul

William W. Austin, Psy.D.
Private Practice
Chicago

Stanley N. Ballard, Th.M., Ph.D.
Chairman and Professor of Psychology
Cedarville College

Dean E. Barley, B.S.
Graduate Student
Brigham Young University

Clark E. Barshinger, Ph.D.
Codirector
Barrington Counseling Associates
Lake Zurich, Illinois

Rodney L. Bassett, Ph.D.
Associate Professor of Psychology
Roberts Wesleyan College

James R. Beck, Ph.D.
Valley Psychological Center
Carmichael, California

David G. Benner, Ph.D.
Professor of Psychology
Wheaton College

Allen E. Bergin, Ph.D.
Professor of Psychology
Brigham Young University

C. Markham Berry, M.D.
Department of Psychiatry
Emory University School of Medicine

William G. Bixler, Ph.D.
Oklahoma Christian Counseling Center
Oklahoma City

Martin Bolt, Ph.D.
Professor of Psychology
Calvin College

Bruce E. Bonecutter, Ph.D.
Coordinator of Mental Health Services
Department of Psychiatry
Cook County Hospital
Chicago

Jeffrey M. Brandsma, Ph.D.
Professor and Director of Clinical Psychology
    Internship
Department of Psychiatry
Medical College of Georgia

T. L. Brink, M.B.A., Ph.D.
College of Notre Dame
Western Graduate School of Psychology

David W. Brokaw, Ph.D.
Assistant Professor of Psychology
Azusa Pacific University

Christine V. Bruun, Ph.D.
DuPage County Mental Health Center
Westmont, Illinois

Rodger K. Bufford, Ph.D.
Chairman and Associate Professor of
    Psychology
Western Conservative Baptist Seminary

Richard E. Butman, Ph.D.
Assistant Professor of Psychology
Wheaton College

Contributors

Alphonse F. X. Calabrese, Ph.D.
Executive Director
Christian Institute for Psychotherapeutic
  Studies
Hicksville, New York

Rudolph D. Calabrese, Ph.D.
Christian Institute for Psychotherapeutic
  Studies
Hicksville, New York

Paul Cameron, Ph.D.
Chairperson
Institute for Scientific Investigation of
  Sexuality
Lincoln, Nebraska

Clark D. Campbell, Ph.D.
Dammasch State Hospital
Wilsonville, Oregon

Michael A. Campion, Ph.D.
Private Practice
Decatur, Illinois

Brian L. Carlton, Ph.D.
DuPage County Medical Health Center
Wheaton, Illinois

Diane Carolan, M.S.W.
Central Kansas Mental Health Center
Salina

John D. Carter, Ph.D.
Professor of Psychology
Rosemead School of Psychology
Biola University

James F. Cassens, Ph.D.
Cassens & Associates, P.C.
Park Ridge, Illinois

Paul W. Clement, Ph.D.
Professor of Psychology
Graduate School of Psychology
Fuller Theological Seminary
Director
The Psychological Center
Pasadena, California

Bonnidell Clouse, Ph.D.
Professor of Educational and School
  Psychology
Indiana State University

Arlo D. Compaan, Ph.D.
Executive Director
Center for Life Skills
Chicago

David M. Cook, M.A.
Graduate Student
Rosemead School of Psychology
Biola University

Mark Coppenger, Ph.D.
Associate Professor of Philosophy
Wheaton College

Mark P. Cosgrove, Ph.D.
Associate Professor of Psychology
Taylor University

John H. Court, Ph.D.
Associate Professor in Psychology
The Flinders University of South Australia
Director
Spectrum Psychological and Counseling
  Centre
Bedford Park, South Australia

James R. David, Ph.D.
Adjunct Associate Professor
National Catholic School of Social Service
Catholic University of America

Creath Davis, M.Div.
Executive Director
Christian Concern Foundation
Dallas

A. Robert Denton, Ph.D.
Director
Victim Assistance Program
Furnace Street Mission
Akron

Quintin R. DeYoung, Ph.D.
Emeritus Professor of Psychology
Chapman College

John B. Dilley, Ed.D.
Private Practice
West Des Moines, Iowa

Carl B. Dodrill, Ph.D.
Associate Professor of Neurological Surgery,
  Psychiatry, and Behavioral Sciences
University of Washington School of Medicine

Charles D. Dolph, Ph.D.
Professor of Psychology
Cedarville College

David Dowell, M.S.W.
National Jewish Hospital
Denver

Warren C. Drew, Psy.D.
USAF Medical Center
Wright-Patterson Air Force Base

William L. Edkins, M.Div., Psy.D.
Assistant Clinical Professor
Rosemead School of Psychology
Biola University

J. Harold Ellens, Ph.D.
Executive Director
Christian Association for Psychological Studies
Farmington Hills, Michigan

Craig W. Ellison, Ph.D.
Professor of Psychology and Urban Studies
Alliance Theological Seminary
Nyack College

James F. Engel, Ph.D.
Professor of Communications Research
Wheaton College

Ronald Enroth, Ph.D.
Professor of Sociology
Westmont College

Truman G. Esau, M.D., F.A.P.A.
Medical Director
Old Orchard Hospital
Chicago

C. Stephen Evans, Ph.D.
Associate Professor of Philosophy and Curator
of the Hong Kierkegaard Library
St. Olaf College

Kirk E. Farnsworth, Ph.D.
Professor of Psychology
Wheaton College

Robert R. Farra, Ph.D.
Professor of Family Sociology
Adrian College

Larry N. Ferguson, Ph.D.
Clinical Director
Link Care Center
Fresno

John G. Finch, Ph.D.
Consulting Psychologist
Gig Harbor, Washington

Joy M. Fisher, Ph.D. candidate
Department of Psychology
University of Minnesota

David J. Frenchak, M.Div., D.Min.
Center for Life Skills
Chicago

Eugene S. Gibbs, Ed.D.
Associate Professor of Educational Ministries
Wheaton College

Dennis L. Gibson, Ph.D.
Wheaton Counseling Associates
Wheaton, Illinois

Emory Griffin, Ph.D.
Professor of Speech and Communications
Wheaton College

James D. Guy, Jr., Ph.D.
Assistant Professor of Psychology
Rosemead School of Psychology
Biola University

John A. Hammes, Ph.D.
Professor of Psychology
University of Georgia

Linda B. Hardy, D.O.
Assistant Professor of Psychiatry and Director
of Medical Student Education
Department of Psychiatry
Medical College of Georgia

Charles E. Henry, Ph.D.
Vice President
VMS Realty
Chicago

William Colyn Hill, Ph.D. candidate
Northwestern University

Elizabeth L. Hillstrom, Ph.D.
Associate Professor of Psychology
Wheaton College

Kenneth A. Holstein, Ph.D.
Bell Labs
Lisle, Illinois

Gary S. Hurd, Ph.D.
Assistant Professor of Psychiatry
Medical College of Georgia

Cedric B. Johnson, Ph.D.
Director
Bethesda Counseling Clinic
Santa Monica

Lucie R. Johnson, Ph.D.
Professor of Psychology
Bethel College, St. Paul

Ronald B. Johnson, Ph.D.
Midlands Psychological Associates
Council Bluffs, Iowa

Theodore M. Johnson, Ph.D.
Philhaven Hospital
Lebanon, Pennsylvania

G. Archie Johnston, Ed.D., Ph.D.
Executive Director
California Behavioral Science Institute
San Francisco

Stanton L. Jones, Ph.D.
Assistant Professor of Psychology
Wheaton College

Brenda Joscelyne, M.A.
Graduate Student
University of South Africa

Donald M. Joy, Ph.D.
Professor of Human Development and
Christian Education
Asbury Theological Seminary

Contributors

Richard D. Kahoe, Ph.D.
Christian Haven Homes
Wheatfield, Indiana

William T. Kirwan, D.Min., Ph.D.
Psychiatric Associates
St. Louis

Haddon Klingberg, Jr., Ph.D.
President
Klingberg Family Centers
New Britain, Connecticut

Rodger D. Kobes, M.D., Ph.D.
Associate Professor of Clinical Psychiatry
Veterans Administration Medical Center
University of Texas Health Science Center

Jane Kopas, Ph.D.
Associate Professor of Theology
University of Scranton

Ronald L. Koteskey, Ph.D.
Professor of Psychology
Asbury College

Kevin R. Kracke, Ph.D.
Director of Children and Adolescent Services
Central Kansas Mental Health Center
Associate Professor of Psychology
Marymount College of Kansas

Michael J. Lambert, Ph.D.
Professor of Psychology
Institute for Studies in Values and Human
  Behavior
Brigham Young University

Reginald Larkin, Ph.D. Candidate
University of Texas at Austin

Lojan E. LaRowe, Ph.D.
Barrington Counseling Associates
Deerfield, Illinois
Assistant Professor of Psychology
Trinity College

John A. Larsen, M.Div., Ph.D.
Director of Consultation and Education
Midwest Christian Counseling Center
Kansas City, Missouri

Kathleen M. Lattea, M.A.
Brentwood, Maryland

Earl A. Loomis, Jr., M.D.
Professor of Child and Adolescent Psychiatry
Medical College of Georgia

H. Newton Malony, Ph.D.
Professor of Psychology and Director of
  Programs in the Integration of Psychology
  and Theology
Graduate School of Psychology
Fuller Theological Seminary

Rod A. Martin, Ph.D.
Assistant Professor of Psychology
University of Western Ontario

Michael L. Marvin, Ph.D.
Clinical Psychologist
Federal Prison System
Lompoc, California

George Matheson, Ph.D.
Chief of Psychology
Etobicoke General Hospital
Rexdale, Ontario

Larry McCauley, Ed.D.
Christian Clinic for Counseling
Oklahoma City

Donald S. McCulloch, Ph.D. candidate
Nova University

M. E. McCurdy, Ph.D.
Director
Elbert County Mental Retardation Services
  Center
Winder, Georgia

John McDonagh, Ph.D.
Private Practice
Huntington, New York

Marvin J. McDonald, Ph.D.
Pine Rest Christian Hospital
Grand Rapids, Michigan

Jeffrey J. McHenry, Ph.D.
Research Psychologist
Personnel Decisions Research Institute
Minneapolis

Rodney B. McKean, Ph.D.
First Alliance Church
Tucson

D. Douglas McKenna, Ph.D.
Research Psychologist
Personnel Decisions Research Institute
Minneapolis

Clinton W. McLemore, Ph.D.
Associate Professor of Psychology
Graduate School of Psychology
Fuller Theological Seminary

Steven P. McNeel, Ph.D.
Professor of Psychology
Bethel College, St. Paul

Mary Jo Meadow, Ph.D.
Associate Professor of Psychology and of
  Religious Studies
Mankato State University

Dan Motet, Ph.D.
Private Practice
Honolulu

S. Bruce Narramore, Ph.D.
Professor and Dean
Rosemead School of Psychology
Biola University

Melvin R. Nelson, Ph.D.
Private Practice
Wauwatosa, Wisconsin

Mary Ann Norfleet, Ph.D.
Professor of Psychology
Western Graduate School of Psychology

Gary Jackson Oliver, Ph.D.
Director of Counseling and Family Ministries
Christian Resource Center
Giltner, Nebraska

Steve R. Osborne, Ph.D.
Senior Research Scientist
Allen Corporation of America
Dallas

E. Mansell Pattison, M.D.
Professor and Chairman of the Department of
    Psychiatry and Health Behavior
Medical College of Georgia

David Pecheur, Ph.D.
Claremont Psychological Services
Claremont

Peggy Perry, M.S.W.
Department of Psychiatry
University of Kentucky

James E. Plueddemann, Ph.D.
Chairman and Associate Professor of
    Educational Ministries
Wheaton College

L. Rebecca Propst, Ph.D.
Assistant Professor of Psychology
Lewis and Clark College /

George A. Rekers, Ph.D.
Professor of Family and Child Development
Kansas State University

Dennis R. Ridley, Ph.D.
Research Associate
Department of Human Service Studies
Cornell University

John H. Robertson, M.A.
Mercy Center for Health Care Services
Aurora, Illinois

Michael D. Roe, Ph.D.
Associate Professor of Psychology
Bethel College, St. Paul

James L. Rogers, Ph.D.
Associate Professor of Psychology
Wheaton College

Ronald H. Rottschafer, Ph.D.
Private Practice
Oak Brook, Illinois

Timothy J. Runkel, M.Div., Ph.D.
Consulting Psychologist
Zion, Illinois

Robert J. Salinger, M.D.
Madison Psychiatric Associates
Madison

John A. Sanford, M.Div.
Certified Jungian Analyst
Private Practice
San Diego

Onas C. Scandrette, Ed.D.
Emeritus Professor of Psychology
Wheaton College

Nathan Schroer, Ed.D.
Department of Counseling and School
    Psychology
Texas A & M University

David C. Schutz, M.D.
Assistant Clinical Professor of Psychiatry
Loyola University Medical School

Donna Lynne Schuurman, Ed.D. candidate
Northern Illinois University

Leigh S. Schaffer, Ph.D.
Associate Professor of Psychology
West Chester State College

Bethyl J. Shepperson, Psy.D.
Claremont Psychological Services
Claremont

Vance L. Shepperson, Ph.D.
Associate Adjunct Professor
California Graduate Institute
California State University at Los Angeles

Dale Simpson, Ph.D.
Clinical Director
Family Life Counseling Services
Bryan, Texas

Stan Skarsten, D.S.W.
Stan Skarsten Consulting
Toronto

Don Smarto, M.A.
Program Director
Sunburst
Wheaton, Illinois

Darrell Smith, Ph.D.
Professor and Director of Training
Counseling Psychology Program
Department of Educational Psychology
Texas A & M University

Contributors

Glenn G. Sparks, Ph.D.
Assistant Professor of Communication
Cleveland State University

Mark W. Stephens, Ph.D.
Southwestern Indiana Mental Health Center
Evansville, Indiana

Brenda G. Stone, Ph.D.
Private Practice
Houston

Adrin C. Sylling, Ph.D.
Private Practice
Pasadena

Andrzej Szutowicz, M.D., Ph.D.
Research Assistant Professor of Psychiatry
University of Texas Health Science Center

Joseph E. Talley, Ph.D.
Staff Psychologist
Counseling and Psychological Services
Clinical Associate
Department of Psychiatry
Duke University

Siang-Yang Tan, Ph.D.
Director of Counseling
Ontario Bible College

Glenn C. Taylor, M.Th., M.Ed.
General Director
Yonge Street Mission
Adjunct Faculty
Ontario Theological Seminary

Randie L. Timpe, Ph.D.
Chairperson and Professor of Psychology
Mt. Vernon Nazarene College

Harry A. Van Belle, Ph.D.
Professor of Psychology
Redeemer College

Hendrika Vande Kemp, Ph.D.
Associate Professor
Graduate School of Psychology
Fuller Theological Seminary

James H. Vander May, M.A., F.T.E.P.
Chairperson
Activity Therapy Department
Pine Rest Christian Hospital
Grand Rapids, Michigan

Bryan Van Dragt, Ph.D.
Private Practice
Gig Harbor, Washington

Henry A. Virkler, Ph.D.
Adjunct Faculty Member
Psychological Studies Institute
Georgia State University
Director of Counseling Services
Ministry Counseling Center
Atlanta

Paul C. Vitz, Ph.D.
Associate Professor of Psychology
New York University

Edwin R. Wallace IV, M.D.
Director of Psychotherapy Education and
  Associate Professor of Psychiatry
Medical College of Georgia

Richard Welsh, M.S.W.
Professor of Clinical Social Work in Psychiatry
University of Kentucky Medical Center

Floyd Westendorp, M.D.
Professor of Psychiatry
Michigan State University

William T. Weyerhaeuser, Ph.D.
Private Practice
Gig Harbor, Washington

Frances J. White, Ph.D.
Professor of Psychology
Wheaton College

Frank B. Wichern, Ph.D.
Director of Counseling
Dallas Theological Seminary

Rod Wilson, Ph.D.
Dean of Students and Director of Counseling
  Program
Ontario Theological Seminary

R. Ward Wilson, Ph.D.
Professor of Psychology
Palm Beach Atlantic College

William P. Wilson, M.D.
Professor of Psychiatry
Duke University Medical Center

Ellie L. Wright, B.S.
Graduate Student
Brigham Young University

H. Norman Wright, M.A.
Director
Family Counseling and Enrichment
Santa Ana, California

Category Index

In the list that follows all articles in the encyclopedia are grouped into twelve categories. Two of these categories, "Psychopathology" and "Treatment Approaches and Issues," are further subdivided.

Fields of Specialization and Professional Organizations

Abnormal Psychology

American Association of Pastoral Counselors

American Board of Professional Psychology

American Psychiatric Association

American Psychological Association

Applied Psychology

Association for Clinical Pastoral Education

Christian Association for Psychological Studies

Clinical Psychology

Clinical Social Work

Community Mental Health

Community Psychology

Comparative Psychology

Consulting Psychology

Consumer Psychology

Counseling Psychology

Cross-Cultural Psychology

Developmental Psychology

Differential Psychology

Educational Psychology

Environmental Psychology

Experimental Psychology

Forensic Psychiatry

Forensic Psychology

Gerontology

Health Psychology

Health Service Providers in Psychology

Industrial/Organizational Psychology

Instructional Psychology

Mathematical Psychology

Media Psychology

Neuropsychology

Parapsychology

Personality Psychology

Philosophical Psychology

Physiological Psychology

Professional Schools of Psychology

Psychiatrist

Psychoanalyst

Psychohistory

Psycholinguistics

Psychologist

Psychology, History of

Psychology, Methods of

Psychology of Religion

Psychopharmacology

Psychophysics

School Psychology

Social Psychology

Social Work

Sociobiology

Sport Psychology

Eminent Contributors to Psychology

Abraham, Karl

Adler, Alfred

Allport, Gordon Willard

Ames, Edward Scribner

Angyal, Andras

Aristotle

Bandura, Albert

Beers, Clifford Whittingham

Binet, Alfred

Bleuler, Eugen

Boring, Edwin Garrigues

Breuer, Josef

Bruner, Jerome Seymour

Cannon, Walter Bradford

Cattell, James McKeen

Cattell, Raymond Bernard

Charcot, Jean-Martin

Clark, Walter Houston

Coe, George Albert

Descartes, René

Dewey, John

Dix, Dorothea Lynde

Ebbinghaus, Hermann

Ellis, Albert

Ellis, Henry Havelock

Erickson, Milton Hyland

Erikson, Erik Homburger

Eysenck, Hans Jurgen

Category Index

Category Index

Psychopathology

Psychosexual and Sex-Related Disorders

Category Index

Category Index

Pressure of Speech
Pseudocyesis
Rehearsal, Obsessional
Screen Memory
Self-Injurous Behavior
Shame
Shyness
Sleep Disorders
Somnambulism
Stereotypy
Stress
Stupor
Suicide
Syncope
Temper Tantrum
Tension
Verbigeration
Vertigo
Word Salad
Workaholism

Treatment Approaches and Issues

Systems of therapy are listed according to their most common format. However, some can be applied in several formats (individual, group, etc.).

Individual Therapies

Actualizing Therapy
Adlerian Psychotherapy
Adolescent Therapy
Allo-Centered Psychotherapy
Anamnesis
Antabuse Therapy
Applied Behavior Analysis
Assertiveness Training
Autogenic Therapy
Aversion Therapy
Behavior Therapy
Biblical Counseling
Biocentric Therapy
Bioenergetic Analysis
Biofeedback Training
Broadspectrum Psychotherapy
Cancer Counseling
Child Therapy

Christian Counseling and Psychotherapy
Cognitive-Behavior Therapy
Conditioned Reflex Therapy
Conditioning, Operant
Coping Skills Therapies
Daseinsanalysis
Direct Decision Therapy
Direct Psychoanalysis
Ego-State Therapy
Electroconvulsive Therapy
Existential Psychology and Psychotherapy
Flooding
Geriatric Psychotherapy
Gestalt Therapy
Growth Counseling
Guidance
Hypnosis
Hypnotherapy
Hypnotherapy, Indirect
Insulin Shock Therapy
Integrity Therapy
Jungian Analysis
Life Skills Counseling
Logotherapy
Morita Therapy
Multimodal Therapy
Naikan Psychotherapy
Narcotherapy
Neurolinguistic Programming
Nouthetic Counseling
Object Relations Therapy
Orgone Therapy
Orthomolecular Psychiatry
Paraverbal Therapy
Pastoral Counseling
Personal Constructs Therapy
Person-Centered Therapy
Phenomenological Therapy
Poetry Therapy
Primal Therapy
Problem-Solving Therapy
Provocative Therapy
Psychedelic Therapy
Psychoanalysis: Technique
Psychoanalytic Psychotherapy
Psychodrama
Psychoimagination Therapy
Psychopharmacology

Psychosynthesis
Rational-Emotive Therapy
Reality Therapy
Reconstructive Psychotherapy
Reeducative Psychotherapy
Regressive Therapy
Short-Term Anxiety-Provoking Psychotherapy
Short-Term Dynamic Psychotherapy
Short-Term Therapies
Spirituotherapy
Structural Integration
Supportive Psychotherapy
Systematic Desensitization
Tranquilizer
Transactional Analysis
Vocational Counseling
Will Therapy
Z-Process Attachment Therapy

Group Therapies

Activity Therapy
Assertiveness Therapy
Dance Therapy
Encounter Groups
Gestalt Therapy
Group Psychotherapy
Psychoanalytic Group Therapy
Psychodrama
Sensitivity Training Group
Theme-Centered Interactional Groups

Couple Therapies

Behavioral Marital Therapy
Creative Aggression Therapy
Marital Contract Therapy
Marital Enrichment
Marital Therapy
Premarital Counseling
Relationship Enhancement Therapy
Sex Therapy
Strategic Therapy

Family and Social System Therapies

Behavioral Family Therapy
Biopsychosocial Therapy

Category Index

Aa

Abnormal Psychology. This specialized area defies exact definition because of the powerful influence of values, attitudes, and beliefs. Simply defined, abnormal psychology is the study of behavior which is maladaptive, disordered, or abnormal. However, significant problems arise in the interpretation and application of words such as *maladaptive* and *abnormal*. Related terms, often used interchangeably with abnormal psychology, include psychopathology, mental illness, mental disorder, and abnormal behavior. Insanity, a legal term, typically refers to a serious state of mental incompetence.

The scope of abnormal psychology includes the etiology, diagnosis, treatment, and prevention of mental disorders. Etiology denotes the systematic search for causes underlying abnormal behavior. Diagnosis involves the description and classification of such behavior. Treatment refers to the application of various therapeutic techniques to modify maladaptive behavior and to promote adaptive behavior. Prevention includes all of those strategies designed to reduce the possibility of mental disorder and to foster good mental health.

Estimates of the incidence of abnormal behavior suggest that between 10 and 20% of the people in the United States will experience serious emotional problems in any given year. Over 40% of our nation's hospital beds are occupied by patients with mental disorders. The National Institute of Mental Health estimates the cost of mental disorder in the United States to be about $25 billion per year for treatment services, operation of mental hospitals, and loss of productivity.

History. Archaeological evidence suggests that mental disorders were known in prehistoric times. Many of our modern treatment techniques as well as many of our popular misconceptions regarding abnormal behavior have their roots in man's early history. It is convenient to divide the history of abnormal psychology into seven periods.

Primitive Period. Prehistoric man believed that everything was controlled by spirits or supernatural beings. Flowers blossomed, grass grew, and rivers flowed because of the spirits which resided within them. This belief is known as animism. Animistic thinking permeates the early history of most ancient civilizations. Bizarre or unusual behavior tended to be explained by evil spirits. Many historians of abnormal behavior conclude that animistic beliefs provided early man with a rationale for treatment. If evil spirits were the cause of abnormal behavior, the logical solution was to drive out those spirits.

According to some historians early medicine men exorcised evil spirits by using starvation, purgatives (putrid-tasting laxatives), floggings, and other forms of torture. A large number of skulls found in Peru with small holes cut through the forehead suggest that Stone Age man may have had other ways of permitting the evil spirits to escape. This kind of opening is called a trephine. Some of the skulls show evidence of healing around the trephine, indicating that the patient survived the operation and lived for a considerable period afterward (Coleman, 1976).

Preclassical Period. Egyptian and Babylonian manuscripts dating back to 5000 B.C. describe abnormal behavior as the result of evil spirits or demons. References to mental disorder are also found in the early writings of the Chinese, Hebrews, and Greeks. The Chinese established institutions for those with mental disorders as early as 1100 B.C. The Bible (1 Sam. 21:12–14) tells how King David escaped from Achish, king of Gath, by faking abnormal behavior. His technique included scribbling on the doors and letting his saliva run down onto his beard.

Even before the Golden Age of Greece and Rome efforts were being made to find a more rational treatment for psychopathology. As early as 860 B.C. the Greeks reserved torture for the more difficult patients. The priests, who were responsible for treating abnormal behavior, tried music, suggestion, recreation, and kindness as a supplement to the usual prayers and chants.

Classical Period. The humane, rational approach to abnormal behavior which emerged during this period originated in the thinking of three men: Pythagoras, Hippocrates, and Plato. Some of their original assumptions have been confirmed by modern research. Significantly, modern psychiatry traces much of its terminology to the Golden Age of Greece. Pythagoras (ca. 580–500 B.C.), a Greek philosopher and physician, believed the brain to be the center of intelligence and the focus of mental disorder. Pythagoras also developed some of the first principles of physical and mental hygiene.

Hippocrates (ca. 460–377 B.C.) combined the speculations of the philosophers of medicine with firsthand observations; for this reason he is called the father of modern medicine. While most of his contemporaries believed that mental disorder was a punishment for offending the gods, Hippocrates sought to explain all diseases, physical and mental, on the basis of natural causes. He followed Pythagoras in the belief that brain pathology was the major cause of abnormal behavior. His treatise *The Sacred Disease* illustrates his unequivocal belief in natural causes. If you cut open the head, he wrote, you would find the brain "humid, full of sweat, and smelling badly." This would prove that it is not a god which injures, but disease. Unfortunately, Hippocrates and the other Greek physicians knew very little about anatomy at this time. They deified the human body and for this reason could not dissect it.

Hippocrates classified the mental disorders he observed into three major categories: mania (abnormal excitement), melancholia (abnormal depression), and phrenitis (brain fever). His writings give detailed descriptions of many specific disorders, including migraine headaches, alcoholic delirium, convulsions, epilepsy, phobias, and postpartum psychosis. Hippocrates was primarily a clinician with a strong interest in the symptoms of his patients. Consequently his daily clinical records are remarkably thorough.

Hippocrates did not include a fourth disorder, hysteria, in his classification of mental disorders because he thought it was restricted to women. He believed hysteria (physical symptoms such as paralysis in the absence of organic pathology) was caused by the wandering of the uterus in search of moisture or humidity. At that time it was believed that the uterus was unattached in the female body and free to float about. Hippocrates recommended marriage as the best remedy.

According to Hippocrates some personality disorders stemmed from an imbalance of four humors, or vital fluids, in the body: blood, phlegm, black bile, and yellow bile. For example, an excess of phlegm would cause a person to be listless, sluggish, and indifferent. Little physiological evidence was available to support the theory. Unfortunately, medical treatment based on such theories continued for several centuries.

Hippocrates also recognized the importance of the environment, and he often removed patients from their families. For melancholia he prescribed rest, exercise, a vegetable diet, abstinence from alcohol, celibacy, a tranquil life, and bleeding if necessary. In order to ensure that such a regimen was followed, he often moved patients into his home where he could supervise their treatment.

Anticipating modern psychoanalysis, Hippocrates realized that the analysis of dreams might be useful in understanding a patient's personality. He also suggested the importance of heredity and a predisposition to mental disorder.

Plato (ca. 427–347 B.C.) identified three possible factors to account for mental disorder: organic factors, moral factors, and divine factors. In the latter case he shared the belief of many of his contemporaries that some forms of mental illness were due to the intervention of the gods. One of his most original contributions was his idea that criminals are mentally disturbed. This concept has led to one of modern psychiatry's most controversial issues: the use of insanity as a legal defense for criminal acts.

Plato's pupil, Aristotle, hindered the development of a naturalistic approach to mental disorder when he rejected the possibility that mental illness might develop from psychological causes.

Some of the most advanced medical practices of this period were found in Alexandria,

Egypt, which became an important center of Greek culture after it was founded in 332 B.C. by Alexander the Great. Mental patients experienced comfortable surroundings in the temples dedicated to Saturn which served as sanatoriums. Treatment consisted of a variety of activities that show striking similarity to modern occupational therapy. For example, musical concerts, walks in the temple gardens, dances, parties, and rowing along the Nile were typical activities. Gymnastics, hydrotherapy, and massage were used by some of the later Greek and Roman physicians working in Alexandria.

Several Greek physicians traveled to Rome during this period to practice medicine. Asclepiades and Aretaeus were two of the most notable. Asclepiades recognized the difference between acute and chronic disorders. Because of his sympathy for those with mental disorders, he developed treatments for their comfort and relaxation. One pleasurable treatment involved the drinking of chilled vintage wine while immersed in a warm tub. Asclepiades also differentiated delusions and hallucinations.

Aretaeus (50–130) followed closely the teachings of Hippocrates. He carefully observed the mentally ill and described in vivid detail a number of important disorders. Aretaeus was probably the first to suggest that some types of mental illness were only extensions of normal personality traits. He viewed manic and depressive states as phases of the same illness and recorded detailed descriptions of the prepsychotic personalities of some of his patients. Finally, he noted that some people with serious mental disorders do not experience intellectual deterioration. This was an idea which received little attention until the twentieth century (Alexander & Selesnick, 1966).

Another devoted follower of the Hippocratic tradition was Galen (131–200), who moved to Rome in A.D. 162. Galen organized and systematized a large amount of data concerning mental and physical disease. He conducted studies of human and animal anatomy in order to understand the relationship between the nervous system and behavior. In addition to recognizing that mental disorders had both physical and psychological causes, Galen suggested a variety of specific causes, including alcoholism, fear, head injuries, love affairs, menopause, and economic difficulties.

The darkest period in the history of abnormal psychology began with the death of Galen. One notable exception was Trallianus (525–605). Trallianus followed the teachings of Galen and was an early advocate of the impor-

tance of constitutional factors in mental disorders. In one of his more interesting clinical histories, he recorded the case of a man who was deeply depressed by the belief that someone had amputated his head. Anticipating contemporary behavioral treatments, Trallianus devised a leaden cap for the patient's head. When this cap was suddenly placed upon the man's head, he felt the weight and thought his head had been replaced.

The contributions of the Greek and Roman physicians were forgotten during the medieval period, when most physicians turned to superstition and some form of demonology.

Medieval Period. The fall of Rome to the barbarians near the end of the fifth century brought a resurgence of ancient superstitions. Naturalistic explanations for abnormal behavior gave way to the revival of demonology. Unfortunately, contemporary theological thinking did little to discourage those trends.

Peculiar manifestations of mass madness occurred periodically from the tenth to the seventeenth century. The most prominent example of group mental disorder was known in Italy as tarantism (because it was thought to be caused by the bite of the tarantula) and in the rest of Europe as St. Vitus's dance. Also called the dancing mania, this phenomenon involved large groups of people who engaged in epidemics of wild dancing and jumping until they collapsed from exhaustion. It is difficult to know whether these epidemic manifestations have been greatly exaggerated as successive generations have related them. The cause of mass madness is not known. A few people may have had neurological conditions which produced uncoordinated movements of the head and the extremities. Fear of the disease and mass suggestion may have caused the spread of this phenomenon throughout Europe.

The medieval period represents a sorry chapter in the history of psychopathology. Mental disorders were generally ascribed to possession by the devil. Treatment techniques concentrated on making the body of the possessed person an undesirable place for the devil to inhabit. Initially attempts were made to insult the devil by calling him obscene and foul names. If this failed, torture was the accepted method for trying to drive the devil out. Immersion in hot water, flogging, starving, and similar techniques were accepted treatments, but they were hardly distinguishable from punishment.

While some people were thought to be possessed unwillingly as a punishment by God for past sins, it was generally accepted during the fifteenth century that most possessed people had made a bargain with the devil in exchange for supernatural powers. Such a view justified all sorts of cruel practices. Late in the fifteenth century two Dominican monks, Johann Sprenger and Heinrich Kraemer, published *Malleus Maleficarcum* (*The Witches' Hammer*). With backing from Pope Innocent VIII, Maximillian I, and the theology faculty at the University of Cologne, this book became the handbook of the Inquisition.

The *Malleus* was adopted by both Roman Catholic and Protestant countries as the definitive guide for dealing with witchcraft and for conducting witch hunts. By definition a witch might be a dissenter or a person who behaved in an unusual or abnormal manner. Undoubtedly many so-called witches were psychotic or severely depressed. Proof of witchcraft involved torturing the person until a confession was obtained. The penalty for witchcraft might be strangulation, mutilation, beheading, or being burned alive, but ultimately the witch's body was always burned. One French judge boasted that in 16 years on the bench he had burned 800 women. In Geneva 500 witches were burned in the year 1515. The persecution of witches continued sporadically until the eighteenth century. In the United States the famous Salem witchcraft trials occurred in 1692.

Greek and Roman medicine survived into the medieval period in the work of Avicenna, an Arabian physician (980–1037). His treatment of the mentally ill was free of the demonology which permeated European thinking. In one case Avicenna told of a man who was suffering from melancholia and the delusion that he was a cow. The man not only bellowed like a cow, he also demanded that he be killed so that a good stew might be made from his flesh. When he refused to eat, Avicenna sent a message telling him to rejoice because the butcher was coming. Shortly afterward, Avicenna arrived at the hospital, entered the man's room holding a knife, and said, "Where is the cow that I may slaughter it?" The sick man lowed like a cow to indicate his whereabouts. However, when Avicenna felt all over the man's body, he said, "This cow is too lean to be slaughtered; he must be fattened up." When food was offered to the patient, he now began to eat willingly and regularly. As he regained his strength, the delusion disappeared and the cure was complete.

Within recent years some historians (Kroll, 1973; Spanos, 1978) have found reason to believe that the superstition and cruelty of the medieval period may be greatly exaggerated. Nevertheless, there remains strong evidence that this was a period of frightening torture and inhumanity for the mentally disordered.

Renaissance Period. While the mentally ill were being burned at the stake by the tens of thousands, isolated voices were being raised against the ignorance and superstition of the times. One of the earliest voices was that of an unconventional Swiss physician, Philipus Aureolus Theophrastus Bombastus von Hohenheim (1493–1541), who called himself Paracelsus.

Paracelsus openly rejected demonology and insisted that the epidemics of abnormal behavior during the Middle Ages were due to disease and curable by proper medication. Because of his arrogance as well as his ideas, Paracelsus was hounded and persecuted until his death.

Johann Weyer (1515–1588) published a scientific analysis of witchcraft in which he repudiated demon possession as the cause of abnormal behavior. His *The Deception of Demons* has been called the first textbook of psychiatry, and some regard him as the father of modern psychopathology. Weyer's thesis was simple. He believed that most of those who were imprisoned, tortured, or burned for witchcraft were actually sick in mind or body. Unfortunately, his ideas were two hundred years ahead of his time. The church banned his writings until the twentieth century.

Following Weyer's lead Reginald Scot (1538–1599), an Englishman, published a scholarly book in 1584 detailing the evidence for psychopathology in those who were being persecuted for witchcraft. His *The Discovery of Witchcraft* was seized and burned, and King James I wrote a refutation entitled *Demonology*.

During the Renaissance period a few mental hospitals were established in some of the larger cities of Europe. Henry VIII founded one of the most famous hospitals by converting the monastery of St. Mary of Bethlehem in London. Bethlehem was soon contracted to "Bedlam," and this term became synonymous with any wild mob scene. On Sundays Bedlam was a popular sightseeing attraction for Londoners who paid a penny to see the bizarre behavior of the violent patients in their chains. The harmless patients begged for charity on the streets of London. Shakespeare refers to them as the "Bedlam beggars" in *King Lear*. Little treatment was given at Bedlam other than emetics, purgatives, and bloodletting. In other hospitals patients were caged, preyed upon by rats, deprived of the basic necessities of life, and left to lie naked in their own excrement for months at a time.

Perhaps the most encouraging sign of humanity during this period was the Gheel Shrine in Belgium. Because of a long tradition involving cures for the insane, the town of Gheel became a popular center for pilgrimages as early as the fifteenth century. Many of the disturbed were left behind by their families to live in the homes of the inhabitants of Gheel. It was hoped that a cure might be effected if they stayed in Gheel for a period of time. Eventually the entire town became a colony where mental patients lived in private homes, worked in the community, and experienced few restrictions other than abstinence from alcohol. After more than five hundred years the colony at Gheel continues to thrive as one of the most enlightened treatment programs in the history of abnormal psychology. In 1975 over 2,000 certified mental patients were living in this family and community setting (Aring, 1974, 1975). Most of the major mental disorders are represented, including schizophrenia, psychopathic personality, and mental retardation. Patients normally remain in Gheel until a supervising therapist considers them to be recovered.

Humanitarian Period. The general trend toward humane treatment for the mentally ill came in the wake of the social, political, economic, and scientific reforms that characterized the latter half of the eighteenth century. Perhaps the most significant event of this period was the appointment of Philippe Pinel (1745–1826) as physician-in-chief at Bicêtre Hospital for the Insane in Paris. This hospital was widely recognized as a national disgrace. Grudgingly, the Revolutionary government gave Pinel permission to remove the chains from some of the patients as an experiment to test his view of mental illness. He believed that mental patients were normal people who had lost their reasoning ability due to serious personal problems. To treat them as vicious beasts and criminals retarded the recovery process. Pinel believed that kindness and consideration were the most appropriate treatment. Some of his experimental patients had not seen the light of day for 40 years. The results were dramatic. Even the most excited, unruly, and maniacal patients became manageable. Many patients recovered and were released.

Pinel instituted a number of additional reforms. Dungeons were replaced by airy, sunny rooms. Promenades and workshops were built. He also introduced the maintaining of case histories on patients and the training of

attendants. Many of the less desirable treatments, such as bleeding and purging, were discontinued.

The humanitarian reform was instituted in England by William Tuke, a layman and a Quaker, who believed that the mentally disordered would improve most in a quiet and supportive religious atmosphere. Tuke moved a group of mental patients to a rural estate, York Retreat, where they worked, rested, talked about their problems, prayed, and took walks through the countryside.

While Pinel and Tuke encountered vigorous resistance from some contemporaries, their ideas caught on and became known as moral therapy. This approach sought to relieve psychological and social stresses, which were believed to be the cause of mental disorder, by the development of friendly relationships, discussion of the problems, and pursuit of meaningful activity on a daily basis. In modern therapeutic terms moral therapy was social therapy, individual therapy, and occupational therapy combined into a total milieu. One hundred years before the advent of antipsychotic drugs moral therapy was amazingly effective. In some hospitals which used moral therapy during the first half of the nineteenth century, more than 70% of those who had been ill for less than one year prior to admission were discharged as improved or totally recovered.

Humanitarian reforms came to the United States through the efforts of Benjamin Rush (1745–1813), the founder of American psychiatry. He wrote the first book on mental problems in the United States and organized the first medical course in psychiatry. While Rush advocated many reforms similar to those of Pinel, his theories were tainted by astrology, and his treatments included bloodletting and purgatives.

Some of Rush's reforms were extended by the work of an unknown but energetic schoolteacher, Dorothea Dix (1802–1887). Forced into early retirement by tuberculosis, Dix campaigned across the United States for 40 years on behalf of the mentally ill who were suffering inhumane treatment in jails, asylums, and almshouses. She raised millions of dollars, established 32 mental hospitals in the United States, and helped to reform the asylum systems of several other countries.

Ironically, moral therapy declined and almost disappeared during the latter half of the nineteenth century. Several factors contributed to the decline. The large, centralized state mental hospitals which resulted from the campaigns of Dorothea Dix were one important factor. These huge warehouses were inundated with chronic cases. The focus of attention shifted from moral therapy to the physical well-being of the patients. Diet and room temperature were more important than relationships and meaningful activity. An increasing immigrant population also contributed thousands of patients to an overcrowded system. Finally, a series of advances in medical science led many to believe that all mental disorders would soon be explained by physical or organic causes. The medical establishment considered psychosocial factors to be unimportant or irrelevant. As moral therapy declined, the discharge rate dropped to 30%, where it remained until the advent of antipsychotic drugs in the mid-1950s.

Present Period. Several developments have contributed to our modern view of abnormal behavior. Some of these have their roots in the medicine of Hippocrates or in the philosophy of Aristotle. Other developments are of more recent origin.

The development of a systematic classification scheme has been a persistent problem for at least 2,500 years. Currently the American Psychiatric Association classifies mental disorders according to the *Diagnostic and Statistical Manual of Mental Disorders*, Third Edition (1980). This classification scheme first appeared in 1952 and has received substantial revision over the last 30 years.

While the organic viewpoint is a development traceable to the naturalistic views of Hippocrates, the emphasis on biological factors received significant impetus from the work of Emil Kraepelin (1856–1926), a German psychiatrist. His organic theory generated significant hope that all mental illnesses could be shown to have manageable organic causes. In fact, at the turn of the century several mental syndromes—senile psychoses, cerebral arteriosclerosis, toxic psychoses, and certain types of mental retardation—had been shown to be associated with brain pathology. Perhaps the most important success for the organic viewpoint was the discovery that a devastating mental syndrome, general paresis, results from the syphilitic spirochete, which passes through the bloodstream and into the central nervous system. This viewpoint continues to be the impetus for the biochemical research into the causes of schizophrenia and other disorders.

The development of the psychosocial viewpoint resulted from the repeated failures to find organic pathology in the majority of cases of mental disorder. While the role of psycho-

logical factors in mental illness had received some attention, it was not a widely accepted viewpoint prior to the turn of the century. A number of individuals were instrumental in making early contributions, but Sigmund Freud is usually given major credit for establishing the viability of this point of view.

Several other developments are worthy of mention: 1) biologically based therapies, including electroconvulsive therapy (ECT), psychosurgery, and chemotherapy; 2) psychological therapies; 3) community-centered treatment facilities to reduce the chances of long-term disability; 4) emphasis on prevention; and 5) holistic and interdisciplinary views, which recognize that any disorder is a disorder of the whole organism, necessitating an awareness of biological, psychosocial, and sociocultural factors.

Theoretical Models of Abnormal Behavior. The models discussed in this section represent the variety of perspectives that have been taken to explain and treat abnormal behavior. Seven representative models will be briefly discussed.

Medical. This model is virtually synonymous with the organic viewpoint and is often referred to as the disease model. While it exerts a powerful influence today, it reached its peak of influence around the turn of the century. By that time the importance of brain pathology in mental disorders was well established. Mental illness was on a more or less equal footing with physical illness, and the medical sciences were pressing ahead to clarify the role of organic factors in other disorders. Kraepelin played a dominant role in the early development of this model. Today the medical model receives most of its support from the field of psychiatry. Under the medical model the focus of therapy is on physical treatments (chemotherapy, shock therapy, etc.) supplemented by psychotherapy.

Psychoanalytic. Sigmund Freud, Alfred Adler, and Carl Jung are recognized as the major developers of this model. In the United States, Karl Menninger has been a leading figure in the promotion of psychoanalytic thought. This was the first model to demonstrate how psychological processes could cause mental disorder. Psychoanalytic thought views persons as dominated by instinctual drives and unconscious motives which produce conflict and anxiety. Mental disorders result when one is unable to resolve these conflicts or alleviate anxiety by the use of ego defense mechanisms or other means. According to the psychoanalytic model early childhood experiences condition much of one's behavior. In this rather negativistic and deterministic view, rationality and freedom for self-determination are minimized. The focus of therapy in this model is on the development of insight into the unconscious by free association, dream analysis, and other techniques.

Behavioral. While the other theoretical models developed in the clinical setting, this model initially evolved out of laboratory research. The behaviorists strongly opposed the study of subjective experience. For them the only valid scientific data were those which came from the study of observable behavior. Ivan Pavlov, John B. Watson, and B. F. Skinner are regarded as the most important developers of the behavioral model. Their laboratory studies of learning eventually produced new ways of explaining and treating abnormal behavior.

For the behaviorist mental disorders result from the learning of ineffective or maladaptive behavior patterns and/or the failure to learn the essential adaptive behavior patterns and basic competencies. In addition, abnormal behavior may result from conflict situations that require the individual to make discriminations or decisions of which he feels incapable. Behavior therapy focuses on changing behavior. Undesirable behaviors are eliminated by using one or more behavior modification techniques, including counterconditioning (systematic desensitization, implosive therapy, and aversion therapy), operant conditioning (token economies and biofeedback), modeling, and cognitive restructuring.

Humanistic. The humanistic perspective emerged during the 1950s as a "third force" in psychology, opposed on most issues to the other two "forces," psychoanalysis and behaviorism. Gordon Allport, Abraham Maslow, Carl Rogers, and Fritz Perls are usually regarded as the major developers of the humanistic approach. While humanism recognizes the importance of the traditional subject matter of psychology, it focuses on topics which are seldom the subject of laboratory research—self-actualization, wholeness, creativity, rationality, goodness, love, and hope.

Humanistic psychologists believe that abnormal behavior results from those situations that block personal growth and fulfillment, including unfavorable social conditions, excessive stress, faulty learning experiences, and the overuse of defense mechanisms. Humanistic therapists try to help individuals move in the direction of self-fulfillment by facing reality, dropping defenses, getting in touch with their inner selves and developing the essential competencies. While humanists may use encounter groups and awareness training to foster personal growth, they usually tend to deemphasize techniques.

Existential. Existential psychology developed out of the European existential philosophies of Kierkegaard, Heidegger, and Sartre. Victor Frankl, the Austrian psychiatrist, and Rollo May, the founder of existential therapy in the United States, represent two of the major proponents of the existential perspective.

This model, like the humanistic model, emphasizes personal growth and self-fulfillment. Existentialists also discuss the importance of responsibility, freedom for self-direction, and the search for meaning and value in life. In comparison to humanism, existential psychology tends to present a less optimistic view of human nature, stressing the anxieties of making existential choices and the irrational tendencies in behavior. Psychopathology results from alienation and depersonalization in a mass society, along with the loss of meaning in life and the weakening of traditional values. The existential therapist offers support and empathy as he helps the client to confront the past, to clarify values, to relate authentically to others, and to work out a meaningful way of life.

Interpersonal. Harry Stack Sullivan, an American psychiatrist, developed the major ideas underlying this model. Eric Berne, the author of *Games People Play*, elaborated on Sullivan's ideas in his development of transactional analysis. According to interpersonal therapists, abnormal behavior results from faulty communication and poor interpersonal relationships. The therapeutic process includes learning new interpersonal skills, changing maladaptive relationships, and developing more fulfilling relationships.

Moral. Within the last 25 years there has been growing interest in the relationship between psychology and religion. A symposium entitled "The Role of the Concept of Sin in Psychotherapy" at the 1959 convention of the American Psychological Association helped to create some of the interest. O. Hobart Mowrer's *The Crisis in Psychiatry and Religion* (1961) sparked additional interest.

A broad range of viewpoints is included in the moral model. The basic idea that brings them together is the belief that sin may be an important factor in the development of abnormal behavior. Mowrer, for example, believes that guilt, caused by sin which is unacknowledged and uncorrected, may lead to neurotic or psychotic problems. Jay Adams, author of *Competent to Counsel* (1970), takes the extreme position that all so-called mental and emotional problems result from organic diffi- culties or personal sin. Most moral therapists take a less extreme position. Therapy in the context of the moral model often involves confession and restitution along with more conventional therapeutic techniques.

Summary. While abnormal psychology may be approached from several perspectives, this article has elaborated on two important ones, the historical and the theoretical. The histori- cal perspective gives context for our current thinking about the causes, treatment, and prevention of abnormal behavior. The theoreti- cal perspective shows the diversity of our modern ideas about psychopathology.

References
Alexander, F. G., & Selesnick, S. T. *History of psychiatry.* New York: Harper & Row, 1966.
Aring, C. D. The Gheel experience: Eternal spirit of the chainless mind! *Journal of the American Medical Associa- tion, JAMA,* 1974, *230*(7), 998–1001.
Aring, C. D. Science and the citizen. *Scientific American,* 1975, *232*(1), 48–49; 52–53.
Coleman, J. C. *Abnormal psychology and modern life* (5th ed.). Glenview, Ill. Scott, Foresman, 1976.
Kroll, J. A. A reappraisal of psychiatry in the middle ages. *Archives of General Psychiatry,* 1973, *29,* 276–283.
Spanos, N. P. Witchcraft in histories of psychiatry: A critical analysis and an alternative conceptualization. *Psycho- logical Bulletin,* 1978, *85,* 417–439.

C. E. HENRY

See PSYCHOPATHOLOGY IN PRIMITIVE CULTURES; PSYCHOLOGY, HISTORY OF.

Abortion. Since the 1940s abortion has be- come an increasingly popular method of birth control. In the 1940s it would appear that about 7% of the pregnancies of white 15- to 19-year-old females ended in elective abortion. By 1979 about 37% of the pregnancies in this group of women ended in elective abortion (O'Connell & Moore, 1980; Zelnik & Kantner, 1980). These figures are estimates which at- tempt to include legal and illegal abortions. Limiting the figures to legal abortions, the Center for Disease Control (1980, 1982) reports a total of 485,816 abortions in the United States in 1971, rising to 1,238,987 in 1979. While somewhere between a quarter to a third of elective abortions are had by women previ- ously having had one or more abortions, it seems clear that an increasing proportion of women are choosing abortion.

In a random-probability-based study of the phenomenon, Cameron (1981) asked 2,251 women whether they had ever obtained an abortion. Thirteen percent replied "yes." Re- spondents classified themselves as Protestant, Catholic, Jewish, other, or nonreligious, and Christians designated themselves as "very de- vout," "moderately devout," "not very de- vout," and "not at all devout." Eight percent of those claiming to be very devout Christians, 15% of the moderately devout, and 23% of the remainder claimed to have obtained at least one abortion, while 21% of the Jews and 25% of the secularists made the same claim. The possible psychological consequences of abor- tion have been only partially explored, and the studies that have been done have generally yielded inconclusive data. Areas that deserve attention include the effects upon the woman, the "almost father," immediate and extended family members, and society. Of these only the effects upon the woman have received careful study. These possible effects include her psy- chological adjustment, attitudinal changes, and behavioral changes. Most of the studies have examined psychological adjustment fol- lowing the abortion.

Osofsky and Osofsky (1972) reported that following an abortion 15% of women have an unhappy mood and that 24% had a negative feeling about the abortion. This was contrasted to 65% who were happy and 63% who were positive. Baluk and O'Neill (1980) reported on 18 patients about one year after their abortion. Most tested within the normal range on meas- ures of anxiety, guilt, and depression. How- ever, they estimated higher levels of all emo- tions on the the day after the abortion. Simon, Senturia, and Rothman (1967) followed 46 women over almost a ten-year period. Half had a "positive reaction" to the abortion in both the short and the long term. About half the remainder developed psychiatric illnesses or were hospitalized, the rest experiencing vary- ing degrees of guilt and depression. The Fried- man, Greenspan, and Mittleman (1977) study involving over 500 women who obtained abor- tions led them to estimates that appear gener- ally reasonable: postabortion psychiatric ill- ness in between 2 to 10%, immediate negative reactions in about 23%, and longer-term nega- tive reactions in 11% of women receiving an elective abortion.

Attitudinal changes per se have not been investigated. However, Cameron (1981) re- ported that women who have obtained abor- tions and those who favor legalized abortion tend to differ from nonaborters and those who oppose abortion by more frequently 1) endors- ing euthanasia, infanticide, legalization of sui- cide, and more extensive use of capital punish- ment, 2) believing that homosexuality should be legitimized, 3) regularly smoking and using drugs and alcohol to get high, 4) claiming lower life satisfaction, and 5) claiming lessened love for humanity.

Since one of the strongest arguments for legalized elective abortion has been the assumption that it would reduce the number of unwanted children, one very significant research area for the future would be to examine the relationship between wantedness of pregnancy and wantedness of the child after birth. One study addressing this area (Cameron & Cury, 1977) produced data which suggest that while there is a slight relationship between the father's reaction to the pregnancy and his reaction to the child after birth, no such relationship exists for mothers. Further research will be needed to settle this issue. At present it appears unlikely that the availability of abortion has significantly reduced unwanted children.

References

Baluk, U., & O'Neill, P. Health professionals' perceptions of the psychological consequences of abortion. *American Journal of Community Psychology*, 1980, *8*(1), 67–75.

Cameron, P. Abortion, capital punishment, and the Judeo-Christian ethic. *Linacre Quarterly*, 1981, *48*(4), 316–332.

Cameron, P., & Cury, D. Do unwanted pregnancies produce unwanted children? In P. Cameron (Ed.), *The life cycle: Perspectives and commentary*. Oceanside, N.Y.: Dabor Science Publications, 1977.

Center for Disease Control. *Abortion Surveillance 1978*. Atlanta: Author, 1980.

Center for Disease Control. *Morbidity and Mortality Weekly Report 31 4*. Atlanta: Author, 1982.

Friedman, C. M., Greenspan, R., & Mittleman, F. The decision-making process and the outcome of therapeutic abortion. In R. Kalmar (Ed.), *Abortion: The emotional implications*. Dubuque Iowa: Kendall/Hunt Publishing, 1977.

O'Connell, M., & Moore, M. J. The legitimacy status of first births to U.S. women aged 15–24, 1939–78. *Family Planning Perspectives*, 1980, *12*, 16–25.

Osofsky, J. D., & Osofsky, H. J. The psychological reaction of patients to legalized abortion. *American Journal of Orthopsychiatry*, 1972, *42* (1), 48–60.

Simon, N. M., Senturia, A. G., & Rothman, D. Psychiatric illness following therapeutic abortion. *American Journal of Psychiatry*, 1967, *124*(1), 59–65.

Zelnik, M., & Kantner, J. F. Sexual activity, contraceptive use and pregnancy among metropolitan-area teenagers: 1971–1979. *Family Planning Perspectives*, 1980, *12*, 230–237.

P. CAMERON

Abraham, Karl (1877–1925). Pioneer German psychoanalyst and founder of the Berlin Society of Psychoanalysis (1908). Abraham was born in Bremen into a well-established and highly cultured Jewish family. His father gave up being a teacher of Hebrew religion for economic reasons, and Karl early abandoned the Jewish faith. His writings reflect no interest in religion, this being in marked contrast to his friend and mentor, Sigmund Freud.

Following the standard German preparatory education Abraham received his medical degree from the University of Freiburg in 1901. Thereafter he became deeply interested in philology and linguistics, and learned to speak five languages, read several others, and even analyzed some patients in English.

Abraham's first position was at Burgholzi Mental Hospital in Zurich. He became assistant to Eugen Bleuler and studied with Jung, who in 1907 introduced him to Freud. In that same year Abraham published his first paper, which began with the phrase, "According to Freud." It was a prophetic beginning. Abraham, among all Freud's disciples, never deviated either from personal loyalty to Freud or from the classical principles of psychoanalysis. However, he was soon alienated by Jung's personality and by what he saw as Jung's threats to the scientific status of psychoanalysis. Despite Freud's pleadings the two men were never reconciled, and Abraham soon left Zurich to establish a practice in Berlin. This practice flourished, and among his analysands were several who became respected analysts, including Karen Horney, Sandor Rado, Helene Deutsch, Melanie Klein, and two American physicians, James and Edward Glover. Thus Abraham brought to the fledgling psychoanalytic movement considerable prestige, and his contributions have lasted far beyond his own brief lifetime.

Abraham's total literary output was less than 700 pages, consisting of 4 short books and 49 papers, all but 8 of which dealt with the theory and practice of psychoanalysis. Nevertheless, he made important contributions to the psychology of sexuality, character development, myths, dreams, symbolism, and folk psychology. His most important theoretical contribution was his delineation of the etiology and dynamics of manic-depressive disorder.

Q. R. DEYOUNG

Abreaction. The term refers to a psychotherapeutic process wherein previously repressed feelings are brought to conscious awareness and given expression. These feelings are usually associated with past traumatic experiences. Their expression, therefore, is usually accompanied by considerable emotional discharge. Getting rid of these pent-up emotions may provide the patient with insight into the causes of unrealistic or immature behavior and allow these behaviors to be modified or eliminated.

9

The reliving of the repressed experiences is sometimes aided by HYPNOSIS or by drugs such as sodium amytal (*see* NARCOTHERAPY). Specialized techniques in Gestalt therapy, primal therapy, and psychodrama are also often very useful in achieving abreaction.

The method used to bring about abreaction is called CATHARSIS. Abreaction refers to the end result. Abreaction and catharsis are, however, often used synonymously.

G. A. JOHNSTON

Abstinence, Therapeutic Rule of. The therapist should abstain from meeting the unconscious infantile and neurotic emotional demands of the patient; this is the rule of therapeutic abstinence. The procedure is of central importance in the psychoanalytic technique, but it is used in some form in all systems of therapy.

When a person submits himself to the care of a psychotherapist, he comes to the therapeutic setting with mixed feelings. Seemingly the patient seeks to be cured or somehow improved. But in fact the psychotherapy patient is desperately afraid of being discovered and is afraid of change. Paradoxically the patient both wants to change and wants not to change. He unconsciously wishes to avoid personal change; instead, he wishes for the world to change to accommodate his unrealistic expectations and fantasies. Furthermore, either unconsciously or consciously he seeks to have the therapist meet these irrational and unrealistic needs and thus protect his neurosis from the onslaught of reality. The psychoanalytic approach proposes that the therapist refrain from meeting these emotional demands but rather help the patient to understand them. Thus the patient should have an unencumbered opportunity to see the unrealistic nature of his view of the world.

The strictest application of this rule results in the analyst not responding to (gratifying) any of the patient's attempts to relate socially. Thus Brenner (1976) advises against shaking hands or engaging in social conversation or other social amenities within therapy. Colby (1951) somewhat moderates this absolute rule, saying that the therapist is also a person and that rigid attempts to avoid social and practical interaction with the patient artificially induce neurotic symptoms rather than bring them to the surface.

Colby agrees, however, that there is a tremendous temptation for the therapist to fall into the trap of seduction. While the patient's seducing includes sexuality, it is not exclusively sexual. More often the patient simply wants the therapist to agree with him, and seeks this agreement by covert seduction and overt asking for approval. The therapist's own narcissistic needs, including the need to be seen as kind, reasonable, and beneficent, often make it difficult to resist such attempts to enter into a neurotic alliance with the patient. However, he enters such an alliance at the expense of a therapeutic alliance.

References
Brenner, C. *Psychoanalytic technique and psychic conflict.* New York: International Universities Press, 1976.
Colby, K. M. *A primer for psychotherapists.* New York: Ronald Press, 1951.

R. B. JOHNSON

See PSYCHOANALYSIS: TECHNIQUE; also, PSYCHOANALYTIC PSYCHOLOGY.

Abulia. A rare symptom, occurring mainly in schizophrenia, characterized by an impairment in the ability to carry out decisions. The absence of will power may include a desire to settle on a plan of action but no power or energy to actually perform it. The person feels unable to channel his thoughts into behavior and exhibits extreme apathy and indecisiveness. The term is usually reserved for extreme cases where a person cannot perform even the most routine functions such as dressing or walking. A counterpart symptom to abulia is hypobulia, which connotes an impairment, not an absence, of will power.

D. L. SCHUURMAN

Acalculia. A learning or language disturbance in which the person cannot perform arithmetic operations. This inability to calculate mathematically is the result of a loss of capacity for numerical ideation, often associated with brain injury or disease. Of three types of acalculia, two are associated with speech and verbalization disturbances. One type involves the loss of previous ability to grasp the meaning of symbols or to write numbers and figures. A second type is anarithmia, a disturbance in the actual performance of arithmetic operations. A third type involves the inability to spatially organize numbers, so that the person cannot read or understand what is read. Acalculia is found in persons with brain lesions. It is also associated with spatial dyslexia, spatial agnosia, sensorikinetic apraxia, somatospatial apractognosia, and some oculomotor disorders.

D. L. SCHUURMAN

See LEARNING DISABILITY.

Acathisia. The term, meaning literally "not sitting," was first used in 1955 by Haase to describe the inability to sit still and other hyperkinetic symptoms arising as side effects of the phenothiazine group of major tranquilizers. Intense anxiety, motor restlessness, and muscular quivering are provoked even by the thought of sitting down. In severe cases of acathisia spastica the thought or act of sitting provokes hysterical convulsions. The condition is accompanied by irritability and insomnia, and the acathisia sufferer may pace constantly or rock back and forth.

D. L. SCHUURMAN

Achievement, Need for. Murray's (1938) taxonomy of human motivation included the need for achievement, conceived as the desire to accomplish something difficult. To assess an individual's motivational concerns Murray designed the THEMATIC APPERCEPTION TEST, in which the respondent is presented with ambiguous pictures and asked to write a brief story about each. Presumably these invented stories reflect the respondent's own needs. Although the Thematic Apperception Test has shortcomings, it continues to be the instrument typically used for the assessment of the achievement motive.

Research has indicated that the need for achievement is often positively related to success in school, particularly in courses that are perceived as relevant to the student's future career, and also to the ability to delay gratification to obtain a greater reward later. High need for achievement has been associated with the preference for a high-status occupation and with interests similar to those of successful business people.

People who vary in achievement motivation also differ in the explanations they give for their own successes or failures. Individuals high in achievement need take personal responsibility for success and perceive themselves as high in ability. They may attribute failure to insufficient effort. In contrast, people with a low need for achievement have a tendency to attribute their success to external factors such as ease of the task or good luck. They may attribute failure to a personal lack of ability.

Atkinson (1964) proposed one of the most influential theories of achievement motivation. He suggested that in every achievement-related situation both the need to achieve success and the need to avoid failure are aroused. A person's behavior is determined not only by the relative strength of these motives but also by the expectancy and the incentive value of success and failure.

One of the predictions derived from Atkinson's theory is that people high in achievement motivation will prefer tasks of intermediate difficulty rather than those that are very easy or difficult. Research has confirmed this prediction. In one study investigators measured how far subjects chose to stand from the target when playing a ring-toss game. Those high in achievement motivation stood at an intermediate distance at which the game was challenging but not impossible. Other studies have also indicated that people with high need for achievement may set challenging but realistic goals. Some have argued that tasks of intermediate ability provide the performer with the most information about his or her competence. Performance on easy or difficult tasks is more likely to confirm one's knowledge of the external world.

McClelland (1961) has attempted to explain the economic development of societies in terms of achievement motivation. He reasoned that the link Weber saw between the Protestant Reformation and the growth of capitalism was mediated by a changed pattern of child-rearing practices that encouraged independence and the need for achievement. In an important study McClelland determined the achievement scores of different societies through an analysis of their written material, particularly of children's readers, and related these scores to the societies' economic growth as assessed through such indices as electric power consumption. Results indicated that an increase in the achievement need of a society preceded economic development, while decreases in achievement motivation were followed by subsequent economic decline. Other studies suggest there may be negative consequences when a society emphasizes achievement. For example, achievement scores also correlate with psychosomatic illness.

Early research found that achievement motivation did not predict the behavior of females as well as that of males. Although different explanations have been offered for this finding, the most intriguing has been that women may be motivated to avoid success. Presumably they have learned from childhood that successful achievement is unfeminine and thus leads to social rejection. While initial research seemed to indicate that the motive to avoid success was greater in women than in men, more recent studies have failed to replicate this finding. Some psychologists have suggested that women are not necessarily motivated by a fear of success itself but that both males and females may have a set of expectations regarding the negative consequences that may occur if they deviate from accepted sex-role norms.

Psychologists have generally viewed the need for achievement as a learned motive, with parents playing a major role in shaping their children's later strivings. Some have suggested that parents may foster achievement motivation through independence training, by setting high but realistic standards for their children and by being appreciative of their children's successes. Achievement motivation has been raised in adults through special training in the creation of success fantasies and through role-playing exercises.

References

Atkinson, J. W. *An introduction to motivation.* Princeton, N.J.: Van Nostrand, 1964.

McClelland, D. C. *The achieving society.* Princeton, N.J.: Van Nostrand, 1961.

Murray, H. A. *Explorations in personality.* New York: Oxford University Press, 1938.

M. Bolt

See MOTIVATION; PERSONALITY.

Achievement Age. The chronological age at which a specific achievement is usually attained. This age is established by achievement tests. Educational age is sometimes used synonymously with achievement age but is a more imprecise term.

Achievement Tests. An achievement test is a measure of proficiency in a specific area obtained by testing performance or knowledge in that area. Achievement tests are a type of ability test. Many writers have attempted to distinguish among ability, achievement, and aptitude tests. Most agree that, in the main, the achievement test is a measure of past learning, the ability test is a measure of an individual's present status, and the aptitude test is an estimate of future performance (English & English, 1958). Anastasi (1960) asserts that an aptitude test, which attempts to predict future performance, measures learning from broad and uncontrolled areas of influence. An achievement test, which attempts to evaluate past performance, measures learning from more known and specific sources. While such distinctions among the three are useful, there remains a considerable amount of overlap. How can we test achievement without also testing ability? In a purely theoretical sense we cannot.

Achievement tests measure the effect of some kind of training, narrow or broad. For example, an instructor may conduct a two-day instructional unit on the Battle of Vicksburg and then give a test that may or may not be sophisticated and well constructed. Many achievement tests, however, measure a much broader area, such as high school mathematics or college German. Those tests that measure school performance or vocational training are the most popular.

Achievement tests are used for many different purposes. Students can receive helpful feedback on their educational progress from the results of achievement tests, even though critics assert that discouraging results can have a detrimental effect on future achievement. Achievement tests of the survey type will give the student a single score; a diagnostic achievement test will yield several scores, helping the pupil identify various discrete strengths and weaknesses; and a readiness achievement test will tell the pupil if he or she is prepared to enter the next level of training in that field (Brown, 1976). Teachers and instructors can often obtain valuable information regarding the effectiveness of their teaching, but, it is hoped, the practice of "teaching for the test" is relatively rare. A final major use of achievement tests involves administrative evaluations. School officials can gauge the effectiveness of various curricula, the value of supplemental programs, or the benefit of allocating funds by the achievement scores of pupils.

A vast array of standardized achievement tests is available. Buros (1978) is the best source for information on each test's reliability and validity, age range, topics covered, scoring procedures, and cost. The *Mental Measurements Yearbook* series also includes major reviews by test construction experts as well as bibliographic citations of research regarding the tests. Many publishers offer an age-graded series of achievement batteries which can be used by a school district over a span of years on the same group of pupils.

During the 1970s a major movement by advocates of minority and disadvantaged children began to question the validity of testing, including achievement tests (Williams, Mosley, & Hinson, 1979). Because the results of achievement tests are often used as a criterion for further education, children who have suffered from educational deficits not of their making tend to suffer discrimination. Some have advocated the use of criterion-referenced achievement tests rather than norm-referenced tests as a way of minimizing the discriminating aspects of achievement tests (Gorth, O'Reilly, & Pinsky, 1975). Other researchers are exploring cultural-specific achievement tests.

References

Anastasi, A. Standardized ability testing. In P. H. Mussen (Ed.), *Handbook of research methods in child development.* New York: Wiley, 1960.

Brown, F. G. *Principles of educational and psychological testing* (2nd ed.). New York: Holt, Rinehart & Winston, 1976.

Buros, O. K. (Ed.). *The eighth mental measurements yearbook* (2 vols.). Highland Park, N.J.: Gryphon Press, 1978.

English, H. B., & English, A. C. *A comprehensive dictionary of psychological and psychoanalytic terms.* New York: Longmans, Green, 1958.

Gorth, W. P., O'Reilly, R. P., & Pinsky, P. D. *Comprehensive achievement monitoring.* Englewood Cliffs, N.J.: Educational Technology Publications, 1975.

Williams, R. L., Mosley, E., & Hinton, V. Critical issues in achievement testing of children from diverse ethnic backgrounds. In M. J. Wargo & D. R. Green (Eds.), *Achievement testing of disadvantaged and minority students for educational program evaluation.* New York: McGraw-Hill, 1979.

J. R. BECK

See PSYCHOLOGICAL MEASUREMENT.

Acrocephaly.
A birth disorder characterized by severe MENTAL RETARDATION and an exceptionally high skull. It is believed to be caused by a dominant gene.

Acting Out.
The concept of acting out was first developed by Freud to describe the tendency of patients in psychoanalysis to respond to unconscious conflicts by action. Instead of remembering and understanding, the individual circumvents insight by reliving the repressed emotional experiences through direct discharge of tension. Acting out is therefore a defense against the unconscious conflict. It also frequently serves as resistance against the therapeutic process.

An example of acting out would be the man who reacts to his unconscious hostility to his father with aggression toward his boss. This behavior begins, or intensifies, when therapy starts to focus on the unconscious conflict. When these feelings are acted out upon the person of the therapist, it is called TRANSFERENCE. Acting out that occurs within the therapy situation is referred to as acting in. Although it is still a defense against remembering and verbalizing, it is generally seen as closer to symbolization or verbal expression and is therefore easier to work with. It is also less disruptive to therapy because it can be observed by the therapist and analyzed.

Acting out does not occur only in psycho-analysis. However, many therapies fail to deal with its defensive functions and some may even encourage it. The term *acting out* is often applied indiscriminately to all aggressive or antisocial behavior. Such usage has led to a confused understanding of the concept.

D. G. BENNER

See RESISTANCE IN PSYCHOTHERAPY.

Active-Ambivalent Personality Pattern.
Sometimes described as the negativistic personality pattern, this is one of the eight basic personalities described by Millon (1981). Clinically what distinguishes such people is their sullen and contrary attitude toward almost every aspect of life. They are easily set off, quarrelsome and jealous, and often very unpredictable. Within the span of a single morning mood can fluctuate from despondent and distraught to spiteful and accusatory, then back to despondent and self-deprecating. They cannot decide to be dependent or independent of others, active or passive in their approach to life. Pessimism prevails: no course is worth pursuing for long. In the less severe range of pathology active-ambivalent men are often described as tyrannical, women as spiteful, and both sexes as being impossible to please. In the more severe levels of pathology such individuals may evidence paranoid features.

The most frequently cited family background of individuals displaying an active-ambivalent pattern is a schismatic family. In such families parents are manifestly in conflict with each other. In addition to constant fighting these parents undermine each other through disqualifying and contradictory statements (Millon, 1981). The active-ambivalent patient may be an incorporation of the familial environment, allying with one side then the other, but never experiencing compromise or even victorious dominance by one side.

Unpredictability of mood and high likelihood of ACTING OUT give active-ambivalents a certain coping advantage. People will often avoid confronting them and quickly give them their way. However, in situations where persistence, productivity, or teamwork are required, the active-ambivalent patient has few if any effective coping mechanisms. In longer-term relationships such as at school, at work, and even in psychotherapy, the brooding negativistic experiences of the active-ambivalent build up a history of perceived failures and putdowns which eventually make relationship building odious to the patient and others. This cycle of self-fulfilling pessimism and repeated failures leads to a later life depression which, when mixed with the impulsivity of the active-ambivalent, makes suicide a marked risk.

The active-ambivalent personality pattern is particularly insidious because it is so easily self-perpetuating. Not only are active-ambivalents in inner turmoil, vacillating between approach and avoidance, but they act out their discontent so vociferously and dramatically that they fulfill their pessimistic prophecy of personal failure. Millon (1981) notes that in this pattern of self-perpetuating failure negativistic and unpredictable behavior wastes energy and makes goal attainment difficult or impossible. Furthermore, active-ambivalents anticipate failure and stop short of seeing tasks or relationships through to a successful outcome.

The therapeutic prognosis for such people is not good. Typically the active-ambivalent will seek out therapy after a breakup in some attempted relationship. Such persons appear anxious, self-deprecating, and guilty. The distorted cognitive filters and the likelihood of acting out against self and others make both cognitive-behavioral and affective-experiential techniques limited in therapeutic power. Psychotropic medication regimens need close monitoring due to the rapid emotional shifts and the real suicidal risk.

It is often helpful to remove the patient from major environmental pressures, particularly family pressures. If inpatient care is appropriate it can involve highly structured cognitive-behavioral approaches which may facilitate the learning of new behaviors. Group therapy can also often be of help in learning alternative interpersonal styles. An economically more costly alternate is the extensive and prolonged personality reconstruction techniques of psychoanalytic psychotherapy. However, the therapist must be able to successfully challenge the tendency of active-ambivalents to use long-term therapy as a simple ventilation of pent-up hostility, thus solidifying a pessimistic view of themselves and the rewards of life.

Reference
Millon, T. *Disorders of personality.* New York: Wiley, 1981.
B. E. BONECUTTER

Active-Dependent Personality Pattern.

One of the eight basic personality types described by Millon (1981). Closely related to the HISTRIONIC PERSONALITY DISORDER, this pattern is characterized by social gregariousness, dramatic but superficial expression of emotion, and manipulative and attention-seeking behavior. It is apparently widely prevalent. One reason for this may be the Western societal emphasis on individual marketability and popularity. On the well-adjusted end of this personality style people are gregarious and sociable. However, the active-dependent personality pattern refers to persons who are not merely initially friendly and outgoing but who are driven to solicit praise and market themselves regardless of the audience.

Active-dependent personalities are externally focused in the extreme. This external locus of reinforcement usually leaves them bereft of an independent identity and inexperienced at processing their genuine emotional responses. It is as if their lifelong orientation toward reading the reactions of others prevents them from learning to deal with their own cognitive and emotional selves. Their reliance on massive repression and their overwhelming dependence make them prime candidates for hypochondriasis and conversion disorders. Dramatic illness unconsciously represents repressed emotion and buys care and attention from others.

Given this external orientation and their history of practice at charming others, it is little wonder that active-dependent personalities have a fairly successful set of interpersonal coping strategies. Typically their cybernetic skills are remarkable. They are able to sense what will sell to their audience. They are usually very successful in eliciting stimulation and capturing the attention of others. These strategies are considered pathological because active-dependent personalities fail to limit their manipulations to situations in which they are appropriate. Furthermore, despite their ability to please the crowd they lack the inner substance to maintain long-term relationships. Therefore they frequently develop strategies for sabotaging relationships at points where commitment or closeness develops. Over the years this often produces loneliness and depression.

The family background of active-dependent personalities frequently involves parental modeling and reinforcement of attention-seeking behavior and some degree of sibling or peer group competition. In such a family one learns that pleasing the parent produces significant rewards. Millon speculates that attractive persons may be at greater risk in developing the active-dependent personality pattern. Athletic boys and aesthetically appealing girls receive rewards and approval from others quite readily. However, if they do not develop any other source for reward, they will likely become disenchanted as aging limits their earlier simple attractiveness.

The active-dependent pattern is self-perpetuating largely because of its coping value in current Western society. Yet in spite of this, these persons have a good treatment prognosis. A therapeutic relationship is usually established easily, often beginning with positive transference and countertransference features. This usually passes quickly as the work of therapy begins. FLIGHT INTO HEALTH and premature termination are frequent occurrences, and the major therapeutic challenge is keeping the person in therapy after the initial honeymoon period wears off.

Regardless of therapist style, the therapeutic focus must move beyond the overdramatized superficial affect toward the more genuine and indirectly expressed emotions at the core of the active-dependent person. Given sufficient motivation these clients are good candidates for psychoanalytic psychotherapy. Medication is rarely needed over long periods of time and, given their external locus of control, may be counterindicated due to their tendency to become psychologically drug dependent. Group therapy is potentially effective once the client has some awareness of a need to establish genuine interpersonal communication.

Reference
Millon, T. *Disorders of personality.* New York: Wiley, 1981.
B. E. BONECUTTER

See DEPENDENCY; DEPENDENT PERSONALITY DISORDER.

Active-Detached Personality Pattern. One of the eight basic personality styles described by Millon (1981). The active-detached person is overly sensitive to various aspects of interpersonal interaction and thus actively avoids others by apparent detachment, inactivity, withdrawal, and restraint. Hypervigilance to cues of rejection or humiliation creates a high degree of anxiety, making interpersonal contact unrewarding. Yet these people experience a great need for contact and affection and thus feel their isolation and loneliness very deeply. However, this is more than matched by their fear and mistrust. Since their interpersonal coping and rewards are minimal, they often have excessive dependence on intrapsychic mechanisms such as a rich fantasy life. Over time these intrapsychic mechanisms may become increasingly nonconsensual or nonfunctional, thus fading into a schizotypal pattern of egocentricity.

Behaviorally, these people are seen as timid, shy, withdrawn, perhaps evasive and strange. They are very introspective and will report being usually tense, anxious, fatigued, and lonely. The key intrapsychic conflicts revolve around attachment versus mistrust. They also experience low self-esteem. Interpersonally they are experts at using distancing techniques, but especially in their younger years their tense and fearful demeanor often brings ridicule from others. Etiologically both temperament and experience are thought to contribute to this pattern in various degrees. The pattern tends to be self-repeating, self-fulfilling, and self-destructive. It is generally resistant to therapeutic intervention.

Reference
Millon, T. *Disorders of personality.* New York: Wiley, 1981.
J. M. BRANDSMA

See AVOIDANT PERSONALITY DISORDER.

Active Imagination Technique. *See* IMAGERY, THERAPEUTIC USE OF.

Active-Independent Personality Pattern. The active-independent or aggressive personality is one of the eight basic personality patterns proposed by Millon (1981). It is closely related to what has been termed antisocial personality. However, this label places too much emphasis on delinquent behavior and does not properly focus on the personality pattern that underlies the antisocial behavior. The active-independent personality pattern is more often expressed in socially acceptable behavior, and these personalities are often very successful in business, the military, and politics.

In Millon's system of classification, personality disturbances of mild severity are divided into detached, dependent, independent, and ambivalent patterns; the independent patterns are subdivided into passive (narcissistic) and active (aggressive) types. Both active and passive independents turn inward for their gratifications, are fearful of dependency, and are overly concerned with matters of status, superiority, power, and control. However, for the active-independent this turning inward is not from a belief in one's own self-worth, but rather a protection against an environment perceived as humiliating, exploitative, and hostile.

Historically the problem of dramatic antisocial behavior has consistently muddled the understanding of this personality type and its etiology. People with this type of personality pattern were frequently labeled with "moral insanity" or "constitutional psychopathic inferiority." A study of the evolution of these concepts shows a varied collection of referent behaviors because social standards of acceptable behavior have changed over time. Thus Millon proposes a semiabstract conceptualization (rather than behavioral delineation) of the themes that characterize these personalities. These themes are hostile affectivity, social rebelliousness and vindictiveness, assertive self-image, fearlessness, and the use of projection—at least three of these themes will have been consistently notable since adolescence.

On an intrapsychic level active-independent personalities are intolerant of distress for any length of time. Whenever able, they will externalize the problem and act out their impulses in a way that is intimidating and vindictive. In situations where this is not appropriate they will use the defense mechanisms of rationalization, sublimation, and projection. Thus in behavior they will seem to be brusque, competitive, argumentative and dogmatic, at times cruel and vicious, guarded and resentful, but often very clever. They are consistently suspicious of the "softer" emotions such as warmth and compassion, seeing them as manipulative devices to be used to gain control over others.

Perceptually these personalities are alert to the moods and feelings of others, but only to use this sensitivity manipulatively for their own ends. Yet they view themselves as honest, strong, realistic, and cynically able to deal with "the world as it really is." Because of their basic adaptation patterns active-independents will usually have few, if any, other symptoms. They are unwilling to experience distress for long and seem unable in an open environment to work out their conflicts intrapsychically. Under extreme conditions they can exhibit brief periods of paranoid rage which may be quite delusional.

Interpersonally all behaviors are built on a basic stance of mistrust. Before others can do negative things, one must aggregate power and block them, never displaying weakness or compromise, acting decisively, using preemptive counterattack. These persons show no loyalty and must dominate others (before being dominated). Basic hostility will be used vindictively, but rationalization will often be able to justify these actions. Inflexibility characterizes all personality disorders; these people do not have the variability and balancing of affect characteristic of more normal patterns. Despite some superficial charm and affectivity, there is always an underlying theme of suspiciousness and hostility evident upon more prolonged contact.

Both biological and psychological factors have been consistently implicated in the etiology of this disorder. From very early in development active-independent personalities are described as being highly energetic and having a low threshold for activation. As children they are described as venturesome and not deterred by punishment. As adolescents they seem to need intense forms of stimulation to create pleasurable experiences. These probably biological dispositions interact with their upbringing to produce the various forms of aggressive personality. Partly because they are nonresponsive and hard-to-manage infants, parents may get off to a bad start with these children. But usually the parents go much further than this in contributing to the pathology by being both dominating and cruel. The meanness, abuse, and irresponsible behavior of parents engender a certain view of the world and great counter-hostility in these children, and the parents do not provide them with appropriate social models. These children learn that they can feel powerful by using their anger and ability to cause trouble in their families and society. Thus biological responsivity and parental rejection interact with social conditions to produce the characteristics of this personality.

These patterns are not readily altered in therapy because they are often successful and protect the person intrapsychically from many painful memories. Active-independents will rarely accept blame or guilt, will have trouble being submissive patients, and will often do battle or "play games" with the therapist. Directive and punitive methods will not work because the whole defensive structure is oriented toward resisting this type of rehabilitation. In contrast, cognitive reorientation and channeling toward more constructive outlets are useful, as well as group therapy. Often this has to occur in conditions providing external control, i.e., hospitals or prisons.

Reference
Millon, T. *Disorders of Personality.* New York: Wiley, 1981.
J. M. BRANDSMA

See ANTISOCIAL PERSONALITY DISORDER.

Activity Therapy. A combination of action-oriented therapies used in mental health inpatient and partial hospitalization programs. Often misunderstood as mere time-structuring efforts, activity therapy is in reality a potent treatment method that is effective in providing therapeutic experiences for persons of all ages.

During the past 50 years several types of

activity therapies have emerged. Occupational therapy, therapeutic recreation, and art, dance, and music therapies became the leading innovations in what was called adjunctive therapy, meaning therapy which is additional to individual and group psychotherapy. Within the last ten years the term *adjunctive* has more often been replaced by *activity*, reflecting the importance activity therapy has achieved as a therapeutic modality.

The therapeutic impact of each type of activity therapy is heightened by their collective use. Many activity therapists use combinations of dance, art, music, recreation, and occupational therapy to provide a well-rounded, highly personalized approach to treatment. Activity suggests action, and action is a major characteristic of the many therapies included within this approach. The patient is engaged in doing. The hands manipulate the brush, the clay, or the musical instrument. Larger muscles move the body in sports activities, dance, or creative movement. In addition to action is interaction. Many of the activity therapy experiences involve interaction with another person or a group. In activities such as art and dance two or more individuals may co-create. Thus, interaction develops into an even higher level of functioning, co-action.

Activity therapists generally use a here-and-now orientation in their work. Some attention is given to the patient's past experiences, but these are generally integrated with what is happening in the present. Emphasis is on what the patient is experiencing at the moment. What is he or she learning during the activity? How does the activity compare to other life situations where similar feelings are experienced? How does what the patient experiences now relate to future situations? These are questions that the activity therapist considers.

The goals of activity therapy obviously differ for each patient. However, the following are some of the general changes often seen: enhanced creativity, better use of leisure time, improved physical and interpersonal skills, and increased self-esteem. It is also often helpful as a diagnostic aid in determining the patient's strengths, weaknesses, and interests.

Activity therapists work as members of a treatment team in conjunction with other mental health professionals. Some are employed in private practice. They are certified through national organizations in the major specialty areas—occupational, recreation, art, dance, and music therapy. Each provides a unique contribution to the overall holistic treatment of the patient.

Occupational Therapy. This was the first well-developed activity therapy, and was the forerunner of modern activity therapy. In this form of treatment media which can be manipulated with the hands are used to assist patients in their recovery from emotional disabilities and psychosocial dysfunction. In nonpsychiatric settings such as general hospitals and schools it is used primarily as a treatment for physical rehabilitation and sensory motor development.

Traditionally occupational therapy has been associated with leather, art, metal craft, ceramics, sewing, woodworking, personal hygiene, and instruction in everyday living skills. Classes in remotivation are offered to patients who need moderately stimulating experiences in reality orientation. Some of the creative arts are helpful in increasing attention span while reducing anxiety.

Although some attention is given to the finished product, the focal point is the treatment process, that is, the experience of the patient in the activity. Psychodynamic activities are developed to deal with the patient's unconscious conflicts. Conflict themes center around issues such as aggression, self-image, and social relationships. The activity is a catalytic agent toward the development of meaningful relationships and helpful intrapsychic learning experiences.

In addition to the activity, the personality of the occupational therapist is an important part of the therapy. Occupational therapists have extensive training in treatment approaches, evaluative methods, and group dynamics, and have been leaders in developing state licensing programs.

Therapeutic Recreation. This professional service provides recreational activities appropriate to the therapeutic needs of specific groups of people. These services are prevalent in psychiatric hospitals, day care agencies, homes for the aged, and penal institutions. The process of therapeutic recreation is directed toward a positive change in the individual.

The therapeutic recreation professional begins by assessing the patient's level of dysfunction. With the assistance of the treatment team, goals are established and specific recreational activities selected as interventions. The recreation therapist provides services on three levels—rehabilitation, leisure education, and independent recreation participation. As the patient moves up through these levels, the therapist becomes less directive and more facilitative. This therapeutic strategy promotes autonomy and independence in the patient.

Activity Therapy

The image and function of the recreation therapist have evolved considerably. Initially the job required organizing parties and recreational events. This was an outgrowth of programs provided for American armed service personnel in stateside military bases during World Wars I and II. Today in most settings for the mentally ill and handicapped therapeutic recreationists occupy an important place in the overall treatment program. Instead of helping the patient pass time by playing games, the therapist focuses on ways the individual can change and creatively designs the experiences which will facilitate this.

An important part of treatment receiving recent attention is the opportunity to provide patients with aftercare experiences in recreation activities. Such an emphasis requires active leadership on the part of therapeutic and municipal recreation professionals, who must combine efforts to provide meaningful activities for these special groups. Leisure counseling is also becoming an important skill of the therapeutic recreation professional.

Art Therapy. This is a human service profession which assists individuals in dealing with personal problems and conflicts through the media of art. Art therapy programs are often included as one of the activity therapies in psychiatric centers, schools, prisons, and other mental health-oriented settings.

The art therapist uses the visual arts as a means to assist integration or reintegration of personality. Art is seen as a form of symbolic speech promoting the direct expression of fantasies and dreams. From a psychoanalytic point of view spontaneous art expression releases unconscious forces and attitudes which may be interpreted initially by the therapist and eventually by the patient.

In addition to the evaluative use of art therapy it also provides healing through the creative process. In the creative act of the art experience conflict is reexperienced, resolved, and integrated. The atmosphere in the art therapy session is supportive and caring. The patient is invited to share thoughts and feelings activated by the art experiences. The goal is to serve the total personality by developing a fusion between reality and fantasy, unconscious and conscious; to discover both the self and the world and thereby establish a rational relationship between the two. Through the creative processes these inner and outer realities are fused in a new entity.

Art therapists are trained in a combination of art and the psychodynamics of individuals and groups. Although many are skilled artisans, their major focus is not on the finished product but rather is aimed toward a healing experience for the patient.

Dance Therapy. Dance, or movement, therapy involves the therapeutic utilization of movement in order to help an individual integrate his physical and emotional aspects. Dance therapists view the body as a manifestation of the personality. Thoughts and emotions are closely connected to physical movement, and therefore the healing process uses the body as the instrument for its own restoration.

The particular goals of the dance therapist often determine the nature of the movement experience. An initial broad objective is an increase in body awareness. New movements expand the body's repertoire of actions. Tensions are recognized and relieved. The body is recognized as a potential source of joy. Another goal is the catharsis elicited through movement. Dance therapists believe that the expression of feelings through shaking, kicking, or pounding provides a purging and therefore results in renewal. They strongly encourage the verbal identification of feelings so that a more complete integration is achieved.

The results of successful dance therapy go far beyond improved dancing skills. Much more significant are the frequent gains in interpersonal communication, both verbal and nonverbal. Dance and other group movement activities bring people together in relaxed positive contact so that natural social interactions develop.

Music Therapy. Here music is employed as the major treatment medium. The music therapist adapts sound and rhythm to create an environment in which the patient will respond by developing healthy attitudes and responsible decision making. The patient is drawn to others and experiences structure and organization as well as self-confidence and mind-body stimulation.

Music has therapeutic benefits because it is a nonthreatening medium through which the patient may express feelings, develop creativity, increase self-esteem, learn to work with and trust others, and express himself nonverbally. Learning how to play an instrument is a practical side benefit.

The therapy experience is a combination of music listening for reflective relaxation and music participation for the experience of learning and growing. The relaxing qualities of listening to music are therapeutic for all ages of people who experience the high stress levels of everyday living.

The major therapeutic goal is positive behavior change and insight into one's self. The therapist places most attention on the experience of the patient during the music therapy session. As in the other activity therapies, music therapy seeks to develop not great musicians but whole people.

Additional Readings
Bonny, H. L., & Savary, L. M. *Music and your mind.* New York: Harper & Row, 1973.
Feder, E., & Feder, B. *The expressive art therapies.* Englewood Cliffs, N.J.: Prentice-Hall, 1981.
Mosey, A. C. *Activity therapy.* New York: Raven Press, 1973.
O'Morrow, G. S. *Therapeutic recreation.* Reston, Va.: Reston Publishing Co., 1980.
Ulman, E. [*Art therapy*] (E. Ulman & P. Dachinger, Eds.). New York: Schocken Books, 1975.

J. H. VANDER MAY

Act Psychology. Two competitive schools dominated nineteenth-century German psychology. The less rigorous approch was advocated by Franz Brentano (1838–1917) at Vienna and by Carl Stumpf (1848–1936), his student, at Berlin and was known as act psychology. The rival school, STRUCTURALISM was centered in the work of Wilhelm Wundt at Leipzig. While Brentano and Wundt agreed on making psychology a science, there were differences in the definition of the subject matter and its method. Wundt conceived of psychology as the experimental study of the contents (structure) of consciousness, while Brentano stressed it as an empirical study of the act of experiencing.

For Brentano act psychology was the view that every mental event referred to an event other than itself. This process of referring defined the subject matter of psychology and took the act-forms of ideating, judging, and feeling. Attention was directed toward understanding the nature and process of referring. This stood in opposition to Wundt's assertion that psychology was directed toward the elements of that object which was experienced.

Brentano suggested the act of perceiving color was mental, while color itself was a physical quality. The act of perceiving could not occur without the object, but the act was more than a simple reflection of the physical properties of the object. The sensory content of a color was different from the act of sensing color. The act of sensing was meaningless without something being sensed, yet the act was more than the objective qualities. The subjective act was dependent on the experiencer, not solely on the experience.

Wundtian introspection was a highly structured, disciplined experimental technique. Orthodox introspection was a trained method in which the reporter was instructed to guard against committing the cardinal sin of stimulus error. Rather than reporting the experience of an apple as an apple, one was to report its objective, contentual properties of intensity, protensity, and extensity. But to the act psychologists this trained approach destroyed the act. Stumpf favored using native or naïve introspection, introspection as it occurred in the common folk.

Due to Wundt's prodigious publication rate, structuralism won out as the leading German psychology in the latter decades of the nineteenth century. However, the influence of act psychology did not die out. Brentano's doctrine made a positive impact on his students, who included Stumpf, Christian von Ehrenfels, and Sigmund Freud. Edmund Husserl, one of Stumpf's students, founded the philosophy of phenomenology. Other of Stumpf's students, Marx Wertheimer, Kurt Koffka, and Wolfgang Köhler, were instrumental in founding Gestalt psychology. The tenets of act psychology are found in the works of Fritz Heider, Kurt Lewin, and Carl Rogers. Act psychology was antecedent to Gestalt, psychoanalytic, and phenomenological psychologies.

R. L. TIMPE

See PSYCHOLOGY, HISTORY OF.

Actualization. *See* SELF-ACTUALIZATION.

Actualizing Therapy. Socrates claimed that the destiny of humans is the "perfection of the soul." By that he meant that humans are invested by their Creator with a magnificent and nearly infinite set of creative potentials for growth in body, mind, and spirit. The reason for the life of every person, he thought, was the grateful and thoughtful actualization of all those productive possibilities for humanness. Believing human personality to be essentially rational in nature, he concluded that the way to self-actualization was through thoughtful and rational living.

In modern psychology the challenge of self-actualization has not been championed so much by the rationalists as by those who have assumed that human personality is essentially emotional and dynamic in nature. Abraham Maslow brought the notion of self-actualization back into focus with his work on the hierarchy of human needs and his study of self-actualized individuals (1954). It was left for Everett Shostrom to translate these ideas into a system of therapy, which he has done in his book, *Man the Manipulator* (1967). His more recent work, *Actualizing Therapy* (1976), contains the most systematic presentation of the theory and practice of this approach.

Shostrom views actualizing therapy as a creative synthesis of many schools of theory and practice in psychotherapy (Shostrom & Montgomery, 1981). From conjoint family therapy he took the emphasis on the feeling polarities of anger-love and strength-weakness. From client-centered, or person-centered, therapy comes the focus on feelings and the importance of the therapist's nonjudgmental respect for the client. From Gestalt therapy Shostrom took the focus on the client's awareness in the here and now, and from bioenergetic analysis the focus on the client's body as a primary diagnostic and therapeutic tool. This sort of borrowing from other traditions was facilitated by Shostrom's close personal relationship with the founders of these approaches as well as with Abraham Maslow, Rollo May, Victor Frankl, and Albert Ellis. These relationships, as well as Shostrom's personal synthetic style, account for the broad and integrative quality of his approach.

Actualizing therapy deals systematically with the problem of helping people become more actualizing. It may be conducted within an individual or group therapy format. It can also function within the framework of any school of therapeutic preference. When it is offered within a group format, the emphasis is on the perception and expression of inner feelings, thoughts, needs, strengths, and weaknesses that function in the self and others. The intent is to achieve honesty and growth-inducing coping responses to one's inner world and outer world. Comparably, individual therapy endeavors to achieve the same process with a therapist.

The actualizing therapy model sees the client moving through eight stages from manipulator to self-actualizer and instigator of self-actualization in others. Persons may enter therapy at any stage of their own self-actualization. They should then experience some growth in self-actualization, and they may leave therapy at any one of the stages at which they are functioning.

The actualizing process consists, according to Shostrom, of "aiding the person to become aware of core pain, to express feelings that have been rigidly held back, to experiment with actualizing behaviors, body awareness and feeling expression, . . . [and] to develop a sense of core trust in being oneself" (Shostrom &

Montgomery, 1981, p. 7). This process is facilitated by twelve basic therapeutic strategies. *Caring* as unconditional positive regard or as care-filled confrontation, addresses active and passive manipulators respectively. *Ego-strengthening* develops the thinking, feeling, and perceptive ability of the client in positive directions, enhancing the belief that he or she is capable of coping. Behavior modification is usefully employed in this regard. *Reflection of feeling* involves the reexpression, in fresh words, of the essential attitudes expressed by the client. *Reflection of experience* involves observing the client's nonverbal behavior and feeding back certain information in order to expand the client's self-awareness. This technique is most effective for focusing on contradictions between verbal and nonverbal behavior.

Interpersonal analysis clarifies for the client how he or she misperceives and manipulates the therapist and others. The client is also confronted with the relationship-defeating games he or she plays. *Pattern analysis*, a corollary to interpersonal analysis, examines the client's self-defeating coping techniques. Therapy identifies alternative constructive patterns that may be chosen. *Reinforcement* is a process of therapeutic rewards for socially adaptive, self-actualizing behavior. Healthy responses replace bad psychological habits and bring rewarding gains. *Self-disclosure* is the process in which the therapist as wounded healer acknowledges his or her own defenses and pathologies and incarnates the evidence that life can be lived wholesomely despite these. *Value reorienting* helps the patient to choose more functionally operational values, and *reexperiencing* is the process of reviewing past perceptions and their pathological consequences so that their impact on the present may be acknowledged and they can be changed. *Body awareness* techniques assist the client in learning to attend to the messages from the body, and *interpretation* is the therapist's way of presenting hypotheses about relationships which should serve to bring a new perspective on familiar behavior.

Actualizing therapy contrasts with the medical model of psychotherapy, which moves a patient from illness to normalcy, in that it expresses the expectation of moving the person to growth beyond mere elimination of symptoms. Shostrom developed the Personal Orientation Inventory (Shostrom, 1963) to measure growth in self-actualization. This instrument has proven useful in providing an objective measure of the client's level of actualization as well as positive guidelines for growth during therapy. It has also been useful in researching the effectiveness of actualizing therapy. In one study Shostrom and Knapp (1966) showed actualizing therapy to be effective in helping clients become more emotionally spontaneous and expressive, less interpersonally withdrawn, more competent in effective time use, more present oriented, more inner directed, and less socially constrained. Compared to other therapeutic processes the patient's achievement was more that of growth than mere cure of symptoms. Shostrom's judgment is that actualizing therapy is most effective with normal or mildly disturbed individuals. It has not been used extensively with severely neurotic or psychotic persons.

The perspective of actualizing therapy expresses well the essential elements of Judeo-Christian anthropology. As imagers of God we are described in the Bible as endowed with majestic and immense potential for growth, creativity, productivity, and communion. Humans are just a "little less than God," according to Psalm 8. Humans, then, are destined to magnificent growth in the actualization of their full range of possibilities as divine imagers. Illness is anything that obstructs or curtails that growth. To be in a state of such curtailment is, by definition, to be sick. Health is the state of being self-actualized or of being at a place on the continuum of self-actualization appropriate to one's stage in life. Healing is any process that removes the curtailment of growth. Therapy is any formal strategy for the production or enhancement of the healing process. Therefore, Paul can say with confidence that the whole creation is standing on tiptoe, waiting for the children of God to come into their own.

References

Maslow, A. H. *Motivation and personality.* New York: Harper & Row, 1954.
Shostrom, E. L. *Personal orientation inventory.* San Diego: EdITS, 1963.
Shostrom, E. L. *Man the manipulator.* Nashville: Abingdon, 1967.
Shostrom, E. L. *Actualizing therapy.* San Diego: EdITS, 1976.
Shostrom, E. L., & Knapp, R. R. The relationship of a measure of self-actualization (POI) to a measure of pathology (MMPI) and to therapeutic growth. *American Journal of Psychotherapy,* 1966, *20,* 193–202.
Shostrom, E. L., & Montgomery, D. Actualizing therapy. In R. Corsinsi (Ed.), *Handbook of innovative psychotherapies.* New York: Wiley, 1981.

J. H. ELLENS

See SELF-ACTUALIZATION; HUMANISTIC PSYCHOLOGY.

Adaptive Behavior Scale. *See* SOCIAL MATURITY TESTS.

Adjustment Disorders. Maladaptive reactions of individuals to the psychosocial pressures of life, adjustment disorders are often labeled developmental and situational stressor events. Since everyone is repeatedly exposed to these stressors in varying degrees throughout the life span, the adjustment disorders are relatively common.

A maladaptive reaction is one that is severe enough to hinder adequate social or occupational functioning or to evoke symptoms beyond the normal range of responses to a specific stressor. The reactions are experienced within three months of the onset of the stressor event. They last until the stressor ends or, in cases where it is more chronic, until the individual develops more effective coping mechanisms.

Reactions to particular psychosocial tensions are conditioned by the quality and quantity of the changes and therefore losses inherent in the precipitating event; the intrapsychic nature of the individuals experiencing the stressor; the timing of the event; and the nature of the milieu in which it occurs. The intrapsychic variable contributes to individuals' vulnerability to stress reactions, especially when there is a preexisting personality or organic mental disorder.

The interrelationship of all the determining factors has been emphasized by family system therapists. In assessing the import of a reaction to a stressor, they consider the effect of each family member's life-cycle stage upon every other individual in the family system. In addition, the dimensions of the inherent qualities of the family system in which the individual functions (e.g., rules, myths, communication patterns, intimacy patterns) are seen to impact positively or negatively upon reactions to stressors according to the degree of tension they generate within the family (Carter & McGoldrick 1980). The higher the tension, often in the form of anxiety, the greater the possibility of a maladaptive reaction to the stressor event (Bowen, 1978).

The *DSM-III* gives eight categories of adjustment disorders, each with a description of its own predominant symptoms—depressed mood, anxious mood, mixed emotional features, disturbance of conduct, mixed disturbance of emotions and conduct, work or academic inhibition, withdrawal, atypical features.

Treatment approaches vary from those applicable to crisis intervention and undue stress, wherein the therapist uses a more supportive and/or problem-solving approach until the symptoms remit, to more educative strategies that facilitate a new level of adaptation. In some cases a core conflict must be dealt with in order to permit a healthy resolution of the disorder. When it is necessary to deal with deeper issues, it is important not to confuse the goal of resolving the adaptation disorders with the aims of treatment of the underlying or related disorders.

Crucial factors in working effectively with adjustment disorders are the need for the therapist to: 1) understand the theoretical base of the different situational and development stressors; 2) recognize the varying effects the stressors have upon individuals and the systems in which they function; 3) be familiar with the treatment strategies and techniques found to give the best results in dealing with particular stressors. This background for differential treatment of unhealthy reactions to identified stressors is available in an ever growing number of professional journal articles and books. Treatment of adjustment disorders of specific ethnic groups is the subject of more recently published literature.

References

Bowen, M. *Family therapy in clinical practice.* New York: Aronson, 1978.

Carter, E., & McGoldrick, M. *The family life cycle: A framework for family therapy.* New York: Gardner Press, 1980.

Additional Readings

Golan, N. *Passing through transition: A guide for practitioners.* New York: Free Press, 1981.

McGoldrick, M., Pearce, J. K., & Giordano, J. *Ethnicity and family therapy.* New York: Guilford Press, 1982.

F. J. WHITE

Adler, Alfred (1870–1937). The major developer of the concepts of inferiority feeling, social interest, life style, and fictional goals, Adler was also the founder of the theory of personality known as INDIVIDUAL PSYCHOLOGY. His life, especially his early childhood, portrays many of the concepts he later developed.

Alfred Adler was the second child in a large Jewish family. His mother appears to have embodied what her son later referred to as the martyr complex: gloomy and self-sacrificing. The father was cheerful and self-confident, and Alfred strongly identified with him. The senior Adler believed in avoiding both punishment and overt physical affection with his children, but he believed in giving them encouragement. As a prosperous grain merchant he could afford to provide his family with a suburban rather than a ghetto residence. The children grew up more influenced by Viennese than by Jewish culture.

Alfred's childhood was marred by several close encounters with death and disease. When he was three, a younger brother died in the next bed. When he was five, he contracted pneumonia and barely survived. Twice he was in street accidents. One of his earliest childhood memories was of sitting on a bench, incapacitated by rickets, while an athletic older brother played. In school he tasted defeat several times. He could not draw well and had to repeat an arithmetic class. One counselor told his father that the boy should be apprenticed to a shoemaker. One day Alfred figured out an arithmetic problem that could not be solved by anyone. He told the teacher, felt proud, and from then on did well in math. His later school years were remarkable for the number of friends that he made.

Adler met Raissa Epstein at a political rally. She was the daughter of Russian intelligentsia, and had come to Vienna to complete her education. When she returned home, Adler scraped together enough money to visit her in Russia, and finally married her in 1897. A strong-willed woman with a social background different from Adler's, Raissa influenced her husband's positive views on the equality of women. Although the marriage had a few conflicts, it served as the basis for Adler's positive view of monogamous matrimony. Two of their four children became psychiatrists.

Adler received his medical degree in 1895. He first specialized in ophthalmology, but broadened his practice to general medicine. His interest in psychiatry grew around the turn of the century, but he maintained his general practice until after the First World War. From his clinic in a lower-middle-class neighborhood he worked with a broad range of patients and diseases. This experience convinced him that the organic and psychological dimensions of disease were not separate, and that many individuals' special mental or physical abilities arose as overcompensations for childhood inferiorities.

After the war he was given the special task of establishing a system of guidance clinics for youth. Every child from 6 to 14 was screened, and those with learning disabilities, emotional disturbances, or behavioral problems received counseling. This project reduced the level of delinquency and served to convince Adler of the importance of child-rearing practices.

Adler never considered himself a pupil or disciple of Freud's. He first heard Freud lecture in 1899 and was invited to join the latter's discussion group in 1902. Adler was never psychoanalyzed himself, as were the other members of the inner circle. Nevertheless, the general practitioner won the respect of the early psychoanalysts and was selected as the editor of their journal and elected president of the Vienna Psychoanalytic Society. Adler's intellectual independence led to a widening rift with Freud. Early in 1911 Adler delivered three lectures to the Vienna society. He clearly enumerated the differences which set him apart from Freud. The subsequent discussion factionalized the group into a Freudian majority and an Adlerian minority. The former group declared that Adler's views were not psychoanalytic and the latter group withdrew, forming the Society for Free Psychoanalysis, which later became known as the Society for Individual Psychology. Freud and Adler remained on poor terms from then on.

Although individual psychology has religious implications, little is known about Adler's personal views on religion. He has been accused of being a radical atheist, but he had himself baptized a Protestant at age 34. This could have been due to a conversion experience, but more likely it was an attempt to escape the vestiges of Judaism, which he consistently criticized. Politically Adler was socialist. He attended rallies and discussion groups in his student days. His first publication, *A Health Book for the Tailor Trade*, in 1898, proposed sweeping social reforms to improve the workers' environment at home and work.

Adler was a lively public speaker who richly sprinkled his lectures with clinical anecdotes. However, his writings suffered because he never mastered the rules of formal scholarship. There were insufficient allusions to knowledge in other disciplines. For this reason, of all the early psychological theorists Freud remained the most remembered and Adler has been the most rediscovered. Since he wrote many books, articles, and pamphlets, the repetition of content is enormous. Two posthumously compiled anthologies (Adler, 1956, 1964) give a sufficient introduction to his writings.

References
Adler, A. *The individual psychology of Alfred Adler.* New York: Basic Books, 1956.
Adler, A. *Superiority and social interest.* Evanston, Ill.: Northwestern University Press, 1964.

Additional Reading
Sperber, M. *Masks of loneliness: Alfred Adler in perspective.* New York: Macmillan, 1974.

T. L. BRINK

Adlerian Psychology. *See* INDIVIDUAL PSYCHOLOGY.

Adlerian Psychotherapy.
"It would not be easy to find another author from which so much has been borrowed from all sides without acknowledgment than Adler" (Ellenberger, 1970, p. 645). Fifty years after Alfred Adler's death present-day thinkers are coming up with ideas similar to Adler's without apparent awareness of his work. Cognitive behavior therapy and rational-emotive therapy view personality and approach psychotherapy much as did Adler, yet have not derived their theories from his body of work. Adlerians regard this as proof that Adler drew his concepts from a well of truth self-evident to any alert student who takes an uncomplicated, commonsense approach to understanding human nature.

Psychology textbooks routinely list Adler as a dissident disciple of Freud. Adler's disciples view his years with Freud (ca. 1902–1911) as a collegial relationship of two genius physicians in search of psychological truth. They attribute the subsequent dominance of Freud's ideas to his more voluminous writing, his greater elegance of expression, and his choice to orient to the intelligentsia of the medical profession. Adler opted instead to popularize his views. He wrote rather loosely organized materials for the lay public and eschewed arcane jargon in favor of commonsense terms.

Theoretical Roots. The primary precursor who shaped Adler's views was the philosopher Vaihinger (1924). Vaihinger taught that none of us can know truth exactly; we all formulate our own approximations of reality, then live by these fictions as if they validly represent the truth. Adler expanded this basic idea into his concept of life style, by which he meant the particular arrangement of convictions each person establishes early in life concerning self, others, and reality (*see* STYLE OF LIFE). Adler emphasized life style as something a person uses rather than something the person possesses. He called it the person's unique law of movement. His view of the uniqueness and holistic cohesiveness of each individual's personality resulted in the term INDIVIDUAL PSYCHOLOGY for his school of thought.

Theory of Psychotherapy. To the Adlerian therapist the primary problem with any person seeking therapy is low social interest. The neurotic preoccupied with striving for glory thus evades the normal tasks of life: love and sexual adjustment, work, and friendship. The primary goal of therapy is to arouse the patient's social interest, or sense of commonality with all fellow humans, who, by the very nature of human limitations, need each other's cooperation in order to live.

Adlerian therapists function as educators. In supportive therapy they identify and build on strengths the client already shows. They encourage the person to use those talents for the benefit of other persons. In more intensive therapy they seek to identify and revise crippling perceptions of self, others, and the world in the client's life style. Since there is no perfect cognitive map for people to follow, the goal of life-style revision is to replace big mistakes with smaller ones.

Process of Psychotherapy. From the first contact Adlerians work to establish a friendly relationship with their clients. They make themselves models to follow in being humorous rather than anxious, unimpressed by their own mistakes rather than perfectionistic, and curious rather than defensive about flaws in thinking or acting. They realize as educators that much of what clients take away with them will be caught rather than taught. Adlerian therapists are seldom sphinx-like and passive; they are usually active and talkative.

Many Adlerians do a formal life-style assessment early in therapy. Part of this assessment focuses on the family constellation in which the person grew up. Adlerians ask more about birth order and sibling relationships than do therapists of most other persuasions, who tend to emphasize parental influences in the person's childhood.

A second aspect of life-style assessment is early recollections, which Adlerians use as a projective technique. Analyzing these much as they do dreams, therapists distill themes that indicate what directions of movement a client considers important vis-à-vis the tasks of life.

Therapists make this assessment an actively therapeutic process. They involve clients thoroughly in refining the final, written life-style formulation. They offer an interpretation and ask, "Does that seem to fit you?" Clients who say, "Yeah, that's me all right," take responsibility for the guidelines they follow in living. In reviewing the life-style assessment findings over the course of one- to three-hour-long therapy sessions, therapists teach that people form their fundamental beliefs about life, themselves, and other persons early in life as they strive to find a place of significance in their families of origin. Thereby therapists set the stage for future repeated references to cognitions and the purpose they serve for the client's felt sense of security and significance.

Adlerian therapists rely largely on interpretations to promote insight. Insight implies that a person grasps some bit of self-knowledge with the zest of an "aha" experience. This energizes behavioral change in the direction of social interest. Ideally an interpretation of a thought or action should illuminate its purpose and dynamic effects as well as the use the client makes of it. Purpose, movement, and use, three central Adlerian constructs, are thus the three criteria for a good interpretation. For example, an interpretation may sound something like this: "You use your tears as water power to arouse sympathy in others, to get them to excuse you from tasks you agreed to take on but at which you don't want to look inadequate. A skill you began using with your mother long ago you still use today even with your own grown children."

The Adlerian typically embeds such an interpretation in good-natured humor and in back-and-forth talk with the client. An interpretation like the above might arise in a group setting in which the therapist comments on a client's here-and-now behavior. One such group setting which Adlerians like involves multiple therapists with one client.

Long before the cognitive behavior therapies flourished in the late 1970s Adlerians directed their clients to do tasks outside of therapy that would change their beliefs, feelings, and habits. They often assigned roles for clients to play: *as if* they were successful, *as if* they were beautiful, or courageous, or happy, or whatever clients said they lacked.

Adler loved paradoxical tactics. He often prescribed that clients do more of some resistant action they were already doing, so that they could continue resisting him only by doing less of the prescribed action. For example, a depressed client who was hardly doing anything more than getting out of bed each day might ask desperately at the end of the first interview, "But Doctor, what can I do till next time?" Adler characteristically might answer, "Don't do anything you don't want to do."

Adler is reported to have said that neurosis, in a word, is vanity. Both he and Karen Horney repeatedly cited the godlike strivings behind the neurotic's vain search for glory. In this they echo biblical views of pride as the central human sin (Gen. 3:5; Isa. 14:14).

Adler saw no basic clash between his views and those of Christian theology. He wrote that individual psychology and religion have things in common, often in thinking, in feeling, in willing, but always with regard to the perfection of mankind (Adler, 1979, p. 281). This quotation comes out of 37 pages of exchange between Adler and a Lutheran clergyman,

Ernst Jahn. Adler agreed heartily with Christian teachings that we must love our neighbors as ourselves. His concept of social interest was the bedrock of his own humanistic rather than theistic faith.

References
Adler, A. *Superiority and social interest: A collection of later writings* (3rd ed.) (H. L. Ansbacher & R. W. Ansbacher, Eds.). New York: Norton, 1979.
Ellenberger, H. F. *The discovery of the unconscious.* New York: Basic Books, 1970.
Vaihinger, H. *The philosophy of "as if."* New York: Harcourt, Brace, 1924.

Additional Readings
Adler, A. *The practice and theory of individual psychology.* New York: Harcourt, Brace, 1924.
Mosak, H. H. Adlerian psychotherapy. In R. J. Corsini (Ed.), *Current psychotherapies* (2nd ed.). Itasca, Ill. Peacock Publishers, 1979.

D. L. GIBSON

Adolescence. While adolescence may be defined as beginning with the onset of pubescence, its character and tasks are primarily psychosocial in nature and extend until the arrival at full adult status and responsibility. Biologically triggered and socially terminated, the period of adolescence is therefore a flexible time span contingent upon 1) initiatives made by the emerging adult as to how quickly or late full adult responsibilities will be grasped, and/or 2) initiatives permitted by the immediate family and social matrix for such grasping of adult status and responsibility, and/or 3) social, civil, and legal definitions and regulations which govern the transition from "minor" to "major" status and responsibility.

Stone Age cultures tend to move the child to adult status in a rite of passage which coincides with or actually precedes arrival at the sexual maturity denoted by puberty. Technological cultures tend to delay the granting of employment, establishment of marriage, and full adult status until the mid-20s. Complicate any of the above by economic depression or military rule and the age may be delayed into the 30s. In such situations males are prevented from taking adult status, but females are more likely to marry and to bear children in union with older males. Since girls arrive at puberty more than a year earlier than males, peer marriages are uncommon in most of human history. Economic depression or military intervention delays marriage primarily for males, and a similar pattern of nonpeer marriage occurs. As older males dip into the pool of younger females even for second marriages, fewer peer marriages are possible even for those who prefer to marry the high school sweetheart.

In this discussion it will be important to identify the three stages of adolescence common in the Western and especially the North American environment. This will be followed by a discussion of a series of adolescent tasks and some common complications which face adolescents in their journey through these tasks.

Early Adolescence. We can equate the junior high school years as roughly equivalent to this developmental period. In 1980 the mean age for arrival at first menarche (menstrual period) was 12.2. Males tend to arrive at first ejaculation a little more than one year later, on the average. This means that the average female arrives at first menarche during the sixth grade of public school, while the average male would achieve first ejaculation near the end of seventh or in the early eighth grade. (For physiological changes accompanying puberty *see* PUBESCENCE.)

The primary task facing the early adolescent is coping with physiological changes. Hormonal changes in the body tend to complicate problems with the skin and complexion. Some studies show as high as 80% of males and females worry about pimples and other skin problems. Early arrival at pubescence tends to enhance a boy's self-image, but it has been shown to be a disadvantage to a girl. Early-maturing girls tend to register as lacking in poise, being submissive, even listless, and are frequently rejected by their female peers (Jones, 1963). The boy who matures slowly is under the most severe social disadvantage. The early-maturing girl may be fully developed sexually and physiologically by 9 or 10, while the late-maturing boy may lag behind at age 15 or 16. Unless the late maturing boy adapts socially to make friendships with much younger pseudo peers, he may have to pay high prices for winning the approval of his age mates and may be into a life-long pattern of such accommodation.

Middle Adolescence. We can equate the senior high school years with middle adolescence. In the more rural parts of North America adult status and privileges come close on the heels of the high school diploma, a sort of rite of passage for Americans who live close to the soil. As is historically established, this is more likely for females than for males; it is more common with males only when economic and military conditions are supportive of early establishment in vocation for the male.

Signals of arriving at adult status which strike during the senior high school years include being licensed to drive an automobile, registering for the draft, and arriving (in some states) at voting age. Many will seek part-time employment at age 16 and a few will have jobs during the senior year as a part of vocational training.

The most critical task facing the middle adolescent is the synchronizing of sexual potency, affectional feelings, self-image, and full responsibility for the self in both public and private behavior. These are basic components within the so-called identity crisis, and unless they are positively synchronized, the intimacy crisis of later development will tend to be flawed by unfinished business from the middle adolescent years. None of these components can be adequately handled unless the adolescent has a clear sense of personal history, or roots, and the beginning of a sense of destiny, or life vision. If these two polarities are forming in a positive way, the self-image tends to begin to flourish and integrity in behavior begins to develop.

Recent experiments with making birth control and abortion easily accessible to high school students may be depriving them of an essential component in arriving at a healthy self-identity. These social interventions are electives chosen by adults for their children as alternatives to dealing with the pressing demands of the young for intimacy and release from the pressures of culturally contrived extended adolescence. In some other cultures families take more responsibility for the intimacy needs of their young and help the adolescent manage these needs through a timetable negotiated between parents and children. It is for this reason that the Old Testament dictates nothing about sexual intimacy between young lovers; families handled such matters. But the Old Testament exacts extreme penalties for rape and against sexual predators. To the extent that Christians demand late marriage for their young, they are likely rejecting the Judeo-Christian way of dealing with the intimacy needs and adult status needs of youth and are endorsing a pagan American experiment. That experiment says, in effect: "You may not consummate your love in marriage, so we will look the other way. Don't get pregnant/Don't get anybody pregnant. Come back when you are 25 and we'll get you a job and then you can get married."

A sensitively Christian family approach might sound far different: "We are glad that you are dating. Let us help you keep it cool so that you don't get to sexual intimacy before the wedding night. We want to 'get you to the church on time.' So we are on your side. Keep your relationship always developing before public eyes; avoid absolute privacy whether in the car or anybody's house, apartment, or room. And let us know when you sense that you are nearing the point of no return, that you expect to be together for the rest of your lives, and we'll help you plan the wedding date to match the stage of your relationship." Launching a marriage or a new family is always the responsibility of the parents. It is important that economic assistance be regarded as a present sharing of the family's resources, not as monetary manipulation of the decisions and behavior of the young. Delayed marriage beyond the early adult transition period of 17 to 23 assumes a higher priority on vocation than on integrity in sexual intimacy, and often presumes the sacrifice of chastity and virginity in that exchange.

Late Adolescence. This period is usually associated with the college years, or approximately 17–22. A final marker for males having completed sexual development is the appearance of pigmented hair in the ears and nostrils, commonly around age 25. By this time many males tend also to begin hormonally related male pattern baldness—receding hairline or thinning top hair. Testosterone is produced not only in the testicles but also in the epidermis, especially of the scalp. But the major features of the late adolescence agenda are psychosocial.

According to some studies middle adolescent girls are more likely to have had sexual intercourse experience than are males. But once out of high school, socially active males without an anchor point in their identity and values tend to be highly susceptible to sexual intercourse with female partners. This frequent investment of sexual energy and appetite in intercourse during the late adolescent years tends to detour the male's identity work into experimentation with pseudo intimacy, resulting in serious negative effects on both his sense of identity and his capacity for intimacy. Females who begin early with intercourse and who continue through late adolescence with intercourse outside of marriage tend to even more seriously impair their capacity for lifelong monogamous intimacy. Yet males and females at this stage find themselves in a culturally charged pressure cooker which pushes them toward sexual intercourse without the option of consummating a relationship in marriage.

Erikson's (1950) caution that frustrated or deformed intimacy leads to isolation signals a major pathology of our time. The rising specter of single housing and of live-in partners who are unmarried and of homosexual couples in a parade of changing partners are all signals of actual isolation. Isolation is characterized by the inability to take full responsibility for oneself and another person. It is rooted in Erikson's previous negative task resolutions of role diffusion, inferiority, guilt, shame, and mistrust. Given the feelings of economic dependency, of vocational confusion, and of fears of nuclear war, it is not uncommon that late adolescence is extending beyond age 40 for many, who then, faced with their own mortality, often retreat in their isolation into depression and despair.

Satellization and Identity. Ausubel (1954) traces the movement toward adult maturity as beginning with "satellization" in early childhood. This refers to the attachment through identification that characterizes healthy psychological functioning in this period. The child has limited or nonexistent consciousness of being a self separate from his or her mother or the family. Young children who fail to have these intimate bonds with parents tend, according to Ausubel, to become troubled adolescents, in trouble with civil authority and often incarcerated as adults. The well-satellized child, however, moves during adolescence to a necessary desatellization phase during which an identity separate and distinct from parents is established. Often this requires the use of parent surrogates. The adolescent tends to temporarily identify with, imitate, and invest time in relationships with admired adults who are often younger than his or her parents. This phase of identity development finds the adolescent experimenting with modified values and life styles exhibited in the admired temporary parent surrogates. These models are most often found in the schools, churches, and other highly visible places. Musicians, coaches, youth ministers, and Sunday school teachers are among the most common models. Ausubel notes that most adolescents resatellize as they assume full adult status and responsibilities; they tend to return to a value base and life style that have a high degree of consistency with the original parent-child satellization period.

Effects of Divorce. Adolescence is a particularly vulnerable time to experience parental stress, separation, and divorce. The aftereffects tend to persist in subtle ways throughout adulthood (Rubenstein, 1980). Children of divorce are more prone toward marital problems in their own marriages, males tending to be less involved in fathering behaviors toward their own children and females tending to be more heavily involved in parenting behaviors, perhaps anticipating the possibility of having to do the parenting alone. Children of divorce are measured as more lonely as adults. They also have lower self-esteem, and the lowest scores come from those whose parents divorced when the child was very young. Children of divorce, as adults, are more likely to experience crying spells, insomnia, constant worry, feelings of guilt, worthlessness, and despair. They are more anxious, afraid, and angry, and are highly prone toward separation anxiety.

In extensive studies (Parish, Dostal, & Parish, 1981) it has been established that both male and female children attach negative ratings to remarriage families. Male children, but not females, who find themselves in an "unhappy divorced family" tend to evaluate themselves very poorly—more so than children from intact or remarried families. Males are specifically more negative in their evaluations of their fathers than are females. Evaluations of the mother are correlated with whether the present family circumstances have improved or worsened. Lowest self-esteem for all conditions is found in boys whose mothers' fortunes improved following the divorce, suggesting that the boy's value of himself as a male is seriously lessened by what he perceives to have been negative effects of his natural father's behavior and presence. (*See* DIVORCE and CHILD CUSTODY for further discussion of this area.)

Effects of Father Absence. For many adolescents divorce and father absence are virtually synonymous. Early studies on the effects of father absence were triggered by high verbal scores and low numerical scores among entering males at Ivy League universities following World War II. Only much later was it discovered that father absence was the cause that correlated with these differing effects. It is during adolescence that many of the predictable effects become visible, but research indicates that the earlier the father was removed from the family, the more pronounced the effects are likely to be. Hetherington and Deur (1971) provide a good summary of this research.

Father-absent boys tend to be more impulsive, less under self-control, and less able to delay gratification than are father-present boys. They are more likely to be convicted of crimes, to be homosexual in preference, and to be exploitive of females. Father-absent boys at adolescence tend to adopt exaggerated and macho male behaviors, mere caricatures of healthy masculinity. Father-presence, on the other hand, tends to foster gentleness, high investment in parenting behaviors, and more positively masculine behaviors, with little tendency toward criminal or delinquent behavior. It remains true that father-absent boys do, in fact, score higher on verbal tests and lower on numerical tests at college entrance.

Father-absent girls, on the other hand, tend to cluster in two groups. One syndrome appears to be more frequent when the father separation was caused by death: severe sexual anxiety, shyness, and discomfort around males. The second syndrome seems more correlated with father-absence caused by desertion and divorce: inappropriately assertive behavior toward male peers and adult males, and sexual promiscuity. Girls without fathers have missed the interaction time and have not developed skills for coping with and interacting with males. The unique combination of security in knowing her father's goodwill and of receiving feedback from him regarding her acceptability as a woman evidently establishes an adolescent girl with positive self-regard and with the skills necessary to relate appropriately to male peers. Beyond this, her father's goodwill and admiration provide her with an assurance that he will be her advocate and will demand high accountability from her male peers for their care of her (See FATHERING).

Effects of Family Cohesiveness. Set over against effects of divorce and father-absence is a further predictable set of outcomes. Glueck and Glueck (1950) attempted to unravel potential causes of juvenile delinquency by studying 500 persistently delinquent boys and 500 nondelinquents who were matched by age, intelligence, ethnic derivation, and neighborhood conditions. They used five prediction factors developed from analysis of the 1,000 boys: 1) discipline of the boy by his father, 2) supervision of the boy by his mother, 3) affection of father for the boy, 4) affection of mother for the boy, and 5) cohesiveness of the family. While replications of the Gluecks' work have used as few as three of the factors, cohesiveness of the family stands as the highest single predictor of juvenile delinquency, 96.9% of boys from unintegrated family patterns of relating being delinquent. The elements of integration were such things as at least one meal each day taken together, family vacations together, the presence of family rituals, and the celebration of birthdays and holidays as a family group.

Response to Faith. While most Judeo-Christian groups process their children into adult status through prepubescent or early adolescent rituals, the changes of middle adolescence demand a faith transformation if faith is to be owned in a personal and voluntary way. These early rites of passage include such things as bar mitzvah, believer's baptism, going forward to be saved, and confirmation.

Given the physiological changes of pubescence, the susceptibility to surrogate parent models outside the home, and the urgency of the identity and intimacy agendas of the middle and late adolescent, responses to faith during these years are often pivotal (See FAITH). The autonomy of faith responses during adolescence is given its privacy and its power by the awakening of sexual pleasure and by the sense of responsibility for managing sexual energy with integrity. The high demand for privacy during middle adolescence and beyond often gives parents a sense of being abandoned by their children. Staffing of youth programs is most effective when parents are not included, since youth of 13 to 25 have high needs for alternative parent models. If these are available and are trustworthy, they will serve as confidential mentors to the highly valued young, and the value base of the next generation is more likely secured.

References

Ausubel, D. P. *Theory and problems of adolescent development.* New York: Grune & Stratton, 1954.
Erikson, E. H. *Childhood and society.* New York: Norton, 1950.
Glueck, S., & Glueck, E. *Unravelling juvenile delinquency.* New York: Commonwealth Fund, 1950.
Hetherington, E. M., & Deur, J. L. The effects of father absence on child development. *Young Children,* 1971, *25*(4), 233–246.
Jones, M. C. Self-conceptions, motivations and interpersonal attitudes of early- and late-maturing girls. In R. E. Grinder (Ed.), *Studies in adolescence.* New York: Macmillan, 1963.
Parish, T. S., Dostal, J. W., & Parish, J. G. Evaluations of self and parents as a function of intactness of family and family happiness. *Adolescence,* 1981, *16*, 203–210.
Rubenstein, C. The children of divorce as adults. *Psychology Today,* 1980, *13*(8), 74–75.

Additional Reading

McCandless, B. R. *Adolescents: Behavior and development.* Hinsdale, Ill.: Dryden Press, 1970.

D. M. Joy

See LIFE SPAN DEVELOPMENT; PSYCHOSEXUAL DEVELOPMENT; PSYCHOSOCIAL DEVELOPMENT.

Adolescent Therapy. With the recent advances in biological psychiatry there are exciting changes occurring in the treatment of the adolescent patient. Some of these findings challenge long-standing theoretical concepts of certain aspects of psychopathology and, consequently, the treatment of the adolescent with these clinical pictures.

One of these advances is the development of the Dexamethasone Suppression Test (DST), which is proving to be of great benefit in the identification of depression in children and adolescents (Poznanski, Carroll, Banegas, Cook, & Grossman, 1982). It is difficult to make the diagnosis of depression in adolescents on a clinical basis, since the behavior which they utilize to cope with their depression often masks the depression itself. Traditionally these patients have been treated with psychotherapy and/or behavioral therapy. Current data derived from use of the DST suggest that these patients should be treated with antidepressants concomitantly with psychological therapies.

Another biological advance is a clearer delineation of panic disorders (Sheehan, 1982). The new findings indicate that panic disorders may manifest first by a clinical picture previously called separation anxiety or school phobia. These clinical syndromes were perceived as purely psychological phenomena and classified as a neurosis. The new data suggest that this may be a distinct biological syndrome with phobias as a by-product. The studies also suggest that the best treatment is not psychotherapy, which has been utilized in the past with minimal benefits. Rather, the recommended treatment is specific antidepressant medications.

These illustrations support the need for a comprehensive evaluation prior to beginning any treatment. The essential components of this evaluation include a developmental and family history as well as a history of the present problem. From a biological perspective what is needed is a physical examination, a mental status examination, and biological tests such as the DST and other endocrine tests. The third component of the evaluation is psychological testing. Which tests are to be utilized depends on the nature of the problem.

Treatment of the adolescent ideally should be conducted within a multidisciplinary framework. At best this is carried out by a team that has representatives from the medical, social, and psychological disciplines. Fragmentation must be avoided. If all components are not addressed, the results will be inadequate. If each component is addressed in isolation, one representative may work against another or a situation may exist in which the adolescent can manipulate one against the other. There must be close collaboration between all members of the treatment team, with one member serving as the primary therapist

whose responsibility is to orchestrate the therapeutic input of the team members. The team members need not all be from the same agency. For example, the biological input may be from the adolescent's family physician, while much of the social input, as well as psychological evaluations, can come from school personnel—teacher, school social worker, and school psychologist. Often if an adolescent comes for therapy, another member of the family has been or is being seen by another social agency. Here it is important to have a collaborative relationship with this agency.

A variety of treatment modalities are available in the treatment of the adolescent. No one of these needs to be used in isolation, nor is one invariably the preferred treatment. Rather, the multidisciplinary team generally utilizes a combination of treatment modalities under close coordination of the primary therapist. The most common treatment modalities are behavioral, biological, social, and psychotherapy. This article will focus on psychotherapy with adolescents.

Therapist qualifications. Work with adolescents requires somewhat different qualifications from those required for work with adults, since most adolescents do not come to therapy of their own accord. Rather, they are coerced by the family, the schools, or the court. A second reason for this difference lies in the dynamics of the adolescent. Generally adolescents are in a state of strong ambivalence between dependence and independence, and this conflict is closely linked with their self-esteem. This often makes the therapeutic relation difficult to establish and accounts for the powerful transference and countertransference features encountered in treatment.

The therapist must be able to develop a warm, friendly relationship in which good rapport is established as soon as possible. He or she must also be able to accept the adolescent as he is. It is also important that the therapist be able to establish a feeling of permissiveness in the relationship so the adolescent feels free to express his feelings. Additionally, the therapist must be alert to feelings and be able to reflect them in such a manner that insight is gained. The therapist must also maintain respect for the ability the adolescent has for solving his own problems if given the opportunity. Consequently, adolescents must be helped to realize that it is their responsibility to institute changes and not that of the therapist. Finally, the therapist must be able to assist adolescents in setting limits, in order to anchor the therapy to the world of reality, and to make adolescents aware of their responsibility in the relationship as well as responsibility for all their behavior.

Short-Term Therapy. Most psychotherapy with adolescents is relatively brief, either by design or because of premature termination. However, brief therapy is often both successful and the treatment of choice due to the nature of adolescence and the types of problems which lead adolescents to seek help. Adolescence is a time of rapid growth and maturation; consequently, much of the behavior patterns of this period are not a fixed part of their personality. This makes adolescent problems more adaptable to change, often rather rapid change.

One form of brief psychotherapy frequently utilized is advice and provision of an organizational framework. This consists of assessing the problem and providing concrete advice, especially to the family. The approach enables the patient and family to place an ill-defined vagueness about what is wrong into a well-formulated problem with structure, which enables them to find their own solution to the problem. It not only assists the family in coping with the present problem and making appropriate resolutions, but it also helps mobilize them to cope with subsequent problems in an adapted fashion that leads to positive resolution. The approach is most effective when it enables the family's current anxieties and preoccupations to be placed in a relevant conceptual framework, where they are able to see their own positive qualities that will assist them in successfully coping with the stress. This approach is most successful when dealing with an adolescent showing a healthy response to a self-limiting problem but where, due to misjudgment on the part of the family, a self-perpetuating state of anxiety appears to be established with the prospect of a prolonged disturbance from which the family cannot extricate themselves.

This approach accomplishes two therapeutic tasks. First, through the family assessment process the family members are able to hear each other out and ventilate their feelings, consequently altering their communication network. Second, it assures the family that the behavior of the adolescent is a variation of normality and can be self-limiting, provided that the family's anxieties do not perpetuate it.

The second brief psychotherapeutic approach is crisis intervention, which represents an intermediate approach between advice and the provision of structure and insight-oriented psychotherapy. Crises usually arise when persons are confronted by important life problems from which they cannot escape and which they cannot solve in their usual coping manner. The cause of the crisis can be internal (i.e., physiological or psychological) or it can be environmental. Adolescents' crises generally are not as dramatic as those of adults; therefore, agencies tend not to be as responsive. During crisis adolescents tend to reach out more readily and are much more easily influenced; consequently it is a good time to make a significant impact. The timing is important. It is during the second phase of a crisis—i.e., during the time of increasing tension and disorganization—that an individual is most susceptible to seeking help and making changes.

Crisis intervention is reality-based and focuses on the here and now, utilizing new problem-solving techniques to bring about resolution. In crisis intervention one does not seek insights into the how or why of the problem but rather focuses on mechanisms for surmounting the difficulties. It is important to provide a supporting environment that aids in problem resolution or a structure that allows decisions to be made.

Medication and hospitalization should never be utilized as a solution to a problem but rather as a means to assist in mobilization of inner resources. The danger is that these treatments may actually postpone problem solving or lead to premature closure. However, either one must be used, when necessary, in order to protect the individual, the family, the social agency, or the therapist, or when it provides the necessary means to mobilize inner resources.

Long-Term Therapy. Long-term insight-oriented psychotherapy should be utilized only by experienced therapists who have a comprehensive knowledge of both psychodynamics and normal growth and development. It is utilized with adolescents who have experienced long-term problems. It must be understood that the insight produced through this approach is not necessarily curative. However, it does frequently alleviate stress and misery and often serves to establish continuity and a sense of order in the individual's life. Ideally the insight gained from such an experience will also bring mastery of the problems the adolescent is experiencing. Some of the common goals in long-term psychotherapy include the achievement of age-appropriate maturation, improved object relationships, improved capacity to tolerate frustration, improvement of reality testing, a modification of defenses and reduction of anxiety, removal of fixations, and the recovery of repressed memories.

There are certain components of long-term psychotherapy that are common to all such therapies regardless of theoretical orientation. These include concern, the provision of a stress-surmounting structure, the provision of a corrective emotional experience, interpretation, and limit setting.

Concern enables the therapist to maintain an interest in the adolescent until the adolescent acquires insight which allows therapeutic intervention. It permits intimacy without being intrusive. It permits the therapist to be accepting and respectful of the adolescent, yet still free to state his or her own views.

The provision of a stress-surmounting structure involves the establishment of an environment that is safe for both the therapist and the adolescent. The therapist is responsible for providing the language and concepts for the adolescent to use, as well as the interpretation, confrontations, and necessary controls. Much of the adolescent's anxiety regarding psychotherapy can be relieved by having a comprehensive understanding of the rules of the game.

Provision of a corrective emotional experience can best be accomplished by assisting the adolescent in disentangling his feelings and helping him to understand them. This is especially true with respect to his ambivalence toward significant adults in his life. Often the best timing for addressing these issues is when the therapist experiences similar reactions of the adolescent toward the therapist.

The goal of interpretation is insight and the learning of new, more adaptive ways of coping with anxiety and conflicts. The therapist must be aware of the patient's anxiety and of his general coping mechanisms, as well as the quality of his object relations. The communication of the interpretations must be in language that is meaningful to the adolescent; it must be given in an acceptable dose so that it does not precipitate more anxiety than is necessary to facilitate the patient in developing his own solution. Interpretations of transference should be made very cautiously with adolescents.

It is of utmost importance for the therapist working with adolescents to set limits through controls and confrontations. Many inexperienced therapists want someone else to set the controls and let them do the therapy, since they want to maintain emotional rapport with the patient. However, this is always counterproductive. Setting of limits assists in ego development by inhibiting direct primitive expression of aggression. Also, during the session, if limits are not set, the therapist may be preoccupied with self-defense rather than with conducting therapy. A passive, nondirective approach by the therapist ultimately leads to treatment failure. Limit-setting does not imply rejection of the adolescent but rather, rejection of the deed along with expectations of the adolescent.

All long-term therapy is a learning experience. This is facilitated by three factors. First, learning through conditioning takes place by means of the repetitive working through of material. Second, the patient develops an awareness of the connection between motivation and behavior, diminishing the gap that exists between one's emotional and intellectual life. Third, and most important, is that learning occurs by the adolescent identifying with the psychotherapist.

References
Poznanski, E. O., Carroll, B. J., Banegas, M. C., Cook, S. C., & Grossman, J. A. The dexamethasone suppression test in prepubertal depressed children. *American Journal of Psychiatry*, 1982, *139*, 321–324.
Sheehan, D. V. Panic attacks and phobias. *The New England Journal of Medicine*, 1982, *307*, 156–158.

Additional Readings
Evans, J. *Adolescent and pre-adolescent psychiatry*. New York: Grune & Stratton, 1982.
Holmes, D. J. *The adolescent in psychotherapy*. Boston: Little, Brown, 1964.
Malmquist, C. P. *Handbook of adolescence*. New York: Aronson, 1978.
Meeks, J. E. *The fragile alliance: An orientation to the outpatient psychotherapy of the adolescent* (2nd ed.). Huntington, N.Y.: Krieger, 1980.

F. WESTENDORP

Aerophagia. An excessive swallowing of air, observed in the hyperventilation syndrome, which produces an expanded abdomen and rapid-breathing attacks. Literally "air-eating," aerophagia may be associated with unconscious conflicts or desires, such as a pregnancy wish in women or cannibalistic impulses.

Affect. A term often used loosely as a synonym for feeling, emotion, or mood. A more precise definition places affect closest to feeling, additionally requiring, however, that the feeling state be observable. It should be distinguished from mood, which is a more pervasive and often longer-lasting state. Common examples of affect are anger, sadness, and joy.

In describing an individual's affective functioning, clinicians frequently employ the dimensions of range, stability, and appropriateness. The range of affects experienced may be either broad or constricted. Although there is considerable variability between people, normal affective functioning usually involves the expression of a range of affects with variability in facial expression, voice quality, and body movements. Restrictions of this may show in terms of either a limited range of affects experienced or a reduction in the intensity of their expression. The stability of an individual's affects describes the persistence of affective states. Affect is labile when it is characterized by rapid and abrupt changes. The appropriateness of affect describes the concordance between the individual's speech or thoughts and the affect.

D. G. BENNER

See EMOTION.

Affective Disorders. The essential feature of this group of disorders is a disturbance of mood. When mood is understood to be a more pervasive and longer-lasting emotional state than AFFECT, it is clear that the term *mood disorders* would be a more exact designation. The term *affective disorders* has, however, been most commonly used and is the term adopted by *DSM-III*.

In this most current diagnostic classification system six disorders are included: BIPOLAR DISORDER, major depression (*see* DEPRESSION: CLINICAL PICTURE AND CLASSIFICATION), CYCLOTHYMIC DISORDER, DYSTHYMIC DISORDER, atypical bipolar disorder, and atypical depression. Manic disorder is not included in this classification but is now a subclassification of bipolar disorder.

D. G. BENNER

Affiliation, Need for. Research clearly indicates that human beings have a pervasive tendency to seek out the company of others. The need to associate and interact with other people is perhaps most evident in reactions to isolation. After reviewing the anecdotal accounts of those alone at sea or locked in solitary confinement, Schachter (1959) concluded that "one of the consequences of isolation appears to be a psychological state which in its extreme form resembles a full-blown anxiety attack" (p. 12). Feelings of anxiety are often followed by apathy and extreme withdrawal, with prolonged isolation even producing hallucinations in some people.

While some psychologists have suggested an innate basis for the affiliative tendency, others have regarded it as a learned need. According to this view infants may come to associate other persons, particularly their parents, with the satisfaction of basic needs for food, warmth, and security. As a result of these repeated pairings most children learn to seek out the company of others. Presumably when others have not been a source of pleasure in early life, the child may develop as a loner who prefers to engage in relatively solitary activity.

Individual differences in the need to affiliate are evident from both anecdotal accounts and laboratory studies. In an attempt to understand more fully the need to affiliate, Schachter (1959) paid student volunteers $10 a day to remain alone in a locked, windowless room. Of the five male subjects who participated, one reported a strong desire to leave after 20 minutes. Of the three who remained in their rooms for two days, one said that he had become uneasy and would not repeat the experience, while the other two appeared relatively unaffected by the isolation. The fifth student, who remained alone for eight days, admitted that he had grown uneasy, but no lasting effects of the isolation were evident. Very likely the short period of social deprivation as well as the students' knowledge that they could terminate the experience at any time played a role in their relatively mild reactions to isolation.

Several attempts have been made to measure individual differences in the need to affiliate. The concept was included in Murray's (1938) list of motives and, like the need for achievement, has been measured with the Thematic Apperception Test. More recently Mehrabian (1970) designed a scale consisting of 31 statements to assess the need for affiliation. Research on individual differences in affiliation need has indicated that interpersonal behavior may vary as a function of the strength of the motive. Not only are those high in this need more likely to initiate conversation and to attempt to establish friendships, but they also seem to have a greater desire to be accepted and liked by others.

Situational factors also influence the desire to affiliate. In a series of classic experiments Schachter (1959) tested the hypothesis that fear may be an important determinant of affiliation. Female subjects were led to believe that after a ten-minute delay, in which the necessary equipment would be set up, they would receive either painful electric shocks or mild, virtually painless stimulation. Each subject was then allowed to choose whether she wanted to wait alone or with some of the other subjects. In the low-fear condition only one-third of the women desired to wait with others, while in the high-fear condition two-thirds of the women preferred to wait with others. Other research has confirmed that fear increases the desire to affiliate.

One explanation for why stressful situations increase the affiliative tendency is that people in these situations may be uncertain of their reactions and want to compare their experiences with those of others in an attempt to reduce anxiety. An alternative explanation has been that others simply serve as a distraction. Schachter found that fearful people had no desire to wait with others unless the others also expected to receive shock. These results indicate that mere distraction does not explain the link between fear and the desire to affiliate. Support for the social comparison hypothesis is also found in another study in which, relative to control groups, subjects anticipating electric shock spent more time interacting and discussing the frightening experience.

The positive relationship between fear and affiliation holds true primarily for firstborns and only children. Such children have likely had the undivided attention of their parents, who offered comfort in times of difficulty. Thus they continue to seek out others when they are afraid. In contrast later-born children have had more competition for their parents' attention and perhaps siblings who were not particularly sympathetic to their distress.

References

Mehrabian, A. The development and validation of measures of affiliative tendency and sensitivity to rejection. *Educational and Psychological Measurement*, 1970, *30*, 417–428.

Murray, H. A. *Explorations in personality.* New York: Oxford University Press, 1938.

Schachter, S. *The psychology of affiliation.* Stanford, Calif.: Stanford University Press, 1959.

M. Bolt

Aggression. The first recorded incident of aggression in the Bible is Cain's murder of Abel (Gen. 4). Since then violence and aggression have been significant social problems. Although there is some disagreement among authorities on the nature of aggression, the dominant social psychological analysis focuses on the intent to harm another. When viewed in this way, aggression is closely akin to violence, where violence is conceived as the deliberate attempt to seriously injure another person. Understanding the origins and consequences of aggression becomes important in solving social problems of violent crimes (e.g., assault, homicide, rape), racial hostilities, family discord, and war.

Three threads run through the definition of aggression as intent to inflict injury on another.

First, the intention may originate from emotional arousal, particularly negative responses like anger and frustration. Second, the person's intention constitutes the motivational component. Third, if the instigation is sufficiently intense, and if the situation permits, the motivational element is enacted in behavior which delivers an unpleasant stimulus to the other individual. The primary target is the person who originally induced the negative emotion. The injury may be physical (e.g., slap) or psychological (e.g., sarcasm, innuendo) in nature.

Intrapersonal Origins. For convenience' sake the origins of aggression may be considered as lying in innate or personal factors or as deriving from some aspect of social interaction. In his theoretical writings of the 1920s Sigmund Freud sought to understand the atrocities of the First World War. He concluded that humans are driven by two instincts: eros (the drive to life) and thanatos (the drive toward death). Eros was manifested in the pleasure principle and actions geared toward self-preservation. Thanatos spoke of the constant march toward death and involved the death wish and aggression. Aggression was a "turned around" death wish. To Freud a significant part of socialization was given over to displacing or sublimating the death wish and aggression.

A second approach that considers aggression as an innate instinct is the ethological and evolutionary theory of Konrad Lorenz (1966). Intraspecies aggression and fighting serve to distribute the species over a greater territory. Greater territory provides greater resources with which to ensure the survival of the species. Furthermore, it ensures that only the strongest will mate. Interspecies aggression is merely an example of predation or defense. These findings were then applied to humans. This particular approach has been popularized by Desmond Morris (1967). However, the anthropologist Ashley Montagu (1976) critiqued the scientific data available and concluded that there is little evidence for aggression being an instinct in humans, a view most behavioral scientists share.

A third theory of intrapersonal origins has a hedonistic base. The psychologists Dollard and Miller developed the frustration-aggression hypothesis (Dollard, Miller, Doob, Mowrer, & Sears, 1939). In their original view frustration always led to aggression; aggression always resulted from frustration. The relationship between the two was linear. Frustration was understood as a blocked goal response, and aggression as intended harm. This restrictive view was later modified to suggest that frustration leads to the instigation of aggression rather than overt acts per se. The effects of frustration were strongest when the individual was attacked rather than the goal blocked, when the frustration was unexpected and arbitrary, when aggressive stimuli were present in the environment, or when the aggression might be positively reinforced.

An interesting derivative of this approach was the catharsis hypothesis. Acting out one's aggression "cleansed" one of the accumulated aggressive instigation. It was also suggested that vicarious participation in aggression (e.g., watching aggression on TV) lessened subsequent aggressive action. Experimental findings on these suggestions have been mixed and inconsistent (Middlebrook, 1980).

Interpersonal Origins. Modification of the frustration-aggression hypothesis suggested that certain environmental cues facilitate aggression. Berkowitz (1962) theorized that individuals are conditioned to act aggressively in the presence of specific environmental cues. Classical conditioning was believed to be responsible for teaching aggressive responses. This conditioning occurs in a social context as symbols for aggression are communicated from individual to individual. In Berkowitz's view certain symbols (e.g., weapons) trigger aggression. In a classic study Berkowitz and LePage (1967) demonstrated that the presence of a gun increased the level of aggressiveness.

An alternate view was developed by Bandura (1973). According to his social learning theory, two separate aspects of learning affect the production of aggression. Aggression, like most complicated behaviors, is first learned by imitation. Whether this learning leads to aggressive action depends upon the anticipated consequences. Vicarious reinforcement of aggression leads to aggression in the imitators; vicarious punishment for aggression suppresses aggression in imitators.

The importance of the Berkowitz and Bandura perspectives is that not only does aggression have interpersonal and social consequences (i.e., injury to another human), but it has interpersonal and social origins as well. Aggression is communicated and taught in the process of socialization, especially when the prevailing sex role equates maleness and aggressiveness.

Other psychological observations strengthen this view. In certain segments of society aggression and violence operate as a subcultural norm (e.g., specific military units, professional hockey, juvenile gangs). Manifestation of aggressive norms are especially likely under intense economic competition for limited resources. This economic competition hypothesis predicts aggression is probable to the extent that the rival group is seen as a hostile, dissimilar outgroup and to the extent that resources are limited and unjustly distributed (e.g., strikes, wars). This may be further accentuated if there is a reduction in the restraining forces against aggression (e.g., anonymity as a factor in looting, or shared guilt in the passing around of a murder weapon by members of the Ku Klux Klan). However, it must be recognized that within the individual members there normally would exist frustration and emotional arousal as personal instigating forces.

These approaches do not provide an altogether adequate explanation for violence as a transaction, as in cases of domestic violence and abuse or war. According to Toch (1969) aggression is a predictable series of events. One member of a dyad is provoked and confronts the other person. The other reacts through defense and counterattack. Then the argument escalates to issues other than the original provocation. If the confrontation-escalation sequence is not halted, the original verbal dispute may result in physical attack. The provocation-confrontation-escalation view provides insight into the origins and dynamics of domestic disputes and international incidents of an ideological nature.

Social and Clinical Syndromes. There is considerable evidence that males in Western cultures are socialized to be aggressive through sex-typing mechanisms of imitation, identification, and reinforcement (Maccoby and Jacklin, 1974). However, recent studies suggest that genetic factors may also contribute to male aggressiveness. It has been hypothesized that aggression may be linked in some fashion to the Y chromosome. Especially important are the studies of chromosomal abnormalities. One of the chromosomal aberrations found in males is the existence of an additional Y chromosome, making the genotype XYY. Several studies have found that the incidence of XYY males is greater in prison populations than in the population at large. The XYY inmates are more likely to be charged with violent crimes against persons than with property crimes like burglary and forgery.

Disturbances involving aggression characterize both the personality that is undercontrolled and the one that is overcontrolled. In the undercontrolled personality inhibitions against aggression are weak, so that the individual typically reacts impulsively when slightly angered or disturbed. Aggression in the undercontrolled is no surprise. But when the silent, introverted individual erupts in a violent display of anger, everyone is horrified and questions how it happened. Megargee (1966) suggested that in this overcontrolled individual the expression of emotion is normally inhibited. The person stores up aggression over a long period of time. Then at some point the normal inhibitory brake fails and the individual explodes in a sudden violent outburst. The outburst is often out of proportion to the triggering event. In both types of personality the ability to handle aggression-arousing emotions in socially acceptable ways has never been learned.

Another clinical hypothesis can be advanced. Horney (1937) asserted that personality is motivated by hostility and anxiety. Hostility stems from a sense of injustice and unfairness in life. It seems that the connection between hostility and injustice is particularly acute in males. This is likely to be exacerbated if in the socialization of the male he is not able to differentiate between the various negative emotions: frustration, fear, anger, anxiety, etc. Anger and hostility become the undifferentiated response to any situation that arouses an unpleasant or negative emotional state. This seems likely in cultures and family units where males are expected not to cry and where the discipline styles are punitive and authoritarian.

In summary, aggression is a perverse and pervasive phenomenon covering a wide gamut, from indirect expression in racial jokes and gossip to direct expression in crimes of passion and international warfare. Accounts of its origins range from instinctual and genetic predispositions to cultural conditioning; personality dynamics play a significant role.

References
Bandura, A. *Aggression: A social learning analysis.* Englewood Cliffs, N.J.: Prentice-Hall, 1973.
Berkowitz, L. *Aggression.* New York: McGraw-Hill, 1962.
Berkowitz, L., & LePage, A. Weapons as aggression-eliciting stimuli. *Journal of Personality and Social Psychology,* 1967, 7, 202–207.
Dollard, J. Miller, N. E., Doob, L. W., Mowrer, O. H., & Sears, R. R. *Frustration and aggression.* New Haven: Yale University Press, 1939.
Horney, K. *The neurotic personality of our time.* New York: Norton, 1937.
Lorenz, K. *On aggression.* New York: Harcourt, Brace, & World, 1966.
Maccoby, E., & Jacklin, C. *The psychology of sex differences.* Stanford, Calif.: Stanford University Press, 1974.
Megargee, E. Undercontrolled and overcontrolled personality types in extreme antisocial aggression. *Psychological Monographs,* 1966, 80(3), Whole No. 611.
Middlebrook, P. *Social psychology and modern life* (2nd ed.). New York: Knopf, 1980.
Montagu, A. *The nature of human aggression.* New York: Oxford University Press, 1976.
Morris, D. *The naked ape.* New York: McGraw-Hill, 1967.
Toch, H. *Violent men: An inquiry into the psychology of violence.* Chicago: Aldine, 1969.

R. L. TIMPE

Aging. *See* GERONTOLOGY.

Agitation. A state of anxiety and marked restlessness, manifested by psychomotor activities such as pacing, insomnia, handwringing, continuous talking, and constant movement. Often feelings of worthlessness and hopelessness are present, and in severe cases of agitated depression, talk of death or suicide is frequently observed.

Agnosia. The loss of ability to recognize a symbol despite intact functioning of the sense organs. Nonrecognition of linguistic symbols, auditory or visual, is classified as aphasia. The term *agnosia* therefore is reserved for symbols in the nonlanguage sphere. The most common agnosias are astereognosis or tactile agnosia (the inability to identify familiar objects by touch); visual agnosia (the inability to recognize familiar visual symbols); and auditory agnosia (the inability to recognize familiar noises or melodies). Agnosia is usually the result of neurological damage or disease.

Agoraphobia. An abnormal or exaggerated dread of being in open spaces. The person suffering from agoraphobia is panic-stricken even at the thought of going outdoors, and usually remains at home.

See PHOBIC DISORDERS.

Agraphia. A subdivision of aphasia, agraphia is the state of being unable to communicate one's thoughts or ideas in writing. The inability may involve individual letters or entire words and phrases. While commonly attributed to cerebral disorders, agraphia may also be psychically or emotionally induced as a result of melancholic inhibition.

Alcohol Abuse and Dependence.
History. The human race has used and abused alcohol from the time of its earliest recorded history. Alcoholic beverages, until about 500 years ago, were made exclusively by fermentation of organic juices. These beverages were used for their mood-altering effects and also as food, since the beverages retained (as do some modern fermented beverages) many of the nutrients of the raw materials. In

addition to social and private consumption, alcoholic beverages were also widely used in the religious rituals of primitive cultures. About 500 years ago the process of distillation was developed in Europe. This produced a stronger alcoholic beverage, distilled spirits. Distilled beverages can far exceed the 14% absolute alcohol content of fermented beverages; in modern times beverages containing up to 99% absolute alcohol can be purchased.

Abuse of alcoholic beverages seems to be as old as their use. Genesis 9 records the drunkenness of Noah. Ancient writings of other cultures record similar anecdotes, as well as admonitions which parallel those in Proverbs to refrain from excessive use of wine and strong drink (e.g., Prov. 23:29–35). There are a variety of indications in several cultures that a distinction has been made between occasional drunkenness and a more habitual inebriation with a corresponding lessened personal responsibility. Keller (1976) noted that the first-century Roman philosopher Seneca "distinguished sharply between 'a man who is drunk' and one who 'has no control over himself, . . . who is accustomed to get drunk, and is a slave to the habit'" (p. 1698). In addition, the writers of the Talmud concluded that the "person who consumed half a log of undiluted wine must be a drunkard and hence could not be convicted of a capital crime" (Keller, 1976, p. 1698). This distinction between the person who drinks, perhaps even to drunkenness, and the drunkard, with an implied loss of control over drinking and lessened personal responsibility, is a core issue in the "disease" debate of alcoholism, and will be discussed at length later.

Effects of Alcohol Consumption. Ethyl alcohol, often called ethanol or absolute alcohol, is the active pharmacological agent in alcoholic beverages. As a very crude rule, most "drinks" (e.g., a 12-ounce can of beer, one 4-ounce glass of wine, one ounce of most distilled spirits) contain about a half-ounce of ethanol. The nature of the physiological and psychological effects of alcohol consumption is a function of a number of variables. These include the amount of ethanol in the drink, the ratio of ethanol to carrier (mixer), foods and other liquids consumed along with the alcohol, the rate of alcohol consumption, body weight, and body chemistry. Contemporary research also suggests that one of the strongest determinants of the psychological effects of alcohol consumption is the expectation of the consumer of what the effects will be. These expectations are communicated through families, peer groups, cultures, and past experience.

When alcohol is consumed, the ethanol in the drink is absorbed rapidly into the bloodstream, principally through the walls of the stomach. It stays in the bloodstream until the liver removes the toxin. The adequately functioning liver of an average-sized person can remove the amount of ethanol in one average drink from the bloodstream in about two hours. Thus, the consumption of more than one drink every two hours for the average healthy person leads to a gradual buildup of the level of absolute alcohol in the blood with a correspondingly increased time needed for the liver to complete detoxification.

Alcohol has its primary effect upon the central nervous system, where it acts as a depressant. The subjectively experienced stimulant effect of alcohol is thought to be due to the inhibitory effect that alcohol has upon higher cortical centers, which are thought to function to inhibit primitive, impulsive, or antisocial behavior. Thus, where these centers are themselves inhibited, the person experiences a release of inhibitions.

Extent and Cost of Use and Abuse. *Consumption.* When measured by official records of alcohol sales, consumption patterns show some variation over time. Since the end of Prohibition in the 1930s an overall trend of increasing consumption has been evident over all three major classes of alcoholic beverages (beer, wine, and distilled spirits). This rate of increase was very sharp during the 1960s, but slowed considerably in the 1970s. Average alcohol consumption in the 1950s stood at two gallons of pure ethanol per every person over 14 years of age. This rose to 2.7 gallons per person per year by 1978. This average is a bit misleading, however, as the one-third of the U.S. adult population which is totally abstinent was included in that average. In addition, the National Institute on Alcohol Abuse and Alcoholism (1980) estimates that "more than 16 million adults 18 years and older (approximately 11 percent of the adult population) consume about half of all beverages sold" (p. 15).

Abuse. There does not appear to be a trend in recent self-report survey statistics indicative of increasing prevalence of drinking problems for American adults. Behaviors associated with alcohol dependence and loss of control are shown by 20% of male drinkers and 10% of female drinkers (NIAAA, 1980). This includes such behaviors as morning drinking, shaky hands, and drinking to get over a hangover.

The same study showed that 9% of the male drinkers and 5% of the female drinkers experience adverse social consequences such as legal, vocational, and/or family problems. It should be noted that only a small percentage of persons described as alcoholics fit the "Skid Row" stereotype.

Even conservative estimates of the dimensions of the alcohol abuse and dependence problem in the United States suggest that there are over five million persons with a severe dependence upon alcohol, ranking it among the foremost health problems of this country and of the world. Estimates of abuse of alcohol among adolescents reflect only drinking rates, as very few adolescents report signs of alcohol dependence, loss of control, or adverse social consequences. Approximately 31% of 10th through 12th graders report drunkenness at least six times in a year (DeLuca, 1981).

Costs of abuse. "Problem drinking and alcoholism cost the nation $43 billion in 1975. This figure includes $19.64 billion in lost production, $12.4 billion in health and medical costs, $5.14 billion in motor vehicle accidents, $2.86 billion in violent crimes, $1.94 billion in social responses, and $0.43 billion in fire losses" (NIAAA, 1980, p. 19). The human cost is impossible to quantify. The medical risks to abusing drinkers include increased incidence of liver damage, heart disease, hypertension, stroke, sexual impotency, and cancer of the mouth, pharynx, larynx, and esophagus. Pregnant women who abuse alcohol expose their unborn children to increased risk of mental retardation and a variety of other disabilities. The abusing drinker affects the physical, emotional, and spiritual well-being not only of himself or herself but also that of family, friends, and vocational contacts. Alcohol consumption has been significantly tied to increased incidences of motor vehicle accidents and fatalities, murders, suicides, drownings, divorces, and child abuse (NIAAA, 1980).

Diagnostic Criteria and Definitions. The term *alcoholism* has over the last century been a standard medical term for the condition of habitual drunkenness conceived of as a disease. This term has become common in public usage. Alcoholic refers to the person exhibiting that disease. Because this disease model has not been universally accepted, the more theoretically neutral terms *alcohol abuse* and *dependence* have become more popular in professional literature and will be used here.

American Psychiatric Association Definitions. DSM-III breaks the spectrum of alcohol consumers into three groups: those whose use of alcohol is nonproblematic, those whose use is extremely problematic and who exhibit signs of physical addiction to ethanol (i.e., alcohol dependence), and the intermediary group whose use is problematic but who do not show signs of physical addiction (i.e., alcohol abuse). Physical addiction is defined by two criteria: tolerance and withdrawal. Tolerance is the need for increased amounts of an addicting drug to obtain a "standard effect" or a decrease in the subjective effect caused by a standard drug administration. Withdrawal refers to the physical disturbance that results when administration of an addicting drug is interrupted. "Morning shakes" and DTs (delirium tremens) are the most well-known forms of alcoholic withdrawal.

The defining criteria for alcohol abuse are: 1) a pattern of pathological alcohol use (e.g., the need for daily use of alcohol for adequate functioning); 2) impairment of social or occupational functioning; and 3) duration of disturbance for at least one month. The first two diagnostic criteria for alcohol dependence are the same as for alcohol abuse (pathological use and impairment of functioning). The third criterion is the presence of either tolerance or withdrawal to alcohol.

Disease versus Nondisease Model Definitions. Other definitions of alcohol abuse and dependence might be grouped roughly into two major camps: those advocating a disease model of alcoholism and those not advocating a disease model.

The disease model definitions of alcoholism include the World Health Organization's (1977) definition of alcohol dependence syndrome: "A state, psychic and usually also physical, resulting from taking alcohol, characterized by behavioral and other responses that always include a compulsion to take alcohol on a continuous or periodic basis in order to experience its psychic effects, and sometimes to avoid the discomfort of its absence; tolerance may or may not be present" (p. 198). Keller (1976), in his definition of alcoholism, added the notion that alcohol consumption interferes with the health or personal adjustment of the drinker. Further, he perceptively identified the core of the disease model as the idea that "the condition constitutes a physical or mental disablement of the person" (p. 1696). The critical disablement in alcoholism as a disease is thought to be the loss of control over alcohol. Those who advocate a disease model generally separate those who abuse alcohol into prealcoholics and alcoholics. Prealcoholics abuse alcohol without loss of control. The abuse of alcohol by alcoholics is complicated by a diminished ability to control or limit their intake of alcohol. The alcoholic may or may not exhibit physical addiction to alcohol.

Nondisease model theorists reject this strict dichotomization of abusers into two groups. For example, Wanberg and Horn (1983) state that "there is no such single-disease process and alcoholism is merely a label for a mixed collection of several distinct conditions that have distinct etiologies" (p. 1056). The core commonality among nondisease theorists is their belief that alcohol abuse represents a common behavioral outcome of a number of psychosocial disorders.

The question of whether or not alcohol dependence is a disease is a complex and emotional one. It should be recognized that this issue is to some degree independent of the question of etiology of the disorder, as thinkers in this area can frequently share common ideas about the origins of the disorder and yet disagree on whether or not it is a disease.

The issues involved in this debate can best be explicated by presenting the essentials of the arguments on each side of the debate (see Keller, 1976, and Marlatt, 1983, for more extended presentations of the contrasting views). The disease model adherent argues that, due to either (or both) physiological and psychological abnormalities, the alcoholic was predisposed to develop a dependency upon alcohol, including loss of control over alcohol consumption. Thus, when the internal (biological and/or psychological) causes of the compulsion to drink occur, the person has no control. In this view alcoholism is "a disease like tuberculosis or diabetes. . . . Alcoholics cannot be blamed for drinking too much any more than tuberculosis victims can be blamed for coughing too much" (Finn & Lawson, 1976, p. 3). The disease is viewed as incurable and irreversible. The alcoholic remains either a drunk alcoholic or a "recovering" or sober alcoholic throughout life. Disease model adherents argue that the alcoholic needs treatment, not moralistic platitudes or punishment, to stop drinking.

Nondisease model adherents in turn argue that alcohol dependence is not a disease because it has no clearly defined biological etiology. While the disease model served well to educate the public that alcohol dependents need treatment to overcome their drinking problem, it has created problems of its own. It robs the alcohol abuser of his or her responsibility for the abusive drinking. It provides an

excuse for further drinking ("after all, I can't help it; I've got a disease"). They suggest that the medical establishment has acted in its own self-interest in defining the problem as a disease. Finally, it is argued that the central concept of loss of control is hopelessly circular. ("How do you know when someone has lost control?" "When they drink too much." "Why do they drink too much?" "Because they can't control their consumption.")

A disease model which releases the drinker from moral responsibility for his or her drinking would not be a valid option for the Christian, as it would be inconsistent to argue that individuals can be morally excused for behavior that violates direct commands of Scripture (Eph. 5:18). On the other hand, it must be recognized that this does not mean that the individual who abuses or is dependent upon alcohol could decide not to drink as easily as someone who has been abstinent throughout life. Adams (1979) has developed the idea that the term *flesh* in Scripture refers to "the body plunged into sinful practices and habits" (p. 160). The Bible contains many passages referring to the possibility that one can increase one's propensity to sin by immersing oneself in sinful practices (e.g., 2 Peter 2:13–14; Jer. 13:23). Thus, Christians must compassionately recognize the difficulty of change for one whose life has been immersed in abusive drinking. To argue, however, that when one has been immersed long enough in sinful behavior that the person's moral culpability disappears seems to be contrary to the scriptural view of sin and responsibility. Either a nondisease model or a modified disease model that retains the concept of personal responsibility despite the hypothesized diminished control over drinking would be a valid starting point.

Causes and Development of Abuse and Dependence. *Causal Factors.* Theories of etiology can be grouped into genetic/biochemical, psychodynamic, behavioral, and sociological perspectives. The causes of the problem undoubtedly transcend disciplinary boundaries.

There is some evidence from studies of adopted children of alcoholic parents that there may be a genetic predisposition toward alcohol dependence. It is unclear as to whether this predisposition is a generalized vulnerability to development of emotional distress due to heightened emotional reactivity, an increased physiological tolerance of the high levels of alcohol intake necessary to develop dependence, or is attributable to as yet undetermined factors. Biochemical theories argue that prolonged intake of high levels of alcohol produces biochemical lesions, that is, alterations in brain chemistry which produce the loss-of-control/compulsion phenomena. There are a variety of other genetic/biochemical theories, none of which are backed by unequivocal empirical support.

Psychodynamic theories suggest that conflicts and unmet needs from childhood development produce a person vulnerable to alcohol abuse. Hypothesized developmental factors include parental overindulgence or lack of love and inconsistencies in parental rearing practices. Traditional psychoanalytic theory suggests alcohol abuse to be the result of lack of gratification of oral dependency needs. Alcohol consumption is seen as a behavior which compensates for unmet needs and aids in repression of unacceptable impulses by acting as an outlet for unconscious tendencies toward homosexuality, self-destructiveness, power or autonomy, or hostility (McCord & McCord, 1960).

The behavioral theories basically view alcohol abuse as a coping response that functions in the place of more adaptive coping responses which the abuser either never developed or is not currently using. In addition, alcohol consumption is seen as possibly intrinsically reinforcing for some individuals, and as being extrinsically reinforced in most social circles. Behavioral theories focus more on explaining current alcohol abuse than on explaining hypothesized factors in the origin of an alcohol dependence problem. In one model (Miller, 1976) a variety of stressors, including social (e.g., a nagging spouse or aggressive friend), situational (e.g., a cocktail party with alcohol available), cognitive (e.g., thoughts such as "I'm no good"), physiological (e.g., pain or withdrawal symptoms), and emotional (e.g., anxiety or anger) stressors, are thought to act to set the stage for alcohol consumption. Drinking is then reinforced by the reduction in the adversiveness of the stressors, the pleasantness of the effect of alcohol, the overt social approval, the ability to behave in a more uninhibited manner, and the knowledge that one is doing the socially accepted thing. Alcohol problems can be expected to be more severe for those individuals who lack other more adaptive ways for coping with stress, who find the state of inebriation or alcoholic "high" inherently reinforcing, who believe that alcohol consumption is an acceptable way of coping, and who are enmeshed in social systems which reinforce excessive alcohol consumption.

Sociological theories focus on larger demographic variables that seem to partially account for alcohol abuse. Miller (1976) cites evidence that the highest rates of alcohol abuse are associated with "low socioeconomic status, urban residence, history of broken home, Catholic or liberal Protestant religious church affiliation, and unmarried status (either single or divorced)" (p. 7). In general, the research suggests that low rates of abuse are associated with the following familial/cultural patterns: the presence of clear norms concerning the acceptable contexts of alcohol use and amount of consumption; drinking is viewed as neither positive nor negative while excessive drinking is clearly not sanctioned; abstinence is socially acceptable; parents present consistent models of moderate alcohol use; and alcohol is not a primary focus for activities (NIAAA, 1980; Miller, 1976).

The most important studies for answering the question of etiology of abuse are those which trace a group of individuals from childhood onward to observe the development of alcohol abuse. This type of study (Vaillant & Milofsky, 1982) tends consistently to show that individuals who later become problem drinkers do not significantly differ from their peers in terms of childhood emotional problems, environmental strengths and weaknesses, or family stability. The best predictors of less alcohol abuse are Southern European ethnic background (e.g., Italian, Greek) and absence of alcohol abusers among immediate ancestors. Absence of adolescent antisocial behavior is a less powerful but significant factor. Thus, it may be that alcohol abuse produces emotional and interpersonal conflict, not that emotional conflicts later produce alcohol abuse.

Development. Jellinek (1960) conceived of alcoholism as a progressive disorder. By progressive he meant that if the disorder goes unchecked, it necessarily progresses on a natural course of four stages: 1) the prealcoholic stage, characterized by drinking for periodic psychological relief; 2) the prodromal stage, characterized by more frequent relief drinking coupled with blackouts, surreptitious drinking, guilt, and denial; 3) the crucial stage, characterized by uncontrolled drinking leading to frequent intoxication, hangovers, ineffective attempts to control drinking, and vocational disturbance; and 4) the chronic phase, characterized by daily intoxication, a gradual erosion of tolerance as the liver deteriorates, possible psychosis, and an eventual drift into Skid Row. Jellinek reserved the term *disease* for only those alcoholics who reach the fourth stage.

Cahalan (1978) has summarized evidence suggesting that this progressive model of development is inaccurate. Cahalan's studies surveyed alcohol abusers at different times and found that the problems reported at one point were of little value in predicting the type of behavior reported at a later time, suggesting that a reliable progression of a disease was simply not present. Thus, while there are many theories of the development of alcohol abuse and dependence, all are lacking empirical evidence to support their claims.

Treatment Principles. Three critical steps may need to be taken in the treatment of the alcohol abuser: 1) medical management of acute intoxication to save life and detoxify the abuser: 2) medical treatment to deal with health problems associated with abuse; and 3) changing the long-term patterns of abusive drinking. The first two steps are not the focus of the present work, so only the third step will be closely examined.

Emrick (1974), in an exhaustive review of existing studies of psychological treatments of alcohol dependence and abuse, concluded that no single treatment approach had emerged as superior to others. Regardless of method of treatment, about two-thirds of those treated improved significantly in the year following treatment, including one-third who remained abstinent for the entire year. No clear evidence of a superior mode of treatment has emerged since Emrick's review, notwithstanding the extravagant claims of some alcoholism treatment programs. Almost every treatment in existence has been used with alcohol abusers.

The most common contemporary form of treatment for alcohol abuse is a multimodal three- to six-week inpatient treatment package followed by continued therapeutic contact and involvement in Alcoholics Anonymous or some related abstinence support group. In these multimodal programs the first treatment principle is that the abuser must recognize his or her problem with alcohol. To accomplish this task the abuser is exposed to alcohol education programs and confrontive group therapy where she or he is forced to examine the dysfunctional aspects of his or her life. Next, it is important to reduce emotional or interpersonal conflicts. For this purpose individual, family, and vocational counseling are vigorously pursued. It is also common for the program to focus on developing the abuser's other more adaptive capacities for coping with stress. Thus, it is becoming increasingly common for programs to include such behavioral skills training modules as relaxation training, assertiveness training, drink refusal training, etc. Finally, it is absolutely critical that the abuser acquire a social context supportive of abstinence. Most alcohol abusers are then encouraged to join Alcoholics Anonymous or related groups.

A final issue in treatment is the choice of abstinence or controlled drinking as a goal of treatment. The suggestion in some circles that alcoholics can return to controlled or social drinking has elicited a negative and emotional reaction from most adherents to the disease model of alcoholism. Marlatt (1983) summarized the unequivocal evidence that a substantial portion of problem drinkers have returned to controlled drinking following long periods of abuse. Miller and Caddy (1977) suggest rigorous criteria for selecting an appropriate treatment goal for each problem drinker. Overall, they conclude that as drinking problems become more severe and long-standing and as the person's personal, familial, and vocational resources decline, controlled drinking treatments become less appropriate for the person.

Prevention. There are two major approaches to prevention of alcohol abuse and dependence. The first is prevention through education about the use and abuse of alcohol. Most programs of this type are targeted at young people or persons identified as at risk for the development of abuse. The evidence for the effectiveness of such programs is at best mixed. The underlying assumption is that education can significantly influence the unknown developmental process that leads to alcohol abuse; many writers question the validity of such an assumption. It should be noted in passing that the family is undoubtedly the most powerful preventive force in the growing child's life. Parents should model responsible alcohol use for their children through either abstinence or controlled social drinking.

The other major approach to prevention of abuse is social control of the availability of alcohol. Prohibition was the most notable example of such a preventive attempt, and opinion is split as to whether Prohibition was a failure or a qualified success. Several current thinkers in the area of prevention support increased taxation of alcoholic beverages as a means of decreasing consumption; a few others are pushing for some sort of governmentally controlled rationing system. The latter program would undoubtedly be even more difficult to implement than Prohibition.

References

Adams, J. *More than redemption*. Phillipsburg, N.J.: Presbyterian and Reformed Publishing, 1979.

Cahalan, D. Implications of American drinking practices and attitudes for prevention and treatment of alcoholism. In G. Marlatt & P. Nathan (Eds.), *Behavioral approaches to alcoholism*. New Brunswick, N.J.: Rutgers Center of Alcohol Studies, 1978.

DeLuca, J. R. (Ed.). *Fourth special report to the U.S. Congress on alcohol and health from the Secretary of Health and Human Services*. Rockville, Md.: National Institute on Alcohol Abuse and Alcoholism, 1981.

Emrick, C. A review of psychologically oriented treatment of alcoholism. *Quarterly Journal of Studies on Alcohol*, 1974, *35*, 523–549.

Finn, P., & Lawson, J. *Alcohol—pleasures and problems*. Washington: National Institute on Alcohol Abuse and Alcoholism, 1976.

Jellinek, E. M. *The disease concept of alcoholism*. New Haven: Hillhouse Press, 1960.

Keller, M. The disease concept of alcoholism revisited. *Journal of Studies on Alcohol*, 1976, *37*, 1694–1717.

Marlatt, G. A. The controlled drinking controversy: A commentary. *American Psychologist*, 1983, *38*, 1097—1110.

McCord, W., & McCord, J. *Origins of alcoholism*. Stanford, Calif.: Stanford University Press, 1960.

Miller, P. M. *Behavioral treatment of alcoholism*. New York: Pergamon Press, 1976.

Miller, W., & Caddy, G. Abstinence and controlled drinking in the treatment of problem drinkers. *Journal of Studies on Alcohol*, 1977, *38*, 986–1003.

National Institute on Alcohol Abuse and Alcoholism. *Facts about alcohol and alcoholism*. Rockville, Md.: Author, 1980.

Vaillant, G. E., & Milofsky, E. S. The etiology of alcoholism. *American Psychologist*, 1982, *37*, 494–503.

Wanberg, K. W., & Horn, J. L. Assessment of alcohol use with multidimensional concepts and measures. *American Psychologist*, 1983, *38*, 1055–1069.

World Health Organization. *International classification of diseases*. Ann Arbor, Mich.: Author, 1977.

S. L. Jones

Alcoholics Anonymous (AA). A nonprofit voluntary self-help organization of current and former alcoholics whose aim is to help themselves and others overcome their problem of alcoholism. The first AA group was founded in Akron, Ohio, by a stockbroker and a physician in 1935. The broker, known to AA as Bill W., traced his sobriety to being confronted by a friend who had achieved sobriety by "getting religion." Bill W. could not accept the idea of God, though he could accept a "Universal Mind or Spirit of Nature," so his friend challenged him to "choose your own conception of God" (Alcoholics Anonymous, 1939, p. 22). Thus Bill W. came to see that "it was only a matter of being willing to believe in a power greater than myself. Nothing more was required of me to make my beginning" (p. 22).

The concept of loss of control over alcohol and that of the efficacious belief in a "Higher Power" of the person's choosing form the foundation of AA's twelve steps to recovery.

Alcoholics begin these steps by admitting their loss of control over alcohol and their lives and by believing that a Higher Power can restore them to sanity. Persons are encouraged to make a "decision to turn our will and our lives over to God" *as they understand Him* (p. 71), to make a moral inventory of themselves, to admit to God, self, and others those defects found, to be ready for God to remove those defects, and to ask him to do so. They are to list all persons they have harmed, be willing to make restitution to all, and to proceed to make restitution where appropriate. Finally, the recovering alcoholics are to improve their conscious contact with their Higher Power through prayer and meditation. This spiritual awakening is to result in reaching out to help other struggling alcoholics.

The only requirement for involvement in AA is a desire to stop drinking. Typical problem drinkers might attend their first AA meeting during a period of discouragement or defeat. AA meetings are usually structured to include recovering alcoholics, who identify themselves by only their first names. Several members will then give a testimonial of their struggle with alcoholism and their pilgrimage in the AA program. The troubled drinker can ask for more assistance after the meeting. If he or she is serious about stopping drinking, a recovering alcoholic would volunteer to be the person's "sponsor," someone who can be called on for advice and guidance and, of particular importance, who can guide the person through AA's twelve steps. An integral part of the person's recovery program is continued attendance at AA meetings.

Members of AA strictly adhere to a disease conceptualization of alcohol abuse, defining themselves as alcoholics who have the disease alcoholism. Alcoholics are seen as being different from normal individuals. While the alcoholic might have been able to control his or her drinking earlier in life, that person at some point comes to lose control over alcohol consumption, thus becoming an alcoholic. This loss of control is most cogently summarized in the frequently heard AA adage, "one drink, one drunk." The disease is viewed as permanent and as progressive and irreversible. It may be halted in its course by abstinence, but upon any alcohol consumption the alcoholic will reinitiate the chain of abusive drinking at the same level at which he became abstinent unless the twelve steps are started over again. Alcoholics who are sober are termed "recovering alcoholics" rather than "recovered alcoholics," since the former implies that the disease has only been arrested in its progress rather than cured or reversed.

AA grew enormously in its popularity in the first few decades following its founding, and its members have exerted tremendous effects upon the views of American society regarding the problem of alcoholism. Today there are said to be about 40,000 chapters throughout the world, with membership estimated at one million men and women.

The effectiveness of AA is difficult to gauge. Recovery rates of up to 90% have been claimed. Several factors make the estimation of effectiveness problematic. First, recovery rates differ with differing definitions of success, and no consensus has been achieved on a single definition. Second, success rates are drastically influenced by the parameters set for the population to be studied. Does one include only those who really commit themselves to the AA program (a very select group), or should all drinkers who have ever attended an AA meeting constitute the sample? Finally, AA meetings and philosophies have been absorbed as supports for many alcoholism treatment programs which also include other treatment methods. How are alcoholics going through these programs to be considered when studying the effectiveness of AA?

There are elements of AA philosophy and practice which are compelling parallels to Christian faith and practice: submission to God, confession of and restitution for wrongdoing, reliance upon God for the shaping of personality and behavior, and diligent prayer and meditation to facilitate personal contact with God. Based upon these parallels, many orthodox believers have unequivocally endorsed AA.

There are, however, fundamental problems in drawing too close parallels between AA and the evangelical Christian faith. AA was established and its basic philosophies set under the influence of modernist theological thought (Kurtz, 1979), and this influence is strongly reflected in its prescribed belief system. AA adherents are encouraged to believe in a transcendent entity of their own choice. This flexibility in choice of a faith object suggests a basic confidence in faith *qua* faith rather than confidence in faith based on a reliable and benevolent transcendent Being. Also consistent with classical liberal thought is the assumption that the Higher Power is known only through its felt impact and not through external referents such as inspired Scriptures. A third major problem concerns the concept of powerlessness over

alcohol. While Scripture addresses the influence of environmental events upon persons (e.g., the exhortations to avoid contact with immorality), we are not pronounced powerless over these influences. In Scripture the description of drunkenness as a moral problem implies responsibility for refraining from alcohol abuse. It appears that AA would state that a recovering alcoholic is responsible for refraining from taking the first drink, but cannot be held responsible for subsequent drinking over which he has no control. This philosophy is responsible in part for the prevalent conceptualization of alcoholism as a disease rather than a moral or legal problem. Finally, AA appears to be a religious way of life, including a conversion (Kurtz, 1979, p. 184). The question is whether such a system should be regarded as a secularized religion not incompatible with orthodox faith, or as a potentially dangerous mix of near-truth and untruth.

References
Alcoholics Anonymous. *Alcoholics Anonymous.* New York: Works Publishing Co., 1939.
Kurtz, E. *Not God: A history of Alcoholics Anonymous.* Center City, Minn.: Hazelden Educational Services, 1979.
                                                                    S. L. JONES

See MUTUAL HELP GROUPS.

Alcoholism. *See* ALCOHOL ABUSE AND DEPENDENCE.

Alcohol Organic Mental Disorders. The brain is the organ which produces mental activity. When that activity is interrupted by alcohol, disordered mental activity occurs. Even small amounts of alcohol will have effects on brain activity. However, with excessive, prolonged consumption of alcohol, serious organic changes are observed. The basic characteristic of recent or prolonged ingestion of alcohol is maladaptive behavior, which may include slurred speech, aggressiveness, or hallucinations.

It is important to differentiate alcoholic organic mental disorders from ALCOHOL ABUSE AND DEPENDENCE. Alcohol abuse is a pattern of regular excessive use of alcohol beyond acceptable limits. Alcohol dependence occurs when the abnormal consumption is more serious, when more must be consumed to get the same effect and there are clear signs of withdrawal if drinking is reduced or stopped. It is after considerable excessive and dependent use that alcoholic organic mental disorders are evidenced.

Intoxication. When alcohol is ingested, mental activity at first may show a disinhibiting effect, and the person may appear expansive, alert, and experience a sense of well-being. With continued drinking, however, the depressing effect of alcohol on the central nervous system is evidenced by slower movements, depressed and withdrawn behavior, and even unconsciousness. With intoxication the individual's usual behavior may be exaggerated or altered. An aggressive person may become even more aggressive, or a quiet person may become socially involved.

Factors affecting intoxication include the person's weight, whether he has eaten or not, how rapidly the alcohol is consumed, and the type and amount of alcohol drunk. As the blood alcohol level reaches 30 mg %, effects may be noticed. Many states accept 150 mg % as intoxication. Death may occur at levels ranging from 400 to 700 mg %. Four ounces of whiskey or one and a half quarts of beer, taken with food, will produce from 30 to 50 mg % alcohol blood level.

Alcohol intoxication is diagnosed when the following criteria are met: alcohol has recently been drunk in sufficient quantity to cause intoxication in most people; maladaptive behavioral effects are noted (such as fighting or interference with social functioning); at least one of these physiological signs is evidenced—slurred speech, incoordination, unsteady gait, nystagmus, flushed face; and at least one of these psychological signs is present—mood changes, irritability, loquacity, impaired attention.

Alcohol idiosyncratic intoxication is diagnosed when a marked behavioral change is observed, yet the amount of alcohol consumed is not sufficient to induce intoxication in most people. The behavior is usually not normal for the person when he is not drinking. While fairly rare, alcohol idiosyncratic intoxication, sometimes called pathological intoxication, is dramatic since the behavior is so extreme and unexpected. The person may harm self or others during this episode. After a few hours the person returns to a normal state.

Withdrawal. After a dependency on alcohol has developed, cessation of drinking will bring on a set of symptoms characteristic of alcohol withdrawal. The basic features of withdrawal are coarse tremors of the hands, tongue, and eyelids, nausea, vomiting, malaise or weakness, anxiety, depressed mood, and irritability. Withdrawal symptoms begin within a few hours after cessation of drinking and almost always disappear within five to seven days. Sleep is often fitful and disturbed by bad dreams. Brief hallucinations may be experienced.

Alcohol withdrawal is diagnosed when a cessation of or reduction in heavy prolonged drinking is followed by the above symptoms. After five to fifteen years of heavy drinking, even if it is episodic heavy drinking, delirium may occur when withdrawal takes place. Often called DELIRIUM TREMENS, this begins two to ten days after drinking stops. Unless complicated by other conditions, the symptoms usually last three to six days.

The basic characteristics of alcohol withdrawal delirium are clouding of consciousness, disorientation, and memory impairment. Early in the course of delirium tremens nightmares, anxiety attacks, panic, illusions, and vivid hallucinations are noted. As the symptoms progress, agitation, disorientation, visual hallucinations, restlessness, and dizziness occur. The symptoms may fluctuate during the day.

While only 5% of patients being treated for alcohol withdrawal develop delirium, the severity of the delirious state warrants immediate medical attention. The inability to pay attention to the surroundings, reduced capacity to shift, focus, or maintain attention, and the presence of hallucinations create possible endangerment to the person. Seizures may occur and head injuries may result from falling.

Excessive Alcohol Use. Three specific problems associated with the excessive use of alcohol are alcohol hallucinosis, alcohol amnestic disorder, and dementia.

Alcohol hallucinosis has been reported in persons in their early to mid 20s, but the most typical onset is about age 40, after 10 or more years of heavy drinking. The essential feature is a persistent hallucination that develops after an individual has recovered from the symptoms of alcohol withdrawal and is no longer drinking. The condition is rare and occurs one to two weeks after the person has stopped drinking. Four times as many men as women experience this syndrome. The symptoms may last from a few days to several weeks or months. A chronic form may develop and is associated with repeated episodes. The hallucinations occur in a normal state of consciousness and are unpleasant and disturbing. Usually auditory hallucinations come as accusing or threatening voices. The person may act in a way to protect himself and may attack others as a defense. Ideas of reference and other poorly systematized persecutory delusions often become prominent.

Alcohol amnestic disorder is a result of vitamin deficiency associated with prolonged, heavy use of alcohol. It is sometimes referred to as Korsakoff's syndrome or Wernicke's syndrome. The thiamine deficiency results in both short-term and long-term memory impairment. Immediate recall is undisturbed, but twenty minutes later the person cannot recall even three items. No clouding of consciousness is noted and the person remains alert. However, the individual is unable to learn new information or recall information that was known in the past.

Dementia associated with alcohol use is characterized by a loss of intellectual abilities, memory impairment, and impairment of social or occupational functioning. The excessive use of alcohol has been going on for many years before this disorder develops. This diagnosis will not be made until at least three weeks have passed since the cessation of alcohol use, in order to rule out the transient effects of withdrawal and intoxication. By then it is evident that abstract intellectual capacities, judgment, and other higher cortical functions are impaired. Persons with this disorder may become lost, are unable to care for themselves properly, and may harm themselves or another. The gross deterioration of the brain means these individuals will require care.

L. N. FERGUSON

Alexander Technique. A method of improving the use of the body by modifying what Reich has called the MUSCULAR ARMOR. The technique was developed by Frederick Alexander, an Australian actor, who discovered that his periodic voice loss while performing was caused by tension in his neck and rib cage. His self-treatment consisted in changing his muscular-skeletal habits through careful awareness of faulty existing patterns and the practice of new ones. This was the birth of the Alexander technique.

The technique is basically quite simple. The patient gives commands to his own body (e.g., "Let the neck muscles loosen and lengthen") while the therapist uses his hands to assist the body in complying with the command. Neck and head muscles receive the first attention, as Alexander felt that if the individual's head is balanced properly on the spine, the rest of the muscular-skeletal system can then be more easily balanced.

Perls was greatly influenced by Alexander in his development of Gestalt therapy. Bioenergetic analysis and other body therapies are the most common psychotherapy systems utilizing the Alexander technique. It is also often used in the training of actors, and general medicine has shown some interest in the technique for the treatment of stress disorders.

Additional Reading
Barlow, W. *The Alexander technique.* New York: Knopf, 1973.

D. G. BENNER

See BIOENERGETIC ANALYSIS.

Alexia. The loss of ability to read, thought to be caused by a cortical lesion.

See READING DISABILITIES.

Alienation. The word is derived from the Latin *alienatio,* which comes from the verb *alienare,* meaning to transfer something to another, to remove, or to take away. In addition to this connection with property the term in both Middle English and Middle High German usage also meant alienation of mind, or mental disorder, and personal estrangement (Schacht, 1970). A summary of the validity and reliability of 14 scales purporting to measure this concept may be found in Robinson, Rusk, and Head (1968).

Alienation is a theme in many works of literature, from Plato and Sophocles of classical Greece to Dante of the Middle Ages down to writers of modern times (Josephson & Josephson, 1962). Existentialist philosophers dwelt heavily on human estrangement. Twentieth-century art, sculpture, and music reflect the discordant, the bizarre, and the grotesque, all symptomatic of contemporary alienation (Cole, 1966).

In the modern age alienation has come to have many meanings, including loss of self, anxiety states, anomie, despair, depersonalization, rootlessness, apathy, social disorganization, loneliness, atomization, powerlessness, meaninglessness, isolation, depression, and the loss of beliefs or values (Josephson & Josephson, 1962). Many authors have considered alienation in terms of four ruptured relationships: between man and God, between man and man, within man himself, and between man and nature. Guinness (1972) has referred to this fourfold breach as theological, sociological, ecological, and psychological alienation. The first three of these will be discussed in the present article (*See* SELF-ALIENATION for a discussion of psychological alienation).

In the Judeo-Christian tradition the basis for theological alienation, the rift between man and God, is the Adam and Eve story. Original humankind rebelled against its Creator, resulting in expulsion from the Garden of Paradise and a disruption of the divine friendship. Although Christians are to establish God's kingdom on earth (Matt. 6:10), that kingdom nonetheless is not of this world (John 18:36). Indeed, Jesus Christ himself was the portrait of alienation. He emptied himself of divinity, so to speak, in order to become incarnate (Phil. 2:6–7); he was not received by his own people (John 1:11); he was rejected, despised (John 10:31), finally crucified, and buried in another's grave (Matt. 27:60). In Judaism also the individual is not supposed to feel at home on earth. The Jewish people were to be a people apart from other nations. The prophets Moses, Elijah, Amos, Hosea, and Jeremiah were themselves thoroughly alienated from society, strangers among their own people (Kaufmann, 1970).

Sociological alienation, the rift between man and his fellows, has been treated extensively. Karl Marx conceived of work as the means of self-realization and consequently of ultimate importance to fulfillment. The worker can become alienated in two ways: when he is separated from the product of his labor and when he loses control over work itself (Schacht, 1970). The values of our technological society have been held largely accountable for sociological alienation today. Keniston (1965) discusses three characteristics of a technological society: 1) fragmentation of tasks—i.e., specialization that leads to work without a seen purpose or final achievement; 2) shattering of community—i.e., life in organizations rather than in communities; 3) ascendancy of technological values—i.e., concern with instrumental rather than final values, the preoccupation with the how rather than the why of things. Additionally, technology has produced awesome weapons for nuclear destruction, creating the specter of world annihilation.

Ecological alienation, the rift between man and nature, is illustrated in the so-called energy crisis, the alarm over the rapid depletion of natural energy resources by ever-increasing technological consumption. Furthermore, pollution, the result of energy abuse, has risen to the extent that major cities report daily atmospheric pollution indexes. Our earth, streams, and oceans are increasingly despoiled by the influx of nonbiodegradable refuse. Modern man has lost the concept of stewardship and now proclaims absolute domain over all he surveys.

Various humanistic solutions to contemporary alienation have been proposed. However, from the Christian perspective any resolution espousing relativism, the rejection of absolute and certain truth, negates the very possibility of finding ultimate answers to human origin, purpose, and destiny. Only a return to absolute values can resolve the plight of man (Hammes, 1978). The Christian would further contend that the fourfold rupture between man and God, between man and man, between man and nature, and within man himself has been healed in the reconciliation accomplished by Christ, and it will be only through following the example of Jesus that alienation can be finally resolved.

References

Cole, W. G. *The restless quest of modern man.* New York: Oxford University Press, 1966.
Guinness, O. *The dust of death.* Downers Grove, Ill.: Inter-Varsity Press, 1972.
Hammes, J. A. *Human destiny.* Huntington, Ind.: Our Sunday Visitor, 1978.
Josephson, E., & Josephson, M. (Eds.). *Man alone: Alienation in modern society.* New York: Dell Publishing, 1962.
Kaufmann, W. The inevitability of alienation. In R. Schacht (Ed.), *Alienation.* Garden City, N.Y.: Doubleday, 1970.
Keniston, K. *The uncommitted.* New York: Harcourt, Brace & World, 1965.
Robinson, J. P., Rusk, J. G., & Head, K. B. *Measures of political attitudes.* Ann Arbor, Mich.: Institute for Social Research, 1968.
Schacht, R. *Alienation.* Garden City, N.Y.: Doubleday, 1970.

J. A. HAMMES

See EXISTENTIAL PSYCHOLOGY AND PSYCHOTHERAPY.

Allo-Centered Psychotherapy. This takes its name from the Greek allos, meaning "others." It advocates a change in emphasis from self-centeredness and introspection to others and empathy. It was developed in the early 1970s by Motet (1981), who sees it not so much as another unique system of therapy but as an approach that can be used in conjunction with more traditional therapies. The main psychological roots of the approach are in the work of Adler, Frankl, and Allport. From Adler, whose influence has been greatest, it takes the idea of SOCIAL INTEREST. However, Motet does not see social interest as inborn, and his approach focuses more on orientation toward another individual rather than toward society as a whole. From Frankl it takes and further develops the idea of self-transcendence, and from Allport it adopts the idea of becoming, as well as the emphasis on a philosophy of life.

The allo-centered personality is an ideal to aim for; very few actually reach it fully. Allo-centered therapy gives recommendations for moving toward the ideal. One of these is the development of awareness of others through learning to understand their cognitive, affective, and behavioral uniqueness. One way of accomplishing this is to analyze the client's interaction with some significant person from the perspective of this other person. Both the uniqueness and the sameness of people are emphasized. The individual is seen as a mosaic of characteristics shared by many but combined in a unique way in each individual.

Self-knowledge is enhanced by the understanding of others in that it allows comparison. Thus, paradoxically, self is found not by searching for it but by turning to others. The awareness of sameness also helps to produce a sense of belonging and to alleviate alienation and loneliness. The main question to ask is not "Who am I?" but "Who am I becoming; for whom and for what?" This sense of purpose and of meaning is the basis of the resulting strong personal identity.

Motet's emphasis on the importance of an other-centered orientation to personality is clearly in accord with the Christian virtue of love. His criticism of our culture's NARCISSISM and of the ways in which traditional psychotherapies can reinforce this is also important. Allo-centered psychotherapy is not advanced as a major system of therapy but rather as a corrective emphasis to much in contemporary therapy.

Reference

Motet, D. *Allo-centered psychotherapy and counseling.* Paper presented at the annual meeting of the Western Psychological Association, 1981. (ERIC Document Reproduction Service No. ED 217–319)

D. MOTET

Alloplasty. An adaptation to a stressful situation by altering or manipulating one's external environment. It is contrasted to AUTOPLASTY, which is adaptation through changing oneself. The most common forms of alloplasty are flight and defensive behaviors.

Allport, Gordon Willard (1897–1967).
American psychologist who established personality as a legitimate psychological study and resurrected the American psychology of religion.

Born in Montezuma, Indiana, Allport was the last of four sons of physician John Edwards Allport, who soon moved his practice to Ohio. Gordon's maternal grandmother was a founder of Free Methodism; his mother, Nellie Wise Allport, strongly influenced his quest for ultimate religious answers. Gordon finished Cleveland public schools in 1915.

Floyd Allport, later an eminent social psychologist, suggested that his brother follow him to Harvard University. Gordon did and stayed there the rest of his life, save seven years. He earned his A.B. in economics and philosophy in 1919. Gordon was inclined toward social service, but took an opportunity to teach one year at Robert College in Constantinople (now Istanbul). Unexpectedly comfortable with teaching, he accepted a fellowship to return to Harvard. His 1922 Ph.D. thesis was titled "An Experimental Study of the Traits of Personality: With Special Reference to the Problem of Social Diagnosis." His first article, also on personality traits, was coauthored with Floyd in 1921. After graduating, Allport studied two years in Germany and England. The German experience enabled him to interpret German psychology to America and assist in the immigration of many academic refugees from Nazism.

At Harvard, 1924–1926, Allport taught the first recorded personality course offered in America. He delivered his first professional paper, "What Is a Trait of Personality?" while at Dartmouth College, where he taught for the next four years. He returned to Harvard in 1930.

Gordon Allport is best known as a personality theorist. As presaged by his thesis and initial papers, he held a trait view of personality, but, emphasizing the uniqueness of individuals, he stressed personal dispositions over common traits. Nonetheless he collaborated on two popular tests of common traits: the A-S Reaction Study (his second and last publication with Floyd) and A Study of Values. Allport used the term *proprium* for his central concept of self. He believed that an individual's conscious thinking and present life are more important for personality and behavior than the unconscious and childhood or other historical events. He posited his principle of FUNCTIONAL AUTONOMY of motives in *Personality: A Psychological Interpretation* (1937). The concept holds that adult motives may develop from basic drives of infancy and childhood, but they become self-sustaining and no longer depend on the baser motives. *Personality* was one of two 1937 books that stimulated introduction of personality into psychology curricula. It was standard reading in personality until Allport's 1961 revision, *Pattern and Growth in Personality.*

Although personality theory was Allport's primary intellectual love, half of his work was in social psychology. Research in mass communication led to work on rumors and morale during World War II, including a daily newspaper feature countering harmful war rumors. Attitudes in general and prejudice in particular were prolonged concerns, with *The Nature of Prejudice* (1954) the germinal work in the field.

As an undergraduate Allport had tried to replace childhood dogmas with a humanistic religion. Soon that position appeared to "exalt one's own intellect and affirm only a precarious man-made set of values. . . . Humility and some mysticism, I felt, were indispensable for me" (1968, p. 382). He became an Episcopalian, active in Boston's Church of the Advent.

Allport wrote little on psychology of religion before the 1940s, when seven articles (10% of his publications for the decade) had religious implications. That rate increased to 22% in the 1960s. *The Individual and His Religion* (1950), more than any other work, reopened American psychology to a serious study of religion.

Allport wrote, "A narrowly conceived science can never do business with a narrowly conceived religion" (1950, p. x). Rather, he brought to religious studies the openness he demanded for personality theory, never forsaking the quest for ultimate meanings his mother set him on. In a mature religion, he said, a belief is heuristic—"held tentatively until it can be confirmed or until it helps us discover a more valid belief" (1950, p. 81).

Mature faith also has a "derivative yet dynamic nature" (1950, p. 71). Its motivations are separate from the organic cravings that underlie the religious life; "a mature religious sentiment supplies its own driving power, and becomes dynamic in its own right" (1950, pp. 71–72). This statement simply applies functional autonomy to religion. As early as 1946, Allport's studies of prejudice found churchgoers to be more prejudiced than the nonreligious. This apparent violation of the Christian principle of brotherhood received further attention in *The Nature of Prejudice*. Allport gradually transformed his distinction between immature and mature religion into concepts of extrinsic and intrinsic religion, which became the most influential constructs in the new American psychology of religion. His last research paper (1968, pp. 237–268) presented these widely used measures. The larger number of extrinsic, immature, self-serving churchgoers tended to be prejudiced; the intrinsic minority were relatively free from prejudice.

Allport served as president of the American Psychological Association (1939), Eastern Psychological Association (1943), and the Society for the Psychological Study of Social Issues (1944); he received the American Psychological Foundation gold medal and the American Psychological Association distinguished scientific contribution award. He edited the *Journal of Personality and Social Psychology* (1938–1949), helped found the interdisciplinary Department of Social Relations at Harvard (1946), and in 1966 was appointed the first Richard Cabot Professor of Social Ethics at the university. The bibliography in *The Person in Psychology* cites almost 250 publications.

References

Allport, G. W. *Personality: A psychological interpretation.* New York: Henry Holt, 1937.
Allport, G. W. *The individual and his religion.* New York: Macmillan, 1950.
Allport, G. W. *The nature of prejudice.* Reading, Mass.: Addison-Wesley, 1954.
Allport, G. W. *Pattern and growth in personality.* New York: Holt, Rinehart & Winston, 1961.
Allport, G. W. *The person in psychology.* Boston: Beacon Press, 1968.

R. D. KAHOE

See PSYCHOLOGY OF RELIGION; RELIGIOUS ORIENTATION; PREJUDICE; PERSONALITY.

Altered States of Consciousness. *See* CONSCIOUSNESS.

Altruism. *See* HELPING BEHAVIOR.

Alzheimer's Disease. A presenile DEMENTIA characterized by progressive mental deterioration, leading to severe language impairment and eventually death. The disease was described in 1907 by the German neurologist Alois Alzheimer. Its early stages include gradual loss of memory, carelessness, inability to perform everyday tasks, and poor perception and reasoning. As it progresses, intellectual functioning and emotional expression become impaired, and the person laughs and cries without known cause. In the final stages complete disorientation and incoherency occur, and speech deteriorates from extreme talkativeness to isolated words and phrases. Ultimately the person degenerates to a vegetative state. The average duration of the disease before death is 6½ years, although it ranges from several months to 10 years. Alzheimer's disease is 2½ times more frequent in women than in men and usually strikes between the ages of 40 and 60. The physiological changes in Alzheimer's disease involve atrophy of the frontal lobes of the cortex. The cause is unknown, although it has been suggested it may be due to an acquired or inherited metabolic defect. There is no known treatment.

D. L. SCHUURMAN

See GENETIC AND BIOCHEMICAL FACTORS IN PSYCHOPATHOLOGY.

Ambiguity, Intolerance of. An ambiguous situation may be defined as one that is unclear because of a lack of meaningful cues. Intolerance of ambiguity is the tendency to perceive (or interpret) ambiguous situations as sources of threat. There are basically three types of situations that may fit this definition: 1) a novel situation in which familiar cues are totally lacking; 2) a complex situation in which many disparate cues must be organized; and 3) a contradictory situation where existing cues suggest mutually exclusive solutions.

More than 30 years ago Adorno, Frenkel-Brunswick, Levinson, and Sanford (1950) found that authoritarian personalities had more difficulty in coping with ambiguity than did people in general. Since that time hundreds of studies of intolerance of ambiguity have been conducted by means of questionnaires, interviews, projective tests, systematic observation, and experimental research. Several tests of tolerance-intolerance of ambiguity have been developed, the most frequently used being that of Budner (1962). The focus of most of the research studies has been the attempt to determine how intolerance of ambiguity relates to other personality characteristics. It has been found to be positively related to rigidity, closed-mindedness, dogmatism, anxiety, repression, religious fundamentalism, conformity, prejudice, racism, negative attitudes toward employment of the handicapped, negative attitudes toward homosexuals, dislike for abstract art, lack of curiosity, low creativity, and aesthetic insensitivity.

Although the dynamics of intolerance of ambiguity are not altogether clear, Frenkel-Brunswick hypothesized that this trait is the result of repression and projection. When a person represses an unacceptable emotion, he tends to project this emotion to others. Stimuli which fail to support his perception (are ambiguous with respect to his projection) are threatening. Frenkel-Brunswick (1949) documented a strong correlation between intolerance for ambiguity and hostility, power orientation, externalization, and rigid stereotyping.

Budner (1978) believes that the confusion about tolerance-intolerance of ambiguity results from the fact that research has largely taken the form of correlations between specific variables rather than longitudinal studies of the development of individual predispositions. In one longitudinal experimental study (Harrington, Block, & Block, 1978) measures of intolerance of ambiguity were obtained on the same group of subjects at three, four, five, and seven years of age. Information about parents

and parent-child interactions was also obtained. Reliable independent ratings of intolerance of ambiguity were obtained from nursery school teachers. Subjects who were intolerant of ambiguity were hesitant to enter, narrow in deploying attention within, and premature in imposing structure upon three ambiguous experimental situations. Early intolerance of ambiguity in boys was related to later intolerance of ambiguity, general anxiety, structure-seeking behaviors, and less effective cognitive functioning at age seven. Fathers of boys intolerant of ambiguity described themselves as relatively distant and authoritarian. In a standardized teaching situation fathers of boys intolerant of ambiguity tended to be impatient, critical, and less resourceful when interacting with their sons. Early intolerance of ambiguity in girls related to later stable peer relationships in which girls played nonassertive roles. Mothers of girls who were intolerant of ambiguity described themselves as nurturant, and in the teaching situation were emotionally supportive and task structuring.

In summary, the most readily observable attitudinal and behavioral characteristics of people who are intolerant of ambiguity are 1) low self-regard, 2) inability to understand the feelings of others, 3) strong ethnocentrism, 4) strong needs to receive support from authority figures, 5) tendency to see issues as black or white, 6) preference for the known and routine, 7) tendency to jump to conclusions without adequate data, 8) acceptance of what they have been taught, regardless of inconsistencies, 9) repression of impulses, and 10) rigidity in thinking.

Research findings on intolerance of ambiguity have implications for Christian leaders. In the first place, many Christians have been reared in the kind of homes from which persons intolerant of ambiguity come. In the second place, there are many ambiguities within Christian theology and life. Hard-to-understand passages of Scripture, differing theological viewpoints, and conflicting views with regard to the proper life style for the Christian all demand high tolerance for ambiguity.

Persons who are intolerant of ambiguity are emotionally insecure. Consequently, anything that will make the individual feel more secure will increase his ability to cope with ambiguity. Obviously, the more a person can feel forgiven, accepted, and loved by God, the more secure he will feel. However, unless the individual can experience the love of Christian people, he will find it difficult to believe in and accept God's love.

DOUBT may be regarded as a form of intolerance of ambiguity since the doubter is threatened by cues which seem contradictory and suggest mutually exclusive responses. An important factor in resolving doubt is an atmosphere of openness and honesty. Where this is lacking, doubters are afraid to voice their doubts for fear of being condemned or ostracized. Many college students who are exposed to ideas which challenge their faith hesitate to discuss their doubts with parents, pastor, or members of their church for fear of censure. Christians who have repressed their own doubts instead of resolving them often are shocked when young people raise the same questions. When young people raise disturbing questions with their elders, they are sometimes rebuked for entertaining sinful thoughts, given proof texts, or prayed for. Too infrequently are they listened to with understanding and love. The person who is bothered by ambiguities with regard to his faith must be given the assurance that it is not sinful to have sincere doubts. Christ's attitude toward the sincere doubter is instructive. Although Christ harshly condemned the insincere scribes, Pharisees, and Sadducees who asked questions in an attempt to trap him, his treatment of the sincere questioner was quite different.

When John the Baptist, who was then in prison, sent two of his disciples to inquire of Christ, "Art thou he that should come or do we look for another?" one might have expected Christ to be justifiably exasperated. Instead, he answered, "Go and shew John again these things which ye do hear and see; the blind receive their sight, and the lame walk, the lepers are healed, and the deaf hear, the dead are raised up, and the poor have the gospel preached to them" (Matt. 11:4–5).

Thomas had not been present when the risen Christ appeared to the other disciples and showed them his hands and side. When the other disciples told Thomas that they had seen the Lord, Thomas doubted their report, saying, "Except I shall see in his hands the print of the nails and thrust my hand into his side, I will not believe" (John 20:25). Eight days later Christ appeared to the disciples again, but this time Thomas was with them. Instead of upbraiding Thomas for his lack of faith, Christ invited Thomas to examine his hands and side.

Doubts can often be resolved in intimate dialogue with fellow believers. Scripture exhorts us to "confess our faults one to another"

(James 5:16), "bear one another's burdens" (Gal. 6:2), and "rejoice with those who do rejoice and weep with those who weep" (Rom. 12:15). Leslie (1971) has shown that encounter-like groups within the church setting can be effective in resolving both psychological and spiritual problems. Formal groups organized around another objective, such as Sunday school classes, ordinarily do not provide the right atmosphere for intimate sharing. Consequently, special groups composed of individuals who feel the need for intimate sharing must be formed.

References

Adorno, T. W., Frenkel-Brunswick, E., Levinson, D., & Sanford, R. N. *The authoritarian personality.* New York: Harper & Row, 1950.

Budner, S. Intolerance of ambiguity as a personality variable. *Journal of Personality*, 1962, *30*(1), 29–50.

Budner, S. Intolerance for ambiguity and the need for closure. *Psychological Reports*, 1978, *43*(2), 638.

Frenkel-Brunswick, E. Intolerance of ambiguity as an emotional and perceptual personality variable. *Journal of Personality*, 1949, *18*, 108–143.

Harrington, D. M., Block, J. H., & Block, J. Intolerance of ambiguity in pre-school children: psychometric considerations, behavioral manifestations and parental correlates. *Developmental Psychology*, 1978, *14*(3), 242–256.

Leslie, R. C. *Sharing groups in the church.* Nashville: Abingdon, 1971.

O. C. SCANDRETTE

See RELIGION AND PERSONALITY.

Ambition. The strong desire for achievement or success, ambition is viewed psychodynamically as a defense against shame. Success proves that there is no need for shame. Apart from these psychoanalytic speculations there has been little systematic study of ambition. The closely related concept of need for achievement has, however, been extensively studied (see ACHIEVEMENT, NEED for).

Ambivalence. The psychic activity whereby a person has two apparently opposite, contradictory, or complementary feelings. The experience of ambivalence can be normal and rewarding or pathological and damaging, depending on the depth to which one integrates his infantile demands and resolves childhood conflicts.

Traditional psychoanalytic understanding of the concept of ambivalence as it relates to personality development is best represented by Fenichel (1945), who proposes that the origin of ambivalence is in infancy. The infant develops, or has by nature, ambivalent feelings because it has as its primary function the activity of eating. Eating is viewed as ambivalent in that it is both aggressive (biting, sucking) and receptive (swallowing). Fenichel and others (Klein, 1975) suggest that this aggressiveness while eating is the seed of the adult experience of hate and aggression, and this receiving (swallowing, digesting) is the origin of adult love and tenderness. As the individual moves from infancy to late childhood, those early ambivalent feelings can develop into active loving/giving on the one hand or aggression/protection on the other.

The manner in which the infant relates to its environment, most importantly the mother, predicts relationships in adult life. The infant's primary object in early life is the food it ingests, namely milk, and this primary object is represented by the mother's breast or breast substitute. As the infant develops in relating to this primary breast object, so will he relate as an adult. Some persons remain fixated at the so-called anal-retentive stage of infancy in their personal psychology, and become greedy and passive in adult life. Such neurotic persons tend to cling to others as their primary means of loving, and do not progress to a more fully developed capacity to love by giving and receiving. Likewise, jealousy can originate in this early retentive stage.

Such concepts as the oedipus complex and penis envy proposed by Freud and developed by his followers are classic examples of ambivalence in early childhood. In the oedipus complex the child loves the opposite-sex parent and hates or envies the same-sex parent. Fenichel believes that envy is more prominent in women than in men, and originates in penis envy and the related ambivalent feelings about being female and "incomplete."

Most adult sexual disorders are seen as resulting from unresolved childhood ambivalent feelings. Thus, homosexuality is related to the "anal eroticism" characteristic of the second year of life, as the rectum ambivalently is used to both retain and reject feces. Feces in infancy become an ambivalently loved object, first retained, then expelled, and adult homosexuality similarly shows desires for reception and expulsion. Other evidence of ambivalence predominating in homosexuality is seen in the love and hatred of men in adult life, a result, it is suggested, of desire for intimacy with an unavailable father and a resulting hatred of the father. The passive submission to another male is an unconscious desire to rob him of his masculinity and is a displacement of the homosexual's ambivalent feelings.

Compulsive neurosis is seen as a result of too early toilet training whereby the infant does not naturally move in his development from the feeling that he is "giving" something to his mother to a more mature understanding of his bodily elimination processes. Undue altruism is a denial of one's hate side, an evidence of poorly integrated or synthesized love and aggression. Inhibitions are evidences of early conflicts of ambivalence which have been avoided. Thus, one could be socially inhibited due to his failure to accept his sexual fantasies as normal.

Sometimes ambivalent feelings can be displaced into neurotic fears, such as fear of animals, dark, or sex. Phobias such as these represent a lack of acceptance of one's normal fears and compensating aggressive/angry tendencies.

Jacobsen (1971) suggests that the heart of depression, schizophrenia, and psychopathy originate in ambivalence. One is first ambivalent toward other objects (people) and then toward oneself. Thus, one can neither love well nor hate well. The subtle arrogance of depression is that "someone should take care of me because I deserve it," but the depressive appears humiliated. He has not learned to love a person without devouring him, and his inability to devour depresses him. The paranoid person, accurately perceiving the unconscious desires of others, fails to see his own aggressive tendencies.

The most devastating element of unresolved infantile ambivalence for adequate adult functioning is the retention of separate hate and love. Thus, in adult life there are good people and bad people, and this goodness or badness is largely defined according to the pleasure they induce. The neurotic person has not synthesized his own love and aggressiveness enough to see both good and bad in everyone.

Ambivalence, adequately developed and accepted, can become the hallmark of the mature person. The acceptance of one's sinful nature as well as the capacity to love is the basic ingredient of adult humility and happiness.

References
Fenichel, O. The psychoanalytic theory of neuroses. New York: Norton, 1945.
Jacobsen, E. Depression. New York: International Universities Press, 1971.
Klein, M. Love, guilt, and separation and other works, 1921–1945. New York: Delacorte Press, 1975.

R. B. Johnson

See Psychosexual Development; Psychoanalytic Psychology.

American Association of Pastoral Counselors. This association was formally organized

in 1964 in response to the need for standards for involvement of religious organizations in mental health care. Since that time the association has provided leadership in pastoral counseling practice and training, criteria for religious institutions in pastoral counseling ministry, and coordination with other mental health professionals.

AAPC establishes standards for training and supervision in pastoral counseling. Fulfillment of these standards leads to certification of individuals for practice as pastoral counselors and accreditation of institutions which provide counseling service and education. The association also provides opportunities for continuing education, professional dialogue, and ongoing consultation.

AAPC defines a pastoral counselor as a minister who practices counseling at an advanced level, integrating religious resources with insights from the behavioral sciences. Three basic kinds of individual membership are available: certified, affiliate, and training. Certified membership requires B.A. and M.Div. degrees, good standing in a recognized denomination or faith group, one unit of clinical pastoral education in an accredited center, three years as a minister, and 375 hours of pastoral counseling together with 125 hours of supervision of that counseling. Affiliate and training membership standards are less stringent.

C. DAVIS

See ASSOCIATION FOR CLINICAL PASTORAL EDUCATION; PASTORAL COUNSELING.

American Board of Professional Psychology.

An independent organization which certifies the special competence of professional psychologists in both the United States and Canada. After World War II the American Psychological Association initiated steps to help develop and guide the rapid emergence of professional psychology by creating the independently incorporated Board of Examiners in Professional Psychology. Established in April, 1947, the board first held written examinations in 1949; it became the American Board of Professional Psychology in 1968. The board currently awards diplomas in four professional fields: clinical psychology, counseling psychology, industrial and organizational psychology, and school psychology. In 1983 there were approximately 3,000 ABPP diplomates with the majority, 2,200, in clinical psychology. About 80 to 100 diplomates are added per year.

Psychologists must voluntarily apply for the·

ABPP diploma and meet the following requirements: 1) a doctoral degree in psychology from an approved institution; 2) membership in the American Psychological Association or the Canadian Psychological Association; 3) an internship of at least 1,800 hours; 4) five years of acceptable experience; 5) present work in one's field of specialization; and 6) evidence of continuing postdoctoral education in psychology. The candidate's credentials are then examined on the basis of adequacy and extent of training, quality of professional experience, special competence, and impeccable professional reputation.

Once these requirements are met, the board requests work samples that typify the candidate's practice in assessment and intervention. A committee of five diplomates examines these materials and the candidate. The panel tries to evaluate the candidate's knowledge and skill, awareness of relevant research and theory, and sensitivity to the ethical aspects of the profession. The candidate may repeat the examination if he or she fails, and the ABPP reserves the right to revoke the diploma if the individual no longer represents professional standards.

W. C. DREW

See AMERICAN PSYCHOLOGICAL ASSOCIATION; PSYCHOLOGIST.

American Psychiatric Association.

A rising tide of humanism at the end of the eighteenth century gave rise to the moral treatment of the insane. An outgrowth of this movement was the establishment of mental hospitals, usually founded and financed by the state. When enough of these hospitals had been established in America, it is not surprising that the superintendents of these institutions found it desirable to assemble to discuss their mutual problems and to share their discoveries. The prime movers of the first meeting were Samuel B. Woodward of Massachusetts and Francis T. Stribling of Virginia. The first meeting was held at the Jones Hotel in Philadelphia on October 16, 1844. This group became known as the Association of Medical Superintendents of American Institutions for the Insane, later renamed the American Medico-Psychological Association and finally the American Psychiatric Association.

Since its inception the association has worked to improve hospital design and construction, the training of physicians and mental health professionals, medical jurisprudence, and the understanding of the causes, prevention, and treatment of mental disease. As was the case in the rest of medicine, little real progress was made until the turn of the century.

The American Psychiatric Association has instigated and promoted community psychiatry, leading to the current emphasis on community care. It has encouraged better understanding of the mentally ill prisoner, leading to increased utilization of psychiatrists in prisons. It has insisted on better management of the delinquent child, leading to the development of the specialty of child psychiatry. It has encouraged the treatment of psychologically disturbed soldiers, leading to the Veterans Administration assuming responsibility for their care.

The American Psychiatric Association has also encouraged research. Its annual meetings and journal (*American Journal of Psychiatry*) have provided a forum where research findings are disseminated to the profession. It has also been a leader in the education of physicians, nurses, psychologists, and social workers. It has encouraged the development of competence in psychiatry by participating in the approval of training programs and the establishment of the American Board of Psychiatry and Neurology (a certifying agency) and by requiring continuing education for all its members. Undergraduate medical education has not been neglected, for the association has insisted on the inclusion of adequate psychiatric education for all physicians.

W. P. WILSON

See PSYCHIATRIST.

American Psychological Association. On July 8, 1892, at the invitation of G. Stanley Hall, 18 psychologists met at Clark University in Worcester, Massachusetts, to form the American Psychological Association. Hall was elected the first president. The first meeting of the new association on December 27, 1892, saw the installation of 31 members: 26 charter members and 5 regular members. Membership dues were $1.00 per year.

In 1929 there were 680 members. However, the rapid expansion in membership came after the Second World War and was associated with the general growth of psychology in this era. In 1947 membership stood at 4,400. By 1959, only 12 years later, this had risen to 17,000, and to approximately 58,000 in 1983.

Three classes of membership exist: member, fellow, and associate. Members must have a doctoral degree in psychology, while associates need have only two years of graduate work in psychology plus a year's acceptable psychological work experience. Fellows are members who have distinguished themselves by making an outstanding contribution to or performance in the field of psychology. Fellows are nominated after a minimum of five years of postdoctoral experience.

In order to provide for the many varied and specialized interests of different psychologists, the American Psychological Association has a number of divisions. In 1983 there were 40 such divisions:

1. Division of General Psychology
2. Division on the Teaching of Psychology
3. Division of Experimental Psychology
5. Division on Evaluation and Measurement
6. Division on Physiological and Comparative Psychology
7. Division on Developmental Psychology
8. The Society of Personality and Social Psychology
9. The Society for the Psychological Study of Social Issues
10. Division of Psychology and the Arts
12. Division of Clinical Psychology
13. Division of Consulting Psychology
14. Division of Industrial and Organizational Psychology
15. Division of Educational Psychology
16. Division of School Psychology
17. Division of Counseling Psychology
18. Division of Psychologists in Public Service
19. Division of Military Psychology
20. Division of Adult Development and Aging
21. The Society of Engineering and Applied Psychologists
22. Division of Rehabilitation Psychology
23. Division of Consumer Psychology
24. Division of Theoretical and Philosophical Psychology
25. Division for the Experimental Analysis of Behavior
26. Division of the History of Psychology
27. Division of Community Psychology
28. Division of Psychopharmacology
29. Division of Psychotherapy
30. Division of Psychological Hypnosis
31. Division of State Psychological Association Affairs
32. Division of Humanistic Psychology
33. Division of Mental Retardation
34. Division of Population and Environmental Psychology
35. Division of Psychology of Women

36. Psychologists Interested in Religious Issues
37. Division of Child and Youth Services
38. Division of Health Psychology
39. Division of Psychoanalysis
40. Division of Clinical Neuropsychology
41. Division of Psychology and Law
42. Division of Psychologists in Private Practice

(There are no Divisions 4 or 11.) Members of the association usually join one or more of these divisions according to their areas of training and interest.

The association publishes 18 scientific and professional psychological journals. In addition, nine of the divisions also publish a journal, and the majority of the divisions publish a newsletter or bulletin. The association also holds an annual convention to aid communication and exchange of new knowledge among psychologists. Additionally the divisions hold their own meetings and continuing education experiences.

In 1983 the American Psychological Association purchased *Psychology Today*, a popular magazine, as a major step toward increased public knowledge of psychology. That year also saw the association first produce and televise public service announcements designed to increase awareness of who psychologists are and what services they offer. These steps represent the association's increasing efforts toward public education, the previous focus being more exclusively on psychologists themselves.

D. G. BENNER

See PSYCHOLOGIST.

Ames, Edward Scribner (1870–1958). Professor, pastor, author, and psychologist of religion, Ames was born in Eau Claire, Wisconsin. His father, Lucius Ames, frequently moved the family to pastor churches of the growing Disciples of Christ. A practical, commonsense, nontheological faith pervaded the home.

Edward received his A.B. (1889) and A.M. (1891) from Drake University, his B.D. from Yale Divinity School (1892), and his Ph.D. in philosophy from the University of Chicago (1895). He then taught at Chicago's Disciples Divinity House (1895–1897) and at Butler University in Indianapolis (1897–1900).

From 1900 to 1940 Ames ministered to the Hyde Park Church of Christ (later renamed University Church of Disciples of Christ). He had been a charter member of the six-year-old church, still under 100 membership when he accepted the challenge of a liberal, university

community congregation. It grew fivefold and erected a new sanctuary under his leadership. During the same period Ames was associated with the University of Chicago until retirement in 1935 and Disciples Divinity House (1927–1945).

With no thought of university service when he came to the Hyde Park church, Ames almost immediately began teaching in the Philosophy Department, which included psychology and education. His appointment expanded to two-thirds time. The works of William James and anthropologists' writings on religion led Ames to introduce probably the first psychology of religion course, in 1905. Teaching, reading, and forging ideas in the practicum of the pastorate produced the widely regarded *Psychology of Religious Experience* (1910). Ames emphasized the roles of symbol and ceremony and the centrality of mystical experience in religion. He was convinced that scientific and psychological analyses enriched faith: "Reflection helps religious practice to be sane and precious, showing its true function and importance. . . . Psychology and philosophy of religion renew religion. A religion without their benefit will not satisfy a modern critical mind" (Ames, 1959, p. 96). Ames wrote six more books and contributed to at least four others.

References
Ames, E. S. *The psychology of religious experience.* New York: Houghton-Mifflin, 1910.
Ames, V. M. (Ed.). *Beyond theology: The autobiography of Edward Scribner Ames.* Chicago: University of Chicago Press, 1959.

R. D. KAHOE

See PSYCHOLOGY OF RELIGION.

Amnesia, Psychogenic. Psychogenic amnesia, or memory loss, is usually associated with the diagnosis of a dissociative disorder. Persons suffering from this syndrome have one of four types of memory loss: 1) localized amnesia, 2) generalized amnesia, 3) systematized amnesia, or 4) continuous amnesia. Localized and generalized amnesia are characterized by a total loss of memory for all events and cover a period of time of several hours to many years or even a lifetime. The onset of the memory loss usually occurs after a long period of stress is finally punctuated by some trauma.

Typical of patients responding to a long period of stress was the wife of an army physician who in wartime was moving from the West to the East Coast after her husband had been transferred. She had lower extremity paralysis from polio but functioned well with braces. Accompanied by her two small children, she set out to drive from the West Coast to the East. In Kansas City, after much car trouble, she was found sitting in a hotel not knowing where she was going, where she had come from, or where her husband could be reached. The police eventually located her husband, who brought her to the hospital. She remained amnestic for several days but rapidly recovered. In wartime acute combat experiences frequently precipitate amnestic episodes, especially after traumatic battle experiences.

Acute stress can produce an amnesia for a short period. This is sometimes observed in patients who are involved in auto accidents but not injured. At the accident site they are often amnestic. They cannot remember the accident and, at times, a period before or after the accident (retrograde or auterograde). In other instances a generalized amnesia can develop. Persons with generalized amnesia behave like infants, since all their memories are blotted out. They do not recognize even close family members, do not know who or where they are, and are not even able to recognize the significance of familiar objects. If they are carefully observed, many amnestic patients do not behave as if anything is amiss, sometimes giving the impression that they are malingering.

The two other types of amnesia are systematized and continuous. In the former the person loses memory for specific and related past events usually surrounding a person or situation. Other events simultaneously experienced are adequately remembered. The person with continuous (anterograde) amnesia forgets each event as it occurs, although he is alert and aware of what is transpiring. These two forms of amnesia are rare.

Another form of amnesia is called a fugue state (see FUGUE, PSYCHOGENIC). In this dissociative state the person blots out his past, wanders off and starts a new life. Sometimes the patient wakes to find himself with a new vocation, a new wife, or even a new family. Others are "found" by relatives or friends even though they deny their past life. Many have been declared dead.

The mechanism of psychogenic amnesia is repression. Here the mechanism protects the person's ego against the painful feelings that are generated by the conflict or emotional trauma. In other instances repression provides a defense against undesirable drives and impulses that the person cannot control.

Learning theory predicts that the repression occurs because intense emotion generated by the memory motivates the person to stop remembering. Inhibiting the memory thus relieves the painful affect. When persons lose their ability to remember, they also lose their ability to make fine discriminations, including those of realistic and unrealistic dangers. They cannot think creatively or solve problems. They therefore appear childlike in the area of thinking that is repressed.

Treatment of these syndromes requires that the dissociated memories be uncovered as quickly as possible and help given to develop new coping mechanisms to resolve conflicts. The memories can often be uncovered in a free association interview, but some require sodium amytal interviews (see NARCOTHERAPY) or hypnosis. Reconstructive psychotherapy is desirable in most instances.

W. P. WILSON

See MEMORY.

Amnestic Syndrome. In 1881 Wernicke described a syndrome of paralysis of the eye muscles and staggering gait with other neuritic symptoms. In 1887 Korsakoff, a Russian physician, described these same symptoms but also noted that they are often accompanied by a psychosis which peculiarly affects memory.

Most commonly this syndrome develops in chronic alcoholics who have nutritional problems. After a period of abstinence the person often develops DELIRIUM TREMENS. With adequate treatment, which includes restoration of a proper nutritional state, there is an improvement and recovery from these symptoms. The person is, however, seen to be irritable, capricious, and demanding, or depressed and apathetic. Attacks of severe confusion or violence can also occur. Consciousness is preserved, and persons are attentive although distractable. The symptoms gradually give way to the peculiar disturbance of memory, an amnesia that is distinctive of this syndrome.

Korsakoff, as a result of his clinical observations, described a wide variety of memory changes that characterize this symdrome. Recently Talland (1965) has used modern psychological tests to examine persons and has more precisely categorized their defects as follows: 1) retention of newly presented information is markedly impaired, so that short stories are not retained; 2) new associations are not made; and 3) there is a loss of the capacity to reproduce chronological sequences.

The clinical picture presented by these persons is one of partial disorientation, especially as to time. They seem to be unaware of the passage of time. They live in a past that is confused because of their inability to sequence past events. This, coupled with some retrograde and lacunar memory defects, gives rise to a thinking disorder known as confabulation. This confabulation has been described by Talland as an internally consistent story about the patient which is false but which is presented without awareness of its distortions. Its content is drawn from the patient's recollections, and confabulation is the attempt to reconsruct the disjointed content.

Although the mood in the acute syndrome may be one of fear or depression, apathy or a loss of affective tonus is most common in the chronic form of the disease. The cause is usually chronic alcoholism, but it may occur in patients with chronic infection or in the aged. Treatment with multivitamins will facilitate recovery in some patients.

Reference
Talland, G. A. *Deranged memory.* New York: Academic Press, 1965.

W. P. WILSON

See KORSAKOFF'S SYNDROME; ALCOHOL ORGANIC MENTAL DISORDERS.

Amok. A culture-specific syndrome of Malay in which an individual attacks murderously anyone he encounters. This state of frenzy continues until the individual collapses. Running amok has frequently been thought to be a manifestation of psychomotor epilepsy. Others have viewed it as hysterical behavior.

See PSYCHOPATHOLOGY IN PRIMITIVE CULTURES.

Amusia. The loss of ability for either perception or reproduction of vocal or musical sounds. Motor amusia involves the memory and interpretation of melodies, so that a person loses the ability to play an instrument or reproduce tunes. Sensory amusia is characterized by an inability to recognize tunes. The person may be able to reproduce notes, but he can't understand what he's singing or playing. Amusia may be a result of a tumor, blood clot, or lesion in the temporal lobe of the brain.

Amytal Interview. *See* NARCOTHERAPY.

Anaclitic Depression. First described by Spitz, anaclitic depression refers to the syndrome observed in infants separated from their mothers for long periods of time. The infant initially gives indications of distress. However, after approximately three months of separa-

tion the infant begins to withdraw, and psychological contact after this point is progressively more and more difficult.

See MATERNAL DEPRIVATION; REACTIVE ATTACHMENT DISORDER OF INFANCY.

Anal Stage. According to Freud, the anal stage is the second stage of a child's psychological development, consisting of approximately the period between 18 and 30 months.

See PSYCHOSEXUAL DEVELOPMENT.

Analytical Psychology. A school of psychology founded in 1913 by Jung following the break of his close association with Freud. Jung named his approach analytical psychology to distinguish it from Freud's psychoanalysis. Trained as a psychiatrist, Jung did not limit himself to the traditional methodology of science. He allowed other sources of knowledge— art, religion, anthropology, the myths of a variety of cultures—to inform his understanding of human nature. His involvement in the physical science was thus balanced by an equally vital commitment to the humanities.

Analytical psychology is a way of viewing human nature in its widest possible context. Its focus is not just psychopathology but human expression, particularly as seen in religion, myth, and art. In fact, Jung's interest in the religious aspect of psychic experience was a contributing factor leading to his break with Freud. Jung's interest in religion enabled him to be a strong advocate for the reality of the soul and the importance of a healthy soul for psychological well-being.

Analytical psychology is based, first, on Jung's own experience with human beings, normal, neurotic, and psychotic. His theories are, in his own words, "suggestions and attempts at the formulation of a new psychology based in the first place upon immediate experience with human beings" (Fordham, 1953, p. 15). Jung's thought is also closely connected with his own personal life. Each new discovery was intimately connected to the preceding ones. His findings are therefore in this sense empirical; however, they are not systematic. The paradox of analytical psychology is that Jung's work is highly individual, yet it also reaches into general principles drawn from the history of human consciousness and experience and is, therefore, applicable to the wide spectrum of human nature.

Personality Theory. Jung postulated that the psyche has both a conscious and unconscious dimension, the conscious constituting merely the tip of the psychic iceberg. Consciousness is the part of the psyche that is knowable and has at its center the ego. It is that part which regards itself as in charge and in control.

Consciousness. Jung identified four main functions of consciousness: the thinking function, concerned with objectivity and rationality; the feeling function, sensitive to the value or agreeableness of things; the sensing function, attentive to the way things feel, sound, smell, and appear; and the intuitive function that ponders the whither or why of things. As the ego develops in the first half of life, it tends to embrace one of these functions as the dominant mode of operation.

Jung was the first to use the terms *extroversion* and *introversion* to describe the general flow of one's libido or psychic energy as being either outward from oneself or inward toward oneself. According to analytical psychology one's psychological type is based on the dominant function combined with either the extrovert or introvert attitude. During the second half of life the functions and the direction of psychic energy that remain underdeveloped begin to emerge in a compensatory manner that brings balance and wholeness to the individual.

The Unconscious. The more significant dimension of the psyche in analytical psychology is the unconscious, which is divided into two parts: the PERSONAL UNCONSCIOUS and the COLLECTIVE UNCONSCIOUS. The personal unconscious incorporates everything that Freud described as the preconscious and the subconscious, including all the material relating to one's personal life as well as thoughts or feelings too objectionable to the conscious mind and therefore repressed.

The concept of the collective unconscious is peculiar to analytical psychology. It makes up the bulk of the psychic iceberg and consists of material more remote from individual personal experience and more related to the collective experience of humankind. The collective unconscious cannot be controlled; one can only observe its manifestations in ARCHETYPES. Jung spent much research on this, and named some of the principal archetypes that affect human thought and behavior: the persona, the shadow, the anima or animus, the wise old man, the earth mother, and the self.

Dreams. Archetypes manifest themselves in various ways but particularly through an individual's dreams. Dreams are the natural reaction of the self-regulating psychic system. They are the unconscious mind's way of compensat-

ing for the conscious mind. The archetypes as manifested in an individual's dreams give clues to those functions and archetypes of the psyche pressing at the moment for attention.

It is through dreams that one comes to understand and incorporate into consciousness the archetype of, for instance, the shadow, that inferior being in each one of us, the one who wants to do all the things we do not allow ourselves to do. It is through dreams that one comes to understand the anima (if he is male), that female aspect of himself that may produce sudden and strange moods. A female may come to understand and incorporate into her consciousness the animus, and thus become a fuller person because she understands a part of her total self that formerly controlled her at times.

Dreams are also compensatory. They produce a point of view that runs counter to the stance of conscious ego; for example, a person who in conscious life has an excessive inhibition of sexual feelings might have explicitly sexual dreams. Dreams compensate in three ways: 1) by adding information from the interpreted dream to the knowledge of the waking ego; 2) by showing a self-representation of the state of the psyche, which may vary from the view of the waking ego; 3) by a direct alteration of the structure of the waking ego itself. One purpose of dream analysis in analytical psychology is to understand what function a dream, or dream series, has and to incorporate that into the conscious waking ego.

Analytical psychology defines several categories of dreams. The initial dream occurs frequently at the beginning of analysis. It usually provides a broad portrait of the individual's unconscious and often a preliminary insight into the secret that is disturbing the person seeking therapy. The recurrent dream is the second type which Jung found to be broadly experienced. It is a dream which reoccurs at intervals over the course of weeks, months, or years. Recurrent dreams are familiar; many people have had the same dream such as missing a train, flying, failing an examination, being caught before an audience without clothes, discovering an unknown room in one's house, or being chased by a dark figure.

Less common is the anticipatory dream, which seems to suggest an event that will take place in the dreamer's future. A fourth type is the lucid dream, frequently described by individuals who are attempting to solve a complex problem. This involves the presentation of either the resolution to the problem or in some cases a new idea essential to the resolution. A fifth type is the great dream, which speaks to the larger community and is subject to the scrutiny of that community because it is descriptive of the community's destiny. Such dreams are usually evident in the leaders of the people.

Symptoms and Symbols. Jung believed that every psychosis is an attempt to compensate for a one-sided view of life, and a voice, as it were, drawing attention to a side of the personality that has been repressed or re-flected. Symptoms are not simply effects of long-past causes but attempts at a new synthe-sis of life. Though often unsuccessful, they have a core of value and meaning. The symptoms need to be understood, via the symbols, dreams, and fantasies, and then incorporated into consciousness.

Myth is a very important element in analyti-cal psychology. Individual consciousness is only a manifestation of a larger whole, a whole the individual may ignore only at the expense of his own spiritual development. Defining myth as that which has always been believed everywhere by everyone, Jung went on to say that anyone who thinks he can live without myth, or outside it, is "like one uprooted, having no true link with the past, or with the ancestral life which continues within him, or yet with contemporary human society" (Camp-bell, 1971, p. xxi).

The archetypes and symbols of the collec-tive unconscious, evidenced in both dreams and myths, express common human needs, instincts, and potentials. The individual's per-sonal unconscious chooses specific images con-sistent with the archetypal themes in the surrounding culture. If the manner of life and thought of an individual departs from the norms of human culture, then a pathological state of imbalance may occur and the individ-ual will begin to have dreams and fantasies analogous to fragmented myths. These dreams and fantasies can be interpreted by the analyst, not by referring to repressed infantile memo-ries, but by comparison to the analogous mythic forms. The disturbed individual may thus learn to see himself depersonalized in the mirror of the human spirit and discover by way of analogy the way to his own larger fulfillment.

Analytic Goals. This confrontation and in-corporation of the contents of the unconscious by the conscious ego is the goal of analytical psychology. The approach is a way not only of healing but also of developing the personality through a process Jung termed INDIVIDUATION.

Individuation is the conscious realization of all the possibilities inherent in the self.

Precisely when individuation takes place continues to be a matter of discussion in analytical psychology. Initially Jung postu-lated that it occurred only in the latter half of life. Most analytical psychologists now under-stand that individuation processes are evident in early childhood and that these processes are blocked by pathological influences. If these processes are not blocked, individuating expe-riences may occur early in life. If, however, psychic energy is used to reinforce the ego rather than for identification and development of the self, these experiences are not reinforced or integrated, contributing to a more dramatic experience of individuation in the latter half of life.

The primary therapeutic goal of analytical psychology is for the analysand to come to terms with the unconscious so that he or she may gain insight into the specific structures and dynamics that emerge out of the uncon-scious. Once named and understood, these structures and dynamics affect the structures and dynamics underlying ego consciousness, producing a tension between the opposites. Change occurs as an individual in therapy integrates into consciousness the more uncon-scious structures and dynamics. The individ-ual's focus of identity then shifts from ego to self.

Analysis and Pastoral Care. In a paper entitled "Psychoanalysis and the Cure of Souls" (Jung, 1936) Jung drew some parallels and contrasts between analysis and pastoral care as he saw it at that time. He noted that both share the goal of "curing souls." Jung conjectured that a major difference in the process was that analysis worked at this goal by reinforcing and supporting the natural drive toward wholeness and salvation that exists within each individ-ual, while pastoral care professionals worked at this goal by supplying answers and meaning that were external to the person. Since the publication of that paper many pastoral care and counseling professionals have concluded that there is more compatibility than conflict between analysis and pastoral care. The large number of certified Jungian analysts who are theologically trained or who are ordained ministers attests to this commonly perceived compatibility.

Jung described four stages of treatment in analysis: confession, interpretation, education, and transformation. While these stages are not necessarily sequential, they are descriptive of the process that occurs between the analyst and analysand. Psychotherapy in analytical psychology departs from the Freudian model of a closed system analysis in which the analyst maintains an impersonal and essentially passive position in respect to the analysand. Therapy in analytical psychology is based on the dialectical relationship established between the analyst and the analysand as it moves in and out of the various stages of treatment. Both the stages and the dialectical relationship are familiar to pastoral care professionals. In the first stage the dialectic may be seen in the professional's ability to be an empathic mirror. The second stage involves the professional's ability to confront the analysand and support the message which comes to the imbalanced ego from the self. The third stage requires the professional to make connections for the analysand of his individual truth to the collective truth manifested in religion and myth. The final stage may be one of literal or symbolic celebration, which includes testimony to the change that has occurred. This final stage, more than any other, requires a commitment to the dialectic process by both analyst and analysand.

Since coming to terms with the unconscious is the goal of analytical psychology, and since the unconscious has two parts, therapy includes gaining insights in both the personal and collective unconscious. It means mastering the personal complexes and grasping the symbolic meaning of the emerging archetypes from the collective unconcious. Analysis, or therapy, is the intentional structured dialectic between the ego and the unconscious and is mirrored in the dialectical relationship between the analyst and the analysand.

Analytical psychology regards the soul as the quintessence of the self, the inner person, the center of creativity and source of religious feeling. Jung stated, "The soul possesses by nature a religious function. . . . Supreme values reside in the soul.. . . . [The soul] contains the equivalents of everything that has been formulated in dogma and a good deal more. . . . I did not attribute religious functions to the soul, I merely produced the facts which prove that the soul is *naturaliter religiosa*, i.e., possesses a religious function" (Jung, 1967, p. 90).

The biblical references to the reality of the soul as an entity apart from an individual ego identity are significant when one attempts to correlate analytical psychology and Scripture. Equally important to this correlation is a study of the symbols and archetypes in Scripture. Jung expressed the view which analytical psychology strongly emphasizes—that within every individual there is an ever-present archetype of wholeness which often disappears from the purview of consciousness or may never be perceived at all, an archetype that needs to be both awakened and illumined. Jung suggested that Jesus Christ occasions such an awakening and illumining by imparting to the soul an image of that self for which it has been longing. For Jung, Christ exemplified the archetype of the self. Jung held that the ultimate purpose of the Bible was not information but transformation and that the power of Scripture lay in its ability to symbolically capture the dynamics and structure of the struggle for the soul.

Analytical psychology can be a useful approach to the understanding of psychology and religion, particularly for those who are interested in understanding primary religious experience and for those who see the study of theology to be in tune with the world of art, sculpture, music, and poetry. While analytical psychology fails to provide a clearly defined system of understanding the divine, it welcomes the ongoing exploration of the divine in human existence and provides a structure and system that not merely allows but expects a spiritual experience to be part of one's coming to wholeness.

References

Campbell, J. (Ed.). *The portable Jung.* New York: Viking Press, 1971.

Fordham, F. *An introduction to Jung's psychology.* Baltimore: Penguin Books, 1953.

Jung C. G. Psychoanalysis and the cure of souls. In N. Read, M. Fordham, & G. Adler (Eds.), *The collected works of C. G. Jung* (Vol. 11). Princeton, N.J.: Princeton University Press, 1936.

Jung, C. G. *The spiritual problems of modern man.* Princeton, N.J.: Princeton University Press, 1967.

Additional Reading

Rollins, W. G. *Jung and the Bible.* Atlanta: John Knox Press, 1983.

D. J. Frenchak

See Jung, Carl Gustav; Jungian Analysis.

Anamnesis. A term meaning literally recollection. In psychiatry it usually refers to the life history of the patient. Psychologists have often been guilty of neglecting a thorough anamnesis during assessment. It has, however, traditionally been a central component of the Psychiatric Assessment.

Anger. An intense emotional reaction, sometimes directly expressed in overt behavior and sometimes remaining a largely unexpressed feeling. It is not a disease but rather a social event that has meaning in terms of the implicit social contract between persons. Being angry is an emotional readiness to aggress. It is caused and maintained by multiple factors and is best viewed as an interpersonal process.

Most of the professional literature related to anger is dealt with under the rubric of aggression. This literature, dealing with the theories of its origins and the patterns of its display, is reviewed in a separate article (*see* AGGRESSION). The more popular literature has focused primarily on the positive value of expressing anger, with Christian popular authors often dealing with the question of the ethics of anger as well as its value (Cerling, 1974; Pederson, 1974). The ethical questions are important since many, especially conservative Protestant Christians, frequently have been explicitly taught that anger is a sin and should be avoided at all costs. This article will present three major theories about anger within the popular and professional literature and will discuss appropriate ways to manage anger.

Konrad Lorenz presents what many authors term the hydraulic model of anger (Lorenz, 1966). He suggests that anger is instinctual. If it is not discharged it will accumulate from within like water behind a dam. In other words, anger comes from within the individual rather than from the environment. Although there is physiological evidence to suggest that aggression is influenced by heredity, blood chemistry, and brain diseases (see Myers, 1983), this position probably represents a distortion of the well-recognized relationship between repressed anger and certain psychophysiological disorders. The bulk of the evidence, however, does not support this view (Tavris, 1982). Warren (1983) presents a popular Christian version of the position.

A second broad theory about anger contends that frustration creates anger (see Berkowitz, 1978). This theory holds that when appropriate aggressive cues are present, anger may be released as aggression (verbal or physical) or turned inward against oneself. Frustration is inevitable in the human experience, and the larger the gap between one's expectations and one's achievements, the more likely one is to become angry. Especially vulnerable to such frustrations are those persons who drive themselves hard and set increasingly high expectations for self and others, and who by nature are intensely competitive. Much of the research on cognitive strategies in psychotherapy (see Ellis & Harper, 1975) tends to support this theory. Hart (1979) presents a popular Christian version of this position.

A final major view contends that anger is a socially learned behavior (Bandura, 1979). This position is well documented in the research literature. Bandura, for example, has observed that the socialization of angry feelings is affected by experience and by observing others' success with aggressive behaviors. Anger, then, is a state of arousal that can be experienced differently depending on how the source is perceived. In other words, arousal can be shaped by the environment into anger. Anger is a particular response to arousal, one which can be redirected into affection, humor, or compassion. Humans have the capacity, social learning theorists contend, to rechannel unacceptable impulses (e.g., the desire to aggress) into acceptable, even creative, actions. Gandhi and Martin Luther King, Jr., are two examples of individuals who put anger to such socially constructive uses.

A frequent source of anger is the sense of demand or obligation ("The world must be good to me on my terms"). Such persons feel unloved, unworthy, and often angry, and their unrealistic expectations for self and others contribute to diminished self-esteem and frustration (Ellison, 1983). Fearful and anxious, such individuals are much more likely to lash out at those who do not give them what they feel is rightly owed. Self-protective strategies develop lest others discover their anger and punish or reject them. Anger may be disowned but indirectly expressed in cynicism, sarcasm, projection, or more directly in explosive episodes. Destructive repressive mechanisms develop and become firmly entrenched, keeping these individuals from experiencing and owning their anger, and denying them the opportunity to explore it, seek to understand it, confess it, experience healing, and seek reconciliation where needed.

Anger is a complex emotional reaction, and clinicians must be cautioned against implementing techniques which fail to reflect an appreciation for the many factors that cause and maintain it. Explosive outbursts may have an initial calming effect on the individual, but in the long run they tend to reduce inhibition and may even facilitate the expression of aggressive behaviors. Such tantrums are often imitated by others if the results obtained from such behaviors are deemed successful. In contrast, there is a need in all societies to acknowledge and affirm role models that exhibit nonaggressive ways to express their feelings and inform others how certain behavior affects them (i.e., responsible assertiveness). Learning how to recognize one's own feelings and those of others can also be helpful, as well as training in the recognition of the many subtle and overt manifestations of anger (see Augsburger, 1973).

Minimizing aversive stimulation, rewarding nonaggressive behavior, and eliciting reactions that are incompatible with anger are all strategies that have been suggested in the literature (see Myers, 1983).

For the Christian, self-control is a fruit of the Spirit. Anger appears to be a symptom instead of a cause of the basic problem—the inability to love self and others. The key, then, is to properly deal with anger, to develop a growing capacity to accept God's love for us, and to so experience that love that we can genuinely respond to others with compassion and sensitivity.

References

Augsburger, D. *Caring enough to confront.* Scottsdale, Pa.: Herald Press, 1973.

Bandura, A. The social learning perspective: Mechanisms of aggression. In H. Toch (Ed.), *Psychology of crime and criminal justice.* New York: Holt, Rinehart & Winston, 1979.

Berkowitz, L. Whatever happened to the frustration-aggression hypothesis? *American Behavioral Scientist,* 1978, *21,* 691–708.

Cerling, C. E. Anger: Musings of a theologian/psychologist. *Journal of Psychology and Theology,* 1974, *2*(1), 12–17.

Ellis, A., & Harper, H. *A new guide to rational living* (Rev. ed.). Englewood Cliffs, N.J.: Prentice-Hall, 1975.

Ellison, C. W. *Your better self.* San Francisco: Harper & Row, 1983.

Hart, A. D. *Feeling free.* Old Tappan, N.J.: Revell, 1979.

Lorenz, K. *On aggression.* New York: Harcourt, Brace & World, 1966.

Myers, D. *Social psychology.* New York: McGraw-Hill, 1983.

Pederson, J. E. Some thoughts on the biblical view of anger. *Journal of Psychology and Theology,* 1974, *2*(3), 210–215.

Tavris, C. *Anger: The misunderstood emotion.* New York: Simon & Schuster, 1982.

Warren, N. C. *Make anger be your ally.* Garden City, N.Y.: Doubleday, 1983.

R. E. Butman

Angyal, Andras (1902–1960). One of the major proponents of the holistic point of view in psychology. As a European he shared in the phenomenological tradition of his time, and his thinking concerning human nature, health and illness, and death resembles that of contemporary existential writers.

Born in Hungary, Angyal spent his youth in rural Transylvania. He received his Ph.D. in psychology from the University of Vienna in 1927 and an M.D. from the University of Turin in 1932. After coming to the United States in 1932, he focused his early research on the physiological and psychological aspects of schizophrenia. Angyal's first book, *Foundations for a Science of Personality* (1941), developed a detailed conceptual framework for approaching each personality problem from a consistently organismic, holistic standpoint. A major shift in emphasis occurred in 1945, when he focused his efforts entirely on his private practice in Boston. Although he continued to write and lecture, his primary interest remained his therapeutic work with neurotics. His final and perhaps most important work was *Neurosis and Treatment: A Holistic Theory* (1965), published posthumously. This summarized his conceptualizations based on his many years in clinical practice.

Angyal developed an intricate theory of personality and neurosis that avoids a mind-body, subject-object dichotomy. Instead, life is viewed as a continuous interplay of organismic and environmental influences. Two observable forces, autonomy and homonomy, constantly interact to direct a person's behavior. Autonomy refers to the striving for control over one's environment. Homonomy refers to the striving to be a part of something larger than self. Neurosis is a way of life resulting from a self-protective isolation which has grown out of an individual's anxiety and diffidence caused by early traumatic experiences during the individuation process.

Angyal advocated a therapeutic stance that seeks to make holistic interpretations which uncover the patient's patterns of isolation, conflict, and anxiety. More than leading one to insight, such interpretations attempt to return the patient to a healthy "real self" by carefully unearthing and fostering the repressed healthy pattern which existed prior to the development of the neurosis.

Angyal considered religion to be an important aspect of the human experience. He was particularly interested in the aspects of human existence expressed by the wide variety of religious philosophies and world views present in numerous cultures, and through these he countered attempts to dispel the importance of religious beliefs and experience which characterized much of the scientific writing of his time.

References

Angyal, A. *Foundations for a science of personality.* New York: The Commonwealth Fund, 1941.

Angyal, A. *Neurosis and treatment: A holistic theory* (E. Hanfmann & R. M. Jones, Eds.). New York: Wiley, 1965.

J.D. Guy, Jr.

See Organismic Theory.

Anhedonia. The absence of pleasure in acts that are normally found pleasurable, such as sexual activity, intellectual stimulation, and athletic involvement. In general, a person loses enjoyment for previously pleasurable activities and appears apathetic, emotionally flat, and indifferent. Anhedonia can be a symptom of depression, and is frequently observed in schizophrenia.

Animal Psychology. *See* COMPARATIVE PSYCHOLOGY.

Anorexia Nervosa. Unlike its name implies, this is not a disorder of appetite. Rather, it is the fear of gaining weight, with the accompanying misperception that one is grotesquely fat, this persisting even in the presence of indisputable evidence to the contrary. Interestingly, many anorexics report normal sensations of hunger and are frequently preoccupied with food, so much so that they do a great deal of cooking, baking, or gathering of cookbooks. The loss of appetite does not occur until late in the starvation process.

Accompanying the weight loss is the postponement of menses and possibly hypothalmic dysfunction. Medical complications may arise from laxative abuse and self-induced vomiting. For those individuals in the later stages of the starvation process who frequently use vomiting or laxatives to rid themselves of unwanted calories, the following must be monitored: hematologic indices; electrolytes; and hepatic, cardiac, and renal functioning.

Along with the medical complications there are also psychosocial complications that arise. Frequently anorexics become social isolates, which only confirms their deep sense of self-loathing and unacceptability. Many become very meticulous and perfectionistic as a means of reclaiming some self-worth or as an attempt to establish some artificial boundaries within the family. One 16-year-old anorexic kept her bedroom meticulously clean and was an excellent student. For her, good grades were not easily achieved, so she spent a great deal of time studying; this was a way to obtain excellent marks as well as a means of establishing her autonomy within the family. Many anorexics also display compulsive patterns of exercise and an obsession with the topic. Some report a sense of power, mastery, and control that becomes equated with losing weight. For them this sense of mastery is a pocket of control which establishes them as important, providing some sense of autonomy and self-esteem.

Bruch (1973) relates anorexia nervosa to severe ego deficits which she called perceptual and conceptual disturbances. They are 1) distortion of body image; 2) distortion of internal states and sensations (such as hunger, satiety, and emotion); and 3) the persuasive sense of personal ineffectiveness. According to Bruch these deficits are a result of dysfunctional interactional patterns that arose between the mother and infant.

Garfinkel and Garner (1982) see anorexia nervosa as a multidimensional disorder, viewing it as a heterogeneous disorder with a multidetermined nature. It is a consequence and interaction of 1) those factors (individual, familial, and cultural) that predispose one to the disorder; 2) a precipitating event that acts as a stressor to bring about the onset of the disorder; and 3) factors that maintain or sustain the disorder.

Therapeutically each of the three clusters needs to be addressed in the course of treatment. Thus therapy may include medical maintenance, nutritional counseling, individual therapy, family therapy, behavior therapy, rational-emotive therapy, or group therapy in order to address those factors that predisposed, precipitated, or are functioning to sustain the disorder. This may best proceed from a multidisciplinary perspective which should include a physician, nutritionist, psychiatric social worker, psychiatric nurse, dietician, and clinical psychologist. Their cooperative effort is most significant for cases on the inpatient ward.

The younger the age of onset and treatment, the better the prognosis. Usually those individuals who also suffer from BULIMIA have a much poorer prognosis than those who do not. Individuals who have both anorexia nervosa and bulimia have frequently been associated with borderline character structures. Though the disorder is relatively rare in males, it is likely to be an indication of severe psychopathology.

References
Bruch, H. *Eating Disorders.* New York: Basic Books, 1973.
Garfinkel, P. E., & Garner, D. M. *Anorexia nervosa: A multidimensional perspective.* New York: Brunner/Mazel, 1982.

K. R. KRACKE and D. CAROLAN

Anosognosia. A denial or nonrecognition of physical illness in one's own body. Its most common manifestations are cases of blindness or deafness. Phantom limb has been described as a transitory form of anosognosia. This unawareness of sickness or disease may be a method of adaptation to stress which enables a person to cope by denying the illness. It is also interpreted as a defense mechanism which serves to make the victim of an illness feel better about himself. In some cases the denial is based on a view of sickness as failure or weakness.

D. L. SCHUURMAN

Antabuse Therapy. Antabuse is one trade name for the generic compound disulfiram. It was first used in the treatment of alcohol abuse in the late 1940s after it was noted that patients taking the drug exhibited an extremely unpleasant physical reaction following ingestion of any product containing alcohol. The symptoms of a typical disulfiram-alcohol reaction for a person on a daily regimen of the drug begin within 15 minutes following alcohol ingestion. The symptoms typically appear in the following order: flushing, sweating, heart palpitation, hyperventilation, decreased blood pressure, nausea, vomiting, and finally drowsiness. The intensity and duration of symptoms of the reaction depend on the daily dosage of disulfiram ingested, the amount of alcohol consumed, and individual physiological variables. When disulfiram was first introduced, physicians administered much larger doses than is common today, and dangerous side effects of the drug were much more common. These side effects, which are possible even at lower doses, include psychosis and degeneration of peripheral neural fibers. Extreme reactions, caused by individual hypersensitivity or by larger doses of disulfiram or alcohol, can result in psychosis, shock, or cardiac arrest. Most authorities feel, however, that when properly administered at today's lower dose levels, disulfiram is a relatively safe drug to use as an adjunct to the treatment of alcohol abuse.

There is still some question as to the mode of effect of disulfiram. It is well established that disulfiram blocks the metabolism of alcohol in the liver at a point when a major alcohol by-product is a toxin. The buildup of this toxin may directly cause the symptoms of the reaction. It is also possible that the drug has other effects involving the central nervous system when combined with alcohol, though the evidences for these secondary modes of action are just beginning to accumulate.

When first introduced, disulfiram was viewed by many as a cure for alcoholism. It then became popular to use it as the primary ingredient in a fear-conditioning treatment of alcohol abuse. Following this model, abusive drinkers were put on large doses of disulfiram and then made to repeatedly drink alcohol in the hospital to induce multiple reactions. Repeated experiences of reaction were viewed as necessary to condition a fear of drinking. This view of the utility of disulfiram is now in disfavor. Disulfiram is currently viewed by most professionals as a helpful component of a comprehensive, psychologically based treatment program. Taking disulfiram is viewed as a form of self-control whereby the patient is able to decide once daily whether or not he will drink during the next 24 hours, rather than having to make constant decisions on a moment-by-moment basis. It is seen as an excellent temporary way to limit impulsive drinking, thus giving other aspects of the treatment program the opportunity to be effective. The goal is the eventual termination of the use of disulfiram. There is some empirical evidence that use of disulfiram does increase the effectiveness of psychological treatment of alcohol abuse (Kwentus & Major, 1979). It should be noted that Antabuse therapy is opposed by most members of ALCOHOLICS ANONYMOUS, as it is seen as a continuance of the pattern of reliance upon chemical substances by the recovering alcoholic.

Reference
Kwentus, J., & Major, L. Disulfiram in the treatment of alcoholism. *Journal of Studies in Alcohol,* 1979, *40,* 428–446.

S. L. JONES

See ALCOHOL ABUSE AND DEPENDENCE.

Antiexpectation Technique. *See* PARADOXICAL INTERVENTION.

Antisocial Personality Disorder. As defined in *DSM-III* this disorder describes a person who is lawless and manipulative. *DSM-III* lists a series of specific behaviors which must be evidenced and also requires that the disorder have been manifest before age 15 and have persisted at least until the patient has reached age 18. In current terminology this disorder includes disorders previously described as sociopathic or psychopathic personalities.

In addition to these criteria there are two other general characteristics of the antisocial personality. There is a loss of respect for the rights of others and for society itself, coupled with an apparent lack of shame or guilt. These result in an absence of loyalty or an inability to make consistent commitments to other people, and a parallel failure in maintaining a coherent course in life.

In the childhood of the antisocial personality lying, cheating, stealing, truancy, disobedience, fighting, and running away are commonly seen. In adolescence destructive sexual behavior and the illicit use of drugs and alcohol are usually added. In adulthood these behaviors usually continue, and an inability to establish a permanent marriage relationship also becomes manifest, coupled with a failure to constructively continue in a given occupational course. Antisocial behavior continues, apparently compulsively, usually evidenced by a growing police record.

Antisocial persons do not actually go to prison as often as one would expect, due to their skilled interplay of manipulation, charm, ingratiation, and blatant lies. As a last resort, eloquent protestations of remorse and promises of reform often get them off.

Although antisocial personalities may appear normal and occasionally even intelligent, urbane, and altruistic, when one knows them a little better they seem callous, emotionally immature, and so shallow that their personality is seen as a façade covering emptiness. Whether this emptiness is real or a manifestation of their failure to normally sense and respond to emotions is difficult to say.

Responses to stimuli by the antisocial personality are immediate, simple, and animal-like, apparently directed more by impulse and the needs of the moment than by any consideration of future consequences. These persons have a peculiar lack of shame and fear as well as guilt, although they might talk about these emotions as though they were familiar. Underlying this callous exterior there is a disturbing tension and dysphoria, together with an intolerance of boredom, depression, and the thought that others are hostile toward them.

The antisocial characteristics are usually manifest in childhood in the male. In the female, where the disorder is much less common, it usually appears as disturbed sexual behavior at puberty or soon thereafter. There are strong suggestions from both research and common experience that the disorder is genetically transmitted (Winokur & Crowe, 1975). Estimates of prevalence cluster around a figure of 3% in males and less than 1% in females.

Antisocial personalities fall along a continuum ranging from the charming con man to the habitual criminal. When a diagnosis is made on the basis of illegal or antisocial behavior alone, a distinction must be made from a "dyssocial" disorder, or delinquency which is socially determined by group norms that might differ from those of the general community. True antisocial behavior must also be distinguished from conduct arising out of other psychiatric conditions. The psychotic person may create a disturbance in a public place, or even assault someone, but in the true antisocial personality the acts are stubbornly repeated and other conditions are not manifest.

True sociopathic behaviors are usually not stereotyped (as are impulse disorders, such as kleptomania, exhibitionism, etc.) and apparently serve no sensible purpose. This lack of reasonable motivation plus the strange absence of guilt and concern for consequences make this disorder something of an enigma. It would appear that the only motivation is the pleasure of manipulating others or the excitement of the crime itself. The sociopath seems unaware that the reason he is so successful, and appears so clever, is that normal people function with a reasonable confidence in the word and goodwill of those they deal with and they thus tend to believe others. The antisocial person might consider himself more intelligent than he really is, not being aware that he is missing the richly rewarding mutual confidence and cooperation that are a part of normal life.

The interpersonal relationships of those suffering from the antisocial personality disorder are as disturbed as they are in the narcissistic personality, but there is a distinct difference. In the antisocial personality one is impressed by the stark lack of any kind of emotional attachment beyond direct and immediate needs. In narcissistic pathology there is a similar self-centeredness and even manipulativeness, but emotional interactions are characteristically intense, if ambivalent.

Efforts by psychologists to understand the dynamics of this disorder are varied and inconclusive. Cleckley (1976), an author who has given the fullest description of this group, felt they experienced almost no feelings toward others, and that statements such as "I'm sorry I hurt you" really are devoid of meaning and mock-ups of normal communication. He calls this "semantic dementia" and considers it to be the central defect.

Many theories have been developed which relate the antisocial personality to social learning theory (see McCord & McCord, 1964). The hard evidence which suggests this is the strong correlation between sociopathy and violent homes in poor, turbulent neighborhoods. Most antisocial children also have been shown to have sociopathic or alcoholic fathers (Robbins, 1966). The condition invites a sociological explanation, but none has been convincing to date.

There seems to be little question as to a familial influence in the antisocial personality disorder (Winokur & Crowe, 1975). This has stimulated a search for other organic expressions of such a genetic error. Hare (1970) gives a comprehensive review of an impressive number of neurological defects often found in these patients. But again, these data have not yet been helpful in understanding clearly the psychopathology of the illness.

It is tempting to consider that the antisocial personality suffers primarily from an inability to feel or respond to emotions, particularly anxiety, empathy, and guilt. Clinically one gets this impression clearly, and Quay (1965) has even proposed an integration of clinical and research data in which antisocial behavior is seen as stimulation-seeking, an effort to fill an internal world which is pathologically arid. Vaillant (1975) disagrees and suggests that the problem actually comes from overwhelming internal anxiety. The debate between these alternate conceptualizations continues.

Viewed phenomenologically these patients seem to have a central and severe deprivation of normal affective experience. Since brain defects of other kinds are so common, one might suspect that this deficit is organic at base. This defect then would be expected to produce profound disturbances in the development of the personality, particularly in primary object relationships.

In addition, antisocial personalities organize the data of their environment around patterns of dramatic manipulation (Bursten, 1972). Restlessness becomes oppressive when there is no movement in their lives, and movement is thought of as the caper or confidence game.

For these reasons the most logical approach to therapy would be to stabilize the patient with controlled confinement, deal promptly with the resultant anxiety, and then begin a long-term therapeutic effort to understand successively the borderline and narcissistic difficulties that will also be present.

Actually, patients suffering from antisocial personality disorders are seldom seen in private practice and are usually charges of governmental agencies. Incarceration in prison is the only treatment most receive. Though they are often offered less rigid individual and group therapy, they seldom avail themselves of it. This is understandable when one considers that these therapies depend on a relationship that involves trust, hope, and at least some degree of warmth and stability, which are usually lacking in the antisocial personality. One might expect that the results of ordinary therapies will be dismal.

Follow-up studies from incarceration (Arendson Hein, 1959) indicate a maximum rate of improvement from imprisonment of somewhere around 50%, with a slight advantage going to those programs which are highly structured and rigid (Craft, Stephenson, & Granger, 1964). The effectiveness of this treatment is usually measured by recidivism, and one is left to question whether these people changed or simply became more skilled at avoiding prison sentences. There does seem to be an amelioration of antisocial behavior as the patient grows older, though again there is no evidence that there is a change in intrapsychic structure.

People who suffer from antisocial personality disorder are occasionally encountered in church life. They apparently find the hopeful optimism of the Christian community appealing, and often ensnare kindly church people who are sympathetic to their childlike need. Whether they seek this kind of naïvete or whether they think the church offers true hope for relief for their internal pain is difficult to determine. Suffice it to say that church leadership and the clergy would be well advised to identify these people before they create disturbing confusion within the congregation.

References

Arendson Hein, G. Group therapy with criminal psychopaths, *Acta Psychotherapeutica*, Supplement, 1959, *7*, 6–16.

Bursten, B. The manipulative personality. *Archives of General Psychiatry*, 1972, *26*, 318–321.

Cleckley, H. *The mask of sanity: An attempt to clarify some issues about the so-called psychopathic personality* (5th ed.). St. Louis: Mosby, 1976.

Craft, M., Stephenson, G., & Granger, C. A. A controlled trial of authoritarian and self-governing regimes with adolescent psychopaths. *American Journal of Orthopsychiatry*, 1964, *34*, 543–554.

Hare, R. D. *Psychopathy: Theory and research*. New York: Wiley, 1970.

McCord, W., & McCord, J. *The psychopath: An essay on the criminal mind*. Princeton, N.J.: Van Nostrand, 1964.

Quay, H. C. Psychopathic personality as pathological stimulation seeking. *American Journal of Psychiatry*, 1965, *122*, 180–183.

Robins, L. N. *Deviant children grow up*. Baltimore: Williams & Wilkins, 1966.

Vaillant, A. E. Sociopathy as a human process. *Archives of General Psychiatry*, 1975, *32*, 178–183.

Winokur, G., & Crowe, R. R. Personality Disorders. In A. M. Freedman, H. I. Kaplan & B. J. Sadock (Eds.), *Comprehensive Textbook of Psychiatry, II* (Vol. 2). Baltimore: Williams & Wilkins, 1975.

Additional Readings

Craft, M. *Psychopathic disorders and their assessment*. New York: Pergamon Press, 1966.

Reid, W. (Ed.). *The psychopath: A comprehensive study of antisocial disorders and behaviors*. New York: Brunner/Mazel, 1978.

C. M. Berry

See PERSONALITY DISORDERS; ACTIVE-INDEPENDENT PERSONALITY PATTERN.

Anxiety. Of all the unpleasant emotions anxiety probably ranks as the most common. All humans experience it at times. Even though science and technology have reduced many of life's dangers, our present age is still often described as "the age of anxiety."

The psychological study of anxiety has not been an easy task. The subjective nature of emotions makes them difficult to define. Even more difficult is the development of a comprehensive framework that sufficiently explains cause. The potential variables that affect anxiety are numerous and often hard to measure. The interaction of these factors creates a spider web of possibilities.

Anxiety may be defined as a subjective feeling of tension, apprehension, and worry, set off by a particular combination of cognitive, emotional, physiological, and behavioral cues. It is generally thought to differ from fear in that it is not tied to a realistic threat from the environment.

Following Spielberger (1966), anxiety is generally viewed as taking one of two forms. Acute, intense discomfort, usually in reaction to a perceived threat, is called state anxiety. The momentary state lasts for a relatively short period and can occur from time to time during a person's life. In contrast, trait anxiety is thought to be the more chronic, ingrained response of a person who has adopted an anxious life style. Such an individual attempts to cope with life using worry and anticipation of a frightful future. These people develop long-standing muscle tension as if to protect themselves physically from the anticipated blows of life. Giving up such habitual anxiety is not usually successful without treatment because the fear has taught the sufferer to avoid unpleasant situations. This avoidance reduces the anxiety, rewarding passivity and increasing the likelihood that avoidance will occur in the future.

It is now possible to distinguish state and trait anxiety by means of psychological tests (i.e., Spielberger, Gorsuch, & Lushene, 1970). This is a significant improvement over earlier assessment procedures where all anxiety was lumped into a single category, often underestimating the amount of state anxiety.

Physiological Research. Anxiety states are related to physical changes within the individual. This includes both parasympathetic and sympathetic activities of the autonomic nervous system, with sympathetic involvement being more pronounced. These changes are related to the fight or flight reaction, seen in such processes as rapid heart rate, perspiration on the hands and feet, increased blood pressure, and bodily coldness. Muscle tension increases as the person braces for a feared

onslaught from the environment. Epinephrine and norepinephrine are secreted into the blood by the pituitary-adrenocortical system. Anxious people can trigger these metabolic changes more quickly than nonanxious individuals. Those who show trait anxiety can even maintain increased levels of metabolic arousal for long periods of time (Martin, 1971).

Genetic studies have been done to examine the role heredity plays in anxiety. It is clear that anxious parents tend to beget anxious children, but the relative contributions of heredity and learning are not obvious. Monozygotic twins seem to show higher concordance of anxiety than dizygotic twins. However, the number of studies examining this question is too small for confident conclusions to be drawn (Burrows & Davies, 1980; Klein & Rabkin, 1981).

Another potentially fruitful area of research concerns the biochemical changes related to anxiety. Several research investigations have examined the metabolic changes that occur during the anxious state, as well as the possible chemical causes of the problem (Matthew, 1982). Abnormality in lactate metabolism has been put forward as an explanation, but to date only correlational evidence exists. High blood levels of lactic acid can produce symptoms of anxiety, but proof has not surfaced that these high levels are the cause of anxiety.

Psychological Theories. *Intrapsychic Theories.* Freud was the first theorist to differentiate the concepts of fear and anxiety. He viewed anxiety as the specific, unpleasant state that resulted from intrapsychic conflict between the person's concept of the self and an unacceptable wish or impulse (Freud, 1936). Anxiety was seen by Freud as an unconscious ego reaction to the danger of disrupting impulses. However, the anxiety itself was often disrupting, thus causing ego defenses to be directed against it. Thus, anxiety frequently comes to be central in the neuroses.

Existential theorists (e.g., May, 1950) retain a basically intrapsychic view of anxiety while rejecting most of Freud's theory. They see anxiety as the result of an inner struggle of being. Man, as the creator of meaning, is any moment on the edge of nonmeaning either from despair or death. From this perspective anxiety is the result of the inner struggle of self-assertion and self-validation and is a necessary part of life lived responsibly and authentically.

Probably the central weakness of intrapsychic models of anxiety is their reliance on theoretical constructs that are difficult to test scientifically. This is particularly a problem when anxiety is seen to be rooted in unconscious mental processes, as is the case in the psychoanalytic model.

Social/Interpersonal Theories. Social theorists such as Sullivan (1953) see anxiety as the result of interpersonal forces and conflict. The emphasis here is on a perceived threat to one's acceptance and value in the eyes of a significant other. People need love and security from significant others. Threat of rejection is therefore a major cause of anxiety.

Social theories tend to downplay the biological roots of anxiety. Tension between the self and other selves or threats to one's social needs are suggested as the underlying dynamic of anxiety. Perhaps, rather than viewing insecurity as the product of interpersonal experiences, it could be that inherited predispositions propel a person into socially inferior behaviors. Phobias are examples of anxieties sometimes difficult to explain on the basis of threats to one's social needs. While some anxiety is alleviated by attention from significant others, often such payoff is not apparent or even plausible. Anxiety produced in impersonal situations with little apparent social meaning is difficult to explain from the social viewpoint.

Cultural-Political Theories. According to cultural-political theorists such as Laing and Fromm (see Fromm, 1941), political and economic forces exert pressures on people to behave in sick ways and are the cause of anxiety. Anxiety is the natural result of conforming to a crazy or unhealthy world. Elkind's *The Hurried Child* (1981) documents the way in which technology and the values of Western society are rapidly eliminating childhood. Children are pressured to be little adults. According to Elkind, the developmentally hurried child is a person forced to be someone he or she is not, leading to inner conflict, depression, and despair.

For some thinkers in this category societal repression of human drives produces the conflict within the individual. To those theorists society is seen as an enemy, inhibiting people in unnatural ways. The therapeutic goal is to break the bonds of society that have a hold on us, releasing the natural order within each individual.

Cultural-political theories broaden our understanding of anxiety. However, to say that humans are anxious because anxiety-producing environments make them so is to ignore that some humans in these settings are not anxious and that the environment which shapes humans is itself shaped by humans. Single-factor theories of causation appear quite limited. Christian or Freudian models seem to fit the data better because man's evil side is acknowledged. Social structures become inherently flawed because all individuals are inherently flawed.

Cognitive-Behavioral Perspectives. Paul and Bernstein (1973) have attempted to synthesize behavioral views of anxiety by proposing a useful distinction between two types of anxiety. The first type, conditioned anxiety, is most frequently identified as *the* behavioral view of anxiety. Conditioned anxiety is thought to occur by the process of classical conditioning, wherein a previously neutral stimulus (such as the interior of an automobile) becomes associated with an unconditioned stimulus (physical injury caused by an automobile accident) which produces an unconditioned response (anxiety, fear, etc.). When subsequently faced with the stimulus previously associated with the very negative emotional reaction, the person will experience elements of that original response, i.e., anxiety. Such anxiety responses do not easily extinguish, because people typically try to avoid or escape from anxiety-producing situations, thus interfering with the extinction of the anxiety reaction.

Many forms of anxiety reactions have no such focal incident by which the occurrence of anxiety can be explained. Redd, Porterfield, and Anderson (1979) note, however, that research suggests that conditioned anxiety can be established by means other than a single traumatic trial or series of trials. In addition, such a conditioned response could be established by exposure to a series of subtraumatic events or by vicarious conditioning. Thus, the mail carrier exposed repeatedly to growling, snarling dogs might experience enough fear arousal to develop a conditioned anxiety response, or a child exposed to his mother's distress and worry about spiders might develop a phobia or other anxiety-based disorder.

The second type of anxiety, reactive anxiety, occurs when a person becomes anxious due to his appraisal of his circumstances. Lazarus (Lazarus & Launier, 1978) has been a major theorist in this area, suggesting that people's anxiety reactions are mediated by their appraisals or judgments of threat and capacity to cope when faced by any sort of demand. Thus, reactive anxiety may be the result of a true environmental threat to safety (the sight of flames and smoke in a restaurant), by misappraisals of demands on the person ("I must do perfectly on this exam or my life is over"), by real or perceived skill deficits ("I'm so shy, I'll probably make a fool of myself on this date"), or by any process whereby the perceived demands on the person tax or exceed the person's perceived capacity to cope. The concept of reactive anxiety is a more cognitive counterpart to conditioned anxiety. Most behavior therapists see them as relatively distinct and complementary types of anxiety.

These conceptions of anxiety are quite flexible and are capable of explaining the most specific conditioned reaction (i.e., phobias) as well as the broadest and vaguest forms of anxiety (i.e., existential anxiety). The latter might be seen as the natural reaction of persons who come to view their lack of understanding of their meaning and purpose as threatening and indicative of helplessness and powerlessness. Another advantage of these views is their implicit acceptance of the existence of reasonable and unreasonable forms of anxiety reactions. The complementary weakness is that behavioral writers typically construe healthy anxiety as occurring only in response to survival or pleasure-threatening events; other types of anxiety, such as the anxiety of the individual struggling with alienation from God, are more frequently viewed as due to "irrational beliefs." Irrational beliefs are too frequently defined merely in terms of their failure to enhance survival or pleasure rather than their compatibility with transcendent truth. These views of anxiety have been integral parts of the foundation for the development of the effective behavioral treatments of many forms of anxiety, especially conditioned and social anxiety.

Biblical Perspectives. Among Christians there is a wide range of views about anxiety. At one end of the continuum some Christian writers are almost indistinguishable from the existentialists, emphasizing man's search for identity, self, and meaning, and the resulting existential angst. They seem to deemphasize both Scripture and the idea of a personal God who holds the answers to the human condition. On the other end of the spectrum are the writers who focus upon the sins of fear and doubt of God's provision, calling people to repentance, deliverance, and an end to anxiety through prayer and meditation. All problems result from sin, they would say, so one should call the troubled persons to change their lives. Those in the middle accept the Christian ideal of a life free from worry as well as the fact of fallenness in ourselves and the creation. Neurotic anxiety may be viewed as ultimately the result of sin, but

whose sin and how that should be dealt with are often unclear. They would argue that even though anxiety may not be desirable, the route to eliminating it is not repression and denial but rather the acceptance of our anxious feelings as real.

Although the Bible is silent about unconscious mechanisms of anxiety, fewer things are clearer in Scripture than Jesus' view regarding worry and earthly care. In Matthew 6:25–32 Jesus announces that because of God's love and omnipotence, worry is a needless waste of energy. The implication is that only God can run the world, so worry about things not under our control is senseless. Jesus also contrasted two categories of life experiences we can focus upon: the material or the spiritual world. Both masters cannot be served simultaneously. One focus leads to worry and care, the other to peace. The emotional consequences of the two choices are predictable.

Paul was an intense man who at times experienced "fear and trembling" (1 Cor. 2:3). Yet he echoes Jesus' position regarding the uselessness of worry. In Philippians 4:6 he urges his readers to "be anxious for nothing," entreating us instead to pray with thanksgiving. Peter joins Paul's call, exhorting us to humble ourselves before a mighty God, "casting all your anxiety upon him, because he cares for you" (1 Peter 5:7).

As it was with the Israelites (e.g., 1 Sam. 17:47), our "battles are the Lord's." If he is for us, why should we fear? Yet knowing this intellectually is only the first step. The Holy Spirit must work into believers God's peace. This peace results from a relationship with him and not simply from positive thinking or some other cognitive technique.

According to the Scriptures, our attention should be fixed on the ultimate spiritual realities. Over 300 biblical passages tell us not to fear. Narcissistic self-preoccupation, besides being unnecessary and unrealistic, is a form of self-reliance, and self-reliance is, according to Scripture, sin. The consequence of seeking God's kingdom and righteousness first is that our needs are guaranteed to be met (Matt. 6:33). When we seek anything other than God as first priority in our lives, the meeting of our needs is not assured.

References

Burrows, G. D., & Davies, B. (Eds.). *Handbook of studies on anxiety.* New York: Elsevier North-Holland Biomedical Press, 1980.
Elkind, D. *The hurried child.* Reading, Mass.: Addison-Wesley, 1981.
Freud, S. *The problem of anxiety.* New York: Norton, 1936.

Fromm, E. *Escape from freedom*. New York: Farrar & Rinehart, 1941.

Klein, D. F., & Rabkin, J. G. (Eds.). *Anxiety: New research and changing concepts*. New York: Raven Press, 1981.

Lazarus, R. S., & Launier, R. Stress-related transactions between person and environment. In L. A. Pervin & M. Lewis (Eds.), *Perspectives in interactional psychology*. New York: Plenum, 1978.

Martin, B. *Anxiety and neurotic disorders*. New York: Wiley, 1971.

Matthew, R. J. (Ed.). *The biology of anxiety*. New York: Brunner/Mazel 1982.

May, R. *The meaning of anxiety*. New York: Ronald Press, 1950.

Paul, G. L., & Bernstein, D. A. *Anxiety and clinical problems*. Morristown, N. J.: General Learning Press, 1973.

Redd, W. H., Porterfield, A. L., & Anderson, B. L. *Behavior modification: Behavioral approaches to human problems*. New York: Random House, 1979.

Spielberger, C. D. *Anxiety and behavior*. New York: Academic Press, 1966.

Spielberger, C. D., Gorsuch, R. L., & Lushene, R. E. *Manual for the state-trait anxiety inventory*. Palo Alto, Calif.: California Consulting Psychologists Press, 1970.

Sullivan, H. S. *The interpersonal theory of psychiatry*. New York: Norton, 1953.

D. Simpson

See Coping Skills Therapies.

Anxiety Disorders. In this group of disorders anxiety is either the predominant symptom or is experienced if the individual attempts to master the other symptoms. The major disorders in this classification category are Phobic Disorders, Posttraumatic Stress Disorder, Panic Disorder, Generalized Anxiety Disorder, and Obsessive-Compulsive Disorder. It is estimated that from 2% to 4% of the general population suffer from one or more of these disorders.

Anxiety Hysteria. The name given by Freud to the syndrome now classified as Phobic Disorder. Although sometimes still used by psychoanalysts, the term is now largely obsolete.

Anxiety Neurosis. This disorder was dropped from the most recent diagnostic classification system *DSM-III* and replaced by two separate disorders, Panic Disorder and Generalized Anxiety Disorder. This differentiation of two separate disorders was made on the basis of research (Zitrin, Klein, & Woerner, 1978) which suggested the two disorders show unique treatment responses.

Reference

Zitrin, C. M., Klein, D. F., & Woerner, M. G. Behavior therapy, supportive psychotherapy, impramine and phobias. *Archives of General Psychiatry*, 1978, *35*, 307–316.

D. G. Benner

Aphasia. A general term for all speech disorders that involve a loss of ability to comprehend, manipulate, or express words in speech, writing, or signs. More peripheral disorders of speech that affect only the motor activity or the phonation process are not classified as aphasias, which necessarily involve a disruption of symbolic activities. Aphasic speech disorders are usually caused by localized brain lesions in the dominant cerebral hemisphere.

See Speech Disorder.

Applied Behavior Analysis. Applied behavior analysis has its historical origins in operant conditioning and the experimental analysis of behavior. Skinner introduced the basic concepts of operant conditioning in 1938 in *The Behavior of Organisms*. He insisted that observable behavior is the proper concern of psychology and that individual variability in behavior can be accounted for in terms of environmental variables without making reference to unobservables such as thoughts or feelings. He did not deny the presence of covert processes. He simply denied that they are necessary in giving an account of what controls behavior.

Fifteen years after publishing his first book on operant conditioning Skinner wrote *Science and Human Behavior*. In this work he tried to illustrate how to account for complex human processes in terms of environmental factors. Among the topics covered were self-control, thinking, the self, social behavior, government, religion, psychotherapy, education, and cultures. The book was a catalyst for many investigators and theorists. Skinner's approach to psychology was distinctive in at least two ways. First, he insisted on the possibility and importance of analyzing even the most complex behaviors in terms of their publicly observable controlling variables. Second, he insisted on studying individuals rather than data averaged across groups of subjects. This focus on the individual led to research designs and methodologies not used by most other psychological investigators. At least partially because the Skinnerian approach to research was different from that used by most other psychologists, journal editors were often not receptive to publishing articles by operant investigators. In 1957 this publishing problem was alleviated by the introduction of the *Journal of the Experimental Analysis of Behavior*. The title of this new journal communicated the essence of operant conditioning. Skinner's followers were committed to analyzing behaviors of individual animals or persons by systematically manipulating those variables which may have a controlling influence. Rather than first developing a comprehensive theory and then experimentally testing the validity of the theory, the operant investigators were committed to gather experimental data, determine trends in those data, and repeatedly replicate those trends before articulating laws or principles.

Another landmark in the development of the experimental analysis of behavior was the publication of Sidman's *Tactics of Scientific Research* in 1960. Prior to this there had been no comprehensive text explaining how to do intensive experimental studies on individual subjects. Sidman's book made the concepts and procedures of the experimental analysis of behavior available to a broader audience.

At the same time these methodological advances were occurring, other researchers were beginning to explore means of applying the procedures that had been developed with rats and pigeons to people and their problems in living. These early explorations were part of the beginning of a major movement within education, medicine, and psychology.

Behavior Modification and Behavior Therapy. Beginning in the 1950s an increasing number of researchers became interested in applying the experimental analysis of behavior to problems that occur in the "real world." For example, Bijou and Baer of the University of Washington analyzed the behavior of developmentally disabled persons as well as that of normal children. In the process of experimentally analyzing what variables controlled the individual's behavior, they discovered ways of helping the person behave more effectively or appropriately. Obviously persons responsible for the care of individuals with problems did not want simply to know what environmental variables control what behaviors. They wanted a psychological technology that could be used to strengthen appropriate behaviors and to weaken inappropriate behaviors. They wanted methods for changing behavior. They were interested in behavior modification.

Other investigators began in the 1950s to explore how to apply findings and procedures discovered in learning laboratories to alleviate the kinds of problems faced by clinical psychologists and psychiatrists. A. Lazarus and Wolpe were two such persons. They began their clinical research in South Africa and both eventually came to the United States, where they continued their clinical research and writing. They too were interested in focusing on observable behavior. Since they were psychotherapists, they were responsible for treating their patients. As clinicians they had a natural interest in therapy. A combination of these two concepts produced behavior therapy.

Although early behavior therapists such as Lazarus and Wolpe seemed to emphasize the concepts of theorists such as Hull and Pavlov more than those of Skinner, there was no fundamental incompatibility in the approaches of the behavior modifiers and the behavior therapists. Behavior modifiers tended to be persons who had come out of operant conditioning laboratories. Behavior therapists tended to be persons who had trained and worked in mental health settings and then turned to findings from laboratory research for help in treating their patients more effectively.

Most contemporary behaviorally oriented psychological practitioners treat behavior modification and behavior therapy as synonyms. Whether they are talking about modification or therapy, the emphasis is placed on interventions and their outcome. In contrast, applied behavior analysis places the emphasis on analyzing what environmental variables control a given behavior rather than focusing primarily on outcome.

Strategies for Analyzing Behavior Change. Behavior analysts have developed a large number of strategies for evaluating the effects of environmental variables on individual subjects. The strategies are usually referred to as single-subject, $N = 1$, or intensive experimental designs. Hersen and Barlow (1975) have provided comprehensive descriptions and evaluations of most of these designs.

Perhaps the best known single-subject strategy is the ABAB design. Each letter represents a treatment phase, with "A" usually indicating baseline or nontreatment conditions and "B" indicating treatment conditions. Each phase lasts a number of days, weeks, or sometimes months. The investigator records the subject's behavior throughout each phase. Normally at least 5 to 10 observations are made within each phase. Following the initial baseline phase the investigator introduces a treatment for a period of time equal to the first baseline period. Assuming the treated behavior changes during intervention, the next step is to restore the original baseline conditions. Most typically the target behavior worsens during this third phase. The final phase is a return to intervention. If the applied researcher can systematically increase and then decrease the target behavior as the conditions are changed from phase to phase, experimental control is demonstrated and a controlling variable is identified.

Another widely used single-subject design is the multiple baseline strategy. For example, a behavior analyst may begin by observing three behaviors (such as on task, raising hand before speaking, and disruptiveness) in the same subject without applying any treatment. Then the investigator may apply an intervention to on task while keeping the other two behaviors on baseline conditions. If only on task improves and the other two behaviors stay the same, there is evidence that the treatment controlled the behavior. Next the analyst can apply the treatment to both on task and raising hand but not to disruptiveness. If raising hand then improves but disruptiveness does not, additional evidence accrues regarding the impact of the treatment. Finally, the investigator can apply the intervention to disruptiveness. If disruptiveness then improves, still more evidence is obtained about the power of the intervention.

A basic concept underlying the preceding designs is replication. Treatment effects are replicated within a single subject. Then those effects are replicated across many subjects taken one at a time. When the same effects can be repeatedly demonstrated within and across individuals, experimental control is demonstrated.

Applications. Interest in adapting the concepts and procedures of the experimental analysis of behavior to practical problems grew rapidly during the 1960s. This interest led to a new journal in 1968, *The Journal of Applied Behavior Analysis.* Its purpose as stated in the initial issue was "primarily for the original publication of reports of experimental research involving applications of the analysis of behavior to problems of social importance."

Applied behavior analysts have spent much time determining what factors enhance or hinder academic performance. They have investigated variables that control classroom behavior—sustained attention, disruptiveness, handwriting, hyperactivity, learning disabilities, doing homework, tardiness, truancy, and underachieving.

Another focus has been health-related behaviors, including drug addictions, alcoholism, asthma, headaches, smoking, auto accidents, high blood pressure, pain, cerebral palsy, adjusting to deafness, diabetes, exercise, nutrition, obesity, rumination in infants, self-injurious behavior, recovery from head injuries, and chronic vomiting.

A third area of exploration has been social and relational skills, including altruism, assertiveness, isolate behavior, marriage, parenting, oppositional children, cooperative play, sexual behavior, sexual deviations, and sharing.

Behavior analysts have identified ways to affect a wide range of personal problems, including aggression, anxiety, articulation disorders, autistic behavior, snoring, child molesting, excessive crying, delusions, enuresis, encopresis, echolalia, gambling, gender identity problems, head banging, homosexuality, incontinence, insomnia, phobias, stuttering, stealing, throwing tantrums, thumbsucking, tics, and difficulties in toilet training.

Applied behavior analysis has also been used to identify ways of promoting athletic performance, energy conservation, creativity, driver safety, personal goal setting, happiness, job interviewing skills, prayer, room-cleaning behavior, self-care, swimming, time management, and work output.

Effectiveness. Applied behavior analysis is not a set of treatment techniques. It is an approach to analyzing the impact of any environmental variable that might influence behavior. Psychological treatments constitute one broad category of environmental variables. Applied behavior analysis has been useful in evaluating the effects of a wide range of treatments. Behavior analysts have clearly demonstrated the possibility and value of experimentally analyzing which interventions are most effective for a particular type of psychological problem.

Applied behavior analysis bridges the gap between traditional laboratory research and clinical practice by merging experimental research with practical problem solving. The development of single-subject experimental designs has made it possible to do controlled research with individual subjects in their own homes, schools, playgrounds, offices, athletic fields, or hospital rooms. This particular approach seems to have some effect on most problem areas to which applied psychologists have paid attention.

Current Issues and Future Directions. The first two decades of applied behavior analysis involved primarily demonstrations of how various interventions could influence the targeted behaviors. The demonstrations were usually made with a limited number of subjects, on a limited number of problems, in a limited number of settings, and over a relatively short period of time. In contrast, the next few decades should see greater attention paid to a few major issues. One issue concerns GENERALIZATION—i.e., how to get primary treatment effects to generalize to untreated behaviors, untreated settings, and into the future. A second issue concerns how to increase the potency of available interventions so that they will not make impaired persons simply better but will make the suffering individual perform at the same level as "normals." A third problem is how to promote the assimilation of those treatment procedures which are validated by experimental analyses into the practice of all psychologists, psychiatrists, and other psychological practitioners regardless of their theoretical orientations. A final major problem is how to get society at large to adopt the approaches and programs which behavior analysts have demonstrated to have social value.

References
Hersen, M., & Barlow, D. H. *Single case experimental designs.* New York: Pergamon Press, 1975.
Sidman, M. *Tactics of scientific research.* New York: Basic Books, 1960.
Skinner, B. F. *The behavior of organisms.* New York: Appleton-Century, 1938.
Skinner, B. F. *Science and human behavior.* New York: Macmillan, 1953.

P. W. CLEMENT

See BEHAVIORAL PSYCHOLOGY; BEHAVIOR THERAPY.

Applied Psychology.

The human mind seems to have a need to organize and name the parts of its world. For example, we name ourselves, our pets, and our occupations. One way to name psychologists is to use the applied/basic distinction. Typically, applied psychologists are interested in helping people while basic psychologists are interested in understanding people. Among psychologists in the American Psychological Association (Boneau & Cuca, 1974) the majority tend to be applied: clinical (33%), counseling (12%), school (9%), educational (7%), industrial and organizational (6%), community (2%), and engineering psychologists (1%). The others are generally labeled basic: experimental (9%), social (5%), developmental (4%), personality (2%), and quantitative psychologists (1%).

The problem with the applied/basic distinction is that it represents a dimension rather than two discrete categories. Almost all psychologists reflect a blend of applied and basic orientations. In addition, today's esoteric laboratory research may become tomorrow's solution to an important human problem. Therefore, although naming psychologists as basic and applied may satisfy some human need, it can in fact distort our understanding of psychologists and what they do.

With the above qualifications in mind, this article will discuss two current areas of psychological study that are bearing significant applied fruit but have basic roots: the psychology of the courtroom and behavioral medicine. Both areas are new and rapidly growing, and both hold the potential for producing wide-ranging changes in people's lives.

Forensic Psychology. As psychologists have entered the courtroom they have focused primarily on three issues: eyewitness testimony, "irrelevant" attributes of the defendant affecting judgments of guilt or innocence, and the dynamics of jury deliberation.

Probably the major contribution of psychologists regarding eyewitness testimony has been to disabuse us of the notion that people are walking videotape machines. A basic Gestalt principle is that when faced with an event, such as a crime, people interpret, organize, and transform what they experience. Among other things this means that we tend to see what we expect to see, going beyond the facts to produce a more understandable and organized picture of what happened. More recent evidence (Loftus, 1979) suggests that how we recall an event may alter our memories. Thus, biased questioning of a witness may distort a witness's memory/testimony (e.g., "Wasn't it true that the defendant spoke to the victim in an angry tone of voice?").

Research into the impact of defendant attributes suggests that jurors are affected by more than just the facts of a case. For example, pretty defendants are less likely to be judged guilty than ugly ones (Cash, 1981). Presumably jurors, and people in general, attribute fairly positive characteristics to beautiful people. However, there is a limit to the benefits of beauty. If a defendant used his or her good looks in the commission of a crime, jurors seem to be less understanding (Sigall & Ostrove, 1975).

The study of jury deliberations is a natural extension of the research in group dynamics. Perhaps one of the more interesting pieces of information to come from this work is that with split juries the minority has a better chance of their view prevailing if they argue for acquittal rather than a guilty verdict (Kalven & Zeisel, 1966).

Behavioral Medicine. A second major current application of psychology is behavioral medicine. It has been argued (Miller, 1983) that before the introduction of antibiotics medicine really had no inherently therapeutic methods or substances. In other words, people were healed through medical interventions simply because they believed in medicine. This suggests that the human mind has tremendous power to heal the human body. If this is so, then there is certainly room for the application of psychology in the world of medicine.

One possible application is in the area of patient compliance with a doctor's requests. Oftentimes a patient is asked to take medicine or participate in some therapeutic process which will have long-term benefits and short-term costs. The classic example is the use of medication to reduce high blood pressure. In the long run the patient may be protected from a heart attack or stroke, but the immediate consequences of the medication include tiredness and other side effects. Under these conditions patients often do not follow doctors' orders. Psychology could be helpful in making doctors more persuasive.

A second area of application concerns the relationship between personality and health. For example, people vary in the degree to which they believe they control what happens in their lives. Those people who feel they have lost control are likely to feel helpless, and this can have a tremendous impact upon health (Seligman, 1975). A broader understanding of the interface between personality and health should help us to more effectively predict and control health problems.

The placebo effect has interesting implications for medicine. Procedures having no inherent therapeutic benefit heal people simply because people expect to be healed. Apparently sugar pills and other related devices release the healing power of the human mind. This mechanism may provide a natural explanation for some of the "miracles" that have been accomplished through faith healing.

Finally, psychology has provided specific technologies for medicine. Biofeedback allows patients to consciously control "involuntary" processes. Blood flow to the hands can be increased to avoid migraine headaches. Heart irregularities can be reduced. Brain activity can be controlled to promote relaxation. What began as a series of studies with white rats has evolved into a major medical tool.

In conclusion, psychology has much to say about important areas of our lives. These contributions and insights often begin as part of basic psychology and evolve into significant tools for applied psychology. Therefore, basic and applied psychology are more like Siamese twins than normal siblings.

References

Boneau, C. A., & Cuca, J. M. An overview of psychology's human resources. *American Psychologist*, 1974, *29*, 821–840.

Cash, T. F. Physical attractiveness: An annotated bibliogra-phy of theory and research in the behavioral sciences (Ms. 2370). *Catalog of Selected Documents in Psychology*, 1981, *11*, 83.

Kalven, H., Jr., & Zeisel, H. *The American jury*. Boston: Little, Brown, 1966.

Loftus, E. F. *Eyewitness testimony*. Cambridge, Mass.; Harvard University Press, 1979.

Miller, N. E. Behavioral medicine: Symbiosis between laboratory and clinic. In M. R. Rosenzweig & L. W. Porter (Eds.), *Annual Review of Psychology* (Vol. 34). Palo Alto, Calif: Annual Reviews, 1983.

Sigall, H., & Ostrove, N. Beautiful but dangerous: Effects of offender attractiveness and nature of the crime on juridic judgment. *Journal of Personality and Social Psychology*, 1975, *31*, 410–414.

Seligman, M. E. P. *Helplessness: On depression, development, and death*. San Francisco: Freeman, 1975.

Additional Reading

Myers, D. G. *Social Psychology*. New York: McGraw-Hill, 1983.

R. L. BASSETT

Apraxia. The impairment of learned purposeful movement which is not attributable to paralysis or other motor or sensory disorder. In apraxia of gait, for example, the individual has difficulty in coordinating limb movements necessary for walking. There is currently no comprehensive understanding of the causes of apraxia. It is undoubtedly related to neurological lesions. However, the specific areas of the brain involved remain unclear.

Aptitude Tests. An aptitude test is a standardized battery or set of batteries designed to produce a score which is predictive of future performance in a given area. An aptitude is generally defined as a capacity to acquire proficiency in a specific or general area after the person has received training. For example, a person's potential to become an automobile mechanic could be measured by a mechanical aptitude test. Or a high school senior's potential to do well in college could be measured by a scholastic aptitude battery. The former is a type of specific aptitude testing and the latter illustrates a general aptitude test.

Aptitudes are one kind of ability. An ability is a present or actual capacity to perform a certain task or group of functions. Hence one's current ability to perform certain manual dexterity tasks with speed and precision might also be an aptitude for future high performance in mechanics once training was obtained. A test of manual dexterity would be called an ability test if the aim was to measure current functioning, an aptitude test if the intent was to predict future performance in mechanics, or an achievement test if the intent was to measure the adequacy of past learning or training.

The development of aptitude testing was one of the early achievements of psychology as a discipline. The initial impetus came during World War I when it became necessary to identify men with the potential to become pilots.

The success of the Otis-based Army Alpha tests of aptitude in directions, arithmetic, practical judgment, synonyms, disarranged sentences, number series, analogies, and general information launched the new field of aptitude testing. Hull (1928) was a pioneer in developing a solid theoretical and statistical base for aptitude testing. The development of correlation coefficients gave this infant science a much stronger means of identifying how closely two sets of numbers were related to one another than had previously been possible. Thus research could proceed to identify correlations between various tasks needed in the performance of certain jobs and simple tests which might be good predictors of future performance.

The theory behind aptitude testing assumes that all individuals differ. The differences may be congenital, acquired, physical, or mental. The theory is supported by the fact that training often highlights the natural differences among people to perform certain tasks and that some people do not seem to achieve well in certain tasks no matter how well they have been trained.

Aptitude tests are frequently used in schools "to give the counselor and, indirectly, the student and his parents more definitive information about the student's potentialities than is possible with an intelligence test alone" (Lyman, 1968, p. 13). Another major user of aptitude testing is the industrial personnel field in testing present or future employees for potential achievement in various skills. The General Aptitude Test Battery is a widely used battery of tests emphasizing the measurement of motor skills needed in various nonprofessional occupations.

The major criticisms of aptitude tests revolve around their questionable predictive value for long-term performance (Wigdon & Garner, 1982) and problems in test construction. Critics claim that most aptitude testing relies so heavily on verbal skills that serious contamination results.

References

Hull, C. L. *Aptitude testing*. New York: World Book Co., 1928.
Lyman, H. B. *Intelligence, aptitude and achievement testing*. Boston: Houghton Mifflin, 1968.
Wigdon, A. K., & Garner W. R. (Eds.). *Ability testing: Uses, consequences, and controversies*. Washington, D.C.: National Academy Press, 1982.

J. R. BECK

See PSYCHOLOGICAL MEASUREMENT.

Archetypes. As described by Jung, archetypes are inborn images or encapsuled symbols that suggest the most fundamental motifs and themes of human existence. The very same archetypes exist in people of all times and from all places. Since they are universally experienced, the archetypes form what Jung called the COLLECTIVE UNCONSCIOUS. This home of the archetypes, the collective unconscious, is the deepest, most primitive stratum of the human mind and as such is hidden from us. Therefore pure pictures of archetypes remain masked from full awareness.

However, representations of archetypes are available through symbols and metaphors, particularly as revealed in fairy tales, legends, myths, and folklore. These representations are distorted by both the culture in which they emerge and the personal histories of authors or storytellers. Culture and personal history serve as filters through which the image of an archetype must pass. Therefore archetypes are best glimpsed through symbols that distill the commonalities of similar legendary figures in different cultures. The wise old man, the trickster, the great earth mother, and the hero are examples of such distillations.

As a student of archaeology and anthropology Jung found these characters in every culture. The stories of King Arthur, Columbus, Homer's Odysseus, George Washington, and Rama (the hero warrior of Hindu scriptures) are all variations on the theme "the hero." In the Bible, David fits this role well. The elusive essence of this archetype is a "hero-ness" which seems to require questing. It is almost as if the hero's identity is the quest. Here conscious verbal explanations fade. Sometimes a painting or sculpture goes further to communicate such archetypal ideas.

Jung observed archetypes to be active forces in the lives of his patients as well as in his own life. In a sense the archetypes represent the many potential aspects of the self or the numerous subpersonalities common to every personality. Thus, a part of each of us wishes to see the self as questing heroically, and therefore we can identify with stories of those who act this role to the utmost. A person who cannot identify at all with a particular archetype may have alienated that part of the self.

Such denying from awareness prevents harmonious functioning of the various components of the personality and hence may cause psychological problems.

Although Jung popularized the term *archetype*, he acknowledged that the concept was not new and viewed St. Augustine's *ideaes principales* as the equivalent. Plato's Forms, described as existing before, above, and apart from all actual things, are similar to archetypes. Most familiar in the Christian tradition is the *imago Dei*, or image of God, which is imprinted in every person. This is the God archetype. Jung is saying that we also have many other images imprinted in our minds. The Christian task in this framework is to make the God image dominant in the personality and to weave together archetypes representing all other parts of the self, including the less palatable or "daemonic" aspects, under the image of God within us.

J. E. TALLEY

See ANALYTICAL PSYCHOLOGY.

Aristotle (384–322 B.C.). A student of Plato who eventually broke with his master on a number of key issues. Specifically Aristotle contended that the Forms which Plato had accepted existed not separately from the physical world but only as the essential structures of that world. Aristotle's philosophy dominated the late medieval period, and many of his ideas and insights continue to be lively centers of controversy. Among his many achievements Aristotle virtually invented formal logic.

The general tendency of Aristotle's psychology is away from Plato's dualistic separation of soul and body toward a more unified view of the "soul as the form of the body," the two together forming one substance. Aristotle viewed the main functions of the soul as the nutritive, the perceptive, the power to initiate movement, and the power to reason. These he arranged in a hierarchy, with lower forms of life sharing the lower functions but only humans fully possessing the power to reason. This laid the basis for his famous definition of man as a rational animal.

In an obscure passage in *On the Soul* Aristotle distinguished between an active and a passive intellect or reason, and stated that the active intellect is in some sense "separable" and, when separated, is eternal. This passage enabled Christian Aristotelians like Thomas Aquinas to interpret Aristotle as allowing for personal immortality. Other commentators, such as Averroes, interpreted the active intellect as identical with a universal or divine reason, a view which does not allow for personal immortality.

Aristotle taught that all human beings aim at happiness, which is therefore the supreme good, but he denied that happiness could be equated with pleasure in a hedonistic fashion. For Aristotle the good for anything involves the fulfillment of its nature or actuality; hence happiness for humans is found in actualizing the characteristic functions of the soul. Since man's most distinctive characteristic is seen as reason, the happy life is a rational one. Practically this requires moral virtue, which consists in developing habits of choosing the mean course between extremes. The highest form of happiness, for Aristotle, was the life of theoretical reason, the disinterested contemplation of truth, a life which is lived most perfectly by God.

C. S. EVANS

Artificial Insemination. A technique whereby sperm, obtained by masturbation, is placed by a syringe into the vagina. It can occur by one of three processes. Artificial insemination donor (AID) refers to mechanically introducing sperm into a woman from a man other than her husband. Artificial insemination homologous (AIH) refers to a similar process using the husband's sperm. A third form of artificial insemination involves mixing the husband's sperm with a donor's and is referred to as biseminal artificial insemination (BAI). Artificial insemination of a donor's sperm (AID) is the most common procedure. It is employed when the couple desire a child and the husband is infertile. It is also used when the husband is a carrier of some serious hereditary disease such as Huntington's chorea or Hoffman's atrophy.

The first recorded artificial insemination was performed at Jefferson Medical College in Philadelphia in 1884. Currently between 5,000 and 10,000 infants born each year are conceived by artificial insemination. It is effective about 60% of the time. This compares to 75% of couples who conceive after six months of unprotected intercourse. Usually one or two inseminations are performed per cycle in the fertilization effort.

There are several concerns involving artificial insemination. The most obvious possible complication is infection. The infection can be locally caused by contaminated sperm or disseminated venereal infection. Some of the local infections could include viruses, parasites, or bacterial infection. Disseminated infection includes venereal diseases such as gonorrhea.

The chance of disease is lessened when the donors are carefully screened.

Psychological complications following artificial insemination may include a husband subconsciously feeling threatened, inferior, or jealous of the unknown donor. Such complications can be lessened by careful screening by the physician using the procedure. The assistance of a psychologist is essential to help analyze the dynamics of the couple's relationship. The psychologist can help the couple carefully explore the reason they want a child and can also help them consider why they wish to choose artificial insemination over adoption as a means of obtaining a child.

The possibility of genetic selection or manipulation can occur as a result of artificial insemination if the procedure is used on a large scale. There is, for example, an increase in the male to female sex ratio in pregnancies resulting from artificial insemination, a slightly higher percentage of children thus conceived being males. However, as long as the procedure is not widespread, genetic selection or manipulation should be a minor factor.

Currently there is a lack of adequate legislation to cover artificial insemination. This means that the area is open to litigation that may occur from complications such as chromosomal abnormalities, infection, and congenital disease. There may also be grounds for complaint if the couple believe the child's appearance is too different from the father, or if there has been a break in confidentiality. There is, therefore, a need for legislation to deal with these possible legal complications.

Artificial insemination is not an issue dealt with directly in the Bible. Physical adultery is not involved in the procedure; therefore, it is more a question of one's motivation rather than the physical act. A couple should be in total agreement regarding the decision and should be clear as to the reasons for their choice of artificial insemination over adoption or continuing without children.

Additional Reading
Waltzer, H. Psychological and legal aspects of artificial insemination (A.I.D.): An overview. *American Journal of Psychotherapy.* 1982, *36*(1), 91–102.

M. A. CAMPION

Artificial Intelligence. *See* INTELLIGENCE, ARTIFICIAL.

Art Therapy. *See* ACTIVITY THERAPY.

Assertiveness Training. The first systematic discussion of assertiveness training was by Salter in *Conditioned Reflex Therapy* (1949). Salter believed many psychological disorders were caused by excessive inhibition, and he prescribed assertive (his term was "excitatory") procedures as the treatment of choice.

For a variety of reasons Salter's views did not gain wide acceptance at that time, and it was not until the writings of Wolpe and A. Lazarus in the 1950s and 1960s that assertiveness training became accepted as a useful therapeutic technique. Since then several hundred articles, at least 50 books, and several assertiveness training inventories have been published. Assertiveness training has become widely accepted by both behavioral and humanistic clinicians as a useful adjunct to individual therapy.

Assertiveness can be defined as the ability to express disagreement, to defend oneself against unfair or inaccurate accusations, to be able to say "no" to unreasonable or inconvenient demands from others, and to ask for reasonable favors and help when these are needed. It also encompasses a number of friendship skills, including the ability to initiate, maintain, and terminate conversations, and to give and receive compliments comfortably. In all of these there is an emphasis on respecting the needs, feelings, and rights of the other person while expressing one's own.

Assertiveness, Passivity, and Aggression. Assertiveness can be differentiated from three other interpersonal styles: passivity, aggression, and passive-aggression. The passive life style is illustrated by the person who fails to stand up for his own thoughts, feelings, needs, or rights, or communicates these so ineffectively that others easily take advantage of him. People frequently adopt a passive life style because they fear they would be rejected if they were assertive. However, some Christians adopt this stance because they believe passivity is required by the biblical commands regarding humility and personal submission.

Aggressiveness is the opposite of passivity. While the passive person counts other people but not himself, the aggressive person counts himself without adequate regard for the rights or feelings of others. Aggressive people use physical or psychological intimidation in order to achieve their objectives. They often achieve their immediate goals, but repeated aggressiveness usually destroys any significant relationships they may have.

Passive-aggression, or indirect aggression, is an interpersonal style midway between passivity and aggression. Often the passive-aggressive person agrees to go along with something even though he does not want to, and then expresses his anger indirectly through silence, sarcasm, or cynicism. The recipient usually knows that *something* is wrong, but frequently is unaware of the issue that is actually causing the problem. Christians sometimes respond passively because they believe this is the biblical thing to do; but as their needs are repeatedly ignored, their frustrations build and they become passive-aggressive, often against their own wishes.

Training Process and Objectives. The process of assertiveness training is highly variable. Some people learn assertiveness in the context of individual therapy; others attend an assertiveness training group. Groups generally meet once or twice a week for three to twelve sessions. Topics covered usually include several of the following: 1) a theoretical understanding of assertiveness, passivity, aggressiveness, and passive-aggressiveness; 2) individual analysis of each person's typical mode of responding, either through self-analysis or one of the assertiveness inventories; 3) helping people identify the personal assumptions (often unconscious or preconscious) that cause them to respond passively, aggressively, or passive-aggressively; 4) modeling assertive interactions; and 5) role playing assertive responses with feedback from the instructor and group.

Even as the format for assertiveness training is highly variable, so also are the skills taught in any given assertiveness group or book. Most assertive skills presently taught would fit into one of the following five categories: conversational skills, nonverbal assertive skills, methods for making initial assertive statements, methods for deflecting those who try to detour persons from following through on their initial assertive statements, and types of workable compromises.

Conversational skills include those behavioral skills needed to initiate, maintain, and close a conversation comfortably. They also include learning to give and receive compliments graciously.

Nonverbal assertive skills include learning to use eye contact, facial expressions, body posture, gestures, timing, voice tone, inflection, and volume to increase the probability that a person's message will be "heard" and acted upon. Nonassertive people often invite rejection of their requests because of timid nonverbal behavior.

There are a number of models for making initial assertive statements, many of which use some combination of three components: affirmation, assertion, and action. The affirmation component includes some way of affirming the person, such as "I've appreciated the effort you've been making to clean your room recently." The assertion component specifies the problem behavior and indicates how the speaker feels when the problem behavior occurs. It avoids name calling or attacks on the other person's personality. Thus, instead of saying, "You're a slob!" or "You treat me as if I were your maid!" the individual would be coached to say, "There's one thing that still bothers me. After you finish showering you leave wet towels and dirty clothes all over the bathroom floor." The action component usually prescribes the specific action the person would like to have occur. This may involve an invitation to a talk about the issue or a proposal of specific behavioral change. If it specifies an action, the speaker may include a positive consequence (reward) if the person performs the requested behavior or a negative consequence if he does not.

Whenever a previously nonassertive person attempts to be assertive, it is common for someone in his environment to try to detour him back into his previous nonassertive style. These detouring attempts occur in various ways, such as put-off detours ("Not now"), distracting detours (picking up on some incidental part of the assertive statement and shifting the focus to that area), and blaming detours (blaming the speaker or someone else for one's behavior). In order to follow through on an initial assertive statement, people need to be taught how to evaluate such responses and how to deflect those detours that are purely manipulative.

A final set of skills included in some assertiveness training classes or books might be labeled workable compromises. Workable compromises are used if, after each person has expressed his or her thoughts and goals, the goals are dissimilar. Workable compromises include finding an alternative that includes both persons' wishes, developing a quid pro quo (this for that) contract, taking turns deciding, mutually agreeing to temporarily separate in order to accomplish both persons' goals, letting an involved third party decide, and positive yielding (yielding to the other person's wishes out of love or consideration).

Evaluation. There appears to be both a biblical basis for assertiveness and some biblical criticism of assertiveness. For example,

Matthew 18:15–17 seems to recommend assertively attempting to restore broken relationships rather than allowing frustration to remain unspoken and build into resentments. "Speaking the truth in love" (Eph. 4:15) suggests a balance that is neither passive nor aggressive. Perhaps the strongest passage endorsing assertiveness is Ephesians 4:26–32, which says; "In your anger do not sin [don't be aggressive]. Do not let the sun go down while you are still angry [don't be passive]." Verse 31 then goes on to list the entire range of passive-aggressive emotions that are likely to result if persons fail to deal with their anger, and says that Christians are to put away all of these feelings. In addition, Proverbs contains indictments against angry (aggressive) behavior, and the New Testament clearly says that resentment and unforgiveness (the hallmark of the passive-aggressive person) are not to be part of the believer's life (Matt. 6:12–15; Mark 11:25; Eph. 4:32).

However, wholesale adoption of assertiveness is not appropriate for the Christian. The primary goal for the non-Christian is self-actualization; the Christian's primary goal is building God's kingdom in the hearts of people. Therefore the Christian may sometimes choose to suspend expression of his own needs or desires in order to be a testimony to the non-Christian (Matt. 5:38–48) or to build up a fellow believer (Rom. 14:1–21). Secondly, assertiveness often helps one become only a more polite narcissist. The biblical message is that we are to strive to become as concerned about the needs of others as we are about ourselves (Phil. 2:3–8). Finally, assertiveness rarely encourages people to examine their motives before being assertive. James 3:13–4:4 teaches that often our frustrations arise because we have selfish, self-centered motives. In these cases the biblical answer is not assertiveness but examination and modification of those motives.

Reference
Salter, A. *Conditioned reflex therapy.* New York: Creative Age Press, 1949.

Additional Readings
Bower, S. A., & Bower, G. H. *Asserting yourself.* Reading, Mass.: Addison-Wesley, 1976.
Faul, J., & Augsburger, D. W. *Beyond assertiveness.* Waco, Tex.: Calibre Books, 1980.

H. A. VIRKLER

See BEHAVIOR THERAPY; BEHAVIORAL PSYCHOLOGY.

Association for Clinical Pastoral Education.

An ecumenical, interfaith association composed of clinical pastoral educators, theological school representatives, representatives of church agencies, health and welfare institutions, and interested individuals. The purposes of the association are to define standards for clinical pastoral education; accredit clinical pastoral education centers; certify supervisors; promote clinical pastoral education as a part of theological education and as continuing education for ministry; and provide conferences, publications, and research opportunities for its members.

Clinical pastoral education can be described best as professional education for ministry. It brings theological students and ministers into supervised encounter with persons in crisis. Out of an intense involvement with persons in need, and the feedback from peers and teachers, students develop new awareness of themselves as persons and of the needs of those to whom they minister. From theological reflection on specific human experiences they gain new understanding of the human situation. Within the interdisciplinary team process of helping persons they develop skills in interpersonal and interprofessional relationships. There are over 350 clinical pastoral education centers throughout the United States.

C. DAVIS

See AMERICAN ASSOCIATION OF PASTORAL COUNSELORS; PASTORAL COUNSELING.

Associationism.

While historians of psychology seldom ascribe to associationism the status of a school, its adherents worked from a common point of view and saw the major problems of psychology in the same way (Heidbreder, 1933). The classical principles of association were postulated by Aristotle in partial response to two related paradoxes articulated in Plato's *Meno:* "We cannot learn anything *new* unless we already know it (by some other means), and we cannot know *anything* unless we have already learned (come to know) it" (Weimer, 1973, p. 16). Aristotle felt that memory processes were explainable through processes of association. These follow the laws of similarity, contrast, and contiguity. When one thing is recalled, the recall is usually followed by the recall of another thing which is like it, different from it, or accompanied by it in the original experience. From the differences between Plato and Aristotle emerged two lines of explanation in philosophy/psychology: explanations based on mental faculties (*See* FACULTY PSYCHOLOGY) and explanations based on processes of association.

Associationism had its roots in British

EMPIRICISM. Thomas Hobbes distinguished between regulated, orderly "trains of thought" and those which were unguided and without design. John Locke coined the phrase "association of ideas," viewing ideas as either simple or complex and arising either in sensation or reflection. The compounding of complex out of simple ideas was one of the operations of the mind, and errors of understanding resulted from wrong connections. George Berkeley, the Anglican Bishop of Cloyne, was more explicit in his assertion that "ideas are associated when they are connected in experience" (Watson, 1968, p. 194). Berkeley described simultaneous and successive association, and distinguished among association by similarity, causality, and coexistence. Abstract ideas resulted from particular ideas becoming associated with one general idea. David Hume marked the culmination of this phase when he argued that causality is a special case of resemblance (similarity) and spatial and temporal contiguity.

Associationism as a school was founded by David Hartley, who published its systematic principles in the first part of his *Observations on Man* in 1749. Hartley emphasized the principle of contiguity as an explanation for the passage from sensation to idea and from one idea to another. He formulated parallel laws for mental and bodily associations, and posited a controversial physiological psychology based on Newton's theory of vibrations to account for the neurophysiology of sensation, motion, and ideation.

The Scottish psychologists tended to oppose both the extreme empiricism and associationism of the British. The work of James Mill epitomized the notion of association as an essentially additive principle. He asserted that all complex associations could be analyzed into multiple elementary associations and that the notion of their compounding was an absurdity. He also specified conditions of association and criteria for specifying associative strength. In his assertion that words accrue their meaning by association, he articulated an associative theory of meaning later much elaborated in Titchener's context theory. John Stuart Mill rejected the atomistic, additive associationism of his father and stressed the mind's activity. He also asserted that the combination of mental elements gave rise to quality not present in the originals, thus articulating what Wundt later termed "creative synthesis." Alexander Bain systematized the classical associationist position at its apex, added his own ideas on creativity and repetition, and made associa-

tionism the basis for the newly emerging physiological psychology. Herbert Spencer added an evolutionary touch by claiming that complex traits in the human race evolved in the same way that the complex ideas evolved from simple ones in individuals.

While Aristotle's associationism involved a clear rejection of the soul and the transcendent, this antitheological bias did not extend to all these psychologists. Hartley was "a zealous champion of scriptural authority and seriously concerned with theological teachings" (Klein, 1970, p. 616). Associationism also had a strong influence on nineteenth-century theological education. Psychology was at that time included in the college curriculum as mental philosophy, a course generally taught by the college president, who was usually trained for the Christian ministry.

References
Heidbreder, E. *Seven psychologies.* New York: Appleton-Century-Crofts, 1933.
Klein, D. B. *A history of scientific psychology.* New York: Basic Books, 1970.
Watson, R. I. *The great psychologists: From Aristotle to Freud* (2nd ed.). Philadelphia: Lippincott, 1968.
Weimer, W. B. Psycholinguistics and Plato's paradoxes of the *Meno. American Psychologist,* 1973, *28*(1), 15–33.

H. VANDE KEMP

See PSYCHOLOGY, HISTORY OF.

Asthenic Personality. A personality type characterized by a low energy level and a seeming incapacity for enjoyment or enthusiasm. Formerly classified as a personality disorder, it was dropped from the most current diagnostic classification system, *DSM-III.*

See PASSIVE-DETACHED PERSONALITY PATTERN.

Asthma. A disorder characterized by recurrent periods of breathlessness, wheezing, and cough. The experience of being unable to breathe results from a narrowing of the large and/or small airways in the lungs that can be caused by muscle spasms, mucus secretion, mucus plugs, or a swelling of lung tissue. These may be triggered by a multitude of factors, including allergens, seasonal changes, exercise, dust, pollen, and animal dander. Some view emotional perturbation as another trigger.

The question as to the presence of psychosomatic factors in asthma has been the object of much controversy. According to Ferguson and Taylor (1981) there is no clear and convincing evidence that a direct correlation exists between asthma and psychosocial influences. However, others (Knapp, Mathe, & Vachon, 1976) have found research that has linked psychological factors such as stress, environmental changes, and learned responses to quantifiable pulmonary changes. Opponents of the psychosomatic theory question if small but statistically significant changes in pulmonary action due to psychosocial factors are massive enough to produce or exacerbate the clinical symptoms of asthma. In light of the equivocal evidence to date, it may be best to view asthma as a disorder with multiple interactional factors, psychological influences possibly being one of these.

Medical treatment generally consists of the use of oral bronchodilators, inhaled bronchodilators, and corticosteroids, the latter being used only when necessary because of the numerous and adverse side effects. When the asthma is not controlled by an adequate medical regimen, emotional factors are frequently involved in the exacerbation of the symptons. For example, Liebman, Minuchin, and Baker (1974) contend that poorly controlled asthma in children is perpetuated—but not necessarily caused—by chronic, unresolved conflicts in the family.

Relaxation, airways biofeedback, and systematic desensitization have shown positive results in decreasing breathlessness. Even more conclusively these approaches have been found to decrease the anxiety associated with the panic of an asthma attack. Behavior modification, group therapy, individually oriented psychoanalytic psychotherapy, and family therapy are all being used with favorable results. Because these therapies are reporting some positive outcomes, their use could be a valuable adjunctive therapy in the medical management of this debilitating disorder.

References
Ferguson, J., & Taylor, C. *The comprehensive handbook of behavioral medicine*, (Vol. 2). New York: SP Medical and Scientific Books, 1981.
Knapp, P., Mathe, A., & Vachon, L. Psychosomatic aspects of bronchial asthma. In E. Weiss and M. Segal (Eds.), *Bronchial asthma: Mechanisms and therapeutics*. Boston: Little, Brown, 1976.
Liebman, R., Minuchin, S., & Baker, L. The use of structural family therapy in the treatment of intractable asthma. *American Journal of Psychiatry*, 1974, *131*, 535–540.

K. R. KRACKE AND D. DOWELL

Attachment Theory. Developed by Bowlby, this theory explains the propensity of human beings to develop strong affectional bonds with significant others and to experience emotional distress when those ties are disrupted (Bowlby, 1977). Attachment, distinguished from dependency, is viewed as a normal necessary ingredient of emotional health. The ANXIETY that results when separation from the attachment object is real or threatened is experienced to some degree by everyone.

An undue fear of losing the meaningful object, known as anxious attachment, results from a traumatic experience with loss particularly during the first years of life. Individuals anxiously attached tend to develop unhealthy emotional reactions especially during periods of stress. Therefore, Bowlby perceives attachment experiences as critical factors in determining the etiology as well as the treatment considerations of pathological anxiety.

Reference
Bowlby, J. The making and breaking of affectional bonds. *British Journal of Psychiatry*, 1977, *130*(Mar.), 201–210.

F. J. WHITE

See LOSS AND SEPARATION; GENERALIZED ANXIETY DISORDER.

Attention. A mental process of focusing on a specific portion of the total stimulation impinging on a person. Since our sensory receptors are being bombarded by a large number of stimuli simultaneously, something is needed to avoid total chaos and confusion. Attention allows us to actively detect and experience the myriad of stimuli.

The internal determinants of a person's attention include past experience, ongoing behavior, and physiological condition. The past history of a geologist leads him to attend to different stimuli than a farmer would. During a fierce battle a soldier may not notice the pain of a wound. A hungry person attends to the sights and smells of food. External determinants of attention include the repetition, size, movement, intensity, novelty, contrast, and complexity of stimuli. In all these factors affecting attention the reticular activating system, a network of cells extending from the upper part of the spinal cord to the brain stem, plays an important role in alerting the brain to process sensory information.

Selective attention has been explained in terms of a hypothetical filter located in the brain. The filter is presumably interposed between the initial sensory registration and later stages of perceptual analysis. If information is allowed through the attentional filter, it can then be further analyzed and stored in memory. If it does not pass through, it is not remembered. Information that has some special significance to the person may be processed, even if it is not attended to. The best example of this is the sound of one's own name. We are often not aware of a nearby conversation until our name is mentioned. This suggests that the attentional filter attenuates irrelevant stimuli but does not block them completely. Related to the filter theory of attention is the deviant filter theory. This theory holds that schizophrenics are the victims of a malfunctioning filter system that floods the brain with more signals than it can handle, thus producing the delusions that characterize schizophrenic behavior.

It is obvious that people experience or attend to only a small fraction of the total neural activity in the brain at any one moment. In their shifting attention people are able to separate themselves from their total brain activity. This fact does not necessarily imply a dualistic view of the person, but it does limit the usefulness of reductionistic, materialistic views which equate personality with neural activity.

M. P. COSGROVE

See MIND-BRAIN RELATIONSHIP; PHYSIOLOGICAL PSYCHOLOGY.

Attention Deficit Disorder. The contemporary diagnostic label for the syndrome that has been more commonly known as minimal brain dysfunction, hyperkinetic syndrome, or developmental hyperactivity. The syndrome has its onset in childhood, with the early signs appearing between the time the child is a toddler to when he enters school. In making the diagnosis the clinician compares the child's behavior to that of typical children who are the same age.

Clinical Picture. The syndrome is called attention deficit disorder because inattention is the central problem. Inattention is manifested by 1) failing to finish tasks after they are started, 2) behaving in a manner which causes adults to conclude that the child often does not listen, 3) becoming distracted easily by extraneous events, 4) having difficulty sticking to an assigned task such as schoolwork, and 5) tending not to stick with a single, constructive play activity. The child must exhibit at least three of these five problems in order to be diagnosed as having attention deficit disorder.

Impulsivity is the second major problem area that defines this syndrome. The specific clinical signs relating to impulsivity are 1) frequently acting without thinking about the probable consequences of the actions, 2) changing activities at an excessive rate, 3) failing to organize work at an age-appropriate level, 4) behaving in a way that causes adults to provide the child with excessive supervision, 5) excessive speaking or yelling out in the classroom, and 6) refusing to take turns or to wait for one's turn in games or other group activities. The diagnosis requires the child to manifest at least three of these six signs.

The third problem area is hyperactivity. Attention deficit disorder may occur with or without hyperactivity. The child must show at least two of the following signs in order to be diagnosed as hyperactive: 1) running around or climbing objects excessively, 2) fidgeting excessively or failing to sit still, 3) tending not to stay seated in those situations calling for seated behavior, 4) tossing and turning excessively during sleep, and 5) being in continuous motion, as though having a mainspring which never unwinds.

All these clinical signs must be present for at least six months before the diagnosis of attention deficit disorder is made. The diagnosis should not be made if the child meets the criteria for profound mental retardation, conduct disorder, schizophrenia, or affective disorder with manic features. Stressful environments can also produce many of the behaviors which define attention deficit disorder; therefore, another diagnosis may be more appropriate when the child lives in a highly stressful situation.

Children who suffer from attention deficit disorder often perform poorly in school, have difficulties in peer relationships, and do not do well with authority figures. This is a very common disorder, occurring in approximately 3% of American children; it is about 10 times more common in boys. The family histories of these children show that often the parents, particularly the fathers, manifested similar problems in their childhoods.

Etiology. There are several theories regarding the etiology of attention deficit disorder. One theory argues that the disorder represents a "seizure equivalent"—that attention deficit disorder is best conceived as a mild form of epilepsy. A slightly different approach proposes that there is a biochemical defect or dysfunction underlying the syndrome. These theorists have proposed the term "minimal brain dysfunction" as the most appropriate indentifier of the syndrome. Both these theoretical orientations consider children with attention deficit disorder as being qualitatively different from "normal" children.

Other theorists conceive the primary differences as quantitative rather than qualitative. One of these focuses on the concept of temperament. Temperament refers to the style in which a child behaves rather than what the child does. Temperament relates to *how* a child behaves—such as activity level, rhythmicity, approach/withdrawal in new situations, adaptability, intensity, threshold for responding, mood, distractability, attention span, and persistence. Everyone would fall somewhere along a continuum in each of these dimensions. A fourth theoretical orientation focuses on the child's behavior itself. This approach assumes that behavior is behavior—i.e., one behavior is no more abnormal than another and all behaviors are susceptible to the same controlling variables. Social expectations, rather than some hidden, underlying process, are what define a particular behavior as normal or abnormal.

Treatment. Available clinical research has failed to demonstrate that child psychotherapy, including play therapy, has a positive impact on the primary symptoms of attention deficit disorder; however, there are three additional approaches to treatment which do appear to provide clinical benefits.

The first of these is family/parent counseling. (*See* BEHAVIORAL FAMILY THERAPY.) Children who receive the present diagnosis often come to perceive themselves as bad. They, their siblings, and their parents need assistance in developing positive coping strategies and weakening troublesome behaviors without attacking the child's character. The family counseling usually covers effective methods of discipline, a clear plan for the parents to follow at home in dealing with their child, clarification of what to expect from a hyperactive child, techniques for not blaming others, and ways to relate effectively to school personnel.

The second useful treatment strategy is BEHAVIOR THERAPY. Most typically there are two therapy programs, one for the home and one for school. The treatment program in both settings may incorporate a written contract which spells out the primary target behaviors, the consequences for each, who will deliver the consequences when and in what amounts, and how the contract may be amended. These treatment programs lean heavily on the principles and procedures of CONTINGENCY CONTRACTING, APPLIED BEHAVIOR ANALYSIS, and CONDITIONING, OPERANT. These procedures have proved effective in increasing sustained attention, improving impulse control, reducing hyperactivity, and improving academic performance and social relations. Behavior therapy may be combined with the third treatment approach to obtain even greater effects.

Physicians may prescribe stimulants to help the child with attention deficit disorder. These drugs are fast acting. Their effects usually become apparent within 30 minutes following ingestion, but the effects of many of the drugs are short-lived, i.e., a few hours. The more commonly used drugs are amphetamine (Benzedrine), dextroamphetamine (Dexedrine), methamphetamine (Desoxyn), methylphenidate (Ritalin), pemoline (Cylert), and deanol (Deaner). The most widely used and best known of these is methylphenidate (Ritalin). Available evidence suggests that from 65 to 85% of children diagnosed as having attention deficit disorder can benefit from such stimulants. The primary benefits are increased attention and impulse control, decreased restlessness, and improved social relations; however, the stimulants do not appear to improve these children's academic achievement.

Additional Readings

Safer, D. J., & Allen, R. P. *Hyperactive children: Diagnosis and management.* Baltimore: University Park Press, 1976.

Stewart, M. A., & Olds, S. W. *Raising a hyperactive child.* New York: Harper & Row, 1973.

P. W. CLEMENT

See MINIMAL BRAIN DYSFUNCTION.

Attitude Assessment. Although some researchers approach attitude assessment using ad hoc, single-term indices of individuals' attitudes, most experts advocate the use of carefully constructed attitude scales to maximize the validity of attitude measurement. Among the wide variety of available techniques for attitude assessment three have gained widespread acceptance: the method of equal-appearing intervals, cumulative scaling, and the method of summated ratings.

The method of equal-appearing intervals was developed by Thurstone as an extension of psychophysical scaling. A Thurstone scale consists of a number (usually nine) of statements expressing sentiments across the range of possible attitudes toward an issue. These statements are chosen to represent equal-appearing intervals in order to form the analogue of a yardstick. For example, there may be four statements favorable to the issue which appear to give measurement in units for varying degrees of positive attitude. Similarly, the range of negative attitude willl be represented as units, with the midpoint of the scale being a statement of neutral affect. Individuals indicate their attitude by choosing the statement most similar to their own position.

Cumulative scaling was developed by Guttman. Items in Guttman scaling are like attitude-related performances that vary in terms of the strength necessary to endorse them and also represent an individual's attitude by a single score. Metaphorically, Guttman items are hurdles ordered according to the strength needed for endorsement. Since performance is, within limits, mathematically cumulative, the total range of a person's performance can be reconstructed from knowledge of his greatest performance. For example, a high jumper capable of clearing seven feet can be expected to make a six-foot jump but to fail at a height of eight feet. Similarly, persons who are strongly prejudiced could be expected to endorse any sentiments of mild or moderate prejudice and to fail to endorse only those statements that are more extreme than their own position.

The most familiar technique is the method of summated ratings developed by Likert. A Likert scale consists of a series of statements of belief accompanied by the Likert response format—strongly agree; agree; no opinion; disagree; strongly disagree. Each Likert response option is given an integer value (e.g., strongly agree equals 5, agree equals 4, etc.); a person's attitude is then summarized by a single score obtained by summing the person's ratings for each statement. A Likert scale, in which all statements are used to generate a single score, must not be confused with simple questionnaires in which each statement examines a separate issue.

Complete descriptions of these and other techniques are available in Fishbein (1967), including exact procedures for developing and validating each type of scale.

Reference

Fishbein, M. (Ed.). *Readings in attitude theory and measurement*. New York: Wiley, 1967.

L. S. SHAFFER

Attitude-Behavior Relationships. Attitude has been historically the most important explanatory concept in social psychology. This is true because social psychologists have chosen to study the influence of social learning on behavior, and attitudes are the most conspicuous product of social learning. Further, nonscientists have been in general agreement that attitudes are important, citing social attitudes as reasons for their behavior and making attitude change an important target for educational and political programs. Recently, however, social psychologists were forced to reassess the adequacy of their views of attitudes when empirical studies attempting to predict individuals' behavior from relevant measures of attitude proved disappointing. The result has been a recognition that there is a more complex relationship between attitudes and behavior.

While there are a number of technical distinctions made in defining attitudes for scientific purposes, most definitions include the following elements. Foremost, attitudes are evaluative feelings individuals have formed about social objects. Attitude measurement must, therefore, in some way include the dimension of evaluation. Attitudes studied by social psychologists have typically been social attitudes (attitudes held by many people or groups) rather than idiosyncratic, personal attitudes. Attitudes are always about something (a group, an individual, a place, or a practice) which is called the attitude object. Finally, most social psychologists describe attitudes as having three components: a cognitive component (beliefs or ideas), the evaluative component (feelings), and a behavioral component (tendencies of approach or avoidance).

It is the presumed correlation between evaluative feelings and social motivation that is at the heart of the historical theory of attitude-behavior relationships. The classical view of attitudes can be described as follows. Attitudes are formed in the context of daily social interaction. They may form in a variety of ways—direct experience with the object, verbal transmission of beliefs and evaluations about the object, etc. But once formed, attitudes are relatively enduring predispositions to respond to a general class of social objects. That is, it was thought that once individuals had formed attitudes toward a religious group, for example, they possessed a generalized motive that would predispose their social actions toward any member of that group or its possessions. The presumed explanatory power of attitudes in this conception is broad. Knowing individuals' attitudes would mean that it is possible to predict their overt social behavior in a variety of situations. It was thought that individuals would be consistent in their social behavior, both in the sense of avoiding behavior that would contradict attitudes (e.g., vandalizing a valued religious relic) and performing comparable behavior across situations (e.g., verbalizing a prejudiced attitude irrespective of occasion or audience). In this classical view it is obvious that attitudes are presumed to be the most powerful determiner of behavior; stated in terms of precise measurement, scores on valid attitude scales should correlate highly with measures of overt social behavior.

Almost from the beginning there were empirical findings which did not square with the classical conception. While the design of many of those early studies can be faulted, by the close of the 1960s it was clear that empirical assessment of the classical view was disappointing. In a highly influential review of the best research available, Wicker (1969) reported attitudes had fared very badly in predicting social behavior; in precise terms, the correlations reported between measures of attitude and behavior rarely exceeded .3. The result of Wicker's review and comparable work was a scientific crisis, called the attitude-behavior problem, in which attitude theory was opened for serious criticism.

Fortunately, the "problem" resolved itself relatively quickly. First, it was discovered that consistency is a matter of individual differences; some individuals express their attitudes more clearly than others, and this is now an active topic for personality researchers. Second, it was found that where correlations of attitude with single acts were disappointing, correlations between attitudes and multiple-act criteria are much better. That is, religiosity may correlate poorly with any single act of religious behavior, such as church attendance, but correlate highly with combined indices of attendance, financial contributions, and activity. More importantly, attitude theory now recognizes that attitudes are only one of many influences on social behavior, and often a secondary influence at that. Most social psychologists now accept what is called the theory of reasoned action (Fishbein & Ajzen, 1975), in which attitudes directly affect behavioral intentions (individuals' intentions to perform specific acts). It is the behavioral intentions, formed in the context of the realities of the individual's situation, that best predict overt behavior.

References

Fishbein, M., & Ajzen, I. *Belief, attitude, intention, and behavior: An introduction to theory and research.* Reading, Mass.: Addison-Wesley, 1975.

Wicker, A. W. Attitude versus actions: The relationship of verbal and overt behavioral responses to attitude objects. *Journal of Social Issues,* 1969, 25(4), 41–78.

L. S. Shaffer

Attitude Change. Though the study of attitude change or persuasion has been marked with a wide diversity of theories and approaches, three basic questions have always permeated the field: 1) What are attitudes? 2) Why are attitudes important? 3) How is attitude change determined?

What are attitudes? Allport (1935) defined an attitude as a "mental or neural state of readiness, organized through experience, exerting a directive or dynamic influence upon the individual's response to all objects and situations

with which it is related" (pp. 804—810). This definition has enjoyed wide acceptance and is typical of definitions which hold that attitudes prepare people for actions, are learned from experience, and exert a motivating force on behavior. However, other approaches to the attitude concept have also been influential.

One popular view of an attitude, having its roots in the writing of Plato, emphasizes three components. The first is cognitive and refers to all the beliefs or ideas that a person has about some attitude object. The second is evaluative or emotional and refers to all the feelings, favorable or unfavorable, a person has about the attitude object. The third component is behavioral and refers to the behavioral tendencies a person has toward some attitude object.

One implication of this view is that for any given attitude there should be an underlying consistency among the three components. It was precisely this implication that prompted Fishbein and Ajzen (1972) to define attitude in a slightly different way. They define the cognitive component as "belief" and the behavioral component as "behavioral intentions." In their view an attitude is the evaluative or emotional feeling toward an attitude object. Fishbein and Ajzen see no necessity for an underlying consistency among beliefs, attitudes, and behavioral intentions. For example, the belief that a given car is inexpensive might have little to do with a person's feelings about owning the car. Likewise, a person's feelings about owning the car may have little relationship to the person's intention to buy the car.

Fishbein and Ajzen used this redefinition of attitude to develop the theory of reasoned action (Fishbein, 1980). This development alone indicates that concern over the definition of attitude is not misplaced. Though there is no single definition of attitude that persuasion researchers unanimously share, a perusal of the research indicates that most often a person's feeling toward an attitude object has been taken as the best indicator of attitude.

Why are attitudes important? In addition to their key role in persuasion theory, attitudes are important because of the various psychological functions they have for the individual. But the attitude concept derives most of its importance from its presumed close relationship to behavior. Social scientists have generally viewed attitudes as crucial in explaining, understanding, and predicting human behavior. The precise nature of ATTITUDE-BEHAVIOR RELATIONSHIP has been a source of controversy that is of interest in its own right. Though as a result of that controversy some theorists are beginning to question the utility of the attitude construct, there is little doubt that attitudes and attitude change will continue to be important in the study of human behavior.

How is attitude change determined? Before social scientists could study attitude change effectively, ways of measuring attitudes had to be devised. Currently there is a wide range of instruments that the persuasion researcher can select from in order to measure attitudes (*See* ATTITUDE ASSESSMENT). Typically the researcher is interested in testing a given theory of attitude change. This involves documenting the presence or absence of attitude change from one time to another. But in addition, the specific reason for the change is of prime importance. The most common method used to indict any particular reason for attitude change is the experimental method. A carefully designed experiment often allows the researcher to make a statement about the causes of any attitude change observed. Because the researcher in attitude change seeks to describe, explain, and predict human behavior, and because the experimental method is the keystone of the search, the study of attitude change is properly construed as a scientific endeavor.

Theories of Attitude Change. *Conditioning theories.* One approach to the study of attitudes, more popular in the 1950s and 1960s than it is today, was a direct result of the behaviorist movement that dominated the social sciences. Razran (1940) is typical of early researchers who used the classical conditioning paradigm to show that an attitude could be conditioned. He was able to show that by repeatedly pairing some new attitude object with an old object that already elicited a favorable or unfavorable response, people would begin to respond to the new object in the same way they responded to the old one.

Another principle of behaviorism, which states that people act to maximize rewards and minimize costs, serves as the underlying principle behind the operant conditioning of attitudes. For example, Scott (1957) showed that when debaters won their case, they were more likely to change their attitude to conform to the position that they had argued. In contrast, debaters who lost their case were more likely to change their attitude in the opposite direction of the position they had argued. Presumably winning debates is rewarding and losing debates is psychologically costly. The person's attitude toward the issue becomes conditioned as a result of the favorable or unfavorable experience.

Studies done in the conditioning paradigm have often been criticized for flaws in experimental design. However, research has clearly shown that attitudes can indeed be conditioned. The overall contribution of this approach to the study of attitudes must be tempered by the fact that the underlying assumptions of behaviorism regarding basic human nature differ radically from those of cognitivism, which currently dominates psychological theory. In addition, these conditioning effects seem to apply for the most part to the formation of new attitudes rather than to changing existing ones.

The message-learning approach. Hovland, Janis, and Kelly (1953) fashioned an approach to persuasion which focused on the importance of attending to the message, comprehending it, and yielding to its arguments. This focus resulted in fairly intense research activity on the characteristics of both the message and the source of the message that would tend to increase attitude change.

The credibility of the source has received more research attention than any other source characteristic. Early research on credibility examined the persuasiveness of sources that possessed high levels of expertise and/or trustworthiness in relation to a given topic. This research almost always concluded that high credibility sources were more persuasive than low credibility sources. However, as Petty and Cacioppo (1981) point out, this effect is significantly reduced when the message is personally relevant to the recipients. Presumably this is due to the increased attention and closer scrutiny people give to messages that are personally relevant.

Researchers have also examined the persuasiveness of particular types of messages. One variable of special interest to practitioners of religious persuasion is the level of fear induced by the message. Generally high fear appeals are more persuasive (Leventhal, 1970). However, this effect is observed only if people are convinced that negative consequences are very likely if they do not adopt the message's recommendation *and* if they are convinced that adopting the recommendation will completely ward off the danger. Griffin (1976) agrees that fear is a powerful motivator but cautions the Christian persuader to use the technique carefully and "to err on the side of too little fear than too much" (p. 77).

While the message-learning approach to persuasion proposed no formal theory, it helped to generate a large body of research findings that has served as a firm foundation for understanding attitude change processes.

Cognitive dissonance theory. No other single theory has generated more controversy and research than Festinger's (1957) theory of COGNITIVE DISSONANCE. The heart of the theory for persuasion research is Festinger's contention that people strive for consistency or harmony among their various thoughts. When two thoughts are dissonant, a person will work to reduce that dissonance. One way to reduce dissonance is to change one of the thoughts. Thus, cognitive dissonance is a strong motivating force for attitude change.

One application of cognitive dissonance theory is to situations in which people must choose between two or more alternatives. According to the theory, once a person chooses, the negative aspects of the chosen alternative are dissonant with the fact that it was chosen. Likewise, the positive aspects of the unchosen alternative are dissonant with the fact that it was not chosen. Consequently, the theory predicts that immediately after such a decision, if the person does not revoke the decision, he will reduce dissonance by changing his attitude toward the alternatives. The chosen alternative will be viewed more favorably while the unchosen alternatives will be devalued. The research evidence supports this application of the theory.

Another area of application for dissonance theory is situations in which people have little justification for engaging in a certain behavior. As a result, dissonance is aroused, and one way persons may reduce it is to change their attitude toward the object of their behavior. Zimbardo, Ebbesen, and Maslach (1977) suggest that this process of persuasion is often at work in religious cults. Potential converts find themselves in a position where they have invested a fair amount of time and effort with little justification or reward for their actions. Consequently, they begin to conclude that the justification for their action resides internally and that their attitude toward the cult must be favorable.

According to Festinger, dissonance is something that exists inside a person. Only the effects of dissonance can be observed. This is one of the reasons that dissonance theory fell out of favor in the 1970s. However, the cognitive revolution in psychology has brought about a renewed interest in dissonance theory. While the new research often attempts to document the specific nature of dissonance (e.g., Higgins, Rhodewalt, & Zanna, 1979), it is clear that the research community is more comfortable with this cognitive concept than it was years ago.

The cognitive revolution. The heavy emphasis in psychology on cognitive structures and processes has served to rekindle interest in persuasion. It is difficult to speculate on the ultimate contributions that the cognitive revolution will make to the field. But cognitive theorists have already shown the potential for their work to yield new insights and offer satisfying explanation of attitude change processes.

Petty and Cacioppo (1981) point out that simply how much a person thinks about something is a key variable in the persuasion process. If a person thinks a lot on any given issue, persuasion in general becomes more difficult. But any persuasion that does occur after a great amount of thought is likely to last over time. This approach to persuasion holds promise for unifying different approaches and theories of attitude change under one general framework.

Cappella and Folger (1980) contend that some of the major theories in attitude change—e.g., dissonance—are really "closet" cognitive theories. In focusing on the relationship between messages, attitudes and behaviors, they typify a new hard-core cognitivism in stating that "it is certainly beyond time that these relationships were explained by mechanisms and processes permitting a meeting of cognitive theories of attitude and behavior change and more general theories of cognitive information processing" (p. 187). There are some faint signs that the logical end of the cognitive revolution will see the dawning of a focus on neurophysiology. It remains to be seen whether or not such pursuits will yield rich payoffs in terms of understanding attitude change.

Ethics. In pointing out that God is concerned about more than just the success or failure of attempts to influence, Griffin (1976) argues that Christians can rely upon a general ethical standard in their attempts to influence others: "Any persuasive effort which restricts another's freedom to choose for or against Jesus Christ is wrong" (p. 28). Griffin also urges Christians to weigh their persuasive tactics on the scales of love and justice, carefully considering how any appeal affects the other person and at the same time determining whether or not the appeal violates standards of Christian conduct.

In addition to these ethical concerns in the practice of persuasion, attitude change theories provide a rich terrain for ethical analysis. Some of the assumptions underlying purely behavioristic theories of attitude change are clearly not in harmony with the traditional Christian view. Perhaps the most pervasive of these is the basic denial of the importance of the human mind. Because of this, the emergence of cognitive psychology with its basic assumption that human beings are active processors of information may be seen as a favorable development from the Christian perspective.

But cognitive theories often give rise to some of the same ethical concerns that arose in the wake of behaviorism. Woelfel (1980), a cognitive theorist of attitude change, refers to the "moral outrage caused some workers by a 'physical' theory of human behavior" (p. 95). As cognitive psychology matures and leads, perhaps, to neurophysiology, theories of attitude change may grow increasingly "physical" in terms of the structures that lie behind the explanations of behavior. To the degree that such theories imply little free choice on man's part, they may be just as devastating to human autonomy as the most radical behaviorist theory. Since there is a dearth of writing on ethics and attitude change, Christians will have a great opportunity to contribute to ethical thinking in persuasion during the coming years.

References

Allport, G. W. Attitudes. In C. Murchison (Ed.), *Handbook of social psychology* (Vol. 2). Worcester, Mass.: Clark University Press, 1935.

Cappella, J. N., & Folger, J. P. An information-processing explanation of attitude-behavior inconsistency. In D. Cushman & R. McPhee (Eds.), *Message-attitude-behavior relationship*. New York: Academic Press, 1980.

Festinger, L. *A theory of cognitive dissonance*. Evanston, Ill.: Row, Peterson, 1957.

Fishbein, M. A theory of reasoned action: Some applications and implications. In H. Howe & M. Page (Eds.), *Nebraska symposium on motivation* (Vol. 27). Lincoln: University of Nebraska Press, 1980.

Fishbein, M., & Ajzen, I. Attitudes and opinions. *Annual Review of Psychology*, 1972, *23*, 487–544.

Griffin, E. *The mindchangers*. Wheaton, Ill.: Tyndale House, 1976.

Higgins, E. T., Rhodewalt, F., & Zanna, M. P. Dissonance motivation: Its nature, persistence, and reinstatement. *Journal of Experimental Social Psychology*, 1979, *15*, 16–34.

Hovland, C. I., Janis, I. L., & Kelley, H. H. *Communication and persuasion*. New Haven: Yale University Press, 1953.

Leventhal, H. Findings and theory in the study of fear communications. In L. Berkowitz (Ed.), *Advances in experimental social psychology* (Vol. 5). New York: Academic Press, 1970.

Petty, R. E., & Cacioppo, J. T. *Attitudes and persuasion: Classic and contemporary approaches*. Dubuque, Iowa: W. C. Brown, 1981.

Razran, G. H. S. Conditioned response changes in rating and appraising sociopolitical slogans. *Psychological Bulletin*, 1940, *37*, 481.

Scott, W. A. Attitude change through reward of verbal behavior. *Journal of Abnormal and Social Psychology*, 1957, *55*, 72–75.

Woelfel, J. Foundations of cognitive theory: A multidimensional model of the message-attitude-behavior relationship. In D. Cushman & R. McPhee (Eds.), *Message-attitude-behavior relationship*. New York: Academic Press, 1980.

Zimbardo, P. G., Ebbesen, E. B., & Maslach, C. *Influencing attitudes and changing behavior*. Reading, Mass.: Addison-Wesley, 1977.

G. G. SPARKS

Attribution Theory. How do people make sense out of the world? Under what conditions do we decide that someone intended to cause a particular consequence, and how do we use this information to ascribe personal characteristics to others? How do we decide what our own intentions are? These are the kinds of questions addressed by attribution theory.

There are actually many different attribution theories, but they all have roots in the phenomenological psychology of Heider in the 1940s and 1950s. Heider developed a systematic understanding of the commonsense, implicit theories people use in explaining the causes of events in their lives. His followers built on this foundation, developing and empirically testing systematic hypotheses focusing on personal intentions (Jones & Davis, 1973), self-perception (Bem, 1972), and perception of both self and others (Kelley, 1967). Each line of research builds upon Heider's major distinction between internal attributions (personal intentions or dispositions) and external attributions (to other persons or the physical environment).

These theories all assume that people seek to understand the environment, particularly the personal environment, in ways enabling them to predict and control it. This emphasis on understanding has led to a focus on what people think, to the detriment but not the exclusion of what they feel. While there is a certain amount of overlap, each approach has made important and unique contributions, including identification and increased understanding of some important biases in how people make attributions.

Intentions of Others. The first attribution theory to yield extensive empirical research was the work of Jones (Jones & Davis, 1973) on the intentions which an observer attributes to an actor in situations of free choice. Sometimes behavior is very informative about the intentions of the actor. In such situations, called high correspondence situations, people will be very confident in inferring that an actor had a particular intention (personal attribution), usually one consistent with the behavior. An example is an observer's strong feeling that a person who made a hostile remark has hostile intentions or is a hostile person. In other situations observers are less sure of the person's intentions or infer intentions that are less extreme. These inferences are called low correspondence inferences and may involve the conclusion that the behavior was caused by persons or objects in the environment (environmental attribution).

Several factors strongly influence the correspondence of attributions. Higher correspondence, i.e., the confident assumption of a particular intention behind the behavior of another person, is expected when the behavior's consequences are less desirable. Higher correspondence is also likely when the act produces noncommon consequences, i.e., consequences different from those which alternative acts would produce. Higher correspondence is also likely when the results of the act affect the observer. Finally, higher correspondence is expected when the observer sees the act as particularly conditioned by his presence.

While the last two factors provide a way for the theory to examine how observers' needs, wishes, and motives influence attributions, the theory and research have tended to focus on the rational aspects of attribution. This is confirmed by the more recent extension of the theory to include the notion of expectancy. When a person's free behavior is more unexpected, it carries more information about his or her intentions or personal characteristics. This expectancy effect is offset by yet another rational factor, skepticism, if the discrepancy between what is expected and what occurs is too great.

Jones and his colleagues have shown that both actors and observers tend to make biased attributions. Observers tend to overestimate the importance of personal factors in others' behavior without considering sufficiently the circumstances in which the behavior occurred. In contrast, people tend to overestimate the importance of situational factors in their own behavior. This actor-observer difference often produces situations of interpersonal conflict. For example, in a marriage having difficulty, the wife may tend to blame the husband's lack of attention on the "clear fact" that he is a workaholic (person attribution), while the husband blames it on the unavoidable pressures of his job (situational attribution).

One explanation of these biases focuses on the different perspectives involved. The actor's attention is focused outward, toward the environment, so environmental attribution is natural. In contrast, the observer's attention is focused on the actor, so attribution to the actor as a person is natural. A second explanation of actor-observer differences focuses on the differing amounts of information which they have. For example, the actor knows what he or she has usually done in this type of situation, whereas the observer may not.

These explanations of actor-observer differences in inferences can be applied in therapy; reattribution training counters inaccurate attributions and encourages more effective living. For example, Brehm (1976) suggests the following when a client makes too many personal attributions to another, such as incorrect or too-strong attribution of hostile intent. First, personal attributions of hostility can be minimized by emphasizing to the client the other person's lack of choice due to strong environmental pressure. Attributions of hostility would also be reduced by showing the client that the outcomes of the other person's behaviors were too variable to allow confident inference of hostile intent. Finally, in some contexts the therapist could reduce attributions of hostility by using techniques such as role playing to encourage the client to empathize with the other person.

Reattribution training procedures such as these should be effective in modifying attributional biases that are due mainly to rational processes. However, when misattribution also serves ego defensive or ego enhancing purposes (as suggested by such biblical passages as Ps. 19:12–13), then reattribution training procedures are less likely to be completely successful.

Self-Perception. Bem (1972) was the first to develop an explicit theory of how people interpret their own behavior and internal states. He argued that the internal cues to our attitudes, emotions, and inner experience are often weak, ambiguous, or uninterpretable. Hence, a person comes to know his own internal states partly by using the same method he uses to know other people; he looks at the relevant behavior (his own in this case) and the context in which it occurs and makes a reasonable attribution about what his internal state is likely to be. If there are no strong external conditions influencing the behavior, an internal (personal) attribution is likely. For example, a child may effectively say to herself, "Since I failed the math test, I must not be good at math." In contrast, the presence of strong external factors, such as strong extrinsic reward or punishment, leads toward external attributions.

The therapeutic implications of self-perception theory are important. Strong external incentives may produce immediate behavioral accommodation, but only at the cost of cognitive changes within the client which minimize long-term behavior change. Therefore, attributional retraining should be effective if it strongly encourages a client's positive internal attributions. For example, research shows that self-esteem and academic performance increased when adults attributed children's success in academic situations to the internal factors of ability or motivation. Such changes tend to be longer lasting than persuasion-induced changes, partly because the behavior change is intrinsically located or motivated. Similar applications to chronic problems in adults need to be examined further.

Bem's theory dovetails nicely with Schachter and Singer's (1962) theory of emotions, which focuses on both arousal and cognitive states. Emotional states can be intensified by arousal caused by an irrelevant source but mistakenly attributed to one's own emotional state. For example, arousal from physical exercise or from reading about arousing events can intensify emotions such as hostility in response to provocation, males' liking of an attractive female (or disliking of an unattractive female), appreciation of music, or funniness of cartoons.

Perception of Self and Others. Kelley (1967) has developed the most comprehensive attribution theory. His view holds that persons (self or others), entities (things or environmental stimuli), and times (occasions or situations) are all possible causes of behavior. His general principle of attribution is covariation; in deciding upon a cause for a given behavior, he assumes people search for a set of conditions associated specifically with the occurrence of that behavior. For example, an employee might argue frequently with other people, whether at home, at work, or at play (his behavior is not distinctive); he might do this over a period of time and with reference to many different issues (his behavior is consistent); and yet other people do not usually argue (there is low consensus among various actors). Under these conditions an observer would probably conclude that the employee is an argumentative person (person attribution). Other patterns of distinctiveness, consistency, and consensus lead to stimulus attributions and to situational attributions. The major attributional bias in Kelley's model is that people tend to underuse consensus information and rely too heavily on their own experience

with a limited number of cases. Testimonials of a few others or a very limited amount of personal experience are often more persuasive than broadly and carefully collected information which is more accurate.

Kelley's model is appropriate for situations in which people can perform a relatively complete causal analysis. When this is not possible, Kelley argues that several factors influence the attributions which people make. First, through extensive experience people develop causal schemata; they learn that certain types of events are associated with certain causes. A particular causal scheme is brought into play when the situation makes it seem relevant. Misunderstandings can easily result when an inappropriate causal schema is used, as might occur in a crosscultural situation, in the attributions of a paranoid person, or in attributions about the intentions of someone of the opposite gender. Second, people often discount potential causes if other plausible causes are present. A rich woman may disbelieve her suitor's avowals of love, thinking instead that he is after her money. Third, an augmentation principle seems to operate when an event occurs despite some inhibiting factor. For example, a person who helps someone in spite of great cost to herself will be judged to have particularly strong motivation to help. Knowledge of factors influencing attributions should be helpful in many situations in therapy.

References
Bem. D. Self-perception theory. In L. Berkowitz (Ed.), *Advances in experimental social psychology* (Vol. 1). New York: Academic Press, 1972.
Brehm, S. S. *The application of social psychology to clinical practice.* New York: Halsted Press, 1976.
Jones, E. E., & Davis, K. E. From acts to dispositions. In L. Berkowitz (Ed.), *Advances in experimental social psychology* (Vol. 2). New York: Academic Press, 1973.
Kelley, H. H. Attribution theory in social psychology. In D. Levine (Ed.), *Nebraska symposium on motivation* (Vol. 15). Lincoln: University of Nebraska Press, 1967.
Schachter, S., & Singer, J. Cognitive, social, and psychological determinants of emotional state. *Psychological Review*, 1962, 69, 379–399.

Additional Reading:
Antaki, C., & Brewin, C. (Eds.). *Attributions and psychological change: Applications of attributional theories to clinical and educational practice.* New York: Academic Press, 1982.

S. P. McNeel

Authoritarian Personality. In the aftermath of World War II many social scientists attempted to explain how individuals, or even whole societies, could resort to such intense prejudicial and aggressive attitudes as were demonstrated by the fascist forces of Europe.

Though many theories and lines of research have been developed over the past four decades, few have received as much attention as the theory of the authoritarian personality. Psychologists Adorno, Frenkel-Brunswik, Levinson, and Sanford, in their 1950 book entitled *The Authoritarian Personality*, proposed the notion that there is a certain personality type that is especially prone to develop and display prejudicial and/or aggressive attitudes and behaviors. Such individuals seem particularly predisposed to engage in "scapegoating," or blaming their personal or societal difficulties on a certain class of people or an ethnic or religious minority.

For Adorno and his colleagues there are four major characteristics that, taken together, help define the authoritarian personality. The first is that of *fascism*. They define fascism as a trait in which a person focuses upon the importance of demonstrating respect for, and showing obedience to, established authority persons and structures. The leader (or master) is all-important, all-powerful, and all-good, and should be accorded due honor and respect. A person with fascist tendencies is likely to show blind and unquestioning devotion and loyalty to his or her leader (whether it be a führer, president, premier, king, commanding officer, or simply an older sibling) and to be highly outraged at hearing criticism of this leader. The fascist person is overly influenced by the position of authority itself. No honor can be greater than to have served the authority well, and to have been faithful to the end to all of the leader's commands and wishes; the virtue comes in having served authority simply for authority's sake. Another tendency of fascist individuals is to divide the world's people into two rather simplistic groups. The "good" group serves authority well and is physically, spiritually, and morally strong. The "bad" group consists of immoral, crooked, and feeble-minded people who can never be trusted, who never learned respect and reverence for tradition, and who are responsible for most of the world's problems. Finally, there is a tendency in fascism to enjoy and respect symbols of power, authority, and mass conformity—guns, swords, flags, insignias, uniforms, etc.

The second major characteristic of the authoritarian personality is the tendency toward *ethnocentrism*. An ethnocentric attitude holds that one group or culture or nation is best, and all others are inferior ("My country is the greatest one on earth!"). Political pluralism and ethnic or religious diversity are not societal qualities to be admired or desired.

Third, the authoritarian personality tends to be quite *anti-Semitic*. Such an individual is likely to possess many stereotypes of Jews (e.g., "Jewish power and control in money matters is far out of proportion to the number of Jews in the total population") and is likely to blame "the Jewish element" for a myriad of social and economic problems.

Fourth, the person with an authoritarian personality is seen by Adorno as being *politically and economically conservative*. This person will believe in the notion that determination and hard work are the only requirements for success in life (ignoring racial or gender barriers), that "children should be taught the value of the dollar," and that tradition is usually superior to innovation in both the political and economic arenas.

Adorno and his associates established a paper-and-pencil inventory of authoritarianism and used the tool to isolate authoritarian individuals for research and study. One important finding is that subjects with authoritarian personalities tend to have grown up in homes characterized by strict and punitive child-rearing practices; the subjects often report that their fathers, in particular, demanded obedience and unquestioning loyalty.

Lest Americans think that authoritarianism was to be found only in Hitler's Germany, many theorists have pointed to the United States' own brand of authoritarianism. For example, it has been suggested that the Ku Klux Klan, many individuals in the nation's intelligence and/or military agencies, and, quite simply, many Americans in general seem to demonstrate several traits of the authoritarian personality (the trait of anti-Semitism may be broadened to include scapegoating of any cultural, religious, ethnic, or gender group, be they "hippies," Catholics, blacks, illegal aliens, "gays," feminists, etc.). Individuals who possess such a personality constellation have even been portrayed as major characters on popular television programs, such as Archie Bunker in *All in the Family* or Major Frank Burns in *M*A*S*H*.

The popularity of many of the religious cults in America today has been explained in part by the ability of charismatic and power-oriented leaders to capture the hearts and minds of potential followers who have an authoritarian bent. Of even greater concern to many Christians is the opinion expressed in some quarters that elements of the "new right" in American politics and religion represent a special kind of Christian authoritarianism where blind devotion and loyalty is accorded to fast-speaking preachers as much as, if not more than, to Christ himself.

The concept of, and the research on, the authoritarian personality is not without its critics. One concern, for example, is that the existing research only presupposes a right-wing authoritarian personality. Could there not also be a political and religious left-wing counterpart personality type? Finally, social scientists who study so-called authoritarian personality individuals might be somewhat prejudiced themselves in the way they describe the personality traits of their subjects; e.g., the authoritarian person is often described as being "intolerant of ambiguity" and "rigid." Perhaps others might see such a person as being "decisive" and "stable."

References

Adorno, T. W., Frenkel-Brunswik, E., Levinson, D., & Sanford, R. N. *The authoritarian personality*. New York: Harper & Row, 1950.

D. E. ANDERSON

See PREJUDICE; AMBIGUITY, INTOLERANCE OF.

Autism, Infantile. A rare disorder (two to four cases per 10,000) that commences within the first 30 months of age. It is usually marked by an inability to relate to people or situations from the beginning of life, severely impaired communicative skills, and a compulsive insistence on consistency or sameness. This article describes the clinical picture, outlining diagnostic criteria as they pertain to this disorder. There are varying opinions about the etiology of autism; some of these opinions are discussed in addition to a variety of treatment suggestions for working with the autistic child.

Clinical and Diagnostic Criteria. Significant impairments in sociability, including relatedness with others, the ability to play, and communication skills, are the major clinical features of infantile autism. While autistic children can appear normal, with appropriate alertness and good motor coordination, symptoms of autism may be noticed rather quickly. They avoid eye contact and lack visual and/or auditory responsiveness to other people. Mothers may say, "He was never cuddly," or "He never noticed when I came into or left his room." These children are described as "good" babies who cooperate quietly with being left alone and do not fuss at bedtime or other times of separation. On the other hand, they show no normal imitative gestures such as waving good-bye or playing social games like peekaboo or pattycake.

Another major symptom is gross deficits in language development. Speech may be either totally absent or sound strange, having a mimicking-like quality. Repetitious, stereotyped phrases are used, and the child is not involved in any communicative give-and-take. The autistic child does not respond with a "yes" or "no" answer but typically may reiterate the question. Personal pronouns are repeated as heard; thus, the child refers to his or her own person as "you" and the other individual as "I." While these children usually ignore verbal requests or comments to the extent of seeming to be deaf, they frequently respond to sound rather normally. They often have a strong, positive response to music. Their nonverbal communication skills—e.g., socially appropriate facial expressions or gestures—also seem to be grossly lacking.

Bizarre responses to the environment are another outstanding characteristic of autism. Ritualistic, repetitive behaviors and rhythmic movements are characteristic. Changes, even such minor ones as a different place setting at the table or moving furniture around, can be met with extreme responses such as screaming and crying. It seems as if the child's internal world is held together by obsessive sameness in the external world. Frequently there is attachment to unusual objects; e.g., the child may insist on always carrying a string or rubber band. Play items are important, not because they have been given by a parent, but because the toy is something to which the child can cling; it can be manipulated as the child so desires. Essentially the child prefers to live in a static world where he or she can relate to objects, making the learning of something new quite difficult.

As odd as their behavior and mannerisms may be, these children do not have delusions, hallucinations, loosening of associations, and incoherence as is characteristic in schizophrenia. Autism is chronic. A few of these children go on to lead independent lives, manifesting minimal signs of the disorder. However, most remain severely handicapped and in need of care and supervision. Special education facilities are almost always required.

Etiology. There are many theories about the etiology of infantile autism. These range from organic causes on one end of the spectrum to parent-child relationship factors on the other. While the current trend of research emphasizes organic causations, there have been strong tendencies in the past to place certain familial interpersonal factors as the primary cause.

Current literature suggests that such diseases as maternal rubella, phenylketonuria, encephalitis, meningitis, and tuberous sclerosis may lead to this disorder. One source views the symptoms as a consequence of an impairment in the brain. Studies have indicated that an impairment in the function of the reticular formation of the brain stem may prohibit the appropriate flow of oxygen, which could lead to autism. Any impairment in this area of the brain could lead to serious neurophysiological disturbances (Kessler, 1966). One theoretical orientation suggests that these children are constitutionally vulnerable and predisposed toward autism. This basically means that the child tends to be vulnerable and hypersensitive in his or her responses to both inner and outer stimuli. The child is unable to discriminate between relevant and nonrelevant stimuli and therefore becomes overwhelmed. Whereas most children can respond to trauma without falling apart, the supersensitive, autistic child seems to collapse beneath it.

The role of the parents is another consideration in the causative factors of autism. Some studies have suggested that a lack of emotional warmth, detachment, obsessiveness, and a more mechanical type of mothering is representative of the parents with autistic children. These studies are frequently criticized for their lack of rigorous investigation and their tendency to make generalizations that have not been either thoroughly tested or followed up.

Most researchers in this area agree that autism cannot be attributed to a single cause. Most likely the impairments are due to a combination of several contributing factors.

Treatment Suggestions. The approach to treatment will be determined by the view one takes of the etiology and by the specific problems presented by each individual case. As previously mentioned, special education facilities are usually necessary for these handicapped children. The first step in remedial education is to provide the child with warm, caring experiences until he or she feels comfortable and safe in the setting. Following this, training commences. Frequently a behavioral approach is used to teach the child to perform certain new responses which will replace the old autistic habits. Rewards and punishments are used to reinforce newly acquired and more appropriate skills.

Most therapists who treat children with this disorder emphasize that the patient-therapist relationship needs to be relevant and immediate in a way the child can experience and appreciate. The relationship cannot be merely symbolic; it must be experienced by the child as real and concrete. The therapist must have a great amount of endurance and patience to provide the child an experience in emotional consistency and understanding. The pace of therapy is extremely slow. Goals include increased socialization, postponement of immediate gratification, and the establishment of a positive, warm personal relationship. Any movements toward these goals must be supported. It is possible the child will need this constant support for his or her lifetime to maintain the progress of the steps taken toward these goals.

Another approach that may be taken would include treatment of the child and family. The child is kept at home and seen on an outpatient basis. The parents are seen either individually or together, with the goal being to strengthen their functions as parents, especially in relation to their autistic child.

Reference
Kessler, J. W. *Psychopathology of childhood.* Englewood Cliffs, N.J.: Prentice-Hall, 1966.

B. J. SHEPPERSON

See PERVASIVE DEVELOPMENTAL DISORDER OF CHILDHOOD OR ADOLESCENCE.

Autochthonous Idea. An autochthonous (literally "sprung from the soil") idea is a DELUSION or false idea which appears to an individual to have come from outside influences, even though it actually springs from his own unconscious. The ideas are experienced as foreign or strange and may lead to undirected behavior uncontrolled by conscious thought. This may include obsessional thinking, primary delusions, or a feeling of being possessed. Autochthonous ideas are commonly observed in paranoid schizophrenia.

Autoeroticism. Usually defined as self-stimulation of any kind short of orgasm. Some have differentiated this from MASTURBATION, which has historically been defined as self-stimulation to the point of orgasm. In contemporary discussion, however, these words are often used interchangeably, along with others like self-exploration, self-pleasuring, and self-arousal. The distinction between any of these terms no longer seems helpful either clinically or theoretically.

R. E. BUTMAN

Autogenic Therapy. Prominent approach among the therapies oriented toward the treatment of both psychological and physical aspects of the person. It is much more popular in Europe and Japan than in America, and many of the empirical studies of its effectiveness have been published in non-English professional journals. Autogenic therapy bears many similarities to relaxation training, hypnotherapy, biofeedback, and meditation techniques.

Autogenic therapy (or training) has its roots in studies of hypnotic suggestion and autohypnosis in Germany at the turn of the century. Schultz and Luthe (1969), the major proponents of autogenic training, attempted to remove what were seen as the negative aspects of hypnotherapy (i.e., the passivity and dependence of the patient on the therapist) from the suggestion process by developing standardized procedures for self-suggestion. Their final result was a series of six standardized self-suggestion exercises which combine suggestion of the experience of calmness or peace with suggestion of particular physical experience related to absence of anxiety. Examples of such suggestions are heaviness and warmth in the extremities, regulation of cardiac activity and respiration, abdominal warmth, and cooling of the forehead (Ramsay, Wittkower, & Warnes, 1976). A typical single script might have patients suggesting to themselves three times, "My right arm is very heavy," followed by the suggestion, "I am completely calm." This whole sequence may then be repeated a number of times. The exercises are to be practiced regularly by the patient and integrated into the person's normal daily routine.

Autogenic therapy is most frequently applied to anxiety-based psychosomatic disorders such as peptic ulcers, ulcerative colitis, a number of psychologically based cardiovascular disorders (including angina pectoris, paroxysmal tachycardia, and essential hypertension), migraine and tension headaches, and asthma. The clinical efficacy of autogenic therapy is difficult to judge. When compared to other variants of relaxation training, autogenic training seems to be as effective as other methods. Autogenic therapy is probably a useful adjunct to the psychotherapeutic treatment of anxiety-based disorders, though it is unquestionably not as efficacious as other methods when used as the sole treatment modality. Some form of relaxation training can provide substantial benefit in the treatment of psychosomatic disorders and is likely to be of use as an adjunct in the treatment of other anxiety disorders.

References

Ramsay, R. A., Wittkower, E. D., & Warnes, H. Treatment of psychosomatic disorders. In B. B. Wolman (Ed.), *The therapist's handbook*. New York: Van Nostrand, 1976.

Schultz, J. H., & Luthe, W. *Autogenic therapy*. New York: Grune & Stratton, 1969.

S. L. JONES

See RELAXATION TRAINING.

Automatic Writing. The hypnotic operator has at his disposal a variety of ideomotor signaling systems. Ideomotor signals from the subject to the operator give the operator necessary feedback about the subject's internal events, which allows for tailoring of future suggestions. One of the most frequent ideomotor signaling systems, in addition to head nodding and finger lifting, is automatic writing.

Following trance induction and deepening, the operator who wishes to utilize automatic writing will frequently suggest to the subject that he will develop an awareness of all the sensations in his upper extremities, particularly in the (right or left) hand. The subject is to become curious about how these sensations of energy or tingling may change as time goes by. The operator may then go on with other, unrelated suggestions to allow this idea to incubate at various levels within the subject's mind. After a suitable period of time has elapsed, usually several minutes, the operator may place a writing pad in the subject's lap and put a pen in his hand. If some regressive suggestions have been made, the subject may be given a crayon or chalkboard with chalk.

The actual suggestions for automatic writing may well go as follows: "I would like you to gaze at your right hand with your eyes open, or with your eyes closed, as you imagine quite clearly your right hand resting on that writing pad (pause). What I would like for us to do next is to let our conscious minds be curious as to how your hand will begin moving, and what it will scribble, or doodle, or write, and what information your unconscious mind will share with your conscious mind, like giving it a gift or a treasure. You can let your conscious mind be surprised or puzzled as the pen begins to move across the paper—as though it were moving in a preshaped groove and could move in no other direction. Or you might have the pleasurable feeling of standing behind another person and watching his hand move across a page and filling it with markings."

This approach is a rather direct one. Creative permutations for suggesting automatic writing are endless. For example, the operator can have the subject sit and carefully watch as he points to his right hand and begins writing automatically. One could also tell an anecdote about another person who happened to sit and write an important letter while watching curiously as little drops of ink dribbled out onto the paper a bit at a time and formed curious shapes, letters, words, and sentences.

Before attempting this or any other hypnotic technique one should have a solid foundation in the basics of the theory and practice of therapeutic hypnosis.

V. L. SHEPPERSON

See HYPNOSIS; HYPNOTHERAPY; HYPNOTHERAPY, INDIRECT; ECSTATIC RELIGIOUS EXPERIENCES.

Automatism. Automatisms are acts performed without intent or conscious control on the part of an individual, often without realization that one is exhibiting the behavior. The actions tend to be of short duration, but may last one or two days. Most catatonic symptoms and compulsive behavior are considered automatisms. It is also common in clinical states such as FUGUE, where a previous activity is abandoned and the person takes up another activity without apparent knowledge he is doing so. In some cases of brain damage a person may perform automatisms, including complex motor acts such as driving a car, without conscious knowledge.

D. L. SCHUURMAN

Autonomy, Functional. According to Allport's principle of functional autonomy, motives or behaviors can become independent of their origins. The man who learned frugality during his childhood years of economic depression and who continues its practice in spite of present prosperity illustrates this principle.

Autoplasty. The process of adapting to stress by changing oneself intrapsychically. It is contrasted to ALLOPLASTY, which involves adaptation through the manipulation of external factors in the environment. In some cases autoplasty is a normal and healthy process, as in psychoanalytic treatment or other methods of internal change. Autoplasty can also be a neurotic adjustment to stress, as evidenced in symptom formation or psychosomatic disorders.

Auxiliary Chair Technique. The auxiliary chair, or empty chair as it is sometimes called, is used in PSYCHODRAMA to represent a person or thing significant to the protagonist. The protagonist vividly fantasizes the image in the chair and encounters it. Unspoken thoughts and feelings are vented, yielding a cathartic release. This technique is particularly useful if the protagonist chooses not to use auxiliary egos to play the role of the person or thing.

The auxiliary chair technique is similar to the empty chair used in Gestalt therapy, where it is referred to as the "hot seat." The basic difference is in application. Psychodramatists encourage the protagonist to confront persons, things, and self. The Gestalt therapist uses the hot seat to help the client encounter parts and dimensions of the self.

J. H. VANDER MAY

See GESTALT TECHNIQUES.

Aversion Therapy. This therapy consists of a number of techniques utilizing a variety of stimuli. Common features include the use of unpleasant stimuli and the goal of weakening or eliminating undesirable behaviors.

There are two major groups of aversion procedures. First are punishment procedures, in which the frequency of a behavior is reduced directly through contingent presentation or removal of a stimulus. Second are aversive counterconditioning procedures, in which the undesirable response is changed indirectly through altering the functions of the discriminative and reinforcing stimuli. In practice this distinction is somewhat blurred, since most aversion procedures have both punishing and stimulus-altering effects.

Contingent Punishment. Although Skinner and others argue that punishment is ineffective and has undesirable side effects, there is a growing consensus that it is highly effective and that its side effects are beneficial rather than harmful. Punishment by electric shock has proven effective with excessive vomiting, self-mutilation, dangerous climbing, and sexual behavior such as transvestism and fetishism (Rimm & Masters, 1974).

RESPONSE COST CONTINGENCY is another commonly employed punishment technique. This procedure involves withdrawing material reinforcers contingent upon the occurrence of some undesirable behavior. Response cost procedures are effective in reducing verbal and physical aggression, stuttering, and obesity. Their effects are quite durable, and most investigators report few undesirable effects. One potential problem is incurring a debt such as might occur when monetary fines exceed income; debt seems to reduce effectiveness of response cost.

Aversive Counterconditioning. In COUNTERCONDITIONING the discriminative and reinforcing stimuli that maintain the problem behavior are presented to the person and an unpleasant stimulus is presented simultaneously, so that discriminative and reinforcing stimuli acquire aversive properties through association.

Two basic forms of aversive counterconditioning are escape and avoidance training.

Often escape training is used initially, then modified into avoidance training. A third form of aversion training involves presenting the unpleasant stimulus without permitting escape or avoidance.

In escape training the target stimulus is presented, then an unpleasant stimulus such as electric shock occurs. After brief exposure to the two stimuli the individual terminates the stimuli by making some specified response. For example, a transvestite is given an article of women's clothing to put on, then administered electric shock. When the clothing is removed, the shock is terminated.

In avoidance training the individual is presented with the target stimulus. If an avoidance response is made quickly enough, the unpleasant stimulus may be avoided entirely. Typically, the response is one in which the target stimulus is removed. In the above example, removing the article of clothing during the warning stimulus prevents receiving shock. The advantage of the avoidance procedure is that the client learns to be anxious in the presence of the target stimulus (women's clothing) and is negatively reinforced for actively avoiding it.

COVERT SENSITIZATION is a form of aversive counterconditioning in which the client imagines an unpleasant event following the undesired behavior rather than actually experiencing aversive stimulation. For example, he imagines taking a large bite of hot fudge sundae topped with whipped cream and nuts, then imagines himself grossly fat, unable to fit into his clothes, and socially ostracized. In the avoidance phase he imagines becoming increasingly anxious as he approaches the ice cream shop. He then imagines turning away and experiencing immediate relief.

Stimuli used in aversion include drugs, electric shock, aversive imagery, and response cost. The ideal stimulus is one that permits sudden onset, prompt termination, controlled intensity, and rapid recovery so that repeated trials may be administered in a brief time. Electric shock is readily controlled in these ways but drugs are not. Drug administration also requires medical personnel, sometimes hospitalization, and is medically contraindicated for many individuals. It also may have side effects that impair conditioning. Shock is widely applicable except for persons with heart conditions. For these reasons shock has replaced drugs as the principal aversion technique.

Aversive counterconditioning has been found to be quite effective with transvestism and fetishism. Results with homosexuality are more modest; they are better for homosexuals voluntarily seeking treatment and for those with prior heterosexual experience. Although drugs have sometimes yielded promising results, shock is used almost exclusively with sexual behaviors.

Drug aversion continues to be used for alcohol abuse. Initially it is successful, but as time passes, an increasing percentage of clients resume drinking. Booster treatments reduce this frequency.

Research studies of covert sensitization have unfortunately produced disappointing results. Thus cognitive theorists such as Meichenbaum (1974) currently prefer stress inoculation (see COPING SKILLS THERAPIES).

Ethical Issues. Guidelines for aversion emphasize informed consent and minimal exposure to painful stimuli. Persons voluntarily seeking treatment respond better than those sent by the courts or family members. For both these reasons, use of aversion on reluctant patients is questionable (Bufford, 1977). Practically, the individual will avoid treatment if the experience is sufficiently unpleasant. Aversion to the target stimulus or elimination of the problem behavior must thus be accomplished without causing aversion to the treatment process.

Research evidence indicates that problem behaviors are most effectively eliminated when constructive behavioral alternatives are developed simultaneously. This raises two concerns. First, too often aversion techniques are used without establishing suitable alternate behaviors. Second, problems arise in selecting alternatives, especially for sexual deviances such as homosexuality, voyeurism, and transvestism. From a Christian perspective heterosexual activity outside of marriage is unacceptable. Alternate sexual behaviors which are morally acceptable are, then, often difficult to identify. The biblical concept of love suggests a direction for consideration. Learning to experience and express love, especially God's love, may be the alternative to the deviant sexual behavior. For those whose sexual behavior is motivated by seeking interpersonal closeness the alternative might be learning to experience the love of others. For those primarily motivated by desire for sexual gratification the alternative might be helping them learn how to express love in more acceptable ways.

Theoretical Issues. Covert sensitization is appealing for both theoretical and practical reasons (see Lazarus, 1976). However, lack of empirical evidence of treatment effectiveness raises doubt about the effectiveness of aversive imagery, and may suggest some practical limitations to the cognitive-behavioral approach.

There is considerable evidence that an aversion procedure combined with a specific alternative response works better than either procedure alone. Interestingly, Adams (1970) notes that a number of biblical teachings are consistent with the idea of replacing responses rather than simply eliminating them.

A promising suggestion by Lazarus is that it is important to match modalities of the aversive stimulus and the stimulus controlling the problem response. Thus, use of a whiff of ammonia might prove more effective than shock in controlling obesity and alcohol abuse because of the important role of taste and smell in these responses.

Finally, avoidance procedures are generally preferable to escape or unavoidable aversion procedures since avoidance is highly resistant to EXTINCTION.

Summary. Aversion therapy uses contingent punishment, aversive counterconditioning, and covert sensitization to eliminate undesired behaviors. Research indicates contingent punishment and aversive counterconditioning are effective, but casts doubt on covert sensitization. Aversion procedures are generally more successful when coupled with procedures for establishing a desirable alternative behavior.

Electric shock therapy is now the preferred aversion therapy approach for a number of practical reasons, although theoretical considerations suggest that matching the aversive stimulus to the target behavior may be more effective.

Finally, as applied to sexual behavior, aversion therapy poses a number of unique problems from a Christian perspective.

References

Adams, J. E. *Competent to counsel.* Philadelphia: Presbyterian and Reformed Publishing, 1970.

Bufford, R. K. Ethics for the mass application of behavior control. In C. W. Ellison (Ed.), *Modifying man.* Washington, D.C.: University Press of America, 1977.

Lazarus, A. A. (Ed.). *Multimodal behavior therapy.* New York: Springer, 1976.

Meichenbaum, D. *Cognitive-behavior modification.* Morristown, N.J.: General Learning Press, 1974.

Rimm, D. C., & Masters, J. C. *Behavior therapy.* New York: Academic Press, 1974.

R. K. BUFFORD

See PUNISHMENT; COGNITIVE-BEHAVIOR THERAPY; BEHAVIOR THERAPY.

Avoidant Disorder of Childhood or Adolescence.

A relatively uncommon disorder manifested by a persistent and excessive shrinking from contact with strangers. This avoidance behavior severely disrupts social functioning in the child's interpersonal relationships. The condition develops after age 2½ and after the time when the normal developmental tendency to be afraid of strangers should have disappeared. At the same time, however, the child clearly desires affection and acceptance; family members and other familiar people generally experience warmth and acceptance with the child. It is as though familiarity in a relationship relaxes the child whereas a lack of personal knowledge of an individual causes the child to freeze and become scared.

Such children or adolescents can be observed clinging or whispering to their caretakers, becoming tearful and anxious with even the slightest demand for contact with someone they do not know. They tend to lack assertiveness and self-confidence and show embarrassment and timidity in social relationships. Adolescents may avoid normal psychosexual activity (e.g., socializing with peers or dating). If their social anxiety is particularly high, these children may seem unable to talk; there is, however, no impairment of their skills to communicate.

While there is little information available regarding what contributes to this disturbance, it appears to have many characteristics consistent with an enmeshed family. In this view the child who has difficulty making contact with strangers or separating or being different from the family is fearful that any contact outside the perimeters of the nuclear family unit will be interpreted as a violation of family unity. This excessive concern with obedience to unspoken but very real family rules regarding inclusion and exclusion of significant others promotes the fear of stranger contact. A similar rule, often unspoken in a direct fashion, addresses the issue of safety inside the family and outside of it. The child is taught that to venture outside the family's boundaries is a high risk enterprise.

This intense loyalty to the family system seems to be particularly focused on the mother. Each time the child is presented with the opportunity to individuate and include nonfamily members in his life, it is as if the child is betraying the family's basic interests. The child's fear of strangers ensures loyalty and commitment to remain in the family circle. This meets the needs of the family for closeness, intimacy, affection, and acceptance; the child receives these in return and thus experiences satisfaction. Stepping outside the family, i.e., making contact with strangers, threatens the unhealthy family system. Anxiety and fear of being left become intolerable. Unfortunately in this situation the child's probability of individuating the self from the nuclear "undifferentiated family ego mass" is severely hampered (Bowen, 1978).

A serious complication of this inability to form social bonds beyond the family can be feelings of isolation and depression. The adolescent and older child may benefit from individual psychotherapy focused on lowering anxiety when faced with contact with strangers, exploration of the patient's feelings and permission to have these feelings. The relationship with the therapist serves as a bridge between the family and the outside world, thus enabling the patient to work through the severe anxiety of contact with strangers. With increased levels of awareness and comfort the person can separate from the family and experience more comfort with others.

Treating the family is another approach. An attempt is made to make family members aware of their unconscious needs for acceptance and affection as well as fear of loss and rejection. As the child, parents, and other family members become aware of their needs and how they are using one another to meet these, there is more opportunity for the utilization of other alternatives in meeting genuine needs. One goal may be to have parents relate with each other about their needs and concerns. As the parental coalition strengthens, there is less need to hold the child to them.

Reference

Bowen, M. *Family therapy in clinical practice.* New York: Aronson, 1978.

B. J. SHEPPERSON

Avoidant Personality Disorder.

The person diagnosed as having this disorder displays, as the name suggests, an avoidance of interpersonal relationships. The diagnostic features include low self-esteem, social withdrawal, desire for affection, hypersensitivity to rejection, and an unwillingness to enter relationships unless guaranteed open acceptance. Such persons devalue their achievements and become overly concerned with their personal shortcomings. They withdraw from social opportunity because of marked fear of being rejected, belittled, shamed, or humiliated. The slightest disapproval from someone devastates them and may cause self-anger for failing to relate effectively.

Avoidant personality disorder results in depression, anxiety, and self-anger. Impairment in social relationships may preclude marriage or meaningful relationships. Also, occupational goals may not be met if job interaction requires interpersonal involvement. At best, job performance will be impaired due to social withdrawal.

Differential Diagnosis. A key difference between avoidant personality disorder and schizoid personality disorder is that while the latter involves social isolation, it is without a desire for social interaction. The individual with an avoidant personality disorder strongly desires acceptance and affection from others and is very sensitive to criticism.

Avoidance disorder of childhood or adolescence, 18 years and under, has similar features to the adult version. It may develop as early as 2½ years of age and may become chronic and continue into adulthood. Children with this disorder are inhibited in normal psychosexual activity, unassertive, experience severe interference with social functioning with peers, and lack self-confidence. They desire affection and acceptance. They have satisfying relationships with family members and others with whom they are very familiar. The problem is only noticed when it comes to relationships outside the family or outside close familiar friendships.

Separation anxiety in children differs from avoidant personality disorder in that the former is due to separation from home or a special person rather than fear of contact with strangers. Schizoid disorder of childhood or adolescence differs in that there is little or no desire for social interaction. In the case of overanxious disorder, the anxiety is not limited to social contact with strangers. In other words, it is not focused on a specific situation or object.

Treatment. Treatment is difficult because it requires individuals with avoidant personality disorder to meet a stranger for therapy. When they do come for treatment, it is usually at the encouragement of a family member. In fact, the treatment of choice often is family therapy. Whether or not the person has left home, family therapy helps the avoidant person to understand his or her response pattern and move toward increased healthy social contacts.

Individual therapy is often an important part of the total treatment process and, in many cases, is the sole format. A major goal of individual therapy is to build a therapeutic relationship and, through the relationship, gain insight into the dynamics of the problem. Group therapy is also often helpful in that it provides social interaction experiences with strangers in a protected environment. It thus serves as a testing ground for new behavior under the protection of the group leader.

Chemotherapy may be appropriate in some cases if the depression and anxiety are severely impairing the therapy process. Drug therapy must be approached with caution because it can easily be used as a means of further avoiding relationships by retreating into dependency on medication.

M. A. CAMPION

See PERSONALITY DISORDERS; ACTIVE-DETACHED PERSONALITY PATTERN.

Bb

Bandura, Albert (1925–). Known for his development of a social learning theory of personality and abnormal behavior. Bandura grew up in the tiny hamlet of Mundare in northern Alberta. His undergraduate study was done at the University of British Columbia, and at his graduation in 1949 he received the Bolocan Award in Psychology.

Bandura chose the University of Iowa for graduate study, influenced by the presence of Kenneth Spence. The Iowa program emphasized theories of learning and rigorous experimentation. Following completion of his Ph.D. in clinical psychology in 1952 under the direction of Arthur Benton, Bandura took a postdoctoral internship at the Wichita Guidance Center. He joined the Stanford University faculty in 1954, and has remained there since, except for one year at the Center for Advanced Studies in Behavioral Science.

Bandura's professional activities and awards have been numerous. Among the more prominent ones are serving on the editorial boards of about 20 journals, editing the Social Learning Theory series for Prentice-Hall, receiving a Guggenheim Fellowship and a Distinguished Scientist Award from the American Psychological Association's Division 12 in 1972, being elected president of the association in 1974, receiving the J. McKeen Cattell award in 1977, and being elected president of the Western Psychological Association in 1981.

When Bandura went to Stanford, he brought with him interest in learning and in abnormal behavior. Under the influence of Robert Sears he began investigation of social learning and aggression with his first doctoral student, Richard Walters, culminating in their books on aggression and personality. Further studies of observational learning and symbolic modeling led to several more books. More recent work involves self-regulatory mechanisms and self-percepts of efficacy. He is currently involved in study of the mechanisms by which self-referent thought mediates action and affective arousal.

R. K. BUFFORD

See SOCIAL LEARNING THEORY; MODELING.

Basic Youth Conflicts Seminar. The media attention that Bill Gothard's Basic Youth Conflicts Seminar received during the middle 1970s has disappeared, but the seminars themselves have not. These 30-hour, 6-day seminars have continued on a biweekly basis in various cities, often in videotape format, with roughly 25,000 or more attending each seminar. In addition to the Basic Seminar the Gothard organization gives an annual one-week Advanced Seminar for pastors and male church officers that includes some separate sessions for pastors only.

In spite of the size and continuance of these seminars, surprisingly little has been written on Gothard himself, though most denominational and all major evangelical magazines have had at least one article on the Basic Seminar. Gothard discourages seminar attendees from discussing the material. He also strongly discourages public criticism of any Christian person or action, including his teaching, seeing this as a violation of Matthew 18:15–18 and Galatians 6:1, which enjoin direct confrontation of a Christian brother who is at fault.

The Basic Seminar is taught topically as follows: self-image, chain of command (family hierarchy), conscience, rights, freedom, success, purpose, friends, dating, and commitment. Each of the areas is rooted in a fundamental principle which is viewed as supernatural and universal. The violation of these principles is assumed by Gothard to lead to problems in the life of the believer and nonbeliever alike. These principles are the implicit conceptual structure of the seminar and make up the content of the seminar. Thus the entire Basic Seminar is directed to teaching the nature of and obedience to these principles.

In addition to this general theory Gothard has a specific theory of problems. He specifies psychopathology in terms of four levels of conflict, each level considered to be more fundamentally causative than the previous one: 1) problems perceivable to others (surface problems), 2) inner tensions (surface causes), 3) basic personality conflicts (root problems), and 4) the person's response to God (the root cause). Examples of surface problems are hostility, lying, stealing, and sensual habits. Surface causes include rebellion, insecurity, worry, and nervousness. Bitterness, temporal values, and moral impurity are the only three root problems. For Gothard there is only one root cause, which is rejecting God's grace through the violation of one of the basic biblical principles.

Although Gothard does not have an explicit statement on therapy, there is an implicit therapeutic emphasis throughout his work. Obedience and right response to each of God's principles is the general procedure stressed. A brief discussion of two of these principles, design and authority, may give the flavor of his approach. The principle of design is primarily concerned with the acceptance of oneself and one's situationally determined experiences. Negative attitudes toward the self are described as bitterness toward God, who is the designer of the self. The first step to self-acceptance is to start a new and intimate relationship with God. The second is to thank him for his work, what he has done up to the present. This means accepting God as the designer of all non–self-determined events—e.g., one's body, parents, and environmental events (even hurtful events such as rape)—as part of God's design for the person. The third step to self-acceptance is cooperating with God by developing qualities of the self in any given circumstances according to his values. The fourth and final step is to reproduce Christ's life in others.

Another implicit therapeutic procedure grows out of the principle of authority described as the chain of command. A diagram illustrating the chain of command in the family shows God, depicted as a triangle, holding father, who is depicted as a hammer, coming down on mother depicted as a chisel, who in turn is chipping on the teen-ager, depicted as a diamond in the rough. Gothard strongly emphasizes the importance of each person recognizing his or her place in the chain of command. The person is not responsible for his position or for the behavior of those above. Rather he is only responsible to obey those above in the chain of command. Rebellion and self-direction are not options for the individual. Nonobedience to an authority is permitted only if participation in overt sin is demanded. Even non–church attendance is required if a non-Christian parent forbids such attendance. If overt sin is commanded, the teen-ager is told to offer a constructive alternative. If the alternative is not accepted, the teen-ager may then be called upon to suffer for Christ's sake. Gothard's heavy emphasis on authority is undeniable. It and related concepts of submission permeate the entire seminar.

The Basic Youth Conflicts Seminar contains a vast amount of material (160 pages) and is so concentrated that a comprehensive evaluation would have to involve considerable specific detail (see Carter, 1974, and Bockelman, 1976, for more complete evaluations). Nevertheless, the strength and weakness of the seminars themselves can be summarized. The phrase "Have the right attitude"—toward God, self, family, sensuality, and all of life—is probably the most general thrust. Another pervading emphasis is obedience to authority. While this theme is needed in a society which is characterized by individualism and rebellion, this pervasive vertical thrust of obedience dwarfs what can be called the horizontal personal character of human life. Interpersonal experience is viewed almost totally in terms of God's design and purpose for classes of individuals. For example, the wife is never described as a co-parent but only as under her husband's authority. In addition, the whole biblical concept of fellowship and love is simply not discussed. The whole inner dimension of joy, freedom, and liberty in Christ is ignored. Instead there is a constant stress on obedience and the numerous reasons why some action should or should not take place. God seems to be a distant being who has enumerated a vast number of rules to be obeyed, rather than a loving Father who in Christ has forgiven us our sin and who asks us to walk in loving fellowship with his Son and each other. The seminar overemphasizes the vertical rule-keeping dimension of obedience to God and neglects the horizontal relational aspect of the Son and fellowship of his people and the spontaneous joy and liberty in the Holy Spirit.

However, the strength of Gothard's system should not be ignored. He has developed a dynamic model of both pathology and human functioning which has biblical and psychological aspects. Gothard's discussion of prayer, fasting, and meditation calls attention to some often neglected biblical therapeutic processes, and his collation of vast amounts of scripture focuses on many important biblical principles relating to life.

References

Bockelman, W. *Gothard: The man and his ministry: An evaluation.* Santa Barbara, Calif.: Quill Publications, 1976

Carter, J. The psychology of Gothard and Basic Youth Conflict Seminars. *Journal of Psychology and Theology,* 1974, 249–259.

J. D. CARTER

B-Cognition. *See* PEAK EXPERIENCES.

Bedwetting. *See* ENURESIS.

Beers, Clifford Whittingham (1876–1943). Founder of the mental hygiene movement. After his graduation from Yale University in 1900 Beers suffered a "mental breakdown" at the age of 24. He attempted suicide by jumping from a fourth-floor window. After a year of depression he was committed to the Hartford Retreat. In 1902 he experienced feelings of exaltation and decided to describe these feelings, writing at a rate of 12 feet of manila wrapping paper an hour. An assistant physician confiscated the manuscript, and Beers spent 21 nights in a straitjacket in a padded cell. Later he was transferred to the Connecticut State Hospital at Middletown, and was released in September, 1903.

Beers resolved to write about his experiences and to organize a movement to help the mentally ill. He knew that he had to prove his sanity, so he married and took a position in business. His autobiography, *A Mind That Found Itself,* describes his experiences. William James read the manuscript in 1906 and wrote a letter of approval which became part of the introduction when the book was published in 1908. Beers also enlisted the aid of Adolf Meyer, a leading psychiatrist. Meyer suggested that the movement be called mental hygiene. In May, 1908, Beers founded the Connecticut Society for Mental Hygiene, the first such organization in the United States. In 1909 he founded the National Commission for Mental Hygiene and became its secretary. In 1928 he organized the American Foundation for Mental Hygiene and was its secretary until his death.

He also helped Clarence Hincks found the Canadian National Committee for Mental Hygiene in 1918 and the International Committee for Mental Hygiene in 1920. Later he organized the first International Congress on Mental Hygiene in 1930. His work to help the mentally ill and prevent mental illness had a worldwide impact.

R. L. KOTESKEY

See PSYCHOLOGY, HISTORY OF.

Behavioral Assessment. Advocates of behavior modification and behavior therapy in the 1960s and earlier had departed widely from the mainstream of clinical and counseling psychology. They attacked not only the dominant conceptions of human personality and of treatment but also the predominant modes of psychological assessment, claiming that unreliable and frequently invalid methods of assessment and diagnosis were used. They also claimed that assessment was intrapsychically oriented and thus tended to ignore important environmental causes of behavior, and that traditional assessment looked for symptoms of underlying disturbance rather than dealing with the person's behavior as behavior. The result of this was a diagnostic judgment which really had little to do with shaping subsequent treatment.

Behavioral assessment was proposed as an alternative system to more traditional techniques. Its major distinctives are associated with a greater concern for an individualized formulation of the problems and assets of the client as opposed to a description of the client in terms of broad diagnostic categories. More balanced attention is given to environmental determinants of the problems, focusing on what is causing and maintaining the behavior. This also involves a primary focus on the present rather than the past. Finally, the attempt is made in behavioral assessment to define the problem of the client in concrete, observable terms. Given these distinctives, it was hoped that behavioral assessment would be more directly relevant to the development of a comprehensive treatment plan to alleviate the focal distress of the client.

The actual process of behavioral assessment can be understood best by distinguishing between the information which the assessment is designed to generate and the methods used to gather the information. Goldfried and Davison (1976) distinguished four major classes of variables that must be carefully assessed. The first is the maladaptive behavior itself. What characteristics or qualities of the behavior lead to it being labeled a problem? How can the problem be concretely defined so that it can be monitored throughout treatment? Second, the antecedent environmental stimuli related to the problem must be assessed. Under what environmental conditions does the problem occur and not occur? Third, the behavior analyst looks at organismic variables. What personality variables are related to the occurrence of the problem behavior? The behavior therapist would look especially at the distinctive ways in which the client is interpreting his or her world which might be related to the occurrence of the problem. Finally, the behavior therapist would look at consequence variables—i.e., the results of the client's problem and nonproblem behaviors. Generally, the ways in which the client's maladaptive behavior is actually reinforced by events in his or her life, and the way in which more adaptive behavior is not reinforced or perhaps even punished would be closely examined.

Many methods of gathering these data have been used. The most widely used technique is the clinical interview. The client is asked to be very concrete about the nature of the problem behavior and the factors relating to or causing it. Clients also might be observed directly to uncover relevant information. This observation might take place in natural settings (e.g., observing a troubled couple in their home or an emotionally disturbed child in the classroom) or in contrived settings (e.g., when the client is asked to role-play a situation where the problem would occur, or the attempt is made to observe the maladaptive behavior in the therapist's office). Psychophysiological recordings might be taken to provide additional information about the physiological dimension of the client's responses. The therapist might instruct the client in the nature of the relevant information which would be beneficial to planning treatment and then help the client keep careful self-monitoring records to yield usable data. Finally, self-report methods might be used, with these techniques ranging from specially constructed behavioral inventories that ask about the occurrence of specific behaviors (e.g., feared stimulus inventories, assertive behavior inventories, marital behavior inventories, etc.) to use of the more empirically validated psychological tests.

The overall goal of behavioral assessment is to gather specific, concrete information that will be maximally relevant to treatment planning. Behavioral assessment is no longer as

distinct from other broadly accepted assessment approaches as might once have been the case. With the increased societal emphasis on professional accountability, most assessment approaches are becoming more problem oriented and are requiring higher levels of empirical validity for specific assessment methods. Behavior therapists, on the other hand, recognizing the tendency for certain problem behaviors to be highly correlated (e.g., reported sadness and loss of energy), are becoming more willing to use diagnostic classifications (e.g., depression) than in the past. The most important criticism of behavioral assessment is that with all of the emphasis on empirical validation of technique, the behavior therapist still uses largely unvalidated assessment methods. The primary diagnostic tool of the behavior therapist is the old standby of mental health practice, the clinical interview. Many of the existing self-report instruments are psychometrically crude, with little attention paid until recently to assuring that they measure what they purport to measure. Behavior therapists have also developed complex systems for rating behavior, but again have only recently begun to examine the validity of these systems. Overall, the field of behavioral assessment provides an alternative to many forms of traditional assessment; its distinctiveness, however, flows more from its theoretical base than from any firm empirical demonstrations of its superiority.

Reference
Goldfried, M. R., & Davison, G. C. *Clinical behavior therapy.* New York: Holt, Rinehart, & Winston, 1976.

Additional Reading
Barlow, D. H. (Ed.). *Behavioral assessment of adult disorders.* New York: Guilford Press, 1980.

S. L. JONES

See APPLIED BEHAVIOR ANALYSIS; BEHAVIOR THERAPY; PSYCHIATRIC ASSESSMENT.

Behavioral Family Therapy. As with all forms of family therapy, the major purpose of behaviorally oriented family therapy is to help the family become a better functioning interdependent group. Ideally this should result in improved communication, autonomy and individuation, empathy, more flexible leadership, reduced conflict, individual symptom improvement, and greater individual task improvement. The key differences in the varied approaches to family therapy are in how the problem is best conceptualized and in what specific ways change can best be implemented.

The behaviorally oriented family therapist sees the family situation as an opportunity to encourage behavioral change in the family members by restructuring their interpersonal environments (Lieberman, 1970): Specifically, they study how the various family members act on each other in terms of their contingencies of reinforcement (i.e., what behaviors they choose to reinforce, extinguish, or punish, and how often they do this). Reinforcement patterns, then, are the best way to conceptualize family interactions.

After these patterns are carefully studied by the therapist, the therapeutic task is to induce family members to reinforce desirable behaviors rather than negative, attention-getting behaviors. This assessment of the problem, also called a behavioral analysis, is central to the behavioral approach in family therapy. The therapist and the family members then decide upon mutually agreeable target behaviors to increase (behavioral deficits) or decrease (behavioral excesses). The therapist also encourages the family members to verbally reinforce desirable traits (behavioral assets) in each other. By helping the family set realistic goals for its members the therapist guides them toward intentionally altering reinforcement contingencies. A variety of reinforcers has been used, including verbal praise, physical contact, food or treats, and tokens, depending on the nature of the problem and makeup of the family unit.

The applications of behavioral approaches have been diverse and exciting in the past 15 years. Behavioral parent training (Gordon & Davidson, 1981) was the early focus, followed by application of social learning principles to working with the families of juvenile delinquents (Patterson, McNeal, Hawkins, & Phelps, 1967). More recently the emphasis has been on behavioral marital therapy (Jacobson, 1981) and the treatment of sexual dysfunction (Herman, LoPiccolo & LoPiccolo, 1981). All these approaches share the viewpoint that family therapy is a learning experience, with the therapist best functioning in the role of educator, model, coach, and social reinforcer. On the surface the approach appears deceptively straightforward. In reality it can prove to be a highly sophisticated, technique-oriented strategy that aspires to nothing less than restructuring the interpersonal environments of families. Behaviorally oriented family therapy is rapidly becoming a significant minority viewpoint in the family therapy movement.

References

Gordon, S. B., & Davidson, N. Behavioral parent training. In A. S. Gurman & D. P. Kniskern (Eds.), *Handbook of family therapy*. New York: Brunner/Mazel, 1981.

Herman, J. R., LoPiccolo, L., & LoPiccolo, J. The treatment of sexual dysfunction. In A. S. Gurman & D. P. Kniskern (Eds.), *Handbook of family therapy*. New York: Brunner/Mazel, 1981.

Jacobson, N. S. Behavioral marital therapy. In A. S. Gurman & D. P. Kniskern (Eds.), *Handbook of family therapy*. New York: Brunner/Mazel, 1981.

Lieberman, R. P. Behavioral approaches to family and couple therapy. *American Journal of Orthopsychiatry*, 1970, *40*, 106–118.

Patterson, G. R., McNeal, S., Hawkins, N., & Phelps, R. Reprogramming the social environment. *Journal of Child Psychology and Psychiatry*, 1967, *8*, 180–195.

R. E. BUTMAN

See FAMILY THERAPY: OVERVIEW; BEHAVIOR THERAPY.

Behavioral Marital Therapy. Marital therapy is a relatively recent development within the field of behavior therapy, with behavioral marital therapy increasing dramatically in its influence and sophistication during the late 1970s. In the late 1960s behavioral marital therapy typically involved teaching spouses to reward (through attention or tokens) those behaviors they desired from their partners. While the basic theoretical conceptualizations behind behavioral marital therapy are consistent with those of early researchers, the theories have been better elaborated and the therapeutic techniques rendered much less artificial and mechanical.

Generally, behavioral marital therapy contends that each person's behavior can best be seen as a function of that person's social environment and past learning history. Since one's spouse is a powerful part of one's social environment, it follows that marriage "is best thought of as a process of circular and reciprocal sequences of behavior and consequences, where each person's behavior is at once being affected by and influencing the other" (Jacobson & Margolin, 1979, p. 13). This conceptualization has received some empirical support. Because of their belief that each spouse's behavior in the marriage will be in part a function of the behavior of the other spouse, researchers predicted and demonstrated that marriages are characterized by reciprocity— i.e., the tendency for spouses to exchange positive (rewarding) and negative (punishing) behaviors at about the same rate. Spouses tend to treat each other in similar manner over time, though this should not be taken to imply an immediate reciprocity in a reflexive sense.

Behavioral marital therapists view marriage as being rule governed, with the relationship rules (implicit and explicit expectations regarding roles, duties, acceptable behavior, etc.) serving to structure and define the exchange of positive and negative behaviors. Change is inevitable in marriage relationships. Unfortunately, many persons are more likely to influence their spouses to change through aversive means than positive means. Aversive control techniques (nagging, yelling, threatening) are more successful in producing immediate behavior change (compliance) than positive means (compromise, praise, reason). However, the aversive means create complicating problems by their very use. Behavioral marital therapy is directed at developing positive change patterns in a dissatisfied couple.

Marital distress is viewed as occurring for a variety of reasons. Spouses may lack positive behavior change skills such as basic communication and problem-solving skills. The "reinforcement value" of each spouse for the other can decay over time, so that one spouse seems to have little or nothing to offer the other. This may occur due to a gradual buildup of grievances or a failure of each person to grow and develop, thus bringing fresh life to the relationship. There may also be undiscussed rules or unresolved expectancy conflicts in the marriage. Finally, situational changes (e.g., a new job, new social or romantic relationships) may undermine motivation to put necessary time and work into the relationship.

Behavioral marital therapy is almost always conducted with both partners present. It tends to be brief, more directive than many forms of marital therapy, and maintains a strong focus on specific changes that must occur in the relationship. Critics suggest that it is mainly a group of techniques without a good theory of the overall conduct of the therapeutic process. While this criticism seems overdone, it is undoubtedly the case that the techniques are the main focus of behavioral writers. The other less specific aspects of the therapy process are more difficult to conceptualize behaviorally.

There are three major forms of behavioral marital therapy interventions, each of which has numerous variations. The first class of interventions, probably the most widely used, focuses on increasing the clients' positive change skills. This most often takes the form of communication skills training. One variant is training in problem-solving or negotiation skills. Spouses might also be taught active listening skills to facilitate understanding, or possibly new skills for clearly expressing affection and emotions. In the process of learning these skills spouses come to see more clearly the impact they have on each other, thus setting the stage for the start of positive change in the relationship.

The second general class of interventions are those which serve to structure and increase the couple's positive interactions, thus serving to increase relationship satisfaction. These techniques might be useful where spouses have gradually habituated to each other or where situational factors (lack of time, money, etc.) have prevented them from sharing pleasant interactions. The most common form of this intervention is for the therapist to negotiate with clients to observe special days or periods of time when they strive to dramatically increase their positive interactions, either on a unilateral or bilateral basis. Writers term these times "love days" or "caring days." There are numerous other techniques for increasing positive interactions.

The final major class of interventions are the contracting methods which aim to make explicit the expectations and rules affecting the marital relationship. Behavioral therapists once emphasized the use of quid pro quo contracts, which specifically link the behavior of the spouses in an "if I do this for you, then you do that for me" fashion. Because of the numerous difficulties with this approach, therapists are now much more likely to use good faith contracts, which mainly serve the purpose of clarification of expectations.

At this time there are numerous studies documenting the beneficial effects of behavioral marital therapy in increasing marital satisfaction. The approach has not been shown, however, to be significantly more effective than other therapies. Behavioral marital therapy research has been criticized as having been conducted with atypical couples (e.g., those responding to newspaper advertisements) and for lacking long-term follow-ups of treated couples to verify the stability of the treatment gains.

Behavioral marital therapy's strengths include its directness, specificity, action orientation, and apparently shorter time span of treatment. The directness of scriptural injunctions for changes in marital relationships may suggest the frequent suitability of such direct approaches with many couples. The focus on relationship patterns rather than personal problems frequently helps clients be nondefensive and receptive to change. One prominent Christian author and marriage counselor (Wright, 1981) feels that the cognitive-behavioral framework is largely compatible with revealed truth.

Behavioral marital therapy suffers from all

the limitations inherent in the field of behavior therapy. The approach has an inadequate philosophical groundwork of materialism and strict determinism. This gives it a somewhat mechanistic flavor. Its basic principles (reinforcement, punishment) are defined tautologically, and there are very real problems with reducing all interactions into either reinforcers or punishers. Also, the limited number of documented interventions could lead the naïve therapist to push clients through a standardized treatment package rather than individualizing the approach. It should also be noted that most of the approaches classified as behavioral marital therapy were in existence under other names before being labeled as behavioral techniques. Finally, a major problem with behavioral marital therapy is its lack of a model of healthy marriage. Overall, the approach promises to enrich the field of marital therapy. However, as it currently stands it is very likely inadequate as an overall model of marital therapy.

References

Jacobson, N. S., & Margolin, G. *Marital therapy*. New York: Brunner/Mazel, 1979.

Wright, H. N. *Marital counseling*. Denver: Christian Marriage Enrichment, 1981.

S. L. Jones

See Marital Therapy; Behavior Therapy.

Behavioral Medicine. *See* Health Psychology.

Behavioral Psychology. It is generally recognized that there are three broad schools of theory within psychology: psychoanalytic, behavioral, and humanist-existential. Of the three, behavioral psychology most clearly traces its roots to the psychology laboratory and empirical research.

Historical Introduction. Behavioral psychology springs directly from the tradition of laboratory experimentation in learning theory that has characterized psychology from its inception. Thus, while applications of behavioral psychology to applied problems are a relatively recent development, the history of behavioral psychology can be traced back to the end of the nineteenth century.

The Russian physiologist Pavlov is generally recognized as one of the earliest forerunners of modern behavior theory. Pavlov's original work involved the study of the digestive system. However, coincidental to that work he noticed that the dogs he was studying secreted saliva at the sight of food as well as the presence of food in the mouth. Pavlov soon discovered that the mere presence of the lab attendant was sufficient to produce salivation and that other stimuli such as the ringing of a bell or sounding a tone preceding the presence of food also could elicit salivation.

The process which Pavlov discovered came to be known as classical, respondent, or Pavlovian conditioning. Shortly after Pavlov's initial discoveries John B. Watson, an American psychologist, became aware of Pavlov's work. Watson vigorously objected to such concepts as mind, consciousness, volition, and emotion, believing that psychology should be the science of directly observable behavior. He adopted the conditioned reflex method of Pavlov and played a major role in initiating the development of behavioral psychology in America. Watson's influence was sufficiently great that he is generally recognized as the founder of American behaviorism.

Another major contribution made by Watson was his emphasis on comparative psychology; Watson was firmly convinced that principles of animal behavior could be extended to higher-order animals and to humans. As a result, it seemed reasonable to conduct laboratory research on lower organisms in order to learn something about more complex human behavior.

A contemporary of Watson, E. L. Thorndike, shared Watson's emphasis on naturalistic and mechanistic approaches and on comparative psychology. Thorndike also shared the emphasis on psychology as a science of observable behaviors which should be developed through rigorous experimentation. He conducted studies of learning and concluded that human and animal learning took place by trial and error. Thorndike's major contribution was the development of the law of effect. The law of effect states that responses followed by reinforcement will be repeated, while responses followed by nonreinforcement or punishment will not recur.

While many others, including Guthrie, Hull, and Tolman, made contributions that were significant in developing psychology of learning, for our purposes B. F. Skinner is the next theorist of major significance. Although Skinner introduced new terminology, his work can be seen as basically an extension of Thorndike's law of effect.

Skinner's early work was characterized by an intrepid individualism in choosing to go his own way even though this was inconsistent with the more prominent theories of his time. He studied the laws of operant behavior through ingenious laboratory techniques which he originated and for which he developed the necessary laboratory environment and apparatus. Over the next three decades Skinner, and later his students, contributed prolifically to the growing knowledge of operant behavior. Whereas Watson had conceived respondent behavior as the sole form of learned response, under Skinner's influence the point of view gradually shifted until by the 1950s respondent behavior was seen as a minor form of animal and human behavior, and most behavior of social interest was conceived of as operant.

Modern Behavior Theory. Where early theorists emphasized the exclusive role of respondent behavior (classical conditioning), and later theorists emphasized the predominant role of operant behavior (operant conditioning), more recent work has suggested that both views oversimplify the issues. It has become apparent that operant and respondent processes interact continuously in complex and significant ways. Further, the traditional distinctions between operant and respondent behavior have been blurred through research on operant conditioning of respondent behaviors conducted by Neil Miller and his colleagues.

Respondent behavior. Respondents are behaviors elicited or controlled primarily by preceding events. They are involuntary, involving the autonomic nervous system and the smooth muscles and glands. Respondents occur automatically following the appropriate eliciting stimulus unless the organism is exhausted or incapacitated; thus, respondents are sometimes referred to as reflexive. While respondents are initially under control of a limited range of stimulus events determined by biological and genetic factors, through presenting a new stimulus followed by the eliciting stimulus, new eliciting stimuli can be developed. This process is known as respondent or classical conditioning. Conditioned respondents can be eliminated by presenting the new controlling stimulus in the absence of the natural eliciting stimulus until the organism ceases to respond; this process is called respondent extinction.

The range of respondent behavior is limited for several reasons. First, respondents are determined by biological factors; essentially the responses are given with the biological characteristics of the organism. Second, learning simply brings the existing respondents under control of the new stimulus; no new responses are developed. Third, conditioned stimuli lose their eliciting capability very

quickly. Fourth, much behavior is not respondent in nature.

Operant behavior. Operant behavior involves the organism acting on the environment to produce an effect. Operants are controlled primarily by events which follow them; these are generally called consequences. However, once the response-consequence relationship has been established, the response can then be brought under control of events which precede it; these events are termed discriminative stimuli and the process is called stimulus control. Since much of human behavior is operant, the principles of operant behavior are extremely important in understanding the behavior of humans and other organisms.

Although theorists like Bijou and Baer (1965) hold that operant behaviors are determined by the biological characteristics of the organism, much like respondent behaviors, operant behavior is vastly more variable than respondent behavior, and the initial number of operants is much larger as well. Operant behaviors include walking, throwing, talking, thinking, bicycle riding, and piano playing.

Operant learning involves a variety of processes. Complex operant performances may be thought of as an integrated set of basic response units under precise stimulus control. Complex operants are synthesized out of the basic performances by the processes of operant learning and stimulus control. These processes include 1) strengthening and weakening of responses by altering their consequences, 2) shaping, 3) establishing stimulus control, 4) chaining.

The most basic operant processes are those which increase or decrease the frequency of a response by altering its consequences. A positive reinforcement is a consequence which increases the strength of a behavior (i.e., giving verbal praise after a desirable behavior). A negative reinforcement has the same effect by virtue of the removal of a negative consequence (i.e., allowing a child to come out of his room when his behavior has settled down). Punishment involves the presentation of an undesirable consequence following the occurrence of an undesirable behavior (i.e., spanking a child after he misbehaves). Another basic process affecting the strength of operants is extinction, which involves terminating a previously established response-consequence relationship.

In shaping, the form or topography of a response is progressively altered from an existing form to a desired form. This is accomplished through systematically reinforcing successively closer approximations to the desired performance. For example, in teaching a child to say "daddy" one might begin by reinforcing the vocalizations "da-da-da" and then gradually shift to reinforcing only two-syllable vocalizations: "da-da." Gradually reinforcement would be provided only when the "da-dee" sequence occurred.

Stimulus control is a second process of operant development. It is accomplished by presenting a stimulus before a response. When the stimulus reliably predicts that a particular consequence will follow a given response, the response gradually comes under control of the stimulus. For a young child, if the word "hot" reliably predicts pain when an object is touched, the child soon learns to avoid touching objects when Mom or Dad says "hot." Similarly, bringing the vocalization "daddy" under stimulus control involves reinforcing the vocalization "daddy" only when Daddy is present or when objects or events related to Daddy occur.

Chaining is the process by which discrete response elements are linked into integrated sequences. Through this process longer and more complex sequences of behavior may be developed. Saying "da-dee" is an example of an elementary chain composed of two response elements.

Operant and respondent interactions. Initially behavior theory viewed respondents as the exclusive form of human and animal behavior. With the discovery of operant behavior respondents were accorded an increasingly minor role, and operant behavior came to be viewed as the predominant form of behavior. Recently it has become clear that both these formulations are inadequate and that operant and respondent processes continuously interact in an intricate fashion. These interactions can be seen in at least four ways. First, the consequences following operant responses—reinforcement, punishment, and extinction—not only affect the frequency of a preceding operant but also simultaneously elicit various respondent behaviors. When Johnny runs an errand and completes it, Mother's comment, "Thank you, Johnny, that's a good boy," not only strengthens Johnny's errand running but also produces pleasant emotional respondents.

A second way in which operants and respondents interact is in the form of setting conditions. Setting conditions are stimulus-response interactions which, simply because they have occurred, affect a wide range of subsequent stimulus response interactions

(Bijou & Baer, 1961). There are many kinds of setting events—being ill, having eaten a good meal, or smashing one's thumb with a hammer. For purposes of understanding operant-respondent interactions it is important to remember that the respondents elicited by the consequences of an operant will also function as setting conditions. In the example given above, when Johnny's mother compliments him for errand running, the emotional responses produced will affect his response to other people and events for a period of time. Contrast the effects of the compliment she gave with the effects that might have occurred if Mother had said, "Johnny, you dummy, you never get things right." The emotional effects thus elicited are an essential concomitant of each operant-consequence interaction. Depending on which of these interactions has just occurred, Johnny's response to a wide range of stimuli will be dramatically different.

A third area of interaction among operant and respondent processes is in the operant conditioning of presumed respondents conducted by Neil Miller and his colleagues. Miller and his co-workers have demonstrated that such autonomic nervous system functions as peripheral vascular dilation, heart rate, blood pressure, and kidney output can be influenced by operant conditioning processes. While the precise mechanisms involved are a subject of controversy, these findings clearly blur the traditional distinction between operant and respondent processes (Swenson, 1980).

A fourth area of overlap between operant and respondent processes is seen in the area of what has come to be known as species-specific behavior. Species-specific behaviors include such phenomena as the well-known process of imprinting in young ducklings. Characteristics of species-specific behavior include a learning experience, a critical time period in the development of the organism, and a relatively permanent or lasting effect often from a single exposure to a stimulus event. Because these processes are so unusual, some theorists consider them a third type of learning (Swenson, 1980).

Applications. During its early history behavioral psychology was closely associated with laboratory research in learning. Thus many years passed before practical applications of behavior theory were developed. Early hints of this movement are reflected in the work of Watson and Raynor on conditioning of fear responses, and by Jones in the elimination of conditioned fear. Other early work included the development of the negative practice technique by Dunlap (Ullmann & Krasner, 1965).

The early application studies were isolated and had little impact until around 1950. Dollard, Miller, and Mowrer contributed to relating psychoanalytic concepts to learning theory. More significantly, Skinner's book *Science and Human Behavior* (1953), although largely theoretical, clearly advocated application of behavior theory to practical human concerns. In the following decade two additional books were published (Eysenck, 1960; Wolpe, 1958), and journal articles applying behavioral principles to human problems began to appear more regularly. At the same time, a number of behavioral psychologists began to shift their work from basic to more applied concerns.

By 1963 the interest in behavior modification and behavior therapy had become sufficiently widespread that the first journal devoted exclusively to this subject, *Behavior Research and Therapy*, was started. In the ensuing 15 years research in applied behavior theory has grown phenomenally. By 1980 dozens of journals had appeared that dealt with a broad range of applied behavioral research.

At present, applications of behavior theory have been extended to institutionalized retarded persons, institutionalized psychotics, the public school system, outpatient practice of psychotherapy with adults and children, the prisons, business and industry, and a variety of other settings. The scope of behaviors addressed is equally broad, including such things as elimination of tantrums, establishment of basic social skills such as toileting, the educational process, and such social concerns as conservation of resources and reduction of litter. There have even been some initial applications of behavior principles to Christian education and pastoral ministries in the church (Bufford, 1981).

Many specific behavioral techniques have been developed. Among these are: cognitive therapy for depression; aversion therapy for alcohol and drug abuse and for sexual offenders; token economies for use with institutionalized psychotics and retarded persons; systematic desensitization and a variety of other approaches for elimination of anxiety and phobic behaviors; and numerous cognitive interventions such as covert sensitization and desensitization, implosion, flooding, and negative practice.

Issues from a Christian Perspective. Behavioral psychology has been highly controversial for Christians. Perhaps the key issue is related to the fact that Skinner, one of the most prolific and prominent behavioral spokesmen, is a militant reductionist, determinist, and materialist. Because many Christians reject Skinner's views in these areas, they tend to reject behavioral psychology as well. However, Skinner's world view is not essential to behavioral psychology; in fact, behavioral psychology can be shown to be compatible with a biblical world view in many ways. The reinforcement principle is consistent with the biblical teaching that one must work to eat and that the laborer is worthy of his hire. Biblical teachings about social influence indicate that association with wise persons or with foolish or angry persons results in learning their ways; these are paralleled by Bandura's (1969) concepts of modeling and vicarious learning. Biblical teachings that self-control is a desired characteristic are comparable to the behavioral emphasis on self-control (see Bufford, 1981, pp. 29ff.).

Although many parallels exist, critics from a Christian perspective are quick to point out the numerous contrasts between behavior theory and biblical teachings. It is important to note that most of the controversy surrounds the philosophy of behaviorism rather than the science of behavioral psychology. These issues include the emphasis by many behaviorists on materialistic reductionism, naturalism, scientism, determinism, evolution and related views of the nature of man, the focus in early behavioral work on overt motoric behavior to the exclusion of mental and emotional aspects of behavior, and a strong antireligious bias. In addition to these issues some Christians take exception to the behavioral emphasis on reinforcement or reward. Finally, at times empirical findings have been reported that seem contrary to biblical teachings, such as the findings which led Skinner and others to conclude that punishment was both ineffective and undesirable.

That man is a material being is clearly acknowledged in Scripture, and it is clear that human beings share with other animate creatures many common characteristics. However, Scripture is clear in attaching a special significance to humans. Of all creatures created by God, only mankind was created in God's image. It is this quality that many behavioral psychologists reject, and it is to such a materialistic reductionism that many Christians object. However, it is important to keep in mind that such a viewpoint is not intrinsic to behavioral psychology. One can study the behavior of man as a material being in relationship to his environment without assuming that this is the entire story. This identifies an important limitation of behavioral psychology discussed below. Yet this limitation does not invalidate the behavioral approach; it simply limits it (Koteskey, 1980).

Another criticism of behavioral psychology is its implicit scientism. Scientism is the view that science is the only legitimate way of knowing. Such a perspective rejects propositional biblical revelation. However, it is possible to be committed to the scientific enterprise and to view science as a legitimate approach without presuming that it is the exclusive means of knowledge.

Closely allied to scientism is naturalism, the view that reality is limited to the natural order. Naturalism is implicit in scientism and is a logical corollary of a position that denies the existence of a creator God. While repudiating naturalism, however, we must be careful not to deny the existence of the creation which God pronounced as good and over which he charged men and women with custody.

Another closely related issue is the view regarding the nature of man associated with behavioral psychology. Many behavioral psychologists view man as "nothing but" an animal—certainly a sophisticated and complex animal, but no more. From a Christian perspective the biblical teaching that man is created in the image of God requires that humans be viewed as different from other creatures in some radical way. Underlying the behavioral view is a basic assumption of evolution. While such an assumption is commonly held by many behaviorists, it is not essential to behaviorism as a scientific approach. It is possible to view man as unique, yet also as an animal-like being who shares many features in common with other creatures, without assuming evolution. Indeed, comparative psychology, that branch of psychology concerned with exploring the parallels among various species, is entirely defensible without assuming evolution. For example, if man and other animals are made by a common creator and share a common environment, it is reasonable to expect similarities. However, the Bible is clear that as God's image bearer man is also a spiritual being.

Perhaps the most fundamental issue for many Christians is the behavioral emphasis on determinism. In contrast, many Christians affirm freedom of choice. While a number of definitions of freedom may be offered, the extreme one is the view which holds that free will is an uncaused cause of human behavior. Such a view is antithetic to science since it implies that human behavior is not predictable. At the other extreme determinism suggests that responsible choice is an illusion.

Both these positions are inconsistent with biblical teaching.

In the New Testament freedom is not used in the philosophical sense mentioned above, but rather in terms of one's relationship to God in Christ. The New Testament idea of freedom is linked to the Old Testament idea, which sees freedom as connected to God as giver. This freedom is a freedom from the bondage of sin and its inescapable compulsion. Liberation from the compulsion to sin opens up the hitherto impossible possibility of serving God (Bufford, 1981).

Thus freedom in the sense of human will as an uncaused cause of human actions is not a biblical concept. Indeed, the Bible seems to imply that no future event is indeterminate relative to God, for he foreknows and foreordains all things. The Bible contrasts freedom with slavery to sin and its consequences; freedom is an act of God in relationship to man and involves freedom from the penalty, the power, and ultimately from the presence of sin. It also involves freedom to serve God and receive his blessings. Paradoxically, the Bible suggests that to be free from sin is to be a slave to Christ.

The often criticized behavioral position of affirming determinism and the common reaction to it of asserting free will are both inconsistent with biblical teaching. Rather, the Bible seems to suggest a paradoxical point of view in which man's behavior is influenced by cause and is completely predictable by God, and yet each person makes choices for which he is called to account before God. Overarching all of this are the biblical teachings regarding the sovereignty and providence of God.

In many ways materialistic reductionism, naturalism, scientism, and determinism are intricately interrelated. If one is committed to a naturalistic world view which rejects the notion of a creator God, these viewpoints are easily adapted, especially for persons involved in contemporary academic communities where such viewpoints are widespread and rarely subjected to critical evaluation (VanLeeuwen, 1982). In psychology this is true not only among behaviorists but also among adherents of the other major theoretical systems as well. In summary, it is possible to adopt a methodological behaviorism while holding a Christian world view. Conversely, it is possible to hold unchristian world views whether or not one is a methodological behaviorist.

Objections have been raised regarding the behavioral emphasis on reward; some have equated reward with bribery. However, the notion of reinforcement, or reward, is a common theme in Scripture. We are told that God is a rewarder of those who diligently seek him, that on his return he will come quickly and that his reward will be with him. Similarly, the elder who serves well is worthy of a double reward. At a more general level Scripture teaches that one must work in order to eat and that laziness leads to want and poverty.

Another criticism is that behavioral psychology neglects the central essence of man. The Bible is clear in its teaching that persons function as unified wholes. This means that it is supportive of a behavioral perspective which emphasizes the role of what one does. At the same time, it strikes a balance and thus takes exception to early forms of behavior theory which tend to deemphasize the role of thinking and feeling. As noted above, recent developments extend behavior theory to include thought and emotion.

Central to the discussion of a Christian perspective on behavioral psychology is the notion that God's normal method of working is through the natural means of the created order. The Bible affirms that God created and continuously sustains the universe, and that God's normal method of working in the created order is through the natural processes which he ordained. In contrast to the naturalistic viewpoint of many behavioral psychologists, which holds that all events may be explained completely in terms of natural causes, this view implies that most events in the created order can be explained at two levels: first, in terms of natural cause; second, in terms of divine activity. Miracles are a special class of events, at least some of which may be explainable only in terms of divine activity (e.g., creation *ex nihilo*). This implies that while God's normal action is through means of the natural processes of the created order, God's activity is not limited to this mode; it also implies that science, the study of the created order, is simply one method of knowing and understanding these natural processes through which God normally moves. As such, science in general and behavioral psychology in particular pose no insurmountable problem for a Christian world view.

The notion that all truth has its source in God suggests that ultimately there should be consistency between good science and good biblical interpretation. While the world view of many behavioral psychologists is incompatible with a biblical world view, behavioral psychology per se is fundamentally consistent with biblical teachings.

References

Bandura, A. *Principles of behavior modification*. New York: Holt, Rinehart & Winston, 1969.

Bijou, S. W., & Baer, D. M. *Child development* (Vol. 1). New York: Appleton-Century-Crofts, 1961.

Bijou, S. W., & Baer, D. M. *Child development* (Vol. 2). New York: Appleton-Century-Crofts, 1965.

Bufford, R. K. *The human reflex: Behavioral psychology in biblical perspective*. San Francisco: Harper & Row, 1981.

Eysenck, H. J. *Behavior therapy and neurosis*. New York: Pergamon Press, 1960.

Koteskey, R. L. *Psychology from a Christian perspective*. Nashville: Abingdon, 1980.

Skinner, B. F. *Science and human behavior*. New York: Macmillan, 1953.

Swenson, L. C. *Theories of learning*. Belmont, Calif.: Wadsworth Publishing, 1980.

Ullmann, L. P., & Krasner, L. (Eds.). *Case studies in behavior modification*. New York: Holt, Rinehart & Winston, 1965.

VanLeeuwen, M. S. *The sorcerer's apprentice: A Christian looks at the changing face of psychology*. Downers Grove, Ill.: Inter-Varsity Press, 1982.

Wolpe, J. *Psychotherapy by reciprocal inhibition*. Stanford, Calif.: Stanford University Press, 1958.

R. K. Bufford

Behavior Genetics. *See* Heredity and Environment in Human Development.

Behavior Modification. *See* Applied Behavior Analysis; Behavior Therapy.

Behavior Therapy. This term is typically applied to an exceptionally broad group of approaches to enhancing human welfare. The terms *behavior therapy* and *behavior modification* are increasingly regarded as synonymous. For simplicity, only the former term will be used here.

History. The rise of behaviorism in the first half of the twentieth century set the stage for an application of this perspective to the clinical practice of psychology and psychiatry. The philosophy of behaviorism provided a view of persons as exclusively physical beings who necessarily acted in accordance with universal behavioral laws and a view of science which eschewed all knowledge not empirically verifiable. Applications of operationistic, quantitative, experimental scientific methods in psychology produced what were seen as remarkable advances in scientific knowledge about animal and human behavior.

The typical practices of clinical psychology and psychiatry at this time were also influential in the rise of behavior therapy because of their disparity with academic psychology. Kazdin (1982) called the predominant model at this time the "intrapsychic disease" approach. This approach tends to look for psychological disease processes underlying behavioral symptoms. Further, this view encourages the search for symptom syndromes (or clusters), implying a common underlying cause for each syndrome. Treatment approaches based on these conceptions (e.g., psychoanalysis) were preeminent during this period.

Kazdin (1982) has documented that many treatment methods essentially behavioral in practice had been used before 1900. For example, Lancaster in the early 1800s developed and used what was essentially a token economy system for the classroom, and Brissaud developed a precursor to systematic desensitization in the 1890s. Use of expressly behavioral methods of treatment began to increase steadily in the first half of the 1900s. Watson, Jones, and others worked at conditioning and deconditioning fear. The Russian psychologist Kantorovich and Americans Voegtlin and Lemere used aversive shock conditioning to treat alcoholics. In his *Conditioned Reflex Therapy* (1949) Salter proposed conceptualizations of and treatment methods for abnormal behavior which were based primarily on Pavlovian conditioning models of habit.

In 1952 Eysenck published his famous article in which he argued that there was no convincing evidence that psychotherapy as commonly practiced produced any benefits for clients above that which would normally accrue to them without formal treatment. This article scandalized the professional community and became a rallying point for the search for more effective (behavioral) methods for treating maladjustment.

Major developments began to emerge on three continents in the 1950s. In South Africa, Wolpe began to report his pioneering development of systematic desensitization for the treatment of anxiety-based disorders. In Britain, Eysenck, Rachman, and others at Maudsley Hospital in London were vigorous proponents of behavioral treatment methods similar to Wolpe's. In the United States an increasing number of applications of operant methods were reported. Ayllon, Lindsley, and Skinner worked with psychotic inpatients, and Bijou, Staats, and Ferster did pioneering work with disturbed children.

The behavior therapy movement has continued to grow. The character of the movement has evolved remarkably with its growth. The publication of Bandura's influential *Principles of Behavior Modification* (1969) marked an increased openness to the consideration of mediational variables (discussed below) and highlighted the diversity of views that might be called behavioral. Lindsley and Skinner in the United States and Lazarus in South Africa

were the first to use the term *behavior therapy* in the 1950s. The first behavior therapy journal began publication in 1963; now over 15 journals are devoted to that one topic and many others publish a substantial number of behavioral articles. A large number of books on the approach have been published. Most graduate schools of psychology teach specialized courses in the practice of behavior therapy, and several major national and international associations exist for the promotion of behavior therapy, the largest of which is the Association for the Advancement of Behavior Therapy. Given the relatively recent development, it is remarkable that Smith (1982) showed that behavioral and cognitive-behavioral orientations are together the most frequent orientation of practicing psychologists who identify themselves as adhering to a specific approach.

Distinctives. Erwin (1978) struggled to define behavior therapy and came to the surprising but compelling conclusion that "no such definition is possible because behavior therapies do not share a set of illuminating defining properties" (p. 38). He proposed rather that there is a group of characteristics that tend to be associated with what we call behavior therapy approaches. The more of these characteristics an approach exhibits, and the more clearly they characterize the approach, the more likely the approach is to be considered behavioral. The following list of characteristics is derived from Erwin (1978) and Agras, Kazdin, and Wilson (1979).

First, behavior therapy is fundamentally oriented toward the alleviation of human suffering and the promotion of human growth. Second, it is a psychological rather than biological form of intervention. Third, it is usually used to modify problem behaviors directly rather than to modify hypothesized psychological disorders. For example, the behavior therapist would attempt to modify a person's unassertive behavior directly rather than exploring a hypothesized inferiority complex. Fourth, behavior therapy expahsizes current determinants of behavior rather than historical antecedents. If a problem is shown to be clearly related to a series of childhood events, the behavior therapist would focus on how these events are still active in the person's life today rather than concentrating on retrospection. Fifth, behavior therapy can be used sequentially (i.e., different problems in the same person tend to be viewed as independent, thus allowing for different methods to be brought sequentially to bear on each problem). Sixth, assessment, problem conceptualization, and treatment are individualized. In behavior therapy diagnostic groupings are used at most for economy of communication; the behavior therapist tends to doubt that such categorizations are the best way to group disorders, questioning whether they represent real "species." Seventh, the therapist's role in relation to the client is that of behavior change consultant. Eighth, many behavior therapy techniques are closely related (at least on a metaphorical level) to classic learning theory research. Finally, behavior therapists are typically committed to an applied experimental science approach to clinical practice. Empirical confirmation of treatment effectiveness is emphasized and is the major criterion for judging the value of a technique.

Agras et al. (1979), noting that modern behavior therapy cannot be considered monolithic, differentiated four major perspectives on behavior therapy. The first they termed APPLIED BEHAVIOR ANALYSIS. This approach is most heavily influenced by Skinner's operant psychology. Its practitioners emphasize the alteration of the functional relationships between overt behaviors and their antecedents and consequences. Intensive analysis of individual cases is the major form of empirical investigation utilized.

The second school was labeled the *neobehavioristic mediational S-R model.* Typified by Eysenck, Wolpe, and Rachman, this perspective tends to emphasize classical conditioning processes (to which "S-R" refers) while also using operant methods. Neobehavioristic mediational refers to the willingness of its adherents (unlike the Skinnerians) to use hypothesized intervening psychological states in their conceptualizations (e.g., fear, anxiety). Their treatment techniques frequently assume the reality of mental events (e.g., systematic desensitization assumes that the person can really imagine a feared scene). These mental events are, however, viewed as being simply another type of causally determined behavior which operates according to the same laws of conditioning as all other forms of behavior.

The final two groups are dominant in contemporary behavior therapy. The third major group is the *social learning* group. Exemplified by Bandura and Mischel, this approach suggests that operant and classical conditioning processes occur primarily via cognitive mediation. Beliefs, thoughts, perceptions, and other cognitive processes are viewed as the major determinants of behavior. Modeling and other forms of vicarious learning (learning by indirect rather than direct experience) are empha-

sized. Humans are assumed to be capable of limited self-direction, in that people can exert some control over the environmental and cognitive determinants of behavior. (*See* SOCIAL LEARNING THEORY.)

The fourth major perspective is COGNITIVE-BEHAVIOR THERAPY. This perspective was inspired by Ellis's rational-emotive therapy. Mahoney, Meichenbaum, Beck, and others drew from Ellis the emphasis on cognitions as a major influence upon behavior, but attempted to develop more broadly applicable and less philosophically loaded methods for changing human cognition. The differences between these last two perspectives is primarily one of emphasis on thoughts and behavior, with this last group almost exclusively emphasizing the mediating cognitive variables that are frequently described as an "internal dialogue."

Practice of Behavior Therapy. In her or his relationship with the client the behavior therapist is primarily a consultant in behavior change who serves as a supporter and motivator in the process of change, as a resource in clarifying the problem and designing change strategies, and as a model of more functional behavior. Therapy usually begins with behavioral assessment, in which the attempt is made to understand the client's unique problems in light of their current psychological and environmental determinants. Treatment is carefully tailored to the results of the assessment process. Since client problems are frequently complex, treatment tends to be multifaceted.

The process of treatment varies with the specific orientation of the behavior therapist and the problems of the client. Applied behavior analysts are likely to use such techniques as material or social reinforcement, punishment, shaping, time-out, token economies, prompting, and contingency contracting. Applied behavior analysis seems to be most widely used with the retarded, children, and institutionalized populations. Neobehavioristic mediational S-R therapists utilize conditioning techniques such as systematic desensitization, flooding, covert sensitization, and aversive conditioning. The first two techniques are widely used with anxiety-based disorders (phobias, obsessive-compulsive disorders, impotence) whenever a stimulus for the anxiety can be identified. The latter two are used to create aversions to stimuli in order to decrease the occurrence of such problem behaviors as sexual deviations and drug or alcohol abuse.

Social learning therapists emphasize methods that utilize modeling and competency building—such as training in coping skills, social skills, assertiveness, and communication skills—to deal with social interaction difficulties, anxiety-based disorders, and depression. Self-control is also a focus in this model; it can be taught by teaching the skills of self-monitoring, self-evaluating, and self-consequating behavior. Cognitive-behavior therapists frequently use such exclusively cognitive methods as cognitive restructuring, problem solving, thought stopping, or covert sensitization. These cognitive-behavioral methods are used particularly in treating affective disorders (anxiety, depression, and anger), stress disorders, and pain; in children they are used to decrease impulsivity and increase academic skills.

There are few purists in any of these schools, and almost all the techniques listed for one group are used by practitioners in the other groups. The overall effectiveness of behavior therapy is difficult to judge. Some suggest that it is no better than other approaches. Reports suggest that it is extremely valuable in the treatment of specific anxiety disorders, behavior and cognitive disorders of childhood, interpersonal skill deficits, unipolar depression, sexual dysfunction, stress reactions, and schizophrenia (in tandem with pharmacotherapy). Lanyon and Lanyon (1978) provide a very readable introduction to the practice of behavior therapy.

Views of Human Nature. A major distinctive of a behavioral view of human nature is its emphasis on universal processes of human change, in contrast to other schools' emphasis on universal psychological structures, stages of development, or motivations. Because it is the "laws of learning" that are emphasized, there is greater readiness to appreciate the idiosyncratic nature of human life. Behavior therapists are less likely to emphasize commonalities of experience (e.g., Rogers's proposed tendency toward self-actualization) but rather to focus on the way in which learning can lead to the development of practically any pattern of human behavior imaginable, depending upon the person's learning history and biological potential. One implication of this is that behavior therapists tend not to employ a standard diagnostic nomenclature, which is judged to be rooted more in theory than reality.

Secondly, the behavioral view of humankind (except perhaps for the applied behavior analysis group) is interactional in nature; that is, it gives serious consideration to both personal and environmental (physical and social) determinants of human behavior. To the behavior therapist dynamic views of personality underemphasize the pervasive effect which external events have upon persons. They believe instead that behavior originates primarily from intrapsychic causes.

In the most general terms the behavior therapist views people in terms of their "person variables" (Mischel, 1973), their biological heritage, and their environment. Person variables (also termed organismic variables or learning history) include the person's acquired response capacities, expectancies, and the myriad of other cognitive variables. Biological variables include physical assets and deficits, physiologically based emotional responsiveness, and conditionability. Social and physical environmental variables must be considered at all levels, from the most immediate and specific (the parent reinforcing the noncompliant child's misbehavior with attention) to the most broad and indirect (e.g., culture and language). If the pressure cooker is a metaphor for understanding human behavior from a psychoanalytic perspective, then we might say that behavior therapists would use the computer as a metaphor for understanding the human person. Input (environmental variables) is processed through the software (person variables), which is built upon the existing hardware (biological variables) to produce the behavioral output.

Most behavior therapists would argue that humans are basically hedonistic in nature. Behavior therapy, therefore, is maximally responsive to requests to end or decrease suffering and to promote growth toward greater pleasure and enjoyment of life. Behavior therapists have no a priori model of optimal human functioning toward which clients are led. On one hand, this allows them greater flexibility in attending to client complaints, since they have no prior commitments to a concrete definition of normality. On the other hand, this inevitably leads behavior therapy to be pathology oriented, especially in its research literature, because people typically come for treatment wanting relief from a specific problem or problem complex.

Conclusion. Erwin (1978) has suggested that behavior therapy neither needs nor is consistent with the philosophical behaviorism that was part of its ancestry. Many Christians reject behavior therapy on philosophical bases (i.e., the unacceptability of materialism, determinism, ethical relativism) that have little impact on its practice and effectiveness. The behavioral emphasis on the potential for beneficial change of one's thoughts and actions is consistent with a scriptural emphasis on similar changes as critical to sanctification (Rom. 12:1–2; Eph. 4:20–32). Biblical injunctions to avoid bad company (1 Cor. 15:33) and to build the community of believers (1 Thess. 5:11–22) show an environmental as well as intrapersonal focus of Christian faith. Habit is a theme of human life in the Scriptures (Heb. 5:13–14). On the negative side, the ever-present reductionism of behavioral analysis can undermine our understanding of such critical human capacities as love and will, as when the former is described in terms of reinforcement history and the latter as the possession of self-management skills. More fundamentally, the Scriptures suggest that both behavior and thoughts issue out of the heart, which is that central part of human life allied to or in rebellion against the Lord God. For the behavior therapist, thoughts and actions are purely functional; there is no human capacity akin to the biblical doctrine of heart. Overall, the behavior therapies warrant serious study by the Christian counselor.

References

Agras, W. S., Kazdin, A. E., & Wilson, G. T. *Behavior therapy: Toward an applied clinical science.* San Francisco: W. H. Freeman, 1979.

Erwin, E. *Behavior therapy: Scientific, philosophical, and moral foundations.* New York: Cambridge University Press, 1978.

Eysenck, H. J. The effects of psychotherapy: An evaluation. *Journal of Consulting and Clinical Psychology,* 1952, *16,* 319–324.

Kazdin, A. E. History of behavior modification. In A. S. Bellack, M. Hersen, & A. E. Kazdin (Eds.), *International handbook of behavior modification.* New York: Plenum, 1982.

Lanyon, R. I., & Lanyon, B. P. *Behavior therapy: A clinical introduction.* Reading, Mass.: Addison-Wesley, 1978.

Mischel, W. Toward a cognitive social learning reconceptualization of human personality. *Psychological Review,* 1973, *80,* 252–283.

Smith, D. Trends in counseling and psychotherapy. *American Psychologist,* 1982, *37,* 802–809.

S. L. JONES

Belle Indifference. A term originally used by Janet to characterize the appearance of unconcern manifested by hysterical patients toward their physical symptoms. Instead of anxiety there is an air of calm indifference. This may be a coping mechanism in that it can bring secondary gains of attention and sympathy which may help the individual cope with the conflict.

Bender-Gestalt Test. The Bender Visual-Motor Gestalt Test, commonly known as the Bender-Gestalt test, is widely used by clinicians as a screening device for the assessment of brain damage. It is often included in a standard psychological test battery along with a measure of general intelligence (e.g., the Wechsler Adult Intelligence Scale), one or more projective tests (e.g, the Thematic Apperception Test or the Rorschach), and an objective test of personality (e.g., the Minnesota Multiphasic Personality Inventory).

The study of the behavioral effects of brain damage deeply interests clinicians for several reasons. First of all, they want to describe more precisely the cognitive or perceptual loss that often accompanies organic impairment. Secondly, they administer tests of perceptual-motor-integration or spatial visualization like the Bender-Gestalt to determine whether or not brain damage (also called organicity) exists. Thirdly, clinicians need to assess the possibility that cerebral dysfunction might be a contributing factor in the client's clinical symptoms.

The test itself was first introduced in 1938 by Bender and reflected psychology's concern at that time with Gestalt perceptual theory. The test consists of nine simple geometric designs which are shown to the subject one at a time and are removed after the subject has reproduced them. A number of objective scoring systems have been developed for both children and adults (Marley, 1982). Some clinicians, however, prefer to score the results intuitively, both as a measure of brain damage and as a type of projective device. In the latter, the individual's approach to the task is hypothesized to reflect a certain cognitive and perceptual style.

To successfully complete the task the subject must evidence visual acuity and adequate motor control. If these can be assumed, errors in reproduction would be attributed to cerebral impairment. An exception would have to be made, however, for an individual who reproduces the figures in an impulsive and haphazard manner. This is highly relevant information, but it more often reflects the person's style of approach to the task at hand. With younger children immaturity can be a significant factor as well. The sensitive and intuitive clinician is often able to discern the relevance of these factors for differential diagnosis.

Classic errors on the test include rotation of the geometric designs, partial reproduction, and perseveration (the individual draws more than is in the stimulus design). The frequency of these errors is thought to be a rough measure of the type and degree of cerebral dysfunction.

There is an impressive body of research on the Bender-Gestalt test. It is a moderately reliable and valid screening device for the assessment of cerebral dysfunction. Recently there have been attempts to increase its validity by using a background interference procedure whereby the subject is asked to reproduce the designs on paper which already has randomly drawn curved black lines (Malony & Ward, 1976).

If, after using this test in conjunction with additional tests and observational data, the clinician suspects the possibility of brain damage, he should consider referral to a neuropsychologist who is familiar with the Halstead-Reitan Test Battery, a promising new approach to assessing the complex effects of damage to the brain. This should help refine or rule out the diagnosis. A referral to a neurologist should also be considered. Careful assessment is prerequisite for most effective psychotherapeutic interventions.

References
Maloney, M. P., & Ward, M. P. *Psychological assessment*. New York: Oxford University Press, 1976.
Marley, M. L. *Organic brain pathology and the Bender-Gestalt test*. New York: Grune & Stratton, 1982.

R. E. BUTMAN

See NEUROPSYCHOLOGICAL ASSESSMENT.

Bestiality. *See* ZOOPHILIA.

Biblical Anthropology. The study of the biblical view of man has been somewhat confusing, since a multitude of terms are used to refer to humanity. *Soul, spirit, body, heart,* and *mind* are a few of the key words which refer to man in his psychospiritual functioning. In the past much debate has centered on the so-called dichotomistic versus the trichotomistic models of man. However, more recent biblical scholarship suggests that anytime the Bible speaks of an aspect of man (soul, spirit, or mind) it is always talking about the whole person (Berkouwer, 1962). Biblically, man is never fragmented or divided into parts; he is always viewed as a totality. This separates biblical thought from Greek thought, where knowledge was seen as cognitive; to the Greeks, the accumulation of facts was something that could be abstractly discussed apart from the knower or the context of a personal commitment to that knowledge by the knower. Biblical thought knows nothing of such an idea, but sees knowledge as something to be acted upon and demanding commitment by the person. Thus in the Bible *mind* and its

ability to know refers to a response that involves the whole person.

It seems clear that the key biblical term for the psychospiritual nature of man is *heart*. More than any other biblical term heart refers to the absolute inner center of man in that it suggests a depth view. All the other biblical terms may often be used interchangeably with heart. They may give a different light on man in totality, but they do not indicate a part of man that is separate from or not included in his heart. A brief examination of a few of these other terms will help interpret the biblical concept of heart.

Soul, Spirit, and Mind. The words soul (*nephesh; psuche*) and spirit (*ruah; pneuma*) are often used as parallel expressions and probably should be viewed as synonymous. Matthew 27:50 reads, "And when Jesus had cried out again in a loud voice, he gave up his spirit (*pneuma*)." However, in contrast, in John 10:17 Jesus says, "The reason my Father loves me is that I lay down my life (*psuche*), only to take it up again." Here both soul and spirit refer to the laying down and giving up of Christ's life and seem to be used interchangeably.

Also it should be noted that the highest experiences of life can be ascribed to either the soul or the spirit. In John 12:27 Jesus said, "Now my soul (*psuche*) is troubled and what shall I say? Father, save me from this hour?" In contrast John 13:21 says, "After he had said this, Jesus was troubled in spirit (*pneuma*) and testified, I tell you the truth, one of you is going to betray me." To attempt to differentiate soul and spirit based on these examples would be extremely difficult. Those who make a distinction suggest that soul refers to the individual's personal life, while spirit refers to the principle of life—i.e., the sense of man's being a spiritual being.

With the term *mind* (*nous; dianoia*) we find the same emphasis. The total man is always in view. In Deuteronomy 6:5 God says, "Love the Lord your God with all your heart and with all your soul and with all your strength." There was no technical word in Hebrew for the mind, so we have the word *strength*. In repeating this commandment Jesus says in Matthew 22:37, "Love the Lord your God with all your heart and with all your soul and with all your mind (*dianoia*)." Clearly his reference to loving God with the mind implies the whole personality is to be committed to an intimate and personal relationship with God.

Heart. Heart is emphasized as the more absolute center, the core of psychospiritual life. "Above all else guard your heart, for it is the wellspring of life" (Prov. 4:23). In some of his harshest teachings Jesus rebuked the Pharisees, and in doing so picks up the theme of the heart as central to human personality: "But the things that come out of the mouth come from the heart, and these make a man unclean. For out of the heart come evil thoughts, murder, adultery, sexual immorality, theft, false testimony, slander" (Matt. 15:18-19). The heart refers to the person's inner essence. It represents the ego or the person. "Thus the heart is supremely the one center in man to which God turns, in which the religious life is rooted, which determines moral conduct" (Kittel, 1976, p. 608). Brandon notes that the heart is the source of motives, the seat of passions, the center of the thought processes, and the spring of conscience. He further notes that this incorporates what is now meant by the cognitive, affective, and volitional elements of personality (Brandon, 1967).

It is interesting to note that the uses of *heart* which refer to thinking, feeling, and acting are balanced enough so as to represent nearly equal emphases. The heart can then be said to contain cognition, affect, and volition. Delitzsch (1867/1977) states that the heart is the center of the pneumatico-psychical life, the life of thought and perceptions, the life of will and desire, and the life of feelings and affections. According to Scripture the heart is not the seat of emotion only, but also of the will and thought; all three spiritual activities converge in the heart (Delitzsch, 1867/1977, p. 307).

This biblical perspective underlines the importance of the heart and its key role in Christian life and thought. It is upon the heart that God looks (1 Sam. 16:7), with the heart that we believe unto salvation (Rom. 10:10), and from the heart that obedience springs (Rom. 6:17). It is the heart which is wicked and evil (Jer. 17:9), and finally the heart is the internal source for all that is external in us (Luke 6:45). As the center of the person, the internal source of one's life, it is the core and seat of emotions, the center of emotional reaction, feeling, and sensitivity. The full spectrum of emotions, from joy to depression and from love to hatred, are ascribed to the heart. Says Delitzsch, "The heart is the laboratory and place of issue of all that is good and evil in thoughts, words and deeds" (p. 148).

If God views the heart as the central influence in the Christian life, then how is the heart transformed from being "deceitful above all things" to "white as snow"? How is the condition of the heart altered? Perhaps no more important question can be asked in philosophy as well as in psychology. The biblical answer is quite clear. The heart is changed only through relationship with Jesus Christ. All theology which deals with a person's change, salvation, sanctification, and glorification ultimately focuses upon the simple relationship that an individual can have with Christ. Biblically, neither the heart nor the human person is ever changed in any other way. Evidence for this cardinal truth can be seen throughout Scripture. In the Old Testament only a personal relationship with Jehovah, the covenant God, changed a person. David says, "Create in me a pure heart, O God, and renew a steadfast spirit within me" (Ps. 51:10), and again, "Search me, O God, and know my heart; test me and know my thoughts" (Ps. 139:23). The primacy of the heart is also set forth in Ezekiel. God says, "I will give them an undivided heart and put a new spirit in them; I will remove from them their heart of stone and give them a heart of flesh" (Ezek. 11:19). Paul repeats the same thinking in the New Testament (Eph. 4:16-19).

Implications for Psychology. This meaning of the biblical use of heart has several implications for the study of psychology. First is the emphasis on the hiddenness of the heart. It is presented as that which lies at the root of thinking, feeling, and acting, the core of man's psychic processes. Its depth and unknowability strongly hint at the modern concept of the unconscious. This is substantiated by David's prayer, "Search me O God and know my heart, . . . and see if there be any wicked way in me" (Ps. 139:23-24). Again, "The heart is deceitful above all things and desperately wicked; who can know it?" (Jer. 17:9). The primacy of the intellect versus the primacy of the inner man or his heart needs to inform the direction of Christian thought in psychology.

Second, the heart shows the importance of affect or feeling. Clinically the power of feelings is easily observable, but to have the Bible point to emotions and feelings as a key and important part of man is significant. Since Christians have often tended to downplay emotions or make them subordinate to other functions, the heart stands as a corrective against such views.

Third, the importance of relationships can be seen by the fact that the heart is changed only by relationship with Christ. This emphasis is found through the entire Bible, and it too has tended to be overlooked by Christian thought. The heart calls relationships to the fore in any discussion of Christian theology or psychology.

Fourth, the heart serves to inform us about the use of psychological thought today. If a person's chief areas of functioning are knowing, being, and doing, it can be seen that congnition, feeling, and behavior correspond closely to these. Therapy should therefore involve all three if it is to be biblical.

Last, the heart must be the core which corresponds to the modern concept of identity. Cognition would emphasize self-image or one's rational view of himself. Affect would emphasize self-esteem or one's feeling about his worth, value, or image. Volition would emphasize self-control or one's ability to control his impulses and feelings. The biblical emphasis on heart suggests that all three components would apply to man as an observer of himself. Thus a comprehensive psychology of identity must include self-image, self-esteem, and self-control mechanisms and structures.

References
Berkouwer, G. C. Man: The image of God. Grand Rapids: Eerdmans, 1962.
Brandon, S. G. F. Jesus and the zealots. New York: Scribner's, 1967.
Delitzsch, F. J. A system of biblical psychology (2nd ed.). Grand Rapids: Baker, 1977. (Originally published, 1867.)
Kittel, G. Kardia. In G. Kittel (Ed.), Theological dictionary of the New Testment (Vol. 3). Grand Rapids: Erdmans, 1976.
W. T. KIRWAN

Biblical Counseling. Developed by Crabb, biblical counseling is an attempt at a biblically based theory of personality, psychopathology, and counseling. It received its first presentation in Basic Principles of Biblical Counselling (1975), where Crabb argued that man has two basic needs: significance and security. Difficulties stem from sinful thinking concerning how these needs can be met. Concurrently counseling focuses on the restructuring of these cognitive patterns. Effective Biblical Counselling (1977) develops the philosophical base of Crabb's approach, with particular emphasis on the integration of psychology and theology as well as a delineation of the etiology of personal problems. His most recent book, The Marriage Builder (1982), applies his model to the marriage relationship.

Crabb argues that, prior to the fall, man was loved and accepted (security) and regarded himself as worthwhile (significance). However, when man sinned and separated himself from God, his capacity for love was no longer filled and a need for security was produced. Similarly Adam lost his worth in terms of his relationship with God, and a need for significance was created. In his natural state, then, man develops beliefs about how his needs for

security and significance can be met, sets goals in light of those beliefs, and lives accordingly. Operating constantly from deficit motivation the natural man strives to gain something that will meet his personal needs. The Christian, in contrast, does not operate from a deficit but from fullness, since his needs for significance and security are completely met in a relationship with Jesus Christ.

Crabb's understanding of the image of God in man is that we are personal beings who have a cognitive, volitional, and emotional component. Although the fall has distanced man from God, the image has not been lost completely. According to Crabb, man still has the capacity to think, choose, and feel. From this he concludes that true biblical counseling must be carried out with a recognition that man is composed of these various facets. This is presented in contrast to typical counseling models that tend to stress one or two aspects to the exclusion of the others.

Based on the foundation that man is created in the image of God, Crabb's model of counseling purports to take that into account. Because we are personal beings and have a need for security and significance, our natural tendency is to develop beliefs about how these needs can be met. When the belief has been established, behavior will be engaged in that will presumably fulfill this belief. So the wife who believes her security depends on her husband's love will always be trying to win his love. When his love diminishes, she will become frustrated because her need for security is not being met.

When this woman comes for counseling she will probably express feelings of resentment and reactive behaviors such as withdrawal of affection or angry outbursts. Crabb suggests that some Christian counselors would intervene at this level and ask her to confess her sinful response and change her behavior toward her husband. In contrast he argues that while clients tend initially to describe feelings and behavior, it is the task of the counselor to move to the identification of wrong thinking patterns. Why does this woman want her husband's unchanging affection? She believes that it will meet her need for security and its loss is deeply personal. The counseling process then moves from the identification of negative feelings and behavior to the identification of wrong thinking. Ultimately Crabb would contend that wrong thinking is anything that denies the fact that God is sufficient for meeting one's personal needs of security and significance.

After this three-step diagnostic stage, help

occurs by promoting right thinking, planning right behavior, and identifying satisfying feelings. The crux of this lies in the changing of the assumptions. The first step is the identification of their origin. The belief has been developed in the person's history and needs to be understood from that perspective. Also the counselor needs to help the client work through the feelings surrounding the cognitive assumptions and encourage him as he goes through the painful process of change. The real work of counseling, however, occurs when new cognitions or beliefs replace old ones. Crabb encourages clients to write out biblical assumptions on 3×5 cards and behave in accord with them. To the criticism that this may be hypocritical Crabb replies that behavior is not judged on the basis of whether our feelings are in accord with it but on the basis of whether it is biblical or not.

Crabb's overall counseling approach is based on an integration perspective that he has called "spoiling the Egyptians." Referring to the experience of the children of Israel in Exodus 12, he argues that the Christian can "spoil" (take from) the world (i.e. secular psychology) provided the principles are carefully screened through Scripture. In light of this Crabb freely acknowledges the influence of Ellis (importance of thinking), Mowrer (stress on responsibility), Frankl (meaning in life), Sullivan (social side of man), and Skinner (environmental influence) on his own thinking. Of these Ellis's contribution is clearly the most influential.

In sum, Crabb argues that the core of all psychopathology is our attempt to meet our needs independently of God, an attempt that is based on a satanically inspired belief (Crabb, 1981a p. 419). In articulating this approach Crabb seeks to be loyal to Scripture as it pertains to the nature of people, problems, and solutions. For this he is to be commended. However, two potential limitations may be noted.

Crabb (1981b) argues that many Christian counselors aspire to a "two-book view" of revelation and do not give the Scriptures the place they deserve. He suggests that ultimately this approach may weaken our view of the Bible and lead to a questioning of its authority. Three responses to this issue (Breshears & Larzelere, 1981; Ellens, 1981; Guy, 1982) raised questions about Crabb's view of Scripture, particularly in terms of its intent, and his lack of separation between biblical and theological inerrancy. This issue needs to be addressed in more detail, especially in light of the fact that Crabb's system purports to have a biblical base.

Another area of concern relates to the biblical substantiation for the basic security and significance needs. Crabb cites Paul's response to God's love in Romans 8 as an illustration of our need for security. Abraham's desire to find a city (Heb. 11:8–10) is used as an example of our need for significance. At a descriptive level these passages show one man who is responding to God's love and another who is responding to God's direction. The imputing of need, and the implicit message that these are the two basic needs do not appear to be well defended biblically. On top of that, the fact that these needs can be met only in Christ, and not in people, appears to deny the horizontal dimension of Christianity. While Crabb does argue that spouses may make us feel significant and secure, he adds that only Christ meets our needs in this area. Again theological backing for the distinction between being secure in Christ and feeling secure with others is not given.

References

Breshears, G., & Larzelere, R. E. The authority of Scripture and the unity of revelation. *Journal of Psychology and Theology*, 1981, 9, 312–317.

Crabb, L. J. *Basic principles of biblical counselling*. Grand Rapids: Zondervan, 1975.

Crabb, L. J. *Effective biblical counselling*. Grand Rapids: Zondervan, 1977.

Crabb, L. J. Biblical counselling: A basic view. In J. R. Fleck & J. D. Carter (Eds.), *Psychology and Christianity: Integrative readings*. Nashville: Abingdon, 1981. (a)

Crabb, L. J. Biblical authority and Christian psychology. *Journal of Psychology and Theology*, 1983, 9, 305–311. (b)

Crabb, L. J. *The marriage builder: A blueprint for couples and counselors*. Grand Rapids: Zondervan, 1982.

Ellens, J. H. Biblical authority and Christian psychology II. *Journal of Psychology and Theology*, 1981, 9, 318–325.

Guy, J. D. Affirming diversity in the task of integration: A response to "Biblical authority and Christian psychology." *Journal of Psychology and Theology*, 1982, 10, 35–39.

R. WILSON

See CHRISTIAN COUNSELING AND PSYCHOTHERAPY; PASTORAL COUNSELING.

Biblical Psychology. *See* CHRISTIAN PSYCHOLOGY.

Biblical View of Man. *See* BIBLICAL ANTHROPOLOGY.

Bibliotherapy. The term refers to the use of literary materials as a treatment technique aimed at the reparation of a psychological disorder or the inducement of change toward growth. Discussions and research in this area almost always refer only to printed material (books, stories), but in this revolutionary age of media diversification it is quite likely that a discussion of books alone is too limited. There are innovative programs involving theater, movies, television, and other single or combined media presentations currently being used as adjuncts to or substitutes for therapy. These more innovative programs have not been explored thoroughly in the literature. Thus, bibliotherapy as the use of printed matter alone will be discussed here, but this discussion should hold for other forms of media as well.

Bibliotherapy has a long history. Sclabassi (1980) notes that the concept of growth through reading is an ancient one. Certainly the great moral writings of antiquity (e.g., the proverbs of the Hebrews, the ethical handbooks of the Greek Stoics) represent an attempt to codify rules for life conducive to enhancement of human welfare. The concept of bibliotherapy as understood today dates back to the emergence of the mental health professions. Benjamin Rush in the early 1800s and Alfred Adler in the early 1900s were pioneers in the use of bibliotherapeutic methods.

There are two major approaches to bibliotherapy, the didactic and the catalytic, which can respectively be identified with more cognitive and behavioral approaches to therapy versus dynamic and humanistic approaches. The didactic approach attempts to facilitate change by providing information helpful in analyzing a problem being faced, formulating new approaches to problem resolution, and motivating the reader to implement and evaluate change procedures. Glasgow and Rosen (1979) have reviewed the self-help behavior therapy manuals that are but one subgroup of literature in this area. These works are generally intended to be used by the reader without professional help, but many behavior therapists use them on an adjunct basis during the process of behavior therapy. A survey of the self-help section of any bookstore reveals an incredible array of such materials. Didactic books have been developed in the areas of fear reduction, weight reduction, smoking cessation, enhancement of assertive responding and social skill, parenting and child management, physical fitness, sexual dysfunction, marital enrichment, depression, and problem drinking, among others. Unfortunately, writers of these works frequently do not document the effectiveness of their programs. Potential problems with such self-help works include extravagant claims for effectiveness, high noncompliance rates with the suggested techniques (one empirical study of such a manual

failed to find a single subject who fully completed the recommended self-treatment procedure), and the negative impact which the reader's "failure" after following an "expert's" program might have on future commitment to and expectations for psychotherapy.

Catalytic bibliotherapy is substantially different, involving the use primarily of imaginative literature for the purpose of facilitating identification, catharsis, and insight on the part of the client (Sclabassi, 1980; Schrank & Engels, 1981). Identification with book or story characters can reduce the client's sense of isolation from others due to perceived uniqueness of his or her problems and can pave the way for catharsis. Catharsis, or therapeutic release of affect, can occur as the reader vicariously shares the powerful experiences of the literary characters. Finally, insight occurs as parallels between the reader and story characters are explored. There are few specific guidelines for method of presentation in this area, and there are no guidelines for choice of materials. Catalytic bibliotherapy has been used with children and adults, individually or in groups, as an elective adjunct to therapy and as a mainstay of the therapeutic content. Schrank and Engels (1981) reviewed the research in this area and concluded that positive recommendations for bibliotherapy far exceed conclusive demonstrations of its merit. But they feel that "catalytic bibliotherapy appears effective for developing assertiveness, attitude change, helper effectiveness, self-development, and therapeutic gains" (p. 145).

Atwater and Smith (1982) recently surveyed Christian psychologists, documenting their wide usage of bibliotherapeutic materials and providing an annotated bibliography of commonly used resources. Bibliotherapy is a potentially useful but underdeveloped approach to enhancing human growth.

References
Atwater, J. M., & Smith, D. Christian therapists' utilization of bibliotherapeutic resources. *Journal of Psychology and Theology*, 1982, *10*, 230–235.
Glasgow, R. E., & Rosen, G. M. Self-help behavior therapy manuals: Recent developments and clinical usage. *Clinical Behavior Therapy Review*. 1979, *1*(1), 1–20.
Schrank, F. A., & Engels, D. W. Bibliotherapy as a counseling adjunct: Research findings. *Personnel and Guidance Journal*, 1981, *60*(3), 143–147.
Sclabassi, S. H. Bibliotherapy. In R. Herink (Ed.), *The psychotherapy handbook*. New York: New American Library, 1980.

S. L. JONES

Binet, Alfred (1857–1911). Pioneer in the development of intelligence tests. Born in Nice, France, Binet obtained a law degree from the

Lycée Saint-Louis in 1878, but his real interest was in the biological sciences. Even while studying law he was attracted to the Sal-pétrière Hospital, where he was influenced by Charcot. He studied medicine and began a career in medical research. In 1890 he obtained a degree in the natural sciences, and in 1894 he earned his doctorate in science with a thesis on the insect nervous system.

In 1889 Binet and Henri Beaunis founded the first experimental psychology laboratory in France. When Beaunis retired in 1895, Binet became director of the laboratory. That same year the two men founded the first French psychology journal, *Psychological Year*, with Beaunis as editor. This became the major vehicle for publication of Binet's research on intelligence. Binet himself became editor in 1897 and continued his research in intelligence until his death.

Binet conducted research in several areas, but he is most widely known for his development of intelligence tests. In the late 1880s and early 1890s he used tests measuring sensory and motor capacities, but soon realized that these did not measure intellect. He then began to use tasks to measure attention, comprehension, memory, judgment, etc. In 1903 he published his most important work, *The Experimental Study of Intelligence*.

In 1904 the Minister of Public Instruction in Paris appointed a commission to recommend procedures by which mentally retarded children could benefit from their education. Binet and Simon (a psychiatrist) were commissioned to develop a test that would pick out children who would not profit from the regular classroom. Such children could then be put in special classes. The first Measuring Scale of Intelligence (1905) had 30 items arranged in order of increasing difficulty. The second one (1908) had 59 tasks grouped at age levels from 3 to 13 years. This test has been revised several times, standardized in different countries, and is still widely used today (*see* STANFORD-BINET INTELLIGENCE SCALE).

In addition to his work in intelligence Binet published such important works as *The Psychology of Reasoning* (1886), *Changes in Personality* (1892), *Intellectual Weariness* (1898), and *Suggestibility* (1900). Although he was productive in many areas, the concept of mental age was his most lasting contribution. That concept was later used by others to determine an intelligence quotient, the IQ. IQ tests became very popular during the first half of the twentieth century.

R. L. KOTESKEY

Biocentric Therapy. In the 1960s Nathaniel Branden developed a system of psychology and therapy in response to the limitations of the deterministic view evident in both psychoanalysis and behaviorism. Called biocentric therapy (biologically oriented and life centered), this cognitive and experiential approach has its roots in the philosophies of Aristotle and Rand (1964) and stresses the importance of fully actualizing all of man's capacities to achieve maturity and maintain mental health. Basic to Branden's thinking is the belief that the individual plays a vital and active role in his personal psychological development and achievement of self-esteem. The essential elements in this self-creative process are the ability to reason, the decision to either use that faculty or suppress it, and the conscious and subconscious value judgments that influence one's emotions and behavior. Anything that blocks or distorts one's reason, volition, values, and emotions results in maladaptive behavior and decreased self-esteem. In biocentric therapy the failure to achieve a healthy sense of self-esteem is the basis for all neurotic disorders, and symptoms are viewed as undesirable solutions to real problems.

The goal of therapy (Branden, 1969, 1971) is to improve the thinking process and to eliminate the blocks to awareness so that new alternatives become available. Biocentric therapy makes use of a wide variety of techniques, such as psychodrama, hypnosis, homework assignments, and breathing exercises, which are meant to incorporate the best aspects of both cognitive and emotive therapies in dealing with the whole person. Unique to biocentric therapy is the use of sentence completion tasks, which serve as a powerful tool in eliciting a client's repressed feelings and images and which bring about a reintegration of his cognitive and affective experience.

According to Branden, the more one is aware of all aspects of oneself and the world outside, the better one can responsibly function to meet unique needs and enhance well-being. Throughout his works he stresses the survival value of the virtues of rationality, independence, honesty, integrity, justice, productiveness, and pride. However, he defines all of these in terms of the objectivist's ethics of rational self-interest, which hold that every person is an end in himself and that the attainment of one's own happiness is one's highest moral purpose. There is no room in this philosophy for self-sacrifice or for the dynamics of faith, as reason in the pursuit of self-interest is the only reality.

References

Branden, N. *The psychology of self-esteem*. Los Angeles: Nash, 1969.

Branden, N. *The disowned self*. Los Angeles: Nash, 1971.

Rand, A. *The virtue of selfishness*. New York: New American Library, 1964.

W. C. DREW

See SELF-ACTUALIZATION.

Bioenergetic Analysis. A form of psychotherapy founded by Alexander Lowen. Lowen was a student for many years of Wilhelm Reich (*see* ORGONE THERAPY), who was a contemporary of Sigmund Freud and the originator of body psychotherapy. Lowen continued the work of Reich in the analysis of bodily-muscular expressions of mental illness and in the development of techniques for releasing those tensions.

Bioenergetic Theory. In the theory of body psychotherapy it is believed that the person experiences the reality of the world primarily through the body (Lowen, 1975). The sense of individual identity stems from a feeling of contact with the body. To know who one is, an individual must be aware of what he or she feels. Without this awareness of bodily feeling and attitudes, a person becomes split into a disembodied spirit or mind and an increasingly inflexible, deadened body (Lowen, 1967).

The problem in mental health, according to body psychotherapy, is the tendency to repress or "implode" (i.e., to hold within and refuse to express) viscerally experienced feeling. The source of this repression of bodily experienced feelings is the growing child's desire to avoid the loss of love by conforming to what the child perceives to be the expectations of others. The child relies upon his mind to figure out what is expected and then attempts to perform those behaviors that will ensure love. A result of this process is that the cerebral cortex struggles to gain control over the naturally experienced body emotion. The intelligence of the individual is funneled into ego, and the ego is increasingly split off from the needs and experiences of the body. This split is viewed as neurotic since mind (the cognitive functions) and body (the visceral feelings and responses) are one unitary process.

The result of long-term repression of bodily experience in favor of adaptation to the demands of society can be rigidification of the body. This is referred to as increasing MUSCULAR ARMOR. Muscular armoring is accompanied by physical tension and the experience of deadness and isolation. Increasingly the cerebral cortex censors and controls as much of the experience of life as possible. Knowledge becomes increasingly intellectual, cut off from the inner depths of the person. Other personality characteristics include self-consciousness, self-doubt, competitiveness, conformity, striving and yet holding back, and frustration.

Control becomes the key in the life of such individuals. They are turned inward. Thoughts and fantasies replace feeling and action. Exaggerated mental activity substitutes for contact with the real world, and belief systems replace aliveness. Faith, hope, and love are increasingly superstitious, pietistic, legalistic, and/or authoritarian. Belief becomes objectified rather than experienced from within. Interpersonal relationships also suffer as other people become objects to be navigated around in life rather than persons to be intimately engaged. The rich inner life of emotions is squeezed to a trickle except for moments of sentimentally or vicariously experienced strong emotion such as through films, sports, and mass behavior. The individual relates more and more to his or her body as a machine to be used and pushed to its limits. The body is weighed, measured, and pushed to meet some idealized sense of proportion, rather than enjoyed for the feeling of aliveness and vitality for its own sake.

The healthy individual has the ability to adjust harmoniously to the demands of society while remaining open and responsive to needs, information, and experience coming from within one's own body (Lowen, 1970). Most individuals have trouble doing this. They lose touch with their inner experience. Bioenergetic analysis attempts to alleviate this alienation between ego and body and thereby assist them in their pursuit of faith and happiness. According to Lowen, faith comes from the heart, which is literally surrounded by flexible and nonrigid muscles. Thus, the pursuit of faith and happiness entails the releasing of energy throughout the body. The healthy individual experiences the freedom of thought and sensation that is rapidly and freely passed throughout the body without the resistance of chronically tight muscles inhibiting such an experience of vitalness.

Bioenergetic analysis also theorizes that different childhood developmental experiences result in different types of muscular armoring and thereby different personality or character types. Lowen devoted much attention to the analysis of and the therapeutic intervention with the different character types (Lowen, 1958). For example, very early life experience that is inadequate in nurturing love may result in what is called the oral character type. Such a person is characterized by feelings of deprivation, inner emptiness and despair, extreme fluctuations in mood, great dependency, and strong fear of loss of love objects. Another character type is the masochistic. The underlying quality of this person's life is the fear of self-assertiveness. Masochism is characterized by intense muscular tension, often resulting in muscle spasms and pain. Other character types include the hysterical, the schizoid, and the "rigid character structures" which include the phallic-narcissistic, the passive-feminine, and the compulsive. In each of these different character types childhood developmental issues differ, and the resulting muscular armoring, in both its intensity and location in the body, also differs. The different character types are treated therapeutically in often very different ways.

Bioenergetic Therapy. Therapy in bioenergetic analysis centers on increasing the internal unity of body and psyche in a context of safety, acceptance, and understanding. Body psychotherapy is a combination of physical exercises and more traditional verbal interactions. The physical exercises are aimed at stretching, relaxing, and opening the tensions in the body so that the deeper emotions and repressed memories of the individual can be reintegrated.

A safe environment is a key since the person in pain learned early that uncensored expression of feeling was fundamentally dangerous. Often the therapist will touch the patient in a nurturing way. At times he will encourage the patient to express some emotion strongly. This might take the form of pounding on a pillow with a tennis racket for the release of anger long denied expression. The expression of feeling in a physical and deeply honest verbal way begins the reintegrative process of allowing the ego and the body to once again communicate freely. To Lowen this is the beginning of faith and the emergence of the true self. Feelings are usually logical long before the intellect understands the rationality of the response. In other words, feelings may emerge that at first seem to be unjustified or irrational but which, upon closer examination and more information, become thoroughly understandable and logical.

One of the therapist's important functions in bioenergetic analysis is helping the patient to understand and accept the message of his feelings and body states. The final goal of body psychotherapy, then is a unitary, holistic response to life, where deep inner wells of being are free to be brought to bear on life. The heart is working in cooperation with the head and the head in cooperation with the heart. The individual is increasingly able to focus on life and its real problems rather than being self-absorbed.

Evaluation. One of the major strengths of bioenergetic analysis is its attempt to avoid the sterile and passive verbal reflections which have tended to characterize much traditional psychotherapy. The holistic goal of working with both body and mind often allows for a more vital sense of treatment and well-being. Body-oriented psychotherapies have proliferated recently. The popularity of these therapies could be argued to suggest that the inclusion of direct body movement and touch is experienced by the patient as more satisfying and releasing than traditional therapies which focus exclusively on verbal interchange.

One of the major criticisms of body psychotherapies is the tendency among some practitioners to be anti-intellectual. In such a case the client is often encouraged into emotional experiences and bodily movement without much sense of their purpose or meaning. The release of emotion in the therapy process is seen as an end in itself rather than a purposeful step in the unification of mind and body. Such an attitude can lead to the valuing of the expression of feelings regardless of the social context. The result is an insufficiently integrated and balanced individual. Such a person's credo is doing his or her own thing regardless of its impact on others.

Another criticism of body psychotherapy is that it often tends to create an unnecessary amount of confusion and disorientation in the patient. As the "de-armoring" process continues, there is a good deal of confusion and disorientation as the person attempts to get a new sense of who he or she really is. During this process it is important that a great deal of nurturance and support be given in order to provide the patient with a sense of trust and security.

Bioenergetic analysis and other body psychotherapies are fundamentally compatible with the teachings of Scripture. Throughout the history of Christianity there has been a tendency to disconnect the Christian faith from the body and to reduce the Christian message to abstract theology. A theology that flows only from a detached intellect is more likely to be a statement of the status quo than a compassionate, courageous spirituality. The Pharisees, for example, were condemned not for carnal sins of the flesh but for an egoistic perversion of the truth in which the letter rather than the heart of the law was worshiped. In the many scriptural references regarding the dangers of the flesh the reference is never to materiality and sensuousness as such, but to materialism and sensualism. In other words, it is not money and pleasure that the Bible condemns, but the lifting of these aspects of life to improper status within our lives. In short, the materialistic and sensualistic pursuit is fundamentally a *mental*, not a *material* process. It is the distortion occurring in hearts and minds that turns the body and its sensual pleasure from gifts of God to be enjoyed into sinful preoccupations.

Faith is the ability to surrender the more secure, predictable, and safe life of an ego-dominated existence in favor of an open responsiveness to the needs and desires of the true inner self. Faith and life become integrated because the person is integrated. Knowledge itself, Lowen reminds us, is a surface phenomenon and belongs to the ego, while truth flows through the whole being. We are advised in Ephesians 5 to know the love of God though it is beyond knowledge. Lowen postulates that knowledge becomes understanding when it is coupled with feeling. The Scriptures argue that the devil knows the truth and yet does not embrace it.

It is possible to argue that the problem of spirituality is knowing one's real needs. Most of us are unconsciously shaped to assume that our needs are related to consumption, status, and esteem. But our deepest needs are for touch, warmth, relatedness, and love. In its purest form bioenergetic analysis is committed to helping individuals become aware of these needs and then meet them in healthy ways.

References

Lowen, A. *Physical dynamics of character structure.* New York: Grune & Stratton, 1958.

Lowen, A. *The betrayal of the body.* New York: Macmillan, 1967.

Lowen. A. *Pleasure.* New York: Coward-McCann, 1970.

Lowen, A. *Bioenergetics and the language of the body.* New York: Coward, McCann & Geoghegan, 1975.

C. E. Barshinger and L. E. LaRowe

See Physical Contact in Psychotherapy; Primal Therapy.

Biofeedback Training. Biofeedback training consists of reporting back to individuals, through instrumentation, information about their physiological functions in order to help them modify or regulate their biological responses. The goals are twofold: to develop increased physiological self-awareness in order to control specific internal functions, and to transfer that control from therapy to the other areas of one's life.

Self-regulation through such techniques as progressive relaxation and autogenic training was developed 50 years before clinical biofeedback training, but the clinical results were not well substantiated until instrumentation was developed to record the data. This prevented biofeedback training from making an impact on psychology and medicine until the 1960s. Since then biofeedback training has emerged as a new frontier in the treatment of stress diseases, which have emerged as the leading cause of illness and death.

Most modern medical textbooks attribute between 50 to 80% of all diseases to psychosomatic or stress-related origins. Stress causes inappropriate heightening of arousal that includes increased heart rate, muscle tension, blood pressure, palm sweating, and peripheral vascular constriction. In many cases there is also rapid respiration. This stress reaction is theorized as a contributing factor to many serious diseases.

The underlying principle behind biofeedback is that stress and nonstress states cannot exist in the human organism at the same moment. Biofeedback training uses such instruments as the electromyograph, skin surface thermometer, and electrodermalgraph (or galvanic skin response) to help train individuals to monitor and reduce their stress levels. The immediate feedback, either by a tone, light, or observing a needle on a panel, allows patients to immediately know if they are relaxing or becoming more tense.

The electromyograph measures the electronic activity of muscles. Electrodes are attached to various parts of the body (e.g., to the forehead and/or back of the neck in the treatment of tension headaches). The instrument has been shown to be quite successful in the treatment of tension headaches and has shown some promise in the treatment of generalized tension (Katkin & Goldband, 1980). The thermal unit measures skin (peripheral) temperature. The sensors are usually attached to the fingertips. As the smooth muscles around peripheral blood vessels dilate during relaxation, the skin temperature rises. The thermal unit is frequently used in the treatment of migraine headaches, Raynaud's disease, and hypertension (Fuller, 1977). The electrodermalgraph measures the level of skin conductance. It is used to show the client areas of stress which need to be dealt with, such as fear or anger as well as anxiety. It can also be used to aid the therapist in creating a hierarchy for systematic desensitization and guided imagery.

The stress management program asks individuals to initiate physiological change through focusing their attention on their biological functioning. Many times this is accomplished by relaxation exercises that focus on relaxing various parts or the whole body. The instrumentation gives feedback as to the effectiveness of the relaxation effort.

Not all patients respond to biofeedback training, nor should all individuals be considered for such treatment. The training aspects of treatment can be discouraging, especially to individuals who expect a quick cure. Persons suffering from myocardial infarction or diabetes should not be considered for biofeedback training on an outpatient basis. Psychological conditions in the psychotic range, especially paranoia, are also inappropriate for biofeedback training.

Although the most frequent applications of biofeedback training have been to stress-related disorders, other applications have emerged. Biofeedback has become a central focus of behavioral medicine (see HEALTH PSYCHOLOGY) and has shown much promise in such areas as muscular rehabilitation, epilepsy control, and the treatment of cardiac dysfunction. In fact, some research seems to suggest that biofeedback training may be even more successful in these areas than in the more traditional psychological areas such as anxiety reduction (Katkin & Goldband, 1980).

Applications of biofeedback continue to expand. Dentists, alcohol treatment programs, and mental retardation facilities are all exploring uses of the method. Increasing numbers of psychotherapists incorporate biofeedback into their practice, and training workshops in the approach abound. With this trend, quality control in training and practice becomes an increasing problem. The Biofeedback Society of America began in 1981 to administer a certification test to biofeedback personnel. Although this is a step in the right direction, large numbers of therapists continue to adopt biofeedback procedures with minimal training and no certification.

References

Fuller, G. D. Biofeedback. San Francisco: Biofeedback Press, 1977.

Katkin, E. S., & Goldband, S. Biofeedback. In F. Kanfer & A. Goldstein (Eds.), Helping people change (2nd ed.). New York: Pergamon Press, 1980.

M. A. CAMPION

See STRESS; TENSION; HEADACHE, MIGRAINE; HEADACHE, TENSION.

Biopsychosocial Therapy. An approach to family therapy developed by Nathan Ackerman, considered by many to be the founding father of family therapy. Ackerman approaches family therapy from a psychoanalytic framework that is a result of his early training. However, his approach is extremely flexible and quite broad as he integrates social and cultural perspectives with those of personal and family development. Family life is seen as a cornerstone of personal as well as cultural survival.

Although the approach is called a biopsychosocial theory, there is very little emphasis placed on the biological aspect of human development. Occasional reference is made to the perpetuation of the species and to heredity. An important factor for the family therapist is to identify the history or presence of organic difficulties, as this is a powerful influence on how the family system operates. Yet this is not discussed in any detail by Ackerman. Rather, he immediately discusses how biological functions interrelate with social and psychological variables (Ackerman 1958).

According to Ackerman, flexibility in family therapy is necessary because family problems are seldom clear-cut. Family sessions should be problem oriented and not oriented to a particular technique. The sessions may involve continuous participation of three generations in a family system or individual psychotherapy of a family member accompanied by family therapy. Throughout the family's treatment, the participants may change from family therapy to marital therapy, to single parent or child therapy, depending on the problems. In spite of this diversification the emphasis is on the whole family and not segments of the family. Whatever has thrown the family into an unstable way of functioning needs to be identified and resolved. Usually there is a history of family pathology which surfaces during the age of adolescence, and the youth becomes the symptom-bearer of historical family conflict (Ackerman, 1970a).

The family interview places tremendous pressure on the therapist (Ackerman, 1970b). The pressure to encourage the family to stay in therapy is met with the fear of sharing family secrets which have never been discussed. The therapist must identify how each family member relates to the others as well as the coalitions, patterns of withdrawal, and verbal nuances of anger, fear, and frustration. Also, methods of communicating affection, warmth, and concern need to be identified. Individual stages of development reflect areas of conflict, such as parents asking their children for parenting and marital advice instead of asking adult peers or professional therapists. Pushing a child's independence or discouraging it adds considerable family conflict. Each person in the family needs to assess his or her own direction for growth and interaction with the family and beyond. Ackerman describes the therapist as being like a conductor pulling together the separate talents of family members into a working whole without destroying individuality (Ackerman, 1958).

The training of the therapist is critical, according to Ackerman. Knowledge of intrapersonal and interpersonal dynamics is imperative. Accompanying this is the need for a clear understanding of patterns of communication that are healthy and those that are pathological. A good background in sociology and/or anthropology would be most helpful in order to identify different external sources of pressure for each family. The therapist's use of self is repeatedly acknowledged as a catalyst to facilitate family interaction. He or she must be prepared to be extremely flexible. At times the therapist is incorporated into the family, often as a wise grandfather figure. Similarly the therapist will withdraw from the family interaction and facilitate the problem-solving skills as a professional observer. At times the therapist is firm, confrontive, direct and incisive, and at other times warm and compassionate. Because of the flexible model for meeting with family members, there are multiple levels of conflict occurring simultaneously within the family. The therapist must explore these conflicts periodically with the whole family in order for them to build better understanding of one another (Ackerman, 1972).

Because Ackerman sees each family therapist functioning differently in family therapy, it is difficult to build a general theory from his approach. His model is an attempt to build a picture of the family as the cornerstone for human survival and provides us with some perceptive insights into the components of family pathology and family well-being. It also serves as an important reminder of the flexibility required on the part of the family therapist.

References

Ackerman, N. W. *The psychodynamics of family life.* New York: Basic Books, 1958.

Ackerman, N. W. Adolescent problems. In N. W. Ackerman (Ed.), *Family process.* New York: Basic Books, 1970. (a)

Ackerman, N. W. Family interviewing. In N. W. Ackerman (Ed.), *Family therapy in transition.* Boston: Little, Brown, 1970. (b)

Ackerman, N. W. The growing edge of family therapy. In C. J. Sager & H. S. Kaplan (Eds.), *Progress in group and family therapy.* New York: Brunner/Mazel, 1972.

T. M. JOHNSON

See FAMILY THERAPY: OVERVIEW.

Biosocial Theory. The comprehensive, integrated formulation of human behavior developed by Gardner Murphy. It is comprehensive in its reliance on diverse data bases, including clinical experience, physiological and animal experimentation, and social science research. Murphy strove to use all reliable empirical data. It is integrated to the extent that Murphy attempted to specify the interrelations and interdependencies of the biological and social substrata of behavior.

By biosocial Murphy meant "what is biological is at the same time social" (Murphy, 1947, p. 138). Biological processes have antecedent and consequent social impact. "The only thing that can be socialized is a biological process, and in man most biological processes are to some degree socialized" (Murphy, 1947, p. 139). Most biological events can be visibly altered by social control.

Personality denotes 1) affective and volitional qualities that distinguish persons from one another, and 2) general characteristics that distinguish persons from nonpersons. The latter is the focus of Murphy's major theoretical interest, though he did not deny individual differences. To Murphy, personality can be studied at three levels of complexity: personality as distinct individuals, personality as structured whole with defined parts, and personality as structured organism-environment field in which the components of each interact. Biosocial theory considers personality at the highest level of complexity. Murphy developed his propositions logically, methodically, and meticulously. As a consequence, he has been called a "theorist's theoretician."

Murphy conceived of personality as having its prime mover in a biological field. The organic systems of the body are tension or energy systems with complex interactions designed to achieve homeostasis. Energy moves from an area of excess to one of deficit in response to changing needs and environments. A hierarchy of interdependent organs exists to ensure survival. Each organic system (e.g., sympathetic nervous system) is responsive to endogenous needs, needs of other systems, and exogenous stimulation. Organic needs involve the visceral needs for food, water, air, etc., activity needs of exploration and preservation, and needs to avoid pain, death, and threats. Needs operate to motivate behavior and are produced from the interplay of inner and outer pressures. Murphy's theory of personality is essentially a motivational one (cf. Maslow's hierarchy of needs).

Biosocial theory can be considered in light of five major postulates: 1) field theory wherein the person is an organism in a time and space energy system; 2) evolutionary development following the homogeneous to heterogeneous to structured organization sequence; 3) canalization as the process by which needs become more specific when satisfied in a specific manner; 4) autism by which cognitive processes work in concert with need satisfaction; and 5) feedback which provides a basis for testing reality and avoiding self-deception.

Following the Gestalt heritage of Lewin, Murphy believed the person to be a nodal point in an energy field. This *field theory* was a "psychological approach which regards the barrier between individual and environment as indefinite and unstable, and requires the consideration of an organism-environment field whose properties are studied as field properties" (Murphy, 1947, p. 986). The perceptual redefinition of organism and environment results from the exchange of materials through the skin and other membranes. The same relation holds between the person and the social environment, in which social forces become internalized and the person alters the environment.

Human development follows the three-stage *evolutionary theory* advocated by Herbert Spencer. In this view the organism begins as a homogeneous, undifferentiated unit, but specialized structures form to accomplish specialized functions. The second stage is one in which the organism is composed of heterogeneous units with unique roles. The third stage is marked by further specialization in structure-function relations, with special structures performing the function of integrating the others (central nervous system and self). This integrating mechanism maintains the structural unity of the whole. This conception of development is applied to biological development from ovum through senescence. It is also descriptive of cognitive development as theorized by Piaget, and of socialization of individuals into substructures of society.

Social differentiation is accomplished largely through conditioning and *canalization*. C. S. Sherrington (1857–1952) had asserted that responses were of two major types, preparatory or consummatory, each modifiable through specific forms of learning. Murphy held that conditioning applied only to preparatory responses (e.g., Pavlov's dog which salivated in anticipation of meat powder) and that conditioning was reversible, subject to extinction. However, consummatory responses (e.g., eating, drinking, sexual behavior) are canalized. Once canalized stimuli are associated with the consummatory response, they cannot be modified or extinguished (cf. Allport's functional autonomy). Murphy borrowed Janet's term *canalization* to describe the "process by which general motives . . . tend, upon repeated experience, to become more easily satisfied through the action of the specific satisfier than of others of the same general class" (Murphy, 1949, p. 162). Canalization forms the basis of acquired tastes. The choice of satisfier goes to the familiar one, so that a progressive shift is made in preference to specific means of satisfaction. Murphy asserted that those preferences did not change much once formed.

The life of the organism is geared toward need satisfaction. Canalization makes certain satisfiers more emotionally appealing or desirable than others. To maintain internal integrity cognitive processes are altered to conform to emotional predispositions regarding satisfiers. Murphy termed this tendency *autism*, and defined it as "the movement of cognitive processes in the direction of need satisfaction (1949, p. 980). Feelings are justified in thinking, in that "the best is the norm" (1949, p. 377) and "needs keep ahead of percepts" (1949, p. 378). This autistic-type thinking is evidenced in rigid and defensive reactions (cf. Freudian rationalization). To prevent autistic self-deception from destroying it, the organism tests its percepts against reality.

In summary, Murphy's concept of personality is that it is a point in a biological and social field. It draws and returns energy to that field, being interdependent with the field. Personality development is a process of progressive differentiation. The future of human personality is positive, provided conflicts are resolved (Murphy, 1953).

References

Murphy, G. *Personality: A biosocial approach to origins and structures.* New York: Harper & Brothers, 1947.
Murphy, G. *Historical introduction to modern psychology* (Rev. ed.). New York: Harcourt, Brace, 1949.
Murphy, G. *Human potentialities.* New York: Association Press, 1953.

R. L. TIMPE

See MURPHY, GARDNER.

Bipolar Disorder. A subclassification of the affective disorders, more specifically the major affective disorders. Its central feature is a disturbance of mood which influences the entire psychic life. The bipolar disorder (also known as manic-depressive illness) is subdivided into mixed, manic, or depressed.

The clinical picture of mania is represented by a cluster of symptoms in which the principal mood is elevated. This results in pressure of speech, flight of ideas (accelerated speech with abrupt change from topic to topic), irritability, distractability, and rapidly developing involvement in activities that can be destructive. There is usually poor insight and judgment in a manic episode. Characteristic symptoms involve spending sprees, grandiose plans, and expansiveness. Superficially such a patient appears humorous and dramatic. As the syndrome develops, delusional grandiosity emerges, including special relationship to God or other prominent figures. Sleep seems irrelevant and unnecessary. There is no sensation of tiredness. Hallucinations may be present; they coincide with the grandiose self-esteem. Depression may be intermingled with the apparent elation.

The first attack of a manic episode usually occurs in the 20s and typically begins suddenly, with a rapid development over a short time span. The episodes may last a few days to as long as months. Often the manic episodes end abruptly. The course of the illness usually has interspersed depressive episodes.

In bipolar disorder the initial attack is commonly a manic episode. Persons who have repeated manic attacks will also usually have major depressive episodes which are characterized by depressed mood. Bodily functions are affected in that weight loss or gain, appetite disturbance, sleep disturbance, feelings of worthlessness, and motor changes (either slowed up or agitated) are present. There may be suicidal ideas and/or intent. This mood disturbance is recognized by the individual, but he is unable to talk or think his way out of the problem. Delusions or hallucinations, if present, involve depressive themes such as being punished for sinfulness. A major depressive episode may occur at any age.

Bipolar disorder involves a cycle between manic and depressive episodes, the current attack being labeled by the predominant recent symptomatology. A mixed bipolar disorder presents both manic and depressive episodes, intermixed or rapidly alternating within days.

The course of bipolar disorder is variable. There are usually lucid periods of varying frequency and duration between attacks. Twenty to 30% present a chronic course with

residual symptoms and impairment. Impairment includes social and occupational areas and results from the poor judgment or withdrawal. The most serious complications are substance abuse, financial or legal problems, and suicide. Prevalence studies suggest 0.4% to 1.2% of adults have had bipolar disorder, equally distributed between the sexes.

Bipolar disorder needs to be differentiated from other diagnoses. Organic affective disorders from medications or such illnesses as multiple sclerosis may appear to be a manic episode. Paranoid schizophrenia may be difficult to separate from a manic episode. A diagnosis of schizoaffective disorder is used at times when it is impossible to distinguish between a manic episode and schizophrenia. Hypomanic episodes are seen in a cyclothymic disorder, but the full-blown manic symptoms are absent.

Kraepelin distinguished dementia praecox (later called schizophrenia) from manic depressive illness (bipolar disorder), noting a "family taint" in the latter. Abraham viewed manic depressive illness as an overaccentuation of oral eroticism and related it to repetitive love disappointments with the mother, reinforced by later losses. Freud focused on the decreased self-esteem in melancholia. He postulated the introjection of a lost object and viewed the rage turned against the self as a central dynamic in depression. Beck has considered the cognitive defect the primary one, leading to a negative interpretation of one's own experience and self. (See COGNITIVE-BEHAVIOR THERAPY). Bowlby and Spitz developed observations about early loss and anaclitic depression. (See LOSS AND SEPARATION).

Psychobiological perspectives have come to the fore more recently. There is as yet no conclusive information regarding a biochemical basis of affective disorders. However, mounting clinical evidence along with genetic studies of bipolar disorder suggest this possibility (Rainer, 1975).

Several genetic observations are worthy of review. For bipolar disorder the morbid risk of first-degree relatives of those affected may be 25 to 50% (Winokur, 1973). Twin studies show significantly greater concordance rates for bipolar disorder in one-egg twins than in two-egg twins, whether they were raised separately or together. The concordance rates are greater for bipolar disorder than unipolar disorder (manic or depressed). However, the concordance rates for one-egg twins are less than 100%, clearly implying environmental or learned factors in addition to genetic ones.

Adoption studies in Belgium (Mendlewicz & Rainer, 1977) show results supporting an inherited predisposition. These same studies give evidence of an x-linkage of bipolar disorder, but this is a tentative finding.

Bipolar disorder therapy represents a remarkable advance in psychiatry with the availability of lithium carbonate, a simple salt that interchanges with sodium in the body. Its distribution in the body is roughly that of water. It is concentrated more highly intracellularly in the brain and the reverse in other organs. Also there is relatively more lithium in the nerve ending fraction of brain cells. Although lithium has been used with limited success in other biological disorders, it was not until 1949 that Cade in Australia used lithium as a sedative with manic patients. This discovery was not recognized in Europe until the 1950s and the United States until 1970. By then the climate for utilization of psychopharmacological treatment of emotional problems was low. Further, the toxic hazards of lithium led to only cautious investigations. At this time lithium therapy is the standard chemotherapy of mania, and its applicability to other mood disturbances is being investigated (especially schizoaffective disorder and depression). Therapy with bipolar disorder patients requires a physician's involvement, first for diagnosis and then for chemotherapeutic management. For some patients lithium therapy is unacceptable, and other agents must then be attempted.

Several significant psychotherapeutic issues tend to emerge with bipolar disorder. These patients have often learned to live with the "high" state; the exhilaration is experienced as ego-syntonic, and mood stabilization is thus experienced as a deprivation of a desired euphoria. Involvement of the spouse and/or the family may be useful so they may appreciate the pain and turmoil experienced by the loved ones. Marital disturbances frequently follow the untreated cycling; marital therapy is valuable for understanding and resolution. Genetic counseling is advised for family planning of bipolar patients.

Extensive failures of psychotherapeutic management alone mark the literature prior to the advent of the chemotherapy agents. To rely solely on psychotherapy in the bipolar disorder deprives the patient of truly remarkable medical means for effective management. Yet, since persons with bipolar disorder are subject to the usual human needs and ills, the management of the disorder by medication alone is insufficient.

References

Mendlewicz, J., & Rainer, J. D. Adoption study supporting genetic transmission in manic-depressive illness. *Nature,* 1977, *268,* 327–329.

Rainer, J. D. Genetics and psychiatry. In A. M. Freedman, H. I. Kaplan, & B. J. Sadock, (Eds.), *Comprehensive textbook of psychiatry, II.* Baltimore: Williams & Wilkins, 1975.

Winokur, G., Diagnostic and genetic aspects of affective illness. *Psychiatric Annals,* 1973, *3*(2), 6–15.

Additional Reading

Cole, J. O., Schatzberg, A. F., & Frazier, S. H. (Eds.). *Depression: Biology, psychodynamics and treatment.* New York: Plenum Press, 1978.

T. G. Esau

See articles on Depression; Psychopharmacology.

Birth Order. The ordinal position of the child within the family has been studied extensively, and researchers conclude that a number of personality characteristics can be linked to order of birth. Being the oldest child or the youngest child or a child in between affects the psychological relationship the child has with parents and siblings. As each child comes into the family, he or she is given a special place in the family constellation and is treated accordingly. To be sure, the characteristics attributed to children in each of the three positions—oldest, middle, youngest—will not apply to every child, but they will hold true generally for the population as a whole.

Galton (1869) was among the first to record that men of genius are more apt to be firstborns, a conclusion supported by studies since that time, including Terman's (1925) well-known observation of almost 1,500 very bright children and Zajonc and Markus's (1975) study that the oldest child is more apt to do well in school. The firstborn is more apt to be listed in *Who's Who,* to become a doctor, a lawyer, or an astronaut, and to show leadership ability. Other characteristics include superior language ability, higher achievement motivation, a greater sense of responsibility, and a sensitivity to social expectations. On the negative side firstborns are less warm and more anxious than their siblings, are more apt to be brought to the attention of mental health professionals (Abram & Coie, 1981), are sometimes bossy, and tend to feel superior to other people.

These characteristics, both positive and negative, are attributed to the fact that parental concern and attention are greater for the first child than for later-born children. More pressure is put on the oldest child to achieve and to act responsibly. Parents are excited when the first child arrives, but they also are tense and feel personally responsible for the kind of adult the child will become. More directives are given to this child to ensure successful development, giving him or her the incentive to do well but also creating anxiety when things go badly. The superior language skill exhibited by firstborns is directly related to the fact that the first child has adults as models of speech whereas later-born children imitate siblings as well as parents.

The middle child refers to any child between the first and the last, and although less research has been done on the middle child than on either the oldest or the youngest, it is generally agreed that the middle child is sociable, well liked, adapts to new situations easily, and is seldom spoiled. Middle children also make better marriage partners. However, their easy-going manner and diplomatic ways are in contrast to their general lack of self-esteem. These are the "sandwich kids" who are bossed by an older brother or sister and have to vie for the attention given to the baby. Often they are lost in the shuffle and their self-concept suffers accordingly. This is more apt to occur if the middle child is a second female (Jacobs & Moss, 1976). The more relaxed attitude of the parents to the second child contributes to the child's gregarious nature yet takes its toll in fewer accomplishments and lower self-esteem. It would seem that, in all fairness, parents should spend more time with the middle child, showing affection and finding ways to appreciate the child's unique abilities.

The youngest child is usually more dependent, less mature, and less oriented to parental and peer approval than older brothers and sisters. Being the youngest means no one will ever take his or her place, and the child can continue to enjoy the attention reserved for the last one in the family. Parents tend to be less exacting, less punitive, and less demanding with the youngest, and sometimes parents are too weary to work with this child as they did with the others, giving the child the reputation of being spoiled. This greater permissiveness on the part of parents makes the child more difficult to live with and is a source of irritation to siblings, who feel discriminated against when rules do not apply to all alike. Yet because of the increased freedom, the youngest may become the inventive one in the family, going in a direction quite different from the others.

Part of the confusion in studies on birth order comes because other variables enter into the picture and affect the outcome. The sex of the child, the spacing between children, the education of the parents, the socio-economic status of the family, and the family size are all relevant and must be taken into account. However, controlling for these factors is difficult, especially when the very nature of the topic mandates that the research method be observational rather than experimental. As one might expect, the only girl in a family of boys and the only boy in a family of girls will be given a special place regardless of ordinal position. Girls with older sisters are more feminine than girls with older brothers, and boys with older brothers are more masculine than boys with older sisters (Lamke, Bell, & Murphy, 1980), an understandable finding in the light of the toys and other interests shared by children within the same household.

The spacing between children also has an effect on the child. There is more sibling rivalry and a greater bid for parental attention if children are close to one another in age, whereas a space of six or seven years may mean that a later-born child is raised in much the same way as the oldest child and so will take on the same characteristics as the oldest child. The education of the parents and the socioeconomic status of the family also affect child-rearing procedures. If the family income changes appreciably between the first child and the last, this may make a difference. Overall family size also has repercussions, larger families being more strict and expecting children to take more responsibility than do smaller families.

Although research on birth order is relatively recent, an understanding of personality characteristics as related to ordinal position has been known for centuries. In the parable Jesus told of the prodigal son (Luke 15:11–32), the behavior and attitude of the older brother were typically those one would expect from the oldest child, whereas the actions of the younger brother were not surprising in the light of the fact that he was the younger one. What is so unusual in this parable is not the dispositions of the two brothers, but the behavior of the father to the younger son. In Bible times it was expected that only the eldest son would receive such attention. Mosaic law gave the firstborn male a status not shared by any other child, and because he was "the firstborn of thy sons" he was to be given to the Lord (Exod. 22:29) and blessed with a double portion of the inheritance. What Jesus was saying is that every child has worth, even the youngest who may take a wrong turn. Every child is a part of the family of God and will be welcomed into that family by the Father.

References

Abram, R. S., & Coie, J. D. Maternal reactions to problem behaviors and ordinal position of child. *Journal of Personality*, 1981, *49*, 450–467.

Galton, F. *Hereditary genius: An enquiry into its laws and consequences*. London: Macmillan, 1869.

Jacobs, B. S., & Moss, H. A. Birth order and sex of sibling as determinants of mother-infant interaction. *Child Development*, 1976, *47*, 315–322.

Lamke, L. K., Bell, N. J., & Murphy, C. Sibling constellation and androgynous sex role development. *The Journal of Psychology*, 1980, *105*, 139–144.

Terman, L. M. *Genetic studies of genius*. Stanford, Calif.: Stanford University Press, 1925.

Zajonc, R. B., & Markus, G. B. Birth order and intellectual development. *Psychological Review*, 1975, *82*, 74–88.

B. CLOUSE

Birth Trauma. The experience of being born is a unique experience in the life of a human being. Psychoanalytic theories suggest that all anxiety and pleasure may originate in this experience called birth trauma.

While it is in the safety, warmth, and care of the uterus, the experience of the fetus is presumably pleasant, or at least peaceful. All bodily functions are cared for to such an extent that it does not even have to breathe for itself. There is little or no variation in temperature, and the fetus has hardly any need for activity requiring energy. Conjecture is that there is either no thinking and feeling or that these functions are so primitive as to be nonexistent.

During the birth process the fetus experiences more change in a matter of the relatively few hours of labor than it has experienced during the nine months of incubation. The new elements of light, sound, cold, and absence of contact might bring fear to the newborn. Gone forever are the constant contact of mother's uterus, 98° warmth, and near-perfect protection and provision.

Freud (1936) believed that all anxiety of adult life was due to this flooding with stimulation in the absence of adequate defense apparatus. Thus, Freud viewed all attempts to reduce anxiety as symbolic of returning to the warmth and safety of the womb. Anxiety, which is a symptom of displeasure, is evidence of the adult feeling separate from mother.

Similarly, pleasure is felt whenever there is a creation of a womblike experience or a reminder of the safety of the womb. Thus, according to Rank (1929), the mourning for a lost loved one represents the desire to join the dead person, as death is safe like the womb. Likewise, the playing of hide-and-seek by children is symbolic of the womb in that when hiding, one is alone, crouched as if in a fetal position, and covered.

Thumb sucking, rocking, wetting, soiling, and clinging may all be symbolic of the care of the womb. When symptoms predominate to impair daily functioning, anxiety is indicated, which in turn points to the trauma of birth.

The concept of birth trauma has been most closely associated with the writings of Otto Rank. Most psychoanalytic theorists agree with Rank that birth is probably the most important psychological event in life. His assumption that all anxiety and pleasure are related back to the birth experience has, however, not been so widely accepted.

References

Freud, S. *The problem of anxiety*. New York: Norton, 1936.
Rank, O. *The trauma of birth*. New York: Harcourt, Brace, 1929.

R. B. JOHNSON

Blended Family. A blended family is formed by the merging through marriage of two or more subsystems of broken families. At least one spouse has been previously married and brings to the family a child or children from that union.

Blended families vary considerably in composition. For example, children may belong to the wife and/or the husband by a previous marriage or may be theirs by the present marriage. Inasmuch as custody is ordinarily awarded to the mother, the typical unit consists of a wife, her children, and the husband (whose children, if he has any, reside with the ex-wife).

With the growing popularity of joint custody and the rising number of serial marriages, blended family configurations are becoming increasingly varied. Many children now belong to two households, dividing their time equally between both. In other families children from two or more previous marriages retain their paternal surnames. Hence, three or more last names may be used within the same family.

The principal challenge of the blended family is to develop into a cohesive unit. Yet it must be defined by boundaries that allow appropriate contact with what frequently is a large, disjointed network of relatives. Experts generally agree that these families must negotiate several critical developmental tasks in order to coalesce.

One such task faced by all members is to mourn the lost family. Though commonly denied after the fact, the breakup of one's family is emotionally traumatic for most persons. Grieving this loss is essential to making a positive investment in new relationships.

Countless blended families are products of rebound marriages—unions motivated by a desire to escape the pain of a recently terminated relationship. These spouses may cognitively accept the inevitability of their divorce or their partner's death, but they still grieve at the point of remarriage. Usually they will consciously shut off their grief in an act of loyalty to the new spouse. But instead of going away the grief festers underneath, only to surface later.

Children also grieve, sometimes long after the family breakup. This is seen in the persistent longing to be reunited with the absent parent and in the enduring fantasy that mother and father will eventually remarry. It is also manifested in the refusal of some children to form a relationship with the stepparent. To the extent that a child's mourning is unfinished, he or she will remain loyal only to the natural parent.

Unresolved grief is poison to the blended family. It produces intrafamilial tension and siphons off emotional energy that could otherwise be channeled into strengthening family relationships. Because of its insidious character, professional help is frequently needed to resolve this type of mourning.

A critical developmental task for spouses is to form a strong marital bond. Continued contact with the ex-spouse (child visitation) and ex-in-laws can be disruptive to their developing relationship. Issues of jealousy, trust, and loyalty are easily activated by these continuing contacts. Yet, as in the nuclear family, the cornerstone of the blended family is the marriage.

Additionally, the couple must develop a co-parent partnership that is strong enough to withstand repeated testing by children. Because parent-child relationships predate the marital bond, such a partnership is not easily forged. It requires a strong marital commitment, good communication, and general agreement on matters of child management.

Another blended family task is to develop functional stepparent-stepchild relationships. Children are more likely to accept a stepparent if the natural parent displays an unwavering commitment to the marriage. If the marriage is tenuous, children are wont to provoke marital conflict as a means of getting their own way. They do this by facing off against the stepparent and maneuvering for the natural parent's support. Feelings of loyalty and guilt (for failing the child by failing in the first marriage) prompt the parent to side with the child.

Maintaining a "mine/yours" view of the children should be avoided as it greatly undermines the stepparent-stepchild relationship. It places the stepparent in the untenable position of having to borrow authority from the natural parent when dealing with stepchildren. This arrangement also precludes their working out their own relationship. When tension develops between the child and the stepparent, the natural parent invariably steps in to mediate, thus setting up a destructive triangling pattern (*see* TRIANGLE). Loyal to both parties, the mediating parent is in the stressful position of having to take sides. He or she is typically the one who initiates a counseling request.

Finally, a task specific to children is to develop functional stepsibling relationships. The ordinal position among siblings can change dramatically with the merging of two families. The oldest child in the first family, for example, may now have to contend with older stepsiblings. While rivalry with siblings may diminish, it often increases with stepsiblings.

Another seldom mentioned problem in families with adolescents is that children who could be dating are suddenly living together. Sexual boundaries are usually weak, as blended families do not have a well-established incest taboo. Conflict is one way in which teen-age stepsiblings unconsciously define a boundary to protect themselves from getting too close.

The challenges faced by blended families are not insurmountable. Many families do adjust and eventually enjoy harmonious relationships. But it takes time—usually two to four years—before the critical adjustments are made.

J. A. LARSEN

See DIVORCE; CHILD CUSTODY; FAMILY SYSTEMS THEORY; FAMILY COMMUNICATIONS THEORY.

Bleuler, Eugen (1857–1939). Swiss psychiatrist who has had a profound influence on the development of the dynamic view of psychopathology. Born in Zollikon, Bleuler served as the director of the Burgholzli Hospital in Zurich from 1889 until 1927, succeeding August Forel. Burgholzli was the first mental hospital to accept psychoanalysis as a means of treatment, due in large part to the work of Bleuler, along with Jung and Binswanger.

Like most of his contemporaries Bleuler considered mental illness to be primarily an organic process. However, unlike others of his day he did not endeavor to explain the neuropathology of mental illness itself, but rather the meaning of the symptoms as the result of psychological events. Bleuler combined Kraepelin's systematic classification of mental illness with Freud's dynamic approach to the unconscious to redefine psychosis, aligning himself with neither a purely organic nor a psychoanalytic model.

In 1911 Bleuler coined the term *schizophrenia* to replace Kraepelin's *dementia praecox*, disagreeing with Kraepelin's belief that premature dementia was the ultimate outcome and viewing schizophrenia as a group of treatable psychotic reactions rather than one distinct and incurable disease. He used the term schizophrenia (from Greek words meaning split mind) to describe the dissociation of thoughts and affects that he observed in these patients.

Bleuler considered the primary symptoms of schizophrenia to be disturbances of affect, volition, and associations, viewing the symptoms described by Kraepelin (hallucinations, delusions, negativism, and stupor) as secondary. He observed the inappropriate expression of affect and the circumstantial and tangential verbal associations of these patients, and noted that certain psychotics seemed to experience the simultaneous presence of two opposing tendencies (i.e. love and hate) more intensely than did normals or neurotic patients, a condition which he termed ambivalence. He also coined the term *autistic thinking* to describe the schizophrenic patient's primitive cognitive processes, which were characterized by wishful symbolic thinking rather than conformity to logic or reality. Thus, Bleuler's system of schizophrenia is often referred to as the four A's: disturbances in affect and associations, autism, and ambivalence. Bleuler divided schizophrenia into four basic subtypes—catatonic, hebephrenic and paranoia (described by Kraepelin), and schizophrenia simplex.

Although Bleuler's 1911 monograph *Dementia Praecox or the Group of Schizophrenias* was not translated into English until 1950, his *Textbook of Psychiatry*, published in 1923, became well known and helped to disseminate his ideas. Bleuler is best remembered for his contributions in the field of schizophrenia, and many of his theories and observations remain clinically relevant today in the dynamic understanding of this mental disorder.

L. B. HARDY

Blocking. A sudden obstruction of speech in the middle of a thought or sentence, to which no specific external influence can be ascribed. Following the interrupted action the person may indicate he cannot find words to express himself, is unable to explain why, and cannot remember what he has been saying prior to the obstruction. The inhibited train of thought may be a reaction to the emergence of unconscious material of a threatening nature. A temporary form may occur in healthy individuals who are suddenly overcome by powerful feelings. Blocking is also referred to as thought obstruction or thought deprivation.

D. L. SCHUURMAN

Body Image. The term refers to the body as a psychological experience, focusing on the individual's feelings and attitudes toward his own body. It is concerned with the individual's subjective experiences with his body and the manner in which these experiences are organized (Fisher & Cleveland, 1968).

Historically, neurologists were among the first to be confronted with persons suffering from body image distortions. Brain-damaged individuals sometimes report the following: the denial of certain body parts, the belief that new parts exist, difficulty distinguishing between left and right sides, the conviction that their body has completely disappeared, hallucinations of a double of themselves, and the feeling that certain parts of their body are thickened, shortened, enlarged, or artificial.

Body image distortion has also been evident in schizophrenia. Some schizophrenic patients report feeling as if parts of their body have changed in shape or size, while others feel as though their body has been penetrated in some manner, that they have exchanged their bodies with another person, that their bodies are half man and half woman, or that their whole body is deteriorating.

Body image distortion has also been reported as a result of drug usage. Use of LSD has led to the following reported experiences: a preoccupation with one's body, a sensitivity to bodily feelings, feeling that one's body is charged with energy, or that body parts are dislocated (i.e., limbs are detached and floating). Others report alteration in or breakdown of body boundaries, describing themselves as experiencing movements or events that are happening in others.

Body image distortions are experienced by individuals under hypnosis. Depending upon the suggestion, subjects may report increasing awareness of the body, feelings of numbness, the sensation that one is shrinking or swelling, difficulty determining the right and left sides of the body, disturbances in body equilibrium, or changes in size, especially in the face and extremities.

One final area of considerable importance

concerns body image and the normal person. Although body image distortions here do not appear to be as radical as those described by pathological individuals or by those in altered states, one's perceived body image can often involve distortion. For example, whether a person believes that his body is attractive or ugly, big or small, masculine or feminine, strong or weak can potentially be a powerful determinant of his behavior. Some become obsessed with creating and maintaining the perfect external body image and spend an exorbitant amount of time exercising or body building. There is a visible distortion of external body image in those who are extremely obese and those suffering from anorexia nervosa.

A number of measurement devices have been used to assess body image. One method has been the questionnaire where individuals may be asked on a scale of 1 to 5 whether they agree or disagree with such statements as, "I have often been self-conscious with people I am attracted to because of my body appearance." Another measure has been the Draw-A-Person test; it is assumed that an individual's drawing of a human figure represents a projection of his own body image. The body cathexis scale is another measure. This scale asks subjects to rate approximately 40 different areas of their body. They approximate the size of certain parts of their body and indicate what size they ideally would like them to be. Another tool used to measure body image is the body image boundary score, which is derived from projective responses to ink blocks. This score is intended to assess an important function of the body image, i.e., its action as a psychological structure which separates and protects itself from the environment. These assessment scales as well as others are described and summarized by McCrea, Summerfield, and Rosen (1982).

References

Fisher, S., & Cleveland, S. E. *Body image and personality* (2nd ed.). New York: Dover, 1968.

McCrea, C. W., Summerfield, A. B., & Rosen, B. Body image: A selective review of existing measurement techniques. *British Journal of Medical Psychology*, 1982, *55*, 225–233.

M. L. MARVIN

Body Language. *See* COMMUNICATION, NONVERBAL.

Boisen, Anton Theophilus (1876–1965). Founder of the clinical pastoral education movement. Born in Bloomington, Indiana, where his father was a professor of modern languages at Indiana University, he graduated from Indiana University in 1897 but could not find a teaching position. The next 24 years of his life were ones of struggle and frustration. He entered graduate school in 1897 but suffered a severe anxiety attack on Easter morning of 1898. He was a part-time teacher of German and French, attended the Yale Forest School of Forestry, and entered the Forestry Service in 1905. He attended Union Theological Seminary from 1908 to 1911, served churches in Kansas and Maine, did surveys for the church, spent time in Europe with the United States Army, and was unable to find a pastorate when he returned to the United States in 1919.

In October, 1920, he suffered a psychotic episode and spent 15 months in mental hospitals. After he recovered, he began an experiment in religious ministry to the mentally ill. In July, 1924, he began as chaplain at Worcester State Hospital in Massachusetts. He also wanted to train seminary students in such work, and in 1925 he had his first four students, the beginning of the clinical training movement. He became chaplain at Elgin State Hospital in Illinois in 1931 and lived there the rest of his life. He retired officially from Elgin in 1938 and taught three years, but returned to Elgin for research and writing.

His major books are *Exploration of the Inner World* (1936), *Religion in Crisis and Custom* (1945), and his autobiography, *Out of the Depths* (1960), which details five psychotic episodes occurring between 1908 and 1935. He describes these as problem-solving experiences, leaving him not worse but better. Much of his original thinking came from his efforts to test the insights formed during these periods of acute conflict. Out of these experiences has come the clinical pastoral education movement. (*See* ASSOCIATION FOR CLINICAL PASTORAL EDUCATION). In 1930 the Council for the Clinical Training of Theological Students was incorporated.

Boisen used clinical case studies, sociological surveys, and his own experiences as a participant observer keeping company with the patients and staff of the old custodial mental hospital. He made contributions to psychology, religion, and the psychology of religion. Unfortunately, he is more often remembered for his idiosyncrasies and schizoid personality than for his contributions—contributions made both because of and in spite of his personal experience of mental illness.

R. L. KOTESKEY

Borderline Personality Disorder. A new category that has been added to the American

Psychiatric Association's classification system in *DSM-III*. It has been under discussion for some 40 years, during which time it has aroused a good deal of controversy, but has at the same time stimulated much research into normal human development. It has now reached general consensus, largely because of the clinical pressure of many patients who are best understood under this heading (Gunderson & Singer, 1975).

In the *DSM-III* definition borderline symptoms cluster around four centers. 1) *Behavior* is marked by impulsivity and physically self-damaging acts. 2) There is marked *affective instability* with rapid mood swings and a tendency toward severe depression and bewildering anxiety. 3) *Identity disturbance* is experienced, manifested by uncertain self-image, gender, and vocational issues. These persons have difficulty being alone and express chronic feelings of emptiness and boredom. 4) There is a pattern of intense, *unstable relationships* with those who are close to them, with marked shifts of attitude, idealization, devaluation, and manipulation.

History of the Concept. Deutsch's paper in 1934, "Some Forms of Emotional Disturbance and Their Relationship to Schizophrenia" (Deutsch, 1942), is generally considered as initiating the discussion of the borderline personality disorder. She described the borderline individual's whole relationship with life as having something about it that is lacking in genuineness, and yet outwardly the individual functions as if he or she were complete. This peculiar paradox of the person who on first appearance seems to be normal and who on better acquaintance elicits the comment, "What's wrong with him?" has remained a hallmark of the borderline.

Zilboorg introduced the term *ambulatory schizophrenia* in 1941 since he also considered the borderline a special category of schizophrenia. Psychoanalysis was the treatment he recommended for these people, though he warned prophetically that unstructured free association would be disorganizing to the borderline, as are projective tests such as the Rorschach.

Hoch and Polatin (1949) described disconcerting polymorphous sexuality in borderlines. Both the fantasies and the behavior of these persons may take homosexual, autoerotic, sadistic, or any other form, even in those who are clearly heterosexual in their fundamental sexual orientation.

Knight's (1953) description of borderline pathology as defensive maneuvers has been particularly helpful. Knight took the famous metaphor Freud used to describe libidinal regression, that of a retreating army, and extended it. Instead of a single, coherent force, the borderline's defense breaks up, he says, into a variety of detachments, each of which might hold different ground in different ways. This is demonstrated clinically as the mercurial polyneuroses so frequently encountered in the borderline syndrome.

The first major empirical study of these patients was done by Grinker, Werble, & Dye (1968). They concluded that the category was indeed distinct, and a follow-up study of the same patients by Werble some 10 years later (Werble, 1970) indicated that the condition was stable, without sliding toward schizophrenia.

Contemporary Theories. The contemporary literature on the borderline personality disorder is dominated by the thinking of Kernberg. The disturbed ego of the borderline, as Kernberg sees it, manifests a lack of anxiety tolerance, poor impulse control, and a defective capacity to effectively sublimate aggressive drives. The resulting regression unveils a rather primitive substrate, particularly seen in unexpected primary process thinking. This latter, he states, is "still the most important single structural indicator of borderline personality organization" (Kernberg, 1975, p. 25).

In order to effectively define the borderline condition without having to prematurely decide on etiology, the syndrome can be conceptualized as a disease of limits. The borderline fails to establish essential and reasonable internal limits.

A clinical example will clarify this definition: A young man borrows his girl's car "to go down to the corner store for some cigarettes." He keeps it longer than she anticipates. A normal man would predict his girl's feelings with reasonable accuracy and be considerate of them. The narcissist might keep it an extra hour or two, visit someone else in the meantime, even another girl, without really anticipating or understanding how the owner will feel about this. The borderline might decide to take the car to Mexico for an excursion.

In order to understand how these persons differ, one can hypothesize that the normal man has a means of sensing how his girl will respond to his actions and is willing to sublimate his wishes to hers. The narcissist usually lacks both the sense and the will. However, the narcissist still maintains certain internal limitations which do not permit him to do more than he does. The borderline lacks both sensitivity and limits.

To carry this thinking still further, we might hypothesize that there is in the normal person some psychic structure around which normal awareness of reasonable limits forms. The internalization process of moral values which takes place during adolescence would depend on there being such a structure in the psyche. For some reason, either by a genetic or biological error, because of brain injury, or by distortion or failure in the environment of the developing infant, this essential component of the machinery of ethical growth is lacking or inadequate in the person suffering from the borderline personality disorder.

Treatment. Viewing borderline personality disorder as a disorder of internal limit setting also serves to organize most of the thinking about the treatment. Analytic thinkers deal with the distorted or split internal models, or representations of self and other and the way these relate. They universally consider this pathology to be deeply embedded and strongly defended. All recommend psychoanalysis, modified in one way or another, but warn that the process is demanding and long, and the outcome unpredictable.

There are two other modalities open to the therapist which are more familiar and more generally accepted. The first of these is to treat the oppressive anxiety and depression of the borderline with medications. They respond less predictably than do neurotic patients, but often can be given helpful relief. The internal instability of these patients sometimes responds to medication. Longer courses of major tranquilizers or antidepressants are often stabilizing.

Supportive treatment remains the best ordinarily available form of psychotherapy (Zetzel, 1971). Sessions can often be interspersed with relatively long time intervals. The goal is to present explanations which clarify the various components of daily conflicts and pain and help the borderline understand why other people act as they do, what is going on inside them, where reasonable limits should be set, and how they can manage their affairs better. Such supportive interventions are very often unexpectedly helpful. Supportive therapy does not get to any known center of the illness, but supportive assistance will often make the difference between a reasonably normal life and the destiny of a life like that of Vincent van Gogh.

A modification of supportive treatment is used in some adolescent inpatient facilities. The patient is immersed from the first hour in an environment where the limits are clear, precise, and firm. His or her adjustment to this artificially vivid limit-world is gained in a series of stages or "levels." The patient is expected to master life within the rules of each stage before moving on to the next, where the space is a little larger. By small progressions the principle of limits is taught, and the moral underpinnings of the outside world are imprinted a little at a time. By the time the entire stairway has been ascended, the patient is able to deal with life more effectively, even if only by cognitively mastering the concept of limits and learning to live within them. A more rational approach would be to begin this same process earlier. We might hope one day to identify the borderline in childhood, so that this training could be more intensely reinforced in the home training.

It is interesting to ponder the spiritual implications of this disorder. In a very graphic way these people seem to be "without law." The believer is free from the law in Christ, but the borderline will teach us the serious implications of living completely without its influence. Watching the pathos of these lives we come to realize that the law was given by the same hand which fashioned man's own nature. Because of this, one disregards it at great risk, and finds his way smoother when he lives within its limits.

References

Deutsch, H. Some forms of emotional disturbance and their relationship to schizophrenia. *Psychoanalytic Quarterly*, 1942, *11*, 301–321.

Grinker, R. R., Werble, B., & Dye, R. C. *The borderline syndrome.* New York: Basic Books, 1968.

Gunderson, J. G., & Singer, M. T. Defining borderline patients: An overview. *American Journal of Psychiatry*, 1975, *132*, 1–10.

Hoch, P. H., & Polatin, P. Pseudoneurotic forms of schizophrenia. *Psychiatric Quarterly*, 1949, *23*, 248–276.

Kernberg, O. *Borderline conditions and pathological narcissism.* New York: Aronson, 1975.

Knight, R. Borderline states. *Bulletin of the Menninger Clinic*, 1953, *17*, 1–12.

Werble, B. Second follow-up study of borderline patients. *Archives of General Psychiatry*, 1970, *23*, 3–7.

Zetzel, E. R. A developmental approach to the borderline. *The American Journal of Psychiatry*, 1971, *127*, 867–871.

C. M. BERRY

See PERSONALITY DISORDERS.

Boredom. The feeling of unpleasantness and restlessness experienced by the individual who desires to do something but does not know what. In mild forms it results from prolonged exposure to an unchanging environment (such as repetitive monotonous tasks) or from an absence of external stimulation. More pathological forms exist in the presence of external stimulation and are experienced as the inability to become stimulated.

The psychodynamic understanding of boredom assumes that it represents a defense against some unacceptable drive. Fenichel (1953) suggests that it is a state of excitement in which the aim is repressed. Accordingly, bored persons are looking for distraction from their disruptive and unacceptable unconscious urges.

Reference

Fenichel, O. On the psychology of boredom. In H. Fenichel & D. Rappaport (Eds.), *The collected papers of Otto Fenichel.* New York: D. Lewis, 1953.

D. G. BENNER

Boring, Edwin Garrigues (1886–1968). Experimental psychologist and historian of psychology. Born in Philadelphia, he received an M.E. degree in engineering from Cornell University in 1908. He returned to Cornell for an M.A. degree in psychology in 1912 and a Ph.D. in 1914. He taught at Cornell from 1911 to 1918, at Clark University from 1919 to 1922, then began his long career at Harvard. He taught at Harvard from 1922 until his retirement in 1957 and was director of the psychological laboratory there from 1924 to 1949. Under his direction the departments of psychology and philosophy were separated in 1934, and in 1945 the divisions of experimental and physiological psychology were separated from those of social and clinical psychology.

Boring was an experimental psychologist in the broadest sense of the term. Between 1912 and 1929 he published research on audition, animal behavior, dementia praecox, educational psychology, organ and alimentary sensations, thermal sensitivity, the psychology of testimony, cutaneous sensations, psychophysics, vision, sleep, psychometrics, statistics, psychological examining, intelligence, facial expression, psychic research, the psychology of science, olfaction, and memory.

This wide background prepared him to write *A History of Experimental Psychology* in 1929, which became the definitive work on the history of psychology. Revised in 1950, it continued to be a leading textbook in the history of psychology in American colleges and universities. He became the leading historian of psychology, also publishing *Sensation and Perception in the History of Experimental Psychology* (1942). He emphasized an intertwined *Zeitgeist* and Great Man theory of history.

In addition to the history of psychology, he wrote much on epistemology. Two of Boring's students selected his most important papers

and classified them into five categories: 1) history; 2) the psychology of science, the problem of how the beliefs and motivations of the scientist help or hinder scientific progress; 3) the scientific method, especially operationism; 4) the mind-body problem; 5) the communication of science, the psychological and strategic problems of criticism.

Boring served as co-editor of the *American Journal of Psychology.* He was one of the founders of *Contemporary Psychology: A Journal of Reviews*, and its editor for the first six years. In his regular monthly feature, "CP Speaks," he called attention to a variety of current issues, many of them the problems of the psychology of communicating science.

R. L. KOTESKEY

Brain and Human Behavior. *General Organization of the Nervous System.* The *encephalon*, or brain, and the *medulla spinalis*, or spinal cord, together form the central nervous system. The peripheral nervous system consists of 12 pairs of cranial nerves and 31 pairs of spinal nerves. The cranial nerves arise from the base of the brain and serve a variety of functions including olfaction, vision, gustation, and sensation and motor activity of the head and neck. As with the spinal nerves, the cranial nerves consist of both afferent and efferent conductors (nerves bringing in information and nerves taking out commands to various organs and muscles). Although this article focuses on the central nervous system, one should bear in mind that the peripheral nervous system is also important in execution of even the most simple acts.

The spinal cord occupies most of the vertebral canal. It is protected by vertebral bones. Like the brain, it is enclosed in three membranes (meninges): the dura mater, the arachnoid mater, and the pia mater. In width it varies from level to level and shows a general tapering as it proceeds from the brain downward. Ascending and descending tracts transmit neural information between the brain and spinal nerve roots. These emerge at all levels to innervate body parts. A great deal of study of the tracts has been undertaken, and highly specialized information is available in textbooks of functional neuroanatomy and related resources (e.g., Netter, 1962; Williams & Warwick, 1975).

The spinal cord comes to the attention of psychologists most frequently when its functioning has been adversely affected by some event. Commonly, an accident has resulted in a crushing or severing of the spinal column, with paralysis below the level of injury. Spinal tumors may also occur and require surgical treatment. In addition, congenital defects such as spina bifida may affect functioning. The extent to which functioning is decreased will depend on the nature of the problem and the level at which it occurs. In general, more widely distributed deficits are associated with higher levels of spinal cord damage, since lower levels of the cord are usually also adversely affected. Problems with respect to the spinal cord may be particularly frustrating, since persons experiencing them may be entirely intact intellectually and have the will to produce certain actions but are unable to do so. Physical therapy may be helpful in maximizing residual functioning capabilities, but psychotherapy may be required to help the person accept and cope with the dysfunction.

Basic Divisions of the Brain. The brain may be divided into three basic parts. These are, in ascending order from the spinal cord, the hindbrain (*rhombencephalon*), the midbrain (*mesencephalon*) and the forebrain (*prosencephalon*). In general, the more basic or vegetative functions are handled by the hindbrain and the midbrain, with structures more related to higher-level mental abilities in the forebrain.

Hindbrain. The hindbrain consists of the medulla oblongata, the pons, and the cerebellum. Taken together, these parts are often called the brain stem.

The *medulla oblongata* is the most caudal part of the brain stem, and it connects directly with the spinal cord. Its dorsal surface forms the floor of the fourth ventricle. The medulla is involved in basic activities such as the control of breathing and blood pressure regulation.

The *pons* is the portion of the brain stem between the medulla and the midbrain. It contains many nerve fiber tracts including certain cranial nerves and fibers related to the cerebellum. The tracts pertain to movement of the face and eyes and other related functions. The reticular formation is found in the dorsal portion of the pons; this contains neurons and fibers with many different connections which mediate both somatic and visceral functions.

The *cerebellum* is the largest part of the hindbrain, and it lies dorsal to the pons and medulla. It consists of two cerebellar hemispheres and a midline vermis. The cerebellum receives impulses from the spinal cord and vestibular impulses from the inner ear. The cerebellum functions in close harmony with the forebrain in the production of smooth motor movements and in helping to control posture.

Midbrain. The midbrain connects the pons and cerebellum with the forebrain. It is a vital conduction pathway and a reflex control complex. Ocular reflexes and eye movements are mediated by the midbrain, and it is a relay center for auditory and visual impulses. Nuclei serving postural and righting reflexes are also found in the midbrain region.

Forebrain. The forebrain consists of two basic groups of structures. First is the diencephalon, or "interbrain," which consists of the thalamus, the epithalamus, and the hypothalamus. These structures surround the third ventricle and are rostral to the midbrain. The second basic group is known as the telencephalon; it includes the limbic system, the basal ganglia, and the cerebral cortex.

The *diencephalon* has often been called the interbrain because it is between the cerebrum, which is responsible for higher-level cognitive functions, and the somatic and autonomic nervous systems, which are responsible for lower-level functions.

The thalamus is the subcortical sensory center for all sensory stimuli except taste. Sensory neural impulses arriving at the thalamus are transmitted to the cerebral cortex. The thalamus also mediates emotional activities and instinctive responses. With its many interconnections with the frontal lobes, the temporal-parietal cortex, and the limbic area, the thalamus is also important in tasks requiring attention.

The epithalamus includes the pineal body, which has hormonal influences.

The hypothalamus lies just caudal to the thalamus but rostral to the pituitary gland. It has five major divisions. Major nuclei derive their names from their locations in relation to these divisions. The hypothalamus is the motor control center for the autonomic nervous system, and it is also responsible for integrating and regulating appropriate autonomic-somatic behavioral responses. To do this, it utilizes many interconnections with the thalamus, the medulla oblongata, the spinal cord, the pituitary body, the limbic system, and the reticular system. The hypothalamus is important in the secretion of endocrines and other substances affecting the nervous system. It is also involved in temperature regulation, in the regulation of food and water intake, in sexual behavior and reproduction, in biological cycles, and in the development of certain emotions such as fear, rage, and pleasure. Lesions of the hypothalamus can cause alterations in these functions according to which portion is damaged.

Since the *telencephalon* consists of those structures most typically associated with higher levels of functioning, it is the portion of the nervous system of greatest interest to psychologists. Although the division of the telencephalon has been made in various ways, it may be identified as having three general parts.

The limbic system consists of a series of structures which develop in the base of each cerebral hemisphere. The most commonly cited parts include the hippocampus, the amygdala, the cingulate gyrus, and the olfactory bulb. The olfactory bulb and olfactory nerve and related structures are associated with the sense of smell. Other functions of the limbic system are complex and include the integration of coded events from environmental perception and past experiences stored by the hippocampus. These structures may provide a basis for establishing semiautomatic responses to the environment, including individual behaviors as well as physiological reactions. Furthermore, related responses may be fairly complex and include behaviors pertaining to sexual activity, eating, drinking, aggressive, affective, and emotional activities. The hippocampus also subserves recent memory, whereas distant memories are more likely stored in the cerebrum, particularly in the temporal lobe. The limbic system is also involved in arousal and attentional mechanisms. It is clear that the limbic system plays a number of important roles in the overall behavior of human beings.

The *basal ganglia* consist of four principal nuclei which are situated deep within the cerebral hemisphere. These structures are the caudate nucleus, the lentiform nucleus, the amygdaloid body, and the claustrum. The basal ganglia subserve important coordinative connections between the diencephalon and the telencephalon, and are regulated by neuronal systems arising in the cerebral cortex. The basal ganglia are connected with the supplementary motor areas of the brain and are involved in refining intricate movements and complicated inherent motor responses. The basal ganglia are also involved in emotions and in refining body tonus important for voluntary and automatic motor capabilities. Their connections with other portions of the brain make them important in everyday human behavior.

The *cerebral cortex*, or neocortex, is of greatest interest with respect to behavior and cognition. The cerebral cortex consists of two cerebral hemispheres, the right and the left.

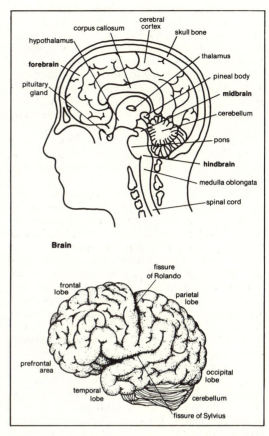

Brain

These hemispheres appear to be approximately the same, but there are differences between them. The hemispheres have a convoluted appearance and have two major fissures.

The central fissure, the fissure of Rolando, serves as a major landmark and separates the anterior and posterior portions of each cerebral hemisphere. Anterior to the central fissure is the frontal lobe and immediately posterior to it is the parietal lobe. The sylvian fissure runs laterally across the lower, lateral portion of the cerebral hemisphere with the temporal lobe inferior and the frontal and parietal lobes superior to this fissure. The occipital lobe is in the far posterior portion of the cerebral hemisphere. The anatomical and functional descriptions of each of the cerebral lobes are briefly given below:

The *frontal lobe* is a large mass which consists of a precentral gyrus ("motor strip") just anterior to the central fissure and several gyri anterior to the motor strip. The motor strip is important in initiating voluntary movement, and each portion of the gyrus is distinctly related to a particular part of the body. The lower portions of the body are related to the upper parts of the gyrus. Lesions in the area of the motor strip will result in decreased motor skills, the magnitude depending on the extent of damage and the part of the body affected, which in turn depends on the location of the damage. In addition to its obvious and very important motor functions, the anterior portion of the frontal lobe is related to more complex human functions, probably including motivation, judgment, abstract thinking, and foresight. In terms of psychological functions this portion of the cerebral cortex is probably the least well defined.

Broca's speech area is in the posterior, inferior aspect of the frontal lobe on the side of the brain related to speech functions (the dominant hemisphere). In combination with related areas it is responsible for expressive speech.

The large *parietal lobe* is situated just behind the central fissure. Its most anterior aspect consists of a sensory strip parallel but posterior to the motor strip of the frontal lobe. Sensory perception is integrated in this area. Lesions in the sensory strip can result in defective processing of information, which, of course, represents a handicap to ultimately generating appropriate responses. The posterior portions of the right and left parietal lobes do not appear to serve the same functions; they will be discussed under hemispheric specialization.

The *temporal lobe* has a number of functions that are incompletely understood. It receives and processes auditory information. It is also involved in memory, although the type of memory varies (see below on hemispheric specialization). On the speech-related side of the brain (dominant hemisphere), the posterior portion of the temporal lobe is more related to receptive functions and the anterior portion more to expressive functions. It is likely also that the temporal lobe is involved in important aspects of emotion. The frontal, parietal, and temporal lobes are all involved in cognition in one way or another, and it is evident that they interact with one another in producing thoughts and many behaviors.

The occipital lobe is the portion of the far posterior aspect of each cerebral hemisphere. Its most commonly recognized function is visual perception. It receives information from the visual pathway system which begins in each eye and terminates in the occipital visual cortex. Lesions of the visual cortex or the visual pathways result in visual defects or blindness.

Blood supply of the brain. The brain needs a continuous supply of oxygenated, cleansed blood in order to function and maintain life. The blood supply to the brain is primarily by means of the internal carotid and vertebral arteries which come up in each side of the neck. The internal carotid artery is the larger of these vessels and serves much of the cerebral cortex after it branches into the anterior, middle, and in some instances the posterior cerebral arteries. Of these, the middle cerebral artery is especially important since it furnishes blood to critical areas of the temporal, the frontal, and the parietal lobes, including the sensory-motor strip. These areas are important for a variety of human abilities.

Ventricular system. Four ventricles or spaces are found within the brain and brain stem. The two largest of these are within the cerebral hemispheres themselves, and consist of laterally situated elongated cavities, one per hemisphere. The ventricles communicate with each other and with the subarachnoid space which surrounds the brain and which lies between the dura mater and the pia mater. The subarachnoid space and the ventricles are filled with cerebrospinal fluid secreted by the choroid plexus. The spinal fluid provides a cushion for the brain.

Hemispheric Specialization. Although in some respects corresponding areas of the two cerebral hemispheres perform similar functions, in a number of instances different functions are performed, and these differences are of great interest. However, one should never disregard the fact that human behaviors are complex and that in all probability most involve several portions of the brain. Thus, the parts of the brain do not usually act in isolation from one another. Much of the interhemispheric coordination is served by the corpus callosum, which is a substantial group of nerve fibers connecting the two cerebral hemispheres.

One important aspect of cerebral hemisphere specialization results from the crossing over of most ascending and descending motor and sensory tracts from right to left and from left to right. Thus, functions related to the right side of the body are associated almost entirely with the left cerebral hemisphere, whereas similar functions pertaining to the left side of the body are related almost entirely to the right cerebral hemisphere. This finding is of great importance in evaluating individuals with neurological deficits and in setting up neuropsychological tests (*see* Neuropsychological Assessment). By comparing responses to similar stimuli given to each body side, information is provided concerning whether or not there is brain damage and where such damage may be.

A second very important aspect of hemispheric specialization is that typically the left cerebral hemisphere is associated with language functions and the right cerebral hemisphere with visual-spatial functions. This is true for almost all right-handed individuals, and it is true for the majority of left-handed persons as well. Occasional exceptions are found, as documented by the intracarotid sodium amytal injection procedure (Wada & Rasmussen, 1960). On the side of the brain related to speech, the posterior inferior aspect of the frontal lobe (Broca's area) is typically involved in expressive (motor) speech. The temporal areas and surrounding structures are related to various aspects of language, with the receptive functions tending to be posterior and expressive functions anterior. Some aspects of the inferior parietal lobe relate to speech as well. Typically, there is no speech relatable to corresponding areas of the opposite cerebral hemisphere. With respect to visual-spatial functions, the right parietal area is especially important. Thus, the left cerebral hemisphere is typically related to speech and language (verbal) functions, whereas the right cerebral hemisphere is typically related to visual-spatial (nonverbal) functions.

In addition to the verbal versus nonverbal differences summarized in the previous paragraph, it is likely that the language versus visual-spatial distinction is of importance in other ways. For example, whereas both temporal lobes involve memory functions, it is clear that the left temporal lobe is especially related to memory for verbal information and the right temporal lobe to memory for visual-spatial matters (Milner, 1972). There may be other verbal versus visual-spatial specializations elsewhere in the cerebral hemispheres that are not as easy to identify.

The verbal versus visual-spatial differentiation is of particular interest to psychologists. One reason is that the Wechsler scales are divided into verbal and performance sections which happen to correspond fairly well to the left and right cerebral hemispheres respectively (Matarazzo, 1972). A number of studies have in fact shown that Verbal IQ scores on the Wechsler scales are likely to be decreased when there are lesions of the left cerebral hemisphere, whereas the Performance IQ scores are likely to be decreased when there are lesions of the right cerebral hemisphere. Thus, the hemispheric specialization implies that brain lesions located in one part of the brain may result in significant deficits in certain respects, but in other ways there may be few or no difficulties.

This can be of considerable importance in the day-by-day adjustment of people with brain lesions, since they may appear very capable to themselves and others in certain respects while at the same time they may have substantially lowered performances in other areas. The result is likely to be significant emotional distress as well as a tendency on the part of other people to conclude that the individual is "lazy" or not really trying in certain areas. Counseling to deal with these concerns is often required after a neurological problem resulting in brain injury has been experienced.

The difference between the cerebral hemispheres with respect to verbal versus visual-spatial functioning is often of great importance in school and work placement. Typically, children with brain damage involving the left cerebral hemisphere do poorly in school. The identification of the extent and nature of the difficulties by means of a neuropsychological evaluation is often helpful in understanding the troubles experienced and in setting expectations for the future. For adults, jobs can often be defined in terms of their relative verbal versus visual-spatial requirements. Knowledge of strengths and weaknesses in these areas can be of immeasureable help in terms of successful job placement.

In recent years attempts have been made to establish one additional general difference between the functioning of the two cerebral hemispheres, and this is with respect to emotional maladjustment. The position has perhaps best been articulated by Flor-Henry (1976). According to this viewpoint, emotional problems reflecting defective cognition (such as schizophrenia) are related to dysfunction of the left cerebral hemisphere, whereas disorders of affective nature (such as depression) are related to dysfunction of the right cerebral hemisphere. Language symbols are believed very important in cognition, and thus any defects in the language-related area might result in emotional difficulties characterized by defective thinking. Problems that are not well expressed verbally, but which are nevertheless experienced, may relate to the more subjective aspects of the person, including the right cerebral hemisphere. Occasionally, data appear in support of this position, but equally often the data available are not supportive.

Pathology of the Brain. Several common sources of brain damage have implications for intelligence and emotional adjustment.

Hydrocephalus is a disorder in which there is an abnormal accumulation of cerebrospinal fluid within the ventricles or over the surface of the brain. It may occur when there is a partial or complete blockage of the pathways which normally permit cerebrospinal fluid to exit from the ventricles. As previously indicated, the choroid plexus in each ventricle produces cerebrospinal fluid, and it continues to produce this whether or not the fluid can exit from the ventricle normally. In hydrocephalus the ventricles are typically substantially enlarged and the brain mass may be compressed. The result is usually generalized dysfunction. If hydrocephalus occurs in childhood, the increased pressure may result in an enlarged head and mental retardation. When this condition is identified, efforts are made to correct it by inserting a shunt or tube to allow the escape of the fluid.

Craniosynostoses are sometimes found in childhood when there is a premature closure of one or more of the sutures between the bones of the calvarial vault. Depending upon which suture closes early, the head may be exceptionally long, high, or wide. Without surgical intervention, normal growth of the brain is restricted and adverse mental effects may result. Surgical treatment designed to alter the skull and allow more room for brain growth is usually successful.

Birth injuries occur which can have adverse effects on later growth and development. If for any reason the child does not breathe at the time of birth, brain damage may result from the anoxia. In addition, injuries may also result from external pressure exerted on the skull at the time of birth, resulting in compression of the brain.

Head injuries can occur at any time during life but are especially common in older children and young adults. They may be divided into two groups. Closed head injuries are most common and typically occur when the cranial vault comes in contact with a stationary object or one that is moving at a different speed than the individual. The brain is bounced back and forth within the hard skull, resulting in a contusion (bruising of the brain) or a concussion. The point on the head where the injury occurred is not necessarily a good indicator of possible brain damage, because the brain is battered within the skull rather than being injured on one side only. Open head injuries occur when something goes through the skull into the brain, such as a bullet. Both open and closed head injuries can be severe. Typically, recovery begins following the immediate effects of the accident and may continue for one to two years or longer. During this time the person may experience significant distress if the injury has adversely affected abilities such as memory. An incomplete recovery may result in a need for the person to adapt to residual limitations, which may in turn require psychotherapeutic intervention.

Vascular disorders affecting the brain can take several forms. An aneurysm is a vascular dilatation or enlargement of a blood vessel so that an area resembling a small balloon develops. If this bursts, a hemorrhage occurs; if the bleeding is not stopped the person dies. An arteriovenous malformation consists of an abnormal mass of arteries and veins. It is congenital by nature and may require surgical intervention. Another major type of vascular problem is the occlusion of one of the major arteries going into the brain, which can result in death of a portion of the brain ("stroke") and substantial deficits. In addition, cerebral arteriosclerosis may result in arterial breakage because of brittleness with consequent hemorrhage. All of these vascular difficulties may be associated with substantial decreases in brain functions and intelligence, often with increased emotional problems.

Tumors or neoplasms may be found in various parts of the cranial vault and are of two basic types. The most common form of extrinsic tumor is the meningioma. It is said to be extrinsic because it arises and remains outside the brain tissue itself and because it compresses that tissue rather than invading it. Astrocytomas are the most common of the intrinsic tumors and are very destructive and invasive lesions. They are very difficult to remove completely. Both extrinsic and intrinsic tumors may result in increased pressure within the cranial vault, causing a number of problems in functioning, including visual difficulties and headaches.

Infectious disorders include diseases such as meningitis and encephalitis. In meningitis, the meninges (pia mater, arachnoid mater, dura mater) become inflamed, and the infection may spread around both the brain and the spinal cord. Permanent neurological damage may result. In encephalitis the brain itself is infected and inflamed.

Individuals who have suffered any of the above may have residual deficits which persist despite all forms of physical therapy or other steps toward remediation. Frequently such persons need help in identifying what are realistic goals for themselves and in learning to deal with deficits. A neuropsychological evaluation is often helpful in setting realistic goals, particularly since some abilities may be much stronger than others and since the individual may be confused concerning where strengths and weaknesses lie. Often the person seems very bright and capable in certain respects, and it is therefore presumed by everyone involved that the individual should be equally capable in all areas. When deficits actually exist, however, this leads to failure and to emotional distress, feelings of guilt, etc. Psychotherapy by a skilled therapist is often required to help the person with brain injury come to grips with the limitations and to effectively work with them.

References

Flor-Henry, P. Lateralized temporal-limbic dysfunction and psychopathology. *Annals of the New York Academy of Sciences*, 1976, *280*, 777–797.

Matarazzo, J. D. *Wechsler's measurement and appraisal of adult intelligence* (5th ed.). Baltimore: Williams & Wilkins, 1972.

Milner, B. Disorders of learning and memory after temporal lobe lesions in man. *Clinical Neurosurgery*, 1972, *19*, 421–446.

Netter, F. H. *The CIBA collection of medical illustrations* (Vol. 1). New York: CIBA Pharmaceutical Company, 1962.

Wada, J., & Rasmussen, T. Intracarotid injection of sodium amytal for the lateralization of cerebral speech dominance. *Journal of Neurosurgery*, 1960, *17*, 266–282.

William, P. L., & Warwick, R. *Functional neuroanatomy of man*. Philadelphia: Saunders, 1975.

Additional Readings

Brodal, A. *Neurological anatomy in relation to clinical medicine* (3rd ed.). New York: Oxford University Press, 1981.

Goldberg, S. *Clinical neuroanatomy made ridiculously simple*. Miami: MedMaster, 1979.

C. B. DODRILL

See NEUROPSYCHOLOGY.

Brainwashing. The emergence and increased visibility of "new age" CULTS and other religious movements during the late 1960s and 1970s have engendered considerable discussion and debate regarding allegations of brainwashing and mind control on the part of these new cultic groups. The controversy continues, at both professional and popular levels, as to whether or not "mind bending" techniques are employed, consciously or unconsciously, by a variety of new religious movements and self-improvement groups whose primary appeal seems to be to young, middle-class adults.

The term *brainwashing* is a useful though scientifically imprecise concept which refers to an array of complex phenomena resulting in the impairment of the individual's cognitive and social functioning. Such synonymous terms as thought reform, coercive persuasion, resocialization, and mind control are frequently used in the literature.

According to the research findings of sociologists, psychologists, and other mental health professionals, extremist cults employ recruitment and indoctrination procedures that effectively induce behavioral and attitudinal changes in new recruits. Such changes are usually described as relatively sudden and dramatic, resulting in diminished personal autonomy, increased dependency, and the assumption of a new identity. Psychospiritual conditioning mechanisms used by the cults have reportedly affected members' ability to remember, to concentrate, and to fully exercise independent judgment. Members are subjected to intense indoctrination pressures which include the manipulation of commitment mechanisms so that new recruits assume a posture of rigid loyalty and unquestioning obedience to the leadership.

The brainwashing view of cult recruitment posits that new adherents are isolated from the outside world in order to minimize contacts with persons holding conflicting views as well as to reinforce commitment to the group and its particular world view. Typically, external ties with all familiar social support systems are severed, including family, friends, and former church connections. Especially evident is the disruption of normal family bonds and the redefinition of past frames of reference. The cult becomes the convert's new "spiritual family."

Members are placed into a socially and psychologically dependent state where decisionmaking is minimal. Leaders maintain a taut organizational structure by suppressing dissent and managing group loyalty. The convert is able to function relatively independently (and securely) within the cult's social and ideological structure but is often dysfunctional outside the totalistic milieu.

In addition to residential isolation and the suppression of alternative views, control-oriented cults are also characterized by a vigorous regime of work, fund-raising, recruitment, and participation in various sorts of ritual and worship. When this intense level of activity and the resulting sensory deprivation (particularly sleep) is combined with a low protein diet, limited self-reflection, reduced privacy, and a highly idealistic orientation, the brainwashing potential of any given group becomes increasingly plausible. This is especially true when strong affective ties are encouraged toward a living person who is the charismatic leader/inspirator of the group.

Many of the newer cultic movements, especially the Eastern mystical groups, stress the use of various forms of spiritual technology in order to achieve desired altered states of consciousness. These conditioning mechanisms include meditation, repetitive chanting, and various forms of yoga. They are employed to eliminate all consciously directed thought and to heighten awareness levels. From the Christian perspective, such spiritual technologies also open the individual to the possibility of demonic involvement.

Brainwashing cults are able to utilize commitment-building processes which bind the individual to the group and which foster an unquestioning devotion to the cause. Themes of sacrifice and renunciation are pervasive. True believers must be willing to sacrifice a college education, a career, or even a potential mate for the good of the group. An austere life style and disengagement from the outside world may be called for. Frequently, new names and a new manner of dress are cultural insignia which identify the person with his or her newly found life style.

Thought reform is reinforced by the threat of sanctions should one ever consider leaving the group. The use of fear, guilt, and various forms of psychospiritual intimidation are effective means of ensuring conformity and limiting defections. Physical punishment is rare but not unknown. Dissenters are viewed as rebellious detractors from the cause and are encouraged to submit their individual wills to group goals.

Critics of the brainwashing argument maintain that it is a simplistic concept with little scientific evidence to support its claims. Such critics point to the absence of physical coercion in virtually all the major religious cults and to the fact that voluntary exit from these groups is not uncommon. They argue that the manipulation that undoubtedly occurs in cults has been exaggerated and is nothing more than extensions of basic principles of group dynamics and psychological conditioning which are routinely applied in less emotionally charged situations of everyday life. The accusation of brainwashing, it is claimed, is applied to unfamiliar new religions by those who disapprove of such groups (and fear them) or by those seeking a scapegoat (including parents who are no longer able to exert influence over their offspring).

It is difficult for the Christian observer to remain neutral and value free in the face of accumulating evidence of the destructiveness of cults on human lives. Certainly the Scriptures make frequent reference to spiritual brainwashing as a device commonly employed by God's adversary, Satan. It should not be surprising, then, that false teachers and self-appointed "spiritual masters" have achieved considerable success in undermining and subverting the autonomy of many people who have joined cults.

Additional Readings

Appel, W. *Cults in America: Programmed for paradise.* New York: Holt, Rinehart & Winston, 1983.

Bromley, D. G., & Shupe, A. D. *Strange gods.* Boston: Beacon Press, 1981.

Enroth, R. *Youth, brainwashing and the extremist cults.* Grand Rapids: Zondervan, 1977.

Lifton, R. J. *Thought reform and the psychology of totalism.* New York: Norton, 1961.

R. ENROTH

Breuer, Josef (1842–1925). A highly respected and successful Viennese neurologist-scientist whose considerable contributions tend to be veiled in the shadow of Freud. Freud himself credited Breuer with the creation of psychoanalysis. However, even before their collaboration Breuer had made fundamental and far-reaching discoveries in mammalian physiology.

Religiously Breuer was influenced by the *zeitgeist* of the physicalistic science then dominating the medical faculty of the University of Vienna. A skeptic, Breuer described himself as one who had religious needs but found himself utterly unable to satisfy them within the faith of popular religion. Although his writings reveal little interest in religion, he was neither irreligious nor antireligious.

Breuer early manifested a talent for experimental science. With Ewald Hering, he identified the mechanism regulating respiration. A second major contribution was his elucidation of the differing functions of the labyrinth. Over a 40-year period he published some 20 purely physiological articles. But his primary loyalty was to his large and very lucrative practice, serving the illustrious and the indigent alike.

Freud's acquaintance with Breuer, an older and highly respected physician in Vienna, came as a result of his fascination with Breuer's reported treatment of a hysterical young woman named Anna O. To Breuer's great surprise he found that, after the patient reported the details of the onset of her hysterical symptoms (paralysis as well as sight and speech disturbances), these symptoms disappeared. His treatment evolved from this discovery and placed a major emphasis on catharsis and hypnosis, techniques of much interest to Freud at this early point in the development of psychoanalysis.

In the course of his work Breuer arrived at two important principles which were to become the cornerstone of psychoanalysis. First, neurotic symptoms arise from unconscious processes. Second, these symptoms disappear when their causes are made conscious through verbalization. Freud and Breuer published their observations in "Psychic Mechanisms in

Hysteria" (1893) and their practical and theoretical conclusions in *Studies on Hysteria* (1895). Psychoanalysis and a new era of psychotherapy was born.

In his obituary of Breuer, Freud expressed regret that Breuer's brilliance had been directed toward psychopathology for only a brief time. All the eulogies published after Breuer's death emphasize that the range and depth of his cultural interests were as unusual and important as his medical and scientific accomplishments.

Q. R. DeYoung

Brief Reactive Psychosis. In *DSM-III* brief reactive psychosis has been distinguished from other psychotic disorders. The diagnosis of brief reactive psychosis is based on at least one of the following symptoms: incoherence or loosening of associations; delusions; hallucinations; or behavior that is grossly disorganized or catatonic. Also the person must show emotional turmoil. Usually the person is dangerous to himself or others. The condition is distinguished from other psychotic disorders by being preceded by a stressful life event. Prior to this stress there was no evidence of increasing psychopathology. The timing of this disorder is crucial to its diagnosis. The symptoms last more than a few hours but less than two weeks. An eventual return to prepsychotic personality functioning marks the disorder as well. Associated features include perplexity, inappropriate affect, poor insight, and incapacitation, rendering the person dependent on others.

In the differential diagnosis schizophrenia is ruled out by the situation-specific nature of the brief reactive psychosis, as is schizophreniform disorder by the greater duration of the illness. Previously brief reactive psychosis was known as acute schizophrenic disorder or other variants of schizophrenia. It has also been referred to as hysterical psychosis. Acute hallucinogenic disorders may appear in a similar form. Lack of a history of drug ingestion and absence of organic-type hallucinations distinguish this disorder. The disorder increases in the presence of wartime conditions or disaster. It may be more frequent in less developed areas of the world.

Treatment consists of those measures required to protect the person from self-harm, either through suicidal impulses or misjudgment while in a state of confusion. This may necessitate brief hospitalization. Brief therapy with psychoactive medications speeds recovery, but continued medication is rarely necessary after a period of readaptation. Psychotherapy (individual, family, and/or marital as needed) is essential to aid the person in evaluation of the illness, identification of those stressors that could repeat the illness, and strengthening of his defenses. Reassurance that he is not suffering from a genetic disorder or schizophrenia is helpful.

Persons under extreme stress are susceptible to brief reactive psychotic episodes. The family, friends, therapists, and significant others will be of special value in helping the person see the episode in this context without more dire labels.

T. G. Esau

See Adjustment Disorders.

Brief Therapy. *See* Short-Term Therapies.

Briquet's Syndrome. *See* Somatization Disorder.

Broadspectrum Psychotherapy. An expression that denotes an open-mindedness regarding the practice of psychotherapy. It has more to do with attitude than with preference for any particular theoretical orientation. Some psychotherapists are likely to consider the term synonymous with eclecticism. Although the same basic frame of reference characterizes both eclecticism and broadspectrum therapy, the latter tends to be more precise in conceptualization, to be treated more systematically, and to possess greater breadth and comprehensiveness.

Multidimensionality in problem analysis or diagnosis and treatment modalities is the central theme of broadspectrum therapy. A stronger emphasis is usually placed on the applied and practical aspects than on the philosophical and theoretical issues. A major assumption is that the best clinical treatment is provided when the presenting problem is defined from the widest possible perspective and interventions are made by carefully selecting appropriate methods and strategies from a storehouse of well-refined techniques. The methodological options are dictated by an accurate diagnosis, an integration of the various components of the problem situation, and a compatibility of the techniques with the personality of both the therapist and the client.

Broadspectrum therapy has been articulated most clearly by Lazarus (1971, 1976) under the term Multimodal Therapy. Other advocates of the broadspectrum approach, though they might not use the specific term to describe their position, include Ivey (Ivey & Simek-Downing, 1980), and Goldfried (1982).

References
Goldfried, M. R. *Converging themes in psychotherapy.* New York: Springer Publishing, 1982.

Ivey, A. E., & Simek-Downing, L. *Counseling and psychotherapy.* Englewood Cliffs, N.J.: Prentice-Hall, 1980.

Lazarus, A. A. *Behavior therapy and beyond.* New York: McGraw-Hill, 1971.

Lazarus, A. A. *Multimodal behavior therapy.* New York: Springer Publishing, 1976.

D. Smith

Bruner, Jerome Seymour (1915–). Best known as a child psychologist who has had significant impact on the field of education. Born in New York, Bruner completed the Ph.D. degree in psychology at Harvard in 1941 after completing a bachelor's degree at Duke in 1937.

His first interests in psychology were animal perception and learning. These interests shifted to human psychology with the outbreak of World War II. During the war Bruner studied human perceptions and propaganda, and wrote his doctoral thesis on Nazi propaganda techniques. He served with General Eisenhower's headquarters, working on psychological warfare.

After the war he returned to Harvard, where he began his work on children's perceptions. His studies indicated that needs and values strongly influence human perceptions. Bruner soon became a main force in cognitive psychology, and by 1960 he had helped establish the Center for Cognitive Studies at Harvard.

After Russia launched Sputnik in 1957, America placed new emphasis on education. Various types of experts were consulted, and Bruner became involved in educational psychology. In 1960 he wrote *The Process of Education*, in which he makes his famous statement, "Any subject can be taught effectively in some intellectually honest way to any person at any stage of development." He was quickly misquoted and criticized as saying that anything could be taught to anybody regardless of the person's age.

Bruner's hypothesis was based upon the concept of structure. He maintained that any subject matter or field of knowledge has an inherent structure, and that normally a person learns the structure of a subject before learning all the propositional details of the subject. His ideas can be illustrated by how a person learns the rules of grammar. Most four-year-olds can select the proper case for a pronoun depending on whether it is the subject or the object of the sentence. There are dozens of other rules of grammar that four-year-olds can use appropriately in speech, and thus they could be said to know those rules of grammar. However, few if any know the rules as stated propositionally. Bruner calls the first level of knowledge illustrated above "intuitive knowledge" of the

subject matter, in this case of grammar. His suggestions are that we should learn how children intuitively learn the structure of various subjects before they learn those subjects verbally, and then we should design curriculum and instruction in order to coordinate with this natural way of learning.

Bruner also came to be known for his emphasis on inquiry, problem solving, and discovery as modes of school learning. This emphasis led him to develop an elementary school curriculum called Man: A Course of Study, in which the entire curriculum is based around answering the question, "What is human about humans?"

In 1963 Bruner received the Distinguished Scientific Award by the American Psychological Association, and in 1965 was elected president of the association. In 1972 he left Harvard and took up a new post at Oxford University in England.

R. B. McKean

Bruxism. A tension symptom where an individual grinds or gnashes his teeth, typically at night during sleep. It is an indication of hostility, resentment, or repressed aggressiveness, common in adolescents and older children, and especially in alcoholics.

Bulimia. An eating disorder characterized by episodic binge eating accompanied by an awareness that the eating pattern is abnormal, fear of not being able to stop eating voluntarily, and depressed mood with self-deprecating thoughts following the eating binges. Although it is often found among those with a history of Anorexia Nervosa, a willful pursuit of thinness which often leads to life-threatening weight loss, most researchers view bulimia as a distinct subgroup among eating disorders. The exact incidence of this disorder is unknown, although recent studies estimate that at least 4% of the general population may be bulimic. Bulimics are typically females between the ages of 20 and 40 (Stangler & Printz, 1980).

Until very recently little was known about bulimia and those who evidence this disorder. However, recent research suggests that bulimic eating binges involve the rapid consumption of high caloric foods whose texture permits quick swallowing (Mitchell, Pyle, & Eckert, 1981). Foods such as ice cream, bread, candy, doughnuts, soft drinks, and a variety of dairy products are often included. As many as 11,500 calories may be consumed in one episode, although the mean average tends to be around 3,000 to 4,000. These episodes may occur as often as 10 times a day, although such a high frequency is rare. Studies indicate that between 40 to 65% report at least one episode per week, while 15 to 35% report binge eating on a daily basis. The average frequency is estimated to be three to four episodes per week. While some describe episodes which last an entire day, it is reported that most binge eating episodes last less than two hours. A binge is usually terminated by the onset of abdominal pain, sleep, social interruption, or, most frequently, induced vomiting. Although the eating binges may be experienced as pleasurable while they are occurring, depression and self-hatred typically follow.

Recent attempts have been made to provide a clinical description of those who develop bulimia. Bulimics tend to be quite labile in mood, although they are frequently depressed. They are often anxious, overly sensitive individuals who experience strong feelings of guilt and hopelessness. Bulimics typically display a variety of impulsive behaviors, such as alcohol and substance abuse, kleptomania, self-mutilation, and multiple suicide attempts. Not surprisingly, bulimics evidence marked impairment in social functioning. Finally, not only is there a high frequency of obesity in the mothers of bulimics, but they themselves often have a history of premorbid obesity (Casper, Eckert, Halmi, Goldberg, & Davis, 1980).

Little is known about the actual etiology of bulimia. Some have hypothesized that our culture's pursuit of thinness and high performance expectations of women may be factors precipitating the development of eating disorders like anorexia nervosa and bulimia. Others have suggested that, rather than the pursuit of thinness, bulimia results from various symbolic misrepresentations of the eating function. It may also reflect a disturbance regarding mastery over one's body, body image, and internal sensations (Bruch, 1973). It has also been reported that bulimics experience feelings of comfort and well-being from the sensation of "fullness" that results from the binge eating episodes, thus motivating them to binge at times when they are feeling particularly depressed, withdrawn, and vulnerable.

Clinically, bulimics are very difficult to treat. Because of the shame they typically experience regarding their disorder, they tend to be quite secretive about the actual symptoms they experience. As result, bulimics may remain unidentified, even after months of psychotherapy. Once diagnosed, they tend to underestimate the severity of their problems, and they may avoid providing the psychotherapist with details about the frequency and duration of the binge eating episodes (Pyle, Mitchell, & Eckert, 1981). As a result, the therapist is left with the uneasy feeling of knowing very little about what the binges actually involve. This is particularly worrisome since frequent binges can lead to electrolyte imbalance, dehydration, and gastric dilation, especially when these are followed by vomiting (Mitchell et al., 1981). In very rare cases death can result from gastric rupture. Thus, it is important for the psychotherapist to obtain as much information about the frequency and duration of the binges as possible in an attempt to assess the severity of the patient's condition. It is also important for the therapist to suggest that the suspected bulimic patient obtain a thorough physical examination. This allows the clinician the opportunity to consult with a physician concerning the physical features of the disorder.

Perhaps because bulimics often come for psychotherapy showing moderate to severe depression, it is this constellation of symptoms which typically becomes the focus of treatment (Russell, 1979). Insight-oriented long-term psychotherapy which facilitates the formation of a therapeutic alliance of trust, support, and acceptance has been demonstrated to be quite helpful in reducing the depression, self-hatred, and shame that bulimics often experience. It may also help the patient to gain insight into the underlying dynamics that led to the development of the disorder. As the depression lifts and the patient begins to feel more in control of his or her emotions and behavior, the frequency of the binge eating episodes sometimes decreases. Group therapy has been found to be somewhat successful, particularly time-limited, symptom-focused groups consisting totally of bulimic patients. Finally, it has been reported that the use of antidepressant medications has proved somewhat helpful when it is combined with psychotherapy.

References

Bruch, H. *Eating disorders.* New York: Basic Books, 1973.

Casper, R. C., Eckert, E. D., Halmi, K. A., Goldberg, S. C., & Davis, J. M. Bulimia. *Archives of General Psychiatry,* 1980, *37,* 1030–1035.

Mitchell, J. E., Pyle, R. L., & Eckert, E. D. Frequency and duration of binge eating episodes in patients with bulimia. *American Journal of Psychiatry,* 1981, *138,* 835–836.

Pyle, R. L., Mitchell, J. E., & Eckert, E. D. Bulimia. *Journal of Clinical Psychiatry,* 1981, *42*(2), 62–64.

Russell, G. Bulimia nervosa. *Psychological Medicine,* 1979, *9,* 429–448.

Stangler, R., & Printz, A. DSM-III: psychiatric diagnosis in a university population. *American Journal of Psychiatry,* 1980, *137,* 937–940.

J. D. GUY, JR.

Bystander Intervention. *See* HELPING BEHAVIOR.

Cc

California Psychological Inventory. Harrison Gough developed the California Psychological Inventory (CPI) for the purpose of measuring "folk concepts" of personality—traits that are so much a part of our personal and social experience that they are symbolized in the natural language of virtually all cultures and societies. The CPI focuses on the positive or normal aspects of personality rather than the negative or pathological. Although popularity is not an indicator of a test's scientific merit, the 1,362 CPI references in Buros's *Mental Measurement Yearbook* (Editions 5–8) attest to its practical utility in a wide variety of research and applied settings.

The CPI is composed of 480 true-false items which are scored as 18 separate scales. Items ask the respondent to report typical feelings, behaviors, opinions, and attitudes toward moral, ethical, and family concerns. To facilitate the interpretation of the scales, Gough clusters them into four classes. Class I includes the dominance, capacity for status, sociability, social presence, self-acceptance, and sense of well-being scales. Responsibility, socialization, self-control, tolerance, good impression, and communality are the scales in Class II. Class III measures are achievement via conformance, achievement via independence, and intellectual efficiency. Class IV scales include psychological-mindedness, flexibility, and femininity.

The CPI can be administered individually or in groups and takes about one hour for most people to complete. Although the test has been used with individuals ranging in age from 12 to 70, its content is most appropriate for high school students through young adults. Scoring is done either by hand with templates or by using several available computer scoring services. Standardized scores based on normative samples of over 6,000 men and 7,000 women are reported in profile form. The CPI manual (Gough, 1975) and the handbook (Megargee, 1972) provide detailed instructions for the interpretation of each scale and the overall profile.

Evidence for the psychometric quality of the CPI scales ranges from very strong to nonexistent, depending upon the scale in question. Test-retest reliabilities with intervals up to one year range from .38 (communality) to .87 (tolerance). The CPI handbook gives a review of validity studies. While several of the scales need research attention, it should be noted that the socialization, dominance, sociability, and achievement via conformance scales are among the most well-validated measures in the personality test literature.

The CPI's uniqueness as a general personality test lies in its method of construction. As in the Minnesota Multiphasic Personality Inventory and the Strong-Campbell Interest Inventory, CPI items were selected according to their correlation with an external criterion. For example, items that differentiate high versus low socioeconomic status respondents were selected for the capacity for status scale. Scales that will predict "real-life" behaviors are the goal of this procedure. In settings where prediction of such behaviors from common personality traits is desired, the CPI merits serious consideration.

References

Buros, O. K. (Ed.). *Mental measurements yearbook* (Eds. 5–8). Highland Park, N.J.: Gryphon Press, 1938–1978.
Gough, H. G. *Manual for the California psychological inventory*. Palo Alto, Calif.: Consulting Psychologists Press, 1975.
Megargee, E. I. *The California psychological inventory handbook*. San Francisco: Jossey-Bass, 1972.

D. D. McKENNA

See PERSONALITY ASSESSMENT.

Cancer Counseling. Because of recent medical advances, having cancer does not necessarily mean an immediate death. Rather, when one is working with a cancer patient in a counselor-client relationship, a more likely goal than preparing for death is that of adapting to the illness. Since adaptation to illness requires two separate tasks—coping with the illness and its accompanying problems and coping with life as it is changed by the illness—there are several aspects of this adjustment process that can be facilitated by a counselor.

For patients the task of dealing with the illness itself and its accompanying problems, such as pain, may be foremost (Moos & Tsu, 1977). During treatment the patient is usually placed in a hospital where he must adjust to a variety of new procedures and situations at a time when his resources are at a low level. The patient must also learn to relate to a group of health-care givers. Also, for many patients any of the major treatment methods for cancer—surgery, radiotherapy, chemotherapy—cause a great deal of apprehension and dread.

There are additional general life-related tasks that must be accomplished by patients. They must preserve relationships with family and friends in order to maintain sources of social support, and they must engage in maintenance tasks of preserving emotional stability and self-image.

Given the wide variation in individual behavior, it is difficult to specify which patient responses are adaptive in nature and which are nonadaptive. For example, Weisman and Worden (1976) demonstrated that newly diagnosed cancer patients have a high level of distress at the time of diagnosis which usually tapers off later. Therefore, to assume that high levels of anxiety at the time of diagnosis indicate maladjustment would be erroneous. However, it is important to recognize when the patient's behavior ceases to be healthy or productive and begins to be destructive. Senescu (1963) has offered the following conditions as indicative of potential poor adjustment: 1) when the patient's emotional reactions interfere with treatment by preventing his seeking treatment or cooperating with treatment; 2) when the patient's responses cause more pain and distress than the disease itself; 3) when the patient's emotional responses interfere with the accomplishment of everyday tasks; 4) when the patient's emotional responses are manifested as psychiatric symptoms—e.g., distortion of reality.

The several psychosocial responses that patients can make to cancer seem to fall into four categories (Moos & Tsu, 1977). First, patients may deny or minimize the severity of the illness. While there is some controversy regarding the healthy use of denial, it is clear that this response does accomplish useful goals of providing time needed to assimilate information and of reducing emotional distress. Second, patients may employ intrapsychic defenses of repression of affect, dissociation, or projection. Third, they often find some meaning for the illness in the context of their lives—e.g., attributing the illness to divine intervention or retribution. Last, patients may think through alternative outcomes of their illness. They may prepare for death, or change in employment or other results of the illness.

In general, counseling the cancer patient can be conceptualized as task-oriented assistance or as process-oriented assistance. If the counselor adapts a task facilitation approach, there are several tasks that could be undertaken by both patient and family members. For example, learning specific illness-related procedures, such as changing dressings, may be important to help the patient be an active participant in his medical treatment. The patient and family should also seek accurate medical information. In many cases a lack of information and an attention to cancer "myths" have caused patients needless grief as relatives and friends have avoided them for fear they might "catch" cancer.

Counseling which focuses on process may deal with several types of issues. First is the need for patients to be able to "tell their stories," to relate at some length the histories of their illness and their responses. There are also self-esteem needs for the patient to be discussed, particularly in light of the patient's separation from everyday mechanisms of feeling good about himself, such as employment and family relationships. Finally, there are process issues having to do with fear of dying and management of that fear. Keeping hope alive among cancer patients appears to be a crucial aspect of psychosocial care (Cassileth, 1979).

In summary, while issues of death and dying may be relevant for cancer patients, issues of growth and adjustment are also important to consider. Within these issues are tasks that can be facilitated by the counselor among the patient and his family and psychological adjustment processes that can be initiated by the counselor for the patient.

References

Cassileth, B. R. (Ed.). *The cancer patient.* Philadelphia: Lea & Febiger, 1979.

Moos, R. H., & Tsu, V. D. The crisis of physical illness. In R. H. Moos (Ed.), *Coping with physical illness.* New York: Plenum Medical Book, 1977.

Senescu, R. A. The development of emotional complications in the patient with cancer. *Journal of Chronic Diseases,* 1963, *16,* 813–832.

Weisman, A. D., & Worden, J. W. The existential plight in cancer: Significance of the first 100 days. *Psychiatry in Medicine,* 1976–77, *7,* 1–15.

E. M. ALTMAIER

See HEALTH PSYCHOLOGY.

Cannabis. *See* MARIJUANA.

Cannon, Walter Bradford (1871–1945). Physiologist whose research on physiological factors in motivation and emotion is important for psychology. Born in Prairie du Chien, Wisconsin. His early education was in the public schools of Milwaukee and St. Paul, but his father took him out of school because he was not applying himself. After two years of work in a railroad office, Cannon returned to school with a new appreciation for it and completed high school in three years. He won a Harvard scholarship and graduated *summa cum laude* in 1896. He received his M.D. from Harvard in 1900 and taught there from 1899 to 1942.

Cannon introduced the concept of homeostasis, and believed that organisms were motivated to maintain themselves at an optimal level of functioning. In his peripheral (or local) theory of motivation, stimuli such as stomach contractions or dryness of the mouth prompt searching for food and water. When homeostasis is restored, messages from the periphery stop, and the organism is no longer motivated. His most important book on this is *The Wisdom of the Body* (1932). Although such local factors cannot account for all motivation, they have some effect.

In his *Bodily Changes in Pain, Hunger, Fear and Rage* (1915) he reported his work on the emergency functions of the sympathetic nervous system. Critical of the James-Lange theory of emotion, he and Bard proposed an alternative theory of emotion in an attempt to explain the behavior of brain-damaged cats. Cannon and Bard suggested that the thalamus (or hypothalamus) contains centers for the emotions; these are responsible for organizing both the autonomic responses and the overt behavior patterns in rage. These centers also stimulate the cerebral cortex to give rise to the conscious experience of emotion.

R. L. KOTESKEY

Capgras Syndrome. First described in 1923 by the French psychiatrist Capgras, this syndrome is the delusional belief that other individuals are not really themselves but imposters or doubles. French psychiatrists consider the syndrome a disorder in itself. American thought has generally viewed it as a part of the paranoid schizophrenic disorder. It has also been reported in organic disorders and affective psychotic disorders.

Cardiovascular Disease. Everyday expressions and folk sayings recognize the close link between the heart and psychological states. The disappointed are referred to as downhearted or brokenhearted; when happy, one's heart leaps for joy; when frightened, one's heart stands still; it goes out to those for whom one has compassion, and the heart is given in love. Proverbs notes, "A merry heart maketh a cheerful countenance," and "He that is of a merry heart hath a continual feast" (15:13, 15).

Personality factors related to heart disease began to receive widespread attention in 1974 when two cardiologists, Friedman and Rosenman, published their now classic *Type A Behavior and Your Heart.* In it they described the Type A and Type B behavior patterns and showed that Type A people had much higher incidences of heart attacks than the calm, easygoing Type B's. The Type A's were aggressive, ambitious to accumulate material goods, and always on the go. They were excessively competitive, seemed always to be laboring under a sense of urgency in an attempt to meet deadlines, and they were impatient. They became frustrated if someone took too long to complete a task and would frequently interrupt in an effort to accomplish things more quickly.

The Type B's may be just as ambitious as the Type A's, but ambition in the Type B person seems to steady and give confidence and security rather than to goad, irritate, and infuriate. These people are able to enjoy their leisure, tend to have well-thought-out, longer-term goals, and lack the time urgency that is characteristic of Type A's.

There is a strong correlation between the degree of Type A personality behavior and the level of serum cholesterol in the blood. The serum cholesterol increases in response to stress. Type A men studied by Friedman and Rosenman were seven times more likely to have clogging of the heart arteries than Type B men. They also exhibited the blood, fat, and hormone abnormality that the majority of coronary patients also showed, leading Friedman and Rosenman to conclude that the behavior pattern itself gives rise to the abnormalities.

Other researchers have noted that people with cardiovascular disturbances tend to show chronic anxiety and hostility, although these people are often not aware of their hostility and anger (Alexander, 1950). Both anxiety and anger activate the sympathetic nervous system, which in turn increases the body's output of adrenalin. These physiological changes prepare the person to run from danger or fight an attacker. In our stressful society we don't usually run or fight, but the body prepares for this when we feel threatened and it stays in a continual state of arousal when these feelings are present. An increase in fear, anxiety, anger, or other activating emotions causes the heart to work harder. For example, a man who does not like his job or his employer may stay in a frustrating situation for years because he is afraid he will lose the job if he speaks out, and he fears not securing as good a job if he quits. When chronic, the constant stress of fear and frustration can contribute to high blood pressure or to heart pains (angina).

Preventive efforts can be greatly enhanced if people with Type A behavior learn to be more relaxed and to cope more effectively with frustrations. This is a difficult task because personality and behavioral traits are well ingrained. In addition, our culture encourages and rewards many of the behaviors that define the Type A personality. Friedman and Rosenman have noted that Type A behavior cannot be changed unless the Type A person is first motivated to change. This requires a certain level of awareness of one's total life. Such awareness would lead the Type A person to realize that he can be successful without continuing to jeopardize his life by persisting in behaviors that can ultimately kill him.

Programs are currently under way to teach stress reduction to Type A's. They learn to relax, become more patient and less competitive. Preliminary results indicate that those who actively participate in such programs show significantly lower incidence of heart attacks. In contrast to telling people to slow down, these programs teach people active ways of coping with stress. They learn to feel in control rather than helpless, as they might if they just took it easy. In addition to relaxation skills people learn more effective means of communicating so they can express feelings, wants, and needs directly rather than indirectly or competitively.

As scientists learn more about changing the behaviors related to cardiac disease, people will be able to focus more accurately on what they must do to prevent heart disease. In the meantime, one can positively influence one's own cardiovascular health by learning to cope more effectively with stress. A merry heart does more than make a cheerful countenance; it promotes happiness, good health, and long life.

References
Alexander, F. *Psychosomatic medicine.* New York: Norton, 1950.
Friedman, M., & Rosenman, R. H. *Type A behavior and your heart.* New York: Knopf, 1974.

Additional Reading
Pelletier, K. R. *Mind as healer, mind as slayer.* New York: Dell, 1977.

M. A. NORFLEET

See HEALTH PSYCHOLOGY.

Casework. *See* SOCIAL CASEWORK.

Castration Complex. In psychoanalytic theory the castration complex is a normal part of the process of psychosexual development for both males and females. It is hypothesized to be most prominent during the oedipal crisis, which occurs in late infancy, beginning at approximately age 3 and usually lasting until age 6 or 7. It is assumed that the manner in which the castration complex is handled determines in large part the adequacy of the resolution of the oedipus complex; failure to resolve this latter complex is hypothesized to lie at the root of adult neurotic disorders.

Freud's assumption was that children of both sexes believe that everyone is born with a penis. When the female child discovers that she does not have one and that boys do, she responds with what he called penis envy and blames her mother for her deprivation. This is felt to lead to the onset of the oedipal crisis as she then moves her primary attachment from her mother to her father. For the male child the discovery that some people (girls) do not have a penis is assumed to confirm his own fear that he might lose his, just as in the past he lost other valued possessions. In particular, he fears that his father might inflict this on him as punishment for his secret incestuous longings for his mother (the oedipus complex). Thus, in the male the castration complex is assumed to lead to the resolution of the oedipus complex in that the male represses his oedipal longings and moves to a primary attachment to and identification with his father.

D. G. BENNER

See PSYCHOSEXUAL DEVELOPMENT; OEDIPUS COMPLEX.

Catalepsy. A spontaneous or hypnotically induced trancelike state in which an individual maintains a semirigid or rigid physical posture. It is a disorder of the muscular system. The two types of catalepsy are waxy (or flexible, sometimes called *flexibitas cerea*) and rigid. In waxy catalepsy a person assumes postures that someone else places him in. Limbs can be positioned and the individual will maintain the position until he is moved by another. In rigid catalepsy the person assumes self-selected postures and is resistant to changing them. Catalepsy is most common in catatonic schizophrenia, epilepsy, and hysteria, and may also occur as a result of organic brain damage. It is often associated with amphetamine toxicity.

D. L. SCHUURMAN

Cataplexy. A temporary attack of paralysis or powerlessness provoked by an emotional experience or intense excitement. The physical loss of muscle tone results in a collapse of the body, most commonly triggered by laughter but also by anger or anxiety. Cataplexy is associated with narcoleptic attacks.

Catharsis. The word, which comes from the Greek, means purification. Aristotle used it to refer to the emotional purgation which spectators experience while viewing a tragic play. Many of the healing rituals of primitive peoples involve an emotional intensity which seems to be followed by a sense of release and restoration to normal functioning. The same tendencies could be found in Mesmer's "animal magnetism cures." For almost two hundred years religious conversion in some Protestant groups has been accompanied by a great emotional outpouring and sometimes followed by dramatic behavioral changes (*see* ECSTATIC RELIGIOUS EXPERIENCES).

In the nineteenth century M. Allen treated agitated patients at his asylum by allowing them to ramble (accompanied by an attendant) and scream in the forest the whole day long. The greatest advance in the application of catharsis to the treatment of mental disorder occurred at the close of the century when Freud and Breuer used hypnosis to remove hysterical symptoms. Although French alienists had used these techniques for over a decade, Freud must be credited with developing the theoretical framework for understanding the therapeutic value of the abreaction. The early psychoanalytic model was homeostatic and hydraulic. The mind was viewed as a steam kettle or water balloon. If too much emotional pressure builds up, the vessel may become stretched out of shape, spring a leak, or completely rupture. The abreaction obtained during therapy serves to discharge excessive tension and return emotional pressure to tolerable levels.

Although the homeostatic, hydraulic understanding of catharsis has persisted, the nature of the abreacted emotions and degree of reliance on catharsis has varied widely in psychotherapy. Freud, who understood catharsis as a discharge of painful memories from early childhood, abandoned the technique of hypnosis for free association and began to understand cure in terms of insight and ego strengthening. Rank and Janov (*see* PRIMAL THERAPY) developed their forms of psychotherapy by emphasizing the need to have a catharsis of painful early memories. Later Rank moved away from this when he replaced his emphasis on the birth trauma with that of the need to strengthen the will. Reich conceived of catharsis as sexual orgasm and emphasized physiological factors, especially muscular rigidities. BIOENERGETIC ANALYSIS continues this emphasis. In the last quarter century catharsis has been a central feature of several popular therapies, including Gestalt therapy, psychodrama, and encounter groups. While these approaches include catharsis of feelings in general, including those resulting from sexual experiences and painful memories, the focus is frequently on the ventilation of anger.

There are several problems with the reliance on catharsis in psychotherapy. One is that the proof of its efficacy is founded more on metaphor, analogy, introspection, and anecdotal case studies than on carefully designed experiments. A difficulty here is that the therapists who are quite skilled in cathartic therapy are usually not precise designers of quantitative research. Indeed, the operational definitions of catharsis have been imprecise and varied. One researcher may use GSR (galvanic skin response) measurements and another might use "blind" raters who evaluate the patient's degree of emotional intensity in a taped therapy session. The measurement of the criterion for treatment success has likewise varied between physiological measures (e.g., blood pressure) and subjective reports. The area of catharsis research in which there have been several well-designed studies has been that of anger (the emotion) and aggression (verbal or physical catharsis). Here the weight of the evidence is that catharsis, in whatever form, does not reduce the likelihood of future anger and aggression.

In general, neither catharsis nor its hydraulic way of understanding human mental processes has been popular with cognitive or behavioral psychologists. The former reject the concept of emotion as something that can be stored in favor of seeing emotion as a by-product of cognitive structures. Many cognitive therapists would agree that the controlled expression of hostility may be therapeutic, but because it enhances the perception of control and power, not because of emotional discharge per se. The behaviorists also reject the model's emphasis on unobservable, internal processes. Many behaviorists echo James's concern that emotional discharge may become habit-forming rather than purgative. Although one form of behavioral modification, FLOODING, involves great emotional intensity, the behaviorists describe its efficacy in terms of conditioning.

Until there is improvement in both the quantity and quality of research on the use of catharsis in psychotherapy, therapists must proceed with some caution. Catharsis may sometimes be useful, though it is only rarely essential and is certainly not a self-sufficient treatment. Catharsis may be most appropriate in the kinds of patients that Freud and Breuer saw: somatoform and dissociative disorders. Many therapists have found that bereaved patients seem to benefit from abreaction. It is usually best that the therapist *permit* the patient to engage in intense emotional expression, rather than compel it (or contend that it is an absolute requirement for cure). Catharsis seems to work best when the patient believes in its therapeutic value and has a great faith in the therapist. One danger of catharsis is that the therapist (and/or patient) may come to see it as the purpose of therapy rather than an adjunct. Another danger of catharsis is that it tends to leave patients in a highly vulnerable state. In order to protect them against the possibility of becoming psychiatric casualties, it is important to provide them with a supportive therapist and/or group.

Additional Reading
Nichols, M. P., & Zax, M. *Catharsis in psychotherapy.* New York: Gardner Press, 1977.

T. L. BRINK

Cathexis. In psychoanalytic terminology cathexis signifies a concentration of psychic energy upon some person or object. This concept plays a central role in the process of PSYCHOSEXUAL DEVELOPMENT where psychological maturation is traced in terms of shifting patterns of cathexes.

Cattell, James McKeen (1860–1944). Pioneer in testing and practical application of psychology. Born in Easton, Pennsylvania, where his father was professor of classics at Lafayette College, Cattell received his bachelor's degree from Lafayette in 1880. After graduate study at Göttingen, Leipzig, and Johns Hopkins, he returned to Leipzig to receive his doctorate in 1886.

Cattell was lecturer at the University of Pennsylvania, Bryn Mawr College, and Cambridge University. He received the first professorship of psychology in the world at the University of Pennsylvania in 1888. In 1891 he became professor and head of the department at Columbia University. After long-time difficulties with the administration, Cattell was dismissed from Columbia in 1917 because of his pacifist activities. He never took another academic appointment, but devoted himself to the public promotion of psychology and the other sciences.

Although he did studies on reaction time, his major early interest was in individual differences. He developed a rank order method of evaluating persons, was the first psychologist to teach statistics in his course, and coined the term *mental tests* in 1890. He also conducted research in association, perception, reading, and psychophysics.

Although his bibliography includes 167 items, Cattell is most widely remembered as an editor, creating channels to disseminate psychological information. He was cofounder of the *Psychological Review, Psychological Monographs,* and *Psychological Index.* He bought *Science* in 1894, and five years later it became the official journal of the American Association for the Advancement of Science. He published *Popular Science Monthly,* which became *Scientific Monthly,* and was editor of *School and Society* and the *American Naturalist.* Between 1906 and 1938 he edited six editions of *American Men of Science.* He also founded *Leaders of Education* and the *Directory of American Scholars.* In 1921 he organized the Psychological Corporation to promote the application of psychology to industry and make it available to the public through psychologists.

R. L. KOTESKEY

Cattell, Raymond Bernard (1905–). Developer of the trait approach to personality. Cattell was born in Staffordshire, England, and received his B.S. degree in chemistry and physics from the University of London in 1924. He changed to psychology because of his concern for social ills, and in 1929 received his

Ph.D. from the University of London, where he studied under Charles Spearman.

From 1928 to 1937 Cattell held a variety of "fringe" jobs in psychology because there were few full-time jobs for psychologists in England. He lectured at Exeter University and set up a psychological service and clinic in Leicester while he continued to conduct research and write. Finally, in 1937, he was offered a full-time position in the United States. He went to Columbia University in 1937, Clark University in 1938, Harvard University in 1941, and became research professor at the University of Illinois in 1945. He retired in 1973, and is currently visiting professor at the University of Hawaii.

Cattell sees personality as a structure of traits which can be identified by using the method of factor analysis on data gathered from masses of human subjects. He distinguishes between surface and source traits, environmental-mold and constitutional traits, ability and temperament traits, and dynamic traits in individuals. He also proposes a concept, syntality, which refers to traits characteristic of a group of people.

Cattell's writings include some 30 books and 350 journal articles, making him one of the most prolific of personality theorists. His major works include *Personality and Motivation Structure and Measurement* (1957) and *The Scientific Analysis of Personality* (1965) as well as two handbooks he edited, *Handbook of Multivariate Experimental Psychology* (1966) and *Handbook of Modern Personality Theory* (1977). In 1973 he established the nonprofit Institute for Research on Morality and Self-realization, through which he hopes to integrate his interest in science with social and religious concerns.

R. L. KOTESKEY

See FACTOR THEORIES OF PERSONALITY; PERSONALITY.

Celibacy. The abstinence from sexual intimacy. Celibacy has a long history in Christianity, but virtually no precedent in Judaism; marriage and child-bearing are high-priority religious values in the Jewish community. While the sacred duties of priests (Lev. 21:1–15) and the rigorous ascetic requirements placed on Nazirites (Num. 6:1–21) detailed many abstinences, there is no hint of celibacy. Rabbinic law required priests and religious leaders to be married. Josephus reports that celibacy was practiced among the Essene groups, yet rabbinic law prevented the unmarried from holding public office. Celibacy was evidently tolerated among the Jews on rare occasions. In the Talmud Ben Azzai wrote: "My soul is fond of the Law; the world will be perpetuated by others" (*Yev.* 63b). Even here celibacy is tolerated only because the scholar is so fully absorbed in his sacred work and he is not experiencing sexual temptation. In the Jewish understanding religious maturity and perfection could be reached only in the married state.

The teaching and the practice of Jesus provide the ambiguous base on which the Roman Catholic Church eventually made celibacy an institution. On the one hand, the teachings of Jesus consistently echo the "one flesh" quality of marriage (Matt. 19:4–6), and he was fond of the metaphor of weddings, in obvious reference to his activity and mission (Matt. 9:15). Beyond these metaphoric images, but consistent with them, is the vision of the eschaton as culminating in a marriage banquet, a spotless bride dressed up for her husband (Rev. 19:7–9; 21:2; 22:1–7). Thus, in Jesus there are combined the princely groom and the pure and spotless bride—the church; they are temporarily separated (since the ascension) but will be reunited in eternity. All of this suggests the image of "one flesh" projected from Eden to the eternal kingdom.

On the other hand, Jesus of Nazareth lived and died single, thus seeming to validate celibacy by his personal practice. And his teachings contain terse sayings which seem to downgrade family and marital obligations. The excuse of having married a wife is not sufficient to draw back from following him (Luke 14:20). "Leaving all" to follow Jesus suggests that the single life style is, however, perhaps more adapted to being a disciple. One must not even hold back to care for the burial of members of the family (Matt. 8:21; Luke 9:59). Yet some of the apostles, perhaps all, were married (Matt. 8:14; 1 Cor. 9:5).

Paul, who could not have been a member of the Sanhedrin without being married, recommended marriage for church leaders (1 Tim. 3:2), but held up his present unmarried state as the better way of consecrating oneself to the work of God (1 Cor. 7:26–35). And his bottom line for justifying marriage is difficult to align with the elegance of the creation: "But if they cannot control themselves, they should marry, for it is better to marry than to burn with passion" (1 Cor. 7:9).

Only once does Jesus address the issue of celibacy directly. In Matthew 19, in the context of responding to the question about divorce, Jesus expounded on the miracle of the sexual bond which, he said, should be protected at all costs: "Therefore what God has joined together, let man not separate" (19:6). This new insight, that marriage is absolutely permanent, led the disciples to exclaim, "If this is the situation between a husband and wife, it is better not to marry" (19:10). This exchange sets the stage for Jesus to speak of celibacy. First he stated that "not everyone can accept this teaching." What is unclear is whether he is referring to his own words about the permanence of marriage or to his disciples' expression of their fear of being permanently married and their statement that it is better not to marry. Either way, he then cites three kinds of "eunuchs": 1) those who were born sexually dysfunctional, hence eunuchs without capability of reproduction; 2) those who were made eunuchs by the surgeon's knife, sexually altered usually for the purpose of being household domestic servants; and 3) those who "have made themselves eunuchs" for the sake of the kingdom of heaven. Then he ends with, "Not everyone can receive this teaching, only the one to whom it has been given" (19:11).

Based on the teaching in Matthew 19 and 1 Corinthians 7, the Roman Catholic Church, largely through the tendency towards literalism of early devout believers, formulated the requirement of celibacy for clergy in the Roman church. One of the church fathers, Origen, castrated himself as a literal response to the teaching of Matthew 19. By the fourth century most of the bishops from Greece, Egypt, and Europe either had remained unmarried or had placed their wives in monasteries upon being consecrated bishop. During the first three hundred years, however, deacons and priests married.

Canon 33 of the Council of Elvira (*ca.* 305) reads: "We decree that all bishops, priests, and deacons, and all clerics engaged in the ministry are forbidden entirely to live with their wives and to beget children: whoever shall do so shall be deposed from the clerical dignity." Hosius of Cordova brought celibacy to the Council of Nicaea hoping to make it the law of the clergy in general. When the council refused to enact such a law, the popes decreed it: Damascus I, Siricus, Innocent I, and Leo I required celibacy and dissolution of marriages of all clergy. Gregory VII, pope at the zenith of the Hildebrandine reform, made every effort to establish celibacy for all clergy. But actual adherence to sexual and marital abstinence was still far from universal. It was the Council of Trent (1545–1563) which clarified that celibacy is the law of the church and not the law of God.

Fueled by the literalism of Origen's self-castration, the young church was vulnerable to a Gnostic dualism: the body itself is evil, while with the mind and spirit one may truly serve God. This dualism undergirded and distorted the significance of the virgin birth of Jesus by making sexual intercourse earthly and an accommodation to the dark side of the dualistic view of humans that was emerging. To this was added the dogma of the immaculate conception of Mary, by which the "Mother of God" was protected at the time of her own conception from the transmitted earthly evil. Augustine codified the life of true sanctity as lying beyond this life, a belief that lasted until Bernard of Clairvaux and, later, John Wesley reunited the body and spirit and called for sanctity in this present life. The traces of fourth-century Gnostic dualism are present in much late-twentieth-century Protestantism. These are most visible in low views of redeeming grace; "spiritualizing" salvation issues while taking a casual view of the human condition; creedal and cognitive formulations as a test of membership, with a relatively casual concern for life style evidences of obedience to Jesus; and hierarchical views of institutions, with the corresponding low view of women and children.

Today, the Roman Catholic case for celibacy is based on the desire for devotion of high levels of sexual energy to the service of God. In some orders a review of sexual orientation and appetite prior to ordination is required to establish that the priest to be is not sexually deformed but that he is, indeed, making a "living sacrifice." It is also based on the desire to protect the priesthood from the family vocation tradition, hence drawing, in each generation, a supply of freshly called ministers from the homes of the laity. Celibacy also serves to protect against the potential conflict of priority between family and ministry.

Protestantism returned to the Jewish pattern of a married priesthood, and it was common for the Reformers, most of whom were trained as Roman priests, to marry soon after separating themselves from the Roman church. Zwingli, Luther, Cranmer, and Calvin each married. The Lutheran, Anglican, and Calvinist focus has consistently been on the quality and structure of family life. Each parsonage, rectory, or manse has felt a clear obligation to display a model of the Christian marriage, family, and home.

Even so, in the late twentieth century there is renewed interest in celibacy for the sake of the kingdom of God. It revolves around unusually high risk vocations, ethical considerations regarding population control, and perhaps fear. It will be important to distinguish between celibacy for Jesus' sake and mere singleness experienced by choice or by failure to find a relationship that leads to marriage. Singleness, a rising phenomenon among young adults in North America, tends to be characterized by sexual promiscuity and may serve as a reminder of Jesus' caution that only those who are able should attempt to take the lonely road, and of Paul's concern that those with high sexual appetite should marry rather than burn. The rising number of singles and previously married adults may signify for us the trend toward privatism, toward isolation, and thus away from fulfillment through responsible relationships. Jesus and the creation seem to focus clearly on the high vision of a "one flesh" fulfillment of human personhood. That vision continues to be the standard to define both the cost of celibacy and the despair of being left alone in the world.

Additional Readings

Blenkinsopp, J. *Celibacy, ministry, church.* New York: Herder & Herder, 1968.

Frein, G. H. (Ed.). *Celibacy: The necessary option.* New York: Herder & Herder, 1968.

Hermand, P. *The priest: Celibate or married.* New York: Libra, 1965.

Lea, H. C. *The history of sacerdotal celibacy in the Christian church.* New York: Russell & Russell, 1957.

Thurian, M. *Marriage and celibacy.* London: SCM Press, 1959.

D. M. Joy

See SEXUALITY.

Cerebral Hemispheric Specialization. *See* BRAIN AND HUMAN BEHAVIOR.

Character Disorder. *See* PERSONALITY DISORDERS.

Charcot, Jean-Martin (1825–1893). The leading French neurologist and psychiatrist of his time. Becoming a professor of pathological anatomy in 1878 and later director, Charcot made the Salpêtrière Hospital in Paris the first postgraduate institute for psychiatric education.

Charcot was widely acclaimed for his research in localization of function in cerebral disease and hysteria. By means of his experiments in hypnosis, he distinguished hysterical phenomena from organic neurological disorders. Although he believed, as did most of his contemporaries, that hysteria has a neurological basis and was due to degenerative changes of the brain, he also believed that the symptoms manifested in hysteria were also psycho-

genic in origin and were produced by a specific set of ideas held by the patient. By the same token he reasoned that hysterical symptoms could be cured by ideas. The basic theory of disassociation originated with Charcot's teachings that the stream of consciousness breaks up into diverse elements in cases of hysteria.

In 1885 Freud went to Paris to study with Charcot. He was most impressed by Charcot's innovative approach to hysteria through the use of hypnosis. As a result of Charcot's influence, Freud became deeply interested in the problem of hysteria and came to believe that the phenomenon was genuine. Charcot was able to precipitate hysterical paralysis, seizures, and other symptoms through hypnotic suggestion. Freud returned to Vienna in 1886 with the intention of giving up his laboratory studies so that he might devote all of his time to the clinical practice of neurology.

Because of Charcot's prestige at the Salpêtrière, hypnosis soon acquired wide popularity, together with an equal amount of opposition from the medical profession. Charcot was the first modern physician to make a serious attempt to treat emotional disorders on an individual psychotherapeutic basis.

G. A. Johnston

See HYPNOSIS.

Child Abuse. *See* DOMESTIC VIOLENCE.

Child Custody. The historical and religious background of child custody reveals varied practices and few clear principles. The earliest biblical reference to the Jewish certificate of divorce (Deut. 24:1–2) omits any mention of children. The oldest known copy of such a document also does not mention the status of the children. The New Testament and other early Christian writings continued this silence, although Christ emphatically values children and their welfare (Matt. 18:1–6; 19:14; cf. James 1:27). Subsequently the Talmud advised that mothers routinely receive child custody, although fathers could claim custody of boys age 6 or older. However, Roman law gave fathers sole custody, and this practice influenced English common law, which in turn influenced United States law. Although in 1839 U.S. law began giving equal consideration to parents in deciding custody, by 1900 sole custody was being regularly awarded to mothers. Now emphasis is returning to equal consideration (Salk, 1977). Given this flux of historical approaches and the biblical silence, one might conclude that child custody is

determined better by careful consideration of individual cases than by rigid rules preferring one parent or the other.

Currently about 60% of divorces in America involve children. Although courts settle custody arrangements in only a minority of such cases, these decisions greatly influence the arrangements that are agreed on outside the courts. There are four basic types of arrangements: sole custody, in which one parent receives all the children; split custody, in which one parent receives some of the children and the other parent receives the rest; divided custody, in which one parent has control over the children part of the time and the other parent has control the rest of the time; and joint custody, in which both parents share in care and decisions affecting the children. Visitation rights may be granted and subjected to renegotiation under each form of custody. Over 30 states even have laws protecting visitation rights for grandparents. Child support payments are also subject to various arrangements, yet studies have found that payments average less than half the cost of child raising and are often made irregularly or discontinued (Gardner, 1982).

Although the Uniform Child Custody Jurisdiction Act of 1969 established the child's best interests as the supreme criteria in determining custody, it has devolved on the states to establish the methods of determining these best interests. The Michigan Child Custody Act of 1970 has been considered a model act for specifying the factors to be evaluated: love and emotional ties between parent and child; capacity of parent to give guidance, continue any religious education, and provide food, clothing, medical care, remedial care, and other material needs; continuity of a stable environment; a parent's health and moral fitness; a child's records in home, school, and community; and the child's preference if the child is of sufficient age (Woody, 1978). As the adequacy of judges and lawyers to assess such information has been questioned, the expertise of mental health professionals has been increasingly called on. The American Psychological Association has officially recommended that equal consideration be given to fathers and mothers for custody (Salk, 1977). Nevertheless, despite mental health professionals' strong endorsement of family mediation counseling to agree on custody and of joint custody, the public's response to these new approaches has been less than enthusiastic.

Children's initial reactions to divorce and custody vary greatly with the children's age

and maturity. Those under 6 years old are usually bewildered by divorce, strongly opposed to it, and inclined to blame themselves for it. Their adjustment to custody often progresses through denial with fantasies of their parents' reuniting, apprehension about abandonment or their daily needs going unmet, and increases or decreases in their activity level. Such grieving may resolve itself after a period of depression. Children age 7 to 8 are more likely to think simplistically and blame one parent or the other. However, when such children are interrogated in court hearings, they usually experience stress, feel guilt over rejecting a parent, and may subsequently regret their actions. The most distinctive reaction of children age 9 to 12 is awareness and expression of their own anger. Children age 13 to 18 view the changes in their families more objectively yet may worry about their own sexual expression and future marriages. The majority of children of all ages wish for unrestricted access to the noncustodial parent. Relationships with visiting fathers often improve for sons under 8 years of age but often deteriorate for older sons. Father-son relationships appear to be much more likely to change than father-daughter relationships (Levinger & Moles, 1979; Wallerstein & Kelly, 1980).

Although acute, disruptive reactions to divorce and custody usually subside within 18 months after the separation, other characteristics appear over the long term. National surveys reveal that such single-parent children achieve less academically, are absent from school more, and have more disciplinary problems than do similar children living with two parents. The financial hardships of single parenthood contribute to these problems but do not account for all of them. Faced with so many family issues and often serving as confidants of the single parents, these children may display a pseudo-maturity which masks low self-esteem over inability to adequately handle such adult tasks. The children may experience extra trouble in relationships with authorities and peers. Boys may be uncertain about their own masculinity, yet there is little evidence that these boys are at special risk of becoming homosexual. As adolescents both boys and girls appear prone to act out sexually, especially when confronted with their single parents' sexual activities. Adolescents' compensation for affection in this manner sometimes breeds a later caution about intimacy. The high incidence of remarriage by the divorced parent introduces additional variables in the children's adjustment to stepfamilies, a process in which the children may benefit or suffer (Levinger & Moles, 1979).

Many parents hesitate or feel awkward telling their children about divorce and explaining custody arrangements. Parents may attempt to justify themselves while they vilify their partners. At the very time they must adjust to new relationships with their children parents are also faced with the stress of legal proceedings, economic hardships, and the probable loss of relationships with in-laws. Custodial parents often depend on their children for increased emotional support, a normal process if it is temporary. The custodial parent must also deal with scheduling time to meet children's needs which were once met by the second parent and with introducing the children to the parent's succession of dates with new people. Over half the parents are initially stressed by contact with former spouses during child visitation. The visiting parents often begin with a fear of rejection by the children and with an awkwardness over where to go and what to do on visits. The customary "reasonable visiting hours" are often felt to be too short by visiting parents and children. Visiting parents' depression, guilt, or provocativeness may interfere with the visits. Nevertheless, by 18 months after the separation most of the parents have become more approving of the divorce and more established in some pattern of visitation. The personal adjustments of the parents range from a number who feel a need for therapy to a few who report an increased gratification in parenting (Levinger & Moles, 1979; Wallerstein & Kelly, 1980).

Clergy, educators, and other helpers can assist these parents and children in many ways, especially when the helpers themselves accept that custody arrangements sometimes can be healthier than bad marital environments. Helpers should encourage both parents to together inform children honestly of plans for divorce and custody. The children should understand they are not responsible for either the divorce or efforts to reunite the parents. Helpers can teach parents about the responses of children of different ages, their usual need for relationships with both parents, and the option of mediation rather than adversarial proceedings to settle custody. Noncustodial parents need extra support in their first year of establishing visitation. Custodial parents and children need the support of an extended family, friends, or other adults who serve as role models for the children. Helpers can instill hope that children can adjust well to

custody and that those still disturbed 18 months after a divorce may benefit through therapy.

Unfortunately the quantity of research on children of divorce has exceeded the quality of the research. Caution should be used in inferring cause and effect from studies which merely examine correlations between divorce and other factors. Furthermore, the representativeness of the families studied has limited the generalizability of many findings. Divorce and custody have been studied too long as uniform phenomena when they in fact vary in many significant ways, such as the history and quality of family relationships, the mental health of family members, the age and maturity of the children, the types of custody, family socioeconomic status, external sources of support, and formation of stepfamilies. Research is needed which recognizes these variables and asks specifically what troubles children about custody and what helps them adjust to it.

References

Gardner, R. A. *Family evaluation in child custody litigation.* Cresskill, N.J.: Creative Therapeutics, 1982.

Levinger, G. K., & Moles, O. C. (Eds.). *Divorce and separation.* New York: Basic Books, 1979.

Salk, L. On the custody rights of fathers in divorce. *Journal of Clinical Child Psychology*, 1977, 6(2), 49–50.

Wallerstein, J. S., & Kelly, J. B. *Surviving the breakup.* New York: Basic Books, 1980.

Woody, R. Family counselors and child custody. *International Journal of Family Counseling*, 1978, 6(2), 81–88.

T. J. RUNKEL

See DIVORCE; BLENDED FAMILY.

Child Management. See PARENT TRAINING PROGRAMS.

Child Psychology. See DEVELOPMENTAL PSYCHOLOGY.

Child Therapy. Until the turn of the century child therapy was a neglected field, and even now its potential has hardly been tapped. However, it is becoming increasingly popular with the rise in incidence of childhood disorders and childhood suicides.

Most often child therapy takes the form of play therapy, as play is considered the child's natural means of self-expression. Inhelder and Piaget (1958) believe that the symbolic activity of play serves to meet the affective needs in the young child's life, needs which cannot yet be met through his or her active interchange with the social and physical environment.

The goal of child therapy can be seen as the process of moving the child, through play, from the indirect expression of needs and conflicts, to the direct verbalization of these issues. It is believed that through play and, eventually, talking, the child is helped to become consciously aware of thoughts, feelings, and conflicts. This in turn will eventually lead to a change in his or her behavior and interaction with the environment.

The main role of the therapist in play therapy is to facilitate the child's growth, and this can be achieved in two ways: directive therapy, where the therapist assumes responsibility for guidance and interpretation, or nondirective, where the therapist allows the child to take responsibility and direction during the session. In general, however, the sequence of therapy moves from the passive participation of the therapist in play to a more active involvement. Interpretations by the therapist gradually shift from indirect to direct, and the predominant content of the sessions should move from play to verbalization.

Like most other forms of therapy child therapy, and play therapy in particular, grew out of psychoanalysis. It seems that the majority of child practitioners and theorists base their approaches on these foundations with some modifications and improvements. Child therapy appears to have begun when S. Freud (1909/1955) attempted to alleviate the phobic reaction of "Little Hans" by advising the child's father rather than by treating the child directly. It was only in 1919 that therapy directly with children was introduced. Hug-Hellmuth (1921) used play as her medium for analysis with children, and strongly recommended that play sessions be held in the children's homes with their own toys. However, she did no work with children under the age of 6.

Both A. Freud (1928) and Klein (1932) adapted traditional psychoanalysis for use with children by adopting play into their sessions. Although their use of play is psychoanalytic, they used it also for different purposes. Freud used play as a direct means to communicate with children in therapy and establish a therapeutic alliance between therapist and child. The techniques of free association and dream analysis used with adults were considered foreign to the child's natural way of relating. Thus, she developed a relationship with the child through play and then directed the child to verbalization. At this stage she would encourage free association by the analysis of the child's daydreams. Klein saw play as a direct substitute for verbalization and, therefore, equivalent to the free associations of adult patients. Thus, play activities became the

primary data on which she based her interpretations of the child's unconscious processes. Both these therapists placed great value on the role of transference and the interpretation of what was happening between analyst and child.

Arising directly out of the psychoanalytic model of child therapy, a technique known as structural therapy was developed. This was a goal-oriented approach, in which the therapist would devise a series of specific stimulus situations that the child could then freely play out. Structured play therapy was developed by Levy in the late 1930s and expanded further by Hambridge in 1955. Levy (1938) also developed a technique called release therapy to help children overcome a specific traumatic event. Through this method the event could be restored in the child's play and thereby release the anxiety that the child had been unable to release by himself.

In 1947 Axline developed a nondirective approach to play therapy with children, which was the first major shift from the psychoanalytic view. This method focused on the child as the source of his or her own positive growth and therapeutic direction. The play situation was such that it allowed the child to be himself or herself without facing criticism or pressure to change. Axline's rationale was that play allows feelings to surface so that the child can face them and thereby learn to control them or abandon them. Her model of play therapy parallels the client-centered, or person-centered, approach to adult therapy developed by Rogers.

An offshoot of the Axline school was that of limit-setting therapy introduced by Bixler (1949). He believed that the development and enforcement of limits was the primary vehicle of change in child therapy sessions. This approach contended that limits allowed the child to express negative feelings without hurting others, and also helped the therapist to maintain a positive attitude toward the child. Both the psychoanalytic schools and Axline's nondirective approach have dealt primarily with the child in therapy. Axline (1947) and others sometimes allowed parents to be passively present in the playroom, but the basic tenet has mainly been "children only." In contrast, the behavioral approach to child therapy as propagated by Russo (1964) emphasized the essential nature of parental involvement. Behavioral therapy with children is firmly grounded in operant learning, where the focus is on building up adequate patterns of behavior by using reinforcement or the extinction of undesirable behavior by negative reinforcement. For this to be effective the parents need to be directly involved in therapy. Parental play begins passively, gradually leading to a more active participation by parents, until finally the therapist withdraws and parents take over all play activities. In this way the parents learn how to generalize activity from a simulated environment to everyday life.

Family therapists have emphasized the fact that children exist within a family system, and therefore therapeutic intervention must involve the entire family. Safer (1965) introduced the conjoint play therapy technique where the main focus of each session is on family play rather than discussion. The child is allowed to choose his or her play at random and the parents, siblings, and therapist are required to participate. The role of the therapist in family play therapy is a multifaceted one and includes educator, play facilitator, role model, and player, as well as interpreter when needed. Griff (1983) sees family play therapy as an adjunct to other kinds of intervention techniques rather than a therapeutic entity in and of itself.

References

Axline, V. M. *Play therapy*. Boston: Houghton Mifflin, 1947.
Bixler, R. H. Limits are therapy. *Journal of Consulting Psychology*, 1949, *13*, 1–11.
Freud, A. *Introduction to the technic of child analysis* (L. P. Clark, trans.). New York: Nervous and Mental Disease Publishing, 1928.
Freud, S. Analysis of a phobia in a five-year-old boy. In J. Strachey (Ed. and trans.), *The Standard edition of the complete psychological works of Sigmund Freud* (Vol. 10). London: Hogarth Press, 1955. (Originally published, 1909.)
Griff, M. D. Family play therapy. In C. E. Schaefer, & K. J. O'Connor, (Eds.), *Handbook of play therapy*. New York: Wiley, 1983.
Hug-Hellmuth, H. On the technique of child analysis. *International Journal of Psychoanalysis*, 1921, *2*, 287–305.
Inhelder, B., & Piaget, J. *The growth of logical thinking from childhood to adolescence*. New York: Basic Books, 1958.
Klein, M. *The psycho-analysis of children*. New York: Norton, 1932.
Levy, D. Release therapy in young children. *Psychiatry*, 1938, *1*, 387–390.
Russo, S. Adaptations in behavioural therapy with children. *Behaviour Research and Therapy*, 1964, *2*, 43–47.
Safer, D. Conjoint play therapy for the young child and his parent. *Archives of General Psychiatry*, 1965, *13*, 320–326.

Additional Reading

Schaefer, C. E., & O'Connor K. J. (Eds.), *Handbook of play therapy*. New York: Wiley, 1983.

B. JOSCELYNE

See ADOLESCENT THERAPY.

Christian Association for Psychological Studies.

An international society of Christian professional and paraprofessional persons in the helping professions. It was founded in 1952 in Grand Rapids, Michigan, by a small group of psychologists, psychiatrists, and pastoral counselors and has held an annual convention each year since then. From 1952 to 1974 the organization published annual proceedings of its conventions. From 1974 to 1981 it replaced these proceedings with a quarterly professional journal, *The Bulletin of CAPS*, which in turn was replaced in 1982 by the *Journal of Psychology and Christianity*. The association also publishes monographs in a series called Christian Perspectives on Counseling and the Behavioral Sciences.

The association is committed to the exploration of the relationship between Christian faith and responsible professional life and work, between theological sciences and psychological sciences, between the church and the scientific and academic institutions, and between wholesome spirituality and psychological health. Its purpose is to promote 1) the development and communication of thought regarding theoretical and applied relationships between Christianity and the psychosocial disciplines; 2) fellowship among Christians in psychologically related professions; 3) professional and educational services in relation to the general Christian community; and 4) witness and expression of views and values regarding Christianity and psychology-related issues to the secular community.

Members of the Christian Association for Psychological Studies adhere to a statement of faith which, as presented in the organization's by-laws, requires "belief in God, the Father, who creates and sustains us; Jesus Christ, the Son, who redeems and rules us; the Holy Spirit, who guides us personally and professionally, through God's inspired Word, the Bible, our infallible guide of faith and conduct, and through the communion of Christians." Regular members (including psychologists, psychiatrists, psychiatric nurses, marriage and family counselors, chaplains, pastoral counselors, and social workers) must hold master's degrees in their fields; they have full rights of membership. Associate members (such as students and paraprofessionals) hold restricted rights of membership. An *International Directory* is available for the entire regular membership.

J. H. ELLENS

Christian Counseling and Psychotherapy.

One of the more visible products of attempts to integrate psychology and Christian theology has been the development of a number of systems of counseling and psychotherapy qualifying themselves with the adjective *Christian*. While many have viewed these developments with enthusiasm, some have argued that it is ridiculous to describe psychotherapy as Christian. To do so, they feel, suggests that there is a unique procedure that a Christian should employ for every action. If it is appropriate to talk about Christian psychotherapy, then why not Christian plumbing or Christian penmanship? However, the focus of psychotherapy is obviously much closer to that of Christianity than is the case in activities such as plumbing or penmanship. Also, the value-laden nature of the therapy process (*see* VALUES AND PSYCHOTHERAPY) necessarily makes it either more or less Christian.

A more serious criticism is raised by Bobgan and Bobgan (1979), who view psychotherapy and Christianity as fundamentally incompatible. Contrasting the psychological way to health to the spiritual way, these authors assert that psychotherapy is not a neutral set of scientific techniques but rather a religious system, and a false one at that. The attempt to "Christianize" psychotherapy is therefore seen as a further erosion of the spiritual ministry of the church.

While agreeing that psychotherapy cannot be seen as a value-free set of techniques, a good many Christian mental health professionals and lay persons have seen that this is precisely why it is imperative that Christians subject their theories and practice of therapy to rigorous biblical evaluation. Others have gone further than this, arguing that since existing secular theories of therapy are built upon non-Christian presuppositions, a truly Christian approach must begin (and in some cases end) with the biblical view of persons. Concepts and techniques are then drawn from secular systems if they are found to be compatible with the new foundation. (For a more complete discussion of these and other ways of relating psychology and theology, *see* CHRISTIAN PSYCHOLOGY.)

Current Approaches. One factor that makes it difficult to overview and classify current Christian approaches to therapy is the often unclear line of differentiation between pastoral counseling and other forms of Christian therapy. Hiltner and Coltson (1961) demonstrated that the context of pastoral counseling (usually a church) and the symbols and expectations attached to the role of the clergy all serve to make it somewhat different from therapy offered outside an explicitly pastoral context. However, as pastoral counselors have sometimes moved physically out of the church to secular centers of pastoral psychotherapy, and as some psychotherapists have made a more explicit and visible identification with Christianity and its values, the differences are often less apparent. Since pastoral counseling is dealt with in a separate article, the primary focus here will be nonpastoral therapy.

In a recent summary of the major current approaches to Christian therapy Collins (1980) identifies 17 systems, including 4 that are explicitly pastoral, which he suggests to be distinctively Christian. While these vary tremendously in their sophistication, for the most part they are quite simplistic and fall far short of being a comprehensive system or model of therapy.

Ford and Urban (1963) suggest that a system of therapy needs to include a theory of personality development, a theory of psychopathology, a statement of the goals of therapy, and the conditions and techniques for producing behavior change. These ideals of a comprehensive system are met imperfectly by most, if not all, models of psychotherapy. For example, Gestalt therapy and reality therapy are usually seen to be deficient in terms of their assumptions about both normal and abnormal personality development. Existential therapy has most commonly been judged to be weak in terms of its therapeutic techniques.

The current approaches to Christian counseling are no more adequate in terms of these criteria. In fact, in the majority of cases they are much less comprehensive. For example, relationship counseling (Carlson, 1980) includes assumptions only about the conditions for change, ignoring personality development, psychotherapy, and goals of therapy. Similarly growth counseling (Clinebell, 1979), love therapy (Morris, 1974), and integrity therapy (Drakeford, 1967) all give only very minimal treatment to the processes of normal or abnormal personality development, focusing on goals and techniques of therapy. Only biblical counseling as developed by Crabb (1977) explicitly sets forth a model of personality development and psychopathology and then relates goals and techniques of therapy to this foundation. In this regard it stands as probably the most comprehensive of the existing Christian approaches. However, in comparison to psychoanalysis, client-centered (person-centered) therapy, or behavior therapy, it still must be seen as simplistic and far from a comprehensive model.

To be fair, however, it is important to realize that it was probably not the intention of these authors to present their ideas as a comprehensive system of counseling but rather as an *approach* to counseling. For example, Carlson (1980) states that his intent is to present a style of counseling that is based on Jesus' style of relating. He goes on to assert that "there is no recognized set of techniques that are exclusively Christian" (p. 32) and that there is "no agreed-upon focus of change" (p. 33). His focus, therefore, is on a style of relating, which he feels is the point where a counselor or therapist is most able to be explicitly Christian.

There is one additional point that should be noted in evaluating existing Christian approaches to counseling. With the exception of biblical counseling and nouthetic counseling none of the other approaches have been explicitly developed from Christian theology. Rather, they are adapted forms of existing secular theories which the authors argue are consistent with Christian truth. Thus, we find transactional analysis (Malony, 1980), reality therapy (Morris, 1974), and family systems therapy (Larsen, 1980) at the basis of approaches to therapy which are argued by respective advocates as being basically compatible with biblical theology.

This leads to the question of how these approaches differ from others that are not called Christian. Is Christian psychotherapy anything more than a Christian doing psychotherapy? Vanderploeg (1981) argues that "there is no difference between Christian and non-Christian therapy. The goals are the same, . . . the means are the same. . . . The difference lies not within therapy but within the therapists themselves. One group is Christian and the other is not" (p. 303). Those who have disagreed with this position and have argued for an approach to psychotherapy that is uniquely Christian have usually done so on the basis of either uniqueness in theory or uniqueness in role and/or task. These two major arguments will be considered separately.

The Bible and Personality Theory. For a number of authors the answer to the question of what makes a particular approach to counseling Christian has been quite simple and direct. They assert that Christian counseling is based on the biblical model of personality. In other words, they assume that Scripture contains a unique anthropology and theory of psychotherapy. Adams (1977) argues that the Bible is the only textbook needed for the Christian to learn all that is needed for counseling. He asserts that "if a principle is new to or different from those that are advocated in Scriptures, it is wrong; if it is not, it is unnecessary" (p. 183).

Others (Carter, 1980; Crabb, 1977) have avoided the assumption that nothing useful can be learned about counseling apart from the Scriptures but have retained the expectation that Scripture does contain a unique personality theory and implicit model of counseling. The striking thing, however, is that seldom do these people agree as to just what Scripture suggests to be this unique model. This is reminiscent of Berkouwer's (1962) assertion that the failures to find a system of personality or psychology in Scripture "have only made clear that because of the great variety of concepts used in the Bible, it is not possible to synthesize them into a systematic Biblical anthropology in which the structure and composition of man would be made clear. . . . It is obviously not the intention of the divine revelation to give us exact information about man in himself and thus to anticipate what later scientific research on man offers" (p. 199).

Although the Scriptures should not, therefore, be expected to provide a comprehensive theory of personality or psychotherapy, they obviously do contain a view of persons that is most essential to the individual wishing to provide Christian therapy. In fact, whatever else Christian counseling is, surely it must be based on and informed by these biblical perspectives on human nature. Three biblical themes seem particularly relevant: the unity of personality, creation in the image of God, and the reality of sin. (*See* BIBLICAL ANTHROPOLOGY; COUNSELING AND PSYCHOTHERAPY: BIBLICAL THEMES; COUNSELING AND PSYCHOTHERAPY: THEOLOGICAL THEMES.)

Psychospiritual unity. Historically, attempts to understand what Scripture teaches about human personality have often begun with a discussion of the so-called parts of persons (heart, soul, mind, etc.). In fact, one long-standing debate in biblical anthropology has been over whether man is best seen as a dichotomy (body-soul) or trichotomy (body-soul-spirit). Significantly, this debate is now receding into history, as the consensus of many theologians has increasingly been that the primary biblical emphasis is on the unity of personality. The suggestion is that while Scripture does present a number of characteristics of persons, these were never intended to be interpreted as components or parts. Always they are to be seen as perspectives on the whole.

The implication of this is that man does not *have* a spirit, man *is* spirit. Similarly, man does not have a soul or a body, but *is* soul and *is* body. Further, this means that since we do not have spiritual or psychological parts to our personality, neither do we have problems that are purely spiritual or purely psychological. All problems occur within the common substrate of psychospiritual processes and affect the totality of a person's functioning. The Christian therapist must therefore resist the temptation to artificially separate problems and people into psychological and spiritual parts. Similarly, the Christian therapist cannot ignore a problem just because it has a superficial religious or spiritual appearance.

Created in God's image. The second aspect of the biblical view of persons that needs to be considered is the concept of the *imago Dei.* Although Scripture directly discusses the fact of our creation in God's image in only a few passages, theologians have usually given it a central place in their doctrine of man. Vanderploeg (1981) has similarly argued that it must be seen to be foundational to any understanding of psychotherapy. The fact that we were created in God's image establishes human beings as essentially relational, called to relationship with God and with each other. Viewing the major goal of psychotherapy as helping individuals deal with and enhance their relationships, Vanderploeg then argues that this represents helping people expand and explore the *imago Dei* within them.

The doctrine of the *imago Dei* also helps us understand man's religious nature. Hart (1977) has argued that because we were created in the image of God, our whole life is intended to mirror God. We were created to serve God and to lose ourselves in joyous fellowship with him. By his gift of free will he allows us to choose whether we will, in fact, serve him or not. However, we will serve someone or something, and that is the heart of our religiosity. Religion therefore defines mankind. It is not something added on to an otherwise complete being. It describes our essential meaning, our need to be self-transcendent and to lose ourselves in service to God and others.

The reality of sin. While the fact of our creation in God's image validates the good and noble aspects of human functioning, the Christian view of persons must be balanced by the reality of sin. More than just a tendency to fail to meet our personal expectations or those held of us by others, sin has traditionally been viewed by Christian theology as active rebellion against God and his holy law. This rebellion results in alienation from God, self, and others. These consequences of sin are therefore ultimately, although not necessarily personally or directly, at the root of all our problems.

This reality informs a Christian approach to counseling. If sin is real, then guilt may not always be neurotic. Sometimes it will be real, and forgiveness and repentance will then be necessary. Pattison (1969) states that "the task of the psychotherapist, then, is not to assuage guilt feelings, although that is often a necessary preamble to successful therapy. Rather, the therapist seeks to help the patient see himself and his relationships with others in the light of how the patient violates the relationships to which he is committed. . . . Patients would quite willingly settle for pacification of their superego, but they are reluctant to undergo the pain of changing their pattern of relationships so that they no longer need to feel guilty" (pp. 106–107).

When combined with other equally important biblical themes such as grace, the incarnation, and life after death, the concepts discussed above should be at the foundation of any theory of personality that calls itself Christian. However, they are far from adequate as a complete personality theory. While we therefore may conclude that the Scriptures should not be expected to yield a comprehensive system of therapy, it is clear that they contain perspectives on persons that ought to be foundational for Christian therapy.

Roles and Tasks. The second possible basis for the uniqueness of Christian therapy is the role and tasks of the Christian therapist. In his sociological analysis of psychiatry and religion, Klausner (1964) suggests four different ideological positions based on the differentiation of the task and role in counseling or psychotherapy: reductionist, dualist, alternativist, and specialist. Reductionists maintain that there is only one role and one task. This is because there is only one type of personal problem and only one type of person equipped to address it. Material reductionists view this problem in scientific psychological terms and see the person trained in this system as the only one equipped to handle such problems. Spiritual reductionists view the problem in spiritual or religious terms and see the minister as the only one equipped to handle such problems.

Dualists believe that there are both psychological and spiritual problems. However, they also believe that one qualified person can address both these types of problems. Alternativists are opposite to the dualists, claiming only one basic type of problem but allowing for the two separate roles in the treatment of this problem. Mental health professionals and clergy are viewed as equally valid, functionally equivalent alternative roles, both groups being appropriately involved in the treatment of the one basic problem experienced by people. Finally, specialists argue that there are two discrete tasks and therefore there must be two roles. Ministers and therapists are, respectively, spiritual specialists and psychological specialists, each dealing with one of the two basic types of problems.

All four of these positions are represented in the contemporary Christian counseling literature. The spiritual reductionist position is probably best represented by Adams (1977) and Bobgan and Bobgan (1979). These authors argue that nonorganic psychological problems are really mislabeled spiritual problems. The one person equipped to provide help for such problems is the Christian who draws his mandate, goals, and techniques from the Bible and from this source alone. While this position has been well received by many conservative Protestant pastors, most Christian mental health professionals have viewed it as providing an inadequate account of psychological functioning and a limited understanding of the role of the therapist.

This assumption of one basic type of problem is shared by the alternativists. Benner (1979) represents this position, arguing that all emotional or psychological problems are at core both spiritual and psychological. Because of the fundamental unity of personality, depression is as much an issue of spiritual significance as guilt is a matter of psychological significance. The challenge is for the Christian therapist to view people as spiritual beings regardless of their religiosity and to be sensitive to spiritual dimensions of their functioning. The challenge to the minister is to similarly view a person as a psychospiritual unity and to resist the tendency to either reduce psychological problems to spiritual problems or to ignore psychological problems since these are beyond their competence. This is not to suggest that all ministers or psychotherapists will be adequately equipped to handle the broad range of problems encountered in pastoral counseling and in psychotherapy, but rather to encourage both groups to view problems within the matrix of psychospiritual unity and to respond accordingly.

The alternativist position is attractive to many because it seems to combine something of the simplicity of the reductionist model with a more adequate understanding of psychological processes. Its major weakness lies in its difficulty in explaining what often appear to be differing levels of psychological and spiritual

health within a person. If psychospiritual processes are as unified as argued, the parallels in psychological and spiritual functioning should be even more pronounced than those often seen.

The dualist position is perhaps the most popular in contemporary Christian therapy. Tournier (1963) has been a very influential representative of this position. Minirth (1977) is perhaps an even better representative, arguing that Christian therapy must be responsive to the unique problems of body, soul, and spirit. The first step is therefore the differential diagnosis of the problems of each sphere. Each type of problem is then treated by appropriate and unique methods. Advocates of this position view it as a psychology of the whole person in that the therapist is prepared to respond to both spiritual and psychological problems. Critics view it as more a total treatment approach than a whole-person approach in that the person is not viewed as a whole but rather as the sum of a number of different parts.

A related criticism questions the possibility of differential diagnosis and treatment of spiritual and psychological problems. When is depression a psychological problem and when is it a spiritual problem? Perhaps more difficult to resolve are the technical questions associated with the different tasks required for work with explicitly religious issues versus nonreligious issues. For example, Pattison (1966) asks when the therapist should treat religious questions as grist for the therapeutic mill and when he or she should enter into either a Socratic dialogue or perhaps an explicit instructional role. Also, what are the effects of such movement between roles on transference and countertransference? These questions do not as yet seem adequately answered.

The specialist model has been argued by Pattison (1966), who suggests that different roles are appropriate for the unique tasks of the therapist and minister. The role of the minister, who works as a definer of social and moral values and behavior, is best served by a close social-emotional relationship with the parishioner. In contrast, the task of changing personality argues for the therapist to remove himself from a direct involvement in the patient's social value system and maintain more personal and emotional distance.

The problem with this position is that the distinction which it makes between the goals of therapists and ministers may be exaggerated. Perhaps personality change and changes in social values and behavior are not as discrete as presented. However, if the goals are as represented, Pattison's conclusion as to the role that best supports each set of goals appears helpful.

Goals. What goals should then guide Christian therapy? Ward (1977) suggests that the ultimate goal of Christian therapy must always be to assist the client in becoming more like Jesus Christ. Arbuckle (1975) claims that the desire of the Christian to convert and to change others to his own personal faith appears to be contradictory to general counseling philosophy, which values client self-determination. But are these incompatible? First we must realize that therapy is never value free and that all therapists either implicitly or explicitly communicate their values and personal religion. Therefore, the question is not whether the therapist has certain personal values or goals but how these influence the therapy process. A therapist who uses the therapy relationship to force his or her beliefs on another person is obviously behaving in an unprofessional manner. Christ clearly had the goal of bringing people into relationship with the Father, but his relating to individuals was never characterized by coercion. He clearly was willing to allow people their right of self-determination.

This suggests that while the Christian therapist will have the ultimate spiritual welfare and growth of the client as a part of his concern and goals, he will be willing to work with less ultimate concerns if this is most therapeutically appropriate. Again, Christ's own behavior illustrates this. His frequent healings of individuals apart from an explicit verbal proclamation of the gospel show his concern to meet people at their point of need. His ministry was not always in ultimate dimensions, even though he never lost sight of those ultimate concerns.

Ellens (1980) points out how easy it is for Christian therapists to substitute private philosophy for demandingly sound psychotherapeutic practice. He states that "the practice of the helping professions which is preoccupied with the final step of wholeness, spiritual maturity, will usually short circuit the therapeutic process and play the religious dynamic of the patient or therapist straight into the typical religious patient's psychopathology" (p. 4).

The goals of the Christian therapist will also be guided by the picture of the whole mature person that is presented as the goal of Christian growth in Scripture. Thus, for example, the Christian therapist would seek to encourage the development of interdependence, this in contrast to the autonomy and independence valued in many therapeutic approaches. Other aspects of Christian maturity are also readily translatable into therapeutic goals for the Christian counselor. The Christian therapist will be likely, therefore, to share many of the goals of his secular counterpart. However, the goals that direct Christian therapy should grow out of the overall Christian view of persons discussed earlier.

Techniques. Is Christian therapy unique by virtue of its employment of certain techniques? Are there uniquely Christian or non-Christian techniques? Adams (1977) answers these questions affirmatively and, assuming techniques to be dependent on their presuppositional base, has judged the techniques of secular therapies to be inappropriate for the Christian therapist. The relationship between most techniques and the theory with which they are primarily associated seems, however, to be very loose indeed. One has only to note the very diverse theoretical orientations laying claim to the same techniques to see this point.

Most techniques seem to be neither Christian nor non-Christian. Therefore, they should be judged not on the basis of who first described them but rather their function. Do they support the therapeutic goals? Also, they should be evaluated for their consistency with the overall theoretical framework guiding the therapy. The Christian therapist will thus be cautious of pragmatic eclecticism as the sole guide to which techniques to employ.

Some Christian therapists do employ explicitly religious resources such as prayer, Scripture reading, or even laying on of hands. While any of these interventions may well be appropriate under some circumstances, the responsible therapist would want to understand clearly the significance of using them for the client and the therapy process (*see* RELIGIOUS RESOURCES IN PSYCHOTHERAPY).

Summary. Christian therapy is clearly not a monolithic development. Little consensus exists on such basic questions as the role and task of the therapist and even the question of whether Scripture should be expected to yield a definitive model for Christian counseling. A recent survey of the membership of the Christian Association for Psychological Studies (Cole & DeVries, 1981) indicated that 48% of the Christian mental health professionals responding do not expect Scripture to yield a unified biblical model of counseling. The same percentage do expect such a development. Also, 87% see an eclectic approach as most faithful to Scripture, which they see as consistent with a great diversity of styles of counseling.

If Christian therapy is not simply the application of some biblical theory of personality and therapy, what then is it? This article has suggested that it is an approach to therapy offered by a Christian who bases his or her understanding of persons on the Bible and allows this understanding to shape all aspects of theory and practice. This suggests an ongoing process rather than a finished product. Seen thus, the Christian therapist is not one who practices a certain type of therapy but one who views himself in God's service in and through his profession and who sees his primary allegiance and accountability to his God, and only secondarily to his profession or discipline.

References

Adams, J. E. Lectures in counseling. Nutley, N.J.: Presbyterian and Reformed Publishing, 1977.

Arbuckle, D. S. Counseling and psychotherapy. Boston: Allyn & Bacon, 1975.

Benner, D. G. What God hath joined: The psychospiritual unity of personality. The Bulletin of the Christian Association for Psychological Studies, 1979, 5(2), 7–11.

Berkouwer, G. C. Man: The image of God. Grand Rapids: Eerdmans, 1962.

Bobgan, M., & Bobgan, D. The psychological way/the spiritual way. Minneapolis: Bethany Fellowship, 1979.

Carlson, D. Relationship counseling. In G. R. Collins (Ed.), Helping people grow. Santa Ana, Calif.: Vision House, 1980.

Carter, J. D. Towards a biblical model of counseling. Journal of Psychology and Theology, 1980, 8, 45–52.

Clinebell, H. Growth counseling: Hope-centered methods of actualizing human wholeness. Nashville: Abingdon, 1979.

Cole, D. T., & DeVries, M. The search for identity. The Bulletin of the Christian Association for Psychological Studies, 1981, 7(3), 21–27.

Collins, G. R. (Ed.). Helping people grow. Santa Ana, Calif.: Vision House, 1980.

Crabb, L. J., Jr. Effective biblical counseling. Grand Rapids: Zondervan, 1977.

Drakeford, J. W. Integrity therapy. Nashville: Broadman, 1967.

Ellens, J. H. Biblical themes in psychological theory and practice. The Bulletin of the Christian Association for Psychological Studies, 1980, 6(2), 2–6.

Ford, D. H., & Urban, H. B. Systems of psychotherapy. New York: Wiley, 1963.

Hart, H. Anthropology. In A. DeGraaff (Ed.). Views of man and psychology in Christian perspective. Toronto: Institute for Christian Studies, 1977.

Hiltner, S., & Coltson, L. G. The context of pastoral counseling. New York: Abingdon, 1961.

Klausner, S. Z. Psychiatry and religion. New York: Free Press, 1964.

Larsen, J. A. Family counseling. In G. R. Collins (Ed.), Helping people grow. Santa Ana, Calif.: Vision House, 1980.

Malony, H. N. Transactional analysis. In G. R. Collins (Ed.), Helping people grow. Santa Ana, Calif.: Vision House, 1980.

Minirth, F. B. Christian psychiatry. Old Tappan, N.J.: Revell, 1977.

Morris, P. D. Love therapy. Wheaton, Ill.: Tyndale House, 1974.

Pattison, E. M. Social and psychological aspects of religion in psychotherapy. Insight: Quarterly Review of Religion and Mental Health, 1966, 5(2), 27–35.

Pattison, E. M. Morality, guilt, and forgiveness in psychotherapy. In E. M. Pattison (Ed.), Clinical psychiatry and religion. Boston: Little, Brown, 1969.

Tournier, P. The strong and the weak. Philadelphia: Westminster, 1963.

Vanderploeg, R. D. Imago dei as foundational to psychotherapy: Integration versus segregation. Journal of Psychology and Theology, 1981, 9, 299–304.

Ward, W. O. The Bible in counseling. Chicago: Moody Press, 1977.

D. G. BENNER

See SPIRITUAL AND RELIGIOUS ISSUES IN THERAPY.

Christian Education. See RELIGIOUS CONCEPT DEVELOPMENT.

Christian Growth.
Of keen interest to developmental psychologists of late has been the issue of adult growth and maturation. Traditionally developmental psychology has focused almost exclusively on child and adolescent growth and maturation, with limited attention given to adulthood and old age. Now, however, developmental theorists are very interested in LIFE SPAN DEVELOPMENT, with some seriously studying the implications of human development for the maturation of faith and the quest for human meaning. There is a need for careful reflection on the relationship between spiritual and psychological maturity and the processes of growth in each. Recent efforts by Malony (1978, 1983), Carter (1974a, 1974b), Oakland (1974), and Nouwen (1972) are examples of such integrative thinking.

Mature Religion. A major work by Strunk (1965) has attempted to define mature religion, a task that is needed in order to give a sense of perspective to the maturation of faith and reason. He sees religion as a dynamic organization of cognitive-affective-conative factors, suggesting that the characteristics of mature religion be analyzed in terms of beliefs, feelings, and actions. Mature religious beliefs are characterized by 1) lack of contamination by childish wishes; 2) deep involvement in the world in terms of one's attitudes; 3) a high awareness of one's convictions; 4) the conviction of the existence of a Being greater than oneself; and 5) comprehensiveness and articulation in a manner that serves well in the search for meaning. Religious feelings that are mature, according to Strunk, are characterized by profound experiences of mystical oneness resulting in feelings of wonder and awe, elation and freedom. Mature religious actions are characterized by 1) good integration with the religious factors of the psyche; 2) the presence of love as a comprehensive action with productiveness, humility, and responsibility as natural signs of this love; and 3) a dynamic balance between commitment and tentativeness. Strunk believes that in the analysis of mature religion one will find these factors dynamically organized both horizontally and in depth, yielding a religious motive of master proportion. He argues that individuals will not be "mature" or "immature" but will fall on a continuum somewhere between.

According to Strunk, the questions the Christian helper should be asking are: 1) What am I doing personally to foster my own religious growth and development? 2) What am I doing personally to foster that maturation process in the persons with whom I work? 3) How are the religious organizations and systems of which I am a part facilitating development on a corporate level?

Faith Development. Fowler (1981) has written a seminal work on the stages of development through which the faith aspect of a human life may pass. He is a stage theorist, seeing moral/faith development as progressing through invariant and sequential stages. Fowler is careful to distinguish between religion and faith in discussions of Christian growth and development. Faith should not be confused with creed (i.e., the listing of one's theological beliefs in a creedal statement should not be equated with a confession of faith). Faith is answering the basic question, "On what do you set your heart?" Making certain theological assertions part of the furniture of the mind is not the same as faith. Rather, Fowler sees faith as an active mode of being and committing which has a strong relational component of trust in or loyalty to someone or something else. Such a faith, in its more mature form, becomes imaginative in that it allows the person to see everyday life in relationship to the issues of ultimate meaning and in the broader context. Faith, then, is dynamic, evolving, and relational, not static and cognitive.

Building on a theoretical foundation of Erikson, Piaget, and Kohlberg, Fowler presents a six-stage model of faith development which clearly reflects these significant psychosocial, cognitive, and moral theorists. Stage 1, *intuitive-projective*, is the fantasy-filled, imitative phase in which the child can be powerfully and permanently influenced by other models and their visible faith. Stage 2, *mythic-literal*, is the stage in which the individual

begins to make personal the beliefs, observances, and stories that symbolize belonging to his or her community support system. This is followed by Stage 3, *synthetic-conventional*, which provides a coherent orientation in the midst of a more complex and diverse range of involvements. It synthesizes values and information; it provides a basis for identity and outlook. Also, it is a conformist stage in that it is acutely tuned to the expectations and judgments of others and does not yet have enough independence to construct and maintain an autonomous perspective.

Stage 4, *individualistive-reflective*, is marked by a double development. The self, previously sustained in its identity and faith by a network of significant others, now claims an identity no longer built by the compositive of one's roles or meanings to others. Fowler suggests that "self (identity) and outlook (world view) are differentiated from those of others and become acknowledged factors in the reactions, interpretations and judgments one makes on the actions of self and others" (p. 182). Stage 5, *conjunctive*, involves the integration of much that was suppressed or unrecognized in the interest of Stage 4's self-certainty. Faith in this stage reunites symbolic power with conceptual meaning. Stage 6, *universalizing*, is a disciplined making real and tangible of the "imperatives of absolute love and justice of which Stage 5 has partial apprehensions. The self at Stage 6 engages in spending and being spent for the transformation of present reality in the direction of transcendent actuality" (p. 200). In any of these stages faith development can be facilitated or retarded by the quality of the communities of faith of which one is a part. These potentially nurturing bodies hold great importance for the believer in terms of assisting him or her in the working out of faith.

Fowler has a high view of persons, one that places the quest for meaning at the core of human existence. He also makes a valuable contribution to the discussion of faith development by offering an important perspective on the critical distinction between faith and creed. Much of the research by conservative Christians in the past decades has been crippled by potentially static and overly cognitive notions of faith. Although we must be careful not to see all of faith development in terms of invariant sequential stages or to use a stage model to categorize persons in a legalistic manner, the idea of developmental milestones is invaluable in the study of faith growth and maturation, since it forces us to reflect on those factors that might facilitate or retard the process of deepening one's commitments. Finally, Fowler's model is longitudinal in its outlook, which encourages us to study the maturation process in a participant-observer manner, a study approach increasingly being advocated by integrative thinkers (e.g., Farnsworth, 1981; Van Leeuwen, 1982).

Psychospiritual Wholeness. Summarizing the existing literature on spiritual and psychological health, the following qualities would seem to characterize the psychospiritually whole person: a strong religious faith commitment expressed both individually and corporately; the ability to resist conformity pressures, especially in uncertain situations; a small circle of close, intimate friends; a deep appreciation of God's handiwork; the ability to generate novel solutions to problems (i.e., creativity); self-acceptance and openness toward others; the desire and the ability to confront others openly, directly, and honestly; a good balance between the rational and the emotional; involvement in helping those less fortunate than oneself; interdependence; good decision-making ability; a tolerance for ambiguity in life; the ability to see through the petty conflicts of life; a high level of moral development; and a belief that one's actions make a difference and that one is not simply the victim of forces beyond one's control.

Probably no one meets all these criteria all the time. Certainly we are limited by our own finiteness, fallenness, and humanness. Spiritual maturity, not unlike psychological normality, is a matter of one's batting average. While we can reasonably expect that a deeply internalized faith commitment will enhance a person's psychological well-being, we cannot expect Christians ever to become fully self-actualized and/or sanctified (McLemore, 1982). The doctrine of sin implies the utter impossibility of such perfection. Persons bring to their Christianity their own "raw material." Without a reliable standard to measure anyone's faith except our own, we should be careful not to judge others. Rather, our energies should be geared toward creating opportunities and settings in which spiritual growth and development can be maximized and regression can be minimized. The skillful administration of grace by nurturing Christian communities with a clear sense of direction with regard to faith development will truly be an important part of the process.

References

Carter, J. D. Maturity: Psychological and biblical. *Journal of Psychology and Theology*, 1974, 2, 89–96. (a)

Carter, J. D. Personality and Christian maturity: A process congruity model. *Journal of Psychology and Theology*, 1974, 2, 190–201. (b)

Farnsworth, K. E. *Intergrating psychology and theology.* Washington, D.C.: University Press of America, 1981.

Fowler, J. *Stages of faith.* San Franciso: Harper & Row, 1981.

Malony, H. N. *Understanding your faith.* Nashville: Abingdon, 1978.

Malony, H. N. (Ed.). *Wholeness and holiness.* Grand Rapids: Baker, 1983.

McLemore, C. W. *The scandal of psychotherapy.* Wheaton, Ill.: Tyndale House, 1982.

Nouwen, H. J. M. *The wounded healer.* Garden City, N.Y.: Doubleday, 1972.

Oakland, J. A. Self-actualization and sanctification. *Journal of Psychology and Theology*, 1974, 2, 202–209.

Strunk, O. *Mature religion.* New York: Abingdon, 1965.

Van Leeuwen, M. S. *The sorcerer's apprentice: A Christian look at the changing face of psychology.* Downer's Grove, Ill.: Inter-Varsity Press, 1982.

R. E. Butman

See Faith; Religious Health and Pathology.

Christian Psychology. Although the term is not widely used at the present (for an exception see Myers, 1978), Christian psychology refers to a movement within psychology which seeks to integrate the evangelical understanding of biblical doctrine with scientific and applied aspects of psychology. The critical focus of the movement is to reconceptualize psychology in such a way as to be consistent with the tenets of an orthodox, Protestant cosmology and anthropology. However, the general purpose is broader than purely cognitive reconceptualization; theological and psychological insights are applied to bolster one's personal faith.

The Desacralization of Psychology. The past century of psychology has witnessed the gradual but complete secularization of concepts about human personality which had theological origins (Roback, 1952). During the first half of the twentieth century psychologists were more disposed to discuss sexual matters (unheard of in the Victorian period of 1830–1900) than religion (except for the noble examples of James and Allport). In spite of recent antipathy between psychologists and theologians there is a close historical link between them. The Latin term *persona*, from which the English term *personality* developed, denoted both the mask used to indicate a particular theatrical role and the real self or actor. *Persona* suggested that the inner nature may be split from outward action. But the Latin word *religio* meant a binding or fastening, especially in the form of reverence or fear of a more powerful being. Thus the person had internal integrity because of the religious nature of personality (Oates, 1973).

The ancient Greeks used two words to portray the essence of human nature. *Psychē* originally meant the breath or spirit which distinguished the animate from the inanimate. Later it developed connotations of soul and mind, and the study of psychology ensued. *Pneuma* was a close parallel to psyche; *pneuma* referred to life, but in its relationship to the eternal. From the study of the *pneuma* came theology; religion was a human expression of *pneuma*. The secularization of *psychē* inevitably led to the development of psychology as a discipline distinct from philosophy and theology.

The language of psychology has been desacralized at other points. The Hebrews used the word *nepeš* to describe the whole person, a union of inner and outer aspects of *lēb* and body. In the old Testament *nepeš* is commonly translated *soul*. However, when *soul* gradually developed connotations of transcendency and eternity, psychologists adopted the term *self* to refer to human wholeness. Self to the holistic psychologists is essentially the rebirth in a desacralized form of the Hebraic concept of soul. Secularization of will is recounted by Roback (1952) and Kantor (1963).

The Integration of Psychology and Christianity. Christian psychology originates from a drive to construct a more adequate psychology by reconnecting the severed relationships with theology; the drive embodies a desire to adopt the best of science and faith. The goal is to integrate faith and reason by linking theology and science. The reassertion of biblical orthodoxy as the basis of one's science is a reaction to modern psychology's endorsement of the religion of secular humanism (Collins, 1977; Vitz, 1977). Although the relationship between theology and psychology has been strained and one of mutual suspicion and denigration, this need not be the case (Ellison, 1972).

The attempt to integrate psychology and theology strives for "the unity of truth." The task of integration involves an explicit relating of truth gleaned from general or natural revelation to that derived from special or biblical revelation, of interrelating knowledge gained from the world and knowledge gained from the Word. Of critical importance are the issues regarding the nature of reality (metaphysics) and the nature of knowledge (epistemology). The conflict between science (e.g., psychology) and theology at this point stems from variations in original assumptions. The naturalistic, objective, and inductive biases of scientists are juxtaposed to the supernaturalistic, subjective, and deductive premises of the theologian. The integration movement offers a rapprochement by proposing the adoption of two premises: 1) God is the source of all truth no matter *where* it is found; 2) God is the source of all truth no matter *how* it is found (Timpe, 1980).

To the integrationist, natural revelation supports special revelation instead of being a rival methodology. That is, if God is consistent (i.e., immutable) as the Scriptures suggest (e.g., Mal. 3:6), then knowledge based in revelation should parallel and complement that derived from reason. Both will complement that founded in replication and observation. Underlying this approach is a faith statement common to scientist and theologian alike: the laws that govern the operation of the world are discoverable.

Models of integration. Those who seek to understand the relationship between psychology and theology employ one of four strategies (Carter & Narramore, 1979). Some models of integration have sacred and secular versions. Perhaps the oldest and most familiar description is the *against* model, in which psychology and theology are portrayed as mortal enemies. Each defines one exclusive approach to truth (empiricism vs. revelation), one cause for human discomfort and misfortune (environmental conditioning vs. sin), and one solution to problems (psychotherapy vs. salvation). Freud and Ellis espoused a secular version of this approach; Adams adheres to the sacred version.

The *of* model (e.g., the psychology of religion) holds that human beings are moral-spiritual creatures not reducible to a collection of naturalistic forces. Humans are fundamentally good, and whatever pain is experienced is attributed to environmental or psychological factors rather than sin. Psychological insights aid persons in spiritual development. In the secular version human personality tends to be deified, while in the sacred version the divine is desupernaturalized. The works of James, Allport, and Hiltner exhibit this mode of thought.

In the *parallels* model psychology and theology are held to be separate disciplines with separate goals, contents, and methods of inquiry to describe separate dimensions of human nature. There is a dualism in which spiritual dimensions constitute the province of theology, while physical and social dimensions concern psychology. Psychological insights parallel those of theology, but neither purports to offer a comprehensive description of human totality. In one respect psychology and theology have chosen to limit the focus of their study; both attempt to conceptualize the given aspects of human nature.

Etymologically, the word *psychology* has origins in two Greek words, *psychē* and *logos*, so that literally psychology is human words about life and personality. Simlarly, the term *theology* comes from the Greek *theos* and *logos*. Theology is human words about God. Individuals who favor the parallels model suggest that psychology and theology are theory and conceptualization, regardless of what evidence each is based on. Psychology and theology are free to change when new facts are discovered or when old facts are reinterpreted. Humans are not obliged to act as psychologists have constructed them, nor is God obligated to correspond to theological ideas.

Moreover, the parallelists have defined different goals. Psychology is often described as the science which seeks to understand, predict, and control behavior. The choice of following the scientific model has had the effect of limiting study to regular, lawful, and aggregate events. Theology has sought to reason and deduce the nature of God and his laws aided regularly by divine revelation via the Scriptures. The focus in theology is often on unique, one-time events (e.g., incarnation, miracles). Psychology may be described as a science that tells the "how" of personal motivation and social relationships, whereas theology explains the "why" of creation and redemption (Jeeves, 1976; Timpe, 1980). Psychology is horizontal, theology is vertical in perspective. Each discipline couches its insights in a separate set of linguistic conventions, with parallels between conventions being mentioned (e.g., personality theory and anthropology, psychopathology and hamartiology, developmental psychology and soteriology). Furthermore, the parallel model holds that the Bible was inspired to be not a science book but rather history (i.e., the story about God's redemptive efforts to save his people). As history it contains all truth necesary for an individual's salvation.

According to Carter and Narramore (1979), the *integrates* model is to be preferred, since it is the most comprehensive. Psychology is not treated as a system of thought about human nature but rather about the actuality of created humanness. In like fashion theology is more than a body of thought about God; it takes on the character (or caricature) of cosmology. Knowledge is not pigeonholed into discipline-defined units, but all sources of knowledge are interrelated into one body of truth. Of necessity, the integrationist must be competently knowledgeable in both fields, and then be able to transcend the traditional limits of each. Tournier seems to have been able to accomplish those ends in much of his writing.

Levels of integration. The various models of integration may be applied at several levels (Larzalere, 1980). The broadest level of analysis is cosmological, in which assumptions about one's world view are articulated. These are in essence faith statements, since neither psychology nor theology can prove the correctness of their assertions about the nature of reality. Embedded within the world view is the second level of special assumptions; those assumptions pertain to content (e.g., human personality) and approved methodologies. Most of the tension existing between psychology and theology occurs at these two levels.

Foundational presuppositions in large measure determine the shape of the superstructure (i.e., theory). The central and nonnegotiable assumption for the Christian psychologist is that God exists and is Creator-source of all truth and power (i.e., omniscience and omnipotence). Furthermore, God has chosen to reveal to humans, individually and collectively, some of his nature through the created world, through the inspired Scriptures, and through Jesus Christ as agent of creation and redemption. Various positions are taken on a number of peripheral assumptions. The central assumption deals with the *Christian* in Christian psychology while the peripheral assumptions may reflect Christian *psychologies*. The peripheral assumptions deal with such issues as the mind-brain relation, the nature-nurture controversy, the priority of general or special revelation, the extent of the pervasiveness of sin, and determinism and freewill; they may distinguish one integration from another. Integrationists take a position on each, however implicit or explicit, but peripheral assumptions remain secondary and subservient to the supernatural one.

The third level of analysis is that of theoretical proposition and hypothesis. The fourth and final level constitutes data. While conflict between psychology and theology may exist at these levels, it is not as pronounced as at the first two levels.

Examples of integration. Conflict between psychology and theology is most prominent at the world view and special assumptions levels. The credo of the secular psychologist is: "I believe in the efficacy of empiricism, the divinity of determinism, the reality of relativism, the revelation of reductionism, and the necessity of naturalism" (adapted from Collins, 1977). Collins (1977) spent considerable time and effort addressing the issues of world view and special assumptions. He found the traditional behavioral assumptions of empiricism, determinism, relativism, reductionism, and naturalism problematic in an integration of psychology and theology (*see* PSYCHOLOGY, PRESUPPOSITIONS OF). Since these do not correspond well with traditional theological tenets, he suggested the faulty assumptive foundations be rebuilt. He proposed an expanded empiricism that allows God to reveal himself through sense impression and other means. Expanded empiricism permits more subjectivity in observation and knowledge than does the more radical version of scientism (Bufford, 1981).

In lieu of the traditional behavioral assumption of determinism, Collins substituted freedom and determinism. His solution was a soft determinism where the laws of the universe limit the number of alternatives, yet within those alternatives the individual is free to choose the course of action. The alternatives are not equally attractive or probable, because heredity and past environmental influences affect their relative likelihood. Among direct influences on behavior the supernatural work of the Holy Spirit and angels must be included.

As a replacement for unlimited relativism Collins upheld a biblical absolutism, in which the individual searches the Scriptures for absolutes. Absolutes as general principles guide behavior and increase knowledge. Where the Bible appears to be silent, value judgments are deduced from biblical principles.

A modified reductionism is also proposed, permitting the individual to gain further information about nature, but not asserting that nature itself can be reduced to "nothing but" basic elements. Christian supernaturalism is inserted in the place of naturalism. There is a sovereign God who created the natural order, and his laws account for the orderliness of nature. However, God is a transcendent being, not bound to the created order.

While the work of Collins was at the world-view level, Koteskey (1980, 1983) addressed the general theoretical level. The integrative mechanism he employed is a variant of Schaeffer's (1968) view that God is personal and infinite. Humans are like God in having personality (soul, spirit, etc.), but a chasm exists between God, the Creator and created mankind relative to infiniteness. Thus the personal dimension emphasizes the ways in which humans mirror God's image and are different from animals, while the infinite aspects point to human-divine differences and a commonality with animals. In this way

perspectives and ideas from structuralism, Gestalt psychology, and humanistic psychology illustrate likenesses between the divine and human. Behaviorism and functionalism point to the similarities of humans and animals, while psychoanalysis marks how unlike God humans are.

Koteskey's (1983) position is not that psychology and theology need to be integrated, but that theology (i.e., Schaeffer's discussion of the personal and infinite dimensions) should serve to integrate a fragmented secular psychology. The content areas in psychology are ordered into this pattern. For example, physiological studies in structure, motivation, emotion, sensation, and conditioning describe similarities between humans and animals. Godlikeness is seen in the areas of perception, cognition, and cognitive aspects of motivation, emotion, and social relationships. Psychiatric disorders can be ordered similarly. Organic mental disorders, disorders appearing in childhood or adolescence, somatoform disorders, phobic disorders, psychosexual disorders, and anxiety disorders are at the animal end of the continuum. Personality disorders, paranoid disorders, schizophrenic disorders, narcissism, and affective disorders are failures to achieve human potential at the Godlike end of the continuum.

At the general theoretical level Bufford (1981) examined behavioral psychology and its relation to Scripture. His basic position is that there is little in behavioral psychology and its practice (i.e., methodological behaviorism as a way of knowing and changing) to contradict current biblical understanding. However, when behavioral psychology takes a more radical view (i.e., radical or metaphysical behaviorism), the naturalistic and reductionistic premises pose problems at the philosophic level for a classical theologian. This tension is due in large measure to Platonic dualism, with an exaggeration of naturalism by Enlightenment scientists and a corresponding exaggeration of supernaturalism by theologians of the Middle Ages. Neither exaggeration is consistent with the biblical record.

Bufford conceptualized causation of events in an intriguing way. The two causes, divine and natural, could either be present or absent. When these are combined into a 2×2 matrix, 4 possible types of causation emerge. When both divine and natural causes are absent, there is chaos. When divine cause is absent but natural cause is present, a naturalistic explanation is given. In the event that a supernatural cause is present and the natural cause is absent, there is said to exist a supernatural explanation or miracle (e.g., creation *ex nihilo*). Providential explanation is the divine employing natural mechanisms as sources of causality. The Christian scientist or psychologist must endorse the providential explanation, since chaos and miracles are not predictable nor are they recurring events. Natural explanations must also be ruled out on the basis of the assumption of divine causation.

Providential explanations have an impact on how human freedom is construed. In the behavioral literature freedom is not so much an attribute of human nature as a behavior. It is not the absence of control, but it is absence of *effective* (most often aversive) control. An individual acts free when he removes himself from an aversive control situation. In this way freedom is predictable in that an observer could predict an individual's behavior without causing it, simply by foreknowing the nature of freedom. God can foreknow an individual's freeing actions without causing the action.

Human freedom is a constrained or limited freedom, wherein the limits are determined by divine intervention or providential process. The individual is free to choose only from those options known. Only God as a sovereign, infinite being has "free will in the sense of unhampered or uncaused choice" (Bufford, 1981, p. 54). Bufford contends that the behavioral view expressed above is consistent with the Westminster Confession of Faith.

Several writers have attempted to present Christian perspectives on specific propositions or hypotheses. Both Custance (1980) and Jones (1981) argue that there is biblical and scientific support for a dualistic solution to the mind-brain problem. Their hypothesis is a modernization of Cartesian interactionism. Citing the works of the neurosurgeon Penfield, the physiologist Eccles, the brain researcher Sperry, and the philosopher Popper, they assert that consciousness cannot be equated with brain state and that full humanness, in the biblical perspective, is described only when physical and mental dimensions of the person are recognized. Furthermore, human dignity has its fullest meaning when the physical and spiritual (i.e., mental) dimensions are viewed as God's creation. However, Myers (1978) reviewed the same literature and holds a monistic (i.e., holistic) view of human nature in which mental conditions (e.g., thoughts, feelings, and beliefs) are identical to brain states.

At the data level of analysis Myers (1978, 1980) has reported a remarkable parallel between experimental studies in social psychol-

ogy and biblical concepts. It seems that pride (i.e., undue concern for self) is manifested in a number of social psychological processes of self-serving biases. From a theological point of view pride would distort the way the individual responds to experience in the world. Similar processes are reported in laboratory experiments. Persons attribute positive consequences to their own good action but blame environmental forces such as fate or task difficulty for bad behavior or outcomes. The individual asserts that he had freedom and responsibility when the outcomes of acts are good, but avoids personal freedom and responsibility when outcomes or behaviors are bad. Self-serving biases induce individuals to change attitudes and values to be consistent with behavior, because attitudes are derived from behavior. Self-serving biases are present in the way one makes causal attributions in altering memory to fit one's basic beliefs, in overreliance on anecdotal evidence, in overestimating the accuracy of one's own perception, and in "I knew it all along" after-the-fact analysis.

In addition to the theoretical and conceptual works of the type cited above, there is a plethora of applied works from Christian perspectives. These address a multitude of topics such as self-esteem, child rearing and discipline, personality development, husband-wife relations, and counseling.

Christian psychology, or the movement to integrate psychology and theology, meets all the criteria to be considered a school or system. Its general perspective and theoretical assumptions have been articulated. It is an explicit institutional goal in graduate psychology programs at Fuller School of Psychology (Fuller Theological Seminary), Rosemead School of Professional Psychology (Biola University), Psychological Studies Institute (affiliated with Georgia State University), and Wheaton college. Professional organizations recognize and emphasize aspects of integration and interface of psychology and religion: the Christian Association for Psychological Studies, American Scientific Affiliation, and Psychologists Interested in Religious Issues (Division 36 of the American Psychological Association). Several professional journals publish integration works—e.g., *Journal of Psychology and Theology, Journal of Psychology and Christianity, Journal of the American Scientific Affiliation.* Integration is an important activity in a number of Christian liberal arts colleges. The integration of psychology and theology has also had an impact on seminaries, and is seen in recent rises in pastoral psychology and pastoral counseling programs.

References

Bufford, R. K. *The human reflex: Behavioral psychology in biblical perspective.* San Francisco: Harper & Row, 1981.

Carter, J. D., & Narramore, B. *The integration of psychology and theology.* Grand Rapids: Zondervan, 1979.

Collins, G. R. *The rebuilding of psychology.* Wheaton, Ill.: Tyndale House, 1977.

Custance, A. C. *The mysterious matter of mind.* Grand Rapids: Zondervan, 1980.

Ellison, C. W. Christianity and psychology: Contradictory or complementary? *Journal of the American Scientific Affiliation,* 1972, 24, 131–134.

Jeeves, M. A. *Psychology and Christianity.* Downers Grove, Ill.: Inter-Varsity Press, 1976.

Jones, D. G. *Our fragile brains.* Downers Grove, Ill.: Inter-Varsity Press, 1981.

Kantor, J. R. *The scientific evolution of psychology* (Vol. 2). Chicago: Principia Press, 1963.

Koteskey, R. L. *Psychology from a Christian perspective.* Nashville: Abingdon, 1980.

Koteskey, R. L. *General psychology for Christian counselors.* Nashville: Abingdon, 1983.

Larzalere, R. E. The task ahead: Six levels of integration of Christianity and psychology. *Journal of Psychology and Theology,* 1980, 8, 3–11.

Myers, D. G. *The human puzzle.* San Francisco: Harper & Row, 1978.

Myers, D. G. *The inflated self.* New York: Seabury, 1980.

Oates, W. E. *The psychology of religion.* Waco, Tex.: Word, 1973.

Roback, A. A. *History of psychology and psychiatry.* New York: Philosophical Library, 1961.

Schaeffer, F. A. *The God who is there.* Downers Grove, Ill.: Inter-Varsity Press, 1968.

Timpe, R. L. Assumptions and parameters for developing Christian psychological systems. *Journal of Psychology and Theology,* 1980, 8, 230–239.

Vitz, P. C. *Psychology as religion.* Grand Rapids: Eerdmans, 1977.

R. L. Timpe

Circumstantiality.

Speech that is indirect and encumbered with unnecessary details and parenthetical remarks. Unlike Loosening of Associations, where there is an absence of a meaningful connection between the various parts of the sentence, circumstantial speech is organized and the speaker never loses sight of the original focus of the conversation. The problem is that the speaker fails to suppress extraneous thoughts and the essential message gets lost. Circumstantiality is frequently seen in schizophrenia and compulsive personality disorder. It also sometimes occurs in epileptic dementia.

Clang Association.

Nonsensical talk on the basis of an association of words or ideas by superficial sound similarity. In manic states and schizophrenia the rapid speech is considered part of a thought disturbance (*see* Flight of Ideas). Without any apparent meaning the individual carries on a one-way conversation; for example, he may say, "We went to the land ... there was a band ... bang, bang ... dam broke ... we caught kites."

Clark, Walter Houston (1902–).

Known for his contributions to the advancement of the scientific study of religion and, more specifically, for his work in the psychology of religion.

Clark took his Ph.D. degree at Harvard University in 1944, studying under Allport. His doctoral dissertation was a study of the moral rearmament doctrine of the Oxford Group, a social movement of interest both to social psychology and to religious studies. Using a case study approach, Clark studied the manner in which the movement contributed to the personal religiosity of its members. He served as professor of psychology and dean of the Hartford School of Religious Education at the Hartford Seminary Foundation and later as professor of the psychology of religion at Andover Newton Theological Seminary, from which he retired in 1969.

Clark was one of the founders of the Society for the Scientific Study of Religion, serving as a member of the editorial board of the *Journal for the Scientific Study of Religion* and serving the society in various capacities, including its presidency in 1964. He also chaired the committee on research of the Religious Education Association, which convened a commission in 1961 to provide methodological guidelines for researchers of religious phenomena. The publication resulting from the work of this commission has been widely influential in guiding empirical research in the last two decades.

Clark has produced many articles and book reviews in the area of psychology of religion, but he is best remembered for three books. The first, *The Oxford Group, Its History and Significance* (1951), was an elaboration of his doctoral dissertation. *The Psychology of Religion* (1958) was a textbook updating and reconceptualizing the whole field. This book also presented a concerted plea for greater methodological rigor in psychology of religion research. His best known book, *Chemical Ecstasy: Psychedelic Drugs and Religion* (1969), was also his most controversial. In this book he explored the relationship between religious and drug-induced experience. Clark's arguments in support of the value of mystical experience, including drug-induced mystical states, were provocative and led to accusations that the book was merely a defense of Timothy Leary and illicit drugs.

L. S. Shaffer

Classification of Mental Disorders.

For the Christian the concept of mental disorder is closely associated with the disorder introduced into the whole of nature as a result of the fall. As Berkouwer (1962) has observed, the fall left each human being thereafter living in an imperfect body within an imperfect environment. Other consequences of the fall include the disrupted relationship of man to God, to other people, and to himself. Paul classifies some of the resulting disorders in 1 Corinthians 6 and Galatians 5. His list includes adultery, idolatry, hatred, envy, murder, and drunkenness.

The Christian is forced, therefore, to admit this personal and universal state of disorder. Everybody is disordered to some degree. The mental disorders identified and classified by psychology or psychiatry are a subset of this total disorder. Yet not all personal disorder, even mental disorder, warrants classification as a clinical disorder. *DSM-III* defines a mental disorder as: "a clinically significant syndrome or pattern that occurs in an individual and that is typically associated with either a painful symptom (distress) or impairment in one or more important areas of functioning (disability). In addition, there is an inference that there is a behavioral, psychological, or biological dysfunction, and that the disturbance is not only in the relationship between the individual and society" (p. 6).

Ethical and Scientific Accountability. In classifying mental disorders, the classifier should be precise both from a scientific need for reliability and from an ethical imperative not to apply demeaning labels to people. One ethical and scientific practice, frequently recommended but not easily regulated, is to assume psychological normality until able to justify a diagnosis of mental disorder. One should assume the person to be normal and prove this assumption wrong. It is true that some character styles put persons out of order with themselves, others, and God. In fact, some diagnostic systems focus on character defects (Millon, 1969, 1981). However, the usual meaning of mental disorder is an extreme of mental, social, or interpersonal style. Such extreme labels require scientific specificity and ethical caution when applied to persons.

One needs to keep in mind the purpose of classification in the scientific and mental health professions. The purpose of labeling persons according to a diagnostic system is to construct treatment interventions appropriate and effective with that specific type of problem. Unfortunately, it is tempting to see the diagnosis as the end rather than a means to an end. If a diagnosis does not lead to appropriate treatment, precise labeling is of no real value to the client. The diagnostician has the respon-

sibility to be accurate in diagnosis and then to prescribe the best available treatment for that disorder.

Adequate data collection is also obviously essential for making responsible diagnostic judgments. Psychodiagnostic systems differ on the data from which a diagnosis is drawn. Most, however, gather data from cross-time, multidimensional, multimeasure testing and observation of a client's behavior. Comprehensive diagnostic assessments may use a battery of psychological tests; structured interviews with the client, family and significant others; and observations of the client made by various professionals over a period of time.

History and Development of Classification Systems. Classifications of mental disorders date as far back as 2600 B.C. when the syndromes of hysteria and melancholia appear in Egyptian literature. However, the understanding and classification of psychopathology developed very little over the next 4,000 years (*see* ABNORMAL PSYCHOLOGY). The first official system developed in the United States was prepared for the census in 1840. It contained only one category for all mental disorders, lumping together the mentally retarded and insane.

The first major effort at classification of mental disorders was done by the German psychiatrist Kraepelin. His *Textbook of Psychiatry* was published in 1883 and presented his earliest attempts at classification. Here he identified two basic disorders: dementia praecox (schizophrenia) and manic-depressive psychosis. His book underwent eight revisions over the next 40 years and his classification efforts came to be the basis of most later developments in psychodiagnostic classification.

World War II brought a need for more precision in diagnosis for the purpose of screening draftees and for developing syndrome-specific treatments for those soldiers suffering from mental disorders. From 1940 to 1951 the Standard Nomenclature of Diseases of the Psychobiological Unit was the major system used. It had three major categories: mental deficiencies; mental disorders including psychosis, psychoneurosis, and primary behavioral disorder; and organic diseases affecting mental functioning.

The first *Diagnostic and Statistical Manual* (*DSM-I*) of the American Psychiatric Association was published in 1952. It provided the standard nomenclature in the mental health professions until 1968. *DSM-I* was collected and codified by one psychiatrist. Its revision, *DSM-II* in 1968, was the work of a committee of psychiatrists. Both *DSM-I* and *DSM-II* were developed by only one of the mental health professions (psychiatry) and assumed predominantly a disease model of psychopathology. Both *DSM-I* and *DSM-II* were also qualitative/subjective rather than quantitative/objective in their major focus.

DSM-III (1980), the most recent revision of this classification system, is a major departure from the preceding two efforts. It was compiled mainly by psychiatrists, but also drew contributions from psychologists, social workers, and nursing specialists. Departing from a disease model of psychopathology (*see* MENTAL ILLNESS, MODELS OF), *DSM-III* became more objective, quantitative, and descriptive. Finally, and most noticeably, *DSM-III* requires evaluation on several axes, thus viewing mental disorders as multidimensional phenomena rather than single-disease entities. Even with these improvements, work on *DSM-IV* is already beginning.

DSM-III includes more than 200 specific disorders organized into 18 major groups: disorders usually first evident in infancy, childhood, or adolescence; organic mental disorders; substance use disorders; schizophrenic disorders; paranoid disorders; other psychotic disorders; affective disorders; anxiety disorders; somatoform disorders; dissociative disorders; psychological factors affecting physical condition; personality disorders; specific developmental disorders; factitious disorders; psychosexual disorders; adjustment disorders; conditions not attributable to a mental disorder; and other disorders of impulse control.

A complete diagnostic evaluation, according to *DSM-III*, requires that an individual be evaluated on several axes, each of which represents a different class of information. *DSM-III* has five such axes, the first three constituting the official diagnosis and the last two being research scales. Axis I contains most of the major clinical syndromes, excluding only personality disorders and developmental disorders which are coded on Axis II. Axis II is also used for other personality traits even in the absence of a personality disorder. The rationale for the separation of these two axes is that it ensures that consideration is given to the presence of disorders that are frequently overlooked when attention is focused on the more apparent disorder listed on Axis I. The clinician may list multiple diagnoses on either Axis I or II, in which case they are listed in estimated order of treatment.

Axis III is used to record medical conditions potentially relevant to understanding or treating a client. Once again, multiple diagnoses are permitted. Axes IV and V are the research scales related to the client's life stressors and level of functioning in the recent past. Axis IV consists of a seven-point ordinal scale for ranking levels of severity of stressors within the past year of the client's life. Adult and child/adolescent examples of stressors are given as an aid in reliability. Axis V is a seven-point ordinal scale designed to indicate the highest level of adaptive functioning in the past year. Three areas of functioning are considered: social relations, occupational functioning, and use of leisure time. This information frequently has prognostic value and is therefore important in treatment planning.

Throughout *DSM-III* specific criteria are outlined which must be present or which rule out giving a specific diagnosis. Frequently five out of eight symptoms must be present and must have been present for more than six months or a year in order to legitimately permit using a mental disorder label. A complete DSM-III classification for an adult client in a partial hospitalization program might look like this:

Axis I. Major Affective Disorder, Bipolar Mixed, in remission (controlled with $LiCO_3$)—Secondary.

Axis II. Paranoid Personality Disorder; Fears of Homosexuality—Primary.

Axis III. No significant medical problems.

Axis IV. Severity of Psychosocial Stressors: 3—Mild; argument with family; does not live with family.

Axis V. Highest Level of Adaptive Functioning in the Past Year: 5—Poor; Trouble keeping friends; held two jobs for three to four weeks each during past year.

The *DSM-III* diagnostic system affords a fairly succinct view of the client at a number of levels without oversimplifying the biological-cognitive-emotional-social complexity of the human condition. Inasmuch as it is a secular system, no attempt is made to determine the client's moral or spiritual functioning. One might wish to add axes VI and VII with specifically ordered ranking scales for moral and spiritual functioning.

Alternate Approaches. Although *DSM-III* has rapidly become the major classification system currently used in North America, it is not the only one. Each of the alternatives grew out of a different set of assumptions about mental disorder. Therefore, each reflects a critique of *DSM-III*. Some systems infer cause in the etiology of psychopathology, some are merely descriptive of psychopathological behavior, and some are really little more than a general view of psychopathology.

Biophysical systems. The basic notion in these systems is that disorders in genetic code or biophysiology are the key elements of mental disorder. Theorists in this tradition usually do not claim that biophysiological explanations will account for all mental disorder, but often do suggest that far more is determined by biophysiological phenomena than our current level of science can identify. This tradition has made key contributions to neurology, psychoneurology, and psychopharmacology.

Theorists in this tradition differ from the symptom-descriptive system of *DSM-III* in that they focus on organic causality in attempting to construct a diagnostic system. The focus is on what biophysical theorists would call primary causes of mental disorder, rather than on the more confused array of secondary symptoms which *DSM-III* attempts to classify. The appeal of such an argument is considerable. The question remains as to ultimately how much psychopathology can be explained by such biological reductionism.

Developmental systems. Erikson's eight stages of life (*see* PSYCHOSOCIAL DEVELOPMENT) is a good example of the psychodiagnostic systems in this category. Here the basic notion is that the degree of mental disorder is the degree of difference between chronological age–appropriate behavior and the client's current behavior. For example, an 8-week-old child's inability fully to distinguish self from environment and fully to trust the environment is not pathological. However, a 21-year-old's inability to consistently distinguish self from objects and persons in the environment and his struggle with basic trust issues is very pathological.

These systems offer a natural observational and conceptual outline on which to build a theory of psychopathology. In comparison to the atheoretical approach of *DSM-III*, proponents of developmental systems of diagnosis feel that their theory permits better predictive value and, even more importantly, provides guidelines for therapeutic intervention.

Phenomenological and humanistic systems. This loose collection of approaches is associated with phenomenological, existential, and humanistic traditions within psychology. A basic tenet of these systems is that each individual is unique and that attempts to know (diagnosis) this unique individual must not rob him of his uniqueness. Grouped classification systems such as *DSM-III* are eschewed, since

they are viewed as treating individuals as categories or diseases. Humanistic psychologists argue that the task of diagnosis is for the therapist to experience the world as closely as possible to the way the individual client experiences it. They argue that to achieve successful treatment individual phenomenology is needed. Their challenge is to view clients as people and not as clinical entities. This tradition has been an important corrective balance in psychodiagnostics.

Cognitive and linguistic systems. The essence of these systems' hypothesis is that a defect in a client's language system will result in a defect in his perception of the world and in his problem-solving capabilities in a broad range of situations (Whorf, 1956). The greater the cognitive and/or linguistic error in representing the world and manipulating symbols, the greater the mental disorder. Bandler and Grinder (1975) use neurolinguistic systems to diagnose the client's preferred sensory and cognitive representational system.

DSM-III focuses on disordered thought as one symptom of a disorder. Cognitive theorists focus on a much more extensively defined range of cognitive and linguistic systems. Unlike the *DSM-III* descriptions of disordered thought, these systems of defining "wrong thinking" suggest therapeutic interventions which guide the therapist in learning the client's language and communicating alternate ways of thinking to the client.

Behavioral systems. BEHAVIORAL ASSESSMENT and APPLIED BEHAVIOR ANALYSIS have become important alternative diagnostic systems. Such systems as those developed by Kanfer (1965) have proven beneficial in assessing a wide range of psychopathology from stress disorders to psychotic depressive withdrawal. Currently some third-party payers (insurance companies, etc.) and quality assurance programs mandate behavioral statements defining the client's problem. This requirement serves to objectively inform the client and third-party payer about the goals for therapy. Behavioral diagnostic systems are also quite important for clinics offering time-limited therapy as an option.

DSM-III picks up some of the behavioral tradition in its insistence on observable symptoms. However, as a more eclectic system it is acceptant of intrapsychic processes in its definition of these observable symptoms. For example, in a behavioral diagnostic system the delusional speech produced by a client is the symptom. In a more dynamic system an inferred intrapsychic symptom such as delusional thought process might be identified as the major symptom. *DSM-III* attempts to classify symptoms arising from several dimensions—social, cognitive, emotional, biological, etc. Behavioral diagnostic systems argue that only the client's behavior is precisely measurable and, therefore, treatable.

Multidimensional systems. Two rather sophisticated systems, unrelated to each other apart from the fact that both combine a number of dimensions in assessing psychopathology, are INTERPERSONAL DIAGNOSIS (Leary, 1957; McLemore & Benjamin, 1979) and Millon's (1969) system. Interpersonal diagnosis is the classification of psychological disorders in terms of observable social behavior. Leary's approach to such a classification views an individual in terms of two axes: love-hate and dominance-submission. Other interpersonal diagnostic systems are even more complex.

Millon views psychopathology within a framework of three interacting dimensions. The first dimension relates to severity of disturbance, problems being viewed as either mild, moderate, or markedly severe. The second dimension specifies four interpersonal styles associated with different ways of gaining rewards and avoiding punishment: independent, dependent, ambivalent, and detached. The third dimension specifies two styles of behavior involved in gaining these reinforcements: active and passive. The second and third dimensions yield a 4×2 matrix involving eight basic personality styles: active-independent, passive-independent, active-dependent, passive-dependent, active-ambivalent, passive-ambivalent, active-detached, and passive-detached. (See separate articles on each of these personality patterns for additional details.)

The multidimensionality of *DSM-III* is only a nominal listing–two parts mental disorder, one part physical disorder, and two parts situational disorder. There are no rules for mixing these ingredients. Several of the other multidimensional systems offer interactive mathematical models of diagnosis that enable the diagnostician to locate clients at the intersection of their scores on two or more interactive dimensions. *DSM-III* urges attention to the whole person by calling attention to five parts of humanness separately, and other multidimensional systems call attention to several dimensions of humanness in concert.

References
Bandler, R., & Grinder, J. *The structure of magic.* Palo Alto, Calif.: Science and Behavior Books, 1975.
Berkouwer, G. C. *Man: The image of God.* Grand Rapids: Eerdmans, 1962.
Kanfer, F. Behavioral analysis. *Archives of General Psychiatry*, 1965, *12*(6), 529–538.
Leary, T. *Interpersonal diagnosis of personality.* New York: Ronald Press, 1957.
McLemore, C., & Benjamin, L. Whatever happened to interpersonal diagnosis? A psychosocial alternative to DSM-III. *American Psychologist*, 1979, *34*, 17–34.
Millon, T. *Modern psychopathology.* Philadelphia: Saunders, 1969.
Millon, T. *Disorders of personality.* New York: Wiley, 1981.
Whorf, B. L. *Language, thought and reality.* Cambridge: Massachusetts Institute of Technology Press, 1956.

B. E. BONECUTTER

Claustrophobia. The fear of confinement, of being locked or trapped in enclosed places such as elevators, classrooms, boats, planes, or narrow streets. This phobia may represent fear of yielding to a desired temptation, or it may serve as a type of self-inflicted punishment for giving in to an ego dystonic temptation. Most commonly it is a reaction based on a combination of both fear and punishment.

See PHOBIC DISORDERS.

Client-Centered Therapy. *See* PERSON-CENTERED THERAPY.

Clinical Pastoral Education. *See* ASSOCIATION FOR CLINICAL PASTORAL EDUCATION; BOISEN, ANTON THEOPHILUS.

Clinical Psychology. As a distinct specialty clinical psychology is less than 50 years old. During and immediately after World War II a critical shortage of psychiatrists brought more and more psychologists into the arena of applied mental health services. Psychologists had already developed a reputation as testing specialists in the decades preceding the Second World War, but it was only in the aftermath of this war that they were accorded anything like true parity with psychiatrists in the practice of psychotherapy. Moreover, only in the past two decades have psychologists established themselves as fully autonomous mental health practitioners.

The identity struggles of clinical psychologists have had both positive and negative consequences. On the negative side, some psychologists still show what seems to be a cavalier disregard for the medical expertise of psychiatrists, who are without question the mental health professionals best equipped to handle psychiatric hospitalizations, psychotropic medications, and physical evaluations. On the positive side, as a direct result of clinical psychology's successful battle for professional independence, the general public now has access to professionals who are equipped to render high-quality helping services grounded in behavioral science.

While the psychiatrist is unquestionably master of the physical domain and is often the expert best suited to manage psychiatric emergencies, clinical psychologists also have unique qualifications. For one thing, whereas psychiatrists ordinarily are not trained in the logic and methods of psychological science, all psychologists from reputable training programs have had exensive training in psychological research. Specific areas in which this empirical orientation affects their work include the construction and validation of assessment methods such as psychological tests, the study of treatment regimens such as hospital programs, and the analysis of organizational structures. This training also equips and encourages them to evaluate rigorously the effectiveness of all psychological treatments. Psychologists, therefore, are typically less reliant on intuition and more likely to be tough-minded about what they do.

Another unique qualification possessed by the clinical psychologist relates to the extensive background in psychology gained through four years of undergraduate and four to six years of graduate study. The study and practice of medicine ordinarily has little if anything to do with the ability of one human being to help another through psychological means. Freud himself believed that, because of the differences in thought forms between psychological and physiological disciplines, medical training was an obstacle that had to be overcome in order to provide good psychological treatment.

Clinical psychologists are engaged in a wide variety of activities, ranging from management consulting to working in pain clinics. However, the principal activities of clinical psychologists usually concern the diagnosis and treatment of mental disorders. While many psychologists take exception to terms such as "diagnosis" and "treatment," viewing them as archaic metaphors from psychiatry's medical heritage, it cannot be doubted that clinical psychology is focally concerned with understanding and alleviating human psychological misery.

Although a number of persons with master's degrees are regarded by their respective states as clinical psychologists, most members of the American Psychological Association (APA) regard the possession of an earned doctorate in psychology from an accredited institution as a critical criterion. Furthermore, this doctorate will ideally have been earned in an APA-approved clinical training program. Such programs demand at least one year of internship work beyond preinternship level "clerkships," and most states require an additional year of clinical experience beyond the doctorate for licensure. It should be noted that at least one state has abolished its psychologist licensing statutes, with the result that in that state anyone can hold himself or herself up to the general public as a "clinical psychologist." Guild issues aside, most psychologists view this as highly undesirable.

It should also be noted that the American Psychological Association has expressly disapproved of persons with doctorates in nonclinical areas simply doing an internship and then representing themselves as clinical psychologists. The import of this disapproval is to highlight the special educational requirements for clinical specialization.

The major journals of interest to clinical psychologists, and those in which they tend most often to publish, are *Journal of Abnormal Psychology, Journal of Consulting and Clinical Psychology, Professional Psychology Psychotherapy: Theory, Research and Practice*, and a number of behavioral psychology journals, most notably *Behavior Research & Therapy*.

Regarding the relationship of clinical psychology to Christianity, it must first be said that the doing of good in any form is, at very least, a vehicle for the expression of common grace. Clinical psychologists minister to human hurts, miseries, and tragedies. It must also be said, in the interest of candor, that while clinical psychology is grounded in and informed by behavioral science, psychotherapy is heavily saturated with applied philosophy. Stated differently, the conduct of verbal psychotherapy is an art form that relies on science, philosophy, and at least an unspoken theology.

The belief systems and values held by therapists are bound to influence clients (*see* VALUES AND PSYCHOTHERAPY). The idea of an ethically neutral psychotherapy is quite simply naïve (London, 1964). At the same time, the psychological results produced even by atheistic therapists must not be disparaged. Indeed, it may sometimes be difficult to decide whether to have a loved one treated by a professionally incompetent believer or a competent unbeliever. While this issue is unlikely to confront those who live in urban areas, it does arise for persons who live in rural parts of the country. The power of persuasion that psychotherapists sometimes seem to hold over clients must be considered in this decision.

As we move toward the end of this century, society is witnessing the exponential growth of clinical psychology. This growth is perhaps an anomaly of human history, in that clinical psychology has expressly to do with helping human beings cope with problems in living, which of course is precisely what the church purports to do. It is vitally necessary, at this juncture, for Christians to embrace what is good within clinical psychology and to use it in every way they can to augment the well-being of persons. At the same time, the danger of psychology becoming a new religion for many people, as it seems to have done for some (Vitz, 1977), is a danger that should not be ignored.

References

London, P. *The modes and morals of psychotherapy.* New York: Holt, Rinehart & Winston, 1964.
Vitz, P. *Psychology as religion.* Grand Rapids: Eerdmans, 1977.

Additional Readings

Garfield, S. L. *Clinical psychology: The study of personality and behavior.* Chicago: Aldine, 1974.
Goldenberg, H. *Contemporary clinical psychology.* Monterey, Calif.: Brooks/Cole Publishing, 1973.
Korchin, S. J. *Modern clinical psychology.* New York: Basic Books, 1976.
Weiner, I. B. (Ed.), *Clinical methods in psychology.* New York: Wiley-Interscience, 1976.

C. W. McLEMORE

See PSYCHOLOGIST; PSYCHOLOGY, HISTORY OF; PSYCHOLOGY AS RELIGION.

Clinical Social Work. This term has become inreasingly popular since 1970, and is used by social workers to describe a newly defined practice and new nomenclature.

The late 1960s and early 1970s saw great hopes for social change. Money and personnel became available to fight social ills of various kinds. The war on poverty was one such example of a concerted effort to fight poverty. The historical term *casework* became associated with a view in which people were helped to adjust to a harsh social reality. Casework was seen as inadequate in terms of changing social-structural problems, or in helping people to mobilize their own resources and regain morale, faith, and mental health through actively restructuring their own lives and environments. Casework was often identified with psychoanalysis and the past history of social work. The need for the term *clinical social work* was brought about due to the change in client unit from a single individual to couples, families, and groups, as well as a new theoretical base for social work. Related

to this was also an increase in interest in the client's social environment, as well as a wish to develop an empirical basis for practice.

Increasingly, the direct-service practitioners started to form their own societies and study groups and publish their own journals. The National Federation for Clinical Social Work was founded in 1971. The purpose was to establish standards for direct-service practitioners as well as a peer review system. Their association journal, *The Journal of Clinical Social Work*, was founded in 1972. Two obvious reasons for the founding of this organization were 1) the feeling shared by many direct-service practitioners that the regular professional organization, the National Association of Social Workers, was not paying enough attention to them, and 2) the growing awareness by social workers going into private practice that they had much to offer which the other mental health professions did not, such as expertise in marital and family therapy. As a result, the National Association of Social Workers was forced into recognizing clinical social work as a legitimate area of professional activity for social workers. In 1976 they issued the *Register of Clinical Social Workers*, defining a clinical social worker as one who is, "by education and experience, professionally qualified at the autonomous practice level to provide direct, diagnostic, preventative and treatment services to individuals, families and groups where functioning is threatened or affected by social and psychological stress or health impairment" (p. xi). The educational requirements were a doctoral or master's degree and two years or 3,000 hours of qualified supervised experience.

Two books which outline the status, history, and promise for the future of clinical social work are Strean (1978) and Rosenblatt and Waldfogel (1983). Both books show an increased sophistication in direct social work practice and point toward what Strean calls "psychotherapy plus," where, in addition to the usual concerns with internal processes, the clinical social worker is also vitally concerned about the client's interaction with his social environment. Additionally, there is an emphasis on research for clinical practice, effects of practice settings, and education for clinical social work.

In conclusion, clinical social work has become the increasingly accepted term for an expanded and research-based direct intervention approach by social work practitioners with individuals as well as groups and families. It goes beyond but includes normal psychotherapy in that it stresses the client's environment and his transactions with this environment.

References

National Association of Social Workers. *Register of Clinical Social Workers*. Washington, D.C.: Author, 1976.

Rosenblatt, A., & Waldfogel, D. (Eds.). *Handbook for clinical social work*. San Francisco: Jossey-Bass, 1983.

Stream, H. S. *Clinical social work*. New York: Free Press, 1978.

S. Skarsten

See Social Work.

Cluttering. Also known as agitolalia, cluttering is hasty, erratic, and jumbled speech, associated with personality and behavior changes such as hyperactivity, untidiness, and disorganized and impulsive behavior. Motor awkwardness and poor academic ability in reading, spelling, and language may also be apparent. The clutterer is often unconscious of his defective speech, which may include jumbling words, omitting syllables, transposing parts of words, and delays in beginning to speak. Hoarseness and stammering are also frequent. Cluttering is similar to stuttering, but unlike stuttering appears to be hereditary, coming on gradually and with a tendency to persist throughout life. Cluttering is more common in boys than girls, and may range in severity from poor articulation to total incomprehensibility. In some cases cluttering seems to reflect minimal brain dysfunction.

D. L. Schuurman

See Speech Disorders.

Coe, George Albert (1862–1951). One of the most important contributors to religious education in the United States. Coe was born in Mendon, New York, and was educated at the University of Rochester, Boston University School of Theology, and the University of Berlin. His academic career spanned five decades and included faculty appointments at the University of Southern California, Northwestern University, Union Theological Seminary, and finally at Teachers College of Columbia University, from which he retired in 1927. His retirement was honored by a special edition of *Religious Education* in 1927, but retirement did not terminate his productivity. Two of his most notable books *What Is Christian Education* (1929) and *What Is Religion Doing to Our Consciences*, were published after his retirement. In all Coe published 11 books, nearly 60 book reviews, and over 250 articles.

Coe was one of the founders of the Religious Education Association in 1903 and was generally recognized as the leader of that movement. His view of Christian education was quite broad; he argued that it is a process of systematic, critical study of interpersonal relationships guided by two theological assumptions—the existence of God (conceived as the "Great Valuer of persons") and the infinite value of the individual (which Coe specifically identified as the teaching of Christ). Yet Coe avoided being dogmatic in his views and encouraged constructive debate among various theological views. He remained active in the Religious Education Association throughout his life and was honorary president of that body at the time of his death.

Coe is perhaps best known for his pioneering study of the psychology of religion. *The Psychology of Religion* dealt with issues in the methodology of the fields. His best-known work, *The Spiritual Life: Studies in the Science of Religion* (1900), is often mentioned along with the contemporary work of James and Leuba as one of the seminal books in that field. In this work Coe analyzed the cases of 27 converts and tried to explain the character of their conversion experiences with the psychological theories of the day. On the basis of his cases Coe related sudden, striking conversions to an active "subliminal self," and suggested that such conversions usually occur in people who are emotionally suggestible, passive, and show a tendency toward automisms. Coe's work in the psychology of religion remains influential to this day.

L. S. Shaffer

Cognition. The debate over the role of cognition in psychology is a long-standing one. The early schools of psychology, structuralism and functionalism, defined psychology as the study of conscious experience. The advent of Watsonian behaviorism in the second decade of this century redefined psychology as the investigation of behavior, not conscious experience. Behaviorism was the predominant school in the field for decades. However, since the late 1960s there has been a resurgence of interest in cognition and, attendantly, a growing realization of its power in understanding and explaining behavior. In short, "man's cognitive processes must be included in any theory of personality or in any method of therapy" (Brown, 1967, pp. 858–859). As used in this article, the term *cognition* includes both thoughts and visual images in the stream of consciousness.

Cognitive Theory. Humans, as language-creating beings, start to learn from early childhood to formulate thoughts, perceptions, and feelings in words, phrases, and sentences

(Ellis & Harper, 1975). After approximately the age of 5, children attain the initial verbal control of motor behavior; they become capable of regulating certain actions by internal verbal rules and of utilizing the significative aspect of their own external speech to help organize their behavior in complex situations (Wozniak, 1972). By the time they reach adulthood practically all people appear to do most of their important thinking, and consequently emoting, in terms of self-talk or internalized sentences (Ellis & Harper, 1975).

The crux of cognitive theory can be capsulized in the assertion that our self-verbalizations essentially determine our emotional and behavioral responses. In other words, what an individual says to himself governs the way he feels and acts (Rimm & Masters, 1974). This has been conceptualized by Ellis in his ABC theory of emotion. A refers to some external event to which the individual is exposed. B refers to the particular chain of thoughts (self-verbalizations) that he emits in response to A; and C symbolizes the emotions and related behaviors that are a result of B. In the theory of emotion as a response, cognitive activity is therefore emphasized as the mediator of stimulus reception and the concomitant behavioral-emotional response (Morris, 1975).

It is not the environmental stimulus per se that is of primary significance, then, but what the individual says to himself about that stimulus (Beck, 1976). Accordingly, what a person says to himself about a specific situation can differentially determine his emotional and behavioral reactions to that situation (Goldfried, Decenteceo, & Weinberg, 1974). For example, depending on whether someone assesses a stimulus as beneficial or detrimental to his personal domain, he experiences a positive or negative reaction, respectively. "This is good for me" leads to emotions such as joy, pleasure, and happiness. Something assessed as "bad for me" induces sadness, anxiety, or anger (Beck, 1976).

It should be pointed out that when an individual is confronted with real-life situations, he is unlikely in many of these situations to literally "tell himself" various things consciously or deliberately. Because of the habitual nature of one's expectations or beliefs, it is likely that such thinking processes become as automatic and seemingly involuntary as any overlearned responses (Meichenbaum, 1976).

Summary of Research Evidence. Compelling evidence attesting to the viability of the cognitive perspective in psychology abounds. However, it is beyond the scope of the present

article to systematically examine the massive amount of data which provide cogent support for the theoretical underpinnings and the therapeutic efficacy of the cognitive approach. It will suffice to summarize the conclusions of the research studies assessing the tenability of key aspects of the cognitive position.

Self-talk and physiological arousal. According to Schachter and Singer's (1962) theory of emotion, "emotional states may be considered a function of a state of physiological arousal and of a cognition appropriate to this state of arousal" (p. 398). A number of studies (e.g., May & Johnson, 1973) have clearly indicated that even the state of physiological arousal, necessary to emotional states, is a function of cognition (i.e., covert self-statements).

Self-talk and emotion. A cardinal feature of cognitive theory states it is the content of a person's thinking that influences the person's mood. Numerous studies (Goldfried & Sobocinski, 1975) have been conducted which demonstrate that the self-verbalizations we emit in response to an event mediate our emotional response.

Self-talk and behavior. The other cardinal feature of cognitive theory posits that an individual's self-statements determine his behavioral responses. Meichenbaum and his colleagues have rigorously tested this hypothesis by performing a series of studies designed to evaluate the role of cognitive factors in behavior modification. In the case of impulsive children and schizophrenic patients appropriate self-instructional statements appeared to be missing from their repertoires. Consequently, self-instructional training was employed to develop the "interiorization of language" in these persons. The findings (Meichenbaum, 1969; Meichenbaum & Cameron, 1973; Meichenbaum & Goodman, 1971) showed that a cognitive self-guidance program which explicitly trains a subject to appropriately talk to himself was capable of bringing impulsive children's nonverbal behavior under their own cognitive control and of modifying schizophrenic patients' behavior in a variety of attentional, thinking, and language tasks.

In contrast to the lack of appropriate self-instructional statements in the vocabularies of impulsive children and schizophrenic patients, a large number of clients, who usually fall under the rubric of neurotic, seem to emit a diversity of maladaptive, anxiety-engendering self-statements. The goal of intervention here would not be to remedy the absence of self-statements, but rather to make the neurotic individuals aware of the self-statements which mediate maladaptive behaviors and to train them in new self-statements that are incompatible with the undesirable behavior (Meichenbaum & Cameron, 1974). Self-instructional training procedures designed to accomplish this goal have been successfully employed with a variety of neurotic clients, including speech-anxious, test-anxious, and depressed persons. As a result of these people being taught to efficaciously talk to themselves, self-control was engendered and behavior change was facilitated.

Cognitive Therapy. To the cognitive therapist mental illness is fundamentally a disorder of thinking by which the client consistently distorts reality in a self-defeating manner. The client's idiosyncratic thought processes adversely affect his view of the world and result in unpleasant emotions and behavioral difficulties. Consequently cognitive therapy is aimed at modifying the faulty pattern of the client's thinking and his underlying premises, assumptions, and beliefs. In the words of Ellis: "Human emotions and behavior are importantly affected (and even created) by cognitions. If, for almost any reason, the individual significantly changes his beliefs, attitudes, and values, he will concomitantly change his emotional and behavioral reactions" (Ellis, 1971, p. 617).

Cognitive therapy can be viewed as learning a new language, a process in which the client acquires the ability to speak to himself in new and appropriate ways so as to control his conduct. Cognitive therapy, therefore, is designed to alter the internal dialogues in which clients engage in order to effect therapeutic change (Meichenbaum, 1974). Cognitive therapy can be conceptualized as a four-stage process.

Stage 1: Presentation of rationale. The client is presented with the idea that what we think determines how we respond to situations. Relevant examples can be offered to illustrate the point that our feelings and behaviors are the result of what we tell ourselves about situations rather than the situations themselves. In describing and illustrating the basic rationale, it is helpful for the therapist to indicate that in many situations our self-statements may have reached the stage where this labeling process is more or less automatic.

Stage 2: Self-observation. The next stage of cognitive therapy involves the client's becoming an observer of his own behavior. It is recognized that the force and prominence of maladaptive thoughts tend to increase with the severity of the client's dysfunction. In severe disorders the thoughts are typically conspicuous and may, in fact, occupy the center of the ideational field, as in acute cases of depression, obsession, anxiety, or paranoid states. Clients experiencing a mild to moderate disturbance in their feelings or behavior, in contrast, may not be aware of their maladaptive thoughts even though these occur within the realm of consciousness. By shifting their attention to these thoughts the clients become aware of them and can specify their content.

A fundamental procedure for helping a client identify his "automatic" thoughts is to train him to observe the sequence of external events and his reactions to them. Generally there is a gap between the stimulus and response. The emotional and/or behavioral response becomes understandable if the client can recollect the thoughts that occurred during this gap (Beck, 1976).

Through heightened awareness and deliberate attention the client monitors with intensified sensitivity his thoughts, feelings, and behavior. One important by-product of this increased self-awareness is that the client gains a sense of control over his emotional state and behavior; he sees himself as an active contributor to his own experience and not as a defenseless victim of his thoughts and feelings and the reactions of others. A sense of hopefulness is engendered. The client's experience of having increased his control over his own emotions and overt behavior is an essential component of effective psychotherapy (Meichenbaum, 1976).

Stage 3: Assessment and modification of cognitions. Once the client has become an effective observer of his behavior, the third stage is introduced by the preliminary therapeutic objective of delineating the client's underlying belief system from which his self-defeating cognitions are derived. His erroneous beliefs or assumptions can be inferred from an enumeration of cognitions and events that lead to dysfunctional emotions or behavior. The faulty cognitions and underlying beliefs are then discussed and assessed for logic, validity, adaptiveness, and enhancement of positive behavior versus maintenance of maladaptive behavior. Finally, as these cognitions and beliefs are convincingly disputed, the client becomes willing to substitute more reality-oriented appraisals and interpretations for them, resulting in the development of rational, adaptive thought and behavior patterns. Cognitive therapy is thus more accurately described as the power of realistic thinking as opposed to the power of positive thinking.

Stage 4: Cognitions concerning change. The last stage of cognitive therapy focuses on what the client says to himself about his newly acquired cognitions and beliefs, since these self-verbalizations determine whether the therapeutic changes will be maintained. As the client endeavors to behave differently, he will frequently elicit different reactions from significant others (Meichenbaum, 1976). If these reactions are primarily negative, they may cause the client to waver in his convictions regarding his newly acquired beliefs and tempt him to return to his old, dysfunctional beliefs in an attempt to obtain immediate reinforcement (e.g., to obviate rejection and to ensure acceptance or approval from these significant others). Subsequently it becomes necessary for the client to be helped to see clearly the long-term deleterious effects of holding on to these erroneous beliefs. If this is successfully accomplished, then the stability and generalizability of the therapy will have been safeguarded.

Christian Sanctification. God created man in his own image. Despite the fall, in which man rejected God's purpose for his life and in which the image of God in man was consequently marred, God's purpose for humanity did not change. His purpose has remained the same: to conform each human being into one image—the image of his Son, Jesus Christ. In sanctification one is "being renewed in a full knowledge in the likeness of him who created him" (Col. 3:10). This renewal begins in regeneration, but it is continued in sanctification (Thiessen, 1949). Accordingly, sanctification is the process of the restoration of the image in each Christian; it enables the Christian to be what he was created to be, to become what he is—a child of God.

As the image in each Christian is being renewed, his cognitions become progressively more Christlike. Furthermore, this process of change in sanctification can be conceptualized with the same four stages that conceptualized the process of change in cognitive therapy.

Stage 1: Presentation of rationale. The Scripture verse which most patently corroborates the theoretical framework of cognitive therapy is found in Proverbs: "For as he [a man] thinketh in his heart, so is he" (23:7). It follows then that "the thoughts of the righteous are right, but the counsels of the wicked are deceit" (Prov. 12:5), "for they that are after the flesh do mind the things of the flesh; but they that are after the Spirit, the things of the Spirit" (Rom. 8:5). Since Scripture teaches

that what we as Christians think reflects either our old nature or our new nature, it behooves us to become aware of the type of self-talk we actually engage in.

Stage 2: Self-observation. The psalmist evidently recognized the importance of self-observation, for he appears to have been actively involved in the process of becoming aware of his covert verbalizations when he prayed, "Search me, O God, and know my heart; try me and know my anxious thoughts; And see if there be any hurtful way in me, and lead me in the everlasting way" (Ps. 139:23–24). An invaluable implement which God has given us to help discern our thoughts and underlying beliefs is his word, which the writer of the book of Hebrews describes as the "discerner of the thoughts and intents of the heart" (4:12). The biblical concept of heart denotes the center of the intellectual and volitional life of a person (Holloman, 1976). A salient point is that the Bible indicates that the thoughts which emanate from our hearts fall within the realm of consciousness. This means that a person who is motivated to know himself can become an accurate observer of the thoughts which come from his heart.

In conclusion, identifying the operative sinful cognitions and beliefs that are sources of problems and impediments to growth precedes assessing and replacing them with Christlike attitudes and their salutary behavioral consequences.

Stage 3: Assessment and modification of cognitions. The word of God is utilized to assess the veracity of the Christian's sinful cognitions and underlying beliefs because it is the embodiment of knowledge and of truth (Rom. 2:20) and is "inspired by God and profitable for teaching, for reproof, for correction, for training in righteousness" (2 Tim. 3:16). As Christians are convicted through God's word and the agency of the Holy Spirit that certain of their cognitions and beliefs are sinful, they are in a viable position to modify them, "bringing into captivity every thought to the obedience of Christ" (2 Cor. 10:5).

The modification of sinful cognitions and beliefs is central to the process of sanctification. The Scriptures enjoin Christians to be transformed by the renewing of their minds (Rom. 12:2). The renewal referred to means the adjustment of thinking to the mind of God, which is designed to have a transforming effect upon life. The Christian plays an active and vital role in the process of renewing his mind and, concomitantly, in restoring the image of God within himself. The Christian's responsibility to be actively involved in modifying his sinful cognitions and beliefs is also evident in Paul's instruction to the Colossians: "Set your mind on the things above, not on the things that are on earth" (3:2).

Stage 4: Cognitions concerning change. A Christian's self-statements about his growth toward Christlikeness are most likely to be positive if he continues to appropriate the resources available to him as a Christian, namely, the word of God, fellowship with God, and corporate fellowship. The actualization of these resources will not only maintain the Christian's growth but will foster it as well. If, however, a Christian begins to stumble in his walk of faith and returns to setting his mind "on the things that are on earth," he needs to recognize the essentially self-defeating consequences of this decision: "But now that you have come to know God, or rather to be known by God, how is it that you turn back again to the weak and worthless elemental things to which you desire to be enslaved all over again" (Gal. 4:9). He then needs to heed Paul's admonishments: "It was for freedom that Christ set us free; stand fast therefore, and do not submit again to a yoke of slavery" (Gal. 5:1).

It should be noted that the conceptualization of the process of change delineated in this article does not consist of a mechanical or intellectualized set of techniques that ignores feelings and subsitutes a sterile dialectic for a vital interpersonal relationship. On the contrary, in both cognitive therapy and sanctification this process of change in cognitions and beliefs occurs in the context of an accepting and loving relationship, the kind of relationship in which the emotions are most freely and abundantly expressed and most positively and beneficially experienced. This process of change, then, is truly a holistic one.

References

Beck, A. T. *Cognitive therapy and the emotional disorders.* New York: International Universities Press, 1976.
Brown, B. M. Cognitive aspects of Wolpe's behavior therapy. *American Journal of Psychiatry,* 1967, *124,* 854–859.
Ellis, A. Review of behavior therapy and beyond by A. A. Lazarus. *Behavior Therapy,* 1971, *2,* 616–619.
Ellis, A., & Harper, R. A. *A new guide to rational living.* Englewood Cliffs, N.J.: Prentice-Hall, 1975.
Goldfried, M. R., Decenteceo, E. T., & Weinberg, L. Systematic rational restructuring as a self-control technique. *Behavior Therapy,* 1974, *5,* 247–254.
Goldfried, M. R., & Sobocinski, D. Effect of irrational beliefs on emotional arousal. *Journal of Consulting and Clinical Psychology,* 1975, *43,* 504–510.
Holloman, H. W. *Theology 2.* La Mirada, Calif.: Talbot Theological Seminary, 1976.
May, J. R., & Johnson, H. J. Physiological activity to internally elicited arousal and inhibitory thoughts. *Journal of Abnormal Psychology,* 1973, *82,* 239–245.
Meichenbaum, D. H. The effects of instructions and reinforcement on thinking and language behavior of schizophrenics. *Behavior Research and Therapy,* 1969, *7,* 101–114.
Meichenbaum, D. H. *Cognitive behavior modification.* Morristown, N.J.: General Learning Press, 1974.
Meichenbaum, D. H. Toward a cognitive theory of self-control. In G. Schwartz & D. Shapiro (Eds.), *Consciousness and self-regulation: Advances in research.* New York: Plenum Press, 1976.
Meichenbaum, D. H., & Cameron, R. Training schizophrenics to talk to themselves: A means of developing attentional controls. *Behavior Therapy,* 1973, *4,* 515–534.
Meichenbaum, D. H., & Cameron, R. The clinical potential of modifying what clients say to themselves. *Psychotherapy: Theory, Research and Practice,* 1974, *11,* 103–117.
Meichenbaum, D. H., & Goodman, J. Training impulsive children to talk to themselves: A means of developing self-control. *Journal of Abnormal Psychology,* 1971, *77,* 115–126.
Morris, N. *A group self instruction method for the treatment of depressed outpatients.* Unpublished doctoral dissertation, University of Toronto, 1975.
Rimm, D. C., & Masters, J. C. *Behavior therapy: Techniques and empirical findings.* New York: Academic Press, 1974.
Schachter, S., & Singer, J. E. Cognitive, social, and physiological determinants of emotional state. *Psychological Review,* 1962, *69,* 379–399.
Thiessen, H. C. *Introductory lectures in systematic theology.* Grand Rapids, Eerdmans, 1949.
Wozniak, R. H. Verbal regulation of motor behavior: Soviet research and non-Soviet replications. *Human Development,* 1972, *15,* 13–57.

D. PECHEUR

Cognitive-Behavior Therapy.

Cognitive-behavioral therapies have enjoyed an immense popularity these past 10 years as effective approaches to psychotherapy. Essentially, a cognitive-behavioral approach to psychological treatment is, as its name suggests, a combination of two treatments: the cognitive and the behavioral. Cognitive refers to the thoughts of the individual. A therapy treatment with a cognitive emphasis thus consists of an emphasis upon the modification of the individual's conscious thoughts about himself or his environment. The implication of this concept is that psychological disorders, and in particular affective disorders such as depression or anxiety, result from thinking the wrong kind of thoughts; this must then be corrected. Behavioral, on the other hand, refers to an emphasis on the individual's external behaviors. A behavior treatment for any disorder is usually focused on changing the individual's overt behaviors, with the assumption that the behavior itself is the problem. Cognitive-behavior therapy refers to the use of both behavior and cognitive techniques to change the way an individual thinks about himself or herself.

At present there appears to be ample evidence that one's thoughts have an impact on one's emotions (Kendall & Hollen, 1979). In addition, current theories of emotions suggest that while physiology may determine the intensity of the emotions, the content of the emotions (sad vs. happy, e.g.) is determined by the cognitions or thoughts of the individual.

The behaviorism of cognitive-behavior therapy is not metaphysical behaviorism but methodological behaviorism. The distinction between these is crucial for the Christian. The former makes strong statements about determinism, and may imply in its more radical varieties an absence of responsibility and freedom on the part of the individual. Methodological behaviorism, however, implies only that there will be an emphasis on experimental rigor in the analysis of behavior. One will deal with publicly observable events such as behaviors in the discussion of changes in the individual.

The combination of the cognitive and the behavioral appears to have come about because, while on the one hand the efficacy of performance-based therapeutic procedures had been recognized, on the other hand behavioral explanation which defined change totally in terms of environmental contingencies did not seem to be sufficient. The internal thoughts and assumptions of individuals obviously mediate how they respond to the environment.

Philosophical Foundation. One underlying assumption of cognitive-behavioral therapists is the concept of *reciprocal determinism.* This implies a transactional approach to behavior, in which the individual is active in creating his own environment. For example, a person may perceive his environment in a distorted fashion, as is the case with depression (*see* DEPRESSION: COGNITIVE PERSPECTIVE). Such a person may then think negative thoughts about the environment and act on these thoughts. His actions may then engender certain changes in the interpersonal environment, which in turn will further influence his cognitions and subsequent behavior. This entire process is called reciprocal determinism because individuals' perceptions and thoughts about their environment or the environment they have constructed in their heads are in fact the environment they respond to. Thus they determine the environment. Likewise, the environment in the external world has an impact on their thoughts and behaviors.

Some more radical theorists have attempted to extend the notion of reciprocal determinism, to posit some sort of monism inherent in the universe. That is, because the individual determines his environment

through his thoughts, the environment and the individual have an identity. This is a reaction to the dualism that exists in Western psychology, which insists that not only are the individual's cognitions (mind) and his body totally separate, but so also are the individual and his environment. The distinctions become blurred, however, in cognitive therapy, because one's thoughts about the environment often make up the environment to which the individual responds.

For the Christian it is not necessary to move from complete dualism to monism (complete identity of everything). Not only does the Hebrew concept of the individual include both the physical and the spiritual (or mental), but there is also found throughout Scripture the theme of the unity of the world. Creation and the individual are inextricably bound up with each other. For example, because of the fall of the human race, "all creation groans, and waits to be delivered." Thus, the reality in which the individual finds himself is the reality which he has in some sense helped to create through his perspective.

Essential Characteristics of Cognitive-Behavior Therapies. Meichenbaum (1976) asserts that the basic postulate of the cognitive-behavioral therapists is that the final way to all behavior change is the internal dialogues in which clients engage. He further states that there are basically three stages in any cognitive-behavior therapy. The first stage involves teaching an individual skills in self-observation. There are two processes involved in this stage. First, individuals are given a conceptual framework in which they are told that indeed their thoughts have an impact on their feelings of depression and anxiety, and they need only change their thoughts in order to change their emotions. Essentially the idea communicated is that they can have some control over their emotions. The second process involved in this phase teaches individuals to monitor their thoughts. Essentially they are to ask, along with the psalmist (Ps. 42), "Why are you cast down, O my soul?" What are you thinking about that makes you seem so depressed? Individuals are usually given the assignment to monitor their thoughts when their mood changes.

The second stage of any cognitive-behavior therapy asks individuals to modify or restructure their thoughts (*see* COGNITIVE RESTRUCTURING). The way in which this is done usually varies with the therapist. Whereas Ellis in rational-emotive therapy may ask clients to realize why certain of their ideas are irrational,

Beck (Beck, Rush, Shawn, & Emery, 1979) may ask his clients to present evidence that their cognitions are incorrect. Clients may be challenged to change certain irrational thinking styles such as selective inattention to certain things in their environment or overgeneralization of a situation. In some cases clients may be given a behavioral assignment that will serve to actually disprove some of their negative thoughts. Some problem-solving therapies may ask the individual to substitute a problem-solving inner dialogue for an ongoing negative dialogue (e.g., "Let's see, after I do this first step, I must then do this next step . . ."). Finally, certain self-reinforcement therapies would encourage clients to monitor their performances in an area and then say positive things to themselves when certain behaviors occur.

An additional group of cognitive models are the covert conditioning models. These models consist of a number of techniques, such as covert counterconditioning, thought stopping, or covert sensitization. They posit the idea inherent in the classical conditioning model of pairing a negative stimulus (such as a negative thought) with a positive stimulus (such as a positive thought). For example, if an overweight individual continually thinks about food so that these thoughts represent a positive stimulus, certain therapists may ask the patient to imagine a negative scene every time he or she imagines food. One example of a negative scene is an image of getting sick and vomiting. Thought stopping may merely ask patients to verbalize the word "stop" every time they start to think something that they do not want to think, such as anxiety-provoking thoughts.

A number of cognitive techniques have a third stage wherein the individuals begin to look for underlying themes in their thoughts. After they have learned to monitor their thoughts and modify them, they then may be asked to review thoughts which they have recorded in order to look for the common theme. For the depressed or anxious individual, some of the underlying themes may be irrational and may consist of ideas such as "I must always be perfect." Meichenbaum, however, also emphasizes such ideas as ideosyncratic thought patterns that keep individuals from more effectively coping with their environment.

Treatment Efficacy. An important issue that must always be raised in evaluating any approach to therapy is treatment efficacy. Does the treatment do what it claims to do? Fortunately, cognitive-behavioral therapies

fare better here than some of the more traditional approaches such as psychoanalysis because the efficacy of these cognitive-behavioral approaches has in fact been confirmed (Mahoney & Arnkoff, 1978).

In evaluating the efficacy of cognitive-behavioral treatments, all approaches can be divided into two large categories: the covert conditioning therapies and the cognitive learning models. The covert conditioning therapies do not fare as well as the cognitive learning models. The literature is mixed in its evaluation of both thought-stopping and covert sensitization techniques. Essentially, the effectiveness of both these techniques has yet to be demonstrated. Covert counterconditioning, however, seems to have some effectiveness. In this approach the individual is taught to relax and then asked to imagine progressively more aversive scenes or performances, such as speaking in front of a group, if that is a difficult problem for the individual.

Cognitive learning therapies have been shown to be fairly effective. This category includes cognitive restructuring therapies such as rational-emotive therapy, Beck's cognitive therapy (discussed above), and Meichenbaum's cognitive model (*see* SELF-INSTRUCTION). These approaches have been shown to be quite effective in the treatment of a number of disorders ranging from depression to childhood behavioral problems.

Also in this second category are the COPING SKILLS THERAPIES. The distinguishing feature of these strategies is their emphasis on helping the client to master a repertoire of skills that will facilitate adaptation. Numerous procedures, such as training the patient to imagine the steps in solving a problem, have all been found to be effective. One procedure, which has been termed covert modeling, has been found to be especially effective with phobias and subassertiveness. A third type of approach in this category is the PROBLEM-SOLVING THERAPY, in which patients are taught the rudiments of problem solving. A number of studies have reported the success of this therapy with various categories of individuals. Mahoney and Arnoff (1978) state that research support for the problem-solving therapy shows it to be one of the most promising of the cognitive-behavioral therapies.

Evaluation. The cognitive-behavioral therapies offer some exciting potentials for the Christian for two reasons. First, they have been found to be consistently effective. Second, their central notion, that the individual's intellectual construction of the world and his or her attitudes about that world are a major determinant of the individual's mental health, is a notion familiar to Christian theology. Certainly Scripture points out a close connection between thoughts and mental health. (Prov. 23:7; Phil. 4:4–9, 11, 13; Mark 7:20, 23).

There are, however, two cautions in regard to cognitive-behavioral therapy. First, one must guard against baptizing any one approach to psychotherapy as the Christian approach. Also, while one's thoughts and perspectives are important for one's spiritual well-being, some theologies have held that the intellect can never be the central basis of a theology. A second caution is that some Christians tend to be too simplistic in their use of these therapies. Because the focus of these treatments appears to be on helping the individual gain a more healthy adaptive perspective on the world, many Christian counselors have felt that such a perspective could be gained by lecturing the individual or sermonizing during the therapy hour. However, cognitive therapy involves two processes which differentiate it clearly from simply lecturing to the client. First, the clients learn to monitor their own thoughts before they work on modifying them. Both counselor and client must be aware of what the client's thoughts are. Second, cognitive therapy places a larger emphasis on emotions than is usually realized (Beck, et al., 1979). Not only does the individual need to be tuned into his emotions, so that bad emotions or sudden changes in emotions become a cue indicating thought changes, but the counselor must continually make the link between the client's emotions and thoughts in the therapy session. If the above mentioned cautions are kept in mind, however, the cognitive-behavioral therapies can be effective and useful tools for the Christian counselor.

References
Beck, A. T., Rush, A., Shawn, B., & Emery G. *Cognitive therapy of depression*. New York: Guilford Press, 1979.
Kendall, P. C., & Hollen, S. D. (Eds.). *Cognitive-behavioral interventions*. New York: Academic Press, 1979.
Mahoney, M., & Arnkoff, D. Cognitive and self-control therapies. In S. L. Garfield & A. E. Bergin (Eds.), *Handbook of psychotherapy and behavior change*. (2nd ed.). New York: Wiley, 1978.
Meichenbaum, D. Towards a cognitive theory of self-control. In G. E. Schwartz & D. Shapiro (Eds.), *Consciousness and self-regulation: Advances in research*. New York: Plenum Press, 1976.

L. R. PROPST

Cognitive Development.
Cognitive development concerns man's intellectual and mental ability to learn and to understand the world.

As a topic in psychology, it is most usually associated with the work of Piaget. Piaget's studies led him to believe that there is a link between genetically based human development and the way people come to know, or "make sense" of, their world. Thus, he often referred to his work as genetic epistemology. Piaget suggested that a system of four stages developed through a process of adaptation explains cognitive development.

Foundational Components. Piaget's views rest on three foundational components: an organismic view of human beings, a developmental view of biology, and a structural view of human intelligence.

An organismic view is contrasted to a mechanistic or physicalistic view in the same way that a living organism is contrasted to a machine or a piece of rock. In this sense a living organism is "active" on its own; it is a living force with an internal ability and power to act. The cognitive developmentalist believes that since man is an organism, he is involved in bringing about his own learning and development by actively trying to make sense of the world.

Piaget's background in developmental biology and his view of man as an organismic/biological being led him to believe that man is a developmental organism. Developmental biologists believe that the processes and patterns of human development are rooted in man's genetic/biological make-up. Thus, as a developmental organism, a person is believed to possess a genetically based pattern of cognitive development, and it is as normal and natural for one to develop mentally as it is for one to develop physically. It is also believed by the cognitive developmentalists that just as an organism has to interact with its environment through eating, breathing, and exercise in order to develop physically, so the organism actively interacts with the environment in order to bring about its biologically based pattern of cognitive development.

A structural view of human intelligence states that the person actively constructs or structures his mental understanding of the world rather than merely absorbing or adopting someone else's understanding of the world. It is believed that perceptions and pieces of information are not objectively and purely stored as in a deep freeze, but are subjectively transformed and interpreted into a holistic structure of the world. It is through such structuring that an individual is actively involved in making sense of the world.

The Christian must critique these foundational concepts from a theistic view of creation, man, and truth. That a person is an organismic/biological being is certainly not inconsistent with a biblical view of man as part of God's creation. That man is actively involved in contributing to his own maturity is more likely to be questioned by evangelicals. At first appearance it seems that the cognitive developmentalist has too optimistic a view of human nature. But it should be noted that the developmentalist is talking only about man's biological nature as having a pattern and capacity for development, not man's disposition to do good things, nor man's spiritual nature. Thus, if the developmentalist is saying that biologically human beings are adequately equipped to learn and make sense of the world, such a statement could easily be seen as consistent with what we would expect to find in God's good creation.

That people may be viewed as being in a process of development is also not inconsistent with biblical ideas of growth and maturity. Many of the metaphors used to describe what God demands of people are taken from gardening or animal husbandry. Implied in the use of these metaphors is that maturity is something that is approached through a process of growth. Paul often used the contrast between babes and adults as if he assumed that everyone understood that people developed.

That people subjectively construct a mental understanding of the world rather than possessing knowledge or truth objectively and absolutely is also sometimes contested by evangelicals. But the statement does not necessarily claim that absolute truth does not exist. It is a statement about epistemology rather than a statement about metaphysics or ethics. Subjective epistemology does not need to be seen as inconsistent with theistic ideas about objective and absolute truth (Holmes, 1977).

The Process of Adaptation. As an organism actively making sense of the world, an individual uses a process of adaptation to construct his cognitive structure of the world. The process of adaptation is a dual process. Either the individual adapts perceptions of the world and information from it in order that they may be assimilated into his already existing cognitive structure of the world, or else the individual adapts his cognitive structure in order to accommodate the perceptions and information from the world. The processes of assimilation and accommodation are employed in order to maintain a relative state of cognitive equilibrium.

Usually each person subjectively perceives the world in ways that are easy to assimilate. This subjective perceiving often involves misinterpreting the facts of the world so they can be easily assimilated. The process of accommodation usually is employed only when the individual is in a state of cognitive disequilibrium, that is, when the perceptions and facts of reality cannot be assimilated into the present cognitive structure. Because accommodation involves an overhaul of one's structure of the world, it is entered into only when the individual perceives a strong need for it.

Stages of Development. As Piaget studied the development of intellectual ability in people, he developed a system of four stages which identify major categories of cognitive structures by which people make sense of their world. These stages display four characteristics: invariant sequence, hierarchical integration, structured wholes, and qualitative difference.

Piaget maintains that people develop through the stage system in an *invariant sequence* and that no stages are skipped. He also maintains that there is no movement backward through the stages. Each stage builds upon the abilities of the previous stage. This is the principle of *hierarchical integration*. Each stage is cognitively more adequate since it has helped resolve some cognitive disequilibrium that the previous stage could not. However, it does not contradict the contributions of the previous stages. In this sense the stages are not airtight boxes that people move through, but each stage represents the development of a new cognitive capacity. Furthermore, each stage is comprehensive enough to help interpret all reality and all of life's experiences. Thus, each stage is viewed as a *structured whole*. The stages are not content or context specific but are general stages. Finally, as alluded to in the three previous characteristics, each stage represents a *qualitatively different* way of structuring the world. This is to be contrasted to a quantitative difference in knowledge, which is a more typical way of understanding the nature of intellectual growth of people.

Sensorimotor stage (ages 0–2). This is the stage of infancy. As with all other stages, the ages given are aproximate, corresponding to the emergence and dominance of the stage. The infant makes sense of the world primarily through physical observations ("sensori-") and manipulations ("motor"). A true description of most infants' mental capacity is "out of sight, out of mind." Infants tend to operate only on those things that they can see, hear, or touch.

During the sensorimotor stage of development the infant develops the mental capacity to 1) realize that objects still exist though they cannot be seen, 2) coordinate muscular movements with sight and hearing, 3) intentionally act upon objects rather than merely react reflexively, 4) anticipate future movements of objects and people, 5) experiment with new ways of acting on objects and people. The final element of sensorimotor development is the capacity of the infant to mentally represent the world internally to himself. This allows for the development of language in the next stage.

Preoperational stage (ages 2–7). This is the stage of the toddler and the preschooler. The primary ways of making sense of the world involve language and fantasy. The new development of internal mental representations, which emerged at the end of the sensorimotor stage, allows for the development of language during the preoperational stage. However, the child still does not possess adultlike logical thinking.

Though preoperational children have the capacity for internal mental representations (what we normally call thinking), they are still strongly influenced by the appearance of an object or event rather than by a logical explanation of it. Preoperational thinking also makes it difficult to 1) understand that other people might think differently from oneself, 2) distinguish between "real" and "pretend" people and events, 3) logically think backward to the beginning of a physical or mental sequence of events.

Concrete operations stage (ages 7–11). This is the stage of the elementary school-aged child. The primary way of making sense in this stage is through the use of concrete thinking. Concrete operations give the child the opportunity to use adultlike mental logic for the first time. But the child's use of mental logic is limited only to situations and problems that are real and observable. This is in contrast to situations and problems that are primarily verbal or hypothetical.

Because of the ability to do logical operations such as addition and subtraction, the child tends not to be fooled by the appearance of an object or event but can logically compare several aspects of something before making decisions. Thus, the child's decisions are more influenced by logic than by perceptual appearance.

Concrete thinking makes learning facts very easy. Concrete thinking also leads children to 1) be very literal about interpretations of rules, instructions, and other verbal language, 2) concentrate on details, 3) emphasize black and white, right and wrong answers to questions and social situations.

Formal operations stage (ages 11 and up). This is the stage of adolescence and adulthood. The primary way of making sense of the world is through the use of abstract thinking. For the first time the person is capable of solving hypothetical and verbal problems. In Piaget's terminology, the person is able to think about the form of an object or problem without having it physically present or concretely represented. With formal operations the person has fully developed the mental skills for completely logical thinking.

With the new capacities of formal operations come the ability to 1) recognize several points of view simultaneously and identify conceptual (rather than merely functional) relationships between them, 2) see gray areas in solving social and other problems, 3) participate in mental reflection (thinking about thoughts and feelings), 4) understand cause-and-effect relationships (no longer are various areas of study, such as history and science, merely factual information, but there is an understanding of the relationships between the facts).

Factors Influencing Development. Piaget suggested that the transition from one stage to another is influenced by four factors which, as they work together, bring about the opportunities for the accommodation necessary for the structural development from one stage to the next. These four factors are maturation, direct experience, social interaction, and equilibration.

A minimum amount of biological *maturation* of the central nervous system is necessary for the various types of mental operations which characterize each stage. For example, until puberty the brain does not contain the kind of make-up necessary for abstract thinking. Thus, the normal rate of biological maturation limits the rate at which cognitive development can occur.

Each individual also needs a certain amount of *direct experience* with the world in order to fully exercise the mental operations of each stage and to come into contact with problems and situations that require a qualitatively more adequate way of understanding those problems and situations. This includes the *social interactions* which help stretch and challenge the child's perspective-taking ability. Social interaction also includes the use of language, which is important for developing operational thought.

Equilibration is sometimes known as the "motor" for cognitive development. It is the organism's biological drive for equilibration that motivates the individual to construct a new cognitive structure of the world when the previous one is seen to be inadequate. But equilibration also acts as a limiting force in development. Equilibration is not something that can be manufactured in order to induce or speed up development.

Reference

Holmes, A. F. *All truth is God's truth.* Grand Rapids: Eerdmans, 1977.

Additional Readings

Piaget, J. *The origins of intelligence in children.* New York: International Universities Press, 1952.
Piaget, J. *The construction of reality in the child.* New York: Basic Books, 1954.
Piaget, J. *Science of education and the psychology of the child.* New York: Viking Press, 1970.
Singer, D. G., & Revenson, T. A. *A Piaget primer: How a child thinks.* New York: New American Library, 1978.
Wadsworth, B. J. *Piaget's theory of cognitive development* (2nd ed.). New York: Longman, 1979.

R. B. McKean

See Thinking; Intelligence; Culture and Cognition.

Cognitive Dissonance. In the 1950s Festinger proposed the theory of cognitive dissonance, which had a greater impact on social psychology than any other theory except attribution theory. Festinger had observed that when an individual held a cognition (e.g., belief or expectation) that was later disconfirmed, the individual afterward held the cognition more strongly. Festinger studied a religious group that had predicted the end of the world on a particular day. Anticipating the end, which included a daring rescue from outer space, they sold all possessions and waited on a mountaintop. When the predicted end and rescue did not occur, they held their beliefs even more strongly. These findings stimulated Festinger (1957, 1964) to examine the cognitive and social factors in belief and behavior change.

As the most famous of the cognitive consistency theories, the theory of cognitive dissonance is deceptively simple; its implications are provocative and widespread. An individual holds beliefs or cognitive elements that do not fit with each other (e.g., I believe the world will end, and the world did not end as predicted). Nonfitting beliefs give rise to dissonance, a hypothetical aversive state the individual is motivated to reduce, or at least not increase. This aversive stimulation initiates changes in the individual's behavior (e.g., undoing) or beliefs (e.g., the world was saved because of our fervent prayer) or limits exposure to discrepant information.

Cognitions relate to other cognitions in three ways: they may be irrelevant, dissonant, or consonant. Dissonance exists between two beliefs when one is the opposite of the other, yet both are held simultaneously; consonant relations exist when one belief follows from the other. Dissonance may arise from logical inconsistency of beliefs, when beliefs are against the prevailing cultural mores, or when beliefs are inconsistent with past experience.

The amount of dissonance indicates the importance of the beliefs to the person. Beliefs that are held more strongly are capable of arousing more dissonance than less important beliefs. When the dissonance level rises to equal the resistance of the least resistant element, that element will change and the dissonance will be reduced.

Dissonance may be reduced by changing behavior, altering a belief, or adding a new one. When the person makes a decision where the alternate choices each have positive and negative aspects, dissonance may result from the decision. Dissonance will be greater when the decision is important and when the unchosen alternative is attractive. This may lead to revoking the decision, denigrating the unchosen one, and postdecision justification.

The theory has generated much research by advocates and opposition. Research has addressed the role of volition and commitment, the ability to tolerate dissonance, and the limits under which the theory works best. It has been applied to self-persuasion, forced compliance, exposure to information, and social support. It has been used in cognitive psychotherapies to initiate personal change. Its attraction seems to lie in counterintuitive predictions.

References

Festinger, L. *A theory of cognitive dissonance.* Stanford, Calif.: Stanford University Press, 1957.
Festinger, L. *Conflict, decision and dissonance.* Stanford, Calif.: Stanford University Press, 1964.

R. L. Timpe

Cognitive Restructuring. This technique, refined primarily by Goldfried (Goldfried & Goldfried, 1980), is a translation of Ellis's Rational-Emotive Therapy into a social-learning framework. Many behavior therapists have seen the utility of Ellis's conceptualization of psychopathology and psychotherapy, especially with anxiety disorders, but have been leery of the system because of its heavy philosophical trappings and because of Ellis's advocacy of a rather combative model of therapist influence. At the theoretical level Goldfried grounded the concept of "irrational ideation" in the broader experimental literature dealing with cognitive mediation of stress reactions and the social learning concept of expectancy.

Goldfried conceptualized the process of doing cognitive restructuring as involving four steps. First, the therapist helps the client recognize how unrealistic thoughts can be involved in emotional upset. The therapist also discusses with the client how such beliefs can become so habitual that the client is no longer aware of these automatic thoughts. Second, the therapist helps the client recognize the obvious irrationality of some exaggerated unrealistic beliefs that the therapist supposes might be relevant to the client's distress. Having the client role play being a therapist who is persuading a client of the irrationality of the exaggerated beliefs is frequently used here. The third step is to help the client see the unrealistic thoughts that are causing his own distress. At this stage Socratic questioning, requests for evidence in support of specific beliefs, and examination of the long-term implications of the client's way of thinking may be used to help the client see the relationship between his thoughts and his distress. The final stage of the process is to help the client think more realistically when confronted with problem situations.

Role-playing practice is the primary mode of change. Goldfried's research suggests cognitive restructuring to be an effective treatment intervention, particularly with persons suffering from discrete anxiety disorders (Goldfried, 1979).

References
Goldfried, M. R. Anxiety reduction through cognitive-behavioral intervention. In P. Kendall & S. Hollon (Eds.), *Cognitive-behavioral interventions.* New York: Academic Press, 1979.
Goldfried, M. R., & Goldfried, A. P. Cognitive change methods. In F. H. Kanfer & A. P. Goldstein (Eds.), *Helping people change* (2nd ed.). New York: Pergamon Press, 1980.
S. L. JONES

See COGNITIVE-BEHAVIOR THERAPY.

Cognitive Science. *See* INTELLIGENCE, ARTIFICIAL.

Cognitive Style. *See* CULTURE AND COGNITION.

Cognitive Therapy. *See* COGNITIVE-BEHAVIOR THERAPY.

Colitis. An inflammation of the lining of the large intestine. This condition is a form of chronic inflammatory disorder of the colon referred to as chronic nonspecific ulcerative colitis. Another less common type of inflammatory bowel condition is called Crohn's disease of the colon. In both, small ulcers form throughout the lining of the colon, but they tend to be deeper in Crohn's disease. The incidence of ulcerative colitis is not high but is more common in urban settings and in white people, particularly Jews. Colitis occurs both in children and in adults.

The major symptom of colitis is frequent bloody diarrhea, which may be accompanied by stomach pain or cramps, fever, and loss of weight. Complications may be local, such as perforation of the wall of the colon, or systemic, such as anemia, vitamin deficiencies, arthritis, or skin lesions.

The causes of colitis are unknown. Possibilities are genetic, bacterial or viral, allergic reactions, immune mechanisms, or, most likely, some combination of these factors. Current understanding places a strong emphasis on psychological contributions. Many people with colitis are depressed and have feelings of hopelessness and despair. They may exhibit underlying hostility with unexpressed chronic resentment. People who develop colitis have often experienced major psychological stresses within six months prior to its onset. These include death of a family member, a change in residence, or other distressing situations.

Mild attacks of colitis can be treated on an outpatient basis; acute attacks are usually treated in the hospital where the inflammation can be controlled and nutritional losses can be replaced. In addition to bed rest, treatment often includes only clear liquids for food and intravenous feedings to replace lost fluids. This also allows the bowel to rest. In order to correct anemia blood transfusions are required for those who have extensive bleeding. Corticosteroids are administered to reduce inflammation, pain, and fever. Steroid medication is gradually reduced over a 2- to 6-month time period, although some people have to take it indefinitely. Sulfasalazine is given concurrently with the steroid medication. Surgery is required for perforation, severe bleeding, or failure to improve after 2 to 3 weeks of intensive medical treatment. Psychotherapy is often also prescribed.

Colitis is a highly variable condition. About three-fourths of the people who develop colitis have recurrences, with 10 to 15 years elapsing before the next attack. Others have chronic and unremitting symptoms over long periods of time. Most have periods of good health interspersed with intermittent symptoms. If the condition is properly treated, the prognosis is favorable.

M. A. NORFLEET

See PSYCHOSOMATIC DISORDERS.

Collective Unconscious. In Jungian or analytical psychology the unconscious division of the psyche consists of two distinct domains or levels. One level is composed of a more or less superficial layer of repressed and/or forgotten contents that have been derived from personal experience. This part of the personality is referred to as the personal unconscious. The other domain of the unconscious is a much deeper layer that does not derive from personal experience and is not a personal acquisition but is inborn or inherited. This domain of the psyche is known as the collective unconscious and owes its existence totally and exclusively to heredity.

The term *collective* expresses Jung's belief that, in contrast to the personal psyche that is individually acquired or developed, part of the unconscious has contents and modes of behavior that are nearly the same everywhere in all individuals. That is, there is a common or universal psychic substrate of a suprapersonal/transpersonal nature that is present in everyone. The collective unconscious can be viewed as being impersonal, supraindividual, and objective due to its belonging to all members of the human species.

While the personal unconscious is made up of complexes or feeling-toned trains of thought, the collective unconscious consists of ARCHETYPES. Archetypes are preexistent, inherited dispositions to apperceive typical or nearly universal situations and figures. They are not inherited ideas but a priori possibilities phylogenetically transmitted from one generation to the next. Archetypes are not determined innately in terms of specific contents but only in regard to their form. The archetype itself is empty and purely formal, only a possibility of representation in consciousness. These preexistent forms lie deeply in the unconscious and require cultural influence to activate and symbolically structure or clothe them in order to attain conscious reality. There are as many archetypes as there are typical situations in life, and when a situation occurs that corresponds to a given archetype, that archetype becomes activated and takes the color from the

individual consciousness in which it happens to appear. Thus the contents of an archetype develop from being filled out with the material of conscious experiences.

Archetypes can be seen from two points of view. On the one hand, they are predispositions to have certain experiences. This suggests the notion of potential without any concrete or measurable existence. On the other hand, archetypes may be considered as idea-forms that can become a part of actual experience. These two perspectives complement each other, since an individual cannot have experience without the preexisting potential for such. For example, the mother archetype requires an actual mother experience in order to take definite shape; but at the same time there must be the innate potential to have this mother experience.

The collective unconscious, with its storehouse of archetypes, contains the building forms and blueprint for the entire personality and indeed the whole of life. As the archetypes for the ego—e.g., persona, shadow, anima/animus, self, and God—become activated, symbolized, and actualized, the person matures and moves toward the individuated state.

The philosophical roots of archetypes can be detected in such sources as Plato's conception of the universal Idea as supraordinate and preexistent to all phenomena, and Kant's categories of meaning. From a theological perspective Irenaeus, a leader in the early years of Christianity, alluded to archetypes in his belief that the Creator of the world fashioned things according to preexisting patterns or archetypes. This theme is seen in God's giving instructions to Moses concerning the construction of the tabernacle according to an already existing pattern (Exod. 25:1–9, 40; Heb. 8:1–5).

Additional Reading
Jung, C. G. *The archetypes and the collective unconscious.* New York: Pantheon Books, 1959.
Jung, C. G. *Man and his symbols.* Garden City, N.Y.: Doubleday, 1964.

D. SMITH

See ANALYTICAL PSYCHOLOGY; JUNG, CARL GUSTAV.

Communication. Language is, perhaps, the loveliest dimension of human nature. A person's ability to share with another person genuine sensations and insights regarding the meaning of things surely is the epitome of God's image reflected in our humanness. Language is the channel of communication and may take the form of verbal or nonverbal expression. Verbal language has two forms: oral-aural symbols and pictographic symbols.

Both allow communication because they have culturally agreed-upon meaning. Nonverbal language involves symbolic gestures which may or may not be accompanied by verbal language. Nonverbal language, frequently referred to as body language, includes posture, facial expression, limb movements, dress, and other symbolic behaviors.

Language is useful because it allows us to communicate such a broad range of experiences. Through language the communicator is able to create in the receiver a cognitive and emotive experience like that which the communicator experiences (Hayakawa, 1949). There is considerable question whether the communicator actually transfers to the receiver a "package of meaning" through the channel of language or whether, as Kant thought, the meaning percept is already latently present in the receiver and is stimulated into experience by the impact of language upon the receiver (Keltner, 1969).

The communication process is structured in terms of the dynamics of who says what to whom, in what channel, and with what effect. In that process numerous elements function in an interactive manner (Ross, 1974). Within the sender an emotive need is sensed, probably subconsciously at first. The psyche raises that need to a semiconscious or conscious level and then raises it, as a notion or budding thought, to the cognitive level. The cognitive function of the person evaluates the need sensation and the idea it generates, and begins the process of conceptualizing a formal thought. That thought may be either pictorial or linguistic, depending in part on whether the person is right or left hemisphere dominant. The formal thought is then encoded in verbal or body language and prepared for expression. The encoded percept is then broadcast in the language channel to the receiver. That person's receptor grasps the signal, decodes the symbology, interprets the cognitive material, and registers it in the psyche.

In this total process a number of subprocesses are functioning. As the sender is sensing, encoding, and broadcasting the message, he or she is also experiencing an intrinsic feedback loop by which each stage of the sender's experience is being internally evaluated. This evaluation is influenced by previously stored memory, rational reflection, learned defenses, and the monitoring which the superego brings to bear upon the matter. Moreover, as the broadcasting of the message is in process, an extrinsic feedback loop is also functioning by which the sender is evaluating the setting and responses of the receiver and the communications environment and is modifying the message accordingly. The same may be said conversely about the receiver.

The communication process is never free from distraction. This is referred to as static. It may be static generated by incongruence between the sender's verbal and nonverbal language, offensive elements in the language, noise or uncongenial activities in the environment, or behavior of the receiver. Static is usually an activity or condition that emotionally overloads some aspect of the communication process. This aspect then attracts all the attention and energy away from the main message. If a preacher used scatological language in a sermon, the congregation would remember the scatology rather than the sermon. This is because the scatology would incite emotions of great intensity which would absorb all the energy and attention that should be concentrated on the sermon. That scatology is, therefore, static in the communication system and obstructs communication.

It is evident, therefore, that there are numerous junctures in any communication process at which breakdown can occur. It may occur in the sender or receiver at each of the points of perception transition. Moreover, the sender and receiver may not "speak the same language," since our cultures today are filled with jargon and are vocationally and therefore linguistically tribalized. In such a situation sender and receiver have different communication channels and cannot therefore communicate.

Finally, it is clear from this communication theory why the first chapter of Hebrews emphasizes the importance of God's shift in history from speaking to humanity in the diatribes of the prophets to the incarnate visit in his Son, Jesus Christ. Dialogic communication is more effective than monologic. Therefore, a visit is better than a lecture (Wheelwright, 1954). Also, a combined verbal and nonverbal communication is more efficient than an exclusively verbal one. This is evident in Jesus' teaching combined with ministries of healing. Thirdly, the communication mission of the believing community is to incarnate the gospel in word and deed, since that heals humans most effectively and enlightens them best (Wheelwright, 1962).

References

Hayakawa, S. I. *Language in thought and action.* New York: Harcourt, Brace, 1949.

Keltner, J. W. *Interpersonal speech communication.* Belmont, Calif.: Wadsworth Publishing, 1969.

Ross, R. S. *Persuasion*. Englewood Cliffs, N.J.: Prentice-Hall, 1974.

Wheelwright, P. E. *The burning fountain*. Bloomington: Indiana University Press, 1954.

Wheelwright, P. E. *Metaphor and reality*. Bloomington: Indiana University Press, 1962.

J. H. ELLENS

See FAMILY COMMUNICATIONS THEORY.

Communication, Nonverbal. Verbal communication has its complexities and confusions, but nonverbal communication is practically limitless. Our faces can make 250,000 different expressions (Birdwhistell, 1970). More than 100 hand acts have been observed (Ekman & Friesen, 1975). In spite of the inherent difficulty of defining or describing nonverbal communication, study of the visible and invisible messages we send and receive is crucial to effective communication.

Essentially, a nonverbal message functions in one of four ways; it replaces, reinforces, regulates, or contradicts a verbal message. Most often we resolve contradictions by believing the nonverbal portion of the total message (Mehrabian, 1971). Knapp (1978) offers an alternate classification scheme that includes seven factors which may contribute to a nonverbal communication: environmental factors (i.e., furniture, lighting, temperature); proxemics (use and perception of one's social and personal space); kinesics (body motions); touching behavior (physical contact); physical characteristics (physique, height, weight); paralanguage (vocal cues surrounding speech such as pitch, volume, tempo); and artifacts (manipulated objects in contact with interacting persons such as eyeglasses or clothes).

Research on proxemics has shown four kinds of distance at which people place themselves from another (Hall, 1959). Intimate distance is 18 inches or less. Personal distance is 1½ to 4 feet. Social distance ranges from 4 to 12 feet. The largest of the zones, public distance, denotes 12 feet or more, and it exists only in human relationships. One study of ethnic differences reveals that Mexicans stand closest to one another, Anglos are intermediate, and blacks tend to stand most distant (Keltner, 1973). Age and sex variables influence proxemics. Younger persons stand closer than older persons, and male-female groups stand closer than male-male groups.

In spite of the impeccable clarity with which performers such as Marcel Marceau or Buster Keaton have communicated a vast array of emotions and thoughts, nonverbal language is far too complicated to be reduced to simple rules for understanding. A frequently believed myth surrounding the psychology of nonverbal behavior is that every movement has its own meaning and that the observer can always discover the "true" person by "reading" the nonverbal messages. While often true, this belief leads the gullible observer to overinterpret cues which may be incidental or tied to a contextual meaning unavailable to the observer. Therefore, one must cautiously view the total message rather than zealously dissect its parts.

On the other hand, Gestalt therapists have demonstrated the importance of attention to body language. Incongruence between nonverbal and verbal messages is often a signal to the therapist that further probing is warranted. Individuals emitting conflicting messages may not be consciously aware of their inner feelings. Counselors must choose whether to deal directly with the incongruence or to maintain an awareness themselves and gradually draw out the client's emotions.

Wenburg and Wilmont (1973) note four of the axioms of communication postulated originally by Watzlawick, Beavin, and Jackson (1967) which are important for a counselor to keep in mind. The first of these is that one cannot *not* communicate. When we are in contact with another human being, we are always communicating. Our very presence and sometimes our absence communicate. Second, every communication has both content and relationship aspects. Verbally we emit cues of information which are interpreted by the contextual meaning provided by nonverbal messages. "I hate you!" delivered with a smile and squeeze on the arm suggests teasing.

The third axiom is that a series of communications can be viewed as an uninterrupted sequence. The way in which a message is "punctuated" nonverbally influences its interpretation. Wenburg and Wilmont (1973) state that "the essence of many marital struggles is a disagreement over how communication interchanges are punctuated. Take the couple that has the following punctuation of events. The wife says, I nag my husband because he withdraws and won't communicate with me and the husband says, I withdraw because my wife nags me. They are stopping the process at different points and, as a result, are assigning different causes and effects" (p. 104). Finally, the fourth axiom states that all communication relationships are either symmetrical or complementary, depending on whether they are based on equality or difference. Symmetrical communicators treat each other as equals and mirror each other. Complementary communicators maintain one as superior to the other.

Nonverbal communication occurs in so many varied ways that the perception process forces us to select out those deserving attention. Counselors must become keen observers of both content and relationship as they communicate. Recognition of incongruities and punctuation in messages can help to more accurately interpret the messages received and formulate useful hypotheses about the counselee. Strategic utilization of one's own body language to communicate genuineness, warmth, empathy, and positive regard for the counselee can increase effectiveness.

References

Birdwhistell, R. L. *Kinesics and context.* Philadelphia: University of Pennsylvania Press, 1970.
Ekman, P., & Friesen, W. V. *Unmasking the face.* Englewood Cliffs, N.J.: Prentice-Hall, 1975.
Hall E. T. *The silent language.* Garden City, N.Y.: Doubleday, 1959.
Keltner, J. W. *Elements of interpersonal communication.* Belmont, Calif.: Wadsworth Publishing, 1973.
Knapp, M. L. *Nonverbal communication in human interaction.* New York: Holt, Rinehart, & Winston, 1978.
Mehrabian, A. *Silent messages.* Belmont, Calif.: Wadsworth Publishing, 1971.
Wenburg, J. R., & Wilmont, W. W. *The personal communication process.* New York: Wiley, 1973.
Watzlawick, P., Beavin, J. H., & Jackson, D. D. *Pragmatics of human communication.* New York: Norton, 1967.

B. G. STONE

See FAMILY COMMUNICATIONS THEORY.

Communication Skills Training.

Programs that teach people skills for communicating with each other have become a conspicuous part of popular applied psychology. These programs usually are directed toward married or engaged couples, parents, teachers, employers, managers, or lay and professional counselors. Two conspicuous training programs with widely publicized textbooks typify the field. One is Parent Effectiveness Training (Gordon, 1970), with its offshoots for teachers and for leaders in business and government. The other is the Couples Communication Program (Miller, Nunnally, & Wackman, 1979).

Parent Effectiveness Training rests on the cornerstone of empathic listening skills Gordon learned from his mentor, Carl Rogers. The Rogerian imprint shows throughout the communication training literature, including that for counselors (Carkhuff, 1969) and for encounter group participants (Egan, 1973).

The format for a Parent Effectiveness Training course includes 10 weekly sessions 2 or 3 hours long for up to a dozen persons. The instructor follows a course outline replete with exercises for the class members to use in role playing problem situations. The pinnacle skill is active listening. That means I as receiver say back to you, the sender, in my own words what I sense you have just communicated to me in your words and nonverbal feeling tone. When your behavior bothers me, I use the second skill: confrontation. This involves what are called "I-messages," so named because they start with the nonjudgmental self-disclosure of "I," rather than the critic's rapier "you."

Parent Effectiveness Training emphasizes *hearing* the messages of a partner or child who is not necessarily committed to the communication process. By contrast, the Couples Communication Program stresses *telling* one's messages to a cooperating partner (e.g., spouse) so as to help that partner understand one. The approach places heavy emphasis on self-disclosure and on the distinction between content and process (i.e., *what* we say and *how* we say it). Instructors typically lead groups of about 4 couples in 4 weekly 3-hour sessions. The couples practice skills in front of the group, using actual issues between them. The leader keeps the emphasis on learning the skill rather than on solving particular problems.

Marriage enrichment programs of many kinds also emphasize communication skills. Like the other training programs they do not rehabilitate the sick, but aim to make good relationships better. The prototype is Marriage Encounter, which is conducted in an intense weekend experience using written dialogues between spouses. This technique controls the flow of words, so that eye contact and voice tones do not intimidate shy partners or inflame conflictual ones.

Although research on the effectiveness of these programs is minimal, typically participants look back on the training sessions as rich experiences. But they quickly apologize for not having followed through as diligently as they intended. They generally seem to approach everyday situations with the confidence of knowing they can draw on the skills they have filed away if problems arise. Trained couples committed to not separating or divorcing return to carefully using the structures they learned as a kind of portable referee when things get sticky between them. The key ingredient in the effectiveness of these programs is not, therefore, the skill but the will to use the skill.

References

Carkhuff, R. R. *Helping and human relations* (Vols. 1 & 2). New York: Holt, Rinehart, 1969.

Egan, G. *Face to face.* Monterey, Calif.: Brooks/Cole, 1973.
Gordon, T. *Parent effectiveness training.* New York: Wyden, 1970.
Miller, S., Nunnally, E. W., & Wackman, D. B. *Talking together: Couple communication I.* Minneapolis: Interpersonal Communication Programs, 1975.

D. L. GIBSON

See MARITAL ENRICHMENT; PARENT TRAINING PROGRAMS.

Community Mental Health. 1) A social/political philosophy, 2) a model for providing mental health services, and 3) an academic subdiscipline. It emerged in the early 1960s as a reaction to the cultural rejection and mistreatment of the mentally ill. Witch-hunts and snakepits had been eliminated; however, their replacement, the state mental hospital, was commonly located in remote rural areas where its existence could be forgotten as much as possible.

Moral horror at this situation was the primary fuel for the development of the community mental health movement. But there were other factors as well. By the 1950s there was increasing awareness that, in addition to the seriously mentally ill, a very great number of people were in need of psychotherapy or counseling. The great numbers of psychiatric casualties of World War II crowding the Veterans Administration hospitals and clinics could not be ignored. Except for the wealthy who could afford to pay private psychiatrists, and the lucky who were eligible for veterans' service or had access to one of the few existent child-guidance or university-based clinics, little help was available. This contributed a political dimension to the advocacy for an alternative. There was also a call to refute the cultural attitude of rejection of mental health problems and those who bear them. Then in the 1950s great advances in psychopharmacology emerged, and with the new wonder drugs of psychiatry state hospital patients who had been incurable no longer were. New assumptions and solutions were needed.

The ideology of community mental health developed from this combination of factors. It encompassed both a set of political values concerning the community's responsibility to its members, with special reference to the poor and the hurting, and an organizational model for addressing these values.

Conceptual Basis of Community Mental Health Centers. Although community mental health goes far beyond what community mental health centers actually do, the domain of community mental health remains best defined by the federal Community Mental Health Centers Act of 1963. This act set forth four key concepts in establishing the network of federally subsidized community mental health centers. First was that mental health services should be available to all people regardless of their ability to pay. It is important to note that the services were not to be free, except for the truly indigent, but only that they were not to be inaccessible either geographically or economically to anyone. Second, the centers were to be rooted in the community. Each center was to serve an area including ordinarily 100,000 to 250,000 people but varying with population density and was to be identified in every sense with that area. Third, each center was to provide all mental health services needed, that is, to be comprehensive. Finally, the services were to be coordinated by having them provided by the same rather than by different organizations. This was designed to ensure continuity of care to clients who needed more than one kind of service.

These concepts reflect several premises that can be grouped into three categories: the role and responsibility of the *community*, the scope of the *mental health* needs and services, and the mechanism of mental health *centers*.

Community Responsibilities. *Acceptance.* The first premise concerning community responsibility is that communities cannot banish their mentally ill but must care for them within their borders. Community mental health centers are designed to keep the individual in his own community. If the person requires hospital care, that hospital should be as near as possible to his home, not on the other side of the state. Alternatives to hospitalization should also be employed whenever possible. Partial hospitalization treatment was from the outset one service a mental health center had to provide if it were to qualify for federal support. Individuals who need more than weekly, or even daily, counseling sessions but who do not present a danger to themselves or others should continue living in their homes; they should receive intensive treatment as necessary but otherwise live normal lives. Finally, to whatever degree the individual must be removed from normal functioning in the community, he should be returned to it as soon as possible.

Civil rights legislation and litigation since 1963 have greatly elaborated the legal aspects of the mandate to provide the least restrictive effective treatment (i.e., that which least removes the individual from the community). A person may not be confined against his will, no matter how mentally ill he is, unless he presents a danger to himself or to others or is incompetent to care for himself. As a result of this, many chronically mentally ill individuals have been returned to their communities. Previously they would have been kept confined simply because they seemed somehow strange or frightening to others. Despite their strangeness, even if they openly have hallucinations and delusions and are indeed diagnosed mentally ill, their danger to others is often less than that of the average citizen, and courts have affirmed that the community may not banish them.

Financial base. A second premise is that the community should accept responsibility for providing and paying for mental health care. It was argued that providing these services would ultimately repay the community by reducing later expenditures for hospitalization, criminal justice, welfare, and education (by lowering discipline problems, etc.) and increasing worker productivity and stability.

The federal government underwrote the initial expense for building community mental health centers and much of the initial expense of hiring mental health professionals to staff them. Federal support was designed to decrease through the years. It was thought that the need for and value of these services would become so obvious that local communities would willingly take over their cost. This proved naïve. Some states have provided substantial support for community mental health centers, but others have not, and local tax dollars have not taken up the slack. Only about half of the originally planned network of centers, serving slightly more than half the population, have been established.

The early 1980s saw the Reagan administration largely remove the federal commitment to assure community mental health services. It greatly reduced federal outlays for mental health services and changed the funding mechanism to "block" grants to states. The block grants allow states flexibility in use of these federal funds instead of committing their use to community mental health centers, thus inviting states to use the funds to support other demanded services and thereby reduce state tax commitments.

Pressure to reduce tax expenditures on social programs at all governmental levels was, then, added to the failure of almost half the communities in the United States to have made the commitment to provide full mental health services for its members. The financial basis of community mental health services has become threatened. Increased concern with containing health care costs and cutback on Medicare and Medicaid have in fact reduced the economic accessibility of services to many in the community.

Governance. A third premise is that communities should have authority, as well as responsibility, over provision of mental health services to its citizens. Community mental health centers are established not as governmental services, either federal or state, but as nonprofit corporations. They are governed by boards of directors representing the community. Their revenues include fees paid by clients and insurance carriers as well as tax dollars from federal, state, and local sources. These governmental units may set conditions on their funding; in fact, until the Reagan administration the primary vehicle for assuring the standards for and scope of community mental health services was the contingency of federal grants on centers' meeting federal standards. Still, localities were free, within limits, to set their own priorities via their boards of directors and free to choose not to accept the federal or state money with its standards and mandates.

Services Needed. *Basic services.* Another premise is that the community has the responsibility to provide all the mental health services needed by its members. Before 1963 there were essentially just two kinds of services: hospitalization and outpatient psychotherapy. These were the ones most obviously needed and the ones that mental health professionals of the time were trained for and preferred to provide. To qualify for federal grants a community mental health center from the beginning had to provide at least three more basic kinds of service. One was partial hospitalization. The second was a 24-hour emergency service that would provide help when needed, not just during routine working hours. Prior to 1963, rarely if ever was such a service available. The third was referred to as consultation and education services. These entail several premises of their own.

Consultation and education. The Community Mental Health Centers Act assumed that all of the community profits from increasing the emotional well-being of each. Community mental health should therefore include serving not just those with especially serious problems, but serving all. Consultation and education services were mandated in part to extend needed care, at least indirectly, even to people who do not seek services of the mental health center.

A related premise is the proposition that prevention is preferable to treatment. The only two questions regarding preventive mental health services have been 1) are they possible and 2) who should pay for them?

The answer which has emerged to the first question is that preventive mental health services can indeed be effective, and that their focus should be on stress. Stress demonstrably precipitates or exacerbates essentially all mental health problems, from the most to the least severe. Many sources of stress can be prevented and the impact of stress can be lessened in various ways by teaching people how to cope with, or avoid, serious stresses and providing supports to help them through stress periods. Prevention services have included helping start support groups, providing supportive services for the chronically mentally ill, teaching skills in parenting, offering Children-of-Divorce groups, teaching relationship skills to children, and many others. Many efforts at prevention have no doubt been ineffective, but many others have clearly shown their effectiveness.

As for who should pay, the answer is once again that it must be the community, not the individual, which pays. Community mental health centers were therefore given the mission of doing what could be done to prevent, as well as treat, mental health problems in the community.

Regardless of the success of preventive mental health efforts, many in the community will continue to develop mental health problems and will need help. The next premise was that the number of such people will always far surpass the number who can be directly served by mental health centers. Repeated surveys conclude that, on average, 15–20% of all people in the community need mental health services each year. From the start it was estimated that no more than 2–3% of the population of any community could be served directly in any given year. Many of those remaining, who need help but are not getting it, are in contact with pastors, teachers, counselors, caseworkers, or physicians whose mission is to help them. These other caregivers, if they have enough skill and understanding, may often be able to give the needed help. It may often, in fact, be preferable for all concerned if the individual can get the help he needs without having to become a client of a mental health center. A prime mission of a mental health center, then, is to help these other caregivers be effective in their roles through providing them consultation and education.

Mandated specialized services. As mental health centers began meeting their initial mandate, some additional needs were identi-

fied. These were later added to the list of services centers were obligated to provide. They include specialized treatment and other services for people with alcohol and other drug abuse problems, for children and adolescents, for the elderly, and for victims of rape. They also include specific services for the chronically mentally ill, and consultation to courts and law enforcement agencies confronted with individuals who need treatment instead of or in addition to incarceration. Other specialized services could also be added. The community should actively seek to identify the people being missed by its services, not passively accede to the demands of those seeking service. The disenfranchised, the timid, and the intimidated are a special responsibility of the community and therefore of community mental health centers.

Centers. There were at least two reasons for specifying that mental health services should be provided through some centralized authority in the community. One was that otherwise communities or service providers might choose to provide only the services they wanted and leave serious needs unmet. The second was that clients often need several services, and transitioning from one to another must be effective.

This centralization has been better accomplished in some states than in others. In some, county politicians have insisted on being the coordinating agents by distributing to separate care-providing units the federal and state tax funds provided for the services. This procedure can leave the services themselves and the service providers largely uncoordinated. In some instances private professionals have been rewarded with contracts to perform the more lucrative services, while the services most dependent on tax support, especially prevention services and services to the chronically mentally ill, are neglected.

Finding the most effective means of providing community mental health services is, then, both a technological and a political problem. Even without the obvious intrusion of politics, observers agree that in most communities there is still need for more coordination of services.

Community Mental Health and Christian Ministry. The ministry of the church, in all but its narrow spiritual aspects, and the mission of community mental health could be said to be virtually the same. Indeed, a great many Christians have been attracted to the mental health professions as vehicles for ministry. There are abundant opportunities for mutual facilitation of the church's ministry and the community mental health center's mission. Yet there often is substantial distrust between the church and mental health agencies, and between many Christians and many mental health professionals.

This distrust undoubtedly comes from many sources, not the least of which may be an unexamined feeling of competition. Just as some Christians view secular mental health therapy as an alternative to Christian healing, similarly the unchurched therapist may view faith as an inferior substitute for the kind of self-understanding therapy can bring. Such perceptions produce mistrust and competition rather than the cooperation that is possible if spiritual growth is seen to be essential for emotional growth, and vice versa.

Just as Christians have from the beginning helped lead the advocacy for community mental health centers, many mental health authorities have recognized the church as particularly important in community mental health. Those serving the elderly and the chronically mentally ill, in particular, have seen how crucial a social support system is for those who would otherwise be isolated. An adequate support system may prove to be the most important of all preventive mental health resources. Next to the family, the church can provide that resource better than any other institution in the community.

Also, church memberships include their own share of alcoholics, dysfunctional marital relationships, depressed or undisciplined children, pregnant teen-agers, and victims and perpetrators of spouse and child abuse. There is little to support the hope that these problems occur much less frequently among the churched than among the unchurched; all the problems are likely to occur frequently in the average church, although often without the knowledge of the pastor or the rest of the congregation. If the church does not serve these people by reaching out and helping (or referring) them, then it can scarcely be effective in its ministry. In addition to these obviously needy people other mental health needs abound in the church membership—those dealing with the crises of aging or of mid-life; adjusting to the disillusionments of new marriage, new parenthood, or the blow of divorce or widowhood; children and teen-agers and their parents confronting the realities of emerging sexuality, etc. These are the transitional-stress issues for which preventive mental health services have proved especially important and effective. What more appropri-

ate setting to address these issues is there than the church? What better means is there of strengthening the church and for serving the community?

Additional Reading
Bloom, B. *Community mental health.* Monterey, Calif.: Brooks/Cole, 1977.

M. W. STEPHENS

Community Psychology. A relatively new subdiscipline which straddles the hazy boundaries between clinical psychology and social work, sociology, ecological psychology, and related disciplines. Numerous authors have noted the difficulty of defining precisely what community psychology is, and the definitions that have been offered to date have shared few commonalities. Community psychology tends to be characterized by the attempt to understand and intervene with human psychological maladjustment at group levels (i.e., organizational, institutional, or societal), and to intervene earlier in the development of psychopathology. Thus, community psychology is distinguished by several conceptual emphases in the understanding of human maladjustment and by several functional distinctives regarding methods of intervention and research.

History. The development of community psychology cannot be understood apart from its historical context. The treatment of the emotionally disturbed during the time of the development of clinical psychology was heavily institutional in nature and was dominated by the medical model (i.e., the belief that the disturbed are stricken by a disease which must be treated by a qualified professional). County and state mental hospitals housed huge numbers of the chronically disturbed during this period before and after World War II. Resident patient census in these institutions peaked at 559,000 in 1955 (Bassuk & Gerson, 1978).

In 1949 a conference on professional training in clinical psychology was held in Boulder, Colorado. The conferees there set the standard of the Ph.D. as the necessary degree for the professional practice of psychology and mandated the clinical psychologist to be a "scientist-practitioner," competent in academic and professional worlds. As the discipline grew, psychologists were employed in hospital and outpatient clinic settings, frequently training and working under the direction of medical personnel.

The quarter of a century following the Boulder conference was a period of tremendous social change. In reaction to a variety of influences, including the New Deal precedent for governmental social service, the growth of the social sciences and the understanding of social forces influencing emotional disturbance, the emergence of the civil rights movements, and the development of more effective psychoactive medications (especially the antipsychotic medications), national policies on the treatment of mental disturbance began to change. In 1955 the federal Joint Commission on Mental Health and Illness was formed. This commission issued a series of evaluative and prescriptive reports on the practice of mental health treatment in the United States. As a result of its recommendations Congress passed legislation in 1963 calling for and providing funding for the establishment of community mental health centers designed to detect and treat mental illness in the community early in its development, thus avoiding hospitalization in large geographically removed treatment centers. Each community mental health center was mandated to serve a specific geographic area, called the catchment area. In addition, the centers were mandated to coordinate the stabilization of the more chronically mentally ill in the community and thus to end the need for the large insane asylums of the first half of the twentieth century.

A group of psychologists met in Boston in 1965 to discuss the professional training of psychologists to work in the community mental health center movement. Great concern was expressed about the limitations of the existing legislation. It was felt that the institutional structure of the mental health centers and the manner in which services were to be delivered had simply moved the medical model from inpatient hospitals to outpatient clinics, with no real revolution in the way emotional disturbance was understood or treated. Dissatisfied with the medical model and what was perceived as clinical psychology's acceptance of it, conferees pressed for the rejection of the medical model and the development of a distinctly communal, distinctly psychological approach to dealing with emotional maladjustment and enhancing human welfare. Thus, the term *community psychology* was adopted at the conference and in subsequent publications. Conferees urged greater attention to basic research in the understanding of maladjustment as a cultural-sociopsychological (rather than medical) phenomenon. They called for the "community psychologist to be a social change agent, a political activist, and a 'participant-conceptualizer'" (Rappaport, 1977, p. 13).

Several years after the Boston conference

Division 27 (Community Psychology) of the American Psychological Association was officially formed. Most graduate departments of clinical training today provide some training in community psychology or community mental health. Many departments have identifiable community or clinical-community tracks within the professional training program. A second major conference on graduate training in community psychology took place in 1975 in Austin, Texas. (See Iscoe & Spielberger, 1977, and Rappaport, 1977, for a further discussion of the historical development of community psychology.)

Community Psychology and Community Mental Health. The distinctions between community psychology and COMMUNITY MENTAL HEALTH are not universally agreed upon. Goodstein and Sandler (1978) have provided a helpful heuristic model which distinguishes among four models of psychological service delivery: clinical psychology, community mental health, community psychology, and public policy psychology.

Clinical psychology is aimed at helping troubled individuals through the application of knowledge about remedial behavior-change techniques. Its basic style is professional (practitioner accountable to the profession and to the client) and passive (the "sick" or distressed client comes to the office or hospital for treatment). *Community mental health* practitioners serve troubled individuals and their significant others (family, clergy, employers, community leaders) in a catchment area, largely by applying the same knowledge base as the clinical psychologist. Community mental health practitioners are more active in marketing their services than are clinical psychologists and consult with significant others to speed recovery and help prevent relapses of those who have been identified as disturbed. The community mental health center is accountable primarily to the catchment area it serves. Rappaport (1977, pp. 75–79) has summarized research suggesting that while these centers have provided needed services in their catchment areas, they have not produced a revolution in the understanding and care of the psychologically disturbed. Despite some discussion, very little attention has in fact been paid to prevention.

Community psychology is characterized by Goodstein and Sandler (1978) as aimed at understanding and changing social systems rather than individuals. The focus, they suggested, is changing the system which controls deviance and socialization. So, instead of working with a single troubled child, for example, the community psychologist would work with the school, the church, the neighborhood, or the local community mental health center of that child. The goal of this intervention is to increase the likelihood that the child would be able to make a more satisfactory adjustment in life as a result of his contacts with these institutional systems. The skills of the community psychologist are then unique, consisting largely of system analysis and organizational design skills, as opposed to individual behavior-change skills.

The final model of Goodstein and Sandler is *public policy psychology*, which aims at the formulation and implementation of public policies that will yield the maximal returns in terms of the enhanced welfare of the citizens of the society. The public policy psychologist needs all the analytic skills of the community psychologist but a different set of intervention skills in the area of political participation.

This heuristic model is extremely helpful in understanding some of the differences between community mental health and community psychology. It should be remembered, however, that these pure types exist only in theory. Community mental health and community psychology usually differ in terms of emphasis rather than being clearly and qualitatively distinct.

Conceptual Distinctives. The first distinctive of community psychology has been called the *ecological perspective*, the assertion that all behavior, including abnormal behavior, must be understood as resulting from the interaction of the person with the social and physical environment. Unlike more traditional understandings which locate the entire responsibility for behavior within the individual, the ecological perspective proposes an interdependence between each of us and our environment. Thus, the causes of the emotional disturbance of a person must be located in both the person and the environment.

There is an overwhelming mass of evidence supporting this assertion, especially the studies of the epidemiology of mental disturbance, which show that disturbance is strongly affected by social class, the occurrence of stressful life events, and the presence of social support systems. Lower social class status and more frequent or more severe life stress increase incidence of psychological disturbance; the presence of social support ameliorates the effects of stress and reduces incidence of disturbance. Overall, the community psychologist emphasizes environmental causes of distur-

bance; he also looks to the social environment of the disturbed individual to understand the significance of that person's behavior. This environmental emphasis includes a distinct appreciation of political, cultural, and economic factors which influence adjustment.

Second, many community psychologists reject a defect model of human disturbance in favor of a *competency model of human potential*. Albee (1982) has defined the defect model as the belief that human disturbance is the relatively unmodifiable result of enduring genetic or biochemical defects within the disturbed person. Rappaport (1977) and Albee (1982), following others, call such a position "blaming the victim"; the person is branded as unworthy and despicable because of his problem, when it is obvious from an ecological perspective that the person has been the victim of outside forces. In place of the defect model community psychologists emphasize the enhancement of strategic competencies of the individual and adjustment of the person's environment to better enhance personal welfare. Persons are viewed as experiencing problems not because they are flawed by a defect, but because they have failed to develop competencies and are in a dysfunctional environment.

Finally, many community psychologists emphasize the *value of diversity*. "In value terms, an ecological viewpoint implies that differences among people and communities may be desirable" (Rappaport, 1977, p. 3). They recommend creation of alternative settings which allow variant groups to exist to their personal satisfaction. As examples of the way traditional psychology has not allowed such a coexistence, community psychologists have pointed to the cultural imperialism implicit in the elevated diagnoses of mental disturbances and mental retardation among new immigrant groups and cultural or racial minorities. Community psychologists would argue that by and large such diagnostic patterns represent intolerance of cultural differences and the stress produced by such intolerance.

Functional Distinctives. Current research in community psychology is of two major types. The first is basic research into the determinants of psychosocial distress and life satisfaction for aggregates of people. This research is distinguished from more traditional research on psychopathology by 1) its concern with community aggregates (e.g., residents in a community, employees of a company) as opposed to individuals or diagnostic group aggregates (e.g., schizophrenics) and 2) a relative lack of concern for the specific form that the psychopathology takes. The concern is for overall levels of symptomatology as opposed to occurrence of a specific disorder. Current research is emphasizing the role of stress (emotional, physical, economic, etc.) in the etiology of emotional disturbance and of personal resources such as social support networks and coping skills in the amelioration of the effects of stress.

The second major type of community research is the development and evaluation of prototype intervention programs. Community psychologists have emphasized the prevention of emotional disturbance, particularly primary prevention, the goal of which is the reduction of the occurrence of new cases of disturbance in a population. Advocates for this approach argue convincingly that no disorder has ever been eradicated by treating those afflicted with the problem. Cowen (1980), following the President's Commission on Mental Health, discusses five major types of preventive interventions: mental health education of the public and of specific groups, interventions to change social systems such as schools and vocational settings to be more humane, competence training aimed at the development of important life skills, stress reduction and coping interventions, and work to enhance the effectiveness of a person's social support system and informal helping networks.

There are several critical distinctives of community psychology interventions as contrasted to clinical psychology and community mental health. The first is its lack of specific focus on a particular individual. Groups of persons are frequently the target, as are organizations or institutions, which are changed to enhance the functioning of anyone happening to interface with that institution. An increasing emphasis in community psychology is the enhancement of human effectiveness rather than the reduction of psychopathological symptomatology. The preventive rather than remedial emphasis of community psychology is another distinctive. The intentional and intensive focus on psychological health and disturbance distinguishes community psychology from other disciplines and professions that also aim to promote human welfare. Finally, community psychology has been characterized by its continued struggle to resist premature professionalization. There has been much greater openness to utilization of paraprofessional resources and a greater emphasis on continual empirical revaluation of interventions than in traditional clinical psychology.

Evaluation comments. The fact that community psychology is so difficult to define is troublesome and probably reflects the lack of a true consensus within the field regarding its defining properties. Given this ambiguity, the present article may suggest a greater unity than in fact exists. There is also a good deal of continuing disagreement over training and professional practice in this area. Because of the complexity of the problems addressed by this field, community psychology is probably on even less sure footing regarding its knowledge base than its parent discipline, clinical psychology. Community psychology is no longer quite as distinctive as in its early years, given the steady ascendancy of behavioral and family systems models within clinical psychology, which emphasize person-environment interactions and relational definitions of psychopathology. This may represent a significant triumph of the community psychology movement in making these perspectives acceptable to the professional community.

The greatest contributions of community psychology are its emphasis on prevention and on large-scale interventions (with their hopefully greater efficiency) and its appreciation of the environmental (especially cultural and political) influences on the person. Christian theology is compatible with a view of persons which sees the person's adjustment as a function of both person and environment. This is seen in the Scriptural emphasis on the maintenance of purity in the church and other social relationships (i.e., one's social environment) in service of personal piety.

The church has historically been deeply involved in social ministry at all levels, from individual acts of charity through large-scale societal/political reorganization (e.g., Calvin's Geneva). The church has not historically focused intensively on psychological adjustment, and such a focus from community psychology would surely be of benefit to the church. The church undoubtedly is a major resource for enhancing human adjustment through its inherent emphasis on community, support, and ministry.

References
Albee, G. W. Preventing psychopathology and promoting human potential. *American Psychologist*, 1982, *37*, 1043–1050.
Bassuk, E. L., & Gerson, S. Deinstitutionalization and mental health service. *Scientific American*, 1978, *238*(2), 46–53.
Cowen, E. L. The wooing of primary prevention. *American Journal of Community Psychology*, 1980, *8*, 253–284.
Goodstein, L. D., & Sandler, I. Using psychology to promote human welfare: A conceptual analysis of the role of

community psychology. *American Psychologist*, 1978, *33*, 882–892.

Iscoe, I., & Spielberger, C. D. Community psychology: The historical context. In I. Iscoe, B. L. Bloom, & C. D. Spielberger (Eds.), *Community psychology in transition.* Washington, D.C.: Hemisphere, 1977.

Rappaport, J. *Community psychology: Values, research, and action.* New York: Holt, Rinehart, & Winston, 1977.

S. L. JONES

See PREVENTION OF PSYCHOLOGICAL DISORDERS.

Comparative Psychology. The scientific study of the behavior of animals that is oriented toward identifying similarities and differences in animal behavior. Comparative psychology also involves a special concern for the comparison of human and animal behavior.

Comparisons between human and animal behavior occurred with some regularity during the seventeenth and eighteenth centuries. The majority of these comparisons emphasized the major differences that existed between man and animal. However, the emergence of theories of evolution and the influence of Darwin's work, which emphasized the similarities between human and animal behavior, provided sufficient impetus for the development of a distinct comparative psychology.

Comparative psychology is based on an evolutionary view of behavior and proceeds according to the following assertion: Because animals have evolved along different evolutionary pathways and have adapted to different environments, differences should exist in structure, function, and behavior among animals, including humans. Observed differences and similarities presumably can be accounted for and explained in terms of evolution and heredity.

Evolution is believed to act only on traits that are inherited. Consequently, early comparative psychologists emphasized the instinctual nature of animal behavior. Because humans were assumed to have evolved from animals, it was reasoned that humans must also have instincts, some of which may be the same as those of animals. One early trend involved examining human behavior to find signs of its instinctual determinants and to catalog instincts for every observable human behavior. This approach gave way, over time, to a more systematic, scientific set of procedures. The methods of contemporary comparative psychology are drawn primarily from learning and physiological psychology. A typical study might involve comparing the performance of two different species on an artificial learning task conducted in a controlled laboratory environment.

Comparative psychology has had only a limited impact on the overall psychology of learning and behavior. This has occurred for several reasons. First, investigating a representative sample of behaviors across a representative set of species presents an overwhelming task. Second, the influence of comparative psychology has been overshadowed by the behaviorists' position, which minimizes the role of heredity on behavior and asserts that learning processes in all organisms are essentially the same except for some quantitative differences. Behaviorists have also tacitly assumed that general principles of behavior could be identified by investigating a small number of species. Over the last decade or so, however, there has been a resurgence of interest in the biological and hereditary determinants of behavior, and even behaviorally minded psychologists are increasingly evoking evolutionary explanations of behavior.

S. R. OSBORNE

Competition. *See* COOPERATION AND COMPETITION.

Complex. A group of ideas or memories which are repressed but which have a strong emotional charge. This term was first used extensively by Jung, who called his approach "a psychology of complexes." In psychoanalytic thought the complex is always partially unconscious even though the content of the complex may be partially conscious. Nonpsychoanalytic writers sometimes use the term to refer to overemphasized ideas, without any implication of unconscious source.

Compliance. The art of getting someone to do a favor. Often this involves only a simple and straightforward request. Sometimes, however, a simple request is made more powerful by adding subtle social pressures. These more manipulative methods have attracted the attention of most social psychologist researchers (Baron & Byrne, 1981). Of these techniques the majority fall into one of two groups: those that rely on multiple requests and those that take advantage of our notions of fairness.

Of the multiple-request techniques the most common is the foot-in-the-door. With this technique the request of real interest is preceded by a smaller and less costly request. For example, successful panhandlers often lead into a request for money by first asking directions or the time of day. A biblical variation of the foot-in-the-door is Abraham's plea before God for Sodom (Gen. 18:16–33). Apparently, at least with finite beings, the technique works because it produces a change in self-concept. After saying yes to the small favor, the person perceives himself as someone who does favors for the requester. He is then more vulnerable to the second request.

Another multiple-request technique is the door-in-the-face. Someone using this technique begins with an outrageously large request. When the target refuses, the person counters with a more moderate request (the request of real interest). Because the requester appears to compromise, the target feels pressure to reciprocate by agreeing to the smaller request. When a TV evangelist, for instance, first appeals for large donations and then suggests that even small amounts will help, he is using the door-in-the-face.

Low-balling is a very effective variation on the foot-in-the-door. In low-balling the cost of compliance is increased after the person says yes. Thus, the second request is simply a costlier version of the initial request. A biblical example is provided by the negotiations between Jacob and Laban (Gen. 29:15–30). Jacob was low-balled into working twice the original agreed-upon time for obtaining Rachel as his wife.

The second group of techniques revolve around our commonly accepted notions of fairness. It has long been acknowledged that favors beget favors. When someone does us a favor, our notions of fairness typically obligate us to reciprocate. Publishers send complimentary copies of books to educators. Of course, such a practice serves an informational function. But it also exerts pressure upon the teacher to adopt the text for his or her class.

Another example of a technique that takes advantage of our notions of fairness is guilt induction. If we feel we have harmed someone, we become more vulnerable to a request. By saying yes we may be attempting to restore equity, make ourselves feel better, or even make ourselves look better. Charitable organizations often accompany requests for donations with graphic depictions of human hurt and anguish. To the extent that we feel part of this world, and thus at least indirectly involved, we may be induced by guilt to donate.

A thought-provoking issue for Christians is the extent to which such techniques should be used in evangelism and fund raising. The easy answer is to assume that those who use manipulative techniques are simply interested in selfish gain and thus are wrong. However, a more serious look at the issue forces one to acknowledge that there are good-hearted Christians who use manipulative techniques

simply to advance the kingdom of God. For these individuals, since intention is not an issue, the question becomes, How do we know when they have gone too far? Basinger and Bassett (1982) suggest that the boundary line is a respect for personhood. Such a respect means a recognition that, though fallen, we are created in the image of God. We can feel, think, are responsible, and have value. Thus, any technique which seriously thwarts one or more of these attributes is wrong.

References

Baron, R. A., & Byrne, D. *Social psychology: Understanding human interaction* (3rd ed.). Boston: Allyn & Bacon, 1981.

Basinger, D., & Bassett, R. L. Ye shall be manipulators of men. *Eternity*, 1982, *33*(7–8), 20–23.

R. L. BASSETT

Compulsion. An urge to perform an act or ritualized series of acts which if not completed leads to intolerable anxiety. Hence, the urge feels irresistible. The anxiety, according to psychoanalytic theorists, is the result of ideas or desires that are unacceptable to the person but are nevertheless surfacing into conscious awareness. The compulsion serves to defend against the anxiety by displacing attention from the unacceptable ideas or desires onto the irrational but acceptable compulsion. The allaying of anxiety serves to reinforce the performance of the act, thus making its repetition even more likely. An example of a compulsion is the individual who feels forced to wash his hands every time he touches anything. Compulsions are characteristic of obsessive compulsive disorder and may also be seen in schizophrenia.

J. E. TALLEY

See OBSESSION.

Compulsive Personality Disorder. As a personality type the compulsive prefers to organize his experience around rule, order, and standards. When functioning at their best, these people are hardworking, diligent, and responsible. They are the workhorses of the world, grinding out the systematic and detailed tasks on which a modern technological society depends. While doing this they tend to be "black and white" people who are less sensitive to the subtleties of interpersonal relationships, who find it difficult to accept human frailties and compromise.

When these traits become pathological, a characteristic triad of cold perfectionism, preoccupation with detail, and indecisiveness appears. Should these people come to the therapist to seek aid for their personality problems, their chief complaint is usually this indecisiveness and procrastination. More commonly they come complaining of more specific symptoms which seem to originate in the personality. Profound depression is not unusual, and specific obsessions and compulsions can become disturbing in their daily lives.

Their coldness seems associated with a sense of responsibility for order, as though they must establish and defend rightness. They tend to be conventional, moralistic, and overly scrupulous and to exact standards of perfection from themselves and others that are unreasonable or even impossible. They are often considered "stiff" and deal with emotions awkwardly. The expression of tender feelings, compliments, or even giving gifts is to them a struggle. They seek pleasure in a heavy-handed manner and have trouble relaxing. Their hobbies, when they have them, seem psychologically overdetermined, tasks rather than fun.

Their concern for detail and procedural minutiae often is associated with a loss of the bigger picture. They become inefficient when bogged down in making lists and ruminating about priorities. They usually overcompensate for this ineptness by working longer and using more deliberate methods. A resentment of the demands made on them and the slackness of others usually simmers under the surface of their apparent zeal.

The person suffering from a compulsive personality disorder characteristically finds decision making an ordeal. It is as though he must find a perfect answer to every choice. A patient once described a compulsive father as "the world's master of second-guessing." By this she meant that he always rethought, rehashed every decision, trying to find a faultless course in places where he had to settle for the lesser of evils. This overconscientiousness and difficulty in accepting the myriad of small compromises of each day make the lives of compulsives miserable. They seem anxious and restless with anything short of absolute perfection.

Rappaport (1951) has called this a disease of cognition or of the intellect. Indeed, therapy with these people seems to bog down endlessly in repetitive thought patterns which circle around guilt over real or imagined transgressions and efforts at expiation. This intellectualization is generally considered by analysts since Freud to be defensive, protecting against rage hypothesized to originate in the anal stage conflict between a harsh and punitive superego and the ego's demand for control and dominance.

Primitive anger and frustration not adequately worked through can result in several kinds of pathology in the compulsive adult. In a passive person an obedient, fear-ridden pattern might develop. Another person, more aggressive in nature, by reaction formation might become parsimonious, untidy, and critical. More effective sublimation could produce a person devoted to the principles of the Scout Oath, though at the cost of his being overcontrolled, ingratiating, and lacking in self-confidence and self-esteem.

Within the Christian community people suffering from compulsive personality disorder tend to be excessively legalistic, falling into the profound error of the Pharisee. Their icy correctness is often ministered without love or understanding, empowered by the fundamental biblical concern for righteousness. In the course of their treatment themes of righteousness, law, order, and standards very soon boil down to issues of control. It is essential that these be dealt with firmly and compassionately so that the focus can get down to the more fundamental struggles over primitive fear, helplessness, and rage. Nothing much seems to change in the life of the compulsive until this level of experience is dealt with. Weintraub (1974) gives a succinct discussion of the treatment of the compulsive and makes the interesting observation that treatment can be complicated by the compulsiveness of the therapist.

DSM-III allows a helpful distinction between the compulsive personality disorder and an anxiety disorder designated the OBSESSIVE-COMPULSIVE DISORDER.

References
Rappaport, D. *Organization and pathology of thought.* New York: Columbia University Press, 1951.
Weintraub, W. Obsessive-compulsive and paranoid personalities. In J. R. Lion (Ed.), *Personality disorders.* Baltimore: Williams & Wilkins, 1974.

Additional Reading
Salzman, L. *Treatment of the obsessive personality.* New York: Aronson, 1980.

C. M. BERRY

See PERSONALITY DISORDERS.

Computer Applications in Mental Health.

Increasingly sophisticated technological advances have brought a new wave of uses for computers in the field of mental health. Glueck and Stroebel (1975) define five general areas in which these uses fall: data collection, diagnosis, treatment, evaluation of progress, and referral information.

Data collection may be simplified in several ways through the use of the computer. Initial history taking and admission processing can be handled quickly by the computer, saving time when caseloads are full and additional cases waiting. Psychological tests like the Minnesota Multiphasic Personality Inventory may be coded and evaluated more efficiently by computer than by hand. Some computer programs conduct the interviewing process itself (Angle, Johnsen, Grebenkemper, & Ellinwood, 1979). Slack (1977) demonstrated that some people prefer the computer to a live interviewer, particularly when discussing extremely personal material for the first time. When this is the case, a therapist may benefit from allowing the computer to handle the data collection process. Most existing diagnostic computer programs are intended for such problem-oriented objective questions as sleep patterns, relational inquiries, drug and alcohol use, and other patterns of behavior. Obviously, less problem-focused objective questions would be more difficult, though not impossible, to handle through the computer interviewer.

Diagnostic uses of the computer ordinarily fall into the symptom cluster design. That is, symptoms are fed into the computer's memory, which has already been coded for recognizing patterns of psychological disturbances. There are some distinct advantages to this method of diagnosis, but it is not without critics. On the positive side proponents argue that the computer diagnosis eliminates interviewer biases and subjective imposition of problems on the client. It can use larger samples of information than one counselor can possibly personally deal with in a lifetime, and it can handle much more information than the human mind can process. The computer is also more flexible in that information can be easily changed to reflect new learning, and it handles information processing quickly, with explicit rules. Critics argue that the procedure is depersonalizing and that the intuitive element of initial interviewing and diagnosis is absent. The use of computers in this area, as well as in actual treatment, seems to be more conducive to cognitive approaches to therapy than person-centered approaches.

Following on the heels of diagnostic use of the computer are treatment uses, usually taking the form of recommendations for treatment based on symptoms. Again, these treatment recommendations are preprogrammed into the computer based on large samples of studies. Prognosis and evaluation of progress of therapy can also be handled by the computer based on symptom clusters and treatment recommendations.

The use of computers for therapy itself is one of the most controversial areas in mental health today. It is a threatening, though often misunderstood, idea for mental health workers who fear that their skills will be replaced by the computer. The idea is not to replace therapists with computers, but to find ways in which they can work together to the benefit of the client. The Plato DCS (Dilemma Counseling System) at the University of Illinois links with over a thousand computer terminals at colleges, businesses, and communities across the United States and Canada, as a counseling program for personal use for a variety of problems. Its highly structured and logical problem-solving approach has helped thousands of people in decision making, particularly as related to career choices and other important decisions (Wagman, 1980). Other uses of the computer for therapy include systematic desensitization, administering positive and negative reinforcement, and psychotherapeutic dialogue.

Computers can effectively be used for referral data, simplifying this procedure immensely. The computer system allows easy access to collection of agency information, specialty clinics, names, addresses, and other relevant data. In addition, computers have such wide-reaching uses as vehicles for training of mental health workers, research compilation, and even suicide prevention (Barnett, 1982).

Legal and ethical considerations such as confidentiality and professional liability need to be addressed, but these issues are evident in the field of mental health whether computers are used or not. With the continuing trends toward computerization, new uses for computers in the field of mental health will continue to evolve.

References

Angle, H. V., Johnsen, T., Grebenkemper, N. S., & Ellinwood, E. H. Computer interview support for clinicians. *Professional Psychology*, February 1979, pp. 49–57.

Barnett, D. C. A suicide prevention incident involving use of the computer. *Professional Psychology*, August 1982, pp. 565–570.

Glueck, B. C. & Stroebel, C. F. Computers and clinical psychology. In A. M. Freedman, H. I. Kaplan, & J. B. Sadock (Eds.). *Comprehensive textbook of psychiatry, II* (2nd. ed.). Baltimore: Williams & Wilkins, 1975.

Slack, W. V. Talking to a computer about emotional problems. *Psychotherapy: Theory, Research and Practice*, 1977, *14*, 156–164.

Wagman, M. Plato DCS: An interactive computer system for personal counselors. *Journal of Counseling Psychology*, 1980, *27*, 16–30.

D. L. Schuurman

Concretizing Technique. Concretization, a technique of PSYCHODRAMA, involves the use of sculpting (see FAMILY CHOREOGRAPHY; FAMILY SCULPTURE TECHNIQUE) to describe the dynamics involved in interaction. Much of the content for concretizations comes from symbolic language used by the person to describe his or her plight. The spacial dimension is seen in the nearness of the person to significant others. High and low often represent power and weakness. The others in the scene are sculpted according to their relationship with the person.

An example of the concretizing technique is a scene in which a person feels alienated and powerless in the presence of a parent. The individual might assume a 20-foot distance and be on his or her knees. The parent (played by another member of the psychodrama group) might stand on a chair pointing derisively.

In a more general way, the concretizing technique is also used within other therapeutic traditions when the therapist asks for concrete details to move a highly abstract and generalized discussion toward specifics. Therapists must also model this dimension through their own use of concrete and specific terminology. When they avoid vagueness and ambiguity, clients tend to do the same.

J. H. VANDER MAY

Condensation. In psychoanalysis, condensation refers to the process whereby a single idea in consciousness contains all the emotion associated with a number of unconscious ideas. The single idea, word, or phrase is described as overcathected in that it has attached to it the psychic energy of all the fused ideas. This process is best seen in dreams, where details in the dream are each condensations of a number of unconscious elements. The dream itself, therefore, is a condensation of a vast complex of unconscious ideas.

Conditioned Reflex Therapy. The current name for this approach is ASSERTIVENESS TRAINING. Conditioned reflex therapy is the name used by Salter (1949) when he first described the treatment of inhibition, assumed to be at the core of all neurotic problems, through training in expressive behavior. The approach has generally been viewed as one of the first clinical applications of the principles of conditioning, and Salter thereby earned his place as one of the pioneer behavior therapists.

Reference
Salter, A. *Conditioned reflex therapy.* New York: Creative Age Press, 1949.

D. G. BENNER

Conditioning, Avoidance. In avoidance conditioning the occurrence of an aversive event is postponed or prevented by performing the appropriate response prior to its onset. Most laboratory studies of avoidance conditioning have used the following procedure. A stimulus, such as a light, is presented some time (e.g., 30 seconds) before the presentation of the aversive event (e.g., painful electric shock). If the appropriate avoidance response is performed during the light and prior to the aversive event, shock does not occur, the light is terminated, and there is a pause of specified length before the light is presented again. If the avoidance response is not performed, shock is presented.

A critical factor in the acquisition of an avoidance response is the nature of the response itself. For example, rats readily learn to press a lever for food pellets, but a lever-press avoidance response is acquired very slowly and sometimes incompletely. Alternatively, rats rapidly acquire a running response to avoid shock. Aversive stimuli often elicit innate defensive behavior. If the required avoidance response is compatible with the general form of the defensive behavior, then it normally will be learned easily. Otherwise, learning may occur slowly or not at all.

Variables that affect avoidance conditioning, other than the nature of the response, include the interval between the onset of the conditioned stimulus and the presentation of the aversive event, the interval between successive conditioning trials, intensity of the aversive event, the nature of the conditioning stimulus, the type of organism (e.g., rat, pigeon, etc.), whether or not the aversive event can be escaped, and, if so, the nature of the escape response.

Apart from laboratory investigations of avoidance conditioning the learned ability to avoid potentially harmful situations is clearly adaptive; for many animal species such learning is critical to their very survival. For humans the effects of avoidance learning go well beyond mere survival. Most people learn to avoid unpleasant social situations and to adapt their behavior to avoid the potentially aversive consequences of unlawful, immoral, or unacceptable social behavior.

The outcome of avoidance learning, however, is not always adaptive. Phobias—extreme, irrational fears—often result in maladaptive or debilitating avoidance behavior. For example, a person with a chronic fear of hospitals may avoid seeking needed medical help. Avoidance responses also may generalize beyond the original situation. For example, a child who has experienced aversive (emotional) consequences because of failing a particular academic subject may try to avoid school altogether. Finally, avoidance learning may limit future behavioral flexibility. That is, avoidance learning may have originally taken place under a set of circumstances that no longer 'exist. However, inappropriate avoidance behavior may be maintained because the avoidance response itself prevents the person from coming into contact with the new contingencies.

Fortunately, maladaptive avoidance behavior often is corrected naturally by the behavioral consequences that exist in our everyday lives. In more extreme cases (e.g., phobias) some form of behavioral therapy may be required.

S. R. Osborne

See Learning.

Conditioning, Classical.

Conditioning, Classical. Classical, or respondent, conditioning represents a simple form of learning that results from the pairing of stimuli. In a well-known experiment Pavlov, who was studying the digestion of dogs, noticed an unusual phenomenon. A metronome that was associated with the placement of food in the dogs' mouths caused the dogs to salivate in much the same manner as did the food itself. This simple observation became the basis for the theory of classical conditioning.

Some stimuli have an innate ability to elicit a response; i.e., they automatically produce a response without any special training or previous experience. Such a stimulus is termed an unconditioned stimulus and the response it elicits is termed an unconditioned response. Eye blinks to a puff of air, knee jerks to taps below the knee cap, perspiration to warm temperatures, and salivation to food are all examples of unconditioned responses and stimuli.

If a stimulus that normally has no effect on behavior is repeatedly paired with an unconditioned stimulus, it will come to elicit the same response as the unconditioned stimulus, even if presented in its absence. The previously neutral stimulus is then called a conditioned stimulus, the response a conditioned response, and the process itself classical conditioning. For example, if a tone (neutral stimulus) is repeatedly paired with a puff of air (unconditioned stimulus) to the eye, the tone will become a conditioned stimulus and elicit the eye-blink reflex even if the air puff is not presented. Similarly a neutral stimulus, after

sufficient pairing with a painful electric shock, can come to elicit an emotional fear response similar to that elicited by the shock.

Conditioned responses can be classified according to the type of unconditioned stimulus used and the nature of the response that is conditioned. An unconditioned stimulus is appetitive if it is generally attractive to the organism (e.g., food) and aversive if it is generally unpleasant (e.g., a loud noise). Responses are classified as skeletal if they involve the musculature of the body, organic if they involve internal organs, and glandular if they involve the glands. All these types of conditioning have been demonstrated in the laboratory. A conditioned response also can be developed if the unconditioned stimulus is presented at regular and predictable time intervals (temporal conditioning). In this case the time interval separating successive presentations of the unconditioned stimulus comes to serve as the conditioned stimulus.

Classical conditioning has many properties that are important in determining how it affects behavior. First, conditioned responses tend to be anticipatory. When a conditioned response is fully conditioned it typically precedes the occurrence of the unconditioned stimulus or occurs before the unconditioned stimulus would have been presented. Therefore, the conditioned response is not simply a substitute for the unconditioned response but a particular learned reaction in its own right. Second, conditioned responses generalize from one stimulus to another. Stimuli that are similar to the conditioned stimulus will elicit the conditioned response; the greater the similarity, the greater the likelihood that generalization will occur. For example, in an early experiment a young infant was conditioned by repeatedly pairing a white rat with a sudden loud noise. Eventually the white rat came to elicit a fear response similar to that produced by the noise. However, fear responses also were elicited by other white, furry objects (e.g., a white rabbit) even though these objects had never been paired with the loud noise.

A third property of classical conditioning is that discriminations between stimuli can be developed. Discriminations are the behavioral opposites of generalizations; they enable an organism to narrow the range of generalization. The process can be demonstrated by the following example: If the conditioned stimulus (white rat) is presented with the unconditioned stimulus (loud noise) and a similar stimulus (white rabbit) is presented without the unconditioned stimulus, the conditioned response (fear reaction) that initially occurred to both stimuli will soon become more frequent to the conditioned stimulus that is paired with the unconditioned stimulus and the fear response to the other stimulus will eventually cease.

Finally, conditioned responses are not necessarily permanent. If the conditioned stimulus is repeatedly presented without the unconditioned stimulus, it will eventually lose its power to elicit the conditioned response. The number of unpaired presentations required for this extinction process to occur depends upon, among other things, the strength of the original conditioning.

The implications of classical conditioning extend far beyond the laboratory curiosity of learning psychologists and Pavlov's dogs. The conditioned reflex is regarded by many as the basic building block of behavior. Moreover, the critical conditions necessary for conditioning to occur are present in the normal environment of every person.

The role of classical conditioning in our lives is not trivial. Simple conditioned responses make a significant contribution to our behavior. For example, people close their eyes when something is about to hit them in the face and they flinch when threatened by a blow. Many internal body reactions also are partially controlled by a wide variety of conditioned stimuli. These stimuli have functional significance in preparing us for events to come. The heart rate and blood pressure changes and increased adrenaline flow that characterize fear are often elicited by stimuli that are not inherently threatening. Such stimuli acquire their power through conditioning.

Classical conditioning procedures also form the basis of some psychotherapies. Systematic desensitization is one method psychologists have developed for overcoming such undesirable, long-lasting emotional responses as phobias. The objective of desensitization is to condition the patient to relax in the presence of anxiety-arousing stimuli. Because relaxation and anxiety are incompatible, as the patient learns to relax he simultaneously learns not to be anxious. Although the success rate of desensitization depends on the specific anxiety, systematic desensitization has been shown to be a very effective treatment and is a standard approach of most behavioral clinicians.

S. R. OSBORNE

See LEARNING.

Conditioning, Higher-Order. Within classical conditioning there are many ways in which a neutral stimulus can acquire conditioning properties. One method, known as higher-order conditioning, involves the pairing of two or more stimuli in a situation in which an unconditioned stimulus is not directly involved.

The standard conditions under which classical conditioning normally occurs consist of the repeated pairing of a neutral stimulus (e.g., a tone) with an unconditioned stimulus (e.g., food) so that the previously neutral stimulus comes to elicit a response similar to the one elicited by the unconditioned stimulus. In higher-order conditioning a second neutral stimulus is repeatedly paired with an established conditioned stimulus. After a number of pairings the neutral stimulus will elicit the same response as the conditioned stimulus, even though the new stimulus has never been paired with the unconditioned stimulus. For example, the tick of a metronome when paired with the presentation of food will eventually elicit a salivation response similar to that elicited by the sight of food itself. If the sound of the metronome is then preceded by a second stimulus (e.g., a light) this stimulus initially will have no effect on the salivation response. However, after repeated pairings of the light and the sound of the metronome, without any presentation of food, the light alone will come to elicit the salivation response. This process of higher-order conditioning has been demonstrated with as many as three conditioned stimuli, counting backward from the unconditioned stimulus.

The importance of higher-order conditioning is that it shows that conditioning can take place in situations in which an unconditioned stimulus is not directly involved. It also highlights the complex relationships that can be developed between stimuli through the conditioning process.

S. R. OSBORNE

See LEARNING.

Conditioning, Operant. Learning based on the relationship among a discriminative stimulus, a response, and a reinforcer, plus those variables that affect the power of a reinforcer. A discriminative stimulus is a cue which signals what reinforcer is likely to be delivered when a particular response occurs. The response in operant conditioning consists of emitted behaviors. Emitted behaviors are actions which technically are known as operants. Reinforcers are stimuli which are produced by an operant and which change the rate of that operant (see REINFORCEMENT).

An example of operant conditioning would be the employee who works with extra diligence and enthusiasm when the boss is in the office. The presence of the boss is here the discriminative stimulus and the extra productivity in work is the operant, or response. The reinforcer in this example would be the boss's approval (perhaps expressed in a smile or a greeting) or at least the absence of the boss's disapproval, which could be expressed in dismissal or reprimand.

Skinner introduced the basic concepts of operant conditioning to the psychological world in *The Behavior of Organisms* (1938). His system and the type of behavior that he studied may be contrasted with that of Pavlov. Pavlov focused on reflexive responses, which are elicited by stimuli which immediately precede them (*see* CONDITIONING, CLASSICAL). Skinner labeled such reflexive responses respondent behaviors.

Operant conditioning involves a process analogous to Darwinian natural selection. In operant conditioning those behaviors which are reinforced by the environment survive; those behaviors which are not reinforced by the environment do not survive. Since operant conditioning focuses on actions, and since actions constitute that category of behavior of most importance to human behavior, the way the environment "selects" behaviors has great significance.

In order to study behavior an investigator must choose a particular measure. Early in his career Skinner chose rate as his primary response measure. Much of his work has used simple responses such as pecks by a pigeon or lever presses by a rat. To study such behaviors in laboratory animals Skinner developed what he called the operant chamber; most of the rest of the psychological world has referred to the operant chamber as the Skinner box.

Researchers have used the Skinner box to explore the effects of reinforcers on operants. There are two basic types of reinforcers—positive and negative. Positive reinforcers are stimuli which will strengthen a response if the response produces the reinforcer. Examples are food, water, or sexual stimulation. Negative reinforcers are stimuli which will strengthen a response if the response removes the reinforcer. Examples are a loud noise, extremes of temperature, or an electric shock. These are examples of primary reinforcers—i.e., these reinforcers are relatively universal in their effects and they do not acquire their power through prior learning. Secondary reinforcers, in contrast, are conditioned or learned

reinforcing stimuli. Words of praise are commonly used secondary reinforcers. Behaviors either producing or removing positive or negative reinforcers involve four basic reinforcement contingencies: positive reinforcement, negative reinforcement, punishment type I, and punishment type II. Positive reinforcement is the name of the contingency when an action produces a positive reinforcer. For example, when the rat presses the lever, the dispenser drops a pellet of food in the animal's food dish. Actions which produce positive reinforcers are strengthened. Negative reinforcement occurs when an action removes a negative reinforcer. For example, a cat escapes from an electric shock by jumping from the shocked side to the safe side of a shuttle box. Actions which remove negative reinforcers are strengthened.

Punishment type I is the contingency in which an action produces a negative reinforcer. For example, when a toddler runs into the street, the parent spanks the child. The effects of punishment type I are not the opposite of those for reinforcement. Punishment type I may temporarily suppress an operant, but the organism is not likely to stop responding permanently. Punishment type II is the contingency in which an action removes a positive reinforcer. Examples of this contingency are when an operant produces a fine or time-out from positive reinforcers. Actions which produce a response cost or time-out tend to be weakened (*see* PUNISHMENT).

In addition to these four contingencies, a fifth possibility exists: the organism acts, but the actions do not produce or remove any effective reinforcers. Such a situation is labeled EXTINCTION. Actions which have been effectively reinforced but are then switched to extinction conditions tend to decrease in rate. Actions which have been effectively punished but are then switched to extinction conditions tend to increase in rate.

The power of a reinforcer is affected by operations such as depriving the organism of the reinforcer, satiating the organism on the reinforcer, administering certain drugs, applying physical restraints, noncontingently administering positive or negative reinforcers, and providing or removing choices.

Previous reinforcement, punishment, and extinction contingencies are not the only events that can alter response rates. The motivational operations mentioned above as well as age, emotional arousal, illness, and rest may alter response rates.

Investigators of operant conditioning have spent much time determining the effects of different schedules of reinforcement (*see* REINFORCEMENT, SCHEDULE OF). The most common have involved continuous reinforcement schedules, fixed-interval schedules, variable-interval schedules, fixed-ratio schedules, and variable-ratio schedules. Each schedule of reinforcement produces a distinctive pattern of responding. Variable-ratio schedules tend to produce the highest rates of responding. In addition to these commonly used schedules of reinforcement there are a number of more complex schedules.

Research on operant conditioning has covered a wide range of problems. Among the generic issues explored have been discrimination, differentiation, and generalization. Discrimination research focuses on the role of cues (discriminative stimuli) in operant conditioning. Discriminative stimuli signal whether a particular response will produce a particular reinforcer. Differentiation of a response refers to the shaping of a response pattern by making reinforcement contingent on gradual changes in one dimension of responding. Generalization refers to one of many processes: stimulus generalization, response generalization, temporal generalization, subject generalization, or combinations of two or more of these processes.

Operant conditioning developed concurrently with a particular approach to psychological research that is known as the experimental analysis of behavior. This approach emphasizes the intensive study of single subjects rather than comparing groups of subjects. Operant conditioning and the experimental analysis of behavior have had a profound impact on applied psychology. The earliest attempts to apply operant conditioning to problems in the real world occurred in the 1950s. By the 1960s applied behavior analysis was being practiced in a wide range of human service settings including mental hospitals, schools, institutions for developmentally disabled persons, correctional facilities, rehabilitation medicine, and special education. Programmed instruction, teaching machines, and behavior modification are direct outgrowths of operant conditioning.

Reference

Skinner, B. F. *The behavior of organisms.* New York: Appleton-Century, 1938.

P. W. CLEMENT

See APPLIED BEHAVIOR ANALYSIS; LEARNING.

Conduct Disorders. A group of diagnoses commonly given to children and adolescents who are referred for psychiatric evaluation and treatment because of antisocial behavior. To qualify for this diagnosis the antisocial behavior must have been present for at least six months, and must be more serious than the ordinary mischief and pranks associated with these age groups. The seriousness of the disorder is not manifested only in the quality of the antisocial behavior; other essential features include its repetitiveness and its persistent pattern. In this disorder the basic rights of others or the major age-appropriate societal norms or rules are violated.

Categorization. DSM-III categorizes conduct disorders according to the presence or absence of aggression in the antisocial behavior, and as to whether or not the individual is socialized. The aggressive conduct-disorder child violates the rights of others by either physical violence against persons or property (e.g., vandalism, rape, fire setting or thefts outside the home which involve confrontation with the victim). The nonaggressive conduct-disorder child violates the rights of others, or major societal norms (e.g., by chronic school truancy, substance abuse, repeated running away from home overnight, serious lying, and stealing not involving confrontation with a victim).

The second level of categorization determines whether or not the individual has been socialized. To diagnose a child as undersocialized there must be evidence that the child has failed to establish a normal degree of affection, empathy, or bonding with others. This is seen by the undersocialized demonstrating no more than one of the following and the socialized at least two of the following: has one or more peer group friendships that have lasted at least six months; extends himself or herself for others when no immediate personal advantage is likely; apparently feels guilt or remorse when such a reaction is apropriate; avoids blaming or informing on companions; shows concern for the welfare of friends or companions.

The undersocialized disordered individuals frequently come from families who overtly rejected the child or where the child blatantly was unwanted. Consequently there is no history of bonding or a satisfactory period of early attachment. This dynamic prevents the child from forming other meaningful relationships. Therefore, the undersocialized disorder would generally be prepubertal in its first manifestations. Other factors that contribute to early manifestation are the associated presence of an ATTENTION DEFICIT DISORDER, inconsistent management with harsh discipline, and early institutional living.

The socialized disordered individual's onset is usually pubertal or postpubertal. These adolescents often come from large families where the father is frequently absent or has alcohol-related problems. The individual often associates with a delinquent subgroup.

Associated features of conduct disorders can be categorized in two primary classifications: neurological and social. Neurological features include a history of attention deficit, poor frustration tolerance, irritability, temper outbursts, provocative restlessness, and enuresis. These are often accompanied by academic underachievement, which may result in school dropout. Some associated social features seen with conduct disorders include behaviors that can be considered attempts to compensate for feelings of low self-esteem. These include early drinking, early sex, early smoking, and involvement in other substance abuse.

Some of the predisposing factors tend to overlap with the associated features. There is a definite socioeconomic linkage. Poverty, with a lack of community cohesion and family solidarity, seems to be a significant predisposing influence. Within the family there is a lack of adequate bonding, preventing a child from developing a capacity for affection and trust or adequate socialization. Also seen is faulty parental attitude and child-rearing practices. Finally, a definite neurologic linkage seems to be present. This is manifested by the high number of conduct disorder children with borderline IQs and with learning disabilities.

In considering conduct disorder diagnosis, one must rule out the following: borderline symptom, affective disorders with manic features, oppositional behavior, and childhood or adolescent antisocial behavior which cannot be attributed to a mental disorder.

Description of the Various Subgroups.

Undersocialized, aggressive. These patients will be seen to have a high degree of egocentrism with no meaningful relationships. Their orientation toward others is in terms of what they can get from the other person, giving nothing in return. The aggressive antisocial behavior may take the form of bullying, physical aggression, and cruelty toward peers. Toward adults they may be hostile, verbally abusive, defiant, and negative (nongoal directed). It is not uncommon for them to be involved in persistent lying, frequent truancy, and vandalism. In severe cases there is destructiveness and stealing accompanied by physical violence.

These individuals have often experienced parental rejection, frequently alternating with unrealistic overprotection, especially from the consequences of their behavior. Deficient socialization expresses itself both in excessive aggressiveness and in the lack of sexual inhibition. The child is labeled a "bad kid," and punishment at this time invariably increases the maladapted expression of rage. There is also persistent enuresis to an advanced age. Typically these individuals are described as hostile, provocative, and uncooperative.

Undersocialized, nonaggressive. In this classification we see two basic patterns. In one, individuals are fearful and timid and engage in self-protective lying as well as manipulative lying. They generally are perceived as fringe members of delinquent groups. They are seen as childish, immature, whining, demanding, and having temper tantrums. They complain of feeling rejected and having been treated unfairly and are consequently very mistrustful of others. They have low self-esteem and are frequently victimized and submissive sexually because of pressure, especially in return for protection and material gain.

The second type is more ingratiatingly and casually friendly. However, if there is no payoff for this, they are quick to lose their friendliness. They also may appear detached and sly. They generally will appear anxious when caught, but their anxiety will clear when they are out of danger. They present major behavior problems in the schools.

The undersocialized nonaggressives differ from the undersocialized aggressives in that they respond to frustration and anger with devious techniques and flight. They feel weak, abandoned, mistreated, worthless, helpless, and hopeless. Even though they may associate with a gang, they remain on the fringe because they lack courage and loyalty.

Socialized conduct disorders. In these individuals there generally is a history of adequate or excessive conformity to parental wishes which ends when the individual becomes a member of a delinquent group. This is usually in the preadolescent stage of development. Frequently these individuals show marginal or poor school performances. They also frequently manifest mild behavior problems, or even neurotic symptoms such as shyness.

Families of such children are generally pathological. Parental discipline is rarely ideal and may vary from harshness and excessive strictness to inconsistency or relative absence of supervision and control. The mother often protects but does not seem to develop a warm relationship with the child, especially in early infancy and childhood. There frequently are marital problems and the absence of genuine family cohesion. The families are generally large and in poor economic circumstances.

Usually these individuals commit their crimes with their peer group. The delinquency is generally minor and stealing is the rule. Stealing in the home is rare. The misdeeds seem bold and almost playful. For example, the individual really doesn't run away. He or she just stays out late. Of primary importance is the membership in the gang.

Theories of Etiology. This disorder raises a basic question: Does a learning disability predispose a child to delinquency, or is the academic problem due to rebellion against authority in all forms? The conflict between these alternate explanations is especially noted in conduct disorder, since the triad of family pathology, difficult socioeconomic situation, and academic deficiency makes up the clinical picture.

There are three basic theories explaining the etiology of conduct disorders—biological, sociological, and psychological. The biological theory is based on the high prevalence of neurological deficits as manifested by learning problems, attention deficit, borderline IQ, and low frustration tolerance. There frequently is a family pattern with respect to temperament, with temperament being a constitutional tendency to react to one environment in a certain way. Also, there is a high frequency of one parent being an alcoholic, with no difference in outcome if the child is raised with or without the alcoholic parent. The sociological theory is supported by the close correlation to poverty, higher incidence in the urban black, the relationship to historical periods, and the lack of community cohesion. The psychological theory is supported by the data on bonding, faulty parental attitude, and the presence of low self-esteem.

It is obvious that no one etiological theory explains the entire phenomenon. All three explain a certain component in each of the subgroups. They therefore show the complexity of this disorder as well as the need for a comprehensive evaluation and treatment plan.

Treatment. For any emotional disorder it is important to begin with a comprehensive evaluation. The evaluation consists of a complete social history that includes the family history, the developmental history of the patient, and the present history of the behavioral problem. Each evaluation should include a physical examination with a special emphasis on the neurological exam. Psychological testing is of importance in looking for strengths and weaknesses, especially evidence of a learning disability.

Approaches to treatment will vary, depending on whether the patient is undersocialized or socialized. With the undersocialized the approach is often empirical, and treatment is very difficult because of the lack of emotional involvement of the patient. The goal in treatment is not only the removal of the symptoms of the behavior disorder; permanent change is more dependent on improvement of self-esteem. Treatment methods most commonly utilized include special education with the goal of assisting the individual to achieve improved self-esteem through academic mastery. Patients are also provided with pleasant and safe social experiences which assist them in improving their self-esteem through affection, acceptance, and approval. Since the patient's behavior often interferes with the educational program and social experience programs, it is necessary to utilize behavioral modification techniques for symptom removal. Frequently it is necessary to move the patient from the home environment into a residential treatment setting. This depends on the nature of the symptoms. Usually the symptoms are of such a nature that the community demands the removal of the patient. Other factors include the home environment and the strength of the family. Also to be considered is the motivation of the patient for change. Most of these patients are coerced into therapy and motivation is at a minimum initially.

Socialized conduct disorders generally respond best to reality therapy or other group therapies that have the goal of helping the individuals to understand their rationalizations, denials, and self-justifications with respect to their behavior. Traditional individual psychotherapy, family therapy, and residential treatment programs have not been highly successful in the resolution of these behavior problems, especially if the behavior disorder is related to participation in antisocial groups.

Both with undersocialized and socialized it is of vital importance that the family be involved in the treatment. Without change in the family it is unrealistic to expect change to occur in the child or adolescent. If change does occur while the patient is in a residential treatment setting, it is likely that there will be rapid regression to previous behavior patterns upon return to the home environment unless the family has been involved in the treatment.

The church community can play a key role in prevention. This occurs at three levels. The first is being sensitive to environmental conditions that are conducive to the development of a conduct disorder in a child or adolescent. The second is early detection of a conduct disorder and making appropriate referrals. The third is assistance to the family and the patient when the patient returns to the community from a residential treatment setting, helping the patient maintain the improved self-esteem that, it is hoped, he developed while in active treatment.

Additional Readings

Aichhorn, A. *Delinquency and child guidance: Selected papers.* New York: International Universities Press, 1964.
Kaplan, H., Freedman, A., & Sadock, B. (Eds.). *Comprehensive textbook of psychiatry, III* (3rd ed.). Baltimore: Williams & Wilkins, 1980.
Malmquist, C. *Handbook of adolescence.* New York: Aronson, 1978.
Robins, L. *Deviant children grown up.* Baltimore: Williams & Wilkins, 1966.

F. WESTENDORP

See PERSONALITY DISORDERS.

Confabulation. The unconscious act of replacing memory gaps by fantasizing experiences with no basis in fact. The gaps are replaced by confabulations which are narrated in elaborate detail with specific events and real people. Confabulations differ from delusions in that the props of the stories are real, but the experiences themselves never took place. The individual believes his stories are factual and will stick emphatically to them. Unconscious motives are evident in that the individual seems to hide his embarrassment over a memory loss by inventing fabrications. Confabulation is found in organic brain diseases and principally in Korsakoff's syndrome.

D. L. SCHUURMAN

Confession. The professionals most often sought for assistance in easing the pain of human anguish and guilt are psychotherapists and the clergy (Frank, 1973). As their roles in the healing process are examined, one may ask how tasks of the psychotherapist differ from those of the priest hearing a confession (Jung, 1938). Such reflection raises at least three basic questions: 1) What are confession and psychotherapy? 2) How is confession comparable to psychotherapy? 3) Can the two be brought together into a single more efficient method? (Worthen, 1983).

One of the great mysteries of faith is the redemptive process. At the heart of God is the desire to forgive, making confession and forgiveness spiritual experiences which transform lives. The Scriptures call us to practice confession both as a private matter between the individual and God and as a corporate discipline between believers (Stott, 1965). Yet practicing confession is a difficult discipline to implement in our lives, partly because, as Bonhoeffer (1954) noted, we have fellowship with one another as believers and as devout people, but do not have fellowship as the undevout and as sinners. Consequently there is a tendency to conceal sin from self and others lest the fellowship be disturbed. We thereby remain alone in our sin, living in lies and hypocrisy. The alternative is to recognize that we are first and foremost a fellowship of sinners needing to hear the unconditional call of God's love, and needing to confess our neediness before our Creator and our brothers and sisters in Christ.

Confession has been understood differently throughout the course of church history. In the Catholic tradition confession or, more correctly, the sacrament of penance is a threefold process. As Worthen describes it, it involves first the acknowledgment on the part of the sinner that a sin has been committed and a strong resolve not to repeat it. Second, the confession proper is to be heard by a priest. Third, there is the willing performance of some task (penance) imposed as compensation and as a token of good faith to accept the consequences of sin. In the Jewish tradition a special day was set aside for confession in which amends were to be made to the person against whom sin had been committed and from whom the offender desired and needed to receive forgiveness. The Reformation tradition has stressed the authority of all believers to receive the confession of sin and forgive it in the name of Jesus Christ (John 20:23). Foster (1978) calls this authority a great gift, an opportunity to manifest God's grace that we dare not withhold. Confession is seen as an essential responsibility of all believers who desire to restore a right relationship between individuals and their Maker and between fellow believers. And as Bonhoeffer noted, hearing such confession is the greatest service of listening that God has committed to us, a trust that is built on listening to one another on lesser subjects.

Psychotherapy is a process in which a trained clinician helps clients resolve emotional difficulties, develop more constructive attitudes, and alter their behavior in the direction of becoming more independent, self-fulfilled, growth-directed individuals (Goldenberg, 1973). Both confession and individually oriented therapy, then, are intimate, one-to-one interpersonal relationships with the aim of reducing subjective distress and restoring emotional and/or spiritual health. In contrast, however, confession stresses conscious motivation and recall, whereas more depth-oriented approaches to therapy aim at finding out whether or not unconscious dynamics might be influencing current functioning. Although the ultimate goal might be the same, the processes often differ. Sin may or may not be viewed differently (see Menninger, 1973). Both see it as having pathological individual and corporate effects. They may differ, however, in viewing it in terms of turning from God, as a break in a code of morality, as a form of egocentrism, or as the development of conflicts (Worthen, 1983). Likewise, the guilt that it produces may or may not be dealt with differently (see Narramore, 1974).

How one approaches the problems of human anguish and guilt has profound implications for diagnosis and treatment (e.g., locus of problem, responsibility for the cure, type of treatment to be used) and prevention (e.g., What is a meaningful philosophy of life?) (Belgum, 1963). In comparing the literature on confession and psychotherapy, Worthen (1983) suggests several conclusions. First, there seems to be more of an emphasis on restoration to the community in confession than in traditional notions of psychotherapy. Second, penance, in the Catholic tradition, is based on an almost universally accepted procedure. Psychotherapy, in contrast, does not have a universal format of procedures to alleviate human anguish and guilt. Third, the priest-confessor generally views sin as the cause of unhappiness. The psychotherapist more often sees sin as egocentrism which is the end result of an involuntary process contrary to the individual's will. Some argue that confession more often deals with the evil of human freedom, whereas psychotherapy deals with the results of human compulsion. It should be noted, however, that problems of human freedom and neurotic conditions can be equally vicious and agonizing.

Another difference is that confession is most often seen as necessary for dealing with willful misdeeds, whereas psychotherapy more often sees itself dealing with the dynamics of unconscious motivation. The psychotherapist is less likely to be concerned with the confession of a moral offense, but rather looks for the causes of problems. In the Catholic tradition the priest is required to act as a judge of subjective moral rightness or wrongness. Confession may help prevent problems if the confessee keeps a continual open heart to the confessor. Similarly, although psychotherapy was not ordained to forgive sins, it can do much to free the individual from certain compulsions that make it difficult to abstain from, and to repent of, sin. Confession tends to see intention as the core and basic cause of sin. Psychotherapy is more likely to see the motivation of the external act as the result of the individual's inability to cope with outside influences. It should be noted that there is considerable difference of opinion not only among psychotherapists as to what techniques best alleviate anguish and guilt, or whether or not religious beliefs should be dealt with in psychotherapy (see Bergin, 1980). Catholic priests also disagree as to the nature of involvement in the penitent's life after confession (i.e., Is pastoral counseling indicated by the same priest who heard the confession?).

A potential resolution to the perceived conflicts is possible. With mutual respect for both confession and psychotherapy, a new direction may be found. It is not enough, for example, to quote Scripture to a brother after you hear his confession. The listener must encounter and speak to that individual in such a way that the message of God's grace and forgiveness for sins is stated clearly and is relevant to his needs. Confession of sin, followed by constructive change and repentance, can certainly contribute toward the wholeness of the person. Psychotherapy can assist the person in developing the psychological freedom to respond to the environment. Confession can assist the person in developing the spiritual freedom to respond to the world and to God (Worthen, 1983). Together, these separate but complementary functions can assist the Christian in the process of being oneself in truth before God and others, wholly integrated psychologically and spiritually.

Many who have written on confession have pointed to the important role of personal preparation in being able properly to hear the confession of another. By coming to grips with the sin that nailed Christ to the cross, we will realize that there is nothing that anyone could say that would disturb us. Bonhoeffer (1954) calls this learning to live under the cross. Such a commitment will convey to others that it is safe to come to us, and that we can receive anything they could possibly reveal. We would thereby demonstrate by our listening and response that we understand and that we do not need to tell others privileged information that has been revealed to us. In other words, we must prepare for this sacred ministry by earning the right to be trusted by those who come to us in godly sorrow. By living under the cross, we approach the other person as an equal, resisting the temptation to control him or straighten him out. What he does need, however, is our acceptance and understanding. We should pray for a deepening of spiritual commitment in ourselves, so that when we are with others we will radiate Christ's life and light into them (i.e., we will act in such a way that our very presence demonstrates the love and forgiving grace of God). Finally, Foster (1978) warns us to discipline ourselves to be quiet and to pray for the other, both during the confession and afterward.

Confession brings an end to pretense; we are all equal under the cross. By openly confessing our sin, we allow ourselves to more fully know the forgiving and empowering grace of Christ. Confession requires commitment and honesty. Confession leads to change in thought, action, and deed. Surely, confession is a grace that needs to be practiced more often in the church.

References

Belgum, D. R. *Guilt: Where religion and psychology meet.* Englewood Cliffs, N.J.: Prentice-Hall, 1963.

Bergin, A. E. Psychotherapy and religious values. *Journal of Consulting and Clinical Psychology*, 1980, *48*, 95–105.

Bonhoeffer, D. *Life together.* New York: Harper & Row, 1954.

Foster, R. J. *Celebration of discipline.* San Francisco: Harper & Row, 1978.

Frank, J. *Persuasion and healing* (Rev. ed.). Baltimore: Johns Hopkins University Press, 1973.

Goldenberg, H. *Contemporary clinical psychology.* Monterey, Calif.: Brooks/Cole, 1973.

Jung, C. G. *Psychology and religion.* New Haven: Yale University Press, 1938.

Menninger, K. A. *What ever became of sin?* New York: Hawthorn Books, 1973.

Narramore, S. B. Guilt: Where theology and psychology meet. *Journal of Psychology and Theology*, 1974, *1*, 18–25.

Stott, J. *Confess your sins.* Waco, Tex.: Word, 1965.

Worthen, V. Psychotherapy and Catholic confession. In H. N. Malony (Ed.), *Wholeness and holiness.* Grand Rapids: Baker, 1983.

R. E. BUTMAN

Conflict. A prominent construct in clinical, motivational, and social psychology, conflict is usually defined as the simultaneous existence of mutually exclusive or opposite desires or response tendencies. It may be intrapsychic, interpersonal, or mental.

In clinical psychology conflict concepts are present in the theories of Freud and Horney. Several types of conflict were considered by Freud. One of the biological impulses, eros (e.g., sexual motivation) or thanatos (e.g., aggression), may confront the prevailing social reality. Libidinal impulses (i.e., id) demand a type of gratification, deemed inappropriate by society. Furthermore, libidinal impulses may bid for expression only to be thwarted by the moral censoring of the superego. Ego defense mechanisms are strategies to resolve intrapsychic conflict. They permit the expression of libidinal energy, but in forms tolerable to one's moral training or social convention.

In Horney's view basic conflict is intrapsychic tension due to competing neurotic trends (e.g., the need for autonomy and independence versus the need for a partner to take over one's life). Basic conflict may stem from incompatible images of self, particularly the idealized self versus the despised real self. Central conflict is an intrapsychic conflict between the healthy, constructive forces of the real self and the neurotic obsessions of the idealized self. In either case, conflict is an underlying force in the etiology of neuroses.

Much of the motivational analysis of conflict originated in Lewin's (1938) field theory. The direction and strength of forces comprise a vector. When two vectors are balanced (e.g., same strength) but are directed in opposite directions, a state of conflict is said to exist. Lewin posited three types of conflict. In the approach-approach conflict an individual experiences two attractive but mutually exclusive goals. Equilibrium is, however, unstable. Movement toward one resolves the conflict, because the equilibrium is upset.

The avoidance-avoidance conflict is more serious. The person experiences two goals, both of which are aversive, but one must be chosen. The equilibrium is stabilized at the point between the goals at which the avoidant forces are equal. At this point there is little movement; the conflict remains unresolved.

In the approach-avoidance conflict one goal object has both positive and negative aspects. The person is both drawn to and repulsed by the goal object. The approach-avoidance conflict has a stable equilibrium point where the positive and negative forces balance. However, the goal object is never experienced.

Building on the work of Lewin, Miller (1959) gathered extensive experimental evidence regarding the nature of conflict. He found that the closer the organism is to the goal, the stronger the motivation; he termed this a *gradient.* The avoidance gradient was found to be steeper than the approach gradient. In approach-avoidance conflicts when the organism is far from the goal, the approach tendency is stronger and the organism approaches the goal. However, as the organism approaches the goal, the avoidance tendency becomes stronger. The approach stops when the avoidance gradient overtakes the approach gradient. At that point equilibrium is achieved.

A more complicated form of approach-avoidance conflict is typical of most life conflict situations. The double approach-avoidance conflict involves two goal objects, both of which have positive and negative aspects. For example, one might be shopping for a new home. One house is very spacious, prestigious, and expensive; the other less spacious and less prestigious, but more affordable.

Miller further demonstrated that when two incompatible responses are in conflict (e.g., approach or avoidance), the stronger motivation occurs. In the case of approach drives, deprivation of the goal object served to strengthen the drive.

The only serious challenge to Miller's theory is that of Maher (1966). Maher questioned the concept of intersecting approach and avoidance gradients, presuming instead that approach and avoidance gradients are parallel. Conflict exists when the relative strengths of these gradients are indistinguishable. Maher also suggested that feedback cues, rather than distance per se, produced the avoidance and approach gradients. However, to date, Miller's analysis appears to have more support than Maher's.

Conflict can be interpersonal as well as intrapersonal. Social psychologists consider conflict to exist when persons in dyads or groups have variant aims. Satisfactory functioning of the group is contingent on resolving conflict through the process of negotiation. Mixed motives exist when one person in the dyad desires to cooperate while the other one views the situation as competitive. A conflict spiral emerges as one person uses a threat to induce conformity and the other responds with a counterthreat.

In summary, conflict is the existence of divergent aims or goals within the person or group. It is normally expected that conflict be resolved or reduced, especially for healthy functioning. The nature of the conflict is determined by the positive and/or negative aspects of the goal object.

References

Lewin, K. *The conceptual representation and measurement of psychological forces.* Durham, N.C.: Duke University Press, 1938.

Maher, B. A. *Principles of psychopathology.* New York: McGraw-Hill, 1966.

Miller, N. E. Liberalization of basic S-R concepts. In S. Koch (Ed.), *Psychology:* (Vol. 2). New York: McGraw-Hill, 1959.

R. L. TIMPE

See COOPERATION AND COMPETITION.

Conflict Management. An applied and interdisciplinary field dealing with the resolution of interpersonal disputes by the application of psychologically and sociologically derived principles. It interests Christians because it represents, in some measure, practical advice that helps them fulfill their biblical mandate to be peacemakers. By utilizing empirical generalization from the behavioral sciences, conflict can be managed.

Drawing upon many fields for concepts, conflict management is an eclectic gathering of ideas. From psychology the concepts of defense mechanisms, intrapsychic conflict, motivation, and anger are drawn. From psychiatry comes the physiology of stress and aggression; from sociology come small group research, power analysis, and communications networks; from organizational theory comes negotiation; and from law come mediation processes. These diverse ideas are integrated by their use for a common purpose, the resolution (or management) of disagreement. Conflict management is therefore a practical art rather than a theoretical science.

Along with intervention techniques is a set of assumptions common to the various emphases in conflict management. First, conflict is viewed as a normal, in fact an inevitable, slice of life. It is therefore not to be avoided or suppressed but rather expected, used, and even celebrated as an expression of rich diversity in human personalities. Second, although conflict is often destructive to relationships, it does not need to be. It can be channeled and even constructively escalated in order to enhance trust and communication. Third, individuals tend to respond or react to conflict in predictable and stable patterns that may be labeled styles. These patterns or styles of action may be productive or unproductive within particular conflicts. Fourth, specific organizational techniques and individual verbal skills offer methods that enable one to become more flexible in handling conflict and directing it to constructive ends.

The work of Simnel (1955) and Lewin (1948) launched the postwar study of conflict in small groups. Coser (1967) contributed significantly toward an empirical understanding of how and why conflict serves a group or the larger society with his 16 propositions (1956). Among his most significant ideas are: 1) conflict permits dissension and dissatisfaction to emerge so that it may be dealt with; 2) conflict allows the emergence of new norms; 3) conflict reveals the strength of current boundaries between groups; 4) conflict releases human energy and summons purposefulness; and 5) the closer the relationship, the more intense the conflict. With these thoughts and others in mind, he analyzed conflicts as either functional or dysfunctional.

In the 1960s conflict research emphasized the application of game theory to international problems and the creation of intrapersonal and interpersonal theories of communication based upon experimental studies. Works representative of these two emphases are Schelling (1960) and Festinger (1964). Deutsch (1973) summarized more than a decade of research on all levels of conflict. More recently, popular psychology has offered conflict management ideas under the rubric of assertiveness training. This approach to interpersonal effectiveness suggests that both avoidance (flight) and aggression (fight) are often important responses to conflict.

Christians have not been idle in the utilization of conflict management ideas. The Christian Legal Society has developed a conciliation service that assists churches, Christian organizations, and even individuals in the resolution of their conflicts. The functions of such a reconciler are to help establish trust, open channels of communication, clarify issues, advocate just resolutions, and offer new alternatives. The handling of ANGER by Christians is another topic receiving much attention. Through many sources Christians are becoming aware of insights and techniques for accepting angry emotions and expressing them appropriately.

References

Coser, L. A. *The Functions of social conflict.* Glencoe, Ill.: Free Press, 1956.
Coser, L. A. *Continuities in the study of social conflict.* New York: Free Press, 1967.
Deutsch, M. *The resolution of conflict.* New Haven: Yale University Press, 1973.
Festinger, L. *Conflict, decision and dissonance.* Stanford, Calif.: Stanford University Press, 1964.
Lewin, K. *Resolving social conflicts.* New York: Harper, 1948.
Schelling, T. C. *The strategy of conflict.* Cambridge, Harvard University Press, 1960.
Simnel, G. [*Conflict*] (K. H. Wolff, trans.). Glencoe, Ill.: Free Press, 1955.

Additional Readings

Filley, A. C. *Interpersonal conflict resolution.* Glenview, Ill.: Scott, Foresman, 1975.
Frost, J. H., & Wilmot, W. W. *Interpersonal conflict.* Dubuque, Iowa: W. C. Brown, 1978.

Walton, R. E. *Interpersonal peacemaking.* Reading, Mass.: Addison-Wesley, 1969.

W. C. HILL

See COOPERATION AND COMPETITION.

Conforming Personality. *See* PASSIVE-AMBIVALENT PERSONALITY PATTERN.

Conformity. The change in an individual's beliefs or behavior as a result of group pressure. While this failure to remain independent of social influence may have negative consequences—e.g., when it leads people to violate their own moral principles—conformity is also an important force for social stability. Without some agreement on what is appropriate behavior, social chaos would result. Psychologists have studied the extent to which people conform, their reasons for doing so, and the factors that influence their responses.

Sherif (1935) reported experiments that dramatically demonstrate how a person's judgments may be influenced by others. His studies utilized an optical illusion known as the autokinetic effect, in which a pinpoint of light shown in a darkened room appears to move. Sherif placed solitary individuals in the room and asked them to make decisions about the movement of the light. In this highly ambiguous situation individual judgments varied greatly. Sherif then brought the subjects together in small groups to repeat the task. After a short time judgments within the group converged. A common norm developed regarding the light's movement. When subjects were again asked to make their judgments alone, they did not return to their individual norms but adhered to the group norm. The influence of others was permanent.

Asch (1956) conducted studies of conformity in which the task was not nearly so ambiguous. In these studies groups of subjects were asked to perform a simple visual discrimination task. They were requested to state which of three vertical lines drawn on a card was closest in length to a comparison line. In each group all but one of the subjects were confederates who had been instructed by the experimenter to make incorrect judgments on certain trials. The real subject responded to the examiner's questions after most of the confederates had made their judgments. Asch reported that, when the confederates unanimously agreed on an obviously incorrect judgment, the subjects conformed in approximately 37% of their choices. Only 25% of the subjects remained completely independent and never conformed to the majority.

Research has revealed two reasons people conform. A person may be influenced by others because they provide important information. Their statements and actions are used as guides to understanding reality. When others are used as a source of information, their influence will be pervasive and will be likely to change both a person's beliefs and behavior. A second reason that a person may conform is the desire to avoid rejection by others or to gain their approval. Groups often reject those who consistently deviate. When a person conforms to avoid rejection, the influence of others may be less pervasive and produce temporary changes in behavior but not in belief.

Many studies have sought to identify factors that influence the extent to which people conform. For example, when the group is unanimous, as was true in Asch's initial study, the person finds resisting group pressure is particularly difficult. If just one ally is present, he is significantly less likely to conform. Another factor is the size of the influencing group. As the number of group members exerting pressure rises to approximately five persons, conformity also increases. Beyond this level increasing size produces little effect. A third factor concerns the person's evaluation of the group. People are more likely to conform to those perceived as attractive, expert, or of high status.

While early studies indicated that females may conform more than males, subsequent research has not found strong differences in conformity between the sexes. However, significant cultural differences have been found in the tendency to respond to group pressure. Such variations suggest that people can be socialized to be more or less conforming. Specific personality characteristics are only moderately related to conformity. For example, higher self-esteem has been associated with less conformity, but the relationship is not as strong as might be expected.

While the degree to which people conform is often surprising, research also indicates that a person may resist being influenced. People are not puppets, and when social pressure becomes blatant, they may act to restore their freedom. This may be expressed in an increased liking for the choice the group seeks to prohibit. Resistance is particularly strong when the issue is important and when people believe they have a right to choose for themselves. Studies also suggest that, while people do not want to appear too different from others, they do not want to appear too similar either. They may resist influence in an attempt to maintain their distinctiveness and sense of individuality.

References
Asch, S. E. Studies of independence and conformity. *Psychological Monographs*, 1956, 70 (9, Whole No. 416).
Sherif, M. A study of some social factors in perception. *Archives of Psychology*, 1935, 187, 60.

M. BOLT

See OBEDIENCE.

Confrontation in Therapy.

An active intervention tool by which the therapist brings a client into face-to-face contact with an issue. Along with questions, probes, and directives, confrontation is in a noninterpretive mode. It is quite different from the less active interventions such as interpretations, reflections, and restatements. When a confrontation is made, the therapist takes on the role of an observer offering a one-sided observation. An interpretation, by way of contrast, is a shared discovery between the therapist and client.

The use of confrontation in therapy is analogous to its use in other interpersonal relationships. In all settings confrontation is most effective when conducted in an atmosphere of mutual trust and openness. The timing of confrontation is also critical. Its overuse may lead to the client taking a passive stance in the relationship just as might happen if confrontation were overused in a friendship.

Jesus frequently used confrontation in his relationships and was also confrontive when dealing with people in need. Hence the model Jesus provides as a counselor encourages its use.

The role of confrontation varies in different schools of therapy. Generally, the more directive and active therapies advocate a greater use of confrontation. All advocates of confrontation emphasize the need to be accurate and discerning in its use. One danger in the therapeutic use of confrontation is that the therapist may assume an authoritarian role or a condemnatory stance toward the client. A major benefit of confrontation is its facility in helping the severely disturbed or the decompensating client.

Confrontation is central to some therapies. Garner (1973) proposes a model called *confrontation problem-solving therapy* in which the therapist confronts the client with directive statements reflecting some aspect of the client's behavior. This is followed by a question to determine the client's understanding of the reaction to the confrontation. The goal of Garner's therapy is to foster good reality testing.

Confrontation is also essential to the theory of Adams (1970). Adams builds his view of counseling around the Greek word *nouthesis*, which is defined as a caring confrontation. The aim of nouthetic confrontation is to effect change in the counselee by encouraging greater conformity to the principles of Scripture (*see* NOUTHETIC COUNSELING).

In the analytic therapies confrontation is an auxiliary intervention used mainly when interpretation is not feasible or when it is insufficient. For example, analysts use confrontation in the face of ACTING OUT behavior, in emergencies, or when a client is decompensating. Analysts feel that confrontation has limitations because it deals with surface resistance and defenses and it interrupts the flow of a session.

Confrontation is also central to many group therapies which advocate helping clients encounter previously unknown facets of their personalities. In this sense confrontation is more than an intellectual interaction; it is a substantive emotional interaction.

References
Adams, J. E. *Competent to counsel.* Grand Rapids: Baker, 1970.
Garner, H. H. Confrontation problem solving therapy. In R. R. M. Jurjevich (Ed.), *Direct psychotherapy* (Vol. I). Coral Gables, Fla.: University of Miami Press, 1973.

Additional Reading
Adler, G., & Myerson, G. (Eds.). *Confrontation in psychotherapy.* New York: Science House, 1973.

J. R. BECK

Congruence. As developed by Rogers (1957) congruence refers to an accurate matching of experience, awareness, and communication. It can be illustrated by a hungry infant who is crying. The baby is experiencing hunger at the visceral level, he is fully aware of being hungry, and he is *communicating* the discomfort of hunger.

Incongruence can be illustrated by a man engaged in an argument whose face is flushed, whose voice is raised, and who shakes his finger at his opponent but who denies being angry. It seems clear that at the physiological level the man is experiencing anger. His denial of anger may be due to lack of awareness of his experience or unwillingness to communicate his experience. In either case there is not an accurate matching of experience, awareness, and communication.

The concept of incongruence can also be used to describe a discrepancy between the perceived self (self-concept) and the experiencing self. For example, a man may have the cherished concept of being a good tennis player

but may be experiencing frequent defeats by mediocre players. Logically this should cause the man to revise his self-concept downward with respect to his tennis-playing ability. However, if skill at tennis is an important part of his self-concept, the man may cling to this belief in spite of his experience. A number of stratagems may be used to maintain this faulty self-concept. He may quit playing tennis, thus becoming the "retiring champ," or he may play only very weak opponents, thus continuing to win.

Congruence on the part of the therapist has been found to be one of the three important therapist interpersonal factors in the success of psychotherapy, the other two being empathy and nonpossessive warmth. These three factors are often referred to as the "therapeutic triad." Congruence in the context of psychotherapy means that the therapist is fully aware of the feelings he is experiencing and is able to communicate them to the client if appropriate. According to Rogers (1961), if the therapist is experiencing persistent negative feelings toward his client, it may be necessary to communicate these feelings to the client. For example, to maintain congruence between his experience, awareness, and communication he may have to say, "I may be wrong but I have the feeling that you are not being honest with me." In a summary of eight studies related to the therapeutic effectiveness of congruence, Truax and Mitchell (1971) found that in seven of the studies overall combined outcome measures favored the hypothesis while none of the overall combined measures were against the hypothesis.

Rogers (1961) believes that congruence is as important in other interpersonal relationships as it is in psychotherapy. He has suggested as a general law of interpersonal relationships that the greater the congruence of experience, awareness, and communication on the part of one individual, the more the ensuing relationship will involve "a tendency toward reciprocal communication with a quality of increasing congruence; a tendency toward more mutually accurate understanding of the communications; improved psychological adjustment and functioning in both parties; and mutual satisfaction in the relationship" (p. 344).

References
Rogers, C. R. The necessary and sufficient conditions of therapeutic personality change. *Journal of Consulting Psychology*, 1957, *21*, 95–103.
Rogers, C. R. *On becoming a person.* Boston: Houghton Mifflin, 1961.
Truax, C. B., & Mitchell, K. M. Research on certain therapist skills in relation to process and outcome. In A. E. Bergin

& S. L. Garfield (Eds.), *Handbook of psychotherapy and behavior change.* New York: Wiley, 1971.

O. SCANDRETTE

Conjoint Family Therapy. A model of therapy in which a therapist sees family members together when just one of them, usually a troublesome child, is identified as the one needing help. The term is most strongly identified with Satir (1967).

Satir took her training in social work, which has a larger-than-the-individual emphasis. In 1959 she brought that perspective to the Mental Research Institute in Palo Alto, where she collaborated with Jackson, Bateson, Watzlawick, and others associated with the communications theory of psychopathology and family systems functioning. Sullivan's earlier work on interpersonal theories of personality significantly influenced this group's leading force, D. Jackson.

Satir indentified with the optimistic, experiential humanism referred to as the "third force" in midtwentieth-century American psychology. She was one of three remarkable therapists (with Perls and Erickson) studied by the founders of neurolinguistic programming, Bandler and Grinder. These two astute observers reduced Satir's effective actions to descriptive terms. *Changing with families* (Bandler, Grinder, & Satir, 1976) semantically analyzed key verbal sequences that Satir used to clarify communications between members of a dysfunctional family system.

In her view of human nature Satir emphasizes that all behavior, no matter how distorted, aims at preserving and enhancing self-esteem. Virtually synonomous with self-esteem is a person's sense of being esteemed, validated, welcomed, and responded to congruently by others. Therefore, behavior that society regards as "sick, crazy, stupid, or bad" is really a message signalling distress and requesting help. Everyone can learn to communicate feelings more effectively and thus escape his or her psychic prisons.

Satir calls her model of therapy a growth model, in contrast to the medical model and the sin model. She caricatures the latter as a critical, moralistic model; it lacks the element of good news that the Bible announces for persons whose values, beliefs, and attitudes make them incongruent with the blueprint by which a loving God created them.

Satir is evidently antichurch, since she sees Christianity causing more guilt than is good for people. She regards pathology as dysfunctional communication by individuals within families and cultures. In this she comes close to the profound insight expressed by an Old Testament prophet: "I am a man of unclean lips and live among a people of unclean lips" (Isa. 6:5).

Illness in a person derives from inadequate methods of communicating in that person's intimate relationships. It follows that the goal of therapy is to improve those methods. That means putting into clear, direct words messages that have been delivered in the past by unclear and indirect nonverbal gestures and nuances. Most of these transactions have been outside the awareness of the participants, so they could never talk about them. Therapists make the covert overt.

One of the primary topics that people can learn to talk about is differentness. Therapists work to immunize family members against the jarring effects of discovering that loved ones think, feel, perceive, and desire in ways different from themselves. A therapist "raises their capacity to give and minimizes their sensitivities to painful subjects, thereby decreasing the necessity for defenses" (Satir, 1967, p. 165).

The conjoint therapist concentrates especially on reducing the threat of blame, so as to build "a safe, understanding framework within which child and mates will be able to comment on what they see and hear" (Satir, 1967, p. 132). Achieving this safety is a primary step toward uncovering the root of all family problems—discord in the husband-wife relationship.

In her role as therapist Satir actively manages the sessions. She structures the first two to four sessions by taking a family chronology. She questions relentlessly and specifically, often repeating her questions as if a little slow to catch on. This repetition simplifies and clarifies what had previously been to the family confusing, overwhelming aspects of their lives.

Absolutely opposed to any hint of faultfinding, Satir speaks of the identified patient's "pain" and says that the whole family hurts. She thus shifts the investigative aspect of therapy from that of a policeman seeking to arrest a villain to that of a curious child seeking to solve a puzzle. She spreads ownership of the problem to the family. She further fosters a "we" orientation in positive ways by citing the strengths of the family, especially the storms they have already weathered in their history. She highlights the relationship-seeking intention behind even the most hurtful actions. At the end of the first interview she assigns each family member to make it known when pleased by what another member does.

Conjoint family therapy is primarily a means for fostering more enjoyable and productive relationships among persons living or working together in systems. Management relations, marriage enrichment, and premarital counseling increasingly use concepts that Satir and her colleagues advocate.

References

Bandler, R., Grinder, J., & Satir, V. *Changing with families.* Palo Alto, Calif.: Science and Behavior Books, 1976.

Satir, V. *Conjoint family therapy* (Rev. ed.). Palo Alto, Calif.: Science and Behavior Books, 1967.

D. L. GIBSON

See FAMILY THERAPY: OVERVIEW; FAMILY COMMUNICATIONS THEORY.

Conscience. The set of personality processes involved in evaluating oneself by one's accepted ideals or standards. Beyond this broad definition, however, there is little agreement on the precise meaning and nature of conscience. Psychological theorists shape their understanding and definition of conscience to fit their theoretical framework. Fromm (1947), for example, spoke of an infantile, fear-based, authoritarian conscience and a more mature, rational, and sensitive humanistic conscience. Allport (1955) wrote of the generic conscience that enhances one's life, and Freud (1927) drew a general parallel between his concept of the superego and conscience.

Theologians also differ in their understanding of conscience. Pierce (1955, p. 111), for example, sees conscience as God-given and the punitive functions of conscience as "the internal counterpart and complement of the wrath" of God. In contrast, Bavinck (1898) and Bonhoeffer (1959) view conscience as a result of the fall and as carrying out fallen humanity's attempt to "know good and evil" apart from God and to solve its moral dilemma on its own.

Conscience in the Bible. The Old Testament has no word fully equivalent to conscience. The Hebrew lēeb (generally translated heart), however is sometimes used to refer to the functions the New Testament calls conscience. Conscience (*syneidēesis*) is used 31 times in the New Testament, but nowhere is it clearly defined. Its functions include 1) bearing witness or evaluating oneself in relation to a standard (Rom. 2:14–15); 2) assuring one of consistent, intergrative living (2 Tim. 1:3); 3) motivating constructively (Rom. 13:5; Acts 24:16); 4) inhibiting unnecessarily (1 Cor. 8:4–8); and 5) producing feelings of guilt and self-condemnation (1 John 3:19–20).

The first three functions of conscience are God-given. As moral beings we are created with the capacity to observe ourselves and to live consistently and responsibly out of a motivation of love. At times, however, the conscience can also needlessly inhibit and become the source of self-punitive, destructive emotions of guilt. Although some assume these functions are also the work of God, Scripture indicates they are not. Paul speaks of those with a weak conscience that is overly restrictive (1 Cor. 8:7). And John indicates that condemnation is not God-given when he writes, "If our heart condemns us, God is greater than our heart" (1 John 3:20). The biblical doctrines of the atonement and justification make it clear that the believer's sins have already been paid for and that the Christian is no longer under condemnation (Rom. 8:1). Seen in this light the condemnation of a guilty conscience actually involves a denial of the efficacy of the atonement. It constitutes an additional, self-inflicted penalty or payment for one's sins.

Biblically conscience functions a great deal like the law. Prior to salvation it serves the useful purposes of showing us a standard to reach for, acting as a schoolmaster (Gal. 3:24), giving moral structure to society (Exod. 21:1–31:18), and showing us our failures and driving us to despair and consequently to God's grace (Rom. 5:20–21). After salvation, however, the Christian must learn to relate to conscience in an entirely different manner just as he does to the law. The attempt to merit acceptance or avoid punishment by living up to the demands of conscience can be as much a legalistic process as the attempt to merit God's approval by living up to the law. This effort to merit approval and avoid the condemnation of conscience must be replaced by a motivation of love growing out of the fact that Christ has fully taken our condemnation and that we are now acceptable through him.

The Development of Conscience. The processes we know as conscience develop out of the complex interaction between 1) one's God-given moral potential, which is rooted in the image of God and progressively unfolds with the development of one's cognitive capacities; 2) one's own desires and attempts to merit self-acceptance and avoid punishment; and 3) the impact of socializing agents, particularly parents. Although the Bible does not elaborate extensively on humanity's moral nature, it does describe us as moral beings, created in the image of God with the "law of God written in the heart" (Rom. 2:14–15). It is this fundamental moral nature that provides the ability for the individual to profit from the socializing process and to develop a set of moral values.

Beyond humanity's innate moral propensity and the law written on the heart, the unique shape of one's conscience is highly influenced by one's interaction with significant socialization agents. This takes place through the process of internalization. From early childhood children take in, or internalize, the ideals and expectations of parents and significant others because they fear parental punishment or rejection if they fall short and because they love and admire these significant adults. In the first five years of life parents are the main source of these expectations. As children grow older, they increasingly look to other authorities and to peers and broader social standards for the ideals they adopt.

As these ideals and expectations are internalized and merged with one's innate moral awareness and individual desires, they come together to form what is generally called the ideal self or the ego ideal. This set of ideals becomes the standard by which one judges himself or herself.

At the same time children are taking in their parents' values and standards they also internalize the corrective attitudes of significant others. When parents rely on angry, punitive corrections, children tend to take in these corrective attitudes as their own. As these punitive attitudes merge with the child's inherent sense of moral justice, they form the essential ingredients of punitive emotions of guilt generally called neurotic or false guilt. By contrast, when children take in predominantly loving disciplinary attitudes, those attitudes merge with the child's inherent moral sense and love to form a set of love-based corrective attitudes. These comprise the essence of godly sorrow, or what is sometimes referred to as true guilt.

With the completion of this process the development of the broad outlines of conscience is largely finished. Individuals have a set of standards, the perceptual ability to evaluate themselves (to bear witness), and two sets of corrective attitudes they can use to motivate themselves.

Pathologies of Conscience. Problems of conscience grow naturally out of disturbances in the function of conscience described above. Some people have problems with the functioning of conscience because they develop inadequate standards. They may have failed to internalize acceptable standards, or they may have repressed their inherent moral nature

and developed antisocial or sociopathic personality styles because they have inappropriate values. Or they may have internalized rigid and narrow standards that inhibit unnecessarily, cause neurotic problems, and do not allow a creative and assertive style of life.

Others develop problems because of inappropriate corrective attitudes and emotions. Internalization of punitive corrective attitudes can result in the severe guilt emotions found in depressive and obsessive compulsive personalities, the two "guilt neuroses." The failure to internalize loving corrective attitudes can lead to a lack of concern for others and consequently antisocial behavior.

Psychotherapy of Problems of Conscience. An understanding of the processes involved in the development of conscience also provides direction for resolving problems of conscience. Effective therapy needs to give attention to the development and adequacy of both one's standards and one's corrective attitudes. People who have developed rigid, neurotic standards need to rework those. Those who have repressed or failed to internalize biblically and socially appropriate values need to develop those. And people who have developed self-punitive guilt feelings need to internalize the fact that they are forgiven and accepted by God and can give up their own self-punishment. In each case this is most effectively carried out within the context of a meaningful personal relationship that provides an emotional bond to help effect deep changes in one's personal values rather than merely an intellectual change of standards.

References
Allport, G. *Becoming: Basic considerations for a psychology of personality.* New Haven: Yale University Press, 1955.
Bavinck, H. *Gereformerde dogmatiek* (Vol.3). Kampen: J. H. Bos, 1898.
Bonhoeffer, D. *Creation and fall.* New York: Macmillan, 1959.
Freud, S. *The ego and the id.* London: Hogarth Press, 1927. (Originally published, 1923.)
Fromm, E. *Man for himself.* New York: Rinehart, 1947.
Pierce, C. A. *Conscience in the New Testament.* London: SCM, 1955.

Additional Reading
Narramore, B. *No condemnation: Rethinking guilt and motivation.* Grand Rapids: Zondervan, 1984.

S. B. NARRAMORE

See GUILT; SUPEREGO.

Consciousness. In contemporary use consciousness usually means conscious experience, a phenomenon so general and so obviously a part of many aspects of psychology that it would seem impossible to describe in one short article. Actually the meaning of the term has shifted with both time and the interests of the people investigating it. Currently consciousness is a topic of great interest to psychologists in at least two different branches of the discipline.

Those who wanted to make psychology into a science in the latter half of the last century believed that they should study conscious experience. In subsequent years attempts to study sensation and even memory by applying the new techniques of the physical sciences were fairly successful, but attempts to study conscious experience were not. In fact, STRUCTURALISM, an attempt to isolate the "elements" of conscious experience and to deduce the rules by which these elements might combine (an idea borrowed from atomic theory), was such a sterile approach that psychologists began to wonder if the scientific study of such phenomena was even possible. About this time Watson (1913) argued very convincingly that conscious experience could not be studied with experimental methods and proposed instead that psychologists confine their investigations to behavior. His arguments helped launch behaviorism, an approach which dominated psychology in this country up to the late 1960s. Behaviorism's influence was so strong and pervasive that for many years consciousness was simply ignored. Now, however, it is being investigated once more.

One group of researchers interested in conscious experience are the new cognitive psychologists who are studying such things as decision making, problem solving, and mental imagery (Block, 1980). A second group is interested in the nature of the mind and how it is related to the brain, in altered states of consciousness, and even in the spiritual nature of man. This second area of consciousness research falls into two categories—mind-brain relationships and the "consciousness movement."

Mind-Brain Relationships. Studies done on the mind-brain issue are currently of great interest to many people besides those aligned with the consciousness movement, especially those who have a vested interest in a materialistic view of human beings. For many years most psychologists have been materialists, assuming that man is nothing more than a physical being, a highly advanced animal who is programmed by past learning, internal physical events, or external environmental events. They either deny that a person has a soul or spirit or claim that these things are merely words we have invented to describe

some of the phenomena we all observe. For them all experience can ultimately be explained by physical or chemical events occurring in the brain. Mind, then, would refer to subjective feelings we experience as a result of certain brain states. Mind does not produce the brain states but instead is produced by them. The brain states, in turn, depend on programming from genetic influences and past experiences, or on one's present physiological state or circumstances.

Recently several scientists have described evidence and produced arguments that are difficult to reconcile with a purely materialistic explanation (see Custance, 1980). One of the most noted of these is Eccles, who was awarded the Nobel Prize in Physiology and Medicine in 1963. Eccles has written and edited several important books on this topic. Although he would be among the first to acknowledge that certain brain injuries can drastically affect the functioning of the mind or even personality, he points out that there are even more drastic injuries which do not seem to affect either. For instance, some individuals with life-threatening tumors in their brains have had their entire nondominant cerebral hemisphere removed and have not been perceptibly changed psychologically. In fact the operation can be carried out under local anesthesia and they do not even lose consciousness as it is being done. (They do suffer loss in their visual fields and weakness in limbs on the opposite side of the body.) If mind is totally dependent on the brain, one would expect some significant change psychologically as a result of the loss of so much brain tissue. When hemispherectomies are done on the dominant hemisphere (the one that is necessary for speaking and apparently self-awareness), they are usually limited to children under 10 years of age because in young brains the entire language and awareness function can shift to the other hemisphere. In older children and adults these functions do not shift and the individual will remain severely aphasic and handicapped. The fact that the hemispheres can shift function is also hard to explain from a strictly physical point of view since the neurons which presumably provided these functions are completely destroyed and are not replaced by new ones. What, then, is left to reorganize the neurons on the other hemisphere to restore these vital functions?

Another interesting paradox observed by Libet (1982) is an apparent time lag between the brain state produced by a sensory stimulus (such as a light touch on the finger) and the conscious awareness of that stimulus. Similarly Kornhuber (1973) has shown that there is a substantial time lag between willing to move some part of the body and the achievement of a brain state capable of initiating that movement. If conscious experience is merely an aspect of a particular brain state, there should be no time discrepancy at all.

Another area of brain research that yields very interesting information about brain-mind relationships comes from patients who have undergone the "split-brain" operation. This operation, done to relieve seizures that cannot be chemically controlled, involves severing the corpus callosum, a broad band of some 200,000,000 fibers that carries visual and tactile information from one cerebral hemisphere to the other. (It is cut because it also transmits the abnormal seizure activity from one hemisphere to the other, causing the person to lose consciousness.) The operation is effective, and after recovery neither the patients nor their families are able to detect psychological or other changes. However, tests in more stringent laboratory conditions do reveal some rather startling differences.

In one type of test patients are seated in front of a screen; while they look straight ahead a word is flashed briefly on the left or right side of the screen. The information travels to either the right or left hemisphere, and since the callosum is cut it is isolated there. When a word is flashed to the left hemisphere (which is also the dominant, language hemisphere in 95% of the population), the person can say the word and use the right hand (also controlled by the left hemisphere) to reach under a screen to pick up the object named. When the word is flashed to the right hemisphere, however, the person is not aware that any word has been flashed. If persuaded to reach under a screen with the left hand to try to identify the object, they can usually do so. Oddly, even when they have the object in their left hands they cannot verbally identify what they are holding.

The results of this and many other types of tests on split-brain patients indicate that when the hemispheres receive different and discrepant visual or tactile information, they seem to act independently, as if they are really two separate minds in one head. (See Springer & Deutsch, 1981, for a comprehensive review of this area.) At first, these results seemed to confirm the materialist's assertion that mind is nothing more than a manifestation of the physical brain. After all, splitting the brain

seemed to split the mind. However, later information has been difficult to reconcile with this position.

One important question is whether the mute right hemisphere is really conscious in a human sense when disconnected from the left, since it seems to have neither the ability to produce language nor self-awareness, depending, of course, on the way self-awareness is defined. Sophisticated research techniques have shown that the right hemisphere excels in some things—e.g., recognizing patterns or faces, directing spatial tasks (drawing, sculpting), or discriminating musical chords. Sperry (1982) indicates that the right hemisphere can also identify its own face, members of the family, pets, and acquaintances, and seems to show appropriate emotional response to all these things. It also seems to be cognizant of the person's daily and weekly schedules, important dates, and the need for fire or health insurance. He argues that these abilities are sufficient to establish self-awareness. Others define self-awareness as our subjective stream of consciousness not only of events, but of our reactions to them, of our thoughts and feelings from moment to moment (James, 1916). If this definition is used, the right hemisphere is not self-aware, because when information is sent to the right hemisphere alone, that part of the psyche that the patient identifies as the self is not aware that anything has happened.

If this argument is valid, it puts to rest the disturbing possibility that a single brain operation could create two persons out of one, but it does not eliminate the fact that a separate, semiautonomous aspect of the person does exist that can interact intelligently with its environment, perhaps with the same level of consciousness available to animals (Gazzaniga & LeDoux, 1978). Gazzaniga has often set up situations in which the right and left hemispheres receive different information and the patient's two hands seem to do contradictory things. When this happens, the patients are very adept at explaining the inconsistencies and do not seem disturbed by them. Gazzaniga proposes that this phenomenon in split-brain patients is not really so strange but rather is a characteristic common to all of us. Human beings can be notoriously inconsistent, intending to do one thing and then doing the opposite, but are then adept at providing rational reasons for the unexpected switch. Perhaps we are inconsistent because we also have a duality. Since we become so accustomed to inconsistency, we also become proficient at covering it up without really wondering about it.

One final observation about the split-brain studies is that they are producing a rather profound change in the way that brain scientists are viewing mind-brain relationships. For instance, Sperry (1982), one of the most noted researchers in the area, has come to the conclusion that conscious experience (mind) is very real and that, besides being different from and greater than the sum of its parts, mind also causally determines the fate of the parts. Sperry believes that as more and more brain scientists accept this perspective, the old conflict between the scientific and humanistic view of human beings will disappear and that the study of the mind and of human judgments and values will become important.

The Consciousness Movement. The individuals contributing to the consciousness movement come from very diverse disciplines and include biologists who specialize in understanding the brain, psychologists, parapsychologists, medical doctors, physicists, and even specialists in Eastern and other religions. A substantial proportion of the authors within this group perceive and present their efforts as scientific attempts to understand man's spiritual nature, yet very few of them accept or will even seriously consider Judeo-Christian beliefs. Instead they embrace Eastern religions, espousing such doctrines as reincarnation. Many have also adopted a modified theory of evolution which proposes that men are evolving mentally and even now are on the threshold of revolutionary change. These changes would include new (or newly discovered) mental powers such as telepathy, psychokinesis (the ability to move objects by mental powers alone), the ability to enter into altered states of consciousness, to heal physical disorders in others by mental means, the ability to experience other "spiritual realities" (i.e., to contact spiritual beings), or even the ability to separate at will from one's body. (See Goleman & Davidson, 1979, for a general collection of readings on this topic.)

Many of these researchers seem to believe that these mental powers may be more accessible through altered states of consciousness and thus are very eager to study them. Some of the specific areas of interest include hypnosis (Bowers, 1979), drug states (Tart, 1969), psychotic states, meditative states (Deikman, 1973), and even possession states (Ludwig, 1967). Comparisons of the characteristics of these altered states reveal surprising similarities among them, including passivity, loss of ability to control one's mental processes, hallucinations, vivid visual imagery, and extreme emotional experiences.

If these experiences were the only gratifications that altered states provided, one might wonder why anyone would repeatedly risk his health to pursue them. The real reasons for their appeal may lie in their more subtle enticements. Any of the altered states can induce people to attach great significance to their subjective experiences, ideas, or perceptions, making them believe that they have been privy to profound insights or have grasped ultimate truths. Unfortunately, however, these insights frequently bear no relationship to reality, but they can and frequently do linger on and influence thinking long after the experience. The various altered states may also provide mystical and transcendent experiences in which supernatural forces or beings may be sensed, seen, or even communicated with. These experiences are especially vivid, and their importance is exaggerated by the hyper-suggestibility and suspension of critical thinking that also accompany altered states. Such experiences have changed people's lives (Ludwig, 1969).

Researchers in the consciousness movement have also been interested in studying psychic healing and other paranormal abilities, including the scientific study of mediums. They have studied the near-death phenomenon, first described by Moody (1975), and some have even been working on scientific methods to help people leave their physical bodies. According to Brooke (1979), who worked on one such project before his conversion to Christianity, the information on how to do this is coming from what the believers call "spirit guides," who are presumably trying to help mankind on to the next stage of spiritual evolution.

From a Christian perspective these developments within the consciousness movement are unsettling because the "spirit guides" sound hauntingly similar to demons, and the "spiritual evolution" they presumably promise seems to be no more than an elaborate scientific cover-up for one more diabolical attempt to deceive and destroy. The movement, whose stated goal is to unite science and religion, is apparently attracting fairly substantial numbers of educated men and women who may perceive it as a way to satisfy their spiritual longings without meeting the costly demands of Christianity. Christians should certainly be made aware of the potential implications and dangers in this new area of study.

References

Bowers, K. Hypnosis and dissociation. In D. Goleman & R. Davidson (Eds.), *Consciousness: Brain, states of awareness and mysticism.* New York: Harper & Row, 1979.

Brooke, R. T. *The other side of death.* Wheaton, Ill.: Tyndale House, 1979.

Custance, A. C. *The mysterious matter of mind.* Grand Rapids: Zondervan, 1980.

Deikman, A. Bimodal consciousness. In R. E. Ornstein (Ed.). *The nature of human consciousness.* New York: Viking Press, 1973.

Gazzaniga, M. S., & LeDoux, J. E. *The integrated mind.* New York: Plenum, 1978.

Goleman, D., & Davidson, R. *Consciousness: Brain, states of awareness and mysticism.* New York: Harper & Row, 1979.

James, W. *The varieties of religious experience.* New York: Longmans, Green, 1916.

Kornhuber, H. H. Cerebral cortex, cerebellum and basal ganglia: An introduction to their motor functions. In F. O. Schmitt & F. G. Worden (Eds.), *The Neurosciences third study program.* Cambridge: MIT Press, 1973.

Libet, B. Subjective and neuronal time factors in conscious sensory experience, studied in man, and their implications for mind brain relationships. In J. Eccles, (Ed.), *Mind and brain.* Washington, D. C.: Paragon House, 1982.

Ludwig, A. M. The trance. *Comprehensive psychiatry,* 1967, *8,* 7–15.

Ludwig, A. M. Altered States of Consciousness. In C. T. Tart (Ed.), *Altered states of consciousness.* New York: Wiley, 1969.

Moody, R. *Life after life.* Atlanta: Mockingbird Books, 1975.

Sperry, R. Some effects of disconnecting the cerebral hemispheres. *Science,* September 1982, pp. 1223–1226.

Springer, S., & Deutsch, G. *Left brain right brain.* San Francisco: W. H. Freeman, 1981.

Tart, C. T. (Ed.). *Altered states of consciousness.* New York: Wiley, 1969.

Watson, J. B. Psychology as a behaviorist views it. *Psychological Review,* 1913, *20,* 158–177.

Additional Reading

Eccles, J. (Ed.). *Mind and brain.* Washington D. C.: Paragon House, 1982.

E. L. Hillstrom

See Mind-Brain Relationship; Self; Personhood; Transpersonal Psychology.

Constitutional Personality Theory.

Constitutional psychology is the study of the relationship between personality and the structure of one's physique. That is, the psychological aspects of human behavior are studied as they are related to morphology (form and structure) and physiology (organs, tissues, etc.) (Sheldon, Hartl, & McDermott, 1949). Though Sheldon is the most noted researcher in this area, others have also attempted to demonstrate a relationship between personality and body structure.

Hippocrates is known for his classification system of body types. For him, people were either short and fat or long and thin. He also proposed four basic temperament dimensions. People characteristically were cheerful (sanguine), apathetic (phlegmatic), depressed (melancholic), or violent (choleric).

In the twentieth century Kretschmer has studied the relationship between body type and mental illness. His body classification system describes people as muscular (athletic), short and fat (pyknic), or thin and long-limbed (asthenic). In his major study investigating body type and mental disorder (1925), he found that persons who experienced emotional highs and lows (manic-depressive) were usually short and fat, and those who experienced bizarre and irrational thinking (schizophrenics) were usually thin and long-limbed. Kretschmer's work was useful but limited due to the type of people studied.

Sheldon undertook the task of further determining what kind of relationship exists between personality and body type. Schooled in both psychology and medicine, he was well equipped to investigate both areas. Using Kretschmer's work as a basis, Sheldon decided to explore more scientifically the apparent relationship. His first task was to determine the various types of human physiques in existence. To do this, he and his associates (Sheldon, Stevens, & Tucker, 1940) photographed and studied nearly 4,000 male college students. After thorough examination, Sheldon determined that three basic body types were adequate to classify all human physiques.

The first type Sheldon called endomorphy, characterized by softness and roundness. The second type was labeled mesomorphy, muscular and rectangular in shape. The athlete best exemplified this body type. The third type of physique was called ectomorphy, usually thin, lightly muscled, and flat-chested.

The process Sheldon used to classify each body type was a numerical procedure referred to as somatotyping (Sheldon, Dupertuis, McDermott, 1954). This procedure described each body component at either its minimum or maximum potential. For example, a somatotype of 7–1–1 would depict an individual who was the highest possible in endomorphy (always the first numeral), the lowest possible in mesomorphy (always the second numeral), and the lowest possible in ectomorphy (always the last numeral). A typical person might be 4–6–2, indicating features of average roundness, developed muscular structure with an absence of frailness. Sheldon further proposed that one's physique remained constant over time. Though a person's weight might fluctuate sharply, his basic body structure (skeleton, shape of head, neck, wrists, ankles, calves, forearms, etc.) did not.

The next step in the development of Sheldon's constitutional personality theory was to devise a means of assessing personality. This procedure was based on the assumption that though there are many surface temperament dimensions, in reality there are only a small number of core personality traits. His task was to determine the character of these basic traits. He first surveyed the literature and extracted 650 traits. These were examined for redundancy, and only 50 were considered essential. To determine the evidence of these 50 traits in people, 33 men were thoroughly studied over a period of one year. The results of this study indicated three major groups of traits. The first group, which Sheldon labeled viscerotonia, was characterized by the desire for comfort, relaxation, sleep, social approval, and dependence. The second group, referred to as somatotonia, was centered around assertiveness, maturity, activity, and the need for exercise. The third group, labeled cerebrotonia, included traits of privacy, rigidity, social restraint, and sleep disturbances. Sheldon considered these trait groups as representative of the human personality.

With the procedures for assessing body physique and personality established, Sheldon was then faced with the question of whether a relationship really did exist. To determine this, he (Sheldon, Stevens, 1942) undertook a major five-year study involving 200 white male college students. Each student was thoroughly examined, somatotyped, and rated on the temperament dimensions. The findings of this study indicated a strong relationship between particular body types and certain trait groups. Sheldon's study was a correlational one—i.e., it indicated the extent to which two variables, in this case body type and personality, occurred together. A positive correlation meant that evidence of one variable was accompanied by evidence of another. Positive and negative correlations theoretically range from $+1.00$ to -1.00. In this classic study Sheldon found a strong correlation between mesomorphy and viscerotonia $(+.79)$, between mesomorphy and somatotonia $(+.82)$, and between ectomorphy and cerebrotonia $(+.83)$. Sheldon himself expressed surprise at finding such high correlations. He concluded that there did indeed exist a marked relationship between particular body types and certain personality temperaments. This study comprises the major evidence in support of constitutional personality theory.

There have been numerous explanations as to why people have particular personalities. One explanation emphasizes a strong environmental influence; one's personality is the result of contact with significant others, early

childhood experiences, and adolescent relationships. One's physique is not considered influential in personality development. This explanation speaks to personality development but not to how a relationship such as that found by Sheldon might exist.

A second explanation proposes a strong environmental influence coupled with the fact that people are born with different body types; a person's physique may change the environment he experiences. For example, an individual born with a frail physique may find it difficult to excel in contact sports or strenuous outdoor activities. Therefore, he may turn to more mental kinds of endeavors and become more private, rigid, and socially restrained. This reasoning could explain the relationship Sheldon reported.

Another explanation involves a strong environmental influence not only on one's personality but also on one's physique. A person may be born with a rather sturdy physique (mesomorph) but through nutritional deficit experience skeletal damage and permanent muscular atrophy. This could explain one's body type and to an extent one's later personality development. As one's physique is altered by nutritional environment, this stimulates changes in the social environment and subsequently one's personality.

A fourth alternative is to explain one's physique and personality in terms of biological-hereditary factors only. This explanation proposes that the same gene or combination of genes influences both physical and personality development, not only initially but consistently throughout life. This alternative could theoretically explain the results reported by Sheldon.

A fifth explanation is to consider some of the aforementioned influences as instrumental to personality development but in varying degrees for each individual. In this case one might consider hereditary factors initially very influential, childhood experiences most influential to core personality development, and an interaction of physique and adolescent relationships as most important to later personality formation. Admittedly, a number of theoretical combinations are possible. Nevertheless, Sheldon's theory seems to reflect a strong biological-hereditary orientation.

Constitutional personality theory appears to be one of the less controversial secular theories. It is not a comprehensive system, offering philosophical assumptions, numerous theoretical constructs, or extensive experimental research. Its strength lies in its straightforward approach to examining personality as this is related to physical body type. It is helpful in that it provides information assisting us to a more thorough understanding of human behavior.

References

Kretschmer, E. [*Physique and character.*] (W. J. H. Sprott, Ed. and trans.) New York: Harcourt, Brace, 1925.

Sheldon, W. H., Dupertuis, C. W., & McDermott, E. *Atlas of men:* New York: Harper & Row, 1954.

Sheldon, W. H., Hartl, E. M., & McDermott, E. *Varieties of delinquent youth.* New York: Harper & Row, 1949.

Sheldon, W. H., Stevens, S. S., & Tucker, W. E. *The varieties of human physique.* New York: Harper & Row, 1940.

Sheldon, W. H., & Stevens, S. J. *The varities of temperament.* New York: Harper & Row, 1942.

Additional Reading

Sheldon, W. H. Constitutional factors in personality. In J. M. Hunt (Ed.), *Personality and the behavior disorders.* New York: Ronald Press, 1944.

M. L. MARVIN

See PERSONALITY.

Consulting Psychology.

In the past this term has referred more to one of several functions of psychology rather than to a type of psychologist. More recently, however, it has been used by some professionals to depict their total identity. Caplan (1970) has described consultation as the service given to a person who seeks help on a given problem by a specialist who has expert knowledge in the area of concern but who is not directly involved in the situation.

Two trends have contributed to the emergence of consulting psychology as a professional speciality subfield. The first is the growing awareness that the need for treatment is far greater than can ever be met by mental health professionals. Thus even in the 1960s consultation became one of the essential services which community mental health centers were required to provide. The second is the new awareness among many varied organizations that their effectiveness can be improved by consultation. Thus it is now the rule rather than the exception for governmental, private, business, and service groups to routinely employ consultants in their work.

The role of the mental health consultant should be differentiated from that of friend or therapist. Consultants are experts with specific knowledge rather than friends with general interests. Furthermore, the consultant is not, nor does he become, the primary therapist. It is the consultant's intent to enlighten the situation from a specialized viewpoint in order that the person or group may become better informed, function more effectively, and acquire skills for use in the future.

Caplan (1970) has identified four types of mental health consultation: 1) client-centered case consultation, in which the focus of the interaction is the individual who is being treated for a problem; 2) consultee-centered case consultation, in which the focus of the interaction is the therapist providing the treatment; 3) program-centered administrative consultation, in which the focus of the interaction is the organization providing the service; and 4) consultee-centered administrative consultation, in which the focus of the interaction is the individual administrator of the service program.

Organizational consultation is much broader than mental health consultation in that here the psychologist is perceived as an expert in human behavior in general, not just in human psychopathology and its treatment. Organizations are understood to be the primary social units in which individuals achieve status and identity. Consultant psychologists see their work as efforts to enhance change in these social systems in order that they may accomplish their goals more successfully while fulfilling their members' lives more completely. Thus, they perceive themselves as "organizational development" specialists and advise groups on a wide range of problems relating both to the processes through which they function and the practical methods they use to achieve their goals. They engage in problem analysis, training, conflict management, personnel selection, and program planning to name only a few of their roles.

Reference

Caplan, G. *The theory and practice of mental health consultation.* New York: Basic Books, 1970.

Additional Readings

Blake, R. R., & Mouton, J. S. *Consultation.* Reading, Mass.: Addison-Wesley 1976.

Lippitt, G., & Lippitt, R. *The consulting process in action.* La Jolla, Calif.: University Associates, 1978.

Schein, E. H. *Process consultation.* Reading, Mass.: Addison-Wesley, 1969.

H. N. MALONY

See APPLIED PSYCHOLOGY; INDUSTRIAL/ORGANIZATIONAL PSYCHOLOGY.

Consumerism.

An orientation toward using rather than producing; an emphasis on buying, on purchasing tangible goods that enhance one's comfort and sense of security. In its extreme form consumerism is a drive to accumulate and possess, without much thought for the ecological, psychological, and spiritual effects.

Traditionally consumer behavior has been

thought of as purely a matter of economics. The danger of this is pointed out by Scitovsky (1976): "Economists . . . accept unquestioningly the consumer's judgment of what is best for him, his tastes as the outcome of that judgment, and his market behavior as the reflection of his tastes. Economists will not analyze the motivation of consumer behavior" (pp. 4–5). Scitovsky, however, is an economist who is an exception to the rule.

In the field of psychology Scitovsky's best-known ally has been Katona. In his *Psychological Economics* (1975) Katona demonstrates graphically how the traditional economic model increasingly fails to predict how consumers actually behave. As an example, he points out that the 1970 recession was in part triggered by deteriorating public confidence based on such noneconomic factors as race riots and the Vietnam War. Also, in the inflation/recession period between 1973 and 1975, when economists predicted that consumers would save less and tap into their savings to buy goods now in anticipation of future prices, what actually happened was that the overall rate of savings went up. People were scared.

The study of consumerism reveals many aspects of consumer motivation and behavior. One aspect is manipulation by advertising. Advertising requires that the consumer be gullible to suggestion and vulnerable to deception. Through continuous bombardment advertising deadens the gullible mind to any type of analysis of the noneconomic side of consumerism. Deception is saying that happiness is having, and then redefining everything as marketable to make possible more and more buying and, therefore, greater happiness.

Another very important aspect of consumer motivation and behavior, however, is satisfaction of a noncommercial nature. To see that happiness cannot always be bought one need only consider such satisfactions as competently managing a home, gardening organically, or praying to God. Yet the thrust of consumerism is to convert as many noneconomic satisfactions as possible to economic ones, to market them. Merton (1964) suggests that this is done by people "who think that what has no price has no value, that what cannot be sold is not real, so that the only way to make something *actual* is to place it on the market" (p. 9).

A psychological critique of consumerism is revealing in other ways as well. Economists, for instance, use the Gross National Product (GNP) as the primary indicator of a society's quality of life. Nonmarketed satisfactions are not included in the GNP. Marketed miseries are, however, included. This is reflected by expenditures for such things as police protection necessitated by crime, pollution control, emergency treatment of accident victims, and methadone maintenance drug treatment programs.

In addition, one of the major contributions of Scitovsky's critique is his analysis of comfort as a primary goal of consumerism. He points out that comforts not only typically fail to carry external benefits, but many of them generate external nuisances as well. To see this, one has only to consider many of those appliances that substitute mechanical power for human effort. In addition to comfort they also often generate noise, chemical air pollution, or both. Further, in consumers' relentless pursuit of comfort they save effort only to run the risk of dying of a heart attack, save time and then waste it, save being bothered and in the process waste resources.

Clearly a Christian response to consumerism is called for. Living freely, unencumbered by materialism, sharing rather than accumulating possessions, and respecting God's creation for what it is rather than a means to selfish ends would be a Christlike response (Farnsworth, 1978; Gish, 1973; Taylor, 1975). Being carefree and yet bored from chasing fleeting comforts in the marketplace would not. Or, in Jesus' words, "Do not worry, saying, 'What shall we eat?' or 'What shall we drink?' or 'What shall we wear?' For the pagans run after all these things, and your heavenly Father knows that you need them. But seek first his kingdom and his righteousness, and all these things will be given to you as well" (Matt. 6:31–33).

References

Farnsworth, K. E. The psychology of consumption. In *Alternative Celebrations Catalogue* (4th ed.). Bloomington, Ind.: Alternatives, 1978.

Gish, A. G. *Beyond the rat race*. Scottdale, Pa.: Herald Press, 1973.

Katona, G. *Psychological economics*. New York: Elsevier Scientific Publishing, 1975.

Merton, T. *Raids on the unspeakable*. New York: New Directions, 1964.

Scitovsky, T. *The joyless economy*. New York: Oxford University Press, 1976.

Taylor, J. V. *Enough is enough*. Naperville, Ill.: SCM Book Club, 1975.

K. E. FARNSWORTH

Consumer Psychology. "That branch of psychology which seeks, through utilization of distinctively psychological concepts and methods, to understand the dynamics underlying and determining consumer behavior" (Jacoby,

1975). More often referred to as consumer behavior, this discipline has its roots in social psychology but focuses on application of theory and method in the context of purchase and use of consumer goods.

Theory and research are based on the assumption of consumer sovereignty—a purposeful and goal-oriented buyer and user. The goal is to understand decision processes in order to help improve effectiveness of marketing strategy in a business firm and to help the consumer behave more wisely (the focus of home economists and consumerists).

Consumer psychology emerged as a distinct field of study in the late 1960s, largely in schools of business, with the publication of two comprehensive models of consumer decision processes (Engel, Kollat, Blackwell, 1968; Howard & Sheth, 1969). This was followed by formation of the Association for Consumer Research in 1970 and by the *Journal of Consumer Research* in 1974. The greatest development continues in business schools and only secondarily in departments of psychology.

The greatest contributions have emerged through applied psychological research in both laboratory and real-world settings. One of these has been the development of comprehensive models of high-involvement purchase decisions (high relevance and deliberation) as contrasted with low-involvement purchase decisions (minimal relevance and deliberation). This has led to important clarification of the ATTITUDE-BEHAVIOR RELATIONSHIP. Major advances have also been made in the areas of consumer information processing and the effects of commercial persuasion. The impact of this has been the development of a tradition of practical consumer research which can inform decisions in business, government, and many other spheres of life.

There have been some surprisingly relevant applications to research on spiritual decision processes. The so-called Engel scale (Engel, 1979), widely used in evangelistic strategy to help understand readiness for response to the gospel, comes directly from this research tradition. Much current understanding of the impact of media and persuasion on spiritual decision making has also come from this research approach. Thus, consumer psychology continues to make direct contributions to enhanced stewardship in world evangelization.

References

Engel, J. F., *Contemporary Christian communication.* Nashville: Nelson, 1979.
Engel, J. F., Kollat, D. T., & Blackwell, R. D. *Consumer behavior.* New York: Holt, Rinehart & Winston, 1968.
Howard, J. A., & Sheth, J. N. *The theory of buyer behavior.* New York: Wiley, 1969.
Jacoby, J. Consumer psychology as a social psychological sphere of action. *American Psychologist*, 1975, *30*, 977–987.

J. F. ENGEL

Contextual Family Therapy. This approach understands human existence in the context of human relationship, emphasizing the covenantal relationship based on having received and having to reciprocate. It is strongly rooted in the Judeo-Christian tradition, and its proponents have sought to integrate family theory and the biblical theologies of both Old and New Testaments. Other roots lie in OBJECT RELATIONS THEORY, which emphasizes the internal images of significant others developed during the earliest years of life.

The first major systematic presentation of the contextual perspective was by Boszormenyi-Nagy and Spark (1973). These authors stress the loyalty commitments in families, invisible fibers holding together the relationship network. Each family member keeps track of his or her perception of the balances of give-and-take in past, present, and future. Affirming the work of Erikson, these authors assert that an environment worthy of trust, the ideal childhood environment, inevitably engenders indebtedness. If the child cannot repay the benefits received, an emotional debt will accumulate. Ultimately several generations of personal relationships may be necessary to build a family environment characterized by an adequate balance of trust and mistrust. When loyalty debts are heavy, the adult child may be unable to transfer loyalty from the parents and the family of origin to a new relationship. Thus, marital commitment will continually be in tension with loyalty to the family of origin. In the future the marital commitment is likely to be in conflict with loyalty to the offspring as the unbalanced relationship ledger seeks to balance itself in the new generation. Vertical loyalty commitments tend always to conflict with horizontal ones, so that the loyalty owed to previous or subsequent generations (to parents, grandparents, and children) will conflict with loyalty owed to husband or wife, brothers and sisters, friends and peers.

The contextual family therapist takes into account four dimensions while assessing the family's dynamics: 1) facts, which are those aspects provided by destiny and include such things as ethnic identity, adoption, survivorship, illness, sex, and religious identity; 2) psychology, which refers to those things occurring within the person, thus affirming the psychodynamic dimensions of drives, psychic development, object relations, and inner experience; 3) transactions or power alignments, those aspects examined especially by the structural and systems family theorists; and 4) relational ethics, concerned with the "balance of equitable fairness between people, . . . the long-term preservation of an oscillating balance among family members, whereby the basic interests of each are taken into account by the others" (Boszormenyi-Nagy & Ulrich, 1981, p. 160). It is this emphasis on relational ethics that is most distinctive to the contextual approach. Entitlement and indebtedness are among the existential givens of life, and relationships are trustworthy only to the extent that they allow these ethical issues to be faced.

The most basic of the existential givens is the fact of one's birth. We do not ask to be born, yet we are born into a family which inherits the invisible loyalties of countless preceding generations. Another given which the therapist must take very seriously is the wish of every family member to establish trustworthy relationships. The assumption of adversary relationships within families violates the basic urge toward relational justice. The family is strengthened by moves toward trustworthiness and weakened by moves away from it. Thus, high levels of individual merit, accumulated by supporting the interests of others, contribute to the health of the whole family.

The concept of legacy relates to the family's bookkeeping system and has two ethical components. The first is based on the debts and entitlements contributed by legacy, to which the child must adapt his or her life. One's actual entitlement is composed both of one's natural due as parent and child, and of what one has come to merit. That the legacies ascribed to different children in one family may be unequal is another existential given. Legacy expectations are perceived by family members as ethical imperatives. Thus, they are perceived as things one *ought* to do rather than things one would *like* to do. The currency in which one's relational debts are paid is also dictated by the family, so that options available to a member of one family may not be available to a member of another. Enlarging the range of options may be one of the tasks of the contextual family therapist.

A situation of grave concern to the contextual family therapist is that of split loyalty, in which the child can offer loyalty to one parent only at the expense of the other. It is imperative for the mental health of the child that in a situation of divorce and remarriage the child

not be asked to renounce loyalty to the noncustodial parent. Also damaging to the child are parents who are unwilling to accept payments on the debt owed by the child. When nothing is acceptable as repayment, the child enters into new relationships with no emotional energy available for the relationship. That which is given to the mate or friend will be regarded as stolen from the parental account. The tragic component of legacy is that "patterns shall be repeated, against unavailing struggle, from one generation to the next" (Boszormenyi-Nagy & Ulrich, 1981, p. 166). Accounts can only be settled in those relationships where they were engendered, and thus it is critical that one's "unfinished business" with parents and brothers and sisters be completed before one enters into a marital relationship, where the same dynamic repeats itself.

In this context family pathology is regarded as the result of exploitation in the realm of relational ethics. Examples of exploitation are the secret marriage contracts in which each partner serves to act out the negative aspects of the other; the scapegoating of a child, in which the child bears the family's pain; the parentification of a child, in which the child tries to give to its parents the nurturance they never received from their parents; and relational corruption, in which one person believes that he or she is entitled to be unfair to anyone, because he or she has never been on the receiving end of a truly nurturing relationship.

In contextual family therapy the goal is always to move the marital partners and family members in the direction of ethical relationships. By involving members of the extended family the chains of invisible loyalty and legacy can be loosened, allowing individuals to give up symptomatic behavior and opening up new options. However, individual goals are always considered in the context of all family members, since "no family member can alone judge whether the ledger is in balance" (Boszormenyi-Nagy & Ulrich, 1981, p. 164).

Integrative efforts focusing on this approach have come primarily from Krasner and her co-workers (Krasner & Shapiro, 1979). Krasner's work, drawing on the rabbinic tradition, has focused on such issues as trust building in religious communities, the idea of a "no-fault" world, forgiveness, and other implications of relational justice. Boszormenyi-Nagy and his colleagues also address the loyalty conflicts inherent in the traditional psychotherapeutic situation, where the therapist challenges the client's loyalty to the parents. Contextual family therapy adds a psychodynamic perspective to God's words that "the iniquity of the fathers shall be visited on the children," and reminds us that the ethical dimension of relationships cannot be escaped.

References

Boszormenyi-Nagy, I., & Spark, G. M. *Invisible loyalties.* New York: Harper & Row, 1973.
Boszormenyi-Nagy, I., & Ulrich, D. N. Contextual family therapy. In A. S Gurman & D. P. Kniskern (Eds.), *Handbook of family therapy.* New York: Brunner/Mazel, 1981.
Krasner, B. R., & Shapiro, A. Trustbuilding initiatives in the rabbinic community. *Conservative Judaism,* 1979, *33*(1), 3–21.

H. VANDE KEMP

See FAMILY THERAPY: OVERVIEW.

Contingency Contracting.

A technique used primarily in behavior therapy, by which an agreement is made between two or more parties and then formalized into a contract (either written or verbal, but always explicit). This contract specifies the behaviors required of the parties to the contract, and spells out the consequences that are to follow those behaviors.

Behaviorists believe that behavior is in large part a function of environmental consequences of the behavior. Contracts are thus a means of clarifying and ordering in a systematic way the consequences of the client's actions. Contracts may focus on the interactions between therapist and client (e.g., specifying consequences for succeeding at agreed-upon changes in the client's behavior), interactions between spouses (e.g., specifying mutual responsibilities in the marriage and the consequences for reneging on those responsibilities), and between parent and child (e.g., defining responsibilities and privileges of the child, including loss of privileges following failure to meet responsibilities). These examples are the most common areas of use for contingency contracts. The use of a contract presupposes, first, the capacity of all parties involved to understand the details of the contract and, second, that the behaviors in question can be adequately defined and the appropriate consequences provided.

S. L. JONES

See BEHAVIOR THERAPY; APPLIED BEHAVIOR ANALYSIS.

Contracts, Therapeutic Use of.

Believing that no productive outcomes arise from therapy that does not work toward specific goals, therapists of several different theoretical orientations employ treatment goals as a contract for therapy. Such contracts sometimes also specify the role or responsibilities of both therapist and client, although a statement of mutually acceptable goals is the most common ingredient. Gestalt, transactional, and behavioral therapists most commonly employ such treatment contracts, but their use is not limited to these modalities of therapy. Their use in these approaches is consistent with the generally more active role of the therapist. Contracts are thus often employed by therapists who might also utilize homework or other structured assignments.

See HOMEWORK IN PSYCHOTHERAPY.

Control Group.

Those subjects in an experiment who do not receive the experimental treatment but who are otherwise as similar to subjects in the experimental group as possible. The experimental group are those subjects who receive the experimental treatment. The results are then interpreted by comparing the degree and direction of the effect on the experimental subjects to that of the control subjects.

See PSYCHOLOGY, METHODS OF.

Conversion.

Webster's dictionary suggests that conversion means to "turn around, transform, or change the characteristics of something." The word is sometimes used to refer to general personality or behavioral changes, such as those that result from education or psychotherapy. However, conversion refers most often to religious experiences in which attitudes or actions are dramatically altered, as when Paul was converted on the Damascus Road or, more recently, when Malcolm Muggeridge converted to Roman Catholicism.

The Paul and Muggeridge illustrations refer to the distinction between "inner" and "outer" conversion as suggested by some theorists. Often the joining of a given church or religious group (termed "outer" conversion) is mistaken for a radical change of perception and outlook (termed "inner" conversion). Although both may occur simultaneously, they are not necessarily synonymous. Gordon (1967) noted this fact in studying converts by marriage to the Jewish faith. Often these are cultural conversions rather than genuine transformations of outlook. Many persons attest that it was this outer conversion in which they participated when they joined the church in early adolescence and that this was followed by an inner conversion at a later time.

Whereas outer conversion refers to a formal

action of identifying with a given faith, inner conversion refers to a newly acquired sense of inner security, unity, peace, and meaning such as is exemplified in Paul. James (1902) gave the classic definition of this experience: "To be converted, to be regenerate, to receive grace, to experience religion, to gain an assurance, are so many phrases which denote the process, gradual or sudden, by which a self hitherto divided, and consciously wrong, inferior and unhappy, becomes unified and consciously right, superior and happy, in consequence of its firmer hold upon religious realities" (p. 157). James's definition has provided many of the themes which have been investigated by psychologists since the beginning of this century. These themes have included 1) whether conversion is a process or an event; 2) the preconversion mental state; and 3) the nature of the inner change that occurs in conversion.

Conversion as Process or Event? James considered conversion to be "a process, gradual or sudden," whereas many religionists have thought of it as a specific event occurring at a given point in time. In fact, many have used the word to apply only to those who can point to a time and place at which they were "born again" in a manner similar to that recommended to Nicodemus by Jesus (John 3:3) and exemplified by Paul (Acts 9). However, James contended that these events were part of a process and used the term "conversion" to apply both to those who could and those who could not point to a specific moment of decision.

Healthy and Sick Minded Converts. James contended that the self-awareness of both sudden and gradual converts was preceded by a period of preparation whether the individuals were conscious of it or not. He paired up sudden conversions with "sick" minded and gradual conversions with "healthy" minded personalities. There was no bias toward the healthy minded in James's theory. In fact, he perceived them as weaker than their sick minded counterparts because they were unable to bear prolonged suffering in their minds and, consequently, had a tendency to deny conflict and to see things optimistically. Thus, they engaged in what the psychoanalysts call repression in an effort to avoid inner turmoil. This led the healthy minded to affirm a given type of religion, namely the idealistic, positive kind, and to be unaware of the time when they adopted such an outlook. James described these persons as "gradual" converts or as "once born" persons.

Sick minded individuals, on the other hand, had a stronger congenital temperament. These persons were, in fact, more realistic about themselves and about the world. They were able to perceive enigmas, injustices, hypocrisies, and evils. They agonized over problems in themselves in much the same fashion of which Paul spoke: "For I do not do the good I want, but the evil I do not want is what I do. . . . Wretched man that I am! Who will deliver me from this body of death?" (Rom. 7:19, 24). From a psychoanalytic point of view, they had enough ego strength to keep opposing impulses in consciousness. They were not neurotic in the sense that they remained aware of the conflict. The resolution of their dilemmas typically came suddenly and the immediate release that occurred prompted James to term these "twice born" persons.

James did not make the distinctions among levels of consciousness that were later clarified by analytic theorists. However, he did suggest that sick minded converts were more aware of their unconscious minds than were healthy minded persons. Nevertheless, there was a sense in which he considered the sick minded persons predisposed toward morbidity and an inability to trust either themselves or the universe. Whereas they were able to tolerate conflict better than healthy minded persons, they also tended to remain weak and fearful after the experience and to rely too intensely on divine power. This tendency toward self-depreciation and immature dependence was characteristic of much religious experience that Freud was later to criticize and denigrate.

Process of Conversion. A model that encompasses both gradual and sudden conversions has been proposed by Tippett (1977). It includes both "periods" of time and "points" in time in alternating sequence. Initially there is a *period of growing awareness*, in which the individual becomes conscious of the possibilities of a given faith answer to problems of life but sees them as peripheral to his or her own concerns. This is tantamount to saying that the answers of faith which are later affirmed by the convert must first become a part of the mind at a subliminal level. This is usually the result of cultural contact with one or more religions.

This period of growing awareness is succeeded by a *point of realization*, at which time the potential convert becomes aware that the faith to which she or he will later accede is not merely an idea but a possibility. Tippett contends that there is such a moment even though persons may not be able to pinpoint it exactly. This is tantamount to saying that the cultural context which had been a backdrop for the thinking of the convert becomes somewhat more focal and results in fleeting ideas that the faith could have some personal meaning in the future.

This point of realization is succeeded by a *period of consideration* during which the individual wrestles with the dilemmas he is facing and also interacts with others who have found an answer to these same problems. The person becomes an active seeker during this period and places himself in settings where the faith which will later be affirmed is talked about and acted upon. As Tippett notes, the change which will later be made is never a change from *no* faith to a faith but a change from *this* faith to *that* faith. The ideas of faith come to the foreground in the mental life of the individual during this time. They compete with other options on an equal basis even though they do not dominate as they will in the future.

This period of consideration ends with a *point of encounter* for the gradual as well as the sudden convert, according to Tippett. Again, although the sudden convert may have a public event to which he can point, if the truth were known there is a day on which the gradual convert also felt sure of the faith which he espouses. However it comes about, it is at this point that most persons would say a conversion has occurred. Often this experience is accompanied by a sense that a problem has been solved and that peace and security have come. The supposed psychological processes that occur at this point will be discussed later in this article. Suffice it to say that a point at which the faith takes over and the individual decisively changes his or her outlook on life does happen and that many persons can indicate the time and place at which this occurs. This means that faith is no longer one among several options cognitively, but it takes over and dominates the other possibilities which the individual was considering as answers to dilemmas.

Although both Tippett and James consider conversion to be a process, Tippett proposes a sequence of events that occur after the point of encounter as well as before it. James also writes about these but calls them "saintliness" rather than conversion. This is an important distinction because Tippett is more aware of the absolute meaning of conversion as complete change of life. He is aware that this by no means occurs simply because a person has made a decision to accept a given faith, which is only the beginning of a change that will itself take time. The point of encounter may signify a "turning around" or a "stopping of going in one direction," but it does not signify that a person has reversed the past to the point where new life is a reality.

These considerations led Tippett to propose another period in the conversion process after the point of encounter. There is a *period of incorporation* during which the new convert is socialized into the new faith. For example, the public confession of faith, typical for the sudden convert, is often followed by a period of training and consultation during which the individual both reconsiders the meaning of the decision and learns more about the religion to which he or she desires to belong. This is followed by a "rite of passage" such as baptism and joining the church, which signifies that the person is now a part of the faith in both its public and private dimensions. Furthermore, after a person has become a new member of the faith group, there are obligations and opportunities which are provided as means whereby the individual can grow in faith. This maturation process is sometimes ritualized into pressure to reach a new point of development and receive a "second blessing," which may express itself in such ways as speaking in tongues and healing powers. Tippett considers this process of growth in faith and practice to be an integral part of conversion. The new faith takes over the mental and physical life of the individual and becomes the dominant life force by which the person exists. Only when this is so can conversion be thought to have fully occurred.

Two contemporary communication theorists (Lofland & Stark, 1965) have translated Tippett's model into terms of traditional Christian categories, which include God's action, the role of the Christian evangelist, and the response of the convert. They begin with God's general revelation whereby persons are aware of a Supreme Being but have no effective knowledge of the gospel. This leads to the proclamation of Jesus as Savior, which is God's special revelation and which leads to an initial awareness of the Christian faith. As the proclaimer begins to influence and persuade the soon-to-be-convert, a grasp of the fundamentals and implications of the gospel begins to grow. Soon the individual begins to have a positive attitude towards the gospel and toward the evangelist. This results in a decision to act, after which the convert repents and places his or her faith in Christ. God's role then becomes that of regeneration, and the convert both becomes and begins to become the new creature in Christ.

After this God's role becomes one of sanctification and the role of the evangelist one of support and cultivation. During this time and throughout the rest of life the convert evaluates his or her decision, is incorporated into the church, grows in Christian knowledge and behavior, begins to daily commune with God, identifies personal gifts of ministry, and begins to witness to others and to engage in social action. This total process is conversion in the same sense that it is for Tippett. It retains an acknowledgment that there is both a point in time at which a person changes direction and a period of time both preceding and succeeding this event wherein a person grows toward the full meaning of conversion.

The Preconversion Mental State. Several psychologists other than James have studied this phenomenon. At the turn of the century much attention was given to the experience of adolescence, which was thought to be accompanied by much stress and strain. Hall (1905) postulated in his theory of recapitulation that each individual went through the experience of the race and that adolescence was parallel to primitive society. Because conversion often occurs during this period, it was natural that it was conceived to be a distinctively adolescent phenomenon. Erikson later proposed adolescence to be a unique period of identity formation during which persons were especially open to a reconsideration of the meaning and purpose of life. Thus, it would seem natural that many conversions would occur in this period during which persons are struggling for independence and are looking for new authority in their lives.

Hall, one of the early pioneers in both developmental psychology and the psychology of religion, offered an apology for the Christian faith based on his understanding of the crucial nature of the adolescent experience (Hall, 1904). He suggested, along with many other theorists, that humans were created innocent and altruistic but became self-centered in the experience of growing up. During adolescence persons began to see both the limits and the possibilities of living selfishly, became torn but attracted by their egotistic tendencies. Their greed turned them against the altruism with which life began. No amount of reason or appeal to conscience changes persons from this greedy track, according to Hall. Only the Christian gospel with its story of a God who loved persons enough to die for them could break through this tough barrier and open persons up to the possibilities of loving again. Hall considered the gospel the most powerful psychological force in converting persons from a life of selfishness to the life of love for which they were created. He offered a psychodynamic explanation wherein the persuasive force of the gospel was powerful enough to interrupt all other mental forces in the conversion process during adolescence.

Whereas Hall conceived the process of Christian conversion as healthy and normal, Freud (1928) suggested that religious conversion is a sign of psychopathology. For Freud, affirming religious faith is a sign that one has resolved psychosexual conflicts inappropriately. Although religion as a mass neurosis was better than individual neuroses, it was still abnormal and immature. Persons should face evil in themselves and in the world in a rational manner. They should solve problems with scientific pragmatism rather than dependent faith.

Salzman (1966), while agreeing with Freud in his basic model, suggested that there could be progressive as well as regressive conversions. Those that were progressive would result in courage and faithful action, while those that were regressive would result in self-doubt and dependency. Progressive conversions would seem to be more what Hall had in mind in his contention that the Christian faith made persons more loving.

In an alternate understanding of the place of psychopathology in conversion Boisen (1936) contended that there was a close affinity between mental illness and religious experience. He suggested that both the mentally ill and the sincerely religious were likely to be deeper thinkers than the average person. They experienced the crisis of life at its most intense and deepest level. He compared the fantasies of psychosis with the supernatural stories of faith and concluded that they were similar. He concluded that some persons came through these experiences with religious conversions while others went the way of mental illness. Thus, unlike Freud, he did not consider the experience itself as abnormal. Quite the contrary, it was a sign of greater depth of personality.

Changes Occurring Through Conversion. James felt that the event of conversion resulted in a shift of mental energy so that it was concentrated in one area of the mind and withdrawn from another. He felt this accounted for the intensity of the feelings and thoughts that accompanied the experience. He contended that there was no such thing as a unique religious emotion and that the feelings differed from normal experience in degree rather than in kind.

An alternative explanation for these phenomena was proposed by Sargant (1957), who compared conversion to brainwashing. Using the Pavlovian model of conditioning-crisis-breakdown-reorientation, he suggested that the individual is worked up into a hyperemotional state he termed "transmarginal inhibition," during which the nerve endings become so exhausted that the individual borders on hysteria and becomes hypersuggestible. At this point the individual becomes more susceptible to ideas which he would resist in a normal mental state. This is coupled with a suppression of previously held beliefs. The new faith is acted upon in a dramatic manner and becomes the new conditioned stimulus for behavior.

Sargant's theory essentially equates the influence process which leads persons to conversion with those who manipulate others in a brainwashing fashion. He is thus negative in his evaluation and suggests that such influence processes have negative value for society in that they induce pathology and dependence. Although many would agree with his evaluation as it applied to some mass meetings, it should be noted that he makes no distinction between the process and the positive results that often occur in people's lives from such experiences.

From a more positive perspective Oden (1966) has equated healing in psychotherapy with the process of conversion. Oden contends that God's grace is always available to humans in that he unconditionally accepts them and has infinite positive regard toward them. Wherever persons experience this, either from a therapist or an evangelist, the result is the same. Persons cease being self-centered, self-protective, defensive, and easily led into wrongdoing. They begin to appreciate anew the purpose for which they were uniquely created and which they have been denying. They discover again the power which is given them to love and to live without pretense. They gain courage to risk themselves and to be loving. They have been converted.

On the question of the life changes resulting from conversion, once again James offered a model for evaluating as well as explaining these phenomena. He concluded that what conversion did was to integrate the personality around a dominant motive. He believed that conversion was the process whereby a divided self became unified. His dictum that religion should be judged by its fruits rather than its roots was a way of saying that if conversion resulted in a less conflicted, less indecisive, less troubled person, then it was valuable regardless of whether it occurred in a sick or a healthy mind. His *Varieties Of Religious Experience* is replete with accounts of lives in which this unification resulted from religious conversion. James was describing in behavioral terms the phenomenon referred to in Scripture as the "new creation" (2 Cor. 5:17). The gospel accounts of Zacchaeus, Nicodemus, and the woman at the well are prime biblical examples of James's description. Charles Colson is representative of many modern examples of lives that have been radically changed by conversion in the manner James depicted.

Ideally the person should feel inwardly less anxious, less confused, more in control, and more energized. The purpose and meaning of life should be more clear. Outwardly the person should become more unselfish, more loving, more just, and more merciful. However, research suggests that typically these life changes are far less radical than might be anticipated. If James was correct in suggesting that conversion should be evaluated in terms of the degree to which these changes occur, then far too many conversions fall short of the ideal. However, if Paul is correct in Romans, these changes are less important than James might have presumed—at least from God's point of view. In fact, the juxtaposition of sin and grace in the Pauline model implies that salvation is less an achievement and more a gift and that righteousness, the biblical term for James's changes, is ascribed to the believer rather than characteristic of her. Furthermore, from a psychological point of view the dilemma of achieving one's life goals of love and justice remains a problem even after conversion. These goals are better conceived as possible when they are understood as the gifts of grace rather than the expectations by which our salvation is proven.

More empirically, Gorsuch, a social psychologist, has concluded that we cannot expect change of mind, the typical kind of change that occurs in conversion, to generalize fully to other types of behavior such as overt actions of love and mercy (Gorsuch & Malony, 1976). Behavioral change will most likely generalize to other similar types of behavior and will less likely generalize to dissimilar kinds of acts. Thus, attitudes and thoughts and feelings would predictably change more than interpersonal behaviors. But, apart from whether change should or should not occur, from a strictly psychological point of view it would not be expected as much for some behaviors as for others.

One of the most recent reconceptualizations of the conversion experience has been that of Richardson (1979), who has proposed that we think less of conversion from a "preordained" than an "interactive" point of view. Taking the conversion of Paul as a focus, he suggested that the preordained model saw the event as planned by God in such a manner that it was *predispositional* from a psychological and *presituational* from a sociological perspective.

A corrective to these points of view might be to conceive of Paul's experience less as occurring on the Damascus Road than as *beginning* there and continuing for a prolonged period of seclusion in which he probably conversed with Jesus again and again. Again, Paul's experience was no surprise to him but instead came as the end result of long years of searching for the meaning of life. He knew the language of faith long before he met the Messiah on the road to Damascus. Paul's dramatic experience with Jesus was but the first of many times that Paul renewed his faith and grew in his understanding of the Good News which changed his life. And finally, in regard to behavioral changes which resulted from the experience, Paul reported "I die daily" (1 Cor. 15:31), as if to say his struggle with sin in his life was an ongoing struggle. He "grew in grace" throughout his life and in many new circumstances.

This interactive view of the changes that occur puts the experience of conversion in a sound sociopsychological as well as theological perspective. It preserves the power of God as well as the activity of persons in the conversion process. It allows for conceiving the behavior change in conversion more as a change of direction than a total change of life.

References
Boisen, A. *The exploration of the inner world.* Chicago: Willett, Clark, 1936.
Freud, S. *The future of an illusion.* New York: Liveright, 1928.
Gordon, A. *The nature of conversion.* Boston: Beacon Press, 1967.
Gorsuch, R. L., & Malony, H. N. *The nature of man.* Springfield, Ill.: Thomas, 1976.
Hall, G. *Adolescence.* New York: Appleton, 1905.
James, W. *The varieties of religious experience.* New York: Doubleday, 1902.
Lofland, J., & Stark, R. Becoming a world saver: A theory of conversion to a deviant perspective. *American Sociological Review,* 1965, *30,* 862–875.
Oden, T. C. *Kerygma and counseling.* Philadelphia: Westminster, 1966.
Richardson, J. T. *A new paradigm for conversion research.* Paper presented at the International Society for Political Psychology, Washington, D.C., May 1979.
Salzman, L. Types of religious conversion. *Pastoral Psychology,* September 1966, pp. 8–20.
Sargant, W. *Battle for the mind.* Garden City, N.Y.: Doubleday, 1957.
Tippett, A. Conversion as a dynamic process in Christian mission. *Missiology,* 1977, *5*(2), 203–221.

Additional Reading
Johnson, C., & Malony, H. N. *Christian conversion: Biblical and psychological perspectives.* Grand Rapids: Zondervan, 1982.

H. N. MALONY

See PSYCHOLOGY OF RELIGION.

Conversion Disorder. Formerly called hysterical neurosis, this is a somatoform disorder in which psychological conflict or severe stress is converted into symptoms resembling a physical condition. Thorough evaluation rules out organic causes or malingering and determines that the symptoms are functional. Most of these disorders mimic neurological impairment with either sensory or motor involvement. Clinicians see conversion symptoms of blindness, deafness, various kinds of pain, lack of sensation, localized sensations, paralysis, loss of coordination, tics, tremors, seizures, and inability to talk or swallow.

Personality characteristics associated with conversion disorder follow a general pattern. Socially the person exhibits superficial warmth and charm. Many are narcissistic and self-centered. Many gain attention through childishly dramatic, exaggerated behaviors, becoming excitable frequently over minor events. Some adjust as dependent and helpless. Others avoid or retreat from stressful events. Most respond to the conversion symptoms with an affect called *belle indifference* (beautiful indifference). In this the person lacks a genuine concern about his or her supposed physical problem. Suggestibility is frequently observed, particularly under hypnosis and with placebos.

One example of conversion disorder is a woman hospitalized with episodes of paralysis. Her condition had deteriorated over two months until she was spending much of her day in bed. Upon hospitalization she showed few signs of distress or concern about her symptoms. Thorough medical consultation revealed no physical basis. The woman had no voluntary control over the paralysis and on one occasion collapsed in the hallway and pulled herself with her hands back to her bed. Careful observation indicated that her paralysis usually occurred when she became exceedingly angry. Further investigation found that she had impulses to strike or attack persons, particularly her husband. She was not a violent person and never had hit anyone. The sudden paralysis prevented her from acting on these intolerable impulses. The symptoms also disarmed whomever she was angry at and elicited help and attention. The paralysis gradually decreased after she identified the impulses and learned appropriate ways of handling anger.

Conversion disorder or hysteria have been observed for centuries. Hippocrates held the theory that hysteria (the Greek word for uterus) resulted from the uterus wandering around the body searching for humidity. He thought hysteria only occurred in women. Because most conversion symptoms resemble neurological impairment, neurologists were the first to conduct detailed studies of the disorder during the late 1800s. Charcot considered the disorder to be neurological but contributed psychological insight by demonstrating that hypnotic suggestion could alter conversion symptoms. From this observation, as well as others, Freud began to treat hysteria and developed his theory of psychoanalysis primarily from his understanding of the disorder. He believed that a repressed oedipal complex was the source of conflict and anxiety resulting in conversion symptoms.

Present-day clinicians know that the dynamics of conversion disorder start with any tremendously threatening anxiety. Conflict over unacceptable sexual or violent impulses may arouse such anxiety. Life-threatening traumas, such as war, are other sources. For protection from the anxiety the person develops defense mechanisms that prevent the conflict or trauma from reaching the consciousness. Repression, or motivated forgetting, provides the first line of defense. If repression is not successful, some persons convert the anxiety into the alleged physical ailments and thereby prevent awareness of the conflict. Clinicians call this memory loss and the resulting anxiety reduction PRIMARY GAIN. SECONDARY GAIN occurs when the symptoms offer the opportunity to elicit attention and help from others. Both the primary and secondary gains maintain the disorder and prevent resolution.

As the dynamics might suggest, conversion disorders are most frequently found in cultures with rigid and scrupulous denial of sexual and anger impulses. Christian groups which exercise a severe Puritan ethic contribute to increased incidence of this disorder. Besides these cultural patterns traumas such as war also increase the frequency. In our own culture, conversion disorders are infrequently seen. This is probably because of the greater sexual and aggressive freedoms, but also because of increased education about physical and psychological disorders. This education limits one's suggestibility. In some southern

states, particularly rural areas, conversion symptoms are still seen with some frequency.

Although conversion symptoms can occur at any age, the most common onset begins in adolescence and early adult life. This is not surprising, since sexual and aggressive impulses are stronger and more personally threatening during these years. Most often the disorder is a singular event with a relatively rapid onset. Prognosis is generally good if it follows this pattern. However, prognosis for habitual or gradually developing symptoms is less predictable. The more mature and independent the adjustment prior to symptom development, the greater the likelihood of rapid and complete recovery.

Treatment begins with a thorough investigation to determine that the symptoms are functional. Next, some estimation should be made as to the purpose of the symptoms and source of anxiety. Individual psychotherapy then should help the person gain insight into the links between conflict, anxiety, and symptoms. Direct interpretation and education regarding the significance of the symptoms may help, but resistance is to be expected. Once the person believes the symptoms are psychological rather than physical, he can quickly learn a more adaptive response to the conflict or trauma. Occasionally suggestion and/or hypnosis may be useful in helping the person learn that the disorder is psychological.

Additional Readings

Janet, P. *The major symptoms of hysteria* (2nd ed.). New York: Macmillan, 1920.
Kolb, L. C. *Noyes' modern clinical psychiatry* (7th ed.). Philadelphia: Saunders, 1968.
Ziegler, F. J., Imboden, J. B., & Meyer, E. Contemporary conversion reactions: A clinical study. *American Journal of Psychiatry*, 1960, *116*, 901–910.

M. R. NELSON

See SOMATIZATION DISORDER.

Cooperation and Competition. Humans have long been concerned with cooperation and competition. Armchair theorizing about these behaviors was prominent in the early political, economic, and social theories of such men as Thomas Hobbes, Jeremy Bentham, and Karl Marx. This thinking led naturally to real-life experiments in groups ranging from families to entire nations.

More recently interest in competition has been stimulated by economists' concern for predicting the consequences of economic competition. Similarly, interest in cooperation has been heightened by the awareness of some of the obstacles created in interpersonal relationships by some forms of competition. Finally, cooperation and competition are interesting because they are social situations encountered by everyone in daily life. These and related factors have led to intensive research in the last 35 years on experimental games, bargaining and negotiation, coalition formation, and related small groups phenomena. This work provides an understanding of the causes and consequences of competition and cooperation that can make the avoidance or resolution of conflict more likely.

Cooperation and competition may each be defined in terms of the goals or motives that underlie a person's actions. Cooperation refers to acting with another for mutual benefit, while competition refers to rivalry. Hence, one may think of cooperation as looking to the interests of others as well as to one's own interests, while competition involves pursuing personal benefit at the others' expense. While much social conflict is based on the adoption of mutually competitive goals, often conflict also reflects a disparity between people's goals. For example, when a husband has competitive and a wife cooperative goals, negative outcomes and feelings are guaranteed.

Cooperation and competition can also be seen as particular types of social situations. For example, many parlor games and sports events are intrinsically competitive, since their meaning is defined in terms of how one stands in relation to the other. In contrast, a cooperative reward structure is one in which it is natural to maximize joint profit; moving toward one's own goal facilitates the other person's movement toward his goal. An example is a work group in which people with complementary skills must all contribute something in order for the overall task to be accomplished.

Finally, from a simple behavioral perspective some kinds of behavior are generally understood to be cooperative and others competitive. These perceptions are often rooted either in assumptions about what people's goals usually are in the situation or in assumptions about the intrinsic nature of the social situation. Both of these assumptions may be wrong. For example, when a Sunday school student receives a prize for learning many Bible verses, other students may assume that she wanted to win (competitive goal), when she may have sought simply to know as much of the Bible as possible (a nonsocial, individualistic goal). The difference in perceived motive is significant. It is clear that such misperceptions can easily lead to social conflict where none is necessary.

Research in cooperation and competition has focused on situations in which there are mixed motives. Motives may be mixed in two ways. First, as indicated, the motives of different people interacting in a given situation may conflict. Second, there may be a conflict of motives within a single person. For example, an act can be performed for more than one reason, leading others to misperceive a person's true intent. In another internal conflict, when a person does something to accomplish a particular goal, she may also have other goals which would lead to contradictory acts. Such mixed motives produce conflict and tensions within the person and may lead to inconsistent behavior, resulting in competition and conflict between the person and others.

Social exchange theory is a central theoretical framework used to understand cooperation and competition. This approach (see Chadwick-Jones, 1976) assumes that people's social behavior can be explained and predicted best from an understanding of how they exchange social reinforcements or rewards. Social rewards are broadly defined and include outcomes such as praise from another, winning in a competitive interaction, and achieving a goal together. The social motives of cooperation and competition are best seen as types of social reward which may be important to people in a given interaction. Hence, based on such factors as prior experiences, personal preference, and situational pressures, people choose what will be socially rewarding to them. These choices have a central influence in determining whether or not the interaction will be conflictual.

A second important theoretical framework is the interdependence theory of Kelley and Thibaut (1959, 1978). This approach gives a detailed analysis of the many types of social interaction, including many types of cooperation and competition, and of the interaction problems which occur. It is based in social exchange theory but draws additionally on social comparison theory (people's tendency to compare with others), attribution theory (how people decide about the motives and intentions of others), equity theory (the desire for fairness in the social world), and theories of bargaining and negotiation.

Competitive interactions need not lead inevitably to social conflict. Many competitive interactions are begun with agreed-upon and socially acceptable purposes. Examples would include parlor games and friendly contests used to motivate high levels of individual or group performance. However, both research and personal experience show that even such friendly uses of competition can set the stage for social conflict. It is easy for invidious comparison to occur in competition leading people to attribute negative intentions or motives to their opponent. Examples can be found easily in casual interactions, in intimate relationships like marriage, and in large group interactions like international negotiations.

In spite of the negative consequences often associated with competition it is used widely as a motivator in schools, churches, and other organizations in Western society. This use seems based on the assumption that competitive rewards are more effective in stimulating learning and group performance. However, there is reason to seriously question this assumption. Much research shows that cooperative situations generally motivate individual learning and group performance as well as (or better than) competitive or individualistic situations. Furthermore, they do so with more positive effects on personal feelings and relationships. While there are conditions in which each reward structure is superior, the research does not yet clarify what these conditions are.

Competitive interactions can be transformed to have fewer negative social consequences. Given the general superiority of cooperative interactions, a key method involves constructing cooperative situations to replace competitive ones (i.e., changing the structure of the interdependence). For example, teachers can make grades dependent on the performance of cooperative work groups in which individuals must learn to work together to reach their common goals. Cooperative situations can often be constructed more easily than people expect, given their training in a competitive culture.

When direct social change is not possible, there remain useful methods of conflict resolution which involve changing something in the situation to encourage cooperation. A first set of strategies involves communication between conflicting parties. A focus on honesty and openness is important, since communication can also be used for deceptive and conflicting purposes. Hence, modes of unilateral influence, such as threats, persuasion, and sometimes even promises, are generally less effective than two-way communication. Communication which enhances awareness of the nature of the interdependency and which clarifies perceptions, attributions, goals, and values is more likely to yield cooperative solutions.

A second set of strategies does not focus on verbal communication between the conflicting parties, though communication may be involved. Examples would be the use of contingent rewards, modeling, and third-party intervention. Finally, role playing and particularly role reversal exercises can be helpful in conflict resolution. By taking the role of the other person, people often can "see" the other's viewpoint, resulting in a new appreciation of the importance of cooperation.

Each conflict resolution strategy has strengths and weaknesses and should be evaluated in terms of the master motive of love; we should consider the other person's welfare as well as our own. Consistent with biblical norms, the strategies which seem most effective show respect for the personhood and dignity of the conflicting individuals.

References

Chadwick-Jones, J. K. *Social exchange theory: Its structure and influence in social psychology.* New York: Academic Press, 1976.

Kelley, H. H., & Thibaut, J. W. *Interpersonal relations: A theory of interdependence.* New York: Wiley, 1978.

Thibaut, J. W., & Kelley, H. H. *The social psychology of groups.* New York: Wiley, 1959.

S. P. McNeel

See Conflict; Conflict Management.

Coping Skills Therapies. Coping skills treatment is conceptually based in behavior therapy and owes its beginnings to a shift in emphasis within behavioral treatments from environmental control to self-control (Bandura, 1969). Coping skills treatments are oriented toward teaching the client a model for stress that emphasizes the role of the individual in coping with the stress and a set of techniques or skills for use in stressful situations.

Coping skills treatments are based in a model of disturbance that has three assumptions. First, it is assumed that humans develop both adaptive and maladaptive feelings and actions through the influence of cognitive processes. For example, our anxiety in a stressful situation comes about as we appraise the situation, think about resources that can be brought to bear on the situation, and decide whether we have sufficient or insufficient resources to cope, thereby determining whether the situation is a challenge or a threat (Lazarus, 1966). If we decide the situation is a threat, we will likely feel anxious and depressed, have thoughts that are fearful and avoidant of the task, and consequently have less adaptive behaviors.

The second assumption behind coping skills is that these cognitive processes (thoughts, feelings, beliefs) are learned according to the same laws of learning that govern the acquisition of behaviors. This assumption is the tie between the cognitive and behavioral theoretical backgrounds of coping skills. The third assumption is that the therapist's task is that of an educator or a trainer, who assesses clients' current levels of coping skills and provides education and direction in the process of altering present ineffective cognitive processes and acquiring new coping skills. Because of these assumptions, coping skills therapy is used in a preventive as well as a remedial context (Mahoney & Arnkoff, 1971).

There are several different treatment approaches which all fit under the label of "coping skills." These treatments all share a common goal of helping the client develop a repertoire of skills which will facilitate his or her adjustment to stressful situations. The four approaches most commonly considered coping skills therapies are 1) covert modeling, 2) coping skills training, 3) anxiety management training, and 4) stress inoculation.

The distinguishing feature of *covert modeling* is that the client mentally rehearses the desired behavior (e.g., making an assertive request) prior to the situation where the behavior will be used. This procedure is very common among athletes and has recently been employed with success in overcoming specific fears, such as interpersonal and social anxieties. Such covert, or imaginal, rehearsal is also an important feature of *coping skills training*, a variation of systematic desensitization in which the client is not instructed to stop visualizing a threatening scene when anxious, but is encouraged to maintain the image and cope with the anxiety by learning to relax it away. *Anxiety management training* uses clients' visualization of different scenes, some unrelated to the target fear, to develop generalization of the coping responses.

Perhaps the most fully articulated method of coping skills training is *stress inoculation* (Meichenbaum, 1974). Stress inoculation has three distinct phases: education, rehearsal, and application. In the education phase clients are presented a model which defines anxiety as having an affective component (feelings), a cognitive component (thoughts and beliefs about the stressful event), and a behavioral component (muscular tension, avoidance behaviors). Clients are also encouraged to view stress and their responses to it as a four-stage process: anticipation of stressor, confronting and handling the stressor, coping with being overwhelmed by the stressor, evaluation and reinforcement of coping. Clients are then taught a variety of coping skills during the rehearsal phase, with an emphasis on restructuring of thoughts and relaxation of tension. Lastly, during the application phase, clients are given opportunities to practice their newly acquired coping skills in controlled stressful situations.

The research on coping skills treatments has not yet included sufficient controlled outcome studies to allow a confident assertion of the effectiveness of these treatments. However, initial reports (see Jaremko, 1979 for review) suggest that the treatments are effective means of teaching coping skills to clients. The very nature of the treatment suggests that it is appropriate for clients with minimal degrees of pathology, who show ineffective behavior in certain aspects of their lives, and who experience depression and anxiety due to these situational problems.

The emphasis on cognitive processes as mediating the effects of the environment on the individual does not conflict with the biblical view of man as a rational person and, in fact, is an expression of the need to consider one's thoughts. Additionally, the emphasis on the individual's need to be an initiator of self-regulatory actions corresponds to a Christian emphasis on personal responsibility. In spite of many Christians' concerns over behavior modification (e.g., Kauffmann, 1977), there seems to be an acceptance of therapies more cognitive-behavioral in nature (e.g., McAllister, 1975). Given the promise of these therapies in general, and coping skills training in particular, such acceptance appears warranted.

References

Bandura, A. *Principles of behavior modification.* New York: Holt, Rinehart, & Winston, 1969.

Jaremko, M. E. A component analysis of stress inoculation: Review and prospectus. *Cognitive Therapy and Research,* 1979, *3*, 35–48.

Kauffmann, D. Behaviorism, psychology, and Christian education. *The Bulletin of CAPS,* 1977, *3*(3), 17–21.

Lazarus, R. S. *Psychological stress and the coping process.* New York: McGraw-Hill, 1966.

Mahoney, M. J., & Arnkoff, D. B. Cognitive and self-control therapies. In S. L. Garfield & A. E. Bergin (Eds.), *Handbook of psychotherapy and behavior change.* New York: Wiley, 1971.

McAllister, E. W. Assertive training and the Christian therapist. *Journal of Psychology and Theology,* 1975, *3*, 19–24.

Meichenbaum, D. *Cognitive behavior modification.* Morristown, N.J.: General Learning Press, 1974.

E. M. Altmaier

See Cognitive-Behavior Therapy; Life Skills Counseling.

Coprophilia. Referring to a love of feces or filth, coprophilia describes a condition in which erotic arousal or orgasm is dependent on the smell, taste, or sight of feces. Generally found among men, the incidence is low, with few reported cases. When it is noted it is often associated with prostitution or homosexual acts.

In some cases smearing or eating feces is part of the act. An individual derives sexual arousal when another person defecates on the body or is watched while defecating. Often the fantasy life is involved, where an individual imagines feces during the sexual act. This is said to enhance the sexual involvement.

There are no clear factors associated with the development of coprophilia. Various case histories have indicated that small children saw the mother or father defecate and drew some pleasure from it. Some theorists suggest that its origins may be in mammalian hygiene whereby infants are licked clean. Why this would continue into adulthood and fixate on feces is unclear.

Psychoanalysts view coprophilia as a carryover from the anal stage when retention or expulsion of fecal material is hypothesized to produce intense sexual stimulation. Sometimes the interest in the product is transferred to other objects where no conscious connection is seen. In coprophilia, however, the feces themselves continue to provide erotic fantasies or arousal.

Treatment will include group therapy where persons are able to learn from each other how to control or regulate the behavior. A cure is difficult because the behavior often goes undetected and is easily hidden.

L. N. Ferguson

Correlation. A statistical expression of the degree of relationship between two or more variables. Correlation coefficients vary between $+1.00$ and -1.00, 0.00 indicating the absence of any correlation and $+1.00$ and -1.00 indicating a perfect negative or perfect positive relationship. Perfect correlations are seldom found in experiments. Positive correlations are found when an increase in one variable leads to an increase in the other. If an increase in one leads to a decrease in the other, the correlation is negative.

See Psychology, Methods of.

Correspondence in Therapy. In psychotherapeutic practice correspondence involves both written communication as a form of psychotherapy and communication with referral sources and other resources for necessary client information. Situations occur where persons needing treatment are unable to ob-

tain help due to psychological or physical obstacles. Written correspondence makes assistance available to such individuals. One study evaluating this approach involved a therapist responding to letters describing problems with behaviorally oriented therapeutic responses (Bastien & Jacobs, 1974). The approach was effective, based on the decrease of problems reported by the clients.

The second use of correspondence involves acknowledgment to a referral source that a client has followed through with the recommendation to seek treatment. This is a brief letter which includes the client's disposition, omitting details of the case, diagnosis, or dynamics. To obtain information or testing from physicians, community resources, or a previous therapist, further correspondence may be necessary. Such letters usually are accompanied by a "release of information" form signed by the client.

Reference:
Bastien, S., & Jacobs, A. Dear Sheila: An experimental study of the effectiveness of written communication as a form of psychotherapy. *Journal of Consulting and Clinical Psychology*, 1974, *42*, 151.

B. J. Shepperson

Cotard's Syndrome. A rare delusional state, identified by the French neurologist Jules Cotard (1840–1887). In this psychotic state, characterized by anxiety, depression, and suicidal tendencies, the patient believes reality has ceased to exist and that he no longer has a body.

Cotherapy. During the past 25 to 30 years there has been an increasing trend toward involving two professionals in a particular therapeutic setting. This has been called cotherapy, multiple therapy, cooperative psychotherapy, and three-cornered therapy. The most common form of cotherapy involves two therapists engaged simultaneously in a given therapeutic context, such as individual, marital, family, or group psychotherapy. As early as 1930 Adler reported success in using cotherapy to treat dysfunctional families (Adler, 1930). This technique was later used by others for marital, group, and individual psychotherapy, with almost universal claims of success but very little empirical data to substantiate such reports (Holt & Greiner, 1976).

Cotherapy has been used for a wide variety of reasons. Sometimes it is used with the intent of simplifying the therapeutic task. For example, cotherapy is often utilized in the treatment of severely dysfunctional families, marital couples, and psychotic patients because it is believed, or hoped, that this will somehow reduce the difficulty of the therapeutic task. Although this position lacks empirical support, several reasons for the belief exist. Psychodynamically oriented therapists believe that the use of cotherapists reduces the intensity of the transference by dispersing it among the two, thereby facilitating the treatment of severely disturbed patients. Others feel that the added strength and support of a second therapist help to balance the power of control, preventing more regressive forms of acting out within the session. Finally, some believe that in cotherapy one therapist is always available to be objective and thereby more helpful while the other is under the gun during a moment of confrontation or heightened emotion.

Cotherapy is often used by psychoanalytically oriented therapists, who believe that the use of two therapists, particularly when they are of the opposite sex, facilitates transference and thereby encourages exploration of family issues and early conflicts. Cotherapy is also used for purposes of training, supervision, and consultation. It is viewed as a particularly valuable way to provide carefully monitored on-the-job training.

The use of cotherapy can be quite successful to all concerned when the therapists are of equal status, competence, and sensitivity. Cotherapists who are comfortable and open with each other, respectful and courteous, and mutually concerned with the needs of the patient can have a profoundly valuable therapeutic impact.

References

Adler, A. *The education of children*. New York: Greenberg, 1930.

Holt, M., & Greiner, D. Co-therapy in the treatment of families. In P. J. Guerin (Ed.), *Family therapy*. New York: Gardner Press, 1976.

J. D. GUY, JR.

Counseling and Psychotherapy: Biblical Themes.

A basic description of counseling is one person relating to another through listening and responding in such a way as to effect change in the one seeking help. Such an interpersonal relationship is intentionally designed to facilitate the growth of the other.

The New Testament church leaders developed a pattern of ministry which was designed to facilitate the spiritual growth and maturity of new believers in Christ. Since these new believers came from a pagan culture, it was necessary that their life style and values be modified to come into line with the values and

life style that were consistent with their newfound faith in Christ. The implications of this newfound faith needed to be worked out over a period of time. It was to this issue that the church leaders addressed themselves in developing a pattern of ministry. This pattern of ministry evolved in the Book of Acts, with the pattern appearing to take on more consistency in the epistles. It provides some guidance for interpersonal functioning in the growth-facilitating ministry of counseling.

Although there may be some dangers inherent in seeking to understand patterns of ministry based on a study of New Testament terminology, it seems that there is profit to be gained from such a study. Understanding the way in which the New Testament leaders described their ministry does provide us with a doorway to understanding their philosophy, approach, and intention in ministry. Even the choice of terms will reflect both their attitude to ministry and their attitudes toward those with whom they ministered. Deducing a face-to-face pattern of relating from a form of relating such as the pastoral letters does require some care. Counsel by letter will be somewhat different from counseling in a person-to-person model. Nevertheless, we do have from these descriptive references to pastoral relationship some patterns that may together indicate a model of the helping relationship as it evolved in the New Testament.

The Community Context. Christians are called into relationship with one another. In the context of this relationship they are to manifest the grace of God operative in their lives. The relationship of believers to one another at once gives evidence of the new birth and bears witness to the dynamic of the Spirit of God in a life related to God through faith in Jesus Christ. It is not the individual alone who bears witness to the grace of God, but the individuals in community who demonstrate in quality relationships the power of God in human lives. The manifold wisdom of God and the power of God in man are made known through the community of faith (Eph. 3:10, 16).

In Acts 9–20 we see the patterns of ministry that grew out of Paul's concern for the new community of faith. "The church throughout all Judea, Galilee and Samaria enjoyed peace, being built up; and going on in the fear of the Lord and in the comfort of the Holy Spirit, it continued to increase" (9:31). Being built up, going on, and experiencing comfort are the three key phrases describing the ministry experienced by the new believers. As one studies other key passages in Acts, other concepts of modes of ministry emerge. Preaching and teaching were central. To edify, encourage, strengthen, admonish, and urge to continuance and steadfastness in commitment describe the ministry of Paul and Barnabas. Of these descriptive terms the three most commonly used are to edify, to encourage, and to admonish.

In the epistles another important concept emphasizing the community context of ministry is that of the mutual responsibility of each believer to others in the community of faith. Related to this is the body imagery developed in 1 Corinthians 12 and Ephesians 4. Each member of the body needs the others. Each contributes to the well-being and maturity in Christ of the others. No one stands alone.

At the end of Ephesians 4 Paul summarizes the qualities that are to characterize relationships within the community—mutual kindness, tenderheartedness, and forgiveness. The Good News is that God desires us to live by the power of his Spirit, and the training ground is the community of faith. The community of faith is to provide the context of love and acceptance where we can grow to the demonstration of such qualities of relationship. Our communications within the community must be such as to invite one another to life and growth in Christ. Their appropriateness will be measured by their effect as well as their truthfulness. Love is the undergirding quality, and that love is poured out in our hearts by the Holy Spirit. The behavior of believers to one another is to be the incarnation of grace. Our demonstration of forgiveness and love may be only a shadow of God's love and forgiveness, but in essence it is one with his because it is of him and through him.

Biblical Themes Defining Ministry. This brief survey of some of the New Testament teaching on the community of faith clearly demonstrates the importance of relationships in the facilitation of growth in Christians. We will now examine more closely some of the biblical themes that relate to these patterns of relationship. Taken in total, they will be seen to provide a style and pattern of relating that will facilitate spiritual growth.

Fellowship: Investing in others. A key descriptive word which brings into focus the quality of relationships within the community of faith is *koinonia.* This word is variously translated as fellowship, communion, communication, and contribution. The key idea seems to be involvement, the participation of a person in a situation in an active and a practical sense. The depth of this involvement or identification may be illustrated by the incarnation of Christ; he

took upon himself flesh and blood so that he might be like unto his brethren whom he would redeem. The fellowship of believers involves something of that kind of commitment and partnership. It reaches through all differences between people. This fellowship of faith involves entrance into another person's existence, an involvement of risk and an identification at the level of need. It is evident that entering into this believing fellowship implies a concerned care for one another. Fellowship in the community of faith is involvement with those in need in such a way that our resources become theirs. Our resources received by God's grace are given freely to supply the need of our fellows in faith.

Edification: Building others. One of the central modes of ministry in the New Testament is that of edifying. This word reminds us of the family dimensions of membership in the community of faith and our mutual responsibility to build each other. This is a very important word in Scripture, and for Paul it becomes the touchstone by which to measure the ministry and behavior of believers. In 1 Corinthians 14 he urges that the exercise of gifts be to the end that the church is edified. The principle is, "Let all things be done for edification" (v. 26). Love edifies, and we are to "pursue the things which make for peace and the building up of one another" (Rom. 14:19). Our communications are to be controlled to the extent that we speak only what will accomplish edification (Eph. 4:29).

An important aspect of this is the relation of the stronger believer to the weaker saint. "Now we who are strong ought to bear the weaknesses of those without strength and not just please ourselves. Let each of us please his neighbor for his good, to his edification" (Rom. 15:1–2). We are to be unselfishly what our brother needs us to be for his benefit, with the result that he will be built up and strengthened. Our interests are to be subjected to his interests so that in our caring for him, he grows. This mode of ministry involves self-conscious effort, planned and deliberate. To summarize, edification is being to another person what that person needs you to be for his good and resultant growth.

Paraklysis: Supporting others. The Holy Spirit, promised by Christ to his disciples, is called the Comforter. Jesus is called the Advocate. Paul speaks of God as the "Father of mercies and the God of all comfort" (2 Cor. 1:3). This noun, *paraklysis,* as well as its frequently used verb forms, indicates another significant mode of ministry of believers to one another— support.

Unfortunately this word is often translated incorrectly as "exhortation." Rather than referring to the giving of an admonition, the word more correctly interpreted focuses on the action of being called alongside. Thus, the emphasis is on a supportive action rather than a verbal exhortation. The picture is of someone in need being ministered to by someone coming alongside, lifting and sharing the burden. Second Corinthians illustrates the ministry envisioned in this word. God is described as *the God of all coming alongside* (1:3), who comes alongside of ourselves so that we may support others in affliction with the same dynamic by which we were supported by God (1:4). In chapter 7 Paul shares his distress in Macedonia which was relieved by Titus coming alongside of him. The ministry of Titus was made possible by his having experienced that supportive undergirding by the Corinthian believers. This ministry is transferable from relationship to relationship. Barnabas is the model and and example par excellence of this ministry. As believers we are to be sensitive to the varied calls of our fellows as they open themselves to us, that we may come alongside and actively encourage them to the fulfillment of their potential and the purposes of God's grace in them. *Paraklysis* may then be defined as coming alongside to bear up another and his needs that he might be encouraged and supported.

Nouthesis: Confronting others. There are several words that bring into focus our responsibility to confront one another with a view to bringing our lives into line with God's revealed will. The most frequently used word in this group is *nouthesis*. This word, often translated "admonish," provides the basis for NOUTHETIC COUNSELING. As used in Scripture it suggests kindly but firmly bringing one another to the awareness of discrepancies between our lives and the will of God. Such confrontation is to lead to changes in our thinking and attitude, resulting in increased conformity to God's will.

Paul expresses confidence in the Roman believers' ability to admonish one another because they were filled with goodness and knowledge (Rom. 15:14). He also urged the Colossian Christians in whom the word of Christ dwelt to use psalms, hymns, and spiritual songs to admonish one another as they expressed their thankfulness to God (Col. 3:16). The community of faith is one in which each exercises the responsibility for the growth and maturity of the other by confronting him in love. The word nouthesis is used to describe the ministry of the apostles, elders, fathers,

and also of all the leaders in their relation to one another. The means indicated include the Scriptures, psalms, hymns, and spiritual songs as well as verbal persuasion. It should be obvious that confrontation is not an exercise of harshness but an exercise of care, expressing tenderness and concern as well as firmness.

Teaching and training. Two words focus on these concepts. One is *paideia*. The emphasis is that of a mature person directing a younger or less mature person toward fulfillment of his or her potential. This involves the provision of a model for the immature person through the attitudes and values of the more mature one. It is related to the phenomena of culture-carriers or the socialization process accomplished through example.

The second word, *didasko*, has specific reference to teaching the word of God. This is done through preaching (1 Tim. 4:11), exhortation (1 Tim. 6:2), and confrontation (Col. 3:16). In our helping relationships the teaching of the word must be central if those relationships are to be described as Christian.

Burden-bearing nurturance and discipleship. There are several other words that present helpful imagery of the relationship of believers to one another. We are urged in Gal. 6:2 and Rom. 15:1 to bear one another's burdens and weaknesses. This is very powerful imagery, which pictures picking up and carrying away the burden of another person so that it in fact becomes our burden. Such mutual sharing of weights and weaknesses is a powerful demonstration of our mutual responsibility for one another. In 1 Thessalonians 5:14 we are urged to "hold on to the weak ones and to be longsuffering with all men." "Hold on" indicates that we come over against another person, taking hold of that person that he may be held up. The word is sometimes translated "cleave" (Matt. 6:24). "Longsuffering" contains the thought of enduring in the exercise of patience for a very long time toward another person. It is used by Peter (2 Peter 3:9) to describe the enduring patience of the Lord toward his children.

There are other passages in the New Testament that present models and images of ministry that would be instructive for one entering into a helping relationship. One enters into a helping relationship that he might serve as a slave (1 Cor. 9:19). One may function within the helping relationship as a nurturing parent (1 Thess. 1:7; 2:7–12). Finally, there is the role of disciple maker. Jesus functioned in this relationship to his followers, providing for their growth and development through a discipling process. Within the Christian community as we enter into helping relationships with one another, we do so as one disciple facilitating growth in another disciple. The model of the servant in Isaiah 50 is appropriate at this point. "The Lord God has given me the tongue of disciples, that I may know how to sustain the weary one with a word. He awakens me morning by morning, he awakens my ear to listen as a disciple. The Lord God has opened my ear and I was not disobedient, nor did I turn back" (vv. 4–5). One who would enter into a helping relationship with another, hoping to sustain that weary one with a word, must speak with the tongue of a disciple representing his Master faithfully. In order to do so he must experience the grace of God opening his ear that he might have the ear of a disciple and demonstrate the obedience of a disciple.

G. C. TAYLOR

See CHRISTIAN COUNSELING AND PSYCHOTHERAPY; COUNSELING AND PSYCHOTHERAPY: THEOLOGICAL THEMES.

Counseling and Psychotherapy: Overview.
Few professional services are as difficult to define as counseling and psychotherapy. Both terms have been used to mean a wide variety of things, from the giving of legal advice to the administration of antipsychotic medications. Except for the vague sense that psychotherapy is somehow a more serious and perhaps professionally respectable service than counseling, few people—including mental health professionals—could summon up clear and nonoverlapping definitions of the two. Even these professionals, if pressed, might fall back on some kind of distinction grounded in credentials: therapy is what doctors do and counseling is what every other psychological helper does. Alternately, a distinction might be drawn on the basis of frequency and duration of sessions: therapy is a long-drawn-out endeavor, sometimes involving several sessions per week, while counseling is a brief and less intense process. Yet another distinction that might be made is that therapy is what sick people get, whereas counseling is for normal people.

Definitions and Clarifications. There is an important difference between counseling and psychotherapy, but it relates only tangentially to the above distinctions. Counseling and therapy are actually opposite points on a continuum. Any particular helping relationship may move all over this continuum as the needs of the client change from moment to moment and session to session.

Psychotherapy is, at root, the process of increasing a person's emotional capacity and self-sufficiency. This implies a more or less permanent change in the personality. Such change often takes considerable time, but it can occur within a matter of minutes—e.g., in response to a life challenge or a catastrophe. Thus, sheer duration of treatment or frequency of visits does not ensure that any real therapy has taken place.

Similarly, the mere possession of professional credentials, however impressive, is no guarantee of the ability to render competent psychotherapeutic service. There are some people with prestigious permaplaques on the wall who probably could not facilitate the psychological growth of anyone. On the other hand, certain persons without very much in the way of formal qualifications are superbly capable of being therapeutic. For the term *psychotherapy* to be specific enough to be useful it should probably be restricted to services that are rendered in a professional setting, under conditions in which there is at least an informal understanding that therapy is to be attempted.

Finally, it makes little sense to try to define psychotherapy as a medical treatment given to the sick, since such a definitional effort only adds one set of ambiguities onto another. Who exactly are the sick? As many writers have pointed out, describing persons with nonorganic psychological difficulties as "ill" is a regressive metaphor that stigmatizes recipients of psychological services. This metaphor once served an important social function in that it markedly decreased the outrageous persecution to which psychologically disordered persons were often subjected. At this juncture in history, when there is little persecution to compare to that of previous centuries, whatever benefits the medical model may afford are heavily outweighed by its inherent stigmatization (see MENTAL ILLNESS, MODELS OF). Part of this stigmatization is the idea that there is a clear qualitative difference between the mentally ill and the rest of us. Persons with profound psychoses tend to blind us to the fact that all people fall somewhere on a continuous scale of psychological functioning. Since psychotherapy is the process of facilitating emotional growth and self-sufficiency, just about anyone could probably profit from it.

At the opposite end of our psychological service continuum counseling is explicitly concerned with exactly what the good therapist tries to avoid: concrete advice giving. The counselor wants to help the client with immediate practical problems. These can range from choosing a career to coping with a tragedy. No permanent change in personality is necessarily expected. If such change occurs, it is a by-product of the counselor's central objective, which is to better enable the person to face a specific situation.

During the process of providing psychotherapy to a person, troubling practical problems may arise in the client's life. At such times the therapist may, without even thinking much about it, offer advice about how to respond to these problems. Some therapists fluidly move in and out of giving the client advice about decisions with respect to money matters, in-law troubles, job difficulties, and the like. Others of a more psychoanalytic persuasion believe that the giving of any advice about how to deal with concrete problems only fosters neurotic dependence and thus undermines the long-term goals of therapy. These therapists tend not to give such advice, even in the face of potential disaster for the client. All therapists probably engage in some advice giving, and it may well be that the best therapists are those who know when to "do therapy" and when to "give counsel."

Basic Dimensions of Psychological Change. Setting aside for the moment the distinctions we have drawn between counseling and therapy, it may be useful to highlight some of the ways in which different people benefit from psychological services.

Actions. As a result of professional services people may learn to behave in new ways, or learn not to behave in old, dysfunctional ways. For example, a shy person who perhaps tends to feel worse and worse during the course of a party may learn to speak up early and thereby interrupt a self-defeating pattern of mounting withdrawal. Or a child may learn to inhibit aggressive behaviors such as hitting other children.

Feelings. As a result of psychological assistance people can develop new emotional reactions or learn better ways of handling already existing feelings. For example, a person may begin to feel tenderness toward others that he or she has never felt before. Or a person may learn to express anger that previously had expressed itself only in unconscious anguish.

Perceptions. Some individuals, as a direct result of help, gradually see things in a new light. For example, a client may decide that the world is, after all, not a hostile place, "out to get you." Or a person may decide that her mother or father is not such a bad person after all.

Physiology. Many persons respond to psy-chological help with an improvement in physiological functioning. A business executive may be less troubled by ulcerative stomach pain after consulting a psychologist. Or a client's blood pressure may go down.

Thoughts. In response to psychological services persons often undergo changes in how they think. Instead of telling themselves all sorts of terrible things—e.g., "I'm no good"—they may come to think of themselves as worthwhile. Or a person may change from thinking in a confused, anxiety-ridden manner to thinking in a clear, relaxed way.

Values. Some people, as a result of psychological interventions, undergo a change in values. They may come to care more deeply about other people and less intensely about occupational success. Or they may esteem certain of their feelings in a way they never did before.

Historical Roots. The roots of psychotherapy and counseling are intricate and lengthy. No doubt from earliest times people have tried to comfort, advise, and nurture each other in countless ways. Nevertheless, within Western society there have been several major turning points on the way to psychological services as they exist near the end of the twentieth century.

While Augustine's *Confessions* and a few lesser volumes will always stand as early examples of brilliant psychological analysis, it was probably the French philosopher and mathematician René Descartes who most encouraged Western civilization in the direction of psychology. Once people turned their attention to the exploration of subjective realities and processes, it was only a matter of time before society attempted to ameliorate psychological difficulties through subjectively oriented helping methods.

The first person to construct an eminent career upon this foundation was, of course, Sigmund Freud. During the latter part of the nineteenth century neurology and psychiatry were essentially one discipline. While Freud wanted to pursue an academic career within medicine and physiology, his marriage forced him to enter clinical practice as a way to support his family. Beginning as a neurologist-psychiatrist, Freud was immensely influenced by one of his teachers to explore the benefits of "talking cures." Always the scientist-researcher-theoretician and only secondarily the practitioner, Freud was intrigued with the workings of the human psyche. His lifetime of clinical investigation has come down to us in what we know as psychoanalysis.

A second major turning point was John Watson's inauguration of behaviorism. Whereas psychoanalysis grew out of medicine, which has continued to dominate its development to this day, behaviorism developed out of academic psychology. Watson came along at the right time to persuade university psychologists of the wisdom of his approach. For many years prior to the publication of Watson's initial and ultimately most influential writings (between 1910 and 1920), introspection had been the main method of psychological research. In this period introspection involved training observers to monitor and report some aspect of their experience. Unfortunately, because of introspection's inherently subjective nature, the "trained observers" of different researchers disagreed on a regular basis. Psychology, which had begun with great promise, threatened to end up in unresolvable arguments. Watson encouraged psychologists to throw out all consideration of mental events in favor of the study of observable behavior. While Watson's excursions into clinical phenomena were few, a great many subsequent psychologists have applied his methods to the remediation of psychological disorders, in the form of what is now known as behavior therapy.

The so-called third force or, as we are calling it, the third turning point was the emergence of what is usually known as humanistic psychology. Carl Rogers, who was raised in a conservative Christian home and who began as a divinity student, left Union Seminary to study psychology across the street at Columbia University. He later held a job for many years at another college, where he provided a great deal of clinical service to students. Out of these experiences Rogers developed what has traditionally been known as client-centered (or person-centered) therapy. While the psychoanalysts focused on unconscious processes and the behaviorists focused on observable actions, Rogers and his followers focused on conscious subjectivity, in particular on feelings.

Many other forms of therapy and counseling have been advanced, so many in fact that it would be ludicrous even to attempt to review them all here. We will, however, mention those which have received the most attention, omitting such specialized forms of counseling as vocational and rehabilitational.

Major Forms of Counseling and Therapy.
Because psychoanalysis has been such a strong influence on psychiatry and psychology for so many decades, it has spawned numerous off-shoots and innovations. Thus, in addition to classical psychoanalysis we find direct psychoanalysis, object relations therapy, ego psychology, and a number of other variations. Still, common to virtually all analytic therapies is an emphasis on the therapeutic benefits of *insight*. Psychoanalysts have traditionally defined insight as the coming into consciousness of that which previously had been unconscious. Good analysts understand that for insight to be helpful it has to be more than intellectualization (i.e., it has to have emotional impact). And into what is the analysand seeking insight? His or her psychodynamics—those subtle mental processes, typically characterized by conflict, which create symptoms. An example of a psychodynamically based symptom is the soldier who, fearing to be called (and, perhaps more importantly, to call himself) a coward, but fearing even more that he might be killed, develops hysterical blindness (a true inability to see without any organic reason for this inability). The classic analytic position is that by allowing the nature of his conflicts into conscious awareness, the soldier will be cured of his visual impairment.

The therapies that have evolved out of Watson's behaviorism have been influenced to a great extent by Harvard psychologist B. F. Skinner and, to a lesser extent, by psychiatrist Joseph Wolpe. Wolpe is the originator of systematic desensitization, in which the patient's fears are, in the ideal, replaced by relaxation responses. The methods that have come from Skinner's work are based on the idea that people do what they do as a result of previous rewards and punishments. While Skinner has never been a clinician, a great variety of techniques have come from his research into operant conditioning. Some of these techniques have yielded excellent results (e.g., with heretofore regressed schizophrenics who, perhaps for the first time in years, learn to attend to personal grooming and to answer when someone else greets them). Operant methods have also been put to use in the classroom. Collectively, these methods are usually known as *behavior therapy*, although the more generic term *behavior modification* is also widely used. A new twist has been given to the behaviorally oriented therapies by the advent of *cognitive-behavior therapy*, which is the name for a group of clinical techniques that are designed to alter behavior by altering thought processes. Moreover, in cognitive-behavior therapy the techniques themselves are more or less patterned along the lines of traditional behavior therapy. For example, a client might be taught to say "I can do it, I am capable" in the face of previously debilitating challenges.

Client-centered (person-centered) therapy, as we have noted, developed out of work with college students. The Rogerian helper tries above all to provide the client with three essential things: unconditional positive regard (i.e., the client is accepted by the therapist no matter what the former says or feels); genuineness (i.e., the therapist accurately portrays his or her own feelings to the client); and accurate empathy (i.e., the therapist places a premium on coming to understand exactly how the client feels and, further, communicating this understanding). A central thesis of Rogerian counseling/therapy has always been that there is an innate growth tendency in people which will be released when these three conditions are met during any human encounter.

These three therapeutic traditions have been most influential. Some other schools of therapy will be described more briefly.

Adlerian psychotherapy, which seems to have decreased in prominence, is concerned with helping the individual clarify constructive life goals and plans, develop proper social interest (concern for others), and better understand his or her life style and how this relates to psychological development.

Jungian analysis, which has often been geared toward persons in their 40s, focuses on the deep unconscious (including one's ancestral unconscious, or what Jungians ordinarily call the collective unconscious) and in particular on the latent unexpressed parts of the person. Almost mystical at times, Jungian therapy is very philosophical in tone compared with most others. Jung was one of Freud's close associates who ultimately broke with him. Adler was another.

Interpersonal psychotherapy derives from the work of Harry Stack Sullivan, an American psychiatrist who was intensely interested in the clinical significance of how people act toward others. Therapists who are interpersonally oriented attend carefully to what causes the client anxiety and to the defensive behaviors this anxiety triggers. These behaviors hinder intimacy and augment idiosyncratic (autistic) thinking.

Transactional analysis (TA) is concerned with helping the client understand, and put an end to, the games he or she plays. Games, according to TA, are anything but light and breezy fun. Indeed, they can be lethal, such as those games that revolve around alcohol or suicide. Transactional analysts use humor,

blackboard diagrams, and group feedback in their work with people.

Family therapy is the general name for just about any clinical method in which the family rather than the individual is the focus of treatment. Specific methods range from psychoanalytically to behaviorally oriented ones. Closely related to family therapy is marital therapy and counseling, but the latter term, like the former, refers more to a "target population" than to a specific school of therapy.

Gestalt therapy is primarily concerned with the client's awareness. Gestalt therapists try to facilitate clients' knowledge of disowned feelings and to encourage them to take responsibility for these feelings and, indeed, for their whole lives. Like interpersonal psychologists, therapists of the Gestalt orientation attend carefully to what is going on in the present between therapist and patient.

Biofeedback typically involves using technological devices, such as EEG (electrical brain activity) monitors, to teach people how to bring under voluntary control physiological processes that were previously automatic. Thus, a business executive with high blood pressure might be taught to lower his blood pressure at will.

Hypnotherapists employ hypnosis—a treatment method with a noble heritage as well as a sideshow reputation—to help people stop smoking, learn to study better, and so forth. There is still much debate among scholars over what hypnosis is, whether an altered state of consciousness, a form of role playing, or something else entirely.

Existential psychotherapy is a philosophically oriented therapy that deals with such issues as what gives the client's life meaning. Emphasis is placed on the thesis that each person creates his or her own life as a project, and that choices are therefore of paramount importance.

Sensitivity and encounter groups are methods for helping people become more aware of their feelings and of their impact on others. Most such groups involve a good deal of confrontation among participants. Sometimes this confrontation is gentle and sometimes not.

There are, of course, many other therapies, but these are the ones most often practiced and, therefore, those the reader is most likely to encounter.

A Three-Dimensional Model for Classifying Therapies. Therapies can be classified according to how much they emphasize thought, feeling, or action. Some therapies—e.g., Gestalt—lay heavy stress on feeling and pay relatively little explicit attention to thought or action. Others, such as behavior therapy, stress action to the relative exclusion of thought and feeling, although the rise of cognitive-behavior therapy has shifted this stress for some practitioners. Still others, such as rational-emotive therapy, place primary emphasis on the client's thoughts.

It is often useful to find out exactly what is stressed by a particular therapist, since there should be at least a reasonably good match between what the therapist offers and what the client needs. Given that there is a finite amount of time and energy to distribute during the course of any therapy session, it is best to make sure that these resources will be wisely spent.

Licensing and Regulation. Most states now have licensing laws governing who can and who cannot hold himself or herself out to the public as a psychologist. *Psychiatrist* has always clearly implied the possession of a medical license, so there has traditionally been fairly tight regulation over who could use this title. The title *counselor* is almost totally unregulated. Thus, just about anybody can advertise as a counselor, as long as terms like "psychological" and "psychiatric" are not used.

What makes matters even more confusing is that psychotherapy is not a profession per se, and psychotherapist is not a formal professional title. A psychotherapist is simply one who conducts psychotherapy. Some states, recognizing the danger of leaving these two terms unregulated, stipulate by law that they cannot be used except by persons who fall into certain professional groups. In certain states, however, there is excessively wide latitude in defining which groups of professionals are included. Thus, a nurse without any training in verbal psychotherapy can be a psychotherapist. This is not to say that some nurses are not excellently therapeutic but merely to point out how loosely regulated the psychotherapy field really is.

State licensing boards are primarily responsible for policing the actions of their licensees, although in certain instances of gross misconduct criminal prosecution may occur. The most the licensing board can ordinarily do is to suspend or revoke the license, but the state attorney general can seek more serious action, if appropriate, by formal prosecution.

Most reputable professionals belong to one or more professional societies, such as the American Psychological Association. Such societies can expel members who fail to conform to their standards of conduct.

Psychological Help as Persuasion. We cannot deal thoroughly here with the subject of counseling and therapy as persuasion. But we should at least note that clients who come for help usually invest in their helpers a great deal of trust, especially if the relationship endures for any length of time. As a result, psychological helpers have more than an ordinary amount of persuasive power. The proper use of this power is the express purpose of nearly all licensing laws and codes of ethics.

Some theorists regard therapy/counseling primarily as a means of giving people new philosophies of life, new ways to make sense of old experiences. If so, therapy may be more of a religious activity than any of us heretofore have been willing to admit.

Additional Reading
McLemore, C. W. *The scandal of psychotherapy: A guide to resolving the tensions between faith and counseling.* Wheaton, Ill.: Tyndale House, 1982.

C. W. McLemore

See Moral and Ethical Issues in Treatment; Psychology as Religion; Values and Psychotherapy; Philosophical Psychology.

Counseling and Psychotherapy: Theological Themes.

Responsible Christian professionals acknowledge a necessary relationship between the art of Christian living and that of psychotherapy and counseling. They recognize that behind those applied arts is an essential interaction between the science of theology and the science of psychology, each science forming and informing the other.

There are four levels at which the two sciences interact: theory formulation, research methodology, data base, and clinical application. At each level the two sciences interact specifically within the anthropology that is functioning in each science. More specifically, it is the personality theory in that anthropology which is the locus of the interaction of the two sciences.

Since Christians acknowledge that all truth is God's truth, no matter who finds it or where it is found, the information derived from both psychology and theology is taken with equal seriousness. God's message in the special revelation of Scripture and God's general revelation in the created world are both sought diligently to ensure the maximum constructive interaction between theology and psychology. The concern in this is not to integrate the two sciences but to acknowledge that each, as science, has its own domain and data base and must be done in the light of or from the perspective of the other.

In this perspectival model (Ellens, 1982) which acknowledges that the science of biblical theology examines special revelation and the science of psychology examines general revelation, the development of sound personality and psychotherapy theory requires careful attention to the cardinal themes of both psychology and theology. In the art of counseling and psychotherapy those theological themes have clear-cut and palpable import.

Principles and Themes. The first theological principle for counseling and psychotherapy is that godliness or Christian authenticity requires thorough responsibility. To be a Christian counselor or therapist means first to be the best therapist it is possible to be. The second principle is that Christian and professional authenticity requires incarnation in the person of the therapist of that grace-shaped redemptive quality which reflects how God is disposed toward humans and how God designs humans to be disposed toward each other. To be a Christian counselor or therapist means to be God's incarnation for the patient or client, as Jesus Christ is for all of us in everything necessary to our redemption.

Eight theological themes crucially shape a Christian personality theory and counseling or psychotherapy. The first is grace: radical, unconditional, and universal. In the creation story humans are never referred to as children or servants of God but are depicted as compatriots, colaborers, and coequals of God in the kingdom enterprise. That royal status is not abrogated by the fall. The *protoevangelium* (Gen. 3:15) affirms that, whereas God recognized that the human predicament had changed and therefore that the divine redemptive strategy had to change, the objective remained the same. Humans exist to grow into the divinely ordered destiny of full-orbed personhood, in the image of God. To ensure that, God's disposition is not one of judgment but of unconditional acceptance of humans as we are, for the sake of what we can become. It is a disposition of grace, freedom, and affirmation. That covenant is "for the healing of the nations." It renders irrelevant all strategies of religious legalism, psychological defensiveness, and self-justification. Grace is God's ambition for all humanity; it cuts through to the center of our alienation and disorder, and outflanks all our techniques for creating a conditional relationship with God and each other.

The second theme is alienation. The fallenness of humanity is obvious. Its psychological consequences are evident everywhere. Humans are as children thrust out of the maternal womb and unable to catch hold of our father's hand. The biblical story of the fall depicts the spiritual and psychological disorders caused by this experience. The confusion of identity, role, focus, and relationship pervades life like that confusion attendant upon all birth trauma and adolescent disengagement. That is undoubtedly why the biblical account of the fall spontaneously seems so authentic. In the face of generic human fallenness and alienation life becomes an endeavor at anxiety reduction. Most human strategies for that, and for increasing control and security, are pathogenic compensatory strategies. All religion is such an anxiety-reduction strategy. Apart from the Judeo-Christian grace theology, all other religions increase the human sense of alienation and disorder because they provide only strategies for self-justification. Unconditional grace cuts through that pathogenesis and affirms humans as God-compatriots, in spite of ourselves. Even in Judeo-Christian history there have been frequent reversions to pagan conditionalism, but the essence of grace theology transcends that.

The third theme is therefore the biblical theology of personhood. From the biblical tradition of the Jahwist, through the theology of the prophets, to the gospel incarnated in Jesus' way of handling people, it is clear that humans are unconditionally cherished by God. Human personhood is rooted in the fact that we are created as imagers of God and arbitrarily assigned the status of coequal with God in keeping the garden kingdom. So human persons have only two potential conditions: to be in a posture which rings true to that God-given status and, therefore, to self; or to be inauthentic, alienated from God and our own true destiny, and suffering the dissonance and disease inherent to our inauthenticity. In all that, since God is God and grace is grace, God remains preoccupied with human need, not naughtiness; human failure of destiny more than duty; and with our redeemed potential, not our wretched past. Health then means not merely absence of disease but freedom and affirmation for growth to our destiny. We are free in spite of ourselves, to be what we are, for the sake of what we can become before the face of God.

The fourth theme is sin, the failure to achieve authenticity to self and the full-orbed personhood in Christ. Sin is a distortion and distraction to lesser achievements. Nothing can compensate for it. One can only be converted from it. Repentance is the only solution: turning from our pathogenic compensatory behavior to acceptance of God's unconditional acceptance of us. God's law, then, is not a threat but a constitution for the life of the kingdom, wholeness in the whole person. Having freed us by his grace, God simply waits for us to achieve the self-actualization which expresses the regal status of God-compatriot. Sin is "falling short of his glory," his glorious destiny for us—true selfhood as imagers and compatriots of God.

The fifth theme is discipline and discipleship. It is the endeavor of beginning down the way of grace: forgiveness and acceptance of self and others and unconditional caring for self and others. It is not structuring life in a controlled legalism of personal purity and piety designed to gain credit with God. Discipleship is a troth with self and God to incarnate that divine grace dynamic that infuses the universe. It is a troth to forsake all other *foci* and keep only to the kingdom destiny of God imager, compatriot, and incarnator of grace.

The sixth theme is that of the suffering servant or wounded healer. Nouwen (1972) suggests that there are four doors through which God and the Christian can touch humans: the woundedness of the world, of a given generation, of the individual, and of the healer. Grace, growth, and healing are communicated through the brokenness of the healer to the person to be healed. The humanness and brokenness of both must be affirmed. The healer's role is not to remove the pain of life but to interpret it. The evidence in the healer of woundedness and pain and of the constructive uses and endurance of it helps to heal the patient. The wounded healer can become the model and the sign of hope, of the risk taking inherent in growth and healing.

The seventh theme is celebration. People who can be grateful can be healthy. People who cannot be grateful cannot be healthy. They do not have access to the psychological and spiritual machinery of health. The Christian life is celebration. The Bible makes it clear that Christianity is not a command to be obeyed, a burden to be labored under, nor an obligation to be met. It is an opportunity to be seized, a relief to be celebrated, and a salvation to be savored. The celebration of gratitude may take the form of the childlike posture of prayer or the exhilarated enjoyment of God's providence.

The eighth theme is mortality. The Bible gives little impetus to the perfectionist notions

that building the kingdom will eliminate mortality. It affirms the world's brokenness and pathology and that we are dying persons in a world of malignancy as well as of magnificence. It is acceptable to age, wrinkle, weaken, become more dependent, and even die. Maturation, not youthfulness, is the focus of meaning. People needing healing need to feel in their counselors the Christian realization that it is a supportable and perhaps even a celebratable condition to be a human mortal before the face of God.

Implications for Therapy. The consequences of these themes for counseling and psychotherapy are direct and practical. First, they imply that the patient possesses a preestablished identity, arbitrarily imputed by God in his grace. The patient is, in spite of himself or herself, an image bearer of God. That identity needs to be recovered. Therapy is the process of recovering it and propelling the patient into the certified and secure destiny of purposeful self-realization as imager and compatriot of God. That may not be overtly explained in therapy but will be implicit in the perspective, goals, expectations, and values inherent in the therapist's incarnational role.

Second, the themes of grace-shaped identity, growth, healing, and destiny introduce into the therapeutic milieu dynamics which can erode neurotic guilt, remorse, grief, hopelessness, self-pity, compulsivity, and rigidity of personality. The Christian perspective potentially decreases the need for the self-defeating processes of denial and self-justification as well as the various compensatory reactions so often produced by them. The biblical perspective frees the patient and the therapist for self-acceptance and a life style of dignity. It is a perspective shaped by God's unconditional positive regard for humans.

Third, the Christian perspective removes the anxiety of the therapy responsibility for the therapist and so decreases the degree of iatrogenic psychopathology (i.e., therapist-induced psychopathology). It also affords a base for wholesome transference and countertransference and frees the therapist to be human and healthily humorful.

Fourth, the Christian perspective can reduce the anxiety and distraction of the patient. This may come by means of the sense of relief and affirmed self-esteem implied in the fact that his or her worthiness is imputed and inherent rather than a worthiness earned and dependent upon his or her health or behavior.

Fifth, this Christian perspective of freedom and affirmation expands the potential for risk taking toward growth by its constructive anxiety-reduction value. It affords relief from constraints that distract the patient from Christian self-actualization. It releases persons to accept humanness and mortality, and thereby it mollifies that ultimate threat which stands behind all pathology: the fear of death and meaninglessness.

Theology and faith are cognitive-emotive processes. Their functions for good or ill are relevant to all cognitive and emotive disorders, even those of an organic or body chemistry source. Therefore, concerns about theological perspective, faith commitment, religious experience, and spiritual maturity are vital therapeutic issues. The concern to be a *Christian* professional is a crucial one.

References

Ellens, J. H. *God's grace and human health.* Nashville: Abingdon, 1982.
Nouwen, H. J. *The wounded healer.* Garden City, N.Y.: Doubleday, 1972.

J. H. ELLENS

See CHRISTIAN COUNSELING AND PSYCHOTHERAPY; COUNSELING AND PSYCHOTHERAPY: BIBLICAL THEMES.

Counseling Psychology.

One of the four traditional applied specialties of psychology, the other three being clinical psychology, industrial/organizational psychology, and school psychology. The American Psychological Association recognizes these distinct specialties by accrediting their training programs; a similar recognition is made by the American Board of Professional Psychology, which awards diplomate status to outstanding practitioners in these specialties. Counseling psychology, as a specialty, overlaps with each of the others but is distinguished by its focus on issues of development and decision making across the life span among relatively adequately functioning individuals (Delworth, 1977).

Specialty Guidelines for the Delivery of Services by Counseling Psychologists delineates the services of counseling psychology as those "principles, methods, and procedures for facilitating effective functioning during the life-span process" (APA, 1981b, p. 654). The goal of counseling psychology practice, therefore, is to help individuals resolve life crises, make effective choices, and build on personal strengths. Particular techniques which a counseling psychologist might employ include assessment and testing, counseling and therapy, consultation, teaching and training, and research and evaluation.

The distinction between counseling and clinical psychology is often a puzzling one. Indeed, as shall be discussed later, there has recently been a blurring of the traditional practice areas of counseling and clinical psychology. However, as defined by *Specialty Guidelines for the Delivery of Services by Clinical Psychologists*, goals of clinical psychology services are to "understand, predict, and alleviate intellectual, emotional, psychological, and behavioral disability and discomfort" (APA, 1981a, p. 642). Thus, clinical psychology, in contrast to counseling psychology, focuses on individuals' pathology or disturbances and uses remedial techniques to remove or alleviate the dysfunctions.

History. This distinction between clinical and counseling psychology is easily understood in light of the specialties' histories. When clinical psychology developed within medical settings, the primary task of the specialty was to do assessment and provide diagnoses for patients who would then receive therapy from psychiatrists. However, after World War II, with the development of various "schools" or kinds of psychotherapy, clinical psychologists began to be trained in the delivery of therapy services as well as in assessment. Their services were still delivered in medical settings (although some clinical psychologists started private practices), and their patients were still primarily persons with severe psychological disturbances.

Clinical and counseling psychology came into being officially in 1946 as charter divisions (12 and 17 respectively) of the newly merged American Psychological Association and the American Association for Applied Psychology. Counseling psychology's division was entitled Counseling and Guidance. This title reflected the common interests of early counseling psychologists who taught in colleges and universities and who were active in developing models of vocational decision making. The primary task of counseling psychology was vocational guidance and counseling, and many of the counseling psychologists who were charter members of Division 17 were also members of the American College Personnel Association, whose members were involved in student personnel work in colleges and universities, and the National Vocational Guidance Association, whose members were involved in providing vocational counseling in secondary schools.

During the 1950s the division changed its name to Counseling Psychology, and its members became known as counseling psychologists. Funding for training programs became available through the Veterans Administration, and these programs were developed with the goal of the doctoral degree as the minimal level of training (APA, 1952). An invitational conference at Greyston Center further contributed to the specialty's development by providing a common specialty definition and by separating counseling psychology from the related but separate practice of counseling, which was also developing during this time period (Thompson & Super, 1964).

Counseling psychology rapidly expanded through the 1960s into the mid-1970s. Most graduates of the increasing number of training programs took jobs either in the Veterans Administration system or in college and university counseling services. During this period there was also a proliferation of research on the process of counseling, on issues in testing and measurement, and on vocational and career development. This research was published in the major counseling psychology journals, *Journal of Counseling Psychology, The Counseling Psychologist, and The Journal of Vocational Behavior.*

Current Status. Changing population trends put an end in the mid-1970s to this period of expansion and ushered in a period of change in the specialty. As the number of counseling center and Veterans Administration positions stabilized, counseling psychology graduates began to seek positions in community mental health centers and private practice settings, where for the first time they directly competed with clinical psychologists for jobs for which counseling psychologists believed they had comparable training. This state of affairs came about for several reasons. Since the 1960s the American Psychological Association had accredited training programs in psychology and therefore had established basic educational requirements which made training in clinical and counseling psychology comparable. Second, clinical psychology had begun responding to criticisms of its medically oriented service delivery model and had broadened the focus of treatment approaches to include those clients who had concerns which were more developmental and crisis oriented in nature. (It was during this time that community psychology developed from clinical psychology, as many clinical psychologists began to apply their skills toward prevention, rather than only remedial purposes, within the community.) Counseling psychology, in parallel fashion, had broadened its service delivery beyond vocational decision making to include psychotherapy, behavior therapy, marriage and family counseling, and other more "clinical" procedures as means of reaching the goal of facilitating normal growth and development. Therefore, many counseling psychologists and clinical psychologists, trained in programs which closely resembled each other in content and method, were claiming similar competencies. Third, counseling psychologists were beginning to be more active in the consideration of private practice issues of credentials, licensing, and third-party payment (insurance reimbursement for health care services such as therapy).

As these pressures, generated by changes in the specialty, have intensified, there has been a corresponding conflict among counseling psychologists concerning their rightful role in the profession of psychology (Fretz & Mills, 1980; Osipow, 1977). As Ivey (1979) noted, counseling psychology may be the most broadly based specialty in psychology. Although a common emphasis on development of positive and adaptive functioning among clients is stressed, there is among counseling psychologists a wide diversity of educational backgrounds, experiential areas, skills, and identities. Counseling psychologists do vocational counseling, develop career interest inventories, train medical students in listening skills, provide therapy in community mental health services, train hospitalized cancer patients in coping skills, and so on. The difficulty of such diversity is that, although remaining faithful to the goal of dealing with clients in a developmental and growth-oriented framework, counseling psychology has lost any certainty of self-definition. It is this fact which caused Weigel (1977), in considering current confusion over the definition of the specialty of counseling psychology, to assert, "I have seen the enemy—and they is us."

Future Trends. For counseling psychology, or indeed any area, to exist as a specialty, certain criteria need to be met. A specialty practice area indicates that a knowledge base has increased to the point where specification of training, practice, users, and the "state of the art" is possible. Counseling psychology faces a difficult series of choices in this regard. Should counseling psychology reaffirm its roots of vocational guidance? Should it broaden its practice to include more disturbed clients for whom intensive therapy is appropriate? Or is there a middle ground of practice which reaffirms counseling psychology's tradition of building on strengths but which expands service delivery to new and varied settings? Many counseling psychologists believe the latter is the best choice, and foresee increased involvement with psychological, social, and vocational rehabilitation of the chronically and severely disabled; the development and delivery of mental health services for underserved populations (e.g., minority, rural); outreach activities such as consultation; and research relating to all these new directions.

References

American Psychological Association, Division of Counseling and Guidance. Recommended standards for training counseling psychologists at the doctoral level. *American Psychologist,* 1952, *7,* 175–181.

American Psychological Association. Specialty guidelines for the delivery of services by clinical psychologists. *American Psychologist,* 1981, *36,* 640–651. (a)

American Psychological Association. Specialty guidelines for the delivery of services by counseling psychologists. *American Psychologist,* 1981, *36,* 652–663. (b)

Delworth, U. Counseling psychology. *The Counseling Psychologist,* 1977, *7*(2), 43–45.

Fretz, B. R., & Mills, D. H. Professional certification in counseling psychology. *The Counseling Psychologist,* 1980, *9*(1), 2–17.

Ivey, A. E. Counseling psychology. *The Counseling Psychologist,* 1979, *8*(3), 3–6.

Osipow, S. H. Will the real counseling psychologist please stand up? *The Counseling Psychologist,* 1977, *7*(2), 93–94.

Thompson, A. S., & Super, D. E. (Eds.). *The professional preparation of counseling psychologists: Report of the 1964 Greyston Conference.* New York: Teachers College, Columbia University, Bureau of Publications, 1964.

Weigel, R. G. I have seen the enemy and they is us—and everyone else. *The Counseling Psychologist,* 1977, *7*(2), 50–53.

E. M. Altmaier

See Clinical Psychology; Community Psychology; Applied Psychology.

Counselor Training. *See* Training in Counseling and Psychotherapy.

Counterconditioning. In counterconditioning, a maladaptive response is eliminated by establishing a new response in the presence of the stimulus which initially controlled occurrence of the maladaptive response. In a classical study crying in the presence of a rabbit was eliminated by feeding the fearful child and gradually bringing the rabbit into his proximity while he ate.

The critical components in counterconditioning are the maladaptive stimulus-response pattern and a new stimulus-response interaction. This new pattern is usually developed through replacing the maladaptive response with a more acceptable response—in other words, response substitution. By contrast, punishment and extinction weaken present responses without developing alternative responses to the controlling stimulus.

Although rarely discussed in recent behavioral literature, counterconditioning is a basic process underlying many behavior therapy techniques, including such procedures as covert sensitization, differential reinforcement of alternative behavior, aversion therapy, systematic and in vivo desensitization, assertion training, and sex therapy.

Despite recent neglect of the concept, there is general agreement that the research evidence indicates that replacing problem behaviors with adaptive behaviors is an effective treatment approach. An interesting parallel noted by Adams is that a number of biblical teachings suggest the value of replacing sinful practices with godly behavior (Adams, 1973, pp. 176–216).

Reference

Adams, J. E. *The Christian counselor's manual.* Grand Rapids: Baker, 1973.

R. K. Bufford

See Behavior Therapy.

Countertransference. Freud was the first to identify and develop the concepts of transference and countertransference. Both emerged from his clinical observations and insights into the dynamic interplay between the therapist and patient. He described countertransference as the therapist's neurotic reactions to the patient (Freud, 1910/1961, 1912/1961). He was aware of the fact that an awareness of countertransference was essential for successful therapeutic work. But he viewed it as a constant danger to effective therapy and felt that it contained the potential for catastrophic consequences in the therapeutic relationship.

Freud's insights into transference are the foundation for understanding countertransference. While transference is concerned with the patient's unrealistic image, feelings, and impulses toward the therapist, so countertransference is concerned with the therapist's unrealistic reactions to the patient or to the patient's transference manifestations toward the therapist. Just as we refer to the pathological manifestation of the patient's transference to the analyst as the "transference neurosis," so we might in the same way view the pathological expression of the therapist's unresolved problems toward the patient as the "countertransference neurosis."

Freud was, of course, not the only psychoanalytic theorist to deal with this topic. Lorand (1946) wrote of the potential hazards of countertransference, pointing out the tendency for a therapist to seek solutions for his own problems in the therapeutic relationship. He suggested that it was dangerously easy for the therapist to derive narcissistic gratification from the therapeutic relationship and that this, or any other meeting of personal needs in therapy, has an undesirable effect on the therapeutic experience. Racker (1968) considers the destructive effects of countertransference but also discusses its potential value when perceived and understood. He felt that countertransference reactions had characteristics that helped the therapist understand the specific character of psychological patterns in the patient. For instance, a strong sexual response by the therapist may be the consequence of sexual signals emitted by the patient. Knowledge of the base for his response enables him to avoid being ensnared in acting out episodes. Langs (1976) provides a summary of these and other psychoanalytic writings on transference and countertransference as well as his own synthesis of this literature.

Development and Management. As with the patient, part of the therapist's libido remains fixated, in fantasy, to the introjected objects in his past. To the degree that his psychic conflicts remain unresolved, a solution will be sought by a pathological transfer and attachment of the libido to external objects in the present. It is 'important to note that countertransference reactions are always pathological and consequently destructive. If not perceived and understood they will at the least hinder the therapist in his perception of pathological processes in the patient's behavior, and at worst will ensnare the therapist in a bind that will defeat the very purpose of the therapeutic encounter.

Every therapist should be aware of the fact that he or she is not fully free of unresolved infantile dependencies, of distortions in object relations, and of basic neurotic anxieties resulting in pathologic defense mechanisms. This insight may be handled in one of two ways. He may resort (unconsciously) to denial of inappropriate reactions to the patient. This results in resistance to an examination of the reason for his reaction to the patient, and to attitudes or behavior that will abort the patient's free flow of feeling. Examples of this would include the therapist who considers prayer or Scripture as the only necessary therapeutic tool in Christian-oriented psychotherapy or counseling; the therapist who adopts a pedantic attitude toward the patient; or the therapist who prevents emotional catharsis from taking place by resorting to reprimand, communicating displeasure, or merely changing the subject. These are all

examples of reactions toward patients that betray the existence of countertransference.

The second, and more constructive, way of dealing with countertransference, once the therapist admits its existence, is to adopt one or all of the following solutions. He may seek therapy for himself; involve himself in a good training program; seek out sources of information such as lectures, tapes, professional literature, or workshops concerned specifically with countertransference; or seek out a good professional supervisory experience preferably with a psychodynamic therapist who is well versed in the concepts of transference, countertransference, and resistance.

In order to avoid the neurotic traps inherent in therapeutic relationships, it is essential that therapists understand the phenomenon of countertransference and realize that his reactions are always destructive if not understood and properly handled. Anyone engaged in counseling, whether in-depth therapy such as psychoanalysis or less intense approaches such as pastoral counseling, should have a good knowledge of his own unresolved problems as well as the ways these problems affect his functioning in therapy. Such a knowledge will prevent personal catastrophies and will increase the probability of successful therapy.

References

Freud, S. *The future prospects for psycho-analytic therapy.* In J. Strachey (Ed. and trans.), *The complete psychological works of Sigmund Freud* (Vol. 11). London: Hogarth Press, 1961. (Originally published, 1910.)

Freud, S. *The dynamics of transference.* In J. Strachey (Ed. and trans.), The complete psychological works of Sigmund Freud (Vol. 12). London: Hogarth Press, 1961. (Originally published, 1912.)

Langs, R. *The therapeutic interaction* (2 vols.). New York: Aronson, 1976.

Lorand, S. *Techniques of psychoanalytic therapy.* New York: International Universities Press, 1946.

Racker, H. *Transference and countertransference.* New York: International Universities Press, 1968.

A. F. X. CALABRESE

See TRANSFERENCE.

Couvade Syndrome. A psychogenic disorder in which expectant fathers are afflicted by symptoms resembling those experienced by their wives during pregnancy or labor. The name denotes the similarity to couvade ritual, a custom found in some primitive tribes. In this ritual the expectant father gives pretense of childbirth by taking to his bed immediately after his wife delivers. The mother usually immediately returns to work.

Unlike the ritualistic form, the couvade syndrome is not a pretense. Nausea and vomiting, food cravings, abdominal swelling, and spurious labor pains are frequently experienced by these males. Although the development of the full range of symptoms is relatively rare, estimates of incidence suggest that 20 to 25% of expectant fathers give evidence of some of the symptoms (Trethowan, 1972).

Couvade syndrome males give prominent display of anxiety. Generally the cognitive content of their anxieties revolves around what might be called pseudo-obstetrical concerns such as "her mother had such a hard time in childbirth" rather than more realistic fears of genuine obstetrical hazards. This superstitious quality has been noted by a number of theorists of the disorder who have viewed it as a hysterical disorder. Other theorists have viewed it as a mask for hostility experienced by the husband toward the wife. Still others have viewed it as an expression of the man's envy of his wife's ability to bear children. This has been referred to as parturition envy. A final hypothesis suggests that the syndrome is the result of identification and empathy. Trethowan (1972) notes that none of these possible explanations necessarily excludes the others and all could conceivably be operative to varying degrees in any given case.

Reference

Trethowan, W. H. The couvade syndrome. In J. Howells (Ed.), *Modern perspectives in psycho-obstetrics.* New York: Brunner/Mazel, 1972.

D. G. BENNER

Covert Modeling.

A cognitive process in which the individual changes response patterns through imagining himself engaging in the desired responses rather than by means of observing another person model the responses. Since these new responses are weak, even at the imaginal level, it is essential that they be reinforced in order to strengthen and maintain them. Normally this reinforcement is self-administered. Covert modeling thus involves a combination of modeling and self-control procedures, all conducted internally in the form of thought and fantasy.

Although covert modeling is a fairly new concept, it has been used in assertiveness training, the development of athletic skills, and reading comprehension enhancement. Research on its effectiveness has been encouraging, although the number of well-controlled studies is quite small.

A basic limitation with covert modeling is that it requires prior exposure to the desired behaviors in some manner, such as by instructions or by observing a live model. Thus covert modeling is effective in releasing responses

already available to the individual, such as assertive responses that are inhibited by unrealistic expectations of social responses to them, but is not effective for teaching new responses. A second limitation is that the performance must ultimately come under reinforcement control of events mediated by the environment, much as with other self-control procedures. Finally, it seems a bit strained to term this process modeling, since it does not involve observing another's behavior at all.

R. K. BUFFORD

See MODELING; SELF-CONTROL; COGNITIVE-BEHAVIOR THERAPY.

Covert Sensitization.

A form of aversion therapy in which a covert response such as a thought or image is followed by an imagined aversive event. The individual may imagine himself relaxing in front of the TV and eating a large bowl of hot buttered popcorn, enjoying the smell and taste; he then imagines the rolls of fat accumulating around his waist, having to buy new clothes, and being rejected by his girlfriend because of his weight. In covert sensitization the cognitive elements of the stimulus-response sequence are dealt with rather than overt responses and external stimuli. The goal is to block the thoughts and fantasies that precede undesired overt behaviors and increase their probability.

Although it is possible for the individual to self-administer covert sensitization in an aversive self-control procedure, it is more common for covert sensitization to be conducted in a structured therapy interaction. Often relaxation procedures are used to heighten the relief following termination of the imagined aversive stimulus.

Covert sensitization has been employed with homosexuality, pedophilia, obesity, and smoking. Initial studies of its effectiveness have been encouraging.

Covert sensitization offers some advantages over aversion therapy. Since the events are imagined, pictures, slides, projectors, shock apparatus, and other equipment are not required.

However, covert sensitization has two disadvantages. First, because the scenes, behavior, and aversive stimulation are all imagined, they are not amenable to precise control. Second, there is the problem of finding a suitable aversive stimulus which the individual is able to imagine. Since most behaviors that are candidates for this approach are highly motivated, intrinsically reinforcing, and under strong stimulus control, it is essential to locate a powerful aversive stimulus.

Finally, covert sensitization shares a limitation common to all the aversive procedures: the failure to establish alternative and more desirable forms of behavior. For this reason some theorists object categorically to all forms of aversive procedures. The majority of professionals, however, agree that the preferred intervention strategy is to use aversion procedures in conjunction with procedures designed to establish positive alternative behaviors. Thus, in many applications of covert sensitization the individual terminates the aversive scene and then imagines initiating an alternative, more desirable response.

R. K. Bufford

See Aversion Therapy; Behavior Therapy.

Creative Aggression Therapy. A skill-building, educative type of short-term endeavor originated by Bach (Bach & Goldberg, 1974). The approach tends to be highly structured and requires the therapist to be quite active and flexible, shifting from role to role as teacher, cajoler, coach, referee, and antagonist. It is built on the assumptions that 1) nice people get themselves into emotional trouble by blocking the expression of negative emotions such as anger and rage; 2) people change by doing something different rather than by gaining insight into something different; 3) the verbal and physical expression of negative affect acts as a curative change agent within the client.

According to Bach, current Western culture emphasizes the prohibition of anger. As a result of not being allowed to directly vent their aggression many individuals pay a heavy price: depression (or anger indirectly expressed at one's psyche), psychosomatization (anger indirectly expressed at one's own body), passive-aggressive life styles (anger indirectly expressed toward others), impulsive life styles (anger indirectly breaking out through action rather than through talking), and psychotic behavior (anger vented toward others that is simultaneously disqualified through "crazy talk," so that one cannot be held responsible for the anger). This premise is extended further to a political level on which the escalating level of violence within cities and between nations is viewed as a partial product of our cultural proscription of clean, direct expression of anger between individuals.

Much of creative aggression therapy is based on an avoidance learning paradigm. It is hypothesized that many individuals are afraid of the disastrous consequences that will certainly follow the direct expression of anger. One learns as a small child that it is not smart to be directly angry at one's parents; they are far more powerful and wield a vast array of positive and negative reinforcers not available to the child. As an adult, this avoidance of the expression of anger becomes an anachronistic albatross around one's neck. However, as long as one avoids aggression, one will never learn that the contingencies have changed and that it is now more safe to vent anger.

From this perspective it does little good to inform an individual that he or she is angry. It is assumed that at some level the client already knows about this anger. The knowledge of that internal state of *being* without appropriate *doing* produces an iatrogenic effect: the individual becomes more and more furious without finding any way of releasing that aggressive feeling directly. Insight does not prove to be curative from this point of view. Instead, the client needs to be taught how to directly vent aggressive feelings in an appropriate fashion.

The creative aggression therapist will typically operate in the following fashion: first, one teaches clients (individuals, couples, or families) something of the above theoretical perspective; second, one instructs these clients regarding the mechanics of how to appropriately discharge aggression using a ritualistic type of procedure, assertiveness skills, and/or a fair fight format; third, one sends the clients home to practice the new skill; and fourth, one follows up on the new learning by rewarding progress verbally or with other prearranged reinforcers in future sessions.

As an example of aggressive ritual, a couple might be encouraged to stand nose to nose and scream vindictives simultaneously. In this fashion neither can hear the other and both can experience a catharsis. In a similar way an individual might be encouraged to vent his anger by pounding on a pillow with fists or a bataca bat. While physically pounding, the client might also be encouraged to scream out his anger toward an imagined significant other in his current or past experience.

Creative aggression therapy is best known by many for its fair fight ritual. A fair fight is useful both for families who are sufficiently inhibited so that they never risk a cross word and for families whose constantly destructive uproar pattern needs to be contained by appropriate structuring. When using the fair fight the therapist determines who is the "heavyweight" and who is the "lightweight" in the relationship (i.e., who is most and least powerful). The lightweight is given the job of setting a time and place for the fight when the couple is least stressed and most relaxed. Once the appointment is made, the couple is instructed to initially keep within a 15- to 20-minute limit. Each individual defines for the therapist and partner what are sensitive areas, or "zaps," not to be mentioned (e.g., "You act just like your mother when you say that!"). A "zap tolerance" for each person is established beyond which the fight is terminated even if the time limit is not completed. Once the fight has finished, the couple is given "fight style" score sheets to rate each other. These score sheets assign values to each of 10 different dimensions thought to be critical in fighting.

This type of therapy has distinct potential applicability within that Christian sector where aggressive displays of behavior are thought to be unspiritual. The Christian therapist is faced with the task of teaching clients to "be angry and sin not" (Eph. 4:26). The danger in this therapy lies in encouraging undisciplined, inappropriate lashing out toward others in a destructive manner; the benefit lies in more open, honest communication between intimates. Thus, as in most therapy, discernment and good judgment on the part of the therapist are essential.

Reference
Bach, G., & Goldberg, H. *Creative aggression.* Garden City, N. Y.: Doubleday, 1974.

V. L. SHEPPERSON

See AGGRESSION; ANGER; ASSERTIVENESS TRAINING.

Creativity. Creativity has been defined in many ways, depending on psychologists' theoretical and philosophical persuasions. Stein (1975) suggests that it is a process that results in a novel product or idea which is accepted as useful by some significant group of people.

A key point in this definition is that a creative product or idea must be more than merely novel or original. Creativity occurs within real-world settings and is thus subject to various constraints. For example, creative scientific acts must either contribute to new theories or, more commonly, advance established theories in such a way that fellow scientists who are qualified to judge will acknowledge that the contribution "works" well. These decisions depend on more or less established criteria, explicitly or tacitly applied. Controversy and change in these standards can occur, occasionally resulting in belated assessments that creativity has occurred. However, solitary appraisals are of little note unless they are validated later on by a significant group of people. Creativity does not occur in a social vacuum.

This definition also suggests complexity. Creativity involves both the private perception and thinking of individuals during its genesis (the intrapersonal) and the broader social setting in which products and ideas are introduced and tested (the interpersonal). Many discussions of creativity focus on only one of these aspects. It is necessary to use the broad framework implied by this definition to evaluate creativity.

Not surprisingly, theories of creativity have been likened to the fabled blind men who described the same elephant in radically different ways (Yamamoto, 1965). The differences stem in large measure from theorists' identification with one of the major systems of psychology. Yet, as the following survey reveals, each makes provocative and valid points.

Associationist Approach. This approach arose from the theory which dominated psychology until recently—ASSOCIATIONISM, which explains the acquiring of behavior in terms of associations or bonds between stimuli and responses. In this view the problem of creativity is to explain how responses which are only weakly associated with a given situation—e.g., creative solutions to a newly encountered problem—are evoked. A well-known example is Maier's two-string problem, where two strings are suspended from a ceiling more than arms' length apart and subjects must tie them together using no more than a few implements lying close by. The solution is to use an object to make one string a pendulum and swing it close to the other string. Exposure to objects being used in untypical ways enhances the likelihood of solving the problem.

The associationist approach makes detailed analyses of experimental situations and practical suggestions for facilitating solutions in these situations. An outgrowth of the approach is an idea also associated with the group technique known as brainstorming. This technique encourages the rapid production of a large number of proposed solutions to a problem with a minimum of criticism. An associative explanation is that when a large number of responses to the same stimulus are made in rapid succession, stereotyped, uncreative responses are used up first, allowing weaker, remote associations to appear. These enhance the likelihood of creative solutions.

This perspective has lost influence recently despite its usefulness in some experimental situations. Perhaps the greatest difficulty is the need to make enormous leaps from the experimental setting to creativity in art, science, engineering, and so forth. Additionally, the assumption that the basic elements of creative acts consist of associations to environmental stimuli appears overly restrictive in the light of other perspectives.

Psychometric Approach. The psychometric approach of Guilford and others has stimulated much research, particularly the measurement of creative performance and the identification of intellectual abilities that influence it. Psychometric refers to the basic research tool used. Paper-and-pencil tests are devised to measure separate facets of creative performance (e.g., subjects are asked to name unusual uses for a brick and other common objects). Scores on these tests (e.g., the number of nonstandard uses for a brick) are correlated to discover to what degree the tests measure the same or different things. A statistical technique known as factor analysis reveals underlying patterns in the ways various tests are correlated, and these suggest the intellectual abilities or other traits that best explain individual differences on test scores.

Probably the most significant avenue of research stemming from this approach relates to the distinction between creativity and intelligence. Early on, Guilford (Guilford & Merrifield, 1960) distinguished between two types of questions assessing intellectual performance. Standard intelligence tests ask questions which require convergence toward one best answer, whereas questions most relevant to creativity allow many different responses, as in the unusual uses example above. Guilford proposed that creativity, like intelligence, is not simple, but is rather a domain consisting of a host of divergent thinking abilities. However, the issue of whether creative abilities are distinct from intelligence as traditionally measured became doubtful when tests designed to measure these abilities were found to be at least as highly related to intelligence scores as they are to each other. This contrasts to the subtests of an intelligence test battery, which tend to be highly correlated. But other investigators found that when the context of evaluation normally associated with test taking is relaxed and time restrictions removed, performance becomes more consistent across divergent thinking tests. To recall the argument of associative theorists, removal of these artificial restrictions allows more creative

responses to appear after the stereotyped ones are used up.

Findings such as these supported the argument that there is a creativity domain, measured by divergent thinking tests, which is distinct from intelligence. Indeed, good divergent thinkers proved different in many ways from those high in IQ alone—e.g., in social adjustment and occupational preference. But are these performances associated with complex, long-term, or outstanding examples of creativity? While controversy on this issue is ongoing, it is at least clear that other personality variables comparatively ignored in this approach are also relevant.

Psychoanalytic Approaches. Psychoanalysts beginning with Freud have preoccupied themselves with the internal dynamics of creative persons, and frequently have tried to relate creativity and abnormal behavior. For Freud (1916) creative works, like cultural achievements in general, are suspect. They arise from the artist's attempt to derive gratification in fantasy, like a child in play. Unlike his followers, Freud presumed only to illuminate motives behind the creative work, not the shape taken by the work itself.

Psychoanalysts since Freud generally have taken a less cynical view of creativity. Kris (1952) theorized that creative works evidence, not neurotic trends within the creator, but rather a mature form of adaptation which he called "regression in the service of the ego." This is an ability or tendency to relax the boundaries of the ego, or conscious self, to permit material not accessible to conscious recall to influence the creative work. Similarly, Schachtel (1959) proposed that creative work demands a mature form of perception characterized by radical openness to experience. The value of these capacities for creativity stems from the greater availability of material often barred from conscious awareness. These ideas call attention to interference with the creative process due to a certain inflexibility—an over-insistence on keeping a conscious grip on oneself. They also suggest that creative artists succeed in part through eliciting uncharacteristic modes of awareness in their audiences.

Cognitive-Developmental Approach. Still other psychologists place creativity in the perspective of cognitive development. An important theorist is Werner (1957), who described an invariant sequence in development. Infants can make little differentiation between themselves and the external world; their various psychological processes—sensory, affective, motoric, etc.—lack organization or differentiation from one another. For example, objects are first perceived as inseparable from the feelings they evoke in the infant. By adulthood the individual clearly separates between the technical properties of objects and internal psychological processes. A great deal of empirical work supports the notion that creativity is marked by flexible functioning or integration of the developmentally mature and developmentally primitive modes of perception. The similarity between this idea and the psychoanalytic concept of "regression in the service of the ego" is obvious. However, the emphasis is on a developmentally ordered sequence of stages rather than on unconscious sources of creative ideas. The cognitive-developmental approach may be faulted however, for not having enough to say about other types of development such as social, affective, and personality development.

Toward a Comprehensive Model. The foregoing brief overview reveals so much theoretical ferment and pluralism that it is probably premature to attempt a comprehensive theory. Nevertheless, some broad dimensions which any comprehensive theory must account for can be sketched. There is some consensus regarding many of these dimensions, and without keeping them in view, theorizing is likely to flounder over merely semantic difficulties.

First, creativity can be studied in relation to at least four components: process, product, person, and situation. As the survey revealed, different theories are involved with some components more than others. For example, the associative approach is more concerned with situational analysis than are the other approaches. When attention is focused on only one area, there is greater consensus at least in regard to description. For example, the creative process is described in much the same terms regardless of the approach. Wallas (1926) describes four stages of the creative process: prior preparation, incubation or relaxing of conscious effort, illumination or discovery, and verification or testing of the result. While slight variations have been proposed, these stages are still frequently cited. There is also consensus regarding what creative persons are like. Their attributes include flexibility and productivity of ideas; uniqueness and originality of ideas and perceptions; intuitiveness, empathy, and perceptual openness; preference for complexity; independence of judgment; and aesthetic sensitivity.

A second dimension is the field of endeavor. Although there is surprising consistency in the description of both creative processes and

persons regardless of field, it appears likely that different fields place different demands on creative work. Roe (1952) has elucidated such differences among the branches of science.

Third, the level of creativity is crucial. Many key studies used subjects selected for their high level of creativity. Still unclear is what relationship exists between creativity on this level and that on lower or even higher levels. One suggestion is that while creativity and intelligence may be meaningfully separated at lower levels, eminent accomplishment depends on a happy coincidence of both.

Finally, the relationship between divine and human creativity should be considered. The biblical revelation shows us that we are made in God's image. Sayers (1941) has suggested that a characteristic common to both God and humanity, the divine or image-bearing quality indicated in the Genesis account, is the ability and desire to make things. In her analysis, striking parallels between human creativity and the trinitarian nature of God are revealed. However, humble recognition that, unlike us, God is an uncreated spirit and the author of life itself helps us to render our own finite creativity in his service.

References

Freud, S. *Wit and its relation to the unconscious.* New York: Moffat, Yard, 1916.

Guilford, J. P., & Merrifield, P. R. *Structure of the intellect model.* Los Angeles: University of Southern California, 1960.

Kris, E. *Psychoanalytic explorations in art.* New York: International Universities Press, 1952.

Roe, A. *The Making of a scientist.* New York: Dodd, Mead, 1952.

Sayers, D. *The mind of the maker.* New York: Harcourt, Brace, 1941.

Schachtel, E. G. *Metamorphosis.* New York: Basic Books, 1959.

Stein, M. I. *Stimulating creativity.* New York: Academic Press, 1975.

Wallas, G. *The art of thought.* New York: Harcourt, Brace, 1926.

Werner, H. *Comparative psychology of mental development.* New York: International Universities Press, 1957.

Yamamoto, K. Research frontier: "Creativity"—A blind man's report on the elephant. *Journal of Counseling Psychology,* 1965, *12,* 428–434.

D. R. RIDLEY

See INTELLIGENCE; THINKING.

Creativity Tests. Creativity is a theoretical concept in psychology that is defined in a variety of ways and thus is measured with a variety of methods. Since these methods are often fraught with problems of reliability and validity, tests of creativity need to be applied and interpreted with much caution.

Traditional measurement approaches to

creativity have included achievement performed, ratings of specific productions, prediction of future creative behavior from biographical information, and tests of divergent thinking. Today, an even wider variety of tests is being developed or adapted to creativity research to correspond with the lessened emphasis on logical, rational thinking and the greater interest in insight and intuitive processes. For example, the focus of current research includes such topics as transcendental meditation, image making, and incubation. Even so, divergent thinking tests continue to be the most widely applied and researched.

Many divergent thinking measures originate in Guilford's model, in which divergent production is performed on a variety of contents with a variety of outcomes (Guilford & Merrifield, 1960). Divergent thinking does not lead to a single correct answer but goes off in a multitude of directions, leading to numerous solutions. For example, tests such as Guilford's Creativity Tests for Children and Torrance's Tests of Creative Thinking include items requiring the examinee to provide as many meanings as possible for ambiguous words (e.g., hand), to propose possible outcomes for novel situations (e.g., if people flew rather than walked), and to produce pictures combining geometric figures (e.g., a boat, using squares and triangles only). Responses are evaluated according to fluency, flexibility, originality, and elaboration.

Although extensively used, measures of divergent thinking have been criticized for their questionable predictive validity, their reliance on time, and for not acknowledging the importance of convergence in creative productions. That is, to be recognized as creative, processes and/or products must conform to some social expectations.

Reference
Guilford, J. P., & Merrifield, P. R. *Structure of the intellect model.* Los Angeles: University of Southern California, 1960.

M. D. ROE

See CREATIVITY; THINKING; PSYCHOLOGICAL MEASUREMENT.

Cretinism. A congenital condition associated with complete absence or defective functioning of secretion in the thyroid gland. Mental and physical development is retarded, and the disease becomes evident in approximately the sixth month of life. A disturbance in the central nervous system, skeleton, and skin leads to general underdevelopment, distorted posture and gait, and a bloated appearance. Other

symptoms include lethargy, defective speech and hearing, apathy, protrusion of the tongue, and thickening of the features. The cause of cretinism is unknown, but it is thought to be related to birth injuries, an iodine deficiency, or infectious diseases in childhood. The use of iodized salt in the first six months of life has reduced the incidence and severity of the disease.

D. L. SCHUURMAN

See MENTAL RETARDATION.

Crime and Mental Disorder. Perceptions of the role of mental disorder in criminal behavior have varied over the past century. This variety roughly corresponds to the development and popularity of behavioral science models. It may be summarized as an evolution from the early ideas about mental deficiency, through the influence and popularity of psychometric testing, to the psychoanalytic models and, finally, the qualifying influences of social psychology and behaviorism.

Intelligence and Criminality. Mental deficiency has been a popular explanation of crime. It has had various interpretations throughout the development of criminology. Early treatment of the mentally deficient lumped them together with the insane in prisons, workhouses, and asylums. Moral insanity was seen as imbecility and moral perversion. This was said to cause the individual of "bad blood" to behave in patterns which were morally unacceptable.

With the advent of psychometric testing, defective intelligence became the hypothesized cause of crime. The estimated extent of causation varied from about half of all crimes to almost all such behavior. Subsequent research has failed to substantiate such contentions. Research has, however, shown that offenders with high intelligence tended to commit securities violations, forgery, robbery, and auto theft, while those with lower intelligence were convicted of homicide, rape, aggravated assault, and perjury (Johnson, 1964). It may be that the feebleminded who are convicted for criminal acts are less capable of foreseeing future consequences of present actions. Hence, they are more easily prompted to criminal behavior due to impulsive activity in an opportune situation. However, this may be more indicative of lower class culture than simply of mental impairment.

Subsequent research on the relationship between intelligence, crime, and cultural background has suggested a lessened contributing effect of intelligence. It appears that persons of all intelligence levels commit crimes. Those of lower intelligence may have more difficulty in planning, committing, and escaping detection, but criminal motivation per se is not related. Johnson suggests that lower intelligence may actually prevent criminal behavior by insulating the individual from the frustrations of modern social life.

Studies of personality traits and attitudes relating to criminal behavior have produced mixed results. The confusion is often a result of the studies' failure to develop a set of traits or attitudes which are clearly defined, mutually exclusive, and exhaustive.

Psychoanalytic Theories. Psychoanalytic explanations of criminal behavior attempt to identify some variable within the individual which produces the criminal behavior. There is considerable disagreement on the etiology of criminality and even on the approach to its study among those who share this framework. Some focus exclusively upon the individual and organic aspects of criminality, while others have developed more social-psychological perspectives. Alexander and Staub (1956) suggest that all infants are born criminal. They become noncriminal during the years between four and adolescence by repression of instinctual drives in order to gain social acceptance (p. 31). Crime thus is really a defect in development rather than some inborn trait.

For most psychoanalysts conflict between the child and parent for the affection of the parent of the opposite sex represents the basic problem which must be managed. Toilet training introduces the child to the crime-punishment complex as primitive instinctual drives are frustrated. Inadequate resolution prompts criminal behavior through the resultant fear, aggression, and irrationality that become characteristic of adult mental activity.

Three sources of crime are posited by the psychoanalytic model: psychoneurosis, psychosis, and psychopathy. Psychoneurosis results from the unleashing of the id as it struggles under the ego's subjection to the superego. When this occurs, physical and mental disturbances are possible. Since neuroses are basically suppressive, it is believed that they are not typically involved in delinquent behavior except for such crimes as kleptomania and pyromania.

Psychoses represent the second pathology potentially related to criminal activity. Psychoses are said to originate from early fixations or severe regressions in personality devel-opment or from organic brain disease. Very few criminals are actually psychotic. The most common estimate is 1½ to 2% (Johnson, 1964). Among these offenders schizophrenia is most common. The manic depressive will more likely commit crimes when melancholic. The paranoiac, reacting to delusions with retaliation, is most likely to get even through nonviolent means. In spite of the fact that some psychotic individuals do commit crimes, it is generally believed that psychoses are not causative factors of crime. Rather, both the crimes and the psychoses stem from some personal maladjustment.

Psychopathy occurs when the superego fails to develop adequately, a result of deprivation of deep and nurturing affection during early life. In order to cope, the individual acts out aggressively and insensitively. There are no symptoms of neuroses or psychoses, and the person, though verbally warm, is callous, unaffected by punishment, and capable of any behavior. This diagnostic category has lost favor in current thinking but continues in popular use. The term lacks agreement in definition and illustrates a fundamental problem for these models that have more recently been eclipsed by cognitive and behavioral approaches: failure of precise definition of terminology.

Social-Behavioral Theories. Current considerations of crime have become more social-psychological and behavioral in orientation. These approaches have moved professional attention and interest away from understanding behavior as solely a product of the person. Interactionists, who believe behavior to be a function of the person interacting with the environment, see crime as an external process. Cressey writes, "Criminality is not in people; . . . it is a status conferred upon certain persons for certain acts at certain times in certain places." (Cressey & Ward, 1969, p. xiv). Behavioral approaches are not concerned with internal mental states, and their popularity has reinforced the general deemphasis of the mental illness approaches.

Psychological explanations of criminal behavior have generally been limited in usefulness. The major reason for this is that they have tended to be too individualistic, viewing criminal behavior as a function of the person in isolation from the influences of broad social activity. While helpful in understanding some aspects of crime, they have been unable to provide a unified explanation. Most research in the past decade has increasingly qualified the role of mental disturbance in criminal activity and has placed more emphasis on the individual in interaction with the enviornment.

References

Alexander, F., & Staub, H. *The criminal, the judge, and the public* (Rev. ed.). Glencoe, Ill.: Free Press, 1956.

Cressey, D. R., & Ward, D. A. *Delinquency, crime, and social process.* New York: Harper & Row, 1969.

Johnson, E. H. *Crime correction and society.* Homewood, Ill.: Dorsey Press, 1964.

A. R. DENTON

See FORENSIC PSYCHIATRY.

Criminal Insanity. *See* FORENSIC PSYCHIATRY.

Crisis Family Therapy. *See* FAMILY CRISIS THERAPY.

Crisis Intervention. A short-term therapeutic approach to the common human experience of emotional crisis. In recent years it has become increasingly popular among mental health professionals. As practiced today, it has its roots in the work of Lindemann (1944), who developed a program to aid in the healthy resolution of the grief of the survivors and relatives of those who perished in the Coconut Grove nightclub fire of 1943. During the 1940s and 50s, when little professional attention was given to crisis intervention, Caplan (1964) and his colleagues followed up Lindemann's work, advancing the understanding of crisis and its healthy resolution. Since the middle 1960s— spurred by the community mental health movement, increased consumer demand, and limited professional resources—the helping professions have turned more and more to crisis intervention as an effective mode of providing care for those in emotional crisis.

In theory and practice crisis intervention is still developing. It is strongly eclectic, corralling insights and techniques from a variety of mental health disciplines. At the heart of its current theory and application is Caplan's (1964) concept of homeostasis. Borrowed from physiology, the term, as understood in crisis theory, refers to the healthy balance between the emotional and cognitive experience and functioning of the individual, allowing him to relate effectively to his environment.

Each person has a homeostatic stability that is "normal" for himself. However, he constantly faces situations that disrupt that homeostasis. These "emotionally hazardous situations" (Caplan, 1964)—changes in environment, interpersonal relationships, or oneself that entail loss and are perceived as negative—give rise to painful emotions, sometimes accompanied by decreased cognitive ability. In the face of this stress the person calls

forth habitual coping mechanisms (both conscious and unconscious) and problem-solving activities in an effort to restore homeostasis. If they fail to restore homeostasis, an emotional crisis may ensue.

Because individuals cannot tolerate stress indefinitely, emotional crises have a limited life span, usually resolving themselves, for better or for worse, within four to six weeks (Caplan, 1964). If the person receives help and learns new, effective coping skills, the crisis will resolve healthily, strengthening him for future events. In the absence of help or of acquiring effective coping skills, the crisis resolution will be maladaptive, leaving the individual more vulnerable to similar crises in the future.

Crises are a normal part of life and are not in themselves an indication of psychopathology. Everyone, even the well-adjusted, experiences emotional crises in stressful situations for which coping behaviors are weak or absent. Crises may be triggered by relatively predictable developmental events—life transitions such as birth, adolescence, and old age—and by the more unpredictable situational upsets such as illness, unemployment, divorce, or moving to a new home. Crises always involve either actual or symbolic conflicts with a significant other person. Developmental and situational changes lead to crisis when they reawaken unresolved conflicts and traumas from the past.

Because of the limited duration of crises, crisis intervention, to be effective, must take place as soon as possible after the precipitating event. The goal of crisis intervention is to restore the person as quickly as possible to at least a precrisis level of functioning, whether or not that level was ideal. Solving all the client's problems, restructuring personality, bringing about major changes, and resolving deep-seated, long-standing conflicts—goals common to long-term therapy—are outside the scope of crisis intervention. Any gains in those areas are considered a therapeutic bonus, not a goal to be pursued.

In crisis a person is more open than usual to receiving help and support from others and learning new ways of functioning. The therapist's role is to guide the client, over the 4- to 6-week duration of the crisis, toward an adaptive resolution. Unlike long-term insight-oriented therapy where the therapist may be passive and maintain a professional distance, crisis intervention calls for an active, personal encounter. The therapist must be direct and flexible enough to use a variety of techniques.

The therapist provides hope and support to the client, presenting himself as interested, caring, and willing to understand and help. Through empathy the therapist both communicates support and helps the client to ventilate and understand those negative emotions that are preventing him from coping with the situation, thereby restoring some cognitive mastery.

Since the goal of therapy is to restore the client's own functioning, the therapist, while supportive, does not foster dependency but seeks to mobilize the client's own internal strengths and external resources (e.g., family or friends) in defining the problem, identifying the event that precipitated the crisis, addressing and at least partially resolving the underlying conflict that has made the client vulnerable to that event, and planning ways of dealing with the situation. In the process the therapist seeks to help the client avoid learning or using maladaptive coping responses; learn new, adaptive coping skills; reconcile himself, both emotionally and intellectually, to the changes brought about by the crisis; and anticipate and plan for future similar situations.

The focus of therapy is the present situation, not the historical origin of the client's conflicts. Attention is given to past events only as they relate to the current crisis, helping the client to understand and act in his present situation. In the course of therapy the therapist gradually shifts responsibility for dealing with the problem to the client, building his hope, independence, and self-esteem. When crisis intervention is successful, the client's anxiety is replaced with genuine hope for the future as his supportive interpersonal relationships are strengthened and he gradually regains his capacity for independently planning ways to meet his needs.

Crisis intervention offers one way of answering Scripture's call to help those in need. Its balance between supportive help and encouragement of the client's own independent functioning is reminiscent of Paul's teaching that we are to bear one another's burdens, yet each is responsible to carry his own load when he is able (Gal. 6:2, 4–5). Its emphasis on hope is also consistent with Scripture's teaching on coping with difficulty (Rom. 5:3–5; James 1:2).

References

Caplan, G. *Principles of preventive psychiatry.* New York: Basic Books, 1964.

Lindemann, E. Symptomatology and management of acute grief. *American Journal of Psychiatry,* 1944, *101,* 141–148.

Additional Reading

Aguilera, D., & Messick, J. *Crisis intervention, theory and methodology* (4th ed.). St. Louis: C. V. Mosby, 1982.

Baldwin, B. A. Crisis intervention: An overview of theory and practice. *The Counseling Psychologist,* 1979, *8* (2), 43–52.

Ewing, C. P. *Crisis intervention as psychotherapy.* New York: Oxford University Press, 1978.

F. J. WHITE

Critical Period. *See* SENSITIVE PERIOD.

Cross-Cultural Psychology. Recent years have seen the growing awareness that the psychology developed mostly in Europe and North America should expand its field to the understanding of other cultures. The interest in Eastern cultures, the rise of economic, political, and cultural influences of the Third World, the impact of refugees, and the need for preparation of missionaries and Peace Corps workers—all have stimulated research in cross-cultural psychology. The publication of the 6-volume *Handbook of Cross-Cultural Psychology* (Triandis et al., 1979–1980) is a reflection of the developments in this field. From a Christian point of view Hesselgrave's *Communicating Christ Cross-Culturally* (Hesselgrave, 1978) is an important work. The domain of cross-cultural psychology is the study of intracultural and intercultural behaviors and experiences of people from different cultures.

Cross-cultural psychology has contributed much toward understanding such issues as the use of tests and research methodologies in different cultures; the correlation between language and thought; the cultural influence on perception, cognition, memory, emotion, and motivation; the developmental factors in different cultures; psychopathology, psychotherapy, and counseling; and issues of social psychology such as organizational psychology, acculturation, values, attitudes, and beliefs. Much of the knowledge acquired has great importance for the Christian pastor, missionary, Bible translator, and lay worker.

Research. Although it is now generally accepted that psychological tests cannot be completely culture free, psychometric instruments have been able to provide valuable information when adapted to the local culture and when the results obtained are interpreted with caution. Issues of valid communication and observer bias are important factors to consider. The controversy between the use of naturalistic versus experimental studies is relatively settled, with an acceptance that each has its appropriate use and the results can complement each other.

There is little hard experimental data in cross-cultural psychology. Manipulating variables in an unfamiliar environment is very difficult, and errors can easily be made. Presently, people working in the applied areas have to rely mainly on the information provided by observation. However, there has been some important research that will be very briefly summarized (see Triandis et al., 1979–1980 for further details on these research areas).

Perception. Ways in which people of different cultures perceive subjective and even objective events are learned, therefore ecologically determined. Also, although the sensory systems are physiologically the same, the degree of reliance upon one system or another is different across cultures. For example, European-originated cultures rely mainly on visual cues, while African cultures rely more upon auditory and kinesthetic cues.

Cognition. The older views differentiating primitive, inferior cultures from superior cultures have been abandoned by most researchers, who now consider cultural differences in cognition to be a diversity in cognitive styles created by varied environmental demands. The fact that youngsters transplanted from one culture to a different one adapt to the new environment and cognitive styles validates this latter approach. People tend to focus their attention on what is most important in their way of life, and in different cultures they associate things in different ways, give different meaning to concepts, and memorize easier what is more familiar to them. Cross-cultural studies on intelligence have begun to consider these factors. While a Bushman may perform poorly on an IQ test, an European or American genius would fail the survival test that Bushmen pass in their environment every day.

Emotion. The nonverbal, facial expression of emotions seems to be universally similar. Anger, disgust, fear, happiness, sadness, and surprise are easily identified in photos by people of different cultures. On the other hand, the degree and form (overtly, covertly, verbally, nonverbally) in which emotions are expressed are different. One dimension that seems to hold across cultures is the affective meaning. Osgood's dimensions of evaluation, potency, and activity account for most human metaphorical meaning (Osgood, Suci, & Tannenbaum, 1957).

Motivation. Such motives as dependency and aggression are universal, yet their strength and form of expression differ with the culture. Even the achievement motive seems to be universal. Its strength seems to depend on the degree to which each culture has a standard of excellence. Its manifestation differs in different cultures.

Aesthetics. Involving perception, aesthetics is culturally bound. Yet the way the aesthetics of one culture penetrates another culture (e.g., the influence of African aesthetics in modern Western art) demonstrates that learning is a significant element in its development. This accounts for why art, music, and literature are such powerful means of cross-cultural communication and even influence. The old-time missionaries who, with great hardships, carried their organs with them to the most remote areas of the world were obviously aware of this.

Developmental psychology. The main motor and mental competencies seem to develop in children in a similar manner in all societies. Small variations exist concerning the age at which they are expressed. In later development it seems that at least the sequence of Piagetian stages and substages is universal. There are strong indications of critical periods for language acquisition, and the ages at which children develop certain abilities is quite similar in all cultures studied so far.

Differences in development have also been reported by some researchers. For instance, African babies have an earlier motor development than European or American babies. In the area of intellectual maturation it seems that the development of acquisition and retrieval strategies are culture-dependent, probably due to differences in training.

Social psychology. The complexity of phenomena covered by social psychology creates additional difficulties for cross-cultural research. Most studies have been directed toward the question of whether results obtained in the United States also hold for other cultures. Topics such as attitudes, beliefs, values, interpersonal relationships, small group behavior, and organizational psychology have been studied. While most results are still insufficiently verified and some data are contradictory, the future is promising and of great value for applied cross-cultural psychology.

Applications. In addition to psychotherapy and counseling, cross-cultural psychology can bring important contributions to fields such as adjustment to a foreign culture, business, tourism, cultural relationships, politics, and Christian missionary activities. Great errors, sometimes with potential catastrophic consequences, can be made if we do not become more aware of cultural differences. For instance, some people in positions involving Soviet-American relationships make the mistake of inferring that the Soviet leadership, raised in and committed to a materialistic dialectic philosophy, thinks the same way and has the same ideals as Americans, whose thinking was shaped mostly by a Protestant-democratic or a humanistic-democratic ideology.

In any cross-cultural interaction the way we are perceived by others, as well as the way we perceive them (whether objective or subjective, true or false), has a great influence upon the relationship. It is essential also to consider that we have to deal with relative rather than absolute perceptions. An American, for instance, will tend to be seen as too loud and talkative by a Japanese and too distant, cold, and uncommunicative by a Latin.

The ability to adjust to a new cultural environment is facilitated by factors such as education, allocentrism (other-centeredness), and flexibility. If we do not have an elementary knowledge of the geography, history, leadership, and heroes of a country we visit, we risk being looked upon as uneducated and may also offend our hosts for whom these issues are important. Allocentrism creates a more favorable condition for the understanding of people who are different from ourselves. Finally, flexibility is required in order to adapt to the new cultural demands.

Communication is the most important factor in cross-cultural relationships. While lack of language mastery is an obvious barrier, the necessary level of this mastery is frequently underestimated. A crash course provides for what is needed in elementary communication but not for becoming an active agent of change, whether in relationships or beliefs. Languages contain subtleties that differ not only from textbook usage but also from subculture to subculture within the same language speaking population. In many societies the knowledge of these subtleties spells the difference between being accepted and trusted, or not. Most cultures are more ethnocentered and emphasize stronger interpersonal relationships than does the more heterogeneous American culture, which is probably the most individualistic among all presently studied societies. In nearly any other society it is more important that one first develops an interpersonal relationship before one proceeds to any other important transaction.

Poor mastery of a language leads to a tendency to take words literally. Our misunderstanding of other cultures can at times be equivalent to the misunderstanding of our culture by a foreigner who takes literally the sports broadcaster saying that team A bombed team B, or that player X was praised for stealing so many bases.

Attention should be paid to the difference in the value of concepts. Americans tend to use the word *friend* much more liberally than most other cultures, who reserve it for what we would call intimate friend. Foreigners, after an initial period of elation produced by the rapidity with which we call them friends, experience a feeling of betrayal and of being deceived because our actions do not reflect the value they give to the concept *friend*. This misunderstanding leads to one of the most frequent and unfortunate conclusions at which many foreigners arrive, that Americans are not loyal and reliable friends. Likewise problems arise from our devaluation through overuse of the word *love*. We love God, our spouse, ideas, and objects. This is very confusing for the foreigner. Similarly, in other cultures we have to be aware of the value of concepts. If we use English in communication, we have to be careful to use the words within the textbook limits and not colloquially.

For missionaries and Bible translators communication is even more complicated. As Nida (1960) points out, they have to communicate an adopted culture (the Christian culture) to a foreign culture in a way that is not distorted by the influence of the missionaries' own culture. They need first to have an active understanding (to the point of being able to communicate it) of the biblical culture, and not only of a Westernized version of it. Secondly, they need a good understanding of the recipient's culture. A close cooperation between local pastors and missionaries is helpful. Care should be taken that locals maintain their culture and not copy Western teachers, borrow Western style, and alienate themselves from their own people.

According to Hesselgrave (1978), in cross-cultural communication a variety of dimensions should be considered: ways of perceiving the world (world views), ways of thinking (cognitive processes), ways of expressing ideas (linguistic forms), ways of acting (behavioral patterns), ways of interacting (social structures), ways of channeling the message (media influence), and ways of deciding (motivational resources).

In presenting the Christian message it is well to start from the point where the audience is. Paul's ministry presents many such examples. For hierarchically structured societies it is beneficial to first address the respected elements in the society (i.e., older people or community leaders). When Moses tried to become the leader of the Jews by directly addressing the grass roots, he failed. Later, when returning from the Midianites, he first contacted Aaron, according to God's command, and was introduced to the leaders. Then the people followed him.

The means through which the message is communicated is also very important. For some societies preaching is much less effective than group discussion in which the people are encouraged to speak, questions are raised, and better answers suggested through Christianity. The knowledge of and sensitivity to the culture of the recipient is the key to message acceptance, or at least to sympathetic and respectful attention given to it.

References

Hesselgrave, D. J. *Communicating Christ cross-culturally.* Grand Rapids: Zondervan, 1978.
Nida, E. A. *Message and mission: The communication of the Christian faith.* New York: Harper, 1960.
Osgood, C. E., Suci, G. J., & Tannenbaum, P. H. *The measurement of meaning.* Urbana: University of Illinois Press, 1957.
Triandis, H. C., et al. (Eds.), *Handbook of cross-cultural psychology.* (6 vols.). Boston: Allyn & Bacon, 1979–1980.

D. MOTET

See CULTURE AND COGNITION.

Cross-Cultural Therapy.

Most therapeutic systems were devised to be used within the European-derived societies. The automatic use of these systems cross-culturally can be counterproductive. The therapist must be aware of differences along dimensions such as dependency versus self-reliance, cooperativeness versus individualism, respect for hierarchy versus equalitarianism and challenge of authority, elder versus youth orientation, submissive versus assertive and activist role of women, and indirect versus direct communication. These differences are expressed consciously or unconsciously, overtly or covertly, and in different degrees, depending upon the person and the strength of traditionalism.

While being sensitive to the individual differences and avoiding stereotypes, the cross-cultural therapist should also be attuned to cultural influences which are especially persistent in members of group-oriented societies. For example, such influences are sometimes present up to the third generation in Japanese-Americans, and may create conflicts with the dominant American cultural elements. To the unaware therapist such conflicts may be misdiagnosed as pathology.

These cultural patterns are even harder to recognize because they do not belong to the present-day foreign culture, but to the one transplanted three generations ago and then transmitted to the descendant. Thus cross-cultural therapists must ideally know not only the present-day foreign culture, but also the changes that have occurred in the last two or three generations, since culture tends to change more slowly in immigrants than in nationals who live in the midst of historical changes in their society. Besides the internal conflict previously mentioned, a second or third-generation American may also have familial conflicts with parents or grandparents who maintain strong elements of the old-country culture.

Cultures Within a Culture. It is important to realize that it is not necessary to travel to another country in order to be involved in cross-cultural therapy. In our pluralistic society much therapy involves cross-cultural elements. Besides the obvious cases of nonresident foreigners, resident aliens, immigrants, and other minorities, are the more subtle cases such as the meeting of subcultures within the same race and nationality. When the parents of a child raised on the East Coast move to the West Coast or the Midwest, the whole family, but especially the child, faces a cross-cultural adjustment. Or when a person raised in the Bronx marries one raised in Manhattan, there is a good chance that cross-cultural problems will emerge. Therapists involved with such families need to be conscious of these cultural influences.

In doing adjustment counseling with immigrants, the encouragement of total rejection of the old culture in an attempt to rapidly "Americanize," is to be avoided. It will seldom succeed and will frequently produce an identity crisis. Neither does the attempt to start by blending elements of both cultures seem advisable. If such a blending is to develop, it is better to let it happen naturally after the immigrant has developed a true biculturalism, being able to function in both the old and the new culture and, aware of the differences, being able to shift from one to another at will. The old culture is needed because it protects the identity and maintains a sense of continuity. This adjustment, through cultural enrichment rather than replacement, also enlarges the horizon of the immigrant. This approach is strongly recommended in the case of temporary sojourners, such as students, in order to reduce the reentry problems.

American Cultural Distinctives. It is important for the cross-cultural therapist to be aware of some main differences between the typical mainstream American culture and other major world cultures. For instance, we tend to stress self-reliance and individualism to the point of considering them an index of mental health. Almost all other cultures value relationships more highly, with a corresponding valuing of reliance upon others, whether family, friends, organizations, or institutions. This means that the cross-cultural therapist must emphasize more strongly than usual the building of relationship in the beginning stages of treatment. Furthermore, the goal of autonomy and independence, so common to much contemporary North American therapy, will need to be modified to reflect the importance placed in most other societies on interdependence.

While we tend to be equalitarian and frequently antagonistic to authority, many other societies are hierarchically organized on the basis of status, rank, or age. In these cultures therapists are more effective if they are rather directive and are perceived as authorities by the patients. However, younger therapists should use this directiveness and authority with deference toward older patients. Similarly, in most foreign countries women are less emancipated yet sometimes more respected than in the United States.

Clinical Implications. In the initial interview the culturally sensitive therapist should ask questions concerning the cultural background of the patient's parents, the cultural environment in which the patient grew up, and cultural bonds and allegiance. Information on the cultural influences and affiliations that may have contributed to the development of personality and life style can provide explanations for many internal and external conflicts. Further, correct diagnosis is facilitated and the most efficient therapeutic approach can be instituted.

Most therapeutic systems require some modifications in order to be used in different cultures. For example, psychoanalysts may encounter difficulties with Orientals, Arabians, and even Latins if the therapist insists in remaining impersonal and detached. Uncovering defense mechanisms may make the patient (especially the Japanese male) feel that he is losing face and therefore forced to quit therapy. With Latins, Arabians, and to a certain extent Filipinos, therapists should refrain from labeling the cultural tendency to debate issues as intellectualization or defensiveness. Such factors as these require fine-tuning of the traditional psychoanalytic technique.

Client-centered therapists find that people from many other cultures often lack the patience and tolerance for the therapist's apparent inactivity necessary for work within this approach. Reflection of feeling and insistence that the clients express deeper and deeper feelings can be efficient with Latin, Arabian, and even Polynesian patients. However, it may alienate Japanese and Southeast Asians, who would respond better to initial focusing on behavior and physical symptoms rather than on feeling.

Behavior therapy appears generally suitable in all cultures. However, the choice of reinforcement must be made carefully. For example, there are cultures in which the social reinforcements are very efficient, while a token economy would be considered outright offensive.

Whichever specific therapeutic approach is used, the Christian therapist has an advantage when working with a Christian patient of any origin. Regardless of their cultures of origin, they now have a common culture as a basis for relating—Christianity. With a common system of values and beliefs, the relationship and trust are more easily established. Similarly, they have at their disposal mutually acceptable ways of dealing with guilt, meaninglessness, hopelessness, and despair.

Additional Readings

Marsella, A. J., & Pedersen, P. B. (Eds.). *Cross-cultural counseling and psychotherapy.* New York: Pergamon Press, 1981.

McGoldrick, M., Pearce, J. K., & Giordano, J. (Eds.). *Ethnicity and family therapy.* New York: Guilford Press, 1982.

Pedersen, P. B., Draguns, J. G., Lonner, W. J., & Trimble, J. (Eds.). *Counseling across cultures* (2nd ed.). Honolulu: University Press of Hawaii, 1980.

Walz, G. R., & Benjamin, L. (Eds.). *Transcultural counseling: Needs, programs, and techniques.* New York: Human Sciences Press, 1978.

D. Motet

Cross Dressing. *See* Transvestism.

Cults. Religious cults are not a new phenomenon on the human scene. Since 1965, however, there seems to have been an upsurge in the growth of new religious movements, aberrational Christian groups, and so-called mass therapies or self-improvement cults. Although most of these cultic movements have emerged in the West, many of them have been heavily influenced by an Eastern/mystical/occult world view. This is true not only of the specifically religious movements but also of those groups which claim to be nonreligious in nature and whose stated objective is human transformation or the realization of human potential.

The definition of the term *cult* depends largely on the frame of reference of the definer. Most definitions stress the unconventional and nonnormative dimensions of the word. There is usually negative connotation and stigma associated with its usage. Most cults are groups that are outside the mainstream of the prevailing, established religious tradition of any given society. Cult members view themselves as a minority group who share a common vision and who are dedicated to some person, ideology, or cause. Traditional churches are generally considered to be culture-accepting organizations whereas cults tend to avoid accommodation to the dominant social realities and are, in fact, culture rejecting. The degree to which they are separatist in orientation varies from group to group. They are often targets of suspicion and distrust.

A psychosocial approach to cults includes a consideration of group dynamics (especially leader-follower roles), recruitment and indoctrination practices, the assumption by a member of a new identity and its management by the group, and the various methods of ego destruction and thought control which characterize the more extreme cultic groups.

A theological approach to the identification of a cult focuses on the group's belief system and its relation to a standard of Christian orthodoxy. From this perspective a cult is a religious movement which has doctrines and/or practices that are in conflict with the teachings of biblical Christianity as represented by the major Catholic and Protestant denominations. Primary focus is on issues of truth and error as theologically defined.

Cult Membership: Predisposing Factors. Any serious consideration of cult dynamics must include an examination of the reasons why people are attracted to cults and what factors make some people more vulnerable to cultic involvement than others. While there is always a danger in generalizing, the existing literature—both popular and professional—suggests that certain patterns characterize the recruitment/joining process.

The target population for most recruitment efforts by the newer cults is the age bracket 18–28. Persons in this age grouping are frequently experiencing changes in their life situations and are in various stages of transition. They may be between high school and college, between college and career, or between love affairs. They may be the victims of other forms of situational contingencies that increase their vulnerability.

Cult recruits are usually normal people who are experiencing specific and transitory difficulties in life. They may be disenchanted with a sociopolitical cause, or suffering from academic frustration, or encountering career uncertainty or job dissatisfaction. There may be a recent history of disruption in relationships, such as a breakup with a boyfriend/girlfriend or spouse, or a troubling relationship with a parent.

Unlike the typical member profile of cults from the past, those who are joining the newer cults and self-improvement groups are more highly educated and tend to come from middle- and upper-middle-class surroundings. Few racial and ethnic minorities (with the exception of Jews) are found in the new cults. Rather than coming from the margins of society, the typical cult recruit today is from the white, affluent suburbs.

Prospective cult members are also individuals who can be characterized as seekers—people who are searching for religious experiences and for truth. Typically, the person who joins a cult has a very nominal religious background or no religious background at all. The fulfilling of perceived spiritual needs is an obvious component in the decision to explore alternative religious options. Those individuals who are attracted to aberrational Christian groups frequently are young Christians lacking in discernment skills or members of evangelical churches who become dissatisfied or disillusioned with their traditional church life.

There are also emotional and interpersonal factors which predispose some people to cult membership. Among the converts to cults are those individuals who show some evidence of developmental and emotional problems over a period of time. Frequently this type of recruit also has experienced some kind of disjuncture in family relations, such as conflict with parents.

Sometimes the decision to join a cult reflects a need to escape the family. Some clinicians who have worked with ex-cult members report a family background pattern that includes a passive father and a relatively domineering mother, or parents who are overly possessive and protective.

Cults appeal to persons who are experiencing a sense of personal inadequacy, loneliness, or disappointment with life in general. There are also those individuals who exhibit strong dependency needs and who are attracted to the more totalistic and communal groups. The cultic milieu thus becomes a haven of security where decision making is minimal and life's basic necessities are provided. Contact with the larger society is regulated and the demands of conventional existence can be bypassed or at least deferred.

Cults also appeal to people who have a strongly idealistic orientation. Such people are sincerely desirous of being a part of a group or organization which is focused on change—personal transformation or societal change. To join such a group is to affiliate with a cause, to become linked with a network of true believers who are determined to achieve their objectives. In the process any individual goals that may have been present merge with or are transcended by the goals of the group.

Commitment Mechanisms. Among the most significant psychological dynamics at work in the cultic milieu are the various commitment mechanisms which help bind members to the group and which militate against easy departure from the cult.

Most cultic organizations exercise control over members by requiring total loyalty to the group, its particular ideology, and its leadership. Unquestioning loyalty can result in forms of unhealthy commitment, in fanatical commitment. Often legitimate and acceptable biblical concepts such as loyalty and commitment are completely redefined and distorted to suit the needs of the leadership.

Another effective commitment mechanism involves the suspension of supportive ties with the member's precult life, a severing of ties with families, friends, and all other familiar social support networks. There is a dying to the past, a conscious distancing of oneself from the "outside" world and its attendant evils. There may well be a requirement to surrender one's personal and material resources to the group out of a sense of devotion to the cause.

Themes of sacrifice and investment pervade the cultic life style. There is frequently a willingness to forsake family, education, or career in order to advance the objectives of the group. Whether the decision to invest all of one's energy (and material resources) in the group is a decision freely entered into is a matter of controversy. Critics contend that informed consent is not always fully operative in totalistic cults and that considerable psychological and spiritual pressure is exerted on members to be committed to the group to a point beyond what is normative for conventional religious organizations. The demands for zealous commitment, as evidenced by interrupted life patterns, are a major focus of concern for parents and other observers critical of the manipulative aspects of cult existence.

A related pattern seen in many cults and aberrational Christian groups is the tendency to adopt a simple, often austere life style. While this is not an inherently negative characteristic, it is often accompanied by a whole syndrome of drastic life changes which, viewed as a whole, represent a radical and unconventional shift from the expectations of the larger society and give substance to the sometimes bizarre image of cultic groups. Various cultural insignia such as specialized clothing styles, speech patterns, cosmetics, and other identifying symbols help set off the group from more traditional religious groups.

Fervent commitment to the group is also enhanced by a deliberate devaluing of the individual in favor of the group. Drastic personality shifts are often observed in individuals who become involved with cults. The person tends to be more rigid and less autonomous. The individual personality is submerged in the group and a collective/communal orientation predominates. Life's basic necessities as well as one's emotional needs are met within the group. The imagery of the family is evident and recognized. A new "spiritual" family often replaces the natural family. Cult leaders assume the role of surrogate parents.

Along with the adoption of a new life style and the acquisition of a new identity there is the assumption of a radically new world view. Ideological conversion, however, usually is secondary to the gratification of basic human needs represented by the act of joining. In short, most individuals are attracted to cultic groups because of the need for acceptance, community, fellowship, a sense of belonging, a need for purpose and direction rather than by the particular ideological propaganda of the group. Cults are successful because they meet human needs. Conversion to the ideological position of the group follows the decision to join, and the indoctrination process is often gradual.

The nature and scope of the indoctrination process varies from group to group. Some cults have rather elaborate theological systems; others are unsophisticated in this area. In any event, indoctrination is almost always wedded to elitist thinking: we alone possess the truth. Such thinking reinforces other aspects of cult life which emphasize an exclusiveness, a separateness, demarcating the group from unenlightened outsiders.

A crucial dimension of transformation and commitment is the process by which the human will is subverted. This mechanism is also related to a strong sense of group identification. It involves submission to the leadership and to the belief system of the group.

There is considerable debate among scholars and other observers as to whether the subjugation of the individual member's will to the requisites of the cult involves the loss (or diminishment) of personal autonomy. Cult critics maintain that, especially in the more totalistic groups, members' ability to think for themselves and to make independent decisions is impaired.

Cult defenders claim that allegations of brainwashing and thought control leveled at new religious movements are questionable and unfounded. Scholars are divided as to whether such charges are substantiated in the professional literature. Concepts of brainwashing and mind control are said to be vague and elusive. Some observers maintain that whatever manipulative techniques may be present in the controversial groups are simply extensions of basic principles of psychological conditioning and group dynamics. The changes that are often reported in the behavior of cult members are seen by these observers as the result of manipulated attitude adjustment rather than the effect of coercive persuasion.

Leadership Dynamics. Many feel that the most crucial factor in any approach to the psychology of cults is the role played by leaders. In the newer cultic movements as well as in the cults of the past there is always a single, living person (usually male) who is the founder/leader of the group and who occupies a position of respect and prominence within the organization. Almost without exception cult leaders are highly authoritarian and extract from their followers a loyalty and devotion that are probably due to a combination of awe, charisma, and psychospiritual intimidation.

Controversy surrounds the assorted gurus and self-appointed messiahs who represent the motivating force behind all cults. Existing evidence suggests that the leaders of most cults and aberrational Christian groups are strong-willed individualists. They frequently are ecclesiastical loners who find it difficult to conform to established, traditional religious systems and who therefore found groups that tend to be spiritually elitist and culture rejecting. Many of the leaders and their followers also tend to be very conservative in their sociopolitical leanings.

Similarly, there is some evidence to indicate that charismatic cult leaders are insecure individuals who need to exercise power over people and who find it easier to do so within a tightly structured environment. There is some debate as to whether their motives include any or all of the following: the exploitation of members for financial gain; political ambition; ego need for recognition and acceptance; genuine religious conviction that their own role is central to truth and the unfolding of history; the building of self-serving religious empires.

Cult critics claim that leaders use fear, intimidation, and guilt to control members' lives. In extreme cases physical punishment is employed as a sanction and control mechanism. The degree to which leaders are able to exercise control and directly impact individual members' lives varies from group to group.

There are those who argue that cult leaders exhibit varying degrees of psychopathology, particularly paranoia. The latter trait is linked with the frequent assertion by leaders that they and their movements are targets of attack and persecution by the media, parents, governmental agencies, and anticult activists.

In some cultic organizations the leader is granted special sexual access to the membership. Such access is either explicitly sanctioned by the group and its teachings or looked upon with indifference or resignation. Besides the sexual and material benefits that accrue to the role of leader, there are ego needs that are satisfied by virtue of the special status accorded leaders, not the least of which is the realization that one is recognized as a spiritual master, a religious pioneer, even a messianic figure. In most instances cult leaders sincerely believe in their spiritual mission. From their perspective, and certainly from the perspective of their loyal followers, they are not charlatans.

Postcult Adjustment. Most cults employ highly sophisticated techniques for inducing behavioral change and conversion to their ideological systems. The life situation of most cult members is all-encompassing and highly intense. It therefore follows that the period following separation from the cult is often traumatic and unsettling. Sensitivity to the special problems of former members is especially needed by helping professionals who might be called on for counseling.

The early transition period following the cult experience is frequently characterized by episodes of depression and feelings of confusion. There is often uncertainty and indecisiveness regarding the future and feelings of anger and embarrassment about the past. Ex-members should be encouraged to sort things out regarding their cultic involvment. They need to understand their particular vulnerabilities and that they were not abnormal or "strange" because of their entry into a cult experience.

Depending on the particular person and

specific cult involved, a considerable amount of time may be required for the process of resocialization following exit from an extremist cult. Opportunity should be made available for persons to rest, reflect on their experience, and reconnect with old friends as well as family members. Unresolved problems that may have precipitated entrance into the cult will have to be confronted.

Leaving a cult is like leaving the bosom of a family. Friends and meaningful experiences will be left behind. New friendships will have to be formed. Difficulties in decision making may be anticipated. Former cult members need to understand that family and friends will be watching them, looking for signals that might indicate a desire to slip back into the security of cult days. The cult veteran as well as relatives and friends will need encouragement and assistance in handling the difficult postcult period. Outsiders need to recognize that not all that happened in the cult was negative; former members may, in fact, want to recount some of their positive memories.

The reconstruction activity following the cult experience is incomplete if it fails to deal with the spiritual vacuum resulting from the exit from the group. The Christian counselor should be especially sensitive to the possibility of "spiritual burnout" that frequently characterizes the ex-member. A relationship of trust must be established in view of the likelihood of extreme distrust of religious authority of any kind. The individual therapist, like the Christian church at large, must be an agent of healing, restoration, and reconciliation.

Additional Readings
Appel, W. *Cults in America: Programmed for paradise.* New York: Holt, Rinehart & Winston, 1983.
Enroth, R. *Youth, brainwashing and the extremist cults.* Grand Rapids: Zondervan, 1977.
Enroth, R. *The lure of the cults.* Chappaqua, N.Y.: Christian Herald Books, 1979.
Enroth, R. (Ed.). *A guide to cults and new religions.* Downers Grove, Ill.: Inter-Varsity Press, 1983.
Stoner, C., & Parke, J. *All god's children.* Radnor, Pa.: Chilton, 1977.

R. Enroth

See BRAINWASHING.

Culture and Cognition. The search for human universals is a task with significance for theory and practice. Theories generated from data of a single culture must be verified cross-culturally or our theoretical assumptions may in fact be localized phenomena. The increasing interaction and interdependence of people from vastly different cultures add practical urgency to the study of culture and its effect on cognition.

Historical Development. Psychologists and anthropologists have long been interested in cross-cultural cognitive differences. In 1899 a study team went to Torres Straits Islands to conduct comparative studies on the perception and memory of primitive people. Some of the findings showed that the natives had better sensory functions than did their European counterparts, but had less facility in abstract functions. In attempting to explain the differences the researchers suggested that highly developed sensory functions focus predominant attention on concrete things and may act as an obstacle to higher abstract mental development (Rivers, 1901, p. 45). The issue was, "Why do non-Western people seem to think differently from Western people?" The debate centered around causes of differences and similarities between human beings in different cultural settings.

Boas (1911) wrote that the laws of mental activity are the same for all people, but the manifestations of the mind depend on individual experience. Both Western and non-Western thought patterns are useful for understanding the world. Both systems can find unity in a world of seeming diversity, and both use an interplay of theory and common sense. Wundt (1916) argued that though intellectual potential is the same for all mankind, the intellectual capacities of primitive people have remained on a low plane because of isolation, few environmental pressures, and the limited nature of their wants.

Levy-Bruhl, in his books, *How Natives Think* (1926) and *Primitive Mentality* (1923), argued that both mental preferences and mental competencies of primitive people were different from those of people in more advanced cultures. He gathered data by looking at "collective representations" or systems of belief among primitive societies. He concluded that "primitives perceive nothing in the same way as we do" (1926, p. 43). He further stated that primitives are prelogical, mystical, and entwined with emotional life. They are at a lower evolutionary stage of cultural development. Boas (1911) disagreed with Levy-Bruhl, both in the methodology and in the findings of his study.

Levi-Strauss (1966) studied indigenous categorizing systems of non-Western societies and concluded that differences in systems were the result of different problem-solving needs. He found that primitives used both complexive and superordinate rules in classifying animals and that they often classified people into hierarchical totem groups and subgroups. He discovered that primitive classification systems were based on characteristics that were easily seen and experienced, in contrast to the classification systems of modern science which focus on necessary relationships in the structure of objects. Levi-Strauss assumed a basic human unity, with differences explained in terms of different needs in problem solving.

Cognitive Development. Piaget (1966) stressed the need for and significance of cross-cultural studies to test his theories of cognitive development. According to Piaget, four important factors affect cognitive development: 1) biological or epigenetic systems, 2) equilibration or autoregulation factors, 3) social and interpersonal factors, and 4) educational and cultural factors. It is impossible to test Piaget's theory of development without cross-cultural studies. Piaget summarized the findings of cross-cultural studies and concluded that the order of stages in cognitive development was the same in all cultures and was thus biologically controlled. The rate of development appeared to be dependent on social, educational, or cultural factors. He commented that there was a need for cross-cultural studies which would measure formal operational thinking, since in many cultures there does not seem to be much progress beyond the level of concrete operations.

Dasen (1972) presented a summary of cross-cultural Piagetian research that appeared to verify the sequential order of the stages of development. He identified several factors that seem to interact to influence the rate of development: test materials, urban-rural differences, schooling, European contact, and nutrition. His studies also showed that one cannot assume that adults of all societies reach concrete operational thinking or formal operational thinking. Piaget (1972) recognized the importance of relevant experience when he admitted that adults may reach the formal operations stage only in the specialized areas of their aptitudes and professional specialization. The development of formal structures may be more closely related to cultural factors than to biological factors.

In summary, Piagetian cross-cultural research indicates that whatever stages are achieved are usually developed in the same sequence and may be tied to genetic patterns or potentialities for development. But environmental factors appear to limit or promote both the rate and the limits of the developmental process. No single environmental factor has consistently been shown to determine cognitive development.

Brunner developed several hypotheses on cognitive development which have been tested in many parts of the world (Greenfield & Brunner, 1966). He argued that the stages of development are seen in the manner in which the child represents reality, or events. Young children represent the world through actions (i.e., an enactive mode). Next they progress to an ikonic or picture representation stage, and finally to the symbolic stage. There are two kinds of pushes toward growth, the internal and biological unfoldings and the external or cultural amplifiers.

Language is the most important tool for promoting cognitive development. Language provides the "temptation" to form concepts. Grammatical structures encourage hierarchical structures of experiences. Words can be used to hypothetically change the real world, which encourages symbolic modes of representation.

Cognitive Style. A large and growing body of cross-cultural literature is emerging from studies on cognitive style by Witkin (1967). Results of his studies on development factors in cognitive style support some of the Piagetian cross-cultural studies. Witkin developed and verified several hypotheses through research conducted around the world. He described cognitive style as a stable, self-consistent mode of intellectual functioning that is organismic, developmental, and related to age and the socialization process.

Variables which interact to either promote or hinder the developmental process are parental, societal, ecological, and nutritional. For example, mothers in a Temne society are authoritarian, and societal structures are tight and well-defined, thus not encouraging the development of the child's articulated cognitive style. Factors which promote development of articulated cognitive style in a child are mothers who have developed an articulated body concept, mothers who punish consistently and less harshly, tribal structures that are less dominating, a balanced diet, and an occupation such as hunting, cattle herding, or sailing (in that these encourage individual mental resourcefulness). Schooling is often an important variable in the development of an articulated and differentiated cognitive style.

Witkin argued that both global and articulated cognitive styles may be adaptations to social needs. Thus one cannot make a value judgment as to which is better. Global, or field-dependent, styles have a social orientation that is more sensitive to the needs of group members, while the orientation of articulated, or field-independent, styles is more impersonal. Possibly there is a need for the global style when one lives in close contact with many people and a need for an articulated style when one must make independent decisions in order to survive.

Cognitive Differences or Deficits. Typically, anthropologists do descriptive studies that provide insights into events in a society, but they do little to investigate internal cognitive structures. Psychologists, on the other hand, provide insights into internal cognitive structures but pay little attention to everyday manifestations of cognitive development in a given culture. Cole and Schribner (1974) did much to bridge the gap between psychology and anthropology. After ethnographic studies among the Kpelle of Liberia, Cole (1975) concluded that 1) all people can carry out complex mental tasks: 2) people are good at the kinds of tasks they do most often; 3) cross-cultural measurement techniques do not measure cognitive process, only cultural skills.

For example, Cole contrasted the effective, though subtle, interpersonal communications among the Kpelle with their poor, seemingly egocentric performance on a stick description task. He concluded that the test was not measuring the cognitive process but was merely measuring the cultural skill of stick description. Cole is eager to disprove the deficit theory of cognitive development, which resulted from the difficulty researchers have encountered in attempting to design instruments. Differences do not mean deficits (Cole & Bruner, 1971). Cole believes that persons in all cultures have equal potential for cognitive capacity, whereas differences in cognitive preferences are explained in terms of the needs, interests, and values of the particular culture. Traditional peoples apply complex cognitive skills in social situations but fail to use them in an experimental task. Studies of cognitive development need to take into account the situational variations in which the cognitive process is manifested.

Berry (1976), a cultural relativist and a developmentalist, emphasizes the appropriateness of adaptation. The goal of cognitive development is not to reach the "highest" stage of development but to achieve the most appropriate stage for the natural and cultural environment. Empirical data may show a consistent order of development, but that does not mean that each individual in each society should always move in that direction.

Current Trends in Research. Early research in cognitive development hypothesized that developmental structures would be the same in all cultures. Findings in cross-cultural studies generally showed the same sequence of development as in European children. However, differences were found in the rate of development. In some cultures a high percentage of adults do not seem to reach concrete operational thought, and in a few cultures no adults used formal operational thinking (Dasen, 1972).

The similarities and differences in markedly different cultures led researchers to investigate the possibility of universal cognitive structures with cultural differences influencing the rate and end point of development. The search for an explanation of differences led away from descriptive research to a quasi-experimental search for independent variables. De Lacey (1970) investigated the influence of the social and physical environment on mental development. Findings demonstrated a relationship between contact with European-enriched environment and optimal cognitive development.

Other studies investigated the relationship of schooling and literacy to cognitive development and cognitive style. Relationships have also been studied between urban/rural differences, social class, linguistic differences, degree of industrialization, nutrition, occupation, child-rearing techniques, tightness of social control, and the level of cognitive functioning.

Recent studies have become more experimental, more tightly controlling the independent variables. Such studies are beginning to hypothesize relationships between appropriate teaching styles, curriculum materials, and cognitive development. For example, Mackie (1983) explored the relationship between the type of sociocognitive conflict in children and increased ability to conserve space. The implications of this study have practical significance for the classroom.

Research questions began with a descriptive analysis of the applicability of the theories to other cultures. Studies then investigated factors correlated with differences. Now researchers are investigating cause-and-effect relationships to either better match curriculum with cognitive style or to better promote cognitive development.

Distinctive Issues from a Christian Perspective. An unresolved question is, Should we adapt our teaching or counseling to culturally appropriate cognitive styles, or should we attempt to foster higher levels of cognitive development? We cannot answer the question of whether differences are deficiencies until we ask a basic question. How does cognition relate to our assumptions about the nature of persons?

Many Christians see the basic purpose in life being to glorify God and enjoy him forever. We might assume that Christians who are more spiritually mature would be better able to glorify God. Are Christians with an articulated cognitive style and the ability to do formal operational thinking more capable of glorifying God? The answer is unclear, but very significant. It may seem that there is no relationship between cognitive development and spiritual maturity. Yet large amounts of Scripture cannot be properly understood from a concrete operations, or immature cognitive developmental, perspective. Perhaps then there is a relationship between the understanding of Scripture and spiritual development.

Kohlberg's studies in the growth of moral reasoning and Fowler's faith development studies hypothesize that cognitive development is necessary but not sufficent for the development of moral reasoning and higher stages of faith. It seems that God would be more pleased when people glorify him and trust him for higher moral reasons. A person at a lower level of reasoning might love God out of fear of punishment. A person at a higher level of reasoning might love God not for what he might receive for such love, but because of a deeper abstract understanding of the holiness, justice, and goodness of God.

Levels of human development are only one dimension of the nature of persons. Physical, social, cognitive, ego, and moral development may be interrelated and may be similar processes for all human beings from all cultures, Christian or non-Christian. Human development is not an adequate factor in our ability to glorify God. If human development is seen as a horizontal continuum, trust in God may be a vertical continuum, making a matrix. Children may be adequately glorifying God at a lower level of human development. Adults capable of a higher level of cognitive functioning may not be adequately bringing glory to God if they continue to function at a child's level of cognitive development.

Such a concept does not answer the question of the goodness or badness of cultural deficits, but it does allow for cultural relativity in cognitive functioning. Cultures could be different in their cognitive functioning and equally pleasing to God. Because we believe that God made all people, we are not surprised by cross-cultural universals of cognition. And because of the effects of sin, we are not surprised with differences of functioning affected by environmental pressures and social interactions. While it is helpful and necessary to study the effects of culture on cognition, Christians need to see the study of human development as only one set of factors relating to spiritual development.

References
Berry, J. W. *Human ecology and cognitive style.* New York: Halsted Press, 1976.
Boas, F. *The mind of primitive man.* New York: Macmillan, 1911.
Cole, M. An ethnographic psychology of cognition. In R. W. Brislin, S. Bochner, & W. J. Lonner (Eds.), *Cross cultural perspectives on learning.* New York: Halsted Press, 1975.
Cole, M., & Bruner, J. S. Cultural differences and inferences about psychological process. *American Psychologist,* 1971, *26,* 867–876.
Cole, M., & Schribner, S. *Culture and thought: A psychological introduction.* New York: Wiley, 1974.
Dasen, P. R. Cross-cultural Piagetian research: A summary. *Journal of Cross-Cultural Psychology,* 1972, *3,* 23–39.
De Lacey, P. R. A cross cultural study of classificatory ability in Australia. *Journal of Cross-Cultural Psychology,* 1970, *1,* 293–304.
Greenfield, P. M., & Bruner, J. S. Culture and cognitive growth. *International Journal of Psychology,* 1966, *1*(2), 89–107.
Levi-Strauss, C. *The savage mind.* Chicago: University of Chicago Press, 1966.
Levy-Bruhl, L. *Primitive mentality.* New York: Macmillan, 1923.
Levy-Bruhl, L. *How natives think.* London: Allen & Unwin, 1926.
Mackie, D. The effect of social interaction on conservation of spatial relations. *Journal of Cross-Cultural Psychology,* 1983, *14,* 131–151.
Piaget, J. Need and significance of cross-cultural studies in genetic psychology. *International Journal of Psychology,* 1966, *1*(1), 3–13.
Piaget, J. Intellectual evolution from adolescence to adulthood. *Human Development,* 1972, *15,* 1–12.
Rivers, W. H. R. Introduction and vision. In A. C. Haddon (Ed.), *Report of the Cambridge Anthropological Expedition to the Torres Straits,* (Vol. 2). Cambridge: Cambridge University Press, 1901.
Witkin, H. A. Cognitive styles across cultures. *International Journal of Psychology.* 1967, *2,* 233–250.
Wandt, W. *Elements of Folk psychology.* London: Allen & Unwin, 1916.

J. E. PLUEDDEMANN

See COGNITION; COGNITIVE DEVELOPMENT.

Culture and Psychopathology. The main objective of the study of culture and psychopathology is reflected in the following questions which have dominated research in this area: Are concepts of mental illness and the Western system of psychiatric diagnosis universal and applicable to other cultures? Are the incidence of mental illness and its symptoms the same across cultures? Are there culture-bound syndromes? If culture-bound syndromes do exist, are they the same type of syndromes familiar to Western psychiatrists but expressed differently, or do they represent different psychiatric entities? Answers to these questions are important to one's understanding of the etiology of psychopathology, particularly the relative influence of genetic and environmental factors in different cultural contexts. If psychopathology is found all over the world, this would support the view that it is part of human nature and cannot be eliminated in any human society. However, finding psychopathology in some cultures but not in others would suggest that it is culture-bound rather than an inevitable factor of human existence.

Proponents of the medical view of psychopathology believe that mental disorders are universal and their rates are the same in quite dissimilar cultures. Early in this century Kraepelin, the father of modern psychiatry, traveled to Southeast Asia and to other parts of the world to observe the incidence of mental illness across cultures. He reported that mental disorders known in the West, such as dementia praecox (his term for schizophrenia) and manic-depressive illness, do exist in non-Western countries. More recently, Berne found striking similarities among patients in mental hospitals he visited in several African countries, North America, and Australia. He concluded that "clinically, differences can be treated as mere dialects or accents of a common language; the Italian schizophrenic speaks schizophrenic with an Italian accent; the Siamese manic speaks manic with a Siamese accent" (Berne, 1959, p. 108). Murphy (1976) reported community studies of the rates of mental illness among Canadian villagers (18%), the Eskimos (19%), and members of the Yoruba tribe in Nigeria (15%) in order to demonstrate similarity in the rates of psychopathology despite wide differences between these cultures.

In contrast to the medical concept, the cultural approach accepts the concept of cultural relativity as a guide for research. Cultural relativity implies that each culture has its own mental disorders, and normality and abnormality are defined within a specific social and cultural context. The classical version of this approach was expressed in the 1930s by the anthropologist Ruth Benedict, who suggested that what is regarded as abnormal in one culture may be considered as normal or may constitute highly desired behavior in another culture. Whereas psychiatrists believe that the diagnostic system of mental disorders can be universally applied regardless of culture, the cultural relativists, who are mainly anthropologists, emphasize that diagnosis should not be divorced from understanding the habits and beliefs of the group, and that psychopathology should be viewed within a social system.

One notion that became popular among proponents of the cultural approach is that only complex Euro-American cultures cause serious mental illness; uncomplicated "primitive" cultures produce no neuroses or psychoses. It is implied that advances in civilization increase tension as well as the rates of mental illness. An early example of this notion was expressed by the "nature cult" of the eighteenth century, which attributed the increase of insanity in Europe to a degeneration from a golden age of natural virtue, and which idealized the Noble Savage who was in previous generations free of greed, egotism, envy, and the like. The concept of the Noble Savage in the study of culture and psychopathology is consistent with anthropological reports in the 1920s and 30s—e.g., the well-adjusted Trobriand Islanders described by Malinowski and the contrast between the carefree Samoan adolescents and the storm-and-stress of European and American youth made by Mead. In *Civilization and Its Discontents*, published in 1930, Freud conceptualized neurosis as the result of a conflict between instincts and the repressive processes of civilization: individuals are better off in a simpler culture with fewer restrictions on their instincts. A survey of cross-cultural research by Benedict and Jack (1954) does not support the hypothesis that a non-Western life style provides an immunity against mental illness; the major psychoses occur in all human societies.

An intermediate position between the medical and the cultural approaches suggests that psychopathology is comparable across cultures, but it is also variable in its incidence and expression. Both common cross-cultural patterns and local cultural differences in psychiatric syndromes coexist. This position is well demonstrated by Edgerton (1966) in a study of four East African tribes. He found considerable agreement among the four tribes in the conception of psychosis. Their conception of psychosis was also much similar to that in the West, but there were some differences. Going naked was considered an aspect of psychotic behavior by the East African tribes; murder, attempted murder, or serious assault were emphasized more than in the West. However, hallucinations, which are basic to the diagnosis of psychosis in the West, were seldom mentioned as aspects of psychotic behavior.

The following sections discuss the influence of culture on depression and schizophrenia, two major diagnostic psychiatric categories which are well established on a worldwide basis. Culture-bound syndromes which are expressed quite differently from traditional psychiatric syndromes are also discussed.

Depression. Early studies suggest that true depression is rare or even nonexistent in some parts of Africa and Asia; if the disorder occurs, it tends to be relatively mild, with a short duration and no guilt feelings or suicide. Recent studies, however, suggest that true depression in non-Western patients may appear in some other form; for example, patients may emphasize the physical aspects of their trouble to such an extent that they would not see a psychiatrist, or if seen by a psychiatrist, their condition may be considered a physical rather than a depressive illness. Later studies, in fact, reported high rates of depression among non-Western patients. Depression is found to be the most common mental illness among women who seek help in shrines in rural Ghana. Leighton et al. (1963) compared the results of two field surveys of depression using the same procedure in Nigeria and Canada; depressive symptoms were about four times more common among the Nigerian sample than among the Canadian sample.

An opinion survey of psychiatrists in 30 countries reveals that depression is present in widely different cultures. The survey indicates that the most common form of depressive illness includes the following symptoms: a mood of depression or dejection, diurnal mood change (e.g., more depressed in the morning than in the evening), insomnia with early morning waking, diminution of interest in the social environment, and fatigue. Other symptoms seem to be less frequent in some cultures: weight loss (Scandinavia), despondency and hopelessness (West Africa), and loss of sexual interest (Japan). Self-depreciation and guilt feelings were reported as the most frequent among devout Roman Catholic communities and rare among Moslems and Hindus, but it is unclear from the data whether the association is truly with Christian belief or with modern European civilization.

Other attempts to find links between religion and depression were inconclusive. For example, a higher prevalence of depression in Jews than in Christians was found in hospital admissions in New York, but studies in Israel did not reveal such a trend. Eaton and Weil (1955) found higher rates of depressive illness with guilt feelings among the Hutterites, but

patriarchal family structure and community pressure on the individual rather than religious beliefs are felt to be contributory factors to the development of both depression and guilt feelings. However, religious beliefs may influence both the conception and treatment of depression among the Hutterites. Symptoms of depression are not considered as an illness but as a socially patterned expression called _anfechtung_, meaning "temptation by the devil"; the victims are suffering because they have sinned and questioned basic religious beliefs. Confession is expected to restore the patient to God's favor. The Hutterite way of life seems to provide an atmosphere within which emotionally disturbed members are encouraged to function within the limits of their handicaps, thus avoiding the negative effects of institutionalization (such as extreme social withdrawal and mental deterioration).

Schizophrenia. Studies by anthropologists suggest that chronic psychosis and schizophrenia are rare or even absent among some tribes, but these reports are based on small populations. Studies of large samples of communities report schizophrenia everywhere. However, some groups tend to have unusually high rates of schizophrenia (Republic of Ireland, Croatia in the northwestern corner of Yugoslavia, the Singapore Indians, certain tribes in Ghana and Liberia), whereas others tend to have low rates (the Hutterites, some Pacific islands). Torrey (1980) undertook extensive research to gather support for the view that schizophrenia is a disease of civilization. He reported that studies in India in the 1930s indicated greater prevalence among highly educated and/or Westernized castes such as Anglo-Indians, Parsees, and the educated section of the Hindus and Moslems. Schizophrenic patients were also found to be much more common in regions in Africa which had more missions, schools, and towns.

Cultural variation in the prevalence of schizophrenia seems to be well established (for example, 6.2 per 1000 in Ireland vs. 1.0 per 1000 in Tonga in the South Pacific). Are classical symptoms of schizophrenia universal? The International Pilot Study of Schizophrenia carried out by the World Health Organization (WHO, 1973) identified a core of symptoms of schizophrenia in nine countries of Europe, Asia, Africa, and the Americas. The features most characteristic of "typical" schizophrenia are seen to be lack of insight, auditory hallucinations, delusions of reference, and flatness of affect.

Cultural effects on the content of symptoms tend to be superficial and may only reflect secondary features of the disease. For example, some familiarity with European history or Christianity is necessary for arriving at the delusion that one is Napoleon or Christ. A common delusion among Western patients is that of being controlled by rays or electricity, but this is found only among Westernized Africans. Similarly South American Indians who move to the cities develop delusions of radio waves and secret police instead of the more traditional delusions about saints, witchcraft, and jungle spirits. Hospitalized schizophrenic patients are less violent and aggressive in India, Africa, and Japan than in the West. Catatonic rigidity, negativism, and stereotyped behavior are more often reported in India than in other countries. Differences in the contents of symptoms are found among schizophrenics in Western nations: for example, Irish patients show preoccupation with sin and guilt related to sex, but this is not true of Italian patients, who are more emotionally expressive (elation, overtalkativeness, grinning, laughing, assaultiveness).

A diagnostic label like schizophrenia carries a different meaning even to psychiatrists trained in quite similar cultures such as Great Britain and the United States. Cooper et al. (1972) found that identical patients were five times more likely to be diagnosed as schizophrenic by American than by British psychiatrists. American psychiatrists tend to have a broader concept of schizophrenia and see more severe pathology in their patients.

The International Pilot Study of Schizophrenia (WHO, 1979) found that schizophrenia has better outcome in non-Western cultures. Prognosis was more favorable among Nigerian and Indian patients than among British, Czechoslovakian, Danish, and American samples. It is still not known why non-Western patients with the same level of pathology as their Western counterparts recover faster from schizophrenia, but support from social networks such as the extended family and the tolerance of deviance in the culture may facilitate the social recovery of patients.

Culture-bound Syndromes. Some forms of psychopathology tend to appear in some societies but not in others. These culture-bound syndromes demonstrate how myths, thoughts, wishes, and fears of normal members of society are expressed in psychiatric symptoms by the disturbed individual. The Windigo psychosis, for example, takes its name from a mythical man-eating giant which is a source of anxiety for the Algonquin-speaking Indians in northeastern Canada and the Ojibwa Indians of the United States. The person with Windigo psychosis feels himself changing into a Windigo or being possessed by it with an increasing desire to consume human flesh. Isolation and starvation during the winter is a culture-specific source of tension and could explain both the myth of the man-eating Windigo and the desire of disturbed individuals for eating human flesh.

Koro occurs in Chinese and Malayan cultures of South and Southeast Asia. It consists of the experience or perception of the shrinking or retraction of the penis into the body which would eventually result in death. The patient also expresses guilt and anxiety over sexual excesses, particularly masturbation. This syndrome may be linked with cultural preoccupation with masculine sexual potency and with the cultural emphasis on producing heirs in the family.

Waswās is an obsessive compulsive behavior that is associated with the Islamic rituals of cleansing and prayer, which are particularly important in the religious practices of Islam. The sufferer from waswās finds it difficult to terminate the ablution because he is afraid that he is not yet clean enough to carry out the prayer; or he may repeat the introductory invocations and the raising of arms many times because of doubts of not being fully concentrated on the worship of God. At the end of the prayer he may have doubts about whether he has carried out the ritual correctly, and thus repeats the prayer over and over again. In the Moslem world waswās is not considered a deviance, but only an individual peculiarity; the waswās victim is respected because of his meticulousness in religious matters.

Windigo, koro, waswās, and many other culture-bound syndromes are considered by some researchers as atypical forms of psychosis or neurosis, even though they are different from these mental illnesses in their symptoms, causes, and outcomes. The exotic culture-bound features of syndromes should provide a striking example of the plasticity of psychopathology as known in the West.

References

Benedict, P. K., & Jack, I. Mental illness in primitive societies. *Psychiatry,* 1954, *17*, 377–389.

Berne, E. Difficulties of comparative psychiatry. *American Journal of Psychiatry,* 1959, *116*, 104–109.

Cooper, J. E., Kendell, R. E., Gurland, B. J., Sharpe, L., Copeland, J. R. M., & Simon, R. *Psychiatric diagnosis in New York and London.* New York: Oxford University Press, 1972.

Eaton, J., & Weil, R. *Culture and mental disorders: A comparative study of the Hutterites and other populations.* Glencoe, Ill.: Free Press, 1955.

Edgerton, R. B. Conceptions of psychosis in four East

African societies. *American Anthropologist,* 1966, 68, 408–425.

Leighton, A. H., Lambo, T., Hughes, C., Leighton, D., Murphy, J., & Macklin, D. *Psychiatric disorder among the Yoruba.* Ithaca, N.Y.: Cornell University Press, 1963.

Murphy, J. M. Psychiatric labeling in cross-cultural perspective. *Science,* 1976, *191,* 1019–1028.

Torrey, E. F. *Schizophrenia and civilization.* New York: Aronson, 1980.

World Health Organization. *Report of the International Pilot Study of Schizophrenia.* Geneva: Author, 1973.

World Health Organization. *Schizophrenia: An international follow-up study.* New York: Wiley, 1979.

Additional Reading

Al-Issa, I. (Ed.). *Culture and psychopathology.* Baltimore: University Park Press, 1982.

Murphy, H. B. M. *Comparative psychiatry.* New York: Springer Verlag, 1982.

Triandis, H. C., & Draguns, J. G. (Eds.). *Handbook of cross-cultural psychology* (Vol. 6). Boston: Allyn & Bacon, 1980.

I. AL-ISSA

See PSYCHOPATHOLOGY IN PRIMITIVE CULTURES.

Culture and Psychotherapy. Although there are vast differences between modern and folk psychotherapies in both style of operation and goals, there are universal elements in all kinds of healing practices: mobilization of hope for recovery, faith in the therapist, active participation of the clients and their families, providing the authority figure and warm personality of the therapist, and facilitation of emotional arousal as a prerequisite of changes in attitudes and behavior. Frank (1961) suggested that confession and suggestion are also universal therapeutic experiences.

Altered states of consciousness involving dreams, mystical experience, shamanistic ecstasy, and dissociation states are frequently used for therapeutic purposes in non-Western cultures (Prince, 1980). A sick person among the Australian aborigines, for example, may dream of a supernatural visitation and be cured. Dreams are used in diagnosis in West Africa, where disturbed women dream of killing their children; they are then diagnosed as witches who must confess their evil witchcraft in order to be healed of their symptoms. Almost all major world religions prescribe exercises or meditation techniques aimed at achieving mystical experiences. Growing interest in the integration of concepts of meditation and mystical experience into psychotherapy in North America is indicated by the setting up of a special subsection on Mysticism and Religion in 1974 by the American Psychiatric Association.

Shamanic ecstasy is a visionary state in which the healer's "soul" journeys out of the body to the upper world of spirits or to the underworld of demons to obtain information about the illness of the patient or to search for his lost soul. Singing, drumming, and smoking culminate in the shaman's falling into an unconscious state. After a few minutes to an hour, the shaman regains consciousness and reports his journey. The shamans' contact with the realm of spirits enhances their suggestive power and endows them with enormous prestige.

Dissociation states are also often utilized in therapeutic systems. Dissociation states are achieved through dancing and music, or may follow a period of starvation and/or overbreathing which culminates in convulsive jerks and unconsciousness. Both healer and patient may experience dissociation during the therapeutic sessions. The spirit speaks through the healer (the medium), whereas the dissociated patient experiences catharsis—i.e., acting out forbidden emotions and behavior (aggressive, sadistic, cross-sex behavior). Cult ceremonies, such as in the Zar cult in Ethiopia and the Middle East or the Pentecostal services in Africa and Caribbean countries, seem to be widely used for therapeutic purposes in non-Western cultures.

Many elements may be identified with regard to the therapeutic effects of these non-Western healing procedures (Wittkower & Warnes, 1974): 1) fears of an unknown origin are rationalized (e.g., "Sopono, the smallpox god, has inflicted this on you"); 2) suggestion by a prestigious traditional healer results in the repression of stressful conflicts; 3) projection of personal wickedness onto malicious deities; 4) displacement of sin or sickness on a scapegoat or a sacrificial animal; 5) displacement of aggression by killing an animal rather than a person; 6) penance by sacrifice.

References

Frank, J. D. *Persuasion and healing: A comparative study of psychotherapy.* Baltimore: Johns Hopkins Press, 1961.

Prince, R. Variations in psychotherapeutic procedures. In H. C. Triandis & J. G. Draguns (Eds.), *Handbook of cross-cultural psychology* (Vol. 6). Boston: Allyn & Bacon, 1980.

Wittkower, E. D., & Warnes, H. Cultural aspects of psychotherapy. *Psychotherapy and Psychosomatics,* 1974, *24,* 303–310.

Additional Reading

Kiev, A. (Ed.). *Magic, faith and healing: Studies in primitive psychiatry today.* New York: Free Press, 1964.

Torrey, E. F. *The mind game: Witchdoctors and psychiatrists.* New York: Emerson Hall, 1972.

I. AL-ISSA

See CROSS-CULTURAL THERAPY.

Cybernetics. *See* INTELLIGENCE, ARTIFICIAL.

Cyclothymic Disorder. A specific affective disorder in which the essential feature is chronic mood disturbance (more than two years) involving periods of depression and hypomania. These prominent alterations of mood and activity are not of sufficient severity and duration to meet the criteria for a major affective disorder. The depressive and hypomanic periods may alternate, intermix, or be separated by periods of normal mood lasting for several months. Delusions, hallucinations, incoherence, or loosening of associations are absent. Although the cyclothymic disorder may precede a bipolar disorder, it is not due to any other mental or emotional disorder. Finally, according to DSM-III, during depressive periods there must be at least three classic signs of depressed mood or lost interest or pleasure (e.g., insomnia or hypersomnia, social withdrawal, low energy, or chronic fatigue) and at least three classic signs of expansive, elated, or irritable mood (e.g., inflated self-esteem, more energy than usual, physical restlessness).

The disorder is first seen in early adulthood without a clear onset. It is more common in females and shows a familial pattern. Since there is no severe thought and mood disorder, the clinician is more likely to see evidence of cyclothymic disorder in outpatient settings. The disorder tends to run a chronic course resulting in impaired occupational and social functioning. Recent theorists (Akiskal, Djenderedjian, Rosenthal, & Khani, 1977) argue that it is a milder form of the bipolar affective disorder.

As with the major affective disorders, theories of etiology vary considerably. Psychoanalytic theory stresses inverted anger as a contributing factor in depression, whereas cognitive theorists stress the crucial importance of thoughts and beliefs in the same mood state. Seligman's (1973) theory of learned helplessness and Lewinsohn's (1974) assertion that depression is a result of a reduction in reinforcement are explanations that are favored by behaviorally oriented clinicians. It is interesting to note, however, that there is no major psychogenic theory of mania except psychoanalytic assertions that mania is a defense against depression.

Physiological theories have received a great deal of attention in recent years. Genetic evidence for the bipolar affective disorder is suggestive, so it is assumed that genetics would play a predisposing role in certain cyclothymic disorders. Biochemical theories relate depression to low levels of neurotransmitter—norepinephrine and/or serontonin. As with the genetic data, however, there is contradictory evidence. It would probably be most helpful to view the cyclothymic disorder as a product of behavioral, environmental, and physiological factors.

Therapy for the cyclothymic disorder follows that for the major affective disorders. Somatic treatments include tricyclics and monoamin oxidase (MAO) inhibitors to control depressive episodes and lithium carbonate to control both hypomania and depression. Electroconvulsive therapy would rarely be used with the cyclothymic disorder. More psychological approaches would stress the importance of uncovering and rechanneling the anger (psychoanalytic), increasing reinforcement contingencies (behavioral), helping a person find meaning (logotherapy), and changing cognitive self-talk statements (cognitive-behavior therapy). Standard psychotherapeutic approaches would probably all be used in the treatment of the milder forms of the cyclothymic disorder.

References

Akiskal, H. S., Djenderedjian, A. H., Rosenthal, R. H., & Khani, M. K. Cyclothymic disorder. *American Journal of Psychiatry*, 1977. *134*(11), 1227–1233.

Lewinsohn, P. H. A behavioral approach to depression. In R. J. Friedman & W. M. Katz (Eds.), *The psychology of depression*. Washington, D. C.: Winston-Wiley, 1974.

Seligman, M. E. P. Fall into helplessness. *Psychology Today*, 1973, 7(1), 43–48.

R. E. Butman

See the articles on Depression.

Dd

Dance Therapy. The psychotherapeutic use of movement. Its earliest systematic clinical applications appear to have been in the early 1940s at St. Elizabeth's, a large federal hospital in Washington, D.C. The American Dance Therapy Association was formed in 1964, and a register of qualified dance therapists was developed in 1972.

See ACTIVITY THERAPY.

Daseinsanalysis. A method of existential psychotherapy developed by the Swiss psychiatrist Medard Boss. Analyzed by Freud, Boss then studied under such eminent psychoanalysts as Reich, Jones, and Horney before beginning private practice as a psychoanalyst at the age of 32. As a result of a close personal friendship with existential philosopher Martin Heidegger, he gradually moved from classical Freudian thought toward an existential psychology. His method of therapy focused on the individual's existence or his specific way of "being-in-the-world" (*dasein*).

See EXISTENTIAL PSYCHOLOGY AND PSYCHOTHERAPY.

Daydreaming. A form of mental activity which, although nearly universal in human experience, has eluded systematic investigation until fairly recently. One reason for this is simply that daydreams are so personal, private, and often fleeting that they are difficult to study with objective methods. Nevertheless, considerable progress has recently been made through the convergence of data from different methods, yielding clues to the functions of daydreaming, how it changes over development, what conditions favor its expression, individual differences, and its relation to mental health.

Daydreaming is characterized by a shift of attention away from ongoing activity in the immediate environment toward one's internal thoughts and images. These may comprise more or less imaginary persons and sequences of events. Accompanying these experiences, commonly called "fantasies" or "reveries," is usually some affect, often pleasure or excitement. Daydreaming tends to be thought of as a form of irresponsibility or even mental instability showing an inability to cope with life's circumstances. However, this stereotype must be questioned in light of current research.

Freud contributed substantially to this common view of daydreaming as irresponsibility or even a sign of mental disorder. Although he acknowledged that daydreams can represent preparation for action, he felt that in most cases they represented a neurotic avoidance of action. In essence, psychoanalytic theory states that all thought and imagination grow out of instinctive desires. These are in conflict with reality constraints and must therefore be suppressed. However, if a person lacks an acceptable outlet for these desires, he or she may find a substitute fulfillment in fantasy. The daydreamer derives pleasure vicariously through the exploits of fantasy characters.

The cognitive-affective view of Singer (1975) emphasizes a much more positive, adaptive interpretation of daydreaming. It is also derived from a much broader research base than was Freud's view. Singer views daydreaming as essentially a "trial action." It is a process whereby individuals anticipate and plan for a range of possible future actions without committing themselves in action.

Despite the unrealistic quality of many daydreams, the content is practical. Surveys reveal that daydreaming is reported by virtually every category of persons, regardless of age, status, or sociocultural background. Most daydreams are future oriented (although elderly persons often report reminiscent daydreams as well), and they deal with possible actions bearing some relation to the daydreamer's circumstances. Frequently there is a definite correlation between the content of early daydreams and actual accomplishments, suggesting that they helped the individual prepare and plan for future roles.

The cognitive-affective interpretation of daydreaming rests on Tomkins's (1962) theory of emotions, in which the individual is viewed according to the analogy of information processing. In essence, people are oriented toward understanding the environment, and thus tend to assimilate new information into categories that have worked for them in the past. However, information that is very novel can evoke fear. The positive character of daydreams or fantasies lies in their permitting one to anticipate and deal with possible future situations and thus conquer debilitating fears at the same time.

Relaxed states of awareness, such as just before falling asleep, are often times of increased daydreaming. However, a surprising amount of daydreaming occurs during periods of mental productivity through a kind of "time-sharing," or rapid shifting of attention and mood. Experiments have also shown that eye shifting occurs frequently when questions are posed which demand reflection. Apparently in some mental activity attention must be diverted away from the task in order to attend to one's private store of associations. As in daydreaming, the process is adaptive to the situation.

Singer's research has provided a good deal of support for a more positive interpretation of daydreaming. He has shown that daydreaming is frequently adaptive. His research also suggests that daydreaming can under some circumstances even be associated with decreased reliance on drugs and less resort to aggression (1975).

The psychoanalytic interpretation, on the other hand, is not well supported. Daydreams do not appear to automatically reduce the level of a need such as aggression through substitute fulfillment. According to the psychoanalytic view, one might expect TV portrayals of violence to reduce tendencies toward aggression. On the contrary, people tend to respond more aggressively under certain conditions following the TV portrayals. This and other evidence suggest that daydreaming is not well explained

as discharge of pent-up emotion. Therefore, whatever positive benefits might accrue from the activity are probably better explained as a consequence of shifting one's mood and attention toward future possibilities.

Christians can be challenged to take a broad view of daydreaming as one capacity that God has given us for our good. The lack of an obvious, immediate return on the investment should not necessarily cause one to scorn the activity as unprofitable. In this regard, one recalls the scorn of Joseph's brothers in Genesis 37:19 ("Behold, the dreamer cometh") in contrast with God's favor upon Joseph.

References

Singer, J. L. *The inner world of daydreaming.* New York: Harper & Row, 1975.
Tomkins, S. S. *Affect, imagery, consciousness* (2 vols.). New York: Springer Publishing, 1962.

D. R. Ridley

Death and Dying. Life is animate being, and once it begins it inexorably leads to death. Death is a cessation of life, an irreversible state that is characterized by the cessation of all those processes that sustain life.

Life begins with conception, an event that is the starting point of its trajectory. At conception an organism possesses all the potential that it will ever have, although growth is necessary for the realization of the potential. The process of growth continues to a point called maturity. At maturity the organism can maintain its integrity by replacing cells that are injured and die. This capacity to replace cells is, however, finite, and in time the process of repair cannot continue. At this point the organism reaches the senium. Just as growth decelerates, decay accelerates. The accelerating decay in time affects the brain or cardiovascular system. As the adequate functioning of these two systems are essential to life, the failure of either eventually results in death.

There are many things that can interrupt the trajectory of life. Spontaneous or induced abortion, trauma, infection, cancer, as well as many other diseases can occur during the period of growth to end life prematurely. These interruptions to a great extent determine life expectancy. In prehistory man's life was short. Disease or trauma ended life at an average age of 18 years. Even in ancient Greece and Rome one could not expect to live beyond 20 to 22 years. At the time of the colonization of America life expectancy had not increased beyond 35 years. The major increase has occurred in the last century, rising from 47 years at the turn of the century to 71 years in 1971.

This has increased even further in the last decade to just less than 80 years. This dramatic change has come about because of the control of infectious disease through immunization and treatment with antibiotics.

Medical Death. Throughout the centuries the determination of death was simple. If a person fell unconscious, someone would feel for the pulse, determine whether there was breathing, and look at the pupils. If there was no pulse or breath and the pupils were fixed, death was assumed to have occurred. These criteria were called the heart-lung criteria. Over time, physicians have been given the primary responsibility for the determination of death.

In recent years medicine has developed techniques to prevent the rapid death that was inevitable when a person became comatose. At present many persons appear to be dead even though their hearts continue to beat and their vital organs function well enough to keep the largest part of the cells of the body alive. Although they have some appearances of being alive, they are insensate and do not carry on those intellectual functions that characterize life. It has therefore been necessary to establish new criteria for a kind of death that is called brain death.

Brain death has been the subject of much discussion during the last 30 years. This discussion was the outgrowth of the need to determine the point at which life support systems could be discontinued with the certainty that there was absolutely no hope for life. Later, with the advent of transplant surgery, first with kidney and later with heart and liver transplantation, the need for definite criteria to determine brain death increased because intact viable organs were necessary if transplantation was to be successful. As a result, a study was conducted in 1968 at the Harvard Medical School to establish criteria for brain death. A subsequent cooperative study conducted in several institutions has further refined these criteria. They are 1) unreceptivity and unresponsivity, 2) no spontaneous or stimulated movements or breathing, 3) no reflexes, 4) a flat electroencephalogram in absence of drug intoxication and hypothermia. (The flat electroencephalogram indicates the absence of brain metabolic activity.)

When a patient meets these critera for 24 hours, or when there is obviously no hope, such as in traumatic lesions of the brain that are irremediable, brain death has occurred. When it is determined that brain death has occurred, it is permissible to discontinue life support systems and to harvest organs for transplant. Most countries in the Western world have enacted legislation to legally define brain death. The medical profession and the law have become increasingly comfortable with the concept of brain death.

Persons who have died and have subsequently been resuscitated have reported the experience as pleasant. It is dying that they consider unpleasant.

Some Non-Christian Views of Death. The secular world and medicine have viewed death as an enemy, something to be avoided at all costs but which is, nevertheless, accepted as inevitable. Most persons have conflicts about dying. Some are afraid of "not being," or being a coward, of being punished, or of pain. Others dislike the interruption of their goals, or are concerned about the impact of their death on their survivors. Scientific humanism, a philosophy to which most physicians subscribe, sees it as dissolution and destruction.

Since physicians have seen death as an enemy, their entire training and efforts are directed toward the preservation of life. As a result, physicians and other medical personnel maintain an attitude of detached concern for the dying and a matter-of-fact attitude about death.

Ancient Greeks, following Plato's teaching, believed in immortality of the soul. In their view the preexistent soul resumed its incorporeal existence after separation from the body and hopefully ascended toward truth through a process of education. Hindus and Buddhists teach that man is caught on the wheel of circumstance and is born, suffers, and dies only to start the cycle over again in reincarnation. The only way to escape is to merge into the ultimate, an act accomplished either through meditation or good works or both. These latter religions deny death.

Judeo-Christian Views of Death. In the Judeo-Christian religions death is also an enemy and is related to sin. It is the outgrowth of man's rebellion. It was because of Adam and Eve's rejection of God's command that men have been appointed to die. In early Old Testament writings the body decayed and the soul ceased to be (Pss. 6:5; 88:10–12). Later, in the writings of the prophets, there was hope of resurrection (Isa. 26:19; Dan. 12:2). In the New Testament resurrection is not just a hope; it is a reality attested by the reality of Jesus' resurrection (John 5:28–29; 1 Cor. 15:1–32).

In the New Testament death is contrasted to life, so that time and eternity have different dimensions. In life there is conflict; in eternity there is harmony. In life there is strife; in eternity there is peace. In life and eternity there are other contrasting qualities such as work versus rest, search versus discovery, suffering versus wholeness, faith versus strife, yearning versus fulfillment, and, finally, imperfection and brokenness versus wholeness. In eternity there is no separation, and knowledge is complete.

These qualities are to be attained at the resurrection, which is to occur at the establishment of the new order. Souls are to sleep until it occurs. The Scriptures are, however, not clear on when this new order is to be established. Jesus' promise to the thief that "today you will be with me in Paradise" suggests an immediate transition. Paul seems to have held a similiar view, although in his description of the return of Christ he notes that the dead will be raised to life at the sound of the last trumpet. Paul did, however, believe that the return of Christ was imminent. In the teaching of both Jesus and Paul there is a retention of the unity of body, soul, and spirit, although the resurrection body has different dimensions from the one occupied in time.

The early church fathers held to the resurrection view of death, although Origen accepted the Platonic view. Tertullian, on the other hand, was the first to propose a purgatory where a prejudgment was to occur prior to the doomsday judgment. Augustine supported this view, which in time became a doctrine of the church. Interestingly enough, the doctrine is in accord with the Greek Platonic view instead of the apocalyptic view of Jesus and Paul. It was made official doctrine by the Council of Trent.

The Protestant view, as set forth by Luther and Calvin, denied the existence of purgatory and affirmed the reality of the resurrection. Protestant doctrinal positions are either vague or do not speak to the whereabouts of the soul from death until the resurrection, at which time the eternal destiny of every soul to life or death will be decreed.

Dying. Every person comes to the knowledge that death is final and inevitable. When this realization occurs, whether in the process of meditating on one's life, when faced with imminent death, or when a loved one dies, there is the development of what is known as death anxiety. Death anxiety is separate and distinct from general anxiety. It occurs when it is impossible to discern meaning to death. Persons who are involved in the world and who have a sense of purpose in life have less death anxiety. Persons who go to church are no different from those who do not go, but those who are involved in their religion tend to have less death anxiety. The terminally ill, mentally ill, and aged do not have more death anxiety than persons who are not ill or aged. Those who are likely to have high levels of death anxiety are those who are uninvolved with life and have no well-defined purpose in life and those who are highly motivated to achievement.

Death anxiety can progress to a despair of death, one of the existential predicaments that human beings must face. Despair of death occurs if a person cannot discern meaning when he examines his life and then contemplates his certain death. Such despair can be a moment or a way of life.

When death is imminent, persons have needs which if not met can result in despair. These needs are 1) to control pain, 2) to retain dignity and self-worth as they participate in decisions that affect outcomes, and 3) to receive love and affection from others in the environment. The despair that occurs is characterized by depression and feelings of hopelessness, helplessness, and withdrawal. The emotional trajectory of death has been described by Kübler-Ross (1969). Her five stages of dying are denial, anger, bargaining, depression, and acceptance. Other investigators have not confirmed her findings. In contrast, they find that initially there are two general responses to imminent death—despair and withdrawal.

The response to death by those who survive the death of a loved one is grief, which is resolved by decathexis of the lost love object. This process is accomplished by mourning. Facilitation of mourning is accomplished by talking about death of the lost loved one to sympathetic listeners and if the mourner is a Christian, by committing the eternal destiny of the dead person to God and surrendering one's love for the person to him. The empty spot in life can be filled with God's love.

References
Kübler-Ross, E. *On death and dying.* New York: Macmillan, 1969.

Additional Readings
Brooks, D. *Dealing with death.* Nashville: Broadman, 1974.
Gatch, M. M. *Death.* New York: Seabury, 1969.
Shulz, R. *The psychology of death, dying and bereavement.* Reading, Mass.: Addison-Wesley, 1978.
Winter, D. B. *Hereafter.* London: Hodder & Stoughton, 1972.

W. P. WILSON

See LOSS AND SEPARATION; GRIEF; ANXIETY.

Decision Making. Two branches of psychology, mathematical and clinical, have contributed to our understanding of decision making.

Mathematical psychologists have developed normative models and optimal decision strategies from statistical concepts, while clinical and counseling psychologists have concentrated on models and techniques more applicable to the needs of clients.

From the statistical perspective an optimal decision is one that maximizes gain and minimizes loss. One technique which achieves this is the maximum expected value model (Coombs, Dawes, & Tversky, 1970). This model assumes that for every decision there are two or more alternatives and that each alternative will be followed by one or more potential consequences. Each consequence has a probability of actually occurring ($p_1, p_2, \ldots p_n$) and an overall value ($v_1, v_2, \ldots v_n$) which can be positive or negative depending on whether it represents a gain or loss. The expected value (EV) for each alternative can be calculated by multiplying the probability of each of its consequences by its corresponding value and adding these products ($EV = p_1v_1 + p_2v_2 + \ldots + p_nv_n$).

For example, imagine that you want to buy a TV and that a salesman has offered you a demonstrator, over the phone, for $50 less than the regular price. However, since a sale is in progress he can only promise to hold it for 15 minutes. When you get to the store, 10 minutes later, you cannot find a legal parking space. You have two choices: to park illegally, getting the TV for sure ($v_1 = \$50$, $p_1 = 1$) but risking a fine ($v_2 = -\$20$, $p_2 = .5$) or to look for safer parking, avoiding the fine ($v_1 = -\$20$, $p_1 = 0$) but perhaps missing the bargain ($v_2 = \$50$, $p_2 = .5$). (Since you don't actually know the probability of getting a fine or missing the bargain, a safe strategy is to set it at .5.) Considering only this set of consequences, the expected value of parking illegally, $40, is greater than that of parking legally, $25, and thus is the optimal choice.

A modification of this technique, the subjective expected utility model, allows one to also consider more subjective consequences such as feeling guilty and ashamed for breaking the law. Using this technique, the probabilities of consequences can be objective or subjective and the values attached to consequences would be estimated on a uniform scale (e.g., from -7 to 0 to 7, representing extremely undesirable to neutral to extremely desirable). In this case individuals who would feel guilty for parking illegally or ashamed if ticketed would find that their optimal choice would be to park legally, whereas the opposite choice might be optimal for someone else. Since both models allow the simultaneous evaluation of large numbers of alternatives, they are very valuable for complex decisions and have been used for that purpose by government and industry.

Research indicates that people do not actually use these methods unless trained to do so. Simon (1976) found that people often "satisfice" rather than optimize. They approach decisions with a set of minimum requirements and accept the first alternative that meets those requirements. This strategy requires much less thought and energy than optimizing, since alternatives can be considered one at a time with a simple set of criteria.

Sometimes very important decisions are made on the basis of a single criterion or decision rule. For example, people in serious difficulty have been known to consult a doctor or lawyer recommended by a trusted friend and unhesitatingly follow whatever course of action the counselor recommends. Sometimes people use a single moral precept as their only rule when deciding to help someone in trouble (Schwartz, 1970). If they realize that someone requires aid and they give it, they do so without further deliberation. They may in fact think it immoral to consider any other choice.

Another common strategy (or lack thereof) has been termed *incrementalism*—making choices or changes by small, slow steps to alleviate some present problem or commitment rather than making choices consistent with an overall plan or goal. Sometimes people make very important life decisions this way (e.g., marriage or career choice) and find that by refusing to consider long-term priorities they have been forced into alternatives they really do not like. Habits also strongly influence decisions.

Many of the difficulties treated by counselors either originated with, or are increased by, poor decisions or an unwillingness to make decisions. Janis and Mann (1977) and others have demonstrated the benefits of teaching some clients better problem-solving and decision-making skills. Clients can benefit by being taught to recognize the possible implications and consequences of events (to overcome inertia and denial), to consider a greater number of alternatives and their consequences (to overcome hasty decisions or very limited deliberations), to develop skill and confidence in their ability to make decisions (overcoming panic and excessive worry), and to learn to accept and live with potential negative consequences of decisions. Some successful intervention techniques include decision counseling, the use of systematic balance sheets, outcome psychodrama, and emotional inoculation against postdecisional regret (see Janis & Mann, 1977, for further clinical applications).

References
Coombs, C. H., Dawes, R. M., & Tversky, A. *Mathematical psychology: An elementary introduction.* Englewood Cliffs, N.J.: Prentice-Hall, 1970.
Janis, I. L., & Mann, L. *Decision-making.* New York: Free Press, 1977.
Schwartz, S. Moral decision-making and behavior. In J. Macaulay & L. Berkowitz (Eds.), *Altruism and helping behavior.* New York: Academic Press, 1970.
Simon, H. A. *Administrative behavior: A study of decision-making processes in administrative organization* (3rd ed.). New York: Free Press, 1976.

E. L. HILLSTROM

Decompensation. A breakdown in the operation of defense systems which previously maintained the person's optimal psychic functioning. An example of such a breakdown of the defense system is a relapse in the schizophrenic patient.

Defense Mechanisms. However negative Freud may have been toward religion, no honest and competent scholar can deny the monumental contributions he made to psychological thought. Among his greatest achievements was the careful way in which he documented the complexity of the human heart. Freud, the founder of psychoanalysis and consequently of all psychodynamic approaches to psychotherapy, systematically studied the incredibly subtle ways in which people try to fool themselves and others. Psychological defense mechanisms can be viewed as forms of dishonesty.

Freud ignored the moral implications of his insights by claiming that defense mechanisms were, by definition, unconscious. The person defending is neither aware of the defensive process nor purposely invoking it. According to the orthodox Freudian view, if the person is aware of what he or she is doing, one cannot correctly speak of the operation of a defense. Thus, while repression is one of the cardinal Freudian defenses, suppression—consciously putting material out of one's mind—is not.

From the vantage point of contemporary behavioral science, defense mechanisms are a subset of a broader class of phenomena: coping strategies. They are those coping strategies we engage in without awareness, in order to keep ourselves from experiencing anxiety. Anxiety is prompted by unwanted thoughts, feelings, and impulses. To prevent or "bind" our anxieties, we try to keep these thoughts from entering consciousness.

There has been much debate among psychodynamically oriented theorists over which of the defense mechanisms is primary, the progenitor of all the others. While some have contended that the prototypical defense is projection and others have suggested that it is denial, the traditional psychoanalytic view has stressed REPRESSION. Accordingly, repression is said to be the most primitive of all the defenses. It is the simple exclusion from awareness of troubling psychic contents.

A psychological disorder in which repression can be seen pivotally to operate is PANIC DISORDER. People with this diagnosis have acute attacks of anxiety, often quite severe, which seem not to be triggered by any specific event. They sweat, shake, have rapid heartbeats, and so on. Typically and significantly, such persons have little understanding of what underlies their anxiety. Psychotherapy usually reveals that the person is troubled by certain ideas, sentiments, or inclinations that he or she simply does not want to face. The anxiety attacks occur when repression fails to keep these unwanted contents completely out of consciousness.

Closely related to repression is DENIAL. While many clinicians use the two terms interchangeably, there is a technical difference between them. Repression is keeping from awareness that which is inside one's own psyche. Denial, on the other hand, is refusing to admit into awareness that which comes from one's environment—e.g., what others say or do. Some people, for instance, will not acknowledge, even to themselves, that someone else is behaving in an unfriendly manner. They are said, unkindly, to be "too stupid to be insulted." In reality, of course, their failure to comprehend hostility has nothing to do with their intellectual endowment or the lack of it. Another example would be the husband or wife who does not see what all the neighbors can—that his or her spouse is involved with someone else.

PROJECTION is refusing to come to terms with our own attributes—e.g., anger or lust—by seeing them in others but not in ourselves. On days when you feel irritable, for example, others may seem excessively irritable to you. Sometimes disturbed persons will claim that others are trying to seduce them when, in fact, such persons are merely projecting their own libidinal inclinations. Although it is usually unfavorable characteristics that we project onto others, it is also possible to see in them our own favorable qualities, such as trustworthiness and valor.

RATIONALIZATION is the process of trumping up justifications for ourselves—for what we do, think, and feel. Rationalizations are, at root, excuses, offered sometimes to others but perhaps even more often to ourselves. The business person who, sensing potential advantage, unethically dissolves a partnership may view himself or herself as taking this action for a good reason—e.g., the incompetence of the disenfranchised partner. A more primitive example of rationalization is the delinquent who maintains that he stole the car because its owner left the keys in the ignition.

INTELLECTUALIZATION is closely related to rationalization and involves the substitution of safe intellectual concerns for dangerous ideas and impulses. Acting almost as verbal magic, intellectualization is an attempt to control the world and to cope with inner conflicts through thinking. What intellectualization in fact does is to prevent us from turning our attention toward unpleasant mental material—e.g., feelings of injury, grief, or anger. People who intellectualize often seem to others to have no feelings. In actuality such feelings as they do have are defensively blocked out by excessive cogitation.

While intellectualization involves an exaggerated reliance on words—thinking is carried along on a train of words—ISOLATION is the defense of compartmentalizing troublesome aspects of our mental life without necessarily doing a lot of thinking. Upsetting mental conflicts can be stripped of their emotional power by separating them from their natural affective significance. These conflicts become detached from the rest of the personality.

DISSOCIATION is a related defense that involves splitting off some aspect of ourselves. Sleepwalking is a well-known form of dissociation. A less well-known form is FUGUE, in which a person may suddenly travel to another city, amnesic with respect to his or her ongoing life, and begin another existence. One patient, for example, would blank out and find herself in a phone booth, many miles from home, telephoning the police.

UNDOING is the attempt to nullify or cancel out the significance of an earlier action. Everyday apologies often serve an undoing function. We say "I'm sorry" to make it almost as if we had not done whatever it is for which we claim to be repentant. One advantage of such apologies, of course, is that they make us less likely to pay for the social consequences of our actions. A more pathological form of undoing can be seen in Lady Macbeth's washing the imaginary blood from her hands. Undoing can take a compulsive form. Pathological repentances are also extreme versions of undoing.

REACTION FORMATION is the substitution in consciousness of what is unconsciously true. Schoolchildren provide us with a particularly charming example of reaction formation when, embarrassed by their budding romantic sentiments, they suddenly "hate" members of the opposite sex. Adamant social reformers are also sometimes defending against their own deeper wishes and impulses. Note, however, that one should not assume that a defense is necessarily operating in all social reform. Not all persons who crusade against pornography can be said to be enacting psychological defenses against their own lust. Reaction formation is also used to defend against anger. Sometimes, for example, we witness people whom we know to be quite angry acting inordinately nice.

AMBIVALENCE is regarded as a defensive maneuver by certain theorists. Preventing ourselves from making psychic or behavioral commitments by endlessly posing reasons "why not" is a common strategy for guarding against the anxiety that often attends commitment. As soon as one thinks of doing such-and-such, reasons for doing the opposite may come to mind. Dialectic thinking is of course characteristic of intelligent human beings, but it can become a way of life—a way to avoid making a mistake.

DISPLACEMENT is attaching to a neutral object mental contents that were originally attached to someone or something else. The man who kicks the dog on the way into the house is probably angry at his boss or coworker. Parents often take out on the kids what they feel toward each other. The payoff in displacement is obvious. Telling off one's boss can be hazardous. Fighting openly with one's spouse can also lead to more retaliation than children are immediately able to mete out.

IDENTIFICATION can operate as a defense against one's own powerlessness or lack of perceived virtue. An especially tragic example of identification is when prisoners of war internalize the antisocial values of their captors. Beyond such tangible payoffs as avoiding torture or acquiring more rations, identification with the aggressor serves to diffuse the awfulness of the experience as well as to bind one's own (dangerous) counteraggressive impulses. Most identifications are far less dramatic. Children growing up normally identify with their parents, one result of which is internalization of the parents' values.

Identification is sometimes closely tied up

with another defense, *compensation*. Our culture is replete with stories of skinny or afflicted youths turning themselves, through herculean efforts, into wonders of athletic prowess. Teddy Roosevelt is one example. Compensation is ordinarily used as a defense against felt inadequacy.

Although most treatises on defense mechanisms do not discuss MANIA, frenetic activity is probably used by many people to ward off a lurking depression. One theory of psychotically manic individuals is that they too are using activity as a defense against depression. Activity may serve to distract one from inner misery.

Freud maintained that there is at least one defense mechanism that is usually constructive: SUBLIMATION. This is the changing of baser desires into socially acceptable ones. An example would be the artist who takes out his aggression by constructing highly creative and aesthetic paintings. A more neurotic form of sublimation is the individual who makes up for lack of marital intimacy by working 16 hours a day instead of having an affair.

Depending on the literature one reads, lists of defense mechanisms vary from just a few to over 20. This article discusses those that are common to most lists. Theorists making finer discriminations among the defenses also write about other mechanisms, such as insulation, substitution, PROJECTIVE IDENTIFICATION, INTROJECTION, and INCORPORATION.

It is important to keep in mind that defense mechanisms are metaphors. Mental health professionals often forget this and regard the classical defenses almost as physical realities. In fact, defenses are models, approximate representations of how human beings deal with anxiety-provoking material.

Additional Readings

Fenichel, O. *The psychoanalytic theory of neurosis.* New York: Norton, 1945.
Freud, A. *The ego and the mechanisms of defense.* London: Hogarth Press, 1937.
Laughlin, H. P. *The ego and its defenses* (2nd ed.). New York: Aronson, 1979.

C. W. McLEMORE

See ANXIETY; PSYCHOANALYTIC PSYCHOLOGY; RELIGIOUS DEFENSE MECHANISMS.

Déjà Vu. The déjà vu experience is the illusion of familiarity. The individual experiencing this encounters some new situation with the distinct feeling of having had the same experience previously. It is not an illusion of the senses but rather of memory. It occurs in healthy normal individuals, particu-

larly in a state of exhaustion, but more frequently in neurotics and psychotics. Freud suggested that the déjà vu feelings correspond to the memory of an unconscious fantasy. Others have viewed it as an example of generalization from past experience. Plato took it as evidence of a previous existence.

D. G. BENNER

Delinquency. *See* JUVENILE DELINQUENCY.

Delirium. A psychiatric syndrome of transient disorganization of cognitive and perceptual functions due to metabolic disturbance of the central nervous system. In simpler terms, this means that delirious patients are confused because there is something wrong with the brain's functioning. Some terms that are used almost synonymously with delirium are acute brain syndrome, acute confusional state, and toxic psychosis.

Although it was one of the first mental disorders to be recognized by medical science, delirium remains the most common of all the psychoses and may be even more prevalent today than ever before. Studies on the incidence of delirium are lacking in quality and quantity. It is estimated that about a fifth of all general hospital patients become delirious, and this proportion rises to half of the aged patients.

In delirium the patient initially complains of several of the following symptoms: anxiety, restlessness, irritability, fatigue, hypersensitivity to light and noise, disturbing dreams, and brief hallucinations. Examination of the patient will discover cognitive impairment that may range from a mild bewilderment to a complete insensibility. There is an inability to orient oneself in time and place. Memory, especially the recall of recent events, is faulty. If given instructions for a simple task, the patient will have difficulty maintaining attention and directing thought in a purposive manner. Some cases of delirium also involve psychopathological changes of personality, usually extreme anxiety, but depression and mania are also possible.

The cause of delirium is always organic and most frequently related to toxic effects of drugs and poisons. The range of poisons that can produce delirium is wide: plants, mushrooms, venom from reptile bites or insect stings, industrial chemicals (e.g., lead, gasoline, bromides, solvents, glue, exhaust fumes). The drugs include those that are intentionally abused (e.g., alcohol, LSD, angel dust) and also prescription medications that have adverse side effects in a small percentage of patients. Arthritis and heart medications (e.g., digitalis, diuretics) are frequent offenders. Drugs such as alcohol, sedatives, and tranquilizers can also lead to delirium if an addicted patient undergoes withdrawal syndrome.

One reason why delirium is more prevalent in the aged is the reduced ability of the body to tolerate certain medications (and combinations of medications). While they account for only a tenth of the population of the United States, the aged receive a quarter of the prescription medications. The average nursing home patient ingests four or five different drugs every day. The heart and arthritis drugs are commonly dispensed in nursing homes, but the most commonly used drugs are those which act directly on the central nervous system: sedatives and tranquilizers. In order to avoid toxic buildup, the staffs of nursing homes must carefully monitor the side effects of medication.

Nutritional disturbances can bring on delirium. A deficiency of B vitamins or an overabundance of A or D is common. Potassium metabolism, which is frequently disturbed by medication for controlling blood pressure, can cause delirium if there is either too much or too little of the mineral. The delicate balances of fluids and sugars are also important. Dehydration is likely to lead to delirium. The failure of liver, kidney, pancreas, thyroid, or parathyroid functioning can impair the assimilation of nutrients and bring on delirium. Anemia or protein deficiencies are other possibilities.

Physical disease is one of the most frequent causes of delirium in hospital patients. Infectious diseases that result in a high fever can disturb central nervous system functioning, making the patient delirious. Cardiovascular disorders (e.g., heart attack, stroke) which interrupt the flow of blood to the brain can cause delirium. Any tissue abnormality around the brain (e.g., tumor, abscess, cyst) can exert a pressure or chemical disturbance which makes the patient delirious. Delirium is also experienced in the wake of seizures.

Environmental causes are also possibilities. Severe blows to the head can produce concussion or contusion. Temperature extremes can lead to heatstroke or hypothermia, a lowering of the body's core temperature. Electric shock, radiation, and even food allergies can disrupt cerebral metabolism. All these conditions can cause delirium.

The diagnosis of an acute brain syndrome is twofold. One step is to verify that the patient is merely delirious rather than suffering from some other psychiatric disorder. Schizophrenia, depression, mania, and anxiety all exhibit symptoms similar to those of delirium, but the overlap is not as great as the key differences. The severe overall cognitive impairment found in serious cases of delirium indicates an organic brain syndrome. Neurologists can recognize the telltale changes on the electroencephalogram. Perhaps the greatest difficulty is distinguishing delirium from DEMENTIA. The key factors for delirium are rapid onset (dementia is gradual), hallucinations, disturbed sleep cycle, short duration, and a fluctuating course with lucid intervals (dementia's course is progressively downward). One factor that complicates the differential diagnosis is that delirium and dementia are two separate disorders which are not mutually exclusive. About a third of demented aged admitted to psychiatric hospitals have an acute brain syndrome superimposed on a preexisting chronic brain syndrome.

The next step involves the identification of the cause of the delirium. Medical records indicating known diseases, prescriptions, and allergies are most helpful. So are reports about the onset of the delirium. One of the most helpful facts is the patient's age, because certain causes are more likely at different points in the life cycle. When the answer cannot be provided by external data, extensive medical laboratory investigations can usually find the cause.

The prognosis for delirium is generally favorable. Most patients recover from the organic cause and regain normal brain functioning. If recovery does not take place, the most likely course is a progression to stupor, coma, and death. If there is neither recovery nor death, it is likely that the diagnosis of delirium was in error.

Management of delirium is usually best accomplished in a medical environment. The most important aspect of treatment is the elimination of the underlying organic cause. If the body's own recuperative powers are not sufficient, medication or surgery might be indicated. Whatever the cause of the delirium, it is important to take care of the patient's needs for sleep, comfort, nutrition, and fluid intake. Certain of these physiological processes may have to be monitored closely, depending upon the cause of the disorder. The optimal environment for recovery is a quiet, well-lighted room and the provision of unambiguous, orienting, reassuring information. Any attempt at psychotherapy with a delirious patient should fit into this mold and be supportive and directive.

Additional Reading
Lipowski, Z. J. *Delirium*. Springfield, Ill.: Thomas, 1980.

T. L. Brink

See Geriatric Psychotherapy; Psychotic Disorders.

Delirium Tremens. An acute brain syndrome characterized by terrifying hallucinatory delirium and tremors of the hands, tongue, and lips. Caused by alcohol or drug intoxication, delirium tremens rarely occurs before the age of 30 and follows at least a 3- to 4-year history of alcoholism or drug addiction. It was first named and described by Thomas Sutton in 1813. Delirium tremens may occur any time in chronic alcoholism, but usually follows a prolonged drinking spree or infection.

The initial signs of delirium tremens include rapid pulse, confusion, headache, fever, loss of appetite, nausea, perspiration, and dehydration. The delirium which follows may last from three to six days and frequently involves visual hallucinations, particularly of animals like snakes or rats. Auditory hallucinations are generally of a derogatory nature, with references to persecution or castration. The resulting memory impairment and disorientation may lead to suicide or homicide. The alcoholic's emotional state may waver from panic, anxiety, and terror to complete indifference. Often the delirium is followed by a deep sleep and amnesia, and the person returns to the same cycle of alcohol or drug abuse. Pathologically, repeated alcohol intoxication leads to nuclear destruction of nerve cells and frequently death. If the condition is untreated, mortality rate may be as high as 15%, although this is now rare. However, death can occur suddenly as a result of hyperthermia or vascular collapse.

D. L. Schuurman

See Alcohol Organic Mental Disorders.

Delusion. A false belief held by a person who disregards explicit evidence to the contrary. A delusional person intertwines fantasy with reality, distorting events and interpreting them to support the false belief. Usually a delusion is based on a false premise which, if accepted, then makes the delusion reasonable. Psychopathological disorders in which delusions occur include some schizophrenias, bipolar disorder, psychotic depression, paranoid personality, and paranoid psychotic disorders.

Speculations about the causes of delusions range from a genetic/biochemical basis or predisposition to strictly psychological/environmental factors. In vulnerable persons delusions usually originate under overwhelming stress triggered by real or imagined dilemmas such as rejection, inadequacy, inferiority feelings, guilt, and fear of one's own impulses. Delusions reduce anxiety resulting from these dilemmas and thereby become somehow more acceptable than facing such difficulties directly.

Distinctions should be made between systematized and nonsystematized delusions, and between fixed and nonfixed delusions. A person experiences a systematized delusion when he interprets events to fit a rather tight cohesive story or central false belief. Nonsystematized delusions are more common and occur as loosely organized, sometimes vaguely defined, false beliefs. No central theme is evident.

The distinction between fixed and nonfixed delusions is significant for prognosis. Fixed refers to the degree of tenacity with which the person holds to an idiosyncratic interpretation of events. As fixedness increases, there is greater disregard of reality and less willingness to hear what others say. Therefore, fixed delusions generally suggest a poor prognosis.

There are numerous types of delusions, but delusions of persecution are the most frequent, with the central ideation of others inflicting harm on oneself ("Communists are plotting against me; neighbors are trying to poison me; the pastor is attempting to destroy my reputation; and God wants me dead"). The underlying dynamic of persecutory delusions is the psychological defense called Projection. Because of anxiety about feelings, thoughts, or impulses, the person disowns the threatening personal quality and attributes it to some other source. Hostile impulses toward one's wife are denied, but she is perceived as angry and plotting. The dynamic of projection also occurs in delusional jealousy. A person attributes his own sexual impulses to his spouse, who is then perceived as unfaithful. Circumstantial evidence is then used to support the false belief.

Delusions of influence also result from projection. Here the person does not disown having the personal quality but believes external forces control him. Anxiety is reduced by attributing the responsibility for the thoughts, impulses, or behavior to someone else.

Delusions of grandeur occur when someone believes he is a special person. Examples are someone believing he is going to be accorded worldwide recognition, or someone believing he possesses special knowledge that others are trying to get. Occasionally a person with this type of delusion will assume the identity of someone important or powerful because he is so threatened by feelings of inadequacy, inferiority, or dreaded impulses within himself. Those who believe they are Christ, the Antichrist, Mary, or a special agent of God suffer from delusions of grandeur.

Delusions about self-accusation, as well as those of sin, guilt, impoverishment, and disease, are commonly found in psychotic depression. These delusions may lead persons to question such things as their salvation, their relationship to God, or their health. Delusions of self-accusation result after controls over forbidden impulses weaken. The person then becomes very self-accusatory and depressed. A need to punish oneself for some unacknowledged forbidden impulse is seen in delusions of guilt, impoverishment, and disease. Occasionally nihilistic delusions indicate the severity of the condition. The person believes he is dead, without feelings, or that certain aspects of reality do not exist.

Sometimes shared delusions can be seen in cults. Frequently persecutory in nature, such shared false beliefs are not uncommon. These beliefs may not arise from a pathological condition, but nevertheless are dangerous. A future mass delusion is referred to in Scripture regarding belief about the "man of lawlessness," probably the Antichrist (2 Thes. 2:3-12).

Problems for churches can be found in some of the above examples. Occasionally pastors are plagued by someone whose psychopathology affects the way he interprets events. The more bizarre delusions are not difficult to identify. However, the borderline delusional states are troublesome. All accusatory statements require careful evaluation. Claims of special understanding of Scriptures or personal revelations must be investigated. Persons frequently bolster their delusion with quotations from Scripture, misleading many others. Extreme reformers, prophets, and accusers often cause severe rifts in a church. Moreover, many pastors and church members have had their reputations ruined by unfounded accusations of infidelity, romantic intentions, or of not measuring up to someone's specially revealed standards.

M. R. NELSON

See ORGANIC DELUSIONAL SYNDROME; PSYCHOTIC DISORDERS.

Dementia. This psychiatric term denotes a deterioration of mental condition. Before the

term *schizophrenia* became popular 60 years ago, *dementia praecox* described that psychotic disorder characterized by delusions, hallucinations, and bizarre patterns of communication, and beginning in adolescence or early adulthood. Later life mental disorders, especially those characterized by a diminution of cognitive capacity, were referred to as *dementia senile*. Today, *senility* has become a popular term that connotes physical as well as mental decline. Many gerontologists believe that senility has become a wastebasket category for all the unsolved cases of mental disorder in the aged. While senility may be a prejudicial or useless term, dementia has remained a technical, psychiatric term denoting a certain mental disorder (or group of mental disorders). The adjective *senile* is sometimes affixed to dementia in order to indicate that the disorder is associated with later years, while *presenile* refers to dementias that usually strike before age 60. Terms which are almost synonymous with senile dementia are *organic brain syndrome* and *chronic brain syndrome*. One term that is gaining in popularity is *senile confusional state*.

The incidence of dementia in the United States is about one million cases, or only 5% of the population over age 65. (In nursing homes, however, the majority of the patients suffer from dementia.) Chronic brain syndrome is neither the most common psychiatric disorder in old age nor an inevitable consequence of aging. Many individuals are able to preserve cognitive functioning to the very end. Pablo Casals, who had led a turbulent life, died at the age of 96, having conducted a concert only a few weeks before.

The onset of dementia tends to be gradual. The first mental changes to be noticed may be mood changes, especially spells of depression, heightened rigidity, and suspiciousness. Some elders become aware of their diminishing mental capacities and respond by avoiding situations which tax their brain power—giving up work, a home, or driving. As the disorder progresses, memory deficits become pronounced. The loss of short-term memory is the most distinctive feature of dementia in later life. Many patients can tell you in great detail what happened years ago but cannot recall what happened a few minutes ago. One demented patient played a piano piece that she learned almost 70 years ago. When the other nursing home patients applauded and requested another, she obliged by playing the same one. Although she could remember how to play the piece (long-term memory), she had forgotten that she had just finished playing it (short-term memory). As the chronic brain syndrome progresses, there is increasing disorientation of time and place, perseveration, apathy, and inability to relate to the demands of the environment, both physical and interpersonal. In advanced stages the patient may lose control over bowel and bladder functions or require spoon feeding.

Dementia is different in kind rather than degree from the forgetfulness which most elders complain of at times. Such forgetfulness, therefore, does not by itself offer any serious prognostic implications. Neither is dementia analogous to regression to a second childhood. Childish playfulness stems from a lack of knowledge about proper adult behavior, whereas demented elders may manifest such behavior because of impaired memory, confusion, or sensory/motor limitations. Some patients may act more like children if the staff rewards such behavior with attention, especially affection.

Etiology. Many gerontologists, especially those with a behavioral science background, have attempted to demonstrate that senile behavior can be explained as the result of environmental variables. Earlier in their lives senile patients in general had lower socioeconomic status, less formal education, fewer social and recreational skills, and fewer social roles when compared with normal elders. Seniles were also more likely to be immigrants and unmarried. Experiments have demonstrated that physical environments that are barren and featureless routines make it difficult for nursing home patients to orient themselves. If the staff insists on doing everything for the patients, their capacity to cope with the environment's demands progressively erodes. Meacher (1972) concluded that some senile behavior is really an adaptive response to the demands of institutional life. When an "enriched" environment is provided, with increased stimulation and demands, the patient's performance on several measures of senility improves.

The evidence is surely sufficient to demonstrate an important environmental component in senile confusional states. Unfortunately, in their zeal to be reformers (or to sell books), some popular gerontologists have claimed that senility is a myth, that old people act in a confused fashion solely because of an inauspicious environment. Such writers do a great disservice if they lead lay persons to refuse to accept a diagnosis of organic brain syndrome in an aged parent. Although there is an environmental component in many cases, and some cases can be due totally to environmental factors, the chief cause of dementia is a structural problem with the brain.

There are over 50 different diseases that can cause the symptoms of dementia. Huntington's chorea is due entirely to the presence of a single dominant gene. Creutzfeldt-Jakob disease is caused by a viral infection, perhaps due to the consumption of bovine brains. Hydrocephalus is due to the pressure of cerebrospinal fluid impairing the functioning of the cortex. The majority of the demented geriatric patients suffer from *Alzheimer's disease* (also known as *senile dementia: Alzheimer's type*), which results in specific degenerative changes in the brain's tissues. These changes can be observed postmortem or via computerized tomography.

For several decades it was assumed that the principal cause of dementia was cerebral arteriosclerosis, a hardening of the brain's arteries resulting in less oxygen being supplied to the brain's tissues. The current consensus is that diminished blood flow is a significant causal factor in less than a fifth of the cases of dementia in later life. Reduced oxygen consumption may exist in a majority of dementia cases, but it is more of a result than a cause. The new theory is that the greatest danger posed to the brain by the vascular system is multi-infarct dementia, many tiny strokes which have the composite effect of diminishing mental capacity without bringing on the paralysis characteristic of larger strokes.

Diagnostic Issues. The diagnosis of dementia cannot be based solely on the patient's memory complaints. There is no correlation between the degree of self-reported memory capacity and memory capacity indicated by objective means. Many of the elders who complain the most about diminishing memory are well within the normal range. Some thoroughly demented patients perceive no difficulty with their memories. The first step in the diagnosis should be brief psychological tests. Use of the Bender-Gestalt test, IQ tests, or any test devised for other purposes or other age groups should be avoided. Questions which test the patient's capacity for orientation in space and time are useful. Focusing the examination on short-term memory tends to neutralize some confounding environmental variables and give a truer indication of organic brain syndrome. Most of these psychological tests have a greater sensitivity than specificity; it is more likely that some normal elders will be misdiagnosed as having dementia than that seniles will score in the normal range. Whenever the tests suggest the presence of dementia, a comprehensive neurological examination should be given.

One great diagnostic difficulty is to distinguish organically based dementia from a pseudodementia caused by depression. True dementia is characterized by gradual onset, while depression may have a rapid progression of symptoms in the wake of some environmental stress or loss. Depressed patients are more likely to complain of memory loss and give "don't know" answers to orientation questions. Purely demented patients are more likely to attempt to conceal cognitive deficits or give ludicrous answers rather than admit that they do not know the answer. One factor complicating the differential diagnosis is that depression and dementia are not mutually exclusive. Indeed, the awareness of cognitive decline can produce a depressive reaction, and a sizable minority of demented patients have a clinically significant depression.

Another possibility is that the cognitive impairments are the result of DELIRIUM rather than dementia. This is the case with the majority of confused elders admitted to general hospitals. The details relating to the onset can be helpful here. However, neurological tests are usually required in order to differentiate a chronic brain syndrome from the acute ones found in delirium.

The diagnosis of dementia, even with appropriate psychometric tests, electroencephalograms, and computerized tomography, is far from exact. Psychologists and psychiatrists trained in the field still disagree with each other on a quarter of the diagnoses. Organic brain syndrome is probably overdiagnosed in the United States, more depressed and conversion reaction patients being diagnosed as demented than the other way around. However, there are cases of patients who were diagnosed as having a purely functional disorder who demonstrated a massive organic brain syndrome when an autopsy was performed.

Treatment. Treatment for dementia can be both medical and psychosocial. About a fifth of chronic brain syndrome patients have dementia due to a treatable organic cause (e.g., hydrocephalus, which is treated by surgery). A much debated therapy in the last few years has been the use of medication (e.g., vasodilators, Hydergine) to improve cerebral circulation and metabolism. The drugs occasionally produce dramatic results, but perceptible mental improvements are generally seen in only a minority of the patients. (However, greater effectiveness might be found with newer drugs

or higher dosages.) An even more recent trend has been the use of antidepressant therapy (medications and electroconvulsive therapy) to treat whatever degree of depression the patient may have. This has cured several patients who really had depressive pseudodementia.

Psychotherapy, especially in groups, can be a real help in treating depression or in getting a demented patient to fully utilize remaining potential. Therapeutic milieus which seek to motivate, stimulate, and orient the patient to reality can be highly successful (Folsom, 1968).

A most important aspect of a comprehensive treatment approach is work with the families of demented patients. Many of them fail to understand the organic basis of dementia and wonder if their treatment of an aged parent or spouse was the cause of the confused behavior. The families that attempt to keep a demented patient in the home need support and consolation for the sacrifices they undergo. The families that decide on the option of institutionalization may have unresolved feelings of guilt.

References

Folsom, J. C. Reality orientation for the elderly mental patient. *Journal of Geriatric Psychiatry*, 1968, *1*, 291–307.

Meacher, M. *Taken for a ride*. London: Longman, 1972.

Additional Readings

Brink, T. L. Brief psychiatric screening of institutionalized aged: A review. *Long Term Care and Health Services Administration Quarterly*, 1980, *4*, 253–260.

Wells, C. E. Chronic brain disease: An overview. *American Journal of Psychiatry*, 1978, *135*, 1–12.

T. L. BRINK

See GERONTOLOGY; GERIATRIC PSYCHOTHERAPY.

Dementia Praecox. The term, coined in 1857, originated from a term signifying a psychosis with a poor prognosis, often ending in complete deterioration and incurability. Dementia refers to a mental disorder, and praecox refers to the origin of the disorder in early life, frequently adolescence. Included under this term are the symptom complexes of catatonia, hebephrenia, and paranoia. Although some European psychiatrists continue to use dementia praecox to describe an incurable type of schizophrenia, the term is largely obsolete following Bleuler's introduction of the term schizophrenia in 1911.

D. L. SCHUURMAN

See SCHIZOPHRENIA.

Demonic Influence and Psychopathology. Belief in demons and demonic possession has been a worldwide phenomenon from earliest recorded history. Incantations, various forms of demonic phenomena, and exorcisms abound in archaeological discoveries from Sumer, Babylonia, Egypt, and Assyria. The religions of India, China, and Japan contain elements of demonism, as do the animistic religions of Africa and South America (Hitt, 1973).

Throughout the Old Testament, Moses and other prophets repeatedly warned against involvement in demonically energized activities such as divination, sorcery, and idol worship. At the time of Jesus belief in demons was widespread among the Jews. From the New Testament record it is clear that Jesus and the New Testament writers regarded demons as personal, fallen, spiritual beings, stronger than men but weaker than God. Demons were viewed as being able to oppress and possess human beings.

Jesus and the New Testament writers were more conservative than surrounding pagan cultures in that they did not ascribe all physical and mental illness to demonic causation. The scriptural writers repeatedly distinguished the state of being demon-possessed from that of illness. In at least 17 places in the Gospels and Acts this distinction is made (e.g. Matt. 4:24; 8:16).

Furthermore, Jesus and the New Testament writers underscored the difference between demonically caused and nondemonically caused illness in their discussion of healing. Both kinds of illnesses were healed, but by different means. Demonically caused illnesses were healed by casting the demon out of the person, whereas nondemonically caused illnesses were never healed by exorcism or binding of demons.

The church throughout most of its history has maintained these same views—i.e., that demons are real and do inflict physical and mental illness, but that not all illness is of demonic causation. In the early church converts from pagan and Jewish backgrounds were usually exorcised before baptism, and throughout the Middle Ages exorcism was included in the rite of infant baptism. There has been an office of exorcist in the Roman Catholic Church until the present day. However, there has also been a place for physicians who heal natural illnesses by natural means.

In recent years some Christian theologians have attempted to demythologize the New Testament characterization of demons and possession, claiming that either Christ was a product of the prescientific thinking of his day or else he accommodated himself to it. It is difficult to reconcile such theories with orthodox views of Christology or the inspiration of

Scripture. If Christ's teachings on demons were erroneous, then his teachings in other areas may also be in error. If Christ knew that people were not demon-possessed but knowingly accommodated his teachings to what he knew to be false, he could not serve as a sinless atonement for humanity. If God inspired an erroneous Scripture, than either his omniscience or his truthfulness is jeopardized. The only view that leaves the orthodox doctrines of Christology and inspiration intact is to believe that demons exist and that they do at times tempt, oppress, or possess people.

Levels of Demonic Involvement. For heuristic purposes we may consider four levels of demonic involvement in human temptation. These levels represent a continuum ranging from no demonic involvement to significant involvement. They should not be taken to refer to discrete categories.

No involvement. Scripture makes it clear that temptations may come from our sinful nature without the necessity of demonic intervention. Jeremiah 17:9 says, "The heart is deceitful above all things and beyond cure." Jesus said, "From within, out of men's hearts, come evil thoughts, sexual immorality, theft, murder, adultery, greed, malice, deceit, lewdness, envy, slander, arrogance and folly. All these evils come from inside and make a man unclean" (Mark 7:21–23). And James 1:14–15 states that "each one is tempted when, by his own evil desire, he is dragged away and enticed. Then, after desire has conceived, it gives birth to sin; and sin, when it is full-grown, gives birth to death."

Temptation. Scripture speaks of a second category of temptation that is demonic in its origin. Christ was tempted directly by Satan (Matt. 4:1–11). Satan apparently tempted Ananias to lie (Acts 5:3); he incited David to take a census in Israel in a way that was displeasing to God (1 Chron. 21:1). An evil spirit also is spoken of as somehow involved in the treachery of the men of Shechem against Abimelech (Judg. 9:23). Finally, Paul reminds believers that they battle against evil supernatural forces, and thus must be fully equipped (Eph. 6:10–18).

It seems likely that in many cases yielding to one's sinful human impulses provides an opening for demonic temptation. For example, David's pride in the growing strength of Israel probably made him more easily susceptible to Satan's temptation to take a census for the wrong reasons. Judas's love of money made him susceptible to Satan's temptation to betray Jesus. Scripture repeatedly affirms that the practice of yielding to sin makes one less and less able to resist its temptations (e.g. John 8:34). This suggests that yielding to sinful temptations arising from one's own nature makes one increasingly susceptible to demonic temptation as well.

Oppression. A more intense level of demonic involvement in human life is variously referred to in the literature as demonic influence, demonic oppression, demonic subjection, or demonic obsession. Within this category demons exert considerable influence over a person's life short of actual possession (Unger, 1971, p. 113). Oppression may range from a simple form of occult subjection that may go unnoticed for years until a particular event uncovers it, to a moderately intense form of oppression where a negative reaction occurs toward any form of Christian counseling, to a state where the person is continually surrounded and oppressed by the powers of darkness (Koch, 1971, p. 32). Since demonic temptation, oppression, and possession form a continuum rather than discrete categories, extreme forms of oppression share much in common with possession.

The tragic end of King Saul's life illustrates well the phenomenon of demonic oppression. Saul began to lose favor with God following his intrusion into the priest's office (1 Sam. 13:8–15) and then in his deliberate disobedience in the war with the Amalekites (1 Sam. 15:1–9). Saul apparently continued his disobedience toward God until God removed the Holy Spirit from him and an evil spirit came to tempt him episodically for the rest of his life (1 Sam. 16:14).

Unger (1971, p. 114) summarizes the biblical data regarding manifestations of demonic oppression as blindness and hardness of heart toward the gospel (2 Cor. 4:4), apostasy and doctrinal corruption (1 Tim. 4:1), and indulging in sinful, defiling behavior (2 Peter 2:1–12). This is roughly paralleled by Lechler's (1971) description of symptoms he has seen in his European psychiatric experience with cases of oppression. Wilson (1976, pp. 226–228) reviews three contemporary cases from his American practice which also seem to fit the characteristics of oppression.

People usually seem to become demonically oppressed in one of two ways—either through personal, continued involvement in sin, or through family involvement in the occult (Koch, 1971). In the latter type of situation the oppressed person himself may not have been involved in the occult but may have had a spell put on him by a relative or acquaintance.

While the above discussion has focused on the psychological and spiritual aspects of oppression, Scripture mentions briefly that demonic oppression sometimes results in physical illness also (Luke. 13:10–16).

Possession. Some Christians have objected to the translation of *daimonizomai* as demon-possessed, preferring instead the word *demonized.* Lexically the word means to have a demon, to be possessed by a demon, or to be exercised by or under the control of a demon. It is never used to refer to someone who is demonically tempted or oppressed. Thus there seems to be no clear lexical objection to the use of demon-possessed to translate *daimonizomai.*

In several instances where demon possession is described in the biblical record, no specific symptoms are mentioned. Identifiable symptoms that are noted include the possessed individual manifesting supernormal strength; going about naked; being unable to speak, hear, or see; experiencing self-destructive convulsions with attendant symptoms such as rigidity, foaming at the mouth, and bruxism; and saying things that evidence a supernatural knowledge. In some cases the symptoms caused by the demon seem to be continuously present. In other instances the manifestation of the demon's presence seems to be episodic.

While some have questioned whether demon possession continues today, large numbers of missionaries who work in countries where demonic (idol) worship is prevalent testify that demon possession continues to exist there with symptoms quite similar to the biblical characterizations (Nevius, 1968; Peters, 1976; Tippett, 1976).

Possession occurs through idol worship, occult involvement, spells cast by another person, or by receiving healing through sorcery (Koch, 1971). Possession is sometimes by a single demon and sometimes by multiple demons.

There is continued debate among Christians about whether believers can be possessed or not. A number of accounts from experienced missionaries assert that this does occur. It is particularly noteworthy that the highly respected biblical scholar Merrill Unger, who in 1952 had written in *Biblical Demonology* that true believers cannot be demon-possessed, says that he has received so many letters from missionaries all over the world documenting this kind of occurrence that he now believes that it does happen (1971, p. 117). The common means by which this seems to happen is through believers arrogantly attacking demons or through continued practice of sin.

Demonic Influence and Mental Illness. Differentiation of demon possession from mental illness is immediately beset by several problems. The foremost of these is that the symptoms arising from psychopathology and demonization overlap to a considerable extent; nearly every symptom thought to be an indicator of demon possession is also found in psychopathology of nondemonic origin. The same phenomenon is found in the biblical record: blindness sometimes had a demonic etiology (Matt. 12:22) and at other times only a natural base (Mark 8:22–25). Deafness and dumbness were likewise found to have sometimes a natural and sometimes a demonic base.

Second, diagnosis is always forced to contend with the problem of role enactment. People continuously fulfill a variety of roles in which they behave as they consciously and unconsciously believe persons in these roles should act. There is strong evidence to suggest that the role a person adopts modifies his or her perception of reality in ways consistent with that role. Thus, a person who experiences unusual mental events and begins to believe that he is demon-possessed may begin to act in ways that are consistent with demon possession without actually being demonically possessed. If such a person receives feedback from his environment that his perception of being possessed is correct, his experience is further reinforced.

A third complicating problem in differential diagnosis is that demon possession does not occur on a blank personality. Psychopathological states and demonic possession may coexist within the same person, with a consequent blending and overlapping of the symptoms resulting from each state (Jackson, 1976, p. 263).

Fourth, we have no guarantee that the relatively brief descriptions of demonically caused symptomatology found in Scripture were intended to be normative examples of possession across time and cultures. All that the narrative accounts of demonization found in the Gospels and Acts claim is that they are accurate descriptions of demonization of that time, not normative descriptions of demonization that can be used for all successive generations. Hermeneutically it is more correct to accept the biblical descriptions as suggestive criteria for diagnosis than as normative criteria.

Fifth, most Christian workers faced with diagnosis will be well trained in psychology *or* theology, but rarely in both. We tend to underestimate the contribution of a field that we do not understand well. Thus psychologists and psychiatrists, heavily influenced by the antisupernaturalistic bias of their secular training, may tend to underdiagnose demonic oppression and possession. Conversely, theologically trained workers may underdiagnose mental illness originating in the natural realm. Mallory states that "there seems to be a tendency in this [deliverance] literature, to attribute to demons what is not understood by the author's limited knowledge of mental illness" (McAll, 1976, p. 322).

There are a number of reasons why proper diagnosis is important. Many Christians have observed the damaging effects that occur when a person in the midst of a brief reactive psychosis or suffering from severe depression has been told that he is demon-possessed. In addition to the stress that produced the actual psychological disorder, the person now has the added guilt and anxiety that demons have taken up residence in his body.

There are at least three unhealthy aspects to the practice of considering sins that arise primarily from our own human natures to be the result of demonic forces. First, it tends to remove the responsibility of recognizing and confessing one's own sinfulness. Scripture clearly teaches that God will not allow believers to be tempted beyond what they are able to withstand, meaning that when we do sin, we are responsible for that action. As Montgomery (1976) rather bluntly states: "The devil made me do it is not an acceptable theological stance, but rather a demonic form of escapism to avoid confrontation with personal sin within" (p. 22).

Second, to view ourselves as a battleground upon which forces of good and evil alternately rampage without volitional control robs us of a sense of potency. We may fail to make needed changes in our lives because we believe such changes are beyond our control. Further, by suppressing and repressing our own urges, viewing them as demonic by-products rather than as parts of ourselves, we are building an unhealthy personality structure. Large portions of our selves remain dissociated rather than integrated.

Accurate differential diagnosis is important in order that truly demonically oppressed or possessed people can receive appropriate treatment. Traditional psychotherapeutic and chemotherapeutic methods have no demonstrated efficacy in the treatment of possession. Diagnosis can proceed in a manner similar to the way other medical or psychological diagnoses are made. This includes taking a history, analyzing the constellation of presenting symptoms, observing epiphenomena or related activity within the person's social system, and evaluating the person's response to treatment.

History taking would focus on the person's spiritual history and involvement with the occult, and on immediate precursors of the present situation. Many who write in this area emphasize that even casual interactions with occult practices may result in long-standing effects. In addition it seems to be important to investigate family involvement in the occult back as far as three or four generations. Evidence of occult involvement in the past does not prove that the present problem is demonic but increases the probability that it may be so. An analysis of the immediate precursors to the present situation may be helpful in differentiating role-enactment behaviors from genuine possession.

Some writers have concluded that diagnosis of demon possession on the basis of symptom analysis is indeterminate, since each individual symptom found in demon possession is also found in some kind of mental illness. Such a conclusion seems needlessly pessimistic. In most diseases it is the complex of symptoms, rather than any individual symptom, that is the basis of a diagnostic decision. Thus while various mental illnesses share one or two symptoms in common with demon possession, there are none that share the entire symptom complex.

The symptom complex may be described in terms of physical symptoms, psychological symptoms, and spiritual symptoms. Physical symptoms often include 1) preternatural (more than natural) strength, 2) change in facial demeanor (usually to one of intense hatred and evil), 3) change in voice tone and pitch (usually the voice deepens and becomes harsher or takes on a mocking tone), 4) epileptic-like convulsions with attendant symptoms, and 5) anesthesia to pain.

Psychological symptoms may include 1) clairvoyance (seeing things that could not be seen through normal means), 2) telepathy (communication from one mind to another by other than normal means), 3) the ability to predict the future, 4) the ability to speak in languages not known by the possessed person, 5) clouding of consciousness while in the trance state, and 6) amnesia for things which happened while in the trance state.

Spiritual changes may include 1) a significant change in moral character (a previously modest person will dance naked), 2) becoming

verbally or physically aggressive or falling into a trance if someone prays, and 3) an inability to say Jesus' name reverently or to affirm that he is God's son in the flesh (1 John 4:1–2).

An important epiphenomenon of diagnostic significance in demon possession is that possession is often accompanied by poltergeist ("noisy ghost") phenomena. These may include such things as unexplainable noises, furniture or household goods inexplicably overturned, pungent odors, and showerings of damp earth.

If the preceding criteria do not yield a diagnosis, the person's response to treatment may also be used. If standard psychotherapy and chemotherapy do not produce expected results, it would be possible to conduct a trial ceremony to bind or exorcise any demons who might be involved. If it was believed that it might be clinically disadvantageous to involve the client in the process, it is possible to conduct such a ceremony without the client's knowledge or presence (McAll, 1976).

Two classes of mental illness that some have viewed as having overlapping symptomatology with demon possession are the disorders of multiple personality and undifferentiated schizophrenia. In multiple personalities and demon possession there are voice changes, abrupt personality changes, and frequently amnesia for some of the other personalities and their behavior. However, in multiple personalities there are usually not epileptic-like convulsions, anesthesia to pain, clairvoyance, telepathy, ability to predict the future, ability to speak in languages not learned by at least one of the personalities, or the spiritual changes that usually occur with demon possession. In addition, the various personalities identify themselves as human personalities rather than demons.

In undifferentiated schizophrenia there are also some similarities to demon possession. The person may speak with words or syntax that is not part of his native language. He may claim to be someone other than who he is normally known to be. He may occasionally possess unusual strength. There may be changes in his voice tone, and pitch and facial expressions. He may claim to have unusual telepathic powers. There may sometimes be clouding of consciousness, and he may sit as if in a trance for long periods of time. Personal hygiene often deteriorates, and occasionally such persons will even walk about naked.

However, there are significant differences between the person with undifferentiated schizophrenia and the demon-possessed person, even within the above-mentioned similarities. There is a vast qualitative difference between the word salad and neologisms of the schizophrenic, and the sometimes eloquent speaking in foreign languages of the demon-possessed person. Within the demon-possessed person we usually find two or more well-organized, goal-directed personalities, each episodically taking control of the body they inhabit. The delusion of the schizophrenic in which he believes himself to be someone he is not is easily seen by others to be patently false and a product of his own distorted perceptions. The schizophrenic may claim to have clairvoyance or telepathy, but his claims usually prove groundless. In the case of the demon-possessed person, the demon actually has supernatural access to such information and the clairvoyance and telepathy may be genuine.

The person with schizophrenia may or may not be a believer, but even if he is not, he generally will not demonstrate the radical negativism toward prayer that characterizes the demon-possessed person. Furthermore, poltergeist phenomena happen with the demon-possessed person but not the schizophrenic. The schizophrenic will often respond to antipsychotic medication, whereas the demon-possessed person does not. The schizophrenic person may respond to exorcism with a symptomatic remission, but the psychotic symptoms generally return in a short period of time.

Treatment. In cases of actual demon possession pagan and church history reveal three basic classes of exorcism. One means of exorcism used at various times and within various cultures has been physically beating the possessed person. The theory behind this practice was that if one were to inflict enough pain on the body which the demon was possessing, the demon would choose to leave. A second class of exorcism methods involves the use of magic formulas. Such formulas have been used from the time of the ancient Assyro-Babylonian cultures (or before) until the present day (Norvell, 1974).

Jesus presents a definite break with both these two methods. He needed neither scourging nor magic rituals. His exorcism method was powerful, direct, and brief. Frequently Jesus exorcised demons with a single word, "Go." At other times he used a slightly longer command, "Come out of him." Jesus' longest recorded exorcism was: "You deaf and dumb spirit, I command you, come out of him and never enter him again" (Mark 9:25). Jesus commanded his followers to continue the ministry of exorcism and empowered them to do

so. Their instruction was to cast out demons in his name.

There is no instruction given that Christian exorcists must force the demon to name himself so that they could exorcise him by name. Furthermore, the biblical record suggests that exorcism can be done without the presence or cooperation of the person possessed (Mark 7:25–30). They do, however, admonish those involved in deliverance ministry to have a firm faith in Jesus' power to exorcise the demon and to prepare for exorcism by prayer. Scriptures also warn that it is dangerous for unbelievers to attempt to exorcise demons in Jesus' name (Acts 19:13–16).

A similar list of suggestions has been made by those Christians who have been actively involved in deliverance ministry in the twentieth century. The following recommendations represent the consensus of the authors listed in the references: 1) Remember that the power to exorcise demons lies in Jesus' name, not in a prescribed procedure or ritual. 2) Faith in Jesus' ability to exorcise demons is essential. Prayer beforehand is important preparation. 3) Self-examination and godly living is essential. More than one would-be exorcist has been embarrassed by a demon publicly revealing his private sins. 4) Exorcism should be done by a group of believers whenever possible. 5) Exorcism can be performed without the presence or cooperation of the possessed person. When the possessed person is able to be involved, it strengthens the process for him or her to let the demon know that he or she wants the demon to leave. 6) The possessed person should make a full confession of sins, pray a prayer of renunciation, and make a clean break with sin by burning occult books, breaking mediumistic contacts or friendships, etc. 7) More than one demon may possess a person simultaneously. It is important that all demons be cast out before the exorcism process is discontinued. 8) Relapses can occur after exorcism. On more than one occasion demons have reported that they have been enabled to reenter a believer's life because of lapses into pre-Christian ways of living. Therefore the exorcised persons should fill their lives with Bible reading and the Holy Spirit. 9) A follow-up support group of two or more people who can meet regularly for prayer and fellowship is recommended.

References

Hitt, R. *Demons, the Bible and you.* Newtown, Pa.: Timothy Books, 1973.
Jackson, B. Reflections on the demonic: A psychiatric perspective. In J. W. Montgomery (Ed.), *Demon possession.* Minneapolis: Bethany Fellowship, 1976.

Koch, K. (Ed.). *Occult bondage and deliverance.* Grand Rapids: Kregel Publications, 1971.

Lechler, A. What is the demonic. In K. Koch (Ed.), *Occult bondage and deliverance.* Grand Rapids: Kregel Publications, 1971.

McAll, R. K. Taste and see. In J. W. Montgomery (Ed.), *Demon possession.* Minneapolis: Bethany Fellowship, 1976.

Montgomery, J. W. *Demon possession.* Minneapolis: Bethany Fellowship, 1976.

Nevius, J. L. *Demon possession* (8th ed.). Grand Rapids: Kregel Publications, 1968.

Norvell, A. *Exorcism.* West Nyack, N.Y.: Parker Publishing, 1974.

Peters, G. W. Demonism on the mission fields. In J. W. Montgomery (Ed.), *Demon possession.* Minneapolis: Bethany Fellowship, 1976.

Tippett, A. R. Spirit possession as it relates to culture and religion. In J. W. Montgomery (Ed.), *Demon possession.* Minneapolis: Bethany Fellowship, 1976.

Unger, M. F. *Demons in the world today.* Wheaton, Ill.: Tyndale House, 1971.

Wilson, W. P. Hysteria and demons, depression and oppression, good and evil. In J. W. Montgomery (Ed.), *Demon possession.* Minneapolis: Bethany Fellowship, 1976.

H. A. VIRKLER

Denial. An unconscious mental mechanism in which refusal to perceive or admit the existence of something serves as an ego defense against some unpleasant, unacceptable aspect of reality. Thus, when some internal or external perception is judged by the unconscious ego as potentially threatening, the perception or memory of that reality is filtered out of conscious awareness. This process generally operates within a weak ego, functioning most successfully in the denial of painful or threatening internal realities. Denial, also known as negation in the psychological literature, is seen in the example of a woman faced with the news of her impending death from cancer, who believes that there must be some mistake, that such an event could not be happening to her.

R. LARKIN

See DEFENSE MECHANISMS.

Dependency. There is nothing inherently wrong with depending on others. Healthy interdependence differs, however, from symbiotic relationships wherein one's psychological need for a stable self-esteem is dependent on others. Such behavior is best viewed as pathological dependency. It is often present in members of conservative religious groups.

Healthy cooperation, or depending on one another, is the foundation of human social life. Yet truly dependent individuals in the pejorative sense are characterized by a willingness to allow others to assume major responsibility for their lives. One can see the extreme of such behavior in the dependent personality disorder where diminished self-esteem and autonomy are accompanied by a panicky need for protection and eventual learned helplessness. In other words, excessive dependency is an infantile refusal to accept responsibility for managing one's life, making decisions, and acting on them (Willis, 1982). Such patterns reflect, for a variety of reasons, a preference for symbiotic relationships over against ones based on healthy mutual cooperation.

Dependency begins developmentally in the familial context and is eventually shaped by the larger social network. A measure of dependency is normal and natural in childhood, but as the person grows and develops, it can be distorted in an effort to mold oneself to gain the approval of others at great cost to one's personhood. Persons remain dependent because they crave security or prefer to engage in self-protective and anxiety-reducing strategies to allow themselves to remain childlike. In short, pathological dependency is the failure to grow up psychosocially, cognitively, and maturationally.

All persons who desire to promote wholeness in others must come to grips with the subtle and overt ways people hang on to outside sources of affirmation, identity, and security. Certain parental, leadership, interactional, and teaching styles are clearly antidevelopmental in that they fail to foster autonomy and interdependence. As the clinician knows, deeply ingrained habits develop, and abandoning these can be an intensely painful and anxiety-producing experience. Since helping persons discover true autonomy and interdependence is an important goal in therapy, therapists must sensitize persons to the freedom and responsibility that is theirs, and cultivate within them a sincere desire to develop their inner resources for problem solving. Their choices must become their own choices within the context of their communities. Without coercion or manipulation, they must be helped to develop a more adequate philosophy of life, so that authentic living can increasingly replace their fearful self-protectiveness.

There are several dangers in regard to pathological dependency in the clinical or helping relationship. It is very tempting for the therapist to use the therapeutic relationship to serve personal dependency needs and thereby to retard the development of the patient. Freeing the patient to choose and to take full responsibility for decisions is certainly anxiety-producing for the therapist (Fromm-Reichman, 1950). Although the therapist may be

299

perceived as accepting and nurturing, he must be careful to set clear limits so that pathological dependency is not simply transferred to him. An integrated person lives by his or her own standards, not by those of the therapist. What the patient takes from the therapist must, therefore, be incorporated within the fabric of his own personality and not remain an alien parcel. More specifically for the Christian, holy values need to be fully assimilated so that they become a part of one's being, and not merely an unassimilated set of moralisms—i.e., a concern for surface behavior.

References
Fromm-Reichman, F. *Principles of intensive psychotherapy.* Chicago: University of Chicago Press, 1950.
Willis, E. The politics of dependency. *Ms.,* 1982, 7, 181–214.
R. E. BUTMAN

See ACTIVE-DEPENDENT PERSONALITY PATTERN; PASSIVE-DEPENDENT PERSONALITY PATTERN.

Dependent Personality Disorder.
The diagnostic criteria for dependent personality disorder include lack of self-confidence, allowing others to assume responsibility for one's life, allowing one's own needs to be second to others, and the inability to function independently. Such individuals feel inadequate and helpless and put their own needs second so as to avoid offending the person on whom they are dependent. They believe that if they offend that person they will be rejected, leaving them to rely on themselves. Thus they will even suffer humiliation and physical abuse from a mate in order not to lose the relationship. They are preoccupied with the thought of being abandoned. If they are married, their spouses will assume all responsibility regarding where they live, who they should be friends with, and what job they should take.

Physical illness in childhood may contribute to the development of this disorder. Such children allow their parents to decide who they should play with, how to spend their free time, and what they should wear. Separation anxiety and avoidance disorder of children or adolescents are often the precursors of dependent personality disorders in adults. Dependent personality is found more frequently in women. It is frequently associated with other personality disorders such as avoidant, histrionic, narcissistic, or schizotypal. Also, depression and anxiety are commonly associated with this disorder.

Persons with a dependent personality disorder are impaired in social relationships. Their contacts become limited to only the person on whom they are dependent and the individuals who are acquaintances of that person. There are also vocational limitations. The dependent person has difficulty making decisions and asserting himself, and the autonomous functioning required by some jobs poses impossible demands.

Dependent personalities may be mistaken for agoraphobics. In both, dependent behavior is prominent. In the dependent personality disorder, however, persons passively maintain a dependent relationship, while in agoraphobia they actively insist that the other take responsibility for them.

Persons with this disorder will often benefit from insight therapy. The goal is to help them gain an understanding of how the disorder developed and learn to utilize assertive skills. The person on whom the client is dependent should also participate in the therapeutic process. Such persons need to understand how they can encourage the client to gain self-confidence and independence. These persons may also need the dependent relationship in order to meet their own needs, and thus present a problem which can be addressed more productively with their involvement in the therapy process. If anxiety and depression interfere with therapy, medication may also be a helpful component of a total treatment approach.

M. A. CAMPION

See ACTIVE-DEPENDENT PERSONALITY PATTERN; PASSIVE-DEPENDENT PERSONALITY PATTERN.

Depersonalization Disorder.
One of a class of disorders known as dissociative disorders, which are characterized by "sudden, temporary alterations in the normally integrative functions of consciousness, identity, or motor behavior" (*DSM-III,* p. 253). The disorder must be distinguished from symptoms of depersonalization which are much more prevalent than the disorder.

Symptoms of Depersonalization. The symptoms of depersonalization usually develop rapidly and are characterized by a sense of alienation and estrangement from one's self. Self and the environment may appear dreamlike and unreal. Persons who have experienced depersonalization may report feelings of being outside one's body and observing it from a distance. These persons may also report feeling detached, numb, mechanical, disjointed, or dead inside. Some feel as though they are floating. While these feelings are unpleasant, depersonalization is usually accompanied by diminished rather than heightened emotion.

Depersonalization is marked by a qualitative change in experiencing. It is as though consciousness dissociates from the body and the person steps outside the physical boundaries of the body. The person's ability to perceive self and the environment are not grossly impaired, but the perceptions do not "feel right." Although the person may have a difficult time communicating what was experienced during the episode of depersonalization, the report may be distinguished from the hallucination of a psychotic because the content is organized, accurate as to the physical details of the setting, and free from delusional content. The person with depersonalization disorder does not demonstrate the extreme anxiety and disorganization of the psychotic or schizophrenic person. Mild to moderate anxiety or depression sometimes accompanies depersonalization.

Symptoms of depersonalization (but not depersonalization disorder) may be secondary to many other medical or psychological disturbances. Symptoms of depersonalization frequently are reported by schizophrenics. Episodes of depersonalization also frequently accompany chronic alcohol intoxication and alcohol withdrawal. Prolonged depersonalization has been noted after marijuana use. Epileptics, especially those suffering from temporal lobe epilepsy, occasionally report depersonalization shortly before or after seizures. In each of the preceding cases depersonalization is incidental to other significant disorders and depersonalization disorder would not be diagnosed.

Depersonalization Disorder. Depersonalization disorder is diagnosed only when the person's symptoms are unaccompanied by any evidence of another significant psychological or medical problem. While depersonalization disorder may be accompanied by some anxiety or depression, the anxiety and depression are alone insufficient to warrant a diagnosis other than depersonalization disorder. Persons with depersonalization disorder are not psychotic. They do not lose touch with reality, although their experience of reality may be episodically altered. In addition, the diagnosis of depersonalization disorder is not made unless the symptoms are severe enough to impair social relationships or occupational competence.

Depersonalization disorder occurs most frequently among adolescents and young adults. It tends to run an intermittent but chronic course. Episodes of depersonalization tend to be elicited by stress. Depersonalization disorder does not appear to result in marked personality deterioration, and persons may function adequately between episodes. Symptomatology probably diminishes with age and adjustment. Sex differences in the incidence of depersonalization disorder have not been reliably established.

Normal persons may infrequently experience some symptoms of depersonalization. It has been speculated that as many as 70% of all adolescents and young adults experience mild and temporary depersonalization. A study of persons in life-threatening situations revealed that two-thirds experienced some temporary symptoms of depersonalization. The "life after death" experiences that are being reported and are beginning to receive research scrutiny seem to be a type of depersonalization experience.

As ubiquitous as symptoms of depersonalization are, depersonalization disorder is a seldom diagnosed and little understood problem. The cause is unknown. Some explanations have suggested brain lesions in memory-related structures of the brain as the cause. Most theories have suggested that depersonalization reflects difficulties during development, either in infants' failure to develop a unified sense of self and world or adolescents' inability to forge a coherent identity and assume healthful roles in family and society.

Treatment of depersonalization disorder has also varied widely and depends largely on the theoretical orientation of the clinician. Many medical treatments have been tried and discarded. Major tranquilizers, minor tranquilizers, amphetamines, and antidepressants have been used with relatively little success, although there still seems to be considerable interest in the use of antidepressants. Supportive psychotherapy has been frequently used, with mixed results. Behavioral approaches have included recording symptoms, stress management, relaxation and assertive training. Milieu therapy has been recommended for adolescents in an attempt to help them develop a sense of identity. In spite of these recommendations there has been little research on the treatment of depersonalization disorder, and a clearly superior method of treatment has yet to be determined.

C. D. DOLPH

Depression: Behavioral Perspectives. Most behavioral theorists see depression as a syndrome which is the final common endpoint of a variety of possible etiological pathways. In general, behavioral theories of depression are distinguished by their focus on the interaction of the behavior of the depressed person with the responses of his or her environment. Behavioral models differ from cognitive models in proposing that the distorted thinking of the depressed person is largely the result, rather than the cause, of depression.

The most comprehensive and best researched behavioral model of depression is that of Lewinsohn. He argues that the "key notion is that being depressed results from too few person-environment interactions with positive outcomes for the person" (Lewinsohn, Sullivan, & Grosscup, 1980, p. 324). He argues that it is reinforcement, as defined by the quality of the person's interaction with the environment, that maintains normal affective behavior. When reinforcement decreases or becomes overshadowed by overwhelmingly negative events, depressive behavior results. There are three general reasons in Lewinsohn's model why this would ever occur: 1) Reinforcement may not be as available as would be desired (as when a loved one dies, or a person takes a new job or moves to a new area where few positive satisfactions are available, or the environment may have acquired many negative properties). 2) The person may lack the life skills to obtain available reinforcers or cope with negative stressful events (e.g., the individual who is socially anxious and thus unable to take advantage of opportunities for meaningful relationships). 3) The positive value of certain reinforcers may have been eroded or the negative impact of certain other events heightened (as when a painful experience with a friend sensitizes one to criticism and makes the friendship less satisfying).

Low rates of reinforcement directly cause dysphoria (or sad feelings) and extinguish normal behavior, leading to further reduction in reinforcement, a cycle which Lewinsohn has described as a downward spiral. To complicate matters further, it is suggested that depressive behavior is reinforced by the sympathetic attempts of friends and family to encourage the depressed person, and that the rejection and avoidance of the depressed person by others also complicate the picture by further decreasing the reinforcement available to the person.

Lewinsohn's model has received a fair amount of empirical support, though this support cannot be interpreted as supporting Lewinsohn's model alone. Depressed persons have reported lower frequencies of engaging in pleasant activities and experiencing less enjoyment of these activities when they do engage in them. It has been shown that people usually

initially respond to the depressed person with supportive statements but tend to avoid him whenever possible. Depressed people are consistently rated as less socially skilled and less attractive interpersonally.

The behavioral theory of Ferster (1973) is very similar to that of Lewinsohn, the major difference being that Lewinsohn focuses outward, emphasizing low rates of reinforcement received, and Ferster focuses inward on depression as "loss of reinforcible behavior." Ferster attributes this loss of behavior to either 1) low rates of reinforcement, ineffective schedules of reinforcement, or sudden environmental changes, or 2) the supplanting of normal behavior with escape or avoidance behavior such as whining and crying.

The LEARNED HELPLESSNESS model of depression has historically been called a behavioral model of depression, but in its present form it is more a cognitive model.

Finally, Rehm (1977) has proposed a self-control model of depression. Following the work of Kanfer, he suggests that persons regulated their behavior by self-observation, by self-evaluation or judging the adequacy of their behavior, and by self-consequating their behavior, either reinforcing ("I did that well") or punishing ("I really blew that") themselves for their performance. Rehm suggests that disruptions in any of these three stages of self-control can lead to depression. Depressed persons are thought to selectively attend to negative aspects of their behavior and of environmental events, as well as to attend almost exclusively to immediate outcomes of their behavior. They evaluate their behavior by very harsh standards and tend to attribute their successes to luck or fate. They reinforce themselves very sparingly and punish themselves frequently and harshly for failing to meet their standards. This model does not have the breadth of support of Lewinsohn's model.

Sociological studies such as that of Brown and Harris (1978) relate the occurrence of depression to the occurrence of stressful life events or provoking agents (e.g., poverty, loss of loved one or job) in the absence of protective factors (i.e., factors which serve to attenuate the harmful impact of a stressor, such as familial or general social support systems). The people most likely to experience stress without such protective factors are those most likely to get depressed—groups such as blacks, females, the aged, and the poor. Brown, Bhrolchain, and Harris (1975) found that 38% of their subjects who experienced severe stress without a trusted confidant experienced depression as a result, while only 4% who experienced a similar stress with a confidant became depressed. Brown and Harris also suggested that age, past loss of a significant other, and previous episodes of depression influenced the severity of depression experienced. These findings are easily subsumed within the behavioral model of Lewinsohn, with the interaction between provoking agents and protective factors being interpreted as one way of understanding the relative reinforcing and punishing effect of environmental events. Variables such as past loss and previous episodes of depression probably represent critical events which influence the individual's skills for coping with stress and obtaining reinforcement.

The common theme among all behavioral models is the idea that in the depressed individual life satisfaction is not sufficient to support normal affective states. Depression is either the inevitable (unconditioned) response to such low rates of life satisfaction, or it represents a particular style of coping with the low rates of reinforcement. The behavior therapist, then, must influence the client to move actively toward taking greater control of his or her life, including taking constructive steps toward the goal of increased life satisfaction. The major work of therapy is removing obstacles to obtaining these satisfactions. Almost any of the standard BEHAVIOR THERAPY techniques might be used in this process. These would include ASSERTIVENESS TRAINING to help a person become more socially active, anxiety-reduction techniques to allow the client to be more relaxed and thus better able to enjoy available reinforcers, and PROBLEM SOLVING training to equip the depressed client to deal more effectively with problems in living.

Piper (1977) has argued persuasively that humans were made by God to live in a perfectly good and pleasing relationship with him, our fellow humans, and with the creation at large. Because we were designed for this, it is reasonable and natural that a major motive of life would be the pursuit of happiness, though this pursuit is now distorted by sin, resulting in most individuals seeking that which ultimately does not satisfy. Christians should not reject the pursuit of happiness as a motive of life per se, but rather reject the pursuit of pleasure along paths that are perversions of God's original designs for our lives. Thus, it is possible that the behavioral view of depression is broadly compatible with a biblical view of human motivation. Further, the depression experienced by David in the Old Testament (e.g., Pss. 32 and 51) is understandable from a behavioral perspective. The self-control interpretation of the depression following his adultery with Bathsheba would be that the depression followed a harsh self-evaluation of and self-punishment for his adultery. However, such a view ignores God's supernatural dealing with David over this issue. A further limitation of the behavioral models might be their trivializing of the spiritual/existential aspects of our human struggle, which can sometimes result in depression and despair.

References

Brown, G. W., Bhrolchain, M. N., & Harris, T. O. Social class and psychiatric disturbance. *Sociology,* 1975, *9*(2), 225–254.

Brown, G., & Harris, T. *Social origins of depression.* New York: Free Press, 1978.

Ferster, C. A functional analysis of depression. *American Psychologist,* 1973, *28,* 857–870.

Lewinsohn, P. M., Sullivan, J. M., & Grosscup, S. J. Changing reinforcing events: An approach to the treatment of depression. *Psychotherapy: Theory, Research, and Practice,* 1980, *17*(3), 322–334.

Piper, J. How I became a Christian hedonist. *His Magazine,* 1977, *37*(6), 1, 3–5.

Rehm, L. A self-control model of depression. *Behavior Therapy,* 1977, *8,* 787–804.

S. L. JONES

Depression: Clinical Picture and Classification. The clinical picture of the depressed person can vary widely from complaints of localized pain to problems with motivation. The various depressive syndromes seem to manifest themselves among sufferers in endless ways. Because of this variety, most descriptions of the typical depressive symptoms focus on those symptoms which best differentiate depression from other mental disorders. Beck (1967) lists four symptoms as core signs: low mood, pessimism, self-criticism, and retardation or agitation of movement. Emotionally, depressed patients will often report dejection, inability to appreciate humor, lower levels of pleasure from previously pleasurable pursuits, and difficulties in being involved with people. Crying is also a frequent complaint.

Depression also makes inroads into the thought life of the victim. Recurring thoughts of self-deprecation, low self-esteem, and gloomy outlooks are common. The depressed person will often be indecisive, sometimes to the point of being unable to function. Suicidal thoughts are found among those whose depression is strong.

Depression usually also has somatic manifestations. Kiev (1974) lists gastrointestinal tract complaints, sleep disturbances, pain, and sexual dysfunction as major physical features of depression. A loss of appetite for food and a lack of energy are frequent problems. Many depressed patients exhibit facial sadness and slowed motor activity.

The American Psychiatric Association officially divides depression or mood disorders into three major classifications (*DSM-III*): major affective disorders, other specific affective disorders, and atypical affective disorders. The two major affective disorders are bipolar disorder (formerly manic-depressive illness) and major depression. A diagnosis of bipolar disorder is made whenever a manic episode has occurred, whether or not a depression has accompanied it. A major depression is one which exhibits severe depressive symptoms that persist over time. The category called other specific affective disorders includes two moderate forms of the major disorders: cyclothymic disorder (characterized by mood swings) and dysthymic disorder (formerly depressive neurosis). The atypical classification is reserved for depressions that cannot be categorized elsewhere.

Some researchers tend to see depression as a unitary phenomenon spread out on a continuum from mild to severe. Other theoreticians see at least two major categories of depression: endogenous and exogenous. These two types are differentiated on the basis of where the cause of the depression is located: inside the person (endogenous) or outside the person (exogenous). Endogenous depressions are psychotic, tend to respond best to pharmacotherapy because of their biological base, and are influenced by heredity factors. Exogenous depressions are neurotic, reactive, and are thought to be most amenable to psychotherapy. The debate between the unitary schools and the exogenous versus endogenous theories continues. *DSM-III* maintains a neutral stance on this issue.

References

Beck, A. T. *Depression: Causes and treatment.* Philadelphia: University of Pennsylvania Press, 1967.

Kiev, A. (Ed.), *Somatic manifestations of depressive disorder.* New York: American Elsevier Publishing, 1974.

J. R. BECK

Depression: Cognitive Perspective.

The cognitive model of depression assumes that the nature and characteristics of one's thinking determines how one feels. Cognition is a broad term that refers to both the content of thought and the processes involved in thinking.

Many of the complex processes subsumed under the term *cognition* are still poorly understood. Therefore, in the absence of a clear, comprehensive theory of cognition, the existence of cognitive structures, or schemata, has been postulated. Cognitive structures, or schemata, are relatively enduring patterns of organization of one's prior experiences. They suggest a code or a framework into which individuals organize their experiences.

Contrary to common belief among clinicians, the cognitive approach to depression does not assume that a well-adjusted individual is one who thinks more logically and solves problems more rationally, or has a more reasonable cognitive schemata. What is rather assumed is that depressed individuals organize their thoughts in a manner that is not adjustive. Their particular way of viewing the world does not allow them to adjust in a reasonable manner. The depressed way of ordering one's thoughts interferes with one's emotional well-being and general functioning.

The cognitive view of depression contradicts the popular assumption that mood alteration is central in depressive syndromes. The focus of this view is rather on the thinking and preoccupations of the depressed individual. The central thoughts of the depressed individual center around the theme of loss. This loss may be in regard to the individual's own person, such as a loss of self-confidence or self-esteem or a loss of valuable traits. This loss may also be in regard to a loss of pleasure in one's surroundings. The theme here is often, "I do not enjoy anything anymore. Nothing is worthwhile." Finally, the loss may be a loss of hope for the future, a loss of hope that circumstances will improve.

The theme of loss regarding the future relates also to a phenomenon of time distortion which the cognitive model posits for depressives; namely, the depressed individual has a highly constricted time perspective. The depressed individual is often so preoccupied with the pain of the present that there is no focus on the future. Often the individual will say that he or she has "no future" or "nothing to look forward to."

An additional characteristic of the thought processes of the depressed individual is distorted recall. Depressed individuals selectively recall material with negative content or implications and ignore positive or neutral material.

A third characteristic of the thinking patterns of the depressed individual is the strong tendency to assign negative global and personalized meanings to events. For example, from one minor occurrence, the depressed individual extrapolates global judgments regarding his or her overall worthlessness as an individual.

Beck (1979) assumes that each of those thought patterns arises from silent assumptions that depressed individual holds. These assumptions were probably formed during the person's earlier years and have not been modified. Furthermore, these assumptions are more likely to be activated by conditions that resemble the circumstances in which they developed. For example, an assumption or scheme that originally developed as a consequence of the death of a close relative during the patient's childhood may be readily reactivated by any death the patient confronts during adulthood. Usually these assumptions involve all-or-nothing attitudes or black-and-white issues—e.g., "I must be totally successful, otherwise I am a failure," or "I must please everyone around me or I am nothing but a failure."

At present there seems to be research support for the cognitive model of depression from a number of different sources (cf. Hollon & Beck, 1979). Some of the evidence includes findings such as the tendency of depressed individuals to expect more negative outcomes on expectancy measures than nondepressed individuals. Depression has also been found to be correlated with various irrational beliefs tests. Depressed individuals tend more often to use all-or-none thinking or other forms of more rigid thinking. Also, a number of studies have found that depressed individuals perceive themselves as having less skills needed to complete a certain task. In the actual study 'they had skills equal to those of the nondepressed individuals. Other studies have found that depressed individuals were more likely to recall negative events than were nondepressives. Finally, a number of studies have been able to use cognitive induction procedures to induce negative mood states, complete with physiological changes consistent with the relevant mood state. That is, asking individuals to think sad thoughts led not only to increased dysphoric mood but also to the physiological concomitants of clinical depressives.

Taken together, the above brief summary of research in this area suggests that indeed there is a close relationship between what one thinks and his mood state. This appears to corroborate the statement in Proverbs 23:7: "As a man thinks within himself, so he is." One must be careful, however, in positing any one cause for depression. Craighead (1980) has stated that depression is probably multidimensional and thus may have many causes. However, it does appear to be the case, that at least in some cases of depression the thoughts of the individual are a causative factor of that depression.

References

Beck, A., Rush, A., Shaw, B., & Emery G. *Cognitive therapy of depression.* New York: Guilford Press, 1979.
Craighead, W. E. Away from a unitary model of depression. *Behavior Therapy*, 1980, *11*, 122–128.
Hollon, S., & Beck, A. Cognitive therapy of depression. In P. C. Kendall & S. D. Hollon (Eds.), *Cognitive-behavior interventions.* New York: Academic Press, 1979.

L. R. PROPST

See COGNITIVE-BEHAVIOR THERAPY.

Depression: Dynamic Perspective. A dynamic perspective on depression is a way of understanding depression as a product of one's mental life, in particular as an outgrowth of one's conflicts and motivations. Most psychodynamic theorists regard depression as the result of inverted anger—i.e., anger that one turns on oneself. The depressed person is angry but, fearing the results of expressing this anger toward someone else, expresses it toward himself. Careful scrutiny of the depressive experience will reveal that there is a qualitative as well as a quantitative difference between depression and sadness. Even pronounced grieving does not necessarily have the pathological features of true clinical depression.

A clinically depressed person is in agony. Sometimes this agony shows up as agitation and sometimes as a kind of shutdown of one's psychological system. When the depression is intense and the person is without a sense of hope, ruminations of worthlessness coupled with a wish to die can lead to suicide, this being a rather transparent manifestation of anger turned against self. Guilt, which can be viewed as a form of self-punishment, usually also plays a significant role in depression.

Depressed persons typically feel a loss of self-esteem. Yet, ironically, they are unable to accept from others that which they most need: emotional nourishment. As Fenichel notes, "Depression is a desperate attempt to compel an orally incorporated object to grant forgiveness, protection, love and security" (Fenichel, 1945, p. 396). This means that depressed people are trying, as it were, to purchase love from imaginary persons existing within their own minds. These imaginary people are typically mental representations (introjects) of significant others from childhood, such as a mother or a father. All people have such introjects. Depressed individuals differ from normals not by the existence of the introjects but rather by the neurotic expectations attached to them.

One example of how this can develop is the

child who loses a parent through death or divorce. In such a situation the lost parent is often introjected (made a part of the child's mental apparatus) and becomes the object of an intense wish for love. Since the introjected person is only imaginary, he or she cannot supply this love, and consequently the child becomes depressed. The child is thus in an untenable psychological position that is not easily resolved without psychotherapeutic intervention.

According to psychoanalytic theory, the harsh self-punishing attitude toward oneself that undergirds serious depression is energized by highly primitive (id) forces. The depressive not only "gets down" on himself or herself but does so with almost a primal passion.

It is impossible within the compass of a short article to present adequately all of the various psychodynamic views of depression. While the above classical psychoanalytic view is not the only dynamic perspective on depression, it is certainly the wellspring from which all others have come.

Reference

Fenichel, O. *The psychoanalytic theory of neurosis.* New York: Norton, 1945.

Additional Reading

Menninger, K. *Man against himself.* New York: Harcourt, Brace, 1938.

C. W. McLemore

See Psychoanalytic Psychology.

Depression: Physiological Factors.

Many depressed patients have significant changes in neurobiological regulatory functions. In order to make the diagnosis of major depressive episode, evidence of these changes must be present. Such changes would include a decreased appetite with a significant weight loss (apart from dieting) or an increased appetite with weight gain, insomnia or hypersomnia, psychomotor agitation or retardation, loss of energy and easy fatiguability, along with impaired ability to think or concentrate as manifested by slowed thinking or indecisiveness or memory disturbances. Many patients also have significant loss of sex drive. These activities are all regulated by midbrain structures in the limbic system and reticular activating system of the central nervous system. Considerable investigation is currently under way into the nature of these changes. The conclusions from this research will be briefly summarized here.

There is some evidence that major depressive illness is at least in part mediated by genetic factors (Gershon, 1979). Studies of families with bipolar affective disorder indicate a risk to siblings of approximately 40%. Studies of twins show that 65% of identical twins will both manifest major depression if one does. In fraternal twins the concordance rate is only 14%. The fact that there is not 100% concordance between identical twins points toward a variable penetrance of a genetic influence. However, while severe depression tends to be familial and fits genetic models, the milder forms of depression have not been found to fit genetic models in family studies. There may be a sibling to sibling cultural effect or a social learning effect in some of these families.

There has been much investigation of changes in sleep in patients with major depressive illness (Mendels & Amsterdam, 1980). In contrast to normal patients, where there is usually a lag of approximately 90 minutes between the onset of sleep and the first period of rapid eye movement (REM) sleep, in depressed patients there is a decreased time between the onset of sleep and the first REM period. In addition, normal patients tend to begin with a brief REM period with progressively increasing duration during the night for the first four periods. In depressed patients the first REM period tends to be the longest. Also, depressed patients have a significant decrease in the total amount of stage 4 sleep.

Clinically, it has long been noted that patients with major depression have sleep difficulties. Sometimes there is difficulty falling asleep, but most typically the problem is remaining asleep. Patients have a sleep pattern characterized by frequent early morning awakenings. Artificial changes in the sleep cycle and sleep deprivation often are able to produce a transient elevation of mood in some depressed patients.

Investigation into circadian rhythms (daily fluctuations in body temperature, activity and arousal levels, and various hormonal levels) has shown that these activities may be related to depression. When the circadian activity cycle is disrupted in normal patients, many of them experience a marked decrease in REM latency and a long initial REM period. In addition, these patients tend to become irritable and dysphoric in mood and have poor performance of work tasks, all characteristics shared by depressed patients. This is commonly observed in the phenomenon of jet lag. It has been noted that these rhythms take two to three weeks to adjust to a new situation. Experimentally, many patients have improved when their sleep cycle has been altered. Confirming this intervention, many bipolar depression patients spontaneously move toward an altered sleep cycle as they emerge from a depressive episode.

Various neurotransmitters have been shown to be involved in the regulation of sleep and may be involved in depression as well. These include norepinephrine, acetylcholine, and serotonin. Various studies have implicated these neurotransmitters in the control of affective disturbance. Many antidepressant drugs have effects on norepinephrine reuptake in the presynaptic cell and on postsynaptic receptors. Other antidepressant drugs have been shown to have effects on reuptake of serotonin. Acetylcholine systems have been implicated in depression by studies wherein cholinergic drugs, such as physostigmine, which inhibits the metabolism of acetylcholine, have produced depressive symptoms in patients and have exacerbated depressive mood in patients who already experienced depression.

The evidence is far from complete in the area of neurotransmitter research. The precise mechanism of action of antidepressant drugs has yet to be determined. Many of the newer antidepressant drugs do not appear to act by blocking the reuptake of neurotransmitters, although they are equally effective in the treatment of depression. The implication is that these drugs may be doing more than affecting reuptake of neurotransmitters. The further elucidation of the mechanism of action of the antidepressant drugs will help to provide an explanation of the neurobiology of affective illness. Some newer studies have shown an effect of these drugs on cerebral capillary permeability, which would have far-ranging effects on brain metabolism.

Neuroendocrine regulation is also disturbed in major depressive illness. Various studies have shown impairments in the regulation of thyroid hormone, growth hormone, and cortisol release. Depressed patients demonstrate a decreased growth hormone response to insulin tolerance test. In addition, when a depressed patient is given TRH (a thyroid releasing hormone), there is a decrease in the usual release of thyroid-stimulating hormone by the pituitary. This occurs in anywhere from 25 to 50% of patients with endogenous depression.

There is also a change in the regulation of the hypothalymic-pituitary-adrenal axis which regulates cortisol levels. This has been demonstrated experimentally by the administration of dexamethazone, a synthetic steroid (Brown, Johnson, & Mayfield, 1979). This drug would normally cause a suppression of cortisol levels

for a day or two following its administration. However, depressed patients often do not show this suppression. This test is now being used extensively on a clinical basis to confirm the diagnosis of depression. Under carefully controlled circumstances, the failure to suppress cortisol levels following the administration of dexamethazone (now called the dexamethazone suppression test) is a 95% reliable confirmation of endogenous depression, indicating the need for aggressive biological treatment with antidepressant drugs and/or electroconvulsive therapy. The presence of suppression does not rule out endogenous depression, since there is approximately a 40% false negative response, where patients with clear-cut endogenous depression will have normal suppression of the adrenal gland. It has also been shown that adequate treatment of depression causes a return of suppression of cortisol levels following dexamethazone.

References

Brown, W. A., Johnson, R., & Mayfield, D. The 24-hour dexamethazone suppression test in a clinical setting: Relationship to diagnosis, symptoms, and response to treatment. *American Journal of Psychiatry*, 1979, *136*, 543–547.

Gershon, E. S. Genetics of the affective disorders. *Hospital Practice*, 1979, *14*, 117–122.

Mendels, J., & Amsterdam, J. D. (Eds.). *The psychobiology of affective disorders.* New York: Karger, 1980.

R. J. SALINGER

See GENETIC AND BIOCHEMICAL FACTORS IN PSYCHOPATHOLOGY.

Deprogramming. *See* CULTS.

Depth Psychology. Systems of psychology which address the realm of the unconscious rather than just the conscious aspect of mental life. The term is used much more frequently in Europe, less frequently in England and America. Some authors simply equate it with PSYCHOANALYSIS. More broadly understood, it also includes the systems of INDIVIDUAL PSYCHOLOGY, ANALYTICAL PSYCHOLOGY, and much of European EXISTENTIAL PSYCHOLOGY.

Dereistic Thinking. A thought process that deviates from the normal laws of logic, reality, and experience. An example is the person who believes he is Jesus Christ. Such mental activity, characteristic of autistic and schizophrenic thinking, is called dereistic in that it is out of harmony with the facts.

Descartes, René (1596–1650). French philosopher and mathematician who is justly renowned as "the father of modern philosophy." Descartes's importance for psychology lies in his promulgation of a dualistic view of the human person, in which the true self is viewed as an immaterial soul which is distinct from the body. Though his position is widely rejected in the twentieth century, Descartes's formulation of the mind-body problem continues to be a starting-place for contemporary discussions of the issue (*see* MIND-BRAIN RELATIONSHIP).

Descartes lived in a period of scientific upheaval and social change. He attempted to overcome the resulting threat of skepticism by a method of doubting all beliefs that were not truly certain. The one thing which he felt could withstand such a doubt was his own consciousness of himself as a conscious being. Hence he laid down *Cogito, ergo sum.* (I think, therefore I am) as the ultimate foundation for knowledge. Descartes reasoned that even if all his perceptual experience was illusory, even if he had no body, at least *he* must exist as the subject of the illusory perceptions.

From this basis Descartes argued that he, as "thinking thing" or soul, must be an immaterial substance, distinct from any body. His argument is as follows: Whatever can be clearly and distinctly conceived as separate could exist separately (at least by God's omnipotence). Descartes can clearly and distinctly conceive himself as a conscious being (soul) existing separately from a body (e.g., existing even if his body is a perceptual illusion). Therefore, soul and body could exist separately. Since whatever can exist separately is distinct, therefore soul and body are distinct.

This argument, even if sound, proves only that soul and body are *separable*, not that they are separate, a position we might call minimal dualism. Minimal dualism is a position many Christians have accepted for theological reasons, and it continues to be a defensible philosophical position. However, Descartes went on to assume that soul and body were *separate* and to postulate that soul or mind interacts causally with the body. The difficulty in understanding and explaining such interaction has led many to accept parallelism, which denies any interaction, or simply to reject dualism altogether.

Descartes's conception of thinking was a very broad one, encompassing such diverse forms of mental activity as doubting, perceiving, willing, imagining, and feeling. Although the soul was thought of as a free spiritual entity, the body was conceived by Descartes as "extended stuff" which operates in a machine-like manner. At some places Descartes suggested that animals were purely physical machines which lacked consciousness. Contrary to his intentions, this suggestion that apparently conscious behavior in animals could be explained in mechanistic terms eventually led to the suggestion that consciousness in humans could be explained along the same lines. This discussion of animals highlights the poor fit of Cartesianism, which draws such a sharp line between the human and the subhuman, with evolutionary theory. Contemporary dualists have usually been emergentists, who attempt to work out a view of consciousness that allows more continuity with the higher animals.

C. S. EVANS

Descriptive Psychology/Psychiatry. The descriptive approach to psychology or psychiatry is based on the study and classification of behavior without attempts to explain why the behavior occurs. It contrasts with the dynamic approach (*see* DYNAMIC PSYCHOLOGY), which focuses on the underlying causes of behavior.

In psychology the descriptive approach had its beginning in Germany with the work of Franz Brentano (1838–1917). Brentano opposed STRUCTURALISM as an approach to psychology and became the founder of its major contemporary rival, ACT PSYCHOLOGY.

In psychiatry the descriptive approach is most commonly associated with the work of Emil Kraepelin. Kraepelin was also a German, and in spite of the overlap of their lives, there is no clear indication that he and Brentano had any awareness of each other or the similarities of their approaches. Kraepelin's classification of psychopathologies was in essence a descriptive approach. His assumption was that groups of symptoms which occur regularly together should be regarded as a specific psychopathology. This approach remains in current classifications of mental disorders. In fact, *DSM-III*, the most current classification system for psychopathology, differs from its predecessor, *DSM-II*, primarily in its attempt to remove the dynamic assumptions contained in some of the classifications of *DSM-II* and make the system more exclusively a descriptive one.

D. G. BENNER

See CLASSIFICATION OF MENTAL DISORDERS; DYNAMIC PSYCHOLOGY.

Desensitization. *See* SYSTEMATIC DESENSITIZATION.

Determinism and Free Will. The question of whether or not a person's choice of behavior is free, and to what extent, has plagued thinkers for centuries. Each answer has its defenders and critics. The position supporting free will or free-choice behavior has been called libertarianism (D'Angelo, 1968), or voluntarism (Hammes, 1971). Freedom here refers to the absence of intrinsic necessity in the performance of an act. That is, given alternatives among which to choose, one can select freely, without coercion. Freedom in behavior does not mean absence of causality. The libertarian does not contend that human behavior is uncaused, but rather that there is a cause (the self) which can operate in a free manner to produce effects (choices).

Freedom is not the same as variance, as some would contend (Boring, 1957). The statistical variability of accumulative behavioral responses, referred to as the standard deviation of a distribution, does not constitute human freedom. Animals lower than man, even the earthworm, possess behavioral variability. However, the voluntarist does not attribute freedom to such behavior. Human freedom can induce variability, but the presence of variability does not necessarily infer freedom.

There are certain prerequisite conditions that must be met before a free choice is possible. The first is awareness, or a normal state of attention. A second condition is deliberation. The person must have opportunity to consider choices of action prior to decision. When awareness and deliberation are lacking, either in degree or in entirety, there is corresponding attenuation of freedom and responsibility—e.g., in actions of the retardate or the psychotic, and in spontaneous emotional impulses (Hammes, 1971).

Evidence for Free Will. Various kinds of evidence have been adduced to support freedom in human choices. First, there is the capacity for voluntary attention, the act of directing the focal point of awareness to some object (Bittle, 1945). At this moment, the reader's attention is on this page. Since the present behavior is deliberate, the state of attention is called voluntary. If, however, a sudden noise were to draw this attention aside, the interruption would illustrate involuntary attention. The fundamental awareness that attention is at times under personal control, and in other instances is not, demonstrates human freedom and is the basis for differentiating the two states of attention. Indeed, the experience of intentionality itself is evidence for freedom and is a basic theme of humanistic-existential authors.

Libertarians also point to the experience of moral consciousness and conscience to support their belief in freedom (Bittle, 1945). The experience of guilt is indicative of the fundamental awareness that in the area of moral behavior one can be responsible for evil acts which need not have been done, or which could have been freely avoided. The experience of guilt is so universal that persons lacking such feelings are diagnosed as psychopathic. Libertarians also cite the experience of moral effort in support of the conviction of human freedom (Dworkin, 1970), as well as personal achievement and the pride of accomplishment (Hammes, 1971).

Another argument in defense of free will is the conviction "I could have done otherwise" (D'Angelo, 1968). For the libertarian this statement means, "If I had so freely chosen, I would have done otherwise." It would seem the original statement could be compatible with determinism, if interpreted to mean, "If the determining conditions were different, I could have chosen otherwise" (Lamont, 1967). However, the belief in free will is based on the grounds of practical experience, whereas the determinist's objections are primarily theoretical and therefore not as weighty (Dworkin, 1970).

Another defense of freedom of choice is based on the observation of indeterminancy at the subatomic level. As expressed in the Heisenberg principle, which points out that it is impossible to make a simultaneous determination of the position and momentum of atomic particles, this indeterminancy is understood to be in the very fabric of nature rather than mere uncertainty or limitation in knowledge (Bube, 1971). However, libertarians vary on this interpretation of Heisenberg.

Determinist Objections to Free Will. Determinism has been classified by some observers into hard determinism and soft determinism. Hard determinists assert that freedom is illusory, that every event has a cause and is predictable, and that all human acts occur necessarily as effects of causes. Soft determinists attempt to introduce some element of freedom while still recognizing determinism. Humanistic-existential writers such as Rollo May and Carl Rogers are sometimes placed in the category of soft determinism. Others disagree with this division within determinism. They consider soft determinism an evasion of the issue and logically reducible to either libertarianism or hard determinism. Hard determinism has been presented in a number of different ways. Each will be examined here, followed by the libertarian's response.

A primary objection to freedom is that of *skeptic determinism*. The common basis for testimony of freedom is awareness, or the consciousness of this capability. Skeptic determinism strikes at the root of this conviction by asserting consciousness to be an invalid informational source. For example, an amputee may attribute sensation to a foot no longer present; a straight stick placed partly in water appears bent, although it is not. In both instances the skeptic contends that consciousness has lied.

However, the converse is true. Past learning accounts for the discrepancy between fact and judgment in the first example, and in the second example advantage has been taken of the structure of the human eye, which does not naturally correct for refraction of light in two media. The skeptic therefore attempts to use abnormal settings to discredit the testimony of consciousness in normal circumstances. A similar argument would be that if a blind person cannot see, no one can.

A more critical reply to the skeptic, however, concerns the validity of his own positiveness. Can he doubt the trustworthiness of consciousness while using that consciousness as a basis for his doubt? Obviously not. The skeptic, in removing the basis for the validity of any doubt, consequently discredits his own. He can only hold to a doubt which is in itself doubtful.

A second form of determinism, *cause-effect determinism*, is based on law and predictability. It is contended that freedom is a conclusion based on ignorance of the causes actually present but unknown. These causes act necessarily to produce behavior as an effect. In response, the voluntarist concedes that all behavior is caused, but disagrees that all causes act necessarily to produce effects. In the instance of free choice he contends that the person, as cause, freely initiates effects (behavior). Furthermore, the principle of causality states that effects are necessarily brought about by causes, but does not demand that all causes necessarily act to produce effects. Neither is predictability a problem for the libertarian, for a person may, and usually does, choose to act consistently, since by nature we are ordered human beings. A person freely choosing to lead a good moral life, for example, can be predicted to act in ways consistent with this resolve. Predictability, being compatible with both freedom and determinism, cannot be used as an argument against freedom.

A third expression of determinism is *mechanistic determinism*. This grows out of the monistic view that man is merely a complex machine whose mental processes are neurological only, reducible to physiochemical forces subject to the determining laws of matter. However, the evidence that mind and brain are distinct within the human person, and that the mind cannot be reduced to matter, makes possible the exercise of freedom in human behavior (*see* MIND-BRAIN RELATIONSHIP).

Fourth is *biogenetic determinism*. Heredity, temperament, glands, and emotions are supposedly the architects of human personality and the dictators of action. Sociobiology is a contemporary example of the emphasis on genetic structure as a determinant of character traits and presumably choice behavior as well. The libertarian responds that these factors are not self-evidently deterministic and can be considered influences rather than determinants.

A fifth variety of determinism is based on learning theory and could be termed *stimulus-response determinism*. This is illustrated by Pavlov and other classical conditioning learning theorists. Conditioned behavior is sometimes used to arrive at the sweeping generalization that all human behavior is conditioned and that consequently freedom is precluded. However, some learning patterns require concentrated effort (e.g., learning to play golf or mastering algebra). The attempt to reduce all human learning to simple conditioning is, in the opinion of the libertarian, arbitrary and unwarranted.

A closely related but broader theory is that of *reinforcement determinism*. This is illustrated by Skinner and other operant conditioning learning theorists. Whatever reinforces behavior determines its repetition. However, the fact that reinforced behavior is repeated does not necessarily infer a determined relationship. It is only logical for one to choose pleasurable experiences over unpleasant ones. Knowledge of the action taken sheds no light on whether or not the choice was free or determined.

Wider still is the theory of *sociocultural determinism*, the view that behavior is shaped by forces such as home, school, church, and community. These environmental variables purportedly indoctrinate the individual and structure his choice behavior. For example, slums are said to breed criminals. Clarence Darrow believed prisoners could not help being criminals, just as those outside of jail could not help but be there (Dworkin, 1970). Skinner contends human behavior can be engineered and controlled through cultural design. The libertarian would respond that social forces should be considered as influences rather than determinants of behavior. Criminals come from high as well as from low socioeconomic levels, and good citizens as well as delinquents emerge from slum conditions. Although socioeconomic factors most certainly limit the kind and number of available opportunities, the choice among these alternatives can nonetheless be free (Hammes, 1978).

An eighth objection to free will is *motivational determinism*. This is expressed by the statement, "The stronger motive prevails." Neo-Gestalt field theorists illustrate this position (Lewin, 1935). The fault in motivational determinism is akin to that in the Monday morning quarterback. The prevailing motive is not labeled until after the decision is made. Thus, no matter what alternative is selected, the determinist would obligingly designate it as the stronger one. To do so proves nothing. The knowledge that a decision has been made gives no information on whether or not there was freedom or lack of freedom existing prior to the decision.

Another example offered by motivational determinists is that of reactive inhibition. After a person has pressed a red-light button for a hundred trials, and has then been given the opportunity to push a light button other than red, it can be predicted that the individual will invariably select the alternative, which was thereby necessitated, according to the determinist. The reader may have recognized reactive inhibition as a term equivalent to monotony. A repetitive behavior pattern will usually induce the impulse or tendency to alternate activity, a response natural to life forms, one which has survival value and which in man may even be consciously experienced. Even in such circumstances, however, the voluntarist would consider these behavioral tendencies to be influences rather than compulsive determinants.

Unconscious motivation is used as the basis for a ninth objection to freedom, termed *unconscious determinism*. This is illustrated by Freud. Some psychoanalysts, on the evidence of unconscious defense mechanisms, deny freedom of choice. Even though on the conscious level man is convinced of freedom, it is contended that there are unconscious forces unknowingly manipulating the decision-making process.

The defect in this line of reasoning is that the unconscious, being unconscious, is un-knowable. The voluntarist, by the same token, could argue that the unconscious force of the rejected alternative was actually the stronger, and the chooser exerted great self-effort in his decision to overcome that option. Since the role of motivation below the level of awareness is an unknowable variable, it is arbitrary to assign various strengths of influence to one alternative over another. Unconscious motivation, therefore, cannot be used to prove or disprove freedom of choice.

A tenth theory of determinism involves the relationship between God and man and can be called *theological determinism*. Three variants of this perspective are creationistic determinism, omniscient determinism, and predestination, based respectively on God's creative power, his knowledge, and his will.

Creationistic determinism is based on the law of causality, which states that effects are utterly dependent on their causes. If so, it follows that man (as an effect) created by God (his cause) would be completely dependent upon the Creator in all human activity, including decision behavior. According to this idea man is a divinely manipulated puppet.

Defenders of human freedom consider this view to be an unnecessary application of a law in the physical world to the world of the spiritual. In the material cosmos it is true that effects are completely dependent upon, and determined by, their causes. But is it not possible that different cause-effect relations exist on the nonmaterial, or spiritual, level? God could, if he so desired, create in his image a being with free will, utterly dependent upon him for existence, but nonetheless possessing the capacity for freedom of choice. In no way would this concept do violence to the laws governing the material universe. Freedom exists as an immaterial, or spiritual, behavior pattern, since such activity is a function of the mind, itself immaterial. It could thus be argued that God created man not just "to be" but rather "to be free."

A second expression of theological determinism is *omniscient determinism*. Since God is all-knowing, he knows every human choice before it is made. Consequently, it is contended that his knowledge determines that choice. The problem here lies in man's inability to experience outside of time, since the human creature is time-bound, and can only experience events as they occur. God, being independent of time, is not so bound. However, we can understand by analogy how his knowledge need not be causative. A person having seen a football game, and then reviewing it on film, could predict during the film exactly what the players would do next. Now, if one were not bound by time, he could also have predicted the play at the time of watching the actual game. In neither instance would such knowledge be the cause of the players' reactions.

Therefore, it should be apparent that knowledge of behavior, even divine knowledge, is not necessarily the cause of that behavior. God could, of course, if he so desired, control human activities completely. The question here is not whether or not God possesses this power; it is rather whether or not his knowledge alone predetermines human choice.

A final variant of theological determinism is *predestination*, the position that God chooses those to be saved. Although both Luther and Calvin, representative of this view, believed in free will in everyday choice activity, they did not extend this ability to the matter of cooperating in personal salvation. Moreover, Luther believed in single predestination, the saving of the just, whereas Calvin held to double predestination, which included the eternal perdition of the reprobate. Predestination, however, is compatible with human freedom if interpreted to mean the promise of salvation to those who freely respond to God's redemptive grace. Since we are dealing here with matters of Christian faith, determinists and voluntarists will be divided in accordance with their understanding of divine redemption.

Alternative Approaches. In addition to libertarianism and determinism, there are two other options in the argument over free will. There are those who believe the controversy to be an unresolvable paradox with which one must learn to live, and there are others who consider the controversy a pseudoproblem, reducible to semantic confusion. Some have applied Bohr's principle of complementarity, borrowed from physics, to the freedom-determinism controversy. According to this view both perspectives, being complementary, are true. Such attempts have been described as reconciliationism (Berofsky, 1966). However, voluntarists perceive the problem as involving contradictions, not mere complementarities, and resolvable only in terms of one side or the other, not both.

The linguistic analyst sees the solution in terms of describing behavior in diverse languages, descriptions which present different aspects unrelated to each other (Barbour, 1966). Thus man can supposedly be both determined and free in the same behavioral act, dependent on whether he is being de-scribed in terms of spectator language (determinism) or actor language (voluntarism). However, this approach would appear to be an evasion of the issue. For example, the preference of a scientist for spectator language or of an existentialist for actor language is irrelevant to the objective, ontological nature of the act, which in itself is independent of any descriptive language.

Resembling linguistic analysis is the multilevel systems approach (Bube, 1971), which contends that description on one level may be deterministic and yet on another level be indeterministic. All such approaches deny the determinism–free will problems. However, for reasons already considered in this article, many observers conclude that a real controversy exists, one that cannot be dismissed so easily and one that requires resolution.

References

Barbour, I. G. *Issues in science and religion.* Englewood Cliffs, N.J.: Prentice-Hall, 1966.
Berofsky, B. (Ed.), *Free will and determinism.* New York: Harper & Row, 1966.
Bittle, C. *The whole man: Psychology.* Milwaukee: Bruce Publishing, 1945.
Boring, E. G. When is behavior pre-determined? *Scientific Monthly*, 1957, *84*, 189–196.
Bube, R. H. *The human quest.* Waco, Tex.: Word Books, 1971.
D'Angelo, E. *The problem of freedom and determinism.* Columbia: University of Missouri Press, 1968.
Dworkin, G. *Determinism, free will, and moral responsibility.* Englewood Cliffs, N.J.: Prentice-Hall, 1970.
Hammes, J. A. *Humanistic psychology.* New York: Grune & Stratton, 1971.
Hammes, J. A. *Human destiny: Exploring today's value systems.* Huntington, Ind.: Our Sunday Visitor Press, 1978.
Lamont, C. *Freedom of choice affirmed.* New York: Horizon Press, 1967.
Lewin, K. *A dynamic theory of personality.* New York: McGraw-Hill, 1935.

J. A. HAMMES

Detriangulation. The process of family therapy by which a triangle (three people stuck in repetitive maladaptive patterns of interaction) is broken up. This can occur by the removal of one member of the triangle, as in the case of an adolescent who leaves home for college. Where removal of an individual is not feasible, detriangulation can be brought about by realigning relationships among the three. Essentially this process involves moving from enmeshment to interdependence. Because behavior patterns within triangles are frequently rigid and because the emotional forces among the three are so powerful, psychotherapy may be needed to effect a complete detriangulation.

J. A. LARSEN

See TRIANGLE; FAMILY SYSTEMS THEORY; FAMILY SYSTEMS THERAPY.

Developmental Psychology. This branch of psychology is concerned with the aspects of animal and human behavior that change from conception to death and with the processes that account for these changes. The length of time required for mature development is in relation to the position of the species on the phylogenetic scale, higher forms of life taking longer to reach reproductive capacity than lower forms.

The processes that account for behavioral change include growth, maturation, and learning. Growth is primarily quantitative and is seen in an increase in size. As children grow older, they also get bigger. Maturation is a more nebulous term but generally is used in connection with the unfolding of genetic potential. Programmed within every organism is a sequence and direction of behavior needed to adapt to the environment. What sets humankind apart from all other forms of life is a "biological given" that provides for intellectual, emotional, social, moral, and spiritual attainments not seen in any other species. The worth of the human infant is based not on competencies present at birth but on possibilities that will be realized as the child matures.

Learning connotes relatively permanent changes in behavior as the result of experience. All beings are influenced by the environment and learn as they are rewarded and punished. People learn not only by the consequences of their actions but by imitating others and by responding to verbal instruction. Concept formation, problem solving, and language acquisition allow for complex understandings that enrich life and render the human experience unique. All three processes of development may combine to produce a given behavior. Playing basketball, for example, is possible only after the body has increased in size, muscles have matured, and the proper way to handle the ball has been learned. Psychologists who hold a behaviorist position tend to emphasize the role of learning in development, whereas psychologists who take a humanistic view are more apt to stress the potential within each person.

Development proceeds in a series of stages that correspond with chronological age. Infancy, early childhood, middle childhood, adolescence, early adulthood, middle age, and old age comprise the major groupings. The research focus traditionally has been on the child rather than on the adult. Changes occur more quickly in the young and are easier to observe and record. Furthermore, the earlier stages are critical in that they take place during the formative years and affect succes-sive stages. However, the more recent interest in the life span has produced considerable information on developmental processes during middle age and old age. Each period is unique, representing the optimal age for the development of specific skills, cognitions, and personality characteristics.

All development is an interaction of heredity and environment. The fetus is affected not only by genes inherited from the parents but also by an intrauterine environment that is sensitive to whether the expectant mother smokes, consumes alcohol, is malnourished, or contracts particular diseases such as rubella (German measles). The extent and nature of the insult to the developing organism depend on the characteristic that is changing most rapidly at the time. For example, European babies born with deformed limbs in the 1950s were so afflicted because their mothers took Thalidomide during the early weeks of pregnancy when limb buds were forming.

The emphasis of American psychology has been on the environment rather than on heredity, especially after the child is born. It is attractive to the Western mind to believe that with proper care and education every child can become a happy and useful adult. Attention given to individual differences present at birth which restrict the limits of development in such areas as intelligence (Jensen, 1969) and temperament (Thomas & Chess, 1977) has met considerable resistance.

The Scriptures present a number of comparisons between the development of the child and development in the Christian life. Salvation is described as a new birth (John 3:1–8) and spiritual growth as a consequence of feeding on "the sincere milk of the Word" (1 Peter 2:2). Parents are enjoined to diligently teach their children the commandments of God (Deut. 6:6–7) since the early formative years affect the direction and pattern of behavior as children grow older (Prov. 22:6). "Growing up in Christ" brings new understanding and communications (Eph. 4:18, 29), development which, for the Christian, will someday be complete when "we shall be like him" (1 John 3:2).

References
Jensen, A. R. How much can we boost IQ and scholastic achievement? *Harvard Educational Review*, 1969, *39*, 1–123.
Thomas, A., & Chess, S. *Temperament and development.* New York: Brunner/Mazel, 1977.

B. CLOUSE

Dewey, John (1859–1952). The life of John Dewey is an example of his theory. He was influenced by the rural democratic Vermont environment, and he in turn did much to modify the environment of American education.

Dewey was born in Burlington, Vermont, the son of a grocery store owner. His deeply pious mother required that he attend Sunday school, church services, and properly observe the sabbath. Dewey reacted against this training and rejected the supernaturalism of his mother. He felt the idea of God hindered creative intelligence. After attending the University of Vermont, he taught high school for three years, then began doctoral studies at Johns Hopkins in 1882. He studied under Gordon S. Hall, became interested in the writings of Hegel, and wrote his dissertation on Kant.

In 1884 Dewey became an instructor of psychology and philosophy at the University of Michigan. Ten years later he took over the chair of philosophy, psychology, and pedagogy at the University of Chicago. He began a philosophical shift from Hegel's idealism to a pragmatic instrumentalism while at the University of Chicago. He saw ideas as instruments for solving problems encountered in the environment. Nature, he believed, is ultimate reality, and people find meaning in the present.

Dewey's educational psychology was tested and developed in the laboratory school he and his wife began in Chicago. This was a functional psychology that focused on all aspects of the student as the student worked to adjust to the environment. Schools must begin with the interest of the child and provide opportunity for the child to interact between doing and thinking. While Dewey reacted against the content transmission of traditional schools, he also reacted against the kind of progressive education that failed to teach the disciplined use of intelligence.

In 1904 Dewey moved to Columbia University, where he was associated for the next 47 years. He attracted thousands of students and published enough books and articles to fill 125 pages of bibliography.

Dewey believed that maturing people are constantly being faced with challenges from the environment, challenges which stimulate the use of intelligent action by the individual, which in turn promotes more maturity. Problems in experience are the stimuli that generate interest in growing.

While Dewey wrote little about therapy techniques, it would not be unreasonable to assume that he would advocate the exploration of problems through intelligent action. He had faith in the self-correcting process of creative intelligence. The counselor probably would 1) help the individual articulate and analyze a problem situation, 2) help the individual to project possible courses of action, and 3) allow the individual to act, then help the person to scrutinize the consequence of the action. Since Dewey believed that people grow and mature when they interact with a community of inquiries, he most likely would facilitate problem solving in groups.

Dewey is often rejected by evangelical Christians because of his antipathy toward supernaturalism and special revelation. He rejected institutional religious dogma of any kind. Yet several aspects of his psychology seem consistent with Scripture and may be helpful to Christians. First, as the Christian struggles to find a view of the person which takes into account both the image of God and fallen human nature, Dewey can give valuable insight. His psychology would not accept a mechanistic view of the person, nor would he accept a romantic view that overlooks the selfishness of the child.

Second, to better understand the process of maturity we can learn from Dewey's psychological understanding of growth. Scripture illustrates God's use of the problem-posing experiences to stimulate maturity. Often God's chosen people were given difficulties that encouraged them to learn by reflecting on the consequences of their actions.

Some of Dewey's views of human nature and his views on the process of growth can be helpful to the Christian psychologist. While Christians need to beware of his antisupernaturalism, we can learn from Dewey as we seek to promote Christian growth.

J. E. PLUEDDEMANN

Dextrality–Sinistrality. *See* HANDEDNESS.

Differential Diagnosis. Most simply, differential diagnosis is the process of determining which of a number of similar-appearing disorders a patient actually has, while ruling out those which do not apply (Gallatin, 1982). In reality this is an extremely difficult task, particularly when the disorder is emotional rather than physical. In order to better understand the complexity of this task, it is necessary first to briefly review the purpose and technique of diagnostic formulation.

When a therapist is confronted with an individual seeking psychotherapy in order to find solutions to problems, relief from distressing symptoms, or guidance in formulating meaningful short and long-range goals, a diagnostic formulation is sometimes helpful in assessment as well as in treatment planning. Rather than providing a snapshot of the present emotional state, a thorough diagnostic formulation serves as a road map that outlines the entire journey, past and present, as well as providing information on the likely directions of future functioning. This formulation takes into account constitutional factors which may have predisposed an individual toward certain forms of psychopathology; past significant traumatic experiences; and particular factors of interest in the early family environment. This information leads to what is called a genetic diagnosis, a summary of early, possibly predisposing, factors and forces which have formed the background for the present problems. A thorough diagnostic formulation may also include a dynamic diagnosis, which is typically a summary of the mechanisms and techniques unconsciously employed to manage anxiety and enhance self-esteem (Kolb & Brodie, 1982). The dynamic formulation focuses on the pattern of human transactions, resultant intrapsychic structures, and possible unresolved conflicts that have led to rigid, ineffective, self-defeating patterns of thought and behavior. Finally, a thorough diagnostic formulation includes a clinical diagnosis, a recognized system of classification which provides general information regarding associated symptoms, probable course, prognosis, and useful methods of treatment. *DSM-III* is the nationally recognized classification system in this country. It is when trying to determine the appropriate clinical diagnosis that the issue of differential diagnosis becomes paramount.

DSM-III contains 18 major classifications and more than 200 specific disorders. (*See* CLASSIFICATION OF MENTAL DISORDERS.) Due to the similarity of symptoms and the sometimes vague and confusing presentation of symptoms, determining the appropriate diagnosis can be a difficult task. (For example, it may be difficult to differentially diagnose a conversion vs. organic or psychophysiological disorder, dissociative vs. malingering or organic-mental disorder, multiple personality vs. schizophrenia, affective vs. organic-mental disorder, or affective disorder vs. schizophrenia. It may also be difficult to determine whether the underlying personality structure is that of a borderline, narcissistic, or histrionic personality disorder.) Differential diagnoses are sometimes made on the basis of symptoms described, history of previous func-

tioning, response to treatment, psychological test data, neurological exam data, physical exam data, presence or absence of current stressors, family history, and current level of functioning.

Studies of the accuracy of differential diagnosis have demonstrated such decisions to be often quite inaccurate and unreliable. For example, in one study there was less than 40% agreement concerning the diagnoses in a group of psychiatric inpatients (Beck, Ward, Mendelsohn, Mock, & Rebaugh, 1962). While attempts to differentiate among major diagnoses (such as psychosis vs. nonpsychosis) ranged as high as 70 to 85% in agreement (Gallatin, 1982), more narrow differential diagnoses, such as the specific form of schizophrenia or affective disorder, resulted in embarrassingly little agreement beyond that expected by pure chance. Even more interesting, although 80% agreement could be obtained when clinicians indicated that they were "certain" of the diagnosis, the infrequency of such moments of certainty and the low level of agreement at other times seriously undermine confidence in either the reliability or validity of present diagnostic systems for accurate differential diagnosis.

Why is differential diagnosis so difficult? Several reasons are typically given. Some attribute it to failure to apply uniform methods for collecting data in the interview process, as well as a lack of quantification of principal symptoms and signs recorded by different interviewers (Kolb & Brodie, 1982). Others attribute it to the complexity, ambiguity, and uncertainty inherent in the available diagnostic classification systems such as the *DSM-III* (Gallatin, 1982). Still others point out the inherent complexity of sorting through confusing, vaguely presented symptoms reported by the patient (Woodruff, Goodwin, & Guze, 1974).

It is encouraging to note that Spitzer, Williams, and Skodol (1980) report improving reliability in differential diagnosis with the adoption of *DSM-III* during the past few years. However, regardless of how precise classifications become during the years ahead, the ambiguity of emotional problems and symptoms, as well as variance in the styles and experience of clinicians, will continue to make differential diagnosis a difficult task fraught with errors.

References
Beck, A. T., Ward, C. H., Mendelsohn, M., Mock, J. E., & Rebaugh, J. K. Reliability of psychiatric diagnosis. *American Journal of Psychiatry*, 1962, *119*, 351.

Gallatin, J. E. *Abnormal psychology*. New York: Macmillan, 1982.

Kolb, L. C., & Brodie, H. K. *Modern clinical psychiatry* (10th ed.). Philadelphia: Saunders, 1982.

Spitzer, R. L., Williams, J. B., & Skodol, A. E. DSM-III: The major achievements and an overview. *American Journal of Psychiatry*, 1980, *137*, 151–164.

Woodruff, R. A., Goodwin, D. W., & Guze, S. B. *Psychiatric diagnosis*. New York: Oxford University Press, 1974.

J. D. GUY, JR.

Differential Psychology. "The objective and quantitative investigation of individual differences in behavior" (Anastasi, 1958, p. 1). As a branch of psychology it examines the types, amounts, antecedents, and consequences of differences, whether between individuals or groups (e.g., sexes or races). Measurement of differences is a key concern, as are the related issues of reliability and validity (*see* PSYCHOLOGICAL MEASUREMENT). As a consequence differential psychologists rely on statistical theory, particularly correlational and normative statistics. For this reason, sometimes differential psychologists have been called quantitative psychologists.

Differential psychology is best contrasted with general psychology (Cronbach, 1957). General psychology (e.g., experimental) studies individuals with the purpose of formulating general laws describing how individuals are alike. Differential psychology (e.g., ethnic, psychometric, genetic, comparative, or individual) asks how individuals differ. These branches employ different research strategies. The controlled experiment where the psychologist manipulates one variable (independent variable) to determine its effect on another variable (dependent variable) while all other influences are constant is the method adopted by the general psychologist. But differential psychologists conduct multiple measurements on variables under nature's control to determine their interrelations.

The forte of general psychology is the discovery of general laws of behavior through the methods of isolation and control. Differential psychology searches out reliable relationships between variables through correlational methods, such as factor analysis. In general psychology individual differences are considered to be noise and become a significant component in the composition of experimental error. General psychologists attempt to minimize individual differences through controlling experiential histories and use of powerful treatments. Differential psychologists seek to maximize individual differences, which increases the reliability of their measurements. Maximization of variance and use of large samples become important in use of the normal distribution.

Differential psychology may have originated in Adolph Quetelet's (1796–1874) application of the normal curve to biological and social data. Previously it had been applied only in the physical sciences. Quetelet coined the phrase *l'homme moyen*, "the average man," to indicate that when measurements were taken from a large, randomly selected sample, they approached the normal distribution, with a concentration of scores near the mean and only a few extreme cases.

Galton applied the normal curve to hereditary genius and other individual differences such as reaction time and sensory thresholds. This work was conducted in his famous Anthropometric Laboratory. He developed the concepts of "co-relation" and regression toward the mediocre (i.e., mean). The symbol *r*, signifying correlation, came from regression. Karl Pearson (1857–1936) developed the present statistical formula, product-moment correlation, to measure Galton's concept.

Further developments came from J. M. Cattell, who coined the phrase "mental tests." Cattell investigated reaction time as a significant part of mental abilities. The study of reaction time stemmed from an incident at Greenwich Observatory. The royal astronomer Maskelyne dismissed Kinnebrook for observing stellar movements a consistent one-half second later than himself. Other contributions to differential psychology include Binet and Simon's work on intelligence testing, Spearman's two-factor theory of intelligence, Thurstone's theory of primary mental abilities, and R. Cattell's factor analytic work on personality and mental abilities (*see* FACTOR THEORIES OF PERSONALITY).

In recent years differential psychologists have concentrated on personality and intellectual differences. However, a number of other domains have been examined in the past. These include a study of the nature-nurture controversy (*see* HEREDITY AND ENVIRONMENT IN HUMAN DEVELOPMENT), psychological differences between the sexes (*see* WOMEN, PSYCHOLOGY OF), and age and class differences.

References

Anastasi, A. *Differential psychology* (3rd ed.). New York: Macmillan, 1958.

Cronbach, L. J. The two disciplines of scientific psychology. *American Psychologist*, 1957, *12*, 671–684.

R. L. TIMPE

Direct Decision Therapy. A loosely formed approach to counseling and psychotherapy founded by Greenwald (1967, 1973). It has its roots in psychoanalytic theory, in which Greenwald was originally trained, but it tends to be open-minded and eclectic in nature. The approach has not achieved the status of a major system of psychotherapy. It appears to be little known and remains primarily the interest of its founder.

Greenwald defines direct decision therapy as a brief therapy that is in essence a philosophy of living. The main objective is to help individuals make decisions to change their lives. "Direct" has reference to the fact that clients are made aware that they indeed are making decisions in therapy as well as in everyday living. "Decision" depicts the choices that can be made regarding alternative behaviors, ways of organizing information, or modes of perceiving the world.

Direct decision therapy is built on some basic assumptions about human beings and their behavior. People are free to decide and change. Yet there exists the tendency to remain and act like infants in the desire to be taken care of. But with professional guidance individuals have the ability to deal with their problems, make constructive choices, and take charge of their lives.

An individual life style is shaped by the decisions one makes. Basic decisions include deciding to be perfect, to be different, to suffer, to please, to live or die, to be indecisive, to be nonexpressive of feelings, to be "crazy" or "normal," and so forth. It follows that problems in living—e.g., psychoses, depression, homosexuality, anger, loneliness—are the consequences of an individual's decisions. Environmental influences do serve to condition certain problems, but decision making accounts for most of the causation. Organic conditions such as congenital defects and mental retardation impede adaptive decisions.

Direct decision therapy places a strong emphasis on the relationship between the therapist and the client. The therapeutic encounter is marked by the therapist's authenticity, honesty, and nonjudgmental attitude. The therapist also seeks to have an empathic understanding of the client and his or her problem, to respect the individual as a person, to provide an accepting atmosphere for therapy, and to demonstrate consistently the firm belief in the client's ability to decide and change for the better.

A set of essential guidelines are followed to give structure to the procedures in the therapy process. The client first is asked to state the problem clearly. Next the client is guided in

examining past decisions that have helped to create and maintain the problem. Third, the payoffs for each of the decisions are identified. Fourth, a profile is sketched of the context in which the original decision was made. Then the client identifies and explores alternatives to the past decisions. After identifying alternative options, the client is asked to choose one of the alternatives and to decide to put it into practice. The therapist's encouragement and support are used to reinforce the client's carrying out of the decision.

A wide variety of therapeutic methods and strategies are used to supplement the decision-making model. Examples of the eclectic blend are psychoanalytic free association, Gestalt, behavior modification, paradoxical intervention, humor, and hypnosis.

Direct decision therapy is offered by the founder as a therapy that is applicable to the gamut of problems in living. However, Greenwald himself seems to have a penchant for cases of sexual deviancy. Perhaps this stems from his original research with female prostitutes. While the decision-making paradigm appears to be down-to-earth and useful, the approach lacks depth and comprehensiveness. Also, the Christian counselor or therapist is likely to look askance at Greenwald's free-spirited and sometimes risqúe style of doing therapy. The appealing qualities of direct decision therapy are its simplicity, practicality, and stress on the therapist as a genuine, self-disclosing person.

References

Greenwald, H. *Active psychotherapy.* New York: Atherton Press, 1967.

Greenwald, H. *Decision therapy.* New York: Wyden, 1973.

D. SMITH

See SHORT-TERM THERAPIES.

Direct Psychoanalysis. This therapeutic approach was developed by John Rosen in his attempt to understand and communicate directly with the unconscious of psychotic patients. It utilizes in modified form many of the psychoanalytic insights and techniques in an effort to make them most useful for work with psychotics.

Rosen's approach is based on the assumption that the behavior of the psychotic patient, no matter how bizarre it may appear, is actually an attempt to communicate. The challenge for the therapist is, therefore, to understand the logic of the unconscious in an attempt to decode the psychotic communication. In essence the treatment consists of having the patient relive early traumatic experiences with the mother. In this process the therapist makes a head-on attack on the patient's delusions. Thus, for example, if a patient claims he is God, Rosen might say "Prove it." Or he might squeeze the hand of a mute patient until he screams and then use this to prove to him that he can communicate vocally.

Rosen adopted the term *direct psychoanalysis* to contrast his approach to that of Freud, whose classical method he saw as too indirect for work with psychotics. He reports his procedures to be quite successful, but the majority of psychoanalysts remain skeptical about his methods and their effectiveness.

D. G. BENNER

Disorientation. A breakdown in the awareness and understanding of time, people, and places. Temporal effects include an impairment in the individual's understanding of where he is in time and space. He also loses perception of who he is and of his body image. Disorientation occurs in psychosis, organic conditions, mental disorders such as hallucinations and delusions, and neurotic disorders such as hysterical fugue.

Displacement. The unconscious transference of emotional charge or symbolic significance from one object or set of ideas to another. This ego defense process serves to protect against the threat or pain of associating the feelings or meanings with their original ideas. This may be seen in the case of a schizophrenic patient who has displaced all the anxiety and emotion originally associated with his conflicted relationship to his mother onto a word, phrase, or mental image apparently unrelated to his mother, reacting to that idea as he otherwise would react to mother. Displacement may also operate toward the self, as when anger at another is turned inward. This results in irrational self-denigration, depression, guilt, and perhaps suicidal impulses.

Displacement may also refer to the redirection of id impulses. This would be seen when sexual impulses, denied direct genital satisfaction, find expression through talking about intimate sexual matters. This form of displacement, called SUBLIMATION, is viewed by psychoanalysts as a healthy and often socially constructive activity.

R. LARKIN

See DEFENSE MECHANISMS.

Dissociation. The segregation or separation of a group of mental processes so that their normal relationship to the rest of the personality is lost. This generally results in the almost independent functioning of the isolated processes. In this context dissociation is also often referred to as SPLITTING. The ego defense mechanism of ISOLATION is one form of such dissociation.

Dissociation also applies to the formation of double or MULTIPLE PERSONALITY. In this state a person seems to exhibit two or more distinct subpersonalities, capable of gaining full consciousness and motor control only one at a time. Each subpersonality possesses its own set of thoughts, memories, attitudes, and personality characteristics, each dissociated from the others and from the main personality.

The splitting off of some ideational system, not subject to control by the remainder of the personality, is also a form of dissociation. This may be seen in the person who maintains a strong and fearful delusion despite his ability to perceive its irrationality or inconsistency. Another facet of dissociation is modeled by the person who exhibits gaiety while describing a painfully potent and personally significant experience; here a group of ideas has become separated from the appropriate emotions.

R. LARKIN

See DEFENSE MECHANISMS.

Dissociative Disorders. This group of disorders all share as the essential feature an alteration of consciousness, identity, or motor behavior. Included are MULTIPLE PERSONALITY, DEPERSONALIZATION DISORDER, psychogenic amnesia (*see* AMNESIA, PSYCHOGENIC), and psychogenic fugue (*see* FUGUE, PSYCHOGENIC).

Divine Guidance. *See* GUIDANCE, DIVINE.

Divorce. An important part of the larger picture of rapid change in nearly all aspects of our lives in America today is the tremendous rise in divorce rates. The current rate of divorce in the United States is one of three marriages. Another significant phenomenon is that older couples, those married 10, 20, or 30 years are representing the highest rise in the incidence of divorce (Glieberman, 1981, p. 53). Remarriage rates are also high, as are rates for second divorces, with second marriages ending sooner than first marriages.

The Christian community is not exempt from divorce. There no longer appears to be any significant difference in the divorce rate among the major American religious groups. Today Protestant and Catholic divorce rates are converging, and there seems to be little difference between the devout and the nondevout, although the rate is still a bit lower for the devout (Hunt & Hunt, 1977).

Some factors contributing to the increase in divorces include unreasonable expectations from marriage, mismating, neurotic personality manifestations, personal turmoil projected onto the marriage, poor communication, loss of friendship between couples, an inability to tolerate discomfort and imperfections, increasing societal approval of divorce, and a frantic increase in pursuit of personal happiness.

Marriage and Divorce in the Bible. In the Old Testament there are a number of different kinds of passages regarding divorce. The primary legislative statement on divorce and remarriage is found in Deuteronomy. 24:1–4. This is a passage Jesus cites in his teachings. The prophetic message decrying the frequency of divorce among the Hebrew people is found in Malachi 2:13–16, with verse 16 calling attention to the cruelty that divorce inflicts on women. Metaphorical passages where divorce is used as an analogy for the relationship of God to Israel are found in Jeremiah 3:1–8 and Hosea 1–3.

These passages enable us to take for granted the practice of divorce in ancient Hebrew culture. God's primary concern seemed to involve attempts at controlling and humanizing the practice. In the Old Testament it seems that divorce is nowhere officially instituted and the right to remarry is nowhere officially granted. Both were practiced as a commonly accepted privilege.

In the New Testament the references indicate that divorce is still a possible course of action for some, but the primary emphasis is on the nature, sanctity, purpose, and permanence of marriage. Marriage is viewed as unique and sacred; it is seen as a covenantal relationship ordained by God. Thus the partners are not free to dissolve the marriage if it no longer pleases them to continue in it. The word *covenant* refers to a partnership of wholeness, a relationship that fully embraces the lives of the two persons into a lifelong and life-embracing union.

One important New Testament passage on marriage is Mark 10:2–9. It is here that Jesus proclaims the "one-flesh" principle, in which marriage is rooted in creation and man must not separate married couples. Although various interpretations of these verses are possible, they seem to indicate that the man who remarries commits adultery against his first wife and the woman who remarries commits adultery against her first husband. Matthew 19:9 seems to teach that a man who divorces a faithful wife may cause her to commit adultery, perhaps by forcing her to remarry. A man who remarries after a divorce from a faithful wife also commits adultery (Matt. 5:32; 19:9). In 1 Corinthians 7:39–40 Paul tells us that remarriage is possible where the former marriage is broken by death. In 1 Corinthians 7:8–9 Paul expresses concern for those who attempt celibacy without the ability to maintain it.

Both Jesus and Paul see marriage as a binding covenant from which no one is ever totally released apart from the death of the spouse. Thus neither seems approving of remarriage after divorce; at least neither directly recommends it. Jesus' basic teaching is the principle of one flesh and permanent marriage. This appears to be God's normative premise for Christian marital morality. We may, however, infer that since divorce was permitted in the Old Testament for "hardness of hearts," and since that statement was not retracted by Jesus, he may accommodate today to tragic situations as well. The wrong in divorce is not simply obtaining a legal decree, but the destruction of the partnership in which the terms of the marital covenant can no longer be fulfilled.

The Divorce Process. *The preseparation period.* In a marriage that ends in divorce there is usually a period of increasing tension and adjustment difficulties that build prior to the actual separation. This period has been termed the stage of emotional divorce. Most couples who are in this phase present themselves to relatives, friends, and even to marriage counselors as if they are in the process of deciding with respect to continuation of the marriage. Ostensibly they need help in making a decision regarding the future of their marriage. However, often one partner has already made a decision to terminate the marriage. In that case marital therapy amounts to helping this decision become conscious and verbalized.

In retrospect couples often describe the partner's decision to leave the marriage as the point when that individual's emotional investment began to be withdrawn from the marriage. Not being consciously aware of this decision this partner will often continue in the marriage, stating a desire to improve the marriage. The partner may even seek marriage counseling, believing that he or she wants the marriage to continue. As a result, the marriage may continue for years, appearing to outsiders to be troubled but intact.

This process indicates that one spouse has passed a psychological point of no return. The no-return concept is a hypothetical construct that has been pieced together from the retrospective accounts of numerous divorced persons. The person who has passed the point of no return basically has given up on the marriage, and begins to act out his or her decreased investment in the relationship. In order to realistically help the troubled couple the marital therapist should be able to assess when this line has been crossed.

Although the point of no return may be a point beyond which the relationship may be maintained, it usually reflects one person's personal dynamics more than the dynamics of the marriage. It may reflect the displacement of the provoker's own inner dissatisfaction with himself or herself onto the marriage. If so, the therapist will have to shift the focus from the marriage to the individual. The individual may mistakenly feel that divorce will bring improvement in the area of these vague dissatisfactions, and this error in reasoning will have to be identified.

In order for the therapist to make this assessment, both parties should be present, since the process will require knowledge of the behaviors of both. When one partner wants to end the marriage but continually denies this fact, he will begin to engage in actions that reflect increasing dissatisfaction with and withdrawal from the marriage. In nonverbal ways he will communicate his desire to leave the marriage. He cannot openly admit it, so he engineers it indirectly, with strategies that are unconsciously calculated to force the other spouse to terminate the marriage.

The primary strategy used in this forcing process is provocation. It consists of a series of acts which serve to damage the relationship and provoke the other spouse to declare that the marriage is over. The provocations consist of a series of threatening behaviors of increasing severity, followed by accommodations by the other spouse until the other spouse is no longer able to accommodate. Thus, most often the person seeking marital therapy is not the person who really desires a divorce, but the one who has been provoked into terminating the marriage.

The dissolution of a marriage is a long process involving interacting dynamics and a series of actions and reactions. The therapist needs to help the couple determine on which side of the point of no return each spouse is located. If, despite continued therapeutic attempts at alleviating and resolving dissonance, one spouse continues the provoking behavior over a period of time, it is reasonable to suspect he or she has crossed over the line of no return regarding the marriage. This needs to be confronted in terms of clarification and directions for continued therapy. If, however, when confronted, the provoker stops the acting-out behaviors, he or she may well still be committed to improving the marriage. Hence, the key for the therapist becomes the behavioral responses to the therapist's confronting the provoker with his behavior and its possible meaning for the marriage. Federico (1979) believes that if the provoker has indeed crossed the point of no return, he will not stop the provoking behaviors but will rather be driven to accelerate those behaviors, despite any therapeutic intervention aimed at eradicating them, until the accommodating partner takes steps to terminate the marriage.

The preseparation period is one of the peak stress periods of the divorce adjustment process. It often leaves deep psychic scars that take the form of depression, anxiety, low self-esteem, anger, guilt, or self-doubt, particularly for the spouse who wants the marriage to continue.

The emotional suffering and pain involved in divorce is intense and severe. Therapists, friends, and family need to be aware of the intensity of these difficult feelings in order that the help they offer may be effective. Therapeutic help needs to include hope, personal validation, support, reassurance, and tolerance of some of the aberrant behaviors often exhibited during the adjustment process.

The litigation period. Overt action taken to terminate the marriage ushers in the litigation period, in which the couple are adversaries, working out the best possible deal for themselves through the courts.

The litigation period is often fraught with frustration, fear, and anger. Legal costs are usually commensurate with such factors as the length of the marriage, the number and ages of children involved, and the amount and complexity of community property the couple has accumulated. Experience reveals that the husband is usually worried that he will be assessed too high an economic settlement, and the wife fears that her settlement will be too little to enable her to maintain a decent standard of living. Thus the couple now, if not before, usually become adversaries.

The primary therapeutic task in this period is to help the couple put their accounts together. The usual pattern is that initially the client feels the other spouse is almost totally at fault. With therapeutic understanding, patience, and help, the client ultimately moves through a phase where he or she admits to some participation in the marital failure to a phase of considerable objectivity where the concern is to learn fully the involvement in the failure process and move toward a greater understanding of his or her own needs and motivations.

The couple then moves to a period in which they change their mental outlook from being mentally married to being mentally divorced. The rate at which they move through this process is directly related to the amount and effectiveness of their therapeutic involvement and their mental health state, as well as the length and intensity of their marriage and previous commitment to each other. Therapeutically, group therapy has been demonstrated to be the most effective modality to meet the emotional needs of those involved in divorce, although any kind of personal growth therapy can also be effective.

Children and Divorce. Each year there are more than one million children involved in divorce in the United States. More than 60% of divorcing couples have children at home. Previously, conventional wisdom decreed that couples, no matter how unhappy, should remain together for the sake of the children. Research and experience no longer support that principle. In one study mothers reported that after the children had adjusted, half of them were not damaged and one third may have become improved (Gardner, 1977).

Studies indicate that most children do have at least a one-year adjustment period following divorce. Some of the symptoms exhibited during this time are signs of regression, acting out, truancy, fighting with siblings, running away, nail biting, and nightmares. The extent to which children suffer in divorce is affected by several factors: age, nature, custodial agreement, and the nature of the custodial parent's adjustment.

Children who are older and younger have fewer problems than those ages 6 to 14, who seem to have greater adjustment difficulties. The better adjusted the child, the fewer adjustment problems he will have following separation of his parents. The nature of the custodial parent's adjustment seems to be the key consideration in the child's adjustment, which depends in part on the extent to which the child resembles the custodial parent. The greater the similarity of the child to the custodial parent (i.e., sex, physical appearance, behaviors, etc.), the better the adjustment that can be anticipated. Another factor involving

the adjustment of children is time with the father. The more time lost with the father, the higher the maladjustment of the child in the first year following the divorce.

Initially all children, regardless of age, are affected by divorce. As parents demonstrate their ability to manage the postmarital situation, remain appropriately related to the child, and keep the postmarital situation free of turmoil, the child's adjustment will be positively facilitated. Since the custodial parent's adjustment is such an important factor in the child's future adjustment, it is of utmost importance that those custodial parents who are experiencing severe adjustment problems seek professional help, not only for themselves but for the sake of their children (*see* CHILD CUSTODY).

The Church and Divorce. It is important that the church, in the light of God's Word and the rise in the divorce rate, should not attack the divorced but rather should promote its vision of marriage. Thus the church needs to rethink divorce in the light of the Christian view of marriage and in the light of a realistic view of human nature.

Throughout Scripture there is a realistic view regarding humanity's ability to achieve God's intention for marriage. The Old Testament assumes that some marriages will fail, and thus the Old Testament seeks to achieve justice for those involved in divorce and remarriage. Jesus viewed the permanence of marriage as the ideal, but he also indicated the ideal is not always achieved. He recognized marriages would fail, and thus biblical teachings indicate the possibility that human shortcomings will thwart God's intentions. This is the harmony of idealism and reality.

Since divorce is a thwarting of God's purpose, it is a sin. Not sin in the sense of having done something wrong, but sin in the sense of the human predicament of distorting God's original intention for life. This means that not only divorce but every failure of marriage to achieve God's purpose is sinful. The biblical treatment of this reality makes it clear that marital failure is only one of many instances of human sinfulness. Also, nowhere is it reported that violations of God's creative intention in marriage and divorce are more serious than any others.

Another theme in Scripture is the acknowledgment that great injustice is liable to occur in divorce. The Bible acknowledges that divorce can be one of the most dehumanizing and shattering experiences in life, and God is concerned about our suffering. The church should also be concerned about humanizing social practices in our society.

There are two extreme views taken by churches regarding remarriage: there are those governed by law and those governed by grace. Law without compassion becomes legalism, and compassion without law becomes flabby sentimentalism. The redemptive act of God in Christ is the good news that no person need be denied a harmonious relationship with God, no matter what the offense. Also, we are enlisted in God's redemptive plan. Hence, those who are divorced and remarried can be accepted by God's forgiving love.

In summary, the church needs to teach God's intention for marriage as a moral law. The church needs to concern itself with learning ways of greater moral nurturing. The church needs to recognize that some Christian marriages are beyond repair, that the decision to divorce is usually not an impulsive act but the result of a process. When divorce happens, the marriage is dead. When this occurs, the calling of the church is for renewal for the divorced person.

References

Federico, J. The marital termination period of the divorce adjustment process. *Journal of Divorce*, 1979, *3*, 93–106.

Gardner, R. *The Parents Book about Divorce*. Garden City, N.Y.: Doubleday, 1977.

Glieberman, H. A. Why so many marriages fail. *U.S. News and World Report*, July 20, 1981, pp. 53–55.

Hunt, M., & Hunt, B. *The Divorce Experience*. New York: McGraw-Hill, 1977.

Additional Readings

Barnhart, J., & Barnhart, M. Divorce counseling for devout Christians. *Journal of Divorce*, 1977, *1*, 141–151.

Levinger, G. K., & Moles, O. C. (Eds.). *Divorce and separation*. New York: Basic Books, 1979.

Loewenstein, S. F. Helping family members cope with divorce. In S. Eisenberg & L. E. Patterson (Eds.), *Helping clients with special concerns*. Chicago: Rand McNally College Publishing, 1979.

Small, D. *The right to remarry*. Old Tappan, N.J.: Revell, 1975.

Weinglass, J., Kressell, K., & Deutsch, M., The role of the clergy in divorce. *Journal of Divorce*, 1978, *2*, 57–82.

A. C. SYLLING

Dix, Dorothea Lynde (1802–1887). A major force in mental health reform, Dorothea Dix has a secure place in the history of psychology. She was born in Hampden, Maine. Her parents treated her so harshly that she left them to live with her grandparents in Boston. At the age of 14 she began teaching school in Worcester, and by the age of 20 she was running a school that catered to the daughters of prominent Bostonians.

Soon she was the victim of recurring attacks of tuberculosis. During this time, from 1824 to 1840, she wrote stories and books for children. She became financially independent when she received her inheritance from her grandmother. In 1841 she began teaching a Sunday school class for women prisoners in Boston. She was horrified at the neglect, brutality, and the mixing of the mentally ill and the retarded with criminals.

Between 1841 and 1881 she aroused the public and the state legislatures to an awareness of the inhuman treatment of the mentally ill. New Jersey was first to respond by building a hospital for the mentally ill in 1848. More than 20 states built or enlarged more than 30 state mental hospitals. Dix directed the opening of two institutions in Canada, reformed the asylum system in Scotland, and brought about reform in 14 other countries.

During the Civil War she organized the nursing forces of the Northern armies. Later she heard of the dangerous shores of Sable Island, Newfoundland, visited the region, and got officials to provide life-saving boats. A resolution presented by Congress in 1901 described her as "among the noblest examples of humanity in all history."

R. L. KOTESKEY

Dogmatism. The concept of dogmatism in psychology is most closely associated with the work of Milton Rokeach and is discussed most fully in his book *The Open and Closed Mind* (1960). The Dogmatism Scale developed by him promoted and popularized research on the subject. Hundreds of published studies relate dogmatic tendencies to attitude, personality, and behavior variables, including religion.

Political extremes of World War II inspired theories and research about authoritarian personalities, most notably *The Authoritarian Personality* (Adorno, Frenkel-Brunswik, Levinson, & Sanford, 1950). Whereas these studies emphasized fascist, conservative authoritarianisms of the "right," Rokeach observed that liberals or "leftists" can be equally authoritarian or dogmatic.

Any communication includes both relevant and irrelevant information. The relevant facts concern the immediate problem to which one must react. Irrelevant facts indicate the source of the message, authority figures, rewards and punishments for alternative actions, and relationships of these to our belief systems, defenses, and motivations. Open-minded people, Rokeach said, discriminate and respond primarily to the relevant information. Dogmatic or closed-minded persons fail to discriminate the relevant facts and tend to respond to irrelevant factors, such as the authority and personal needs. The dogmatic tend to see the world as threatening and hold a narrow, future-oriented (contrasted with broad) time perspective. They are also prone to hold their beliefs in isolation, without logical integration, and tend strongly to reject and to be ill-informed about belief systems other than their own. The Dogmatism Scale was based on such definitions of dogmatism.

Rokeach's theory and research related the development of closed-mindedness to an inability to express ambivalent feelings about one's parents and, by a defensive constriction, a dearth of influence by adults outside the family. Subsequent research on the origins of personal dogmatism has related open-mindedness to higher social class, larger family size, and later birth order.

Situational threat as a factor in dogmatism was demonstrated by an investigation of conversions to authoritarian or dogmatic denominations. In two studies (nationwide for 1920–1939 and Seattle, Washington, for 1961–1970) times of economic prosperity were associated with relatively more conversions to non-authoritarian groups and economic depression with more conversions to authoritarian faiths (Sales, 1972). Rokeach (1960) said that institutions, like individuals, respond to threat with increased dogmatism. Religions are not inherently dogmatic, but dogma may be invoked to defend the institution against heresy and ensure its continuation. Rokeach demonstrated this in a study of 12 Roman Catholic ecumenical councils from A.D. 325 to 1563. The degree of threat or heresy preceding each council was strongly related to dogmatism of the resulting canons, both in degree of authority invoked and in the punishment ordained for violators.

Subsequent research supports dogmatism as generalized authoritarianism—political and religious, left and right. Dogmatism is associated with racial prejudice, sex-role stereotypes, and rejection of unconventional music. Persons with dogmatic personalities tend to show anxiety, low self-esteem, the need to receive support from others, general maladjustment and instability, defensiveness, impatience, timidity, and conformity (Vacchiano, Strauss, & Schiffman, 1968).

Catholics were more dogmatic than Protestants in Rokeach's (1960) midwest studies, but some Protestants are more dogmatic, particularly in the south. Churchgoers tend to be more dogmatic than the nonreligious, but radical atheists are also dogmatic. Dogmatism tends

to accompany an extrinsic or self-serving religion, but usually it is not related to an intrinsic or committed religious orientation. If, as Allport said, mature, intrinsic faith develops out of self-serving religion, dogmatism may be a normal phase in the development of religious faith. The theories of Kohlberg, Fowler, and Loevinger (in development of moral judgment, faith, and ego respectively) all include rigidly held beliefs and reliance on authority at early developmental stages. Similarly, in the growth of a personal religious faith, openness to relevant new information tends to replace defensive reliance on authority as the faith becomes more committed, mature, and secure.

References

Adorno, T. W., Frenkel-Brunswik, E., Levinson, D. J., & Sanford, R. N. *The authoritarian personality.* New York: Harper & Row, 1950.

Rokeach, M. *The open and closed mind.* New York: Basic Books, 1960.

Sales, S. M. Economic threat as a determinant of conversion rates in authoritarian and nonauthoritarian churches. *Journal of Personality and Social Psychology,* 1972, *23,* 420–428.

Vacchiano, R. B., Strauss, P. S., & Schiffman, D. C. Personality correlates of dogmatism. *Journal of Consulting and Clinical Psychology,* 1968, *32,* 83–85.

R. D. KAHOE

See AUTHORITARIAN PERSONALITY; AMBIGUITY, INTOLERANCE OF; RELIGION AND PERSONALITY; RELIGIOUS ORIENTATION.

Domestic Violence. Those activities of a threatening or violent physical nature within the context of what is commonly called a home environment. Most laws enacted in recent years address both the mental and physical aspects of violence and usually define domestic in terms of legal and common-law relationships. Further, they apply to all members of a family who are or have lived together within a domicile. The counselor should consult local and state codes for precise definitions and provisions.

Incidence of domestic violence is uncertain. It is currently addressed in terms of known cases and hence represents a minimum assessment. One study shows that 1.7 million Americans faced a spouse wielding a knife or gun during a one-year period. Another study indicated that over 28% in the sample had engaged in at least one violent incident against a family member in that particular year. Generally, one out of eight American couples indicates the incidence of violence during their marriage. In one study an investigation of 8,800 divorces produced evidence that physical abuse was the complaint in 90% of the cases. Boston City Hospital has reported that 70% of the assault cases treated in the emergency room were attacked in their home by husband or lover.

Police reports indicate that domestic violence (disputes and disturbances) account for the greatest percentage of all calls. Police in Kansas City indicate that in 1977, 85% of the domestic homicides had previously been visited by officers and that 50% of that group had been visited five times prior to the killing.

While the exact incidence of domestic violence is uncertain, the problem appears to be considerable both in terms of its destructiveness in the home and the pressures placed upon the various public institutions who must deal with it. Counselors and pastors are increasingly facing the problem across their desks, in homes, and in emergency rooms. Domestic violence shelters report that the phenomenon is not limited by race, profession, or income, and clergy and counselors may struggle with the problem in their own places of residence.

Predictive Factors. Recognizing the presence of domestic violence is often difficult. It is covered in a variety of ways, and even doctors often fail to diagnose it correctly. Hospital officials are told the physical symptoms are accidents. Clothing is worn which conceals bruises, scratches, and cuts. Social events are shunned, and life styles retreat to the inner sanctum.

Certain groups, however, have shown a high propensity for domestic violence. Children who are raised in a context of such violence more often introduce it into their own marriages. Young children in violent homes have been observed to utilize the violence in manipulative ways to gain greater freedom; some adopt the hostage syndrome and identify with the violent marriage partner. Young males tend to adopt certain attitudes of superiority over females and relate to their mothers and sisters in domineering ways. The phenomenon thus tends to be self-perpetuating.

A high incidence of alcohol and drug usage is correlated with domestic violence. It is also likely that if the husband has a history of violent relationships outside the home, particularly in a criminal context, he will be violent in the home interactions.

Types of injury sometimes are helpful in identifying victims of battering. It has been found that deliberate physical assault manifests itself in what is described as a "body map" whereby injuries may be distinguished from household accidents. Battered women tend to have injuries to the head, face, chest, breasts, and abdomen, whereas nonbattered women are more likely to injure the forearm, hand, lower legs, and feet.

Several studies have indicated that domestic violence appears to increase during pregnancy. Violence increases miscarriage rates from 1 in 15 to 1 in 4. There is also an increased frequency of abortion.

These predictive factors, however, in no way limit the problem. It is well known, for example, that middle-class victims of various social ills seldom come in contact with the agencies that normally identify and label official deviants.

Dynamics of the Violent Relationship. The battering interaction may be described in terms of three distinct phases or stages. The first phase is seen as the tension-building stage where stress increases and coping techniques become less effective. The violent party or parties react negatively to the stress, and psychologically the violence begins at this point.

It is in the second phase that the violence erupts. In this acute battering stage the impending violence is inevitable and the attack occurs. Activities are irrational, and intervention is limited to separation of the couple.

The third phase may be referred to as the warm and loving stage. Immediately after the abuse the batterer typically expresses repeated feelings of remorse and promises that it will never happen again. The offender may shower his mate with affection and gifts. Such behavior has a strong tendency to reinforce the victim to stay in the relationship. It also has produced overly optimistic prognoses among clergy and counselors who come into contact with the couple at this stage.

Repeated violence extends itself beyond the narrow circle of the nuclear family. At some point the battered spouse will often look to her family for support. Inevitably the ensuing violence alienates close family and friends, leaving the wife alone and increasingly vulnerable. More victims are thus turning to available agencies that offer specialized services, and these agencies tend to recommend physical separation and divorce as a solution.

Recent research indicates that the socioeconomic role of the woman affects her role in the second and third stages. In states where the socioeconomic index for women was low, the women tended to be more passive during the violence. In those states where the woman had a higher status, she was more aggressive and equal in the violent episodes. Furthermore, these women more often left the marriage through divorce, thereby prompting some observers to optimistically note that a solution to the increasing rise in violence may have been realized.

Causative Factors. Many myths have been generated about the nature of domestic violence, the appreciable number of persons who continue to live within the context of repeated attacks, and the unconscionable suffering which is often extended to the children involved. Often the wife has been accused of having some deep-seated need for such abuse or is described as "asking for it." Considerable research has dispensed with such easy descriptions, and pat answers should be seriously questioned by anyone who deals with the problem.

Domestic violence lends itself to oversimplification. Some blame the wife, which is simplistic. But it is equally simplistic to put the entire blame on the husband. Domestic violence occurs in a variety of instances having diverse causes. It might currently be best understood as a continuum from incidental to pathological.

Incidental violence often appears under unusually stressful situations and surprises both partners. Each may say, "I never thought I would do this!" The counselor seems to have greater potential to help such clients, since both parties may be more sensitive to their responsibility.

Pathological violence should be seen as the opposite end of the continuun from incidental domestic violence. Typical of issues in family research, more is known about the "sick" families involved than the relatively healthier. Profiles have been created for both the pathological batterer and the victim. The batterer, usually the male, possesses characteristics that make it relatively easy to predict future occurrence of attack. The batterer usually shows major mood shifts wherein he is alternately charming and vicious. Further, he tends to have an extremely low self-concept, perhaps linked to the probability that he either witnessed or was the object of such abuse in his own family. Another characteristic commonly observed is exaggerated jealousy coupled with an uncanny ability to project both blame and guilt onto the other principle individuals. The crippling effects of the violence often come more from this ability to make the victims feel responsible than from the physical damages inflicted. It has further been noted that the pathological batterer has a tendency to utilize sex in aggressive ways. Occasionally the offender will utilize his spouse in a duplicate mother relationship, resorting to violence when the stresses placed on the relationship begin to break the marriage.

Wives of pathological batterers often complement the husband. The battered wife tends to have an equally low self-concept and to maintain a very traditional view of husband-wife roles. She usually accepts both the responsibility and the guilt for her husband's actions. Most have experienced severe psychological abuse. Many have endured bizarre and often incestuous sexual patterns from their husbands. The counselor should note that wives in this context of abuse often have tolerated repeated violence (known as the secondary battering syndrome) because they were convinced that they had to solve the problem by themselves since no other help was known. The relationship is often extended by the batterer's frequent projection that his emotional well-being and life depend on her.

Intervention. The counselor should recognize certain difficulties inherent in initiating therapy with such clients. The wife from a pathological relationship will be singly available when she discovers help may be obtained in a safe manner. Most often this will occur just before or just after she physically moves from the relationship, thereby bringing a multitude of social needs into the counseling milieu. The husband is the least likely partner to seek such help. His view is that she has the problem, and the proximity of an outsider who may indicate he has certain responsibilities is too threatening. Voluntary treatment for the husband is rare.

The counselor will have to deal with the self-blame brought into therapy by the battered client. Real responsibilites and problems must be separated from those projected by the batterer. Often she will have adopted a multitude of excuses designed to cover the physical damage as well as social behavior. One young wife who was employed asked a crisis intervenor in a refuge center, "What am I going to tell my employer?" The intervenor, herself a former battered wife, replied, "You tell him your husband did it. For if you can't, you're likely not prepared to break the vicious cycle."

Therapeutic goals will be set by the client and tend to involve two choices: 1) return home to either survive or work toward improvement, or 2) leave home via separation and divorce. It is crucial that the counselor not recommend solutions with which the client will have to live. The choice must be that of the client, since either choice will be painful and the impact of the counseling will be limited if the client feels the therapist "got her into this."

Successful resolution in either direction depends on the client's ability to assume responsibility for her survival.

The counselor must remain sensitive throughout the intervention to issues of incest and child abuse. There is considerable physical and sexual child abuse linked with domestic violence. If such abuse is detected, the abused child and the abusing parent should both also be referred for help. In some cases the woman may refuse to press this referral herself. The counselor should be prepared to do so, an action required by law in many states. This problem is an eventuality for those counselors who deal with domestic violence.

A thorough knowledge of the laws and social resources available will be necessary to properly assist victims. Shelters are of particular benefit for those who can develop a working relationship with such agencies. These are sometimes better suited to helping meet the needs of long-term reorientation cases who opt for separation or divorce.

The counselor who practices from a Christian framework will need to be clear about his or her role. It is critical that the counselor be a means of grace and specifically an agent of redemption who can meet the client where she is and bring healing. Biblical teaching about the role of husband and wife, the advice to wives to stay with their husbands so that they might be saved, and God's will concerning divorce may easily be misinterpreted and misused. The possibility of greater damage is always present. The counselor and the church must develop a clearer response to this delicate problem or forfeit this area as a field of redemptive activity.

Additional Readings

Fleming, J. B. *Stopping wife abuse.* Garden City, N.Y.: Doubleday Anchor, 1979.

Roy, M. (Ed.). *Battered women: A psychosociological study of domestic violence.* New York: Van Nostrand Reinhold, 1977.

A. R. DENTON

See VICTIMS OF VIOLENT CRIMES.

Double Bind. The double bind hypothesis was first formulated to describe a communication phenomenon observed in schizophrenic families (Bateson, Jackson, Haley, & Weakland, 1956). The elements of the double bind are two or more people having repeated experiences in an important relationship, at least one of whom is sending messages with a primary injunction coupled with a secondary injunction which conflicts at a different level. Additionally there is a perceived inability to escape from the relationship or comment on the incongruity. Reactions to this pattern of communication include anxiety, ambivalence, defensiveness, withdrawal, paranoia, shifts between concrete and abstract thinking, and disqualification of the other, the message, or the self. In summary, the double bind describes or underlies several of the symptoms of schizophrenia, and it is thought to have a progressive and cumulative effect on psychic functioning.

As an example, a mother has a fear of intimacy and dislikes children but, through the defense mechanism of reaction formation, shows loving behavior toward her child. The child is in a double bind; if he discriminates accurately, he will realize that his primary love object and best hope for survival does not love him (or does so ambivalently at best). If he does not discriminate accurately, he will approach her and be rebuffed by more or less conscious hostility. If he then withdraws, she will punish him verbally because the withdrawal indicates that she is not a loving mother. In this situation, the child cannot win. The only escape from this situation is to talk with the mother about the bind, but the child is unable to do so because of age or a history of punishment. Thus, over time this child fails to learn to talk about his binds. He too begins to give distorted messages, feels ambivalent, does not do well outside his family, and eventually becomes symptomatic.

The best theoretical formulation of this hypothesis has been in terms of a conflict of logical types, a paradox involving the inappropriate use of concepts drawn from two different conceptual levels or categories but sent in the same message (Gootnick, 1973). This understanding has often proved to be too abstract; it is also too easily extended to areas where in fact it has no logical explanatory power, even though it seems applicable. Thus it has been difficult conceptually and empirically to specify accurately what is indeed a double bind and to determine whether the effects will be negative or positive. However, the hypothesis remains very useful with regard to generating research and sensitizing clinicians to communicational subtleties in family interaction patterns. It has directly contributed to the popularity of family therapy, especially for schizophrenics. It has also come to play an important role in some forms of hypnotherapy (*see* HYPNOTHERAPY, INDIRECT), especially those associated with the work of Erickson. Weeks and L'Abate (1982) have developed an approach called paradoxical psychotherapy in which the double bind plays a prominent role.

References

Bateson, F., Jackson, D. D., Haley, J., & Weakland, J. H. Toward a theory of schizophrenia. *Behavioral Science*, 1956, *1*, 251–264.

Gootnick, A. T. *The double-bind hypothesis: A conceptual and empirical review*. Journal Supplement Abstract Service, 1973, *3*.

Weeks, G. R., & L'Abate, L. *Paradoxical psychotherapy*. New York: Brunner/Mazel, 1982.

J. M. BRANDSMA

See PARADOXICAL INTERVENTION; FAMILY COMMUNICATION THEORY.

Double Technique. The double technique, used in PSYCHODRAMA, involves a person (the double) whose purpose it is to mirror the protagonist (the one being helped) and facilitate the expression of unsaid feelings and thoughts. The double begins by mirroring the body of the protagonist, then seeks information about who the protagonist is and what he or she is feeling. This information assists the double in enlarging on the role and speaking what is not being spoken. Often during the psychodrama the double is directed to become a specific part of the protagonist—e.g., self-condemning, confused, nurturing. Although most commonly employed in group settings, this technique is also useful for individual therapy. Doubling does require some training and experience in psychodramatic methods.

J. H. VANDER MAY

Doubt. A state of mind characterized by an absence of either assent or dissent to a certain proposition. It is a suspension of commitment to belief or disbelief, either because the evidence pro and con is evenly balanced (positive doubt) or because evidence is lacking for either side (negative doubt, exemplified by the apostle Thomas). Doubt is thus an integral part of each person's belief system, since it is impossible for anyone to firmly believe or fully disbelieve all propositions of which he or she is aware. Yet in spite of the natural occurrence of doubt in human cognition, many people view doubt as a negative mindset to be avoided if at all possible.

Doubt is a topic of interest to scholars from three academic disciplines. Philosophers study doubt because of its epistemological implications in relation to knowledge, truth, and awareness of existence. Theologians are concerned with doubt because it often occurs as a prelude to belief or as a precursor of disbelief. Psychologists investigate doubt because of the emotions which often accompany it (anxiety, depression, or fear) and because in certain pathologies doubt can become obsessional and debilitating.

Doubt, Unbelief, and Ambivalence. Doubt should be differentiated from unbelief. Unbelief is a positive conviction of falsity regarding an issue and hence is a form of belief. Doubt does not imply a belief in a contrary position; it is simply being unconvinced. If, however, doubt becomes pervasive and dominates the thinking of a person regarding all issues, it is more appropriately called skepticism (or definitive doubt). The skeptic despairs of ever knowing truth with certainty.

Doubt can also be distinguished from ambivalence. Ambivalence is a state of mind characterized by the concurrent presence of two or more differing feelings toward the same object. Ambivalence, in massive quantities, is classically seen as a primary indicator of schizophrenia, whereas massive doubt is more often a part of obsessional disorders. Indecisiveness and vascillation, although related to doubt, refer more to a lack of commitment to a proposition or to a frequent change of opinion.

Normal doubt can be differentiated from abnormal doubt chiefly by the degree to which the doubt impairs daily living. Doubt is normal when it does not dominate a person's thinking, when it is overshadowed by stable beliefs, and when the goal of the doubt is resolution into belief or disbelief. Doubt is also normal when employed, as Descartes advocated, for the purpose of seeking truth. Normal doubt is a type of mental clarification and can help a person better organize his or her beliefs. Developmental theorists have noted several phases of life when doubts are characteristically found: in adolescence, when the teen-ager moves from childhood credulity toward a personalized belief system, and in the middle years, when issues of competence and direction predominate (Grant, 1974). Abnormal doubt focuses on issues having little consequence or issues without grave implications of error.

Religious Doubt. Religious doubt has been a concern of believers from biblical days to the present. In the Garden of Eden the serpent used doubt as a tool to move Eve from a position of belief to one of disobedience. Abraham, Job, and David all had times of doubt which were painful yet growth-producing. The best-known example of doubt in the Bible is Thomas, who was absent when Jesus made a postresurrection appearance to the 10 apostles. Jesus showed the 10 his hands and his side (John 20), evidence that dispelled their doubt as to his identity. When told of Jesus' appearance, Thomas replied that he would not believe until he too had seen the evidence. Eight days later Jesus reappeared, showed

Thomas his wounds, and made a gracious plea for faith.

By way of contrast, Jesus consistently condemned unbelief wherever he found it. Presumably, Jesus tolerated doubt because it was a transitory, nonpermanent state of mind, whereas he condemned unbelief because it was a fixed decision often accompanied by hardness of heart. In general, the evidence seems to indicate that Jesus showed a tolerant attitude toward doubt and a negative view toward unbelief. Guinness (1976) cautions, however, that Scripture sometimes uses the word *unbelief* to refer to doubt (Mark 9:24). Hence exegetical care is needed when interpreting the Bible's teachings regarding doubt.

Doubt is a problem in theological systems committed to inscripturated truth. For example, evangelical Christians are generally not tolerant of doubt if it is prolonged, unyielding, and centered on cardinal truths. Doubt is not so much a problem in liberal theologies since truth is more relative and less certain. Thus, the conservative Christian community sees doubt as risky and dangerous, whereas the liberal Christian community sees doubt as a sign of healthy intellectual inquiry. Doubt is resolved into belief or disbelief in any of four ways: through conversion, through liberalization, through renewal, or through emotional growth (Helfaer, 1972).

Normal doubt tends to appear when a person's belief system "does not protect the individual in his life experiences and from its more painful states" (Helfaer, p. 216). Even so, it is possible for someone to construct rigid defenses designed to ensure belief and prevent doubt at all costs. Cults are noted for such an approach, which discourages any reexamination of beliefs (Cohen, 1972).

Doubt and Psychopathology. In psychopathology doubt often occurs as a prominent symptom in the obsessive-compulsive disorders. Earlier in the twentieth century a special diagnostic category was created called *folie du doute,* or doubting mania. The disorder was described as an extreme self-consciousness and a preoccupation with hesitation and doubt. The condition was frequently considered progressive and incurable. Eventually the disorder was seen as but one variety of an obsessive-compulsive disorder, since the doubting mania was accompanied by overconscientiousness, fears of contamination, and other obsessive-compulsive characteristics.

The obsessive doubter is one whose symptoms have taken a cognitive rather than a predominantly behavioral form. In other words, the doubter is usually more obsessive than compulsive, although the dynamics behind either form is similar. The obsessive doubter usually centers his or her thinking on some imponderable issue which is just beyond the pale of provability. For example, the doubter may fret over issues of existence (Do I really exist?) or over issues of reality (Did I actually put a stamp on the letter I just mailed?). As the doubter becomes more and more proficient in his or her ruminations, an elaborate network of essentially futile mental operations is created. This network of doubts serves several secondary purposes usually described as secondary gains. For example, decisions can be delayed, responsibilities can be laid aside, and action can be postponed. Obsessive doubters with high intellectual capacity can create such doubts that their friends are likewise captivated by the issues. Other issues over which doubters can obsess include paternity, memory, and length of life.

If the obsessive doubter is religious, the doubts will likely involve issues of God's existence, God's involvement in human affairs, salvation, security, and one's eternal state. Doubters who are serious students of Scripture will find an ample supply of issues that qualify for genuine obsessing—i.e., issues that are essentially unanswerable or imponderable. For example, the obsessive doubter who reads Jesus' statement, "If anyone is ashamed of me and my words, the Son of Man will be ashamed of him" (Luke 9:26), will worry about a specific time of embarrassment or shame in the past. Soon all confidence and security disappear, and the doubter fears eternal damnation.

There are several characteristics of the teachings of Jesus which seem to aggravate the obsessive doubter (Beck, 1981). Jesus frequently used themes of exclusivity (Matt. 10:33), absoluteness (Luke 18:22), abstractness (Mark 9:43, 45), impossibility (Mark 10:25), and prohibition (Luke 13:28). Any of these themes can aggravate the obsessive's tendency to be overconscientious, rigid, and concrete, resulting in doubts.

The etiology of obsessive doubting is similar to that of the obsessive-compulsive disorder in general (Salzman, 1968). Professional help is indicated in cases of obsessive doubting. If treatment commences soon enough in the process, the prognosis is generally favorable. Therapy can help the sufferer to learn new channels for coping with anxiety and new patterns of effective decision making.

In summary, doubt can be a valuable part of one's life if its goal is resolution and if it results in deeper commitment to existing beliefs and less commitment to extraneous or harmful presuppositions (Pruyser, 1974). All belief has about it a feeling of resolved doubt. Hence as the doubter moves toward belief, his or her life is enriched by the resulting relief and satisfaction.

References
Beck, J. R. Treatment of spiritual doubt among obsessing evangelicals. *Journal of Psychology and Theology*, 1981, *9*, 224–231.
Cohen, J. *Psychological probability.* London: Allen & Unwin, 1972.
Grant, V. W. *The roots of religious doubt and the search for security.* New York: Seabury, 1974.
Guinness, O. *In two minds: The dilemma of doubt and how to resolve it.* Downers Grove, Ill.: Inter-Varsity Press, 1976.
Halfaer, P. M. *The psychology of religious doubt.* Boston: Beacon Press, 1972.
Pruyser, P. W. *Between belief and unbelief.* New York: Harper & Row, 1974.
Salzman, L. *The obsessive personality.* New York: Science House, 1968.

J. R. BECK

Down's Syndrome. A type of MENTAL RETARDATION first described by J. Langdon-Down in 1866, also known as Langdon-Down disease and previously called mongolism. It is caused by an extra chromosome (No. 21) which triples instead of the usual pairing, leaving 47 chromosomes instead of the normal 46. It is not an inherited disorder but the result of an error in cell division, and the occurrence of the disease increases in frequency with advanced parental age. Down's syndrome occurs once in approximately every 700 births, with 1 per 1,000 to mothers under 30 and 1 in 40 to mothers over 45.

Mentally, the Down's syndrome child is usually docile and imitative, with a mental age of between 4 and 7 years. Some are hyperactive, and a small percentage may have destructive tendencies. The term *mongolism* was first applied due to the resemblance in facial appearance to members of the Mongolian race. Down's Syndrome is associated with a short nose, flabby skin, hypotonic muscles, and a large tongue that is fissured and often protrudes. Less than 60% of Down's syndrome children live more than 5 years after birth, and the approximate life span is 35 to 40 years. There is no known effective medical treatment.

D. L. SCHUURMAN

Dreams. *See* SLEEP AND DREAMING.

Dreams, Therapeutic Use of. The therapeutic potential of dream interpretation has been a basic assumption of depth psychologies and dynamic psychotherapies ever since Freud developed the method of free association. The publication of Freud's *The Interpretation of Dreams* in 1900 marks a second major turning point in the historical status of, and approach to, dream interpretation.

As summarized elsewhere (Vande Kemp, 1981), the nineteenth-century psychology of dreaming represented a transitional period between the Christian/classical oneiric traditions and the interpretive/investigative traditions of the twentieth century. Dreams of the classical period had a supernatural or transpersonal significance: they were regarded as messages from the gods to men (in the Christian tradition, from God to men). During the nineteenth century they took on an interpersonal significance: they were regarded as messages from one person to another, or as mere epiphenomena of physiological states. In the twentieth century their significance is intrapersonal: they constitute a message from the person to the self.

In each of these periods the dream interpreter represented a different type of "community." During the transpersonal or supernatural era the dream interpreter was an inhabitant of the social community. The dream characters (whether gods or wandering souls) were considered real, and the meaning of the dream could be consensually validated. When the interpersonal period emerged, both dreamer and interpreter were moved to the pseudocommunity, in which some of the dream characters were considered real and at least some others validated the dream's meaning. The remaining content was a product of imagination, and its meaning of a nonconsensual nature. During the intrapersonal period both dreamer and interpreter reside in the autistic community. The dream characters are all imaginary, though they represent the real, and the dream's meaning is strictly personal, or limited to the relationship between the dreamer and the interpreter. It is to an understanding of this latter meaning that most therapeutic uses of dreams are directed, and methods of dream interpretation are as diverse as the multiple psychotherapies.

Freud. Freud's therapeutic approach to dreams involved the critical distinction between manifest and latent dreams. The manifest dream is the dream "story" that we relate to others. The latent dream is transformed into the manifest dream through the dreamwork, which consists of essentially four mechanisms: condensation, displacement, dramatization, and secondary revision.

Condensation reflects the fact that dream elements are overdetermined so that each element in the manifest dream represents several elements of latent content, and vice versa. Thus, a person in the dream may be constituted by fusing traits belonging to several actual persons. *Displacement* reflects the fact that the psychic intensity, or the emotional content, of the dream thoughts is placed on the less essential aspects of the dream, so that the most important content of the latent dream is present in the manifest dream only as a weak allusion.

Dramatization is based on the fact that regression occurs in dreams. Because the dream is primarily a visual and auditory experience, like a play enacted on stage, logical relationships between ideas must be expressed through spatial or temporal proximity or through fusing several features. Similarity may thus be represented through identification, and causal relationships by making one group of elements follow another, as when one movie scene fades into another. Opposition and contradiction are depicted through inverting the two corresponding elements or scenes. *Secondary revision* or elaboration refers to the alteration in the dream processes when they are perceived by consciousness: the originally fragmented parts of the dream are transformed into a whole by inserting connecting words or scenes during the recollection or retelling of the dream. Freud's method of dream interpretation through the process of free association may be regarded as the reversal of this process in order to unveil underlying conflicts.

Probably the most popularized aspect of Freud's theory involves the role of symbolization. The much-popularized sexual symbolism of Freudian dreams may be found in the Song of Solomon, where the meaning of the sexual symbols reaches back to antiquity. When the association between symbol and idea symbolized appear widely discrepant, Freud attributes this to the work of the censor, a hypothetical function of the ego whose job it is to see that the sleeper's sleep is not disturbed by the dream. Because of the censor's work the meaning of a dream element can only be discovered through the process of free association; seldom is such a meaning discernible merely through intuition. For Freud the ultimate meaning of the dream lay in the fulfillment of a wish.

Several contemporaries of Freud emphasized other aspects of the therapeutic use of dreams. Prince (1910) utilized a method of dream interpretation which incorporated free association as well as dissociation into various states of consciousness. In each of these hypnotic states his patient had memories that differed from those of her waking state and from those in the other hypnotic states. When awake, she could not remember her dreams at all, or remembered them only imperfectly. In one hypnotic state they were remembered in vivid detail. The other hypnotic states were used to obtain associations for dream analysis. Others who discussed the therapeutic uses of dreams included Charles Fere, Arnold Pick, and Bronislaw Onuf. Pick published several studies showing how intense hysterical states resulted from previous reveries. Onuf pointed to the striking similarity between dreams and the somnabulistic and trance states of hysterics.

Jung and Adler. Freud's dream theory was empirically based in his own dreams and those of his patients. Dream interpretation, because it unearthed secret, disguised wishes, was regarded as the royal highway to the unconscious. Major shifts in the depth psychology of dreaming came with the work of Jung and Adler. With Adler there was a shift to the interpersonal level of meaning, and dreams comprised the royal highway to consciousness. Jung, relying on the rich traditions of mythology, mandala symbolism, and alchemy, shifted the focus to the transpersonal or suprapersonal realm, and dreams offered a royal road to the collective unconscious.

As Jones (1970) summarized Jung's position, it is distinguished by three specific interpretive procedures: 1) The interpretive method should be exegetical rather than associational. 2) The dreamer should be asked "what for" rather than "why," so that the excessive or inadequate conscious experience represented by the dream can be corrected. 3) The dream should be regarded as a real experience rather than a merely symbolic one.

Underlying this method was, first of all, Jung's assumption that the dream's manifest contents must be taken seriously, that they can give an accurate picture of the dreamer's psychological state. The exegetical method requires that before we attempt to understand and interpret, we first "establish the context with minute care" (Jung, 1974, p. 96). This requires shedding a spotlight on the complexes, or the interconnected associations grouped around particular images. Jung emphasized that this is very different from Freud's method of free association to randomly picked dream images.

Jung also emphasized the dreams should not be viewed as a mere façade concealing the true meaning. The dream, like the façade on most houses, follows the building's plan very carefully and provides major clues to the interior arrangement. For Jung the manifest dream *is* the dream. It contains the whole meaning. The dream seems obscure because we lack understanding. Jung prefers that we treat the dream as an anthropologist or linguist treats a text in an unknown language, not by trying to get behind it to its "real" meaning, but rather by simply learning to read it.

Rather than serving as a protector of sleep, the dream's function is compensatory. Thus, Jung states that in beginning to interpret a dream it is always helpful to ask: What conscious attitude does it compensate? Jung defines compensation as "balancing and comparing different data or points of view so as to produce an adjustment or a rectification" (1974, pp. 73–74). In discussing how compensation takes place in dreams, Jung considers three possibilities. When the conscious attitude toward a life situation is primarily one-sided, the dream will take the opposite side. If the conscious position is more nearly a median one, the dream will simply present some mild variations. If the conscious attitude is adequate, the dream will reinforce this tendency, identifying with it and emphasizing it.

Using the patient's dreams as a guide, the therapist seeks for a balancing of conscious and unconscious factors in the patient's life, thus leading to mental health. Jung cited the dream of Nebuchadnezzar in Daniel 4:10–16 as an early example of a dream interpreted as compensatory. Daniel interprets the dream so that the tree, which becomes personified, is the dreaming king himself. Daniel interprets the dream in this manner so that "its meaning is obviously an attempt to compensate the king's megalomania which, according to the story developed into a real psychosis" (Jung, 1974, p. 37). According to Jung, psychosis is possible when there is a lack of harmony between the conscious and the unconscious.

Adler's therapeutic use of dreams was consistent with his emphasis on the person's LIFE STYLE. Adler regarded dream symbols as protective devices for the threatening problems of life, and the dream was "rehearsal for life" and a compensation for inferiority feelings. Three ideas stand out in Adler's theory: "(1) Dreams express the unity of personality, i.e., the dreamer's 'lifestyle.' (2) Dreams are forward looking and problem solving experiences. (3) Dreams produce emotions which can carry over into waking life with possible adaptive consequences" (Jones, 1970, p. 79).

Other Contributions. Wilhelm Stekel, an early disciple of Freud, regarded dreams as a struggle between good and evil. In the dream the dreamer searches for a compromise between the katagogic ego (leading to life on the lower levels) and the anagogic ego (leading to the idealistic, loftier peaks of life). Stekel regarded the dream as a signpost to the life conflict.

Herbert Silberer, another early Freudian disciple, contributed through his dream research to the classification of dream symbols, thus aiding in their interpretation. The regressive symbols of most dreams could be classified into three categories: material, functional, and somatic. Material symbols refer to what the person was thinking. Thus, for example, objects of thought are transformed into symbols. Functional symbols refer to how the person was thinking. Here experiences such as joy, restraint, or defiance are represented in symbols. Finally, somatic symbols reflect the bodily states and sensations. Silberer concluded that "the stimulus of the dreams is always an emotional factor of high valence" (Jones, 1970, p. 83). In his method he attempted to steer a middle course between placing emphasis on manifest and latent dream contents and between relying on associative materials and direct interpretations.

Calvin Hall, often regarded as the empiricist of dream psychology, devoted himself to the collection, classification, scoring, and interpretation of thousands of dream accounts. Preferring the dream series to a single dream, Hall used the spotlight method of dream interpretation wherein a single conflict isolated from one dream is used to scrutinize other dreams in the series for projections of the same basic conflict. While accepting Freud's assumption that dreams serve as the fulfillment of a wish, he rejected the notion of disguise.

Related to the spotlight method of Hall is the focal conflict theory of Thomas French, who assumes that the dreamer is attempting to solve interpersonal problems. In the dream analogous problems are posed in such a way that they are amenable to the nonverbal thinking that takes place during sleep. Usually one of the problems making up the manifest dream involves a problem which is a reaction to a recent emotional dilemma of the dreamer. Congruent earlier problems converge around this, as do similar contemporary problems. French refers to this as the focal problem. Preferring to work with dream series, French uses the methods of direct symbol translation, functional analysis, and literal interpretation to attempt to identify the focal conflict and help the patient respond to it more directly.

Leaving the psychoanalytic tradition, there are a number of other approaches to dream interpretation. Medard Boss, expanding on the existential framework of Ludwig Binswanger, is concerned with experiencing dreams to the exclusion of either study or interpretation. A similar position is taken by the Gestalt therapists: "In gestalt therapy we don't worry about understanding, we concentrate on experience. The experience becomes discovery, which is deeper and more complete than understanding because it is not limited to the level of intellectualization" (Downing & Marmorstein, 1973, p. 11). Also critical to this approach is the assumption that every part of the dream is the dreamer.

Summary. Regardless of the theoretical perspective adopted, dreams can serve a variety of therapeutic purposes. Hersh and Taub-Bynum (note 1, 1982) suggest eight uses of dreams in short-term therapy: 1) they aid in setting a focus for treatment and planning its course; 2) they aid in assessing the quality of object relations or interpersonal relationships; 3) they aid in facilitating the expression of repressed affect; 4) they aid in assessing the nature of transference; 5) they provide a here-and-now focus emphasizing the affective component; 6) they assist the patient in the search for meaning; 7) they may actually serve as a form of resistance when dream reporting is substituted for the confrontation of primary affect; and 8) they may be used to translate insight into behavioral strategies. Hall (1977, pp. 183–212) lists a number of clinical uses of dreams similar to those cited above. He also lists four areas in which dreams may serve as indicators without being used interpretively. The dream may indicate past conflicts that are incorporated into complexes and other current functioning and relationships. It may also point to unrecognized current causes of conflict. It may help focus transference and countertransference problems in psychotherapy. And it may point to troublesome family and social configurations.

Several Christian writers have made dreams the focus of integrative efforts. Meseguer (1960), a Jesuit priest, summarizes the history of dream interpretation and incorporates recent principles into the spiritual direction process. Kelsey (1968), an Episcopal priest, asserts that "the sheer givenness of the religiously significant dream removes the current doubt that something other than physical reality can invade consciousness di-

rectly" (p. 15). Similarly, Sanford (1968) applies a Jungian understanding within a Christian framework.

References

Downing, J., & Marmorstein, R. (Eds.). *Dreams and nightmares.* New York: Harper & Row, 1973.

Freud, S. *The interpretation of dreams.* New York: Macmillan, 1913. (Originally published, 1900.)

Hall, J. A. *Clinical uses of dreams.* New York: Grune & Stratton, 1977.

Jones, R. M. *The new psychology of dreaming.* New York: Grune & Stratton, 1970.

Jung, C. G. *Dreams.* Princeton, N.J.: Princeton University Press, 1974.

Kelsey, M. T. *Dreams: The dark speech of the spirit.* Garden City, N.Y.: Doubleday, 1968.

Meseguer, P. *The secret of dreams.* Westminster, Md.: Newman Press, 1960.

Prince, M. The mechanism and interpretation of dreams. *Journal of Abnormal Psychology,* 1910, *5,* 139–195.

Sanford, J. A. *Dreams: God's forgotten language.* Philadelphia: Lippincott, 1968.

Vande Kemp, H. The dream in periodical literature: 1860–1910. *Journal of the History of the Behavioral Sciences,* 1981, *17,* 88–113.

Note

1. Hersh, J. B., & Taub-Bynum, E. B. *Use of dreams in brief therapy.* Paper presented at the annual meeting of the American Psychological Association, Washington, D.C., August, 1982.

H. Vande Kemp

See Sleep and Dreaming.

Drive. An aroused state resulting from a biological need. The concept of drive is a major one in the field of motivation. When an animal or a person is deprived of essentials, such as food, water, or air, it is said to be in a state of physiological need. This need state leads to the state of arousal known as the drive state. The energized drive state then pushes the organism to do something to reduce the need. After the need is satisfied, the drive subsides.

Although Freud used the German word *Trieb* similarly in 1915, Woodworth first used the word *drive* to describe this hypothetical force or energy in 1918. Within a few years nearly all psychologists believed in some form of the drive concept. The logic of drive theory was advanced by Cannon's concept of homeostasis introduced in 1932. According to Cannon, whenever the internal physiological conditions deviate from their normal state, a state of disequilibrium is set up and the body attempts to return to an equilibrium.

Drive theory reached its fullest development in Hull's learning theory in 1943. Hull said there were many sources of drive, but they all contributed to the total pool of arousal. The resulting drive energized behavior but did not direct it. Instead, the direction came from the habits operating in the given situation. The drive simply multiplied the habits present at the time. When the drive was reduced following response to a stimulus, the connection between that stimulus and response was strengthened.

In 1948 Miller showed that fear could become a learned drive. Rats learned to press a lever or turn a wheel when the only drive present was the fear of the box in which the rats had been shocked. Simply escaping from the box led to learning to make the pressing or turning response. Psychologists then began proposing all kinds of learned secondary drives, such as a drive for money and a drive for achievement. The concept of homeostasis was essentially broadened to include psychological as well as physiological imbalances.

During the 1950s psychologists began to question the drive theory as a means of explaining all kinds of behavior. They realized that organisms were not pushed into activity just by internal drives. External stimuli, called incentives, also play an important part in determining behavior. People may not even be hungry until they smell the food cooking. They may eat more dessert if it tastes good, even though they are full from dinner. People and animals are not only pushed (drives) but pulled (incentives) as well.

The mechanistic philosophy underlying the original drive concept is now outmoded. Most psychologists do not hold the idea that people or even animals are inert and have to be driven into activity. They see movement as intrinsic to life. However, the word *drive* continues to be used. Drive theory does help explain some behavior, but it is not adequate as a complete theory of MOTIVATION as many psychologists tried to make it in the 1940s.

R. L. KOTESKEY

Drug Addiction. *See* SUBSTANCE-USE DISORDERS.

Drugs, Therapeutic Use of. *See* PSYCHOPHARMACOLOGY.

DSM-III. The standard abbreviation for the *Diagnostic and Statistical Manual of Mental Disorders, Third Edition* (1980). Prepared and published by the American Psychiatric Association, *DSM-III* is the standard classification system used in North America.

See CLASSIFICATION OF MENTAL DISORDERS.

Dynamic Psychology. This branch of psychology encompasses the various psychologies

of motivation as they emphasize the role of the will, affects, and the unconscious rather than the psychophysiological components. Dynamic psychology emerged independently in several different countries, at different periods, and includes such schools as psychoanalysis and purposive psychology as well as the dynamic psychologies proper. Its principal source lies in the work of Freud as well as that of Mesmer, Charcot, Bernheim, and Janet. Another source lies in the act psychologies of Leibnitz, Herbart, Brentano, and others, with the notion of active ideas or motives being basic to the conflict and psychological mechanisms of motivation. A third source lies in the motivational doctrine of hedonism, which can be traced from Hobbes through Locke and Hartley to Bentham and the Mills, culminating in Thorndike's law of effect and Freud's pleasure principle.

Four elements are basic to all dynamic psychologies (Roback, 1952, p. 248): 1) the analysis of motives rather than causes, thus shifting the emphasis from "how" to "why;" 2) a shift of interest from cognition to affect; 3) an interest in drives, instincts, and complexes; 4) a rejection of the introspective method in favor of clinical material as a base for inference. Most dynamic psychologists also share the assumption that one drive can be changed into another without the conscious effort of the individual, as epitomized in Freud's mechanisms of sublimation and conversion. Freud adopted the concept of the unconscious and constructed a personality theory based on unconscious psychic tensions that were often sexual in nature. The unconscious was conceived as active, striving, and powerful, and repression was viewed as evidence of the deep-seated conflict between the ego and unconscious desires. While Freud was primarily an affectional dynamist, Prince was an ideational dynamist, retaining the role of cognition in the psyche. Giving a dynamic turn to abnormal psychology, Prince illuminated the process of dissociation and the phenomenon of multiple personality, studied hallucinations and visions, and elaborated a doctrine of purpose and meaning. A motivational emphasis was retained in the neo-Freudian psychologies.

While Freud was probably the greatest dynamist, McDougall rates a close second. As early as 1923 he pleaded for a "purposive behaviorism," of which his hormic psychology was a prime example. McDougall asserted that there was "an end or purpose which goads us on to action without any real knowledge of its nature, although a dim or vague foresight or prescience may be there" (Roback, 1952, p. 259). He called his dynamisms instincts, urges, and finally propensities. Instincts, being goal directed, consisted of the liberation of energy guiding the organism toward a goal. Adopting McDougall's concept of purposive behaviorism, Tolman's learning theory included many purposive terms (demands, goal objects, and means-end readiness) and assumed that purpose could be observed. Holt's cognitive psychology was also purposive. Holt termed the dynamic principle a wish, and spoke of both negative and positive purposes, though these were conceived in causal rather than teleological terms.

The dynamic psychologies proper include those of Woodworth, Lewin and Murray. Woodworth began using the phrase *dynamic psychology* around 1910 and probably coined the term. His dynamism consisted in his belief that the organism was an important intervening variable between the stimulus and response, and that the organism's activity might be seen in its conscious processes as well as in its behavior. Lewin regarded the person as a locomotor organism whose desires could be represented as valences and vectors which push the person toward or away from objects. He used the concept of tension to describe motivations and needs. Murray articulated his dynamic theory in terms of needs, presses, themas, and regnancies, and formulated a list of needs very similar to McDougall's list of instincts.

Also in the dynamic camp is Allport, who defined personality as the dynamic organization within the individual of those psychophysical systems that determine his unique adjustments to the environment.

Of special interest to the Christian psychologist is the dynamic psychology of Moore (1948), the Benedictine monk who became a leader in the psychology department at the Catholic University in Washington, D.C. Moore blended dynamic psychology, functional psychology, the techniques of factor analysis, and the traditional Thomistic psychology. Dynamic psychology also inspired the integrationist efforts of Hiltner (1972), who states that theological doctrines themselves always exist in a dynamic relationship, containing tensions and equilibriums and the temptation to distortion" (p. 201). Dynamic psychology stands in contrast to descriptive psychology and psychiatry, which focuses on a classification of behaviors without regard for motives or other underlying dynamics.

References
Hiltner, S. *Theological dynamics*. Nashville: Abingdon, 1972.
Moore, T. V. *The driving forces of human nature and their adjustment*. New York: Grune & Stratton, 1948.
Roback, A. A. *History of American psychology*. New York: Library Publishers, 1952.

H. Vande Kemp

See Psychology, History of.

Dyslexia. An impairment of reading ability most commonly associated with parietal lobe lesions or minimal brain dysfunction.

See Reading Disabilities.

Dyspareunia. A medical term for painful sexual intercourse. It is usually used in reference to women (as it is here) rather than men.

The pain experienced during penile-vaginal intercourse may have physical or emotional bases. If the dyspareunia is physically based, it is often brought about by a semiperforated hymen, ulceration of the fourchette, urethritis, vaginitis, and other inflammatory conditions in the pelvis (Taber, 1940).

If, after physical examination by a physician, no organic basis for the presence of dyspareunia is found, the condition is generally assumed to be emotionally based. It is frequently referred to as functional dyspareunia, referring to disorders that are without known organic basis.

Pain at the beginning of intercourse generally indicates an absence of vaginal lubrication. Normally lubrication and swelling of the vaginal canal begins less than one minute after the beginning of sexual stimulation. The lack of lubrication is generally due to a lack of sexual desire on the part of the wife, fear of becoming pregnant even though sexual desire is present, or other emotionally based resistances to experiencing sexual excitement (Hinsie & Campbell, 1970).

Functional dyspareunia may be symptomatically overcome by using various lubrication jellies. Establishing the capacity for natural vaginal lubrication and swelling, which will eliminate painful intercourse, is very difficult, since the requisite vasocongestion is governed by the parasympathetic portion of the autonomic nervous system, which is beyond conscious, decisional control. (*See* Inhibited Sexual Excitement.)

As with other aspects of human sexual response, the presence of painful intercourse (functional dyspareunia) may vary in frequency, duration, and degree. Generally there is no overt marital discord to account for the lack of vaginal lubrication. The absence of vaginal lubrication and swelling associated with functional dyspareunia is sometimes labeled general sexual dysfunction.

No definitive figures are available for the incidence rate of dyspareunia. Some approximation is contained in a study by Biggerstaff, David, and Lloyd (1982). Upon taking a sexual history of 100 consecutive women presenting themselves for routine gynecologic examination, they found that 17% had no organic basis for their reported dyspareunia while 7% had gynecologic pathology upon examination.

Overcoming functional dyspareunia may be accomplished by spending more time in sexual play prior to insertion of the penis. Coaching the couple would involve advice to enjoy present or "now" feelings rather than focusing on intercourse itself. Penetration should not be attempted until it is ascertained that adequate lubrication is present. No direct conscious effort by the wife should be made to lubricate; instead, allowing sexual excitement to occur will spontaneously bring about the desired lubrication.

It is suggested that wives experiencing difficulty with lubrication and accompanying painful intercourse use the female superior position and insert the husband's penis into the vagina only when sufficiently aroused and adequately lubricated. Using the weight of her body to slowly introduce the penis into her vagina gives the wife greater control and reduces fear of pain or discomfort (Hartman & Fithian, 1974).

Wives should be counseled to not accept dyspareunia as an untreatable condition. Whether organically or emotionally based, it is subject to resolution. As in the treatment of most all sexual dysfunctions, the crucial process involves relaxed touching without pressure or demand for sexual performance or intercourse. It is a paradoxical situation—like the Christian sayings, "It is in giving that we receive," and "It is in dying that we are born to eternal life." We will become sexually aroused if we do not consciously strive for it to happen.

References

Biggerstaff, E. D., David, J. R., & Lloyd, A. J. Female sexual dysfunction incidence rate in a military medical center. *Medical Bulletin*, 1982, *39*(6), 17–21.

Hartman, W. E., & Fithian, M. A. *Treatment of sexual dysfunction.* New York: Aronson, 1974.

Hinsie, L. E., & Campbell, R. J. *Psychiatric dictionary (4th ed.).* New York: Oxford University Press, 1970.

Taber, C. W. *Taber's cyclopedic medical dictionary.* Philadelphia: Davis, 1940.

J. R. DAVID

See SEX THERAPY.

Dysthymic Disorder. The essential feature of this disorder is a chronic disturbance of mood involving depression and loss of interest and pleasure. Under older terminology the disorder was called neurasthenia or depressive neurosis. It is differentiated from the more serious depressive disorder, major depressive episode, on the basis of severity and symptom duration.

See DEPRESSION.

Ee

Eating Disorders. This subclass of disorders is characterized by abnormal eating behavior. Included are ANOREXIA NERVOSA, BULIMIA, and PICA. OBESITY is not formally classified as an eating disorder since it is not generally associated with any distinct psychological or behavioral syndrome. It is not, therefore, included in *DSM-III*.

Ebbinghaus, Hermann (1850–1909). Pioneer in the study of memory. Born in Barmen, Germany, Ebbinghaus studied history and philosophy at Bonn, Berlin, and Halle between 1867 and 1870. He received his doctorate in philosophy in 1873 from Bonn after serving in the army during the Franco-Prussian War. For the next seven years he lived as a private scholar, visiting England and France, where he ran across Fechner's work.

In 1880 Ebbinghaus began teaching at the University of Berlin. He became professor in 1886 and remained at Berlin until 1894, when he accepted the chair of philosophy at Breslau. In 1905 he went to Halle, where he remained until his death. He founded or expanded laboratories at all three universities.

The best known of Ebbinghaus's accomplishments is his experimentation on memory. He invented the nonsense syllable in an attempt to get verbal material without previous associations. With the combinations of three letters (consonant, vowel, consonant) he developed 2,300 meaningless syllables which he could use in memory studies. He served as his own subject in his experiments and memorized hundreds of lists. His results have been verified by other research and are still cited in general psychology texts today.

Although Wundt had stated that it was not possible to experiment on the higher mental processes, Ebbinghaus opened up this new field. He applied Fechner's methods of psychophysics to memory rather than just to sensation. He also devised a sentence completion test as a method of mental measurement.

Ebbinghaus was a careful researcher, but his desire to check, recheck, and revise his work resulted in fewer publications (and fewer promotions) for him than for many of his colleagues. His classic book *On Memory* (1885), is still frequently cited a century after its publication. He also published a successful general textbook, *The Principles of Psychology* (1902), and a more popular text, *A Summary of Psychology* (1908). In 1890 he was cofounder of the *Journal of Psychology and Physiology of the Sense Organs*, a journal publishing experiments different from those done by the structuralists at Leipzig.

Ebbinghaus made no theoretical contributions, did not create a formal system, had no important disciples, and did not found a school, but his research findings have stood the test of time. He brought objectivity, quantification, and experimentation to the study of learning and memory. The nonsense syllable has been widely used in the study of memory; however, psychologists have found that such materials do have associations, so they are used less today.

R. L. KOTESKEY

Echolalia. A pathological reaction characterized by the mechanical imitation of the speech of another. The repetitive echoing of words or phrases tends to be persistent, and the tone is mumbling, mocking, or stilted. In some cases there is guarded hostility, perhaps as a regressive childhood behavior. Echolalia is not to be confused with habitual repetition of questions.

In echolalia a person may reply to the statement, "It's a rainy day outside," with the words, "Rainy day outside, rainy day outside." The reaction is noted in organic mental disorders, catatonic schizophrenia, Pick's disease, Alzheimer's disease, and some pervasive mental disorders.

Echopraxia. A pathological reaction and a common symptom in catatonic schizophrenia, in which a person acts as a mirror image of another by imitating movements. The term is reserved for those with brain disease or functional psychosis. The imitation of actions of another is known as echokinesis, and the imitation of the gestures of another is echomimia.

Eclecticism in Psychotherapy. Professional psychotherapy had its beginning with the work of Freud at the turn of the twentieth century. A number of eager disciples were attracted to the founder of psychoanalysis, but Freud was unable to hold the loyalty of most of these equally ambitious men. Surprisingly soon, individuals such as Adler, Jung, Rank, and Reich proceeded to launch their own schools of psychotherapy. Since the founding of Freudian psychoanalysis and the various neo-Freudian spin-offs there has been a proliferation of theoretical approaches to psychotherapy. Each new system of therapy has faulted, to some degree, all of its predecessors and claimed a status superior to them on one ground or another. Although adherence to a particular school of psychotherapy often appears to be more prestigious, many psychotherapists have shown a consistent disenchantment with exclusive systems of psychotherapy and a preference for an eclectic orientation that integrates the essential features of the various theories about human behavior into a more comprehensive theory.

The word *eclectic* has its origin in the Greek verbal root *eklego*, a composite of *ek* (from or out of) and *lego* (to pick, choose, or select). Eclectic literally means then to pick out or to select from. A typical definition of eclecticism emphasizes the practice of choosing what appears to be best from the doctrines, works, or styles of others. English and English (1958) define it as "the selection and orderly combination of compatible features from diverse sources, sometimes from otherwise incompatible theories and systems; the effort to find valid elements in all . . . theories and to combine them into a harmonious whole. The resulting system is open to constant revision even in its major outlines" (p. 168).

Brief History. Theoretical eclecticism is not a new phenomenon either in psychology or the practice of psychotherapy. James (1907) sought to bring together the thoughts of tender-minded rationalists and tough-minded empiricists via the pragmatic method. He considered pragmatism as being a mediator and reconciler that eschewed fixed principles, rigid dogma, pretense of finality in truth, and closed systems. He viewed it as marked by openness and a flexible empiricist attitude that invites the application of any and all principles, concepts, and methods that can be assimilated, validated, corroborated, and verified in reality.

Woodworth (1931) referred to himself as a "middle-of-the-roader" who saw some good in every school of psychology and believed that none of them was ideal. He maintained that each school or system makes its special contribution to the whole of psychological knowledge but no single one possesses the final answer. For a half-century Woodworth encouraged rapprochement of overtly competitive factions.

Allport (1964, 1968) was a self-described "polemic-eclectic" who was theoretically open, yet prepared to challenge any psychological idol. His concept of a theoretical system was "one that allows for truth wherever found, one that encompasses the totality of human experience and does full justice to the nature of man" (1968, p. 406).

Numerous eclectic approaches to psychotherapy have been developed in the last half century. The psychobiology of Meyer (1948) is generally accepted as the first serious attempt at an eclectic psychotherapy. Meyer wanted an integration of the psychological, sociological, and biological dimensions of human behavior. He insisted on a comprehensiveness that included the life history of the individual, a thorough diagnosis of the clinical situation, and the application of a variety of techniques that fitted the person and the problem presented.

Dollard and Miller (1950) endeavored to integrate the psychoanalytic concepts of Freud, learning theory, and cultural influences. Their aim was "to combine the vitality of psychoanalysis, the vigor of the natural science laboratory, and the facts of culture" (p. 3).

Wolberg (1954) made an initial effort to extract methods from the field of psychoanalysis, psychobiology, psychiatric interviewing, casework, and therapeutic counseling and to blend these into an eclectic system of methodology. He has broadened the scope of the inclusions in two subsequent editions of *The Technique of Psychotherapy*.

For better than 30 years the late Fredrick

Thorne was the prince of the eclectics. He wrote prolifically on eclecticism, and each of his several major works is encyclopedic in content. A quote from his *Psychological Case Handling* well illustrates his position: "to collect and integrate all known methods of personality counseling and psychotherapy into an eclectic system which might form the basis of standardized practice; . . . to be rigidly scientific . . . [with] no priority given to any theoretical viewpoint or school . . . [but] to analyze the contributions of all existing schools and fit them together into an integrated system . . . [that] combines the best features of all methods" (Thorne, 1968, Vol. 1, p. vi).

The *Therapeutic Psychology* of Brammer and Shostrom, published in 1960 and now available in the third edition, is a landmark in the evolution of eclectic psychotherapy. They use the term *emerging eclecticism* to define their efforts to develop a comprehensive and dynamic perspective on personality structure and change as a basis for clinical practice. They assimilate extractions from psychoanalytic, humanistic, existential-phenomenological, and behavioral approaches to form a multidimensional system of therapy.

Another substantial work on eclectic theory, *Beyond Counseling and Psychotherapy* by Carkhuff and Berenson, appeared in 1967. These authors sought to build around a central core of facilitative conditions an armamentarium of clinical methods judged to be compatible with the facilitative core. The methods were derived from client-centered, existential, behavioral, trait-factor, and psychoanalytic orientations.

The work of Lazarus (1976, 1981) represents some of the latest, and perhaps best, efforts to craft an eclectic psychotherapy. His multimodal therapy approach espouses a technical rather than a theoretical emphasis. Starting with social learning theory and behavioral principles Lazarus develops a broad-spectrum system that deals with the clients' "salient behaviors, affective processes, each of his/her five senses, basic images, cognitions, and intrapersonal relationships" (1976, p. 4).

Several other psychotherapists have presented excellent eclectic themes, though these have been less substantial in nature than those cited above. A sample of these titles and their authors include *Psychological Counseling* (Bordin, 1968), *Psychobehavioral Counseling and Therapy* (Woody, 1971), *A Primer of Eclectic Psychotherapy* (Palmer, 1980), and *Psychotherapy: An Eclectic Approach* (Garfield, 1980).

Criticism. A mixed audience exists regarding eclecticism in psychotherapy. Some of the attitudes toward the eclectic approach from both the pro and con perspective are given below.

Positive views. 1) Since there is no single "best" kind of psychotherapy, an eclectic alternative is essential if maximum assistance is to be offered to each and every client (Wolberg, 1954).

2) As desirable and necessary as particular systems might be, the only way to comprehend the nature of human beings and their situation in life is by a reasoned and systematic eclecticism marked by a conceptual and theoretical openness. A comprehensive metatheory is preferred to a plurality of dogmatized and separatistic particularisms (Allport, 1964).

3) Individuals, as free beings, cannot be confined to monolithic systems. In order to enable clients to live effectively, the therapist must select from many systems those elements that promise to be most useful in given situations. Empirical data suggest that the most effective approach is an open-ended, systematic, eclectic model fashioned around a central core of caring relationship conditions and complemented with a variety of techniques derived from several theoretical orientations (Carkhuff & Berenson, 1967).

4) A psychotherapist can hardly afford to ignore any technique proven to be effective, regardless of its theoretical origin. The therapist who maintains a strict adherence to a particular school of thought arbitrarily excludes from his or her repertoire many effective procedures. Technical eclecticism has decided potential to enrich the practitioner's therapeutic effectiveness without jeopardizing his or her position (Lazarus, 1967).

5) Eclecticism is the prerequisite for complete or total psychotherapy that serves best the needs of clients at various stages or phases in the therapy process. Therapy must match the personality needs of the particular client, and sectarianism unavoidably limits therapeutic efficacy (Slavson, 1970).

Negative views. 1) Eclecticism is a namby-pamby process in which directionless eclectics are comparable to jackdaws who aimlessly carry anything and everything to their nests (Goethe, as cited by Allport, 1964).

2) Essentially eclecticism is a bag-of-tricks and trial-and-error approach that has no adequate information regarding the criteria to govern what techniques to use when and with what clients. It has no general principles of counseling and lacks a logical rationale; it is simply a random collection of techniques held together in a manipulative manner (Patterson, 1959).

3) Eclecticism makes it easy for lazy or inept

individuals to choose bits and pieces indiscriminately from a wide spectrum of counseling theories and methods and to concoct a hodgepodge of contradictory assumptions and incompatible techniques (Brammer, 1969).

Current Status. Surveys of counseling and clinical psychologists indicate that the majority of therapists identify with some form of eclecticism (Garfield & Kurtz, 1976; Smith, 1982). At the same time there seems to be a growing dissatisfaction with the traditional label, since *eclecticism* suggests laziness, undisciplined subjectivity, mediocrity, and poor systemization (Smith, 1982). The current trend in labeling such approaches appears to be in the direction of such terms as masterful integration (Smith, 1975), creative synthesis (Shostrom, 1976), general systems theory (Ivey & Simek-Downing, 1980), and systematic multimodal therapy (Lazarus, 1981).

References

Allport, G. W. The fruits of eclecticism: Bitter or sweet? *Acta Psychologica*, 1964, *23*, 27–44.

Allport, G. W. *The person in psychology*. Boston: Beacon Press, 1968.

Bordin, E. S. *Psychological counseling* (2nd ed.). New York: Appleton-Century-Crofts, 1968.

Brammer, L. M. Eclecticism revisited. *Personnel and Guidance Journal*, 1969, *48*, 192–197.

Brammer, L. M., & Shostrom, E. L. *Therapeutic psychology*. Englewood Cliffs, N.J.: Prentice-Hall, 1960.

Carkhuff, R. R., & Berenson, B. G. *Beyond counseling and psychotherapy*. New York: Holt, Rinehart & Winston, 1967.

Dollard, J., & Miller, N. E. *Personality and psychotherapy*. New York: McGraw-Hill, 1950.

English, H. B., & English, A. C. *A comprehensive dictionary of psychological and psychoanalytic terms*. New York: Longmans, Green, 1958.

Garfield, S. L. *Psychotherapy: An eclectic approach*. New York: Wiley, 1980.

Garfield, S. L., & Kurtz, R. Clinical psychologists in the 1970s. *American Psychologist*, 1976, *31*, 1–9.

Ivey, A. E., & Simek-Downing, L. *Counseling and psychotherapy*. Englewood Cliffs, N.J.: Prentice-Hall, 1980.

James, W. *Pragmatism*. Cambridge: Harvard University Press, 1975. (Originally published, 1907.)

Lazarus, A. A. In support of technical eclecticism. *Psychological Reports*, 1967, *21*, 415–416.

Lazarus, A. A. *Multimodal behavior therapy*. New York: Springer Publishing, 1976.

Lazarus, A. A. *The practice of multimodal therapy*. New York: McGraw-Hill, 1981.

Meyer, A. *The common sense psychiatry of Dr. Adolf Meyer*. New York: McGraw-Hill, 1948.

Palmer, J. O. *A primer of eclectic psychology*. Monterey, Calif.: Brooks/Cole, 1980.

Patterson, C. H. *Counseling and psychotherapy*. New York: Harper & Row, 1959.

Shostrom, E. L. *Actualizing therapy*. San Diego, Calif.: EDITS Publishers, 1976.

Slavson, S. R. Eclecticism versus sectarianism in group psychotherapy. *International Journal of Group Psychotherapy*, 1970, *20*, 3–13.

Smith, D. *Integrative counseling and psychotherapy*. Boston: Houghton Mifflin, 1975.

Smith, D. Trends in counseling and psychotherapy. *American Psychologist*, 1982, *37*, 802–809.

Thorne, F. C. *Psychological case handling* (2 vols.). Brandon, Vt.: Clinical Psychology Publishing, 1968.

Wolberg, L. R. *The technique of psychotherapy*. New York: Grune & Stratton, 1954.

Woodworth, R. S. *Contemporary schools of psychology*. New York: Ronald Press, 1931.

Woody, R. H. *Psychobehavioral counseling and therapy*. New York: Appleton-Century-Crofts, 1971.

D. SMITH

See COUNSELING AND PSYCHOTHERAPY: OVERVIEW.

Ecstatic Religious Experiences. Ecstatic experiences play important roles in many Christian and non-Christian traditions. Other committed believers and religious subcultures find no need for such expressions.

Scope. Religious ecstasies (notably speaking in tongues, or glossolalia) are recorded in the New Testament, and some are reported throughout church history. The most consistent expressions, however, have been within the Pentecostal movement, beginning in the first decade of the twentieth century, with influences from southern black Christian traditions. Starting about 1960 ecstatic experiences, especially glossolalia, have found expression in Catholic and mainstream Protestant churches.

Perhaps the prototype of ecstatic religion is the possession trance in African animism, Haitian vodou (voodoo), and numerous other folk religions. Possession trance refers to an alteration of personality, consciousness, or will that is attributed to possession by an alien spirit, which might be the spirit of an animal or another person. In some primitive cultures possession trance is cultivated as an important part of the religious expression. Sometimes possession is seen as an experience to be avoided or terminated, as in Catholic exorcism rites. In some Pentecostal, charismatic, and black churches glossolalia, shouting, dancing, and fainting are interpreted as manifestations of possession by the Holy Spirit—i.e., as possession trance. Others consider them gifts of the Spirit or simply "blessings." Almost invariably, though, such experiences are perceived as supernatural or beyond mere human will—in psychological terms, a trance or an altered or alternative state of consciousness.

Automatic writing, as claimed by some prophets and religious founders, has trancelike if not overtly ecstatic features. Much snake handling, fire handling, and fire walking are similarly trancelike and/or ecstatic. Some faith healing rituals and mystical experiences involve ecstasy and, especially in mysticism, altered states of consciousness, but they have significantly different religious functions and psychological causes or dynamics.

Functions. Considerable speculation and some firm evidence indicate that ecstatic religion functions in part as a compensation or outlet for frustrated or conflicting needs. Possession trance is more likely to occur in societies that have rigid, fixed status distinctions, including slavery. Trance behavior represents a "safety valve" for stresses caused by such social rigidities (Bourguignon, 1976). Pentecostalism has made its greatest inroads in American lower classes and African countries that have anxiety-producing status differences and class conflicts. Glossolalia is often associated with anxiety states and a need to discharge built-up tension, and is related to personality measures that give credence to this function (Smith, 1976).

A related function, beyond mere compensation, is actual personality integration. Do ecstatic experiences actually prove therapeutic to their anxious and frustrated subjects? Ritualized possession trance does not solve any of the social differences that spawn it, but it can give new structure and meaning to individual lives (Bourguignon, 1976). It is hard to separate the ecstatic expressions themselves from the belief and social support system of which they are a part. Most studies of glossolalia suggest that the total religious context, not just the ecstatic experience, is redemptive. Nonetheless, the emotional release and personal interpretations of ecstasies are part of the religious system that provides hope and meaning to many desperate lives.

Probably the most fundamental function of ecstatic religious experiences was suggested by James: "Beliefs are strengthened whenever automatisms corroborate them. Incursions from beyond the transmarginal have a peculiar power to increase conviction" (1902, p. 372). Speaking in tongues or other public display of "irrational" behavior irrevocably sets people apart from secular society, affirming their religious identities and belief systems. In the 1960s the disruption of traditional Roman Catholic practices by Vatican Council II changes and the secular drift of liberal Protestant denominations set the stage for the need to reaffirm spiritual identity and dependency. Visions, automatic writing, and other charismatic gifts have lent credence and impetus to the revelations of major religious leaders for centuries. Sometimes ecstasy functions as testimony to unbelievers of God's power. Appalachian Holiness fire handlers avow that their purpose is to convince sinners of God's power and produce re-

pentance. Miracles in both Testaments frequently served these belief functions.

Dynamics of Ecstasy. To the uninitiated, religious ecstasies often look like psychiatric disorder—hysteria, schizophrenia, or even perhaps epilepsy. Consequently most serious psychological studies of the ecstasies have used personality measures like the Minnesota Multiphasic Personality Inventory (MMPI). The results have been minimal and sometimes inconsistent. Glossolalists (the most widely studied group) and snake handlers have usually shown fewer signs of pathology than nonecstatic religious groups. In general they show somewhat different personality patterns but no greater indication of personality disorder per se. Ecstasy practitioners tend to be less socially conforming and more pleasure oriented—i.e., less inhibited and more expressive. Usually they show signs of lower autonomy and more dependence on other individuals, especially trusted religious leaders. They are more trusting in general. Hysteria—the MMPI scale indicating tendency to express inner conflicts through physical means—consistently has not been related to ecstatic behaviors. As a group glossolalists are apparently less intelligent and lower in educational levels than comparable nonglossolalists (Smith, 1976).

Glossolalists frequently have experienced some personal stress or crisis (financial reversal, family or personal illness, marital discord, e.g.) not long before they first spoke in tongues (Kildahl, 1972; Smith, 1976). A few studies have failed to find this effect. Perhaps it may be that in groups who use glossolalia in a more playful manner, for "ego enhancement," the gift is less likely to be related to stress, anxiety, or other psychiatric factors.

To a substantial extent religious ecstasy is more a matter of learning than of psychiatry. People who grow up in a culture or church where such experiences are routine are, in effect, imprinted to accept and enact such behaviors at an appropriate age and circumstance. Social learning has been explicitly observed for possession trance in Haitian vodou. Children who hear adults talk about the clan's favorite possessing spirits accept the spirits as virtually part of the extended family. Discussion and observation of the rites leading up to trance teach the children how to induce the trances and how to respond when in them (Bourguignon, 1976). Similar observations could surely be made in Pentecostal churches.

More individualized learning is sometimes observed. While glossolalia is not learned in the way one learns a foreign language, coaching has been noted at charismatic meetings—e.g., "Come on now. Speak out. You're still begging. There you are. Keep talking. Come on. Hallelujah. He's praying a new language" (Samarin, 1969). Once an individual has experienced glossolalia, possession trance, or Pentecostal ecstatic expressions, these can be repeated with relative ease in the appropriately sanctioned religious setting.

Glossolalic utterances have frequently been claimed as real foreign tongues that the speaker has not learned. Scientifically verifiable, firsthand reports of such events have not been produced. Nor do glossolalic utterances show linguistic characteristics common to human languages.

Expression of trancelike religious ecstasies resembles hypnosis. Induction has been related to loud, rhythmic, repetitious, and/or stupefying music and other environmental and physical factors—a hot, stuffy room high in carbon dioxide, social isolation, and fasting (Aylland, 1962).

Other unconscious factors undoubtedly play roles in glossolalia. Christian tongues speaking sometimes occurs spontaneously, without explicit social modeling or learning, but probably never without knowledge of such events in the New Testament record. Occurrence of glossolalia also in non-Christian religions and in psychosis suggests that the structure of the central nervous system enables nonrational use of language. The brain appears to have neurological structures that promote development of a natural language, given normal linguistic experience in a family or human community. Similarly various neural inhibitions, disinhibitions, and "switches" controlling them are consistent with current knowledge of the central nervous system. These brain mechanisms are probably involved in the practice of speaking in tongues.

Psychologists increasingly recognize various altered states of consciousness, and they frequently consider trancelike religious ecstasies from this perspective. Fire walking and handling fire in many religious traditions can involve a trance state or altered state of consciousness. Southern Appalachian Holiness fire handlers report an "anointing" that enables them to expose bodily parts to intense flames and heat for up to 15 seconds without pain or burning. The anointing is variously described by practitioners: "Just don't feel much at all. I get numb. Feels like my skin crawls." "A shield comes down over me. I know when it's around me. It's cold inside. My hands get numb and cold" (Kane, 1974, p. 119).

Hypnotic experiments spanning more than half a century demonstrate psychological control of heat pain. With few exceptions, hypnotic suggestion eliminates or minimizes the effects of heat stimuli applied to a limb. Similarly, given the suggestion that the experimenter's finger is a red-hot iron, the finger can produce pain and blisters like those normally produced by heat. When subjects are hypnotized to be insensitive to heat pain, their blood vessels constrict in the affected body parts, and they report numbness and coldness strikingly similar to reports of "anointed" Holiness fire handlers. Given either hypnosis or spiritual motivation, the central nervous system can control the effects of intense heat for as long as 15 seconds.

Every religious experience occurs in the context of an individual who is at once a physical, psychological, and social as well as spiritual being. Ecstatic religious experiences in particular serve a variety of functions, some primarily religious, some more psychological. Each such occurrence is grounded in a human personality with distinctive individual and cultural experiences, with neurological capabilities that are not fully understood. No single dynamic, cause, or factor explains any form of ecstatic religious experience. Even taken together they to not fully account for any individual's ecstatic behavior or feelings. Psychologists slowly and imperfectly seek better to understand and explain these factors and their interacting effects on human behavior. However, no psychological explanation, however complete, can "explain away" or determine the spiritual value of any religious experience.

References

Aylland, A., Jr. "Possession" in a revivalistic Negro church. *Journal for the Scientific Study of Religion*, 1962, *1*, 204–213.

Bourguignon, E. *Possession*. San Francisco: Chandler & Sharp, 1976.

James, W. *The varieties of religious experience*. Garden City, N.Y.: Image Books, 1978. (Originally published, 1902.)

Kane, S. M. Holiness fire handling in Southern Appalachia. In J. D. Photiadis (Ed.), *Religion in Appalachia*. Morgantown: West Virginia University, 1974.

Kildahl, J. P. *The psychology of speaking in tongues*. New York: Harper & Row, 1972.

Samarin, W. J. Glossolalia as learned behavior. *Canadian Journal of Theology*, 1969, *15*, 60–64.

Smith, D. S. Glossolalia: The personality correlates of conventional and unconventional subgroups (Doctoral dissertation, Rosemead Graduate School of Psychology, 1976). (University Microfilms No. 77–21,537)

R. D. KAHOE

ECT. *See* ELECTROCONVULSIVE THERAPY.

Ectomorph. In Sheldon's system of constitutional types the ectomorph is a person with a thin, frail, and angular body. This body type, comparable to Kretschmer's asthenic type, is contrasted to the ENDOMORPH and MESOMORPH types. Sheldon's research suggested that ectomorphs tend to be restrained, inhibited, and self-conscious.

See CONSTITUTIONAL PERSONALITY THEORY.

Educational Psychology. Educational psychology deals with 1) learning and cognition and the conditions that influence them, particularly within educational settings; 2) the psychological development, social relationships, and adjustment found within educational settings. Additionally, the attention of educational psychology has broadened to encompass nontraditional subjects and contexts—i.e., those lying outside the institution and age boundaries most frequently associated with education of the young. Interests in lifelong learning and on learning in work and other nonstandard educational settings are but two examples of these expanding boundaries. Similarly, the study of cognitive outcomes associated with school curricula is now only one concern, albeit the major one, among others. Attitudes, career awareness, and creativity are also prized outcomes. In short, while continuing to focus primarily on school learning and instruction, educational psychology includes many other considerations relevant to teaching and learning.

Considering its full scope, disparities among characterizations of the field do not seem surprising. For some it is a branch of applied psychology, the goal of which is to identify the educationally relevant concepts and findings of psychology and demonstrate their applications, much as engineering uses basic principles of physics to solve practical problems. Others place more emphasis on educational psychology as a discipline in its own right.

The roots of this ambiguity go back to the establishment of educational psychology as a scientifically respectable discipline by Thorndike around 1900–1910. This beginning was actually a manifesto promising that laws of learning would be identified and education would be founded at last upon a secure scientific foundation. Thorndike's positive contributions were his insistence on objective, empirical methods and his stress on the role of environmental influences. These set the field forever apart from armchair philosophizing about learning. However, in retrospect the price of this rigor was methodological narrowness and an impoverished view of the learner and the learning process. This view, which saw learning in terms of forming bonds between

stimuli and responses, was enormously significant in stimulating the behaviorist school of psychology. While many practical applications eventually resulted from this movement—techniques of behavior modification and programmed instruction, to name only two—the major consequence was failure to fulfill the original promise of a "science" of education. It also led to a widening gap between theory and experimentation on the one hand and educational practice on the other. Educational psychologists were placed in the position of trying to bridge this gap; hence the confusion as to what their role should be.

Another significant activity of many educational psychologists is the testing of individual differences, particularly intelligence and special abilities, and identifying their components. The testing movement does not fit the above characterization, since tests have gained their prominence primarily as a response to urgent practical needs—e.g., selection and placement in education, industry, and the military. The thriving test industry demonstrates the popularity of tests for many practical purposes. Nonetheless, testing has not in general been undergirded with a psychological theory of learning and performance, and thus the gap between theory and practice in educational psychology has not been significantly closed by this movement.

Currently the dominant theoretical force in educational psychology is cognitive psychology. This approach is concerned with the neglected hyphen in the stimulus-response formulation—i.e., the active, internal mental processes of thinking, remembering, problem solving, etc., which underlie instruction and learning. Modern computers have provided powerful tools for simulating many complex mental operations and testing the model's correspondence to human subjects' performance. The view of the learner as an active information processor has also spurred a great deal of experimental research resulting in an enriched understanding of reading, mathematical comprehension, the acquisition of subject matter competence, and more.

A closely related phenomenon has been the ascendancy of cognitive developmental psychology under the influence of Piaget, Bruner, and others. The interaction between cognitive developmental stages and instruction has been of paramount interest.

Finally, the field of testing and individual differences is undergoing a great deal of ferment through the impact of these developments. Several trends now challenge the static view of individual differences as permanent fixtures to which instruction must simply accommodate. First, intellectual abilities are being closely analyzed to reveal the actual mental operations which contribute to test performance. Second, achievement tests are being designed as adjuncts to instruction, to facilitate learning rather than merely report the results of previous learning. "Mastery learning," as this approach is called, suggests that many individual differences, regarded as fixed when tests are used to classify students, diminish sharply when tests are used as learning devices. A third trend is the analysis of ways in which learners' attributes do appear to make a difference in the type of instruction that is optimal. The focus here is on students' typical cognitive processes and how they interact with instruction (i.e., a conceptual grasp of what is happening rather than formula prescriptions for different types of students).

Educational psychology can now be identified, with more justification than heretofore, as a distinctive field of inquiry with many potential implications for practice. However, the field still has not developed into the kind of prescriptive science Thorndike envisioned, and few can say confidently that it will do so in the foreseeable future.

Although the Bible does not explicitly set forth principles of educational psychology, when one reads it with educational psychology in mind, numerous points of contact emerge. For instance, Jesus as the teacher par excellence demonstrated in his manner of teaching several important principles. One is that of engaging the active curiosity of listeners by asking probing questions ("Who do you say that I am?" "To what shall I liken the kingdom of God?" etc.). Jesus' model would seem to support the current cognitive emphasis more than a strictly behavioral emphasis. Another principle is illustrated by his patient nurturance of learning, extending over his three-year ministry and coordinated with the readiness of his disciples to receive his teaching. Finally, Jesus dealt with the whole person, not with cognitive understanding alone. In this respect, a strictly cognitive approach may eventually turn out to look as impoverished as the stimulus-response approach now looks from the perspective of cognitive instructional psychology.

D. R. RIDLEY

EEG. See ELECTROENCEPHALOGRAPHY.

Ego. The Latin word meaning "I." The technical usage of the term has been around for quite some time in psychology. As early as 1867

William Griesinger, who published a text in psychiatry, and a French contemporary, Durand, used the term to describe the conscious areas of personality which have to do with self-control and self-observation. They viewed pathology as occurring when there is a vast discrepancy between what a person is in his unconscious and in his conscious ego. About the same time Meynert, a German psychiatrist, also developed a theory of personality based on the psychology of the ego.

It was one of Meynert's students, Sigmund Freud, who would go on to revolutionize psychiatry with his psychoanalytic theory of the ego. Freud avoided using the Latin *ego* in his theory but accepted the term used by his mentors, the German *Das Ich* ("the I"). This is remarkable because it demonstrates his intent to use the term in a way that was consistent with the technical, psychiatric definition of ego at that time, namely, the self-conscious, controlling aspect of personality. As Freud worked with his patients he expanded this concept of the ego and saw it as part of a topographical model of the mind. In this model he viewed the conscious ego as a repressor which overlays unconscious forbidden memories and impulses that might seek to surface into consciousness.

However, by the time Freud wrote his monumental work on the structure of the psyche, *The Ego and the Id*, in 1923, he significantly expanded the role of the ego in mental functioning. Instead of using ego to refer loosely to consciousness, he more clearly defined it as a mental structure comprising those aspects of the psyche which function to regulate the interaction between the demands of external reality and the demands of internal instinctual drives. The ego arises out of the raw instinctual mass of the id. Through the impact of the external world the child learns the prominence of the reality principle: that instinctual gratification and pleasure must at times be postponed or relinquished and that the realities of consequences must be taken into account. Thus, the ego is made up of the aspects of mental life that have become tamed, in that it seeks to achieve gratification of id impulses within the limits of reality. It employs secondary process, or rational thinking, in the pursuit of gratification in place of the id's primary process, which is more immediate and irrational. In *The Problem of Anxiety* (1926) Freud went on to give the ego even more prominence by stating that it was capable on its own of mounting a defense against id impulses when these were too threatening.

Nevertheless, it was left up to other psychoanalytic theorists to study the role of the ego in its own right, apart from the id, as a conflict-free aspect of personality beyond Freud's more restricted, conflict-oriented understanding of the ego. Actually, the history of psychoanalysis since Freud's death has been dominated by the study of the ego to the point that contemporary psychoanalysis is often called EGO PSYCHOLOGY. This has contributed greatly to an understanding of ego defenses (repression, denial, rationalization, etc.), ego functions (perception, reality testing, relationships), how the ego develops from birth through relationship, and how to treat patients with severe ego defects in their ability to test reality, relate to others, or moderate self-esteem.

W. L. EDKINS

See PSYCHOANALYTIC PSYCHOLOGY.

References

Freud, S. [The ego and the id.] In J. Strachey (Ed. and trans.), *The standard edition of the complete psychological works of Sigmund Freud* (Vol. 19). London: Hogarth, 1975. (Originally published, 1923.)

Freud, S. [The problem of anxiety.] In J. Strachey (Ed. and trans.), *The standard edition of the complete psychological works of Sigmund Freud* (Vol. 20). London: Hogarth, 1959. (Originally published, 1926.)

Ego Dystonic. An urge, symptom, or personality trait which is rejected by the ego as unacceptable is known as ego dystonic. These may include obsessions or compulsions that are viewed as undesirable and are prevented from reaching the ego for behavioral consideration. Some common examples of ego dystonic impulses include homosexual urges, oedipal and incestual arousal, and criminal tendencies associated with intense anger or provocation. The term ego alien is often used synonymously with ego dystonic, and both terms describe the opposite of EGO SYNTONIC.

Ego Psychology. Ego psychology refers to the development of psychoanalytic theory in terms of the impact of early relationships on the adaptive aspects of personality. As Freud began his career in psychiatry and neurology, he observed the crucial role sexual instinct, or libido, played in the etiology of his patients' symptomatology as well as in normal infancy (Freud, 1905). At a time when the rest of psychology was mostly concerned with how consciousness functions, Freud devoted the next two decades to understanding and treating the instinctual, unconscious aspects of personality. During these years he sought to bypass the more conscious functioning of his patients by using hypnosis and free association so that he could treat the more hidden unconscious material and conflict areas. At this point Freud viewed the ego as this

more conscious domain of personality which stood in the way of reaching the unconscious. However, as he continued to work with his patients, he noted that the resistance evoked by each patient's ego to the psychoanalytic process of exploring the unconscious was, for the most part, unconcious. However, if the ego is synonymous with consciousness, ego defense mechanisms should also be conscious. Freud also observed the ego's role in symptom formation. He noted that symptoms were really unconscious compromises between a forbidden impulse and the ego. For example, hysterical blindness might express a compromise between the impulse to view parental intercourse and the attempt to control the impulse by the experience of blindness.

From these experiences Freud concluded that the ego, as well as the instinctual aspect of personality, the id, had an unconscious aspect to it and that this also had to be dealt with in the course of psychoanalysis. In 1923 he proposed a model of the psyche which consisted of the id, ego, and another structure, the superego, which develops out of the ego by the child's identifying with the moralistic aspects of the parental figures. This model emphasized the unconscious ego and its role in symptom formation and in treatment. It also placed the ego in a prominent position in psychoanalysis and gave birth to ego psychology.

Freud's daughter, Anna Freud, carried her father's work on ego psychology even further. She was primarily interested in the way people master their conflicts by means of ego defense mechanisms such as rationalization, repression, and denial. She believed that instead of viewing these defenses as being hindrances to treatment, they should be seen as a means of getting to the unconscious by giving a clue to the analyst that there was an unconscious conflict emerging. She found that as the defense itself was analyzed as to its origin and history, the ego would be strengthened and the person would feel strong enough to allow the unconscious material underneath to emerge. Thus, she changed the focus of analytic treatment from the id to the ego.

Heinz Hartmann, an influential and innovative psychoanalytic theorist, made the next major contribution to ego psychology. In his major work, *Ego Psychology and the Problem of Adaptation* (1939), he proposed that the earlier psychoanalytic emphasis on unconscious conflict and the id gave psychoanalysis a slanted picture. It was like trying to understand a country by observing it only during a wartime economy. According to Hartmann, psychoanalysis also needed to observe the more regular and normal ego functions in personality. He thus expanded psychoanalysis to become more of a general psychology concerned with perception, thinking, development of relationships, and human coping processes. Also, he saw the ego as being as basic to human development as the id. Instead of the ego arising later in development out of the id, as Freud had posited, Hartmann saw certain necessary ego functions being present from birth.

Close to the time of publication of Anna Freud's (1936) and Hartmann's (1939) major works, Sigmund Freud died in 1939. This threw psychoanalysis into a crisis. There was no longer a central person to orchestrate the development of psychoanalysis, and there was question whether the theory would continue to develop within the boundaries of orthodoxy. At this same time World War II was breaking out on the Continent, and there was an influx of European psychoanalysts into Great Britain and the United States. These countries became hotbeds of theoretical controversy. In England psychoanalysts such as Melanie Klein and W. R. D. Fairbairn proposed sweeping revisions of psychoanalysis with their OBJECT RELATIONS theories. Harry Stack Sullivan, Karen Horney, and Erich Fromm in the United States rejected traditional theory for more interpersonal and cultural dimensions.

Also as a result of the war Anna Freud fled to England and Hartmann immigrated to the United States. Hartmann, along with other influential analysts who had immigrated, founded the New York Psychoanalytic Society and Institute. The work of the New York group and Anna Freud was distinct in that these theorists continued to expand Sigmund Freud's ego psychology while maintaining orthodox emphases on instincts, psychosexual stages, and the structural model of personality. They also stressed the role of interpersonal, or object, relations, but they did this in the context of Freud's ego psychology, hence the name for this school, ego psychology.

The next major contribution to ego psychology came through the work of a colleague of Hartmann at the New York Psychoanalytic Society, Rene Spitz. He undertook the task of observing infants to establish the validity of ego psychology's theory of development. He found (Spitz, 1965) that the role of mothering object, or person, was crucial to the development of instincts, language, perception, and affects. He noted that disturbances in the mother-infant relationship even resulted in various physiological diseases. Under extreme circumstances such disturbances could even lead to the death of the infant in spite of adequate food and shelter.

This emphasis on the role of relationship has prevailed in ego psychology. Edith Jacobson pursued the process of how the actual, external mother becomes represented as an object, or image, within the infant's mind and how the ability to function depends on the healthiness of this representation. Margaret Mahler also conducted observational research of infants with their mothers. She found that infants go through definite stages in their "psychological birth" as persons. Infants start off life in an unattached, autistic mode. By approximately two months of age they progress to an intensely close, symbiotic dependence on their mother. From six months through the third year they then are involved in separating from their mothers and establishing a basic sense of their own identity.

These discoveries about early object relations and ego development have enabled ego psychologists to make great gains in the ability of psychoanalysis to treat more severe psychological disturbances. Freud saw his treatment as primarily geared to oedipal issues—i.e., conflicts the child had over his or her sexual desires for the opposite-sex parent. Now ego psychologists are able to treat conflicts that have their etiology during the first years of life, such as certain forms of severe depression (Jacobson, 1971), borderline schizophrenic personalities (Kernberg, 1975), and narcissistic personalities (Kohut, 1971).

Despite its adherence to a common theoretical base of psychoanalysis and general agreement on most major issues, ego psychology is plagued by terminological confusion and points of conflict between theorists. The conflicts even involve very crucial treatment implications, as seen in Kohut's (1971) and Kernberg's (1975) different suggestions for the treatment of narcissistic personalities.

The theory has certain points of conflict with biblical theology. It does not hold to the existence of moral absolutes, and its emphasis on ego mastery and coping could become counter to a healthy dependence on God. However, there are many places where theology and ego psychology can be integrated, such as the teachings of both disciplines on relationship, the process of internalization, pride and narcissism, and maturity.

References

Freud, A. *The ego and the mechanisms of defense.* New York: International Universities Press, 1946. (Originally published, 1936.)

Freud, S. [Three essays on the theory of sexuality.] In J. Strachey (Ed. and trans.), *The standard edition of the complete psychological works of Sigmund Freud* (Vol. 7). London: Hogarth, 1975. (Originally published, 1905.)

Freud, S. [Ego and the id.] In J. Strachey (Ed. and trans.), *The standard edition of the complete psychological works of Sigmund Freud* (Vol. 19). London: Hogarth, 1975. (Originally published, 1923.)

Hartmann, H. [*Ego psychology and the problem of adaptation.*] (D. Rapaport, trans.). New York: International Universities Press, 1958. (Originally published, 1939.)

Jacobson, E. *Depression.* New York: International Universities Press, 1971.

Kernberg, O. F. *Borderline conditions and pathological narcissism.* New York: Aronson, 1975.

Kohut, H. *The analysis of the self.* New York: International Universities Press, 1971.

Spitz, R. A. *The first year of life.* New York: International Universities Press, 1965.

Additional Readings

Blanck, G., & Blanck, R. *Ego psychology: Theory and practice.* New York: Columbia University Press, 1974.

Blanck, G., & Blanck, R. *Ego psychology II: Psychoanalytic developmental psychology.* New York: Columbia University Press, 1979.

Mahler, M., Pine, F., & Bergmann, A. *The psychological birth of the human infant.* New York: Basic Books, 1975.

Rapaport, D. A historical survey of psychoanalytic ego psychology. *Psychological issues,* 1959, *1*(1), 5–17.

W. L. EDKINS

See PSYCHOANALYTIC PSYCHOLOGY.

Ego-State Therapy.

Ego-state theory and therapy was created and developed by a husband and wife team, John and Helen Watkins (Watkins & Watkins, 1979; Watkins & Johnson, 1982). The basic tenet of this approach is that one's personality is not unified but consists of a variety of parts within the self which they call ego states. These internal subentities are made up of psychological elements of behavior and experience held together by boundaries that are more or less permeable. Within and between individuals one may find varying levels of dissociative permeability. Minimal levels of dissociation are revealed in relatively normal mood changes, this reflecting easy movement between ego states. More extreme levels of dissociation are manifest in multiple personalities, which reflect less permeable boundaries between ego states. The primary theme of this theory is that one's personality is something of a "family of the self" and can be worked with as such using techniques adapted from group and family therapies within a primarily hypnotic modality.

Some historical background to this approach is helpful. The splitting off of semi-autonomous parts of the self has traditionally been considered only in reference to hysterical dissociation and has been viewed by most clinicians as something of a rarity. The Watkins appeal to some of the notions of Paul Federn (Berne's psychoanalyst), who spoke of the ego as having organized subpatterns (Federn, 1952). Berne furthered these ideas with his development of transactional analysis. Other writers, such as Kohut and Hartmann, have recognized the existence of such entities but have attributed to them only minor significance. The Watkins's work differs from these theorists in that they attribute major significance to this organization of the self and do not limit the entities to preformed categories such as Parent, Adult, and Child. Instead the therapist is free to explore all those parts within the client that are relevant to the current symptomatic picture. Conflicts between any one of an individual's ego states and others extant within the self may result in a broad range of symptoms, including various neuroses, psychoses, multiple personality trends, phobias, anxiety reactions, and habit control disorders.

The practice of ego-state therapy is a test of one's ingenuity and flexibility. The therapist typically will employ a type of internal "shuttle diplomacy" between conflictual ego states while using a variety of systemic, suggestive, supportive, confrontive, desensitizing, abreactive, and interpretative techniques. These techniques are best utilized within a hypnotic modality. Nonhypnotic techniques which utilize a relaxed state (e.g., free association) are also useful but appear to be less potent (Watkins & Watkins, 1979).

When these ego states are activated, each refers to itself in the first person and the rest of the self in third person. The ego state which is being addressed at the moment is said to be executive. Once a particular ego state has been activated the therapist must be careful not to contaminate the client's internal organization of self through the inadvertent use of hypnotic suggestion. The Watkins hold that one may minimize this influence by working as carefully and objectively as possible to elicit information regarding an ego state's origin, content, function, and goals. The ego state will also inform the therapist of its name and sexual identity to the degree these attributes have been defined.

The therapist's goal is not to fuse the various ego states, since each jealously guards its own identity and existence. The goal is rather to increase cognitive cooperation and consonance among the parts of the self so they become better integrated. This is true even for that part of the self that seems malevolent or self-destructive; in this situation one strives to positively rechannel its activities and functions. As a result of this approach one finds that the client typically moves toward the less dissociated end of the continuum, where greater permeability exists among the various ego states. Clients reaching successful termination of therapy still possess covert, autonomous ego states that can be elicited hypnotically. One typically finds these functioning as cooperative subparts of a normal personality.

Ego-state therapy still remains in its infancy. Its applications have thus far not been extensive, and research on its effectiveness is virtually nonexistent. However, as a creative, primarily brief therapy its clinical potential seems great. Furthermore, its theoretical contributions to the understanding of disorders such as Multiple Personality and fugue states as well as the defense mechanism of dissociation seem promising.

References

Federn, P. In E. Weiss (Ed.), *Ego psychology and the psychoses*. New York: Basic Books, 1952.

Watkins, J., & Johnson, R. J. *We, the divided self*. N.Y.: Irvington Publishers, 1982.

Watkins, J., & Watkins, H. In H. Grayson (Ed.), *Short term approaches to psychotherapy*. New York: Human Sciences Press, 1979.

V. L. Shepperson

See Hypnotherapy.

Ego Strength. A term commonly used by psychodynamically oriented psychotherapists to describe the level of effectiveness with which the ego accomplishes its various functions. The ego is that part of the personality which establishes a relationship with the world in which we live.

The group of functions which we metaphorically refer to as the ego deals with the environment by means of conscious perception, thought, feeling, and action. It contains the evaluating, judging, solution-forming, compromising, and defense-creating aspects of the personality which form the basis for reality testing, intermediary synthesizing, and the executive functions of the personality. The ego must mediate between the blind, instinctual drives of the id and the sometimes rigid demands and aspirations of the superego, all within the context of the reality principle. The ego seeks to channel the instinctual drives of the id into patterns of thought and behavior that will bring lasting satisfaction and fulfillment.

Good ego strength is present when the ego is able to accomplish these goals in a flexible, adaptive manner, without becoming restricted by inflexible, repetitive defenses that limit the personality's ability to cope with stress. Good ego strength allows for the presence of extra energy that can be channeled into creative, satisfying tasks and interests, while poor ego strength requires that all energy be rigidly channeled into basic survival. Where there is poor ego strength, the ego is likely to be underdeveloped, dominated by unconscious factors, prone to regression or even disintegration, and overwhelmed by mounting repression. This typically leads to symptom development and marked distress.

In psychodynamically oriented psychotherapy, ego strength typically becomes a focus. First, there must be sufficient ego strength present to withstand and adapt to increasing stress as the therapy uncovers and dismantles ineffective, restrictive defenses. Thus, assessing ego strength becomes a focus of determining suitability for insight-oriented psychotherapy (Paolino, 1981). Second, some forms of therapy specifically focus on strengthening the ego, increasing its flexibility, and improving its useful defenses. This is especially true when it is determined that ego strength is poor and more classical psychoanalysis is inappropriate.

Where ego strength is good, the personality will be capable of exhibiting such traits as commitment, responsibility, loyalty, perseverance, integrity, empathy, likability, humor, playfulness, flexibility, curiosity, dedication, and courage. Through the course of psychotherapy, as rigid and restrictive defenses are surrendered freeing up energy for other purposes, it is common to see the emergence of such traits almost spontaneously, without direction from the therapist.

Reference

Paolino, T. J. *Psychoanalytic psychotherapy*. New York: Brunner/Mazel, 1981.

J. D. Guy, Jr.

Ego Syntonic. Personality traits, impulses, or urges deemed acceptable to an individual are known as ego syntonic (literally "invigorating with" or "together"). This compatibility with the ego is the opposite of Ego Dystonic.

Eidetic Imagery. See Imagery, Eidetic.

Ejaculation, Premature. Premature ejaculation is difficult to define, and sex therapists have often used quite different criteria for prematurity. Masters and Johnson (1970) base their definition on whether or not the man ejaculates before his wife reaches coital orgasm more than 50% of the time. Others use as their basis the amount of time between vaginal insertion and ejaculation. Others use as their criterion the number of penile thrusts.

Kaplan (1974) believes that the key issue in arriving at an adequate definition of premature ejaculation is ascertaining the degree of voluntary control the man is able to exert in regard to his ejaculatory reflex. She speculates that premature ejaculators do not perceive the erotic sensations which occur prior to orgasm and are thus unable to develop adequate control of the ejaculatory reflex. A parallel example would be the inability of young children to develop urinary continence until neural sensory capacity is developed.

Premature ejaculation is most likely the result of prior conditioning and anxiety. For treatment purposes, ascertaining the exact roots of the dysfunction is not necessary unless significant resistance to treatment is encountered.

While it is believed that the vast majority of men could be termed premature ejaculators, the precise incidence rate is unknown. Some authorities, such as Kinsey, believe that it is normal to ejaculate quickly. Others assert that early conditioning through masturbation conditions males to ejaculate quickly.

In any event, the most commonplace attempts to overcome premature ejaculation also are the least effective. A widespread, mistaken belief involves the application of various salves or ointments which serve to numb the penis; unfortunately, they have no effect on the male's ability to control ejaculation. Other equally common and ineffectual approaches involve concentrating on thoughts totally removed from the sexual experience, forbidding the wife to touch the husband's genitals, and distracting techniques such as tensing other muscles throughout the body.

A somewhat superficial but effective suggestion is to encourage the couple to increase the frequency of sexual intercourse. Telling the couple that the first encounter will likely be rapid but thereafter the length of time prior to ejaculation will lengthen brings about a lessening of anxiety and greater confidence in the ability to last longer. A deficiency in this approach, if not used in concert with the optimum treatment method, is the tendency to return to prematurity upon lessening of sexual frequency.

Until the pioneering work of Semans in the 1950s, the psychoanalytic techniques of free association, interpretation of dreams, and analysis of transferences were the major avenues for treating premature ejaculation. Treatment was rarely successful and only after several years of treatment with 2 to 5 interviews each week. The Freudian theory holds that the male harbors intense, unconscious, sadistic feelings toward women and expresses hostility through rapid ejaculation. Research fails to support this theory.

Systems theory formulations which contend that the prematurity is a manifestation of the couple's interpersonal difficulties are ill supported because resolution of spousal conflict does not necessarily end the prematurity. The same rationale applies to the use of the behavioral technique of systematic desensitization; it is an effective tool for reducing sexual anxiety, but it is not often effective in treating prematurity. Pharmacological approaches produce only temporary cures, with the duration dependent upon continued use of the medication.

The treatment of choice for premature ejaculation involves several methods which focus the male's attention on the sensations preceding orgasm. Treatment is generally effective after 4 to 6 weeks for 98% of those treated. Without treatment, prematurity may last an entire lifetime.

The most effective method of treating premature ejaculation was pioneered by Semans (1956). It consists of extravaginal stimulation of the penis by the wife until the sensations indicative of imminent ejaculation are present. The husband than signals the wife to cease penile stimulation until the sensations end. Stimulation is then resumed, and the pattern is continued several times until the husband can tolerate the extravaginal stimulation for an indefinite period. Once this point is reached, the prematurity is permanently cured. This method is called the "stop-start" technique. The "squeeze" technique developed by Masters and Johnson (1970) is a variation of the Semans stop-start technique and simply requires the wife to squeeze the penis just below the rim of the glans until the erection partially subsides.

As is the case in most treatment regimens involving the modern behavioral approach to sex therapy, a gradual series of progressively more erotic homework assignments are given to the couple. The initial assignment usually has the couple engage in limited sexual activity at home. The instruction is to proceed to the point of the husband developing an erection but to stop short of ejaculation. The next step is to begin the start-stop technique. As an increase in ejaculatory control is attained, intercourse is suggested. Specific coital positions are sequentially prescribed, such as female superior position, lying on sides position, and male superior position.

It is important to note that varying degrees

of resistance to changing or altering sexual patterns will surface in virtually all couples. Therapist skill in guiding couples past their hesitancy to change the very behaviors they profess to want to eliminate is frequently a key factor in successful treatment.

The wife's willingness to participate in the treatment plan is also crucial. She must temporarily give more than she receives. For both spouses difficult steps are realizing and accepting their individual self-responsibility for the outcome of their mutual lovemaking. Once this elusive truth is understood and implemented, the human tendency to look for causes outside of oneself and to blame the other person are able to be set aside.

The man's ability to overcome and to continue mastery of the tendency toward premature ejaculation will be related to the amount of pressure to perform exerted by the wife. Both spouses must strive to create a climate of mutual acceptance. Pressuring the other to perform sexually most often increases the tendency toward dysfunction.

References
Kaplan, H. S. *The new sex therapy*. New York: Brunner/Mazel, 1974.
Masters, W. H., & Johnson, V. E. *Human sexual inadequacy*. Boston: Little, Brown, 1970.
Semans, J. H. Premature ejaculation: A new approach. *Southern Medical Journal*, 1956, *49*, 353.

J. R. DAVID

See SEX THERAPY; PSYCHOSEXUAL DYSFUNCTIONS; SEXUAL RESPONSE PSYCHOLOGY.

Ejaculation, Retarded. See INHIBITED ORGASM.

Elective Mutism of Childhood or Adolescence.
A persistent refusal to talk in almost all social situations despite an ability to speak and understand spoken language is the most significant characteristic of elective mutism disorder. While there may be some articulation dysfunction and delayed language development, the refusal to speak is not due to any mental disorder or language insufficiency. The child may communicate through gestures—e.g., nodding or shaking the head—or by monosyllabic or short, monotone utterances. This rather rare disorder is found in less than 1% of referrals to clinical and child-guidance centers.

There also may be evidences of more than usual shyness, clinging behavior, refusal to attend school, and the tendency to withdraw or be socially isolated. The child may experience encopresis or enuresis, and controlling oppositional behavior may be manifested, especially at home. The onset of elective mutism is usually before age 5 but may not come to clinical attention until the child begins school. While it can last for several years, generally the duration is for only a few weeks or months.

This disorder may stem from an overprotective mother, a trauma or hospitalization prior to age 3, immigration to a country of a different language, mental retardation, or the entrance into school. In most of these predisposing situations a strong sense of security is lacking. Either the mother binds the child to her to relieve her own anxiety or the child's bond with the mother is disrupted by circumstances, thus leaving the child vulnerable to intense fear, threat of rejection, or loss of the love object.

To determine the appropriate treatment modality and goals, there needs to be a careful evaluation of the precipitating causes, duration, family dynamics, and the quality and characteristics of the mother-child relationship. Family therapy or individual (play) therapy may be used depending on the evaluation findings.

B. J. SHEPPERSON

Electroconvulsive Therapy.
The idea of using electricity to cure disease can be traced back at least as far as the ancient Romans, who used shocks from eels. In the 1920s and 1930s European psychiatrists experimented with drug-induced convulsions as a treatment for schizophrenia. In 1938 Cerletti and Bini developed an apparatus which used electricity to induce convulsions. Although it proved to be of limited benefit for schizophrenia, electroconvulsive therapy (ECT) achieved remarkable success in the rapid alleviation of depression.

In the decade after the discovery of ECT its use was widespread and indiscriminate, perhaps excessive. This was undoubtedly due to the fact that it was a highly effective treatment, easy to administer, and frequently superior to alternative therapies. Since the advances in psychiatric medication during the 1950s the use of ECT has declined. During the last dozen years the political strength of patients' rights organizations has resulted in certain barriers to ECT, including legal limitations. Due to these factors and technical constraints, less than a fourth of American psychiatrists regularly perform ECT on their patients.

How ECT Works. The patient is prepared for ECT in several ways. Usually psychiatric medication has been discontinued. No food is given during the 4 hours prior to treatment.

The bladder must be voided. Patients are given injections of muscle relaxants in order to reduce the physical expression of the convulsion (and prevent fractures of vertebra). General anesthesia is given and supplemented with forced respiration of pure oxygen. In order to protect the teeth and tongue, a plastic protective block is inserted just prior to turning on the current.

The standard procedure for ECT is to apply electrodes to the forehead. Skin resistance is decreased by a solution or jelly. The amount of current is usually between 70 and 130 volts, but only continues for a fraction of a second. Convulsions occur and may last up to a minute. Oxygen is given until the patient resumes normal breathing. The patient regains consciousness in a few minutes, but may not be fully alert and able to leave the treatment area for an hour. During this recovery period the patient has a clouded consciousness and may experience a headache.

What is not precisely known is the mechanism which accounts for ECT's efficacy. No one theory is comprehensive enough or has led to hypotheses which have been validated using appropriate research. Various psychological explanations have been advanced: that patients needed punishment to alleviate guilt complexes, that ECT is a technique for breaking through psychic defenses, that ECT serves to destroy the painful memories behind the mental disorder. Such psychological theories are at best speculative, and certainly do not assist psychiatrists in the selection of patients for ECT. Most psychiatrists believe that ECT works because it succeeds in altering the functioning of the brain, in some way serving as a "diencephalic stimulation," probably via increased catecholamines.

Indications. Today ECT is regarded as a treatment reserved for serious cases of depression and catatonia. While the efficacy of ECT for schizophrenia or unipolar mania may be questioned, there is little debate about its impact on depression. Five to ten treatments, administered over a period of two weeks, will secure a dramatic remission of symptoms in almost 90% of the cases of depression. The superior efficacy of ECT compared to other treatments for depression (e.g., medication, psychotherapy) has been demonstrated in dozens of studies using different kinds of research designs in different countries. Indeed, it can be said that ECT has the best-documented efficacy of any psychiatric treatment, bar none.

Patients who pose an imminent suicidal risk are important candidates for ECT. The dramatic drop in suicide rates (espicially among institutionalized patients) after 1940 must be attributed to ECT. The advent of newer forms of psychiatric medication has not changed the fact that ECT is the treatment of choice for suicidal depressives. Tricyclics, MAOIs and lithium may take weeks to alleviate depressive symptoms and suicidal ideation. Because many of these medications can be fatal if taken in overdose, there is a danger that they can be used as the tools of suicide.

Another group of patients for whom ECT should be given early consideration are those who are especially susceptible to the side effects of antidepressant medication. Certain cardiovascular conditions may make the use of tricyclics or MAOIs risky. Liver or kidney problems may preclude the use of lithium. These factors, and the poor response of elders to these antidepressant medications, make ECT an appropriate consideration in geriatrics.

Several studies have attempted to correlate response to ECT with background and personality factors in hopes of identifying predictors of ECT response. Sudden onset, weight loss, low salivation, and low galvanic skin response have been correlated with subsequent favorable response to ECT. Hypochondriasis seems to be the best predictor of poor response to ECT. However, the correlations here are low, and even complicated weighings of numerous factors do not achieve valid and reliable predictions of ECT response. If the depression cannot be successfully treated by other means or if there is a serious risk of suicide, ECT is indicated.

Problems and Controversy. ECT is not the dangerous procedure that the lay person might imagine. Spontaneous seizures occurring after the completion of treatment have an incidence of less than 1 in 500 cases. Deaths occur in less than 3 in 10,000 cases. (This is the same rate for general anesthesia without ECT.) The one absolute contraindication is brain tumor. Another relative contraindication is postpartum depression. Cardiovascular problems are not a contraindication; indeed, ECT is less risky here than some antidepressant medication. (Even patients with cardiac pacemakers have received ECT after certain precautionary measures were taken.) Pregnancy is not a contraindication, for there is no evidence of harm to mother or fetus. While ECT is not contraindicated in children and adolescents, studies of the effects of ECT on this age group are few in number and questionable in design. Many child psychiatrists have doubts about the appropriateness of ECT for younger patients.

One limitation of ECT is that it is not a permanent cure. There is always the danger that the patient may become depressed again. While other psychiatric treatments short of lobotomy have the same problem, the relapse rate seems to be higher with ECT. (This could be related to the fact that only the most difficult cases of depression receive ECT in the first place.) One suggested way of handling the problem of relapses would be to give an ECT treatment every two months or so as maintenance therapy, but this idea has not really caught on. A more common technique is to use long-term lithium therapy as a maintenance for patients who were formerly treated with ECT.

The most frequently reported side effect of ECT is memory loss, both in the form of retrograde amnesia (especially forgetting what happened just before the treatment) and anterograde amnesia. Almost half of all ECT patients complain that their memory ability is impaired right after treatments, but this proves to be temporary. Although objective tests rarely document permanent loss of memory 6 months after treatment, some patients do make such complaints. What has not been adequately researched is the effect of many (over 50) ECT treatments on memory.

In an attempt to get around the problem of memory loss, several modified procedures of ECT have been developed. One has been to use unilateral ECT (electrodes placed only on the right side of the head). The research clearly demonstrates that such unilateral ECT leads to significantly fewer memory problems without a significant decrement in the remission of depressive symptoms. A newer technique is the use of multiply monitored seizures. Unfortunately, many psychiatrists practicing ECT are older and somewhat disinclined to try these new procedures.

Perhaps the greatest problem with ECT is not that it is cruel or barbaric, but that the public (and many patients) regard it as such. Although the patient experiences no pain during the seizure, the clouded state of consciousness when the patient slowly comes to is not pleasant. When the patient notices memory problems, she or he may begin to worry that ECT is doing some permanent damage to the brain. Therefore, many former ECT patients develop a disgust and/or fear of the procedure.

The public's position on ECT seems to be quite negative, due to a combination of ignorance, sensationalistic movies, and the dramatic stories of a few dissatisfied patients. Therefore, several states (e.g., California) have enacted strict laws that put a number of obstacles in the path of the prescription of ECT. As a result, some hospitals have abandoned the procedure and fewer psychiatrists administer it. Many psychiatrists now view ECT as a treatment of last resort.

Additional Readings

American Psychiatric Association. *Electroconvulsive Therapy: Report of the task force on electroconvulsive therapy of the American Psychiatric Association.* Washington. D.C.: Author, 1978.
Fink, M. *Convulsive therapy.* New York: Raven Press, 1979.

T. L. Brink

Electroencephalography. The recording of electrical currents developed in the brain by means of electrodes applied to the scalp. Commonly called EEG, it is a procedure used primarily by neurologists and other medical doctors, and the recording is typically done in a hospital or clinic setting. The test is usually ordered when a neurological problem pertaining to the brain is suspected, especially when the problem suspected might result in abnormal brain waves.

The procedure is accomplished by applying electrode disks to the scalp with a type of paste. Wires run from these disks to the electroencephalograph. Since the electrical signals from the brain are very weak, the electroencephalograph must amplify them many times and send them on to pens which provide a written record of the brain waves. Recordings may be made during wakefulness or sleep or both. Extended recordings lasting for several days or more are sometimes done, particularly with individuals with suspected epilepsy. Such extended recordings can be very helpful in identifying whether or not epilepsy exists, and if so, from what part of the brain seizures arise. Much has been learned about this test since it was introduced by Hans Burger in 1929, and it is routinely accomplished with no significant risk or discomfort.

Typically, an EEG is given as part of a larger workup in an attempt to identify whether or not a neurological problem exists, and if so, to make it more specific. Other parts of the neurological evaluation may include the taking of a neurological history, a physical neurological examination, and the use of additional tests, including a computerized tomographic (CT) scan, cerebral angiography, and in some instances a neuropsychological evaluation.

EEGs are typically interpreted as normal or abnormal. If abnormal, the nature of the abnormality is usually specified, including the part of the brain involved. The use of serial EEGs permits the physician to identify any changes in brain condition that may occur over time.

C. B. DODRILL

See BRAIN AND HUMAN BEHAVIOR; NEUROPSY-CHOLOGY.

Ellis, Albert (1913-). American psychologist who developed RATIONAL EMOTIVE THERAPY. Born in Pittsburgh but raised in New York City, he had a difficult childhood. As he put it in his autobiography (Ellis, 1972), much responsibility for his brother and sister helped him become a "stubborn and pronounced problem solver." At the age of 12 he became "an unregenerate atheist." In junior high school he decided to become a renowned writer, but to make a fortune in business so he could retire in his 30s and write what he pleased, without having to worry about it selling.

He received a degree in business administration from the City College of New York in 1934. By the time he was 28 he had 20 unpublished full-length manuscripts in his files. He decided to abandon fiction, to use nonfiction to propound his revolutionary views, and to devote much of his life to furthering the sex-family revolution. While he was gathering material for a manuscript he called *"The Case for Sexual Liberty, "* his friends started coming to him for information and advice. He then realized he could be more than a "sex writer and revolutionist." He could be a "sex-love-marriage counselor."

Believing that psychoanalysis was the most effective therapy, he entered analysis himself. In 1943 he received an M.A. and in 1947 a Ph.D. from Columbia University. During the late 1940s and early 1950s he taught at Rutgers University and at New York University, and was a clinical psychologist at Greystone Park State Hospital, the New Jersey Diagnostic Center, the New Jersey Department of Institutions and Agencies, while maintaining a private practice.

However, Ellis's faith in psychoanalysis was crumbling. Patients he saw only once a week, or even every other week, did as well as those he saw daily. He began to take a more active role in therapy, and by 1955 he had given up psychoanalysis entirely and originated rational-emotive therapy. By 1957 he had published a book

on this therapy, and in 1959 he organized the Institute for Rational Living, where he held workshops to teach his principles to others. In 1968 he founded the Institute for Advanced Study in Rational Psychotherapy.

Ellis has made two major contributions to psychology, both of which conflict to some extent with Christianity. He encourages all kinds of sexual experimentation. At first he was labeled a sensationalist and a sexual radical, but now his views are accepted by a large part of our society. The titles of some of his books about sex express his views on the subject: *The American Sexual Tragedy, Sex Without Guilt, Creative Marriage, If This Be Sexual Heresy, Sex and the Single Man, The Intelligent Woman's Guide to Manhunting, Nymphomania: A Study of the Oversexed Woman, The Case for Sexual Liberty, Suppressed: Seven Key Essays Publishers Dared Not Print, The Search for Sexual Enjoyment, The Art of Erotic Seduction, The Civilized Couple's Guide to Extramarital Adventure, The Sensuous Person: Critique and Corrections, Sex and the Liberated Man,* and *The Intelligent Woman's Guide to Mating and Dating.* These books advocate both premarital and extramarital sex.

His other major contribution is rational-emotive therapy. This uses an ABC approach to human personality and its problems. The A refers to activating experiences from the outside world which keep people from reaching their goals, such as failing at tasks or being rejected. B refers to people's belief systems, through which they draw conclusions about A. Many people have sets of irrational beliefs, such as "I must always succeed in everything I do." C refers to the emotional and behavioral consequences of evaluating A by B. People may conclude that failing one task means that they are failures. The goal of the therapist is to eliminate the irrational beliefs.

Many Christians find several aspects of Ellis's practice of rational-emotive therapy disturbing. First, he places humans at the center of the universe and gives people almost full responsibility for their own fate. Second, he lists such things as needing "some supernatural power on which to rely" as irrational beliefs (Ellis, 1980). Third, he advocates the use of strong language during therapy to loosen up the client, to show that the therapist is a down-to-earth person, and to give the client an emotive jolt or shock.

In addition to more than 50 books, Ellis has written more than 300 journal articles and more than 100 articles in popular magazines. *A Guide to Rational Living* (1961) and *Humanistic Psychotherapy: The Rational-Emotive Approach* (1973) give his approach to life and rational-emotive therapy.

References

Ellis, A. Psychotherapy without tears. In A. Burton (Ed.), *Twelve therapists*. San Francisco: Jossey-Bass, 1972.

Ellis, A. Overview of the clinical theory of rational-emotive therapy. In R. Greiger & J. Boyd (Eds.), *Rational-emotive therapy*. New York: Van Nostrand Reinhold, 1980.

R. L. Koteskey

Ellis, Henry Havelock (1859–1939). Pioneer in the study of human sexuality. He was born in Croydon, Surrey, England, the son of a sea captain, and educated at private schools in South London. In 1875 he went to Australia on his father's ship and taught school there until 1879, when he returned to England. In 1881 he began the study of medicine at St. Thomas Hospital, London, living on a small legacy.

Ellis received his M.D. degree in 1889, but did not practice medicine. While studying, he met G. B. Shaw and Arthur Symons at meetings of the Fellowship of New Life. He conceived and was editor (1887–1889) of the Mermaid Series, a collection of works by lesser-known Elizabethan dramatists. He held no academic or official medical position but supported himself through his writings and editorial jobs. In 1890 he published a study of Ibsen, Whitman, and Tolstoy, *The New Spirit*. From 1889 to 1914 he was editor of the Contemporary Science Series. During this same time he was working on his most influential contribution, *Studies in the Psychology of Sex*, which appeared in seven volumes between 1897 and 1928.

Although he could be described as an essayist, editor, physician, or literary critic, it was his study of sexual behavior that made him famous. And while he worked in areas studied by Freud, he drew his material from medical, anthropological, and historical data as well as interviews and questionnaires. Krafft-Ebbing had dealt with sexual abnormality or perversion, but Ellis dealt with normal sexual behavior in both humans and animals.

The first volume in *Studies in the Psychology of Sex* was *Sexual Inversion* (1897), in essence an apology for homosexuality. It was a part of his lifelong effort to broaden the spectrum of acceptable sexual behavior. In the second volume, *Auto-Eroticism* (1899), he sought to do for masturbation what he had for homosexuality. In later volumes he treated topics ranging from sadism and masochism to erotic symbols, perfumes, and dream imagery. He opposed censorship in regard to public discussion and literary treatment of sexual practices.

A legal dispute over the first volume resulted in the judge calling his claims for the scientific value of the book "a pretense, adopted for the purpose of selling a filthy publication." The remaining volumes were published in the United States and were available only to those in the medical profession until 1936, when publishing rights were taken over by Random House.

R. L. Koteskey

Emotion. The word is derived from the Latin *emovare*, meaning "to move." Affect, passion, and mood are other words that describe some aspect of the same phenomenon. In common usage emotion refers primarily to perceived feelings, while affect includes the drives that are presumed to generate both conscious and unconscious feelings. Passion is intense emotion, and mood is emotion of long duration.

Psychology of Emotion. James (1890) was quite correct when he stated that emotions were reflexes. They arise as a result of stimuli that have symbolic meaning to the individual. They usually are elicited by extrapsychic events that occur in the environment, either activities of other living organisms or natural phenomenon that threaten the individual's control of his environment. The stimuli that arise as a result of the behavior of other people have both cognitive and emotional qualities. The display of an emotion by one person may elicit the same emotion in the observer. This process is called empathy. If it elicits sorrow, it is called sympathy.

Autopsychic stimuli also elicit emotions. Past events may arouse emotions when they are recalled in memory. The recall may be spontaneous or elicited by events in the environment that are similar to the emotionally significant memory. The process whereby emotional responses are attached to and stored with memories is called cathexis.

Because emotions are compound reflexes, they normally possess the properties of reflexes. They can be facilitated or occluded. They summate, are graded in intensity, and are subject to fatigue. Early in life they are likely to dramatically display the properties of irradiation and generalization, which become more limited as stimulus specificity develops. They do not, however, lose these properties with maturation.

Emotions are composed of sensory, skeletal, motor, autonomic, and cognitive components. The early theorists focused on the autonomic and skeletal motor phenomena because they were observable. McLean added the cognitive aspect. Recent work strongly suggests that the feeling of the emotion, the sensory component, may be reflexly elicited at the rhinencephalic level. The observation that certain experiences (e.g., chills running up and down one's spine or the sensation of one's hair standing on end) are not associated with observable autonomic change lends credence to this idea.

There are many autonomic motor and sensory phenomena that are common to several specific emotions. One may tear with sorrow, anger, pain, awe, joy, or love. In a like manner, epigastric tightness, a sensory phenomenon, may be experienced in anger, fear, jealousy, and sorrow. Motor responses are more variable, but almost all unpleasant emotions are associated with increased muscular tension in all or some muscles, whereas pleasant emotions are associated with decreased tension in all or some muscles. It would appear then that emotions are synthesized from a number of autonomic, sensory, and motor responses to provide their specificity. It is believed by most authorities in the field that the cognition of the specific emotion is concomitant with the autonomic, sensory, and motor responses.

The Varieties of Emotions. Lindsley (1951) in his discussion of emotion linked the drives for sleep, sex, nutrition, and psychomotor activity to emotion. He did so because of their relationship to the reticular activating system. Psychopathological observations would support this linkage. Emotional states that are prolonged almost always result in aberrations in the intensity of these biological functions. These functions or drives give rise to behaviors that are specific for the drive. Thus, they can be considered tonic emotions, since they move the organism to specific behaviors.

James emphasized that there was nothing immutable about an emotion and that emotions were not to be described and classified rigidly. Although there is truth in his statement, most persons who have studied emotion have attempted to develop a taxonomy. Twelve fundamental emotions have been repeatedly mentioned in the natural philosophical literature. These are divided into nine unpleasant and three pleasant emotions. The unpleasant are sorrow, fear, anger, jealousy, shame, disgust, pain, confusion, and emptiness. The pleasant ones are love, joy, and awe. There are, however, other terms that are used to describe these same emotions. These terms further indicate differences in intensity or duration, or refer to the stimulus that elicited the emotion.

An example of some words that refer to anger but also indicate intensity are irritation, fury, and rage. One that includes duration is hate. Examples of words that relate to the stimulus are jealousy and envy, the former being elicited by desire to have or maintain a relationship with other beings and the latter relating to the desire to have or maintain possession of material things.

Included in the list of emotions are three that are not usually encountered—disgust, emptiness, and pain. The first two have been emphasized by the existentialists, who consider them to be the most common emotional responses to the predicament of being. Pain is not usually included because of the specificity of its exciting stimulus. It is nevertheless a real emotion, since the sensation of pain elicits specific behaviors that are recognized by observers as symbolizing the pain state and elicit empathy or sympathy in the observer.

Human beings have always desired rationality; however, they generally do not behave rationally but are driven by emotions. Ideas are of no value until emotions are attached to them, since the emotion provides the force for action. It is imperative, then, that as one accumulates a body of knowledge, appropriate emotions be cathected to ideas in order that they may have value. Values are ideas—with cathected emotions—that make a favorable difference in life.

Learning is a conditioning process that involves the cathexis of emotion. Operant conditioning occurs when a behavior is elicited and is rewarded by the eliciting of a pleasant emotion or the satiation of an appetite. Love or joy are the emotions that are primary in operant conditioning. Avoidance conditioning occurs when a behavior elicits an unpleasant emotion or fails to produce satiation of an appetite. Fear or pain are commonly elicited emotions that produce avoidance, but anger may also serve to produce avoidance.

The capacity for emotion is inherent. Some emotions may be recognized at birth. The Perez reflex elicited by rapidly stroking the spine of a newborn child with a gloved finger will produce fear, which is immediately followed by anger. Evidences of joy are revealed in the smiles of the infant before three months of age. Jealousy has been observed as early as nine months, and shame within the first year. Love is probably present as a diffuse feeling tone at birth but can be recognized as a specific emotion by six months. The entire human emotional repertoire is recognizable by two years of age.

As the child develops, the process of cognitive and emotional training begins. The exercise of volition is manifest early. It becomes more channeled as the infant develops intellectual and motor functions. Discipline is directed toward achieving an appropriate channeling of the child's spirit by his knowledge and its cathected emotions. His emotions vector his spirit by facilitating or inhibiting its direction. It is imperative, then, that the child be taught emotional control. This is begun in the first year by the conditioning process. Neither pleasant nor unpleasant emotions should be expressed unrestrainedly, nor should they be overly inhibited. There are inappropriate expressions of emotions that profoundly handicap a person in relating to the environment and other people. Personality is built on a foundation of emotional expression.

Neurophysiological Theories. Because they produce sensations of bodily change as well as behaviors, emotions have always been thought to have their genesis in some biological process. The humors of the ancient Greeks were presumably chemical. Recently, when the means to study the physiology of the brain became available, behavioral scientists have focused on the neurophysiology of emotion while at the same time continuing to investigate the neurohumoral mechanisms. The neurohumors that have been implicated are epinephrine, norepinephrine, acetylcholine, gamma aminobutyric acid (GABA), serotonin, and enkephlins.

Neurophysiological theories were first proposed by James and Lange, who believed that emotions were reflexes and that emotional feeling was the perception of changes in the activity of the viscera and skeletal muscles. They believed that emotion or feeling was the result of, rather than the cause of, the reflex response. According to this view, our body reacts first and we feel the emotion later. Developed independently by James and by Lange, this theory came to be known as the James-Lange theory. It is most clearly presented in James's *Principles of Psychology* (1890).

One problem with this theory was the observation that animals seemed capable of experiencing emotion even when deprived of sensory input. As a result of this seeming inadequacy of the James-Lange theory, Cannon proposed that there was a tonic force in the brain stem that was released from cortical inhibition by signals from the thalamus. This process added to the perception in the peculiar quality of emotion while at the same time

adding in motor response. Bard elaborated the theory to make it a corticothalamic process. In what came to be known as the Cannon-Bard theory, the thalamus acts as a relay station transmitting impulses to the cortex (which are the "feeling" of the emotion) and to the visceral organs (the response pattern of emotion).

Subsequently the work of Hess brought about a further modification of the theory, moving the emphasis from the thalamus to the hypothalamus. More recently the discovery of the significance of the ascending reticular system in the integration of cerebral activity led Lindsley to include it as an important part of the system that elaborates emotion. Papez proposed a theory of emotion that makes the limbic system of prime importance. McLean built upon this view, arguing that the limbic system (part of the "old brain") serves to interpret emotion in terms of feeling, while the neopallium (or "new brain") gives it symbolic meaning.

Most recently Gellhorn (1963) has elaborated these theories even further. Although his work has not been widely accepted, recent neurophysiological research has added increasing evidence to support his theory. To Gellhorn emotions are reflexes that are mediated and controlled through two systems that balance one another. There is an activating system composed of part of the hypothalamus, the mesencephalic reticular system, the thalmic reticular system, and the paleocortex. Opposing this system is an inhibitory system composed of part of the hypothalamus, the head of the candate nucleus, the globus pallidus, and the neocortex. The balance between these two systems is a tonic one, but it is unbalanced by sensory stimuli. Once the balance in this system has been shifted, the rhinencephalic mechanisms elaborate the pleasant or unpleasant response to provide the feeling while neopallial mechanisms provide the symbolic or cognitive aspect. One can see that Gellhorn's approach is an integration and extension of the earlier theories. (See Wilson & Nashold, 1972, for a more detailed discussion of these theories.)

Psychopathology and Emotion. Thinking and feeling are inextricably linked. Thus, it is not surprising that all mental disorder is characterized by disturbances of both. Etiologically, many view psychopathology as consisting of two distinct classes of problems: those that are learned and those that are a result of dysfunction of the brain. In the former category are the personality disorders and neuroses. In the latter are the major mental disorders, including depressive illnesses, schizophrenia, and those diseases that are due to anatomical or physiological disease of the brain.

The personality disorders represent dysfunctional exaggerations of normal personality attributes. It is only when personality traits are inflexible and maladaptive and cause either significant impairment in social or occupational functioning or subjective distress that they constitute personality disorder. When persons with such disorders become dissatisfied with their inability to function effectively, some may become depressed or suffer considerable anxiety. Others have emotional disturbances that are symptoms of the disorder. Anger is often expressed intensely or inappropriately by persons who have a histrionic, narcissistic, antisocial, or borderline personality disorder. Persons with paranoid disorders may display pathological jealousy, while those with histrionic, narcissistic, and borderline disorders may suffer exaggerated shame.

The neuroses are no longer considered diagnostically as a group but have been subdivided under various headings such as affective disorders, anxiety disorders, somataform disorders, and dissociative disorders. These disorders, which have as their etiology disturbed learning in early life, all have marked disturbances of affect. The dysthymic disorder is characterized by pervasive depression accompanied by irritability (anger) and changes in biological function. The anxiety disorders are all characterized by intermittant or continuous severe anxiety. The term *anxiety*, defined here as fear without an object, is often used as a synonym for fear. Although fear is the predominant affect in these disorders, depression is also a concomitant. Somatization disorder, conversion disorder, psychogenic pain disorder, and hypochondriasis are characterized by the emotions of fear, depression, and pain. A lack of emotion (belle indifference) in conversion disorder accompanies the ideational distortions that lead persons to believe that they have some physical disease. The dissociative disorders are characterized primarily by disturbances of memory function. As these disorders defend the person from overwhelming fear, they are characterized by a lack of emotion.

Of the major mental disorders, major affective disorder is the one most characterized by a gross disturbance of affect. This illness, which usually has a well-defined onset, involves a pervasive alteration of mood that is either pleasant or unpleasant. The most frequent unpleasant emotion is sorrow; the most frequent pleasant emotion is joy. That this tonic disturbance of affect may be expressed in other terms is undeniable; anger, fear, confusion, pain, shame, or emptiness can occur as the primary expression of the pathologically unpleasant affective tonus. Similarly, in those disorders in which the exaggerated tonus is abnormally pleasant, love and awe as well as joy can be the primary expressions.

Although most major affective disorders are characterized by a continuing presence of unpleasant or pleasant emotion, some may have sudden shifts from one emotion to another. It is not uncommon to find sorrow and either shame, anger, fear, or emptiness occuring intermittantly in the illness. Similarly, one may observe intense expressions of love and awe in the patients who have joy as their primary emotion. In bipolar disorder there may be longer or shorter periods of depression followed by a period of elation. The transition from one to the other may be abrupt or gradual, or it may be punctuated by periods of euthymia. In some instances one of the two states may be brief and/or mild in its severity.

Schizophrenic disorders disturb every aspect of mental functioning and are characterized by a splitting of thinking from emotion. Two major disturbances of emotion are seen. One is a loss of emotional tonus; the other is a concomitant loss of emotional responsiveness or an inappropriateness of emotional expression. The loss of emotional tonus usually manifests itself in a loss of will. The person cannot be motivated into activity. The loss of emotional responsivity gives rise to what is called emotional flatness. In the schizophrenic patient there is usually a loss of both emotional tonus and responsivity, whereas in the major affective disorder of the depressed type there is no loss of emotional tonus. In schizophrenia the emotional inappropriateness is mainfest in the expression of the wrong emotion in response to a stimulus or in the partial expression of an emotion, or even in the simultaneous expression of parts of two emotions. This latter phenomenon is called emotional ambivalence.

In organic brain disease disturbances in intensity, duration, and appropriateness of emotion can occur. Patients with delirium may be extremely fearful, angry, sorrowful, or even joyful. It is not uncommon to see patients with delirium frightened or angered to the point of defending themselves by their hallucinations or delusions, or they may be quite amused by the conversations or behavior of hallucinated persons or animals. In dementia there may be a blunting of emotional expression or its replacement with jocularity. Depression and anxiety sometimes occur early in the course of dementing diseases, especially if the person is aware of his loss of mental capacity. In other patients an inability to modulate emotions may result in sudden outbursts of anger, progressing to rage or exaggerated expressions of fear, sorrow, or joy. Some persons who have had encephalitis between the ages of 5 and 15 are particularly susceptible to outbursts of rage to the point of becoming homicidal. This may occur occasionally in persons with dementia.

Epileptics are believed to be unusually susceptible to emotional dyscontrol. There is, however, no scientific evidence to support this contention.

Finally, it is important to recognize that all persons can be stressed to the point of developing transitory emotional disorders. Life's problems cause anxiety that may temporarily interfere with living. Grief is a normal response to the loss of a loved one, whether it be by divorce or death. If one accumulates enough stress within a limited period of time, symptoms will develop. Symptoms that occur with any specific stress are dependent on the significance of the stress to the individual and the coping mechanisms for the specific stress. It is true, of course, that some individuals have low thresholds for stress and thus respond to seemingly minor problems, whereas others have high thresholds and manage overwhelming problems without decompensation. (*See* STRESS.)

Christianity and Emotion. In contrast to the Stoics, who viewed emotion as irrational, and Epicureans, who acquiesced to the inevitability of emotion, Jesus realistically faced the role of emotion in human life and provided guidelines to control negative and facilitate positive emotion. The remarkable message in his teaching is that love is the most powerful positive emotion and anger the most powerful negative emotion. He understood that love drew men together in harmony and that anger drove them apart in strife. He further understood that these two emotions were antithetical and that the existence of one precluded the occurrence of the other. He taught, therefore, that we are to love God, our neighbor, and one another. He knew that we would have an inherent love for our children and spouse and used them as an example of how we should love other persons.

The language of the Bible describes how love is an installation of persons in one another. A psychospiritual union occurs in love that creates various degrees of oneness—the greatest being the total union of God's Spirit with our spirit and the total union that is to occur in marriage as man and woman become one. To emphasize this union Jesus said that he and the Father would come and live *in* us if we lived (abided) in him. The same language was used to describe the indwelling Holy Spirit received at Pentecost. As God is considered to be love, a person is given an emotional tonus of love when he receives Christ into his life.

The Bible has many instructions that help persons to cognitively structure their emotional life. It was noted earlier that emotion does not exist by itself but is always attached to ideas. Therefore, the command to love becomes significant if ideas have love cathected to them. Likewise, the commands to not be angry or hate also become effective if love is cathected to them. But people cannot avoid being angry, for they are human, and so a derivative of God's love was given so that persons could decathect anger from ideas and replace it with love. This derivative was forgiveness (John 20:23). As God is the final judge, only he can forgive; so it is that true forgiveness is possessed only by those in whom God lives.

Unpleasant emotions are also addressed. Sorrow is to be overcome by the promise of eternal life; fear by the knowledge that God attends to our every need and watches over and protects us; emptiness by his glory and the wonder of his love; shame by the acceptance of our inadequacy and the forgiveness of our sin. Jealousy is destroyed by the trust that we have for others when we love them rightly. Other less frequently experienced unpleasant emotions are also dealt with in the teaching of Jesus.

Our Lord also recognized the need to control the biological drives with their behavioral concomitants, which we have described as emotions. To control them he provided attitudinal guidelines that call forth suitable inhibiting emotions to prevent inappropriate expression, and suitable exciting emotions to facilitate appropriate expression.

Paul addressed emotional life with equal vigor. He taught that the control of biological drives as well as the more specific emotions is only accomplished by the office of the indwelling Holy Spirit, who provides power to effectuate right values. Paul provided practical guidelines for the avoidance or control of unpleasant emotional expression as well as direction on how to resolve the consequences of its expression. Finally, he emphasized the role of forgiveness in the resolution of damaging emotional interactions.

Only in Christianity is man's emotional life given such a place of prominence. God certainly recognized that love, joy, and awe had to be the predominant emotions if persons were to have happiness, so he gave us himself that this might be accomplished.

References

Gellhorn, E., & Loofbourrow, G. N. *Emotions and emotional disorders: A neurophysiological study.* New York: Harper & Row, 1963.

James, W. *The principles of psychology* (2 vols.). New York: H. Holt, 1890.

Lindsley, D. B. Emotion. In S. S. Stevens (Ed.), *Handbook of experimental psychology.* New York: Wiley-Interscience, 1951.

Wilson, W. P., & Nashold, B. S. The neurophysiology of affect. *Diseases of the Nervous System,* 1972, *33,* 13–19.

Additional Reading

Eccles, J. C. *The human psyche.* New York: Springer International, 1980.

W. P. WILSON

Emotional Insulation. An unconscious process in which the ego seeks to avoid tensions through reduced emotional involvement. When a situation is perceived as threatening pain, disappointment, or extreme anxiety, the individual responds by withdrawal into a protective passivity. This may be seen in the concentration camp prisoner who loses all conscious hope, becoming resigned and apathetic. He becomes a passive recipient of any treatment or punishment given him, rather than endure the emotional pain of continual frustration and debasement.

See DEFENSE MECHANISMS.

Empathy. The contemporary usage of this term grows out of a heritage rich with varied meanings. The Greek concept of *em-pathein,* "animation of the inanimate," can be traced to Aristotle. The German *enfuhlung* referred to an aesthetic response to a work of art until the beginning of the twentieth century, when Lipps and Wundt applied the term to a basic psychological process. This usage was translated by Titchener with the English word *empathy* meaning "feeling into."

Although therapists such as Freud, Reik, and Sullivan discussed empathy, Rogers was the first to make it a major therapeutic concept. Rogers's emphasis on empathy as "accurate perception of another's internal frame of reference" was amended by Truax to explicitly include "verbal facility in communicating this understanding to the other" (Hackney, 1978). Empathy is related to sympathy by the same

Greek root, *pathos,* "suffering" (e.g., Heb. 2:18), but differs in that sympathy entails harmony or agreement in feelings. Compassion, derived from the Latin root *pati,* "suffering," differs from empathy by stressing sorrow for another's misfortune and one's desire to alleviate the other's pain (cf. Matt. 9:36).

The natural occurrence of empathy provides the background for its function in therapy. Most theorists hold that humans have automatic mimicry and visceral responses to others' expressions of emotions. An infant's ability is reinforced as it enjoys nurturant parents' responsiveness to it. A child grows to recognize similarities between its own and others' experiences. Understanding arises from both nonverbal and verbal cues, with the latter becoming a primary channel for adults. Mature empathy includes cognitive analysis of another's experience. Social philosophers have long considered such empathy to be a basic prosocial motivation and bond.

Most therapists agree that empathy helps in understanding a client and building a working rapport. Rogers's (1957) distinctive claim was that a therapist's attitudes of empathy, genuineness, and positive regard for the client were necessary and sufficient for client change and growth. Empathy was said to facilitate the client's self-exploration and resolution of conflicted feelings. Although Rogerian, or client-centered (person-centered), therapists were to show nonjudgmental acceptance of clients' feelings, it became apparent that skilled practitioners used considerable psychological judgment in selecting which part of clients' messages to show empathy for. Thus therapists reinforced clients' examining certain deeper issues and feelings.

Counselor education often includes training in empathy skills—i.e., perceiving others' experience and communicating that understanding. Exposure to interviewing begins to expand one's awareness. Role playing with feedback gives one the experience of being in another's shoes. Method acting can reawaken one's emotional experiences as clues to others' similar reactions. Supervisors can identify trainees' hesitations and encourage them to attend to feelings which are avoided in social conversations but must be recognized in therapy. Supervisory feedback can also help distinguish one's experience from a client's and thus reduce distortion from projection or attribution of one's views to the client. Communicating empathic understanding includes nonverbal and verbal messages. Verbal responses include reflecting, paraphrasing, restating or accenting, and summarizing main points of another's message. A therapist's disclosure of similar experiences should be done cautiously. The phrase "I understand how you feel" may be presumptuous and risks clients' retorting "You do not!" The common expression "That must make you feel . . . " is also of limited value in that it reinforces the misconception that outside factors decisively determine people's reactions.

The concept and use of empathy continue to develop. Matching client language and characteristic ways of perceiving the world is receiving increased attention. Visual, auditory, and kinesthetic perceptions expressed with phrases such as "I see," "I hear," and "I feel" may be best responded to with similar terms and imagery (Harman & O'Neill, 1981). In group and family work the therapist's empathy can identify interactive patterns shown by collective behavior but understood only partially by the individuals involved.

Research confirms therapist empathy is correlated with client self-exploration and improvement of disturbed clients. However, empathy research raises some doubts. First, research has not supported the belief that empathy facilitates outcomes with normal clients facing developmental concerns (Hackney, 1978). Second, measures such as Truax's Accurate Empathy Scale have been found to have questionable validity and reliability. Third, the sufficiency of empathy, positive regard, and genuineness for client improvement has not been consistently demonstrated (Matarazzo, 1971). Other theories suggest empathic reflection of feelings should be supplemented by intervention and instruction covering beliefs and behavior.

References

Hackney, H. The evolution of empathy. *Personnel and Guidance Journal*, 1978, *57*(1), 35–38.
Harman, R., & O'Neill, C. Neurolinguistic programming for counselors. *Personnel and Guidance Journal*, 1981, *59*(7), 449–453.
Matarazzo, R. Research on the teaching and learning of psychotherapeutic skills. In A. B. Bergin & S. L. Garfield (Eds.), *Handbook of Psychotherapy and behavior change: An empirical analysis.* New York: Wiley, 1971.
Rogers, C. The necessary and sufficient conditions of therapeutic personality change. *Journal of Consulting Psychology*, 1957, *21*(2), 95–103.

T. J. RUNKEL

Empiricism. A philosophical commitment to sensory experience as the true source of knowledge. This perspective, particularly in the guise of those nineteenth- and twentieth-century movements that have variously been labelled "positivisms," has probably had more influence on contemporary psychology than any other philosophy. The advocates of psychology as science have from the beginning held a conception of science that is deeply influenced by empiricism, a fact that is evident in the high value academic psychology places on experimental research.

Historical Development. Although there were empiricists in ancient times, and although there is a sense of the term in which Aristotle and his followers must be regarded as empiricists, the most influential stream of empiricism must be traced to the British philosophers John Locke, George Berkeley, David Hume, and John Stuart Mill.

Locke (1632–1704), in his famous *Essay Concerning Human Understanding*, mounted a strong attack on the claim that human beings possess any innate ideas or knowledge. In contrast to the rationalist tradition, which held that some truths could be known in an a priori fashion, Locke argued that at birth the mind is like a blank tablet and that experience is the source of all human ideas. He held that sensory experience was the source of simple ideas, which could be combined in various ways by the mind to form complex ideas. Locke believed that our ideas of primary qualities (which included such quantifiable aspects as mass, velocity, size, and shape) corresponded to real qualities in the physical world, while secondary qualities (such as smell and color) were subjective qualities produced by physical bodies when they impact our sensory organs.

Berkeley (1685–1753), an Anglican bishop, extended Locke's ideas in a consistent, if sometimes counterintuitive manner. Berkeley argued that not only do all our ideas come from experience; we only have knowledge of experience. The idea of a material or physical world that exists independently of perception is a useless and even meaningless notion. Berkeley's limitation of knowledge to what is directly experienced contains the seeds of the later positivist suspicion of theoretical, unobservable entities and the demand for operational definitions of terms—though not many have followed Berkeley's mentalistic view of the material world.

Hume (1711–1776) extended Berkeley's skepticism about material substances to the mental realm as well. He challenged the idea that humans experience themselves as a unified soul or ego and claimed that he was only aware of himself as a "bundle of perceptions." Hume also divided all human knowledge into two areas: "relations of ideas" and "matters of fact." Relations of ideas, such as "all bachelors are unmarried males" and "$2+2=4$" can be known with intuitive or deductive certainty because they only concern our own conceptions. All knowledge dealing with matters of fact (i.e., "the earth is round") is grounded in experience and can never be absolutely certain. This distinction clearly underlies the common twentieth-century distinction between analytic or conceptual truths which are grounded in conventional definitions and empirical or synthetic truths which are grounded in experience.

One of Hume's most influential doctrines was his empiricist interpretation of cause and effect. Hume denied that we have knowledge of any real connections between events that are regarded as causally linked. Rather, our knowledge of causality is a knowledge of constant conjunctions, or natural regularities. To know that A causes B is simply to know that A regularly precedes B in our experience. Causal knowledge therefore reduces to knowledge of empirical regularities that must be discovered experimentally.

James Mill (1773–1836) and his more famous son, John Stuart Mill (1806–1873), built on their empiricist predecessors to develop what is called associationist psychology, which was an attempt to develop empirical laws explaining all mental phenomena as the result of the association of basic mental elements. The associationists clearly foreshadowed the dominant view of learning in twentieth-century psychology.

Logical Positivism and Behaviorism. In the twentieth century, empiricist thought has been most strongly represented by the philosophy of logical positivism. Positivism arose in the nineteenth century from such thinkers as Auguste Comte, who developed a view of science which is expressed in his law of three stages. According to Comte all human sciences pass through an early theological stage, through a metaphysical stage, to a final stage of positive science, which consists of knowledge of natural regularities known by experience. Comte's view of the history of science is still influential and can be clearly seen in Skinner (1971).

Twentieth-century logical positivists differed from their nineteenth-century predecessors chiefly in the greater appreciation they had for formal logical techniques. Originating in a group of philosophers who met in Vienna for discussion, the logical positivists put forward the verifiability theory of meaning. In this theory all statements that are not intended as analytic statements (which hold because of definitions) must be empirically verifiable (Ayer, 1936). Their slogan was, "The meaning of a sentence is its method of verification." This led to a program of giving operational definitions of scientific terms and to a suspicion of unobservable, theoretical entities.

Although logical positivism was not the only influence on behavioral psychology, its period of dominance in philosophy coincided with the development of behaviorism in psychology, and the two movements clearly supported each other. The influence of positivism is very clear in the work of psychologists such as Hull, whose conception of science closely follows the hypothetico-deductive method developed by such positivists as Schlick. In this view a genuine scientific theory is one from which testable consequences can be deduced. The general behaviorist emphasis on measurability and on the notion of a purely factual data base also reflects clear empiricist influences. The major nonempiricist influence on behaviorism that accounts for some of the major differences between behaviorism and associationist psychology is the behaviorist acceptance of physicalism.

At least three major tendencies in contemporary psychology, particularly in its behaviorist forms, can be traced to empiricism. These include 1) a rejection of a priori theorizing and suspicion of all theories not experimentally testable; 2) an emphasis on the passivity of the human organism, not in the sense that humans do not operate on their environment, but in the more basic sense that they are ultimately shaped by their environment; 3) an atomistic tendency to explain what is complex in terms of what is simple and what is later in terms of what is earlier. Allport (1955) discusses some of these tendencies and traces them to Locke.

Critical Evaluation. Empiricism, especially in its positivist forms, has suffered much criticism in the latter part of the twentieth century. Much of this criticism is directed to the empiricist view of science and much of it is relevant to psychology.

One area of criticism pertains to the aims of science. The positivist sees science as aiming at predictive power, which centers on the discovery of testable regularities. However, philosophers such as Toulmin (1961) have argued convincingly that science aims at understanding and theoretical intelligibility, not just predictive power. If this is correct, then theorizing has a greater and different role in science than positivists have allowed.

A second area of concern pertains to the nature of experience and observation itself. Many empiricists have spoken of experience as if it involved a simple registering of bare, uninterpreted facts. However, philosophers of science such as Hanson (1958) have stressed that scientific observations are "theory-laden" and that "all seeing is seeing something *as* something." If this is correct, then theory and interpretation cannot simply be *derived* from experience because they are *involved* in experience.

Many of these points have come to focus in Kuhn's influential book, *The Structure of Scientific Revolutions* (1970), which stresses the way in which scientific activity presupposes a shared framework of assumptions, which Kuhn calls a "paradigm." Philosophers who have accepted these ideas, even in modified form, have concluded that scientific theories are holistic systems which make contact with experience selectively and as a whole, and thus that it is harmful to demand that all scientific concepts be operationally defined. With the recognition of the historical character of science and the theory-laden and interpretive character of observation, they have also been forced to recognize the problematic character of verification and falsification, understood as straightforward testing of isolated elements of theory.

References
Ayer, A. J., *Language, truth, and logic.* New York: Oxford University Press, 1936.
Allport, G. *Becoming.* New Haven: Yale University Press, 1955.
Hanson, N. R. *Patterns of discovery.* Cambridge: The University Press, 1958.
Kuhn, T. S. *The structure of scientific revolutions.* (2nd ed.). Chicago: University of Chicago Press, 1970.
Skinner, B. F. *Beyond freedom and dignity.* New York: Knopf, 1971.
Toulmin, S. *Foresight and understanding.* Bloomington: Indiana University Press, 1961.

C. S. EVANS

See PSYCHOLOGY, METHODS OF; PSYCHOLOGY, HISTORY OF.

Encopresis. Functional encopresis is usually defined as incontinence of feces that is not due to organic defect or illness. *DSM-III* gives the following three diagnostic criteria: 1) repeated voluntary or involuntary passage of feces into places not appropriate for that purpose in the individual's own sociocultural setting; 2) at least one such event after the age of 4; and 3) not due to a physical disorder. In this manner functional encopresis is distinguished from encopresis resulting from organic causes, such as an anal fissure, Hirschprung's disease, rectal defect, neurological impairment, or an aganglionic megacolon (Kolb, 1973).

Functional encopresis is further subdivided

into primary and secondary encopresis. It is thought to be primary when a child who has not achieved fecal continence for at least one year reaches the age of 4. Secondary encopresis involves cases where the incontinence has been preceded by at least one continuous year of fecal continence. Thus, by definition primary encopresis begins by age 4, while secondary encopresis usually occurs between the ages of 4 and 8.

It is thought that primary and secondary encopresis generally occur with about the same frequency, although primary encopresis may occur more frequently in the lower socioeconomic classes. Encopresis is more common among males. The overall incidence is estimated to be about 1% of all 5-year-olds. Thus, it is quite rare, and its presence is often disturbing to parent and child alike. On the part of the parent there may be anger, disgust, and acrid recrimination often aimed at the child. The child on the other hand may experience shame, embarrassment, and anxiety. Attempts may be made to hide the problem, causing the child to dispose of the soiled clothing or to hide it in his bedroom. However, when the incontinence is deliberate, more serious psychopathology is suggested.

The etiology of encopresis is unclear. It is generally believed that primary encopresis is due to inadequate or inconsistent toilet training, while secondary encopresis is often the result of psychosocial stress which encourages regressive behavior. Examples of such stressors might be the birth of a sibling, sickness or death in the immediate family, the onset of school, or the separation or divorce of the parents.

While psychoanalytic treatment has had at least minimal success, the most popular treatment utilizes behavioral techniques such as positive reinforcement, modeling, and structured bathroom times. This may also be combined with the use of mineral oil or a very mild laxative in the case of an impacted rectum. Before treatment is initiated, it is mandatory that the child receive a thorough physical examination in order to rule out possible organic etiology. If the condition persists, formal psychological treatment should be considered.

References
Kolb, L. C. *Modern clinical psychiatry (8th ed.).* Philadelphia: Saunders, 1973.

J. D. GUY, JR.

Encounter Groups. A term applied to various types of organized intensive group experiences that became popular, especially in the

United States, in the 1950s. They developed into a significant social movement, peaking in popularity in the late 1960s and continuing in mutated forms. The term eventually achieved a much broader usage. It currently includes group experiences ranging from bizarre, hedonistic experiments in instant group intimacy sponsored by encounter gurus, to interpersonal relations training sponsored by educators and business and marriage enrichment retreats sponsored by churches.

Social Context. The social context of encounter groups has been called the encounter culture (Schutz, 1971). This is distinct from the counter culture which, though part of the same era, was characterized by political dissent and a call for the redistribution of power.

The focus of the encounter culture was the small group experience aimed at interpersonal confrontation, feedback, expression and intensification of feelings, heightened personal awareness, and behavior change. This subculture within American society gathered loyal followers who were antiestablishment to varying degrees and who worked to counteract sexual repression, the depersonalizing influences of industrial society, and the alienation of individuals from self and others. A more positive manifestation of this social force is the human potentials movement, which stresses helping persons realize their fullest individual potential to experience life and relationships and to live out personal uniqueness in creative, fulfilling ways.

As the encounter culture was diffuse, so was its outworking in encounter groups. A similar confusion surrounded the simultaneous development of what were called T-groups. T-groups emerged in Britain and the United States. A major American center was the National Training Laboratories Institute (NTL) at Bethel, Maine, part of the National Education Association. NTL developed T-groups ("T" for training) as a tool for interpersonal relations skills applied to business and education. Its creators made clear distinctions between therapy (making sick people well) and training (making well people better) and ultimately were dismayed that encounter groups, T-groups, and therapy groups blended into one another and even became synonymous in the public mind.

Important factors caused medical and mental health professionals to resist the spread of encounter groups. The absence of research and experimental controls, the failure to screen participants, and the unprofessional zeal of encounter leaders were among these. Propo-

nents presented methods as entirely new, showing a naïveté about history, and the movement lacked the backing of any major establishment such as education, business, or religion. Popular reports of encounter group casualties raised public concern and professional criticism (Maliver, 1973).

Basic Characteristics. Though there were no clear lines distinguishing the varieties of encounter groups, there were vast differences in the way groups operated, in their goals, applications, settings, participants, and methods (Solomon & Berzon, 1972).

Most groups were composed of 8 to 12 persons. Some groups were leaderless—at least at the outset—and others had leaders who tightly controlled the events. Time spans for encounter groups ranged from single 2- to 3-hour sessions, to multiple sessions, to the "marathon," which might continue nonstop for 12 to 36 hours with the same participants.

What took place in the groups varied according to sponsor and members. The groups might be described in three broad categories, though mutating was increasingly an obstacle to definition. First, there was a variety of radical encounter experiences for sale. While not all programs at Esalen Institute, Big Sur, California, could be described as radical, Esalen still became their best-known source. Its personal growth programs included nude swimming pool encounters, Sufi tales, body sandwiches, vomit training, experiences of loving the body or leaving it, ski encounter, rapture workshops, yoga, massage, and seminars in sex, celibacy, passion, and trance states. These encounter groups attracted persons who often sought out one intensive experience after another. They were called encounter addicts and groupies because of their pursuit of the "group grope." Reports of radical experiments aroused the suspicion of many citizens, lay and professional. Particularly, persons with traditional values and religious commitments came to regard encounter groups negatively and even as a threat to both church and society.

Second, there was a tamer and more benign use of small group experiences which came under the encounter label. These groups were used in business, education, and in nonprofit organizations as a tool for improving interpersonal relations and promoting organizational development. NTL and other centers refined group techniques for these purposes. There tended to be more control of group experiences by leaders, more focused goals, and more natural or designed selection of participants.

Third, the small groups movement arose in American religion in the same era, and "encounter," though less descriptive of religious groups, became a designation for these also. The popular marriage enrichment program promoted by Roman Catholics is still called Marriage Encounter (Bosco, 1972). Small group prayer and Bible studies, combining discussion with self-disclosure and personal caring, flourished in the Christian community during the encounter era, and these gatherings continue in widespread use. Most church-sponsored group experiences have been clearly tied to traditional values and have been aimed at enhancing corporate and individual spirituality. Many participants testify to personal renewal as these groups have taken on an ecumenical character, drawing in persons from many denominational backgrounds, all in search of a lively and relevant experience of shared faith.

It is interesting that a majority of American Protestant theological seminary catalogs listed group interpersonal experiences as part of the curriculum or as voluntary student opportunities during the late 1960s (Klingberg, 1973). Earlier, such offerings were rare in these graduate schools, and by 1980 the catalogs again reflected far less use of small group encounter experiences. This pattern in a peak usage of groups is similar to that in secular education and in the encounter culture.

Encounter Group Process. Despite the generic use of the term *encounter* and the diversity of group experiences to which it refers, it is possible to summarize the phases of an encounter group. Rogers (1970) described 15 stages in the experience. These stages are observed, not prescribed, as the relatively open agenda of the encounter group unfolds. 1) A period of polite surface interaction and confusion about who is in charge; 2) showing of public selves, hiding of private selves, and resistance to expression of feelings; 3) cautious expression of some past feelings; 4) some negative feelings expressed, often toward the facilitator for not giving leadership; 5) negotiation of negative feelings and exploration of personally meaningful materials, with a sense of responsibility for the group experience; 6) immediate feelings, positive and negative, expressed toward other group members; 7) helpful and constructive dealing with pain and suffering of group members; 8) increased acceptance of self and feelings; 9) impatience with defenses of members, and the cracking of façades; 10) feedback given and received as members learn about their impact on others; 11) confrontation and conflicts; 12) attempts to help one another outside the group meetings; 13) feelings of being totally with and for one another; 14) expression of positive feelings and closeness; 15) positive behavioral changes.

The sense of leaderlessness often experienced and objected to in encounter groups should not suggest that there were not specific techniques in general use. In fact, a repertoire of group exercises came to be expected by purchasers of encounter adventures. These included the blind walk, in which persons wandered among the group, eyes closed and arms outstretched for touching. Another trust exercise was carried out by a small circle with one member, blinded, in the center. The blinded person would relax, without verbal communication, and fall toward the circle, where others would catch her and break the fall to prevent injury. A nonverbal anger exercise was the hand-push. A member could express anger by pushing his hands against the hands of another person, using that force to express the degree of outrage toward that person.

Perspective. As encounter groups came into extensive use, there was little to guide the public, general institutions, or churches. The zealous proponents of encounter behaved like prophets ushering in a new era for humankind. The severest critics warned that the encounter movement would undermine civilization. The enthusiastic testimonies of participants conflicted with reports of group casualties. Through all of this very little was done on a sufficient scale or with adequate care to give reliable guidance on the movement.

Two studies are of particular significance in gaining a perspective on encounter groups. One is a massive research project by Lieberman, Yalom, and Miles (1973). The other is a historical, theological review by Oden (1972), which is of special interest to the Christian community.

Encounter Groups: First Facts (Lieberman et al., 1973) was published after a detailed, carefully designed study of 17 different encounter groups (T-groups, Gestalt, psychodrama, transactional analysis, Esalen eclectic, marathons, etc.). Extensive use of rating scales attempted to measure the outcome of group experiences, including change according to self, leaders, and other participants; types of change; maintainance of change (six to eight months later); and differences among groups. Findings of the study were many, and the interrelationships of various factors were explored. Somewhat over 60% of participants saw themselves, immediately following the experiences, as having benefited; but six months later 10 to 20% of these were less enthusiastic about the changes. The groups showed a modest positive impact, although the amount of this impact was much less than suggested by supporters or participants. The groups differed from one another significantly: some were innocuous, others highly productive, and still others were, on balance, destructive, doing more harm than good.

Oden (1972) calls the intensive group experience "the new pietism." His perspective of history is very different from that of the developers of contemporary group procedures. Among the earliest connections seen by mental health professionals is Pratt's group treatment of tuberculosis patients beginning in 1905. Others trace the movement to World War II psychiatric treatment of casualties, when circumstances demanded group treatment (Bennis, 1960). T-group proponents root its emergence in the 1940s. Oden takes exception to the accepted idea that the encounter group is an invention of this century. Instead, it is his hypothesis that the encounter movement is traceable to the 1600s and 1700s and the dissenting pietism of Jewish and Protestant traditions.

Oden also criticizes encounter practitioners who portray the movement as the inculcation of Eastern philosophy and practices into the West. We remain Western, and the encounter movement is a Western phenomenon. Oden ingeniously discloses the career links among Perls and Reich (innovators in the encounter movement), Buber (Jewish philosopher), and Tillich (Protestant theologian)—all of whom were in Frankfurt in the first half of this century. Rogers (American psychologist and encounter proponent), Lewin (group process researcher), and others were influenced by this group. The encounter movement flourished in America, but its leadership may be traceable to the earlier era in Frankfurt.

From Oden's point of view, the contemporary Frankfurt group was related to what preceded it by 300 years. Then, in the same city, was launched the pietistic movement under Philip Jacob Spener and August Hermann Francke. The modern American encounter movement is strikingly similar, Oden proposes, to the small gatherings of pietists advancing their "religion of the heart," feeling and experience, the relevance of faith for life, and the practice of love, confrontation, confession, and forgiveness—in small groups.

There are Christians and Christian groups who make efforts to distance themselves from the contemporary encounter movement. Yet it may be that the spirit of, need for, and practices of encounter are rooted in the rich ecumenical, practical, and experiential faith of classical pietism (as distinguished from the deteriorating pietism of the nineteenth and twentieth centuries). This seems consistent with the testimonials to the renewal of active faith among persons, neighborhoods, and churches who frequently claim that this renewal is the result of rediscovery in the shared experience of small groups.

References

Bennis, W. G. A critique of group psychotherapy research. *International Journal of Group Psychotherapy*, 1960, *10*, 63–67.

Bosco, A. *Marriage encounter*. St. Meinrad, Ind.: Abbey Press, 1972.

Klingberg, H. An evaluation of sensitivity training effects on self-actualization, purpose in life, and religious attitudes of theological students. *Journal of Psychology and Theology*, 1973, *1*(4), 31–39.

Lieberman, M. A., Yalom, I. D., & Miles, M. B. *Encounter groups: First facts*. New York: Basic Books, 1973.

Maliver, B. L. *The encounter game*. New York: Stein & Day, 1973.

Oden, T. C. *The intensive group experience: The new pietism*. Philadelphia: Westminster, 1972.

Rogers, C. R. *Carl Rogers on encounter groups*. New York: Harper & Row, 1970.

Schutz, W. C. *Here comes everybody: Bodymind and encounter culture*. New York: Harper & Row, 1971.

Solomon, L. N., & Berzon, B. (Eds.). *New perspectives on encounter groups*. San Francisco: Jossey-Bass, 1972.

Additional Readings

Burton, A. (Ed.). *Encounter*. San Francisco: Jossey-Bass, 1969.

Gustaitis, R. *Turning on*. New York: Macmillan, 1968.

Houts, P. S., & Serber, M. (Eds.). *After the turn on, what?* Champaign, Ill.: Research Press, 1972.

H. KLINGBERG, JR.

Endomorph. In Sheldon's system of constitutional types the endomorph is a person whose body is soft, round, and flabby in appearance. This body type, comparable to Kretschmer's pyknic type, is contrasted to the ECTOMORPH and MESOMORPH types. Sheldon's research suggested that endomorphs tend to be warm and affectionate.

See CONSTITUTIONAL PERSONALITY THEORY.

Enuresis. Involuntary discharge of urine, most commonly during sleep. According to DSM-III, in order to receive a formal diagnosis of functional enuresis, the following diagnostic criteria must be met: 1) repeated involuntary voiding of urine by day or at night; 2) at least two such events per month for children between the ages of 5 and 6, and at least one event per month for older children; 3) the disorder cannot be due to a physical disorder, such as diabetes or a seizure disorder.

Functional enuresis is subdivided into primary enuresis, where there has not been a preceding period of urinary continence of at least one continuous year, and secondary enuresis, where there has been at least one year of urinary continence preceding its onset. Enuresis is most often nocturnal, occurring during sleep, although a child may evidence diurnal enuresis, occurring during waking hours, or both nocturnal and diurnal enuresis. Estimated prevalence is as follows: at age 5, 7% for boys and 3% for girls; at age 10, 3% for boys and 2% for girls; at age 18, 1% for boys and almost nonexistent for girls. By definition the onset of primary enuresis is age 5, while most cases of secondary enuresis occur between the ages of 5 and 8. Most children with this disorder become continent by adolescence, although some rare cases have continued into adulthood.

It is typically believed that primary enuresis results from inadequate, delayed, or inconsistent toilet training, delayed development of bladder musculature, or impaired bladder ability to adapt to urinary filling. Secondary enuresis is thought to result from a variety of psychosocial stressors, including the birth of a sibling, sickness or death in the immediate family, marital discord and/or divorce, the onset of school, and hospitalization prior to age 4. In addition, there is a large body of psychoanalytic literature which attributes functional enuresis to a variety of early factors, such as the oedipal conflict, lack of proper identification with the same-sex parent, and sibling rivalry (Kolb, 1973).

In most cases of nocturnal enuresis, the most common form, the urination occurs during the first third of the night, during non-REM sleep. The child awakes with no memory of having urinated and with no memory of a dream. In other, more unusual cases it has been found that the urination occurs during non-REM sleep typical of later phases of deep sleep, preceded by marked electroencephalographic arousal (Ritvo, 1970).

Enuresis is often the cause of shame, humiliation, embarrassment, and social isolation. Such children may avoid overnight visits to friends, camping trips, and so forth. The individual's self-esteem may suffer as a direct result of social ostracism by peers, and anger, punishment, and rejection by parents. Fortunately, treatment interventions have been developed which have been quite successful. In particular, behavioral techniques utilizing classical conditioning paradigms, such as the "bell and pad"

apparatus available in some department stores, have been especially successful. With this device urination completes an electrical circuit which results in the sounding of a buzzer or alarm, awakening the child, who then immediately stops urinating and arises and goes to the bathroom to finish voiding. It is thought that the feeling of fullness in the bladder immediately preceding urination is then paired with arousal and appropriate voiding, causing the child to eventually awaken prior to urinating. Other useful techniques have included the use of low doses of Tofranil, an antidepressive drug whose anticholinergic side effects often reduce the likelihood of nocturnal enuresis. Finally, more traditional psychodynamic forms of psychotherapy have been somewhat successful over extended periods of treatment. If the condition persists into early adolescence, professional psychological treatment should be sought.

References
Kolb, L. C. *Modern clinical psychiatry* (8th ed.). Philadelphia: Saunders, 1973.
Ritvo, E. R. Contributions of sleep research to understanding and treatment of enuresis. *International Psychiatric Clinician*, 1970, 7(2), 117–122.

J. D. GUY, JR.

Environmental Psychology. A subfield of social psychology associated with the study of the ways in which people are affected by their environments. For example, environmental psychologists are interested in the portable, invisible bubble we all carry around with us called personal space. They have demonstrated that the size and shape of this space varies as a function of the culture, sex, and personality of the individual. In addition, by keeping people at a distance we are able to control and express the level of intimacy of a relationship.

Environmental psychologists are also interested in the psychological impact of such natural phenomena as weather. Admissions to mental hospitals (north of the equator) peak during summer and spring. Sunshine often makes people more helpful, but a long hot summer facilitates aggression. And there is evidence that, despite the term *lunacy* and the many portrayals found in the media, the lunar cycle is not linked to emotional disorders.

Our man-made environment can also affect us psychologically. The architectural design of some low-cost housing projects has made them virtually uninhabitable. The colors blue and green do have a calming effect. And the arrangement of a room can profoundly affect the extent to which we feel crowded.

It is important to note that throughout these findings, and environmental psychology in general, there runs a common thread: the distinction between subjective and objective reality. Perhaps this distinction is clearest in the area of crowding. Research results have forced investigators to distinguish between physical density and the perception of crowding. Having a large number of people in a room does not guarantee feelings of being crowded. A well-attended party may lead to a sense of anticipation and success rather than uncomfortableness and a desire to withdraw. Environmental psychologists, therefore, explicitly or implicitly emphasize subjective experience. Further, research has demonstrated that of all subjective experiences, perhaps the most debilitating is the perception of loss of control. Feelings of helplessness have been linked to everything from feeling crowded to dying (Seligman, 1975).

Reference

Seligman, M. E. P. *Helplessness.* San Francisco: W. H. Freeman, 1975.

R. L. Bassett

See Social Psychology.

Envy. A bad feeling stirred up because of the presence of something good in another person but lacking in oneself. This emotion has received considerable attention from the authors of Scripture, theologians, and psychologists. A surprising degree of unanimity characterizes both the secular and sacred views of envy; namely, envy is universal in its occurrence, is destructive in its impact on the human personality, and can become a dominant, invasive emotion if left unchecked. While not a part of the well-known pantheon of vices such as greed, wrath, or jealousy, envy is a powerful emotion that deserves more attention than it usually receives.

Envy has several components. First, at least two persons are involved: the envier and the person being envied. The presence of envy can be completely unknown by those around the envier, since no verbal communication regarding the envy must occur in order for it to be present. Second, the envier must be aware of some feature or facet of another's life which he regards as good and which he feels is missing in his own life. In other words, envy can only occur when a person perceives himself or herself in a position inferior to another. Hence the issue of self-esteem is related to the problem of envy. Third, the envier experiences a sadness that the missing feature is not present in his or her own life. When envy is a major feature of one's own personality, life becomes a constant, dreary calculation of how others are better, and the self is saddened because of it.

Emulation is the positive counterpart of envy (Davidson, 1908). Emulation similarly involves at least two people and a sense of inferiority or lack on the part of one of the two. But the component of sadness is replaced by a desire to obtain the missing feature of life by achievement or growth. Emulation sees the other person as a friend; envy sees the other as a rival. Envy is selfish; emulation is constructive and geared toward change. Envy often wishes harm to the other or rejoices if bad fortune befalls the envied person; emulation has a positive force to it.

Authors disagree on the precise difference between envy and Jealousy. Although they are related emotions, jealousy often involves three persons, is based in fear, and includes the strong desire to possess exclusively the item or person of desire. Jealousy is wanting to hold on to what one already has, and envy is a sadness regarding what one does not have (Walker, 1939).

In the Old Testament envy is described as a powerful enemy (Prov. 27:4) and a destructive force (Job 5:2; Prov. 14:30). The insidious emotion of envy was powerful in the life of Saul (1 Sam. 18:9), Rachel (Gen. 30:1), and the brothers of Joseph (Gen. 37:11). (Many versions substitute "jealousy" for the proper "envy" in these passages.) In the New Testament the verb form for envy occurs one time, in Galatians 5:26, where the exhortation to avoid envy is strongly given. Envy appears in lists of the acts of a sinful nature (Gal. 5:21; Rom. 1:29; Titus 3:3; 1 Tim. 6:4, and 1 Peter 2:1). Christian ministry can be prompted by envy (Phil. 1:15), and envy was a driving emotion behind the actions of those who called for the death of Jesus (Mark 15:10).

Catholic theologians have regarded envy as a capital (deadly or cardinal) sin because it leads a person to other sins (Meagher, O'Brien, & Aherne, 1979). Because it was regarded as a cardinal sin it was treated extensively by Dante and Chaucer. Envy is described as a sin because it is opposed to benevolence, an essential ingredient in charity (Herbst, 1967).

In psychology the theoreticians who have had the greatest interest in the emotion of envy are those of psychoanalytic persuasion. Envy was early recognized as a harmful and detrimental emotion by psychoanalysts. Freud gave extensive treatment to the concept of envy in his theory of penis envy as a factor in the development of the female personality, a concept which many recent authors dispute extensively. Freud also saw envy as a powerful factor in the sociopsychological development of a sense of community. More recent analysts such as Klein (1957) postulate a very early developmental origin for the emotion. Klein feels that an infant receives a supply of mother's milk with either a sense of gratitude (necessary for the later task of love) or with a sense of envy (the base for later pathology).

VanKaam (1972) has aptly integrated the destructiveness of envy in a moral sense (as described in Scripture) with the psychologically harmful impact of envy as documented by the analysts.

References

Davidson, W. L. Envy and emulation. In J. Hastings (Ed.), *Encyclopedia of religion and ethics.* New York: Scribner's, 1908.
Herbst, W. Envy. Editorial Staff at Catholic University of America (Eds.), In *New Catholic encyclopedia.* New York: McGraw-Hill, 1967.
Klein, M. *Envy and gratitude: A study of unconscious sources.* New York: Basic Books, 1957.
Meagher, P. K., O'Brien, T. C., & Aherne C. M. (Eds.). *Encyclopedic dictionary of religion.* Philadelphia: Sisters of St. Joseph of Philadelphia, 1979.
vanKamm, A. *Envy and originality.* Garden City; N.Y.; Doubleday, 1972.
Walker, W. L. Envy. In J. Orr (Ed.), *The international standard Bible encyclopaedia.* (Rev. ed.). Grand Rapids: Eerdmans, 1939.

J. R. Beck

Epilepsy. A neurological disorder which manifests itself in the form of recurrent seizures. Seizures are episodic disruptions of functioning which are the products of abnormal brain wave patterns. In particular, seizures may appear in connection with a paroxysm of synchronized overactivity of a group of nerve cells in the brain. Seizures may take a variety of forms ranging from major convulsions, through minor alterations and peculiarities in behavior, to attacks which are so small that they would never be noticed and are only known to the individual experiencing them.

Epilepsy is extremely common, and it occurs in at least 1% of the general population (Epilepsy Foundation of America, 1975). The International Classification of Epileptic Seizures (Commission on Classification and Terminology of the International League Against Epilepsy, 1981) is the most widely recognized classification of seizures. According to this system there are two basic types of seizures. The first is partial seizures, which are those attacks involving only a part of the brain at the outset. There are two basic types of partial seizures. Simple partial seizures involve limited motor movements and/or somatosensory impressions, but there is no impairment of consciousness and the person is usually able to hear and to talk normally during the seizure. Complex partial seizures on the other hand involve at least some impairment in consciousness, either at the beginning of the seizure or as the seizure continues. Individuals with complex partial seizures may demonstrate repetitive movements called automotisms, such as fingering their clothing, wandering about, or performing other nonpurposeful actions. Partial seizures of either type may progress to involve the entire brain and to result in convulsions. Partial seizures are extremely common in adults with epilepsy and are found in perhaps 60 to 70% of this group.

Generalized seizures are the second basic type recognized by the International Classification of Epileptic Seizures. Absence seizures (previously called petit mal) are short episodes of loss of awareness which appear without warning and which are most commonly seen in children. The child may simply stare momentarily, or there may be slight motor movement. Tonic-clonic seizures (previously called grand mal) represent convulsions which may manifest themselves initially with rigidity of the entire body (tonic phase) followed by rhythmic and frequent violent jerking of all body parts (clonic phase). Other types of generalized seizures also exist.

In Christian circles epilepsy has often been confused with demon possession or demonic influence. A review of relevant biblical passages does not reveal a single instance in which it is unquestionably true that an individual had epilepsy, and in fact the Authorized Version does not use the term. Probably the instance most commonly thought to indicate epilepsy is that of the healing of a boy which appears in Matthew 17, Mark 9, and Luke 9. Some of the behaviors described, particularly in the passage in Mark, could be consistent with a tonic-clonic seizure, but in view of Christ's response a spiritual rather than a neurological explanation appears most likely. It is, of course, entirely possible that demons could manifest themselves in violent ways which to some extent could mimic epilepsy in certain cases. However, it is important to differentiate clearly between these two types of problems and not to conclude that the presence of one implies the other.

Individuals with suspected epilepsy should be referred to physicians, preferably to neurologists, for evaluation and treatment. Evaluation typically consists of the taking of a history, a physical neurological examination including basic testing of mental, motor, and perceptual skills, and typically an EEG (see ELECTROENCEPHALOGRAPHY). The establishment of a diagnosis is routinely followed by treatment with antiepileptic medications such as Dilantin, phenobarbital, Tegretol, Depakene, and Mysoline. It is of great importance that such medication be taken regularly. If this is not done, a condition of continuous seizures may emerge (status epilepticus) that may result in death. Furthermore, although the person may feel some side effects of the medication, these tend to resolve over time, and the effects of seizures are routinely worse than the effects of medication given at customary doses. If a tonic-clonic seizure does not resolve in approximately 5–10 minutes, emergency medical treatment is indicated. Shorter seizures which resolve on their own typically require no medical treatment unless the attack recurs or unless an injury has been sustained.

Epilepsy is a definite indication that at least at the time of a seizure the brain is not functioning well. Even between seizures the majority of individuals with epilepsy demonstrate abnormalities on their EEGs. Since the brain is the basis for all mental skills, one might expect mental skills to be at least somewhat decreased between seizures, and this has been found to be the case in many instances (Epilepsy Foundation of America, 1975). When abilities are decreased, performance in life is also likely to be at less than the expected levels and a person's coping abilities are also frequently decreased. Because of this, a number of emotional and psychosocial problems frequently appear. These have been described along with resources to help deal with these concerns (Sands, 1982). Such resources include a number of organizations that help the person with epilepsy to find appropriate medical care, medication at minimal cost, employment, insurance, information concerning epilepsy, and support groups for people with seizures. The Epilepsy Foundation of America provides all these services and is a substantial source of assistance to people with seizures. In instances where individuals with epilepsy seem impaired in terms of functioning, a NEUROPSYCHOLOGICAL ASSESSMENT is desirable.

References

Commission on Classification and Terminology of the International League Against Epilepsy. Proposal for revised clinical and electroencephalographic classification of epileptic seizures. *Epilepsia*, 1981, *22*, 489–501.

Epilepsy Foundation of America. *Basic statistics on the epilepsies*. Philadelphia: Davis, 1975.
Sands, H. (Ed.). *Epilepsy: A handbook for the mental health professional*. New York: Brunner/Mazel, 1982.

C. B. DODRILL

Erhard Seminar Training. *See* EST.

Erickson, Milton Hyland (1901–1980). Erickson was born with a number of congenital sensory-perceptual difficulties that led him to perceive reality in a rather different fashion from most normal children. In addition to struggling with these difficulties he also was called upon to manage the painful effects of polio, which struck him at ages 17 and 51. These effects left him without clear speech, in much pain, and unable to walk.

It was probably this combination of liabilities in conjunction with an iron determination to rehabilitate himself that led him to become one of the real pioneers in hypnosis as well as the field now known as neurolinguistic programming. Over a span of more than 50 years Erickson published literally hundreds of scientific articles and co-authored a variety of books. (See Rossi, 1980, for a collection of many of his works.) He became something of a guru because of his innovative, intuitive, and authoritative uses of language in the area of hypnotherapy. He took particular pride in being able to subtly and indirectly intervene in the lives of individuals considered too resistant to work well in psychotherapy. Hence, his approach to therapy has often been described as utilizing indirect applications of hypnosis. Erickson's careful and colorful use of language wove metaphors, created double binds, and presented other paradoxical interventions that puzzled the conscious mind and allowed other parts of the client's person to become therapeutically mobilized.

During his amazingly productive professional life, Erickson founded and edited *The American Journal of Clinical Hypnosis;* was president of the American Society of Clinical Hypnosis; and was life fellow of the American Psychiatric Association and American Psychopathological Association.

Reference

Rossi, E. L. (Ed.). *The collected papers of Milton H. Erickson on Hypnosis* (4 vols.). New York: Irvington Publishers, 1980.

V. L. SHEPPERSON

See HYPNOTHERAPY, INDIRECT; UTILIZATION TECHNIQUE.

Erikson, Erik Homburger (1902–). Psychoanalyst Erik Erikson, born in Germany, was educated in the traditional manner for the child of a middle-class family. An important part of his early experience was traveling throughout Europe during his adolescence— a period in his life he later described as his "moratorium." His developmental theory was to include moratorium as an important aspect of the adolescent stage.

Before committing himself to a career, Erikson spent much time painting. Because he had obvious talent, he gained a minor reputation as a promising artist. Portraits of children became his speciality. A key point in his life came when he was commissioned to paint the portrait of the child of an Austrian doctor, Sigmund Freud. This work allowed him time for lengthy, informal discussions with Freud. Within a few weeks Freud invited Erikson to join the Psychoanalytic Institute of Vienna. He did so and focused on the analysis of children, under the direction of Anna Freud. His moratorium had come to an end.

Following the completion of his training in Vienna in 1933, Erikson emigrated to the United States. He began a private practice in Boston as that city's first child psychoanalyst. He also held positions at Massachusetts General Hospital and Harvard Medical School. He served from 1936 to 1939 as a research associate in psychiatry at Yale, and during this time he also worked with Henry Murray at Harvard. He then moved to positions at the University of California and to the Austen Riggs Clinic in Massachusetts, where at the same time he held an appointment as visiting professor with the University of Pittsburgh School of Medicine.

Soon after studying children on a Sioux reservation in South Dakota and on a Yurok reservation in California, Erikson published *Childhood and Society*, an influential book that helped establish him as a writer of literary as well as scientific ability. In 1958 he wrote *Young Man Luther*. This book made an important contribution to both psychohistory and psychobiography. In 1960 he wrote *Gandhi's Truth* for which he received the Pulitzer Prize, the Melcher Award, and the National Book Award. In *The Life Cycle Completed* (1982), he reviewed, with modest revision, his whole developmental outline.

Three key concepts identified with Erikson are epigenesis, referring to growth and development; the life cycle, with eight ages of human life; and the search for identity, heightened during adolescence. Every stage in the life cycle presents the individual with potential hazards and potential for renewed growth, with a central focus for each. Erikson's insight

has been that while persons are shaped by environmental and historical events, each one contributes to the environment and to the course of history.

Erikson's career, in a real sense, came full circle when he returned to Harvard University as a professor of psychology, achieving emeritus status in 1970. Since 1972 he has been a senior consultant in psychiatry at Mt. Zion Hospital in San Francisco. It should be noted that he has had an exemplary career in psychology and psychiatry without the benefit of any earned college degree.

Erikson has been awarded honorary degrees from the following institutions: Harvard (M.A. and LL.D.), University of California (LL.D.), Brown University (LL.D.), Loyola University of Chicago (D.Sc.), Yale (D.Soc.Sci.), and the University of Lund. He received the Foneme prize in Milan in 1969, the Aldrich award of the American Academy of Pediatrics in 1971, the Montessori medal in 1973, and the McAlpin Research award of the National Association for Mental Health in 1974. He is a fellow of the American Academy of Arts and Sciences, an emeritus member of the National Academy of Education, a fellow of the Division of Developmental Psychology of the American Psychological Association, and a life member of the American Psychoanalytic Association.

E. S. GIBBS

See PSYCHOSOCIAL DEVELOPMENT.

Erotomania. A delusional state occurring almost exclusively in females wherein the woman is convinced that some man is deeply in love with her. The man is usually older and of higher status than the woman. The delusion is usually seen as a defense against a narcissistic injury that has made the patient feel unloved or unlovable. The term is also sometimes used to refer to excessive sexual desire.

EST (Erhard Seminar Training). A controversial training program in expanding and transforming consciousness, created in 1971 by Werner Erhard. His aim is to change the world through the transformation of different levels of society, beginning with individuals, relationships, and institutions. Not quite a therapy per se, EST has been described as a form of participatory theater, based on a blend of Zen, Gestalt, European and Eastern influence, encounter, Carl Rogers and Dale Carnegie, scientology, and hypnosis. It uses techniques from many traditional psychotherapeutic disciplines in an effort to create a "space" where people can deal with their own problems and troubles.

The training program takes place during two long weekend sessions, with 15–20 hours each day spent in a hotel ballroom with approximately 250 people, each of whom has paid $300 or more for the experience. During this time the participants are not permitted to eat, smoke, drink, chew gum, talk unless given permission, use the rest room, wear watches, or leave the room, even to vomit (they're to raise their hand and a trainer will bring them a bag for that purpose). During the 60–80 hours of the training, trainers shout at, order around, insult, and lecture the attendees in order to bring about a life-changing experience of enlightenment, known in EST terms as "getting it." In this intense emotional confrontation three main techniques are employed. The first consists of talks by the trainer, who gives information, definitions, and philosophical analyses of life—such as "Your lives don't work!" and "In life, understanding is the booby prize—life must be experienced." A second process is the sharing and questioning by participants, which is encouraged but not required. Finally, exercises are incorporated into the sessions, such as guided meditation and the "truth process" technique, which probes into bodily sensations, emotions, and memories.

Based on the thesis that we all hold painful experiences and are trapped and controlled by our minds, EST seeks to transform people from the state of mind to the state of self—i.e., to free individuals to experience fully. EST maintains 1) that there are barriers preventing us from experiencing and expressing our perfection as human beings; 2) if you try to resist or change, behavior becomes more solid; and 3) the re-creation of an experience makes the experience disappear. In that framework participators experience the following: awareness of belief systems that define or limit one's world; emotional patterns like resentment, guilt, and righteousness; specific thoughts; and repressed traumatic incidents. It is assumed that this process destroys the hold these experiences maintain over the individual. Erhard has more recently created an advanced seminar series for graduates of the EST standard training.

D. L. SCHUURMAN

Ethics and Psychological Practice. *See* MORAL AND ETHICAL ISSUES IN TREATMENT.

Etiology. A division of medical science dealing with the systematic study of the causes of mental and physical diseases. It is concerned with both the physiological response of tissues to the disease and the psychological reaction of the individual to the results of the disease. In psychopathology theories of etiology are much more speculative. Seldom are they built on sufficiently uncontestable data so as to be universally accepted by clinicians or psychopathology theorists.

Excessive Sexual Desire. In contrast to a lack of interest in sex or an inability to function adequately sexually, excessive sexual desire is not generally recognized as a psychological disorder. The great difficulty in dealing with the concept lies in determining how much sexual desire is excessive and to whom it is excessive. Tremendous variations exist within the boundaries of normal sexual desire. Some persons desire sexual intercourse only a few times per year, while others desire sexual intercourse several times per day. While both these variations are unusual, they are not necessarily pathological or sinful. Surveys have shown that most married couples engage in sexual intercourse between two and three times per week. The frequency is higher among younger couples and decreases as age increases. Neither the Scriptures nor contemporary psychologists prescribe the optimal amount of desire.

Often a person's sexual desire is labeled excessive by his or her spouse, who does not wish to engage in sexual intercourse as frequently and who may feel pressured by the partner's desires. In this situation it is the couple's responsibility to communicate with each other about their feelings and beliefs and work out a compromise that will be fair to each. Scripture makes it clear that the sexual relationship between spouses is very important and is of mutual concern, since both spouses are one flesh. Decisions about the frequency of sexual intercourse must not be made unilaterally (1 Cor. 7).

Sexual desires are a normal and healthy part of life. Human sexual desire can and should be used to image and glorify God through cementing the marriage relationship and procreation. If a person believes his or her own sexual desire is excessive, a psychologist or physician should be consulted to get information on normal sexual desire. Ignorance of normal human sexual desire sometimes results in a person feeling as though his or her own sexual desire is excessive, when in fact it is quite healthy and normal.

If one has learned about human sexual

desire and consulted a professional and still believes one's sexual desire to be excessive, he or she may decide to decrease it. It can be changed. While the foundation of sexual desire is biological, specifically hormonal, many aspects of it have been learned and therefore can be modified. Sexual desire depends on both stimulation and inhibition. Excessive sexual desire may be decreased by either avoiding stimulators or increasing inhibitors. Many forms of psychological therapy are currently available to change sexual desire.

Scriptural directives must be followed to avoid the degeneration of sexual desire into lust, which is a sexual desire or action that dishonors God. Scripture commands that Christians put off the old nature and put on the new nature through a transformation of their thoughts. God promises to help his children endure sexual temptations. In addition to depending on God for strength and the renewing of their minds, Christians are commanded to flee fornication and to avoid making provisions for fulfilling sexual lusts.

Clinical evidence indicates that a few people do have a psychological problem characterized by excessive sexual desire. In females this affliction is known as nymphomania; in males it is called satyriasis (nymphs and satyrs are mythological creatures who were known for their sexual appetites). These disorders are so rare that the current classification system of psychological disorders does not treat them as independent disorders but classifies them with other unspecified sexual disorders.

Persons with nymphomania or satyriasis possess a constant, compulsive, and uncontrolled desire to engage in sexual intercourse with many partners. In spite of this high level of sexual activity they invariably find little or no satisfaction in the sexual act. Genuine personal and emotional relationships between the nymphomaniac or satyriac and the sexual partner are nonexistent. These persons feel unhappy, dissatisfied, and out of control, yet they are unable to stop. They are perceived by others to be exploitive and self-centered. Most psychotherapists believe these problems stem from childhood conflicts that were never resolved and which resulted in faulty personality development. Psychotherapy is often effective in helping the person regain control.

Usually an abnormal increase in sexual behavior (hypersexuality) is secondary to some other problem. Masturbation in adolescents is often secondary to extreme anxiety and feelings of inadequacy. This behavior does not reflect excessive sexual desire as much as an attempt to reduce tension. Some men masturbate or engage in intercourse frequently in an attempt to reassure themselves that they are sexually potent.

Most frequently hypersexuality is secondary to a mood state known as hypomania, which is one of the phases of bipolar disorder. Hypomanic persons feel excited, tireless, self-confident, and impatient. During this state they are prone to be grandiose, unrealistic, irresponsible, and abrasive. They may also initiate an unusual number of sexual contacts.

Much less frequently hypersexuality has been noted in the opposite emotional state—incipient depression. These persons apparently attempt to ward off feelings of depression by increasing sexual activity. As depression progresses, however, sexual activity falls below normal levels or may cease. Schizophrenics sometimes develop sexual obsessions, but these are rarely accompanied by sexual activity. A few instances of hypersexuality have been reported following brain surgery for temporal lobe epilepsy.

C. D. DOLPH

Exhibitionism. A self-display of the genitals without the consent of others. It is very prevalent in that one-third of all sexual offenses are for indecent exposure (MacDonald, 1973). Cox and McMahon (1978) further report that one-third of the female college students surveyed have come in contact with an exhibitionist. Almost all exhibitionists are male. The onset is in puberty, and the peak incidents are between the ages of 15 and 30. Exposures usually are to a single adult female. The few reported cases of female exhibitionism were performed by women diagnosed as retarded or psychotic.

Exhibitionists do not usually desire sexual involvement with the audience but use the exposure to elicit a particular reaction such as flight, fear, abuse, indignation, or pleasure. Most exhibitionists do not undress completely, and almost one-half of the exposures are performed in cars. The most common times for exposure are between 8:00 A.M. and 9:00 A.M. and between 3:00 P.M. and 5:00 P.M. The exposures are mainly during the months of May to September and are usually in the middle of the week (MacDonald, 1973).

Most exhibitionists feel urged to exhibit in conjunction with conflicts regarding females in their personal life. In adolescents it is conflicts with the mother, while in adulthood it involves the fiancée or wife. Exhibitionism is also precipitated by interpersonal stress or by a period of intense conflict over some problem involving authority figures which causes a person to feel inadequate.

The exhibitionist is usually a loner at school and therefore isolated from other children. He has few friends and has difficulty handling aggression. Many times he is bullied by others or involved in fights. Exhibitionists' intelligence scores are lower than the general population and higher than that of other sexual offenders (Ellis & Brancale, 1956). Their educational achievement is poor even though they are usually hard workers and conscientious.

The family background of the exhibitionist usually involves an emotionally distant father who is often industrious, passive, ineffective, and meek. His mother is usually either an aggressive and masculine woman or a "clinging vine" (Rickols, 1950). The mother forms a strong bond with the child and rejects her husband. The dynamics in the home often result in divorce, more than 50% of all exhibitionists coming from broken homes. Many exhibitionists are raised in homes with a strict sexual moral code and where modesty is stressed. The child gains acceptance only if he is well-behaved and passive. He grows up to be a very insecure and sexually immature individual.

Most exhibitionists are married. Even so, their major form of sexual release, along with exposure, is masturbation. Masturbation may or may not precede, accompany, or follow the act of exposure.

Most exhibitionists do not graduate to more severe sexual offenses. Their recidivism rate of 20% (Mohr, Turner, & Jerry, 1964) is the highest among sexual offenders. There is some thought that the reason exhibitionists are apprehended and continue to get caught is a feeling of guilt and a need to be punished.

It should be noted that other forms of exhibitionism may or may not be considered psychological deviance. Some examples would be nudist camps, female striptease acts, streaking (running naked as a prank), or mooning (exposing one's posterior). The motivation for these acts is important as well as the intended reaction from the viewer. In the case of the streaker or mooner, it is usually part of youthful thrill seeking, while striptease dancers exhibit for monetary consideration. In the case of the nudist, the viewers are willing, and therefore it does not bring the individual into conflict with the law.

In our culture today there is a double standard between male and female exposure. Society passively condones a woman going braless with a see-through blouse or wearing microscopic beachwear, while similar behavior involving men's genitals would be promptly reported as exhibitionism. Perhaps the reason there are not very many female exhibitionists is because society passively condones their behavior and provides outlets such as go-go dancing and striptease work for those females so inclined.

Comprehensive treatment for exhibitionism includes insight therapy, group therapy, and behavioral treatment. The insight therapy is directed to help the individual gain insight into the causes of his maladaptive behavior. Group therapy should provide effective sex education, as well as help the individual develop more assertive or typical heterosexual behavior patterns.

The behavioral component of treatment includes aversion therapy and systematic desensitization. Aversion therapy usually involves presenting the exhibitionist with slides or pictures that call up images of heterosexual behavior or exhibitionist activities. The slides with exhibitionist material are accompanied with electric shock. When the subject changes to a slide describing normal sexual response, the shock is stopped. Aversive conditioning attempts to condition the patient away from exhibitionism by making it unpleasant.

Desensitization to the stress that precipitates the indecent exposure is another type of behavioral treatment. The patient builds a hierarchy of stress situations and then is helped by the therapist to become less sensitive to the stress-producing stimulus. Exhibitionists who receive treatment have a good chance of recovery. Cox and Daitzman (1975) found that if the exhibitionist behavior is stopped for 18 months after treatment, it is unlikely that it will recur.

References

Cox, D. J., & Daitzman, R. J. Behavior therapy, research and treatment of male exhibitionists. In I. M. Hersen, R. Eisler, & R. Miller (Eds.), *Progress in behavior modification* (Vol. 7). New York: Academic Press, 1975.

Cox, D. J., & McMahon, B. Incidents of male exhibitionism in the United States as reported by victimized female college students. *International Journal of Law and Psychiatry*, 1978, *1*, 453–457.

Ellis, A., & Brancale, R. *The psychology of sex offenders.* Springfield, Ill.: Thomas, 1956.

MacDonald, J. M. *Indecent exposure.* Springfield, Ill.: Thomas, 1973.

Mohr, J. W., Turner, R. E., & Jerry, M. B. *Pedophilia and exhibitionism.* Toronto: University of Toronto Press, 1964.

Rickols, N. K. *Exhibitionism.* Philadelphia: Lippincott, 1950.

M. A. CAMPION

Existential Psychology and Psychotherapy.
The word *existential* comes from the Latin

ex sistere, meaning literally to emerge or to stand out. True to this emphasis, existential psychologists seek to understand human beings not as static, but always in the process of becoming or emerging.

The beginnings of existential philosophy are usually identified with the Danish philosopher and theologian Søren Kierkegaard. Kierkegaard argued that knowledge can only be discovered via existence, and existence is incapable of further reduction. His major protagonist was Hegel, who identified abstract truth with reality. Against this, Kierkegaard argued that truth cannot be found in abstract theory but only in existence. In contrast to Descartes's dictum, "I think, therefore I am," Kierkegaard answered, "I exist, therefore I think." Existence precedes essence.

Defining Characteristics. As a system of psychology the existential tradition stands in opposition to those approaches which view persons reductionistically. Scientific psychology is viewed as treating people as objects rather than as human beings. Existential psychology rejects this subject-object cleavage. Rather than deal with human essence, the abstraction which has become the focus of traditional scientific psychology, existential psychology focuses on human existence. One's essence is one's existence; that is, the essence of man is his power to create himself.

In 1963 James Bugenthal, then president of the American Association of Humanistic Psychology, delineated five basic points which summarize the existential position: 1) Man supersedes the sum of his parts and cannot be understood from a scientific study of part-functions. 2) Man has his being in a human context and cannot be understood by part-functions which ignore interpersonal experience. 3) Man is aware and cannot be understood by a psychology which fails to recognize his continuous, many-layered self-awareness. 4) Man has choice and is not a bystander to his existence. 5) Man is intentional; he has purpose, values, and meaning. This understanding of human nature, or ontology, puts a completely new light on psychotherapy. The goal is not to communicate with the other in terms of presuppositions and expectations, but rather to set aside our world and enter into the other's world as he lets us in. The therapist's concern and attention are focused on the phenomena themselves. In this way the therapist does not abstract himself or become objective about what is going on, but is very much involved in the process. Disclaiming the protective veneer of objectivity, the therapist is continually in

the mainstream of the other's search for meaning and values. This might be described as a double-mirrored relationship. The therapist himself must be in quest of his destiny to better understand the process of searching.

Although existentialism is related to PHENOMENOLOGICAL PSYCHOLOGY, most existentialists feel that the two traditions are separate. The Swiss psychiatrist Binswanger notes that while the existential therapist enters into the phenomena present before and with him, existentialism does not confine itself to states of withness. It includes the existence of the whole being. Binswanger likewise points to the conflicting "worlds" in which the individual lives as opposed to the phenomenologist's notion of the unity of the individual's inner world of experiences. Again, while phenomenology limits itself to the immediate subjective worlds of experience, existentialism takes in the whole existence of the individual. This is where the individual's history comes into play.

View of Persons. In order to better comprehend the whole person, Binswanger (1958) divided his concerns around three aspects of a person's exisence, his mode of being in the world. He saw three worlds in which human beings live. These he termed *Umwelt*, *Mitwelt*, and *Eigenwelt*. By *Umwelt* he meant the biological world, including one's own body, the animal world, and, as a matter of fact, the entire physical existence. *Mitwelt* includes man in relation to other persons and emphasizes the more than biological interplay between persons. The aspect he termed *Eigenwelt* deals with the person in relation to himself—the self relating itself to its self and thus becoming a self. This is what Kierkegaard termed *spirit*.

In this understanding of persons several important factors stand out. Since man is seen as being, the implication is that he is moving toward becoming. This implies that man is a creature who is going in a certain direction to fulfill his destiny. On this journey he encounters certain distractions and diversions which attempt to mislead him in his questing. While his chosen strategies for dealing with the obstacles are rooted in his history, his ontology informs him, via anxiety, of his waywardness, and this reminds him of his responsibility to be himself in truth and to fulfill his destiny. This realization in turn implies that he has the freedom to choose. If he does not choose his destiny, he experiences guilt. Boss (1956) points out that guilt is not for things done or not done, but for who we refuse to be. Nor, says Boss, is guilt responsive to any other form of relief. Resolution of guilt comes about as the result of a change of direction in our lives toward the fulfillment of our destiny. In this view of personality symptoms are viewed as roadblocks that the human being throws up to avoid and evade his destiny. Psychopathology is a means of communicating. It is the purpose of the therapist to understand the language of the symptoms-symbols because symptoms are symbolic communications of what ails man.

Existential Psychodynamics. In his book *Existential Psychotherapy* Yalom points to death, freedom, isolation, and meaninglessness as the corpus of existential psychodynamics. He suggests these are the givens of existence and may be discovered by a "method of deep reflection. The conditions are simple: solitude, silence, time and freedom from the everyday distractions with which each of us fills his or her experiential world" (1980, p. 8).

Heidegger's (1962) discussion of death suggests that man lives on two levels: a state of forgetfulness of being and a state of mindfulness of being. To live in the former state is to live in continual distraction and diversion, in a preoccupation with things, abstractions, and impersonal concerns. Self-awareness is a very low priority in this existence. In the latter state one is continually aware of being. This awareness keeps one in touch with one's existence and the world of being. Living in awareness of one's being produces authenticity but is also fraught with anxiety. Anxiety increases when one who is aware of being is confronted with the reality of nonbeing, or death. An extraordinary sense of accountability is initiated with the realization of one's death. This limitation of time also urges one on to greater fulfillment or authenticity. Any experience that suggests a lessening of our individuality or a loss of our unique identity is in many ways reminiscent of our death, and this becomes a challenge to a fuller, more authentic existence.

The second major existential psychodynamic is freedom and its corollary, responsibility. The awareness of being has two dimensions, the awareness of our objective ego and the awareness of a transcending ego. This ability to transcend self not only reminds a person of his possibilities and his freedom, but it places on him the necessity to accept that responsibility. To be fully aware of this is what Kierkegaard describes as dizziness. Failure to accept and discharge our responsibility is what leads to guilt and a sense of groundlessness.

A third concern of the existentialist is isolation. This may be likened to a schizoid state—a condition in which a fundamental separation portrays the nonrelational character of the existent. Rogers describes this condition as the separation from one's own real wishes or desires. I am so unaware of who or what I am that I do not know who I am or what I want. All that confronts me is a sense of nothingness. Man is urged to discover his identity, his destiny. But this is the most awful calling of being separate and alone. On these twin possibilities man spends his entire life. Yalom (1980) describes this as the oscillation between life anxiety, the fear of self-affirmation and authenticity, and death anxiety, the fear of loss of autonomy.

The fourth major concern of the existentialist is meaning. This dimension opens up the whole world of values. Questions such as "What is life all about?" "Why do we exist?" "What meaning in my life makes existence worthwhile?" are singularly and significantly relevant to existentialists. These are likewise most pertinent questions in therapy.

The elements of faith and commitment are both integral to the existentialist's notion of meaning. The question is, "Faith in what or whom?" The existentialist answer is that we begin with commitment to ourselves and our being, and only then do we find meaning. This is what is understood by reaching toward our destiny.

Yalom draws on Maslow when he speaks of the self-actualization process involving a person striving toward what most people would call good values—i.e., toward kindness, honesty, love, unselfishness, and goodness. These values, according to Maslow, are "built into the human organism and . . . if one only trusts one's organismic wisdom, one will discover them intuitively" (Yalom, 1980, p. 438). Thus values and meaning are both seen to be rooted in existence.

Psychotherapy. While there is no single theory or approach to existential psychotherapy, May (1959) has summarized the major common elements in all existential approaches to treatment. He first points out that to look to existential psychology textbooks for techniques will be disappointing. The techniques used by existential psychotherapists are much like those used by other therapists. They are not, however, emphasized in existentialists' discussions of therapy. This is in reaction to the overemphasis on techniques in our Western culture, which is viewed as objectifying and "thing-ifying" persons.

According to May, the essential task of existential therapy is to "seek to understand the patient as a being and as being-in-his-world" (p. 77). Understanding a person is contrasted to analyzing an object. To understand a person means to relate to him as a person. The relationship of the therapist and patient is taken as a real one, not merely a professional role. Within this relationship the therapist attempts to help the patient experience his existence as real. The quintessence of existential therapy is to enable the person to become more fully aware of his existence. Involved in this is helping the patient develop an orientation to commitment. The patient must be brought to a decisive attitude toward existence. "The points of commitment and decision are those where the dichotomy between being subject and object is overcome in the unity of readiness for action" (May, 1959, p. 88).

Christian Existential Psychology. This section explores a Christian alternative to existential psychology and, as such, constitutes a critique of that psychology from a Christian perspective.

As noted above, existential psychology has largely abandoned any concern for an ultimate reference point for the spirit or self. Adopting a relativism that virtually rejects any unifying purpose or meaning to existence, modern existentialism has cut itself off from the vital taproot of which Kierkegaard spoke when he asserted that spirit must be grounded in Spirit. Christian existential psychology returns to this basic theme in Kierkegaard as its central tenet.

As a distinct system, Christian existential psychology has been developed in numerous articles and books over the past quarter century by Finch (1980b, 1982). These writings represent the meeting ground between his religious experience and his psychological awareness—a search that led him first into the pastorate and later into clinical psychology. Finch's approach represents an intentional integration of existential depth psychology and the Christian faith. The focal point for this integration lies in the Christian existential view of the nature of man.

Personality and Psychopathology. In concert with other existentialists, Finch affirms that man is essentially what Kierkegaard called spirit. That is, man is not mere machine, as Freud and others proposed, but rather man has a definite potential and the freedom and responsibility to actualize that potential. But what is this potential? In Kierkegaard's terms, it is the "absolute of all that a man can be." The secular existentialist speaks of man's destiny. But to what do these terms refer? It is here that the Christian, in contrast to the logical positivist or "pure" scientist, is free to

respond in absolute terms: the self, the absolute of all that a man can be, is defined by the *imago Dei*, the image of God in man.

Although made in God's image, man has allowed that likeness to be obscured by a network of defenses which, while purporting to protect the self, actually suffocates it. Enveloping the true, authentic self like a shroud, this "false self" prevents the spirit from coming to expression. The false self develops as a result of sin. Sin may be characterized as both a defense and a sickness, a sickness created by our egocentric tendency to assert that we are the captains of our fate, the masters of our souls. This act of pride cuts us off from the very Source of all life.

Man's spirit cannot be grounded or find meaning in itself, but only in the Spirit which created it. Freedom, responsibility, and the transcendent quality of the self have meaning only as they relate to God. It is this relation which is the core of Christian existential psychology, and it is in the life, death, and resurrection of Christ that this relation is elaborated most fully. It is therefore in the choice to invest oneself in the way modeled by Christ that one truly undertakes the task of becoming oneself. Finch recognizes that placing Christ at the center of psychology is a philosophical assumption. But he claims that his experience as well as that of innumerable others throughout the ages validates the assumption.

In fact, Finch asserts that following Christ is the supreme corrective to psychological disturbance. Insofar as man was created to be one with God, any deviation from this path creates an intolerable inner tension, for one is then at war with one's own being. This conflict must inevitably be expressed in physical and emotional distress. When one sets about becoming like Christ, one becomes aligned with one's ontology, the tension is eliminated, and the entire being—body, mind, and spirit—is once again integrated. This leads to another central theme in Finch's approach: the concept of anxiety.

Like other existential psychologists Finch sees anxiety in all its forms as demonstrating one's alienation from one's own being. Finch, however, puts the case even more unequivocally in his characterization of *all* anxiety as good. He sees anxiety as an inherent, positive, "creative directive to be oneself in truth, relentlessly" (Finch, 1980b, p. 154). When one makes life choices that are aligned with one's being as a child of God, anxiety is maintained at a creative level. However, when one violates one's nature, one blocks that creative flow and, like the waters of a dammed river, the pressure of anxiety intensifies and overflows into physical and psychological symptoms. By interpreting these symptoms and their causes biologically rather than ontologically or spiritually, we misconceive anxiety and increase it.

At the heart of anxiety we find the conscience. Where anxiety is "a nebulous power that activates and drives the being to fulfillment" (Finch, 1980b, p. 162), conscience is the focal point, the "eye of anxiety." Conscience may be defined as the spirit's potential for urging in one's consciousness its authoritative actualization in relation to Spirit. Conscience is ontological. That is, it is vital to man's being rather than contingent. It is not to be confused with the Freudian superego, which is the result of parental introjects and therefore potentially alien to one's ontology (consider the inner parental voice that may urge a woman "never to trust a man"), or with cultural norms or environmental influence, all of which conscience mediates and filters.

Failing to heed the call of conscience involves one in guilt. Viewed existentially, guilt consists not in what one has done or not done, but rather in one's failure to fulfill one's possibilities in the moment—i.e., in one's refusal to *be*. Virtually all physical and mental or emotional disorders have their genesis in our attempts to avoid the reality of our guilt. The only way to dissipate guilt is to choose to be. This choice is the essence of repentance and forgiveness. When we choose to be authentic, "the whole order of things cooperates with us to annul the past which has produced the guilt, and to affirm the present." Here we are in the realm of grace—that divine, patient, loving "acceptance which both pulls and pushes our development, using every condition of existence to facilitate the emergence of the self" (Finch, 1980a, p. 249).

Human development. Christian existential psychology views human development in terms of the struggle between the true and false selves. Already in the womb the fetus begins to react to parental anxieties by assuming a defensive posture. This defense eventually takes the form of an egocentric mistrust of and withdrawal from the milieu and an inner commitment to "go it alone," using everything and everyone for one's own ends—in short, a commitment to make the world good on one's own terms. This response is inevitable. It is one's foremost developmental task (and therefore also the work of therapy) to shed these defenses in order to be revealed *as one is*. It is

only in the extremity of this openness and vulnerability that one relates genuinely to God.

Finch conceives the developmental process in terms of four stages. Progression through the stages is a lifelong journey marked by frequent setbacks.

The first stage is that of dependence, the authentic or natural state of the neonate and infant. As natural growth processes carry the self farther from the security of the womb, the dizzying freedom and responsibility of one's increasing abilities and possibilities create an anxiety from which the self tries to escape by contorting itself and distorting reality. All such tactics constitute an attempt to re-create the security of the womb by enticing (e.g., placation) or by coercing (e.g., tantrums) from the environment the nurturance one either does not trust to come freely or does not wish to procure in an honest fashion.

The second stage, that of independence, is actually a variation of the first stage. In it one seeks the privileges of freedom without the attendant responsibilities. Characterized by the bullying, pouting, blackmail, and other tactics typically associated with the adolescent's masquerade of selfhood ("I'm old enough to drive, but you'd better pay for the gas"), independence is actually a way of spreading anxiety to the environment so that it will allow one to be dependent.

After an intense struggle one comes to the painful discovery that one's attempts to remain dependent only increase anxiety. As the self acts on this realization and gives up its vise-like grip on the defensive strategies by which it has imprisoned itself, the self is born in true freedom and responsibility. This is the stage of self-dependence, in which the self becomes self-caring, self-creating, self-affirming, and self-supporting.

Self-dependence is not to be confused with the idea of needing nothing. As Finch notes, we all need blood to survive. Self-dependence is analogous to producing one's own blood, while dependency is like receiving an endless series of blood transfusions because one's organism has lost the ability to produce its own. Nor is self-dependence to be confused with a schizoid withdrawal from, or inability to depend on, others. Rather, one functions in such harmony with oneself and the milieu that one is able to recycle and draw sustenance from what is offered rather than insisting on having things one's own way. Being in such spiritual harmony one is able to find meaning and value in even the harshest of life circumstances, even in the pain of a crucifixion or the irritations of an uncooperative spouse. This "selflessness" is possible because the self-dependent person is rooted both within and outside himself in God.

Finally, when two selves are able to relate to each other with "a mutuality and sharing that assumes full responsibility for oneself but no less responsibility for the other" (Finch, 1980b, p. 172), we reach the stage of interdependence or interrelation. In this stage anxiety is manifest in concern, and the source of motivation is a quiet inner serenity rather than a desire for satisfaction of one's needs at the other's expense.

One observes, then, that spiritual growth is marked by adoption of a mature *Weltanschauung*, or philosophy of life. This philosophy is not merely cognitive, but is rather inclusive of one's whole existence. The highest value of philosophy of life, asserts Finch, is expressed in the concept of *nishkamakarma*. Literally translated as "desireless action," this Sanskrit word conveys the idea of "doing one's duty with faith in God, without attachment to the fruit of the action" (Finch, 1982, p. 45). This stance of nonattachment (which is not to be confused with uncaring detachment) allows one to focus on the requirements of spirit rather than being pulled and pushed by the vagaries of time and circumstance.

Therapy. The fundamental task of Christian existential therapy is to facilitate spirit's encounter with Spirit. To this end the therapist seeks to dismantle, through loving confrontation, the strategies of the false self. The therapist guides the person into his anxiety rather than away from it, appeals to the individual's sense of responsibility, unclutters the conscience, and encourages a healthy perspective on guilt. The therapist's own values invariably become part of the therapeutic process as he enters deeply into the person's struggles. Because the relationship with the therapist becomes the vehicle by which the person experiences grace and a more mature *Weltanschauung*, it is critical that the therapist be actively engaged in his own search for authentic existence.

As the person's facade disintegrates and the props of dependency are removed, the individual experiences the dread associated with what has been called the *abyss*. This is a radical and ineffable confrontation with one's own being which becomes at the same instant an experience of the infinite love of God. For, having abandoned one's feeble attempts to constitute one's own universe and thus ensure one's own security, one finds that he or she is and always

has been held. One does not fall, as one fears, *out* of existence, but rather *into* it.

Such a journey requires the most focused concentration. Integral, therefore, to Christian existential therapy is the ages-old concept of the monastic retreat for the purpose of spiritual direction. This retreat takes the form of a three-week intensive therapy, in which one lives alone and seeks oneself under God, with the therapist's direction. Writing and talking in absentia to one's significant others is one aspect of this process, which often resembles the primal therapies in its emotional intensity.

In conclusion, while existential psychology is not incompatible with a Christian world view, Christian existentialism asserts that it falls short of a complete understanding of man by virtue of its lack of a reference point for man's spirit. In bringing a theologically informed perspective to bear on this problem, Christian existential psychology finds this reference point in Spirit—i.e., in God. And, giving fresh meaning to the doctrines of sin, guilt, grace, and forgiveness, an existentially informed Christianity offers new promise for healing in depth.

References

Binswanger, L. The existential analysis school of thought. In R. May, E. Angel, & H. Ellenberger (Eds.), *Existence*. New York: Basic Books, 1958.
Boss, M. "Daseinsanalysis" and psychotherapy. In J. H. Masserman & J. L. Moreno (Eds.), *Progress in psychotherapy*. New York: Grune & Stratton, 1956.
Finch, J. G. Guilt and the nature of the self. In H. N. Malony (Ed.), *A Christian existential psychology: The contributions of John G. Finch*. Washington, D.C.: University Press, 1980. (a)
Finch, J. G. The message of anxiety. In H. N. Malony (Ed.), *A Christian existential psychology: The contributions of John G. Finch*. Washington, D.C.: University Press, 1980. (b)
Finch, J. G. *Nishkamakarma*. Pasadena, Calif.: Integration Press, 1982.
Heidegger, M. [*Being and time*] (J. Macquarrie & E. Robinson, Eds.). New York: Harper & Row, 1962.
May, R. The existential approach. In S. Arieti (Ed.), *American handbook of psychiatry*. New York: Basic Books, 1959.
Yalom, I. D. *Existential psychotherapy*. New York: Basic Books, 1980.

J. G. FINCH and B. VAN DRAGT

Experiential Focusing. Developed by Gendlin in the 1960s, experiential focusing is a technique for introspection and change. Gendlin, a professor of psychology at the University of Chicago and past editor of *Psychotherapy: Theory, Research, and Practice*, discovered that patients who would succeed in therapy could be quickly identified by how they talked about their experiencing. That internal process is called focusing. The focus is a concrete, "felt sense" which Gendlin describes as a preconceptual experiencing that can be symbolized in many ways. For example, the name of a friend may release rich inner associations, the whole of which is one's felt sense about that person. Gendlin has investigated how focusing can be taught to a wide range of people for use in various therapies and in everyday situations when alone or with another.

Focusing proceeds through six movements (Gendlin, 1978). After pausing quietly, one first asks, "How do I feel?" One lists the problems mentally and steps back from them. Second, one asks, "Which problem feels the worst right now?" and attends to the whole felt sense of it. Third, one finds the crux of it by asking, "What is the worst of it?" and refraining from deliberately answering. Fourth, one lets words or images come from the feeling and label it. Fifth, one checks these words against the feeling until a match occurs that is experienced as a felt shift, a pleasant, physical release. After pausing with this felt sense, one may begin the sixth movement by repeating this process to unlock the body message under the felt sense just experienced.

The Bible asserts both the importance of one's inner impressions and the limitations of relying on them (e.g., Prov. 4:23; 28:26; Rom. 7:22–23). Accordingly, focusing can be most useful when balanced with objective orientations.

Reference

Gendlin, E. T. *Focusing.* New York: Everest House, 1978.

T. J. RUNKEL

Experimental Group. Those subjects in an experiment who receive the experimental treatment. They are then compared to the CONTROL GROUP, which consists of matched subjects who did not receive the treatment.

See PSYCHOLOGY, METHODS OF.

Experimental Neurosis. *See* NEUROSIS, EXPERIMENTAL.

Experimental Psychology. The application of the experimental method to the study of behavior and mental processes. Although experimental psychologists initally studied only a few subject areas, they are currently identified not so much by what they study as by how they study it. They receive special training in research design, methodology, and the logic of the scientific approach. Experimental psychology is on the borderline between the physical sciences and the behavioral sciences. It is the most self-consciously scientific area of psychol-

ogy, sharing much methodology with such areas as physics.

Although psychologists can make observations or do demonstrations on only one group, the experimental method logically demands comparing at least two groups. In some instances these two groups may actually be different groups of individuals which are treated the same in every respect except one, a between-subject design. In other instances experimenters use the same group of subjects but test them under different conditions, a within-subject design. In either case the different conditions must be compared.

Experimental psychology emerged from structuralism, functionalism, behaviorism, and Gestalt psychology during the latter part of the nineteenth and first half of the twentieth centuries. Since behaviorism became the dominant school of psychology in the United States during the first half of the twentieth century, experimental psychology came to be identified with behaviorism. The subject area of learning came to be the dominant one studied, with a major emphasis on classical conditioning and operant learning. Other traditional subject areas studied were psychophysics, sensation, perception, memory, thinking, motivation, and emotion. These subject areas are reflected in the four parts of the *Journal of Experimental Psychology.* Published as separate issues of this journal are *Human Learning and Memory, Human Perception and Performance, Animal Behavior Processes,* and *General.*

Experimental psychologists frequently work with animals as well as with humans. Although rats and pigeons are the most common, at one time or another almost every kind of animal has been subjected to behavioral study. Animals are used because they are simpler and because some types of experiments simply cannot be done on humans. Furthermore, animals are inexpensive, have a short life span (thus allowing for experiments of relatively short duration), and can be kept in a completely controlled environment. Variables such as brain operations and breeding experiments, which cannot be studied in humans for ethical reasons, can be manipulated with animals.

Although some Christian psychologists tend to reject animal research and other aspects of experimental psychology, it can contribute to Christian psychology. Since humans are created beings, like animals, there are many similarities between humans and animals, especially in terms of their physiology, their sensations, their learning, and their biological motives. Phenomena found in animals in these areas have frequently, but not always, been generalized to humans. The experimental method is one of the best ways of investigating creation, so Christians should not reject it, but remember that it is only one way to knowledge about creation. Unfortunately, some experimental psychologists imply that it is the only way leading to valid knowledge.

Experimental psychology has traditionally been defined as the study of the relatively restricted set of subject areas mentioned above. However, since mid-century the trend has been to define it as study involving scientific methodology, especially the experimental method. Experimental psychologists are no longer confined to a few areas, but conduct research in almost the whole of psychology. One can easily find material on experimental child psychology, experimental social psychology, experimental clinical psychology, and many other such areas. In fact, the most widely accepted model for clinical psychology training programs is the scientist-professional one. In addition to their professional training, clinical and counseling psychologists receive training in statistics, research design, and methodology. Although the actual membership in the Division of Experimental Psychology of the American Psychological Association is relatively small, most psychologists have training in this branch of psychology.

Finally, experimental psychology should not be thought of as opposed to theoretical psychology. Experimental psychologists usually place a great emphasis on theory as well as the experimental method. While the results of their experiments are scientific facts, such facts cannot be left in isolation. Theory serves two functions. First, theory serves to integrate the results of past experiments, to show how the facts are related. Theories are not opposed to facts, but serve to summarize facts. Second, theories serve the function of generating hypotheses to be tested by experiments. They guide the experimenter in predicting what new facts may be found. Although some research is the "I wonder what would happen if . . . " type, most of it is tied to theory in some way.

Additional Readings
Elmes, D. G., Kantowitz, B. H., & Roediger, H. L. *Methods in experimental psychology*. Boston: Houghton Mifflin, 1981.
Kantowitz, B. H., & Roediger, H. L. *Experimental psychology*. Chicago: Rand McNally College Publishing, 1978.
Sheridan, C. L. *Fundamentals of experimental psychology* (2nd ed.). New York: Holt, Rinehart & Winston, 1976.

R. L. KOTESKEY

Explosive Disorder. DSM-III regards the explosive disorder as a disorder of impulse control. Together with pyromania, kleptomania, and pathological gambling, the explosive disorder is fundamentally characterized by a failure to contain an impulse which is destructive to self or others. Other pathologies with this lack of impulse control would be the substance abuses and the sexual perversions.

Central to the explosive disorder is the impulse to strike out to harm, to hurt, or to destroy. Hence there is a rather direct link between the behavior and its hostile antecedents as opposed to the indirect linkage found in the other disorders of impulse control. Persons with an explosive disorder will act out far more aggression than the precipitating event would normally evoke in others. For example, a man may experience anger because of a comment made by a family member and proceed to break up two entire rooms of furniture. The explosion may last from minutes to hours; once the acting out has ceased, the explosive person will return to his or her "normal" self. Mental health personnel rarely see an explosion in progress, although law enforcement personnel may witness the acting out (Barrett, 1980). Because destruction of property and injury to persons are often the results of the acting out behavior, this disorder is most likely to be seen in a correctional institution.

The explosions often have the quality of a fit, or the person seems to be seized by some uncontrollable force. (Earlier diagnostic systems referred to this disorder as an epileptoid personality.) Once the incident is over, the patient may report that he or she does not remember what happened and may express puzzlement over the event. Many persons with this disorder have a strong sense of remorse once the incident is finished. Yet their repentance is insufficient to prevent a recurrence.

The explosive disorder is thought to be relatively rare. A mild form, the explosive personality, was eliminated as a diagnostic category in the latest American Psychiatric Association diagnostic system. There is some evidence that the disorder occurs more frequently in family members than in the population as a whole. Statistics reveal that more males than females receive the diagnosis.

Evidence that the disorder has an organic base is sketchy and inconclusive. Some sufferers have vague EEG abnormalities or minor neurological symptoms. The disorder occurs more frequently among people with an epilepsy disorder than among the general population.

The disorder is called intermittent if several separate incidents occur over a period of time and isolated if only a single incident has occurred.

Persons with explosive disorders experience difficulty in relating to the opposite sex and may have other disruptions in their social network as well. Therapy with these persons often reveals an inner vulnerability and a pervasive sense of inadequacy which is covert. Treatment is difficult and carries a poor prognosis (Pasternack, 1974).

References

Barrett, C. L. Personality disorders. In R. H. Woody (Ed.), *Encyclopedia of clinical assessment.* San Francisco: Jossey-Bass, 1980.

Pasternack, A. A. The explosive, antisocial, and passive-aggressive personalities. In J. R. Lion (Ed), *Personality disorders: Diagnosis and management.* Baltimore: Williams & Wilkins, 1974.

J. R. BECK

Extinction. The term can refer to any of three experimental operations or to the corresponding behavioral changes produced by these operations. The three types of extinction are extinction occurring in classical conditioning, extinction occurring in operant conditioning, and vicarious extinction. Usually the changes involve weakening some behavior, but there are circumstances in which the target behavior does not change or even increases in strength. Extinction is only relevant to previously conditioned or learned responses; the concept has no meaning in terms of original learning.

In classical conditioning a previously neutral stimulus (such as a bell) is consistently followed by an unconditioned stimulus (such as a squirt of food powder in the mouth). Prior to conditioning the bell cannot produce salivation, but the food powder can. The bell is the conditioned stimulus and salivation is the conditioned response. Following many pairings of the bell and food powder, presentation of the bell alone will elicit salivation; however, continuous presentation of the conditioned stimulus (bell) without the unconditioned stimulus (food powder) constitutes the operation of extinction. This operation will normally result in a weakening and eventual disappearance of the conditioned response (*see* CONDITIONING, CLASSICAL).

Emotional behavior seems to follow the principles of classical conditioning. Since emotional reactions can be classically conditioned, they can be weakened via extinction processes as just outlined. An infinite variety of environmental events can function as conditioned stimuli. If the effective stimulus for a given emotional reaction can be identified and presented in the absence of the relevant unconditioned stimulus, the power of the conditioned stimulus can be extinguished. Such a conceptual analysis is consistent with treatment effects achieved through clinical procedures such as systematic desensitization and flooding.

Operant conditioning deals with emitted behaviors which are controlled by their consequences. Consequences can consist of producing a positive stimulus (positive reinforcement), removing an aversive stimulus (negative reinforcement), producing an aversive stimulus (punishment, type 1), or removing a positive stimulus (punishment, type 2). When an action has produced one of the above consequences but now does not do so, the behavior is on extinction. What will happen to response rate during extinction will depend on what consequence had followed the action prior to the extinction phase. Previously reinforced behaviors will tend to be weakened during extinction, but previously punished behaviors will tend to be strengthened during extinction (*see* CONDITIONING, OPERANT).

For extinction to work, *all* positive reinforcers for the target behavior must be removed. Since carrying out such a prescription in the natural environment is usually difficult, programmed extinction is used sparingly in treatment programs. When parents are encouraged to ignore their children's misbehavior, the consultant probably is assuming that the parents' attention has been serving as the positive reinforcer for the misbehavior. Having parents ignore the tantrums of their toddler is a common example of extinction applied to an everyday problem.

Intermittent schedules of reinforcement or punishment constitute the most common approach to training for resistance to extinction.

Human observers may exhibit extinction effects of both a classical and operant variety without being directly exposed to the extinction conditions. Social models may produce extinction vicariously just as classical or operant conditioning may occur through observational learning (*see* LEARNING).

P. W. CLEMENT

Extrasensory Perception. *See* PARAPSYCHOLOGY.

Extraversion-Introversion. *See* INTROVERSION-EXTRAVERSION.

Eysenck, Hans Jurgen (1916–). Noted for his introversion-extraversion theory of personality, Eysenck was born in Germany but has spent his professional life in England. Although he received his early education in Germany, both his B.S. degree in 1938 and his Ph.D. degree in 1940 are from the University of London.

During World War II, Eysenck served as psychologist at the Mill Hill Emergency Hospital. Following the war he was appointed reader in psychology at the University of London and director of the Psychological Department at the Institute of Psychiatry there. The institute includes Maudsley and Bethlehem Royal Hospitals, with which he has been affiliated since 1945 and 1948 respectively, and where much of his research has been carried out. His entire professional life has been spent at the University of London, where he set up the first psychology department in England offering training in clinical psychology.

Eysenck has been a persistent critic of all types of psychotherapy, but especially psychoanalysis. He has characterized such therapy as an art form and has questioned whether it does any good. While accusing other personality theorists of being subjective storytellers with theories based on conjecture and unfounded assumptions, he has attempted to develop a theory based on empirical data and experimental procedures. He has obviously been a very controversial figure.

He has searched for the basic dimensions or traits of personality and has found two major ones. His introversion versus extraversion dimension, like Jung's, refers to the degree to which a person is passive and quiet or outgoing and active. Neuroticism, which has anxious restlessness, can be contrasted with emotional stability, which has carefree calmness. More recently Eysenck has investigated a psychotic versus nonpsychotic dimension in which the psychotic is unable to distinguish between reality and fantasy.

Eysenck has developed a research method, criterion analysis, which is like factor analysis but more deductive. In criterion analysis one begins with a hypothesis about underlying variables and does the statistical analysis to test the hypothesis rather than letting the factors appear by themselves in the statistical analysis. Since Eysenck has advocated the use of behavior therapy, his approach bridges the gap between trait and learning approaches to personality.

He has written many books, ranging from scientific volumes to popular bestsellers. His most important are *Dimensions of Personality* (1947), *The Scientific Study of Personality* (1952), *The Causes and Cures of Neurosis* (1965, with Rachman), and *Uses and Abuses of Psychology* (1953). He was also editor of the comprehensive *Handbook of Abnormal Psychology* (1961).

R. L. KOTESKEY

See FACTOR THEORIES OF PERSONALITY.

Ff

Factitious Disorders. Factitious, or factitial, disorders refer to a category of behavior involving various physical and psychological complaints or symptoms that an observer would suspect to be simulated and subject to voluntary control. Thus, the term has become a synonym for self-induced diseases. Although they are voluntarily controlled and produced with the conscious awareness of the individual, the repeated use of these behaviors has a compulsive quality suggesting that they have been adopted involuntarily and maintained to serve the personal dynamics of the individual.

Moral and social disapproval of these illnesses has always existed despite the existence of systems within society to compensate and even encourage their development and maintenance. These self-induced diseases also evoke frequent negative emotion and reaction from physicians.

Factitious disorders may encompass practically the entire range of medical nosology. Dermatological concerns might involve the excoriation of skin and insertion of parasites. Surgical issues include bleeding from various orifices. Medical problems include metabolic and hematological disturbances, such as diabetics tampering with their diets and insulin regimen. Many times these feigned illnesses do considerable and often irreparable damage to health.

The discrimination of these symptoms from those associated with the real disorders that they masquerade is a judgment of the outside observer. The conclusion that the behavior simulates illness is determined through assessing the intellectual abilities of the patient to know the appropriate signs, the timing or process of the symptoms, and the lack of any positive gain through the behavior. The pro-

duction of the symptoms, while concealing the voluntary control, requires an appreciable level of intellect and judgment. Simulation requires not only the production of appropriate signs but the sequencing of these to be consistent with the real disorder. Further, the identification of any environmental gain such as avoiding work or getting insurance payments would indicate a malingering, while the lack of such gain supports the diagnosis of factitious disorder.

Frequently less specific disorders are masqueraded so that concealment can be more easily maintained. Occasionally chemicals or drugs are ingested to produce supportive symptoms or test results for the simulated physical disorders. The simulation of nonorganic mental disorders (e.g., Ganser syndrome) may also be facilitated by stimulants, hallucinogenics, and hypnosis. Approximate or vague answers also can serve to protect from discovery.

The lack of environmental or secondary gain suggests that factitious behavior is a maladaptive response in which the assumption of the patient role somehow serves the dynamics of the individual. The limited literature available suggests that these patients are generally dependent and demanding. Frequently they are single women with poor psychosexual adjustment and numerous hysterical traits. Fras (1978) characterizes these patients as immature, with persistent, primitive oral and tactile needs. They were very dependent on their mothers, but generally had their dependency need unfulfilled due to its intensity and extent. Frequently their fathers were sick or in some other way unable to provide the needed emotional gratification. Furthermore, such patients usually possess poor verbal communication skills, thus rendering illness behavior suitable as a mode of communicating needs.

Due to the real risk to health, therapy must initially be cautious and involve support and establishment of the relationship. Confrontation of the characteristic denial must be postponed generally, with the exception of immediate intervention and interpretation in crisis situations. Occasionally these patients need to be hospitalized to prevent further damage. Only after a secure rapport is achieved can traditional psychotherapy be commenced. Even then it must be with the awareness of the existence of a brittle ego with weak defenses. The therapist can often be caught between a frustrating patient with few health responses and a frustrated, impatient medical profession lacking in understanding. Such a role calls for a mature, secure, and patient therapist.

References
Fras, I. Factitial disease: An update. *Psychosomatics*, 1978, *19*, 119–122.

Additional Readings
Berney, T. P. A review of simulated illness. *South African Medical Journal*, 1973, *47*, 1429–1434.
Crabtree, L. H., Jr. A psychotherapeutic encounter with a self-mutilating patient. *Psychiatry*, 1967, *30*, 91–100.
Fras, I., & Coughlin, B. F. The treatment of factitial disease. *Psychosomatics*, 1971, *12*, 117–122.

G. MATHESON

See MALINGERING.

Factor Theories of Personality.
Many theories of personality exist side by side, each employing its own definition of personality. Psychologists fail to reach a consensus in this matter because the concept of personality is based on subjective insights.

Factor analysis is an attempt to give psychological concepts a more objective basis. Human behavior could be compared to a jungle. The psychologist is the hunter. How does the hunter decide whether the dark blobs he sees are two rotting logs or a single alligator? (Cattell, 1965, p. 56) Movement will tell: If the blobs move together, a single structure can be inferred. In the "psychological jungle" factor analysis looks for behaviors, test results, or other data which "move together" with enough reliability to allow for the inference of a unitary trait (e.g., anxiety).

Essentially, factor analysis is a mathematically sophisticated technique using John Stuart Mill's principle of concomitant variation in order to reduce a large number of behavioral data to a small number of factors. One might start, for example, by gathering 50 test results for each individual in a group and observe that

tests 1, 3, 5, 23, and 49 are highly intercorrelated. Performance on any one of these tests is a good predictor of performance on any of the other tests. Hence, these tests could be grouped into one factor. Naming and interpreting that factor, however, is a more subjective process, the result of analyzing the similarities between tasks involved and linking them through the use of a theoretical label such as imagination or ego strength.

Early Applications. The use of factor analysis in psychology started with Spearman in 1904, in relation to his work on the nature of intelligence. Spearman taught at London University, where both R. B. Cattell and Eysenck, two major contributors to the factorial analysis of personality traits, did their doctoral work. Eysenck later taught at London University, while Cattell spent the major part of his professional life in the United States, at the University of Illinois.

In the United States the first psychologist to apply factorial analysis to the study of personality was Guilford in a 1934 study on the Jungian concept of introversion and extraversion. Guilford's (1949) main contribution to the field of personality is the Guilford-Zimmerman Temperament Survey, in which 10 personality traits were identified: general activity, restraint, ascendance, emotional stability, sociability, objectivity, friendliness, thoughtfulness, personal relations, and masculinity-femininity.

R. B. Cattell. While Guilford deserves credit for being first in the field, the distinction for the most voluminous output of research undoubtedly belongs to R. B. Cattell, who by 1964 had already authored 257 chapters and articles and 22 books, and has been writing ever since (Cattell, 1964, p. ix).

Cattell believes that to study personality one has to start by examining language. In his study of temperamental traits, for instance, his point of departure was a list of 4,500 descriptive adjectives compiled by Allport and Odbert (1936). Through a process of eliminating synonyms and intercorrelated traits, he reduced them to 46 surface traits (Cattell & Kline, 1977, p. 31).

Cattell then looked at real-life data, questionnaire data, and test data analyzed on the basis of these traits, intercorrelated them, and found 16 temperament source traits, on the basis of which he constructed his SIXTEEN PERSONALITY FACTOR QUESTIONNAIRE (Cattell, Saunders, & Stice, 1950).

The names Cattell chose for his factors reflect his fondness for neologism. They are: sizia (reserve) vs. affectia (outgoingness), intelligence, ego strength (emotional stability), submissiveness vs. dominance, desurgency (taciturn) vs. surgency (enthusiastic), superego strength (expedient vs. moralistic), threctia (shy) vs. parmia (venturesome), harria (tough-minded) vs. premsia (tender-minded), alaxia (trusting) vs. protension (suspicious), praxernia (practical) vs. autia (imaginative), alertness (forthright) vs. shrewdness, guilt proneness (self-assured vs. insecure), conservatism vs. radicalism, group-adherence vs. self-sufficiency, strength of self-sentiment (careless of social rules vs. controlled), ergic tension (relaxed vs. tense) (Cattell & Kline, 1977, pp. 342–343).

In addition to the above temperamental traits, which describe the *how* of behavior, Cattell has also addressed the *why* of behavior through his study of dynamic traits. These traits fall into three categories: strength of interest traits related to the Freudian concepts of id, ego, and superego; basic drives or ergs, such as fear, sex, exploration; and sentiments (environmentally based interests) (Cattell & Kline, 1977, pp. 160–184).

The development of traits across the life span and their application to particular situations occur within a complex network of drives, attitudes, and sentiments: the dynamic lattice. Pathways within the lattice change over time as the result of learning, especially through rewards or favorable consequences (instrumental conditioning).

However, aside from these developmental changes, an individual's trait configuration is not perfectly stable. Day-to-day variations in performance occur because of what Cattell calls state changes. Some of the states Cattell considers are exvia (extraversion), anxiety, depression, arousal, fatigue, guilt, stress, and regression (Curran & Cattell, 1974). This aspect of Cattell's theory is more recent and is still developing.

Cattell's work is impressive. He has tried to test and incorporate insights from sources as diverse as Freud, Guilford, Eysenck, Skinner, Murray, and McDougall. His work touches on most areas of psychology. Some aspects of his theory that have not been considered here are his concept of abnormal behavior traits and his study of genetics vs. environmental components of behavior. Cattell often leaves the reader waiting for a more centralized theoretical statement.

H. J. Eysenck. While Cattell's theory is remarkable for its scope, incisiveness is the hallmark of Eysenck's approach. Eysenck started his research career at a military psychi-atric facility, the Mill Hill Emergency Hospital. He became interested in Jung's idea that introversion and extraversion lead to different types of mental illness.

He selected 700 patients, analyzed their intake and treatment histories according to 39 categories, intercorrelated them, and discovered that they could be explained in terms of two independent factors: the introversion-extraversion factor, describing the individual's temperament, and the neuroticism factor, reflecting the degree of mental maladjustment. Jung had been right: Introverts high on the neuroticism scale showed symptoms associated with high anxiety. Neurotic extraverts showed bodily symptoms without organic basis, lack of energy, sexual difficulties (hysteria-like illness) (Eysenck, 1947, pp. 36ff.).

Eysenck sees a correspondence between his two factors and Galen's classical temperament categories. The choleric temperament characterizes the neurotic extravert, while the neurotic introvert is melancholic. The former is more apt to acquire a criminal record, the latter a psychiatric one (Eysenck, 1967). Stable introverts are of the phlegmatic type, a type often encountered in successful industrial managers. Stable extraverts correspond to the sanguine type, which is often found in the armed forces (Eysenck, 1970, pp. 427–430).

Eysenck ascribes the introversion-extraversion dimension to the ascending reticular system (ARAS) in the brain. The ARAS is like a central switchboard with a double function—activating the cortex and inhibiting it. Introverts are very sensitive to incoming stimulation, extraverts less so. Extraverts are more likely to disregard irrelevant or repeated stimulation because of their strong inhibition functions. This understanding of introversion and extraversion has interesting practical applications. Introverted students need quiet to study because they are easily disrupted. Extraverted students need some background noise to maintain concentration; they fall asleep in quiet libraries. It may take very little of a stimulant drug to arouse an introvert, but it will take quite a bit of a depressant to quiet him down. The individual who goes to sleep easily after drinking several cups of coffee is probably an extravert (Eysenck, 1967). Extraverted children do not pick up easily the cues and subtle rules that govern social and ethical behavior; they need firm rules, clearly enforced. This type of treatment, however, would probably render an introverted child overly anxious.

Both introverted and extraverted individuals may be either neurotic or stable. For Eysenck, neuroticism is associated with strong emotionality. Strong emotions, according to Eysenck, are controlled by the visceral brain, an area of the brain comprising hypothalamic and limbic structures and connected to the activation of the autonomic nervous system.

When strong emotions are produced—which occurs fairly rarely in normal people—the visceral brain is activated, and through it the sympathetic system. Cortical arousal follows automatically. Hence, when introverts already characterized by a high level of arousal become neurotic, they may become immobilized because the excess arousal has finally triggered their cortical inhibition mechanisms. Neurotic extraverts, more aroused because of their neurosis, might react in a manner reminiscent of normal introverts. At higher levels of stress, however, the pattern reverses; neurotic introverts become very agitated as their inhibition systems break down, and neurotic extraverts become immobilized (as neurotic introverts are at lower levels of stress) (Eysenck, 1970, p. 437).

More recently Eysenck has studied the dimension of psychoticism (Eysenck & Eysenck, 1976), which he views as a two-level genetic trait composed of small effect genes (e.g., schizoid tendency, tendency toward drug addiction), and large effect genes more directly related to the occurrence of an actual psychosis.

Although the neurological mechanisms related to psychoticism have not yet been discovered, Eysenck and Eysenck (1975) have designed an instrument, the Eysenck Personality Questionnaire, which measures introversion, extraversion, and psychoticism. A person scoring high in psychoticism, while not necessarily psychotic, would definitely be different. High psychoticism scores would be present in psychotics, but could be present also in persons of unusual ability.

While Cattell's and Guilford's contributions are mostly in the area of the classification of traits, Eysenck reaches the level of causal explanation for personality differences and opens the possibility of practical applications in the area of diagnosis and treatment.

References
Allport, G. W., & Odbert, H. S. Trait names: a psycholexical study. *Psychological Monographs*, 1936, *47*, 63, 171.
Cattell, R. B. *Personality and social psychology*. San Diego, Calif.: Knapp, 1964.
Cattell, R. B. *The scientific analysis of personality*. Baltimore: Penguin Books, 1965.
Cattell, R. B., & Kline, P. *The scientific analysis of personality and motivation*. New York: Acedemic Press 1977.
Cattell, R. B., Saunders, D. R., & Stice, G. F. *The sixteen personality factor questionnaire*. Champaign, Ill.: Institute for Personality and Ability Testing, 1950.
Curran, J. P., & Cattell, R. B. *The eight state questionnaire*. Champaign, Ill.: Institute for Personality and Ability Testing, 1974.
Eysenck, H. J. *Dimensions of personality*. London: K. Paul, Trench, Trubner, 1947.
Eysenck, H. J. *The biological basis of personality*. Springfield, Ill.: Thomas, 1967.
Eysenck, H. J. *The Structure of Human Personality* (3rd ed.). London: Methuen, 1970.
Eysenck, H. J., & Eysenck, S. B. *Eysenck personality questionnaire*. San Diego, Calif.: Educational and Industrial Testing Service, 1975.
Eysenck, H. J., & Eysenck, S. B. *Psychoticism as a dimension of personality*. New York: Crane, Russak, 1976.
Guilford, J. P., & Zimmerman, W. S. *The Guilford-Zimmerman temperament survey: Manual of instructions and interpretations*. Beverly Hills, Calif.: Sheridan Psychological Services, 1949.

L. R. Johnson

See Personality.

Faculty Psychology. Within philosophy a number of theories have been put forward to account for various mental activities. Many of these have taken the form of faculty psychologies. A faculty psychology is a philosophical doctrine that ascribes a number of powers to the mind. These powers, or faculties, are the method by which the mind exercises its influence. They represent not so much substructures as forces for implementing mental activity. Normally it is assumed that the mind is unitary but accomplishes its ends through multiple faculties. Originally faculties were descriptions of mental activity; later they became explanations. The existence of the faculties was deduced from observations of behavior that resembled the assumed underlying faculty.

A primitive faculty psychology is found in Plato's *Republic*. The mind was tripartite and its powers prioritized. Of highest value was intellect—located in the head—which was desired in rulers. Volition (spirit) was housed in the chest and was the source of courage for warriors. The lowest one, appetite, was located in the abdomen and was found in largest measure in artisans, tradesmen, and slaves. The relative development of faculties and the resulting division of labor ordered society (Heidbreder, 1933). The intellect strove for understanding, the spirit motivated one toward success, and the appetite sought bodily pleasure (Watson, 1978). These were revised by Augustine as reason, memory, and will. Imagination was a lesser faculty which mediated between memory and reason.

Aristotle suggested the psychic functions

were nutrition, sensation, and reason. Like expanding sets of rings, growth defined living nature, sensation highlighted animal nature, and reason defined human nature. Thomas Aquinas, in the Aristotelian tradition, held that the soul exercised its powers through the faculties of reason, sensing, and appetite. The senses were divided into the five exterior senses and the four interior senses of common sense, estimation and cogitation, imagination, and memory.

In the work of Descartes the mind retained its unity, but the faculties were reduced to two. Volition was unlimited; it provided for freedom of choice and was a means to account for error. Understanding, on the other hand, was limited; it was aided by imagination, memory, and the senses.

Faculty psychologies reached their highest influence in the eighteenth century in "the systematization of mental science" (Kantor, 1969, p. 134). The German Christian von Wolff and the Scottish school of Thomas Reid, Dugald Stewart, Thomas Brown, and William Hamilton reacted to the atomizing and naturalizing of the mind advocated by British associationists David Hume and David Hartley. The mental scientists abhorred the fragmentation of mind into a collection of associations and maintained rather the unity of mind (soul). Further, they attempted to incorporate classical theological dogma into the new psychology and adjust theological accounts to fit the newly acquired scientific data regarding the mind.

The soul, according to Wolff, was the entity which made one aware of self and outside events. Activities of the soul were accomplished through the faculties of cognition (which included sensing, perceiving, apperceiving, attending, imagining, and remembering) and volition (which included affections, appetites, and aversions). What marked cognition as distinct from volition was the former's clarity (cf. Descartes's analysis).

Reid extended the system by defining the mind as that which thinks, remembers, reasons, and wills. The body had certain properties, but mind had its operations. "*Faculty* is most properly applied to those powers of the mind which are original and natural, and which make a part of the constitution of the mind" (Reid, cited by Kantor, 1969, p. 150). This stood in direct opposition to the British associationists' empiricism. The mind's faculties were listed as consciousness, sensation, perception, attention, association, memory, reason, feelings, passions, instinct, and will. In Reid's return to mentalism even bodily forces were faculties of the mind.

Hamilton represents an eclecticism of Scottish faculty psychology and British associationism. Each of the five mental faculties had one or more processes. The presentative faculty was evidenced in sensation and perception. Attention and memory constituted the processes of the conservative faculty. Association was the basis for the reproductive faculty, while imagination was instrumental in the elaborative faculty. The regulative faculty subsumed the processes of abstraction, classification, and conditioning.

As more came to be known about mental capacities and the structure of the brain, the number of faculties multiplied. In the phrenology of Franz Joseph Gall and Johann Kaspar Spurzheim, the brain was conceived of as the secretory organ for mental processes. Highly developed mental processes were dependent on localization of mental function and specialization of brain structure. Cortical structures were the sites for some 37 mental faculties. The charlatanlike activities of Gall and Spurzheim and the multiplicity of faculties made phrenology the last faculty psychology. Furthermore, studies by Thorndike and Woodworth failed to demonstrate broad powers of learning and limited transfer of training, both of which were assumed in faculty psychology.

References

Heidbreder, E. *Seven psychologies*. New York: Appleton-Century-Crofts, 1933.

Kantor, J. R. *The scientific evolution of psychology* (Vol. 2). Chicago: Principia Press, 1969.

Watson, R. I. *The great psychologists* (4th ed.). Philadelphia: Lippincott, 1978.

R. L. TIMPE

See PSYCHOLOGY, HISTORY OF.

Failure, Fear of. *See* LEVEL OF ASPIRATION.

Fair Fight Training. *See* CREATIVE AGRESSION THERAPY.

Faith. A term that has been alternately defined as a set of beliefs or a set of actions. Of course, believing is itself an act, but the distinction between faith and work is as old as the New Testament book of James, which seems to opt for one side of the dilemma in identifying faith as a set of beliefs over against faithful behavior (James 2:14ff.). However, it should be added that the writer of James was arguing for a combination of belief and practice, as suggested by the statements, "Be doers of the word, and not hearers only, deceiving yourselves" (1:22) and "faith by itself, if it has no works, is dead" (2:17).

This is a more balanced viewpoint than might be initially supposed, and it is consonant with the import of the 11th chapter of Hebrews, where faith is depicted as launching out into life on the basis of "the assurance of things hoped for, the conviction of things not seen" (11:1). In the illustrations that follow, the writer of Hebrews mentions numerous biblical personages who "by faith" engaged in heroic, riskful action. The Thorndike-Barnhart dictionary affirms this combination of belief and action by defining faith as "believing without proof; trust."

It is this trust dimension, embedded in the Latin *credo*, that was the original connotation of the English word *believe*. The word *creed* came from the word for heart. To believe meant to set one's heart on. It had an active, behavioral component, similar to the implication of "entrustment" inherent in the Greek *pistis* used commonly in the New Testament to refer to faith.

Psychological Contributions. Early in this century Delacroix, a psychologist of religion, added a third dimension to the understanding of faith, namely culture or institutional religion. He termed this authoritative faith and distinguished it from reasoning faith (belief) and trusting faith (action). This third dimension provided for a person's accepting a given religious tradition as *the* faith for that person. Religious institutions in a culture provide this dimension with their creeds, rituals, and traditions. Delacroix's differentiation provided a basis for understanding people who identify themselves as members of the Christian faith, for example. He suggested that adjustment and conformity are the dynamic processes operating in this dimension of faith, just as reason and emotion are inherent in the other dimensions.

Most psychological understandings of faith have depended heavily on the proposal of the theologian Schleiermacher who, early in the nineteenth century, suggested faith was "a feeling of dependence" in which the individual had an intense experience of powerlessness coupled with an absolute reliance on the strength of a transcendent reality—i.e. God. Kierkegaard continued this emphasis with his depiction of faith as based on a "sickness unto death" which propelled a person to make the "leap of faith."

In this century Leuba built on the ideas of Schleiermacher and Kierkegaard and detailed the components of what he termed the "faith state." Faith is always preceded by a period of self-dissatisfaction and a yearning for enlightenment. He compared this prefaith period to that of symptoms in a disease in which a person fears a breakdown. The higher state is envisioned but seems out of reach. The resolution of this turmoil becomes the dominant preoccupation of the individual's mental life. Leuba suggested that when faith arrives, it is characterized by two inner experiences. First, the person feels that nothing else matters now that faith has come. Second, the intensity of joy and peace which results from surrendering to God is greater than any before experienced. Leuba believed that faith is primarily an emotion and that it is these faith feelings which provide the certainty with which people assert the truthfulness of their beliefs.

Leuba's ideas are similar to the "shift of energy" theory proposed by James as an explanation for religious experience—which has been identified with faith by many theorists. James suggested that in religion the mind focused its energy on the experience and excluded much else that might be distracting or troubling it. This theory provided the basis for his assertion that religious experience could integrate a person and provide a central purpose for life.

The most recent theorizing about faith has been done by developmental psychologist/theologian Fowler, who has defined faith as the "making and maintaining of meaning in life" (1981). He follows H. R. Niebuhr and Tillich in asserting that faith is a universal human concern in that one of the unique aspects of being human is a need to find meaning. Thus faith is the experience of becoming "ultimately concerned" in the sense that faith is that which ties life together finally or ultimately.

Stages of Faith Development. Fowler has been primarily concerned with delineating the developmental stages by which faith develops. In this endeavor he has relied heavily on the thinking of Erikson, a neoanalytic ego psychologist who has written about the several stages of identity formation; Piaget, a cognitive psychologist who has written about the development of the mental structures that make thinking possible; and Kohlberg, a philosophical psychologist who has applied Piaget's theory to moral development.

Fowler proposes six stages of faith plus infancy, which he describes as an "undifferentiated faith" period. He suggests that the theorists noted above contributed to his understanding of these stages by their emphasis on 1) how people know what they know (epistemology); 2) the structure, rather than the content, of faith; and 3) the interactional, as contrasted with the behavioral or the maturational, dimensions of development. As contrasted with these theorists, Fowler emphasizes a spiraling, as opposed to a hierarchical, model of development and perceives faith as dealing primarily with the logic of conviction, as opposed to the logic of rational certainty.

Following Erikson, Fowler sees infancy as a prefaith stage in which basic trust is the chief result of good parent-child interaction. The mutuality, hope, and love that emerge from such experiences provide the basis for faith in the later stages and can be distorted either by overindulgence, leading to narcissism, or negligence, leading to isolation and distrust.

Stage 1 typically occurs from ages 3–7 and is termed intuitive-projective faith, in that the need for meaning is fashioned by fantasy-filled, imitative interactions with the overt faith of the primary adults in the child's life. Self-awareness comes into being during this time, and the child becomes aware for the first time of death, sex, and taboos that are central to cultural faith. The emergent strength of this stage is imagination, while the danger is that the child's mind will be filled with terror.

Stage 2 typically occurs at about 10 years of age and is termed mythic-literal faith, in that the need for meaning is fashioned by the child affirming for himself the stories, beliefs, and observances that indicate belonging to the community of faith with which he is soon to identify. The imagination of the previous stage is curbed and channeled into an almost literal acceptance of the symbols of the faith-culture in which he lives. The emergent strength of this stage is the ability to live through story and drama, which give coherence to experience, while there is danger in the overliteral acceptance of the factual truth of the stories.

Stage 3 is typical of the adolescent years and is termed synthetic-conventional faith, in that the need for meaning is fashioned by identification with others beyond the family and an affirmation of the interpersonal dimension of the faith experience. The literalness of the previous stage is replaced with the vitality of present experiences with others. The emergent strength of this stage is that the individual begins to form a personal story of faith identity, while the dangers lie in a possible overconformity to others' wishes and a too intense reliance on other persons who may betray such trust.

Stage 4 is typical of the adult years 20–30 and is termed individuative-reflective faith, in that the need for meaning is fashioned by the assumption of responsibility for fashioning one's own commitments, life style, beliefs, and attitudes. Although many persons remain at stage 3, those who move to stage 4 have to face the tension of individuality and the reality of personal feelings that may have been suppressed. The emergent strength of this stage lies in the critical capacity to reflect on identity (self) and on outlook (ideology), while there is the danger of becoming overconfident in one's ability to critically examine one's faith.

Stage 5 is typical of middle adulthood and is termed conjunctive faith, in that the need for meaning is fashioned by acquisition of the ability to do both/and rather than either/or thinking. In this stage, when it occurs, the individual becomes able to both trust others and the traditions they represent and to reflect in a critical manner on any and all conventions. Fowler calls this "dialogical" knowing. It involves a new reworking of one's past and an integration of convictions and feelings in a new unity. The emergent strength of this stage is the acquisition of ironic imagination in which one can be in, but not of, one's surroundings, while the danger is the possibility that one will become passive and inactive due to this newfound insight.

Stage 6, which does not usually appear before late adulthood—if it appears at all—is termed universalizing faith, in that the need for meaning is fashioned by an overcoming of the paradoxes of stage 5 and an active involvement in the imperatives of love and justice as an expression of faith. The emergent strength of this stage is the perception of the truths beneath the creeds of traditional religion and the willingness to become involved in bringing about the order to which these religions point—e.g., the kingdom of God. The danger of this stage is possible disillusionment that may result when success does not come.

In all of the above stages there is the implicit assumption that faith is a universal necessity and that it can be more or less mature. Numerous investigations are presently being undertaken to assess whether Fowler's stages can be validated empirically.

References
Fowler, J. W. *Stages of faith.* San Francisco: Harper & Row, 1981.

H. N. MALONY

Faith Healing. In American culture faith healing is most commonly associated with miracles and religion. One imagines an emotionally charged gathering in which an enthusiastic, charismatic preacher exhorts members of the audience to trust in God, throw down their crutches, and "claim their cure." The "miracle services" led by Kathryn Kuhlman followed this pattern. Healing obtained in such a setting is usually attributed by the participants to a divine intervention which sets aside the natural laws governing the course of physical illness. The sufferer's belief or faith in God is seen as the key to this miraculous event.

In the popular and scientific literature the term *faith healing* is used in a variety of contexts. Psychic healing, chiropractic, folk medicine, and shamanism—as well as religious or sacramental healing—have all been referred to as faith healing. Some authors seem to use the term interchangeably with nonmedical treatment. Others use it in a pejorative fashion to connote quackery or primitive or unscientific technique.

Faith healing has, in fact, long been one of the more controversial topics in both the medical and religious communities. Nor has the debate over the validity of the phenomenon raged solely between the two camps, for each has been divided within its own ranks. The lines of argument have often been drawn quite absolutely, leading to incredible claims for the healing efficacy of religious faith on the one hand and, on the other, to blind rejection of genuine extramedical healing phenomena.

The resolution of at least some of this conflict has come in the research on psychosomatic relationships, which has made the concept of faith healing acceptable to the religious- and scientific-minded alike. Studies in such areas as biofeedback and meditation have demonstrated the mind's ability to influence bodily function. Among others, Simonton's cancer research suggests that visual imagery and positive changes in attitude can alter the course of illness, even to the point of total remission of cancer symptoms (Simonton, Matthews-Simonton, & Creighton, 1978). There is by now a host of research findings correlating changes in attitude, feeling, or belief with changes in the body, thus providing an empirical base for what has been observed phenomenologically for millennia; namely, that faith healing often "works."

However, what is known of psychosomatics fails to account for the rare but well-documented cases of instantaneous and total cure of diseases otherwise thought to be incurable and the rejuvenation of organ systems thought to be beyond repair (cf. Clapp, 1983).

Two concepts of faith healing will be addressed here. First, the term *faith healing* often refers to any process whereby positive physical change correlates with and is apparently caused or mediated by changes in the individual's values, attitudes, or beliefs. While virtually every healing is probably affected by the person's disposition toward it, faith healing in this first sense refers to healing in which the *primary* cause or mediating influence appears to be "faith," understood psychologically.

Note that this is a psychological rather than a religious or theological understanding of faith healing and that the content of one's beliefs may or may not relate to the divine. Faith healing in the psychological sense is differentiated from medical or surgical healing, in which the presumed cause is chemical or physical, and from psychic healing, in which the presumed cause is some power transmitted from or through the healer.

This first concept of faith healing is further differentiated from a second common usage, in which the term relates to "miraculous" healing, or healing occurring in contradiction to what is considered possible through medical/surgical or psychological intervention. Within the Christian religious community the presumed cause of such faith healing is God.

History. Healing by faith is an old tradition. In antiquity it often centered around religious ritual. The Greeks, for instance, believed that disease was the work of the gods and that cures required the intervention of other gods, such as Asclepius. Accordingly, people would journey far to one of his temples, there to sleep and, they hoped, to receive a healing vision of the god. Testimonial plaques left by some pilgrims attest to cures of blindness, lameness, paralysis, baldness, and a multitude of other ailments. Old Testament Hebrews also placed healing within the province of religion, believing that sickness was a result of sin, and therefore healing was a task reserved for the Levites and other religious figures.

Healing was an integral part of Jesus' ministry, and he also taught his followers to heal. Faith seems to have been a critical ingredient in at least some of these healings, in that Jesus often used the phrase, "Your faith has made you whole" (Mark 10:52). By contrast, on other occasions the utter disbelief of his audience apparently prevented healing from occurring (Mark 6:5–6).

Since the time of Christ there have been groups and individuals within the Christian church who have continued Jesus' emphasis on healing through faith. For example, since the mid-nineteenth century thousands of pilgrims yearly have journeyed to a shrine in Lourdes,

France, in search of healing at the spring there. The shrine was constructed at the site of a young girl's vision of a woman calling herself the Immaculate Conception. The Roman Catholic Church has since carefully documented numerous cures (actually a very small fraction of the cures sought) obtained there which defy medical explanation.

Until recently, however, the church as a whole had largely departed from the ministry of healing. Kelsey (1973) traces this official departure to about the tenth century, when the service of unction for healing was gradually transformed into extreme unction, a rite of passage for the dying. Subsequently a whole theology arose to show why the "gift of healing" disappeared and is no longer a proper concern of Christianity. As Kelsey demonstrates, however, more recent theology and practice have reinstated healing by faith into the fabric of the church. Today it is practiced widely across the Christian denominations.

Psychological Approaches to Faith Healing. Psychological studies of faith healing have approached it from many directions, including the interpersonal, situational, psychophysiological, and intrapersonal dimensions of the phenomenon.

Social factors have been shown to have a powerful influence on healing, as is clearly demonstrated in research on the placebo effect in medicine. Placebo medications (usually saline or lactose), which have no specific chemical activity for the condition being treated, bring symptom relief in about a third of the cases in which they are used (Beecher, 1955). The "active ingredient" appears to be the patient's belief in the medication, which is affected in turn by the doctor-patient relationship (Shapiro, 1964). In general, the doctor who is warm, empathic, friendly, reassuring, and not conflicted about the patient or the treatment elicits positive placebo reactions, whereas the doctor who is angry, rejecting of the patient, or preoccupied with personal problems is more likely to elicit negative placebo reactions. Presumably any interpersonal variables affecting the doctor's ability to persuade the patient (cf. Frank, 1961) would be relevant here. The doctor's own belief in the medication's efficacy also effects the patient's response, since the placebo effect increases if the doctor is told that the agent is active and not a placebo.

Patient variables thought to influence faith, and thereby healing, have often been studied under the rubric of suggestibility, or susceptibility to interpersonal influence (Calestro, 1972). One broad area of research has tested hypotheses linking suggestibility to personality traits, various neurotic disorders, or other patient variables such as sex and age (Shapiro, 1964). Another line of research has studied the elements of communication that enhance attitude change. Compatibility of the patient's assumptive world or system of belief with that of the doctor or healer is one important factor here.

Still another relevant area of study is that of psychosomatic research, which addresses the broad question, "Under what conditions will what thoughts, feelings, beliefs, or attitudes produce what sorts of physiological changes and by what psychophysical mechanisms or pathways? For example, placebos have been hypothesized to act via the cerebral cortex, which activates elements of the endocrine system, thereby producing specific chemical changes in the body which promote healing.

Still, understanding the factors that enhance faith or the pathways by which it operates does not necessarily bring one to an understanding of faith itself.

Phenomenologically, we observe that one has faith that something is the case when it does not occur to one to doubt it. A nearly parallel expression is that faith is the lack of resistance to that which one hopes to receive. These expressions imply two things. First, faith has cognitive content. That is, there is some situation or event that is anticipated, based on a specific set of beliefs about the way things are—beliefs that may or may not have religious content. Second, faith involves an openness or a positive expectation that this event or situation will occur or is already occurring.

It is at this point that existential psychology further illuminates our understanding of faith. To the existentialist faith is more appropriately conceived as "faithing." That is, it is an act which one undertakes with the totality of one's being. Faith may be seen as the decision on the part of the self to open itself to the possibility of completion or growth. Such an act is the response of the person to life itself. It is the will to live—one's willingness to *be*. This act of opening oneself may be the key that unlocks the body's own healing resources. Indeed, faith healing is often seen simply as a facilitator of spontaneous remission.

A Transpersonal Approach to Faith Healing. There is quite possibly yet another aspect to faith healing; namely, a transpersonal dimension. One is forced into considering such a possibility by those cases of "miraculous" or instantaneous healing that apparently go beyond psychosomatics.

Viewed in this fashion faith is understood as that internal state of being "in which alone God can get near enough to man to do *his* work. The power of faith is, in one sense, nil. It is the state of personality in which God can exert *his* power" (Weatherhead, 1951, p. 431). In this religious concept of faith man may be conceived as essentially spirit and healing as resulting from his faithing response to, and joining with, Spirit, or God. Faith, then, is an existential openness, a "thirst and a desire that moves man toward the Absolute" (Panikkar, 1971, p. 223).

This view of faith does not supplant psychological approaches to faith healing, since the transpersonal dimension of faith is seen either as orthogonal to its psychosomatic dimension or as prior to it in the sense of being an ultimate cause, with the psychosomatic relationship being the proximate cause of the healing.

A Christian Critique. Misunderstanding of the nature and purpose of faith in healing has led to serious distortions within the church. While there is a relationship between health (conceived holistically rather than purely physically) and holiness (conceived as right relationship with God), some Christians believe that failure to be healed implies some fault on the sufferer's part (namely, a lack of religious faith) and consequently stigmatize those who are not cured. Others will die refusing medical or other physical assistance, believing that sickness is sent from God to punish sin and must therefore be endured unless and until one can "please" God with appropriate "faith."

Yet the concept of healing by faith is clearly rooted in the teachings of Jesus. Faith, whether considered in its psychological or religious aspect, is integral to healing. A balanced perspective on faith and healing would accept the help that psychology and medicine can afford, while at the same time being open to the possibility of miracles.

Whether such anomalous healing is the result of an unknown psychophysical mechanism, the direct intervention of the Deity, or something akin to the "inner shift" of which *A Course in Miracles* (Foundation for Inner Peace, 1975) speaks is yet unknown. The research problems inherent in any attempt to answer this question are enormous and probably insurmountable, although one may, of course, venture to discover the answer experientially.

References
Beecher, H. K. The powerful placebo. *Journal of the American Medical Association, 1955, 159,* 1602–1606.
Calestro, K. M. Psychotherapy, faith healing, and suggestion. *International Journal of Psychiatry, 1972, 10* (2), 83–113.
Clapp, R. Faith healing: A look at what's happening. *Christianity Today, 1983, 27*(19), 12–17.
Foundation for Inner Peace. *A course in miracles* (3 vols.). Tiburon, Calif.: Author, 1975.
Frank, J. D. *Persuasion and healing: A comparative study of psychotherapy.* Baltimore: Johns Hopkins Press, 1961.
Kelsey, M. T. *Healing and Christianity.* New York: Harper & Row, 1973.
Panikkar, R. Faith—A constitutive dimension of man. *Journal of Ecumenical Studies, 1971, 8*(2), 223–254.
Shapiro, A. K. Factors contributing to the placebo effect. *American Journal of Psychotherapy, 1964, 18* (Supplement No. 1), 73–88.
Simonton, O. C., Matthews-Simonton, S., & Creighton, J. *Getting well again.* Los Angeles: J. P. Tarcher, 1978.
Weatherhead, L. D. *Psychology, religion, and healing.* Nashville: Abingdon, 1951.

Additional Reading
Frazier, C. A. (Ed). *Faith healing: Finger of God or scientific curiosity?* Nashville: Thomas Nelson, 1973.

B. Van Dragt

False Pregnancy. *See* Pseudocyesis.

Family Choreography. A variation of the family therapy technique known as sculpting. The method involves asking family members to physically arrange themselves in various positions to create a picture of how they perceive themselves as a group. Individuals are requested to place themselves in the family tableau and to assume postures and expressions that describe their feelings about being in the family (Papp, 1976).

An angry, domineering father, for example, might stand on a chair angrily pointing at a rebellious son below. The son is facing the door as if he were about to leave the family. The mother has hold of the back of his shirt while looking toward the father with a pleading look.

Choreography is ordinarily used at the beginning of therapy as a diagnostic aid. The family can also be choreographed according to the ideal of each of its members. Choreographing the family as it is and as it ideally would like to be helps to identify relationship changes needed within the family.

Reference
Papp, P. Family choreography. In P. J. Guerin, Jr. (Ed.), *Family therapy: Theory and practice.* New York: Gardner Press, 1976.

J. A. Larsen

See Family Sculpture Technique; Family Therapy: Overview.

Family Communications Theory. "Toward a Theory of Schizophrenia" was the title of a paper (Bateson, Jackson, Haley, & Weakland, 1956) and the beginning of a conceptual revolution in psychology and psychiatry. It set forth the DOUBLE BIND theory of schizophrenia. It vaulted four men and their associates into prominence in the field of abnormal psychology. It proposed interpersonal rather than intrapsychic roots for the genesis and maintenance of human psychopathology. It promoted a family-oriented therapy at the expense of individual psychoanalytic therapy. And it announced a wedding between general systems theory and human mental health, a relationship which has since then blossomed.

Essential Characteristics and their Development. Family communications theory grew out of research mainly on the families of young adults diagnosed schizophrenic. The principles evolved there were soon applied to a wider range of disorders, especially those brought to therapists by married couples having troubles between themselves or with a misbehaving child. The theory highlights the nature of communications in families of origin as the most important factor in personality development. Ongoing relationships in later adult life, such as marriage and parenting, continue to be expressed and determined by patterns of communications. How things are said, both verbally and nonverbally, reveals the kind of relationship two or more persons have and the kind of identity each has in the other's eyes.

The 1956 double bind paper represented a research project on human communications headed in Palo Alto, California, by the noted anthropologist Gregory Bateson. He brought there with him from Columbia University two able research assistants, John Weakland and Jay Haley. A brilliant psychiatrist, Don D. Jackson, joined the team and later founded the Mental Research Institute and its brief therapy center in Palo Alto. Out of a welter of early research directions the team focused on the nature of schizophrenic transactions.

The team resolved not to be shackled by prevailing conceptions of psychopathology, which in general followed the epistemology, and largely unexamined philosophical assumptions that Freud used. They labeled themselves "clinical anthropologists." They repeatedly asked themselves, "*What* is going on here?" rather than "Why?" as they watched people interacting. They struggled to answer a fundamental question: What would be their basic unit of observation? Previous thinking had somehow selected individual persons and what they said as the units of study. That choice produced datum statements like "Mr. X said Y." The new researchers took a larger view, selecting a system in operation as its unit

of study. Their datum statements took the form "Mr. X said Y to Mrs. X in context Z."

One concept emphasized in almost all family communications theory literature is that people send messages on several levels at once. A grade-school boy, taunted by playmates, with tears in his eyes shouts angrily at them, "You can't hurt me. I don't care what you say." His tears say he is hurt. His words say he's not. His angry manner says he wants to hurt his playmates. Erickson studied and masterfully applied such multilevel messages in his version of indirect hypnotherapy (Haley, 1973). The Palo Alto group frequently consulted him.

Virginia Satir also worked with the Palo Alto group at one time. Her *Conjoint Family Therapy* (Satir, 1967) stands as a classic in family communications theory. It stresses ways to help family members clarify their communications. She later collaborated (Bandler, Grinder, & Satir, 1976) to apply rules of semantic analysis to family therapy. In 1977 three of the authors of the 1956 double-bind paper joined with four other family therapy theorists for a conference entitled Beyond the Double Bind. A book by the same title (Berger, 1978) carries the proceedings of that conference, telling what effects the double bind theory had in 20 years, where research has gone since 1956, and what changes have been made in the theory.

Communication. Family communication theorists emphasize that we cannot *not* communicate. This rule derives from the view that all behavior between people is communication. Therefore, it is inappropriate even to say that I communicate. That is, I cannot originate communication with you; anything I say or do merely participates in the communication that is already happening between us (Watzlawick, Beavin, & Jackson, 1967). This means that I have no choice *whether* to respond to you, only *how*.

Every message is both information from sender to receiver and a comment on the kind of relationship the sender considers them to have. These are the report or content aspect—the "what" of a message, and the command or relationship aspect—the "how" (Watzlawick et al., 1967, p. 51). For example, a man barks to his wife, "Pick up a gallon of milk on your way home." On the report level he is informing her that their milk supply is low. On the command level he is defining their relationship as one in which he gives her orders and expects her to comply. If his wife answers, "Get it yourself," she is not indicating an aversion to milk, but rather is proposing a redefinition of their relationship.

The next principle is that of message levels. Messages may contain both communication and metacommunication (Watzlawick, Weakland, & Fisch, 1974). A metacomment is an editorial comment, a comment about a comment. In order to clarify our meanings we must be able to talk about how we talk. In the above exchange the wife could have responded to the milk message with a metacomment such as, "I'm not sure if that's an order or a request." Such a request for clarification regarding incongruence in a message is essential for good communication.

A final rule about communicating is that we do it in two modes: digital and analogic. Digital communication is verbal and conveys primarily the content of a message. Analogic communication is nonverbal and carries most of the relationship aspect of a message. Each of these either reinforces or disqualifies the other. A man says to a woman, "We've got to stop meeting like this" and winks. She knows he wants to continue the relationship.

Personality. Family communications theorists frequently note that the concept of an individual is of less and less use in attempting to understand human behavior. They view persons as fragments of families. The aspect of behavior that they emphasize is its intended impact on others (i.e., its communicative nature). They imply therefore that personality consists of an individual's characteristic communicating styles. People learn these styles as they do their native tongue, in their early years in their families of origin.

Language is rule-governed behavior, even when speakers do not consciously recognize the rules they are following. So it is with a family's communication patterns that each member internalizes. Adults look for partners who "speak their language"—i.e., who function by rules of communication similar to the ones they themselves adopted early in life. To the extent that their partners do not follow the same rules, people try to make them do so. Many marital feuds trace back to disputes over communication rules which each partner holds to be self-evident truths. However, neither one can articulate the rules, nor do they realize that such rules are often the basis of their relationship conflicts.

Psychopathology. The ability to metacommunicate is essential to healthy interaction. Some families have unspoken yet rigidly enforced rules against the children commenting on how someone else has communicated. It is

as if there is an elephant in the room and a covert agreement to keep it secret by acting as if it's not there. "There's an elephant in the room and nobody is acknowledging it" would make the covert overt.

Families that have a young adult or teen-age member who is diagnosed schizophrenic have a peculiar way of dealing with a metacomment like the above. They disqualify the speaker, or the fact that the speaker spoke, or the pertinence to them of what the speaker said. Such families are said to be in schizophrenic transaction. This description has come to replace the term *schizophrenogenic*, which arose soon after the 1956 paper and usually inferred that the mother in such families made the child schizophrenic. The way she did this was said to be by creating double binds on the child.

The term *double bind* is often used incorrectly for any difficult situation. Its precise definition involves six conditions: 1) two or more persons, 2) interacting repeatedly in such a way that 3) one of them becomes the victim or target of a negative injunction or warning of the form, "If you do X, I will punish you"; 4) the victim also receives a secondary prohibition contradicting some aspect of the primary injunction (e.g., "Do not think of me as a punishing person or I will punish you"); 5) the victim cannot escape the field; and 6) the victim cannot comment on what is happening.

The authors of the double bind theory (Bateson, et al., 1956) further stated that victims come to perceive their universe in double bind patterns. Then the full set of original conditions is no longer necessary to provoke the predictable reaction of panic or rage. Psychotic behavior beomes a rather creative way to respond to the double bind, since it avoids violating any of the conditions while at the same time forsaking the impossible task of resolving their contradictions.

Double bind as a theory for the development of schizophrenia stands unproven and largely discarded. There simply have never been found the droves of schizophrenogenic mothers which the theory postulates. Schizophrenia remains a phenomenon of keen research interest along multicausal lines. The theory lives on as a rich and valued concept for viewing dysfunctionally communicating systems and for designing therapeutic interventions to improve family interaction patterns.

Psychotherapy. Although the double bind theory was never intended to be a theory of therapy, many practitioners took it as a starting point for much that they began to do. Since the theory said pathology originates in families, therapists began meeting with whole families when one young person was the identified patient. Since the theory said pathology is interactional, therapists began to focus on interactions in the family and on how they could improve these.

Subsequent refinements do not as rigidly require that whole families be present at each session. The very concept of an interacting system implies that a change made in any one member or in any one relationship within a family cannot help but alter the entire system.

Haley (1976), more than the other theorists mentioned here, has continued working with schizophrenics since his Palo Alto work in the 1950s. He has become even more adamantly against individually focused, insight-oriented therapy than he was in 1956. He now trains therapists to direct parents to manage their child's specific behavior so that the child does not act crazy. Haley even downplays communication training and marital therapy in favor of concretely solving problems that keep families from emancipating their young persons into socially useful adult independence.

Satir (1967) makes a strong communications focus in family therapy sessions. A statement she might offer would be this: "Mrs. X, as you were telling about your sadness over your son's accident, your husband's eyes filled and he reached for a Kleenex. I wonder what you think he was telling you about *his* feelings."

Paradoxical techniques are strongly identified with double bind theory and with therapies that derive from it. The heart of therapeutic paradox lies in encouraging patients to do more of the behavior you want them to stop. A therapist might urge a conflicting couple to have a fight right in the office and to raise their voices louder than usual. The couple then laughs instead of fighting. Why? Theory says that symptomatic behavior is the only spontaneous action a person sees possible when feelings are caught in a double bind. When the therapist prescribes the symptom, the persons can no longer do it spontaneously. The artistry of creating therapeutic double binds (blessed if you do, blessed if you don't) is described in detail in *Paradox and Counterparadox* (Palazolli-Selvini, Boscolo, Cecchin, & Prata, 1978) and the many writings of Erickson.

Relationship to Christianity. Although the fact is not acknowledged by its proponents, family communications theory shares several emphases in common with biblical Christianity. Communication is fundamental to God, both among the three persons of the Godhead and between God and humanity. Human be-

ings were created for communication with God and with each other. In fact, the social and communicative nature of mankind is so fundamental to personality that God gave Adam a partner, Eve, so that he could relate to another person and not just to God.

The Godhead can thus be seen as an interactive system. Man, created in God's image, is therefore created for interaction and communication. The New Testament concept of the church as the body of Christ is distinctly that of an interacting system regulating itself for the benefit of all concerned.

The concept that we cannot *not* communicate epitomizes the biblical view of humans as capable of responsibility. Joshua challenged, "Choose this day whom you will serve." Clearly, not to choose God was to choose rebellion. Not to decide is to decide.

References

Bandler, R., Grinder, J., & Satir, V. *Changing with families*. Palo Alto, Calif.: Science and Behavior Books, 1976.
Bateson, G., Jackson, D. D., Haley, J., & Weakland, J. H. Toward a theory of schizophrenia. *Behavioral Science*, 1956, *1*, 251–264.
Berger, M. (Ed.). *Beyond the double bind*. New York: Brunner/Mazel, 1978.
Haley, J. *Uncommon therapy: The psychiatric techniques of Milton H. Erickson, M. D.* New York: 1973.
Haley, J. *Problem solving therapy*. San Francisco: Jossey-Bass, 1976.
Palazolli-Selvini, M., Boscolo, L., Cecchin, G. & Prata, G. *Paradox and counterparadox*. New York: Aronson, 1978.
Satir, V. *Conjoint family therapy* (Rev. ed.). Palo Alto, Calif.: Science and Behavior Books, 1967.
Watzlawick, P., Beavin, J. H., & Jackson, D. D. *Pragmatics of human communication*. New York: Norton, 1967.
Watzlawick, P., Weakland, J. H., & Fisch, R. *Change*. New York: Norton, 1974.

D. L. Gibson

See Conjoint Family Therapy; Family Systems Theory.

Family Context Therapy. *See* Family Group Therapy.

Family Crisis Therapy. A technique developed by Langsley and Kaplan (1968) to relieve acute psychiatric reactions in family members by seeing the entire family together on an outpatient basis rather than hospitalizing the identified patient. The presupposition is that the crisis is precipitated by all the family members' maladaptive responses to the increased stress that can result from developmental or situational changes. Immediate psychiatric help is sought when unresolved conflicts result in highly dysfunctional behavior in the most susceptible member, thereby increasing the tension of the entire family to what it perceives as an unmanageable level.

The interventions in the technique differ from individual crisis counseling by guiding the family members to conjointly contribute to the resolution of the crisis. The principles of the therapy are: 1) the immediate availability of around-the-clock help; 2) the presence of all family members in the initial session and the possible involvement of members in subsequent contacts; 3) an emphasis on the present, with history taking limited to the events leading to the crisis; 4) the use of highly supportive types of interventions; 5) the assignment of specific tasks that lead to renewed functioning and the gradual resolution of the crisis state; 6) instructions about future crises and the assurance that help will be available, even if only in the form of a telephone call.

The technique is especially valuable for those families prone to repeated crisis reactions where one or more members react with severe symptoms such as a psychotic episode or suicidal threat.

References

Langsley, D. G., & Kaplan, D. M. *The treatment of families in crisis.* New York: Grune & Stratton, 1968.

F. J. WHITE

See SHORT-TERM THERAPIES; CRISIS INTERVENTION.

Family Diagram. Sometimes called a genogram, the family diagram is a shorthand used in family therapy for mapping three or more generations of a family. It provides the therapist with an overall structural picture of the family by delineating membership and boundaries.

Symbols are used to represent people and relationships. A circle denotes a female, a square a male. A horizontal line between two people indicates marriage. A vertical line drawn downward from a horizontal line (marriage) to an individual denotes offspring.

Constructing a family diagram is a low-threat method of obtaining a family's history. Basic identifying information (names, ages, careers) is gathered along with transitional events (marriages, deaths, moves). Issues of therapeutic significance (quarrels, secrets, crises) may also surface in the course of constructing a family diagram.

J. A. LARSEN

See FAMILY THERAPY: OVERVIEW.

Family Group Therapy. While most other approaches to family therapy are clinically derived, John Elderkin Bell developed family group therapy based on group dynamics theory. Using social psychology research on small group interaction, he found several parallels between small group interaction and family dynamics, particularly the process of problem solving as a group task. Unlike persons in group therapy, the family members are involved in a long-term relationship both prior to and following completion of psychotherapy. Between sessions there is continuous interaction that relates directly to the family's problem-solving skills. Actually the family is in the best position to identify and solve the family problems, and family group therapy is an approach designed to help them do that (Bell, 1970).

Instead of focusing on communication problems and content analysis, Bell stresses functional analysis. This is an emphasis on the family's use of "purposes or motivations, evaluations, resolutions and decisions, interpersonal adjustments, rehearsals, and other elements of the total action process" (Bell, 1976, p. 131).

Bell identified seven stages of family group therapy. First, therapy is initiated by some family concern or an external recommendation for the family to get help. The family seeks out the therapist and the terms of their relationship are discussed. At the first session the family members discuss expectations for themselves and the therapist, as well as who will attend the sessions. The second stage involves the family testing the firmness and flexibility of the therapy rules. This often involves expression of intense feelings as well as challenges for control of the session.

The third stage involves a more explicit struggle for power. This challenges the therapist's ability to work with the family without being drawn into their difficulties. The therapist must maintain a position of process leader in order for the family to pursue its priorities. This means that the selection of a common task, the fourth stage, agreed upon by all family members, becomes the focus of the sessions. The family becomes a group, focusing on a common task that utilizes the resources of each family member.

The fifth stage, struggling for task completion, necessitates family members developing creative ways to utilize each other's strengths in order to work out their problems. Intrusions, interruptions, and other events which slow or impede work on the common task become opportunities for family members to practice new ways of working with each other. The common task provides a continuous focus throughout the difficulties of learning to work together effectively. Task completion, the sixth stage, is reached when the family members agree that they do not need any further work on the common task. Each family member gives evidence of his or her satisfaction with the results either through personal insights, support of other members, or other means. The final stage, separation, is usually accompanied by the strengthening of the familial bond. The desire to function without the therapist may be stated clearly, or the family may try to push the therapist away by strong negative statements. The therapist likewise must separate from the family and support their move toward independence (Bell, 1976).

Bell describes healthy and efficient families as those which have mutual satisfaction of their members, complementary aims and support of the family as a group, and flexibility to adapt to individual demands of the group. The healthy family also has a variety of patterns to deal with conflict and can evaluate "the consequences of its achievements of accommodations" (Bell, 1971, pp. 869–870).

The therapist's purposes play a pivotal role in the family group therapy process. Not only is the therapist a leader, but the direction of leadership must be clear. The family is encouraged to be as autonomous as possible. Keeping the family on target with their agreed-upon task minimizes diversion into low-priority concerns. The hope is that the family will experience successful problem solving during the sessions and will be able to generalize these experiences and techniques to other family situations. The therapist must remain free of emotional entanglements with the family in order that the family will learn to maximize its resources and to rely on each other to assist in problem solving. Because each family is different, each must work out its own problem-solving methods, with the therapist guiding them through this process.

According to Bell, it is important that the therapist have no relationship with family members other than during the sessions. There are no private sessions with family members and no conjoint sessions. It is strictly a group process, and this must be adhered to throughout work with the family.

It is the therapist's role to attempt to bridge gaps between family members, model effective listening, affirm the value of each family member, and work with the family at a pace that facilitates development of their boundaries as well as their autonomy. Families are encourged to experiment, to try different ways of working on problems in order to increase their flexibility and their aware-

ness of the resources within the family system (Bell, 1976).

Family group therapy addresses many different aspects of family functioning and in general seems to balance the significance of individual growth and learning with working together effectively as a group. Its utilization of small group processes and dynamics is an interesting alternative to clinically derived family therapy approaches.

References

Bell, J. E. A theoretical position for family group therapy. In N. W. Ackerman (Ed.), *Family process.* New York: Basic Books, 1970.

Bell, J. E. Recent advances in family group therapy. In J. G. Howells (Ed.), *Theory and practice of family psychiatry.* New York: Brunner/ Mazel, 1971.

Bell, J. E. A theoretical framework for family group therapy. In P. J. Guerin (Ed.), *Family therapy.* New York: Gardner Press, 1976.

T. M. JOHNSON

See FAMILY THERAPY: OVERVIEW.

Family Life Cycle. A concept employing ideas from developmental psychology for analysis of family units. It is based on the idea that just as individual human organisms develop through a successive series of stages as they interact with the environment, so the family as a unit also develops through a set of predictable stages.

The family life cycle concept was articulated by E. Duvall in the 1950s when she built on Havighurst's (1949) concept of developmental tasks. Developmental tasks are understood as culturally defined needs based on a person's stage in his or her own development. Havighurst and others suggested that there is an identifiable list of developmental tasks that each person must resolve at each stage of human development.

Building on this idea, Duvall (1977) developed a list of developmental tasks that each family faces at each stage of its development. Those tasks are to establish and maintain 1) an independent home, 2) satisfactory ways of getting and spending money, 3) mutually acceptable patterns in the division of labor, 4) mutually satisfying sex relationships, 5) an open system of intellectual and emotional communication, 6) workable relationships with relatives, 7) ways of interacting with associates and community organizations, 8) competency in rearing children, and 9) a workable philosophy of life.

Duvall has suggested that eight stages in the family life cycle can be identified. Each stage can be described by approximate ages of the family members during this stage, the relative length of the stage, and specific developmental tasks of that stage. Since stages are often based on the point of development of the oldest child, a family may actually overlap into more than one stage at a time. Duvall's descriptions of these stages are based on American norms and may differ with any particular family for a number of reasons, though each family will still have its own developmental cycle.

Stage 1: Married couples. During this stage there are no children. The husband and wife are usually in their 20s. On an average this stage lasts about 2 years. For the typical couple who will bear and rear children this is a stage of orientation, establishing a base upon which the family will be built. Not all the tasks of this stage are forward-looking. Wives and husbands are themselves already members of the family, and their own individual developments are being influenced by how they, as the married couple, resolve the tasks of the first stage of their family life cycle.

Stage 2: Childbearing families. A family is in this stage until the oldest child is 30 months old. Childbearing families must face radical changes in their life style from the married couple stage. Maintaining the strength of the base from stage 1 is a major task of stage 2.

Stage 3: Families with preschool children. This stage lasts about 2½–3½ years, until the oldest child is school age. As the oldest child develops more independence socially and physically, the family takes on a new character. By this time parents are usually in their late 20s and early 30s and are settling down more in social and occupational roles.

Stage 4: Families with school-age children. For about 7 years the family faces tasks created by an ever-widening world when their oldest child enters school. The child is also at a peak time in terms of achievement and mastery, and much of the family's resources will be directed toward these needs.

Stage 5: Families with teen-agers. The family will experience this stage for another 7 years as the oldest child develops more emotional and ideational independence.

Stage 6: Families launching young adults. Duvall suggests that this stage lasts about 8 years—from the time the oldest child leaves home until the youngest leaves and all children have established themselves as independent of their parental family living unit.

Stage 7: Empty nest. This stage usually lasts for over 15 years—from the time the last child leaves home through retirement years for the parents. The parents must learn to adapt to a new life style. There is often new strain on the

married couple who have kept themselves together by child rearing. Children too must learn to adjust to any new life styles and values that their parents might develop.

Stage 8: Aging family members. For 10 or 15 years the family is in its last stage as the parents age and as each spouse dies. This stage is marked by decreases in many resources— money, energy, health, and friends.

The family life cycle concept is useful for analyzing families. How the developmental needs, tasks, and processes of individual family members affect the family as a unit can be identified, as can the effect of the family unit's stage upon individual development. Thus the concept is useful in identifying how to be helpful to individual family members or to the family as a unit.

References
Duvall, E. M. *Marriage and family development* (5th ed.). Philadelphia: Lippincott, 1977.
Havighurst, R. J. *Developmental tasks and education.* Chicago: University of Chicago Press, 1949.

R. B. MᶜKᴇᴀɴ

Family Network Therapy. See Sᴏᴄɪᴀʟ Nᴇᴛᴡᴏʀᴋ Iɴᴛᴇʀᴠᴇɴᴛɪᴏɴ.

Family Scapegoating. Also described by some as the family projection process, this is a process whereby an individual is unconsciously selected to carry the symptoms of a disturbed family. While some scapegoating occurs naturally in most "normal" families without serious symptomatology, in more troubled situations the scapegoated member develops a behavioral and/or emotional disorder. In family therapy this person is commonly referred to as the "identified patient."

Scapegoating takes various forms, but the process essentially involves one or both parents projecting their emotional problems onto a child. Unable to protect themselves against parental pathology, these children eventually accept the role and try to make the most of it.

The willingness of scapegoats to accept the symptom-bearing role is surprising to those who do not see the reinforcement involved. Parents, for example, often focus on and express overconcern about the child's problems. In some cases attention is negative, but it is nevertheless attention. The scapegoat also enjoys considerable power in that family stability depends on his or her staying in the role. To break out is to give up attention and power and to run the risk of producing considerable disruption within the family.

Scapegoats play a sacrificial role in troubled families. They do this by absorbing stress so that others may function with less tension and conflict. Also, locating the problem in one person distracts from the dysfunctions of other members, thus allowing them to appear "normal" at the expense of the scapegoat.

Because the benefits derived from the scapegoat role often outweigh the emotional stress that accompanies it, getting out can be a formidable task. Intrapsychic factors within the individual along with family pressure combine to keep the scapegoat locked in. Family therapy is ordinarily required if one's symptoms are a function of family scapegoating.

J. A. LARSEN

See FAMILY COMMUNICATIONS THEORY; FAMILY SYSTEMS THEORY.

Family Sculpture Technique. Sculpture is a body of action-oriented methods and strategies that help members of human systems to live out spatially the meanings, images, and metaphors they hold about their interpersonal relationships within the system. Sculpting taps these internal images or metaphorical maps to make them externally visible to everyone who participates in or observes the system. Thus the private conceptualizations of interpersonal patterns become accessible to all members of the family or system. Sculpture seeks to provide experientially and nonverbally the behaviors previously represented by word descriptions or verbal metaphors. For example, sculpture would map spatially and actively a wife's language metaphor of "My husband and I are not close at all." The sculpture process would use real physical distance to symbolize the perceived emotional distance.

Family sculpture has its historical and methodological roots in the work of Jacob Moreno, the founder of psychodrama. Other mental health professionals with interests in human relations and family therapy—e.g., David Kantor and Virginia Satir—have built on the efforts of Moreno.

The sculpting procedure involves four different roles that parallel those observed in the enactment of a psychodrama. First, the *sculptor* (protagonist or client) is the one who volunteers to disclose his or her private view of the family or system. Second, the *monitor* (director or therapist) is the professional who assists the sculptor in carrying out the sculpture. Third, the *actors* (other members of family or group) are those individuals who make themselves available to portray members of the sculptor's family as the sculptor perceives them. Finally, the *audience* (the same term used in psychodrama) consists of members of other families or the group who observe and give feedback to the sculptor at the appropriate time in the sculpting process.

Similar to psychodrama, three developmental stages are required for a complete sculpturing process. The initial phase focuses on the sculptor's establishing the specific situation or family event he desires to explore. This includes mapping out the physical space and the sculptor's associating his kinesic and sensory experiences to this space. In the simplest terms, the first stage is concerned with setting the stage with its topography and atmosphere. The second stage involves the actual sculpting in which the therapist has the sculptor bring the actors on stage to fill out his family space. The sculptor, without talking, places the actors bodily in the family space to give external reality to his private experiences of familial relationships. The final stage involves processing, discussing, and giving feedback. All participants in the sculpture, including members of the audience, become active in the feedback and processing of experiences.

Sculpture can be used with individual clients, couples, entire families, family subsystems; extended families or kinship networks, multiple families, groups, and even corporations or organizations. When sculpture is used with an individual client, it is necessary for the therapist either to assume also the roles of family members or to substitute objects such as chairs. Dyadic or boundary sculpture is particularly useful in working with couples to help them clarify the issues of territoriality, kinesics, and proxemics. Each person is required to become aware of both his own personal space and that of the other person, including the "rules" and "laws" that govern the control of that space. This negotiating of space can be extended to a variety of relationships. Family or group sculpture is essentially an extension of dyadic and relationship sculpture that involves a larger number of people in a more complicated system.

A sculpture can be linear in nature or it might be a matrix. Linear sculpture lends itself to both unipolar representations (members of a system placing themselves on a continuum assessing some theme, e.g. "frequency of initiating conversation") and bipolar situations (e.g. "introverted vs. extraverted" or "passive vs. aggressive"). Matrix sculpture allows for the simultaneous sculpting of the relationship between two variables. For example, on one line or dimension the "frequency of intimate behaviors" can be portrayed, while on a second line or dimension, perpendicular to the first line, the "importance of intimacy" can be featured.

Sculpture has unusual potential for both diagnosis (or evaluation) and therapeutic intervention. It allows room for the therapist to be resourceful, using his individuality and creativity in fitting a sculpting style to his personality and values. It also provides an opportunity for the client to deal with life situations and relationships as they really are and to experiment with them the way he or she would like them to be.

Additional Readings

Constantine, L. L. Family sculpture and relationship mapping techniques. In G. D. Erickson & T. P. Hogan (Eds.), *Family therapy* (2nd ed.). Monterey, Calif.: Brooks/Cole, 1981.

Duhl, F. J., Kantor, D., & Duhl, B. S. Learning, space, and action in family therapy: A primer of sculpture. In D. A. Bloch (Ed.), *Techniques of family psychotherapy.* New York: Grune & Stratton, 1973.

D. SMITH

See PSYCHODRAMA.

Family Systems Theory.

The person given credit for originating and initially developing general systems theory in the 1920s was the biologist Ludwig von Bertalanffy. He was reacting against the trend toward mechanistic or reductionistic thinking in which science investigated only empirically verifiable relationships between two variables (e.g., stimulus and response). These variables were connected in a linear, stepwise fashion to form a final explanation for whatever product resulted at the end of the reasoning chain. This reactive, chainlike process resulted in a progressive narrowing of one's focus.

This type of "funnel" reasoning did not explain well such phenomena as increasing complexity within an organism. In order to tap such a process one needed more than mechanistic thinking. As a result, von Bertalanffy focused on organismic principles of perceiving and organizing data. The concepts of organization, and the patterning of relationships within the whole organism or system became central to his thinking. A system became defined as a set of elements or persons standing in some consistent relationship to one another over time (von Bertalanffy, 1969).

Since its inception general systems theory has been used primarily as a tool to understand interpersonal systems. The primary relational system of interest to systemic thinkers in the social sciences is the family unit.

Central Systems Concepts. *Organization within the system.* When discussing such a central property of a system as its organization, it seems best to break this idea down into some important subdivisions. The first and most important idea in understanding systemic organization has traditionally been the notion of *wholeness.* It is axiomatic within this perspective to think of the whole as more than the sum of its parts; no system can be adequately and completely understood once it has been broken down into separate segments. Further, all of these parts are interdependent.

The second concept helpful in understanding systemic organization is that of *boundaries.* A system's boundaries are modified by the qualities of permeability and internal patterning. The nature and degree of internal patterning reflect the uniqueness and complexity of a system. To the degree that a system's patterning is different from its surroundings and more or less complex than those surroundings it can be defined clearly by outside, objective observers. An interpersonal system jeopardizes its own existence if its boundaries are too highly permeable or too closed. It can become wide open to members entering and leaving indiscriminately, thereby losing its identity. Or it can become so inbred that it "dies on the vine."

A final important idea about systemic organization has to do with its *hierarchical structure.* Different levels of complexity and power primarily determine a system's internal structuring. Often within interpersonal systems there is an overt and covert hierarchical ordering. Within a family, for example, the father and mother overtly compose a parental subsystem; the children, a sibling subsystem; and grandparents, uncles, aunts, and cousins, the extended family subsystem. One currently popular perspective organizes elements within the system into groups of three (or triangles), thus forming a different, covert coalition structure with different power relationships than what the overt structuring would suggest (Haley, 1980). It is important to note that any one person can belong to many different subsystems simultaneously.

Patterning within the system. The patterning of a system's growth, functions, and activities is reflected in two central ideas: homeostasis and feedback loops. *Homeostasis* essentially refers to a system's capability to achieve a balance or steady state within its boundaries. Jackson (1965) and his associates at the Mental Research Institute are credited with the innovative application of this concept to interpersonal systems from the province of medical physiology. Preset rules within the system act as a filter to determine the acceptability of any new behavior by members within the system. These rules may or may not be congruent with social and cultural mandates; as a result, it is possible that relatively bizarre behavior (according to other norms) might be required to balance out any one system.

The realization that symptoms can equilibrate families as well as intrapsychic forces has momentous theoretical and practical implications. Multiperson systems, whereby one person carries part of the motivation and behavior of another person, are only beginning to be understood; the close other can become a structural part of the self. Whenever two or more persons are in close relationship, they collusively carry psychic functions for one another. It is thus important to understand that everyone derives an emotional income from the behavior of others within one's own system. Within each system this emotional sharing of symptoms balances itself out over time into a unique homeostasis.

The concept of *feedback loops* is a second interdependent explanatory construct. One of their functions is to help regulate or control the homeostatic balance within the system. Feedback loops are traditionally grouped into two categories: positive and negative.

Positive loops, or deviation-amplifying loops, are defined as causally connected events in which an increase in one leads to a similar increase in the other. If unchecked, this type of loop will typically lead to unregulated growth which may destroy the system. Positive feedback loops also serve a more adaptive function in the service of systemic transformation: the desire to minimize systemic pain or maximize systemic pleasure allows for growth from a pathogenic homeostasis.

Negative loops, or deviation-minimizing loops, functionally police the homeostasis in a very protective fashion. Within the family system it has been postulated that a fear of unrelatedness or abandonment fuels the negative loop cycle, thus helping to preserve the status quo.

Patterning within the system occurs across the dimensions of time and space. Family systems theorists give different priorities to these dimensions. Those theorists more concerned with family structure and organization typically give most of their attention to spatial issues. On the other hand, those theorists concerned with communication flow, information exchange, and behavioral sequencing are more apt to study temporal variables. It is important to note the trade-off between these variables, since theorists concerned with one dimension typically do not give much written recognition to the other.

It should be noted that a systemic way of thinking suits itself well to integrative issues seeking to bridge psychology and theology. Rogers (1981) and Shepperson (1982) illustrate the applications of systems theory to psychological-theological integration.

Major Schools of Family Systems Theory. Systems theories can be roughly divided into two major camps: psychodynamically based theories and communication-oriented interpersonal theories.

Psychodynamically oriented systems theories. The key attribute of psychodynamically oriented systems theories is their focus on the temporal variable of historicity and the spatial-structural variable of the unconscious. In addition theorists from this school, in varying degrees, endorse concepts from the traditional psychoanalytic orientation. Major family theorists in this camp are Bowen (1978), Framo (1981), Sager (1981), and Boszormenyi-Nagy and Ulrich (1981).

The emphasis on the unconscious was, of course, a hallmark of Freud's writings. Although he focused primarily on individuals and their personal intrapsychic functioning he was aware that the unconscious of one person seems to be able to react to the unconscious of another without the conscious state of either being involved. This same theme is developed by contemporary psychoanalytic family system theorists. Bowen (1978), for example, speaks of an "overadequate-underadequate reciprocity" in which a strong family member automatically compensates for the weak or symptomatic behavior of the system's identified patient (e.g., a dominant wife married to an alcoholic husband). On the other hand, it is also possible that a covert collusion may exist within any one system in which members share the same symptom together (e.g., the classic *folie à deux*). This concept is similar to a psychodynamically oriented notion of the undifferentiated family ego mass, which is characterized by a relative lack of individuation by members within the system (Bowen, 1978).

Another unconscious force with strong power is the concept of pseudomutuality. This was originally defined as "the internalized family role structure and associated family subculture which serves as a kind of primitive superego which tends to determine behavior directly, without negotiating with an actively perceiving and discriminating ego" (Wynne, 1958, p. 216).

An emphasis on historical data is the second key characteristic of psychodynamically oriented systems theories. The concern for history does not limit itself to the study of recurrent patterns in the identified patient's lifetime but examines similar patterns in the lives of parents and grandparents as well (Boszormenyi-Nagi & Ulrich, 1981). This multigenerational emphasis is based on the idea of an intergenerational balance sheet, a different variety of homeostasis. Members within the extended family system keep track of this emotional accounting system at some conscious or unconscious level (Framo, 1965). Integral to this orientation is the notion that all systems are basically conservative: what is given by one generation will eventually be repaid by the next generation. No energy ever leaves the system; instead, all debts are balanced in the long run.

This notion also aids the understanding of why we as adults remain so strongly attached to introjections of our parents. It is the unconscious clinging to disturbing internal objects that perpetuates circular patterns of currently unsatisfying interpersonal relationships. From a dynamic systems orientation this process of unconscious clinging to the past is the major obstacle to change in the present.

The psychodynamic systemic orientation was the first to develop historically (Ackerman, 1938). Currently many theorists within this camp endorse a blend of systemic and linear concepts. Communication-oriented theorists are often quick to renounce the validity and utility of psychodynamic systemic thought and therapy.

Communication-oriented systems theories.
Adherents to the communication-oriented approach to systems theory tend to focus on temporal variables within the present such as interaction sequence analysis and problem-solving process analysis. Spatial variables such as family structure are also typically considered within the present. Little interest is taken in "psychoarchaeology" or other data from the past.

Compared to the more psychodynamic position, theorists of this orientation tend to see themselves more as systemic "purists." The main theoretical contributors to this broadly defined school currently are Haley (1980); several individuals from the Mental Research Institute in Palo Alto, California (Watzlawick, Weakland, & Fisch, 1974; Sluzki, 1978); four psychiatrists from Milan, Italy (Palazzoli-Selvini, Boscolo, Cecchin, & Prata, 1978); and Minuchin (1974).

Most of these theorists might be surprised or even troubled by such a grouping, since each has a unique approach. Haley and others have associated themselves with strategic therapy; Minuchin originated structural therapy; the Mental Research Institute associates go by various labels, a common one being interactional therapy; and the Italian group focus on paradoxical therapy. (It should be noted that Boscolo and Cecchin now have their own institute in Calgary, Canada.) However, despite differences among them, their approach to systems conceptualizations remains more alike than different.

The primary commonalities among these schools consist of their emphases on 1) present tense analysis of intrafamilial control mechanisms, 2) social learning processes within the family, and 3) concern with relatively concrete microanalyses of behavior as opposed to more abstract macroanalyses of behavior such as the psychodynamic systems approach might use.

Each school emphasizes how a family system controls its environment as opposed to adapting itself to its environment (Steinglass, 1978). This process of control applies both to members within its system and to other systems surrounding it. In this same regard, symptomatic behavior is largely viewed as a way of controlling others without having to be responsible for that bid for control. When one is sick, he or she cannot very well be criticized for failure or shortcoming in any particular area.

Various strategies for bringing about change without threatening the family's need for control are of primary interest to the strategic and paradoxical therapies (Haley, 1980; Palazolli-Selvini, et al., 1978). Typically resistance is handled in an indirect fashion; head-to-head clashes between therapist and family are considered poor form and avoided by the use of more efficient and effective techniques such as the directive.

Each school within this approach also has a demonstrated interest in how family members learn from one another in circular and interlocking fashion. The use of hypothesis testing, problem-solving strategies, and behavioral validation of one's interpretations and attributions regarding another's behavior are all of importance in varying degrees to different theorists within this general approach.

Communication-oriented systems approaches typically value specific, "micro" information that can be gathered by the questions: Who? What? When? Where? and How? "Why?" on the other hand, is not often asked because the type of information it yields is more vague and given to psychodynamic explanations. Insight per se is not valued as a curative agent as highly as *doing* something. One first changes the (temporal) interactional processes, which eventually calcify into (spatial) structural changes. Once these organizational variables have been effected through the use of behaviorally oriented directives or prescribed rituals, it is hoped that some level of heightened insight will occur. However, the therapy is viewed as complete with or without insight occurring.

Specific differences between these schools may be examined by referring to the appropriate article within this volume (*see* Category Index). All of these theoretical approaches are outwardly shifting their boundaries in the current mental health megasystem, which is changing its rules and homeostases through the use of circular growth patterns, positive feedback loops, and organismic evolution.

References

Ackerman, N. The unity of the family. *Archives of Pediatrics*, 1938, *55*, 51–62.
Boszormenyi-Nagy, I., & Ulrich, D. Contextual family therapy. In A. S. Gurman & D. P. Kniskern (Eds.), *Handbook of family therapy*. New York: Brunner/Mazel, 1981.
Bowen, M. *Family therapy in clinical practice*. New York: Aronson, 1978.
Framo, J. L. Rationale and techniques of intensive family therapy, In I. Boszormenyi-Nagy & J. L. Framo (Eds.), *Intensive family therapy: Theoretical and practical aspects*. New York: Harper & Row, 1965.
Framo, J. L. The integration of marital therapy with sessions with family of origin. In A. S. Gurman & D. P. Kniskern (Eds.), *Handbook of family therapy*. New York: Brunner/Mazel, 1981.
Haley, J. *Leaving home: The therapy of disturbed young people*. New York: McGraw-Hill, 1980.
Jackson, D. The study of the family. *Family Process*, 1965, *4*, 1–20.
Minuchin, S. *Families and family therapy*. Cambridge: Harvard University Press, 1974.
Palazzoli-Selvini, M., Boscolo, L., Cecchin, G., & Prata, G. *Paradox and counterparadox*. New York: Aronson, 1978.
Rogers, M. L. The call of Abram: A systems theory analysis. *Journal of Psychology and Theology*, 1981, *9*(2), 111–127.
Sager, C. Couples therapy and marriage contracts. In A. S. Gurman & D. P. Kniskern (Eds.), *Handbook of family therapy*. New York: Brunner/Mazel, 1981.
Shepperson, V. L. Systemic integration: A reactive alternative to "the conduct of integration." *Journal of Psychology and Theology*. 1982, *10*(4), 326–328.
Sluzki, C. Marital therapy from a systems theory perspective. In T. Paolino & B. McCrady (Eds.), *Marriage and marital therapy: Psychoanalytic, behavioral, and systems theory perspectives*. New York: Brunner/Mazel, 1978.
Steinglass, P. The conceptualization of marriage from a systems theory perspective. In T. Paolino and B. McCrady (Eds.), *Marriage and marital therapy: Psychoanalytic, behavioral, and systems theory perspectives*. New York: Brunner/Mazel, 1978.
Von Bertalanffy, L. General systems theory. In W. Gray, F. S. Duhl, & N. D. Rizzo (Eds.), *General systems theory and psychiatry*. Boston: Little, Brown, 1969.
Watzlawick, P., Weakland, J. H., & Fisch, R. *Change*. New York: Norton, 1974.
Wynne, L. C., Ryckoff, I. M., Day, J., & Hirsch, S. I. Pseudo-mutuality in the family relations of schizophrenics. *Psychiatry*, 1958, *21*, 205–220.

V. L. Shepperson

See Family Communications Theory.

Family Systems Therapy.

Approach to the treatment of families most often associated with the work of Murray Bowen. Other approaches also associated with a family systems model are described in Family Systems Theory.

Bowen's Theory. Bowen began his work in the early 1950s in association with the National Institute of Mental Health. Working first with severely disturbed children, he was struck by the ways in which patients were assigned psychiatric diagnoses that were not at all helpful in the treatment of these patients. Additionally, Bowen was not satisfied with the psychiatric definition of schizophrenia, which held that the emotional disturbance of this disorder was contained within the individual.

As Bowen treated schizophrenic children, he became aware of an emotionally close relationship between the patient and the patient's mother. He observed that this relationship had taken on a symbiotic quality that seemed to rob the patient of a solid identity. As his theory developed, Bowen saw that this relationship between the patient and mother provided the inadequate mother with a great deal of power over the patient. Further, there appeared to be an emotional struggle between mother and child. Whenever the child attempted to break away from the symbiotic relationship, the mother would become extremely anxious and the child would, in turn, give up attempts to become autonomous.

As Bowen further developed his family theory, he began to look at the father's relationship to the mother and child. He observed that the father seemed removed, cut off from the highly emotional relationship between mother and child. Bowen discovered that parents of schizophrenic children were unable to achieve authentic emotional closeness in the marital relationship. Instead, this relationship was marked by undifferentiation (inability of couples to be emotionally separate) or pronounced marital fusion which, according to Bowen, manifests itself in one of three ways: intense marital conflict, sickness or dysfunction in one spouse, and the projection (triangulation) of unresolved marital problems onto one of the children. Bowen discovered that if therapeutic attention was focused on the parents of schizophrenic children and if the couple began to address their unresolved conflicts, through a process of differentiation of self, the patient's psychotic symptomatology disappeared.

Later Bowen found that children achieve varying levels of differentiation of self from the family ego mass in their families of origin. Differentiation is similar to Erikson's (1963) concept of identity. Individuals marry others of equal level of differentiation of self. If individuals possess low levels of differentiation of self, emotional fusion is likely to manifest itself in the marital relationship.

Key Concepts. *Differentiation of Self Scale.* This scale is an effort to classify all levels of human functioning, from the lowest possible levels to the highest potential level, on a single dimension. The lowest score, which is 0 on the scale, indicates total undifferentiation and 100, the highest score, indicates the greatest degree of differentiation.

Differentiation of self. This is the degree to which an individual will negotiate and compromise his basic beliefs and convictions in order to gain approval or increase position in relationships, particularly in the marital relationship. Individuals who possess low differentiation of self regard feelings and subjectivity as dominant over the objective reasoning process (Bowen, 1972). Individuals who possess high differentiation of self "have an increasing capacity to differentiate between feelings and objective reality" (Bowen, 1978).

Fusion. This concept refers to the emotional "stuck togetherness" of a family. According to Bowen, the level of differentiation of self determines the degree of emotional fusion. There are three areas in which fusion is expressed in the nuclear family: in marital conflict, in dysfunction in one spouse, and in projection to one or more children.

Triangle. Triangle refers to the most basic unit of any emotional system. A two-person emotional system is unstable in that it forms itself into a three-person system or triangle under stress. As tension increases in the dyad, it is common for one person to "triangle in" another to relieve some of the tension. This shifts the focus of tension away from the first two and onto the third, and this prevents the resolution of conflict in the dyad.

Family projection process. This occurs when parents fail to deal effectively with their marital conflict and triangle in one of their chil-

dren. This shifts the focus from the marriage and projects it upon the child. The child exhibits the marital conflict by developing psychological problems.

Multigenerational transmission process. This concept describes the pattern that develops over multiple generations as children emerge from the parental family with higher, equal, or lower basic levels of differentiation than the parents. According to the theory the most severe emotional problems, particularly schizophrenia, result from the lowering levels of differentiation of self over multiple generations.

Emotional cutoff. This concept refers to the process by which individuals handle their unresolved emotional attachments to their parents.

Therapy. According to Bowen, the overall goal of therapy is to help individual family members rise up out of the emotional togetherness (fusion) that binds them and to help the motivated family member to take even a small step toward a better level of differentiation.

Bowen identified nine therapeutic techniques that promote differentiation. First the therapist serves as a coach rather than as a traditional therapist interpreting behavior. He constantly questions one spouse, then the other. The purpose of such questioning is to temporarily inhibit emotional responsiveness, thus allowing each spouse to hear the other. Second, the therapist serves as a model by using "I" statements. This provides an example for an individual, couple, or family. Third, the therapist avoids becoming triangled by refusing to take sides. Fourth, the therapist encourages each family member to work toward a greater level of differentiation from his or her own family of origin. Fifth, the therapist uses a coaching model rather than a model based upon transference.

Sixth, the therapist avoids emotionality. Bowen suggests that the more the therapeutic relationship is endowed with high emotionality, the less likely it is to be long-term. The lower the emotionality and the more the relationship deals in reality, the more likely the change will come slowly and be solid and long-lasting.

Seventh, the therapist works with the strongest person in the family or couple. Eighth, the therapist avoids the emotionality of a crisis and refuses to be pulled into the conflict of a crisis. Finally, the therapist uses reversals and humor to detoxify an emotional situation, to allow the family to look at their own dysfunctional behavior, and to permit a family member to get "unstuck" from what seemed to be an unchangeable position.

References

Bowen, M., Toward the differentiation of a self in one's own family. In S. L. Framo (Ed.), *Family interaction: A dialogue between family researchers and family therapists.* New York: Springer Publishing, 1972.

Bowen, M. *Family therapy in clinical practice.* New York: Aronson, 1978.

Erikson, E. H. *Childhood and society* (2nd ed.). New York: Norton, 1963.

R. R. FARRA

See FAMILY THERAPY: OVERVIEW.

Family Therapy: Overview. During the past 15 years the treatment of whole families in emotional crisis or conflict has become an established clinical procedure. This article will review basic aspects of family dynamics and consider some biblical concepts that relate to family structure and function.

Basic Concepts of Family Therapy. Family therapy differs from individual therapy in several important respects. Instead of an individual with a problem, the therapist focuses on the individual within his family and defines the problem as a relational one. The therapist relates to the whole family rather than to one member of the family and observes the interaction of the family members rather than relying on the report of one member. Therapy is directed toward changing the structure of the family. This in turn leads to changes in the behavior and the inner experience of all the members of the family. These changes include changes in the ways the members relate.

Family therapy is such a new field that theories and techniques of treatment have been tremendously diverse, with a large number of schools of treatment. These have been grouped into four basic approaches by Gurman and Kniskern (1981): psychoanalytic and object relations, intergenerational, systems theory, and behavioral. There are several theories and techniques within each of these approaches.

The family itself is not a static entity. It is a constantly evolving system with its own set of developmental phases. The family can be seen as adjusting to the presence of young children, as coping with the emergence of adolescent members, or as working through the empty nest syndrome. Each of these developmental tasks requires changes in the pattern of the members' interactions with one another and threatens the personal security of each member.

The interactional style of the family will determine the way these developmental problems are resolved, depending upon the freedom of the family members to communicate stress to one another and resolve conflict. High stress and poor conflict resolution ability may result in the precipitation of psychiatric or medical symptoms in one of the members. Stress may come from contact of one or more members with extrafamilial stressors, a natural transitional phase in development, or an idiosyncratic problem in a member.

A family is defined as a psychobiological group of people with a boundary that separates them from the other people in their environment. Families are divisible into structural (e.g., marital or sibling) and functional (e.g., parental) subsystems—i.e., groupings of family members designed to meet certain needs or carry out their functions. It is possible for a man to be an effective husband in his functioning in the spouse subsystem and an ineffective father in his function in the parental subsystem.

The ability of a member of a subsystem to develop the skills necessary for effective functioning in the family depends on that member's freedom and the freedom of the whole subsystem from interference by other subsystems. When the boundaries around various subsystems are not clearly defined, confusion within the family will result. Members of the various subsystems will not know what is expected of them, and they will not be able to achieve competency in the various tasks required of them.

All families have power and authority hierarchies. Parents and children have different levels of authority in the family. In a normal generational delegation of authority, parents in general have authority over their children, and there is a complementary function between the husband and wife in an interdependent relationship. In pathological families power patterns almost invariably differ from this. Identified patients generally tend to wield a great deal of covert power in their families.

Family members develop a predictable set of responses to interactions between other family members. The basic pattern involves at least three members of a family and is called triangulation. In the presence of anxiety any two-person system will tend to involve the closest vulnerable other person to form a triangle. In addition, when the tension in a triangle is too great for a threesome, it will involve others, forming a series of interlocking triangles. Eventually the interactions stabilize and anxiety is passed through the family along predictable channels. This process of triangulation is the process of symptom formation. Usually the person least able to pass on the emotional tension in the most stable triangle develops a symptom or expresses overt conflict with the other involved members of the triangle.

General systems theory posits the development of an equilibrium with a certain range of tolerated variability in any system. When behavior or interactions occur which deviate beyond the threshold of tolerance of the system, the distress level of the system rises. Corrective mechanisms will also be invoked to restore equilibrium. Given the levels of stress in our society and the tasks that face the family developmentally, it is inevitable that the family's interactional pattern will be frequently confronted with the necessity for change. This change may occur in an adaptive or maladaptive way depending on the freedom of the system to be flexible. General systems theory also posits an inherent resistance to change in the system because it is set up to maintain itself in equilibrium.

The family exists to provide support for its members. It is intended to function as a shelter from impinging forces outside it, all of which make various demands on family members. It is the site of the growth and development of its members, both children and adults. In order for growth to occur, family members must experience two things. They must develop a sense of belonging, initially to one other person and later to other family members, and they must be able to individuate and establish a sense of separateness within the context of belonging. Throughout life the individual must develop competent responses to the variety of situations encountered in life. These situations present constant challenges to self-esteem and personal security. A sense of belonging is necessary in order to risk adaptive behavior. The freedom to be separate is critical in order to succeed adaptively outside the family of origin.

Biblical Concepts of Family Functioning. The model of family functioning and development discussed above is consistent with biblical concepts of family functioning. The Bible provides clear guidelines for family structure and function, and a model for relationships that mitigates against triangulation. Biblical values foster personal responsibility, growth, and individuation in the context of belonging to a family group.

Structure and roles. Paul delineated the basic concepts of family structure in his letters to the churches at Colossae and Ephesus. Each marital partner makes a covenantal commitment to the other. There is an ordered mutuality in the marital relationship, one which is intended to transcend convenience and personal satisfac-

tion. The man is the spiritual, emotional, and administrative head of the family. Husbands are encouraged to relate to their wives as equals, participants with them in the grace of God (1 Peter 3:7). The analogy of the marital unit to the union of Jesus and the church reflects both the intensity of investment required in the marital relationship and the high regard given to the marital relationship by God (Eph. 5:25–30).

Having established the marital pair, Paul goes on to delineate parental authority over children. In addition, the subsystems are given different tasks. Children must learn obedience, a lifelong socialization process. The family is the source of learning about the necessity for negotiation and compromise between the needs and desires of the individual and the needs and desires of those around him. The parental subsystem has the task of providing a sense of belonging and personal value and setting necessary limits in such a way that children do not become overly frustrated or resentful and alienated from the family.

Both parents are to provide discipline, instruction, and affection, not leaving child rearing to mothers alone. Discipline here refers to a consistent pattern of training for the imparting of certain skills, not merely punishment. Parents are able to teach their children social skills, housekeeping skills, skills in having fun, and to provide practical spiritual instruction, teaching them about God and his ways.

Triangulation and conflict resolution. Application of basic scriptural values to family relationships will release forces in the family that promote growth, individuation, cohesiveness, and stability. These forces mitigate against triangulation and scapegoating. Every member of the family stands equal before God (Acts 10:34). There should be a growing awareness of God's concern for and valuing of each member of the family. It is difficult to continue to blame someone and to consistently attribute negative qualities to them when one realizes that the person is highly valued by God and is his creation. Furthermore, everyone in the family falls short of God and has his or her own problems to be solved (Matt. 7:1–5; Gal. 6:1–5). Families are a place where people should not need to hide for fear of being rejected, judged, or criticized.

Jesus gave instructions for conflict resolution in the church (Matt. 18:15–16). He prescribed honest confrontation between the two parties involved in the conflict, with a bona fide attempt to resolve the conflict before involving another party. When an outside person is involved, the involvement should be forthright and open, with a chance for each party to speak and be heard. The purpose is to move to an open expression and resolution of the conflict. Triangulation occurs when an outside person is brought into the relationship to detour the conflict and avoid a confrontation. For example, a mother will tell her daughter about her husband's criticisms of her. She may then feel better, but her daughter's relationship with her father has been undermined. The daughter may act out her mother's anger and be labeled a "brat" by her parents.

The scriptural solution to this situation requires the wife to honestly confront her husband about his criticisms, despite the anxiety that might be provoked by such a confrontation. Should the two of them be unable to reach a resolution, they could agree to go together to seek an outside opinion. This maintains the mutuality of the relationship, keeps the tension in the dyad, and enables the outside party to be used for conflict resolution rather than tension reduction. Tension reduction will follow clear discussion of differences and resolution of conflicts.

Biblical injunctions to forgive do not mean that one must overlook intolerable situations, deny conflict, or minimize interpersonal stress. In fact, the call to forgiveness often uncovers long-suppressed conflict requiring a confrontation with self and others. Often this is more difficult than continuing the resentment. The willingness to forgive is a statement of concern for the other, a realization that the relationship is more important than who is right or wrong.

Boundaries. Adam's attempt to blame Eve for his own disobedience is the first example of many recorded attempts to avoid accountability. Accountability to God means one must be willing to be an individual in one's own family despite strong emotional forces in other directions at times. There is a call to personal integrity in the midst of the intense emotional pressures of family life. Jesus showed his willingness to withstand these pressures at the same time that he honored his family (John 19:25–27).

Jesus was careful to point out that an undue tie with one's family (i.e., the lack of individuation) is a serious obstacle to serving God. God must be seen as even more important than one's parents and children. One must be willing to accept the possibility of conflict in order to be faithful to the call of God (Matt. 10:34–39). The conflict will be a tension of priorities.

In addition, Christians are called to extend their involvement beyond family boundaries. The church is a sharing community, with its members involved in an unusually intensive way with one another beyond the limits of family boundaries. This biblical pattern of stressing the importance of family along with extrafamilial involvement is also reflected in Christ's own extension of his personal family boundaries to all who love and obey God (Matt. 12:50).

Summary. Biblical concepts of family functioning are consistent with current family theory and clinical practice. There are clear guidelines for family structure, including a firm marital coalition and generational boundaries. These provide guidelines for a Christian therapist and for a family seeking God's order, which transcends cultural and individual idiosyncrasies. Furthermore, scriptural guidelines for the resolution of interpersonal conflict, coupled with respect and valuing of all family members, provide strong forces against triangulation and scapegoating processes. Scriptural values of openness, caring, and sharing in the midst of order and structure are those traits which the research of Lewis, Beavers, Gossetl, and Phillips (1976) found to be associated with optimal families. Healthy Christianity should be a force toward increased family cohesiveness as well as individual growth of family members, thus adding a potent force for change to the family system.

A family therapist dealing with a religious family must consider the influence of religious values on both family structure and family functioning. These values may be serving the family in either healthy or dysfunctional ways. A Christian family with problems may be involved more fully in a therapeutic endeavor by engaging the healthy aspects of its religious system. Distorted values that are hindering the growth of the family can be addressed as trust in the therapist develops.

References

Gurman, A. S., Kniskern, D. P. (Eds.). *Handbook of family therapy.* New York: Brunner/Mazel, 1981.
Lewis, J. M., Beavers, W. R., Gossetl, J. T., & Phillips, V. A. *No single thread: Psychological health and family systems.* New York: Brunner/Mazel, 1976.

R. J. SALINGER

Family Types. Family researchers and therapists have classified families according to at least five variables. These variables identify different significant features of families; consideration of each contributes to a fuller understanding and diagnosis of the family. The following typologies include both functional and dysfunctional family types. Distribution and use of power is a critical variable in family styles. Jackson and Kramer have each proposed a typology of families based on power dynamics. Each suggests three types: the symmetrical, the complementary, and the parallel (Jackson & Lederer, 1968); the overadequate-underadequate, the united front, and the conflictual (Kramer, 1980).

The symmetrical family is "one in which the spouses continually need to state to each other behaviorally, 'I am as good as you are'" (Jackson and Lederer, 1968, p. 161). These spouses are status strugglers. Each seeks at least equal control, equal power. Spouses are competitive, not collaborative. This pattern is close to what Kramer calls the conflictual family, where continual conflict and disagreements occur. Usually the avoidance of intimacy is one objective of the constant conflict, even though each spouse may verbally express a desire to be closer. Parents in these families may often involve the children by choosing favorites. Some parents will pick on a child because that child is more like the disliked spouse (scapegoating the child). Children in intensely conflictual families frequently manifest significant problems.

The complementary relationship is "one in which one spouse is in charge and the other obeys" (Jackson & Lederer, 1968, p. 161). This complementarity may be divided according to the areas of competence or responsibility, or it may characterize the majority of spousal interactions. Kramer describes this type as the overadequate-underadequate family. The overadequate spouse appears efficient, super-responsible, totally capable, while the underadequate spouse seems to be always demonstrating incompetence. Children in these families often seek to identify with the apparently more competent parent and/or sympathize with the underadequate parent. Occasionally the underadequate parent uses this to wield significant power in getting sympathy and help.

The third type for Jackson is the parallel family, where the parents alternate between symmetrical and complementary relationships in response to the demands of different situations. Flexibility in the use of power characterizes these families.

For Kramer the third type is the united-front family, where parents and often also children use their power to present a unified picture of the marriage or the family to the outside world. Often the children experience significant problems either emotionally or physically as a result of the hidden conflicts. The parents are usually resistant to seeing the children's problems as related to the marital dynamics.

A second system of classification proposed by Jackson is based on the two variables of spousal satisfaction and stability of the marriage. Four combinations are possible: the stable-satisfactory, the unstable-satisfactory, the unstable-unsatisfactory, and the stable-unsatisfactory. In the rarely observed stable-satisfactory marriage differences are considered variations of "tastes and values, not as symbols of a hostile relationship" (Jackson and Lederer, 1968, p. 131). In the unstable-satisfactory relationship, which describes most marriages that last more than 10 years, the spouses believe they have a comfortable relationship, but their disappointments on occasion are obvious. There may be periodic outbursts of aggression, but both spouses see sufficient positives to want to remain married.

In the stable-unsatisfactory marriage conflict is ever present but always avoided, and no one is really happy with the situation. "In a quiet socially respectable manner the people in this group suffer more pain, hate more profoundly, and cause more discomfort to others than do the members of the other three groups" (Jackson & Lederer, 1968, p. 153). This is the type most often seen in therapy. The final type is the unstable-unsatisfactory relationship—the infamous "I can't live with you, I can't live without you" relationship. Tremendous hostility is observed by others, but the family members are often unaware of it. In the last two types the children often experience emotional or physical problems.

A fourth variable used for classification is the intimacy level of the family. Glick and Kessler (1980) suggest five levels of intimacy: the conflict-habituated marriage, where both spouses stay together because of fear of alternatives; the devitalized marriage, where extrinsic reasons such as children or moral or legal principles keep the spouses together, while each lives a fairly separate life; the passive-congenial marriage, where interests are shared and life is pleasant, but interactions lack intensity; the vital marriage, where one major area is intensely satisfying to both spouses; and finally the total marriage, where many areas are intensely satisfying to both spouses.

The fifth variable is the amount of individuation permitted in the family. Bowen (1978) describes the schizophrenogenic family as characterized by an "undifferentiated ego mass."

The boundaries between individuals are unclear, and children do not develop a clear sense of themselves in distinction from other family members, especially parents. Families can thus be classified according to the amount of individuation present.

Additional variables suggested as bases for typing families include the personality style (Glick & Kessler, 1980) and the developmental stage of the family (Hill & Rodgers, 1964).

References

Bowen, M. *Family therapy in clinical practice.* New York: Aronson, 1978.

Glick, I. D., & Kessler, D. *Marital and family therapy* (2nd ed.). New York: Grune & Stratton, 1980.

Hill, R., & Rodgers, R. H. The developmental approach. In H. Christensen (Ed.), *Handbook of marriage and the family.* Chicago: Rand McNally, 1964.

Jackson, D. D., & Lederer, W. *The mirages of marriage.* New York: Norton, 1968.

Kramer, C. H. *Becoming a family therapist.* New York: Human Science Press, 1980.

A. D. COMPAAN

Fantasy in Therapy. *See* IMAGERY, THERAPEUTIC USE OF.

Fasting. The voluntary abstinence from food. Fasting has been advocated as a means for weight loss, a religious exercise, and a way to prevent bodily diseases. It has also been implicated as a symptom of anorexia nervosa. For whatever reason, fasting has been the focal point of a great deal of controversy and deserves serious attention.

Fasting is often criticized for being a crash diet that may produce fast initial weight loss with equally rapid rebound gain. It is not a sound program of self-management that requires a long-term commitment and emphasizes gradual weight loss. Effective weight loss, researchers argue (Williams & Long, 1983), requires one to change one's style of eating permanently. This is accomplished through the development of weight managment skills. Fasting, although it may achieve quick and dramatic weight loss, fails to teach these skills.

In addition, fasting is not without possible physical risks. Berland (1974), after an extensive review of the literature, concludes that there are potential hazards with fasting that necessitate continuous medical supervision. Agreeing with the U.S. Public Health Service, he argues that a fasting diet should never be self-administered. Fasting for more than a day, even for religious or meditative reasons, can be dangerous to one's health.

Any discussion of fasting must mention the life-threatening eating disorder ANOREXIA NERVOSA. Here fasting (self-starvation) leads to serious weight loss and is coupled with an intense fear of becoming obese and a refusal to eat sufficiently to gain or maintain body weight. Effective intervention includes individual and family therapy, together with biological and behavioral interventions to reestablish normal eating patterns.

Claims for the use of fasting as a means to prevent bodily disease have been numerous, but they are generally not substantiated by carefully controlled research.

An excellent example of a nondogmatic and biblically balanced treatment of fasting as a spiritual discipline can be found in Foster (1978). He contends that fasting has developed a bad reputation both in and outside the church because of the excessive ascetic practices of the Middle Ages and the constant propaganda that implies that unless we eat three large meals a day, with snacks in between, we are on the verge of starvation. We make the mistaken assumption that the hunger urge must be satisfied.

Foster goes on to state that the Bible has much to say about fasting, and that if it is done correctly, one can fast with beneficial physical effects for up to 40 days. All major religions, he contends, see the value of fasting as a spiritual discipline.

Many Christians wonder if fasting is a commandment. Foster argues that Jesus expected his disciples to fast after he was gone, although in the strictest sense he did not command fasting. But it is obvious that Jesus "proceeded on the principle that the children of the kingdom of God would fast" (Foster, 1978, p. 47). Giving money has long been recognized as an element in Christian devotion, but fasting has been widely disputed. Strange indeed, says Foster, since fasting has far more of a biblical basis than does giving. Perhaps it is indicative of which is the larger sacrifice for contemporary Christians.

Foster concludes his discussion with suggestions about the practice of fasting. He is careful to warn diabetics, expectant mothers, and heart patients not to attempt to fast. To this list should be added growing children and adolescents, and persons who are described as well-behaved, conscientious, and perfectionistic (i.e., high risk for developing anorexia nervosa).

References

Berland, T. (Ed.). *Rating the diets.* Chicago: Rand McNally, 1974.

Foster, R. *Celebration of discipline.* San Francisco: Harper & Row, 1978.

Williams, R., & Long, J. *Towards a self-managed life style* (3rd ed.). Boston: Houghton Mifflin, 1983.

R. E. BUTMAN

Fathering. Both lay persons and academics have shown an increasing interest in the contribution made by fathers to the psychosocial development of their children. The father's involvement with children is as important as the mother's, yet it has not received nearly as much attention in the literature as mother-child relationships. One can only hope, therefore, that psychology's long history of neglecting fathers may be about to end.

The recent literature on fathers has focused primarily on two areas: the role of the father in child development (Parke, 1979, 1981) and the effects of father absence (Lamb, 1981). Other areas which have received some attention are father surrogates (in cases of absent fathers) and the divorced father. Research in these latter areas is, however, still minimal.

Lamb (1981) is one of the recent researchers whose work has challenged the long-held assumption that infants were incapable of forming attachment to their fathers. He and others have shown that, although such attachments are qualitatively different from those in mother-infant bonding, they do exist. Furthermore, available research suggests that the infant who establishes close relationships with both parents is at an advantage in the acquisition of important socialization skills.

One of the best-established findings concerning childhood is that the masculinity of sons and the femininity of daughters are greatest when the father is both nurturant and active in the child-rearing process. Further, the child is most likely to imitate a father about whom it feels positively than one of whom it is afraid.

It has sometimes been assumed that since most fathers spend less daily face-to-face contact time with their children than do mothers, they must have less influence on them. But this does not necessarily follow, since it is not the amount of time spent with a child that is the critical variable, but how that time is spent. Obviously, however, there can be no quality without a reasonable amount of quantity. One recent study estimated that an average employed American father spends 20 hours a week in the presence of his children but only 2 hours actively interacting with them (Szalai, Converse, Feldman, Scheuch, & Stone, 1972). Besides the variable of quality interaction time the father's emotional expressiveness and encouragement are important variables for promoting the psychosocial and cognitive development of his children.

One way that researchers have sought to understand paternal influences is to study children raised without fathers and then to compare them to children raised with fathers present. Although the research on father absence is extensive, it is not always methodologically rigorous. Much of it is clinically oriented and based on retrospective analysis. Still, there is developing consensus in these findings in several areas, including how father absence influences sex-role development, morality, achievement, and psychosocial adjustment.

Boys raised without fathers are reported to be less masculine or to exhibit compensatory hypermasculinity. Such boys also have a much higher probability of juvenile delinquency. The greatest impact appears to be on those boys who are separated from their fathers in early childhood. The effects can be reduced by the presence of other male models. For girls the effects are not as clear, but it seems that father absence might affect interaction with males or the girl's developing sense of femininity. But these are controversial assertions. It does appear that the impact of father absence is not as harsh for females as it is for males.

Achievement in boys appears to be adversely affected by father absence as measured by school performance and intellectual capacity. However, the effects can be lessened by an involved mother. Cognitive styles also appear to be influenced, with boys raised in father-absent homes being less analytic and more field dependent. These effects are not pronounced in girls and seem to be specific to lower- and middle-class families. Finally, father absence is associated with greater difficulty in establishing satisfying peer relationships, behavioral adjustment, and successful heterosexual relationships, particularly in boys. All these effects appear both in homes where the father is physically absent and those where he is physically present but psychologically absent. However, children of psychologically absent (distant and inaccessible) fathers experience less extreme effects.

Recent research is focusing on ways to distinguish adaptive and pathogenic responses to father absence. The existence of the effects is clear, but the evaluation of the effects may differ. The importance of the age of separation, the availability of father surrogates, and the role of cognitive variables is receiving increasing attention in the literature.

References

Lamb, M. E. (Ed.). *The role of the father in child development* (2nd ed.). New York: Wiley, 1981.

Parke, R. D. The father of the child. *The Sciences*, April 1979, pp. 12–15.

Parke, R. D. *Fathers*. Cambridge: Harvard University Press, 1981.

Szalai, A., Converse, P. E., Feldman, P., Scheuch, E. K., & Stone, P. J. (Eds.). *The use of time: Daily activities of urban and suburban populations in twelve countries*. The Hague: Mouton, 1972.

Additional Readings

Cath, S. H., Gurwitt, A. R., & Ross, J. M. *Father and child: Developmental and clinical perspectives*. Boston: Little, Brown, 1982.

MacDonald, G. *The effective father*. Wheaton, Ill.: Tyndale House, 1977.

Rubin, Z. Fathers and sons: The search for reunion. *Psychology Today*, 1982, *16*(6), 22–33.

Stevens, J. H., & Mathews, M. (Eds.). *Mother-child, father-child relationships*. Washington, D.C.: National Association for the Education of Young Children, 1978.

R. E. Butman

See Mothering.

Fear. This most constricting emotion contrasts with other intense negative states—anger, anxiety, phobia. Anger incites attack against a threatening event; fear incites withdrawal from the threat. Fear is related to an identifiable object or event; anxiety is usually interpreted as "free-floating" apprehension. Anxiety probably incorporates other emotions with fear. Normal fear apprehends a realistic danger; phobia implies an irrational fear.

Fear ranges from uneasiness to total insecurity, with threats to one's physical and/or psychological self. Intense fear constricts perception, thinking, and motor processes. The frightened person simultaneously wants to investigate the threat and to escape from it; the conflict may cause one to freeze or panic. Compared to anger, fear is more strongly associated with increases in respiration rate, skin conductance, and peaks in muscle tension. These physiological measures are related to arousal of the sympathetic nervous system and the hormone epinephrine (adrenalin). However, physiological characteristics of different emotions vary widely among individuals and are less studied than in past decades.

Facial expressions are more reliable. These display fear with eyebrows relatively straight and raised, inner corners of the brows drawn together, horizontal wrinkles over two-thirds to three-fourths of the forehead. Eyes are wide, lower eyelids tensed and upper lids slightly raised; the mouth is open, lips tense and drawn back tightly.

Fear typically differentiates from generalized distress in the child's sixth month as an innate response to sudden, intense stimuli. Fear responses to strange stimuli (particularly to objects that differ strikingly from a very familiar object) are maturational, not learned. A year-old child has not learned to fear father in a hat when he first so appears; the image of hatless father just has to be internalized first.

Children pass through a sequence of fear stages. In the first year loud noises, strange or unexpected stimuli, and threats of bodily harm are mostly feared. Mother's departure becomes feared in the second year. The third year ushers in many fears, mostly auditory but also large objects, rain, wind, animals, and the dark (which often persists through the sixth year). In the fourth year visual fears predominate, but in the fifth auditory fears again prevail. Five-year-olds show less fear, but the end of the sixth year may bring many fears—especially auditory stimuli and sleeping alone. Some of the numerous fears at age 6 may be learned; fears of ghosts, witches, large wild animals, loud weather, and bodily injury abound. At 7 fears become increasingly personal: wars, new situations, being late for school, burglars. As coping with fears begins, 8-year-olds have fewer and more variable fears, with school failure and other self-esteem threats most frequent (Ilg & Ames, 1955).

Fears are learned several ways. Children may identify with adults or peers who model fears of objects or events. Classical conditioning may develop fear reactions to an originally neutral stimulus when the latter is associated with a stimulus that already produces fear. However, some neutral stimuli are much more prone to formation of classically conditioned fear responses than others. Some differences among people in intensity and number of fears are related to temperament and proneness to emotional conditioning.

Fear occurs naturally in virtually every neocortical animal species and serves adaptive functions. An animal without fear is likely to become some predator's dinner or a "road kill." In humans moderate fear is psychologically adaptive; patients with moderate fear before surgery respond to the scheduled operation better than those with little or great fear. Fear also keeps social mammals in protective groups and bonds infant primates more tightly to their mothers. This maternal bond paradoxically provides a security that allows the infant more effectively to explore its world. However, extreme fear produces an exaggerated bond that interferes with formation of other social relations (Suomi & Harlow, 1976).

Some parents try to control children's behavior by recourse to fear—of the bogeyman, the devil, or "your father." Adult versions of socialization by fear (e.g., slowing your car when you see a patrolman) usually mix guilt, shame, or other emotions with fear. Instead of threatening with fear, parents who can tolerate fear may teach children to accept and master their fears. A further step encourages positive action in the face of fear—facing the dentist courageously despite apprehension. Intense, irrational fear—phobia—generally is treated by behavioral methods. Excessive fear may also be controlled cognitively by reinterpretation of supposed threats, assurances of security, and by strengthening of incompatible behaviors: "Do not fear, for I am with you" (Isa. 41:10); "perfect love drives out fear" (1 John 4:18).

References

Ilg, F. L., & Ames, L. B. *Child behavior.* New York: Harper Bros., 1955.

Suomi, S. J., & Harlow, H. F. The facts and functions of fear. In M. Zuckerman & C. D. Spielberger (Eds.), *Emotions and anxiety.* Hillsdale, N.J.: Lawrence Erlbaum Associates, 1976.

Additional Reading

Izard, C. E. *Human emotions.* New York: Plenum Press, 1977.

R. D. KAHOE

See PHOBIC DISORDERS.

Fechner, Gustav Theodor (1801–1887). Founder of psychophysics. He was born in Gross-Särchen in southeastern Germany, where his father had followed his grandfather as the Lutheran pastor in the village. Since his father died when Fechner was only 5 years old, he, his mother, and his brother spent the next nine years with his uncle, who was also a preacher. He started medical school at Leipzig at the age of 16 and received his degree in medicine in 1822.

Rather than practicing medicine, he began translating French handbooks of physics and chemistry into German. In 1824 he began lecturing in physics at Leipzig and received the prestigious appointment of professor in 1833. Following great intellectual activity and overwork, he had a severe breakdown in 1839. He was extremely depressed, could not sleep, could not digest food, and was oversensitive to light. For three years he spent most of his time in a darkened room, listening while his mother read to him through a narrow opening in the door. His neurosis lasted until 1851. In 1844 Fechner was given a small pension from the university and thus was officially established as an invalid. However, every one of the remaining years of his life resulted in a serious scholarly contribution, and his health was good until his death.

During his illness Fechner became deeply religious, spending many hours in meditation and reflection. Concerned with the problem of the soul, he set out to investigate the relationship between the mind and the body. On the morning of October 22, 1850, it occurred to him that the solution was to be found in a statement of the quantitative relationship between mental sensation and material stimulus. This was the beginning of PSYCHOPHYSICS, the relationship between the mind and the material world. He believed that the mind quality or sensation (S) was equal to a constant (K) times the logarithm of the stimulus (R). Thus Fechner's law is $S = K \log R$. His psychophysical methods of average error, constant stimuli, and limits are still used today.

Fechner wrote widely in many fields, but his most important work in psychology was *Elements of Psychophysics* (1860). His interest in religion is reflected in the title of another work, *Zend-Avesta, or The Things of Heaven and the Hereafter* (1851). In all, Fechner was a physiologist for 7 years, a physicist for 15, an invalid for 12, a psychophysicist for 14, an experimental esthetician for 11, and a philosopher for at least 40 of those years.

R. L. KOTESKEY

Fees for Psychotherapy. One important aspect of the delivery of psychological services that has received relatively little attention is the setting of fees for service. For the most part individuals or institutions have established fees based on subjective judgments of the worth of the service relative to that provided by others. For individual psychotherapists this would usually reflect training, years of experience, and competency. However, in the absence of guidelines and standards this involves to a large extent abiding by prevailing rates or a judgment of what the market will bear.

Although there has been a considerable amount of clinical folklore regarding the setting and handling of psychotherapy fees, relatively little research has been conducted on the issue.

Clinical Considerations. One guiding notion in the history of fee assessment has been the assumption that psychotherapy must involve a sacrifice for the patient if it is to be maximally effective. First expressed by Freud, this view has been a cornerstone of psychoanalytic thought since then. Dewald (1969) argues that if the fee is set too low, the patient may depreciate the therapy and not take it seriously. The patient may also have to feel grateful to the therapist for the low fee, which in turn makes the expression of anger toward the therapist difficult. The acceptance of a reduced fee may also lead the patient to feelings of guilt and the feeling of having gotten something unfairly.

On the other hand, setting too high a fee may also produce complications in therapy. In an effort to please the therapist patients may agree to an unrealistically high fee that may jeopardize their financial resources and place them under a significant additional burden. In such situations patients may be more prone to expectations of a magical cure or to transference reactions related to their perception of specialness to the therapist by virtue of their paying more than other patients.

From the standpoint of the therapist the fee will also have a variety of meanings. Too low a fee may be set by a therapist wishing to be liked or seen as kind and beneficent. However, this may later lead to feelings of resentment and other negative countertransferential responses. Such a therapist may also feel the patient should be appreciative and may therefore have a more difficult time handling negative transference reactions in the patient. Setting too high a fee will also have consequences for the therapist. Often this produces a feeling of guilt or a sense of pressure to do an extra good job, either of these reactions being counterproductive to good therapeutic work.

These considerations led Langs (1973) to advise that therapists should carefully set a fair fee for their services and communicate this directly to the patient. The patient should then be allowed time to react. If he feels he cannot afford the stated fee, the therapist should be ready to either offer a lower one, indicating that this is an acceptable fee to himself, or offer to refer him to someone else who will accept a lower fee. Langs also feels that it is the therapist's responsibility to be as certain as possible that the agreed-upon fee is realistic for the patient. He should also ensure that it will be acceptable to himself for the duration of treatment. Langs believes that the raising of a fee during therapy always produces seriously undesirable complications.

One final clinical issue related to the fee is that of insurance. Some psychoanalysts refuse to accept insurance payments out of concern for the loss of confidentiality involved in such arrangements or the feeling that such coverage removes the necessary financial sacrifice from the patient. However, the acceptance of insurance payments is standard practice for most therapists. The availability of insurance should not influence the therapist to charge a larger than usual fee. Similarly, therapists must be careful never to participate in any of the devious fee arrangements which patients sometimes suggest in conjunction with insurance coverage. (See Langs, 1973, for a nonmoralistic discussion of why therapists must avoid such arrangements.)

Research. Research on fees in therapy has been limited to a small number of studies that have investigated the relationship between fees and outcome. Evidence reported by Rosenbaum, Friedlander, and Kaplan (1956) indicated that fee-paying clients improved significantly more than nonpaying clients. Goodman (1960) found a similar relationship. Several more recent studies have, however, contradicted this finding. Dightman (1970) found no relationship between fee and improvement, appointment-keeping behavior, or length of treatment.

Pope, Geller, and Wilkinson (1975) reviewed the records of 434 psychotherapy cases, distinguishing four fee arrangments: no payment, welfare, scaled payment, and full fee. They also controlled for two potentially confounding variables: socioeconomics status and diagnosis. Their results showed fee arrangement to be unrelated to outcome, session attendance, and length of therapy. Balch, Ireland, and Lewis (1977) report the same conclusion.

These studies suggest that fee payment may not serve as the source of motivation which clinical thought has suggested. Their limited number, as well as some methodological problems, would suggest caution in drawing any conclusions until further research is carried out.

Christian Perspective. Principle 6 (Welfare of the Consumer) of the *Ethical Principles of Psychologists* (APA, 1981) indicates that psychologists should "contribute a portion of their services to work for which they receive little or no financial return" (p. 6). This public service ideal is easily ignored or forgotten. However, for the Christian it is ignored at the expense of the fundamental Christian virtue of charity, or self-sacrificing love and service of others with special concern for the poor.

Danco (1982) develops a Christian perspective on fee practices in psychotherapy, suggesting that churches should assist Christian professionals in providing psychological services to lower socioeconomic clientele. They could do this by providing office space and support staff and by underwriting therapy costs. Christian therapists involved in such an arrangement would usually need to accept less total income than that which could be generated by traditional private practice. This would be one way, however, of demonstrating Christian charity and a way of involving the church in the provision of psychological services. Regardless of how it is done, the Christian psychotherapist should demonstrate concern for those needing but unable to afford his or her services. Fees will be set, therefore, with this in mind.

References

American Psychological Association. *Ethical principles of psychologists.* Washington, D. C.: Author, 1981.

Balch, P., Ireland, J. F., & Lewis, S. B. Fees and therapy: Relation of source of payment to course of therapy at a community mental health center. *Journal of Consulting and Clinical Psychology,* 1977, *45*, 504.

Danco, J. C. The ethics of fee practices: An analysis of presuppositions and accountability. *Journal of Psychology and Theology,* 1982, *10*, 13–21.

Dewald, P. A. *Psychotherapy: A dynamic approach* (2nd ed.). New York: Basic Books, 1969.

Dightman, C. R. Fees and mental health services: Attitudes of the professional. *Mental Hygiene,* 1970, *54*, 401–406.

Goodman, N. Are there differences between fee and non-fee cases? *Social Work,* 1960, *5*, 46–52.

Langs, R. *The technique of psychoanalytic psychotherapy* (Vol. 1). New York: Aronson, 1973.

Pope, K. S., Geller, J. D., & Wilkinson, L. Fee assessment and outpatient psychotherapy. *Journal of Consulting and Clinical Psychology,* 1975, *43*, 835–841.

Rosenbaum, M., Friedlander, J., & Kaplan, S. M. Evaluation of results of psychotherapy. *Psychosomatic Medicine,* 1956, *18*, 113–132.

D. G. BENNER

Festinger, Leon (1919–). Social psychologist whose major contribution has been in the study of cognitive dissonance. Born in New York City, he earned a B.S. degree from the City College of New York and a M. A. and Ph.D. from the State University of Iowa.

Festinger taught and did research at many universities during the early years of his career. He was at Iowa until 1943, Rochester until 1945, the Massachusetts Institute of Technology until 1948, Michigan until 1951, and Minnesota until 1955. He taught at Stanford from 1955 to 1968, then went to the New School for Social Research in New York City.

Festinger views humans as essentially thinking beings who try to bring order and coherence into their lives. In his SOCIAL COMPARISON THEORY he holds that individuals are motivated to evaluate their opinions and abilities, to know the truth about themselves. If no objective standards are available, persons can judge themselves by comparing themselves with other appropriate people.

Although Festinger has conducted research

in various areas of social psychology, no recent concept has stimulated more research than his theory of COGNITIVE DISSONANCE. In *A Theory of Cognitive Dissonance* (1957) he states that two cognitive elements (beliefs, opinions, understandings) "are in a dissonant relation if, considering these two alone, the obverse of one would follow from the other." For example, assuming that they want to live a long, healthy life, cigarette smokers experience cognitive dissonance when they know 1) that they smoke and enjoy doing so, and 2) that smoking is hazardous to their health.

Cognitive dissonance is regarded as being an uncomfortable state which people are motivated to reduce or eliminate. Such dissonance can be reduced in several ways. Smokers can quit smoking, avoid information reminding them of the dangers of smoking, emphasize the pleasures that smoking brings, reinterpret the information about health hazards so that the risk seems small, and so forth.

Festinger applied cognitive dissonance theory to situations ranging from a cultist group waiting for the end of the world (*When Prophecy Fails,* 1956) to rats running in a maze getting partial reinforcement (*Deterrents and Reinforcement,* 1962). Social psychology has changed a great deal since 1957, and much of that change can be directly traced to Festinger's theory, to elaborations of it and reactions against it. The most consistent results have been obtained when the dissonance was between one's self-concept and cognition about a behavior that violated this self-concept.

R. L. KOTESKEY

Fetishism. Sexual fetishism is the use of nonliving objects to obtain erotic arousal. The object must be used repeatedly, and it must be the exclusive or preferred method of achieving sexual excitement. Objects usually include women's underclothing, boots, shoes, or sometimes unrelated items such as plastic bags, automobile tailpipes, or baby carriages. Occasionally the fetish involves parts of the body such as hair or fingernails.

The fetish is usually fondled, kissed, smelled, or tasted to achieve sexual excitement. This may accomplish orgasm in itself, but it is usually accompanied by masturbation. Sexual fetishism most commonly involves males.

Fetishism is usually part of a larger pattern of maladjustment. The individual may have doubts about his masculinity and potency. He may fear humiliation or rejection by the opposite sex. The mastery over inanimate objects compensates for his feelings of inferiority and failure at mastery in relationships.

The mere involvement of objects in the process of sexual excitement is not necessarily fetishistic. The smell of perfume or the viewing of attractive articles of clothing for the purpose of stimulating sexual arousal are not considered a fetish unless the article becomes a sexual end in itself and precludes normal male-female sexual relationships.

The individual engaging in fetishism sometimes comes in conflict with the law in the pursuit of the desired object. This situation is illustrated by a man who had a fetish for large plastic bags. He was arrested by the police while coming out of a dry cleaning store carrying two rolls of plastic bags he had just stolen. Most referrals for treatment of fetishism come through such contact with the law.

The age of onset of fetishism is childhood. However, the object really begins to be a trigger for erotic excitement during adolescence. The original conditioning process may be accidental, but it becomes paired with sexual excitement and orgasm over time.

The effects of the overall environment on the child and adolescent must not be excluded when the conditioning process is considered. A maladaptive environment often blocks the child from progressing normally through exploration and experimentation as he develops toward sexual maturity and appropriate behavior.

The treatment of sexual fetishism is difficult because of the chronic nature of the sexual deviation and the reluctance of the individual to seek treatment. Even after they are apprehended and referred by the court, such individuals usually deny the fetish and its sexual connotations. Behavior therapy is often effective. Adversive conditioning is utilized to decondition the client by pairing unpleasant stimuli such as an electric shock with the fetish. The patient receives a mild shock while viewing slides of the fetish object, the theory being that the unpleasant stimulus will be paired with the sexual object, thus decreasing its attractiveness. Systematic desensitization can also be employed to lessen the fears associated with heterosexual relationships.

M. A. CAMPION

Fictional Goals. Hans Vaihinger was a turn-of-the-century philosopher who developed the concept of fictions. He contended that there were two spheres of reality: a world of motion and a world of consciousness. Human behavior can only be comprehended in the world of consciousness. Things in themselves do not explain behavior as causes. Behavior can be understood only when psychologists comprehend the way in which people find meaning and relevance in things (Vaihinger, 1935).

Fictions do not exist in the world of things. Fictions are abstractions which consciousness finds meaningful or relevant. In mathematics the concepts of zero, empty space, negative numbers, and infinity are all fictions. In science theories that cannot be conclusively proved (e.g., atomic structure) are fictions. People use fictions *as if* they were accurate representations of things in themselves. When Britain was on a metallic money standard, people accepted pound notes and counted them as if they were pounds of sterling.

The natural world is discovered by observation. Machines and instruments are invented by human creativity. Fictions are mental instruments, and as such they are created, not discovered. Hypotheses about the natural world are verifiable (provable by observation). Fictions are not verifiable, and indeed they are known to be false. However, fictions are "proved" by means of vindication (justification). Justifiable fictions are those that are useful, that are means to an end. They are errors, but they are retained and acted upon because they are fruitful errors. Fictions that do not justify themselves (i.e., cannot be proved useful or necessary) should be eliminated.

Notions of categories and causes are not observable aspects of the natural world. We retain these notions because they have utility, giving order and facilitating communication. The idea of free will is an extremely important fiction. It allows us to act as if our actions were the product of independent reason, and allows us to treat others as if they were responsible for their actions. Even though we shall never have the evidence to verify free will, the fiction is vindicated by its value.

Adler (1956) read Vaihinger in 1911 and was greatly influenced by the concept of fictions. Indeed, the concept enabled Adler to clarify some of his basic differences with Freud. Adler accepted the idea that human behavior is determined by fictions, not by mechanistic forces. He then modified Vaihinger's theory in several ways. First, he emphasized that human behavior is determined by goals rather than reactions to events. Goals are fictions because they do not exist, yet individuals behave as if the goal was the most important factor in behavior. Second, he suggested that each person is unique and has his own set of fictions for guidance. What is vindicable for one person is not necessarily vindicable for another. Third, the purpose of the fiction is to preserve self-esteem against inferiority feeling. Fourth, most fictions are unconscious. The individual will not admit that they are fictional. Fifth, when the individual adheres rigidly to a fiction, there is a danger that lack of relevant contact with reality and other people will result in a neurosis.

Psychotherapy along the lines of INDIVIDUAL PSYCHOLOGY focuses on understanding the patient's fictional goals, helping the patient to achieve these insights, and assisting the patient to change those fictions that are dysfunctional.

References
Adler, A. *The individual psychology of Alfred Adler.* New York: Basic Books, 1956.
Vaihinger, H. *The philosophy of as if: A system of the theoretical, practical, and religious fictions of mankind* (2nd ed.). New York: Barnes & Noble, 1935.

T. L. BRINK

Figure-Drawing Tests. Tests often used by psychologists to assess emotional maturity or the presence of psychopathology in children, adolescents, and adults. In one form of the test procedure the examinee is asked to draw a person (Draw-A-Person or Draw-A-Man Tests) or to draw a house, tree, and a person (House-Tree-Person Test). The examiner observes as the figures are drawn and notes how the subject executes the task. After the drawings are complete, the examiner will often interview the subject to obtain verbal information about the drawings. Later the drawings are evaluated as to their content, quality, and overall characteristics.

Interest in using drawings as a guide to assess a person's psychological nature began in the nineteenth century with evaluations of art by persons labeled insane. Early in the twentieth century Goodenough (1926) developed a version of the human figure-drawing test to assess intelligence in children. Later researchers (e.g., Koppitz, 1968) expanded the assessment of children's drawings to encompass other psychological dimensions. Buck (1966) has expanded the technique so that the test can be administered to adults.

Figure-drawing tests are projective in nature. That is, the drawings are assumed to contain some inner elements of a person's psyche that are projected into the drawing task. Drawings are said to have value because they give the examiner a look at what otherwise might be a private, unrevealed world. Figure-drawing tests are valuable because they do not require verbalization and because their purpose is somewhat obtuse to the examinee. Faking good or bad behaviors may thus be minimized, since what constitutes a good or bad response is usually unknown to the examinee. However, the figure-drawing test does require a cooperative attitude from the subject.

The interpretation of figure drawings is predicated on the assumption that "normals" will include all the essential components of the figure, will add only a few nonessential details, and will not exaggerate or overelaborate any one element of the drawing. For example, Buck (1966) defines the essential elements of a human figure drawing as a head, a trunk, two legs, and two arms. Essential facial details are two eyes, a nose, a mouth, and two ears. The absence of one or more essential elements in a figure drawing is considered serious.

Extensive guides help the examiner score the test. Various researchers have agreed on the meaning of certain features. For example, in an adult's drawing an outlined human figure that is not filled in suggests serious problems. Drawing internal organs on the trunk of a human figure is indicative of psychotic functioning (Ogdon, 1967). Other details are not uniformly interpreted. Heavy shading of human hair has been seen as indicative of anger, anxiety, sensuality, or concern with sexual excitement (Ogden, 1967).

Such ambiguity of interpretation is a central criticism of the tests. If advocates of the tests cannot agree on interpretation, critics argue, how can such tests be valid? Roback (1968) cites other weaknessess of the assessment procedure: a paucity of solid research substantiating the procedure, reliability problems, and other concerns regarding validity. Even the staunchest advocates of the tests warn that conclusions regarding a person's functioning should never be drawn solely from figure drawings but rather from data gathered from all measurement tools in the assessment battery.

References
Buck, J. N. *The house-tree-person technique: A revised manual.* Beverly Hills, Calif.: Western Psychological Services, 1966.
Goodenough, F. L. *Measurement of intelligence by drawings.* Yonkers-on-Hudson, N.Y.: World Book, 1926.
Koppitz, E. M. *Psychological evaluation of human figure drawings.* New York: Grune & Stratton, 1968.
Ogdon, D. P. *Psychodiagnosis and personality assessment.* Beverly Hills, Calif.: Western Psychological Services, 1967.
Roback, H. B. Human figure drawings: Their utility in the clinical psychologist's armamentarium for personality assessment. *Psychological Bulletin,* 1968, 70 (1), 1–19.

Additional Readings

DiLeo, J. H. *Children's drawings as diagnostic aids.* New York: Brunner/Mazel, 1973.

Schildkrout, M. S., Shenker, J. R., & Sonnenblick, M. *Human figure drawings in adolescence.* New York: Brunner/Mazel, 1972.

J. R. Beck

See Psychological Measurement; Personality Assessment.

Figure-Ground Relationship. A perceptual phenomenon in which one part of a perception stands out as a unified object (figure) while the rest is relegated to background (ground). This phenomenon is most clearly manifest in the visual sense but occurs in all senses. It was an important object of study in the early stages of Gestalt psychology.

Filial Therapy. A specific psychotherapeutic technique designed for use with children exhibiting a variety of psychosocial disorders. It was developed by B. Guerney and his colleagues (see L. Guerney, 1980). Like B. Guerney's other major contribution to therapeutic technique, Relationship Enhancement Therapy, this approach attempts to teach Rogerian interactional skills via the common four-step behavioral process of didactic presentation, modeling, rehearsal/practice, and feedback.

In the case of filial therapy the goal is to teach the nondirective helping skills of unconditional positive regard, empathy, and genuineness to parents in a group training process. Parents are taught in essence to be their child's play therapist. They are initially encouraged to conduct weekly play therapy sessions with their children. After the nondirective therapy skills become well established, parents are encouraged to utilize the skills in their day-to-day interactions with their children. Other skills may be added to the parents' repertoire. One goal of this approach is to enhance the psychosocial adjustment of the child through the beneficial effects of the play therapy sessions. Another benefit is effect the approach has on other areas of parenting.

Filial therapy was ahead of its time in its use of parents as change agents, a procedure now common in child behavior therapy. The research supporting this particular approach is spotty, however, and in general filial therapy is neither a well-recognized nor widely used treatment method.

Reference

Guerney, L. Filial therapy. In R. Herink (Ed.) *The psychotherapy handbook.* New York: New American Library, 1980.

S. L. Jones

Fixation. In psychoanalytic thought fixation refers to the arrested personality development associated with the persistence of strong energy attachments (cathexes) to memories and experiences in an earlier stage of development. Fixation generally implies psychopathology, as it assumes that the energy left behind at the earlier developmental level results in a weakening of the ego. It is therefore closely related to the concept of Regression, which suggests that, when facing a serious trauma or stress in the present, the individual will tend to regress back to the point where energy, or ego resources, were left behind.

In both normal and abnormal functioning earlier levels of personality development persist alongside each other. Thus the mere presence of some residual aspects of infantile functioning is not in itself sufficient to indicate the presence of fixation. When fixation is present, the energy retained at the earlier levels of development exceeds that seen in more normally functioning individuals and therefore is thought to be indicative of a weak spot in the psychic structure. This weakness may manifest itself either as a Neurosis or as a character trait.

Predisposing factors relative to the formation of fixations include hereditary and constitutional factors, excessive gratification, excessive frustration, or some combination of these factors. Most commonly, fixations seem to develop as a result of a traumatic experience of early childhood.

Sometimes the concept of fixation is used in a less technical manner to describe an aberration of affection in which an individual experiences exaggerated attachment to someone else (e.g., a father fixation).

D. G. Benner

See Psychoanalytic Psychology.

Flight into Health. A psychoanalytic concept referring to apparent improvement in psychological functioning that is a defense against further therapeutic exploration. Because the improvement is not based on a resolution of the neurosis, it is not seen as a real cure. In many cases such rapid improvement is based on the patient's passive-dependent relationship to the therapist, who is idealized and endowed with omnipotence. For this reason it is often also called a transference cure.

Flight of Ideas. A disturbance of thinking characterized by a continuous flow of rapid speech jumping abruptly from topic to topic. Although there is no common theme or continuity of thought, each idea is superficially related to the former idea, usually through common word sounds or play-on-word associations. In severe cases the speech is elated and incoherent, and the person is unable to retain any logical train of thought. While most frequently observed in manic episodes, flight of ideas may also be seen in organic mental disorders, schizophrenia, and psychotic disorders.

Flooding. A behavioral approach used in elimination of unwanted fears or phobias. In flooding the client imagines or is directly exposed to highly frightening events in a protected setting. Presumably the fear-inducing stimuli will lose their influence once the individual is fully exposed to them and discovers that no harm occurs. Thus an individual who is fearful of elevators is asked to imagine boarding a glass-enclosed high-speed elevator, then watching through the glass as the elevator rapidly rises from the ground level to the 20th floor.

Following a discussion of the person's fears, in a typical flooding procedure the person is then asked to imagine the most feared situation. The therapist describes the salient fearful elements to enhance visualization. Scenes are presented for extended periods, often several minutes at a time, so that the individual experiences the full fear response and it begins to abate. For extinction of the fearful response to occur, it is important that the scene not be terminated until the anxiety abates; terminating too soon may actually strengthen rather than alleviate the fearful response. Unfortunately, it is sometimes difficult to judge this, and facial and body cues must be carefully observed. Although there are widespread individual differences in the timing, it is typical that the client shows an initial increase in anxiety response, then a gradual abatement of anxiety.

The theoretical rationale for flooding is based on two-factor learning theory. According to this theory individuals learn to escape from situations in which they are presented with unpleasant stimuli. When a warning stimulus (e.g. a light) reliably predicts the unpleasant stimulus (e.g. shock), the individual gradually learns to escape when the warning stimulus is presented, thus avoiding the unpleasant one. If Dad beats Johnny when he comes home drunk, Johnny soon leaves the house whenever Dad comes in drunk, thus avoiding beatings.

According to two-factor learning theory the warning stimulus, through pairing with the unpleasant stimulus, comes to produce anxiety responses in anticipation of the unpleasant stimulus. Escape from the warning stimulus eliminates these anxiety responses, hence is negatively reinforcing. Research has shown that avoidance behaviors learned in this way are extremely resistant to extinction, evidently because the person is so effective in avoiding the unpleasant stimulus. Normally, this is an adaptive response, as when the sight of fire comes to produce the caution appropriate to fire's capacity to cause painful burns. Not infrequently, however, through a variety of unfortunate experiences persons learn to be anxious or fearful in the presence of relatively harmless stimuli. According to behavior theory, this is how phobic responses are initiated.

In animal studies of two-factor learning theory one effective method for eliminating fear responses to conditioned aversive stimuli when they are no longer followed by the unpleasant stimulus is preventing the animal from escaping the warning stimulus. Prolonged exposure to the warning stimulus without opportunity to escape weakens the escape response. Flooding is analogous to this procedure, since the person is exposed to the unpleasant phobic stimulus without opportunity to escape.

Systematic desensitization and implosion share similar treatment goals with flooding but use different approaches. In systematic desensitization the individual is first taught to relax; treatment then begins with minimal anxiety-inducing stimuli, presents them briefly, and progresses gradually to more threatening stimuli, maintaining relaxation throughout. In this way anxiety is minimized throughout treatment. The elevator scene described above might serve as the final step in systematic desensitization but be the beginning point in flooding.

Some theorists use the terms *flooding* and *implosion* interchangeably. There are similarities in the two procedures, but important methodological and theoretical distinctions suggest that this confusion is unfortunate. Implosion, as developed by Stampfl, draws heavily on psychoanalytic theory. It is assumed that the basis for phobias is unresolved conflicts involving rejection, dependence, orality, anality, sexuality, loss of impulse control, and guilt stemming from the childhood stages of psychosexual development. Thus the imagery used in implosion focuses on these presumed underlying conflicts rather than concentrating on the identified phobic stimulus. In addition, in implosion it is common to dramatize the scenes to make them as traumatic as possible even though the individual may never have experienced such events. The individual may be asked to imagine climbing into bed with hundreds of snakes, feeling the snakes crawling over his body, squeezing and biting the snakes, and so on.

The results of experimental studies of flooding are mixed. The procedures are not standardized; thus, procedural variations may account for inconsistencies in results. Comparative studies suggest that systematic desensitization probably is as effective as flooding, though results are inconsistent. Horrifying scenes may actually impair the effectiveness of flooding. (For a review of research on flooding see Morganstern, 1973.)

Finally, flooding is generally unpleasant. This could result in premature termination of treatment. Therefore, most practitioners prefer systematic desensitization and related procedures.

Reference

Morganstern, K. P. Implosive therapy and flooding procedures: A critical review. *Psychological Bulletin*, 1973, 79, 318–334.

R. K. Bufford

Focusing. *See* Experiential Focusing.

Folie à Deux. First described by Frenchmen Lasèque and Falret in 1877, folie à deux, or insanity of two, is a relatively rare condition where two persons share the same mental disorder. Usually having a paranoid psychosis of a persecutory type, they believe the same reality distortion to the extent that even delusions are held in common.

The persons usually belong to the same family and have been closely related for years. They live rather socially isolated, excluding others and having few outside interests. Women are more susceptible than men. Two sisters or a mother-daughter combination are most frequent, but occasionally a husband and wife share the disorder.

One of the pair usually dominates and may be paranoid regardless of the relationship. The other person follows in a dependent, submissive, and suggestible manner. The follower's identity is so intertwined with that of the dominant person that reality distortions are accepted uncritically. If the relationship ends, the follower's adherence to the delusions and faulty beliefs will usually decrease. Terminating the relationship is usually sufficient treat-ment for the follower. The more dominant person requires treatment similar to that given for paranoid psychosis.

M. R. Nelson

Forensic Psychiatry. The branch of psychiatry that concerns itself with the common ground shared by the law and psychiatry. According to Slovenko (1980), forensic psychiatry may be broadly categorized into matters of credibility, capability, competency, compensation, and custody. Although forensic psychiatry is often thought of as a relatively new arrival compared to more traditional areas of psychiatric involvement, it becomes apparent that what is unique to the twentieth century is legal involvement in the practice of psychiatry. Psychiatry's input into legal issues, on the other hand, is not new. Physicians in general and psychiatrists in particular have been asked to explain, or attempt to explain, deviant behavior as an illness which could then ostensibly be "treated."

Although the terminology has changed, psychiatry's main interface with the law remains that of attempting to alternately explain, justify, or excuse behavior caused by mental illness. The overlap with theology immediately becomes apparent. In 1973 the prominent psychiatrist Menninger asked the question, "Whatever became of sin?" (Menninger, 1973). Menninger expressed the belief that perhaps we have gone too far in attempting to "psychopathologicalize" deviance, stating that much of the behavior which mental health professionals view as sickness might better be understood as plain old-fashioned conscious wrongdoing or, bluntly, sin.

It has been in this century that external legal controls have played an increasingly large role in the psychiatric profession, questioning such areas as civil commitment, malpractice, breach of confidentiality, and the rights of the mentally ill, among others. This legal involvement has markedly altered the psychiatric profession as a whole, and brought about change in many procedures regarding treatment of the mentally ill.

Historical Roots of the Law/Psychiatry Interface. A review of the historical roots of forensic psychiatry reveals two major themes. The first involves an attempt at determining responsiblity for criminal behavior and, within this context, delineation of those types of disorders that would mandate the individual's exemption from responsibility. The second involves the requirement of involuntary commitment of those individuals deemed injurious or potentially injurious to themselves or others. Both attempt to reconcile societal needs for order and stability with the individual's rights to freedom of behavior which must be protected from arbitrary and unconstitutional restrictions. This tension between societal needs and individual rights colors the entire process of decision making within the realm of forensic psychiatry.

Early Greek law accepted the premise that in order to be held legally and morally responsible for his actions an individual must demonstrate the capacity for free choice. The Greeks made a distinction between intentional and unintentional crimes. Aristotle further stated that moral blameworthiness requires an individual's capacity for freedom of choice. He noted that such capacity was lacking in animals, children, and in the insane.

Roman law held that if an offender was felt to be incapable of assuming responsibility for his behavior, he must therefore be regarded as unable to assume civil rights. Thus, he and his property were placed under control of a guardian. Deutsch (1949) notes that Roman law emphasized that this responsibility for criminal action required the presence of a "guilty mind" in addition to an evil act.

During the Middle Ages the insane were technically judged to be responsible for and therefore guilty of crimes, though in certain cases the individual could receive pardon. In certain regions of Europe insanity was perceived as evidence of sin and punishable by law.

An important legal defense emerged early in the fourteenth century which recognized impairment of mental capacity, including both insanity and mental retardation, as grounds for exempting the offender from responsibility for his actions. This defense resulted in a verdict of guilty along with a special petition of insanity that was presented to the king in hopes of his granting a pardon. From increased frequency of such pardons grew the concept of insanity as a valid defense, which by the sixteenth century was well established in the law.

Originally it was held that a person must be totally deprived of reason for the insanity defense to be valid. In 1736, however, Matthew Hale made the distinction between "total" and "partial" insanity. Partial insanity was defined as being limited to "particular discourses, subjects, or applications; or else partial in respect to degree." The case of Rex vs. Hadfield furthered this attitude in 1800 by pointing out that a single symptom of a mental disorder

ought to be sufficient to warrant a defense of insanity. This case was a forerunner to the concept that an individual may be insane in one respect (e.g., a circumscribed delusional system) while perfectly sane in others.

Conversely, it was held in 1791 that "the business of the court is to try the cause and not the man; and a very bad man may have a very righteous cause" (Thompson vs. Church). This would imply that an individual could be considered "bad" or morally unsound or even insane in certain aspects of his thinking or behavior, but that the character evidence has only remote bearing on the particular offense in question.

These areas of criminal responsibility and competency continue to be debated in psychiatric and legal circles and, along with issues of testamentary capacity, child custody, and civil law, comprise the majority of psychiatry's input into law.

In the twentieth century there has been an upsurge of concern in the United States for those persons in society labeled mentally ill. Cries of outrage were evoked by what was considered inhumane treatment of the mentally ill in state hospitals and asylums. Psychiatrists and other mental health professionals were increasingly asked to explain their diagnostic procedures, research protocols, and treatment plans. The legal system became involved by setting external regulations regarding such issues as the right to treatment and the right to refuse treatment, civil commitment procedures, and confidentiality. Gross failure to safeguard individual rights and acts of commission where rights were violated resulted in stricter ethical codes and legal regulation within the profession. Those areas of concern include civil commitment, malpractice, assessment of dangerousness, rights of the mentally ill to receive treatment, and rights of the mentally ill to refuse treatment.

Psychiatry's Involvement in the Law.
Criminal responsibility. We have already seen that it has long been considered unjust to hold an individual blameworthy unless his offense was voluntary and unless the individual professed guilt. In the now famous M'Naghten trial in England in 1843, Daniel M'Naghten was found not guilty of murder by reason of insanity and was thereby certified to be of unsound mind and detained for the remaining 22 years of his life in a lunatic asylum. M'Naghten had attempted to kill Sir Robert Peel, the prime minister, but instead mistakenly shot Edward Drumner. The jury's decision created a furor, as it was speculated that

M'Naghten, a Scot, was a political assassin. Queen Victoria and other influential political figures were outraged at the acquittal and demanded clarification and revision of the concept of criminal responsibility. The consequence of this process came to be known as the M'Naghten rule, which reads: "The jurors ought to be told, in all cases, that every man is presumed to be sane, and to possess a sufficient degree of reason to be responsible for their crimes, until the contrary has been proved to their satisfaction; and that, to establish a defense on the ground of insanity, it must be clearly proved that at the same time of the committing of the act, the party accused was labouring under such a defect of reason, from disease of the mind, as not to know the nature and quality of the act he was doing; or if he did know it, that he did not know that what he was doing was wrong."

Thus the M'Naghten rule asks if the defendant understood the nature and quality of his act and if he knew the difference between right and wrong within the confines of that particular offense. This is a somewhat narrower question than had been previously asked—i.e., whether the accused knew the difference, in general, between right and wrong.

The question of exactly how to determine criminal responsibility remains, as evidenced by continuing debate. In 1962 the American Law Institute recommended the following test of responsibility for criminal action [§ 4.01]: "(1) a person is not responsible for criminal conduct if, at the same time of such conduct, as a result of mental disease or defect, he lacks substantial capacity either to appreciate the criminality (wrongfulness) of his conduct or to conform his conduct to the requirement of the law; (2) as used in the Article, the terms mental disease or defect do not include an abnormality manifested only by repeated criminal or otherwise anti-social conduct."

The attempt in 1982 to assassinate the President of the United States, and the finding of the offender to be insane, has again fueled debate regarding when a person can be called insane, if insanity should be grounds for negating blameworthiness, and what action—e.g., treatment, punishment, or incarceration—should be taken.

Competency to stand trial. There have long been provisions to ensure that an individual may not be subjected to a criminal trial if he lacks the capacity to understand the nature of the proceedings against him, to consult with counsel, and to assist in preparing his defense. The Supreme Court has stated that "the prohibition [against trying a mental incompetent] is fundamental to an adversary system of justice" (Drope vs. Missouri, 1975).

This prohibition has been utilized in the past to prevent an individual's participation in a criminal trial on grounds of insanity. It has also been attempted (usually unsuccessfully) when the offender is on psychotropic medications, or when the offender claims that the stress of trial will cause physical or mental breakdown. Generally the definition of the incompetency plea has narrowed over the past few years. However, the question remains as to what to do with the psychiatrically ill (and perhaps potentially dangerous) individual declared incompetent to stand trial. Traditionally these individuals have been held for varying lengths of time in special buildings for the criminally insane, which also house those individuals found not guilty by reason of insanity or guilty but insane.

Child custody. Frequently, psychiatrists are asked to participate in situations where custody dispute arises. Court action in a child custody dispute attempts to establish custody rights in the best interest of the child. Early English common law gave the father an absolute right to the custody of his children. Over time, the rights of mother and father equalized, and currently the mother is favored as the primary parent. Within the last decade, however, increasing numbers of fathers have been asserting custodial claims, citing that since increasing numbers of women are now working, the traditional rationale for maternal custody is less relevant. Although rights of the natural parents are paramount over third parties, a natural parent's claim may be superseded by foster parents or other relatives. The primary difficulty lies in defining the "best interest" of the child. This takes into account, among other things, consideration of the "moral fitness" of the competing parties; their mental and physical health; the emotional ties between the child and the competing parties; the ability of the competing parties to provide material needs, guidance, education, and religious instruction; and the reasonable preference of the child, if the child is deemed old enough to make such a choice.

Simpler divorce laws and changing life styles have made child custody disputes more frequent and have increased debate over exactly what constitutes the best interest of the child. Controversial areas include joint custody, a homosexual parent, and circumstances in which the parent is living in what is considered to be a nontraditional life style.

Every state today has a statute allowing the child to be removed from the parental home if there is legitimate evidence of abuse or neglect. If this occurs, the child is then supervised by a legal organization (e.g., welfare, probation department) and placed in a foster home, an institution, or with relatives. This process may lead to further dispute, as when the natural parents seek to regain custody.

Legal Involvement in Psychiatry. *Civil commitment.* It is perhaps in the area of civil commitment that the tension between individual rights and societal needs is most acute. Civil commitment involves involuntary confinement of an individual for either a specifically defined time or an indefinite period. Generally civil commitment can be classified as: 1) emergency commitment (usually initiated by law enforcement officers); 2) temporary or observational commitment (initiated by relatives, physicians, hospitals); 3) indeterminate commitment (authorized by a court, medical doctors, or an administrative tribunal).

Although states differ in their statutes regarding commitment procedures, a fundamental requirement is that the person to be committed must be mentally disabled. Obviously this is not sufficient cause for commitment. Virtually all states require that one of five other conditions must also be present: 1) the need for hospitalization; 2) the need for care or treatment; 3) impaired judgment; 4) disablement; 5) dangerousness to self or others (Brooks, 1974).

The mental disability is defined variously as illness, disorder, feeblemindedness, insanity, mental deficiency, etc. The commitment may be predominantly for the benefit of society (dangerous to others) or predominantly for the person's own benefit (dangerous to self). Current debate involves the "benefits" of civil commitment and the misuse of commitment procedures for authoritarian purposes by the state.

Critics point to poorly defined criteria for commitment, confinement disproportionate to the behavior exhibited, and failure to provide adequate protection for the individual. Some argue for the abolition of civil commitment. Others wish to retain the procedure but minimize potential abuse by defining stricter criteria for commitment, improving conditions while in confinement, and educating mental health professionals and legal personnel as to the potential abuses involved.

Malpractice. A major area of legal input into psychiatry involves malpractice, a term used to refer to professional negligence. According to law the psychiatrist, like other professionals, has a legal duty to exercise the degree of skill ordinarily used by other members of his profession under similar circumstances. Slovenko (1980) notes that psychiatrists have been sued for malpractice mainly for 1) faulty diagnosis or screening; 2) improper certification for commitment; 3) suicide of the patient; 4) harmful effects of convulsive treatments and psychotropic drugs; 5) improper divulgence of information; and 6) sexual intimacy with patients. Malpractice law regulates the physician's behavior and helps define standards of practice. If the physician (in this case, psychiatrist) harms a patient, either intentionally or through negligence, he may be sued. To establish negligence several conditions must be met. First, a standard of care must be established. Next, the psychiatrist must be shown to have had a duty owed. Third, the duty must be shown to be owed to the plaintiff; and fourth, the breach of duty must be shown to be the legal cause of the claimed damage.

Right to treatment. The right to treatment doctrine was introduced by Birnbaum (1960) and refers to the legal right of the state mental hospital patient to adequate care and treatment. The doctrine was introduced to guard against inadequate care due to understaffing, overcrowding, and other factors. Treatment is generally defined as providing a humane environment, adequate staffing, and an individual treatment plan for each patient.

The right to treatment statute arose from the realization that hundreds of thousands of mentally ill persons are hospitalized annually in state mental hospitals, and that often they receive only minimal custodial care, usually due to lack of funding. Patients in state hospitals are disproportionately poor, black, and uneducated, and frequently are involuntarily committed. The right to treatment sets forth a moral argument for adequate care.

Right to refuse treatment. In other medical specialities the imposition of treatment on a competent patient against his wishes is likely grounds for battery. Because of the inherent differences involved in treating the mentally ill, it was not uncommon in the past for hospitalized psychiatric patients, voluntary or committed, to have treatment forced upon them. This has changed recently, and some courts have ruled that even committed patients have the right to refuse treatment. This doctrine arose from the outrage surrounding invasive procedures such as psychosurgery, electroconvulsive therapy, and aversive behavioral therapy being used on nonconsenting patients. Since then more traditional treatments, such as psychotropic drugs, have also been questioned.

This doctrine is currently a controversial one in regard to traditional forms of treatment. The ultimate question arises from having the ability to commit patients to a hospital where treatment is available but cannot be given. Stone (1977) notes that this policy, taken to the extreme, threatens to return our mental hospitals to their barbaric state of a century ago, before appropriate treatment was available.

Assessment of dangerousness. The psychiatrist may be liable in some instances where a patient under his care commits suicide or harms another person. The psychiatrist is not expected to prevent every patient from committing dangerous acts to himself or others, but is expected to exercise reasonable caution. Standards of care regarding the suicidal patient are vague. Suits may be brought against the psychiatrist by a patient who made an unsuccessful suicide attempt or by family members of a patient who committed suicide. Further complications are added by the rulings that require patients to be treated in the least restrictive environment. Generally speaking, the psychiatrist would not be liable unless marked indications of suicidal intent had been communicated to him, and he had not taken their seriousness into account in diagnosis and the planning of treatment.

The patient who harms others presents a somewhat similar problem. Here the psychiatrist is liable for both restraining the patient and also warning the potential victim.

The Tarasoff ruling of 1976 set the groundwork for psychiatrists' obligation to inform third parties about their patient's dangerousness. In this case, Miss Tarasoff was killed by a psychiatric patient who had admitted his homicidal intent to his therapist. No effort was made to inform Miss Tarasoff, and her parents brought an action for wrongful death against the therapist, the campus police, and the University of California. In ruling on the decision the California Supreme Court stated, "When a therapist determines or pursuant to the standards of his profession should determine that his patient represents a serious danger of violence to another he incurs an obligation to use reasonable care to protect the intended victim against such danger" (Tarasoff, 1976). This issue must be weighed against breach of confidentiality. The court decided in favor of preventing risk of life of another

person over violation of confidence, stating "the protective priviledge ends where the public peril begins."

Theological Implications. Psychiatry has been asked through the ages to explain deviant behavior. Through these efforts certain standards have been set to establish when a person may be excused from responsibility due to mental incompetence or insanity. If a person is judged insane, law prevents him being held responsible for his actions.

Mowrer (1961) notes that many therapists excuse deviant behavior on the grounds that it is merely a symptom of an illness that was present before the offense occurred. However, he also notes that this makes it difficult to find any basis for moral responsibility or social accountability. If any wrongdoing is judged as due to illness, the implication is that treatment from an external source is necessary, and that the individual himself cannot be expected to change his behavior based on conscious choice.

In primitive cultures deviant behavior was believed to be caused by demonic forces and evil spirits. No distinction was made between criminality and mental illness, and both resulted in punishment. With the identification of psychiatric illness in modern times, society has aimed to make this distinction, to treat those with illness and to punish those who are morally "bad." Menninger (1973) points out that it became the custom to attempt to legislate morality and to coerce virtue by law. Currently we seem to be turning full circle, with religious and moral leaders pleading to return deviant behavior to its original status as sin. Some see modern society's tendency to excuse deviant behavior based on psychopathology as indicative of collective social irresponsibility.

Socrates stated well the age-old question with which psychiatry, law, and theology continue to grapple. He wonders how it is that men know what is good, but do what is bad.

References

Birnbaum, M. "The right to treatment. *American Bar Association Journal*, 1960, *46*(5), 499–505.

Brooks, A. *Law, psychiatry and the mental health system.* Boston: Little, Brown, 1974.

Deutsch, A. *The mentally ill in America* (2nd ed.). New York: Columbia University Press, 1949.

Drope v. Missouri, 420 U.S. 162 (1975).

Menninger, K. *Whatever became of sin?* New York: Hawthorn Books, 1973.

Mowrer, O. H. *The crisis in psychiatry and religion.* Princeton, N.J.: Van Nostrand, 1961.

Slovenko, R. Forensic psychiatry. In H. I. Kaplan, A. M. Freedman, & B. J. Sadock (Eds.), *Comprehensive textbook of psychiatry, III.* Baltimore: Williams & Wilkins, 1980.

Stone, A. Recent mental health litigation: A critical perspective. *American Journal of Psychiatry*, 1977, *134*(3), 273–279.

Tarasoff v. Regents of the University of California, 131 Cal. Rptr 14 1976.
Thompson v. Church, 1 Root 312 Conn. 1791

Additional Readings
Bromberg, W. *The uses of psychiatry in the law.* Westport, Conn.: Quorum Books, 1979.
Halleck, S. L. *Law in the practice of psychiatry.* New York: Plenum Medical Book, 1980.
Rosner, R. *Critical issues in American psychiatry and the law.* Springfield, Ill.: Thomas, 1982.

L. B. Hardy

See Malpractice; Crime and Mental Disorder.

Forensic Psychology. A branch of psychology that deals with legal issues pertaining to mental health. This may include courtroom testimony, treatment, consultation, and research.

The late 1800s marked the beginning of psychologists in the courtroom. The first psychologist to enter the witness stand was believed to be Karl Marburg of Germany (Farrington, Hawkins, & Lloyd-Bostock, 1979). Hugo Munsterberg was the first, however, to draw attention to the psychologist in the courtroom with his research concerning the problems of witnesses' perceptions. His work, published in 1899, on the time interval between two gunshots is still used today, and was of theoretical value in the double bullet controversy in the assassination of President John F. Kennedy.

Yet forensic psychology has been slow to gain acceptance from the courts of the United States. This is not true in Great Britain and some other countries where, after World War II, psychologists have been accepted without question as experts in the courtroom.

Currently there is no recognized degree or licensing in the speciality of forensic psychology in the United States. Most specialized training comes after the Ph.D. or Psy.D. in psychology has been earned and a license to practice psychology has been granted. The training includes attending seminars, reading the relevant literature, and adapting previous training and experience to the courtroom. Some universities offer courses in forensic psychology, and students can take them on an elective basis.

Roles and Functions. Currently the role and function of the psychologist in a court setting can involve pretrial, trial, and posttrial tasks. The pretrial question of competency of the defendant to cooperate with the attorney and understand the charges is usually determined by a combination of clinical interviews and tests such as intelligence tests, projective tests, and tests for literacy.

The psychologist may also be asked to determine the state of the defendant's mind at the time of the crime. This is a rather controversial aspect of the competency evaluation because the psychologist is asked to determine the defendant's mental state not at the time of evaluation, but at some previous point in time. Questions to be determined are: Was the defendant's act at the time of the crime the product of mental illness, and can he therefore be held responsible for his behavior? Did the defendant know right from wrong, or was his behavior the result of an "irresistible impulse" that precluded his ability to control his behavior at the time of the alleged crime?

The defendant may be diverted into treatment in lieu of a trial, and will not stand trial for the alleged crime if the treatment is successful. However, if the person does not cooperate with the therapy process, he may be returned to stand trial.

Forensic psychologists also are called upon to determine the risk potential of the defendant before possible commitment decisions are made. A very dangerous defendant may be committed to a mental hospital, possibly against his will. Psychologists may also be asked to recommend other appropriate treatment measures to be taken.

The potential for rehabilitation of a first offender or repeater is another question the courts ask the psychologist to address. This also includes recommendations for specific treatment or treatment programs. Whether or not the individual would profit from the treatment is particularly pertinent for persons accused of alcohol or drug abuse, or where injury to family members has occurred.

Currently child custody cases are demanding more of the forensic psychologist's clinical time. Attorneys and judges are asking for information to help decide which parent should have custody of the child. Through the clinical interview, home study, and projective techniques, the psychologist is able to make the necessary recommendation in custody cases.

In juvenile cases involving serious crimes the psychologist may be asked to help the judge in determining whether the defendant should be tried as a juvenile or as an adult. This is determined after considering the circumstances of the crime and the emotional factors contributing to the alleged criminal act. The psychologist would also, in juvenile cases, offer opinions as to the possibility for rehabilitation.

Attorneys occasionally ask the forensic psychologist to assist in jury selection. The attorney and psychologist together determine the most appropriate jury members to weigh testimony in behalf of their client.

Pretrial assistance to the court also includes inpatient or outpatient treatment of persons accused of a crime where competency to stand trial is in question. The goal of the treatment would be to restore the person to competency in order to allow him to stand trial.

During the trial forensic psychologists testify as expert witnesses. The testimony is based on their evaluation of the defendant through testing and clinical interview. The opinion is given in the context of accepted psychological principles and within the mainstream of psychological research. Testimony may include such topics as "perception, sensation, confessions, eye-witness identification, mental state; or about the results of their clinical evaluation of the defendant on such topics as motivation or mental status at the time of the alleged offense, or at the time of the trial" (Fersch, 1979).

The psychologist may consult with the attorney during the trial. The consultation could include the testimony of the opposing side's psychological or psychiatric expert witness. There may be questions as to the appropriateness of the research cited, the psychologist's or psychiatrist's credibility as an expert, or the appropriateness of the testimony presented from the tests and individual interview of the defendant.

When the trial is finished, the psychologist's work might not be. The posttrial professional duties may involve treatment as part of probation or as a condition of a suspended sentence. The treatment is usually stipulated by the court for a period of time or until marked improvement is noted. The psychologist is usually asked to report to the judge or probation officer as to the progress toward rehabilitation.

Forensic psychologists also conduct research in legal-mental health areas; offer training to probation officers, counselors, and social workers; and provide consultation to lawyers and judges in order to help clarify mental health issues.

Ethical Issues. In forensic psychology ethical issues involve both the professional and spiritual level. The American Psychological Association Code of Ethics (APA, 1977) defines the professional ethical limits within which a psychologist must function. Principle 4 of the ethical standards states that "psychologists who interpret the science of psychology or the services of a psychologist to the general public accept the obligation to present the material fairly and accurately, avoiding misrepresentation through sensationalism, exaggeration, or superficiality." If a psychologist is not presenting the material fairly, and therefore distorting it to the advantage or disadvantage of a particular defendant, he or she is in violation of the ethical code. The problem is that it is difficult to legally determine violations, which means much of the responsibility to be honest in one's testimony rests with the individual forensic psychologist's personal moral value system.

The "opinion for hire" is a constant problem among forensic psychologists. The temptation is great to bias the testimony to assure continued use of a psychologist's expertise by a particularly generous law firm. Without a personal relationship with Christ and the indwelling of the Holy Spirit it is very difficult to withstand the monetary temptations and maintain a consistent stand of honest behavior.

Another ethical issue for the forensic psychologist is stated in Principle 5, Subsection B of the Ethical Standards of Psychologists: "The psychologist is responsible for informing the client of the limits of the confidentiality." If he has been appointed by the court, the psychologist has an ethical responsibility to inform the defendant that some or all of the psychological evaluation may be presented in open court as testimony. It is important to inform the defendant that he is essentially waiving his confidentiality as a result of a court-ordered examination.

The Future. The future of forensic psychology appears to be rather optimistic. The courts appear to be using expert psychological testimony with greater frequency, due to a greater awareness of emotional and mental health issues regarding the individual's criminal behavior.

The courts also are more concerned with rehabilitation than with punishment. Therefore, they are more willing to use psychologists to help determine the best course of action to take in the rehabilitation process. In addition, with more divorces occurring, there is more opportunity to testify in child custody cases.

With the greater use of forensic psychologists, greater controls will be placed on them. In the future degrees will probably be granted in forensic psychology, and, of course, licensing and certification will be part of the requirement to practice this specialty in psychology.

References

American Pscyhological Association. "Standards for providers of psychological services." *American Psychologist*, 1977, *32*, 495–505.

Farrington, D. P., Hawkins, K., & Lloyd-Bostock, S. M. (Eds.). *Psychology, law and legal processes.* Atlantic Highlands, N.J.: Humanities Press, 1979.

Fersch, E. A. *Law, psychology and the courts.* Springfield, Ill.: Thomas, 1979.

Additional Readings

Cooke, G. (Ed.). *Role of the forensic psychologist.* Springfield, Ill.: Thomas, 1980.

Fersch, E. A. *Psychology and psychiatry in courts and corrections: Controversy and change.* New York: Wiley, 1980.

Gordon, R. *Forensic psychology: A guide for lawyers and the mental health professions.* Tucson: Lawyers and Judges Publishing, 1975.

Lloyd-Bostock, S. M. (Ed.) *Psychology in legal contexts.* Atlantic Highlands, N.J.: Humanities Press, 1979.

M. A. CAMPION

Forgetting. *See* MEMORY.

Forgiveness. Even though it has been a continuing problem throughout history, modern psychological literature does not offer much discussion of the concept of forgiveness. Yet it is crucially important in interpersonal and intrapsychic functioning. Moreover, it is one of the key ideas bridging psychology and theology.

One possible exception in the psychology literature is Mowrer (1972), who has written extensively on the subjects of guilt, confession, and restitution. He is opposed to privatism, the idea that sin can be remitted through private prayer, sacraments, or psychotherapy. In his view there must be overt action with significant others involving self-disclosure in order for these processes to be completed. In contrast to this interpersonal emphasis the view developed in this article is that forgiveness has both intrapsychic and interpersonal elements and that these will vary in each case.

To deal with forgiveness conceptually it is necessary to first describe the context in which it occurs. The situation is one wherein a person experiences a violation of his or her sense of fairness—i.e., in a context of an implicit need or an explicit agreement one person is wronged by omission or commission. What was expected (or needed) was not forthcoming. These actions or lack thereof can be inadvertent or completely conscious on the part of the violator; the effect on the violatee can be consequential or trivial. In the extreme case the violator will take no action to undo any of his violations.

In the situation described the one who is wronged experiences both frustration and loss. The loss is experienced as a diminishment of the self in terms of esteem, possessions, a dream, or one's sense of adequacy. An important concomitant of this dysphoria is that the person is brought closer to awareness of various needs, some of the most important of which are survival, dependency, vulnerability, and adequacy. The psyche responds quickly and automatically to protect itself by generating anger at the violator, thus externalizing the problem.

The Anger Defense and Its Consequences. Anger has both positive and negative possibilities. On the positive side it generates energy and a sense of power; it protects the self and initiates strivings that may be used to master or constructively change the situation. Anger creates distance and boundaries between people, and thus defines one's autonomy and values. In an angry situation it usually becomes clearer what one stands against and thus what one stands for. On the negative side excessive energy can be channeled into the generation of many nonconstructive fantasies, and often an emotional commitment is made to "do justice" or "get even, if it is the last thing I do." This feels quite appropriate in the heat of the moment, but as time goes on this decision and the dedication of a portion of one's energy to it tends to become preconscious and overgeneralized. From then on it produces much bitterness and unfocused hostility. The effects of the experience on personality will differ with the age of the person engaged in this process as well as with the number of past similar experiences. In general, the younger the person and the more past similar experiences, the more insidious and pervasive the effects will be.

In a state of threat and anger the self tends to become rigid in relationships and exercise hidden agendas. Generalized trust in others decreases, and a pattern of not giving until one first gets, and of being hypersensitive to this, emerges. Thus, a self-perpetuating process in relationships is begun.

Perhaps because restitution is often not possible, desirable, or even necessary, the wronged person often never becomes aware of what would be appropriate restitution or does not think through possible resolutions. As emotional generalization and overdetermined secondary gain occur, the situation soon develops wherein it seems that there could never be enough done, or the right amount at the right time, etc., to undo the wrong. With no awareness, no request, and no restitution forthcoming, interpersonal contact is broken, and one is likely to begin retribution in passive or active ways. Soon this is sensed as hostile by the violator, and an escalation (continued or new omissions or commissions) may occur in responses from the original violator. This provides the interactional basis for a vendetta or feud, a game without end.

In such a dyadic state there soon comes to exist a willful, competitive conspiracy between both parties to nurture their anger and wounds in order to pay back greater than they have received, even though the ostensible purpose may be to get even. In transactional analysis terms both persons then devote much of their energy to collecting anger stamps, organizing them into books, and waiting to cash them in when the external environment allows or when the internal pressure grows too great.

Basically there can be one of three responses to violation: retribution, love, or ignoring the act. The last option may involve forgiveness if ignoring the wrong is not used as a strategy to punish the other person by indifference—e.g., by not responding to a spouse's needs. A loving response does, however, involve forgiveness, and it is to that process that we now turn our attention.

The Process of Forgiveness. To forgive, a person must reexperience the hurt caused by the violator in a different context, one that allows less threat and more availability of resources like cognition and empathy. One basis for forgiveness is an awareness of ownership of a need in the situation of violation. If we didn't want anything from anyone, they couldn't hurt us, we wouldn't get angry, and they wouldn't need forgiving. Thus one's own need is critical in the depth of the hurt, and thus the hurt is not attributed quite so much to the other person's behavior, no matter how despicable. To ascertain this truth often requires a humbling of the self to admit a dependency or to give up a defensively held grandiose view of the self. Reexperiencing a hurt in the context of a therapeutic relationship while owning one's needs usually heals and broadens the self, even if it is a humbling experience.

A second basis for forgiveness is to abandon the egocentric position of seeing others only in terms of one's own needs. A broader appreciation of another's motives, needs, and reasons for acting helps one to be more magnanimous. For example, one could depersonalize the violation not as a defense, but as a perception of reality—"It's not you personally; he does it to everybody." Another example: "Father, forgive them, for they know not what they do." It

is helpful in this regard if the person who is wronged can understand in some way that the violator was trying to protect or enhance his or her interests or self, albeit in a misguided fashion. Some might label this as being more objective, but it is not that. It is taking a more empathic and subjective view of the other's behavior, but at the same time detaching oneself personally from the other and the consequences. A broader view of parents as people, for example, often helps children, when older, to forgive their parents' mistakes.

Often it is useful to look at the empirical basis for one's expectation that another "should" have acted in a different way. If no expectation is explicit or contractual, it again points to one's own needs projected onto the situation. If there were an explicit contract, one could become assertive and request an appropriate resolution or retribution. When one has laid this groundwork, he or she is more nearly in a position to give up anger. This is the point of having no emotional push toward retribution. To come to this position often requires support, because in admitting one's need and putting aside the anger defense, one is again becoming vulnerable to hurt.

Outcomes of Forgiveness. Even if a person is able to give up his anger and its distilled bitterness, if he judges the probability of the violator's changing in a positive direction to be slight he may decide to continue to avoid the violator. In this case the outcome is a basic affective neutrality toward the violator. Included in successful avoidance and neutrality is also a commitment not to look for retributive opportunities or to take advantage of those that might present themselves.

With others, spouses in particular, the situation will demand contact and the person will need things from the other. Here forgiveness implies a commitment to risk again the possibility of being hurt. However, this does not have to imply complete vulnerability; it probably will mean a more discriminating trust and vulnerability and perhaps an agreement to work together with the other to see that the violation does not occur again. An example would be one spouse agreeing to be more sensitive to the other's needs so that the other does not have to get into entangling relationships outside the marriage.

Certain persons may have difficulty forgiving because they think that to forgive is to condone an action. This false deduction is probably a consequence of refusing to give up self-protective anger. This often leads them to demand that the other person change before being forgiven, thus giving them a guarantee that they will not be hurt again.

The closely related problem of forgiving oneself is similar. It requires an expanded awareness of one's motives and impact on others, repentance, and, if possible, restitution. It is often the "end of innocence" wherein one must accept a humbler view of the self and a more complicated view of reality. Rigidly high standards for self must be lowered or tempered even as rigidly high standards for others must often be lowered in forgiving them.

Theological Perspective. A theological perspective adds a necessary and unique set of dimensions to any understanding of forgiveness. It helps in dealing with the extreme cases where forgiveness seems humanly impossible—i.e., those who consciously wrong others and remain unrepentant.

Unlike the recent psychological literature the Bible does provide extensive discussion of forgiveness. In stories and examples and particularly in the life, work, and teachings of Jesus we find principles of forgiveness set forth. In Christian theology *agape* love is the ultimate principle of the universe. By *agape* is meant a love of persons and an existential commitment to their whole being. Christian values provide an imperative to forgive and, if possible, to reestablish a loving relationship, even if this involves a struggle.

An added and crucial corollary to this imperative is that a person does not in any sense deserve to be forgiven. Man has been corrupted by his heritage, pride, willfulness, and alienated relationship from God. He has chosen to disregard his relationship to his Maker and his fellows. There is no human way to undo this ontological condition of estrangement, and God's standards continue to be unfaltering. This situation was irreconcilable until God acted in a historical context to forgive through and indicate his forgiveness in the Christ events. The incarnation and resurrection remain great mysteries, but one clear meaning of God's action is quite evident—we are indeed forgiven.

The Old Testament indicates that vengeance belongs to God ("I will repay"), but the New Testament indicates that the slate of violations is wiped clean for the individual who will accept his provision. This is achieved through no inherent goodness of our own, but rather through God's action in coming to us. An unconditional loving action produces reconciliation and breaks through estrangement. It is a great gift wrapped in a humiliating judgment. Justification occurs through personal acceptance of this fact, which then leads to a life stance that responds to and becomes an instrument of this love. We have been surprised by undeserved love; if this can be experienced in some human fashion, perhaps then, in some feeble way, we can pass this grace on in our forgiving of others. We are unable to do this on our own. However, to the extent that we can participate in God's love, an experience transcending our self and selfishness, to that extent we can pass on forgiveness to others, trusting God to help us with our vulnerabilities.

Therapeutic Applications. In therapy directed toward intrapsychic forgiveness, it is important to remember that forgiveness must occur on at least two broad levels: the anger defense and the narcissistic insult to the self. Appropriate therapy must resolve both levels or the problem will soon return.

Forgiveness points to an emotional change away from anger and implies both behavioral and cognitive elements. More specifically, forgiveness implies behaviorally that the person has a low probability of emitting retributive behaviors. Cognitively it implies that the person will learn to accept what happened without continuing to obsess over retributive fantasies.

Once the problem is framed and agreed upon, the therapist can work to help the client understand his own individual needs and projections in the troubling situation. If successful, this may result in a reexperiencing of the hurt and anger in a context of exploration. The therapist might ask the client to specify what exactly he wanted or didn't want, how it affected him, and what (if anything) could be done by either party to undo the violation. Often useful is homework in which the client makes a list of all his "angers"—i.e., the violations of the other. The list can be discussed to see which are forgivable and which are not, and why.

A good intermediate goal is neutrality. One can work toward emotional desensitization. This is usually accomplished by some sort of rehashing of the situation and an altered understanding of the other's actions. Thus, for example, alternative explanations might be suggested that would account for the behavior but not frame it as a premeditated personal attack. Forgiveness may then be achieved after this first goal of neutrality, or partial forgiveness, is reached.

In the case where there has been an explicit contract between the parties, a counselor can work toward having the wronged person assert himself to claim some form of restitution. Role playing can be done in the office and later, with some modification, in reality. An important aspect of office work would be the therapist prophylactically engineering the situation wherein the client asserts himself clearly and then does *not* get what he asks for. This is very difficult for the client, and many feelings need to be discussed throughout the process, but particularly at the point of frustration. However, as a result of working through this frustration, a personal strengthening and constructive resolve is likely to occur.

A natural outcome after a violation of some magnitude is to avoid contact with the violator. This is often an excellent strategy (the notable exception being a spouse) *if* the time is used to work on forgiveness rather than retribution. The therapist's role during this crisis would be to clarify the avoidance, interpret its utility and function, and perhaps comment on its desirability. This might involve working toward making it a flexible, more cognitively controlled coping device, not a rigid permanent solution.

Usually at several points in this process the focus can shift to forgiving one's self for such things as being so stupid, having unacknowledged needs, misreading a situation, making bad decisions, etc. This of necessity involves a reworking of one's self-image into one that is less prideful, more human, and more in tune with a broader internal and external reality. Indeed, this process of self-forgiveness is basic to the process of forgiving another and to the whole process of living. The tears that are shed in this kind of therapy are for the injured self, which must be forgiven and healed as well.

As an ideal, the therapist should help the client in this process to participate in the activity of God and the personality of Christ. This is to say that the client does not condone wrongdoing, still has high standards, and knows that the other does not deserve forgiveness. However, in spite of this, he is still able to maintain an ongoing attitude of forgiveness and to seek rapprochement with himself and others in the future because of the model of and implicit imperative contained in God's forgiveness. What the client and therapist often cannot accomplish on their own they can still strive for with the help of God's Spirit. And the business of reconciliation, of returning good for ill, goes on.

References
Brandsma, J. M. Forgiveness: A dynamic, theological, and therapeutic analysis. *Pastoral Psychology*, 1982, *31*(1), 40–50.

Mowrer, O. H. Conscience and the unconscious. In R. C. Johnson, P. R Dokecki, & O. H. Mowrer (Eds.), *Conscience, contract, and social reality*. New York: Holt, Rinehart & Winston, 1972.

J. M. BRANDSMA

Formication. Derived from the Latin word for ant, formication is an abnormal subjective sensation of ants or other tiny insects creeping in or under the skin. Formication is most common in narcotic addiction, primarily alcohol, cocaine, or morphine deliriums. It may also occur in psychogenic mental states.

Frankl, Victor Emil (1905–). Existentialist psychiatrist and the founder of LOGOTHERAPY. He was born in Vienna, receiving his M.D. (1930) and Ph.D. (1949) from the University of Vienna. He is professor of psychiatry and neurology at the University of Vienna, professor of logotherapy at the United States International University, and visiting clinical professor of psychiatry at Stanford University. His system of therapy, logotherapy, is often referred to as the third Viennese school of psychotherapy (Freud's being the first and Adler's the second).

Although it is generally believed that logotherapy began with Frankl's own experience of imprisonment during the holocaust of World War II, his concentration camp episodes were actually the proving grounds of his evolving existential theory. Frankl developed the fundamental concepts of logotherapy as a medical student and as a physician in Vienna. The exact birthday of logotherapy could be identified as an evening in 1909 when Frankl thought while falling asleep, "One day, I too will die. I will no longer be alive. What, then, is the meaning of my living?" It is around the pursuit of the answer to this question that both Frankl's life and the development of logotherapy revolve.

At the age of 14 Frankl wrote a school paper entitled "We and the World Process." At 15, while in high school, he attended adult education classes in applied and experimental psychology. At 17, he lectured in a philosophy seminar in the adult education classes on the meaning of life. He delineated the two main concepts that later developed into logotherapy: 1) life does not answer our questions about the meaning of life, but rather puts those questions to us, leaving it for us to find the answers by deciding what we find meaningful; 2) the ultimate meaning of life is beyond the grasp of our intellect, but is something we can live by without ever being able to describe it cognitively. Frankl's high school graduation paper, "About the Psychology of Philosophical Thinking," came about as the result of his correspondence with Freud and reflected his interest in psychoanalysis as well as in the individual psychology of Adler.

Frankl is the author of 27 books, including the best seller, *Man's Search For Meaning*, in which he describes his brutal experience in four Nazi concentration camps and in which he outlines the basic concepts of logotherapy. He considers his death camp experiences a validation of the concepts on which logotherapy is based. He has remarked that he is the product of the school of medicine, the school of philosophy, and the school of life.

J. B. DILLEY

Free Association. Introduced by Freud after he became disillusioned with the results of hypnosis, the technique of free association was used to help discover—rather, uncover—subconscious or repressed thoughts, ideas, and complexes. Although the occurrence of association has been observed and described by writers of psychologically related thought since ancient times, Galton was the first to experimentally investigate the phenomena in 1879.

When free association is used as a therapeutic technique, the patient is typically asked to respond with the first thing that comes to mind and to continue to describe aloud any and every thought that is associated with it. Further, the patient is encouraged not to censor or edit the material, but to flow with the streams of thought that spontaneously arise. Frequently the patient is instructed to lie on a couch, facing away from the therapist so as to minimize likely visual or interpersonal interruption of this flow. The analyst then takes this fundamental psychic information and synthesizes it into an analytic interpretation, later feeding it back to the patient in order to enhance insight. In psychoanalysis it is assumed that the accumulation of such insight will eventually lead to a healthier or more well-adjusted personality.

Although one might assume that most associations occur at random, and that basing a theory of one's personality on such randomness is artificial, evidence indicates that one's associations are determined by previous experience and are idiosyncratic or very personal. Free association, therefore, has become the basic tool of classic psychoanalysis. Jung used a related tool, the word association test, as a quick means of detecting complexes; that is,

the more peculiar the word content as well as the longer the subject took to give a response to a stimulus word, the more likely that the stimulus-response word pair suggests a related psychological conflict.

J. B. DILLEY

See PSYCHOANALYSIS: TECHNIQUE; PSYCHOANALYTIC PSYCHOTHERAPY.

Free Will and Determinism. *See* DETERMINISM AND FREE WILL.

Freud, Sigmund (1856–1939). The founder of psychoanalysis. Freud was born to Jewish parents in Freiberg, Moravia. In 1859 the family moved to Leipzig and a year later to Vienna, where Freud later attended medical school. Possessing a broad liberal education, with special interests in philosophy, the classics, and antiquity, as a university student Freud nevertheless soon opted for the physiological research that occupied him for much of early adulthood. In the laboratory of the great physiologist Brücke he imbibed the mechanistic tenets of German materialistic science that held him, to some degree, for the rest of his life.

The Early Years. In 1882, reluctantly acknowledging the financial nonfeasibility of a research career, Freud became a resident in the General Hospital of Vienna. There he studied internal medicine, neurology, and psychiatry, while continuing to pursue neuroanatomical studies. In the fall of 1885 he completed his residency, was given the academic title *Privatdozent* (on the strength of his histological publications), and journeyed to Paris to study with the eminent neurologist Charcot. There he was introduced to the fascinating world of hysteria and hypnosis. Also in the early 1880s Freud had heard the internist Breuer speak several times on his psychotherapeutic treatment of Anna O, the now famous hysteric. Breuer and his patient discovered that when she recollected and related the affects and events surrounding each symptom's initial appearance, it would disappear.

Upon returning to Vienna in 1886, he married Martha Bernays (who became his lifelong helpmate), opened his private practice, published some important papers on neuroanatomy and the classic monograph *On Aphasia* (1891), and concerned himself for a while with research into the therapeutic properties of cocaine. During this time, it must be remembered, psychiatrists confined themselves to the universities and hospitals, and outpatient psychiatric treatment was primarily in the hands of neurologists like Freud. Consequently, much of Freud's practice consisted of hysterical symptoms masking as neurological disease. Like most other neurologists of the day Freud initially interpreted hysteria as the epiphenomenon of underlying neurological disorder or degeneration. Also like his colleagues Freud's treatments of this condition were generally somatic—tonics, electrotherapy, massage, and diet.

Nevertheless, through his work with Charcot and his conversations with Breuer, Freud had become convinced that hysterical symptoms, whatever their etiology, could be approached psychotherapeutically. This, coupled with the poor results from somatic therapies, led Freud to hypnotic suggestion in 1887. In 1889 he returned to France to improve his hypnotic technique under the tutelage of Liébault and Bernheim.

Gradually, from 1889 to 1895, Freud's psychotherapeutic technique evolved from hypnotic suggestion through hypnotic catharsis to free association in waking consciousness. From his clinical work and collaborations with Breuer, Freud concluded that the etiology of hysteria was a psychical one—the repression or strangulation of painful, disagreeable memories and affects associated with traumatic experiences. The treatment consisted of undoing the repression of the unconscious memories and affects through the free association method.

Psychoanalytic Psychology. In *Studies on Hysteria* (1895) Freud clearly recognized the role of repressed sexuality in the etiology of neurosis. From 1895 to 1900, through his clinical work and self-analysis, he would become more and more convinced of the importance of sexual factors. The turning point occurred in 1897. In this year Freud discovered that his hysterics' accounts of seduction, which he had hitherto believed to be literally true, were fantasies. This awoke him to the importance of psychical reality. He also uncovered, in his patients and himself, the oedipus complex—an unconscious constellation of sexual longing for the parent of the opposite sex and rivalrous hatred toward the one of the same sex.

The year 1899, when *The Interpretation of Dreams* was published, is generally considered the birthdate of psychoanalysis. Here Freud introduced the topographic theory of the mind (the conscious, preconscious, and unconscious), the concept of primary and secondary process mentation, of dreams as the disguised fulfillment of unconscious wishes, and of dreams and neurotic symptoms as compromise formations.

Soon afterward Freud advocated the significance of transference—the patient's repetition of historically determined patterns of behavior in the present. The interpretation of the historical roots of the patient's transferential behaviors came to be viewed as the cornerstone of psychoanalytic treatment.

From 1900 to 1926 Freud's ideas underwent considerable development and modification. However, he seldom totally discarded his earlier conceptions but usually incorporated them into—or allowed them to lie alongside—his later ones. Freud's growing appreciation of the defensive operations of the psyche, as they manifest themselves to the therapist in the form of the resistance, led him to lay the foundations of ego psychology from 1920 to 1926. *Group Psychology and the Analysis of the Ego* (1921) and *The Ego and the Id* (1923) flesh out the structural theory of the psychic apparatus—id, ego, and superego. Along with this came the understanding that defensive maneuvers and moral ideals and prohibitions can be quite as unconscious as the impulses which they oppose.

Inhibitions, Symptoms, and Anxiety (1926) presented the seminal theory of the relationship between unconscious intrapsychic conflict, anxiety, and symptom formation. In conflict an unconscious affect-laden fantasy (id impulsion), disagreeable to the demands of the superego or society, threatens to rise into consciousness, raising the possibility it might then be translated into action. The unconscious ego experiences this as an imminent danger situation. In order to prevent the feared response from superego or society, the ego generates anxiety. This *signal anxiety*, as it is termed, is unpleasurable. Since the psyche moves toward pleasure and away from pain (in accordance with the pleasure principle), the ego blocks the offending impulse from awareness and removes the need for signal anxiety. When the defense mechanism fails, a symptom results. A symptom is therefore a compromise between the unconscious fantasy striving for expression and the defense against it.

In tandem with these conceptual innovations Freud's therapeutic writings take increasing cognizance of the importance of analyzing the resistance. In other words, it becomes just as important to know why a patient is withholding a fantasy or feeling (i.e., to discern the fear that motivates the resistance) as it is to uncover the unconscious feeling or fantasy itself.

Sociocultural and Religious Writings. After 1926, though Freud continued to write on psychoanalytic psychology, the bulk of his original thinking shifted to culture. Among the most important contributions of his sociocultural work are his ideas on social cohesion. He came to view the bonds that unite the members of society as aim-inhibited (or sublimated) libido and the mutual identification of individuals with one another through their incorporation of a similar set of ideals. Repression of aspects of both sensuality and aggression was viewed as vital to maintaining group cohesion.

Foremost among these cultural concerns is religion, a subject with which Freud was ambivalently preoccupied his entire life. Freud used the psychological mechanisms he had encountered in his work with patients to elucidate religious behaviors. In *The Psychopathology of Everyday Life* (1901) he introduced his conceptualization of religion as a projective system. He understood God, Satan, and the spirit world as personifications of man's projected unconscious fears and fantasies.

In his famous essay, "Obsessive Actions and Religious Practices" (1907), Freud explained religious ritual on the model of obsessive-compulsive symptomatology. The religionist's rituals, like the obsessional's symptoms, were viewed as compromise formations between the repressed impulse and the repressing forces, as simultaneous defenses against unconscious strivings and disguised gratifications of them.

The omnipotence of thoughts, a mechanism particularly favored by obsessive-compulsives, was recruited in *Totem and Taboo* (1913) to explain animism and religion. The omnipotence of thoughts is the unconscious presupposition that the wish is equivalent to the deed and that wishing can effect, independently of any action, changes in one's environment. Freud believed that in the animistic-magical stage people ascribe omnipotence to themselves, while in the religious stage they transfer it to a deity and yet retain the idea that they can influence him, through prayer and ritual, according to their wishes.

Freud believed that one's attitude toward God derives from one's childhood attitude toward one's father; that one's attitude toward the Deity is a displacement of one's stance toward the parent. In short, the heavenly Father is conceptualized as an exalted version of the earthly one. Not being content to account for this with ontogenetic factors alone, Freud introduced phylogenetic ones as well. In man's dawn he was said to have lived in a horde, dominated by a tyrannical "primal father" who maintained jealous possession of

the women and excluded the sons to a life of celibacy and impotence. One day the young men, overcome with dissatisfaction, united and slew and ate the primal father. This was no sooner accomplished than remorse and longing for the father set in. The unconscious memory of, and guilt over, this deed, genetically transmitted, were then posited to determine each subsequent religion, including Christianity. Religious rituals as diverse as the totem meal and the Eucharist were explained as simultaneous reenactments of the eating of the primal father and expressions of remorse over it.

In *The Future of an Illusion* (1928) Freud developed his thesis of religion as infantile dependency and illusion or wish fulfillment: "When the growing individual finds that he is destined to remain a child forever, that he can never do without protection against strange superior powers, he lends those powers the features belonging to the figure of his father; he creates for himself the gods whom he dreads, whom he seeks to propitiate, and whom he nevertheless entrusts with his own protection. Thus, his longing for a father is identical with his need for protection against the consequences of human weakness" (p. 24).

Elsewhere Freud emphasized the role of primary process in myth and religion, comparing them to dreams. He conceptualized religious behaviors as sublimations of sexual and aggressive drives. Religious mysticism was explained as a reactivation of the infant's experience of oceanic oneness with its mother's breast.

Wallace (1983a, 1983b) has criticized Freud's work on religion on several grounds. First of all, there is a good deal personal bias implicit in his characterizations of religion as infantile dependency and in his many comparisons of it to psychopathology. References to religion as "neurotic relics," "mass delusions," and "blissful hallucinatory confusion" evidence the presence of hidden moral judgments. Second, Freud's treatment of religion ignores questions of history and sociocultural context. Third, it makes no distinction between the concept of the individual and that of the institution, presupposes the existence of a mass mind, relies on an exaggerated concept of psychic unity, and gives insufficient attention to the conscious aspects and phenomenology of religious behavior and experience. Fourth, Freud pays insufficient attention to adaptiveness as a point of differentiation between psychopathology and religious behavior. Fifth, in his work on religion Freud failed to use his most powerful tool—the clinical method of psychoanalysis. His concepts of religion were derived not from actual clinical work with religionists themselves but from a speculative transfer of psychoanalytic ideas to groups of people (and whole cultures) whom he had never analyzed. Finally, Freud presumes to give "scientific" answers to metaphysical questions.

Nevertheless, to conclude from the speculative excesses and methodological weaknesses in Freud's work on religion and culture that he makes no contribution to the psychology of religion would be disastrous indeed. However, it is in his psychological writings rather than those specifically addressed to religious issues that we find the greatest contribution.

There is a great deal that Freud's psychoanalysis can contribute to the elucidation of religious phenomena. It can clarify the relationship between one's religious belief and the rest of his psychical structure, including the quality of the integration with the rest of his personality. It can disclose conflicts for which religious convictions and practices serve as the vehicle of expression or defense, or in which they contribute force to one side or the other. It can uncover the history of each individual's religious beliefs, the childhood object cathexes and identifications that are associated with these beliefs and which help determine their final form. It can comment on the role of one's religion in his overall adaptation (or maladaptation) to the internal and external environments. Finally, it can contribute to the ethical sphere of religion. Broadened awareness of one's motivations and enhanced ego strength can lead to a broadened sense of responsibility, the avoidance of easy rationalizations, and a more subtle form of self-control.

In sum, psychoanalysis is on most solid ground when it investigates the psychological meaning of the religious beliefs of an individual. Only from the cumulative results of such laborious, clinically based studies can psychoanalysis make meaningful statements about religion and religionists in general. What Freudian psychology can of course never do is determine whether, after all the psychodynamic factors are removed, there is a transcendental justification for religious faith; such a question remains forever beyond the range of a theoretical and empirical psychology.

References

Wallace, E. R. Freud and religion: A history and reappraisal. In L. Boyer, W. Muensterberger, and S. Grolnick (Eds.), *The psychoanalytic study of society* (Vol. 10). Hillsdale, N.J.: Lawrence Erhlbaum Associates, 1983. (a)
Wallace, E. R. Reflections on the relationship between psychoanalysis and Christianity. *Pastoral Psychology*, 1983, *31*, 215–243. (b)

E. R. WALLACE IV

See PSYCHOANALYTIC PSYCHOLOGY.

Frigidity. *See* INHIBITED SEXUAL EXCITEMENT.

Fromm, Erich (1900–1980). Along with Erikson, Horney, and Sullivan, Fromm introduced into orthodox psychoanalytic thought careful and detailed considerations of social processes. Of the four, he was the most concerned with large-scale social forces.

Trained as a psychologist (Ph.D. from Heidelberg in 1922), Fromm was an avowed Marxist. He denounced all extant forms of government, including capitalism and communism, as incapable of fulfilling human needs. At the same time he staunchly believed that an adequate social organization could be achieved, and much of his writing is laced with utopian hopes and ideals.

For Fromm it was society that perverted human behavior. His proposal of five basic character types (receptive, exploitative, hoarding, marketing, and productive) also reflects his socioeconomic orientation. Only the last of these types is healthy, according to Fromm. However, there can be combinations of the five. Thus, a particular individual might be productive-exploitative. Such a person might be an opportunistic building contractor who constructs houses and creates jobs.

Escape from Freedom (1941) is perhaps Fromm's most famous book, written as the Nazis controlled his native Germany and World War II was accelerating. Writing from the United States, Fromm saw the German people embracing fascism because it seemed to offer security. Freedom and the alienation and isolation that come with it is aversive. Social structures which offer people a sense of belongingness can be powerfully appealing, regardless of how heinous they may be.

Indeed, rootedness, relatedness, and identity are three of the five needs that Fromm argues are fundamental to the human condition. The others are the need for transcendence (to rise above one's animal nature and to create) and the need for a frame of orientation or reference (a way of making sense of the world and of one's experience in it). These uniquely human needs stem from the fact that we are part of nature yet separate from it. We are animals, but we have reason, imagination, and the capacity to self-reflect.

Fromm, who called himself a dialectic

humanist and who promoted a form of government he termed "humanistic communitarian socialism," was a learned and articulate writer. Over the span of his career he acquired a considerable following, perhaps more among the liberally oriented literati than among the ranks of behavioral scientists. His thought bears a resemblance to that of Rosseau and other proponents of Noble Savage ideology. Despite what may have been Fromm's blindness to personal evil and to evil's diabolical quality, he was the first well-known psychological writer to draw attention to the relationship between societal structure and personality.

From the vantage point of Christian theology Fromm is to be commended for his honest admission that he *was* engaging in philosophical speculation. He did not try to hide behind the authority of physical science. Moreover, he clearly saw that people are more than animals. On the other hand, there is a hopeless circularity to Fromm's ideas on mental health and morality: that which is healthy is good, and vice versa. Ultimately, what is healthy *and* good must be taken to be what Fromm thinks they are. Christians appeal to revelation as the solution to such circularity.

C. W. McLemore

Frustration-Aggression Hypothesis.

Proposed in 1939 by Dollard and his colleagues at Yale University, the frustration-aggression hypothesis has provided one of the most popular explanations of human AGGRESSION (Dollard, Miller, Doob, Mowrer, and Sears, 1939). In its original form it stated that the occurrence of aggressive behavior always presupposes the existence of frustration and that the existence of frustration always leads to some form of aggression. In other words, aggression is always the result of frustration, and frustration always leads to aggression. Frustration was defined as the blocking of goal-directed behavior, and aggression was considered to be action intended to cause injury to another. While aggression might be directed at its source, the authors maintained that fear of punishment may result in a displacement in which attack is directed toward a substitute, safer target.

The suggestion that frustration always leads to aggression was quickly challenged, and the authors of the hypothesis clarified the point by postulating that frustration creates the *instigation* to aggression. Whether it finds expression depends on the relative strength of the instigation and inhibitions. Research indicates that frustration does not always produce aggressive behavior. For example, some people become depressed and inactive in response to frustration. The nature of frustration also seems to be important in understanding how people respond. When it is severe, deliberate, or arbitrary, people are more likely to respond with aggression. When it is accidental or understandable, a hostile response is less likely.

Berkowitz (1978) has proposed an important revision of the original frustration-aggression hypothesis. He argues that frustration produces ANGER and thereby an emotional readiness for aggression. Whether this readiness results in hostile behavior, however, depends on the presence of environmental stimuli or cues which release the bottled-up anger. One such aggressive cue is a weapon, and the sight of a gun may provide the necessary stimulation for aggression to occur.

The other part of the original hypothesis—that aggression is always the result of frustration—has also been challenged. Research clearly indicates that frustration is one of several possible causes. People act aggressively for many different reasons and in response to many different factors. A variety of biological, social, and personal factors contribute to aggression. A popular alternative to frustration-aggression theory is that people learn aggression through experience and through the observation of aggressive models.

References

Berkowitz, L. Whatever happened to the frustration-aggression hypothesis? *American Behavioral Scientist*, 1978, *21*, 691–708.

Dollard, J., Miller, N. E., Doob, L. W., Mowrer, O. H., & Sears, R. R. *Frustration and aggression.* New Haven: Yale University Press, 1939.

M. Bolt

Fugue, Psychogenic.

The unexpected travel of a person who cannot later recall the trip. It is classified among the dissociative disorders by the American Psychiatric Association (*DSM-III*). In a dissociative state the affected person temporarily is unable to integrate all the elements of personality into a unified whole; the result is fragmentation or splitting. Other examples of dissociative disorders are psychogenic amnesia, multiple personality, and depersonalization disorder.

A fugue is a flight: in music, of notes and melody; in psychopathology, of persons and personalities. Often the sufferer will assume a new identity while on his or her trip and be genuinely unable to recall the former, true identity. An elaborate or full-blown example of psychogenic fugue would include the person assuming a bolder, more outgoing personality during the fugue state than would normally be characteristic of that person. More often, however, the fugue state is relatively short.

Spitzer, Skodol, Gibbon, and Williams (1981) cite as an example of psychogenic fugue the case of a 42-year-old male brought to a hospital emergency room by police. The man had been involved in a minor incident, but the police became concerned because he could not properly identify himself. He had no memory of how he had arrived in town a few weeks earlier when he began his work as a short-order cook. A fingerprint check identified him as a missing person from a city 200 miles distant. His wife later identified him and told of an increasing amount of work and family pressure immediately prior to his sudden disappearance.

There is some evidence that heavy use of alcohol can predispose a person to the development of this disorder. The condition is quite rare, although it tends to be seen more frequently during war or after a natural disaster. Technically a fugue state can be differentiated from other similar pathologies by careful observation. For example, a person in a fugue state is unaware that he has forgotten anything, whereas a psychogenic amnesiac is well aware that true identity is beyond recall (Nemiah, 1980). Also, the casual observer of a newcomer to town who may actually be in a fugue state will not necessarily suspect that something is drastically wrong. People who observe sleepwalkers, in contrast, can usually detect something amiss in the person's behavior. If a person's travel is nonpurposeful and appears to be aimless wandering, an organic mental disorder is the more likely diagnosis. Psychogenic fugue can be feigned so that the distinction between a genuine fugue state and malingering is difficult to make.

Most theoreticians view the etiology of fugue states as similar to the origins of hysterical reactions. "The patient carries out literally the wish that many a harassed normal person expresses when he says, 'I'd like to get away from it all, just go away and forget everything!'" (Cameron, 1963, p.357). The powerful defense mechanisms that enable such escape are repression and denial.

Treatment can not commence until the true identity of the fugue victim is established. Gradual reexposure to the normal environment plus careful therapy to help the victim learn more constructive pressure-coping strategies will enhance recovery. Recurrences are rare.

References

Cameron, N. *Personality development and psychopathology: A dynamic approach.* Boston: Houghton Mifflin, 1963.

Nemiah, J. C. Dissociative disorders. In H. I. Kaplan, A. M. Freedman, & B. J. Sadock (Eds.), *Comprehensive textbook of psychiatry* III, Baltimore: Williams & Wilkins, 1980.

Spitzer, R. L., Skodol, A. E., Gibbon, M., & Williams, J. B. W. *DSM III casebook.* Washington, D.C.: American Psychiatric Association, 1981.

J. R. BECK

Functional Autonomy. As defined by Allport (1961), the originator of this concept, functional autonomy refers to any acquired system of motivation in which the tensions involved are not of the same kind as the antecedent tensions from which the acquired system developed. In other words, in functionally autonomous behavior the motives for present behavior are independent (autonomous) of the conditions which first caused the behavior.

This initial conceptualization was later developed into two levels of functional autonomy. The more primitive level was perseverative functional autonomy. This referred to acts or behaviors that are repeated even though they have lost their original function. For example, an adolescent female may, due to rebelliousness, begin to smoke cigarettes because she knows it will irritate her parents. As the girl matures and becomes an adult, she may continue to smoke. This primitive level included activities such as compulsions, addictions to drugs and alcohol, and ritualistic behavior.

The second level of autonomy is what Allport called propriate functional autonomy. This referred to acquired interests, values, dispositions, sentiments, and life styles. Allport contended these and other adult life choices exist because a self-image, gradually formed, demanded this particular motivational focus.

Allport's conceptualization of motivation provided an alternative to the psychoanalytic paradigm (i.e., being motivated primarily by conflicts rooted in childhood) and the radical behaviorist explanation (i.e., a strict stimulus-response model).

Reference

Allport, G. W. *Pattern and growth in personality.* New York: Holt, Rinehart, & Winston, 1961.

M. L. MARVIN

Functional Disorder. Any abnormal behavior or disorder that has no known organic basis but is rather the result of emotional or psychological causes. This includes psychoneuroses, psychosomatic disorders, and stress reactions.

An example of one type of functional disorder is hysteria, which is unrelated to actual pathological change in organic structure. Another type of functional disorder is the psychosomatic illness, where the problem is not due to tissue or organ pathology but where physical changes result from emotional factors. Some disorders are classified as functional because to date no organic causality has been found. However, medical discoveries sometimes result in a recategorizing of a disorder as organic.

D. L. Schuurman

Functional Family Therapy. This therapy (Alexander & Parsons, 1982) has been used chiefly in the treatment of families with a delinquent member. Developed from theory, research, and clinical experience, the model focuses on the specific relationships ("functional outcomes") that family members are seeking from each other. Adaptive behaviors are substituted for "inefficient," problematic ones to achieve the same relational goals. For instance, adolescents seeking independence (relational distance) are trained to negotiate with their parents for this outcome rather than to engage in delinquent behavior to gain it.

This model combines systems theory with a behavioristic approach. From a systems perspective behavior is meaningful in the ways it is linked to the behavior of all the other family members, rather than individual stimulus-response sequences. The behavioral emphasis is seen in the concept that individual actions are rewarded by producing desired relationships with others in the family. Specifically, each person in the family chooses behaviors that are reinforced for him or her by relational distance or intimacy.

Functional family therapy differs from traditional orientations, which regard the individual as responsible for his actions and behavior as good, bad, or healthy. Instead, the model makes the assumption that all behavior is adaptive in terms of its functional relationship properties. This means that behavior is not inherently good or bad, or even healthy or sick. Behavior is simply a vehicle for producing and maintaining specific outcomes from interpersonal relationships. These outcomes are conceptualized as distance, intimacy, or a moderated combination of both. To illustrate, an adolescent's running away is an inefficient, rather than an unhealthy, method to gain the outcome of distance.

Criteria for ideal functioning are not used in functional family therapy. Instead, maladap-

tive processes in delinquent families are altered to correspond more closely with the adaptive, problem-solving capacities of nondelinquent families. As nondelinquent families have been shown to communicate with more reciprocal supportiveness and less reciprocal defensiveness, have less silence, more equal talk time, and more constructive interruptions for feedback and clarification (Alexander, 1973), these specific processes are targeted for intervention.

A complete assessment is considered essential for successful treatment. In particular, three critical levels of analysis are necessary: 1) relationships among all family members which result in regular, ritualized sequences of behavior; 2) the functional "payoffs" (distance or intimacy) that each member receives in the behavioral sequence; and 3) individual strengths, weaknesses, and behavioral styles. "Functional family therapists must understand how the behavior change of an individual must be embedded within the powerful processes of family relationships, and how these behavior or other changes will consistently meet each family member's outcomes or functions" (Barton & Alexander, 1981, p. 417).

Intervention consists of therapy and education. Therapy prepares the family members for behavioral change by redefining the negative views that they hold toward each other. The therapist accomplishes this "reattribution" by addressing each person (rather than focusing on the identified patient), speaking in nonjudgmental terms, and helping the family understand how their actions are interdependent. Another powerful tool of reattribution is relabeling objectionable behavior, putting it in a more acceptable framework. For example, a truant teen-ager may be described as "seeking his own way to be independent" and a possessive mother may be recast as an "involved" parent.

Education implements the behavior change strategies. The therapist selects behavioral techniques consistent with the family's interpersonal and individual styles. The new behavior modality must fit 1) the relational outcomes that individuals were previously seeking (i.e., the outcomes stay the same, but the means of achieving them change) and 2) the reattributions of the therapy phase. For instance, an "independence-seeking" adolescent would be better served by the flexibility of negotiating a behavioral contract with his parents than having a contingency management program closely monitored by them.

Research data (Alexander, Barton, Schiavo,

& Parsons, 1976) have shown that a key factor in family change is the therapist's interpersonal skills. Therefore, Barton and Alexander emphasize that the functional family therapist must possess relationship and structuring skills. Relationship skills include the ability to link the feelings of family members with their behaviors, the use of nonblaming language, interpersonal warmth and humor, and self-disclosure. Structuring skills, necessary to implementing change, include directiveness (coaching and modeling effective communication), self-confidence, and clarity.

The functional family model has been shown to be particularly effective with families of delinquent adolescents. A comparison of delinquent families in treatment using this model with the delinquent member treated individually or receiving no treatment showed an improvement in family communication processes when the functional model was used (Alexander & Barton, 1980). When compared to psychodynamic and client-centered family therapy, recidivism rates for delinquents treated by functional family therapy were significantly lower (Parsons & Alexander, 1973); and in a follow-up study several years later, sibling delinquency rates in the families of the same treatment groups were also significantly lower for the functional therapy group (Klein, Alexander, & Parsons, 1977).

This model of family therapy diverges from Christian thought in the positions that 1) the individual is not considered responsible for his behavior since behavior is a message about relationships rather than being "good" or "bad" in itself, and 2) "the therapy process in the functional family model is admittedly very manipulative and does not reflect 'reality' or 'truth'" (Barton & Alexander, 1981, p. 423). Both these positions provide a relativistic view of behavior and personal responsibility. However, the intent of this approach seems to be to give persons an acceptable perception of themselves in order to help them attain goals they have chosen as important to them. This intent is congruent with the Christian faith's respect for the integrity of the person.

References

Alexander, J. F. Defensive and supportive communication in normal and deviant families. *Journal of Consulting and Clinical Psychology*, 1973, *40*, 223–231.

Alexander, J. F., & Barton, C. Intervention with delinquents and their families: Clinical, methodological, and conceptual issues. In J. P. Vincent (Ed.), *Advances in family intervention, assessment, and theory*. Greenwich, Conn.: JAI Press, 1980.

Alexander, J. F., Barton, C., Schiavo, R. S., Parsons, B. V. Systems-behavioral intervention with families of delin-quents: Therapist characteristics, family behavior, and outcome. *Journal of Consulting and Clinical Psychology*, 1976, *44*, 656–664.

Alexander, J. F., & Parsons, B. V. *Functional family therapy*. Monterey, Calif.: Brooks/Cole, 1982.

Barton, C., & Alexander, J. F. Functional family therapy. In A. S. Gurman & D. P. Kniskern (Eds.), *Handbook of family therapy*. New York: Brunner/Mazel, 1981.

Klein, N. C., Alexander, J. F., & Parsons, B. V. Impact of family systems intervention on recidivism and sibling delinquency: A model of primary prevention and program evaluation. *Journal of Consulting and Clinical Psychology*, 1977, *45*, 469–474.

Parsons, B. V., & Alexander, J. F. Short-term family intervention: A therapy outcome study. *Journal of Consulting and Clinical Psychology*, 1973, *41*, 195–201.

C. V. BRUUN

See FAMILY THERAPY: OVERVIEW.

Functionalism. Chronologically functionalism was the first of the major schools of psychology reacting against structuralism. It focused its critique on the structuralist's definition of the subject matter of psychology as "the structure of the mind." Functionalism was unique primarily in its stress on function or usefulness of mental processes. Thus it served as a transitional movement between structuralism and behaviorism, and its pragmatic emphasis continues to characterize contemporary American psychology.

In its broadest sense any psychology may be described as functional if its main objective is the study of mental processes, operations, or functions. Thus early American psychologists used the term *function* in several ways—to denote a mental activity such as perceiving or calculating or imagining; a use for some end; or the dependency relationship between antecedents and consequents or stimuli and responses, using the term in its mathematical sense. A focus on any of these characterize functional psychology in its broader sense. In a narrower sense functionalism refers to the psychological school emerging at the University of Chicago in the late nineteenth century under the influence of John Dewey and James R. Angell.

The roots of functionalism may be traced to several British sources. The Darwinian focus on the observation of animal behavior and morphology and a hypothesized continuity between human beings and animals became the justification for the extended study of animals, strongly identified with the work of George John Romanes and C. Lloyd Morgan. The evolutionary emphasis on adaptation to the environment was regarded as perhaps the most significant function of human behavior. Galton's studies of hereditary genius became the impetus for both the American emphasis on individual differences and the mental testing movement.

Other roots are found in some American predecessors. The leading functionalist antecedent was James, a vehement critic of the "mind-stuff" theory of structuralism. James argued for pragmatism as a criterion for the validity of knowledge: knowledge must be judged in terms of its consequences, values, and utility. Human beings must be considered in terms of their adaptation and readaptation to the environment, and psychologists must explore the conditions and purpose of consciousness. The functionalist agenda, with its evolutionary, genetic, and psychometric emphases, was also implicit in the works of George T. Ladd, Edward W. Scripture, James Mark Baldwin, Edward L. Thorndike, James McKeen Cattell, and G. Stanley Hall.

Functionalism was officially launched in 1896, when Dewey published an article on the reflex arc concept in psychology in the *Psychological Review*. Dewey protested against the reductionism and elementism implicit in breaking the reflex or any other behavioral act into sensory, motor, and associative components or into other units such as stimulus and response or sensation and movement. Dewey, whose attention turned toward education and philosophy, left it to Angell to crystallize the functionalist psychology. Angell addressed the American Psychological Association on "The Province of Functionalism" in 1906, stating its three primary assertions: 1) the subject matter of psychology was mental operations and their ends; 2) mind was a means of mediating between the needs of the organism and its environment; 3) psychology must be psychophysical, taking both mind and body seriously.

Several other characteristics of functionalism can be stated. The method of introspection, involving the subject's own report of his experience, was only gradually replaced by observation and other objective methods. A biological orientation directed the functionalist to the theory of evolution; an interest in the nature-nurture controversy; the concept of the person as organism; the study of animal behavior; and genetic, comparative, and psychophysiological studies. Practical applications encouraged the study of differential and social psychology and psychometric theory.

Harvey A. Carr succeeded Angell at Chicago and introduced an emphasis on motivating factors, thus adding a component of dynamic psychology to functionalism. C. H. Judd, also at Chicago, authored the most systematic

textbook version of functionalism. Columbia University was also a stronghold of functionalism under the leadership of Cattell, Thorndike, and Woodworth. Columbia emphasized the importance "of curves of distribution, of individual differences, of the measurement of intelligence and other human capacities, of experimental procedures and statistical devices, of the undercurrent of physiological thought" (Heidbreder, 1933, pp. 291–292). At Columbia functionalism also became foundational to educational psychology, as it freed the psychologist to study what was helpful to both the individual and society.

Criticisms of functionalism focused on its multiple definitions, its utilitarian motives, its theoretical and methodological eclecticism, and its teleological emphasis. Teleological explanations, which explain behavior by appealing to its ultimate consequences or final causes, have characteristically been criticized by twentieth-century psychology. Christian theology has consistently been teleological in its orientation, and thus a functional component may be regarded as a necessary aspect of any adequate psychology.

Reference
Heidbreder, E. *Seven psychologies.* New York: Appleton-Century-Crofts, 1933.

H. Vande Kemp

See Psychology, History of.

Future Projection Technique. A Psychodrama technique involving a manipulation of time so that the person may experience a future situation. The psychiatric inpatient, nearing discharge, who explores the problem of his co-workers' attitudes toward his having been in a psychiatric unit is one example of this technique. A scene is set using the available knowledge about what might occur. As a practice session for future difficult situations this technique is very useful.

Another use of the technique is to explore what events might occur in the individual's life if certain self-defeating behaviors are not alleviated. An awareness of the consequences may provide the person with the necessary energy and motivation needed for change. Role training also may be projected into the future to develop skills in parenting, marital communications, and overall personal effectiveness. Such behavior rehearsal and the associated verbal discussion provide a deep experiential learning for the individual.

J. H. Vander May

Gg

Galton, Francis (1822–1911). Few characters in the history of psychology can match the color and creativity of Sir Francis Galton. His scientific contributions range across geography, meteorology, criminology, biological statistics, behavioral genetics, and psychology. His intellectual brilliance and intense curiosity were apparent at an early age. By the age of 2½ years he could read and write, and by 5 he could read any English book. Such accomplishments led Terman (1917) to estimate Galton's IQ at around 200.

Galton's contributions to psychology sprang largely from four key questions: 1) What are the major psychological differences between individuals? 2) How can these differences be accurately measured? 3) How are these differences related to each other? 4) To what extent are such differences attributable to hereditary and/or environmental factors? Quite appropriately, Galton is often called the father of differential psychology, a discipline that is still directed at these basic questions.

Galton's interest in individual differences was stimulated by the work of his cousin, Charles Darwin. When Darwin proposed that such differences fueled the process of natural selection, Galton was quick to recognize that these characteristics must be identified, measured, and understood, if not merely for the sake of science, for the sake of determining the future direction of the human race. His concern for mankind's future and the role of genetics in that future led him to found the controversial field that later became known as eugenics, which examines ways of moving human evolution along a more desirable path through selective breeding of individuals.

The foundations of differential psychology were established primarily in four of Galton's books: *Hereditary Genius* (1869), *English Men of Science: Their Nature and Nurture* (1874), *Inquiries into Human Faculty and Development* (1833), and *Natural Inheritance* (1889). Throughout these works we see almost religious commitment to the notion that critical human differences are largely attributable to heritable factors. In *Hereditary Genius*, Galton tried to substantiate this hypothesis by showing that "eminence" ran in families. When critics argued that persons from eminent families may have benefited from similar enriched environments as well as similar genes, Galton developed a self-report questionnaire designed to trace the environmental and hereditary roots of 200 English scientists. Thus, the questionnaire method, so widely used in psychology today, was born.

Galton pursued the problem of measuring individual differences in his 1883 book. Here he describes the development and use of the Galton whistle for measuring auditory acuity; instruments measuring simple reaction time, breathing power, and color sense; and the first tests of mental imagery and word association. Many of these instruments and tests were put to use in his Anthropometric Laboratory, which attracted many subjects and spectators at London's International Health Exhibition of 1884.

Perhaps Galton's two most important contributions to psychology were methodological in nature. Through keen observation Galton identified two types of twins, which later became known as monozygotic (MZ) and dizygotic (DZ) twins. By looking at the relative similarity of MZ and DZ twins on various psychological characteristics, Galton was able to estimate the contributions of hereditary and environmental factors to these traits. The twin-study method is now a cornerstone of modern behavior genetics.

Prior to Galton psychologists and biologists struggled with the problem of mathematically summarizing the association of variables that tend to go together. Working with data from his measures of individual differences, Galton developed bivariate scatter plots, noted the "regression to the mean" phenomenon, and observed that the "slope" of the regression line corresponded to the degree of association between the variables. From there, Karl Pearson developed Pearson's r coefficient, the r referring to Galton's regression phenomenon. The fundamental ideas underlying this important statistical tool are attributable to Galton.

Although the fruits of Galton's efforts can be found throughout most contemporary psychology, they are most clearly seen in areas where the measurement of individual differences is important—e.g., personnel psychology, behavior genetics, clinical assessment, and educational psychology.

Reference
Terman, L. M. The intelligence quotient of Francis Galton in childhood. *American Journal of Psychology*, 1917, *28*, 208–215.

D. D. McKenna

Gambling, Pathological. Not all gambling is pathological. Social gambling is usually engaged in with friends, mainly on special occasions and with predetermined acceptable losses. In contrast to this, pathological gambling involves a chronic and progressive failure to resist impulses to gamble, which disrupts or damages personal or family life. Characteristic problems that often accompany pathological gambling include such things as arrest for embezzlement or income tax evasion due to attempts to obtain money for gambling, default on debts or other financial responsibilities, borrowing money from illegal sources, and often loss of work due to absenteeism in order to pursue gambling (*DSM-III*).

Most of the clinical literature on pathological gambling is written from a psychoanalytic perspective, which classifies the disorder as a character neurosis as differentiated from a symptom neurosis. In the character neuroses the psychopathology is expressed not in neurotic symptoms but in social behavior. In contrast to this, in the symptom neuroses the individual responds to unconscious impulses by neurotic mechanisms (symptoms) rather than by giving overt expression to them. One further contrast is that in the symptom neurotic the defensive symptom alleviates anxiety that would otherwise be even more distressing than is the case, whereas the character neurotic perceives little, if any, anxiety.

Discussion of the dynamics of pathological gambling should begin with Freud, who felt that gambling represented a substitute for masturbation. According to Freud (1924/1950), the irresistible nature of the temptation, the solemn resolutions (which are nevertheless invariably broken) never to do it again, and the passionate activity of the hands all betray the nature of the underlying dynamic.

Bergler (1957) presents a more detailed discussion of pathological gambling and suggests two basic dynamics: unconscious aggression and an unconscious tendency toward self-punishment because of that aggression. The act of gambling is a denial of the reality principle; that is, it is not consistent with rational judgment about how to maximize gain and minimize loss. In this act of denial the gambler is expressing his neurotic aggression toward those who taught him the reality principle—his parents. In losing he is simply paying the penalty for this aggression. This tendency toward self-punishment parallels Freud's equation of gambling and masturbation in that both provoke intense guilt, which is a major mental mechanism of self-punishment.

Another dynamic postulated by Bergler is the gambler's infantile megalomania. Nowhere is this primitive mental state more clearly demonstrated than in the attitude the gambler displays while gambling. Just like a child he expects that he will win because he wants to win. Bergler states that "when a gambler places his stake on a card or a color or a number, he is not acting like a person who has adapted himself to reality; he is 'ordering' the next card to win for him, in the complete illusion that he is omnipotent" (Bergler, 1957, p. 23).

In summary, the pathological gambler may be seen psychodynamically to display unconscious masochism wherein he produces situations in which he will be punished. Unaware that he himself has been responsible for his losses, he often strikes out in righteous indignation against the world's cruelty and injustice. This is then followed by profound self-pity; fate has handed him a raw deal. It is also followed by guilt, the ultimate psychic mechanism of self-punishment.

References
Bergler, E. *The psychology of gambling*. New York: Hill & Wang, 1957.
Freud, S., *Collected papers* (Vol. 5). New York: Hogarth, 1950. (Originally published, 1924.)

R. D. Calabrese

Game Analysis. One of the major techniques of TRANSACTIONAL ANALYSIS. Games are a set of ulterior interactions (having double motives) between persons that lead to predictable bad results. Initially game analysis involves noting repetitive interactions in the life of the client. Usually these appear to be rational, straightforward behaviors (i.e., complementary transactions). The task of the therapist is to intuit the concealed or hidden motive beneath the surface. Games are usually "played" to confirm feelings of low self-esteem.

A game begins with the con (the invitation to play) and the gimmick (the response of the other indicating he or she is hooked into playing). This leads to a response (a series of interactions), followed by a switch (changes in ego states indicating the hidden message has been sent and received), and a crossup (confusion as to what happened). The result is a payoff (bad feelings).

H. N. MALONY

Gender and Psychopathology. In contrast to sex, which refers to the biological expression of maleness and femaleness, gender indicates the social aspects of being a male or a female. However, these two terms are often used interchangeably with no regard for their original biological or social meaning.

Gove and Tudor (1973) reported extensive statistics on gender differences from both psychiatric facilities and community studies in the United States. In support of the conclusion that among adults (age 18 and over) women are more often mentally ill than men, was the finding that women receive more treatment for psychosis and neurosis. However, the definition of mental illness did not include alcoholism, addiction, antisocial personality and psychosexual disorders that are higher in men than women.

In child psychopathology the overall rates are higher in boys than in girls, but the sex ratio becomes nearly equal in adolescence. Changes in the sex ratio of psychiatric disorders from childhood to adolescence are the result of an increase in emotional disorders among females as they pass from childhood to adulthood. Boys are consistently higher than girls in the various types of psychoses, including childhood schizophrenia. Other disorders that are higher in boys are infantile autism (M to F ratio 3:1), attention deficit disorder with hyperactivity (M to F ratio 10:1), conduct disorders (M to F ratio 4:1 to 12:1), chronic motor tic disorder (M to F ratio 3:1), and mental retardation (M to F ratio 2:1) (*DSM-III*). Gender differences in the subtypes of adult psychopathology are not as consistent as in child psychopathology.

The Major Psychopathologies. *Depression.* There are about two depressed females to one male (Weissman & Klerman, 1977). However, higher depression among females is limited to a specific group: young adults, relatively uneducated, formerly married, and employed in low-income jobs. Women who are in higher status occupations and who are relatively educated do not usually report more depression than their male counterparts. Gender differences in depression may be related to the mode of symptom expression, which results in different consequences. Men report inability to cry, various somatic concerns, social withdrawal, and a sense of failure. Women will report a depressive mood which can be easily identified as depression, whereas men's experience could be seen as based on overwork or physical illness. Helplessness and crying displayed by women could be construed as appropriate sex-role actions. Thus, depression in men may elicit more negative reaction from others, which in turn may discourage men from reporting depressive complaints.

Phobias. Simple phobias that involve specific fears, particularly animal phobia, have higher incidence among females (95% female incidence). Males and females are more equally represented in social phobia (F to M 3:2). Agoraphobia, the most frequently reported phobia among patients, is consistently higher among women (F to M 3:1). Agoraphobia has often been referred to as the housewives' disorder, due to its high incidence among young married females. In particular, it was found that discontented housewives (who wanted to work outside the home but did not) tended to be more symptomatic, more agoraphobic, and needed more help for their phobias than contented housewives (content only with housework).

Schizophrenia. It is generally reported that the treated incidence of schizophrenia in the general population is equal. There is a sex-age pattern for hospital admission; age of onset is earlier for males than females. This sex-age pattern has been found in many countries. Clinical observations of schizophrenic patients in hospital wards and in psychotherapy indicate that schizophrenic women tend to be more aggressive and more sexual than schizophrenic men. Schizophrenic men tend to be more passive and withdrawn than normal men, whereas schizophrenic women appear more active and domineering than their normal counterparts. The presence of heterosexual interest and affect in females and passivity and withdrawal in males is compatible with the tendency of females to develop less severe types of schizophrenia.

These gender differences raise the question whether men are more vulnerable to schizophrenia, particularly its severe type, than women. One major issue is whether genetic and environmental factors are involved to the same degree in the development of schizophrenia in males and females or whether these factors are gender-specific and have different impact on the sexes. Twin studies reveal that genetic factors are equally involved in the development of schizophrenia in the two sexes. However, family disturbance (loss of a parent, psychiatric illness) and interpersonal relationship are more associated with schizophrenia in women.

Alcoholism. A current estimate, derived from general population surveys, indicates that in North America about 120 men drink for every 100 women who do. The heavier the drinking level reported, the greater the difference between males and females. There are three men who are problem drinkers for every woman; gender ratios are a little higher (M to F, about 4:1) when based on clinically defined alcoholics. In both sexes problem drinking and heavy drinking are higher among the unemployed. However, employed married women have higher rates of problem and heavy drinking than single women or housewives not in the labor force. These facts may not support the stereotype of the female alcoholic as a housewife who drinks secretly.

Women may be more vulnerable than men to the physical effects of alcohol; health problems in association with alcohol are reported twice as often by women as by men. In men increases in aggression, sexual response, sociability, and even laughter and eating are related only to the assumption that alcohol has been consumed and occur even when the drink contains none. This evidence contradicts the notion that pharmacological effects of alcohol cause disinhibition. The assumption of having consumed alcohol increases social anxiety in women, which may reflect beliefs regarding alcohol effects on women. Women become more intoxicated than men by the same dose of alcohol; they tend to be smaller in size and have lower proportion of body fluid to fat and thus a smaller volume in which to absorb a given amount of alcohol.

Explaining Gender Differences. *Gender role.* One theory explaining gender differences postulates that female rates of mental illness are comparable to those of males, but because of their gender role women become more involved with the psychiatric profession. According to this theory high rates of mental illness among females are the result of two major factors. 1) The sick role is more compatible with the role obligation of women. They may have more contact with services because of the relative accessibility and convenience of health service for them. Housewives have more time and incur less loss than working men who lose time from work when attending health clinics. 2) Women may report more illness than men because it is culturally more acceptable for them to be ill. Men are expected to "grin and bear it" and avoid the public display of emotional behavior.

Stress. It is suggested that sex differences seen in psychopathology are caused by stresses related to gender role. It is assumed that because the female role is more stressful than the male role, women tend to have more mental illness than men. However, research on stressful life events indicates that women report about the same number as men. One gender difference may be in the subjective experience of stress; women tend to rate the same life events as more stressful than men. Also, some events tend to be more traumatic for women than for men, such as changing residence, especially moving to another city or state. In contrast, stressors related to low socioeconomic status are more strongly associated with mental illness in men than women.

Female sex hormones. It is assumed that there is a causal relationship between low hormonal levels during the premenstrual period and anxiety, depression, and hostility. However, a causal relationship between hormonal levels and psychiatric disturbance is not well established. Hormonal changes seem to affect negatively those women who are vulnerable to psychiatric disturbance. Also, women who believe that menstruation is debilitating report significantly more symptoms for the premenstrual phase of the cycle.

It is also believed that the menopause is linked with psychological and somatic complaints. Symptoms that are consistently reported during the menopause are physical ones such as hot flashes (flushes and episodes of perspiration). Psychological symptoms such as insomnia, irritability, depression, reduced sexual drive, headache, dizzy spells, and palpitation do not occur consistently during the menopause. Contrary to common belief, psychiatric disturbance is not more common among middle-aged women, who have a hormonal depletion during the menopause.

The rapid fall in hormonal levels after childbirth seems to increase the risk of psychiatric disturbance. The "baby blues," which involve mood swings and crying episodes, are experienced during the first 10 days after childbirth by 50–80% of women. Psychotic states and more severe depression occur in only 1–2 cases per 1,000 deliveries. Some women taking contraceptives may report psychiatric symptoms, but the pharmacological basis of their complaints has not been established. It is still uncertain whether the reaction of these women is the result of suggestibility and psychological reaction to the pill (conflict and guilt over sexual freedom or desire for more children) or due to the pharmacological agent.

References
Gove, W. R., & Tudor, J. F. Adult sex roles and mental illness. *American Journal of Sociology*, 1973, *78*(4), 812–835.
Weissman, M. M., & Klerman, G. L. Sex differences and the epidemiology of depression. *Archives of General Psychiatry*, 1977, *34*, 98–111.

Additional Reading
Al-Issa, I. (Ed.). *Gender and psychopathology*. New York: Academic Press, 1982.

I. Al-Issa

Gender Identity.
The concept of identity popularized by Erickson (1959) is a description of eight stages of the life cycle during which we experience and express different styles of being a person. Identity combines the senses of who I am, what I do, and how I do it. The sense of identity may be quite inchoate, affective, and inarticulate in the young child, while the introspective adult may articulate very precise descriptions of his or her identity. Gender identity is only a part of the whole sense of identity, yet at the same time a core component around which nongender aspects of identity are crystallized. Failure to achieve precise gender identity may impair the development of mature, complex adult identity, whereas the mature normal adult accepts gender identity as a given quality and elaborates other identity attributes.

Experience and Identity. Several aspects of personal experience must be identified and separated: the "me" experience, the "I" experience, and the "self" experience. Each is a part of the sense of identity, but not necessarily gender-linked. The "me" experience refers to the sense of being alive, of possessing what happens to "myself." Such experience is present probably in early infancy, later cognated upon, and then verbalized as the sense of "me." The experience of "me" precedes and is distinct from the acquisition of sense of gender. The experience of "I" is the conscious appreciation of ego operations such as cognition, affect, and perception. That is, one experiences the sense of "I" am thinking, seeing, doing, feeling, deciding, acting. Again, the sense of "I" precedes and is distinct from the acquisition of sense of gender.

The term *ego* shall be construed operationally to describe mental operations—i.e., cognition, perception, affect systems. Ego operations are experience and directed. But ego operations are impersonal. We acquire different styles of ego operation that may become part of our identity formation. For example, "I am a fuzzy-thinking person" versus "I am a clear-thinking person." Ego styles are gender-linked. In a given culture males and females are differentially socialized in different styles of ego operations. We may say, for example, "You think like a woman" and thereby make an accurate observation of cultural influence on gender-linked ego style (Spence & Helmreich, 1978).

Self is the image of "who am I?" It is a complex mental construction, including my "ideal self" or what I ought to be (the combined psychoanalytic ego ideal and superego), my "desired self" (a consciously constructed self-model), and my "actual self" (the observation of my person in action). Self-identity is neither innate nor epigenetic, as is true of "me" and "I" experiences. Rather, self-identity is learned, constructed, formulated, modified, and elaborated on throughout life (Gergen, 1971). Gender plays a major role in the development of self-identity. In brief, one can experience me, I, and ego operations apart from a sense of gender, but one does not experience self apart from a sense of gender.

It is obvious that sexual impulse, desire, and behavior are entwined with gender identity. Freud interpreted sexuality as a basic determinant of identity. However, a century of research has demonstrated that sexuality is a reflection of gender identity rather than a determinant. That is, sexuality is acted out in terms of impulse, arousal, desire, and action on the basis of one's gender-identity formation (Stoller, 1968).

Anatomy and Destiny. A major question is raised by the obvious differences between male and female appearance, behavior, and role functions. Is this biological determinism or cultural artifact? It is appealing to assume that innate biological instincts account for male-female differences. In animal species we observe highly complex social behavior that is gender-linked. However, the biologic determinants of behavior shift with animal complexity. In brief, basic instincts are the same in man, monkey, pigeon, or worm. These generate drives, which become less directive as we ascend the phylogenic ladder, so that when we reach the level of man, instinctual drive stimuli no longer determine specific behavioral complexes.

An example of this is the sexual instinct. The amoeba reproduces asexually at a predictable rate of fission. The earthworm has both male and female sex organs and copulates with another earthworm by matching male and female genitalia in random fashion. Frogs and birds only mate during a mating season, with gender-linked stereotyped courtship behavior and with a partner for the season. Higher mammals, such as the gorilla, form generational families, choose specific mates, mate during estrous seasons, and care for the young within the family structure. Young monkeys who are reared apart from the mother do not successfully copulate or care for their own young. In the human sexuality may never be expressed, in that celibate persons may live a normal and psychologically healthy life without significant sexual experience. On the other hand, persons may use sexual behavior to quell loneliness, anxiety, or conflict without experiencing any sexual pleasure. At the same time, human sexual behavior is not necessarily linked to reproductive mating.

To conclude, in terms of biologic principles we cannot appeal to differences in male and female instincts to account for male-female variations in behavior per se.

The influence of genetic variation and hormonal influences on behavior must be considered. Persons with abnormal gender chromosomal patterns may exhibit genetic defects of deformations of skeleton, muscle formation, etc. But their behavior may not differ from persons with normal gender chromosomes. If we administer sex hormones to a person, what will happen? In the average person—nothing. However, in some experiments, if one administers hormones to homosexual persons, they increase their homosexual activity level. That is, sex hormones increase the drive stimuli but do not change the sexual orientation of the person. Clearly then, gender behavior includ-

ing sexual behavior, cannot be accounted for primarily on biological grounds (Money & Musaph, 1977).

Facets of Gender Identity. The development of identity is biopsychosocial. We can truly speak of psychosexual identity, but more accurately we should speak of *psychogender* identity, since sexuality is an expression of gender sense. Eight variables contribute to psychogender identity (Money & Ehrhardt, 1972).

Variable 1: Chromosomal gender. In the normal pattern the female has an XX sex chromatin pattern, the male an XY. In genetic abnormalities there may be 5–6 sex chromatin gene patterns, each giving rise to different clinical syndromes and involving different hormonal, musculoskeletal, and genital patterns and different levels of sexual potency. Yet a person with a female chromosome pattern may be born with male-appearing genitalia, be reared as male, and behave as male, and vice versa. Obviously the sex chromatin pattern does not determine gender behavior.

Variable 2: Gonadal gender. This refers to the presence of either testes or ovaries. In embryo the human is bisexual, and under hormonal influence one set withers and the other grows. Yet in some cases of aberrant chromosomal and/or hormonal influence, the external genitalia may develop of one gender while the gonads are of opposite gender. Thus an infant may be born with female-looking genitals along with well-developed undescended testicles, or vice versa. Again, the primary gonads do not determine gender orientation or behavior.

Variable 3: Hormonal gender. Males and females do have distinctive hormonal systems, produced by both the gonads and other body organs. Malfunction or disequilibrium in the hormonal systems may influence the male-female balance of hormones. In turn this may result in masculinization or feminization of body traits, such as voice, hair pattern, breast development, fat deposition, skeletal growth, and development of external genitalia in embryo. In children this may result in a chromosomal and gonadal male with a female hormone balance that causes feminization of body structure, or vice versa. Nonetheless, the person will act male or female in accord with that person's rearing, regardless of the hormonal balance or body habitus.

Variable 4: Internal genitalia. This refers to the vagina and uterus in the female and prostate in the male. These internal organs develop in accord with embryonic hormonal patterns.

Variable 5: External genitalia. These organs are the most visible evidence upon which we first assign gender. Yet they may be misleading. As noted, variations in chromosomal, gonadal, and hormonal variables may produce external genitalia that appear of one gender, yet are opposite to all other previous gender variables. A male may not develop closure of the bilateral pubic genital tissues and appear to have a vulva. A female may have overdevelopment of the clitoris which looks like a penis. But the external genitalia do not determine gender identity.

In the case of *Transsexualism* the person has the identity of one gender (I experience my identity as female), while having all the normal body attributes of the other gender (I live in a male body). In this instance the distinction between gender body attributes (biological) and gender identity (psychological) is clearly seen.

Variable 6: Gender of assignment and rearing. This refers to the label the parent gives the child as either male or female. Boys and girls are handled differently as infants by their parents. They are treated differently long before they can talk or cognate on their own gender identity. The child is socialized into a basic gender identity long before language acquisition. In fact, such gender acquisition precedes language. The threshold for fixation of gender identity is about 18 months, while the point of no return for change in gender reassignment is about 30 months. After 4 years of age it is almost impossible to change gender assignment without severe psychological conflict in the child.

Variable 7: Core gender identity. This is the first basic sense of identity that is crystallized via cognition as part of self-identity. The child cognitively is able to state, I am a boy or girl. This appears to be organized as a cognitive construct between ages 3–4. In contrast, the gender assignment has already been well established. It appears that when parents assign the child one gender (male) and treat the child as the other gender (female), the psychological conditions for transsexualism are created (I have been labeled a male, but treated and expected to be a female). In psychotic regressive states we can observe similar confusion about core gender identity in patients who demonstrate no gender confusion in normal states. Similarly, persons with primitive character disorders demonstrate gender identity confusion.

Variable 8: Gender role identity. This refers to the social patterns of appearance, behavior, and role performance associated with the sociocultural definitions of masculinity or femininity. There is probably some degree of psychological linkage between the sense of maleness or femaleness and behavior in masculine or feminine roles as defined by the culture. For example, in cultures with weak male roles the males demonstrate a higher incidence of identification with women, as in couvade (male pregnancy fantasies). On the other hand, one can experience a strong sense of maleness or femaleness and not behave in traditional or expected gender-linked roles. For example, a feminine woman can be a police officer; a masculine man can knit doilies (Munroe & Munroe, 1977).

In the area of social gender roles there has been much confusion about the difference between gender identity and gender roles. The concept of androgyny has been promoted to do away with gender distinctions. This misses the point that gender identity is ineluctably a part of personal identity, but that many social roles and behaviors need not be gender-linked (Sargent, 1977). The mature person with a secure gender identity is in fact free to elaborate a wide variety of social role behaviors that become part of personal identity apart from gender.

Gender and Self-Identity. Although self-identity need not be tied to gender in many aspects, in another sense self-identity is always linked to gender. There are eight stages of psychological development of identity, according to Bemporad (1980). Each stage is not left behind but is incorporated into the next developmental level. Thus in the mature adult we continue to see reflections of each stage of identity.

Stage 1. In what is called an oral incorporative mode the newborn engulfs everything encountered. This style of relating to the world is to take it in and make it part of himself. The young infant does not differentiate between self and other. The lack of body boundaries, the timeless sense of fusion with the other, the experience of engulfing and being engulfed is reexperienced in adult life in sexual orgasm. The theme of incorporative identity is reflected in love play with nibbling or biting and in courtship with the primordial declaration:"I love you so much I could eat you up!"

Stage 2. Between 15–36 months the young child identifies his body as part of self, and body image becomes a major nidus of self-identity. Possession of body is possession of identity. The same motif is seen in adults who experience a sense of loss of identity when accident, surgery, or illness results in loss or immobilization of body parts. Where body is still a major source of self-identity and sexualized, the loss of genitalia (gonads, breasts) or sexual function may be experienced as a major loss of identity. Such statements as, "I don't feel like a man or a woman anymore," reflect a sexualized fixation on body as a source of identity and of gender identity.

A bit later the child extends the body boundaries to objects, clothes, playthings, as body extensions. My things are my body, are part of me. Again, in adults we see identity rooted in possessions as a source of identity, or gender identity reinforced through possessions: "I have a gun, ergo I am a male!" or "I have a house, ergo I am a woman!"

Stage 3. In the 3–5 age group the child differentiates self from other objects. There is generic identification with children of the same gender. Boys and girls reinforce gender identity by modeling and emulating behavior and social roles of the same-gender parent. Play helps the child to learn how to be an adult person. Identity is related to how one looks, acts, behaves. Playing house is modeling behavior that reinforces gender identity. Identity is developed in terms of social custom that differentiates men and women. Little girls cook, bake, and sew. Little boys pound nails and mow grass. This need not, and should not, be preparatory role behavior for adulthood, but some gender-linked role modeling is necessary to reinforce the sense of "I am becoming a man or a woman." This is identity through same-gender comparison.

Stage 4. Ages 5–7 is the oedipal period. Here identity development occurs through opposite-gender comparison. The child elaborates gender identity by modeling behavior of the same-gender parent with the opposite. The boy tries to behave with mother like father does. The girl treats father like mother does. Naturally children will emulate erotic and seductive behavior of the parent. Children act "sexy" not because of infantile sexual strivings, as Freud suggested, but rather because they are modeling the sexy behavior of their parents. At this stage children need affirmation from both parents that these early strivings toward adult behavior are not bad, and that in adulthood they will find mates to replicate the behavior of mother and father. Disapproval of either parent, fear of either parent, or failure to successfully identify with the parent of the same gender all lead to failure at this stage of identity development, resulting in homosexual orientation. Thus, homosexuality is not a problem of sexuality but a failure in maturation of

identity development at the oedipal stage (Stoller, 1968).

Stage 5. In latency, 7–12 years, the child elaborates personal identity via doing things. Skill acquisition enables the child to define personal abilities and ego coping style unique to him or her. Again, skill acquisition is in part linked to gender: learning male skills and female skills. But at this stage it is possible to also offer children androgynous skill acquisition not linked to gender but instead adding to development of unique individual skills and identity.

Stage 6. In adolescence the sense of self is heightened. Sexual drive stimuli are increased, and attraction to the opposite gender occurs. But what is the nature of the attraction? It is an exchange of mutual ideal images. The teen-ager falls in love with a projected image of an ideal, which is reciprocated. When the ideal image is tarnished by harsh reality, the "puppy love" dissolves. The attraction is reciprocated appreciation of an ideal self. When this is then eroticized, one feels a sexual attraction. Sexual interaction becomes a vehicle for reinforcement of self-identity.

Stage 7. In young adulthood a major transmutation of identity must occur from "what I do gives me identity" to "who I am gives meaning to what I do." That is, external attributes have given value to self-identity. Now the young adult must invest in internal attributes, an internal constructed sense of self, and identity apart from external exigencies. Failure to accomplish this task results in persons who seek others, sexually or not, to reinforce their own identity, self-esteem, value, and self-worth. So-called identity crises may occur in adults who lean on external definitions of identity and therfore lose their sense of self when those externalities diminish or disappear.

Stage 8. Mature adulthood involves the capacity to share one's identity with another. Mature love involves the capacity to retain one's own autonomy and identity but also acquire a shared identity with a partner. Marriage and sexuality can occur without sharing the intimacy of identity. On the other hand, mature love involves "growing together" (Curtin, 1973). Here gender identity merges into a joint male-female identity of a marital pair.

In summary, the biblical observations that "male and female created he them" and "the two shall become one" represent the journey of psychogender development. The child begins with genderless fusion, acquires a gender identity, and moves on to an autonomous unique personal identity. But the mature adult shares gender identity with a mate of the opposite-gender identity in a new fusion that is a gender and sexual union, two unique self-identities, and a conjoint mutual marital identity. Thus there is the sense of paradox, in that identity is on the one hand profoundly rooted in a distinct sexual gender, and on the other hand unites and transcends gender.

References

Bemporad, J. R. (Ed.), *Child development in normality and psychopathology.* New York: Brunner/Mazel, 1980.
Curtin, M. E. (Ed.). *Symposium on love.* New York: Behavioral Publications, 1973.
Erickson, E. H. *Identity and the life cycle.* New York: International Universities Press, 1959.
Gergen, J. J. *The concept of self.* New York: Holt, Rinehart, & Winston, 1971.
Money, J., & Ehrhardt, A. A. *Man and woman, boy and girl.* Baltimore: Johns Hopkins University Press, 1972.
Money, J., & Musaph, H. (Eds.). *Handbook of sexology.* New York: Excerpta Medica, 1977.
Munroe, R. J., & Munroe, R. H. *Cross-cultural human development.* New York: Aronson, 1977.
Sargent, A. G. *Beyond sex roles.* St. Paul: West Publishing, 1977.
Spence, J. T., & Helmreich, R. J. *Masculinity and femininity.* Austin: University of Texas Press, 1978.
Stoller, R. J. *Sex and gender:* London: Hogarth, 1968.

E. M. PATTISON

See SEXUALITY; PERSONHOOD; SELF.

Gender Identity Disorder of Childhood.

Occurring before puberty, this disorder is a rare condition in which the child reports a chronic feeling of belonging to the other sex while persistently rejecting the appropriateness of his or her own sexual anatomy. A gender identity disorder may be first suspected when a predominantly effeminate behavior pattern in boys or an extreme form of tomboyishness in girls is seen. But the disorder involves more than unconventional sex-role behavior patterns. It is a profound psychological disturbance of the normal sense of maleness or femaleness.

More than 90% of all diagnosed cases of gender identity disorder of childhood reported in the clinical literature have been boys, suggesting a higher incidence in males than in females and/or a relatively more complex task of detecting disorders of gender identity in girls (Rekers, 1981). Cross-gender-identified boys are associated with a persistent and compulsively stereotyped pattern of preoccupation with feminine sex-typed activities, with some combination of several of these behaviors:

1) The boy frequently dresses in girls' or women's clothing, or in fantasy play improvises feminine clothing with other materials if actual clothing is unavailable. Sexual excitement has not typically been reported to be associated with this cross dressing in children, unlike many adult cases of transvestism.

2) The boy often displays gestures, arm movements, gait, and standing and sitting postures that are culturally recognized by others as stereotypically feminine. These behavioral mannerisms appear to occur unconsciously, with the child usually unable to inhibit them, even at times of severe male peer group ridicule for acting like a "sissy."

3) The boy tends to avoid boy playmates and rough-and-tumble play, while feeling compelled to play with girls and with toys exclusively associated with female roles or with girls' pastimes. Baby dolls and female Barbie-type dolls are often preferred toys, with which the boy fantasizes delivery or breast feeding or rehearses other maternal roles with an infant. In playing house with girls, the boy may surprise the girls by rigidly insisting on a female role most of the time for himself. In other play role-taking, a female role is frequently preferred, even in imaginary games where a male role would have been possible (e.g., as when playing teacher). There is a keen interest in play or real cosmetic items.

4) The boy may prefer to be called by a specific girl's name.

5) He may talk predominantly about feminine topics, such as pregnancy, female undergarments, beauty parlors, shaving legs and underarms, flirting with boys, earrings, or cosmetics. In some cases the boy regularly or occasionally projects his voice into a high femalelike voice inflection while talking.

6) Less often, a gender-identity disturbed boy will display overt deviance regarding his male sex organs (a) by refusing to urinate from the standing position, insisting on sitting "like girls" on the toilet; (b) by claiming that his penis, testes, and/or scrotum are disgusting or will disappear; (c) by insisting that he would prefer not to have his penis or testes; or (d) by tucking his penis between his legs in the bath to appear to look like a girl.

7) In addition to some pattern of these overt cross-sex behaviors, the diagnostic criteria for this disorder require that the boy make strong, direct, and persistent verbal statements that he actually is or would prefer to be a girl or woman, and that he will develop to become a woman and/or become pregnant when he grows up. The diagnostic criteria also require onset of the disturbance before puberty.

The diagnosis of gender identity disorder in girls is not only more rare but is a more difficult clinical task, since the symptoms must be carefully differentiated from the common tomboy phase of a large percentage of normal girls (see Rekers & Mead, 1980, and Rekers, 1982b, for a detailed differentiation of abnormal from normal tomboyishness). The essential features of a gender identity disorder in a girl involve a chronic, predominant, and persistent pattern of some combination of the following behavioral characteristics:

1) The girl avoids girl playmates and stereotypically feminine play activity, such as play with dolls or playing house (unless she plays father or other male roles). She rejects feminine sex-typed toys as inappropriate for her and desires toys appropriate for either sex or toys usually preferred by boys. This is coupled with a preference for boy playmates and a keen enthusiasm for athletic and rough-and-tumble play with boys.

2) She wants to be considered "one of the boys" in her relationship with male peers, or she insists on being called by a boy's name or a boy's nickname.

3) She displays masculinelike gestures, mannerisms, gait, standing and sitting postures.

4) She talks predominantly about masculine topics, such as army combat duty, shaving one's facial beard, being a football player, or being a father. In some cases the girl regularly or occasionally projects her voice into an artificially low, masculinelike voice inflection while talking.

5) The girl regularly and chronically rejects feminine clothing, feminine hair styling, and play cosmetic sets. This is coupled with a preference for wearing clothing that is normally appropriate for boys only or for both sexes.

6) In addition to some pattern of the above overt masculinelike behaviors, the diagnostic criteria for this disorder require that the girl insist that she is a boy or strongly and persistently state her desire to be a boy or man (over and above any statements about perceived cultural advantages proscribed to males). In addition, the disturbance must have an onset before puberty and must include a persistent repudiation of her female anatomy, as evidenced by at least one of the following types of repeated assertions: (a) that she will grow up to be transformed into a man (not merely in role), (b) that she will not be able to become pregnant biologically, (c) that she cannot develop breasts, (d) that she actually has no vagina, or (e) that she has, or will grow, a penis.

The diagnostic criteria for a gender identity disorder, therefore, require more than behavioral deviance in culturally stereotyped sex-role behaviors. The assessment of cross-sex behavior involves measurement of frequency, setting, cultural context, and developmental context of the sex-role behaviors, and the psychological significance of the behavior to the child. It is the ratio of feminine to masculine behavior rather than the sheer frequency of cross-sex behaviors that is of diagnostic significance (Rosen, Rekers, & Friar, 1977).

Almost all cases of this disorder have been diagnosed in children with normal physical and genetic sex status as measured by currently available genetic, physical examination, and medical history measures (Rekers, Crandall, Rosen, & Bentler, 1979). The age of onset of the disorder is in the preschool years in most cases, when cross dressing and cross-sex play behavior patterns begin. In later grade school years many of the public cross-sex behaviors decrease in frequency, even though the cross-gender identity likely persists in the absence of treatment.

Both retrospective and longitudinal studies indicate that at least one-third to one-half of boys with untreated gender identity disorders feel tempted in adolescence to masturbate to homosexual fantasies and to seek homosexual relationships with boys or men (Rekers, 1982a). Certain homosexually inclined adolescent and adult males may make more homosexual advances toward the effeminate, gender-identity-disturbed adolescent boy than to normally masculine-behaving teen-aged boys. A minority of girls with this disorder persist with a masculine identification, with some also developing homosexual temptations and practices. The limited data available suggest that from 5 to 12% of untreated cases of childhood gender identity disorder develop adulthood Transsexualism, which is accompanied by severe depressive episodes and a high risk for suicide attempts. Another 5 to 12% appear to become continuous with adult Transvestism. Apparently, only a minority of untreated cases of this disorder eventuate in a normal, unconflicted heterosexual adjustment.

Although very little reliable scientific data exist on the etiology of this disorder and its most common adulthood correlates of homosexuality, transsexualism, and transvestism, plausible developmental theories have been postulated (see Rekers, 1981, 1982a, for details). The formation of gender identity normally requires the child's appropriate identification with his or her genital anatomy and its eventual reproductive potential. Psychosexual differentiation is theoretically conceptualized as a complex sequential interaction among biological development variables and the social contributions of parents and others to the child's growing psychological understanding of sex role and sexual distinctions. While biological abnormalities could theoretically contribute to sex role or sexual identity disorders in rare cases, social learning variables have been considered to be the main cause of gender identity disturbances.

Child-rearing experiences normally contribute to a child's identification with the parent figure and peers of the same sex and to the development of complementary role relationships with members of the other sex. Some evidence suggests that physical or psychological absence of the father during early childhood years, coupled with an excessive, exclusive, and extremely prolonged physical and emotional closeness between mother and infant, may contribute to gender identity disorders in boys. Similarly, disturbed relationships between a young girl and her mother and father could contribute to a cross-gender identification.

From a theological perspective the available scientific data and theories and Scriptures (e.g., Prov. 22:6) place a moral responsibility upon fathers and mothers (Eph. 6:1–4; Titus 2:3–5) to teach their children the essential sex-role distinctions and thus assist their normal gender identity development (see Rekers, 1982a, 1982b, for details). Many sex-role distinctions are culturally defined, (a) based on biological sex difference (e.g., wearing a dress is feminine; shaving facial hair is masculine); (b) based on arbitrary but benign assignment (e.g., wearing lipstick is feminine; opening doors for women is masculine); or (c) based on arbitrary and harmful stereotypes that should be abolished (e.g., being a nurse is feminine; being a doctor is masculine). Other sex-role distinctions are biologically defined—e.g., breast-feeding an infant is feminine, and impregnating one's wife by sexual intercourse is masculine. Still other sex-role distinctions are morally defined, based upon sex differences created by God (see Braun & Rekers, 1981)—e.g., modest clothing of the upper torso (1 Tim. 2:9–10) and being submissive to one's husband's leadership at home (1 Cor. 11; Eph. 5; 1 Tim. 2:11–12; Titus 2:3–5) are feminine; while providing moral and spiritual leadership in the home (Eph. 5:22–6:4) and abstaining from sexual relations outside of marriage are masculine (1 Cor. 7:1–2; Titus 2:6–7; 1 John 2:13–17). It is a parental responsibility to teach these sex-role distinctions to sons and daughters (Rekers, 1982a, 1982b)

Experimental studies have demonstrated that specific child behavior therapy techniques are successful in treatment of gender identity disorders. These techniques include 1) positive reinforcement of normal sex-typed play, speech patterns, and behavioral mannerisms in the clinic, home, and school settings, and 2) behavioral extinction procedures and response-cost reinforcement contingencies for eliminating cross-sex behavior patterns (Rekers, 1977; Rekers & Mead, 1979). Parents can be trained and supervised to carry out the behavior-shaping procedures in the home environment (Rekers, 1982b). If the disorder is untreated in childhood and develops into a problem with homosexuality in adolescence, a variety of counseling and Christian ministry approaches can be successful in helping the adolescent or adult resist the temptation to homosexual lust or homosexual behavior (see Rekers, 1982a).

References

Braun, M., & Rekers, G. A. *The Christian in an age of sexual eclipse*. Wheaton, Ill.: Tyndale House, 1981.

Rekers, G. A. Assessment and treatment of childhood gender problems. In B. B. Lahey & A. E. Kazdin (Eds.), *Advances in clinical child psychology* (Vol. 1). New York: Plenum, 1977.

Rekers, G. A. Psychosexual and gender problems. In E. J. Mash & L. G. Terdal (Eds.), *Behavioral assessment of childhood disorders*. New York: Guilford Press, 1981.

Rekers, G. A. *Growing up straight: What every family should know about homosexuality*. Chicago: Moody Press, 1982. (a)

Rekers, G. A. *Shaping your child's sexual identity*. Grand Rapids: Baker, 1982. (b)

Rekers, G. A., Crandall, B. F., Rosen, A. C., & Bentler, P. M. Genetic and physical studies of male children with psychological gender disturbances. *Psychological Medicine*, 1979, *9*, 373–375.

Rekers, G. A., & Mead, S. Early intervention for female sexual identity disturbance: Self-monitoring of play behavior. *Journal of Abnormal Child Psychology*, 1979, *7*(4), 405–423.

Rekers, G. A., & Mead, S. Female sex-role deviance: Early identification and developmental intervention. *Journal of Clinical Child Psychology*, 1980, *8*, 199–203.

Rosen, A. C., Rekers, G. A., & Friar, L. R. Theoretical and diagnostic issues in child gender disturbances. *Journal of Sex Research*, 1977, *13*(2), 89–103.

G. A. REKERS

General Adaptation Syndrome. First described by Selye, the general adaptation syndrome refers to the various changes in the body that occur in response to stress. Selye distinguishes three stages to this response: the alarm reaction, the state of resistance, and the stage of exhaustion.

Generalization. The process of spreading or transferring the effects of education, training, or treatment from the circumstances under which learning initially took place to other settings. Generalization is the opposite process to that of discrimination. Whereas generalization expands responding, discrimination restricts or limits the range of responding along one or more dimensions.

Types. There are many types of generalization, but the best known is *stimulus generalization*, also known as *setting generalization*. In stimulus generalization cues that were not used during prior learning experiences become effective cues for signaling the acquired response. For example, a brown terrier bit 4-year-old Bobby. Prior to being bitten, Bobby showed no signs of fearing the terrier or other dogs. One week after the biting incident Bobby manifested much distress and avoidance behavior when any dog was nearby.

Response generalization is the second-best-known form. This is the process in which a single stimulus comes to control more responses than those targeted during prior teaching, training, or treatment. For example, a mother has used the oral command "Stop!" under three circumstances in the past: when her toddler ran toward the street, when he reached toward the hot stove, and when he reached to touch a bee sitting on a flower. In each instance she shook her child by the shoulders. Subsequent observations demonstrated that the mother's saying "Stop!" would inhibit climbing, jumping, and throwing hard objects, even though she had not provided negative consequences for these actions in the past.

Temporal generalization is a third type, in which a subject makes a particular response in the training setting even though the response no longer produces a consequence. Temporal generalization occurs under EXTINCTION conditions. When a subject manifests resistance to extinction, this third form of generalization is present. Although they probably don't think about the technical issues involved, parents often seek to produce temporal generalization in their children. For example, Proverbs 22:6 is speaking to temporal generalization by admonishing, "Train up a child in the way he should go; and when he is old, he will not depart from it."

A fourth important category is *subject generalization*, in which treatment, training, or correction are applied to one subject who acquires the desired response, but untreated subjects also acquire the response. When untreated subjects change as though they had been treated, the concept of subject generalization is applicable. For example, in talking to teachers about their misbehaving children, some parents have said, "Don't yell at my kid when he acts up. Reprimand the student who sits next to him, and my son will shape up." Such parents are predicting that their children will manifest subject generalization.

These four types of generalization may be combined to produce more complex forms, but relatively little research has been done on these complex forms of generalization.

Methods of Producing Generalization. One approach is to teach only those behaviors which the person's natural environment is likely to reinforce after the treatment or formal lesson ends. Teaching a shy child how to make social greetings and to enter play with other children would be an example, because the other children are likely to reinforce the shy child's friendly gestures. If the subject identifies which behaviors he or she wants to strengthen and asks family, friends, or others to provide appropriate reinforcers for the occurrence of those behaviors, the change will be even greater.

Second, generalization itself can be treated as a response. The trainer can reinforce the learner for generalizations as they occur. Doing so will promote more rapid generalization.

Third, training or treatment settings should contain many of the stimuli that will be present in those settings to which generalization is desired. On the average, the amount of generalization increases as the number of stimuli common to the training and generalization settings increases.

Fourth, although initial learning may be most rapid under tightly controlled training conditions, generalization is promoted by loosening the training conditions—e.g., by using a variety of cues, responses, and consequences.

A fifth method for promoting generalization is to train the learner in strategies for solving a particular type of problem. Presenting diverse examples of the type of problem to be mastered and approaches to solving the problem facilitates generalization.

Sixth, procedures that blur the differences between training and generalization settings also help. For example, gradually thinning the frequency of reinforcement promotes resistance to extinction (i.e., temporal generalization). Delayed reinforcement may have similar positive effects.

A final useful approach to promoting generalization is to employ self-regulation procedures by having the learner serve as his own teacher through self-observation, self-recording, self-evaluation, self-reinforcement, self-prompting, or self-modeling.

During most of the history of modern psychology theorists have viewed generalization as involving passive, automatic processes. More recently many psychologists have asserted that generalization is just as active a process as discrimination. This assumption has produced an emphasis on developing revised conceptual models of generalization and a methodology for producing the process. On a practical level parents, teachers, and therapists cannot assume that generalization will automatically follow initial learning. They must carefully engineer into the learning situation those conditions that will promote generalization.

P. W. CLEMENT

See LEARNING.

Generalized Anxiety Disorder. ANXIETY may be defined as the felt experience of apprehension, tension, or dread. It is a universal human experience that can be brought on by an almost limitless number of real or imagined stresses. Most individuals handle the stresses of everyday living with a minimum of anxiety. In fact, a certain amount of tension or anxiety may be not only helpful but necessary in order to perform efficiently certain stressful tasks. For example, the mild anxiety which a confident driver experiences while traveling along a busy freeway serves a useful function. The increased tension accompanying the adrenalin flow may enhance reaction time and decision-making ability, thus helping the driver to respond more quickly to dangerous traffic situations than if he were totally relaxed. Therefore, one must be careful not to assume that all anxiety is harmful and in need of swift extinction.

However, anxiety is harmful when it becomes intense, persistent, and pervasive. An individual experiencing this type of anxiety may be said to be suffering from generalized anxiety disorder. In order to be correctly diagnosed as having this disorder a person must have been experiencing the anxious mood continuously for at least one month, manifesting symptoms from three of the four following categories: 1) motor tension (shakiness, fatigability, or restlessness); 2) autonomic hyperactivity (sweating, heart pounding or racing, dizziness, or light-headedness); 3) apprehensive expectation (worry, fear, or anxious rumination); 4) vigilance and scanning (hyperattentiveness resulting in distractability, difficulty in concentrating, or insomnia) (*DSM-III*).

Generalized anxiety disorder should not be confused with either phobic disorder or panic disorder. Phobias are irrational fears of specific objects or situations with an accompanying need to steadfastly avoid the feared object or situation. In contrast, generalized anxiety disorder is characterized by vague, ill-defined feelings of fear or dread. Panic attacks are discrete episodes of terrifying apprehension separated by periods of relative emotional stability. Both are in contrast to the continuously experienced apprehension characteristic of generalized anxiety disorder.

Treatment. Different systems of therapy advocate differing strategies for dealing with debilitating anxiety. A psychodynamic understanding would hold that the intense anxiety is caused by inner conflicts such as fear of death, hostility, or separation. These fears are unconscious and can be triggered by threatening external events such as death in the family, illness, catastrophe, or major life change. Given this understanding of the disorder, the treatment of choice would be an uncovering therapy utilizing the transference relationship, making interpretations, and developing insight on the part of the client into the unconscious determinants of the anxiety.

In contrast to the uncovering model of psychodynamic therapy, behavioral and cognitive therapies tend toward a coping skills model in treating this disorder. That is, instead of examining the unconscious, these therapies attempt to deal solely with the symptoms of the disorder. Clients are thus taught specific skills to combat and eliminate, or greatly minimize, the anxiety symptoms.

The most sophisticated cognitive-behavioral approaches have moved beyond utilizing only one technique to deal with the complexity inherent in generalized anxiety disorder. Instead they incorporate a wide variety of cognitive and behavioral techniques within one treatment plan. An example of this is Richardson's (1976) anxiety management training. This is a treatment strategy designed for groups. The members engage in the following activities: 1) an initial discussion of common sources of stress and the nature and symptoms of anxiety and fear; 2) completion (at home) of a fear- and social-anxiety inventory; 3) keeping a diary of stressful situations, successes and failures in coping with them; 4) training in deep muscle relaxation; 5) identification and discussion of irrational beliefs and self-statements causing anxiety; 6) development of more rational, calming beliefs coupled with adaptive self-talk; 7) a session to self-induce anxiety followed by relaxation or competency scenes; 8) imagination rehearsal of coping with stressful situations; 9) homework assignments to try out some new behavior during the week.

Another approach that has been found to be effective is supportive therapy. This modality utilizes reassurance, persuasion, and inspiration on the part of the therapist. Unlike psychodynamic therapy it attempts to rebuild shattered defenses or erect new ones rather than working through existing ones. It involves active guidance and direction on the part of the therapist and explicitly attempts to use the relationship to help heal the client. An attempt may be made to alleviate guilt and fear via reassurance or through therapist-imposed prohibitions and restrictions (Wolberg, 1977).

Occasions may arise in which the client's anxiety inhibits his concentration, verbalizing, or ability to follow even simple directions to such an extent that therapy of any kind is not feasible. In those instances it may be helpful for the client to take antianxiety medication (minor tranquilizers) until the anxiety has decreased to a level that will allow therapy to be beneficial.

A number of medications, including Tranxene, Librium, and Dalmane, have been found to be effective in temporarily reducing anxiety. However, caution should be exercised when utilizing these drugs because, as Marks (1982) points out, the effects tend to wear off a few hours after the medicine is discontinued, and addiction is a very real possibility with prolonged use. Antianxiety medications provide only temporary relief and thus should always be considered adjunctive to some other method of treating the anxiety.

References

Marks, I. M. Anxiety disorders. In J. Griest, J. Jefferson, & R. Spitzer (Eds.), *Treatment of mental disorders*. New York: Oxford University Press, 1982.

Richardson, F. C. Anxiety management training. In A. Lazarus (Ed.), *Multi-modal behavior therapy*. New York: Springer Publishing, 1976.

Wolberg, L. R. *The technique of psychotherapy* (3rd ed.). New York: Grune & Stratton, 1977.

Additional Readings

Marks, I. M. *Living with fear: Understanding and coping with anxiety*. New York: McGraw-Hill, 1978.

Meichenbaum, D., & Turk, D. The cognitive-behavioral management of anxiety, anger, and pain. In P. Davidson (Ed.), *The behavioral management of anxiety, depression, and pain*. New York: Brunner/Mazel, 1976.

W. G. BIXLER

General Paresis. The brain syndrome associated with syphilitic meningoencephalitis, a disorder produced by progressive degeneration of brain tissue. Clinically general paresis is a comprehensive, but variable, syndrome characterized by a variety of neurological and mental disturbances that increase in severity, leading to eventual death when left untreated. Prior to 1920, about 8 to 10% of the patients committed to public hospitals in the United States were suffering from general paresis (Kolb & Brodie, 1982). In contrast, today less than 1% of all first-time admissions are due to this syndrome. Paresis occurs four times more frequently in men than in women, although the probable ratio of initial infection is thought to be about 2 to 1. The reasons for this gender-related difference in susceptibility are unknown.

The microorganism involved in general paresis is one of the few that can penetrate the bloodbrain barrier with relative ease. The actual infection is transmitted during sexual contact. The basic pathology of paresis involves two components—inflamation and eventual degeneration. The process of progressive degeneration typically begins in the frontal region and usually spreads to other areas, such as the cortex and cerebellum. Although it is not known whether the destruction of brain tissue is due to the action of the spirochetes or their toxic products, the damage can be quite widespread and severe. Following initial infection general paresis develops after an incubation period of 5 to 30 or more years. In about half the cases the incubation period is from 10 to 20 years, with an additional 25% of cases involving less than a 10-year incubation period and the remaining cases incubating for more than 20 years. The peak curve of incidence occurs between the ages of 35 and 45 (Kolb & Brodie, 1982).

The personality changes associated with general paresis are typically the first identifiable signs of the illness. Unfortunately, these initially involve only an exaggeration of previously existing personality traits, so they are quite insidious and hard to identify. They may involve irritability, difficulty in concentration, depression, periods of confusion, impairment in judgment, and impulsivity. In more advanced stages psychoticlike symptoms may appear, such as delusional thinking and grandiose and expansive behavior (Buss, 1966). The eventual dementia may be characterized by impairment in memory, logical reasoning, and learning. Physical symptoms often include fatigue, drowsiness, headaches, body aches, various somatic complaints, and general lethargy. Disturbances in eye movement or reflexes often occur, as well as retinitis or ocular atrophy. A progressive weakness and incoordination of voluntary muscles typically result from advanced stages of the syndrome. Enunciation, facial movements, and handwriting may also evidence deterioration. Three quarters of all cases suffer from convulsions at some time.

Diagnosis is done primarily through the use of clinical analysis of spinal fluid, using the Wassermann test and the colloidal gold test (Kolb & Brodie, 1982). Although early identification of suspected cases may result from the slow, pervasive degeneration which is brought to the attention of mental health professionals or physicians, the ultimate diagnosis will almost certainly be based on the results of these serologic tests. Because of the constellation of certain symptoms, a diagnosis of general paresis may include a reference to the particular associated mood, affect, and behavior, leading to the identification of four subtypes: simple, expansive, depressed, and circular.

Penicillin is the treatment of choice for syphilitic meningoencephalitis. In the absence of treatment death usually occurs from 2 to 5 years after the onset of identifiable symptoms. The prognosis in treated patients depends on the promptness and thoroughness of treatment. If proper treatment is begun before symptoms appear, in 85% of the cases further deterioration is arrested. If treatment is begun during the early stages of identifiable symptoms, improvement or stabilization occurs in about 60% of the cases. When considering all hospitalized cases, the number actually recovering is less than 30%, the death rate is 20 to 30%, and further deterioration is arrested in only 30 to 50%.

The drop in incidence, due to marked improvements in early identification and treatment, makes it unlikely that the typical clinician will be confronted with a case of general paresis. If such a client does appear for outpatient psychotherapy or counseling, a focus on providing a supportive, structuring treatment that enlists all available environmental resources will likely be the most helpful, in conjunction with penicillin treatment managed by a physician.

References
Buss, A. H. *Psychopathology*. New York: Wiley, 1966.
Kolb, L. C., & Brodie, H. K. *Modern clinical psychiatry*, (10th ed.). Philadelphia: Saunders, 1982.

J. D. Guy, Jr.

Genetic and Biochemical Factors in Psychopathology. In the last 25 years several chemical compounds have been developed that are very useful in the treatment of psychiatric disorders. These have dramatically changed the treatment of psychiatric patients and have stimulated an intensive search for biochemical abnormalities which might explain these disorders. The results have helped to identify some of the possible underlying biochemical mechanisms and have provided a rationale for several current therapeutic approaches.

Most of the research has concentrated on schizophrenia and affective disorders, since these are serious problems. Several organic brain syndromes, such as Alzheimer's, Huntington's, and Parkinson's diseases, which are accompained by fairly specific mental disturbances, have also been studied. In addition, epidemiological and genetic studies have enabled researchers to study the frequency with which particular illnesses occur, to identify high-risk groups, and to discover the links between genetic and environmental factors in the etiology of these diseases.

Schizophrenia. This disorder, whose cause is still unknown, is characterized by disturbed thinking, disorted perception, altered mood, and peculiar behavior. Schizophrenics may have paranoid delusions in which external powers or people are plotting against them, or they may believe that they possess extraordinary powers or have a mission to fulfill. They may experience auditory or, less frequently, sensory or visual hallucinations, and their moods and actions are often entirely inappropriate for the situation they are in. All of these factors interfere with the schizophrenic's ability to function normally at work, in a family, or in social situations.

Schizophrenia is a common problem, occurring in 1% of the population. Because it is also practically incurable, schizophrenics occupy about one-fourth of all hospital beds in the United States. Epidemiological studies indicate that genetic factors are involved in the etiology of the disease, but they do not show a simple and unequivocal inheritance pattern. Schizophrenia occurs more frequently among relatives of schizophrenics than it does in the general population and more frequently in close relatives than in more distant ones. For instance, Kessler (1980) found that siblings of schizophrenics whose parents were not affected had a 7% chance of developing schizophrenia. If one parent was also affected, the risk rose to 13% and if both parents were affected, that risk rose to 35 to 46%. This is much higher than the 1% risk in an average population.

Twin studies have commonly been used to study genetic relationships in schizophrenia. In general these studies have shown that identical (monozygotic) twins of schizophrenics are themselves affected 3 to 5 times (14 to 50%) more often than fraternal (dizygotic) twins. Fraternal twins are also affected 4 to 19% of the time.

Other convincing information has been provided by studying the frequency of schizophrenia in adopted children. When children of schizophrenic mothers are reared in foster homes, 10 to 30% develop schizophrenia or schizophrenic type disorders. No cases of schizophrenia were found in the other children in these foster homes whose mothers were normal, but schizophrenic spectrum disorders were detected from 0 to 17% of the time. Children who are related to schizophrenics and who are also raised by foster parents with psychiatric disorders run a greater risk of developing schizophrenia than those with normal foster parents. However, psychiatric disorder in foster parents does not increase the risk of schizophrenia in children from nonschizophrenic mothers (Kessler, 1980).

These data clearly indicate that genetic factors are involved in schizophrenia. The percentages obtained do not support a single trait explanation but are compatible with a polygenic theory. This theory postulates the existence of several pathogenic genes which could make the person inheriting them more susceptible to the development of the disorder. Schizophrenia could be triggered in such individuals by different biological and psychological life stresses associated with their social and economic situations. However, just how these genetic and environmental factors might combine to produce the disease is still unknown. One thing that can be deduced from the genetic relationships is that part of the problem is physiological, most likely due to enzymatic or metabolic abnormalities.

The two major biochemical hypotheses of schizophrenia suggest that the disorder is due to some abnormality in nerve impulse transmission in brain tissue. Brain cells, called neurons, are intricately interconnected by structures called synapses. Nerve impulses travel along the neuron axon and then cause the release of a chemical, called a transmitter substance, into the synapse. Transmitter substances cross the synapse and attach themselves to special structures (receptor sites) on the receiving neuron, thereby stimulating or inhibiting the activity of that neuron. The receptor sites are thought to be shaped like the molecules of transmitter substance and to be activated only when a molecule of the same or similar shape is present. Some substances,

which are very similar chemically to neurotransmitters, can themselves actually stimulate or block these receptor sites. In order for nerve transmission to go smoothly, the very complex chemical events at the synapse must also occur with precision. If neural transmission is garbled or disrupted by biochemical abnormalities or imbalances, or by the presence of exogenous chemicals which interfere with normal synaptic function, perception, thinking, and emotion may also be distorted.

Two very similar neurotransmitters (both referred to as catacholamines) that are currently implicated in schizophrenia are dopamine and norepinephrine. Norepinephrine is actually synthesized from dopamine by the enzyme beta-hydroxylase, and dopamine is synthesized from tyrosine by tyrosine hydroxylase. Since the two transmitters are so similar, research attempting to differentiate between the two types of synaptic activity is fairly difficult. One fact that has aided such research is that synapses utilizing dopamine as a transmitter also contain tyrosine hydroxylase, whereas those utilizing norepinephrine contain both tyrosine and beta-hydroxylase. After these transmitters cross the synapse and stimulate or inhibit the receiving neurons, they are pulled back into the sending neuron (a process known as reuptake) and chemically deactivated.

One current explanation of schizophrenia, the dopamine hypothesis, suggests that symptoms are produced by too much activity at dopaminergic synapses. Support for this hypothesis comes from indirect pharmacological data. For instance, when normal individuals take large or repeated doses of amphetamines, they develop symptoms that are very difficult to distinguish from acute paranoid schizophrenia. Furthermore, when schizophrenics are given amphetamines, their symptoms are exacerbated. Amphetamines increase the activity of dopaminergic synapses in two ways: by increasing the amount of dopamine released after a nerve impulse and by inhibiting reuptake.

Another line of evidence comes from the effects of drugs which alleviate the symptoms of schizophrenia. Chlorpromazine and other phenothiazines can selectively reverse the psychotic symptoms produced by schizophrenia or by amphetamines (Snyder, 1976). These drugs are also known to block dopaminergic receptor sites, thereby stopping or reducing the flow of information along dopaminergic pathways. Experiments done on animals have shown that phenothiazines do in fact block dopaminergic receptors sites and that the neurons apparently try unsuccessfully to compensate by increasing the amount of dopamine they release into the synapse. As a consequence the levels of dopamine and of its breakdown products in the brain and body fluids increase. The strength of the blockade and consequent increase in dopamine also correlate well with the clinical effectiveness of various antipsychotic drugs.

Another class of drugs that are even more effective against schizophrenic symptoms are the butyrophenone neuroleptics, which include haloperidol. There is evidence that these bind to, and hence reduce activity in, one of the two types of dopamine receptors (type 2). Postmortem studies of three major dopaminergically innervated brain areas (nucleus caudatus, putamen, and nucleus accumbens) have shown that schizophrenics have greater numbers of dopamine type-2 receptors than patients dying with different diseases. So far this is the only significant documented difference between schizophrenic and nonschizophrenic brains (Snyder, 1976; Crow, 1982).

Although there is good evidence for the dopamine hypothesis, there is some discrepant evidence as well. If, for example, the symptoms of schizophrenia are due to overactivity at dopaminergic synapses, then one should expect to find greater concentrations of dopamine, its breakdown products, or of dopamine hydroxylase in the brains or body fluids of schizophrenics than in nonschizophrenics. So far no such differences have been found. Another problem is raised by the fact that these drugs have to be administered for three to four weeks before they begin to have a therapeutic effect, even though some of their physiological effects can be seen soon after they are taken.

Another explanation of schizophrenia, the transmethylation hypothesis, suggests that one or both of the catacholamine neurotransmitters, dopamine or norepinephrine, are abnormally converted (methylated) in the brain to toxic hallucinogenic substances similar to mescaline (Osmond & Smythies, 1952). A mescalinelike substance was discovered which appeared in the urine of schizophrenics but not in that of nonschizophrenics; however, it did not prove to be hallucinogenic. Methionine is a substance which increases methylation in animals and which worsens schizophrenic symptoms in humans. However, methionine probably does not worsen symptoms by increasing methylated catecholamines, since it does not increase the concentrations of these substances in the body fluids of schizophrenics. Another way to test the transmethylation hypothesis is to see if schizophrenic brains have greater concentrations of enzymes which could facilitate methylation than the brains of nonschizophrenics. Unfortunately for the hypothesis, Elliot and Barchas (1979) looked for such differences but could not find them.

One final attempt to explain why dopaminergic systems might be overactive in schizophrenics stems from the discovery that dopaminergic (and other) neurotransmitter systems are controlled, in part, by an inhibitory transmitter called gamma-aminobutyric acid. Perhaps schizophrenics are deficient in this inhibitor and the lack of inhibition causes increased dopaminergic activity. Once again the research fails to support the hypothesis. Studies of concentrations of gamma-aminobutyric acid or of activity levels of glutamic acid decarboxylate (an enzyme that produces gamma-aminobutyric acid) fail to show any differences between schizophrenics and nonschizophrenics (Van Kammen, 1977).

Another group of substances in the body that may be linked to schizophrenia are the endogenous opioid peptides (endorphins or enkephalins). These are the brain's own pain killers, which are similar in structure to morphine. Several investigators have observed increased beta-endorphin levels in schizophrenics, which returned to normal when patients were successfully treated. Hemodialysis, a process of filtering the blood, sometimes improves schizophrenic symptoms. It has been suggested that this process may be removing beta-endorphins. On the other hand, some derivatives of gamma-endorphin have apparently relieved schizophrenic symptoms, especially in acute patients. While some studies link endorphins with schizophrenia, many others do not. Berger and Barchas (1981) suggest that the evidence more strongly implicates endorphins in depression than in schizophrenia. It is probably too early to tell whether or not endorphins play an important role in schizophrenia because research has only been going on for the last seven years and the physiological significance of these substances is, at present, not clearly understood.

Affective Disorders: Depression and Mania. We have all experienced feelings of sadness, grief, discouragement, disappointment, or loneliness during difficult or stressful moments. In primary depressive disorder these emotions are more profound and enduring. Patients may experience piercing attacks of guilt, worthlessness, fear, and anxiety. They often feel hopeless, suicidal, and unmotivated to maintain relationships or to continue to work. Their thinking is often distorted and unrealistic. Patients characteristically speak and move slowly and lethargically and may suffer somatic disorders such as weakness, loss of appetite and weight, disturbed sleep, pain, feelings of tightness in the chest, constipation, etc.

There are two major forms of affective disorder: unipolar, characterized by recurring bouts of depression, and bipolar, in which depression alternates with mania. (Bipolar disorder is less frequent, occurring in approximately one-fifth of the cases.) During a manic phase depression gives way to an excited, even jovial mood, in which the patient may feel clever, efficient, carefree, or overconfident, and lethargy gives way to boundless energy, excited movement, and restlessness. Manic patients generate ambitious ideas and projects but abandon them quickly as other possibilities divert their attention.

Depression is very common. It is estimated that up to 15% of the population has had at least one depressive episode. Twin and family studies suggest that depression has a genetic component and that this component may be passed along on the X chromosome. It is commonly observed that depression occurs more often in women than in men, that it is often associated with color blindness (another sex-linked trait), and that it also occurs frequently in persons with the red blood cell antigen Xga, which is carried on the short arm of the X chromosome.

Twin studies indicate that 50 to 100% of the monozygotic twins and nearly 40% of the dizygotic twins of depressives have experienced depression, and family studies indicate that relatives of depressives are more likely to become depressed than those whose families do not include a depressive. Data from these studies do support a genetic hypothesis, but they are not totally compatible with the hypothesis that depression is passed on the X chromosome because there are several cases of sons inheriting the problem from fathers. These results suggest that there is more than one genetic mechanism for transmitting depression, which fits well with the fact that there are at least two types of depression. This conclusion is further supported by twin studies in which 81% of the twins who develop affective disorder develop the same type (Berger & Barchas, 1981; Angst, 1974).

Research into the biochemical mechanisms in depression has been influenced heavily by the biogenic amine theory, which proposes that depression is related to underactivity at monoamine synapses (dopamine, norepinephrine, and serotonin) in the central nervous system. The theory originated with the observation that reserpine, an alkaloid from the plant *Rauwolfia serpentinia*, causes sedation and motor retardation in experimental animals and also caused depression in some patients who took it for hypertension. Reserpine depletes monoamine stores in both the central and peripheral nervous system.

If depression is related to underactivity at monoamine synapses, depressives should not have as much of the breakdown products of these transmitters in their bodies or their urine as nondepressives. Unfortunately, however, studies of these breakdown products have not revealed many clear differences in depressed patients. One substance, 3-methoxy-4-hydroxyphenyl-glycol (MHPG), a breakdown product of norepinephrine which is thought to be produced primarily in the brain, is substantially lower than normal in patients with bipolar depression (but not in primary depressives). There are many other factors besides depression that can effect the levels of monoamines, their derivatives, and MHPG (such as life style, diet, exercise, circadian rhythms, and disease), which means that the MHPG results should be interpreted cautiously. Despite these reservations MHPG excretion levels to help to rationalize current treatments and they do predict the outcome of tricyclic antidepressant therapy. For instance, patients with low excretion levels of MHPG respond better to imipramine, while those with normal or high levels respond better to amitriptyline. These drugs apparently increase activity at monoamine synapses by inhibiting the breakdown of the transmitter and by delaying reuptake.

Other effective antidepressive drugs seem to increase the availability of the monoamines by inhibiting the activity of the enzyme monoamine oxidase, which normally breaks down these transmitters after they have been used and retrieved from the synapse (Leonard, 1982). One thing that seems rather puzzling about these effects is the one- to three-week time lag that intervenes between the initiation of treatment and clinical improvement.

One explanation of this time lag is that it is not the immediate increase in transmitter availability that is responsible for the improvement in depression but rather the long-term effects that are produced at the synapse. One hypothesis is that a long-term deficit at adrenergic synapses (norepinephrine or epinephrine) stimulates the synapse to try to compensate by increasing the number of receptor sites available, and the increased number of receptors increases the overall sensitivity of the synapse. When antidepressive drugs are taken, they increase the amount of transmitter available to the synapse, and it eventually responds by decreasing the number of sites and the sensitivity. According to this hypothesis, oversensitivity at adrenergic synapses is somehow responsible for depression, and when this can be decreased the depression improves.

There is evidence to support the sensitivity hypothesis. For instance, it has been demonstrated that the number of adrenergic receptors in blood platelets in depressed untreated patients is much higher than in a control group of undepressed patients (Berger & Barchas, 1981; Leonard, 1982). It has also been demonstrated that all antidepressants, regardless of their chemical structure, have the ability to decrease the number of adrenergic binding sites in the brains of experimental animals and in blood platelets and leukocytes of normal and depressed people. This decrease is observed after several days of treatment and is compatible with the time course of antidepressant therapy. Electroconvulsive shock therapy may also produce some of its benefits by its effects at the synapse, since it is known to increase the release and turnover of dopamine and norepinephrine in animal brains.

There are some findings that do not fit either of these two theories very neatly—e.g., the existence of effective antidepressants, such as iprimidole, which do not seem to alter monoamine metabolism. Likewise, lithium, an effective treatment for mania, does not affect catacholamine transmission. There is evidence that other transmitters such as gamma-aminobutyric acid (GABA), acetylcholine, or endorphin, or hormones such as cortisol or growth hormones may also be involved. On the whole, however, the present information probably best supports the hypothesis that depression is primarily associated with a deficit at noradrenergic (norepinephrine) synapses.

Alzheimer's Disease. Alzheimer's is a degenerative brain disease which results in senile dementia and appears most frequently between the ages of 40 and 50 (presenile dementia). Alzheimer's characteristically progresses from the loss of memory and disorientation to speech impairment, confusion, and finally the inability to manage even the simplest everyday activities. These symptoms are accompanied by anxiety, irritability, agitation, petulance, and inability to concentrate. Deterioration is

progressive and irreversible, leading to the final stages of severe dementia within a period of 1 to 10 years. The disease reduces remaining life expectancy by 50%. Victims usually die of secondary complications such as pneumonia or circulatory insufficiency.

The incidence of Alzheimer's disease is about 2 to 3% among individuals who are 65 or older but is much higher (7 to 10%) among children or siblings of its victims. Interestingly, the incidence of Down's syndrome is 10 times more likely in families with early onset of the disease than in the general population. The evidence does suggest that genetic factors are important. Other data suggest that virus(es) or immunological factors may also be involved. One such hypothesis came from experiments on animals showing that injections of aluminum salts produced brain lesions similar to those found in Alzheimer's disease. Studies of brain areas most severely damaged by Alzheimer's have found aluminum concentrations that were several times higher than those found in age-matched controls. Part of this aluminum was specifically bound to DNA, a condition that differentiates Alzheimer's dementia from aluminum encephalopathy associated with long-term hemodialysis therapy (Marchbanks, 1982; NIH, 1980).

A number of pathological changes can be seen in the brains of Alzheimer's victims. Neurofibrillary tangles, which consist of densely packed neurofilaments, appear in the cerebral cortex and in the hippocampus, and neuritic plaques replace degenerating brain cells. The most characteristic feature is the appearance of granulovacuolar changes in the pyramidal cells of the hippocampus. Another puzzling change in the hippocampus, a brain area that is crucial to memory formation, is the appearance of Hirano bodies, structures thought to contain inactive ribosomes. Normally ribosomes translate RNA into proteins, a process that may be important in the storage of memory (NIH, 1980).

The fact that Alzheimer's disease has a well-defined biochemical base encourages researchers to believe that someday they can find an effective treatment for it. The main biochemical discovery is that there is a marked decrease in the activity of the enzyme choline acetyltransferase, which normally synthesizes the neurotransmitter acetylcholine. This decrease is found in the cerebral and hippocampal cortex in tissues that show other pathological changes. The enzyme activity in these areas may be reduced by 50 to 90% with the largest decreases in the hippocampus. These percentages are probably also a good estimate of the proportion of cholinergic neurons that have been destroyed. Incidentally, all of the authors who have reported on this type of research have found the same large loss in acetyltransferase activity, dramatic confirmation that the cholinergic neurons that are vital in memory formation are destroyed in Alzheimer's disease (Marchbanks, 1982).

The noradrenergic neurotransmitter system, among others, is also affected by Alzheimer's disease, although to a lesser degree. The activity of dopamine beta-hydroxylase, the enzyme which synthesizes norepinephrin from dopamine, is decreased by 50 to 70% in the same areas of the brain which lose cholinergic function. On the other hand, neither dopamine nor serotonin levels nor their associated enzymes are affected. In spite of a clear understanding of biochemical problems in Alzheimer's disease there is still no effective treatment. Substances which increase activity at synapses utilizing acetylcholine produce some improvement in mental functioning; however, they also have serious side effects and do not halt the progress of the illness (Winbladt, Adolfsson, Carlsson, & Gottfries, 1982).

Other Central Nervous System Diseases. Endogenous panic disorder is characterized by anxiety and phobia which lead to panic attacks. It can be successfully treated with tricyclic antidepressants or with monoamine oxidase inhibitors, clearly implicating one or more of the monoamine neurotransmitters in its etiology.

There are other brain disorders, involving different neurotransmitters, in which mental disturbances are secondary to other bodily impairments. One of these is Parkinson's disease, which starts between the ages of 50 and 60 with tremors in the fingers and hands and progresses to limb stiffness, slowing motor activity, and a decreasing ability to use facial gestures or speech. In this disease dopaminergic neurons in the nigro-striatal area of the brain are destroyed, resulting in a deficiency of dopamine in that area. The deficiency can be treated by giving the patient L-dihydroxyphenylalanine (L-Dopa), the substance from which dopamine is normally produced.

Huntington's chorea is a neurological disorder, transmitted on an autosomal dominant gene, which begins between the ages of 30 and 50. Affected individuals experience progressive involuntary choreiform movements and dementia. This disorder seems to be caused by an imbalance between various neurotransmitter systems in the neostriatum of the brain. There

is apparently a marked loss of function in neurons utilizing GABA or acetylcholine as transmitters, but there are no changes in neurons utilizing dopamine, serotonin, or glutamic acid. The damage seems to be confined to a very small area of the brain and to specific transmitters in that area. In spite of the well-defined biochemical abnormalities in this disease, attempts to treat the disturbance with substances which should help restore synaptic function have been unsuccessful.

References

Angst, J. Genetic aspects of depression. In N. S. Kline (Ed.), *Factors in depression.* New York: Raven Press, 1974.

Berger, P. A., & Barchas, J. D. Biochemical hypothesis of mental disorders. In G. J. Siegel, R. W. Albers, B. W. Agranoff, & R. Katzman (Eds.), *Basic neurochemistry* (3rd ed.). Boston: Little, Brown, 1981.

Crow, T. J. The biology of schizophrenia. *Experientia*, 1982, *38*(12), 1275–1282.

Elliot, G. R., & Barchas, J. D. The transmethylation hypothesis of schizophrenia: Current status and future prospects. In E. Usdin, R. T. Borchardt, & C. R. Creveling (Eds.), *Transmethylation.* New York: Elsevier North-Holland, 1979.

Kessler, S. The genetics of schizophrenia: A review. *Schizophrenia Bulletin*, 1980, *6*(3), 404–416.

Leonard, B. E. Current status of the biogenic amine theory of depression. *Neurochemistry International*, 1982, *4*(5), 339–350.

Marchbanks, R. M. Biochemistry of Alzheimer's dementia. *Journal of Neurochemistry*, 1982, *39*(1), 9–15.

National Institutes of Health. *Alzheimer's disease: A scientific guide for health practitioners.* Bethesda, Md.: Author, 1980. (NIH Publication No. 81–2251)

Osmond, H. & Smythies, J. Schizophrenia: A new approach. *Journal of Mental Science*, 1952, *98*(2), 308–315.

Snyder, S. H. The dopamine hypothesis in schizophrenia: Focus on the dopamine receptor. *American Journal of Psychiatry*, 1976, *133*(2), 197–202.

Van Kammen, D. P. Aminobutyric acid (GABA) and the dopamine hypothesis of schizophrenia. *American Journal of Psychiatry*, 1977, *134*(2), 138–143.

Winbladt, B., Adolfsson, R., Carlsson, A., & Gottfries, C. G. Biogenic amines in brains of patients with Alzheimer's disease. In S. Corkin, K. L. Davis, J. R. Growdon, E. Usdin, & R. J. Wurtman (Eds.), *Aging* (Vol. 19). New York: Raven Press, 1982.

A. SZUTOWICZ and R D. KOBES

Genetic Factors in Personality. See HEREDITY AND ENVIRONMENT IN HUMAN DEVELOPMENT.

Genius. Historically the term *genius* has denoted individuals who possess exceptionally high levels of intellectual or creative ability, often manifested in new approaches to longstanding problems in science, art, philosophy, and other fields. Although the concept has a long history, only within the last hundred years or so have ideas and opinions regarding genius, its identification, and speculations about how it occurs been subjected to empirical study.

The modern phase of empirical study has radically altered or replaced several features of the earlier concept of genius. One assumption was that genius is an intrinsic quality or trait that an individual possesses which is relatively unaffected by education or nurture. A second assumption was that genius has a disruptive influence on society much like that associated with insanity. Common to both of these assumptions was the notion that the appearance of a genius is more or less inexplicable and unpredictable. During the Middle Ages this notion was even associated with the belief that the genius was possessed by supernatural agencies.

An important impetus to the modern study of genius was the work of Galton, who pioneered in the field of mental measurement by elaborating on the assumption that mental traits, like physical traits, could be measured. Through the work of Binet and Terman in developing practical measures of intelligence, genius came to be understood in terms of measurable intellectual abilities. These abilities, in combination with particular personality traits (e.g., drive or persistence), led to real-life achievements and recognition. Speculative opinions about the nature of genius gave way to studies of exceptional, or gifted, children and adults, and the term genius was often restricted to anchoring the extreme end of the IQ scale. Terman's longitudinal studies of a large group of intellectually gifted children demonstrated that exceptional abilities can be fruitfully studied and measured, and that they continue to be manifested in individual achievements across the life span.

Another influence on the study of genius came from intensive investigations of the biographies and current psychological functioning of living individuals who have made outstanding and creative achievements in their respective fields. These studies generally showed that the emergence of those who will become eminent contributors can be illuminated, if not precisely predicted, by obtaining a knowledge of both their intellectual abilities and the dynamics of their development. For example, Roe (1961) found that eminent scientists were characterized by high intelligence as traditionally measured, but also by a confluence of personal and family circumstances which fostered hard work, achievement, and independence. Studies of this type have revealed the importance of early development, which can foster the thinking styles, commitment, and social adjustments required, along with high ability, for significant achievement in various fields. Another factor frequently identified is the availability of role models in a field that is congruent with these abilities and dispositions.

The study of genius has generally proceeded away from the assumption that intrinsic and unpredictable characteristics can account for the achievements that have brought recognition to these individuals. This assumption is unfruitful because it merely labels the phenomenon and then invokes the label as an explanation, begging the question of how and under what circumstances exceptional achievement occurs. Greatest progress toward understanding genius seems to come from a focus on the study of eminent individuals.

Defining genius in terms of eminence, or influence upon a field, capitalizes on the fact that there has always been remarkable consensus as to which persons can be called geniuses. This approach has given rise to a program of research whereby the conditions for the occurrence of genius are better understood. It also has the important consequence that the genius must be viewed not merely as an unusual individual, but as one who has achieved widespread influence on those whose recognition counts toward success in his or her field. Productivity within a field proves to be a key to genius, seen as eminence, since eminent contributors are almost invariably individuals who entered their fields early in life and were prolific in their contributions over a long span of time. There is evidence that productivity is a cause and not merely a consequence of genius as intrinsic ability. Again, the genius must have high abilities, but must also demonstrate extraordinary persistence in order to stay productive, overcome barriers to acceptance of his or her ideas, and eventually win status and recognition.

Ever since Galton's work it has been known that geniuses often appear in the same family. However, the notion that genius is an inherited trait has generally been discredited. The Christian's acknowledgment of a sovereign Creator does not require that an individual's gifts and talents be either inherited or bestowed suddenly. On the contrary, God's sovereignty is shown through his supervision of the family and other environmental circumstances which contribute to exceptional talent. The Christian's response in making these talents available for God's purposes is, in part, an acknowledgment that God was intimately involved in their formation.

Reference
Roe, A. The psychology of the scientist. *Science*, 1961, *134*, 456–459.

See Intelligence; Intellectual Assessment.
D. R. Ridley

Genogram. *See* Family Diagram.

Geriatric Psychotherapy. The care and treatment of problems associated with later life. Psychopathologies such as reactive depression and organic brain syndrome (delirium and dementia) can occur at any time, but are especially prevalent in persons in the last third of the life cycle. A mental health professional specializing in geriatrics has expertise in dealing with dementia and depression, or the biopsychosocial crises commonly encountered in later life (e.g., retirement, widowhood, declining health).

Many psychologists and psychiatrists have negative attitudes toward working with the older client, often preferring not to work in the field of geriatrics. They are generally of the opinion that the prognosis, especially for depression, is less favorable with the aged client. They often view the geriatric patient as "set in his ways" and "unable to change." These prejudicial views are not substantiated by the data. Elder clients tend to be more reliable when it comes to keeping appointments and following homework instructions. Most of them have had a lifetime of successful coping experiences and just need a little professional assistance to help them cope with the special stresses of later life. It is difficult to measure cure rates in psychotherapy, but there is some indication that successful outcome is positively correlated with age. Furthermore, both the length of psychiatric hospitalization and the readmission rate is lower for older patients.

The great American pioneer in geriatric psychotherapy was Lillien J. Martin, a retired university professor. In 1929 she founded the San Francisco Old Age Counseling Center. For the next 15 years she developed her own techniques. The Martin method involved a series of five or six structured interviews emphasizing a directive approach of specific suggestions and motivating slogans. The counselor examined the client's daily routine and goals during the sessions and then worked behind the scenes to help the client find housing, employment, social services, and interpersonal networks. Although the Martin clinic appeared to be successful, her influence in geriatrics never extended to the mainstream of social work or psychotherapy. However, both her basic strategy and many specific techniques have been rediscovered by other psychotherapists.

General Treatment Approach. The psychoanalytic movement has not been very interested or optimistic about geriatric psychotherapy. Freud did not have clinical experience in the field, but believed that persons over 40 were simply too rigid to profit from psychoanalysis. Several of Freud's followers who took on older clients agreed that classical psychoanalytic treatment seemed inappropriate. However, instead of declaring the patient to be beyond help, they decided to modify the psychotherapeutic techniques: eliminating the sofa, making the therapist more active and directive, limiting the goals to specific problems, focusing on the present, and providing flexible scheduling (Rechtschaffen, 1959). Such modified therapy was quite effective.

In order to comprehend the strategy of geriatric psychotherapy, it is necessary to abandon much of classical psychoanalytical and person-centered approaches. The goal in working with older clients is not to facilitate the creation of a growing personality or to resolve a 70-year-old oedipus complex. The starting assumption is that the client's underlying personality is healthy and that the purpose of intervention is to help overcome the particular stressful life events that have temporarily exceeded the client's coping capacities. The therapist will be able to uncover many behaviors which border on the pathological and many long-standing intrapsychic conflicts. The wise geriatric psychotherapist exercises a great deal of restraint and avoids intervention in most of these areas, concentrating the therapeutic efforts on those specific points where the client's responses to the present environment are ineffective and painful.

While most counseling with the aged centers on highly selective intervention geared to concrete problem solving in a brief time frame, a minority of the patients have highly dependent personalities and will require a long-term, supportive therapeutic relationship. Having a confidant is a key to maintaining mental health in later life. Usually the confidant is a friend or grown child (particularly a daughter) to whom the elder can debrief daily routine and receive some degree of empathy. All elders can benefit from such a relationship, and most are able to sustain one on their own. Some individuals have an extreme need for a confidant and yet have difficulty in getting one. With passive-dependent individuals the resources for short-term problem solving may be lacking, and what the patient really needs is someone to lean on in a long-term relationship. Some therapists fit this role well, but they are not necessarily the same therapists who motivate elders to solve their own problems.

Whether the thrust of the therapy is supportive or problem solving, a team approach is essential in geriatrics. The cause of the elder's mental health problems are physical, social, and economic, and the therapist cannot ignore these fronts. Yet face-to-face discussion by itself will do little to improve these aspects. There are numerous resources for elders in the United States—specialized physicians, dentists, opticians, physical therapists, pharmacists, nutritionists, and lawyers. A therapist who is able to put the client in touch with such resources can effect much more in problem solving and emotional support. A therapist who is part of a team of multidisciplinary services can work within a coordinated approach to providing the elder with what is needed.

Transference and Countertransference. Transference is part of the dynamics of every psychotherapeutic relationship. The maintenance of a problem-solving orientation diminishes the prospects for deep transference dynamics, while long-term supportive relationships encourage transference. It is difficult to predict what kind of transference will arise in psychotherapy with an elder. The patient might unconsciously relate to the therapist as if the latter were a parent, child, spouse, or peer. Countertransference, with the therapist unconsciously relating to the client as if the latter were a parent or grandparent, can be countertherapeutic if it leads the therapist to falsely ascribe characteristics to the client. While transference issues can be largely ignored unless a major problem arises, therapists must continuously monitor their own countertransference patterns with each new client.

One of the best ways to avoid problems with either transference or countertransference is the therapist's maintenance of an aura of authority. Most elders are not used to dealing with a counselor whom they address by the first name. The counseling paradigms with which they are most familiar and most comfortable are the physician and clergy, who come into the relationship with a special title (doctor or reverend), special knowledge (medical or spiritual), and special authority (Aesculapian or sacerdotal). All geriatric psychotherapists should strive to maintain the image of authority bestowed by their profession, but physicians and clergy will find it somewhat easier.

There is yet another reason why physicians and clergy might be the best therapists for aged clients. Elders lack the psychological sophistication of the younger generation. Many older people conceive of their mental and emotional problems in spiritual or medical terms, and seek out the family physician, rabbi, priest, or minister. Many elders hold nineteenth-century views on mental health and believe that only insane people would need a psychologist or psychiatrist.

Techniques and Strategies. The first session of therapy should involve the establishment of the therapist's authority combined with a mutual respect for the client's dignity. The client as well as the therapist should be addressed by an appropriate title (Mrs., Deacon, Colonel, etc.) unless the client indicates a preference for informality. The therapist should exercise authority by controlling the time of the session, asking specific questions (about both background and the present situation), and interrupting, politely yet firmly, when the elder strays too far from the topic under discussion. Above all, the therapist must not let the client wallow in self-recriminations or negativisms. The first session should include an opportunity for both parties to express their expectations for counseling, enunciating specific goals and commitments, if possible.

Elders tend to be more rigid than other age groups, and this may result in resistance to the therapist. This is less likely to occur if the therapist maintains an authority position. When resistance does occur, it must be respected. Admit that the patient has a strong will and praise it as a positive force, "strength of character." Concede that there is nothing in all your professional training that is strong enough to counter the client's will. This can increase the elder's self-esteem and preserve the strong will for later use as a motivator.

The content of the sessions should generally focus on current problems and realistic solutions. Homework assignments are especially appropriate for doing this. Certain distressing symptoms might be removed by direct suggestion, hypnosis, or behavior modification. Dysfunctional thought patterns can be challenged directly from the therapist's authority position. For example, guilt complexes are not common among the elderly, but when they occur they can be quite severe. Absolution by a sacerdotal figure can do more for the elimination of a guilt complex than hours of attempting to reason it away.

One popular technique in geriatric psychotherapy is the use of a life review. Cataloging and reliving the past is useful if it serves the function of convincing the client that "I have been through some pretty tough times before, and although the present looks bad, I am tough and resilient enough to see it through." If the patient uses the life review as an escape from the present, it will not achieve the goals of therapy. If the client's past is a series of failures and pain, the life review could intensify depression.

Dreamwork is another possible technique. Even though the aged dream less and are less likely to recall their dreams, they can be motivated to bring them to the therapist. Patients with distressing dreams need to be calmed by an authoritative explanation of the mechanisms and symbols of dreams. Some clients will hanker after insight, but this is less common among the aged, especially the demented or depressed. Dreams can also be used as monitors and rehearsals for coping, and can be combined with a psychodrama in which the client reenacts the dream and changes the ending by substituting more effective behavior (Brink, 1977).

Group therapy offers many potentials in geriatrics, primarily in the area of supportive networks. The only geriatric patients who do not respond well to groups are those with a communication disorder (the deaf or aphasic) and overtly hostile persons. Free-flowing groups left to their own internal dynamics may not succeed with this age group. Clear-cut leadership, structure, and language should be provided by an authority figure.

Suicidal comments and symptoms can never be ignored. When an elder is depressed, it may be wise to directly initiate discussion on the topic of suicide. A nonjudgmental, empathic reaction from the therapist is important, together with an expression of confidence in the outcome of therapy. Many elders believe that suicide is wrong. They do not want to kill themselves, but they find themselves caught up in racing thoughts of pessimism and self-destruction. Helping the patient learn ways of monitoring and stopping racing thoughts is extremely important. Prayer is one of the best ways of doing this. If the risk of suicide becomes high, institutionalization may be necessary. One of the best ways to assess a real suicidal risk is the elder's refusal to promise not to kill himself before the next scheduled therapy session.

Scheduling must be flexible with elder patients. In general, one or two sessions a week for a month or two should be sufficient. Most of the sessions should be brief, under an hour, and become shorter and more infrequent as they become progress reports. Rather than a firm, abrupt termination, the sessions should be phased out as the client regains the capacity to self-direct coping operations. The therapist informs the client that the counseling relationship can be reinitiated at any point in the future, should the client feel it necessary.

The families of elders can become involved in therapy in either of two ways. One is conjoint therapy for the elder and significant family members—spouse, adult children, etc. The entire family must adjust to the elder's physical and mental changes, and the elder's psychological task is to cope with the changing family system. The other way to involve families in therapy is to form a group for the families of dependent aged. Many of them can benefit by the discussion of alternatives with other families in the same situation. An additional benefit is the emotional support and empathy provided by the group.

References

Brink, T. L. Dream therapy with the aged. *Psychotherapy: Theory, research, practice,* 1977, *14,* 354–360.

Rechtschaffen, A. *Psychotherapy with geriatric patients: A review of the literature. Journal of Gerontology,* 1959, *14,* 73–84.

Additional Readings

Brink, T. L. *Geriatric psychotherapy.* New York: Human Sciences Press, 1979.

Brink, T. L. Pastoral care for the aged: A practical guide. *Journal of Pastoral Care,* 1977, *31,* 264–272.

T. L. BRINK

Gerontology. The study of aging, a study which has become a multidisciplinary endeavor. There are biologists, psychologists, sociologists, economists, and political scientists doing research in this field.

There are two basic research designs in gerontological research. Cross-sectional studies compare old people to young people. A cohort is a group of people born in the same time period (e.g., 1890–1900). Cross-sectional research ends up comparing two different cohorts. If cross-sectional research establishes that people over 65 are more religious than people under 40, we do not know if this is due to the fact that people over 65 were from the pre–1915 cohort or whether it is due to a developmental factor in the aging process.

Longitudinal research gets around this problem by studying only one cohort, measuring them as young adults and then again as elders. Longitudinal studies of aging are rare for two reasons. Researchers do not want to wait 40 years for the results, and it is often impossible to locate the original participants in a study 40 years later. Many of the subjects have died, and it is questionable if the survivors are representative of the group. Usually they are healthier and more intelligent, and this can distort the results. So both methods of gerontological research have their drawbacks.

The age of 65 has often been taken as a cutoff point to define old age. The point is arbitrary, and there are some people in their 40s going through several of the problems usually associated with later life, while some in their late 70s have avoided most of the usual crises of aging. Using 65 and over as the definition of old age, the percentage of elders in America has increased from 4% in 1900 to 11% today. By the year 2015 that figure could rise to the 15–20% range.

Two variables are responsible for this growing percentage. One is the lengthening life expectancy, the average age to which a child born today will live. The current life expectancy for white females in America is 70+, with a few years less for males and nonwhites. This figure could be pushed up another 10 years by the conquest of cancer, better control of hypertension, or increased automobile safety. Given the fact that an individual has already made it to age 65, life expectancy is in the 80s. The other factor determining the percentage of elders in the population is the birthrate. In Mexico, a country with a high birthrate, the majority of the population is under 16, and only 3% are over 65.

Biopsychosocial Crises. Each stage of life involves demands for adaptation to physical and social changes. Most of the problems that the aged experience are due to a failure to adapt to these demands. The greatest and most universal problem is physical deterioration. Living longer has not meant living better. Frequently a longer life is merely more years of suffering with chronic disabilites. While old age itself is not a disease, many serious disorders are more common in the aged—strokes, arthritis, deafness, cataracts, and sexual dysfunctions. While constituting only 11% of the population, elders account for a third of the nation's total health bill. Even physical changes that do not constitute medical problems (e.g., wrinkling skin) can have an impact on self-esteem and mental health.

Although elders are closer to death than other age groups, the aged are not generally fearful of it. They worry more about physical suffering or being a burden to others. Many, especially those in poor health or in institutions, look forward to death. A strong fear of death may be taken as a symptom of an underlying neurosis, usually one involving a guilt complex or a sense of failure.

The death of significant others, especially the spouse, is a far more serious threat to mental health. Two-thirds of aged females are widowed. Those who were dependent on the spouse in many key areas often find it very difficult to adjust. Even where the marriage was a stormy one, widowhood can be difficult, due to the loss of a sparring partner or to a nagging sense of guilt. The widows who have the least difficult time after the death of the spouse are those who experienced a great deal of anticipatory grief (e.g., the spouse died from a long and serious disease, making the death an event that was both predictable and a blessing). Otherwise, the first year of widowhood is the most difficult, and the incidence of depressive symptoms, physician visits, and mortality are all higher. Next to time itself, the most helpful aids in coping with grief are bereavement rituals, even if the widow disavows them.

Retirement is a difficult transition for some elders, even those who looked forward to it. After a few weeks of what seems like an extended vacation, life can get boring unless there are absorbing outside interests. A phasing out of one's career is preferable to an abrupt end. Serious difficulties in coping with retirement are most likely when the individual had few interests apart from work, when there are financial problems, or when the wife resents the postretirement frequency of contact.

The statistics on the income of older families is most discouraging. However, most have some savings or other assets, and the liquidation of these assets permits about three-fourths of elders to maintain their previous life style. The greatest stress that financial problems can present is a forced relocation to a less desirable residence.

The greatest fear of most American elders is crime. Some of this fear is an overreaction to the news media's reports of crime, but the poorer elders who have to live in urban areas are easy prey for street criminals. Widows and wealthy elders are prime targets for confidence artists.

"Ageism" refers to any prejudiced or negative stereotypical attitude toward elders. While our society is clearly ageist, there is no evidence that this in and of itself presents a problem for older people. Obviously, if prejudiced views lead to discriminatory behavior against the aged, there is harm. However, the stereotype of the feeble elder helps most aged believe that they are exceptionally spry for their age.

Various socioeconomic developments make aging more difficult today than in previous centuries. The extended family has lost its importance. Industrialization has made the factory and office, rather than the home and farm, the centers of production. Education and the mass media, not old storytellers, are the custodians of culture. It is simply harder for the aged to participate in our society and have a significant productive or interpersonal impact.

Institutionalization is the fate of one million elders in the United States. By age 85 almost 15% live in long-term care facilities. The percentage has increased fivefold in 40 years. Most institutionalized elders are widowed or single and have grave physical problems (e.g., less than half can walk). The majority are seriously confused. Nevertheless, a great many older people end up in institutions for purely socioeconomic reasons. There is no place else to go. The development of alternate levels and forms of care (e.g., day care, home care) can reduce institutionalization.

Mental Changes. Existing psychological theories about aging can be summed up in one word: inadequate. Erikson and Jung had virtually no clinical experience with the older client, yet they presented speculative, highly romanticized pictures of later life which are virtually useless in dealing with some of the more common psychopathologies. Cumming and Henry (1961) developed from survey data the disengagement theory. This theory suggests that the elders who adjust best are those who progressively and gracefully relinquish their roles and withdraw from interaction. Subsequent research has been inconsistent, but slightly more in tune with the opposing theory: that best adjustment occurs when high levels of activity are maintained (Lipman & Smith, 1968).

One theory suggests that psychopathology in later life is an outgrowth of long-term maladjustment and fundamental deficiencies in the personality (Livson & Peterson, 1962). However, there is much data to indicate that mental disorder in later life often occurs in people who were normal adults but who have now experienced a reaction to the stress occasioned by specific biopsychosocial crises. While broad theories about aging have been poorly substantiated, a great deal of survey, experimental, and clinical data exist on several points.

IQ scores decline with age. The difference is slight with longitudinal research, since the more intelligent subjects live longer and are easier to locate for the follow-up study. The difference is pronounced with cross-sectional studies, perhaps indicating some cohort effect. The decline is greater for those subtests involving abstract or creative abilities. Declining IQ could be attributable to many factors: lack of familiarity with test-taking procedures, declining sensory acuity, slower reaction time, depression, lack of intellectual stimulation, or dementia.

Rigidity is a psychological construct which refers to measures of dogmatism, impulse control, cautiousness, and resistance to persuasion. Rigidity correlates positively with age, even when variables such as education, IQ, and social class are controlled. There is also a negative correlation between mental health and rigidity, but clinical experience suggests that rigidity is the result of neurosis rather than its cause. Indeed, rigidity may be the only way the many elders with limited mental resources can cope with crises that would otherwise overwhelm them.

Introversion, a shift of attention away from the external world, has been investigated by projective tests. The data indicate that old people become more introverted. Introversion, like rigidity, may be a defensive response to environmental stress.

Inferiority feeling, rather than guilt, seems to be the major factor eroding self-esteem in later life. In addition to the inferiority feeling generated by physical disabilities and the loss of productive roles, elders must cope with a society that is both youth oriented and moving away from some of the traditions they cherish.

Senility is a popular term describing general mental decline, especially confusion and disorientation. The causes can be organic brain syndromes (*see* DELIRIUM; DEMENTIA) or depression.

Depression has a higher incidence in old age than in any other part of the life cycle. Although biochemical changes can be a predisposing factor, most geriatric depressions are reactions to the stresses of widowhood and physical disability. Many depressed elders do not recognize that they are depressed, and many physicians who examine them fail to diagnose the affective disorder. Untreated depression is the main reason why the geriatric suicide rate is higher than that of any other age group. If discovered and treated, however, geriatric depression is usually reversible.

Schizophrenia, mania, and personality disorders rarely have their onset in later life.

Delusional disorders, such as hypochondriasis and paranoia, are easy to observe but difficult to treat. Geriatric hypochondriasis is not fundamentally different from that observed in younger patients, except that the older hypochondriac probably has some real physical problems along with the imagined ones. Geriatric paranoia is different from the delusions of persecution found in young schizophrenics. Diminishing sensory and memory capacity leads to inability to account for various changes, especially lost objects. The delusion that a neighbor or relative is stealing or exchanging the patient's property is one way to account for these gaps. Many paranoids do a good job of meeting their environmental demands in other ways, so that the disorder is largely a problem only for the people who have to listen to the patient's complaints.

Religion in Later Life. Older people have more traditional religious beliefs, including scriptural literalism and obedience to the commandments. However, the aged are less superstitious than the general population. The percentage of adults who affirm a belief in God rises steadily with age. Elders are more likely to describe themselves as religious, moral, conservative, and fundamentalist.

The aged are the most frequent Bible readers. They more often pray and listen to religious broadcasts. Attendance at religious services is higher for older Roman Catholics, Episcopalians, and Eastern Orthodox Christians, but lower for Protestant and Jewish denominations. Despite a virtual gerontocracy in the Catholic and Mormon churches, there is a tapering off of leadership roles, especially among the laity, with advancing age.

Most measures of adjustment correlate positively with most measures of religion. The happiest elders attend church the most often. Poor adjustment is found in those with low or declining attendance. Geriatric admissions to mental hospitals and psychiatric wards are more frequent for elders with little religious affiliation. Prayer and religious belief seem to be a solace for the problems of later life, especially death and bereavement. The chief exceptions to this trend are in members of fringe sects, where the strength of belief and degree of participation is slightly correlated with neurosis.

There are few studies of the aged who have pursued a religious vocation. Compared to the laity they have the same problems when it comes to physical decline and loss of mental powers. Members of a religious community would have fewer worries about finances, widowhood, or institutionalization. There is also the strong probability of a greater sense of fulfillment in having lived a life of service.

References
Cumming E., & Henry, W. E. *Growing old: The process of disengagement.* New York: Basic Books, 1961.
Lipman, A., & Smith, K. J. Functionality of disengagement in old age. *Journal of Gerontology,* 1968, *23,* 517–521.
Livson, F., & Peterson, P. G. *Aging and personality.* New York: Wiley, 1962.

Additional Readings
Bahr, H. M. Aging and religious disaffiliation. *Social Forces,* 1970, *49,* 59–71.
Brink, T. L. *Geriatric psychotherapy.* New York: Human Sciences Press, 1979.
Gray, R. M., & Moberg, D. O. *The church and the older person.* Grand Rapids: Eerdmans, 1962.
Williamson, J. B., Evans, L., & Munley, A. *Aging and society; An introduction to social gerontology.* New York: Holt, Rinehart & Winston, 1980.

T. L. BRINK

Gesell, Arnold Lucius (1890–1961). Pioneer in child psychology. He was born in Alma, Wisconsin, and spent two years at the University of Wisconsin. He then studied psychology at Clark University, where he received his Ph.D. in 1906. After teaching psychology for several years, he became convinced that medical training was necessary for the proper study of child development. He studied medicine at Yale while teaching there and received his M. D. in 1915.

After receiving his Ph. D. he taught psychology at Los Angeles State Normal School. In 1911 he was appointed professor of education at Yale, where he founded the Yale Clinic of Child Development. He remained director of the clinic until 1948, when he became director of the Gesell Institute of Child Development, continuing the work begun by the Yale clinic. He was active as a research consultant until 1958.

Initially Gesell was concerned with retardation, but came to the conclusion that an understanding of normal infant and child development is necessary for an understanding of abnormality. By 1919 he was studying mainly the development of normal infant mentality, developing methods of observing and measuring behavior. After 1926 the movie camera became his principal tool, and he filmed about 12,000 children of all ages and levels of development through a one-way screen.

The results of his studies are in the form of minute descriptions of the films and other records, comparing the results with findings on other normal subjects. Rather than attempting to formulate a theory of mental development or analyze the factors influencing it, Gesell remained purely descriptive. He concluded that mental development proceeds in a predictable and measurable sequence, although the timing is not identical in all children. He believed that the emerging behavior patterns have as much structure as the growing physical organism, that the behavioral patterns are basically determined by internal forces rather than environmental ones. His emphasis on maturation was not widely accepted in psychology because it was proposed when behaviorism was dominant and psychology was taking an extremely environmentalistic position.

Gesell published over 400 papers and books. His most important books are *The Mental Growth of the Preschool Child* (1925) and *Infancy and Human Growth* (1928). In these he presented his developmental schedules, containing items to evaluate child development during the first five years of life. Later he turned his attention to older children, publishing *The Child from Five to Ten* (1946) and *Youth: The Years from Ten to Sixteen* (1956).

R. L. KOTESKEY

Gestalt Psychology.

The movement that sprang up in Frankfurt and Berlin as a protest against the analysis of consciousness into elements and the exclusion of values from the data of consciousness. It is most closely associated with the founding triumvirate of Wertheimer, Köhler, and Koffka, but is also strongly rooted in the act psychology of the Austrian school. Other roots lie in the phenomenological movement, the holistic psychologies, the revolt against positivism, and the more general tension between the *Naturwissenschaften* and *Geisteswissenschaften*. The Gestalt psychologists sought a system that permitted both understanding and scientific explanation.

The Austrian school contributed to the Gestalt movement both its name and the major problem of perception. The elementism of structuralism and associationism regarded perception as a composite of sensations, and even Wundt's famous experiments in fusion and complication did not resolve the complexity of space and time perception. Ernst Mach first addressed these issues in 1886 by positing "sensations of time-form" and "sensations of space-form," with *form* an experience or sensation independent of quality. Mach's ideas were systematized in 1890 by Christian von Ehrenfels, who spoke of "form quality," which he regarded as a new or secondary quality rather than a combination of primary qualities.

Alexius Meinong added the Gestalt production theory, which was later rejected by Gestaltists. This theory perception is a two-step process, the first leading from stimuli to sensations, the second from sensations to a whole perception in an act of production. Hans Cornelius regarded the form quality as a founded attribute rather than an act of production. Thus, he claimed that the attributes are disestablished by analysis, while initial experience tends to be of wholes: attention to the parts destroys these wholes and their founded attributes. Within this tradition Vittorio Benussi was the first experimentalist, testing Meinong's act of production through the study of ambiguous figures.

While Gestalt psychology was one among many holistic psychologies, it proposed the radical view that the whole is psychologically, logically, epistemologically, and ontologically prior to its parts. The wholes were emergent qualities which inhered in no single element. Adequate knowledge of the whole could only come from observing the whole itself and must never be inferred from the parts and their relations. The most striking example of such an emergent whole was Wertheimer's phi phenomenon—i.e., the illusion of movement produced when stationary stimuli are presented in rapid succession in slightly different positions.

In contrast to the structuralists the Gestaltists felt that the distinction between description and inference could not be clearly made and that all objects which are perceived immediately, without an inferential process, should be regarded as phenomena. Thus, they adopted the phenomenological method, involving a free description of immediate experience rather than introspection. Their arguments were more often based on the *experimentum crucis*, a convincing single demonstration or illustration of a phenomenon, than on statistical analyses. Familiar illustrations of this sort are the ambiguous figures used to demonstrate the shifting nature of figure and ground, and the lines and dots often used to illustrate the laws of form or principles of organization (which include nearness, quality, closure, common destiny, good continuation, and symmetry, simplicity, and order).

Wertheimer, who was the leader of the Gestalt group, contributed primarily to the psychology of perceived motion. He was also the epistemologist of the group, being the first to challenge Meinong's production theory and also challenging Benussi's interest in ambiguity (as opposed to the compelling stimuli which could be regarded in only one way).

Köhler, who was a physicist and animal psychologist, contributed the most experimental research. On the basis of his experiments with anthropoid apes on the island of Tenerife, he challenged trial-and-error learning and concluded that it was the perception of relations that distinguished intelligence, terming the sudden perception of useful or proper relations *insight*. Köhler also articulated the principle of transposition, asserting that when parts change while their relations remain the same, the form or object remains constant. Thus we recognize a melody when it is transposed into a new key. Köhler also formulated the principle of isomorphism, postulating a structural correspondence between the external perceptual field and the internal, physiological field of the brain and nervous system. This extension of the physical dynamic concept of field theory into psychology became the foundation for Lewin's topological field theory, extending Gestalt psychology into the fields of personality theory and motivation, thus placing it in the realm of dynamic psychology.

Koffka, whose interests lay primarily in developmental and educational psychology, became the systematizer for the school. His books and articles made Gestalt theory clear especially to American psychologists. With Köhler he founded *Psychologische Forschung* (Psychological Inquiry), the Gestalt journal which circulated from 1921 to 1938. Serving as co-editors of the journal were Hans Gruhle and Kurt Goldstein, whose major contributions were in the area of psychopathology and neurology.

Others associated with Gestalt psychology include several phenomenologists. Erich Jaensch made contributions in the areas of visual acuity, depth perception, and eidetic imagery. David Katz demonstrated the interrelationship between space and color perception and discriminated among surface, volumic, and film colors. Edgar Rubin extended Benussi's studies of figure-ground perception. His studies of ambiguous figures emphasized the fact that these involved phenomenal change rather than retinal changes induced by neurological factors. Gestalt principles also found their way into E. C. Tolman's sign-gestalt theory of learning.

Gestalt psychology, especially after the publication of Koffka's *Principles of Gestalt Psychology* in 1935, constituted a comprehensive system deeply rooted in philosophy. While it was originally founded to combat the traditional psychology of the structuralists, it soon found an even stronger challenge in behaviorism, to which it was diametrically opposed. The Gestaltists asserted that organisms do not merely respond to the environment but have transactions with it. And the environment itself is an outcome of the interaction between physical objects and perceptual dispositions of organisms, so that stimuli are transformed in the perceptual process.

Of considerable interest for the Christian is the Gestalt psychologists' interest in values. Meinong and his associates debated whether the experience of value was based on will or desire or should be reduced to feeling. This led to research on the theory of value and validity. In this area of values Köhler's William James Lectures, published as *The Place of Value in a World of Facts* (1938), have become classic. Gestalt psychology was also heavily influenced by twentieth-century religious history. Nearly every major theorist was Jewish, and it was the Nazi persecution (and American sympathy for the Jews) that was responsible for its Americanization. The Gestalt therapy of Fritz Perls, while borrowing its language, "has *no* substantive relation to scientific Gestalt psychology" (Henle, 1978, p. 31).

Reference
Henle, M. Gestalt psychology and Gestalt therapy. *Journal of the History of the Behavioral Sciences,* 1978, *14,* 23–32.
H. Vande Kemp

See Psychology, History of; Gestalt Therapy.

Gestalt Techniques. The Gestalt approach to counseling and psychotherapy offers techniques that emphasize the here and now, the immediacy of experience, and both verbal and nonverbal expressiveness. Gestalt therapy is characteristically experiential in nature and is concerned more with being and doing than with thinking and talking. These experience-oriented strategies are used by the therapist to assist the client in making better contact with both self and the environment, to focus attention on particular situations that emerge within the organism-environment field, to integrate attention and awareness, and to restore organismic control and balance. Core Gestalt techniques are discussed under the following three categories.

Communication Strategies. *Here and now.* Communication in the here-and-now present tense is encouraged in order to promote awareness and immediacy of experiencing. This mode of communicating helps also to integrate past material into the personality of the client. The historical moment is relived in the existential now.

I and thou. Authentic communication and interpersonal experiencing involve the *I* of the sender making direct, personal contact with the *thou* of the receiver. This intersubjectivity facilitates better social contact and a keener sense of self.

I language. Clients who refer to their body and behaviors in objective, second and third person, you-and-it language are asked to substitute *I* for *you* and *it*. This facilitates the individual's perception of self as an active, dynamic agent rather than a passive, acted-on object. *I* expressions also help the client to assume personal responsibility, involvement, and control regarding his or her total behavior.

What and how of behavior. The therapist instructs the client to focus on the *what* and *how* of behavior in order to guide the individual in making good contact with his sensorimotor self and away from the interpretive *why* of behavior. The *why* tends to lead to intellectualizations, explanations, and defensiveness.

Gossip is forbidden. Often in group therapy a member will "gossip" or talk about another member rather than address the member directly. Usually gossip serves to protect the gossiper from strong feelings provoked by the other person. The therapist uses the no-gossiping principle to facilitate direct confrontation of the client's feelings.

Statements versus questions. Rather than serving as helpful and supportive measures, questions frequently represent passivity, laziness, lack of personal involvement, manipulation, cajoling, and/or indirect advice giving. The therapist asks the client to change inappropriate questions into statements in order to personalize and optimize communication effectiveness.

Experiments. *Dialogue.* Individuals typically experience discordant polarization in their personality functioning at one time or another. These splits or dualisms include situations such as masculine versus feminine, aggressive versus passive, commanding versus resisting, etc. When the therapist detects the discordant poles in the experience of a client, one strategy to effect integrated functioning of the fragmented parts is to have the client engage the two disagreeing components in actual dialogue. The discordant parts confront and encounter each other until the two elements merge into a new, balanced realization. For example, the outcome of a dialogue between aggression and passivity is assertiveness. Two popular modes of dialogue are the use of two empty chairs or the two hands. One chair or hand can represent one pole, while the other chair or hand represents the opposing side. The client takes turns in speaking for the two sides of the polar conflict. The dialogue may be between two differing psychological attitudes or feelings, two parts of the body, or between the personality of the client and some significant other person who is in some type of unresolved conflict with the client.

Completing unfinished business. Clients bring unfinished business or unresolved feelings such as hurt, anger, guilt, or resentment to the therapy setting. When unfinished business surfaces in the therapy process, the client is asked to complete the task by living it out in the here and now. Role playing, psychodrama, pillow therapy (expressing attitudes and feelings regarding some other person by using a pillow or cushion as a substitute for the other person—verbal statements are addressed to the pillow and physical contact is made), and dialogue are some of the specific techniques used for the resolution of unresolved feelings.

Playing the projection. Quite often what is understood by the client to be a perception is really a projection. That is, a trait, attitude, feeling, or a mode of behavior that actually belongs to the client's personality is attributed to another person and then experienced as directed toward the client by the other person. Whenever a client expresses a projection disguised as a perception, he is encouraged to play the role of the personification involved in the projection to discover his own conflict in this area. For example, a client who says to the counselor, "You don't really care about me," may be asked to play the role of a noncaring person. Following the role playing the client could be asked to determine to see whether this is a disowned trait that he possesses personally.

Reversals. The reversal technique is used to help the client realize that manifest behavior often represents the opposite of the underlying impulse. For example, the client who fears being rejected by other people might be asked to play the role of a hermit or recluse who could care less about other people and how others perceive and accept him.

Exaggeration. When a client makes a significant gesture or statement in a casual, feeble, or underdeveloped manner, indicating a lack of awareness of its importance, he is invited to repeat it again and again with amplified movement, loudness, and/or emphasis. This facilitates the client's achieving better contact with self and putting more of himself into integrated communication and experiencing.

May I feed you a sentence? Frequently a client will present significant messages that are implied but might not be in his full awareness. The therapist proposes a sentence for the client "to try on for size and fit" and to amplify if desirable. Although interpretation is present, the primary objective is to enable the client to experience more of self through active participation. A spontaneous development of the sentence should follow if the statement proves to be an accurately relevant one.

Stay with it. Sooner or later in the therapy process the client will hit on a feeling, mood, or state of mind that is unpleasant and will prefer to run from rather than encounter it. Instead of making it easy for the client to avoid the unpleasant situation, the therapist encourages him to stay with it. If the client is able to confront the painful moment, he will advance in the maturation process. Both healing and growing are bedfellows in human existence together with pain and suffering.

Guided fantasy. An excellent opportunity for clients to explore, clarify, and come to grips with feelings and themes in their life situations is provided by fantasy journeys. They may project themselves into numerous fantasy situations, such as becoming an acorn and going through all the developmental processes from being planted to growing into a mature tree, or hiking in the mountains to visit a wise old man in a cabin who has gifts and insights into life to share with his visitors. Rather than being mere fantasies these experiences become genuine expressions of an individual's existence, what he or she is really concerned about or values. The fantasy trip is best done with the eyes closed while the client is deeply relaxed. The fantasy journey can be guided either by the therapist or by the clients themselves after some basic instructions regarding the procedure.

Dreamwork. Gestalt theory considers the dream to be an existential-phenomenological self-revelation of the person. In a very real sense the individual *is* his dream. But from another perspective, every image in a dream represents an alienated, disowned, discordant, and projected part of the self of the dreamer. Therefore, as Perls has observed, the dream is the "royal road to awareness and integration."

In Gestalt dreamwork an experiential rather than an analytical approach is followed. The client first tells his dream and then plays the part of the various images, be they persons, animals, or objects. By reexperiencing and enacting the dream in the present tense from the vantage point of each image, the client can begin to reclaim and integrate the alienated parts of the personality. Interpretation of the dream is left to the client. The therapist assists by 1) suggesting the order in which the images are played, usually from the less to the more vivid ones, 2) helping the client deal with avoidance and resistance in playing the disowned parts of self; and 3) suggesting when the client might relate the images and feelings of the dream to his current life situation. Dialogue and other techniques identified above can be used in dreamwork to facilitate the integration of the discordant elements of the personality revealed in the dream.

Additional Readings
Fagan, J., & Shepherd, I. L. (Eds.). *Gestalt therapy now.* Palo Alto, Calif.: Science and Behavior Books, 1970.
Passons, W. R. *Gestalt approaches in counseling.* New York: Holt, Rinehart, & Winston, 1975.
Zinker, J. *Creative process in Gestalt therapy.* New York: Brunner/Mazel, 1977.

D. Smith

Gestalt Therapy. Developed by Perls in the 1940s, Gestalt therapy has rapidly evolved into an important and popular form of treatment. It attracts many because it represents a genuine alternative to more traditional insight-oriented approaches.

The major goal in Gestalt therapy is to teach the client to be more aware of what is happening both within and without. Perls thought that problems develop because people fail to maintain this awareness. Therapy attempts to restore awareness by focusing primarily on the here and now and by avoiding the twin traps of what Perls referred to as "obsessive remembering of the past" and "anxious anticipation of the future."

Theoretical Roots. Generally viewed as an existential-humanistic form of therapy, the approach has come to be considered a mainstream within humanistic psychology. Its roots reach beyond this orientation, however, and include three major systems: psychoanalytic psychology, Gestalt psychology, and existentialism.

Perls's training and early practice was as a psychoanalyst, and this system exercised considerable influence on his subsequent development. Though psychoanalytic roots are clearer in his early writings, they continue to show in his use of such concepts as superego, repression, introjection, and projection. While he believed he had completely abandoned his psychoanalytic heritage, classifying Gestalt therapy as an existential therapy, some still classify it as a form of psychoanalytic therapy.

As for the influence of Gestalt psychology, Perls initially intended to use the basic concepts of this movement as a foundation for a comprehensive system of personality, psychopathology, and psychotherapy (Perls, Hefferline, & Goodman, 1951). This ambitious goal went largely unfulfilled. He did borrow some of the basic concepts (most notably that of the figure-ground relationship) and the essential spirit of the movement (the desire to understand behavior and experience without analytic dissection), but he failed to do more than marry these to the other major concepts borrowed from psychoanalytic psychology and existentialism.

The third and perhaps most important influence was the existential movement in philosophy and psychology. Gestalt therapy's stress on such concepts as the expansion of awareness, freedom, the immediacy of experience, and the here and now all demonstrate its close relation to existentialism. Nowhere is this more clear than in the so-called Gestalt prayer: "I do my thing and you do your thing. I am not in this world to live up to your expectations and you are not in this world to live up to mine. You are you and I am I and if by chance we find each other, it's beautiful. If not, it can't be helped." (Perls, 1969, p. 4)

Basic Assumptions and Therapeutic Task. Proponents of Gestalt therapy begin with the humanistic assumption that individuals have within themselves all they need to achieve personal wholeness and live effectively. The essential ingredient missing from most people's lives is courage, the courage to become aware of their feelings and of the ways they characteristically avoid experiencing the present in its fullness.

Living fully in the present is most difficult. It demands choice and therefore responsibility. Human beings tend to avoid choice by limiting awareness and consequently limiting freedom. This results in anxiety and a suspension of personal growth.

The heart of the therapeutic task lies in increasing one's awareness. Gestalt therapy assumes that awareness mobilizes energy within the person and enables him to act. Until a person becomes aware that he is hungry, he does not seek food. The awareness of hunger leads naturally to action. Similarly, if a person is unaware of being angry, he takes no action. Awareness of anger makes action possible.

Acting on an awareness is described as finishing an experience. This produces a Gestalt, or a completed experience. Unfinished business results from failing to act on an important past awareness. Generally these experiences involve unexpressed feelings of anger, pain, guilt, and other negative emotions. Because they remain unexpressed, they linger on, continuously pressing for expression. Increasing awareness in the present not only stops the accumulation of unfinished experiences but allows the individual to act on those of the past that are the most pressing.

Gestalt therapy does not suggest, as some critics have alleged, that it is either possible or desirable to act on every awareness. Perls recognized that in any moment the individual is confronted with thousands of possibilities for awareness, only a small number of which can be followed by action. Selective awareness operates constantly.

Perls also recognized that action is sometimes inappropriate. Not every feeling of anger should be expressed, both to preserve social order and to achieve personal mental health. He assumed, however, that most people err on the side of too little awareness and consequently too little expression of feelings. He noted that we fail to be aware of those things within us which we wish were not there. Only after we become fully aware of them can they be changed.

This pursuit of heightened awareness requires the Gestalt therapist to function in an active manner, continuously calling attention to present experience. The therapist does this primarily through the use of *what* questions (e.g., What are you aware of now?) and *how* questions (e.g., How do you experience your fear?). He never employs *why* questions because they lead to rationalizations and intellectual rumination.

The goal is neither analysis nor understanding; it is integration. Lost parts of self are found when channels of awareness are reopened. Perls's dictum, "Loose your mind and come to your senses," captures well this sensory focus of Gestalt therapy. He believed clients must once again learn to use their senses fully if they are to grow.

Related to this is the emphasis on action rather than mere talk. Therapy techniques often require the behavioral involvement of the client. Sometimes the client will reenact an important past situation during which he failed to take the necessary action (e.g., crying at a parent's funeral). Other times he may portray a dream or fantasy in a role play. This emphasis on action is reflected in the designation of many therapy techniques as games. The most common of these include the game of dialogue, the rehearsal game, and the exaggeration game (*see* GESTALT TECHNIQUES).

Gestalt therapy usually follows a group format. The therapist customarily works with one group member at a time, with individuals volunteering to take the "hot seat" and work on some issue. In the pure form of Gestalt therapy spontaneous interaction among group members is minimal. Members observe the therapist's work with one member and contribute only after completion of the therapeutic work. Other styles of Gestalt groups allow more spontaneous interaction. While the group has emerged as a favored medium and probably represents Gestalt's most potent context, individual therapy is also appropriate and commonly practiced.

Evaluation. Because of the paucity of research on Gestalt therapy, gauging its overall effectiveness is difficult. The few studies that have been done have been generally encouraging. Foulds and Hannigan (1976) have shown Gestalt therapy to be effective in decreasing introversion and neuroticism; Nichols and Fine (1980), in increasing self-concept. These and most other existing studies, however, are therapy analogues conducted with student experimental subjects rather than clients seeking help.

Because Gestalt therapy has most frequently been applied to individuals who function relatively normally, little is known about its usefulness with more typical clinical populations. Most Gestalt therapists seem to agree with Shepherd that it is "most effective with overly socialized, restrained, constricted individuals—often described as neurotic, phobic, perfectionistic, ineffective, depressed, etc.—whose functioning is limited or inconsistent, primarily due to their internal restrictions" (1970, p. 235). She cautions against its use with psychotic or more severely disturbed individuals, and this caution seems sensible in the light of the degree of frustration and confrontation normally inherent in Gestalt therapy.

The most common criticism of Gestalt therapy is that it lacks a theoretical foundation. Initially Perls set out to develop an overall theory of personality, both normal and abnormal. He soon abandoned this pursuit, however, asserting that theoretical speculation interfered with creative clinical work. The theory that was developed consists of little more than a few hypotheses about psychopathology attached to one concept of normal personality development—the concept of awareness. The absence of a unifying theory reduces Gestalt therapy to an assorted collection of techniques with an overall philosophy of life. This theoretical deficiency constitutes a major weakness.

Related to this is the system's anti-intellectual bias. The mistrust of thinking, together with the consequent deemphasis on the cognitive factors in the therapy process, confines the therapist. It also conflicts with the biblical view that a person's thinking is an expression of one's heart or core (Prov. 23:7). Christian theology has historically understood rationality as one aspect of the image of God in which mankind was created. This suggests that a therapy system ought to take seriously the cognitive aspects of human functioning.

The biblical view of persons also stands in contrast to the strikingly independent person depicted as the healthy ideal of Gestalt therapy. The philosophy that "I do my thing and you do your thing" reflects an inadequate notion of our interdependence on each other. At least as described by Perls, Gestalt therapy denies our responsibility to others, and this fails to square with the Christian understanding of human relatedness to others and to God. The emphasis on personal responsibility and the refusal to accept helplessness as an excuse for not changing do reflect the Christian understanding of human nature. The emphasis on one's responsibility for oneself must also be joined, however, by an emphasis on responsibility to others.

References

Foulds, M. L., & Hannigan, P. S. A Gestalt marathon workshop: Effects on extraversion and neuroticism. *Journal of College Student Personnel,* 1976, *17*(1), 50–54.
Nichols, R. C., & Fine, H. J. Gestalt therapy: Some aspects of self support, independence and responsibility. *Psychotherapy: Theory, research and practice,* 1980, *17*(2), 124–135.
Perls, F. *Gestalt therapy verbatim.* Lafayette, Calif.: Real People Press, 1969.
Perls, F., Hefferline, R. F., & Goodman, P. *Gestalt therapy: Excitement and growth in human personality.* New York: Julian Press, 1951.
Shepherd, I. L. Limitations and cautions in the Gestalt approach. In J. Fagan & I. L. Shepherd (Eds.), *Gestalt therapy now.* Palo Alto, Calif.: Science and Behavior Books, 1970.

Additional Readings

Hatcher, C., & Himelstein, P. (Eds.). *The handbook of Gestalt therapy.* New York: Aronson, 1976.
Perls, F. *In and out of the garbage pail.* Lafayette, Calif.: Real People Press, 1969.
Polster, E., & Polster, M. *Gestalt therapy integrated.* New York: Brunner/Mazel, 1973.

D. G. BENNER

Gifted Children.
Traditionally, gifted children have been recognized as those who have outstanding intellectual ability compared with

their agemates, as measured by standard tests of intelligence or IQ. The Stanford-Binet test, for example, used in pioneer studies of giftedness conducted by Terman and his associates, continues in its revised form to be used as a reliable and valid means of identifying intellectual precocity. However, as the concept of giftedness has broadened to embrace creativity and various types of special talents, so have current techniques of identifying the gifted become more flexible. Generally, at least a minimal level of superior general intelligence is expected in all those labeled gifted (the cut-off level being an arbitrary or conventional matter). Recently, however, other indicators have been used with good results. One example is the development and use of difficult mathematics tests to identify mathematically precocious children for accelerated programs. The specific criteria adopted depend on the desired focus, available resources, and judged likelihood that those identified will profit from instruction tailored to their special needs.

The more than 60 years of research on gifted children has resulted in the revelation of much more about what they are like than can be captured by test results alone. Some of this research has contributed to criticism of intelligence tests in particular. Placing too much emphasis on one global measure such as the IQ may contribute to neglect of other characteristics that are significant in various types of real-life achievements. These previously overlooked characteristics include wide-ranging and versatile interests, superior adjustment and leadership among peers, curiosity, productive thinking (proposing many solutions to a problem or task), and relating well to older companions. Many of these characteristics appear to clash with stereotypes of the gifted child as invariably bookish, introverted, and poorly adjusted. Indeed, in many respects the gifted child proved to be much more "normal" and less an object of curiosity than was commonly supposed. In sum, detailed qualitative descriptions of gifted children have given parents and teachers an informed basis for identifying the gifted child.

Notwithstanding the general acknowledgment that it is imperative to develop the nation's intellectual resources, discussion of public education of gifted children betrays a persistent ambivalence. Much of this ambivalence is based on the feeling that it is inherently antidemocratic to concentrate on developing the potential of the ablest. The common misconception that the gifted will succeed regardless of their opportunities ("the cream

always rises") has been used to rationalize this attitude. Only slightly more sophisticated is the oft-expressed concern that the gifted, if accelerated ahead of their age mates, will suffer from socioemotional maladjustment, resulting eventually in waste rather than actualization of their potential. A program of "enrichment," as opposed to acceleration, is often proposed along with the latter viewpoint. This may consist of relevant and worthwhile educational experiences—planned, however, within a traditional age-segregated program. Research on acceleration (grade skipping, advanced placement, early graduation, etc.) reveals generally superior results as compared to enrichment without any substantial evidence of long-lasting adjustment problems. In contrast, there may be too little concern over adjustment problems resulting from inadequate intellectual challenge to gifted individuals who must adapt to lock-step advancement through the grades.

Gifted children may be found in all ethnic and racial groups and in different socioeconomic strata. However, failure to identify many of these individuals and provide educational opportunities commensurate with their promise helps ensure that intellectual talent is most likely to be actualized among the relatively privileged. This reality refutes the notion that the cream always rises.

The term *giftedness* still connotes an unmerited bestowal of talents, either through the genes, divine favor, or some other agency. In psychology the notion that giftedness is to some degree genetically determined has had its advocates ever since the earliest studies were done. Anecdotes regarding child prodigies such as Mozart apparently support this view. It is equally certain, however, that favorable environments are essential to intellectual growth in general. A balanced review of the evidence would concede that heredity probably establishes broad limits for intellectual growth. Such a view does not take away from the individual the responsibility to develop and use his or her abilities to the fullest, to the glory of God—to be a profitable steward (Matt. 25:14–30). Nor does this conclusion give any warrant to parents or their surrogates to set preconceived limits on any child's potential on the basis of which they might withhold crucial stimulation or encouragement. A child's readiness for learning and intellectual growth comes from having the most favorable environment possible: it may not be dogmatically determined beforehand. In this perspective, education of the gifted is not elitist but merely the logical consequence of lovingly helping each child to realize his or her possibilities to their fullest.

D. R. RIDLEY

See CREATIVITY; INTELLIGENCE; INTELLECTUAL ASSESSMENT.

Globus Hystericus. A hysterical symptom in which the sensation of a ball or lump rises from the abdominal area to the throat, where it produces the feeling of choking or strangulation. Psychoanalysts hypothesize that this symptom is based on unconscious rejection of aggressive impulses, frequently of a sexual nature. The connection between these impulses and swallowing plays an important role in the symptom formation, as does disgust, which may be seen as a combination of temptation and rejection.

Glossolalia. An unintelligible conglomeration of sounds that simulates normal speech in that the utterances contain distinctions of words, sentences, and even paragraphs. It is most often seen in states of religious ecstasy, although it sometimes is also present in schizophrenic speech.

See ECSTATIC RELIGIOUS EXPERIENCES.

Goldstein, Kurt (1878–1965). Originator of ORGANISMIC THEORY. Born in Kattowitz, Germany, he received his M.D. degree at the University of Breslau in 1903. In 1933 he came to the United States, where he held academic and clinical positions in a variety of institutions in addition to maintaining a private neuropsychiatry and psychotherapy practice in New York City for many years. Goldstein's work on brain-injured soldiers during the First World War made him famous and enabled him to develop much of his organismic theory.

Organismic theory emphasizes the unity, integration, and consistency of the normal personality. The organism (person) is viewed as an organized system. The person behaves as a unified whole and not as a series of differentiated parts. Rather than being motivated by a number of drives, the individual is motivated by the one sovereign drive of self-actualization. The inherent potentialities of the organism for growth is a prominent point in Goldstein's theorizing. Intense study of the individual rather than group studies accounted for many of his views.

Goldstein's major works were *The Organism*, (1939), *Human Nature in the Light of Psychopathology*, (1940), *After-effects of Brain Injuries in War*, (1942), and *Language and Language Disturbances*, (1948).

S. N. BALLARD

Graphology. The study of handwriting as an expression of the writer's character and personality, also known as the psychology of handwriting.

The primitive interpretation of handwriting dates back to the second century, with the first real systematic approach linked to an Italian doctor, C. Baldi, in 1622. The term *"graphology"* was first coined in the 1800s by the French priest Jean-Hippolyte Michon. Early theories of graphology were based on an intuitive approach to dissecting and interpreting individual pieces of writing, such as the location of letters, size of loops, connections between letters, size, consistency and other minute differences. These variables were then correlated with specific character traits or states of emotion, such as frustration, anger, insecurity, and joy. A chemist, L. Klages (1872–1956), was influential in broadening the base to look not just at individual parts of writing, but at the whole, which he called form level. He also recognized the limitations and cautions involved in handwriting analysis and viewed the procedure with more balance than many of its most ardent advocates.

While many psychologists would be prepared to accept the general assumption that one's handwriting probably contains a good deal of information about one's personality, few view graphology as a serious clinical tool. The reason for this has been the inability to discover a valid method of analyzing handwriting. Although numerous systems have been proposed, none has yet been validated. It should be noted that the general pessimism of American psychologists regarding the usefulness of graphology has not been shared by Europeans, who accept it more commonly and use it rather widely in personnel selection.

D. L. SCHUURMAN

Grief. The cognitive and emotional process of working through a significant loss. The removal of anyone or anything that has emotional value to an individual will precipitate a grief reaction.

Grieving is to the emotional system following a loss what healing is to the physical system after surgery. Just as an operation traumatizes the body, a loss jolts the emotional system, producing disruption and upheaval. While grieving is painful, it is to be viewed as a healthy response, for without it a complete emotional recovery is not possible.

The most salient symptom of grief is acute psychological pain. Emotional turmoil; wide fluctuations in mood; and feelings of hurt, guilt, depression, helplessness, anger, sadness, love, rage, loneliness, resentment, and hopelessness are commonly reported. A frequent perception of the normal grief-stricken individual is, "I'm losing my mind." This fear of disorganization threatens one's self-confidence and is perhaps the most debilitating aspect of grief.

Secondary symptoms may also emerge, though frequently their causes are wrongly attributed to factors other than loss. Eating, sleeping, and sexual disturbances, for example, may accompany grief. Somatic complaints—headaches, low energy level, ulcers, dizziness, colitis—may be present. The inevitable heightening of an individual's stress disturbs family relationships, which may become more distant or laden with conflict.

Stages of Grief. The notion that grief progresses in definable stages has gained wide popularity through the writings of Kübler-Ross (1969). On the basis of studies with dying patients she postulated five stages of grief—denial and isolation, anger, bargaining, depression, and acceptance. The survivor's grief, according to Kübler-Ross, generally parallels that of the dying patient.

While the vague outlines of stages can be seen in the experiences of many, grieving is hardly an orderly, sequential process. More typically it is chaotic, with feelings coming and disappearing only to reappear later. Some feelings are specific, others vague.

The course of grief varies considerably from person to person, depending on several factors. Cause of death, for example, will affect the survivor's reactions. A sudden, accidental death brings on an acute grief reaction, whereas a gradual demise through lingering illness allows for anticipatory grieving to occur.

Other factors that influence the course of grief include the individual's emotional stability, the social support system, age of the deceased person, and the degree to which he or she was at peace with self, God, and family. Because troubled relationships are more unfinished at the point of separation than positive ones, they are especially difficult to get over. Hence, contrary to popular opinion, loss of a good relationship is more easily grieved (with fewer complications) than a conflicted one.

Abnormal Grieving. Under normal circumstances grief is time limited. It is a self-limiting emotional process that runs its course and is completed after several months. Growing evidence suggests, however, that certain losses such as suicides are never completely resolved. While the survivor's pain might diminish over time, it is never completely eliminated as it normally is with other types of death.

Abnormal grief reactions may occur immediately following a loss, as in the case of the person who becomes psychotic and is totally unable to cope. The opposite extreme is to completely disown the pain and proceed with a business-as-usual attitude. Neither reaction is a healthy coping response.

Sometimes signs of abnormal grief are not evident until months after the loss. Enshrinement is a good example. This refers to the practice of leaving the deceased person's room and possessions untouched long after he or she is gone. Creation of a "shrine" becomes symbolic of the survivor's inability to let go of the loved one.

For others, abnormal grief is evidenced by persistent physical symptoms, angry withdrawal, intense loneliness, obsessing over the loved one, and lingering depression. If after a year to 18 months following a loss grief continues to interfere with one's overall functioning, professional help is indicated.

Christians and Grief. The Christian's spiritual experience is not unaffected by grief, especially when a tragic loss is involved. Some will react defensively with an overdevotion to God and the church, to the neglect of all else. Others will accuse God of being distant and will eventually leave the church. None of these individuals effectively mobilizes faith resources in coping, because of a deep and unconscious anger toward God. So long as God-directed anger is unnamed, denied, and contained, spiritual paralysis is inevitable. In the healthy Christian response all the pain typical of grief is present, and anger at God is recognized, accepted, and appropriately released.

Because death is not an ultimate tragedy for Christians, their grief is without the sting experienced by those who have no hope. Yet this same belief can support an unhealthy denial of the very real emotional pain brought on by the death of a loved one. Christian faith, with its emphasis on eternal life, in no way exempts one from the normal, human process of grieving.

Some Christians are in need of having their experience normalized by others who can give reassurance of the right to grieve. Those who feel pressure to be "strong" and a "good and cheerful witness" are especially in need of such support to prevent their grief and God-directed anger from being contained and allowed to fester inside. Biblical models like Job can be helpful in this regard.

The principal challenge for those dealing with loss is to release their grief. This involves respecting, specifying, and expressing painful thoughts and feelings associated with the loss. To get beyond grief one must go through it, not around it. Nor are there any painless short-cuts.

Good models for handling grief, a strong faith, an understanding of what is involved in mourning, and a caring support system can facilitate the working through of a difficult loss. Because grief is a social event, it cannot be resolved in isolation. Those who grieve must be willing to risk sharing their pain, and those who minister must be willing to risk the discomfort of being with the persons in their pain.

Reference
Kübler-Ross, E. *On death and dying.* New York: Macmillan, 1969.

J. A. Larsen

See Loss and Separation; Death and Dying.

Group Dynamics.

Although all psychologists maintain that a group is more than a collection of individuals, they have not always agreed on its essential characteristics. In defining a group some have emphasized the importance of a common goal, while others have suggested that its members must perceive themselves as belonging together. Still others stress the organizational characteristics of a group, including its unitary functioning. Probably the most widely accepted definition is that a group consists of two or more persons who interact with and influence one another (Shaw, 1981).

People join groups for a variety of reasons. They may be attracted to the members of a group, and the factors that influence interpersonal attraction have been studied more extensively than any other determinant of group formation. People may also be drawn to a group's activities. For this reason they join discussion groups, social clubs, and athletic teams. Perhaps most importantly individuals form and join groups to attain some goal they could not achieve by themselves. They organize political groups to protest injustice, labor unions to improve working conditions, and neighborhood associations to combat crime. In certain cases people perceive group membership as the means to some goal that lies outside the group. For example, a person may join a church because such membership will be "good for business." Finally, some psychologists maintain that people have a basic need to affiliate that is satisfied only in the context of the group.

When people join together to form a group, their first task is to organize. The group establishes norms (shared rules of conduct) which serve to maintain behavioral consistency. These norms guide each individual's actions and also help each group member to anticipate the behavior of others. Associated with each place or position in the group may be a role, a set of norms that defines how a person occupying that position ought to behave. Psychologists have noted how role performance often comes to shape one's attitudes and values. Zimbardo (1972) found that role playing influenced both behavior and identity when he randomly assigned male college students to be inmates or guards in a simulated prison. Within six days the prisoners became servile, dehumanized robots while the guards became brutal and tyrannical. Status, another important element in group structure, refers to the respect or prestige that is accorded a person occupying a particular position. Those positions that contribute most to the achievement of the group's goal are typically granted the highest status.

Group Leadership. Researchers in group dynamics have been particularly interested in understanding the nature and impact of group leaders. The trait approach, often referred to as the "great man" theory of leadership, assumes that all leaders have certain personal characteristics that distinguish them from other group members. Empirical support for this theory has been weak. Studies indicate that the necessary abilities and skills for effective leadership depend largely on the context in which group interaction occurs. The situational theory of leadership assumes that certain individuals become leaders because they possess the unique knowledge and skills needed at the moment. Thus various situations call for different leaders, and presumably anyone could become a leader in the right situation. A limitation of both trait and situational theories is that they assume leadership is unidirectional and thereby fail to recognize that leaders are also influenced by their followers. Contemporary theories of leadership maintain that effective leadership is a complex interplay involving the characteristics of the leader, of other group members, and of the situation.

Fiedler's (1964) contingency theory has provided one of the most influential models of leadership effectiveness. Fiedler suggests that in most cases persons adopt one of two leadership styles. Some leaders are task oriented—i.e., they are primarily concerned with getting the job done; others are relationship oriented, focusing first of all on the social-emotional climate of the group. The style that is more effective depends on the situation. A directive, task-oriented approach presumably produces better results when the situational conditions are either very favorable or unfavorable to the leader. In contrast, a relationship-oriented style is more effective when the conditions are moderately favorable. According to Fiedler, three factors determine the favorability of the situation: 1) the leader's power over the group, 2) the degree to which group tasks are clearly structured, and 3) the quality of the leader's personal relationships with other group members.

Communication and Cohesion. Group interaction involves communication among members. In the late 1940s and early 1950s several investigators examined the effect of communication networks on group dynamics. The degree to which communication flows freely through a group can influence morale, productivity, and various aspects of group structure. A decentralized or open communication network in which group members may converse freely with each other is associated with greater member satisfaction and with improved efficiency in the solution of complex problems. In contrast, a centralized network in which all communication must be directed to one person, and thus in which members are unable to converse with each other, may be more efficient for solving simple problems. Organizational development, including the emergence of a leader, also occurs more rapidly in a centralized network.

Cohesiveness, the degree to which members are motivated to remain in the group, has been one of the most researched variables of group dynamics. Simply assigning individuals to different groups typically produces some degree of group loyalty. Cohesiveness may be further increased if the members are placed in intergroup competition or are exposed to some external threat. Highly cohesive groups exert greater influence over their members and are often more effective in achieving their goals than are less cohesive groups. People in highly cohesive groups communicate more, tend to be friendlier, more cooperative, and also feel more secure than members of less cohesive groups. However, cohesiveness may also have negative effects. People may spend more time socializing than working on the group task. And since people in highly cohesive groups are particularly responsive to each other's influence, norms that regulate productivity may occasionally lead some individuals to reduce their output.

Groups and Performance. The experimental investigation of group phenomena can be traced back to Triplett's (1898) studies of how the mere presence of others may influence an individual's performance. Intrigued by the finding that bicyclists' times were faster when they raced together than when they raced against the clock, Triplett conducted one of social psychology's first experiments. He reported that children wound string faster when they worked with others than when they performed alone. Other investigators also found this social facilitation effect when people solved simple multiplication problems, crossed out designated letters, or performed simple motor tasks.

At the same time, however, some studies failed to obtain this positive effect. In fact, the presence of others hindered people's performance in learning nonsense syllables, in completing a maze, and in solving complex multiplication problems. Zajonc (1965) finally reconciled these contradictory findings with a well-known principle from experimental psychology: Arousal enhances whatever response tendency is dominant. Since other research indicates that the presence of others arouses us, it follows that observers or co-actors should improve the performance of easy tasks, for which the correct response is dominant, but hinder performance of difficult tasks, for which an incorrect response is dominant. Subsequent research has supported this hypothesis.

Improved performance in the presence of others may occur when people work toward their own goals and when their efforts can be individually evaluated. However, when people pool their efforts toward a common goal, and when individual contributions cannot be monitored, psychologists have often found "social loafing." In one study people who worked alone or in groups were asked to pull as hard as they could on a rope attached to a meter that measured the strength of their pulls. Contrary to the common notion that in unity there is strength, results indicated that as group size increased, the amount of effort exerted by each person dropped. More recent experiments have also indicated that group members often work less hard when performing "additive" tasks. One explanation for this finding has been provided by social impact theory. Briefly, this states that the effect of any external force on a group is divided among its members. Thus, according to this theory, the pressure to work hard is divided among all group members so that as group size increases, each person exerts less effort.

Decision Making. While decisions by groups are often thought to be more cautious than those of individuals, research has shown that group discussion often actually enhances risk taking. This finding, which has been successfully replicated in dozens of studies, is known as the risky shift phenomenon. However, the risky shift is not universal. In some cases people became more cautious after group discussion. Analysis of these apparently contradictory findings led investigators to postulate the group polarization hypothesis: Discussion generally strengthens the average inclination of group members before discussion (Myers, 1983). Thus if the average inclination is toward risk, group discussion will enhance risk taking. On the other hand, if the inclination of individuals is toward caution, group discussion will strengthen that tendency. More generally research has shown that the initial average position of individuals is enhanced through group discussion. In short, groups intensify the opinions of like-minded people.

At least two social influences account for group polarization. Through group discussion individuals become aware of more arguments favoring the viewpoint they are already inclined to support. Secondly, individuals discover that others are more supportive of the socially preferred tendency than they expected, and in order to be perceived favorably by others they themselves express stronger opinions.

Often two heads are better than one, and thus group decision making may be superior to that of individuals. However, in analyzing the decisions that led to several political fiascoes Janis (1972) concluded that a group's desire for harmony may sometimes lead to the loss of critical judgment, a phenomenon he called groupthink. He argued that the conditions that breed groupthink include high cohesiveness, isolation of the group from outside contact, and a directive leader. Janis also identified the major symptoms of groupthink: the group's illusion of invulnerability, an unquestioned belief in its own morality, direct pressure on dissenters to conform, an illusion of unanimity, collective rationalization, a stereotyping of out-groups, the presence of self-appointed mind guards, and individual self-censorship.

To prevent groupthink Janis recommends that group leaders remain impartial during group deliberation, that they encourage group members to express their reservations, that they assign one or more members the role of devil's advocate, and that after the group reaches a preliminary decision they call a "second-chance" meeting at which each member is asked to express any remaining doubts. Janis further suggests that on occasion independent groups be assigned the same problem. After each has reached a decision, they should come together to air any differences. All these procedures, Janis argues, will serve to stimulate critical thinking and prevent groupthink.

Deindividuation. Psychologists have long observed that persons in large groups frequently display behaviors they would not exhibit if they were acting alone. Looting by rioters and the violence of the lynch mob provide just two examples. Persons in groups may experience both loss of self-awareness and evaluation apprehension, a process called deindividuation. The individual's submergence in the group leads to a decrease in his or her inhibitions about performing certain behaviors. The lessening of inner restraints allows individuals to seek satisfaction for certain needs or impulses which they could not otherwise satisfy. Group situations that produce anonymity and draw attention away from each person seem most likely to foster the deindividuation process.

References

Fiedler, F. E. A contingency model of leadership effectiveness. In L. Berkowitz (Ed.), *Advances in experimental social psychology* (Vol. 1). New York: Academic Press, 1964.

Janis, I. L. *Victims of groupthink.* Boston: Houghton Mifflin, 1972.

Myers, D. G. *Social psychology.* New York: McGraw-Hill, 1983.

Shaw, M. E. *Group dynamics* (3rd. ed.). New York: McGraw-Hill, 1981.

Triplett, N. The dynamogenic factors in pacemaking and competition. *American Journal of Psychology*, 1898, *9*, 507–533.

Zajonc, R. B. Social facilitation. *Science*, 1965, *149*, 269–274.

Zimbardo, P. G. Pathology of imprisonment. *Transaction/Society*, 1972, *9*(6), 4–8.

M. BOLT

See LEADERSHIP; DECISION MAKING; GROUP PSYCHOTHERAPY.

Group Homes. The history of group homes is embedded in the history of child welfare, which in turn is very much related to the social, economic, and educational philosophy espoused in Western culture. In antiquity there was no room for any child outside the kinship system. There was no term in the biblical or classical literature for foster homes or institutions. The early Christian church did attempt to care for abandoned children and adults who were sick or aged. During the Middle Ages monasteries and convents accepted abandoned children. Finally, during the Elizabethan period the Poor Laws came into effect. These regulated the care of abandoned children, placing them into two categories: those who were given out for indenture and those placed in almshouses. Indenture was the early beginning of the foster home, and the almshouse was the early beginning of the children's institution.

In the United States two figures are particularly well known for their work with unwanted children: Charles Loren Brate in New York and Charles Birtwell in Boston. During the 1800s these two men greatly encouraged the development of foster home care and were in large part responsible for the transformation of the old-fashioned almshouses. The controversy between foster homes and institutions grew to an alarming proportion and culminated in the 1909 White House Conference on Children. The conference decided that the child's own home was the best place for the child to be. This became the early beginning of the deinstitutionalization of dependent children.

Group homes are distinguished from foster homes in that foster homes tend to have one or more children living in an already established home, and a group home tends to be one in which a group of unrelated children all live together in one house with a couple or some single people acting as houseparents. Further, the group home usually has more of a treatment focus.

The development of the group home accelerated in the 1940s when Jacob Kepecs of the Jewish Children's Bureau in Chicago set up a chain of group homes to take children who were moved out of institutions and foster homes. Since that time the number of group homes has increased tremendously all over the country—so much so that, according to Gula, a new group home is probably established each day somewhere in the nation (Gula, 1973). Although there has been a general decline in the total number of children in care, due to the decline in the number of children generally as well as other related factors, the group home movement has continued.

Group homes are generally divided into family group homes, peer group homes, and group residences. Family group homes are usually homes in which group home parents, with or without their own children, take care of from 4 to 6 other children. These group home parents are usually the employees of an agency, or they may do their work on a service fee basis. A peer group home is usually a home which is rented or owned by an agency and in which a child care staff supervises the living arrangements of anywhere from 5 to 10 children. Usually the child care workers are younger persons. A group residence is usually owned or rented by an agency, and a child care staff looks after approximately 10 to 15 children. A group residence is distinguished from an institution in that it is integrated into the community and the children attend school in the local community.

The purpose of a group home is to provide treatment while keeping the children in an environment which is as close to a normal family environment as possible. The children therefore usually attend schools in the neighborhood and are involved in other community activities such as church, clubs, and YMCA. It is imperative that the children are healthy enough to live in a normal community. Much damage has been done to the concept of group homes because overly aggressive and disturbed children were placed in a group home that was not capable of controlling the child.

The staff of a group home are either trained child care workers or mature, dependable married persons who are interested in helping children. Owing to the difficult nature of the work and the frustrations involved, there is need for careful supervision as well as in-service training. Without this kind of service support, staff members tend to burn out quickly. In many group homes the average length of stay for staff is as low as six months.

HALFWAY HOUSES are also called group homes.

References

Gula, M. Community services and residential institutions for children. In Y. Bakal (Ed.), *Closing correctional institutions*. Lexington, Mass.: Lexington Books, 1973.

Additional Reading

Mayer, M. F., Richman, L. H., & Balcerzak, E. A. *Group care of children*. New York: Child Welfare League of America, 1977.

S. SKARSTEN

Group Psychotherapy. The practice of persons forming into groups for purposes of mutual protection, support, and understanding is as old as mankind itself. However, the scientific investigation and utilization of the healing powers of groups is less than a hundred years old.

The beginning of modern group therapy can be traced back to 1905 when Joseph Pratt, a Boston internist, set up special classes for tuberculosis patients. These "classes" not only involved instruction to the patients about the treatment of their common malady, but it also provided them opportunity for interpersonal support and encouragement. As Pratt increased his work with these patient groups, he came to realize the psychological benefits that resulted from them.

Pratt's work became known to psychiatrists, including Edward Lazell and L. C. Marsh, who in the 1920s and 30s adapted the group method for use with psychotic patients. Although they were methodologically unsophisticated, these men helped awaken the mental health professions to the therapeutic value of working with the psychologically disturbed in group settings.

The first group therapists were psychoanalytic in theory and technique. However, they were soon challenged by nonanalytic clinicians who saw this particular treatment modality fitting well with their own psychotherapy theories and methodologies. Thus the models of group therapy began to proliferate, with many, such as psychodrama and Gestalt group therapy, moving far afield from the psychoanalytic approach to groups.

The proliferation of group therapy models became a veritable explosion in the late 1960s and 70s, with a new form of group therapy seeming to spring up almost daily. Despite the faddishness often associated with such groups, it could not be denied that many persons experienced emotional and psychological healing by participating in therapy groups.

This same period saw the emergence of the encounter group movement, which emphasized the use of groups for enhancing the emotional growth of psychologically healthy people. Groups were no longer considered useful only to mentally ill persons; rather, they could be used to teach principles of group dynamics, increase interpersonal intimacy, help persons get in touch with their emotions, etc. While encounter, or growth, groups have many adherents and are often used in businesses and industry, group therapy remains the primary focus for most mental health professionals who work with the psychologically disturbed.

It is somewhat of a misnomer to speak of group therapy in the singular, given the vast number of models in existence. These models often differ markedly in their methodology and theory, and in their understanding of human nature. Despite these differences, almost every type of group therapy can be defined at its most basic level as treatment of "several emotionally disturbed people who meet with the therapist as a group for the purpose of helping find a more comfortable and effective adaptation" (Halleck, 1978, p.387).

Major Models of Group Therapy. *Psychoanalytic.* That the first group therapists were psychoanalytic in orientation may seem paradoxical, given Freud's emphasis on understanding and treating the individual psyche. However, pioneering therapists such as Burrow, Wender, and Schilder recognized that many of Freud's concepts were applicable not only to individuals being treated by classical psychoanalysis but also to persons in therapeutic groups.

Psychoanalytic group therapy uses traditional Freudian concepts and treatment techniques, modifying them for use in a group context. Therapists engaging in this form of treatment see their patients as suffering from psychological problems due to conflicts experienced at various developmental stages. Not only are these conflicts unconscious, but the patient resists their emergence into awareness.

The group therapist asks the members to comment on any and all things said and done in the group, similar to the technique of free association in individual analysis. During this process the therapist attempts to help the various members understand their resistance to unveiling internal conflicts. This is accomplished by the therapist pointing out to the member the defense mechanisms he is using as these are manifested in interactions with other group members and with the therapist.

The relationship between an individual group member and the therapist leads to TRANSFERENCE. This transference of feelings from a parental figure to the therapist is not only permitted but encouraged by the therapist, based on the assumption that insight into the historical reasons for transference will free a person from its grip. Often a group member will also manifest transference toward other members. This "multiple transference" provides more opportunities for interpreting the transference to the patient than would be the case in individual analysis. Also, the numerous interactions between members will highlight the defense mechanisms habitually used by each participant.

While not ignoring group dynamics, psychoanalytic group therapy primarily focuses on the unconscious intrapsychic experience of individuals within the group. It moves from the level of interpersonal interaction to that of investigating unconscious motivation. Because of this individual focus Wolf and Schwartz (1962) prefer to call it "psychoanalysis in groups" rather than psychoanalytic group therapy. (*See* PSYCHOANALYTIC GROUP THERAPY for a discussion of this approach.)

Group Dynamic. Group dynamic theorists do not deny the validity of psychoanalytic theory when applied to individuals. However, they argue that an individualistic perspective is not adequate to fully understand what occurs in a therapy group. Thus they look to social psychologists, such as Lewin, to help explain precisely what happens when patients meet together for therapy. Lewin held that all elements in a social field, or environment, whether persons, motivations, drives, etc., could not be fully comprehensible apart from their context.

Thus from the standpoint of group dynamic theory the individual words and actions of each group members are no longer conceptualized as being independent of the group process. Rather, all behavior in the group is seen as embedded in the context of the group, with the group viewed and treated as if it were an organism with its own peculiar traits and characteristics.

A representative example of a group dynamic model of therapy is that of Whitaker and Lieberman (1964). They hold that seemingly independent and unrelated behaviors of group members actually refer to an implicit here-and-now concern. There is thus an underlying coherence to members' verbalizations which is unconscious even to the members.

The covert concern or theme of the group is conceptualized by Whitaker and Lieberman as always taking the form of a conflict, termed the focal conflict. This is usually a conflict between a wish motive and a fear motive. For example, one group's focal conflict may be between a shared wish to gain the attention and approval of the therapist and a fear that gaining the attention would result in feelings of rejection by other group members (Yalom, 1975).

The group will experience tension when confronted with the focal conflict. They will then work toward a group solution that will allay the fear while allowing for partial satisfaction of the wish. In the example cited above, the group might share their desire for approval from the therapist with each other, while supporting those in the group who are most fearful of rejection.

The group therapist has the task of dissipating unrealistic fears of members of the group that they will be rejected by him. Another responsibility is to increase the group's sense of psychological safety while helping them to circumvent restrictive solutions to the focal conflicts.

Each individual group member becomes increasingly involved in the group as more of the group's focal conflicts touch on his or her own unresolved emotions. Although the conflicts are frightening, a certain amount of security is provided as consensually arrived-at solutions emerge that promise to keep anxiety and conflict at manageable levels (Shaffer & Galinsky, 1974).

Existential. Existential psychology blends the thinking of philosophers such as Sartre, Heidegger, and Kierkegaard with the therapeutic approaches of men such as Binswanger and Boss. The first sympathetic presentation in the United States of existentialism as a movement relevant to the mental health professions came in 1958 with the publication of *Existence*, edited by May, Angel, and Ellenberger. The aim of existential psychology is to understand a person in his total existential reality, which includes his subjective relationship to himself, to his fellow humans, and to the world (Misiak & Sexton, 1973).

The subjective, phenomenological experiences of each member of an existential therapy group are held in the highest regard and are generally not viewed as needing to be interpreted or analyzed for deeper, hidden meanings. The explicit denial of psychic and biological determinism carries with it an emphasis on the ultimate responsibility of each person for his own meaning in life. Life has no inherent meaning; mankind is free and responsible to make choices; thus meaning must be chosen and created by each person.

Psychopathology is viewed as stemming from inauthentic modes of being. Inauthenticity may come from fear of responsibility and from not acting, even in the face of the ultimate absurdity of one's finiteness and eventual death.

Existential group therapy provides its members with many and frequent opportunities for I-thou encounters, relationships which reflect authenticity and "beingness." The group therapist is to live the therapy rather than do it; that is, he is to be himself without role or façade. Group members are treated as subjects to be experienced rather than as objects to be analyzed. There is no attempt on the part of the therapist to force his own world view on the group, for this would be treating the members as objects to control, change, or manipulate. The group provides support for its members as they struggle to relate to one another more authentically, to create their own sense of meaning in the universe, and to take absolute responsibility for their own actions.

Nondirective. Nondirective, or group-centered, group therapy takes its theory and methodology from the work of Rogers, who asserts that a therapist must manifest nonpossessive genuineness and empathy to provide the proper therapeutic environment for change on the part of the patient or client.

In the same way, a nondirective group provides an atmosphere of acceptance, openness, and empathy for its members so that they can then mobilize their own inner resources to help them change. Since each member enters the group with anxiety due to an inability to relate effectively with others, the proper group atmosphere will lessen the anxiety and accompanying defensiveness.

The group provides opportunity for self-discovery and self-disclosure. More positive and satisfying ways of relating to others are highlighted as each member becomes increasingly free and adept at self-examination, with assurances that the group will not condemn or reject. Persons who are blind to positive aspects of themselves gain clarity of self-perception, and with it an increase in the sense of self-worth.

The therapist models genuineness, empathy, and warmth for the group with no attempt to coerce or persuade members to change their value system. Members are exposed to values other than their own as they interact in the group; however, they are responsible for themselves in choosing and changing their values or beliefs. Thus the therapist, while maintaining a nondirective role, is nevertheless quite active as he responds to group members in a way that will help them to become increasingly aware of their deep feelings. The group usually deals with whatever problems come up in a session; there is no particular agenda or attempt to analyze beyond the level of emotional expression.

Here-and-Now/Process. This model is not associated with any one method of individual psychotherapy, as is the case with psychoanalytic and nondirective group therapy. Despite the handicap of not having a parent therapy, it is one of the most widely used models of group therapy. It is presented by Yalom in his widely read text, *The Theory and Practice of Group Psychotherapy* (1975).

Yalom argues that the therapeutic power of a group resides in two "symbiotic tiers," here-and-now activation and process illumination. In the first tier the group members must focus their attention on their feelings toward one another, the therapist, and the group as a whole. The immediate events in the session thus take precedence over events both in the distant past and in the current outside life of the members. This here-and-now focus enhances the development and emergence of each member's social microcosm; it also facilitates feedback, catharsis, meaningful self-disclosure, and the acquisition of socializing skills. The vitality of the group is greatly intensified, and each member becomes deeply involved in the session.

However, the second step, process illumination, is necessary for any real therapeutic gain. The group must recognize, examine, and understand process—i.e., it must understand itself, study its own transactions, transcend pure experience, and apply itself to the integration of that experience.

The group lives in the here and now, and then doubles back on itself in order to examine the here-and-now behaviors that just occurred. The therapist steers the group into the here and now while guiding the self-reflecting process. The group can assist the therapist in focusing on the here and now, but the self-reflection, or process commentary, remains the responsibility of the therapist (Yalom, 1975).

Psychodrama. PSYCHODRAMA is one of the oldest models of group therapy extant. Jacob Moreno, credited with coining the term *group therapy*, began to develop this treatment modality in the 1920s. Despite its long history psychodrama has not been as widely accepted and utilized as its creator hoped it would be. However, many of the techniques used in psychodrama, such as the empty chair technique and role reversal, have been adopted by individual and group therapists of diverse theoretical orientations.

Psychodrama emphasizes action or behavior rather than mere verbalization. Instead of talking about life problems, group members are asked to act them out in spontaneous dramatization. The dramatization, or psychodrama proper, takes place on a stage in front of an audience consisting of group members and assistants to the therapist, who is called the director.

In order to emotionally prepare the audience to benefit from the psychodrama, the director engages in preliminary warm-up exercises to decrease the various levels of anxiety and defensiveness found in the members. Once the group is warmed up, a group member is chosen to be the protagonist, the central character in the psychodrama. The director helps the protagonist determine the problem to be dramatized; as much information as possible is obtained in order to get an accurate picture of the problem and of the significant persons in the protagonist's life who are part of the problem. Auxiliary egos are chosen from the other group members or from the director's assistants to play the significant persons in the protagonist's life, to play intrapsychic elements of his psyche, or to play the protagonist himself.

The purposes of the spontaneous dramatization are to help the protagonist achieve an emotional catharsis or total emotional release, to break down emotional blockages due to repression and suppression, to desensitize the protagonist to intense expression of affect, and to help the protagonist become comfortable with new ways of responding behaviorally to old conflictual situations.

The session often ends with a wrap-up time in which the audience is provided opportunity to be supportive to the protagonist while also sharing how they benefited via identification with the various characters in the psychodrama.

Gestalt. Gestalt therapy, created by Fritz Perls, become an exceedingly popular form of group therapy in the late 1960s and early 70s. Like psychodrama it emphasizes action rather than words. Gestalt group therapy may take two forms. In the first, therapeutic work is done between the therapist and one participant within the group setting. The other group members are encouraged to observe and experience what is going on without interaction until the work is over. After the work is complete, they are free to interact and share what they experienced during the one-to-one work. The second method involves all participants interacting within the group.

The methods and techniques of Gestalt group therapy find their source in the philosophy and psychology of its founder. The major focus is on the enhancement of awareness of the group members. Being in touch with one's flow of awareness is considered an essential aspect of a Gestalt therapy group. However, the object of this awareness is not facts or cognitions but sensory data, feelings, and emotions. Talking about the past, asking questions, making psychological interpretations are all

considered futile exercises that cannot help persons change their behavior.

Numerous techniques are used to enhance awareness and decrease intellectualizations. For example, group members are asked to turn questions into first-person statements, to talk to persons directly rather than talking about them, and to eschew discussion of their personal histories (*see* GESTALT TECHNIQUES).

The Gestalt group therapist holds that each person is solely responsible for his own behavior, and that behavior is only in the here and now. Each group member has the potential for greater self-reliance and for therapeutic change if the blockages to self-awareness, such as intellectualizing, can be removed (Greenwald, 1975).

Encounter Groups. The term ENCOUNTER GROUP is a generic label for a wide variety of experiential, humanistically oriented groups. T-groups, sensitivity groups, personal growth groups, marathon groups, truth labs, and human relations groups are all considered encounter groups (Yalom, 1975).

The encounter group movement began in the 1950s with the human relations training established by the National Training Laboratory. The basic skill training groups, or T-groups, were created to teach persons about interpersonal behavior, to explore group dynamics, and to discuss group members' problems in their home organization. Gradually the emphasis moved away from group dynamics to group work for the sake of self-fulfillment and self-realization. Encounter groups became, in essence, group therapy for normals.

Goals within encounter groups are often vague and ill-defined, but are usually shaped by a belief that even psychologically healthy people experience a certain degree of isolation and alienation from others and from themselves. Thus, these groups will strive for goals such as increased emotional intensity, heightened sensory awareness, increased self-disclosure, and a reexamination of one's basic life values.

There are a number of important differences between encounter groups and therapy groups. Encounter group members are generally psychologically healthier than group therapy members. They are able to communicate better, learn more quickly, and to apply what they have learned to life situations. Group therapy members, on the other hand, are usually fearful, suffer low self-esteem, are pessimistic about their ability to change, and desire safety rather than growth as a primary goal.

The encounter group leader is perceived as a

guide or facilitator for the group. The group usually does not hold the leader in awe, tending to see him as a peer. Group therapy members, however, deal with the distortions in relationships that are symptomatic of psychological disorder. Transference reactions toward the group therapist are unavoidable. For better or worse, the therapist is most often seen as a healer, someone to be looked up to for guidance, insight, and safety.

Lastly, the atmosphere of encounter groups is usually less tense and disquieting than that of therapy groups. Encounter group members look forward to learning more about themselves and others in the group; they eagerly anticipate getting more "in touch with themselves." Group therapy members often fear and loathe the idea of getting to know themselves better; they may be suspicious of other group members and resistant to change.

Research. Yalom (1975) has done a considerable amount of research attempting to identify the therapeutic aspects or elements common to all the group therapies regardless of their theoretical or methodological differences. He has divided these common elements or "curative factors" into 11 primary categories: 1) Instillation of hope—the creation of a sense of optimism and positive expectation. 2) Universality—decreasing each group member's sense of being alone in his misery and psychopathology. 3) Imparting of information about mental health and illness. 4) Altruism—the creation of a group climate of helpfulness, concern, support, and sharing. 5) Corrective recapitulation of the primary family group—helping group members to see that their interactions in the group recapitulate their interactions with primary family members. 6) Development of socializing techniques—increasing group members' ability to relate to one another in positive and mature ways. 7) Imitative behavior—helping group members to change via observation of functional, mature behavior on the part of the therapist and other group members. 8) Interpersonal learning—utilizing transference, corrective emotional experiences, and insight to assist members in changing themselves. 9) Cohesiveness—the sense of togetherness that causes a group to see itself holistically rather than as a collection of individuals. 10) Catharsis—the open expression of affect within the group process. 11) Existential factors—dealing with such issues as personal responsibility, contingency, basic isolation, and mortality.

The curative factors of group therapy are not static or autonomous, but can be influenced by a variety of forces. Different types of groups may emphasize different clusters of curative factors, depending on the methodology of the group and the leadership style of the therapist. Also, various factors may be more salient at one stage of therapy than at another. For example, instillation of hope and universality may be more important in the early stages, whereas catharsis and the corrective recapitulation of the primary family group may be much more therapeutically valuable in the later stages of treatment.

Orlinsky and Howard's (1978) comprehensive review of research comparing the efficacy of group therapy versus individual therapy found that a majority of studies showed no significant difference in outcome between the two modalities. A few studies found group to be more effective than individual treatment, while other research found the combination of both types of treatment to be superior to individual therapy alone. Two studies indicated that persons in individual therapy sometimes had better outcomes than those who had only group therapy. However, group treatments have been shown often to be effective in helping people achieve more healthy, positive evaluations of themselves and others, as evidenced by instruments measuring self-concept assessment, attitude change, and positive personality development (Bednar & Kaul, 1978).

The available research data do not strongly support the notion of differential effects or superiority of any one type of group therapy. This lack of confirmation does not eliminate the possibility that some types of groups are more effective. The problem may lie with the research tools and methodologies, which may not be precise enough to separate out differential effects. Further research may discover that significant differential effects do, in fact, exist.

Biblical/Theological Perspectives. A critique of group therapy per se will not be found in Scripture, since the Bible was not written as a psychotherapy textbook. However, the assumptions and goals of the group therapies need to be critically examined from a biblical perspective.

One of the basic working assumptions of all group therapies is that human relationships are not only important but essential for healthy functioning. This assumption is shared by Scripture; in Genesis it is the impetus for the creation of Eve. Adam's isolation was declared "not good," implying the goodness of the husband-wife relationship and, by extension, all human relationships. The goodness of relationships is confirmed throughout Scripture, from the story of David and Jonathan to Paul's plaintive lament that "no one supported me, but all deserted me" (2 Tim. 4:16).

Further, the doctrine of common grace would support the notion that psychological healing can occur via group therapy as a function of God's general care and concern for all humanity. God, who causes rain to fall on the just and the unjust (Matt. 5:45), may also send penultimate healing via group therapy relationships, without diminishing the ultimate healing that is effected by faith in Christ.

Still it is necessary to critique and reject unbiblical assumptions and goals that are associated with certain therapies. A Christian world view stands in opposition to the existential notion that man creates his own meaning in a meaningless universe. The psychodrama goal of achieving godlike autonomy is likewise antithetical to a biblical understanding of man as dependent on the Creator. Also, the Freudian notion that religious beliefs are nothing more than neurotic projections must be summarily rejected.

Despite these criticisms the emphases of group therapies on honesty, empathy, individual responsibility, mutual support, and personal integrity cannot be gainsaid. While group therapy is not a substitute for Christian fellowship, there are many fearful, anxious, insecure Christians who may benefit greatly from it.

References
Bednar, R. L., & Kaul, T. J. Experiential group research. In S. L. Garfield & A. E. Bergin (Eds.), Handbook of psychotherapy and behavior change (2nd ed.). New York: Wiley, 1978.
Greenwald, J. A. The ground rules in Gestalt therapy. In F. D. Stephenson (Ed.), Gestalt therapy primer. New York: Aronson, 1975.
Halleck, S. L. The treatment of emotional disorders. New York: Aronson, 1978.
Misiak, H., & Sexton, V. S. Phenomenological, existential, and humanistic psychologies: A historical survey. New York: Grune & Stratton, 1973.
Orlinsky, D. E., & Howard, K. I. The relation of process to outcome in psychotherapy. In S. Garfield & A. E. Bergin (Eds.), Handbook of psychotherapy and behavior change (2nd ed.). New York: Wiley, 1978.
Shaffer, J. B. P., & Galinsky, M. D. Models of group therapy and sensitivity training. Englewood Cliffs, N.J.: Prentice-Hall, 1974.
Whitaker, D., & Lieberman, M. Psychotherapy through the group process. New York: Atherton, 1964.
Wolf, A., & Schwartz, E. K. Psychoanalysis in groups. New York: Grune & Stratton, 1962.
Yalom, I. The theory and practice of group psychotherapy (2nd ed.). New York: Basic Books, 1975.

Additional Readings
Kaplan, H. I., & Sadock, B. J. Comprehensive group psychotherapy. Baltimore: Williams & Wilkins, 1971.

Naar, R. A primer of group psychotherapy. New York: Human Sciences Press, 1982.

W. G. Bixler

Growth Counseling. An approach to counseling developed by Howard J. Clinebell. As a model for therapy, growth counseling focuses on a person's positive potentials rather than on their failures or weaknesses (Clinebell, 1979). As such, it can be seen as one of several approaches typically grouped together as part of the human potential movement of the late 1960s and early 1970s.

Clinebell has obviously been greatly influenced by the works of Rogers, Maslow, May, and Fromm; as a result, growth counseling incorporates the optimistic, humanistic orientation of their thinking. As Clinebell states it, "Growth counseling is a human-potentials approach to the helping process that defines the goal as that of facilitating the maximum development of a person's potentialities, at each life stage, in ways that contribute to the growth of others as well as to the development of a society in which all persons will have an opportunity to use their full potentials" (pp. 17–18). As part of this process growth occurs in six major areas: the mind, the body, relationships with others, the biosphere or environment, relationship to groups and institutions with which one is associated, and the spiritual dimension. Growth counseling further focuses on facilitating and accelerating "potentializing," the ongoing process of actualizing one's inner potential. This potentializing is enhanced by incorporating the "dynamic power of hope," encouraging "intentionality," and focusing on caring and confrontation within the therapeutic relationship (pp. 42–73).

The counselor seeks to communicate this hope-growth perspective in a supportive, largely nondirective manner. Clinebell maintains that helping the client to focus on his or her need for spiritual growth and transcendence is the key to enhancing true, lasting growth. This spiritual growth focuses on reestablishing communion with God, which provides a meaningful philosophy of life, socially responsible values, a sense of transcendence to one's higher self, a love for all of nature, a sense of unity with the universe, self-esteem, a sense of celebration, and movement away from the destructive alienation of guilt. This helps one to overcome the existential anxiety which Clinebell feels is characteristic of our age. For Clinebell, the Bible is full of uplifting messages of hope, growth, freedom, and transcendence that can be usefully incorporated into the process of growth counseling. Growth counseling may appear to be best suited for individual therapy, although Clinebell asserts that it can be used with couples, families, and groups.

In evaluating Clinebell's growth counseling approach, one is initially struck by its obvious similarity to the nondirective, client-centered (person-centered) approach developed by Rogers, whom Clinebell mentions only once in passing. Thus, it is difficult to view this approach as uniquely different from others that incorporate an optimistic, humanistic, self-actualizing philosophy into a therapy model. This leaves Clinebell open to the same criticisms that have resulted in movement away from such approaches. Many question the human potential for growth, wholeness, self-direction, and tranquillity, on historical, sociological, and theological grounds. Some consider this optimistic view of human nature as quite idealistic and unrealistic.

Beyond disagreements concerning this philosophical foundation, some may take exception to Clinebell's portrayal of spiritual growth as "an integrating, energizing, growing relationship with that loving Spirit that religions call God" (p. 107). The absence of such concepts as rebellion, judgment, repentance, and true redemption in Clinebell's view of the relationship between God and humankind reduces spiritual growth to a concept of little meaning or biblical relevance in which God becomes nothing more than a mirror of human wholeness and potential.

Reference
Clinebell, H. J. *Growth counseling: Hope-centered methods of actualizing human wholeness.* Nashville: Abingdon, 1979.
J. D. GUY, JR.

Growth Groups. *See* ENCOUNTER GROUPS.

Guidance. A form of supportive psychotherapy in which the client is provided active help through advice and direction. Such help is given in employment (*see* VOCATIONAL COUNSELING), religion (*see* PASTORAL COUNSELING), education, and a number of other areas.

While giving advice has a place in psychotherapy, a reliance on this mode of relating makes the relationship much more like that of friends or acquaintances. Because similar advice has frequently been given by others and found to be of minimal use, many people resent receiving advice from a psychotherapist. Others, however, are always willing to be told what to do and sometimes seem able to constructively use such advice.

Properly used, guidance is a supportive technique that can help people adjust and grow. In many cases it is the only type of intervention to which an individual will respond. However, it should not be expected to produce deep changes in underlying conflict or basic personality organization.

D. G. BENNER

See SUPPORTIVE PSYCHOTHERAPY.

Guidance, Divine. Divine guidance presupposes what has been traditionally called the will of God. Being guided implies a destination, tangible or intangible, and divine guidance implies the revelation of some part of the divine intention. To state specifically how divine guidance works would be presumptuous of any psychologist. However, discussion of some of the psychological complications associated with divine guidance is appropriate, as it represents an aspect of religious life open to psychological examination.

The concept of divine guidance is biblically based. Many passages of Scripture support this—e.g. Ps. 32:8, "I will instruct you and train you in the way you shall go; I shall counsel you with my eye on you." Once we acknowledge that divine guidance exists, we must face the problematic questions of when and why this guidance is sought and how it is recognized as divine guidance. This is a move toward the psychological realm.

Such guidance shows itself in Scripture surely, but what of problems such as vocational and marital choice? Here many persons engage in prayer, in listening for a divinely inspired thought or feeling, or in looking for a sign—some event that is interpreted as having a special meaning. As one listens to inner thoughts and feelings, how can one single out a God-given directive? Packer (1973) warns Christians against a reliance on inner promptings and advocates depending on Scripture. Nevertheless, inner promptings still influence how we interpret Scripture, and many personal questions are not directly answered biblically.

Misattribution of Inner Promptings. It is important to realize that the mind is full of many promptings that come from different sources. Christian tradition has often dichotomized inner "voices" into the voice of the "flesh" and the voice of the "spirit." Oversimplifying the problem in this manner may lead to worse confusion. If these two voices, also seen as God versus the devil, are believed to be the only ones, then all voices that are not in some obvious way "fleshly" may be presumed to be of God.

An example would be the young person who prays for guidance about vocational choice and subsequently has the idea of becoming a missionary. This idea may be accepted uncritically as divine guidance, without giving consideration to the fact that the person's parents are missionaries and that they are hoping their child will make the same choice. In short, the importance of internalized parental voices often is ignored or even unrecognized, since such voices may sound similar to how we imagine divine guidance might sound.

Until internalized parental voices can be recognized as such and separated from the individual's self, the analyzing and observing ego, there is always doubt as to the true source of what is attributed to divine guidance. Until this separation is accomplished, divine leading toward almost anything not thought correct by the parents' convention would be assumed incorrect or even a demonic temptation. Thus, in this situation one is not truly open to God's leading. This separation is an aspect of "being born again," as it dethrones the parents as gods (or as devils) and allows God to now be Father.

Parental internalizations comprise the superego. This includes the ego ideal, that which we strive to be, and the conscience, the internal threat of punishment for not acting in accord with the ego ideal. Parental voices may often be identified as divine directives because they often carry this threat with them. It is a "do this, or else" thought. However, if it is God guiding, the feeling should be one of peace. Although the recognition of possible negative consequences for not following through may be present, fear should soon be quelled. In Scripture, particularly in the opening chapters of the Gospel of Luke, when the Spirit of God reveals something the receiver is initially afraid but is told not to fear. The anxiety then subsides.

Personality Types and Their Vulnerabilities. When and why does one seek divine guidance? Since any action is influenced by a variety of motives, it is not productive to ask if we seek divine guidance to serve God or to satisfy ourselves. It is likely that in seeking divine guidance we are motivated both to serve God and to fulfill certain psychological needs. Some of these needs, such as wanting to see ourselves as "good" people, may be relatively benign. However, other needs reflect more pathological personality traits that can contaminate the whole process of seeking divine guidance.

In such situations the needs of the individual so predominate that what is thought to be a desire for guidance is often a wish to indulge a hidden pathological need. In the extreme, such needs are associated with personality disorders. However, most people have tendencies in the direction of at least one of these disorders. Therefore, each person should identify his or her own tendencies or vulnerabilities in the hope that knowing the self better will allow for a more mature discernment of divine guidance. Otherwise one risks confusing one's own wishes with divine guidance.

Histrionic personality. The histrionic personality is characterized by overly intense, reactive behavior. Such persons are prone to exaggeration and often act out a role, such as the victim, without being aware of it. They crave stimulation and excitement and tend to be impressionable and easily influenced. Being suggestible, they show an initial positive response to any strong authority figure who might be able to provide a magical solution to their problems. The individual with a significant histrionic tendency might search for divine guidance in the hopes of avoiding the normal frustrations encountered in life and would use the search for guidance or its results to gain attention. Any search for divine guidance that seems to draw attention to the self must therefore be carefully examined to see whether it reflects underlying histrionic qualities rather than a search for God's will.

Narcissistic personality. The traits of the narcissistic personality can also negatively influence the search for divine guidance in that grandiosity, preoccupation with attention and admiration, and characteristic responses to threats to self-esteem may result in utilizing a relationship with God to feel more important than others. When narcissism predominates, the person feels an inflated sense of self-esteem. This is due to an identification with God to the point that one might see the self as merged with God and above the human experience. The power, strength, and goodness of God are wished for by a self that senses a lack of these qualities. Since everyone has some narcissism, one must suspect the temptation to interpret divine guidance in a way that makes one more special or important than others.

Dependent personality. The excessively dependent person allows others to assume responsibility for major areas of his or her life. Such persons lack self-confidence and the ability to function independently. They leave major decisions to others. Overly dependent persons may want God to decide daily minutia for them (e.g., what to wear that day, etc.). The overly dependent person hopes that divine guidance will enable him to avoid being a thinking, responsible adult with the option of choice regarding his actions. It is hard to believe that God would not have us accept responsibility for utilizing our own judgment at times. Perhaps God even sometimes withholds guidance in order to encourage appropriate self-confidence, independence, and adult growth.

Compulsive personality. Traits of the compulsive personality include excessive perfectionism, the insistence that things be done in his or her own way, and indecisiveness. In seeking divine guidance a person with compulsive traits might insist on guidance that conforms to a human notion of perfection, which may well not be identical to God's perfection. The compulsive would also be inclined to conclude that a leading in one direction must mean no subsequent changes. This definition of divine guidance is quite narrow and not necessarily God's view, but the compulsive clings to it out of fear of losing control of the situation.

The issue of indecisiveness is related to the importance of knowing the various voices of the mind. The more compulsive one is, the more doubting, obsessing, and ruminating there will be as to whether a prompting is indeed divine guidance. There will be a reluctance to follow a leading without some proof that this course will lead to good things. God has never promised to show all aspects of a path, but the compulsive person resists taking the first step without being able to see the whole path. Obviously such persons greatly limit the divine guidance they might receive by maintaining such stringent requirements.

Faith and Wisdom. Thus, the paradox emerges that we are to ultimately follow God's leading on faith without guarantees or proofs, while at the same time we must attempt to discern which of the voices we hear is the divine voice guiding us. It is essential that we know ourselves, the instruments through which divine guidance is received, well enough to have confidence that what we interpret as divine guidance comes from outside the personality itself. Recognizing internalized parental voices and being aware of various motives of the personality for seeking divine guidance help us identify and interpret divine guidance more accurately.

Reference
Packer, J. I. *Knowing God.* Downers Grove, Ill.: Inter-Varsity Press, 1973.

J. E. TALLEY

Guided Imagery Technique. *See* IMAGERY, THERAPEUTIC USE OF.

Guilt. *Guilt* can be used either as a judicial term referring to violation of a law or to designate an emotion that follows judging oneself in violation of a standard. The first usage refers to an objective state or condition. When individuals break a civil law, they are objectively guilty whether they feel guilty or not. The second usage refers to a subjective experience. People may feel guilty even though they are not legally guilty.

Objective and subjective guilt can be further divided into two types. Objective guilt can refer to one's condition in relation to either a human law or to God. In reference to God all persons have been judged guilty (Rom. 3:23; Isa. 53:6), whereas only some people are guilty before human law. Subjective guilt can be divided into self-condemning emotions called neurotic guilt (false guilt, punitive guilt, or simply guilt feelings) and love-based corrective feelings variously called true guilt, ego guilt, existential guilt, or constructive sorrow.

Much confusion has been created by the failure to distinguish among these four types of guilt. Theologians have sometimes been alarmed by psychologists' efforts to eliminate neurotic guilt feelings because they were not aware that psychologists wanted to replace these punitive feelings with healthy love-based moral motivations. Similarly, some psychologists have viewed Christianity as a neurotic, guilt-inducing religion because of its stress on humanity's guilt before God. Not realizing the difference between objective and subjective guilt, they assumed that the concept of guilt before God meant that people should experience punitive feelings of guilt. Unfortunately, some Christians have also failed to differentiate between objective and subjective guilt and have assumed that since they are objectively guilty before God, they should experience feelings of guilt.

Guilt and Neurosis. An understanding of guilt feelings is central to the understanding of psychological maladjustment. Guilt is one of the major emotions (anxiety being the other) that sets in motion the various psychological defense mechanisms. Because anxiety and guilt are painful emotions, people attempt to repress the wishes and experiences surrounding them. This repression is one of the first steps in the formation of neurotic symptoms. It is also the main reason why many therapists promote a value-free approach to therapy in which they attempt to make no moral judgments of their clients. They believe any moral judgments in therapy will create further guilt feelings, motivate greater repression and rigidity, and move the client further into neurosis.

Development of Guilt Feelings. Punitive guilt emotions are usually referred to by psychologists simply as guilt. These feelings are based on attitudes of self-punishment, self-rejection, and low self-esteem; they develop over a period of years within the context of the child's relationships with parents and significant others. Four dynamics appear to be central in their development: 1) the child's innate capacity for self-observation and judgment, 2) the taking in of the standards and expectations of others, 3) the taking in of the punishments and corrective attitudes of others, and 4) the child's anger over the frustration of his or her needs and wishes.

Although theorists vary in their understanding of the development of guilt feelings and other aspects of moral functioning, all agree that the child's innate potential for cognitive development is central to the process. Without the unfolding of these cognitive abilities children would be unable to accurately evaluate their actions and the consequences of them or to profit from the socialization process. It is this process that sets humanity's sense of right and wrong on a totally different level from animals. Animals have the capacity for some simple learning of right and wrong through rewards and punishments but not the capacity for self-observation that can result in true moral judgments.

Although most psychologists view the human potential for mature morality as simply the ability of an amoral individual to profit from socializing influences of parents and others, the scriptural assertion that we are created in God's image suggests that we are born with more than simply the capacity to profit from experience. It suggests that every person has at least some ability (or potential ability) to know whether his deeds are good or evil apart from (or in addition to) what he is taught. Paul's reference to the law written on the heart (Rom. 2:14–15) also suggests we are not born morally neutral but have some inherent sense of right and wrong.

The second factor in the development of guilt feelings is the child's taking in of the standards of parents and significant others. This process, called internalization, takes place as children begin to adopt parental and societal values. Since children admire and look up to their parents and because they fear punishment or rejection for disobedience, they gradually take their parents' standards as their own. These standards, when merged with the child's inherent moral capacity and own wishes and desires, form the core of the standard of conscience, or the child's ego ideal or ideal self. This set of ideals becomes the criterion by which the child judges his or her level of morality and accomplishment. After it is well established it will operate much as an internal law, and the child will tend to feel guilty any time its standards are violated.

At the same time children are taking in their parents' ideals and standards they also take in their corrective attitudes and actions. Consequently, if parental punishment is severely punitive or rejecting, children soon adopt these attitudes toward themselves and begin to mentally inflict similar punishments on themselves when they fall short of their ideals. These punitive and self-rejecting emotions form the core of neurotic guilt feelings.

The other contributor to the development of guilt feelings is the child's anger. When children become angry at parents and others, they naturally assume their parents are angry with them in return. Consequently, when parents punish children, children tend to see the parents as angrier than they really are. As children take in their parent's punitive attitudes, they take them in as they perceive them to be rather than as they are in reality. The strength of the child's punitive feelings of guilt, in other words, is not simply a reflection of the punitiveness of parental discipline. It is actually as strong as the combination of the parents' anger and the child's own anger. This is one reason why many people with loving parents still have serious problems with guilt.

Guilt in the Bible. Although the Bible has a great deal to say about humanity's objective guilt before God, it has surprisingly little to say about punitive feelings of guilt. In fact, not one of the three Greek words translated as *guilt* in the New Testament refers to the subjective experience of guilt feelings. They refer instead to our objective condition of guilt before God or to being under judgment or indebted to another person. This fact and the scriptural teaching on the atonement has led some (Bonhoeffer, 1955; Narramore, 1984; Thielicke, 1966) to conclude that guilt feelings are not a divinely ordained type of motivation. Since Christ has already paid for the believer's sins and made us acceptable to God, there are no grounds for continuing to punish and reject oneself by feelings of guilt (Rom. 8:1).

Since the believer's sins have been paid for by Christ, any further self-punishment can actually be seen as a form of self-atonement, which is ultimately based on a rejection of the efficacy of Christ's atoning death. From this perspective guilt feelings are seen as legalistic efforts to satisfy the demands of conscience apart from Christ. This perspective is supported not only by biblical teachings on justification and forgiveness but also by John's explicit statement that "we shall know by this that we are of the truth, and shall assure our heart before him, in whatever our heart condemns us; for God is greater than our heart, and knows all things" (1 John 3:19–20).

The Alternative to Guilt. While psychologists from a variety of theoretical perspectives point out the harm caused by punitive guilt emotions, most also see the need for an alternative form of motivation. Variously labeled true guilt (Tournier, 1962), existential ego guilt (Pattison, 1969), or constructive sorrow (Narramore, 1984), this type of motivation is set off from punitive guilt feelings in several ways. Whereas punitive guilt feelings are a self-centered form of punishment designed to atone for one's failures, constructive sorrow focuses on the damage done to others and the desire to make things right. Feelings of guilt are focused more on past failures, whereas constructive sorrow is oriented toward future changes. And feelings of guilt are based on anger, whereas constructive sorrow is motivated by love. Paul wrote of this type of motivation when he spoke of the sorrow that is according to the will of God "that produces repentance without regret in contrast to the sorrow of the world that produces death" (2 Cor. 7: 8–10).

Much as punitive guilt feelings develop out of the interaction of the child's innate capacity for moral functioning and internalized parental punitiveness, feelings of constructive sorrow grow out of one's innate moral capacities and the internalizing of loving parental corrections. When parents and significant others correct children with firm but loving and respectful discipline, children learn to respond to their failures not with punitive self-rejection but with a genuine desire to do better based on a concern for others and a desire for personal integrity. For Christians this constructive sorrow (or true guilt) is encouraged by God's loving care and provision. Before Paul wrote of a godly or constructive sorrow in 2 Corinthians 7:8–10, he reminded the Corinthians of a number of God's Old Testament promises (2 Cor. 6:16–18) and then wrote, "Therefore, having these promises, beloved, let us cleanse ourselves from all defilement of flesh and spirit, perfecting holiness in the fear of God" (2 Cor. 7:1). His appeal was not to avoid the pain of guilty condemnation, since that issue was already settled. Instead it was to respond in love to the work of God. It is this positive motivation that is the biblical alternative to guilt feelings.

References

Bonhoeffer, D. *Ethics.* New York: Macmillan, 1955.
Narramore, B. *The condemnation: Rethinking guilt and motivation.* Grand Rapids: Zondervan, 1984.
Pattison, E. Morality, guilt, and forgiveness in psychology. In E. Pattison (Ed.), *Clinical psychiatry and religion. Boston:* Little, Brown, 1969.
Thielicke, H. *Theological ethics* (2 Vols.). Philadelphia: Fortress, 1966.
Tournier, P. *Guilt and grace.* New York: Harper & Row, 1962.

S. B. NARRAMORE

See SUPEREGO; SHAME.

Hh

Hair Pulling. This behavior, called trichotillomania, is typically associated with severe psychopathology in childhood, although it is occasionally found in adolescence and adulthood. The hair is usually pulled from the head in a compulsive, violent fashion that removes clums, even fistsful, of hair from the patient. At times there is a ritualistic, repetitive quality to the behavior. This has lead psychodynamic theorists to view it as a masturbatory substitute or a denial of castration, particularly when the hair is pulled from the pubic area. Others have considered such behavior to be an expression of aggressive or exhibitionistic impulses.

Clinically, hair pulling in children often suggests a pervasive developmental disorder, such as infantile autism or childhood schizophrenia. In such cases hair pulling may appear at an early age, between ages 3 to 12. It is often associated with other self-destructive or self-mutilative behaviors, such as head banging, biting or hitting parts of the body, or eye gouging.

Behavioral techniques have often proven effective in the treatment of trichotillomania. Typically, an incompatible behavior such as finger painting is positively reinforced while the hair pulling is followed by an aversive consequence such as a mild electric shock or a time-out. In cases where the child does not respond to contingencies such as these, he or she is fitted with a helmet that prevents this behavior.

J. D. GUY, JR.

See SELF-INJURIOUS BEHAVIOR.

Halfway House. A mode of assistance to some group of individuals involving a shared living arrangement and a program focused on the problems of that particular group. Halfway houses are also called group homes, community treatment centers, and shelters.

Halfway houses assume a nonpermanent state of living arrangement and address the needs of a person in transition from one situation to another. For instance, a parolee or probationer may be moving from an institution or partially back into a state of custody. A juvenile delinquent may be placed in a group home for treatment. A convict may reside in a community treatment center while on work or study release from a prison. A victim of domestic violence may stay in a shelter for temporary protection or support while establishing a new residence. Halfway houses are also utilized for persons who are mentally retarded, emotionally upset, or chemically dependent.

Historically the concept developed in conjunction with the criminal justice system, and has applied to assistance provided to the offender. The idea dates back to 1817 when the Massachusetts legislature recommended that a lodging system be established for destitute ex-convicts. Switzerland has operated such homes or "hostels" since 1905, and religious and humanitarian organizations have operated such residences for decades. Further development came with the establishment of Dismus House in St. Louis and St. Leonard's House in Chicago, which employed professional staff and specialized programs. Subsequent developments reflect increased policy and program activity within the field of corrections.

Halfway houses proliferated during the 1970s when emphasis was placed on community treatment as opposed to incarceration.

Rising prison populations and costs in conjunction with a correctional optimism focused on rehabilitation made community treatment centers attractive. Funding was available, and the facilities became popular. With the wane in community corrections programs and the questions concerning the efficacy of rehabilitation raised by research, some of the initial enthusiasm for such centers has died down (Abadinsky, 1977). The surviving facilities are left with an ongoing task.

Programs tend to operate from two philosophies. One presumes a minimum of structure, allowing considerable freedom of the individual resident concerning program requirements, independence, responsibilities, etc. The other assumes a maximum of structure with regard to personal activities, freedom, and responsibility by emphasizing authority, security, and supervision. The more highly structured programs appear to be more effective in generating behavior change than those that are less authoritarian.

In addition to the various provisions made through staff and program, the climate generated by individuals in a context of community living seems to be one of the critical independent variables. Therapeutic intervention is not limited to a certain time or place but occurs in all the interactions of a group living arrangement. Thus the influence is multifaceted. A positive group climate is therefore necessary, or else the living context can become counterproductive.

The success of halfway houses depends on what criteria are used. If recidivism is the criterion, the results require qualification. Some homes work with offenders who have higher rates of recidivism than the normal offender population. Some are more selective than others and may choose those whose needs are more easily met.

Ascertaining the rate of recidivism is currently a problem due to insufficient evaluation research. In some cases this is due to incomplete data, lack of sufficient control groups, a dearth of baseline information, and reports which do not lend themselves to tests of statistical significance. Most information to date indicates that recidivism is not higher among residents of halfway houses and tends to be lower in terms of percentile comparisons (Allen, 1979). Some argue, however, that definitions used to describe recidivism may be incompatible with what is commonly referred to as rehabilitation.

If practicality, implementation of specific treatment methods with certain populations, and an alternative to incarceration are criteria, then such centers may be considered successful.

References

Abadinsky, H. *Probation and parole: Theory and practice.* Englewood Cliffs, N. J.: Prentice-Hall, 1977.

Allen, H. E., Carlson, E. W., & Parks, E. C. *Critical issues in adult probation.* Washington, D.C.: U.S. Department of Justice, National Institute of Law Enforcement and Criminal Justice, 1979.

A. R. DENTON

Hall, Granville Stanley (1844–1924). Pioneer psychologist who founded America's first psychology laboratory, the American Psychological Association, the classic American psychology of religion, and four journals. Nurtured in New England Congregationalism, he evolved a humanistic theology that scandalized the orthodoxy of his time.

A descendant of Puritans John Alden and William Brewster, Hall grew up on the Massachusetts farm where he was born. After graduating Phi Beta Kappa from Williams College in 1867, he followed his mother's influence toward the ministry and attended Union Theological Seminary. There he soon found himself in lessening sympathy with religious orthodoxy. After Hall preached his first sermon at Union, his professor, despairing of mere criticism, knelt to pray for the skeptic.

Hall studied philosophy in Germany (1868–1870) and finished his Union divinity degree in 1871. While he was teaching at Antioch College (1872–1876), Wundt's psychology text captivated him. En route to Germany to study psychology, Hall detoured to Harvard, where he tutored English and in 1878 took America's first psychology Ph.D., under William James. He became Wundt's first American student during another two years abroad.

Back at Harvard in 1881 Hall gave a popular series of Saturday lectures on education that led to a professorship at Johns Hopkins University. There he founded the first American psychology laboratory (1883) and started the country's first psychology journal, *American Journal of Psychology* (1887).

Hall spent most of his career as president of Clark University, Worcester, Massachusetts, beginning in 1889. Although the university's benefactor, Jonas Clark, frustrated Hall's expectations for financial support, Hall kept his position until his retirement at 76.

Stanley Hall knew personal tragedy. In 1890 his wife and 8-year-old daughter were asphyxiated by a gas lamp that was turned on but failed to light. His second wife, within months after their marriage, developed a mental disorder that required Hall to maintain her in a nursing home until her death.

Hall's fertile mind leapfrogged from interest to interest, stimulating students and leaving new enterprises at each stop. He brought what he called his "child-study craze" from Johns Hopkins to Clark, founded the *Pedagogical Seminary* (now *Journal of Genetic Psychology*) in 1891, and produced his monumental two-volume *Adolescence: Its Psychology and Its Relations to Physiology, Anthropology, Sociology, Sex, Crime, Religion and Education* (1904). His interest in the psychology of religion overlapped the developmental studies and in 1904 spawned the *Journal of Religious Psychology*, which lapsed after a decade of irregular publication. Hall founded the *Journal of Applied Psychology* in 1915. He was the first president of the American Psychological Association, organized in his home in 1882.

Hall's earliest journals published his and his students' pioneering questionnaire studies of religious phenomena. Chapter 14 of *Adolescence*—"The Adolescent Psychology of Conversion"—forms his major early work on psychology of religion. The 82 pages range over and beyond the growth of conversion theology in New England, ages at conversion for 5,524 cases, conversion in literature, and comparisons of Christianity with "alien faiths." Obviously Hall's psychology of religion transcended the recitation of numerical questionnaire data. Some followers were less creative, and by 1920 psychology of religion was waning, weakened within and attacked by psychoanalysis and behaviorism.

Personally Hall retained his Puritan mysticism while abandoning orthodoxy and the institutional church. He believed the insights of other major religions reflected different stages of psychological development, but Christianity—with its emphasis on love and service—formed the highest revelation. He considered the Bible the greatest textbook in psychology, reflecting the needs of human souls.

Hall's late infatuation with psychoanalysis led to *Jesus, the Christ, in the Light of Psychology* (1917), his final major statement of his psychology of religion and personal theology. He believed that literal belief in Christ's miracles was a necessary early stage of faith but that they ultimately possess higher spiritual truths. Christ's supreme sacrifice produced the resurrection—not a literal fact, but a firmly held belief that motivated mankind to the highest spiritual levels. Hall was keenly disappointed that the book received damnation from the orthodox and scant attention from scholars.

After retirement Hall scrutinized his latest life stage in *Senescence* (1922). Elected to the presidency of the American Psychological Association a second time (an honor shared only with James), he died before the term expired.

Additional Reading

Pruette, L. *G. Stanley Hall: A biography of a mind.* Freeport, N.Y.: Books for Libraries Press, 1970. (Originally published, 1926.)

R. D. KAHOE

Hallucination. A perception in the absence of a stimulus to a sensory organ. The hallucinated individual assumes this perception represents a true sense of reality. A hallucination is distinguished from an illusion, in which a real external stimulus is misperceived or misrepresented. In the strictest sense hallucinations are seen as psychotic only when accompanied by a gross impairment of reality testing.

Some experiences akin to hallucinations are generally not included under the term. These include false perceptions occurring during sleep, while falling asleep (hypnagogic), or while awakening (hypnopompic). Also those intense religious experiences of a shared group nature are excluded from the definition.

Hallucinations may be a perception in any sensory modality. Thus there are auditory (sound), gustatory (taste), olfactory (smell), tactile (touch), and visual (sight) hallucinations. In addition, a somatic hallucination involves the perception of a physical experience in one's body.

Hallucinations may have organic or functional roots. The nature of the hallucination is only suggestive of its cause. Thus visual, gustatory, and olfactory hallucinations have been considered more commonly organic in origin. Appropriate medical and neurologic investigations are necessary to identify the source of such organic hallucinations. Often alcohol and drug abuse have been associated with organic hallucinations. Delirium tremens with vivid visual hallucinations is noted in alcohol withdrawal. In the current drug culture LSD and other hallucinogens induce hallucinations (usually visual). Brain tumors, irritative lesions in the temporal area, and temporal lobe epilepsy may be present with hallucinations.

Most commonly hallucinations are associated with psychosis, principally schizophrenia. Auditory hallucinations predominate in schizophrenia. Three characteristics present themselves: 1) The schizophrenic has gone from thought or concept to percept; thus he has perceptualized his thoughts. 2) This is complicated by heightened projection, a distortion in which the inner experience is assigned to external reality. 3) The hallucinated person has extreme difficulty in distinguishing and separating these experiences from reality. So we understand the schizophrenic as creating an external representation of his inner conflict, perceiving as reality the embodiments of his inner life.

Hallucinations in schizophrenia are best viewed from their content. Often the experience is a conretization of a fantasied or real interpersonal or intrapsychic conflict. For example, the concept of being harmed by someone's attitude is transformed into the concrete paranoid notion that one is being plotted against. Very often the original concept has some basis in fact. However, it is concretized into a paranoid certainty and then into an accusing voice. This requires adoption of PRIMARY PROCESS thinking.

Insight into the unreality of the hallucination often is present early in its development. A listening attitude, an expectancy, is integral to the experience and can be used in the treatment process. Such patients are usually able to distinguish those anxiety-provoking experiences that precede the hallucination. Psychodynamic work involves enlarging the patient's time perception, moving him from being locked into the present to a consideration of the past and the future. In this way, the hallucination's meaning may unfold and its function and purpose become apparent. Dynamic work may then undo the underlying cause of the fearful projection. Developing trust in the therapeutic relationship is an essential before this can occur.

Present-day psychopharmacology has provided psychiatry with many antipsychotic agents that rather rapidly reverse an acute schizophrenic hallucinatory experience. Such agents as chlorpromazine (Thorazine) and haloperidol (Haldol) have this capacity in common. They differ more in side effects than in therapeutic benefit to the psychosis.

Often hallucinated individuals require psychiatric hospital care, not because of the misperception alone but from the attendant poor reality testing, impaired judgment, and potential danger to themselves. Some current psychiatric practice is content with resolution of the experience of the hallucination through chemotherapy. Attention to its content and context are often minimized, leaving the patient susceptible to subsequent attacks without the advantage of psychotherapeutic work leading to insight and self-protective awareness of those stresses likely to endanger him.

There are no biblical references to hallucinations. Mental illness itself was not conceptualized by the writers, and so we are not surprised to find little in regard to these experiences. This is not to say that biblical perspectives are irrelevant to the treatment of psychotic disorders. The biblical contributions are more in regard to underlying presuppositions about human nature than specific methodology in treating specific disorders.

T. G. ESAU

Handedness. The consistent tendency that most people demonstrate to use one hand or the other on tasks requiring only one hand (e.g., writing, using a hammer, turning a doorknob). The vast majority of individuals are right-handed (they demonstrate *dextrality*) and use the right hand for essentially all unimanual tasks. Left-handedness (*sinistrality*) is much less common, and its incidence is substantially dependent upon how it is defined. In general, individuals who are identified as left-handed typically are not as strong in their hand preference as are persons who are identified as right-handed. That is, the majority of these persons usually perform some unimanual tasks with the left hand and some with the right hand. Such individuals have frequently been identified as ambidextrous, but almost certainly incorrectly so, since this term implies ability to use both hands with equal ease. In point of fact, there are probably very few people who are truly ambidextrous, with successively more who are strongly left-handed, mixed in handedness, and strongly right-handed.

Left-handedness has been noted for centuries. The first statistical study of it was, in fact, reported in Judges 20:16. In the tribe of Benjamin it was noted that 700 of the 26,000 swordsmen (2.7%) were either fully left-handed or as effective using the left hand as the right. Over the course of history a number of reasons for left-handedness have been offered, a summarization of which is given by Harris (1980). Data bearing on a number of these theories are summarized by Herron (1980). In general, it may be said that the data are more supportive of a biological theory of handedness than a sociological approach. Among biological factors of importance are heredity and early brain injury. In the former case one may be left-handed merely because others in the family are left-handed. In the latter instance individuals with early damage to the left cerebral hemisphere show an increased incidence of left-handedness (the left and right hemispheres control the opposite sides of the body). The right cerebral hemisphere may take over functions associated with speech and/or the preferred hand. Thus, it appears that there is more than one type of left-handedness.

Handedness is of special interest because of its potential relationship with other psychological characteristics. In general, left-handedness has always been looked upon in a negative way, with the more normal and preferred hand being the right hand. Some of the earliest references to this are in the Bible (Gen. 48:17–18; Ps. 137:5; Rev. 5:7). A number of theories have also appeared over time relating decreased intelligence, increased learning problems, and increased emotional difficulties to left-handedness. It is probably true that neurological disorders of the brain arising early in life are associated with left-handedness and other problems of various types, but left-handedness due to other causes is likely not associated with substantial problems.

References

Harris, L. J. Left-handedness: Early theories, facts, and fancies. In J. Herron (Ed.), *Neuropsychology of left-handedness.* New York: Academic Press, 1980.

Herron, J. (Ed.). *Neuropsychology of left-handedness.* New York: Academic Press, 1980.

C. B. DODRILL

Handwriting Analysis. *See* GRAPHOLOGY.

Headache, Migraine. Headaches are one of the most frequently occurring pain syndromes. Two of the most common types are migraine (vascular) and tension (muscle contraction).

The migraine headache can vary in its symptoms and may be of a classic, common, cluster, or hemiplegic and opthalmoplegic nature. The clinical features vary somewhat, depending on the type of migraine. Generally a pronounced neurological or visual prodromata, commonly called an aura, precedes by several hours the onset of the classic or common migraine headache. Early in the headache phase the sensation is one of a throbbing or pulsating pain, followed by a more generalized dull, steady pain lasting generally from 2 to 24 hours.

Cluster migraines occur in clusters of shorter duration, usually without warning signs, and are strictly in one side of the head. The pain is severe and may disturb vision and involve nasal congestion and tearing. "Weekend" and menstrual headaches are sometimes considered to be of a vascular or migraine nature. All forms of this headache often are accompanied by mood disturbances.

The basic physiology of a migraine headache involves initial constriction of an artery and associated capillaries in the carotid system with resulting minimal anoxia and neurological signs. This accounts for the reports of olfactory, auditory, and gustatory hallucinations or visual disturbances. Arterial dilation follows with concomitant reaction of the surrounding tissue. The accumulation of tissue substances produces an extension of the arterial walls and edema and tenderness. The causes of this mechanism are not known, but triggers such as allergies, air pressure, pollutants, alcohol, and stress have all been associated with the occurrence of the migraine.

Psychologically a migraine-prone personality has not been isolated or identified. However, the obsessional personality who controls anger and rage through suppression or repression has been associated with the migraine syndrome. Migraine sufferers are usually more intelligent, more ambitious, and more prone to compensatory perfectionistic behaviors.

Episodes of vascular headaches often occur during periods of significant life stress or major phases of adaptation such as adolescence, marriage, parenting, separation, and loss. Often the occurrence of migraines at these points in the life cycle is associated with difficulties in adapting and with resulting depression which cannot be successfully defended or repressed. Of those patients who seek psychological help with the pain, a rigid, proper, proud, and controlled personality is common. Such persons put excessive demands on self and severe restriction on verbal or direct expression of anger or aggression.

The recurrent patterns of the migraine headache and the anticipation of its onset can frequently lead to social withdrawal and the avoidance of personal responsibility. This effect plus the frequently existing family pressures to inhibit emotion and hostility often produce additional tensions and complications.

Migraine headaches are most frequently and successfully treated with ergotamine tartrate with caffeine. Maximum effect of this medication is achieved when it is taken in the prodromal stage. The variants of the vascular headache which lack this early stage (e.g. cluster headaches) are less responsive to ergotamine. The associated symptoms in all types of migraine headaches—nausea, vomiting and disequilibrium—may be treated with antispasmodics, antiemetics, or sedatives. Because of the recurrent nature of the migraine narcotics are generally to be avoided. Tricyclic antidepressants such as imipramine or amitriptyline hydrochloride may be prescribed for the treatment of any migraine-related depression.

An alternative intervention is hypnosis. The combined effect of relaxation and redirection of blood flow into the lower periphery serves to reduce the pain and may help to avoid the headache if applied during the prodromal phase. Psychotherapy, when included with hypnosis or medication, is helpful in exploring and developing alternative means of dealing with the life stress, the repressed emotions, and any existing depression.

G. MATHESON

Headache, Tension. Four basic types of headaches have been identified: tension headaches, classic migraines, common migraines, and cluster headaches. Tension headaches are stress related and may be caused by a tightening of the muscles in the neck and head. The other types are characterized by increasing pain, caused by contraction of arteries to the head followed by dilation and swelling. This produces a symptom described as "pounding." Frequently these more severe headaches debilitate the person for a few hours to several days. A significant factor in differentiating the stress headaches from other types is that the latter usually run in families, suggesting a genetic tendency toward the disorder.

No matter what the type of headache, it is important to be aware that this disorder is psychobiological in origin. This means that the person is responding to complex interactions of physiological and psychological variables that become manifest in the presence of stress-related events. The individual actually is experiencing pain and discomfort regardless of the etiology.

Research and treatment of all types of headaches largely followed a medical model up until the 1970s. Biochemical and genetic models were primarily used. Recently the appearance of clinical biofeedback and research on applications of relaxation training to stress responses have greatly changed current theories of etiology and, most importantly, treatment.

The research of Sargent, Green, and Walters (1972) reported considerable success in reducing headaches by having subjects raise their finger temperature with the aid of biofeedback. Their hypothesis was that the voluntary increase in finger temperature is correlated with an increase in blood flow to the peripheral regions and with a decrease of blood flow to the cranial regions. Budzynski, Stoyra, Adler, and Mullaney (1973) found that training in electromyogram biofeedback could reduce headache activity in people suffering from muscle contraction headaches.

Biofeedback training involves the simultaneous regulation of mental and somatic functions to reduce muscle tension and raise skin temperature. Patients are encouraged to envision themselves in calm, safe, secure places. They imagine themselves at peace, without pain. With practice they can produce a pleasant, relaxed feeling. The advantage of biofeedback is that patients can see what thoughts and relaxation methods enable them to relax muscles that cause headaches.

Unfortunately, present research by medical scientists continues to search for biochemical precursors. Personality and emotional aspects are receiving less attention, although they are still cited as the major trigger of tension headache. Also, many patients do not believe their attacks are precipitated by emotional episodes. Therefore, although psychological aspects may be primary factors, they are often ascribed secondary status.

Bakal (1980) suggests optimism for a holistic approach combining biochemical, environmental, and behavioral treatment strategies. A number of studies reported by Bakal indicate success in reducing the frequency and severity of chronic headache attacks with biofeedback, relaxation training, and cognitive-coping training. It should be noted that the exact action of these interventions is not known. However, the hypothesis has been offered that positive success in coping with less severe headaches or stressful life events may lead to confidence in being able to deal with more difficult life situations or greater intensity of pain.

Many medical schools and treatment centers offer a pain treatment clinic. These pain or headache clinics are capable of evaluation and treatment. Counselors should refer to these resources or other competently trained professionals, since significant relief from tension headaches is available.

References

Bakal, D. A. Headache. In R. H. Woody (Ed.), *Encyclopedia of clinical assessment.* San Francisco: Jossey-Bass, 1980.

Budzynski, T. H., Stoyra, J. M., Adler, C. S., & Mullaney, D. J. EMG biofeedback and tension headache: A controlled outcome study. *Psychosomatic Medicine*, 1973, *35*, 484–496.

Sargent, J. D., Green, E. E., & Walters, E. D. The use of

autogenic feedback training in a pilot study of migraine and tension headaches. *Headache*, 1972, *12*, 120–124.

F. B. WICHERN

Head Banging. *See* SELF-INJURIOUS BEHAVIOR.

Healing of Memories. *See* INNER HEALING.

Health Psychology. Disorders of the mind and of the body, once considered clearly different are not now so clear and distinguishable. The clinical psychologist, who was once generally relegated to a subsidiary role in the area of mental disorders, is now beginning to assume an active role in the assessment and treatment of persons with physical disorders.

Historical Development. The history of mankind has always recorded the existence of illness. Various understandings as to the source of these illnesses have existed. Sometimes they were believed to be from the gods or evil spirits, sometimes from worms, and sometimes from physical or dietary excesses. Often, as with the Egyptians of 2000 B.C., the practice of hygiene was combined with magic and exorcism.

The Greek physicians of 500 B.C. believed that nature held within it a strong healing force, and that illness was a disruption of the harmonious mixture of humors. However, in the second century A.D. this holistic view was called in question by another Greek, Galen, who sought more local origins of illness.

Galen's view held sway for the following 1500 years, with little further clarification or advancement. The scientific and technological advancements of the late 1700s and 1800s furthered the understanding of the mechanisms of bodily function and the role of microorganisms in disease transmission. The Industrial Revolution also brought with it the disease of urbanization and the awareness that social factors such as pollution, crowding, poverty, and working conditions affected health. The force of social medicine, which focused on the ill person as well as the individual illness, had begun to develop in Europe.

In the United States, Rockefeller and Carnegie, both having benefited from industrialization, were interested in contributing financially to medical education. The Flexner Report of 1910, arranged and financed by them, determined that only recognized schools which endorsed the concepts of specific etiology or the "germ theory" should be endowed. This decision and the subsequent direction of funds served to determine the focus of medical education and practice in North America for the following 50 years or more.

Psychology in 1900 was a fledgling profession that was generally considered to address in an acedemic fashion such issues as introspective processes or reaction-time measurement in normal persons. Thus, it appeared to have little to offer to the treatment of pathological functioning. The study of psychopathology was thought to be the domain of psychoanalysis, which was separate in its orientation from psychology and which was also seen to have little to offer to medicine. A small segment of applied psychologists practiced their skills apart from the mainstream of academic psychology. However, their contribution received little recognition until after World War II. The Boulder Conference of 1949 established the definition of the clinical psychologist as one who combined the skills of research and the practice of the profession.

As the limitations of bioscientific medicine began to be recognized, more attention was paid to the the patient in regard to psychological makeup, interpersonal relationships, and social and physical environment. Regrettably, psychology was initially slow to respond to this emerging interest. A marked change occurred subsequent to Schofield's significant paper (1969) on the need for psychological research and service in general medical settings. Psychologists from various theoretical backgrounds today take part in the application of behavioral interventions to general health problems.

Initially this activity was referred to as medical psychology, a term sometimes confused with the British psychological medicine, which connotes psychiatry. Subsequently *psychosomatic medicine* was used interdisciplinarily to describe the effect of emotional states on the development of somatic symptoms and illness, and until recently included a rather limited number of diseases (Weiner, 1982). The later term *behavioral medicine* grew out of the application of behavior techniques to physical problems. It expanded to include the development and application of behavioral science knowledge and techniques relevant to the understanding of physical health and illness (Schwartz & Weiss, 1977; Davidson & Davidson, 1980).

Current Status and Applications. Health *psychology* is a term which lately has gained more common usage. It has distinct advantages over its predecessors. The term defines the practice within the perspective and profession of psychology, without any unnecessary association with medicine. It also describes its scope as within the broad spectrum of health, which includes wellness and preventative activities as well as illness and treatment (Ardel 1977). The domain which has historically interested medicine, that of physical pathology and dysfunction, is only part of that area which interests the health psychologist. The psychologist's scope includes the means of health factors, both human and environmental, as well as psychobiological effects and illness behavior. The health psychologist addresses not only factors influencing health or illness but also the factors or conditions under which a person utilizes and benefits from health care services.

Stone, Cohen, and Adler (1979), in providing a schema for the role of psychology in the health system, identified several separate categories. One is the psychobiological study that addresses both the unintended effects of behavior on body tissues and processes and the effects of abnormal body function on behavior. Included in the former are such patterns of behavior as Friedman and Rosenman's (1974) "Type A" behavior relating to cardiac function and pathology, and LeShan's (1959) study of the relationship of cognitive and emotional appraisals to immune dysfunction. The latter considers the specific effects on behavior of bodily changes induced by disease, surgery, drugs, and other agents, and includes such things as the effects of drugs on driving and working and the specific adaptations involved in using a prosthetic device.

Another health psychology category is that of health behavior, which subsumes all behavior in well or ill persons that has immediate or delayed effects on their health such as drug use, exercise, utilization of health services, compliance with medical regimens, and coping with disease. Within this category attention is also directed to the relationship between personality and coping styles and the emergence of various illnesses and the sick role behavior (Millon, Green, & Meagher, 1982). Also falling in this category is the study of the effect of various stressors such as recent life changes and intrapsychic phenomena such as pessimism, somatic anxiety, and social alienation.

Alternative to the study of the individual, the clinical health psychologist may focus on the health process from the perspective of the health care system. Issues such as treatment methods, therapeutic relationships, and health equipment and settings may be investigated. Illich dramatized the issues of medical treatment, claiming that as medical technology advanced, some aspects not only lost their humanistic value (as in the undesired extension of the dying process) but also constituted a major threat to health through iatrogenic diseases and medicine's "structurally health-denying effect" (1979, p. 27).

The psychologist can both identify the iatrogenous risks and seek methods of treatment that reduce this possibility (e.g., the development of relaxation and biofeedback methods as alternative strategies to pharmaceutical intervention and possible addiction). The psychologist's interest may also focus on the doctor-patient relationship, specifically its effect on the process of diagnosis, on the course of medical decision making, and on the preparation for and compliance with treatment. Or the psychologist may assist in the medical setting in terms of the organizational aspects of information and responsibility and of the physical environment and equipment.

Basic Issues in Practice. Central to understanding and intervening in health issues is an awareness of the complexity of factors and the individuality of the patient. The age, sex, personal history, intelligence, cultural beliefs, social practices and customs, as well as adaptive styles, defense mechanisms, and stressors all influence the maintenance of well-being and the development of illness (Cohen, 1979a). The manifestation of pain, for example, is not a singular phenomenon but varies in its expression and the role it plays in health care utilization. The frequently occurring case of low back pain combines organic and functional components with issues of secondary gain, therapist pessimism, and available vocational options.

A second psychological consideration is the role of adaptive and defensive mechanisms in the expression of symptoms and in the utilization of available treatment. A controversial aspect of this is whether the individual should be an active participant or a passive patient in the process. Historically the person has been expected to remain passive and compliant. Some interventions (Simonton, Matthews-Simonton, & Creighton, 1978) seek to encourage a more active involvement of the patient, assuming that the increased sense of responsibility and activity will decrease the stress and help to avoid any depression associated with inactivity. However, the risk is that increased responsibility may boomerang with a heightened sense of past responsibility and blame for the illness or increased worry and stress responses.

Thus, no one stance can be held in all situations. A more active involvement and heightened sense of control may be appropriate with some diseases, such as myocardial infarction, and may be difficult, if not impossible, with others, such as advanced cancer.

Another psychological concept, again complicated by controversy but important to the understanding and treatment of health problems, is the intrapsychic processes of vigilance and avoidance. Janis and Rodin (1979) have argued that vigilant strategies are most suitable in pain states where attention may have future benefits. In contrast, avoidant and denial strategies are seen to have advantages for those awaiting surgery or recovering from burns (Cohen & Lazarus, 1979b). Cassem and Hacket (1971) have demonstrated that myocardial infarction patients benefit most from education and psychological treatment aimed at increased health awareness if their defensive style is consistent with vigilance. Deniers, on the other hand, have equally good prognoses but are not benefited by education. Those caught with an undeveloped or inconsistent defensive style have a significantly greater risk of recurrence and a poorer prognosis.

A related issue involves the strong adaptive capabilities for survival of the total person. This is evident in "the will to live" and is scientifically demonstrable in the belief component of the placebo effect. The health psychologist must consequently attend to those things that support this striving and maintain this sense of control. The medical environment can be examined as to its impact, whether supportive or interruptive, on this adaptive capacity. It may be in this area of medical activity that the concept of the patient as a participant-partner is best understood.

Psychotherapy literature contains a variety of strategies and techniques for the treatment of clients with physical symptoms. These approaches range from the psychoanalytic concepts of symptoms in the service of the ego (i.e., "How is this problem helping the patient in some way?"), to systems theory constructs of the identified patient as the "person who is willing to be sick for the family," to behavioral models of malingering and conditioned pain.

Each therapeutic approach has its rationale, its supporters, and its successes, and the choice for utilizing is closely linked to the personality and style of the individual clinician. However, as Stone (1979) noted, one principle underlies all these theories: that of irrationality. Many health care models assume rationality in behavior, in decision making and

in the acquisition and assimilation of information. But people are subject to the limits of the rational and are unable to process all the information that is available. The clinician's role in intervention, therefore, is not only to provide the appropriate information or service but to provide it within the context of the individual person and with an awareness of the limits of the rational and the role of the defenses. Thus, the clinician with the experience of the irrational has his or her place in health care alongside the scientist of the rational.

In conclusion, psychologists historically have contributed extensively to the medical and health care literature. But they have often done this with little attention to their own professional identity. This does not mean that a role does not exist for the psychologist interested in health issues. On the contrary, no other profession is better suited or more professionally equipped to address the issues of the person in the health care system. Whether it be through attending to normal processes to enhance well-being, understanding of psychopathology and psychobiology, intervening in illness and sick-role behavior, or developing adaptive strategies, the psychologist has a special role. Health psychology requires both the investigator and the clinician, the former to identify and evaluate new factors and the latter to apply the knowledge and skill.

References

Ardel, D. B. *High level wellness: An alternative to doctors, drugs, and disease.* Emmaus, Pa.: Rodale Press, 1977.

Cassem, N. H., & Hackett, T. P. Psychiatric consultation in a coronary care unit. *Annals of Internal Medicine*, 1971, *75*, 9–14.

Cohen, F. Personality, stress, and the development of physical illness. In G. C. Stone, F. Cohen, & N. E. Adler (Eds.), *Health psychology.* San Francisco: Jossey-Bass, 1979. (a)

Cohen, F., & Lazarus, R. S. Coping with the stresses of illness. In G. C. Stone, F. Cohen, & N. E. Adler (Eds.), *Health psychology.* San Francisco: Jossey-Bass. 1979. (b)

Davidson, P. O., & Davidson, S. M. (Eds.). *Behavioural medicine: Changing health lifestyles.* New York: Brunner/Mazel, 1980.

Friedman, M., & Rosenman, R. H. *Type A behaviour and your heart.* New York: Knopf, 1974.

Illich, I. Medical nemesis. In C. Garfield (Ed.), *Stress and survival.* St. Louis: Mosby, 1979.

Janis, I. L., & Rodin, J. Attribution, control, and decision making: Social psychology and health care. In G. C. Stone, F. Cohen, & N. E. Adler (Eds.), *Health psychology.* San Francisco: Jossey-Bass, 1979.

LeShan, L. Psychological states as factors in the development of malignant disease: A critical review. *Journal of the National Cancer Institute*, 1959, *22*, 1–18.

Millon, T., Green, C., & Meagher, R. (Eds.). *Handbook of clinical health psychology.* New York: Plenum, 1982.

Schofield, W. The role of psychology in the delivery of health services. *American Psychologist*, 1969, *24*, 565–584.

Schwartz, G. E., & Weiss, S. M. What is behavioural medicine? *Psychomatic Medicine*, 1977, *39*, 377–381.

Simonton, C. O., Matthews-Simonton, S., & Creighton, J. L. *Getting well again*. New York: St. Martin's Press, 1978.

Stone, G. C. Psychology and the health system. In G. C. Stone, F. Cohen, & N. E. Adler (Eds.), *Health Psychology*. San Francisco: Jossey-Bass, 1979.

Stone, G. C., Cohen, F., & Adler, N. E. (Eds.). *Health psychology: A handbook*. San Francisco: Jossey-Bass, 1979.

Weiner, H. Psychobiological factors in bodily disease. In T. Millon, C. Green, & R. Meagher (Eds.), *Handbook of clinical health psychology*. New York: Plenum, 1982.

G. MATHESON

Health Service Providers in Psychology.

The National Register of Health Service Providers in Psychology is a listing of approximately 15,000 psychologists in the United States and Canada who are trained in the provision of health services. To qualify for inclusion an applicant must voluntarily apply, be currently licensed or certified by the state board of examiners of psychology, have a doctorate in psychology from a regionally accredited institution, and have two years of supervised experience in health service.

Because of the wide variety in training in graduate psychology programs and the diversity of licensing and certification requirements in different states and provinces, a licensed or certified psychologist is not necessarily one whose expertise lies in providing direct assessment and therapeutic intervention services. In order to identify those qualified psychologists the American Psychological Association together with the American Board of Professional Psychology developed the National Register. Since its inception in 1975 the National Register has grown to list approximately 60% of all eligible psychologists and is used as an important resource in federal and state legislation concerning professional psychology as well as a guide for the general public.

The National Register is published biannually with semiannual cumulative supplements. It consists of two sections—an alphabetical list of health service providers in psychology with descriptive information, and a geographic index which lists psychologists by city within each state.

W. C. DREW

Healthy Personality.

Until recently psychologists who described human personality focused a great percentage of their efforts on identifying the pathological aspect of personality. The diagnosis and classification of various forms of mental illness as well as the development of numerous psychotherapies constitute a large portion of psychology. Within the last 25 years there has been a growing attempt to describe the positive potential of human nature. This positive potential does not refer to the normal personality or the personality of the average person. Rather than focusing on the normal, psychologists have attempted to define the highest characteristics of human functioning.

Most psychologists use the term *maturity* rather than *healthy personality* to describe the positive potential of human beings. Occasionally the terms *self-actualized, transcendent,* or *authentic* personality are used by some psychologists. Since these concepts are relatively equivalent, the more frequently used concept of maturity or mature personality will be used throughout this article to describe the healthy personality.

Rogers (1961) lists 10 characteristics of the "self that truly is"; Maslow (1954) names 14 characteristics of self-actualizers; Allport (1961) cites 6 aspects of the mature person; and Jahoda (1958) summarizes 6 aspects of positive mental health. In spite of the difference in terminology and length of their descriptive lists, these and other psychologists agree substantially on the nature of maturity. The differences are essentially over the degree of detail each author wished to address. Therefore, maturity will here be described in terms of 5 basic dimensions: 1) having a realistic view of oneself and others; 2) accepting oneself and others; 3) living in the present but having long-range goals; 4) having values; and 5) developing one's abilities and interests and coping with the task of living. While the list could be extended or elaborated upon in more detail, these dimensions cover the basic aspects of maturity.

Psychologists are not the only ones to speak of maturity. The New Testament repeatedly uses the concept to describe the character of Christian experience. The biblical word for mature is *teleios*, which is translated "perfect" in the King James Version and "mature" in most recent versions. Its basic meaning is mature, complete, or fully developed, and it refers to the potential of the person or thing to grow, develop, or become complete.

Psychological Perspective. *Realistic view of self and others.* This dimension involves an accurate, objective evaluation of oneself and others. Maslow (1954) lists this dimension first in describing self-actualizing people. Allport (1961) calls it self-objectification—the ability to know and understand oneself, to recognize how one's present behavior and reactions were influenced by similar experiences in the past. This dimension also represents the whole development of the ego in Freudian thinking (Freud, 1927).

A realistic view of the self often may be obtained by asking oneself such questions as, "What kind of things can I do best?" "What are my strengths and weaknesses?" At the same time it is necessary to ask, "Would others agree, and have I had some success in my area of strength?" It is important to realize that people often have more than one real talent and a host of lesser abilities. In addition, one's talents and abilities are often related to one's interests (Allport, 1961). Often a person finds that he is good at doing the things he likes to do, or can learn to do them more quickly than someone who does not share those interests. The variety of interests an individual has is related to the variety of his abilities. Consequently, in gaining a realistic view of the self, an examination of one's interests may be very helpful in discovering one's abilities and potential.

The immature person often makes one of two errors in gaining a realistic view of himself. The first is to assume he is very capable or talented in one or more areas when he is not. Coupled with this error is the assumption that others have little or no real ability, having achieved their office, job, or position of responsibility by coincidence. This first error is often observed in children and particularly in adolescents who seem convinced that they can do things much better than just about anyone. This is also the error of the "armchair" or "Monday morning quarterback," who is certain he could have done a much better job than the real player. The second error is the reverse of the first. This person says he is untalented and really can't do anything very well. In fact, he says most anyone can do almost anything better than he can.

A person with realistic self-perception avoids both errors. He know his strengths and his weaknesses and does not over- or underestimate either. He can also laugh at himself (Allport, 1961). Just as there was a correlation between one's view of himself and others in both errors of immaturity, so there is a close relationship in a realistic view of self and a realistic view of others. When a person can perceive his own strengths, abilities, and talents as well as his lack of ability in certain areas, he can then also perceive the talents of others accurately.

One may see that his friends and neighbors have similar strengths or weaknesses or quite different ones. (Since an accurate view of self and others is related, one can begin to grow by starting with either. However, since everyone spends more time with, and has more information about himself, it is often easier to begin with oneself.)

Accepting self and others. This second dimension of maturity is closely related to the first. Rogers (1961) so stresses the importance of this dimension that he divides it into its components and discusses each separately. Adler (Ansbacher & Ansbacher, 1956) repeatedly stressed the acceptance of others, calling it social interests and social feeling—a feeling of brotherliness toward one's fellows. To Sullivan (1953) relating to others in a healthy way and mutually meeting each other's needs is the very nature of personality.

Accepting means allowing, believing, or recognizing that something is true or real in one's inner experience. It does not imply that whatever needs to be accepted is good, valuable, or right, but only that it really exists. For example, everyone has a variety of hopes, fears, desires, and aspirations. These are not all good or desirable, but they are all real. Their reality must be accepted if one is to be mature. They must be accepted as existing now in order for change or improvement to occur. Suppose a child gets in trouble with the neighbors by walking on their grass and picking their flowers, but his parents say to the neighbors he is a good boy and wouldn't do such a thing. The longer the parents fail to accept the reality of the child's bad behavior (and thus their relationship to it), the more likely the child is to continue and the more the relationship with the neighbors will degenerate.

In addition, acceptance means that the self or other selves are approved as persons or personalities apart from however many imperfections exist. The immature individual often confuses some specific habit, attitude, or action with the total person and rejects the person, rather than accepting the total person as worthwhile and more important than the undesirable aspect.

Living in the present. The third dimension of maturity is living in the present but having long-range goals. For Adler (Ansbacher & Ansbacher, 1956) maturity involves living in the world of others and finding meaningful work. The productive orientation described by Fromm (1947), which touches on several dimensions, includes meaningful work for the person and for the common good. Rogers (1961) calls the multitude of feelings that are related to the network of interaction patterns involved in living "being complexity"—i.e., one is involved in many interpersonal relationships, both in the home and occupationally, with both positive and negative feelings. A person is all of these feelings; he is a complex being in the present.

Living in the present means facing and coping with one's present circumstances and situations. This involves dealing with and acknowledging the importance of one's self, job, church, friends, family, etc. Each and all of these situations could be described as "where I am." Each has some positive and negative qualities; it meets some needs but not others. The mature person is aware of these qualities and his needs. He is able to see what is good and bad as well as what can and cannot be changed in each situation. In each the mature person has some goals that he would like to see accomplished and is aware of the present state of progress toward these goals. The immature person tends to live with the "if only" or the "when" attitude—"if only it were as good as it used to be" or "won't it be grand when." In either case there is little or no acceptance of the present situation and the person's responsibility in it and for it, or for changing it.

In addition, the mature person is aware that the present is not all that it could be or all that he would like it to be. Consequently he develops goals toward which he directs the course of his activity and life. Maslow (1954) refers to this quality in terms of mature people being characterized by a high degree of autonomy—i.e., the ability to set their own goals. White (1959) describes a related aspect of goal setting as competence, the learned ability to cope with life tasks and to establish one's own goals in the situation. These goals usually are spread over several areas of life, such as familial, vocational, economic, and personal. The goals vary as to their clarity, permanence, and desirability. As he moves toward them, the mature person assesses his progress and directs or redirects his effort as needed. He may even change his goals. He remains master of his goals, and they remain flexible. The immature person tends to be mastered by his goals, becoming rigid and rejecting others or himself for not obtaining or making satisfactory progress toward his goals.

Having values. At first this may not appear to be a very psychological concept, but most psychologists recognize implicitly, if not explicitly, the existence of values for the mature or healthy person. Frankl (1963) describes having values as having "the will to meaning" which organizes all of one's life. Similarly Allport (1961) speaks of mature people having a unifying philosophy of life, while Maslow (1954) says the mature have a strong ethical sense and are able to resist the cultural pressure to conform. May (1953) speaks of values in terms of choice and the courage to decide how one is going to live. According to the psychologist, therefore, values must be self-chosen. They are not values the individual accepts because he is coerced by a society or a religion. Rather they are chosen by the mature person and integrated in the person's self-concept and behavior. They are thus not external but internalized values. Internalization and integration of values in the person implies harmony within the personality and purposefulness of his plans and actions. The immature person operates without values (e.g., a psychopath or a child) or with a rigid, threatening set of moral values (e.g., an obsessive-compulsive individual or a preadolescent) (White, 1964). Some immature persons alternate in various ways between these polarities of no values whatsoever on the one hand and rigid values on the other. The mature person is free of coercion because his values are self-chosen, and he acts accordingly. His values may be those of society or religion, but they have become his own by choice and internalization. Having values is clearly related to the long-range goals described above.

Developing one's abilities. Developing one's abilities and interests and coping with the problems of living is the final characteristic of maturity. The first characteristic focused more on self-perception, while this last one focuses on developing one's potential and skills and then utilizing them to create, make, and do things, both from necessity and for fun. This characteristic has a certain global and integrative quality which Freud would call reality orientation. In general, Rogers and Maslow call it self-actualization. More specifically Maslow (1954) refers to mature people as problem-centered, while Schactel (1959) refers to this ability to be involved in life as allocentricity, the ability to concentrate intensely on problems outside of oneself. Mature people are interested in their job, home, family, community, church, themselves, etc. Of course their degree of interest may vary from area to area, but they have interest. They are not only capable of purposeful, creative action but they like to do things. They have a high degree of ability to concentrate on the task at hand but also to leave it when necessary. The immature person seems to have more dislikes than likes and has not developed his creative abilities nor the interest or ability to cope with life's daily tasks.

Coleman (1960) summarizes this final aspect of maturity as a task-oriented approach to life versus a defensive orientation. The immature person is trying to protect or defend himself from life, the world, others, and himself as well, while the mature person is involved in the tasks of life. He is able to modify his approach and try an alternate approach, and to accept a substitute goal and make compromises when necessary.

The Biblical Perspective. The biblical parallel to the psychological perspective becomes evident. The Bible asks man to have a realistic or objective view of himself and others. The basic requirement is to perceive the self, others, and the world from the divine perspective. God views each and every person as fallen and in need of a savior (Rom. 3:23). Once a person recognizes his need for a savior and responds, he becomes a new creature, with a new relationship to God, other men, and the world (2 Cor. 5:17). Another aspect of a realistic biblical view of self and others is the recognition of natural traits and abilities as well as one's spiritual gifts (1 Cor. 12:14–25) and his place in the spiritual body (1 Cor. 12:14; Eph. 4:4). A realistic perception of the need of others, both believers (Gal. 6:2) and unbelievers (Matt. 25:34–40), is the biblical expectation as well as a divine view of the social order (Rom. 13:1–3).

A second aspect of biblical maturity involves accepting oneself and others. Perhaps the clearest statement of this principle is given by Jesus: "Love your neighbor as yourself" (Matt. 22:39). It is important to note that the love of neighbor depends in quality and amount on love of self in the sense of acceptance, as described above. Acceptance means allowing the biblical view of sinfulness and fallenness to be true or real in my inner experience both before and after I become a Christian. Sinfulness and fallenness are not eliminated by being saved. Righteousness always belongs to Christ and is legally attributed to the person by God. It does not become a personal quality so the person can brag (Phil. 3:9) either before God or others. A corresponding view of others is also characteristic of the spitiually mature.

In accepting self and others one must recognize that both self and others are sinful and fallen. Each person is created in God's image (Gen. 1:27) and is also fallen (Rom. 5:12); each is redeemed or in need of redemption. God loves everyone whom he created, which means that everyone is worthwhile as a person. Hence, everyone should be accepted as a person. Acceptance as a person does not imply approval of all the person's behavior or motives. However, the Bible calls the mature believer to a very high level of love for other believers (1 John 3:16), to a deep sensitivity to their weaknesses (Heb. 12:12), and to the whole body as brothers and sisters in Christ (1 Cor. 12:25–26). The biblical words *agape*, *philia*, and *koinonia* call for a greater depth of warmth and maturity in a relationship than perhaps any psychologist emphasizes, other than Carl Rogers, who came from a Christian home (Rogers, 1961).

Third, living in the present with long-term goals is basic in the Scriptures. Now is the day of salvation, for the believer as well as the unbeliever. Salvation has an eternally present aspect. While the Bible describes the future life with God, there is a very heavy emphasis on present actions and attitudes. The believer is to manifest the fruit of the Spirit in his life. Christ makes an observable difference in the believer's ongoing action. It is the carnal or immature who does not show an observable change. In fact, believers are warned not to long to leave the world but to live in it now (1 Cor. 5:9–10). "Abide" and "grow up in Christ" are repeatedly used to emphasize the current ongoing focus of the Christian. However, the Christian life is also described as a race with a prize (Phil. 3:14). Most clearly Paul makes the third aspect of maturity the model of the mature Christian life: "As many as would be perfect [mature—*teleios*] be thus minded" (Phil. 3:15). He describes his previous life in Judaism (Phil. 3:4–6), which he then gives up for Christ (Phil. 3:8), but the process does not end at that point. In verse 10 Paul goes on describing the model: "That I may know him, the power of his resurrection, the fellowship of his suffering, being conformable to his death." This last verb is a present participle and is the strongest possible way of stressing ongoing action—the focus is on the present. However, Paul further elaborates the model of maturity by saying, "Not as though I am already perfect [mature] but . . . I press to that which is before. . . . I press toward the mark of the high [upward] calling of God" (Phil. 3:14). Thus the model of the Christian has a present focus with long-range future goals.

A fourth characteristic of Christian maturity is having values which are self-chosen. Joshua in the process of conquering and possessing the land appeals to the Israelites, "Choose this day whom you will serve" (Josh. 24:15). Values are a "package plan" because they involve an integrated set of motives and actions, not just something one says he thinks is right. The value packages are clearly indicated in the descriptions of the flesh and the works of the Spirit. Paul in Philippians 3:8 describes a complete value rethinking, and accompanying actions are reinterpreted and reversed. However, the value reassessment is an ongoing process: "Not as though I had already attained or were already perfect, but this one thing I do, forgetting those things which are past, I press toward the mark" (Phil. 3:13–14). Thus the process of reassessing is an ongoing process that merges with the realistic evaluation of the self and the focus on the present, but is pulled forward and clarified by the long-range goal of high calling of God. It is the commitment of the self to a set of values that reorganizes the person and gives him an identity. For the Christian this is union with Christ, which is so characteristically described by Paul with the phrase "in Christ."

The final characteristic of the mature Christian is developing one's abilities and interest in everyday living. The development and use of one's talents and gifts (Eph. 4:7) is a necessary part of Christian maturity, since they are given to the church for the work of the ministry (Eph. 4:12). Timothy is encouraged to rekindle the gift of God within him (2 Tim. 1:6). The encouragement of growth toward Christian maturity seems to be the purpose of the gifts and the goal of the ministry (Eph. 4:15–16). Interest in everyday living involves working to support oneself (1 Tim. 5:8). The daily tasks are not to be neglected or done grudgingly (Eph. 6:6; Col. 3:22). Thus, the developing of one's abilities, talents, and gifts begins to merge with Christian values and a biblically appropriate perception of oneself and others. This merger produces congruence in the mature Christian of all that he says and does (James 2:26; 1 John 3:18).

Perhaps this is best illustrated in the First Epistle of John where the apostle describes three criteria of mature Christian faith: believing the truth (Jesus is the Christ), loving the brotherhood, and practicing righteousness. These three criteria are repeated three times in the epistle. They tend to focus on three different aspects of the human person. Believing the truth has a strong cognitive component, while practicing righteousness has a strong behavioral focus and loving the brothers involves the emotional-motivational aspects.

These joint criteria thus emphasize the unified or integrated aspect of Christian maturity in the personality. The mature Christian's behavior, beliefs, and emotions are thus organized in a consistent, congruent, and unified pattern. He is interested in his daily life because this is where God has placed him (Phil. 4:11; Heb. 13:5; 1 Cor. 7:20) and he acts as unto the Lord (Eph. 6:8). Every task or sphere of activities is infused with spiritual meaning and interest. He recognizes that every good thing in life is from God (James 1:17) and that there is much that is worthy of his attention and enjoyment in this life (Phil. 4:8). Furthermore, the mature believer is aware that the mandate to subdue the earth (Gen. 1:28) has never been revoked. On the other hand, the immature Christian is torn by conflict because he is pulled in two directions (James 1:8; 4:8) and because he is unclear about his identity; that is, he has not reckoned himself dead to sin and alive to God (Rom. 6:11). He has not embraced his identity as a new man or self but rather tries to operate as the old man which he is not.

By way of summary, five aspects or dimensions of maturity have been outlined. The parallel between the psychological and biblical implications has been developed and illustrated. However, when all five aspects of maturity are taken together, two new higher dimensions emerge: actualization and congruence. In discussing the five aspects a certain degree of overlap was evident. The overlap occurs because a mature person in either a psychological or biblical sense is integrated, has a purposeful or goal-directed quality about his life, and is open to himself and others; the immature person is disorganized, having either conflicting goals or no goal, and is unaware and unaccepting of various aspects of himself and others.

Christian Maturity and Actualization. As each of the aspects of maturity has a psychic and biblical parallel, so the processes of self-actualization and congruence have parallels. Psychologically, actualization means developing one's body, mind, and emotions into a fully functioning person. Biblically it is the same; the process is parallel but the content is different. The non-Christian may actualize his full potential as a person made in God's image but fallen. The fall limits the potential and direction of self-actualization. It does not prevent the person from becoming a good, healthy, kind, and developed person, since the image is more fundamental than the fall. The fall marred the image of God in man (Berkhof, 1941). Some Christians seem almost to reverse the pattern, emphasizing the fall so much that it appears that fallen man is only tainted by the image. Counts (1973) calls this latter view "worm theology."

Many non-Christians show varying degrees of behavior and attitudes similar to the fruit of the Spirit. An individual may develop his humanity (the God-given divine image) by utilizing the principles of psychology and mental health, with or without the aid of a therapist, to become a more mature, healthy, self-actualized person. However, the most fully functioning non-Christian will not be characterized by a relationship to Christ or the body of believers, nor will he be motivated by *agape* love, and his self-perception and perception of the cosmos will not be Christlike in character.

The Christian, on the other hand, actualizes his potential as created, fallen, and redeemed. In the Christian the image is being renewed (Eph. 4:24; Col. 3:10). Christ becomes the model or ideal for the Christian and the Scriptures his guidelines. Since the Christian is related to the God of the universe, he becomes more in harmony (if he is growing and maturing) with the divine purpose and pattern in both himself and the world. This is the meaning of the renewing of the image; but note that it is a process—the removal of the effects of the fall on the image. Christian self-actualization moves toward perfection after Christ (Phil. 3:10–14). The non-Christian can become complete as a created and fallen person, while the Christian becomes complete (or rather, perfected) as created, fallen, and renewed.

The image here is the Greek long-distance runner moving through the race to the finish line. The runner forgets what is behind and does not consider himself to have arrived but presses forward toward the goal. This is similar to the growth process of self-actualization. The past becomes irrelevant because the person is moving forward, realizing that his goals are not yet achieved. Thus there is an awareness of one's progress without a sense of either failure or arrival. The focus of Christian maturity is the present, but with the knowledge that one is currently moving toward the goal. This goal is self-chosen. The mature believer wills or chooses to follow Christ, and Christ becomes his choice. Thus the biblical concept of salvation in its various facets parallels the psychological process of self-actualization described by Rogers (1959), Gendlin (1964), and Jung (1970).

Christian Maturity and Congruence. The dimension of congruence, consistency, or balance is also a biblical principle, and it is related to salvation and Christian maturity. While the Bible does not use the language of personality theory, it does describe human congruent functioning in its own terms. The congruence emphasized in Scripture usually involves a consistency between cognitive, affective, and/or motivated behavior. For example, "Faith without works is dead" (James 2:26); "Let us love not in word or tongue but in deed and in truth" (1 John 3:18); "If you love me keep my commandments" (John 13:34); "Out of the abundance of the heart the mouth speaks" (Matt. 12:34). In each of these examples consistency between inner aspects of the person and outer behavioral aspects is either described or encouraged as part of Christian living.

Furthermore, congruence in the Christian life is described by such concepts as fruit of the Spirit (Gal. 5:22–23) and the new man (Eph. 4:24; Col. 3:10). In each case a consistent pattern of behavior, attitudes, traits, and/or motives is described. Each is also contrasted with an antithetical pattern of the works of the flesh or the old man. In addition there is strong biblical exhortation and encouragement to try to live congruently. Regular incongruent living is biblically described as carnal (1 Cor. 3:3), or double-minded (James 1:8; 4:8). Finally, congruence in the Christian life is one of the major themes of 1 John. While more evidence could be cited, enough has been given to indicate that Scripture represents the mature Christian as living a congruent or consistent life in which his thoughts and beliefs, motives and feelings, and attitudes and behavior are consistent with each other and with Scripture.

Summary. To summarize, Scripture grounds Christian maturity in two process dimensions: actualization and congruence. Actualization has two aspects: 1) the process of salvation, which is described in terms of being saved, sanctified, glorified, and made like Christ; and 2) Scripture also uses the word *teleios* (perfect, mature, complete) to describe maturity. The process of salvation focuses on something that God causes to happen to the believer, while *telios* seems to focus on the believer's choice or will (Phil. 3:14–15). Hence, the mature Christian becomes what he is—a son being renewed after the image—and becomes what he chooses, pressing toward the mark of the high calling of God.

The second process of Christian maturity is congruence, integrity, or consistency. The mature believer is characterized by the fruit of the Spirit. His actions and words flow consistently out of an inner thought and emotional life which has been committed to Christ. Since the mature believer lets the mind of Christ dwell in him, his actions follow congruently (Phil. 2:5–8)—i.e., they are both Christlike and self-congruent.

References

Allport, G. W. *The pattern and growth of personality.* New York: Holt, Rinehart, & Winston, 1961.

Ansbacher, H. L., & Ansbacher, R. R. (Eds.). *The individual psychology of Alfred Adler.* New York: Basic Books, 1956.

Berkhof, L. *Systematic theology* (2nd rev.). Grand Rapids: Eerdmans, 1941.

Coleman, J. C. *Personality dynamics and effective behavior.* Chicago: Scott, Foresman, 1960.

Counts, W. M. The nature of man and the Christian's self-esteem. *Journal of Psychology and Theology,* 1973, *1,* 38–44.

Frankl, V. *Man's search for meaning.* Boston: Beacon Press, 1963.

Freud, S. *The ego and the id.* London: Hogarth, 1927.

Fromm, E. *Man for himself.* New York: Holt, Rinehart, & Winston, 1947.

Gendlin, E. T. A theory of personality change. In P. Worchel & D. Byrne (Eds.), *Personality change.* New York: Wiley, 1964.

Jahoda, M. *Current concepts of positive mental health.* New York: Basic Books, 1958.

Jung, C. G. The structure and dynamics of the psyche. *The collected works* (2nd ed.). (Vol. 8). Princeton, N.J.: Princeton University Press, 1970.

Maslow, A. H. *Motivation and personality.* New York: Harper & Row, 1954.

May, R. *Man's search for himself.* New York: Norton, 1953.

Rogers, C. R. A theory of therapy, personality and interpersonal relationship, as developed in the client-centered framework. In S. Koch (Ed.), *Psychology: The study of science* (Vol. 3). New York: McGraw-Hill, 1959.

Rogers, C. R. *On becoming a person.* Boston: Houghton Mifflin, 1961.

Schactel, E. G. *Metamorphosis.* New York: Basic Books, 1959.

Sullivan, H. S. *The interpersonal theory of psychiatry.* New York: Norton, 1953.

White, R. W. Motivation reconsidered: The concept of competence. *Psychological Reports,* 1959, 66 297–333.

White, R. W. *The personality* (3rd ed.). New York: Ronald Press, 1964.

J. D. CARTER

Heart Disease. *See* CARDIOVASCULAR DISEASE.

Helmholtz, Hermann Ludwig Ferdinand von (1821–1894). One of the preeminent figures of intellectual history, whose career blurred the distinction between vocation and avocation. Helmholtz was born in Potsdam, Germany. From childhood he was interested in mathematics and physics, but his capacities were not recognized in the gymnasium, which emphasized training in classical literature. With an undistinguished academic record he entered the Royal Friedrich-Wilhelm Institute of Medicine and Surgery because he could train to be an army surgeon without paying tuition. Upon graduation he used his position as a surgeon to do research in physiology and write about physics, mathematics, and philosophy. These works earned him a position in physiology and anatomy at Königsberg. Then in 1871 he achieved his childhood dream when he was named professor of physics at the University of Berlin, a position he held until his death.

Helmholtz was not an advocate of a separate science of psychology, but his three editions of the *Handbuch der physiologisches Optik* with its pioneering research on vision and hearing would by themselves place him with Wundt and Fechner as a contributor to the establishment of experimental psychology. Yet according to Boring (1950), Helmholtz's contributions to psychology rank only third behind his contributions to physics and physiology. Helmholtz published more than 200 books and articles; a partial listing of his accomplishments includes the invention of the opthalmoscope, measurement of the speed of the neural impulse, mathematical formulation of the principle of the conservation of energy, preliminary statements of the Faraday-Maxwell conception of electrical phenomena, and pioneering papers on non-Euclidean geometry.

Helmholtz's impact on religion was unintentional but not inconsequential. He argued in favor of empiricism and against metaphysics. More importantly, he was an active opponent of vitalism, the doctrine that life can only be explained by postulating a supernatural "vital entity" that animates the physical bodies of living beings. In 1845 he entered into a pact with three other young scientists (Emil duBois-Reymond, Carl Ludwig, and Ernst Brucke), who pledged themselves to the promulgation of this statement: "No other forces than the common physical chemical ones are active within the organism" (Boring, 1950, p. 708). The success of these men has had an indirect impact on religion by contributing to the advance of secularism and by supporting a mechanistic, materialistic view of human behavior. Both these trends are seen in the work of one of Brucke's students—Sigmund Freud.

Reference

Boring, E. G. *A history of experimental psychology* (2nd ed.). New York: Appleton-Century-Crofts, 1950.

L. S. SHAFFER

Helping Behavior. Since the late 1960s much research has focused on helping behavior—i.e., voluntary behavior benefiting others. It has also been called bystander intervention and prosocial behavior. The intensive research was triggered by the 1963 murder of Kitty Genovese. Thirty-eight people watched her being murdered and were very upset by it, but no one intervened or called the police.

Most recent research has addressed the general question of what factors facilitate or inhibit helping behavior. Darley and Latane (1968) showed that choosing to help involves a series of separate decisions. First, one must notice that help is needed. With the demands of a bustling city or of one's own priorities, a rational strategy may be to not notice when help is needed. Second, one must interpret the event as an emergency. Is this just a family quarrel or does someone really need help? Help is less likely in ambiguous situations. ATTRIBUTION THEORY describes processes that operate during this step. Third, potential helpers must decide that they are responsible for helping. Fighting children may be ignored if their father is present ("It's not my responsibility to intervene in family affairs"). Fourth, one must decide what form of assistance is appropriate. A clear answer makes helping more likely. Finally, one must decide to implement the action. If such factors as fear of bodily harm or psychological discomfort intervene, help may not be offered. Assessments of rewards and costs are important in this step. Clearly, helping in emergencies occurs only if one decides appropriately at each step. In nonemergency situations an additional factor, evaluation of the needy person's motives, is especially important. If a person has shown irresponsible behavior, others may be less likely to help.

Bickman (1972) has focused on the factors involved in assuming personal responsibility for helping. When others are available to help, people share responsibility, which results in diffusion of responsibility. With less personally felt responsibility people also help less. This means that the greater the number of people who witness an emergency, the lower the probability any one of them will intervene. Many other environmental factors also influence felt responsibility for helping. For example, if someone has relevant skills (a nurse is nearby during a medical emergency), others feel less responsibility and are less likely to help. Similarly, many characteristics of the needy person also influence people's tendency to feel responsible for helping.

Social exchange theory (Foa & Foa, 1975) identifies other factors that influence helping. According to this theory human social behavior depends on anticipated and received social rewards and costs. Analysis of costs helps explain why people might sometimes avoid helping. For example, costs to the helper for helping and costs to the victim of lack of help both influence the amount and type of help given. Many situational factors can be understood as rewards or costs which influence degree of helping. For example, individuals are more likely to help people they like; people of their own race; people holding similar beliefs, attitudes, or values; and people who have previously rewarded them.

According to equity theory (Berscheid & Walster, 1967) people want equitable or fair relationships with others. When they perceive unfairness, they seek to reduce the resulting discomfort. If we assume we live in a just world (people get what they deserve), the existence of needy people implies they lack worthiness. Such people may therefore be considered lazy, unintelligent, or even sinful. Hence, paradoxically, belief in a just world can lead to blaming victims and refusing to help them.

Helping behavior is also influenced by social norms. One widespread norm is reciprocity: help should be returned for help, and in the long run we expect a balance in help given and help received. However, reciprocity is sometimes overriden by a social responsibility norm: we should help those who cannot reciprocate or are dependent on us. For example, people may give self-sacrificially to children or the disabled.

Personal characteristics can also influence helping behavior. People like Mother Theresa of Calcutta stimulate the thought that a person's enduring personality traits are related to helpfulness. No clear personality traits have been identified as uniformly connected with helpfulness, though some specific traits, such as empathy, social approval, or need for understanding, influence helping in certain situations. However, several personal factors do relate to helping: guilt, mood states, and personal norms.

Numerous studies show that people do whatever they can to expiate their guilt, including helping others. For example, people who do well on a test because of information they surreptitiously received from someone else are more likely to help the test giver on an extraneous task. Helping seems to restore one's personal and public self-image. Other negative mood states, such as sadness, can yield increased helping: helping is often an intrinsic reward that neutralizes bad feelings. Similarly, positive moods, whether produced by task success, receiving a gift, thinking happy thoughts, listening to pleasant music, or even being in the sunshine, can increase helpfulness.

Finally, people possess personal norms which influence their helping. For example, if one feels a personal obligation to help a depressed person, he is more likely to help when confronted with an actual depressed person. General social norms sometimes do not affect behavior because of contradictions; norms for helping are often contradicted by norms for minding one's own business. Hence, it is important to recognize that personal norms do exist and influence subsequent helping.

The reactions of recipients vary considerably and are also an important part of helping behavior. Recipients do not always respond with gratitude; they may dislike the helper or feel resentment toward him. Receiving help implies indebtedness that may seem unfair. In many cultures gift giving and humiliation are directly linked. Unless the perceived unfairness is resolved (e.g., through opportunity to reciprocate), permanent negative feelings may result. Attribution theory suggests that a further condition producing negative recipient reaction occurs when recipients attribute the helping behavior to donor needs such as selfishness or manipulativeness. Further, negative self-perceptions may result if the recipient attributes his or her own need for help to personal characteristics such as weakness or incompetence.

Finally, reactance theory (Baer, Hinkle, Smith, & Fenton, 1980) suggests that people value their behavioral freedom and react against its limitation. If proffered help seems threatening to one's freedom, negative reactions or a refusal of the help may be a means of reestablishing one's sense of behavioral freedom. These reactions can be minimized by encouraging the recipient's choice regarding when, where, and how help is given. In summary, while help is often appreciated, there are conditions that produce resentment and resistance.

Research in helping behavior has particular value for the Christian community, since there is strong evidence that Christians are not always helpful. For example, Rokeach (1969) has shown that people who place a high value on salvation are generally more indifferent to the plight of disadvantaged groups. Further, ignoring the church's recent history of social action (e.g., antislavery, prohibition), some twentieth-century Christians have argued that the church should not be involved in social concerns, fearing a degeneration into an unacceptable "social gospel." These attitudes and behaviors contrast sharply with Christ's clear model of self-sacrificial giving. Further, the Scriptures command Christians to help those in need and connect helping behavior directly with personal salvation (Matt. 25:31–46). Knowledge of the factors facilitating and inhibiting helping can show individuals seeking a biblical life style how to be more responsive to the needs of others.

References

Baer, R., Hinkle, S., Smith, K., & Fenton, M. Reactance as a function of actual versus projected autonomy. *Journal of Personality and Social Psychology*, 1980, *38*, 416–422.
Berscheild, E. E., & Walster, E. When does a harm doer compensate a victim? *Journal of Personality and Social Psychology*, 1967, *6*, 435–441.
Bickman, L. Social influence and diffusion of responsibility in an emergency. *Journal of Experimental Social Psychology*, 1972, *8*, 438–445.
Darley, J., & Latane, B. Bystander intervention in emergency situations: Diffusion of responsibility. *Journal of Personality and Social Psychology*. 1968, *8*, 377–383.
Foa, U. G., & Foa, E. B. *Resource theory of social exchange*. Morristown, N.J.: General Learning Press, 1975.
Rokeach, M. The H. Paul Douglass Lectures for 1969 (Part 2): Religious values and social compassion. *Review of Religious Research*, 1969, *2*(1), 24–39.

S. P. McNeel

Helping Relationship. *See* Human Relations Training.

Hemispheric Specialization. *See* Brain and Human Behavior.

Heredity and Environment in Human Development. The question of whether heredity or environment contributes more to behavior has been a source of debate in psychology and biology for many years. It has given rise to decades of research, thousands of pages of writing, and even to a specialized field of psychology called behavior genetics.

The heredity-environment question is not really, Which is most important? but rather. What are the relative contributions of "nature" and "nurture" to a specific characteristic? It is generally acknowledged that physical traits such as height, eye color, and skin pigmentation are substantially influenced by one's heredity. However, researchers agree much less about the relative influence of heredity on psychological traits such as extraversion, phobias, and intelligence.

Research into heredity, environment, and human development has generated passionate debate. The conclusions of researchers in this field carry important social policy applications in areas such as education, family roles, and equal employment opportunity. For example, one of the intents of the Head Start program established during the 1960s was to reduce social class differences in academic achievement by providing disadvantaged children with a head start of one or two years in school prior to kindergarten. One of the questions addressed by heredity-environment researchers of the 1960s and 1970s was whether an environmental intervention like Head Start could eliminate these achievement differences. The results of this research were discouraging and contributed to funding cutbacks for this program in the mid and late 1970s.

The Hereditarian Viewpoint. The hereditarian argues that differences in genetic endowment are primarily responsible for shaping behavior. For example, McDougall (1920) pondered what would happen if, at birth, every English child were exchanged for a French child. He concluded that within a century England would become overwhelmingly Catholic while France would turn to the Protestant religion.

The possibility that all our choices and actions are controlled by our genetic endowment is very threatening to most individuals. However, few serious scholars are in agreement with this extreme position. Moreover, many individuals who do believe that genes are the source of most differences between individuals often misunderstand some of the implications of their position.

First, those who attribute group differences (e.g., sex and race differences) to genetic factors often focus on group averages while ignoring the similarities and overlap between groups. For example, psychologists have found that, on the average, males tend to score quite a bit higher than females on tests of spatial ability (Maccoby & Jacklin, 1974). On the basis of these findings employers might be tempted to conclude that they should interview only males when they are attempting to fill jobs that demand high levels of spatial ability. However, in spite of this average spatial ability difference between males and females, almost one-third of all women score higher than the male average on tests of spatial ability. Thus, any employer who chose not to interview females for such jobs would be ignoring a large pool of potentially successful job candidates.

Second, contrary to popular belief genetic causation does not imply that a characteristic cannot be altered. An example is the genetic disorder phenylketonuria (PKU), which can be controlled very effectively through proper diet if it is detected at birth. Also, genetic causation does not necessarily mean that a characteristic is present at birth. There is a 50% chance that a parent with Huntington's chorea will pass this disease on to the next generation, but the disease does not usually manifest itself until around middle age.

Third, genetics is not always equivalent to heredity. Down's syndrome is a genetic disorder. It is caused by an extra 21st chromosome. However, only a small percentage of families in which it occurs have any history of the disorder.

Fourth, there appears to be much confusion concerning the degree to which studies of heredity, environment, and group differences can reveal information about God. For example, some advocates of a hereditarian position assume that observed differences between groups reflect nature's (or God's) intended order. Inevitably these observed differences are linked to genetic differences between the groups, regardless of whether empirical data exist to support such a linkage. Thus, if some groups score higher than others on IQ tests, it is because they were "intended" to be the more dominant race. This reasoning has been called the natural fallacy by philosophers and social scientists. As the name implies, the natural fallacy is the belief that the natural (i.e., current) state of nature and society is God's intended order of nature and society. This view fails to recognize that we live in a fallen state, where natural man often perverts God's original intent at creation. Therefore, Christians must be extremely careful when we attempt to infer from "what is" to "what ought to be." Further, we must heed our divine instructions to regard each individual as God's special creation.

The Environmentalist Viewpoint. The environmentalist view holds that behavior is largely shaped by one's upbringing and one's surroundings. Advocates of this position believe that large and consistent environmental forces, such as socialization into one's culture and one's generation, are the most powerful determinants of behavior and attitudes.

Most environmentalists believe that social inequities were created and are perpetuated by society. An important implication of this view is the environmentalist belief that if we now do all that we can to correct for past injustices, then everyone will be "equal" again. Perhaps the most famous advocate of this position is B. F. Skinner, who has called for a "technology of behavior" as a means of solving society's problems (Skinner, 1971).

Skinner and other behaviorists emphasize the malleability of human behavior. Early behaviorist John Watson boasted that if given a dozen healthy infants and a specified world in which to bring them up, he could take any one at random, regardless of his talents or abilities, and train him to become any type of specialist (Watson, 1926).

Many of the same scientists and philosophers who object to the radical hereditarian position also find fault with the radical environmentalist position. The environmentalist view implies that we are mere puppets of our environment and upbringing. No allowance is made for individual duty, responsibility, or will. However, it is difficult for even the most casual observer to overlook the many similarities in temperament and behavior that occur within families. To totally ignore the role of heredity in human development would simply be folly.

Toward a Compromise. Research and personal experience both indicate that neither of these extreme views is correct. Genetic endowment and environmental experiences no doubt set limits on development. However, an individual's behavior is a complex product of both his heredity and his environment. Indeed, the developmental outcome resulting from comparable hereditary and environmental forces may vary greatly during the course of development. A crisis experienced at age 5 may affect one quite differently from the way that same crisis would affect that same individual at age 25 or 65. Therefore, many psychologists interested in human development have argued that we should no longer be content to study the isolated effects of heredity and environment on development. Rather, we should attempt to understand the mechanisms of development in an effort to identify which interventions are most effective at shaping behavior during the various stages of development.

Perhaps the best model of this complex interaction between heredity and environment is the "epigenetic landscape" model proposed by Waddington (1962). An individual's epigenetic landscape consists of inherited penchants and tendencies. The shape of this landscape can be likened to a hill containing dips, grooves, gullies, and gentle slopes. Development, according to Waddington, can be viewed as a ball rolling down this hill. The course followed by the ball is largely determined by the features of the landscape. However, at critical points in the maturation process a particular environmental influence may divert development, just as the ball might be diverted by the wind or rain into a path other than that which it might otherwise have followed. Obviously the new path taken by the ball depends on the features of the landscape encountered during the diverting environmental influence

as well as the intensity and duration of that influence. The implication is that the course of an individual's development is jointly determined by genetic predispositions and tendencies, the forces encountered in the environment, and the timing of those environmental forces during development.

Measuring Genetic and Behavioral Similarity. Since genetic similarity can be measured much more easily than environmental similarity, most heredity-environment research designs have been adapted from designs employed by geneticists. A common theme running through all these designs is the assessment of behavioral similarity among individuals of varying degrees of genetic similarity. To the extent that close relatives are more similar than distant relatives and unrelated individuals, evidence is accrued for the influence of heredity on development.

Genetic similarity follows a relatively simple mathematical pattern. Each child obtains half his genes from each parent. Consequently first-degree relatives such as siblings share on the average one-half of their genes, second-degree relatives such as half-siblings or grandparents and grandchildren share on the average one-quarter of their genes, and third-degree relatives such as cousins share on average one-eighth of their genes. Identical twins, of course, share all their genes.

The statistic used to assess behavioral similarity is the correlation coefficient, r. The correlation coefficient measures the strength of the relationship between two variables. In behavior genetic research designs, r is used to quantify the degree of similarity between individuals. The range of r is from -1.00 to $+1.00$. As r approaches 1.00, it indicates that the individuals under investigation are very similar to one another. A correlation of 0.00 would indicate that the individuals under investigation are no more similar to one another than two individuals selected at random. A negative correlation would not ordinarily be expected in genetic research, since it would indicate that the individuals under investigation (usually close relatives) are *less* similar to one another than people selected at random.

The simple genetic model makes predictions about the degree of similarity between individuals based solely on their degree of relationship. According to this model, the more genes two individuals share, the more similar they should be.

This simple genetic model is usually adequate for estimating the degree of similarity between individuals. However, the model makes many assumptions concerning how genes shape development. Sometimes these assumptions are incorrect. First, the model assumes that all the genes affecting a particular trait simply come together to produce a particular genetic tendency or predisposition. However, we know that certain genes have more of an influence on development than others (genetic dominance) and that the predispositions produced by particular combinations of genes can be quite different from the sum of their individual contributions (genetic epistasis). Second, the model assumes that people marry randomly. However, we know that this is not true because people tend to marry people to whom they are similar. The result is that spouses' genes for certain characteristics are more similar than one would expect by chance alone. Finally, the model assumes that there is no relationship between one's genes and the type of environment in which one lives. However, we know that this too is incorrect. People tend to migrate toward environments that are compatible with their interests and temperaments.

Behavior Genetics Research Designs. Psychologists employ a wide variety of research designs in their study of the contributions of heredity and environment to development. By and large, heredity-environment researchers are most interested in the predictions of the simple genetic model. That is, they seek to determine if individuals who share many genes in common will be more similar than those who share few or no genes.

Each of the research designs involves comparisons among individuals of varying degrees of genetic and environmental similarity. Built into each design are controls to measure or eliminate the sources of bias (i.e., dominance, epistasis, etc.) noted above. Of course, some designs are more successful than others at controlling certain types of bias. It is therefore important to integrate the findings from all these designs in order to draw accurate conclusions.

Family studies. Perhaps the most popular reseach design used to identify the relative contributions of heredity and environment is the family study method. Researchers who employ this method measure the degree of behavioral similarity among relatives of varying degrees of relationship. If close relatives who share many genes in common are more similar than distant relatives who share only a few genes in common, it is likely that those characteristics are under genetic control.

In spite of the popularity of this design most researchers recognize that this is the least effective method for identifying genetic and environmental contributions to development. This is because of the gene-environment correlation described above.

An example of this correlation may help to explain why it is often difficult to interpret results uncovered through this design. It has been found on numerous occasions that children whose parents smoke cigarettes are themselves more likely to smoke than children of nonsmokers. And if both parents smoke, the children are even more likely to smoke. Similarly, grandchildren of smokers are slightly more likely to smoke than grandchildren of nonsmokers, though the difference is not as great as the difference between children of smokers and nonsmokers. This pattern of smoking is the exact same pattern that would be predicted by those who believe that smoking is genetically influenced. However, many studies have also demonstrated how modeling and imitation influence the development of behavior, so it is equally possible that children of smokers are more likely to smoke simply because they are imitating their parents' example. The family study design makes it very difficult to determine which of these viewpoints is correct.

In spite of the problems caused by the gene-environment correlation, this design can still address several important research questions. First, children typically have more contact with their mother than with their father. Therefore, if the environment and socialization contribute significantly to the development of behavior, children should be more similar to their mother than to their father. However, Rimland (1969) has found that schizophrenic fathers and schizophrenic mothers are equally likely to parent schizophrenic children. In addition, Bouchard and McGue (1981) found that average mother-child and average father-child correlations for IQ were .41, indicating that children were equally similar to both parents with respect to IQ. Second, this design can be useful for identifying sex-specific genetic and environmental effect. If the characteristic under investigation is influenced by sex-specific environmental or genetic factors, then same-sex parent-child correlations should be higher than opposite-sex pairings. Again, this was not found for IQ (Bouchard & McGue, 1981). However, Grotevant, Scarr, and Weinberg (1977) found that same-sex siblings had more similar interests than opposite-sex siblings.

Most psychologists agree that the chief

usefulness of family studies is to serve as a complement to other research methods. Results from family studies can suggest behavioral characteristics that should be investigated in more detail by other research designs. Used alone, the method has little explanatory power.

Adoption studies. Researchers who use the adoption study method seek to discover ways in which adoptive children are more like their biological family members than their adoptive family members, and vice versa. To the extent that children are more similar to their biological family members, psychologists can conclude that heredity plays a significant role in development. To the extent that children are more like their adoptive family members, researchers accrue evidence showing the importance of environment and socialization in the development of behavior.

Psychologists using the adoption method often claim that it eliminates the gene-environment correlation that weakens the family study method. In reality, however, adoption agencies often try to utilize information about a child's biological parents in order to place the child in an environment that will match the characteristics of the child's biological parents. This matching results in selective placement and raises the possibility that similarities between a child and his adoptive family are simply a product of temperamental similarities between biological and adoptive parents. However, researchers who have focused on this selection factor suggest that because it is often difficult to obtain information about the child's biological parents, particularly the father, the influence of selection placement is probably minimal (Scarr & Weinberg, 1978).

Another problem with adoption studies is that adopted children and their adoptive parents are not truly representative of people in general. Severely retarded babies and very poor families are typically not selected in the adoption process. Consequently the mean IQ of adopted children and the mean socioeconomic status of adoptive parents are higher than the means in the general population.

Scarr and Weinberg (1978) attempted to control for these problems in their adoption study of intellectual attainment. They compared similarities found in a group of adoptive families to similarities found in a comparable group of biological families. Their results showed that social and environmental factors play very little part in intellectual development. In a related adoption study Scarr, Web-

ber, Weinberg, and Wittig (1981) studied intrafamilial similarity in personality. Their analyses of a broad range of personality traits and characteristics yielded average correlations of .20 for biological siblings and .07 for adopted siblings. Grotevant, Scarr, and Weinberg (1977) studied similarities and differences in interest theme scores and profiles in samples of biological and adoptive families. They found that the biological parent-child correlations on the various interest themes ranged from −.13 to .4, while the correlations between adoptive parents and children ranged from −.15 to .25. They concluded that the interests of adoptive families were no more similar than the interests of randomly paired individuals.

Twin studies. Twin studies are particularly helpful in separating the relative contributions of heredity and environment to behavior. Identical, or monozygotic, twins develop from a single fertilized egg. Since a fertilized egg carries an individual's entire genetic code, monozygotic twins will share an identical genetic heritage. This means that the twins will be identical with respect to all of the physical, intellectual, and emotional characteristics that are controlled by one's genes. It also means that monozygotic twins will be very similar with respect to characteristics that are heavily influenced by one's heredity.

Psychologists who study twins generally study fraternal, or dizygotic, twins as well as monozygotic twins. Dizygotic twins arise from two different fertilized eggs. Genetically they are no more alike than brothers and sisters. On the average dizygotic twins share 50% of their genetic heritage. Thus they are likely to share many common physical and psychological characteristics that are under genetic influence, just as brothers and sisters resemble one another. However, they will probably not be nearly as similar with respect to these genetically influenced traits and features as monozygotic twins would be. Therefore, they provide an important reference or control group for researchers attempting to identify genetic influences on behavior.

Like any research method the twin study method has weaknesses. First and foremost, many researchers interested in identifying behavioral characteristics under genetic control have questioned whether dizygotic twins provide a valid control group for monozygotic twins. The major rationale for using dizygotic twins as a control group is that parents tend to treat twins more similarly than brothers and sisters. But some researchers, such as Brooks and Lewis (1974), have noted that parents tend to treat opposite-sex dizygotic twins differently. Since monozygotic twins would always be the same sex, this probably means that parents do not treat dizygotic twins as similarly as monozygotic twins. To eliminate this potential source of bias from their research some psychologists eliminate opposite-sex dizygotic twins from their control groups. Still, many critics are not satisfied by this concession. They argue that parents are still more likely to treat monozygotic twins more similarly than dizygotic twins.

A second criticism of twin studies is that twins are not a representative sample of the population as a whole. If true, this limits the ability to generalize twin research findings to other groups of individuals. Indeed, researchers have identified several ways in which twins differ from the general population. For example, the average IQ of twins is a few points lower than the average IQ of members of the general population. Moreover, the special psychological bond between twins is a feature of their environment which most of the rest of the population does not share. Twins also seem to be especially susceptible to prenatal and perinatal trauma. In addition, there is a much higher incidence of birth complications for twins. However, in spite of these potential problems, most researchers still view the twin study method to be the most effective tool for addressing the heredity-environment interaction question.

Perhaps the most frequently cited study of twins is the National Merit Twin Study (Loehlin & Nichols, 1976). The study was begun in 1962, when all the 600,000 students who completed a nationwide test sponsored by the National Merit Scholarship Corporation were asked to indicate if they were a twin. Based on responses to this question approximately 1,500 sets of twins were identified. Each of these sets of twins was asked to complete a series of questionnaires dealing with physical characteristics, behaviors, attitudes, goals, interests, and personality. In addition, ability data (results from the National Merit test) were also available for these twins. A total of 850 sets of twins provided complete data for the research.

Loehlin and Nichols were primarily interested in determining which psychological characteristics were most influenced by the environment and which were most influenced by heredity. They analysed their data for seven different areas: general ability, special abilities, activities, interests, personality, goals and ideals, and self-concept. They found that genetics and environment contributed approximately equally to variability between the twins in each of these seven areas.

Loehlin and Nichols also asked the twins and their parents a series of questions related to the twins' upbringing and rearing environment. They then attempted to relate these rearing variables to the twins' psychological characteristics. Even though they assessed rearing variables that they assumed would be strongly related to psychological development and behavior, none of their rearing variables was significantly related to any of the major trait dimensions they studied. Loehlin and Nichols concluded that the environment appears to be acting randomly in shaping behavior.

The National Merit Twin Study is most noteworthy because it was a large-scale, well-controlled study that replicated results found previously by almost 100 other sets of twin researchers. In his summary of these studies Nichols (1978) concludes that they are consistent with the findings from the National Merit Twin Study that heredity and environment each account for approximately half of the variability in human behavior.

The twin study method has also been useful for studying the etiology of certain forms of psychopathology and antisocial behavior. For example, Bertelsen, Harvald, and Hague (1977) reported concordance rates of 58% for monozygotic twins for bipolar disorder, while the concordance rate for dizygotic twins was only 17%. Such data reveal the strong influence of heredity on bipolar disorder. Rosanoff, Handy, and Rosanoff (1934) found that criminality also appeared to be under at least moderate genetic influence. A twin study by Slater and Shields (1969) revealed that the tendency to suffer from neurotic anxiety is influenced by one's heredity, though there was no evidence of a genetic predisposition for hysteria or neurotic depression.

As noted above, critics of twins studies have charged that monozygotic twins are more similar than dizygotic twins because monozygotic twins are treated more similarly. However, this variable could be eliminated if researchers could study the behavior of twins who were separated at birth and raised in different environments. If monozygotic twins reared in totally separate homes were more similar to each other than dizygotic twins reared apart, it would be powerful evidence for the importance of genetic factors in development. If, on the other hand, monozygotic twins reared apart were not very similar, it would indicate that genetics has very little to do with behavior.

To date researchers have completed two major studies of twins reared apart. Newman, Freeman, and Holzinger (1937) studied 19 sets of monozygotic twins reared apart. They obtained a number of physical, cognitive, and personality measures from their twins, which they then compared to data obtained from samples of 50 monozygotic twins reared together and 50 dizygotic twins reared together. Their data led them to two conclusions. First, they concluded that the effects of heredity are very powerful. In spite of the fact that they had been raised in disparate environments, their monozygotic twins reared apart were remarkably similar to each other—as similar as fraternal twins who had been reared in the same family. Second, they concluded that the environment can also be a very powerful influence on behavior. They based this conclusion on the fact that their monozygotic twins reared apart were not nearly as similar to each other as those reared together.

Shields (1962) conducted his research in England on 88 sets of monozygotic twins, half reared together and half reared apart. He found that identical twins reared apart were even more alike than identical twins reared together on measures of extraversion and of neuroticism. This was interpreted as strongly supportive of a hereditarian position.

In summarizing the data from these two studies Jensen (1970) concluded that heredity contributes approximately 85% of the total variability in IQ, with environment and IQ test error contributing the remaining 15%. This conclusion is very similar to that put forward by Burks (1928) based on a study of adopted children she conducted in the 1920s.

One final major study of twins reared apart, still under way at date of writing, is Bouchard's Minnesota Twin Study. Studying monozygotic and dizygotic twins raised together and apart, the research involves the twins spending a week in Minnesota, during which time they undergo rigorous medical examinations and psychological assessment. In total, the twins respond to over 15,000 multiple choice questions during the week, and they spend approximately 60 hours in over a dozen different laboratories.

Thus far Bouchard has analyzed only a comparatively small amount of the data he has amassed. However, his tentative results (Bouchard, 1983) indicate that monozygotic twins reared apart are much more similar to each other than are dizygotic twins reared apart. The Minnesota Multiphasic Personality Inventory (MMPI) profiles for the monozygotics raised apart are remarkably similar. In addition, Bouchard has uncovered some unexpected similarities between monozygotic twins reared apart for psychological variables that researchers previously believed were independent of genetic influence. Final results of this important study are eagerly awaited by behavior genetics researchers.

Conclusion. We are still a long way from understanding many of the mechanisms of human development. Most researchers agree that the influence of heredity is quite powerful—much more powerful than was assumed even a decade ago. The accumulated research evidence indicates that physical characteristics such as eye color are relatively invulnerable to environmental influence, while attitudes and values are the most strongly influenced by one's upbringing. Intelligence, psychopathology, personality, interests, and weight seem to be influenced significantly by both heredity and environment.

There still remain a number of unresolved research questions, however. Even though we know that heredity has a strong influence on human development, we understand very little about how genes operate. And we understand even less about which environmental pressures are "trait-relevant." Future examination of genetic and environmental processes will require greater interaction between psychologists and geneticists. Both disciplines have a great deal to contribute to the development and exploration of more sophisticated developmental models. However, answers to important research questions are likely to require fewer quantitative studies dealing with the relative contributions of heredity and environment and more complex studies of developmental mechanisms. Such studies will likely be much more fruitful if psychologists and geneticists pool their expertise and creatively combine their best research methods.

References

Bertelsen, A., Harvald, B., & Hague, M. A Danish twin study of manic-depressive disorders. *British Journal of Psychiatry*, 1977, *130*, 330–351.

Bouchard, T. J. Twins: Nature's twice told tale, *1983 yearbook of science and the future*. Chicago: Encyclopaedia Britannica, 1983.

Bouchard, T. J., & McGue, M. Familial studies of intelligence: A review. *Science*, 1981, *212*, 1055–1059.

Brooks, J., & Lewis, M. Attachment behavior in thirteen-month-old opposite-sex twins. *Child Development*, 1974, *45*, 243–247.

Burks, B. S. The relative influence of nature and nurture upon mental development: A comparative study of foster parent–foster child resemblance and true parent–true child resemblance. *27th Yearbook of the National Society for the Study of Education*, 1928, Part I, 219–316.

Grotevant, H. D., Scarr, S., & Weinberg, R. A. Patterns of

interest similarity in adoptive and biological families. *Journal of Personality and Social Psychology*, 1977, *35*, 667–676.

Jensen, A. R. IQ's of identical twins reared apart. *Behavior Genetics*, 1970, *1*, 133–148.

Loehlin, J. C., & Nichols, R. C. *Heredity, environment and personality: A study of 850 sets of twins.* Austin: University of Texas Press, 1976.

Maccoby, E. E., & Jacklin, C. N. *The psychology of sex differences.* Stanford, Calif.: Stanford University Press, 1974.

McDougall, W. *The group mind.* New York: Putnams, 1920.

Newman, H. H., Freeman, F. N., & Holzinger, K. J. *Twins: A study of heredity and environment.* Chicago: University of Chicago Press, 1937.

Nichols, R. C. Twin studies of ability, personality and interests. *Homo*, 1978, *29*, 158–173.

Rimland, B. Psychogenesis versus biogenesis: The issues and the evidence. In S. C. Plog & R. B. Edgerton (Eds.), *Changing perspectives in mental illness.* New York: Holt, Rinehart, & Winston, 1969.

Rosanoff, A. J., Handy, L. M., & Rosanoff, I. A. Criminality and delinquency in twins. *Journal of Criminal law and criminology*, 1934, *24*, 923–934.

Scarr, S., Webber, P. L., Weinberg, R. A., & Wittig, M. A. Personality resemblance among adolescents and their parents in biologically-related and adoptive families. *Journal of Personality and Social Psychology*, 1981, *40*, 885–898.

Scarr, S., & Weinberg, R. A. The influence of "family background" on intellectual attainment. *American Sociological Review*, 1978, *43*, 674–692.

Shields, J. *Monozygotic twins.* London: Oxford University Press, 1962.

Skinner, B. F. *Beyond freedom and dignity.* New York: Knopf, 1971.

Slater, E., & Shields, J. Genetical aspects of anxiety. In M. H. Lader (Ed.), *British Journal of Psychiatry*, Special Publication No. 3. London: Headley, 1969.

Waddington, C. H. *New patterns in genetics and development.* New York: Columbia University Press, 1962.

Watson, J. B. Experimental studies on the growth of the emotions. In C. A. Murchison (Ed.), *Psychologies of 1925.* Worcester, Mass.: Clark University Press, 1926.

J. J. McHenry and J. Fisher

Hermaphroditism and Pseudohermaphroditism.

A hermaphrodite is a person who possesses both male and female sex glands. The hermaphrodite may have an ovary and a testicle, or a modified sex gland that contains both ovarian and testicular tissue. The cells of most hermaphrodites manifest the typical XX female chromosome pattern. Some hermaphrodites' bodies contain some cells with female chromosomes (XX) and other cells with male chromosomes (XY).

Most hermaphrodites manifest developed breasts and a penis above a vaginal opening. Both the penis and vagina are likely to be rudimentary and incompletely developed. Reproductive organs are usually only partially developed and nonfunctional. Hermaphrodites are characterized by an unusual mixture of sex glands, hormones, organs, and genitals.

True hermaphrodites are extremely rare. Less than 100 cases have been documented in modern times. A similar hormonal disorder that occurs more frequently than true hermaphroditism is known as pseudohermaphroditism. Pseudohermaphrodites, like hermaphrodites, may have a combination of male and female genitals and reproductive organs. Unlike true hermaphrodites, pseudohermaphrodites do not have both male and female sex glands or both testicular tissue and ovarian tissue. Pseudohermaphroditism is also very rare.

Most instances of pseudohermaphroditism are caused by hormonal abnormalities during prenatal development. If the infant developing within the womb is a chromosomal female (XX), an excess of male sex hormones (androgens) can disrupt her normal sexual development. Too much androgen will result in the enlargement of the clitoris so that it resembles a penis and in the fusion of the labia to resemble a scrotum. In spite of the fact that the infant may have internal female organs, her genitals may resemble a male's more than a female's. As a result many of these children have been raised as males even though they are females.

At least three causes exist for excessive androgen levels during prenatal development. The first is genetic. In advenogenital syndrome a recessive gene stimulates the child's adrenal glands to produce excessive androgen. (All persons produce both male and female sex hormones.) Since this genetic defect is present throughout life, the masculinizing effect continues after birth. A second cause for excessive androgen during pregnancy is traceable to the ingestion of progestin, a synthetic form of the hormone progesterone, a female hormone secreted by the ovaries which may stimulate androgen. Progestin was prescribed to some women in order to minimize the risk of miscarriage. This practice has since been discontinued. A third androgen-related cause for pseudohermaphroditism in females is a maternal tumor which stimulates androgen secretion.

If the fetal child is a genetic male (XY), he may become pseudohermaphroditic through a failure to secrete androgens, or if these are secreted, a failure of the body tissue to respond to them. Testicular feminization is an example of this condition. Ample supplies of male sex hormones are produced, but due to a genetic anomaly the receptor sites are blocked. As a result prenatal development follows a feminine course and the infant's genitals look more female than male. These persons usually have a fairly typical feminine physique with developed breasts, undescended testes, a closed-ended vagina but no uterus, and sparse body hair. Not surprisingly, most of these persons have been raised as women.

The psychological impact of hermaphroditism and pseudohermaphroditism on the patient and his or her parents is tremendous. The prospects for successful adjustment are much greater today than previously for several reasons. Today physicians are able to make a rapid diagnosis and determine the genetic sex of the infant. Previously parents and physicians could only guess at whether they should raise the child as a male or female, and sometimes they guessed wrong. Second, surgery can be performed at a very early age to reconstruct the child's genitals. This can be done before gender identity is established, thus minimizing the trauma. Hormone therapy can be initiated to enable the child to develop more normally, especially through puberty. Finally, counseling can be provided to help the parents assign the proper gender and cope with the shock and guilt. Supportive developmental counseling for the child can also be of great benefit.

Psychologist John Money, who has done extensive research on these disorders, has indicated their value in demonstrating that a person's sex is actually based on six characteristics: chromosomal gender, gonadal gender, hormonal gender, internal accessory organs, external genital appearance, and assigned gender (Money, 1980). The life histories of hermaphrodites and pseudohermaphrodites make this clear. Most of the persons studied conformed to the sex role to which they were assigned and in which they were raised. While the contribution of social environmental factors to gender identity is significant, the degree to which they interact with the person's biological state is still undetermined.

Reference

Money, J. The future of sex and gender. *Journal of Clinical Child Psychology*, 1980, 9(2), 132–133.

Additional Reading

Overzier, C. (Ed.). *Intersexuality*. New York: Academic Press, 1963.

C. D. Dolph

See Sexuality.

History of Psychology. *See* Psychology, History of.

Histrionic Personality Disorder. The essential features of the histrionic personality disorder form a triad of an immature, overdramatic person with intensely expressed but shallow feelings and seriously disturbed interpersonal relationships. This classification incorporates the older hysterical character disorder.

It is usually the intense affective overreactions to relatively minor stimuli which bring the hysteric to the attention of the therapist. The complaint of profound depressions or pseudomanic episodes is expressed. Hysterical emotionality is considered shallow because it is usually inconstant and unreasonable. The angry outbursts and deep melancholy of these persons characteristically are loud and draw significant others around them into a dramatic turmoil.

At other times these patients can be charming and appealing, though they are rarely seen as genuine even then. This shallow affect and the tendency of the hysteric to be demanding and manipulative keep friendships from deepening into intimacy. Casual relationships are frequently passionate but deteriorate rapidly under the assault of what appears to be self-centered, childish, and self-defeating behavior.

Hysteria and Sexuality. Traditionally the hysteric's difficulty with intimacy has been understood in terms of disordered sexuality. At worst this was seen as a frustrating paradox of seductiveness and frigidity. A little more kindly, Chodoff and Lyons (1958) call hysterics "caricatures of femininity." Blackner and Tupin (1977) refined this to "the caricature of the sexual role." In fact, the widespread impression that these people have specific sexual problems has not held up under the scrutiny of statistical analysis (Slavney & McHugh, 1974). Perhaps for this reason there has been a theoretical shift away from sexuality and toward a focus on the dramatic.

DSM-III has chosen the term *histrionic* which is derived from the Latin *histrio*, actor. *Hysteric*, on the other hand, comes from *hystericus*, womb. This latter term reflects an ancient tradition of associating various complaints, occurring particularly in excitable women, with a wandering uterus. For example, *globus hystericus*, or choking sensation in the throat caused by strong emotion, was thought to be caused by the pressure of the womb in the chest. Even though this association with the woman's womb and reproductive function makes the hysteric among the first patients to be described in medical history (Veith, 1965), it has introduced a good deal of confusion in our understanding of the condition.

"Hysterical," for example, can describe a

highly excitable person who dramatically overreacts in social situations. More technically, a number of flamboyant paralyses, sensory losses, or muteness which come on under psychological stress and have no physiological explanation, have been labeled hysterical. These are now called *conversion phenomena*.

The association with the womb also served to tightly link hysteria with females. If one has this preconceived conviction, his clinical experience tends to reinforce it when flighty, childish, or naïve people are seen. It has been a myth of the profession that hysteria occurs only in females or homosexual males—yet how it occurs in males remains to be clarified. Some have suggested a parallel between hysteria in the female and sociopathy in the male (Halleck, 1967).

Another ancient idea is that the hysteric is hypochondriacal. This too was supposedly caused by the wandering womb, and medical treatments which attempted to lure the organ back into the pelvis and drive it away from the chest were used as late as the nineteenth century. It has only been with the criteria of *DSM-III* that both the hypochondriacal and the conversion symptoms have been completely separated from this disorder.

Psychoanalytic Theories. The concept of the hysteric as a personality disorder is much more modern, though it was implicit to some extent in the earliest psychoanalytic writings (Lazare, 1971). Freud's work before the turn of the century was concerned with understanding and removing symptoms, mostly conversion complaints. Later he associated these with what he called "the erotic libidinal type." In 1925 Abraham demonstrated how the symptoms were precisely associated with stages of libidinal development, and it was then that the idea of the "hysterical character" began to develop. He connected this with fixations or regressions to the early phallic (genital) organization. Neither he nor Freud had actually used the term *hysterical character*, but it became common terminology almost immediately.

The first thorough psychoanalytic discussion of the hysterical character was that of Wittels (1930). He clearly linked the symptoms to character and described these patients as infantile and feminine. He thought that the pathology occurred before the genital phase and was therefore more serious. Much later Marmor (1953) amplified this, noting that although hysterical symptoms are usually among the easiest of all clinical symptoms to resolve, the underlying hysterical character is often one of the most difficult to alter. He

worked out in detail the oral dynamics involved.

The field was to remain somewhat muddled until a paper by Chodoff and Lyons (1958) at last clearly distinguished the personality disorder from conversion symptoms. The personality disorder, when studied independently, has since then been seen as occurring in both a "good" form (Zetzel, 1968) and a much more severe state. The difficult hysteric presents some special problems in analysis, particularly in the transference. These problems have not been clarified in terms of oral dynamics. Rather, they are now being studied in terms of the even earlier dynamics of object relationships (Kernberg, 1976; *see* OBJECT RELATIONS THEORY).

Efforts to define the disorder more precisely have been even more frustrating. Statistical analysis and even the Minnesota Multiphasic Personality Inventory have failed to clearly distinguish hysteria from the pervasive depression that seems to accompany at least its clinical presentation. Again, about the only distinguishing quality that stands out is that histrionic personalities organize their experiences around a dramatic axis (Slavney & McHugh, 1974).

Cultural and Phenomenological Perspectives. The dramatic or narrative quality of life has been almost obscured in Western thought for a long time, and this has made the hysteric often difficult for the social scientist to understand. In the form of myth, fable, and history drama has an important, fundamental role for human beings, both individually and culturally. It has always been appreciated by thoughtful therapists (Spense, 1982). Its deep roots in the biblical tradition of both Jews and Gentiles are also currently being reexplored in terms of narrative theology.

At best, the histrionic personality might serve to keep more compulsive persons aware of the dramatic cause of events. This adds a distinct grace to the ordinary and mundane. Hysterics are frequently found matched with more methodical personalities for just this reason. When they become disordered, a rather predictable series of events will follow. Their insight becomes too narrow, and they become undependable, inconsistent, and wild. Other equally valid dimensions of reality to which they seem blind surface to haunt them. The mate who marries the histrionic personality for liveliness may end up enmeshed in irresponsibility and chaos, and desiring peace at any price.

The histrionic personality, on the other

hand, frequently becomes anxious when the action stops. Lack of movement is oppressive stasis and boredom, compelling them to set something in motion, even if it is a furor. The life history of the hysteric often takes on the pattern of a soap opera, one crisis after another.

Treatment. Effective therapy would serve to widen the perceptual scope of the histrionic personality to appreciate the reality and value of law, of consistency, of the group or community, and of stable intimate relationships. At the same time, the therapist would hope also to find a place where the distinct gift of this person to the group could be appreciated and exercised. It would seem that working within a group, such as an understanding religious fellowship, would be the most effective means of healing. It does seem evident that the traditional approaches of trying to restructure underlying dynamics or attempting to change these persons by experiential efforts are long and arduous, without a great deal of hope.

This most ancient of disorders still attracts a great deal of professional interest. Should this research bring, in the future, a deeper understanding of the pain and possibilities of this personality, we will all be richer for it.

References

Blackner, K. H., & Tupin, J. P. Hysteria and hysterical structures: Developmental and social theories. In M. J. Horowitz (Ed.), *Hysterical personality.* New York: Aronson, 1977.

Chodoff, P., & Lyons, H. Hysteria, the hysterical personality and "hysterical" conversion. *American Journal of Psychiatry,* 1958, *114,* 734–740.

Halleck, S. L. Hysterical personality traits. *Archives of General Psychiatry,* 1967, *16,* 750–757.

Kernberg, O. *Object-relations and clinical psychoanalysis.* New York: Aronson, 1976.

Lazare, A. The hysterical character in psychoanalytic theory. *Archives of General Psychiatry,* 1971, *25,* 131–137.

Marmor, J. Orality in the hysterical personality. *Journal of the American Psychoanalytic Association,* 1953, *1,* 656–671.

Slavney, P. R., & McHugh, P. R. The hysterical personality: A controlled study. *Archives of General Psychiatry,* 1974, *30,* 325–329.

Spense, D. P. *Narrative truth and historical truth.* New York: Norton, 1982.

Veith, I. *Hysteria: History of a disease.* Chicago: University of Chicago Press, 1965.

Wittels, F. The hysterical character. *Medical Review of Reviews,* 1930, *36,* 186–190.

Zetzel, E. R. The so called good hysteric. *International Journal of Psycho-Analysis,* 1968, *49,* 256–260.

Additional Reading

Easser, B. R., & Lesser, S. R. The hysterical personality: A re-evaluation. *Psychoanalytic Quarterly,* 1965, *34,* 405.

C. M. Berry

See Personality Disorders; Active-Dependent Personality Pattern.

Holistic Health and Therapy. The holistic health movement is based on a philosophy of treatment that utilizes a broad array of therapeutic techniques to help persons attain and maintain health. It has become popular in the past two decades because it provides an alternative to more traditional models of health care, particularly the medical model.

The medical model has come under considerable criticism recently for a variety of reasons. It has often been criticized for being too molecular and impersonal. Health care providers have frequently treated the body but neglected the whole person. The role of psychological, environmental, social, life style, and spiritual factors and their contributions to health problems or recovery have often been ignored because the physical condition received exclusive attention. In addition to being impersonal and limited in scope, traditional health care has been illness oriented rather than health oriented. The focus has been more on remediation than prevention. More is known about disease than health.

The medical model of health care has also been criticized for implicitly encouraging patients to take passive roles in maintaining their health. Medical treatment has been perceived as a unilateral effort on the part of the physician, who takes responsibility for restoring the patient to health, rather than a mutual effort in which the patients have primary responsibility for their own well-being and work with the health care provider. To some degree this imbalance in responsibility and roles has been due to physicians' extensive use of medications and surgery. These interventions are things that are "done to" patients; they are largely nonparticipative treatments. Since physical problems are almost the sole focus of physicians' attention and are treated by medication or surgery administered by experts, patients passively take their bodies to doctors to be fixed much as they take their automobiles to mechanics to be repaired.

The holistic health movement may be more clearly understood against the medical model. The central feature of this movement is holism, the belief that persons must be viewed in their entirety as complex and integrated beings who exsit in an environment. Any attempts at understanding, diagnosing, or treating persons must be based on a macroscopic perspective that recognizes the significance of all aspects of personhood, not just physical symptomatology in isolation. Therapists must consider persons' psychological, social, environmental, and spiritual aspects as well as their physical status because they are all related. They influence one another. A change in one component will result in changes in the others. The holistic approach to personhood is a systems approach. According to the holists, the goal of the organism is health.

The holistic health movement views health as a dynamic process of development that includes all aspects of the person, not just the body. Pelletier states that "health is not the absence of disease but a state of optimum functioning about which we have very little information" (1979, p. 5). He makes the point that persons are not healthy by default (the lack of a discernible disease), but rather they are healthy when they are functioning up to their potential, experiencing inner harmony, and interacting effectively with their environment. Holistic health requires effective functioning physically, psychologically, socially, and spiritually plus the successful integration of all these components.

Holistic health requires continuing, conscious awareness and effort. It is best accomplished by developing a healthy life style. The primary responsibility is upon the individual, not the medical establishment. The person must learn methods of self-control such as relaxation techniques, incorporate healthful habits such as regular exercise, and avoid destructive behaviors such as smoking and overeating. A heavy emphasis is placed on preventive medicine, especially through health education. Teaching lay persons about their bodies and how they function is an attempt to get persons more actively involved in assuming responsibility for attaining and maintaining their own health. The hope is that teaching will supersede the need for treatment.

The holistic health movement has gained momentum from research on stress and psychosomatic disorders which clearly demonstrates the effect of the mind (used in its broadest sense to include cognitive, emotional, volitional, and spiritual components) on physical health, especially on persons' vulnerability to disease. Human beings' unique possession, their minds, can be their undoing physically because it enables them to experience stress beyond their physical capability to endure it. Excessive stress leads to psychosomatic diseases that are caused or aggravated by stress. Pelletier (1977) estimates that 50 to 80% of all diseases are psychosomatic or stress related. But the power of the mind can be used for good as well as for ill if properly harnessed. As surely as the mind can slay, it can also heal.

Since optimal health depends on the harmo-nious integration of many components of life (mind, body, and environment), it follows that most health problems will be relatively complex because they involve several of those components. For example, a spiritual problem such as a sense of meaninglessness may lead to a psychological problem such as anxiety, which may have physical concomitants such as an ulcer. These problems may require complex or multileveled solutions. The spiritual, psychological, and physical problems may all need attention simultaneously. To treat the ulcer medically without addressing the other aspects of the problem would be a shortsighted and most likely ineffective approach. A holistic view of the person would lead to a comprehensive, multidimensional treatment approach.

The holistic health movement has cautioned the public to be very careful about submitting to potentially dangerous therapies such as surgery and medication, which may themselves cause a variety of problems. Instead, holistic health advocates have championed a host of more participative and preventive therapies that are aimed at helping persons cope better, regulate themselves more effectively, and change maladaptive life styles. The goal is to use the mind to foster health rather than illness. Through the optimal development of persons' cognitive, emotional, spiritual, and social resources stress can be significantly reduced and better managed, and resistance to psychosomatic diseases can be significantly enhanced.

Holistic therapists vary widely in their training and their therapeutic methods. A partial listing of techniques used or suggested in the holistic health movement includes nutritional therapy, vitamin therapy, massage, acupressure, aerobics, exercise, biofeedback, meditation (of various types), autogenic training, assertiveness training, self-hypnosis, values clarification, imagery therapy, and support groups. The two that have probably received the most attention are nutrition and biofeedback. Note that all these techniques are programs which require active participation on the part of the persons receiving the treatment and that all the treatments involve some sort of education and self-regulation.

While holistic health practitioners do reject the medical model, most do not totally eschew conventional medical or psychological treatment. Many recommend psychological therapy to resolve marital, familial, or relational discord. Psychotherapy is often viewed as an important mind-expanding tool in changing personality and helping persons to change a stress-prone personality type and find their optimal style of living. Psychological and medical technology have proven very helpful in developing stress profiles, which identify individuals' characteristic physiological and psychological responses to stress. Through analysis, individuals' particular vulnerabilities can be determined and individually tailored health maintenance programs can be developed. The holistic health movement has reacted mainly to the limited views and abuses of the medical establishment.

From a Christian perspective the strengths of the holistic health movement include its rich and holistic view of persons, its openness to spiritual concerns, its acknowledgment of the importance of a world-life view in health, and its emphasis on prevention, health, and personal responsibility. These values are consistent with Scripture.

However, several Christian authors (Reisser, Reisser, & Weldon, 1983) have pointed out that in spite of these more superficial compatibilities with Christianity the "new consciousness" world view behind most of the writings in holistic health make it necessary for Christians to examine this movement very critically. These authors identify the roots of the movement in "a loose synthesis of various elements of mysticism, occultism, spiritism and animism" (Reisser et al., 1983, p. 12). They note, however, that not all writers or organizations promoting health for whole persons are based on a new consciousness world view. The writings of Westberg (1979) and the network of Wholistic Health Centers founded by him are explicitly grounded in Christianity.

Since the holistic health movement is neither a discipline nor a professional association, its weaknesses reside in the lack of ethical and minimum training standards. Holistic health therapists, while sharing some common assumptions, vary widely in their education, competence, therapeutic approaches, and views on spiritual issues.

In conclusion, the holistic health movement has highlighted some valuable concepts, but its practitioners and their methods must be carefully evaluated on an individual basis in light of Scripture.

References
Pelletier, K. R. *Mind as healer, mind as slayer.* New York: Delacorte Press/S. Lawrence, 1977.
Pelletier, K. R. *Holistic medicine.* New York: Delacorte Press/S. Lawrence, 1979.
Reisser, P., Reisser, T., & Weldon, J. *The holistic healers.* Downers Grove, Ill.: Inter-Varsity Press, 1983.
Westberg, G. R. (Ed.). *Theological roots of wholistic health care.* Hinsdale, Ill.: Wholistic Health Centers, 1979.

Additional Reading
Allen, D. F., Bird, L. P., & Herrmann, R. (Eds.). *Whole-person medicine.* Downers Grove, Ill.: Inter-Varsity Press, 1980.

C. D. Dolph

Homeostasis. A term coined by the American physiologist Walter B. Cannon, referring to the tendency of any organism to maintain a state of relative internal constancy. Homeostasis is seen as operating at different hierarchical levels based on motivational influences that can range from basic organic needs to complex psychological adaptive mechanisms. Homeostasis is thus applied to any system's (individual or group) maintenance of the status quo.

The concept of group maintenance of relative internal constancy is foundational to family therapy. It was noted in family practice that when one member would decrease his or her dysfunctional symptomatic behaviors, a different family member would concomitantly become dysfunctional, so that the overall level of family functioning would remain the same. This has been termed the homeostatic cycle, and often involves more than just two family members. When the homeostatic cycle involves three members, such as a dysfunctional adolescent and her parents, it has been called a family Triangle.

D. S. McCulloch

See Family Systems Theory.

Homework in Psychotherapy. Many therapies utilize task assignments. Those who consider counseling and psychotherapy to be primarily educational, skill-building endeavors write most extensively and helpfully about this tool. Therapy based on homework became a conceptual model with the work of Shelton and Ackerman (1974) and later of Shelton (1979). In his recent writings Shelton refers to his approach as instigation therapy, which he sees to be a close ally of behavior therapy.

Homework in therapy is defined as "assignments given to the client which are carried on outside the therapy hour" (Shelton & Ackerman, 1974). Various theoretical positions use homework differently. Some offer occasional, nondirected and/or open-ended tasks; others, consistent, well-defined, and systematic tasks. The systematic, consistent use of homework tasks is a part of therapy throughout the intervention in most behavioral models (Wells, 1981). In some longer-term therapies the desire and need to write often emerge as an expressive and creative act (e.g., keeping a diary or journal of one's thoughts and dreams).

The primary intention of this adjunctive therapy tool is to extend the work of the therapy hour. Therapy hours are simply not enough time for growth. Homework tasks are one way to reach beyond the session time to assure the impact of the therapy.

The homework assignment format includes one or more of the following five instructions: 1) a *do* statement (e.g., read, say, observe); 2) a *quantity* statement (e.g., talk three times about or give five compliments); 3) a *record* statement (e.g., count and record the number of compliments or mark on a chart each time . . .); 4) a *bring* statement (e.g., bring your chart, observations, child . . . to your next appointment); 5) a *contingency* statement (e.g., call for your next appointment after you have done . . .) (Shelton & Ackerman, 1974). Toward the end of the therapy hour the reason for and nature of the homework assignment is explained to the client. Summarized homework instructions are usually written down, with both client and therapist keeping a copy.

Successful homework is a result of well-planned treatment. The client's cooperation in carrying out homework tasks is emphasized at the time of the assignment. Contingency statements, rewards, and other reinforcements act to ensure completion of the task. If clients fail to carry out their assignments, the therapist should take this seriously and never overlook the issue. If the task has been given simply and clearly and has been acknowledged, the therapist should never take responsibility for its unsuccessful completion; instead, the responsibility should firmly and kindly be placed on the client's shoulders.

Not all clients can benefit from task assignments. Clients with magical expectations, individuals who refuse to accept any personal responsibility, clients who just need time to ventilate in an accepting environment, and clients coming under external duress do not work well in this modality.

References

Shelton, J. L. Instigation therapy: using therapeutic homework to promote treatment gains. In A. P. Goldstein & F. H. Kanfer (Eds.), *Maximizing treatment gains.* New York: Academic Press, 1979.

Shelton, J. L., & Ackerman, J. N. *Homework in counseling and psychotherapy.* Springfield, Ill.: Thomas, 1974.

Wells, R. A. *Planned short-term treatment.* New York: Free Press, 1981.

B. J. Shepperson

See Bibliotherapy.

Homosexuality: Classification, Etiology, and Treatment.

In its broadest sense homosexuality is defined as erotic attraction toward persons of the same gender. Thus at root homosexuality is a psychological/emotional orientation. Gender orientation varies in degree in the general population. Kinsey, Pomeroy, and Martin (1948) developed a simple 0–6 rating scale. At the 0 level there is exclusive heterosexual attraction; at the 6 level there is exclusive homosexual attraction; the 3 level would be equal bisexual attraction. About 90% of U.S. adults are at the 0–1 level, less than 5% at the 5–6 level. Gender orientation is not fixed, but may vary over time and age in the life cycle.

It is crucial to distinguish between gender orientation and sexual behavior. They are not necessarily closely related. Actual sexual behavior is more determined by social expectations, personal values, and morals than by gender orientation per se. In turn, actual sexual experience significantly influences psychological orientation.

Types of Homosexual Behavior. There are many variants of homosexual arousal. But the point can be made that homosexuality is not merely one stereotyped behavior pattern.

Experimental homosexuality usually refers to adolescent experimentation with degrees of sexual interaction with both genders. At a minimal level many adolescents engage in same-gender sexual activity. Among males this is commonly mutual urination or masturbation contests, among females breast and genital hair comparisons. Strictly speaking this is "homoerotic" activity rather than homosexual activity. That is, there is sexual arousal in association with the same gender, but the ultimate aim is heterosexual. At the extreme end among adolescents is experimentation in sexual intercourse with both sexes. This experimentation usually leads to a heterosexual resolution. Troiden (1979) reports that a relatively large number of males consciously test the extent to which they may be sexually attracted to men. As a result of this experimentation a substantial number may decide that homosexuality is not for them and choose exclusive heterosexuality. It is therefore quite likely that only a small portion of the males who have ever engaged in homosexual behavior take on gay identities. Kinsey et al. (1948) report that about 15% of youthful exclusive homosexuals became exclusive heterosexuals by age 30.

Situational homosexuality involves homosexual behavior when heterosexual relations are not available. This frequently occurs in prisons, isolated military bases, and isolated work areas. Homosexual experience is primarily for sexual release without affection or relationship. It appears that a more immature personality structure may be necessary to participate in such situational sexuality.

Defensive homosexuality refers to a situational variant, often seen in prisons, where aggressive homosexual behavior is used to demonstrate that one is *not* homosexual, i.e., a passive victim. Heterosexuality is the desired norm, and the aggressive homosexual acts represent a defensive demonstration that one retains heterosexuality.

Reactive homosexuality represents fear of heterosexual encounter as dangerous (often castration anxiety). Although heterosexuality is preferred, homosexual behavior is chosen as less dangerous. For example: A 30-year-old engineer was highly stimulated by women, but backed away from heterosexual experiences. He repetitively dreamed of entering a large cave whose entrance was guarded by huge teeth that would bite him. He fantasized of his penis being bitten off. He did not feel threatened by homosexual relations.

Social role homosexuality involves the adoption of homosexual behavior as part of a required social role. Throughout history some societies have reared persons to enter special roles, such as actor, warrior, or priest, in which homosexuality is required as part of that role. The clearest example of socially required homosexuality is a recent anthropologic study of a New Guinea tribe in which all males from 8–16 are required to play a passive homosexual role and from 16–22 an active homosexual role. Then they are required to marry and remain heterosexual thereafter. Over 95% of the tribal males successfully follow these socially prescribed sexual role behaviors. Of great theoretical import is the fact that sexual orientation and behavior can be so strongly socially determined (Herdt, 1981).

Obligatory homosexuality refers to the sense of sexual orientation which a person comes to experience as an internal necessity. The person experiences no heterosexual response, but instead experiences homosexual arousal. This is usually a source of considerable anxiety and conflict because we are reared to anticipate heterosexual interest and arousal. Often such persons find little pleasure in typical adolescent dating, although they may have excellent social relations with the opposite gender. They just feel no attraction. When they begin to experience homosexual arousal, usually in later adolescence, they are surprised, as if against their will. Hence the concept of obligation; they feel obliged by their own feelings to

respond to the same gender. This pattern describes perhaps the majority of homosexual persons.

Preferential homosexuality occurs in those with bisexual arousal. Many homosexual persons experience heterosexual impulses and arousal, and may well perform heterosexual acts with satisfaction. In a large survey sample of homosexuals Bell and Weinberg (1978) reported that 45% did not consider themselves exclusively homosexual, 76% behaved in more homosexual fashion than they actually felt, 33% had heterosexual dreams, 23% had heterosexual masturbatory fantasies, and 72% experienced heterosexual arousal. Nevertheless, this group preferred to choose homosexual experiences over heterosexual.

A variant of this pattern is manifest in homosexuals who marry. This may occur before explicit awareness of homosexual arousal or as an attempt to eradicate homosexuality via marriage. Such marriages usually end in unsatisfying and unstable relations because the person prefers the homosexual relationship even in the face of satisfactory marital sexuality. Where such marriages survive, it is because the partner is permitted to engage in homosexual liaisons as part of the marital life (Saghir & Robins, 1973).

Homosexual panic is a phenomenon often seen in young adults. Typically, a college student may encounter nude persons in an athletic shower room and suddenly experience sexual arousal. He fears this represents homosexuality and develops an acute anxiety attack. Usually this does not represent homosexual arousal, but merely generic sexual arousal from seeing nude bodies.

Generic sexual arousal describes the almost universal phenomenon of small degrees of fantasized sexual interest or response to many persons of both sexes. Personal interest, involvement, attraction, and intimacy are the psychological bases for any close personal relationship. We then can eroticize and attach sexual meaning and value to that relationship. Even small intimations of familiarity or closeness may evoke an eroticized response. We learn to inhibit and repress such erotization— we call them taboos. Nevertheless, in most normal persons the repression barrier may occasionally be slightly breached, resulting in erotic responses to mother, father, brother, sister, grandfather, grandmother, infant boy or girl. Such responses are usually ignored, but may cause anxiety if noticed. Rarely are they acted upon to any degree. But this does indicate the ubiquitous nature of our capacity to respond erotically to many persons regardless of gender, age, or relationship. This type of homosexual arousal is generic and does not indicate sexual orientation.

Neurotic regressive homosexuality appears in persons as a retreat from personal conflict in a heterosexual relationship. In this instance the person has a heterosexual orientation but regresses to homosexual levels of identity development (*see* GENDER IDENTITY). Resolution of the interpersonal and identity conflict allows the person to return to the heterosexual orientation. For example: A 35-year-old married couple had a happy, active heterosexual marriage for 10 years. During 5 years of marital conflict they both had numerous heterosexual affairs which also became unsatisfactory. Both began to experiment with homosexual liaisons which were nonconflictual. After 4 years of successful marital therapy they gave up all types of extramarital sex and resumed a satisfying monogamous marriage.

A variant of this pattern is *latent* homosexuality and *pseudohomosexuality*. These are psychodynamic terms used to describe persons who have developed a heterosexual orientation, which is not consciously appreciated because of neurotic conflict. They consciously experience homosexual arousal or seek homosexual liaisons to resolve neurotic conflicts. In latent homosexuality the person may uncover homosexual fantasy, ideation, or impulses in the process of resolving neurotic conflict. In pseudohomosexuality the person acts as if the homosexual orientation were dominant (Ovesey, 1969).

In sum, homosexual impulses, fantasies, and behaviors demonstrate wide variation. Homosexual orientation itself varies and is changeable. Homosexuality is therefore not a fixed state or process. Rather, variations of homosexuality are part of the dynamic complex of human function. When we speak of homosexuals, we usually refer to obligatory and preferential homosexual orientation. However, even then a person may not behave in homosexual fashion. For example, a person with strong homosexual orientation may remain celibate; or a bisexual person may choose to engage only in heterosexual relations.

Related Sexual Variants. In the panoply of sexual behaviors there are closely related syndromes that are not strictly homosexual but are related to some degree.

TRANSSEXUALISM is the phenomenon where a person has a gender identity opposite to body gender (I am a man in a woman's body). This is thought to represent a failure in development of core gender identity at years 2–3 (*see* GENDER IDENTITY). Such persons may seek "sex change" treatment, involving hormonal treatment and surgical transformation of their genitalia. Such persons are not considered homosexual, but clinical experience has revealed high failure rates because many persons who are seen as transsexuals are actually homosexual.

TRANSVESTISM is a variant which involves a person wearing the clothes of someone of the opposite sex and sometimes assuming the role or behavior of the opposite sex. According to *DSM-III* transvestism occurs in heterosexuals who experience sexual excitement through the cross-dressing. Some, however, use the term to refer to persons of homosexual orientation who mimic the opposite gender. These are the "impersonators." A lesser degree is seen in the assumption of some opposite gender attributes—dressing in "drag" for males or "butch" for females. Less obvious is the subtle imitation seen in masculinization or feminization traits. All these variants represent a hostile identification with the opposite gender, which is caricatured while retaining same-gender identity. For example: The male "drag queen" exaggerates feminine traits, reflecting both identification with women and hostility toward women. But he says, "I prefer men." The majority of homosexual persons do not exhibit these traits and usually exhibit culturally typical male and female roles and male and female mannerisms.

FETISHES or PARAPHILIAS represent neurotic mechanisms of sexual arousal. For example, a male may be unable to achieve an erection unless his female partner is wearing spike-heel shoes. (Symbolically, the female now has a penis and therefore he need not fear castration during intercourse.) Common fetishes or paraphilias are sadomasochistic types of foreplay (beating or being beaten, chaining the partner or being chained, etc.). It appears that homosexuals participate in fetishes and paraphilias more often, although there is not reliable empirical data. There is no evidence of more pedophilia among homosexuals (Karasu & Socarides, 1979).

Homosexuality versus Gay Style. The major social problem of the homosexual in society is stigmatization and prejudice. It is true that in most modern Western societies homosexual persons have suffered persecution and loss of civil liberties solely because they are homosexual in orientation, regardless of behavior. The "gay lib" movement has sought to redress this social injustice. Democratic societies affirm the right to personal liberty and personal privacy. Thus the person of homosexual orientation has the right to practice homosexual behavior in private. At the same time, the homosexual person has the right to enjoy civil liberties without prejudice or persecution due to sexual orientation (Marmor, 1980).

The above does not imply that society approves or condones homosexuality or that homosexuality represents an acceptable social norm. Hayek (1960) observes that the fact that conduct within the private sphere is not a proper object for coercive action by the state does not necessarily mean that in a free society such conduct should also be exempt from the pressure of opinion or disapproval. No society has ever accepted homosexuality as a "normal alternative" (Karlen, 1971). In turn, it is unrealistic to expect that the homosexual person will not experience disapproval of homosexual behavior.

But decriminalization of homosexuality does not justify the social institutionalization of homosexuality which the gay lib movement seeks. A pluralistic democratic society must accommodate to many forms of private behavior, but this accommodation must be clearly differentiated from the necessity for a society to provide behavioral and sexual norms. As Geis (1972) notes, the absence of criminal sanctions does not necessarily mean that a society is obligated to view all forms of behavior with moral indifference.

Another serious problem with the gay lib movement is that in its attempt to overcome the deviancy of being a member of the social class labeled "homosexual," it forces the homosexual person to assume a social class identity as "gay." Thus to be heterosexual or homosexual in private is replaced by a public homosexuality. The homosexual person is stripped of personal identity without regard to sexual orientation, and instead is given a "gay identity" in which sexual orientation and sexual behavior become the major nexus of identity. Personal identity is tied to a social label. Sagarin (1973) states that because homosexuals want to believe that they are not worthless (which they are not), and because they confuse the worth of a person with that of a characteristic, they go the next step and say that gay is good.

The rhetoric of the gay-is-good position may have clinical significance in that homosexuality is defined as desirable and unchangeable, thus locking persons into a sexual orientation that may be neither desirable nor immutable for that person. Recent research suggests that moving into a gay identity may preclude change in sexual orientation, while movement out of a gay life style may augur potential change in sexual orientation (Troiden, 1979; Pattison & Pattison, 1980).

Associated with the gay lib movement is the concept of homophobia, defined by Weinberg (1972) as the revulsion toward homosexuals and the desire to inflict punishment as retribution. The concept is employed in gay lib rhetoric to label as neurotic anyone who disagrees with or expresses emotional repugnance to homosexual behavior. There may be true homophobia—i.e., a neurotic fear of association with homosexual persons. However, such a state is clinically very rare. It is a misuse of labels to suggest that disagreement on social value is a phobia. Even more important is the fact that sexual taboos do carry a negative emotional tone. One does experience an emotional revulsion at the idea of sexual relations with one's parents or children. Even so, there is a normal emotional revulsion experience by heterosexuals to the idea of engaging in homosexual relations. The concept of homophobia has been widely misunderstood, employed as political rhetoric, and incorrectly defined.

Etiologic Variables. It would be difficult to pinpoint the causes of homosexuality through the study of homosexuals alone, but in combination with the abundant data on gender development and sexual development there is reasonable scientific agreement on etiology (Gagnon & Simon, 1973).

There is no evidence that homosexual traits, tendencies, or orientation are hereditary. Neither is there convincing evidence that any biological factors per se contribute to the development of homosexuality. Chromosomal and hormonal aberrations may result in differences in masculinization or femininization of body traits, but that is not sexual orientation. Administration of sex hormones increases sexual drive but does not change the direction of the drive (Money & Musaph, 1977).

Psychological development themes in identity formation offer the clearest indication of causal factors. In a large nonclinical population study of homosexual developmental history, Bell, Weinberg, & Hammersmith (1981) report that adult homosexuality is the predictable consequence of detectable childhood preference and feelings about oneself and relationships to significant others. They conclude that homosexuality is the product of an extraordinarily strong conditioning effect. They demonstrated a homosexual orientation in latency-age children, 7–12 years, long before manifest sexual behavior. It is in late adolescence, with increased sexual drive, that the orientation is experienced as homosexual arousal.

What are those childhood conditioning effects? Here we can examine both preoedipal and oedipal identity development themes. In the preoedipal period, ages 3–5, the child strongly identifies with the parent of the same gender. Failure to successfully identify, due either to a hostile relationship, absent or distant relationship, or other conflict, leaves the child with an incomplete and inadequate sense of gender identity. Although other aspects of personality develop, the child continues on into adulthood with the sense of being an "incomplete" male or female. These children continue to seek same-gender relations to strengthen their internal search for gender identity. When those relations are eroticized, same-gender sexual arousal occurs. Sexual relations provide a symbolic expression and experience of becoming a whole person of the same gender.

The following cases illustrate homosexuality as a symbolic acquisition of gender identity. First, a 30-year-old artist could not achieve erections, although aroused, unless he inserted a wooden penis in his rectum. His fantasy was that he possessed only half a penis and needed the missing half. Homosexual relations provided the same sense of having a complete penis. The penis symbolized his whole physical body and whole sense of identity. Second, a 35-year-old woman with large breasts had a self-image of being a prepubescent ugly girl. During lesbian intercourse she would suck on her partner's breast. At that point she experienced the fantasy of being a grown person who was physically well developed. She hated her mother and refused to acknowledge that she had a face and body build like her mother. She felt she had never become a woman, and did not want to become a woman like her mother.

A second dynamic occurs in the oedipal period, during which the child identifies with the parent of the same gender in learning to relate to the opposite gender. Hostility of one parent toward the other may impair cross-gender modeling, as when the father hates the mother. Hence the son learns that male associations are more desirable than relating to women. Or there may be competitive jealousy. For example, a mother may become jealous of her daughter relating to men. Therefore the girl learns that she must restrict her relationships to women. A variety of complex dynamics involving parents (or parent substitutes) of both genders can come into play.

In addition, there are sociocultural circumstances that promote or inhibit the development of homosexuality. Is homosexuality found as a universal cultural practice? Homosexual behavior has been recorded in almost every culture, and to that extent is universal. But does universal imply natural? Karlen (1971) observes that we must distinguish between casual homosexual acts and homosexual identity. Further, he says, we must determine how a culture views homosexual practices, whether they are enthusiastically praised, neutrally accepted, shrugged off as a misdemeanor, or seen more with pity than anger. Karlen concludes that predominant or exclusive homosexuality is seen negatively everywhere. Further, he concludes that homosexual acts are accepted only in special situations or times of life, and to the extent that they do not impair heterosexual functioning or loss of sexual identity.

There is also the question of whether different cultures produce different rates of homosexuality. The cultural heritage of Greek asceticism produced a "sex-negative" value system in Western cultures. Sexuality among women was concomitantly minimized, repressed, or denied. Homosexual practice among women was therefore minimal. On the other hand, covert homosexual practice and homosexual identity among men has been subtly encouraged at points in Western history, as in Victorian upper-class England. In contrast, "sex-positive" cultures, such as the Indian subcontinent, China, and American native tribes, tolerated many forms of casual homosexual practices among both men and women, insofar as basic family structure was not threatened and the heterosexual marital bond was maintained. However, the Muslim world provides an interesting study of contradictions. Although this is a religiously sex-positive culture, male homosexual practice and homosexual identity are widespread. This so-called Arab homosexuality is attributed to a religious tradition that valued sexuality yet strictly segregated men and women through all of social life, with harems that made female spouses unavailable to many men.

Every culture has rooted sexual practice in marital and family function, to provide progeny, to provide an heir to look after the parents in their old age, to take care of necessary rituals, to keep the family going. In different cultures, however, homosexual identity may be selectively encouraged in institutional forms, as in eunuchs, actors, priests, shamans, warriors, etc., whose social role is demarcated from normative social roles of sexual identity and practice. Thus different cultures do promote or inhibit homosexual identity formation or behavior, although in none is homosexuality an acceptable normal alternative to heterosexuality enacted in marital bonding (Bullough, 1976).

Mental Health and Homosexuality. The issues of whether homosexuality is abnormal or normal and whether homosexuals are mentally healthy or not have been hotly debated. Apart from ideological polemics there are conceptual issues and issues subject to scientific investigation.

First is the question of whether homosexuality is normal or not. The answer revolves around our definition of normality (Pattison, 1974). The first definition of normality is that of health. Health here is reasonable function; it is the antonym of illness. If you are reasonably free of pain, discomfort, and disability, you are healthy. In this view homosexuality does not brand a person as abnormal unless the person experiences untoward symptoms as a result of homosexuality.

The second definition views normality as an ideal fiction, a utopia. Yet a set of ideal behaviors, attitudes, and values is the measure of normality. In this view homosexuality is almost invariably defined as a gross abnormality of development and behavior.

In the third definition normality is average, a statistical concept. Normality is the middle range of behavior of most people observed. In this view homosexuality would be defined as abnormal in the general population but normal within a specific subculture or homosexual community.

The fourth, normality as process, is an adaptive view. Normality is the overall adaptation of the person at this point in time. Here homosexuality per se is not at issue. Rather, homosexuality is normal or abnormal in terms of adaptation to one's homosexual orientation.

The next issue is whether homosexuals are mentally healthy. From a broad population standpoint, homosexuals do not demonstrate different rates of psychosis or neurosis from heterosexuals. Homosexual persons demonstrate as good adaptive and coping capacity as heterosexuals. On the other hand, homosexuals do have a much higher rate of alcoholism, and probably of drug abuse (Brandsma & Pattison, 1982).

A third issue is whether homosexuals are psychologically mature. This is a complex problem because maturity is not a uniform process. We may be mature in some areas of

life but not in others. To generalize, in overall life skills and abilities homosexual persons are as mature as the general population. However, in terms of identity development they demonstrate immature development and immature capacities for stable intimate relationships. This is reflected in the fact that homosexual intimacies are notoriously unstable and long-term homosexual liaisons are rare. Where homosexual "marriages" do endure, they are relatively asexual and assume the form of "good friend" relationships. It is unclear whether children raised in a homosexual family structure suffer adverse effects.

Treatment Alternatives. A major issue concerning treatment is the goal of treatment. That in itself is controversial. The gay lib movement has argued that treatment of the homosexual should be geared toward affirmation of homosexual orientation, acceptance of homosexual identity, and engagement in a gay life style (Gonsiorek, 1982). This approach to treatment is ideologically opposed to the goal of change in sexual orientation.

A second goal is an adaptive one, which neither approves nor disapproves of homosexuality but seeks to help the homosexual person adopt a life style that minimizes personal and social conflicts.

A third goal is to change the sexual orientation of the homosexual. This is exceptionally difficult among the persons who seek professional help to change. But this may be characteristic only of homosexuals seeking treatment, not necessarily of all homosexuals. As Bancroft (1974) states, "If in fact we had evidence that either a homo- or a hetero-sexual identity was an immutable and fundamental aspect of an individual's nature, then any attempt to modify such an identity would be inappropriate and unjustifiable. But there is no such evidence, and we know that many individuals pass through a phase of homosexuality or bisexuality into a stable heterosexual role" (p. 191).

Methods to change gender orientation are numerous. However, on the whole, none are remarkably successful. Bancroft (1974) reports that the best predictors of change are fewer traits of the opposite gender, persons under 35, first homosexual experience after age 16, and evidence of heterosexual arousal. To that list Pattison and Pattison (1980) added the presence of sexual ideals and values, moral attitudes toward homosexuality, and opportunity for normal interactions of nonerotic intimacy with adults of both genders.

The suppression of overt homosexual behavior or involvement in heterosexual activity does not constitute cure in the sense of change in sexual object choice. The criterion for a cure by Saghir and Robins (1973) is "a reversal of psychological responsiveness from a predominantly homosexual to a primarily heterosexual one. Thus a 'cured' homosexual would not only disengage from homosexual activity but he/she would also disengage emotionally to a large extent from homosexual attachments, including homosexual fantasies, dreams, and physical arousal by sight or touch" (p. 319).

Treatment methods can be summarized in the light of the above. Hormonal treatment will change sexual drive level but not influence object choice. Behavior conditioning treatment can change arousal stimulus responses, and even evoke heterosexual behavior, but does not change the internal psychological object choice (Feldman & MacCulloch, 1971). Interpersonal training in intimacy techniques has been reported as successful in a small sample (Masters & Johnson, 1979). Psychoanalytic psychotherapy is modestly successful with motivated patients (Bieber, Dain, Dince, Drellich, Grand, Gudlach, Dremer, Rifkin, Wilbur, & Bieber, 1962). The most recent approach has been through religious peer counseling, so-called ex-gay ministries. Pattison and Pattison (1980) report that 8 of 11 subjects had changed from exclusive homosexual orientation to exclusive heterosexual orientation through a process of religious fellowship. Although there are no published evaluations, such religious ex-gay programs have spread throughout the world. Their efficacy remains to be determined.

In sum, homosexual orientation is much more malleable than has been considered. Homosexual behavior is quite variable. Change in homosexual orientation, attitudes, and behavior probably is strongly related to moral considerations about homosexuality.

Theological Issues. The biblical view of human nature is sex-positive. Sexuality is proclaimed as an integral part of the person. The aim of sexuality is not merely pleasure or procreation, but sexual union unites the male and female such that together they reflect the image of God. Physically, emotionally, psychologically, the marital union symbolizes the human reflection of God's nature.

The expression of sexuality is clearly limited to and defined as part of marital union. Premarital, extramarital, and homosexual expressions of sexuality are proscribed as a violation of the meaning of sexuality, of marriage, and of family. Similarly, homosexual marriage is a violation of the meaning of gender union and of family.

Although the Bible is unclear about the morality of homosexual orientation, the historic Christian message has affirmed the redemption, sanctification, and graceful acceptance of all believers without specification of psychological structure of the person. The fact that a person has a homosexual orientation or any other variety of sexual orientation does not per se preclude Christian fellowship and leadership.

Appeal to the concept that all people need to engage in sexual behavior to be mentally or physically healthy is contravened by the simple observation that many normal, mature, healthy people are sexually celibate. Sexual activity has no correlation with mental or physical health. Similarly the appeal that homosexuals love each other and therefore are entitled to a loving sexual relationship ignores the distinction between love and sex. We have loving relations with parents, children, relatives, and friends, but this does not justify sexual relations with them. Love and sex are two different aspects of human relations.

In conclusion, the Christian church accepts the person of homosexual orientation as any other person but rejects homosexual behavior.

References

Bancroft, J. *Deviant sexual behavior: Modification and assessment.* Oxford: Clarendon Press, 1974.

Bell, A. P., & Weinberg, M. S. *Homosexualities.* New York: Simon & Schuster, 1978.

Bell, A. P., Weinberg, M. S., & Hammersmith, S. K. *Sexual preference: Its development in men and women.* Bloomington: Indiana University Press, 1981.

Bieber, I., Dain, H. J., Dince, J. R., Drellich, M. G., Grand, H. G., Gudlach, R. H., Dremer, M. W., Rifkin, A. H., Wilbur, C. B., & Bieber, T. *Homosexuality: A psychoanalytic study of male homosexuals.* New York: Basic Books, 1962.

Brandsma, J. M., & Pattison, E. M. Homosexuality and alcoholism. In E. M. Pattison & E. Kaufman (Eds.), *Encyclopedic handbook of alcoholism.* New York: Gardner Press, 1982.

Bullough, V. L. *Sexual variance in society and history.* New York: Wiley, 1976.

Feldman, M. P., & MacCulloch, M. J. *Homosexual behavior: Therapy and assessment.* New York: Pergamon Press, 1971.

Gagnon, J. H., & Simon, W. *Sexual conduct: The social sources of human sexuality.* Chicago: Aldine, 1973.

Geis, G. *Not the law's business?* Rockville, Md.: National Institute of Mental Health, 1972.

Gonsiorek, J. C. (Ed.). *Homosexuality and psychotherapy: A practitioner's handbook of affirmative methods.* New York: Haworth Press, 1982.

Hayek, F. A. *The constitution of liberty.* Chicago: University of Chicago Press, 1960.

Herdt. G. H. *Guardians of the flutes: Idioms of masculinity.* New York: McGraw-Hill, 1981.

Karasu, T. B., & Socarides, C. W. (Eds.) *On sexuality: Psychoanalytic observations.* New York: International Universities Press, 1979.

Karlen, A. *Sexuality and homosexuality: A new view*. New York: Norton, 1971.

Kinsey, A., Pomeroy, W., & Martin, C. *Sexual behavior in the human male*. Philadelphia: Saunders, 1948.

Marmor, J. (Ed.) *Homosexual behavior*. New York: Basic Books, 1980.

Masters, W. H., & Johnson, V. E. *Homosexuality in perspective*. Boston: Little, Brown, 1979.

Money, J., & Musaph, H. (Eds.). *Handbook of sexology*. New York: Excerpta Medica, 1977.

Ovesey, L. *Homosexuality and pseudohomosexuality*. New York: Science House, 1969.

Pattison, E. M. Confusing concepts about the concept of homosexuality. *Psychiatry*, 1974, *37*, 340–349.

Pattison, E. M., & Pattison, M. L. "Ex-Gays": Religiously mediated change in homosexuals. *American Journal of Psychiatry*, 1980, *137*, 1553–1562.

Sagarin, E. The good guys, the bad guys, and the gay guys. *Contemporary Sociology*, 1973, *2*, 3–13.

Saghir, M. T., & Robins, E. *Male and female homosexuality*. Baltimore: Williams & Wilkins, 1973.

Troiden, R. R. *Becoming homosexual: A model of gay identity acquisition*. *Psychiatry*, 1979, *42*, 362–373.

Weinberg, G. *Society and the healthy homosexual*. New York: St. Martin's Press, 1972.

E. M. PATTISON

See SEXUALITY.

Homosexuality: Social Psychological Consequences.

The Bible is reasonably clear in its condemnation of homosexuality (Lev. 20:13; 1 Cor. 6:9–11). The Judeo-Christian community generally assumes that God condemns the kinds of activities and life styles that are harmful to those who do them or to the human community. Sexuality's basic function is to bond persons and generate progeny within a family context. If sexual practice detracts from family bonding, then the practice is sinful. Thus, while the Bible does not present a theory of why homosexuality is sinful, the Judeo-Christian ethic would lead us to expect that it is condemned because practicing it would generally lead to personal and social harm, or to less good in both these spheres than would result from the practice of heterosexuality.

One significant consideration in judging the personal and social adequacy of a life style is the assessment of those involved in that life style. The Kinsey Institute survey (Gebhard & Johnson, 1979) asked white, nondelinquent homosexuals, "If an adolescent who was just beginning both hetero and homosexual activity came to you and asked your advice as to whether to continue or stop homosexual activity, what would you tell him (her)?" (p. 617). Thirty-eight percent of the males and 30% of the females said they would advise to cease, against 9% of both genders who would advise to continue. Thirty-six percent of these homosexuals said that they regretted being homosexual, compared to 52% of the white homosexuals in the Bell and Weinberg (1978) study. Fifty percent of white homosexuals in the latter study claimed that they "would be upset if their child became a homosexual" (p. 339), and 25% claimed to regard homosexuality as an emotional disorder (p. 339). Realizing that these replies were given to highly sympathetic investigators, one would conclude that a large proportion of homosexuals are substantially dissatisfied with their sexual orientation.

Personal Consequences. The question of personal consequences of the practice of homosexuality is very difficult to answer. The debate over whether homosexuals are psychologically healthy or not has been hot and has been fueled more by rhetoric than research data. The limited evidence that is available suggests that homosexuals are less mentally healthy. However, because this data is correlational, caution must be taken in drawing causal conclusions.

Saghir and Robins (1973) report that both male and female homosexuals were more frequently diagnosed as possessing a psychiatric disorder. These authors also report a higher incidence of attempted suicide. Bell and Weinberg (1978) also indicate that homosexuals more frequently report suicidal ideation and attempts, and that male homosexuals more frequently report psychosomatic symptoms, loneliness, depression, worry, tension, paranoia, and lower self-acceptance. Female homosexuals report lower life satisfaction, lower self-acceptance, and more frequent tension. Cameron and Ross (1981) report that homosexuals were more frequently self-abusive or self-destructive and were somewhat less apt to claim high morale. Finally Brandsma and Pattison (1982) report much higher rates of alcoholism in homosexuals.

Social Consequences. The practice of homosexual behavior would also seem to have consequences for human community in that the sexual activities of homosexuals appear less frequently to involve significant human bonding. One evidence of this is the reported higher frequency of more impersonal sexual contacts such as prostitution (Gebhard & Johnson, 1979), bestiality (Gebhard, Gagnon, Pomeroy, & Christenson, 1965; Gebhard & Johnson, 1979), and masturbation (Saghir & Robins, 1973). A higher percentage of homosexuals report having engaged in orgies (Saghir & Robins, 1973), and although comparable statistics for heterosexuals were not provided, Bell and Weinberg (1978) report 99% of homosexual males to have had sex with total strangers. In the case of males this often involves the so-called "glory hole," a small hole in a wall between two rooms where sexual contact is made without any face-to-face contact whatsoever.

Homosexuality is also associated with less permanent sexual relationships. In the Bell and Weinberg (1978) study, male homosexuals claimed an average of about 100 sexual partners in their lives to date. Female homosexuals reported an average of 10. The only direct comparisons were reported by Saghir and Robins (1973); homosexuals reported about three times the number of sexual partners as heterosexuals. Furthermore, the duration of homosexual relationships is brief. Gebhard and Johnson (1979) report that the longest continuous affair averaged two years for men, three for women. The average length of heterosexual marriage that ends in divorce is seven years, and about two-thirds of heterosexuals manage to stay married until one of them dies. Cameron and Ross (1981) report that the median number of psychological intimates (i.e., "persons for whom you care deeply and vice versa" for both in- and out-of-closet homosexuals was three, while for heterosexuals the figure was six. Homosexuals' intimates were more apt to be of the same gender and same age. All in all, the bonding qualities of homosexual relationships appear considerably weaker than those of heterosexuals.

What would be the social consequences of widespread, perhaps even openly accepted and legitimized homosexuality? Since no known civilization or society has granted equal social status to homosexuality and heterosexuality (Karlen, 1971), an absolutely certain answer is not available. However, the Judeo-Christian tradition would suggest a number of possible consequences (Cameron, 1978).

The first of these is that, since homosexuality and heterosexuality are learned gender orientations and because homosexuality offers more certain immediate sensual gratification, in a sensually charged society homosexual availability may well make heterosexuality a difficult choice. This may place family-centered, procreative sexuality at hazard. The heightened sensual enjoyment of homosexuality has been reported by a number of authors. Gebhard and Johnson (1979) and Schofield (1965), for example, report a higher percentage of homosexuals than heterosexuals rating the enjoyment of their first coital experiences as high. Furthermore, Gebhard and Johnson (1979) report that a higher percentage of homosexual as opposed to heterosexual females regularly (91–100% of the time) experienced orgasm, while a smaller percentage reported

never experiencing orgasm. In a society in which immediate gratification and heightened sensual pleasure are so frequently sought as the ideal, the question is whether heterosexuality can effectively compete.

A second possibility is that since homosexuality is basically self- rather than humanity-centered, Christian thought charges that those in the social system championing equivalency of heterosexuality and homosexuality are more apt to espouse other human life-threatening social policies. Cameron and Ross (1981) reported evidence supportive of this contention, with those favoring social acceptance of homosexuality also more frequently being in favor of greater social acceptance of abortion, suicide, infanticide, and forms of euthanasia. These same people were also more apt to engage in activities of self-abuse, such as drug abuse or suicide attempts.

Finally, homosexuality tends toward short bondings and immediate sensual reward. Therefore a host of short-perspective and family and stability threatening social policies, attitudes, and life styles might be expected to emerge or be reinforced by more widespread acceptance of homosexuality as an equal and alternate life style.

References
Bell, A. P., & Weinberg, M. S. *Homosexualities.* New York: Simon & Schuster, 1978.
Brandsma, J. M., & Pattison, E. M. Homosexuality and alcoholism. In E. M. Pattison & E. Kaufman (Eds.), *Encyclopedic handbook of alcoholism.* New York: Gardner Press, 1982.
Cameron, P. A case against homosexuality. *Human Life Review,* 1978, *4,* (3), 17–49.
Cameron, P., & Ross, K. P. Social psychological aspects of the Judeo-Christian stance toward homosexuality. *Journal of Psychology and Theology,* 1981, 9(1), 40–57.
Gebhard, P. H., Gagnon, J. H., Pomeroy, W. B., & Christenson, C. V. *Sex offenders: An analysis of types.* New York: Harper & Row, 1965.
Gebhard, P. H., & Johnson, A. B. *The Kinsey data.* Philadelphia: Saunders, 1979.
Karlen, A. *Sexuality and homosexuality: A new view.* New York: Norton, 1971.
Saghir, M. T., & Robins, E. *Male and female homosexuality.* Baltimore: Williams & Wilkins, 1973.
Schofield, M. *The sexual behavior of young people.* Boston: Little, Brown, 1965.

P. CAMERON

Hope. A desire accompanied by the expectation that the desire will be obtained. It is partly cognitive (it is a thought), partly emotional (it involves anticipation and other positive affects), and partly volitional (it contains belief). Hope has traditionally had spiritual or religious connotations. For this reason hope has not been a major focus of psychological study in spite of its obvious emotional components. It has, however, been very present in literature and is a prominent concept in the Bible.

In Scripture hope is a major theme in both testaments. The psalmist often spoke of hope as a major resource for coping with defeat, discouragement, and danger (e.g., Pss. 119:116; 146:5). The hope of the Old Testament was but a foreshadow of the hope found in Jesus Christ (1 Tim. 1:1; Col. 1:27). Hope is prominent in Acts and the Epistles and is described as a central element of the Christian's resources.

Theologically hope serves the function of linking the believer to the future promised by Christ. As the follower of Christ experiences a new spiritual life, there is a keen awareness that the earthly enjoyments of faith in Christ are incomplete. What has begun on earth will continue into eternity. Hope links the believer's present with a glorious future.

Biblical anthropology does not give an exhaustive commentary on the psychological value of hope to men and women. Psalm 22:9 reads in the Authorized Version, "Thou didst make me hope when I was upon my mother's breasts." At first glance the verse appears to suggest that hope is innate or is a part of human experience reaching back into infancy. More recent translations suggest that the more probable interpretation is that the Lord caused the psalmist to trust as an infant, thus referring to the mother-child bonding phenomenon. However, the Bible emphasizes the strategic role of hope in the human personality. Faith seems to answer to the human need for spiritual meaning, love relates to the intrapersonal and interpersonal needs of humans to relate to self and others, and hope reflects the motivational needs of humans to find meaning and purpose in the future. Hope is clearly portrayed as a significant motivator of human endeavor (Titus 2:11–14; 1 John 3:3). Hope longs for the resurrection body (Jeeves, 1976).

Psychology has indirectly studied the concept of hope from three different vantage points: 1) the role of hope in human motivation theory; 2) the importance of hope in human personality (as inferred from the absence of hope in certain pathologies); and 3) the curative power of hope in the recovery of severely disturbed persons.

Several important personality theories emphasize the significance of purpose as an ingredient in the human system. Hall and Lindzey (1957) describe purposive or teleological qualities as those which are goal seeking and future oriented. The classical analytic theories of Freud, Jung, and Adler all empha-

size purpose, as do Fromm and Sullivan. In fact, so many contemporary theorists emphasize the purposive side of human personality that Hall and Lindzey suggest this aspect of personality is almost taken for granted and is no longer an issue of debate in psychology, as it was in the early twentieth century. Purpose is related to hope in that both are future oriented and both assume the attainment of some longed-for desires.

Hopelessness, or the lack of hope, is a prominent feature of the various depressive syndromes and of suicidal persons. Beck (1967) notes that hopelessness is a clinical feature of moderate and severe depressions and is present in about one-half of mild cases. Furthermore, Beck states, "In our studies we found that suicidal wishes had a higher correlation with hopelessness than with any other symptom of depression" (p. 58). It seems reasonable to conclude that if hopelessness is so highly associated with the desire to kill oneself, then the presence of hope in the human psyche must be vitalizing and central to survival.

The final avenue of psychological investigation into hope, exemplified by Stotland (1969), confirms the above deduction. Stotland views hope as a mediating variable that helps explain data regarding the recovery of hospitalized schizophrenics and depressives. When optimism and hopefulness are conveyed by the staff and the milieu, he concludes, people recover.

References

Beck, A. T. *Depression: Causes and treatment.* Philadelphia: University of Pennsylvania Press, 1967.
Hall, C. S., & Lindzey, G. *Theories of personality.* New York: Wiley, 1957.
Jeeves, M. A. *Psychology and Christianity: The view both ways.* Downers Grove, Ill.: Inter-Varsity Press, 1976.
Stotland, E. *The psychology of hope.* San Francisco: Jossey-Bass, 1969.

J. R. BECK

Hormic Psychology. The major characteristic of hormic psychology was the assumption that all behavior is purposive. It was introduced in 1908 by WILLIAM McDOUGALL, who further felt that goals are sought for their own sake, not just for the pleasure that might result from their attainment. Hormism is thus opposed to hedonism, which assumes that goals are pursued exclusively for the pleasure they produce. McDougall believed that individuals possessed certain instincts and that each of these leads to a specific end. He identified seven primary instincts: escape, combat, curiosity, repulsion, self-assertion, self-abasement, and the parental instinct.

This school of thought has never attained the status of a major system. Because of its emphasis on the teleological aspects of behavior, it became aligned with psychoanalysis, which shares its dynamic quality but which is built on a much more comprehensive theoretical base.

D. G. BENNER

Horney, Karen (1885–1952). Widely influential American psychoanalyst, born in Hamburg, Germany. Her father was a devoted Christian, but her mother was a freethinker and ridiculed his Bible reading. Dominated by her mother, Horney followed her in eventually renouncing her Christian beliefs during adolescence. She trained in medicine and psychoanalysis in Berlin, where she not only studied and interacted with many famous pioneers of psychoanalysis but also supervised, analyzed, and taught at the Berlin Institute.

Primarily an interpersonal theorist, Horney has played a crucial role in establishing the importance of interpsychic as well as intrapsychic forces in the personality. Because of her interpersonal orientation she has been criticized for not dealing with the depth of the psyche, a criticism that probably has some justification. Early on, she criticized Freud's biological emphasis, not only for its negative implications for women, but also for its inadequacy as a base for personality structure.

Neurotic Needs and Personality Types. First presented in 1942 in *Self Analysis*, Horney's list of 10 basic neurotic needs has been her best-known contribution. The development of these needs begins with the child being subjected to a stressful environment, which produces anxiety. The child responds to this by developing a strategy to cope with the stress. Because the strategy reduces anxiety, it becomes highly significant for the individual. It actually becomes a need. Horney feels these needs become so strong that they actually determine the person's basic orientation toward others and his or her environment. Thus, they actually determine a person's personality. In *Our Inner Conflicts* (1945) Horney classified the 10 neurotic needs according to three basic interpersonal styles with which they are associated: moving toward, against, or away from people. She described these as the major solutions to the problem of basic anxiety.

Moving toward. Overt or covert rejection leads the child to feel that he or she does not belong and produces neurotic or exaggerated belongingness needs. There are two such needs: the neurotic need for affection and the

neurotic need for a partner who will take over one's life. The neurotic need for affection and approval involves an indiscriminate need to please others and to be liked and approved by everyone. Pleasing others is seen as the way to win the desperately needed love. The neurotic need for a partner to take over one's life involves the individual looking to some one person, often a spouse, to fulfill all expectations and needs. The successful manipulation of this person becomes the predominant life task.

These two needs combine to produce what Horney calls the moving toward, or self-effacing, personality. Such individuals feel compelled to be loving and lovable, self-sacrificing, sympathetic, and dependent. They hope that these virtues will produce the sought-for intimacy and sense of belonging. Their basic life slogan is, "If you love me, you won't hurt me."

Horney lists three attitudes held by this personality type: the feeling that he or she is weak and helpless, a tendency to subordinate self to others, and a general dependence upon others. This dependence includes clinging to others not just to meet nurturance needs but also to try to achieve a sense of identity. The identity comes from being an appendage to the partner or stronger person.

Moving against. The second basic personality style is that of moving against people. Associated with this personality type are the neurotic or exaggerated self-esteem needs. There are five such needs: the need for power, for exploitation, for recognition, for admiration, and for achievement.

The neurotic need for power involves the person craving power for the purpose of dominating others, keeping them in a subordinate position. Power and strength are glorified and weakness is despised. This need takes two forms: the control of others through reason and foresight, and control through omnipotence of the will.

The second need is the neurotic need to get the better of other people. This person uses others for his own gain and dominates them by exploitation. The third need is the neurotic need for social recognition or prestige. For this person all things are judged by their competitive value.

The fourth neurotic need is the need for personal admiration. As this individual maintains an inflated picture of himself or his idealized image, he needs to have this image admired. His self-evaluation depends on adequate admiration of his image by others. Finally, the neurotic need for personal achievement is reflected in the drive to surpass others in all activities. Such individuals must be the very best in all pursuits.

These five needs combine to form the moving against, or expansive, personality type. This person takes it for granted that everyone is hostile and refuses to be convinced otherwise. His or her slogan is, "If I have power, no one can hurt me." The person must therefore dominate and control others while maintaining an inner sense of self-glorification. While this personality may present very manipulative façades and use all the right words, he or she is simply exploiting in order to control. Affection, sympathy, and trust are seen as weakness to be shunned. The person is afraid to admit to error, imperfection, or even illness, for these represent limitations. Other people are mistrusted and seen as competitors.

Moving away. The third personality type is that of the person moving away from other people. Three needs are associated with this type: the need for self-sufficiency, the need for perfection, and the need to restrict one's life within narrow borders.

In the neurotic need for self-sufficiency and independence, distance and separateness are seen as the only source of security. Such an individual can never need anybody, yield to any influence, or be close to anyone. The neurotic need for perfection and unassailability involves a relentless driving for superiority. The resulting feeling of actually being superior gives one a sense of being infallible. Finally, the neurotic need to restrict one's life within narrow borders involves being undemanding and contented with little. The need is to be ultraconservative and retire to the background.

These needs form the moving away from, or resigned, personality. Such people strive to be free of all emotional feelings. Therefore, both the first two basic orientations must be repressed as the person moves away from others as well as from his or her own feelings. Such a person's slogan is "If I withdraw, nothing can hurt me."

The moving away style can be visualized as a person building an emotional fort in which he lives alone. Retreating behind huge emotional walls which shut all others out, he can communicate only by yelling over the walls of the fort, since he can never be coaxed to come out of its safety and security. Life in the fort, though lonely, feels unassailable and invulnerable. In order to maintain such an attitude this person needs to feel superior and strong compared with others. Detachment allows

such feelings as "I'm stronger" or "I'm better" to go unchallenged, thus reinforcing a sense of safety and security.

This need for detachment means that close ties with others are impossible. The attitude toward oneself is one of objective interest and numbness. The moving away can take one of three forms: the person who is persistently resigned, with an aversion to activity; the rebellious person whose passive resistance becomes active and is directed against environmental factors or inner restrictions; and the person whose shallow living causes emptiness and despair, driving him or her to avoid the pain of loneliness through sex, constant activity, or other escapes.

The Idealized Image. In order to deal with feelings of anxiety and insecurity people also develop what Horney calls an idealized image. This corresponds closely to Freud's ego ideal and Adler's striving for superiority. However, Horney's idealized image is more clearly and completely expounded, and here lies what may be her most valuable contribution to the understanding of abnormal psychology.

The idealized image is a false self that is developed when living with one's actual self becomes too painful. If the actual self is hated or despised, a flight into fantasy can relieve the awfulness of living with it. Initially, the idealized image is conscious, as in the case of a child who envisions herself as a beautiful princess living in a huge castle with a handsome prince. Later the image becomes more and more inclusive of the total personality, until the individual so identifies with his or her idealized image that it becomes the glorified self. This identification with the idealized image is, for Horney, narcissism. The individual is driven to keep this image actualized because it relieves anxiety, satisfies his or her exaggerated needs, and transforms the despised qualities of the actual self into the glorious ones of the idealized image.

In the "moving toward" person, compliance and submission become goodness, love, saintliness, and service. The "moving against" person transforms his or her aggressiveness into strength, heroism, leadership, and power. Finally, the "moving away" person transforms aloofness into wisdom, self-suffering, and independence.

Horney felt that the idealized self represents the perfect person and as such is never attainable. Because of this she called the image "a devouring monster." In *Neurosis and Human Growth* (1950) she laments the abandonment of the actual self for the idealized image. Surveying the ravaging forces unleashed by the idealized self, she stated that "we cannot help but see in it a great tragedy, perhaps the greatest of the human mind. Man in reaching out for the Infinite and Absolute also starts destroying himself. When he makes a pact with the devil, who promises him glory, he has to go to hell—to the hell within himself (p. 154). She points to Christ's successful resistance to Satan's promise to give him the kingdoms of the world as an example of not abandoning one's actual self (who Jesus really was) in favor of the idealized image (ruling over the kingdoms of the world). She comments that it is a testimony of true greatness when one person can resist such temptation. Identification with one's idealized image constitutes what she calls the devil's pact, since it costs the individual so dearly in the alienation from who he or she really is.

It is interesting to note that we have here an excellent picture of the Pharisees whom Jesus so vehemently denounced because of their false standards of righteousness. Indeed, the whole thrust of the Sermon on the Mount is Christ's attempt to get the religious leaders of the day to see their real selves below their idealized selves, which consisted of a righteousness based on ritual, rules, and regulations. Jesus' dispute was with their distortion of the teachings of Moses by presenting them as a means of appearance and office rather than as a way to God. They held up the idealized image of righteousness both to God and to other people. Jesus' message was that one must acknowledge one's actual real self because it is genuine and acceptable to God. But, he says, God will never accept the false self with its pride, hypocrisy, and alienation of self and God.

Implications for Therapy. Horney's insights can inform the task of counseling or psychotherapy. First, the counselor must ascertain which movement a troubled person is using in attempting to cope with his or her insecurities, anxieties, and depressions. Second, the counselor must see what kind of form the idealized image is taking. This, as has been seen, will be based primarily on the interpersonal style. The idealized image causes the person to be alienated from his or her real self and to live under a standard of perfection with its systems of oughts and shoulds. It also causes the person to utilize externalization. Through this defense mechanism he betrays the alienation from his actual self by blaming his failures on outside forces. This not only shifts the responsibility toward some other object but actually leads the individual to feel

that all these things actually take place outside of self.

In dealing with a person's idealized image a counselor must gradually show that it is a "search for glory" which drains away one's whole life. Horney compares it to the creation of Frankenstein's monster, which in time usurped the creator's best energies. It eventually strangles the drive to grow. All energy is directed toward actualizing the idealized self. "It entails not only the compulsive drive for worldly glory through success, power and triumph but also the tyrannical inner system by which he tries to mold himself into a godlike being; it entails neurotic claims and the development of neurotic pride" (Horney, 1950, pp. 367–368).

The idealized image also demonstrates a basic self-hatred and nonacceptance of self. The reconciliation of the idealized image and the actual self must occur so that the real self can emerge. This is the ultimate goal of counseling for the Christian. If the actual self is in Christ, nothing about it should be avoided or denied. In principle the Christian should have no need for the idealized image, nor should he or she use one. Such a use betrays an inward rejection of his or her real being. Based on Christ's death and unconditional acceptance, the Christian can face self without the use of Pharisaism and its futile flight from truth.

As reconciliation with the real self takes place, the particular interpersonal style, whether it is toward, against, or away, will also be diminished in intensity and strength. Since these movements are rooted in the despised and hated actual self, they serve their weak and cowardly master by attempting to protect. If the actual self is reconciled, its acting-out methods will gradually diminish and be eroded.

References

Horney, K. *Self analysis.* New York: Norton, 1942.
Horney, K. *Our inner conflicts.* New York: Norton, 1945.
Horney, K. *Neurosis and human growth.* New York: Norton, 1950.

W. T. Kirwan

Hull, Clark Leonard (1884–1952). American psychologist best known for his attempt to construct a general theory of behavior. Hull was born near Akron, New York. Several years later his family moved to a farm in Michigan, where he grew up and received his education at Alma College and the University of Michigan. Since his family had little income, he had to drop out of school several times to work. He was also plagued with illnesses, crippled from polio at the age of 24, and had poor eyesight. He finally received his Ph.D. degree from the University of Wisconsin in 1918 at 34 years of age.

Hull remained at the University of Wisconsin until he became a professor in the newly founded Institute of Human Relations at Yale in 1929. He remained at Yale until his death. His famous open seminar attracted many students who performed the experimental work necessary to test his theory.

Hull did research in concept formation, the effects of tobacco smoking, hypnosis, suggestibility, and aptitude testing. He began to develop his theory of behavior while still in graduate school, but worked on it in earnest from 1929 until his death. He wanted to develop a hypothetico-deductive theory in which he could begin with a small set of postulates and corollaries, then logically deduce the behaviors that would occur when a given stimulus was presented.

Hull's theory was a mechanistic, reductionistic, objective behaviorism. It was essentially a theory of learning inspired by Pavlov's work but extended to all behavior of all species, including humans. This approach dominated the psychological conceptions of learning for nearly 30 years, and continues to be influential.

Although his books on hypnosis and aptitude testing were well received, it was those works developing his theory of behavior which have had a lasting impact. *Principles of Behavior* (1943) was his major contribution, first setting forth his overall theory. He revised his theory in *Essentials of Behavior* (1951) and *A Behavior System* (1952), but neither of these had the impact of the 1943 book. His contribution to psychological theory building in general is much more than his own theory. Although many parts of his theory are questioned, many psychologists respect and admire the methods he used to develop it. It is to his credit that his theory is stated specifically enough to be shown incorrect. Although well known in the psychology of LEARNING, he is almost unknown to the general public.

R. L. KOTESKEY

Humanistic Psychology.

Broadly conceived, humanistic psychology is a movement within psychology that in its psychological theorizing and research emphasizes what it perceives to be the distinctly human characteristics of man.

Though not devoid of a number of articulate theories or a respectable body of knowledge, humanistic psychology is characterized less by its theoretical stance or research orientation than by its attitude toward human beings. Its emphasis is on spontaneity, internal locus of control, uniqueness, wholeness, personality, and capacity for self-actualization. Thus, it seeks to humanize what today is a predominantly mechanomorphic psychology and to replace it with a psychology based on a concept of persons as creative, self-transcending beings, controlled not by outside or unconscious forces but by their own values and choices alone.

The movement counts a large number of prominent psychologists as its adherents. Among them are Buhler, Fromm, May, Frankl, Murray, Allport, Rogers, and Maslow. These by no means agree with each other on every point. In the broadest sense humanistic psychology includes theorists and practitioners who operate from a phenomenological and existentialistic tradition as well as those who work from a predominantly holistic, pragmatistic, and Darwinian tradition. What unites all of these into one movement is their opposition to the mechanistic, deterministic view of man, positivism in philosophy, and behaviorism in psychology.

In the literature phenomenology and existentialism are frequently described separately as systems of philosophy and psychology, next to humanistic psychology. Thus, it is perhaps more accurate to characterize humanistic psychology in the broadest sense as a humanistic *movement* in psychology and philosophy. This allows us to reserve the name *humanistic psychology* in the strictest sense for that branch of psychology proper of which Maslow and Rogers are the chief proponents.

History and Development. Humanistic psychology has had great impact on psychology as a whole. It is an American product that has incorporated many of the typically European phenomenological and existentialistic themes. But in doing so it has nevertheless remained firmly rooted in the American individualistic and evolutionistic tradition.

The origin of humanistic psychology as a school dates back to 1954, when Maslow described its adherents as "people who are interested in the scientific study of creativity, love, higher values, autonomy, growth, self-actualization, need gratification, etc." (Misiak, 1973, p. 127). In subsequent years there followed a series of publications by various authors, each taking humanistic psychology as their point of departure. In 1961 the *Journal of Humanistic Psychology* was founded by Anthony Sutich. One year later the American Association for Humanistic Psychology was established. In 1970 the American Psychology Association approved the establishment of a Division of Humanistic Psychology (Division 32). During that same year the First International Conference on Humanistic Psychology was held in Amsterdam, with Charlotte Buhler as its president, and from then on the movement was off and running.

By now the movement has generated a veritable troupe of second-generation adherents, all of them busily applying humanistic psychology principles in therapy, education, family life, business, interpersonal and international relations. Through the use of encounter groups the movement currently offers a smorgasbord of growth-enhancing workshops that is so diverse that it makes one wonder whether anything short of behaviorism cannot be included under its banner. Indeed, the ability to incorporate whatever is new and creative is one of the hallmarks of this school of psychology.

Philosophical Roots. Philosophically, humanistic psychology has several roots. This accounts to a large degree for the inner tensions which the movement is currently experiencing.

Phenomenological-existentialistic Tradition. The first root lies in what may loosely be called the phenomenological-existentialistic tradition. Its history goes back to Franz Brentano (1838–1917), who is the acknowledged father of both Husserl's philosophical phenomenology and Stumpf's empirical phenomenology.

Brentano's chief contribution was his notion of intentionality. This notion implies that consciousness is not a matter of contents impressed upon our minds by some external reality, but that it can only be understood with reference to the subjective activity of human intentions. Conscious content is what human subjects intend there to be. At the same time intentionality also implies that consciousness is always consciousness of something. Intentionality is always directed toward, and stands in relation to, some intended object. When he forms, intends, or intuits the object, the human subject must therefore always be guided by the nature or the essence of the object.

This makes the intended object simultaneously the product of the intentional act of the human subject and the object toward which that act is directed. From that intentional vantage point investigation can go one of two ways. It can go in the direction of Husserl's philosophical phenomenology, which investigates the intentional act of the human subject that constitutes consciousness. It can also go in the direction of Stumpf's empirical phenomenology, which investigates the relation of human intentionality to the intended object. In either case, however, phenomenology consists of the investigation of psychic acts rather than psychic contents.

Via Stumpf's empirical phenomenology Brentano became the grandfather of Gestalt psychology in general and of Lewin's field theory in particular. His influence is evident in the Gestalt notion of perception. It manifests the ambivalence of phenomenology in that perceiving is clearly viewed as a constructive act, but nonetheless an act that is governed by the laws of perception inherent in the perceptual object or percept. Similarly, the self in Lewin's field theory functions as the subject pole of every perceptual act that constitutes the phenomenal field. But also as perceived object in the phenomenal field it regulates, if not determines, the nature of the perceptual acts of the self as subject.

Humanistic psychology borrows from Brentano and Husserl the notion that the human subject (i.e., the organism) is active in the sense that it organizes the world that surrounds it. The organism responds only to an environment that it itself has perceived (Rogers, 1961). But the human subject also finds its organizing purpose or direction in the phenomenal field. It incites the organism to perform its perceptual activity. Experience (here understood as experiential field) has meaning, and the organism must let experience tell it its own meaning (Rogers 1961). The organism must be open to, and receptive of, the phenomenal field. More than that, it must seek to enhance the phenomenal field, particularly that part of it which constitutes the self.

Thus a number of the basic notions of humanistic psychology such as the self, experience, perception, the phenomenal field—all of which it views as distinctly human characteristics—are directly derived from the phenomenological-existentialistic tradition.

Pragmatism. But humanistic psychology is also rooted in the pragmatism of James and even more firmly in that of Dewey. Dewey's main importance for humanistic psychology was that he served as the conduit for the influence of Darwinism on the movement. Darwinian thought held that reality is dynamic, that living things develop in adaptive interaction with their environment.

Following Darwin, Dewey too saw change rather than stasis as the primary characteristic of reality. This dynamic notion allowed him to conceive of the order of the different kingdoms in reality (i.e. rocks, plants, and animals) as one of different levels of interactive complexity. For Dewey reality originally consisted of an infinite number of interactions. Things emerged, or came into being, when series of these interactions grouped themselves into organized wholes. When these wholes, in turn, began to interact with other wholes, they made it possible for even more complex wholes to emerge.

For Dewey this ongoing process is characteristic of all that exists in nature. No organized interactive whole, or thing, is ever complete in itself. Its meaning lies perpetually in the consequences it engenders in subsequent, more complex interactive wholes. Things are always in the process of becoming integrated into more complex things. Reality is thus perpetually (re)ordered or (re)constructed in a process that runs from lower to higher differentiation and integration. This dynamic order of ongoing, naturally occurring differentiation and integration is what Dewey called growth.

Humanistic psychology owes a great deal to Dewey's pragmatism and, via Dewey, to Darwin's theory of evolution. Notions such as becoming, growth, actualization, organism, and the hierarchical structure of human activity are all derived from this philosophical root.

However, on one significant point humanistic psychology parts company with Dewey. This concerns the formative influence of human subjects on the process of growth. Dewey held that on the human level of interaction the innovative activity of the human subject can shape the process of growth and redirect it to its own human ends. Thus at that level of interaction the naturally occurring growth process becomes a historically formative process, governed by changes that have their purpose in a source outside the growth process itself. Simply put, Dewey held that people can form growth.

While humanistic psychology certainly recognizes the existence of subjects, it denies that they exist external to the process of growth, and thus it also denies that subjects can form growth to their own human ends. On the contrary, the growth process itself has formative power, and it naturally shapes the human subject rather than the reverse.

Humanistic psychology holds that everything that exists, including human beings, is taken up in this total evolutionary process of becoming. This becoming, or growth process, has its own ends in view and its own organizational principle within itself. It has morphological properties. It forms itself dynamically. Individuals, as microcosms of this total process, each uniquely have the capacity to form themselves or to actualize their potentials. But they have this capacity only insofar as they are open to and receptive of this evolutionary process of becoming, thus only insofar as they function as the organisms that they are.

This morphological principle hails back all the way to Aristotle's doctrine of entelechy. He defined it as the impulse of an organized body (or organism) to become what it is. The vitalist Hans Driesch defended this principle as late as the beginning of this century against the predominantly mechanistic view of mainstream biology.

The problem with the entelechy doctrine is that it implies a teleology—i.e., it implies that the growth process is directed by goals. And once these goals are fulfilled, they can conceivably stop the growth process, thus endangering its status as a total, perpetually ongoing process of becoming. To avoid such negative consequences humanistic psychology rejected the notion of entelechy and opted for the notion of directionality.

This notion, originating with Goldstein, is derived from a biological version of holism developed by the South African philosopher-biologist Jan Smuts. Angyal, following Smuts, has suggested that the goal does not "define the direction of an activity, but rather the intrinsic pattern of a direction of behavior determines what object is a suitable goal" (Angyal, 1958, p. 53–55). This notion of directionality safeguards the dynamic self-motivation and self-direction of the growth process at every level of differentiation and integration.

Essential Characteristics. Humanistic psychology is often called the third force in psychology because it pits itself against the deterministic picture of persons evident in both psychoanalysis and behaviorism. Thus it presents itself as an alternative to both these systems of psychology. It rejects the pessimistic view of psychoanalysis, which holds that one's actions are wholly driven by the libidinal energy of an unconscious, irrational id. It also rejects the behavioristic view that human behavior is wholly determined by environmental forces. Thus it rejects the internal determinism of psychoanalysis as well as the external determinism of behaviorism because both reduce persons to something lower than human.

Over against the position of traditional psychology that man is nothing but an animal or a machine it posits the view that man is human. Over against the view that behavior is nothing but a response to a stimulus it states that human behavior is purposive. Over against the view that culture is nothing but a sublimated, covert attempt at gratifying dark sexual urges it emphasizes the view that culture is the expression of humanity's higher aspirations. Over against the elementarism of Wundt and Watson alike it argues that a person is a totality. Over against the determinism of mainline psychology it stresses human freedom, creativity, spontaneity, and playfulness. Over against a preoccupation with needs and drives that drag people down to the level of animals it talks about goals that draw people up to the height of the gods. Over against mechanism, which depicts human behavior as randomly governed by perilous chance, it steadfastly maintains the orderly, organized character of human acts. Over against a depth psychology it proposes a psychology of heights. In short, it states that a human being is always more than the reduced picture that traditional psychology has given of him.

Humanistic Psychology is a "more than" psychology; "more than" is its basic paradigm. Traditional psychologies are viewed as all being reductionisms. But humanistic psychology, with its emphasis on all things human, is a thoroughgoing, dynamic transcendentalism in which one's reach must exceed his grasp. It is a celebration of human potentiality and possibility. Its motto is *semper excelsior* and its key is transcendence. Moreover, to guarantee the perpetuity of this process of transcendence or growth, and to avoid the stultifying effects of finalism, it stresses that the direction of the process is primary and its goals secondary.

Basic Themes and Their Implications. Growth. Humanistic psychology is primarily a growth psychology as opposed to a depth psychology or a stimulus-response psychology. This emphasis on growth and actualization represents its first and major theme. It characterizes its view of human reality as dynamic, with its constant emphasis on novelty. The picture of man in humanistic psychology is that of *homo novus*.

Personhood. A second theme stresses the importance of such notions as person, autonomy, uniqueness, self, experience, and (inter) subjectivity. This theme states, first of all, that man is unique. This not only means that as a species man is distinctly human as opposed to other creatures, but more importantly it means that it is in the nature of man to be unique. Every human being alive is first and foremost universally unique, thus wholly unlike his fellows (Rogers, 1961).

Second, it stresses that every human being, without exception, is a person. This means that every man is the initiator, the director, and the evaluator of his own development. Personal growth, actualization, and enhancement are not externally controlled but occur internal to the human person. Every man is in that sense autonomous—i.e., a law unto himself.

Third, it stresses that every person is uniquely the subject pole of his own experience, of his own perception, of his own awareness, and indeed of his own reality. This means that no one's experience, perception, or reality is identical to that of any other. A reality that holds for every person does not exist. There are as many realities as there are persons. Quite literally, all that exists or occurs in the world exists or occurs within the internal frame of reference of persons.

Fourth, it stresses that man is aware of himself as a person. This self-awareness makes that part of a person's experience which constitutes his own being—i.e., the self—the most important element in his entire experiential field. The self functions as the reference point to which all other parts of the field are centrally and directly related.

Finally, every person meets with others in his experience. These others are like himself, unique, thus principally unlike himself. These others are persons who are the masters of their own destiny, who have their own experience and their own world. It behooves all of us, therefore, in the spirit of the best of empiricism, not to treat others as extensions of ourselves. Rather than manipulate them, or explain them as objects in our experience, we must be open to them, receive them, and understand them as autonomous subjects. The other can never be counted, measured, or manipulated as our object, because he is a subject. For this reason there is no such thing as objectivity among people. Man is indeed man-with-man, but this human fellowship is always a fellowship of subjects, an intersubjectivity.

Taking these two themes together we can state that each person is a unique principle of self-actualization or self-transcendence. This formulation characterizes humanistic psychology both in its depth and in its breadth. This formulation further implies that the only viable stance anyone can ever take toward one's fellow is to be receptive and even reverent of his capacity to grow, to transcend himself. We must always be open to his newness and, what is more, allow ourselves to be changed by his dynamic uniqueness.

While this ultraempiricism has its good points, it results in such particularization of experience that one loses sight of the woods for all the trees. In the field of personal growth this has resulted over the past two decades in a burgeoning of all kinds of growth-promoting methods and approaches. However, it is a diversity, where the point of unity that connects each of them to the other is lacking. Humanistic psychology is thus faced with the problem of finding unity in its diversity. It needs a common denominator. This brings us to its third theme, which stresses wholeness, universality and being.

Wholeness and universality. Under the guidance of Ockham's principle of parsimony traditional psychology had found its point of unity in science, and it realized this unity in science by reducing all created activity, including human activity, to nothing but physical states of affairs. Thus it achieved wholeness and universality by insisting that at bottom everything is matter—i.e., physical being. This door is closed to humanistic psychology because it commits itself to a dynamic view of reality (everything "is" in a state of becoming). It rejects the static view of matter as being, in favor of potentiality and becoming. Thus it can locate its point of unity only in the human subject and in the growth process. In its view, therefore, each person is whole insofar as he remains true to himself *and* continues to evolve.

While this formulation satisfies the need for wholeness, it does nothing for universality. The assertion that everyone is universally unique, far from solving the problem, in fact propagated the bewildering particularism and individualism that characterizes humanistic psychology today.

Maslow was the first to recognize this problem and began to stress his concept of "B-(eing) cognition." Persons who have transcended to a kind of superconsciousness are said by him to be capable of B-cognition. It involves a person in rising to ecstatic peak experiences of cosmic wholeness, where one can stoically contemplate and stand in awe of the colorful particularity "below." That level of cognition is universal, unified wholeness personified. It exists above and beyond the lower dichotomies, such as those of good and evil. Similarly Rogers, the lifelong champion of persons, has in his later years begun to stress the need for persons to dissolve themselves into the universal stream of life as a further

step in their actualization process (Van Belle, 1980).

This latest development seems to suggest that humanistic psychology is drifting toward the universalism, mysticism, and spiritualism of transpersonal psychology. In the first issue of the *Journal of Transpersonal Psychology*, Sutich, who is also the founder of the *Journal of Humanistic Psychology*, calls transpersonal psychology the fourth force in psychology. Its adherents are described as people who are interested in studies of ultimate human capacities and potentialities. Sources for these studies are Eastern religions, parapsychological phenomena, and phenomena typically studied by humanistic psychology.

The term *fourth force* is apt, for it is likely that humanistic psychology as the unique champion of persons will be superseded if it persists in its movement toward transpersonal psychology. Yet, given its dynamic, transcendental character, one may wonder whether it can do anything but exchange its personalism for a transpersonalism. In doing so it will lose its ability to fruitfully engage in culture formation, since mysticism and universalism of any kind have always thrived on withdrawal from the rip and tear of concrete culture and society into the ethereal realm of pseudoreligious spirituality (Roszak, 1975).

Humanistic psychology has always had a particularly seductive pull for Christians. It has loosened the antispiritual, materialistic, and reductionistic grip of psychoanalysis and behaviorism on psychology. In doing so, it has made talk of persons, purpose, values, and spirituality, all topics dear to Christians, once more respectable. But its transcendentalism seems to lead to a subjectivistic, pantheistic and world-denying spiritualism, where wholeness is the highest good to be attained. Moreover, if one sees that the path to this wholeness implies that good and evil, as commonly understood, must be seen as structural parts of creation rather than its postfall continuum of direction, then one wonders whether humanistic psychology is not more Christianity's bane than its boon.

References

Angyal, A. *Foundations for a science of personality* (2nd ed.). Cambridge: Harvard University Press, 1958.

Misiak, H. *Phenomenological, existential, and humanistic psychologies.* New York: Grune & Stratton, 1973.

Rogers, C. R. *On becoming a person,* Boston: Houghton Mifflin, 1961.

Roszak, T. *The unfinished animal.* New York: Harper & Row, 1975.

Van Belle, H. A. *Basic intent and therapeutic approach of Carl R. Rogers.* Toronto: Wedge Publishing Foundation, 1980.

Additional Readings

Dagenais, J. *Models of man*. The Hague: Nijhoff, 1972.

Maslow, A. H. A Theory of human motivation. *Psychological Review*, 1943, *50*, 370–396.

Maslow, A. H. Cognition of being in the peak experience. *Journal of Genetic Psychology*, 1959, *94*, 43–66.

Maslow, A. H. *The farther reaches of human nature*. New York: Viking Press, 1971.

Rogers, C. R. *Carl Rogers on personal power*. New York: Delacorte Press, 1977.

Tart, C. T. *Trans-personal psychologies*. New York: Harper & Row, 1975.

H. A. Van Belle

Human Relations Training.

Systematic human relations training is a program of learning experiences designed to teach lay people to relate to others more helpfully. As most commonly used the term refers to the approach developed by Carkhuff (1969). This approach grew out of his association with Carl Rogers and his subsequent identification of core dimensions of a helping relationship. He then placed these dimensions, or helper characteristics, within an overall model of the helping relationship and developed training procedures and assessment devices for the development of the core skills.

Carkhuff outlined three goals of helping relationships. The first is to encourage the person's self-exploration. The helper listens as the one seeking help talks and explores the problem areas. This leads to the second goal, self-understanding. The third goal is action or problem resolution. This is not a natural consequence of understanding but must be planned for and actively pursued. It is important to note that not all helping interactions lead through all these steps and achieve the desired outcome of problem solution; often the helper is just one link in the chain of life of a person.

The Core Dimension.

The first phase of the helping process as conceived by Carkhuff is directed toward establishing a sound caring relationship with the person seeking help. Before any action dimensions are employed in the helping process, the helper utilizes the safe, less threatening facilitative dimensions that are deemed necessary to prepare the person to accept and thus benefit from the more threatening action dimensions.

The helper begins building the base by responding with empathy, respect, and warmth. Empathy is judged to be the most important dimension in the helping process. Empathy involves the helper's understanding of both content (the facts of the situation) and affect (how the person feels about it). Persons are never quite able to put into words all that they feel; no word is so powerful that its meaning is completely clear. Thus, the helper's initial responses should reflect back to the person the information and feeling the helper perceives (e.g., "You sound angry because your husband doesn't seem to care about your problem at work").

Respect is another facilitative dimension. Respect involves faith in the person's ability to solve the problem. Hastily given advice communicates disrespect for his or her intelligence. Warmth, or caring, is closely related to empathy and respect. People tend to love or have concern for those whom they understand (empathy) and in whom they believe (respect). Warmth is communicated primarily through nonverbal means, such as eye contact, posture, gestures, etc.

These first three dimensions are a restatement of Rogers's necessary and sufficient conditions for therapy. Carkhuff views their role as facilitating the establishment of a therapeutic relationship which, once established, will then involve other dimensions.

The facilitative dimensions encourage the person to self-explore. With repeated empathic reflection of content and feeling a point will eventually be reached where no new feelings or information will be forthcoming. At this point the helper needs to encourage the person to risk more self-exploration. Thus, the dimensions of concreteness, genuineness, and self-disclosure are added. These three dimensions are action oriented as well as facilitative.

To achieve concreteness the helper must encourage discussion of specific feelings and experiences. Generalities and vague discussions are avoided. Genuineness refers to the helper's honesty in the relationship. Genuineness does not mean brutal honesty but rather honesty timed so that it can be of assistance to the other person. It also means not being dishonest in what is communicated. Self-disclosure of the helper can also enhance the relationship if the disclosure is appropriate. When helper self-disclosure is premature or irrelevant to the other's problem, it may confuse him or shift the focus to the helper.

Human relations trainers view the action phase as the ultimate goal, since it is in this stage that some type of problem resolution is reached. Action dimensions are *confrontation* and *immediacy*.

Confrontation refers to dealing with a discrepancy between what the person has been saying and what he has been doing. One should use confrontation only when that right has been earned through empathic responses. Immediacy is closely related to confrontation. It refers to the helper commenting on important aspects of what is happening in the relationship. The timing of immediacy is critical if it is to be used beneficially by the helper.

There are many courses of action for problem solution or achievement of goals. The important thing is the identification of possible courses and consideration of the consequences and their ramifications. Then the chosen course of action can be broken down into steps to allow for intermediate success experiences that offer encouragement and reinforcement along the way to problem resolution.

Evaluation. Extensive research has been done on the effects of systematic human relations training. Aspy and Hadlock (1967) found that during one school year students with teachers possessing the highest levels of warmth, empathy, and genuineness gained an average of 2½ academic years, while students with the lowest level teachers gained only an average of 6 academic months. Further, the association between marital communication and adolescent self-esteem suggests that unfacilitative communication affects all relationships in the family (Matteson, 1974). In a study by Carkhuff and Banks (1970) systematic human relations training was effective in shaping more facilitative levels of communication and understanding among people of different races. A study conducted to evaluate the effects of human relations training on members of church groups revealed significant improvement in both perceiving and responding skills (McCurdy, 1976).

Polls have indicated that the influence of the church on society may be diminishing. As Christians live in the home, school, and business arena, as they live in every relationship of life, they are the church in the world. If the church's influence is decreasing, it would appear that there must be some deficit in the personal relationships within the church and the world. Ellens (1973) emphasizes that worship is essentially a horizontal experience of communication with other people about the facts of grace shared and lived. In order to facilitate worship, then, and to sensitively minister to people in need, it seems appropriate for the church to train people in human relations as a major response to God's call to serve our neighbors.

References

Aspy, D. N., & Hadlock, W. The effects of high and low functioning teachers upon student performance. In R. R. Carkhuff & B. G. Berenson (Eds.), *Beyond counseling and therapy.* New York: Holt, Rinehart, & Winston, 1967.

Carkhuff, R. R. *Helping and human relations* (Vols. 1 & 2). New York: Holt, Rinehart, & Winston, 1969.

Carkhuff, R. R., & Banks, G. Training as a preferred mode of facilitating relations between races and generations. *Journal of Counseling Psychology,* 1970, *17,* 413–418.

Ellens, J. H. Psychological dynamics in Christian worship: A beginning inquiry. *Journal of Psychology and Theology,* 1973, *1*(4), 10–19.

Matteson, R. Adolescent self-esteem, family communication, and marital satisfaction. *Journal of Psychology,* 1974, *86,* 35–47.

McCurdy, M. E. Human relations training with a church related population. *Journal of Psychology and Theology,* 1976, *4,* 291–299.

M. E. McCurdy

Hume, David (1711–1776). An influential Scottish philosopher. One of his most important doctrines was his interpretation of cause and effect. He argued that the apparent connection between cause and effect may be based on an illusion produced by repeated temporal contiguity of the two events.

See Empiricism.

Humility. To persons attempting to integrate their personal faith with psychology, humility is an issue of great concern. Christians frequently ask, "How can I avoid pride, as the Bible commands, and still feel good about myself?" "How can I be truly humble and assertive at the same time?" "Isn't it more biblical for me to feel badly about myself than to be proud?" Humility, then, is a spiritual virtue that appears to be at odds with much of the emphasis in modern psychology.

Most modern English dictionaries list a two-pronged definition of humility including 1) an attitude, quality, or state of being free from pride or arrogance, and 2) having a low opinion of one's importance or the attitude that others are superior. The second part of the definition is more frequently referred to as inferiority feelings or an inferiority complex by modern authors. The first part is most often seen by Christians as a positive Christian value highly commended in Scripture.

This dichotomous view of humility has its roots, not in Scripture, but in developments subsequent to the close of the canon. Christian mystics, in their zeal for purity of spirit and heart, viewed humility as an active process of debasing self in order to glorify God. For example, Bernard of Clairvaux worte in *The Steps of Humility* that humility is an important monastic virtue that helps the Christian see his own miserableness. The Benedictine Rule gives 12 steps of humility: fear of the Lord, ignoring desire, submission to superiors, perfect obedience, complete · confession, admission of inferiority, belief in one's inferiority, conventionality, silence, gravity, restrained speech, and downcast eyes. All in all, the monastic or mystical view of humility incorporated selflessness, a sense of inferiority, and a docile physiognomy.

The New Testament presents a much different picture of humility. Two central passages unfold a simple definition of this important Christian grace. The first, Matthew 11:28-30, is a self-description of our Lord: "I am meek and lowly in heart." As with all biblical virtues, humility is seen most clearly in the life of Christ, who was fully aware of his dependence on God. There is no painful introspection or self-debasement seen in Christ, only a single vision to serve God. In Augustinian thought humility is a complete bowing of the sinner and creature before God.

The second major passage is Philippians 2:1-11, a Pauline description of Christ. "Have this mind in you, which was also in Christ Jesus: who ... emptied himself, taking the form of a servant, ... and he humbled himself, becoming obedient even unto death, yea, the death of the cross." The servant heart of Jesus is the prime scriptural figure of humility, and Jesus' servant heart was nowhere seen more clearly than in his washing of the disciples' feet as recorded in John 13. "The feeling of obligation for all one is or has, and of shortcoming in the use of those gifts which we cannot even praise ourselves for having well employed, is a mark of humility" (McClintock & Strong, 1867, p. 403). "To be humble means to put the interests and needs of others before your own, and to put yourself at others' disposal as a servant" (Kinzer, 1980, p. 69). The practical difficulty of living as a servant for others is evident to all, even to the fictitious Screwtape and his trainee Wormwood (see Lewis, 1942, pp. 62-63).

Humility, however, does not loom large as a topic of investigation for modern psychology. Freud used the word *humility* nine times among his millions of words (Guttman, Jones, & Parrish, 1980). In most of the nine occurrences the word itself was not the topic of consideration. Similarly, *humility* is rarely found in abstracts of research, in indices for journals, or in personality textbooks. The Christian concept of humility is indirectly measured by certain personality inventories, but never under the label of humility. For example, certain features of the deference scale ("to accept the leadership of others") and the nurturance scale ("to treat others with kindness and sympathy") on the Edwards Personal Preference Schedule are components of humility (Edwards, 1959). Likewise some scales on the California Psychological Inventory (Gough, 1969) touch on the Christian virtue of humility. But for the most part humility is seen as a spiritual or religious concept and not a worthy topic for psychological investigation.

Humility may indeed represent a feature of personality that runs counter to the spirit of twentieth-century thought with its emphasis on individuality, assertiveness, independence, and introspection. For the Christian, however, the example of Christ's footwashing on the night before his death and the obedience of his death itself make humility an obligatory goal and a worthy aim.

References

Edwards, A. L. *Edwards personal preference schedule manual.* New York: Psychological Corporation, 1959.
Gough, H. G. *Manual for the California psychological inventory.* Palo Alto, Calif.: Consulting Psychologists Press, 1969.
Guttman, S. A., Jones, R. L., & Parrish, S. M. (Eds.). *The concordance to the standard edition of the complete psychological works of Sigmund Freud* (Vol. 3). Boston: G. K. Hall, 1980.
Kinzer, M. *The self-image of a Christian: Humility and self-esteem.* Ann Arbor: Servant Books, 1980.
Lewis, C. S. *The Screwtape letters.* London: G. Bles, Centenary Press, 1942.
McClintock, J., & Strong, J. *Cyclopedia of biblical, theological and ecclesiastical literature* (Vol. 4). New York: Harper & Bros., 1867.

J. R. BECK

See SELF-ESTEEM; NARCISSISM.

Humor. Humor is a ubiquitous, multifaceted human phenomenon. Smiling and laughter as expressions of pleasure and mirth appear very early in the development of the infant and, although the stimuli and thought patterns that evoke them change dramatically over time, continue throughout the individual's lifetime.

Humor represents a unique combination of rather complex higher-order cognitive processes with the set of seemingly bizarre physiological-behavioral responses called laughter (e.g., facial grimaces, autonomic arousal, explosive vocalization, altered patterns of respiration). What is the psychological function of this uniquely human phenomenon? This question has for centuries occupied the attention of a wide variety of thinkers, and numerous theories of humor and laughter have been proposed. None of these theories encompasses all aspects of humor, and many contradict one another at various points. Part of this contradiction stems from the fact that humor seems to represent a curious mixture of the base, ugly, and aggressive aspects of human nature with the sublime, innocent, and joyful. Various theorists have differed in the degree to which they emphasize one or the other of these facets of humor.

References to humor and comedy in the writings of Plato, Aristotle, Bacon, and Descartes, for example, focus on the derisive qualities of laughter, which, they argued, is directed toward ugliness and deformity and is always accompanied by a tinge of venom. Some more recent theorists, such as Henri Bergson, have seen in humor and laughter a powerful social corrective that is used to humiliate and correct the one who does not conform to social expectations.

In contrast, writers such as Voltaire, Jean Paul Richter, and Max Eastman have disagreed sharply with this negative view, contending that humor is an expression of tolerance, acceptance, and sympathy, since it involves an identification of the laughter with the foibles and weaknesses of all humans. This view of humor sees it as a liberating force that frees individuals from the often stifling constraints of social pressures.

Theories of Humor. In general, the many theories of humor may loosely be categorized into three main types: tension relief, superiority, and incongruity.

Tension relief theories. These are best exemplified by Freud (1916/1960). Freud drew a distinction among three types of humorous experience: wit (or jokes), the comic, and humor. He postulated that each of these is characterized by a "savings" or "economizing" of psychic energy which, having become unnecessary for its normal purposes, is dissipated in the form of laughter. The three types of humorous experience are distinguished according to the form of psychic energy that is thus economized: 1) jokes (wit) involve a savings of inhibitory energy that is normally used to repress unconscious sexual or aggressive drives or childish tendencies; 2) the comic, a savings of ideational or mental energy; and 3) humor, a savings of emotional energy. Freud viewed humor, which he described as a "rare and precious gift," as one of the highest and healthiest of the defense mechanisms. Many more recent psychologists, such as Allport, May, and Maslow, have reaffirmed Freud's emphasis on the value of humor in contributing to psychological health.

Superiority theories. This second group has perhaps the longest history of the three, dating back to Plato and Aristotle. It is epitomized in Thomas Hobbes's famous dictum that "the passion of laughter is nothing else but sudden glory arising from some sudden conception of some eminence in ourselves, by comparison with the infirmity of others, or with our own formerly" (from *Leviathan*, 1651). In these theories humor is perceived as a means of increasing one's own self-esteem by making light of the weaknesses of others. This approach is thus most closely associated with the school of thought that emphasizes the aggressive, derisive aspects of humor.

Incongruity theories. The third major category is currently enjoying increasing support in the context of the cognitive revolution in contemporary psychology. This approach, originally propounded by such writers as Pascal, Kant, and Schopenhauer, regards humor as essentially comprising a sudden shift in cognitive perspective. It has been most fully elaborated in recent times by Koestler (1964), who contends that all forms of humor involve a process which he has termed *bisociation*. This expression refers to the juxtaposition of two normally incongruous frames of reference, or the discovery of various similarities and analogies implicit in concepts normally considered remote from each other.

Several psychologists who espouse this theoretical approach to humor have suggested that humor serves as an effective coping strategy because of the rapid perceptual-cognitive switches in frames of reference which it embodies. The flexible ability to shift perspective is thought to allow the humorist to "distance" himself from the immediate threat of a problem situation, to view it from a different perspective, and therefore to reduce the often paralyzing feelings of anxiety and helplessness.

Humor and Therapy. Recent research findings have lent support to the hypothesis that humor serves as an adaptive coping mechanism. Researchers have found, for example, that individuals identified as having a strong sense of humor are less likely to experience depression and other forms of mood disturbance following stressful life experiences than are those with a less marked sense of humor. Evidence has also accumulated suggesting that laughter has important physiological effects on the body, protecting organs such as the heart from the effects of stress and possibly stimulating the production of endogenous analgesic substances (endorphins) in the brain. Accounts have been published of individuals recovering from serious illnesses through a regimen of comedy and laughter or surviving extremely stressful situations, such as those encountered in wartime, by means of humor. In this regard recent research has found that subjects who appreciate and produce humor in their lives tend to have fewer symptoms of illness which are treated by a physician than do those who are less humorously oriented. Although more research is needed to explore the physiological concomitants of laughter, it appears at this point that humor and laughter play an important stress-buffering role in human functioning.

The view of humor as an adaptive coping mechanism, supported on both theoretical and empirical grounds, has prompted a number of psychotherapists to advocate the use of humor in therapy (e.g., Mindess, 1976). One application of humor in therapy has been to make use of the client's favorite jokes as a sort of projective technique in assessment. Drawing from Freud's notion that jokes are a means of expressing repressed impulses, it has been suggested that the jokes which a client most enjoys are likely to betray unconscious issues that are particularly salient for him or her.

Apart from diagnostic uses humor may serve two broad purposes in psychotherapy: 1) humor for its own sake may be therapeutic because of its elevating effect on moods and because it provides an acceptable way of expressing repressed thoughts and feelings; 2) it may be used as a means of providing alternate perspectives on the client's life situation and communicating ideas that might otherwise be disturbing to the client. It is recognized that humor, like any therapeutic technique, may be misused in the hands of an inexperienced or inept therapist and must be carefully and judiciously employed. Therapeutic humor goes beyond wit and represents a flexible, confident attitude toward the world and toward oneself. Perhaps the most effective use of humor in therapy is for the therapist to provide the client with a model of such a humorous attitude.

Humor and the Christian Faith. The role of humor in Christian life has generally received very little attention from theologians and the clergy. Indeed, the many humorous themes in the Scriptures are frequently overlooked by lay readers and scholars alike. Trueblood (1964) has noted numerous examples of humor in the ministry of Christ. He has argued convincingly that many of the sayings and parables of Christ that have puzzled Bible scholars for centuries may be clarified when they are recognized as instances of humor. It has also been pointed out by others that hundreds of humorous puns are to be found throughout the Bible, most of which are lost in translation. In many cases very serious truths are expressed through such vehicles of humor.

The negative, derisive aspects of humor as well as the positive, joyful aspects are represented in the Bible. Humor is often used by the prophets and others in a sarcastic or ironic manner to deride hypocrisy and idolatry (e.g., the story of Elijah and the prophets of Baal in 1 Kings 18:16–46; Jesus' denunciation of the Pharisees in Matt. 23). God himself is represented in several passages as laughing at his enemies (e.g., Ps. 2:4). On the other hand, the positive, therapeutic effects of humor are also recognized in such passages as Proverbs 17:22 ("A merry heart doeth good like a medicine"). Despite the suffering and persecution which believers may have to endure, the Scriptures frequently emphasize that joy and laughter characterize those who have placed their faith in the Lord (e.g., Ps. 16:11; 1 Peter 1:8). Indeed, the blessings of the Kingdom include Christ's promise, "Blessed are ye who weep now, for you shall laugh" (Luke 6:21).

References

Freud, S. *Jokes and their relation to the unconscious.* New York: Norton, 1960. (Originally published, 1916.)

Koestler, A. *The act of creation.* New York: Macmillan, 1964.

Mindess, H. The use and abuse of humour in psychotherapy. In A. J. Chapman & H. C. Foot (Eds.), *Humour and laughter: Theory, research and applications.* New York: Wiley, 1976.

Trueblood, E. *The humor of Christ.* New York: Harper & Row, 1964.

Additional Reading

Chapman, A. J., & Foot, H. C. (Eds.). *It's a funny thing, humour.* New York: Pergamon Press, 1977.

R. A. Martin

Huntington's Chorea. Identified by American neurologist George Huntington (1850–1916), Huntington's chorea is a chronic degenerative disorder characterized by irregular and spasmodic involuntary jerking and stretching movements of the limbs and facial muscles. This rare hereditary disease of the central nervous system affects adults between the ages of 30 and 50, and terminates in 10 to 20 years in mental deterioration and dementia. Physical symptoms include facial grimacing, speech impairment, smacking of the tongue and lips, and an erratic jerking gait. Mental symptoms include poor attention span, irritability, memory impairment, apathy, and suicidal tendencies. There are usually no delusions or hallucinations in Huntington's chorea.

Hydrocephaly. The increase in the volume of cerebrospinal fluid in the skull, usually associated with an increase in pressure. Hydrocephaly may result from an injury or an obstruction to the flow of fluid within the system or a decrease in absorption of the fluid. In children the size of the head frequently increases, but in adults this enlargement is rare. Neurological and mental symptoms develop, sometimes leading to severe MENTAL RETARDATION, convulsions, or loss of sight and hearing. Drainage operations to relieve the volume of fluid in the skull are possible.

Hyperactive Child Syndrome. *See* ATTENTION DEFICIT DISORDER.

Hypersexuality. *See* EXCESSIVE SEXUAL DESIRE.

Hypertension. A condition in which the blood is pushed against the arterial walls with greater than normal force. Hypertension, or high blood pressure, affects 15% of the adult population in this country. If not treated, it can cause serious and irreversible damage to the brain, heart, kidneys, eyes, and blood vessels themselves. It can prove fatal by causing a stroke, heart attack, or kidney failure.

Although hypertension is due to defined physical disease in some cases of kidney disorder, toxemia of pregnancy, adrenal tumor, or ovarian tumor, 95% of all high blood pressure is diagnosed as essential hypertension. In this condition the physician cannot find an exact physical cause. Essential hypertension is usually attributed to a complex of physiological, genetic, and emotional factors. High blood pressure is a particularly difficult medical problem because it is often asymptomatic. Most people do not know they have it.

People with hypertension respond to stress with elevations in their blood pressure. They hold tension in their nervous, muscular, and vascular systems. In hypertension the blood vessels contract excessively and eventually lose their elasticity. These constricted vessels are more resistant to fluid moving through them, so greater pressure is required to pump blood through the vascular system. Under these conditions the heart has to work harder to pump blood. With time, this causes the heart muscle to thicken and the heart enlarges. The increased pressure on blood vessel walls can cause them to weaken or even tear. The body attempts to heal these tears by patching them with fatty deposits called cholesterol plaques. Large amounts of such plaques can block the vessels supplying the heart or brain at critical areas. Rigid, inelastic blood vessels require even higher pressure to pump blood through the body. This can lead to further tears and progressive complications.

Blood pressure is expressed as two components, with a larger top number (systolic pressure) and a smaller bottom figure (diastolic pressure). These readings are measured in millimeters of mercury. The systolic pressure reflects the heart's contraction as blood is forced out of the heart; the diastolic measure reflects the pressure during the heart's resting stage when its chambers are filling with blood in preparation for the next contraction. Normal blood pressure depends on age and other variables but is usually considered high if it is above 140/90.

It is mandatory that high blood pressure be medically treated. The person with hypertension is normally treated with medication that reduces the contractility of the heart. As an alternative a diuretic may be administered to remove some of the sodium and water from the body and thus decrease the total volume of blood. Other medications reduce the tension in the blood vessel walls or directly affect the central (brain) control of blood pressure. Salt restriction is almost always prescribed in addition to medication; dietary change is as important as taking medication. Medications used to treat hypertension can be expensive and can cause unpleasant side effects such as lethargy, weakness, sexual impotency, depression, dry mouth, bad dreams, and sleep disturbance. However the long-term problems resulting from hypertension are much worse than the side effects of medication.

Many people now use relaxation techniques, including biofeedback and meditation, in conjunction with their antihypertensive medication and salt restriction. Often these adjunctive therapies can help reduce the dosage levels of medication required, and in some cases medication can be discontinued completely. This must always be monitored by a medical doctor since high blood pressure frequently has no symptoms. Ongoing medical supervision is required for adequate treatment of this dangerous and potentially life-threatening condition.

Research has shown that people who attend church regularly tend to have lower incidence of hypertension than the general population. Possibly regular churchgoers have lower levels of anxiety and anger, both of which activate the nervous system and increase blood pressure.

Because high blood pressure does not produce noticeable symptoms, it has been termed the "silent killer." It is quite important to have one's blood pressure checked at least once each year and more frequently if high readings have ever been obtained. If hypertension is diagnosed, working closely with the physician and following his treatment prescriptions will minimize the effects of this condition. Although untreated hypertension is potentially lethal, if it is caught early and treated the hypertensive can live a long and productive life.

M. A. NORFLEET

Hypnosis. This curious phenomenon has captured the interest, imagination, and apprehension of individuals and cultures for centuries. In an article entiled "Hypnosis Comes of Age," Goleman (1977) notes the changing attitude toward hypnosis. From parlor stunts and quackery hypnosis has become a respectable therapy solidly allied with psychology and medicine. The American Society of Clinical Hypnosis, which began in 1957 with 20 members, now boasts an annual membership of over 2,600. In 1956, the American Medical Association pronounced that hypnosis was "valuable as a therapeutic adjunct." Other professional associations have given similar recognition to the validity of hypnosis, including the British Medical Society, the American Psychiatric Association, and the American Psychological Association.

History. The history of hypnosis as an identifiable clinical process goes back about 200 years, finding its origins with Mesmer and the animal magnetists. However, its history as a natural phenomenon and a cultural manifestation is as old as mankind.

Wolberg (1972) interprets the Genesis 2:21–22 passage, in which God caused a "sleep" to come over Adam so that his rib could be removed to create Eve, to refer to hypnosis. Given the modern use of hypnoanesthesia in major surgical procedures (Hilgard & Hilgard, 1975), this is a reasonable possibility. In the early sixteenth century a controversial physician, Philippus Paracelsus, suggested that the magnetic fluid emanating from the stars produced hypnotic effects. Soon it was claimed that similar magnetic forces could be radiated at will by some individuals, and magnetic cures become famous. The reputation of an Irishman, Valentine Greatrakes, "the Stroker," drew thousands to him, including eminent philosophers and theologians. In 1646 the German mathematician Athanasius Kircher proposed a force in nature, "animal magnetism," as being responsible for disease. Its cure, he claimed, was through "magneto therapeutics."

Franz Anton Mesmer (1734–1815) is often considered to be the inventor of animal magnetism as a therapeutic tool of medicine;

hence, "mesmerism." Initially his cures became fashionable with the wealthy and influential who thronged to his apartment where, around a baquet, they held onto iron rods which spread from the tubelike spokes, serving to convey the magnetism from the magnetized water. Mesmer added his touch of atmosphere by appearing in a long silk robe and touching his patients as they fell into a stupor or trance. It was upon recovering from this state that the cure was to have been evidenced.

With the growing popularity of mesmerism came the exaggerated claims, charges of fraud, quackery, and the growth of a skeptical segment of the population. A commission of investigation appointed by the king of France and headed by Benjamin Franklin concluded that magnetic fluids did not exist and that any reported effects were only due to suggestion.

Fluidists persisted in their belief in magnetic forces, but gradually the claims fell away as the suggestionists gained support for their theory. By the mid-1800s the psychological theory had gained major acceptance through the research activities of Braid and the surgical work of Esdaile in India. The latter reported more than 300 painless major surgeries conducted solely under hypnosis. Bernheim, a professor at the Nancy Medical School, extended the suggestion theory, publishing a book in which he claimed cures for hysterical paralysis, aphonia, gastric difficulties, depression, loss of appetite, pain, tremors, and a host of other functional diseases.

The effects of Bernheim's teaching concerning the efficacy of mental suggestion alone is still evident in the practice of hypnosis. It was first with Charcot and later Bernheim that Freud studied to develop his hypnotic technique. Contrary to popular opinion, Freud never repudiated hypnosis; rather he put it aside for the free association process, an outgrowth of his hypnotic technique, which he found to be more personally effective. Despite Freud's written statement that hypnosis had a place in medicine and that the future of analysis lay in hypnosis, hypnosis was virtually abandoned after the turn of the century as hopes rose for the new psychoanalytic methods. This continued until the two world wars, which created a demand for psychiatric and medical treatment that could not be met by the traditional therapies. Hypnosis was revived as a means to abbreviate treatment.

Myths of Hypnosis. Several myths are so commonly believed that they deserve examination at this point. They are mainly the products of ancient superstitions maintained by vaude-

543

villian demonstration and fictional stories of books or television. The myths add to the entertainment value of hypnosis but fail to represent a more factual understanding.

The myth of induction. The first popular error is that the hypnotist has the power to *put* the patient or subject into hypnosis. This belief presumes that the power for hypnosis resides in the therapist, much as magnetism was previously believed to exist in Mesmer and travel out through his iron wand. The caricature of the hypnotist frequently shows extended fingers and staring eyes, from which power in the form of lightning is seen flashing. The hapless victim is thought to be overcome by the hypnotist's superior power through the mere thrusting of a hand. Any individual difference in the subjects is ignored, since the critical variable is considered to be the "mesmeric" quality of the hypnotist.

Benjamin Franklin's royal commission of 1784 concluded that no such power existed and that the hypnotic trance, or mesmerized state, was due to the willingness of the individual and his cooperation with the suggestions implied or given. More recent investigations into hypnotic susceptibility have revealed that individuals do vary in their ability to enter into hypnosis, that these differences are measurable and reliable over time, and that in fact the degree of response is a function of the individual. The hypnotist is seen as part of an environment that facilitates this induction into trance. Some environmental qualities that are generally considered to be conducive to trance attainment are: 1) the restriction of sensory input through removal of distracting stimuli (a quiet, relaxing situation); 2) the narrowing of attention to an external object (a spot, a pendulum, a cross, etc.); 3) talking in a quiet, often monotone manner; and 4) the suggestion of internal images or sensations for increased restriction of attention.

A second aspect of hypnosis which refutes the "power of the hypnotist" myth is the field of self-hypnosis. It is of continual amazement to those believing the myths that one can learn to induce one's own trance safely and effectively. This procedure is frequently employed by the clinician in the treatment of habits, anxiety, and even pain states.

However, the assurance given to counteract this myth of power, that "you can never be hypnotized against your will," is only a half truth. A hypnotic induction does require the cooperation of the individual, and a trance can be resisted. Nevertheless, the individual's participation may not be a conscious response,

and people can enter into hypnosis without knowing that they did so. Erickson (Haley, 1967) is famous in this regard, due to his skill in using the naturally available stimuli of external objects and nonverbal behaviors to induce a trance without preparation or awareness by the subject. The ethics of this may be debated, but as an event it should not be so surprising if hypnosis is viewed as a natural process available to most people in differing degrees.

The myth of control. Another myth is the fear of what one will do under hypnosis and the fear that the hypnotist can cause anything to happen. This is generally a fear generated from contact with hypnosis as represented by stage, television, and fiction, where one sometimes sees a hypnotized subject act like a zombie, make a fool of himself, or commit a criminal act.

This issue of coercion and control is another field receiving considerable research attention. The nature of hypnosis is such that people will respond more readily and less critically to suggestions given to them while in trance. This hypersuggestibility has been a prominent characteristic of hypnosis. However, it appears that while individuals will respond to suggestions that at other times and out of trance they think are ridiculous or irrational, there does appear to be some limit to the extent to which these suggestions can go before the person refuses to cooperate and/or spontaneously awakens. Considerable debate still continues regarding the point at which this limit is imposed. Some believe that one will never do in hypnosis anything that they would not do otherwise, while others believe it creates the potential for very irrational if not immoral and criminal acts.

It is this view of hypnosis as a potentially dangerous tool, if improperly or unprofessionally employed, that has sparked moves for legislation restricting its use. Research continues to attempt to understand this issue. At present most clinical hypnotists tend to agree with Thorton (1976), who stated that "when people inquire whether mesmerism is not a dangerous thing, I always reply that I am happy to say it is—a nonentity, an unreal, though alleged power of nature can do no harm; but all the real powers of nature will work readily for evil if misapplied" (p. 110).

The myth of getting stuck. Another erroneous concern is that one may get stuck in hypnosis and not be able to come back to the alert state. No such occurrences have ever been documented. However, many times people in hypnosis enjoy the ecstasy or the relaxation to such an extent that they are reluctant to alert. Once they are aware of the fact that this is a state they can produce at will, the need to hold on is reduced.

In both hetero- and self-hypnosis, one is capable of alerting at any moment or at a prearranged signal. Failure to do so will result in either spontaneous arousal at a later time or a conversion into natural sleep from which the person will awaken naturally.

The myths of an altered sensorium and amnesia. As a natural psychological process, the shift into the hypnotic state probably occurs quite frequently. However, due to mistaken impressions of what that state is like, most instances go unrecognized. Erroneous expectations often include an anticipated altered state of consciousness such that the person will not know what is going on (i.e., unconscious, stuporous) and will not have remembrance of anything that occurred (amnesia).

Concerning the issue of subjective trance sensations, the awareness of the environment was assumed to contraindicate a trance state, and depth of trance was judged to be negatively associated with degree of mental activity. Hence, the development of metaphorical terms such as *alert*, *sleep*, and *hypnosis*. In fact, however, the profound and dramatic effects of hypnosis occur in a state in which one senses some degree of awareness of the environment, and it is specifically this awareness that contributes to hypnosis's relevance to clinical problems (e.g., natural childbirth, in which hypnosis functions to relieve the pain while allowing full contact with the birth experience).

The forgetting of trance events is no longer viewed as an inevitable characteristic of a hypnotic episode. Suggested forgetting (hypoamnesia) does remain as a valid phenomenon and evidences the person's genuine inability to remember material that was once learned but is now temporarily unretrievable due to the effects of hypnosis. It is worth noting in regard to amnesia and forgetting that hypnosis is frequently employed to assist one in recovering forgotten or repressed material. As such a tool it is of significant value in the treatment of functional illnesses and in psychotherapy.

The phenomenon of age regression has generated a related myth. This is the belief that we can regress through life, past birth, to an earlier existence. Concrete evidence for such an occurrence is unavailable. Available research suggests that such phenomena are the product of the creative imagination of the subject rather than the experience of a prebirth existence or former life.

The Hypnotic State and Its Phenomena. If hypnosis is not what most people think it is, then what is it? The scientific foundations upon which the understanding of hypnosis is based have become firmer in the past two decades. A much clearer description of hypnotic processes is now available. However, divergent psychological and physiological theories exist to explain phenomena. Physiologically, considerable research has been conducted in attempts to uncover physical mechanisms and responses, including shifts in cerebral activity, selective inhibition of certain brain centers, and changes in vasomotor responses. Hypnosis has also been investigated as a possible by-product of a neural pathology such as epilepsy. Psychologically, hypnosis has been explained as a role-playing response, a primitive phylogenetic response, a conditioned response, a special form of transference, or a regressive phenomenon. Research continues on all these theories, and currently none can be eliminated. (See Fromm & Shor, 1972, for an overview of this research.)

Hypnosis is clearly not a power or force that one possesses to control another. Rather, hypnosis appears to involve a shift in concentration, executed in a passive manner (such as occurs in daydreaming or sleeping), resulting in a state of consciousness distinguishably different from alertness or ordinary sleep. It is characterized by narrowing of attention, reduced rational criticalness, and increased responsiveness to suggestion. It appears to provide a clearer access to the functioning of the mind, allowing understanding of that which is subconscious or dissociated. Additionally, it seems to play some role as a mediator or transducer (Hilgard & Hilgard, 1975; Bowers, 1976) between cognitions and physiological functioning.

Although the myth of power radiating from the hypnotist has been refuted, there is considerable information concerning those environmental variables that do influence trance performance. Barber (1969, 1972) identified positive attitudes, motivation, and expectancies as important situational influences that allow the person to let go of extraneous thoughts and enter into hypnosis.

The beginning phase of hypnotic session is referred to as the induction stage. Many styles of induction exist, all incorporating a gradual shift in attention with a reduction in external awareness. This is done in a manner compatible with the expectations and values of the patient. Frequently the induction encourages the subject to focus his attention, either through focusing his eyes on something external (eye fixation technique) or through focusing internally on breathing or any other sensation (e.g., muscle tension). Further suggestions of comfort, relaxation, or rest are then clearly and calmly given along with compatible visual, auditory, or physical images such as a beach, stairs, or floating on clouds. Following this induction phase therapeutic strategies can be introduced.

A more complete discussion of the uses of hypnosis can be found in HYPNOTHERAPY. Each of the uses (e.g., pain control) reflects one or more of the phenomena of the state (e.g., hypnoanesthesia). A brief, highly selective overview of some of these phenomena follows.

Collison (1975) reported a retrospective analysis of 121 asthmatic patients treated with hypnotherapy, indicating that 54% made a good to excellent (significant decrease to symptom free) reponse. Similar findings have been reported by Maher-Loughnan (1970). Numerous dermatological disorders have also been treated by hypnosis. The most commonly reported is that of warts, which are epidermal tumors with an apparent viral cause. In that they can come and go spontaneously, it becomes difficult to claim therapeutic success. However, Sinclair-Giebens and Chalmers (1959) used hypnotic suggestions to treat warts *on one side* of the body only. Nine of the 10 patients judged to be hypnotically susceptible and thus treated were virtually free of warts within 5 to 12 weeks, but only on the treated side, with no improvement on the other half. Replication (Surman, Gottlieb, Hackett, & Silverberg, 1973) has yielded support for this finding, but with reduced success rates.

Hypnotic control of blood flow has been documented by many sources. Clawson (Clawson & Slade, 1975) records how, under general anesthesia and during emergency surgery, suggestions given to his own grandson resulted in the stoppage of bleeding and completion of the operation. Dubin and Shapiro (1974) report similar results with a severe hemophiliac. Such evidence is used to explain changes in skin temperature and the treatment of Raynaud's syndrome (in which blood supply to the extremities is severely reduced, with a resulting drop in hand temperature), as well as treatment of migraines, hypertension, and other problems related to the cardiovascular system. In fact, Raginsky (1959) acknowledges one experimental situation in which suggestions to recall faintness and cardiac distress related to Stokes-Adams disease resulted in sudden limpness, paleness, and heart stoppage of 5 seconds, as measured through an electrocardiograph.

The medical and psychological disorders reported to be responsive to hypnosis appear endless. They include many forms of pain (e.g., pain due to surgery, headache, or cancer), obesity, sexual dysfunction, enuresis, constipation, insomnia, obstetric problems, labor phobias, smoking habits, gagging, bruxism, stuttering, depression, and gastrointestinal disorders. Current evidence suggests that hypnosis is, in some manner and in some susceptible people, effective as a transformer of cognitions into physiological responses.

Bowers extends this concept of hypnosis to suggest that "highly susceptible people are better able to process and appraise information outside of awareness ... without being distracted from their primary involvement" (1976, pp. 137–138). This absorption in the task and its dissociative qualities facilitate some of the introspective and analytical aspects of psychotherapy, helping the individual to divorce himself from his experienced rationalized reality in order to entertain and comprehend new alternatives and understandings.

References

Barber, T. X. *Hypnosis: A scientific approach.* New York: Van Nostrand, 1969.

Barber, T. X. Suggested ("hypnotic") behaviour: The trance paradigm versus an alternative paradigm. In E. Fromm & R. Shor (Eds.), *Hypnosis: Research developments and perspectives.* Chicago: Aldine-Atherton, 1972.

Bowers, K. S. *Hypnosis for the seriously curious.* Monterey, Calif.: Brooks/Cole, 1976.

Clawson, T. A., & Slade, R. H. The hypnotic control of blood flow and pain: The cure of warts and the potential use of hypnosis in the treatment of cancer. *American Journal of Clinical Hypnosis,* 1975, *17,* 160–169.

Collison, D. R. Which asthmatic patients should be treated by hypnotherapy? *Medical Journal of Australia,* 1975, *1,* 776–781.

Dubin, L. L., & Shapiro, S. S. Use of hypnosis to facilitate dental extraction and hemostasis in a classic hemophiliac with a high antibody titer to Factor VIII. *American Journal of Clinical Hypnosis,* 1974, *17,* 79–83.

Fromm, E., & Shor, R. (Eds.). *Hypnosis: Research developments and perspectives.* Chicago: Aldine-Atherton, 1972.

Goleman, D. Hypnosis comes of age. *Psychology Today,* 1977, *11*(2), 54–60.

Haley, J. *Advanced techniques of hypnosis and therapy: Selected papers of Milton H. Erickson, M.D.* New York: Grune & Stratton, 1967.

Hilgard, E. R., & Hilgard, J. R. *Hypnosis in the relief of pain.* Los Altos, Calif.: William Kaufmann, 1975.

Maher-Loughnan, G. P. Hypnosis and autohypnosis for the treatment of asthma. *International Journal of Clinical and Experimental Hypnosis,* 1970, *18,* 1–14.

Raginsky, B. B. Temporary cardiac arrest induced under hypnosis. *International Journal of Clinical and Experimental Hypnosis,* 1959, *7,* 53–68.

Sinclair-Giebens, A. H. C., & Chalmers, E. Evaluation of

treatment of warts by hypnosis. *Lancet*, Oct. 3, 1959, pp. 480–482.

Surman, O. S., Gottlieb, S. K., Hackett, T. P., & Silverberg, E. L. Hypnosis in the treatment of warts. *Archives of General Psychology*, 1973, *28*, 439–441.

Thornton, E. M. *Hypnotism, hysteria and epilepsy: An historical synthesis*. London: Heinemann Medical, 1976.

Wolberg, L. R. *Hypnosis: Is it for you*. New York: Harcourt, Brace, Jovanovich, 1972.

G. Matheson

See Hypnotic Aspects of Spiritual Experience.

Hypnotherapy. Hypnosis is often shrouded in such mystery that it evokes, in lay persons and professionals alike, curiosity about its real effects and the exaggerated claims. Although it has often been difficult to sort out the fact from fancy regarding hypnosis, the practice has become scientifically respectable and has secured an accepted place as a valuable tool in the practice of psychology, medicine, and dentistry. However, in these professional practices hypnosis is recognized as an adjunct and not as a separate profession or therapy. Hypnosis by itself does not contain the body of knowledge or theory to make it an independent therapy. Thus, the term *hypnotherapy* refers to the use of hypnosis as a technique to be employed in conjunction with other skills by a trained psychotherapist, physician, or dentist.

Basically the breadth of hypnotherapy is the combined territories of these three professions. Its use as a therapeutic technique relies on its nature and characteristics and the phenomena that can be produced through it. A central feature of hypnosis is the ease with which an individual under hypnosis can produce very deep relaxation. The simple effect of this can alter many clinical symptoms. For instance, the anxiety one experiences prior to a performance (e.g., an interview, a sporting event, a recital) can be greatly reduced and made manageable through hypnotic relaxation, particularly when it is combined with self-hypnosis so that the individual can do it for himself or herself when needed. Similarly, relaxation can modify the anxiety and experienced discomfort in medical and dental procedures where the pain is often heightened by the anticipatory arousal and anxiety (e.g. pelvic examinations, dental cleaning and repair, inoculations, and blood taking). Also, the after effects of anxiety and physical arousal such as tension headaches, asthma, gastric ulcers, and insomnia can be influenced by hypnotic relaxation.

When hypnotically produced analgesia, or in some instances anesthesia, is combined with relaxation, the outcome can be even more dramatic. Hypnosis is often used in this way to facilitate the birth process by reducing the experienced discomfort of labor while allowing the mother to be alert and to enjoy the experience. Hypnosis has also been employed to produce sufficient anesthesia to allow a caesarian section to be performed on an otherwise unanesthetized woman. In a similar fashion hypnotic analgesia can be used in other surgical procedures where chemical anesthetics are unavailable or too risky to the patient. Barber (1977) demonstrated that a single hypnosis experience was sufficient to produce analgesia of a strong enough nature to allow for various dental procedures without other anesthetics in over 95% of his subjects. The analgesic effects of hypnosis are often employed in the treatment of pain due to injury or burns and with chronic pain states such as tension headaches, low back pain syndrome, arthritis, and myofacial pain.

Hypnosis also serves as a transducer in that suggestions and images can through hypnosis be transformed into physiological responses. Thus, the migraine headache, which involves excessive blood flow to the head, can be significantly altered in most patients by hypnotically suggesting that the blood will flow more into the limbs and leave the head cool and comfortable. The same procedure can have therapeutic effects with Raynaud's syndrome, where the hands and feet become very cold due to insufficient blood flow to the periphery. Other alterations in physiological functioning include the shrinking of warts, the altering of the immune response in oncological disorders, and the changing of the physical response in sexual dysfunctions such as impotence.

Direct suggestive effects and guided hypnotic imagery have been used extensively, particularly in the treatment of habit disorders such as smoking, bruxism, nail biting, hair pulling, and some eating disorders. The combination of specific suggestions with supportive imagery and ego-enhancing experiences has been found to be most effective in the reduction of these undesirable habits. In cases where positive habits are being created (i.e., study habits, dental routines, and performance tasks) the combination of direct suggestions, images which enhance mastery, and autohypnotic techniques work most effectively together.

Hypnosis is also extremely valuable in psychotherapeutic activities. The hypnotically achieved relaxation can often enhance rapport and facilitate conversation. The dissociative aspects of the hypnotic state can facilitate cathartic experience as well as the exploration of material too psychically painful for immediate conscious awareness. The hypernesic effect can permit recall and, on occasion, revivification of past, forgotten material, while the amnesic effect can allow the forgetting of material discovered through hypnosis but too threatening for conscious retention at the moment. Hypnotic imagery can create the situation for projection of psychic material into fantasy or hypnotic dreams either for analysis or Gestalt dreamwork. Also, the hypnotic relationship between therapist and patient is one which can often facilitate strong transferential qualities that can be either explored or used profitably in ways that will advance therapy.

Hypnosis is very effective and valuable in pediatrics. By their nature children are generally better hypnotic subjects and can use hypnosis very naturally for pain control, to alter symptoms or habits, to imagine and change situations or outcomes, or to adjust physical functioning. Enuresis and encopresis respond well to hypnotic interventions of suggestions and images that enhance mastery and self-confidence. Hypnotic control of pain for the suturing of lacerations, setting of fractures, inoculations, and other medical and dental procedures is available to most children. Additionally, hypnotic techniques can be useful in dealing with habits such as thumb sucking and nail biting.

Increased use of hypnotherapy has recently begun in areas peripheral to the main three professions. Hypnotic enhancement of athletic performance is being developed, and has been used by a number of teams in various professional sports, both to manage pre-event arousal and to better integrate the functions of the body and mind. In education hypnotic techniques for "superlearning" exist that involve improving attention, concentration, memory, and recall. In business the relaxing and creative problem-solving aspects of hypnosis have been used to manage existing stress, avoid burnout, and develop new aspects of the job.

Reference

Barber, J. Rapid induction analgesia: a clinical report. *American Journal of Clinical Hypnosis*, 1977, *19*(3), 138–147.

Additional Readings

Crasilneck, H. B., & Hall, J. A. *Clinical hypnosis.* New York: Grune & Stratton, 1975.

Erickson, M. H., & Rossi, E. L. *Hypnotherapy, an exploratory casebook.* New York: Irvington Publishers, 1979.

Gardner, G. G. & Olness, K. *Hypnosis and hypnotherapy with children.* New York: Grune & Stratton, 1981.

G. MATHESON

Hypnotherapy, Indirect. Traditional hypnotherapy has emphasized the use of straightforward, direct suggestions to effect an altered state of awareness within a client. This can be done in either an authoritarian or permissive fashion. For example, an authoritarian approach to arm levitation would be: "Your arm is getting lighter and lighter, like a balloon tied to your wrist is pulling it up." A more permissive form of direct suggestion would be: "Isn't it delightful how you don't have to do anything but wait for that lightness in your arm to start it lifting up and up all by itself?"

In contrast to these direct approaches a more subtle means of suggestion was developed by Erickson (Rossi, 1980). Indirect approaches, described in this article, employ an anecdotal or metaphoric format utilizing a number of techniques: embedded suggestions and commands, paraverbal shifts of tone, voice directionality, enunciation, syntax, and pacing; the use of truisms, binds, double binds, and other semantic variations derived from the field of neurolinguistic programming (Bandler & Grinder, 1979). Due to the subtle quality of indirection, a resistant, oppositional client—or merely a scared, unsure client—can be enticed more readily into cooperating with the therapist toward resolving whatever issues are problematic.

The indirect hypnotherapist also will capitalize on the attributes of universality and individuality in his metaphoric process in order to enhance the probability that his suggestions will be accepted and utilized by the client. *Universality*, as used in this context, refers to the process of relating anecdotes that tap experiences common to the average subject from a particular culture. *Individuality* refers to the process of tailoring a story in order to allow the client to utilize his own store of personal life experiences as he becomes more and more deeply absorbed in his inner reverie.

These and other principles of indirect hypnotherapy are illustrated in the induction to trance in Table 1. This metaphor is intended to facilitate arm levitation. Often the therapist will also use subtle nonverbal cues, such as gentle lifting of the wrist while talking. For purposes of illustration it will be assumed that the client in this example experiences his world primarily through kinesthetic sensory channels.

Throughout the induction procedure in Table 1 the metaphor was phrased in such a manner as to appeal individually to a kinesthetically oriented individual (e.g., feel, touch

Table 1

Metaphor	Principles Of Hypnotherapy Induction
Once, when I was quite young . . . and just learning . . . how to swim in the shallow end . . . of a warm pool of water . . . I had a most fascinating experience.	Evocation of childhood memories; suggestion to learn something new; introducing such learning as being safe; ideosensory suggestion to feel warmth; suggestion to build an expectancy set of curiosity.
I was spending my time playing, splashing, lightly floating. Every once in awhile I would touch bottom . . . just to make sure it was really there, as do most children. As I was exploring gradually deeper and deeper . . . areas of the pool . . . I began to feel more and more comfortable . . . with floating and didn't have to touch bottom quite so often.	Repetitious suggestion for levitation, experiencing of comfort and security and a trance. Suggestions for comfort and levitation in unspecified fashion. Embedded command to go deeper in trance.
I continued to drift quietly in the warm water for some time. . . . At some point in this period of drifting—and I don't know exactly when—I became consciously aware of something that had been happening outside of my awareness for some time.	Nonspecific suggestion for drifting into deeper relaxation; suggestion to feel warmth; building expectancy set for change; client given permission to proceed at his own pace.
As I had been floating so pleasantly . . . watching fleecy clouds to my right drift by in interesting, curious patterns . . . I had been playing intriguing little games in my mind, imagining shapes of birds or gliders or balloons in the clouds . . . as children are prone to do. During this time I had not been aware consciously that the arm on my right side had been slowly floating from down deeper . . . to the surface of the water. It was as if the arm had a mind of its own. What a pleasant surprise this was to me! I suppose this was when I first began to learn about trusting my own unconscious mind for new and different gifts.	Indirect suggestions for: developing a conscious-unconscious split; levitation of the right arm; dissociation of right arm from self (arm becomes object instead of subject); further work on maintenance of expectancy set for comfort and pleasure.

bottom, float, warmth, splash). Suggestions were also phrased in a manner that would tap common universal experiences in most individuals' memory banks. Combined with this induction were suggestions for deepening the level of trance at a pace with which the client felt comfortable (e.g., exploring deeper areas of the pool). Regardless of whether or not the client's arm actually levitated, the operator would probably have succeeded in inducing a light to moderate depth trance state.

Once the induction and some form of trance-deepening procedure has been accomplished, it is then up to the therapist to construct a series of suggestions that will indirectly address the client's problems. It is advised that the therapist first develop a metaphor that matches the client's problem statement and then bring in a resource that the client would find helpful in resolving his or her difficulty (see Gordon, 1978, for an excellent discussion of how one builds such a metaphor).

The example in Table 2 briefly illustrates the development of such a process in addition to all the earlier stated principles of indirect hypnotherapeutic suggestion. The client's

problem is sexual frigidity. The client was the second of eight siblings in a poor rural family which offered her no privacy physically or emotionally. She married a highly driven man who attempted to apply the same high pressure business principles that had allowed him to be very successful to his sexual life. His lack of gentleness and other earlier marital trauma between them had totally alienated his wife sexually. Both were committed, evangelical Christians. The metaphor in Table 2 was offered to them conjointly following a relaxation induction and a quiet, gentle, lulling period of trance deepening.

This trance process was taped for them and they were asked to play it three or four times a week for several weeks. Following the intervention the couple reported an improvement in their level of emotional and sexual intimacy (as well as a greater enjoyment of church-related activities).

Christian Integrative Potential. This particular therapeutic style of intervention lends itself well to use by therapists who wish to convey to clients their own beliefs and values. By telling clients metaphors or parables in this

Table 2

Metaphor	Principle Of Hypnotherapy Intervention
There was once a small clapboard church building out in the middle of nowhere, or so it seemed to the church. The people in the small town nearby mainly ignored the church unless they wanted her to somehow meet *their* needs. They came to her all in a rush to come and go away.... And no one ever knocked or asked her permission to come ... in. It was kind of like she felt no one in the local *body* ... of believers really respected her for what *she* had to offer.	Appeal to Christian beliefs; indirect reference to childhood loneliness and lack of attention; veiled reference to sexual intercourse and matching that reference with a set of equally negative feelings.
Everyone just seemed to rush in regularly and then pull out to go conduct business as usual. Well, very gradually, the small community prospered. And they gave her a new coat of paint; a new tall, proud steeple pointing upward: and they fixed the leaks in her roof so no one could see her tears on the inside. They even stuck in stained glass windows. Some of them had jewels in them so that people could press their eyes up close and get a really good look.	Reinforcement of the matching between the church and sexual intercourse with negative feelings; continued development of matching metaphor through indirect reference to prosperity, sexuality, a lack of privacy, and her husband still not understanding her emotional needs.
This went on for some time, ... pretty on the outside but yearning for something more on the inside, ... wanting to be a place of worship.	Reference to her need to be cherished and given free choice in sexual matters.
One day something strange happened. It was an unpredictable happening. Someone actually knocked. He knocked before coming in. It was the familiar face of an old admirer but with something different about him, something changed about his face. It was as though he really cared about her needs ... *now*.... He came in and out, back and forth, taking care of all her needs that no one else had seemed to notice. He oiled the hinges on her doors; he ran his hands over her walls to make sure they were smooth and not rough; he straightened the candle on the high altar, and did all manner of caring things.	Introduction of resource metaphor. More explicit references to sexuality but in a changed, caring context with emotional insight and commitment.
At first she was suspicious. But over time, as days went by and he continued to come to her and minister to her real needs, she began to look forward to his coming very much. Often when he walked by she felt like stretching out and coming to *him*. Often she didn't understand why she wanted him and his visits so badly. Yet, slowly, she just learned to accept the fact that consciously her spirit did not have to understand the changes going on inside of her ... all the new feelings stirring within her ... because after all she was just a simple country church being cared for deeply by a man who understood her and loved her in a new and different way. She thought often to herself about how the Holy Spirit worked in ways she didn't understand, and yet that was okay for her. She could just accept that and forget everything else, since it wasn't important anyway.	Indirect suggestion that change will take time. Development of a conscious-unconscious split in her awareness. Encouragement to just relax and accept change without questioning how or why it was taking place. Indirect connection of the Holy Spirit and her own spirit working together as a team; final suggestion for amnesia which was developed in subsequent suggestions.

manner the therapist communicates to the client on multiple levels of awareness. The method is similar to the style of speaking that Jesus used in communicating so effectively to the people of his day (Shepperson, 1981; TeSelle, 1975). Jesus aimed his messages at different levels of awareness. At one level of awareness a listener was having his physical needs attended; on another, his emotional; at still another, his spiritual needs. What he received depended on the relative press of his different needs or drives.

An example of Jesus' astute ability to communicate in this metaphoric manner is seen in his command to eat his flesh and drink his blood (John 6:54ff.). Some listeners were intrigued, some disgusted, some puzzled. The behavioral result was that some went away, some gained a significant insight into Jesus' primary intervention plan for their lives, and others shrugged their shoulders and waited for something they could understand.

The Christian therapist seeking to intervene on multiple levels in his clients' lives would do well to model the basic method Jesus presented in his work. The mechanics of this method are as follows. First, one must listen to the primary representational modalities used by a client (e.g., visual, auditory, kinesthetic, etc.) and talk his language back in the same modality (see Bandler & Grinder, 1979). Second, one must tailor one's metaphor to fit the specific aptitudes and interests of the client. When talking to a nature lover, speak in terms of the particular elements familiar to that person's environment. It is interesting to note in this regard that Jesus talked to crude sailors in terms of the sky and sea and wind. When dealing with scholars he moved to their intellectual environment, the Scriptures.

A further step toward effective metaphoric communication has to do with "seeding the unconscious." Basically this means just grazing an issue in passing with an indirect allusion to the insight one desires the client to reach at a later point when he is more ready to respond appropriately. This process of seeding was developed in more recent times by Erickson (Rossi, 1980). The technique may involve nothing more than a pregnant pause following a significant idea before one continues with the metaphor at hand. For example, if one wishes the client to go deeper into trance, a common seeding tactic might be a statement such as: "As he walked . . . *deeper and deeper* . . . into the woods he became more *self-absorbed*."

These techniques allow a therapist to redefine or reframe the client's problem in such a fashion that a previously insoluble dilemma can now be viewed from a different, more workable perspective. The metaphor is essentially parallel to the client's life situation except in a few critical elements. These changes allow the client to recognize or develop resources within himself that were previously discounted or unavailable (Lankton, 1980). These resources can be spiritual, emo-

tional, or relational. For example, one can be allowed to get in touch with the presence of one or more benevolent introjects from one's childhood through metaphor (e.g., "And so the little ragamuffin, hair all mussed and soot streaking her face, finally came to the startling realization that indeed she *was* a princess. All she had really been required to do was see her father pass by in the parade and call out as loud as she could, *Daddy!*").

Summary. Indirect hypnotherapy combines elements of neurolinguistic programming, traditional hypnotherapy, and an applied understanding of psychodynamic theory. It is recommended for those practitioners who have or wish to develop the gift of weaving therapeutic parables into the fabric of everyday life for both themselves and their clients.

References

Bandler, R., & Grinder, J. *Frogs into princes.* Moab, Utah: Real People Press, 1979.

Gordon, D. L. *Therapeutic metaphors.* Cupertino, Calif.: Meta Publications, 1978.

Lankton, S. R. *Practical magic: A translation of a basic neuro linguistic programming into clinical psychotherapy.* Cupertino, Calif.: Meta Publications, 1980.

Rossi, E. L. (Ed.). *The collected papers of Milton H. Erickson on hypnosis.* New York: Irvington Press, 1980.

Shepperson, V. L. Paradox, parables, and change: One approach to Christian hypnotherapy. *Journal of Psychology and Theology*, 1981, 9, 3–11.

TeSelle, S. *Speaking in parables.* Philadelphia: Fortress, 1975.

V. L. SHEPPERSON

Hypnotic Aspects of Spiritual Experience.

Since its modern inception in the practices of Mesmer, hypnosis has frequently been associated with the spiritual and the occult. Because it appeared to be something magical, it was presumed to depend on unknown forces or powers. Since, on many occasions, hypnosis was employed to help people achieve things beyond the normal (e.g., avoid pain, sudden recovery of lost vision or sensation), it was seen as involving the supernatural. This association has unfortunately persisted despite the fact that the scientific foundations upon which the understanding of hypnosis is based have become firmer in the past two decades (Hilgard & Hilgard, 1975). The current conceptions of hypnosis remove the magical, occult characterization and allow hypnosis to provide another perspective on the understanding of religious experience (Matheson, 1979).

Hypnosis and Religious Events. Religious experiences are admittedly very personal and varied in their nature, but generally they are considered to be the effect of some being outside of the person or external to the self (Lindblom, 1962). However, religious experiences are usually the result of religious events, the close observation of which reveals processes and phenomena equivalent in nature to those generally known as hypnotic. This is not to imply that all religious experiences are the result of hypnotic effects, nor is it intended to suggest that hypnosis is the sole contributing factor to any religious experience. Rather, the intention is to consider the role hypnotic experience plays in extending the religious experience beyond that of the rational.

Tappeiner (1977), in examining prophetical utterances, acknowledged the divine source of these prophecies but stressed that certain characteristics of the hypnagogic state—specifically vividness, originality, changefulness, and independence of conscious control—made it the most suitable channel for divine communication. Matheson (1979) in an examination of salvation, healing, and public prayer, also compared the systemic characteristics of these religious events to the formal and traditional styles of hypnosis. For example, the repetition, imagery, cadence, movement, and focus of the singing and the preaching induce a trancelike state in the listener which can then facilitate the spiritual response independently of mere rational thought. With these qualities, a religious experience is likely to have the subjective sense of having originated outside of the self.

The initial implications of this view of religious experiences as hypnotic phenomena are of two types: those that are complementary and those that clash with the implied religious intentions. This conceptualization supports a view of religious experience which is not merely rational in nature but which also integrally involves images and sensations. Thus, believing precedes knowing, as sensory experience precedes rational thought. Further, this view sheds light on theological conflicts that frequently have led to division. If the basis of faith resides in perceptual form, and if creed is a verbal description of this image, then attempts to debate doctrine without at least acknowledging and clarifying the perceptual models involved are destined to difficulty.

However, the effect of a hypnotic state can, at least in some people typically called high susceptibles, lead to behavioral responses that are not well grounded in the person. A response may be forthcoming but may extinguish over time, resulting in an apparent change in beliefs or loss of faith. In addition, the hypnotic process can be involved in the formation of various emotional states that can be pleasant and satisfying to the person. Associations between these pleasant affects and the producer of these

feelings can then occur; if so, an intimate rapport develops in which the person is likely to respond to further suggestions, however incompatible they may be to the person's established personality. This effect is most noticeable in cults and sects established on very strict rules that are rigidly observed and enforced. Thus, the initial "good feeling" serves to create the fertile environment for later responses (Sargent, 1957; Stoner & Parke, 1977).

In summary, the traditional concept of hypnosis provides a means for examining many religious activities and the resulting religious experiences. The hypnotic process can lead to an expanded experience through imagery and sensation and does not restrict the event to a cognitive one. However, it also raises the risk that some may respond because of the pleasant affect and in a way not compatible with their existing selves. The above considerations briefly address the relationship of hypnotic processes to religious experiences. Religion is generally defined as any system of faith and worship of a supreme being, God. When compared with "spiritual," religion is generally seen as having an external focus on practice and form. In contrast, the essence of spiritual is that of soul or life, immaterial and yet at the centre of one's being. The consideration of the relationship of hypnosis to spiritual experience involves an examination of the hypnotic facilitation of spiritual experience and the spiritual aspect of hypnotic experience.

The Spiritual and the Unconscious. As opposed to the religious, which usually finds its origin in the conscious and the deliberate, the spiritual is usually the gift of the unconscious. Religion is by nature something of form and structure, in which behavior is a product of tradition and deliberate intention, and content is thought and verbal recordings. In contrast, spiritual experiences seem to have their origin in darkness, breaking through into one's consciousness, often producing surprise and ecstasy.

As rich as the Age of Enlightenment was in its treasury of art and music, it also served to establish the preeminence of the conscious and the rational over that of the mystical, the imagined, and the unconscious. Consequently, that which could be decided or reasoned was valued and that which was dreamed or imagined was discredited. Concurrent with this thinking was the church's affirmation of Augustinian theology and the emergence of an approach to the Christian life that stressed the literal aspects of the Bible along with the logical understanding of one's faith. This emphasis promoted the rational and the conscious, and devalued the intuited and the unconscious. (This suspicious view of the unconscious was further enhanced by the Freudian concept of the unconscious as the seat of sexual and aggressive urges.) The emphasis on salvation as an act of personal decision and the continuing suppression of the inner world of feelings and creativity in favor of the mental world of thought and volition have focused on a particular side of Christian truth and exaggerated it out of proportion.

However, this deemphasis on the unconscious has not always been present. Prior to the so-called Age of Enlightenment the unconscious was more typically seen as the creator, the motivator, and the source of spiritual experiences which achieved expression through the services of the conscious mind. The unconscious was understood as the source of spiritual experience: of visions, prophecies, "the still small voice." Such a view of unconscious functioning sees it not as a bound or closed system driven by previous experience and instinctive and antagonistic urges, but as an open system, receptive to creative and imaginary (nonrational) input. The unconscious processes serve to receive this input from within, from others, from the cosmos, and from God. Once received, the input is unconsciously perceived through a process of searching and organizing, and may then be made available to conscious awareness through a number of means including bodily sensations, dreams, daydreams, and behavior.

The visions of the Old and New Testaments all have elements of this creative unconscious. Ezekiel's wheels of fire and Jacob's ladder, as well as the dreams of Joseph and the revelations of John, are all consistent with the view of a receptive and perceptive unconscious. Similarly, Christ's teaching that we become as little children (implying, among other things, a reduction of the adult's rational thinking) and that we know in our hearts (in contrast to the knowing of the mind) are consistent with the role of the unconscious in the spiritual. Similarly Christ's use of parable, metaphor, and paradox also reflect his way of often bypassing the rational and analytical processes of consciousness in favor of communicating more directly with the unconscious mind. (See Shepperson, 1981, for a more detailed discussion of the place of unconscious hypnotic dynamics in Christ's communication patterns.)

Hypnosis and the Spiritual. Because hypnosis is an inborn ability and a naturally occurring process, it can be seen as relevant to the spiritual experience. Hypnosis is not to be considered as an invasive technique which imposes on human integrity and sanctity, but rather as an available resource for experience and growth. Once the spiritual can be seen as integrally involved in the receptive, perceptive, and creative processes of the unconscious, it can be seen as relevant to hypnosis. The spiritual is not a rational system of rules and thoughts but the intimate awareness and experience of the creation and the Creator.

Hypnosis, particularly as it is used to open up and expand experiences, can be a vehicle to approach the spiritual aspects of persons. Hypnosis can also be employed in such a way as to free up the sensory experience, to stimulate new perceptions, to activate unconscious searches, and to openly access unconscious phenomena. This experience of hypnosis is commonly achieved in self-hypnosis when the individual willingly and openly proceeds with images and techniques in order to facilitate new sensory occurrences such as visual images and altered physical perceptions. However, this same type of response may be evoked in heterohypnosis (i.e., with another person doing the hypnosis).

Self-hypnosis and heterohypnosis are both characterized by absorption and the fading of a general reality orientation. However, as Fromm, Brown, Hurt, Oberlander, Boxer, and Pfeifer (1981) noted, significant differences between these two forms of hypnosis lie in areas of attention and ego receptivity. While concentrative attention and receptivity to stimuli coming from the hypnotist characterize heterohypnosis, expansive, free-floating attention and ego-receptivity to stimuli coming from within are characteristic of self-hypnosis. Many religious activities bear considerable similarity to the characteristics of heterohypnosis; there is increased absorption and narrowing of focused concentration and responsiveness to one external stimulus who may be the preacher, the healer, or the prophet. The result is an increase in responses consistent with what is suggested by the external source. In contrast, the spiritual experience is highly compatible with the nature of self-hypnosis in that the perceived events are expansive, freely changing or floating, and emerging from some place that seems to be within or independent of any objectively external source.

This does not reduce spirituality to some natural psychological process; rather, it aids in understanding the spiritual experience and even provides means to facilitate this part of one's life. Hypnosis, particularly in its self-experienced form, can be the process in which one achieves a state receptive to material from the unconscious. It may also be receptive to the intimate awareness and experience of the creation and the Creator. Such an understanding is foreign neither to the experiences described in Scripture nor to writings about prayer, contemplation, or spirituality.

The Bible and the Unconscious. The Bible contains many examples which attest to the creative role of the unconscious and the involvement of self-hypnotic activities in the experience of the Deity. The role of visions is prominent throughout Hebrew and Christian Scripture. "The word of the Lord came to Abram in a vision" telling him not to fear (Gen. 15:1). This was probably not an externally audible sound but one woven into a vision to which Abram could respond, suggesting that he was not asleep. Similarly, Samuel experienced the voice of the Lord calling him while he rested. Initially he responded as if it were the voice of Eli, but was then guided by his mentor (who apparently could not hear it) to attend to this voice as the voice of God (1 Sam. 3). Further examples exist throughout the Old and New Testament, including Daniel, Joseph, Job, Elijah, Ezekiel, and the revelation of John.

Christ's examples of prayer are also indications of unconscious and hypnotic activities. Not only did he suggest a structure to prayer (Matt. 6:9–13), but he also went apart where he struggled with visions and experienced his praying physically. Paul addresses this nonrational, unconscious element of prayer when noting the basic inability of people to pray (Rom. 8:5–8, 26). This inability is not due to any psychological difficulties. Rather, it is because Christian prayer must begin by maintaining the fundamental mystery of God, and consequently not knowing how we ought to pray (Rom. 8:26) is paradoxically the condition that makes all true prayer possible. It is the focusing of both conscious and unconscious mental processes on God that results in expressions of "unutterable groanings."

Here the parallel to self-hypnotic techniques can be seen most closely, for the self-hypnotic abilities allow nonrational, nonverbal attention to symbols and mysteries. These can be perceived and experienced outside of consciousness but may culminate in images, words, or voices reappearing in the arena of consciousness. A structured technique for the utilization of unconscious resources in self-hypnosis is to ask oneself one important or focused question before commencing self-hypnosis. This is assumed to direct the unconscious search processes, perhaps resulting in a hypnotic response or an "answer" sometime later (Erickson & Rossi, 1976).

Implications and Conclusions. A theology which overcomes the Augustinian dualism and declares all of creation to be of God, to be experienced and enjoyed, can accept hypnosis as a part of that creation, a naturally occurring phenomenon which is neither inherently evil or good. The value of hypnosis is that it provides a means of achieving a special state in which the person can go beyond the bounds of usual rational thinking to affect both mental and physical processes. Sensations and experiences which were previously considered to be beyond access can be influenced, and unconscious processes and responses can be stimulated.

Self-hypnosis is particularly effective, since the resulting trance state is expansive, free-floating, and internally responsive in nature. Consequently, this state is a desirable means for individuals to approach and utilize their own unconscious resources.

According to Jung (1936) the unconscious psyche contains both a personal part, which holds an assembly of past, repressed content, and a collective or universal part, the product of heredity and creation. This latter part contains the archetypes or models for development and can be seen as that aspect of the person which is initially subject to synchronistic influence and communication with God. Thus, the activity of the unconscious can be experienced as the "still, small voice," or the awareness of God within, and can be the source of our spiritual experience. Similarly, the contemplative experience can be viewed as the achievement of a self-hypnotic state which is furthered by an activation of the unconscious in ways that defy verbal description, and yet have a real and appreciable effect on the individual.

Self-hypnosis is a learnable process that is generally available to anyone; it can be the means for the achievement of trance, the transcendence of the rational, and the entrance into the mystical. Such experience taps into the spiritual and unconscious resources of the individual and also into that part of the psyche that is open to the influence of God and the cosmos. Hypnosis has in reality always been integral to the experience of spirituality; its use can enhance spiritual growth.

References
Erickson, M. H., & Rossi, E. L. Two-level communication and the microdynamics of trance and suggestion. *American Journal of Clinical Hypnosis*, 1976, *18*(3), 153–171.

Fromm, E., Brown, D. P., Hurt, S. W., Oberlander, J. Z., Boxer, A. M., & Pfeifer, G. The phenomena and characteristics of self-hypnosis. *International Journal of Clinical and Experimental Hypnosis*, 1981, 29(3), 189–246.

Hilgard, E. R., & Hilgard, J. R. *Hypnosis in the relief of pain*. Los Altos, Calif.: William Kaufman, 1975.

Jung, C. G. The concept of the collective unconscious. In C. G. Jung, *The archetypes and the collective unconscious*. Princeton, N.J.: Princeton University Press, 1936.

Lindblom, J. *Prophecy in ancient Israel*. Philadelphia: Fortress, 1962.

Matheson, G. Hypnotic aspects of religious experience. *Journal of Psychology and Theology*, 1979, 7, 13-21.

Sargent, W. *Battle for the mind: The physiology of conversion and brainwashing*. Garden City, N.Y.: Doubleday, 1957.

Shepperson. V. L. Paradox, parables, and change. *Journal of Psychology and Theology*, 1981, 9, 3–11.

Stoner, C., & Parke, J. *All God's children: The cult experience—salvation or slavery?* Radnor, Pa.: Chilton, 1977.

Tappeiner, D. A. A psychological paradigm for the interpretation of the charismatic phenomenon of prophecy. *Journal of Psychology and Theology*, 1977, 5(1), 23–29.

G. MATHESON

Hypoactivity. A state of depression characterized by hopelessness and helplessness. It is frequently the result of a loss of self-esteem or ego depletion and involves a nonreactive and passive lack of activity.

Hypochondriasis. A technical medical term which describes the behavior of the hypochondriac. Such behavior involves an exaggerated, morbid preoccupation with health and the false belief that one is suffering from physical disease. These patients frequently consult physicians and vigorously complain about physical disorders. Although no physical function has been lost or impaired, the patient is convinced that there is a dire illness that previous medical examinations have been unable to detect. The complaints usually involve the head, chest, and abdomen, but the complaints are usually as vague as they are urgent and the disorder easily shifts. When extensive medical investigations reveal no organic pathology, the patient refuses to accept a verdict of health. Instead, the hypochondriac insists on more testing or even treatment. If the physician refuses, the hypochondriac will probably look for another clinic. Eventually the patient becomes a chronic attender at several clinics, perhaps simultaneously. Many hypochondriacs also fall prey to quacks.

Whether or not hypochondriasis constitutes a primary psychiatric disorder is a much debated topic. *DSM-III* finally classified hypochondriasis with a code of 300.70 (the same given to atypical somatic disorders). Kenyon (1976) recommends that we stop talking about hypochondriasis as a separate disorder and speak only of hypochondriacal behavior. The hypochondriac usually has some other psycho-pathology (e.g., depression, anxiety) to which the hypochondriasis is secondary. Several studies have shown that the majority of hypochondriacs suffer from a clinically significant depression. In a third of later life depressions the classic mood symptoms are masked by bodily complaints. The patient's focus on the body not only serves to hide the depression from the physician, it also succeeds in limiting the depression. Patients can reinterpret their dismal situation and avoid a more serious break with reality. The unconscious focus on physical illness also provides an excuse and serves to absolve the hypochondriac of some feelings of guilt or failure.

The diagnosis of hypochondriasis is largely the outcome of extensive medical tests, negative findings, and the patient's continued refusal to accept assurances of health. There is a hypochondriasis scale on the Minnesota Multiphasic Personality Inventory (scale 1, abbreviated Hs), but it is largely a symptom checklist. Its validity is suspect, especially with hospital and nursing home patients, who have many real physical symptoms (Pilowski, 1967). Pilowski (1967) and Brink, Belanger, Bryant, Capri, Janakes, Jasculca, and Oliveira (1978) have devised scales measuring health attitudes rather than specific physical complaints. However, the precise relationship between hypochondriacal attitudes and hypochondriacal behavior has not yet been established.

Hypochondriasis is easily distinguished from other psychological disorders involving physical complaints. In psychosomatic illness the cause is also mental, but the physical symptoms (e.g., ulcer, migraine) are real and can be treated medically. In conversion reaction (e.g., hysterical paralysis or blindness) the cause is also an unconscious defense against anxiety or a stressful environment, but the physical complaints are limited to the loss of an active function. In malingering the patient consciously feigns a particular physical disorder in hopes of escaping from some undesirable situation or cashing in on an insurance policy or personal injury suit.

There are several theories regarding the origin of hypochondriasis. Sullivan (1953) contended that hypochondriacs unconsciously focus on physical explanations as a way of avoiding their interpersonal problems. Adler (1956) saw hypochondriasis as the result of the patient's pampered childhood; what the patient really seeks is to have the medical staff give the kind of elaborate attention that the patient enjoyed as a child. The behaviorists have a similar explanation: sickly behavior has been rewarded with special attention (positive reinforcement) and release from normal obligations, such as not having to go to school (escape conditioning).

Research on the epidemiology of hypochondriasis has not been conclusive. The disorder is equally common among males and females. Although it can be found in every age, socioeconomic, and ethnic group, it tends to be more prevalent among the aged, poor, and ethnic minorities, where psychological sophistication is less and there is a tendency to construe mental stress as the result of physical disorders. Hypochondriacal behavior may be the result of an underlying personality that is apprehensive, unstable, dependent, and timid. There may also be an environmental component: hypochondriacal behavior may be the response to a certain degree and kind of environmental stress in certain individuals.

The treatment of hypochondriasis is difficult and the prognosis is poor. The patient steadfastly believes that the disease is physical and so considers psychiatric treatment inappropriate. Many clinics speak of managing such patients rather than curing them. Such management of these cases involves firm policies and limit setting enforced by the entire staff, starting with the receptionist. The goal is to prevent the hypochondriac's demands from overtaxing the staff or disrupting the operations of the clinic.

One approach to treatment is to attempt to alleviate the underlying depression. Placebos rarely have a positive impact. Of all the tricyclic antidepressant medications, doxepin seems to be the best tolerated, giving the patient less opportunity to complain of side effects. Sulpiride, an antidelusional compound, has also proved useful in some cases of hypochondriasis. Although electroconvulsive therapy is highly effective in most cases of severe depression, this is generally not the case with hypochondriacs, because the patient is looking for a cure that is not overtly psychiatric.

Most hypochondriacs do not accept counseling or psychotherapy with someone designated as a mental health professional. The most appropriate psychotherapist is the primary care physician. The physician should neither explain that the symptoms are delusional nor attempt to treat such symptoms with medication or surgery. What the physician must do is listen attentively to the patient's problems, avoid the temptation to refer the patient, and schedule a follow-up appointment. The visits are kept in a medical setting so that the

hypochondriac is allowed to retain his security blanket. The physician's posture must be that of the benevolent authority who uses a controlled, directive, yet patient approach. With these regular, brief (15- to 20-minute) appointments the patient's complaints gradually shift from the physical to the psychosocial.

The role of pastoral care in hypochondriasis is unclear. The patient is seeking help in a medical context, not a spiritual or psychological context. While cases of conversion reaction frequently respond to faith healing, this is not the case with hypochondriasis. Perhaps the best thing a psychologist or pastor can do for a hypochondriac is to make a referral to a physician who is willing to establish the firm, caring, listening relationship that the patient needs.

References

Adler, A. *The individual psychology of Alfred Adler.* New York: Basic Books, 1956.
Brink, T. L., Belanger, J., Bryant, J., Capri, D., Janakes, C., Jasculca, S., & Oliveira, C. Hypochondriasis in an institutional geriatric population: Construction of a scale (HSIG). *Journal of the American Geriatrics Society,* 1978, *26,* 557–559.
Kenyon, F. E. Hypochondriacal states. *British Journal of Psychiatry,* 1976, *129,* 1–14.
Pilowski, I. Dimensions of hypochondriasis. *British Journal of Psychiatry,* 1967, *113,* 89–93.
Sullivan, H. S. *The interpersonal theory of psychiatry.* New York: Norton, 1953.

T. L. BRINK

Hypoglycemic States. Physiologically, hypoglycemia is a somewhat chronic state of low blood glucose. Commonly associated physical symptoms include exhaustion, insomnia, headache, dizziness, sweating, tremor, rapid heart rate, and muscle pain. Psychological symptoms may include depression, anxiety, irritability, crying spells, phobias, and difficulty in concentrating. Hypoglycemia has frequently been associated with depression and with hyperactivity in children. The psychological symptoms decrease or disappear as the hypoglycemia is successfully treated.

Hypoglycemics have frequently been misdiagnosed as neurotics or psychotics. For example, Airola (1977) described what happened to one of his patients, an actress who began feeling weak, exhausted, and depressed, especially in the morning. She had numerous crying spells, began having difficulty memorizing scripts, and finally fainted on the job. Neither a complete medical exam nor a subsequent three-year period of psychotherapy helped. She began drinking, her husband left, and she was finally admitted to a psychiatric hospital. Drug and shock therapy were ineffective and she was released from the hospital. Fortunately she visited Airola, a nutritionist, as a last resort and was able to recover completely with a change of diet.

Blood glucose levels are normally controlled by a hormone, insulin, which is secreted from the pancreas in response to increased blood glucose. Insulin reduces the level of glucose by facilitating its entry into cells or its storage as fat or glycogen. Blood glucose levels normally rise after meals and fall as time passes since the last meal. (We have all experienced minor symptoms of hypoglycemia, perhaps a headache, tiredness, or irritability after a prolonged period without eating.) In the hypoglycemic the pancreas responds to increased glucose levels by releasing more insulin than needed (hyperinsulinism) so that too much glucose is removed from the blood, depleting the amount immediately available to the brain (Fredericks & Goodman, 1969).

A number of things can contribute to hypoglycemic symptoms. Probably the most important in American diet is the abundance of refined carbohydrates, such as sugar and white flour, which enter the blood as glucose very quickly and copiously, triggering a pancreatic overreaction. One way to quickly alleviate the consequent hypoglycemic symptoms is to raise blood glucose by eating more refined carbohydrate. Unfortunately, this only perpetuates the problem by causing the pancreas to overreact once more.

Caffeine, from coffee, tea, colas, and some pain remedies, can drastically lower blood glucose in hypoglycemics. Nicotine produces a rapid rise in blood glucose followed by an equally rapid drop immediately after smoking stops (which might contribute to chain smoking). Symptoms can also be increased by emotional stress and by nutritional deficiencies in vitamins B1, B6, C, and E, pantothenic acid, magnesium, potassium, chromium, and zinc, which are abundant in whole grains and nuts.

Treatment usually includes eliminating refined carbohydrates, alchohol, tobacco and caffeine from the diet and supplementing certain vitamins and minerals. Weight loss and exercise may also be recommended.

Medical authorities still disagree on the criteria for diagnosing hypoglycemia, about its actual frequency of occurrence, about its symptomatology, and even about its treatment. Nevertheless, enough evidence has accumulated to encourage therapists to watch for hypoglycemic symptoms while treating depressed clients.

References

Airola, P. *Hypoglycemia*. Phoenix, Ariz.: Health Plus Publishers, 1977.

Fredericks, C., & Goodman, H. *Low blood sugar and you*. New York: Constellation International, 1969.

E. L. HILLSTROM

Hysteria. *See* SOMATIZATION DISORDER.

Hysterical Personality. *See* HISTRIONIC PERSONALITY DISORDER.

Ii

Iatrogenic Psychopathology. An iatrogenic disorder is one that is inadvertently induced by the doctor. Thus, iatrogenic psychopathology is psychopathology induced by the psychotherapist. This concept has been explored mainly within the psychoanalytic tradition, where a number of theorists have argued that the therapist's involvement in the life of a patient can be for good or for bad.

Langs (1980) has been the major spokesman for this position, pointing out that the unresolved neurotic problems of the therapist readily lead to a contamination of the therapeutic relationship. This not only blocks therapeutic progress but, according to Langs, can lead to the patient introjecting aspects of the therapist's psychopathology. This leads to Langs's focus on the interactions, conscious and unconscious, between therapist and patient. His approach is therefore often identified as an interactional one in that it emphasizes not just the one-way transmission of healing from therapist to patient, but rather the two-way conscious and unconscious interchange of health and pathology.

Reference
Langs, R. *Interactions*. New York: Aronson, 1980.

A. F. X. CALABRESE

Id. A concept from psychoanalysis representing a realm of the mind that functions in terms of instinctual drives. Freud postulated that the mind could be described by three functional realms: the id, the ego, and the superego. This postulation, called the structural hypothesis, views these realms, or structures, not as concrete entities but as metaphorical representations.

The id is best understood as a container of instinctual drives or energy (libido) seeking discharge. It is wholly part of the unconscious, hence can be defined only in relationship to its opposite structure, the ego, which is conscious and knowable. An independent description of the id was attempted by Freud (1933), but he only talked in terms of images. He pictured the id as a "cauldron of seething excitement" that somehow connects with one's biological substratum and is there filled with instinctual energy and a corresponding impulse to obtain satisfaction for those instinctual needs. This is all directed by what he called the pleasure principle. Freud felt that the id is innate, the other mental structures (ego and superego) developing in the first few years after birth.

The human mental state at birth is described in terms surprisingly reminiscent of those used by some theologians to describe the native state of man. The mental makeup of the young child, composed solely of the id, is described by Freudians as amoral, not knowing good from evil, seeking only selfish gratifications. These childlike demands for gratification of the drives are never outgrown. The mind continues throughout life to seek immediate discharge (cathexis) of id impulses. These operations of the id are labeled the PRIMARY PROCESS. This process ultimately brings a person into conflict with the environment. These conflicts further stimulate the id to supply its own energy to the development of the other mental structures, as well as to the development of their corresponding mental maneuvers that serve to provide either neurotic or healthy means of id impulse discharge.

The id is commonly thought of as representing a person's darker side. For Freudians this darker or unknown aspect of one's being is a major factor in explaining pathology. Today id

558

psychology has been replaced to a large part by ego psychology, which focuses on man's knowable ego in the formation of theories of psychopathology. Although this contemporary relative deemphasizing of the id is viewed with concern by some psychoanalysts, ego psychology does probably represent a more balanced total psychology in that it more adequately addresses all three basic mental structures.

Reference
Freud, S. *New introductory lectures on psychoanalysis.* New York: Norton, 1933.

D. S. McCulloch

Idealization. An ego DEFENSE MECHANISM whereby another person or love object is idealized, elevated, and overvalued in the mind of the individual. Perhaps a common example would be the young man who sees in his newfound companion the perfect lover. In this state of idealization she seems to fill all that he lacks, and the faults that others see in her are to him merely endearing facets of her engaging but flawless personality. Such romantic idealization is, according to Freud, the root of the human experience of being in love.

Idealization is often preliminary to IDENTIFICATION. Both play a vital role in superego development and in character formation. As a defense mechanism, idealization often is a response to dissatisfaction with one's self through the transfer of libidinal attachment to the new ideal. Therefore, it is also used in the aid of DENIAL. Finally, it may be used to replace a lost love object, facilitating the emotional "rebound" to a new love object.

R. Larkin

Idea of Reference. The notion that conversations or actions of people relate to oneself. Such a belief is held less firmly than is the case in a DELUSION.

Identification. A generally unconscious DEFENSE MECHANISM in which the person identifies himself with some object, person, or institution, seeking to think, feel, and behave in a manner consistent with his incorporated mental picture of that object. The purpose of this process is to protect the individual from threatened self-devaluation and to increase feelings of self-worth.

Identification is seen in psychoanalytic thought as one of the most primitive methods of recognizing external reality. It begins with the infant's identification of the mother's breast as part of his own body, transforming what is external and potentially uncontrollable or threatening into something internal, safe, and familiar. Identification also operates during the oedipal phase of development, when identification with the father serves to resolve fear of the father as the omnipotent rival for the mother's affections. An example in adulthood might be seen in the generally ineffectual person who draws feelings of self-worth from identification with the powerful, prestigious multinational corporation for which he works.

R. Larkin

Identity. *See* SELF; PERSONHOOD.

Identity Disorder of Childhood or Adolescence. An emotional disorder of childhood or adolescence in which an individual suffers distress due to an inability to reconcile certain aspects of himself or herself into a relatively coherent and acceptable sense of self. In *DSM-III* diagnostic criteria for identity disorder focus on five main areas: there is severe subjective distress regarding uncertainty about at least three issues relating to identity; there is impairment in social or occupational functioning as a result of these symptoms; the disturbance has lasted at least three months; it is not due to another mental disorder; and if the person is 18 or older, the disturbance does not meet the criteria for borderline personality disorder.

Associated features of identity disorder are related to one of the three following symptoms: mild anxiety and/or mild depression not related to external events; self-doubt and doubts about the future, with difficulty in decision making; and negative and/or oppositional behavior, often transient. This could be considered the "Who am I" syndrome, since the individual is suffering serious self-doubts. He is unable to integrate various aspects of the self into a whole and therefore lacks a coherent identity.

In considering identity disorder one must rule out borderline syndrome, an affective disorder, and a schizophreniform disorder. The more common mistake is to label it as normal adolescent turmoil. This is dangerous because individuals with identity disorder will not "grow out of it," as they would with normal adolescent turmoil.

Causes. It is commonly accepted that there are two primary factors contributing to the development of an identity disorder. The first is the failure of an individual to satisfactorily complete previous psychosocial stages of development. The second is the stress placed on young adults during this time of their life. This developmental phase represents a transitional stage during which the individual is attempting to make a separation from a nurturant protective family. The disorder is more common today than several decades ago. Contributing sociological factors include a society that fears it has no future and, consequently, is not likely to give much attention to the needs of the next generation; replacement of rugged individualism and religion with an excessive reliance on therapy; and loss of parental authority in the family.

Since identity disorder involves societal stress superimposed on stress related to normal developmental stages, we can expect the symptomatology to be related to the developmental tasks normally accomplished during the identity formation stage. Psychoanalytic theorists (e.g., Freud and Erickson) consider the necessary tasks to include 1) resolution of identity diffusion and acquisition, through experimentation, of a realistic and clear sense of self; and 2) ability to achieve genuine love for others as persons in their own right. Cognitive developmental theorists (e.g., Piaget) expect an individual to become autonomous, to internalize rules, to learn that wrongdoing depends on intention, to see that justice is retributive and permits some mercy, and to understand that obligations extend to peers as well as to adults.

Moral developmental theorists (e.g., Kohlberg) expect the individual in the identity formation of adolescence to perceive "being good" to mean liking and helping others and living up to what others have a right to expect, as well as conforming to ideals and to conditions necessary for group functioning. From a faith development perspective the individual should have an individuality-reflection faith. This means that the individual takes on responsibility for his or her own commitments, life style, beliefs, attitudes, and a facing up to certain polarities. These include individuality versus belonging to a community; subjectivity versus objectivity; self-fulfillment versus service to others; the relative versus the absolute (Fowler, 1981).

Clinical Course and Treatment. Although identity disorder may have a sudden onset, the more usual course is a very gradual onset. This will manifest itself by mild anxiety and/or depression accompanied by a loss of interest in friends, school, and activities. Often the individual will appear very irritable and complain of difficulty sleeping and a loss of appetite. If there is not early recognition and treatment,

these problems may progress to a severe identity crisis. This will manifest itself by severe doubting together with an inability to make decisions, a sense of isolation, a feeling of inner emptiness, a growing inability to relate to others, a disturbance in sexual functioning, and a feeling of urgency.

If appropriate intervention is made, the episode is of relatively short duration. If there is no resolution within one year, there should be further diagnostic evaluation, and more than likely the disorder will become chronic. The patient will then be unable to either establish a career commitment or form lasting emotional attachments. Frequent shifts in jobs, relationships, and career directions may result.

There are two basic principles involved in the treatment of these young people, both relating to the fact that this illness is the result of difficulty in emotional development. First, infantization should not be fostered; rather, attempts must be made to prevent regression. Second, growth and development should be encouraged. Four practical applications of these principles are implied. First, experimentation should be encouraged. Anxiety may cause a natural tendency to revert to a previous mode that was sure and secure— e.g., being a conformist, living up to what others expect, seeing beliefs as absolutes. Second, these patients should be treated as adults. They should not be "preached at" when experiments fail or appear counter to their background. Third, these young people should receive acceptance and approval as persons. Fourth, feelings and wishes must be recognized, and the patient should be encouraged to examine his or her longings and feelings of deprivation with an empathic therapist in order to obtain understanding.

Reference
Fowler, J. W. *Stages of faith.* San Francisco: Harper & Row, 1981.

F. WESTENDORP

Idiot Savant. An individual diagnosed as mentally retarded who performs unusual, often incredible mental feats, usually involving complicated puzzle solving or calculations based on numbers or calendar dates. The term *idiot* originally referred to a mentally retarded individual whose mental age was less than 3 years. *Savant* is the term for a person of exceptional learning. Thus the name *idiot savant* was applied to a person of low mental age who could perform an unusual mental feat.

Such unusual abilities among the retarded are rare. In occasional cases, however, seriously retarded persons may show a high level of skill in some specific aspect of behavior that does not depend on abstract reasoning. Cases have been reported where an individual was able to remember the serial number on every dollar bill he was shown or had ever seen. Another was able to instantly name the day of the week for any date for any year without the use of pencil and paper. A musical prodigy with a diagnosed IQ of 54 could play 11 different musical instruments by ear. A famous Japanese painter had an assessed IQ of 47. One woman could recall the birthdates of any person whose birthday she had ever been told.

The classic example of the idiot savant was the "Genius of Earlswood Asylum." Admitted to the asylum at age 15 with personality and speech defects, this mildly retarded man constructed model ships of masterpiece quality. In one 10-foot model, he used more than a million tiny wooden pins and pegs. He wore a navy uniform, and when his models were admired by visitors to the institution, he would express his pleasure by patting his head and repeating "very clever, very clever."

L. N. Ferguson

See Mental Retardation.

Illusion. A distorted perception which misrepresents external stimuli. Illusions always involve the perceptual distortion of stimulus patterns, unlike hallucinations, which are false perceptions, and delusions, which are mistaken beliefs.

There are illusions of apparent movement, such as the phi phenomenon, in which apparent movement is generated by two spatially separated flashing lights. There are illusions that misrepresent spatial figures, such as the Müller-Lyer illusion. In the Müller-Lyer illusion a line that is bounded by two arrowheads pointing outward appears shorter than a line of equal length bounded by two arrowheads pointing inward. Other familiar illusions include reversible figures, such as the Peter-Paul goblet and the staircase illusion. There are also illusions of smell, taste, temperature, time, and touch. A solid representation of the Müller-Lyer illusion, for example, works for the sense of touch.

According to Gestalt theory illusions are the result of innate processes of organization in the brain. However, learning and experience must play some role in illusions, since people of different cultures vary in their susceptibility to specific illusions. Attitudes, instructions, and repeated exposure will also affect one's experience of an illusion.

Most geometric illusions appear to be due in part to certain expectations that people have governing relationships among perspective, distance, shape, and size. In the familiar distorted-room illusion people in a room with distorted dimensions appear distorted in size because viewers expect walls, ceilings, and floors to meet at right angles. In the moon illusion the moon looks considerably larger at the horizon than when it is up in the sky. The main reason is that the horizon looks farther away than the overhead sky. Since the perceptual system compensates for perceived distance, the horizon moon is seen as larger.

The study of illusions supports the viewpoint that the behavioristic, stimulus-response view of the person cannot be entirely correct. This was the emphasis of Max Wertheimer, the founder of the Gestalt school of psychology and a contemporary of John Watson, the founder of behaviorism. Illusions demonstrate that perception (and ultimately personhood) is not just a passive product of sensory input, but that a person's attention, motivation, expectation, memory, and perceptual processes actively filter and alter sensory input. This Gestalt view is in agreement with the Christian view of the person, which describes the person as more than a collection of behavioristic, stimulus-response connections.

M. P. Cosgrove

See Perceptual Development.

Imagery, Eidetic. Vivid visual images of objects not present in actuality. It is sharper in detail and more brilliant in coloration than ordinary memory images. It also differs from an after-image in these same ways as well as in its availability through voluntary recall. It occurs most frequently in children; 60% of those under 12 report the experience. Ahsen (1977) has developed a method of training adults to be able to experience eidetic imagery and has suggested ways to use these images therapeutically.

Reference
Ahsen, A. Eidetics: An overview. *Journal of Mental Imagery,* 1977, *1* (1). 5–38.

D. G. Benner

Imagery, Therapeutic Use of. The term *imagery* here refers to a seeing with the mind's eye, or the formation of mental pictures. The image may be a literal representation of some concrete aspect of reality or a representation that is symbolic. Such mental pictures may appear in a variety of forms. Dreams during sleep, daydreams, paintings that remain vividly in the memory, and hallucinations are all images. Certain images, especially if they occur repeatedly, may indicate strivings or conflicts that are important.

Further, imagery may be thought of as a type of information processing that begins during infancy and functions as a form of language in the preverbal child by giving pictorial representations of objects and events. The preverbal child then "thinks" with images (Singer, 1974, p. 218). Another distinction between the verbal and pictorial modes of thinking exists. Verbal language and logic are controlled primarily by the brain's left hemisphere, whereas imagery, particularly when it is creative, is dominated by the brain's right hemisphere. Since emotions also appear to be controlled primarily by the right hemisphere, Singer (1974, p. 218) suggests the possibility that working with imagery increases accessibility to affect.

Access to affect and to early experiences via imagery are compelling points favoring the use of imagery in psychotherapy. Moreover, an image permits the simultaneous assimilation of many aspects of a situation into a whole experience, thus allowing an intellectual and emotional reaction to the "big picture." This all might happen in the same amount of time a patient could verbalize one small aspect of what heretofore had been viewed as a host of separate problems.

Of course, some verbal dialogue is necessary for an intellectual understanding of the emotional experience produced via imagery. Verbal exchange must also precede the use of imagery for the patient and the therapist to know how the imagery might best be used and to see how comfortable the patient is in working with imagery. Thus, a therapy process that incorporates some imagery work with the verbal components of treatment would appear most effective. However, the therapeutic strategy must be tailored to the individual patient's ability to work with imagery.

Methods of psychotherapy may be categorized according to the way they most often employ imagery. Two dimensions aid in this comparison. The first is the concrete or literal image versus the symbolic image. The second is the guided image (suggested by the therapist) versus the receptive image (spontaneously coming to the patient's mind). This offers four categories as a basis for comparing approaches to psychotherapy utilizing imagery: symbolic-receptive, concrete-guided, symbolic-guided, and concrete-receptive.

The early psychoanalytic approaches that encourage the interpretation of dreams as symbols and work with images as they occur spontaneously to the patient might be categorized, for the most part, as symbolic-receptive. Even though much psychoanalytic method involves the patient recalling early experiences, the symbolic importance of the memory is usually more significant than the concrete facts.

Systematic desensitization, aversive counterconditioning, implosion, and modeling techniques all rely on specific images that the patient and therapist have usually agreed on, although the therapist suggests the images during the actual procedure. Therefore these techniques may be defined as concrete guided. This is in keeping with the behavioral approach, which minimizes the value of the symbolic and typically encourages the therapist to be active.

European imagery methods, such as that of Leuner's (1969) guided affective imagery, are symbolic-guided procedures. The therapist suggests the general situation, and it is understood that what the patient constructs is a symbolic projection. Leuner's approach begins with relaxation training. This is followed by asking the patient to imagine a series of 10 scenes which the therapist suggests in general; the patient is to give a verbal detailed description of the imagery and the associated feelings. Obviously this procedure is receptive in part, since the scene is a projection. However, the therapist does provide some direction and structure through the preset series of 10 scenes, and therefore the process is primarily guided.

The first scene that the therapist asks the patient to imagine is a meadow, any meadow that comes to mind. The next scene is of a landscape while climbing a mountain and the view from the top. In the third scene the imager is to follow a brook upstream to its source or down to the ocean. The subsequent scenes are of a house (including the inside details), a close relative and the associated affect, situations designed to evoke sexual feeling, a lion, a fantasy of the ego ideal, looking into a dark forest or the opening of a cave, and finally a figure emerging from a swamp.

During this process the therapist should discover the qualities of the different themes, factors inhibiting progress, the presence of seemingly contradictory situations, and the nature of the emerging symbolic figures as well as their behavior. For more understanding the patient may be encouraged to free associate verbally and with images to the situations.

Leuner suggests six methods to alter therapeutically the images and the unconscious material they represent. The methods consist of feeding the hostile symbolic figures, calling on an "inner psychic peacemaker" to govern the direction and speed of treatment, confronting hostile figures by holding ground while attempting to suppress anxiety (avoiding running or struggling), reconciling the hostile figures (including making friends with them and perhaps physically touching them), exhausting a hostile figure by exercise and killing it, and finally utilizing "magic fluids" for fatigue or pain. Treatment times vary from 1 to 160 hours with an average length of 40 hours.

Autogenic therapy (Schultz & Luthe, 1969) may be used as a specific-guided or symbolic-guided approach depending on the concreteness of the problem. Finally, contemporary American methods such as transactional analysis, Gestalt therapy, psychodrama, and Shorr's (1974) psycho-imagination therapy combine all categories, including concrete-receptive, in which a specific act may be acted out as it comes to mind.

Shorr's use of imagery in psychotherapy varies more with each patient than Leuner's does, since Leuner employs the same basic procedure with everyone. Shorr believes that problems result from an individual being falsely defined by others and that he or she must find a more independent definition of self. In psychoimagination therapy the therapist attempts to identify the patient's major conflicts by asking the patient to complete such sentences as, "I feel ... ," "The best adjective to describe me is ... ," "I wish ... ," "I must ... ," "I secretly ... ," and "I will ...." The patient would most likely be asked to imagine and describe certain scenes, such as "What do you hear yourself saying if you imagine whispering in your father's ear?" and "What do you see, feel, and do if you imagine dancing with your mother?" It may appear that Shorr focuses more on images for diagnosis than for treatment; however, when the therapist discovers a significant conflict, it will be worked with via imagery. If the patient experiences intense conflict between thoughts and emotions, the therapist might suggest that the patient, with eyes closed, imagine an animal coming out from the head and another from the stomach or heart. Then the patient is to describe what happens as the two animals walk down the road together.

All but certain behavioral approaches appear to be descendants of Jung's active-imagination technique. Jung assumed that all images represent some part of the personality and that the integration of these parts into an organized and balanced unity would reduce the intensity of inner conflict (Singer, 1972). Jung considered patients' associations to dominant images that represented these parts to be important working material.

Jung might suggest that the patient imagine a dialogue between himself and a representation of a specific part of the personality, or that he imagine a dialogue between two such parts. The objective of establishing a comfortable relationship between the various parts is similar to Leuner's idea of reconciliation.

Ignatius of Loyola constructed a series of spiritual exercises utilizing imagery in 1543. In his colloquys Ignatius would speak to the Christ he pictured before him and go through a ritual of confession, repeating of certain prayers, and listening for God's direction. PSYCHOSYNTHESIS and INNER HEALING also utilize imagery in psychospiritual approaches. Both also appear to operate in all four categories discussed here.

An example of the power of imagery to capture a complex problem is evident in the case of a male graduate student who came for therapy because he frequently had been told that his aggressive bravado was offensive. In the third session the therapist asked him to close his eyes, take a few deep breaths, and see if he could form a mental picture to represent, perhaps symbolically, his current situation. He described the image of a huge armored warrior fighting his way forward with a large sword, challenging the world. However, a frightened crying infant was on the warrior's back, holding the warrior around the neck, and as the warrior pushed forward the frightened infant would attempt to hold him back with a choke. Simultaneously the warrior was trying to kill the infant on his back with the sword so that he would be free of the burden it imposed. The student realized that the infant represented his feelings of dependency and helplessness that he was hoping to mask with bravado.

A therapist might follow the sequence just described, asking the patient to take another minute to form an image in the mind's eye of how he or she would like the situation to be, perhaps again in symbolic or metaphoric form. After a description of this ideal image a third image depicting the obstacles impeding movement from the current situation to the desired situation might be repeated. Finally a mental image of the resources and personal qualities that would enable these obstacles to be overcome might be elicited.

In conclusion, imagery may be incorporated as part of psychotherapy in a number of ways, all of which may be described by the categories discussed in this article. These categories then are helpful in matching the patient and the problem with the best technique. Nevertheless, imagery is always only one aspect of the psychotherapeutic process.

References

Leuner, H. Guided affective imagery. *American Journal of Psychotherapy*, 1969, *23*, 4–22.

Schultz, J., & Luthe, W. *Autogenic therapy*. New York: Grune & Stratton, 1969.

Shorr, J. E. *Psychotherapy through imagery*. New York: Intercontinental Medical Book, 1974.

Singer, J. L. *Boundaries of the soul*. Garden City, N.Y.: Doubleday, 1972.

Singer, J. L. *Imagery and daydream methods in psychotherapy and behavior modification*. New York: Academic Press, 1974.

J. E. TALLEY

See DREAMS, THERAPEUTIC USE OF.

Imaginary Friends.

Fictional persons created by a child, usually between the ages of 2 and 4, but often persisting over several years. Bounding out of the creative minds of children, such imaginal creations represent one of the most sophisticated forms of symbolic play. Imaginary friends may assume a variety of roles—e.g., another child, an animal, or some other type of creature. This friend may have a unique and consistent personality quite different from the child creating the character.

Imaginary friends serve a number of functions. For example, if there are no other playmates around, the imaginary friend is a constant companion. The child talks to the imaginary friend, tells it what to do, and behaves with this companion just as he or she would with any real friend. Generally the imaginary friend is about the child's own age or younger. The imaginary playmate becomes a confidant in whom the child can confide matters of great importance.

Frequently the imaginary playmate is involved in a child's attempts to work out the difference between what is right or wrong. Many parents have heard a young child say something like, "Oh, I didn't do that; Tommy did it." Here the imaginary friend becomes a scapegoat for the child, who seems to be communicating the internal struggle he or she is having distinguishing between personal will and obedience. Excuses of this kind are clear indications that the child has a definite idea of what is right and wrong. But, they also show that the child could or did not stop committing the wrong action and is not yet willing to assume personal responsibility for the misdeed.

In summary, "the imaginary friend can be seen as evidence of the child's ability to differentiate himself from others and as evidence of his attempts to gain control over his impulses" (Newman & Newman, 1975, p. 71). Not all children create such friends. Those who do manifest the capacity to deal not only with reality but with what may be possible or not possible. It is a most private expression of the child's attempt to gain self-control.

Reference

Newman, B. M., & Newman, P. R. *Development through life: A psychosocial approach*. Homewood, Ill.: Dorsey Press, 1975.

B. J. SHEPPERSON

Immediacy.

As defined by Carkhuff (1969) and used in his approach to human relations training, the term *immediacy* refers to a person's ability to perceive what is happening in a present interpersonal interaction. In therapy immediacy provides the link between empathy and confrontation. Until a good working alliance is established, the interaction should be focused on the client and his or her experience, rather than on the therapeutic relationship (Gazda, Asbury, Balzer, Childers, Desselle, & Walters, 1973). However, once the therapist has established an empathetic, understanding relationship, the use of immediacy is necessary in order to provide a full growth experience.

Immediacy means perceiving and interpreting in the moment what is transpiring between the client and therapist. Carkhuff argues that in responding immediately to his experience of the relationship with the client, the therapist not only allows the client "to have the intense experience of two persons in interaction but also provides a model of a person who understands and acts upon his experience of both his own impact upon the other and the other's impact on him" (1969, p. 192). Individuals who communicate with immediacy share of themselves openly, honestly, in the moment. Thus, for Carkhuff one of the ultimate goals of a helping relationship is to model such full communication between persons.

It is the therapist's utilization of both positive and negative experiences of the relationship that provides for maximal understanding and growth. Frequently when the client is experiencing difficulty in communicating, this resistance is due to feelings about the therapist or the relationship, feelings which the therapist must identify through immediacy if the therapeutic process is to continue profitably. The therapist will often find that it is most effective in interpreting immediacy to employ the frustrating, directionless moments of therapy to search the question of immediacy. Sensitivity is required in order to discriminate when such interpretation will enhance a meaningful experience and when it will interfere with the communication at hand.

The term *immediacy* has not been widely used in the literature of psychotherapy, although the concept is obviously crucial. The narrower concept of TRANSFERENCE has been more commonly employed.

References
Carkhuff, R. R. *Helping and human relations* (Vol. 1). New York: Holt, Rinehart, & Winston, 1969.
Gazda, G. M. Asbury, F. R., Balzer, F. J., Childers, W. C., Desselle, R. E., & Walters, R. P. *Human relations training: A manual for educators.* Boston: Allyn & Bacon, 1973.
M. E. McCurdy

Implosive Therapy. *See* FLOODING.

Impotence. *See* INHIBITED SEXUAL EXCITEMENT.

Impression Formation and Management.
In attempting to understand other people we carefully note their physical appearance, style of dress, manner of speech, and behavior. From our observations we typically begin to form judgments about their qualities or traits. The process through which we combine this diverse information into a unified picture or impression of another has received considerable attention from social psychologists.

Asch, one of the first psychologists to study impression formation, suggested that our perception of another is not simply a collection of specific pieces of information but an organized, integrated conception of that individual's personality. In a highly influential study Asch (1946) presented college students with a list of seven traits that characterized a hypothetical individual. He asked the students to write a general description of the individual as well as to select other traits they felt would characterize that person. For one group of students the individual was described as "intelligent, skillful, industrious, warm, determined, practical, and cautious." For a second group the list was the same, except that the trait "cold" was substituted for "warm." Two major findings of the study were 1) that students experienced little difficulty in integrating the various traits into a coherent whole, and 2) that manipulation of the warm-cold variable produced a striking difference in the overall impression formed. Asch concluded that certain traits such as warm and cold may be central organizing traits, while others, such as polite and blunt, may be of secondary importance.

While Asch's conclusions have been questioned, his research fostered the development of implicit personality theories. Presumably through experience we develop intuitive notions about what traits are associated with each other in personality. Thus, knowing that a person is intelligent may lead us to conclude that he or she is also industrious. Another example of this process is the halo effect, in which knowing something favorable about a person typically leads us to infer other desirable qualities. For example, a large number of studies have indicated that physically attractive persons are perceived as being more sensitive, kind, strong, poised, and sociable than those less attractive.

Considerable attention has been given to the issue of precisely how we combine different kinds of information about a person into an overall evaluative impression. Both additive and averaging models assume that we assign values to each trait, but the models differ in regard to how we ultimately integrate these values into a general impression. The additive model assumes that we total the trait values so that, for example, the more positive input we have about another person, the more favorable our impression will be. The averaging model suggests that we use the mean value of the traits to form an impression. Thus, learning additional positive information about another does not necessarily improve our overall impression of that person. Research suggests that our impressions actually consist of a weighted average. That is, they are composed of an average of all available information about that person with each item weighted by its relative importance.

Studies indicate that not all information is equally important in our judgments of others. A primacy effect often occurs in which greater weight is given to information that is obtained first. This demonstrates that first impressions are indeed important and also explains why impressions may be hard to alter once they are formed. We also seem to assign greater weight to negative than to positive traits.

Clearly many people strive to influence the images others form of them. One of the basic assumptions of impression management theory is that individuals may present different sides of themselves to different people in different situations. High self-monitoring persons (Snyder, 1979) are particularly likely to exercise control over their self-presentations and to tailor them to fit the circumstances confronting them. They may present themselves as conformists or as independent as the situation demands. Interestingly, high self-monitoring persons are not only effective at practicing impression management but also at detecting such attempts by others.

Ingratiation involves a variety of tactics by which one seeks to increase his or her attractiveness to another person. Flattery, conformity, or rendering favors may be used for purposes of self-gain or self-protection. To be most effective these tactics must conceal manipulative intent as well as any deceit that may be involved.

One of the most important ways in which we may influence another's impression of us is through self-disclosure. Both its timing and nature, however, influence its effect on others. Gradual disclosure of oneself, which moves from the superficial to the intimate, seems to produce the most positive effects and the most stable relationships. Many psychologists also believe that self-disclosure is essential to effective psychological adjustment.

References

Asch, S. E. Forming impressions of personality. *Journal of Abnormal and Social Psychology*, 1946, *41*, 258–290.
Snyder, M. Self-monitoring processes. In L. Berkowitz (Ed.), *Advances in experimental social psychology* (Vol. 12). New York: Academic Press, 1979.

M. BOLT

Imprinting. The phenomenon where the newly born offspring forms an attachment relationship to the caregiver (usually the mother). It was initially identified by Lorenz around 1935 in his observation of the attachment process of the female greylag goose and her offspring. Lorenz observed that as each gosling hatched, the mother engaged in an obviously patterned series of dance steps, wing movements, and calls. The fruition of all this behavior was a gaggle of goslings following and imitating their mother in walking, swimming, and eating behavior. Lorenz became more interested in this phenomenon after he observed the same imprinting phenomenon in an abandoned duckling reared by an adult female chicken.

This experience led Lorenz to consider other mother-absent imprinting conditions (Lorenz, 1961). In the experiment for which he is most famous, Lorenz incubated geese eggs, and while the eggs were hatching, he danced dramatically so that each newborn had an opportunity to observe him. Lorenz recorded that each of the newly hatched goslings imprinted on him. They followed him wherever he went and, perhaps most surprisingly, later refused to accept an adult female goose as a substitute. As a result of these observations, Lorenz concluded that this imprinting phenomenon was genetically based, ensuring that as a result of the attachment to the caregiver the newborn gosling received protection, food, and training in the ways of being a goose. It had survival value for the species. Lorenz and others have found imprinting in other species (e.g., fish, guinea pigs, deer, and some farm animals) and have suggested that the emotional bonding between a human mother and her child is the human equivalent of the phenomenon first reported in the greylag geese. Although serious debate has resulted from this contention, Lorenz's observations have forced psychologists to consider the possible impact of genetic factors in the attachment relationship.

Reference

Lorenz, K. Z. Imprinting. In R. C. Birney & R. C. Teevan (Eds.), *Instinct: An enduring problem in psychology*. Princeton, N.J.: Van Nostrand, 1961.

K. A. HOLSTEIN

Impulse Control Disorders. In *DSM-III* this is a residual class of disorders of impulse control that are not classified elsewhere (e.g., paraphilias or substance use disorders). The essential feature of these disorders is an ego syntonic symptom or impulse that is experienced as irresistible. There is also an increasing sense of tension before committing the act and an experience of release, pleasure, or gratification when the act is committed. Five specific disorders make up this general category: pathological gambling (*see* GAMBLING, PATHOLOGICAL), KLEPTOMANIA, PYROMANIA, and two forms of EXPLOSIVE DISORDER (intermittent explosive disorder and isolated explosive disorder).

Incest. Currently the term refers to any sexually arousing contact within a family except that between husband and wife, whether members are blood related or not. It is often referred to as intrafamily child sexual abuse. As a universally prohibited behavior, incest has been recognized and reported in almost every civilized society. Leviticus 18:6–18 cites 16 prohibited intrafamily sexual involvements. The most common forms of incest are father/daughter, stepfather/stepdaughter, uncle/niece, and brother/sister. Incest may also be homosexual.

The frequency of incest is difficult to assess and varies with the research group. Studies seem to indicate, however, that between 3 and 6% of all females have experienced some type of sexual molestation. Some research suggests as many as 25% of college age females engaged in sexual activity with family members during childhood or adolescence. There are no cultural, economic, geographic, racial, or religious barriers to incest.

Studies of families where incest occurs suggest complicated interaction patterns and may include at least five causal factors. One factor is the family dynamic. Poor communication patterns, unhealthy alliances, inadequate methods of handling conflict, and dependency are seen. A second factor is the inability to deal with sexual issues and intimacy. In many cases the strongly religious homes have more difficulty talking about sexuality. Needs or urges are not discussed. Behaviors begin subtly and remain hidden. A third factor is a strong authoritarian milieu as found in many religious homes. The men in the families believe they "own" their women. The fourth factor is the unconscious dynamic of unresolved hostilities or wishes toward parents. Coming from a family where incest occurred, either as a victim or a witness, may predispose the person to unhealthy interaction patterns with a spouse or children that reflect anger, fear, or distrust. A fifth factor is the emotional immaturity and poor impulse control often noted in the men who commit incest.

Incestuous fathers present a mixed picture as good provider; religious; actively involved in church; dependent on the family for emotional needs; lacking intimacy in life; having a poor self-concept; having an unsatisfying marriage; often abused or emotionally neglected as a child. The daughter, or victim, may be attractive; well-developed; affectionate; the eldest daughter; an obedient girl; one who takes responsibility for household chores. The mother may be a passive, dependent person, incapable of protecting her children from a domineering husband; she may have been a victim herself as a child; or she may be absent from the home frequently due to work or illness.

Generally the development of incest is subtle and slow. When pathology is already present within the father, the behavior may occur sooner. But often the complicated nature of causal factors finds incest beginning innocently. There may be tickling, wrestling, and friendly play. Then these acts become more exploratory and frequently coercive. Incest may begin with fondling and proceed to masturbation or intercourse. Once begun, the acts tend to continue and become more involved. The father usually approaches the girl when he thinks she is asleep. The girl, confused and scared, feigns sleep. She may then pretend to waken, at which time father may leave.

In other more involved cases the father rapes or has intercourse with the daughter, bribing or threatening her to prevent disclosure. The father may have a pattern he follows when the mother is away or sleeping. The girl generally dreads these times but feels powerless to do anything. Fear of family disruption, rejection, punishment, and even guilt, may enter in. She may believe she is at fault and the cause of this. Who would believe her, anyway?

If the girl finally tells someone, the consequences are multiple. Disbelief on the mother's part, denial from the father, and relief from the daughter are seen. The daughter sometimes retracts her accusation because the family disruption may include jail for father, divorce, or foster home placement. In cases where the girl is already rebellious, reporting incest could be viewed as a weapon, which then backfires when the family is separated.

Treatment must begin with prevention. Marital communication and positive, intimate relationships are critical. Understanding one's own sexual feelings, processing those feelings without guilt, and focusing sexuality to the spouse are vital. Intimacy and affection toward the children must be nonsexual, treating the children as persons, not objects. Training families in appropriate means of expressing intimacy and affection and in building strong marital ties is one step churches could take to strengthen the family. Individuals who were abused as children should seek treatment or talk it out with the spouse to reduce the potential of behaving the same way.

In many states reporting incest results in the father's going to jail or the daughter's placement in a foster home. Treatment must include therapy for each individual as well as for the family unit. The family treatment issues are often complex in that incestuous families typically show many maladaptive patterns, poor conflict resolution, or a long history of marital discord. The alliances that developed between mother/daughter or father/daughter must be treated. The daughter needs support to believe that she was not at fault. Fear, guilt, and anger must be handled. Even if there was a hint of seductiveness by the daughter, it was the father's responsibility to avoid incest.

Fathers give many reasons for incest. Sex

education, preventing promiscuity, the daughter's seductiveness, and frigidity of the wife must all be seen as rationalizations. These must be challenged and personal responsibility admitted for healing to take place.

In many states the law requires mental health professionals to report to the appropriate authorities, in writing and by phone any case of incest that is exposed in therapy or treatment. Pastoral counselors are sometimes included in this requirement.

Additional Readings.
Meiselman, K. C. *Incest.* San Francisco: Jossey-Bass, 1978.
Mrazek, P. B., & Kempe, C. H. *Sexually abused children and their families.* New York: Pergamon Press, 1981.

L. N. FERGUSON

Incongruence. *See* CONGRUENCE.

Incorporation. The instinctual aim toward "swallowing" or taking in and making part of the ego external objects that are desirable or pleasurable. It is an ego DEFENSE MECHANISM. Though occurring symbolically in later years, the process has its roots in the oral phase of infancy, in which the attempt to ingest pleasurable external objects is quite literal. This is viewed in psychoanalytic theory as the original form of instinctual satisfaction, from which all sexual expressions are derived. An example may be seen in the person who seeks to envelop his spouse, incorporating her to the extent that he sees her largely as an extension of his own life and ego.

Individual Psychology. The theory of personality and method of diagnosis and treatment formulated by Adler. The term itself has a dual implication; *individual* refers both to the fact that each person has a unique personality and to the fact that the personality is an indivisible unit that cannot be separated into mental structures (e.g., drives, habits, or traits) that have an existence apart from the whole. Therefore, individual psychology is a personality theory that is both humanistic and holistic.

Historical Development. Individual psychology arose out of Adler's clinical practice and represented a synthesis of five basic intellectual roots. These influencing systems and persons provided Adler with many of his basic concepts. Janet spoke of inferiority feeling as the cause of neurosis. Nietzsche emphasized both the importance of the individual and the striving for perfection as a universal goal. Vaihinger contended that people were motivated by fictions (goals and interpretations) rather than reality. Marx identified social forces as the prime determinants of human behavior and urged reforms promoting equal opportunity regardless of birth or gender.

By far the greatest impact on individual psychology was that of Freud, with whom Adler collaborated for almost a decade. Freud's emphasis on the importance of early childhood and parental factors was adopted by Adler. One psychoanalytic perspective on determinism, that all behavior results from and reflects the underlying personality, was never doubted by Adler. However, he did dispute the claim that neither hereditary nor environmental forces could completely determine an individual's personality.

Adler's initial theoretical formulation came in 1907, after 10 years of general medical practice and five years of association with Freud. Adler sought the secret of the mind in the morphological and functional tendencies of the body. Specifically, he was impressed by the fact that if heredity, disease, or injury produced inferiority or damage to any organ or organ system, the body's health-oriented forces went to work to compensate either by rebuilding that organ or by increasing the organism's functional capacity in some other way. If a bone is broken, it heals in such a way that it is stronger at that point than it was before the break. Adler believed that this process of compensation was achieved because the organic inferiority became a stimulus to the central nervous system, which in turn stimulated the rebuilding of the affected organ and resulted in the kind of training which helped the organism meet the environment's needs despite the organic deficiency.

Because the central nervous system has a central role in this process, the dynamics of inferiority and compensation are bound to have an impact on the personality. The central psychological problem in humans is *Minderwertigkeitsgefühl*, inferiority feeling. Everything that a person does, thinks, and feels reflects that person's efforts to overcome inferiority feeling. Adler was a great optimist and firmly believed that although inferiority feeling was universal, all persons could successfully compensate and find happiness.

A year later, in 1908, Adler attempted to reduce compensation to a drive for power or aggression. He discarded the theory of the universality of this drive soon afterward, but kept the idea that all people strive for perfection. Later he termed this drive *masculine protest* and contended that only maladjusted people seek compensation via aggression, power over others, or blind rebellion.

Adler gradually increased his emphasis on social and interpersonal factors, such as the need for affection. By 1911 his view of humans as social rather than sexual beings led to a rift with Freud. Although Adler conceded that sexual components existed in most neuroses, he viewed them as being more symptomatic than casual. The oedipus complex, for example, was to be found only in little boys who felt inadequate to the challenges of the external world and therefore clung closely to their mothers. Any sexual attachment to the parent is secondary and the result of this clinging.

Also in 1911 Adler discovered the writings of Vaihinger, and soon adapted the latter's concept of fictional goals to individual psychology. Each person has a private logic through which objective reality becomes phenomenal reality. We cannot understand behavior in terms of causes but only in terms of goals and strivings. It is not the fact that someone has an organic inferiority or a traumatic experience in the past but the individual's interpretation (which is idiosyncratic or even unconscious) of the fact that determines behavior. The individual's general pattern of interpretation is a style of life, a guiding whole to which specific judgments and behaviors are subordinate. The tenacity with which an individual clings to a given behavior or thought reflects its centrality to the style of life or the degree to which it enables private logic to assuage feelings of inferiority. In general, the greater the feeling of inferiority, the more one holds to fictional goals. The small country has great passport formalities, reflecting the fictional belief that ceremony bespeaks (or compensates for) lack of) greatness.

Adler's later works developed the concept of *Gemeinschaftsgefühl*, which is usually translated as social interest. This is the degree to which the individual overcomes self-boundedness (*Ichgebundenheit*), the hold of private logic, and compensates for inferiority feeling via cooperative and constructive interaction with others. Social interest is the barometer of mental health and is manifested in three areas: friendship, family, and career. Having friends helps one overcome inferiority feeling because friendship allows one to be important to someone else. The interpersonal exchange between friends establishes objective, consensually validated reality that supplants some of the more rigid and dysfunctional aspects of private logic. Marriage is intended to supply the affection and approval that everyone needs

to avoid serious inferiority feeling, and also an opportunity to overcome self-boundedness by focusing on the needs of the spouse and offspring. Career is the opportunity to overcome inferiority feeling with a sense of accomplishment and contribution.

Before Adler's death in 1937 individual psychology had become an international movement with local societies in three dozen nations. Most of Adler's followers have been practitioners. Few have had any interest in revising his major precepts. Unlike the Freudians and Jungians, the Adlerians have not sought interaction with other disciplines, nor have they attracted historians, anthropologists, or literary critics into their fold.

Brachfeld (1951) carried individual psychology to Hungary and Spanish-speaking countries. He focused on inferiority feeling and reformulated it as auto-estimative instability, which is found to vary from one individual to another and even from situation to situation, being determined by the interaction of environmental demands and maturity.

Dreikurs (1950) was the chief apostle of individual psychology in the United States and Brazil. Most of his innovations and improvements were in the area of clinical practice, but several of his insights had theoretical import as well. Many of the parental mistakes in child rearing are due to the parents' own private logic. Dreikurs emphasized the principle of an impersonal order, rather than interpersonal power struggles, in discipline.

Low (1950) was closely associated with individual psychology in Vienna, but went his own way in the United States. He developed a peer group therapy that has grown into a self-help movement known as recovery. The basic principle is training in self-monitoring and will power.

One of the more creative offshoots of individual psychology was the "we" psychology of Kunkel (Kunkel & Dickerson, 1940). His attempt to synthesize individual psychology (Adler) and analytical psychology (Jung) was appreciated by neither Adler nor Jung. Kunkel deemphasized the organic basis for compensation. The newborn child lives in the world of the "primal we." This is disrupted by a breach-of-the-we experience in which the parent becomes seen as an other imposing demands upon the child: a white giant (fostering dependency) or a black giant (punishing). Everything in the child's personality that the parents reject becomes rejected by the child also and forms the basis for inferiority feeling (the shadow). The solution is the we-experience and anything that serves the developing we-group.

Clinical Applications. *Psychopathology.* Neurotics are to be understood as persons who have not managed to achieve compensation through social interest. They do not continue on the path of social interest because they have lost courage. The neurosis is not a mere reversion to an infantile form. It can be a creative attempt to find a sham superiority. Obsessive thoughts and compulsive behaviors are attempts to defend the private logic from the encroachments of reality. Other neurotics (e.g., the depressives) love to wallow in inferiority feelings because it renders them pitiable and occasionally provides the sympathy that meets their need for affection.

Psychotics handle the conflict between reality and fiction by severing contact with reality. In his delusional world the paranoid is the most important person on earth, for how else could he be the target of international and interstellar conspiracies? Some schizophrenics believe that they are famous persons or have special creativity. All these delusions serve to provide the feeling of superiority not given by social interaction.

Psychosomatic, hypochondriacal, and conversion reactions illustrate what Adler called organ dialect. These physical disorders, real or imagined, bespeak the individual's improper life style. Physical disorder can serve as an excuse for failure and a plea for sympathy. Sexual dysfunctions fall into this category and manifest a failure in overcoming self-boundedness—i.e., a lack of social interest.

Personality disorders, delinquency, crime, etc. spring from masculine protest, the attempt to overcome inferiority feeling through rebellion and violence instead of participation and production. Prostitution and addictive behavior are due to strong and unresolved inferiority feeling coupled with an ambivalent approach to dependency.

Diagnostic techniques. Adler and Dreikurs developed several methods of discovering the patient's style of life. Early childhood recollections were elicited by the question, "What is the farthest back that your memory can go?" The patient's response may be inaccurate, but that is not important. The technique is essentially projective. The patient unconsciously distorts the situation recalled in order to have it reflect chosen life goals.

Dreams are another projective technique, but focus more on the current situation and short-range goals. The dream is a rehearsal for coping in real life. The dream content reflects the present challenges in the environment. The dreamer's behavior in the dream is the key to coping strategies. Adler contended that successful coping in waking life removed the need for rehearsal; he mistakenly believed that mentally healthy people did not dream.

Another technique for understanding the style of life is a thorough history of the patient's childhood. Adler believed that the style of life was fairly fixed by age 6 and that such factors as parental relations, sibling relations, and physical diseases had an impact. The Adlerian psychologist asks about childhood illnesses and the family constellation. Of special interest is birth order and any evidence of pampering or neglect by the parents.

Because all behavior is determined by fictional goals, Adlerians are also interested in body language—firmness of handshake, eye contact, slouching, etc. Adler once said that you could observe a patient as you would a mime, ignoring all his words, and render an accurate diagnosis. Even current physical disorders are a tip-off. Adler would ask his patients something like this: "If you were cured of this disorder, what would happen to you?" The answer reveals what the disease is a defense against.

Treatment. Both Adler and Freud probed the patient's childhood, trying to understand central conflicts and to convey this insight to the patient. Adlerian psychotherapy differs from psychoanalysis in several basic respects. The client sits in a chair and faces the therapist. Progress should be apparent in weeks, and treatment should be completed in less than a year. The therapist does not attempt to get the client to have an abreaction, but to build the capacity for self-control.

Adler was a precursor of Rogers in advocating that the psychotherapist accept the patient as human being, without conditions or restrictions. (Giving this gift freely models social interest.) Adler analogized the therapist's role to the maternal function: providing emotional support and encouragement but moving the patient along to an eventual independence. However, he cautioned therapists to be on guard against giving a patient sympathy that would provide reinforcement for being inferior. Furthermore, therapists must try to prevent the development of any transference relationship that would prolong childish dependency. Finally, the therapist must be optimistic and concerned, and yet not express too much personal interest in the recovery of patients, lest they be tempted to demonstrate their (fictive) power by proving that they can still decide to fail despite the therapist's best efforts on their behalf.

Adler was a master at developing insight in patients by responding with the unexpected. When one patient called at three in the morning, desiring his attention over some trivial matter, she apologized for awakening him. Adler replied that he had been sitting at his phone for half an hour waiting for her call. She gained the insight that she was behaving like a pampered child. A syphilophobe saw Adler and explained that every other physician in Vienna had failed to diagnose the dreaded disease, but the patient was certain that he had it. Without any further examination Adler agreed with the patient, who immediately began arguing with Adler, citing the prior medical tests as evidence.

Dreikurs had a technique called antisuggestion. If a patient told Dreikurs about an uncontrollable urge that the patient was attempting to hold in check, the suggestion was to practice that which the patient was making an effort against. Another technique would be to concede that if the therapist had the same goal and private logic that the patient had, the former would have the latter's problems as well.

The first phase of therapy is devoted to developing empathy and insight. The cultivation of the patient's social interest is the subsequent phase. If the foundations of empathy and insights about self-boundedness have been established, the social interest develops easily. Many therapists find that it is helpful to assist the clients with specific opportunities for the expression of social interest.

Child rearing. Because the style of life is harder to change after age 5, the process of child rearing has a great impact on mental health. Adler viewed child rearing as the process of directing the emerging strivings for superiority into social interest channels. Adler's great optimism was due to the fact that he believed parents could be educated in the proper techniques of cultivating social interest in their children.

When the child's inferiority feeling is great, it becomes difficult to promote proper guidance. All children start off with some degree of inferiority feeling due to the fact that they are born into an adult world. They are smaller, weaker, and lacking in learned skills and adult privileges. This is why children pretend to be adults. Children who are also inferior compared to other children due to handicaps, athletic inability, appearance, or lower intelligence have their inferiority feelings intensified.

Another factor that can intensify these feelings is a faulty parent-child relationship. Children are good observers but poor interpreters. Harshly treated or neglected children wonder why their parents mistreat them and conclude that the fault lies within themselves. Parents who are too demanding make the child feel inferior to what is expected. At the other extreme overprotective parents convey to the child their belief that the child is too weak to fend for himself. Parents who spoil the child convey the message that the child is entitled to receive without giving, and this makes true social interest harder to cultivate.

Adler also emphasized the importance of birth order and sibling relations in the development of personality. Oldest children were prone to have overly demanding parenting. Later borns usually compared themselves unfavorably with older siblings. If a later born actually surpassed an older sibling in something, the effect on the older sibling was devastating. Youngest and only children ran a high risk of being pampered. Whenever one child receives more attention than the others, an unfortunate rivalry could be the result.

The best atmosphere is one that is supportive and encourages the child to develop independence. Discipline is a necessary aspect, but it is best accomplished by an all-embracing impersonal order to which everyone, including parents, is subject. This begins with regular feeding schedules. Misbehavior is due to an attempt to gain attention, demonstrate defiance of overly dominating parents, or seek revenge. Adlerians do not favor corporal punishment because it reconfirms the belief that children are powerless and all others are against them. Nagging and scolding are likewise counterproductive. Identify the problem behavior, but never ridicule or prophesy a bad end for the child.

Aging. Many of the adjustment problems at the other end of the life cycle can also be comprehended from the perspective of individual psychology. The increasing physical disability brought about by chronic diseases coupled with changing appearance can yield an intensified feeling of inferiority. This is compounded by a youth-oriented society that no longer respects the knowledge of the elders. The reduced income of the aged adds a financial dimension of inferiority.

Simultaneously with the increase of inferiority feeling, many changes in later life reduce the opportunities for healthy compensation through family, friends, and career. Old friends die, move away to institutions, or become deaf.

The elder's mobility becomes reduced, and there is less chance to see friends. Children grow up, leave the nest, and move away. The loss of a spouse is the greatest blow to the family. Retirement brings an end to the productive participation in one's career. The opportunities for finding new friends, family, or productive endeavors are quite limited in later life.

Many elders, for financial and/or physical reasons, become dependent on their adult offspring or on institutions. Dysfunctional relationships can arise from this. In certain institutions where the staff discourages independent behavior on the part of the patients they are overprotected, though not exactly pampered. More frequently the aged's needs are neglected, and sometimes older people are harshly treated by those charged with their care.

The intensified inferiority feelings, reduced opportunities for compensation, and dysfunctional relationships distort guiding fictions, resulting in excessive rigidity and even senile behavior. The way to prevent many geriatric problems is to make sure that elders have adequate opportunity to express their social interest.

Religious Implications. Adler regarded the idea of God as a fiction that embodied the ideals of perfection, power, superiority, and social interest. Hall (1971) described Adler as rejecting the God of the prophets and the God of the philosophers and substituting a synthesis of being and value, a final goal that can serve as a transcendent basis for the ideal community. Adler criticized atheists for trying to bolster their own sense of superiority by conquering God.

Adler's view of the social aspect of religion was positive, insofar as it is a technique of increasing social interest. Unlike Freud, Adler did not analogize religion to a neurosis, but he was critical of the way in which neurotic individuals perverted religion to serve their faulty styles of life. Anyone who claims a private pipeline to heaven is seeking a sham superiority. This is also the case with highly moralistic people who are eager to note sinfulness in others.

Yet individual psychology offers a framework within which we may gain new insights about Christian theology. The fall is the realization of inferiority feeling, especially the knowledge that one lacks immortality. The fall is necessary for salvation in that it is our defects that spur compensation. The law brings a guiding fiction against which men are

measured. Those who live under the law either feel inferior because they cannot live up to it or proud because, like the Pharisees, they believe they have fulfilled it, and claim a sham superiority. But the motivating factor under the law is self-boundedness: the individual attempts to protect himself from God's wrath or win a place in heaven. Life under works is the piecemeal attempt to deny inferiority. The essence of Christianity is a call for the individual to transcend his self-boundedness and develop a wholesome social interest, manifested in love and charity. The inferiority feeling does not condemn one who lives under grace. Life in the Spirit is the realistic evaluation of one's shortcomings and a commitment to their improvement.

Critique. There are several bases for the evaluation of any school of psychology. Internal consistency in individual psychology is adequate, but some of the interrelations of the internal mechanisms are not clear. Does inferiority feeling counteract social interest, or vice versa? Does the adherence to an inappropriate fiction cause inferiority feeling, or vice versa? Adlerians seem to argue it both ways, depending on the situation.

A further test of any theory is its ability to comprehend phenomena. Individual psychology, like psychoanalysis, is a remarkably flexible system that can be used to understand the dynamics of almost all clinical material, child development, aging, art forms, religion, social and political phenomena. Adler's critics contend that his capacity to facilitate understanding is broad but not very deep, and the resulting level of understanding is little more than common sense or naïveté (Ewen, 1980). Adler (Dreikurs, 1950) has responded that people are misled by the apparent simplicity of individual psychology, and that most people who dismiss it as common sense do not fully comprehend it. Szasz (1973) lauded the direct, commonsense approach in individual psychology and lamented the fact that people have an innate tendency to follow the mystification employed by would-be leaders.

The fact that a theory can generate empirically verifiable predictions is often taken as a touchstone for the scientific status of that theory. Prediction is not the strength of individual psychology. Adler's theory does not enable us to make any prediction about how a person will behave as an adult if he is treated a certain way as a child. An inferiority feeling makes some people excessively shy and others boastful and aggressive. Adult neuroses could be due to pampering or to neglect. Clinicians are not able to use early recollections or dreams to predict what the patient will do next. Indeed, there is scant evidence on the reliability and validity of those procedures. On the positive side, Adler's theory of the impact of birth order has received a great deal of confirmation from correlational studies (Altus, 1966). Adler's basic assumptions about man's evolutionary history are endorsed by other disciplines (Montague, 1970).

Perhaps the greatest testimonial to Adler's theories has been the extent to which other theorists have accepted them, although in slightly altered form. Freud's ideas have been the best remembered, but Adler's have been the most rediscovered. Jung (1953) agreed that the inferiority complex was a major factor in introverts and admitted that he used Adlerian techniques in treating younger patients. The existentialists have emphasized the importance of uniqueness and fictions. Maslow's self-actualizers have gotten over the need to defend against inferiority feeling. The Adlerian duty of making a contribution to the whole parallels Fromm's idea of the productive character. Rogers's emphasis on empathy is an outgrowth of one aspect of Adlerian therapy. Beck's (1976) cognitive therapy is a development of another. Wilder (1959) commented that the question is no longer whether one is an Adlerian, but how much of an Adlerian one is.

References
Altus, W. D. Birth order and its sequelae. *Science*, 1966, *151*, 44–49.
Beck, A. T. *Cognitive therapy and the emotional disorders.* New York: International Universities Press, 1976.
Brachfeld, O. *Inferiority feelings.* New York: Grune & Stratton, 1951.
Dreikurs, R. *Fundamentals of Adlerian Psychology.* New York: Greenberg, 1950.
Ewen, R. B. *An introduction to theories of personality.* New York: Academic Press, 1980.
Hall, R. W. Alfred Adler's concept of God. *Journal of Individual Psychology*, 1971, *27*, 10–18.
Jung, C. G. [*Psychological reflections: An anthology from the writings of C. G. Jung*] (J. Jacobi, Ed.). New York: Pantheon, 1953.
Kunkel, F., & Dickerson, R. *How character develops: A psychological interpretation.* New York: Scribner's, 1940.
Low, A. *Mental health through will-training.* Boston: Christopher Publishing, 1950.
Montague, A. Social interest and aggression as potentialities. *Journal of Individual Psychology*, 1970, *26*, 17–31.
Szasz, T. *The second sin.* Garden City, N.Y.: Anchor, 1973.
Wilder, J. Alfred Adler's influence. In K. Adler, & D. Deutsch, (Eds.), *Essays in individual psychology.* New York: Grove Press, 1959.

Additional Readings
Adler, A. *The individual psychology of Alfred Adler.* New York: Basic Books, 1956.
Adler, A. *Superiority and social interest.* Evanston, Ill.: Northwestern University Press, 1964.

Brink, T. L. Adlerian theory and pastoral care. *Journal of Psychology and Theology*, 1977, *5*, 143–149.
Mosak, H. H., & Mosak, B. *A bibliography for Adlerian psychology.* Washington, D.C.: Hemisphere, 1975.

T. L. BRINK

Individuation. A Jungian concept that denotes the process by which a person becomes a psychological individual—i.e., an indivisible unity or whole. This process of self-realization involves differentiating a totality called the self from all the components of the personality. Thus, individuation is a synthetic process of integrating the various components of personality to the point that the parts, especially the conscious and the unconscious, begin to complement rather than oppose one another. The result is a self that is supraordinate even to the conscious ego.

According to Jung the process of individuation takes place typically during the last half of life. Throughout the first half of one's life the concern is with developing the distinct personifications such as ego, persona, shadow, conscious, unconscious, and anima or animus. These separate subpersonalities are oppositional to each other. For example, the conscious, opposes the unconscious, and the ego opposes the shadow. The data of one component of personality are often threatened by the data of its counterpart. Individuation means, then, the breaking up of these separate components, transcending their oppositional forces, and coming to unique selfhood.

The mechanism for the transformation of a network of subpersonifications into a unified, whole person is a dialetical encounter between and among the various partial personalities. To illustrate, the conscious can be seen as the thesis, the unconscious, the antithesis, and the new self as the resulting synthesis. When individuation is complete, the components no longer suppress, oppose, and injure one another; instead, the dynamic forces of personality are harmonized, balanced, and centered. The person has become a true self and experiences wholeness and inner peace and quiet.

Jung's concept of individuation should not be confused with Mahler's concept of separation-individuation, which refers to a much earlier developmental process occurring in the mother-child relationship.

Additional Reading
Jung, C. G. Conscious, unconscious, and individuation. In C. G. Jung, *The archetypes and the collective unconscious.* New York: Pantheon, 1959.

D. SMITH

See ANALYTICAL PSYCHOLOGY.

Industrial/Organizational Psychology. For most people work is one of life's central and most time-consuming activities. Industrial/organizational psychology uses psychological principles and research methods to further our understanding of this very important human activity. As a basic scientist the industrial/organizational psychologist is concerned with developing general theories or models that help us organize and make sense of the often confusing and complex pattern of worker behavior (e.g., identifying effective leader behaviors). As an applied scientist the industrial/organizational psychologist puts these theories and models to use in solving specific work behavior problems (e.g., helping an organization reduce turnover).

Contemporary industrial/organizational psychology is composed of three overlapping areas: human factors, personnel psychology, and organizational psychology. The human factors area, sometimes called human engineering, focuses largely on the problem of developing machines that are compatible with the sensory, perceptual, and information-processing capabilities of human beings. Human factors psychologists, for example, have been involved in the development of instrument systems that enable aircraft and nuclear power plant personnel to operate their machines more safely and efficiently. Researchers in this area are also involved in the design of work environments, taking into consideration the effects of such factors as heat, noise, and work schedules on worker performance and satisfaction.

Personnel psychology has its roots in three key ideas: 1) People differ with respect to significant psychological and behavioral characteristics (e.g., technical knowledge, social skills, mathematical ability). 2) Jobs differ with respect to the psychological and behavioral demands they make on the worker (e.g., deadlines, resolving staff conflicts). 3) People and organizations are most satisfied and productive when people are placed in jobs that match their abilities and interests. Using psychological tests and measures to assess individual differences and job analysis procedures to assess job differences, the personnel psychologist assists organizations in selecting new employees, identifying optimal career paths for current employees, and appraising worker performance on the job. Where employees need further knowledge or skills to meet present or future job demands, the personnel psychologist is often involved in the development and evaluation of training programs for an organization.

Organizational psychology is basically the social psychology of work. With its historical roots in the famous Hawthorne study at General Electric, organizational psychology emphasizes the importance of interpersonal relations in the work setting. Recognizing that social motives (e.g., fellowship, recognition) play a crucial role in work behavior, organizational psychologists are keenly interested in basic questions of worker motivation and satisfaction. Leadership, power, and conflict in work groups are also important problems in the organizational psychology domain.

Industrial/organizational psychologists are employed in a variety of settings, including industry (35%), universities (25%), consulting firms (25%), and government (15%). Preparation for working as an industrial/organizational psychologist typically involves completion of the Ph.D., but a number of schools do offer master's degrees in the field. Primary resources for research and practice are the *Journal of Applied Psychology, Personnel Psychology, Academy of Management Journal*, and *Organizational Behavior and Human Performance*. Most industrial/organizational psychologists are members of the Society for Industrial/Organizational Psychology, which is a division of the American Psychological Association. The membership directory of this division is an excellent resource for organizations interested in obtaining the specialized services of an industrial/organizational psychologist. Although many industrial/organizational psychologists are licensed as consulting psychologists in their state of residence, there is no special credential for practicing industrial/organizational psychology. For this reason organizations should be very careful in selecting consultants who claim expertise in this area and should contact the Society for Industrial/Organizational Psychology when questions arise.

D. D. McKenna

See Applied Psychology.

Inferiority Complex. The idea that every person feels inferior and that this complex underlies all human behavior forms the core of Adler's system of Individual Psychology. However, the idea of the inferiority complex did not begin or end with Adler. Similar concepts can be found in literary and philosophical sources: Montaigne, Shakespeare, Hobbes, Rousseau, Mandeville, Stendahl. Several authors, including the Swiss theologian Haberlin, have attempted to classify inferiority feelings.

Psychologists have speculated about the

relationship between internal and external factors in the inferiority complex. James spoke of an innate craving to be appreciated, and attributed mental anguish to the feeling that one was insignificant or unworthy of appreciation. Janet spoke of an obsessional impulse of self-shame. Adler initially believed inferiority feeling to be due to myelodysplasia, organ inferiority, but later broadened the concept of inferiority to include social factors, especially interpersonal relations in early childhood. Freud reduced the inferiority complex to the girl's penis envy and the boy's feeling of inadequate genitals after a comparison with his father. Jung believed that inferiority feelings were especially characteristic in the introvert and resulted in dissociation of the personality via repression and projection of everything dark and culpable (the shadow).

The empirical study of inferiority feelings has been hampered by problems with operational meaning. Several self-esteem scales exist, but both validity and reliability are questionable. Murray (1938), after using a comprehensive battery of tests to examine 50 normal, young male adults, concluded that 68% had suffered from inferiority feelings. Numerous factors have been correlated with low self-esteem: physical defects (handicaps, obesity, ugliness, stature, weakness, or poor coordination); parental factors (pampering, neglect, ridicule, contrasts with other children, favoritism); teasing; defeat or failure (academic, athletic, sexual, social); poverty; lack of group acceptance. The correlations are far from perfect because inferiority feeling is a negative emotional reaction, not an objective evaluation of a deficiency. The degree of inferiority feeling is heavily determined by subjective factors and standards of comparison. A man who earns $50,000 a year has a comfortable income but may feel inferior to an entrepreneural sibling who has amassed a fortune. No one makes us feel inferior without our consent.

Inferiority feelings may induce different kinds of behavior in different persons. One response (the true inferiority complex) is resignation, conscious acceptance of the inferior role, and the attempt to use it to gain sympathy and avoid responsibility. One alcoholic who had not worked for 25 years told everyone about his condition, blaming war injuries from the Korean conflict. Another reaction is to deprecate others, especially those persons who somehow make us feel inferior. Employees who are passed over are quick to accuse the promoted co-worker of being a yes-man. Another response is to attempt to overcome the factor responsible for the inferiority feeling, and in so doing, many persons overcompensate and become superior. Glenn Cunningham, whose legs were badly burned as a child, ran in order to rehabilitate his limbs and became a champion distance runner. Theodore Roosevelt, a nearsighted and sickly child, learned boxing and horseback riding in order to toughen himself. Able-bodied motorists have an accident rate almost 20 times that of handicapped drivers. Ray (1957) contends that people do not succeed in spite of an inferiority complex but because of one. She gives many heartwarming and inspiring examples of how inferiority feelings spur people on to success through overcompensations. The treatment of an inferiority complex is generally best accomplished by the techniques of individual psychology, where the emphasis is on encouraging compensation through useful contributions to others (social interest).

Inferiority feeling can be a useful tool in explaining many social phenomena. An advertisement states that sophisticated people use a certain product and then relies on the audience's inferiority feeling to generate sales. Various authors have contended that ethnic stereotypes have a kernel of truth, and describe characteristic behaviors that developed in societies and subcultures as a response to inferiority feeling. The Americans' drive for wealth was an attempt to respond to their feeling inferior about Europe's culture. The Mexicans' machismo is a response to feeling inferior to Europe's culture and America's wealth (Ramos, 1962). Some blacks drive large automobiles, wear flashy clothes, and use big words as a compensation for inferiority feelings. Many strikes (especially the violent ones) are largely unnecessary for economic gains, yet they give workers a feeling of power to compensate for their normal feelings of inferiority with respect to management.

Theologically, inferiority feeling can be seen as the result of pride and refusal to accept the status of creature. Humans are inferior to the Creator; but once humans accept that role, and realize that all other humans are mere creatures, they need feel inferior to no one else.

References

Murray, H. A. Explorations in personality. New York: Oxford University Press, 1938.

Ramos, S. Profile of man and culture in Mexico. Austin: University of Texas Press, 1962.

Ray, M. B. The importance of feeling inferior. New York: Harper & Row, 1957.

Additional Reading

Brachfeld, O. Inferiority feelings. New York: Grune & Stratton, 1951.

T. L. BRINK

Inhibited Orgasm. In the male inhibited orgasm is called retarded ejaculation (Kaplan, 1974) or ejaculatory incompetence (Masters & Johnson, 1970); in the female, commonly used terms are orgastic dysfunction or anorgasmia.

Male orgasm is brought about by stimulation of the penis. The ejaculatory reflex involves involuntary .8-second spasms of the muscles at the base of the penis. Female orgasm is produced by stimulation of the clitoris and also involves involuntary .8-second muscle spasms.

There are several differences in male and female orgastic responses. In contrast to the male, the female does not ejaculate. The amount of time that must elapse between orgasms is much longer for men than for women. This refractory period varies with men of different ages, but women are able to experience repeated, multiple orgasms if desired. Lastly, the female orgasm is far more vulnerable to inhibition than the male's. While the exact reasons are not known, conjecture includes cultural conditioning, the differences in size and sensitivity between the penis and clitoris, and hormonal characteristics.

While retarded ejaculation entails selective impairment of the ejaculatory response, the ability to achieve a firm penile erection is not diminished, nor is the capacity to respond to sexual stimuli with erotic feelings. Although they definitely want to ejaculate and have adequate penile stimulation men suffering from retarded ejaculation have trouble experiencing the orgastic reflex. The range of inhibition varies from occasional and mild to constant and severe. The man may be unable to ejaculate during intercourse with a particular woman but may be successful with another woman who does not evoke anxiety. Some men may not be able to ejaculate in the presence of a woman but are able to successfully masturbate alone. The most severe ejaculatory inhibition includes those men who have never experienced orgasm under any circumstances.

Orgastic dysfunction in the female is termed primary if the woman has never experienced an orgasm. It is termed secondary if the condition develops after a period of being able to reach orgasm. A further distinction is made as to whether the incidence pattern is absolute or situational. If it is absolute, the woman is unable to achieve orgasm under any circumstances. In situational orgastic dysfunction the woman may reach a climax but only under certain conditions.

The amount of direct or indirect clitoral stimulation required to bring about orgasm in the female varies a great deal not only between persons but also in the same woman under different circumstances. For example, the same woman could conceivably climax as a result of mental imagery or fantasy in a given time and place but only upon direct, intense clitoral stimulation on another occasion. The range seems to be between the extremes of no orgasm to orgasm with fantasy, with a mid-range of orgasm with clitoral or coital stimulation.

Etiology. In contrast to erectile dysfunction an organic or physiologic basis for retarded ejaculation is very rare. However, even when circumstances clearly point toward psychological bases, a physical examination is appropriate. At the same time, the genesis of most cases of retarded ejaculation involves an involuntary, unconscious, and conditioned psychological inhibition. The bases might be a home environment that engendered sexual guilt, some type of unresolved intrapsychic conflict, suppressed anger, resentment toward the sexual partner, or a symbolic fear of abandonment, to name just a few.

A commonplace theme for women with orgastic dysfunction or anorgasmia is fear of losing control over feelings and behavior. This tendency to hold back or overcontrol is central to the orgastic dysfunction and varies in its susceptibility to change. The condition may or may not be related to the quality of the couple's relationship. Most often it is rooted in other factors, such as fear of imagined sexual intensity, fear of abandonment (wanting to please the spouse by being a "good girl," meaning not sexual or promiscuous), fear of being assertive, sexual guilt, or ambivalence about the spouse.

Traditional Christian moral teaching finds ample support when anorgasmia is viewed as the end result of a conditioning process involving not letting go. If the young woman ignores the injunction to avoid sexual arousal prior to marriage, the orgastic inhibition may originate with a conscious holding back of sexual feelings lest they become overpowering. In this way control over sexual arousal is reinforced by the reduction of anxiety accompanying desired but prohibited sexual feelings. When this conscious control of sexual arousal is mastered, the inhibition may become automatic so that orgasm is impeded even under the most ideal conditions. In short, it would be preferable to have not engaged in the sexual activity that requires conscious restraint of emotional, sexual involvement.

Treatment. Clinical psychotherapeutic treatment of inhibited orgasm will vary with each practitioner's orientation. However, a trained and certified sex therapist will most likely employ an integration of psychoanalytic, behavioral, and systems theories. In practical terms this means that the therapist will explore past events as a means of understanding the orgastic inhibition, examine the quality of the couple's relationship, and assign specific, behavioral, homework tasks for the individual and/or couple to accomplish.

Treatment procedures will not follow a set outline. Basic principles will be selectively applied by experienced therapists to meet the unique needs and situation of a particular client. Modern sex therapy consists largely of variations or modifications of the basic behavioral techniques developed by Masters and Johnson (1970). The key ingredient is the willingness of the couple to complete assigned tasks to be accomplished in the privacy of their home. A basic assumption is that the person experiencing inhibited orgasm has a partner willing to undergo sex therapy with him or her.

In cases of retarded ejaculation the ultimate goal is for the man to achieve intravaginal ejaculation. The couple is assigned a series of progressively more stimulating sexual tasks to reach the goal. Commonly they would first be instructed to engage in whatever sexual activity they enjoy together but not to attempt ejaculation or have sexual intercourse. In mild cases this paradoxical instruction may be sufficient to overcome the orgastic inhibition. Pivotal variables are the skill and power of the therapist, the level of compliance and motivation of the couple, and the strength of the therapist-client relationship.

The next step is for the couple to continue the satisfying nonejaculatory experiences. The objective is to experience heightened sexual arousal while gradually extinguishing thoughts or fears of sexual failure. The man is then told that he may attempt to ejaculate only under circumstances where he knows he will succeed. After this has been frequently and effortlessly accomplished, the couple is instructed to have the wife manipulate the husband's penis until ejaculation occurs. A gradual transition is then made until the husband is able to ejaculate inside his wife's vagina. This process is often much more difficult and complex than what is outlined here for the sake of brevity.

In female anorgasmia the goal and the manner in which orgasm is reached will vary among couples. Some women are content only if they are successful in achieving orgasm during coitus, while others are satisfied to reach orgasm only with an electric vibrator. The key issue is for the wife, husband, and therapist to be satisfied with the method of attaining orgasm. Overcoming orgastic inhibition is well within the reach of any reasonably motivated woman.

Whether the woman is experiencing primary or secondary orgastic dysfunction, the first, crucial step after establishing a therapeutic, trusting relationship with the therapist and extinguishing as many inhibitory factors as possible is to coach the woman on how to achieve orgasm through masturbation. This approach is necessary for the wife to gain self-knowledge about the steps she must experience to attain orgasm. After resolution of any unconscious fears of orgasm, development of pubococcygeal musculature, and abandonment of overcontrol mechanisms, orgasm is usually achieved. If not, use of an electric vibrator may be employed for a time before tasks are assigned to achieve orgasm with the husband. (See Kaplan, 1974, for a full discussion of treatment procedures for both female and male inhibited orgasm.)

Finally, it should be kept in mind that sexual arousal takes time. Research indicates that most married couples have sexual intercourse two to three times per week for an average of eight minutes per session (Reichert, 1981). This is an inadequate amount of time for many women to achieve sufficient vascular engorgement of the genitalia to allow the orgastic reflex to occur. With sufficient time, adequate knowledge, and a caring relationship, anorgasmia is surmountable.

References

Kaplan, H. S. *The new sex therapy: Active treatment of sexual dysfunctions.* New York: Brunner/Mazel, 1974.
Masters, W. H., Johnson, V. E. *Human sexual inadequacy.* Boston: Little, Brown, 1970.
Reichert, R. *Sexuality and dating: A Christian perspective.* Winona, Minn.: St. Mary's Press, 1981.

J. R. DAVID

See SEX THERAPY; SEXUAL RESPONSE PSYCHOLOGY.

Inhibited Sexual Desire. Human sexual response consists of three separate but interconnected phases: sexual desire, excitement, and orgasm. Their differentiation is based on distinct physiological occurrences in both sexes. Sexual dysfunction may involve one or more or all three of the phases.

Sexual desire dysfunction is generally present due to unconscious psychological factors, the removal of which are tenaciously guarded against. The prognosis for spontaneous recovery is extremely poor. With psychotherapeutic treatment from even the most expert and gifted of clinicians, successful outcome using brief sex therapy currently approximates only 10 to 15% (Kaplan, 1979). The search for more effective psychosexual modalities is ongoing.

The absence of sexual desire is believed to be the most prevalent of all the sexual dysfunctions in the American population. *DSM-III* defines inhibited sexual desire as persistent and pervasive absence of sexual desire. Understandably, determining the presence of inhibited sexual desire must be weighed against recognized norms of sexual behavior and the individual's total life situation. It is not usually symptomatic of another psychiatric condition.

Kaplan (1979) uses the term *inhibited sexual desire* for low libido or sexual appetite due to psychic factors. The term *hypoactive sexual desire* is used when specific causation is undetermined. The Masters and Johnson term, *sexual avoidance*, is imprecise, and is different from inhibited sexual desire in that an appropriate level of desire may coexist with phobic avoidance.

Primary hypoactive sexual desire is rare and is defined as a lifelong history of asexuality, being totally devoid of sexual interest. Secondary hypoactive sexual desire is relatively common and is present when there is a loss of sexual appetite after a history of normal sexual interest. It may be associated with physical ailments or psychological crises such as developmental stress, severe rejection, loss, anger or disillusionment with spouse, or work related pressures.

The loss of sex drive may also be total (global) or situational. A global loss involves the complete absence of erotic ideation and is commonly seen with depression, severe stress, and physical causes. Situational hypoactive sexual desire has a psychogenic basis in that the person feels desire only in situations that are psychically safe for them. A typical example of this is absence of sexual desire with one's regular, appropriate sexual partner but normal desire with strangers, prostitutes, or persons of a lower social class. The key issue is that the sexually appropriate situation, on a symbolic and unconscious level, is seen as dangerous and threatening.

Careful differential diagnosis is essential to ensure correct treatment measures. Physiologic and psychiatric bases must be ruled out prior to ascertaining psychogenic inhibited sexual desire. Also, in some situations sexual desire is appropriately inhibited or not encouraged. Persons suffering from inhibited sexual desire are unaware of the roots of their condition and are generally powerless to change it without professional intervention. While they are probably functioning well in other areas of life, referral to a competent clinician is appropriate if requested.

Reference
Kaplan, H. S. *Disorders of sexual desire and other new concepts and techniques in sex therapy.* New York: Brunner/ Mazel, 1979.

J. R. DAVID

See SEXUAL RESPONSE PSYCHOLOGY, SEXUALITY.

Inhibited Sexual Excitement. In both sexes inhibited sexual excitement involves some degree of impairment of the genital vasocongestive reaction. This psychophysiological lessening of the vascular system's effort to increase the genital blood supply results in a diminished or absent penile erection and reduction of vaginal lubrication and swelling.

The partial or total impairment of the male's capacity for penile erection was formerly termed *impotency* but is now labeled *erectile dysfunction*, thus avoiding the negative or pejorative connotation of the earlier term. The same reasoning has prompted replacing female *frigidity* with *general sexual dysfunction* (Kaplan, 1974) when referring to reduced or total absence of vaginal lubrication and swelling.

Prior to the pioneering research of Masters and Johnson human sexual response was little understood by both professionals and the general populace. There was a tendency to group any type of sexual dysfunction under the single heading of either male impotency or female frigidity. Masters and Johnson (1966) divided male and female sexual response into four stages: excitement, plateau, orgasm, and resolution. The excitement stage has several features. Generally it begins with the presence of erotic feelings. Physiological responses include heavier breathing, increased heart rate and blood pressure, genital vasocongestion manifested in penile erection or vaginal swelling, and temporary rigidity of musculature (myotonia). In women an uneven coloration of the skin (mottling) is often marked. The breasts swell in size and the nipples become erect.

The predominant aspect of the female sexual response during the excitement phase is vaginal lubrication. The vascular engorgement of the female genitalia, brought about by the increased supply of blood, causes the vaginal lubrication to pass through and form on the vaginal walls within 10 to 30 seconds after initiation of sexual stimulation. In some women the clitoris may become erect due to vasocongestion. At the same time the vaginal area enlarges to accommodate the penis.

During the course of clinical practice the Masters and Johnson four-stage description of human sexual response was questioned when it became apparent that the orgastic and vasocongestive responses in men and women were not unitary phenomena. For women orgasm may occur without vaginal lubrication and swelling, or vice versa. The same distinct, separate psychosexual functioning is evident in men in that ejaculation may occur without penile erection, and ejaculation may be retarded even though penile erection is attained.

Thus, human sexual response may be viewed as a two-phase process involving two separate physiologic components. The first is the genital vasocongestive reaction, which is governed by the parasympathetic portion of the autonomic nervous system. The second is the orgasm or orgastic reaction governed by the sympathetic portion of the autonomic nervous system (Kaplan, 1974). Later, this descriptive schema was expanded to include sexual desire as the initial step (Kaplan, 1979). For present purposes, inhibited sexual excitement is manifested by and includes impairment of male erectile functioning and female vaginal lubrication.

Erectile Dysfunction. Erectile dysfunction may be caused by physical or psychological factors. Erection fails to occur when the vascular reflex mechanism pumps insufficient blood to render the penis firm and erect. The person having an erectile dysfunction may feel aroused and excited during sexual contact, but his penis does not become erect. Ejaculation may occur with a flaccid or nonerect penis.

Erectile dysfunction is classified as *primary* or *secondary*. Primary erectile dysfunction is defined as never having experienced a firm penile erection while engaged in mutual heterosexual activity. The person may or may not experience erections by masturbating or due to other stimuli. Secondary erectile dysfunction is present when a person has a history of successful erectile functioning prior to the onset of the dysfunction. Ease of resolution of either primary or secondary erectile dysfunction is directly related to the length or duration of the impairment. In general, the treatment prognosis is better for secondary.

Every person experiencing erectile dysfunction should have a medical examination prior to entering psychological treatment. Penile erection depends on the complex interaction of hormonal, vascular, and neural mechanisms. Erectile dysfunction may be caused by general fatigue, diabetes, androgen deficiency, substance abuse, various prescription medications, and other medical conditions.

Psychological causes of erectile dysfunction may be relatively superficial and amenable to treatment, or they may be at a deeper, unconscious level and resistant to treatment. Several possible causes are performance anxiety, castration anxiety, interpersonal discord, guilt about sexuality, fear of failure, pressure of sexual demands, and the person's inability to abandon himself to his sexual feelings.

General Sexual Dysfunction. Of the female inhibitions general sexual dysfunction is the most resistant to treatment. This is largely due to its mediation by the parasympathetic portion of the autonomic nervous system, which is beyond conscious control. The two principal characteristics of general sexual dysfunction are absence of erotic pleasure from sexual stimulation and slight or no vaginal lubrication and swelling. Orgasm may occur without any of the physiological signs of arousal.

As with erectile dysfunction, general sexual dysfunction may be classified as either primary or secondary. Primary is defined as never having experienced erotic pleasure with any partner in any situation. Secondary is present when the woman has responded at one time to sexual stimulation to some extent. Quite often women with secondary general sexual dysfunction were aroused by sexual activity prior to marriage but have lost that ability when coitus became the principal focus of sexual expression.

Many women with general sexual dysfunction cope as best they can without seeking assistance from their spouse or a professional person. The husband's reaction to the wife's lack of responsiveness ranges from acceptance to feelings of inadequacy and self-blame. For the wife to achieve the relaxation and abandonment that are essential for sexual responsiveness, professional assistance is almost always necessary.

References

Kaplan, H. S. *The new sex therapy: Active treatment of sexual dysfunctions.* New York: Brunner/Mazel, 1974.

Kaplan, H. S. *Disorders of sexual desires and other new concepts and techniques in sex therapy.* New York: Brunner/ Mazel, 1979.

Masters, W. H., & Johnson, V. E. *Human sexual response.* Boston: Little, Brown, 1966.

J. R. DAVID

See SEXUALITY; SEXUAL RESPONSE PSYCHOLOGY.

Inner Healing. A contemporary form of spiritual healing. As described by its advocates, it is a process wherein the Holy Spirit restores health to the deepest aspects of life by dealing with the root cause of hurts and pain. Basically it involves a twofold procedure in which 1) the power of evil is broken and the heritage of wholeness that belongs to the Christian is reclaimed, and 2) memories of the past are healed through prayer.

Forms of Healing. According to McNutt (1974), one of the leading figures in the field, inner healing is one of four forms of healing and is directed primarily toward the healing of memories. He concludes that there are three major types of sickness: sickness of the spirit caused by personal sin; sickness of the emotions caused by psychological hurts from the past; and sickness of the body caused by physical disease or accidents. Prayer can be directed toward any one of these. The prayer of repentance asks forgiveness for sin; the prayer for bodily healing is directed toward physical healing; and the prayer for inner healing is concerned with healing the effects of painful memories. There is a fourth kind of prayer mentioned by McNutt: the prayer for deliverance from demon oppression, or exorcism, in which symptoms of each of the other three sicknesses can appear.

Betty and Ed Tapscott, other leaders in this movement, agree with McNutt's model but do not include exorcism as one of the primary forms of healing (Tapscott, 1975). They suggest that "breaking the power of Satan" is the first step in any healing but feel that this is accomplished through spiritual healing, which means coming to know Jesus as personal Savior. This involves confession of sin, renunciation of occult power, being willing to forgive in the same manner that one has been forgiven, being honest, and being humble. Spiritual healing is the foundation for inner healing of the mind and physical healing of the body.

The other side of breaking the power of Satan is reclaiming one's Christian inheritance, according to the Tapscotts. This means reaffirming what was true in creation and what has been provided in salvation; namely, that God wants people to be whole and has given many spiritual riches to his followers if they will but claim them. These acts of renouncing evil and reaffirming faith in God's goodness become the basis for inner healing, which is accomplished by prayer for the healing of memories. They are also the foundation for physical healing, which occurs through prayer for God to make the body whole again.

Most, if not all, inner healers agree that the several types of sickness and their remediation often occur together. Therefore, even though they emphasize one form of healing (e.g., inner

healing), they are aware of, and utilize, the other types as well.

Of special interest is their attitude toward secular healers such as physicians and psychologists. After noting that millions of dollars are spent each year going to physicians, psychologists, and psychiatrists, one writer suggests that divine healing is the best. The old adage, "Doctors treat but Jesus heals," is offered as an unquestioned truth. Removing symptoms (which doctors do) is not the same as healing the cause (which Jesus does through inner healing). This same writer praises God for Christian psychologists but concludes that "inner healing is psychotherapy, plus God!" Another writer puts it thus: "Psychiatrists bring a degree of healing by probing into the past and bringing understanding of our weak and vulnerable spots and our angry and fearful reactions, but only the Holy Spirit can move into these areas and remove the scars" (Stapleton, 1976, p. x).

Among contemporary inner healers only McNutt accords an equal place to secular healers such as physicians and psychiatrists. He states that he always prefers to work as a team with them rather than by himself. But even he qualifies this approbation by saying that whereas in the 1950s he, like so many priests, discounted his own abilities to heal and referred most psychologically disturbed persons to professionals, he has come to believe that psychiatry does not always help and that prayer for the healing of memories is often the treatment of choice (McNutt, 1974).

Techniques. Prayer for the healing of memories is the core of inner healing. Memories are the residues of experience. Practically everyone has memories from the past from which he or she needs release, even if these are only minor hurts or childlike fears. Others have memories of being unwanted or neglected, of evil deeds or unexpected accidents, or even of events that happened while they were still in their mothers' wombs. Breaking the power of unresolved and oppressive memories is a prime component of inner healing.

This understanding is the major diagnostic model for the prayer that releases persons from the tyranny of the past. It is presumed that the fears, guilts, lethargies, and depressions that result from oppressive memories are against the will of God and, as such, are susceptible to being remedied by him if the person is willing. Of particular import to inner healers has been Hugh Missildine's *Your Inner Child of the Past* (1963). Inner healers feel that they are talking sound psychology because many models of psychopathology put similar emphasis on past experience. They see themselves as legitimate, even though they insist that they do not pretend to be psychologists.

Although there is a basic similarity in approach among those who practice this form of healing, there are some distinctions. The specific approaches of three prominent practitioners—the Tapscotts, Francis McNutt, and Ruth Carter Stapleton—will be examined here.

The Tapscotts. The Tapscotts feel that memories can be healed by the individual himself as well as by the ministrations of another who has the power of healing. They encourage the person to begin with a prayer for the forgiveness of sins and a reaffirmation of Jesus as personal Savior. They suggest that the person next renounce all the forces of evil or Satan that have become a part of his life, asking the Holy Spirit to reveal these forces. At this point the person is to trust the Holy Spirit to bring to mind the images and memories that are handicapping. Even though no release is apparent, the person is to vocally renounce the power of these memories and images. Then he is to ask Jesus to fill the void that is left if the memories should leave. Jesus is asked to give his peace, his joy, and his love.

It is important to note that up to this point persons will quite likely have experienced no healing. Instead they are restating their faith and asking for God's power in their lives. Then they are requested to visualize Jesus walking hand in hand with them back through every moment of their lives. As the Holy Spirit lifts up memories of unpleasant situations, they are to take Jesus into these events. Jesus will redeem the painful memories, set the person free from them, and heal the past. The person is asked to thank God in advance for the miracle that will be worked through inner healing.

The Tapscotts provide printed prayers to be used with or by persons at every stage of the process. Although they do not say so, they seem to imply that these are once-for-all events. However, they recognize the possibility that the release from such experiences might fade, and they prescribe a set of acts designed to keep the inner person healed. These include daily prayer and Bible reading, conscious praise, regular commitment to the Lord, dedication of one's home to God, standing firm against Satan, becoming part of a spirit-filled fellowship, finding a prayer partner, and constantly forgiving others.

Francis McNutt. McNutt begins with the assumption that the basic need of life is for love; if we are ever denied it at any time in our lives, our ability to love and trust others may be seriously affected. The wounds resulting from loss of love fester and handicap us. The first step in inner healing is for Jesus to heal these wounds. The second step is for Jesus to give us the love we want and thus to fill the empty spaces once they have been healed and drained of the poison of past hurts and resentment. Whenever the person becomes aware of fears, anxieties, resentments, hates, or inhibitions, that is the time to seek inner healing.

Before the prayer for healing is offered, two questions are explored with the person. First, when can you remember first feeling this way? Second, what was happening that caused you to feel this way? If the person cannot remember an incident, then God is asked to reveal it. After the time and place of the hurt has been identified, a prayer for the healing of the hurt is offered. In as imaginative and childlike manner as possible, the healer prays that Jesus will go back into the experience and heal the person of the wound that resulted from it. McNutt states, "Jesus, as Lord of time, is able to do what we cannot. . . . The most I was ever able to do as a counselor was to help the person bring to the foreground of consciousness the things that were buried in the past, so that he could consciously cope with them in the present. Now I am discovering that the Lord can heal these wounds . . . and can bring the counseling process to its completion in a deep healing" (1974, p. 187).

After the memories have been healed, the person prays God to fill the void in his life with love. Because of the basic need for love, full healing cannot occur until the person is given what he has been missing, namely love. McNutt notes that this part of inner healing is often more difficult than the healing of the wounds of the past. The person is so accustomed to being without love that he does not know how to receive it. If the person says he does not feel the love of God, Jesus is asked to speak to the person at the depth of his soul and to call him by name. Since the nature of the wounds is known to the healer, he or she prays that God will provide the specific kind of love that the person did not have. Again, the prayer is very childlike and imaginative.

Ruth Carter Stapleton. Of note is Stapleton's emphasis on inner healing as a process, not a one-time event. Her accounts are replete with long-term relationships in which the person returns to the healer again and again. In only a few cases does she report immediate results. Further, she places an emphasis on the fact that inner healing is something more than sound doctrine or even insight into traumatic events. She suggests that most people act as though they want help when they do not really want to change.

Stapleton suggests that the desire to be whole often comes as a result of some inspirational experience with an evangelist or healer. After this the motivation toward healing changes and becomes the basis on which inner healing can occur. She postulates an "inner child" that lives in most of us and has an insatiable need for approval and love. This inner child needs to be "revealed and healed." Although she agrees with other healers that there are real past traumas that need to be faced and healed, there are in many people fantasized hurts grounded in the child within us. Thus, she seems to have an implicit model of evil which must be faced or revealed in the healing process. Finally, she emphasizes group experiences of inner healing much more than do others. Members of the group were often used in role play of other members' situations and much mutual insight occurred.

Stapleton's term for the process of inner healing is *faith imagination therapy.* In this process she recommends that persons visualize as vividly as possible Jesus coming into the experiences that have been identified as troublesome. They are encouraged to allow Jesus to respond to the situation and to take over their own behavior. She contends that forgiveness lies at the heart of all inner healing, and she encourages persons to use each situation as an opportunity to forgive and build. As Jesus dominates the visualization, persons are encouraged to allow themselves to develop into the persons God intended them to be.

Although Stapleton relies heavily on intuitive insights given her by the Holy Spirit, she leaves to the person the task of filling in the details of the visualization. In this process of faith imagination with Jesus at the center, healing deep inside the person occurs. The final step in the process is when the individual ceases being too proud or too self-depreciatory to begin some kind of ministry of service to others. As noted, for Stapleton this process is one that requires prolonged contact over an extended period of time.

Relationship to Guided Imagery. The psychotherapeutic technique most similar to the procedures in inner healing is that of guided imagery (Leuner, 1969). Stapleton is in accord with many practitioners of this technique in asserting that faith imagination is a way of inducing positive changes deep within the mind. According to Leuner guided imagery attempts to replace regressive and defensive mental habits with more mature, adaptive ego functioning. The core method in both guided imagery and faith imagination is that of suggestion. Several aspects of these procedures should be noted.

Initially the role of the therapist or healer is definitely an active one. Although many inner healers listen long and empathically (as would many psychotherapists using guided imagery), when they begin to treat the person they become very active. They are not client centered in their approach or their presumptions. They act on a great deal of intuition, and once they intuit a dynamic, they assertively lead the individual in a fantasy designed to induce healing.

However, it would seem that neither inner healers nor therapists employing guided imagery exert quite the control that hypnotists do, although their methods are similar. Neither faith imaginations or guided fantasies are hypnotic suggestions. They have more fluidity to them. In many hypnotic situations the hypnotist provides most, if not all, the details. In inner healing and guided imagery the individual is encouraged to imagine the action and elaborate the basic situation in fantasy.

There is yet another similarity in the two methods that should be noted. They both use archetypal personages in their fantasies. Guided imagery as a psychotherapeutic technique usually relies on Jungian understandings of psychic structure and dream analysis. For example, roads are life lines, mountains are ambitions or problems, crossroads are decision points, caves are suppressed memories or fears, witches are denied impulses, and old men are inner wisdoms. Inner healers confine themselves to two figures in the Trinity—the Holy Spirit and Jesus Christ. They encourage the individual to allow the Holy Spirit to reveal the incidents that provoked trauma and to allow "Jesus" to be present in the reliving of those events and to heal them.

One could say that the inner healer's Jesus is most like the "old man" of guided imagery. However, there is a radical difference. The guided imagists assume that the old man is the source of inner wisdom, which was there all along but which had been denied due to the pressures of living and to defenses against trauma. The inner healers make a different assumption. Although they rely heavily on reclaiming the inheritance of the image of God in creation, they emphasize much more the gifts of salvation that have been made available through the cross of Christ. Furthermore, Jesus is not inner wisdom but transcendent personal power. He exists outside the person and is much more than denied power. He brings insight and healing that are unavailable to personal resources no matter how suppressed. He is a person, not simply an insight.

Finally, there is a common presumption among inner healers and guided imagists that something more than insight is needed for healing to occur. Both groups are action therapists in the sense that they agree that reexperiencing is the prime means of psychological change. In this they resemble both Gestalt therapists and psychoanalysts, although their presumptions of the dynamic processes involved are somewhat different. Gestalt therapists are more inclined to induce the reexperience of past processes, such as feelings, while psychoanalysts are committed to a spontaneous working through of the transference with the therapist.

Guided imagists and inner healers deal with total events, although the former typically induce standard classical fantasies while the latter encourage reliving of actual personal situations. Yet in both, the participation of the person in present experiencing is the vital component of healing. However, it should be said that here again the inner healers assume that inner resources will not, in and of themselves, accomplish the task. What is needed is the presence and power of the living Christ, who will do for the person what he could not do for himself—namely, heal the memories and heal the person so that he can live anew.

Critique. Several critiques of inner healing have been given. The most recent is that of Alsdurf and Malony (1980), who have analyzed a number of the assumptions underlying the work of Stapleton. Although inner healers differ in some crucial ways, the Alsdurf and Malony critique seems to apply to all in general.

Initially Stapleton is accused of engaging in a simplified psychotherapy, although she denied this. In fact, she claimed that her approach is not counseling in the sense that this word is used among mental health professionals. Yet it is hard to deny that she was indeed engaged in such when one examines her accounts of her work. She met with persons in periodic sessions over extended periods of time. She led group meetings that included sharing, role playing, guided fantasies, and interpersonal catharsis. In spite of her denial she seemed to evidence a cavalier reliance on serious psychodynamic theorizing

and an overreliance on semipopular authors such as Missildine.

While her basic presumption that Jesus can heal quickly and deeply allowed her to expect miracles, she used many standard psychotherapeutic methods without acknowledging them. Furthermore, she seemed naïvely free from the caution that most psychotherapists have in approaching some problems optimistically while recognizing great difficulties inherent in others. Again, her too easy acceptance of one model, Missildine, caused her to assume an almost photographic memory of the past while almost reifying a psychic structure, the inner child of the past, that most theorists would find problematical.

Perhaps the basic problem is that while Stapleton provided fairly intensive psychotherapy, she did not seem to acknowledge the manner in which students of psychopathology have come to understand these issues. To deny this reality is to remain free from self-criticism while evoking the discount of those who know better. This is not to say that her (and other inner healers') basic belief in the power of Jesus to heal needs to be subjected to such analysis by secular theory. It does not. It is to say that this tradition of healing would be strengthened if inner healers could be better informed about how human beings function and what causes them to be as they are.

Another critique, which may be more attributable to Stapleton than to other inner healers, is that she lacked a thorough doctrine of sin. In some comments made to secular groups of therapists, it seems as if she were willing to identify her approach too simplistically with holistic healers who may be operating under Eastern presumptions that do not include a basic propensity toward evil. Thus, while using Christian terminology she may be implicitly utilizing basic assumptions more like secular therapists who have concluded that humans have the resources for self-healing. It should be noted that McNutt and the Tapscotts put great emphasis on the importance of the forgiveness for sin in their methods and that Stapleton denies any such omissions when confronted with this critique. However, her words in certain settings belie this denial and denote a possible naïve reliance on a methodology that seems to bypass the need for the individual to face personal evil in an effort to affirm the power of Jesus to heal hurts resulting from traumatic past events.

All in all, however, inner healing should be looked upon as a unique and powerful form of therapy currently held in wide respect by a large part of the Christian world. Christian psychotherapists should study it deeply and attempt to learn from its bold use of Christian resources in the helping process.

References

Alsdurf, J. M., & Malony, H. N. A critique of Ruth Carter Stapleton's ministry of "inner healing." *Journal of Psychology and Theology,* 1980, *8*(3), 173–184.

Leuner, H. Guided affective imagery. *American Journal of Psychotherapy,* 1969, *23,* 4–22.

McNutt, F. *Healing.* Notre Dame, Ind.: Ave Maria Press, 1974.

Missildine, W. H. *Your inner child of the past.* New York: Simon & Schuster, 1963.

Stapleton, R. C. *The gift of inner healing.* Waco, Tex.: Word Books, 1976.

Tapscott, B. *Inner healing through healing of memories.* Houston: Tapscott, 1975.

H. N. Malony

See Imagery, Therapeutic Use of.

Insanity. See Forensic Psychiatry.

Insight in Learning. In the study of problem solving insight refers to the act of apprehending the principles involved in a task or the relationships involved in a puzzle. The result is a solution to the problem primarily arrived at by cognitive, as opposed to trial-and-error, means. Although this type of problem solving is usually associated with human beings, it was first systematically studied in apes by the Gestalt psychologist Köhler and reported in *The Mentality of Apes* in 1927.

In the most famous experiment Köhler's brightest ape named Sultan was able to discover how to use objects like sticks and boxes to extend his reach and obtain food that was outside the cage or suspended above the cage floor. After he failed to reach the food by repeated efforts of stretching and jumping, the solution to the problem came to the ape following a period of exploration of the cage and a long pause in which the ape appeared to be "thinking" about the elements of his problem. Köhler's interpretation was that the ape did not solve the problem until he grasped it as a whole (or Gestalt) and considered using the objects in the cage as implements to extend his efforts.

Descriptively, when the ape solved the problem, his actions were immediate, purposeful, direct, and effective; he seized the implement and used it without hesitation to extend his reach by dragging food toward the cage with a stick or climbing on a box to stretch high enough to reach food suspended from the ceiling. In contrast to trial-and-error learning, Köhler found that once the ape had solved the problem he could readily repeat the solution

effectively. That is, where trial-and-error learning is gradual, insight seemed to be instantaneous. Further, the insight seemed to be transferable; that is, the ape was able to apply the same approach to solving new but similar problems.

Insight in human beings seems descriptively similar to Köhler's account in apes. The process by which insight occurs seems to be mental transformation of the setting and elements of a problem until the elements are set in a relationship to one another that permits the solution to be recognized. But while this general description is widely accepted, more detailed understanding of the factors that promote insight has not been forthcoming. This is because insight has not been an active topic of research in the last three decades in American psychology. Rather, the results of the earlier study of insight served to lessen the emphasis on repetitive forms of learning (e.g., rote memorization), which had been encouraged by the study of trial and error, and to assert the importance of understanding, especially in formal education. Today insight is primarily a descriptive term, and the investigation of the ability to solve perceptual and linguistic problems has shifted to cognitive psychology.

L. S. Shaffer

See Learning.

Insight in Psychotherapy. As applied to psychotherapy the term *insight* is found most frequently in the psychoanalytic literature. Within this context it can be defined as "a state of knowledge about one's own conscious and unconscious thoughts, feelings, or psychic processes that is the result of deeper genetic understanding of one's behavior and a constructively altered self-perception in which new facts about oneself are learned and some old facts are perceived more beneficially" (Paolino, 1981, p. 146). Insight also refers to the general extent to which the patient is aware that he or she is emotionally troubled, recognizes the nature and extent of the problem, and understands the special underlying factors that have helped to produce this psychological disturbance. Finally, insight refers to the patient's ability to observe himself or herself, reflect retrospectively on feelings and experiences, and understand how the past interferes with present functioning.

Insight-oriented psychotherapy, such as psychoanalysis, emphasizes the central importance of insight in the overall therapeutic process. The main goal of insight-oriented psychotherapy is that the patient be helped to gain sufficient insight into the unconscious roots of his or her problems that changes in the dynamic structure of the personality will result. This becomes the main focus of the psychotherapy, with all the therapist's interpretations directed at increasing the patient's insight. It is generally believed that such insight alone will not cure underlying psychopathology unless it is actually applied by the patient. However, it is also generally felt that true insight inevitably results in profound changes in how patients regard themselves, followed by almost irresistible applications of this newfound understanding, resulting in personality change.

The use of insight is not limited to psychoanalytic psychotherapy. Many psychotherapists representing a wide variety of psychotherapeutic modalities seek to improve the level of insight of their patients. While they may not seek to alter unconscious dynamics and conflicts, it is usually hoped that a patient's insight into the underlying causes of psychological symptoms will result in conscious changes and willful decisions to think, feel, or behave differently in the future.

There are several means of determining a patient's capacity for insight during the early stages of therapy. The patient is asked his reasons for seeking treatment, his thoughts concerning the causes of present symptoms, and his assessment of the possible patterns related to the present difficulty. The more the patient is able to reflect upon his thoughts, feelings, and behavior, and demonstrate some understanding of possible underlying causes and related patterns, the more likely will be his capacity for insight. Where such ability for insight is demonstrated to be present, the patient can be encouraged to examine his psychological functioning quite closely, both within and without the therapy session, to determine possible underlying causes. This helps the patient to feel more in control of his behavior, and his thoughts and feelings become less mysterious and more easily understood. On the other hand, where the patient demonstrates a marked lack of insight or even an inability for such insight to develop, it may be preferable for therapy to be conducted in a more directive and/or behavioral manner.

The use of insight has some important limitations. Perhaps most important is the point made earlier, that insight alone is not always enough to produce desired change. In chronic behavior problems, character disorders, and addictive behaviors, a patient's insight may not be sufficient to bring about a cure. In such case other therapeutic techniques, such as behavior modification, may be necessary to help the patient apply insight and retrain automatic responses. Another limitation is that a patient may have intellectualized rationalizations for his behavior that may be mistakenly regarded as true psychological insight. In such cases these intellectualizations actually hinder attempts at increasing true insight. Rather than resulting from true change-producing understanding, these rationalizations are more often excuses for behavior typically given to release the person from responsibility and confuse the therapist, thereby hindering attempts at confronting the patient's true problems.

When used properly, insight can be a powerful therapeutic tool for producing personality change in a patient capable of such self-understanding.

Reference
Paolino, T. J. *Psychoanalytic psychotherapy.* New York: Brunner/Mazel, 1981.

J. D. GUY JR.

Insomnia. *See* SLEEP DISORDERS.

Instigation Therapy. An educational, skill-building approach to therapy that is built around the systematic use of homework assignments. It is associated with the work of Shelton (1979), who views the approach as closely allied to behavior therapy. Because of its reliance on the completion of assignments in the client's natural environment, it has been seen by many as a promising approach to the enhancement of the transfer of treatment gains back to that primary environment.

Reference
Shelton, J. L. Instigation therapy. In A. Goldstein & F. Kanfer (Eds.), *Maximizing treatment gains.* New York: Academic Press, 1979.

See HOMEWORK IN PSYCHOTHERAPY.

Instinct. An unlearned, species-specific behavior that appears fully developed at a certain point in the growth of an organism. Some examples include nest building in birds, web spinning in spiders, and mating patterns in rats and other lower animals. Freud used the term *instinct* in a different way to mean an inborn primitive force or drive such as hunger, thirst, or sex. He also described thanatos, the death instinct, and eros, the life instinct, as important factors behind human motivation.

James expressed his belief in human instincts, but the psychologist most famous for espousal of the instinct concept in humans was McDougall. He felt that human instincts were related to the emotions and saw fear, repulsion, curiosity, self-assertion, and gregariousness as examples of instincts. However, use of the term *instinct* nearly reached absurd levels early in this century with most types of behavior claimed as instinctively motivated.

The belief in human instincts by psychologists declined after this time because the work of the behaviorists left little doubt that human behavior was not primarily the result of instincts. The view of a human instinct as an innate, hereditary response not modifiable by environmental factors had to yield to the evidence in favor of learned behavior. By 1919 Watson argued that one may safely disregard virtually all innate factors in accounting for individual differences in the behavior of adults.

The concept of instinct began again to influence American psychology in the 1960s through the field of ethology and its nominal founder, Lorenz. The strict definition of instinct, however, was dropped in favor of the concept of biological predisposition. Such a predisposition represents an inherited tendency toward a certain behavior. To psychologists this meant that no behavior would develop independently of the organism's hereditary predisposition. Research showed that species differed with regard to the range and kind of stimuli to which they were particularly sensitive, and with regard to the range and kind of responses they were capable of making.

While the concept of instinct is not a major theme in psychology today, psychologists do recognize inborn propensities without at the same time feeling obliged to accept the proposition that there is a class of behaviors completely directed by heredity and entirely immune to environmental factors.

M. P. COSGROVE

See DRIVE; MOTIVATION.

Instructional Psychology. A relatively new subfield of educational psychology, concerned with the application of learning theory to human problems. It considers clients in their roles as learners, and therefore intervention is viewed primarily as some form of teaching. It differs from educational psychology by its inquiry into the vast wealth and diversity of human interaction considered as teaching-learning processes. Its scope of contribution thereby lies well beyond the boundaries of schooling. Indeed, the broad range of therapeutic interaction may also be fruitfully analyzed in terms of learning and teaching, which are thus a legitimate part of the domain of the instructional psychologist.

W. C. HILL

See EDUCATIONAL PSYCHOLOGY.

Insulin Shock Therapy. One of several types of psychiatric treatment using chemical agents or electricity to induce comas in patients in the hope of "shocking" them into their right minds. Shock treatment was first used as early as the sixteenth century when Paracelsus fed a patient camphor to induce therapeutic convulsive seizures. Other agents that have been used to induce shock include metrazol (a camphor derivative), nitrogen, and guanidine hydrochloride.

Manfred Sakel introduced insulin or hypoglycemic shock treatment in 1933. Some of Sakel's psychiatric patients were also diabetics who sometimes would go into hypoglycemic coma when they took too much insulin. When they recovered, their mental state also improved. Sakel then used insulin to induce coma in other patients with the same salutory results. Insulin shock therapy rapidly gained popularity, and for a few years was the treatment of choice in hospitals with the equipment and manpower to use it. Treatments often required 60 to 90 hours of coma, spread over three months, sometimes also accompanied by electroconvulsive therapy (West, Bond, Shurley, & Meyers, 1954). Because insulin coma therapy took so much time and carried fairly high risks, it was eventually limited to severe schizophrenics (Millet, 1959).

In the early 1950s several well-controlled studies indicated that insulin therapy was no more effective than psychotherapy alone, ELECTROCONVULSIVE THERAPY, or treatment with the newer and safer barbiturates. It was also becoming apparent that the effects of treatment were only temporary (Bourne, 1958). By the 1960s insulin shock therapy had largely been replaced by more effective techniques.

No one really knows why insulin or other shock therapies can improve the functioning of psychotics, but there is at least one promising hypothesis. Selye (1956) has observed that a number of early nonspecific treatments besides shock therapy, such as bloodletting, flogging, or deliberately inducing fevers, have been known to produce beneficial effects. These treatments all cause severe physical stress, and the body tries to protect itself with widespread hormonal and physical changes.

Selye believes that these changes also temporarily improve the psychological condition.

References

Bourne, H. Insulin coma in decline. *American Journal of Psychiatry*, 1958, *114*, 1015–1017.

Millet, J. Shock therapies, old and new. *Pastoral Psychology* 1959, *10*(97), 44–50.

Selye, H. *The stress of life*. New York: McGraw-Hill, 1956.

West, F. H., Bond, E. D., Shurley, J. T., & Meyers, C. D. Insulin coma therapy in schizophrenia. *American Journal of Psychiatry*, 1954, *111*, 583–589.

E. L. HILLSTROM

Integration of Psychology and Theology.
See CHRISTIAN PSYCHOLOGY.

Integrative Approaches to Therapy. *See* BROADSPECTRUM PSYCHOTHERAPY.

Integrity Therapy.
A moral approach to psychotherapy that places a critical emphasis on the interrelationship between mental health and behaviors concerned with honesty, responsibility, and involvement with others. Its fundamental principles were formulated by Mowrer, who is best known for behavioristic research on learning theory. He proposed that emotional disturbance is a symptom of concealed guilt, which in turn emerges from violations of the individual's conscience. In Mowrer's view a return to psychological well-being requires confession of one's moral failures to significant others and subsequent acts of restitution. This approach is distinguished from more orthodox deterministic therapies by its insistence on the individual's personal responsibility for his or her psychopathology.

Integrity therapy is an innovative synthesis of diverse clinical and philosophical traditions. Its principal roots include Sullivan's interpersonal psychiatry, the Judeo-Christian religions, and behavioral psychology.

Mowrer's core assumption is that "human personality is primarily a *social* phenomenon" (1972, p. 22). Since we are social creatures by nature, our moral and psychological integrity depends on community with other persons. Mowrer holds, as do the interpersonalists, that psychopathology and mental health are intimately related to the quality of one's relationships with others.

A second major root is found in the Judeo-Christian tradition. Mowrer finds in the early Christian church an excellent model of healing; in it he identifies precedents for the form, process, and goal of integrity therapy. In terms of form, Mowrer's group format is modeled after the intimate house churches of early Christianity. The therapeutic process involves Mowrer's accommodations of spiritual disciplines such as confession of sin and penance (restitution). As for the goal, group members are called to strive toward moral ideals compatible with the Judeo-Christian ethic.

Behavioral psychology makes up a third root of integrity therapy. Paraphrasing an E. Stanley Jones aphorism, Mowrer endorses the behavioral principle that "it is easier to *act* yourself into a new way of feeling than to *feel* yourself into a new way of acting" (Drakeford, 1967, p. 116). Mowrer's theory of neurosis, attributing emotional disturbance to specific transgressions of social norms, draws heavily from learning theory (London, 1964). His technique of cure—i.e., prescribing acts of restitution—clearly involves the learning and reinforcement of new behaviors, leading some to describe the integrity approach as an action therapy.

The integrity philosophy of neurosis and treatment may be contrasted with psychoanalytic theory. Freudians maintain that anxiety is partially a result of an overly strict conscience, termed the superego. Treatment is thus directed toward reforming the superego along less punitive lines. Mowrer, on the other hand, posits that anxiety reflects the moral "dis-ease" of an appropriately guilty conscience, driven by fear of community reprisal. From his perspective treatment must facilitate personal growth, such that the individual behaves more responsibly vis-à-vis the reality demands of conscience and society.

Mowrer further postulates that neurotics are alienated from others as a consequence of breaking societal rules. He insists that treatment must therefore facilitate the individual's return to community. This process occurs within the context of a subcommunity or therapy group. Such groups offer the added advantage of holding individuals responsible for their misbehavior and rewarding more mature life choices.

Integrity therapy specifies a clearly delineated technique of cure involving two primary client activities: confession and restitution. The former requires the client to accept personal responsibility for wrongdoing and is distinguished from complaining or blaming. Confession is directed toward the significant others who have been wronged.

The technique of restitution follows from Mowrer's contention that symptoms reflect the punishment of a guilty conscience. Integrity therapists insist that guilt must be resolved through restorative actions. This action principle includes giving up one's current misbehavior, rectifying past injustices, and serving others. Mowrer emphasizes that confession without restitution is simply cheap grace and is ineffective for dealing with real guilt.

In addition to confession and restitution Mowrer encourages emotional honesty. This involves activities such as verbalizing feelings or physically touching other group members. Such practices serve to facilitate emotional release and to promote greater interpersonal involvement.

Due to the scarcity of research on the results of integrity therapy, its benefits are difficult to assess. Practitioner observations suggest that integrity techniques are applicable to a wide variety of psychological problems, including marital conflict, anxiety, and depression. Three groups in particular, however, appear nonamenable to this approach: antisocial (psychopathic) personalities, paranoid personalities, and persons whose emotional difficulties are due to physical causes.

Apart from the issue of treatment efficacy, integrity therapy may be assessed in terms of its compatibility with biblical principles. Despite Mowrer's frequent use of religious terminology his approach to persons is clearly nontheistic. For example, words such as *sin*, *confession*, and *forgiveness* have no transcendent referent: these terms refer exclusively to the horizontal dimension—i.e., what persons do to one another. Mowrer clarifies his humanistic emphasis: "Our assumption is that our first obligation is to be good human beings . . . and that in pursuing that end we cannot be displeasing whatever Higher Power or Divine Intelligence one may or may not believe to exist" (1972, p. 11). Although Mowrer rightly points out the individual's responsibilities to other persons, his perspective ignores biblical teachings that: 1) individuals are ultimately responsible to God; 2) moral failures involve transgressions of divine standards; and 3) forgiveness comes from God through Christ.

On the other hand, many concepts and principles of integrity therapy appear compatible with Christian thought: the importance of community (Heb. 10:25), confession (James 5:16), honesty (Exod. 20:16), and restitution (Lev. 5:16). Mowrer's emphasis on acting out moral behaviors is not inconsistent with the exhortation in James 2 that believers demonstrate faith through good actions. Integrity theory is also consonant with Christianity in advocating some crucial Judeo-Christian standards of right and wrong. Because of these areas of convergence, this approach may be accommodated to a biblically based therapy approach (cf. Drakeford, 1967).

References

Drakeford, J. W. *Integrity therapy*. Nashville: Broadman, 1967.

London, P. *The modes and morals of psychotherapy*. New York: Holt, Rinehart, & Winston, 1964.

Mowrer, O. H. Integrity groups: Principles and procedures. *The Counseling Psychologist*, 1972, *3*(2), 7–33.

Additional Readings

Mowrer, O. H. *The crisis in psychiatry and religion*. Princeton, N.J.: Van Nostrand, 1961.

Mowrer, O. H. *The new group therapy*. Princeton, N.J.: Van Nostrand, 1964.

D. W. BROKAW

See MOWRER, ORVAL HOBART.

Intellectual Assessment. One important practical aspect of the more general enterprise measuring individual differences in human performance. The task of intellectual assessment is the measurement, description, and interpretation of the differences between individuals on those skills and abilities which we define as relating to the person's capacity to solve problems, to learn from and adapt to new experiences, to think abstractly, and to synthesize and utilize new information. Cronbach (1960) noted that intellectual assessment tends to be concerned with measurement of the person's maximum possible performance in an area where there are right and wrong answers (such as memory), while personality assessment is typically concerned with measurement of average or habitual responses where there are no right and wrong answers (such as need for affection). The task of intellectual assessment is made quite difficult by the confusion as to what exactly constitutes intelligence, by the limitations of our means for measuring it, and by the frequent misunderstandings and misuses of legitimate intellectual assessment.

Important Concepts. To be useful a test must be reliable. Reliability refers to repeatability and stability of scores. We use a metal tape measure rather than an elastic strap to measure lumber for a carpentry project because the tape measure is more likely to produce relatively unvarying (i.e., reliable) measurements. An intelligence test that rates a person a genius on one day and retarded the next is of little use. No psychological test is perfectly reliable because there is always some fluctuation in human performance. Generally speaking, the more reliable the test of intelligence, the better. Psychologists have developed a diversity of methods for measuring reliability.

An intelligence test must also be valid.

Validity refers to the extent to which the assessment instrument measures what it was intended to measure. Reliability is a necessary but not wholly sufficient condition for validity; one can have a reliable measure (such as temperature) that is unrelated to what one wants to measure (intelligence). Psychologists have differentiated many types of validity. The three main types important in the area of intellectual assessment are content, construct, and criterion validity. Content validity refers to whether or not one can conclude, based upon systematic rational examination, that a particular test appropriately samples what it intends to measure. If our conception of intelligence prominently includes memory, then an intelligence test that does not assess memory would not have content validity. Construct validity refers to the correlation of the test results with results from other tests designed to measure the same attribute. If a new intelligence test fails to correlate with established measures of intelligence such as the Stanford-Binet, this would be evidence against its construct validity. Finally, criterion validity refers to the test's utility in predicting some objective index of what you are trying to measure. Thus, a criterion valid intellectual test might predict with some accuracy future school performance or vocational success, or it might differentiate clearly between those known to be retarded, normal, and gifted.

Measurement of intelligence is inherently relative. No absolute reference point exists against which we can scale persons regarding intelligence. Thus, intellectual assessment always utilizes normative comparison—i.e., the relative ranking of an individual compared to other similar persons (typically similar in terms of age and sex). The intelligence quotient, or IQ, used to be calculated by comparing a person's mental age (based on normative comparison with what an average person can typically do at a specific age) with the person's chronological age. Today IQ is usually calculated based on how close or far from average the person's abilities are. For example, if one's composite raw score on a test was about average for one's age and sex, then one would be assigned an IQ of 100 (the arbitrary designation of average). If one's performance was better than 85% of all persons taking the test, then one's IQ would be 115, and so forth.

Thus it is critical to the accurate interpretation of the results of an intelligence test that it be appropriately standardized; i.e., that it would have been administered to large numbers of persons who are representative of the type of person the test is designed to be used with. The results of these administrations become the norms against which individual performance is compared. If the test has been standardized on a small number of people, the norms are not firm estimates of average scores, making the results of a specific testing less likely to be interpreted accurately. If the standardization sample differs significantly from the person being tested (e.g., a black child is given a test normed only on whites), then again the assessor is at risk of drawing erroneous conclusions from the test.

Intellectual assessment is also inherently probabilistic. When we measure a person's height, we measure all of their height. To measure all the components of intellectual ability and knowledge for the average person, on the other hand, would perhaps require a lifetime. Thus, an intelligence test samples aspects of the person's abilities and knowledge, and bases the estimate of intelligence on that sample. Estimates based on sampling are always probabilistic. Because of this probabilistic nature of intellectual assessment, all intellectual measurements are presented in a format that in some way indicates a probability range of scores, such as "John Doe's tested IQ was 105, suggesting a 95% chance of accuracy in predicting that his IQ lies between 95 and 115." Responsible intellectual assessment is always tentative and relies on other data sources than test performance.

Finally, we should briefly note the impact of theoretical and pragmatic concerns upon test development. The major impetus for the development of most tests has been pragmatic social concerns centering around the efficient yet fair estimation of intellectual capability, in order to allow for optimal distribution of educational resources and planning and implementation of educational programs. There is little correlation between the major theories of intelligence and the major intellectual assessment tools available today. Further, since there is no one monolithically accepted theory of intelligence, "it happens that no IQ test is known to measure the best (in theory) construct of intelligence, and different IQ tests in effect measure different 'intelligences'" (Carroll & Horn, 1981, p. 1017). One theoretical and pragmatic concern that has shaped the face of intellectual assessment is the continued lukewarm acceptance of the theorized "general" intellectual factor and the practical desire to be able to sum up the results of one's testing in one focal number, the IQ. If the theories of intelligence most widely accepted today were forcefully translated into tests, we would see results only in terms of profiles of relative strengths of differing abilities, not one summary number of overall intelligence.

Practical Issues. There are many types of intellectual assessment devices. The most widely used individually administered tests are the WECHSLER INTELLIGENCE TESTS. Many tests have been constructed for use with special groups such as infants; physically, visually, or hearing handicapped; and others. Nonverbal tests of intelligence have been developed. There are many group-administered tests of intelligence. Finally, there are a number of specialized tests for assessing specific abilities without estimating overall intelligence (see Anastasi, 1976, for more information).

Several precautions can help ensure valid and responsible use of intellectual assessment tools. First, the referring source should clearly articulate what question it desires to answer with the testing. Intellectual testing should be performed only when it will significantly assist in answering that question. Mode of testing should be determined and executed by qualified professionals adequately trained in test evaluation, administration, interpretation, and consultation with referral sources. Confidentiality of assessment results and the right to privacy of the person tested must be of preeminent concern. The assessor must exert great effort toward putting the client at ease in the testing situation and building rapport. It should be noted that accurate testing depends on the client's lack of knowledge regarding the tests administered, and this is why exposure to intellectual tests is restricted by test publishers. Open access to public inspection of test methods would damage their validity. Finally, when discussing assessment results with nonprofessional persons the responsible professional discusses the results in general terms only (e.g., John's overall intellectual ability is in the above-average range) and always in reference to the referral question. These guidelines help prevent misunderstandings in the complex matter of test interpretation.

In closing, the issue of test bias should be considered. Racial, cultural, and gender groups have differed significantly in their scores on some intelligence tests. Do these results indicate that some groups (e.g., Orientals) are inherently more intelligent than others (e.g., whites), or do they indicate the presence of cultural bias in testing that unfairly predisposes one group to finish ahead of another? At the risk of gross simplification, those who see cultural bias in testing are frequently committed to the necessary equality of all racial, cultural, and gender groups on the variable of intellect. Therefore, it follows that any measure indicating stable group differences must be biased. Such a position can represent premature closure on value issues and an exaggerated view of the utility of assessment methods.

On the other hand, those committed to defending group differences frequently overlook the somewhat arbitrary nature of the choice of one index of intellect over another (Carroll & Horn, 1981). More specifically, they fail to acknowledge that the typical assessment instrument is validated (criterion validity) against some measure of success (e.g., school or vocational performance) in a society dominated by one major group (white Anglo-Saxon Protestant males). That is, tests are validated by showing that people who score high on the test do well in the white, middle-class-dominated school system and professional world. It is possible that the true index of intelligence has nothing to do with these standards. Cole (1981) concluded that tests are not consistently biased against minority groups, but that tests are only one part of a complex sociopolitical process of decision making regarding the minority person, and that the very real existence of bias must continue to be taken extremely seriously.

References

Anastasi, A. *Psychological testing* (4th ed.). New York: Macmillan, 1976.

Carroll, J. B., & Horn, J. L. On the scientific basis of ability testing. *American Psychologist*, 1981, *36*, 1012–1020.

Cole, N. S. Bias in testing. *American Psychologist*, 1981, *36*, 1067–1077.

Cronbach, L. J. *Essentials of psychological testing* (2nd ed.). New York: Harper & Row, 1960.

S. L. JONES

See PSYCHOLOGICAL MEASUREMENT.

Intellectualization. A DEFENSE MECHANISM whereby the ego attempts to achieve insulation from emotional pain or undesirable impulses through blocking or distorting the emotions normally associated with some thought or event. Also known as brooding, this process involves escaping one's emotions through a focus on intellectual concepts, abstract and insignificant details, or rational explanation devoid of personal significance. This may be seen in the example of the person who, having suffered a major career setback, discusses with apparent detachment all the ways his debacle could have been more devastating. This defense mechanism is closely related to both emotional insulation and rationalization, and is common in obsessive-compulsive disorder.

R. LARKIN

Intelligence. The field of intelligence has long been one of the most popular areas of research in psychology. Since so many important day-to-day decisions, such as job hiring decisions and placement into school programs and classes, are based on an understanding and accurate assessment of abilities and intelligence, it is easy to understand why psychologists are so interested in studying intelligence.

Binet was one of the first to attempt to study intelligence scientifically, developing and validating the first IQ test. Binet's test, currently known as the STANFORD-BINET INTELLIGENCE SCALE, has been revised several times since it first appeared in 1905 and continues to be among the most popular intelligence tests. In large part this popularity is due to Binet's conceptualization of intelligence. Binet viewed intelligence as the ability to adapt oneself in order to solve complex problems. This conceptualization of intelligence as a generalized problem-solving/reasoning ability continues to permeate research on intelligence today.

Psychologists interested in intelligence have generally approached their research from one of two perspectives. Developmental psychologists have studied the unfolding of intelligence as children and adults mature and develop. Perhaps the most famous of these researchers was Piaget, who identified four major stages of cognitive development representative of the intellectual capabilities of children of different age ranges. On the other hand, differential psychologists (psychologists who study individual differences) have been more interested in examining the structure of intelligence. Differential psychologists point out that what we call intelligence actually consists of a number of different abilities (e.g., verbal ability, numerical ability, memory, perceptual/clerical ability, spatial ability, mechanical ability). Differential psychologists seek to determine whether these various abilities are completely independent or simply different manifestations of a single underlying general intellectual ability.

This article will examine the competing theories of intelligence advanced by differential psychologists. For the research of Piaget and other developmental psychologists, see COGNITIVE DEVELOPMENT.

Research Methods. Before the various theories of intelligence can be understood, a short introduction to the research methods of differential psychologists is necessary. Over the years psychologists have developed hundreds of tests to assess different types of abilities. To determine whether these many abilities are truly separate and unique, psychologists will give a battery of these tests to a large sample of subjects. They will then attempt to identify tests that are highly correlated. For example, if subjects who score high on a reading comprehension test also score high on a vocabulary test, and subjects who score low on reading comprehension also score low on vocabulary, psychologists would say that the two tests are highly correlated. To the extent that two tests are highly correlated, psychologists infer that there must be a single ability underlying performance on both tests that causes subjects to score either high or low on both. Thus, psychologists often find that two tests purported to measure two quite different abilities are highly correlated, and the two quite different abilities are really just one single underlying ability.

Psychologists often administer a large battery of 20 to 40 tests to their subjects. Obviously it would be very tedious to examine the correlations between each pair of tests in order to identify the underlying abilities. Fortunately, in the early 1900s psychologist Charles Spearman devised a procedure that simultaneously examines all these many correlations. Spearman's procedure is known as factor analysis. One of the results from a factor analysis is a list of the groupings of tests that are highly correlated with one another. These groupings, or factors, can then be studied in order to identify the common underlying ability represented by the tests included in that factor.

Most of the results and theories that follow are based to a large extent on factor analyses of different test batteries. Given such a straightforward statistical procedure, it may seem surprising that there are several competing theories. However, there are at least two reasons why psychologists using factor analysis have obtained differing results and developed competing theories. First, there are many different methods of doing a factor analysis. These different methods often lead to quite different results. Second, psychologists often include very different sets of tests in their test batteries. For example, a psychologist might exclude all mathematics and numerical ability tests. Of course, if he does this, no numerical ability factor will emerge from his factor analysis. However, this problem probably has only a slight effect on the differences between the well-researched theories outlined below.

Spearman's Two-Factor Theory. Spearman, who devised the statistical technique factor analysis, was a contemporary of Binet's. During the early 1900s, when these two men were conducting their pioneer research into intelligence, there was great debate among psychologists concerning what constitutes intelligence. Binet emphasized adaptation and an underlying problem-solving ability. Other researchers argued that there were many distinct, more specific abilities. Spearman believed that this dispute could only be settled empirically. He assembled a small battery of diverse ability tests and applied his new factor analytic method to subjects' test scores (Spearman, 1904). Spearman found that all the tests were correlated with one another, but the correlations among the tests were not perfect. Thus, there appeared to be a single common ability underlying performance on all the tests, which Spearman called g for general intelligence. However, there also appeared to be unique abilities contributing to performance on the various tests. He called these latter abilities s because they were specific to each test.

Spearman's discovery of g was compatible with Binet's theory of intelligence. Indeed, for his early intelligence test Binet simply compiled a rather jumbled collection of items representing a wide variety of mental tasks. Binet could now cite Spearman's work in support of this approach to mental testing. Given Spearman's finding that g was general to all ability measures, Binet could confidently claim that his test was indeed tapping general intelligence. Spearman himself remained somewhat aloof from the controversy surrounding the nature of g. His primary interest was in defining g statistically; he cared much less whether or not g was the same as problem-solving ability. However, Spearman's work lent credibility to Binet's views.

Thurstone's Theory of Primary Mental Abilities. Spearman believed that the various component abilities comprising s were all uncorrelated with one another. That is, in Spearman's view there was one broad general ability and many unrelated specific abilities. However, during the four decades following Spearman's initial research many psychologists found that things were not quite so simple as Spearman had suggested. For example, Burt found that the s portions from many different types of memory tests tended to be correlated with one another. Similarly, other factors were

found underlying the s portions of verbal, reasoning, number, and spatial tests.

This research culminated in the 1930s and 1940s in a new series of factor analytic studies conducted by Thurstone. In his first study Thurstone (1938) factor analyzed a battery of 56 ability tests and found no evidence of a g factor in this study. Instead, he claimed, there were seven or eight independent primary abilities (e.g., verbal ability, number ability, reasoning, perceptual speed, spatial relations) underlying these 56 tests. However, in subsequent studies (e.g., Thurstone & Thurstone, 1941), he backed down from his claim that the abilities were independent. In the 1941 study he found that his primary abilities were somewhat intercorrelated with one another. This correlation, Thurstone allowed, was evidence that g was present in each of the primary abilities. However, he argued that g alone was not sufficient to explain the structure of intelligence. Any discussion of intelligence, he claimed, must also consider the role of the primary mental abilities.

Since Thurstone's landmark studies, research has been directed toward identifying a more exhaustive list of primary abilities. In general, there was an agreement that overly test-specific abilities should not be included on this list; only abilities that could be measured by two or more distinct types of tests should be considered. Psychologists also generally agreed that the abilities included should be ones that had previously been identified in major factor analytic research efforts. Far and away the most popular ability list to date is that assembled by French, Ekstrom, and Price (1963, 1976). Their kit of cognitive reference tests includes 72 tests designed to measure 23 different abilities. While some psychologists may quibble about the inclusion or exclusion of one or two abilities, almost all researchers who have conducted major studies of intelligence over the past 20 years have used French et al.'s list of abilities to ensure that their studies did not omit any major aspects of intelligence.

Guilford's Structure of Intellect Model. A distinguishing feature of primary abilities models of intelligence is that all abilities are believed to be correlated with one another because they all in part reflect g. However, at least one influential psychologist continues to dispute the existence of g. Over the past four decades Guilford has integrated elements from Piaget, information processing theory, and many other disciplines within psychology into his structure of intellect model of intelligence (Guilford, 1967).

Guilford has identified three major dimensions of intelligence: contents (verbal, figural, symbolic, behavioral); operations (cognition, memory, divergent thinking, convergent thinking, evaluation); and products (units, classes, relations, systems, transformations, implications). These three dimensions can be crossed to define the 120 different factors comprising intelligence. For example, Guilford's cognition of semantic units would correspond to the more familiar ability, verbal comprehension. Guilford asserts that all 120 of his factors are independent. Thus, he rejects any underlying g factor. As proof he claims that the correlations among the various abilities are all very low or zero. He also claims that the abilities all have different developmental histories.

Many have disputed Guilford's claims and assertions. In particular, Guilford's critics charge that his abilities are not as uncorrelated as he would like to believe. For example, Horn and Knapp (1973) state that Guilford has used inappropriate methods of factor analysis— methods that are so weak they virtually ensure that Guilford will find the factor structure he is looking for regardless of the actual correlations among his ability tests. Other psychologists have questioned how Guilford could assert that two abilities would be uncorrelated if they shared common operations and products but differed only in contents. It seems only logical that these two abilities should be more highly correlated than two abilities that share no common dimensions.

Because of criticisms such as these Guilford's model seems to be falling into increasing disfavor. However, his extensive list of 120 ability factors has challenged researchers to consider and investigate many new types of abilities. Over the coming years researchers must attempt to integrate Guilford's abilities into their own schemes of intellectual structure.

Cattell's Theory of Fluid and Crystallized Intelligence. Many psychologists have suggested that there may be some intermediate ability levels between the g factor identified by Spearman and the 23 multiple abilities identified by French et al. These psychologists have proposed hierarchical ability models for organizing the multiple abilities into broad major group factors. These broad group factors would likely be at a level just below g in the ability hierarchy.

While there are a number of different hierarchical theories, the one that has received the most research attention over the past 10 years is Cattell's theory of fluid and crystallized intelligence (Cattell, 1971). Cattell defines fluid intelligence as the biologically determined aspect of intelligence that allows us to identify relationships and solve problems. Thus, Cattell's fluid intelligence is not unlike Binet's problem-solving/reasoning conceptualization of intelligence. Cattell's crystallized intelligence represents the skills, strategies, schemes, and concepts developed as fluid intelligence is applied to the problems of one's culture and environment.

A number of interesting predictions can be made on the basis of Cattell's theory. First, factor analyses of ability tests should result in separate factors for fluid intelligence and crystallized intelligence. The research conducted to date suggests that this is indeed the case. Second, Cattell suggests that the developmental courses of fluid intelligence and crystallized intelligence should be quite different. Since fluid intelligence is largely biologically determined and is thus susceptible to biological trauma, it would be expected to decline somewhat with age. Crystallized intelligence, however, should continue to grow and expand as one ages and has contact with more cultural and environmental situations and problems. Again, the evidence to date is fairly supportive of this prediction. Third, since fluid intelligence is biologically determined, it should be largely determined by one's genes. Crystallized intelligence, on the other hand, is determined by the interaction between fluid intelligence and the environment, and thus, should be less determined by one's genes. The evidence on this third prediction does not appear to be very favorable toward Cattell's theory. However, Horn (1981) claims that this third prediction is not necessarily a logical prediction on the basis of Cattell's theory, and he suggests that psychologists withhold judgment pending further examination of both the theory and the data.

Summary. Research on the structure of intelligence has progressed greatly in the past century. There is general agreement among psychologists that intelligence is composed of a number of interrelated multiple abilities. These abilities are likely organized in some hierarchical fashion, similar to that specified by Cattell's theory. At the highest level, permeating virtually all mental abilities is an underlying general ability factor g.

In the future differential psychologists are likely to borrow more extensively from developmental and experimental psychologists in order to clarify a number of remaining issues regarding the structure of intelligence. Cattell's theory represents one step in that direction. In addition, many other differential psychologists are investigating abilities from an information-processing perspective. These psychologists are interested in how people perceive, encode, store, recall, and retrieve information. Some differential psychologists feel that they will someday be able to understand the structure of intelligence more clearly if they can explain the various mental abilities in terms of these processes. By the end of the 1980s it may be that these processes will provide the structure for new models and theories of intelligence.

References

Cattell, R. B. *Abilities: Their structure, growth and action.* Boston: Houghton Mifflin, 1971.

French, J. W., Ekstrom, R. B., & Price, L. A. *Manual for kit of reference tests for cognitive factors.* Princeton, N.J.: Educational Testing Service, 1963.

French, J. W., Ekstrom, R. B., & Price, L. A. *Manual for kit of factor-referenced cognitive tests.* Princeton, N.J.: Educational Testing Service, 1976.

Guilford, J. P. *The nature of human intelligence.* New York: McGraw-Hill, 1967.

Horn, J. L. The aging of human abilities. In J. Wolman (Ed.), *Handbook of developmental psychology.* Englewood Cliffs, N.J.: Prentice-Hall, 1981.

Horn, J. L., & Knapp, J. R. On the subjective character of the empirical base of Guilford's structure-of-intellect model. *Psychological Bulletin*, 1973, *80*, 33–43.

Spearman, C. "General intelligence," objectively determined and measured. *American Journal of Psychology*, 1904, *15*, 201–293.

Thurstone, L. L. Primary mental abilities. *Psychometric Monographs*, 1938, *1*.

Thurstone, L. L., & Thurstone, T. G. Factorial studies of intelligence. *Psychometric Monographs*, 1941, *2*.

J. J. McHenry

Intelligence, Artificial. Artificial intelligence is the central concern of the growing field of cognitive science, a discipline in which philosophers, psychologists, and computer scientists are cooperatively involved. Artificial intelligence focuses on the claim that mind can be understood as a computational or information-processing system and the attempt to actually construct such a system. It sees mind as a type of cybernetic system, a system governed by feedback mechanisms of a certain type.

As Haugeland (1981) has pointed out, artificial intelligence does not refer to any conceivable attempt to synthetically produce an intelligent being. Attempts to produce an intelligent being by cloning a human or by biologically "brewing" an intelligent creature from a "protoplasm soup" would not be involved; a sophisticated robot with a supercomputer for a mind would be. The guiding principle underlying artificial intelligence (and cognitive science generally) is that mind must be understood as a computational pro-

cess, a process that can be described and explained in the same manner as a complicated digital computer.

Most work in artificial intelligence can be classified under one of two categories, *man-focused* and *machine-focused* inquiries. In both kinds of inquiries human beings are compared with machines. Man-focused inquiries attempt to understand some area of human functioning, such as perception, by constructing theories that are inspired by the manner in which computers function. Machine-focused inquiries attempt to deal with such questions as whether computers are (or could be) conscious, do (or could) feel pain, do (or could) understand language, etc.

An important distinction in machine-focused inquiries is between simulating and replicating some area of human functioning. Simulation involves a reduplication of input-output relations. That is, a machine simulates a given area of human behavior if, given the same input as a human, it reproduces the responses humans would give, regardless of how this is achieved. Replication, however, requires a machine to simulate behavior by doing it in the same manner as a human being; not only the input-output relations are the same, but the mechanisms or processes by which this is accomplished are in some sense the same. Thus a checker-playing computer program can simulate a human player if, given the same board position, it makes the same move or same type of move as a human player would. Obviously it does not necessarily choose that move in the same way the human player does. The computer program may select the move by consecutively considering every possible move (or very many moves) and analyzing likely results of each so as to choose the best. The human player may, however, consider only a few of the possible moves and make a choice based in part on an intuitive feel for the relative strength of certain positions. It is important to recognize, then, that simulating behavior is not equivalent to replicating the mental process involved in the behavior.

History. The history of artificial intelligence stretches back to Hobbes, who claimed that "reasoning is but reckoning," and Descartes, who taught that animals lacking reason, as well as the human body apart from the soul, are simply machines. Although later materialists did not wish to make the exception for soul or mind which Descartes did, for a long time no promising way appeared to explain mental functioning in machinelike terms. A step toward the realization of this mechanistic program was taken by Leibniz's attempt to invent a universal precise symbolic system that could be used for expressing all truths and their relationships. Leibniz believed that such a symbolic system, with precise symbols and grammatical transformation rules, would make it possible to solve all rational disputes by calculation.

Leibniz had himself invented a binary mathematical system, the type of system that underlies the modern digital computer. In the early 1800s George Boole (1854) employed a binary system of mathematics to express elementary logical functions such as "or" and "and," which can then be used to combine and manipulate propositions. Employing these notions Charles Babbage designed in 1835 an "analytic engine" to perform logical and mathematical operations (Dreyfuss, 1979, pp. 70–71). Because of the limitations of the technology of his day, Babbage's engine was never built. The modern electronic digital computer, operating with discrete states, is essentially a realization of Babbage's dream.

Computers as Automated Formal Systems.
To understand how a modern digital computer can be viewed as a thinking machine it is essential to understand the notion of a formal system. A formal system is really a type of game, in which particular tokens can be changed from one state or position to another by a system of rules. To qualify, a game must have definite states or positions for the tokens to occupy, as well as precise rules indicating what states a token in a given state can or must be changed to. Chinese checkers could be viewed as an example of a formal system. Games which appear to be and are different in many ways can still be formally equivalent, which means, roughly, that a position in one game always has a corresponding position in the other, and that the rules of the two games are such that there is always a legal move in one game that corresponds to every legal move in the other game.

Logic and mathematics can be viewed as formal systems, games in just this sense, though we normally think of tokens of this game as more than formal symbols since numbers and logical connectives have for us a meaning. A digital computer can be thought of as an automated formal system, a formal game which in a sense plays by itself (Haugeland, 1981). The game the computer plays is a binary form of mathematics, physically realized in the machine by electrical circuits with only two definite positions, on and off. Using Boole's logical algebra, such a game can be played

with propositions as the tokens. The interesting thing is that this logic game, played through binary circuits, can be used to mimic any formal system whatsoever; every formal game that can be played at all can in theory be played on (or by) a digital computer (Turing, 1950). The digital computer then is a universal machine; every such computer is formally equivalent to every other such machine.

Could a Digital Computer Be Conscious?
Questions as to whether digital computers can (or could) think, be conscious, have feelings, and so on, as well as more exotic questions about whether computers could have rights, have been raised more and more frequently since the early 1950s. These questions have been inspired partly by science fiction; a notable example is the malevolent computer HAL from Stanley Kubrick's 2001. Even more significant, however, are the actual accomplishments of computers. Computers can play creditable if not master's-level chess, compose music, prove logical theories, assist in translation of scientific papers from one language to another, conduct psychotherapy of sorts, and provide the "brains" for robots capable of at least limited interaction with their physical environment.

In light of such accomplishments an argument for the mentality of computers can be constructed. Since our evidence that other people are conscious consists in their behavior, if a computer could be constructed which would simulate human behavior in relevant respects, it would be irrational or at least provincial to deny that it is conscious. Hardly anyone claims that current computers achieve the requisite complexity of behavior, so hardly anyone claims that current computers are conscious. The debate is rather whether or not it is possible, both theoretically and practically, to construct computers that could be called conscious.

Many researchers in artificial intelligence exhibit a striking confidence that it will be possible to construct such a conscious automaton. Part of the grounds for this confidence is the claim, rooted in the fact that digital computers are universal machines, that whatever behavior can be clearly and logically described can be accomplished by a computer. Our inability to simulate a given behavior on a computer is due not to a limitation on the part of the computer, but to our poor understanding of the behavior. As soon as a logically precise and unambiguous description of the behavior can be given, then that formal description can be physically realized.

Suppose that artificial intelligence researchers are right, and that a conscious automaton is possible. What would this imply? Many have assumed that it would be a conclusive proof that a materialistic view of human beings is correct and that dualism is false. Naturalistic philosophers have therefore tended to support both the view that such a conscious automaton could be constructed and its corollary, that human beings are "natural automatons" of this sort, presumably the product of evolution.

That the success of artificial intelligence would lead to reductionism is not accepted by all, however. Although everyone would agree that a computer is in one respect a physical entity, thinkers such as Sayre (1969) have pointed out that the unique character of a computer program is its logical structure or form, which is not a physical characteristic, and have thus drawn the conclusion that a conscious machine would not be a material entity in a reductionistic sense. One leading researcher, MacKay (1979), sees artificial intelligence as lending support for a nonreductive holism, which distinguishes the level of meaning from the level of the physical realization of meaning without regarding the two as distinct entities. One leading materialistic critic, Searle (1981), has actually charged that artificial intelligence is dualistic, since it views the essence of mind to be a logical structure that is essentially independent of any specific physical realization.

Criticisms. Criticisms of artificial intelligence for the most part center around the philosophically loaded presuppositions or conclusions drawn by its researchers rather than the empirical research itself. Generally speaking, critics fall into two major types: those who claim that machines have not simulated and cannot really simulate the kinds of behavior that would be required as evidence of mentality, and those who claim that even if a computer could simulate human behavior, it still would lack the kind of mind that humans possess.

The first strategy is most prominently exemplified in the work of Dreyfuss (1979). Dreyfuss argues that most significant human behavior is made possible by a "tacit understanding," which is possessed in a bodily, visceral manner. Human understanding is contextual and holistic and cannot be stated in a finite set of formal rules. Dreyfuss cites the failures and difficulties of artificial intelligence researchers in fields such as natural language translation and recognition of cursive script as empirical evidence for his view.

The second critical strategy, dubbed the "hollow shell" view by Haugeland (1981), argues that even if computers are able to simulate human behavior, they could never truly replicate it. A computer can act *as if* it were a mind, but it can never truly be a mind, though it is natural for humans to metaphorically project their own traits onto the computer. One reason given for this is that computers lack consciousness. We know "what it is like" to be a human being; we wonder "what it would be like" to be a bat; we do not think that in this sense it would be "like anything" to be a computer (Nagel, 1981). A second reason for denying that computers are conscious is that their formal symbols lack meaning. A computer as a formal system plays by syntactic rules, but its tokens have only a semantic dimension when we interpret them, assign them a meaning.

References

Boole, G. *Laws of thought.* London: Walton & Maberly, 1854.
Dreyfuss, H. *What computers can't do* (Rev. ed.). New York: Harper & Row, 1979.
Haugeland, J. Semantic engines: An introduction to mind design. In J. Haugeland (Ed.), *Mind Design.* Montgomery, Vt.: Bradford Books, 1981.
MacKay, D. M. *Human science and human dignity.* Downers Grove, Ill.: Inter-Varsity Press, 1979.
Nagel, T. What is it like to be a bat? In D. Hofstadter & D. Dennett (Eds.), *The mind's I.* New York: Basic Books, 1981.
Sayre, K. M. *Consciousness: A philosophic study of minds and machines.* New York: Random House, 1969.
Searle, J. Minds, brains, and programs. In D. Hofstadter & D. Dennett (Eds.), *The mind's I.* New York: Basic Books, 1981.
Turing, A. M. Computing machinery and intelligence. *Mind*, 1950, *59*, 433–460.

C. S. Evans

Intensive Journal Workshop. A method of personal and spiritual growth where the individual works by and for himself through the medium of a workbook. Developing out of a synthesis of the later work of Freud, Jung, Adler, and Rank, intensive journal workshops were the creation of Progoff (1975). Progoff developed the concept after using notebooks to record inner thoughts in conjunction with psychotherapy. Finding that this practice depended on outside approval or disapproval from the therapist, he sought to develop a method whereby the individual could go deep into his own unconscious and probe the collective unconscious without a therapist. From 1959 to 1971 Progoff was the director of the Institute for Research in Depth Psychology at the Graduate School of Drew University, and in 1966 the intensive journal workbook was born.

The principles and techniques of this holistic approach where the individual draws on his own resources for becoming whole are taught at basic intensive journal workshops conducted by a journal consultant. The workshop teaches the individual to answer the question, "Where am I going in the movement of my life?" in a nonjudgmental, nonanalytic, nondiagnostic manner. Using the 20 sections of the notebook the individual logs inner and outer experiences and does exercises that build self-reliance and lessen dependence on outside sources for answers to the issues and problems of life.

While direct results are not precisely defined, or even sought after, indirect outcomes of the process include drawing life into focus, enlarging capacities, clarifying where the individual is now in his life, determining both internal and external resources, and developing new directions for more productive living.

Reference

Progoff, I. *At a journal workshop.* New York: Dialogue House Library, 1975.

D. L. SCHUURMAN

Interest Measurement. Interests are the likes or dislikes a person feels for objects and activities either thought about or actually encountered. These likes and dislikes may be held fleetingly, or they may be more enduring. The most effective way to measure one's likes or dislikes is the interest inventory. This technique differs from the direct expression of preferences for various work activities and occupations that could be listed on a questionnaire. In addition to listing a variety of personal values and items related to one's overall life style, the inventory assigns each possible response an empirically determined weight. Weighted scores are then added up to yield a pattern of interests rather than a single subjective estimate of interest.

Interest inventories can help people develop general strategies for life planning as well as making specific curricular and occupational choices. They can also be useful in providing information for personnel managers, supervisors, and administrators who must make career-related decisions about others (Campbell & Hansen, 1981).

The theoretical foundation for the conception and measurement of interests was most clearly provided by Fryer (1931). The story of interest measurement since then has primarily been that of the interest inventory. The first standardized interest inventory was the Carnegie Interest Inventory, conceived in 1921, from which practically every subsequent inventory is derived. E. K. Strong, Jr., who was associated with the Carnegie project, published the Strong Vocational Interest Blank in 1927, and thereby began an undertaking that continues to this day as the Strong-Cambell Interest Inventory.

The Strong-Campbell is not only the oldest interest inventory in current use but also the most extensively researched and developed instrument of its kind. It is characterized by comparisons of respondents with men or women in general, with the likes and dislikes for a full range of jobs, and with a wide variety of aspects of everyday life of persons who are stable, satisfied, and successful in particular occupations. Differing significantly from the Strong-Campbell is the much newer Jackson Vocational Interest Survey. Rather than focusing on specific occupations this inventory utilizes only two broad interest areas. The Career Assessment Inventory is patterned after the Strong-Campbell but is designed specifically for persons seeking careers that do not require a four-year college degree.

Probably the most significant issue presently facing these and other interest inventories concerns their sex fairness. Large discrepancies in the proportion of men and women in certain occupations are usually reflected as social realities in the norming tables. Therefore, interest inventories must be constructed in ways that reduce the likelihood of possible sex bias in the interpretation process. This can best be done by following the guidelines developed by the National Institute of Education (see Diamond, 1975) and through ongoing research into the structure of women's vocational interests (Farnsworth, 1969).

References

Campbell, D. P., & Hansen, J.-I. C. *Manual for the Strong-Campbell interest inventory* (3rd ed.). Stanford, Calif.: Stanford University, 1981.

Diamond, E. E. (Ed.). *Issues of sex bias and sex fairness in career interest measurement.* Washington, D.C.: Department of Health, Education, and Welfare, National Institute of Education, Career Education Program, 1975.

Farnsworth, K. E. Vocational interests of women: A factor analysis of the women's form of the SVIB. *Journal of Applied Psychology,* 1969, *53* (5), 353–358.

Fryer, D. H. *The measurement of interests in relation to human adjustment.* New York: Holt, 1931.

K. E. FARNSWORTH

See PSYCHOLOGICAL MEASUREMENT.

Interpersonal Attraction. Considerable attention has been given to the study of factors that influence our liking others. Psychologists have often utilized reinforcement theory to explain interpersonal attraction. That is, we like those who are in some way rewarding to us or who have been associated with rewarding events. Some theorists further argue that, while we are governed by self-interest in our interpersonal relationships, we have learned that rewards are maximized only if we follow the principle of equity in which each receives benefits from a relationship in proportion to what he or she has contributed to it. Thus we are distressed by relationships in which we are exploited and also by those in which we exploit others.

One of the best predictors of whether two people will be attracted to each other is their proximity. In studying the development of interpersonal relationships in a new housing project for married students, Festinger, Schacter, and Back (1950) found that one of the major factors affecting the formation of friendships was the sheer distance between houses. Research also indicates that the closer eligible men and women live, the more likely they will meet and marry.

Another factor that influences our initial attraction to another is physical appearance. While most people seem to believe that physical attractiveness plays an insignificant role in their evaluation of others, research indicates otherwise. Walster, Aronson, Abrahams, and Rottman (1966) found that the one determinant of whether college students who were randomly matched for blind dates liked each other and repeated the date was their physical attractiveness. Research suggests the presence of a physical attractiveness stereotype in which what is beautiful is assumed to be good. The stereotype is evident not only in the judgments dating partners make but in the evaluations members of the same sex make of each other, in adults' evaluations of children, and in children's liking for one another.

Research also indicates that the more similar two people are on any of a variety of attributes, the more likely they will form a friendship. The "likeness leads to liking" principle holds true for children, college students, the elderly, people of various occupations, and for those in different countries. Agreement may promote attraction because those who share our opinions provide us with social validation of our beliefs. Research is much less supportive of the notion that opposites attract or that we are likely to form close relationships with those whose needs and personalities complement our own.

Another important determinant of whether we will like another person is whether that person likes us. This is particularly true if we are experiencing self-doubt or if our self-esteem has been temporarily lowered. We are especially attracted to those whose attitude has reversed from disliking to liking.

References
Festinger, L., Schacter, S., & Back, K. *Social pressures in informal groups: A study of human factors in housing.* New York: Harper, 1950.
Walster, E., Aronson, V., Abrahams, D., & Rottman, L. Importance of physical attractiveness in dating behavior. *Journal of Personality and Social Psychology*, 1966, *4*, 508–516.

M. BOLT

See LOVE.

Interpersonal Diagnosis. The classification of psychological disorders in terms of observable social behaviors. To the interpersonal diagnostician the most important aspect of any nonorganic psychological dysfunction is the way an individual acts in relation to other people. For example, to what extent is the patient dominant or submissive? Friendly or hostile? Dependent or independent?

Traditional psychiatric diagnosis suffers from a number of defects, not all of which have been remedied by the most recent revision of the American Psychiatric Association's nomenclature, *DSM-III*. Some of these defects are an emphasis on symptoms, which tend at times to be dramatic, rather than on basic personality characteristics; a bias toward viewing psychological disorders as "diseases," which most clearly they are not; an overreliance on the clinician's subjective impressions; little if anything in the way of prescriptions for treatment (which, after all, is the most important function of any diagnostic system); and the near total neglect of social-psychological variables.

It has been suggested that there are at least six interacting psychological "systems," any one or combination of which could be used for diagnosis. These systems are motoric, perceptual, biological, cognitive, emotional, and social. Behaviorists, for example, diagnose largely in terms of the motoric system, while organically oriented clinicians stress the biological system. Interpersonal diagnosticians emphasize the importance of the social system but not to the point of ignoring the other five. It is social *behavior*, after all, that the interpersonalist attempts to classify, along with socially relevant cognitions, perceptions, and emotions. Moreover, interpersonal psychologists well recognize that many psychological disorders have a demonstrable organic etiology. Nonetheless, in the opinion of the interpersonal diagnostician, those cognitions, emotions, perceptions, and behaviors that carry the most clinical significance are the ones that relate to people.

It is important to note that mental events can be interpersonal. For example, probably all of us carry on, inside our own minds, conversations with others. Even a person marooned alone on an island would have interpersonal relationships if he or she had ever been around other people. Significant others from the past populate our psyches, a reality well captured in the opening line of a recent movie: "Death ends a life, but it does not end a relationship."

To arrive at an interpersonal diagnosis the clinician needs some kind of diagnostic scheme, some framework into which to fit the patient's data. Several such frameworks have been advanced, the two most notable of which are Leary's (1957) interpersonal circle and Benjamin's (1974) structure of social behavior. (*See* INTERPERSONAL PSYCHOLOGY.)

Leary's pioneer work was of sufficient merit to earn him an appointment to the Harvard faculty. His involvement with psychedelic chemicals began later and should not be allowed to obscure the sheer brilliance of his earlier work on interpersonal assessment. The Leary circle, as it is informally called, is constructed around two axes at right angles to each other: love-hate and dominance-submission.

To arrive at a diagnosis on the basis of the Leary circle the clinician needs first to specify carefully the level of personality from which any particular bit of information has been obtained. Leary articulated five levels: 1) the patient's impact on another, i.e., how others respond to him or her; 2) conscious self-report, i.e., how the patient conceives of and perhaps describes himself, even on such psychological tests as the Minnesota Multiphasic Personality Inventory; 3) symbolic or thematic material, e.g., what might be revealed through the Thematic Apperception Test or the Rorschach inkblots; 4) the unexpressed or avoided, i.e., those interpersonal themes that are conspicuously absent from the other levels; and 5) values. Leary's own research and most contemporary diagnosis based on it deal only with levels 1, 2, and 3.

Benjamin's system is somewhat more complicated than Leary's and is constructed around three axes: affiliation (similar to Leary's love-hate), interdependence (autonomy vs. dominance and submission, both forms of high interdependence), and focus (either on oneself or on the other person). One advantage of Benjamin's model is its versatility. It can be used globally—in terms of such general categories as "invokes hostile autonomy." It can be used molecularly—in terms of such highly specific points as "uncaringly lets go." Or it can be used in a fashion intermediate between the global categories and the molecular behaviors—in terms of such behavior clusters as "ignores and neglects."

Interest in interpersonal diagnosis, either as a supplement to traditional diagnosis or even as its replacement, seems to be mounting. From the point of view of Christian theology the interpersonal orientation has much to recommend it. For one thing, it emphasizes the importance of relationality to human personality, and it is a basic tenet of most Christian theologies that people were created for the express purpose of relating to God and to each other.

References
Benjamin, L. S. Structural analysis of social behavior. *Psychological Review*, 1974, *81*, 392–425.
Leary, T. F. *Interpersonal diagnosis of personality.* New York: Ronald Press, 1957.

Additional Reading
McLemore, C. W., & Benjamin, L. S. Whatever happened to interpersonal diagnosis? A psychosocial alternative to DSM-III. *American Psychologist*, 1979, *34*, 17–34.

C. W. McLemore

Interpersonal Psychology. An approach to basic and applied behavioral science that rests on the foundational assumption that one's personality is best defined by how one characteristically behaves toward other people. Sullivan, who was renowned for his work as both a theoretician and a teacher of psychotherapeutic practice, was the force behind the crystallization of interpersonalism. He went as far as to suggest that, apart from one's typical interactions with others, the word *personality* has no meaning. Sullivan was famous for saying, "It takes people to make people sick and it takes people to make people better."

To the interpersonally oriented psychologist the most clinically significant observation about people is how they structure their relationships. Are they dominant? Submissive? Loving? Hateful? Controlling? Freeing? Interpersonal therapists pay careful attention to what their clients attempt to do in relation to them during the therapy session as it unfolds. They also want to know everything they can about how the client interacts with people outside the consulting room. How has the patient done with others? Did the patient have a close friend during childhood? Has he or she ever been in love and, if so, at what age(s)?

What about occupational history? Relationships with parents and siblings?

Psychoanalysis and Behaviorism. Interpersonal psychology stands between the mentalism of psychoanalysis and the positivism of behaviorism, and in this sense functions for many psychologists as a unifying theoretical framework (see Wachtel, 1977). Although behaviorists in recent years have become increasingly receptive to the significance of internal events, what they call covert behaviors, the traditional behaviorist stance has been to eschew anything with a subjective cast to it. Thus, the concept of mind has enjoyed very little status among classical behaviorists, who still tend to view the new cognitive behaviorism with suspicion.

Psychoanalysts, on the other hand, have often been criticized for neglecting concrete behavior in favor of the study and alteration of psychodynamics. It is not uncommon to find analysts so immersed in the dynamics of the analysand's psychic life as to neglect what he or she might be doing to perpetuate those problems that brought the person into treatment in the first place. Interpersonalists want to retain the richness of psychodynamic study without sacrificing the rigor of methodological behaviorism—in other words, of careful behavioral science.

Intrapsychic Interpersonal Transactions. The interpersonal psychologist believes that even a person on a desert island has interpersonal relationships so long as that person had previous experience with people. Memories of these people populate the islander's mind, just as we all carry around inside mental personifications of significant people from our past. Freud referred to these personifications as introjects. When in the privacy of our own minds we hear our mother or father say "Well done," it is our mental representations of them who are silently speaking. Alternatively, we may hear someone, sounding perhaps like our grade school teacher, decry us for being "dumb."

It is not only other people's voices that we carry around inside of us, but also our stored perceptions of and reactions to them. Consequently, when we encounter someone we have never seen before, we rarely if ever respond to them in anything like a pristine way. Almost always how we perceive them and, by implication, how we react to them is conditioned by our previous experiences with persons of whom they may remind us.

Anxiety, Avoidance, and Self-defeating Cycles. Interpersonal psychologists, like many other students of human behavior and its dysfunction, are explicitly concerned with sources of anxiety. Who or what triggers insecurity? How are these stimuli prompting the person to behave in ways that may be self-defeating? Efforts to avoid anxiety are precisely what get people into psychological trouble. What a person says or does—or, perhaps, fails to say or do—evokes in other people negative responses, which in turn perpetuate dysfunctional behaviors. For example, someone who whines a great deal is likely to prompt others to respond with persecution. A person who is persecuted will, more often than not, respond by whining. Much abnormal human behavior is maintained by cycles such as these, where what Person A does both prompts and maintains what Person B does, and vice versa.

As a concrete clinical illustration of how behavioral circularity works, suppose Mary comes to therapy complaining that her husband Jim continually messes up their finances. Their bills are months in arrears and the collection agencies are beginning to harass them. She is so distraught by all this that she is seriously contemplating divorce.

Upon careful inspection it becomes evident that Jim and Mary have gone through the same behavioral cycle many times before. Like most neurotic behavior, such interactions tend to repeat themselves, even though they do not work. The cycle in this case may be that Jim neglects paying the bills for several months until the notices of default begin to pour in. Mary ignores them in the hope that Jim will finally take responsibility and straighten out their money problems. Eventually the bill collectors call her at work. When she gets home that evening, she blows up at him and takes the check-book, telling him that if he can't manage it, she will have to. She then handles the money for the next few months and, during this time, manages to restore order to their fiscal situation. However, after some time she again asks Jim if he would not like to take back control of the bills. He consents, and the cycle begins again.

The interpersonally attuned clinician will want to know what is in Mary's mind when she tries to get Jim to do their finances, what is going on inside Jim when he fails to do them adequately, and so on. Breaking this kind of dysfunctional cycle is no easy task and requires a solid understanding of what the payoffs are for each person involved. It may be that Mary very much wants a traditional home in which the man takes care of the money. Her need for this, which in turn may be motivated by a desire to gain her parents' approval of her marriage, may override the clear implication of her past experience, which is that Jim is not going to manage their finances effectively.

Jim, on the other hand, may feel inadequate to handle the finances, and this leads to procrastination. As he delays dealing with their bills, they pile up, he forgets exactly what he owes and thus overspends, and they are again in the clutches of the collection agency. Moreover, he may also employ a passive-aggressive strategy of lousing things up as a way to irritate his wife. Perhaps he bears her some grudge which, in his passivity, he has not expressed to her.

Even this analysis may not be the whole story, and obviously any attempt to make sense of such complex interpersonal behavior is dangerous. On one side, the clinican can spin out endless "psychomythologies" that simply do not correspond to reality. On the other side, the clinician may underestimate the complexity of what is going on, and his therapeutic efforts will fail when he makes too superficial an intervention.

Models of Interpersonal Behavior. Interpersonal psychologists attempt to make systematic sense of how people act in relation to one another, believing that social behavior has a certain degree of regularity and is therefore to some extent rule governed. Persons who do not say "Hello" when greeted, for example, are behaving in an unusual manner. It may be that they have poor hearing, or they may be distracted at the moment. But a person who routinely does not respond to a simple social overture is acting in a way that is sure to impair his or her intimacy with others. The interpersonal researcher wants to know what behaviors in Person A lead to what behaviors in Person B. For example, what has been the interpersonal experience of a person who refuses to respond to an ordinary social greeting. And, how are others likely to respond to this refusal? How will different responses affect the probability of future refusals?

Addressing such questions as these has led interpersonal researchers to develop and validate models of interpersonal behavior. While Sullivan was the progenitor of the interpersonal orientation, he did little to develop a scientific formulation of exactly which behaviors lead to which other behaviors during the course of social transactions. Nor did he come up with much in the way of a scheme for describing what has come to be known as a person's interpersonal style.

Timothy Leary was the first researcher to systematize interpersonal behavior. For nearly 10 years he and his colleagues worked at the Kaiser Hospital in Oakland. The fruit of their work was published in *Interpersonal Diagnosis of Personality*, which remains a classic and which obtained Leary's appointment to the Harvard faculty. Leary's model of social behavior is such that, as you proceed through the range of the behaviors it portrays, you eventually return to the place from which you began. The Leary interpersonal circle is constructed around two axes: dominance-submission, and love-hate.

Another important model was developed by Benjamin (1974), a mathematical psychologist at the University of Wisconsin Psychiatric Center. While Benjamin's model, like Leary's, has love-hate (affiliation) as one of its primary axes, it treats both dominance and submission as two kinds of highly interdependent behavior. Two further axes are therefore included in the system. On the second (interdependence) are behaviors reflecting either the giving or taking of autonomy. The polarities on this axis are autonomy versus dominance or submission, either of the latter two reflecting high interdependence. The third axis (focus) reflects the extent to which the individual's focus is on self or on others. The Benjamin model for observable behavior is portrayed on two diamonds, each of which is composed of many individual "charts points." Each of these points corresponds to a particular kind of interpersonal action. Benjamin has also provided a third diamond to account for interpersonal behavior with oneself as the object.

Both Leary and Benjamin specify rules of human social behavior. For example, both refer to complementarity—behaviors that tend to evoke each other. Within the Leary framework, for example, "guide, advise, teach" tends to prompt others to "respect, admire, conform." Both theorists also specify ways to counteract social behaviors. From the vantage point of Leary's model, the way to stop "punitive, sarcastic or unkind" action is to "support, sympathize, treat gently" or even to "pity, dote on, treat soft-heartedly." Benjamin refers to such counteractions as "antidotes." Within her model the antidote to "whine, defend, justify," for example, is "friendly listen."

(*See* INTERPERSONAL DIAGNOSIS.)

Evaluation. The great strength of interpersonal psychology is its ability to accommodate both behavioral and psychodynamic concepts and findings. Benjamin's structural analysis of social behavior model, for example, allows one to encode both observable social interactions and introjected psychological processes (those in which one's own self is the object). Some interpersonalists would argue that an even greater asset of their approach is that it explicitly focuses attention on that which lies at the heart of almost all functional psychological disturbances: what actually goes on (or has gone on) between people.

Unfortunately, however, interpersonal conceptions have always been a minority voice within psychology, and only recently has the interpersonal perspective received mainline visibility through journal articles and books. This relative neglect of the interpersonal view seems to stem from fears by behaviorists that an interpersonal orientation is insufficiently operationalized and excessively mentalistic, and fears by psychodynamists and phenomenologists that an interpersonal framework is insufficiently sophisticated with respect to mental events and excessively behavioristic.

Recent works, such as Anchin and Kiesler (1982), have served to make clinicians more alert to the importance of relationships to mental health. McLemore and Benjamin (1979) have argued that therapists can no longer afford to ignore a client's social context. This emphasis on relationships seems to be an important component of the biblical perspective on persons and is, therefore, an important movement in contemporary psychology.

References

Anchin, J. C., & Kiesler, D. J. (Eds.). *Handbook of interpersonal psychotherapy*. New York: Pergamon, 1982.

Benjamin, L. S. Structural analysis of social behavior. *Psychological Review*, 1974, *81*, 392–425.

Leary, T. F. *Interpersonal diagnosis of personality*. New York: Ronald Press, 1957.

McLemore, C. W., & Benjamin, L. S. Whatever happened to interpersonal diagnosis? A psychosocial alternative to DSM-III. *American Psychologist*, 1979, *34*, 17–34.

Wachtel, P. C. *Psychoanalysis and behavior therapy: Toward an integration*. New York: Basic Books, 1977.

Additional Reading

Carson, R. C. *Interaction concepts of personality*. Chicago: Aldine, 1969.

C. W. McLemore

Interpretation. The process whereby the psychotherapist presents to the patient an understanding of behavior, events, dreams, or other psychological material in the pursuit of the resolution of the patient's psychological distress.

The psychotherapeutic use of interpretation was initiated primarily by Freud (1913). Freud wished to provide the patient an understanding of the event or dream, an interpretation of the symbolic material present therein, an understanding of the psychic conflicts that are represented in the symbols, and finally a resolution of the patient's internal primitive desires and frustrations. Freud was principally interested in four phenomena requiring interpretation: the transference relationship between therapist and patient, somatic ailments arising from anxieties and unresolved desires, parapraxes (slips of the tongue and accidents), and most importantly dreams.

In his work Freud endeavored to establish a safe relationship with the patient in which the patient could regress to his infantile feelings and allow himself to feel like a child in the presence of the therapist. The patient would then transfer his feelings from his parents to the therapist, albeit in symbolic form. The task of interpretation, then, was to help the patient understand that the feelings he was having were the same feelings he had as an infant or young child. This interpretation then would serve as the beginning of the resolution of the patient's early unfulfilled primitive longings.

Somatic complaints and symptoms would be interpreted by Freud and his followers as representations of displaced drives. Parapraxes likewise are seen and interpreted as substitute or displaced drive gratification, inasmuch as all slips or accidents are viewed as being caused by unconscious desires.

Beyond the interpretation of the transference experience, Freud's most intense interest in interpretation came regarding patients' dreams. Freud worked toward understanding the dream by interpreting otherwise unintelligible content as symbolic. The unconscious would encode its processes in dreams as a way of hiding this material from the conscious, and the person would dream as a means of relieving the anxiety caused by repressed feelings and strivings. Most of Freud's interpretations were highly sexual in content. Thus buildings represented men (or male genitals) and landscapes represented women. A death in a dream represented a death wish, and being naked was the fear of the unconscious being discovered.

The psychoanalytic writers who have elaborated on Freud's method of interpretation offer some additional elements. Giovacchini (1979) asserts that all nontransference interpretations are not only nonessential but usually harmful. He asserts that a patient always feels depreciated when his behavior and feelings are interpreted outside of the transference relationship.

Spotnitz (1976) points out the importance of uncovering resistance before other interpretative work is begun. Spotnitz adds that the interpretation process should be consistently maturational and that one should offer an interpretation only when the patient asks for it. Interpretation is ineffective unless the content of the therapy warrants it; thus, to interpret external behavior or make a judgment about a patient may be premature and harmful. Spotnitz favors having the focus of interpretation on the feelings and thoughts that encompass the therapeutic relationship. Having fun, anger, grief, or joy in a therapeutic hour can, and should, be interpreted.

Jacobson (1971) asserts that depressive patients have extreme reactions to therapeutic interpretations and will alternatively perceive them as seductive promises, severe rejection, lack of understanding, or sadistic punishments. Like Spotnitz, Jacobson suggests the appropriate response of the therapist is his honest one: anger, grief, joy, or whatever, followed by still another interpretation. Obsessional patients will have a detached, overly logical acceptance of interpretations while perhaps not really digesting them. Dependent patients might accept all interpretations without digesting them. Character disorders may reject all of them.

The interpretive process is seen by analysts as a splitting of the ego into an observing and an experiencing part so that the former can judge the irrational character of the latter. Timing of interpretations is therefore critically important. If premature, an interpretation can strengthen resistance. No interpretations should be given until a good therapeutic alliance exists. Finally, all writers agree that the correctness and value of an interpretation should be the change that occurs in the patient's life, not merely his acceptance or rejection of it.

Psychoanalysts are not the only therapists who utilize interpretation as a therapeutic technique. Therapists of other traditions also regularly engage in meaning attribution. Behavior therapists may identify reinforcement value in symptoms, and Gestalt therapists might suggest the meaning of nonverbal behavior to be in repressed parts of self or experience. Yet the literature on interpretation is dominated by psychoanalytic thought, and it is hard to avoid recognizing the accuracy of the observations lying behind many of the analytic interpretations.

References
Freud, S. *Interpretation of dreams.* New York: Macmillan, 1913.
Giovacchini, P. L. *Treatment of primitive mental states.* New York: Aronson, 1979.
Jacobson, E. *Depression: Comparative studies of normal, neurotic and psychotic conditions.* New York: International Universities Press, 1971.
Spotnitz, H. *Psychotherapy of preoedipal conditions.* New York: Aronson, 1976.

R. B. JOHNSON

See PSYCHOANALYTIC PSYCHOTHERAPY; PSYCHOANALYSIS: TECHNIQUE.

Intimacy. There are many kinds of intimacy. Those who share a prison cell or submarine are spatially intimate. Their closeness will necessitate a certain amount of cooperation and accommodation between them. While this may lead to psychological intimacy, it is just as likely to work against it. Close friends are frequently psychologically intimate with each other, knowing and caring about the psychological functioning of the other. But friends are seldom physically intimate with each other, except, perhaps, for short visits or while they go somewhere together. Those who are married or who are members of a family are sociologically intimate with each other. That is, their fortunes are linked together in social functioning. What befalls one has direct bearing upon others in the relationship.

In tribal societies (as with the bulk of Old Testament societies) there would have been little reason to distinguish between spatial and sociological intimacy. Those related to each other shared both, and usually one's psychological intimates were also from one's family, either immediate or extended. In many such societies there is no concept "friend." In contemporary societies one typically chooses where and with whom one will share sociological intimacy. Generally persons are even more careful about where and with whom they establish psychological and sexual intimacy.

As the meaning of marriage has changed from dutifully obeying one's family or tribe to that of a free choice of mate, the kinds of intimacy idealized as occurring within marriage have increased. There is little hint of psychological intimacy between husbands and wives in the Old Testament and similarly little, if any, in the times of the New Testament. But modern marriage is idealized as providing a structure for all four kinds of intimacy; that is, the "perfect marriage" is to feature spouses who live together (spatial intimacy), personally enjoy each other's company (perhaps even as best friends), and choose to share sexual intimacy with each other and no one else.

Empirical indexing of the kinds of intimacy reported by persons in Western society suggests that the marital reality falls considerably short of this ideal in most cases. Cameron, Weber, Klopsch, Gangi, and Naramore (1977) report that the spouse is less apt to appear in the intimacy pool as age increased. Of young adults surveyed (age 18 through 25) 93% included their spouse, while only 35% of the older group (aged 65 or over) did the same. More striking is their observation that the spouse is even less apt to be regarded as a close friend as couples age (74% of young adults nominated their spouse as a close friend, and only 19% of the old did likewise).

The intimacy pool appears to change drastically over the life cycle. In the teen years friends tend to comprise a majority of the nominated intimates; thereafter they decline and typically occupy more peripheral positions in the intimacy pool. In young adulthood the spouse has the best chance of being nominated as the number-one intimate. Over time the spouse's chances of being number one dwindle, and after 40 years of marriage children are more apt to occupy high rankings in intimacy. But in quite longevous marriages children start to lose out to grandchildren and, at times, to great-grandchildren. However, with the exception of the teen years, kin are far more apt to occupy positions of psychological intimacy than are friends.

Even as marital intimacy typically falls short of the expectations generally present in our society, so too does intimacy within the family. Improvements in transportation have spread families out. Similarly the telephone has encouraged communication without physical nearness. The average American family now changes residences every five years, and about a third of all meals are fast food productions eaten away from home. The whole family eats together about twice a week. Intimacy within families would therefore appear to be decreasing.

The pattern that seems to emerge is one of gradual separation of the various forms of intimacy over time. Further, intense, long-term intimacy of any variety appears to be on the decline.

Reference

Cameron, P., Weber, T., Klopsch, J., Gangi, J., & Naramore, S. Homophyly of intimacy across the life span. In P. Cameron (Ed.), *The life-cycle: Perspectives and commentary.* Oceanside, N.Y.: Dabor Science Publications, 1977.

P. CAMERON

Introjection. This process involves the incorporation into the ego of a mental picture of an external object (animate or inanimate), transferring psychic energy from the real object to the mental image. The individual then tends to identify with the qualities and values of the introjected object even though these may be inconsistent with previously embraced perspectives. Events affecting the external object may sometimes affect the person's internal experience with the introjected image.

One example of introjection would be the junior executive who, after a drastic change in top management and company policy, takes on values, perspectives, and beliefs he previously opposed in an unconsciously motivated attempt to protect himself. As described in this example, introjection has been referred to in psychological literature as identification with the aggressor. Another example would be that of the widow who continues to direct her thoughts, conversation, and feelings toward the mental image she holds of her late husband, as if that internal picture were really he.

R. LARKIN

See DEFENSE MECHANISMS.

Introversion-Extraversion. The related concepts of introversion and extraversion were first described by Jung in the early part of this century. It represents one of his more important contributions to the description and theory of personality traits. In fact, the terms have become popular in everyday speech and are often used in lay descriptions of personality.

Jung postulated that each individual develops one of two general orientations or attitudes to the world. The first, *introversion*, is inward, toward the subjective life of the individual; the second, *extraversion*, is an outward orientation toward the external environment. Generally speaking, the introverted person will tend to be quiet, cautious, sensitive, ruminative, imaginative, and more interested in ideas than in other people. The extravert, on the other hand, will typically be seen as being sociable, friendly, outgoing, talkative, and interested in people and things. In Jung's own words, "The first attitude [introversion] is normally characterized by a hesitant, reflective, retiring nature that keeps itself to itself, shrinks from objects, is always slightly on the defensive and prefers to hide behind mistrustful scrutiny. The second [extraversion] is normally characterized by an outgoing, candid, and accommodating nature that adapts easily to a given situation, quickly forms attachments, and, setting aside any possible misgivings, will often venture forth with careless confidence into unknown situations" (Jung, 1953, p. 44).

It should be noted that Jung cautioned

against a division of complex human personality into only two rather simplistic and rigid subtypes. He stated that there are degrees of introversion and extraversion, and that the introvert will become more interested in the outer, more objective world when that world in some way affects or reflects his inner life. Conversely, when the extravert has encountered frustration or disappointment with the external world, he or she may turn inward and become more subjective and moody. In a further refinement of his theory Jung postulated that there are several different types of introverts just as there are several types of extraverts. Thus, simply referring to a person as being introverted or extraverted is insufficient and perhaps inaccurate. Finally, Jung stated that either personality orientation is neither good nor bad in and of itself. Any community of persons probably functions best when it is composed of both types. It is only when individuals develop extreme personality patterns that trouble arises. Jung hypothesized that the extreme extravert, due to the fact that he or she is strongly influenced by social surroundings and is shaped by the values and opinions of others, will likely develop pathological dependencies upon people and things. The extreme introvert, because of the emphasis on subjective reactions and internal feeling states, will likely be characterized by intense anxiety reactions, chronic fatigue, and irritability.

Other personality theorists have also been interested in the concepts of extraversion and introversion. Hans and Sybil Eysenck, for example, have constructed a personality inventory, the Eysenck Personality Questionnaire (Eysenck & Eysenck, 1975), that measures in part a person's introversive/extraversive tendencies. Using this inventory as the basis for a great deal of research, these authors and others have generally found that introverts have sensitive and easily-aroused central nervous systems, while extraverts demonstrate less sensitive, less highly aroused, and more inhibitory brain processes. Eysenck (1967) also finds evidence in his studies for a genetic predisposition to introversion and extraversion. Although childhood experiences can influence one's development along one of these personality dimensions, the genetically inherited nervous system will be primarily responsible for introversive or extraversive tendencies.

In addition to the Eysencks' test, an introversion/extraversion scale is included in the widely used Minnesota Multiphasic Personality Inventory. Although the California Personality Inventory and the Taylor-Johnson

Temperament Analysis do not have specific introversion/extraversion scales, the former test's sociability scale and the latter's active-social and quiet scale do seem to measure introversive and extraversive qualities.

References

Jung, C. G. Two essays on analytical psychology. In H. Read, M. Fordham, & G. Adler (Eds.), *The collected works of C. G. Jung* (Vol. 7). Princeton, N.J.: Pantheon Books, 1953.
Eysenck, H. J. *The biological basis of personality.* Springfield, Ill.: Thomas, 1967.
Eysenck, H. J., & Eysenck, S. B. G. *The Eysenck personality questionnaire.* San Diego: Educational and Industrial Testing Service, 1975.

D. E. ANDERSON

See PERSONALITY; PSYCHOLOGICAL TYPES, JUNG'S VIEW.

Intuition. Of the three main lines of thought regarding intuition, one maintains that there is a magical or spiritual "knowing" one can have by dipping into his or her soul. This can be the so-called female intuition and should not be ruled out as completely unscientific. There are psychologists who believe that women have an ability, learned or inherited, that allows them to know what is happening with someone else. In this same line there is much clinical experience to indicate that schizophrenics may not only have a similar ability but also may be able occasionally to know what will happen in the future, sometimes by means of predictive dreams. All these phenomena, however, are poorly researched and must be considered speculative at this time.

The second area of intuition is that used by people in their interactions with one another. This is based on observations one makes of another person in conversation. Kohut (1977) believes intuitions are actually observation conclusions that occur very quickly at an unconscious level. This means they are actually based on identifiable, if subtle, data collection.

Jung (1971) renders a unique and functional use of the term *intuition*. He identifies intuition as one-half of the polarity of sensing versus intuition, one of three such polarities which he uses to identify psychological types. This sensing-intuition polarity indicates how people perceive the world, how they gather information. Sensing types perceive the world in concrete and factual terms, while intuitive types perceive what is more abstract. Sensing is an external function, while Jung's intuition is internal.

Intuitive types in Jung's definition are imaginative, inquisitive, internal, creative, speculative, and perfectionistic. These people are interested in understanding the present in light of the past, function on hunches rather than visible facts, and are inspired by the possibilities of life rather than the present facts. Intuition of this type causes people to be interested in relationships rather than individual elements of a system. Thus intuitives focus on job, marriage, and friendship relationships.

The strength of intuition is that one can sometimes make brilliant observations of the world by looking inward. Such a person can avoid the distractions of external stimulation. The weakness of a dependence on intuition is that one who looks only inward is inclined to be stubborn about his observations, neglecting contradictory visible facts. When one looks inward for insight, one also sees sin, so an intuitive type is often inclined toward undue self-criticism.

References

Jung, C. G. *Psychological types*. Princeton, N.J.: Princeton University Press, 1971.
Kohut, H. *The restoration of the self*. New York: International Universities Press, 1977.

R. B. JOHNSON

See PSYCHOLOGICAL TYPES: JUNG'S VIEW.

Involutional Psychotic Reaction.

Previously called *involutional melancholia*, this is a depressive psychosis that appears during the involutional period of life (40 to 55 years for women, 50 to 65 years for men) in people who have no history of previous mental disorders. Common characteristics of this depression include an obsession with death, sin, and guilt, accompanied by agitation and dejection. Delusions and paranoid thinking are also sometimes present. At one time involutional psychoses were attributed primarily to the physiological changes associated with aging. Today these factors are considered much less important than the psychological reaction to these changes. Concerns over finances, physical illness, retirement, and bereavement are also frequently associated with the onset of the reaction.

Involutional psychotic reactions account for between 5 and 10% of all first admissions to psychiatric hospitals. However, the actual incidence of the disorder is probably much higher since it is frequently treated quite successfully on an outpatient basis. Electroconvulsive therapy has been shown to be very helpful, particularly in the absence of paranoid features. Antidepressant drugs and psychotherapy have also been successful treatment formats.

D. G. BENNER

See DEPRESSION articles; PSYCHOTIC DISORDERS.

IQ. *See* INTELLIGENCE; INTELLECTUAL ASSESSMENT; STANFORD-BINET INTELLIGENCE SCALE; WECHSLER INTELLIGENCE TESTS.

Isolation. An ego DEFENSE MECHANISM wherein thoughts, ideas, or memories are separated from the emotional charge with which they are normally associated. This unconscious process serves to protect the individual from the pain or conflict threatened by that association. The result is thoughts or memories which, despite their real significance in the life of the individual, are experienced as lifeless and free of emotional charge. An example would be the parent who can recount every act of child abuse entirely without conscious awareness of feeling.

R. LARKIN

Isomorphism. A hypothesis of Gestalt psychology, this is the belief that structured psychological events are similar to corresponding physical processes in the brain. It implies that for every perception there is a point-by-point correspondence to some electrical field in the brain; e.g., if there is a perceived difference of size, there will be a corresponding difference in size of the excitatory field in the brain.

Jj

James, William (1842–1910). An important figure in the intellectual history of the United States whose contributions defy simple categorization. He has been called America's first great psychologist, although he preferred not to be called a psychologist at all. James's contributions to modern thought encompass three major disciplines: philosophy, psychology, and religion.

James was born in New York City in 1842. Much has been written about the eminence of his immediate family, especially his brother, Henry, the novelist. But of greater relevance here is the influence of his father, whose writings include both philosophy and theology. Henry James, Sr., studied at Princeton Theological Seminary but turned against what he considered the formality of "professional religion." He found a congenial form of spirituality in the writings of Emanuel Swedenborg, whose writings centered on attempts to synthesize science, philosophy, and biblical doctrine. Until his matriculation at Harvard, William James never had long periods of sustained formal schooling; rather, his family was the locus of his education. Although James's mature thought bears little resemblance to the particulars of his father's views, his ultimate areas of interest clearly seem to have been influenced by his father's interests. His sympathetic attitude toward religious phenomena in a time when secularism was more fashionable also seems traceable to his father.

After periods of study of foreign languages and the arts in Europe, James enrolled at Harvard in 1861. However, he was unable to settle on a career path, studying chemistry, biology, and then medicine. He finally completed a medical degree at Cambridge in 1869 and returned to Harvard as a faculty member in 1872. James stayed at Harvard until his retirement in 1907.

One field of James's contribution is philosophy. He purposely avoided a systematic philosophy; to him the value of asking the right questions was of greater value than any answers. Like his father he eschewed even the appearance of dogmatism. He had also picked up the European custom of writing for popular rather than professional audiences. These twin "vices" of being unsystematic and popular are best expressed by Ralph Barton Perry, who called James "an explorer, not a map maker."

His most famous philosophical work is *Pragmatism: A New Name for Some Old Ways of Thinking* (1907). As an epistemological idea, pragmatism was a position on the character of truth: a statement is true if it leads to correct "uses" of the world or correct "predictions" of what will happen when one acts experimentally. In its popular form, an idea is true if it "works" when tried in a natural setting. Pragmatism was James's contribution to the founding of the functionalist school of psychology, which asserted that the important study of behavior was how an organism adapted itself for survival.

Another important doctrine was James's concept of radical empiricism. In a 1904 essay entitled "Does Consciousness Exist?" James asserted that consciousness, considered as a principle of explanation of behavior, had come to be reified and treated as a "thing" for philosophers and psychologists to discover, describe, and explain. This error represented an intellectual blind alley; James did not deny that individuals have thoughts, but all that could meaningfully be said was that thoughts had the *function* of "knowing." Radical empiricism argued that the old distinction between a knower (subject) and the known (object) was a useless dualism; the elements of the world are pure experience, and "knowing" refers merely to one possible relationship between two episodes in an individual's experience. This doctrine affected later students of epistemology, including Bertrand Russell, and it also affected psychology by reinforcing the conviction that the discipline was wrongly conceived by those who defined it as a study of "the mind."

A second field to which James contributed is psychology. Here the single work to be considered is *Principles of Psychology* (1890). Twelve years in the writing and over a thousand pages in length, the *Principles* was immediately recognized as a milestone achievement for the new discipline of psychology and was widely adopted as a textbook in Europe as well as the United States. James thought of the book as a description of the current state of affairs in psychology, which revealed the discipline to be young, incomplete, and not yet amenable to a global theory. But it might also be said that the book mirrors the years when James was publicly, albeit reluctantly, identified as a psychologist. The *Principles* contains the sum of the physiological psychology which James studied in Europe during his days as a medical student and offered as the first psychology course taught at Harvard in 1875. The *Principles* also contains a summary and critique of the experimental psychology of perception advocated by Wundt and his students. However, even though James established the first American psychology laboratory at Harvard, he professed no great enthusiasm for the results or the methods of the experimental approach to psychology.

The chapter in *Principles of Psychology* entitled "The Stream of Thought" has affected literature as well as philosophy and psychology. Opposing a mental chemistry that divided consciousness into discrete atoms such as images, ideas, or feelings, James described consciousness as having continuity like a stream which exhibits both identifiable substantive parts and transitive parts in which boundaries are blurred and distinctions are made only imprecisely. When his chapters on emotion (propounding what is now called the James-Lange theory), habit, and the multiplicity of the self are added to the list of novel ideas and fruitful reformulations of older ideas, it is clear that the *Principles* is not only James's most important work, but also one of the most influential works in the history of psychology.

Santayana (1920) once remarked that while James's *Principles* represented his best work,

he would be destined to be remembered for three lesser works: *Pragmatism, The Will to Believe* (1897), and *The Varieties of Religious Experience* (1902)—the two latter books containing the substance of his thoughts on religion. James, like his father, fled from religious orthodoxy, but for different reasons. The application of pragmatism to religion specified that beliefs cannot be held to be true on a priori grounds but must prove themselves by pragmatic test. On that score, belief in God was justifiable to James if holding that belief led an individual to better behavior than if that individual had acted from unbelief. Indeed, by objecting to the doctrine or justifying religious beliefs on historical or rationalistic grounds, James opened the door for people to expand the range of their beliefs. One can reasonably choose to believe something if one is willing to believe it conditionally and discard the belief if it fails to work experimentally.

It is no surprise that James actively entertained many nonstandard beliefs, including everything from animistic metaphysics to parapsychological phenomena. The most valuable product of those interests is the *Varieties*, in which James uses historical sources and personal documents as raw materials for a psychology of religion. In addition to discussing the phenomena of conversion, mysticism, and saintliness, James makes two central points. First, the value of religious sentiments and activities cannot be assessed by discussing the rationality of their origins. True to the spirit of pragmatism, James showed that healthy activity occurs even in people moved by questionable doctrine, and he argued that religion's function as a way of knowing life was vitally important to mankind. Second, James sought to demonstrate that one could plausibly explain religious experience by applying psychological knowledge.

Reference
Santayana, G. *Character and opinion in the United States.* New York: Scribner's 1920.

L. S. SHAFFER

See PSYCHOLOGY OF RELIGION.

Janet, Pierre Marie Félix (1859–1947). French neurologist and psychologist who sought to integrate academic psychology and the clinical treatment of mental illness. In 1882 Janet's report of an unusual case of hypnosis and clairvoyance enabled him to become a student of Charcot. He received his Ph.D. from the University of Paris in 1889 with a thesis on the psychology of automatic ideas. Then, at Charcot's invitation, he became director of the psychological clinic at the Salpétrière Hospital, where he completed his M.D. degree in 1892 with a thesis on the mental state of hysterics. He became lecturer in psychology at the Sorbonne in 1895 and professor at the College de France in 1902, while remaining a practicing physician specializing in nervous and mental disorders.

Janet was interested in both therapy and theory. He believed that academic psychology and clinical psychology could enrich each other. He thought that the level of psychic energy and the particular mental level were causes of some neurotic reactions. Janet saw neurotics as having low mental tension, without enough energy to meet life's needs. Both heredity and environment influenced the amount of energy available. Fatigue, malnutrition, disease, and even inadequate education could lead to lowered energy.

Janet proposed that persons have both conscious and unconscious mental levels. Ideas that would normally be under conscious control could split off and even develop their own system. A lack of integration could result in a splitting of the personality into alternating personalities unaware of each other. He claimed that Freud's psychoanalysis was based on his work and that of Charcot, which led to a strained relationship with Freud. Although Janet used the term *unconscious*, he was using it in a descriptive rather than a dynamic sense. He never attributed psychiatric symptoms to unconscious forces, as Freud did.

Although he was the spokesman for French psychology during the first third of the twentieth century, Janet left few followers either in France or elsewhere. He wrote many articles and 16 books, but only *The Major Symptoms of Hysteria* (1907), *Principles of Psychotherapy* (1924), and *Psychological Healing* (1925) were translated into English. He is best known for his study of hysteria. His system of psychology and psychopathology was promoted primarily by Morton Prince, a disciple of his who lived in the United States.

R. L. Koteskey

Jealousy. Variously described as a sin, an emotion, an anxiety state, or a trait, depending on the perspective of the definer, jealousy is almost as old as the human race (Cain and Abel). Perhaps it is because it is such a pervasive ingredient in the human experience that it is so difficult to define. Scripture describes jealousy as cruel (Song of Sol. 8:6), angry (Prov. 6:34), and frustrating (Prov. 27:4), but does not directly label jealousy as a sin. In

fact, most biblical references to jealousy center around God as a jealous God. God's name is jealous (Exod. 34:14); idolatry is banned on the basis of God's jealousy (Exod. 20:5); God views the church with godly jealousy (2 Cor. 11:2); we can provoke God to jealousy through idolatrous behavior (1 Cor. 10:22). These figures of speech point to the intensity of God's affection, fervency, and sincere love for his own (Harris, Archer, & Waltke, 1980).

Jealousy always involves three persons: self, a loved one, and a rival. Feelings of fear arise in the self when there is a threatened (real or imagined) loss of the affection of the loved one. A third person is always involved. "Jealousy is never wholly rational" (Cameron, 1963, p. 490). Fear can be accompanied by hostility toward the rival, and both are often intense emotions because the threatened loss strikes at one's self-esteem and narcissism. Opinions vary as to whether there is a cohesive continuum connecting "normal" jealousy with the extreme instance of morbid or delusional jealousy. Some theories posit similar dynamics for both, while others see them as different.

Jealousy is usually encountered in one or more of five different settings. The first setting occurs in the context of sibling rivalry. An only child of preschool age will often exhibit signs of jealousy when a sibling is brought home for the first time to join the family. The young child is suddenly dethroned from exclusive access to parental affection to a position where all the good emotional supplies in the family must be shared, and with a newcomer at that. Regressive behavior (soiling, thumb sucking, baby talk) may occur, or the displaced child may exhibit aggressive behavior toward the new infant (Anthony, 1970). Sibling rivalry can persist throughout childhood and even into the adult years (cf. Jacob and Esau). The second setting for jealousy is in the peer relationships which children establish in schools and neighborhoods as their social skills develop. The success or failure children experience as these friendships develop can have a powerful impact on their adult social behavior.

Love and romance provide the third major setting for jealousy. Insecure persons who are enjoying the affections of a loved one can become obsessed with losing that affection to another. Jealousy in this context can become insidious, since it preys on the unknowable aspect of a relationship and can grow into monstrous proportions. Jealousy will eventually destroy a relationship, sometimes even creating what it mistakenly suspected initially. In the Old Testament a special provision was made for the jealous husband: the offering of jealousy and the waters of jealousy (Num. 5:11–31). If a husband suspected his wife of adultery and she denied it, they were to go to a priest and present an offering. The wife would drink water mixed with soil, which would produce health in her if she were innocent and would cause her death if guilty.

The fourth occurrence of jealousy is rare but indicative of the destructive quality of jealousy: the morbidly jealous murderer. Mowat (1966) found that morbid jealousy accounted for 12% of insane male murderers incarcerated at Broadmoor in England. The crime was most frequently committed by bludgeoning or strangulation. Most morbidly jealous murderers are male; most victims are wives or mistresses. On the average these murderers had been married 10 years and had been delusional for half that time.

Finally, jealousy is a frequent symptom among the paranoid. Jealousy operates under the defense mechanisms of denial and projection and thrives in personalities with narcissistic wounds and fragile self-esteem structures. Suspicion and mistrust abound in the jealous person (Meissner, 1978), and false judgments, illogical deductions, and misinterpreted trivia feed it. While not the most important symptom of the paranoid person, jealousy is a significant one and one that greatly impairs the quality of life.

References

Anthony, E. J. The behavior disorders of children. In P. H. Mussen (Ed.), *Carmichael's manual of child psychology.* New York: Wiley, 1970.

Cameron, N. *Personality development and psychopathology.* Boston: Houghton Mifflin, 1963.

Harris, R. L., Archer, G. L., & Waltke, B. K. *Theological word-book of the Old Testament.* Chicago: Moody Press, 1980.

Meissner, W. W. *The paranoid process.* New York: Aronson, 1978.

Mowat, R. R. *Morbid jealousy and murder: A psychiatric study of morbidly jealous murderers at Broadmoor.* London: Tavistock, 1966.

J. R. Beck

Jesus Christ. Although he wrote no books on psychology, or any other subject for that matter, Jesus Christ must be counted among the eminent contributors to psychology, his contribution being through his life and teaching. Whatever one may believe about Jesus, it is safe to say that no one, upon a serious reading of the Gospels, can fail to acknowledge his role as a profound teacher. Jesus' role as a teacher derived its power and authority, in part, from the fact that he lived out what he taught. He *was* his teaching. Those who were convinced of the truth of his teaching were grasped by his presence and by the fact that his teaching was simply a verbal expression of the truth manifested by his presence. He not only spoke of love, he was loving. He not only spoke of forgiveness, he was forgiving.

Since his teachings were congruent with the truth of his being, it can be said that they had ontological validity. With respect to human nature, if a statement has ontological validity it expresses a truth about the essence of human nature. As Christians we affirm that as Jesus expressed the truth of his being in his life and teaching, he also manifested what is true for us. Jesus said, "I am the way, and the truth, and the life; no one comes to the Father, but by me" (John 14:6). His truth is our truth. For us to know God means that we have to grapple with the meaning and relevance of Jesus' truth for ourselves.

If we believe that Jesus' teachings are ontologically valid, then we also imply their psychological validity. This is to say that Jesus teaches a way of life that facilitates mental and emotional health, and brings about wholeness within. Jesus calls each one to align with a way of being which brings one inwardly in touch with the deepest possibilities within the self, to be all that one can be. If psychology ignores this way and its potential for those who have mentally and emotionally lost their way, it does so to its own detriment. One might even argue that Jesus' teachings set the agenda for psychology, for he addressed those concerns that are most fundamental to human nature. It is on these concerns that psychology needs to focus in order to contribute to the development of wholeness within persons.

What did Jesus emphasize about human nature that has implications for psychology? What really was the good news? Jesus proclaimed that one is not bound by, or limited by, that which his senses would tell him is reality. The world perceived by the senses is not the real world. The view that sees man as constituted essentially of matter, as beginning with the birth of his body and ending with the death of his body, is not only inaccurate but terribly limiting. Jesus asserted repeatedly in many different ways that there exists an inner dimension to man that is incorporeal. He called this dimension the spirit, and it is in the spirit that the real source of one's personhood and the truth of his being reside. This is the light within that must shine rather than stay hidden. The light within is a much more reliable guide to illuminate one's way than a code of expectations that comes from without, such as human traditions and laws.

This inwardness, the realm of spirit, is the kingdom of God; it is there for persons to inherit if they but seek it. At the time of Jesus the Jews were looking for a Messiah who would restore the kingdom of Israel and reign as God's representative on earth. The Jews anticipated an earthly kingdom with a political leader sent by God. Jesus turned this anticipation inward. The kingdom of God is not external and will not come as a political institution. Rather it is within. Man's connection with God is that of spirit to Spirit.

Since the kingdom of God is within, we are not separated from each other, as our three-dimensional frame of reference suggests, but at the level of being we are one. We are united and together with each other in God. Separation then becomes an illusion, a transitory phenomenon. The truth is that we are in union in spirit though we persist in our illusion of separation. Jesus directed his teachings toward enabling one to discover the nature of his being, his union at the level of being with others and with God, and the nature of his illusions.

From a psychological standpoint the inheritance of the kingdom of God may be viewed as the process of self-discovery. If self and spirit are the same, then the therapeutic process of self-discovery becomes a spiritual quest. On the one hand, the nature of each person's quest is different because each person is unique. On the other hand, since each is essentially spirit, there are challenges or tasks that each quest shares.

Jesus' teachings are most relevant for psychology because he addressed those challenges that are common to everyone's quest. For example, the process of self-discovery has to involve at some point the severing of dependency ties to parents. Jesus addressed this challenge when he said: "Do not think that I have come to bring peace on earth; I have not come to bring peace but a sword. For I have come to set a man against his father, and a daughter against her mother, and a daughter-in-law against her mother-in-law; and a man's foes will be those of his own household. He who loves father or mother more than me is not worthy of me; and he who loves son or daughter more than me is not worthy of me" (Matt. 10:34–37). Jesus did not mean that he had come to foster domestic strife but rather that the process of following him, the quest for the discovery of the truth of one's own being, inevitably involves a revision of the nature of one's parental relationships. This can cause strife, but strife is certainly not the primary goal.

What is it that Jesus taught that is most germane to the tasks we all face in the process of self-discovery? Jesus said that the two most important commandments are, "You shall love the Lord your God with all your heart, and with all your soul, and with all your mind. . . . And . . . you shall love your neighbor as yourself" (Matt. 22:37–39). These commandments put the challenge to be loving at the heart of self-discovery. A close look at the first commandment suggests it can be taken as an exhortation and as a statement of fact. As an exhortation it is a directive. As a statement of fact the first commandment contains the truth that what one has as one's central concern one *will* love with all one's heart, soul, and mind. "Where your treasure is, there will your heart be also" (Matt. 6:21) is another way of saying this. If the pursuit of money has become one's central concern, then that is what will grasp one totally. If another person has become one's central concern, then that relational involvement will grasp one totally. This fact underlines how important it is that one's central concern allow for the fullest and most meaningful growth of oneself. To love anything short of that which calls forth the fullest expression of one's being only violates one's being. Love of God is the only central concern that does not violate one's being.

Too often love of God implies an objectification of God, as though God is out there somewhere and it is one's duty to love him and worship him. Once God is objectified, what becomes emphasized is one's separation from him. As long as one believes there is a separation that must be bridged, he precludes the bridgement. One's belief sustains the separation. To love God without objectifying God is to commit oneself to love. For "God is love." To love God is to love loving. To love loving is to make loving God one's central concern.

To take on the challenge to be loving does not violate one's being. In fact it draws the fullest possible expression of one's being out of oneself. To be loving also requires one to love one's own being. One cannot reject or hate oneself and love another, for since a person relates through himself to another and since his self is the channel for love, self-rejection sabotages his efforts to love. He cannot relate around himself to another. One relates through one's self-hate, and ends up projecting this on the other in such a way that the other comes to be seen as an attacker.

The relationship between love of self and love of another leads to the second commandment, "You shall love your neighbor as yourself." This can also be seen as a statement of fact as well as an exhortation. As an exhortation it is a directive. As a statement of fact it asserts that you *will* love your neighbor as yourself. If you love yourself, you will love your neighbor. If you do not love yourself, you cannot love your neighbor. So love of self becomes the basis for love of neighbor.

This may sound egocentric. However, egocentricity and self-love are antithetical. Egocentricity is self-protectiveness, not self-love. Egocentricity seeks to resolve feelings of insecurity with the erection of defenses around the self. Then these defenses come to be taken for the self and one loses sight of his true self.

Self-love is self-affirming and seeks the nondefensive expression of being. Self-love emerges in the struggle to be loving, for in this effort one has to cull away the inner obstacles to self-love. As one lovingly engages in this culling process, he is brought closer and closer to the beauty of his own being. This is a gradual and lengthy process and requires an ongoing rigorous self-examination to bring to awareness the nature of one's defenses and the myriad ways one substitutes a reliance on them for being true to oneself.

How does one learn to love? This is not a question that can be addressed prescriptively. One cannot really tell another how to love, one can only suggest he go and try it. Jesus did show what it means to love by loving those around him. How did Jesus love? He remained consistently true to himself in all his interactions with others. He insisted on his freedom to be true to his own being and granted the other the freedom to be true to his being. He shared his vision of himself unreservedly and so awoke those around him to their own beings.

Forgiveness as a manifestation of love is crucial to the process of self-discovery. In the struggle to forgive one discovers himself, because in forgiveness he shifts his focus from blaming another for having wronged him back to himself. In blame one can only see another's fault. One loses sight of himself in the challenge to be himself in truth. In blame one says, "I cannot be until you acknowledge the wrong you did to me." As Finch asserts: "How little do we appreciate the fact that what gets the focus of our attention, gets us. The feat of holding some grudge actually has the effect of the grudge holding us. Being unwilling to let go of yesterday retards us. The self becomes stifled in a mode of existence that does not exist" (Malony, 1980, pp. 253–254).

Forgiveness is particularly relevant in working through the blame one holds toward one's parents. As long as one blames one's parents for their failures to care, one continues to hold one's parents responsible for one's being. It is as if one says to one's parents, "You have been bad parents and until you become good parents, on my terms, I cannot be myself." If one cannot be oneself, one cannot love oneself. So the blame one sustains toward one's parents impedes one's self-discovery. Forgiveness is the only antidote. In forgiveness one releases any claim one has on the other to be good on one's own terms.

Forgiveness is not simply an intellectual process. It may necessitate that one experience intense rage in order to allow one to existentially discover the basis for one's blame. Forgiveness, if genuine, is a process of working through one's feelings to a release of a grudge one is holding against the other. The challenge to forgive is ongoing. Any time one turns away from forgiveness, one locks oneself into a grudge and imprisons oneself therein.

The effort to be loving in all love's manifestations facilitates the emergence of authentic selfhood. To live in this effort is to take Jesus' teachings seriously. If psychology ignores what Jesus taught by way of modeling and by way of instructing, it ignores what is crucial to the accomplishment of the clinical task—that of facilitating the development of personhood.

References
Malony, H. N. (Ed.). *A Christian existential psychology: The contributions of John G. Finch*. Washington, D.C.: University Press of America, 1980.

W. T. WEYERHAEUSER

Job Analysis. The process by which a job is defined and its behavioral requirements identified. It provides the personnel psychologist with an empirical basis for selecting predictors of performance, developing performance appraisal measures, diagnosing training needs, planning career paths, anticipating human resource requirements, and coordinating worker roles. Indeed, job analysis is a fundamental tool, useful in practically all aspects of human resource management and development.

Job analysis information can take many forms. Traditional job descriptions document essential job facts such as major responsibilities, procedures, work environment, and conditions of employment (e.g., pay). Modern methods of job analysis, however, go beyond these facts to systematically examine specific job tasks and the behaviors, abilities, and skills necessary for their accomplishment. Thus, the distinction between job description and job analysis is that the latter yields both an overall picture and a fine-grained behavioral analysis of the job.

There are basically three ways to gather information about jobs: observation, performance, and questioning the experts. Job observation, either by a human observer or by mechanical means (e.g., videotape) is particularly useful with manual, short-cycle jobs. Job performance requires the job analyst to actually learn and do the job. This method, like observation, can be useful for simpler jobs, but its utility quickly declines as jobs become more complex. For example, it would be difficult to observe a sample of the many tasks of an attorney within a reasonable amount of time. Furthermore, direct observation of an attorney's behavior would tell you relatively little about the cognitive demands of the job. For the job analyst to actually perform the job would obviously take far more training time than is available. Considering these limitations and the fact that the number of complex jobs relative to simple jobs is increasing, it is not surprising that the use of these methods is on the decline.

Asking job experts—that is, those who know the job well—is the most common approach to job analysis today. Interviews and/or questionnaires are used to elicit this information. Comprehensiveness and efficiency are the primary advantages of this method, but job analysts must be alert to the possibility that job experts, particularly incumbents, may exaggerate the difficulty or importance of the job. One way to counteract this potential bias is to gather information from several experts— e.g., supervisors and incumbents. As with many measurement problems, multiple perspectives allow us to converge on a more accurate picture of reality.

Job information gathered from experts can be broken down into two types. Job-oriented information emphasizes what work is accomplished rather than what the worker does to accomplish it. In addition to work outcomes job-oriented information may describe the purpose, procedures, materials, conditions, and responsibilities of the job. In job-oriented terms, a personnel director must recruit new employees, administer the compensation program, and supervise the assistant personnel director. Note that the descriptors used in the job-oriented approach are fairly job specific. Examples of this approach are the task inventories developed by the U.S. Air Force (Morsh, 1964).

Worker-oriented information focuses on the actual behaviors and worker attributes (e.g., abilities, traits) necessary to accomplish the job's tasks. Worker-oriented analysis is therefore more process oriented than is job-oriented analysis. A worker-oriented description of a personnel director's job might include a behavior like giving specific feedback to subordinates and an attribute like the ability to plan a departmental budget.

The critical incidents technique (Flanagan, 1954) and the Position Analysis Questionnaire (McCormick, Jeanneret, & Mecham, 1969) are noteworthy examples of worker-oriented methods of job analysis. The critical incidents technique asks job experts to describe, in detail, anecdotes or incidents depicting effective or ineffective worker performance. These incidents provide the job analyst with a concrete picture of critical job behaviors, when they should occur, and why they are important. Because the incidents exemplify the differences between effective and ineffective workers, the critical incidents technique is particularly valuable in developing measures for performance appraisal. Its chief disadvantage is that it is time-consuming and therefore expensive.

The Position Analysis Questionnaire presents the job expert with 194 job elements that are then rated on such factors as extent of use, time spent, and importance. The questionnaire is composed of six divisions: information input, mental processes, work output, relationships with other persons, job context, and miscellaneous job characteristics. It is relatively inexpensive to administer, useful in developing job families, and provides job information amenable to quantitative analysis. Its main disadvantage is its requirement of a college graduate reading level (Ash & Edgell, 1975), a fact that makes it difficult for many job experts to use and understand.

Legal issues in personnel management have played an important role in pointing out the significance of systematic job analysis. In the area of personnel selection the courts and the *Uniform Guidelines on Employee Selection Procedures* (1978) have been very explicit in requiring that selection measures and performance criteria be based on a job analysis. Numerous cases of alleged racial discrimination have turned on the fact that employers could not show that their job performance criteria, against which selection tests were validated, were developed from a systematic job analysis. Sex discrimination in pay is a topic of current debate, both in and out of court. One key question here is whether jobs occupied by men and women are sufficiently similar to require comparable pay rates. Such job similarities can be established only by job analysis.

Given these societal demands, and its central role in many personnel functions, job analysis is likely to receive more and more research attention from industrial/organizational psychologists in the future.

References

Ash, R. A., & Edgell, S. L. A note on the readability of the Position Analysis Questionnaire (PAQ). *Journal of Applied Psychology*, 1975, *60*, 765–766.

Flanagan, J. C. The critical incident technique. *Psychological Bulletin*, 1954, *51*, 327–358.

McCormick, E. J., Jeanneret, P. R., & Mecham, R. C. *Position analysis questionnaire*. West Lafayette, Ind.: Purdue Research Foundation, 1969.

Morsh, J. E. Job analysis in the United States Air Force. *Personnel Psychology*, 1964, *17*(1), 7–17.

Uniform Guidelines on Employee Selection Procedures. *Federal Register*, 1978, *43* (166), 38295–38309.

D. D. McKenna

See Industrial/Organizational Psychology.

Journals, Use in Treatment. *See* Intensive Journal Workshop.

Jung, Carl Gustav (1875–1961). Swiss psychotherapist, founder of Analytical Psychology. Eight of Jung's uncles were clergymen; his father was a Lutheran pastor who inwardly struggled with the validity of his faith throughout his life. Jung began to perceive that the religion of his father, and of most Christians, seemed to consist of theological doctrine—i.e., knowledge about God at the expense of the experience of God. He advocated primary knowledge of God. Shortly before his death, when asked the direct question whether he believed there was a God, his response was, "No, I do not believe, I know."

Life's opposites fascinated Jung; his parents exemplified what he later saw as the inevitable nature of things. His mother was earthy, while his father was spiritually removed. His early observations laid the foundation for later extravert-introvert theories.

Jung studied at the University of Basel and the University of Zurich. Though he pursued a degree in medicine, he also studied philosophy and theology. Between the ages of 16 and 25 he read widely in theology and philosophy, moving from Plato, to Kant and Hegel, to the mystic Eckhardt, and to Nietzsche. It was while reading the *Textbook of Insanity* by Krafft-Ebing that he felt his calling. Here was the blending of the spiritual and the biological.

Psychiatry was not a respected vocation in the early twentieth century, however, and Jung went against the advice of teachers and friends when he became Bleuler's assistant at the Burgholzli mental hospital in 1900.

Jung was quickly promoted to senior staff physician there, and in 1902 he went to Paris to study psychopathology with Janet. His fascination with the occult led him to research a young medium's work. His doctoral thesis "On the Psychology and Pathology of So-called Occult Phenomena" included themes that would later be incorporated into his theories. He saw the personalities the medium assumed during her trances as manifestation of the parts of herself buried in her unconscious.

In these initial years Jung produced the thesis that behind all psychosis and its strange manifestations is a story. Therapy, in Jung's perspective, only began after the investigation of that whole story. At the center of that story was a secret that wanted to be revealed. His next experiments were in word association. This work led to his definition of complexes, influential linked ideas or collections of associations that determine behavior.

After being appointed lecturer at the University of Zurich in 1905, Jung published a pioneering work on schizophrenia in 1907, *Psychology of Dementia Praecox*. He theorized that delusions and hallucinations could have psychological origins; Jung was one of the first to attempt psychoanalytic treatment of these cases. After Freud read the book he asked to meet Jung in Vienna. This was the beginning of Jung's seven years of close association with the psychoanalytic movement. A schism developed when Jung published *Psychology of the Unconscious*, in which he proposed that the son's incestuous desire for his mother lay in spiritual roots. Indeed, Jung's growing interest in the unconscious and its relationship to a person's general and religious history diverged from Freud's emphasis on infantile sexuality. These and other differences led to Jung's inevitable break with the psychoanalytical school in 1913. Meanwhile, he was busy in intense studies of his own unconscious. Preceding and during World War I he was troubled by dreams of Europe drowning in blood. He recorded these dreams and even painted them, as an artistic expression of his unconscious drives. During this period Jung formulated important life concepts, namely that one must be aware of and harness both the conscious and the unconscious aspects of the psyche.

Though Jung maintained his practice at his house at Kusnacht on Lake Zurich, he traveled extensively to lecture and received many honorary awards. Though his first lecture tour of the United States was with Freud, he later went back on his own. In 1924 he studied the Pueblo Indians in New Mexico. Looking for lost aspects of the human myth, he also studied a variety of cultures in Europe and Africa. In India he was impressed with the Buddhists' ability to assimilate the nature of opposites more effectively than was evidenced in Western culture.

Jung's lifetime of study, travel, and introspection substantially advanced the study of psychology. His major areas of contribution include definitions and development of personality types (extraversion/introversion, intuiting/sensing, feeling/thinking), the collective unconscious, archetypes, the self, the nature of dreams, word association, the value of myths, individuation, and the psyche's drive toward wholeness.

Jung's emphasis on the reality of the soul and his incorporation of this reality into his analytical psychology enables one to see numerous connections between analytical psychology and religion. Jung had a deep and abiding respect for the Bible and saw it as a book that speaks of the meaning of life, the meaning of death, and of the mysteries of evil and suffering as well as the mysteries of love and healing. It deals with the psychic fact of sin and guilt and the liberation that comes with forgiveness. Above all it deals with the holy, with the realities that are beyond words and simple formulations. Much of the power of the Bible for Jung was in its stories, figures, and symbols.

In 1952 Jung published an essay entitled *Answers to Job*, which touched on the psychological understanding of Scripture. He made some significant connections. He postulated that all religious statements are rooted in the soul, or psyche, and are forms of confessions of the soul. He felt the purpose of religious statements was the tutelage of souls. Jung also saw religious statements as being rooted in the experience of the transcendent. For Jung the psyche/soul is the place where the divine and the human intersect. He understood that Christ was the divine model of that intersection. He also affirmed that the cross is the most appropriate symbol of that intersection between the vertical and the horizontal and that it represents the need for the ego to die so that the soul could come to life.

Jung proved to be one of the most prolific writers in the field of psychology and religion. He left a legacy of material, most importantly,

Symbols of Transformation; Psychological Types; Two Essays on Analytical Psychology; The Archetypes and the Collective Unconscious; Psychology and Religion: East and West; Memories, Dreams and Reflections; Man and His Symbols; and Modern Man In Search of a Soul.

D. J. FRENCHAK

See JUNGIAN ANALYSIS; PSYCHOLOGICAL TYPES: JUNG'S VIEW.

Jungian Analysis. At the turn of this century Jung and Freud independently developed their ideas about the reality and importance of the unconscious. Freud, the older man, was the first to publish some of his findings, and Jung was greatly impressed by Freud's work. The two met and enjoyed a close working relationship and friendship from about 1906 to 1913, when personal and theoretical differences drove them apart.

After he left Freud, Jung worked alone and developed his own depth psychology, which he called analytical psychology to distinguish it from Freud's psychoanalysis. Jung agreed with Freud on the idea of libido or psychic energy, on the existence of the unconscious part of the mind, on repression, and on the importance of dreams. However, Jung believed the unconscious contained not only repressed or forgotten memories and emotions that were personal to an individual but also typical patterns of energy and behavior that were common to everyone. These patterns Jung called archetypes. He called the latter strata of the unconscious the collective unconscious or objective psyche to distinguish it from the personal unconscious.

Jung also observed in people an innate urge toward wholeness. He distinguished between the ego and the self. The ego he regarded as the center of consciousness, while the self was the center of a total personality that embraced both the conscious and the unconscious. He believed the self to be the whole personality that exists from the beginning as a potentiality and strives to be realized through a developmental life process in which the ego must participate. Jung called this process individuation. In this process the center of the personality shifts from ego to self, and as the ego becomes more conscious of the self, the range of consciousness greatly expands.

Process and Style. The cornerstone of Jungian analysis is the individuation process. The Jungian analyst tries to help this process take place in his client in the belief that as a person individuates he becomes more whole and therefore finds healing and a creative solution for his difficulties.

Jung did not prescribe any set treatment methodology. For one thing, he perceived that people are psychologically different. Some are extraverts (more oriented to outer reality), and some are introverts (more oriented toward inner reality). In addition there are four psychological functions: thinking, feeling, sensation, and intuition. Each person uses one of these functions as his or her main function, and this determines one's particular approach to life. For this reason a therapist of one personality type may work differently than a therapist of another type. A therapist may also work one way with a client who is an introverted thinking type, and a different way with a client who is an extraverted feeling type.

In addition, Jungian psychology as it is practiced today is not a monochromatic system. Some Jungian analysts tend to pattern their therapy after Jung's own approach. Others are more eclectic in their approach and may combine Jungian methods with methodologies from other schools of psychology. Still others have altered Jung's original ideas so much that they refer to their psychology as archetypal psychology to distinguish it from Jung's original analytical psychology. In addition, Jungian analysts come from varied professional backgrounds, and this also may influence how they work as therapists.

Techniques. Nevertheless, there are certain typical methods and procedures widely used in Jungian analysis. While Jungian analysts can and do function as marriage counselors, family counselors, and group therapists, the main thrust of Jungian analysis is individual therapy. Because all Jungian analysts are trained first as psychotherapists, generally accepted psychotherapeutic procedures are usually followed. However, in addition there is an attempt to work with unconscious material as it emerges in dreams, fantasies, slips-of-the-tongue, etc. It is the use of unconscious material that distinguishes analysis from therapy or counseling. Viewed in this way all analysis is a form of therapy, but not all therapy is analysis, since a great deal of therapy deals only with the ego.

Dreams are frequently especially important in Jungian analysis. Dreams are seen as manifestations of the unconscious that tend to compensate inadequate or one-sided ego attitudes. They are regarded as emanating from the self, and for this reason they tend to illuminate and heal when they are recognized, contemplated, and (when possible) understood. The language of dreams is symbolic. This means that they use something known and familiar in the everyday world of consciousness to represent something that is unconscious and therefore not yet known. In this way unconscious contents can approach consciousness and thus enlarge and creatively alter a person's conscious viewpoint.

Dreams are pertinent to particular people at specific times in their lives. For this reason no single theory of the meaning of dreams is always applicable. Jung rejected Freud's narrow interpretation of dreams as always symbolic of repressed sexual urges. Instead of imposing a meaning on the dream from some theoretical structure, the Jungian analyst tries to listen carefully to the structure and symbolism of the dream to see what the dream itself is expressing.

Because dreams are, like a tailor-made suit of clothes, so highly individual, one needs to know who the dreamer is and what that person's life circumstances are before a dream can be understood. When a client presents a dream, he is often encouraged to express his associations to the various dream symbols and images. Sometimes the analyst may also amplify the dream by pointing to similar archetypal motifs in myths and fairy tales. It is as important to explore the dream as a living experience as it is to interpret the dream along the lines of psychological theory.

Dream images, and other manifestations of the unconscious as well, may be further developed by the process of active imagination. In this process a person who is fully awake and alert interacts with images that have arisen from the unconscious. For instance, a figure who appeared in a dream may be brought back to consciousness and a dialogue with that figure may develop. By concentrating on dream figures and images they may begin to have a life of their own, and the ego can then interact with the enlivened psychic image. Sometimes a whole story may develop, the dream or fantasy being continued in this way and allowed to evolve. This method allows consciousness and the unconscious to approach each other, and permits the self, as a function of the psyche transcending and uniting them both, to bring about a process of inner unification. Because active imagination requires a certain amount of psychological maturity and development, it is not a recommended procedure with everyone and often is utilized only in later stages of analysis.

Jungian analysis also regards creative expressions of the psyche as important for the healing process. Dancing, painting, sculpting, and writing are often found to be helpful ways to express and integrate the unconscious. When these methods are used, the point is not to become a good dancer or artist, but to use nonintellectual ways of contacting the vital energy of the self. It is also often recommended that a client keep an informal notebook called a journal in which he or she can record and contain dreams, fantasies, thoughts, creative inspirations—in fact, anything that crosses the screen of consciousness.

The Analytic Relationship. Jung regarded the relationship between therapist and client as especially important. It was his belief that in the process of therapy the personality of the therapist could beneficially affect the personality of the client. If this is to happen, the therapist must be a relatively conscious, mature, and ethical person. Because Jung felt the relationship of therapist and client was so important, he rejected Freud's idea that the client should lie on a couch and the therapist sit behind him. Instead he worked with his clients face to face so there could be a direct and equal interaction.

The relationship between therapist and client is called the transference. The transference may be a relatively simple matter of rapport, a warm relationship in which the concerns of the client can be talked over in a friendly and understanding atmosphere. The transference also includes the hopes and expectations that the client brings into the relationship, plus the interest in the client that the therapist brings. But sometimes the transference may include the transferring to the therapist of reactions that come from childhood. For example, the client may unconsciously see in the therapist the figure of the mother or father and repeat patterns of relating that were learned in childhood. The transference may also include the projection onto the therapist of unconscious archetypal images. For instance, the savior archetype may be projected onto the therapist, or the archetype of the anima or animus (the contrasexual side of a man or woman).

Projection is an unconscious mechanism that results in vital aspects of one person being seen in the other person. When projections occur in the transference, it is helpful, and often necessary, to analyze them in order to make conscious the projected images. In this way the client can withdraw his projections, taking them back into himself so to speak, and thereby enlarge the scope of his personality.

Of course, it may also work the other way around, and the therapist may project contents of her own onto the client. This is called the countertransference. It is expected that with the help of her extensive personal analysis the therapist will be aware of this when it happens and will integrate what is taking place within herself.

One reason for the importance of the relationship between the therapist and the client is that it provides a container for the client's personality. Their relationship has been likened to an alchemical vessel in which the various components of the client's psyche can be contained and gradually transformed: projections can be recognized and withdrawn, dreams can be remembered and reexperienced, emotions can be freely expressed and integrated, all within the "closed vessel" of the analytical relationship.

Training. Since so much in the process of Jungian analysis depends on the personality of the therapist, Jungian training programs place a heavy emphasis on the therapist's individuation. The wholeness, consciousness, and integrity of the therapist are thought to be as important as the acquisition of techniques of doing therapy. For this reason the cornerstone of training to be a Jungian analyst is the continuing analysis of the therapist, although many other things are also involved.

Training is undergone at Jungian Institutes in major cities throughout the United States and Europe. While requirements for admission to training programs vary from one institute to another, all require that a person is or will soon be a licensed psychotherapist, and that he have a considerable amount of personal Jungian analysis. Psychiatrists, psychologists, marriage and family counselors, specially licensed social workers, and sometimes clergy may all be eligible for training programs that lead to certification as a Jungian analyst.

Jungian Analysis and Other Traditions. Jungian analysis can be compared to other psychological approaches and to Christianity. As indicated, Jung agreed with many of Freud's ideas, but saw the psyche in a much broader light than Freud and never insisted upon a specific treatment methodology. Like Rogers, Jung believed the psyche was self-healing and that the true "doctor" was in the patient; but unlike Rogers, Jung emphasized the importance of integrating unconscious material. Jungian psychology sees the emphasis transactional analysis places upon the interaction of parent-child-adult as the exploration of an important archetype (that is why it is so universally applicable), but understands that personality includes many other archetypes in addition to this one. Where Gestalt psychology has little personality theory, Jungian analysis rests on an extensive theory of personality. Gestalt therapy also frequently utilizes an extraverted group approach, whereas Jungian work usually is individual and frequently more introverted.

The concepts of analytical psychology can both enrich and challenge the Christian viewpoint. For instance, Jung's theory of the collective unconscious can be viewed as giving a scientific basis for the biblical view of the objective existence and reality of a spiritual world. Likewise, Jung's idea of individuation corroborates and vitalizes the Christian premise that the life of the individual has a meaning. On the other hand, Jung's idea that Christ is a symbolic representation of the self may enrich the Christian doctrine of Christ as the Son of God, but it also challenges the Christian idea of a unique revelation in Christ, since Jung saw the self represented in many different religious traditions. Finally, Jung's treatment of the nature of evil, and its relationship to the self and to individuation, may also prove problematical to the Christian.

Yet some of the methods frequently used in Jungian analysis can be helpful to the Christian counselor or spiritual director. Jung's emphasis on the importance of dreams, for instance, finds ample support in the view of the Bible and early church, where dreams were universally regarded as an important way in which God spoke to people. Jung's symbolic approach to the unconscious also finds a fruitful parallel in the parables of Jesus, for Jesus also taught in the "as if" language of symbols. The Bible also contains several excellent instances of active imagination—e.g., Ezekiel's vision of the dry bones and Isaiah's vision of Yahweh.

J. A. SANFORD

See ANALYTICAL PSYCHOLOGY.

Jungian Psychology. See ANALYTICAL PSYCHOLOGY.

Juvenile Delinquency.
Now a distinct category within the study of criminology and the function of the criminal justice system. Its scope includes particular definitions of certain behavior, a body of theoretical explanations of that activity, and specific treatment of persons caught enacting such behavior.

Definitions. Juvenile delinquency usually defines two types of behavior: 1) violations of law by a juvenile and 2) status offenses, such as

antisocial behavior or incorrigibility, which legally apply to juveniles only. States differ in their criteria for delinquency but generally set the age limit for such designation between 16 and 18. Violations of law by those over the designated age are defined as adult crimes and treated accordingly. Serious violent behavior may be treated as an adult crime, particularly when the death sentence or life imprisonment is the designated punishment. The juvenile may then be tried as an adult.

Official statistics, which do not represent the actual amount of crime on the streets, indicate that one-third of all crimes are committed by those under 18 years of age. Juveniles account for 10% of all murders and two-thirds of all robberies, rapes, and assaults (U.S. Department of Justice, 1978, pp. 180–181).

Separate from these legal violations are status offenses. Status offenses are behaviors which if performed by adults would not be illegal. These include sexual activity, incorrigibility, runaway behavior, and truancy. Such activity is usually brought to the attention of the juvenile court by parents but may also result from social service or law enforcement referrals.

Status offenders are sometimes referred to as persons or children in need of supervision, and juvenile court jurisdiction over such is a much debated issue. Some maintain there is little distinction between youths who commit delinquent acts (breach of law) and those who are status offenders. Juvenile courts are thus argued to be the sole and logical agencies to provide services to both groups.

Opponents of this view point out that the courts fail to provide adequate help and intensify the problems by labeling and stigmatizing children. Introduction to the criminal justice system is believed to determine future delinquent behavior by locking the individual into the system. Diversion from the system into social service agencies is recommended to short-circuit the progression of juvenile delinquency to adult criminal activity.

In addition to the distinction between delinquency and status offenders there is a differentiation of treatment within the status offense itself. Evidence suggests that female status offenders are subject to harsher treatment than males. Almost 75% of all female status arrests and incarcerations are for promiscuity, disobedience, and runaway—offenses for which juvenile males are less often charged (Abadinski, 1982). Despite the fact that female behavior represents less threat to the community, girls are often held in detention for longer periods of time and less frequently placed in community programs than boys. Since most status offenses are products of home problems (reaction to and flight from alcoholic or abusive treatment), some states have decriminalized these offenses, thus eliminating such activity from their criminal codes.

Explanations of Delinquent Behavior. Explanations of juvenile delinquency generally fall into psychological and sociological perspectives. Theorizing has increasingly moved from psychological frameworks to sociological ones.

Sociological theories can be profitably viewed as falling on a continuum between macro theories at one pole and micro theories at the other. The macro view favors a consensus/order view of society wherein equilibrium and social survival are paramount. Social problems are the result of anomie—people who are out of step with the norms of society. The solution to these problems involves the adjustment of such individuals to the prevailing social norms. The individual is a product of the environment and thus is determined by outside stimuli. The individual is a cell in the organism. The role of science is to explain and predict.

The micro perspective is diametrically opposite. Society is the sum of the individuals' interactions. People are free and valuable, and the goal of the social order should therefore be humanistic in providing for self-affirmation. Social problems are the result of a bad social order that alienates certain portions of the population. Solutions to such problems are derived from adjustment or change in the social order. The role of science is to better understand humanity and create a more favorable quality of life.

The major explanations of delinquency fall on both ends and at the middle of this continuum. Characteristic of the micro perspective is the symbolic interaction framework which asserts delinquency is a learned process that emerges from the delinquent's primary or reference group (Sutherland & Cressey, 1960). This group is composed of the youth's significant others to whom the individual looks for acceptance and with whom the associations are learned in early life and are most frequent, long lasting, and intense.

If the group with whom he primarily associates is delinquent, the individual adopts the values and expectations of that group and eventually the concomitant identity, labeled as delinquent by others. At some phase the label is adopted by the individual as a self-concept.

This labeling process also takes into consideration the status allocated by others. For example, a child who is labeled bad, deviant, or delinquent may become bad, defining himself and performing in terms of those expectations. This approach has been utilized to trace alternation of identity from one self-concept to another, referred to as deviant drift, and maps the social and personal reconstruction of delinquent and deviant identity.

Macro theories see delinquency in terms of the functions of a subculture or gang structure which provides what cannot be achieved within the formal institutions of society at large. Miller (1958) suggests that delinquency is a product of lower-class cultural values. These values implicitly affect behavior patterns formed as responses to frustrations with the dominant cultural values. Delinquency is thus an ordering structure for anomic youths who are out of step with the society at large. Cohn (1955) presents a variation on this theme, suggesting that youth may create delinquent gangs in order to cope with the difficulties faced at the bottom of the social ladder. Delinquents are said to take their norms from the culture at large and turn them upside down as a means of defiance.

Cloward and Ohlin (1960) have stated that delinquent members are not only those who have been unable to function within the larger social context but also those who see their failure as a fault of the social order itself. Three distinct subcultures are identified which are characteristic of delinquency: 1) criminalistic—theft-oriented groups which serve to introduce the youth to adult organized crime; 2) conflict—oriented to intergang violence and having little contact with organized crime; and 3) retreatist—composed of those who fail both in society at large and within the criminalistic and conflict delinquent subcultures.

Merton (1957) has attempted to provide a framework that unites the macro and micro perspectives by way of a middle ground theory. His theory of anomie is based on the common goals of a social order (acquisition of goods, status, success) and the socially approved means provided to some persons, but not all, for obtaining them. If, for instance, a person has the legitimate means for obtaining a goal, there is consensus. If, however, a person does not have the socially approved means, that person may obtain the goal through illegitimate means. A youth who desires a Corvette but does not have the means to buy, rent, or borrow one will resort to innovative behavior and steal it. Delinquency is thus explained by studying the ways in which means are blocked for various groups within the social order.

Treatment. Fundamental to the distinction between criminal activity and juvenile delinquent behavior is the assumption that children behave from a different motivational base. Historically it has been presumed that juveniles lack the necessary "criminal intent" required for an act to be labeled a crime. Juvenile law therefore has operated on a different theory in its treatment of youthful offenders, aiming to protect and treat rather than punish.

Based upon the doctrine of *parens patriae* (wherein the state may legally intervene to provide assistance to persons in need of care), separate courts were created to remove children from the criminal process. Illinois, in 1899, was the first state to establish a juvenile court. Reformers of the late nineteenth century quickly mounted a "save the child" movement and augmented the distinction between adult and juvenile courts. This distinction is apparent in the terminology employed by the two courts. A defendant in adult court, for example, is in juvenile court a respondent. A charge or indictment in the one is a petition in the other. An adult is given an arraignment; a juvenile, a hearing. An adult undergoes prosecution or is tried; a juvenile undergoes adjudication. A verdict for an adult is a finding for a juvenile; a sentence, a disposition.

During the first half of this century the nonunitive approach reflected in the terminology of the juvenile process has been heralded as a major reform. Criticism has risen during the past decade on two fronts. First, removing the activity from the criminal court removed the usual protections of the constitution. Supreme Court decisions have forced juvenile courts to provide at least minimal guarantees of due process, thereby returning a portion of the juvenile court activity to the criminal level.

Second, contemporary reaction to the treatment approaches have called into question the efficacy of the treatment model as it has been operationalized within the juvenile court structures. Increased concern of the nature and rise in crime has led to new legislation in some states requiring harsher punishment for certain juvenile crimes.

Juvenile Delinquency and the Helping Professions. Mental health professionals are wise to learn the specific procedures of the juvenile court in their locale. A common process begins with a referral made by the police, school, public and private social service agencies, or parents. The referral is often handled by an intake officer, who evaluates the case and responds in one of the following ways: 1) The case may be rejected. 2) If the offense is not serious and admission of guilt is expressed by the child or parent, the youth may be placed on informal probation or referred to a child care agency. 3) If the offense is serious or there is no admission of guilt, the case is considered official and a petition is filed.

A court hearing is scheduled that results in a finding and a disposition. The disposition may take one of the following forms: dismissal of the case, referral to adult court for trial, placement on probation supervision, placement in foster care, or commitment to a residential facility of private or public operation. If a child is sent to a residential facility, it is normal that upon release a probation or parole officer will provide aftercare supervision. Human services personnel should also be aware of the supportive services provided by public and private agencies which network with the juvenile court and justice system at the local and state levels.

References

Abadinski, H. *Probation and parole: Theory and practice* (2nd ed.). Englewood Cliffs, N.J.: Prentice-Hall, 1982.
Cloward, R. A. & Ohlin, L. E. *Delinquency and opportunity: A theory of delinquent gangs.* Glencoe, Ill.: Free Press, 1960.
Cohn, A. *Delinquent culture.* Glencoe, Ill.: Free Press, 1955.
Merton, R. K. *Social theory and social structure.* Glencoe, Ill.: Free Press, 1957.
Miller, W. B. Lower class culture as a generating milieu of gang delinquency. *Journal of Social Issues*, 1958, 14(3), 5–19.
Sutherland, E. H., & Cressey, D. R. *Principles of criminology* (6th ed.). Philadelphia: Lippincott, 1960.
United States Department of Justice. FBI *Uniform crime reports.* Washington, D.C.: Government Printing Office, 1978.

A. R. DENTON

Kk

Kelly, George Alexander (1905–1967). Developer of the personal constructs theory, a cognitive model of human personality which suggests that the critical dimension of human personality is the way in which the individual views, experiences, and experiments with the world. Frequently using the concept of man as scientist, Kelly stated that the fundamental motivation of human life is to understand, predict, and control events. To meet this need people learn distinctive ways of looking at the world that are pragmatically useful. Human distress occurs when one's "personal constructs," one's way of viewing the world, cease to work well.

Born in Kansas, Kelly received his undergraduate education at Friends University in Kansas and Park College in Missouri. He pursued graduate training at the University of Kansas, the University of Minnesota, the University of Edinburgh, and the State University of Iowa, where he completed his Ph.D. in 1931. He directed a traveling rural psychological clinic in his early career, was an aviation psychologist during World War II, and later succeeded Carl Rogers as director of the Psychology Clinic at Ohio State University, where he was also professor of psychology.

It was at Ohio State that he developed and wrote his most famous work, *The Psychology of Personal Constructs* (1955), a carefully written formal exposition of his theory of personality. Kelly's theory was a rather radical departure from the three major forces in psychology at the time of its writing (behavioral, psychoanalytic, and nondirective theories). Kelly himself was a man whose career reflected great breadth and willingness to experiment.

Kelly published relatively few works (two books and 12 articles); his greatest influence was through his graduate students at Ohio State. For example, the work of his student Walter Mischel, the social learning personality theorist, continues to show the profound influence of Kelly's cognitive view. Toward the end of his career Kelly engaged in a wide variety of activities which furthered the development of psychology as a profession; these activities included serving as a member of numerous federal and professional commissions. For the last two years of his life he served as a professor at Brandeis University.

S. L. JONES

See PERSONAL CONSTRUCTS THERAPY.

Kierkegaard, Søren Aabye (1813–1855). Danish Christian author whose writings continually cross the parochial boundaries that separate psychology, literature, philosophy, theology, and devotional writings. His literary career began with a series of pseudonymous works that were initially prompted by a failed love affair, and ended with a series of pamphlets and newspaper articles in which he attacked the state church in an attempt to "reintroduce Christianity into Christendom." These writings were accompanied by a steady stream of devotional works, which became explicitly Christian in his later years.

Kierkegaard struggled all his life with what he termed his "melancholy," the result no doubt of an upbringing which he himself described as crazy. The dominant figure in his life, besides his disappointed fiancée was his father, a man whose stern religious exterior apparently shrouded an interior life of guilt and anxiety. However, Kierkegaard's acute analytical mind and literary gifts enabled him to wrest insights from his own suffering that have universal power and validity. Much of his struggle revolved around his attempt to actualize a Christian faith in his own life, so his writings have a particular depth and interest to Christians.

Kierkegaard was concerned with an effort to help his reader develop the inward personal concern, or subjectivity, which he saw as the essential precondition for becoming a true Christian. Kierkegaard saw human beings as spirit. This does not mean they are immaterial, but rather that each human being is intended to be a self. To be a self is to be a self-conscious responsible agent who becomes what he is and is what he becomes. Kierkegaard presents many withering critiques of the "mass man" who loses his self in the crowd, being content to be a self like all the others. Selfhood is an achievement, not a birthright; a self is acquired only through free responsible choice.

There are many different ways of attempting to become a self. Ultimately the structure of the human self is such that its destiny—an eternal happiness—can only be realized by using its freedom to relate to God. However, Kierkegaard believed that there were different kinds and levels of God relationships. The Christian view, as he saw it, demands a recognition that man is incapable of truly choosing God because of sin. The Christian is the one who recognizes his inability to truly become the self he was destined to be, and who recognizes his selfhood as a gift made possible by faith in Christ, a gift that is realized by the believer's willingness to die to self with Christ. Thus the Christian view is paradoxical: only the one who is willing to lose his life can save it.

There are three major themes in Kierkegaard's writings that are of particular interest to psychologists: 1) a developmental theory of selfhood, 2) an implicit therapeutic methodological ideal, and 3) a descriptive analysis of certain passions and moods. A brief account of his contributions in these three areas follows.

The stages on life's way. Kierkegaard believed there were three major answers to the question, "How should I exist?" These three answers make up what he termed the three spheres of existence, or "stages on life's way." These are the aesthetic stage, the ethical stage, and the religious stage. The aesthetic sphere is characterized by living for the moment and attempting to enjoy life by cultivating one's natural inclinations. The ethical sphere is marked by a dutiful commitment to ideals that are seen as having eternal validity. The religious sphere, from which the Christian way of

existence is demarcated as a special case, is noted by the struggle to relate properly to God through suffering and repentance.

Although Kierkegaard saw these three stages as a natural progression, in the sense that everyone begins with the aesthetic stage and ideally should progress to the religious, he insisted that this development is far from automatic or even normal. Since human beings are spiritual creatures, this growth toward selfhood is rooted in freedom. Hence each stage can be, and often is, a way of existence which the individual never surpasses. It is for this reason that Kierkegaard termed them spheres of existence as well as stages.

The maieutic ideal. Although Kierkegaard hoped to help his contemporaries achieve moral and spiritual growth, he believed that this ultimately depended on the individual's freedom. Hence he did not think it possible to directly help another person. Rather, he attempted to help his readers indirectly by creating a situation where they might possibly grasp the truth for themselves and choose to actualize it in their lives. To this end he regarded himself, like Socrates, as a midwife who would help others "give birth;" this is the maieutic ideal. According to Kierkegaard even God acts maieutically. When God appears to man, he appears as a humble servant, which makes it possible for human beings to reject God's help and creates the possibility of offense.

Kierkegaard personally attempted to follow the maieutic ideal in a variety of ways. Rather than simply telling his readers about the three stages of existence, he created fictional characters, pseudonyms, who write books representing and embodying these three spheres. In this way he attempts to withdraw from the reader, forcing readers to think about the books in relation to their own lives. These pseudonymous books are permeated by humor and irony, and since their content is supposed to be attributable to their pseudonymous authors, they have often misled unwary interpreters of Kierkegaard.

Passions and moods. Kierkegaard gave detailed analyses of crucial human moods and passions. Certain moods, particularly anxiety (sometimes translated as dread) and despair, have a decisive significance as revelations of the nature and condition of the self. Anxiety is seen as a necessary accompaniment of human freedom. In anxiety the self confronts its own possibilities and recognizes the possibility of its own nothingness. *The Concept of Anxiety* (1844) explains how anxiety plays a crucial role in the psychological explanation of the possibility of sin.

Despair is the mood in which the lack of selfhood reveals itself. *The Sickness Unto Death* (1849) chronicles and analyzes the many forms of despair. Kierkegaard views despair as a universal human condition, though most people are not conscious of this despair. From a Christian viewpoint despair is sin, a failure to ground one's self in God, and the only cure is the passion of faith.

From Kierkegaard's view the achievement of selfhood involves a synthesis of contrasting elements: temporality and eternity, soul and body, necessity and freedom. This synthesis is made possible by the passions. Genuine passions are not transitory emotions that happen to a person but enduring caring concerns around which the whole personality coalesces. Kierkegaard's *Works of Love* contrasts the Christian passion of neighbor love with various natural loves such as erotic love and friendship. The supreme passion from a Christian perspective is faith, which is not mere intellectual assent but a condition in which the whole person is totally rooted in God.

Additional Reading
Kierkegaard, S. [*Kierkegaard's journals and papers* (7 vols.)] (H. V. Hong, and E. H. Hong, Eds. and trans.). Bloomington: Indiana University Press, 1967–1978.

C. S. EVANS

Kinsey, Alfred Charles (1894–1956). A pioneer in the contemporary study of sexual behavior. Born in Hoboken, New Jersey, Kinsey suffered from rheumatic fever and rickets in high school and was known as the "boy who never had a girl." Although raised in a strict Methodist home, he began to lose his faith as a college student (B.S. Bowdoin, 1916, D.Sc. Harvard, 1920). In 1920, at age 26, he began teaching at Indiana University as an instructor in the Zoology Department. That year he met the first girl he ever dated and married her the next. He never attended church after 1921, expressing indignation about what he felt the Judeo-Christian tradition had done to Western culture. He also felt that Christianity was full of inaccuracies and paranoia.

Possibly because he was reportedly always discussing sex with students as a zoology instructor, in 1938 Kinsey was chosen to coordinate a marriage course at Indiana University. He began by taking sexual histories from students. In 1940, under fire from the religious community, he was pressured to resign teach-ing the course but was permitted to continue his sex research.

The research that started with his student interviews in 1938 expanded with funding from the Rockefeller Foundation in 1941. These reports, and the others written by Kinsey and his associates, were based on surveys of 5,300 white males and 5,490 white females conducted over a period of 15 years. All were sponsored by the Institute for Sex Research at Indiana University, of which Kinsey was the director until his death. Kinsey's work on sexuality culminated in *Sexual Behavior in the Human Male* (1948) and *Sexual Behavior in the Human Female* (1953).

The Institute for Sex Research has, since its inception, featured an unusual degree of secretiveness about what was inquired into and from whom. To date a complete list of the questions asked has never been published, and the samples employed are only known in scant outline. As more has become known, serious methodological problems have become apparent, some of which cast doubt on Kinsey's major conclusions.

The most serious of these problems concerns his method of sampling. Kinsey reported being surprised at the high incidence of deviant sexual practice, since he claimed that "no preconception of what is rare or what is common, what is moral or socially significant, or what is normal and what is abnormal . . . entered into the choice of histories" (Kinsey, Pomeroy, & Martin, 1948, p. 7). However, close scrutiny suggests that Kinsey's sampling methods unquestionably skewed his figures toward high incidence of all forms of sexually unusual behavior. Kinsey was not interested in sampling those whose sex lives were dull, but rather those whose were bizarre. Pomeroy relates how he and Kinsey traveled thousands of miles by car to interview one man about whose sexual exploits they had heard (Pomeroy, 1972, p. 122). Similarly, known homosexual communities were included in population samples selected each year but the first of the 15-year project. All these bizarre histories were added together to give the estimates for the general population.

These and other methodological and statistical problems (Cochran, Mosteller, & Tukey, 1953) give a person reason to seriously question the Kinsey data as a description of normal sexual behavior, which is how it is presented. Kinsey's major contribution, therefore, should be seen to lie in the fact that his work opened a new phase in empirical studies of human sexual behavior.

References

Cochran, W. G., Mosteller, F., & Tukey, J. W. Statistical problems of the Kinsey report. *Journal of the American Statistical Association*, 1953, *48*, 673–716.

Kinsey, A. C., Pomeroy, W. B., & Martin, C. E. *Sexual behavior in the human male*. Philadelphia: Saunders, 1948.

Kinsey, A. C., Pomeroy, W. B., Martin, C. E., & Gebhard, P. H. *Sexual behavior in the human female*. Philadelphia: Saunders, 1953.

Pomeroy, W. B. *Dr. Kinsey and the institute for sex research*. New York: Harper & Row, 1972.

P. CAMERON

See SEXUALITY.

Klein, Melanie

Klein, Melanie (1882–1960). Born in Vienna, Klein came across Freud's *Interpretation of Dreams* about the time of World War I. This so impressed her that she entered psychoanalytic training and personal analysis under Sandor Ferenczi. Later she pursued further personal analysis with Abraham in Berlin. Her interest in child development and her clinical work with children led to development of a psychoanalytic treatment approach for children that brought her prominence. In 1925 she was invited to lecture in England and later, because of political instability on the continent, she settled there permanently.

Her work has always been creative but controversial in psychoanalytic circles. Klein is actually one of the first psychoanalytic theorists to seriously develop Freud's theory of object relations. She is considered an object relations theorist because she addresses early human experience by focusing on the development of internal images, or objects, which the infant forms as internal representations of external people.

She identifies two positions from which infants relate to objects: *paranoid-schizoid* (birth to approximately 6 months) and the *depressive* (6 to 12 months). Technically these are not stages that one goes through and completes. According to Klein, no one is ever completely finished with aspects of these ways of relating; thus her use of positions instead of stages.

Paranoid-Schizoid Position. Klein completely accepts Freud's concept of two instinctual drives that are basic to all human motivation: libido, which has to do with the biological need for gratification, and the death instinct, which involves self-destruction and aggression. According to Klein both instincts create fantasies in regard to the infant's first human contact, the mother's breast. The death instinct first becomes manifested in cannibalistic fantasies involving devouring the breast. The infant then perceives frustration or delay while nursing as the breast intentionally withholding nurturance. The infant responds with envy and greed, wishing to spoil this bad breast. On the other hand, libido attaches to the image of a gratifying breast. This gives rise to the experience of gratitude in the infant for the good breast. Klein identifies the good and bad breasts as part objects in that the infant as yet is incapable of relating to his mother as a whole person or object.

This instinctual situation gives rise to the most extreme conflict and terror for the infant. Because of his envy and greed he is faced with the possibility of destroying his internal good breast on which he is completely dependent and annihilating himself along with it.

Klein posits the presence from birth of an ego that intervenes by dissociating the good and bad objects from each other in order to protect the good object. This splitting of the infant's internal world into good and bad is the *schizoid* aspect of this position. The *paranoid* aspect emerges as the ego projects in fantasy the death instinct and its object, the bad breast, outside the ego by a process called PROJECTIVE IDENTIFICATION. However, in creating a bad object that he considers outside himself, the infant then views the source of danger from his bad object as originating outside himself. Klein calls this persecutory anxiety. Thus, instead of fearing that he himself will devour the good breast, the infant now fears an external persecutor which can devour him and his good object.

Depressive Position. In spite of the turmoil in the infant's internal world, in normal development the ego develops through gratifying experiences. These experiences stimulate gratitude in the infant, which begins to outweigh aggression and persecutory anxiety. With this change in the balance of the infant's inner world comes the decreasing necessity for the ego to split itself. Typically, according to Klein, this starts to occur around 3 to 4 months of age. Because of a more integrated ego the infant goes from fantasizing in terms of part objects to perceiving his mothering object as a whole person.

With the commencing of these ego developments comes the *depressive position*. In using the earlier defenses of splitting and projective identification the infant did not feel personal responsibility for the object. The source of attack against his ideal object was seen as coming from outside himself. However, in the depressive position the infant comes to realize that he has been hating the same object he actually loves. Now the infant's anxiety changes from persecutory anxiety to depressive anxiety and guilt.

Normal working through of depressive anxiety involves attempts, sometimes lifelong, at reparation of the perceived injured love object through genuine concern and empathy for others. Pathological ways that infants or adults utilize in an attempt to escape from the pain of hurting the very one whom they love involve either regression to more primitive split relationships or a frantic display of hyperactivity to avoid awareness of feeling.

Critique. Klein's theory continues to be quite controversial. She is considered to be outside the mainstream of psychoanalytic thought because 1) she posits far too complex mental fantasies for the first six months of life; 2) emphasizes instinctual fantasies to the neglect of environmental factors; and 3) bases too much on the concept of an inborn death instinct. However, her emphasis on how internal needs and conflicts color memory of relationships and experiences is invaluable to understanding the human condition. The importance of early object relations, aggression in early development, and projection identification and splitting have all been accepted into psychoanalysis.

The theory is rich in its potential to interface with theology. Its emphasis on relationship and interpersonal contact parallels the heart of the Old Testament's focus on an intimate knowledge of God and of New Testament theology of body of Christ interrelatedness. By identifying the part that the child plays in coloring his experiences she illustrates the role of responsibility in psychoanalytic theory.

Additional Readings

Klein, M. *Love, guilt and reparation and other works* (Vol. 3). New York: Delacorte Press, 1975.

Klein, M. *Envy and gratitude and other works* (Vol. 4). New York: Delacorte Press, 1975.

W. L. Edkins

See Object Relations Theory.

Kleptomania. A disorder of impulse control, the failure to resist impulses to steal objects. The material stolen is not necessarily taken because the person wants its use or because it is valuable. In fact, the objects may be given away, secretively returned, or stored. Most kleptomaniacs steal alone and do not plan their thefts. In concert with other disorders of impulse control (pathological gambling, pyromania, and the explosive disorders), kleptomania features a gradual increase of inner turmoil before the actual impulse appears. After the act

of stealing the kleptomaniac often reports some gratification or release of tension. The pathology of this disorder is even more apparent in the fact that the person stealing the objects usually has the money to pay for them. The motivation for stealing somehow involves the thrill of doing something illegal without being caught.

Most kleptomaniacs show limited insight into the consequences of their behavior. Obviously, law enforcement personnel are often the first professionals to encounter the kleptomaniac. Stealing occurs in the context of other disorders (schizophrenias, conduct disorders, antisocial disorders, and manic episodes) without the central features of kleptomania. Most incidents of shoplifting are not examples of kleptomania because shoplifting is often planned, unresisted, and for immediate use or gain. King Victor of Sardinia and King Henry IV of France are some of history's more notable kleptomaniacs.

Statistics regarding the incidence of true kleptomania and its sex ratio are scarce; the best evidence suggests it is a rare disorder. Sometimes thieves will attempt to feign kleptomania as a defensive legal maneuver. Differential diagnosis must center on whether or not there was a resistance to the impulse to steal and whether or not the objects were of value and for personal use. The disorder sometimes first appears in childhood or adolescence.

Psychoanalytic theorists have given considerable attention to this relatively rare condition. Most suggestions by the analysts link the impulse to a desire to replace lost objects of esteem. For example, Fenichel (1945) writes, "Cleptomania means in principle to take possession of things which give the strength or the power to fight supposed dangers, especially . . . dangers of loss of self-esteem or affection" (p. 370).

Reference

Fenichel, O. *The psychoanalytic theory of neurosis.* New York: Norton, 1945.

J. R. Beck

Koffka, Kurt (1886–1941). One of the three founders of Gestalt Psychology, actually the only one born in Germany. Although he came from a long line of lawyers, he developed an interest in science and philosophy. With the exception of one year in Edinburgh he was educated entirely in Berlin, receiving his Ph.D. from the University of Berlin in 1909.

Koffka took a number of research positions, meeting Wertheimer and Köhler in Frankfurt in 1910. In 1911 he went to the University of

Giessen and remained there until 1924, when he came to the United States. After holding visiting professorships at Cornell and Wisconsin, he was appointed research professor at Smith College. With no pressure on him to publish or teach, he did many experiments in the field of visual perception. He remained at Smith College until his death.

After World War I, American psychologists were only vaguely aware of the new psychology developing in Germany. Koffka wrote "Perception: An Introduction to Gestalt-Theorie" for the *Psychological Bulletin* in 1922. This article was the first formal presentation of the Gestalt approach available to American psychologists. Unfortunately, the title gave rise to the misunderstanding that Gestalt psychology deals only with perception.

While Wertheimer was the originator and leader of the movement, and Köhler was the physiologist and representative to the general public, Koffka was the most productive of the three Gestalt founders. He was the most complete systematizer and organizer of the theory, the selector and integrator of all the experimental evidence. Although he wrote more than either of the other two, he showed less originality. He was an organizer rather than an originator of knowledge.

Koffka first became widely known through his book on developmental child psychology, *The Growth of the Mind* (1921). While recuperating from a fever caught while on an expedition to study the people of central Asia, he began work on a book intended for lay readers. However, *Principles of Gestalt Psychology* (1935) developed into a book very difficult to read and never became the definitive treatment of Gestalt psychology he intended. Koffka was always the most vocal proponent of the Gestalt position. When Americans were wondering if this was just another German philosophy, Koffka's vivid personality and good-tempered debating tactics effectively presented the mass of ingenious and challenging experiments generated by the theory. Soon everyone realized that GESTALT PSYCHOLOGY could not be ignored.

R. L. KOTESKEY

Kohlberg, Lawrence (1927–). American psychologist best known for his work on a theory of the development of moral judgment. He became interested in this work while he was a doctoral student at the University of Chicago, where he completed his Ph.D. in 1958.

Kohlberg's doctoral work involved him in studies of clinical psychology and child development. He also spent some time as a trainee at Children's Hospital in Boston. His final theoretical ideas about the development of moral judgment emerged as he became dissatisfied with traditional psychoanalytic explanations of children's moral reasonings. He then attempted to build on the cognitive development research of Piaget and on Dewey's ideas on philosophy of education.

Kohlberg became an assistant professor at the University of Chicago in 1962. In 1969 he joined the faculty at Harvard, where he has been a leader in a graduate program in human development. While there, he has continued his emphasis on the development of moral judgment by trying to examine the educational implications of his theory. Two particularly significant areas of work have been the level of justice in an educational community and the use of dilemma discussions for promoting moral development in students.

Kohlberg's work on the level of justice in an educational community has involved the study of methods of making formal school settings more democratic. His theory suggests that higher stages of cognitive moral judgment are more democratic, and that the way of promoting this kind of thinking is to allow people to participate in democratic processes of governance. He has also taken this idea into a prison setting in trying to encourage cognitive moral development of prisoners.

His idea of using moral dilemma discussion for promoting moral development has been very influential in contemporary values education. The theory behind such discussion is that while each person in a group uses a particular cognitive structure for trying to solve the moral problem of the dilemma, students at lower levels of cognitive development will hear, understand, and prefer those explanations that are one stage higher than theirs. They will then restructure their own ways of making moral judgments to be more like those of higher stages. This technique and the broader philosophy of moral development lying behind it are both discussed in his recent and most important book, *The Philosophy of Moral Development* (1981).

R. B. MCKEAN

See MORAL DEVELOPMENT.

Köhler, Wolfgang (1887–1967). One of the founders of GESTALT PSYCHOLOGY. He was born in Reval, Estonia, but his family moved to Germany when he was five. He studied at Tübingen, Bonn, and finally Berlin, where he received his Ph.D. in 1909. He then went to

Frankfurt as an assistant in psychology, arriving shortly before Wertheimer.

Köhler remained in Frankfurt until 1913, when he was invited to study chimpanzees on Tenerife, the largest of the Canary Islands. Six months after he arrived, World War I broke out, and he had to remain because he could not get home to Germany. He returned to Germany in 1920, and in 1922 became professor at the University of Berlin, the chief post at Germany's most important university. He left Germany in 1935 because of his continual conflicts with the Nazis and came to the United States. He served as professor of psychology at Swarthmore College until his retirement in 1953.

Köhler took the responsibility of presenting the Gestalt position to the general public. He wrote less than Koffka, but his books were more readable, so they have became the authoritative word on Gestalt psychology. Although it is difficult to separate the contributions of the leaders of Gestalt psychology, Köhler is probably most responsible for the concepts of insight and isomorphism.

It is fortunate for psychology that Köhler was marooned on Tenerife, because while there he did what he called "intelligence tests on anthropoid apes." This work led to the concept of insight as opposed to trial-and-error learning. Insight is a sudden solution to a problem, a reorganization of the total field so that new relationships are seen. The chimpanzees showed this insight in solving various problems, so that once a given problem was solved, they could repeatedly solve it without error.

Köhler was the physiologist and physicist of the movement, and thus most responsible for the concept of isomorphism. Isomorphism says that form and order in perceptual experience correspond to form and order in the physical world and in the physiological processes. Perceptions represent the real world, but are not copies of it.

The Mentality of Apes (1917) reports Köhler's work on Tenerife and introduces the concept of insight. *Static and Stationary Gestalts* (1920) was a very scholarly work and never completely translated into English. *Gestalt Psychology* (1929) was published in English and is the most comprehensive argument for Gestalt psychology.

R. L. KOTESKEY

See INSIGHT IN LEARNING.

Korsakoff's Syndrome. An organic psychosis found primarily in chronic alcoholics. It is also sometimes found in brain damaged individuals and organic deficit states such as are produced by long periods of dieting or vomiting. Characteristic features of the syndrome include a marked disturbance of perception and immediate memory, confabulations, and inflammation of the nerves, particularly in the legs and wrists. The person is disoriented and cannot recall recent behavior or events. Long-term memory is often unaffected. This nutritionally based deficiency in the central nervous system involves vitamin B deficiency alcoholics. Massive doses of vitamin B along with a high-calorie diet and medical care have been helpful.

The term's usage sometimes extends to include all organic psychoses in which memory disorders are a primary dominant factor. Korsakoff's syndrome and AMNESTIC SYNDROME have classically been viewed as separate entities. However, recent studies have suggested that they may share a common basis, possibly a thiamine deficiency.

D. L. SCHUURMAN

See ALCOHOL ORGANIC MENTAL DISORDERS.

Kraepelin, Emil (1856–1926). German psychiatrist who undertook the systematic classification of mental disorders. Born in Neustrelitz, Germany, a village near the Baltic Sea, he recieved his M.D. degree at the University of Würzburg in 1878. After that he studied neuroanatomy in Munich for four years and then neuropathology in Leipzig, where he worked with Wundt, under whom he had studied one summer while in medical school.

Although Kraepelin almost made a career of neurophysiological research, Wundt and others encouraged him to return to clinical psychiatry. He began teaching at the University of Dorpat in 1885, went to the University of Heidelberg in 1891, and was finally appointed professor of clinical psychiatry at Munich in 1903. In 1922 he retired from teaching to become head of the Research Institute of Psychiatry in Munich, where he remained until his death.

Kraepelin made contributions to early experimental psychology by investigating sleep, expectation, work, fatigue, and the effect of drugs on mental processes. However, his major contribution was his systematic classification of psychoses. He was determined to make psychiatry strictly scientific and to make it follow the methods of the biological sciences. He studied thousands of case histories, traveling to India, Java, Mexico, and the United States in search of material. He wanted to look not only at symptoms, but at the full course of the disorder, from its obscure origins to its recurrence, if there was one.

Although he did not originate the ideas, he brought order to classification, recognizing two major types of psychosis. Dementia praecox (now called schizophrenia) was seen as including several types of cases, such as catatonic, hebephrenic, or mixed. He regarded it as being caused by internal factors, with a tendency toward progressive deterioration and permanent disability. Although he admitted that 13% of such cases recovered, he concluded that either a wrong diagnosis originally had been made or that the patient would suffer a relapse.

The other major psychiatric category was the manic-depressive (now called bipolar disorder), characterized by swings of mood from elation to depression. He considered manic-depressives curable, and many of them did recover. His *Textbook of Psychiatry* was first published in 1883 and soon became the standard text. He was revising a ninth edition of it at the time of his death 43 years later. His classification system became the basis for the current ones, as reflected in the recent diagnostic and statistical manual of mental disorders of the American Psychiatric Association (*DSM-III*).

R. L. KOTESKEY

See CLASSIFICATION OF MENTAL DISORDERS.

Kretschmer, Ernst (1888–1964). German psychiatrist best known in the United States for his studies on the relationship between physique and mental disorder. Kretschmer received his education first at Tübingen and then at Munich, where he received his M.D. in 1914. He studied hysteria as a military physician during World War I. He went to the University of Tübingen in 1918, became professor at the University of Marburg in 1926, and returned to Tübingen in 1946. He remained there as professor of psychiatry and director of the psychological clinic until 1959.

Kretschmer's *Physique and Character* (1921) went through 20 editions, nearly one a year. He proposed that schizophrenia was more common among leptosomes (or asthenics), who were tall, frail, thin, pale individuals. Manic-depressive disorders were more likely to be found among persons with pyknic physiques—those who were round, plump, and florid. Persons with an athletic physique were more muscular and least likely to have a mental disorder. Finally, he noted that there was a small group of dyplastics, who were strikingly different in body build and who were usually considered ugly.

Although he is best known for his constitutional approach, he made many other contributions to European psychiatry. He published a new book nearly every year of his professional life. His books ranged over many topics. In *Hysteria, Reflex and Instinct* (1923) he suggested that symptoms are first conscious, then become unconscious. *The Psychology of Men of Genius* (1929) relates to the visual arts, poetry, and music. In *Psychotherapeutic Studies* (1949) he considered problems of ethics and religion. In addition, he studied new methods of psychotherapy, hypnosis, mental illness in children and adolescents, and criminality. Although he is often considered mainly a forerunner of Sheldon, he made a significant contribution in his own right.

R. L. KOTESKEY

See CONSTITUTIONAL PERSONALITY THEORY.

Kunkel, Fritz (1889–1956). Psychotherapist who developed the concept of "we-psychology." Born in Germany, Kunkel studied medicine at the University of Munich, but his broad range of interests also involved him with drama, poetry, and the arts. In World War I he was a battalion surgeon; while tending the wounded at the Battle of Verdun, he was hit by shrapnel and eventually lost his left arm. He was profoundly influenced by the war and the suffering it brought, and from this experience emerged his decision to be a psychotherapist.

After the war Kunkel studied Freudian psychology and became a close friend of Adler. However, he was most influenced by Jung and Jung's ideas of the collective unconscious, individuation, and the self as the center of the whole personality. Kunkel published the first of his many books in 1928, and during the next decade became a well-known psychologist, author, and lecturer in his native Germany.

Kunkel was greatly disturbed by the rise of national socialism. When he was invited to lecture in the United States in 1936, he accepted, and in 1939 he returned and became an American citizen. He practiced psychotherapy in Los Angeles, and was beginning to be as well-known in this country as he had been in Germany when he died on Easter Day, 1956, of a ruptured aorta.

Kunkel developed his own synthesis of Freud, Adler, and Jung, and out of this emerged a distinct theory of personality that he called the "we-psychology." The cornerstone of his thought is the distinction between the sterile life of the egocentric ego and the creative life of what he called the real self. Kunkel believed that because of childhood injuries the ego emerges into adult life as egocentric—i.e., concerned with its own defense and the furtherance of its own ambitions. However, life eventually brings about a crisis which, if a person goes through it honestly and courageously, leads to the destruction of egocentric patterns and the emergence of a new center in the self. His masterful description of egocentricity and how it defeats the process of growth fills a gap in Jungian psychology, while his dynamic idea of the self takes him beyond the boundaries of Freud's thought.

Kunkel's books in English include his psychological commentary on the Gospel of Matthew, *Creation Continues*, and his two most important books, *How Character Develops* and *In Search of Maturity* (recently reprinted under the title *Fritz Kunkel: Selected Writings*). While Kunkel was not a member of any particular denomination, he was a deeply religious person whose ideas have marked parallels in Christian concepts of man.

J. A. SANFORD

Ll

Lacunae, Superego. Defects frequently found in the superego of individuals diagnosed as ANTISOCIAL PERSONALITY DISORDER. Conduct disorder children sometimes show the same holes or gaps in their system of morality. Colloquially such individuals are often described as having a Swiss cheese superego. The psychoanalytic assumption is that the superego defects originate from similar defects in the parents and that the child is thus unconsciously acting out the wishes of the parents. An example would be a 14-year-old boy charged with numerous counts of fire setting. All other aspects of this boy's superego functioning seemed intact. However, in this one area he experienced no guilt and saw nothing wrong with his behavior. Close examination of the family dynamics showed that in spite of his overt condemnation of the fire setting the boy's father was experiencing a good deal of vicarious excitement through his son's behavior.

D. G. BENNER

See SUPEREGO.

Language Development. Language may be defined as a means of communicating thoughts and feelings by the use of vocalized symbols. Sounds (phonemes) are combined to produce meanings (morphemes), which are spoken in accordance with the rules of grammar (syntax). Words representing objects or events are combined with other meaningful sounds (e.g., prefixes, plurals) in a variety of ways so as to convey a message. Oral language is the primary means by which people relate to one another, thereby sharing ideas and experiences. No other species has the vocal apparatus or the intellectual capacity to develop speech as we know it, thus giving the human race an advantage over all other forms of life.

Language has its origins in the cry of the newborn and the babbling of the infant and proceeds to the first meaningful words of the 1-year-old, the two-word phrases of the toddler, and the adultlike sentences of the child of 4 years of age. Such rapid progress in oral communication remains a mystery, baffling the mind of the scholar and delighting the heart of the parent. Piaget, a careful observer of young children, noted that infants will make the same sound over and over, and then will experiment by varying the sound slightly. Babies as young as 2 months of age respond to their own vocalizations by repeating an utterance again and again, and then modifying it by changing the position of the tongue in the mouth or by increasing the volume (Flavell, 1963). Infants also learn by listening to others, so that by the time they are a year old they have restricted their speech sounds to those that correspond to their native tongue.

Repetition with variation continues with the pivot words of the toddler, the chanting of nonsense syllables by the preschooler, and the rhymes accompanying games and activities (e.g., jump rope) of the school-age child. Although monotonous to adults and at times exasperating to teachers and parents, such repetitions appear to be closely linked with learning a language. Pivot words are used by the small child to apply to a range of situations. For example, "allgone" may be a pivot word. When father leaves for work, the child will say, "Daddy allgone." When the dog cannot be found, it is "Doggie allgone." When mother washes the child's face after lunch, it is "Sticky allgone." Sameness with variation enables the child to learn how words are put together to express a thought. Similarly, the chants, jingles, and rhymes of the older child provide a link between the familiar and the novel as clauses are repeated again and again with only a small portion of the cadence being changed with each repetition. The child at play experiments with the language by manipulating parts of speech and exploring both sound and meaning. Gains in language understanding may be greater during play than at any other time (Pellegrini, 1981).

Although individual differences are apparent, the average 12-month-old has a vocabulary of about three words, which increases to 25 words by the age of 18 months. The number of words rises dramatically to several hundred by age 2 and several thousand by age 6. Children understand more than they verbalize, and it may be years before they pronounce some words correctly. Nouns are acquired first (e.g., "baby"), then linked with modifiers ("pretty baby") and verbs ("baby cry"), followed by more complex sentence structures ("Why is the baby crying?"). Language continues to develop after the child begins school but at a slower pace. Girls have a slight advantage over boys, learning to talk sooner, articulating better, and having fewer speech defects.

There are two basically different theoretical viewpoints as to how language is acquired. The first comes from social learning and reinforcement psychology with its emphasis on principles of modeling and conditioning, the second from cognitive and humanistic psychology with its stress on the potential of the human infant. The first looks to the environment as the teacher, the second to the capabilities inherent within the human organism. The learning position is that children imitate the speech sounds of parents and other models, and in this way acquire the native language with its idioms, accents, and intonations. The meaning of words is learned by pairing a word with its concrete referent (e.g., the word *ball* with the object ball), and the pronunciation of words is acquired by being reinforced with parental attention for closer and closer approximations to the correct way of saying a word (e.g., "bah" becomes "ball"). Cognitive psychologists, by contrast, hold that children are able to discover for themselves the rules needed to communicate with others on a verbal level. Children will try out various ways of expressing themselves, keeping those that correspond to the language around them and eliminating those not recognized by others. It is the inborn capacity of the child to make sense of the environment, not the environment

itself, that results in language acquisition. Language is a symbolic representation of events the child experiences in the real world.

Language is closely related to many other areas of a person's life. Language enables each of us to store information, to plan our day, to read a book, write a letter, or say a prayer. By its use we express not only our thoughts but our feelings as we communicate with others and with the God who created us.

References

Flavell, J. H. *The developmental psychology of Jean Piaget.* Princeton, N.J.: Van Nostrand, 1963.

Pellegrini, A. D. Speech play and language development in young children. *Journal of Research and Development in Education,* 1981, *14,* 73–80.

B. CLOUSE

See SPEECH DISORDERS.

Lashley, Karl Spencer (1890–1958). American psychologist noted for a wide range of research. Lashley was born in Davis, West Virginia. He became interested in zoology at the University of West Virginia, from which he graduated in 1910. He continued study in zoology, receiving an M.A. from the University of Pittsburgh in 1911 and a Ph.D. in 1915 from Johns Hopkins University, where he became acquainted with John Watson.

Lashley held teaching and research positions at the University of Minnesota (1917–1926), the University of Chicago (1929–1935), and Harvard, from 1935 until his death. While still under Harvard appointment he worked for many years at the Yerkes Laboratory of Primate Biology.

Scientists then regarded the brain as a switchboard for making connections between stimuli and responses. Lashley set out to find these specific pathways and connections, looking for definite points of localization in the brain. However, rather than supporting the reflex arc as an element of behavior, his work challenged Watsonian behaviorism. He systematically destroyed different parts and different amounts of the cerebral cortex of rats, studying the effect of such destruction on learning and memory. He generally found that it made no difference what parts were destroyed, only how much was destroyed. He discovered as well that the effect was greater when rats faced complex problems rather than simple ones.

Lashley proposed two concepts about brain function to account for his findings. The concept of mass action says that in any fairly complex learning situation the whole cortex, or at least a large area of it, is involved. The more cortical tissue available, the faster and more accurate the learning. The concept of equipotentiality says that one part of the cortex is essentially equal to another in tasks like maze learning. If one part is destroyed, another part can assume its functions. Most of Lashley's work was published in journals, but he summarized his findings in *Brain Mechanisms and Intelligence* (1929), which is now a classic.

R. L. KOTESKEY

Latency Period. In psychoanalysis the latency period is one of the stages of psychosexual development. Its onset is the resolution of the oedipal crisis and its termination is at puberty. It is thus normally thought to begin at age 5 or 6 and to end at approximately age 12.

Freud assumed a period of relative quiescence or inactivity of sexuality during these years. We now know that sexual integrest still exists, but it is no longer at central stage, as is the case during the earlier years of oedipal struggle. The latency period is a time of consolidating and integrating previous attainments in psychosexual development. The most important of these attainments are gender identity and sex roles. Latency years are therefore characterized by a predominance of same-sex relationships that serve to solidify gender identity and basic sex roles.

D. G. BENNER

See PSYCHOSEXUAL DEVELOPMENT.

Law and Psychological Practice. See MORAL AND ETHICAL ISSUES IN TREATMENT; MALPRACTICE.

Leadership. How do people become leaders, and how can they best lead? These questions have stimulated social psychologists since the beginning of the twentieth century. The two issues have usually been lumped together. In like fashion, researchers have often confused actual leader behavior with ideal models of influence—confusing the *is* with the *ought*. Despite this methodological lack of focus, four distinct approaches to leadership have emerged: trait, situation, style, and interactional.

Trait Situation and Style Approches. Up through World War II research efforts concentrated on isolating personality traits that assured selection for the leadership role. Intelligence, extraversion, self-confidence, high socioeconomic status, and dependability were some of the variables that surfaced. This type of field study led many to conclude that some

people were "born leaders," possessing the characteristics necessary for command. But the quest for leadership bench marks is fraught with problems. Separate studies rarely agree on requisite traits, nor do they offer predictive guidance. People who possess "the stuff of which leaders are made" often fail abysmally, while others bereft of the stated qualities rise to the top. The best the trait approach has to offer is to state chronic behaviors that eliminate one from consideration. Lack of desire, ignorance of the issue at hand, minimal participation, and obnoxiousness seem to be qualities that make a group member ineligible for the position of leadership.

By 1950 research strategy had shifted from the person to the situation. No longer did social scientists seek the common attributes of history's great men. Rather they sought to discover a set of circumstances that catapult an ordinary human into a position of power. The situational perspective is mechanistic in that it assumes that the environment automatically calls forth the person who will meet the demands of the situation. Instead of the man making history, history makes the man. If you are in the right place at the right time, lightning will strike. The person in the center of the communication network has proved to be optimally placed. The process of sending and receiving messages appears to attract power.

Although a good corrective to the simplistic trait approach, the situational interpretation is equally unable to predict leadership. Because each set of circumstances is novel, it is impossible to forecast leadership requirements. So leadership research shifted to a consideration of the effects caused by differing styles of behavior. The crucial variable here is the amount of authority the leader relinquishes to the group.

The autocratic or "tells" style is at one end of the spectrum. It vests all decision-making power in the leader, not trusting the group to have a say in their destiny. The "sells" style places a greater importance on voluntary acceptance of the leader's actions. The "consults" style reserves the final authority for the leader but welcomes the group's input as a way of affecting that decision. The democratic, or "joins," style is adopted by leaders who see their vote as only one of many. They are open to the possibility that the end product may not coincide with their personal opinion, but are committed to guiding a process of orderly investigation. At the other end of the continuum is a delegating, or laissez faire, style that outlines the work to be done and then steps back and lets members alone so they can get on with their task.

The bulk of the research reveals that the most effective pattern of leader behavior is one that places confidence in the group but retains some control as a means to keep it moving along—a joins or democratic style. But these findings are not absolute. Response to a leadership style depends greatly on whether the leader is comfortable enacting that style and whether the experience and expectation of group members will allow them to tolerate that style. It seems there is no one style for all seasons.

Interactional Approaches. The last two decades have seen the emergence of an interactionist perspective that draws upon the wisdom of the earlier three approaches. Considerations of trait, situation, and style are combined in an effort to offer advice to the practitioner who desires to meet the needs of the organization. All groups have two sets of needs, variously labeled as task and relational, production and people, locomotion and maintenance. The group must be aided in accomplishing its work, while at the same time it must be assisted to hold together as a cohesive unit.

Interactionists have varied in their prescription of how to meet these needs. Fiedler (1967) recommends matching the personality orientation of the leader with the difficulty of the situation. Difficulty is measured by the amount of control the situation affords the leader. Fiedler's findings suggest that a relationship-oriented leader facilitates the group best when the situation is moderately difficult, but that a task-oriented person leads best when the situation is at either extreme. Circumstances may alter over time, making a different type of leader desirable. Fiedler believes that it is more effective to switch leaders than to try to retrain the established head to shift his whole approach to life.

Hersey and Blanchard (1969) contend that one person can adapt his or her style to fit differing needs. They see member maturity as the crucial variable in defining the situation. Maturity is determined by a person's capacity to set high but attainable goals, willingness and ability to take responsibility, and education and experience relevant to the specific task at hand. People low in maturity require the high task direction of a "tells" style. They would be sidetracked by warm relational concern. As they begin to work successfully, maturity goes up. A "sells" style high in task and

relational activity is indicated. Those with an even higher maturity level work best under a participative or "joins" style that is low on task concerns but high in relational encouragement. High maturity members thrive when both task and relational initiation from the leader is minimal. A delegating or "laissez faire" style points them in the right direction and then stays out of their way.

Hersey and Blanchard place a premium on leaders' ability to diagnose the maturity level of followers and to alter their behavior accordingly. This is similar to the flexibility required of an effective parent who seeks to respond to the changing needs of a maturing child. Others point out that this kind of adaptability is rare and note that the ideal family group typically has two parental leaders—one task oriented, one more relationally concerned.

Whether the needs of the group are met by successive leaders of differing personality, flexible heads who are all things to all men, or by complementary dual leadership, all interactionalists agree that leadership is effective when it serves these needs. Burns (1978) contrasts the mere powerbroker who gives followers what they want in order to gain position, with the true leader who seeks to fulfill genuine needs. True leadership appeals to a member's higher needs that lie dormant until stimulated by the leader's self-sacrificing behavior. Thus the interactionalist approach parallels the biblical view of servant leader modeled by Jesus.

References

Burns, J. M. *Leadership.* New York: Harper & Row, 1978.
Fiedler, F. E. *A theory of leadership effectiveness.* New York: McGraw-Hill, 1967.
Hersey, P., & Blanchard, K. H. *Management of organizational behavior.* Englewood Cliffs, N.J.: Prentice-Hall, 1969.

E. GRIFFIN

See GROUP DYNAMICS.

Learned Helplessness. During the late 1960s and early 1970s M. E. P. Seligman and his colleagues conducted an extensive program of research documenting the debilitating effects on several animal species of inescapable, noncontingent trauma—i.e., trauma (usually shock) that could not be controlled by the animal because its responses could have no influence on the termination of the trauma. They found that animals exposed to trauma that could be controlled typically experienced no ill effects from it. The animals that received the exact same pattern of trauma but could not control the termination of it demonstrated extreme disruption in their subsequent performance. They were noted to be less motivated to perform tasks, took longer to learn subsequent tasks, and seemed generally despondent and passive. This phenomenon of disrupted responding was labeled learned helplessness. It was subsequently demonstrated that the helplessness effect could be alleviated by forcing the animals to respond, and animals could be "immunized" against showing the helplessness effect by previous success in controlling traumatic events.

To explain this phenomenon Seligman (1975) and his colleagues argued that the animal, based on the experiences with noncontingent trauma, formed a global expectation of learned helplessness—an expectation that its responses would have no effect in controlling to an outcome. They proposed that this expectation led to the behavioral manifestations they observed. Their explanations have been vigorously disputed in continuing animal research, and no firm conclusions can be drawn on this question.

During the 1970s helplessness researchers, impressed by the perceived parallels between the behavior of "helpless" animal subjects and depressed humans, proposed that the expectation of helplessness might be a major factor in human depression. They initiated a series of studies with humans using unsolvable problems as the noncontingent traumatic event. These studies generally showed that a subject's performances on tasks following exposure to unsolvable problems were disrupted, and that in fact normal subjects exposed to a helplessness induction performed much like depressed persons without such an induction. The conclusion of the researchers that these and other experimental studies supported a helplessness model of depression has been hotly debated (Depue & Monroe, 1978). Without question, the theory in its early form was much too simplistic to be of much value.

In 1978 Abramson, Seligman, and Teasdale (1978) reformulated the theory to suggest that the expectation of helplessness was much more complex than previously thought. The foundational process of belief in noncontingency between response and outcome remained from the old model, but in the reformulated model this belief was qualified by the person's judgments of the location of the cause of uncontrollability (within the person or outside in the situation?), the permanence of the state of uncontrollability (enduring or temporary?), and the extensiveness of the uncontrollability (global or specific to a limited set of behavior?).

Subsequent research using the reformulated helplessness model has been very complex, focusing on the causal judgments and other cognitive processes of depressed persons. The research support for the reformulated model has been mixed. As the research has continued, it has moved farther away from the basic concept behind the whole theory of helplessness—the concept of noncontingency. The model appears to be evolving into a more sophisticated approach to the cognitive judgments of depressed people, which will take its place as a model of one aspect of human depression.

References

Abramson, L. Y., Seligman, M. E. P., & Teasdale, J. D. Learned helplessness in humans: Critique and reformulation, *Journal of Abnormal Psychology*, 1978, *87*, 49–74.

Depue, R. A., & Monroe, S. M. Learned helplessness in the perspective of the depressive disorders: Conceptional and definitional issues. *Journal of Abnormal Psychology*, 1978, *87*, 3–20.

Seligman, M. E. P. *Helplessness: On depression, development, and death.* San Francisco: W. H. Freeman, 1975.

S. L. JONES

See DEPRESSION: BEHAVIORAL PERSPECTIVES.

Learning. In order to survive and respond to the demands of a changing environment all organisms must be able to utilize and profit from past experiences. For human beings few behavioral processes have a greater impact on life than learning. It is a process that may begin even before birth and normally continues until death. It plays a dramatic role in shaping our lives: the language we speak, the customs and social behavior we practice, our vocation, our self-perception, and even how we relate to one another—all are affected by how and what we learn.

Learning, Maturation, and Performance. To the nonspecialist learning may refer to simply the acquisition of attitudes, beliefs, or knowledge. However, a more precise definition of learning is required to separate it from other related processes and to aid in understanding the scientific study of the learning process. Learning is defined therefore as the process responsible for relatively permanent changes in behavior that result from experience or practice. Learning is distinguished from behavioral changes that are transient or in which different underlying processes are assumed to operate. For example, maturation may result in marked changes in behavior during critical periods of development (e.g., adolescence) by means of changes in body structure and chemistry and without regard for previous experience or practice.

Learned behavior also is distinguished from inherited behavior. At birth all organisms bring with them a set of inborn capabilities as well as certain behavior patterns or potentials. For example, newborn infants exhibit a suckling response and adults are startled by a loud noise, both without any apparent prior experience or practice. For some animals complex patterns of behavior appear to be entirely genetically determined.

Psychologists have long argued the issue of the origin of behavior. At the extremes of this argument one group has sought to explain behavior solely in terms of inborn patterns, whereas another group has sought to explain behavior totally in terms of experience. Although either of these extreme positions may account for some behavior, both are required to explain the majority of human behavior. Intelligence, once thought to be determined totally by genetic factors, is today recognized by most psychologists as being jointly determined by genetic and experience factors.

Learning also is distinguished from performance. Learning is inferred from changes in some measure of performance; however, a lack of performance does not necessarily indicate a lack of learning. Performance is the outcome of the interaction of a number of variables: learning, motivation, perception, physiological state, and others, depending on the particular situation. Poor performance may therefore result from lack of motivation or physiological inability rather than a lack of learning.

Separating performance from learning has practical as well as theoretical implications. The action required to bring about desired changes in behavior depends upon which processes are responsible for the original behavior. For example, trying to improve the academic performance of disadvantaged students by improving the quality of instruction (a learning solution) may have little effect if the cause of poor performance is insufficient motivation or physiological factors such as poor nutrition.

Human behavior is determined by a multitude of variables working together. The learning psychologist seeks to separate and investigate these variables to understand learning as a distinct process and to provide answers to two basic questions: "How do we learn?" and "What do we learn?"

Historical Perspective. The systematic, scientific investigation of learning has been primarily confined to the twentieth century. However, two general philosophical views of human behavior, empiricism (associationism) and rationalism, have had a significant effect on modern approaches to the psychology of learning.

Early philosophical influences. Empiricism is the view that all knowledge of the world is derived solely from experience. Early empiricists believed that our concepts and ideas are derived from sense impressions. However, realizing that isolated sensations cannot convey meaning, these philosophers postulated that sensory impressions become connected (associated) in the mind when they occur closely together in time or in space. Complex ideas were viewed as being formed by connecting together in memory simple ideas that were experienced contiguously.

According to classical empiricism, association by contiguity in experience was the only means by which knowledge could be acquired. This doctrine was further elaborated upon and applied to many different cases by British philosophers such as Hobbes, Locke, Hume, and Mill. Associationism led to the first experimental investigation of learning. Contemporary behavioristic theories of learning, such as those of Thorndike, Pavlov, Guthrie, Hull, and Skinner, are basically associationist in nature.

Rationalism is the philosophical view that reason is the prime source of knowledge. According to early rationalists such as Descartes, Leibniz, and Kant, sense data are simply unstructured input that only provide raw material to an interpretive mechanism, which in turn considers these raw data as clues regarding their probable source and meaning. Sensory experience can be interpreted only according to basic forms inherent in the mind which determine how experience is organized. From this viewpoint the mind shapes experience, rather than experience shaping the mind, as proposed by the empiricists.

Rationalists argued that association by contiguity failed to provide any restriction on what could become associated and therefore was not sufficient to prevent the accumulation of a disorganized mass of accidental associations. The rationalistic viewpoint ultimately led to the development of Gestalt psychology. It is still very much alive in contemporary psycholinguistics, cognitive psychology, and human information processing approaches to learning.

Modern contributions. Ebbinghaus is usually identified as the founder of the scientific study of the learning process. He is credited with showing how gradual changes in behavior could be related to various factors that might hamper learning or make it more efficient. By plotting gradual changes in performance it became possible to relate objectively those changes to possible causal factors under investigation. The work of Ebbinghaus marked the first time that experimental psychology attempted to utilize the safeguards and precautions of scientific procedure.

Two additional influences had a notable effect on the development of learning research and theory. For nearly a half a century the theories of Thorndike dominated all others in America. For Thorndike sense impressions (stimuli) and impulses to action (responses) became associated or "connected." The strength of a connection was believed to be increased if it was accompanied or followed by a satisfying state of affairs and decreased if it was accompanied or followed by an annoying state of affairs. Thorndike's system was the original stimulus-response (S-R) psychology of learning and the beginning of a methodology known as instrumental conditioning.

Another major influence was the methodology and findings of Pavlov, who showed how a previously ineffective stimulus could acquire control over behavior by being paired with an unconditioned stimulus such as food. To Pavlov we owe much of our modern vocabulary in the field of learning, the discovery of the conditioned reflex, and the formal birth of a learning methodology known as classical conditioning. Pavlov's work also had a significant impact on the development of American behaviorism, which saw the conditioned reflex as the basic building block of behavior.

Approaches to the Study of Learning. Most learning research is conducted under laboratory conditions where it is possible to control some of the variables that might affect the outcome of the experiment being conducted. The immediate purpose of learning research is to establish lawful relationships between a variable of interest (e.g., task difficulty) and some measure of performance (e.g., number of errors). The ultimate purpose of such research is to provide sufficient information to formulate a complete theory of learning. In general, theories are sought that require the fewest number of assumptions yet account for all the available learning data.

Nearly all learning research has been restricted to an investigation of four species: man, monkeys, pigeons, and rats. The widespread use of animals in learning research has been dictated by considerations of availability, economics, and ethics. It also is based on the assumption that basic processes of learning are common across species and on the observed

success of other disciplines in using nonhuman subjects to investigate basic processes. The entire modern science of genetics for example, has been developed largely from investigations of the salivary cell of the fruit fly.

Much learning research also has been oriented toward studying relatively simple tasks. Psychologists seek simplicity because they hope that the underlying laws of learning will prove to be simple and that the complexity we observe in everyday life will prove to be the result of the combination of simple basic processes. A similar hope has occasionally been fulfilled in the natural and physical sciences.

Not all learning psychologists agree with this emphasis on simplicity or with the use of animal subjects to identify complex processes that seem to characterize much of human learning. However, theoretical differences in approaches to the study of learning often are reflected in the types of learning that psychologists investigate and the methods they use. Four types of learning may be identified: classical conditioning, instrumental conditioning, modeling, and cognitive organization.

Types of Learning. *Classical conditioning* refers to the type of learning that occurs when a stimulus that has little or no effect on behavior is either paired with or followed by an unconditioned stimulus. An unconditioned stimulus is one that reliably elicits a well-defined reflex without any prior experience or learning (e.g., an eyeblink or knee jerk). Through pairing, a previously neutral stimulus can itself come to elicit the same response as the unconditioned stimulus, although the previously neutral stimulus will lose its control over behavior if it is repeatedly presented without the unconditioned stimulus. Classical conditioning is regarded as the simplest form of learning and is believed to be universal among all learning organisms.

Instrumental conditioning is based on the observation that behavior is influenced by its consequences. It refers to behavior controlled by rewards and punishment that are contingent on behavior. Behavior followed by reward tends to occur more frequently, whereas behavior followed by punishment tends to occur less frequently. Rewards can vary in complexity from food for a hungry animal to praise from a parent. Similarly, punishment may range from a painful electric shock to disapproval of a valued peer. Instrumental conditioning is a method we all use, both intentionally and accidentally, to influence the behavior of others. It also may be a method we use to reinforce our own behavior when we meet or fail to meet a self-imposed standard of performance.

Modeling involves imitation. Modeling is the process of duplicating another's actions or the result of such duplication. It appears to have three clearly different effects. First, an observer may acquire new response patterns that did not previously exist by imitating the behavior of others. Second, observation of modeled actions and their consequences to the performer may strengthen or weaken responses in the observer. Third, the behavior of others often serves as a cue for the observer in facilitating the occurrence of previously learned responses in the same general class. Modeling of behavior is operative throughout most of our lives, although it is perhaps most noticeable and most influential in the behavior of young children and adolescents.

Cognitive organization is a type of learning that comes from insights into the relations among things or events. Sudden insights might come through changes in the way individuals perceive or think. Contemporary cognitive psychologists believe that the brain actively processes information it receives into new forms or patterns that cannot be explained by mere associations through conditioning. Much of our learning may involve the ways in which we restructure or interpret our perceptions and thoughts. When new information is learned, it is added to preexisting meaning structures within the memory system. The problem facing the learner, according to cognitive psychologists, is to determine the conditions that are relevant to the situation, to determine what the appropriate actions are, and to record that information properly for future use.

Contemporary Learning Theories. It is impossible to describe briefly all the learning theories that exist today. However, two major conceptual divisions currently exist within learning research and theory: behaviorism and cognitive learning. The key issue that separates these two approaches is very similar to the issue that divided early empiricists and rationalists: What is learned?

Behaviorism. This is usually the learning model employed by researchers who study animals in simple experimental arrangements. They use the methods of instrumental and classical conditioning and describe their results in terms of the relationship between stimuli, responses, and reinforcement (rewards and punishment). Behaviorists emphasize the reinforcing value of behavioral outcomes and argue that it is the response leading to a particular outcome that is learned.

Behaviorism assumes that complex forms of learning can be reduced to a set of simple components which in turn can be explained in terms of the principles of conditioning. Behaviorism also focuses on the study of observable behavior, and although it does not dismiss the possible operation of cognitive processes, it does claim that behavior can be explained without reference to such unobservable events.

Cognitive learning. The cognitive approach to learning is illustrated by researchers who study how adults utilize their intellectual capabilities in learning and remembering verbal and visual information. Cognitive psychologists argue that the stimulus-response approach of behaviorism is not a sufficient explanation of learning because it attempts to explain learning by a simple description of the responses of an organism without any consideration of the internal cognitive processing of information that also must take place.

Cognitive theorists also recognize that consequences of behavior are critical to learning; however, they believe that the important aspect of a behavioral outcome is its information value—that is, a signal to the organism about the results of its behavior. Hence cognitive psychologists argue that it is information and cognitive structure that are learned rather than responses. Such information can be used to repeat those actions that are related to desired outcomes and to avoid those actions related to undesirable outcomes.

Modern behaviorists (e.g., Skinner) have argued that instrumental conditioning can explain much, if not all, human behavior. A person's behavior at any given point in time therefore is viewed as being determined totally by the individual's past reinforcement history. Thus, knowledge of this history could provide sufficient information to predict and control every aspect of his life.

Evaluation. The deterministic view of human behavior has received skeptical criticism from some social scientists. It also is inconsistent with Christian theology on a number of issues. First, it denies man the freedom of choice and hence removes personal responsibility for one's decisions and actions. Yet Christian teaching holds that each person must decide individually whether or not to accept the gifts and promises of God and consequently must accept the responsibility for those decisions. The Christian concept of responsibility implies an ability to make rational choices that are not totally dependent upon past experiences.

Second, behaviorism implies that the nature of each person, as well as his or her perception of right and wrong, is determined totally through experience, whereas the Bible teaches that man is created in the image of God and therefore is innately endowed with particular characteristics. Moreover, every human has a basic sinful nature due to his fall from grace.

Finally, behaviorism, due to its total reliance on learning from experience, excludes special insight learning and understanding that comes from the work of the Holy Spirit.

The views of behaviorism have been accepted by many because of the effective and widely used technology it has fostered. Instrumental conditioning methods have found broad and successful application in teaching, psychotherapy, industry, prisons, and institutions for the retarded and emotionally disturbed. However, it is important to separate behaviorism—a theoretical statement about human behavior—from instrumental conditioning as an applied technique of learning.

Behaviorism itself has tended to dehumanize man and is patently incompatible with Christian theology. On the other hand, the basic tenets of instrumental conditioning appear to be consistent with Christian teaching. The Bible gives a legitimate and even prominent place to rewards, although such rewards typically are described in moral or spiritual terms. Similarly, punishment is a sure consequence of sinful and unrepentant behavior. Consequences of behavior have a significant and undeniable impact on learning and future behavior, but they do not tell the whole story about learning or human behavior.

Conceptually the approach of cognitive learning is more in line with the Christian view of human nature. It accounts for the findings of instrumental conditioning, but it does not limit learning to a mechanical response to behavioral consequences. The view that cognitive structures are learned and that individuals have the ability to rearrange, organize, and integrate related information at least makes possible the concept of freedom of choice. It also allows some provision for basic human characteristics, especially if we assume that some rules or structures for processing cognitive information are common to all persons and are an inheritance from our Creator. Cognitive learning also accommodates other types of learning (e.g., modeling) and it provides a possible vehicle for special insight learning provided to Christians from the Holy Spirit.

Although many of the specifics of learning are now understood, there are currently no complete theories that adequately explain existing learning data and phenomena. Of the two major conceptual approaches to learning, of which there are many variations, cognitive theories appear to offer a more comprehensive account of human learning and one that at least is not inconsistent with the Christian view of man. Unfortunately, cognitive learning research still is in its infancy, and its progress is made difficult because cognitive processes are not observable and therefore must be studied as inferences made from measures of observable behavior and performance.

Additional Readings

Hilgard, E. R., & Bower, G. H. *Theories of learning* (4th ed.). Englewood Cliffs, N.J.: Prentice-Hall, 1975.

Lindsay, P. H., & Norman, D. A. *Human information processing: An introduction to psychology* (2nd ed.). New York: Academic Press, 1977.

Rachlin, H. *Introduction to modern behaviorism.* San Francisco: W. H. Freeman, 1970.

S. R. OSBORNE

Learning Disability. Frequently of constitutional origin, learning disability is present in 3 to 20% of the school population. This difference in the estimated number is due to varying opinions as to which problems must be evident, how many problems must be present, and how severe the problem or problems must be before the diagnosis is made. The term does not apply to children whose difficulties in learning stem primarily from visual or auditory impairment, physical injury, mental retardation, emotional disturbance, or lack of environmental opportunity. Rather, the designation is reserved for those who, although normal in appearance and possessing average or above average intelligence, are unable to process information in such a way that sights and sounds are stored within the brain, ready to be retrieved and used at the appropriate time.

As an infant the learning disabled child is more apt to be colicky, high in activity level, and negative in mood. As a toddler he displays frequent temper tantrums, poor motor coordination, and slow or irregular language development. The child is unable to complete a task, running from one activity to another, and is sometimes destructive of toys and household furnishings. The child does not seem to profit from experience or from usual methods of discipline. The reaction of parents is one of frustration, often accompanied by hostile feelings toward the child. "He won't listen," "She doesn't mind," "He's a bad boy" are common complaints.

Learning disability takes a different course with each child. Some children experience problems in many areas; others have difficulty in only one or a few. The disability may be so severe as to cripple the child socially and academically or so slight as to be undetected. More than 100 forms of learning disability have been described in the literature and at least 50 names have been given to them, the most common being minimal brain dysfunction, perceptual handicap, dyslexia, congenital word blindness, and hyperkinesis.

The principal abnormalities are: hyperactivity, in which the child is incessantly in motion and unable to concentrate on appropriate tasks; motor awkwardness, visible in a lack of coordination of large and small muscles; orientation defects, seen when the child cannot memorize the route to school or is unable to differentiate left and right; emotional instability, witnessed by bouts of excessive excitement and times of sadness; unsatisfactory interpersonal relationships, demonstrated by a resistance to social demands and a tendency to be demanding; and dyslexia, the inability to store word images in the brain, making it difficult to recognize words and thus affecting the child's ability to read, write, and spell.

Parents may take heart that such well-known figures as Leonardo da Vinci, Thomas Edison, Woodrow Wilson, Albert Einstein, and Nelson Rockefeller were learning disabled. But the usual pattern is not fame. Instead, the learning disabled child becomes the learning disabled adolescent who continues to do poorly in school and is three times more apt to become delinquent than peers of similar age, social class, and race (Rubenstein, 1982). Whether the propensity toward wrongdoing is because of such personality attributes as impulsivity, inability to learn from experience, and poor reception of social cues, or whether it is a reaction to the negative attitude of parents and teachers and because of being labeled and grouped with other problem children is not known (Lane, 1980). Learning disabled adults also have adjustment difficulties, although some manage to cope quite well.

The etiology of learning disability is not known, although many theories have been offered. These range from improper child-rearing techniques to poor diet, from inner ear infection to genetic predisposition, from slow neurological development to cerebral brain damage. Each view has studies to support it. It is true that children may be confused by parental expectations, but this does not explain why other children in the family reared in the same way are not learning disabled.

Eliminating artifical flavors and dyes in foods and reducing carbohydrates has helped some children, especially those who are hyperkinetic. In one study of 200 learning disabled children, 96% were found to have inner ear disturbances ("Report New Theory on Why Child Is Dyslexic," 1974). Learning disability tends to run in families, with boys being affected four times as often as girls. The most commonly held view is that of neurological impairment, with a developmental lag in one or both halves of the brain or injury to brain cells before or during the birth process being cited as the probable cause.

Remedial procedures vary depending on the nature of the difficulty and the orientation of the educator or therapist. Early intervention is more effective than later mediation. Some schools screen all children before they enter kindergarten, but economic constraints mean that only a few receive the needed attention.

Parents find that neither the hard approach of punishing the child for not doing better nor the soft approach of trying to protect the child is effective. Meeting with other parents who have children with the same problem, lobbying for educational programs within the schools, and being familiar with research methods that may be duplicated in the home provide some relief (Brown, 1969; Golick, 1968; Johnson & Myklebust, 1967; Lerner, 1971).

The child needs acceptance and understanding from the Christian community. This is less apt to occur if people within the church are judgmental because the child does not fit their stereotype of what a child should be like. The learning disabled youngster is often the "troublemaker" at church. This is the child who cannot sit still, listen to the sermon, or read the lesson when called on by the Sunday school teacher. Nevertheless, with firmness and patience the child may be helped. Letting the child act out the Bible stories, encouraging individual talents and interests, and providing facilities and volunteers for tutoring and developmental programs are a few of the ways in which the church may be of service (Rowan, 1977).

The extent to which learning disability touches the lives of people within the Christian community is greater than realized, and it behooves pastors, teachers, and counselors to become familiar with the characteristics of the learning disabled child and with ways to alleviate the distress. Turning failure to success and delinquent tendencies to a desire for values in keeping with the Word of God are meaningful endeavors.

References

Brown, G. W. Suggestions for parents. *Journal of Learning Disabilities,* 1969, *2,* 97–106.

Golick, M. A parent's guide to learning problems. *Journal of Learning Disabilities,* 1968, *1,* 366–377.

Johnson, D. J., & Myklebust, H. R. *Learning disabilities: Educational principles and practices.* New York: Grune & Stratton, 1967.

Lane, B. A. The relationship of learning disabilities to juvenile delinquency: Current status. *Journal of Learning Disabilities,* 1980, *13,* 425–434.

Lerner, J. W. *Children with learning disabilities.* Boston: Houghton Mifflin, 1971.

Report new theory on why child is dyslexic. *Today's Child,* 1974, *22*(6), 2.

Rowan, R. D. *Helping children with learning disabilities: In the home, school, church, and community.* Nashville: Abingdon, 1977.

Rubenstein, C. Oops—learning disabilities do get boys in trouble. *Psychology Today,* 1982, *16*(5), 74–75.

B. CLOUSE

See ATTENTION DEFICIT DISORDER; UNDERACHIEVER; MENTAL RETARDATION.

Learning, Discrimination. The process whereby different responses are made to different stimulus situations. It is opposite behaviorally from the process of generalization, in which the same response is made to different stimulus situations. Discriminations can be made between two or more stimuli (stimulus discrimination) as well as between two forms of the same response (response discrimination).

The basic operation for the formation of a stimulus discrimination involves differential reinforcement of the same response under different conditions. Whenever one stimulus is present, the response leads to a positive consequence. Whenever another stimulus is present, the response either fails to produce a positive consequence or it is punished. Over repeated exposure to this situation the response comes to be made only to the appropriate stimulus. For example, a stimulus discrimination has been learned when an infant's generalized response of "da-da," initially given to all men, comes to be given only to the child's father. The formation of response discriminations involve essentially the same process; that is, the form of the response, such as its intensity, amplitude, or latency, is altered by different consequences (reinforcement). Familiar forms of response discriminations are those associated with learning to ride a bicycle or to steer an automobile.

Both humans and animals are capable of making remarkably complex discriminations. In general, discriminations are more easily learned when 1) the difference to be learned is large rather than small, 2) the consequences of responding are consistent, and 3) correct responses are frequently reinforced.

S. R. OSBORNE

Learning, Escape. A response made in order to escape an aversive stimulus. The removal of an aversive stimulus following a response reinforces that response and makes it more likely to occur in the future. In escape learning the punishing stimulus continues to be experienced until the appropriate escape response is made. Therefore, escape learning often is a precursor of avoidance learning, in which punishment is avoided rather than escaped.

For example, a dog will readily learn to jump over a hurdle to escape an electric shock delivered through the floor of his cage. After a number of trials the escape response becomes an avoidance response; that is, the dog learns to jump over the hurdle at the start of the trial before he is shocked at all. Interestingly, if the dog in this situation is prevented from escaping and is repeatedly shocked, he may subsequently fail to try to escape in future situations even when escape is possible. This phenomenon, termed LEARNED HELPLESSNESS, may have a counterpart in human learning inasmuch as people who repeatedly fail to escape from aversive situations sometimes adopt a defeatist attitude that prevents them from learning appropriate escape or avoidance behavior when the opportunities for such learning arise.

In the laboratory the aversive stimulus in escape learning usually is painful electric shock. However, escape and avoidance responses are learned for a broad variety of aversive situations.

S. R. OSBORNE

Learning, Latent. Learning that occurs without any apparent reward but is not revealed in performance until sufficient motivation is present.

In early latent learning experiments (e.g., Tolman & Honzik, 1930) two groups of food-deprived rats were allowed to negotiate a maze. The rats in one group found food in the goal box of the maze, and over successive trails their time to run the maze and the number of entries into blind alleys decreased. Rats in the other group found no food in the goal box, and their performance showed no evidence of learning. The rats in this group then were placed in the goal box and given food there for the first time. Then the performance of both groups was tested again. This time the rats that previously negotiated the maze without food in the goal box began to run as fast, and with as few errors, as the rats who had found food in the goal box in all the previous trials.

The results of latent learning experiments were significant from a theoretical perspective because they challenged some of the basic tenets of early reinforcement theories. For example, "law of effect" theories (e.g., Thorndike) presumed that reinforcement worked directly upon response strength so that all that was learned would be revealed in performance. However, latent learning suggested that learning could occur and be available without being used, until motivational or reward conditions made it profitable.

Tolman, one of the early behaviorists who studied latent learning, emphasized the cognitive nature of learning and described an animal's behavior in terms of its motives, cognitions, expectations, intentions, and purposes. He argued that the nonreward situation was a good one for learning the spatial relations of the maze, but that there was no reason for the rat to show what it had learned. However, when food was placed at the end of the maze, the rat used its previously learned "cognitive map" to find its way through the maze to the goal box.

On the other hand, reinforcement theorists argued that food in the goal box was not the only possible reward for the rat's running of the maze. Consequently, any learning that had taken place was still due to reinforced responses and not to cognitive learning that occurred without reward.

A number of experiments on latent learning were conducted during the 1940's and 1950's to resolve this controversy over the nature of learning. Despite this effort the issue was never really resolved; different latent learning experiments led to different results. However, of 48 studies reviewed by MacCorquodale and Meehl (1954), 30 reported positive findings relative to latent learning, whereas only 18 showed negative findings.

The lasting importance of latent learning research has been threefold. First, it influenced the development of subsequent learning theories. Second, it provided some empirical support for learning theories that suggested that cognitive structure, in addition to responses, is learned. Third, it emphasized the importance of distinguishing between learning and performance. This last point is especially important because it reminds us that learning will be revealed only under appropriate motivational conditions.

References
MacCorquodale, K., & Meehl, P. E. In W. K. Estes, S. Koch, K. MacCorquodale, P. E. Meehl, C. G. Mueller, W. Schoenfeld, & W. S. Verplanck (Eds.), *Modern learning theory*. New York: Appleton-Century-Crofts, 1954.
Tolman, E. C., & Honzik, C. H. Introduction and removal of reward, and maze performance in rats. *University of California Publication in Psychology*, 1930, *4*, 257–275.
S. R. OSBORNE

Learning, Social. *See* SOCIAL LEARNING THEORY.

Legal Psychology. *See* FORENSIC PSYCHOLOGY.

Lesbianism. *See* HOMOSEXUALITY.

Leuba, James Henry (1867–1946). One of the earliest experimental psychologists in the United States, best remembered for his extensive empirical research on the psychology of religion. He was born in Neuchâtel in 1867, living there until he took the B. S. degree from the University of Neuchâtel. He moved to the United States to study with Hall at Clark University, completing his Ph.D. in 1896. He then took an academic position at Bryn Mawr, where he remained until his retirement in 1933.

Among Leuba's first actions at Bryn Mawr was the establishment of one of America's first psychological laboratories in 1898. His interests in experimental psychology included animal learning (particularly the relationship of instincts to learned behaviors) and motivation. In addition to his experimental interests, Leuba could be classified as one of the early dynamic psychologists. He was favorably impressed by the work of Janet and McDougall, but he had little respect for Freud or the other psychoanalysts.

His interest in dynamics was clearly reflected in his work on the psychology of religion, which began with his doctoral dissertation published as *Studies in the Psychology of Religious Phenomena: The Religious Motives, Conversion, Facts, and Doctrine* (1896). Leuba continued to be an active writer in this area until his retirement. By the reckoning of editor J. M. Cattell, Leuba was one of the top 50 eminent psychologists listed in *American Men of Science*.

Leuba's work on the psychology of religion was at once influential and controversial. McBride (1947) characterized Leuba as a reformer whose work was opposed by press and church alike because it questioned, albeit on an empirical basis, traditional religious beliefs. Ironically, his work was used by secular writers and religious fundamentalists alike to buttress their own beliefs. On the one hand, Leuba thought of his research as developing a firm scientific basis to "show man how to mitigate his moral and intellectual perfections." On the other hand, his book *Belief in God and Immortality* (1916) helped persuade William Jennings Bryan to launch his crusade against the teaching of evolution. Leuba used questionnaires to study the traditional religious beliefs of college students and showed statistically that students' acceptance of these beliefs declined with exposure to college course work, findings that confirmed Bryan's impressions of the matter.

In addition to particular beliefs Leuba also studied other elements of Christianity including sin and morality, faith, and the conversion experience. Adopting the nonsectarian stance of comparative religion, Leuba argued that "sin" refers to a general religious sentiment of current moral imperfection and the aspiration for the feeling of personal wholesomeness and peace. His study of conversion led to the conclusion that particular doctrinal beliefs were not crucial to having a conversion experience. Rather, the prior condition of the convert is the feeling of helplessness coupled with a desire for a higher form of help. Such doctrineless conversions occur when the convert feels the presence of such help as a "joyous conviction" that all will be well in one's life. Perhaps most controversial was Leuba's observation that most worshipers are neither concerned about the nature of their deities nor loyal to them, but rather come to use them to meet their intellectual and emotional needs.

Reference

McBride, K. E. James Henry Leuba 1867–1946. *American Journal of Psychology*, 1947, 60, 645–646.

L. S. SHAFFER

Level of Aspiration. In the 1930s Murray developed a theory of personality in which need for achievement was a major motive. Need for achievement subsequently became a major area of research and theory in personality and social psychology. One of the first areas to be examined in the achievement research was level of aspiration.

In the typical level of aspiration experiment the experimenter manipulated the outcome of a game, unbeknown to the subject. After each round the subject was asked to predict the score in the next round. The usual pattern of results indicated that when a person had a high score (i.e., good performance), he expected to do better on the next round. Conversely when the score was lower than expected, the prediction for the next round was reduced. The level of aspiration varied with successes or failures.

Level of aspiration came to be defined as the level of performance the individual expected to achieve. Level of aspiration operates as a criterion by which the individual evaluates whether his performance is a success or failure. The level of aspiration for future events reflects one's achievement history, with the level being modified upward after a series of successes and downward after failures. One's aspiration level serves as the level of performance considered acceptable within one's self-image. Persons with high need for achievement normally exhibit a higher level of aspiration than those less motivated by success and achievement.

More recently level of aspiration has been one component in a broad theory of achievement. Atkinson (1964) developed an expectancy-value model of achievement. Two major constructs in Atkinson's approach are the tendency to success and the tendency to avoid failure. The individual's motivation to engage in achievement behaviors is a multiplicative function of the success motive, the probability of success, and the incentive value of success. When the probability of success is low, incentive is high, and vice versa. Atkinson predicted that persons with high need for achievement would choose medium risk tasks, as this would maximize the tendency to success. This is exactly what was observed, such individuals choosing tasks of moderate difficulty associated with moderate incentives.

In the same way, the tendency to avoid failure is a product of fear of failure, its probability, and its incentive value. The tendency to avoid failure is highest with tasks of moderate probability of failure and moderate incentive, which implies that individuals with high fear of failure would choose either extremely easy tasks (guaranteed success) or extremely difficult ones (cannot be blamed for failure). This prediction has also received experimental support.

Atypical shifts in level of aspiration have been shown in persons with a high fear of failure. In these persons level of aspiration is raised after failure and lowered after success. Atkinson suggests the individual finds he or she is involved in a task with a moderate probability of failure and is motivated to pick an easier task after success or a more difficult one after failure. By this strategy the individual avoids information which directly reflects one's ability.

In summary, level of aspiration is a subjective expectancy of an individual about anticipated performance. It operates as a standard below which the individual would find performance unacceptable. In persons with a high need for achievement the level of aspiration is realistically adjusted upward or downward, depending on previous success or failure. For persons motivated to avoid failure, tasks that enable the person to realistically evaluate skills and performance are avoided.

Reference
Atkinson, J. W. *An introduction to motivation.* Princeton, N.J.: Van Nostrand, 1964.

R. L. Timpe

See Motivation; Personality.

Lewin, Kurt (1890–1947). Seldom do the ideas of one man alter the course of an entire discipline, but Kurt Lewin had just such an impact upon social psychology. Its emphases on rigorous experimentation, cognitive and motivational processes, and the importance of perceived situational factors in the explanation of social behavior can be traced back to Lewin's seminal work in the 1930s and 1940s (see Festinger, 1980). It is for this reason that Lewin is appropriately called the father of experimental social psychology.

Born in Mogilno, Germany, he earned his Ph.D. in psychology in 1914 at the University of Berlin. At the university Lewin became interested in the work of the Gestalt psychologists Wertheimer and Koffka. Through their influence and his own experimental research, Lewin became convinced of the limitations of simple stimulus-response explanations of human behavior and began to develop his "field theory" as an alternative.

Field theory provides us with a view of persons that differs sharply from behavioristic accounts. First, the theory has a distinct phenomenological flavor. It is perceptions and interpretations of stimuli that prompt action, not the objective stimuli themselves. Lewin attempted to capture this perspective with his concept of *life space*. The life space is a dynamic composition of all the perceptions and cognitions—real or unreal; past, present, or future—capable of influencing an individual's current behavior.

Opposing the elementalism of the behaviorists, Lewin also held to the Gestalt notion that the whole is not the sum of its parts but rather the relations between them. The life space is a Gestalt in the sense that it is composed of interconnected psychical regions to which and

through which the individual could possibly move. Locomotion, or movement through the life space, is not determined by a single stimulus but by the complex, changing pattern of psychical regions and their relations. Lewin thought that this view fit the complexity of natural behavior settings better than the stimulus-response approaches, which insisted on isolating the effects of one stimulus at a time.

Field theory also contrasts the environmental determinism of behavioral accounts with an emphasis on the intentionality and goal directedness of behavior. Lewin believed that, once formed, our intentions and goals take on the character of *quasi-needs*. These self-created needs have no necessary linkage to basic biological needs, but nevertheless cause tension in the life space, which the individual seeks to reduce or satisfy through goal attainment. Lewin considered these quasi-needs as more fundamental than biological needs to an understanding of most human behavior. Indeed, most of us know the very real tension that comes from work deadlines or the desire for a new car or to spend time with a friend, none of which may affect our survival but which seem essential to understanding our day-to-day motivations.

While at the University of Berlin, Lewin and his students conducted experiments on a wide variety of hypotheses derived from the basic ideas of field theory. Perhaps most famous were Zeigarnik's studies of recall for completed versus interrupted tasks. Her finding that people remember interrupted tasks better than completed ones has come to be known as the Zeigarnik effect. Other studies examined tendencies to resume interrupted tasks, the effects of substitute activities on tension systems, and the relationship of level of aspiration to experiences of success and failure.

By 1932 Lewin's work was well known, even in the United States, and he decided to spend a six-month leave as a visiting professor at Stanford. In 1933 the Nazi threat prompted him to leave Germany permanently, and he spent two years at Cornell before moving to the Child Welfare Station at the University of Iowa. Although Lewin continued to explore field theory in his research, Festinger (1980) reports that by the time he (Festinger) arrived at Iowa to work as a graduate student, Lewin's interests were firmly in the area of social psychology. "He wanted to understand the behavior of groups" (p. 237).

A classic study of groups operating under autocratic and democratic climates (Lewin,

Lippett, & White, 1939) was among those that began to change the face of social psychology. First, this research demonstrated that complex social interactions could be fruitfully examined in the laboratory. Second, it showed that social psychological interventions can have large, practical results and that these interventions have potential for use in the real world. Both these consequences flow from Lewin's conviction that theory, research, and the real world must come together in the form of "action research"—research directed at the goal of positive social change. During World War II his studies comparing group decisions versus lectures as methods for convincing housewives to buy glandular meats are classic examples of such action research, contributing both to the war effort and to our understanding of group dynamics and behavior change.

In 1945 Lewin and a number of his colleagues and students left Iowa for M.I.T., where they established the Research Center for Group Dynamics. Work at the center ranged from designing interventions to increase worker productivity to the founding of the National Training Laboratories at Bethel, Maine, where the T-group approach to interpersonal skills training was born. Lewin's sudden death in 1947 left the Research Center without a prestigious leader, and it was subsequently moved to the University of Michigan, where it was joined with the Survey Research Center to become the Institute for Social Research.

Lewin's critics typically focus on the formal properties of field theory, arguing that many of its central constructs (e.g., life space, tension systems) are loosely defined and difficult to test. While this is true, Lewin's work must be credited with tremendous heuristic value, having stimulated a whole generation of social psychological research. Furthermore, Lewin's emphasis on the importance of reciprocal interaction between theory, data, and social problems is a legacy that should never be forgotten.

References

Festinger, L. (Ed.). *Retrospectives on social psychology.* New York: Oxford University Press, 1980.

Lewin, K., Lippett, R., & White, R. K. Patterns of aggressive behavior in experimentally created "social climates." *Journal of Social Psychology*, 1939, *10*, 271–299.

Additional Reading

Lewin, K. *A dynamic theory of personality.* New York: McGraw-Hill, 1935.

D. D. McKENNA

Libido. Defined in Freud's earliest formulations as the energy of the sexual drive. How-ever, the term often is used more generally to refer to both sexual and aggressive energy. According to psychoanalytic thought libido can be changed from its original sexual or aggressive nature through a process of neutralization. It is then available for use by the ego, energizing such diverse ego functions as thinking, creative and artistic expressions, and motor activity. Libido is thus the energy source for all human psychic and behavioral activity.

D. G. BENNER

See PSYCHOSEXUAL DEVELOPMENT; PSYCHOANALYTIC PSYCHOLOGY.

Lie Detection. The procedure involves the use of a particular device, often called a polygraph, to measure several physiological responses that are under autonomic control and accompany strong emotions. These include heart rate, blood pressure, respiration, skin resistance (galvanic skin response), and electrical activity of the brain (EEG). The word *polygraph*, meaning literally *many writings*, comes from the use of several pens in a polygraph device to record the autonomic responses. Lie detectors are used by many police departments to question suspects and by some employers in interviewing applicants for particularly sensitive jobs.

The theory behind a lie detector is that if a person is anxious about a lie, his or her breathing, heart rate, and other autonomic responses will increase. The lie detector is thus more accurately a nervousness detector.

The usual procedure in operating a polygraph is to seat the subject so that he cannot see the examiner or the record of the machine. A recording is first made of the subject while he is relaxed, and this recording serves as a baseline for evaluating subsequent responses. The examiner then asks questions that can be answered yes or no. These include neutral questions interspersed with questions critical to the investigation at hand. Sufficient time is allowed between each question for the measures to return to normal. Presumably the suspect's lie is indicated by the increased physiological responses to the critical questions. Since the inflated blood pressure cuff used for the cardiovascular measure may become uncomfortable, the examination is often limited to several minutes and about a dozen questions.

Another type of lie detector has recently been developed to measure minor changes in a person's voice that are undetectable to the human ear. All muscles, including those controlling the vocal cords, vibrate slightly when in use. This muscle vibration, which is transmitted to the vocal cords, is suppressed by the activity of the autonomic nervous system when a speaker is under stress. When a tape recording of a person's voice is played through a device called a voice stress analyzer, a speaker under stress can be detected. Like the polygraph the voice stress analyzer indicates only that an individual is anxious, and not necessarily that he or she is lying.

The voice stress analyzer has an advantage over the polygraph in that the subject does not have to be attached to a lot of equipment. In fact, the subject does not even have to be present. The voice analyzer can work from the telephone, radio, TV, or tape-recorded messages. Since people's voices can thus be analyzed without their knowledge, there is considerable concern over the unethical use of the analyzer. Tests of the voice stress analyzer show its accuracy rate to be equal to or less than that of the polygraph (Rice, 1978).

No lie-detecting device is foolproof. A subject who is telling the truth may be very tense and react emotionally to the content of the questions, and thus appear to be lying. Attempts to defeat the lie detector, on the other hand, usually fail. It is extremely difficult to suppress or augment the autonomic responses by, for example, thinking emotional thoughts or clenching one's teeth or sphincter muscle. The purpose of such behavior would be to increase one's responses to neutral questions, thus creating a baseline comparable to reactions to the critical questions.

It is possible for pathological liars not to realize that they are lying, or not to care, and thus show very little abnormal response to questioning. It is also clear that tranquilizers can be used to reduce the physiological responses to the polygraph test. Because of these problems most courts do not admit lie detector results as evidence, although such tests are used in preliminary criminal investigations.

Recent research suggests that the context of both the lie and the detection of the lie must be considered. The accuracy of the polygraph can be affected by such variables as attentiveness, personality, drugs, and the interaction between examiner and subject. (Waid & Orne, 1982). The subject's belief in the accuracy of the test can also affect his physiological responses. If the examiner gives a subject feedback about his failure to fool the machine, his next lies are even more easily detected. In spite of these limitations lie-detecting techniques are somewhat effective, and thus their use is likely to continue.

References
Rice, B. The new truth machines. *Psychology Today*, 1978, *12*(1), 61–77.
Waid, W. M., & Orne, M. T. The physiological detection of deception. *American Scientist*, 1982, *70*, 402–409.

Additional Readings
Depaulo, B. M., & Rosenthal, R. Telling lies. *Journal of Personality and Social Psychology*, 1979, *37*, 1713–22.
Lykken, D. T. Psychology and the lie detector industry. *American Psychologist*, 1974, *29*, 725–39.
Reid, J. E., & Inbau, F. E. *Truth and deception: The polygraph ("lie detector") technique.* Baltimore: Williams & Wilkins, 1977.

M. P. Cosgrove

Life Script. The term used in Transactional Analysis to refer to the personal plan for life (Steiner, 1974). Out of the interaction with parents, children adopt one of the basic life positions (I'm OK—You're Not OK; I'm Not OK—You're OK; I'm Not OK—You're Not OK; I'm OK—You're OK). Scripts are the themes for life that stem from one of these positions and dictate how the child will survive.

Berne described several types of scripts, such as 1) never scripts—never getting what one wants; 2) always scripts—doing the same thing over and over; 3) until scripts—waiting before a reward is given; and 4) after scripts—having ominous things occur at certain times.

Scripts can be winner's scripts (where outcomes are mostly positive), loser's scripts (where outcomes are mostly negative), and tragic scripts (where outcomes are mostly disastrous). Often scripts can be understood through the themes of fairy tales such as Cinderella.

Reference
Steiner, C. *Scripts people live.* New York: Grove Press, 1974.

H. N. Malony

Life Skills Counseling. A counseling approach developed by Adkins in the middle 1960s. Traditional counseling methods have, for the most part, failed to be effective with clients who are from disadvantaged backgrounds. This failure is especially pronounced when the counseling method employed is one where discussion of feelings is stimulated by an ambiguous or nonstructured relationship between counselor and client. Adkins (Adkins & Wynne, 1966) developed a counseling approach, based on his experiences with a vocational training program, which emphasizes the use of a structured format to help disadvantaged adolescents and adults learn skills related to employment, interpersonal adjustment, and citizenship. He used three criteria for designing this program. First, the counseling should be centered on problems related to living and working in a city environment. Second, the skills that clients brought to counseling should serve as a foundation for newer skills. Third, the program should allow for both group interactions and personal attention.

Adkins worked with counselors to formulate a task analysis of the skill requirements for successful relationships within work, family, and community settings. On the basis of this analysis he developed a list of 50 common life problems, which were then grouped into five areas: developing oneself and relating to others; managing a career; managing home and family responsibilities; managing leisure time; and exercising community rights, opportunities, and responsibilities. Each of these areas, which are titled curriculum tracks in the program, was divided into smaller units (Adkins, 1973). For example, representative units of the managing a career area are 1) interviews, tests, and application blanks; 2) relating to one's boss; and 3) pay check deductions. These units represent competencies or skills needed to succeed in the larger area.

Adkins also developed a process for teaching these skills that was targeted to the needs of his audience. Since he had noted in his work with disadvantaged clients that nondirected group discussions tended to be unfocused and nonproductive, he developed a four-stage process to teach life skills. This process is based on "a fundamental notion . . . that experience followed by reflection, followed by goal-setting, followed by further exploration, reflection, and so forth" (Adkins, 1970, p. 111) was the most productive method for encouraging self-directed change. His four-stage process, therefore, begins with a stimulus, moves to evocation, then objective inquiry, then to application.

During the stimulus stage the counselor presents a problem using a tape recording, a movie, or an interview and thus stimulates the group's interest and involvement in the topic. Once the group begins to discuss the problem, the counselor's objective is to draw from each group member what he or she knows about the problem—the evocation stage. The group's ideas are written on a blackboard or newsprint, and discussion continues until interest lags. Then the ideas are categorized and questions are developed. The third stage, that of objective inquiry, involves having group members obtain relevant information. The counselor uses prepared multimedia kits to direct the members' information-seeking activities both within and outside the classroom. Once the

relevant information has been obtained and presented to the group, the group selects one or several aspects of the problem to work out in the application stage. During this stage projects that allow for the development and application of new skills are devised and completed.

The life skills approach is meant to be flexible. Thus, a counselor might focus on one area in particular (e.g., employment) and spend several sessions going through the four stages, or may choose to cover every curriculum track at a less specific level of involvement. This flexibility is a major advantage of the approach. Another advantage is that the emphasis on life problems and skills translates counseling goals into specific behavioral objectives rather than insight-oriented affective and cognitive outcomes. Transfer of learning from life skills counseling to real-life problems would therefore be heightened. Maintenance of change would also be likely as the newly learned skills would be incorporated and used successfully after the counseling had ended. Finally, the learning process is learner centered rather than teacher oriented. Thus, motivation for learning, as Adkins (1980) reports, is usually high.

In summary, life skills counseling is an alternative counseling approach designed to teach coping skills to underserved populations (people who need but do not make use of traditional counseling services). Both a program design and a learning process model have been developed. Since the research evidence to date is scanty, the effectiveness of this approach must be demonstrated through use and evaluation. However, Adkins (1980) reports on several research projects in progress which indicate that learners and counselors find the program to be effective.

For a Christian counselor this approach may represent an excellent method for education and development among his or her clients. Although conceived as a remedial intervention, life skills counseling could easily be adapted for use in a preventive context and for life problems, such as marriage and parenting, which seem to be frequent client concerns.

References

Adkins, W. R. Life skills: Structured counseling for the disadvantaged. *Personnel and Guidance Journal*, 1970, 49, 108–116.

Adkins, W. R. Life skills education for adult learners. *Adult Leadership*, 1973, 22, 55–58; 82–84.

Adkins, W. R. Life skills counseling. In R. Herink (Ed.), *The psychotherapy handbook*. New York: New American Library, 1980.

Adkins, W. R., & Wynne, J. D. *Final report of the YMCA youth and work project.* Contract 24–64, Department of Labor. New York: YMCA of Greater New York, 1966.

E. M. ALTMAIER

See COPING SKILLS THERAPIES.

Life Span Development. "The child is father of the man," wrote Wordsworth. While there is truth in this, it should be added that development is not limited to childhood but continues throughout life. Developmental psychology focuses on changes occurring in body, thoughts, and behavior across the life cycle. Often development is viewed as positive expansion to some peak during early life, followed by inevitable deterioration in later life. Although this may reflect physical processes, it does not necessarily reflect psychological ones. Positive expansion can describe psychosocial development from birth through old age.

Principles of Human Development. Current understanding of human development is limited by theoretical presuppositions, cultural setting, and historical time. Our knowledge base is in constant flux as new information antiquates what we thought were foundational concepts and continually affirms the intricacies and complexity of human thought and action.

Cultural specificity. Most developmental research and theoretical models are based on Western, technological, often middle-class subjects, norms, and values. Subsequently, formulations often have limited generalizability. For example, order in developmental sequence may vary across cultures, as in the skill acquisitions of crawling, sitting, squatting, standing. Presence or absence of stages may vary across cultures; for example, many cultures do not recognize an adolescent period. Developmentally relevant social roles and expectations may differ across cultures, as in views of child responsibilities. In some cultures girls as young as five years may fill the role of nurse/caretaker for younger siblings.

Sociohistorical specificity. Events and the social context characterizing historical time periods may also affect development. For example, American sociopolitical events of the early 1970s (Vietnam war, student dissent, Watergate) were so salient in personality development that they sometimes masked age differences among adolescents studied. In fact, adolescence in Western society was not viewed as a distinct developmental period until sociopolitical factors relating to job availability and acquisition of adult skills made necessary a period of prolonged dependence and education. Before this time fewer distinctions in norms and expectations between adult and teen-ager existed.

Individual differences. Variation among people has both genetic and environmental origins and exists at the onset, in the rate, and in the outcome of developmental processes. Although generalizations about developing humans can be provided, few individuals actually fit these.

Variation is also relevant to making comparisons between groups, as when comparing males to females, racial groups, socioeconomic categories of people, and so on. In much of developmental research variation among members of a single group (e.g., among females or among males) is so great, and the amount of overlap between groups is so great, that focusing on group differences is of little value to understanding an individual. That is, prediction of a person's behavior may not be enhanced much by knowing his group membership.

The concept of interaction is essential to understanding variability among people. At any one point in time a person is participating in a dynamic system with the psychosocial and physical environment. The person's presence and behavior change the environment, which in turn feeds back to affect the person in ways specific to his or her learning history, dispositions, and so on. Within a person the physical, personal-social, cognitive, and spiritual dimensions are also interacting with each other. To illustrate, consider an ungainly adolescent boy during a growth spurt. He is in contrast to the physical ideal of his peer group. This may lead to some social rejection, which interacts with his self-concept; these may interact with cognitive performances in school; and all of these may interact with attitudes he currently holds toward a God assumed to be in control.

Stage versus continuity. Stages, across which people are characterized as qualitatively different, are useful in building models and communicating information. However, they also connote discontinuity. Psychological development does not proceed by stops and starts; it is continuous, generally progressive and cumulative.

Stability versus change. The life span from adolescence on has been traditionally viewed as stable, with behaviors, attitudes, and motives established during the early "formative" years. This perspective has often resulted in overanxious views of childhood and rather fatalistic views of adulthood. Childhood *is* an important time of foundation laying; however, evidence consistently supports the conviction that an individual has the capacity for change throughout life. Predictability exists as a function of the environment; that is, behavioral consistency is directly related to environmental consistency.

Related to this is the concept of functional adaptation. Positive development is associated with flexibility rather than constancy. Individuals who can adapt their behavior and attitudes so as to be functional in a changing environment are considered psychologically healthy. This is in contrast to individuals with more rigid self-concepts and behavior repertoires, who are compelled to monitor their behavior constantly to ensure it is consistent with their image of themselves.

Theoretical Models of Development. Data and data interpretations are not independent of the theoretical assumptions of data gatherers. Thus, absolute information on optimal development, cause and effect in development, intervention into development, and so on does not exist. Consider, for example, a recently fed, changed, and cuddled infant who is nonetheless vigorously crying. In the multitude of child-rearing guides on the market today, advice varies according to the author-experts. An Eriksonian author may advise that the infant be given immediate attention, for such will help the infant develop a positive, trustful view of the world. On the other hand, a Skinnerian author may advise that the infant's cries be ignored, because parental attention will simply reinforce the crying behavior and thus make it more likely to recur. Same infant, same behavior, yet opposite child-rearing instructions based on different theoretical models.

Psychodynamic models (representative theorists: Erikson, Freud). Psychodynamic models are primarily focused on personality/emotional development. They are stage oriented and tend to rely on psychosexual development for their frameworks. Motivation for movement through stages relates to the dynamics among personality variables, whose objective is to satisfy basic, instinctual impulses (e.g., sexual) but within the constraints of increasingly rigid social expectations. These models tend to be deterministic, with the individual primarily a respondent to internal impulses and external norms. Early childhood is considered very important in setting the course for the life span; maladjustment in adulthood is often considered the result of childhood experiences.

In general, Erikson has provided a helpful model of the life cycle, particularly with his focus on social influences (*see* PSYCHOSOCIAL DEVELOPMENT). Although influential, Freud's

model has been less compelling in developmental research, with little empirical support (*see* PSYCHOSEXUAL DEVELOPMENT).

Learning models (representative theorists: Bandura, Skinner). Learning models of development are primarily focused on observable behavior. Age-related stages of development are irrelevant, since the same principles of stimulus-response relations are applied across the life span. Development is defined as progressive changes in behavior-environment interactions, with behavior a function of the current environment and the learning history of the person. These models are also deterministic, with the individual primarily a respondent to environmental influences. Behavioral models focus on reinforcement and punishment as the motivators of development; thus, a boy's ethnic identity is considered the result of differential reward and punishment of behavior considered socially appropriate and inappropriate by the ethnic group.

SOCIAL LEARNING THEORY also recognizes the importance of reinforcement and punishment; however, this model introduces more cognitive concepts such as vicarious and symbolic processes. Observational learning is a vicarious process; this is a foundational concept, for instance, in the research into the effects of television viewing on child development. Not all observational learning requires imitation of modeled behavior; much occurs through cognitive symbolic processes. For example, language development is described by social learning theorists as abstract modeling; here common features from a variety of modeled responses are extracted and rules are formed for generating similarly structured behavior.

In general, social learning theory has been more influential in explaining life span development than has the behavioral model. Although behavioral principles are useful in predicting some specific developmental outcomes, the complexity of contingencies necessary to explain life span development is so great that this model becomes unwieldy.

Humanistic models (representative theorists: Maslow, Rogers). Humanistic models of development are in many ways a protest against the determinism of the psychodynamic and learning theories. These models focus on such concepts as selfhood, dignity, creativity, and individuality. They are not oriented toward describing stages of development (although Maslow's need hierarchy may be so interpreted), but rather the process of development. This process is purposeful, with the individual actively involved in planning and making rational choices. The motivation for this process is self-fulfillment—not as a static outcome but as a state of being.

Empirically humanistic models are quite weak. They do make important contributions to understanding human development in their high regard for individual differences, their focus on the whole person, and their tenacious guarding against equating the individual with a data point.

Cognitive development models (representative theorists: Kohlberg, Piaget). COGNITIVE-DEVELOPMENT models are primarily focused on problem solving—i.e., how an individual transforms information from the environment into mental structures and how these mental structures are transformed into behavior. Development is described as orderly, sequential, and interactive, with the sequence of stages being biologically based and maturation the driving force. Development is a dialectic process where the individual revises mental structures to account for new information and selects those concepts and behavior options that are most consistent with the existent concept of self. Cognitive development theorists argue that to facilitate development an individual should be confronted with information advanced a bit beyond current structures, thus causing disequilibrium and requiring a restructuring. This has been applied in educational settings with moral reasoning; the results have been mixed.

Cognitive development models are quite useful in exploring the development of conceptual functions—self-concept, moral judgment, and problem solving. They are somewhat weak, however, in explaining how the individual initially acquires the data necessary to form rudimentary structures.

Composite models. It appears that no single model is sufficient to describe and explain life span development; this is not surprising given the complexity of human development and the different focuses of the models discussed. The most compelling explanations of development today are composite models utilizing principles from a variety of sources. A good example combines social learning theory and the cognitive development model. Social learning precedes cognitive development processes to identify distinctive features and devise and revise rules; this is a *bottom-up* framework. Rules are consolidated into concepts, and *top-down* analyses follow according to cognitive consistency striving. For example, throughout infancy and early childhood a girl is reinforced and punished for behaving in ways appropriate and inappropriate for females. She observes male and female models and formulates rules for her own behavior, and based on all this information she develops her gender identity as female. With this identity she uses cognitive development principles to explore the parameters of femaleness, as well as to select behavior and attitudes consistent with her image of female.

Process of Life Span Development. This section will be a brief overview of development from conception to death. Salient features of each time period will be reviewed in terms of physical and psychosocial variables. No single model of development will be exclusively used; rather, elements from a variety of models will be selected according to their empirical support and ease of understanding.

Prenatal/perinatal period. Rapid growth and differentiation describe physical and physiological development during the prenatal period. In contrast, little is known about prenatal psychological development, although the well-integrated state of the newborn indicates that cognitive and perceptual systems are already functioning in the womb.

Labor and delivery is a critical period for survival, with adaptive requirements extremely compressed in time. During this short interval the individual's systems must take over processes they either shared with the placenta or over which the placenta had complete control. Problems during this transition may adversely affect subsequent physical and mental development. For example, improper presentation and premature closure of the umbilical cord may lead to insufficient oxygen reaching the brain, with possible physical and/or mental handicapping conditions resulting.

The delivery process may also have implications for the social and emotional development of the child. Although few data have yet been collected, theorizing has associated positive parent-child attachment with birthing processes where both mother and father feel responsible and are actively involved. Conversely, some theorists have argued that birth is traumatic and can negatively affect personality development. This perspective has led to some recent practices where the newborn is delivered into an environment simulating a womb—e.g., a warm, quiet, dimly lit delivery room. Perhaps such environments do make the physical transition more pleasant; however, there is little support for birthing practices of any kind directly affecting life span personality development. In fact, rather than producing anxiety, a compelling argument can be made that the outside world's "blooms and buzzes [are] reduced in the infant's mind to a unified, global state" (Kastenbaum, 1979, p. 105). (*See* PRENATAL DEVELOPMENT.)

Newborn period. The newborn period extends for about one month following birth. Newborns do possess many primitive reflexes, the timing, presence, and absence of which often provide important diagnostic information. However, newborns are much more than bundles of reflexes. Coordination and integration among systems exist; for example, newborns can hear a sound, turn their heads toward the source, and lock their eyes on it.

The predominant state of newborns is sleep. Over the first four weeks of life the amount of alert time increases from about 10% to over 20%. Obviously it is in alert states that most information on newborn capabilities is collected. Newborns are sexual beings, demonstrating arousal when their genital regions receive stimulation. Cognitively newborns are quite integrated. They show consistent reaction to human speech over other sounds; in fact, within a couple of weeks they can discriminate between parents' and strangers' voices. In learning they demonstrate habituation, respondent conditioning, and operant conditioning. For example, newborns can learn to turn their heads to the left on a bell and to the right on a buzzer to receive milk. When the relationship is reversed, they quickly adjust.

Infancy. Infancy extends from the second month to 18 months–2 years; the boundary between infancy and childhood is the blossoming in language development. In this prelinguistic time of life little is known about thinking processes. It is theorized that infants use perceptual and motor mental structures, rather than language structures, to construct their world. Cognitive development theorists argue that at first an infant does not separate self from the physical environment. It is with sensory and motor experiences that body size, physical limitations, and so on are learned.

Attachment is an important development during infancy; this is the tendency for infants to desire and seek social contact with other persons. Attachment appears to be adaptive in a variety of ways, not the least of which is for the *detachment* process. Infants who have healthy, trusting attachments to their caregivers have secure bases from which to develop independence. Attachments to specific people occur about the third quarter of the first year, with a multiplicity of attached persons the norm. Healthy child-parent attachments develop in a diversity of family styles and child-rearing practices, as, for instance, in Israeli kibbutzim, where child care is communal.

Cognitively and socially, one of the most exciting developments during infancy is the beginning of language. Language requires symbol manipulation and thus substantial cognitive sophistication. Language moves from crying to cooing to babbling to the one-word stage over the first year. Many developmental psychologists hypothesize that by the end of the first year single words are actually carrying full sentences of meaning. Over the second year vocabulary of single words increases, and toward the end of this period rule-governed combining of words occurs. Language development is a predictable process, with consistent types of words acquired earlier than others; even consistent errors are observed across children.

Physically infancy is a time of rapid increases in weight and length, increasing competence in gross, fine, and perceptual motor skills, and the acquisition of the important developmental tasks of head control, sitting, and walking.

Childhood. Childhood extends from infancy until the prepubertal years around 11–12. Physical growth continues, but at a slowing rate. Sexuality continues to be salient. In early childhood genital differences become known, and learning through exhibition and inspection of self and others is common. Contrary to Freud, later childhood is not a time of sexual latency; sexual interest remains high with peeping, sex jokes, and sex-related words common elements in children's social environment. Sex role development also continues throughout this period, with early and rudimentary gender identity solidified by middle childhood. Knowledge of sex role stereotypes increases, as does adherence to sex-typed norms, particularly in boys. Interestingly, current research is indicating that children possessing positive traits from both the masculine and feminine dimensions may be at an advantage over sex-typed peers in their development. That is, they may be more functionally adaptable.

Socially children move from solitary play to parallel play (where children are in close proximity but playing by themselves) to cooperative play, with the complexity of interaction and guiding rules increasing with increasing age. School generally provides the primary peer group for children and is also important as a transmitter of cultural norms and values.

Cognitively children increase in their facility with symbol manipulation, their ability to take on the perspectives of others, their ability to focus on transformation as well as state, and so on. They do tend to limit their cognitive processes to the concrete here-and-now, however. Likewise, moral judgment increases in complexity, with the conventional reasoning of maintaining the system and obeying authority being added to the predominant orientation where reward and punishment determine right and wrong. Such reasoning has interesting implications for religious conversions occurring during childhood. Children's understanding of God may be limited to concrete parallels such as parent, law enforcer, or friend. Likewise, motivation for conversion may reflect orientations of escaping punishment or pleasing authorities.

Adolescence. Adolescence generally extends from puberty until the individual takes on the status of productive adult. These boundaries are not clear, for individuals who experience later than average puberties may still be considered adolescents, as may individuals in their 20s but still in school.

Early adolescence is an important time physiologically, with the growth spurt, the development of secondary sex characteristics, and reproductive maturity. Body image can change dramatically, both in knowledge of physical potentials and limitations, and in satisfaction with what one has.

Cognitively adolescents begin to break out of the limitations of concrete thinking and to explore the abstract, where *real* is but a subset of the possible. Facility with abstract concepts, however, does not usually occur until late adolescence or early adulthood, with greater competence in some dimensions than in others (e.g., numerical over verbal). One interesting outcome of immature abstract reasoning is naïve idealism. Here adolescents recognize what the adult world is (real) and what it could be (possible), and ascribe to themselves essential roles in achieving the ideal.

In moral judgment conventional reasoning predominates, as it will in the majority of adults. Restructuring of world views may occur in later adolescence. This has been described by some researchers as movement from a dualistic (we-right vs. they-wrong) view, to recognizing that relativism exists, to making commitments to causes and values even in a relativistic world. Individuals in this third level often experience crisis; that is, they actively question and seek among alternatives before they personally commit themselves to some course of action and value system.

Identity formation is an important developmental task of adolescents. This is difficult in our society, where the adolescent is a nonchild and a nonadult existing in a changing body in the midst of social flux, pluralistic value systems, and rapidly changing technology. Answering the questions of "Who am I?" and "What will I be as an adult?" is not easy. It is not surprising that the security of totalistic cult subcultures is attractive to some adolescents. These provide clear parameters with a strong leader, authoritarian group norms, and rewards of group acceptance for behavioral and ideological conformity. Adolescence can also be a time of religious awakening, with crisis permitting movement from an inherited set of beliefs to a personal faith, with abstract thought available to analyze metaphysical issues and with formal religion providing assistance in questions of identity.

Adulthood. Unlike previous developmental periods adulthood cannot be structured by internal frameworks that all experience through maturation, such as walking and language development, or external frameworks that most experience, such as formal education. Adulthood must be viewed according to events or developmental tasks. The effect of these events or tasks depends on timing and the social clock.

On-time events are less stressful than off-time events because one can anticipate and prepare for them. For example, being widowed in one's 20s and becoming pregnant in one's 50s are off-time and require substantial psychological coping by the individual and social system. The social clock is an internalized sense of timing through which society and the individual regulate behavior. The clock is based on age norms, status, and social roles. For example, we smile at children who roll in the grass giggling, whereas we censure middle-aged adults doing so. Likewise, young adults who kiss passionately on a park bench are more readily tolerated than an elderly couple doing the same.

Adulthood is conceptualized in a variety of ways. One example model is Havighurst's (1972) developmental tasks. He views the tasks of early adulthood as selecting a mate, learning to live with one's marriage partner, starting a family, rearing children, managing a home, beginning an occupation, taking on civic responsibility, and finding a congenial social group. The tasks of middle age include assisting teen-age children to become responsible and happy adults, achieving social and civic responsibility, maintaining satisfactory performance in one's occupation, developing leisure-time activities, relating to one's spouse as a person, accepting and adjusting to physiological changes, and adjusting to aging parents. Finally, later maturity tasks include adjusting to decreasing physical strength and changing health, adjusting to retirement and reduced income, adjusting to death of a spouse, establishing affiliation with one's age group, adopting and adapting social roles in a flexible way, and establishing satisfactory physical living arrangements.

Aged adults. Contrary to popular stereotypes most aged individuals are not less intelligent, sexless, disabled, and isolated in nursing homes. Cognitively abstract reasoning abilities remain, although aged adults may perform less well on standardized measures of intelligence. This poorer test performance often reflects a slower response on timed items, and/or motivational factors. Memory in general is not lost among the aged, rather, they tend to perform less well on tasks requiring short-term memory, with the apparent problem being retrieval of information stored.

Socially most aged adults live independently in the community. Social relationships are enjoyed, including intimate relationships with sexual sharing; sexual responsiveness is not inevitably lost in aging. Generally, aged adults who are more active socially report greater life satisfaction; however, this is not a simple relationship. Personality types interact with activity levels; thus, some individuals who are socially disengaged also report high life satisfaction.

Physical decline is associated with aging. However, this does not mandate incapacitation. The vast majority of aged in our society experience good health, although this varies with socioeconomic status. In fact, even with increased longevity the trend is toward improved health status among the aged in our society.

Being aged in a youth-oriented culture such as ours can negatively affect self-esteem. However, satisfactory aging is a reality and is generally associated with three variables: good physical health, economic security, and social support. A loss of any two leads to poor prognosis.

Dying. Dying also is a developmental process with psychosocial significance. In fact, the psychological changes that precede death indicate that distance from death, rather than chronological age, is the most useful time frame here.

Psychological changes are noted among individuals whose death is imminent but who apparently are unaware of this. These include major declines in performance on measures of intelligence, decreased levels in personality organization, and more docile self-images. Among individuals who are aware that their death is imminent a variety of reactive patterns are observed, including denial, anger, anguish, and surrender. Rather than a series of stages as proposed in the past, the dying process appears to be a constant coming and going of the various emotions with no set sequence.

References

Havighurst, R. J. *Developmental tasks and education* (3rd ed.). New York: McKay, 1972.

Kastenbaum, R. *Humans developing.* Boston: Allyn & Bacon, 1979.

M. D. Roe

Life Style. *See* Style of Life.

Lithium Therapy. Lithium, a naturally occurring salt, was the first agent in psychiatry to be specifically effective against a major psychotic disorder. Given orally in tablet form, it usually calms psychotic manic states within 5 to 10 days. When taken on a maintenance schedule it has been shown to prevent the recurrence of manic highs. Once stabilized on lithium, even very severe cases of manic disorder can be treated on an outpatient basis. Although its mechanism of action is still unknown, it appears that it may interfere with sodium retention within brain cells.

See Psychopharmacology.

Lobotomy. A surgical procedure consisting of the ablation of the prefrontal area of the frontal lobe of the cortex. Because of the drastic nature of the treatment and the undesirable side effects that are often present, prefrontal lobotomies, as with all psychosurgical approaches, are ordinarily resorted to only after all other methods have failed. At such a point the operation may be considered as treatment for severe and chronic states of affective disorder as well as paranoid and catatonic schizophrenia.

Locke, John (1632–1704). Born in Somerset, England, Locke studied philosophy, medicine, and science. He is best known for his contributions to Empiricism and Associationism. His major psychological work was *Essay Concerning Human Understanding.* Two other works, *Two Treatises on Government* and *A Letter Concerning Toleration,* both had a profound effect on the American Constitution. He also wrote several books on Christianity, the best known being *An Appeal for a Rational Interpretation of the Gospels* and *Reasonableness of Christianity*.

Locus of Control. A concept that grew out of Rotter's (1954) SOCIAL LEARNING THEORY. The phenomena it addresses, however, have attracted attention from many sources. There has been particular interest in the phenomena, as they appear as barriers to the success of psychotherapy and counseling or as part of the affliction of socially disadvantaged groups.

In Rotter's theory locus of control refers to whether a person believes that what happens to him depends on his own behavior (and thus is internally controlled) or on luck, fate, or the uncontrollable whims of others (and thus is externally controlled). When there is an external control expectancy or belief, the consequences of behavior have little effect in changing that behavior. This has been documented in both animal and human research. The implications for psychotherapy, counseling, and other attempts to help people are obvious: where behavior change is needed, the person must believe that his behavior will have important consequences. It was, in fact, this observation about clients' failure to change in therapy (Rotter, 1966) that led to the theory and research related to locus of control.

Many authors have addressed locus of control without identifying it by this term. Mowrer (1960) does so especially cleverly. He points out that viewing people as sick (instead of sinful) absolves them from responsibility for their woes and thereby works against efforts to foster behavior change. Glasser (1965), the Synanon-style therapeutic community treatment for substance abusers (Yablonsky, 1965), and the various behavior therapies (Rimm & Masters, 1974) all make a primary issue of confronting the client with the consequences of his behavior. These, and others, represent the major techniques for dealing with external control problems, even though they do not identify them by that terminology. Their convergence does, however, reflect how much consensus there is among therapists of very different belief and experience that external control problems are common and crucial in counseling and psychotherapy.

There is also consensus among therapists, although this is less often discussed explicitly in print, that a crucial aspect of therapy is the therapist's attitude regarding who is responsible for the successful outcome of therapy. There is a well-recognized pressure, especially felt by counselors without extensive training in

counseling, to take responsibility for the success of counseling in a way that may be self-defeating. It is easy for the therapist to communicate his feeling that the success of counseling is something which reflects his own skill and effort, not the client's. In this way a client's external control expectancies may be greatly, if tacitly and unconsciously, reinforced and the effectiveness of counseling undermined.

There are, of course, complexities. Many authors have pointed out that there are different kinds of both internal and external control expectancies. For example, it may often make a difference whether the person believes success depends on how skilled he is or how hard he tries, although each might be considered an internal control expectancy. Many different attitude tests have been devised to measure how internal or external are an individual's expectancies in general. Scores on these tests agree only moderately well. Sometimes an internal control measure seems to reflect confidence in ability, sometimes willingness to take responsibility, sometimes political philosophy, etc. No doubt locus of control denotes not a single phenomenon or attribute but a category of them. Still, their commonality is undeniably important in attempts to help people change.

It should also be noted that the whole distinction between internal control and external control beliefs cuts across a Christian's creed in a unique way. The distinction between the two permits no recognition of the joint responsibility of the Christian and God. To assume that an event depends *either* on the individual's behavior *or* on external variables (e.g., God's will) forces a distinction that has been the concern of much Christian theology.

In the Christian recognition that man's responsibility does not deny God's or vice versa—that within God's universe what man does *does* make a difference, and that this difference is what God wills—the distinction between internal control and external control is transcended. This realization is essential if one is to behave responsibly, constructively, or indeed realistically.

References

Glasser, W. *Reality therapy, a new approach to psychiatry.* New York: Harper & Row, 1965.

Mowrer, O. H. "Sin," the lesser of two evils. *American Psychologist,* 1960, *15,* 301–304.

Rimm, D. C., & Masters, J. C. *Behavior therapy: Techniques and empirical findings.* New York: Academic Press, 1974.

Rotter, J. B. *Social learning and clinical psychology.* Englewood Cliffs, N.J.: Prentice-Hall, 1954.

Rotter, J. B. Generalized expectancies for internal versus external control of reinforcement. *Psychological Monographs: General & Applied* 1966, *80* (1), 1–28.

Yablonsky, L. *The tunnel back: Synanon.* New York: Macmillan, 1965.

M. W. STEPHENS

Logorrhea. Excessive, rapid, and uncontrollable speech, often incoherent. It is commonly observed in the manic phase of bipolar disorder. Logorrhea is also known as tachylogia, verbomania, logomania, hyperlogia, and hyperphrasia.

Logotherapy. A theoretical approach to psychotherapy developed by Frankl (1962, 1969, 1978). The term is derived from two Greek words, *logos* (word or meaning) and *therapeia* (healing). Logotherapy, then, is providing or experiencing healing through meaning. Logotherapy can be subsumed under existential psychiatry and psychology. Frankl at one time referred to his approach as *Existenzanalysis*, but has subsequently preferred logotherapy in order to distinguish his work from that of Boss and Binswanger, who have also created existential analytic approaches. As do existential orientations logotherapy views the individual as being free, responsible, unique, and holistic. In the therapy process the client is challenged to become decisive in using his or her freedom in order to discover meaning in life.

Frankl views the individual as a self-determining and self-actualizing person. Thus a human being possesses the innate capacity to transcend environmental factors, be they biological, psychological, or sociological. The transcendent ability is possible because of spiritual freedom that characterizes human beings and distinguishes them uniquely from the animal world. This spiritual freedom is not so much freedom from oppressive forces as it is the potential for discovering, deciding, and actualizing one's existence. Such freedom cannot be taken from the individual, and it is this dimension that makes life meaningful and purposeful.

Human personality is a unity composed of three intermeshing realities: the somatic (physical), the mental (psychological), and the spiritual (noölogical). The combined interaction of the physical and psychological components forms what might be called the psychophysicum. Each dimension of the personality is indispensable, but it is the spiritual dimension that gives meaning. The primary motivation in human behavior is the will to meaning. This is in contrast to Freud's idea of will to pleasure and Adler's concept of will to power or superiority. This will to meaning involves a set of ideals and values that pulls rather than pushes an individual in life. It is a fulfillment of spiritual needs in the process of choosing and deciding.

Like Adler, Frankl thinks it is necessary for an individual to first solve some basic life tasks before finding meaning and purpose in life and thus being fully actualized. These tasks include discovering the meaning of love, the meaning of work and mission, and the meaning of death and suffering. Only then can the meaning of life itself be found.

Problems in living can be discussed under three classifications: neuroses; noögenic neuroses, and psychoses. The neuroses are psychogenic and are experienced either as some type of anticipatory anxiety or an obsessional disturbance. The noögenic neuroses have a spiritually based etiology and are manifested as existential boredom and frustration, a vacuum existence, and a loss of meaning and purpose in life. The psychoses are organic or physically based. A diagnosis always seeks to differentiate these three basic types of problems. Most problems, however, tend to be mixed in nature, and seldom does one problem have a single causation and unitary symptomatology. Accurate differential diagnosis work does indicate the appropriate form of therapy. A neurosis is treated with psychotherapy, a psychosis with physical medicine, and a noögenic neurosis with logotherapy.

The relationship between the logotherapist and the client is characterized by warmth and closeness with a consistent concern for scientific objectivity. An ultimate goal of logotherapy is to help the individual accept responsibility for himself through using spiritual freedom to make personal choices and decisions in the discovery of meaning in and to life.

A variety of methods and strategies are used in the practice of logotherapy. Logotherapy in the purest sense consists of Socraticlike dialogue. Another mode of intervention is logodrama, in which the client is guided in narrating and experiencing the events and meaning of his life. A third strategy is paradoxical intention. This involves asking the client to intend that which he fears. The technique is designed to help individuals overcome anticipatory anxiety or hyperintention. The final major strategy is dereflection. This counteracts obsessive ideation or hyperreflection by helping the client stop thinking about the problem. Both paradoxical intention and dereflection are based on the individual's capacity to detach himself from absorption with personal problems. They have a cognitive behavior emphasis but were developed before cognitive behavior approaches existed.

Logotherapy is the most systematic of all the existential approaches to counseling and psychotherapy. It offers a clear perspective on the nature of the human being, a useful theory of personality, a multidimensional answer to the nature and cause of problems in living, a well-articulated set of procedures and processes to follow in doing therapy, and a body of clearly defined techniques. Much of Frankl's thinking is compatible with historical Judeo-Christian theology (Tweedie, 1961).

References

Frankl, V. E. *Man's search for meaning.* Boston: Beacon Press, 1962.
Frankl, V. E. *The will to meaning.* New York: World Publishing, 1969.
Frankl, V. E. *The unheard cry for meaning.* New York: Simon & Schuster, 1978.
Tweedie, D. F. *Logotherapy: An evaluation of Frankl's existential approach to psychotherapy.* Grand Rapids: Baker, 1961.

D. SMITH

See EXISTENTIAL PSYCHOLOGY AND PSYCHOTHERAPY.

Loneliness. Loneliness appears to be basic to the human condition. As awareness of one's self as a distinct entity dawns, a fundamental sense of separation also appears. This is normally experienced as anxiety and fear of abandonment. In order to overcome this frequently frightening sense of separateness, human beings actively seek to transcend their individuality through psychological or physical fusion. Because experiences of intimacy are only momentary or inconsistently maintained, however, loneliness is a universal experience. Although loneliness seems to be more widespread and intense in societies where the values of freedom and individuality are strongly promoted, kinship-focused societies experience it as well. For example, it has been estimated that the Japanese have about 50 words related to loneliness and intimacy (Hartog, Audy, & Cohen, 1980).

Dynamics of Loneliness. Surprisingly little formal attention has been paid to the phenomenon of loneliness by psychologists until recently. Freud only briefly mentioned loneliness in his writings, though his concept of a fundamental "oceanic feeling" (Freud, 1930) implies a self that is fused with the universe and not yet individuated. Neo-Freudian theorist Fromm (1941) suggested that five human needs of relatedness, transcendence, rootedness, identity, and frame of orientation have to be adequately satisfied or loneliness would result. Moustakas (1961, 1972) has written

about both the disruptive effects of existential loneliness and the potentially creative force that it can be if properly perceived.

Loneliness is normally experienced as painful feelings of disconnectedness or isolation combined with intense longing. The person who is lonely is unable to initiate, continue, or experience a desired relationship at a certain point in time. The sense of being cut off stems from two basic dynamics: a feeling of not belonging and a feeling of not being understood. This may be due to the lack of social initiative from a desired person or to active rejection. Loneliness is not only wanting someone, but also wanting to be wanted. Rejection does not have to be experienced in a current relationship to produce loneliness. Rejection by parents or peers during early years of development may produce chronic loneliness by introducing a belief that one is not good enough ever to be valued by and belong to another in a close relationship.

It appears that chronically lonely people are especially sensitive to rejection cues. Loneliness often comes when a person is unable to share intimately with another or to find one to whom intimate concerns may be communicated and who will respond with interest, empathy, and acceptance. The yearning for a particular person or kind of relationship that marks loneliness is highly similar to the expressions of separation anxiety and grief. A related emotion that is commonly, though not necessarily, associated with loneliness is depression.

The intensity and duration of loneliness vary. Some people suffer from long-term or chronic loneliness. This is typically related to developmental background and personality factors such as shyness and low self-esteem. Chronic loneliness may also be related to existential alienation as well. The prevailing sociological characteristics of a society can contribute to chronic loneliness. Most people experience short-term, or acute, loneliness, which is usually associated with specific and temporary events such as physical separation, illness, misunderstanding or conflict, the loss of a loved one, and unconfessed sin.

In sum, loneliness is a perceived social deficit. It is a complex of feelings stemming from the relationship between expectations or desires and perceptions of how well those expectations are being met. Consequently, loneliness is not so much the objective state of being alone as the subjective state of feeling alone and isolated. With regard to types of loneliness, Weiss (1973) has suggested that there are two basic forms: emotional isolation and social isolation. Hartog, Audy, and Cohen (1980) have identified cosmic, cultural, social, and interpersonal dimensions of loneliness. Additional research must be done to empirically verify or revise these conceptions.

Causes. *Developmental factors.* Three basic developmental needs must be satisfactorily met if chronic loneliness is to be avoided: the needs for attachment, acceptance, and adequate social skills. The initial formation and maintenance of affectional bonds with parents has been shown to be vital for proper emotional and interpersonal health throughout life (Bowlby, 1969, 1973). Acceptance of a child by parents is crucial for the child's fundamental self-esteem and resultant ability to successfully seek intimacy. Negative feedback from those emotionally important to a child creates doubt and insecurity. Those with low self-esteem are less open to others, more preoccupied with themselves, and find it difficult to develop close relationships. Children who come from homes where parents model atypical social patterns, or who are not taught acceptable verbal and nonverbal social skills, are more likely to experience chronic loneliness due to peer rejection and inability to develop relationships in socially attractive ways.

Sociological factors. The widespread nature of loneliness in modern society suggests that certain underlying sociological conditions foster loneliness through socialization and living situations. Four such factors are technology, television, values, and urbanization (Ellison, 1980). Technological emphases on production, efficiency, and specialization combined with the development of bureaucracy tend to minimize the potential for truly intimate relationships. Interaction tends to be minimized, standardized, or role specific, resulting in superficial, manipulative, and emotionally empty exchange in most daily relationships.

Television programming tends to model interaction styles and personal characteristics that work against genuine intimacy. In addition, those who watch heavy amounts of television have a distorted view of the real world (Gerber & Gross, 1976). They see it as more dangerous than it really is, and as a result, they tend to be more distrusting and fearful of others. Finally, television usually involves parallel viewing rather than interaction among family members. Opportunities for development of social skills within the family and direct, rather than vicarious, intimacy are greatly lessened as a result.

Among the prevailing values in contempo-rary America that work against intimacy and promote loneliness are secularism, freedom, achievement, acquisitions, and appearance. Humanism has attempted to deny the existence of spiritual reality and the possibility of a personal relationship with God. As a result of secularism many people suffer from cosmic or existential loneliness, in which they feel cut off from any sense of ultimate purpose, relatedness to the cosmos, and relationship with God. For many, psychology has become a substitute religion, and the therapists and theorists their gods. The intense emphasis on freedom in our society has promoted an emphasis on individualism and personal rights that militates against responsible, long-term relationships in which intimacy can be developed. Achievement values tend to depersonalize others into production and profit terms, to translate them into potential competitors. Things become more important than people as a result of the search for self-worth through acquisitions, and people are frequently viewed as merely means to an end. An emphasis on appearance automatically ensures that those who don't make the standard will be less sought out and more likely to experience loneliness. Those who are handicapped or physically debilitated in some way are shunned by most. Relationships disintegrate because they are not based on deeper personality and value considerations.

For most, loneliness is experienced most directly and intensely as a result of loss. Divorce, moves, retirement, and death are common causes of loss and loneliness. In each, special relationships built on the process of sharing are disrupted and cannot be exactly replaced.

Theological Perspective. A complete understanding of loneliness must involve the biblical accounts of creation and sin. Human beings are fundamentally social beings because they are made in the image of an interpersonal God (Gen. 1:26). Further, God recognized our need for human intimacy and created a companion for Adam (Gen. 2:18). Before sin entered in, Adam and Eve enjoyed intimacy with God and with each other. As a result of sin misunderstanding, defensiveness, blaming, and power replaced perfect intimacy. Self-interest intruded on love. Intimacy was crushed by the loss of integrity. Loneliness and isolation became normal and intimacy an ideal. The Bible indicates that to the extent that God is ignored or sin is left unconfessed, loneliness will pervade human life because intimacy with God and other people will be lost.

References
Bowlby, J. *Attachment.* New York: Basic Books, 1969.
Bowlby, J. *Separation.* New York: Basic Books, 1973.
Ellison, C. W. *Loneliness: The search for intimacy.* Chappaqua, N.Y.: Christian Herald Books, 1980.
Freud, S. *Civilization and its discontents.* New York: J. Cape & H. Smith, 1930.
Fromm, E. *Escape from freedom.* New York: Farrar & Rinehart, 1941.
Gerber, G., & Gross, L. The scary world of TV's heavy viewers. *Psychology Today,* April, 1976, pp. 41–45.
Hartog, J., Audy, J. R., & Cohen, Y. A. (Eds.). *The anatomy of loneliness.* New York: International Universities Press, 1980.
Moustakas, C. *Loneliness.* Englewood Cliffs, N.J.: Prentice-Hall, 1961.
Moustakas, C. *Loneliness and love.* Englewood Cliffs, N.J.: Prentice-Hall, 1972.
Weiss, R. *Loneliness: The experience of emotional and social isolation.* Cambridge: M.I.T. Press, 1973.
C. W. ELLISON

Loosening of Associations. A thought disorder characterized by speech that abruptly shifts from topic to topic in a completely unrelated manner. No affective awareness of the unconnected statements is evidenced by the speaker. Phrases may totally shift from one frame of reference to another, or be juxtaposed so that no comprehensive meaning can be formulated. For example, in reply to the question, "When did your father die?" the person may start talking about skiing, shift to a movie he has seen, and comment on recent trends in the weather. When severe, the speech may be incoherent, particularly in manic episodes, schizophrenia, and other psychotic disorders.
D. L. SCHUURMAN

Loss and Separation. Inextricably entwined with change, separation and loss are universal phenomena experienced by everyone. The many kinds of separation can be classified into two general types: developmental and situational. Developmental separations are an inherent part of the maturational stages a human being experiences from birth to death.

Separation in the ever changing stages of the life span inevitably involves a constant series of attachments detachments; closeness distance; togetherness separateness; losses gains. The struggle to maintain an equilibrium between these polarities is particularly accented at certain transitional points of life, such as the passage periods from one psychosocial stage to another (Erikson, 1968). A newborn, for example, experiences the loss of the security of intrauterine life but gains the possibility of a more exciting, autonomous life. The mother at the same time loses a physical part of herself to gain the fulfillment of raising a child. The adolescent gives up the primary

security of depending upon parents in order to consolidate his identity. Parents simultaneously lose the satisfactions of the more intense dependency of their children to eventually gain the pleasures of grandchildren, of new interests, of deeper peer companionship. The maturational separations with their concomitant losses and gains are a predictable part of human development and growth wherein old sources of gratifications are replaced with new modes of need fulfillment and self-perception.

Separations and losses that result from the less predictable, and therefore often more traumatic, situational circumstances are seemingly infinite in number. An accident, a rape, the birth of a deformed child, a young person's cardiofracture, a job change, a natural disaster, a geographic move, are all examples. They could involve such deeply felt separations and losses as valuable possessions, relationships, aspirations, sense of integrity, body parts, functioning levels, and coping skills. Even separation from a hope, an interest, a physical symptom, can be a traumatic loss.

Universal Reactions. A plethora of research reveals that separation with its inevitable losses can be a stressor event eliciting the emergence of a syndrome of reactions that follow a defined pattern. As early as 1872 Charles Darwin perceived that the reactions to separation from a loved one are innate when he observed similar body movements in grieving individuals regardless of their cultural background.

In *Mourning and Melancholia* Freud describes reactions to separation caused by death of a loved one as being dejection, disinterest in the environment, and a detached air toward others. He explains mourning as a period of the gradual withdrawal of libido from the now missing loved object. According to Freud adjustment to the loss must be a process over time to prevent an out-of-control libido with no structuring of direction. He sees the process as self-limiting; the effects of the loss end when the libido completes its withdrawal from the loved object. Ideally the investment of the libido in an alternative object or an internal representation of the lost object concurrently happens.

Bowlby (1969) saw what he believed was a universal specific syndrome of reactions to separation and loss in his studies on the separation of children from their parents. He further observed other kinds of separations and concluded that a similar process goes on in any loss. He identifies (1973) the three stages—protest, despair, and detachment—as essentially the same for all separation.

657

Since separation and loss are generators of stress, field studies of stress, particularly those done in settings of disaster (e.g., war, earthquakes, fires) reveal common reactions to the changes that these circumstances generate. Lindemann (1944), a psychoanalyst and social psychologist, did a classic field study in which he concluded that 1) reactions to loss fall into a syndrome that contains both psychological and somatic symptomatology; 2) the syndrome may start immediately upon a loss, may have a delayed reaction, may be exaggerated, or may be absent; 3) the syndrome may follow the typical course or distorted courses that represent a particular aspect of the grief syndrome; 4) with appropriate interventions the distorted pictures can be directed into normal grief reactions with ultimate resolution.

Lindemann's study gave impetus to other researchers to investigate the effects of loss in situational crises that did not necessarily involve death. For example, Grayson (1970) found some of the same reactions to the loss of unfulfilled hopes. He points out that abreaction and catharsis help the individual more realistically to admit the agonized feelings and relinquish the hope. Burgess and Holmstrom (1974) found that rape victims who had lost a sense of trust also underwent a similar process, as do adults who lost limbs (Parkes, 1972).

Kübler-Ross (1969) popularized the grief syndrome that occurs when one faces death, in her delineation of the stages of denial, anger, bargaining, depression, and acceptance. Other important studies on bereavement are summarized by Parkes (1972). All the studies reveal a pattern of reaction that can be called the separation or loss syndrome.

Separation Syndrome. In its healthiest form the separation syndrome is a self-limiting process of fairly well-defined stages through which an individual passes over a broadly defined time span. The first reaction in the syndrome is a sense of injury and a groping to hold on to the lost object. Particularly in cases where the separation is unanticipated, there can be such unfocused grief responses as a cry of alarm, panic, protestation, or hyperactivity.

Within a relatively short time the task of the first stage, cognitive reorganization, begins. Initially it is characterized by disbelief, denial, or numbness, during which a full awareness of the loss is not permitted. This avoidance of reality serves the purpose of enabling the individual to mitigate the pain of the loss by maintaining a degree of distance from it. The individual can then deal slowly with its cognitive aspects as he starts to work through it. A

pervading lack of interest in establishing an attachment to a new object is evident. There is an attempt to regain what has been lost. This is particularly obvious when the individual, cognitively starting to grasp the reality of the loss, tends to oscillate between conscious and unconscious avoidance of facing it while alternately being flooded by emotionally laden intrusive-repetitive thought representations of the loss. The representations take many forms, including sleep disturbances, hallucinations, ruminations, preoccupations, and disorganizations, which may be accompanied by pangs of fear, guilt, rage, sorrow, and hypervigilance.

Once the individual acquires some cognitive realization of the loss, the affective response to the separation becomes more pronounced. This second stage is often indicated by a general aura of depression or a sense of despair. Since all relationships include some degree of ambivalence, the gradual resolution of the separation process also provokes feelings of anger and guilt that surface particularly during this stage. The emotions permit a gradual reexperiencing of the loss, in increasingly tolerable degrees. When the affect has been sufficiently diffused, the individual enters the next stage, that of identification with the lost object. This involves internalizing the characteristics of the lost object that are most important to the griever. It means that for the healthy individual "grief works itself out through a process of reformulation rather than substitution. Confidence in the original commitment is restored by extracting its essential meaning and grafting it upon the present" (Marris, 1974, p. 91).

This opens the door to the final phase, the acceptance of the loss. It frees the individual to benefit from the new gains in identity, cognitions, and affects by reaching out to form new relationships.

Movement through the stages is not necessarily a clearly defined process. There can be as many variations within the general pattern as there are differences among individuals. The stages may vary in their sequential order, length, and intensity. They may overlap, repeat themselves, or be skipped. Episodic changes may occur within a stage. Often such events as birthdays, anniversaries, and holidays stimulate a repeat of some aspect of the cycle.

Resolution of the separation process is occurring when intervals between stages are longer, reactions within stages are less intense and of shorter duration, and there is an apparent response to new objects. The healthy individual experiences the pain inherent in the separation process and ultimately comes to grip with the loss and restitution with no undue interruption in his daily life. The ability to integrate the loss is considered a mark of maturity.

For some individuals a more pathological reaction results from a significant separation. Indications can be 1) an expansive sense of overactivity that denies any significant loss or need for reintegration; 2) the maintenance of most aspects of the behavior before the separation without any considerable modification; 3) a psychosomatic reaction; 4) a prolonged change in patterns of interaction that may manifest itself in inappropriate hostility, withdrawal, impatience; 5) a display of self-punitive behavior possibly in the form of depression, insomnia, self-accusations, suicidal threats or attempts; 6) a morbid preoccupation with the loss object that may take the form of clinging to symbolic objects; 7) a marked appearance of the traits of the object in the behavior of the griever; 8) the attributing of magical powers to the lost object.

The continual flow of circumstances involving some nuance of separation, loss, and therefore withdrawal and eventual reinvestment of energy are ubiquitous. Each individual should therefore routinely confront the task of restoring an equilibrium between former and present meanings lest he be stagnated in growth. There are identified variables that determine whether a separation with its concomitant losses will be a growth-producing or a growth-constricting experience.

Determiners of Separation Reactions. The determiners of an individual's reactions to separation and loss can be grouped under three main headings: 1) the nature of the person experiencing the separation; 2) the nature or quality and quantity of the loss involved in the separation; 3) the nature of the milieu in which the separation occurs.

Nature of the individual. The quality of an individual's experiences during the separation-individuation developmental phase is the most basic variable in determining responses to life's recurring separations (Mahler, 1975). This separation process refers to the steps in a child's movement from his infant fusion with the mother. Individuation refers to the developmental stages a child goes through to perceive himself as a separate entity from his mother. This requires the development of object constancy whereby the child realizes that the object still exists even when out of sight. Although it is an ongoing process with

reverberations throughout the life cycle, the basic determining foundation for future separation is laid from about the age of 4 months to 36 months. If the child succeeds in this initial differentiation of his internal self-representation from that of the mother figure, he will be able to perceive his ever expanding world as independent from himself and develop a growing sense of self-identity. In subsequent separations he would then have the inner structure to identify with the important elements of the meaningful object while emotionally relinquishing what is necessary, albeit with appropriate grief, in order to make new attachments. On the other hand, to the degree that an individual remains unhealthily attached to his mother, he is vulnerable to neurotic and even psychotic reactions to separation and loss.

Each developmental transitional period—e.g., puberty, marriage, and parenthood—offers the individual the potential to strengthen, enrich, and even modify his individuation experiences as he terminates his present life structure to initiate a new one. At the same time how he has experienced individuation in past transitions conditions his reactions to the new phase.

The second determining factor of separation reactions is the quality of an individual's attachment to a significant object. Bowlby (1969) sees the need to attach to someone as a normal innate propensity of every human being. When this bond with a significant other is threatened or ruptured, separation anxiety in the form of attachment behavior results. In the small child it takes the form of crying, clinging, following, and calling. Although in normal individuals the manifestations become more sophisticated with age and are directed to new attachment figures appropriate to the developmental period, some form of separation anxiety is apparent throughout the life span. It is especially activated when separation with its accompanying threat of loss has or is about to occur. Since there is a continuous stream of experiences in life that involve loss of some kind, all individuals are forever susceptible to separation anxiety. During separation, gratification of this attachment need seems to sustain self-esteem and reduce hostility, making possible the expression and tolerance of painful tension and minimizing abnormal forms of avoiding reality (Hansburg, 1972).

Individuals who are anxiously attached manifest neurotic symptoms in the face of separation. Anxious attachment is the result of an insufficient relationship with a mothering figure because of death, illness, threats of or actual abandonment, parental discord, insufficient attention, and the like (Bowlby, 1969). These experiences can cause a child, adolescent, or adult to live in constant anxiety lest he lose the attachment figure.

Separation reactions tend to be atypically manifested. There is often intense anger, self-reproach, or depression that tends to last longer than normal. Others manifest anxious attachment through compulsive self-reliance. Even so, some strain and irritability do tend to be present and episodic depressions may occur. However, the causal connection is generally not recognized and the resolution could be postponed for months or years (Bowlby, 1977).

The quality of an individual's cognitive development is a third vital internal variable in the separation process. The two cognitive aspects that play the most crucial role in resolving separation experiences are the development of abstract cognitions and thinking modes that permit adaptation to change (Piaget & Inhelder, 1969). The former makes possible object constancy. It means the individual can identify with the object even in its absence. The latter provides the cognitive sophistication whereby the individual can internalize the significant qualities of the object by extracting its essential meanings and integrating them with the new situation into which the separation has thrust him. Since this process demands the use of abstract thinking, an ability that does not develop to its fullest until adulthood, it is imperative that a child have a real object substitute.

A fourth determiner of separation reactions is the quality of parental attitudes, particularly in the child's early years. Individuals whose parents give out messages that are perceived as confidence in his ability to grow and eventually become autonomous will confront life's separations more successfully. Conversely, those individuals whose parents convey a lack of confidence in them often find separations more traumatic. The quality of the expectations an individual picks up from his parents depends on the parent's ability to 1) provide the environment that develops basic trust; 2) promote an appropriate comfortable expression of feelings, including such ambivalent ones as guilt and anger; 3) communicate a deep security in their love that fosters an age-appropriate independence; 4) maintain an open congruent communication pattern that leads to closer and more secure interpersonal relations.

How healthily parents transmit positive messages about separation is conditioned by how they separated from their own parents. Those who had traumatic or poor experiences in breaking from parents tend to pass the conflict of their unfinished issues on to their own children. They therefore interfere with their child's separation through an often unidentified parental expectation conveyed to the child, which militates against his potential for autonomy.

The quality of an individual's previous life experiences is a fifth influencing factor. The individual who experienced comfortable separations in his past tends to be better prepared for successive ones. The child who has had good school experiences, enjoys spending time with his friends, has fun at camp, makes a good transition to the first grade and then to high school, will probably be less anxious in life's new transitions. On the other hand, children who have experienced traumatic separations with deeply felt losses in their early years tend to be more prone to separation anxiety. This is particularly true when the separation occurred during the initial individuation separation developmental period.

The individual who has undergone multiple separations from persons, places, things, ideas, etc., might tend to protect himself from the pain of separations by avoiding new in-depth attachments to other objects. Again, a significant factor is the presence of a consistent nurturing attachment figure in the midst of such changes.

A sixth element in the nature of the individual is the quality of his life philosophy. An individual's beliefs about life have a far-reaching impact on how he perceives a separation from a meaningful object. It affects how he views himself, others, and life events. A deep inner sense of God's sovereignty at work in not only the overall pattern but also the details of life gives a meaning even to loss through death.

Nature of the loss. Inherent in the loss itself are factors that affect reactions. The timeliness of loss, particularly when it comes through a maturational separation such as marriage, empty nest, even a death, often gives it a more appropriate feeling, thereby making it easier to resolve. Although separation through death may never seem timely, the death of an older person who has lived his life is often easier to accept than that of a child. A child's death diminishes the survivor's confidence in the future.

Maturational separations can be anticipated and therefore a gradual adaptation to the losses involved is possible. Unanticipated losses are often followed by longer and more intense stages of denial than are anticipated ones. It is possible that this longer stage of denial allows the individual to go through some of the emotional preparation that takes place when an anticipatory period exists (Hamburg & Adams, 1967). Janis (1958) substantiated this in his studies on patients' previous preparation for surgery. He found that the patients who experienced reasonable stress before surgery had the least amount of distress after surgery. On the other hand, those persons who showed the most distress after surgery denied anticipatory fear or were extremely preoccupied previous to the surgery. He concluded that moderate fear motivates an anticipatory stage of cognitive processing. This affective and cognitive processing has adaptational effects.

The death of a loved one from a chronic disease also permits the family to do some of the work of mourning before the actual death. In other potential life events such as retirement, a geographic move, or a career change, individuals are able to plan ahead and share their expectations, possibly in seminars. This has been found to greatly ease the intensity of the moment when the event actually arrives.

The expected duration of the loss also affects adjustment. A temporary separation, even when painful, is easier to support than a permanent one. Although in a prolonged separation the individual discovers that he needs more time to readapt to the people, places, and such, the processing is not as complicated. In instances where elements of the loss are continually revived, such as in the case of a handicapped child, the working through process is complicated by the fact that there is a forced open-endedness, since new problems constantly arise as the child develops.

Some losses have the potential to trigger a chain reaction of additional losses. For example, a stroke victim not only loses his health but has to face alteration in such areas as job satisfaction, economic security, status, mobility, freedom, and body image. The effect of the changes is exacerbated when the separation has both developmental and situational components. If a father's stroke occurs at the mid-life transitional point with its usual changes such as children leaving home, the adjustment period could become longer in length, more complicated, and more intense. Separation from each former state must be worked through until the many-faceted implications can be handled in tolerable measure.

The extent of the significance of a loss also plays a role. Significant losses imply deep emotional investment. Significance might be centered in more abstract areas such as the investment of time. The parents whose children leave home and the man who loses a job must work through the loss of a habitual time schedule and discover how to use the new time at their disposal. The loss of irreplaceable items such as family photographs or a family heirloom with nostalgic value could be more deeply felt than a large monetary loss. Cultural attitudes contribute to the significance of a loss. In Western culture, where youth, sexuality, and attractiveness are so emphasized, the loss of a breast could be very traumatic and the severity of the reaction can be increased. Such an experience demands not only present adaptation but future changes.

The extent of the changes involved plays a large role in completing a separation syndrome. If considerable differences exist in the new situation, the stages could be prolonged and felt more deeply. A geographic move from the city to a mountain village calls for more adjustment than a change from one city to another. A move to a foreign country where customs, language, and places are entirely different would probably require a longer adjustment period than a move from the United States to Canada.

The nature of the milieu in which the loss occurs. Reactions to losses are also conditioned by environmental and social factors.

Expectations of society play a large role. For example, adolescents, who are expected to start detaching from parents and turning to peers to complete the developmental tasks of this period, have society's approval of their many changes. On the other hand, a divorced person in a community that frowns on this type of separation may experience additional struggles going through the syndrome.

A second environmental factor is the rate at which change takes place. A case in point is the increasing lack of a sense of continuity in the values from one generation to another. This too is evidenced among adolescents, who consequently could find their struggle with individuation a more pronounced experience.

The more clearly defined the separation process, the easier the transition. The growing up process is often more difficult for a young person in a culture where initiation points are not clear-cut. For example, in Western culture, where stages are fuzzier, college students often see themselves as fairly independent, while parents who support them might perceive them as quite dependent.

The support system within the environment

can maximize or minimize the effects of change. Those involved in closer, more supportive groups conceivably have less difficulty. The very stress of separation elicits the attachment behavior described earlier. In adulthood it is likely to be present when one is depressed, ill, or afraid, and leads to seeking the contact and comfort of an attachment figure. This behavior is adaptive and contributes to the successful resolution of a separation syndrome. The attachment source can be in the form of a church group, a school, a work group, or some other organization that gives the security needed at this time. The role of the body of Christ has tremendous implications here in a society where change is rampant and natural support structures often are not present.

Treatment Implications. The majority of separation and loss reactions follow the normal course through the syndrome, with the stages varying in intensity according to the significance of the loss. In some instances there is hardly an awareness of any adjustment. In other cases, however, individuals seek help because of a lack of understanding of their reactions or because of the inordinate amount of pain they are suffering.

The goal of treatment is to help the person work through the stages to a completion of the process. Therapy is usually supportive, with the specific techniques varying to fit the therapist's orientation. The criterion for choosing a therapy should be its efficacy to promote a fairly progressive movement through the stages. The therapy is generally short-term, from one encounter to a series of sessions up to about 6 months.

An educative approach can be helpful to those relatively healthy individuals who are confused over reactions that are normal for their situation. It can likewise benefit those who face a disproportionate share of separations, such as missionaries. Whether therapy is done individually or in a group, the goals in such an approach would be to help these persons understand the normalcy of the separation process, identify and understand their own reactions as well as those of the persons from whom they are separating, and learn how to diffuse the effects of leave-taking for themselves and significant others. A comprehension of the total process can be particularly helpful to missionaries parting from their native country, to new missionaries going through the throes of culture shock, to children and their parents as children go off to school, and returning missionaries who are going through departure in reverse.

The factors that determine the reactions to separation play a decisive role in the time required to resolve the issues successfully. The intradynamic factors have a particularly high potential to stir up latent conflict stemming from previously unintegrated separation experiences. Where a short-term approach is used, these neurotic conflicts are linked to their role in the current separation struggle. However, if deeply rooted core conflicts, particularly those with their genesis in the early separation-individuation developmental stage, seem to be preventing a healthy resolution, a long-term therapeutic approach that deals more concentratedly with the area of conflict may be indicated.

Mann (1973) has developed a time-limited dynamic approach that can provide a corrective emotional experience for individuals who are conflicted about the recurring life crises of separation and individuation and therefore suffer a painful amount of separation anxiety in the face of loss. These individuals tend to hold on emotionally to relationships beyond the appropriate developmental time and are therefore hindered in facing the mature demands of adulthood. The goal of therapy is to enable the patient to master his anxiety about separation. The method is an empathic acceptance of the patient's feelings with a focused emphasis on the termination date. The patient's ambivalence about fusion and separation is thereby stirred up. His comments often oscillate between the magical fantasies of permanence and the harsh realities of separation. With the therapist's consistent empathy the patient continues to experience feelings of closeness in spite of the inevitable impending separation. This allows the patient to internalize the therapist "as a replacement or a substitute for the earlier ambivalent object. This time the internalization will be more positive, . . . less anger laden, and less guilt laden, thereby making separation a genuine maturational event" (Mann, 1973, p. 36).

Although this approach is effective in cases of unresolved or delayed grief, Mann also sees it as tailor-made for adolescents who are painfully conflicted about separating from their parents.

Whatever the therapeutic approach, the termination phase can play a significant role in the healing of separation anxiety. Termination of therapy provokes many ambivalent feelings connected with previous separation issues in both the patient and the therapist. The resulting reaction can be the impetus to promote a corrective emotional experience with its implication for growth for both the patient and the therapist to the degree that the feelings are dealt with rather than ignored (Edelson, 1963).

Successful resolution of separation and loss, with or without professional help, is indispensable to growth. The most potent benefit is its assault on self-centeredness. The person is forced to relinquish degrees of his infantile delusions of immortality and omnipotence, which can lead to the realization that he functions within a greater whole. This is a motivating factor to lead one to come to grips with the larger meaning of life. The depths of emotions are experienced as they might be in no other way. A deeper level of empathy is often developed. A new confidence in facing life's upheavals may result as old coping mechanisms are strengthened and new ones are developed. As a result, overall functioning may well be at a higher, richer level. Therefore, while inevitable separation and loss upset the present moment, the experience of integrating the old into the new permits individuals to go on to fuller lives.

References

Bowlby, J. *Attachment and loss* (Vol. 1). New York: Basic Books, 1969.
Bowlby, J. *Attachment and loss* (Vol. 2). New York: Basic Books, 1973.
Bowlby, J. The making and breaking of affectional bonds: 1. Aetiology and psychopathology in the light of attachment theory. *British Journal of Psychiatry*, 1977, *130*, 201–210.
Burgess, A. W., & Holmstrom, L. L. Rape trauma syndrome. *American Journal of Psychiatry*, 1974, *131*, 981–986.
Edelson, M. Termination of intensive psychotherapy. In C. C. Thomas (Ed.), *American lectures in psychiatry*. Washington, D.C.: American Psychiatric Association, 1963.
Erikson, E. H. *Identity, youth, and crisis*. New York: Norton, 1968.
Freud, S. Mourning and melancholia. In J. Riviere (Ed.), *Collected papers* (Vol. 4). London: Hogarth, 1950. (Originally published, 1917.)
Grayson, H. Grief reactions to the relinquishing of unfulfilled wishes. *American Journal of Psychotherapy*, 1970, *25*, 287–295.
Hamburg, D. A., & Adams, J. E. A perspective on coping behavior: Seeking and utilizing information in major transitions. *Archives of General Psychiatry*, 1967, *17*, 277–284.
Hansburg, H. *Adolescent separation anxiety*. Springfield, Ill.: Thomas, 1972.
Janis, I. *Psychological stress: Psychoanalytic and behavioral studies of surgical patients*. New York: Wiley, 1958.
Kübler-Ross, E. *On death and dying*. New York: Macmillan, 1969.
Lindemann, E. Symptomatology and management of acute grief. *American Journal of Psychiatry*, 1944, *101*, 141–148.
Mahler, M. S., Pine, F., & Bergman, A. *The psychological birth of the human infant*. New York: Basic Books, 1975.
Mann, J. *Time-limited psychotherapy*. Cambridge Ma.: Harvard University Press, 1973.
Marris, P. *Loss and change*. New York: Pantheon Books, 1974.
Parkes, C. M. *Bereavement: Studies of grief in adult life*. New York: International Universities Press, 1972.
Piaget, J., & Inhelder, B. *The psychology of the child*. New York: Basic Books, 1969.

Additional Readings

Bowlby, J. *Attachment and loss* (Vol. 3). New York: Basic Books, 1980.
Schoenberg, B., Gerber, I., Wiener, A., Kutscher, A., Peretz, D., & Carr, A. *Bereavement: Its psychosocial aspects*. New York: Columbia University Press, 1975.

F. J. WHITE

Love. The word *love* is used broadly and has such variety of meanings that the concept, although familiar, is difficult to define. It helps to define love by specifying the context in which it is used. When a person says to an intimate friend, "I love you," there is quite a difference from the meaning of the word in the sentence, "I love your outfit."

Love, then, has specific, contextual meanings. However, in the widest usage it generally refers to a strong attraction toward an object—a desire to reduce the distance between that object and oneself. For example, if one loves either a person or a thing, one exhibits more of a yearning for that person or object, a desire to clasp it excitedly or fondly, than if the object were merely attractive or of some interest. To love always implies personal investment in the object of love; where there is no evidence of such personal caring, one may question whether love exists for the object.

Kinds of Love. The ancient Greeks specified four kinds of love, a classification that is still widely used today. The most general form is brotherly love, *filios*, love for one's fellow humans including care, respect, and some compassion for the plight of others. The most common form is friendship. A second kind of love, *agape*, is seen in our love for God, a reverence for and deep acknowledgement of the divine being of God, including his commandments for mankind. Third, there is erotic love (*eros*), an affectionate, tender hungering for union with the loved one, a passionate yearning for full relationship which, although it may include genital stirrings, does not necessarily have to do so. Both the Latins and the Greeks had different words for love and sex. Eros was made a god, not sex (May, 1969). The fourth kind of love is libido, sexual love, physical and emotional need that ends in the physical release of tensions in the act of sexual intercourse. Erotic love grows on and on; libidinal love builds up and is released.

In modern usage the word *love* most commonly connotes deep feelings between a man and a woman. There is a differentiation between the state of love and the actual feelings of love. The state of love implies a sense of committed caring and responsibility whereby there is concern and action taken for the well-being of the loved one. This state does not necessarily have to include actual feelings within a person toward the love object. When one allows himself or herself to *feel* love, however, there is an inner awareness of affect, of involvement from the heart rather than from habit or obligation. A state of love without corresponding feelings within leaves the persons involved somewhat distant and colorless. Many suspect that such love is not genuine. Whether that is true or not, when one does not feel something within, this may reflect the person's inability to do so. Some persons are not emotionally mature enough to feel the inner stirrings of love.

How We Learn to Love. The study of early mother-child interactions has made clear that infants need a symbiotic acceptance by the mother that conveys adequate nurturance both physically and emotionally. The infant, and later the child, grows best in a climate of unconditional love where the mother's patient responsiveness clearly demonstrates that she is here to take care of the baby, not vice versa. Love grows best when there is no fear of driving the mother away or consuming her with one's neediness.

The purpose of reliable, trustworthy parental love is to provide security and hence maximize the child's growth. It also teaches the baby how to love as he or she imitates the parents. The parents' ultimate purpose is to have the child internalize the love messages so he believes he is lovable. This belief becomes the inner confidence and self-esteem that not only promotes exploration, learning, and growth, but also becomes the grounds for loving others in turn.

As the person grows through the various stages and cycles of life, he or she experiences different needs, and hence differing forms of love are sought (Orlinsky, 1972). Thus, the infant seeks nurturance, the child responsiveness, the preadolescent a close friend, the teen a lover, and the adult a spouse. Personal love relationships foster psychological growth. There is a cyclical rhythm to these relationships all through the life cycle; closeness provides the inner fuel to separate and individuate, and hence climb to a new level where one again develops a new communion before pushing on again. In communion there is cooperation and mutual sharing to satisfy each other's needs. In individuation the love of self is stressed by assertiveness and contest. Love must include mutuality and individuality,

other *and* self. In Judeo-Christian thinking this same theme characterizes the relationship between God and persons.

One of the most difficult aspects of love relationships is to maintain a rich sense of self within the context of loving the other person. Many personal-emotional problems seen in psychotherapy relate to a fear of love based on the loss of self in the relationship (Branden, 1980).

Degrees of love. There are different degrees to which one shows love, that is, various depths of loving interpersonally. Perhaps the most shallow form of love is fearful clinging. Here the person's immaturity includes an overwhelming dependency that bonds lover to loved one out of fear of loss. Up the scale one step from clinging is love by obligation, where one feels stuck with the so-called loved one and thus cares out of duty. This is seen especially in marriages where the mates feel little personal-emotional commitment but stay together for the children's sake. Both these forms of love are noteworthy for their lack of genuine mutuality and the creative joy that love should bring.

Progressing upward in terms of levels of loving, we find unrequited love, the kind of one-way loving where despite the inequality of feelings one person loves another who does not return the love. Often there is frustration for the person not receiving love, but he or she may still choose to demonstrate a genuine loving care for the love object. This may be seen in parental care for seriously retarded children or in a marriage where one mate does all the loving and is relatively satisfied.

Further upward toward full mutual love are relationships that are reasonably stable, partially gratifying, but less than one or both partners would like to have. Whether through carelessness or lack of sophistication the partners are friendly, helpful, and generally affectionate but do not dare risk the deeper revelations of self and the explorations of the full range of emotions. Perhaps most marriages settle for, or degenerate into, this kind of reasonable if not entirely satisfying kind of love.

The quality of love in relationships between persons need not necessarily be impugned because there are problems or troubles. All human relationships have difficulties, hurts, disappointments, and problems. These can, in fact, bind persons closer together as they seek to solve those issues. The worst one can expect, of course, is that the problems will erode the rapport between partners.

Mature Love. In a full sense of mutual human love we should expect several elements to exist. First of all is the willingness of each partner to be involved in the relationship as deeply as possible in four distinct ways: physically, intellectually, emotionally, and spiritually.

Secondly, full love involves both a giving and a receiving of love by each partner. That means that each person is responsible for giving to as well as getting from the other. Serious problems in the relationship can result when either partner is not giving or getting enough out of the relationship. Love is not giving, as popularly thought; it includes both giving and getting (Rottschafer, 1980). There has to be a daily monitoring of the balance between these two plus the willingness to correct the inequalities. The ratio of how much one gives to how much one gets (whether by taking or by receiving) may vary from day to day, but over time the health of the relationship depends on a balance between these two.

Thirdly, mature love includes as full an experiencing of the broad range of human emotions as is possible. Therefore, in full love the partners open themselves to both joy and sorrow, agony and ecstasy, always keeping in mind the needs of both self and other as the experiences and feelings of life are shared. Love is an art that needs to be learned and practiced throughout one's entire lifetime (Fromm, 1956).

Lastly, full love must include a willingness to commit to one's loved object, whether country, home, family, child, mate, or friend. Commitment involves promise, deliberate intention to take the bad with the good, and a willingness to share one's life with the loved one. Commitment brings mutual trust for quality care in the now, plus predictable, responsible, mutual involvement in the future. Many current social, emotional, and physical ills can be seen as directly related to an absence of these qualities of love.

References

Branden, N. *The psychology of romantic love.* Los Angeles: J. P. Tacher, 1980.
Fromm, E. *The art of loving.* New York: Harper & Row, 1956.
May, R. *Love and will.* New York: Norton, 1969.
Orlinsky, D. E. Love relationships in the life cycle: A developmental interpersonal perspective. In H. Otto (Ed.), *Love today.* New York: Association Press, 1972.
Rottschafer, R. H. Giving and getting, a clinical and spiritual evaluation. *The Bulletin of the Christian Association for psychological studies;* 1980, 6(2), 23–28.

R. H. ROTTSCHAFER

See INTERPERSONAL ATTRACTION.

Lying. A normal process during childhood development. It usually peaks between the ages of 5–6 and 8–9, with boys lying more than girls. During the maturation process children first learn not to lie because punishment usually follows, but later learn to internalize reasons for not lying. Children's lies are often make-believe lies ("A teddy bear flew in my window") or lies of confusion, though they develop into a moral understanding through lies of selfishness ("I don't have the toy") and fear of punishment ("I didn't break the lamp").

Pathological lying, however, is characterized by excessive lying that is frequent, vague, and often appears purposeless in that the liar has nothing obvious to gain from the lies. It is a reaction characteristic of people who have failed more than they have succeeded, and these persons often are antisocial or psychopathic personalities. Lying then sometimes becomes a character trait, and the person may use lies to bolster his ego or as a way of resolving a conflict. Often he lies to get praise, to react against psychic pain, or to deceive himself. Compulsive lying is sometimes usefully viewed as a kind of wish fulfillment in that the compulsive liar may half-believe his own lies and often forgets former lies.

D. L. SCHUURMAN

Mm

Macrocephaly. A rare congenital defect which produces an abnormally large head. The actual cause of the disease is unknown, but physiologically it is due to an abnormal growth of the supporting tissue of the brain, resulting in moderate or severe retardation. There is no known treatment.

See MENTAL RETARDATION.

Magical Thinking. This is present when a person views an internal thought as having external significance and power. A thought, although very private and unobservable, becomes a substitute for action. The "logic" of magical thinking says that thoughts are powerful, and therefore thinking certain thoughts will cause various consequences to occur in the outside world. Magical thinking is not confined by normal barriers between thought and actions, between private thinking and public knowledge, between what is internal and what is external. Nor is it limited by the logical connections that "normal" thinking posits between ideas. The best-known example of magical thinking is the young child who, when angry, will close his or her eyes with the thought of making the disciplining parent disappear. The logic in this childish behavior is: If I can't see, I can't be seen.

Magical thinking is common and considered normal in young children. Developmental psychologists have isolated several stages in the development of cognitive processes, including a phase from 18 to 24 months when mental representations are organized (Greenspan, Lourie, & Nover, 1979). The organization is primitive and incomplete. Ideas, feelings, and perceptions can be "combined or distorted according to need or drive state" (p. 161), hence thinking at this level is magical. Magical thinking is considered pathological when it persists beyond the age of its normal occurrence. In older children it can occur in school phobics, anorexics, or psychotic children.

Psychoanalytic thought views the childish magical thought patterns as part of primary process thinking (concretistic, diffuse, pictorial, magical), which later gives way to secondary process thinking (abstract, focused, verbal, logical) (Fenichel, 1945). The prior, primary patterns of thought can again predominate under the influence of alcohol, sleep (dreams), or extreme stress such as in psychosis and schizophrenia (Weiner, 1966). Primary process thought patterns, including magical thinking, are thought to dominate the unconscious thought of neurotics (Brenner, 1973). Magical thinking is an associated feature of schizophrenia and can also be found in schizotypal personality disorders and in schizophreniform disorders.

Obsessive-compulsives also indulge in magical thinking when they feel that their thoughts can cause harm to others. The defense mechanism of undoing is predicated on magical thoughts, since wishing something makes it so (Brenner, 1973). For example, the child who first hits an adult and then kisses the same person is convinced that the second behavior will undo the first; hence it is magical thinking.

Evolutionary theorists often describe magical thinking as archaic or paleological, a remnant of preverbal and prelogical man. Primitive cultures are sometimes described as being permeated by magical thinking. Antireligionists whose world view does not allow for the existence of a supernatural being use the concept of magical thinking to explain belief in God, prayer, and the miraculous.

References

Brenner, C. *An elementary textbook of psychoanalysis* (Rev. ed.). New York: International Universities Press, 1973.

Fenichel, O. *The psychoanalytic theory of neurosis.* New York: Norton, 1945.

Greenspan, S. I., Lourie, R. S., & Nover, R. A. A developmental approach to the classification of psychopathology in infancy and early childhood. In J. D. Noshpitz (Ed.). *Basic handbook of child psychiatry.* New York: Basic Books, 1979.

Weiner, I. B. *Psychodiagnosis in schizophrenia.* New York: Wiley, 1966.

J. R. BECK

See SUPERSTITION.

Mahler, Margaret (1908–). Born on the border of Austria and Hungary, Mahler received her training in medicine, pediatrics, and psychoanalysis in Vienna. In 1941 she migrated by way of England to New York, a refugee from the Nazi holocaust. Her early professional interests in well-baby development, psychotic disorders in infants, the association between the tic syndrome and early parental separation, and the psychoanalysis of children with other kinds of difficulty resulted in formulation of a process in which the child moves from a symbiotic attachment with the mother toward a distinct individual identity. This process begins at approximately 6 months, and proceeds normally for another 18 months. The process has come to be referred to as the psychological birth of the infant. Its description, as well as the identification of its relationship to many adult psychopathologies, is Mahler's most important professional contribution.

Drawing from the work of Klein, Spitz, Piaget, Winnicott, Bowlby, and others, Mahler described this process as consisting of three rather ordered subphases: differentiation, practicing, and rapprochement. *Differentiation* begins at 5 or 6 months and continues for about the same time. It is marked by the first behaviors of interaction with the mother, such as a smile preferential to the mother, pulling her hair, attempting to feed her, and pulling the body away from the mother to see her better. Bodily dependence on the mother decreases during this subphase as awareness of the outside world increases. Exploration of this world expands with the development of sensory capacities and locomotor skills.

This is followed by the second subphase, *practicing.* From about 10 to 16 months of age the infant tentatively experiments with both psychological and physical separation from the mother. The child progressively becomes more interested in people and objects, and with the ability to walk explores the world more actively. During this subphase these movements take place in close proximity to the mother. Intrapsychically there is a parallel increase in the sense of a separate self, or individuation.

The third subphase, *rapprochement,* coincides with the beginnings of symbolic play and more complex speech, eventuating normally in the toddler's awareness of separateness and of the mother's love. This stage begins zestfully, with cautious awareness—of the dangers of the world and the child's need to cope with them on his own—growing over time.

These three subphases culminate in a consolidation period, in which there are firm foundations for the development of a lifelong concept of individuality and object constancy. This latter is understood by Mahler to include not only the ability to maintain an internal representation of an absent love object but also to bring together the good and bad part objects into a realistic whole.

The "labor pains" of this psychological birth are increasing anxiety over fusion, or symbiosis, with the mother. The process moves against a gradually decreasing anxiety over the loss of this primitive security. In Mahler's terminology, separation anxiety is not simply a fear of being apart from the physical presence of the mother, but more a signal anxiety relating to the loss of attachment to the intrapsychic mother-object, occurring at the time when this inner representation has become clearly enough separate and distinct to be meaningful.

Disorders occur primarily as the residuals of symbiosis, or incomplete separation, and are manifested by recurrences of the primitive anxiety and depression as well as splitting of the good and bad objects, both of which Mahler feels occur normally during these phases of development. The focus of the psychoanalytic exploration that Mahler recommends for resolving these difficulties are these primary object relations. She sees the distortions causing pathology as resulting from inadequate or retarded development rather than primary conflicts.

While it appears that the usefulness of this model is considerable, there does seem at present to be pressure for major revisions to accommodate insights coming from two more recently developing fields of research. The first of these is direct observation of the normal infant during these early months, which now seems to encourage the notion that his perceptual world might be much better organized than the fragmentary sea of unrelated sensory and affective experiences conceptualized by the object relations theorists. This is suggested by the relative peace and contentment of many infants, as well as relatively sophisticated interactions with others that demonstrate clear separation and even individuation.

Another difficulty is the concept held by Mahler that maturity is manifested by completely separate and distinct individuals. Social psychologists, anthropologists, and the biblical model of one body with many members all suggest that mature identity is expressed in a profound unity with significant others which is not symbiosis or fusion, but a new union that respects and even enhances individuality. Unhealthiness then could take the form of either residual fusion or excessive isolation.

Whatever the outcome of future explorations into early human psychosocial development, the pioneering work and thought of Margaret Mahler will long be appreciated.

Additional Readings

Mahler, M. S., *The selected papers of Margaret S. Mahler* (2 vols.). New York: Norton, 1979.
Mahler, M. S., Pine, F., & Bergman, A., *The psychological birth of the human infant.* New York: Basic Books, 1975.
Kaplan, L. J., *Oneness and separateness: From infant to individual.* New York: Simon & Schuster, 1978.

C. M. BERRY

See OBJECT RELATIONS THEORY.

Mainstreaming. *See* MENTAL RETARDATION.

Malingering. The conscious and intentional production or maintenance of symptoms in order to feign a disease that is either medical or psychological so that environmental benefits can be obtained and enjoyed. It is to be distinguished from factitious disorders in which the patient simulates or produces illness for no other reason than the desire to be a patient. In malingering the voluntary production of symptoms is associated with a goal that is obviously recognizable with an understanding of the individual's circumstances.

In some cases malingering is the extension of an earlier existing but now improved illness, while in others it is the initial production of symptoms in order to achieve the benefits of illness. The feigned disease may be either medical in nature, such as pain syndromes (e.g., headache, low back pain) or gastrointestinal (e.g., flu symptoms, gastric distress) or psychological (e.g., a psychotic disorder with delusions and hallucinations or a depressive disorder).

Malingering is dependent on a basic intellectual ability to know the suitable symptoms and on apparent environmental gain either through the avoidance of an unpleasant event (e.g., hospital discharge for a lonely or poor patient) or the attainment of economic or social gain (e.g. disability insurance, welfare housing). Treatment intervention often takes the form of social and environmental manipulation directed toward making the gains previously produced by the illness available independent of the illness. An alternate strategy is to attempt to reduce the comfort or gain produced by the illness, thus removing the payoff for malingering. Psychotherapy can also be addressed initially toward support and later, after a relationship is established, toward confrontational approaches directed toward the patient effecting his own changes.

G. MATHESON

See FACTITIOUS DISORDERS.

Malpractice. Litigation against mental health professionals is increasing. Contrary to popular opinion, however, it is not always easy for the person bringing the complaint to prevail in a malpractice suit. Yet large monetary awards have brought a great deal of attention to the whole issue of professional incompetence.

The relationship between law and ethics is complex. Nearly all illegal actions that are relevant to professional functioning are unethical, and would be judged so by established professional societies. On the other hand, many things that are unethical are not specifically illegal. Thus, the range of unethical behavior is much larger than that of professionally illegal behavior. To put it another way, professionals can behave unethically without necessarily violating the law.

Malpractice litigation, however, usually has little directly to do with whether or not the practitioner has transgressed the laws of the land, i.e., behaved criminally. Malpractice suits fall within the province of civil litigation rather than criminal prosecution. It should be noted that some actions can put the practitioner in the position of being liable both to criminal prosecution and to civil suit.

For a plaintiff to prevail in a malpractice suit, he or she has to demonstrate to the court's satisfaction a number of key elements. Before the suit can even be lodged, the plaintiff must have what attorneys call a "standing to sue." This means that the person bringing the action must have some kind of legally recognized basis for doing so. It is not possible for someone merely reading about a professional's bad treatment in the newspaper to sue that professional. This principle parallels the fact that you cannot take out a life insurance policy on someone with whom you have no recognized close and legitimate relationship.

It must first be demonstrated that the practitioner owed the client the duty to behave according to the standard of care prevalent in the community in which the services were rendered. Ordinarily it is not difficult to establish that the practitioner owed such a duty, but the establishment of exactly what constitutes the relevant standard of care can be more difficult. Expert testimony is often employed. Other professionals are brought in to present their views of what would have been the ordinary prudent actions of any reasonable practitioner under the given circumstances. We should note that judgment errors, of themselves, are theoretically an insufficient basis for winning a malpractice suit. Professionals are allowed to make errors—we are all human—so long as the error was one that could *reasonably* have been expected in the situation at issue.

The next thing that has to be established is that the duty was breached. It has to be demonstrated that the practitioner failed, either by omission or commission, to do what he or she should have done.

Next, the plaintiff must prove that the client was in fact injured in some way. When the injury concerns something as tangible as loss of employment, it is not hard to quantify the severity of the loss by translating it into dollars. On the other hand, it is more difficult to assign dollar values to such ambiguous injuries as mental anguish. Finally, it must be proved that the professional who is being sued was the legal (proximate) cause of the injury. This is where many malpractice suits falter and ultimately fail. It is not as easy as one might think to demonstrate causation when it comes to complex human behavior.

In criminal law conviction rests on guilt having been demonstrated "beyond a reasonable doubt." In civil law, however, liability has to be demonstrated only by a "preponderance of the evidence." It is therefore easier in theory for a plaintiff to prevail in a malpractice litigation than it is for the state to secure a conviction in a criminal proceeding.

In order to reduce the risk of a malpractice suit, mental health professionals (and clergy) should ensure that their dealings with clients are benevolent. Stated differently, malpractice suits typically signify a breakdown in the relationship between a service provider and a consumer of services. Beyond maintaining good relationships it is important for providers of services to confer frequently with colleagues in order to keep abreast of legal and ethical principles that bear on what they do and, in general, to make sure that they behave in a responsible manner.

A person who feels that he or she has been mistreated by a professional has a number of options. The most humane and biblical of these is to express the grievance directly to the professional. If satisfaction is not obtained, the individual can then appeal to such sanctioning professional organizations as the American Psychological Association. Beyond this courts of law are available for seeking legal redress. Naturally, when Christians are aggrieved by other Christians, it is a good idea for them to settle their disputes out of court. The Christian Legal Society is an exceedingly good way to do this. Attorneys who are involved in this organization are committed to informal resolutions of differences between Christians and serve more or less as arbitration boards.

Additional Reading
Cohen, R. J. *Malpractice: A guide for mental health professionals.* New York: Free Press, 1979.

C. W. McLemore

Management Theory. Although some managers contend that the core of management is a combination of intuition and experience, the behavioral sciences have contributed much research to the theories and practice of management in this century.

One necessary perspective on management has been descriptive. Early management studies examined the organization of French industries and government offices and emphasized the themes of division of labor, unity of command, authority, and responsibility. A more recent descriptive approach has been to focus on the individual manager instead of the organization's structures and processes, and to describe the managerial role in terms of various functions: planning; decision making; delegating; supervising; coordinating; motivating; communicating; representing; staffing; disciplining; firing; negotiating; mediating; arbitrating; investigating; evaluating; gathering, interpreting, and disseminating information.

However, the behavioral sciences rarely stop with a description of management structures and processes; usually the purpose is to diagnose problems and prescribe optimal managerial strategies. This tradition began early in this century with motion-time experiments conducted by Taylor in an attempt to get the greatest amount of work from the least workers, hours, and materials. The biggest problem turned out to be worker resistance to more efficient methods rather than mere ignorance of them, and Taylor recommended financial incentives as the remedy.

The Humanistic Approach. The period 1930–1960 saw management theory emphasize the human element, especially the need for participation. The roots of this emphasis go back to Owen, who early in the nineteenth century contended that improvements in production required improvements in the condition of the workers, on and off the job. The scientific impetus for humanistic management came from Mayo's (1933) interpretation of the Hawthorne studies. Although there were economic incentives for the workers, Mayo observed the high levels of production that resulted from this experiment and credited these achievements to factors such as group participation and special attention given to the workers by the experimenters.

Most of the research of this period involved sociograms, morale, and the human qualities of the managers. Case studies, surveys, and even experiments generally indicated that there were positive correlations between productivity and variables such as morale, worker participation in decision making, and the amount of consideration shown by managers. The correlation between productivity and the closeness of supervision was negative. Likert (1961) hoped that the bulk of American firms were slowly moving through the phases of exploitive-authoritative, benevolent-authoritative, consultative, and participative management. In the 1960s and 1970s a process known as organizational development was in vogue; this used a participative group experience to redesign managerial structures and processes.

Another aspect of this humanistic approach has been a focus on noneconomic needs of workers. Maslow's theory of higher levels of needs has been widely (though perhaps uncritically) accepted by management theorists. Schein (1969) constructed a typology of workers: rational-economic (motivated by material gain), social (motivated by affiliative needs), and self-actualizing (motivated by the need to be autonomous and creative). Schein suggested that workers are moving away from the rational-economic in the direction of the self-actualizing. Herzberg (1968) presented a "two-factor theory" which claims that job satisfaction and job dissatisfaction are not polar opposites but two distinct factors. Job satisfaction can only be produced by job "con-tent" factors (e.g., achievement, recognition, growth, and intrinsic enjoyment of the work). Job dissatisfaction is produced by "hygiene" factors (e.g., company policies, working conditions, interpersonal relations on the job, salary, and status). These kinds of theories have led managers to experiment with what Herzberg called job enrichment—i.e., intentionally designing jobs to involve greater task variety and complexity in order to maintain worker interest and increase the sense of challenge.

MacGregor (1960) divided managers into two types: those who accept Theory X (workers are inherently lazy and need to be closely supervised, even intimidated, in order to get them to produce) and those who accept Theory Y (workers want to do a good job and only need to be supported and encouraged). Obviously, MacGregor made a case for Theory Y as being the better set of assumptions for achieving the company's objectives. Ouchi (1981) has proposed Theory Z (also known as Theory J), which he claims has been the secret of the Japanese success: collective decision making, lifetime employment, slow evaluation and promotion, nonspecialized career paths, and concern with the quality of work life.

One approach that synthesizes the emphases on participation and production has been management by objectives. Early in this century, Emerson contended that the first principle of effective management was the use of "clearly defined ideals." Drucker (1967) and Odiorne (1965) recommended that superior and subordinate discuss the goals of the latter's unit and mutually agree on the objectives that the latter would strive for, with the support of the former. It is hoped that the process will focus both superior and subordinate on participative decision making and teamwork. Then the former must measure the latter's progress in attaining the objectives, give appropriate rewards if successful, and diagnose underlying problems if not successful. When this is done well, management by objective is an excellent tool. However, some tasks do not lend themselves to clear statements about measurable objectives. What frequently happens, as in performance objectives in education, is that the objective that ends up being easiest to measure is not exactly what is most important to attain. In such a situation management by objective can grossly distort the real goals of an organization.

Interaction of Factors. In the past twenty years the simplistic assumptions of both the efficiency experts and the participative pollsters have become apparent. No one technique achieves all a firm's objectives. Different methods of designing work and compensating employees achieve different objectives. Job enrichment did not work with urban blue-collar workers. A closer examination of Japanese firms has convinced several researchers that Theory Z was not the factor responsible for economic success. Rather, the success was probably the result of the interaction of traditional Japanese values and the postwar economic boom. The chief movement has been an appreciation of the complexity of the interaction between different personalities and different environments.

Indeed, several humanistic theorists were pointing in this direction. Maslow conceded that only a small percentage of people are capable of sustained functioning at the self-actualizing level, and noted the impact of the environment in determining an individual's most pressing needs. Schein concluded that rational-economic, social, and self-actualizing were not distinct and mutually exclusive types, but traits that could be stronger or weaker in given individuals, companies, societies, or eras, depending upon socialization and other environmental factors.

The idea of identifying several different types of situations that call for different managerial approaches has been attempted by theorists in the past two decades. Blake and Mouton (1964) devised a "managerial grid," which looks at concern for people and concern for production not as polar opposites but as two different dimensions; they suggest that different supervisory styles may be appropriate in different contexts. The leadership studies at Ohio State defined the two dimensions as "consideration" and "initiating structure," and attempted to identify the variables that made for each one's effectiveness. Fiedler (1967) considered the interaction of the variables of leader-member relations, task structure, and leader power position and estimated to what degree a task-oriented management style or relationship-oriented style would be effective. Vroom (1964) developed a series of seven branching questions that can help a manager figure out which combination of five managerial styles would be most appropriate for a situation.

Even the idea that all business organizations should strive to develop and maintain the same structure is being challenged. Mintzberg (1979) developed a theory of five types of organizational structures and attempted to describe the specific environments in which each is most appropriate.

The manager's roles are now seen as varying (in terms of the amount of time and importance they have) according to factors such as the age of the company and managerial level. There is a growing realization that performance in these different roles may be somewhat independent, relying upon different sets of skills. A key point of contemporary management consultants is that such skills can be learned using applied behavioral techniques.

In the future specific terms and theories will come and go, but it seems likely that the focus will be neither on production nor on people, but on the interaction between personality and circumstances.

References

Blake, R. R., & Mouton, J. S. *The managerial grid,* Houston: Gulf Publishing, 1964.

Drucker, P. *The effective executive.* New York: Harper & Row, 1967.

Fiedler, F. E. *A theory of leadership effectiveness.* New York: McGraw-Hill, 1967.

Herzberg, F. One more time: How do you motivate employees? *Harvard Business Review,* 1968, *46*(1), 59–62.

Likert, R. *New patterns of management.* New York: McGraw-Hill, 1961.

MacGregor, D. *The human side of enterprise.* New York: McGraw-Hill, 1960.

Mayo, E. *The human problems of industrial civilization.* New York: Macmillan, 1933.

Mintzberg, H. *The structuring of organizations.* Englewood Cliffs, N.J.: Prentice-Hall, 1979.

Odiorne, G. *Management by objectives.* New York: Pitman, 1965.

Ouchi, W. *Theory Z.* Reading, Mass.: Addison-Wesley, 1981.

Schein, E. H. *Process consultation.* Reading, Mass.: Addison-Wesley, 1969.

Vroom, V. *Work and motivation.* New York: Wiley, 1964.

Additional Readings

Maier, N. R. F. *Psychology in industrial organizations* (5th ed.). Boston: Houghton Mifflin, 1982.

Rambo, W. W. *Work and organizational behavior.* New York: Holt, Rinehart, & Winston, 1982.

T. L. BRINK

See INDUSTRIAL/ORGANIZATIONAL PSYCHOLOGY.

Mania. An elevated mood disorder that results in euphoria, exuberance, excessive enthusiasm, and an inflated sense of well-being. It is frequently one syndrome of BIPOLAR DISORDER (formerly called manic-depressive psychosis). Motor activity may increase to a nonstop level, even to the point where sleep is ignored. The person experiences flight of ideas, expansiveness, and occasionally delusions of grandeur. Speech is boisterous and pressured, with abrupt changes from topic to topic. Sometimes speech is incoherent and disorganized, with clang associations in which the sound of words is more important than the meaning.

The mood impairs judgment and reduces

inhibitions so that actions are taken without consideration of consequences. Excessive spending, sexual acting out, grandiose plans, prolific letter writing, and numerous phone calls at any hour may result in embarrassment to the family. Socially the person may appear affable, but he cannot tolerate interruption without irritability. Sometimes when thwarted, the person can become violent towards those who oppose him.

Biological factors apparently predispose a person to this disorder, since manic syndromes run in families. However, psychodynamic factors of denial and reaction formation are also significant. The person attempts to defend against an underlying depression by massive denial of feelings such as sensed inadequacy, hopelessness, and low self-esteem. Hostility springing from a frustrated dependency relationship or blocked goals is often at the root of the depression.

Treatment usually requires hospitalization and chemotherapy. In recent years considerable success has been attained with lithium. This medication requires close monitoring of blood levels to avoid toxicity and to ascertain a therapeutic range. In addition, psychotherapy may help the person understand psychological aspects of the disorder.

M. R. NELSON

Manic-Depressive Psychosis. *See* BIPOLAR DISORDER.

Marijuana. Cannabis, or marijuana, has been used in various forms as an intoxicating drug for centuries. The *Cannabis sativa* plant is used in three preparations: *hashish*, the most potent form of the drug; *ganja*, the Indian term for a moderate concoction equivalent to the type of marijuana imported to the United States from Mexico or Vietnam; and *bhang*, the weakest variety, grown and most often used in the United States (Brecher, 1972).

The cannabis ingredient -9-tetrahydrocannabinol (THC) is generally believed to fall into the sedative-hypnotic pharmacologic group. Smoked or ingested orally it induces the following symptoms used for *DSM-III* diagnosis of cannabis intoxication: tachycardia; euphoria; subjective intensification of perceptions; sensation of slowed time; apathy; conjunctival injection; increased appetite; dry mouth; maladaptive behavioral effects such as anxiety, suspiciousness, and interference with social or occupational functioning. *DSM-III* has three other cannabis diagnoses: cannabis delusional disorder (similar to organic delusional syndrome),

cannabis abuse (pattern of pathological use for at least a month with disruption of social or work functioning), and cannabis dependence (impairment in social or work functioning due to cannabis use and tolerance).

The clinical picture is complicated by reports of a variety of other behavioral and psychophysiological effects. Behavioral effects reported include: 1) amotivational syndrome, where chronic users lose interest in life goals (Jones & Jones, 1977); 2) psychological dependence, with anxiety over self-perceived need for marijuana (Scher, 1970); 3) panic reactions; 4) psychotic reactions; 5) flashbacks; and 6) acute toxic psychosis with delirium and cognitive impairment. Possible physiological effects being studied in humans and in animals include: 1) brain changes, including EEG and chemical changes (Miller, 1979); 2) cognitive deficits (Sulkowski, 1980); 3) tolerance (Hollister, 1979); and 4) withdrawal (Jones, Benowitz, & Bachman, 1976).

Controversy and disagreement surround much of this research. Researchers in the 1960s and early 1970s often saw the drug as a mild, nearly harmless intoxicant, but more recent study leads some to believe both psychological and physical effects were underestimated. Disagreement among researchers stems from differing opinions on the influence of a subject's prior state and psychological predisposition; study design problems such as dosage accuracy, strength of the particular drug preparation used, definition of light or heavy drug use, and study population variables; and social bias both for and against the drug. Thus theories on etiology of cannabis use and adverse reactions are numerous and conflicting, as are treatment ideas. Among those opposed to use of cannabis, emphasis is being placed on prevention of experimentation with the drug through education about its effects and promotion of alternative activities. Teen groups aimed at helping cannabis users quit through peer support are utilized. Some researchers feel only a small percentage of cannabis users experience problems sufficient to warrant treatment, and no dependence is found as a distinct pathology (Brecher, 1972).

Persons more convinced about negative effects of cannabis use are concerned about drastic increases in its use. A national survey by the Federal Alcohol, Drug Abuse, and Mental Health Administration (Miller & Cisin, 1980) found both opportunity for cannabis use and actual use increasing dramatically since 1967. As of 1979, 50% of all American youth (12 to 17 years old) have the opportunity to try marijuana, and 31% actually used it; over 80% of young adults (18 to 25) have opportunity, and 63% have smoked. Opportunity has increased for adults (26 and over), and 20% of all older adults have tried marijuana, but 50% of those between 26 and 34 have used the drug. A look at demographics shows age is the only strong correlate with prevalence of use. An additional frequency statistic pertains to chronicity of use: 15% of youth and 31% of young adults have used the drug 3 to 99 times; 8% and 28% respectively have smoked over 100 times.

The study of effects of cannabis use continues to be an area of controversy. Some maintain that casual, short-term, or light use of the drug incurs few ill effects, although most acknowledge at least some respiratory risk in smoking marijuana. Others feel that even minimal use risks physical and psychological damage. More recent researchers seem to be finding significant detrimental psychophysiological effects with heavy chronic use. Because no study has specifically pinpointed how or why some casual users become chronic users and because even some infrequent users have experienced adverse psychological consequences, experimentation with cannabis cannot be considered a harmless activity.

References

Brecher, E. M., & Editors of Consumer Reports. *Licit and illicit drugs.* Mount Vernon, N.Y.: Consumers Union, 1972.

Hollister, L. E. Cannabis and the development of tolerance. In G. G. Nahas & W. D. M. Paton (Eds.), *Marihuana: Biological effects.* New York: Pergamon Press, 1979.

Jones, H. B., & Jones, H. C. *Sensual drugs: Deprivation and rehabilitation of the mind.* New York: Cambridge University Press, 1977.

Jones, R. T., Benowitz, N., & Bachman, J. Clinical studies of cannabis tolerance and dependence. *Annals of the New York Academy of Sciences,* 1976, *282,* 221–238.

Miller, J. D., & Cisin, I. H. *Highlights from the national survey on drug abuse: 1979.* Rockville, Md.: National Institute on Drug Abuse/DHHS, 1980.

Miller, L. L. Cannabis and the brain with special reference to the limbic system. In G. G. Nahas & W. D. Paton (Eds.), *Marihuana: Biological effects.* New York: Pergamon Press, 1979.

Scher, J. The marihuana habit. *Journal of the American Medical Association,* 1970, *214,* 1120.

Sulkowski, A. Marihuana "high": A model of senile dementia? *Perspectives in Biology and Medicine,* 1980, *23,* 209–214.

K. M. LATTEA

See SUBSTANCE-USE DISORDERS.

Marital Compatibility. A term describing the character of the relationship fit of the two spouses. In the highly compatible marriage both spouses are acting, thinking, and feeling in such a way that their needs and expectations are being met and few blockages exist to interfere in the relationship. In the highly incompatible marriage significant blockages are present that prevent one or both spouses from obtaining satisfaction of their needs and expectations. Most marriages exist between these extremes and have areas of both compatibility and incompatibility.

The general evaluation of marital compatibility involves an assessment of the specific areas of compatibility and incompatibility as well as an assessment of the relative importance of each area. Significant marital incompatibility may exist when many areas of incompatibility exist or when a few highly important areas of incompatibility exist. If a person highly values religious life and experiences considerable need or expectation frustration in this area, the marriage may be threatened. For a person who does not value this highly, it may have little consequence for the overall marital compatibility.

Happiness and satisfaction are the subjectively experienced consequences of marital compatibility. When both spouses experience needs and expectation satisfaction to a significant degree in the marriage, they are likely to report marital satisfaction. Thus the assessment of marital satisfaction has focused on the evaluation of several areas of needs, including affective communication, problem-solving communication, time together, financial disagreements, sexual dissatisfaction, role orientation, family history, and child-rearing practices (Snyder, 1979). Compatibility thus may be expected to correlate highly with expressed satisfaction.

Compatibility is to be distinguished from complementarity and similarity of spousal behavior. Jackson defines complementarity as "one spouse is in charge and the other obeys" (1968, p. 161). This parent-child marital relationship may be quite compatible as long as each spouse needs the other to play the complementary position or role. These spouses are more opposites than similars. In some marriages, on the other hand, the spouses appear to function very similarly and yet also compatibly. The companionate marriage partner lives most compatibly with someone similar to herself (Sager, 1976). Thus compatibility depends upon the fit of the needs and expectations of each spouse rather than upon the similarity or oppositeness of their needs and expectations.

Marital compatibility sometimes is popularly considered to be a function of personality fit or character traits, where both spouses are understood as fairly static unchangeable en-

expectations = demands (handwritten)

tities. Thus incompatibility is beyond the control of the individual, and its absence becomes grounds for dissolution of the marriage. This parallels the legal grounds for divorce in some states. While personality factors or character traits certainly influence compatibility, such a narrow definition eliminates possibilities of change and of individual and therapeutic work to enhance compatibility in the relationship.

This view of compatibility also conflicts with the view that compatibility may change over the life cycle of a marriage (Rollins & Cannon, 1974). As the spouses change and the family changes, needs and expectations also change. A relationship fit thus may be compatible at one time but incompatible at another. The occurrence of an affair may be an indication of changing needs and expectations which one or both spouses do not find fulfilled in the marital relationship, even though earlier the marriage was considered a compatible one. This suggests that the maintenance of compatibility, and hence marital satisfaction, involves continued adjustment and work throughout the marriage.

Mate selection studies have also suggested that the choice of a spouse depends upon the compatibility of the interpersonal needs. Specifically Murstein (1980) suggests that attraction relates to the initial stimulus factors, similarity of values, and agreement on individual role functions. The theory advanced by Centers (1975) even more clearly suggests that spousal attraction depends upon maximum gratification and minimum deprivation of personal needs.

Compatibility is a significant factor in the selection of a spouse, the maintenance of a relationship, and the experience of satisfaction in a marriage.

References

Centers, R. *Sexual attraction and love: An instrumental theory.* Springfield, Ill.: Thomas, 1975.

Jackson, D., & Lederer, W. *The mirages of marriage.* New York: Norton, 1968.

Murstein, B. I. Mate selection in the 1970's. *Journal of Marriage and the Family,* 1980, *42,* 777–792.

Rollins, B. C., & Cannon, K. L. Marital satisfaction over the family life cycle: A reevaluation. *Journal of Marriage and the Family,* 1974, *36,* 271–282.

Sager, C. J. *Marriage contracts and couple therapy.* New York: Brunner/Mazel, 1976.

Snyder, D. K. Multidimensional assessment of marital satisfaction. *Journal of Marriage and the Family,* 1979, *41,* 813–823.

A. D. Compaan

See Mate Choice.

Marital Contract Therapy. Developed by Clifford J. Sager, a psychoanalytically trained psychiatrist, marital contract therapy is a therapeutic approach to marital dysfunction based upon the concept of contracts (Sager, 1976). According to this approach each spouse has an individual, unwritten contract for the marriage. It is the set of expectations and promises, conscious and unconscious, he or she has for the relationship. A third contract, the marital contract, develops as a consequence of the marital interaction. It is the operational, interactional contract created by the marital system and the unconscious and conscious ways the two spouses seek to fulfill their individual contracts.

Sager groups the various individual contracts into seven different types: equal, romantic, parental, childlike, rational, companionate, and parallel. The combinations of the individual contracts become the 48 different marital contracts, or marital types, described by him. Marital discord results from contractual disappointments when the expectations of one spouse are not being met by the other. Most often these expectations have not been clearly expressed and may be largely unconscious.

Therapy primarily seeks to clarify the terms of the two individual contracts and those of their interactional contract. This begins with helping each spouse explain the expectations they have but have not clearly verbalized. It also involves helping each to become more aware of the unconscious expectations they have for the marriage. This process of making conscious what is unconscious requires considerable clinical skill. Finally, once clarification of the contract has been obtained, agreement on its terms must be reached in order for marital satisfaction to continue.

The identification of individual contracts, the diagnostic phase of therapy, is made by collecting information from three categories. First is the expectations each spouse has for the marriage (e.g., my mate will be loyal and devoted, or marriage will be a respectable cover for the expression of my aggressive drive). Second is the intrapsychic and biological drives of each spouse. Sager identifies 13 basic parameters useful in evaluating each spouse (e.g., independence-dependence, closeness-distance, and dominance-submission). The reciprocal nature of contracts is particularly operative in this area: "I want so-and-so and in exchange I am willing to give such-and-such." The third source of information is the external manifestations of marital problems, the problems often presented as the reasons for seeking therapy (e.g., poor communication, sexual dysfunction). These symptoms, according to Sager, are secondary manifestations of problem areas originating in the other two areas.

In examining each of the above three sources of information, three levels of awareness must be considered. The first is the conscious and verbalized level. These are the expectations and needs that both spouses have talked about in their marriage. The second level is conscious but not verbalized. This includes expectations and needs that the spouses know they have, but for a variety of reasons have been unwilling to tell each other. The third level is the needs and expectations that are present and that influence behavior but are beyond the awareness of both spouses.

The interactional contract is the behaviors followed by each spouse in trying to fulfill his or her individual contract. According to Sager, "much of therapy consists of making the interactional contract and the partners' behavior in it more conscious, and of using the consciousness to work toward a new single contract that provides the basis for healthier interactions" (p. 29).

Contract therapy incorporates many methods proposed and utilized by other therapists. What is distinctive is the focus on expectations and the relationship of these expectations to underlying biological and psychological needs. The implications for assessment and diagnosis of mental dynamics are also a significant contribution (See MARITAL TYPES).

Marital contract therapy is psychoanalytic in its emphasis on the levels of awareness and intrapsychic needs. However, systems theory has influenced the concept of interactional contracts and expectations of marriage. Learning theory has also influenced the approach in its use of behavioral observation in order to identify the interactional contracts of the marriage. In the absence of research, it would appear that the approach may be useful for persons with good ego strength, observational abilities, and verbal abilities. It also provides many helpful concepts and techniques that would fit within virtually any other approach to marital therapy.

Marital contract therapy has some basic similarities to the Old Testament concept of the covenant in that it focuses on promises and expectations in the relationship between two contracting or covenanting parties. Problems in the relationship of God to man and woman result from the breaking of covenant, just as marital discord results from unmet contracts. Sager makes clear that such making and breaking of contracts in marriage (as in our relationship to God) occurs significantly at unconscious and unverbalized levels in the relationship.

Reference

Sager, C. J. *Marriage contracts and couple therapy.* New York: Brunner/Mazel, 1976.

A. D. COMPAAN

See MARITAL THERAPY.

Marital Enrichment. When God designed marriage, he planned it to be a nourishing, enriching, and growth-producing relationship, a vital provision in his plan for individuals to grow in sanctification and become conformed to the image of his Son. God's plan for marriage has not changed. Unfortunately, there are relatively few couples today who are experiencing marriage as God intended it to be experienced.

Today marital disharmony is a major social and spiritual problem. Recent statistics indicate that about 50% of all marriages end in divorce. For many years the primary source of help for troubled marriages was to be found at the office of the pastor or marriage counselor, and most of the time help was sought only after the problems had grown to the point of threatening the relationship.

In the past 20 years marriage enrichment has become one of the major solutions to the problem of failing marriages and stagnant and mediocre relationships. Although marriage counseling can be helpful, and will continue to be a necessary option, there are a growing number of people committed to strengthening good marriages and preventing the growth of problems.

Historical Development. The roots of marriage enrichment are varied, and most of the early programs were church related. Some of the earliest structured activity that could be called marriage enrichment can be traced to the pioneer work of David and Vera Mace, begun in 1962 with the Society of Friends (Quakers). In 1964 Leon Smith began the Marriage Communication Labs through the United Methodist Church. In 1967 Catholic Marriage Encounter was brought to the United States from Spain, where it had been started in 1962 by Gabriel Calvo.

In 1973 the Association of Couples for Marriage Enrichment (ACME) was founded by the Maces to provide weekend retreats; offer local, statewide, and national meetings; and publish a monthly newsletter. In 1975 the Council of Affiliated Marriage Enrichment Organizations (CAMEO) was formed under the auspices of ACME. Today CAMEO recognizes some 25 national organizations and groups offering marriage enrichment and provides a forum for exchanging ideas through national meetings.

Several factors contributed to the growth of the marriage enrichment movement. These include; 1) the significant and continuing increase in the divorce rate; 2) the knowledge that many marriages could have been saved if couples had been given insights and skills before the problems grew out of control; 3) the realization that more than remedial counseling is needed; 4) the fact that many stable and surviving marriages are not happy ones; and 5) the growing shift in society's view of marriage from that of a static institution to that of a dynamic, growing relationship that needs to be nurtured and cherished if it is to grow.

Since 1962 marriage enrichment has grown from a few scattered attempts to strengthen marriages to a national movement that has led to a new mindset as to the nature and importance of the marriage relationship. Today there are hundreds of preventative programs involving hundreds of thousands of couples that can be grouped under the heading of marriage enrichment. There are national organizations whose sole purpose is to provide marriage enrichment programs, and there are hundreds of resources that individual couples can use on their own to strengthen and enrich their relationship.

Although the roots go back to 1962, the greatest growth has occurred in the last 10 years. Otto (1976) surveyed 30 marriage enrichment professionals and found that 90% had conducted their first program in 1973 or later. The majority of the more than 100 doctoral dissertations relating to marriage enrichment have been written in the past 10 years (Sell, Shoffner, Farris, & Hill, 1980).

Defining Marriage Enrichment. Marriage enrichment is a term that covers a wide variety of activities. This makes difficult a concise definition that is both precise and comprehensive. A functional definition of marriage enrichment might be any formal or informal program, exercise, or activity designed to build and strengthen marriage relationships. Marriage enrichment can be a program in which couples participate, an activity in which a couple engages, a perspective a couple adopts, and a commitment a couple makes.

It is important to distinguish marriage enrichment from marriage counseling. While marriage counseling has more of a remedial and reconstructive emphasis, enrichment emphasizes primary prevention, promoting growth, and maximizing relational potential. Marriage enrichment is based on the belief that all relationships are functioning at a fraction of their relational potential and that every relationship has potential for growth. Enrichment goes beyond mere maintenance and emphasizes the growth concept of how to develop new, more satisfying behaviors and increase mutual understanding. Most enrichment programs are for couples who perceive their marriage as functioning fairly well and who wish to go beyond the status quo to make their relationship the best it can be. Mace and Mace (1976) suggest that enrichment means refusing to settle for less than a warm, loving, creative relationship. It means determination on the part of both partners to appropriate all the latent potential they possess and to build together the kind of shared life they really want.

Forms of Marriage Enrichment. One of the most positive aspects of marriage enrichment is the wide variety of ways in which it can be experienced. The various kinds of experiences can be grouped into two general categories: formal programs, and informal activities and exercises.

Formal programs. The most common form of marriage enrichment involves structured programs, seminars, and workshops offered on a weekend or over several weeks. The process usually involves a group of couples meeting together and listening to presentations and participating in exercises under the direction of trained leaders. Although the majority are presented live, there are an increasing number of programs available on film and videocassette.

These formal programs can vary along such dimensions as: 1) time format (weekend or several weeks); 2) the number, training, and style of leadership; 3) the composition of participants (by age, socioeconomic status, denominational affiliation, or stages of marriage); 4) degree of structure; 5) content emphasis (communication, conflict resolution, love, sexual fulfillment, intimacy, expectations, differences, roles, decision making, goals, and values); 6) teaching methods used (primarily lecture or using various group techniques); and 7) kinds of follow-up, if any. Three of the most successful programs that illustrate many of these variables are the Marriage Enrichment retreat, Marriage Encounter, and Couple Communication.

The Marriage Enrichment retreat was developed by Mace and Mace and is offered through the Association of Couples for Marriage Enrichment. The leadership of a retreat is a couple whose role is to serve as facilitators. Each retreat is different, depending on the couples involved. The structure is flexible. Participants are told to design the program on the basis of their needs and concerns. At the beginning of the retreat couples are given three ground rules: no confrontation, share experiences not opinions, and don't try to analyze others (Mace & Mace; 1976). From this point the couples collectively make a list of concerns that will become the agenda for the weekend. A sample list might include: 1) making decisions together; 2) lack of intimacy; 3) sexual fulfilment; 4) expressing negative emotions; 5) roles of husband and wife; and 6) showing appreciation. After a weekend retreat couples are encouraged to participate in monthly follow-up groups. Mace (1982) discusses research that has supported the effectiveness of this retreat format.

Probably the best known form of marriage enrichment is the Marriage Encounter. Initially introduced by the Catholic Church, it now includes Baptist, Lutheran, Episcopal, and other expressions of Encounter. Their format is basically the same. The leadership of an Encounter is several couples who give 10 to 12 lectures over the course of the weekend. Each presentation introduces the 20 to 30 participating couples to a basic part of the weekend, the dialogue technique. At the end of each presentation each person is instructed to go somewhere alone and, after a time of personal reflection, to write his or her feelings in a notebook. Spouses then exchange notebooks and read what the other has written. This is followed by the spouses' verbal communication of their feelings to each other in greater depth. Many of the organizations offering an Encounter provide follow-up meetings and regular newsletters. In a recent study Lester and Doherty (1983) found that about 80% of the 129 randomly selected couples surveyed considered the Encounter to have been a totally positive experience. What meant most to them was the private couple dialogue, which opened up new communication and expression of feelings between them.

The Couple Communication program (Miller, Nunnally, & Wackman, 1979) is one of the most widely researched and effective of the formal programs available (Wampler, 1982). The four highly structured three-hour sessions are conducted over several weeks. The content is communication. The trained leadership directs an average of seven couples using lecture and group interaction through the couple communication test (Miller, et al., 1979). The program emphasizes insights and skills to help spouses tune into themselves, tune into their partners, and to increase accuracy in listening to and communicating with their partners.

In addition to these three programs there are a wide variety of other formal programs and a range of resources that can be offered by both professionals and nonprofessionals to groups of couples. Some of the more popular resources include *Communication: Key to Your Marriage* (Wright, 1974), *The Pillars of Marriage* (Wright, 1979), and *Strike the Original Match* (Swindoll, 1980).

Informal activities and exercises. This category differs from formal programs in that it involves individual couples pursuing enrichment on their own. The primary resources are books, tapes, and magazines.

Books such as *How to Have a Happy Marriage* (Mace & Mace, 1977) and *No-Fault Marriage* (Laswell & Lobsenz, 1976) provide couples with insights and specific exercises they can do. Given the lack of interest in reading on the part of many, cassette tapes are proving to be an especially valuable tool for marriage enrichment. Tape series such as *Love-Life* (Wheat, 1979), *Reflections of a Positive Marriage* (Wright, 1982), and *Communication Skills for Christian Couples* (Miller, Wackman, & Nunnally, 1982) can be listened to by both partners at different times and then discussed together at a convenient time. Magazines such as *Family Life Today* and *Marriage and Family Living* emphasize building strong marriages and equipping the Christian home. Each month they offer fresh ideas, insights, and specific activities to help couples strengthen their relationship.

Conclusion. Marriage enrichment is a comparatively young movement that in the past 20 years has had an increasingly significant impact. Many church leaders are starting to understand the significant implications of marriage enrichment to help accomplish what God has called his people to do. Marriage enrichment not only helps to save and strengthen many marriages; it also helps to build strong families and strong churches and provides a powerful witness to the reality of the difference that Jesus Christ can make in a marriage relationship. Aldrich (1981) has noted that "the two greatest forces in evangelism are a healthy church and a healthy marriage. The two are interdependent. You can't have one without the other. It is the healthy marriage, however, which is the 'front lines weapon.' The Christian family in a community is the ultimate evangelistic tool, assuming the home circle is an open one in which the beauty of the Gospel is readily available. It's the old story: when love is seen, the message is heard" (p.20).

References

Aldrich, J. *Life-style evangelism*. Portland: Multnomah Press, 1981.

Laswell, M., & Lobsenz, N. M. *No-fault marriage*. New York: Ballantine Books, 1976.

Lester, M. E., & Doherty, W. J. Couples' long-term evaluations of their marriage encounter weekend. *Journal of Marital and Family Therapy*, 1983, *9*, 183–188.

Mace, D. *Close companions: The marriage enrichment handbook*. New York: Continuum, 1982.

Mace, D., & Mace, V. *Marriage enrichment in the church*. Nashville; Broadman, 1976.

Mace, D., & Mace, V. *How to have a happy marriage*. Nashville: Abingdon, 1977.

Miller, S., Nunnally, E. W., & Wackman, D. B. *Talking together*. Minneapolis: Interpersonal Communication Programs, 1979.

Miller, S., Wackman, D. B., & Nunnally, E. W. *Communication skills for Christian couples*. Minneapolis: Interpersonal Communication Programs, 1982. (Cassette recording)

Otto, H. A. (Ed). *Marriage and family enrichment*. Nashville: Abingdon, 1976.

Sell, K. D., Shoffner, S. M., Farris, M. C., & Hill, E. W. *Enriching relationships*. Greensboro, N.C.: Sell, Shoffner, Farris, and Hill, 1980.

Swindoll, C. R. *Strike the original match*. Portland: Multnomah Press, 1980.

Wampler, K. S. The effectiveness of the Minnesota couple communication program: A review of research. *Journal of Marital and Family Therapy*, 1982, *8*, 345–354.

Wheat, E. *Love-life: For every married couple*. Springdale, Ariz.: Scriptural Counsel, 1979. (Cassette recording)

Wright, H. N. *Communication: Key to your marriage*. Glendale, Calif.: Regal Books, 1974.

Wright, H. N. *The pillars of marriage*. Glendale, Calif.: Regal Books, 1979.

Wright, H. N. *Reflections of a positive marriage*. Santa Ana, Calif.: Christian Marriage Enrichment, 1982. (Cassette recording)

G. J. OLIVER

Marital Health and Pathology. Married life is a mixture of health and pathology, of both life-enhancing and life-destroying behaviors. The message of grace in the Christian gospel frees marriage partners to recognize the pathology in their relationships, while at the same time releasing a Spirit-filled pull toward change. When spouses acknowledge and receive this grace, they then can more easily face the realistic strengths and weaknesses of their marital relationship. The following seven areas of marital life involve dynamics important in assessing the health of a marriage: ideals, commitment, communication, intimacy, dependency, sexuality, and power.

Ideals. The first area for assessment is the relationship between the images of an ideal marriage relationship and the reality of the relationship. All attitudes, feelings, and behaviors in marriage are affected by the ideal image of marriage which the spouses have. These ideal images are shaped by individual experiences in the family of origin, by cultural and religious teaching, and by other life experiences. Thus they are destined to contain both truth and myth. The greater the disparity between the husband's ideal and the wife's ideal, and between each of their ideals and the reality of their relationship, the greater is the distress in the marriage. Marital life is enhanced when both spouses accept the realities of their marriage and are able then to agree on a mutually accepted ideal and collaborate in working toward it. Sager (1976) discusses the distresses present when spouses' ideals are not complementary and describes the variety of ideal marital relationships (see MARITAL TYPES).

While the Bible has a great deal to say about married life, it does not set forth a single ideal marital relationship that can be called *the* Christian marriage. If only one ideal model for marriage is set forth as the Christian model, the diversity of human behavior and the uniqueness of each marriage are denied. A marital relationship must be realistic and unique for each marital pair and at the same time must meet the universal guides for life established by God and communicated to us through Scripture.

The creative effort of both spouses is necessary to lead marriage toward this goal. Spouses will sometimes equate their personal ideal for marriage with a supposed biblical ideal in order to lend credibility and power to their preference. As a power play by one spouse this usually works against the creative work necessary for achieving a mutually acceptable ideal. Since it is inevitable that each spouse will have an ideal, it is important to recognize that many different options are acceptable and can meet the requirements of a Christian life. Health is fostered when both can agree on the ideal they have for the marriage.

Commitment. Christian marriage is a covenantal relationship in which fidelity for life is pledged by each spouse. Fidelity is a commitment to place the other's good above self-interest. Smedes (1976) defines fidelity in partnership as "commitment to an ongoing, dynamic, changing, sensitive facing off of two people bent on the total well-being of each other. And each is faithful to the extent that he is dedicated to the constant growth, healing, and re-growth of the other person" (p. 178). Clearly no spouse consistently meets this high goal of fidelity. Adultery is the breaking of this covenant commitment and may be expressed in many different behaviors and attitudes. The more frequent and the more serious the breaking of covenant fidelity, the more significant the pathology of the marriage relationship.

Erikson (1950) has noted that the ability to make and keep such a commitment is a late young adult achievement. He says that after resolving the crises of identity, the young adult is then ready to develop "the capacity to commit himself to concrete affiliations and partnerships and to develop the ethical strength to abide by such commitments, even though they may call for significant sacrifices and compromises" (p. 263). Rubin and Gertrude Blanck likewise suggest that marriage affords the opportunity to resolve this developmental task (Blanck & Blanck, 1968, p. 19).

Many individuals find the development of such commitment extremely difficult and sometimes impossible. Their efforts are focused on meeting earlier needs—those of identity, acceptance, and trust. This adversely affects their ability to maintain their commitment to do what is best for the other—i.e., to maintain marital fidelity. For these persons the decision to be married and remain married does not include much of a commitment to place the other's good above their own, but is rather made largely out of a desire to satisfy personal needs. These needs may include the need for being secure, for escaping a tension-filled home, or for replacing a parent with a parentlike spouse.

Covenant keeping in marriage, as in our relationships with God, reaches its intended height only as it becomes an ethical commitment or choice of the individual. Persons forced to remain together by circumstances, by parents, by social or communal pressure, or by personal developmental deficits have not thereby met the biblical goals for marriage. In fact, the dynamics of such marriages are often very destructive. Anger and resentment over being forced to be together may be expressed destructively toward the spouse and often also toward the children.

Communication. Fulfilling the marital vow of placing the interests and needs of the other above one's own self-interests and needs requires communication. Understanding of another person's needs comes only as these are communicated. However, the natural tendency is to hide rather than disclose feelings, thoughts, and desires.

One way to hide is to blame the spouse for something and thus avoid personal responsibility and honest self-disclosure. This communication dysfunction is described as far back as Adam and Eve (Gen. 3). Adam blamed Eve and Eve blamed the serpent, both hoping to direct attention away from their own failures. Such a pattern of blame blocks the communication of

one's real thoughts and feelings, this in turn making it difficult for the spouse to relate in such a way that needs can be met.

God's way of relating to us models more healthy patterns of communication. In the covenantal relationships of God to the people of Israel and of Christ to the church, self-disclosing communication is initiated by God and encouraged in the response of his people. The God of Israel, in contrast to the gods of the neighboring nations, is a God with ears to hear and a mouth to speak (Ps. 135:16–17). God is revealed in word and deed, and finally in the person of Jesus Christ. Marital life is enriched by modeling this self-disclosing communication. It is destroyed by defensive communication. (See Miller, Nunnally, & Wackman, 1979 for a more detailed discussion of marital communication.)

Intimacy. A fourth important area in marriage is intimacy. The Bible sees intimacy as both becoming one and maintaining individuality. The one-flesh union presented as the ideal of marriage requires that both husband and wife first become individuals distinct from their families of origin (Gen. 2:24; Matt. 19:5). Marital health is marked by an ability to be intimate with one's spouse without losing one's distinctive and separate self and without destroying the other distinct and separate self.

A pathological marital relationship that sometimes is equated with this biblical description of marriage is a relationship in which ego boundaries of each spouse have been blurred or fused with each other. Each spouse becomes unable to distinguish his or her partial self from the common self. Bowen (1978) describes this situation as "undifferentiated family ego mass." He feels that the level of differentiation of the self of each spouse determines the degree of emotional fusion in the relationship. The way the spouses handle this fusion governs the areas in which the undifferentiation will be absorbed and the areas in which symptoms will be expressed under stress. According to Bowen, the most common symptomatic expressions of this lack of differentiation are marital conflict, dysfunction in a spouse, and dysfunction in one or more of the children. The lower the level of differentiation of each spouse, the greater is the difficulty in responding to stress without manifesting symptoms in one of these areas. The achievement and maintenance of intimacy is made easier by greater differentiation of self both from the family of origin and within the nuclear family.

Often the family of origin will work to keep

679

the person tied into the family and thus unable to separate and begin a new family. Morris and Wynne (1965) refer to this as the "rubber fence" which extends to keep the person tied to the family of origin. Symptoms of such a situation may include financial ties, entangled living arrangements, and parental judgments of decisions made by a spouse. All of these work against the achievement of intimacy.

In American society young adults often marry before they have adequately individuated and before they have formed an identity apart from the family of origin (Blanck & Blanck, 1968). Thus marriage, with its goal of "oneness," is begun while separation is also being sought, and the early years of marriage may be filled with struggles for both separateness and intimacy. Symptoms of this process include the wife sensing she is competing with her husband's mother for him, one spouse accusing the other of being like his or her parent of the same sex, and arguments over time spent with the guys. Usually intimacy is approximated only after seven to ten years of marriage, and even then it continues to develop only with hard work. (See Clinebell, 1970 for further discussion of intimacy in marriage.)

Intimacy is not fusion. Rather it comes as each spouse acknowledges, respects, and empathizes with the joys, successes, failures, and struggles disclosed by the other spouse.

Dependency. Both communication and intimacy are closely connected to a fifth dynamic, managing dependency in marriage. While marriage involves giving to the other and placing the other as more important than self, it also necessarily involves seeking the other for self. No marriage can sustain itself without each spouse both giving and taking. Total self-giving, as altruistic as it may seem, is destructive in a marriage. It saps a partner of the creative independence he or she needs in order to contribute to the other person. Thus one condition of self-giving is self-assertion (Smedes, 1976). Often the greatest gift in marriage is to fully and joyfully receive, just as the greatest gift we can return to God is to fully and joyfully receive his gift in Christ.

Pathology exhibits itself when spouses are unable to ask for or clearly receive the gifts of the other spouse. Often in these relationships one or both persons project an image of adequacy and self-sufficiency. The other spouse is thus demeaned and made of no consequence. As a result, the "unneeded, worthless" spouse may turn to someone else or to a job where he or she experiences being needed, wanted, and valued. Health in marriage requires the ability to seek what one needs from the other spouse as well as to joyfully receive it. However, each must learn to ask for the satisfaction of needs without demanding or smothering the other.

Where dependency is not acceptable to a spouse (e.g., to a male who sees dependency as feminine or an indication of personal inadequacy), he or she is likely to use covert or manipulative behavior in order to obtain satisfaction for these needs. Such manipulation usually generates anger and resistance in the other spouse, who then may not want to give anything. Accepting dependence as a normal, God-created human situation frees the individual to ask and to receive.

Sexuality. A sixth crucial dynamic of marriage is sexuality. The Christian church has consistently viewed the sexual relationship of marriage to be of the highest significance, even though it has often erred in favor of an unbiblical Greek dualistic split of body and soul and an equally unbiblical dichotomy of sex roles (Nelson, 1978). Sexuality in marriage involves the expression of both *eros* and *agape*, seeking and giving love, and thus is crucially related to the spiritual search for God and the spiritual response of loving God and neighbor. The sexual relationship in marriage can thus be seen as a barometer of many of the other dynamics as well as a barometer of a person's spiritual relationship to God.

Healthy sexual relationships involve a delicate combination of desiring and giving. The communication of what is physically pleasurable and satisfying in the sexual experiences is a key part of both experiencing fulfillment in the sexual relationship and of assisting the spouse to give unselfishly (Masters & Johnson, 1966). Sexual inadequacies frequently involve difficulties in both giving and receiving. Healthy sexuality thus requires health in all dynamics of marriage and is in many ways the expression of a healthy marital relationship. Sexual dysfunctions are, however, not necessarily a sign of marital problems, since they sometimes result from nothing more serious than erroneous information or expectations. (See SEXUALITY.)

Power. Christians are sometimes reluctant to see marriage in terms of the use and abuse of power, often considering any use of power to be unacceptable. However, God clearly gave mankind, both Adam and Eve, considerable power. They were to subdue nature and rule over it (Gen. 1:26–31). Furthermore, they were so powerful that each could act in ways counter both to God's desires and to their own best interests. As a result of the abuse of power in eating the forbidden fruit, man and woman became repeated abusers of that power. Man began to dominate woman, and woman began to use her power manipulatively toward her husband (Gen. 3:16). Thus the ideal of jointly exercising their power in dominion over the rest of creation was lost as they exercised their power over each other.

In their marriage spouses often engage in elaborate power struggles. These struggles take a wide variety of forms, and to varying degrees may destroy the life of the marriage. The therapeutic task is to help the spouses get out of the power struggle and begin to use power constructively.

Paradoxically, most often both spouses experience themselves as powerless in the marriage relationship, even while using extremely powerful methods in the destructive conflict. Thus both are disowning the God-given power that is theirs while using that power in maritally destructive ways. Assisting each to recognize that he or she is very powerful helps each to become more responsible in the use of that power.

References

Blanck, R., & Blanck, G. *Marriage and personal development.* New York: Columbia University Press, 1968.

Bowen, M. *Family therapy in clinical practice.* New York: Aronson, 1978.

Clinebell, H. J. *The intimate marriage.* New York: Harper & Row, 1970.

Erikson, E. H. *Childhood and society.* New York: Norton, 1950.

Masters, W. H., & Johnson, V. E. *Human sexual response.* Boston: Little, Brown, 1966.

Miller, S., Nunnally, E. W., & Wackman, D. B. *Talking together.* Minneapolis: Interpersonal Communication Programs, 1979.

Morris, G., & Wynne, L. Schizophrenic offspring and parental styles of communication: Predictive study using family therapy excerpts. *Psychiatry,* 1965, *28,* 32–39.

Nelson, J. *Embodiment.* Minneapolis: Augsburg, 1978.

Sager, C. J. *Marriage contracts and couple therapy.* New York: Brunner/Mazel, 1976.

Smedes, L. *Sex for Christians.* Grand Rapids: Eerdmans, 1976.

A. D. COMPAAN

Marital Stages. *See* FAMILY LIFE CYCLE.

Marital Therapy. A specialized area of therapy that evolved from the general field of psychiatry. As early as 1931 papers were presented to the American Psychiatric Association describing the sequential analysis of married couples (Sager, 1966).

Because psychoanalysis has traditionally concerned itself with the internal dynamics of the human psyche, it seemed heretical to examine any relationship except the patient-therapist relationship. Freud seemed to feel that it was counterproductive and dangerous for an analyst to become involved in working with more than one member of the same family (1943). Consequently, marital therapy did not gain credence among psychoanalysts until the early 1960s. Jackson (1959) coined the term *conjoint therapy* to describe a therapist meeting conjointly with a husband and wife.

In the 1960s and 1970s marital therapy seems to have been incorporated into the more broadly based family therapy movement under the conceptual umbrella of general systems theory. There appear to be negligible systemic differences in working with a married couple as opposed to the entire family. Some theorists have argued that the differences between marital therapy and family therapy are semantic rather than conceptual (Gurman & Kniskern, 1979).

Marital therapy is founded on the epistemological premises of general systems theory, which differ significantly from the individually oriented, intrapsychic, insight therapies. Based on the medical model, psychodynamic theories assume the Aristotelian notion of linear causality (A causes B). The therapist searches for cause-effect relations, focuses on intrapsychic dynamics, and views symptoms as unresolved intrapsychic conflicts.

In contrast, systemic marital therapy originated from the fields of cybernetics and communications theory, which assume a feedback cycle of circular causality (A causes B, which in turn causes A). The marital system is composed of two subsystems, husband and wife. The behavior of each marital partner creates an interactional pattern or symptom maintenance cycle. The work of the therapist is to join the couple and actively devise interventions that will rearrange the dysfunctional patterns of interaction.

Necessarily when one shifts to the study of the two-person system, one is entering the field of communication. The therapist must describe the individual in terms that apply to the exchange of communicative behavior between two or more people. Symptoms, then, are seen from a communicative rather than intrapsychic point of view, and the individual is best described as a person in communication with others. Communication theory conceives of a symptom as a nonverbal message. Moreover, the client's symptoms are perpetuated by the way he himself behaves and by the influence of other people intimately involved with him.

Intrapsychic therapists generally assume a passive or nondirective role in the therapeutic process. Internal mental processes are inferred from behavior, and change is believed to occur through increased self-awareness.

Because distressed marriages are frequently repetitive, resolution-resisting systems, the therapist cannot afford to remain passive. He must be active and must strategically direct the flow of communication if he is to effect change. Communication theorists question the plausibility of nondirective therapy. As Haley points out, "Actually nondirective therapy is a misnomer. To state that any communication between people can be nondirective is to state an impossibility. Whatever a therapist does not say to a patient as well as what he says will circumscribe the patient's behavior"(Haley, 1963, p. 71).

In contrast to psychodynamic theories, marital systems theories postulate that change occurs as a product of the interpersonal context of client and therapist. It is furthermore suggested that exploration of the human psyche or increased self-awareness may be irrelevant to therapeutic change. To be effective change must occur in the overall system, between both partners.

Behavior therapy has also made significant contributions to marital therapy. The theoretical underpinnings of behavior therapy as a strategy for treating couples evolved from behavior exchange theory, which addresses the interdependency of marriage (Jacobson & Margolin, 1979). Exchange theory assumes that couples constantly emit stimuli that have reinforcing or punishing effects on the partner. Each possible combination of behavioral exchanges yields an outcome for each partner. These outcomes collectively determine one's tendency to emit rewarding behavior in future encounters, one's level of satisfaction in the relationship, and one's general tendency to continue in the relationship.

One factor that determines the outcome of a particular interaction is the receiver's appraisal of his or her potential outcomes in alternative relationships or the outcomes accruing as a result of being alone. The more positive each spouse estimates his or her options outside of the relationship to be, the more positive the outcomes in the relationship need to be in order to justify continuance of the relationship. (Jacobson & Margolin, 1979).

It should be acknowledged that marital therapy, like systems theory, is still evolving from its conceptual infancy. It would therefore be premature to offer a critique of marital therapy at this time. However, it is fairly clear that marital therapy has arisen from a need to explain and treat marital distress where psychodynamic theories have failed or proven inadequate. If it is true, as Kuhn (1962) postulates, that progress in science evolves from paradigms that better explain phenomena, then systems theory has altered our conception of human problems in much the same way as the theory of relativity altered our conception of the universe.

References

Freud, S. *General introduction to psychoanalysis.* Garden City, N.Y.: Garden City Publishing, 1943.

Gurman, A. S., & Kniskern, D. P. Marriage and/or family therapy: What's in a name? *American Association for Marital and Family Therapy Newsletter,* 1979, *10*(1), 5–8.

Haley, J. *Strategies of psychotherapy.* New York: Grune & Stratton, 1963.

Jackson, D. D. Family interaction, family homeostasis, and some implications for conjoint family therapy. In J. Masserman (Ed.), *Individual and familial dynamics.* New York: Grune & Stratton, 1959.

Jacobson, N. S., & Margolin, G. *Marital therapy: Strategies based on social learning and behavioral exchange principles.* New York: Brunner/Mazel, 1979.

Kuhn, T. S. *The structure of scientific revolutions.* Chicago: University of Chicago Press, 1962.

Sager, C. J. The treatment of married couples. In S. Arieti (Ed.), *American handbook of psychiatry* (Vol. 3). New York: Basic Books, 1966.

B. L. CARLTON

Marital Types. The grouping of marital systems on the basis of their similarities. Since systemic theory about marriage is relatively new, a number of typologies have been suggested but none has been widely accepted (Sager, 1976; Lederer & Jackson, 1968; Glick & Kessler, 1980; Kramer, 1980). The most extensively elaborated and most helpful typology is that of Sager.

Sager proposes 48 possible marital types, each based on the combination of two of seven identified individual behavioral profiles. Each profile is based on the observations of individual responses in 12 areas of needs and expectations (e.g., independence-dependence, active-passive, closeness-distance). The seven individual profiles are the equal, romantic, parental, childlike, rational, companionate, and parallel partners.

Basic Behavioral Profiles. The equal partner seeks a relationship in which both partners have the same rights, privileges, and obligations. The equal partner is independent and self-activating; capable of close, sustained intimacy midway between submissive and dominant; and disowns possession of, or being possessed by, the spouse.

Romantic partners finds the elements and symbols of love paramount in the relationship. Security and fulfillment come in the presence of the beloved, and the need for assurances of being loved are insatiable. The romantic wishes to be the sole object of adoration and support, is dependent, seeks emotional closeness, fears abandonment to the extent that it determines behavior, is possessive and controlling.

The parental partner is a controlling parent who enjoys caretaking and governing. A specific and frequently found subtype is the rescuer, who enjoys saving the helpless child-spouse. The parental partner tends to appear independent as long as the spouse remains dependent. This partner is active, needs to use power to dominate, is competitive, is afraid of the loss of the mate, and needs to possess and control the mate.

The childlike partner desires to be cared for and protected. While this partner may appear to be the helpless slave, often he or she is the wielder of immense power. The "save me" partner is a subtype who seeks a parental ("rescuer") partner. The childlike partner tends to be dependent and passive, appears to submit but may use the power of helplessness to dominate, is motivated strongly by fears of abandonment, and submits to being controlled and possessed.

The rational partner seeks a logical and well-ordered relationship. Duties and responsibilities are primary concerns. The rational partner may appear to have little emotion, but in crisis can express it freely. The rational partner is pragmatic, down-to-earth, loyal, appears powerful and in charge, and is active in practical matters. This type of person is also usually quite dependent, although he or she hides this through immersion in the practical administration of the relationship.

The companionate partner acts to ward off aloneness. Thoughtfulness and kindness, not necessarily love, are adequate for a satisfying relationship. These persons want someone with whom to share life and see marriage as a realistic arrangement between adults. The companionate partner tends to mix dependence and independence, be more active than passive, avoid extremes of closeness and distance, and use power but not to extremes.

The parallel partner seeks to avoid intimacy and desires a spouse who respects emotional distance and independence. He or she wants all the advantages of marriage, without emotional intimacy. Usually parallel partners fear loss of integrity and being controlled, appear cool and guarded, though charming. Their behavior is often a reaction formation to great dependency needs that cannot be admitted. Hence they appear independent, are active, distant, in charge of self and life, show no fear of abandonment, have no desire to possess or be possessed as long as rules for distance are observed.

Partnership Combinations. These seven partner profiles combine to make 48 partnership combinations, each of which has a characteristic style. The most gratifying and durable relationship is the one in which both spouses accept each other as they currently are and where some compatibility of styles exists. The following more frequently encountered styles describe both the normal and the mildly to moderately pathological marriages.

The equal-equal combination, though idealized by many, is achieved by few. It is the most difficult to maintain, since the spouses stay together "because they want to be together, not because either is afraid not to be" (Sager, 1976, p. 137). No outside forces such as social institutions or children keep them together. Often partners have differing ideas of what is equality, and considerable discussion is required before agreement is reached. The American cultural heritage regarding gender roles and economic differences makes the achievement of this combination difficult, although beginning in the 1960s it has been idealized as the best marriage style.

The equal-romantic combination often makes for a good relationship. The equal partner usually respects the individuality of the romantic in his or her desire for closeness, communication, and dependence. When the romantic can recognize the equal partner's need for distance, a quid pro quo balance is struck. Problems arise when one is unwilling to accept the other's needs and begins to demand changes.

The equal-rational partnership often emerges out of an equal-equal combination where one spouse's anxiety leads toward stronger rational attempts to control the relationship in order to reduce the anxiety. The equal partner soon responds negatively, and a confusing struggle may follow. The combination may be fairly stable because the rational mate is often trying to be an equal partner.

The romantic-romantic combination is the best combination for the romantic partner. The early stages of this relationship are marked by passion, openness, intimacy, and pervasive interdependence. The inevitable reduction of this intensity is often regarded as the loss of love, bringing a crisis in the relationship. The spouse most aware of the change may seek a new romantic partnership in an affair, which may devastate the other, unsuspecting partner. The element of needing the partner to bring completion to oneself is an essential element in this combination. The couple electing not to have children often is of this type.

The romantic-rational combination often does not work well because the romantic partner feels the rational partner is not close enough, too logical, and does not express feelings. Where a childlike parental subtheme exists, the relationship may be stable, though not without tension.

The parental-childlike combination is the most frequently found and most enduring combination for both these partners. The parental partner desires someone to whom he or she can feel superior; the childlike partner seeks a powerful protecter and caretaker. The parental partner stance may mask the more severe pathology that becomes apparent when the childlike partner ceases to function as the needy, helpless one. Successful therapeutic alteration of this combination depends on significant motivation in both partners. Attempting to alter the system when only one partner expresses a desire to change may lead to rapid decompensation by the other spouse. The rescuer–save-me partnership, a specific subtype of the parental-childlike combination, is frequently found in marriages where substance abuse is involved.

The childlike-childlike combination is found in a relationship characterized by fun and play, with little concern for responsibility. Usually it is only a matter of time before each partner experiences frustration over not being able to get the other to function as a parent. If they are able to each accept some parental roles toward the other, a complementary relationship can be successfully maintained.

The rational partner often seeks a spouse who will supply the emotion and spontaneity of which he or she is afraid. A romantic or childlike partner often is chosen; sometimes an equal or companionate partner works out well. The romantic seeks and expresses great emotions and the childlike partner has fun and free play. The rational partner may appreciate both as long as little pressure is exerted for change.

The companionate-companionate combination is the most common and satisfying for the companionate partner. The contract is to respect and take care of each other. Kindness and consideration are expected, but not love. Since the combination is often found among older adults, "living in the past, rather than for the present or future, is often the most destructive element of companionate interactions" (Sager,

1976, p. 159)—e.g., competing over who is more loved by the grandchildren.

The large number of partner combinations possible in this typology suggests clearly the rich diversity of marital systems that can be fulfilling, satisfying, and problematic for spouses. The variety of partner profiles and partner combinations is consistent with a biblical view of the uniqueness and differences of each person. The application of a Christian ethic of love requires that this diversity be taken seriously so that the partners' differences can be respected while a meaningful marital relationship is worked out. Sager's view that a combination is more workable when spouses can accept the basics of their own and their spouse's profile is consistent with a biblical view of self-love and other-love (Matt. 22:37, 39).

References

Glick, I. D., & Kessler, D. R. *Marital and family therapy* (2nd ed.). New York: Grune & Stratton, 1980.
Kramer, C. H. *Becoming a family therapist*. New York: Human Science Press, 1980.
Lederer, W. J., & Jackson, D. D. *The mirages of marriage*. New York: Norton, 1968.
Sager, C. J. *Marriage contracts and couple therapy*. New York: Brunner/Mazel, 1976.

A. D. COMPAAN

See MARITAL CONTRACT THERAPY; FAMILY TYPES.

Marriage Preparation. *See* PREMARITAL COUNSELING.

Maslow, Abraham Harold (1908–1970). Influential humanistic psychologist, founder of the American Association for Humanistic Psychology, known now as the Association for Humanistic Psychology. Maslow obtained the Ph.D. degree at the University of Wisconsin, was departmental chairman at Brandeis University, and in 1967 served as president of the American Psychological Association. He authored some 150 publications over a 38-year period of productivity, culminating in his final work, *The Farther Reaches of Human Nature* (1971).

Maslow sought a theory of human nature beyond the interpretation of psychoanalysis and behaviorism. In 1961 he founded, with Anthony Sutich, the *Journal of Humanistic Psychology*. The humanistic movement within psychology was termed *third force psychology*, and following the lead provided by Maslow has been concerned with such topics as love, creativity, self-actualization, meaning, responsibility, and values.

Maslow's perspective has been variously described as holistic-integrative (Bischof,

1964), holistic-dynamic (Hall & Lindzey, 1978), organismic (Misiak & Sexton, 1966), and self-actualization theory (Cofer & Appley, 1964). His classical article, "A Theory of Human Motivation" (1943), was subsequently reprinted in 22 works by other authors. A complete bibliography of Maslow's works is contained in Appendix E of *The Farther Reaches of Human Nature.*

Basic Theories. Maslow claims his motivational theory fuses the functional tradition of James and Dewey with the holism of Wertheimer, Goldstein, and Gestalt psychology, as well as the dynamism of Freud, Fromm, Horney, Reich, Jung, and Adler (Maslow, 1970, p. 35). He believes there are seven broad classes of basic, instinctual needs, hierarchically arranged in that a person proceeds up the ladder to higher needs once lower needs have been met. At the bottom of the hierarchy are the physiological needs, homeostatic in nature (e.g., hunger and thirst). Next come safety needs, concerned with security, safety, protection, freedom from fear and chaos, as well as the need for structure, order, and law. Next come belongingness and love needs, followed by the esteem needs, the requirement of achievement, confidence, independence, recognition. This is followed by the need for self-actualization and the desire to know and understand. Finally, at the top of the hierarchy, are found the aesthetic needs, the craving to experience beauty (Maslow, 1970).

Convinced that human values can be found within human nature with no need to appeal to external sources, Maslow concluded that a study of supposedly fully actualized people would provide direction for those less self-actualized. He therefore compiled a list of such individuals and studied their character traits. Maslow believed that the negative criterion of self-actualization was the absence of neurosis, psychopathic personality, psychosis, or strong tendencies in those directions, and the positive criterion was the full utilization of talents, capacities, and potentialities (Maslow, 1970).

Analysis of the group of self-actualized people identified by these criteria yielded such characteristics as more efficient perception of reality; acceptance of self and others; having a mission in life; autonomy and independence of cultural thinking; aesthetic appreciation of people and of nature; compassion for and empathy with mankind; strong moral and ethical convictions; creativeness, originality, inventiveness; and frequent enjoyment of PEAK EXPERIENCES. In a later work Maslow (1971) distinguished between two kinds of self-actualizers: transcendent and nontranscendent. Nontranscendent actualizers are pragmatically oriented, whereas transcendent actualizers have higher, mystical, contemplative insights.

In contrasting healthy with unhealthy growth Maslow used the terms *Being-cognition* and *Deficiency-cognition,* and the correlative concepts of B-love and D-love. In B-love, characteristic of self-actualizing people, there are qualities of openness and nondefensiveness, fusion of sex and love, care and responsibility, greater perceptiveness of the one loved, and a nonpossessive, unselfish admiration of the one loved. Peak experiences, common with self-actualizing people, include aesthetic, creative, love, insight, and mystic experiences (Maslow, 1968).

A test of Maslow's self-actualization concept has been devised (Shostrom, 1963), and his theory has been applied to education theory, industrial management, and social reform (Goble, 1970). Maslow himself envisioned a psychological utopia in which all basic human needs would be met, a Taoist, loving society which he called *Eupsychia* (Maslow, 1970).

Critique. From a Christian perspective Maslow's views of human nature, needs, and motivation suffer from several limitations. First, his philosophical position is that of atheistic, naturalistic humanism. Maslow rejects any source of information concerning human purpose that lies outside human endeavor. He dismisses divine revelation, stating that the scientist pays "as little attention" to theological norms as to any other (Maslow, 1970, p. 267). He believes human nature to be intrinsically good, invariably and spontaneously directed to the good, that evil results from the frustration of this nature, and that such frustration is largely due to society (Maslow, 1968).

Maslow overlooks the question of why supposedly good people who make up society frustrate others. He wrestles with the question of whether destructive and evil behavior is instinctual, concluding that we just do not know enough, or the research data is insufficient, to reach a conclusion (1970). For the Christian these difficulties are resolved through divine revelation, wherein the origin of evil is explained as consequent to humankind's rebellion against God (Hammes, 1978).

Maslow's rejection of fallen human nature leads him to believe there is no opposition between head and heart, reason and instinct; the rule to follow is, "Be healthy and then you may trust your impulses" (1970, p. 179). The Christian, to the contrary, recognizes the struggle between the tendency toward good and the inclination toward evil, a continuing battle between the law of the spirit and the law of the flesh (Rom. 7:14–25), a contest that can be won not through natural means but rather through the supernatural strength of life in Christ.

This difference in perception is related also to self-actualization. Maslow endorses growth on the natural plane, whereas the Christian recognizes self-actualization to be necessary and even more important on the supernatural level. For the Christian self-actualization means to become more Christlike, to the point of proclaiming that no longer he, but rather Christ lives in him (Gal. 2:20; 3:27). The concept of love, too, is given greater depth and dimension in Christian thinking, going beyond Maslow's admirable treatise on the natural level to the supernatural height of loving to the point of death and loving one's enemies as well (John 15:13; Matt. 5:44; Luke 6:27–28).

A further contrast lies in the treatment of man's basic needs. To Maslow's seven the Christian would add an eighth, the need for a personal Absolute, the source and embodiment of ultimate truth, beauty, and goodness, in whose image human beings were made, and whom they must eventually love if they are to attain complete and perfect self-actualization.

These observations do not demean Maslow, who has carried naturalistic humanism as far as it can be developed, but rather show that Christian humanism more adequately presents the human condition and its solution. Only through him who is the way, the truth, and the life (John 14:6), as well as the light of the world (John 8:12; 9:5), can humankind attain its perfection on earth and its eternal destiny hereafter.

References

Bischof, L. J. *Interpreting personality theories.* New York: Harper & Row, 1964.

Cofer, C. N., & Appley, M. H. *Motivation: Theory and research.* New York: Wiley, 1964.

Goble, F. G. *The third force.* New York: Grossman, 1970.

Hall, C. S., & Lindzey, G. *Theories of personality* (3rd ed.). New York: Wiley, 1978.

Hammes, J. A. *Human destiny: Exploring today's value systems.* Huntington, Ind.: Our Sunday Visitor, 1978.

Maslow, A. H. A theory of human motivation. *Psychological Review,* 1943, *50,* 370–396.

Maslow, A. H. *Toward a psychology of being* (2nd ed.). Princeton: Van Nostrand, 1968.

Maslow, A. H. *Motivation and personality* (2nd ed.). New York: Harper & Row, 1970.

Maslow, A. H. *The farther reaches of human nature.* New York: Viking, 1971.

Misiak, H., & Sexton, V. S. *History of psychology.* New York: Grune & Stratton, 1966.

Shostrom, E. L. *Personal Orientation Inventory.* San Diego: Educational & Industrial Testing Service, 1963.

J. A. HAMMES

See HUMANISTIC PSYCHOLOGY; TRANSPERSONAL PSYCHOLOGY; SELF-ACTUALIZATION.

Masochism. *See* SEXUAL MASOCHISM.

Mass Evangelism. The use of communications media to convey the gospel of Jesus Christ to large numbers of people in efforts to persuade them to become Christians. The media include television, radio, movies, and newspapers. Mass evangelism is comparatively indiscriminate in its targeting, although selective viewing and the advent of public television have resulted in some narrowing of the audience.

Although there have been some positive results from the use of mass communications, the failure of the church to understand the strengths and weaknesses of these approaches often results in haphazard evangelism strategy that is costly and relatively ineffective.

In general, mass communication rarely brings about major attitude change (Klapper, 1967). People are most likely to expose themselves to presentations with which they agree and to avoid those messages that challenge their beliefs. This is especially true for those attitudes that are central to a person's identity and are expressive of his or her fundamental values. Changing a central belief has change repercussions throughout a person's belief system. Such changes create uncertainty and anxiety until the implications of a new set of core beliefs can be perceived and worked through in the self-image, decisions, and behaviors of the person. As a result, people usually ignore, distort, or forget messages that threaten a centrally important belief.

The implications of this for mass evangelism are significant. The likelihood that those who are uninterested in Christianity, for whatever reason, will choose to be exposed to evangelistic messages is minimal. Second, the probability of causing a major change in the core values of the viewer is small. Those who are not antagonistic to Christianity in general but do not wish to respond positively to appeals for fundamental change will tend to avoid evangelistic programs that are highly persuasion oriented. If their lack of response is due to ego-defensive reasons, some research suggests a boomerang effect may occur in response to persuasive attempts (Katz, 1960). If a communicator is unaware of the recipient's attitudinal base, he may unwittingly stimulate resistance to subsequent presentation of the gospel. Further, the fact that emotional arousal is normally crucial for radical change to occur militates against mass conversions. These factors suggest that the format and content of mass evangelistic appeals need to include channels of persuasion beyond the purely cognitive, and that the content needs to be focused primarily toward those who are interested in Christianity and open to the possibility of change.

The increased use of music and drama as means of connection with the emotional roots of religious belief increases the likelihood that viewers will listen and the possibility that conversion will occur among the interested. The development of content designed to identify with the life context of typical viewers who are interested in Christianity and showing how commitment to Christianity helps meet their needs would be more effective than appeals for change that are abstract and theological. Since mass communication is relatively unsuccessful in effecting a major change in the unsaved person's attitudinal core, it would be better to direct the bulk of mass communication efforts to building bridges of relevancy and aiming toward modification of existing attitudes. Such modification would "soften" a person's attitude for future conversion.

This is not to say that people cannot be converted through mass evangelistic appeals. However, awareness of the fact that spiritual decision making is a process (Engel, 1975) and that those most likely to be saved normally have at least a positive attitude toward the gospel is important for effective programming strategy. Regarding those who are more neutral or uninterested in Christianity, attitude modification and exposure to basic, positive aspects of the Judeo-Christian faith should be the goal.

In cultures where the masses are relatively unaware of the basics of Christianity and have no opinion about it, research suggests that mass communication can be used successfully to bring about radical conversions. This is due to the fact that mass communication has been found to be highly effective in creating attitudes about topics on which a person had no previous opinion (Klapper, 1967). Although the potential for foreign missions may be significant, the actual response of a person to persuasion attempts will depend upon his felt need, the extent to which the message addresses that need, whether the change required is seen as antagonistic to other cultural mores, and whether the mode of communication connects with the person's primary channel of receptivity (abstract vs. concrete thinking; emotions vs. cognition; aural vs. visual). While making

certain that biblical principles are not compromised, missionaries should make every effort to adapt the message of Christ to those values and beliefs that are prevalent in a particular culture.

The fact that mass communication serves as an agent of reinforcement for the attitudes, opinions, and behavioral tendencies that viewers already possess further suggests an important role for mass communications in evangelism follow-up. Programs designed to identify with and nurture the spiritual development of new believers could be highly effective.

References

Engel, J. F. World evangelization: A myth, a dream, or a reality? *Spectrum*, 1975, *1*, 4–6.
Katz, D. The functional approach to the study of attitudes. *Public Opinion Quarterly*, 1960, *24*, 163–204.
Klapper, J. T. Mass communication, attitude stability, and change. In C. W. Sherif & M. Sherif (Eds.), *Attitude, ego-involvement, and change*. New York: Wiley, 1967.

C. W. ELLISON

Masturbation. Also called autoeroticism, masturbation is any type of self-stimulation that produces erotic arousal. As such, it is a sexual behavior that is frequently discussed (with opinions ranging from unqualified condemnation to total acceptance as a gift from God) and universally practiced from infancy through senescence (Oraker, 1980). Further, masturbation is probably the most successful way of developing one's own sexuality. Still, it would be fair to say that masturbation is clouded by controversy and much emotional concern.

Under certain circumstances masturbation should clearly be considered a maladaptive behavior. In some forms of psychosis, mental retardation, and childhood disorders, for example, masturbation can become a stereotyped part of a behavioral repertoire which is self-destructive in that it leads to extreme withdrawal. For less disturbed individuals it can become obsessive (preoccupation with sexual fantasies), compulsive (one's masturbatory habits become highly ritualized), or guilt-producing (fear that one has violated a standard of behavior). Such psychological consequences can be deeply disturbing on a personal level. For others, masturbation can become a problem when it is utilized as the sole method of sexual outlet when other outlets are readily available (i.e., a marital partner). Still others argue that suppression of the natural tendency to masturbate is far more likely to lead to an emotional or sexual problem (McCary, 1978).

The history of professional and popular

opinion about masturbation has been one of ignorance, pseudoscience, and hysteria. The most frequently cited arguments against masturbation are: 1) only the immature person masturbates; 2) it is condemned in Scripture; 3) masturbation is unsocial or antisocial; 4) it violates the divinely intended purpose of sex; 5) it causes fatigue and physical debilitation; 6) it is a manifestation of low self-control; 7) the fantasies associated with masturbation are emotionally unhealthy; 8) it is sexually frustrating and not as satisfying as sex relations with a marital partner; 9) it is an indication of selfishness; and 10) it leads to undesirable feelings (guilt, anxiety, fear, depression, etc.). These arguments have been developed and carefully critiqued in Johnson (1982) and McCary (1978). All are deficient, most being oversimplified or completely false.

Some of the most interesting literature on masturbation concerns its usage as a way to learn about one's own sexuality (Bird & Bird, 1976; Kaplan, 1974). Persons who, because of a lifetime of sexual taboos and restrictions, are not able to respond freely to sexual stimulation are encouraged to explore and experiment with their own bodies to uncover their full sensitivity. This will, it is hoped, lead to clearer communication and increased arousal, responsiveness, and satisfaction in the marital relationship. For those not married yet intending to marry, such self-exploration can help develop their own sensitivities and awareness, and ease the often difficult transition into the shared intimacies of the marital relationship. For many people such acceptance of masturbation is often slow to develop. Although there may be an intellectual understanding that autoeroticism is acceptable, they may continue to feel that it is somehow unacceptable.

Moral concern about masturbation ought to focus on its role in the person's total development toward a more wholesome heterosexual life (Smedes, 1976). Adolescence and the transition into adulthood, in particular, are highly significant stages in personal development, especially for the coalescence of personal integrity and the consolidation of sexual identity (Kennedy, 1977). Masturbation may contribute to the transition from narcissism to relationships with others in a mature, egalitarian, and intimate manner.

For this reason Kennedy (1977) argues that sensitive counseling is extremely significant; overgeneralized advice or ill-conceived stands for or against masturbation may not foster development in the long run. Further, since the Bible says nothing directly about masturbation, it is difficult to take a dogmatic stand (Johnson, 1982). However, since masturbation is usually a solitary activity, it would be seen by many to fall short of the sexual expression intended by God. The Bible has a high view of sexuality as part of a relationship, and excessive masturbation could certainly distract one from the wholeness of relationships.

Masturbation must therefore be seen within the developmental context of the person's drive toward intimate communion, where one has the other person's interest and fulfillment in mind. Counselors must be prepared to respond to persons across the life span who share conflicts, misgivings, or uncertainties associated with masturbation. In order to do this effectively, the counselor must clarify and work through his or her own feelings about personal sexuality, including masturbation, and respond with understanding and compassion. A calm ability to let persons investigate their conflicts and their own shame and anxiety is extremely healing for persons of whatever age or situation. In short, the greatest service that can be done for the person who struggles with concerns about masturbation is to listen without embarrassment or the need to judge. Such a response can help these persons rebuild their self-esteem and propel them into more meaningful and satisfying interpersonal relationships. The counselor should model the assurance of God's grace, confident that it is total and unconditional.

References

Bird, J., & Bird, L. *Sexual loving: The experience of love.* Garden City, N.Y.: Doubleday, 1976.
Johnson, J. R. Towards a biblical approach to masturbation. *Journal of Psychology and Theology.* 1982, *10* (2), 137–146.
Kaplan, H. S. *The new sex therapy.* New York: Brunner/Mazel, 1974.
Kennedy, E. *Sexual counseling.* New York: Seabury, 1977.
McCary, J. L. *McCary's human sexuality* (3rd ed.). New York: Van Nostrand, 1978.
Oraker, J. R. *Almost grown.* San Francisco: Harper & Row, 1980.
Smedes, L. *Sex for Christians.* Grand Rapids: Eerdmans, 1976.

R. E. Butman

See Sexuality.

Mate Choice. The choice of a spouse has become a matter of extreme importance to young adults. With soaring divorce rates and broken families now common, the possibility of marrying the wrong person creates anxiety, well founded or not, among those contemplating marriage.

The terms *mating* and *mating behavior* are often used for the sexual rituals of animals, and one may find some literature on human behavior in which mate selection refers to the choice of casual sexual partners. But most literature and research on mate choice among humans has to do with how and why persons select particular partners for marriage and the enduring commitment traditionally expected.

Cultural differences are striking. It is well known to anthropologists and to Western missionaries in other cultures that many mates are chosen not by one another but by their families. In some Eastern societies it is done traditionally by parents; it is possible that bride and groom never even meet one another before the marriage ceremony. In these arranged marriages there is often bargaining over what each party shall take (Windemiller, 1976). Marriage brokers may be used—professional matchmakers who know the histories of families, what spouse characteristics are most important, and what is likely to bring the best exchange (bride price, groom price, or dowry). Taking into account these cultural differences, it is less difficult to understand mate choice in biblical narratives (e.g., the story of Jacob, Rachel, and Laban in Gen. 29).

Some Amish living in the United States also reflect a very different mate choice pattern from that of their surrounding society. Dating activities common to most Americans are forbidden (movie going, dancing, even athletics), as are drinking and automobiles. Mates may choose each other only from within the Amish community and only with parental permission. Change in mate selection becomes more apparent in most ethnic groups. For example, first generation Italians coming to America experienced only arranged or tightly controlled courtship, mate choice, and marriage. In the second generation young adults began choosing their own mates, with parental approval. Third generation young, while still close and proud of their heritage, have adopted American courting patterns, including selection of non-Italian mates (Kephart, 1981).

In some religious groups only God is to select marriage partners. Anxiety is generated among adolescents who hear that "God has one special person for you." The testimonies of Christian couples regarding their stable marriages may heighten this anxiety: "We know that God made us for one another" may be honest in retrospect, but for those facing mate choice there may be no such confidence. Even if there were scriptural support for divine selection of specific mates, pastoral problems with the teaching are immense. Many marriageable persons do not know how to be sure, nor is there adequate help in the process of discovering the divine choice. They conclude, understandably, that it would be a grave mistake or sin to marry anyone not designated by God. Another problem arises when parents insist that one person is the mate of divine choice, while the daughter or son insists that it is another.

In a society where the partners choose one another, courtship is the process; it may include dating, going steady, and engagement. "Falling in love" is usually the basis for selecting a mate. Falling in love is difficult to define, though there are stages of romantic attraction. While it may have tremendous immediate emotional force, the state of being madly in love seldom endures. It also may produce anxieties at the time of mate choice ("Is this *real* love, or just a feeling? I have fallen in love so many times, how will I ever know whom to marry?").

Where choice is most free and love is the criterion, one might expect random mating—anyone selecting anyone. But in fact falling in love respects limits (Kephart, 1981; Windemiller, 1976). The field of eligibles does not include members of one's immediate family. People tend to marry in their own age range. While interracial marriages are increasing, they are a small minority; we tend to marry persons of the same race. Religion is a selective factor; Catholic and Jewish intermarriage rates are increasing, but there is still substantial opposition in both groups. Protestants intermarry more. Social class (including such factors as intelligence, occupation, income, and education) is very important; most persons marry within their own social class. Geographical propinquity is also highly significant: "The 'one-and-only' may have better than a 50–50 chance of living within walking distance!" (Kephart, 1981, p. 241).

There is a variety of theories about factors in mate choice. Genetic and cultural factors may interact from generation to generation, as Eckland (1968) points out. He divides theories of mate choice into individualistic (Jung's unconscious archetype; parent image of psychoanalysis: like attracts like; complementary needs) and sociocultural (including such factors as propinquity and values).

Winch (1958, 1967) is largely responsible for the popular theory that needs interact in mate selection. Do likes or opposites attract? As noted above, falling in love takes place between persons who are alike in social and cultural ways. Winch urges a concept of "complementary needs": each person, in choosing a mate, seeks one who may best meet his or her needs. Pairs of needs such as dominance-submissiveness and nurturance-receptivity are some of those on which spouses may differ but be complementary. It is not so much that opposites attract, but that different needs make it possible for individuals to complete one another in the intimacy of marriage (*see* MARITAL TYPES).

One final theory of mate choice grows out of the British approach known as OBJECT RELATIONS THEORY and is most fully presented by Dicks (1967). Dicks argues that while mate choice often appears to be based in need complementarity, a deeper dynamic is to unconsciously choose a mate and relate to that person on the basis of the relationship between unconscious introjected representations of parents. According to this view, love is the response of recognition of someone who will serve as a good container for the person's projections and who therefore affords the possibility of working through unresolved unconscious conflicts. Because the mate is chosen as a symbol for a lost part of one's own personality, when this part is recognized in another person it leads to attraction. However, these same initially attractive qualities often later become the source of irritation as they represent, and tend to resurrect, parts of self that are frightening or for some other reason unacceptable. This rather complex theory emphasizes unconscious factors in mate choice but does not eliminate conscious factors suggested by other theories.

References

Dicks, H. V. *Marital tensions*. New York: Basic Books, 1967.
Eckland, B. K. Theories of mate selection. *Eugenics Quarterly*, 1968, *15* (2), 71–84.
Kephart, W. M. *The family, society, and the individual* (5th ed.). Boston: Houghton Mifflin, 1981.
Winch, R. F. *Mate selection: A study of complementary needs*. New York: Harper & Row, 1958
Winch, R. F. Another look at the theory of complementary needs in mate selection. *Journal of Marriage and the Family*, 1967, *29*, 756–762.
Windemiller, D. *Sexuality, pairing, and family forms*. Cambridge, Mass.: Winthrop Publishers, 1976.

H. KLINGBERG, JR.

Maternal Deprivation. Absent or impaired maternal functioning toward an infant between birth and 2 years of age. It may be due to absence of the mother or to attenuation of her mothering functions and skills, and may be continuous or intermittent. Attenuation of mothering skill may result from the mother's own illness or problems or from interference by circumstances or by other family members. On occasion maternal deprivation may be due to the inability of the infant to accept the available mothering, because of either inborn perceptual motor impairment or inborn impairment of the capacity to respond to the mothering. The child may contribute to the problem by failing to meet maternal expectations, hence evoking less response from the mother or inviting less spontaneity or initiative otherwise appropriate to normal mothering.

The realization that mothering is essential to infantile thriving, growth, and development, or even survival, is not new. *The Anglo-Saxon Chronicle* (A.D. 891–924) set forth an account of how Emperor Frederick's curiosity led to an experiment. Upon his command a group of newborns were isolated from human speech in an attempt to see what language they would use spontaneously. Getting wet nurses to perform the difficult task of remaining mute while they cared for human newborns was accomplished. The criteria for the experiment were thus met. However, the emperor's curiosity was never satisfied because all the children died.

A similar phenomenon was reported by Spitz (1945), a pioneer in psychoanalytic developmental psychology. He described a syndrome observed in foundling children that he dubbed "hospitalism." Infants who had been weaned at approximately 4 months of age were separated from their mothers, kept in sanitary cribs with the sides draped with sheets to avoid drafts, fed and changed by nurses, and visited daily by doctors; but they saw no one else and were cut off from toys. Within a month the infants became and remained unresponsive and withdrawn. They lost curiosity and showed a progressive decline in intelligence. The drop was from an average IQ level of 100 at the onset of isolation to 76 one year later, to 46 two years later.

Behavior manifested by these children ranged from extreme anxiety and bizarre stereotyped movements to apathy or even profound stupor. Their play was largely limited to their own fingers and toes. Their physical development was remarkably retarded, as were locomotion and speech. Moreover, despite daily medical and appropriate nursing care, death occurred in about one-fourth of the foundling children. This is in contrast to the record of no deaths in a parallel nursery group with mothers present, and less than ½% in the community at large (Spitz, 1945). In the parallel nursery mothers spent a great deal of time with their children (in contrast with one nurse per eight foundling children). They cuddled, played with, and talked to their babies. The nursery children's developmental quotients rose rather than fell as they grew older. Another syndrome was also described by Spitz (1946). Infants who had been especially close to their mothers and were abruptly cut off from them between the sixth and eighth month reacted to their mothers' departures by becoming weepy and then withdrawn, lying in their cribs with averted faces and refusing to take part in the life of their surroundings. If the mother did not return or was not replaced after about three months, frozen rigidity of expression replaced the weepiness and withdrawal. The children so affected were also much more susceptible to infection. Spitz called this latter syndrome anaclitic depression. Since not all the children developed the syndrome, Spitz deemed maternal separation to be a necessary, but not sufficient, cause for its development.

Some children are judged to be less vulnerable to the syndrome or more readily able to accept substitute mothering from another person. Spitz also noticed degrees of severity of the syndrome or degrees of vulnerability to separation depression. Anaclitic depression was seen as analogous to the trauma of loss of a love object in an adult. However, it is much more severe since it impinges upon an incompletely developed ego.

Spitz concluded that the child under one year of age receives his capacity to appreciate both inanimate and animate objects and their differentiation from each other through the intervention of his mother's face, voice, and touch, as well as through her use of play objects. While the foundling children were isolated from almost all visual experiences through solitary confinement in their cribs, Spitz did not judge the critical deprivation to be general perceptual stimulation. Rather, he believed that they suffered because their perceptual world was emptied of human partners (Spitz, 1945).

Opinions of contemporary researchers on this topic provide a consensus that different children react differently to otherwise comparable maternal deprivation experiences (Rutter, 1980). Furthermore, it appears that the consequences of deprivation are sometimes reversible, depending on the extent of damage and the extent of resistance the child was able to muster to the stress (Bronfenbrenner, 1979; Ainsworth, 1962).

References

Ainsworth, M. D. The effects of maternal deprivation: A review of findings and controversy in the context of a research strategy. In *Deprivation of maternal care: A reassessment of its effects* (WHO Public Health Papers No. 14) Geneva: World Health Organization, 1962.
Bronfenbrenner, U. *The ecology of human development*, Cambridge: Harvard University Press, 1979.
Rutter, M. Maternal deprivation, 1972–1978: New findings, new concepts, new approaches. In S. Chess & A. Thomas (Eds.), *Annual progress in child psychiatry and child development*. New York: Brunner/Mazel, 1980.
Spitz, R. A. Hospitalism: An inquiry into the genesis of a psychiatric condition in early childhood. *Psychoanalytic study of the Child*, 1945, 1, 153–172.
Spitz, R. A. Hospitalism: A follow-up report on investigation described in volume 1, 1945. *Psychoanalytic study of the Child*, 1946, 2, 113–117.

E. A. Loomis, Jr.

See Mothering.

Mathematical Psychology. The use of mathematical methods to investigate psychological problems. It is not defined in terms of content, such as learning, perception, or motivation. Rather, it is characterized by a style of investigation. This style is not uniform; mathematical psychologists use a variety of methods to investigate different content areas.

The use of mathematical methods dates back to the middle of the nineteenth century, to the work of Fechner, who looked for the mathematical relation between the mind and the body. During the first half of the twentieth century mathematical methods were used in the measurement of intelligence by Spearman, in the representation of learning by Hull, and in social psychology by Lewin. However, it was not until the 1950s that many individuals became involved. In 1963 Luce, Bush, and Galanter edited the *Handbook of Mathematical Psychology*. The *Journal of Mathematical Psychology* began publication in 1964.

The use of mathematics involves selecting a phenomenon to observe, finding a mathematical system to represent it, and establishing the relationship between the two. Some models are algebraic, others are geometric, and still others are probabilistic. Some are stated as computer programs, others as systems of equations, and others in axiomatic form. The advantage of using mathematics is that it increases our precision and deductive power. Theories can be stated in a form that is both general and precise. Theorists are forced to state all their assumptions explicitly and derive the consequences of their assumptions logically.

Nearly every area of psychology has been touched by mathematics, but some have been more affected than others. The areas of psychological measurement and scaling are obviously affected by mathematics, as are many learning theories which are often stated as mathematical models. Theories of sensory processes have been formulated in terms of signal detection theory and cognitive theories are often stated in terms of information processing, both models also strongly reflecting mathematical influence.

R. L. Koteskey

Maturity. *See* Healthy Personality.

May, Rollo Reese (1909–). Born in Ada, Ohio, May spent his formative years in Marine City, Michigan. In 1930 he received the A.B. degree from Oberlin College.

As a youth May developed a strong interest in art. After college he went to Eastern Europe with a group of artists, where he painted scenes of country life and simple people. He spent three years in Europe traveling and teaching at the American College at Salonika, Greece. During this time he became acquainted with Alfred Adler and his work. He greatly admired Adler, but later felt that he was guilty of oversimplification in his theorization.

When he returned to the United States in 1934, May served as a student adviser at Michigan State College. In 1936 he enrolled at Union Theological Seminary in New York, and in 1938 he graduated with the B.D. degree. His goal was to seek answers to the questions of human life, not to become a preacher (Harris, 1969). At Union, May was exposed for the first time to existential thought through the influence of Paul Tillich, and was especially impressed with the thinking of Kierkegaard and Heidegger. He became acquainted at this time with Kurt Goldstein, whose theoretical understanding of self-actualization and anxiety were especially important to him. May was later able to use Goldstein's neurological work as supporting data for his own psychological and philosophical insights.

In the year he graduated from seminary, May married and began pastoring a congregation in Montclair, New Jersey. During the summers of 1937 and 1938 he delivered lectures on counseling and personality adjustment to Methodist student workers. In 1939 those lectures, in expanded form, were published as *The Art of Counseling*. The next year May linked his view of the healthy personality to his general liberal perspective on Christian beliefs. The book in which this linkage appeared, *The*

Springs of Creative Living: A Study of Human Nature and God, became one of May's least favorite, and he has not allowed it to reappear (Reeves, 1977). In *The Art of Counseling* he defined religion as "a basic attitude as man confronts his existence" rather than as sectarian dogma (p. 217). "This broad approach to creative or healthy personality development as inalienable from affirmation of meaning and purpose in life as a whole . . . remains characteristic of May's work as a whole. In *The Springs of Creative Living* . . . May seems to assure a close link between such affirmation and the Judeo-Christian God (even proposing a conception of Christ as 'therapist for humanity' and of religion as 'the stream of meaning')" (Reeves, 1977, p. 255).

During 1943–44 May worked as a counselor at the College of the City of New York and studied psychoanalysis at the William Alanson White Institute of Psychiatry, Psychoanalysis, and Psychology. In 1946 he began a private practice in psychotherapy. He became a member of the faculty of the White Institute in 1948 and a fellow in 1952. He completed his doctoral degree at Columbia University in 1949, the school's first Ph.D. in clinical psychology. His dissertation was on anxiety, and the following year he published it as *The Meaning of Anxiety*. May followed Kierkegaard in seeing anxiety as the threat of becoming nothing. In 1953 he published *Man's Search for Himself*, which seems to have been part of his continuing attempt to clarify for himself the quest for maturity in personality and self-realization.

May taught at the New School of Social Research in New York between 1955 and 1960. In 1958 he co-edited *Existence: A New Dimension in Psychiatry and Psychology* with Ernest Angel and Henri F. Ellenberger. In 1959 he became a training analyst at the White Institute and an adjunct professor of psychology in the Graduate School of New York University. *Symbolism in Religion and Literature* (1960) and *Existential Psychology* (1961) both appeared under his editorship during the next two years. His next two books, *Psychology and the Human Dilemma* and *Existential Psychotherapy*, both appeared in 1967. These were followed by *Dreams and Symbols* (co-authored with Leopold Caligor) in 1968, *Love and Will* (1969), and *Power and Innocence* (1972).

While May sees himself as a neo-Freudian of the interpersonal school, he believes that people cannot be understood fully without consideration of the nature of persons. Intellectually he has made a significant impact on both the fine arts and the liberal arts. He has worked with existential ideas apart from their applications in European psychiatry, and can thus be seen as having developed his own approaches to existential psychology. In this he has helped to support basic spiritual considerations somewhat lacking in contemporary American psychological thinking.

References

Harris, T. G. The devil and Rollo May, *Psychology Today*. August 1969, pp. 13–16.
May, R. *The art of counseling*. Nashville: Cokesbury, 1939.
Reeves, C. *The psychology of Rollo May*. San Francisco: Jossey-Bass, 1977.

E. S. GIBBS

See EXISTENTIAL PSYCHOLOGY AND PSYCHOTHERAPY.

McDougall, William (1871–1938). Pioneer in the instinctivist approach to behavior. Born in Lancashire, England, he entered the University of Manchester at the age of 15 and graduated with honors in 1890. He then studied physiology, anatomy, and anthropology for four years at Cambridge, graduating with highest honors. He received a scholarship for medical studies at St. Thomas Hospital in London, and got his degree in medicine because he believed it was a desirable part of a thorough education.

To further broaden his basis for the study of man, McDougall joined the Cambridge Anthropological Expedition to the Torres Straits. He then spent a year studying at Göttingen under G. E. Müller. When he returned to London in 1900, he taught experimental psychology at University College. From 1904 to 1920 he taught "mental philosophy" at Oxford, then moved to Harvard. His final move was to Duke University in 1927, where he was professor and chairman of the psychology department until his death.

McDougall developed what he called a HORMIC PSYCHOLOGY (from the Greek word meaning an "urge"). The basic proposition of this psychology is that all behavior is purposive or goal-seeking. Behind this striving to reach an end is an instinctive energy force striving for some sort of goal. McDougall developed various lists of instincts throughout his career and associated an emotion with each instinct. Any emotion could develop into a sentiment, an organization of feelings and attitudes that causes the person to react to an object.

McDougall wrote 24 books and well over a hundred articles. The most important of his books are *Introduction to Social Psychology* (1908), *Body and Mind* (1911), *The Group Mind* (1920), *Outline of Psychology* (1923), and *Outline of Abnormal Psychology* (1926). His *Introduction to Social Psychology* appeared in 23 editions and has been reprinted 30 times. He was the champion of many unpopular causes. He spoke of the soul and had an antimechanistic attitude when behaviorism was gaining strength. He supported psychic research and a teleological psychology, and attempted to prove the Lamarkian theory of inheritance of acquired characteristics. All these causes lost ground during his lifetime, but he did not give up on them.

R. L. KOTESKEY

Media Psychology. Communication of psychology to the public through involvement of mental health professionals in the electronic and print media. This is becoming increasingly popular and is a new and potentially powerful way to communicate. Television and radio networks have found this type of programming profitable and have sought to employ members of the various mental health professions to provide psychological expertise to their audiences. While the American Psychological Association formerly banned the provision of psychological services through such impersonal modes as public media (APA, 1971), the most recent statement of ethical principles (1981) defines such services as appropriate so long as the psychologist utilizes the most current relevant data and exercises the highest level of professional judgment. Services by means of public media must also meet the same recognized standards that exist for services provided in the context of a professional relationship.

With these revisions of the *Ethical Principles for Psychologists* media psychology was officially sanctioned, even though standards for its practice remained unclear and imprecise. However, a growing number of psychologists have recognized the importance of utilizing public media, a practice which has come to represent not only a significant extension of the provision of psychological services but also a corrective to the long-standing problem of a lack of public understanding of what psychology is and has to offer. Many feel that this may be the major benefit of the involvement of psychologists in the media.

The first steps toward an organization of psychologists involved in the media occurred in 1981 when a group of nearly two dozen psychologists met in Los Angeles to share their concerns. This was followed by a meeting in San Diego in February 1982, when the Association for Media Psychology was formed. In April 1983 the American Psychological Association established an Ethics Task Force on Media, which was charged with the responsibility to review the current practice of psychologists in media by systematically monitoring such programs, to develop a casebook of critical incidents in media psychology, to develop specific guidelines for media psychologists, and to recommend changes in the *Ethical Principles for Psychologists* if these seem necessary. These actions are viewed by most psychologists as an important step in the regulation of a fast-growing field of applied psychology which has tremendous potential but which needs to be protected by maintaining high standards of professionalism.

References

American Psychological Association. *Ethical principles for psychologists.* Washington, D.C.: Author, 1971.
American Psychological Association. *Ethical principles for psychologists* (Rev. ed.). Washington, D.C.: Author, 1981.
L. McCauley

Medical Model of Psychopathology. *See* Mental Illness, Models of.

Medical Psychology. *See* Health Psychology.

Meditation. This practice can include a variety of efforts to produce an altered state of consciousness. Meditation has become very popular in recent years in the Western world with the introduction of Eastern meditative practices such as Zen Buddhism, yoga, and similar disciplines. The reason for this increased interest in meditation has been the growing search in our fast-paced society for peace, spiritual truth, and an expanded awareness.

While there are many Eastern meditative techniques, all seem to share the common view that human beings live their lives at a low level of conscious experience, and that true enlightenment and peace will only come as conscious experience is elevated. A variety of techniques can be used to accomplish this end, including sensory deprivation, biofeedback, and hallucinogenic drugs, but the technique preferred by many is some sort of meditative exercise. All these techniques seek to suppress or alter ordinary sensory experience. Ornstein (1977) describes meditation as a technique for "turning down the brilliance of the day, so that ever-present and subtle sources of energy can be perceived within" (p. 159). It constitutes a deliberate attempt to inhibit the usual mode of consciousness and to cultivate an alternate mode.

The exact methods in such mind-altering meditation can involve a wide variety of practices, including bizarre dancing, gazing at an object, focusing on one's breathing, or concentrating on a meaningless phrase. The knowledge gained in such meditation is intuitive and experiential rather than rational. The experience is ineffable—i.e., defies being put into words—and is often called the mystic experience.

Transcendental Meditation. A clearer picture of meditation can be gained by examining more closely one particular type: Transcendental Meditation. TM, as it is popularly abbreviated, is a commercialized form of meditation taught in the United States by Maharishi Mahesh Yogi. It is also called the Science of Creative Intelligence. Transcendental Meditation became popular in the United States in the 1970s when the Maharishi discovered that Americans would seek to learn his techniques if they were taught devoid of spiritual and religious ideas.

In Transcendental Meditation a mantra, or a sound repeated continuously, is used to increase a person's deep relaxation and refined specialized awareness. The Maharishi's theory behind the choice of a mantra for a person is that each person meditates best with a sound that fits the vibrations that constitute his personality. After a mantra is chosen, the recommended steps in meditation include: 1) sit quietly in a comfortable position; 2) close the eyes; 3) relax all the body's muscles; 4) concentrate on the act of breathing or on the mantra and banish all other thinking; 5) practice these steps twice daily.

Meditators practicing these steps report feelings of peace, well-being, and a deep sense of relaxation. The person is both highly wakeful and relaxed. Experienced transcendental meditators learn to experience a loss of sense of self and a union with things around them. Objects begin to feel as if they are a part of the meditator rather than "out there." It is this oneness experience that is the ultimate goal of the meditation experience. Psychotherapists who use meditation in therapy seek to produce these same results in their clients. They hope that regular meditation will bring a calming peace to the one troubled emotionally, and that the oneness feeling will allow people to better understand and relate to self, others, and the world around them.

The mind-altering experiences in this type of meditation seem to relate to the sensory reduction practices used. With the eyes closed and attention focused on a mantra, the meditator seeks to decrease the amount of incoming sensory information. Eastern meditators have argued that the human brain as a sensory reducer screens out valuable information about the greater realities of the universe. According to this view, what a person eventually experiences is only a fractional part of the total picture of reality, and a misleading picture at that. According to the Eastern meditator's world view, which is panpsychism (all things are one mind or force), the ordinary person has an erroneous experience of physical reality and personal identity. The person who does not meditate, they feel, is not in touch with the greater reality of the immaterial essence of the universe and a nonpersonal identification with all things. The meditative techniques of closing the eyes and narrowing concentration (and experience) to a single sound or feeling serve to allow the greater nonpersonal, nonrational reality to be experienced.

Physiological Research. In a study of the physiological changes during meditation it was found that heart rate slows, respiration is reduced, less oxygen is consumed, and the meditator's brain waves show a marked increase in alpha frequencies (Wallace & Bensen, 1972). These bodily changes are the opposite of what occurs in the body when a person is subjected to stress. Therefore, it is possible that meditative techniques such as Transcendental Meditation can be a useful means of dealing with the stresses of modern life. The brain-wave changes in meditation are also similar to what occurs in the technique of biofeedback, which is also used to ease some of the symptoms of stress. In biofeedback the person learns to control brain waves and autonomic responses because he receives feedback on these states; therefore, it seems likely that the experienced meditator is learning to tune in to his internal bodily states and brain waves in order to control them.

Somewhat countering the claims of Eastern meditators, it has been demonstrated that the physical benefits of meditation are similar no matter what is used for a mantra. It may be that meditation produces an innate relaxation response in the body, a response that counters the body's autonomic stress response. Doubts about this form of meditation being a unique state of consciousness also surfaced when Pagano, Rose, Stivers, and Warrenburg (1976) found that electroencephalograph readings differed from one day to the next. Other research has countered the spiritual enlightenment claims of Eastern meditation by showing that the meditative state is more similar to a resting state than a unique state of consciousness (Michaels, Huber, & McCann, 1976). It was found that the biochemical states of meditators are highly similar to control data from subjects who merely rested. Therefore, it may be summarized that Eastern forms of meditation may produce a sense of peace and relaxation, if practiced regularly, but there is little evidence to support claims for spiritual enlightenment.

Christian Meditation. Meditation can also be practiced as a part of the Christian life of worship, but it is only remotely similar to Eastern meditation. Christian mystics, most of whom regularly experienced meditative states, have adorned church history down to current times, including Augustine, Theresa, Francis of Assisi, George Fox, John Wesley, and Brother Lawrence.

These Christian mystics well understood that human life is meant to be a personal relationship with a personal God, and that Christ is the only way into spiritual knowledge and life. The meditative experience in this context is the act of listening to God, communing with him, and experiencing a love relationship with him. When Christians have a blissful, peaceful experience in the act of meditation, they are not experiencing a cosmic consciousness so much as they are learning to shut out the chatter of a noisy world that can interfere with focusing attention on God. This is not to say that the mystic is more Christian than one who has not had this experience. All Christians experience a relationship with God to a greater or lesser degree and are, therefore, mystical. The differences in the depth of that experience are probably related more to psychological temperament and God's calling than to a person's degree of commitment to God.

The Christian mystic may indeed practice some of the same techniques as the Eastern mystic in order to further his closeness to God. These techniques could involve fasting or focusing one's attention on an attribute of God or a Bible verse. However, the experience gained from these meditative exercises is not the central facet of Christian meditation.

The Eastern meditator seeks to shatter the feelings of self and personhood and to merge with the cosmic consciousness of the universe. The Christian meditator, on the other hand, sees his personhood as a creation of God and not an erroneous experience. A Christian seeks to lose not self, but self-centeredness. The Christian meditator's goal is not to annihilate human nature but to master it with Christ's help.

The Eastern mystic seeks to become one

with the universe because all of the universe is god. The Christian understands that God is a person and humans have become estranged from him. The Christian seeks to draw closer to God while in this life on earth through meditative worship.

The Eastern mystic seeks to become detached from the world and shuns both its pleasures and its evils. In Eastern mysticism there is a longing to be released from the burdens and pains of this life, and to enter into the effortless, blissful state of nirvana. The Christian meditator may also shun some of the pleasures of life and will certainly shun its sins, but for a different reason. The Eastern mystic uses virtue as a tool to achieve a higher cosmic consciousness. The Christian, knowing that unconfessed sins estrange us from both God and man, has as a goal to live in obedience to God. The Christian believes that a practical asceticism may aid in withdrawing from the confusion of life that often dampens the contemplation of spiritual matters. Christians may detach themselves from some of the things of this life, but only as a method of redirecting life toward a richer attachment to God and to other human beings. Therefore, the insights gained in Christian meditation ought to be practical. Christian meditators seek to clear their minds and meditate as a communion with God. Christian meditation, therefore, represents an expansion of the human personality toward the experience of a relationship with God for which they were created.

References

Michaels, R. R., Huber, M. J., & McCann, D. S. Evaluation of transcendental meditation as a method of reducing stress. *Science*, 1976, *192* (4245), 1242–1244.

Ornstein, R. E. *The psychology of consciousness (2nd ed.).* New York: Harcourt Brace Jovanovich, 1977.

Pagano, R. R., Rose, R. M., Stivers, R. M., & Warrenburg, S. Sleep during transcendental meditation. *Science*, 1976, *191* (4224), 308–309.

Wallace, R., & Bensen, H. The physiology of meditation. *Scientific American*, 1972, *226* (2), 84–90.

Additional Readings

Campbell, C. The facts on transcendental meditation. *Psychology Today*, 1974, *7* (11), 37–46.

Foster, R. J. *Celebration of discipline.* San Francisco: Harper & Row, 1978.

McNamara, W. Psychology and the Christian mystical tradition. In C. T. Tart (Ed.), *Transpersonal psychologies.* New York: Harper & Row, 1975.

M. P. Cosgrove

Meehl, Paul Everett (1920–). American psychologist whose career has spanned a remarkable breadth of interests and accomplishments. Meehl completed his A.B. (1941) and Ph.D. (1945) degrees at the University of Minnesota and has spent his entire career at his alma

mater, rising through the ranks to become chairman of the Department of Psychology (1951–1958) and Regents' Professor of Psychology. He is also professor in the Medical School's Department of Psychiatry, in the Minnesota Center for the Philosophy of Science, and in the Department of Philosophy. He is a diplomate in Clinical Psychology (American Board of Examiners in Professional Psychology) and a fellow of the Institute for Advanced Study in Rational Psychotherapy. He is a member of a large number of professional and academic societies in psychology, science, philosophy, and law. In 1958 he received the award for Distinguished Scientific Contributions from the American Psychological Association.

Meehl has made significant contributions in a large number of professional areas. Early in his career he was very active in research in learning theory, co-authoring the influential text *Modern Learning Theory* (1954) along with many empirical and conceptual articles in this area. He was also active in research in psychological assessment, and had particular influence in the development and widespread acceptance of actuarial assessment, wherein test scores are interpreted by standard quantitative rules rather than by more subjective clinical judgment. These procedures eventually gave rise to the computerized interpretation of psychological tests. His writings in philosophy of science and the methodology of the social sciences in particular have contributed substantially to the discipline of psychology. He has continued to contribute numerous articles in the areas of psychoanalysis and of clinical psychology as a professional discipline. Most recently his major area of interest has been the development of new methodologies for the investigation of taxometrics (the assigning of objects to their most appropriate classes), particularly the accurate assignment of individuals into meaningful diagnostic categories.

Finally, Meehl, formerly a Lutheran layman, was an early contributor to the literature relating behavioral science and Christian faith. His co-authored *What, Then, Is Man?* (1958) has continued to be an important monograph. Unfortunately, he did not stay active in this area after the mid-1960s. Overall, Meehl's impact on the field of psychology has been broad, significant, and positive.

S. L. Jones

Megalomania. A type of Delusion in which an individual feels that he has great superiority. Common delusions include the belief that one is Christ, God, or Napoleon. The person may believe he is everything and everyone, omnipotent and omniscient. His ideations are called delusions of grandeur. The term *megalomania* may be misleading in that it implies a presence of mania, which is not the case in the delusion.

Megavitamin Therapy. *See* ORTHOMOLECULAR PSYCHIATRY.

Melancholia. *See* DEPRESSION: CLINICAL PICTURE AND CLASSIFICATION.

Memory. The scientific investigation of memory began with the work of Ebbinghaus. Lists containing meaningless combinations of alphabetical letters, called nonsense syllables, were learned to two perfect recitations and then relearned after various periods of time. Ebbinghaus, assuming that the number of trials to relearn a list was inversely related to memory strength, concluded that a dramatic loss of memory occurred during the first nine hours after original learning, with only minor losses thereafter (Ebbinghaus, 1913).

Studies over several decades have since shown that the shape of Ebbinghaus's retention curve (i.e., dramatic loss followed by stabilization) cannot always be generalized to other types of memorized material or other memory assessment techniques. For example, Bahrick, Bahrick, and Wittingler (1975) have shown that there is a progressive decline over a 50-year period in subjects' ability to recall the names of individuals in their graduating high school class, while a surprisingly small loss over most of that time period occurs in name and picture recognition. Erderlyi and Kleinbard (1978) have demonstrated the heterogeneous nature of the memory curve even more dramatically. They show that under certain circumstances memory content actually increases over time, a phenomenon termed *hypermnesia*. In short, memory strength over time is now known to depend substantially upon the prevailing circumstances.

Theories of Memory. The bulk of the research on memory, as in most other areas of psychological study, has been conducted within the context of some theoretical framework. Interference theory is one such theoretical viewpoint that has enjoyed popularity over much of the history of memory research. This theory contends that we forget because other information learned earlier or later interferes with what is presently known. The key experimental support for this view stems from two phenomena called retroactive inhibition and proactive inhibition.

Retroactive inhibition occurs when future learning interferes with present memory. For example, Briggs (1957) followed the learning of a first list of material by a variable number of trials of second list learning. As the number of second list trials increased, subjects became less able to recall the first list. That is, the second list retrospectively interfered with the recall of the first. Proactive inhibition involves the interference of present memory by information learned in the past. It is studied by having subjects learn successive lists of words. When the percentage of correct recall of later lists is less than that of earlier lists, proactive inhibition is felt to be present in that earlier learned material is assumed to have interfered with the learning of subsequent material.

In the last decade interference theory has fallen into disfavor among many psychologists. Replacing it has been information processing theory. According to this view the brain is a kind of computer that encodes information, stores it, and retrieves it when needed at a future date. A great deal of research in each of these three areas—encoding, storage, and retrieval—has taken place.

Encoding. Encoding refers to the act of transforming external stimuli, such as objects, words, or events, into internal information. Suppose you were asked to remember the word "apple" so that, when asked tomorrow, you could repeat it. There are many different attributes of the word "apple" that might be encoded. These could include such things as the physical properties of the letters comprising the word, the acoustical characteristics of the word, and various attributes that you personally ascribe to the word to make it meaningful, such as the color red, a sweet taste, the autumn season, your mother's homemade pies, etc.

In general psychologists are currently attempting to discern not only the various ways that external stimuli are encoded but also how different types of encoding influence our ability to remember these stimuli. A series of studies by Wickens (1972) illustrates one method used to study encoding and also provides a good example of the interdependency between interference theory and information processing theory that sometimes emerges. A word was displayed for half a second, followed by a retention interval of 11 seconds. During the retention interval subjects were engaged in a distractor task such as counting backward. After this interval subjects were asked to recall the word just displayed. Using this procedure Wickens consecutively presented three different words followed by a fourth with some salient feature changed. For example, three nouns printed in capital letters might be followed by a noun printed in small letters. Wickens noted a systematic decline in subjects' ability to remember an item for 11 seconds across the first, second, and third items, with memory rebounding substantially for the fourth item. Wickens called this rebound in memory "release from proactive inhibition." Apparently, providing a new way to encode the fourth word kept the earlier three items, all encoded identically with respect to each other but differently with respect to the fourth item, from proactively interfering during the recall of the fourth item. By examining the characteristics of words that resulted in a release from proactive inhibition, Wickens contributed greatly to our understanding of the various types of encoding that humans use.

Storage. When considering how humans store information, one question of long-standing debate concerns the permanence of memory. Clearly no one remembers everything, but is that because the information was not stored or because it cannot be retrieved? The essential problem is that a neurological correlate to what happens when an event is encoded has not yet been discovered. Until such a physiological correlate is located and examined over time, whether or not memory is permanent will likely remain an open question. Nonetheless, some interesting studies have been conducted that may provide clues to the answer.

While operating on epileptic patients under a local anesthetic, the Canadian neurosurgeon Penfield (1955) meticulously described his observations when the cortex of the brain was probed with a weak electrical current. Stimulations of the temporal lobes sometimes resulted in the vivid recall of past events, including the auditory, visual, and somatic sensations that accompanied those events. This observation would suggest that events are stored in the brain in a fashion analogous to a tape recording. Other investigators, however, have challenged Penfield's findings (e.g., see Barbizet, 1970).

Another interesting phenomenon that supports but does not prove the permanence of memory is that of hypnotic age regression. Here a subject is transported back in time while under hypnosis and asked to recall life events of that time period. There is a great deal of evidence suggesting that sometimes past occurrences that cannot be remembered in the normal waking state can be recalled with astounding accuracy under hypnosis. Schafer and Rubio (1978) describe how police officials have successfully used hypnotic age regression to gain critical information from witnesses and victims that was apparently unavailable to them otherwise.

Numerous models have been proposed to account for how information is stored. Two general types have received a great deal of attention. The first views the process of memory as involving essentially three distinct systems: sensory memory, short-term memory, and long-term memory. Information is passed from one type of storage to the next. Although there are many variations, perhaps the best-established version is that offered by Atkinson and Shiffrin (1968). The second model, termed the levels-of-processing model, holds that there is essentially one process behind what others see as two distinct memory stores, short-term and long-term. How well an event is remembered, according to this view, depends on how "deeply" it is processed. The strongest proponents of this theory have been Craik and Lockhart (1972).

Atkinson and Shiffrin (1968) postulated that information first enters a sensory register composed of several types of memories, each corresponding to a given sensory modality. Thus visual information enters "iconic memory," auditory information enters "echoic memory," and so forth for taste, touch, and smell. The sensory store, as it is called, holds relatively large amounts of information for a very short period of time. Information turnover is very rapid, with only selective information passing on to the next level of memory (called short-term store). Sperling (1960) has demonstrated that in the case of iconic memory, an image lasts probably no more than one second and that humans actually can see more than they can report verbally. This latter finding is particularly supportive of the notion that sensory store selectively passes information on to short-term store, where it can then be verbalized.

Short-term store is often called *working memory*, while *long-term store*, as the term suggests, refers to information that remains retrievable over long periods of time. Since long-term store is passive and subconscious, it is in short-term store that the active, conscious manipulation of information occurs. The longer information is in short-term store—i.e., the longer we think about the information—

the greater the chance that it will be passed to long-term store. Further, information in long-term store must be brought back into short-term store before it can be consciously used. In other words, short-term store acts as a kind of clearinghouse for information.

Some of the most interesting support for the existence of a short-term store as a distinct entity is provided by the neuropsychologist Milner (1966). She has reported extensively on an epileptic patient, H. M., who had experienced surgery in a part of the brain known as the hippocampal region. H. M. appeared to have an intact long-term memory for events transpiring before surgery and also was able to function normally on short-term memory tasks after surgery. After the operation, however, H. M. could not remember new information for much over five minutes. Apparently the ability to transfer new information from short-term store to long-term store had been destroyed by the operation.

The precise way in which information is processed in short-term store is not understood, but it appears that rehearsal, the overt or covert repetition of information, is instrumental in transferring it to long-term store. It is important to distinguish between maintenance rehearsal and elaborative rehearsal. The former refers to an almost mindless repetition of information just to keep it from disappearing until it is used. An example of this is repeating a telephone number as we run between the rooms containing the phone book and the phone. It appears that maintenance rehearsal does little to transfer information into long-term store. On the other hand, elaborative rehearsal involves "doing something" with information, such as organizing it, associating it with something already known, or constructing a mental picture that involves the information. Elaborative rehearsal greatly aids subsequent recall, apparently by facilitating the transfer of information to and from long-term store.

In their effort to discover what happens during elaborative rehearsal psychologists have unveiled a large number of helpful memory strategies called mnemonic devices. By using these strategies subjects automatically carry out elaborative rather than maintenance rehearsal. For example, one good way (called the method of loci) to memorize a grocery list is to imagine different food items resting in various areas of your living room (e.g., a large egg sitting on the couch, the butter forming a greasy spot on the rug, etc.). Upon mentally examining your living room after arriving at the grocery store, recall of the items on the list will be surprisingly complete. The popular books *The Memory Book*, by Lorayne and Lucas (1974), and *The Mind of a Mnemonist* by Luria (1968), provide further discussion of mnemonic devices.

Craik and Lockhart (1972) originated the concept that, rather than passing between discrete structural components like long- and short-term store, information is processed in one basic manner but to different levels of depth. An experiment by Rogers, Kulper, and Kirker (1977) illustrates the concept. Subjects were required to evaluate 40 adjectives in one of four ways, each hypothesized to result in a different depth of processing. For example, structural processing merely required subjects to identify the size print used; phonemic processing required subjects to determine if each adjective rhymed with a given word; semantic processing required subjects to decide whether each adjective was synonymous with a given word; and self-reference processing, presumed to be the deepest level of processing, required subjects to decide whether the adjective described one of their own personality traits. As the level of processing increased, performance on a subsequent recall test of the 40 adjectives increased, with adjectives that were processed by self-reference showing a marked superiority over all other types of processing. Relating information to your own self appears to be one of the best ways to ensure that it is stored. This fact is quite useful even though there is considerable controversy over exactly how the storage mechanism operates.

Retrieval. There is widespread agreement that the presence of relevant cues greatly aids the retrieval of information from long-term store. This has been demonstrated by Tulving and Pearlstone (1966). Subjects were presented several category names, such as animal or fruit, and then asked to remember specific instances of each, such as horse, dog, or cat (in the case of the animal category). When cues, in this case category names, were provided, subjects could remember 50% more of the specific items than if no cues were provided. When subjects who attempted to recall specific items without cues were later given cues, almost invariably they were able to recall several additional items. Clearly those additional items were stored but not retrievable until appropriate cues were made available. Tulving has advanced the notion that to be effective a cue must be present at the time that information targeted to be remembered is first presented. Thus the word "dirty" is of little benefit in cueing the recall of the word "city" unless it has been linked with city on an earlier occasion. This principle has been termed *encoding specificity*.

Another principle of retrieval is that of *memory location activation*. Once an item in a given memory location has been retrieved, it is easier to recall in the time that immediately follows other items residing near that location. For example, if we search our memory to locate a state beginning with the letter M (like Minnesota), then immediately thereafter it will take less time to locate a second state that begins with, say, the letter I (like Illinois).

Several retrieval models have been theorized, with one of the best known being Collins and Quillian's (1970) network model. These researchers postulated that information is stored in a giant network with information interconnected by links. According to this scheme information is hierarchically organized into nests that are logically subordinate-superordinate to one another. Thus, animal is superordinate to (i.e., inclusive of) such items as bird, fish, and mammal, while each of these is superordinate to specific instances like canary and bluejay for bird, or shark and salmon for fish. A fundamental principle of this model, called cognitive economy, is that descriptive information lies at the highest possible superordinate level. Thus descriptions like "can eat," "can drink," and "can move" reside near the term animal because these describe all animals. Descriptions like "has fins," "can swim," or "has gills" lie near the term *fish* since they pertain to all fish. More specific descriptions like "is pink," "is edible," and "swims upstream to lay eggs" would reside near the term salmon because these are true neither of animals in general nor fish in general, but just of salmon.

In support of their model Collins and Quillian have shown that it takes less time to evaluate the truth of a statement like "a salmon is pink" than one like "a salmon has skin." The presumed reason is that "is pink" is located immediately adjacent to salmon but "has skin" is next to animal. A subject must locate salmon, must then move to the superordinate fish, and finally must move again to the superordinate animal to determine that, indeed, a salmon (which is a fish which is an animal) has skin like all other animals. Thus it takes from 150 to 180 msec longer to evaluate "a salmon has skin" than to evaluate "a salmon is pink."

Although the network model has an appealing simplicity, some researchers have not been able to experimentally verify the principle of cognitive economy (Conrad, 1972). To compensate for some of the shortcomings in the network model, several substantial modifications have since been suggested. Two other models resulting from these considerations, both too complex to describe in this brief space, are the set-theoretical model proposed by Meyer (1970) and the feature-comparison model proposed by Smith, Shoben, and Rips (1974).

Christian Perspectives on Memory Research. Although Christians can almost always agree with the type of experiment carried out by memory researchers, some may question whether it is appropriate to adopt an information-processing framework that views a human being as a computer. It is important to note that for many psychologists this theoretical position merely provides a working assumption that greatly aids in the organization of research data and the formulation of a systematic research program. Viewing information-processing theory in this way, the Christian psychologist may employ the information-processing model and also hold the conviction that man, created in the image of God, is more than a computing machine. A conflict with Christianity emerges only when it is insisted that a person is "nothing but" a computer, an assertion seldom made even by secular psychologists. MacKay (1979) gives an excellent discussion of the biblical perspective on man as an information processor.

References

Atkinson, R. C., & Shiffrin, R. M. Human memory: A proposed system and its control processes. In K. W. Spence & J. T. Spence (Eds.), *The psychology of learning and motivation: Advances in research and theory* (Vol. 2). New York: Academic Press, 1968.

Bahrick, H. P., Bahrick, P. O., & Wittlinger, R. P. Fifty years of memory for names and faces: A cross-sectional approach. *Journal of Experimental Psychology: General*, 1975, *104*, 54–75.

Barbizet, J. *Human memory and its pathology*. San Francisco: W. H. Freeman, 1970.

Briggs, G. E. Retroactive inhibition as a function of the degree of original and interpolated learning. *Journal of Experimental Psychology*, 1957, *53*, 60–67.

Collins, A. M., & Quillian, M. R. Does category size affect categorization time? *Journal of Verbal Learning and Verbal Behavior*, 1970, *9*, 432–436.

Conrad, R. The developmental role of vocalizing in short-term memory. *Journal of Verbal Learning and Verbal Behavior*, 1972, *11*, 521–533.

Craik, F. I. M., & Lockhart, R. S. Levels of processing: A framework for memory research. *Journal of Verbal Learning and Verbal Behavior*, 1972, *11*, 671–684.

Ebbinghaus, H. [*Memory: A contribution to experimental psychology*] (H. A. Roger & C. E. Bussenius, trans.). New York: Teachers College, Columbia University, 1913.

Erdelyi, M. H., & Kleinbard, J. Has Ebbinghaus decayed

with time? The growth of recall (hypermnesia) over days. *Journal of Experimental Psychology: Human Learning and Memory*, 1978, *4*, 275–289.

Lorayne, H., & Lucas, J. *The memory book*. New York: Stein & Day, 1974.

Luria, A. R. *The mind of a mnemonist*. New York: Basic Books, 1968.

MacKay, D. *Human science and human dignity*. Downers Grove, Ill.: Inter-Varsity Press, 1979.

Meyer, D. E. On the representation and retrieval of stored semantic information. *Cognitive Psychology*, 1970, *1*, 242–300.

Milner, B. Amnesia following operation on temporal lobes. In C. W. M. Whitty & O. L. Zangwill (Eds.), *Amnesia*. New York: Appleton-Century-Crofts, 1966.

Penfield, W. The permanent record of the stream of consciousness. *Proceedings of the Fourteenth International Congress of Psychology, Montreal, June 1954*. Amsterdam: North-Holland Publishing, 1955.

Rogers, T. B., Kulper, N. A., & Kirker, W. S. Self-reference and the encoding of personal information. *Journal of Personality and Social Psychology*, 1977, *35*, 677–688.

Schafer, D. W., & Rubio, R. Hypnosis to aid the recall of witnesses. *The International Journal of Clinical and Experimental Hypnosis*, 1978, *26*, 81–91.

Smith, E. E., Shoben, E. J., & Rips, L. J. Structure and process in semantic memory: A featural model for semantic decisions. *Psychological Review*, 1974, *81*, 214–241.

Sperling, G. The information available in brief visual presentations. *Psychological Monographs*, 1960, *74*, 1–29.

Tulving, E., & Pearlstone, Z. Availability versus accessibility of information in memory for words. *Journal of Verbal Learning and Verbal Behavior*, 1966, *5*, 381–391.

Wickens, D. D. Characteristics of word encoding. In A. W. Melton & E. Martin (Eds.), *Coding processes in human memory*. Washington, D.C.: V. H. Winston, 1972.

J. L. ROGERS

Mental Age. An individual's mental age is an expression of the level of mental development. It is determined by comparing the individual's ability with the ability of others of the same age. The concept was first systematically developed by Binet, and is based on the assumption that intellectual ability can be measured and that it increases progressively with age.

See INTELLIGENCE; INTELLECTUAL ASSESSMENT.

Mental Disorders, Classification. See CLASSIFICATION OF MENTAL DISORDERS.

Mental Health. See HEALTHY PERSONALITY; PREVENTION OF PSYCHOLOGICAL DISORDERS; RELIGION AND PERSONALITY.

Mental Illness, Models of. Central to the concept of mental illness is the notion that behavioral disturbances are in some sense diseases. Although clearly no longer the sole model, the disease model remains the most widely accepted view of psychopathology. The difficulty one faces in attempting to refer to phenomena without using terms connoting illness reflects the pervasiveness of the disease/mental illness model.

The Medical Model. *Definition and development*. There is considerable conceptual ambiguity regarding the nature of the medical model. Blaney (1975) suggests that there are four variations of the medical model: 1) mental disorders are in fact diseases (i.e., they are physiologically based); 2) evidences of disorder are manifestations of an underlying condition (though it is not necessarily organic); 3) the individual has no responsibility for his behavior; 4) psychiatric symptoms can be best understood by ordering them into syndromes.

Historically, the view that mental disorders are diseases has been the most common view for about a century. From antiquity until the nineteenth century mental illness was viewed largely as a moral and religious issue. Persons with deviant behavior were considered to be malingerers or to be possessed by spirits. When the spirits were viewed as evil, exorcism and torture were used in an effort to remove their influence; alternatively, special favor was given when the spirits were viewed as benevolent.

Treatment of the mentally ill changed markedly during the period from the late eighteenth century through the time of Freud. The humanitarian reforms under Pinel, Tuke, and Dix resulted in modification of asylums. Greisinger and Morel advanced the disease hypothesis. John Gray, editor of the *American Journal of Insanity* from 1855 to 1885, gave impetus to the disease model by insisting that physical lesions produced insanity. Since he believed that physical disorders were at the root of mental illness, he led in the transformation of mental asylums to treatment facilities. During the same period the work of Charcot, Janet, Bernheim, and Freud led to a conceptual shift, and persons who had previously been considered malingerers were subsequently diagnosed as hysterics. Thus the disease model was extended to persons outside the institutional care setting.

Further credence was given to the disease model by the discovery that advanced syphilitic infection was the cause of general paresis, a psychotic disorder. This was first suggested in 1857; positive identification of syphilitic infection as the causative agent was provided in 1913.

Together these movements culminated in a major paradigm shift in which the disease notion replaced moral-religious explanations.

Implications for individual and society. Several ideas are integral parts of the disease model. The individual with the disorder, generally referred to as the patient, is sick. His sickness is manifested in a number of symptoms presumed to result from an underlying disease that was produced by a more or less specific cause, or etiology. Efforts to identify the etiology are termed *diagnosis*, and serve as a prerequisite to therapy or treatment. The illness is presumed to have a predictable course (or developmental history) and prognosis (or outcome).

Under this model research and treatment are medical specialties. A concept of mental "health" is needed to specify the goal for treatment and the standard against which abnormality is measured.

In the disease model the symptoms are seen as manifestations of the underlying problem, not the disorder per se. Thus concern arises regarding the possibility of symptom substitution when treatment is focused on symptoms rather than on the underlying problem producing the symptoms. Further, since symptoms may change or vanish without correcting the underlying disorder, evaluation of cure requires medical expertise. Since the individual is often unable to provide care for himself, providing care for the mentally ill becomes a social responsibility.

For the patient there are several implications. He is not responsible for his present condition; he becomes a passive recipient of treatment; he may receive special considerations such as financial support at the cost of the state; he can become free from legal responsibility for actions but may also lose legal rights, since he is presumed to be unable to control his own behavior (Szasz, 1961). Finally, the patient is not considered able to evaluate his own problem; failure to recognize the "illness" may be taken as evidence that the person is in even worse condition than previously thought. Further, the problem which the patient presents may not be viewed as the real problem.

Another implication of the medical or disease model is that research focuses on a search for physical pathology such as infections, genetic anomalies, endocrinological malfunctions, and the like. A radical discontinuity is assumed to exist between normal and disturbed processes; since the underlying causes were presumed to be different, research tended to focus exclusively on identified pathological cases rather than studying normally functioning persons.

Evaluation. The disease model has had considerable impact on the development of modern psychology and psychiatry, and it continues to be the most widespread model. It underlays the early versions of the American Psychiatric Association's *Diagnostic and Statistical Manual of Mental Disorders.* However the most recent version, DSM-III, recognizing some of the limitations of the medical model, is much more behavioral in its theoretical foundation.

Many mental disorders clearly fit the medical model. General paresis, many forms of mental retardation, and the organic brain syndromes are prime examples of disorders resulting from diseases, trauma, and the toxic effects of drugs and other substances. At the same time, many mental disorders so far have no known underlying disease process, and may better fit one of the alternative models described below.

A major problem in evaluating the medical or disease model stems from the complexities of doing research in this area and the consequent limits on available knowledge. Maher (1970) points out the diagnosis of mental disorders tends to be descriptive in nature, thus adding little information about etiology or prognosis of the disorders. Further, well-documented problems with reliability and validity of diagnostic categories frustrate the ongoing effort to link descriptive diagnoses with etiological factors (see Ullmann & Krasner, 1969, pp. 219ff.).

Some believe that the medical model made a major contribution to the elimination of earlier abusive and inhumane approaches to treatment of mentally ill persons. However, the role of the medical model in this development has been challenged; it appears that the moral treatment approach was actually responsible for this development, and the rise of the medical model was in some ways a backward step (Bockoven, 1963). A further criticism of the medical model involves its role in the development of the "not guilty by reason of insanity" plea and the movement away from responsibility and accountability for a variety of actions that transgress legal and moral standards (Szasz, 1961).

While some continue to hold out hope for further advances from the medical model, others have given up on it in favor of newer models which they believe hold more promise for explaining those disorders not already explained in terms of the medical model.

Alternative Models. A number of alternative models have been advanced to replace the medical model. Among the more prominent are the sociopsychological and the systems models.

Sociopsychological. Perhaps the most widely

accepted alternative models to the disease conceptualization are the various sociopsychological or behavioral models (for examples see Bandura, 1969; Ullmann & Krasner, 1969; Rimm & Masters, 1974). Where the medical model postulates qualitative differences between normal and disordered mental functioning, the sociopsychological model views the differences as degrees along a continuum. It is assumed that the same processes underlie behavior at all points along the continuum, and that there is no radical discontinuity between normal and disturbed behavior. The underlying mechanisms by which the various forms of behavior develop are the processes of learning and control of behavior. Problem behavior develops in the same manner as normal behavior and may be dealt with by applying the same principles. With such a view, illness concepts are not appropriate, the concept of symptom and underlying pathology are not meaningful, treatment is not a medical specialty, and ethical and value issues become central in determining the criteria for treatment.

The sociopsychological model suggests that diagnosis should focus on identifying the frequencies, topographies, and social or environmental controlling conditions of problem behaviors. It assumes that the individual typically recognizes the problem, actively seeks change, and may be an active participant in the treatment process. Since the behavior is lawful, the individual is expected to face any social consequences prescribed by society, and is neither accorded special status nor deprived of legal rights. The focus of research is on the principles governing acquisition, elimination, and control of behavior rather than on identification of disease processes. This model is based on the extensive body of psychological research gathered over the past 75 years dealing with learning, motivation, perception, social relations, and growth and development.

Systems. Another model of mental disorders locates the problem within family and social systems rather than in the individual. This is in contrast to both the disease and sociopsychological models. The implication of the systems model is to shift research, diagnosis, and treatment into a broader social context. Intervention tends to be at the system level rather than the personal level.

For example, many contemporary family therapists view parent-child problems as problems of the system (Gurman; Kniskern, 1981). Neither the parent nor the child are identified as patients who have the problem. Rather, the problem is seen as arising from the interaction that occurs between the parent and child, and may be significantly affected by interactions with other family members or circumstances as well.

Issues from a Christian Perspective. Since a Christian approach is particularly concerned with ethical and moral issues, the differences between a medical and a sociopsychological conceptualization of mental illness have profound implications for a Christian perspective. In a medical conceptualization the alcoholic, the depressive, the psychopathic, the retarded, and other disordered individuals are seen as victims of processes outside their control. If the problem is viewed as a behavioral disorder, the individual's personal responsibility for his present condition becomes an issue, with clear moral implications. In reality, the issues may be even more complex, since contemporary research increasingly shows that personal-social life style is a major factor contributing to the probability of contracting various physical diseases.

While articulate presentations which are sensitive to complex issues remain rare, the issues involved in choices among these models have not escaped notice of writers within Christian circles. At one extreme Adams (1970) emphatically proclaims that all problems either reflect organic disorder or sin. Others allow for more complexity, recognizing that sin and organic disorders are only two of many potential causes of psychological problems, others being response to existential issues, maladaptive use of defense mechanisms, demonic influence, and learning (Cosgrove & Mallory, 1977).

Briefly, it appears that all mental disorders—indeed all problems in our world—may ultimately be traced to the entry of sin into the world and the subsequent disruption of the created order (cf. Rom. 8:19–22). Thus, at one level it is accurate to say that the cause of psychological problems is sin; at another, however, viewing the problem as sin is too simplistic. The effects of sin are manifested in mental disorders on at least three different levels: 1) the effects of personal sin leading to guilt or anxiety; 2) the effects of sin in the world, resulting in various biological disorders such as genetic disorders, endocrinological malfunctions, disease, and trauma; 3) the effects of the sin of others, such as retardation due to neglect or abuse by a parent, and anxiety or depression following an assault. In addition, we see interactions among these factors, such as when a person's abuse of alcohol or drugs results in brain damage.

Conclusions. Ethical and moral issues have often been viewed as largely irrelevant within the medical model of mental illness. However, it is becoming increasingly clear that moral issues are unavoidable. While the medical model suggests that individuals should not be held responsible for their diseases, the increasing evidence that personal life style habits are a major factor in illness makes the issue of responsibility for disease more complex. Factors such as the extensive use of alcohol, tobacco, and drugs; diet; exercise; sleep patterns; and sexual promiscuity have been shown to contribute significantly to the probability of contracting disease. In addition, compliance with treatment has become an increasing source of professional concern and research. All of this suggests that the distinctions between medical and psychosocial viewpoints may not be as clear-cut as the foregoing discussion might imply.

Perhaps an analogy between the various effects of sin in psychopathology and the theoretical systems that have been described would be helpful. Sin in the world is most clearly reflected in the disease model, which focuses on the physical basis for disorders. The effects of personal sin, and to some extent the sins of others, seem consistent with the sociopsychological model. Finally, the systems model emphasizes phenomena that are most consistent with problems related to the sin of others.

The medical model has led to positive advances in some areas and created problems in others. However, the complexity and diversity of phenomena included in DSM-III require acknowledgment of multiple causal factors in mental disorders, and therefore the medical model is inadequate. A comprehensive system of mental functioning must include the following components: 1) biological factors, including genetic, anatomical, and biochemical causes and infectious diseases; 2) psychological factors, including personal, developmental, and family history, and relationships to others; 3) social factors such as societal and cultural norms and standards; 4) spiritual factors, including personal sin, ethical and moral responsibilities; relationship to God, and spiritual growth and development. At present it is doubtful that any existing system is able to encompass this diversity.

A medical or disease notion is essential to a full understanding of mental disorders, and further advances will likely be made through the medical approach. However, the medical model is not comprehensive enough to encompass all of the phenomena included under mental illness, and hence other models are required as well. Perhaps some form of synthetic model that brings together elements from several of the present models will emerge. Alternatively, a new system that is more comprehensive may eventually develop.

References

Adams, J. E. *Competent to counsel.* Philadelphia: Presbyterian and Reformed Publishing 1970.
Bandura, A. *Principles of behavior modification.* New York: Holt, Rinehart, & Winston, 1969.
Blaney, P. H. Implications of the medical model and its alternatives. *American Journal of Psychiatry, 1975, 132,* 911–914.
Bockoven, J. S. *Moral treatment in American psychiatry.* New York: Springer Publishing, 1963.
Cosgrove, M. P., & Mallory, J. D. *Mental health: A Christian approach.* Grand Rapids: Zondervan, 1977.
Gurman, A. S., & Kniskern, D. P. (Eds.). *Handbook of family therapy.* New York: Brunner/Mazel, 1981.
Maher, B. A. *Introduction to research in psychopathology.* New York: McGraw-Hill, 1970.
Rimm, D. C., & Masters, J. C. *Behavior therapy: Techniques and empirical findings.* New York: Academic Press, 1974.
Szasz, T. J. *The myth of mental illness.* New York: Hoeber-Harper, 1961.
Ullmann, L. P., & Krasner, L. *A psychological approach to abnormal behavior.* Englewood Cliffs, N.J.: Prentice-Hall, 1969.

R. K. Bufford

Mental Mechanism. *See* Defense Mechanisms.

Mental Retardation. This condition affects about 6.5 million people in the United States. As defined by the American Association on Mental Deficiency (Grossman, 1973), it involves significantly subaverage general intellectual functioning which exists concurrently with deficits in adaptive behavior. It is either present at birth or begins before the age of 18. The deficiency interferes with the person's ability to adjust to the demands of life and manifests itself in poor learning, inadequate social adjustment, and delayed achievement.

Assessment. Psychological assessment of intellectual functioning and a social assessment of adaptive behavior are both necessary when retardation is suspected. When an individual is low in one area but normal in the other, the conclusion would likely be that an emotional problem or specific brain damage accounts for the deficits. Both intelligence and adaptive behavior must be low for mental retardation to be diagnosed.

Psychological assessment. Normal intelligence is placed at an IQ of 100. Persons scoring below 70 IQ, two standard deviations below the mean, are considered to be mentally retarded. A person's score is obtained by administering a reliable test of intelligence and determining the mental age of the person. The mental age expresses the intellectual attainment of a person in terms of the average chronological age by which that attainment is usually present. By comparing the mental age with the chronological age, deficits or normality can be seen. Thus a 10-year-old child functioning at a 7-year-old level would be considered retarded. His IQ would be determined by dividing his mental age (7) by his chronological age (10) and multiplying by 100—an IQ of 70.

Psychological assessment can be done at any age. Below the age of 2 the Kuhlman-Binet test will assess developmental behaviors that occur at more or less specific ages. A normal newborn infant should give a startled response to a loud noise, carry the hand to the mouth, and respond to a light with eye movement. At the age of 1 a child should be able to stand, imitate sounds and movements, and make marks with a pencil. By 2 a child should be able to copy a circle, obey simple commands, and point out objects in a picture.

The Gesell Developmental Schedules and the Bayley Scales of Infant Development are the most common tests used for early childhood. These tests employ the same approach as the Kuhlman-Binet but can be applied up to the age of 6. Motor skills, adaptive skills, personal-social skills, and language skills are assessed. Again, all these skills are based on what the normal child at a particular age can perform.

Above the age of 6 tests focus more heavily on the verbal component of intelligence. The Stanford-Binet, Wechsler Preschool and Primary Scale of Intelligence, the Illinois Test of Psycholinguistic Abilities, and the revised Wechsler Intelligence Scale for Children are the most frequently used. If problems such as deafness, blindness, or the inability to use one's arms or hands exist, special tests are available. The Peabody Picture Vocabulary Test, the Columbia Mental Maturity Test, and the Leiter International Performance Scale were designed to allow for these handicaps. They allow pointing, are often untimed, and can be used in quite severe situations.

The assessment of brain damage may be done with the Reitan Battery or the Luria. The Bender-Gestalt and the Benton Visual Retention tests are the most commonly used as an initial screening of brain damage. The Bender-Gestalt requires an individual to reproduce several geometric figures. Noting the type of distortion or difficulty in drawing can indicate the presence of brain dysfunction.

The psychological evaluation must also include assessment of motivational, emotional, and interpersonal factors. The combination of intellectual ability and the emotional aspects will give a fairly clear picture of the person's capabilities and current functioning.

Social adaptiveness assessment. Adaptive behavior refers to how well an individual is able to cope with life expectations. Independent functioning, personal responsibility, and social responsibility are the three major facets of adaptive behavior. By assessing what behaviors a person is able to perform and by comparing these to what is developmentally and socially expected, a social maturity score is obtained. Retardation occurs when the person's score is at least two years below expectation. The Vineland Social Maturity Scale (Doll, 1965) is one of the most frequently used rating scales.

There are at least 12 adaptive behavior scales available. All attempt to determine the individual's ability to function appropriately for the given age. If the person is not able to behave appropriately, obvious difficulties can occur psychologically, socially, and personally.

Classification. Mental retardation may be classified according to the severity of the symptoms, by etiology, or according to the symptom constellation.

Prior to 1954 retardation was generally classified by severity of symptoms. Idiot, imbecile, and moron were used to denote abilities roughly equivalent to the IQ ranges of 0 to 30, 30 to 50, and 50 to 70, respectively. Since then these terms have been replaced with less offensive ones. Today classification by severity is based on the American Association of Mental Deficiency system (Grossman, 1973) of using the standard score obtained by the individual on a reliable test of intelligence. It assumes intelligence is distributed normally throughout the population and that an adequate intelligence test has been used. The terms applied to scores that are more than 2, 3, 4, and 5 standard deviations below the mean of 100 IQ are labeled mild, moderate, severe, and profound, respectively. They are roughly equivalent to an IQ rating of 55–69, 40–54, 25–39, and under 25.

An etiological classification looks for the factor causing retardation. Pathological conditions such as disease, injury, chromosomal aberration, or a discrete genetic disorder may be used to classify retardation. Whether the cause was exogenous or endogenous may be considered. Locating exogenous factors such as injury or infection, however, is sometimes as difficult as finding endogenous causes such as chromosome or genetic involvement.

Classification by symptom constellation uses syndromes that bear strong resemblance to one another. This is sometimes useful when the cause is elusive. For example, microcephaly, characterized by a small brain and skull, may be caused by heredity, environmental factors, or some unknown factor.

Whether an etiological or symptom cluster classification is used to describe the retardation, it is still the intellectual level that must be assessed to determine retardation. Therefore, classification by level of intellectual functioning is probably the preferred system, and this method is endorsed by both the American Association of Mental Deficiency and by the American Psychiatric Association (*DSM-III*).

Causes. There are three major causes of retardation: genetic and hereditary, physical, and psychosocial.

Genetic and hereditary. In some cases retardation can be directly traced to a chromosomal defect, to heredity, or to some other genetic deficiency. Each individual is born with 23 pairs of chromosomes, on which the physical build and appearance of the person is coded. Each parent provides 23 chromosomes. These match up at conception, and the parents' features are passed on to the children. Sometimes an extra chromosome is accidentally present. Other times there are dominant or recessive traits that are passed on to the child. Sometimes there are disorders in the way the body functions which develop from unknown genetic involvement but which suggest deficiencies in genetic makeup.

Down's syndrome, at one time called mongolism, occurs when an extra chromosome in the 21st pair is found. There is no known reason why this occurs, and either parent may contribute the extra chromosome. This common form of retardation is widely known and occurs about once for every 660 births. For women over 35 years of age the chance of giving birth to a child with Down's syndrome is considerably greater. A child with Down's syndrome may have slanting eyes and a tongue that seems big for the mouth. The head may be flattened in the back. The ears are small and sometimes the tops are folded a little. The nose is also flattened and wide. The child is often short. Children with Down's syndrome usually can do most things that any young child can do, such as walking, talking, dressing themselves, and being toilet trained. However, they do these things a little later than other children. Some Down's syndrome children are severely retarded, while others are less so. All are retarded to some degree. These children are often born with heart problems and a susceptibility to colds and pneumonia. While some Down's syndrome individuals can marry, most are too retarded to live alone responsibly and need someone to care for them. Most do not live beyond the age of 40.

There are four other chromosome defects that produce recognizable syndromes. The *cat-cry syndrome* results from a missing part of the fifth chromosome. Due to vocal chord abnormalities the infant gives a characteristic cat cry. Severe retardation and numerous other physical complications are present. *Trisomy 13*, occurring once in 5,000 births, refers to an extra chromosome in the 13th pair. It is characterized by low-set ears, cleft palate, cleft lip, sloping forehead, extra fingers, retardation, and often minor seizures. Of these children only 18% survive the first year; poor growth is evidenced. *Trisomy 18*, with an extra chromosome in pair 18, occurs about once in 3,000 births. Around 80% are females and only 10% survive the first year. Many die before birth. Low birth weight, incomplete development of skeletal muscle, cardiac defects, severe retardation, and numerous other abnormalities are seen. *Trisomy 22* is rare and is characterized by retardation, small head, slanted eyes, slow and delayed growth, and heart defects.

There are several syndromes related to abnormalities in the chromosomes determining the sex of the child. These chromosomes, called X and Y, produce a female when the pair is XX and a male when the pair is XY. If only one X occurs rather than a pair, a girl is born with *Turner's syndrome.* She is short of stature, has no sexual organs, and lacks sexual development. While 95 to 98% of the fetuses with Turner's syndrome fail to survive to birth, some girls may not be diagnosed until adolescence when the failure to develop sexually is noted. Mild retardation may be present, but more notable is a defect in space-form perception.

Klinefelter's syndrome is found in males when the sex chromosome consists of XXY. Retardation is not usually characteristic, although 25 to 50% of reported cases had subnormal intelligence. In some cases as many as five X chromosomes have been found with a Y. The male with more than two X chromosomes has a higher risk of significant mental retardation.

The XYY male appears to be prevalent in the "normal" population with only slight intellectual retardation noted. At one point it was thought that this chromosome combination was associated with criminality, since reports of numerous XYY men in prisons were published. Later studies failed to verify this, but some lowered language ability was found.

Many syndromes are inherited in simple Mendelian fashion. When one parent passes on a dominant gene to the child, the trait carried by the gene will always occur. Recessive traits require a similar gene from both parents before the trait occurs. While rare and isolated, several syndromes resulting in mental retardation have been associated with dominant and recessive genes.

Most dominant gene syndromes that lead to severe retardation produce death before birth. Four of the syndromes related to dominant gene transmission are tuberous sclerosis, neurofibromatosis, Sturge-Weber syndrome, and myotonic dystrophy.

Tuberous sclerosis is a disease manifested by severe mental retardation, seizures, and a peculiar skin condition characterized by butterfly-shaped reddish-yellow tumors, usually on the cheeks alongside the nose. These tumors are nonmalignant and later may be found in the brain or other organs of the body. They may not be observable, and the disease may not be recognized until the child develops seizures around age 3 or facial skin tumors around age 5.

Neurofibromatosis is a condition characterized by light brown patches on the skin, the color of milky coffee (café-au-lait spots), and by tumors on the nerves and in the skin. The tumors may be tiny or grotesque overgrowths. At least six such spots must be present before a diagnosis is made, since normal people may have one or a few spots. Mental retardation and epilepsy occur in about 10% of cases, possibly due to tumors in the brain.

Sturge-Weber syndrome displays a growth the color of port wine formed by blood vessels on the face, usually in the area of the trigeminal nerve on the cheek or forehead. Similar malformations of the blood vessels within the meninges covering of the brain can give rise to mental retardation and seizures.

Myotonic dystrophy affects the whole body. Cataracts, testicular atrophy, frontal baldness, muscle spasms, and muscle wasting are evident. Considerable behavioral abnormality is seen in adults, and retardation may be present. In most cases the child has received the dominant gene from the mother. This suggests that a combination of an abnormal gene and an abnormal prenatal environment is necessary for very early onset.

There are thousands of recessive genes, many of which are harmless, such as the one producing blue eyes. Others are serious, such as the one producing cystic fibrosis. Many recessive disorders that involve retardation produce specific metabolic deficiencies. Metabolism refers to the ability of the body to break down and use particular foods or release energy for use. Some of the more common metabolic disorders are discussed here according to the type of deficiency affected. Several non-metabolic disorders related to recessive genes will also be covered.

Disorders of protein and amino acid metabolism include the much researched *phenylketonuria* (PKU). PKU is the inability of the body to oxidize the amino acid phenylalanine to tyrosine. As a result untreated individuals are severely retarded, often unable to walk or talk. Beside being bedridden, PKU persons are often restless, jerky, and fearful. They may be shy, restless, and anxious, or destructive with noisy psychotic episodes, irritable, and have uncontrollable temper tantrums. In the last 50 years considerable research has demonstrated that most of the severe symptoms can be prevented with a diet that restricts phenylalanine. Prompt diagnosis is essential, including identifying the parent carrier and screening newborn infants. These methods have reduced the frequency of severe PKU effects. Dietary control can reverse all biochemical abnormalities, but structural defects and brain damage cannot be reversed. Early detection is a must in the control of PKU.

Menkes disease, or the *maple syrup disease*, refers to the inability to metabolize the amino acid leucine. The disease gets its name from the distinct maple syrup odor of the urine. Dietary control prevents many severe symptoms. If untreated, the disease is usually fatal by age 2.

Histidinemia is a block in the metabolism of histidine. Abnormal speech patterns or retardation in language development are seen. Dietary control is used. There is some question in the literature about the relationship of this deficiency to retardation.

Several other rare disorders of amino acid metabolism have been researched. In some cases dietary control has proven useful.

Disorders of carbohydrate metabolism, represented chiefly by galactosemia, involve the inability to break down sugars into usable parts. When lactose, the primary sugar in milk, is converted into glucose and galactose, the body must convert galactose into a glucose substance. If the child's body is unable to do this, life-threatening symptoms develop from a milk diet. Jaundice, vomiting, cataracts, malnutrition, and potentially fatal susceptibility to infection occur. Strict dietary control and prompt identification are necessary to prevent severe damage and death.

When the complex carbohydrate substances are not properly broken down, and the resultant mucopolysaccarides are stored, severe physical and mental retardation occurs. *Hurler syndrome* children are dwarfed, deaf, have clouded cornea, widely spaced teeth, short neck, a large and bulging head, and several internal problems with liver, spleen, and hernias. These children tend to be friendly and affectionate. *Hunter syndrome* is less severe but includes gargoyle appearance, stiff joints, dwarfing, and enlarged liver and spleen. These children are characteristically hyperactive and hard to manage.

Several disorders have been identified related to the inability of the body to metabolize complex fats and lipids. The most common of these disorders is *Tay-Sachs disease*, named after a British ophthalmologist, Tay, and an American neurologist, Sachs, who described cases of this disease in the 1880s. This recessive trait is frequent among Ashkenazic Jews, of whom 1 in 30 is a carrier. In all other groups 1 in 300 is a carrier. The presence of this disease can be detected with blood tests or amniocentesis. It usually begins insidiously by age 6 months, with listlessness, weakness, hypersensitivity to sounds, and visual difficulties developing. Blindness occurs and death is frequent by 3 years. A partial deficiency of the same enzyme has been reported with less severe effects.

A final recessive disorder is *microcephaly*, or a small head. The skull is unusually tiny. Severe retardation and blindness are prominent.

Physical. During the normal development of the individual from conception to maturation, interruptions may occur that result in retardation. These exogenous causes will be discussed according to when they occur —prenatal, perinatal, or postnatal.

The primary prenatal physical causes of retardation are infections and trauma. During the nine months of pregnancy the fetus develops from one cell to a fully functioning body with a brain and all organs in proper order. An interruption of this normal development affects the part of the body that is growing at the time. Most infections are prevented from reaching the fetus by the placenta. Rubella, or German measles, is the only acute infection commonly acquired during pregnancy that is not blocked by the placenta. This acute infection disrupts the normal development and results in severe damage and deformity. In one study of 153 children whose mothers contracted rubella during pregnancy, one half evidenced borderline to severe mental retardation. Deafness is the most common symptom, with blindness and heart defects also seen.

Trauma includes drugs; maternal undernutrition; radiation; Rh blood incompatibility; chronic maternal infections such as certain viruses, bacteria, and protozoa; and various disorders such as maternal anemia, high blood pressure, and diabetes. Treatment during pregnancy and at birth may reduce the severity of effects in many of these cases.

Perinatal problems, those occurring during the birth process, include prematurity, anoxemia, and direct injury to the head. Premature infants are those born weighing less than 5½ pounds. Babies weighing about 3 pounds at birth stand a greater chance of developing more slowly and evidencing lower intellectual abilities. Anoxemia, or oxygen deprivation, occurs when the placenta is blocked at birth or spontaneous breathing does not occur. In several studies with rhesus monkeys deprived of oxygen at birth, up to 7 minutes of deprivation had no noticeable effect on later functioning. Direct trauma to the head may arise from a quick birth through a narrow cervical opening. The breech birth or transverse birth may increase the possibility of suffocation. However, the physician is usually able to turn the baby properly. Evidence is scanty for mechanical damage to the head using forceps. It has been suggested that poorly adjusted mothers tend to blame the child's problems on the birth process rather than seeing them as a response to her or the family's tensions.

Postnatal hazards include head injury, asphyxiation, poisons, malnutrition, infections, and brain tumors. Automobile accidents and child abuse are the two most common causes of severe head injury in young children. Meningitis, a viral inflammation of the brain's lining membrane, and high, persistent fever may affect the brain. These are treatable, and it is usually in severe cases that lingering effects will be noted. Asphyxiation may result in brain damage dependent on the length of time of oxygen deprivation.

Psychosocial. Some individuals show retardation even though no known genetic, hereditary, or physical cause can be found to account for it. Two clusters of characteristics that have proven to be convenient descriptive categories and which are related to the underlying cause of retardation are psychosocial disadvantage and emotional disturbance. Some children obviously fit one category, while others have characteristics of both. In all cases the children evidence signs of retardation, slow learning, and poor academic performance.

Psychosocial disadvantage is diagnosed when four criteria are present. First, the person must function at a retarded level. Second, there must be retardation within the immediate family. Third, no clear evidence of brain damage is present. Fourth, the family background must include impoverished living, care, and nutrition. This kind of retardation will probably not show up until the child enters school, at which time the academic and social learning are seen to be slow and below the other children.

Numerous studies have tried to show the relationship of low socioeconomic status to poor learning abilities. Robinson and Robinson (1976) cite many such studies to show the much higher incidence of retardation among families in the poverty class. The home environment may lack adequate heating, water, or safety precautions. Physical health care may be minimal. Lack of exposure to intellectually stimulating opportunities and poor child-rearing practices reduce the child's ability to respond to learning experiences. Family tensions and pressures may create numerous obstacles to adequate interpersonal relationships. It is no wonder that parents become discouraged and that children do not develop properly.

Emotional disturbance can interfere with educational performance. The child may be withdrawn or excessively active. The more severe the problem, the more likely that the normal processes of school attendance, homework, and socialization will be disrupted. Retardation in this case may be clearly due to emotional factors, but is often difficult to assess.

Treatment and Education. *Historical.* Early records tell of Spartan parents exposing their handicapped offspring to the elements to perish. Few other accounts are available, but by the Middle Ages the retarded were exploited as fools or jesters. The Protestant Reformation found the retarded suspected of being possessed with the devil. The common treatment was "to beat the devil out of them."

Despite the poor treatment often afforded the retarded, the churches of Europe, from the thirteenth century on, began to systematically provide asylums for the less fortunate members of society. No treatment or education was provided, but sanctuary was available from the cruel and competitive society.

Prior to 1800 the prevalent belief was that retardation was inherited and consequently not treatable. Then in 1800 Jean Itard, a French physician, began working with the "wild boy of Aveyron." This boy, captured in the forests of Aveyron, was diagnosed as severely retarded. Itard believed that training and practice could reverse some of the effects of retardation. His efforts produced marked changes in the boy's behavior. While the boy never achieved the ability to talk or live independently, this was the beginning of treatment and education for retarded persons.

In 1850 Edward Seguin, a student of Itard, arrived in America. Having expanded Itard's work, Seguin opened residential schools for the retarded. His complex, systematic sequence of training made him recognized as an international leader in the field. By 1900 residential schools were established throughout the country. These schools were intended as training schools, dedicated to curing mental retardation. But cure did not occur, and today the nature of these schools has radically changed. Rather than attempting a cure, they now emphasize the enhancement of social competence, personal adequacy, and occupational skills.

In 1912 Maria Montessori, a student of Seguin, opened her schools for training the retarded. She developed a system of self-teaching that trains through the senses. In 1914 Charles Scott Berry began a teacher training program in Lapeer, Michigan. Soon after, the first college course on mental retardation was offered at what is now Eastern Michigan University.

Current Trends. The movement from viewing retardation as purely hereditary to purely environmental has lead to a contemporary position which views it as usually the result of the interaction of both these factors. Treatment now focuses on training of personal skills to help an individual reach the highest possible level attainable for the deficiency.

One important trend in recent work with the retarded has related to the concept of normalization or "mainstreaming." This refers to the right of retarded individuals to participate in normal activities. Such activities include privacy, dignity, liberty, the right to engage in loving relationships, and marriage. Special classrooms, while designed to provide homogeneous groupings to enhance manageable training, specialized curricula that would be in line with the interests of the group, and special training needs for teachers, have often been seen as dumping grounds and discriminatory.

In 1965 the passage of the Elementary and Secondary Education Act provided special programs of assistance to disadvantaged and handicapped children in the United States. In 1969, 14 regional instructional materials centers were developed to provide ready access to valid materials and information.

The provision of free public education for all mentally retarded citizens within the context of as natural an environment as feasible was mandated by passage of Public Law 94–142 and Section 502 of the Rehabilitation Act of 1973. The presumption is that society is obligated to support efforts to integrate retarded individuals into the total fabric of the community. Mainstreaming attempts to reduce the discriminatory aspect of being retarded.

The implications of these laws for education are drastic. Free education is provided, even if it means special schooling. The least restrictive environment allows a retarded person to study in regular schools if possible. It is necessary for public schools to make allowances for handicaps, with facilities for wheelchairs or other devices. These requirements have given retarded persons an opportunity for "normal" education and interaction in society. Special education is provided for the more severe cases where participation in regular classrooms is not possible. In both cases yearly plans are made specifying what is to be taught. This reduces the possibility of simply ignoring the children and reverting to minimal training.

Likewise, more adequate living situations are provided. Rather than dumping children into institutions, it is mandated that more normal housing be provided. While institutionalization is necessary for some retarded persons, due to the severity of retardation or specific problems involved, these persons are to receive normal treatment as much as possible. Otherwise, group homes, foster homes, nursing homes, even support in one's own home are provided. Residential facilities are designed to be as colorful, warm, and friendly as a typical home.

Where possible, vocational training is given. Providing a means of earning an income gives retarded persons a sense of achievement and worth. It enhances self-esteem to be in a work situation and accomplish a task.

Regular psychological assessments are also required. These occur naturally in normal schools where academic advance is a primary means of assessment. Since retarded persons learn slower, more regular assessments are needed to verify the strengths, determine if there are other underlying problems, and provide direction for educational plans.

Prevention. *Primary prevention.* Any preventive approach must begin with public education. The public must be taught that mental retardation is a handicap that can be studied, treated, and helped. They must know that retarded persons have feelings and emotions and the need for belonging, like the rest of us.

Improvement of socioeconomic standards must occur. Malnutrition, prematurity, and other conditions that seem related to the disadvantaged and which give rise to retardation must be changed. Raising of living standards, vocational training, and education are all necessary.

Medical measures, such as detection of Rh and other blood incompatibilities, restricting the number of pregnancies in adolescence and after the age of 40 to reduce chromosomal aberrations, and control of diet would reduce the number of reproductive casualties. Preventive measures in obstetrics and pediatrics would further reduce retardation associated with birth and neonatal difficulties.

Genetic counseling to reduce the possibility of recessive traits is needed. While this is a complicated procedure, the known facts and uncertainties must be presented to the parents. They must know the chances and decide what to do in the presence of any particular set of odds. Amniocentesis, the study of the amniotic fluid during pregnancy, can reveal genetic defects. Therapeutic abortions are gaining wide acceptance based on these findings.

Secondary prevention. At this level there must be early identification and treatment of hereditary disorders. In some of the metabolic disorders, such as PKU, early identification and dietary control are crucial to prevent severe retardation. Medical and surgical treatment of other conditions is needed. Reduction of the effects of hydrocephaly is but one example. Immunizations and prompt medical treatment can reduce effects of various diseases or traumas that might lead to retardation.

Identification of the mentally retarded child and a building of positve home situations to reduce emotional and behavioral disturbances, handicapping situations, and cultural deprivation are important. Enhancing a retarded child's self-image and providing help for the parents would reduce the possibilities of stigma.

Tertiary prevention. Direct treatment of the retarded individual is indicated. Treatment of the behavioral and personality difficulties through therapy, schooling, or institutionalization is required. Behavior modification has proven effective in many cases. Counseling the parents in both management and acceptance can reduce much guilt and anxiety. Vocational and physical rehabilitation, combined with special education, can meet the direct needs of the retarded individuals for self-sufficiency and self-respect.

References

Doll, E. A. *Vineland scale of social maturity* (1965 ed.). Circle Pines, Minn.: American Guidance Service, 1965.

Grossman, H. (Ed.). *Manual on terminology and classification in mental retardation, 1973 revision.* Washington, D.C.: American Association of Mental Deficiency, 1973.

Robinson, N. M., & Robinson, H. B. *The mentally retarded child* (2nd ed.). New York: McGraw-Hill, 1976.

L. N. FERGUSON

Mental Status Examination. *See* PSYCHIATRIC ASSESSMENT.

Mesmer, Franz Anton (1734–1815).

Born in Iznang, Austria, Mesmer studied philosophy at a Jesuit university in Bavaria and medicine and theology at the University of Vienna. He wrote his doctoral thesis on the magnetic effects of the planets on the human body. Mesmer's thinking was greatly influenced by the Renaissance physician Paracelsus and Flemish chemist Jan Baptista van Helmont. Both these men believed that the human body was inherently polarized into positive and negative, and that if this polarity could be connected with the Universal Spirit, the power resulting from the union would cure any illness. Mesmer believed that the celestial forces could be attracted and applied through the use of magnets. One of his first cases was that of a woman suffering from attacks of neuralgia, convulsions, and agitation. His treatment was to place magnets over her stomach and legs. With a successful outcome in this case he continued his treatment with other patients, believing that somehow the magnets captured magnetic fluids from the atmosphere and rejuvenated the nervous system.

Mesmer began to adopt many of the mannerisms of a showman when treating his patients, and he made many claims about his perfect process of healing. The Faculty of Medicine in Vienna denounced his cures as products of imagination, and he was expelled from the medical profession.

Mesmer left for Paris, where he constructed a "baquet," which was a large tub filled with magnetized water and with metal rods protruding from all sides. Patients were required to sit around the tub with hands clasped while the rods were placed on their ailing body parts. His technique became very popular, but he was challenged by two scientific committees which discredited his claims as being unscientific. His apparent cures were attributed to imagination, whereby a person could be influenced by the power of suggestion and the interpersonal relationship between doctor and patient.

Mesmer withdrew from public view and died in obscurity in Switzerland. Other physicians such as Puységur, and later Elliotson and Esdaile, continued to experiment with mesmerism in their practice but without any supernatural connotations. The practice of mesmerism later developed into hypnosis.

G. A. JOHNSTON

Mesomorph.

In Sheldon's system of constitutional types the mesomorph is a person with a hard, muscular body. This body type, comparable to Kretschmer's athletic type, is contrasted to the ECTOMORPH and ENDOMORPH types. Sheldon's research suggested that mesomorphs tend to be aggressive, adventurous, and courageous.

See CONSTITUTIONAL PERSONALITY THEORY.

Methods of Psychology. *See* PSYCHOLOGY, METHODS OF.

Meyer, Adolf (1866–1950).

Born in Niederwenigen, Switzerland, Meyer received his M.D. from the University of Zurich and did further study in pathology, neurology, and psychiatry in Vienna, Paris, London, Berlin, and Edinburgh before coming to the United States in 1892. He was a pathologist at the Illinois Eastern Hospital for the Insane until 1895, at the Worcester State Hospital until 1902, and at the Pathological Institute of the New York State Hospital Service until 1910. He was also professor of psychiatry at the Cornell University Medical College (1904–1909) and at Johns Hopkins University (1910–1941), where he became director of its Henry Phipps Psychiatric Clinic in 1914.

Meyer was disturbed by the claim of psychologists that their interest was only in the mental life of the person, and by the attitude of psychiatrists whose interest was in the physical or organic condition of the patient. He believed that this was leading to two dead ends, pointing out that humans are wholes and that they respond to social, psychological, and biological influences. He called his approach psychobiology because he wanted to take all these factors into account. Meyer held the "commonsense" view that mental illness is a matter of maladaptive habits and that psychotherapy is a process of reeducation, replacing maladaptive patterns with effective ones.

He encouraged psychiatrists to take case histories and to study the patient's life situations. The psychiatric interview developed from his work. He encouraged his students to look at both the behavioral life history and the present condition of their patients. He also emphasized prevention and became a dominant force in the mental hygiene movement. He encouraged Beers to publish *The Mind That Found Itself* and was instrumental in establishing the National Committee for Mental Hygiene.

As he realized that social factors were important in mental illness, he and his wife began visiting the homes of mental patients. Her interviews in 1904 are considered to be the beginnings of psychiatric social work, and established closer ties between psychiatry and the social sciences.

Although Meyer is called the dean of American psychiatry, he did not produce an appreciable amount of literature, not even a simple textbook. A selection of 52 of his papers was edited by Albert Lief and published as *Commonsense Psychiatry* (1948). His influence was primarily a personal one on the many students who studied under him at Johns Hopkins.

R. L. KOTESKEY

Microcephaly. Literally "small-headedness," microcephaly is a skull deformation characterized by defective development of the brain and premature ossification of the skull. The impaired functioning of the central nervous system usually includes profound or severe mental deficiencies. Approximately 5% of the mentally retarded population suffers from microcephaly. Physically the head is elongated with a receding forehead and chin. The disease may be caused by a single recessive gene or by various prenatal infectious diseases such as rubella or toxoplasmosis. There is no known treatment.

See MENTAL RETARDATION.

Migraine. *See* HEADACHE, MIGRAINE.

Milieu Therapy. A form of psychological treatment based on the modification of the patient's environment. Also sometimes called sociotherapy, the approach is closely related to the concept of THERAPEUTIC COMMUNITY, which is the label applied to a treatment program that utilizes milieu therapy. In such a program the entire environment, including not just the physical environment, but much more importantly the interpersonal environment, is shaped to make life within it a continuous program of treatment.

One important noninstitutional example of milieu therapy is the Belgian community of Gheel. Since the seventh century residents of this town have taken mental patients into their homes, allowing them to live with normal healthy families for as long as needed in order to return to healthy psychological functioning. The systematic application of the principles of milieu therapy to psychiatric treatment did not develop until the 1930s and 1940s.

D. G. BENNER

Mill, John Stuart (1806–1873). The son of Scottish philosopher James Mill, and generally regarded as the most influential philosopher in the English-speaking world during the nineteenth century. Educated by his father and never having attended school, Mill built upon the foundation of earlier empiricist philosophers and did much to contribute to the development of ASSOCIATIONISM.

See EMPIRICISM.

Mind-Brain Relationship. Throughout history human beings have noted a fundamental dichotomy in their experience. On the one hand, there are those aspects of reality characterized by what Hasker (1983) calls physical properties. These are properties that can characterize ordinary physical objects; for example, mass, length, color, electrical charge, and chemical composition can characterize such objects as a baseball, a finger, or a brain. On the other hand, there are aspects of reality characterized by "mental properties . . . which can only characterize an entity which is possessed of some kind of consciousness or awareness" (Hasker, 1983, p. 60). Vibrant hope, ecstatic joy, excruciating pain, or a firm intention to act are examples of this latter category.

If these two aspects of reality were totally separate, there would be no impetus for inquiry into the relationship of mind and brain. But the interrelationships of the two have been noted as often as the two have been distinguished. On the one hand, physical events can result in mental events, as when compression of the tissue of the thumb with a forceful blow from a hammer results in the predictable and unpleasant mental experience of pain and remorse. On the other hand, mental events can result in physical events, as when the mental image in a dream of an ax murderer attacking one's family produces accelerated heart rate and respiration, increased sweating, and other physical reactions.

The contemporary physical and behavioral sciences have further documented this interrelatedness. Neurosurgeons can elicit such mental experiences as vivid memories by electrical stimulation of certain brain tissues. Interference with the functioning of one part of the brain through injury or drugs drastically changes mental functioning. Imagery, hypnosis, and related "mental" practices are used to reduce or moderate physical processes such as skin temperature, blood pressure, or pain produced by documented physical disturbances. Yet contemporary research in brain functioning has not eliminated the question of mind-brain relationship.

The mind-brain (or more traditionally the mind-body) problem can be stated in two major questions: "Does the common distinction between mental and physical events support a further distinction between mind and body?" and "What is the nature of the relationship between mental and physical events in human existence?" Answers to these questions are important both for the understanding of our own natures and for other practical reasons as well. How one answers the mind-brain questions relates to one's position on such issues as determinism, sanctification, and bioethical matters (e.g., when a person should be pronounced clinically dead).

Major Relationship Theories. The major theories can be divided into two groups: monistic and dualistic. For further information on these theories see Hasker (1983), Shaffer (1967), and specific cited works.

Monistic theories. The monistic theories answer the mind-brain question by denying there is any legitimate distinction between mind and body and arguing that one type of event totally explains the other. One group would argue that only the physical is real, while another would argue that only the mental is real.

Materialistic views include many variants. Physicalism (or logical behaviorism) is the view arguing that only matter exists and that statements about mental events must be translated into statements about actual or potential behavior. Statements that cannot be so translated are not meaningful. "He is feeling angry" would be translated into a statement like "He is clenching his fists, yelling loudly, stomping his feet, and is likely to throw that chair" to be meaningful. In extreme versions of physicalism the existence of beliefs, thoughts, and other mental events is simply denied. In general, philosophers have rejected physicalistic theories as unacceptable because there are so many human experiences, such as pain or dreaming, for which no convincing behavioristic account can be given and the existence of which simply cannot be denied.

A more sophisticated materialistic view is the central-state identity theory. According to identity theory, mental events are real. Each mental event or state is, however, "identical with the property of being in a certain neurophysiological state" (Fodor, 1981, p. 116). For example, my belief that God exists is identical with my being in a certain brain state. My belief that God is a triune God is identical with a different brain state. This view has the advantage of allowing for the reality of mental events even when they give rise to no behavioral effects. Its simplicity in proposing only one type of substance (i.e., material substance) eliminates the problems of dualism, which will be discussed later. It allows for the potential explanation of mental events according to the same deterministic causal laws applied to all physical events; this is viewed as a strength by many scientists and a weakness by others who are concerned with avoiding deterministic explanations of human choice.

Two additional problems for identity theory are the implicit notions that every mental event is identical with a *certain* neurophysiological state and that *all* mental events must be neurophysiological states. The theory of functionalism has been proposed recently to remedy these problems (Fodor). Functionalists assert that different neurophysiological brain states and even other types of states, such as specific computer operations, can result in the same behavioral outcome and thus should be viewed as functionally equivalent mental states. Thus, like the identity theorist adherent the functionalist believes that each human mental event is a brain state. Unlike the identity theorist the functionalist emphasizes not the brain state (in computer terms, the hardware) but the functional or causal nature of the operations performed (the software). Mental states in humans are neurophysiological in nature, but two persons experiencing the memory of a specific picture may not be experiencing the identical brain state. What matters is that the result—in this case the memory—is the same. A further implication is the functionalist's willingness to attribute mentality to nonhuman animals, to machines designed to exhibit artificial intelligence, and even potentially to "a disembodied spirit" (Fodor, p. 118). The functionalist's theory is new and not widely critiqued. It seems a useful improvement on identity theory but shares with that theory the problem of how one gets from a purely mechanical event to a self-conscious awareness of a mental event. The functionalist's recognition that a computer can solve an algebraic equation as well as a human is not equivalent to proving that the computer experiences a conscious awareness of the act as a human does.

The final monistic theory is the opposite of the materialistic theories: the idealism of George Berkeley, who proposed that the concept of absolute (i.e., independent) matter or substance was nonsensical. Berkeley proposed instead that "to be is to be perceived" (cited in Hasker, 1983, p. 63); that is, the only meaningful way to discuss existence is in terms of perception or ideas. He did not, as is sometimes said, assert that the world is not real or that objects cease to exist when we close our eyes. He suggested that there are many perceiving human minds, and that an all-perceiving God undergirds the constancy of creation by the pervasiveness of his perceptions. He also asserted that the fact that things exist only as perceptions does not make them any less real. Thus, Berkeley solved the mind-brain problem by reducing matter to a special subset of ideas. All that exists is mental. Berkeley's theory has never been widely accepted as a theory of metaphysics. It has had more effect on epistomology in influencing the rise of empiricism (what we know comes from what we perceive alone) over rationalism. The idea of the absolute existence of matter seems firmly grounded in human experience.

Dualistic theories. Dualistic theories suggest that physical and mental entities are not just different ways of describing the same reality, but that mental and physical are fundamentally different in being distinct substances, events, properties, states, or relations (Shaffer, 1967, p. 341).

The classic dualistic theory is the dualistic interactionism of Descartes. Similar views go back at least as far as Plato. The different proposals vary in their details, but generally assert that mind and body are differentiable entities and that the two different types of entities causally interact in a meaningful way. Thus, when I think "I'd like to scratch my ear," this immaterial mental event is in some way picked up by the physical brain (which acts something like a radio receiver), is processed, and results in the predicted action. A scratch on the knee, on the other hand, is transmitted via the nervous system to the brain, where it is processed. The resulting brain states are picked up by the mind, and at that point (and not before) they become conscious impressions such as pain or discomfort. Mind and brain are viewed as interacting, yet neither is fundamentally dependent upon the other.

A fundamental difficulty for the dualistic interactionist is the need to specify the manner in which mind and brain are supposed to interact. Descartes proposed that the pineal gland deep within the brain was the locus for interaction, but this notion has been firmly refuted. Two prominent scholars recently stunned the scientific community with a reaffirmation of dualistic interactionism. Philosopher of science Karl Popper and distinguished neuroscientist John Eccles, in their 1977 book *The Self and the Brain*, argued forcibly for the reality of supernatural entities not dependent upon physical bodies, and suggested that the mind affects the brain not at a specific point, as proposed by Descartes, but rather at a myriad of synaptic points throughout the central nervous system. They suggest that quantum indeterminancy opens an avenue for the alteration of the purely physical synaptic processes by mental influences, thus not violating the law of the conservation of energy.

The other fundamental difficulty for a dualistic theory is the commonly observed close correspondence between specific brain functions and specific mental events. If mind is supposed to be totally removed (though interactive) from brain functions, then why does a severe lesion in a certain area of the brain's frontal lobe have such regularly observed mental results (e.g., disruption of sequential planning abilities)? If the ability to plan intentionally is a capacity of the separate mind, why does a focal brain injury disrupt that capacity? The answer that has been historically given on this issue is that specific mental faculties are received and acted upon at certain points in the brain, and that impairment of brain tissues prevents that mental capacity from being clearly articulated in neurophysiological or behavioral events.

To many this answer is unsatisfactory. One problem is that it seems unlikely that a specific mental capacity continues in existence after disruption of the related brain tissues. A version of dualism proposed to mend this problem is epiphenomenalism. This view suggests that mental events are indeed real, but that they have no causal force. Epiphenomenalists suggest that only half of the interactionist's theory is correct, that physical events give rise to mental events. Our sense of the opposite sequence, that mental events cause physical events, is merely an illusion. We might suppose that a man could think of his wife and then stop work to call her. The epiphenomenalist would argue that brain processes, under the influence of such environmental stimuli as a picture of the wife on the desk or the wedding ring on the finger, caused both the mental event of a conscious thought about the wife and the behavioral event of calling her.

The final theory of mind-brain, and the most recent, is called emergentism (see Hasker, 1983; Sperry, 1980). Emergentism suggests that the physical and the mental are truly distinct, but that the mental is fundamentally dependent upon (or produced by) the physical, that is, the brain. As analogies Hasker points to a magnet and its magnetic field and the earth and its gravitational field. In both these cases the fields are real and distinct phenomena which nevertheless cannot exist apart from the physical entity from which they arise. The emergentist further believes that mental events can cause physical events. Sperry (1980) suggests that the mental properties supersede the neurophysiological events on which they are based. He illustrates this by noting that molecules of rubber can be organized into a wheel. By virtue of this higher level structure the atoms can be made to move in ways not at all predictable from the constituent parts, as when the wheel rolls downhill, forcing its molecules to move accordingly. Sperry argues that mental events act similarly in being "self determinant" (p. 200), capable of exerting independent causal forces on physical brain events. In summary, then, the emergentist suggests that mind emerges from the brain's functioning to become a distinct, separate, and causally efficacious agency. Brain scientist McKay (1978) has a similar view of mind and brain but stops short of Sperry's position that mental processes can change physical events. He suggests rather that different types of analysis are necessary at the physical and mental levels, and that determinism at the physical level is not incompatible with responsibility at the mental level.

Christian Parameters for Evaluation. Contrary to popular opinion, the Bible does not clearly endorse one option over another. The basic parameters for a Christian solution to the mind-brain problem can be summarized as follows. First, the idea of both physical and mental essences is not anathema to biblical perspectives on this issue. Christians accept the existence of a supernatural realm that includes God and other active beings, as well as the reality of a created world of physical existence of which we are a part (Gen. 2:7). Neither domain can be summarily discarded. Second, these two domains do interact; God is active in this world. Thus, while we may not be able to specify the mode of interaction between different essences, we are nonetheless assured that such interactions do occur. Third, our natural existence is an embodied existence, as testified to by the doctrines of creation (Gen. 1:26–31), resurrection (1 Cor. 15), and incarnation (John 1). Fourth, Christian theology has fairly consistently recognized an intermediate state between death and resurrection, which suggests that in some form human life must not be irrevocably dependent upon bodily existence. Fifth, Christians are universally committed to the human capacity for responsible action, a position that must lead us away from any mind-brain theory which entails mechanistic determination of human choice. This implies that human mental experiences cannot be regarded either as trivial events or as determined results of causal processes. Finally, a Christian view will be one that emphasizes "functional integration" (Cooper, 1982, p. 17) or human unity (McDonald, 1981). A careful exposition of biblical doctrines of creation, salvation, and sanctification reveals that human beings are unified beings and that God does not deal with isolated aspects of us, as is suggested when it is proposed that sanctification occurs by suppressing the body to set the soul free.

Scientific Parameters for Evaluation. Empirical research in the neurosciences forces us to see the physical and mental as intimately interrelated. Basic research with animals and clinical (surgical, psychological, pharmacological) research with humans has documented with increasing clarity how dependent the most complex of mental functions are upon physical brain functions. A well-informed view of mind and brain will take this contemporary research into account.

The neuroscientists themselves are split on these issues. Eccles and others remain staunch dualistic interactionists. McKay and Sperry are emergentists. Fodor (a philosopher) and others have offered the functionalist viewpoint, which many neuroscientists find compelling, especially those active in research in artificial intelligence. If there is a significant trend today, it would appear to be away from views that ignore mental events or explain them away as trivial (i.e., physicalism and logical behaviorism). The behavioral sciences are emphasizing the importance of mental events as real entities. Whether they are real entities that are brain states (identity theory), functional states, real yet spurious states (epiphenomenalism), dependent yet efficacious entities (emergentism), or wholly separate but interacting entities (interactionism) is still widely debated.

Conclusion. Using the parameters developed earlier, Christians would probably be on stable, acceptable ground both philosophically and scientifically in endorsing emergentism, dualistic interactionism, or a nondeterministic functionalism as an attempt to answer the mind-brain problem. At the broadest possible level empirical brain science and solid Christian scholarship are leading to similar conclusions—i.e., an appreciative view of the irreducibility of mental phenomena and a solid emphasis on the fundamental unity of human existence.

References

Cooper, J. Dualism and the biblical view of human beings (2). *The Reformed Journal*, 1982, *32*(10), 16–18.
Fodor, J. The mind-body problem. *Scientific American*, 1981, *244*(1), 114–123.
Hasker, W. *Metaphysics: Constructing a world view.* Downers Grove, Ill.: Inter-Varsity Press, 1983.
McDonald, H. D. *The Christian view of man.* Westchester, Ill.: Crossway Books, 1981.
McKay, D. M. Selves and brains. *Neuroscience*, 1978, *3*, 599–606.
Shaffer, P. Mind-body problem. In P. Edwards (Ed.), *Encyclopedia of philosophy.* New York: Macmillan, 1967.
Sperry, R. W. Mind-brain interaction: Mentalism, yes; dualism, no. *Neuroscience*, 1980, *5*, 195–206.

S. L. Jones

See CONSCIOUSNESS; SELF; PERSONHOOD.

Minimal Brain Dysfunction.

No other diagnostic category has been so widely described and written about in such diverse terms as minimal brain dysfunction. The lack of clarity from the professional community has lead to a great deal of confusion regarding its definition, etiology, treatment, and prognosis. This confusion has resulted in many children being misdiagnosed as having minimal brain dysfunction.

In the past minimal brain dysfunction was defined as deficits in learning and/or behavior in individuals who had average or near-average intelligence. Clements (1966) in an early work reported that the following characteristics were most commonly associated with minimal brain dysfunction: hyperactivity; perceptual-motor impairments; emotional lability; general coordination deficits; disorders of attention (short attention span, distractability, perseveration); impulsivity; disorders of memory and thinking; specific learning disabilities (reading, arithmetic, writing, spelling); disorders of speech and hearing; equivocal neurological signs and electroencephalographic irregularities. Due to this lack of clarity, minimal brain dysfunction has become synonomous with such commonly used terms as minimal brain damage, hyperactivity, hyperkinetic behavior syndrome, and dyslexia.

The underlying pathology in minimal brain dysfunction is assumed to be the presence of some organic weakness in processing, filtering, or assimilating sensory stimuli. The deficit may be in an individual's receptive (visual, auditory) and/or expressive (verbal, tactile) abilities and/or the integration of these modalities. An example of this last point occurs when there is a failure to transfer the written word C-A-T into the verbal expression "cat."

Behavior problems may either arise directly from minimal brain dysfunction or may develop as a secondary consequence of it. They would be viewed as a direct result of minimal brain dysfunction when they interfere with the individual's perception or processing of environmental or internal information. This cognitive deficit may manifest itself as impulsiveness, carelessness, and lack of foresight as to the consequences of one's actions. Behavioral or emotional problems may also arise secondary to, or as an adjustment to, minimal brain dysfunction. Thus, a child may become easily frustrated, anxious, and even hostile when confronted with a situation that he knows will be difficult or impossible. This leads to decreased self-confidence, which compounds a sense of failure and unwillingness to attempt tasks.

Genetic, metabolic, or biochemical conditions or some form of brain injury have been hypothesized as possible etiologies of minimal brain dysfunction. Often children diagnosed as having minimal brain dysfunction have a positive history of prenatal and birth complications (anoxia, prematurity, low birth weight, small for gestational age) and/or developmental delays or abnormalities (slow to walk or talk, overexcitability, over- or underactive motor reflexes, poor fine-motor-coordination). A positive history of such difficulties makes the diagnosis of minimal brain dysfunction more credible but not conclusive. In order to make the diagnosis of minimal brain dysfunction with confidence one must have some evidence of early trauma or insult together with the history of atypical development. Minimal brain dysfunction may manifest itself in atypical development in an infant who incessantly cries, is irritable, demanding, squirmy, or experiences restless sleep. Older children may manifest signs of atypical development primarily in the areas of perception, gross motor hyperactivity, and fine motor incoordination. For example, preschool and school-age childern may be accident prone or clumsy or show difficulty in skipping, hopping, and jumping. A history of some type of cerebral insult along with the preceding behavioral characteristics makes the diagnosis of minimal brain dysfunction more reliable.

Medication (central nervous system stimulants) has become the most frequently employed treatment for children suspected of minimal brain dysfunction. The rationale for its effectiveness has been that a child with minimal brain dysfunction has a neurologically unresponsive inhibitory system within the arousal area in the brain. However, this is only one of many theories that prevail regarding the exact mode of action of the central nervous system stimulants and their paradoxical calming effect. Other treatment approaches include psychoeducation, behavior therapy, and family therapy. It is important that each of these be considered, since any type of handicapping condition has widespread effects personally, academically, and interpersonally.

Minimal brain dysfunction has come to replace the term *minimal brain damage*. This is based on the fact that brain damage cannot be reliably diagnosed solely on the basis of behavioral signs and symptoms. Unfortunately minimal brain dysfunction is not a much better term. It is still too broad and vague, and consequently its usefulness is limited. It would be best if professionals would attempt to delineate specific aspects of behavior that are deficient rather than collapsing them all under the diagnosis of minimal brain dysfunction. Specific interventions could then be targeted for use for each specific type of deficit.

Reference

Clements, S. D. *Minimal brain dysfunction in children: Terminology and identification. Phase one of a three-phase project.* Washington D.C.: U.S. Government Printing Office, 1966.

K. R. KRACKE

See ATTENTION DEFICIT DISORDER.

Minnesota Multiphasic Personality Inventory (MMPI).
A psychological test that inquires into one's preferences, attitudes, feelings, and behavior. It is one of the most frequently used instruments by psychologists interested in personality functioning and diagnosis. The test was originally developed in 1943 by J. C. McKinley and Stark Hathaway, and has remained relatively unchanged since the first publication.

The MMPI consists of 550 statements. The individual is asked to pencil in "T" (true) to those statements that are descriptive of him or her and "F" (false) to those statements that do not personally apply. The test usually takes one hour to complete and can be scored immediately. Due to the pencil-and-paper nature of the test and the standardized scoring system the MMPI is considered to be an objective personality questionnaire.

A psychological evaluation usually involves the administration of several tests. The MMPI is frequently given because it provides the psychologist with a fairly comprehensive profile of one's personality functioning. Fourteen different areas are assessed, and scores can be plotted in graphic form. Four of the areas give an indication of the individual's test-taking attitude, such as the degree of psychological defensiveness in wanting to reveal oneself or the tendency to have answered in a random and haphazard fashion, thereby making the test results invalid. The 10 remaining scales provide clinical information in the following areas: hypochondriasis, depression, hysteria, psychopathy, masculinity-femininity, paranoia, psychasthenia, schizophrenia, hypomania, and social introversion-extraversion. The interpretation of the results requires that the psychologist have an understanding of these clinical areas and also a knowledge of how they interact with each other. For example, a high score on the depression scale must be interpreted in context of how the individual scored on the other scales.

The MMPI also provides information about other areas of one's personality functioning. An integrated analysis of the final profile helps the clinician in understanding such important areas as the individual's needs, reactions to stress, degree of self-confidence, and psychological resources. Hypotheses can be formed about possible psychodynamics underlying the symptoms. All this information is important to correct diagnosis and proper treatment planning.

The MMPI has been extensively researched. Many articles are published each year on this one instrument alone. It requires little professional time to administer and provides a wealth of information. During a thorough psychological evaluation this objective measure is most frequently administered with other tests, and in particular such projective tests as the Rorschach and the Thematic Appreception Test.

W. W. AUSTIN

See PSYCHOLOGICAL MEASUREMENT; PERSONALITY ASSESSMENT.

Mirror Technique. A technique in PSYCHODRAMA in which the patient (protagonist) is removed from the scene being portrayed so that he or she may view it from an outside perspective. An individual (the auxiliary ego) is selected to play out the protagonist's role, mirroring behaviors as closely as possible. Through the more detached observer role the protagonist witnesses the behaviors that are productive and self-defeating in the scene. He may confront the auxiliary ego and offer helpful suggestions for change. When this occurs, the protagonist then returns to the scene to experiment with these new insights.

J. H. VANDER MAY

MMPI. *See* MINNESOTA MULTIPHASIC PERSONALITY INVENTORY.

Modeling. The process of observing and imitating another person's behavior, also referred to as social modeling. Different theorists have referred to the phenomenon as observational learning, vicarious learning, matched dependent behavior, imitation, and identification. Two of the more popular terms have been imitation and identification, which imply the acquisition of both behavior and attitudes. However, imitation has sometimes been viewed as a more temporary copying of behavior, while identification has been considered a more or less permanent acquisition of personality.

Historically, early twentieth century theorists viewed the modeling phenomenon as an innate propensity. In other words, each individual has an inherent tendency to imitate others. Freud's (1927) understanding of modeling involved an extensive identification process. What was identified with ranged from human ideas, attitudes, values, and behavior, to abstract concepts, imaginary characters, and inanimate objects. Holt (1931) proposed an understanding of modeling that emphasized the importance of typical parent-child interaction. A parent would stimulate behavior in the child, imitate that behavior, provide examples of novel behavior, and parent and child would engage in spontaneous mutual imitations.

An explanation provided by Skinner (1953) stressed the necessity of three sequential processes. First, a stimulus had to be provided—that is, someone had to model some type of behavior. Second, an observer had to imitate that specific behavior; third, reinforcement had to immediately follow emulation. Theoretically, if the observer was not reinforced, learning was not considered to have taken place.

A more recent conceptualization of social model learning has been advanced by Bandura (1971). His theory proposes four cognitive-mediational subprocesses. The first subprocess, attention, simply means the observer must visually see the modeled behavior. The second subprocess, retention, states that the observer must be able to recall what he saw, either through imagery or symbolic coding. An example of symbolic coding would be remembering the route through a maze by coding right turn, right turn, left turn, etc. The third subprocess, motoric reproduction, states that the observer must be able physically to reproduce the modeled behavior. The fourth subprocess, the incentive-motivational function of reinforcement, theorizes that reinforcement is a facilitative but unnecessary condition for imitative learning. In other words, an individual can observe a model, learn the new behavior covertly, and, depending on the consequences, decide whether to exhibit that behavior then, at an opportune moment, or not at all.

Research supporting the existence of the modeling phenomenon has been extensive. One of the classic studies is that of Bandura, Ross, and Ross (1961) who examined the effect of aggressive models on the behavior of nursery school children. In one group children observed a model rewarded for exhibiting unusual forms of physical and verbal aggression. In a second group children viewed the same modeled aggressive behavior, only this time the model was punished. A third group, serving as one of the control groups, observed a highly expressive but nonaggressive model. The fourth group, also serving as a control group, saw no model at all. When compared to the control groups, those children who observed the model rewarded for hitting, kicking, slapping, and generally abusing the life-sized plastic doll generally tended to imitate and exhibit more aggressive behavior. Interestingly, children who observed the model punished for aggressive and abusive behavior did not differ significantly when compared with the control groups. This particular study was invaluable in depicting not only the strong influence of models, but also how some children may become overly aggressive.

Another area where models have been influential is through symbolic conveyance methods. Films, audiotapes, videotapes, books, and even pictures, can all be conceptualized as symbolic models. Much of the aggression research conducted by Bandura has been replicated using symbolic models. The Bandura, Ross, and Ross (1963) study was an exact replication of the 1961 study except this time the models were portrayed on film. As evidenced in the live model study, those nursery school children who observed the aggressive model rewarded were found to perform significantly more aggressive behaviors compared to the other three groups. Again it was also found that those children who had observed the aggressive model being punished did not differ significantly from the children in the control groups. Other areas where symbolic models have been influential are in the clinical treatment of phobias and in counseling with adolescents.

The degree to which some individuals are influenced by others seems to depend on the characteristics attributed to those models. High status versus low status, aggressive male versus aggressive female, adult and peer male model versus adult and peer female model, masculine versus feminine model, and peer versus adult model are all instances where the former characteristic, compared to the latter, was more influential in changing people's behavior. Other model characteristics, such as prestige, competence, age, nurturance, social power, ethnicity, and similarity to the model have also been found to influence observer emulation.

These findings are results of studies where this trend appeared to be the case. How people on a day-to-day basis are influenced may vary, depending on one's culture, race, geographical location, or peers. Other research has indicated that the extent to which some persons emulate models is affected by certain subject characteristics; those persons perceived as incompetent, dependent, and lacking in self-esteem were found to be more influenced by models.

The last area where models have been found influential is in covert modeling. Covert modeling procedures have used the imagination to reduce anxiety, eliminate unwanted habits, help establish new patterns of behavior, and increase existing levels of performance. A typical example would be the procedures involved in covert reinforcement (Cautela, 1970). In covert reinforcement clients are instructed to imagine themselves behaving appropriately in situations where usually they would behave inappropriately. Scenes are periodically interrupted with a cue word "reinforcement" followed by pleasureable scenes such as lying on the beach or relaxing at home. It is assumed that these procedures are influential in altering the behavior, attitudes, and feelings of those who utilize them. It would seem evident that live models, symbolic models, model characteristics, and covert modeling procedures all, to some extent, appear capable of influencing our complex patterns of behavior.

A thorough examination of the modeling phenomenon must take into account a biblical perspective. "For you yourselves know how you ought to follow our example. Because we did not act in an undisciplined manner among you, . . . not because we did not have the right to do this, but in order to offer ourselves as a model for you, that you might follow our example" (2 Thess. 3:7, 9; NASV). This passage depicts the very essence of the modeling phenomenon: the fact that people act in certain identifiable ways—in this case, disciplined or undisciplined—and that this can and does affect how we behave.

Paul is even more explicit in other biblical passages: "Brethren, join in following my example and observe those who walk according to the pattern you have in us" (Phil. 3:17); "Be imitators of me, just as I also am of Christ" (1 Cor. 11:1). Even more powerful and exemplary of modeling is Jesus' statement. "If I then, the Lord and the teacher, washed your feet, you ought also to wash one another's feet. For I gave you an example that you also should do as I did to you" (John 13:14–15). These biblical passages support the basic principle of social model learning. People do imitate and model after others, both through real and symbolic modeling, and one's characteristics do affect the degree to which modeling and imitation occur (Marvin, 1980).

References

Bandura, A. *Social learning theory*. Morristown, N.J.: General Learning Press, 1971.
Bandura, A., Ross, D., & Ross, S. A. Transmission of aggression through imitation of aggressive models. *Journal of Abnormal and Social Psychology*, 1961, *63*, 575–582.
Bandura, A., Ross, D., & Ross, S. A. Vicarious reinforcement and imitative learning. *Journal of Abnormal and Social Psychology*, 1963, *67*, 601–607.
Cautela, J. Covert reinforcement. *Behavior Therapy*, 1970, *1*, 33–50.
Freud, S. *The ego and the id*. London: Hogarth Press, 1927.
Holt, E. B. *Animal drive and the learning process* (Vol. 1). New York: Holt, 1931.
Marvin, M. L. Social modeling: A psychological-theological perspective. *Journal of Psychology and Theology*, 1980, *8*(3), 211–221.
Skinner, B. F. *Science and human behavior*. New York: Macmillan, 1953.

M. L. MARVIN

See LEARNING.

Mongolism. *See* DOWN'S SYNDROME.

Monoideism. An obsession or fixation on a single idea and an inability to think about anything other than that one idea. It is frequently observed in schizophrenia and senile personalities.

Mood. A pervasive emotion of sustained duration in which the internal quality of feeling affects the person's perception of himself and his surroundings. Though not necessarily pathological in and of itself, a mood may persist over a length of time and require professional help. The feelings may be unpleasant (such as depression, anger, or anxiety) or pleasant (such as elation or an exaggerated sense of well-being).

See AFFECT.

Mood Disorders. *See* AFFECTIVE DISORDERS.

Moral and Ethical Issues in Treatment. Psychological treatments are inextricably connected with moral and ethical issues. Virtually all forms of verbal psychotherapy, for example, embody some conception of the good life or of how one ought ideally to think, feel, and act. Moreover, Frank (1961) has argued with considerable force that psychotherapy is, at root, persuasion. The patient comes in demoralized, and the therapist assists the patient to a new way of viewing his or her life and of assessing what is and is not desirable. Szasz (1961) argues that even defining mental health is a subjective if not arbitrary enterprise.

London (1964) also emphasizes the great extent to which therapy is a metascientific undertaking, at best an art grounded in bits and pieces of science. The bulk of what therapists do might be best viewed as "clinical philosophy." While attorneys specialize in the use of logic to enhance clients' concrete advantages, most therapists seem to use some combination of metaphysics and ethics to enhance clients' psychological sense of well-being.

The Nature of Ethics. It is important to understand that moral-ethical questions cannot, in principle, be answered by science. Such questions are by nature speculative, meaning that there are no universally accepted standards, no laboratory observations that will certify which answers are correct. Science cannot address such questions as, "Should I put my mother in a nursing home?" or, "Should I leave my husband?" However, such questions are frequently encountered in psychotherapy, and the therapist must realize that at these points he or she leaves the realm of science and enters what is here being called the realm of clinical philosophy.

One might argue that the Bible tells us what is right and wrong, and therefore that its prescriptions and proscriptions are scientific. Such an argument amounts to little more than an expression of one's confidence in the Bible itself, since the word *scientific* is being used here in an unconventional way. Whatever else it may mean in this context, *scientific* cannot mean demonstrable or provable, as is required by the canons of twentieth-century physical science.

Questions of ethics and personal morality are by nature philosophical. If one is a Christian, much of one's philosophy is conditioned by one's understanding of, and level of commitment to, Christ. Thus, for the Christian most if not all of the philosophical questions that touch on ethical issues are also in some way theological questions; they concern the nature of God and the cosmos, including his ways with us and his desires regarding our ways with each other.

The Nature of Psychological Treatment. Almost everything that positively affects human thoughts, feelings, or actions can be held to be a psychological treatment. Drugs, biofeedback, hypnosis, hospitalization, conditioning, talking, reading, and even ordinary education may be included. Note that within this framework of understanding, the defining characteristic of a treatment is its psychological effects.

It is possible, however, to turn this conceptualization around and to define as psychological treatment only those things which, via alterations of thought, feeling, or action, alter something else, whether physical (e.g., level of adrenalin) or psychological (other thoughts, feelings, or actions). Within this framework the defining characteristic of a treatment is the psychological nature of its mode of action.

One important ethical issue in any psychological treatment relates to the presence of coercion. Seldom is coercion as overt as a threat of harm for noncompliance. However, in a great many subtle but powerful ways therapists can act coercively. When, if ever, is such coercive action ethical? Who decides that coercion is appropriate? When should the client be required to provide informed consent? How much comprehension of risks and benefits must the consenter have in order for the consent to be valid? When, if ever, ought society override the will of the individual to obtain or refuse a treatment? These are only a few of the complex ethical questions involved.

To the degree that a treatment is not coercive, a partially overlapping set of issues emerge. There are still the complexities of informed consent. A more important issue, however, involves the kinds of potentially persuasive "advices" that a therapist ought and ought not to give, as well as the manner in which such advice should be given. Therapists seem to have more than an ordinary amount of influence over their clients. How is this power to be used?

Finally, it should be noted that the issue of coercion in treatment is not synonymous with that of the voluntary or involuntary status of the client. Voluntary clients may be persuaded to undergo a certain treatment without full awareness of the alternatives or the advantages and disadvantages of this particular treatment. Many of these ethical issues are examined and standards provided in *Ethical Principles of Psychologists* (APA, 1981). Similar standards exist for other mental health professionals. Ethical standards in involuntary treatment are usually established by legislation (see Schwitzgebel & Schwitzgebel, 1980).

The Interpenetration of the Moral and the Psychological. God, we believe, desires that we do the right. God, if he is who we believe he is, also desires that we be psychologically healthy. If the cosmos is both orderly and benevolent, it seems reasonable to conclude that all of the Creator's intentions are interlocking—that there is, therefore, an intimate connection between goodness and health. God's laws cannot be arbitrary unless we are the victims of a cruel joke. Whatever he commands must on the whole be in our best interests. Striving to live morally must have positive psychological consequences. And striving for true psychological well-being has to lead us in the direction of a higher morality.

However, sometimes what seems to promote our health flies in the face of Christian teaching. Similarly, obeying God's will as we understand it sometimes appears to hurt us psychologically. Just as there is "pleasure in sin for a season," there seems at times to be health in sin for at least a while.

Few human experiences bring these issues and ambiguities into such sharp relief as the psychotherapeutic encounter. When persons come for psychological help, they are typically in turmoil and pain. "Should I get a divorce?" "Should I have an affair?" "Why am I so discouraged?" "What does life mean?" "Why did my 14-year-old son die in that awful car accident?" These are the sorts of questions that bring people to therapists, and not one of them is devoid of theological and therefore moral implication.

On the other side of the health-morality connection there is also a complex and often subtle interpenetration of sin and sickness. While it is possible to be seriously disturbed without being particularly bad morally, and while it seems possible to be immoral without being psychologically disordered in any conventional sense, psychopathology and baseness are sometimes closely related. Thus, a therapist who attempts to ameliorate psychological disorder sometimes seems to end up affecting the moral character of the person as well.

Law and Ethics. As noted earlier, standards of practice relating to many of these ethical areas exist both within each of the mental health professions and within state legislation. Within the professions serious ethical violations result, at worst, in peer censure, expulsion from an association, and loss of one's license or state registration. However, violation of state criminal or civil law can result in prosecution by government attorneys and conviction by the courts, which may impose fines or imprisonment. Harm to clients may result in their lodging a civil suit against the practitioner, who may be ordered to compensate the aggrieved party.

Many things are unethical that are not illegal, but illegal acts that relate to a practitioner's performance of professional duties are routinely unethical. The range of unethical behavior, therefore, is wider than that of illegal behavior.

Conflicts of interest frequently underlie ethical infractions, and in civil proceedings such conflicts as are relevant to the "cause of action" typically cast the practitioner in an unfavorable light. Courts tend to assume that practitioners cannot properly perform their duties when they have an interest in potential conflict with these duties. Accepting stock market tips from clients, engaging in sexual activities with patients, and serving as a therapist to one's students are examples of unacceptable practices. In each case the practitioner's singleness of purpose and, by implication, clarity of judgment fall under suspicion.

MALPRACTICE suits are civil proceedings. Some malpractice actions are brought on the basis of alleged breach of contract. The plaintiff may argue, for example, that the practitioner did not perform what, for a fee, he or she promised. Most malpractice suits are filed on the basis of an alleged wrong—some for malice (deliberate injury) but the vast majority for negligence. Typically the plaintiff will hold that the practitioner did not adhere to the standard of care prevalent in the community in the way that a reasonable person (practitioner) of ordinary prudence would have, thus failing to fulfill a duty that he or she owed the client and thereby causing injury. Taking negligent action (e.g., administering a harmful treatment) or negligently failing to take appropriate action (e.g., not responding to clear signs of suicidal intent immediately prior to a self-destructive act) are grounds for legal action.

Some professional behavior can be grounds for both a civil suit and a criminal prosecution. For example, a psychotherapist who injures a client with a physically damaging treatment may be brought to trial for assault and battery by the district attorney as well as named in a civil suit by the client.

Religion and Cultural Values. The issues surrounding the question of handling religious issues in therapy are complex and are dealt with separately (*see* SPIRITUAL AND RELIGIOUS ISSUES IN THERAPY). When religion (in general, or of a particular sort) is in disfavor in a society, practitioners who offend their clients with religious material are likely to be viewed as negligent or even fraudulent. Since one's professional peers are routinely called upon to render opinions in malpractice actions, a negative disposition toward religion by society at large or by particular professional segments could adversely affect the fate of a religiously oriented practitioner facing a malpractice suit. On the other hand, during times of religious fervor there may be a negative bias toward any practitioner who dares even to question the possible neurotic nature of a religious behavior.

We seem to be at a point in history when esoteric religions (e.g., cults or Eastern religions) or quasi-religions (e.g., astrology) may enjoy more favor than traditional ones. Although there have been a number of important church-state clashes recently, the place of Christianity in psychological services has yet to receive major legal attention; neither has the place, if any, of religious dissuasion in psychotherapy. (See McLemore & Court, 1977, for further discussion of this latter issue.)

Strongly held ethical principles tend to get reflected in laws, which are society's rules for conduct. These rules and the principles from which they derive have more than a casual connection with cultural values—in particular,

with what society views as desirable and healthy behavior. Since the specification of desirable and healthy behavior is fundamentally a philosophical—and, in the opinion of Christians, a theological—activity, laws and ethics are heavily informed by speculative ideas. Christian ideas ought therefore to be injected into the shaping of societal standards (codes of ethics and systems of legislation). Because of the intimate relationship between psychological procedures and ideals of health, which in turn relate directly to morals and thus to theology, ethical and legal issues bearing on psychological treatments are of more than trivial significance to Christians.

References

American Psychological Association. *Ethical principles of psychologists.* Washington, D.C.: Author, 1981.

Frank, J. D. *Persuasion and healing.* Baltimore: Johns Hopkins Press, 1961.

London, P. *The modes and morals of psychotherapy.* New York: Holt, Rinehart, Winston, 1964.

McLemore, C. W., & Court, J. H. Religion and psychotherapy: Ethics, civil liberties, and clinical savvy: A critique. *Journal of Consulting and Clinical Psychology,* 1977, *45,* 1172–1175.

Schwitzgebel, R. L., & Schwitzgebel, R. K. *Law and psychological practice.* New York: Wiley, 1980.

Szasz, T. S. *The myth of mental illness.* New York: Hoebel-Harper, 1961.

Additional Readings

McLemore, C. W. *The scandal of psychotherapy: A guide to resolving the tensions between faith and counseling.* Wheaton, Ill.: Tyndale House, 1982.

Sharkey, P. W. (Ed.). *Philosophy, religion and psychotherapy: Essays in the philosophical foundations of psychotherapy.* Washington, D.C.: University Press of America, 1982.

C. W. McLemore

Moral Development. A theory most often associated with the work of Kohlberg (1971, 1981). It is a theory about the development of moral judgment and is based on the cognitive development theory of Piaget. Piaget's theory emphasizes cognitive structures that help explain the reasoning process a person uses to make sense of his experience and environment. Kohlberg has used Piaget's concept of structure to make a distinction between content and structure in a moral judgment.

The content of a moral judgment is the normative statement of what is right or wrong. "It is wrong to steal" is the content of a moral judgment. The structure of a moral judgment refers to the cognitive structure one uses to make sense of the world in order to reach the content (i.e., that it is wrong to steal). Thus one person might decide that it is wrong to steal because he is using preoperational reasoning and makes moral decisions on the basis of the size and severity of physical consequences.

Another person might decide that it is wrong to steal because her cognitive reasoning is oriented to concrete answers to social situations, and she believes that it is best to obey concrete rules.

Kohlberg suggests that changes in one's cognitive structural reasons for specific moral judgments are a function of normal cognitive development as explained by Piaget. Thus, for Kohlberg, the term *moral development* refers to development within a system of stages of cognitive structure. His research indicates that a system of cognitive structural stages of moral judgment consists of six separate stages, with two stages each representing three of Piaget's stages of cognitive development.

Level I: Preconventional Morality. Kohlberg's first two stages of moral development are characteristic of Piaget's stage of preoperational thinking. Using preoperational thinking a person tends to focus more on the physical appearance of objects and events rather than on logical and verbal explanations. Preoperational thinking tends to be fantasy based and nonlogical; thus moral judgments of this type would also appear nonlogical to adult thinking. In Level I cognitive judgments about right and wrong tend to be based more on the nature of the physical consequences resulting from certain action rather than on the conventionality or ethical appropriateness of the action.

Stage 1: Punishment, avoidance. In the first stage of moral development one usually defines what is right or wrong on the basis of the severity of the punishment associated with the action. Power and size are often the bases on which authority and rightness are attributed to a person or an idea. A person would also consider an action that caused more physical damage to be more wrong than one that caused less, regardless of the ethical intentions of the person who caused the damage. Often persons in this stage do not even realize they have done something wrong until they sense the punishment coming. A person using this kind of thinking might say that it is wrong to steal "because I will get put in jail," or "because my parents will spank me."

Stage 2: Reciprocal hedonism. In the second stage of moral development a person usually defines right and wrong on the basis of benefit or reward. In this stage the benefit or reward is usually perceived only in physical terms (candy, money, sex). This kind of thinking is represented by the statement, "you scratch my back, and I'll scratch yours." Whereas in Stage 1 morality was defined in terms of the "bad-ness" of an act, in Stage 2 it is defined in terms of the "goodness" of an act. Also as in Stage 1, the relative goodness of the act is determined by the relative physical size of the reward or benefit. A person using this kind of thinking might say that it is wrong to steal "because I get to do special things when I have been good."

Level II: Conventional Morality. Kohlberg's third and fourth stages of moral development are based on Piaget's concrete operational stage of thinking. In this stage one can use adultlike logic for solving problems, but only in a concrete black-and-white, right-and-wrong way. Thus, in Level II cognitive judgments about right and wrong are based largely on concrete codes of morality or social conventions.

Stage 3: Interpersonal concordance. Though similar to Stage 2 in terms of seeking a benefit or reward as the basis for judging a particular action to be correct, Stage 3 shifts the emphasis from a physical benefit to an affectional or interpersonal benefit. Kohlberg described this as a "good-boy, nice-girl" stage. The primary motivation for moral behavior seems to be approval or acceptance by some respected authority. From the perception of this stage that authority could be a parent, a peer group, an ethnic tradition, a church, a nationality, or even God. The main objective is to live up to an external standard of goodness. A person using Stage 3 thinking might say that it is wrong to steal "because good girls don't steal," or "good Christians don't steal."

Stage 4: Maintenance of social order. In the fourth stage of cognitive moral development a person usually makes judgments about right and wrong on the basis of keeping a sense of order in society, a particular institution, or the world. The main emphasis of this perception of morality is on maintaining the status quo. It is often represented by the statement, "If we let you have this exception, we'll have to let everyone have it." It is characterized by a fear of setting new precedents. There is also the perception that moral conventions are good for all and that they keep order although in particular instances they may seem unfair. The concern is usually for the good of the majority of people. A person using Stage 4 thinking might say that it is wrong to steal "because we just can't have everybody going around stealing all the time."

Level III: Postconventional Morality. Kohlberg's fifth and sixth stages of moral development are based on Piaget's formal operational stage of thinking. Formal operations is the most abstract form of reasoning.

Using formal operational reasoning a person can easily consider more than one viewpoint at a time. He can look beyond what he is presently aware of, either physically or in terms of social conventions, and speculate about new and hypothetical solutions to given problems. Thus, in Level 3 cognitive judgments about right and wrong tend to involve ethical principles about universal human rights and ethical standards rather than concerns about physical consequences or conventional rules.

Stage 5: Social contract. Whereas in Stage 4 rules are understood as providing for social order, in Stage 5 rules are agreed upon by a group of people in order to protect the rights and welfare of those people. This type of thinking about morality is represented by the Constitution and Bill of Rights of the United States. In Stage 5 structural reasoning rules exist to serve ethical rights of individuals, and rules can be changed collectively by those individuals when they seem to be no longer effective. In Stage 4 reasoning, decisions about maintaining order seem always to favor the majority. In Stage 5 reasoning, decisions about ethical rights tend to be made with concern for the minority. A person using Stage 5 structural reasoning might say that it is wrong to steal "because it would violate someone's right of ownership."

Stage 6: Universal ethical principles. The sixth stage of cognitive reasoning about morality is the most abstract of all. It is not connected either with conventional rules and consequences or with social agreements. Decisions about right and wrong are based on self-chosen ethical principles that are perceived by the person to be universal. Kant's categorical imperative well represents this stage of reasoning. This kind of reasoning requires that a person be able cognitively to take an objective third-person perspective on any given situation or issue. He should be able to come to a conclusion without regard for any particular person's interests but with regard to an ethical principle that is deemed universal. Kohlberg suggests that the kind of ethical principles involved in Stage 6 reasoning include love, justice, truthfulness, and welfare rather than conventional rules or civil and ethical rights. A person using Stage 6 moral judgment might say that it is wrong to steal "because it is unjust for me to advance my welfare at someone else's expense."

Summary. Kohlberg's theory of psychological stages of moral judgment is a specific theory of cognitive structural development resulting from the research of Piaget. It is not a comprehensive theory of how people do in fact act in moral situations at any point in their lives. Many psychologists and educators have speculated that the link between moral judgment and moral actions has something to do with ego strength, will power, emotional stability, or a combination of any of these. However, at this time Kohlberg's theory is the most comprehensive existing psychological theory of moral development.

References:
Kohlberg, L. Stages of moral development as a basis for moral education. In C. M. Beck, B. S. Crittenden, & E. V. Sullivan (Eds.), *Moral education: Interdisciplinary approaches.* New York: Newman Press, 1971.
Kohlberg, L. *The philosophy of moral development.* San Francisco: Harper & Row, 1981.

R. B. McKEAN

See COGNITIVE DEVELOPMENT.

Moral Education. This concept has been an important part of education for centuries. Education as referred to in Scripture focused primarily on religious and moral education. Much of the writing of Plato and Aristotle on education made significant reference to moral education. The development of theology as an academic discipline in the Middle Ages brought a renewed emphasis on moral education. In later centuries Kant, Dewey, Durkeim, and other leading scholars from many disciplines have written about moral education.

The major task of moral education is to determine what values should be taught and the most effective way to teach them so that people will really act upon them. Some educators have focused on the values and character traits to be taught, and then assumed some sort of teaching or instructional procedure without much thought. Others focus more specifically on ethical arguments and rules, and then teach them as they would any other set of facts or line of thinking. Still others put their attention on the actual behavior of people and recommend instructional procedures that either reinforce acceptable behavior or socialize people into habits and customs of socially moral actions. These are only some of the typical solutions to the task of moral education.

The major task and its typical solutions reveal some basic issues involved in thinking about moral education. 1) The nature of values: Are values things? thoughts? beliefs? Are they a set code? Are they abstract principles? Are moral values universal? cultural? religious? political/economic? 2) The appropriateness of teaching values: Should we impose values on others? Should we just let people figure out their own values? 3) The nature of morality: What part do logical/rational thinking skills play? What part does knowledge play? What part do emotions play? Where does intentionality come in? Where do the physical acts and consequences come into play? What influence do normal human developmental processes have (do we judge morality to be the same for people of all different ages)? 4) The process of learning values: Do people learn values by verbal/direct instruction? By practicing them under social control? By discovering them through experience?

Resolving these issues requires combinations of insights and perceptions from various scholarly disciplines. Psychology contributes by offering ideas about how a person comes to possess a certain set of values. There seem to be three major psychological schools of thought which influence ideas about moral education. These will be referred to as association learning, self-actualization, and interactional development.

Schools of psychology that emphasize *association learning* view the learner as someone who is less mature or less initiated than the surrounding society, especially the teacher. The learner's role is to receive from the teacher the knowledge, values, or skills that are deemed by the teacher to be useful in making the learner more mature. Within this school of thought values are typically understood to exist objectively, and they usually exist as propositional verbal statements to be believed or repeated. Values then are something belonging to the environment, and it is the student's task to come to accept or internalize those external values.

Educational programs based on this psychological view of values and morality usually predefine correct values; these are either verbally transmitted from the teacher to the learner, or the learner's behavior is controlled or reinforced until it approximates the kind of behavior prescribed by the defined code of values. Such approaches to moral education often seem to make little distinction between moral/ethical values, social/cultural values, and traits of personality and character.

Schools of psychology that emphasize *self-actualization* and personal meaning tend to view values as mental constructs created by the individual to guide the behavior of the individual. They are not viewed as existing outside of the learner, but are seen to exist subjectively as a result of the learner's thoughts about his or her own experience.

Thus, the learner is viewed as the most active agent in the moral/value learning process. The teacher may be viewed as a guide into experience or as a guardian to protect the right of the individual to come to personal choices about what values to believe and act on. The task of moral education is to help people feel more confident about their moral choices and behavior rather than to help people conform to external standards about such choices and behavior. Thus, the teacher is often viewed, not as more mature or knowledgeable than the learner, but as another person in the process of discovering personal values.

Schools of psychological thought which emphasize *interactional development* and construction learning tend to view the learner as an organism actively attempting to adapt to the environment. Learning is viewed as constructing knowledge (subjectively) by interacting with the concrete (objective) reality of the environment in order to solve problems. Thus, values are viewed as conclusions reached by the organism about the most healthy way to be and act in the environment. The learner is viewed as very active in the learning process by recognizing problems and testing various hypotheses until he comes to a conclusion about what makes most sense. The environment plays a crucial role in helping the learner distinguish between real and perceived problems, identify various potential solutions to the problems, and validate the conclusions reached. The term *interaction* then refers to a very real interaction between the organism and environment—or the learner and the teacher.

Moral education programs that employ these views work on trying to resolve real-life moral cases or hypothetical case studies rather than on transmitting a predefined set of values. It is believed that learners learn best when they are trying to solve moral problems that they are actually facing. Thus, this kind of moral education does not usually consist of a prepackaged curriculum but of a caring relationship between the teacher and learner where problem solving can occur. It is not inappropriate for the teacher to suggest personal or external values as possible solutions for the moral problem being explored. However, the role of the teacher remains that of a co-explorer, not someone who hands ready-made conclusions to the learner.

Along with psychology other academic disciplines also offer ideas that are useful to moral education. Sociology puts an emphasis on social values and the social networks that transmit those values. It has contributed to moral education by defining the socialization process and the impact of imitation of significant models. Philosophy has suggested how to define the moral/ethical content of moral education. Philosophers have also suggested that moral education ought to teach logic as it applies to moral, social, and civic issues. Theology has suggested ways to define the content of moral education. This content has ranged from prescribed codes to rather abstract guiding principles.

It has been suggested that most real moral learning occurs as the result of the "hidden curriculum." The hidden curriculum is understood as the things we do and the ways we treat people, which in turn have a strong impact on the kinds of moral values people learn. Some believe that democratic social institutions are the most healthy kind of environment for moral education. Others feel the interdependent relational atmosphere usually associated with families is the most powerful force for moral education. There seems to be some consensus that typical hierarchical schooling structures that emphasize conformity to external values and deemphasize the involvement of people in developing their own values will have little impact on teaching people to participate in democratic societies or solve emerging moral problems.

If the contributions from psychology and other scholarly disciplines are combined, the options for moral education can be analyzed in terms of both content and methodology. The optional content foci seem to be 1) absolute moral values; 2) social or socially prescribed moral values; 3) individualistic-relativistic values; 4) logical reasoning skills; or 5) the valuing process. The optional methodological foci seem to be 1) indoctrination; 2) verbal propositional instruction; 3) values clarification; or 4) logical problem-solving case studies and moral dilemmas.

Recently moral education in American public schools has most often incorporated the values clarification and case studies approaches. This has been in an attempt to avoid the problem of indoctrination in a pluralistic society. Following World War II moral education was usually a neglected aspect of public schooling, but it received new emphasis as a result of the social protest over industrialistic/materialistic society, the Vietnam war, and Watergate. Prior to that time moral education usually consisted of direct content-centered propositional instruction and character building. This was also the primary approach to moral education in Christian ministry—and still is, though there have been recent emphases on personal internalization and problem solving paralleling these emphases in public schooling.

Additional Readings
Hall, R. T., & Davis, J. U. *Moral education in theory and practice.* Buffalo: Prometheus Books, 1975.
Purpel, D., & Ryan, K. *Moral education . . . it comes with the territory.* Berkeley, Calif.: McCutchan Publishing, 1976.
R. B. McKean

See Religious Concept Development; Christian Growth.

Moral Therapy. An approach to the treatment of the mentally ill which had its development and focus in late eighteenth-century France. The term *moral* was understood as something closer to morale in that it carried the connotations of zeal and hope. The approach was a movement toward a more humane treatment of the insane. It included such reforms as the removing of chains and shackles from patients and the first attempts to train staff in therapeutic care.

In France this movement is primarily associated with Phillippe Pinel, who is usually credited with being the first to remove chains from the insane. Actually this credit should go to Jean-Baptiste Pussin, a tanner by trade, who was the governor of mental patients at a major Paris psychiatric hospital. In the United States, Benjamin Rush (1745–1813) was a major figure in the moral therapy era. His initiatives were responsible for the abolition of mechanical restraints and the betterment of physical care in numerous American hospitals.

In many ways moral therapy was the first psychological treatment for mental illness. It assumed mental illness was primarily an emotional disturbance, which was therefore curable. Furthermore, mental patients were felt to be not fully responsible for their actions. When combined, these assumptions led to a treatment that was primarily psychological. This accounts for the important place moral therapy plays in the history of Abnormal Psychology.

The period of moral therapy is the historical antecedent of Therapeutic Community and Milieu Therapy. It differed from milieu therapy in its assumption of curability. However, most of the basic thrusts of the movement have remained and are now well entrenched in mental health care.

Additional Reading
Bockoven, J. S. *Moral treatment in community mental health.* New York: Springer Publishing, 1972.
D. G. Benner

Morita Therapy. A Japanese psychotherapy for treating neuroses, developed by Shōma Morita in the early twentieth century. It continues to be successfully applied in Japan, and Western psychotherapists are showing increasing interest in the approach.

Morita's goal was to cure the common Japanese neurosis of *shinkeishitsushu*, which is characterized by feelings of inferiority and anxiety, shyness, oversensitivity, extreme self-consciousness, and perfectionism. Morita viewed the neurotic as one who is conflicted by extreme self-consciousness and an excessive desire to live life fully. He observed that the anxiety generated by this conflict often feeds into a vicious circle in which the neurotic becomes increasingly preoccupied with his debilitating anxiety and therefore begins to function less successfully in the world.

Morita theory assumes this conflict to be primarily conscious, and typically therapists do not deal with unconscious factors. While there is no direct relationship between Morita's theory and Zen, there are several correspondences between the two systems. Zen philosophy holds that the self per se does not exist, and Moritist thinking stresses the curative factor of losing oneself by fully attending to the work at hand. Both systems stress the power of personal experience in validating knowledge; rational understanding alone is viewed as insufficient for coping with the challenges of living. Most importantly, Zen and Morita therapy have as their goals the full acceptance of all aspects of oneself, negative and positive, and both require learning to live contentedly in the here and now.

Morita therapy works best with those who suffer from obsessive, depressive, and anxiety neuroses; hypochondriasis; and some of the phobias. The patient should be strongly motivated toward getting better and should have the ability to reflect on his condition. He usually is knowledgeable about Morita therapy and looks to it as the treatment of choice for his problems. Most patients who are accepted for Morita therapy are men ranging in age from 15 to 40, with the younger patients having the better prognosis.

Morita therapy is most successfully carried out in an inpatient setting. It commonly lasts from 40 to 60 days, although twice this length is not unusual. The goal of the therapy is to bring about a fundamental change in the structure of the patient's personality, not merely symptom removal. Ideally this comes about through four stages.

The first stage consists of rest for a week in which the patient is made to lie in bed without any distractions, except a daily visit from the therapist. This forces him to confront directly his escalating anxiety, immerse himself in it, pursue his neurotic conflict to its ultimate end, and eventually accept it all as part of himself. Morita therapists believe that the acceptance that follows such a confrontation is an innate attitude characteristic of human beings. Once the foundation for the attitude of acceptance is established, the patient typically desires physical activity, and the second stage of partial bed rest, also lasting a week, allows the patient to accomplish some light work. At this time he must keep a diary of his everyday behavior, which the therapist uses for the patient's daily personal therapy.

The third stage, or semiwork period, lasts approximately another week and gives the patient more freedom in his tasks. This is designed to enable him to be more fully committed to the here and now of his labor. Finally, with the successful completion of these more solitary exercises the patient is encouraged to associate with others both in and outside the hospital. To be discharged the patient must be able to accomplish his daily activities in spite of any anxiety symptoms he may still have. Morita therapists actively pursue outpatient follow-up to encourage a patient's basic change in personality structure after the initial profound inpatient experience.

Essentially the Morita therapist creates the conditions for the patient to confront his life situation at the most basic existential level. At the heart of successful therapy is the patient's powerful experiential insight that his neurotic conflict is meaningless when compared to the whole of his life. Thus, the patient is able to emotionally disengage from the conflict and its consequent symptoms. Throughout this process the Morita therapist stresses that man is an active being. What one does is more important than what one feels or thinks; and despite disabilities a person can carry on an active, purposive life.

While these principles may not be altogether incompatible with traditional Christian thought, the biblical view of the reality of man's fallen nature and need for redemption and sanctification strongly contrasts with Morita therapy's stress on accepting all aspects of oneself. Morita therapy does enable a person to confront the meaning of his existence. But its answer of self-acceptance through commitment to the immediate task at hand seems to ignore man's longing for a more profound truth about himself which reflects his desire to transcend the natural limitations of this life. This longing for living fully ultimately is one that only a personal faith relationship with Christ can fulfill.

Additional Reading
Reynolds, D. K. *Morita psychotherapy*. Berkeley: University of California Press, 1976.

W. C. DREW

Mother, Schizophrenogenic. Schizophrenogenic mother is a term first used by Fromm-Reichman (1948) and adopted by others who have focused on certain patterns of mothering that seem often associated with SCHIZOPHRENIA. The term is used to describe mothers who are overprotective, hostile, overtly or subtly rejecting, overanxious, and emotionally cold. The assumption is that such a mother's interaction with her child is the basic determinant of schizophrenia in the child.

Arieti (1974) argues that such mothers account for only 25% of schizophrenics. Furthermore, of all the mothers who could be classified as fulfilling the above description, only a small percentage has schizophrenic children.

Since it has been difficult to identify a consistent pattern of family dynamics in schizophrenics, the schizophrenogenic mother hypothesis has fallen somewhat into disfavor. Some form of serious family disturbance seems always present. However, it may be a necessary but not sufficient causative factor.

References
Arieti, S. *Interpretation of schizophrenia* (2nd ed.). New York: Basic Books, 1974.
Fromm-Reichman, F. Notes on the development of treatment of schizophrenics by psychoanalytic therapy. *Psychiatry*, 1948, *11*, 263–273.

D. G. BENNER

Mothering. Those behaviors given by a nurturing member of the species for the sustenance and preservation of the young. In animals mothering is largely instinctual and is focused on the physical care and protection of offspring. In humans there is less evidence for either a prematernal or a postmaternal instinct, although looking forward to the birth of a baby may increase one's desire for a child, and close contact with the newborn appears to enhance mother-neonate bonding (Klaus & Kennell, 1976). The mothering of the human child requires not only that physical care be given but that emotional, intellectual, and social needs be met as well.

Mothering is usually provided by the biological mother. It seems only natural that the one who bears the child and is capable of nursing the child would be the one to meet the dependency needs of the child. However, giving birth does not in itself program a woman for mothering, and nourishment may come from a bottle as well as from the breast. Consequently, mothering is not restricted to the child's mother or even to the female of the species. Fathers, grandparents, foster parents, as well as a variety of other related and nonrelated individuals have shown themselves capable of the task. "Recent studies indicate that highly involved fathers with a warm, nurturing parenting style seem to enhance their children's sex role development, cognitive growth and self-esteem" (Cordes, 1983). Now that over half the women with dependent children are in the labor force, it is essential that mothering be shared by other adults.

An understandable concern is that too many "mothers" may confuse the child, making it more difficult for the child to establish a warm, continuous, and intimate relationship with another human being. This in turn may affect adversely the child's emotional and social development. Early studies on infant-mother attachment and the separation anxiety felt by children whose mothers were absent supported the traditional view that mothers should stay with their young. Freud's ideas that the psychic energy of the baby extends to the mother even before birth and that the first five years of life are critical for the development of a healthy personality also contributed to the belief that the mother should be the one to care for the child.

More recent research, however, questions both the way in which bonding relates to the mother's care of the infant (Chess & Thomas, 1982; Lamb, 1983) and the way in which attachment of child to mother is affected by multiple caretakers (O'Connell, 1983). Although the findings are somewhat equivocal, there is general consensus that good mothering depends more on the personality characteristics of the caretaker than on early bonding, and that children with several caretakers, when given a choice, usually go to the mother for comfort. During the most sensitive period for attachment, occurring between the ages of 6 and 18 months, children feel more secure with only one or two caretakers but will tolerate more as they grow older. It is recognized that the quality of mothering is more important than either the relationship of caretaker to child or the number of caretakers experienced by the child. Needed is a warm, loving, and stable environment in which the child develops a secure attachment to one or more adults.

The term *mothering* is being replaced in the literature with *parenting*. This reflects the trend toward the greater involvement of fathers in the care of children and also serves to minimize sex-role stereotypes. For generations mothers have been praised or condemned for what their children became. Now it is acknowledged that this important force in shaping the lives of our young extends to others as well, and that they too should be recognized for their part in the nurturance of children.

References

Chess, S., & Thomas, A. Infant bonding: Mystique and reality. *American Journal of Orthopsychiatry*, 1982, *52*, 213–222.

Cordes, C. Researchers make room for father. *APA Monitor*, December 1983, pp. 1; 9.

Klaus, M. H., & Kennell, J. H. *Maternal-infant bonding*. St. Louis: Mosby, 1976.

Lamb, M. E. Early mother-neonate contact and the mother-child relationship. *Journal of Child Psychology and Child Psychiatry and Allied Disciplines*, 1983, *24*, 487–494.

O'Connell, J. C. Children of working mothers: What the research tells us. *Young Children*, 1983(2), *38*, 62–70.

B. CLOUSE

See FATHERING.

Motivation. Many psychologists have sought to answer the question of why people behave as they do through the study of underlying motives. The term *motivation* is used to refer to factors that energize and direct behavior. That is, specific motives not only arouse an organism to action but also guide its behavior. Thus, a hungry person seeks food while a thirsty person searches for drink.

Freud's psychoanalytic theory attributed behavior to powerful innate forces. Freud suggested that there are two basic conflicting energies or instincts that determine behavior. Eros (love) enhances life and growth, while thanatos (death) pushes the organism toward destruction. Sex and aggression were postulated as two basic human motives that arise in childhood. Because parents forbid their free expression, these motives are repressed and operate at an unconscious level. Psychoanalytic theory viewed individuals as trapped in a continuing conflict between these instinctive drives, on one hand, and the restraints demanded by society and by internalized ideals, on the other. Unconscious motives were seen as powerful forces that shape behavior in a variety of ways and are evident in a person's dreams, slips of speech, and in the symptoms of mental illness.

One of the most influential views of motivation to appear in this century was Hull's (1943) drive reduction theory. While Freud's theory was a product of his clinical work, the development of Hull's theory involved the utilization of the laboratory experiment. Both theories assumed that actions are undertaken to satisfy unfilled needs. According to Hull a drive is an aroused state that is produced by some biological need such as a need for food, water, air, or the avoidance of injury.

Basic to drive theory was the concept of homeostasis, which refers to the body's tendency to maintain a constant internal environment. Many physiological states must be maintained within fairly narrow limits. The healthy person, for example, maintains a body temperature within a few degrees. Similarly the concentration of blood sugar, the water balance in the cells, and the level of oxygen must be maintained at a constant level. According to drive theory a need is any physiological imbalance or departure from this state of equilibrium. Thus needs initiate behavior that will restore balance and reduce tension. While drives energize behavior, previously established stimulus-response associations, or habits, provide the direction for action. Hull is perhaps best known for the equation stating that drive and habit relate multiplicatively in producing behavior.

Hull later acknowledged that behavior is not always based in some specific tissue deficit. To account for behaviors that occur in the absence of any actual physiological imbalance, Hull distinguished between primary and secondary, or learned, sources of drive. Fear, for example, may be a learned drive, as is evident when a stimulus previously associated with shock comes to produce avoidance behavior in animals.

While drive reduction provides a comprehensive perspective on motivation, a number of objections have been raised to the theory and have contributed to its declining influence. First, drive reduction theory assumed that the goal of behavior is to reduce tension or stimulation. Yet considerable research indicated that both animals and people often strive to increase stimulation. Offered a choice between a short, direct route to food and a longer, indirect path, a rat frequently prefers the longer, more scenic route. Sensory deprivation studies, in which the subject lies alone in a room wearing translucent goggles and receives very limited stimulation, indicate that people need new and changing sensory input. On the basis of this evidence Hebb (1955) hypothesized that organisms are motivated to maintain an optimal level of stimulation. Too intense or too great a change in stimulation may motivate a person to reduce tension, but too little sensory input or variation will move the individual to increase stimulation.

Another objection to drive theory, at least as it was originally formulated, was that it overlooked the importance of external stimuli in arousing behavior. Goal-directed behavior may occur when an organism is not in a drive state at all. The presentation of delicious food may arouse the hunger drive in people who would not otherwise be hungry. Thus while an internal drive may "push" an organism to act, external stimuli called incentives may "pull" an organism into action. It has become clear that motivation is better understood as an interaction between stimuli in the environment and the physiological state of the organism.

Perhaps the major reason why drive theory is no longer the dominant perspective in the study of motivation is that it neglects cognitive or mental processes and assumes that people are merely complicated machines (Weiner, 1980). One popular cognitive approach to motivation is expectancy-value theory. According to this perspective behavior is jointly determined by the strength of a person's expectation that certain actions will lead to goal attainment and by the value that the goal has for the person. Thus goal-directed behavior is strongest when a goal is highly valued and there is also a high expectation that certain actions will result in achieving the goal.

According to Rotter's (1954) social learning theory, expectancy is shaped by one's prior reinforcement history—i.e., by the previous outcomes of the same situation and by experiences in similar situations. The value of a goal is closely linked to the specific needs of an individual and, according to Rotter, most needs are learned. While expectancy and value are viewed as independent constructs, their interrelationships greatly influence personal adjustment. For example, a low expectancy of success in the presence of a highly valued goal may result in serious behavioral problems.

One of the interesting issues raised by the cognitive perspective concerns the distinction between intrinsic and extrinsic motivation. When an action is performed for the sake of a reward, it is extrinsically motivated. When it is undertaken for its own sake, because the task itself is interesting and challenging, it is said to be intrinsically motivated. One cognitive theory states that, when people receive extrinsic rewards for behaviors that were intrinsically motivated, intrinsic motivation may be undermined. A shift in attitude may occur in which the activity is no longer engaged in because it is liked, but because it produces rewards. Research indicates that rewarding children for performing an initially interesting and freely chosen activity reduces the time the children later spend in the task on their own. Rewards may have hidden costs.

The intrinsic-extrinsic distinction has been important in the psychology of religion as well. Allport distinguished between extrinsic and intrinsic religious orientations. Presumably extrinsics use religion to gain social status, business contacts, or relief from feelings of failure. According to Allport they turn to God but not away from themselves. For intrinsics religious faith becomes the master motive in life, with other needs being subordinated to it. Allport and Ross (1967) developed a scale to measure religious orientations, and research indicates that intrinsics tend to be lower in racial prejudice and significantly more consistent in church attendance than extrinsics.

While most theories of motivation have subscribed to the pleasure-pain principle, in which organisms are viewed as maximizing pleasurable stimulation and minimizing pain, recent cognitive approaches have emphasized humans as information seekers who are attempting to understand themselves and their environment. This position is most clearly seen in the work of attribution theorists. Kelley (1967), one of the leading proponents of this perspective, states that humans are motivated to "attain a cognitive mastery of the causal structure of the environment" (p. 193). People desire an understanding of why events occur; humans are not merely driven by hedonic concerns but are seeking meaning in their world. The more recent cognitive approaches, which emphasize human rationality and the importance of thoughts and beliefs in understanding action, seem in certain respects to be more consistent with a biblical view of the person as an image bearer of God who is capable of making choices and who is responsible for his actions.

Humanistic theorists such as Maslow (1954) have emphasized the person's struggle toward self-actualization, which is the tendency to maximize one's inborn potentialities. Maslow distinguished between deficiency needs, which are concerned with physical and social survival, and growth needs, which motivate one to develop his or her full potential. Presumably in order for the growth needs to manifest themselves, deficiency needs must first be met. Maslow proposed a need hierarchy in which physiological and safety needs appear and must be satisfied before love and esteem needs become evident. These are followed by the higher aesthetic and cognitive needs, with the highest of all human needs being self-actualization.

References

Allport, G. W., & Ross, J. M. Personal religious orientation and prejudice. *Journal of Personality and Social Psychology*, 1967, 5, 432–443.

Hebb, D. O. Drives and the CNS. *Psychological Review*, 1955, 62, 243–254.

Hull, C. L. *Principles of behavior*. New York: Appleton-Century-Crofts, 1943.

Kelley, H. H. Attribution theory in social psychology. In D. Levine (Ed.), *Nebraska Symposium on Motivation* (Vol. 15). Lincoln: University of Nebraska Press, 1967.

Maslow, A. H. *Motivation and personality*. New York: Harper & Row, 1954.

Rotter, J. B. *Social learning and clinical psychology*. Englewood Cliffs, N.J.: Prentice-Hall, 1954.

Weiner, B. *Human motivation*. New York: Holt, Rinehart, & Winston, 1980.

M. BOLT

Mourning. *See* GRIEF; LOSS AND SEPARATION.

Mowrer, Orval Hobart (1907–1982). The formulator of INTEGRITY THERAPY, Mowrer had a long and distinguished career in American psychology. He completed his undergraduate work at the University of Missouri (1929) and obtained his Ph.D. from Johns Hopkins University. Further training at Northwestern University and Princeton prepared him for a position at Yale (1934–1940), followed by assistant and later an associate professorship in education at Harvard (1940–1948). In 1948 he became a research professor in psychology at the University of Illinois, Urbana, where he worked until his retirement in 1975. His specialities included learning theory, language, and personality. He held diplomate (clinical) status from the American Board of Professional Psychology.

Mowrer served as president of the American Psychological Association in 1954 and was the recipient of numerous awards and citations. He authored 12 volumes spanning the years 1939–1980. His early work was on learning theory, and he began his career as a behaviorist. Later he moved toward integrating concepts such as fear and hope into his theory of the second signal system, a filtering structure bridging the individual with the surrounding world (Mowrer, 1980). This shift toward incorporating "softer" concepts into the "hard" data of learning theory was later followed by the addition of a major new area to Mowrer's professional interests: therapy and psychopathology. Meanwhile he wrote or edited four major texts on learning theory.

Mowrer's integrity therapy urges neurotics and others to confess past misdeeds as a necessary step toward health. His approach to therapy was developed as part of his attempts to heal himself of severe, periodic episodes of depression. By his own assessment analysis by three of the nation's "best" analysts failed him. His own self-treatment program of confession and restitution helped him greatly, and his theories have found fertile footing.

Mowrer's writings have been of great interest to Christians because of his emphasis on sin and confession. However, although he uses such terms as sin, grace, and confession, he uses them in an ethical rather than a theological sense. "What I hope for eventually, is some sort of synthesis: a continuation of the ethical concern of traditional religionists with the thoroughgoing naturalism of science" (Mowrer, 1966, p. 25).

Mowrer is unmistakably anti-Freudian. He suggests that during the Freudian era (1920–1955) personality disturbance was seen to arise from the excesses and rigidity of conscience. Remediation came from a loosening of standards and from permissiveness. "It is now widely recognized that psychotherapy based on this 'diagnosis' has been conspicuously unsuccessful" (Johnson, Dokecki, & Mowrer, 1972, p. 38). He views conscience and morality as a necessary and normally helpful part of the human personality. "The main reason 'mental illness' has been such a mystery in our time is that we have so assiduously separated it from the realm of personal morality and immorality" (Mowrer, 1967, p. vii).

According to Mowrer the neuroses develop because of undersocialization and faulty interpersonal relationships (as opposed to Freud's oversocialized superego) and the failure of repression to continue to cover up past misdeeds. The neurotic suffers from guilt that is real (as opposed to Freud's guilt feelings). "The condition which we currently refer to as neurosis or psychosis is the same which an earlier era knew as a state of sin or disgrace; and the defining characteristic of both is the presence in one's life of shameful secrets" (Mowrer, 1961, p. 148).

Obsessive-compulsives are driven and tortured people energized by displaced guilt that is terribly real. Paranoids project their own outraged conscience onto others and then perceive the others as "after" or "against" them. Anxiety comes, "not from acts which the individual would commit but dares not, but from acts which he has committed and wishes he had not" (Mowrer, 1950, p. 597). Depression is self-inflicted suffering. "A depression looks very much like an act of 'serving time,' comparable to what happens in those other places of penance [penitentiary].... The question of whether an individual will have one or more later depressions . . . depends upon whether he has really 'connected' crime and punishment" (Mowrer, 1961, p. 100).

Integrity therapy involves acts of confession and restitution so that the troubled conscience can rest and allow normal functioning to begin again. Peace and relief are the benefits of forgiveness and treating the past with integrity.

Observers of the American psychology scene credit Mowrer with opening the discipline for more favorable consideration of values, religion, and morality. He has had considerable influence on such divergent writers as Adams (1970), Glasser (1965), and Menninger (1973). In an edited volume Mowrer (1967) reprinted works that sustained him in times of discouragement. Included are writings of Fulton Sheen, C. S. Lewis, William Glasser, Thomas Szasz, and Anton Boisen.

References

Adams, J. E. Competent to counsel. Philadelphia: Presbyterian and Reformed Publishing, 1970.

Glasser, W. Reality therapy: A new approach to psychiatry. New York: Harper & Row, 1965.

Johnson, R. C., Dokecki, P. R., & Mowrer, O. H. (Eds.). Conscience, contract, and social reality: Theory and research in behavioral science. New York: Holt, Rinehart, & Winston, 1972.

Menninger, K. A. Whatever became of sin? New York: Hawthorn Books, 1973.

Mowrer, O. H. Learning theory and personality dynamics: Selected papers. New York: Ronald Press, 1950.

Mowrer, O. H. The crisis in psychiatry and religion. Princeton, N.J.: Van Nostrand, 1961.

Mowrer, O. H. Abnormal reactions or actions? Dubuque, Iowa: Brown, 1966.

Mowrer, O. H. (Ed.). Morality and mental health. Chicago: Rand McNally, 1967.

Mowrer, O. H. (Ed.). Psychology of language and learning. New York: Plenum, 1980.

J. R. BECK

Multigenerational Transmission Process.

Bowen (1978) is credited with coining this term. The process describes how an individual's level of emotional maturity is a function of family dynamics in previous generations.

In his transgenerational studies Bowen gave particular attention to the transmission of relationship patterns and emotional factors across several generations. He concluded that, in general, three lines of descent can be traced in most families. One line develops a higher level of maturity (differentiation) than parents, another an equivalent level, and another a lower level. Individuals in each line in turn produce offspring who follow a similar pattern; some go up the scale, some remain at the same level as parents, and others go down the scale.

According to Bowen, it is the degree of emotional involvement between parent and child that determines the direction of a child's emotional development. The greater the involvement (lack of differentiation in the relationship), the greater will be the child's impairment. Conversely, the minimally involved (most differentiated) child will achieve the highest level of maturity.

It is a widely accepted view among family therapists that the overinvolved parent is lacking to some degree in emotional maturity. While their emotional problem may or may not be serious, it will be projected onto the child with whom the parent is overinvolved (see FAMILY SCAPEGOATING). The parent, in a sense, passes the emotional problem to the child, thus hampering his or her development.

The transgenerational transmission process is Bowen's explanation for how a serious disturbance develops in an individual. If one starts with "normal" parents and follows their downward line of descent (the line that produces children with lower levels of differentiation), within eight to ten generations a schizophrenic individual will likely emerge. Hence, it is important to appreciate the historic and family-related factors involved in such disabling emotional disorders as schizophrenia.

Reference

Bowen, M. Family therapy in clinical practice. New York: Aronson, 1978.

J. A. LARSEN

See FAMILY SYSTEMS THEORY; FAMILY SYSTEMS THERAPY.

Multimodal Therapy.

An eclectic approach to psychotherapy developed and popularized by Lazarus (1976, 1981). It is not identified with any particular school of psychological thought, nor is it a separate school or system. Multimodal therapy is simply an approach that is integrative, systematic, and comprehensive in providing a workable paradigm for assessment and therapy. It is pragmatic and holds to a scientific empiricism without following a reductionistic style of reasoning. More concern is given to the technical dimensions than to the theoretical. In fact, Lazarus has referred to multimodal therapy as a technical eclecticism.

Although multimodal therapy retains no identification with any specific theoretical orientation, it is rooted in learning theory, cognitive processes, and behavioral principles.

Its roots lie in behavior therapy (Lazarus, 1971). In fact, Lazarus first described the approach as multimodal behavior therapy.

Assessment and treatment focus on seven distinct dimensions or modalities of human activity. Information about an individual's salient behaviors, affective processes, sensory reactions, imagery, cognitions, interpersonal relations, and physiological processes must be included in the comprehensive multimodal assessment. All these modalities are interdependent and interactive. The diagnosis results in a profile that indicates deficits and excesses across each modality. Multimodal therapy stresses that effective psychotherapy depends on an accurate assessment of the problems presented.

Multimodal therapy encompasses three major areas of concern: 1) the specification of goals and problems; 2) the identification of treatment techniques to achieve the stated goals and remedy the problems; and 3) the systematic measurement of the relative success or effectiveness of the techniques used in the therapy process. In the therapist-client relationship therapists are preferably non-mechanistic, flexible, empathic, and genuinely concerned for the total welfare of their clients.

Multimodal therapy offers an armamentarium of therapeutic methods drawn from numerous approaches. However, in order to remain theoretically consistent, all these methods and strategies have some connection with the principles of social learning theory. Examples of techniques that make up this technical eclecticism are assertiveness training, sensate focusing, empty chair dialogue, relaxation training, Gestalt dreamwork, hypnosis, cognitive restructuring, rational-emotive interventions, and behavioral rehearsal. More than 36 major procedures make up the body of central techniques.

A recent survey of trends in counseling and psychotherapy (Smith, 1982) indicates that multimodal therapy is an umbrella term descriptive of the approach of an increasingly large percentage of therapists. Similarly, the books by Lazarus were judged to be among the most representative of the current zeitgeist.

References

Lazarus, A. A. *Behavior therapy and beyond.* New York: McGraw-Hill, 1971.
Lazarus, A. A. (Ed.). *Multimodal behavior therapy.* New York: Springer Publishing, 1976.
Lazarus, A. A. *The practice of multimodal therapy.* New York: McGraw-Hill, 1981.
Smith, D. Trends in counseling and psychotherapy. *American Psychologist,* 1982, *37*, 802–809.

D. Smith

Multiple Family Therapy. A natural outgrowth of two parallel developments in the history of psychotherapy that emerged in the 1950s: group therapy and family therapy. A basic tenet of group therapy is that a person best learns about himself through interaction in a group where he can risk self-disclosure and receive feedback from other group members about the impact of his communication style. Family therapy arose out of dissatisfaction with the limitation of individual therapy that involves contact between one client and one therapist. It also emphasizes the importance of group interaction, specifically within the most intimate of groups, the nuclear family.

Multiple family therapy brings these two streams together. Families are dealt with in a group setting. Thus, the individual member of the group is itself a subgroup, the nuclear family. The acknowledged founder and only true theorist of this form of therapy is H. P. Laqueur, a psychiatrist who began experimenting with this approach with schizophrenic patients and their families at Creedmoor State Mental Hospital in New York in 1950 (Laqueur, La Burt, & Morong, 1964). He found that patients experiencing such therapy with their families had a lower readmission rate to hospitals than those who were not given the benefit of the experience. Since that time the approach has been widely adopted, not only in inpatient psychiatric settings but in schools, clinics, and growth centers as well. It has become a relatively commonplace adjunct to individual and group therapy in many psychiatric hospitals.

When used in a hospital setting, the approach follows a typical pattern. Usually on a weekly basis, families of 10 to 12 patients meet to discuss therapy themes each family is currently working on with its individual therapist. The length of such a session runs to two hours or more and is often combined with social activities such as eating together before or after the session. The experience initially serves a new family by helping them through the "why did this happen to us" crisis. Family members see that other families entered the hospital with the same fear and shame they did. Often an immediate sense of relief and support develops.

As the family becomes more trustful of the group, it often begins to share the themes of therapy it is working on individually. Families begin to see patterns of communication causing other families difficulty that they then recognize as similar to their own. As is the case in group therapy an individual is usually able to spot quickly the pathology in others that he is blinded to in himself. Families that are able to grow into such an awareness often find multiple family therapy critical to the healing that takes place for them and the identified patient of their family in the hospital setting. Families that entered the hospital in deeply disturbed conditions often find themselves eventually encouraging other families going through the same difficult times.

There is no set limit to the number of people who can be effectively helped in one multiple family therapy session. Many ongoing groups can contain 30 or 40 members and three or four cotherapists. Often not only spouses, parents, children, or siblings attend, but also members of the extended family as well. Friends and neighbors sometimes participate, especially if they have an important role in the posthospital adjustment of the individual patient and his family.

Techniques used in this approach vary as much as they do in group or family therapy. Common group techniques such as role playing and psychodrama are popular. Transference often takes place in multiple family therapy. For example a teen-ager who cannot bring himself to confront his own father may be able to express his anger at the father of a fellow patient. Most therapists attempt to keep the families focused on the here-and-now relationships that are developing between family members, rather than allowing each family to report solely on what has happened to them separately. Therapists help families to learn by the examples of others—healthier families modeling for those who are still more pathological. This approach is especially helpful to broken, one-parent families in dealing with the loss of a significant member; for instance, they may find in the group a father figure who is able to deal with some of the experiences of a fatherless home.

Implications of this approach for the Christian community are significant. There are typically very few opportunities available to members of a Christian congregation to share openly their struggles with each other in a safe, supportive, accepting atmosphere. We tend to want to hide the reality of our family problems, out of embarrassment or fear of judgment that such things are not to occur in a Christian family. Such isolation flies in the face of clear biblical models that seem consistent with the opportunity for self-disclosure and feedback that multiple family therapy offers. Paul's description of the body of Christ in 1 Corinthians 12 includes the provision "so it happens that if one member suffers, all the other members suffer with it. If one member is honored, all the members share a common joy." Paul seems to be saying that if a Christian individual or family suffers or rejoices alone, if the experience of elation or pain is totally private, the body of Christ—the Christian community—fails itself and him. The success of multiple family therapy in secular settings bears unfortunate witness to the lack of community in the experience of many Christians.

The church as community has become accepted as a vital part of its function. Local congregations have experimented, often with great success, in structured activities—usually under the leadership of a trained professional—that allow Christian families to share with each other the struggles and joys of their lives (Cassens, 1973). Prayer groups and house church experiences provide this outlet for some, but for many other Christian families suffering and pain are born in isolation and a false sense of shame.

All families, Christian or not, have to deal with parent-child relations, marital conflicts, expressions of feelings, privacy, and individuality. Multiple family therapy has successfully enabled families to compare themselves to other families, to learn from others, and to gain a sense of kinship and belonging to a larger community as a result. This model would seem to ideally fit a basic calling of the Christian church.

References

Cassens, J. *The catalytic community.* River Forest, Ill.: Lutheran Education Association, 1973.

Laqueur, H. P., La Burt, H. A., & Morong, E. Multiple family therapy. In S. H. Masserman (Ed.), *Current psychiatric therapies* (Vol. 4). New York: Grune & Stratton, 1964.

Additional Readings

Raasock, J. W., H. Peter Laqueur—A reflection. In L. R. Wolberg, & M. L. Aronson (Eds.), *Group and family therapy,* 1980. New York: Brunner/Mazel, 1980.

Strelnick, A. H. Multiple family group therapy: A review of the literature. *Family Process,* 1977, *16* (3), 307–325.

J. F. CASSENS

See FAMILY THERAPY: OVERVIEW.

Multiple Impact Therapy. An intensive short-term family evaluation process based on the premise that when a family is in distress and desiring change, they are most responsive to treatment. It is an interdisciplinary approach using a team of mental health professionals to work simultaneously with the family members for a period of 2½ days.

Considerable planning with the referral source is done prior to the beginning of multiple impact therapy. The referral source is usually involved in preliminary evaluations of the problems, which often concern an adolescent who is the identified patient. The family members' attitudes are crucial to this process, so considerable time is directed to promoting the process with family members.

Sessions usually begin on Monday and are completed Wednesday near noon. Prior to the family arrival on Monday team members meet to discuss the data concerning the family and assign team members to see particular family members. Following this, the team meets with the whole family. At the initial conference early interaction focuses on getting the family to make a clear statement about their reason for coming. Usually the response is strained and unclear. A team member then breaks the ice by stating a blunt observation that reflects what he has assimilated from the preliminary data. An example of such a statement might be, "Obviously this boy has to stay childish in that setting. Only by extending childhood could he help mother justify her excessive attention to him" (MacGregor, 1971, p. 893). This usually results in extensive interaction that demonstrates the family's defective communication.

Team members freely discuss family members with each other and with other members of the family. The interaction is open, and all are encouraged to participate. Team members may openly discuss strategy changes that were originally developed in the briefing session. Following this each family member goes to a team member's office. The individual session gives each parent an opportunity to clarify his or her perception of the family and develop a support relationship with a team member. This is termed a *pressured ventilation*. Later, that team member may meet with the other spouse in order to hear another perception and achieve cross-ventilation of the family problems.

Meanwhile the teen-ager has been in an individual session describing his perception of himself and the family. This session usually lasts about half an hour and is followed by diagnostic testing. This adolescent's team member may then join a parental session for an overlapping session—i.e., the team member assigned to the parent describes the session to the adolescent's team member, giving the parent opportunity to clarify and elaborate on the interaction. The youth's team member describes the session with the youth and tries to fit together the parental and youth descriptions of the family.

The following lunch break gives family members a chance to discuss their experiences as well as a chance for the team to confer and plan the afternoon individual and overlapping sessions. After lunch the team members switch family members and explore the family difficulties with their added information. Overlapping interviews with two family members and two team members may continue to occur as well as cross-ventilations. Frequent use is made of overlapping sessions. The task is to clarify perceptions and validate what family members are saying as well as what team members are observing. A team-family conference is held at the end of the first day. Impressions and observations are again expressed to confirm family members' experiences or shed new light on problems. Team members may have experienced the same communication problems family members have complained about with each other. This conference adds more information to the team's expanding experience of the family and is designed to increase communication between family members.

The second day begins with a brief team-family conference to discuss what happened during the evening. Presumably the family members have discussed the previous day's events. If a family member has an urgent need to discuss a personal concern, this morning briefing session is omitted. More individual, overlapping, and cross-ventilation sessions continue through the second day. The second afternoon the focus changes to rehearsals and applications directly related to the problem that initiated their coming. Parental and marital relationships are discussed, with the focus being on problem solving. Information gained from the numerous sessions is directed toward responsible ways of solving problems; e.g., "You came here feeling that your son was being deprived of your participation. Why not start by inviting him to prepare those reports to his probation officer with you?" (MacGregor, 1971, p. 897).

The third day's sessions are directed toward a final team-family conference. Specific plans concerning the youth are discussed such as returning to the same school. The youth may be dismissed from part of the session so that the marital relationship may be focused upon.

This intense therapeutic approach exposes family problems rapidly by using a number of mental health professionals. The overlapping and cross-ventilation conferences clarify perceptions and attitudes, and facilitate improved communication and the use of problem solving techniques. Although research on the approach is limited, it does seem to hold considerable promise as a creative alternative to, or supplement to, more traditional ongoing family therapy.

Reference
MacGregor, R. Multiple impact therapy with families. In J. G. Howels (Ed.), *The theory and practice of family psychiatry.* New York: Brunner/Mazel, 1971.

T. M. JOHNSON

See FAMILY THERAPY: OVERVIEW.

Multiple Personality. The phenomenon of the coexistence of multiple personalities within a single individual has been the object of considerable interest ever since the first reported case in 1817. Described by S. L. Mitchell in *Medical Repository*, this first report presented the strange circumstances of an American woman named Mary Reynolds, who displayed two alternating personalities, each state being amnesic for the other. As in subsequently reported cases, the differences in behavior and even physical appearance of the two states were quite dramatic. This led to Mitchell's diagnosis of "double consciousness: duality of person in the same individual."

Initial interest subsided somewhat when a total of only three additional cases (one German and two British) were reported between 1817 and 1873. The period from 1874 to 1900 saw 28 cases reported. Then in 1906 Morton Prince published his very influential book, *The Dissociation of a Personality*, describing his detailed investigation of Miss Christian Beauchamp. As the founding editor of the *Journal of Abnormal Psychology*, Prince did much to revive interest in this disorder.

In the period from 1906 to the present around 150 cases have been reported, making a total of approximately 200 reported cases. A number of clinicians have questioned whether this small number is a good indication of actual incidence. They have argued that the disorder is much more common than previously suspected and that the paucity of reports has arisen mainly out of clinical oversight. However, while formally reported cases may underrepresent the incidence of the disorder, multiple personality is still generally assumed to be relatively rare.

Public interest in multiple personality has been disproportionate to its incidence. Robert Louis Stevenson's fictional account of *The Strange Case of Dr. Jekyll and Mr. Hyde* (1877), as well as the more recent popularized accounts of Eve White (Thigpen & Cleckley, 1957) and Sybil (Schreiber, 1973), have all contributed to the public's fascination. This has led to the frequent popular confusion of multiple personality and schizophrenia or, more seriously, the basic equation of multiple personality and all other psychopathologies.

Diagnostic Criteria and Clinical Manifestations. *DSM-III* lists three criteria for the diagnosis of multiple personality: "A) The existence within the individual of two or more distinct personalities, each of which is dominant at a particular time. B) The personality that is dominant at any particular time determines the individual's behavior. C) Each individual personality is complex and integrated with its own unique behavior patterns and social relationships" (p. 259).

Clinical signs which are frequently associated with this disorder and which should therefore be investigated carefully include reports of time distortions or blackouts; reports of being told of behavioral episodes which are not remembered by the patient, particularly if these involve notable changes in behavior; reports of the patient describing himself by different names or referring to himself in the third person; the use of we when a collective rather than editorial connotation seems involved; and the reported discovery of writings, drawings, or objects among the patient's personal belongings which he does not recognize and cannot account for (Greaves, 1980).

Although there is a great deal of variability in the relationship of the various personalities to each other some common features are becoming clear. Typically the main personality has no knowledge or awareness of the existence of any of the subpersonalities. Similarly the main personality has no memory of any of the events that occur when subpersonalities control consciousness. This means that multiples usually have large blocks of life for which they are amnesic.

If there is more than one subpersonality, each is aware of the others and of the main personality to varying degrees. At any given moment one personality will interact verbally with the external environment. However, none or any number of the subpersonalities may have co-consciousness—be aware of the external world and the experience of the conscious personality. The total number of personalities may be over 100, although the majority of reported cases have between 2 and 15, with 3 or 4 being most common.

The various personalities differ from each other in a variety of behavioral, psychological, and physiological ways. Changes in voice, facial musculature, posture, gestures, handedness, handwriting, mood and temperament, attitudes, values, interests, aesthetic tastes, and propriety of behavior are all frequently reported. The various subpersonalities also frequently describe themselves as differing from each other in sex and age. Differences have also been demonstrated on a number of psychological tests as well as physiological measures such as electroencephalogram, visual evoked response and galvanic skin response.

The differential diagnostic issues involved in identifying multiple personality are extremely complex. The major complication arises from the fact that the various personalities may differ so much among themselves as to suggest different diagnoses. For example, one or more personalities may be overtly psychotic while the others may retain good reality contact. Similarly, diagnosis of personality, anxiety, or affective disorders may apply to one or more subpersonalities but not to others.

Female multiples are most often misdiagnosed as schizophrenic, while male multiples are most commonly misdiagnosed as personality disorders. While there is some similarity to possession states, the phenomenon does stand as unique and differential diagnosis is also critical in this area. It is also important to differentiate multiple personality from psychogenic fugue, psychogenic amnesia, organic states such as epilepsy, and simulation.

Question of Authenticity. From the earliest accounts of this disorder, there has been widespread suspicion that multiple personality may not be a legitimate psychopathology but rather a clever deception. Others have questioned whether it might be the creation of the therapist, an iatrogenic syndrome arising from selective reinforcement by an unwitting therapist.

These are really separate issues, and each has received considerable attention in the professional literature related to multiple personality. Regarding the question of simulation or deception, it is interesting to note that a large number of reports of the disorder include the clinician describing initial skepticism being slowly dismantled by the clinical experience. Beyond the reports of a widely distributed number of clinicians, most of whom were well accustomed to watching for fraud, the objective documentation of psychological and physiological differences among the personalities of a multiple leads inescapably to the conclusion that the disorder is real (Ludwig, Brandsma, Wilbur, Bendfeldt, & Jameson, 1972).

The question of the therapist creating the disorder by the use of hypnosis or selective reinforcement through attention and interest has also received considerable treatment in the literature. This is an important matter, since due to the rarity of the disorder it is very easy for a therapist's fascination with a case to lead to selective reinforcement. However, the fact that in the vast majority of the cases of multiple personality the existence of separate personalities was first evidenced well before the initiation of any therapeutic work leads to Greaves's (1980) assertion that "from the weight of the present evidence alone it is undeniably clear that some sort of therapist-independent clinical phenomenon is uniquely denoted by the term 'multiple personality'" (p. 581).

Theories of Etiology. At least 10 different theories of etiology have been suggested to explain the causes and development of multiple personality. A detailed discussion of these can be found in Gottlieb (1977), Berman (1974), and Greaves (1980). The focus of the majority of these theories is the childhood traumas experienced by a very high percentage of multiples. Physical and sexual abuse by one parent, often in the presence and seemingly always with the knowledge of the other parent, is reported most frequently. Very often this abuse also has a particularly sadistic and vicious quality. However, it is important to recall Freud's concept of trauma, which suggests that the essence of a trauma is its capacity to produce psychic injury regardless of the actual stimulus intensity. Thus, when some multiples seem to have experienced much more benign forms of trauma, it has been suggested that they may have possessed a constitutional or temperamental sensitivity to trauma.

Usually dissociation begins after the occurrence of the first trauma and seems to represent a defense against the emotional pain. Seldom does that first dissociation occur after age 8, and most frequently it is within the period between ages 2 and 6. In the face of ongoing trauma dissociation is utilized repeatedly and may even come to be adopted more and more easily. The number of personalities is a probable reflection of the range and number of traumas experienced.

This very general statement leaves unanswered several important questions. What, if any, are the constitutional or physiological predisposing factors in the etiology of multiple personality? Also, is the dissociation involved in the creation of new personalities in any way related to self-hypnosis? Is multiple personality related to the frequent childhood phenomenon of imaginary playmates? These and a number of other questions are central to the continuing debate that is reflected in the various etiological models currently under consideration.

Treatment. Despite the complexity of the task, the prospects for successfully treating multiples appear quite favorable. Therapeutic strategies have varied considerably since the earliest cases. Attempts to stabilize the healthiest of the personalities have generally been disappointing, usually resulting in continued amnesia and dissociation. Similarly the strategy of treating each personality separately now seems a potentially dangerous approach in that it probably tends to strengthen the subpersonalities and therefore further reinforces the dissociated states.

The general goal of treatment today is an integration of all the personalities into one. This is not always possible; thus, in some cases the less ambitious goal of co-consciousness of the most important personalities is the objective. If complete integration is possible, it is necessary to determine which personality will remain. Frequently this will not be the main personality. Obviously this decision demands the collaboration of all personalities and the therapist.

Although a variety of treatment modalities has been utilized, the treatment of choice would seem to be one that allows for the recovery of forgotten traumas and their related repressed effects. The role of hypnosis in therapy of multiples has been controversial, yet the fact that multiples are usually excellent hypnotic subjects has led most clinicians to recommend its use in their treatment.

While integration has been achieved through short-term, highly structured therapy, most typically the course of therapy is much longer. Sybil's treatment consisted of 2,354 sessions over 11 years (Schreiber, 1973). Greaves (1980) suggests an average treatment length of two to five years, this under ideal circumstances with a therapist who is both well informed about multiple personality and highly skilled in psychodynamic, hypnotic, or other integrative methods of psychotherapy.

References
Berman, E. Multiple personality: Theoretical approaches. *Journal of the Bronx State Hospital*, 1974, *2* (2), 99–107.
Gottlieb, J. Multiple personality: A continuing enigma. *Current Concepts in Psychiatry*, 1977, *3*, 15–23.
Greaves, G. B. Multiple personality 165 years after Mary Reynolds. *Journal of Nervous and Mental Disease*, 1980, *168* (10), 577–596.
Ludwig, A. M., Brandsma, J. M., Wilbur, C. B., Benfeldt, F., & Jameson, D. H. The objective study of a multiple personality. *Archives of General Psychiatry*, 1972, *26*, 298–310.
Schreiber, F. *Sybil*. Chicago: Regnery, 1973.

Thigpen, C., & Cleckley, H. *The three faces of Eve*. New York: McGraw-Hill, 1957.

Additional Readings
Bowers, M., Brecher-Marer, S., Newton, B. W., Piotrowski, Z., Spyer, T. C., Taylor, W. S., & Watkins, J. G. Therapy of multiple personality. *The International Journal of Clinical and Experimental Hypnosis*, 1971, *19* (2), 57–65.
Coons, P. M. Multiple personality: Diagnostic considerations. *Journal of Clinical Psychiatry*, 1980, *41* (10), 330–336.

D. G. BENNER

Murphy, Gardner (1895–1979). An extraordinary psychologist whose career spanned 40 years. In a study conducted in 1957 Murphy was cited more frequently in the psychological literature than anyone except Freud, making him the most influential psychologist in the twentieth century. Murphy wielded a command of the breadth of psychology which made him outstanding.

Murphy's parents were an Episcopal minister and a high school teacher. They were exemplars of curiosity, intellectual acumen, and humanitarian interests—qualities manifest in Gardner. They lobbied for greater educational opportunities for blacks and whites, child labor reforms, and improved racial relations.

Murphy attended Yale, Harvard, and Columbia universities, and held faculty appointments at Harvard, Columbia, and the City College of New York. He was director of research at the Menninger Foundation and a visiting professor at George Washington University. He was elected to the presidency of the American Psychological Association in 1944. In 1926 he married Lois Barclay, who became a renowned child therapist. She provided intellectual support by reading and critiquing his works and collaborated with him on others.

Murphy's work is innovative and comprehensive in that he attempted to integrate biological and social perspectives. His BIOSOCIAL THEORY of personality sought to incorporate various data bases in psychology. This integration was courageous, as it was a comprehensive theory when the mainstream of psychology was becoming increasingly specialized, narrow, and provincial. He wrote *Experimental Social Psychology* (1931) before social psychology existed, and one of the first histories of psychology (*Historical Introduction to Modern Psychology*, 1929). His biosocial theory is articulated in *Personality: A Biosocial Approach to Origins and Structures* (1949) and *Human Potentialities* (1958). Other professional interests included parapsychology and Asian psychology.

Gardner Murphy is remembered by students and colleagues as an unusually generous man and an advocate of human dignity and world peace.

R. L. TIMPE

Murray, Henry Alexander (1893–). One of the most fertile and wide-ranging minds that American psychology has seen. His thinking has been shaped by early training in medicine, by an avid involvement in the arts and humanities, and by the works of Freud, Jung, Adler, and Rank as well as the academic psychologists Lewin and McDougall. Murray's writings range from his seminal work, *Explorations in Personality* (1938), which presented his initial formulations of personality theory, to a psychological assessment of Herman Melville's self-destructiveness. Murray's creativity in the area of psychological assessment engendered the THEMATIC APPERCEPTION TEST, which draws on an individual's response to a series of ambiguous pictures to assess his motives and the major environmental forces impinging on him.

Murray was a product of private schools, attending Groton and Harvard, where he received a B.A. in history in 1915. He earned an M.A. in biology from the Columbia College of Physicians and Surgeons. Murray then spent two years in a surgical internship at Presbyterian Hospital in New York, followed by two years on the staff of the Rockefeller Institute for Medical Research, where he conducted embryological research. He received his Ph.D. in biochemistry in 1927 from Cambridge.

While Murray was apparently on his way to a career in medical research, he also demonstrated periodic interest in psychology. A number of influences, most significantly reading and later meeting Jung, prepared him to accept an invitation to join the fledgling Harvard Psychological Clinic in 1927 as an instructor. In 1928 he was appointed an assistant professor and director of the clinic. With this appointment began his consuming affair with the study of personality. Murray remained at the clinic until 1943, when he enlisted in the Army Medical Corps. During the remainder of the war he spearheaded an effort to develop techniques to test the qualifications of recruits for the Office of Strategic Services. Out of this experience he wrote *Assessment of Men* (1948).

Murray returned to Harvard after the war and in 1949 established the Psychological Clinic Annex. He was appointed professor of clinical psychology in 1950 and continued his research until his retirement in 1962. Since then, he has devoted his energies to the study of Melville's works and has sought to awaken concern for the current challenges to human survival. In 1979 the Henry A. Murray Research Center for the Study of Lives was founded at Radcliffe College.

In his study of personality Murray shunned the prevailing behavioristic paradigm as too limited. He sought to develop research approaches and a theoretical perspective which took into account man's inner world, the world of conscious and unconscious needs, as well as the external world. It is difficult to appreciate the radical departure that both Murray's willingness to embrace man's inner world and his case study approach to research were from the established tenets of academic psychology.

Murray's investigations focused on the study of motivation or NEED. The concept of need is fundamental to Murray's personality theory. According to Murray a need is a hypothetical construct. That is, it is assumed to have a physiological basis in brain activity, and its operation is inferred from behavioral observation and subjective reports. A need represents "an organic potentiality or readiness to respond in a certain way under given conditions" (Murray, 1981, p. 42). Needs may be evoked by internal events, such as fantasies, as well as by environmental stimuli. Needs arouse the organism and direct behavior until need satisfaction occurs. The development of a taxonomy of needs and the investigation of the manifold ways needs are manifested in behavior have preoccupied Murray.

Murray has not been unmindful of the impact of the environment on the individual. As a correlative to his need theory he developed his notion of environmental press. Press refers to "a property or attribute of an environmental object or person, which facilitates or impedes the efforts of the individual to reach a given goal" (Lindzey, 1957, p. 178). The concept of press classifies a situation as to whether it is beneficial, harmful, or neutral for the individual on the basis of how the individual interprets the situation in relation to his strivings. In addition to need and press Murray developed a host of concepts in his effort to describe the dynamics of personality and the influence of the environment on the development and manifestation of personality. He strongly advocated longitudinal studies of individuals, as he firmly believed that "the history of the personality is the personality."

Certain of Murray's contributions, such as the Thematic Apperception Test, continue to enjoy an impact. But his influence lies more in the perspective he brought to his study of personality and in the students he inspired. His appreciation of the complexity and the uniqueness of the individual, his unwillingness to disregard this complexity to simplify the research task, his appreciation for the workings of the unconscious, and the creativity he brought to the development of assessment techniques provided his colleagues and students a corrective for the oversimplifications and reductionistic tendency of behaviorism. Murray substantially broadened psychology's vision of the nature of its subject matter.

References
Lindzey, G. Murray's personology. In C. S. Hall & G. Lindzey (Eds.), *Theories of personality*. New York: Wiley, 1957.
Murray, H. A. Proposals for a theory of personality. In E. S. Schneidman (Ed.), *Endeavors in psychology: Selections from the personology of Henry A. Murray*. New York: Harper & Row, 1981.

W. T. Weyerhaeuser

See Personology Theory.

Muscular Armor. A concept introduced by Wilhelm Reich, the originator of body psychotherapy. It refers to a pattern of chronically tense and inflexible muscles that represent at an unconscious level the expression of certain personality and character formations.

Reich believed that the structure of the body is not fixed and immutable. In the course of human development the body of an individual is subject to external influences from the family and society which act upon and modify the body's features, expression, and flexibility. These social forces of conditioning result in admonitions and permissions that the developing child learns to accept and follow. Learning how to act or how not to react is a process in the developing child of gaining muscular control and coordination. In time these controls become automatic and result in a fixed pattern of neuromuscular expression.

An example of this might be the child who has become frightened of harsh reprimands and develops a muscular tendency toward slouching, restricted and limited breathing, a "hushed" vocal pattern, and a tendency toward avoiding direct eye contact. These neuromuscular expressions may also be accompanied by feelings of lack of self-worth that would also be expressed in deep body muscular tension. This pattern would represent a muscular armoring for the individual.

Muscular armoring develops gradually over a long period of time and is therefore an unconscious reaction. It is accompanied by fixed patterns of attitude and behavior regarding self and others. These fixed patterns represent the development of character in that the individual's personality is strongly shaped by the muscular tensions that have formed during life development. These muscular tensions continue to limit the individual's perception of reality, both within and without, due to the unconscious nature of the unnatural muscular tension.

According to Reich, muscular armoring is a defense developed by the socialized ego against the external environment and the dangerous impulses that come from within. Personality that is based on muscular armor rather than the free recognition and expression of the internal life of the body is limited in its resourcefulness for healthy and meaningful expression.

C. E. Barshinger and L. E. LaRowe

See Bioenergetic Analysis.

Music Therapy. *See* Activity Therapy.

Mutism. *See* Elective Mutism of Childhood or Adolescence.

Mutual Help Groups. Often called self-help groups, these are peer interaction therapy groups that come together for a special purpose, to serve a common need, without the participation of professional counselors or leaders. This mutual aid is most often to overcome a problem or to change thoughts, feelings, or behavior in individuals or society at large.

These groups can be a powerful therapeutic resource and a catalyst for change. In addition to the common thread of nonprofessional involvement, mutual help groups are voluntary and most often consist of members with a similar problem, as opposed to a heterogeneous grouping of people for encounter or other types of group therapy. They are peer controlled, normally have no fee (though they tend to encourage freewill offerings to cover expenses), tend not to keep records, and have a regular order of business. In these ways they differ from traditional therapy groups. They are also generally available to the public.

Various theories of origin for mutual groups relate to religious, humanitarian, and economic roots. Drakeford (1969) refers to Wesley's Methodist self-support groups in the 1700s, and Hurvitz (1974) emphasizes religious groups of the 1900s. Others point to early church influences and origins, or to basic units of human organization such as tribes, villages, and towns. The Quaker societies of eighteenth-century England organized peer groups for mutual concerns. In the United States mutual aid groups during and following the Depression focused on economic support, developing into trade unions. The concept of mutual aid groups caught fire following World War II, with the development of groups for people such as parents of handicapped children and those suffering particular diseases.

Perhaps the best known, and certainly the largest and oldest group still in existence, is ALCOHOLICS ANONYMOUS, founded officially in 1935. At least 25 other "anonymous" groups have been modeled after AA, including Gamblers Anonymous, Neurotics Anonymous, and offshoots such as Alateen for the children of alcoholics. Alcoholics Anonymous is structured with strict adherence to principles known as the 12 steps. These guidelines for the alcoholic include acknowledgment of a problem that the individual cannot solve alone, a responsibility to self and others to change, and behavioral standards to enforce that change. The organization provides a climate of mutual support and accountability, with a rigid structure for meetings and behavioral expectations developed by two alcoholics. It is entirely lay led. Some of the factors that appear to influence the success of AA include the acknowledgment of a need; identity and intimacy with others who acknowledge the same need; and involvement and interaction with the group, including accountability and responsibility to self and others. Another element that reinforces positive action is the concept of modeling, where those who are staying sober serve as support people to those struggling with the desire to drink.

Katz and Bender (1976) define five basic types of mutual help groups. There are groups primarily focused on self-fulfillment or personal growth; groups whose focus is social advocacy, such as changing policies in government that affect their particular concern; and groups that attempt to create alternate patterns for living. "Outcast" groups form in response to a need expressed by those who have experienced serious physical, emotional, or psychological pain that impairs their ability to function. The fifth type is mixed groups that are not as clearly defined in that they do not focus on one particular issue or illness.

Gartner and Riessman (1977) divide mutual help groups into four categories: anonymous, ex-patient, "living with," and life transition. The anonymous groups (e.g., Alcoholics Anonymous) stress the acknowledgment of a problem and the need for help. Ex-patient groups deal

with difficulties encountered following a hospitalization for emotional or physical problems. "Living with" groups (e.g., Alanon) are auxiliary groups formed to help relatives or others involved with a symptomatic individual learn to cope constructively with the problem. Life transition groups, which grew rapidly during the 1960s and 70s, include members who are going through similar role transitions (e.g., the newly divorced, widowed, elderly, and single parents).

There are several theories as to why self-help groups develop in a society where professional help is so widely available. One theory maintains that inadequate services prompt people to form their own groups in response to unmet needs. Another theory stresses the need to provide alternatives for existing social service institutions, and points out that professional services are often available only to those who can afford to pay for them. A third theory emphasizes the individual need for community and affiliation with others in the same condition. Most likely a combination of all three leads to the generation of mutual help groups.

Because of the complex conceptual and technical problems involved in outcome research with such groups, little can be confidently concluded about their effectiveness. Since most mutual help groups do not keep records and are resistant to professional interference, traditional research designs are not applicable to them. But the growth and behavioral changes evidenced in such groups as Alcoholic Anonymous speak for themselves and indicate the effectiveness of many self-help groups, despite the difficulties of objective evaluation. It is also well recognized that some self-help groups (e.g., Alcoholics Anonymous and Gamblers Anonymous) successfully work with behaviors that have traditionally resisted the usual professional interventions. The proliferation of health-related mutual help groups seems to be beneficial for specific disease-related problems. In fact, most health organizations now have mutual help chapters focusing on rehabilitative, behavioral, or primary care issues, depending on the disease and its implications for the individual (whether curable, terminal, or stable).

One of the most powerful principles in the mutual help design is what Riessman (1965) calls the "helper-therapy" idea, which is that those who help receive help through their involvement. One dimension of this is reflected through the modeling process with its concomitant accountability. It also makes the helper less dependent, enables him to achieve some objectivity regarding the problem, and fulfills the need for social usefulness. Commitment to the group and its objectives also becomes a powerful force as one becomes involved in helping and in the group process.

The potentials for self-help groups are as unlimited as the groups themselves, but there are some cautions and possible limitations. Too much emphasis on self and a particular problem can possibly lead to escape from responsibilities and relationships. The poor also tend to be underserved in such groups. Frequently self-help mutual aid fosters dependence, authoritarianism, and strong antiprofessional stances. Groups may become isolated from each other. Perhaps the groups that concentrate on altering society's view of a problem or push for social change have best integrated the need for helping the individual while also benefiting society. Despite these limitations mutual help is here to stay, and will evolve to meet the changing needs of society.

References

Drakeford, J. W. *Farewell to the lonely crowd.* Waco, Tex.: Word Books, 1969.

Gartner, A., & Reissman, F. *Self-help in the human services.* San Francisco: Jossey-Bass, 1977.

Hurvitz, N. Peer self-help psychotherapy groups: Psychotherapy without psychotherapists. In P. M. Roman & H. M. Trice (Eds.), *The sociology of psychotherapy.* New York: Aronson, 1974.

Katz, A. H., & Bender, E. I. (Eds.). *The strength in us: Self-help groups in the modern world.* New York: New Viewpoints, 1976.

Reissman, F. The helper-therapy principle. *Social Work,* 1965, *10,* 27–32.

D. L. SCHUURMAN

Mutual Storytelling Technique.

A method of child psychotherapy developed by Gardner (1971). Although it has been a time-honored practice in child therapy to elicit stories, Gardner's technique suggests a more systematic method of utilizing these stories therapeutically.

The technique consists of first asking the child to make up a story. After it is told, the child is then asked to tell the moral or lesson that the story teaches. The therapist listens to this story and, in the light of everything else known about the child, makes a surmise of its psychodynamic meaning. The therapist then tells a story containing the same characters in a similar setting but introducing healthier adaptations and resolutions of the conflicts exhibited in the child's story. The therapist then tells the moral of his or her story. By speaking in the child's own language the therapist is more likely to be heard by the child. Furthermore, the child is not burdened by alien interpretations.

Mutual storytelling is not a therapy per se, but rather a technique that is useful in combination with other techniques. Gardner suggests that it is most useful in the latency period, when the products of the child's imagination are too difficult to access. It has been utilized with a wide variety of childhood disorders, the only limit on its usefulness being the creative capacity of the therapist for prompt formulations and improvisation of stories.

Reference

Gardner, R. A. *Therapeutic communication with children.* New York: Science House, 1971.

D. G. BENNER

Mythosynthesis.

The technique of bringing into awareness and taking responsibility for those frames of reference (myths) that mentally filter one's here-and-now experience (Enscoe & Enscoe, 1980). It is believed that the mythosphere, which is the collective system of myths, develops at a very young age and may not be presently adequate for interpreting the here and now.

In terms of Berne's transactional analysis the mythosphere is part of the Child ego state. A controlled regression must take place in order to encourage Child creativity so that the mythosphere can be modified and brought up to date. This usually takes place in small nurturing groups, with the members creatively using fantasies and metaphors in attempting to bring their personal myths into awareness. These myths are never evaluated in terms of right or wrong, but are viewed as relative ways by which one orders one's world. They are affirmed by the other group members.

The goal of this technique is to make one responsible for the reality that he or she creates. It is through responsibility taking that a synthesis between a person's wishes and what a person believes is possible (personal reality) can take place. The idea of taking responsibility for one's beliefs is an appealing one and encourages flexibility, growth, and development in the individual. However, the idea that reality is self-created seems inconsistent with Christian ontological presuppositions.

Reference

Enscoe, A., & Enscoe, G. Mythosynthesis. In R. Herink (Ed.), *The psychotherapy handbook.* New York: New American Library, 1980.

D. S. McCULLOCH

Nn

Naikan Psychotherapy. Developed in Japan in the 1950s by a lay Buddhist priest and former businessman, Isshin Yashimoto, this meditative therapy is based on Buddhist enlightenment practices. As structured by Yashimoto the therapeutic process begins with the client's solitary reflection upon past and present relationships with others. Next the nondirective therapist hears the client's "confession" along three main themes: 1) what was received from others, 2) what was returned to them, and 3) what troubles were caused them. The goal of this process is to simultaneously produce existential guilt and a sense of having been loved in spite of inadequacies.

Therapists at Naikan centers in Japan say that clients with psychosomatic, interpersonal, and neurotic problems as well as addictions and criminal backgrounds have become less self-concerned and more oriented toward service to others. Outcome research for Naikan is lacking; Kitsuse (1965) reported one study showing reduced recidivism rates among prisoners treated with this therapy.

Spiritual underpinnings and goals of this therapy are acknowledged by its Eastern practitioners. Similarities to the Western theories of integrity therapy, logo therapy, and reality therapy are evident. Naikan therapy reflects the Christian ideal of service but lacks the unique concepts of forgiveness and redemption through God's loving plan in Jesus Christ.

Reference
Kitsuse, J. I. Moral treatment and reformation of inmates in Japanese prisons. *Psychologia*, 1965, *8*, 9–23.

Additional Reading
Reynolds, D. K. Naikan Psychotherapy. In R. Corsini (Ed.), *Handbook of innovative psychotherapies.* New York: Wiley, 1981.

K. M. LATTEA

Nail Biting. Also known as onychophagia, this is a common behavioral disturbance, occurring mainly in children and occasionally persisting into adulthood, particularly when the individual is under severe psychological stress. One-fifth of all adolescents bite their nails, and the most widely accepted reason is that it reduces tension and relieves anxiety. Psychoanalytic interpretation views nail biting as a fixation at the oral stage of libido development. The American Psychological Association classifies it as a special symptom reaction under personality disorders. Two other theories view nail biting as a substitute for masturbation or an outlet for hostile impulses. Male nail biters outnumber female nail biters at later ages.

D. L. SCHUURMAN

Narcissism. An ancient myth tells of a handsome youth, Narcissus, the offspring of the river god Cephesus and the nymph Liriope, who fell passionately in love with his own image reflected in a woodland pool. He was loved by Echo, who had suffered problems of her own from previous brushes with deities. Their only communication was his "I love you," addressed to his own image, and her unheard repetition, "I love you." Narcissus pined away and died, leaving behind only a small, sad flower which even today thrives best when bent over cool streams. The tragic, unrequited desire for SELF-ESTEEM and the unperceived hunger for communication with intimate others are so much a part of the human experience that the myth lives on, and narcissism has become a dynamic term in contemporary psychology (Spotnitz & Resnikoff, 1954).

Actually narcissism means many things. In

common terminology it refers to what has been called a triad of vanity, exhibitionism, and arrogant ingratitude. This is similar to the earliest usage of the term by psychologists, who applied it to autoeroticism as a perversion (Ellis, 1927). In general, narcissism refers to self-preoccupation, while NARCISSISTIC PERSONALITY DISORDER refers to a quite specific disorder. Many have narcissistic qualities, but few meet the criteria of the full-blown disorder.

As a cultural phenomenon it describes our age as one which is intensely individualistic, self-centered, and hedonistically devoted to the quest of the peak experience (Lasch, 1978). The motto of contemporary American advertising might be something like the beer ad: "You only go around once, better make it with gusto!" Just as hysteria seems to have been the psychological disorder of Europe at the turn of the century, around which psychological formulations developed, narcissism seems to be the illness serving this function at the end of the century.

Definitions and Dynamics. But to psychologists the term has several meanings. As a personality disorder, *DSM-III* has described it symptomatically, emphasizing grandiosity, self-centeredness, emotional isolation, and manipulativeness. This particular pattern does in fact seem to be a disorder of epidemic proportions in the contemporary West. It is terribly destructive to marriages, and we are yet to feel its full impact on the children reared in homes dominated or destroyed by these personalities.

Other psychologists see narcissism as a disorder of drive, or instinct, as Freud did in his initial formulation (1914/1975). Here a normal grandiose, self-centered phase of development is postulated in which the infant glories in libido invested or reinvested in the self. This period is preoedipal, and becomes pathological in later life as a fixation or regression to this stage. In contemporary psychoanalysis this developmental period is seen less in dynamic, libidinal terms and more as a phase during which the infant forms images, models, or concepts of the self and significant others. Narcissism now ordinarily refers to disorders of these "objects" and the way in which they relate to each other, or object relations.

The picture most widely held by psychoanalysts and many others of the internal world of these early months of life has been developed by a number of thinkers. Melanie Klein (Segal, 1979) and Mahler (1968) describe an early world in which experiences, both good and bad,

begin to coalesce, forming fragmental structures of self and other. These would have four configurations initially: good self, bad self good other, bad other. Normally an effective relationship with the mothering person will encourage these part objects to merge into a distinct self-object and clearly defined other-objects that are seen as both good and bad. This process is referred to as separation and individuation.

There is much less consensus on the details of exactly how this proceeds, just what there is in the early maternal relationship which brings it about, and how pathology develops in the adult. This field of study is at present so diverse as to be confusing. Despite this, everyone who works in therapy is forced to struggle with a new and deeper understanding of these patients since they do not seem to respond to traditional therapies.

Treatment. The warm, supportive therapeutic context of nondirective therapy will soon lose narcissistic patients. Helping them "Get in touch with their feelings" uncovers endless pools of anger, guilt, and despair, a process that apparently aggravates their problems rather than providing catharsis. Free association wanders rather than leading to crucial conflicts as it would in the neurotic patient, and interpretations of oedipal dynamics miss the mark. In fact, interpretations in the therapy of narcissistic patients are often, as Bach (1977) describes, "talking into the wind or writing on the sand, only to have one's words effected moments later by the waves. The patient either welcomes or resents the analyst's words, and frequently does not even register the actual content. A session which seems to have led to a certain understanding or experience of some kind may, 24 hours later, be totally forgotten " (p. 211).

These difficulties in therapy reflect other serious problems of narcissistic patients. There are sudden, disturbing changes in self-awareness, shifting from a self-image of a good person, one who is important and even ideal, to a person who is worthless and destructive. Parallel switches occur frequently in their picture of those who are close to them. Accompanying these shifts are profound changes in mood, involving intense anxiety, guilt, shame, and depression.

What keeps these persons reasonably functional is an internal structure which is generally referred to as a "grandiose self" (Kernberg, 1975). Kernberg describes this self as it is unveiled in psychoanalysis as "a hungry, enraged, empty self, full of impotent anger at

744

being frustrated, and fearful of a world which seems as hateful and revengeful as the patient himself" (p. 233). Desperate efforts to find intimacy with those close by are often futile because "the greatest fear of these patients is to be dependent on anyone else because to depend means to hate, envy and expose themselves to danger of being exploited, mistreated and frustrated" (Kernberg, 1975, p. 235).

Just how this grandiose self is formed and what its vicissitudes in life have been is elaborated by Kohut (1971, 1977) in a fascinating formulation that is receiving a great deal of attention. He describes two normally occurring developmental lines that begin with temporary structures heavily endowed with narcissistic libido. One is the Grandiose, Exhibitionistic Self, which is the focus around which healthy self-esteem and ambition form; the other is the Idealized Parental Imago, around which mature evaluation and admiration of others form. Given reasonably empathic mothering these mature into a Cohesive Nuclear Self, which has the capacity to form loving, long-term unions with others, relationships that augment rather than threaten the experience of uniqueness. In both the self and others there is an appropriate and enriching interaction between the real and the ideal.

Narcissism and the Human Struggle. As the books and articles proliferate around this conceptual model, one begins to realize that narcissism is a good deal more than an esoteric mental condition. Somehow, in the naked pathology of the narcissist we are seeing a bad photograph of ourselves, alien yet undeniably familiar. In the narcissistic world of primary object relations gone sour are clearly seen caricatures of things fundamentally human. The great paradoxes of selfishness and love, vulnerability and risk, self-centeredness in an overwhelmingly vast universe, as well as unease, masochism, and profound loneliness, are all parts of life. Adding sharp poignancy to this struggle is the blazing backdrop of the ideal: inspiring, bearing witness to some fragmented godlikeness, and yet judging, punishing, and leaving us restless and unsatisfied.

Becker (1973) places narcissism in the context of man's desperate effort to cope with existential anxiety: "In man a working level of narcissism is inseparable from self-esteem. From a basic sense of self-worth . . . it is too absorbing and relentless to be an aberration; it expresses the heart of the creature: the desire to stand out, to be *the* one in creation" (p. 3). Becker may well have started his passage with "in Adam," since those familiar with the

creation story will also see in narcissism the glorious, terrible dilemma in which man found himself after biting off a piece of divinity and casting himself, a poor bare creature, into the contest of the powers and principalities of the air. Without armor or weapons he had undertaken the central theme of history, the agonizing interface of good and evil. The ideal garden, experienced in innocence and now denied; the searing passion to love God and others, a pathway which must now be traversed between fusion and aloneness; the confusion of dealing with a threatening existence while being battered by internal anxiety, panic, and depression—all are results of the sin that came upon us through our progenitor.

If the Bible describes the psychopathology of our age and of our human condition so completely, it also tells us about a Savior, and a way of understanding and facing our condition more courageously and effectively. Marin (1975) contends that in current society the self replaces community, relation, neighbor, and God. It is in rediscovering who we really are in Adam and in Christ, who our neighbor is, what community is, and how we can love that we will find real outlets from our narcissistic drives.

References

Bach, S. On the narcissistic state of consciousness. *International Journal of Psycho-Analysis*, 1977, *58*, 209–233.
Becker, E. *The denial of death.* New York: Free Press, 1973.
Ellis, H. The conception of narcissism. *Psychoanalytic Review* 1927, *14*, 129–153.
Freud, S. On narcissism. In J. Strachey (Ed. and trans.), *The standard edition of the complete psychological works of Sigmund Freud.* (vol.14). London: Hogarth, 1975. (Originally published, 1914.)
Kernberg, O. *Borderline conditions and pathological narcissism.* New York: Aronson, 1975.
Kohut, H. *The analysis of the self.* New York: International Universities Press, 1971.
Kohut, H. *The restoration of the self.* New York: International Universities Press, 1977.
Lasch, C., *The culture of narcissism.* New York: Norton, 1978.
Mahler, M. S. *On human symbiosis and the vicissitudes of individuation.* New York: International Universities Press, 1968.
Marin, P. The new narcissism. *Harpers Magazine*, October 1975, pp. 45–56.
Segal, H. *Melanie Klein.* New York: Viking Press, 1979.
Sotnitz, H., & Resnikoff, P. The myths of Narcissus. *Psychoanalytic Review*, 1954, *41*, 173–181.

C. M. BERRY

Narcissistic Personality Disorder. A distressing triad made up of pathological self-centeredness; a repeated pattern of frustrating, damaging efforts to establish intimate relationships; and an insecure, fragile self-concept. Internally an unpredictable emotional lability makes life miserable. The disorder has been newly added to the latest edition of *DSM-III*. The diagnosis is established by a pattern that includes an exaggerated sense of self-importance and grandiose fantasies marked by idealization, exhibitionism and lack of empathy. The affect is turbulent, fluctuating between indifference, rage, shame, humiliation, and empty boredom. Interpersonal relationships are disrupted constantly by excessive exploitiveness, inconsideration, and an alternating pattern of overidealization and devaluation of those who are close.

Once one is alerted to this pattern, narcissism is seen to be a very common contributor to the problems dealt with in counseling practice. Whereas this is often the personality type of the very successful individual, it is also responsible to some extent for tumultuous adolescence, the mid-life crisis, the divorce after years of marriage, or the miserable old age.

Psychoanalytic Theories of Etiology. Understanding the causes and course of narcissism has proved to be difficult, and as yet little consensus has been achieved. Some degree of narcissism is a part of being human. Its features are seen in all other personality disorders, increasing in its influence with their severity. It might be more logical, then, to consider it on a continuum extending from mild to severe, and only consider it as a disorder in its own right when the functions of living are interfered with or the patient is unable to form satisfactory close relationships.

Most of the current books and articles on narcissism have been psychoanalytic in their orientation. Two men, Kernberg (1975) and Kohut (1971), have dominated this literature. They both start with Freud's (1914/1975) description of a normal stage of primary narcissism, or of grandiosity and self-centeredness. Since this occurs sometime between 6 months and 2 years, fixations and regressions manifested in the adult have a very primitive quality. Beyond this Kernberg and Kohut move in rather different directions.

Kernberg pictures this infantile experience of the narcissist as violent and ambivalent, marked by intense envy and rage. These emotional surges of anxiety and depression disperse widely over the life of the infant, leaving a residual state of hostility and resentment. The defenses of the narcissist are similar to those of the borderline, depending primarily on splitting and projection. Kernberg would distinguish the two conditions by the nature of the self-object as it emerges in the transference. In the narcissist the grandiose self, though still highly pathological, is more coher-

ent and integrated than in the borderline (Kernberg, 1966). His approach to therapy is directed toward the conflict, and thus essentially traditional Freudian analysis, though the technique must be modified.

Kohut (1971) sees narcissism as a failure of the earliest internal images or "objects" of self and significant other to develop normally. These should mature into distinct objects that are realistic, stable, and reasonably predictable. These internal structures then encourage healthy self-esteem and the capacity to enjoy and appreciate others. His treatment allows the patient a modification of healthy development by offering another experience that partially reproduces the effective mothering which these patients are thought to have missed (Kohut, 1977).

Other writers organize their understanding of narcissism in other ways. Each considers one or another of the clinical features of narcissism to be central: masochism (Gear, Hill, & Liedo, 1981); perfectionism (Rothstein, 1980); self-love (Lavelle, 1973); existential anxiety (Lichtenstein, 1977); splitting (Volkan, 1976). Many others have been indicated, all seeming to legitimately bear on the complex. To date no one has made a convincing enough case to win broad consensus, though the formulations of Kohut seem to come the closest to doing so at the date of this writing.

A Phenomenological Interpretation. The disorder may be profitably viewed from a phenomenological approach. Narcissistic persons universally have difficulty in the way they experience their feelings. They are extremely sensitive in that they feel their emotions intensely. Fears, threats, and any precipitous arousal of emotions have an explosive quality, ballooning up, and spilling over into the rest of their lives. This storm of feeling is so violent that the patient experiences his entire world in a different way, sometimes for days at a time. This in turn seriously distorts reality testing of all kinds, but particularly the concept of self and significant others. Self and other objects tend to merge, and there is a splitting of the good and bad in each. The self vacillates between being a grandiose object that constantly needs to be admired and satisfied, and, when this fails, a bad, weak self. This splitting seriously compromises self-esteem, regardless of how successful and admired the person might be in reality.

With many repetitions of these waves an anticipatory dread develops, and emotions are avoided as being dangerous. It is not long before intimacy itself is feared and the characteristic narcissistic ambivalence evolves, in which the beloved is both drawn in and abused. It is as if the narcissist is saying, "If you're going to abandon me, do it now before I get too close and vulnerable."

These volatile swings in the narcissistic affective state, from high anxiety to deep despair, are experienced as fear, anger, guilt, and depression. Mid-range feelings are blotted out, leaving a life devoid of tenderness, mild pleasures, and the sense of warming and distancing. Since it is largely these experiences that fine tune intimacy, the narcissist learns to relate more consciously, learning intellectually perceived systems that make people more understandable and predictable. This approach may work satisfactorily outside the home, but closer to the heart it fails.

In response to all this a defensive self-centeredness develops, and important others cease to have any vital existence except as extensions or part objects of the patient. The internal model of others relates entirely to the patient's own needs and desires. Any failure or refusal of the other to respond to this constant demand for service and gratification threatens to set off another affective explosion, an event commonly called a narcissistic injury.

Treatment. There is at present no commonly agreed upon effective treatment of this condition. Experiential therapy has probably been used most extensively, since this is usually the most agreeable to the patient. The outcome of this approach will depend largely on how successful the therapist is in encouraging the patient to deal more effectively with his emotions.

More is written about psychoanalysis as a treatment, and this is anticipated to be prolonged and difficult. However, its effectiveness has not been dramatic or efficient enough to convince nonanalysts.

An ideal treatment approach that would address the most central phenomena of narcissism directly might begin with controlling the affective storms by medications as much as possible. The antidepressants have been the most effective, though the minor tranquilizers and occasionally major tranquilizers are helpful. These will often allow the patient, over time, to begin to repair object relations and come to know and depend on a more stable, predictable experiential world.

After such assistance is given, therapeutic attention is then focused on feelings, making them clear and specific. Here those persons close to the patient can helpfully serve as therapists, so long as they explicitly express emotional responses in situations that are shared with the narcissist. If at the same time the patient is also encouraged to define feelings, maximum help is offered in understanding and correcting narcissistic emotional responses. In addition, a good deal of effort must be applied to teaching the patient more normal ways of relating.

In most cases, the narcissist does not seek treatment. We must accept these persons and love them for what they are and what they contribute. It would be an injustice to discuss narcissism without acknowledging its power and value in human experience. We are all fascinated by the charisma of many narcissistic personalities. At the same time we are wounded by the injuries that are part of being close to such insensitivity. Almost universally this fascinating flaw is at the center of our heroes and heroines. The fiery struggle between Scarlett O'Hara and Rhett Butler displays better than any textbook the agony and ecstasy of narcissism. Even though we would like to treat the patient and restore "normality," somehow life would lose a measure of its wonder and sparkle if we were successful. If Scarlett had been tamed and had married Ashley Wilkes, she would have had a more peaceful life, but no one would have read the book.

Spiritually also one senses in these people a certain special gift. Many of our religious leaders, pastors, evangelists, and teachers suffer from more than their normal share of narcissism. There is something about these leaders that gives them a Godlike aura, yet also speaks to us of Adam, both in his grandeur and agony. In narcissists we see our own struggle with self-centeredness projected clearly and painfully. We cannot completely disown them.

References

Freud, S. *On narcissism*. In J. Strachey (Ed. and trans.), *The standard edition of the complete psychological works of Sigmund Freud* (Vol. 14). London: Hogarth, 1975. (Originally published, 1914.)

Gear, M. G., Hill, M. A., & Liedo, E. C. *Working through narcissism*. New York: Aronson, 1981.

Kernberg, O. Structural derivatives of object relationships. *International Journal of Psycho-Analysis*, 1966, 47, 236–253.

Kernberg, O. *Borderline conditions and pathological narcissism*. New York: Aronson, 1975.

Kohut, H. *The analysis of the self*. New York: International Universities Press, 1971.

Kohut, H. *The restoration of the self*. New York: International Universities Press, 1977.

Lavelle, L. *The dilemma of narcissus*. New York: Humanities Press, 1973.

Lichtenstein, H. *The dilemma of human identity*. New York: Aronson, 1977.

Rothstein, A. *The narcissistic pursuit of perfection*. New York: International Universities Press, 1980.

Volkan, V. D. *Primitive internalized object relations.* New York: International Universities Press, 1976.

Additional Reading
Stolorow, R. D. Toward a functional definition of narcissism. *International Journal of Psycho-Analysis*, 1975, *56*, 179–185.

C. M. BERRY

See PASSIVE-INDEPENDENT PERSONALITY PATTERN; PERSONALITY DISORDERS.

Narcotherapy. A specialized form of psychotherapy during which a physician introduces drugs intravenously in order to create an altered state of consciousness. The therapy is based on the assumption that diagnostic clarifications and therapeutic gains are thus facilitated in a willing subject at the hands of an experienced clinician. Present-day narcotherapy has developed from a confluence of: 1) observations that a narcotized person may be more self-disclosing and expansive, and 2) the widely accepted idea that exploration of preconscious and unconscious memories and feelings is of therapeutic benefit.

Many agents have been used in an attempt to relax patients or to gain access to repressed experiences; opium, alcohol, ether, nitrous oxide, and LSD are a few. Various side effects and undesirable alterations in consciousness have consequently led to their disuse. Since 1930, when it was first used in psychiatric interviewing, sodium amytal (sodium amobarbital) has been widely accepted as the preferred agent. Amytal is a moderately long-acting barbiturate with a moderately rapid induction time.

The procedure is relatively free of hazard, the medical contraindications being those physiological conditions prohibiting the use of barbiturates. Its use in children is medically inadvisable. Postpubescent adolescents and adults have reportedly benefited from the procedure.

Most psychiatrists employ the drug for selected diagnostic and therapeutic indications. The major impetus to its use in psychiatric emergencies came during World War II in the treatment of acute war neuroses. Other acute traumatic psychiatric disorders soon responded to narcotherapy. Two American physicians, Roy Grinker and John Spiegel, expanded the European use of narcotherapy. They went beyond suggestion as a tool under an amytal-induced state of consciousness into what they termed *narcosynthesis*. Abreaction or catharsis of the painful wartime experiences repeatedly allowed discharge of the painful feelings, or affects, until they could be accepted by the person. Today, on occasion, acute hysterical or traumatic psychiatric disorders are successfully treated in this fashion.

Like most treatment modalities narcotherapy then was applied to a variety of resistant disorders. This slowly led to a working consensus of indications for the use of this treatment. Acute panic states following rape, disaster, or traumatic loss are amenable. Temporary complete amnesia, in which the patient is incapable of recall despite conscious effort, may respond to psychotherapeutic exploration during an amytal-induced state.

Diagnostic explorations suitable for amytal interviewing include the differential diagnosis of organic brain disease from functional (emotionally induced) disorders. In the latent brain-diseased person neurological symptoms such as disorientation, memory defects and confabulation appear in an apparently organically intact individual. Diagnostic interviewing under amytal may uncover previously undetected or even unsuspected suicide potential, paranoid ideation, or even schizophrenia. There are times in the course of extended psychotherapy when severe repression blocks progress. At these times an amytal interview may enable the cooperative patient to uncover repressed material and thereby make a fresh psychotherapeutic endeavor.

The distinction between a stuporous mute catatonic condition and a stuporous depressive state is often most difficult to make. Under an amytal interview the depressed patient will tend to withdraw further; conversely, the catatonic will verbalize in a remarkable and revealing manner. In this lucid period psychodynamic information useful for future therapy may be captured.

The implications of such therapy for the Christian must take into account the ethics behind this procedure. Patients' rights must be respected even if the patient may choose to his own detriment. Ethical medical practice calls for clear, detailed interpretation of the nature of the procedure, any hazards for that patient, and the possible benefits to the patient. In this fashion informed consent may be obtained. A common misconception needs to be cleared up. There is no "truth serum" and the function of the amytal interview is not to gain a confession or to probe purposes outside the patients' desire. Usually the patient is asked to prepare an agenda of areas of self-inquiry about which he wishes to know more. Often a spouse or other family member is present during the procedure and the entire process is tape recorded, the tape becoming property of the patient. This is especially useful when partial amnesia blocks some important data. The recording may thus be used as reference material in subsequent therapy.

A Christian view of man is based on biblical sources for understanding man's spiritual nature and sojourn. The Christian is also open to truth from many other sources in his search for understanding himself. The existence of unconscious and preconscious parts of our mental and emotional apparatus seems indisputable. Similarly our motivations and experiences are influenced not only by what we know consciously, but also by those unresolved, painful experiences we thought we left behind because we could forget them. A Christian view would encompass these complexities in the search for truth and the resolution of individual problems.

The amytal interview is one technique for gaining partial access to such unconscious and preconscious material. If one accepts the validity of the existence of an unconscious world and that benefit can accrue from its being explored, then narcotherapy is a possible source of aid.

One last consideration remains: the quality of trust between the doctor and the patient. This trust must be based on common assumptions and mutual openness so that the patient finds his own answers self-convincing and resolving. In the final analysis the benefits of narcotherapy, like any therapy, will be derived from the truth and insights gained.

Additional Readings
Sharoff, R. L. Narcotherapy. In A. M. Freedman & H. I. Kaplan (Eds.), *Comprehensive textbook of psychiatry.* Baltimore: Williams & Wilkins, 1967.
Naples, M., & Hackett, T. P. The amytal interview: History and current uses. *Psychosomatics,* 1978, *19* (2), 98–105.

T. G. Esau

Nature-Nurture Controversy. *See* Heredity and Environment in Human Development.

Near-Death Experiences. Most modern psychologists would probably reject the notion that the human personality survives bodily death, and would likewise reject the idea that a "spirit world" exists. Even if some of these thinkers should acknowledge such possibilities among their personal beliefs, they would most likely rule the study of the psyche after death out of bounds for psychology because such phenomena are considered to be nonobservable. However, since the mid-1970s this whole set of assumptions is being questioned seriously by a group of investigators of the near-death experience.

Basically the near-death experience is a series of phenomena experienced by individuals who were clinically dead for short periods of time (usually 10 or 15 minutes, though sometimes longer). These near-death survivors report extraordinary experiences which, although somewhat variable, are remarkably homogeneous considering the diversity of the individuals studied. The classic description of the near-death experience is outlined by Moody (1975a). First the person sometimes reports hearing himself pronounced dead by his doctor. He then hears a loud ringing or buzzing and feels himself moving through a dark tunnel. He then may suddenly find himself outside his physical body; he may see his own body as though he were a spectator, and may watch as resuscitation attempts are made.

If the near-death experience progresses further, the individual may find others coming to meet and help him. He sees spirits of relatives and friends who have died, and what many describe as a "loving warm spirit" of a kind never encountered before. This spirit asks him nonverbally to evaluate his life and helps by showing him a panoramic, instantaneous playback of the major events in his life. A later stage of the experience may involve approaching some kind of barrier, which apparently represents the limit between earthly life and the next life. The individual finds that it is not time for his death and he must return to earth. But he does not wish to return because of the overwhelming, intense feelings of joy, love, and peace (Moody, 1975a).

The basic elements making up the near-death experience were found by researchers independently of Moody (Grof & Grof, 1980, Rawlings, 1978, Ring, 1980, and Sabom, 1982). This research is the focus of much controversy. The first controversy involves the explanation of the near-death experience. Some researchers have attempted to explain it as resulting from psychological defense mechanisms (Siegel, 1980). Such an interpretation would argue that the dying person, either consciously or unconsciously wishing to deny his or her imminent death, becomes psychologically detached. The experiences that ensue are then viewed as resulting from a depersonalization process. However, Ring (1980) cites cases in which the near-death survivors report seeing dead relatives and/or friends who were not known to be dead at the time of the experience, while no survivor has ever reported seeing a human spirit concurrently alive on earth. Such a phenomenon is not adequately explained by depersonalization or any psychological defense mechanism.

Another set of interpretations focuses on medical rather than psychological factors. These include effects presumed to result from anesthetics or other drugs. However, many near-death survivors did not have any anesthetic or other drug at the time, and those who did tend to report less intense near-death experiences (Ring, 1980). Noyes and Kletti (1972) have offered an explanation of the panoramic playback of one's past as resulting from a seizurelike neural firing pattern in the temporal lobe. Moody (1975a) observes that such temporal lobe firing does not usually result in memory images played back in an orderly fashion, nor are such flashbacks seen at once in a unifying vision. Also, seizure victims typically do not remember their flashbacks after regaining consciousness. Cerebral anoxia is another medical hypothesis that has been offered. However, some individuals have a near-death experience in which no apparent clinical death took place, yet they have essentially the same experiences as those in which there was such a death (Moody, 1975b). Other medical or physiological explanations include the possible release of endorphins (the body's own opiate), which could account for the release from physical pain and the feelings of peace.

Of great significance also are the aftereffects of the near-death experience. Survivors often report a changed world view and a change in their value systems. Ring (1980) sees these phenomena as being related to getting in touch with the "higher self" or "true self" described in various religious traditions. McDonagh (1982) views such changes as being related to a death of the ego and a rebirth of a new self, and points to a similarity between the near-death experience and conversion or "born again" Christian experience.

Investigators of this phenomenon are careful to point out that their research does not prove in any strict scientific or philosophical sense the existence of an afterlife, nor does it specify indisputably the nature of an afterlife. However, even with this qualification it does seem to represent an important development. The survival of the human personality after death is being taken as a serious possibility, and has at least gained the status of a plausible scientific hypothesis—something that would have been dismissed by many as an intellectual absurdity only a generation ago.

References

Grof, S., & Grof, C. *Beyond death*. New York: Thames & Hudson, 1980.

McDonagh, J. *Christian psychology: Towards a new synthesis*. New York: Crossroad, 1982.

Moody, R. *Life after life*. Atlanta: Mockingbird books, 1975. (a)

Moody, R. *Reflections on "life after life."* Carmel, N.Y.: Guideposts, 1975. (b)

Noyes, R., & Kletti, R. The experience of dying from falls. *Omega*, 1972, *3*, 45–52.

Rawlings, M. *Beyond death's door*. Nashville: Nelson, 1978.

Ring, K. *Life at death*. New York: Coward, McCann & Geoghegan, 1980.

Sabom, M. B. *Recollections of death: A medical investigation*. New York: Simon & Schuster, 1982.

Siegel, R. K. The psychology of life after death. *American Psychologist*, 1980, *35*, 911–931.

J. McDonagh

Necrophilia. A rare morbid sexual perversion in which an individual gains satisfaction from performing sexual acts on a dead body or parts of it. The perversion seems to be confined to men, and it is claimed by some researchers that morticians form a high percentage of subjects with necrophilia. In some cases the necrophiliac will mutilate the body. In most recorded instances he has murdered a woman in order to gratify his psychotic desire. This severe disturbance may be related to a fear of failure in sexual relations. By performing sexual acts on a dead body, humiliation and rejection so feared by the individual are impossible. Necrophilia is said to be the rarest sexual behavior in men.

D. L. Schuurman

Needs. A hypothetical construct prominent in several theories of motivation. Generally needs represent internally or externally aroused forces, accompanied by subjective emotions, which serve as an impetus for behavior. Needs are characterized by two motivational properties: 1) a tendency to energize behavior if the strength is greater than its threshold; and 2) a tendency to activate cognitive processes such as imagining, wish-fulfilling fantasies, and long-range planning. The cognitive processes serve to channel bodily arousal toward need gratification.

Two categories of physiological needs have been identified by many theorists: deficiency and excess needs. Both refer to products related to survival. Need is an intervening variable between deprivation or excess on the antecedent side, and health or survival on the consequent side.

Some theories consider need to be equivalent to drive, while others distinguish between them. In the latter view, an excess or deficiency need elicits tension within a physiological system. This tension evokes a drive (i.e., energy mobilization) toward satisfying the need state.

This need-drive-incentive pattern "asserts that physiological needs are created by deprivation, that these give rise to drives which stir to, and may guide, activity until a related goal object (incentive) is attained, and that the response to the goal object (consummatory response) reduces the drive" (English & English, 1958, p. 339).

In experimental studies need is operationally defined as length of deprivation or extent of excess (e.g., hyperoxygenation). Tissue deficiency is assumed to be directly related to the degree of deprivation or excess.

Personality theories have made extensive use of need, especially acquired needs. Lewin was one of the first psychologists to adopt the need construct. He offered it as a replacement for the instinct suggestion by McDougall. Lewin held that need provides arousal without completely prescribing a uniform behavior sequence. He defined need as any motivated state that may have been evoked by a physiological event, a desire for some object, or a will to achieve. Disequilibrium and tensions accompany needs. Disequilibrium exists when there is an uneven distribution of tension. Behavior achieves equilibrium through release of tension. Tensions are dispelled as needs are satisfied (Chaplin & Krawiec, 1974).

The strength and direction of needs were described by Lewin in vector terms. Vectors are either positive—satisfying or attractive to the organism—or negative in threatening or repelling the organism. When vectors are opposite in direction and equal in valence, a conflict is said to exist. Lewin defined three types of conflict: approach-approach, avoidance-avoidance, and approach-avoidance.

The most highly developed need theory is that of Murray, who defined need as a "construct . . . which stands for . . . a force which organized perception, apperception, intellection, conation and action in such a way as to transform in a certain direction an existing, unsatisfying situation" (Murray, 1938, pp. 123–124). He distinguished between viscerogenic and psychogenic needs. Viscerogenic needs are the physiological ones related to survival. The psychogenic needs are those acquired in the process of socialization. The psychogenic needs and the proceedings to satisfy those needs form the basis of personality. Psychogenic needs are categorized as latent or manifest, proactive or reactive, and modal or effect. The relative strength of the personality needs identified by Murray are measured by the Thematic Apperception Test or the Edwards Personal Preference Schedule. The former measures latent needs, while the latter assesses manifest needs.

Needs which represent repressed or inhibited drives are latent, while manifest needs are those which are more freely expressed and consciously recognized. Murray classified needs as to their origins. Needs originating within the organism are proactive, while reactive needs respond to environmental stimulation. Modal needs concern the process of need satisfaction, while effect needs lead to the achievement of some goal. For example, a pianist who strives to play well would exhibit a modal need, while one who plays well to win a prize is responding to an effect need.

Murray believed that needs were organized within personality. When needs are functionally interconnected or fused so they can be satisfied simultaneously, it is termed *subsidiation*. At other times, the degree of organization may be less adequate and one need might be in conflict with another.

Other personality theorists have also employed need concepts. The motivational theory of Maslow conceived personality as a hierarchy of needs. Needs that have the greatest potency at the time demand satisfaction and drive behavior. Once a need has been satisfied, other needs that are less potent manifest themselves. The hierarchy, which includes both physiological and social needs, in order of priority is physiological, safety, love and belongingness, esteem, and self-actualization needs. Maslow differentiated between deficiency needs (e.g., physiological and safety) and growth needs. Growth needs are derived from the motive of self-actualization when all deficiency needs have been satisfied.

In her study of neurotic personality Horney enumerated 10 neurotic needs. If an individual's security is disturbed, anxiety is experienced, in response to which the individual develops strategies of adjustment. Adjustment patterns may assume the character of needs or drives in personality. Needs may become neurotic if they are irrational solutions to the problems of insecurity. Neurotic needs include the need for affection and approval, for a partner to take over one's life, to restrict one's life within narrow borders, for power, to exploit others, for prestige, for personal admiration, for personal achievement, for self-sufficiency and independence, and for perfection and unassailability. In these neurotic needs the more the person has, the more the person wants (Horney, 1942).

In recent years considerable work has been done by personality and social psychologists on three needs: the need for achievement, the need for affiliation, and the need for power.

References

Chaplin, J. P., & Krawiec, T. S. *Systems and theories of psychology* (3rd ed.). New York: Holt, Rinehart, & Winston, 1974.

English, H. B., & English, A. *A comprehensive dictionary of psychological and psychoanalytical terms.* New York: Longmans, Green, 1958.

Horney, K. *Self-analysis.* New York: Norton, 1942.

Murray, H. A. *Explorations in personality.* New York: Oxford University Press, 1938.

R. L. TIMPE

See MOTIVATION; PERSONALITY.

Needs Met by Religion. *See* PSYCHOLOGICAL ROOTS OF RELIGION.

Negative Effects in Therapy. *See* PSYCHOTHERAPY, RESEARCH IN; IATROGENIC PSYCHOPATHOLOGY.

Negative Oedipus Complex. A form of infantile psychosexual development in which the parental love object is the same sex parent, thus being the opposite or reverse of the normal manifestation of the OEDIPUS COMPLEX. The usual oedipal love object for the male child is the mother and for the female child, the father.

See PSYCHOSEXUAL DEVELOPMENT.

Negative Practice Technique. An early behavioral approach used in the treatment of stuttering, tics, and facial grimaces. The technique is now little used and is mainly of historical interest. A survey of a dozen recent behavior therapy texts produced only one that indexed the technique.

Negative practice is a paradoxical procedure in which repetitive practice is used to eliminate an unwanted response. For example, an individual with a twitch of the corner of the mouth would be instructed to repeat the twitch as rapidly as possible for a period of time.

The theoretical rationale for negative practice is based on Hullian learning theory. Hull postulated that repeating a given action produced a certain amount of reactive inhibition (similar to fatigue), which made successive repetitions increasingly effortful. In negative practice, rapid repetition of the response maximizes reactive inhibition and produces boredom. Ceasing to respond results in relief from both reactive inhibition and boredom, hence is negatively reinforcing.

Though relevant for tics and grimaces, the reactive inhibition notion is not applicable to negative practice with stuttering. To maximize reactive inhibition it would be necessary for the person to repeatedly practice the stuttered words as rapidly as possible without pause between repetitions. In practice whole sentences are repeated, including the normally stuttered words, thus resulting in pauses between repetitions of the stuttered words.

Empirical studies of negative practice have produced mixed results. In some cases beneficial effects have been observed; in some no effects have been noted; and in some instances negative practice has exacerbated the problems. A major difficulty in the use and investigation of negative practice is that no formula has been developed to specify the duration of practice or the desired amount of rest between practice sessions. Perhaps the questionable effectiveness and procedural problems account for the current disuse of negative practice.

R. K. BUFFORD

See BEHAVIOR THERAPY.

Negativistic Personality. *See* ACTIVE-AMBIVALENT PERSONALITY PATTERN.

Neologism. A word created by an individual who attaches his own meaning to it. Such words are often condensations of other words and carry a private significance. Overuse of neologisms is often indicative of a schizophrenic disorder.

Nervous Breakdown. A euphemism for acute psychopathologies that require immediate treatment. It does not refer to any particular disorder or clinical entity. It seems intended to imply that the individual has been under strain and has somehow collapsed under the pressure. Since the problem is then seen to be wholly or largely physical, the individual generally escapes the stigma often attached to problems that are recognized to be more of an emotional nature. Usually, however, this inaccurate term has little or no correspondence to the actual etiology of the psychological problem being described.

See ABNORMAL PSYCHOLOGY.

Network Therapy. *See* SOCIAL NETWORK INTERVENTION.

Neurasthenia. *See* DYSTHYMIC DISORDER.

Neurolinguistic Programming. A recent development in psychotherapy founded by Bandler and Grinder (1975, 1976). It is a compilation of their studies of particularly successful psychotherapists, especially Satir, Perls, and

Erickson. Bandler and Grinder, after analyzing these other methods and techniques, developed a model that focuses on how the client processes information and on how to utilize this "internal strategy" for producing desired changes.

Representational Systems. Fundamental to this model are the representational systems—i.e., the ways of experiencing and processing the world. There are three major representational systems: auditory, visual, and kinesthetic. The dominant system employed by an individual is indicated by both eye patterns called accessing cues and linguistic patterns. Bandler and Grinder report that as you face other persons, their eyes will look up and left when they are accessing remembered images visually, up and right when they are visually constructing images, down and right when they are accessing feelings and other kinesthetic sensations, down and left when they are listening to internal auditory sounds such as internal dialogue, level left for remembered auditory sounds, and level right for constructed auditory sounds.

For example, if you were to ask a person with a visual representational system when she last saw a movie, her eyes would move up and left as she searches for a visual representation of herself the last time she attended a movie. Similarly, if you were to ask a person with an auditory representational system when was the last time he heard Handel's *Messiah*, his eyes might well go level and left as he searches for the memory of that experience auditorily. If you ask a person with a kinesthetic representational system when was the last time he felt angry, he very likely would look down and to the right to access that feeling and retrieve that memory kinesthetically.

The other way of determining a person's representational system is through the linguistic patterns they use. For example, persons with a visual representational system tend to use words that are visual (e.g., picture, vague, bright, flash, perspective). Persons with an auditory representational system use words that are auditory (e.g., scream, screech, hear, amplify, harmonize). Individuals with a kinesthetic representational system use words that are kinesthetically oriented (e.g., handle, feel, grasp, warm, tight, rough).

Knowledge of an individual's representational system makes it possible to establish rapport with the individual. For example, if an individual is looking up right and left while talking (using visual linguistic patterns), responding to that person with visual linguistic patterns (looking up left and right oneself) can put the individual at ease since both persons are experiencing the world in the same way. Rapport is also increased by mirroring nonverbal communications. For example, sitting in the same position, using the same voice volume and tone, and employing the same gestures as the client facilitates the sense of rapport that exists in the communication.

Techniques. Having established rapport, the therapist is now ready to use the techniques for intervention. One technique is *overlapping*, the process of connecting a representational system that is ordinarily not used by the client with one that is regularly used. The result is that the client is gradually enabled to use the new representational system.

Another technique is *anchoring*. Based on the principles of classical conditioning, anchoring is a process whereby some behavior of the therapist is connected to an experience for the client. For example, while a client is remembering a very powerful, confident moment in his or her past, the therapist may lean over and lightly touch him or her on the hand. In the future whenever the therapist wishes to bring the resources of that memory into the client's awareness, he or she need only reach over and touch the client in exactly the same way. Anchoring can be used to change negative memories and to create previously unavailable possibilities by mobilizing resources that were previously out of the individual's awareness.

Another tool in neurolinguistic programming is *reframing*. Reframing is based on the principle that every behavior, both internal and external, has some useful and meaningful purpose. Reframing aims to make the client aware of the positive intention of some behavior previously perceived as negative. Perceiving the positive intention of the problem behavior allows the individual to find more constructive ways of fulfilling this intention. Reframing can also refer to simply looking at the problem in a new way and thereby accepting it with more ease.

Neurolinguistic programming makes significant use of *metaphor*. The value of metaphor is that the telling of a parallel story to the problem situation of the client allows the person to change without really trying. Often people's conscious efforts to change actually end up interfering with their ability to change. The use of metaphor allows a hidden example to become available to them so they can follow the lead of the metaphor and resolve their problems without consciously trying so hard.

Two other tools of neurolinguistic programming are *meta model* and *strategies*. The meta model deals primarily with linguistic patterns that in one form or another overgeneralize or distort external reality. The meta model consists of questions aimed at clarifying hidden limitations individuals place on themselves by accepting inadequate information. For example, one category in a meta model is deletion. To the statement, "I'm afraid," a helpful response is, "Of what or whom are you afraid?" To the statement, "He's the best player," the response might be, "He's the best player among whom?" Through a series of such questions the neurolinguistic programmer is able to help a client understand himself better.

Strategies on the other hand put the emphasis on eye patterns. For example, when asked why he can't study a person might look quickly up and to the left (visual recall) and then, looking down and right, say, "I just can't feel confident." The client might be unaware of the visual picture from the past that flashes through his or her mind just before the feeling of discouragement. This strategy can be improved by bringing the picture from the past into the client's awareness and thereby counteracting some of its negative impact.

As with so many of the other newer therapies, research on the effectiveness of neurolinguistic programming is lacking. Because of the absence of a theory of personality or of psychopathology, the approach seems more a collection of therapeutic strategies and techniques than a comprehensive system of psychotherapy. Many of these appear to be very useful, and a number of them are regularly incorporated into family therapy and hypnotherapy approaches.

References
Bandler, R., & Grinder, J. *The structure of magic*. Palo Alto, Calif.: Science and Behavior Books, 1975.
Bandler, R., & Grinder, J. *The structure of magic II*. Palo Alto, Calif.: Science and Behavior Books, 1976.

Additional Readings
Bandler, R., Grinder, J., & Satir, V. *Changing with families*. Palo Alto, Calif.: Science and Behavior Books, 1976.
Lankton, S. R. *Practical magical: Translation of basic neurolinguistic programming into clinical psychotherapy*. Cuppertino, Calif.: Meta Publications, 1980.

C. E. Barshinger and L. E. LaRowe

Neuropsychological Assessment.
Neuropsychology deals particularly with the effects of brain lesions or brain damage on behavior. Neuropsychological assessment refers to formal evaluative procedures designed to determine the extent to which brain damage or impairment in brain functions may exist in any given case and its effect on functioning in everyday life. A good general reference for neuropsychological evaluations is that of Lezak (1983). Usually a neuropsychological evaluation consists of at least 1) the taking of a neurological history in the search for events that may adversely have affected the nervous system; 2) an interview in which current complaints and related matters are explored; and 3) the administration of neuropsychological tests.

Neuropsychological Testing. An important part of the neuropsychological evaluation consists of the administration of formal and sometimes informal tests. The number and types of tests administered vary markedly. An evaluation may be identified by some psychologists as neuropsychological with less than an hour's testing, whereas in other instances 8 to 12 hours of testing are accomplished. In order for an evaluation to be appropriately identified as neuropsychological, it would appear reasonable to require enough tests to be given so that sampling can be made of a variety of aspects of brain functions. The brain is made in a wonderful and complex manner, and it is clear that merely having an individual draw a few figures, for example, cannot possibly result in a complete assessment of how the brain is functioning. More adequate evaluation must include systematic assessments of perceptual functions (visual, auditory, tactual); motor functions (motor speed, strength, and coordination); and a number of cognitive skills (language abilities, memory functions, visual-spatial relationships, problem-solving skills, ability to attend to the task). A complete neuropsychological evaluation typically includes testing in each of these areas as well as assessment of general intelligence and emotional adjustment.

There are two basic batteries of neuropsychological tests commonly used in the United States today: the Halstead-Reitan Neuropsychological Test Battery and the Luria-Nebraska Neuropsychological Battery (*see* NEUROPSYCHOLOGY).

The Halstead-Reitan Neuropsychological Battery is the best established, and many studies have been done that validate its usefulness. It began with a series of tests from the Halstead Neuropsychological Battery (Halstead, 1947). The Halstead Impairment Index summarizes findings from these tests by indicating the proportion of tests falling outside normal limits. Other tests were added by

Reitan (Reitan & Davison, 1974). When a general test of intelligence (such as one of the Wechsler scales) is included as well as a substantial measure of emotional adjustment (such as the Minnesota Multiphasic Personality Inventory), the entire battery typically requires 6–8 hours for administration with adults. Shorter forms are available for children down to about age 5, and these typically require less time.

The Halstead-Reitan approach has a number of features that contribute to its broad acceptance. It employs tests that are based on extensive observations of individuals with known brain problems, and the test battery was put together in a systematic way in order to cover a wide variety of functions. The battery was also assembled in such a manner as to take advantage of various methods of test scores that complement one another. An additional strength of the Halstead-Reitan approach is that it is very well validated.

The Luria-Nebraska Neuropsychological Battery was devised by Charles Golden at the University of Nebraska. It is based on the work of Luria, whose methods have been described in great detail (Luria, 1966). They are quite different from those of Halstead and Reitan. Luria was a physician rather than a psychologist, and he did many bedside examinations of brain-damaged patients. He developed a long series of very simple tests that can be done with a minimum of equipment. He also developed a substantial theory of brain functions upon which the tests are based. Because he used primarily subjective observations and did very little in the way of formal validational studies, his approach originally achieved only limited acceptance by psychologists in the United States. However, Golden and his associates have done a great deal to quantify the results from the many simple tests and have helped to establish reliability and validity for the procedures (Golden, 1981). The result has been considerable interest in the battery, although a great deal remains to be done to establish its usefulness. It has the potential of doing a quicker evaluation and possibly obtaining information which might not be obtained with other approaches.

Referrals for Neuropsychological Evaluations. Individuals should be referred for neuropsychological evaluations when they report that an incident has occurred (e.g., head injury, stroke) which appears to have affected their ability to function. A neuropsychological evaluation will assist greatly in establishing appropriate expectations for the future. The neuro-

psychological evaluation may also point toward appropriate rehabilitation approaches. Neuropsychological evaluations are also in order when a performance is not in line with what appear to be reasonable expectations. Thus, if a child appears quite intelligent and yet is performing poorly in school, a neuropsychological evaluation may identify neurological difficulties which were not recognized prior to that time. Such evaluations would be especially helpful when there are no other obvious causes of such difficulties. At the conclusion of the evaluation a written report should be provided to the referring professional. A personal interpretation to the individual examined and to that person's family is usually given.

References

Golden, C. J. A standardized version or Luria's neuropsychological tests: A quantitative and qualitative approach to neuropsychological evaluations. In S. B. Filskov & T. J. Boll (Eds.), *Handbook of clinical neuropsychology.* New York: Wiley, 1981.
Halstead, W. C. *Brain and intelligence.* Chicago: University of Chicago Press, 1947.
Lezak, M. D. *Neuropsychological assessment* (2nd ed.). New York: Oxford University Press, 1983.
Luria, A. R. *Higher cortical functions in man.* New York: Basic Books, 1966.
Reitan, R. M., & Davison, L. A. (Eds.). *Clinical neuropsychology: Current status and applications.* Washington, D.C.: Winston, 1974.

C. B. DODRILL

Neuropsychology. The study of the relationship between the brain and behavior. In particular, neuropsychology is concerned with abnormalities in brain structure and function and their effects upon a person's ability to deal with problems in everyday life. Neuropsychologists typically use a battery of psychological tests to evaluate how well the brain is functioning and to determine if brain damage or impairment in brain functions exists. These tests evaluate various types of abilities, including cognitive, perceptual, and motor. By studying the test results and by knowing a great deal about the nervous system, valid inferences about the condition of the brain can be made.

The fact that brain damage can produce adverse effects on behavior and emotions has been recognized for centuries. However, formal study of these deficits has been undertaken only in approximately the last 50 years. In the United States the first full-time neuropsychology laboratory was set up at the University of Chicago by Ward Halstead in 1935. He began by observing individuals with brain injuries in many contexts and finding out how their performances in life differed from those of persons with normal brains. He ultimately developed a test battery that is designed to assess the effects of brain injury on performance (*see* NEUROPSYCHOLOGICAL ASSESSMENT). A summary of Halstead's work is found in *Brain and Intelligence* (Halstead, 1947).

Halstead's most notable student was Ralph M. Reitan. He did a great deal of additional work in the development and expansion of the test battery at the Indiana University Medical School from 1950 to 1970. Building on Halstead's basic work he added other tests to make the test battery complete, including measures of general intelligence and emotional adjustment. By developing two additional batteries Reitan made it possible to test children as well as adults. Finally, he developed a system for the interpretation of test scores and made a number of applications to problems in life. For these reasons his name is commonly included in the general title Halstead-Reitan Neuropsychological Test Battery.

The individual who has had the greatest impact on neuropsychological assessment outside the United States is Aleksandr Luria of the Soviet Union. Approaching the problem of brain damage and its effect upon behavior from a very different angle, Luria developed a complex theory of how the brain functions and a large number of simple tests to evaluate various aspects of brain functions. In contrast to the Halstead-Reitan procedure, which emphasizes quantitative variables, the Lurian approach is primarily qualitative by nature. The method has been quantified and made more acceptable to American psychologists by Golden (1981), but the full value of the approach has not yet been established.

In the early years of clinical neuropsychology there was a strong emphasis on developing tests and relating them to actual brain lesions. This was a necessary stage of development in order to generate basic information and methods of evaluating deficits. In recent years, however, it has been recognized that neuropsychologists can make a unique contribution in the care of persons with neurological difficulties by accurately evaluating the effects of such problems on ability to function in everyday life and by making appropriate recommendations. It has furthermore been recognized that in many instances neurological problems may be fairly mild and not necessarily found by a physician using standard procedures such as the physical neurological examination, the electroencephalograph and the computerized tomography scan. Although such problems may appear very mild in certain cases, they may have a considerable effect on a person's ability to adjust to the problems in everyday life. Neuropsychology is uniquely suited to evaluate such problems and to make recommendations based upon such evaluations. In the future it is anticipated that the emphasis of the discipline will be more and more in this direction, with less emphasis on the use of the tests merely to determine if there is organicity, or brain damage.

At the time of this writing neuropsychology is undergoing enormous growth, and many psychologists are acquiring skills in this discipline. In any area where there is such rapid expansion it should be expected that there will be some variation in the quality of services offered. It is therefore important in making a referral for a neuropsychological evaluation to be certain that the neuropsychologist is adequately trained. In keeping with the standards of the International Neuropsychological Society such a person should have a minimum of one year of full-time experience in neuropsychology in a medical setting under the supervision of a qualified neuropsychologist. Although workshops may be helpful, they alone are not adequate to qualify an individual to work as a neuropsychologist.

References

Golden, C. J. A standardized version of Luria's Neuropsychological Tests: A quantitative and qualitative approach to neuropsychological evaluations. In S. B. Filskov & T. J. Boll (Eds.), *Handbook of clinical neuropsychology.* New York: Wiley, 1981.

Halstead, W. C. *Brain and intelligence.* Chicago: University of Chicago Press, 1947.

Additional Readings

Luria, A. R. *Higher cortical functions in man.* New York: Basic Books, 1966.

Reitan, R. M., & Davison, L. A. (Eds). *Clinical neuropsychology: Current status and applications.* Washington, D.C.: Winston, 1974.

C. B. DODRILL

Neurosis. In psychoanalytic thought a neurosis is the emotional disturbance resulting from unconscious conflict. The term was introduced by William Cullen in the 1770s but was not systematically defined or extensively used until Freud. It quickly became standard terminology, representing a broad class of nonpsychotic psychopathologies. The most recent classification of mental disorders, *DSM-III*, has abandoned the term, preferring others more descriptive and less theory-laden. In spite of this official action the term *neurosis* is still used extensively, although with a variety of meanings.

Freud originally divided the neuroses into two categories: actual neuroses and psychoneuroses. The actual neuroses, which included neurasthenia, anxiety neurosis, and hypochondria, were thought to be caused by a holding back of sexual excitation. They are not the result of unconscious conflict but of current sexual behavior. Later Freud abandoned the concept of the actual neurosis, as have most contemporary psychoanalysts.

In this article the term *neuroses* refers to the psychoneuroses. These have their basis in an unconscious conflict between instinctual forces striving for gratification and counterinstinctual defenses seeking to block both gratification and conscious awareness of the instinctual strivings. This conflict, called a neurotic conflict, results in a damming up of tension and leads eventually to the formation of the neurotic symptom. This symptom is a partial, involuntary, and indirect discharge of the tension. It is a compromise between the instinctual and counterinstinctual forces in that it simultaneously affords some gratification and at the same time further reinforces the defense against direct gratification of the instinct.

This process can be illustrated by looking at a neurotic symptom such as obsessive thinking. An individual may describe the thought of killing his wife as a recurrent and persistent idea that does not seem to be under his control or in any way reflective of his real feelings for his wife. Psychodynamically such a symptom would be viewed as the result of unconscious conflict related to aggression. More specifically the obsessive thought would be seen as providing partial and indirect gratification of the aggressive impulses (through thinking about killing), while at the same time providing further defense against such impulses (through emotional isolation and denial, "I don't really feel that way about my wife").

In summary, behavior is viewed as neurotic when it is based on an unconscious conflict between the id (instinctual forces) and the ego (counterinstinctual defenses) that results in a damming up of tension and finally an involuntary partial discharge of this tension through the behavior. Such behavior is experienced subjectively as irrational and beyond voluntary control. It also interferes with the individual's capacity for love and productive work.

This understanding of the development of neurotic behavior is far from universally accepted. A cogent alternative explanation based on learning theory exists within behavioral psychology. The decision to eliminate the term from *DSM-III* was in large part due to the lack of consensus regarding the etiology of the

disorder. Disorders previously classified as neuroses are now therefore officially classified as affective, anxiety, somatoform, dissociative, and psychosexual disorders.

D. G. BENNER

See PSYCHOANALYTIC PSYCHOLOGY.

Neurosis, Experimental. The disturbed and disorganized behavior patterns that can be induced in animals in experimental settings through the use of specialized techniques. It has been suggested that the responses of these animals closely parallel several forms of human neurotic disturbances, and that therefore hypotheses about the development of neurotic behavior in humans, as well as principles of treatment, can be extrapolated from the study of these phenomena (Wolpe, 1958).

The first demonstration of experimental neurosis occurred in Pavlov's laboratory (Pavlov, 1927). Dogs were presented with illuminated circles (a conditioned stimulus), which were followed by feeding (an unconditioned stimulus); subsequently the presentation of a circle elicited salivation in the dog. Flattened ellipses were also presented followed by no feeding, and thus came to elicit no response from the dog. Slowly ellipses that more and more closely approached the shape of a circle were presented to the dog. At a point where the ellipse was very close to the circle the dog's performance began to degenerate rapidly, with the dog even losing the ability to make discriminations that had been easy before that point. The dog's behavior changed in other ways also, most notably in showing obvious agitation and fear when placed in the experimental chamber. It was this type of behavior that was termed experimental neurosis.

Similar behavior has been produced through other experimental paradigms and with other species. Difficult discriminations in other sense modalities have produced similar effects. Pavlov also found that if the time lag between presentation of a conditioned stimulus and the unconditioned stimulus (food) was gradually lengthened, some animals would become "quite crazy, ... howling, barking, and squeaking intolerably" (p. 294). Cats shocked as they were feeding, or with air blown into their ears, developed behavior patterns of yowling, crouching, and clawing in the experimental chamber. In addition, they uniformly refused to eat in the experimental chamber. LEARNED HELPLESSNESS with animals is a contemporary example of experimental neurosis.

The generally accepted explanation of this

phenomenon is the classical conditioning explanation of Wolpe (1958): experimental neurosis represents the acquisition of a generalized conditioned response of anxiety. In explaining Pavlov's original studies it is asserted that anxiety and fear are the unconditioned responses to impossible discriminations (and other aversive experiences). Upon the occurrence of such a response the experimental setting comes to serve as a stimulus to which the response of fear is conditioned. Hence, subsequent exposures to the experimental chambers lead to agitated "neurotic" behavior. It is assumed that neurotic behavior in humans represents similar instances of anxiety reactions, conditioned to certain stimuli.

Fenichel (1945) offered a psychoanalytic interpretation of these phenomena. He suggested that the neurotic behavior occurs when previously gratifying stimuli are associated with aversive stimuli. This leads to the confluence of two conflicting motives: to obtain gratification and to escape. The conflict between the impulses leads to a buildup of tension which is discharged through neurotic behavior.

Wolpe's (1958) studies of persistent experimental neurosis in cats culminated in his development of procedures to alleviate the reaction. He gradually increased exposure to the feared stimuli while the animal was engaged in behavior incompatible with fear (e.g., eating). This process, termed *reciprocal inhibition of fear*, became the basis for the development of systematic desensitization and assertiveness training in behavior therapy.

References

Fenichel, O. *The psychoanalytic theory of neurosis.* New York: Norton, 1945.
Pavlov, I. *Conditioned reflexes.* Oxford: The University Press, 1927.
Wolpe, J. *Psychotherapy by reciprocal inhibition.* Stanford: Calif.: Stanford University Press, 1958.

S. J. JONES

Nightmare.

Both nightmares and night tremors involve a person awaking from sleep in a state of fear and anxiety. A nightmare is usually associated upon awakening with a particular dream. Nightmares occur during the REM stage of sleep and are most frequently experienced by children 7 to 10 years old. The best initial treatment for a nightmare is calm reassurance that there is nothing to be afraid of.

Night tremors, technically known as *pavor nocturnus*, are more dramatic than nightmares, resembling panic attacks. They are not associated with a dream and upon waking are not typically remembered to have occurred. Research has shown that night tremors are a disorder of the slow wave deep sleep stage and do not occur during the REM dream stage. Night tremors are most frequent in children aged 3 to 5 years.

The occurrence of nightmares and night tremors should not be interpreted as being of great psychological significance unless they become chronic. Chronic problems may be a reaction to emotional stress or may indicate a physiological-biological defect.

D. S. McCulloch

See SLEEP AND DREAMING; SLEEP DISORDERS.

Nondirective Therapy. See PERSON-CENTERED THERAPY.

Nonprofessionals as Therapists. See PARAPROFESSIONAL THERAPY.

Noogenic Neurosis.

According to Frankl, a noogenic neurosis is the result of moral conflicts or conflict among values. This is in contrast to the psychoneurosis which Frankl views, in orthodox psychoanalytic fashion, as the result of conflicts between drives and instincts.

Since the noogenic neuroses reflect what Frankl calls a spiritual problem, he argues that what is needed is not psychotherapy in general but LOGOTHERAPY, a therapy which he developed to specifically address spiritual and existential dimensions of existence. It should be noted, however, "that within the frame of reference of logotherapy, 'spiritual' does not have a primarily religious connotation but refers to the specifically human dimension" (Frankl, 1963, p. 102).

Reference

Frankl, V. E. *Man's search for meaning.* Boston: Beacon Press, 1963.

D. G. BENNER

Normality.

Many psychologists consider normality and abnormality together since abnormality is deviance from normality. Normality represents the lack of abnormality. Professional consensus suggests several conditions that define personality as abnormal: self-proclaimed deviance, antisocial action or intent, antisurvival elements, irrationality, subjective distress, social deviance, or psychological handicap.

A more theoretical definition is offered by Allport (1977). Normality is conforming to a given *norm*, an authoritative standard, while abnormality is deviance from that standard.

However, as Allport notes, there are two competing traditions for defining the norm.

The statistical tradition assumes human traits vary along a continuum on which the relative frequencies approximate the normal curve. The norm is the usual value and is expressed by a central tendency measure (e.g., mean, median, or mode). The degree of deviance from the central tendency of the group determines the degree of abnormality. The genius is as abnormal as the retardate. The orientation of this tradition is toward objectivity and value neutrality. It seeks to measure accurately the "isness" of human nature.

In the second tradition, an ethical one, the norm is defined as something valued, an "oughtness" of human nature. Frequently the usual is not the desired. As a values-invested approach this tradition may reflect several positions, one of which is the moral perspective. In reference to some value theory (e.g., the Bible) the norm is morality, while the abnorm is that which is immoral. In describing the normal personality Christ may be held as the norm for human conduct.

The medical perspective provides a second ethical position. Health is to be desired; health is the absence of illness. The norm is that individuals live lives free from the effects of illness, disease, and dysfunction. The current emphasis on holism is one mode of stating this norm.

A third value position is naturalistically derived and suggests that humans should maximize the ways in which they differ from animals (Allport, 1977). Human uniqueness stems from the propositional use of symbols and protracted childhood. These combine as a substratum for responsibility, social interest, ideals, self-control, and guilt. An alternative naturalistic approach specifies the minimum conditions for survival as growth and cohesion. To fall below those levels is to experience the abnorm and tend toward death and destruction.

A fourth position resembles the naturalistic. In the humanistic perspective normality is the attainment of freedom, self-actualization, personal growth, and intimacy. The abnorm is whatever is excessively repressive or demanding and violates the principles of freedom and cohesion.

In summary, there are two competing traditions for defining normality. The statistical one focuses on the "isness" of the individual by referring to a known distribution of traits and is reflected in the use of norm-referenced test scores. The ethical tradition defines normality by what is desired or "ought" to be. These value statements may be generated from several sources. The statistical approach describes what is usual, while the ethical one prescribes what is desired.

Reference
Allport, G. W. Personality: Normal and abnormal. In H. Chiang & A. H. Maslow (Eds.), *The healthy personality: Readings* (2nd ed.). New York: Van Nostrand, 1977.

R. L. TIMPE

See PERSONALITY; ABNORMAL PSYCHOLOGY.

Normalization in Human Services.

The principle of normalization is a basis for planning, providing, and evaluating services to persons who have disabilities such as mental retardation, quadriplegia, cerebral palsy, mental illness, or alcoholism.

The historical roots of normalization can be traced to 1959 when Denmark became the first nation to pass legislation establishing an agency concerned with the health, education, and welfare of people with special needs and particularly designed to help them experience life as normally as possible. In 1967–68 Sweden passed a similar law establishing an agency to unite resources for retarded people based on the normalization principle. Subsequently in the United States, Wolf Wolfensberger, Frank Menolascino, and a few co-workers labored for several years to establish normalization in service systems for the mentally retarded. This culminated in *The Principles of Normalization in Human Services* (Wolfensberger, Nirje, Olshansky, Perske, & Roos, 1972), which summarized the historical background and formulated the philosophical and practical aspects of normalization. Wolfensberger's approach has been expanded to include persons with all kinds of disabilities rather than focusing only on the mentally retarded.

Definition. Normalization can be described as a system for increasing the probability that, over time, handicapped people will more and more live in society as valued neighbors rather than as devalued objects of pity or derision. This could be stated another way: "And as ye would that men should do to you, do ye also to them likewise" (Luke 6:31).

More specifically, Wolfensberger (1980a) defines normalization as the "use of culturally normative means (familiar, valued techniques, tools, methods) . . . to [improve] persons' life conditions (income, housing, health services, etc.) . . . and to . . . enhance or support their behavior (skills, competencies, etc.), appearances (clothes, grooming, etc.), experiences (adjustment, feelings, etc.), and status and reputation (labels, attitudes of others, etc.)" (p. 25). Services designed on this concept of normalization are likely to result in increasing competence and social participation for individuals with disabilities and in increasing social acceptance of them as a group.

Applications. Implementation of the normalization principle requires that people and service systems avoid devaluing responses to persons who have any type of disability. Three frequent responses that are most harmful are: 1) isolation (segregating people with handicaps); 2) dehumanization (treating people with handicaps as if they were less than fully human); and 3) age inappropriateness (treating people with disabilities as if they are, and always will be, children). Understanding each of these patterns of devaluation helps define positive practices to ensure that people with handicaps experience as much participation in the life of the community as possible.

In the past many residential services for handicapped people were founded and grew when isolation was considered the treatment of choice. For a time the belief that people with disabilities needed protection from community life justified isolation. This eventually turned to a belief that the community needs protection from the costs and dangers allegedly posed by people with handicaps. Therefore, many service systems have moved these people away from their age peers; others move them away from their home communities; and some even isolate people from friends, relatives, and immediate family members.

According to advocates of the normalization concept such practices deprive these individuals of a wide variety of learning experiences, the support of valued peer models, many opportunities to exercise choice, the chance to become a part of a natural social network, and the challenge of contributing to community life.

If persons with handicaps are to learn to meet their needs in the least restrictive possible relationship to their community, proponents of normalization believe they must experience that community individually as an essential part of their learning. They assert that there are two dimensions of community life a person needs to experience: 1) the physical world of places and things, and 2) the social world of people and typical human groups. The isolation of handicapped people from community life breeds suspicion, fear, and rejection. If individuals are to develop and mature as normally as possible, a significant number of community members must support their development in

natural communities by getting to know them on a one-to-one basis, inviting them to their homes, taking them to church, taking them to ballgames, and the like. As long as isolation persists, social acceptance cannot develop.

Advocates of normalization allege that dehumanization is fostered through settings that do not allow for personal space and privacy. Examples of such conditions include sleeping arrangements that permit no choice regarding whether or not one will share a room and with whom, lack of privacy in toileting and bathing, food preparation with few choices of menu or option to cook for oneself, and lack of space for personal possessions.

Further, normalization proponents contend that persons are treated as subhuman when people regard them as one of a group rather than as individuals. This is apparent when persons are grouped according to disability and/or functioning level for leisure time activities rather than on the basis of individual performance. This is also observed when persons are not included in decisions about their own lives. Dehumanization can also be signaled by language that fails to promote the integrity of a person (i.e., labels).

The absence of dehumanizing conditions, however, does not automatically guarantee persons dignity and respect. In order to develop a sense of worth as an individual a person needs opportunities for self-expression and time apart from a group. It is believed that persons have the right to privacy and personal space wherever they live. Living space should be comfortable and attractive. Special equipment to aid posture or mobility should be comfortable, well fitting, and designed to minimize stigmatizing appearances. All facilities should be physically accessible to people with mobility limitations. Individuals also deserve some choice regarding activities and the people with whom they spend their leisure time. Community members can provide these opportunities for choice as they relate on a one-to-one basis with these persons.

In order to participate in life fully each person deserves the opportunity to participate in the decisions affecting his or her life. Individuals with handicaps, especially those who have been institutionalized for extensive periods, often need systematic training to develop their ability to choose. Nevertheless, issues affecting a group of people, even when they have disabilities, should be decided by that group when possible. When this is not feasible, decisions should be made only after input from the group has been obtained.

Persons need to be allowed to take appropriate risks. They have the opportunity to realize success only when they also have the opportunity for failure. People have the right to be systematically taught to understand their legal and personal rights and the means of protecting them. Decision-making and citizenship training ought to be available.

Positive interactions are also crucial to enhancing the dignity and individual respect of persons with disabilities. People should not be treated condescendingly, regardless of their disability. Communication needs to be warm and personal, with people genuinely sharing their lives and personal time with disabled individuals. Handicapped adults have the right to experience personal relationships with friends, including those of the opposite sex.

Another area of concern is age-inappropriate practices that treat handicapped people as if they are, and always will be, children. Consciousness of age appropriateness is seen as critical in the selection of learning activities and materials. Activities that are designed to teach skills should be selected according to age-appropriate processes and carried out at appropriate times. For example, a person who needs training in self-care skills should ideally receive it individually at the appropriate times (upon waking or before bed) in his or her own bedroom or bathroom. Similarly, training materials should be selected that are appropriate to a person's chronological age. An adult may need to learn how to pour. If this is taught in a sandbox with pails and shovels, it loudly signals devaluation for the integrity of that individual. The same skill could be appropriately taught through cooking or potting plants.

It is considered important that the rhythms of the day, week, and year be the same for persons labeled "disabled" as for those labeled "normal." Children ought to attend school; adults should go to a place of work, earn money, experience personal leisure time, and so on. Promoters of normalization contend that a disproportionate amount of time is often spent in recreational and leisure activities. Also, there is often little concern for the quality of performance; the expectation is, "It's enough for them just to try." This disregards the status a person can earn by excellence in at least one area of activity. Acceptance of shoddy work by a handicapped person (or anyone else) communicates a lack of respect for the person's abilities. Such practices and expectations are demeaning and hinder individual development.

Critique and Evaluation. One of the most common criticisms of normalization is that people with disabilities cannot be made normal. Defenders of normalization would tend to agree on this point. Some individuals, when provided optimal opportunities for growth and development of personal worth, may achieve a nonhandicapped and/or nondevalued functioning and status. Such, however, is not the essence of the concept. Proponents feel that all handicapped individuals have a right to as normal an environment as they can utilize, regardless of prognosis for future change.

Another criticism develops when those who do not fully understand normalization philosophy place handicapped individuals in normal situations where they have many problems or fail. Mentally retarded persons, blind individuals, or persons possessing certain other disabilities should not be put in an apartment by themselves, for example, without first identifying the needs such a person would have and developing strategies to meet those needs.

Research on the normalization principle has been difficult because of the vast number of components, corollaries, and action implications that fall into a hierarchy of levels in the normalization process. Not all have the same amount or quality of research support. One way of studying these issues has been to look at the ratings provided by the tool called Program Analysis of Service Systems (Wolfensberger & Glenn, 1975). This instrument is a systematic method of evaluation that breaks services down into 48 areas relating to the quality of services provided to handicapped persons. Wolfensberger (1980b) summarizes some of this research as well as other studies conducted with regard to role expectancies, role demands, etc. These provide encouraging support for the application of the normalization principle.

The Bible is filled with pertinent directions about the responsibility persons share for their neighbors and the quality of their lives. Moreover, a church is called to be a model community that will enhance persons. Certainly, therefore, it seems appropriate for Christians to be actively committed to, and give leadership in, efforts to respond to all persons with valuing and respect.

References

Wolfensberger, W. Research, empiricism, and the principle of normalization. In R. J. Flynn & K. E. Nitsch (Eds.), *Normalization, social integration, and community services.* Baltimore: University Park Press, 1980.(a)

Wolfensberger, W. The definition of normalization. In R. J. Flynn & K. E. Nitsch (Eds.), *Normalization, social integration, and community services.* Baltimore: University Park Press, 1980.(b)

Wolfensberger, W., & Glenn, L. *Program analysis of service systems: A method for the qualitative evaluation of human services* (vols. 1 & 2) (3rd ed.). Toronto: National Institute on Mental Retardation, 1975.

Wolfensberger, W., Nirje, B., Olshansky, S., Perske, R., & Roos, P. *The principles of normalization in human services*. Toronto: National Institute on Mental Retardation, 1972.

M. E. McCurdy

Nosology. A branch of medicine concerned with the study and classification of diseases. Discovery of symptoms and consequent grouping into syndromes is the main area of concern. The delineation and definition of diseases perform four major functions in the medical field: classification of terminology, the categorizing of names and codes within each classification, the establishing of reliable and specific procedures for collecting information, and the operationalizing of rules for making classifications. The three main purposes or uses of information gathered by nosology are to serve as a guide to selection of treatment, to make prognoses, and to function as administrative devices for hospital admissions, insurance purposes, and similar medical or legal requirements.

D. L. Schuurman

Nouthetic Counseling. A theory formulated by Adams (1970) based on the Greek word *noutheteō*, translated as "admonish." Adams's most systematic work on counseling appeared in 1973 as *The Christian Counselor's Manual*, and in 1979 he began a theology of counseling, *More than Redemption*. Seminary trained, Adams has a doctorate in speech. After a pastorate and three years of teaching speech, he became professor of practical theology at Westminster Seminary, where he continues a part-time affiliation.

Personality Theory. Nouthetic counseling can be described in terms of its theory of human nature, view of pathology, and model and process of counseling. Nouthetic theory stresses the overt aspects of human nature. Adams maintains that God describes love in attitudinal and behavioral terms in defining it as commandment keeping (John 14:15). Hence nouthetic counseling focuses less on how clients feel than on how they behave. In addition, voluntary changes in behavior are a function of intelligent decisions and affect the emotions as a result, thus reaching the whole man. "People feel bad because of bad behavior: feelings flow from actions" (Adams, 1970, p. 93).

To Adams the sequence is clear: God's commands deal with behavior and attitudes.

The individual chooses to behave consistently or inconsistently with these commands, and good or bad feelings follow accordingly. Somehow the result is communicated to the whole person, but what the whole person means for Adams is never defined. Behavior is defined as responsible conduct. An attitude is a habitual pattern of thought which strongly influences actions.

Attitudes may be changed more easily than feelings, which Adams defines as the perception of a bodily state, either pleasant or unpleasant. He views other emotional responses of the body as "*responses* to judgements made about the environment and oneself" (1974, p. 112). They come in two kinds, good and bad.

Psychologically, the thrust of Adams's theory is that behavior is central and has fundamental significance. Attitudes are second and interior, but as habitual thought patterns they have an external behavioral focus. Feelings are the most internal and least accessible. They follow or are caused by behavior. Adams maintains this sequence is clearly the biblical ideal (1973, p. 135).

Theologically Adams holds a dichotomous view of man, maintaining that the soul and the spirit are used interchangeably in the Bible. The image of God in man is of more central importance in nouthetic theory than is soul or spirit. This image is moral and cognitive. In the fall the image became a "reflection of the father of lies" (Adams, 1970, p. 128). The Christian is described as restoring the image by eliminating disorder and confusion (1973, p. 342). The fall, Adams says, was a fall into loss of control over the environment, and God calls the Christian to master his environment. "In this way he may once again reflect the image of God by subduing and ruling the world about him" (Adams 1970, p. 129). The focus for the Christian is on behaviorally confronting the environment. The cognitive aspect of the image would appear to be related to the attitudinal or judgment process that mediates feelings, though Adams does not integrate his psychological and theological descriptions of man.

View of Psychopathology. The title of chapter 14 of *The Christian Counselor's Manual* summarizes Adams's view of pathology: "Sin is the problem." The chapter begins, "Christian counselors should not need to be reminded that they have been called to labor in opposition to the world, the flesh and the devil." This is elaborated as, "Sin, then, in all its dimensions, clearly is the problem with which the

Christian counselor must grapple." In his analysis of the fall described in Genesis 3 Adams views the basic temptation as the satisfaction of desire rather than obedience to God. The same choice exists today.

According to Adams the choice is between two ways of living: "the feeling-motivated life of sin oriented toward self" or the "commandment-oriented life of holiness oriented toward God" (Adams 1973, p. 118). The choice is reduced to love or lust, God's commandments or the client's desires. In nouthetic counseling feelings appear to be equated with desire, and desire is tied to sinful actions (Adams 1973, p. 120). Hence feelings are not to be attended to or trusted. However, nouthetic theory maintains that feelings do not necessarily lead to sinful actions since commandment living is called for in spite of feelings. God is not opposed to good feelings, but Adams says they always come from him. How this can occur is not explained.

In addition to sin as a cause of pathology, organic disease and demon possession are also possible causes, though the latter, according to Adams, is not really possible in the believer. According to Adams there is no such thing as mental illness or emotional disorder—i.e. there is no pure or partial psychological cause of pathology since there is no such thing as mental illness. Thus sin is the cause of problems (pathology) when there is no demonic or organic problem.

Three levels of problems exist: presenting problems ("I'm depressed"), performance problems ("I haven't been much of a husband"), and preconditioning problems ("I avoid responsibility when the going gets tough"). Presentation problems are often presented as a cause when actually they are an effect. Performance problems are often presented as an effect when actually they are a cause. Preconditioning problems are often presented as an effect when actually they are the underlying cause (Adams, 1970, p. 148). Adams goes on to emphasize that the preconditioning problem is a habitual response which, as the root problem, often clarifies the relationship between the other two problems. Consequently his theory of pathology is consistent with his view of man. Both have a strong behavioral orientation; listening to feelings (desire) leads to sinful action, while obedience to God's commandments leads to good feelings.

Counseling Process. The model of nouthetic counseling is based on the Greek *noutheteō*, which is translated 13 times in the New Testament as "admonish" or "warn." Since Adams recognizes that there is no one-word English equivalent, he speaks of "nouthetic confrontation" and uses this phrase as his model.

The model has four basic characteristics. First, confrontation in counseling is viewed as inseparable from pastoral authority. Second, the goals of nouthetic counseling are stated to be the same as the goals of Scripture. "Nouthetic confrontation is, in short, confrontation with the principles and practices of scripture" (Adams, 1970, p. 51). Third, nouthetic counseling was originally conceived to be team counseling, though the emphasis on the use of a team of counselors with a single client has not been stressed in Adams's later writings. Fourth, nouthetic counseling has a strong similarity to legal counseling—i.e., it is directive, gives advice, and imparts information.

The process of counseling that unfolds from this model is grounded in Adams's basic assumption that people need meaning or hope in their lives. He feels that one way to raise hope is by taking people seriously when they talk of sin (1973, p. 46). Adams also uses Matthew 18:15-29, which he calls the reconciliation/discipline dynamic, to give hope. If a brother transgresses against you, go to him; if he won't hear, take one or two with you; if he still won't hear, go to the church, which he must heed or discipline will result. Counseling is helping the client apply this dynamic correctly.

In addition to these general methods Adams uses the Personal Data Inventory, listed in an appendix of the *Christian Counselor's Manual*, to gather a client's history and to assess the client's present problems. The early sessions may also involve further history gathering. However, by the sixth session the major issues should be clear, and by the eighth to tenth session the problem should be well on its way toward solution (Adams 1973, pp. 233-234). Adams does not specify the exact length of therapy, but it appears to be relatively short.

The main focus of nouthetic counseling is on *what*, not *why*. The counselor directs his attention as needed to the presentation, performance, or preconditioning problem. He imparts information, gives advice, and focuses on problems in a confrontive manner. The assignment of increasingly difficult homework relevant to the client's problem is another method used. A frequent technique is restructuring all areas of a client's life and pressing for change in each so as to prevent relapses.

According to Adams the Holy Spirit is the real counselor. "Ignoring the Holy Spirit or avoiding the use of scripture in counseling is tantamount to an act of autonomous rebellion" (1973, pp. 6-7). Counseling is only truly nouthetic when the counselee is a Christian. Adams maintains that every Christian is called to be a counselor, but counseling is the special calling of the pastor. There is no legitimate place for a psychiatrist or clinical psychologist, since there is no such thing as a psychological or nonorganic psychiatric problem. Adams is absolutely insistent on this point throughout his writings. Consequently he maintains that a good seminary education is more appropriate for a counselor than medical school or clinical psychology training.

Finally the nouthetic counselor cannot listen to or accept the client's sinful attitudes or ventilations, since the "acceptance of sin is sin" (1970, p. 102). Acceptance or support is passive, hence it is wrong for three reasons: 1) the counselor must never support sinful behavior; 2) support is harmful because it acknowledges and approves of the client's handling of his problems; and 3) there is no biblical basis for passively "being" but not "doing" or "saying" (1973, p. 154). Nor is there any room for empathy that is not problem oriented. Admonishing is the evidence of love, since love, for Adams, is responsible behavior (1970, p. 55).

Evaluation. Since Adams has asked to be evaluated biblically, this is a good place to begin. In his strong emphasis on responsibility Adams has underscored a biblical stress on responsible action. However, what he has omitted is the Bible's focus on the heart as the source of actions, whether good or evil. The New Testament uses the word *heart (kardia)* over 150 times to describe the internal source, the deepest level of human nature or cause of actions. From the heart flows good (Matt. 12:35), evil (Matt. 15:19), doubt (Mark 11:23), conviction (Acts 2:37), and belief (Rom. 10:9). Adultery can be an internal desire not yet an overt act (Matt. 5:28). However, Adams ignores not only the specific passages using *heart* but also this whole inner dimension of human beings which is so central to the Scriptures. In spite of its significance heart is only mentioned 12 times in his first two major works. Equally absent are the related internal concepts of soul, spirit, and flesh. These concepts are so central to the Bible that no model of human nature or counseling can claim to be biblical without them.

A second major weakness in Adams's theory is his failure to justify on biblical grounds why *noutheteō* (admonish) should be the basis for a theory of biblical counseling. He does note the relationship between *noutheteō* and *didaskō* (to teach). He argues that since the pastor is called to teach, he is also called to admonish, which he interprets as counseling. However, the problem is not just the selection of one biblical concept without a rationale, but the omission of other more biblically central concepts—e.g., *parakeleō*, translated "comfort," "console," or "exhort" 70 times in the New Testament. In addition *parakeleō* is a gift given to the church for ministering to the body of believers (Rom. 12:7). Hence *parakeleō* clearly makes a better concept on which to build a biblical theory of counseling.

A third weakness in Adams's theory is his omission of biblical thought that is in conflict with his views. Thessalonians 5:14 describes three types of relating to three kinds of problems: admonish (*noutheteō*) the unruly, encourage (*paramutheō*) the fainthearted, help (*antexō*) the weak. Yet Adams argues for the use of one approach—admonish—with everyone, contrary to this passage of Scripture. In addition, nouthetic counseling is in conflict with the whole point of the book of Job: sin is not always the cause of disaster and suffering. While Adams (1979) specifically recognized that Job's problems were not a result of sin, his whole theory asserts that sin *is* the problem.

Another weakness is Adams's failure to understand the psychologists he most severely criticizes, Freud and Rogers. At one point he attributes the concept of transference to "Rogerians and other Freudians" (1970, p. 101). Psychologically, Rogers and Freud are very dissimilar. No serious psychological analysis has ever viewed them as similar. Nor does Rogers discuss transference or make it a part of his therapy. Adams also states, "The Freudian viewpoint boils down to this, that God is to blame for the misery and ruin of man" (1970, p. 214). Since Freud was an atheist, this is a blatant misrepresentation of his theorizing. Adams's failure to understand psychologists is not surprising, since a glance through the pages of his books shows a striking absence of references to the major works of the psychologists he criticizes, though there are many popular and secondary source references.

References

Adams, J. *Competent to counsel.* Philadelphia: Presbyterian and Reformed Publishing, 1970.
Adams, J. *The Christian counselor's manual.* Grand Rapids: Baker, 1973.
Adams, J. *More than redemption.* Phillipsburg, N.J.: Presbyterian and Reformed Publishing, 1979.

Additional Readings

Carter, J. D. Adams's theory of nouthetic counseling. *Journal of Psychology and Theology*, 1975, *3*, 143–155.

Carter, J. D. Nouthetic counseling defended: A reply to Ganz. *Journal of Psychology and Theology*, 1976, *4*, 206–216.

Ganz, R. L. Nouthetic counseling defended. *Journal of Psychology and Theology*, 1976, *4*, 193–205.

Oakland, J. An analysis and critique of Jay Adams's theory of counseling. *Journal of the American Scientific Affiliation*, 1976, *28*, 101–109.

J. D. CARTER

See CHRISTIAN COUNSELING AND PSYCHOTHERAPY.

Nymphomania. *See* EXCESSIVE SEXUAL DESIRE.

Oo

Obedience. In studying conformity, or obedience to social influence, psychologists have found this occurring at three levels. The deepest level involves the personality and value structures of the individual utilizing conformity as a dominant adjustment mode. The internalized conformity becomes a way of meeting personal needs. Conforming personalities have lower self-esteem, greater authoritarian tendencies, and more unquestioning respect for convention than nonconformists.

A second level concerns attitudes privately held and publicly expressed. If an individual finds a certain group attractive and desirable, he or she may change important attitudes to match those of the group. The individual conforms to group opinion through identification (e.g., dress and musical preferences of teen-agers).

Conformity also exists at a surface level. Groups exert pressure on individuals to exhibit a particular behavior. The group's power to change individual behavior lies in its ability to provide rewards for conformity and punishments for nonconformity. Conformity at this behavioral level is termed compliance. If authority is a factor in the administration of rewards and punishments, then compliance is considered obedience.

Milgram (1973) has studied destructive obedience, the ability of an authority figure to induce subordinates to damage property or harm others. Destructive obedience underlies such historical occurrences as the Spanish Inquisition, the Nazi persecution of European Jews, the My Lai massacre in Vietnam, and the Jonestown tragedy. In each case a leader (ecclesiastical, governmental, or military) ordered followers to torture or kill.

Milgram's experiments followed a common format. He advertised for volunteers to help him conduct an experiment in learning. Those who volunteered were cast in the experimental role of teacher. The teacher's task was to punish the learner whenever he or she failed to learn by administering an electric shock. The shock apparatus was labeled for each shock level (e.g., 15 volts, slight shock; 100 volts, severe shock; 450 volts, danger!). The researcher, who stood in the room with the teacher, required the teacher to administer progressively stronger shocks each time there was a failure to learn. Unknown to the teacher, the learner was the researcher's accomplice who was programmed to fail in the learning tasks. The learner was not actually shocked, but staged more violent reactions as the shocks became more intense. If the teacher tried to quit the experiment, the researcher demanded that teacher continue in the name of science. The actual variable that was measured was the level of shock the teacher was willing to administer.

Milgram originally predicted few teachers would administer extreme shocks. He sampled some psychiatrists, college students, and middle-class adults, who concurred with his predictions. However, in the actual experiment he found that no teacher administered less than 300 volts and 65% gave the most severe shock possible. In the experimental setting the teacher could neither see nor hear the learner (i.e., the remote condition). Postexperiment interviews with the teachers revealed that many experienced anxiety from giving extreme shocks.

Milgram conducted other experiments to determine what variables might influence the level of obedience. He manipulated the amount of contact between the teacher and learner.

When the teacher could hear the learner (i.e., voice-feedback condition) only 62.5% administered maximum shocks. When the teacher and learner were located in the same room (i.e., proximity condition), 40% administered maximum shock. If the teacher and learner were seated at the same table (i.e., touch-proximity condition), 30% of the teachers administered the maximum level. Obedience decreased as the distance and contact between the teacher and learner decreased.

The legitimacy of the authority was examined. When the research was conducted at Yale University, there was a higher rate of obedience than when the research was conducted at a private commercial research firm housed in a rundown office building in Bridgeport, Connecticut. In the latter setting 48% delivered maximum shocks as opposed to the 62% at Yale. Nevertheless, there was considerable obedience even when the authority was not particularly reputable. Bickman (1974) reported greater obedience when the authority was legitimized by a uniform.

When the researcher stood closer to the teacher and when there was more than one researcher present, there was greater obedience. When there were multiple teachers, obedience levels decreased. Milgram noted that certain individuals were more likely to be obedient: police and military personnel, individuals who believed the learners deserved and were responsible for their punishment, persons with stronger authoritarian characteristics, and individuals who had less advanced levels of moral development.

In summary, Milgram demonstrated that most people would be obedient to authority in harming others against their own will. Other forms of obedience (e.g., willing obedience to parents or obedience when privately held attitudes support the authority's request) have not been studied as systematically or thoroughly.

References
Bickman, L. Social roles and uniforms: Clothes make the person. *Psychology Today*, 1974, 7(11), 48–51.
Milgram, S. *Obedience to authority*. New York: Harper & Row, 1973.

R. L. TIMPE

See CONFORMITY.

Obesity. In view of the current emphasis on physical health and slim appearance, it is not surprising that few physical conditions carry the social disapproval that accompanies obesity. The media as well as the health care professions have gone so far as to single out obesity as a matter of "national disgrace" (Bruch, 1978). To effectively treat such individuals it is important to understand the etiology, psychological features, and treatment methods associated with obesity.

Although there is little agreement regarding the precise definition and measurement of obesity, general consensus is to define it as a weight that exceeds the "ideal" weight by 20%. More precise, but less popular, is a method of calibrating excess body fat (Seltzer & Mayer, 1965). National statistics on the prevalence of obesity estimate that between 20 to 30% of the adult population falls within this category. While some studies suggest that a greater number of boys than girls are overweight, others have disputed this conclusion. However, by age 30 women do have a greater tendency to be obese than men, at a ratio of three women per two men (Stuart & Davis, 1972). Differences between the sexes disappear by age 60, since both sexes tend to decrease in weight after that age.

Recent research has revealed several etiological factors that may lead to obesity. Such biologically related factors as genetic predisposition, endocrine and biochemical disorders, abnormal neuroregulatory mechanisms, and early adipose tissue development often contribute to the onset of obesity (Bruch, 1978). Most basic, of course, is the thermodynamic model, which attributes obesity to intake that exceeds energy burned (Mayer, 1968). However, such biologically related factors are not the only causes of obesity. Psychological factors such as an inability to identify hunger or distinguish it from other bodily needs or emotional arousal may also contribute to its development. Other related psychological factors include dysfunctional families, disturbances in size awareness, misperception of bodily functions, misperception of sexual role, issues concerning ownership of one's body and its control, and the use of food and eating as a pseudosolution for a variety of personality problems (Bruch, 1978). Recent studies have suggested that serious overeating may result in response to nonspecific emotional tensions, chronic frustration, emotional disturbance such as depression, and actual psychological addiction to food. It may also occur in reaction to specific traumatic events (Bruch, 1978).

Reasons for the higher frequency of obesity among females have been sought. Schachter's (1971) research has demonstrated that many individuals tend to eat in response to external environmental cues rather than internal physiological states. Thus, it is thought that women's typical involvement in menu planning, shopping, preparing and storing food, as well as other related tasks may increase the risk of obesity for the predisposed homemaker (Hall & Havassy, 1981). It has also been suggested that lack of exercise, subtle role expectations, and societal pressure to be extremely slim have differentially influenced the development of obesity among females, in contrast to males.

A wide variety of treatment techniques has been developed during the past decade. Biologically related interventions include special diets, exercise programs, medication, surgery, and intensive hospital programs (Bruch, 1978). Psychotherapeutic approaches include behavior modification (Kingsley & Wilson, 1977), family therapy (Bruch, 1978), group therapy (Wollersheim, 1970), and approaches based on Schachter's externality hypothesis (Weiss, 1977) and on a psychoanalytic model (Orbach, 1978).

It would appear that several special factors must be considered when developing a treatment strategy for such individuals. First, some clinicians question the assumption that a definite height-weight relationship and specific fat-lean tissue ratio are normal for all people just because they are found among the majority (Bruch, 1978). It may be more useful to determine, in consultation with the client and his or her physician, the preferred weight at which the person feels most comfortable. It is also important to avoid being influenced by the gross bias found in current literature, both popular and medical, which abounds with generalized statements about the possible health hazards of being overweight and its ugliness, social handicaps, and psychological damage. Such stereotypical beliefs often lack scientific support and can be quite destructive when allowed to influence treatment goals and methods.

Goals for weight loss must be realistic and very conservative, in view of the low success rate typically reported (Hall & Havassy, 1981). A comprehensive treatment plan must be formulated which directly confronts the possible role expectations and conflicts that may have led to the initial development of the overweight condition. Finally, the psychological symptoms associated with the obesity must be addressed in a way that seeks to relieve distress as well as provide insight into the relationship between the psychological and the physical well-being of the individual. It is only when the obese client is treated with respect, dignity, and understanding, free of subtle prejudice, that treatment has the optimum chance for success.

References
Bruch, H. *Eating Disorders*. Cambridge: Harvard University Press, 1978.
Hall, S. M., & Havassy, B. The obese woman: Causes, correlates, and treatment. *Professional Psychology*, 1981, *12*, 163–170.
Kingsley, R. G., & Wilson, G. T. Behavior therapy for obesity: A comparative investigation for long-term efficacy. *Journal of Consulting and Clinical Psychology*, 1977, *45*, 288–298.
Mayer, J. *Overweight*. Englewood Cliffs, N.J.: Prentice-Hall, 1968.
Orbach, S. *Fat is a feminist issue*. New York: Paddington, 1978.
Schachter, S. *Emotion, obesity, and crime*. New York: Academic Press, 1971.
Seltzer, C. C., & Mayer, J. A simple criterion of obesity. *Post-Graduate Medicine*, 1965, *38*(2) A-101–A-107.
Stuart, R. B., & Davis, B. *Slim chances in a fat world*. Champaign, Ill.: Research Press, 1972.
Weiss, A. R. A behavioral approach to the treatment of adolescent obesity. *Behavior Therapy*, 1977, *8*, 720–726.
Wollersheim, J. P. Effectiveness of group therapy based upon learning principles in the treatment of overweight women. *Journal of Abnormal Psychology*. 1970, *76*, 462–474.

J. D. Guy, Jr.

Object Relations Theory. A development in psychoanalytic thought based on the role of early relationships and how these relationships then continue as objects, or images, within the mind.

The roots of object relations theory are found in classical Freudian psychoanalysis. Freud first used the term *object* in 1905 in his *Three Essays on Sexuality*. In this work a person in the external environment who is the focus of instinctual interest is termed an object. Freud developed the meaning of object further in *On Narcissism* in 1914. Here he discovered that a patient's own ego could become an internal object for his libidinal attachment. These narcissistic patients experience love objects as aspects of themselves so that their external objects are experienced as self-objects. In *Mourning and Melancholia* (1917) Freud expanded the importance of internal objects even further by identifying their role in the process of mourning and in depression. He concluded that mourning involves holding on to the lost love object by internalizing certain of its aspects. In depression anger that is actually against a perceived lost love object is turned inward against an internal representation of the lost object.

British Approaches. From these roots psychoanalytic theorists have expanded Freud's overall theory of personality largely by exploring the role played by object relations, both internal and external. Some of the most significant developments in object relations theory have taken place in Great Britain. These developments are frequently identified as the British School of object relations. MELANIE KLEIN, a Hungarian child analyst who emigrated to England just before World War II, produced the first comprehensive elaboration of Freud's discoveries about object relations (Klein, 1975). Like Freud, she saw the tie between instinct and object. However, Klein identified the connection as primarily internal in that libido and the other basic motivating drive, the death instinct, have the capability of representing themselves mentally by creating internal images, or objects in fantasy.

Klein posited that in the first six months of life the infant's objects are only part objects because he cannot yet comprehend that his experiences of frustration and gratification actually come from the same person. This condition of having split good and bad part objects Klein labels the *paranoid-schizoid position*. The second half of the first year of life involves the beginning of unification of the infant's experience and objects. The frustrating bad-object images and the gratifying good-object images come together. This results in the depressive position because now the infant starts to grasp that the object he has hated and attacked in fantasy is actually the same object he loves and needs. Klein is considered to be outside the mainstream of orthodox psychoanalytic object relations theory. She relatively neglects the role of external object relations, and she attributes improbable cognitive capacities to infants.

W. R. D. Fairbairn was a British psychoanalyst who was greatly influenced by Klein. As Fairbairn developed his theory, he gradually discarded Freud's and Klein's focus on instincts and reinterpreted most of their theories in terms of relationships. For instance, he proposed that libido was a drive for object relationship rather than an instinct for autistic gratification (Fairbairn, 1952). Fairbairn also interpreted Freud's structure of the psyche in terms of object relations. Instead of the impersonal mental processes of id, ego, and superego being the primary explanation for psychological functioning, Fairbairn proposed internal images or objects as the basic structures of the mind. According to Fairbairn, it is the perception one has of his significant others and how they relate to himself that most accurately accounts for a person's emotions, reactions, and behavior.

Fairbairn's differences with Klein actually make the combining of their theories under the label British School somewhat of a misnomer. It is probably more accurate to identify Fairbairn's theory as a complete object relations theory, since he attempted to completely reinterpret psychoanalytic thought in terms of object relations. Klein's theory could be seen as more of an instinctual object relations theory due to her emphasis on the instincts in the formation of objects. Like Klein, Fairbairn is also considered to be outside the mainstream of orthodox psychoanalysis because of his rejection of major psychoanalytic concepts such as instinctual drives and the traditional structure of the psyche: the id, ego, and superego.

Two other major theorists in Great Britain who have made great contributions to object relations theory are Donald Winnicott and Wilfred Bion. Winnicott, a pediatrician, was influenced by Klein, having been analyzed by her. Along with Klein he chose as his focal point the early years of life in the context of the mother-infant relationship. For Winnicott (1965) it is the mother being able to provide a holding environment (a safe, nonintrusive experience of human contact) that allows the infant to begin to experience his own pristine sense of self. When this kind of relationship is disturbed by a mother who continually impinges on the infant, he hides his true self and erects a false "as if" self.

Bion moved to England from India. He underwent a classical analysis, became interested in Kleinian theory, and went into analysis with Klein. He is best known for his attempts to apply Kleinian theory to group functioning, for his work with psychotics, and with the processes of thinking and language (Bion 1967). In his efforts to interface Kleinian and Freudian theory he developed psychoanalytic theory beyond Freud's mechanistic model to include a more philosophical base by integrating the works of Plato and Kant into psychoanalysis.

American Approaches. There was also much being done in the United States to elaborate on and expand psychoanalytic thought. However, here the work tended to be more orthodox. Heinz Hartmann, an immigrant from Europe, probably more than anyone else set the direction for how psychoanalytic thought would develop in the United States. Hartmann (1958) challenged psychoanalysis to become a general psychology by addressing man not only in his conflict but also in his normal capacities and ego functions such as perception, memory, and object relations.

Hartmann's work opened the door for other psychoanalytic theorists to address the important ego function of object relations. René Spitz, a psychoanalytic pediatrician and colleague of Hartmann, undertook observational studies of the first year of life to actually examine the role of object relations. He found that many disorders of infancy were actually due to problems in the mother-infant relationship (Spitz, 1965). He also found that internal representations or objects were crucial to the development of language, to psychological growth in terms of the differentiation of emotions and the neutralization of intense instinctual drives, and to cognitive development. In fact, in cases where infants were deprived of adequate object relations, he found death resulted in spite of otherwise adequate care.

Margaret Mahler is another psychoanalytic theorist who conducted observational research concerned with object relations. Her research emerged out of her interest in childhood schizophrenia and autism. As she observed infants with their mothers, she noted infants going through stages of nonattachment, or autism, to intense attachment, or symbiosis, followed by a process of emotional hatching out of the intense union with the mother, resulting in an internalization of the mother with the ability to tolerate separation from the maternal object (Mahler, Pine, & Bergmann, 1975).

There are many others in the United States who expanded on Freud's initial theories of object relations while following Hartmann's ego psychology. Jacobson (1964) worked out a comprehensive object relations theory by tracing not only the process of how relationships become represented in the internal world but also how the self comes to be represented. Kernberg (1976) has contributed to object relations theory by tracing the development of object and self representations and then demonstrating the relationship between the earliest states of object relations and the more primitive disorders of schizophrenia and the borderline and narcissistic personalities. Kohut (1971) has written from the perspective of the development of healthy and pathological self-representations. He more than anyone else has added to our understanding of narcissistic object relations and the place of a self-object, which Freud had alluded to decades ago.

Summary and Evaluation. Object relations theory has its roots in Freud's theory. Broadly speaking, object relations theory has taken two major paths. One path follows the developments in Great Britain by such theorists as Klein, Fairbairn, Guntrip, Bion, and Winnicott. These theorists have reinterpreted classical psychoanalytic concepts and are consequently considered to be unorthodox. The second path follows the work of Hartmann in the United States and basically stays within the boundaries of classical psychoanalysis.

There are some major points of contention between these two paths as well as among theorists within each approach: how well the theories of such early mental representations fit with what is known of the infant's limited cognitive capacities; the etiology and treatment of some of the primitive disorders (especially narcissism); and the lack of consensus on the meaning of key terms. There is also a lack of empirical data to clarify some of these crucial questions.

Nevertheless, taken as a whole, object relations literature and research have contributed greatly to psychology's understanding of early human development and relationships; the relationship between internal objects and cognitive and affective processes; and the etiology and treatment of the more primitive disorders (schizophrenia, borderline and narcissistic personalities). It has led to the demise of many of the mechanistic and impersonal aspects of Freud's theory.

It is noteworthy that object relations theory, possibly more than any other psychological theory, addresses many of the same aspects of human existence as does Scripture. Its emphasis on relationship, dependency and independency, internalization and narcissism have obvious parallels in Scripture. Object relations theory coincides with harmatology and Scripture by following a depth or dynamic model of motivation; it is from *within* that come the sins that defile a man. It also allows for and explains the effects of sin and the fall being passed down from generation to generation in less than optimal parenting, while not negating the place of personal responsibility and the individual's own sin in distorting parental discipline and relationship.

References

Bion, W. R. *Second thoughts.* London: Heinemann Medical, 1967.
Fairbairn, W. R. D. *An object relations theory of personality.* New York: Basic Books, 1952.
Hartmann, H. *Ego psychology and the problem of adaptation.* New York: International Universities Press, 1958.
Jacobson, E. *The self and the object world.* New York: International Universities Press, 1964.
Kernberg, O. F. *Object relations theory and clinical psychoanalysis.* New York: Aronson, 1976.
Klein, M. *Envy and gratitude and other works* (Vol. 4). New York: Delacorte Press, 1975.
Kohut, H. *The analysis of the self.* New York: International Universities Press, 1971.

Mahler, M., Pine, F., & Bergmann, A. *The psychological birth of the human infant.* New York: Basic Books, 1975.

Spitz, R. A. *The first year of life.* New York: International Universities Press, 1965.

Winnicott, D. W. *The maturational processes and the facilitating environment.* New York: International Universities Press, 1965.

W. L. EDKINS

See PSYCHOANALYTIC PSYCHOLOGY.

Object Relations Therapy. A psychoanalytic treatment associated with object relations theory. Thus, treatment of emotional disorders from an object relations model focuses on the mental representations or objects the patient has construed of himself and of significant others in his life.

Object relations theory was developed by psychoanalysts. Although some of them—e.g., Fairbairn and Guntrip—have significantly deviated from classical psychoanalytic theory, they have for the most part retained psychoanalysis as the method of treatment. Klein would be the most significant exception in that her treatment does come in conflict with various aspects of mainstream psychoanalytic treatment.

As developed by Freud, classical psychoanalytic therapy was primarily geared to the treatment of the oedipus complex. However, through the work of psychologists such as Anna Freud, Hartmann, Spitz, Mahler, Jacobson, and Kernberg, as well as through the findings of object relations theorists who are more on the fringes of psychoanalytic orthodoxy such as Klein, Winnicott, and Fairbairn, the psychoanalytic understanding of the preoedipal years of life has greatly increased. This has enabled psychoanalysts to diagnose and treat more primitive pathologies that have their roots in the breakdown of preoedipal relationships. This treatment of earlier, more primitive disorders entails a focus on the dyadic mother-child object relationship and all the related issues of intense attachment and dependency, separation and autonomy, and fundamental identity. Guntrip (1968) describes this domain of object relations therapy as the unfolding and treatment of the patient's infantile self, which is terrified, retreating from life, and hiding in an inner citadel of his personality.

The therapy is based on the assumption that units of object relations exist within everyone. These are composed of stable and enduring representations or images of the self linked to images of objects by intense affects. For example, a positive internal object relation might consist of a mental representation of the person's self as a vulnerable and trusting child relating to a strong, caring, and nurturing parent, linked together by an affective experience of love and warmth. On the other hand, a negative internal object relationship unit might be characterized by the hatred and rage a victimized child would feel toward a sadistic parent. These images account for why different individuals would experience the same situation in entirely different ways. Thus, the person who has internalized a predominantly benevolent object relating to a healthy self will experience a blow to his self-esteem quite differently from someone who has a basic identity as a victim suffering under a cruel object.

The goal of psychoanalytic therapy from an object relations perspective is to bring these foundational units of personality to the surface so that they can be exposed to further learning and adaptation and be integrated into the entire adult personality in a more healthy way. This is closely related to the classical psychoanalytic concept of transference. Freud noted that in the course of treatment repressed attributes of parental objects that involved intense conflicts would surface and be unconsciously transferred to the analyst. The analysis of this transference would form the kernel of treatment. The transference relationship remains a primary focus of treatment in object relations therapy. However, object relations therapists view the transferred material not merely as aspects of repressed conflicts but as internal self and object representations. Thus the analysis of the transference yields the clearest available information about the patient's internal object relations world.

Actually these repressed infantile relationships, or the more primitive split objects, can surface in all relationships. Sutherland, a noted British object relations therapist, notes that "all kinds of people are made the pegs on which the object of repressed relationships are hung" (1963, p. 119). He goes on to explain that this surfacing continually recurs as people attempt to work through bad relationships and to become whole persons. What makes psychoanalytic treatment distinct from all the other relationships in which a patient transfers or projects these infantile objects and needs is that the therapist is a trained observer who can penetrate the trappings of the patient's false self and can allow contact and participation in these repressed relationships. In this analytic relationship the patient can allow himself to reexperience the repressed or split-off aspects of himself so that he might find an object now, in the therapist, who does have the ability to understand and relate to his intense needs and affects. This provides the opportunity for the patient to internalize his therapist so that he can then provide these necessary functions for himself.

The difficulty with this kind of treatment is that it typically requires a 3- to 5-year period of at least twice weekly therapy in order to effect significant change in the internal object world. On the other hand, it does offer treatment and hope for the seriously disturbed and fragmented levels of personality.

Like psychoanalysis this method of treatment is not based on an absolute moral and ethical foundation, in contrast to Christianity. In fact, certain analysts deal with God for the most part as simply another internal object, without existence in reality (e.g., Milner, 1969). However, the overall process of development and growth which characterizes this approach is quite consistent with the biblical model of sanctification, which is based on an internal relationship, namely "Christ in you."

References

Guntrip, H. J. S. *Schizoid phenomena, object relations and the self.* London: Hogarth, 1968.

Milner, M. *The hands of the living God.* New York: International Universities Press, 1969.

Sutherland, J. D. Object-relations theory and the conceptual model of psychoanalysis. *British Journal of Medical Psychology*, 1963, *36*, 109–124.

W. L. Edkins

See Psychoanalysis: Technique; Psychoanalytic Psychotherapy.

Obsession.

A persistently recurring thought or feeling that is egodystonic; that is, it is not experienced as voluntarily produced but rather as something that invades consciousness. Psychoanalytic thinkers consider it to be the result of denying certain unconscious wishes or fears. While one obsession derived from a fear may restrict action, another obsession may tempt one to act out a certain impulse, and still another may take the form of an all-consuming preoccupation with a particular philosophical question.

An obsession is pathological to the extent that it impairs productive work and loving relationships. When an individual experiences sufficient distress due to obsessions, psychotherapy is recommended in order to uncover the basis of the obsession and reduce its frequency, duration, and intensity. Obsessions are characteristic of obsessive-compulsive disorder and may also be seen in schizophrenia.

J. E. Talley

See Compulsion.

Obsessive-Compulsive Disorder.

Obsessions and compulsions have traditionally been considered classical manifestations of a neurosis. The recent change in *DSM-III*, making obsessive-compulsive disorder one of the anxiety disorders, reflects a rather radical change in thinking about not only diagnosis but etiology and treatment as well.

Obsessions are repetitive, persistent ideas, thoughts, images, or impulses that are not experienced as subject to the will but intrude unwanted into the consciousness. Their content is typically exactly the opposite of what the person might think voluntarily (e.g., a mother may be disturbed by impulses to stab her much-loved child with a knife). Efforts are universally made to wipe these out of the mind or to ignore them, but they persist or recur alarmingly.

Compulsions are repetitive behaviors that also intrude unwilled into the life of the sufferer. A typical compulsion is to wash one's hands excessively. They are often performed ritualistically, according to stereotyped rules, and are purposeful in that they irrationally promise to produce or prevent some future event. Each handwashing, for example, might be done in four stereotyped washes and be performed to prevent some disastrous contamination. The acts are performed in response to inward demands so insistent that even the greatest efforts by the patient cannot deflect them.

Patients do not derive pleasure from compulsive acts, though there is often a distinct release of inner tension. This then promptly mounts again, and can be relieved only by repeating the act. Drinking, gambling, overeating, or sexual disorders can seem compulsive, but the person often derives, or at least anticipates, pleasure from these; thus they are not compulsions in this technical sense.

Both obsessions and compulsions can be mild or so severe that the entire life of the patient is consumed. The process often begins in adolescence or even childhood, and occurs about as frequently in males as females. It is reported as relatively rare, having an overall incidence among clinical outpatients of about 1%.

Many obsessive and compulsive patients also suffer from phobias, pathological indecision, doubting, and procrastination. In addition excessive anxiety, depressions, and typical panic attacks are common enough to make many feel that all of these anxiety disorders have in fact a great deal in common.

The magical, symbolic quality of obsessions

and compulsions has invited demonic explanations since the earliest recorded history. The senselessness of the phenomena, coupled with their ego-alien quality and the universal lack of insight into their causes, have made the unconscious another logical and promising place to search for causes. Freud felt that obsessions were methods, alternative to conversion, used by the psyche to deal with threatening ideas. In the obsessive the affect was separated from the idea and remained free-floating in the psyche. It ultimately attached itself to other ideas that were not in themselves incompatible.

Initially Freud proposed that the primary conflict centered around sexual issues, usually actual incestuous experiences which were intolerable to the psyche (1894/1952). Later he implicated hostile impulses against the parents, explaining the symptoms as regressions and fixations to the anal and anal sadism stage of development (1909/1955). Since that time one line of psychoanalytic thought has emphasized repressed rage originating in unacceptable sexual impulses. Another group postulated that obsessions and compulsions are extreme and excessive efforts on the part of a child to elicit recognition and acceptance from a rigid and critical parent. (See Salzman & Thaler, 1981, for a review of these and other theories of etiology.)

As a treatment for obsessive-compulsive disorder psychoanalysis has not found wide usefulness, probably for several reasons. For one thing, the searching, interpretive approaches of traditional analysis have tended to encourage an introspective, obsessive stance on the patient's part, producing such an abundance of distracting, irrelevant data that the purpose of the therapy is hindered. More important has been the influence of behavioral therapies. Systematic desensitization was applied by Wolpe (1958) to obsessive and compulsive symptoms. A later review by Beech and Vaughan (1978) reported 21 cases with a success rate of 52%. Others have used essentially every behavior modification method described, including modeling, flooding, response prevention, aversive therapy, and even paradoxical intervention. The success rate reported is about the same as above, though all workers report dramatic results in a few difficult patients.

Recent studies suggest a specific brain disorder rather than intrapsychic processes associated with obsessions and compulsions. The earliest of these were reports that brain-injured patients suddenly developed rather typical obsessive symptoms (Hilbrom, 1960). This has

later been reproduced in animals (Devenport, Devenport & Holloway, 1981). Many have reported good results in treating both obsessions and compulsions with antidepressants (Bunney, 1981). More recently several groups of biochemists have been attempting to identify defectively functioning specific neurotransmitters, or brain chemicals, which are associated with obsessions and compulsions. The systems involved appear to be closely identified with those deranged in depressions, phobias, and panic attacks. This research is still in progress at the date of this writing and must therefore be considered as suggestive only.

Anatomically, the hippocampus seems to be the location of internal inhibition that permits the organism to dampen the alarm response from a dangerous stimulus long enough to deal with the threat effectively (Pitman, 1980). It is part of a complex repressing system within the brain which serves in somewhat the same way a governor does on a motor. A normal person might become frightened by a sudden danger but would soon calm down enough to make an appropriate response. In someone suffering from an anxiety disorder these governors could fail, and the result would be excessive anxiety responses even to minor alarms.

This same inhibition is apparently designed to prevent the formation of feedback loops within brain circuits. Uncontrolled, these will act something like the playback howl in a public address system. Clinically this failure of dampening would be seen as obsessively repetitive ruminations.

With all of these observations an intriguing hypothesis develops, seeing obsessions and compulsions as expressions of tendencies of the brain to form repetitive, circular response patterns when the alarm responses are not adequately dampened. Repressing the centers mediating this governing function would encourage excessive anxiety, and anything that would facilitate the neurotransmitters used in this function allows the person to respond more normally to stress.

The best treatment of most cases of obsessive-compulsive disorder will usually begin with an explanation to the patient that his symptoms are relatively mechanical. This often relieves much stress and reduces anxiety. Medication is almost always helpful. The tricyclic antidepressants and the MAO inhibitors have been most frequently used, and many patients will respond to relatively low dosages. These seem to prevent the recurrence of panic attacks or the severe bursts of anxiety that are often associated with the onset and progression of the symptoms. To this is then added whatever behavior modification program seems indicated by the nature of the symptoms and the experience of the therapist. When symptoms have subsided, the patient should be reevaluated as to the need for ongoing insight therapy.

References

Beech, H. R., & Vaughan, M. *Behavioral treatment of obsessional states.* New York: Wiley, 1978.

Bunney, W. E., Jr. Current biologic strategies for anxiety. *Psychiatric Annals,* 1981, *11,* 11–15.

Devenport, L. D., Devenport, J. A., & Holloway, F. A. Reward-induced stereotype: Modulation by the hippocampus. *Science,* 1981, *212,* 1288–1289.

Freud, S. The neuro-psychoses of defence. In J. Strachey (Ed. and trans.), *The standard edition of the complete pychological works of Sigmund Freud* (Vol. 3). London: Hogarth, 1952. (Originally published, 1894.)

Freud, S. Notes on a case of obsessional neurosis. In J. Strachey (Ed. and trans.), *The standard edition of the complete psychological works of Sigmund Freud* (Vol. 10), London: Hogarth, 1955. (Originally published, 1909.)

Hilbrom, E. After-effects of brain injuries: Research on the symptoms causing invalidism of persons in Finland having sustained brain injuries during the wars of 1939–1944. *Acta Psychiatrica Scandinavica Supplement,* 1960, *35,* Supplement No. 142.

Pitman, R. K. The conditioning model of neurosis: Promise and limitations. *Behavioral and Brain Sciences,* 1980, *3,* 262–263.

Salzman, L., & Thaler, F. H. Obsessive-compulsive disorders: A review of the literature. *American Journal of Psychiatry,* 1981, *138,* 286–296.

Wolpe, J. *Psychotherapy by reciprocal inhibition.* Stanford, Calif.: Stanford University Press, 1958.

Additional Readings

Kandel, E. R. From metapsychology to molecular biology: Explorations into the nature of anxiety. *American Journal of Psychiatry,* 1983, *140,* 1277–1293.

Salzman, L. *Psychotherapy of the obsessive personality.* New York: Aronson, 1980.

C. M. Berry

Occupational Therapy. See Activity Therapy

Oceanic Feeling.

A general term signifying a large range of personal experiences in which one feels a profound sense of unity with God and/or his creation. It has been called mystical experience, cosmic consciousness, unity experience, and peak experience, in addition to a variety of specifically religious terms such as *nirvana, satori,* and communion with Christ.

Most typically oceanic feeling is accompanied by a deep sense of peace, reverence, and joy; an intense conviction of realness coupled with a feeling of incommunicability; a transcendence of the normal senses and corresponding unusual sensations and percepts; the transcendence of subject-object duality; and the feeling of unlimited omnipotence. Thus, the core experience of oceanic feeling is similar for different people, but its interpretation depends upon one's world view and religious orientation.

There are basically two different explanations for the phenomenon. First, the psychoanalytic approach views this experience of oneness as a regression to the primary narcissistic stage when the child's sense of self has not yet differentiated from his environment, a period when the ego believes itself to be omnipotent. Second, the oceanic experience could be due to any phenomenon that disturbs the usual processes of perception which limit, select, organize, and interpret stimuli. Therefore, the truthfulness of what one perceives while in this altered state of consciousness depends upon one's beliefs about the nature of reality and the function of the perceptual processes. The question is whether this different way of perceiving is more likely to open up aspects of God and his creation which are under more normal circumstances unknowable, or whether the altered state is more likely to make one more susceptible to deception.

W. C. Drew

See Meditation; Consciousness; Transpersonal Psychology.

Oedipus Complex.

The behavior and feeling in childhood approximately between the ages of 3 and 6, which indicate that the child is erotically and emotionally attached to the opposite sex parent.

The idea that infants have sexual feelings was first developed by Freud, who proposed that a young child was attracted to the opposite sex parent in the natural course of infantile development. He coined the phrase *oedipus complex* after the Greek tragic hero who, through a fated chain of events, unknowingly had sexual contact with his mother. This phenomenon has become a central theme in psychoanalytic theory.

Psychoanalysts have suggested that most neurotic symptoms have their origins in the oedipus complex. If in infancy a child represses his sexuality, these desires and the associated conflicts will surface in later life neuroses.

On the positive side of this theorized experience the infant can develop, through the oedipal experience, a sense of his or her sexual identity, can feel the security of physical love, and can see the need for another in his life. Psychoanalytic theorists suggest that this sexual energy can be sublimated toward such positive activities as work and creative endeavor. The theory holds that the oedipus complex is resolved by the development of the superego, or the natural restriction of primitive impulses. This makes an uncontrolled aggressive infant into a creative and productive adult.

R. B. Johnson

See Psychosexual Development; Psychoanalytic Psychology.

Oligophrenia. Literally "small mentality," this term indicates a mental deficiency characterized by inherited biochemical alterations in the body.

See Mental Retardation.

Omnipotence, Feelings of. Usually symptomatic of either paranoid or manic states, feelings of omnipotence can range from inflated feelings of power, control, and importance to delusions about possessing special communication and authority from God. Occasionally a person might believe he is Christ or God. Such thoughts and feelings betray an unreal fantasy world that somehow is more acceptable to the person than his actual state in life.

Many clinicians find that narcissism, excessive emotional investment in oneself, and an injured self-concept are at root of feelings of omnipotence. The defense mechanisms of identification and denial protect the person from the injured self-concept and support the narcissism. The person cannot tolerate any personal weakness or failure. Therefore, he denies the inadequacy and takes on the identity or qualities of someone ideal, powerful, or good.

If other areas of personality remain intact, such a person sometimes misleads others. He may misuse Christianity or occasionally may start a cult. Churches have been exploited by some of these self-proclaimed healers, prophets, and zealots. Since they view themselves as God's special agents, it is very difficult to reason with them, and sometimes they can be dangerous.

M. R. Nelson

Only Child. Families with only one child have increased in number from 1 in 20 a generation ago to 1 in 5 today, and the trend toward smaller households continues (Feldman, 1981). The rising cost of rearing children, women waiting until their 30s to have their first child, and a high divorce rate have contributed to fewer children being born. There is also a growing concern for ecology, which leads some couples to feel they should have only one child or two children at the most. Other reasons for having a single child

include more freedom for the parents, less family tension, more time to devote to the well-being of the child, and more time for self and spouse. Increasing numbers of women are entering the labor market, and there is increased concern as to how they can contribute financially to their households and establish their own careers while at the same time experiencing the joys and responsibilities of motherhood. For many women having a sole offspring is the answer.

The long-standing prejudice against the only child has lessened somewhat, although "onlies" still have the reputation of being selfish, egotistic, socially maladjusted, and lonely. Parents of the single child also have been criticized for not providing a brother or sister who will give companionship to the child and with whom the child can learn to share. The research, however, does not support the negative stereotype of the only child. When single children are compared with their peers who have siblings, the picture tends to favor the single child (Falbo, 1976; Hawke & Knox, 1978; Mott & Haurin, 1982; Polit, Nuttall, & Nuttall, 1980). Onlies as a group are confident and resourceful, have a heightened sense of responsibility, are more at ease with adults, and are popular with classmates. Furthermore, they possess superior language development, have higher IQs, make higher grades, go further in school, and have a higher occupational status as adults. The greater degree of parent-child interaction and the higher socioeconomic status enjoyed by the only child appear to be related to these positive characteristics. Polit, Nuttall, Nuttall (1980) state: "The data thus do not support the notion that only children are emotionally or personally handicapped by their lack of siblings" (p. 99).

To be sure, there are problems faced by the single child and the parents that are unique to a three-person household. A power structure of two against one may occur in which the child or one of the parents may feel estranged and there is no one in the family to turn to for support. Adult onlies have the sole responsibility for providing companionship and assistance to their parents and may feel overwhelmed when they alone must make decisions regarding the care of aging parents. The parents may express reservations about having only the one child. They have less basis for knowing what to expect of the child at each age level; they may fear for the child's safety, realizing that if something happens they will be left childless. They also may feel that having more children would increase the chances of at least one child bringing them joy and being a credit to the family name.

A new organization, Only Child International, has been founded to provide a forum for people who never had brothers or sisters to discuss their situation and try to come up with answers to some common problems. Members of the group do not consider that being an only child is a big social problem, but they do feel they can profit by sharing their experiences (Greene, 1983).

The only child has a special place in the affection of others, and parents of the only child should enjoy the child without feeling guilty for having a sole offspring. Any loss to the child or the parents for not having more children in the family appears to be compensated for in other ways.

References

Falbo, T. Does the only child grow up miserable? *Psychology Today*, 1976, 9(12), 60–65.

Feldman, G. C. Three's company: Family therapy with only-child families. *Journal of Marital and Family Therapy*, 1981, 7, 43–46.

Greene, B. An only child shares his life with others. *Chicago Tribune*, Nov. 29, 1983, Section 5, p. 1.

Hawke, S., & Knox, D. The one-child family: A new life-style. *The Family Coordinator*, 1978, 27, 215–219.

Mott, F. L., & Haurin, R. J. Being an only child: Effects on educational progression and career orientation. *Journal of Family Issues*, 1982, 3, 575–593.

Polit, D. F., Nuttall, R. L., & Nuttall, E. V. The only child grows up: A look at some characteristics of adult only children. *Family Relations*, 1980, 29, 99–106.

B. CLOUSE

Operant Conditioning. *See* CONDITIONING, OPERANT; APPLIED BEHAVIOR ANALYSIS.

Oppositional Disorder of Childhood or Adolescence.

The pattern representative of a child or adolescent with an oppositional disorder is one of predominant negativistic attitudes toward authority figures. It may begin after age 3, but more commonly the disorder commences in later childhood or adolescence. A disobedient, negativistic, and provocative opposition to authority figures must have occurred for at least six months to meet the criteria for this disorder. The diagnosis is made only if the basic rights of others or major age-appropriate norms and rules of society have *not* been violated. The pattern of opposition one can expect the child to exhibit typically includes violation of minor rules, temper tantrums, argumentativeness, provocative behavior, and stubbornness. The child needs to manifest a minimum of two of these behaviors for diagnosis, according to *DSM-III*.

The oppositional behaviors and attitudes continue despite their detrimental effects on the needs and concerns of the child or adolescent. For example, for the adolescent to stay out past the curfew hour results in a loss of the privilege to go out the next evening; to become argumentative with one's teacher results in extra homework or detention periods. As a result, these youngsters encounter difficulties in their school and home environments. Serious academic problems can arise if the child refuses to learn.

There is a persistent, confrontive style that marks these individuals and their relationships with others. Even when they appear to be somewhat conforming, there remains a provocative edge, isolating them from closeness with others. Usually negativism is directed toward adults, but at times it focuses on other children too.

One theory of etiology suggests that the parental discipline of these children has been strict but inconsistent. Certain guidelines and rules for managing the child are kept or changed depending on the whim of the parent. Never knowing what to expect from the parent or what the parent expects from the child reduces the child's experience of being able to rely, trust, and depend on the parent. This may generalize to other adults such as teachers. Another compounding factor would be a number of parent figures telling the child what to do. This can be confusing and overwhelming. To maintain some inner consistency the child becomes negativistic and stubborn, an attempt to control the external world.

Another theory of etiology views the disorder as reflecting very disturbed relationships in the family group. The child's negativism is a consistent message that he or she will be different from what is expected or required in this family. The refusal to cooperate with the family system raises the question of what is so negative about this family that the child goes to such extremes to avoid it. There is a variety of possibilities. The family may accept only individuals who comply with their rules; those who do not acquiesce are rejected and labeled stubborn. As a result the child lives out the family's label. Another possibility is that the child has become a scapegoat for other relationship dyads in this system that have become dysfunctional. Or if other relationships refuse to work through their difficulties, the child may bear the psychological illness.

One means of dealing with this dysfunction is to treat the whole family system. This involves a careful exploration of family dynamics and relationship bonds. Through this investigation it is possible to determine the implicit and explicit means by which the family functions. As these dynamics are verbalized, perhaps for the first time, the family has the opportunity to talk out their traditionally nonverbalized communication patterns. This offers the possibility of an alternative means of relating. A variety of individual treatment methods may be used to work directly with the child. However, it is important that the family be treated, since it is a vital part of this disturbance.

B. J. SHEPPERSON

Oral Stage. According to Freud this is the first stage of a child's psychological development. It encompasses approximately the first 18 months after birth.

See PSYCHOSEXUAL DEVELOPMENT.

Organic Affective Syndrome. An organic brain disease which produces a pervasive mood disturbance. The term *organic* here refers to dysfunction of the cells of the brain due to an anatomical lesion or to a metabolic disturbance. These dysfunctional states give rise to disturbances of the sensorium and to specific neurological changes.

The changes that occur in all organic brain disease, except the endocrinopathies, are: 1) disturbances of orientation to time, place, person, situation, and space; 2) defects in the retention and recall of new information; 3) defects in the ability to recall recent and remote memories; 4) an inability to perform simple and complex calculations; 5) disturbances of visual-motor coordination; 6) speech and handwriting disturbances; and 7) other neurological signs such as tremor, sensory and motor dysfunction, and reflex changes. These basic symptoms may vary in their severity, but orientation and memory defects must be objectively verifiable if the cause of the disease is organic.

An organic affective syndrome has, in addition to these basic symptoms, a pervasive disturbance of affect. This affective disturbance can have its origin in a neurosis that predates the development of the organic disease, or it may arise as a direct result of the dysfunction of the brain.

Affective disorder occurring as a result of anatomical lesions is usually the result of infections, brain tumors, or vascular lesions in the frontal lobes of the hypothalmus. As these lesions imbalance the system that mediates emotion, they give rise to a tonic emotional state that can be of depressed or elated affect. The type of emotional disturbance that occurs is to some extent determined by the effect of the lesion on the cells of the brain. If the lesion damages but does not kill brain cells, it may produce hyperexcitability of the cells, which results in an excess of information being fed into the system. This condition can produce elation or depression. Lesions that destroy cells also unbalance the system by reducing the ability of the involved part of the system to process information. Depression is more commonly produced by these lesions. Infections such as brain abcess, syphilis, and encephalitis, as well as slow-growing invasive brain tumors, are more likely to produce irritation, whereas rapidly growing or noninvasive brain tumors and vascular lesions are more likely to produce death of cells.

Physiological disturbances of the brain produce affective disturbances. If the presenting symptoms are not associated with disturbances of the sensorium, they are likely to be endocrinopathies. Panhypopituitarism, hypo- and hyperthyroidism, hypoadrenalism (Addison's disease), hyperadrenalism (Cushing's disease), as well as hyperparathyroidism may be accompanied by moderate to severe disturbances of affect, usually depressive. Elation is rarely seen in hyperthyroidism. Delirium or dementia may occur in these diseases if the metabolic changes are severe.

Physiological brain dysfunction secondary to kidney and liver failure rarely produces severe affective symptomatology. Pernicious anemia, a disease associated with a deficency of vitamin B-12 or folic acid, may have severe depressive symptoms. These patients usually have neurological symptoms of involvement of the sensory systems in the spinal cord and are easily recognized. Finally, porphyria, a disease characterized by a defect in the metabolism of hemoglobin, also gives rise to severe organic affective symptoms, but it too has distinctive physical symptoms of abdominal pain and seizures that make it easily recognizable. An examination of the urine, which turns brick red when allowed to sit unrefrigerated for a while, or chemical analysis of the urine will also aid in the diagnosis. When the specific disease causing this syndrome is treatable, indicated interventions should be carried out.

W. P. WILSON

Organic Delusional Syndrome. Organic brain disease is often manifest by DELUSIONS. These false ideas most often occur in patients with the diffuse anatomical degeneration that occurs with Alzheimer's disease, diffuse vascular disease, trauma, or, rarely, as an aftereffect of infection by encephalitis or syphilis. Some persons withdrawing from alcohol and drugs may have only delusions, but most often they have hallucinations accompanying their delusions. Persons toxicated with amphetamines are quite delusional. A few individuals who have chronically used marijuana, LSD, and other hallucinogens develop a syndrome in which delusions may predominate. In all instances, the basic symptoms of organic brain involvement are present (*see* ORGANIC AFFECTIVE SYNDROME) as manifest in a disturbed sensorium.

The delusions that commonly accompany organic brain disease are usually persecutory (paranoid) or of grandeur (megalomanic). The persecutory delusions are expressed as discomfort caused by someone close to them, either a caretaker or relative. Because delusions and tactile, olfactory, or gustatory hallucinations can occur concomitantly, these persons will often think their food is poisoned, or they are being gassed, or something is being put on their skin that makes them itch or burn. Aged patients may believe that the sensory deceptions they suffer are part of a plot to "get their money" or to get rid of them. Many bedridden patients who are incontinent will complain of sexual assaults after they have been cleaned by nursing personnel. Ordinary nursing care may be interpreted as an assault.

Paranoid delusions predominate in patients who have posttraumatic delusional states. Usually these patients have had severe head injuries and have been comatose for periods longer than seven days. When they regain consciousness and as their confusion clears, there is a transitory delusional state that will clear in a few weeks. If, however, the head injury has been very severe and the period of coma and stupor lasts longer than a month, a chronic delusional state can develop with marked paranoid delusions, explosive outbursts of anger, and assaultiveness and combativeness. Most of these patients will have mild to severe disturbances of coordination as well as a variety of other neurological defects.

Individuals who have postencephalitic delusional states usually have both paranoid and grandiose delusions. This is a rare syndrome, but it does occur and is difficult to distinguish from paranoid schizophrenia. Sensorial changes may be quite subtle. Those who have delusional states that are caused by syphilis of the central nervous system (general paresis) are easily diagnosed. Disturbances of the senso-

rium are obvious in the speech and handwriting disturbances that are typical of the syndrome. The presence of the Argyll-Robertson pupil and tremors of the hands, lips, and tongue make the diagnosis certain. Laboratory tests of the blood and spinal fluid are diagnostic. The delusions that occur with syphilis are quite varied. They are often paranoid or grandiose, but hypochondriacal or depressive delusions can also occur.

Persons toxified with stimulants are paranoid. Their delusions are systematized so that again one has difficulty on initial examination differentiating this syndrome from paranoid schizophrenia. A history of stimulant abuse, especially methamphetamine ("speed"), aids in the diagnosis. These delusions clear when the patient is detoxified. In contrast, the delusions that develop with poly-drug abuse, especially with marijuana combined with the hallucinogens, are much slower to develop and clear when the patient is taken off all drugs. These delusions are not as well systematized as those that occur with stimulants and are more often associated with apathy and lack of drive. Megalomania is rarely seen in either of these drug-induced syndromes.

W. P. WILSON

Organic Hallucinosis. Hallucinations are defined as an apparent perception of an external object when no such object is present. They occur in normal as well as abnormal mental states. Hallucinations are a normal part of one's existence as they occur when one goes to sleep (hypnagogic) or upon awakening (hynopompic). They occur in persons who are having religious experiences. These are called ecstatic states, and do not technically qualify as hallucinations. Hallucinations also occur in schizophrenia and major affective disorders.

Organic hallucinosis is quite common and has a number of causes. As in other organic syndromes the causes can be divided into two major groups: those that are symptoms of physiologically determined brain dysfunction, and those that are due to anatomically determined brain dysfunction. In all organic hallucinatory states there is a disturbance of the sensorium with the basic symptoms of organic brain disease (see ORGANIC AFFECTIVE SYNDROME).

The most dramatic of the organic hallucinoses are those that occur as a result of withdrawal from alcohol. The two syndromes that occur most frequently are delirium tremens and alcoholic hallucinosis. Delirium tremens is characterized by vivid visual hallucinations. These are sometimes associated with sensations in other modalities, but not as frequently as in patients with schizophrenia. They are often of animals, usually in large numbers. Hallucinations of people can be menacing and have a paranoid flavor. Accompanying voices often threaten to kill the person and his relatives. Alcoholic hallucinosis, on the other hand, is usually characterized by accusing voices, which commonly accuse the person of being a homosexual. The words used are usually the argot of the street. Withdrawal from sedative drugs can produce the same syndromes.

Hallucinogens are also a common cause of organic hallucinosis in modern society. The most commonly used for many years was LSD, which has now been replaced by methamphetamine and cocaine. The hallucinations occurring with these drugs are usually geometric patterns that are abstract and colored. A few individuals may see patterned objects that are bizarre and gigantic or Lilliputian in size. Sensorium disturbance is not as severe as in other delirious states, but it is nevertheless always present. In some patients recurrent hallucinations, known as flashbacks, occur hours or days after the effects of the drugs have worn off.

Organic hallucinosis can also occur in the aged, and in persons with epilepsy or brain tumors. In the aged, visual, auditory, and tactile hallucinations occur as transient symptoms in some patients. These have the same qualities as hallucinations due to other organic causes. Hallucinations occurring with epilepsy differ in that they are usually monothematic and associated with other epileptic symptoms. The hallucinations in epilepsy arise almost always as a result of temporal lobe lesions, and abnormal electrical discharge is seen in the electroencephalogram when they are occurring. Similar hallucinations are seen in patients with brain tumors. These tumors, however, usually involve the temporal lobes.

Organic hallucinations differ from schizophrenic hallucinations in that they are not as frequent and do not last as long. They occur more often at night, do not have personal significance, are less likely to involve several sensory modalities, and almost always move. Organic hallucinatory syndromes can occur in persons with any systemic disease that impairs the normal functioning of the brain, but they do not often do so except in children who are quite sensitive to systemic disease and high fevers.

W. P. WILSON

Organic Mental Disorders: Overview. The essential feature of organic mental disorders is a psychological or behavioral abnormality associated with dysfunction of the brain. In *DSM-III* this general category includes two groups of disorders: organic mental disorders, whose etiology is known or presumed, and organic brain syndromes, whose etiology is unknown. An example of an organic mental disorder with known etiology is alcohol amnestic disorder (*see* ALCOHOL ORGANIC MENTAL DISORDERS). Some forms of DEMENTIA also fall into this subclassification in that they are due to neurological disease associated with senility. Examples of organic brain syndromes whose etiology is unknown are DELIRIUM, AMNESTIC SYNDROME, ORGANIC DELUSIONAL SYNDROME, ORGANIC HALLUCINOSIS, ORGANIC AFFECTIVE SYNDROME, and ORGANIC PERSONALITY SYNDROME. Since organic mental disorders are such a heterogenous group of psychopathologies, no single description can characterize them all. For a further discussion of the clinical presentation, mode of onset, duration, and prognosis of each, see the separate articles on each of the disorders.

D. G. BENNER

Organic Personality Syndrome. One's personality is determined by all the functions of the mind. These functions are derived from the body (biological drives), soul (intellect and emotions), and spirit (life force). Organic brain disease can affect any of these functions as well as the compound functions that are derived from them, producing a kaleidoscopic array of personality changes.

Two groups of personality changes are observed: those that are transitory and those that are permanent. The commonest causes of transitory changes are alcohol, trauma, epilepsy, and drugs. The commonest causes of permanent change are degenerative disease, strokes, trauma, encephalitis, epilepsy, and other lesions of the brain.

The changes that take place depend on whether the brain is diffusely or focally involved, or both, and whether the lesion destroys brain cells or causes hyperexcitability of the neurones. Destruction of brain cells produces a loss of function, while hyperexcitability produces an exaggeration of function. Thus, we find that destruction of the frontal lobes causes a blunting of emotionality, whereas lesions that cause hyperexcitability of neurones in that area cause exaggerated emotional tonus or reactivity. Destructive lesions affecting the motor and sensory area of the brain cause either paralysis and hypesthesia or focal motor or sensory seizures. The latter are characterized by parasthesias. Destructive lesions in the occipital cortex give rise to blindness, whereas hyperexcitable lesions give rise to scotomata. Temporal cortical lesions give rise to complex disturbances depending on their laterality and location. Loss of speech, memory, and understanding are some of the cognitive disturbances that arise with destructive lesions of the temporal lobes, while hallucinations, hypermnesia, and other complex physical phenomena are perceptual disturbances that occur.

Lesions in subcortical areas of the brain give rise to disturbances similar to those found with cortical lesions or to disturbances of emotion, especially if they are in the lower centers. These changes are most often in the emotional tonus; thus we can observe emotional apathy or prolonged exaggerated emotions of joy, sorrow, or anger.

It is impossible to describe all the various syndromes observed, but a few common ones that may be caused by several different diseases are worthy of mention. Diffuse degenerative disease, posttraumatic disease, or toxication may cause a syndrome in which apathy or lack of will is the primary symptom. The person seems dull and does little except sit, unresponsive to the environment. Most often memory is impaired and attention decreased. The patient is either unresponsive emotionally or smiles emptily at stimuli. These symptoms occur transitorily during and after electroconvulsive treatments or after mild head trauma.

Encephalitis in children between 5 and 15 years and severe head trauma with residual intellectual deficits may give rise to a syndrome of hyperkinesis and explosive outbursts of anger. These individuals may be homicidal. After severe head injuries similar symptoms can develop, and paranoid ideas may also occur. Epileptics are particularly prone to permanent personality disorders. They often have a variety of symptoms, including emotional dyscontrol, sexual deviations, overreligiosity, compulsive behavior, lack of humor, paranoia, and subtle intellectual changes.

It is important to note that any of these more severe disturbances can occur in patients who have ingested alcohol or drugs and are acutely intoxicated.

W. P. WILSON

Organismic Theory. The aim of organismic theory is to put the mind and body back together and to treat the organism (person) as a unified, organized whole. It rejects Descartes's seventeenth-century split of the individual into two separate yet interacting entities, body and mind.

Within recent years this organismic emphasis has also been known as the holistic viewpoint. In psychology organismic theory has been emphasized by Gardner Murphy and Carl Rogers. Other thinkers whose concepts are compatible with the organismic stance are Dewey, Aristotle, Spinoza, and James. The Gestalt movement of Wertheimer, Koffka, and Köhler is also closely related to the organismic position. However, since Gestalt psychology said very little concerning the organism or personality as a whole, organismic psychology may be treated as an extension of Gestalt principles (Hall & Lindzey, 1978).

The primary advocate of organismic theory was Kurt Goldstein, and this article emphasizes his concepts. For Goldstein the organism always is a single entity, behaving as a unified whole and not as a series of differentiated parts (Goldstein, 1939).

The central theme in Goldstein's personality theory is SELF-ACTUALIZATION, which is defined as the fulfilling of one's capacities or potentialities in the best possible way under a given condition. All Goldstein's dynamic concepts and types of behavior are to be viewed as having the ultimate purpose of self-actualization. Self-actualization occurs in the process of coming to terms with the environment. The individual tries to find a workable position between his own potentialities and the demands of the outer world.

In normal functioning all parts of the organism work as a unified whole as each task presented by the environment is mastered, thus enhancing self-actualization. On occasions, however, the environment contains obstructions and pressures that hinder self-actualization. These properties of the environment tend to upset the average state of tension in the organism. Following its actualization tendencies, the organism uses its organic and psychological processes to return to the average state of tension prior to the stimulus (environmental event) that changed the tension level. This return to an average state is brought about by the equalization process. The equalization process is vitally related to Goldstein's master motive of self-actualization and accounts for the consistency, coherence, and orderliness of behavior in spite of disturbances.

Psychopathology comes about when the equalization process is thwarted by strong disturbances in the environment that are too arduous for the individual (Goldstein, 1940). The person will then develop reactions inconsistent with the principle of self-actualization. These inconsistent reactions provide the conditions for the development of pathological states.

Therapy is aimed at helping the person to master the environment and thus achieve self-actualization. If this is not possible, the goal of therapy is to help the person adjust to the difficulties and realities of the external world.

In the last few years a number of Christian psychologists and theologians have been investigating the biblical emphasis on anthropological holism. Being familiar with the comprehensive principles of organismic theory would be of benefit in pursuing this theme, as Goldstein's emphasis on humans as unified wholes seems consistent with the bibical emphasis. However, his position conflicts with Christian theology in its emphasis that there is nothing inherently bad in the organism; it is made "bad" by an inadequate environment.

References
Goldstein, K. *The organism.* New York: American Book Company, 1939.
Goldstein, K. *Human nature in the light of psychopathology.* Cambridge: Harvard University Press, 1940.
Hall, C. S., & Lindzey, G. *Theories of personality* (3rd ed.). New York: Wiley, 1978.

S. N. BALLARD

Organizational Psychology. *See* INDUSTRIAL/ORGANIZATIONAL PSYCHOLOGY.

Orgasmic Dysfunction. *See* INHIBITED ORGASM.

Orgone Therapy.
The therapeutic approach developed by Wilhelm Reich. It is based on orgone (from "organism" and "orgasm") energy, a cosmic force believed to emanate from the sun. A pupil of Freud's, Reich parted paths with his teacher in 1932 with his emphasis on character analysis rather than dealing strictly with symptoms. His approach is based on diffusion of sexual tension through full orgastic potency, defined as a total lack of resistance and more than simply experiencing an orgasm. According to Reich (1942, 1949) full orgastic ability is the only measure of psychological well-being. Neurosis is due to repressed excess energy, which builds up a chronic character "armor" that interferes with normal functioning. This armor often leads to such physical symptoms as spasms, cramps, and muscular tensions, and to such resistances as cynicism, passivity, and arrogance.

Treatment originally involved an "orgone box" or "orgone accumulator." Built like a metal phone booth and lined with wood or fiber, the box was hypothesized to capture energy from the surrounding atmosphere and concentrate it on the sexual organs, thereby releasing repressed energy. Reich went to prison in 1957, dying there eight months later, for violation of the U.S. Federal Drug Administration's injunction against selling orgone boxes. His theory and treatment approach are not generally accepted in the psychological community today.

The three main approaches involved in contemporary orgone therapy are breathing freely, attacking the spastic muscles with direct pressure, and bringing the patient's resistances to therapy into the open. Seven independent muscular segments are "released" or "freed" in the process of therapy in the following order: ocular, oral, cervical, thoracic, diaphragmatic, abdominal, and pelvic. Often direct pressure is applied to the muscles when the patient expresses strong emotions, particularly rage. The basis for repression is anxiety; therefore the client is encouraged to verbalize his fears and resistances. However, there is less emphasis on verbalization in orgone therapy than in most other approaches.

Training and education for orgone therapy are administered by the American College of Orgonomy (an organization, not a school) in New York City, which also publishes the semiannual *Journal of Orgonomy.*

References
Reich, W. *The function of the orgasm.* New York: Orgone Institute Press, 1942.
Reich, W. *Character analysis* (3rd ed.). New York: Orgone Institute Press, 1949.

D. L. SCHUURMAN

Orthomolecular Psychiatry.
A megavitamin, hormone, and diet therapy that approaches psychological symptoms by biological and biochemical means. The term *orthomolecular*, meaning "right molecules," was first used by Linus Pauling in 1968 to characterize the treatment of disease with nutrients that naturally occur in the human body. Initially orthomolecular methods were developed for the treatment of schizophrenia and alcoholic disorders. These methods are now sometimes used also in the treatment of hypoglycemia, symptoms of which often mimic, accompany, or, as some believe, even cause neuropsychiatric diseases. Adherents (Hoffer, 1980; Hawkins

& Pauling, 1973) believe that orthomolecular medicine is a useful treatment for an even broader range of problems including neuroses, autism, learning disorders, and even criminal behavior.

In orthomolecular therapy the body is viewed as two systems: physiometabolism and psychometabolism. Physiometabolism involves the taking in of food and transforming it into psychochemical compounds to meet the needs of the body's machine: bones, muscles, glands, tissues, blood vessels, and cells. Psychometabolism involves internalized subjective experiences. Orthomolecular psychiatry is the wedding of these two concepts, positing that thoughts, feelings, and functioning are related to what we eat. Nutrition is seen as causing changes in behavior and response to stress, and these responses can then feed back to and alter psychometabolism and ultimately behavior. Orthomolecular psychiatry is involved with prevention first and treatment secondarily. In practice it blends psychoallergy, neuroallergy, megavitamin therapy, diet change, orthomolecular therapy, and ecology.

Orthomolecular psychiatry initially views the patient's psychopathology as an effect rendering the patient progressively deteriorated and in disequilibrium. When viewing the patient diagnostically, the practitioner assesses how much of the manifested psychopathology is truly psychological, sociological, or cultural in nature and how much is directly due to hormone deficiencies, hypoglycemia, or neuroallergies. Following the belief that it is impossible to assess the psychological condition of the patient at the initial interview stage and that much of the psychopathology is due to a somatic-psyche (body induced, mental) condition, the orthomolecular psychiatrist begins by ruling out hypoglycemia with a glucose tolerance test. Allergies, food intolerances, and nutritional deficiencies can then be assessed. Once these conditions have been verified, treatment begins.

While treatment regimens vary, the main focus is on megavitamin therapy—the largest subcategory of orthomolecular medicine— followed by a combination of other treatments such as hormones, minerals, and diet change. More infrequently standard drugs and medications are used. Generally the patient is placed on large doses of vitamins. Proponents claim remarkable changes in the patient's level of depression, acting-out behavior, alcohol/drug ingestion, or anger outbursts within 72 hours after commencing the regimen. Most often the patient is removed from coffee, tea, white flour, sugar, dyes, colorings, and preservatives. The diet becomes a natural, high-complex, carbohydrate (unrefined) diet with six daily smaller meals allowing the patient to sustain his energy. Attention is then directed to the residual psychopathology using standard psychotherapeutic techniques, which could include hypnosis, individual therapy, group psychotherapy, or other treatment approaches.

Orthomolecular psychiatry's effectiveness is under debate. Traditional medicine has taken a strong stance against the field. In 1967 the *Psychiatric News* published an editorial attacking megavitamin therapy. The American Psychiatric Association rejected orthomolecular psychiatry on the basis that it was unsubstantiated by research in a task force report in 1973 (Lipton, 1973). Kety (1976) concludes that controlled studies have failed to show significant improvement in schizophrenia through orthomolecular therapy. This conclusion is debated by Hoffer (1980) and others. However, the controversy will continue until further research makes clear the role of vitamins in psychopathology and its treatment.

References

Hawkins, D. R., & Pauling, L. *Orthomolecular psychiatry*. San Francisco: W. H. Freeman, 1973.

Hoffer, A. Megavitamin therapy. In R. Herink (Ed.), *The psychotherapy handbook*. New York: New American Library, 1980.

Kety, S. S. Dietary factors and schizophrenia. *Annals of Internal Medicine*, 1976, *84*, 745.

Lipton, M. A. *Megavitamin and orthomolecular therapy in psychiatry*. Washington, D.C.: American Psychiatric Association, 1973.

G. A. Johnston

Overanxious Disorder of Childhood or Adolescence. The outstanding feature of this common disorder is a generalized and persistent anxiety or worry that is not caused by a recent psychosocial stressor. The disorder is distinguished from separation anxiety disorder in that it does not focus on a specific situation or objects, such as separating from a parent.

In this disorder the child experiences generalized but persistent worry for a minimum of six months in at least four out of the following seven categories: unrealistic worry about future events, overconcern about competence, preoccupation with the appropriateness of one's behavior, excessive need for reassurance, somatic complaints for which no physical basis is found, noticeable self-consciousness, and marked feelings of tension or an inability to relax. It is also common that the child have problems relaxing and being able to go to sleep.

Children with this disturbance take their concerns very seriously, sometimes doubting themselves to an obsessional degree or becoming perfectionistic. Motor restlessness or nervous habits (e.g., nail biting or hair pulling) are also frequently present. An inability to meet realistic expectations at home or school may be the result of unusually severe cases. Such children may also attempt to avoid activities where performance may be evaluated, and this obviously interferes in a major way with school performance.

This disturbance has been found most commonly in eldest children, small families, upper socioeconomic groups, and families concerned with performance even when children are performing at an adequate or superior level. It is likely that parents are attempting to give a child what they never had, or attempting to cope with their own unconscious or conscious feelings of inadequacy through their focus on the child's performance and achievements. For the child to not achieve to the parents' expectation is a negative reflection on these parents, at least on an unconscious level. The child, of course, can never fulfill the parents' expectations if that child chooses to individuate and develop personally chosen goals. For the child caught in such a family's unwillingness to let him or her become a unique individual, this disorder may persist into adulthood, becoming an anxiety disorder or social phobia.

One treatment goal in working with individuals with this disorder is to provide a supportive therapeutic environment. In individual therapy the child's feelings, opinions, and desires should be explored and encouraged. The goal is to restore a more stable sense of self and to provide permission to make mistakes or not be perfect. This can be accomplished through verbal or play therapy.

Another valuable therapeutic modality is family therapy. Within this approach one can examine current family stressors and family rules about the expression of affection, anger, and anxiety. It may then become apparent that the child is expressing parental dysfunction, this making it most appropriate to first focus on the parental relationship. When the tension here is resolved, one typically finds that the child's anxiety disorder is also alleviated.

B. J. SHEPPERSON

Overcompensation. A term used by Adler to describe a process by which an individual overcomes a weakness of the body, a weakness usually located in a particular organ. He proposed that since some people are born with damaged limbs, poor eyesight, or malfunctioning hearts, their physiological system, in an effort to maintain the appropriate equilibrium, would strive to correct the defect. Later Adler theorized that overcompensation occurs psychologically as well as physiologically. That is, one overcompensates for feelings of inferiority generated by parental neglect, sibling rivalry, peer rejection, and for legitimate bodily impairment.

Overcompensation is typically conceptualized as a direct attack on the situation responsible for the inferiority. It is an exaggerated effort to go beyond achieving a balance or removing a defect. Therefore overcompensation may turn the defect into a strength. However it may also become negative in the sense that one could be overreacting or denying reality. In this case it would be considered excessive and harmful. Overcompensation is differentiated from compensation in that compensation is more of an indirect attack on the situation. In compensation one seeks to lessen the deficit feelings of inferiority rather than excessively overreacting.

A number of noteworthy individuals have overcompensated, either physically or psychologically, in the course of their lives. One famous example is Demosthenes, who stuttered as a child but became one of the world's greatest orators. Another example is Teddy Roosevelt. A weakling in youth, through exercise he developed himself into a physically fit and sturdy individual.

M. L. MARVIN

Overcorrection. Like punishment and time-out, overcorrection is a behavioral technique used to decrease the frequency of behavior. In this procedure the individual is required to correct the effects of his own misbehavior by restoring the situation or to practice a desired alternative behavior. For example, a patient who physically assaulted an attendant was required to spend 15 minutes in providing first aid for the resulting injury sustained by the attendant. In a typical application the individual is manually guided in the activity if it is not voluntarily performed. Thus, overcorrection makes behavioral demands of the patient whereas punishment and timeout do not.

Overcorrection is used as an alternative to electric shock in eliminating self-stimulatory and self-injurious behaviors and for aggressive and antisocial behaviors where timeout procedures are ineffective. Overcorrection is particularly effective when used in conjunction with differential reinforcement for desirable responses.

Overcorrection is a relatively recent technique that is not yet widely adopted. So far it has been used largely with institutionalized retarded individuals. Although it appears effective under certain conditions, the element of manually guided training in an alternative behavior is coercive. This raises ethical problems about coercion as well as practical problems, since it may produce counteraggressive behavior. One way to minimize these problems might be to offer overcorrection as an alternative that might be chosen by the individual in preference to contingent punishment.

R. K. BUFFORD

See BEHAVIOR THERAPY.

Overprotection. While everybody is aware that a child is damaged by neglect, few realize how many negative consequences can result from overprotection.

One of the major causes of overprotection is a premature birth or extensive physical illness in the child, either of which requires special care in the first years of life. This often sets a pattern that parents have trouble altering. Such parents often remain very anxious about their parenting responsibilities and perceive their child as more disabled than he or she actually is. The loss of previous children can also produce fear in parents and lead to overconcern with their children's well-being. Overprotection may also reflect reaction formation, through which the parents exaggerate, out of guilt, the care for a child whom they actually resent. Single parents, or parents having poor relationships with their spouses, may also overinvest in a child as a compensation for marital disappointments.

Some of the symptoms that may indicate overprotection are 1) a tendency to do things for the child that he could do himself; 2) interfering with children's relationships and fighting their fights even when there is no threat of serious consequences; 3) sheltering children from life experiences that are good learning opportunities with a low or no price to pay; 4) parental overinvolvement, beyond the necessary supervision and guidance, in all of the child's activities (school, play, relationships, hobbies, etc.). It may also be evidenced by a general watchfulness, control, or over-checking.

Overprotection can have many undesirable consequences on children's development. Through lack of experience the sheltered child's growth is stifled. Furthermore, such children remain unprepared to handle demanding situations. Not having been taught to deal with frustrations and lacking assertiveness they may become overly submissive and accommodating to whoever promises protection and provides structure and leadership. Or they may be resentful for not getting the service they feel everybody owes them. They may display an inclination to be self-centered, inconsiderate, and lacking empathy, qualities creating difficulties in relationships with others. They may also become fearful and insecure, with a demanding, rebellious, or paranoid attitude toward life.

There are several remedial measures that can be taken to prevent or reduce the damages produced by overprotection. For best results both parents and children, if possible, should be involved in therapy. The parents can be helped by being treated for anxiety and obsessions, if these are present. A dynamic exploration of the causes of this attitude can be of help in most situations. An analysis of their life style may reveal areas of conflict and help eliminate the power struggle between parents that may result in one of them turning excessively toward the child. Parenting education (see PARENT TRAINING PROGRAMS) is of great value in that it helps parents understand the consequences of overprotection and makes them more secure in dealing with children.

For Christian parents an important part of therapy can be helping them understand that God himself does not overprotect his children; he lets them grow and learn by facing the consequences of their behavior and choices. He guides, teaches, supports; he intervenes when the demands of the situation surpass our resources; and yet he allows us to make choices and even educates us by entrusting us to do part of his work.

The children are helped by communication and assertiveness training, involvement with peers (through group therapy or church or community organizations), by being given responsibilities, and offered the minimal support needed. It is important to help them build autonomy and confidence in themselves. It is necessary, therefore, to assess their natural abilities and encourage their development.

Additional Reading
Parker, G. *Parental overprotection: A risk factor to psychosocial development.* New York: Grune & Stratton, 1983.

D. MOTET

Pp

Pain. The International Association for the Study of Pain describes it as "an unpleasant, sensory and emotional experience associated with actual or potential tissue damage or described in terms of such damage" (IASP, 1979). Pain is therefore not just a physical sensation; it is a subjective experience and hence a psychological phenomenon, although it is usually described in terms of a local stimulus.

Acute pain refers to pain of limited duration, and chronic pain to that of at least several months' duration. Pain threshold refers to the point at which one first perceives a stimulus as painful, and pain tolerance to the point at which one is not willing to accept stimulation of a higher magnitude or to continue to endure stimulation at a given level. In general, threshold is related more to physiological conditions and tolerance to emotional or psychological variables (Merskey, 1976).

Theories of Pain. Traditional theories of pain essentially view it as a specific sensation with intensity proportional to the extent of tissue damage. Specificity theory proposes that a specific pain system carries messages from receptors in the skin to a center in the brain. However, contemporary conceptualizations of pain challenge such specificity views (see Melzack, 1973; Melzack & Wall, 1982).

Gate-control theory (Melzack & Wall, 1965) emphasizes that pain perception and response are complex phenomena resulting from the interaction of cognitive-evaluative, motivational-affective as well as sensory-discriminative components. The gate-control theory also proposes that information resulting from noxious stimulation is modified as it passes from peripheral nerve fibers to those in the spinal cord by a specialized "gating" mechanism in the region of the dorsal horns of the cord—in particular, the substantia gelatinosa. In simple terms, information reaches the brain only if the gate is open. Whether the gate is relatively open or closed depends on the balance of activity in large and small afferent fibers (large fibers tend to close the gate, whereas small ones tend to open it) and in fibers descending from the higher centers of the brain (see Bond, 1979).

Recently there has been more emphasis on higher levels of pain control, or gating mechanisms in the brain itself. Further detailed information on the anatomical and physiological bases for this theory can be found in Melzack and Wall (1982). Although some of the more speculative aspects of the gate-control theory have been challenged, it nevertheless has proved tremendously heuristic, inspiring both basic research and clinical applications (Liebeskind & Paul, 1977).

Physiology and Psychology of Pain. Research on the biochemistry of pain has suggested that neurokinins, or proteins that increase in concentration as a result of pain, tend to further lower the pain threshold. More recently natural pain-suppressing substances called endorphins have been discovered in some parts of the brain, and seem to act in ways similar to powerful drugs like morphine or narcotics. Some researchers believe that a possible common biochemical or physiological mechanism operating in a number of pain-reducing interventions (e.g., morphine and some kinds of electrical stimulation) involves enkephalin, one type of endorphin (see Feuerstein & Skjei, 1979), but much more research is needed before a firm conclusion can be drawn.

Whatever the physiological or biochemical

bases of pain may be, it is clear that psychological and social factors play a significant role in pain perception and response (see Sternbach, 1978). These factors include ethnic background, socioeconomic status, family size, birth order, present circumstances, meaning of the situation or the pain itself, anxiety and uncertainty, expectation, depression or hopelessness, and stress. Anxiety, for example, may exacerbate or even produce pain. In general, moderate arousal tends to increase pain, whereas extreme arousal or less intensive experiences tend to reduce pain. Pain is therefore a perceptual experience that is influenced by the unique past history of the individual, by his state of mind at the moment, and by the meaning he attaches to the pain-producing situation (Melzack, 1973). Regarding psychiatric aspects of pain, Merskey (1980) has pointed out that depression that is treatable accounts for only a small part of psychiatric illness associated with chronic pain. Most cases are linked more to relatively intractable chronic neurotic conditions, and the more chronic the pain, the more common are hysterical features.

Treatment. A number of pain treatments are available. Some have been developed as a result of the gate-control theory, which suggests that pain can be attenuated by psychological methods or by stimulation interventions to .close the pain gate. Traditional pain treatments include medications, neurosurgery, and nerve blocks aimed at reducing noxious afferent input to the brain. However, these have often not been successful, and debilitating side effects do occur. Other pain treatments now available include electrical nerve stimulation, exercise, diet, acupuncture, hypnosis, biofeedback, relaxation techniques, behavior modification, and psychotherapy. Several recent applications of cognitive-behavioral interventions such as stress-inoculation training, relaxation strategies, distraction, imagery techniques, and calming self-talk have also been reported (see Tan, 1982). While more controlled research is needed to evaluate the effectiveness of these various treatments, preliminary findings suggest that they are potentially useful for at least some patients.

Pain assessment has included a number of self-report measures such as the use of verbal or visual analogue scales of pain intensity and the well-known McGill Pain Questionnaire (Melzack, 1975); behavioral measures such as ratings of actual pain behavior or amount of analgesic medication used; experimental pain tests using a number of noxious stimuli including heat, pressure, ice water, electric shock,

and muscle ischemia; and physiological measures such as evoked potentials.

A biblical perspective on suffering or pain can provide meaning, facilitate psychological and spiritual growth, and help an individual better cope with pain. Prayer for healing may at times bring about complete remission of certain medical conditions and the associated pain.

References

Bond, M. R. *Pain: Its nature, analysis and treatment.* New York: Longman, 1979.
Feuerstein, M., & Skjei, E. *Mastering pain.* New York: Bantam Books, 1979.
International Association for the Study of Pain. Pain terms: A list with definitions and notes on usage. *Pain,* 1979, *6,* 249–252.
Liebeskind, J. C., & Paul, L. A. Psychological and physiological mechanisms of pain. *Annual Review of Psychology,* 1977, *28,* 41–60.
Melzack, R. *The puzzle of pain.* New York: Basic Books, 1973.
Melzack, R. The McGill Pain Questionnaire: Major properties and scoring methods. *Pain,* 1975, *1,* 277–299.
Melzack, R., & Wall, P. D. Pain mechanisms: A new theory. *Science,* 1965, *150,* 971–979.
Melzack, R., & Wall, P. D. *The challenge of pain.* New York: Penguin Books, 1982.
Merskey, H. Pain. In S. Krauss (Ed.), *Encyclopaedic handbook of medical psychology.* Boston: 1976.
Merskey, H. The management of pain. *Weekly Psychiatry Update Series,* 1980, *3,* Lesson 33.
Sternbach, R. A. (Ed.). *The psychology of pain.* New York: Raven Press, 1978.
Tan, S. Y. Cognitive and cognitive-behavioural methods for pain control: A selective review. *Pain,* 1982, *12,* 201–228.

S. Y. TAN

Panic Disorder. A psychological problem in which the afflicted person experiences extreme and intense anxiety. This anxiety is experienced in relatively brief but recurrent episodes known as panic attacks. Panic attacks are very frightening and aversive experiences in which persons are overwhelmed with the physical symptoms of anxiety. They usually come on rapidly and are precipitated by rapid and shallow breathing. Persons may perspire profusely and feel faint or dizzy. Their hands and feet may feel strangely tingley or numb. Muscles in the scalp, face, neck, shoulders, and back become tense. Breathing becomes an effort as the chest muscles tighten and the heart pounds.

Persons experiencing a panic attack become terrified, and their terror increases the severity of the symptoms. These are such powerful and unusual experiences that many individuals report a strange sense of unreality during the attack. Most victims believe they are either having a heart attack or going insane. Frequently they will rush to a hospital emergency room for help, especially if it is the first time they have experienced a panic attack. The attack usually lasts only a few minutes, although for some people it may drag on for several hours.

The paradox of panic attacks is that they are not in themselves harmful. They occur when anxiety triggers hyperventilation (rapid and shallow breathing), which results in too little carbon dioxide in the lungs. This changes the pH level of the plasma and leads to the tingley, light-headed, unreal, panicky feelings previously described. Because the subjects of attacks do not understand what is happening, they become frightened, and this further accelerates their hyperventilation. Eventually their bodies' natural mechanisms will compensate for this, and persons will momentarily stop inhaling or the rate of respiration will be slowed by fainting, yawning, or sighing.

An old and widely used technique for rapidly stopping hyperventilation is to have hyperventilating persons breathe into a paper bag whose top has been crumpled about the person's mouth. In a few moments this will increase the amount of carbon dioxide inhaled and thus eliminate some of the unusual and frightening symptoms. While very frightening, the attack itself will not injure the person. The attacks are dangerous only if they aggravate some previously existing physical vulnerability such as a heart condition, or if the person is motivated to some dangerous behavior such as driving an automobile recklessly.

Panic attacks are so distressing that after experiencing the first one, most people live in fear that they will recur. This fear is known as anticipatory anxiety. While persons who have experienced a panic disorder go to great lengths to avoid another attack, the fear of another attack makes them more susceptible to subsequent attacks. A history of several panic attacks in a month coupled with an acute fear of further attacks is the hallmark of panic disorder.

Because the initial attacks occur so unexpectedly and are so surprising, those who experience them usually search for reasons for the attacks. Many persons persist in looking for physical causes. They may think the problem is a heart problem, or may investigate inner ear and balance problems. Others think hormone problems are responsible. It is not unusual for a person with panic disorder to be referred for counseling by a physician who has failed to find any physical causes after extensive medical tests.

Panic disorder is diagnosed when the panic attacks are the primary presenting problem and are not secondary to some other psycho-logical problem such as schizophrenia, drug addiction, or phobias. If a person's symptoms include much anxiety and avoidance behavior between panic attacks, AGORAPHOBIA should be diagnosed. Before panic disorder is diagnosed, potential physical causes for panic attacks should be ruled out by a careful medical examination. Some physical problems that can produce panic attacks include hypoglycemia, hyperthyroidism, a variety of drugs and medications, heart valve disorders, and excessive intake of caffeine.

Panic disorder is a relatively common disorder that occurs more frequently among women than men (but is not uncommon in men). It may begin anywhere from adolescence through mid-life. Separation conflicts in childhood are generally thought to be predisposing factors. Except during panic attacks, panic disorder is not usually a severely debilitating problem, and the prospects for successful treatment are quite good.

Treatment of persons with panic disorder usually involves a three-faceted approach. The first facet focuses on increasing the person's understanding of how anxiety triggers hyperventilation and panic attacks. The second focuses on teaching breathing exercises, muscle relaxation, and cognitive methods for physically coping with stress and anxiety. The third focuses on the exploration and treatment of the anxiety that initially triggered the panic attacks.

C. D. DOLPH

Paradoxical Intervention. The psychotherapeutic technique of directing a client to do something contrary to one's actual instructions. The technique has been explained and applied in a number of different ways. Some theorists appeal to the notion of reverse psychology as an explanation; oppositional tendencies within the client are seen as being responsible for the success of the technique. Another perspective is that of Frankl (1960), who labels his approach *paradoxical intention;* the success of the directive is due to one not being able to force that which is involuntary (e.g., telling someone to keep stammering kills the symptom).

Systemic theorists traditionally have offered another sort of explanation. These theorists view symptoms as communicative acts that control the behavior of others within either the nuclear family or the family of origin. When ordered to perform the symptomatic behavior, the patient is put in an untenable position. Being ordered to continue what one is already doing in order to control others changes the meaning and strength of the symptom. This is a variant of the DOUBLE BIND explanation; a patient's symptoms are conflictual communications in that on the surface they proclaim helplessness, while at a deeper level they manipulate others into helping them. The systems therapist then comes into the family system and mirrors this behavior. In a benevolent context (one level of communication) he encourages problematic behavior to continue (another, conflictual level of communication). In other words, he benevolently prescribes that the identified patient continue to engage in the problem behavior in such a manner that it is no longer useful to the patient or the system.

Another systemic perspective is that of Stanton (1981). His compression hypothesis states that a pathological family is in a constant process of moving between the extremes of fusion with nuclear family to fusion with family of origin. When fusion at either end of the spectrum becomes experienced as uncomfortably enmeshing, a fission process occurs and moves the system in the opposite direction. Paradox is explained as pushing the family in the direction it is already going and then blocking that movement, reversing the direction. The system is thus forced to add new behaviors to its coping repertoire. Other related explanatory constructs appealing to the balance between homeostatic and transformational tendencies in the system have also been advanced (Watzlawick, Weakland, & Fisch, 1974).

An excellent review of therapeutic applications of paradox has been offered by Weeks and L'Abate (1979). Other applications of paradox, primarily with families, have been put forth by Palazolli-Selvini, Boscolo, Cecchin, and Prata (1978); Madanes (1980); Papp (1980); and O'Connell (1983). Indications and contraindications as well as practical suggestions for usage are detailed in these works.

Regarding the ethics of paradoxical intervention, it has been alleged that the paradoxical practitioner is frequently insensitive, shocking, uncaring, and manipulative. This has undoubtedly sometimes been true. The therapeutic use of paradox or any other powerful technique can be applied unethically by any individual who unwittingly or consciously wishes to systematically enhance his or her own sense of personal power at the client's expense. It is also true that paradox has an equally great potential for constructive use when applied with integrity and skill. The use

of paradoxical injunctions by Jehovah, Solomon, and Jesus in the biblical record is a fascinating study (see Deschenes & Shepperson, 1983). Thus both sides of this double-edged ethical razor would seem to depend on the practitioner rather than the technique itself. In order to ethically and effectively apply paradoxical intervention, one should become thoroughly acquainted with both its theory and practice.

References

Deschenes, P., & Shepperson, V. The ethics of paradox. *Journal of Psychology and Theology*, 1983, *11*, 92–98.
Frankl, V. Paradoxical intention. *American Journal of Psychotherapy*, 1960, *14*, 520–535.
Madanes, C. Protection, paradox, and pretending. *Family Process*, 1980, *19*, 73–85.
O'Connell, D. S. Symptom prescription in psychotherapy. *Psychotherapy: Theory, Research and Practice*, 1983, *20*, 12–20.
Palazzoli-Selvini, M., Boscolo, L., Cecchin, G., & Prata, G. *Paradox and counterparadox: A new model in the therapy of the family in schizophrenic transaction*. New York: Aronson, 1978.
Papp, P. The Greek chorus and other techniques of paradoxical therapy. *Family Process*, 1980, *19*, 45–57.
Stanton, M. Strategic approaches to family therapy. In A. Gurman & D. Kniskern (Eds.), *Handbook of family therapy*. New York: Brunner/Mazel, 1981.
Watzlawick, P., Weakland, J., & Fisch, R. *Change: Principles of problem formation and problem resolution*, New York: Norton, 1974.
Weeks, G., & L'Abate, L. A compilation of paradoxical methods. *American Journal of Family Therapy*, 1979, *7*, 61–76.

V. L. SHEPPERSON

See STRATEGIC THERAPY; PROVOCATIVE THERAPY.

Paralogical Thinking. A false thinking or reasoning in which an individual distorts reality in order to make it conform to his personal desires or delusional ideas. This illogical reasoning is often found in schizophrenic reactions. For example, based on the premises that 1) the President of the United States loves freedom, and 2) the person himself loves freedom, the paralogical thinker may conclude that he is the President of the United States.

Paranoia. The concept bequeathed to modern psychiatry by Kraepelin, who described it as an insidiously developing, relatively unchanging, delusional system that involved no hallucinations and that could exist side by side with clear and orderly thinking. One of the basic problems in dealing with paranoia is that it is usually compounded with schizophrenic manifestations. Freud recognized this, yet still felt there were grounds for distinguishing paranoia on a dynamic basis. Sullivan, on the other hand, imagined schizophrenia and paranoia as imaginary poles of a clinical continuum. He felt that every schizophrenic has some paranoid feelings and can be led to express them from time to time; conversely he felt that every paranoid person also had some period of schizophrenic adjustment in his history.

Currently the concept is employed in several ways. Its primary use is as a diagnostic category including five different paranoid disorders (*DSM-III*). It is also used to describe a personality trait characterized by isolation, hypersensitivity, guardedness, suspiciousness, and the use of projection as a defense. Clinicians therefore may speak of a person as having a paranoid quality, or of the presence of paranoid mechanisms or dynamics. This article will examine psychoanalytic understandings of the etiology and dynamics of paranoid states. PARANOID DISORDERS will discuss each of the specific disorders in which paranoia forms a central part of the clinical picture.

Freud's Views. Freud related the paranoid state to basic conflicts over homosexual impulses. He considered its essential dynamic to be the defense mechanism of projection, wherein impulses and feeling states that are unacceptable within the self are defended by projecting them onto someone in the external environment (Freud, 1966). Projection arises, he said, as a result of normal tendencies to presume that internal changes are due to external causes. This process is normal as long as we remain aware of the internal state, but it becomes abnormal when we lose sight of this. Paranoid projection therefore is really an abuse of the mechanism of projection for the purposes of defense.

Fixation in paranoia was viewed by Freud to be at an early narcissistic level, intermediate between the primitive autoeroticism, where one's own body was chosen as a love object, and a more mature choice of heterosexual love objects. The homosexual object choice and the conflict over it are repressed. The subsequent failure of the repression allows for a return of the impulses, which then have to be handled by the characteristic mechanism of projection. The unacceptable internal homosexual impulses are thus externalized and distorted, and other people are seen as persecutors or in some other way dangerous. Note that this involves transformation of love into hate, or affectionate impulses into hostile impulses. This is a characteristic dynamic of paranoia. Freud explained the common accompanying delusion of being watched as a projection of the supervisory function of the internal criticizing agency, the superego.

One further component of Freud's theory of paranoia was first presented in his paper, "The

Neurotic Mechanisms in Jealousy, Paranoia and Homosexuality" (1922). In pathological forms of jealousy there is a projection of impulses to infidelity onto the partner. The use of projection and the implicit denial of repressed homosexual wishes make delusional jealousy one of the classic components of paranoia. The delusion is supported not merely by projection but by the patient's perception of actual impulses to infidelity in his partner. Sometimes, of course, such actual impulses are at least in part a response to the paranoid spouse's suspiciousness.

Post-Freudian Developments. One of the most significant contributions to post-Freudian considerations was that of Klein (1948). She shifted the emphasis from libidinal (sexual) to aggressive aspects of paranoia, an emphasis that remains in contemporary thought. Following Abraham's formulation of paranoia as a regression to an earlier phase of anal sadism and as involving a partial introjection of the love object, Klein studied paranoid manifestations in young children. On the basis of her extensive clinical experience, she agreed with Abraham's basic position and felt that the paranoid was fixated in the period of maximal sadism in infantile development—i.e., late oral through early anal stage development (approximately the second year of life).

The contributions of several others represent a further fine tuning of Freud's original formulations. Fenichel (1945) gave more emphasis to the role of superego in paranoid delusions. He felt that these cannot be derived from a homosexual basis but may represent a relief by way of projection from the aggression that has been turned inward in the form of shame, guilt, or feelings of inadequacy. Similarly, Hesselbach (1962) has emphasized the regression of the superego in delusion formation in paranoia. The severity of the superego is determined by the severity of early parental authority. In the regression there is a reemergence of certain archaic parental introjects that are then projected onto external objects. These objects then become endowed with all the aggression and sadism with which the original parental introjects were once endowed. The function of the delusion of persecution is that it permits the unbearably guilt-ridden person to become righteously indignant and to struggle against sadistic impulses in the legitimate form of self-defense.

Some have questioned Freud's assumption that the underlying basic conflict is over homosexual impulses. For example, Carr (1963) suggests that even though patients may engage in overt homosexual practices, homosexual conflicts do not seem to play a considerable role in many cases. He feels that the role of hostility is a central difficulty in paranoia. Paranoia, along with homosexuality, may serve as a defense against hostility.

The broadening perspectives on paranoia led to the contributions of Sullivan (1953). He regarded paranoid ideas of persecution as complex processes that were intended to overcome or obliterate the irremediable sense of inferiority and unworthiness and the incapacity to awaken positive attitudes in others. He described the process in which inadequate approbation in the child's early experience produces a prevailing negative self. Feelings of personal inferiority, unworthiness, and loneliness are at times intolerable. The conviction evolves that the individual is not capable of being fully human, and this creates an intolerable insecurity that makes it impossible to sustain any kind of adaptive effort.

Sullivan posits that the patient achieves security by paranoid projection in which the inferior person is turned into a victim of persecution. The feeling of worth is protected by the paranoid transference of blame onto other individuals. Thus the paranoid's security rests on his being persecuted. The transfer of blame, however, covers an intolerable weakness so that the paranoid's self-esteem must continually draw into the projective system anybody who would be critical. The danger flags are continually flying, and relationships can be permitted only with people who do not represent danger in the sense of reminding the paranoid of what really ails him. The awareness of inferiority creates an intolerable anxiety. This represents a fatal deficiency of the self system, which is unable to disguise or exclude the underlying sense of inferiority and consequent rejection and insecurity. This perspective bears strong resemblance to that of Adler (see INDIVIDUAL PSYCHOLOGY).

The concept of masochism later became an additional cornerstone in the understanding of paranoia. Nydes (1963) stated that the masochistic character appears to renounce power for the sake of love, and the paranoid character appears to renounce love for the sake of power. Thus, in the megalomania phase of delusional paranoia the patient renounces love and adopts the position of the powerful figure of God or one who is equated with God. The masochist projects his wishes for power onto the other person and renounces his own power for the sake of the love of the powerful figure. Nydes also contrasts the paranoid orientation

with the sadistic orientation and feels that they must be distinguished even though they may overlap. The paranoid orientation is essentially defensive against the inner feeling of guilt. It involves identification with the victim, the one who is being persecuted, rather than identification with the aggressor, which is characteristic of a sadistic orientation.

The relationship between depression and paranoia has been stressed by Allen (1967). These two states may substitute for each other, and the treatment of the paranoid patient frequently uncovers an underlying depression. The depression is primary, and the paranoia is an attempt to deal with the implicit suicidal impulse. The paranoid patient is extremely sensitive to the suicidal impulse and can deal with it only by projecting it. When the impulse becomes too strong to be handled by mechanisms of denial and projection, a serious suicide attempt may be made. Thus, the paranoid defenses take their place alongside the manic defenses as major strategies to avoid or diminish the pain of depression and lowered self-esteem. The paranoid resorts to mechanisms of denial and flight into activity. At the pathological extremes paranoid psychosis and bipolar disorder are often difficult to differentiate.

Summary. Paranoia is a style of mental life spanning a wide spectrum of pathological states of varying degrees of severity and distortion. Paranoid states can be seen as defenses against anxiety, aggression, hostility, masochism, inferiority, or depression. The paranoid style and the elements that contribute to it can be conceptualized as operating in the service of specific defenses.

References

Allen, T. E. Suicidal impulse in paranoia and depression. *International Journal of Psychoanalysis*, 1967, *48*, 433–438.

Carr, A. C. Observations on paranoia and their relationship to the Schreber case. *International Journal of Psychoanalysis*, 1963, *44*, 195–200.

Fenichel, O. *The psychoanalytic theory of neurosis.* New York: Norton, 1945.

Freud, S. Extracts from the Fliess papers. In J. Strachey (Ed. and trans.), *The standard edition of the complete psychological works of Sigmund Freud*, (Vol. 1). London: Hogarth, 1966.

Hesselbach, C. F. Superego regression in paranoia. *Psychoanalytic Quarterly*, 1962, *31*, 341–350.

Klein, M. *Contributions to psychoanalysis, 1921–1945.* London: Hogarth, 1948.

Nydes, J. The paranoid-masochistic character. *Psychoanalytic Review*, 1963, *50*, 55–91.

Sullivan, H. S. *Conceptions in modern psychiatry* (2nd ed.). New York: Norton, 1953.

Additional Reading

Meissner, W. W. *The paranoid process.* New York: Aronson, 1978.

R. D. CALABRESE

Paranoid Disorders. The term *paranoid* usually refers to a syndrome characterized by delusions of persecution and grandeur. It has also often been extended to include unreasonable jealousy and erotic attachments of a delusional nature.

These delusions may be monothematic or complex systems, but characteristically they involve others who are conspiring to cheat, demean, malign, or spy upon the patient with the intent of damaging, harassing, or frustrating him in seeking important goals. The patient responds to such threats with suspicion, vigilant coldness, and hostility. Those suspected then often react in a way that supports the patient's suspicions.

The patient's convictions, usually reinforced by more "evidence" unearthed by the excessive vigilance, become so rigid that contradictory evidence, however convincing to others, will have no effect. The resulting delusional system may be vague enough, or held secretly enough, to have little effect on the rest of the patient's life. In other cases, fortunately rare, a patient might strike back in rage with truly dangerous aggressiveness. However, in most cases, interpersonal relationships are severely disturbed, and the patient is unhappy and isolated.

This paranoid process may occur in almost any psychiatric disorder. It occurs most often in functional psychoses (paranoid schizophrenia) but is also seen in toxic or other organic psychoses. It occasionally begins abruptly in an otherwise normal person as a result of drastic environmental changes (acute paranoid disorder) and may have no other complications (paranoid disorder). Those close to the patient may have the same erroneous conviction (folie à deux, or shared paranoid disorder).

In what one might assume to be its purest form (paranoia, or true paranoia), a fixed, unshakable system of persecutory or grandiose delusions occurs in a person who is remarkably logical in other ways. In this form it is thought to be rare and essentially untreatable.

In whatever form it appears, paranoia is a most difficult clinical problem. Persons who have become irrationally convinced that their mates are being unfaithful to them, that their employers have blackballed them, or that they are combatting vaguely defined conspiracies of the CIA, Russia, or the Mafia are encountered rather frequently by anyone who works with people. In the counselor's office they usually appear accompanied by frustrated family members who have tried fruitlessly to prove these fears groundless. The experienced counselor also knows that therapy will be difficult and the hope of completely resolving the delusion dim.

One source of the counselor's frustration is that we do not have a clear, generally accepted idea of just how such a fixed and irrational idea becomes implanted in the mind of a patient. Most psychologists feel that paranoid reactions tend to occur in people who are emotionally constricted, relate poorly to others, and tend to be loners. Most would also agree with Polatin (1975) that in childhood this patient was unsuccessful in developing basic trust reactions, particularly to his parents, and that from this there develops a marked hypersensitivity and a tendency to amplify trivial events out of all proportion. (*See* PARANOIA for a more detailed discussion of theories of etiology.)

In describing the paranoid process phenomenologically, several things seem to be involved. In the first place an environmental stimulus, perhaps even a trivial one, must produce an intense anxiety reaction within the patient. In addition, to form paranoid delusions the patient's primary object relations must have been sufficiently disturbed so that unreasonable motives can be attributed to others close by.

The psychopathological process then would proceed in a way similar to that proposed by Cameron (1974). In a person who is either a narcissistic personality or is disordered narcissistically by psychosis, a paniclike reaction is set off by a minimal stimulus. The brain then seeks to resolve stimulus and reaction by a paranoid delusion that ties the suspicious circumstance to a hypothesis ominous enough to explain the massive emotional reaction. The scenario of the delusion would be determined by the personality of the patient as well as his past experiences, but the process would relate more to anxiety itself.

The resulting formulation is formidable enough to create an emergency atmosphere that would in turn create hypervigilance and also sensitize anxiety responses still further. Other events then would fix the delusion, making it less and less accessible to reason. In the paranoid reaction this proliferation takes the form of a developing system, or what Cameron calls a "pseudocommunity" of hostility.

Psychotherapy for paranoid conditions begins with handling effectively the delusion itself. The therapist is always in danger of being cast into the role of enemy, a part of the hostile conspiracy. The usual advice of experi-

791

enced clinicians is to first establish a position of rapport and trust with the patient. From this position one can deal with the delusional system gingerly, gradually urging the patient to question his own formulations. A more direct approach is to address directly the intense conviction that the patient has in his mind. Whether this conviction is warranted or not is not an issue of therapy. How disturbing it is to the patient and to the mate becomes the central issue of therapy. By focusing on the internal experience of the patient and the relationship with significant others, the central pathology of the disorder is addressed directly. This procedure also frequently helps those around the patient to respond more effectively, building and supporting the relationship and the suffering of the patient rather than struggling fruitlessly with the truth or falsehood of the system.

In paranoid conditions the outcome of therapy depends more on the underlying condition than the paranoia itself. In schizophrenic and organic psychoses the paranoia usually vanishes when the psychosis is effectively treated. With paranoia that is associated with depression and other manifestations of anxiety, antidepressants are often helpful as an adjunct to therapy. In these situations the prognosis is more uncertain. In true paranoia there is little hope of completely eliminating the delusion. A more reasonable goal would be to reduce the impact of the psychosis on the life of the patient and to enrich affective experience and the quality of relationships in other areas of life.

References

Cameron, N. Paranoid conditions and paranoia. In S. Arieti (Ed.), *American Handbook of Psychiatry* (2nd ed.). New York: Basic Books, 1974.
Polatin, P. Psychotic disorders: Paranoid states. In A. M. Freedman, H. I. Kaplan, & B. J. Sadock (Eds.), *Comprehensive textbook of psychiatry II*. Baltimore: Williams & Wilkins, 1975.

Additional Readings

Meissner, W. W. *The paranoid process*. New York: Aronson, 1978.
Pinderhughes, C. A. Managing paranoia in violent relationships. In G. Usdin (Ed.), *Perspectives on violence*. New York: Brunner/Mazel 1972.
Will, O. A., Jr. Paranoid development and the concept of self: Psychotherapeutic intervention. *Psychiatry*, 1961, *24*, 74–86.

C. M. BERRY

Paraphilia. A group of sexual perversions in which sexual arousal is persistently achieved by simulated or real suffering, by the use of nonhuman objects, or from a nonconsenting partner. Some of the more common paraphil-

ias include SEXUAL SADISM and SEXUAL MASOCHISM, PEDOPHILIA (children as sex objects), EXHIBITIONISM (exposing genitals in view of an unwilling audience), ZOOPHILIA (sexual activity with animals), telephone scatologia (obscene phone calls), FETISHISM (sexual arousal from nonsexual objects), TRANSVESTISM (cross dressing), and VOYEURISM (exaggerated interest in viewing sexual objects).

Paraphilias cause impairment of social and sexual relationships. Individuals with sexual deviations have difficulty receiving or giving affection and are usually emotionally immature. Males constitute almost all the reported cases of paraphilia. Paraphilias are often triggered by stress in the individual's life. Even though he is married, the person's sexual needs are not met, and to fulfill sexual desires the perverted sexual behavior must be acted out.

The origins of paraphilia are based in learning and pleasurable reinforcement, fueled by humankind's sinful nature. At birth the child is open to a variety of sexual patterns that can be developed. Through environmental conditioning children and adolescents begin to develop what is pleasurable and erotic. These sexual patterns become well developed as they mature into adulthood.

Additional Reading

Lester, D. *Unusual sexual behavior*. Springfield, Ill.: Thomas, 1975.

M. A. CAMPION

Parapraxis. Freud used this term to refer to misactions such as slips of the tongue or mislaying of objects, actions which he assumed reveal something of underlying unconscious dynamics. Thus the person who says "sex" instead of "six" or who suddenly forgets the name of his best friend with whom he had a fight should not be seen as engaging in accidental behavior but rather in behavior that betrays the true state of the unconscious. Because of this assumption psychoanalysts treat parapraxes as important pieces of behavior for analysis.

See PSYCHOANALYTIC PSYCHOLOGY.

Paraprofessional Therapy. Anthony and Carkhuff (1977) define the paraprofessional, or "functional professional" (the term they prefer), as that individual who, lacking formal credentials, performs those functions usually reserved for credentialed mental health professionals. They include in this group such people as psychiatric aides, community workers, parents, college students, and mental health technicians. Pastors and various church workers would also fall in the category.

While functional professionals have been around a long time, they have been legitimatized only since the mid-1960s. A number of reasons have been advanced for the increase in the number of functional professionals in mental health: 1) the demise of the disease model of mental health (newer approaches do not demand as much advanced schooling); 2) the development of the community mental health concept, along with the recognition of the need for change agents who come from the same background as the clients; 3) the availability of federal money to prepare unemployed and low-income persons for positions as functional paraprofessionals.

Even though paraprofessionals have become common in mental health, the question that has repeatedly been raised is whether or not paraprofessional therapists are effective. A review of the research in 1968 found that paraprofessionals could be trained to effect significant constructive changes in the clients they worked with. There has, however, been little recent research on the effectiveness of paraprofessionals. So many people have become involved in paraprofessional training that the idea of its effectiveness seems to have been forgotten.

Anthony and Carkhuff (1977) argue that paraprofessionals should be taught skills that have been found to be effective. It does no good to teach paraprofessionals skills that in themselves are not effective even when used by trained professionals. However, this often seems to have been done, and consequently most paraprofessional training is not very effective. For example, training for lay counselors usually consists of didactic lectures and discussion groups—an approach that has not been shown to make any difference in terms of observable client change. The most effective paraprofessional, therefore, is one who has had specific training in interpersonal skills and program development skills, as well as training in additional therapeutic skills that have been found to be effective.

Two skills that appear to be easily taught to paraprofessional counselors are empathy and basic skill in cognitive behavioral therapy. Training in these skills would consist of a small amount of lecturing on their nature, modeling by the instructor, and an opportunity for the trainees to practice the skills and receive feedback on their development. Practice could occur within the context of the training program by role playing with other participants.

Summarizing the literature, the following principles of paraprofessional counseling seem to be important. First, goals for any program in the church or elsewhere focusing on paraprofessional training should be specifically defined in observable, measurable terms. That is, the individual should be taught some specific skills so that an observer is able to ascertain that he or she indeed has those skills. Second, the training process should be designed to teach trainees skills that previous research has found to be effective. Finally, the selection of trainees for any program should be based on how well they perform in a situation that is similar to that for which they are going to be trained. Not everyone will benefit equally from a paraprofessional training program.

The substantial amount of literature on community mental health suggests that pastors and other church leaders can play an important role in mental health concerns. Haugk (1976) suggests that clergy can play a uniquely important role in primary prevention because they are closer to the members of their congregation. They can disseminate basic mental health information and make sure everyone is integrated into the community. They could also play a role in secondary prevention because they are in a unique position for the early detection of problems. Finally, they could play a unique role in tertiary prevention, not only by being involved in actual counseling but also by encouraging members of their congregations who are in professional counseling to stay in counseling.

References

Anthony, W. A., & Carkhuff, R. P. The functional professional therapeutic agent. In A. Gurman & A. M. Razin (Eds.), *Effective psychotherapy: A handbook of research.* New York: Pergamon, 1977.

Haugk, K. C. Unique contributions of churches and clergy to community mental health. *Community Mental Health Journal,* 1976, *12*(1), 20–28.

L. R. PROPST

Parapsychology. The study of all psychic phenomena, *psychic* referring to either the events or the persons who seem to possess inexplicable abilities to perceive or influence events. *Psi* refers to hypothetical energy forces assumed to mediate psychic phenomena. The subject of parapsychology elicits responses ranging from fervent belief to rabid rejection, from lay persons, religious believers, psychologists, and other scientists alike.

The Scope of Study. In formal study parapsychology encompasses three varieties of extrasensory perception (ESP) and psychokinesis (PK). Telepathy is the ability to read another's thoughts; clairvoyance implies knowledge of inanimate objects or events without use of the known senses; and precognition is knowledge of events before they occur. Psychokinesis is the ability to move or otherwise control an inanimate object or event without known physical energies.

These presumed phenomena are defined negatively: they cannot be explained by scientific laws, principles, or energies. The knowledge, perceptions, or behavior also must not be a product of unconscious mental (brain) processes, employing sensory cues, past or present, however subtle. Parapsychology assumes that the mind is an "unextended substance," not merely a product of the brain, and therefore involves energy separable from the physical body.

Reports and Research. Parapsychology arose from common life situations. Countless stories tell of uncanny premonitions, precognitive dreams, hauntings, and fortune telling that defy explanation. Around this kind of observation many belief systems have developed—spiritualist churches, palmistry, astrology, I Ching, out-of-body experiences (OBEs), and near-death visions. Poltergeists (noisy spirits) break dishes and furniture, propel objects through the air or off shelves. Mystics claim to levitate—rise bodily into the air—by purely mental powers. Healers perform "psychic surgery," removing apparently malignant tissue from a patient with bare hands, leaving no incision. Dowsers "witch" for water or minerals; performers inexplicably bend keys or spoons; Kirlian photography reveals unearthly "auras" around human fingertips and other objects.

Such reports are widely critiqued by scientists (Hansel, 1966), magicians (Christopher, 1970), and other skeptics. Careful investigation of reports usually reveals critical errors of fact. Poltergeists are usually associated with youths playing tricks on gullible adults. Fortune tellers vary from outright frauds to astute observers who lead their clients to reveal what they want to hear. Astrological and other predictions, when carefully checked and tabulated, have negligible validity. Psychic surgeons and metal benders do not withstand the scrutiny of trained magicians. Even prominent parapsychologists see Kirlian photographs as chemoelectrical artifacts. Of course not every case is discredited, and some must be counted as coincidences. But even a few unexplained reports encourage many people to believe that psi really exists.

Some surveys of psychic phenomena include what might better be called pseudo-psychic events—phenomena without clearly mechanistic explanations, including possession, automatic writing and other automatisms, fire walking, faith healing, hypnosis, and biofeedback. The latter two have been accepted into psychology's domain of fact, and, but for its association with religion, faith healing would probably hold such status. The first three phenomena can be explained by suggestion, learning, and unconscious processes (*see* ECSTATIC RELIGIOUS EXPERIENCES).

Formal investigation of parapsychology began with the founding of the Society for Psychical Research at Cambridge University, England, in 1882 and a similar American society a few years later. In 1920 psychologist William McDougall, then president of the British Society for Psychical Research, went to Harvard University and began a study of psychic phenomena. Botanist Joseph B. Rhine joined McDougall as a research assistant in 1926 and followed him to Duke University the next year. Rhine and his wife, Louisa E., founded the Duke Parapsychology Laboratory, which has conducted the most consistent psychical research. During an initial period of disappointing work psychologist K. E. Zener designed ESP (or Zener) cards that were used in many later studies. A deck of the famous cards included five sets of five bold symbols: plus sign, three parallel wavy lines, and outlines of circle, square, and star. The telepathy procedure usually involved one sender, who thought of five Zener symbols in a run, with the subject or receiver making five guesses.

More encouraging results began appearing in the winter of 1931–32 and were published in 1934 and 1935. Statistical probabilities against the Rhines's results being mere chance are astronomical, and most parapsychologists consider the experimental controls to have been tight. However, Hansel (1966) identified a number of weaknesses, including evidence for recognizing the ESP cards from their backs and/or edges. Rhine's best subject, Hubert Pearce, no longer showed clairvoyance when the deck of cards was moved 8–12 feet away. When ESP card guesses were typically checked after every five cards, subjects could rationally infer the last five cards in the deck. Rhine himself was aware of this problem, noting high scores on the last trials with this procedure.

More recent studies control for the Rhines's apparent defects, but they still draw frequent, very damaging criticisms. Contemporary research includes use of sophisticated electronic gadgets and new ventures outside the laboratory. From early psychokinesis research with hand-thrown dice the Rhines progressed to dice mechanically thrown down a corrogated, inclined plane. Now instead of affecting the throw of dice a subject may attempt to alter the outcome of an electronic random number generator. Another psychokinesis subject reportedly was able to raise or lower temperatures on a highly accurate thermister, on a random schedule. Some psychics are said to impress photographic film with images that have no known physical source.

In the Ganzfeld procedure a telepathy subject relaxes in a soundproof room, eyes covered with split table tennis balls. Meanwhile a sender, some distance away, looks at a picture or series of color transparencies and mentally transmits the images to the sensory-deprived receiver. Astonishing claims have been made for this procedure. In remote viewing telepathy a psychic (supervised in a laboratory) describes the journey taken by experimenters who leave the laboratory, randomly select a route or destination, and drive for a half-hour or so. Independent judges attempt to match the psychic's report with descriptions or pictures of the route actually driven. Brain waves of some psychics have been monitored to study optimum mental conditions for the expression of psi. Animals and plants have also been studied for evidence of psi. Even convinced parapsychologists admit that no current research procedure consistently yields positive results.

Research Conclusions. After more than 50 years of research, what facts, laws, or principles of parapsychology have been established? Not many, and none assuredly. Most research merely demonstrates that something can occur beyond statistical odds. One review (Bowles & Hynds, 1978) concluded that everybody potentially has psychic abilities, though some are exceptionally sensitive. Nothing can be affirmed about the relation of psi to intelligence or personality. Some studies relate success in psychic tasks to friendly, outgoing personalities, good visual imagery, and the subject's belief in psi. Some find that hypnosis, dreaming, relaxation, and meditation enhance psychic abilities. Partners with good rapport frequently make better telepathy subjects. Telepathic communication with animals is equivocal, and plant psi has not been replicated beyond a few spectacular reports.

What can psi communicate? If all reports are accepted, practically anything. All sorts of symbols, perceptions, and knowledge have supposedly been received by the various forms of extrasensory perception, and an almost endless list of events have reportedly been affected by psychokinesis. When does the supposed psi force operate? Time presents no barriers. In some Ganzfeld trials the receiver begins to describe pictures before the sender has looked at any. If the pictures match, precognition rather than telepathy has occurred. Many other situations cannot unambiguously be identified among the four prime forms of parapsychology. If the experimenter knows a fact before a clairvoyant subject does, a correct explanation might be telepathy. When the experimenter or a machine selects items to be guessed in telepathy or clairvoyance, the subject might have exercised psychokinesis over the choices. Such ambiguities early led Rhine to disregard the separate categories of extrasensory perception.

Where can psi occur? Again, anywhere. In real life and in laboratories and across virtually any distance. If psi were some as-yet-unknown energy, it would violate the scientifically established inverse square law for the propagation of energy (Reber, 1982). The apparent limitlessness of psi may impress the believer as pervasiveness, but it rouses doubts among skeptics. All natural phenomena are affected or limited by definable parameters; without such limits scientifically oriented observers tend to dismiss parapsychology as illusory, or to investigate the source of the illusions.

Parapsychology critics continue to attack methodologies and reporting of psychic demonstrations. A typical, widely reported case involves platform psychic Uri Geller. A secondary source tells: "Geller was asked to guess which face of a die was up in an opaque box shaken by the experimenter. Geller, who was not permitted to touch the box, was told he could decline to choose when he felt uncertain. The die was shaken ten times, and Geller chose to respond eight of those times. Each time that he chose to respond he was correct, giving a result at odds of 17,500,000 to 1" (Bowles & Hynds, 1978, p. 66). The original report cited the statistical odds as about 1,000,000 to 1. Gardner reports that one of the experimenters said Geller "was allowed to place his hands on the box in 'dowsing fashion'" (1982, p. 34). Further inquiry revealed that the tests actually took place over a three- to seven-day period; records reportedly were kept but were not provided when Gardner requested them. A film was made of one of the trials (on which Geller chose not to guess), and reports of videotapes were never confirmed by actual film documents. One magician thought cheating could have occurred in several ways, but without seeing the records or films he could not confirm his suspicions.

Contradictory reporting, methodological looseness, and withholding of primary experimental records are typical of much parapsychology research. Defenders of the psychic realm accurately retort that few other research areas attract this kind of critical analysis. No known data could convince most skeptics of the existence of psi, nor is any critique of the work sufficiently cogent to persuade a believer that it is all artifact.

Psychologist Reber (1982) cites three canons of science that parapsychology violates, thus prejudicing scientists against the field. 1) Whereas nature is reliable, psychic phenomena are elusive, frequently disappearing under the closest controls. 2) While science is coherent, psi violates the inverse square law for transmission of energy, and precognition itself violates at least three scientific laws: the principle that cause precedes effect, the linearity of time, and the first law of thermodynamics (that anything without substance can have no impact on a material substance). 3) Scientific explanations are mechanistic, but parapsychology has not proposed any mechanism whereby psi might operate—without violating other scientific canons. Admittedly science is conservative with regard to new facts and systems, but it has accepted biofeedback principles, and it is prone to accept acupuncture as a physiological reality.

Since parapsychology meets none of the three canons, it is not accepted by most scientists. Some phenomena now classed with parapsychology probably will find acceptance within psychology. The regularity of near-death visions points toward unconscious and/or brain mechanisms as an explanation; out-of-body experiences may engage similar mechanisms. Some "mind reading" by stage magicians avowedly employs such keen sensitivity to cues from the audience as almost to constitute an altered state of consciousness. Heightened psychic powers associated with hypnosis, relaxation, and meditation may result from sensitization to physical and/or social cues that have eluded experimental control. The unconscious mind and subtle neurological structures hold unplumbed secrets that probably operate in many parapsychology experiments.

Belief and Christian Faith. The psychology of belief offers a different explanation for parapsychology. Adherents tend also to accept unlikely, extrascientific phenomena such as the Bigfoot legends, the Loch Ness monster, UFOs, and Bermuda triangle mysteries. Little research has studied the functions and causes of such belief systems, but many people seem strongly inclined to believe in the psychic. Psychologists arranged for a magic demonstration in several California university classes, explicitly warning students that the performer "does not really have psychic abilities, and what you'll be seeing are really only tricks" (Benassi, Singer, & Reynolds, 1980, p. 338). When questioned about the performance, 58% of the students called it psychic, and only 33% considered it mere magic.

Religious believers tend to believe the nonmaterial claims of parapsychology also, sometimes even citing them as objective evidence for God and the spiritual realm. Rhine left ministerial study because psychology provided no basis for free will; he hoped parapsychology would give evidence for a transcendent aspect of human nature. On the other hand, some Christians reject the psychic realm as blasphemy (Bowles & Hynds, 1978). The Jewish prophetic tradition had roots in the clairvoyant seer (1 Sam. 9:6–9). Jesus himself, being also the omniscient God, seems frequently to have had clairvoyant or telepathic insights into people's lives (Matt. 9:4; John 1:48; 4:17–18). The miracles have psychokinetic implications. However, the practice of sorcery—seeking answers or affecting events by psychic means—was condemned in Old and New Testaments (Lev. 20:6; Deut. 18:10–11; Acts 19:18–19).

Pursuit of the psychic poses dangers for Christians. While psychic evidences may reinforce belief in the nonmaterial, actively "seeking a sign" implies that religious faith needs outside support. Parapsychology claims a degree of technology and truth held by science itself. If psychic claims are eventually falsified by empirical research, religious faith that depends on them will be unnecessarily undermined. On the other hand, if nonmaterial psi were accorded scientific status, religion might be reduced to technology, not a matter of faith. More significantly, focus on the psychic (whether miracle or illusion) courts triviality in religion. When people revel in the marvelous, they may abandon "the search for truth by other more orthodox and more strenuous and more profitable means, calling for a measure of self-discipline" (Moore, 1977, p. 116).

Even though we may remain skeptical about psi, Christians might be humbly open to the claims of parapsychology. After all, our relationship with God implies direct knowledge through nonsensory means; our claim for prayer power implies faith in spiritual effects on the real world (the first law of thermodynamics notwithstanding). However, attempts to prove the nonmaterial or resting our faith on statistical experiments is a poor substitute for faith in God through Christ Jesus.

References
Benassi, V. A., Singer, B., & Reynolds, C. B. Occult belief: Seeing is believing. *Journal for the Scientific Study of Religion*, 1980, *19*, 337–349.
Bowles, N., & Hynds, F. *Psi search*. San Francisco: Harper & Row, 1978.
Christopher, M. *ESP, seers & psychics*. New York: Crowell, 1970.
Gardner, M. How not to test a psychic: The great SRI die mystery. *The Skeptical Inquirer*, Winter 1982–83, 7(2), 33–39.
Hansel, C. E. M. *ESP: A scientific evaluation*. New York: Scribner's, 1966.
Moore, E. G. *Try the spirits: Christianity and psychical research*. New York: Oxford University Press, 1977.
Reber, A. S. On the paranormal: In defense of skepticism. *The Skeptical Inquirer*, Winter 1982–83, 7(2), 55–64.

R. D. KAHOE

Parataxic Distortion. A concept introduced by H. S. Sullivan to refer to distortion in interpersonal perception that is based on an identification of a person with someone from one's past. Although roughly equivalent to Freud's concept of transference, it is a slightly broader term. Sullivan did not agree with Freud that we are bound to repeat our reactions to early significant people by transferring these attitudes to others. Rather, he felt that one develops ways of coping with those people and then tends to apply these same ways in later relationships. Sullivan felt, however, that this results in distortions in our perception of later significant people. The way we learn what is true and what is parataxic in our thinking about others is to compare our evaluations with those of others. Sullivan referred to this process of consensual validation as the syntaxic mode of communication. He regarded it as a mature mode of relating and contrasted it to the more immature parataxic mode.

D. G. BENNER

See TRANSFERENCE.

Paraverbal Therapy. A form of therapy developed by Evelyn Phillips Heimlich in her work with children suffering from communication disorders. Heimlich found that she could use music, art, and dance as a way of reaching children who would not normally respond to traditional verbal therapies. These media are used alongside verbal therapy with the goal of helping the child to communicate and become more emotionally expressive. Paraverbal therapy serves the purpose of moving the child into conventional treatment and building a therapeutic alliance between the child and therapist. It also offers an opportunity for observational diagnosis. Paraverbal therapy goes beyond music therapy, in which the goal is temporary alleviation of symptoms—although this also occurs in paraverbal therapy.

Paraverbal therapy is based on psychiatric principles, and has been found to be useful in helping children who are autistic, withdrawn, disabled, hyperactive, or suffering from a language disorder. It is not the treatment of choice for patients who could respond to traditional psychiatric therapies.

In practice paraverbal therapy uses eight types of activities which the child and therapist perform together. These activities may include the use of speech cadences, singing improvised or familiar melodies and lyrics, or projective use of psychomotor activities such as mime, dramatizations, or art. No activity is longer than three minutes in duration, and the therapist switches from one activity to another in accordance with the child's behavioral cues of restlessness, boredom, or anxiety.

D. S. McCULLOCH

Parentification. The term used by family therapists to refer to the phenomenon in some pathogenic families of parents who reverse roles with one or more of their children. In such cases the parent is usually uncomfortable with the dependence of the child, and the child is not only treated as an adult but is expected to care for the infantile parent. Sometimes such parents attempt to justify their abdication of parental responsibilities under the guise of permissiveness or being democratic or nonauthoritarian.

Parentification may be direct and obviously pathological, as when one of the parents is explicitly allied with a child against the mate or when the parents turn to a child to settle their arguments. Such blurring or denial of generational boundaries always has negative consequences on the psychological development of the child. However, the phenomenon is more and more manifest today when one parent deserts the family, forcing a child to fill the parent role. The consequences of this sort of situation are not necessarily pathological. They are, however, always present, and need to be more clearly understood.

D. G. BENNER

See STRUCTURAL FAMILY THERAPY; FAMILY SYSTEMS THEORY.

Parenting. *See* MOTHERING; FATHERING.

Parent Training Programs. For the simplest jobs today people get training, yet too many become parents without any training. The child tends to be raised the way parents were, even when they did not like it. Many try to improve upon the model provided by their own parents by reading the available books, which range from excellent to outright damaging. Others, more cautious, hire a qualified person as consultant or join a parent training program. There are hundreds of such programs. Some of them have gained a broad acceptance among parents, educators, and professionals.

Representative Examples.

The Parent Involvement Program is based on Glaser's (1965) views. The parents are urged to become more involved with the children in an honest, warm, and personal relationship, mainly through conversation and mutual interests. The children are considered responsible for their behaviors because they can make choices. Feelings are not ignored, yet the main focus is on behavior. The children are asked to look at themselves and see whether their behaviors are constructive; then they are helped to establish realistic goals for responsible behaviors and to make a commitment. Excuses for failing to fulfill the plan are not accepted, but the children can revise the plan or try it again following a commitment renewal. Parents are urged to be nonjudgmental and nonpunitive. If needed, logical consequences can be applied, but the main focus is on praise for success.

Responsive Parent Training (Willis, Crowder & Willis, 1976) instructs parents in the behavioristic methods of recording the children's behaviors and establishing a base line. Desired behaviors are reinforced and undesirable ones are extinguished by ignoring them, using deprivation of reinforcers, or through overcorrection (e.g., repairing the damage the misbehavior has produced). The program strongly recommends the use of reinforcement over punishment. Even when punishment is used, it has to be paired with reinforcement as soon as the positive behavior occurs.

Parent Effectiveness Training (Gordon, 1970) stems from a humanistic philosophy and focuses mainly on communication. It teaches parents how to interact with children at a feeling level and keep the communication flowing. Roadblocks to communication such as advising, blaming, shaming, etc., are avoided. Parents are trained to detect who owns the problem and act accordingly. If the parents own the problem (even though the children may have caused it), an I-message has the best chance of bringing about changes in the problem-causing behavior. The I-message is a non-blaming message describing the feeling of the sender, the behavior that produced it, and the causal relationship between behavior and feeling. By not arousing defensiveness, anger, and resentment, such a message keeps the communication open and stimulates children to do something about the situation.

When the children own the problem, parents reflect back what they suspect to be the children's feelings. Being correct is not essential. Important is that in this way the parents communicate interest and care.

When both parents and children own the problem, there is a conflict. The no-lose method of conflict resolution is then recommended. There are several steps in this method. The conflict is defined; as many solutions as possible are generated in a non-evaluative way; the solution that seems the closest to satisfying both sides' needs is chosen; decisions are made about implementation, including consequences for failure to adhere to the decision; the outcome is evaluated and, if needed, a new solution is chosen and implemented. When the no-lose method fails, there may be a value conflict. While Parent Effectiveness Training accepts value teaching, it is against imposing the parental values on children. The children may keep their values, yet they may not act them out in a way that creates problems for parents.

The Adlerian parent training programs (Dreikurs & Soltz, 1964; Corsini & Painter, 1975; Dinkmeyer & McKay, 1976) are applied in the parent conferences in schools that adhere to Adlerian Principles, in many Adlerian family education centers, and in the Systematic Training for Effective Parenting training centers.

A misbehaving child is considered to be a discouraged child. The misbehavior has four possible goals: to get attention, to win a power struggle, to revenge, or to express inadequacy. The parents should encourage more constructive behaviors by working toward the development of the 4Rs: responsibility, respect, responsiveness, and resourcefulness. For this the children must be encouraged by being trusted with responsibilities and realistic expectations and being allowed to make decisions. Weekly family councils, democratically run, are convened to discuss the problems and make decisions. Misbehaviors are corrected by allowing natural consequences to occur. When there are no such consequences or when they are dangerous, logical consequences can be set.

An important part of the Adlerian programs are the parents' study groups. These provide a deeper understanding of the child-rearing principles and a prolonged contact for exchange of information and for encouragement.

Summary and Evaluation. All of these four representative parent training programs are from a Christian point of view very useful tools. They can be easily complemented with the teaching of Christian spirituality, values, and ethics based on love and respect for God and neighbor.

The Parent Involvement Program, by emphasizing warm relationships and responsibility, sets itself within the scriptural framework. Although broader than the behavioristic program, it still falls short of approaching children as whole persons.

The Responsive Parent Training program agrees with the Bible in the use of reward and punishment. However, the view that the affective and cognitive aspects are products of conditioning is unnecessarily reductionistic. It also eliminates or reduces the child's responsibility in this area. The program works best with very young children, but even there it benefits from being supplemented for a more holistic approach.

Parent Effectiveness Training is an excellent program in the area of establishing communication and improving relationships—important areas for Christians. Issue may be taken with the reluctance to teach values. However the approach has been successfully used in churches, and the Lutheran Church's Concordia Press has published an edition of Gordon's *Parent Effectiveness Training* with biblical quotations added.

The Adlerian parent training programs are complex and flexible, and they teach parents to prepare children to face real life. Responsibility, respect, resourcefulness, and responsiveness are highly valued by Christianity. The Corsini (1977) article on individual education has been adopted in several Christian schools, and clergymen are frequently involved in Systematic Training for Effective Parenting programs and in family education centers.

References

Corsini, R. J. Individual education. *Journal of Individual Psychology*, 1977, *33*(2a), 292–418.
Corsini, R. J., & Painter, G. *The practical parent.* New York: Harper & Row, 1975
Dinkmeyer, D., & McKay, G. *Systematic training for effective parenting (STEP).* Circle Pines, Minn.: American Guidance Service, 1976.

Dreikurs, R., & Soltz, V. *Children: The challenge.* New York: Hawthorn, 1964.
Glasser, W. *Reality therapy.* New York: Harper & Row, 1965.
Gordon, T. *Parent effectiveness training.* New York: Wyden, 1970.
Willis, J. W., Crowder, J., & Willis, J. *Guiding the psychological and educational growth of children.* Springfield, Ill.: Thomas, 1976.

D. Motet

Parergasia. A combination of an impulse to perform an act and a mismatched action corresponding to the impulse. For example, a person desiring to get up and eat something is interrupted by cross impulses before he takes the first step. Instead of getting something to eat, another impulse will suggest getting dressed, and that wish will be interrupted by another cross impulse. At times the individual is rendered totally inactive, not knowing what to do. Parergasia is characterized by deep regression, an abandonment of reality, and hallucinations and delusions. It is a characteristic of schizophrenia.

D. L. Schuurman

Passive-Aggressive Personality Disorder.
This term describes a person who expresses an underlying aggressiveness in a passive way in both social relationships and occupational activities. For this diagnosis to be made, a pervasive and persistent pattern must be demonstrated, serious enough to disturb efficiency at work and to make relationships difficult. In addition, it should be shown that this particular choice of symptoms was made when more direct expressions of hostility were available.

The typical patient dawdles, procrastinates, forgets, and obstructs in a quiet manner while denying that this behavior is intentionally oppositional. By negativism, disinterest, pessimism, and sullenness these persons manage to stubbornly obstruct the intent of others around them. While the behavior is obvious enough to produce a hostile response from those around them, the persons themselves seem unaware either of the nature of their behavior or the fact that it has been responsible for the antagonism they meet in their daily lives.

The consensus seems to be that passive-aggressive pathology is an immature expression of resentment toward excessive dependency. As such it is the same as the oppositional disorder of childhood. In *DSM-III* the only distinction made between the two is age, the demarcating age being 18 years. This combination of marked dependency and hostility toward that dependency is almost universal in adolescence and also in all serious psychopathology. From this one might assume that the underlying conflict itself does not incline a patient toward a passive expression. This would then raise the question as to whether passivity in the face of anger is not more a quality related to temperament than a distinct disease.

This category has been used more frequently in the past than currently, with an incidence in older literature of about 3% of patients seen in mental health facilities and perhaps 20–30% of those with personality disorders. The usefulness of the category will in all probability decrease, and eventually it may be eliminated, despite the frequency of this method of expressing hostility by psychologically disturbed people.

One reason for the decline is that the aggressive component is usually not acknowledged by the patient, and so depends on the clinical impression of the observer. Objective and statistical demonstration is difficult if not impossible. Again, newer categories now more frequently used would describe many of those previously called passive-aggressive. Currently almost nothing is being written about this disorder.

If one looks critically at the patients studied in the few extant publications on this category (e.g., Small, Small, Alig, & Moore, 1970; Whitman, Trosman, & Koenig, 1954), it is clear that many of these would today be classified as antisocial, borderline, or narcissistic personality disorders. The last two of these options were not available in the taxonomy used in these studies. One might assume that the inclusion of the passive-aggressive personality disorder in *DSM-III* represents only an acknowledgement of the historical importance of the term. In the future one might hope that the term would be limited to the name of a symptom rather than a disease category.

References

Small, I. F., Small, J. G., Alig, V. B., & Moore, D. F. Passive-aggressive personality disorder: A search for a syndrome. *American Journal of Psychiatry,* 1970, *126*, 973–983.
Whitman, R. M., Trosman, H., & Koenig, R. Clinical assessment of passive-aggressive personality. *Archives of Neurology and Psychiatry,* 1954, *72*, 540–549.
C. M. BERRY

See PERSONALITY DISORDERS.

Passive-Ambivalent Personality Pattern.

One of the eight basic personality patterns of Millon's (1969) typology. It is the pattern that most closely aligns with the *DSM-III* diagnosis of a compulsive personality disorder. Such individuals are characterized by restricted affect in terms of emotional control; narrow-mindedness; perfectionistic and meticulous behavior; overconscientious self-image, including a legalistic adherence to institutional, national, or religous absolutes; and an ingratiating manner toward superiors.

The qualities possessed by these individuals are often viewed positively. Their trustworthiness, seriousness, fastidiousness, and their general attitude of toeing the line often make them appreciated. At other times they are simply seen as being rigid, picayune, and lacking any real depth of personality.

This pattern of rigidity and respect for authority is a lifelong habit that clearly developed out of the way they were raised. Their behavior was closely monitored by their parents, and they were specifically punished for trangressions of rules and possibly for frivolous or childlike behavior. The main emphasis in the discipline of such children was on punishing negative action, with little emphasis on reward for good behavior since this was expected. As a defense these individuals develop pseudomaturity and become very conscientious and serious-minded children. The clearly defined rules are quickly internalized, and they develop harsh superegos. They are so fearful of punishment that the mere thought of inappropriate behavior stirs up tremendous guilt feelings. Clearly these people are least anxious in environments where expected behaviors are essentially black and white.

These individuals are resistant to change and new ideas. They are also threatened by having to make decisions, since this process involves an element of uncertainty about what can be expected. The conforming personality pattern is thus self-perpetuating in nature. These people take great strides to keep the status quo, which also assures that their personalities will not change.

Psychodynamically these individuals have unconsciously repressed a great deal of hostility and aggression toward the very legalisms and authorities to which they dutifully and outwardly conform. These feelings, which are the most threatening, are defended against in a way that supports the individuals adhering to a life style they unconsciously detest.

A life style built around conformity does not allow for the development of a rich individual personality. These persons devalue individual qualities having to do with feelings, reflectiveness, and insight. They have little use for therapy, and do not enter it unless, in struggling to maintain their conforming life style while repressing their unconscious desires, they develop stress-related disorders or become psychosomatic. Prognosis for changing such long-standing patterns is generally poor. The defense mechanisms that maintain this style and allow them to generally function at an adaptive level tend to be numerous, sophisticated, and elaborate. Attempting to decrease their anxiety level within a short-term and concrete modality is probably the best strategy for treating these individuals.

Reference
Millon, T. *Modern psychopathology*. Philadelphia: Saunders, 1969.

D. S. McCulloch

See Compulsive Personality Disorder; Personality Disorders.

Passive-Dependent Personality Pattern.

One of the eight basic personality patterns of Millon's (1969) typology. Often called the submissive personality, it describes people who allow the majority of the responsibilities, decisions, competitions, and psychological needs of daily life to be assumed by others in return for feelings of acceptance or belonging.

A recognizable clinical picture can be shown for this personality pattern. Insecurity and a general lack of self-confidence are noticeable in the speech, posture, and behavior of these persons. They do not assert themselves either physically or socially, and they avoid engaging in new or stimulating activities. On the surface, because of their desire to please others, these people give an impression of being humble, warm, or thoughtful, but underneath they are anxiously in need of approval and acceptance. Under stress they may exhibit overt signs of clinging and helplessness. Their mood is often one of depression or pessimism.

Passive-dependent individuals maintain their extremely poor self-images by continually belittling themselves, magnifying the slightest failures, and blaming themselves for things over which they have no real control. They constantly minimize their own abilities and point out their inferiorities. This behavior is meant to elicit from others statements to the contrary. Once praise is forthcoming, or they are unburdened of their responsibilities, they feel guilty and undeserving of such treatment.

Usually two major factors in the history and development of these people are parental smothering and failures in competition with siblings or peers. These people cope fairly well

in life as long as they have strong partners who will supply their dependency needs and who will not grow tried of their incessant demands for reassurance that they are loved. If they enter treatment, directive or behavioral therapy to help develop the competency skills needed for self-individuation and increased self-esteem are often useful. Medication to elevate depressed moods and group therapy have also been recommended.

Reference
Millon, T. *Modern psychopathology*. Philadelphia: Saunders, 1969.

D. S. McCulloch

See Dependent Personality Disorder; Personality Disorders.

Passive-Detached Personality Pattern.

One of the eight basic personality patterns of Millon's (1969) typology. It describes persons who are quite indifferent and strikingly impervious to human contact. Seen in every walk of life, they appear untroubled and indifferent. They seem to function adequately but are described by their associates as rather colorless, shy, isolated, and lacking in need to communicate with or relate affectionately to others (Millon, 1981).

This inability to participate in normal give-and-take relationships is the most striking aspect of passive-detached persons. Their verbal expression is perfunctory, impersonal, and formal. They do not socialize in the milieu of work or in normal social groups. They are as emotionally impervious as they are cognitively askew to reality. Events that normally provoke anger, joy, or sadness seem to leave passive-detached individuals unmoved. When they do become involved with the outside world, it is likely to be in low-energy, mental, highly circumscribed ways—e.g., electronics, needlepoint, television watching; nothing interactive, energetic, or ambiguous.

This pattern might be seen as "the noble individualist," except that the isolation from the world is so complete and the failure to learn cognitive and affective coping strategies is so severe that passive-detached persons have little chance for anything other than decompensation as they traverse the life cycle with its normal demands and stresses. They are in sort of a developmentally imposed sensory deprivation condition and fall prey to all the hazards of distorted reality resulting from this condition. If intruded upon by social demands, they may explode with psychotic, fearful, delusional symptoms. If overly protected and understimulated, they may describe themselves as feeling empty, fearfully empty.

The range of speculation on etiology and pathogenesis is very broad. Their sluggish responsivity suggests abnormalities in inherited neural physiology and autonomic-endocrine balance, neurotransmitter disturbances (especially in the cholinergic or parasympathetic system), or nutritional abnormalities (low energy, ectomorphic build, etc.). These biological theories await experimental verification and must therefore be seen as quite speculative.

Unfortunately, developmental and learning history research is also highly speculative. These theories hypothesize a lack of stimulation (cognitive, emotional or perceptual) provided by the infant's caretakers. It is unclear whether constitutionally unresponsive infants elicit little reaction from their environments, or whether distant, rigid parents provide such an impersonal and unaffectionate atmosphere that the infants develop little experience with the world and others. Well-designed research in this area is greatly needed.

Treatment prognosis for passive-detached persons is poor, given their paucity of coping strategies and the increasing delusional dangers encountered in such an isolated existence. Their vagueness, their impoverished thought and feeling, and their tendency to imperviously float along, skimming the surface of interpersonal phenomena, make them incapable of even the most elementary level of insight or affect-oriented therapy.

There are a few treatment strategies with significant promise. A slow, supportive strategy is advised as a low-threat means of providing a positive interpersonal experience. Behavior modification and social learning techniques may help increase social skills to a point that the passive-detached person may experience rewards from some social contact. Once some social reward is perceived, a low-demand group therapy approach may help the person generalize these social skills. Vocational counseling may also be a helpful adjunct, as may psychotropic medication. At the more normal level of functioning, stimulants are sometimes suggested, with the caution that lowering the experiencing threshold may be frightening for the previously impervious passive-detached personality.

References

Millon, T. *Modern psychopathology*. Philadelphia: Saunders, 1969.

Millon, T. *Disorders of personality—DSM III: Axis II*. New York: Wiley, 1981.

B. E. BONECUTTER

See PERSONALITY DISORDERS.

Passive-Independent Personality Pattern.

One of Millon's (1969) eight basic personality patterns. Often called the narcissistic personality, it describes those people who possess an unusually high sense of self-esteem, personal worth, and superiority, enabling them to have all their psychological needs met within themselves. This exaggerated self-evaluation is usually not fully confirmed by objective reality.

A general clinical picture can be shown for the passive-independent personality. Confidence, calm self-satisfaction, and an air of superiority mark the social behaviors of these persons. They appear untroubled by the minor irritations of life since the mundane concerns of life are beneath their consideration. Their mood is often bright, carefree, and optimistic. Passive-independent persons seem unaware of the implicit societal rules for reciprocity in interpersonal relationships. On the basis of their very existence they expect the world and personal relations to gratify their desires, with nothing in return. At times their confidence and optimistic expectations allow these beliefs to be confirmed and rewarded by others, but at other times they are viewed as conceited, arrogant, and snobbish. The passive-independent personality does not understand this latter view.

Millon hypothesizes that early in life the passive-independent person was overindulged by his parents. He was an exceptional child, often an only child, whose life was blissful because all his needs were always met on demand, and he came to expect this pattern as normative. He also developed cognitive functioning that was prone to fantasy and projection. Whenever reality threatened to undo his perfect view of himself, he withdrew into his own imagination or developed rationalizations to excuse his faulty behavior. He protected himself by blaming, faultfinding, and belittling the weaknesses of others. This tended to further alienate him from others and diminish the opportunity for interactions needed to view himself in a more realistic light.

These people do not view themselves as having faults, so they are unlikely to enter therapy unless there is a crisis. Either short-term supportive therapy or long-term, insight-oriented therapy is indicated for the passive-independent personality.

Reference
Millon, T. *Modern psychopathology*. Philadelphia: Saunders, 1969.

D. S. McCulloch

See Narcissistic Personality Disorder; Personality Disorders.

Pastoral Counseling. Relatively new in its modern form but not in its purpose, the care and cure of souls is as old as the believing community itself.

The beginning of the modern pastoral counseling emphasis is identified with men such as Anton T. Boisen, who himself was hospitalized three different times for short-lived but acute mental problems. In 1925 Boisen, who was chaplain at Worcester State Hospital, Massachusetts, began bringing theological students into the hospital for three months of study and work. He viewed the pastor's study of "living human documents" as superior to academic research alone. Having been a patient himself, he realized the necessity of the helper understanding the plight of the one he attempts to help, and he saw how quickly medical trainees could gain knowledge for their task by being involved with patients. Thus the clinical pastoral education movement began with a medical model. Boisen's work gave rise in 1930 to the Council for Clinical Training, and his methods soon became part of the curriculum of many seminaries. (*See* Association for Clinical Pastoral Education.)

Other pioneers in the field include Russell L. Dicks, chaplain, and Richard C. Cabot, chief of staff, at the Massachusetts General Hospital. Dicks's personal experience with hospitalization and surgery gave him added sensitivity to human needs. He describes his struggle with pain; his personal doubts, apprehensions, and fears; the horror of the anesthetic; the confusion of hospital routine; the different attitudes of various doctors and nurses; and the effect this all had on him. Also in the pioneering forefront of the contemporary developments in pastoral counseling are Carroll A. Wise, Seward Hiltner, Paul Johnson, Wayne E. Oates, and Charles Holman. In Great Britain, Leslie Weatherhead was a major figure in pastoral care and pastoral applications of psychology. By 1935 he had established a clinic at the City Temple, London, for those needing psychiatric treatment as well as pastoral help.

Basic Functions and Formative Concepts.
Clebsch and Jaekle (1964) have identified four pastoral care functions from the pages of church history: 1) healing—"a pastoral function that aims to overcome some impairment by restoring the person to wholeness and by helping him to advance beyond his previous condition"; 2) sustaining—"helping a hurting person to endure and to transcend a circumstance in which restoration to his former condition or recuperation from his malady is either impossible or so remote as to seem improbable"; 3) guiding—"assisting perplexed persons to make confident choices between alternative courses of thought and action, when such choices are viewed as affecting the present and future state of the soul"; 4) reconciling—seeking "to reestablish broken relationships between man and fellow man and between man and God" (p. 33).

These functions were shaped by four germinal ideas that were influential in the 1940s and 50s during the formative period of contemporary pastoral counseling (Clinebell, 1966). The first of these was the formal structured counseling interview coming directly from the psychotherapeutic interview (i.e., appointments, definite time limits, a private meeting place with the label "counseling" attached).

Second, the client-centered, or person-centered, method was seen as the normative and often exclusive methodology. Based on the work of psychotherapist Carl R. Rogers, it holds that each person has the capacity to understand himself and his problems and initiate change in the direction of psychological growth and maturity, providing he is treated as a person of worth. The counselor's function is to assume, insofar as he is able, the internal frame of reference of the client and to communicate this empathic understanding to the client. It is an attitude of complete willingness on the part of the therapist to have the center of evaluation and responsibility remain with the client. The counselor's role stresses attitudes and ways of relating rather than techniques. The assumption is that the creation of a climate of warmth, understanding, and freedom from attack will enable the client to drop his defensiveness and explore and reorganize his life style (Rogers & Becker, 1952). This approach is nondirective, with the greatest emphasis being placed on listening.

Third, new insight was viewed as the central goal of counseling. This emphasis represented a giant advance over the advice-giving or merely problem-solving approaches. Finally, the interlocking concepts of unconscious factors in the motivation of behavior and the childhood roots of adult behavior were both accepted as major influences in personality. Man was seen as not totally the master of his psyche. The more emotionally disturbed a person is, the more pervasive the domination of his behavior by unconscious impulses, conflicts, and repressed memories. The genetic emphasis held that present behavior could be understood only by exploring the complexities of a person's early relationships with the need-satisfying adults in his life. These relationships shaped the individual's basic personality structure and profoundly influenced all his relationships, including his relationship to God.

Uniqueness. While psychotherapists look primarily to the healing forces of life within their patients for recovery, pastoral counselors depend on the power of God present in the midst of life for constructive changes (Brister, 1964). All healing forces are seen as God-given; and unless these are released within the person and his relationships, there will be no healing. The counselor is simply a catalyst in a process which he does not create but which he has learned to facilitate. The pastoral counselor's effectiveness depends on an awareness that healing and growth take place through the relationship rather than as a result of psychological cleverness.

Oates (1962) describes pastoral counseling as being more than simply focusing on specific problems that must be solved. It certainly includes problem solving, but even this takes place either implicitly or explicitly within the commonwealth of eternal life as it is known in Jesus Christ. Our past experience, our present needs, and our future destiny all come into focus in the pastoral conversation. The essence of pastoral counseling is to make the Christian faith effective in the lives of people.

Genuine acceptance is essential in effective counseling. Only when love (*agape*) is experienced will growth occur. Accepting the person is not synonymous with accepting irresponsible behavior. A pastoral counselor's accepting love implies, not ethical indifference, but discriminating awareness of human sin, divine judgment, and the need for the mercy, grace, and love of God.

Acceptance or rejection is communicated both verbally and nonverbally in attitudes, voice tones, and facial expressions. The counseling interview will be influenced greatly by the presence of kindness or sternness, sincerity or superficiality, perceptivity or dullness regarding the person's situation. The person who experiences acceptance from his counselor can express his feelings of helplessness, admit his anxiety or hostility, confess his sin, offer his prayer for divine wisdom, and be assured all the while that he is not alone in his struggle.

The pastoral counselor recognizes the physical, spiritual, emotional, and intellectual dimensions of human life as interrelated parts of the whole of personality. Each affects all.

One of the most distinctive elements of pastoral counseling is its theological base. Pastoral counseling is not limited to scientific knowledge for its understanding of persons but brings a perspective that science alone cannot provide. This perspective is derived from the rich heritage of biblical revelation and the Judeo-Christian tradition, which presents clearly the nature of God (the infinite personal God whose character is revealed as love, righteousness, and truth, Exod. 34:6–7); the nature of human beings (created in the image of God with significance and freedom and by willful choice guilty of sin—rebellion acted out in attempting to live apart from God, Gen. 1–3); the nature of the world (God's handiwork that has been affected by man's fall, Gen. 3); and the redemptive drama (God's promise fulfilled in Christ, who "hath borne our griefs and carried our sorrows" and given us his gracious gift of love, forgiveness, reconciliation, and deliverance, Isa. 53:4; Eph. 2:13–16). These are but a few of the theological perspectives that inform the pastoral counselor.

The pastoral counselor seeks guidance from the Scriptures but does not use them or other religious resources in a mechanical or legalistic fashion. This would result in the exchanging of one form of bondage for another. The very essence of these resources is the dynamic interchange (relationship) between God and the pastoral counselor and between the counselor and the people of God. It is God who works (directly and indirectly through other people) through prayer, Scripture, and other religious experiences and through counseling relationships and procedures to bring wholeness. The pastoral counselor is Christ's representative, who enables a person to sense the caring presence of God and to trust him, which is the essence of the Christian life.

Pastoral counseling aids in discovering one's identity. People must tell their own stories if they are to discover themselves and understand their own history, handicaps, emotions, and gifts. A second, deeper look at life, beyond the primary experience of living it, gives people a perspective on its passages, perils, and privileges. The counselee is a learner who narrates his story to a teacher sent from God, who in turn interprets and assists the counselee in gaining meaning from experience. One's identity and destiny are thus linked to a community of promise, expectancy, and fulfillment.

The pastoral counselor has unique resources available for dealing with human brokenness and guilt. True guilt comes because one has violated God's moral law, the greatest of which is to love God with our whole being and our neighbor as ourself. False guilt or neurotic guilt comes from feelings of inferiority, projected rejection of oneself by others, or from a supersensitive conscience that registers all criticism by others as true. The authority inherent in the symbolic role of the pastoral counselor makes him or her uniquely fitted for helping the counselee find forgiveness for true guilt and release from false guilt.

Similarly the pastoral counselor has a unique perspective to bring to the tragedies and sufferings of mankind. Suffering is an undeniable part of the human scene, and will not be permanently avoided by any of us. Yet the difference between Christian faith and unbelief in dealing with suffering is great. The pain and the anxiety may not be lessened, but what becomes of us as we struggle with life's problems will reveal the mystery of a benevolent God who not only uses our suffering to enlarge our capacity for life, but who also participates in our suffering. Suffering can create a fellowship, or an intimacy, that no other experience in life affords, especially an intimacy with God. Nowhere in all the world is the agony and pain that we feel felt as deeply or as keenly as it is in the heart of God, and the promise of the living Christ is never to leave us.

It is this realization that enables us to believe that there is redemptive purpose in our suffering even if we cannot identify or articulate clearly what that purpose is. It helps enormously to know that our suffering is not simply blind happenstance in a cold, impersonal universe.

Goals. The basic goal of pastoral counseling is to put people in touch with God. Life experiences can become so overpowering that unless one can establish a grace/faith relationship with the God who created him and who intervenes in history and in human life, there may be little or no hope. Regardless of how impossible the human equation looks, when God is added to it, hope flourishes.

The pastoral counselor knows from biblical revelation that God in his infinite wisdom, purpose, and love acts uniquely in each person's experience. Sometimes God intervenes in such a way as to rescue us from our difficult situations; at other times he enables us to work through those difficulties and to come out on the other side as better persons. There are also times when he simply enables us to endure a situation that will not change. Thus we can experience his grace as a miraculous deliverance, as a life-changing process, or as the strength to endure. The pastoral counselor does not tell people the particular way God will intervene in any situation, but that God will intervene as one comes to him in faith.

Pastoral counseling also helps one understand and relate properly to himself. The pastoral counselor brings the gift of objectivity along with a perspective of the significance and value of human personality and human life to the counseling process. No person can really know who he is until he understands his origin (created in God's image) and his destiny (the eternal purpose for life and the choice to respond to or resist the claims of God on one's life). The pastoral counselor understands that inherent within Christ's command to love your neighbor as yourself is the mandate for a proper love of one's own self. Christianity affirms life and personal identity and furnishes a genuine basis for self-acceptance and for a healthy egoism.

Pastoral counseling gives balanced attention to both value issues and emotional/interpersonal dynamics. Psychological problems involve value confusions just as frequently as they involve straightforward emotional and interpersonal dynamics. The pastoral counselor works out of a context where clarification and stabilization of value issues are as prominent a factor as any other.

Another goal of pastoral counseling is to improve the quality of one's relationships. In reality a person is as rich or as poor as the quality of his personal relationships. Every maladjusted person is a person who has not made himself known to another human being and in consequence does not know himself; nor can he be himself. More than that, he struggles actively to avoid becoming known by another person. The journey toward wholeness must include healthy relationships.

Pastoral counseling also seeks to help one assume responsibility for himself and to make decisions and commitments courageously. To see oneself as being at the mercy of external circumstances and/or internal urges is to be caught in the psychological posture of a helpless victim. It is true that life confronts us with many circumstances over which we have little or no control, and the same may be true of some inner urges, but as human beings we are far from being helpless victims. We can choose our attitudes and our responses to these pressures and can, by the grace of God, do something redemptive with them.

Yet another goal is to help people learn "burden-bearing" involvement as the means for participating in the process of reconciliation—of healing the wounds of loneliness and grief, and of loving and forgiving in the context of truth and grace. The Christian experience was designed by God to be a community experience.

Pastoral counseling seeks to facilitate growth in the counselee who desires spiritual wisdom and strength for constructive character change. It also seeks to give support to individuals who need to mobilize their resources for life during some crisis. Such support enables persons to work through their pressing problems and not be overcome by them.

In summary, the goal of pastoral counseling is to relate the biblical resources to every human circumstance. Pastoral care is thus viewed as personal and social, preventive and therapeutic, supportive and confrontive. The object of care is nothing less than the person in the full range of his existence. Care does more than operate in crises. Care aids human development and growth and assists in life's transitions as well as in serious spiritual problems.

Methods Employed. Leaders in pastoral counseling are reluctant to identify themselves with any particular method of counseling and generally resist labeling their own approach. The goals listed above show something of the breadth of approaches used. Most attempt to correlate biblical wisdom and psychological insight in an effort to strengthen persons for life, death, and destiny. A disciplined eclecticism that draws on various sources of wisdom in the practice of pastoral counseling is an appropriate model.

The client-centered, or person-centered, approach has helped to rescue pastoral counseling from the overdirectedness of advice giving and has demonstrated the importance of disciplined listening and responding to feelings. But there is a place for the use of one's authority selectively in sustaining, guiding, feeding (emotionally and spiritually), inspiring, confronting, teaching, and encouraging persons to function responsibly in their relationship with God and with others. In the pastoral counselor's interaction with the counselee he will express empathy as he seeks to identify with the counselee. He will invite personal self-disclosure, reflect the counselee's feelings back to him for thought or clarification, affirm what has been said, and help to effect transitions from one pattern of thought to another. When appropriate he will confront the person with Christian truth or with possible consequences of his feelings or plan of action. Finally he will provide support for dealing realistically with the difficulty faced.

A person's guiding values and the resulting behavior should be examined, not just in terms of how one feels about these matters (although this is important), but also how they influence his relationships and sense of worth and what can be done to help one live more constructively.

It is important that the counselor accept his or her own humanity as a rich resource for counseling effectively. Being a real person when encountering others is most essential for establishing a healing relationship. Whatever approach is taken, the pastoral counselor maintains a vision of spiritual wholeness rooted in the promise of the Christian faith.

References

Brister, C. W. *Pastoral care in the church*. New York: Harper & Row, 1964.
Clebsch, W. A., & Jaekle, C. R. *Pastoral care in historical perspective*. Englewood Cliffs, N.J.: Prentice-Hall, 1964.
Clinebell, H. J., Jr. *Basic types of pastoral counseling*. Nashville: Abingdon, 1966.
Oates, W. E. *Protestant pastoral counseling*. Philadelphia: Westminster, 1962.
Rogers, C. R., & Becker, R. J. A basic orientation for counseling. In S. Doniger (Ed.), *The best of Pastoral Psychology*. Great Neck, N.Y.: Pastoral Psychology Press, 1952.

C. DAVIS

Pathocure. The disappearance of a neurosis upon the outbreak of an organic disease. It is seen most often in people who psychodynamically are classified as moral masochists—i.e., individuals for whom suffering pacifies the SUPEREGO and minimizes feelings of GUILT. In such individuals the neurosis represents that suffering but then is replaced by another kind of suffering.

Pathogenesis. A term used to describe the origin and development of diseases and disorders. Other terms used interchangeably include *pathogenesy, pathogeny,* and *nosogenesis.*

Pavlov, Ivan Petrovich (1849–1936). Russian physiologist who developed the concept of the conditioned reflex. Most students become familiar with his work through introductory courses in psychology or learning. However, Pavlov, the son of a poor parish priest, was by training a physiologist, not a psychologist.

Indeed, he is known primarily for his work on the physiology and pathophysiology of the higher parts of the brain. In 1904 he became the first Russian to receive the Nobel Prize for his classical experiments on the regulation of the digestive glands by conditioned reflexes of the nervous system.

After graduating from the University of St. Petersburg, Pavlov spent four years at the Military Medical Academy, where he received his medical degree in 1879. He then spent two years studying with such leading scientists as Emil DuBois-Reymond in France and Johannes Müller, Carl Ludwig, and Hermann von Helmholtz in Germany. For 10 years he worked in S. P. Botkin's physiology laboratory, where he devoted full time to experimental research. He subsequently was appointed professor of pharmacology at the Military Medical Academy of St. Petersburg. In 1891 he was given the responsibility to organize and direct the department of physiology in the new Institute of Experimental Medicine, and he held this position until his death.

An important phase of Pavlov's work grew out of his investigations of digestion. He found that saliva and gastric juices were secreted by dogs not only when food was introduced into their mouths but also when a variety of stimuli appeared. Pavlov initially ignored these effects, but eventually, through systematic study, discovered that nearly any stimulus— sound, sight, or scent—could act as a signal for the same response as did the actual presence of the object being signaled. As he collected additional data and made generalizations, a new science of higher nervous activity took shape. The basis of that science was the division of reflexes into two categories: unconditioned and conditioned. Unconditioned reflexes are inborn responses that are necessary for minimal survival (e.g., reflexes related to nutrition, defense, or reproduction). Conditioned reflexes are the result of experience and enable an animal to adapt to environmental changes throughout the course of its life.

Pavlov further believed that the higher nervous system sorted out signals from the surrounding environment on the basis of reinforcement. If a signal is important to the survival of the organism, it will be reinforced by unconditioned reflex activity.

One outgrowth of Pavlov's work was that scientists began to accept the view that the behavior of an organism could be understood and described in terms of observable and measurable reflexes. Indeed, Pavlov's work had a significant impact on the development of American behaviorism, which saw the conditioned reflex as the basic building block of behavior. To Pavlov we also owe much of our current vocabulary in the field of learning and the formal beginning of the learning methodology known as classical conditioning. This methodology has become the dominant approach in cerebral physiology and pathophysiology as well as in psychiatry and psychotherapy in the Soviet Union and other socialistic countries. Classical conditioning also continues to be a familiar research topic in the psychology of learning.

S. R. OSBORNE

See CONDITIONING, CLASSICAL.

Peak Experiences. Personal moments of great happiness and joy, a concept developed by Maslow. In the 1950s and 1960s Maslow set forth his idea that the study of exceptionally healthy and mature individuals would give psychologists a more complete understanding of human nature. Behaviorism's penchant for reductionism and the Freudian stress on psychopathology resulted in a view of human beings that tended to neglect their positive and higher aspects. Maslow and other humanistic psychologists studied examples of psychologically healthy people, those rare self-actualized individuals who make full use of their potential and who are most wholly and fully human. It was found that these exceptional people typically were creative, spontaneous, independent, accepting of themselves and others, and that most of them had at some time experienced ego-transcendent or mystical experiences.

Maslow (1968) defined these very personal occasions as "peak" experiences. This very broad definition allowed for a wide range of experiences. However, through analyzing a number of personal reports Maslow was able to list 19 characteristics of peak experiences. This led him to conclude that peak experiences comprise a special type of cognition that he called cognition of being, or "B-cognition." Furthermore, he felt that B-cognition is a manifestation of "Being-love," which is a nonpossessive love for the other that is undistorted by the lover's own needs and deficiencies. Thus, for Maslow a peak experience is an intense transitory experience of Being-love in which one suddenly transcends the usual limits of one's identity to perceive the world as it truly is; an integrated and unified whole, full of truth, goodness, and beauty.

Typically this experience involves feelings

of ecstasy, awe, and a loss of fear, anxiety, and inhibition. During peak experiences an individual may lose track of time and place as he gets caught up in the rapture of the immediate present. His attitude is one of passive and receptive attention rather than active and forced vigilance. While in this mode of complete absorption a person is able to give full attention to an object, and his perceptual experiencing is much the richer for it. The peak experience is felt as self-validating and self-justifying. It is an end in itself, and many people state that attempts to justify it only take away from its dignity and worth. Often during the peak experience dichotomies, polarities, and conflicts are viewed from a radically different vantage point that enables them to be transcended or resolved. However, many individuals find great difficulty in describing their peak experiences, as language seems too inadequate a vehicle for such a powerfully profound and personal event.

Maslow and others describe the aftereffects of peak experiences as therapeutically beneficial. They believe that once a person is exposed to the beauty, goodness, and truth inherent in a peak experience, he or she will feel more positive about life as a whole. Some research has shown that peak experiences do indeed result in a better self-concept and a greater capacity for creativity, spontaneity, and expressiveness. Moreover, Maslow notes that in some cases neurotic symptoms have been cured in the wake of a peak experience.

At first Maslow thought that peak experiences were the province of only a chosen few. However, as his research developed, he and his colleagues agreed that many people have peak episodes but are reluctant to acknowledge them. Part of the difficulty in studying peak experiences is in choosing the terms in which to describe them meaningfully. Maslow himself says that his concept of peak experiences is very similar to what are commonly known as religious or mystical experiences. In *The Varieties of Religious Experience* James noted four characteristics of mystical experience—a sense of profound understanding, ineffability, transiency, and passivity—which are also common to peak experiences. Maurice Bucke's term "cosmic consciousness" is descriptive of peak experiences, and Carl Rogers's concept of "fully functioning" in a therapeutic context includes the characteristics of peak experiences that Maslow listed. Even Freud, who was an atheist, acknowledged these religious experiences, but he described them as "oceanic feeling," in which one regresses back to a

period when the ego believed itself to be omnipotent.

Thus it can be clearly seen that Maslow's peak experience lies at the interface of the disciplines of psychology and theology and is subject to many of the debates between the two fields of inquiry. A major issue is the perennial philosophical argument over the validity of mystical experience in finding truth about God and his creation. Faith seems to have both rational and nonrational components, and history has shown that personal subjective experience must be tempered by a more objective form of revelation, especially as this is found in church tradition and God's word. For example, many Christians would not accept as ultimate truth the idealized picture of the world which so often results from peak experiences, a world that is never seen as evil or chaotic.

Another important point is whether or not peak experiences are in the long run beneficial both psychologically and spiritually. While these experiences may be the hallmark of a healthy and self-actualized person, it does not necessarily follow that the forced production of peak experiences will bring about psychological health to those in need. In 1962 Maslow stated that the peak experience happens to people and cannot be generated on command. However, later Maslow (1970) felt compelled to warn that the trend toward a compulsive searching for triggers to peak experiences could result in a selfish and evil attitude toward others and a vicious circle of subjectivity that could further lead to superstition and involvement in the occult. Maslow's concept of peak experiences has however, helped to reacquaint psychology with realms of personal subjective experience that could be empirically studied.

References

Maslow, A. *Toward a psychology of being* (2nd ed.). Princeton, N.J.: Van Nostrand, 1968.
Maslow, A. *Religions, values, and peak-experiences.* New York: Viking Press, 1970.

W. C. Drew

See Consciousness; Humanistic Psychology; Maslow, Abraham Harold.

Pedophilia. Sexual activity, actual or fantasized, with prepubescent children. For the pedophiliac the preferred or exclusive method of achieving sexual arousal is with children. Most incidents are initiated by adult males who are known to the child personally.

If the offender is an adult, the child must be at least 10 years younger. In the case of an adolescent offender no age difference is specified. In general the younger the victim, the more profound the pedophiliac tendencies in the adult and the more the offender fits the diagnosis of pedophiliac.

The heterosexually oriented pedophiliac tends to prefer 8- to 10-year-old girls. Sexual acts involve fondling and exhibiting genitals. Orgasm is sought by only 6% of the offenders. The homosexual pedophiliac more often tries to attain orgasm with the child through masturbation, fellatio, or anal intercourse. Orgasm is sought by 50% of the homosexual pedophiliacs, who prefer slightly older children. The condition in the homosexual pedophiliac tends to be chronic. The recidivism rate is second only to exhibitionism and ranges from 13 to 28%.

Pedophilia occurs over the entire age range of adulthood, with the peak in middle age. The younger pedophiliac is usually psychosexually and socially immature. The middle-aged pedophiliac tends to be maladjusted and have severe marital problems. He tends to abuse alcohol and generally exhibits repressive behavior. The older pedophiliac (mid to late 50s) is usually a lonely, impotent man. In general the pedophiliac's sexual deviancy is triggered by psychological stress such as loss of an important relationship, marital discord, or extreme loneliness.

In formal diagnostic terms, the person is not diagnosed as a pedophiliac if the sexual acts with the child are an isolated occurrence. A single incident with a child may, for example, have occurred as a result of an impulsive act after alcohol intoxication and is not therefore the consistent method of achieving sexual arousal.

The pedophiliac is unable to cope with normal adult stress and may use children as a means of releasing tension. He has feelings of masculine inadequacy and only feels comfortable sexually with children. The pedophiliac usually was raised in a home environment where the father was distant and impersonal and the mother overprotective or rather cold. Pedophiliacs usually come from broken and unhappy homes.

The psychological literature is rather vague as to the recommended treatment modalities for the pedophiliac. In most states pedophiliacs are punished by imprisonment or committed to a mental hospital. This usually does not change behavior, but it does protect society. Some efforts are made to treat the pedophiliac through group therapy and behavior modification.

Additional Reading
Lester, D., *Unusual sexual behavior*, Springfield, Ill.: Thomas, 1975.

M. A. CAMPION

Pellagrinous Psychosis. A metabolic disorder that produces changes in the brain, resulting in skin lesions, delerium, hallucinations, and in some cases permanent mental deterioration. It is caused by a severe vitamin B deficiency. Only 5 to 10% of the victims develop severe or permanent damage. Early symptoms of the psychosis include headaches, overall sluggishness, irritability, and forgetfulness.

See PSYCHOTIC DISORDERS.

Penis Envy. According to Freud, penis envy is a girl's reaction in the early genital stage to the discovery of the anatomical difference between the sexes. Not only does the girl wish she had a penis, but she also blames her mother for her deficiency. This is responsible for the loosening of her relationship with her mother and the movement toward the father. In this way Freud viewed penis envy as responsible for the onset of the oedipal crisis in the female.

See OEDIPUS COMPLEX; PSYCHOSEXUAL DEVELOPMENT.

Perceptual Deprivation. *See* SENSORY DEPRIVATION.

Perceptual Development. Although the essential neural mechanisms for sensation begin to appear early in prenatal life, the neuromuscular mechanisms for sensation and perception are not yet perfected when an infant is born. However, the infant develops a mature perceptual system by the end of the second year of life.

Fantz (1958) developed the "infant looking chamber" to aid in the study of perception in young infants. With this apparatus the experimenter peers through a small hole in the screen and observes the reflected image on the surface of the infant's eyeball. The technique makes it possible accurately to record the amount of time infants look at different patterns.

At birth the infant is able to see light, dark, and color, and has reasonably good visual acuity. Infant visual acuity is estimated by measuring the optokinetic nystagmus, which is a rapid sideways snap of the eye followed by a slower return to normal fixation. Nystagmus occurs in response to the eye following a moving object. By measuring the response of newborn babies to alternate black and white stripes presented at different speeds psychologists estimate that the neonate acuity is between 20/150 and 20/350. The neonate seems to have a fixed focus at about eight inches from its eyes, which limits its visual acuity. Convergence (the rotation of the eyes inward toward a target) and accommodation (changes in the curvature of the lens of the eye in response to a change in distance) are absent at birth but are developed after four to eight weeks.

The newborn is able to respond to the movement of stimuli and to different intensities of light. A baby who is a few days old will momentarily stop sucking if a light begins to move in his visual field, and he will look for different amounts of time at stimuli of different brightness. The infant also reacts to contrast created by brightness contours by focusing more on a contour than other parts of a visual field.

At 2 or 3 months of age infants show clear visual preferences. They will gaze longer at a bulls-eye than at a striped pattern. They are also more attracted to an accurate but simple representation of the human face. Infants look longer at stimuli that are similar to a human face than at patterns with more contour information. They will gaze at a smiling face whose features are in the proper places more than at a jumbled version of the same photograph (i.e., mouth upside down on the forehead, an eye in the chin, etc.).

From 4 to 12 months attention to jumbled stimulus patterns decreases, but it increases toward the end of the second year. Psychologists hypothesize that the 12-month-old has been exposed to more stimuli than the 4-month-old, and so the jumbled stimuli are not as interesting. Two-year-olds, on the other hand, have acquired some language that helps them to analyze what they are looking at. Some ask, "What happened to the man's face? Did someone hit him?"

Visual habituation appears at almost 10 weeks of age, suggesting that the cerebral cortex takes a long time to mature to the point where the infant can remember visual patterns. Up to that time infants do not seem to get bored with the same stimulus.

Since the human infant is not able to crawl or focus its eyes efficiently until it is several months old, it is impossible to find out about its depth perception before it has acquired a backlog of experiences. Visual cliff experiments suggest that children are born with a capacity to appreciate depth (Gibson & Walk, 1960). The visual cliff is a center runway that has a sheet of strong glass extending outward on two sides. On one side a textured pattern is placed far below the glass, thus giving the impression of depth. Both 6-month-olds and land animals avoid the side that appears to have the drop-off. Even a child who cannot crawl shows a marked decrease in heart rate, indicating attention, when he is placed on the deep side. Work with animals such as chickens and goats suggests that some animals are capable of depth perception in the first day of life.

Less research has been done on the development of the senses other than vision. The newborn is capable of hearing at birth and is sensitive to the location of sound as well as to frequency. The newborn is also capable of responding to odors, turning the head away from unpleasant smells. There is little systematic information on pain sensitivity in infants, but it seems that sensitivity to pain is present to some degree at birth and becomes sharper during the first few days of life.

References

Fantz, R. L. Pattern vision in young infants. *The Psychological Record*, 1958, *8*, 43–47.

Gibson, E. J., & Walk, R. R. The "visual cliff." *Scientific American*, 1960, *202*(4), 64–71.

M. P. COSGROVE

Perfectionism. One of those profound paradoxes that constitute human experience is a deeply embossed image of the perfect, which rubs against constant reminders that human life is imperfect. Somehow, without ever having known in experience the completely right, true, beautiful, or pure, we are aware of all of these. A person who believes himself to be perfect is considered deluded, yet one who denies the perfect has sacrificed something that is uniquely human.

The concept of the ideal, that internalized measure of the utterly perfect, is both our noblest friend and greatest tormentor. It forms the focus of much of human motivation and inspiration, and is, in one form or another, the goal of life's quest. Our ideals are larger than life itself. But this same internal structure that inspires the best can also become the anvil upon which the conscience hammers one into depressing, paralyzing feelings of guilt and worthlessness.

Most religions offer some solution to the pain of the shortfall from righteousness, but at the same time insist on a completely righteous God. Christian theologians have attempted to resolve this human dilemma by associating the ideal with love (Wesley, 1821) or with the charismatic (see Flew, 1934), but usually end up in the same dilemma as the psychologist. One is crushed by the demands of an absolute measuring rod, yet ignores it at great risk.

The richest psychological insights into the origin and function of this fundamental human paradox have come from the psychoanalysts. Freud identified two components of this idealizing internal structure: a standard that "finds itself possessed of every perfection that is of value," or the ego ideal, and the "faculty that incessantly watches, criticizes and compares," or the superego (1920/1963, p. 428). Often in his writing the term *superego* is used for both, and has two roots in human experience. The earliest of these is the primary narcissistic bliss of the infant who is entirely cared for, thoroughly loved, and knows no sin. The other is more external, coming from a complex identification with parents as powerful and good. In the conflictual matrix of the oedipal triangle an overtone of anxious danger to parental and societal criticism and norms is added (Freud, 1923/1961; Sandler, 1960).

More recent analytic thinkers relate these structural elements to the object relations of early infantile development, a process of the first two years of life. Kohut (1968) has described this process as the formation of part objects, when good, satisfying, and soothing, experiences tend to form around foci of "good self" and "good mother." These then become developmental lines that are not lost as the infant proceeds through separation and individuation but persist into adult life. One of these, the "grandiose cohesive self," matures into healthy self-esteem and confidence. The other, "the idealized parental imago," is the foundation of one's admiration of others and the ability to relate to them effectively.

Psychologists offer three general approaches to managing this threatening element of personality. 1) The superego becomes less ominous when insight is acquired into its roots in parental and social norms. 2) Some of the harshness can be relieved by behavioral methods, desensitizing responses to guilt and shame. 3) The superego will threaten us less if we can remodel our ideals into measures that are closer to our actual behavior. None of these approaches has been effective enough to be wholeheartedly endorsed by everyone. There is a consensus that the healthy person faces legitimate guilt and shame and struggles to find a way to improve behavior without letting the superego discourage or paralyze (Menninger, 1973).

The Christian therapist offers another insight into this human dilemma. The ideal can be seen as an internal structure designed by God to maintain a constant awareness of him in life. It serves to remind us constantly of our failings and our need for a Savior. We can have confidence and hope in two primary propositions: 1) The developmental process of the believer, while not complete here and now, will be. We will be perfected. 2) For now, our expectation is in Christ, not ourselves. The work that therapists, pastors, and friends do to bring growth, healing, and unity within the body of Christ will be completed one day in him (Eph. 4:7, 16).

References

Flew, R. N. *The idea of perfection in Christian theology.* London: Oxford University Press, 1934.

Freud, S. Introductory lectures on psycho-analysis. In J. Strachey (Ed. and trans.), *The Standard edition of the complete psychological works of Sigmund Freud* (Vols. 15 & 16). London: Hogarth, 1963. (Originally published, 1920.)

Freud, S. The ego and the id. In J. Strachey (Ed. and trans.), *The standard edition of the complete psychological works of Sigmund Freud* (Vol. 19). London: Hogarth 1961. (Originally Published, 1923.)

Kohut, H. The psychoanalytic treatment of narcissistic personality disorders. *Psychoanalytic Study of the Child,* 1968, *23,* 86–113.

Menninger, K. *Whatever became of sin?* New York: Hawthorn, 1973.

Sandler, J. On the concept of the superego. *Psychoanalytic Study of the Child,* 1960, *15,* 128–162.

Wesley, J. *A plain account of Christian perfection.* New York: Harper, 1821.

Additional Readings

Kohut, H. *The analysis of the self.* New York: International Universities Press, 1971.

Warfield, B. B. *Perfectionism* (2 vols.). New York: Oxford University Press, 1931.

C. M. Berry

Performance Appraisal. One of a supervisor's most difficult tasks. Latham and Wexley (1981) suggest that performance appraisal systems are much like seat belts; most people believe they are necessary, but they don't like to use them. Supervisors and subordinates both recognize that appraisals are often based on vague or poorly communicated performance standards, infrequent or haphazard observation of the worker on the job, and personal likes or dislikes. When such ratings are linked to important decisions about pay, promotion, training, and termination, resistance to performance appraisal becomes understandable. As a result, performance appraisal is often treated as a necessary evil, and its potential for motivating and developing employees is lost. Although there is no perfect performance appraisal system, appraisal practice can be improved by evaluating the type of performance measures used and the manner in which performance feedback is given to the employee.

Latham and Wexley (1981) define performance appraisal as "any personnel decision that affects the status of employees regarding promotion, termination, demotion, transfer, salary increase or decrease" (p. 4). This includes not just formal performance evaluations but also informal day-to-day decisions affecting worker status. All organizations practice performance appraisal in one form or another.

Performance appraisal measures can be broken down into three major types: trait, outcome, and behavior. Trait measures are by far the most popular. These measures ask the supervisor to rate the worker on a number of presumably job-relevant characteristics such as cooperation, dependability, initiative, and communication. Trait measures are popular because they appear to measure important aspects of job performance and they are relatively easy to develop.

Unfortunately, trait measures have a key weakness: Each trait can be interpreted in many different ways. For example, Bass and Barrett (1972) cite a study in which 47 executives produced 75 different definitions of dependability. Lacking clear reference to specific things the worker does on the job, trait ratings may be based on the supervisor's impressions of the worker's personality rather than on his or her actual work. Another problem with trait measures is that they do not tell the worker how to improve a low rating. For example, an unsatisfactory rating on cooperation simply tells the worker that he is not cooperating. It does not tell him specifically what he must do to improve his future performance (e.g., volunteer to work extra hours when the office gets busy).

Outcome measures are grounded in job goals and objectives. They are concerned with the results of work rather than the process. Batting averages, production rates, and sales volume are all examples of such measures. While one cannot deny the importance of "bottom line" figures, they are often influenced by factors beyond the worker's control (e.g., lack of resources, poor economy, inept co-workers). When this is true, decisions based on outcome measures may be perceived as unfair and may undermine worker motivation.

Behavior measures focus specifically on what the employee does on the job that makes him or her effective. They are based on the assumption that good results do not come about by chance, that someone must do something to create them. Behavior measures differ from trait measures in that they communicate performance expectations specifically. Two examples are "involves subordinates in planning and forecasting," and "generates new ways of tackling new or ongoing problems." Because they are less subjective than trait measures and more under the control of the employee than outcome measures, behavior measures appear to be the wave of the future in performance appraisal. Latham and Wexley (1981) provide straightforward guidelines for the development of these measures.

Beyond the question of which type of performance measure to use lie many other important issues. One is the question of how frequently to conduct formal performance appraisals. Most experts recommend three to four performance appraisal meetings per year between supervisor and subordinate. Good supervision, however, requires day-to-day performance appraisal, with both positive and negative feedback given as instances of good and poor job performance arise. With this kind of frequent, informal communication between supervisor and subordinate there should be none of the surprises or bombshells that can make these sessions so tense and difficult for both parties.

In their research Burke, Weitzel, and Weir (1978) have identified several factors that affect the quality of formal performance appraisal interviews. Supervisors would be well advised to put these suggestions into immediate practice. 1) Allow the subordinate to voice his or her opinions. 2) Assure the subordinate that you want to help him or her succeed on the job. 3) Set specific goals for the next performance period. 4) Focus the discussion on problems and work toward solutions. 5) Minimize the number of criticisms.

Finally, supervisors should also be aware that performance appraisal practices are increasingly coming before the courts in cases involving various forms of alleged job discrimination. No organization is immune to this very costly kind of litigation, and all should carefully review their appraisal practices, consulting with a qualified professional if necessary.

References

Bass, B. M., & Barrett, G. U. *Man, work and organizations,* Boston: Allyn & Bacon, 1972.

Burke, R. J., Weitzel, W., & Weir, T. Characteristics of effective employee performance review and development interviews: Replication and extension. *Personnel Psychology*, 1978, *31*, 903–919.

Latham, G. P., & Wexley, K. N. *Increasing productivity through performance appraisal.* Reading, Mass.: Addison-Wesley, 1981.

Additional Reading

Lindquist, S. E. (Ed.). Assessment of missionary and minister effectiveness [Special issue]. *Journal of Psychology and Christianity*, 1983, *2*(4).

D. D. McKENNA

Perls, Frederick Salomon (Fritz) (1893–1970). Originator of GESTALT THERAPY. He was born and raised in a Jewish family in Berlin and was educated in Germany, obtaining the M.D. degree with specialization in psychology. He also studied at the Vienna and Berlin Institutes of Psychoanalysis. His work reflects the influence of his Jewishness, his unhappy childhood, two world wars, Nazism, his own genius, his psychoanalytic training, an unhappy and competitive marriage, the opportunities of the freedoms of America, and his ever-present integrity of searching for truth and reality.

Perls's parents were often bitterly unhappy with each other, apparently caught in social upward mobility. One of his two sisters died in a concentration camp. Fritz was unruly at home and in school, although he did well academically. He finished medical school just in time to join the German army and serve as a medic.

After World War I, Perls returned to Berlin and began psychoanalytic training. He worked with Karen Horney, Clara Happel, and other analysts in Berlin and Frankfurt. Sensing the onset of anti-Semitism in Germany he emigrated to South Africa in 1933 and established the South African Institute for Psychoanalysis in 1935. As director of this institute he lived and worked in South Africa as a somewhat traditional analyst for about 10 years.

Perls began to challenge traditional psychoanalytic theory as early as 1936, but his alternative, Gestalt therapy, was not put forward until his emigration to the United States in 1946. Here, together with his wife, who has developed her own approach to Gestalt Therapy, he founded the New York Institute for Gestalt Therapy. Subsequently he was associated with the Gestalt Therapy Institute in Cleveland and was instrumental in the development of the Esalen Institute in Big Sur, California. For the last 10 years of his life his work was mostly conducted in an experimental workshop format at Esalen and other cities. When he died, he was living in Vancouver,

British Columbia, where he had recently established another Gestalt Therapy Institute.

Perls's books include *Ego, Hunger, and Aggression* (1947), *Gestalt Therapy* (with Hefferline & Goodman, 1951), *Gestalt Therapy Verbatim* (1969), and *In and Out of the Garbage Pail* (1969). His earlier works were more theoretical, something he explicitly rejected in his later experiential writings.

Perls's influence on psychotherapy has been substantial. Gestalt therapy has come to be a major experiential therapy, providing a provocative challenge to other theoretical approaches, particularly psychoanalytic approaches.

R. B. JOHNSON

Perseveration. A term first used by psychiatrist F. S. Niesser to denote the involuntary persistence or repetition of the same thought or activity, usually expressed verbally. The person's attention seems to be fixated on a subject, so that no matter what other topics are brought up, his comments remain on this subject. Perseveration occurs most frequently in cases of brain damage but is also found in schizophrenia. It is sometimes defined by experimental psychologists as the general inability to shift from one activity to another.

Persona. The term used by Jung to refer to the external or social aspects of a person's self. The word is taken from the Latin *persona*, which means an actor's mask. Tournier (1957) has written of the same concept but prefers the term *personage*. With Jung he views the choice of social presentations of self to be crucial in that it must be more than a response to the expectations of others. The persona must be a good medium for the expression of the unique and very personal aspects of oneself. This concept is Tournier's major contribution to personality theory.

Reference

Tournier, P. *The meaning of persons.* New York: Harper & Row, 1957.

D. G. BENNER

Personal Constructs Therapy. Personal constructs theory was developed by American psychologist George A. Kelly, who conceived of the human person as an inquisitive, theorizing creature who views the world through a set of individually devised theories. These individual theories, or personal constructs, are formed whether the person involved is aware of the process or not, or whether the theory construction process has used good or poor rules. The individual constructs within any given person may be well integrated and cohesive or independent and unrelated.

The theory was highly abstract when first described by its originator, but has been applied recently to several practical issues such as therapy (Landfield, 1971) and education (Fransella, 1978). Kelly conceived his system as a comprehensive psychology (Kelly, 1955), although most descriptions of his work categorize it as a theory of personality.

A personal construct is an individual's view as to how two things are alike and different from a third thing (Landfield, 1971). A person's system of internally held constructs determines how people, places, and things are viewed and evaluated. It is assumed that individuals can be better understood if their internal theories about the world can be elicited and graphed.

Kelly and his followers developed a test designed to help map out a person's set of personal constructs. The Role Construct Repertory Test, also known as the Rep Test, can be administered in several different ways, but a typical administration would be as follows: The subject is asked to name several acquaintances in various roles such as friend, mother, and others with whom the subject interacts on a frequent basis. The subject then considers any three of these acquaintances as to how two of them are similar and how the same two are different from the third person in the triad. Each time such an operation is performed by the subject, a personal construct emerges. In this manner, a person's internal theories are exposed for observation and analysis. Kelly theorized that these personal constructs are fundamental to the way the individual anticipated events and shaped his or her behavior. Extensive scoring techniques have been developed, and the test is easily adapted to computer analysis.

Kelly proposed that his personal constructs theory could be applied to therapy (Maher, 1969). Personal constructs therapy is a science, and both therapist and client are scientists. The goal is not to produce certain types of behavior but to observe the behavior of the client as a way of uncovering constructs and of testing their validity. The task of therapy is to devise new and better constructs as inadequate or deficient constructs are found. Therapy is an ongoing process, and clients are urged to make this scientific discovery technique a way of life. Kelly wrote, "What, hopefully, the therapy has demonstrated is a way of getting on with one's life, not an

answer to the question of 'How shall I behave?'" (Maher, 1969, p. 220). Personal constructs therapy uses a variety of techniques, such as urging a client to reverse his or her position on a construct, helping a client make preverbal constructs verbal, or expanding the applicability of existing constructs.

Kelly's theory is phenomenological and in the individual psychology tradition of Allport. The theory is respected for its simplicity as well as for its testability. In recent years there has been a revival of interest in Kelly's work, especially in Great Britain.

References
Fransella, F. (Ed.). *Personal construct psychology, 1977*. New York: Academic Press, 1978.
Kelly, G. A. *The psychology of personal constructs* (2 vols.). New York: Norton, 1955.
Landfield, A. W. *Personal construct systems in psychotherapy*. Chicago: Rand McNally, 1971.
Maher, B. (Ed.). *Clinical psychology and personality: The selected papers of George Kelley*. New York: Wiley, 1969.

J. R. BECK

Personality. One of the more abstract terms in English usage, a state reflecting the history of its parent word, *persona*. Personality has its etymological and conceptual origins in the Latin infinitive *personare*, which referred to the mouthpiece or hole in a mask through which an actor spoke. The classical Latin term *persona* began as a theatrical term describing the mask the actor wore in the role he played. Eventually the meaning of persona spanned a continuum ranging from surface externals to the deep identity of the individual. The English term *personality* spans the same range (Allport, 1937).

Implicit in persona was a tension that exists in various definitions of personality. Legend has it that the theatrical mask was invented by a vain actor who designed it to cover up his squinting. When a play was performed, it was common practice for one actor to play several parts that were designated by different masks. Switching of a mask indicated the switching of roles. Thus persona took on the idea of presenting a façade, of acting a role that may belie one's true thoughts or feelings.

Several modern approaches to personality have adopted this external metaphor. Jung's analytic theory made a distinction between ego and persona. The ego was the center of consciousness composed of perceptions, feelings, thoughts, and memories. The ego provided the basis for the individual's identity and continuity. Persona, on the other hand, was a mask the person adopted as a reaction to social convention. It reflected public behavior expected by society and roles demanded in society. Persona presents humans as social animals. If ego identified too strongly with persona, one's true feelings or inner nature became a mere reflection of society instead of an autonomous identity. Many sociological approaches to personality have taken this view whereby personality represents an individual's "social-stimulus value."

Yet behind each of the actor's masks stood a person, an individual with individual thoughts and feelings beyond those demanded by the role. It was possible that the actor's personal thoughts and feelings might affect how the role was played. This belief developed into an approach that viewed personality as something internal, underlying, or latent to the actual behavior. The observer of the drama might question whether the words expressed by the actor, and their mode of expression, indicated the role demands or the actor's inward inclinations. This mode of thought remains a source of variation in the definition of personality (Stagner, 1974).

Many psychological and theological approaches to personality conceive of personality as the locus of personal causality. Personality (i.e., latent structure) causes behavior (i.e., manifest evidence). Personality is not directly observable, but its existence is established by inference from variation in an individual's behavior. Personality is that which gives a person consistency from situation to situation and from time to time. Personality makes it possible to predict behavior.

In this mode of thought personality is demonstrated in the social, emotional, and motivational domains but does not generally include the physical or the intellectual, although personality may tangentially affect them. Personality as an inner structure is that which gives personhood to persons; it makes individuals distinguishable from one another. Personality also differentiates persons (humans) from other animals, particularly other primates. Personality transcends one's biological framework to emphasize the spiritual or mental uniqueness of the human race.

This tension between true self and outer manifestations is present in classical theological analyses of the Trinity. There is one true God (persona as selfhood) who accomplishes his plans by means of one of three persons (persona as roles). Father, Son, and Holy Spirit are external manifestations of an inward unity and identity.

Maddi (1968) integrated these internal-external dimensions into a unifying frame-work. The *core* of personality is that which is common to all humans but not present in subhuman primates. This core does not change much during the course of living. As assumed inherent attributes the core has a pervasive causal effect on behavior by providing direction, continuity, and purpose to life. The *periphery* of personality is the generally learned attributes that make individuals unique. These concrete differences are more readily observable than are core elements. Traits and types illustrate this peripheral view of personality. Maddi assumed that all individuals share the common core, but variations in developmental experience contribute to the peripheral differences among individuals.

In summary, personality as an abstract concept refers to those internal qualities that define personhood and those external characteristics that make individual differences evident.

References

Allport, G. W. *Personality: A psychological interpretation.* New York: Holt, 1937.
Maddi, S. R. *Personality theories: A comparative analysis.* Homewood, Ill.: Dorsey Press, 1968.
Stagner, R. *Psychology of personality* (4th ed.). New York: McGraw-Hill, 1974.

R. L. TIMPE

Personality Assessment. Systematic techniques for examining global characteristics of people or unique aspects of an individual. The companion field of ability assessment examines areas such as vocational skill, intelligence, and academic achievement. By contrast, personality topics include motivational processes, attitudes, emotional states, interpersonal relations, beliefs, psychological adjustment, values, temperament, and character traits. Personality assessment is often characterized by procedures that have no correct response and that obscure the purpose of the assessment from the examinee.

Different applications of assessment procedures emphasize different components. In research the main consideration is often formal measurement procedures. Clinical work emphasizes the assessment processes of interpretation and evaluation as reflected in the judgment of practitioners. Personality assessment for placement in vocational or educational settings involves important ethical considerations. The entire assessment process depends on the interplay between an underlying conceptual basis for personality and a technology for systematizing the actions and report of the examinee.

Historical Development. Historically various cultures assessed personality through techniques such as astrology, palmistry, and physiognomy. McReynolds has noted the "close interplay between kinds of assessment and the world view of the cultures involved" (1968, p. 483). For example, contemporary emphasis on individual assessment may have developed from a cultural foundation of free-will views of human nature. Personality influences on behavior presumably reflect agency.

Modern forms of personality assessment took shape around the turn of the century through the work of Galton, Jung, and others. During the First World War, Woodworth developed the prototype questionnaire while screening men for psychological fitness to serve in the American military. Rorschach's work in Switzerland culminated in the publication of his inkblot test in 1921.

Personality study emerged during the interwar period as a recognized academic field. While assessment approaches polarized into projective and objective camps, a number of methodological and conceptual developments contributed to the growing field. The rise of psychometric theory, performance assessment, empirical keying methods, and assessment centers all had considerable impact.

The demands of mobilizing extensive military operations for World War II promoted the premature application of the nascent assessment technologies. The wartime development of these techniques provided foundations for contemporary personality assessment.

Projective and Objective Approaches. The concept of projection in personality assessment is broader than the Freudian notion. It refers to the unwitting or conscious exhibition of psychological wants, needs, or attitudes in response to ambiguous stimuli such as pictures or inkblots. The many projective formats and rationales frequently focus on the uniqueness of individuals. Projective tasks usually ask for open-ended responses, either written or oral. The strategies for interpreting responses are often less formally structured than are those of other approaches.

The variety of projective techniques include word association tests, sentence completion tests, drawing tests, and inkblot techniques. Murray's personality theory provided the background for the development of the Thematic Apperception Test using ambiguous pictures as the stimuli. This procedure and Rorschach's inkblot test are perhaps the most commonly employed projective techniques in clinical use.

The objective or psychometric tradition is presumably more scientific than the clinically oriented projective tradition. Psychometric methodology is mathematical theory that evolved in the context of questionnaire construction. Structured response formats (e.g., true-false) typify questionnaires. Assessment procedures of this type usually base scores on comparisons of responses between people. The Edwards Personal Preference Schedule is a controversial exception to this norm.

Global personality inventories, such as the California Personality Inventory, assess many dimensions in contrast to scales, which measure one psychological state or trait. These instruments are standardized by gathering information from a large representative sample. Some questionnaires are clearly grounded in psychological theory. For example, Rotter's Internal-External Locus of Control Scale is based on social learning theory.

A number of techniques have been developed to complement the standardized questionnaires. Rating procedures, sociometrics, performance tests, Q-sort techniques, and structured interviews provide a wide range of information. Any of these procedures can be standardized for specific purposes.

Although psychometric and projective assessment traditions characterize the beginnings of personality assessment, additional schools rose to prominence after World War II. Rogers (1946) discounted the use of tests in psychotherapy but admitted their use in personnel selection or in research. Behavioral psychologists minimized the value of traditional personality assessment in either research or applied settings. Humanistic, behavioral, and other streams of critique have developed approaches to assessment more consonant with their outlook, thus enriching the field of personality assessment as a whole.

Test Theory. The basic question in personality assessment is how to tell a good test or assessment procedure from a poor one. In addition to informal standards, one can specify three related sets of formal standards for the construction and evaluation of tests: classical test theory, scaling techniques, and axiomatic measurement theory. The latter two approaches have important applications in personality assessment topics such as attitude scaling. The bulk of research and practice, however, is founded on the mathematical tools and conceptual framework of classical test theory.

Although classical test theory is still an

active field of research, its limitations have stimulated many experts to develop sophisticated alternatives. Generalizability theory extends the usual mathematical basis and synthesizes the traditional notions of reliability and validity. Item response theory uses a different mathematical basis, which relates to scaling techniques. The continued elaboration of construct validity notions joins with these technical developments in transforming the basic principles of psychological measurement (Jackson & Paunonen, 1980).

Contemporary Trends. The field of personality assessment today is characterized by a plurality of perspectives and models. Diagnostic models, salient in clinical fields, are the topic of much debate (*see* CLASSIFICATION OF MENTAL DISORDERS. BEHAVIORAL ASSESSMENT models are increasing in sophistication and importance. The emphasis on rational use of assessment information gave rise to decision theory models. Analytic models are global approaches that emphasize psychological theory and incorporate aspects of the other models. In contrast, empirical models minimize the place of theory in assessment.

The last 15 years have seen an extensive debate among those who stress personal or situational influences on behavior. Current syntheses emphasize both sets of determinants in different forms of interactional approaches.

Some assessment traditions stress the importance of considering people as individuals rather than comparing them with others. Such tools as the Repertory Grid technique support emerging views that give consideration to both these aspects of assessment. This trend is also exemplified in the combination of psychometric and projective methods and in assessment across the life span.

Consumer rights movements are shaping personality assessment by raising ethical issues (Glaser & Bond, 1981). Societal neglect of the aged, ethnic minorities, and the handicapped is reflected in psychology by assessment procedures that fail to adequately represent members of these groups. In addition to the restriction of inappropriate assessment practices, activists also call for the expansion of personality assessment to address, for example, student motivation in educational settings. Examinee control over testing information and obscurity in personality assessment goals are additional issues being raised. Ethical concerns complement formal standards and theoretical views as standards of evaluation for assessment procedures.

The most salient feature of contemporary personality assessment is the blurring of traditional boundaries. The assessment of competence or cognitive style involves both ability and personality components. Psychophysics and psychophysiology become partners with personality assessment in health psychology. The psychometric study of response styles and the social psychology of person perception combine across the boundaries between theory and method. Ecological psychology provides an impetus toward transactional analysis of personality in context.

Experts vary in their predictions for the future of personality assessment. The pluralism of approaches to assessment is a force behind the continued multiplication of available tools. Role-play techniques are being developed into systematic forms of assessment. Simulation of real world situations is also on the rise. The use of biographical approaches is expanding. Assessment centers provide proving grounds for the formalization of additional assessment tools.

The influences of sex, age, or cultural factors on testing results reflect a variety of social and peronality processes beyond the characteristic being assessed. Consequently the assessment context is studied more intensively. Also, methods such as cross-cultural assessment are becoming more broadly applicable. Assessment in the future will probably be increasingly sensitive to social context. The response of experts to current challenges will probably take the form of technological development and greater integration of practice with psychological theory. Computer capacities and mathematical tools combine to broaden the scope of assessment practice. Important trends are reflected in assessment to fit people with appropriate jobs and services and in the appraisal of personal growth. Automated procedures are used increasingly for the administration, scoring, and interpretation of assessment. In addition, future developments may also involve changes in the basic assumptions of the field (Rorer & Widiger, 1983).

Conclusions. Historical observations and contemporary trends illustrate the extent to which personality assessment reflects and shapes prevailing views of human nature. A biblical view of personality emphasizes the image of God as reflected in fallen humanity. The current flux in the field encourages Christian scholars to work out the implications of a biblical anthropology for personality assessment. The challenge of opportunity stands before the entire Christian community in establishing theoretical foundations, supporting responsible applications, and developing appropriate techniques for such biblically informed personality assessment.

References

Glaser, R., & Bond, L. (Eds.). Testing: Concepts, policy, practice, and research. *American Psychologist, 1981, 36,* 997–1189.

Jackson, D. N., & Paunonen, S. V. Personality structure and assessment. *Annual Review of Psychology, 1980, 31,* 503–582.

McReynolds, P. Historical antecedents of personality assessment. In P. McReynolds (Ed.), *Advances in psychological assessment* (Vol. 3). San Francisco: Jossey-Bass, 1968.

Rogers, C. R. Psychometric tests and client-centered counseling. *Educational and Psychological Measurement, 1946, 6,* 139–144.

Rorer, L. G., & Widiger, T. A. Personality structure and assessment. *Annual Review of Psychology, 1983, 34,* 431–463.

Additional Reading

Buros, O. K. *The eighth mental measurements yearbook* (2 vols.). Highland Park, N.J.: Gryphon Press, 1978.

M. J. McDonald

See Psychological Measurement.

Personality Disorders.
Today this term refers most commonly to a group of mental disturbances that relate to the basic personality of the patient. They are distinguished on one hand from affective and neurotic disorders in that they tend to be more fixed and inflexible. On the other hand they differ from the more serious psychoses in that they do not demonstrate the fixed distortions of thought, perception, and reality testing seen in those conditions.

People suffering from these disorders are encountered frequently in clinical practice. Their incidence in psychiatric outpatient clinics is about 20% (Winokur & Crowe, 1974). Yet even when this is not the primary working diagnosis, personality can influence the clinical course enough to make it an important secondary consideration. In order to permit such multiple diagnoses *DSM-III* encourages the use of a separate Axis II for personality disorders, paralleling the primary clinical syndrome recorded as Axis I. This is done to ensure that these personality conditions would not be slighted when attention is directed to the usually more prominent Axis I disorder.

In spite of the clinical usefulness of personality disorders, sharpening the diagnosis in this area has historically been difficult. When assessments of the same patients made by different clinicians have been compared, reliability has been rather consistently poor. In field trials using *DSM-III* this has improved considerably, though accuracy still falls short of Axis I diagnoses (Spitzer, Forman, & Nee, 1979).

Essential Characteristics. By definition personality disorders are abnormalities relating to personality traits. As such, they are relatively fixed, often identifiable in childhood, and may still be a problem in old age. Treatment is generally long term and directed toward a change in basic personality structures rather than the reduction of symptoms. A great variety of treatment methods have been advocated, but the outcome is generally discouraging.

The degree of maladaptation resulting from these disorders usually falls somewhere between the neuroses and the psychoses, but occasionally can be severe. They may be less painful to the patient than affective or neurotic processes, and for this reason are sometimes said to be ego-syntonic. When they are personally distressing, or ego-dystonic, the patient may struggle over long periods of time, with a great deal of effort to modify them. Either way, personality-related conditions have a tendency to be more disturbing to others close to the patient than do affective or neurotic problems.

While most experienced therapists would agree with all of the above statements in principle, they would realize immediately that there are many exceptions. Though these patterns of response are by definition enduring and fixed, they are often strongly modified by what Frances (1980) calls "state and role factors." Changes in the patient's life circumstances, particularly increasing stress, uncertainty, or loss of a supporting person, can make sweeping changes in the clinical picture. The demands made by the person's role in life, particularly as he perceives it in terms of prestige, or the amount of control he has over his destiny can also greatly reduce or increase the symptoms.

Though the pathology of personality disorders relates to underlying structures rather than to more transient perceptual disturbances, neurotic symptoms are frequently described in clinical studies. Anxiety and depression, as well as a host of psychophysiological symptoms, are almost always present. These are usually more explosive than those seen in neurotic or affective illnesses and often are what brings these people into treatment.

Though personality disorders are usually easily distinguished from schizophrenia and other psychoses, transient psychotic episodes are not rare. The two conditions also share a rather impervious lack of insight. In both, the therapist deals with a frustrating conviction on the part of the patient that all would be well if the world were changed and he or she were left alone.

To describe the particular personality patterns more accurately, the kind of disorder must be specified. *DSM-III* describes 11 specific personality disorders that may be divided roughly into three groups. The first group contains the older, more familiar disorders that usually relate more accurately to personality types: paranoid, antisocial, compulsive, histrionic, and dependent personality disorders. The second group would seem to derive more from the temperament of the individual or his expressive style: schizoid, passive-aggressive, and avoidant personality disorders.

Two other conditions are unequivocally disorders of personality but fail to fall neatly under the first two categories, often showing a mixture of temperament and personality traits. They are still in the process of being formulated, but are exciting in that a great deal of research attention is being focused on them. They are narcissistic personality disorder and borderline personality disorder. The final disorder, a category related to schizophrenia but without sufficient criteria to make that diagnosis, is schizotypal personality disorder.

It is apparent that the categories are at present somewhat fuzzy, deriving from several sources. One hopes that as time goes on, this system will be cleaned up; but for the time being, it is the best available and most widely accepted in the United States. In many ways it would be best if we could avoid the problems of labeling altogether and remain more flexible, since people just do not neatly fall into categories. More realistically, however, pressures are building up from governmental and insurance agencies to use such a code universally.

Psychoanalytic Perspective. The statistical emphasis of *DSM-III* has little to say about the etiology or treatment of the personality disorders. Perhaps because this diagnostic approach to mental health problems is essentially medical, the literature that does speak to these concerns is dominated by psychoanalysis.

In psychoanalytic writing these conditions are called character disorders. *Character* is derived from a German word that means the same as the English *personality* and has none of the ethical loading of the English *character*. Human character is formed in the earliest years of life in the process of learning to identify and relate to the self and others who

are close. In traditional Freudian psychoanalysis internal conflicts as well as excessive frustration or permissiveness by the mothering figure induce the distortions seen later as character disorders. In the process of early development the child forms an individual pattern of perception and defense that becomes part of the personality. Since the instinctual forces involved in these internal conflicts are considered by analysts to be similar in all people, the external forces are more influential; or as Fenichel (1945) said, "The character of man is socially determined" (p. 464). For the first half of the twentieth century these conflicts were related almost exclusively to the dynamics of the oral, anal, and phallic or oedipal stages of development.

In more recent years the focus of psychoanalytic thought has largely shifted to even earlier stages of development, toward the pathology of early object relationships. Pressure in this direction has come from the clinical problems encountered by analysts and other psychotherapists. For reasons that are not entirely clear psychiatrists and clinical psychologists are seeing patients whose difficulty seems to be much more complicated and treatment resistant than those neurotic symptoms around which psychoanalysis was first formulated. The analytic material has become more incoherent, and the transference more chaotic. In order to understand these newer disorders research has reached back into the earliest struggles of infants to mold their experience into realistic and useful models of self and other. It was from this work that the borderline personality and the narcissistic personality disorders have been delineated.

As interesting as all these formulations are, they have not been widely understood or accepted within the mental health care system as a whole. Since the caretakers of the mentally ill now work regularly in teams with other professionals who come from widely divergent conceptual worlds, there is a need for a new approach to personality disorders. Ideally this should be simple and easily understood, and should go beyond the description of symptom clusters found in *DSM-III*.

Phenomenological Perspective. The most logical approach to devising such a system might be to begin with the definition of personality disorders given in *DSM-III* (p. 305). Here personality disorders are variations of normally occurring personality traits that become pathological when they are inflexible or maladaptive enough to disturb function. It is generally conceded that personality traits differ from one person to another, and that this diversity is an important component of the social experience. The problem has been that there is no generally accepted system of describing the differences. Were there one, pathology could be referenced to normality. As it now stands, the opposite is true, and the traits are defined by the pathology. An obsessive person, for example, is one who shows milder forms of the behavior that describes the obsessive personality disorder.

Such a system can be conceptualized by using the way an individual organizes the complexity of reality as an essential element of personality. For example, one person might understand things as components of a moving, interacting system that resembles a narrative or story. A person who frames complex events, or reality itself, in dramatic terms would be considered a histrionic personality. When this trait is normal, the person would contribute a deeper understanding of the drama involved in an event to the group as a whole. When this same trait becomes too rigid or narrow, the same person might lose sight of accuracy and truth, possibly seeing significant others more as actors than real persons. When the trait becomes maladaptive enough to disturb function and relationship, the person would be said to suffer from a histrionic personality disorder.

This approach would be more in harmony also with the biblical model of the church as a community composed of diverse members. Each, though one with others in the body, contributes to the unity of the whole by the unique nature of his or her diversity. Perception represents an important diversity that contributes to the unity. When all the diverse perceptions of the community are contributed and appreciated, the body as well as the individual members is enriched in its understanding and function.

References

Fenichel, O. *The psychoanalytic theory of neurosis.* New York: Norton, 1945.

Frances, A. The DSM III personality disorder section: A commentary. *American Journal of Psychiatry,* 1980, *137,* 1050–1054.

Spitzer, R. L., Forman, J. B., & Nee, J. DSM III field trials: Initial interrater diagnostic reliability. *American Journal of Psychiatry,* 1979, *136,* 815–817.

Winokur, G., & Crowe, R. Personality disorders. In S. Arieti (Ed.), *The American handbook of psychiatry.* (Vol. 3). New York: Basic Books, 1974.

Additional Readings

Giovacchini, P. *The psychoanalysis of character disorders.* New York: Aronson, 1975.

Lion, J. R. *Personality disorders: Diagnosis and management.* Baltimore: Williams & Wilkins, 1974.

Stanton, A. H. Personality disorders. In A. M. Nicholi, Jr.

(Ed.), *The Harvard guide to modern psychiatry.* Cambridge: Harvard University Press, 1978.

C. M. Berry

Personality Psychology. The study of individual differences in human cognition, emotion, motivation, and behavior. The general approach has been to examine systematically how people vary in reactions. This individual differences approach (idiographic orientation) has been more prominent than approaches designed to formulate general laws about all individuals (nomothetic orientation). Clinical theories have been more numerous than experimental theories. As a consequence of the therapist's attempt to meet human need, more emphasis has been given to understanding one individual in depth than to generating laws. The experimental theories are more geared to the latter goal than to the intense understanding of one person.

Several subfields in personality psychology can be identified. Mischel (1971) listed these as theory, assessment, development, and deviance and change. Considerable controversy exists among personality theorists. This is due in part to variant definitions of personality, to diverse assumptions about human nature, and to different convictions about the locus and cause of behavior. Most early theories (ca. 1900 through 1950) focused on intraorganismic factors as prime causes of individual differences. This approach was termed *personologism.* But during the 1950s and 1960s a rival viewpoint emerged that focused on situational or environmental causes. This was termed *situationism.* Personality theory in the 1970s witnessed the development of integrated approaches that consider how person and situation interact to produce behavior. The study of person x situation interaction (i.e., interactionism) combines the strengths of clinical observation of individual differences with the experimental study of situational variables, while overcoming the limitations of each.

To make a theory testable and thus more than speculation, accurate data are essential. The methods available are as numerous as theories. Some measurement approaches rely on the subjective insight of the clinician (e.g., clinical observation, interviewing, diagnosis through projective tests), while others use objective tests and behavioral samples.

Most theories of personality recognize that children are not miniature adults in thoughts and feelings. As a result the question of how the child comes to be a socialized adult is addressed through a search for developmental and maturational processes. The source of developmental influence is variously placed in stages (e.g., Freud, Erikson), in infant-parent interactions (e.g., Horney, Sullivan), and in imitation of adults (e.g., Bandura). Maturational theories may rely on instincts, genetic predispositions, and body types.

A number of personality theories were developed within clinical practice where therapeutic intervention was the focus for therapist-client interaction. Personality theories, through reliance on assessment or diagnostic techniques, attempt to define and describe personality deviance or disorder, so that effective therapeutic change can be effected. Therapy becomes an application of personality theory.

For many students personality study is one of the most fascinating facets of psychological inquiry because of potential self-insight and the desire to help others.

Reference
Mischel, W. *Introduction to personality.* New York: Holt, Rinehart, & Winston, 1971.

Additional Readings
Endler, N., & Magnusson, D. (Eds.). *Interactional psychology and personality.* New York: Halsted, 1976.
Stagner, R. *Psychology of personality* (4th ed.). New York: McGraw-Hill, 1974.

R. L. TIMPE

See PERSONALITY.

Personality Research Form. A tool developed by Jackson for the purpose of measuring personality traits of broad relevance for research in personality and applications in academic, clinical, and organizational settings. Twenty-two dimensions of personality are measured in the five versions of the test. Twenty of these were drawn from the work of Murray (1938).

The Personality Research Form's distinctive lies in the psychometrically sophisticated manner in which it was developed. Jackson followed four steps in the construction of each scale. First, each construct (e.g., need for achievement) was explicitly defined according to Murray's work and more recent studies. Then scale items were written in conformity with these definitions. Second, items were empirically selected from these item pools to maximize each scale's homogeneity. Third, response biases, such as desirability, were controlled at the item selection stage by eliminating items showing high correlations with a separate social desirability scale. Finally, item selection and scale development attempted to maximize convergent (consis-

tency of response within scales) and discriminant (discrimination of response between scales) validity. The result of this involved procedure is, as one reviewer put it, a paragon of technical sophistication.

The care with which the Personality Research Form was developed is reflected in the psychometric quality of its scales. Internal consistency reliabilities for the 20 content scales are among the highest in the personality assessment literature. Test-retest stability is also excellent for short time intervals. Validational evidence for the Personality Research Form comes largely from studies in which peers were asked to describe the test taker in terms of adjectives relevant to each of the test's content scales. Correlations produced by this method suggested strong convergent validity. Similar findings were obtained with self-ratings. (See Jackson, 1967, for further discussion of the test's psychometric properties.)

The Personality Research Form can be used with persons ranging from seventh grade to adult. Normative data, however, are based almost entirely on samples of college students. Thus the user must exercise caution in interpreting standard scores derived from these norms where characteristics of the respondents differ significantly from those of college students. The test is designed to be group administered and takes from 30 to 70 minutes, depending on the form being used. It can be easily scored by hand, or, if desired, machine-scorable answer sheets are available. Interpretive descriptions for each scale are given in the manual, but no empirical evidence is offered in their support.

Although the Personality Research Form represents the best in objective personality testing, it is not without its critics. Chief among the criticisms is that the test has not been shown to predict behavior in "real-life" settings. At this point, then, further applied research is necessary to show whether the test's psychometric sophistication will result in practical payoffs. One must certainly conclude, however, that the test represents a promising major contribution to the field of personality testing.

References
Jackson, D. N. *Personality research form manual.* Goshen, N.Y.: Research Psychologists Press, 1967.
Murray, H. A. *Explorations in Personality.* New York: Wiley, 1938.

D. D. McKENNA

Personal Unconscious. In Jungian or ANALYTICAL PSYCHOLOGY the psyche is understood to consist of two broad regions: conscious and unconscious. Both these major components are subdivided into several personifications. The two principal subdivisions of the unconscious are the collective unconscious and the personal unconscious.

The personal unconscious owes its existence to personal experience and is a personal acquisition, in contrast to the collective unconscious, which is accounted for by heredity alone. The contents of the personal unconscious were at some time conscious but have disappeared from the conscious either through repression or having been forgotten. A characterizing feature of the personal unconscious is that it is made up of complexes (feeling-toned trains of thought or emotion-ladened ideas), whereas the collective unconscious is composed of ARCHETYPES.

A central aspect of the personal unconscious is the shadow, which represents the negative side of personality, the sum of all the unpleasant qualities or traits an individual wishes to hide. Along with those characteristics that the person refuses to acknowledge are insufficiently developed functions.

The personal unconscious is thought to lie less deeply in the realm of psychic unconscious than does the collective unconscious. Therefore the contents can be brought into consciousness more easily than the primordial messages contained in the archetypes. Projection is the chief vehicle for tapping the shadow. Since the data of the shadow are uniquely personal in nature, the projections will reflect themes that represent the person.

Although the contents of the personal unconscious, particularly the shadow, are considered to be negative by the individual, this body of knowledge about the person is invaluable. It is only after these parts of personality are integrated with the more positive qualities that the individual can become a whole person.

D. SMITH

Person-Centered Therapy. Developed by Rogers in the 1940s, person-centered therapy (originally called client-centered therapy) is probably the first typically American system of therapy ever formulated. Like all other forms of therapy it is of course historically dependent on psychoanalysis; thus it is not free from imported European influences in its constitutive parts. But the distinguishing characteristic of this approach to therapy as a whole is that it is made in America for Americans.

Philosophical Roots. More than any other form of therapy, person-centered therapy embodies the early American faith in the primacy of the individual. Early American culture held that if individuals are left to themselves, they will naturally exercise their capacity to realize their fullest potential. It insisted on the necessity of allowing individuals the freedom to choose their own course of action. Person-centered therapy reiterates this theme in therapeutic language when Rogers states that the therapist should rely on the client for the direction of movement in the therapeutic process (Rogers, 1959). Rogers's adherence to this cultural notion of the primacy of the individual is responsible for the individualistic stamp of person-centered therapy as well as for the typically nondirective character of its earliest formulation. It represents the influence of Rogers's view of human beings on his approach to therapy.

Rogers is often seen as a spokesperson for that theoretical orientation in psychology called third force or HUMANISTIC PSYCHOLOGY. For that reason person-centered therapy is frequently characterized as a phenomenological approach to therapy—i.e., an approach that shows unqualified respect for the client's perception of reality. While this characterization has some validity, it is one-sided and superficial because it neglects the other, much deeper dimension of Rogers's thought: his emphasis on growth. Ultimately Rogers's reverence for growth is deeper than his respect for individuals. For that reason also it is more correct to call his person-centered therapy a growth therapy rather than a PHENOMENOLOGICAL THERAPY.

This emphasis on growth in person-centered therapy is due to the fact that for its theoretical-philosophical roots, it hails back to a typically American philosophy rather than to some European import. Pragmatism rather than phenomenology or existentialism forms the philosophical backdrop of this approach. There exists a particularly close affinity between Rogers's person-centered therapy and Dewey's pragmatism. Dewey elevated the notion of change and growth to the central characteristic of living existence. Person-centered therapy does the same. Structure is always dependent on process in Dewey's pragmatism. This holds for person-centered therapy as well.

To be sure, there is also a difference between Dewey and Rogers at the human level of functioning reality. For Dewey change requires human forming, or experimentally guided (re)construction, to become growth. For Rogers change is growth. If allowed, growth occurs naturally and has its own formative power. We can obstruct it or surrender ourselves to it, but we can never induce it or (re)form it. Dewey takes a culturally formative attitude to growth. Rogers takes an actively receptive attitude toward it. This makes Dewey the father of all eclectic forms of therapy and Rogers the father of all nondirective, person-centered forms of therapy. However, both forms of therapy are united in their common emphasis on change and growth.

Evolution of Theory. Because of this dynamic emphasis it is difficult to give a systematic description of person-centered therapy. Those systematic descriptions that do exist tend to describe it in terms of one of the stages of its development. For example, strictly speaking it is incorrect to characterize the approach to therapy developed by Rogers as "person-centered" therapy. Person-centeredness is only one of its formulations. At least two other formulations can be distinguished. In order to do justice to the developing character of Rogers's views on therapy, as well as to the dynamic character of his thought, we need to understand person-centered therapy systematically in its development. The central theme running through this developmental description is a movement from fixity to fluidity.

First formulation. Rogers's first formulation of therapy is nondirective (Rogers, 1942). It states in essence that therapy is an autonomous process in the sense that it occurs entirely within the client. The therapist can either facilitate its release or obstruct the occurrence, but he can never cause or induce it. For that reason Rogers repeatedly warns the therapist against interfering with the life of the client. Such intervention would be therapeutically counterproductive.

Instead, he enjoins the therapist to free the process by creating a warm relationship that is maximally permissive of the expression of feeling. By focusing on the feelings of the client, the therapist brings to open expression all the conflicting feelings that the client has regarding himself and his situation. This yields a process of catharsis, or emotional release, in which these feelings are resolved.

The inevitable and spontaneous result of this catharsis is the achievement of insight on the part of the client. Again, this second movement of the process cannot be given to the client by any form of direction or education. It is the inevitable and spontaneous consequence of the first, cathartic movement because it is entirely brought about by the growth forces inherent in the client himself. To be genuine, such insight must be a working insight. It necessarily involves a process of choice and action on the part of the client. For that reason also the client must earn or achieve this insight himself. It cannot be given to him by the therapist.

Since the therapeutic process is autonomous and thus driven entirely by the growth forces within the client, the only stance that the therapist can possibly take is a nondirective, nonauthoritarian, permissive one. The main aim of therapy in this conception is to avoid obstructing the growth process.

Second formulation. In his second formulation of therapy Rogers moves from nondirectiveness to person-centeredness (Rogers, 1951). In doing so he also gives a richer description of the therapeutic process. The fundamental attitude of the person-centered therapist is one of active trust in the client's capacity for self-help. This attitude of trust must be unconditional because it itself forms the condition for therapy. It makes therapy therapeutic. It must also be pervasive. It cannot be a technique that one tries out on the client and modifies or discards depending on the client's response. Herein lies the essential difference between eclectic and person-centered therapy. The attitude of the eclectic therapist changes depending on its effect on the client. But the active trust that characterizes the whole of the person-centered therapist's attitude lasts for the duration of therapy, irrespective of the changes that occur in the client. To be sure, techniques are not without their usefulness for the person-centered therapist. They serve to communicate his attitude of trust to the client. But this also exhausts their function. As a result of this person-centered attitude in therapy the client gradually becomes more and more aware of his potential for helping himself. Thus it leads the client toward a sense of personal autonomy.

The process that elicits this awareness is essentially that of disorganization and reorganization of the client's self-concept. The self-concept of a person who has no need for therapy is, by and large, internally consistent with what he daily experiences and perceives. Yet even such a person is occasionally bound to have experiences that are incongruent with his self, and these tend to threaten the internal consistency of the self. However, a congruent person normally defends his self against these experiences by denying them access to his awareness. When these incongruent experiences become so powerful or numerous that he can no longer keep them from awareness, the person enters therapy.

As the client begins to explore himself in therapy, he is likely to discover even more attitudes, feelings, and experiences that are incongruent with his self-concept. This tends to further threaten his self until he moves into the amorphous state of no longer having an organized self-concept. Emotionally this disorganization process tends to be extremely disturbing for the client. With every new discovery he is forced to ask himself anxiously what this will do to the basis of his life. The actively and unconditionally trustful attitude of the therapist allows him to continue his self-exploration process in spite of his emotional upheaval. The therapist demonstrates his unconditional and pervasive trust in the client by actively following him, without fear, in any direction and toward any outcome that he may determine. If supported by the therapist, this process of self-disorganization will inevitably result in the growth of an enlarged and reorganized self. This self now can much more comfortably include all those experiences that were previously denied.

The sense of growth further forms the backdrop for the despair that the client experiences in therapy, thus making it possible for him to continue the process to its completion. The outcome of this therapeutic process is a reorganized self-concept that now is much more congruent with his experience. As the process of reorganization occurs, the client begins to feel himself more and more in action. In effect, he discovers that by relinquishing his hold on experience, he has gained more control over experience. Once again, however, the force driving this therapeutic process is not the structuring or interpreting efforts of the therapist but the forward-moving growth forces of life inherent in the client himself. Once released in therapy, these forces make the client aware that he is not the mere product of outside influences but in some real sense the maker of himself, his own product.

Third formulation. While Rogers's first and second formulations of therapy deal with the attitude and action of the therapist, his third and final formulation focuses almost exclusively on the therapeutic process. In this conception therapy is that process through which the client becomes a fully functioning person (Rogers, 1961). In therapeutic terms, to become a fully functioning person means to become the therapeutic process which, as a result of therapy, is released in the client. This third formulation differs from Rogers's person-centered description in that the outcome of therapy is now no longer an enlarged, reorganized self but rather the process of therapy itself. The end result of therapy is no longer openness to, and congruence with, experience but rather an identification with the dynamic living experience that a person is.

This process entails first of all that the client lose all control over his experience. He must surrender himself to his organism (which Rogers largely identifies with experience). Rather than impose meaning upon his experiential organism, the client must let it tell him the meaning that it has. This will happen only if he becomes nondirective and receptive toward his own organic experience. The self as thinker about experience must diminish in order for the growth forces of the experiential organism to bear fruit. When this occurs, the client's self is no longer the watchman over experience but an inhabitant in living dynamic experience.

From the point of view of Rogers's third and most mature formulation, therapy is a process that moves the client from fixity to changingness. Since the organism is a perpetual process of change or actualization, dynamic changingness is the inevitable result of becoming one's experiential organism. For Rogers this dynamic changingness is the hallmark of a mentally healthy person. It means that the client's self is at its best when it functions as a fluid Gestalt that changes with the experience of the moment. As a result of this therapeutic movement the client begins to live existentially, literally changing from moment to moment, ever and anew transcending himself. Finally, instead of having a set of values he becomes a valuing process.

This dynamic changingness is not random movement, however. It is constructive movement in a positive direction. It is also realistic because it is open to all the client's impulses and experiences. Thus the client has access to a maximally possible amount of information. For that reason he is in a position to make the best possible choices for himself so that he can live as fully as possible. The change for the better which the client obtains according to this conception of therapy is that he becomes an experiential organismic process and therefore also a more fully functioning person.

Evaluation. For the neurotic client who is torn apart by conflicting feelings and internal inconsistencies, person-centered therapy offers a sense of emotional relief and a renewed sense of personal wholeness and competence. It helps the client become himself more comfortably, and it helps him change himself more freely.

But this enhanced sense of personal autonomy is not without its cost, because it condemns the client to a life of perpetual change, with no chance of anchoring himself to abiding structures either outside or inside himself. The picture of the fully functioning person that emerges at the end of therapy is that of a person who is thrown back upon himself for the task of maintaining his personal integrity and who is driven by a compulsion to grow. It evokes a sense of intense restlessness about human life. The fully functioning person cannot find rest in his dependence on his fellows or on the Person who is the source of his being, nor on the created structures in terms of which he lives and moves and has his dynamic being. To do so would be a violation of his personal autonomy and of the internal growth principle which, according to this conception of humanity, forms the essence of a person's being.

This state of being is the direct result of Rogers's fixation on growth, as exemplified by his lifelong simultaneous preoccupation with the autonomy of persons and the centrality of dynamic growthful experience in human life. The following statement illustrates Rogers's basic intent: "Experience is, for me, the highest authority. The touchstone of validity is my own experience. No other person's ideas and none of my own ideas are as authoritative as my experience. It is to experience that I must return again and again; to discover a closer approximation to truth as it is in the process of becoming in me. Neither the Bible nor the prophets—neither Freud nor research—neither the revelations of God nor man—can take precedence over my own direct experience" (Rogers, 1961, p. 23).

The central thrust of Rogers's view of therapy is decidedly anti-Christian. At the same time, his system of therapy contains many valuable insights that Christians can gratefully use in their own approach to therapy. Such notions as the respect and care for persons together with an emphasis on human freedom are reflections of important biblical themes, albeit that because of their secularized character they are pale reflections. However, in utilizing these moments of truth we do well to carefully re-form them in order to make them conform to the revealed will of the Lord.

References

Rogers, C. R. *Counseling and psychotherapy*, Boston: Houghton Mifflin, 1942.
Rogers, C. R. *Client-centered therapy*. Boston: Houghton Mifflin, 1951.
Rogers, C. R. A theory of therapy, personality, and interpersonal relationships, as developed in the client-centered framework. In S. Koch (Ed.), *Psychology* (Vol. 3). New York: McGraw-Hill, 1959.
Rogers, C. R. *On becoming a person*. Boston: Houghton Mifflin, 1961.

Additional Readings

Kirschenbaum, H. *On becoming Carl Rogers*. New York: Delacorte Press, 1979.
Van Belle, H. A. *Basic intent and therapeutic approach of Carl R. Rogers*. Toronto: Wedge Publishing Foundation, 1980.

H. A. VAN BELLE

See ROGERS, CARL RANSOM; SELF THEORY.

Personhood. Both in ordinary and philosophical usage persons are usually contrasted with mere things. Thus, to say of some human being that she is a person is to emphasize the differences between the human and subhuman orders, and to inquire about the nature of personhood is to inquire about the nature of those differences.

It was probably Kant who most shaped the meaning of the word *person* with his insistence that persons and only persons are ends in themselves, who should never be treated solely as means. Thus, to speak of human beings as persons is, among other things, to speak of them as morally significant beings, the potential bearers of rights and obligations. This moral sense of personhood must be distinguished from the related legal sense, in which infants may not be considered full persons while corporations are. The term *self* often does much of the same work as the term *person*, and some philosophical discussions use the terms interchangeably.

Though there is general rough agreement on the characteristics that distinguish human persons from nonpersons, different thinkers have at various times regarded different characteristics as being most fundamental. Medieval thinkers emphasized rationality as the essential characteristic of persons, following Boethius, who defined a person as an individual substance of a rational nature. In the modern classical period John Locke, while not ignoring rationality, emphasized the quality of self-awareness over time as decisive for personhood, including particularly memory. More recent thinkers have tended to emphasize activity, seeing persons as responsible agents whose decisions reflect values or caring concerns (Macmurray, 1957). These different views should be regarded as complementary perspectives rather than as rivals, since all these characteristics are significant elements of personhood.

Although the term *person* is usually employed to differentiate human persons from the subpersonal order, some thinkers have attempted to reduce or eliminate these differences. The view that human persons are not really unique or qualitatively different from the rest of the natural order is generally called reductionism, since the aim is to eliminate the special status human persons seem to enjoy by reducing them to the status of other animals. Early behaviorism, as developed by Watson (1930), was an avowedly reductionistic program. Skinner's (1971) radical behaviorism continues this reductionistic program, as is evidenced by the title of his popular book, *Beyond Freedom and Dignity*. More recent social behaviorists have, however, modified behaviorism considerably in a nonreductionistic direction.

Historically most thinkers who have defended the uniqueness of the person have been dualists who have held that the self or soul is not a material entity and must be distinguished from the body. Not surprisingly, therefore, most reductionists have been materialists who have identified the person with the body.

Not all materialists are reductionists, however. Some recent thinkers have attempted to avoid both dualism and reductionism. Strawson (1959) developed a view of the person as a unique kind of entity, which must be described in two different ways. To properly describe human persons we must employ both material predicates and personal predicates. Since personal predicates are not reducible to material predicates, Strawson's view should not be regarded as reductionistic.

Most contemporary discussions of personhood have been problem oriented and have tended to focus on one of three areas: 1) the problem of consciousness, or the relationship of mind to body; 2) the problem of the identity of the person over time; and 3) the nature of personal actions. The latter area encompasses the traditional debate over freedom and determinism.

The Mind-Body Problem. Two facts about human persons seem obvious. First, persons have bodies. Second, persons are conscious. The mind-body problem concerns the relationship of these two facts and their relative significance for answering the question as to what kind of entity human persons really are.

Classical positions on the mind-body problem fall naturally into two groups: monistic positions and dualistic positions. Dualistic views regard the mind or soul (roughly equivalent terms), the seat of consciousness, as a distinct nonphysical substance. In this view a human person is a composite of this nonmaterial substance and the body. Some dualists prefer to identify the person exclusively with the soul. Not all dualists agree on the relationship between the soul and body. Most, like Descartes, have been interactionists who hold that body and soul can reciprocally control and influence each other. Thus, dualism is compatible with the obvious ways in which consciousness is affected by and even dependent on the brain and central nervous system. Other dualists have been parallelists, who have denied interaction between soul and body because of the difficulty in explaining interaction between two radically different substances.

Monistic views, which deny that a human person is or has two distinct substances, are an even more varied lot. Idealists or panpsychists believe that the person is a purely spiritual entity, interpreting the body as being in some sense spiritual. Materialists reject the existence of any nonphysical substance; on this view a person is identical with his body. Neutral monists teach that a person is one substance that has both mental and physical characteristics.

Epiphenomenalism is a special case that does not fit easily into any other category. The epiphenomenalist views consciousness as a by-product of the body. Thus the mind is distinct from the body, as dualists affirm, but completely a function of the body, as materialists affirm.

Materialists differ among themselves as to how to describe and explain the mental aspects of persons. Metaphysical or philosophical behaviorism (to be distinguished from methodological behaviorism) holds that the mind consists of certain types of behavior as well as tendencies to engage in behaviors. Central state materialism, or the mind-brain identity theory, holds that conscious events are not just conditioned by, but are strictly identical with, neurophysiological events in the brain and central nervous system. Eliminative materialism takes the bull by the horns and boldly denies that mind or consciousness really exists. On this view a scientific description of the workings of the brain and central nervous system could in principle, if not in practice, replace our mentalistic language altogether.

Christians do not all hold to the same position on the mind-body problem. Traditionally most Christians have been dualists, and many still are. Some contemporary Christian thinkers have attempted to develop dualistic views that do justice to the unity of the person and body and do not devalue the body in

Platonic fashion. In general anyone who believes in an "intermediate state" after death, in which a person continues to exist prior to the resurrection, is committed to dualism. Other Christians today are more drawn to forms of neutral monism or nonreductionistic materialism, which make life after death depend completely on a bodily resurrection (Reichenbach, 1978).

Personal Identity over Time. Over the course of a lifetime persons change enormously, both intellectually and physically. In what sense, then, can a person be said to be the *same* person at one point in time that he was at some earlier point in time? Unless some good answer to this question can be given, it would seem wrong to punish or reward a person for some past action. Surely one is not generally responsible for actions performed by a different person. The choice of criteria for personal identity also has a crucial bearing on the possibility of life after death, for these criteria simply express our beliefs about how much and in what ways a person can change and still remain the same person. For example, could a person leave his body and still remain the same person? Could he receive a new body?

Several different views of personal identity have been defended. One of the most prominent is the memory theory, which was put forward by Locke. In this view a person is identical with a past person if he has memories of that person's actions and experiences. One major difficulty with this theory is that to remember myself doing some past action *presupposes* that I am identical with that person rather than accounts for that identity. A second theory proposes bodily continuity as the criterion of personal identity. This position obviously rules out any possibility of life after the death of the body.

Dualists who believe that the self is a conscious soul which, though embodied, is not identical with its body handle this issue differently. From the dualistic perspective, since the self is a metaphysical reality, a resurrected person can be the same person, even though the body is new, so long as the new body is possessed by the same self or soul. Christians who are nondualists must argue that bodily similarities and memory experiences would be sufficient to regard a resurrected person as the same individual.

Theory of Action. Correlated with the distinction between persons and mere things is the distinction between actions and mere events. If a rock rolls down a hillside and crushes a car, it makes sense to ask what caused the event. However, if a person pushes a rock down a hillside onto a car, it makes sense to ask who did it as well, and to inquire about the meaning of the action. In the case of the action it is not obvious that the action is caused in the way in which mere events are caused, for most human beings believe that at least some of their actions are freely chosen. Making sense of this distinction between actions and mere events has generated a great deal of discussion, which is still largely unresolved. Among the most debated issues is the relation between reasons for action and causes. Unlike most cases of causal explanation, giving a reason for an act does not seem to render the act inevitable but rather to make the act intelligible. One can know the reason for an act without knowing any relevant causal law. Reasons also serve to justify as well as explain actions in a way that ordinary causal explanations do not. Despite these differences between reasons and ordinary causes, reasons do seem to serve as motives, and it is widely held that they must therefore serve as causes in some sense.

Closely related to this dispute about action is the traditional debate over freedom and determinism. Three classical positions on this issue continue to have adherents. The determinist insists that all human actions have antecedent conditions that necessitate their occurrence and that freedom of the will is an illusion grounded in ignorance of the causal factors. The libertarian, or advocate of free will, claims that at least some human actions, usually those involving rational reflection or moral effort, are not completely determined by their antecedent conditions. This position is easily caricatured. The libertarian admits that not all human behavior is free and that even free choices are limited by the past, but he insists, however mysterious it may seem, that human persons are not completely a product of their past.

The compatibilist believes that freedom and determinism must both be accepted. This is possible if freedom is defined as acting in accordance with one's own wants or preferences, yet those preferences are seen as causally determined. On this view a free action is one that is shaped by the person's internal wants and is not compelled or coerced by some external factor. Libertarians object to this on the grounds that the compatibilist view reduces to determinism. Libertarians claim that since the compatibilist admits that our wants are ultimately caused by external factors, this implies that even in the case of uncoerced acts the ultimate responsibility for an action always rests outside the individual. To the libertarian a person can be held morally responsible for an action only if he could have done otherwise, even given his past history.

The debates about personhood have a particular significance to Christians. Not only do Christians believe that human beings have an eternal destiny, they believe that God himself, the ultimate reality and ground of everything else real, is a person. Many twentieth-century theists have termed their whole philosophy *personalism.* For the theist, to explore the nature of personhood is to plumb the depths of the whole of reality, and the unique characteristics that demarcate human persons from other creatures must be seen as forming the image of God in man, an image that has been defaced but not obliterated.

References

Macmurray, J. *The self as agent.* New York: Harper & Row, 1957.

Reichenbach, B. *Is man the phoenix?* Grand Rapids: Christian University Press, 1978.

Skinner, B. F. *Beyond freedom and dignity.* New York: Knopf, 1971.

Strawson, P. F. *Individuals: An essay in descriptive metaphysics.* London: Methuen, 1959.

Watson, J. B. *Behaviorism* (3rd ed.). Chicago: University of Chicago Press, 1930.

Additional Readings

Allport, G. W. *Becoming.* New Haven: Yale University Press, 1955.

Berofsky, B. (Ed.). *Free will and determinism.* New York: Harper & Row, 1966.

Bertocci, P. A. *The person God is.* New York: Humanities Press, 1970.

Borst, C. V. (Ed.). *The mind-brain identity theory.* New York: St. Martin's Press, 1970.

Evans, C. S. *Preserving the person.* Downers Grove, Ill.: Inter-Varsity Press, 1977.

Penelhum, T. Personal identity. In P. Edwards (Ed.), *The encyclopedia of philosophy.* New York: Macmillan, 1967.

Ryle, G. *The concept of mind.* New York: Hutchinson's University Library, 1949.

Shaffer, J. *Philosophy of mind.* Englewood Cliffs, N.J.: Prentice-Hall, 1968.

C. S. EVANS

See SELF.

Personnel Selection in Religious Organizations.

Achieving an optimal fit between an individual's unique characteristics and the requirements of a particular job is always difficult. But the selection of personnel for positions in religious organizations is further complicated by theological issues and specific methodological problems.

First, religious organizations pursue abstract, generally altruistic goals that are difficult to translate into measurable objectives. Hence, it is difficult to know when success has occurred and, by the same token, to identify the particular worker characteristics likely to lead to success. In the face of this problem religious organizations, unlike their secular counterparts, often fall back on the hope that applicant weaknesses can be supernaturally transformed. Unfortunately this kind of thinking can lead an organization to neglect one of its major stewardship responsibilities, its human resources.

Applicants for positions in religious organizations also face unique situations. Recognizing the inherent idealism of the organization, they may be reluctant to ask specific questions about the job. For example, questions about compensation, travel requirements, and working conditions may not be asked for fear that they will be misinterpreted as a lack of organizational or even spiritual commitment. Since an unrealistic job preview is an excellent predictor of subsequent turnover (Wanous, 1980), this failure to ask specific questions can have serious negative consequences for the individual and the organization.

In addition to these theological and interpersonal issues, selection of religious personnel also poses methodological difficulties. The first is the small number of applicants relative to the number of job openings. Most denominations or mission boards reject only about 5% of those who formally apply. This has the practical consequence of increasing the number of subsequent failures, since the organizations may be forced to accept poorly qualified applicants in order to fill the available positions.

The fact that there may be only one or two individuals holding a particular job also complicates the selection problem. Small samples make it difficult, if not impossible, to statistically validate the predictive power of selection procedures. One way around this problem would be to combine job incumbents from different seminaries, denominations, etc. There may be important differences in job requirements across these groups, however, which could obscure the specific strengths and weaknesses of the selection procedures.

Present Practices. Most selection in religious organizations is based on subjective assessments of job applicants through application forms, letters of reference, and interviews. The validity of these tools rests on one of applied psychology's favorite adages: "The best predictor of future behavior is past behavior." Application of this principle, however, may require considerable extrapolation, since past performance in a local church may have to be used to predict cross-cultural adaptation, or seminary grades to forecast ministerial performance.

There does seem to be a convergence of opinion among religious organizations regarding the characteristics that should be assessed during the selection process. These include spiritual commitment, leadership, and ability to get along with others. Unfortunately these qualities are vaguely defined and difficult to assess, thus forcing most candidacy committees to rely heavily on their general impressions of the applicant's potential.

Without a great deal of survey research it is impossible to definitively reproduce the typical selection process in religious organizations. Informal interviews and personal experience, however, suggest that the following sequence may be reasonably accurate in one particular type of religious organization—mission organizations.

First, the prospect submits a preliminary application that usually focuses on determining whether or not the person meets the organization's minimum eligibility requirements—e.g., education requirements (usually at least a college degree), theological beliefs, life style, and marital status. Following this initial screening the prospect would submit a formal application, which usually asks for 6 to 12 references and detailed information on personal goals and life experiences. One or more interviews are also typical, and in some organizations the applicant may be asked to take one or more psychological tests. For applicants under consideration for overseas assignment an intensive medical examination is usually required. Some mission organizations extend the application process by requiring participation in a candidate school, a training camp, or short-term service prior to acceptance as a career candidate. In addition to providing an intensive orientation experience for candidates, such programs can also provide the organization with a more natural setting in which to observe a candidate's interpersonal strengths and weaknesses. Furthermore, since these programs are usually conducted in close quarters, they can also help build team spirit and morale among candidates. Raising financial support is the final hurdle in the selection process before actual departure.

Evaluation and Recommendations. How accurate are the selection decisions made by religious organizations? Again, the absence of research evidence from a broad-based study forces dependence on informally collected data. With this limitation clearly in mind, it appears that the selection procedures of most religious organizations are reasonably accurate. At the same time, there is reason to suspect that religious organizations and the individuals who work in them may be reluctant to identify marginal performers as failures, thus improving "hit rates" by overlooking personnel selection errors.

What are the primary causes of failure in religious organizations? In general, there is agreement that social and motivational rather than technical problems underlie most voluntary or involuntary terminations. Interestingly, this is also the case in secular organizations (Landy & Trumbo, 1980). Most admissions officers and personnel directors in religious organizations would probably welcome better predictors in these areas.

The place to begin improving selection in religious organizations is with systematic job analysis. Too often selection is based on general notions about what psychological, physical, or spiritual factors contribute to successful performance. Job analysis helps to determine the specific knowledge, skills, abilities, and attitudes that affect performance in a particular job assignment. In addition, job analysis may provide information about training needs of workers in particular jobs.

Once the critical requirements of a job have been determined, psychological tests, interviews, and recommendation forms should be selected or developed that focus on these characteristics. Gathering information that is not clearly job related should be avoided. This can help reduce the effects of unfair interviewer biases—e.g., higher evaluations of interviewees who are perceived to be similar to the interviewer. Interviewers can also be made aware of other common interviewing problems—e.g., the tendency for overall evaluations of the candidate to distort judgments about specific qualifications, an error known as the "halo effect." Also, the task of integrating information about the candidate should be divided up among several people in order to take advantage of their different perspectives. Most important of all, selection committees should receive feedback from the field regarding the accuracy of their predictions. Only in this way can they avoid perpetuating false beliefs about the job, the characteristics leading to success, and the selection program itself.

Considering both the tangible and intangible costs of job failure for both the organization and the individual, it is clear that selection decisions must be approached thoughtfully and with a willingness to learn from mistakes. Nevertheless, selection procedures will never be perfect, thus pointing to the need to supplement them with training programs, individual counseling, and career planning. These developmentally focused programs explicitly acknowledge the dynamic nature of jobs, individuals, and organizations, and represent a continuing commitment to human resource stewardship.

References

Landy, F. J., & Trumbo, D. A. *Psychology of work behavior* (Rev. ed.). Homewood, Ill.: Dorsey Press, 1980.

Wanous, J. *Organizational entry.* Reading, Mass.: Addison-Wesley, 1980.

Additional Readings

Cascio, W. F. *Applied psychology in personnel management* (2nd ed.). Reston, Va.: Reston Publishing, 1982.

Dunnette, M. D. *Personnel selection and placement.* Belmont, Calif.: Wadsworth Publishing, 1966.

Lindguist, S. E. (Ed.). Assessment of missionary and minister effectiveness [Special issue] *Journal of Psychology and Christianity,* 1983, 2(4).

J. M. Fisher and D. D. McKenna

Personology Theory. A distinct tradition in the field of personality, concerned with the study of whole persons rather than with more molecular aspects or views of personality. It is associated with Murray and, to a lesser degree, Allport. For Murray personology is "the branch of psychology which principally concerns itself with the study of human lives and the factors that influence their course, which investigates individual differences and types of personality; . . . the science of men, taken as gross units" (Murray, 1938, p. 4). History and biology play major roles.

The personological approach examines the life history of the individual, including traits, needs, and situations. In its approach personology is a field theory that takes into account the interaction of person and environment as a determinant of behavior. The focus is on a comprehensive understanding of an individual.

Murray's personology was a prototype taxonomy of organismic and environmental influences on behavior. These organismic and environmental factors defined Murray's theory as a motivational one. Behavior is motivated by viscerogenic (primary) and psychogenic (secondary) needs. The former represent the impact of organismic survival tendencies, most of which are innate (e.g., need for air, water, food, urination, etc.). Murrary also included some less familiar survival needs such as "nox-avoidance," the need to rid oneself of noxious stimulation by withdrawing or vomiting, and

"sentience," the desire for sensuous gratifications as exemplified in thumb sucking and carrying one's security blanket (Murray, 1938, p. 78). The focus of viscerogenic needs is restoring homeostasis to the organism.

The psychogenic needs represent the social survival motives. They may reflect social habits or rituals of interaction. Murray listed some 28 psychogenic needs, including the need for abasement, achievement, affiliation, aggression, autonomy, defendance, deference, dominance, exhibition, nurturance, order, play, rejection, and succorance.

Influenced by Freud, Murray conceived of psychogenic needs as being latent (i.e., unconscious underlying determinants) or manifest (i.e., evidenced in overt behavior). Murray (1943) developed the Thematic Apperception Test (TAT) to assess latent motives, while the Edwards Personal Preference Schedule (EPPS) measures manifest motives (Edwards, 1959).

Press was Murray's term for the impact of environment on the individual. "The press of an object is what it can *do to the subject* or *for the subject*—the power that it has to affect the well-being of the subject in one way or another" (Murray, 1938, p. 121). A press, then, is an environmental stimulus that motivates behavior. Press can be categorized as a fact of objective reality or a subjective, phenomenological interpretation. In the former case it is termed an alpha press; the latter is designed a beta press. When a wide divergence occurs between a specific alpha press and its beta correspondent, a delusion is said to exist. Press may take on various forms (e.g., danger or misfortune, lack or loss, rejection, birth of a sibling). Often a need emerges as a reaction to a press.

Temporal units are employed in the analysis of person-situation interactions. A single need-press unit constitutes a thema. When a particular thema occurs with great frequency or intensity, especially in infancy, an underlying pattern or habit develops that gives consistency to behavior; this unity thema serves as a central trait.

Murray's personology was influenced by Gestalt psychology (i.e., field theory) in its use of molar units. Patterns of themas combine to form larger behavioral sequences known as serials. Serials constitute the basic datum of the personologist in analyzing personality. Proceedings are sequences of serials leading to the achievement of goals.

Murray's view of personality built on the depth psychology of Freud and Adler. Murray conceived of the id as a repository of primitive instincts and unacceptable impulses, but thought it also possessed socially acceptable impulses. The ego inhibited and repressed the negative impulses but facilitated the positive ones. The superego developed from cultural conditioning and served as an internalized regulation system. Closely associated with the superego was the ego ideal, which represented personal ambitions and aspirations.

Prenatal and early childhood experiences contribute substantially to personality. When an early experience makes a clear and marked effect on later behavior, those experiences constitute a complex. The claustral complex embodies a wish to return to prebirth conditions, to seek protection and nurturance. The fear of insupport complex is seen in fear of open places, loss of family, falling, etc. Behavior designed to escape to fresh air and open places, to avoid suffocation, emanates from the egression complex.

Murray's study of personality was devoted to the whole person, including the individual's history and biology (Kluckhorn, Murray, & Schneider, 1953). The brain was the site of personality, because to Murray personality was not possible if the individual lacked a brain. Brain activity was a regnant process prerequisite for personality functioning. His personology anticipated recent research that has linked personal motives with situational demands (i.e., interactionism).

References
Edwards, A. L. *Manual for Edwards Personal Preference Schedule* (Rev. ed.). New York: Psychological Corporation, 1959.
Kluckhorn, C., Murray, H. A., & Schneider, D. M. *Personality in nature, society, and culture* (2nd ed.). New York: Knopf, 1953.
Murray, H. A. *Explorations in personality*. New York: Wiley, 1938.
Murray, H. A. *Thematic Apperception Test manual*. Cambridge: Harvard University Press, 1943.

R. L. TIMPE

Person Perception. Kelly (1955) has argued that we view life through templates that we create and then attempt to fit over the realities of the world. The fit is not always very good. Yet even a poor fit is more helpful than having no template at all.

Clearly we are not passive recipients of sensory facts from the outside world. Rather, we actively create our physical and social worlds through selective attention, interpretation, and recall of experienced events. While asserting this as a fact of human nature allows us to break away from the mechanistic dogma of radical behaviorism, it also raises the possi-

bility that we can make serious misjudgments about the world in which we live. When these misjudgments are about other people, they can significantly affect the quality of our social interaction and relationships. This article will examine some of the more prominent biases in person perception that have been identified by social psychologists.

Motivational Bias. Schneider, Hastorf, and Ellsworth (1979) maintain that person perception biases can be divided into two general types: motivational and cognitive. Motivational bias occurs when a perceiver's own needs, values, attitudes, or motives unduly influence his or her view of others. Projection, one of the classic psychoanalytic defense mechanisms, is an excellent example of this type of bias. To avoid acknowledging our own fears, anxieties, and impulses, we externalize them by seeing them in others.

The fact that current needs can bias our perceptions of others is illustrated by Carlson's (1967) study of over 400 managers in the insurance industry. Managers who were told that they had fallen behind on their recruiting quotas evaluated job applicants more favorably than did managers who were told they were ahead of their quotas. We may be more willing to overlook others' weaknesses when under pressure to evaluate them favorably.

Another important motivational bias is ego bias (Schneider, Hastorf, & Ellsworth, 1979), also known as self-serving bias (Myers, 1983). We seem to be highly motivated to see ourselves favorably. This tendency is perhaps most clearly revealed by the fact that we are usually more willing to accept personal responsibility for our successes than blame for our failures. Although ego bias relates primarily to the way we perceive ourselves, it may also have an indirect effect on our perceptions of others. Myers and Bach (1976) found that when two people were required to cooperate with each other on an experimental task, they tended to blame their partner, perhaps undeservingly, for failure. As Myers warns: "When others are blamed for their bad deeds while one's own are excused, open hostility is not far away" (1983, p. 85).

Cognitive Bias. Whereas motivational biases are caused by our conscious or unconscious desires to see others as we would like to see them, cognitive biases arise out of the strategies we use to gather, interpret, and recall information about others.

One such bias is our tendency to form quick impressions of others and then hold on to them, even in the face of strong disconfirming evidence. Stringbett's (1958) classic research on the interviewing process demonstrates the power of first impression bias. He found that interviewers' impressions of interviewees were crystallized after a mean interviewing time of only four minutes, and that these early impressions played a dominant role in determining final hiring decisions.

Our perceptions of others can also be biased by the various beliefs we bring to a social situation. In an experiment conducted by Snyder and Frankel (1976), subjects were shown a silent videotape of a woman being interviewed. One group was told that she was being interviewed about sex, while another was told she was being interviewed about politics. Given these mental sets, the former group perceived the woman to be more anxious, both during the interview and in general, than did the latter.

The effects of contextual cues and expectations upon person perceptions are also shown in Rosenhan's (1973) oft-cited study in which he and his graduate students were admitted as patients to a number of mental hospitals. While their sanity was typically detected by the other patients, staff personnel assumed that they were suffering some psychological disorder and accordingly interpreted their behavior as symptoms. Clearly our expectations about what certain kinds of people are like influence our interpretations of their actions.

Expectations and beliefs affect not only what we see in other people but also how we piece together coherent pictures of their traits, abilities, and attitudes—i.e., their personalities. A number of studies have shown that we often infer that the presence of one characteristic, such as physical attractiveness, implies that the person also possesses certain other characteristics, such as intelligence or extraversion. Stereotyping of minority group members would be one instance where such inferences may lead us seriously astray.

Another manifestation of this type of bias is the "halo effect"—the tendency to perceive an individual's characteristics as being consistent with our general impression of them. Nisbett and Wilson (1977) demonstrated this bias by showing college students videotaped segments of an interview with a college instructor who spoke with a heavy foreign accent. Some of the students saw the instructor act in a very cool, aloof manner, while others saw him act in a warm and friendly way. As expected, the students liked the instructor more in the warm and friendly condition. But the significant finding of this study was that students' liking for the instructor affected their response to his physical characteristics, mannerisms, and accent. While those who saw him as cool and aloof found these features irritating, those who perceived him as warm and friendly saw the same features as appealing. These and other similar findings point out the danger of overlooking specific strengths and weaknesses in individuals because we feel generally positive or negative about them.

Another cognitive bias that has recently received a great deal of attention from social psychologists is the "fundamental attribution error." As we observe and interact with others, we often find ourselves searching for reasons for their actions. Typically we will explain their behavior in terms of their personal qualities (e.g., she is a mean person), or qualities of the situation (e.g., anyone would strike back under such conditions). The fundamental attribution error is our tendency to underestimate the impact of situational factors on other people's behavior. The existence of this type of bias should caution us whenever we are tempted to call a person brilliant, lazy, paranoid, etc. It may well be that situational factors are playing a powerful role in the etiology of their behavior.

Since accurate perceptions of others are so critical in both personal and professional relationships, it is important to ask what can be done to mitigate the effects of perceptual biases. An important first step in this direction is to train persons to recognize the various sources of perceptual errors. Further, some researchers have recommended courses geared to helping people learn to minimize perceptual bias. For those whose work depends heavily on accurate perceptions of others—including mental health professionals, ministers, supervisors—such training would seem to be a wise investment of time and energy.

References

Carlson, R. E. Selection interview decisions: The effect of interviewer experience, relative quota situation, and applicant sample on interviewer decisions. *Personnel Psychology,* 1967, *20,* 259–280.

Kelly, G. *The psychology of personal constructs (Vol. 1).* New York: Norton, 1955.

Myers, D. G. *Social psychology.* New York: McGraw-Hill, 1983.

Myers, D. G., & Bach, P. J. Group discussion effects on conflict behavior. *Psychological Reports,* 1976, *38,* 135–140.

Nisbett, R. E., & Wilson, T. D. Telling more than we can know: Verbal reports on mental process. *Psychological Review,* 1977, *84,* 231–259.

Rosenhan, D. L. On being sane in insane places. *Science,* 1973, *179,* 250–258.

Schneider, D. J., Hastorf, A. H., & Ellsworth, P. C. *Person perception* (2nd ed.). Reading, Mass.: Addison-Wesley, 1979.

Snyder, M. L., & Frankel, A. Observer bias: A stringent test of behavior engulfing the field. *Journal of Personality and Social Psychology*, 1976, *34*, 857–864.

Stringbett, B. M. Factors affecting the final decision in the employment interview. *Canadian Journal of Psychology*, 1958, *12*, 13–22.

D. D. McKenna

Persuasion. *See* Attitude Change.

Pervasive Developmental Disorder of Childhood or Adolescence. This rare disorder, more prevalent in boys than girls, is marked by major disturbances in social relations and unusual kinds of behavior. It commences after 30 months of age and prior to 12 years and seems to be common in children with low IQs.

The social relationships of a child with this diagnosis are at a gross level of impairment. Of the following behaviors, three must be present for diagnosis (*DSM-III*): 1) sudden excessive anxiety (free-floating anxiety, a major overreaction to everyday happenings, inability to receive consolation when upset, or unexplained panic attacks); 2) inappropriate or constricted affect (lack of appropriate fear reactions, unexplained rage reactions, and extreme mood lability); 3) inability to tolerate change in the environment (e.g., upset if dinner time is changed) or the demand that activities be repeated exactly every time (e.g., puts on clothes in the same order); 4) unusual posture or hand/finger movements, or walking on tiptoe; 5) speech abnormalities (questionlike melody, monotonous voice); 6) hyper- or hyposensitivity to sensory stimuli (e.g., hyperacusis); and 7) self-mutilation such as biting or hitting oneself and head banging.

While there are often bizarre ideas and fantasies, there is an absence of delusions, hallucinations, incoherence, or marked loosening of associations. This chronic disorder tends to have a better long-term prognosis than infantile autism. Family, hereditary, or organic predisposing factors are at present unknown.

Such children are unable to function independently. Constant supervision and financial support are necessary. Due to the possibility of self-injury, poor interpersonal skills, and tendencies to react without apparent warning, these individuals require continual observation and care. The surrounding environment should provide physical and emotional protection, predictability, defined structure, and loving, firm limits.

B. J. Shepperson

Pfister, Oskar Robert (1873–1956). Protestant minister and pioneer Freudian psychoanalyst. He was cofounder of Swiss Society for Psychoanalysis and remained a loyal follower of Freud even during the interim in which the group disbanded (1914–1919) and the others turned to Jung.

Pfister's father, a liberal Swiss Protestant minister, died while attending medical school, preparing himself for a medical ministry to the parish poor. From an early age his son Oskar identified with the poor in spirit, the troubled and abused, particularly children who were victimized by the neurotic behavior and rigid regimentation of their schoolmasters. He integrated his perceptions of divine and human love with a grasp of personality development derived from psychoanalysis. From this integration he devised his technique of "psychoanalytic paedegogik," a method of psychoanalytic education for children. Testimony to its importance is its impetus and foundation for Anna Freud's child and adolescent psychoanalysis.

Pfister also turned his attention to the "hygiene of religion," by which he meant a two-way interaction between religion and mental hygiene. His approach emphasized the healing force of religion in human development and life as well as the cleansing and clarifying power of psychoanalytic insight in ridding religion of soul-scarring aberrations. He took pains to correct what he deemed to be misinterpretations of the gospel, and to scourge the theologies and moralisms of the church fathers, the Roman Catholic Church, and the Reformers. He was particularly hard on Calvin, gentler with Luther.

Pfister found that graduate studies in the academic psychology of his time offered little help in pastoral work and the cure of souls. Least of all did it assist him with the children in his parish. For him the newly developed psychoanalysis became the answer to his quest for a means through which to express the love of Christ actively. It became not only a technique in fulfilling his Christian aspirations for his ministry but also a way of life for him. Praising Pfister's 1917 publication of *The Psychoanalytic Method*, Freud wrote that such a book "will . . . be able to count on the gratitude of later generations" (Zulliger, 1966, p. 175). Meng, a Swiss psychoanalytic colleague, commented further: "The new psychology awakened in him the clarity of thought and sensitivity of empathy which enabled him to learn the language of demons and gods in the unconscious, and which simultaneously made possible to bring to life the meaning and language of the Bible, without dogma and in the service of pastoral care" (Zulliger, 1966, pp. 175–176).

Pfister managed to conduct his psychoanalytic, theological, and educational explorations while fulfilling duties as preacher, pastor, and administrator of the Prediger Church (Zwinglian) in Zurich. Having met Freud in Vienna in 1909, he maintained a lifelong friendship through visits and correspondence (134 letters exchanged between 1908 and 1937). Some 300 of Pfister's journal entries testify to the fruitfulness of the interaction between these two minds.

Reference

Zulliger, H. Oskar Pfister: Psychoanalysis and faith. In F. Alexander, S. Eisenstein, & M. Grotjahn (Eds.), *Psychoanalytic pioneers.* New York: Basic Books, 1966.

Additional Readings

Brown, S. H. A look at Oskar Pfister and his relationship to Sigmund Freud. *The Journal of Pastoral Care,* 1981, *35,* 220–233.

Meng, H., & Freud, F. (Eds.). *Psychoanalysis and faith: The letters of Sigmund Freud and Oskar Pfister,* New York: Basic Books, 1963.

Pfister, O. R. *Christianity and fear: A Study in history and in the psychology and hygiene of religion.* New York: Macmillan, 1948.

E. A. LOOMIS, JR.

Phallic Stage. According to Freud, the third major stage of a child's psychological development. It lasts from approximately 30 months to 7 years.

See PSYCHOSEXUAL DEVELOPMENT.

Phantom Response. A delusional perception of the presence of any body part subsequent to its removal or loss. The most common and best described and understood of the phantom phenomena is that of an amputated limb or digit. Less frequently the loss of nose, eyes, teeth, breasts, penis, or other body parts can result in a phantom percept. Not only is this response common, it is also considered to be healthy and appropriate as an immediate reaction to such a sudden loss. However, it can proceed to pathological proportions and has been reported to persist as long as 20 years after the surgery.

A phantom limb or digit is a generally universal response to amputation and is estimated to occur in as many as 98% of such surgical cases. This phantom is generally painless and exists for a period of time in one's perception of body image before fading. In proportionately few cases the phantom may be experienced as painful and necessitate various therapeutic interventions. Breast phantoms, usually in response to mastectomies for breast cancer, are less frequent, occurring in 22–64% of the cases (Simmel, 1966).

The phantom delusion usually involves an initial awareness of the whole extremity, with most awareness being on the distal (or outerly) part such as foot or hand. The sensory impression of the phantom generally consists of three general types: 1) mild tingling; 2) momentary, more pronounced pins-and-needles, often triggered by touching the stump; and 3) unpleasant sensations of burning, twisting, itching, or a variety of other disturbing feelings. The phantom percept is generally intermittent, and the associated sensations are ties to this awareness, being felt only when the phantom is experienced.

The phantom is initially experienced as a whole, but this perception is generally modified by experience through time. It gradually becomes more faintly perceived and the awareness fades away, first proximally (closest to the body), then towards the distal. Thus, there can be a period of confused body image when the percept neither matches the original state nor mirrors the true altered state. The distal part sometimes feels as if it were directly attached to the body, as in hand to shoulder, and sometimes as if a space exists between the body and the part. This collapsing in subjective perception over time is called telescoping and generally occurs in the natural course of the phantom response.

Supportive therapy focused toward the larger issue of loss is generally sufficient for the natural adaptation to occur. However, psychological resistance to this process, frequently related to anger and strong resentment, may necessitate more active psychotherapy. The occurrence of painful phantom phenomena often warrants various approaches, including direct intromission of anesthetic locally to the stump, hypnosis for analgesia, or more extensive psychotherapies.

Reference

Simmel, M. L. A study of phantoms after amputation of the breast. *Neuropsychology,* 1966, *4,* 337–350.

G. MATHESON

Phenomenological Psychology. Most basically, an attitude and an approach: an attitude of respect for the dignity and integrity of each person's experience and an approach or methodology for studying the personal meanings of experience. The context for such study is collaboration and trust rather than manipulation and deception. The results of a psychological investigation utilizing a phenomenological method are qualitative descriptions of the personal meanings of particular experiences. These differ significantly in content as well as form from the results of more traditional psychological research—quantitative analyses of impersonal measurements of behavior.

Phenomenological psychology can be viewed as primarily a critique of the more established schools of psychology, a corrective to some of the emphases and methods of contemporary psychology, or an alternative psychological methodology in and of itself. This article presents a concise discussion of each view, preceded by a brief look at the historical development of phenomenological psychology and some of its central concepts.

Historical Development. The dominant figure in the early development of the phenomenological movement was the philosopher Edmund Husserl, during the first third of the twentieth century. The term *phenomenology*, however, was coined much earlier—in the middle of the eighteenth century—and has since then been applied in a variety of directions. The direction that Husserl chose was heavily influenced by another European, Franz Brentano, generally regarded as the main forerunner of the phenomenological movement. The most thorough and competent review of the predominantly European and philosophical side of the phenomenological movement is the two-volume work of Spiegelberg (1969).

A clear distinction must be made between phenomenological psychology and phenomenological philosophy, even though they have many similarities and common inheritances. Misiak and Sexton (1973) have compiled an excellent survey of the development of the psychological side of the phenomenological movement, as has Spiegelberg (1972). Of particular note are the first contribution of a systematic phenomenological psychology to the American psychological literature (Snygg & Combs, 1949) and the first major American symposium on phenomenological psychology, with such notable participants as Sigmund Koch, Robert MacLeod, Carl Rogers, and B. F. Skinner (Wann, 1964).

Also of importance are the highly original and significant works of the French scholar Maurice Merleau-Ponty, especially in the area of perception, and the development of the psychology department of Duquesne University in Pittsburgh. Psychologists at Duquesne and several of their graduates have made diverse and substantial contributions to the ever-developing literature. In addition, in 1971 they founded the successful *Journal of Phenomenological Psychology*. The journal's stated policy characterizes well the emphasis of contemporary phenomenological psychology: "This journal is dedicated to the aim of approaching psychology in such a way that the entire range of experience and behavior of man as a human person may be properly studied. The priority is placed on the fidelity to the phenomenon of man as a whole and all aspects that are studied must be mindful of their human relatedness. The challenge facing us is to invent methods and other types of analyses that will unveil significant aspects of man's relatedness to himself, others and the world."

Central Concepts. There have been several attempts to list the central concepts of phenomenological psychology. Among the clearest are the works of Merleau-Ponty (1969) and Giorgi (1976). A complete listing would have to include at least the following.

Description. A phenomenological study aims basically to describe rather than explain, to understand how rather than why. The goal is to provide reliable guideposts for others to be able to understand their own similar experience. Applied in a Christian context, personal testimonies, for example, would provide guideposts to help others understand their own experience of God better.

Bracketing. In order for a description to be faithful to what someone has actually experienced instead of what he or she perhaps should have experienced, one needs temporarily to leave aside ("bracket") questions of reality, truth, and cause, and any other personal biases. This does not involve valueless tolerance, but it does involve tolerance of ambiguity. That is, can I stand not knowing something for sure or not letting someone else know that I "know for sure"? Can I temporarily leave aside what I know will impede the revelation of actual experience?

Meaning. A phenomenological description is a detailed account of what a particular experience means to someone. In other words, it portrays the significance or value of the experience plus the details of what it was like, or how it was for that person. Applied to interpersonal communication, for example, to share with you how I value our interaction—what you are like for me, how I feel about you—is to tell you what you mean to me.

Experience. It can be said that meaning is to experience as measurement is to behavior. This highlights the difference between experience, the focus of phenomenological psychology, and behavior, the focus of behavioristic psychology. Whereas a phenomenological description relies on verbal and nonverbal behavior, the importance of the behavior is that it represents the underlying experience. Behavior can in varying degrees represent or misrepresent the experience—what the person really means—so the job of phenomenological psychology is to devise methods to facilitate the accurate representation of experience by self-report behavior.

Phenomenal worlds. Phenomenologically, experience is composed of phenomenal worlds and intentionality. Phenomenal worlds are the reflective organization or stucture, the rationality, the individualized perceptions, feelings, and meanings that people refer to as reality—or at least reality as they see it. This is consciousness, which is often spoken of as the object of the phenomenologist's study.

Intentionality. The prereflective, nonrational part of experience is called intentionality. This is the preverbal tending or orienting toward something that we then become consciously aware of. It is our spontaneous, bodily involvement in a situation before we have words for it. For example, one may break out in a cold sweat while talking with a friend and not have any idea why. Or one may be prayerful without uttering words. This is the realm of the unconscious and is an integral part of human experience. As such, it is crucial for understanding what a person means and what a person knows. The apostle Paul may not have been able adequately to put it into words, but he *knew* the love of Christ (Eph. 3:19) and *knew* the peace of God (Phil. 4:7) that passed his mental understanding.

Phenomenological Psychology as Critique. Perhaps the greatest impact of phenomenological psychology to date has been its critique of mainline psychology. Central to the critique is calling into question the professionally orthodox belief in emotionless, uninvolved abstraction from detached observation—the belief that third-person information is more accurate, more objective, than first-person information. This could be called the myth of "immaculate perception." Maslow (1966) calls it "spectator knowledge," or peeping at people through keyholes rather than being in their worlds.

To be truly objective one must participate with the other person. One must be sufficiently involved to be in contact with how the specific individual (object) qualities of the other person present themselves and with the feeling and drama of the situation. This will of necessity involve dialogue rather than deception and help build trust rather than mistrust.

The basic issue is whether psychology is exclusively a natural science founded on an unbending belief in detached observation, experimental manipulation, and statistical analysis, and the assumption that the subject is merely a passive respondent. Or is it also a human science, founded on belief in participant observation, experiential collaboration, and description of personal meanings, and the assumption that the coinvestigator is an active participant in the research process? (See Giorgi, 1970.)

The pressing need for the development of psychology as a human science is indicated by the continuing treatment of persons as objects and personal feelings and meanings as error. Human persons are being assigned "to the same ontological status as weather, stars, minerals, or lower forms of animal life" (Jourard, 1972, p. 7). Psychologists are making molehills out of mountains, making the person over into the image of their childhood erector sets (May, 1967).

Phenomenological Psychology as Corrective. The consequence of having a choice between psychology as a natural science and a human science is that there is an unavoidable trade-off between rigor on the one hand and relevance on the other. To avoid having precision at the expense of significance some psychologists have utilized a phenomenological method as a preliminary step in generating hypotheses to be tested later experimentally. MacLeod in particular championed this approach. Others have developed phenomenologically oriented procedures as correctives to the experiment itself.

The most radical corrective is to take the entire psychological study out of the laboratory—removing manipulation from the methodology—as a supplementary field test for the laboratory findings. This is a type of naturalistic observation (Willems & Rausch, 1969).

Two very important correctives deal with the persistent findings that the personality of the scientist can be a biasing factor in the experiment, and that the subject often responds more to personal agenda and environmental distractions in the experimental situation than to the verbatim instructions. Bakan (1967), for example, points out that the personality type of the experimenter can determine the choice of the statistical test of significance and thereby bias the results. In addition, Rosenthal (1966) warns of experimenter bias, or the unintended communication to subjects by supposedly neutral, uninvolved experimenters of expectations regarding the outcome of the experiment. In both cases awareness of the potential problem can serve in and of itself as a corrective, although Rosenthal also proposes detailed solutions to the expectancy problem.

Concerning the not-so-passive subject, several studies have revealed a wide variety of role enactments determined by the subjects' preconceptions, motives, and suspicions (Weber & Cook, 1972). Orne (1970) has also discovered the pervasive effects of demand characteristics, or the environmental cues that create compelling expectations and demands on the subject. Orne's double corrective of the preexperimental inquiry and postexperimental interview helps with the problem of role enactments as well as that of demand characteristics.

Phenomenological Psychology as Alternative. As a complete methodology in and of itself phenomenological psychology does not try to control but rather utilizes the effects of the personality of the experimenter and the active participation of the subject. The process is called a coinvestigation and is based on dialogue.

Ideally a phenomenological study begins in silence with an attitude of wonder, of quiet, inquisitive respect. It proceeds inductively from dialogue between the coinvestigators to facilitate the self report of an experience, to extraction of related meanings—themes—from the self-report data, back to dialogue for a check on the accuracy of the themes, to an exhaustive description that combines the relevant themes into a concise statement, and finally back to a dialogue for an evaluation of how well the description represents the original self report and any modification that may be needed. The product is a rich description of experience as it is actually lived.

Representative studies would begin with van Kaam's (1966) study of the experience of really feeling understood and include Stevick's (1971) investigation of the experience of anger, Keen's (1975) study of a five-year-old changing her mind, and Colaizzi's (1977) research into the process of existential change occasioned by reading. Although these four studies adequately portray the diversity of methods within phenomenological psychology, each is significantly less than ideal in fully incorporating dialogue into its methodology.

The phenomenological approach should also prove useful in helping us understand religious experience, by inquiring directly into the experience itself rather than merely checking the Bible to see if it is legitimate (Farnsworth, 1981). In terms of attitude, respecting how people present themselves has definite application to the Christian life. It means being nonjudgmental: "Does our law judge a man without first hearing him to find out what he is doing?" (John 7:51); "Let everyone be quick to listen, slow to talk" (James 1:19); "He who answers before he hears, it is folly to him and reproach" (Prov. 18:13).

References
Bakan, D. *On method: Toward a reconstruction of psychological investigation.* San Francisco: Jossey-Bass, 1967.
Colaizzi, P. F. Psychological research as the phenomenologist views it. In R. S. Valle & M. King (Eds.), *Existential-phenomenological alternatives for psychology.* Baltimore: Williams & Wilkins, 1977.
Farnsworth, K. E. *Integrating psychology and theology: Elbows together but hearts apart.* Washington, D.C.: University Press of America, 1981.
Giorgi, A. *Psychology as a human science: A phenomenologically based approach.* New York: Harper & Row, 1970.
Giorgi, A. Phenomenology and the foundations of psychology. In J. K. Cole & W. J. Arnold (Eds.), *Nebraska symposium on motivation* (Vol. 23). Lincoln: University of Nebraska Press, 1976.
Jourard, S. M. A humanistic revolution in psychology. In A. G. Miller (Ed.), *The social psychology of psychological research.* New York: Free Press, 1972.
Keen, E. *A primer in phenomenological psychology.* New York: Holt, Rinehart, & Winston, 1975.
Maslow, A. H. *The psychology of science: A reconnaissance.* New York: Harper & Row, 1966.
May, R. *Psychology and the human dilemma.* Princeton, N.J.: Van Nostrand, 1967.
Merleau-Ponty, M. What is phenomenology? In J. D. Bettis (Ed.), *Phenomenology of religion: Eight modern descriptions of the essence of religion.* New York: Harper & Row, 1969.
Misiak, H., & Sexton, V. S. *Phenomenological, existential, and humanistic psychologies: A historical survey.* New York: Grune & Stratton, 1973.
Orne, M. T. Hypnosis, motivation, and the ecological validity of the psychological experiment. In W. J. Arnold & M. M. Page (Eds.), *Nebraska symposium on motivation* (Vol. 18). Lincoln: University of Nebraska Press, 1970.
Rosenthal, R. *Experimenter effects in behavioral research.* New York: Appleton-Century-Crofts, 1966.
Snygg, D., & Combs, A. W. *Individual behavior: A new frame of reference for psychology.* New York: Harper & Row, 1949.
Spiegelberg, H. *The phenomenological movement: A historical introduction* (2 vols.) (2nd ed.). The Hague: Nijhoff, 1969.
Spiegelberg, H. *Phenomenology in psychology and psychiatry.* Evanston, Ill.: Northwestern Unversity Press, 1972.
Stevick, E. L. An empirical investigation of the experience of anger. In A. Giorgi, W. F. Fischer, & R. Von Eckartsberg (Eds.), *Duquesne studies in phenomenological psychology* (Vol. 1). Pittsburgh: Duquesne University Press, 1971.
van Kaam, A. *Existential foundations of psychology.* Pittsburgh: Duquesne University Press, 1966.
Wann, T. W. (Ed.), *Behaviorism and phenomenology: Contrasting bases for modern psychology.* Chicago: University of Chicago Press, 1964.
Weber, S. J., & Cook, T. D. Subject effects in laboratory research: An examination of subject roles, demand

characteristics, and valid inference. *Psychological Bulletin*, 1972, 77, 273–295.

Willems, E. P., & Rausch, H. L. (Eds.), *Naturalistic viewpoints in psychological research.* New York: Holt, Rinehart, & Winston, 1969.

K. E. FARNSWORTH

Phenomenological Therapy. A form of therapy emphasizing description rather than explanation. Psychotherapies are most often constructed around what each one regards as the essential explanation of the therapeutic process. Such explanations, however, typically reduce the phenomenon of psychotherapy to theoretical abstractions that are something less than, or at least different from, the therapeutic process as it is actually experienced by its participants. For the behavior therapist, for example, therapy works because of the application of selective reinforcement. For the person-centered, or client-centered, therapist the key explanation is unconditional positive regard. For the psychoanalyst it is transference.

The phenomenological therapist, on the other hand, asks how, not why. An attempt is made to understand *how* the client experiences his or her body, self, space, time, and relationships (Keen, 1976). Phenomenological therapy is, then, as much an attitude as it is a method (*see* PHENOMENOLOGICAL PSYCHOLOGY). It is an attitude of respect for the client's experience and of distrust of theoretical conclusions about that experience. It is a suspension of clinical judgment until after the experience, however abnormal it may be, has thoroughly presented itself (Van den Berg, 1955).

Phenomenological therapy historically had no distinct beginning as such, because as part of the more general phenomenological movement it has usually been an applied afterthought of the phenomenological research process. From a new depth of understanding of the human condition has come a new desire to help people experiencing psychological pain. Consequently, technically there is no such thing as phenomenological therapy as in the sense of a complete set of techniques and procedures.

Rather, there are many therapies that either implicitly or explicitly rely on the phenomenological attitude in the client-therapist encounter, interpersonal strategies that can be applied from phenomenological research (van Kaam, 1966; Zinker, 1977), and/or phenomenologically derived conclusions regarding human psychopathology (Fischer, 1970; Keen, 1970). Thus, it is useful to show, as Spiegelberg (1972) has done, the degree to which such therapists as May (existential therapy), Rogers (person-centered therapy), Frankl (logotherapy), Boss (Dasein analysis), and Perls (Gestalt therapy) are or were phenomenological. In order to do so, one must draw on appropriate historical figures in the phenomenological movement, such as Karl Jaspers, Ludwig Binswanger, F. J. J. Buytendijk, Kurt Goldstein, and Paul Schilder.

A completely phenomenological therapy would have to align itself with the work of historical and contemporary phenomenologists to prevent inauthentic detours. Rogers, for example, assumes that the job of the therapist is to provide an atmosphere for, and not interfere with, the natural unfolding of the "organismic self" of the client; this is based on the further assumption that feelings are most important in human functioning. He then assumes that the therapeutic process can be studied by means of pre- and posttherapy tests and measurement by outside observers of the in-therapy behaviors of client and therapist. This is clearly at odds with the consensus of phenomenological understanding that 1) suspends such beliefs as the existence of an organismic self that naturally unfolds in a world awash in feelings (Barton, 1974) and 2) calls for direct interrogation of the experience of both therapist and client rather than relying on extratherapy tests and the judgments of external observers (Smith, 1971).

Rogers does, however, bring a significant phenomenological emphasis to his therapy. Barton (1974) argues that the task of the phenomenological therapist is to express as faithfully as possible only those meanings, feelings, sensings, and interpretations that are given by the client. "Within client-centered practice, this dwelling on the face-presentation, of not leaping to theoretical, explanatory, or high-level interpretive ideas, is lived out in a faithful, plodding dwelling within what the client says" (p. 266).

Gendlin (1966), an early follower of Rogers, takes this even further when he states that the therapeutic change "occurs not from more exact revelation of how the patient is and came to be as he is, not from more and more fully showing him that he must be as he is. . . . It comes from making this now ongoing relationship into a new and different concrete life experience for him, a kind of experiencing he could not be, and was not, until now" (p. 213).

Phenomenological therapy offers exciting possibilities for the Christian. An attitude of respectful and nonjudgmental listening combined with shared experiences, such as praying together (Farnsworth, 1975), representing a faithful living out of the client's expressed needs, can be tremendously freeing.

References

Barton, A. *Three worlds of therapy: An existential-phenomenological study of the therapies of Freud, Jung, and Rogers.* Palo Alto, Calif.: National Press Books, 1974.

Farnsworth, K. E. Despair that restores. *Psychotherapy: Theory, Research and Practice,* 1975, *12,* 44–47.

Fischer, W. F. *Theories of anxiety.* New York: Harper & Row, 1970.

Gendlin, E. T. Existentialism and experiential psychotherapy. In C. Moustakas (Ed.), *The child's discovery of himself.* New York: Ballantine Books, 1966.

Keen, E. *Three faces of being: Toward an existential clinical psychology.* New York: Appleton-Century-Crofts, 1970.

Keen, E. Confrontation and support: On the world of psychotherapy. *Psychotherapy: Theory, Research and Practice,* 1976, *13,* 308–315.

Smith, D. L. Phenomenological psychotherapy: A why and a how. In A. Giorgi, R. Knowles, & D. L. Smith (Eds.), *Duquesne studies in phenomenological psychology* (Vol. 3). Pittsburgh: Duquesne University Press, 1971.

Spiegelberg, H. *Phenomenology in psychology and psychiatry.* Evanston, Northwestern University Press, 1972.

Van den Berg, J. H. *The phenomenological approach to psychiatry.* Springfield, Ill.: Thomas, 1955.

van Kaam, A. *The art of existential counseling.* Wilkes-Barre, Pa.: Dimension Books, 1966.

Zinker, J. *Creative process in Gestalt therapy.* New York: Brunner/Mazel, 1977.

K. E. FARNSWORTH

Phenylketonuria (PKU). A congenital metabolic disorder resulting from the inability of the body to convert phenylalanine, an essential amino acid. Ten to 25 times the normal amount of phenylalanine is found in the blood and urine, causing severe mental deficiency. The average victim has an IQ below 20. The disorder appears in infancy and is transmitted by a recessive gene in 1 in 10,000 births. One-third of the cases have eczema and convulsions. The majority are undersized, light complexioned, with coarse features and small heads. The typical PKU child is hyperactive and unpredictable and may be incapable of verbal and nonverbal communication. The disorder was discovered in 1934 by Folling, and research in the 1950s found an early diagnosis (prior to 6 months of age) and treatment with a low phenylalanine diet could result in significant improvements for the PKU infant.

D. L. SCHUURMAN

See MENTAL RETARDATION.

Philosophical Psychology. A point of view that cuts across all schools of psychology rather than one discrete school of thought or representative of a single method. Its importance is to be seen in the fact that one of the divisions of the American Psychological Association is expressly dedicated to philosophical psychology.

While most psychologists define themselves as scientists, practitioners, or both, much of what psychologists actually do is philosophical in nature. Their work has to do, in one way or another, with questions that are not answerable by scientific methods. Questions about the ultimate nature of reality, how the universe is fitted together and by implication how people fit into it, what is ethically or morally good and bad, the nature of knowledge and consciousness, the nature of beauty, and the logical consistency of conceptual systems will never be answered in the laboratory. It is impossible to perform an objective experiment and thereby come up with definitive answers to such speculative questions. One could discover through psychological surveys what various people *think* about these questions, but one cannot answer the questions themselves through scientific means. Philosophical psychologists are concerned with clear thinking about such philosophically oriented psychological questions to which science cannot provide answers.

Clinical services are particularly fraught with philosophical issues. For example, many patients come to psychotherapists for philosophic guidance. A person suffering from serious depression might very well be interested in the results of scientific studies that elucidate the effectiveness of various antidepressant drugs, but he or she would usually also be concerned with questions about life's meaning, whether it is worth living, and so on.

Psychotherapists who are centrally interested in these sorts of questions frequently call themselves existential therapists or existential analysts. In so doing, they acknowledge that their services are not only open to, but purposely centered upon, the philosophical concerns of their patients. Moreover, psychologists who adopt what they call a phenomenological point of view are also often candid in admitting the philosophical nature of their clinical activities.

Great confusion has been spawned by the sloppiness with which both psychologists and lay persons have approached the definition of psychology. Many persons confuse behavioral science (research psychology) with speculative psychology (philosophical psychology), and much of what gets passed off on the public as psychology is essentially philosophy. There are, in fact, very strong and inescapable links between philosophy, theology, and psychology. Philosophical psychologists make these links their points of study—issues such as Determinism and Free Will, Personhood, Self, and the mind-brain relationship.

C. W. McLemore

See Psychology, Presuppositions of.

Phobic Disorders. A phobia is an irrational fear of presumably harmless objects or situations. A phobia also occurs when the perceived danger of an object or situation is out of proportion to the real danger. Phobic reactions vary from a moderate degree of anxiety or feeling of unpleasantness to panic levels of anxiety with accompanying physical manifestations. Particularly common physical symptoms include palpitations and missed heartbeats; sweating, dizziness, and feeling of collapse; difficulty in breathing and expanding the chest; and difficulty in swallowing. Often psychological and emotional problems accompany these physical symptoms. These may include indecision, loss of confidence, feelings of unreality, obsessive worrying, feeling that one is "going crazy," depression, and low self-esteem.

A phobic condition so restricts an individual's life that he is unable to go places or do things that he would like. Such a person becomes a prisoner of his own imaginary fortress. This provides a false sense of security in that as long as he avoids the potentially fearful or anxiety-producing situations, his anxiety will be reduced. The reduction in anxiety reinforces the avoidant behavior. The individual's futile attempt to resolve the problem by avoiding the phobic situation thus becomes the means of perpetuating the phobic condition.

In the past, specific phobias derived their names from the Greek word that represented the feared object. Those ranged from acrophobia (dread of high places) to zoophobia (fear of animals). The most recent revision of the *Diagnostic and Statistical Manual of Mental Disorders* (*DSM-III*) has classified phobic disorders into three categories: agoraphobia, social phobia, and simple phobia.

Agoraphobia is the fear of open places. However, this phobic condition may manifest itself as panic attacks (severe anxiety with accompanying physical manifestations) when one is alone, when away from the home, left alone, going into stores, or any other situation where immediate help is not readily available. Some agoraphobic patients may become so terrified when confronted with such a situation that they faint.

A *social phobia* is the experience of intense anxiety when an individual is presented with a social situation that is perceived as potentially embarrassing or awkward. The intensity may be so great that the person shuns even family activities and reunions with relatives. The anxiety does not necessarily have to be associated with the individual's fear of doing something humiliating but may consist of a general uneasiness or awkwardness when around others. Treatment approaches with socially phobic individuals typically include training in assertiveness and social skills.

Simple phobias, in contrast to agoraphobia and social phobias, are typically monosymptomatic, meaning that the phobic condition consists of a single, fairly circumscribed object or activity. The specificity of simple phobias simplifies their treatment. The treatment of choice for simple phobias has been systematic desensitization.

The two most prominent explanations for phobic disorders have been advanced by the psychoanalytic and learning theorists. According to psychoanalytic clinicians, the phobic object or situation symbolizes an underlying unconscious conflict. The situation or object to which one is phobic is in some way associated with or represents this underlying conflict. Classical psychoanalytic thinking viewed conflicts of phobic individuals as sexual in nature, resulting from disturbances during the phallic stage of psychosexual development. Treatment entailed uncovering and confronting the unconscious conflict rather than dealing directly with the phobic object or situation.

Learning theory views phobic behavior as a result of a conditioned fear response. Such a response results when intense anxiety becomes associated with a neutral object or situation. This neutral object, which is now paired with anxiety, becomes the phobic object. Wolpe (1958) developed a procedure originally known as reciprocal inhibition, in which either relaxation, assertiveness, or sexual excitement were counterconditioned to the anxiety-producing situation. Reciprocal inhibition allows the extinction of fear to take place by preventing it from occurring in the presence of the feared object. Now known as systematic desensitization, this technique has come to be the treatment of choice for most clinicians working with simple phobias.

Multiple phobias (agoraphobias and social phobias), due to their behavioral, emotional, and cognitive effects, are usually too amorphous to be eradicated solely by desensitization procedures. It may be that in multiple phobias it is not the particular external event that is feared but rather an internal state. This feared internal state may range from the thought of fainting to the thought of having a heart attack. The feared internal state then becomes generalized to many different situations. For the individual this creates a hypersensitivity and hyperarousal to be on guard and vigilant for anxiety-producing situations. This hypervigilance increases the level of anxiety, making the possibility of a panic attack greater and culminating in a vicious, self-defeating cycle.

The first step in a cognitive behavioral treatment of multiple phobias should deal specifically with decreasing or eliminating anticipatory fears. During this phase of the treatment patients may be asked to develop a short phrase that will enable them to better accept their symptoms. These statements are very helpful in shutting off negative thought patterns and decreasing the amount of one's anxiety. The second step involves the use of relaxation to circumvent or decrease the patient's general level of anxiety. Essentially two approaches may be used, somatic and cognitive. The somatic approach relies on deep muscle training and biofeedback in order to teach the difference between tense and relaxed states. The cognitive relaxation approach relies on having the patient visualize a calm and serene scene in his mind, thereby eliminating negative or fearful thoughts. This may be followed with instruction in positive self-statements and coping imagery. Such statements and images should include confronting the phobic situation and coping with the phobic reaction. The final step is the gradual approach of the phobic situations. This step involves each of the three previous steps.

Reference
Wolpe, J. *Psychotherapy by reciprocal inhibition.* Stanford, Calif.: Stanford University Press, 1958.

K. R. KRACKE

Phototherapy. A technique first systematically utilized and described by the English surgeon Hugh Diamond, who began using photographs in his treatment of mentally disturbed patients in 1854. With the growing popularity of projective tests since the 1940s, an increasing number of therapists in the United States and Canada have used photographs with their clients as either a diagnostic or therapeutic technique.

Phototherapy uses personal photographs from family albums as a primary method.

Additional phases utilize patient interaction with videotaped images, projected slides, and motion pictures. The therapist creates a personal atmosphere, inviting the client to give free responses and form stories using photographs. The goal is to help the client discover and express sources of anxiety and pain. This goal is accomplished by using photographs as a catalyst to stimulate the recollection of painful, frequently repressed memories. Clients generally choose to work with family photos, which provides the opportunity to clarify relationships with families.

As a projective methodology phototherapy seeks to identify the personality structure of an individual, with emphasis on a person's developmental history. The chronological order of family photograph albums lends itself easily to this task. The projective procedure is supported by a theory of the unity of personality, which proposes that behind every expression and individual act is a unique personality structure. Phototherapists believe that ambiguous and largely unstructured tasks most readily reveal personality. Unlike other methods of personality assessment, the projective does not present the client with fixed alternatives. Further, phototherapy, by focusing discussion on the photographic images, offers the client a safe means of verbalizing problems and fears.

Compared to other projective diagnostic techniques, phototherapy does not have a standardized procedure, a scoring system, or generalized interpretations. The therapist supports the client's awareness and expression of values, intentions, motives, and feelings, both as catharsis and as a means toward the goal of defining personal strengths, elevating self-esteem, and establishing realistic goals for change and problem solving.

The procedure for phototherapy begins with the request that the client select a number of photographs from family albums or collections. The client is next asked to place the photos in order. With all photos spread out on a table, the subject responds by identifying symbols, relationships, or overall themes. He then responds in spontaneous fashion to each photograph in the order previously selected. In the final phase of phototherapy using family albums, members of the family respond to a recollection of the client's responses to photos. Exchange of perspective regarding family events, social gatherings, and situations is encouraged.

Phototherapy is most effective with subjects

capable of insight, responsive in a counseling situation, and willing to share personal and family photographs with a therapist. Its use with seriously disturbed persons is probably limited, since phototherapists often invite free association and fantasy role plays in conjunction with photographs. It is therefore not appropriate for use with persons who have hallucinations or systematic delusions.

The Christian call to reconciliation through personal contact and the mandate for fraternal forgiveness is in harmony with phototherapy's intent to increase communication and facilitate healing among family members. The phototherapist uses the family album as a means of evaluating the family system, with the hope of supporting family bonds and relationships. The procedure is in harmony with the Christian belief in the integrity and importance of the family.

Additional Readings

Akeret, R. *Photoanalysis.* New York: Wyden, 1973.
Hattersley, R. *Discover yourself through phototherapy.* New York: Association Press, 1971.
Krauss, D., & Fryrear, J. L. *Phototherapy in mental health.* Springfield, Ill.: Thomas, 1983.

D. SMARTO

Phrenology. A psychological theory originated in the early 1800s by Franz Josef Gall and based on the idea that certain mental faculties are related to specific areas of the brain. A contemporary, Johann Kaspar Spurzheim, coined the term *phrenology,* meaning literally the "science of the mind." The theory asserted that personality and character traits could be judged by the location and size of bumps on the skull.

More than a superficial character-reading technique, phrenology proposed the idea that anatomy directly influences mental behavior. Some 37 localized areas of the brain were specified to contain independent and inherited regions relating to such character traits as self-esteem, conscientiousness, and spirituality. Three general character types—mental, motive, and vital—facilitated grouping of personalities. Phrenology "maps" were drawn to indicate the locations of particular faculties and were then used to analyze the corresponding bumps on the skull of a client.

This practice was popular in the first half of the nineteenth century and greatly influenced the treatment of mental illness. Diagnosis consisted of finding the region of the brain responsible for the illness and treating it as a physical problem, with techniques such as

laxatives, exercise, rest, good food, and cutting off the blood supply. This view of mental illness as a brain disease was contrary to the popularly held belief that mental illness was a result of demon possession, and it changed such common practices in mental hospitals as exorcisms, beatings, starvation, and solitary confinement. While phrenology was later proven to be scientifically unverifiable, the theory may be credited with introducing the idea that mental phenomena can be approached scientifically and objectively.

D. L. SCHUURMAN

See PSYCHOLOGY, HISTORY OF.

Physical Contact in Psychotherapy. Physical contact has been the earliest form of communication known to man. It also is the first meaningful interaction between mother and child. Touch conveys warmth, caring, and acceptance; it soothes and heals when it is intended as such and accepted. Human physical contact is a curative language in its own right and therefore has interesting potential for psychotherapeutic treatment. This is especially true if therapy can in part be understood as a corrective emotional experience where emotional pains from the process of growing up are relived, better understood, and integrated into the person's ego. Since touch, whether by its absence or presence, was an important part of that developmental interaction between parent and child, so too in psychotherapy physical contact is used to facilitate growth and to convey safety.

Historical Context. Mythology, art, tribal medicine, and historic religions have all described the importance of touch as a powerful interpersonal communication (Mintz, 1969). With mysticism and magic contaminating the rigorous demands of nineteenth century science, Freud perhaps had no choice but to deliberately distance his emerging theories from touch. There is evidence to suggest that he himself was uncomfortable with physical intimacy, as seen in his posture behind the patient's couch. Historically psychoanalytic technique has maintained neutrality in the therapeutic hour so that the patient's transference can develop in as uncontaminated fashion as possible.

Modern psychoanalysis has realized that treatment does not avoid emotional interaction between therapist and patient. Therapeutic benefits such as reduced superego guilt or expanded ego development are gratifications. Avoiding touch so as to avoid gratification is therefore felt by some analysts to be unjustified. Rappaport (1975) refers to "the end of an era marked by supremacy of control, analysis, rationality and mental events." He observes that therapy is now rediscovering the biological, experiential roots of meaning, and the task of the therapist is one of "awakening the individual's senses and . . . knowledge of the body" (p. 64).

Prior to the 1970s little was written about touch in therapy (whether as an erotic or nonerotic experience) except the early writings of Ferenczi and Reich. Both broke from Freud's touch taboo and advocated physical contact as a means of enhancing progress in treatment. Reich came into public and professional disrepute by also using sexual intercourse as a therapeutic technique.

However, in a 1970 survey Dahlberg (1970) found widespread evidence of both nonerotic and sexual contact in therapy, as did Masters and Johnson (1970). The American Psychological Association referred to the practice as the "new morality in psychotherapy." Kardener's survey of 450 physcians from five areas of specialization revealed that roughly two-thirds believed nonerotic contact may possibly be of some value. Only 20% beleived sexual contact could be helpful, and only 5% admitted having such contact with their patients (Kardner, Fuller, & Mensh, 1973). Holroyd and Brodsky (1977) found approximately the same statistics for 500 male and 500 female Ph.D. psychologists. About 27% admitted to nonerotic contact (hugging, kissing, touching); 4% admitted to genital intercourse.

Since that time a large number of articles have appeared in the professional literature, most of which have encouraged prudent, conscientious efforts at facilitating treatment by including the potential for physical touch. Almost all have advised against sexual intercourse with patients. Both the American Psychological Association and the American Psychiatric Association have made ethical statements against intercourse or any form of sexual exploitation within the therapeutic relationship.

The Purpose of Touch. Touching patients should be done only when the therapist knows what he or she is doing. That is, by virtue of professional training and experience the therapist must assess what is going on within both the patient and the therapist before deciding to make physical contact. Touch is a service to be given; it is not something to be taken. It should spring from a desire to help, comfort, encourage, and reassure. Touching also is used to share genuine joy and the enthusiasm of celebration. It reminds both parties of their humanness. Touching allows a parental kind of loving care to be displayed for both preverbal infantile needs and childlike needs for security, affection, and acceptance. The therapist becomes a substitute parent temporarily to provide contact with the hurt, angry child as well as to foster exploration of those early data.

Brown (1973) refers to touch as conveying warmth, acceptance, and intuitive understanding. He calls it "the essential healing influence." Brown recommends that physical touching should be discontinued after the patient's reflective, intuitive, contemplative skills are brought into therapeutic interaction.

Perhaps the most important use of touch is to enhance self-esteem. It could be argued that at the core of all neurotic symptoms may be the fear of becoming an autonomous, independent person. Most patients have a defective self-concept and are struggling with issues of security, love, and acceptance by others. They have not learned to love themselves and are guarded and evasive. At bottom is a need for but fear of becoming a person. If psychotherapy is done in an atmosphere of mutuality much akin to what ideally should have occurred between parent and child, then the therapist must include the willingness to be physical, much the same as a good parent. In the nursing profession touch is recognized as healing, relaxing, encouraging, and giving hope (Krieger, 1979); why would it not do the same when expeditiously used in psychotherapy?

For many therapists this is hard to do because they prefer to remain safely intellectual and objective rather than allowing themselves to be lovingly human. For some it threatens to remind them of their own childlike needs. For others it risks sexual urges that they cannot handle as clinicians. It is difficult to make oneself truly available to another person, body and soul, mind and heart. Yet, as Marmor (1974) points out, therapists too have needs and in fact respond better to those patients whom they like more and who satisfy some of their own needs. Touching then may also be construed as an act that helps heal the therapist in some way, much the same as parents need encouragement or love from their children. Kernberg (1975) argues that these countertransference needs do not have to be seen as negative in treatment. He suggests the need to view countertransference as "total emotional reaction of a therapist to his patient, . . . including the therapist's own reality needs as well as his neurotic needs" (p. 49). Psychoanalyst Robertiello (1974) describes his use of touching and holding schizoid patients as one of the essentials in developing transference; it minimizes the risks of misinterpretation by the patient.

Touching patients holds dangers even if the therapist's intentions are primarily to help. Spotnitz (1967) illustrates how touching can stimulate anxiety; arouse to violence; or promote feelings of fear, alienation, distrust, loss of control, and infantile craving. He asks, "If touching can have deleterious consequences, why employ it at all in psychotherapy?" His answer: "Because it is essential for human beings to have some natural, physical contact with one another, it strengthens one's sense of reality . . . and can have a strong maturational effect" (p. 457).

Therapists must guard against using their patients to satisfy their own needs for whatever reason—power, affection, or sexuality. Despite the opinions of some writers (Shepard, 1971; Hammer, 1973) there is little justification for sexual intercourse in psychotherapy, not only because of the questionable ethical and moral practice, but also because it violates the incest taboo implicit in the therapist-patient relationship. There may be reported instances where intercourse has had positive effects (Taylor & Wagner, 1976), but such practices are highly questionable and give the profession a bad reputation (Rottschafer, 1979). Yet to refrain from any touch whatsoever because of risks of patient arousal or misinterpretation, may be an unnecessary overreaction. Most important is the intent of the therapist. Regardless of the patient's distortions or misinterpretations, if the therapist's professional judgment determines it may be effective, touch may be worth the risk.

Therapists need further instruction, discussion, and research to guide them in their effective use of this important treatment modality.

References

Brown, M. The new body psychotherapies. *Psychotherapy: Theory, Research and Practice*, 1973, *10*, 98–116.
Dahlberg, C. C. Sexual contact between patient and therapist. *Contemporary Psychoanalysis*, 1970, *6*, 107–124.
Hammer, L. I. Activity—an immutable and indispensable element of the therapist's participation in human growth. In D. Milman & G. Goldman (Eds.), *The neurosis of our time: Acting out*. Springfield, Ill.: Thomas, 1973.
Holroyd, J. C., & Brodsky, A. M. Psychologists' attitudes and practices regarding erotic and non-erotic physical contact with patients. *American Psychologist*, 1977, *32*, 843–849.
Kardener, S. H., Fuller, M., & Mensh, I. N. Survey of physicians' attitudes and practices regarding erotic and nonerotic contacts with patients. *American Journal of Psychiatry*, 1973, *130*, 1077–1081.
Kernberg, U. *Borderline conditions and pathological narcissism*. New York: Aronson, 1975.
Krieger, D. *The therapeutic touch: How to use your hands to help or heal*. Englewood Cliffs, N.J.: Prentice-Hall, 1979.
Marmor, J. *Psychiatry in transition*. New York: Brunner/Mazel, 1974.
Masters, W. H., & Johnson, V. E. *Human sexual inadequacy*. Boston: Little, Brown, 1970.
Mintz, E. E. Touch and the psychoanalytic tradition. *Psychoanalytic Review*, 1969, *56*, 365–376.
Rappaport, B. S. Carnal knowledge: What the wisdom of the body has to offer psychotherapy. *Journal of Humanistic Psychology*, 1975, *15*, 49–70.
Robertiello, R. C. Physical techniques with schizoid patients. *Journal of the American Academy of Psychoanalysis*, 1974, *2*, 361–367.
Rottschafer, R. H. The healing touch: The uses and abuses of physical contact in psychotherapy. *The Bulletin*, Publication of the Christian Association for Psychological Studies, 1979, *5*(2), 1–7.
Shepard, M. *The love treatment*. New York: Wyden, 1971.
Spotnitz, H. The toxoid response. In N. Greenwald (Ed.), *Active psychotherapy*. New York: Atherton, 1967.
Taylor, B. J., & Wagner, N. N. Sex between therapists and clients: A review and analysis. *Professional Psychology*, 1976, *7*, 593–601.

R. H. ROTTSCHAFER

Physiognomy. The attempt to "read" personality and individual traits from outward appearance, particularly facial features such as the shape of the jaw, the size and shape of the eyes, nose, forehead, and even eyebrows. Its origin as a theory of personality is traced back to Aristotle, the supposed author of *Physiognomica*, who suggested that people who resemble certain kinds of animals also possess their temperamental characteristics.

From the end of the nineteenth century to the first quarter of this century the theory was embellished by Ernest Hooten and Katherine Blackford, among others. Hooten related organic inferiority and primitivism to certain groups, races, and nationalities, while Blackford applied the theory to a method for personnel selection that was popular for some time. This typing was extended to social stereotypes, correlating attributes such as close-set eyes and a low forehead with criminal characteristics, and has become a fertile field for quacks and charlatans. Many of the stereotypes are perpetuated by literature and the media, prejudice, and attempts to further understand human nature through rigid categorization. No significant correlations have been established to validate the theory of physiognomy, although it may be that the myth is often perpetuated because people live up to the expectations of others who have placed stereotypical demands on them.

D. L. SCHUURMAN

Physiological Factors in Psychopathology. *See* GENETIC AND BIOCHEMICAL FACTORS IN PSYCHOPATHOLOGY.

Physiological Psychology. The study of the mental and behavioral effects of physical phenomena. The importance of the brain to the human personality has been known for many years. Descartes recognized that the brain is the organ that mediates certain behavioral functions such as sensation and body movements. However, he did not think the rational faculties were localized in the brain but interacted with the body in the pineal gland in the center of the brain.

Modern neuroscience dates from the work of Charles Bell in the early 1800s. Bell, along with Francois Magendi, discovered what has been called the Bell-Magendi law: that sensory and motor fibers enter and leave the spinal cord by separate roots. Bell was also one of the first to observe that different areas of the brain serve different functions. Several decades later Hermann von Helmholtz made important measurements of the neural impulse in a frog's nerve. In the 1860s Paul Broca, a French physician, provided support for the localization of function hypothesis, which said that specific areas of the brain controlled specific behavioral functions. He was able to relate a patient's inability to speak to a damaged portion of the brain.

The guiding assumptions of physiological psychology from this time were much closer to materialistic monism than to the interacting dualism of Descartes. This meant that the functions of mind and behavior were seen to be entirely a product of brain activity. Thus, from its very beginnings physiological psychology has been searching for those brain areas producing all of what we call the person. This view can obviously cause tension with the Christian concept of the person, in which the person is viewed as more than just the material of the brain.

Great advances in physiological psychology have occurred because of the rapid development of sophisticated techniques to study the brain. Most important among these were stimulation and recording techniques in which even single cells of the brain could be electrically or chemically stimulated and their electrical activity recorded.

The neuron has been identified as the primary functioning cell in the brain. It conducts electrical activity along its length. The electrical signal is then passed between neurons via chemicals known as transmitters. Large collections of neurons on the surface of the brain (cortex) are responsible for vision, hearing, body senses, speech, and motor movement. Internal portions of the brain seem to be responsible for motivational and emotional functions.

Recent Nobel Prize winners Hubel and Wiesel (1968) have discovered through single cell recording in monkey visual systems that cortical neurons are sensitive to simple pattern features in the environment. The other sensory systems also seem to process specific information from the stimulus world.

The hypothalamus in the interior portions of the brain seems to be involved in hunger, thirst, and sexual motivation. Lateral lesions, for example, in the hypothalamus produce hyperphagia or overeating in rats. Emotions such as aggression and rage have also been related to the hypothalamus as well as the limbic system of the brain. So-called pleasure centers have been isolated in the interior portions of the brain, and these may relate to both emotions and learning.

The search for the engram, or the physical basis for learning and memory, has produced a challenge to the localization of function theory. Support for specific storage locations for learning and memory was first provided by D. O. Hebb's cell assembly model and later by Wilder Penfield, who found specific localized stores for certain sensory memories. However, Karl Lashley shifted physiological psychology to a more holistic model of learning with research showing that any learned material was stored everywhere in the brain rather than in a specific location. Pribram (1971) recently attempted to delineate how a memory could be stored everywhere in the brain with his model that compares brain activity to a hologram (a three-dimensional photograph).

The clinical research of physiological psychology has included Hans Selye's work on the effects of stress and the human defenses against stress called the general adaption syndrome. Visceral learning studies related to biofeedback indicate that people and animals can learn to control their autonomic nervous system responses and the effects of stress. Biochemical research indicates that some mental and emotional problems seem to be related to abnormal levels of neural transmitters. Treatment emphasizes the use of drugs to increase or decrease the effectiveness of transmitters. The materialistic assumptions of physiological psychology emphasize rather strongly that all human problems can be solved by appropriate techniques applied to the brain.

The central problem with physiological psychology has always been the mind-brain problem. In its attempt to demonstrate materialism, physiological psychology as a whole has believed that the mind is an epiphenomenon of the brain—i.e., a direct product of brain activity. The research of Nobel Prize winner Roger Sperry on the split brain has been interpreted to mean that dividing the brain produces two minds, each half of the brain producing its own epiphenominal mind. This interpretation seems to attack the Christian concept of the soul. However, not all physiological psychologists accept this materialistic view. Nobel Prize winner John Eccles (Popper & Eccles, 1977) and Canadian neurologist Penfield (1975) believe that the physiological evidence points to the existence of a human mind that interacts with the brain. It should also be pointed out that electrical stimulation of the brain does not produce all the essentials of a person. It produces sensation, movement, sensory memory, and vague emotions, but not thinking, willing, complex emotions, or holistic experience. It is the latter functions that are typical of the human personality, and in these functions the brain seems only indirectly involved. Even if brain activity could be shown to correlate totally with the mind, Mackay (1974) argues that the Christian view of human nature does not depend on a lack of relationship between brain and mind activity.

References

Hubel, D. H., & Wiesel, T. N. Receptive fields and functional architecture of the monkey striate cortex. *Journal of Physiology*, 1968, *195*, 215–243.

Mackay, D. M. *The clockwork image*. Downers Grove, Ill.: Inter-Varsity Press, 1974.

Penfield, W. *The mystery of the mind*. Princeton, N.J.: Princeton University Press, 1975.

Popper, K. R., & Eccles, J. C. *The self and its brain*. New York: Springer International, 1977.

Pribram, K. *Languages of the brain*, Englewood Cliffs, N.J.: Prentice-Hall, 1971.

M. P. Cosgrove

See Brain and Human Behavior; Neuropsychology; Mind-Brain Relationship.

Physique and Temperament. See Constitutional Personality Theory.

Piaget, Jean (1896–1980). Swiss psychologist known for his study of the development of intelligence. Originally trained as a biologist, he developed an interest in psychology after his doctoral studies in the natural sciences at the University of Neuchâtel in 1917. He became interested in philosophy of science and in epistemology, which led him to the field of psychology in an attempt to find the connections between history and philosophy of science and epistemology.

His interest in psychology in turn led to study of the ideas and methodology of clinical psychologists. These studies took him to the Sorbonne in France. While in Paris he became involved at the Binet laboratory school, where he worked on standardized tests. As he worked on these tests, he noticed that there were patterns to the kinds of wrong answers children gave to the questions, and that the wrong answers of younger children had a different pattern from that of older children.

Combining his training in biology, his interest in epistemology, and his interest in psychology, Piaget launched himself into a study that he called genetic epistemology. The primary focus of this field is the relationships between biological development and how a person thinks.

In 1929, at the age of 33, he became director of research at Jean-Jacque Rousseau Institute in Geneva. During the first part of his career in genetic epistemology he focused his attention on children's development of various concepts such as language, causality, and morality. He then turned to the intelligence of infants and young children. During the last part of his career he also gave some attention to the meanings of his theory for the enterprises of education. In 1955, with the help of the Rockefeller Foundation, Piaget developed the International Center of Genetic Epistemology at the University of Geneva. At the time of his death he was working on cross-cultural studies under the auspices of UNESCO, with which he had been affiliated since its inception.

Piaget's native language was French, and much of his work went unread by English-speaking psychologists and educators until the 1950s. Since then more attention has been given to his ideas, as most of his many writings have been translated in English. His major works include *The Origins of Intelligence* (1936), *The Psychology of Intelligence* (1947), *Six Psychological Studies* (1964), and *Genetic Epistemology* (1970).

R. B. McKean

See Cognitive Development.

Pica. The desire for and eating of nonnutritive substances, a practice that occurs in humans or animals as a result of nutritional deficiencies or, in humans as a result of psychopathology. Pica is listed in *DSM-III* as an eating disorder typically seen in children and adolescents. Criteria for diagnosing pica include the repeated eating of a nonnutritive for one month and the absence of other conditions in which pica may occur as a symptom, such as mental retardation, infantile autism, or childhood schizophrenia. Substances consumed by children suffering from this disorder include clay, hair, paint, plaster, starch, or cloth. Normal children may consume some of these items for a short period of time without being considered for the diagnosis.

Pica has been observed as a symptom among chronic schizophrenics, regressed senile patients, deprived groups, and pregnant women. Pica is also used as a more general term to refer to unusual food cravings by pregnant women.

This disorder may be rooted in nutrient deficiencies or, according to analytic theory, in unmet oral needs. Pica may also have strong cultural roots, especially when the symptom is observed in adults. Geophagy, the ingestion of dirt, has been observed in Africa among starving peoples as a means of staving off hunger pains and among warriors who eat the soil of their homeland as preparation for battle in a faraway place. In the nineteenth century geophagy was also observed among southern slaves, some of whom maintained a private clay hole from which they secretly ate.

In the Bible geophagy was part of Satan's curse in Genesis 3:14 (see also Isa. 65:25; Micah 7:17). Licking dust off the feet of a conquering warrior is a frequent figure of speech in the Bible depicting the humiliation of defeat (Ps. 72:9; Isa. 49:23).

J. R. BECK

Pick's Disease. A presenile degenerative brain disease defined by the Czech psychiatrist Arnold Pick in 1906. This rare psychosis with unknown etiology usually strikes individuals between 45 and 55 years of age and is fatal within approximately four to six years. It occurs more often in women than in men. Pick's disease is a progressive dementia with severe emotional impairment, and it affects the individual's ability to deal with abstractions. Speech disturbances and apathy are frequent, and symptoms include apraxia, alexia, agraphia, and aphasia. Pathologically, the cortical cells in the temporal and frontal regions of the brain atrophy, and the patient becomes increasingly debilitated.

D. L. SCHUURMAN

Pinel, Philippe (1745–1826). French physician who initiated humane care of the mentally ill. The son of a physician, Pinel was first interested in philosophy and planned to enter the priesthood. Later he became interested in science and mathematics and decided to follow his father's profession. He received his medical degree from the University of Toulouse in 1773. After tutoring Latin, Greek, and natural history for two years, he went to Montpellier for further study in comparative anatomy.

Pinel arrived in Paris in 1778 but for 14 years remained obscure, impoverished, and studious. He tutored, translated books, and wrote papers on medicine, physics, and philosophy. His interest in insanity began in 1785. In 1792 he was appointed a municipal medical officer, and in 1793 he became head of the lunatic asylum, the Bicêtre. Two years later he was transferred to the Salpétrière asylum. He remained in Paris until his death.

His innovations at the two asylums became Pinel's greatest contribution. Finding the usual combination of squalor, cruelty, and neglect, he approached the president of the Commune for permission to remove the chains from the patients. Although his own sanity was questioned for wanting to do this, he was not forbidden. First he removed the chains from a few patients, and eventually from all. Patients were given food and encouragement, were treated kindly, and were not beaten. They began to recover, and one even saved his life when a mob was about to lynch him.

Pinel believed that mental illness was a result of heredity, physiological damage, and excessive exposure to stress. He developed a simple and accurate description of mental illnesses in his *Philosophical Classification of Diseases* (1798), which became a standard text, going through many editions. He developed a psychologically oriented approach in his *Medico-Philosophical Treatise on Mental Alienation or Mania* (1801). His books were simply written and were understandable to the intelligent layman. Rather than using bleeding, purging, and blistering, he advocated close and friendly contact with patients, discussion of personal difficulties, and purposeful activities.

Through Pinel's efforts France became a leading nation in the treatment of the mentally ill. His "moral treatment" became the model for similar movements in England and the United States. A succession of brilliant men, including Esquirol and Charcot, followed him at Salpétrière so that this hospital remained the psychiatric center of the world for nearly a century. Students of mental disorders flocked to it as experimental psychologists did to Leipzig.

R. L. KOTESKEY

Placebo Effects in Therapy. A placebo may be defined as any substance or procedure which, when used as a method of treatment, is incapable of producing any effect whatsoever due to its inert, inactive composition. The placebo effect, then, refers to the psychological and/or physiological changes brought about solely by the expectation that the administered "medicine" would be effective.

The curative power of the placebo effect is evidenced by the fact that prior to the twentieth century virtually all medicines used by physicians and other healers were pharmacologically inert. However, the effects of these inactive substances often were quite dramatic—fevers vanished, pain subsided, sores disappeared—and the reputation of the physician or medicine man as a great healer was enhanced. A medical historian, reflecting on this fact, notes that until recently the history of medical treatment is the history of the placebo effect (Shapiro, 1959).

Undoubtedly some cures seemingly wrought by placebos were actually due to the natural healing processes of the body that would have occured even if the placebo had not been administered. However, scientific investigation of the placebo effect has convincingly shown that this explanation cannot account for all cures associated with placebos. Rather, the evidence suggests that even when the body's healing systems have failed to correct a particular malady, a placebo—or, more accurately, the placebo effect—will often trigger a previously dormant curative response. For example, warts, which are caused by a virus, have been successfully and permanently eradicated by painting them with a colorful, inert dye and telling the patient that they would disappear as the dye wears off. Even though the dye was medically useless, the expectation that it would be effective in some way altered the physiology of the skin to successfully combat the virus and eliminate the warts. This placebo treatment has been found to be as effective as any form of medical treatment, including surgical excision (Barber, 1961). Other controlled experiments have found placebos to be effective in treating a wide range of maladies including nausea and vomiting, bleeding ulcers, angina, and headaches.

Mechanisms of Action. While it is understood that the placebo effect works via the arousal of expectation, the exact nature of that arousal remains unclear. Placebos do not work with everyone, nor do they always work for the same person in the same way. Sometimes they may even precipitate negative effects if accompanied by negative expectation. This was the case in a study in which patients were told the medicine they were taking (actually a placebo) might produce side effects. As a result they developed nausea, headaches, and vomiting (Pincus, 1966).

The arousal of expectation may be so powerful that it actually reverses the pharmacological action of a drug. This occurred in a study in which ipecac, a drug known to cause nausea and vomiting, was given to a patient already suffering from vomiting. The patient was given stong assurances that the medicine would cure her gastric disorder, and as a result the nausea and vomiting ceased after administration of the emetic (Wolf, 1950).

A review of research on the placebo effect (Shapiro & Morris, 1978) indicates that a number of factors have been investigated that might help to explain how and why placebos work. The variables examined include suggestibility, dependency, psychopathology, introversion-extraversion, acquiescence, social desirability, treatment settings, treatment procedures, as well as patient and therapist attitudes. The arousal of expectation has also been examined in terms of concepts such as transference, role demand, guilt reduction, classical conditioning, and cognitive dissonance. The results of such research remain unclear, due in part to conflicting findings and failure to replicate. Very likely the placebo effect is a multifactored phenomenon in which any one element is dependent on a variety of other variables.

Implications for Psychotherapy. The placebo effect has greater implications for psychotherapy than for any other type of treatment, since both function in whole or in part through the arousal of the expectation of help. Research suggests that the healing effects of expectations are enhanced in psychotherapy when the client has confidence in both the process and the outcome of the therapy.

If the client does not understand the process

of therapy—i.e., how and why change will occur—then the expectation of help will be severely diminished and little therapeutic benefit will be gained. A study on the importance of clarifying clients' expectations in therapy involved comparing two groups of psychiatric patients, each of whom received four months of therapy. Only one of the groups received a preparatory role induction interview designed to clarify the processes of treatment, assure the client that treatment would be helpful, dispel unrealistic hopes (to guard against disillusionment), and help the client behave in a way that accorded with the therapist's image of a good client. The results indicated that as a group the clients receiving the role induction interview showed more appropriate behavior in therapy and had a better outcome than the controls (Hoehn-Saric, Frank, Imber, Nash, Stone, & Battle, 1964).

Positive expectations regarding the outcome of therapy appear to be as important as expectations regarding therapy process. Frank, Hoehn-Saric, Imber, Liberman, and Stone (1978) reviewed a number of studies supporting this notion. One such study found that the degree of symptomatic relief in psychiatric patients following a single contact with a therapist was related to the patient's expressed expectation that he would be helped. A similar study found a correlation between psychiatric outpatients' estimates of how well they expected to feel after six months of treatment and the degree of reported symptom relief after an initial evaluation interview.

Studies such as these would appear to buttress the argument that all healing in psychotherapy is due to the placebo effect alone and therefore all techniques would work equally well if accompanied by the client's expectation that he will be helped (Fish, 1973). This viewpoint is partially supported by Frank's (1973, 1978) demonstration that there are certain features shared by all therapies that account for an appreciable amount of the improvement observed and that one of the features is the arousal of the expectation of help. However, he notes further (1982) that there are some conditions in which a particular therapeutic method does seem to make a significant difference in outcome. For example, behavior therapy seems somewhat more effective for phobias, compulsions, obesity, and sexual problems than are the less focused therapies, while cognitive therapy seems to be particularly effective with depression. Further investigation may add to this list other techniques whose efficacy is problem specific. Thus

for certain psychological maladies the arousal of the expectation of help may be a necessary but not sufficient condition for healing to occur.

Ethical Issues. The element of deception involved in placebo research and treatment raises a serious ethical question regarding the appropriateness of deliberately misleading a client about the effectiveness of a medicine or treatment. While deception has been the modus operandi for administering placebos, there is some evidence to suggest that the placebo effect can be operative without any deception whatsoever. This was demonstrated by a study in which psychiatric outpatients were given a placebo and told exactly what it was. After taking the placebo for a week the patients reported improvement on target symptoms (Park & Covi, 1965). In this instance deception was not part of the healing process, yet the placebo effect was present, apparently generated by the therapist's reassurance and encouragement.

Also a therapist believing in the efficacy of a particular therapy technique may recognize that enhancing the client's expectation of help will increase the effectiveness of that technique. To utilize the placebo effect in the service of a technique one believes to have intrinsic merit eliminates the deceptive element.

Placebos and Faith Healing. Attempts have been made to explain FAITH HEALINGS such as those performed by Christ in the New Testament solely in terms of the placebo effect. While this phenomenon may account for some of the cures wrought by present-day healers, objections must be raised to attributing all miraculous healings to the curative power of expectations. Such reductionistic efforts stem from a naturalistic bias that precludes the possibility that the cause-and-effect universe can be subject to supernatural intervention. This bias is not only patently unbiblical but ignores the findings of quantum physics that the causal nexus is not inviolate.

Further, the placebo effect explanation does not square with the scriptural description of a number of Christ's healings. It is recorded that on several occasions Jesus healed persons, including the centurion's servant (Matt. 8:5–13) and the official's son (John 4:46–54), without their knowledge and from a geographical distance. On other occasions Jesus is reported to have raised deceased persons to life, including Lazarus (John 11:1–44) and the widow's son (Luke 7:11–15). In none of these instances were the recipients of the healing capable of having their expectations aroused by Jesus. Thus the placebo effect could not have been the curative force in these experiences. By extrapolation one may conclude that the healings in which Jesus spoke directly to the ill were manifestations of the same supernatural power. Once an affirmation of supernaturalism is made, the door opens to accepting the validity of many modern faith healings. At the same time we can recognize that the placebo effect may play a part in some, but not necessarily all cures.

References

Barber, T. X. Physiological effects of hypnosis. *Psychological Bulletin*, 1961, *58*, 390—419.

Fish, J. M. *Placebo therapy*. San Francisco: Jossey-Bass, 1973.

Frank, J. D. *Persuasion and healing*. (Rev. ed.). Baltimore: Johns Hopkins University Press, 1973.

Frank, J. D. Therapeutic components shared by all psychotherapies. In J. Harvey & M. Parks (Eds.), *Psychotherapy research and behavior change: The master lecture series* (Vol. 1). Washington, D.C.: American Psychological Association, 1982.

Frank, J. D., Hoehn-Saric, R., Imber, S. D., Liberman, B., & Stone, A. R. *Effective ingredients of successful psychotherapy*. New York: Brunner/Mazel, 1978.

Hoehn-Saric, R., Frank, J. D., Imber, S. D., Nash, E. H. Stone, A. R., & Battle, C. C. Systematic preparation of patients for psychotherapy: I. Effects on therapy behavior and outcome. *Journal of Psychiatric Research*, 1964, *2*, 267–281.

Park, L. C., & Covi, L. Non-blind placebo trial: An exploration of neurotic patients' responses to placebo when its inert content is disclosed. *Archives of General Psychiatry*, 1965, *12*, 336–345.

Pincus, G. Control of conception by hormonal steroids. *Science*, 1966, *153*, 493–500.

Shapiro, A. K. The placebo effect in the history of medical treatment: Implications for psychiatry. *American Journal of Psychiatry*, 1959, *116*, 298–304.

Shapiro, A. K., & Morris, L. A. The placebo effect in medical and psychological therapies. In S. Garfield & A. Bergin (Eds.), *Handbook of psychotherapy and behavior change*. (2nd ed.). New York: Wiley, 1978.

Wolf, S. Effects of suggestion and conditioning on the action of chemical agents in human subjects: The pharmacology of placebos. *Journal of Clinical Investigation*, 1950, *29*, 100–109.

W. G. Bixler

Plato (*ca.* 427–347 B.C.). Probably the most influential philosopher in the history of Western thought. Whitehead's famous comment that "the history of Western philosophy is a series of footnotes to Plato" is in many ways no exaggeration. Plato founded the Academy at Athens, the prototype of the Western university. Through such thinkers as Clement and Augustine he has also exercised an incalculable influence on Christian theology. His writings consist for the most part of dramatic dialogues written over a long period of time; hence it is not easy to derive a consistent "system" from Plato's writings.

Plato viewed human beings as a composite of an immaterial, immortal soul and a physical body. Although this idea is probably of religious origin and is certainly older than Plato, he was the first philosopher to develop and defend such a view. His attitude toward the body is somewhat positive in some dialogues, but he is most famous for the view presented in the *Phaedo* that the body is the "prison-house of the soul." The goal of the soul is to escape its embodiment and reach a pure spiritual existence, a goal that requires a disciplined, somewhat ascetic attitude toward the body and bodily desires.

The soul is seen by Plato as both preexistent and immortal, though he apparently believed in the possibility of multiple bodily incarnations. His most famous argument for the immortality of the soul is derived from his theory of knowledge. Plato saw the human soul as capable of knowing truth of an eternal character. Humans are capable of grasping absolute, timeless standards such as beauty, justice, equality, and the good. This is the famous theory of Forms. Since the soul's function is to grasp these eternal truths, Plato reasoned that the soul must share their eternal character. Specifically he held that knowledge of the Forms is innate and is best explained as recollection of truth known prior to birth. Christian Platonists replaced this "recollection" with a theory of divine illumination to explain such innate knowledge.

The functioning soul is described by Plato in the *Republic* as tripartite in character. The soul contains an appetitive part, the element of impulsive cravings and desires; a rational part, whose proper function is to rule or govern the person; and a spiritual element, which is capable of assisting reason by curbing the impulses. A truly virtuous person integrates these elements harmoniously. Much of Western psychology has been influenced by Plato's divisions, which are still reflected in such distinctions as that between the cognitive and affective dimensions of personality.

C. S. Evans

Play, Adults'. *See* Work and Play.

Play, Children's. Voluntary individual or group behavior, accompanied by signs of positive feeling or affect, that has no obvious purpose or goal. Beyond this broad definition investigators of play do not generally agree on a precise behavioral definition, much less on a single theoretical approach toward understanding the phenomenon. However, there is a consensus of opinion that most play exhibits several identifying characteristics, that there are several distinct types of play, and that play undergoes qualitative changes throughout a child's development that relate closely to other aspects of development. The scientific study of play most emphatically suggests that play is not irrelevant or frivolous behavior, as common sense often regards it.

Among the most important characteristics of children's play is its lack of domination by obvious drives or internal need states. Play behavior has a low priority in comparison with other behavior and is easily inhibited by external threats or the internal press of biological needs. Nevertheless, the universality of play across both cultures and species of animals suggests that play is, in some not so obvious way, a built-in necessity for the developing child.

Play is often compared and contrasted with exploratory behavior, which generally precedes play in temporal sequence. Whereas exploration is high priority behavior, the goal of which appears to be to reduce the individual's subjective uncertainty regarding novel objects, situations, or events, play apparently requires a safe context in which to occur. Exploration has an obvious purpose in helping the individual to adapt to the environment, cope with possible threats, and reduce fear. While it is not always easy to distinguish between exploration and play in ongoing behavior, play is the pleasurable activity that occurs seemingly for its own sake after exploration has reduced the individual's uncertainty below a certain level.

According to some investigators play also reveals the individual's preoccupation with challenges to its developing capabilities. The playing child thus actively tries to create new effects or combinations. For example, in verbal play a solitary child creates new combinations of words and sounds, as though trying to achieve a greater mastery of language. The evidence of actual gains in learning through play is sparse, however.

The work of Piaget (1951) has resulted in a widely accepted scheme for categorizing the types of play and describing how play changes throughout the child's development. Piaget's four types of play are functional play, symbolic play, games with rules, and constructive games. Functional play involves the practice of cognitive or behavioral skills (e.g., a child who, after learning to ask a question, continually asks questions solely for the fun of asking). Symbolic play or make-

believe involves pretending that a given object is something other than what it is thought to be (e.g., a thimble as a doll's cup). Games with rules include those with primarily behavioral combinations (e.g., marbles) and those with primarily intellectual combinations (e.g., checkers). Finally, constructive games emerge out of symbolic play to the extent that the games become more realistic (e.g., acting a part in a school play). These types of play also describe an approximate developmental sequence that Piaget has demonstrated convincingly to be closely related to broad stages of intellectual development.

The various theoretical explanations of children's play have centered around at least three distinct approaches. Most psychologists have focused on play from the standpoint of the individual child and have chosen to emphasize the child's cognitive processes (following Piaget, 1951), compensation for inadequacies (following Erikson, 1977), or internal states of arousal (following Berlyne, 1960). A second approach emphasizes the social and cultural context of play and the ways in which play appears to be functional for the culture. A third approach emphasizes the comparison of play across species and seeks to identify a selective advantage of play from an evolutionary point of view. All of this has resulted in a great deal of theoretical ferment but little consensus as to how play is best understood. In particular, the exact relationship between children's play and adult functioning is as yet unresolved. Nevertheless, the strong conviction persists that children's play is extremely important for optimal development.

Historically in Western, nominally Christian cultural settings the play of children has been regarded as irrelevant or frivolous, and children themselves as merely unsophisticated, miniature adults. Since play is nonproductive in these settings, it is merely tolerated or indulged with little regard for its importance in the child's development. However, this commonsense view is not necessarily supported by Scripture. When Paul spoke of his own childhood (1 Cor. 13:11), he tacitly endorsed the validity of children's play as an integral part of the child's experience and mode of being, notwithstanding its general inappropriateness after one has become an adult. In the context of this passage of Scripture, as long as the more perfect understanding of an adult has not yet come, the partial understanding of children is wholly acceptable and appropriate. Thus play, whether as an expression of or means toward such understanding, appears to be essential for the child, as indeed the scientific literature also suggests.

References
Berlyne, D. E. *Conflict, arousal and curiosity.* New York: McGraw-Hill, 1960.
Erikson, E. H. *Toys and reasons.* New York: Norton, 1977.
Piaget, J. *Play, dreams and imitation in childhood.* New York: Norton, 1951.

D. R. Ridley

Play Therapy. *See* Child Therapy.

Poetry Therapy. The Old Testament describes how David soothed King Saul with his poetry and music, and the Book of Psalms contains some of the poems that enabled David to express his innermost feelings and conflicts. Today the same healing potential of poetry is being utilized, but in a more formal therapeutic setting. As a therapeutic tool poetry is best used in a group situation that supplements individual sessions. The poetry therapist may bring written material to the group after carefully choosing it to reflect the moods of the clients in the group, or the group members may elect to present poems that they themselves write. In either case the poem allows the participants to share in the emotions and struggles of the poet, and group discussions of these reactions often precipitates further understanding of their life situations.

The writing of poetry is encouraged because the process of giving expression to one's problems and feelings is at the core of psychotherapy and represents a major step toward the resolution of those problems. The discussion of someone else's work is also therapeutic because the emotional content of the poem instead of the client himself is directly examined. Thus, poetry often provides a less threatening avenue for the analysis of one's feelings, and its shared expression reassures the client that he is not alone in his struggles. Current literature reports that poetry therapy can be a powerful therapeutic supplement in working with almost every emotional disorder in a large variety of settings.

Additional Reading
Leedy, J. (Ed.). *Poetry, the healer.* Philadelphia: Lippincott, 1973.

W. C. Drew

See Activity Therapy.

Pornography. While pornography has existed for centuries, it is only with the recent growth of the mass media that it has impinged significantly on the whole of society.

The terms came from the Greek *pornogra-* *phos*, meaning the writing of harlots, but that no longer provides an adequate definition. With strong pressure from publishers and others to give it First Amendment protection, it has changed in its styles and content so remarkably over the last 20 years that definition has become crucial to any clear discussion of its significance.

The U.S. Presidential Commission on Obscenity and Pornography (1970) favored a general interpretation of pornography as referring to any sexually explicit materials capable of arousing sexual passion. This approach has not been helpful in scientific discussion since it covers an enormously wide range of materials, from medical texts to hard-core presentations of perverse sexuality.

A more precise definition was offered in the Longford Report: "That which exploits and dehumanises sex, so that human beings are treated as things and women in particular as sex objects" (Longford, 1972). This approach enables one to discriminate between various types of material of greater or lesser explicitness, with attention paid more to the meaning of the materials and their effects on behavior than to subjective evaluations of either shock or approval.

The terms *pornography* and *obscenity* are often used interchangeably, but distinctions are necessary. In the United States obscenity has been defined by the Supreme Court as involving patent offensiveness, affronting community standards, and lacking redeeming social value. It commonly, but not necessarily, refers to sexual obscenity. In England obscenity has been closely linked legally with the "deprave and corrupt" test laid down in 1868 (Williams, 1979).

Hyde (1964) explains that while all pornography is obscene, the converse is not always true. Obscene matter may produce disgust (e.g., a description of the act of defecation) but not be normally calculated to arouse sexual desires and therefore not be classified as pornographic.

Not all sexually explicit materials are pornographic or obscene. Artistic presentations in which the beauty of sexuality is portrayed aesthetically, and scientific presentations whose primary purpose is to inform are not commonly considered obscene. Erotica identifies sexual materials of an erotically stimulating type that do not debase sexuality or people.

It has sometimes been argued in its defense that the use of pornography can be therapeutic for sexually disturbed persons. If one accepts the above distinctions, the evidence for this is unconvincing. While certain well-chosen sexually explicit materials (books and films) can educate and reduce fear in those with sexual dysfunctions, it has not been shown that pornography has such beneficial effects.

Just as research into most aspects of sexuality is of recent origin, so too investigation into the nature and effects of pornography was vestigial until the U.S. report of 1970. Until that time it was widely assumed that pornography was socially undesirable, and few users would publicly admit to an interest in it. After that report claimed to be unable to find convincing evidence of harm from its availability, pornographic books, magazines, and films multiplied rapidly and achieved greatly increased public visibility. Concurrently those findings were subject to heavy criticism. The report as published contained a strong minority section expressing detailed dissent, and was subsequently rejected overwhelmingly by the U.S. Senate.

The ensuing decade has permitted a more detailed analysis of the major issues relating to the nature and effects of pornography. First, the parameters have been more clearly defined. Whereas much earlier research failed to identify materials precisely, experimental and clinical studies have focused on precise components of pornography such as explicitness, type of sexual activity, inclusion of aggression, and degree of consent (Malamuth & Donnerstein, 1984).

Second, it has been possible to test competing theories of effects. The catharsis theory, which argued that wide availability of pornography would result in a reduced incidence of sexual crimes, has not found support. Preliminary indications of such a possibility derived from Danish evidence have been shown to be methodologically flawed (Court, 1980).

By contrast, increasing experimental support has emerged for a "shared taboo" hypothesis, which relates the dual themes of sexuality and aggression. It appears that exposure to vividly arousing sexual themes (erotica) can lead to a reduced probability of sexual aggression against others (Baron & Bell, 1977); but when high levels of arousal associated with hard-core pornography are used, there is an increased probability of sexual aggression. This evidence has been derived using normal and clinical populations (Malamuth & Donnerstein, 1984). The presentation of either explicit violence or explicit sex has the potential for breaking social taboos so that both aggressive and sexual behavioral tendencies are increased.

The expression of such probabilities is now seen in the steep increase of rape reports where pornography has become accepted. This is true in Scandinavia, in contrast to earlier optimistic predictions, as well as in the United States. It has been said of hard-core pornography that "given the current marketing of cruelty, one can only conclude that pornography is indeed the 'theory,' and battery, rape, molestation, and other increasing crimes of sexual violence are not so coincidentally the 'practice'" (Morgan, 1978, p. 55).

It was widely argued that liberalization of pornography laws would result in reduced interest, with a consequent withering of the market—the "forbidden fruit" hypothesis. Evidence for this view has been found faulty, and in recent years the trade has escalated to an unprecedented degree. This development has been not only a matter of quantity. The type of material becoming available has changed constantly to meet changing demands. Production has become more sophisticated while the themes presented have become increasingly perverted. Sadomasochism and child pornography have come largely from the liberal orthodoxy that has pushed for First Amendment freedom by claiming there is no evidence of harm. This position has been enhanced by strong financial vested interests, leading to a trade estimated at 4 billion dollars in the United States alone in 1980.

Contrary pressures have emerged predominantly from three directions. The feminist lobby has been increasingly vocal in its protest against the exploitation of women (Lederer, 1980). The feminist critique emphasizes the distortion of power relationships in pornography, seeing them as an extreme expression of a male-dominated society. This has led to special emphasis on themes of aggression and rape in pornography, with evidence of a corresponding growth of such behavior in society.

A philosophical critique of pornography emphasizes how dangerous pornography is to the fundamental meanings of human relationships. The acceptance of pornography implies an acceptance of debased values, impoverishment of cultural ideals, and a significant loss of meaning. This existential critique, highlighting the essential hate and underlying hostility of pornography, has been most fully developed by Holbrook (1972a, 1972b).

In addition, a moral reaction against pornography has developed with Christians allying with many other religious groups. Protest has taken many forms, sometimes based on moral and theological presuppositions and at times based on personal revulsion or moral outrage.

From a Christian standpoint pornography can be understood as epitomizing some essentially alien principles. While some sexually explicit materials can enrich, educate, and, in clinical situations, assist in overcoming irrational fears of sexuality, pornography by its nature debases sexuality. Sex is no longer seen as a God-given means of expressing mutuality and fulfillment in relationships. The Christian emphasis on monogamic, heterosexual relationships based on love and commitment is challenged in favor of hedonistic promiscuity. An inversion of values ensures that goodness and purity are ridiculed in favor of lust and immorality. The biblical taboos against incest, bestiality, and homosexual practices (Lev. 18) are rejected in favor of a moral relativism that goes well beyond secular humanistic values of consent and caring. Economic pressures of an expanded market have generated extreme expressions of sexuality combined with hate and aggression that attack the sensibilities of civilization. Pornography stands not so much as a cause of sexual immorality as a commentary on and symptom of contemporary decadence.

References

Baron, R. A., & Bell, P. A. Sexual arousal and aggression by males: Effects of type of erotic stimuli and prior provocation. *Journal of Personality and Social Psychology*, 1977, 35, 79–87.
Court, J. H. *Pornography: A Christian critique.* Downers Grove, Ill.: Inter-Varsity Press, 1980.
Holbrook, D. *Sex and dehumanization.* London: Pitman, 1972.(a)
Holbrook, D. (Ed.). *The case against pornography.* London: Tom Stacey, 1972.(b)
Hyde, H. M. *A history of pornography.* London: Heinemann, 1964.
Lederer, L. *Take back the night: Women on pornography.* New York: Morrow, 1980.
Longford, L. *Pornography: The Longford report.* London: Coronet, 1972.
Malamuth, N. M., & Donnerstein, E. *Pornography and sexual aggression.* New York: Academic Press, 1984.
Morgan, R. How to run the pornographers out of town. *Ms.,* November, 1978, pp. 55ff.
U.S. Presidential Commission Report on Obscenity and Pornography. New York: Bantam Books, 1970.
Williams, B. *Report of the Committee on Obscenity and Film Censorship.* London: H. M. Stationary Office, 1979.

J. H. COURT

See SEXUALITY.

Positive Connotation Technique. *See* REFRAMING TECHNIQUE.

Positive Thinking. The positivists of the sixteenth through the nineteenth centuries wrote a profoundly significant chapter in the history of philosophy. Particular attention must be paid to the work of Hume, Descartes, and Comte in any appreciation of modern Western thought. It is tempting, therefore, to seek the roots of the contemporary religious positive thinking movement as represented by Norman Vincent Peale and Robert Schuler within the development of the philosophy of positivism. Such an attempt might suggest the link between the classic positivists and the contemporary religious positive thinkers to be the philosophy of John Dewey.

The difficulty with this thesis, however, is that the apparent similarity between modern religious positive thinkers and classic positivism masks a major philosophical or methodological difference. Classic positivism is rooted in the philosophical assumption that the world is coherent and empirically discernible. Truth, therefore, can be arrived at through formal Aristotelian method and its rational consequences. The psychological posture of positivism is hopeful, optimistic, and confident. The positivist's certainty that rational-empirical method will disclose all truth is virtually absolute.

The philosophical assumption of the positive religious thinkers such as Peale and Schuler stands in sharp contrast to this. They begin with the assumption that the spiritual forces of death or deterioration can be overcome by the spiritual forces of life and growth, since the latter are more powerful. It is further assumed that divine revelation is the source of that information.

Philosophically, therefore, the positive thinkers in religion are virtually opposite from classic logical positivism. In fact, the contrast is precisely that of the rational-empiricism of the positivists versus the romantic idealism of the religious positive thinkers. For the positivists the foundation for the search for truth is the claim that the Aristotelian scientific method discloses absolute truth because it corresponds in method to the coherent structure of the universe and its laws of existence and function. For the positive religious thinkers the foundation for the search for truth is divine revelation. It is evident, therefore, that the romantic idealism of the religious positive thinkers looks more like a form of Platonism than a form of Aristotelianism.

Psychologically Peale and Schuler are similar to the classic positivists in that they are imbued with an absolute form of hopefulness, optimism, and confidence. Their optimism is in and about their apprehension of divine truth and its redemptive applicability in human life.

The optimism of the classic positivists is in the rational-empirical method of pursuing truth.

It is interesting to note that both Schuler and Peale stand within the Reformed theological tradition, Schuler developing within that tradition and Peale coming to it later. This fact is not unrelated to their positive thinking perspective, for at its best the positive thinking movement is the result of the Reformed faith taken to its logical and psychological conclusion. In this tradition grace means an arbitrary divine disposition of unmerited goodwill toward unworthy humans, leading to an eternal hopefulness and unquenchable optimism for all who perceive and take seriously this truth.

Schuler (1981) points out that the freedom for growth implied in God's grace invests everything, including our sin and tragedy as well as our health and holiness, with meaning and hope. Taking his cue from Peale he then shapes his message and style in terms of that transcendent optimism. He contends that positive thinking has profound spiritual and psychological consequences. It incites meaning, infuses one with self-esteem, mobilizes healing and growth, evaporates debilitating anxiety, constructively channels misdirected energy, affirms a durable security, and inspires legitimate comfort for life and eternity. For Schuler all of that, and the faith in God's grace in Christ, is to be part of salvation—spiritual, psychological, and social. Clinebell (1979) is an example of this same positive grace orientation applied to psychotherapeutic theory and practice.

Recent research in mind-body relationships in psychosomatic disorders (Gottschalk, 1978) as well as the insights of cognitive behavior therapists on the relationship between cognitions and affect states (Meichenbaum, 1977) suggest that the claims of the religious positive thinkers may have some basis. Persons who can be hopeful and grateful can mobilize physiological, psychological, and spiritual dynamics of health that are unavailable to the person who cannot be hopeful or grateful. The names we put on experiences determine in large part how they affect us (Meichenbaum, 1977). Humans can, by their thoughts and acts of will, considerably influence their feelings, health, and even their chemistry. This is the truth behind the effectiveness of positive thinking.

References

Clinebell, H. J. *Growth counseling: Hope-centered methods of actualizing human wholeness.* Nashville: Abingdon, 1979.

Gottschalk, L. A. Psychosomatic medicine today: An overview. *Psychosomatics,* 1978, *19*(2), 89–93.

Meichenbaum, D. H. *Cognitive behavior modification: An integrative approach.* New York: Plenum, 1977.

Schuler, R. H. Why Bob Schuler smiles on television, *Leadership,* 2(1), 1981, 26–32.

Additional Reading

Meyer, D. *The positive thinkers: Religion as pop psychology.* New York: Pantheon, 1980.

J. H. ELLENS

Positivism. *See* EMPIRICISM.

Postoperative Disorders. Historically surgery was used as a last resort in the treatment of life-threatening illnesses. However, since the development of safer anesthetics and procedures, it is no longer restricted to acute, critical illnesses. Now surgery is done frequently on an elective basis or as a preventative procedure (e.g., tubal ligations to prevent future pregnancies). It is also used as a diagnostic technique (e.g., laparoscopy) and as a reparative or cosmetic procedure (e.g., plastic surgery).

The surgical event alone is not the only stressful aspect for the surgical patient. The prospective patient enters into a stressful environment the moment he or she leaves home to go to hospital. Depending on his or her adaptive capacities to stressful situations, the patient will experience normal or disturbing emotional responses. These reactions, which may begin even as early as admission to the hospital, can affect the postsurgical recovery process.

Generally the patient is minimally knowledgeable about physiological functioning and about how the proposed procedure will affect the body. This lack of knowledge plus the lack of any foreknowledge of the postoperative course (particularly in the case of first surgical experiences) can lead to considerable preoperative anxiety, which may be shown in excessive questioning, irritability, or regression with demandingness and suspicion. Janis (1958) has shown that a moderate amount of anxiety is both appropriate and indicative of a good postoperative recovery in general. Other preoperative factors that enhance postoperative recovery are general emotional support from hospital staff and the availability of supportive family members or close friends.

The common postoperative experiences immediately after surgery are drowsiness, nausea and occasional vomiting, and a lack of appetite. These are the general effects of the systemic anesthetics and usually wear off in a day or two. Analgesics prescribed for pain often produce sleep and some amnesia or mild confusion. After several days, and particularly with nonambulatory patients or those in intensive care, a state of sensory deprivation can set in due to the monotony and the lack of variety in the environment. This may be evident in the form of fantasies, perceptual distortions, hallucinations, or even psychoticlike behavior. Consistent, concerned human contact and sensory stimulation in the form of pictures, tapes, or a radio can frequently alleviate this and speed recovery.

Certain surgical procedures can lead to specific postoperative issues. For example, the amputation of a limb can activate a sense of loss and body disintegration that may result in denial and the temporary sense of a phantom limb. Fisher and Cleveland (1968) have demonstrated that the occurrence of phantom limb phenomena is associated with the surgical removal of a limb rather than with the accidental loss of the body part.

The control of elimination is generally viewed as an indicator of developing maturity. Thus the loss of this control with colostomies and ileostomies often produces doubts about maturity, embarrassment and anxiety, and an impairment in self-confidence. Plastic surgery usually requires a number of stages separated over some length of time and may lead to postoperative depression. This necessitates support and the patient's understanding that the expected result is a product of numerous separate steps.

Postoperative complications in pediatric surgery are a product not only of the nature of the surgery but also of the developmental stage of the child at the time of the operation. This generally involves issues of separation and dependency. For instance, infants in the first few months generally respond with depressed functioning and apathy. After the sixth to eighth month, the separation produces crying and clinging to the mother. Later (years 1 through 4) the hospitalization and surgery are often experienced as abandonment and may be presumed to be a form of punishment. This may result in regression. In years 5 to 10 the child understands the reason for the surgery but fears mutilation. Finally, the adolescent who is asserting autonomy will experience any major surgery as traumatic to this independence. At each stage the crucial issues will come to the fore in the postoperative recovery and will need to be addressed or supported if recovery is to proceed smoothly.

In conclusion, the management of postoperative complications begins at the point of hospitalization. Adequate preparation of the patient both to what is going to happen during the surgery and what can be expected in the days immediately succeeding it is exceedingly important. Some preoperative anxiety is to be expected. The involvement of a well-prepared family and supportive hospital staff is also conducive to the avoidance or management of these postoperative effects.

References
Fisher, S., & Cleveland, S. E. *Body image and personality* (2nd ed.). New York: Dover Publications, 1968.
Janis, I. L. *Psychological stress: Psychoanalytic and behavioural studies of surgical patients.* New York: Wiley, 1958.

Additional Readings
Furst, J. B. Emotional stress reactions to surgery. *New York State Journal of Medicine,* June, 1978, pp. 1083–1085.
Matheson, G. Terror in the ICU: Exercise in hyperbole? *Forum on Medicine,* February, 1979, pp. 102–104.
Thunberg, U. H., & Kemph, J. P. Common emotional reactions to surgical illness. *Psychiatric Annals,* 1977, 7(1), 39–58.

G. MATHESON

Postpartum Psychosis. A psychotic reaction following childbirth. Reported since the time of Hippocrates, it has been frequently studied by clinicians, yet little is known about the condition. Observations in the 1800s found that it is not a single disorder, but rather includes reactions with varied diagnoses such as psychotic depression, bipolar disorder, and even schizophrenia. Several studies have shown 20 to 60% of women report some type of disturbance in early postpartum. This reaches psychotic proportions in no more than 2 out of 1,000. About one-half of postpartum reactions occur with second or later born children, with no effects seen for the firstborn. Another common misconception is that the condition predisposes difficulties at future births.

The symptom pattern often starts with insomnia, restlessness, exhaustion, labile affect, loss of appetite, and depression. If the disorder progresses, psychotic symptoms may then appear. Confusion, incoherence, dreamy states, depersonalization, and occasionally delirium are all possible. Delusions about motherhood, the baby, or the husband may result. The mother may reject the child or believe that the baby is dead or defective. Hallucinations, if experienced, will support the delusions. Voices may tell her to kill the baby, or that the baby is evil. Rarely is the mother dangerous or suicidal, but precautions are necessary.

Researchers do not know the cause of postpartum psychosis. Many clinicians believe the disorder is the same as other severe reactions in times of crises and stress. Some theorists consider the birth of a child similar to other developmental milestones such as adolescence or menopause. Potential for emotional problems always increases when major changes take place in a person's life.

Other theorists believe there is an endocrinological basis such that chemical and hormonal changes due to the birth may result in predisposing a person to psychosis. Studies are not conclusive, and treatment with hormones has not been successful. However, one frequent observation that suggests a biochemical basis is the fact that symptoms usually do not start until the third day postpartum.

A psychological predisposition may also contribute. Conflicts about the mother role may cause identity difficulty. Feelings of adequacy may be challenged beyond limits. An unfamiliar role with few rewards and little help may prove frustrating. Discrepant advice from others may add to the confusion. Feelings of being trapped are common. The degree of flexibility in one's personality and how the mother reacted to her own mother may all add to the psychological stress.

If the disorder is psychotic, treatment requires hospitalization with appropriate chemotherapy. Tricyclic antidepressants are commonly given if the prominant feature is depression. If the disorder is more bipolar (manic-depressive), lithium is often prescribed. For schizophrenic reactions a phenothiazine or an antipsychotic medication may be used. If medication is not successful and suicidal risk is high, electroconculsive therapy (ECT) is sometimes useful. Most clinicians recommend psychotherapy after relief from the acute psychotic symptoms, with particular emphasis on restoring the mother-child bond.

M. R. NELSON

See PSYCHOTIC DISORDERS.

Posttraumatic Stress Disorder. A characteristic group of symptoms triggered by an environmental event that is a severe enough stressor to evoke significant distress in almost any individual exposed to it. These stressful events fall into one of three categories: natural disasters (e.g., famine, earthquake, fire); deliberate human acts (e.g., murder, rape, torture); or unintentionally human-caused trauma (e.g., car accidents, plane crashes, collapse of a building due to faulty construction). They are differentiated from other more common situational stressors such as divorce, bereavement, or business failure by their infrequency, profound intensity and severity, and strong poten-

tial for physically harmful consequences. In addition, experiencing these events tends to trigger a reaction that includes compulsive repetition of varying aspects of the traumatic situation (Schur, 1966). The repetitions are generally involuntary, and strategies to prevent or suppress them are unsuccessful. They take many disguised forms that can invoke any part of the cognitive, affective, or behavioral aspects of the trauma (Horowitz, 1976).

Cognitive reenactments include intrusive-repetitive thoughts in the form of nightmares, illusions, ruminations, unbidden images, or obsessive ideas. Other manifestations of interference in the cognitive sphere include confusion, lack of concentration, overgeneralization, and preoccupation. Affectively, flooding with guilt, rage, fear, shame, or sorrow can occur with or without accompaniment by cognitive representation. Behavioral manifestations are observable in such forms as gestures, startle reactions, hypervigilance, excessive talk, and listlessness. Autonomic physiological signs such as perspiration, tremulousness, and psychosomatic symptoms may accompany the intrusive-repetitive state (Horowitz, 1976).

Periods of denial often alternate with intrusive-repetitive episodes. Cognitively this is evident in extensive ideational suppression. Affectively the denial manifests as emotional numbness. In the behavioral sphere activity is inhibited by tension. Specific indications of the denial phase include any combination of the following symptoms: markedly diminished interest in significant activities (being in a daze, selective inattention, inability to appreciate the significance of stimuli), partial or complete amnesia, sense of detachment, numbness, psychosomatic symptoms, constricted affect, and inflexibility of thought flow (*DSM-III*; Horowitz, 1976).

At times the patient experiences either the denial-numbness phase or the intrusive-repetitive phase. At other times features of both phases are present. There can be an ideational intrusion of specific parts of the traumatic event, with accompanying emotional pangs, while other aspects of the experience are denied (e.g., guilt-ridden intrusive content related to the theme of having survived, with the suppression of fear of repetition of the stressor). The intrusive thoughts, feelings, and denials include multiple themes as the human mind automatically strives to give meaning to the traumatic event.

Horowitz (1976) identifies eight themes that commonly emerge as either conscious or warded-off ideation and affect: fear of repetition, shame over helplessness or emptiness, rage at the source, guilt or shame over aggressive impulses, fear of aggressivity, survivor guilt, fear of identification with victims, and sadness in relation to loss. The specificity and intensity with which these themes intrude or are warded off depend on factors idiosyncratic both to the particular stressors and to the individual's prestress character and history. After any stressful event, however, there is a combination of interrelated conflictual themes that must be resolved.

Course of Symptoms. When symptoms occur immediately or a short time after the precipitating event, the prognosis for recovery is very favorable (Parkes, 1964). *DSM-III* refers to this as acute posttraumatic stress disorder. When symptoms start six months or more after the trauma or persist six months or longer once they have started, the stress reactions tend to become chronic and are labled chronic or delayed posttraumatic disorder.

There is considerable disagreement on the causal relation between stressful events and chronic reactions (Horowitz, 1976). Although some clinicians attribute persistent reactions to severe stress to personality predispositions, the considerable amount of research done on the survivors of the Nazi Holocaust seems to support the hypothesis that prolonged and profound exposure to extreme stressors may produce permanent reactions regardless of the prestress psychological health of the individual (Horowitz, 1976). Lifton (1967) found similar evidence in his studies of the survivors of Hiroshima and Nagasaki. Current research (see Figley, 1978) focusing on the adjustment problems of Vietnam veterans seems to suggest the existence of some unique features in the posttraumatic stress response of those persons.

Treatment. It is important to start treatment as soon as possible after the symptoms appear in order to avoid more severe reactions. The ultimate goal is a meaningful integration of the conflictual experiences and dynamics (e.g., relief, yet guilt for being alive). This involves a process whereby individuals assimilate the meanings of the traumatic event correctly, understand its disrupting effect on their sense of morality, and through appropriate actions are able to accommodate the conflictual aspects to their value system. The complete process should enable individuals to develop more adequate adaptational responses that would serve them well in future traumas.

The actual sequence of intermediary goals that lead to the desired outcome depends on the present state of the victim. If the stressor event is still present, direct intervention to remove the victim from the situation, obtain emergency care, and assist with immediate decisions receives top priority. Individuals are motivated to enter therapy when overwhelming thoughts and feelings that they neither understand nor know how to handle start to occur. The therapist listens for emerging themes. The more threatening ones will remain suppressed longer, while others will emerge quickly. The themes should be dealt with in the order of their appearance.

When an individual under treatment becomes unduly flooded by painful thoughts and feelings, the therapeutic strategy is to temporarily distance him or her from the memories of the stressful event to permit a rest period. The specific techniques, chosen according to the particular orientation of the therapist, are aimed at providing the victim with more control over the painful intrusive-repetitive thoughts and feelings. When the individual seems ready to resume the work of processing the themes, a treatment modality is used that evokes abreaction-catharsis. The possible methods by which to accomplish this are as varied as the techniques that exist in a psychotherapist's preferred orientational repertoire.

The periods of denial and intrusive ideation will continue to alternate as the conflictual themes are being resolved. The integration of the meaning of the themes represented in the ideational and feeling phase is occurring when 1) the oscillations between the two states are reaching increasingly reduced levels of intensity and duration, 2) the individual can voluntarily not think about or experience the affect of the trauma, and 3) the value conflict is less evident.

Repressed core conflicts will probably be aroused by the traumatic event. However, to maintain the priority of the goal of processing the trauma-related themes to completion, any interpretations should be related directly to themes created by the recent stressors. Interpretations relating to the more deeply rooted prestress pathology would be included in treatment only when longer term therapy is indicated.

References

Figley, C. R. *Stress disorders among Vietnam veterans.* New York: Brunner/Mazel, 1978.

Horowitz, M. *Stress response syndromes.* New York: Aronson, 1976.

Lifton, R. J. *Death in life: Survivors of Hiroshima.* New York: Random House, 1967.

Parkes, C. M. Recent bereavement as a cause of mental illness. *British Journal of Psychiatry,* 1964, *110,* 198–204.

Schur, M. *The id and the regulatory process of the ego.* New York: International Universities Press, 1966.

F. J. WHITE

Poverty of Speech. A disorder characterized by a restriction in the amount of speech or conversation of an individual. Replies to questions are brief and unelaborated, and if the condition is severe, the person may speak only in monosyllables or grunts. Poverty of speech is common in schizophrenia, major depressive episodes, and organic mental disorders such as dementia.

Prayer in Counseling and Psychotherapy. *See* RELIGIOUS RESOURCES IN PSYCHOTHERAPY.

Preconscious. Freud divided unconscious mental structures into two categories: the preconscious and the UNCONSCIOUS. The preconscious consists of those psychic elements readily available and accessible to the conscious mind with a minimal effort of thought. Any moment's conscious thought or memory can be brought from the preconscious, and will go back to the preconscious before and after that moment. When one turns attention to a mathematical problem or recalls a favorite aunt's birthday, one is drawing on preconscious thoughts not always present in the conscious mind.

See CONSCIOUSNESS.

Prejudice. Traditionally defined as a STEREOTYPE accompanied by affective reactions that predispose a person to react in a consistent way (usually negative) toward a given class of objects or persons. The actions of the priest and the Levite in the parable of the good Samaritan (Luke 10:29–37) constitute a classic example of ethnic or class prejudice. The concept of prejudice did not receive much attention from psychologists until the racial atrocities of the Second World War came to light. Shortly afterward Adorno, Frenkel-Brunswik, Levinson, and Sanford (1950) published *The Authoritarian Personality*, giving specific correlates of the AUTHORITARIAN PERSONALITY of which prejudice was one. They had developed the California F (Fascist) Scale as a measure of prejudice and ethnocentrism without reference to specific racial groups. Subsequently Allport (1954) published the classic work on the subject, *The Nature of Prejudice.* Following the overwhelming impact of Allport's treatise, only a few systematic writings appeared (Rokeach, 1960; Ehrlich, 1973).

The etymological roots of *prejudice* lie in the Latin noun *praejudicium*, which originally meant a precedent or judgment based on previous experience. Later it denoted a judgment formed before examination of the facts—i.e., a prejudgment. Eventually it took on the emotional connotations of an unsupported judgment. While the emotional tone could be favorable or unfavorable, much greater use is made of the latter. The work of most social psychologists has supported this view.

Allport (1954) suggested that prejudgments become prejudices when two conditions are fulfilled: an *overgeneralization* toward the class produces an *irreversible* misconception. Overgeneralization of the underlying concept to the class of objects makes the judgment irreversible in that it prevents further evidence.

Attitudes serve individuals through two functions. They operate as a summary of past experience to guide individuals in upcoming situations. They also serve as filters to selectively admit sensory experience into consciousness. The filtering function is not random, but systematically biased. The bias of attitude filtering is in the direction of past experience. In prejudice the individual overgeneralizes from past experience, rigidly adhering to preconceptions, which renders those misconceptions functionally irreversible. Prejudices screen the contradictory evidence from awareness and prevent the individual from entering circumstances where the misconceptions would be exposed.

Social psychologists have traditionally conceptualized attitudes as having three components: cognitive or (belief), affective (emotional), and behavioral (action). In the case of racial prejudices the cognitive component is represented in an ethnic stereotype. The affective component is marked by the individual's desire to avoid, malign, or express hostilities toward the ethnic group. The behavioral component constitutes the discriminatory or other action directed toward the ethnic group. Whether the behavioral component will occur depends on the intensity of the emotional component and several parameters of the situation (e.g., the proximity of the rival group, scarcity of resources important to both groups, degree of anonymity, intergroup cultural differences). Discrimination is also more likely with certain personality traits (e.g., authoritarianism).

The cognitive component of prejudice is a belief reflecting the individual's categorization of events. This stereotype contains a kernel of truth that permits the person to prejudge an event or person on the basis of class membership. The process of categorization and generalization is quite normal. When interacting with new persons or objects, the individual abstracts and sharpens essential features that distinguish the person or object. The abstraction is then applied to others that share the same features—i.e., generalization. Categories formed in this way enable the individual to respond to the object. Thus the stereotype as "an exaggerated belief associated with a category" (Allport, 1954, p. 191) leads to stereotypic behavior toward the class. The individual is responded to as a member of the class or category rather than as a unique individual. In the case of prejudices the categories that are formed seem to be based on minimal information and tend to be dichotomous. Stereotypes in a given society tend to be associated with specific ethnic groups, are widely diffused throughout the society, and reflect a high degree of consensus in the society (Ehrlich, 1973). Stereotypes justify or rationalize behavior in relation to the category.

The direction and strength of the cognitive aspects are supported by emotional associations. Some theorists suggest that the cognitive aspects adapt to justify the emotional response. Disliking someone is verified in finding something to dislike about the person. Similar to other emotional responses, prejudices activate the autonomic arousal system. When physiological arousal is accompanied by appropriate cognitions and labeling of affective states, the individual is likely to engage in discriminatory behavior, provided the situation permits it. The emotional component of a prejudice is a heightened state or arousal usually accompanied by feelings of mistrust, suspiciousness, and rejection of the object of the prejudice.

Under certain conditions, the negative stereotypes and feelings are manifested in negative action toward the objects of the prejudice. The negative action includes the maintenance of social distance, discrimination, and various forms of hostility and aggression.

The seminal work on social distance was conducted by Bogardus (1959), whose social distance scale measures the willingness of an individual to admit a member of an identified race to a category: close kinship by marriage, personal friend, neighbor, fellow in one's occupation, citizen of one's country, or a visitor to one's country. Social distance indicates the normative distance advocated by a group toward others, while personal distance is the behavioral intention of the individual. Just as

stereotypes are shared in groups, groups display consensus about social distance norms. Ethnic groups that have different physical appearances or different cultural heritages or are politically estranged are attributed more social distance than other ethnic groups that are more similar (Bogardus, 1959).

Other types of behavioral intentions are seen in ethnic jokes, ethnic slurs, racial hostilities, racial discrimination, rioting and lynching. The hostilities and aggression may be indirectly expressed when intergroup contact is minimal or when competition is relatively weak. They may be expressed more directly and violently in situations of extreme competition for resources, when individual anonymity is probable, or when sanctions against violence are ineffective.

Certain personality types appear to be more prone to develop prejudices than others. Authoritarianism is a personality-attitude complex that "consists of interrelated antidemocratic sentiments including ethnic prejudice, political conservatism, and a moralistic rejection of the unconventional" (Byrne, 1974, p. 86). In the work of Adorno, et al. (1950) nine dimensions of authoritarianism were postulated: conventionalism—rigid adherence to conventional middle-class values; authoritarian submission—uncritical obedience to leaders; authoritarian aggression—tendency to reject and punish those who violate conventional values; destruction and cynicism—generalized hostility; preoccupation with power and toughness; superstition and stereotypy—magical beliefs about one's fate and thinking in rigid dichotomies; anti-intraception—opposed to the subjective, imaginative, and artistic; projectivity—outward projection of unconscious emotional impulses; and exaggerated concern for sexual events. Experimental evidence has provided modest support for these proposed interrelated dimensions.

Authoritarian parents typically adopt autocratic family structures wherein punishment is physical and harsh and relations are generally restrictive in nature. Autocratic family structures tend to produce authoritarian offspring. By way of contrast, equalitarian parents adopt more democratic family structures marked by love-oriented discipline, permissiveness, and absence of punitiveness. The result is equalitarian personalities in children.

Greater social distance has been observed in authoritarians as well as in those of lower intelligence. Rokeach (1960) has argued that prejudice is more likely in individuals with closed minds. He further suggested that authoritarian and prejudiced personalities are drawn to the fundamentalist end of the religious spectrum, because fundamentalist religious dogmas legitimize that attitude and personality while providing definitive answers to critical questions. Intolerance of ambiguity and intolerance of deviance further characterize the prejudiced personality.

Theories of causation of prejudices are numerous and range from Marx's historical exploitation view to the sociocultural forces of urbanization (Allport, 1954). Psychological origins are suggested in the psychodynamic frustration (i.e., scapegoat) theory, in which intrapsychic conflict is projected outwardly in the form of out-group aggression. But most social psychological approaches conceive of prejudice as being maintained and strengthened when in-group cooperation and out-group competition characterize the social situation. While the transmission of prejudice from generation to generation involves the socialization of children by parents, teachers, and other agents of society as well as identification with and conformity to one's own reference group, these mechanisms are most operative when peculiar historical conditions and politicoeconomic structures sustain intergroup rivalries.

References

Adorno, T. W., Frenkel-Brunswik, E., Levinson, D. J., & Sanford, R. N. *The authoritarian personality.* New York: Harper & Row, 1950.

Allport, G. W. *The nature of prejudice.* Reading, Mass.: Addison-Wesley, 1954.

Bogardus, E. S. *Social distance.* Ann Arbor, Mich.: University Microfilms, 1959.

Byrne, D. *An introduction to personality: Research, theory, and application* (2nd ed.). Englewood Cliffs, N.J.: Prentice-Hall, 1974.

Ehrlich, H. J. *The social psychology of prejudice.* New York: Wiley, 1973.

Rokeach, M. *The open and closed mind.* New York: Basic Books, 1960.

R. L. TIMPE

Premack Principle. A behavioral phenomenon observed by Premack (1959). He discovered that the behaviors performed most frequently by an individual who is given the opportunity to choose among various activities will function to reinforce behaviors performed less frequently. In his research Premack let children have free access to pinball games and candy, and he observed that playing pinball was the higher frequency behavior. By changing the contingencies so that playing pinball was allowed only after eating a certain amount of candy, he found he could increase the children's frequency of eating candy. This principle can be applied in personal behavior modification programs. For example, a high frequency behavior such as television watching or socializing can be used to reinforce and thus increase a lower frequency behavior such as jogging or dieting.

Reference

Premack, D. Toward empirical behavior laws: Positive reinforcement. *Psychological Review,* 1959, 66, 219–233.

K. M. LATTEA

Premarital Counseling. The first mention of premarital counseling as a valued service occurred in a 1928 article in *The American Journal of Obstetrics and Gynecology.* Then, and until the mid-1950s, most writing in the area of premarriage concerned physicians and the premarital physical exam. In the 1950s religious literature began to focus on premarital counseling and writings from the mental health profession.

Historical Development. Traditionally there have been three main groups who provide most of the premarital counseling: ministers, physicians, and mental health professionals. Physicians are most concerned about the physical exam and have little time for long-term counseling. Most mental health counselors have received little or no training in the field of premarital counseling and actually see fewer couples than do those in the ministry. Since minsters are involved in performing the ceremony, they have a greater opportunity to prepare couples for marriage, and most couples tend to seek out ministers for this service. Ministerial involvement in this form of counseling arose as an expansion of the pastoral counseling movement in the 1940s and 1950s.

During the early years of premarital counseling the emphasis appeared to be on troubled couples or individual pathology. Then the role of the minister as a screening agent emerged in the literature of the 1950s and 1960s. Johnson (1953) stated that he saw the minister as being responsible for the continuing growth of a couple's marriage. The role of the minister as an examiner of the emotional readiness and maturity of couples for marriage was emphasized by Stewart (1970) and Rutledge (1966).

In order to challenge the ever-expanding divorce rate, some states have become involved in encouraging premarital preparation. California and several other states have passed legislation requiring persons under 18 to obtain not only parental consent but also a court order giving permission to obtain the marriage license. The Superior Court of Los Angeles County, along with courts in many other counties, mandated premarital counseling as a prerequisite for obtaining a marriage license by minors. Many churches and public health agencies offer their services to young couples seeking permission to marry. In 1972, of the 4,000 couples who applied for marriage licenses in Los Angeles County, 2,745 turned to ministers for their counseling. Many of the other couples used community health services.

Even though the law and the program are relatively new, initial conclusions indicate that couples generally found the experience helpful, and many return for counseling after marriage. The findings reinforce the conviction that premarital counseling is a valuable means of offering primary prevention of common problems of marriage.

Many ministers now receive intensive training in premarital counseling in various seminaries throughout the United States. Organizations such as Prepare (Minneapolis, Minnesota) and Christian Marriage Enrichment (Santa Ana, California) are conducting nationwide seminars for the purpose of training ministers and counselors in premarital preparation.

Objectives. There is little uniformity amongst those conducting premarital counseling. Traditionally ministers were concerned with the wedding ceremony and the spiritual relationship of the couple. In the past decade there has been a new trend emerging. This involves: 1) a very thorough preparation program of several sessions prior to the wedding; 2) premarital counseling as mandatory and not an option for the couple; 3) an intensive homework schedule accompanying the sessions with the couple.

Typically there are several basic objectives to be achieved during premarital counseling. One goal is to make arrangements for the procedural details of the wedding ceremony itself. The couple can express their desires, and the minister can make suggestions and provide guidelines. Premarital counseling is an opportunity for the minister or other counselor to build an in-depth relationship with the couple, which could lead to a continuing ministry in the future.

Providing information is another goal. Probably more teaching occurs in this type of counseling than in any other. Part of this teaching involves helping the couple to understand themselves and what each one brings to marriage, to discover their strengths and weaknesses, and to be realistic about the adjustments they must make to have a successful relationship.

Another goal is providing correction. Correction of faulty information concerning marriage relationships, the communication process, finances, in-laws, and sex will be a regular part of the counseling for most couples. One of the main purposes is to help the couple eliminate as many surprises as possible from the impending marriage. By eliminating these and helping the couple become more realistic about the future, marital conflict will be lessened.

The counselor must have expertise in many areas, because the couple is looking to him or her as the conveyor of helpful information. This is an opportunity to provide an atmosphere in which the couple can relieve themselves of fears and anxieties concerning marriage and settle questions or doubts they may have. This may also be a time in which strained and severed relationships with parents and in-laws will be restored.

The final purpose for counseling could be one of the most important goals. This is a time to assist the couple in making their final decision: Should we marry? They may not come with that in mind, but engagement is not finality. Research indicates that between 35 and 45% of all engagements in this country are terminated. Many people do change their mind. Perhaps during the process of premarital counseling some couples will decide to postpone their wedding or completely terminate their relationship. On the other side, there will be some cases in which a minister will decide that he cannot, in good conscience, perform the wedding because of the apparent mismatch or immaturity of the couple.

Format and Techniques. The structure or format of premarital counseling varies considerably. Many couples are seen by the minister or counselor for several sessions. Other programs involve a combination of conjoint sessions with several group sessions. A third alternative is to conduct all sessions on a group basis. One example of this third alternative is the Engaged Encounter Movement, an outgrowth of the Marriage Encounter Movement. Many are using the combination approach of conjoint and group sessions, which can provide a couple with between 10 to 12 hours of preparation. The ideal and most productive of approaches appears to be either the conjoint or the combination of conjoint and group program. The personal involvement and interaction of a guide with one couple for several hours is an element that a group experience cannot produce.

In most premarital settings various evaluation instruments are used. This is done to assist the couple to gain a better understanding of themselves and their relationship. The various approaches to personal and couple assessment cover a broad range of devices, including personality inventories, psychological tests, rating scales, questionnaires, and personal data forms. Instrumentation helps to promote a strong level of couple involvement in the counseling process. It also assists the counselor or minister in obtaining information that otherwise might be missed. Some of the most frequently used tools are the Taylor-Johnson Temperament Analysis, Prepare, Family History Analysis, Myers-Briggs Indicator, and the Premarital Counseling Inventory.

One of the newest trends developing in the field of premarital counseling is an emphasis on each person's family of origin and the ensuing effect upon the couple's forthcoming marriage. Couples are assisted in determining if they have completed the parental separation process and if there is any unfinished business existing between them and their parents. This approach also helps them understand the kinds of marital models they have for their own marriage. This approach is involved in Stahlmann and Hiebert's (1980) Dynamic Relationship History and Wright's (1981) Family History Analysis.

The content of premarital counseling varies, but the comprehensive multisession approach typically covers numerous significant topic areas. Content areas usually include the following: the effect of courtship, the quality of love, the purpose and meaning of marriage, sexual knowledge and expression, timing for marriage, reasons for marriage, fears and concerns of marriage, family background, family dependency, family closeness, separation from family, personality characteristics, self-image, emotions, spiritual relationship and life, anticipating a future together, expectations, needs, roles, goals, decision making, communication, conflict resolution, in-laws, finances, leisure and friendships, and children.

Evaluation. Research on premarital counseling has been very limited. What is needed is long-term follow-up studies of couples who received premarital counseling versus those who did not. Such studies will need to control for the number of sessions couples receive and the approach taken in the sessions. Proper instrumentation must also be established for the purpose of pre- and posttesting.

In the absence of such research anecdotal reports are the only available data as to the effectiveness of premarital counseling. Numerous ministers and organizations attest to very positive results from premarital counseling. These responses are based on self reports from couples, simple evaluation responses from couples, and personal observations and contact with previously counseled couples. A much lower than average national divorce rate has also been used as a criterion.

There does seem to be some evidence that the more sessions couples attend, the greater the results. These results are reflected in the reports of couples on the value of the counseling, the lower number of divorces, and the number of couples who decide to not marry during the process of premarital counseling (Wright, 1981).

Future research will be important in this relatively new field of preventive counseling. However, the potential for increased effectiveness and for the stabilizing of future marriages appears good through carefully conducted premarital counseling.

References
Johnson, P. E. *Psychology of pastoral care.* Nashville: Abingdon, 1953.
Rutledge, A. L. *Premarital counseling.* Cambridge: Schenkman Publishing, 1966
Stahmann, R. F., & Hiebert, W. J. *Premarital counseling.* Lexington, Mass.: Lexington Books, 1980
Stewart, C. W. *The minister as marriage counselor.* Nashville: Abingdon, 1970
Wright, H. N. *Premarital counseling* (Rev. ed.). Chicago: Moody Press, 1981.

H. N. Wright

Premature Ejaculation. *See* Ejaculation, Premature.

Prematurity. The term used to describe a human infant born with a gestational age of less than 37 weeks. Additionally, an infant born prior to 8¼ months gestation period who weighs between 1500–2500 grams (normal birth weight of a full-term infant is approximately 3500 grams) may also be considered premature.

Causes. In the last 20 years or so scientists have attempted to identify the causes of premature birth. Since the greatest proportion of premature infants are born in economically disadvantaged countries or in the poorer sections of the United States, researchers have identified a link between prematurity and poor maternal diet typically found in these environments. Indeed, mothers who have a history of dietary deficiencies are much less likely to carry the child full term. And even if the infant is carried full term, he or she is more likely to be small and of low birth weight.

In addition to diet various chemical substances have been found to be related to early births. For example, mothers who use heroin or methadone during their pregnancy are likely to give birth to infants who are not only addicted to the drug but are also premature and small. It would appear that the presence of the drug in the mother's and child's bloodstream makes it more difficult for the fetus to use nourishment from the mother. Researchers have also discovered that nicotine may affect the developing fetus. Chronic smokers are twice as likely to bear premature infants than are nonsmokers. And although no direct link between alcohol consumption and premature births has been found, if alcohol use is related to maternal malnutrition then an early birth is a more likely occurrence.

While diet and drugs are the most easily identified causes of prematurity, they are not the only determinants. Poor emotional health, particularly if characterized by anxiety and tension, may also be related to prematurity. Apparently mothers who live in a constant state of neurotic anxiety and who generally have fairly chaotic life styles give birth prematurely more often than do mothers who are more or less emotionally stable.

Consequences. None of the above would seem to be of much concern were it not that some long-term negative consequences often result from a shortened gestational period. Physiologically the last trimester of pregnancy (the last three months) are important in at least three ways. First, during the final trimester a large percentage of the cortical neurons (brain cells) are developed. These neurons are related to intellectual processes, the absence of which may lead to deficits in later intellectual functioning, which is what is found with many premature and low birth weight infants. These children, followed into junior and senior high school, were found to have more problems in a number of academic areas such as reading, spelling, and arithmetic. In addition, they were overly represented in special education classes and among the rosters of high school dropouts. It is important to recognize that these findings are correlational; they do not indicate a cause-and-effect relationship between prematurity, a lack of some important cortical neurons, and later problems in school, but they do indicate that a significant relationship exists between these factors.

The last trimester is also important in the development of the lungs. Although the lungs themselves are developed much earlier, the tiny air sacs, the alveoli, do not complete development until the final 12 weeks. Not surprisingly, children born prematurely are more likely to have respiratory problems.

Physiological problems notwithstanding, the real impact of premature births may actually be in the area of the attachment relationship with the caregivers. Research conducted in the early 1970s found that it takes most mothers a period of several weeks before they can report feelings of love toward their newborns (Robson & Moss, 1970). They indicated that the responses of the newborn—the smiling, looking, and vocalizing—were crucial in the development of these feelings. Parents of infants who did not smile or vocalize often took longer to develop strong attachments to the infant.

Mothers of premature infants are more likely to report that instead of feeling positive emotions, they have feelings of guilt, failure, and alienation from their infant; apprehension about handling; and less involvement emotionally in the care of the infant. Since premature infants are kept in incubators and away from their mothers, the mother's opportunity to interact with her newborn is lost. Some research has indicated that the days immediately following birth may be crucial in the attachment relationship. Some mothers (though certainly not most) may find it difficult to make up for the lost time. While it is not certain just how the relationship is affected, research shows that there is a higher rate of negative attachments between mothers and their premature offspring than between mothers and full-term children (Caputo & Mandel, 1970). Further, premature infants represent a disproportionate number of abused children, and are also overrepresented among children who exhibit antisocial and delinquent behavior. While no cause-and-effect relationship can be postulated, it seems that the affectionate relationship between child and caregiver that is important for many areas of later development may be negatively affected in some mother-infant dyads, especially if the child does not respond positively when handled by its caregivers.

Although the focus of this article has been on the potentially negative effects associated with premature birth, it is important to note that most premature infants develop normally and are indistinguishable from their full-term counterparts. Normally parents and children make the necessary adjustments, and the fact that the child was born prematurely is unimportant.

References
Caputo, D. V., & Mandel, W. Consequences of low birth weight. *Developmental Psychology*, 1970, 3, 363–383.
Robson, K. S., & Moss, H. A. Patterns and determinants of maternal attachment. *Journal of Pediatrics*, 1970, 77, 976–985.

K. A. HOLSTEIN

Prenatal Development. Most physical and psychological development can be described as interaction between growth (increase in size and weight) and differentiation (increase in complexity and organization). At no time are these processes more clearly demonstrated than during the prenatal period.

Prenatal development is commonly divided into three phases. The first begins with a sperm fertilizing the egg and ends about three weeks later with a many-celled structure embedding in the uterine wall. By this time the amniotic cavity is formed, and the embryo is attached to its shell by a stalk that will become the umbilical cord. This phase is characterized by rapid cell division.

The second phase (4 to 8 weeks following fertilization) is termed the embryonic phase or the period of organogenesis, since it is the time when all major organs and organ systems are developed. This phase is characterized by differentiation and is the time when the developing individual is most susceptible to factors producing birth defects. By the end of this period motor activity can be noted, and the embryo begins to appear more human with its development of limbs, face, eyes, and ears.

The third phase (3 months to birth) is the fetal phase, and is characterized by rapid growth with little further differentiation except in select systems. During this period head growth slows down relative to body growth, moving from approximately one-third the standing height at 4 months to one-fourth that height at birth. By 3 months eyes and ears become located in their final positions, and genitalia are so developed that external assessment of gender may be made. In the fourth and fifth months the fetus lengthens rapidly, and in the final months weight gain catches up with the lengthening process to provide the rounded shape associated with the newborn.

Numerous physical and social factors during pregnancy have been related to developmental problems, from infectious diseases to radiation, from serious anxiety to chromosomal aberrations. Most frequently the causes of such problems are assumed to work through the mother's system; however, recent research is beginning to implicate the father's system as well. (For a discussion of strength of evidence for such factors, see Ferreira's, 1969, major review and Persaud's, 1979, update.)

Probably the most important principle in understanding congenital problems is that the phase of prenatal development determines the degree of influence of environmental agents. In phase 1 contact with noxious agents will either be so profound as to cause death or, if few cells are damaged, compensation. Phase 2 has the highest risk for developing malformations, with those organs in their earlier stages of differentiation being most susceptible. Finally, little susceptibility to environmental agents exists in phase 3, except in those few systems still differentiating, such as the brain.

To ensure the best possible uterine environment prenatal assessment is routinely performed. Such monitoring provides invaluable information for healthy pregnancies, for dealing with prenatal problems through intervention during pregnancy, and for permitting parents to prepare for a child diagnosed as at risk for developmental disabilities. Most techniques do not intrude into the womb; maternal blood and urine sampling are used to assess levels of hormones and enzymes, and ultrasound monitors fetal heart rate, growth, and location of placenta. Only when some pregnancy concern arises are intrusive techniques performed. These include amniocentesis—i.e., sampling of amniotic fluid to investigate possible chromosomal abnormalities, inborn errors of metabolism, and other conditions—and the very promising fetoscopy, which uses fiber-optic techniques to directly observe the fetus in the womb.

The cutting edge of prenatal study today is intervention into the uterine environment; and although this work is still experimental in nature, successful treatment to block birth defects is now occurring. Techniques include providing medications through the mother's bloodstream that cross the placenta to the fetus, as well as actual surgery on the fetus while still inside the womb. For all its promise fetal intervention focuses even more attention on difficult ethical questions; for example, what do such techniques imply about when human life begins, or when the individual should be afforded civil rights?

References
Ferreira, A. J. *Prenatal environment.* Springfield, Ill.: Thomas, 1969.
Persaud, T. V. N. *Prenatal pathology.* Springfield, Ill.: Thomas, 1979.

M. D. ROE

Pressure of Speech. A disorder character-ized by accelerated and emphatic talking that is difficult or impossible to interrupt. The speech is frequently loud, and the speaker may talk without any stimulation or response from another. This increased speech is found most often in manic episodes but also in organic mental disorders, schizophrenia, and other psychotic disorders, and occasionally as an acute reaction to severe stress.

Prevention of Psychological Disorders.

This subject has received significant attention in recent years. A large body of literature is now available, including review articles (e.g., Kornberg & Caplan, 1980), a series of annual volumes based on the Vermont Conference on Primary Prevention of Psychopathology (e.g., Joffe & Albee, 1977), a textbook on primary prevention (Bloom, 1981), and even a journal, the *Journal of Prevention.* This increased inter-est in prevention is understandable in light of the shortage of mental health professionals to meet the needs of the emotionally disturbed and the great cost of mental illness, estimated recently to be more than $40 billion annually (see Hatch, 1982). Albee (1982) has pointed out that the mental health community actually sees fewer than one in five of the estimated 15% (32 to 34 million) of the American popula-tion who are seriously disturbed emotionally. Christian authors have also begun to focus on the need for Christian counselors and churches to be more involved in preventive interventions.

Prevention of psychological disorders has usually been divided into three types: primary, secondary, and tertiary (see Zax & Cowan, 1976). Primary prevention involves preventing the development of psychological dysfunction and hence reducing the rate of occurrence of new cases of disorder (its incidence) in the general population. Secondary prevention re-fers to the reduction of the prevalence of disorder by shortening its duration and nega-tive consequences. It therefore seeks to stop mild disorders from becoming prolonged or acute, and focuses on early identification and prompt, effective treatment of psychological dysfunction. Tertiary prevention aims at re-ducing the severity, discomfort, or disability associated with psychological disorder that is already well established. A number of authors have suggested that the terms *secondary* and *tertiary* prevention be replaced by *treatment* and *rehabilitation*, respectively, in order to reduce confusion over terminology. The term *prevention* will therefore be used in this article to refer mainly to primary prevention aimed at reducing the incidence of new cases of psycho-logical disorder. Attempts at primary preven-tion, by definition, occur in a population that is free of the disorder being prevented.

Examples of Primary Prevention. There are many excellent examples of preventive inter-vention with a wide variety of populations (see Bloom, 1981). Heber's (1978) study of preven-tion of sociocultural mental retardation is one frequently cited example of successful primary prevention. Children of mothers with IQs less than ·75 were given day care in an intense program from infancy until they entered pub-lic school. The mothers simultaneously re-ceived remedial education as well as training in home management, home economics, inter-personal relations, and child care techniques. At the final assessment (age 6) children's IQs in the group that received the preventive inter-vention averaged 120.7, while children in the control group had an average IQ of only 87.2. The results of this study therefore seem to indicate that it is possible to modify or prevent sociocultural mental retardation. The preven-tive intervention appears to have improved the intelligence and reduced behavior problems of children reared by parents of limited intellec-tual capacity living in disadvantaged eco-nomic circumstances. However, the trustwor-thiness of these findings has recently been questioned (see Sommer & Sommer, 1983).

Another well-known and significant pre-vention program is the Primary Mental Health Project conducted by Cowen and his colleagues in Rochester (see Cowen, Trost, Dorr, Lorion, Izzo, & Isaacson, 1975). This is a program for early detection and prevention of school adjustment problems in children. Cowen found that many of the children identi-fied as high risk but who received no interven-tion continued to have problems or had worse difficulties during the later school years. His intervention involved the use of housewives as nonprofessional child aides who worked di-rectly with high-risk children in the schools. The children were typically seen about twice a week, usually for the entire school year. The housewives provided an empathic and accept-ing relationship with the children on an individual basis. Research has shown that this preventive intervention has provided both immediate and long-term benefit to the chil-dren who received it, and has significantly reduced later school adjustment problems.

More recently Durlak (1977) used teachers and college students to implement a more specific behavioral preventive intervention.

Verbal and token reinforcement were used to modify maladaptive social behaviors in school children. Evaluation of the eight-week intervention program using ratings by teachers and aides showed that children who received the intervention improved significantly in classroom adjustment at both completion of the program and at a seven-month follow-up. However, longer term follow-up is needed to determine whether these short-term effects last.

Shure and Spivack (1980) reported that significantly fewer young children who were trained in interpersonal cognitive problem-solving skills showed signs of impulsivity or inhibition when compared to a control group of children a year after the intervention. They concluded that problem-solving training prevented the emergence of these behaviors as well as helped children who were already having difficulties. Their study was therefore only partly preventive in nature. Attempts by other investigators to duplicate these results with other age groups and settings have not been as successful (see Cowen, 1980).

Another example of a successful and systematic preventive program is the behavioral work done by Poser and his colleagues (see Poser & Hartman, 1979). In a series of studies they have shown the effectiveness of preexposure and symbolic-modeling strategies for the prevention of maladaptive fear responses in children in situations involving dental treatment and handling of snakes (Poser & King, 1975). More recently measures of psychological vulnerability and environmental adversity or "press" have been validated and used to identify asymptomatic school students who may be at risk for psychological disorder (Poser & Hartman, 1979). Hartman (1979) found that students who received an eight-week group intervention of coping and social skills training improved significantly more than those who did not. There was a strong trend for these gains to be maintained at a three-month follow-up. Once again, longer term follow-up is needed before more definitive conclusions can be made. However, the results do suggest that coping and social skills training may be a very effective preventive intervention.

Another recent successful prevention program involved reducing child abuse and neglect with families identified to be at risk by using parent support groups, parent education, school system coordination, and the utilization of other agencies during prenatal, childbirth, and postpartum care (Turkington, 1983a, b). However, it should also be pointed out that not all efforts at prevention of psychological disorders have been successful. Examples of failure include attempts at preventing juvenile delinquency and crime (e.g., McCord, 1978) and "immunizing" children for speech anxiety (Cradock, Cotler, & Jason, 1978).

The Church and Prevention. Several authors have recently proposed that the prevention of mental disorders should be a concern of the church (Collins, 1980; Uomoto, 1982). Uomoto argues that the church is a potent mental health resource because of its proximity in the community, its independent financial set-up, its consistency in providing a stable social environment, and its mission to enhance the physical, emotional, and spiritual well-being of its members. He suggests three levels of preventive interventions as options for the church: individual interventions, social system interventions, and the provision of a healing community.

Individual interventions could include mental health education (i.e., educating church leaders on psychological principles, mental health resources, mental disorders, referral methods, skill training); skills and competence training (i.e., conducting problem-solving workshops, language skills training, and lay counselor training); and the facilitation of stress reduction and coping (i.e., teaching preventive stress inoculation techniques, relaxation training, and cognitive restructuring procedures). Social system interventions might include the development of social support groups for high risk individuals such as divorcees, single parents, business executives, jobless people, families with disabled members, and former mental patients; regular visitations to peripheral members of a church; connecting people with specific needs to appropriate agencies or resources; establishing a telephone network; and working more closely with other community agencies. Finally, the overall goal would be the establishment of a healing climate in which all of the preceding interventions can be optimally undertaken. Uomoto suggests that such a climate can best be developed within a caring community of believers who are experiencing newness of life in Christ, living according to the law of love, and reaching out to the world.

Barriers to Prevention. Albee (1982) has argued that one-to-one psychotherapy is indefensible because of the unbridgeable gap between the large numbers in need and the small numbers of helpers. Furthermore, he argues that support for primary prevention as an alternative derives from the demonstrated role of poverty, meaningless work, unemployment, racism, and sexism in producing psychopathology, and from the demonstrated effectiveness of programs promoting social competence, self-esteem, and social support networks in reducing psychopathology. He therefore asks why most mental health professionals continue to practice an individually oriented approach to treatment, ignoring the arguments for movement from treatment to prevention.

Bloom (1981) suggests several barriers to prevention: the personal tendency to avoid making immediate sacrifices in order to obtain remote goals in the future, which runs counter to what prevention often requires; the professional reluctance to shift one's focus of practice from traditional psychotherapy after having invested years in it; conceptual inadequacies and the lack of more sophisticated and systematic theory in prevention; the lack of data, especially long-term follow-up data, to support the efficacy of preventive interventions; the great costs of some preventive programs; and ethical objections to the invasion of privacy or the tampering with self-choice, especially among minority or disadvantaged groups. Albee (1982) adds to this list the challenge that prevention represents to the traditional defect model (or medical model) of psychopathology. Focusing on social and environmental factors, prevention efforts are grounded in more of a social learning model. Thus they are resisted by those trained in the more traditional model, who are predisposed to see preventive efforts as modifying human unhappiness and misery but not affecting mental illness.

Albee (1982) has also proposed a religious source of resistance to prevention, arguing that opposition to prevention comes as a result of Calvinistic theology. Believing that neither the individual nor society is perfectable because of the stigma of original sin, Calvinists oppose efforts to better society and the lot of the individual sinner, according to Albee. However, while it is true that Christians do not believe that individuals or society can be made perfect by purely humanistic efforts, it is not true that they therefore have to oppose prevention.

The biblical view of prevention is centered in the redemptive work of Christ, since ultimately only Jesus Christ can meet the deepest psychospiritual needs of human beings. However, this does not mean that psychological, social, and environmental changes are not helpful for healthy mental functioning. While they are inadequate without the new birth in

Christ, which alone can deal with the fundamental problem of sin, they are important and legitimate spheres of Christian service.

Bloom (1981) is of the opinion that barriers to prevention can be overcome by rigorous and systematic research. Albee (1982), however, argues that what is needed is something more like ideological reeducation for mental health professionals. He suggests that significant forward movement toward the prevention of psychopathology will come as more and more people line up with those who believe in "social change, in the effectiveness of consultation, in education, in the primary prevention of human physical and emotional misery, and in the maximization of individual competence" (p. 1050).

References

Albee, G. W. Preventing psychopathology and promoting human potential. *American Psychologist*, 1982, *37*, 1043–1050.

Bloom, M. *Primary prevention: The possible science.* Englewood Cliffs, N.J.: Prentice-Hall, 1981.

Collins, G. R. The future of Christian counseling. In G. R. Collins (Ed.), *Helping people grow.* Santa Ana, Calif.: Vision House, 1980.

Cowen, E. L. The wooing of primary prevention. *American Journal of Community Psychology*, 1980, *8*, 258–285.

Cowen, E. L., Trost, M. A., Dorr, D. A., Lorion, R. P., Izzo, L. D., & Isaacson, R. V. *New ways in school mental health: Early detection and prevention of school maladaptation.* New York: Human Sciences Press, 1975.

Cradock, C., Cotler, S., & Jason, L. A. Primary prevention: Immunization of children for speech anxiety. *Cognitive Therapy and Research*, 1978, *2*, 389–396.

Durlak, J. A. Description and evaluation of a behaviorally oriented school-based preventive mental health program. *Journal of Consulting and Clinical Psychology*, 1977, *45*, 27–35.

Hartman, L. M. The preventive reduction of psychological risk in asymptomatic adolescents. *American Journal of Orthopsychiatry*, 1979, *49*, 121–135.

Hatch, O. G. Psychology, society, and politics. *American Psychologist*, 1982, *37*, 1031–1037.

Heber, F. R. Sociocultural mental retardation: A longitudinal study. In D. G. Forgays (Ed.). *Primary prevention of psychopathology* (Vol. 2). Hanover, N.H.: University Press of New England, 1978.

Joffe, J. M., & Albee, G. W. (Eds.), *Primary prevention of psychopathology* (Vol. 5). Hanover, N.H.: University Press of New England, 1977.

Kornberg, M., & Caplan, G. Risk factors and prevention intervention in child psychopathology: A review. *Journal of Prevention*, 1980, *1*, 71–133.

McCord, J. A 30-year follow-up of treatment effects. *American Psychologist*, 1978, *33*, 284–289.

Poser, E. G., & Hartman, L. M. Issues in behavioral prevention: Empirical findings. *Advances in Behavior Research and Therapy*, 1979, *2*, 1–25.

Poser, E. G., & King, M. C. Strategies for the prevention of maladaptive fear responses. *Canadian Journal of Behavioral Science*, 1975, *7*, 279–294.

Shure, M. B., & Spivack, G. A preventive mental health program for young "inner city" children: The second (kindergarten) year. In M. Bloom (Ed.), *Life span development.* New York: Macmillan, 1980.

Sommer, R., & Sommer, B. A. Mystery in Milwaukee: Early

intervention, IQ, and psychology textbooks. *American Psychologist*, 1983, *38*, 982–985.

Turkington, C. At risk: Project helps hard-to-reach parents, kids. *A.P.A. Monitor*, 1983, *14*, 6. (a)

Turkington, C. National center supports prevention efforts. *A.P.A. Monitor*, 1983, *14*, 7. (b)

Uomoto, J. M. Preventive intervention: A convergence of the church and community psychology. *Journal of Psychology and Christianity*, 1982, *1*, 12–22.

Zax, M., & Cowen, E. L. *Abnormal psychology: Changing conceptions* (2nd ed.). New York: Holt, Rinehart, & Winston, 1976.

S. Y. TAN

See COMMUNITY PSYCHOLOGY.

Pride. Unreasonably high self-esteem. Pride is frequently alluded to in Scripture but is not a topic of great interest to contemporary psychology. Perhaps the reason for such neglect of a critical human fault is to be found in the late-twentieth-century Western mind set, which sees less wrong with pride than with inferiority complexes and less offensiveness in pride than in self-effacement. It is not uncommon for American culture to idolize the proud politician or music star and to ignore the humble. Pride has its roots deep in the human soul, however. Payne (1960) wrote what he terms a history of the human soul by studying pride in literature. "Was not pride the soul confronting itself in a mirror, overjoyed at the recognition?" (p. 1).

The Bible describes pride (self-regarding love and self-satisfaction with one's person, status, behavior, reputation, and traits) as sin. Pride goes before destruction (Prov. 16:18), puts one in an undesirable relationship with God (1 Peter 5:5; James 4:6), and will yield a regrettable end (Prov. 29:23). Nebuchadnezzar was judged for his proud spirit (Dan. 4), Haman was beset with pride (Esther 5), and Pharaoh fell because of it. God promises to humble the proud (Matt. 23:12).

Christian theologians have dealt with the concept of pride mainly in the tradition of Augustine, who viewed pride as the first sin and thus spent a considerable amount of his energy on discussing it. The keystone of his argument was a text in Ecclesiasticus that reads, "pride is the beginning of sin." The verse has later been regarded as very questionable in meaning. Nonetheless, on this basis he proceeded to view the fall of Satan as portrayed in Ezekiel and Isaiah as principally motivated by pride. "Your heart became proud on account of your beauty" (Ezek. 28:17 *a*). What led Satan to his fall was likewise the downfall of the human race in the Garden of Eden. Augustine felt that pride in its extreme was the unpardonable sin

(Green, 1949). He wrote extensively about his own struggles with pride, describing it as his greatest temptation.

The study of pride has also been the subject of great interest to Christians in monastic traditions and later to the pietists. Bernard of Clairvaux in his famous book *The Steps of Humility* said that men can take steps upward if they pursue humility; but if they pursue pride, their steps will lead downward, following the course of Satan. Bernard suggests that there are 12 steps that could lead one from the beginnings of pride—curiosity—to its most severe expression, habitual sin. The intervening steps are frivolity, foolish mirth, boastfulness, singularity (going to all ends to prove oneself superior), conceit, audacity, excusing of sins, hypocritical confession, defiance, and freedom to sin. The first step of pride (curiosity) is the last step of humility (downcast eyes). The last step of pride (habitual sin) should be the first step toward true humility (the fear of the Lord).

Bernard's outline is obviously sermonic in tone and designed as an instructive tool for aspiring monastics. But with all its medieval format, his description of pride rings true. Modern psychology does not have much to add to his outline. Pride elevates the self, seeks to have one's worth recognized by others, and is blind to obvious personal faults. The proud person has difficulty functioning interpersonally, since he or she does not receive or process feedback from others in a satisfactory manner. Nor does the proud person fare well in the task of being other-centered. In essence, pride forms a key element in the psychological construct of narcissism.

Pride, psychologically considered, is defensive in nature. By definition pride is not a fair and true estimate of self; it is an overestimate. Hence the proud person is motivated to hide a subconscious feeling of inferiority, or is motivated to overcompensate for actual inadequacies. Pride can be part of an ill-formed approach to social interaction; the proud person may genuinely feel his or her pride to be the best approach to dealing with self and others and may be unaware of any actual flaws that would preclude the pride. Pride thrives on deference and praise from others. It may have its roots in parental overindulgence or in a background that created deep personal insecurities for which the pride is compensating.

References

Green, W. M. *Augustine on pride as the first sin.* Berkeley: University of California Press, 1949.

Payne, R., *Hubris: A study of pride.* New York: Harper & Row, 1960.

J. R. BECK

Primal Therapy. Primal therapies embrace the traditional notion that psychological illnesses are the result of repressing, or removing from consciousness, the feelings surrounding traumatic life experiences. Healing involves reexperiencing and integrating these repressed feelings in as totally uninhibited a fashion as possible. The screaming that often accompanies the release of these powerful emotions has earned the primal therapies their reputation for being a radical treatment approach.

The primal therapies have a complex ancestry that can be traced to the cathartic method of Breuer and Freud (see Swartley, 1979, for primal therapy's family tree). In 1897 Freud first used the term *primal* or *primary* to denote psychological processes that ignore reality and attempt to gratify every wish either by simple motor activity (such as eating or sexual intercourse) or by identifying with the source of previous satisfaction (such as mother's breast). In contrast, secondary processes take external reality into account when seeking to satisfy a wish. Psychodynamic theorists now use the term *primal* (meaning first in time) for a memory or scene from early childhood that is apparently the first stage in the development of a neurosis.

Freud initially attempted to release and work with these primal experiences directly through free association and hypnosis, but he later abandoned this task as too difficult and as potentially damaging to both therapist and patient. Others, however, have resumed where Freud left off, and in 1972, under the leadership of William Swartley, the International Primal Association was formed. Among contemporary versions of primal-type therapy, Janov's primal therapy has drawn the most attention, both for the coherence and breadth of the theory and for its somewhat sensational presentation in his book, *The Primal Scream* (1970).

After 17 years of practicing standard insight therapy as a psychiatric social worker and psychologist, Janov encountered a baffling clinical situation that forced him to change his theories of neurosis. During an otherwise ordinary group therapy session Janov invited a patient to call out, "Mommy! Daddy!" in imitation of a scene from a play which had fascinated the young man. The patient complied and was soon writhing on the floor in an agony that finally ended in a piercing, deathlike scream. This ordinarily withdrawn person was as puzzled as Janov about the experience and could only report, "I made it! I don't know what, but I can *feel!*" (Janov, 1970, p. 10). Analysis of this and similar clinical experiences led to Janov's theory and therapy, which would regard the young man's scream as a product of the primal pains that reside in all neurotic individuals at all times.

Janov believes that all neurotic behaviors and most physical symptoms derive from a single common source: the suppression of feeling. This suppression begins early in life when the child's basic needs go unmet for any length of time. The pain that results from this deprivation continues until the child either gets his parents to satisfy him or shuts off the pain by shutting off the conscious awareness of need.

The thousands of parent-child interactions that deny the child's needs make him feel that there is no hope of love when he is really being himself. The child therefore begins to act in the expected manner rather than out of his own real needs and desires. The primal scene for Janov is the critical point at which the child shifts from being more real to being more unreal. At this juncture the child is said to be neurotic, and the unreal behavior soon becomes automatic. The real, feeling self is locked away behind layers of defense.

What is crucial here is that the child does not eliminate the need simply by splitting off from it. When excessive pain causes needs to be buried, the body goes into a state of emergency alert, which is experienced as constant tension. Because one's real needs have been removed from consciousness, one must pursue the satisfaction of these needs symbolically. Thus, an incessant smoker who was weaned too abruptly or too early may be symbolically expressing the need to suck his mother's breast. This, for Janov, is the essence of neurosis: the pursuit of symbolic satisfactions. And because the satisfaction is only symbolic, there is no end to the pursuit.

The ultimate goal in primal therapy is a tensionless, defense-free existence in which the individual experiences internal unity and is freely and deeply himself. Janov believes that this state is impossible for the neurotic to achieve without eliminating (i.e., experiencing) primal pains. When one feels fully the pain of one's basic unmet needs, when one finally *wants* what one *needs*, the struggle for love is resolved and the unreal self is destroyed. The patient is then said to be normal.

The primal therapist's objective is therefore to dismantle the patient's defenses in order to destroy the barrier between thoughts and feelings. The therapeutic milieu is carefully contrived to facilitate this. For the first three weeks of treatment the patient is seen daily in individual sessions lasting as long as the person needs (usually two to three hours). For at least the first week the individual stays alone in a motel room. Isolation, sleeplessness, and elimination of tension-relieving activities weaken defenses and keep the patient focused on himself.

During therapeutic sessions the patient lies spread-eagle on the couch. He is encouraged to relive early situations that evoke strong feelings. Defensive maneuvers such as intellectualization are confronted immediately and forbidden, so that one comes at last to experience one's feelings and pain—to "have a primal"—rather than simply to discuss these things. The therapist is thus "the dealer of Pain, no more, no less" (Janov, 1970, p. 247).

After the third week the person is placed in a postprimal group composed of people who have been through the treatment. The function of this group is to stimulate its members into new "primals." The patient usually stays in the group for 12 to 15 months.

Many primal therapists reject Janov's "busting" technique, preferring gentler methods such as massage or music to move the person into primal experiences. The role of pain in neurosis is also controversial. Some therapists observe that pleasure is sometimes more assiduously avoided.

The primal therapies usually last from one to two or more years, depending on the patient's readiness to allow his or her chaotic primal feelings into awareness. These therapies should not be used in their radical form with individuals who have fragile ego structures. The experience of primal hurts carries with it the potential for harmfully disrupting the psychotic or near-psychotic personality. Great skill is required of the therapist to avoid what Swartley calls the "insidious accumulation of side effects" (1979, p. 209) in either therapist or patient.

Though Janov has been criticized for going too far, perhaps the most salient critique from the Christian perspective is that he does not go far enough. For although Janov follows his patients into the primal experiences of birth and even intrauterine trauma, he stops short of the final abyss; his reductionistic view of persons as essentially biological entities forces him to consider neurotic those experiences

that arise out of one's spirit dimension. For example, Janov sees the experience of "oneness with God" as irrational and interprets it as a "loss of reality" (1970, p. 222). For the Christian, however, such a transcending experience is the truest expression of the true self, for God is the very ground of reality. Anxiety calls one to reckon not only with repressed childhood feelings but also with one's responsibilities and commitments, both immediate and ultimate. In the oft-quoted words of Augustine, "Thou hast made us for thyself, and our hearts are restless till they find their rest in thee."

Christian alternatives to Janov's primal therapy include Osborne's (1976) primal integration and Finch's Christian existential psychology (Malony, 1980). Though developed independently of Janov, primal integration uses essentially the same concepts, terminology, and techniques, but in a context that is accepting of religious experiences and values.

Christian existential therapy uses many primal techniques, including a three-week intensive therapy which the patient spends in isolation. However, Finch's approach goes beyond "emptying the well" of childhood hurts to an exploration of what lies beneath the well itself, namely, God. Finch views persons as essentially spirit—created in God's image, by God, and for God. Until one comes to know God experientially, as he is revealed in Christ, one is not truly oneself. In such a context primal therapy finds a responsible, holistic, deeply Christian expression.

References

Janov, A. *The primal scream.* New York: Putnam, 1970.
Malony, H. N. (Ed.). *A Christian existential psychology: The contributions of John G. Finch.* Washington D.C.: University Press of America, 1980.
Osborne, C. G. *The art of learning to love yourself.* Grand Rapids: Zondervan, 1976.
Swartley, W. The new primal therapies. In A. Hill (Ed.), *A visual encyclopedia of unconventional medicine.* New York: Crown, 1979.

B. Van Dragt

Primary Gain. Freud theorized that a patient accrues some gains from the formation of a neurotic symptom. The primary gain is obtained when the symptom allows partial instinctual gratification without the incapacitating guilt or anxiety accompanying direct instinctual discharge. The id impulse is kept unconscious while it is also partially indulged. Thus the patient complaining of disturbing and morbid thoughts of killing his wife can honestly claim no conscious desire to perform the act while simultaneously achieving discharge of aggressive instincts through his symptomatic obsessive thoughts.

See SECONDARY GAIN.

Primary Process. A psychoanalytical term referring to the primitive mental activity of young children and some seriously disturbed adults. Freud theorized that psychic functioning consists of two basic modes of operation, primary process and SECONDARY PROCESS. Primary process refers to a type of thinking or a particular way of manipulating psychic energy. The id operates according to primary process throughout life, while the ego gradually gives up primary for secondary process during the first years of life. The two main traits of primary process functioning are 1) drive toward immediate gratification of instincts, and 2) relatively easy shift from one object or method of gratification to another. The first is shown in the child's inability to delay pleasurable gratification, and the second is illustrated by the child's shift to sucking the thumb when the breast or bottle is unavailable. Other characteristics of the primary process mode are a generally illogical quality, thinking in allusion or analogy, visual over verbal representation, compatibility of mutually contradictory ideas, and absence of negatives or qualifying conditionals. Examples of primary process can also be found in normal adults in jokes or dreaming. Abnormality in adults exists only when psychic functioning is dominantly primary.

K. M. LATTEA

See PSYCHOANALYTIC PSYCHOLOGY.

Primary Reinforcer. In the terminology of behavioral psychology a primary reinforcer (also called an unconditioned reinforcer) is a stimulus that functions naturally to increase the probability of the behavior preceding it. A primary reinforcer need not be previously associated with any other stimuli in order to have behavioral reinforcing qualities. For example, food, water, and air are primary reinforcers because an organism will work to receive them without prior conditioning or learning. A thirsty animal or person will perform required behaviors to receive the primary reinforcer of a drink of water.

See SECONDARY REINFORCER; LEARNING.

Prince, Morton Henry (1854–1929). One of the pioneers in psychopathology and abnormal psychology. Born in Boston, he received his M.D. degree from Harvard Medical School in 1879 and continued his studies in France, where he came into contact with the work of Charcot and Janet. When he returned to the United States, he went into private practice, treating disorders of the nervous system. While practicing medicine he taught neurology at Harvard (1895–1898) and at Tufts (1902–1912).

In 1906 he founded the *Journal of Abnormal Psychology*, which became the *Journal of Abnormal and Social Psychology* in 1922. He edited it until his death. It was restored to its original name in 1965. In 1927 he founded the Harvard Psychological Clinic in an effort to bring normal and abnormal psychology into a closer relationship.

As a result of his studies in Paris he became interested in dissociation. He interpreted MULTIPLE PERSONALITY in terms of unconscious conflicts that split one part of the personality from another. Although he was a disciple of Janet, his view was actually closer to Freud's than to Janet's. His *Dissociation of a Personality* (1906) caused a stir because it read more like fiction than fact. Although his colleagues were advocating the "rest cure," he insisted that psychiatry should gear its treatment to the inner dynamics of the disturbance.

Prince believed that the same principles involved in normal learning could be found in pathological behavior. He argued that when the association between ideas is useful, no one becomes concerned; but when it is harmful, then they think it needs treatment. He viewed neurosis as a perversion of memory, or an "association" neurosis. Prince thought that theoretically what was done by education could be undone the same way, and he found this to be true in practice. He concluded that psychotherapies were just different forms of education, implying that people who were not physicians could treat functional disorders.

Prince was the author of more than 100 articles as well as many books on psychological, neurological, and political issues. His best-known psychological works are *The Unconscious* (1913) and *Clinical and Experimental Studies in Personality* (1929). During the war he wrote *The Psychology of the Kaiser* (1915), which was used as a guide by the British to organize their propaganda campaign against Germany. Several Allied governments decorated him for his contribution.

R. L. KOTESKEY

Problem-Centered Family Systems Therapy. Epstein's problem-centered family systems therapy has evolved out of several decades of research and clinical work. It provides a clear, systematic means of understanding and treating the troubled family. Much emphasis is placed on clarifying the major, sequential steps of therapy ("macro" stages) as contrasted with the specific interventions and strategies ("micro" stages) that vary with therapists' preferred styles. Problems are seen as coming from a blockage in one or more of the three basic functions that a family needs to perform for its members: 1) providing survival needs such as food, shelter, and money; 2) managing developmental stages (individual and family); and 3) giving support in stressful situations and crises.

Although Epstein originally took a psychoanalytic position in adult and child psychiatry, his present approach treats the whole family from a systems perspective, incorporating communication, transactional, and learning theory. This shift occurred when his research (Westley & Epstein, 1969) indicated that the emotional health of adolescents reflected the organizational and transactional patterns of their families.

Therapy Process. The focus of the therapy process is on current family problems. Past issues are given minimal attention. Treatment generally requires 6 to 12 sessions. Family members are enlisted as active collaborators in the problem-solving process. The family provides most of the momentum in the treatment process by identifying its own strengths and weaknesses and by devising means to solve its own problems. The therapist serves mainly as a catalyst, clarifier, and facilitator.

The major intervention steps of Epstein's model are assessment, contracting, treatment, and closure. Each step begins with an orientation by the therapist, who explains that particular phase and secures the family's permission to continue. Each step contains substages in which the family and therapist gather and clarify information, decide how to use this material, and then implement their decision. The hallmark of this model is the emphasis on the family's participation and capacity to be aware of its own problems and to act on them. At the end of each step the therapist summarizes his or her views and seeks a consensus with the family and their permission to proceed, a position that shows respect for the family members and reduces resistance to therapy.

Assessment is the most detailed step of this model and includes all family members living at home. Epstein regards a thorough and comprehensive diagnostic survey as the critical factor in the success of therapy. Six dimensions are investigated to give an overall picture of family functioning: problem solving, communication, roles, affective responsiveness, affective involvement, and behavior control. Each of these dimensions is carefully explored to gain understanding of the family's strengths and weaknesses as well as the level of effectiveness at which the family is functioning.

Problem solving concerns the family's ability to identify and discuss problems and to explore and implement alternatives. Communication involves the family's ability to speak clearly and directly to the appropriate person. Roles are predictable patterns of behavior for family members. The family is assessed as to how well the necessary role functions are performed, how appropriately roles are assigned, and how accountable persons are for their responsibilities. Affective responsiveness measures the degree to which the full range of human emotion, positive and negative, is experienced in the family and the level of appropriateness to the situation. Affective involvement explores the level of participation in the interests of other family members, from the extremes of no involvement to overinvolvement. Behavior control concerns the ways the family monitors and sanctions its members' behavior. Styles of control range from effective, flexible control to rigid and chaotic control.

These six dimensions are also used in a careful assessment of the presenting problem. Additional problems concerning individuals (physiological and psychological) are also assessed, as well as those concerning the family and wider social systems (school, church, extended family). The assessment stage is completed when both therapist and family agree on a list of family problems.

Contracting is the second major step. The therapist helps the family decide whether they would like to work alone on their problems or continue in treatment. If the latter, the family specifies what changes they expect from each other and sets concrete goals. Each person in the treatment process, including the therapist, commits himself to meeting these goals by signing a contract agreement.

The third major step is *treatment*. The therapist gives the initiative for action to the family, including identifying problems with the highest priority and the tasks that move toward meeting the goals. Tasks are distributed among the family members and progress towards goals is evaluated. If goals are met, further tasks are assigned. If a task is not completed, or even attempted, in three successive sessions, Epstein advises either outside consultation or termination.

Closure is the final step. Therapist and family summarize what they have learned in treatment, discuss how they can adapt these gains to future problems, and establish long-term goals. A future follow-up session is planned to monitor the family's progress.

Evaluation. Although more research regarding the effectiveness of this approach needs to be conducted, Epstein and Bishop (1981) consider it particularly effective with acute disturbances in previously well-functioning families. It also appears that it may be more effective with single-parent families having a child 6 to 12 years old and with families in which this is the first experience in therapy.

Epstein explicitly states that the underlying value system of this approach is the Judeo-Christian ethic. The individuals in the family are respected for their capacity to generate productive, healthy solutions to their problems, and emphasis is given to the optimal development of each human being. The therapist is not considered as all-knowing and omnipotent but as a co-worker with the family. This approach of regarding the family as the primary experts on themselves seems to restore the dignity the family may feel it has lost by revealing its problems and weaknesses. The humility of the therapist's stance and the belief in the worth of the individual are both consistent with the biblical perspective.

References
Epstein, N. B., & Bishop, D. S. Problem-centered systems therapy of the family. In A. S. Gurman & D. P. Kniskern (Eds.), *Handbook of family therapy.* New York: Brunner/Mazel, 1981.
Westley, W. A., & Epstein, N. B. *The silent majority.* San Francisco: Jossey-Bass, 1969.

C. V. BRUUN

See FAMILY THERAPY: OVERVIEW.

Problem Solving.
The process through which solutions to formal problems are achieved. A problem in the formal sense involves a state of uncertainty regarding how to attain a specific goal from a specific starting place using only certain allowable alternative operations or "moves." Included in this category are such familiar puzzles as Rubik's Cube, where the goal is to create a clearly understood alignment or configuration of faces on a cube by any possible manipulation of the component parts. Also included are practically the whole range of problems in logic, mathematics, science, and engineering, whenever both the givens and the goal may be specified exactly and there are definite constraints on alternative steps toward a solution.

Although problem solving as it has been delimited and studied in psychology has a multitude of obvious applications to practical affairs, clearly there are also numerous practical problems that fall outside of this study—e.g., how to apply oneself in school, whom to marry and when, when to buy a new car (for strategies for solving these informal, or practical, problems, *see* PROBLEM-SOLVING THERAPY).

The current investigation of problem solving has its historical roots primarily in the Gestalt tradition, the influence of which has been combined with, and to a considerable extent displaced by, modern developments from the engineering and computer sciences. The latter influences include cybernetics (the application of principles by which control, or feedback, mechanisms operate) plus the development of computer programs to simulate problem-solving processes.

Beginning with GESTALT PSYCHOLOGY, it was demonstrated that problem solving is best understood not as a process of trial and error but as a goal-directed search. For example, one experiment placed an ape inside a cage with a banana outside just beyond reach. After unsuccessfully trying to reach the banana, the ape suddenly fashioned a tool by fitting two sticks together and used it to capture the prize. Subsequently the ape mastered similar problems in the same way. Such experiments led to the emphasis on sudden insight over gradual, incremental learning. It also led to the restructuring of the whole field of perception. In short, the problem solver was understood as an active inquirer rather than a passive pawn of environmental events (*see* INSIGHT IN LEARNING).

Modern developments in cybernetics and computers have provided a new theoretical framework in which the concepts of Gestalt psychology take on new and more precise meanings. The emerging theory of problem solving also makes an understanding of the development of problem-solving capability more accessible, thus making the educational implications more explicit than they were before.

As proposed by Newell and Simon (1972), contemporary problem-solving theory conceives of the problem solver as analogous to an information processing system. The problem is internally represented in terms of what the initial conditions are, what is the desired state of affairs, and what are the possible operations for taking steps from the given state to the goal. Problem solving is then a process of goal-directed search through the internal representations of the problem, trying to find a sequence of valid steps for moving from the present status to the goal, and testing at every step for progress toward the goal. In this theory individuals may use different strategies, since there may be more than one way to solve a problem correctly. Thus, in place of the earlier concepts of insight and restructuring are found the newer concepts of search, discovery, and strategy shift.

This theoretical approach has been used in the preparation of computer programs that simulate problem-solving processes with applications to a wide range of types of problems. Comparisons can then be made between the simulations and the actual problem-solving processes of human problem solvers, thus providing evidence that generally supports the overall approach and also helps in the revision of specific programs.

One specific way in which the study of individual problem solving has been helpful has been to show that well-developed problem-solving skills in one area may help very little in another area. Expert problem solvers in a given field are distinguished from novices primarily through having a large organized store of relevant concepts and principles that make their problem-solving efforts more efficient and less haphazard.

The study of group problem solving and the solving of informal (practical) problems makes the investigation immeasurably more complicated but at the same time richer in terms of the applications. However, it is helpful to bear in mind that even these extensions have definite limitations, notwithstanding the confidence Western society has traditionally placed in problem solving for the benefit of humanity. It must be realized that problem solving can be carried out for either good or evil ends; that many social problems are intractable in the sense that they appear to have no final solutions; and finally that the universal problems of death, sin, and finitude are wholly beyond the competence of human ingenuity to solve.

Reference
Newell, A., & Simon, H. A. *Human problem solving.* Englewood Cliffs, N.J.: Prentice-Hall, 1972.

D. R. RIDLEY

See DECISION MAKING.

Problem-Solving Therapy.

Solving the practical problems of everyday life is an especially relevant topic for counselors, who are often approached by clients when the clients' problem-solving abilities are inadequate. In fact, D'Zurilla and Goldfried (1971) noted that "much of what we view clinically as 'abnormal behavior' or 'emotional disturbance' may be viewed as ineffective behavior and its consequences, in which the individual is unable to resolve certain situational problems in his life" (p. 107).

Although problem solving might appear to be a unitary process, and therefore easily acquired through counseling, it actually consists of five separate stages (Heppner, 1978). First is a general orientation, or "set." An optimal problem-solving set is one in which the person acknowledges the existence of the problem and behaves as though an effective resolution is possible, neither acting impulsively nor retreating from the problem. The second stage involves formulating an accurate and specific description of the problem. This description is necessary for alternative responses or solutions to be generated, a process which constitutes stage 3. Making a decision by selecting one action from a number of alternatives is stage 4. Finally, stage 5 involves testing the effectiveness of the chosen alternative against some criterion or standard.

Mahoney (1977) compares a client's problem solving to that of a scientist and argues that the scientist's logical skills are applicable in the client's day-to-day situations. Thus, in his "personal science" approach the client is taught steps of problem solving contained in a sequence represented by the mnemonic SCIENCE: Specify general problem; Collect information; Identify causes or patterns; Examine options; Narrow options and experiment; Compare data; Extend, revise, or replace.

Until recently problem solving was studied by using predefined laboratory-type problems such as mazes, anagrams, and puzzles. However, present research is better contributing to our understanding of the role that problem solving plays in normal adjustment by examining events affecting how people solve real-life personal problems. Spivack and his colleagues (Spivack, Platt, & Shure, 1976) have studied problem-solving processes among preschool children, emotionally disturbed children and adolescents, and hospitalized psychiatric patients. In general their findings indicate that "normal" and "deviant" populations show significant differences in problem-solving ability. For example, emotionally disturbed adolescents generated fewer solutions to hypothetical problems than did their normal peers; in addition, their options often had a distinct antisocial (e.g., physically aggressive) character to them.

Recently Heppner (1982; Heppner & Peterson, 1982) has developed and tested a personal problem-solving inventory that allows assessment of three major aspects of problem solving: personal confidence, approach-avoidance style, and personal control. He used this inventory to distinguish between successful and unsuccessful problem solvers in a college student population. Further study of these two groups revealed that successful problem solvers had fewer symptoms of depression, had more of a tendency to enjoy cognitive activities, were more positive in their self-concept, and utilized coping styles that were less blameful and more problem focused in comparison to unsuccessful problem solvers.

It seems clear that successful problem solving is related to better social adjustment. In thinking about training individuals in such skills, it is clear that several questions need to be addressed: Can such thinking skills be taught? Would learning these skills impact the individual's level of adjustment? Would the effects of such training last over time?

Resolving real-life problems, which usually involves a major interpersonal component, involves a series of skills (Spivack et al., 1976). The first of these is an awareness of the variety of interpersonal and other problems in human existence and a sensitivity to their occurrence. Second is the skill of generating alternative solutions to problems. A third skill, which is emphasized in the work of Spivack and his colleagues, is that of means-ends thinking. This skill includes both spelling out the step-by-step means by which a resolution would be achieved and recognizing the obstacles that must be overcome for the means to work. A fourth skill is that of anticipating the consequences of one's actions on others and on oneself. These skills need to be present for successful problem solving to occur. Their absence may be the result of insufficient learning (the person has not been exposed to these skills or has not learned them adequately) or of the situation (the problem-solving situation may engender emotions that inhibit problem-solving success).

A considerable amount of research evidence suggests that these skills can in fact be taught and that their acquisition does impact behavioral adjustment. Many of the problem-solving training programs described by Spivack et al. (1976) incorporate games and dialogues whereby problem-solving skills are acquired in the context of everyday activities. For example, Shure (1981) discussed a training project in which parents and teachers were taught, when children experienced problems in playing with their peers, to elicit the child's view of the problem (e.g., Sally stole my truck), how each child feels about the problem, the child's description of the problem, and alternative solutions. In her study children who were engaged in these dialogues were rated, compared to no-treatment controls, as having learned both solution and consequential thinking and as having improved adjustment behavior after the training period. Follow-ups at six months and one year revealed that these gains were maintained. For example, of the group of children trained in problem solving, 83% were rated as adjusted immediately after training, 86% six months later, and 77% one year later (decrease not significant). For the untrained children the corresponding percentages were 41%, 42%, and 30%.

Mahoney & Arnkoff (1978) suggest that "among the cognitive learning therapies, it is our opinion that the problem-solving perspectives may ultimately yield the most encouraging clinical results" (p. 709). These approaches seem particularly valuable for two reasons. First, they include both a coping and a restructuring orientation, a blend that will help the client control his or her inappropriate responses while operating on the environment to achieve desired goals. Second, problem-solving therapies allow, in fact demand, that individual differences be recognized and utilized in treatment. These approaches therefore show unique promise for the Christian practitioner because they emphasize a built-in individuality of treatment that might include prayer, seeking advice from others, and so on, as problem-solving alternatives for Christian clients. While there are certain clients and psychological disorders for which these approaches would not be suited, they do have particular promise and are a feasible choice for many kinds of developmental concerns.

References

D'Zurilla, T. J., & Goldfried, M. R. Problem solving and behavior modification. *Journal of Abnormal Psychology*, 1971, *78*, 107–126.

Heppner, P. P. A review of the problem-solving literature and its relationship to the counseling process. *Journal of Counseling Psychology*, 1978, *25*, 366–375.

Heppner, P. P. A personal problem-solving inventory. In P. A. Keller & L. G. Ritt (Eds.), *Innovations in clinical practice: A source book*. Sarasota, Fla.: Professional Resource Exchange, 1982.

Heppner, P. P., & Peterson, C. H. The development and implications of a personal problem-solving inventory. *Journal of Counseling Psychology*, 1982, *29*, 66–75.

Mahoney, M. J. Personal science: A cognitive learning theory. In A. Ellis & R. Grieger (Eds.), *Handbook of rational-emotive therapy*. New York: Springer Publishing, 1977.

Mahoney, M. J., & Arnkoff, D. B. Cognitive and self-control therapies. In S. L. Garfield & A. E. Bergin (Eds.),

Handbook of psychotherapy and behavior change: An empirical analysis (2nd ed.). New York: Wiley, 1978.

Shure, M. B. Social competence as a problem-solving skill. In J. D. Wine & M. D. Smye (Eds.), *Social competence.* New York: Guilford, 1981.

Spivack, G., Platt, J. J., & Shure, M. B. *The problem-solving approach to adjustment.* San Francisco: Jossey-Bass, 1976.

E. M. ALTMAIER

See DECISION MAKING; COGNITIVE-BEHAVIOR THERAPY.

Professional Schools of Psychology.

Over the past two decades a trend toward doctoral training in psychology with a more practical orientation led to the development of professional schools of psychology. Studies following students through doctoral-level clinical psychology programs holding to the traditional scientist-professional model emphases on research skills indicated that these students produced almost no publishable research. Rather, they followed applied practice careers.

In 1965 Kenneth Cleark, chairman of the American Psychological Association Committee on the Scientific and Professional Aims of Psychology, recommended practitioner-oriented degree programs leading to the Psy.D., or Doctor of Psychology degree. Subsequently the Vail conference on training in clinical psychology (1976) recommended professional schools as an option for training clinical psychologists. These schools were to provide programs with a primary emphasis on the delivery of professional services and the evaluation and improvement of those services.

The four basic models of professional schools of psychology include: 1) professional psychology programs within existing graduate departments (the National Council of Schools of Professional Psychology adopted the position that such schools must have separate and autonomous administrative structures and be administrated by a dean who is a registered psychologist; 2) autonomous schools, which have tended to be loosely organized with small staffs and inadequate facilities; 3) professional schools under the control of medical centers; and 4) university-based schools with separate administrative structures. In all cases the program leading to the Psy.D. is a 12-month, 4-year program, with one year in a full-time applied clinical internship. The degree is gaining increasing acceptance in the field as programs and licensing procedures become more rigorous.

D. L. SCHUURMAN

Prognosis.

Psychiatric syndromes do not necessarily carry poor prognostic outcomes. The factors influencing outcome include family, societal, biological, and therapeutic interactions. Each disorder must be perceived within its natural course and its susceptibility to influence by these factors.

Most foundational in evaluating treatment prognosis is the natural history of a disorder, the course the disorder would be expected to take without any treatment intervention. This will include any cyclic characteristics, usual response to psychosocial or biological stressors as well as the tendency for remissions and clinical manifestations of the disorder at various life stages.

Sufficient uncertainty remains in the art of psychiatric diagnosis that prognostic studies of treatment outcome are fraught with confusion. Further, the evaluation of treatment outcome is itself a very complex process, one that defies simple conclusions about the effectiveness of most treatment approaches. These factors lead to statements of prognosis that are a consensus of clinicians, avoiding the dramatic and unsubstantiated claims of the fadist.

Schizophrenic disorders, constituting about 1% of the population and leading to a chronic illness for many, have been observed and treated intensively in this century. The factors that suggest a favorable prognosis include acuteness of onset, triggering of the attack by a precipitating life situation, and a first onset later in life. For example, childhood or early adolescent first attacks usually leave a more guarded prognosis. A person who has made satisfactory sexual, occupational, and social adjustments before the illness is more likely to have a better prognosis. Single, widowed, or divorced patients do more poorly. In general, the more affect displayed by the patient, the better the prognosis. Further, an extended illness over two to three years predicts poor outcome. The more intact and supportive the family, the more the patient is likely to remit. Each exacerbation also increases the likelihood of chronicity. It is now clearly established by placebo controlled studies that a drug maintenance program, conscientiously followed, increases the remission rate. In summary, if medication is used judiciously in appropriate psychotherapy, many schizophrenic patients are able to establish therapeutic relationships, maintain a treatment program, and often experience enduring changes in personality.

Affective or mood disorders constitute a wide variety of problems with differing biological and emotional-social etiologies. The major affective disorders commonly have biological roots. Without appropriate chemotherapy the natural course of these illnesses often results in either remission or suicide. It is becoming more possible to predict efficacy of some antidepressant medications through laboratory studies (such as the dexamethasone suppression test). A clinical trial with a tricyclic antidepressant or similar drug, monoamine oxidase inhibitor, or lithium carbonate can be effective.

Repeated attacks would generally suggest the need for maintenance medication. An increasing percentage of even the most staunchly psychotherapeutically oriented therapists now allow for the necessary role of antidepressant therapy. Prognosis is enhanced for the major affective disorders with the appropriate use of medications. However, the use of drugs unfortunately has made psychiatry less personal and more mechanistic. Repeated hospital admissions (although brief) and noncompliance in medication usage follow the neglect of those other aspects of the person's needs that could be met by psychotherapy.

A more chronic depression, now called dysthymic disorder, becomes part of the person's character. Without intervention patients often experience repeated episodes, with gradual psychosocial impairment. Treatment, when intensive and comprehensive, yields improvement in the majority of cases.

The course and prognosis of organic mental disorders depend on underlying causes. If the etiology arises from another bodily system disorder and can be corrected, the outlook is good. However, structural brain change implies chronicity, if not deterioration. Each syndrome or disorder carries its own prognostic outcome.

Neurotic disorders encompass a variety of clinical syndromes, with anxiety a central feature. Anxiety is handled in a variety of ways, leading to differing neurotic states, such as anxiety state, phobias, obsessive-compulsive disorder, and dissociative disorders. The paucity of investigation into the course of these disorders leads to problems in stating prognosis with or without treatment. Some, such as phobic and obsessive-compulsive disorders, tend to be chronic. These tend to resist therapeutic intervention, in contrast to anxiety states, which tend to be more situationally provoked. In general, the prognostic outlook is improved if treatment occurs soon after onset of symptoms, if environmental stress is prominent, if there is social support, and if the patient's pre-illness adjustments were more satisfactory. Some disorders such as hypochondriasis must be considered chronic, and therefore afford less hope for resolution.

The personality disorders have been associated with poor prognosis despite the fact that their natural history has not been carefully studied. They have been viewed as chronic, without any expectation of remission. Until recently there have been no agreed-upon criteria that could serve as a basis for research. The problem has been compounded by the tendency for persons with personality disorders not to seek therapy. There has also been much reluctance among therapists to treat these persons, and there has been little follow-up. We do know that some personality disorders may be outgrown developmentally and that others may be a prelude to other disorders, such as paranoid personality disorder preceding schizophrenia.

The psychosomatic disorders have not yielded to psychological treatment as other disorders have. Despite vigorous investigation and no lack of literature, these psychosomatic disorders have led many to doubt the validity of the concept of psychophysiological medicine. Whatever the merit of this argument, it is now clear that the simple association of personality characteristics and bodily disease is simplistic. As a result, the whole field is undergoing reevaluation and revision. In a special way these disorders illustrate the mind-body problem, philosophically and therapeutically. Much of early psychosomatic ideology gave patients numerous reasons to feel guilty. Often the task of the therapist is to help the person escape the guilt induced by psychiatric doctrine.

T. G. ESAU

Projection. The unconscious process by which an individual attributes to another the desires, impulses or ideas that he finds unacceptable in himself. This ego DEFENSE MECHANISM allows the person to take whatever is internally threatening or conflictually undesirable, whether instincts or their derivatives, and make it part of an external object or person. The conflict over the projected issue can then be dealt with as an attack from without rather than as a more ego-threatening internal struggle.

This defense is employed in externalizing responsibility for one's failures or undesirable behavior (for example, a student may always find something unfair about any test he fails). It may also externalize responsibility for undesirable thoughts, feelings, or impulses. This is illustrated by the rigidly moral person who is sexually attracted to his married co-worker and, unable to consciously admit to or cope with such feelings, claims that she is attempting to seduce him.

R. LARKIN

Projective Identification. A mental mechanism first described in the psychoanalytic writings of Melanie Klein. Its most comprehensive discussion is provided by Grotstein (1981), who defines it as a mechanism whereby "the self experiences the unconscious fantasy of translocating itself, or aspects of itself, into an object for exploratory or defensive purposes" (p. 123). If the purpose is defensive, the intent of this maneuver is believed to be the effort to rid the self of unwanted, split-off aspects while retaining some identification with the externalized contents. Its more positive and most sublimated form is involved in the experience of empathy.

A good deal of confusion exists in many of the discussions of this concept, with some authors distinguishing between PROJECTION and projective identification and other authors viewing them as identical. Still others reinterpret the concept, arguing that it should really be called projective disidentification, since the intent seems to be projection of some part of self and the subsequent severing of any identification or ownership of this part. The point of consensus in these discussions is that it is one of the most primitive mental mechanisms (along with splitting) and that it therefore will most frequently be utilized by patients suffering from borderline and psychotic disorders.

In its most blatant forms projective identification is sometimes recognized in the fantasy that the individual can enter another person so as to (actively) control him or (passively) disappear and evade feelings of helplessness. In more subtle forms it is sometimes hypothesized to be present when the therapist becomes aware of personal inner emptiness or chaos, which is felt to have been disowned and projected by the patient onto the therapist. Implicit in this hypothesis is the belief that therapists can learn to identify the presence of projective identification by carefully monitoring subjective experience in order to differentiate countertransference or other personally idiosyncratic responses from the interactional influence of projective identification.

Reference

Grotstein, J. S. *Splitting and projective identification.* New York: Aronson, 1981.

D. G. BENNER

See DEFENSE MECHANISMS.

Projective Personality Tests. One of the two major groups of personality assessment instruments, the other being self-report inventories (objective tests). Whereas the self-report tests require the subject to describe himself or herself, the projective techniques require the subject to describe or interpret objects other than self. The underlying assumption is that an individual's responses to an unstructured stimulus are influenced by underlying needs, motives, and concerns. Thus, the individual can be assumed to project something of himself into the response to these tasks. The interpretation of the responses should therefore yield important information about a person's basic personality structure and motivations.

The two most commonly used projective techniques are the RORSCHACH INKBLOT TEST and the THEMATIC APPERCEPTION TEST. In addition to those instruments, numerous SENTENCE-COMPLETION TESTS, FIGURE DRAWING TESTS, storytelling methods, and other approaches exist. These differ tremendously in terms of normative samples, amount of reliability and validity data, and objectivity of scoring and interpretation. When used by someone with the necessary training and experience, they are extremely helpful, and have come to be a standard part of the comprehensive psychological assessment.

D. G. BENNER

See PERSONALITY ASSESSMENT; PSYCHOLOGICAL MEASUREMENT.

Promiscuity. A form of sexual delinquency; the practice of transient sexual relations with a variety of partners chosen indiscriminately. It differs from prostitution in that it is not basically commercial, although it often leads to prostitution. It is considered a major factor in the spread of venereal disease.

With the rapidly changing attitudes toward sexual practices the word *promiscuity* takes on different meanings to different people. There is a differentiation between casual sex, premarital and extramarital sex, and promiscuity, in that promiscuity is considered to be complete indiscrimination in the selection of sexual partners, which is not usually found in the other cases. Gagnon and Simon (1970) estimate that half of all married men and one quarter of all married women will have sexual intercourse outside of marriage at some time. Under this definition of promiscuity over 4 million married people alone are promiscuous. However, complete indiscrimination regarding partners is extremely rare and nearly always related to a severe disturbance of a nonsexual nature.

Sexual gratification is not generally considered a motivational factor, since the majority of girls involved in promiscuity are partially or wholly frigid. Factors believed to be involved include the longing to feel loved or wanted and an expression of revenge or defiance. Promiscuity is often a disguised plea for help. Young men may be motivated to prove they are sexually and socially adequate, and may out of fear be avoiding a relationship with someone they know.

Causal factors may include a disturbed family life where the child is neglected and often the mother herself is promiscuous. Many promiscuous young people have alcoholic fathers. Peer pressure from a group holding loose standards may cause the desire for belonging to push an adolescent into promiscuous behavior. The common fear that sexual knowledge leads to promiscuity is unfounded, according to most research. Typically the promiscuous individual is fairly ignorant about sex, and has learned through experience rather than training or education. It is the most common form of delinquency among mentally retarded girls.

Reference
Gagnon, J., & Simon, W. *The sexual scene.* Chicago: Transaction Books, 1970.

D. L. Schuurman

Prosocial Behavior. *See* Helping Behavior.

Provocative Therapy. A type of therapy developed by Frank Farrelly in the 1960s from his work with psychotics and severe character disorders. It has since been used successfully in many different settings with a wide variety of patients and clients. Rogers had seminal impact, especially his concepts of empathy, genuineness, and congruence. At the same time Farrelly's experience in state mental hospitals with the mentally ill convinced him that they were in touch with certain realities, were more responsible and robust than given credit for, and were experts in analyzing social systems for deviant but functional purposes.

A series of clinical experiences led Farrelly away from his initial Rogerian position. One of these involved work with a client who was part of Rogers's research on therapy with schizophrenics. After 91 traditional person-centered sessions Farrelly introjected something new— a humorous style of agreeing with the patient and taking a cynical, negative position that overtly encouraged deviancy and distress. This client's response (and that of most others since) was to quickly disagree with the therapist and improve his functioning. This style has proved

particularly adept at using the patient's resistance in service of prosocial goals as the patient is provoked into disagreeing in an assertive, constructive manner with the devil's advocate therapist.

Like several other systems of psychotherapy provocative therapy emphasizes that choice is crucial to all therapeutic change; that people have more potential than they assume; that current experience is at least as important as the past; and that the client's behavior in therapy is a relatively accurate reflection of his habitual coping strategies. Unlike most other therapeutic systems provocative therapy assumes that people change and grow best in response to a challange, whatever their degree of chronicity or the severity of the problem; that psychological fragility is vastly overrated; that nonverbal expression is crucial in the impact of many levels of therapeutic communication; and that a judicious expression of "therapeutic hate and joyful sadism" (in evaluating behaviors or as related to specific behaviors) can benefit people greatly (Farrelly & Brandsma, 1974).

Provocative therapy differs from most other forms of therapy in its style: a greater degree of directness and confrontation; the use of a paradoxical communicational style; the use of verbal and nonverbal cues; a high level of playfulness on the part of the therapist; and, perhaps most crucial, the deliberate use of humor in many forms. The basic working hypothesis is that if the therapist provokes a client humorously, perceptively, and paradoxically, the client will move away from his negative self-image and behavior toward increased health.

Five major goals of direct provocative therapy are 1) to learn to affirm self-worth both verbally and behaviorally; 2) to learn appropriate assertion in work and relationships; 3) to learn to defend oneself realistically; 4) to learn necessary psychosocial discriminations in order to respond adaptively; and 5) to learn how to take risks in relationships, especially those that communicate with immediacy both affection and vulnerability.

A wide range of freedom is afforded the provocative therapist in applying many different kinds of techniques. The thrust of this variety is to allow the therapist access to more of his experiences in order to increase empathic contact, to employ strategies that counter those destructive adaptations of the client at multiple levels, and to enjoy the therapeutic encounter while dealing with some very difficult problems.

One common technique is provocative or paradoxical verbal communication. Here the therapist amplifies and encourages self-defeating behaviors and attitudes. This is often accompanied by nonverbal communication such as a twinkle in the eye, selective use of touch, type of intonation, and so on. These qualifiers are meant to convey the therapist's empathy and contact with the patient. Humorous techniques, including banter, exaggeration, reduction to absurdity, ridicule, sarcasm, irony, and relevant jokes, are also frequently employed. Confrontation and feedback, both in terms of social consequences and in terms of the therapist's immediate subjective perception of the client, are also frequently employed. Finally, dramatic techniques such as the therapist's role playing various fantasized scenarios, modeling the patient's negative behavior, and "playing along with" the client while suggesting ridiculous solutions are common techniques.

Some Christian therapists would find it difficult to play the devil's advocate or to lampoon religious attitudes and beliefs, even if the purpose is to test or strengthen them. Also, the emotionally loaded and frequently coarse language often used in provocative therapy would offend many Christians. However, the intent and the outcome of the therapy, properly understood, would not offer problems to Christians.

This type of therapy tends to innoculate against despair and inculcate hope and responsibility. It affirms all of life, all one's capacities and experiences to be organized in service of living better internally and, more importantly, in relationships. The therapist strives for a balancing of cognition, feelings, and behavior through the use of humor. It is excellent at puncturing pretensions and at dealing with too low or too grandiose a view of the self.

Provocative therapists take evil seriously and make the awareness of it an integral part of therapy rather than attempting to sidestep it. The encounter helps one learn that evil cannot be avoided but must be transformed through choice, humor, and through one's relationships. Love, on the other hand, is communicated in an indirect way through intense honesty and caring for the individual, his autonomy and growth as a total person.

Reference
Farrelly, F., & Brandsma, J. M. *Provocative therapy*. Fort Collins, Colo.: Shields Publishing, 1974.

J. M. BRANDSMA

See PARADOXICAL INTERVENTION; HUMOR.

Pseudocyesis. False pregnancy. The term was coined by John Mason Good in 1823 to describe a condition observed by Hippocrates centuries earlier. Other terms that have been used synonymously in the past include pseudopregnancy, phantom tumor, and hysterical pregnancy.

The phenomenology of pseudocyesis includes organic signs and symptoms normally seen in pregnancy and the associated belief that one is pregnant. This belief may become a firmly held conviction that remains unswayed even in the face of medical evidence to the contrary. The physiological changes observed, in order of frequency, include menstrual abnormalities, increase in abdominal size, enlarged breasts and galactorrhea, sensations mimicking fetal movements, gastrointestinal signs and symptoms (including nausea, weight gain, and changes in appetite), cervical changes, and uterine enlargement.

Case reports of pseudocyesis have described its occurrence in all nations, races, and societies. Bivin and Klinger (1937) presented a comprehensive report on 444 cases of pseudocyesis from 20 countries dating back to the seventeenth century. Only approximately 100 additional cases have been reported since their publication, suggesting a marked decline in this diagnosis over the past 100 years.

The patients reported in Bivin and Klinger's study ranged in age from 5 to 79 years, with pseudocyesis occurring most commonly in the third and fourth decades of life. The majority were married, and 41% had previously given birth. The pseudocyesis lasted 9 months in 42% of the patients, and spontaneous recovery was most often preceded by labor pains. At least one recurrence was seen in 5% of the patients. Three cases of pseudocyesis have been reported in men. Common features in these patients included abdominal distention or pain and sexual orientation ambiguity.

Dynamic explanations for the occurrence of pseudocyesis focus on unconscious conflict regarding pregnancy and related sexual functions. Some feel it may be a covert expression of a pathological wish for or fear of pregnancy. Other proposed dynamic theories include competition with other women, an attempt to fulfill dependency needs, a struggle to achieve a feminine identity, and conflict in the separation-individuation phase of development. Oral conflict has been seen as central in the etiological dynamics.

The apparent decrease in the incidence of pseudocyesis has prompted researchers to speculate on the cultural and societal influence in its etiology. The high rate of pseudocyesis in South Africa is thought to reflect the cultural belief in that country that a woman's value is determined by her fertility. In modern America the decreasing rate of pseudocyesis is thought to be secondary to the decreased emphasis placed on procreation, a decreased fear of and incidence of infant mortality, a trend toward smaller families, and increased familiarity with sexual and reproductive functioning.

Currently pseudocyesis is listed as a specific conversion disorder in DSM-III under the general category of somatoform disorders. Other cases have been conceptualized as monosymptomatic hypochondriasis, Munchausen's syndrome, or psychosomatic disorders. While it has been postulated that pseudocyesis occurs most often in histrionic and schizophrenic patients, many have noted that it may also occur in persons with no evidence of psychopathology or underlying personality disturbances. Several authors report a dramatic response and cessation of symptoms in response to brief psychotherapy consisting of patient education and an exploration of the patient's attitudes toward reproduction and sexuality.

Reference

Bivin, G. D., & Klinger, M. P. *Pseudocyesis*. Bloomington, Ind.: Principia Press, 1937.

L. B. HARDY

See COUVADE SYNDROME.

Pseudomutuality.

The appearance of mutuality and a close relationship when in fact the marriage or family is characterized by great distance. It is most often seen in families that fear conflict. Pressure is applied to members to present a picture of harmony and intimacy even when conflict is present. Because individual differences are perceived as threatening to group stability, they are not allowed expression.

Christians who fear negative feelings are especially prone to relate in a pseudomutual manner. The polite wife and ingratiating husband are a classic example. A careful look at their relationship shows that the polite but emotionally distant wife is angry at her husband, whose apparent overconcern belies his frustration with her passive-agressive style. While maintaining the appearance of intimacy, this couple avoids making contact at deeper emotional levels. Moving from pseudomutuality to true mutuality involves accepting individual differences and acquiring conflict resolution skills. Genuine mutuality invariably

involves a balance between individual and family group needs.

J. A. LARSEN

See FAMILY SYSTEMS THEORY.

Pseudoneurotic Schizophrenia. *See* SCHIZOTYPAL PERSONALITY DISORDER.

Psychedelic Therapy.

A therapeutic approach that uses a variety of psychedelic or "mind-revealing" substances to treat a wide array of psychological problems. Mescaline, psilocybin, LSD, MDA, MMDA, harmaline, ketamine, and other drugs have been used in a therapeutic context, although LSD is most commonly administered, and each has its own unique set of effects on human beings. Moreover, various techniques require different dosages of these substances, and therapists vary widely in the kind of setting in which their therapy takes place.

In 1943 Albert Hoffman discovered that LSD, which he synthesized five years earlier, produced symptoms that at first seemed to model natural psychoses. This "psychomimetic" effect was the main topic of LSD research until the mid 1950s, when investigators began to discover the substance's therapeutic potential. Two major paths of interest then evolved. It was found that LSD often enabled individuals to experience more easily and fully the process of regression, transference, and insight that takes place in psychodynamic psychotherapy. Also, researchers were receiving reports of positive personality change in subjects who experienced a peak or mystical experience after taking LSD.

In the following years two types of therapy with LSD reflected these developments. Psycholytic, or "mind-loosening," therapy, practiced mostly in Europe within a psychoanalytic context, consists of giving relatively small doses of LSD (150 micrograms) to a patient over a series of sessions. This allows him to gradually deal with and resolve those unconscious conflicts causing his psychopathological symptoms. Psychedelic therapy in the more narrow use of the term is more popular in North America and strives for personality change through a profound transcendental experience. In psychedelic therapy the administration of a large dose of LSD (500 micrograms); the careful manipulation of the patient's surroundings; and the provision of a warm, sensitive, and supportive atmosphere all work together to facilitate the patient's reaching a deeply religious experience that can serve as a turning point in his life. Therapy with psychedelic drugs usually consists of a combination of psycholytic and psychedelic therapy in that both analytic and transcendental aspects are stressed according to each patient's unique personality and therapeutic goals.

Psychedelic therapy has been used in treating character disorder such as psychopathy and sociopathy; psychosomatic and neurotic disorders; alcoholism and other addictions; some types of psychoses and autism; and the psychological distress of the terminally ill. While initial studies on LSD's beneficial therapeutic effects looked promising, later research revealed many methodological shortcomings. LSD's promise as a therapeutic panacea was short-lived. Unfortunately the controversy over the dangers of LSD, the counterculture's predilection for using contaminated street drugs, the wild claims of a number of psychedelic proselytizers, and the polarization of American society in the late 1960s have led to severe bureaucratic restrictions that have essentially killed the research and practice of psychedelic therapy in the United States today.

Even though many researchers believe that the psychedelics have great therapeutic promise and numerous studies have shown that these substances are relatively safe when used in therapeutic or experimental context, few institutions or individuals have the resources and incentive to overcome the barriers to research with LSD. This is especially tragic because psychedelic therapy can serve as an outstanding vehicle for bringing together the disciplines of psychology, religion, and education to more fully understand human nature and to use this understanding to alleviate suffering.

Additional Readings
Grinspoon, L., & Bakalar, J. *Psychedelic drugs reconsidered.* New York: Basic Books, 1979.
Grof, S. *Realms of the human unconscious: Observations from LSD research.* New York: Viking, 1975.

W. C. DREW

See NARCOTHERAPY.

Psychiatric Assessment. The interview of a patient by the psychiatrist is not a random, casual meeting. The patient brings a set of expectations, apprehensions, and ambivalence. The patient's motivation is often limited or clouded by anxiety and other strong affects. The psychiatrist brings his own unique background both as a person and as a professional with theoretical commitments. The psychiatrist's values and experiences need not prejudice clinical judgments but must yield to understanding tempered by professional awareness.

The fact that there is a variety of psychiatric orientations leads to the possibility of interview conclusions that are more influenced by the orientation than the realities of the patient's situation. The seasoned interviewer recognizes these dangers and listens to the patient while resisting any impulse to impose conclusions. The conclusions are consequently neither hasty nor routine. They go beyond description of behavior to the dynamic that encompasses the biological, social, intrapsychic, interpersonal, and value perspectives.

Many factors influence the interview. These include the setting, whether it be at the bedside in a general hospital, in the psychiatrist's office, or in the psychiatric unit. The psychiatrist will be careful to assure his pledge of confidentiality no matter where the interview takes place. These assurances are commonly verbalized during an initial exploration of why this meeting is taking place. Out of the impressions gained in this initial exploration the psychiatrist begins to formulate a plan for the interview. At the same time he must not lose sight of the necessity to observe and inquire about the standard information necessary for a complete evaluation.

Sufficient time is required for the many transactions in the initial interview. Issues such as note taking, placement of chairs, and presence of family are dealt with in a manner that affords the psychiatrist optimum opportunity to fulfill his task in his own manner without invasion of the patient's rights or sensitivities.

Psychiatric History. The two major components of a psychiatric assessment are the history taking and the mental status examination. The inclusion of a history presumes a developmental viewpoint. This does not prejudice the interviewer because all psychological theories view the course of illness in the context of earlier symptoms, experiences, and transactions. Psychiatric syndromes develop over time, with characteristic features at various phases of the illness.

The life cycle to date will need reviewing, as will the illness itself. In the main this history will be provided by the patient. However, because self report includes distortions and selective recall, psychiatrists of interpersonal persuasion often seek consultation with the spouse or family. This is often conducted in the patient's presence and always with the patient's awareness and permission. For a child or adolescent patient this involvement is essential. Psychiatrists have recently become more comfortable and flexible in seeing the patient in the context of his or her family.

Chief Complaint. Traditionally the chief complaint is the patient's reason for seeking professional assistance. It is best recorded in the patient's words. But psychiatric illness being what it is, often the patient is resistant, reluctant, or confused. Consequently the chief complaint may be a report of others about the patient's behavior, verbalizations, attitude, or mood. Therefore the chief complaint may be as much the concern of others about the patient as the patient's own concern. Often there will be a brief description of the patient as part of the chief complaint.

The psychiatric history starts here because the chief complaint is the entrance to the psychiatric syndrome. The psychiatrist immediately searches for the clues that alert one to the natural history of the disorder.

Present illness. One moves logically and readily into an exploration of the present illness. Adequate time is necessary to delineate the common complexities here. Dynamically oriented observers need to exercise care to differentiate present illness from earlier developmental issues that serve as background to the present illness. As the patient unfolds these details, the psychiatrist will start to assess ego functioning, organizational ability, and distractibility, as well as memory, intelligence, and motivation. All aspects of the interview are appropriate resources for evaluation of the patient's mental status. There is a natural overlap between present illness and the mental status examination. Precipitating causes are an appropriate aspect. Sequences of events and temporal connections suggest possible causation of symptoms. Description of the present illness is more than a recitation of symptoms; it is the basis for the exploration of intrapsychic and interpersonal events.

Past illnesses. Any medical history, psychiatric included, examines previous disorders throughout the life span of the patient. This needs to include reference to age of the patient at time of hospitalizations (if any) or other treatment intervention, forms of treatment, including medication usage. It is important that the exact drug and dosage be identified, as a history of successful response to a particular medication may lead to a treatment regimen with the same agent.

Developmental history. This is a personal history of the patient from birth to present,

with a developmental perspective. Often the psychiatric patient is unable to give detailed information because of the disability. Family members are then needed either as a primary resource or to supplement the patient's report. Also psychiatric emergencies do not lend themselves to gaining this information immediately, so later interviews are needed to explore these details. The developmental history encompasses several facets of personality development, including motor, cognition, social, psychosexual, and school and work performances.

Prenatal and birth histories often contain invaluable clues for the diagnosis. Defects or injury evident at birth as well as maternal illness or drug/alcohol use during gestation bear significantly on infant development. Maternal and paternal attitudes about the pregnancy set the stage for bonding, which develops at birth. Inquiry of the mother as to her feeling toward the patient at birth is an important ingredient of a family psychiatric history.

The first three years are perhaps the most important in personality development and interpersonal relatedness. The more that can be learned of the child's need fulfillment, the better. Not only gross maternal rejection but also maternal depression may significantly interfere with the child's bonding and trust. Early illnesses, eating disorders, sleep patterns, maturational milestones, and constancy of human care need exploration. The presence of splitting by bonding to multiple maternal objects should be noted. Experiences of separation anxiety as well as excessive symbiosis with the mother should also be explored. Power issues may become evident around toilet training history. Other expressions of excessive willfulness will be seen in temper tantrums. Regression at the birth of a sibling or loss of a significant object is also important.

Throughout these three years distinctive personality patterns and traits are emerging. These set the stage for subsequent capacity for self-control and socialization. In addition to information about gains in developmental tasks in all these areas psychopathological features can be ascertained by the history of the first three years. Diagnoses such as mental retardation, attention deficit disorder, separation anxiety, and pervasive developmental disorders (including autism) can all become evident in these years.

Ages three through latency extend the issues of early childhood into growing intrapsychic and interpersonal spheres. Gender identification becomes apparent. Early peer relatedness develops. Intellectual capacity or learning disability surfaces. Patterns of aggression or passivity form rather substantially.

Preadolescent and adolescent development see the finalization of the development of adult personality. The adolescent must deal with intimacy-sexuality as well as independence-separation-individuation issues. Adolescence may be viewed as a resurrection and reprocessing of childhood struggles. The defensive structure of the child becomes the adult defenses through the kaleidoscope of adolescence. With the exception of infancy there is perhaps no other time when the child needs his family more than in adolescence. Unfortunately this is commonly the time when parents are all too ready to give their tasks away to community institutions or peers. Presently the despair of youth as well as their rejection of society's values are manifest in adolescent substance abuse. Superficially this is seen as a conduct disturbance having to do with authority conflict, whereas in reality it much more commonly reflects anguish about family patterns. Such a child is best helped through and in his family, whose usefulness is now greater than ever.

Adulthood has its own developmental tasks and issues, and passage through these should be reviewed for the adult patient. Advanced educational experiences, occupational history, sexuality, social relationships, marital history, children, and military experience constitute the most frequently questioned areas. Retirement history for older adults should also be explored.

As hereditary factors are becoming better understood in psychiatric illness, family history must include reference to possible genetic disorders. There is great value as well in a history of interrelationships between the patient and all significant others, and in a careful exploration of family attitudes about the patient and the illness. This provides an early opportunity to influence their attitudes about therapy.

Religious-value history. Historical divergence and conflict between religious and psychiatric thought have contributed to frequent avoidance by psychiatrists of religious and moral development. More recently mutual respect has grown between the fields, and now the psychiatric examiner will more often include this domain within the assessment. Value development usually goes beyond religious background and upbringing but has its roots in these experiences. To understand these complex interactions the psychiatrist needs a wide perspective and a respect for the patient's unique commitments and experiences. A wealth of data concerning motivation, self-perception, and guilt production can follow. The highly value-oriented patient responds with trust toward the therapist who respects his orientation.

Mental Status Examination. *Behavior and appearance.* History taking very readily becomes clinical evaluation. The alert observer lets no occasion pass in gaining data to identify the patient's mental status. The earliest observations are descriptive in nature. These include the patient's appearance and behavior. Observations of gross behavior are possible even in the mute patient. These include various motor behaviors ranging from severe agitation to mute rigidity. The patient's attitudes about the examination should also be noted. These attitudes are best seen as responses to the examiner's own mood and attitudes. The psychiatrist should have a reasonable awareness of his own attitudes and how the patient responds to them and should, from the beginning of the interview, be watchful for manifestations of transference or countertransference.

Affect and mood. Affect, or emotion, is the feeling experience of the patient. Sustained affect is considered a mood. The range of affect goes from flat (shallow or inadequate) to inappropriate (not corresponding to cognition or event), to labile (cycling or changeable). Affect may be vibrant, pleasurable, disagreeable, or any of the human emotions. The interviewer seeks to assess the predominant sustained emotion. To do this he or she observes and inquires into the patient's feelings about a wide variety of subject matter. Facial expression, verbal expression, and bodily movement suggest inner feelings.

Present mood is understood in the context of recent and present circumstances and also is viewed historically. Mood disturbances are of cyclical or recurrent nature and are usually expressive of early life experiences. Disturbances of mood manifest themselves in disturbances of relationships. The bonds of love and care require expressions and feelings of attachment. Mood disturbances interfere with these. The observer detects not only the mood but also its influence on or by significant others.

Thinking. In examining the form of thinking the psychiatrist explores the stream of thought. This is viewed as quantitative in expression; the amount of thinking and the pattern of its production are significant. Ideas may flow rapidly or with agonizing deliberateness or apparent paucity. In extreme, thinking may be so rapid it is termed a flight of ideas. The content may not be illogical, but interconnecting ideas are missed, leaving an impression of scattered associations. The continuity of thoughts suggests logical thinking. Illogical thinking is suggested by associations that are disconnected or that violate Aristotelian logic. Loose associations suggest schizophrenia, whereas flight of ideas suggests mania. Thinking may be described variously as circumstantial, tangential, perseverative, evasive, or blocked. Severe thought disorder may be manifest as incomprehensible speech with neologisms or word salad.

The content of thinking is also vital. It may be characterized by preoccupations of an obsessive, phobic, or some other nature. More specific disturbances of thought disorder include delusions. Here the psychiatrist attempts to ascertain the delusion's organization and meaning to the patient. The psychiatrist also evaluates the patient's ability for abstract thinking. Deviations may be in the direction of being overly concrete or too abstract. These may be tested by interpretation of proverbs or metaphors. More commonly the conversation in the interview suffices for conclusions regarding the capacity for abstract thinking.

The psychiatrist also learns about the patient's education and fund of information. Simple serial subtraction of 7's from 100 yields observations about concentration, cognitive abilities, and perceptual impairment.

Consciousness. Altered states of consciousness suggest brain impairment or disfunction. Clouding of consciousness is a blunting of attentiveness resulting in inattention to stimuli and some disruption to goal-directed behavior. Disorientation in time, place, and person are usually evident only in organic brain disorder. Questions about the specifics of orientation are an essential component of a thorough mental status examination. Memory functions are usually observed in course of the examination, including recent and remote memory as well as immediate retention and recall. If these are not observed in the natural flow of the interview, simple questioning will usually provide gross assessment of memory.

Ego functioning. The voluntary mental capacities are viewed in their adequacy to self-preserve, control impulses, maintain a relationship to reality and to people, and to organize human functioning. As these are commonly impaired in psychiatric illness, they deserve special attention. The psychiatrist will examine the ego defenses, which are characteristically associated with coping mechanisms as well as psychiatric disorders. These defenses are not necessarily pathological.

Social judgment is required for effective human relationships. It involves a capacity to assess the outcome of one's behavior and attitudes. Impaired judgment is characteristic of psychotic disorders. Judgment is usually revealed by the patient's spontaneous report but can be assessed more directly if necessary through psychological testing or through asking what should be done in specific situations (e.g., fire in a crowded movie theater).

Insight refers to the patient's awareness of his psychiatric illness and also needs to be assessed. It may be intellectual only, limiting the ability to alter his experiences. Emotional insight implies readiness to self-explore, looking for newer means of adaptation.

Psychiatric Assessment in Context. The psychiatrist is a physician by training and responsibility. The person and the brain are not clinically separable; the psychiatrist uses the latest mind-body understandings to distinguish organic disorders from those disorders that are thus far best understood in psychodynamic terms. Knowledge of bodily dysfunctions allows a comprehensive assessment and referral in cases of organic illness. A thorough psychiatric history and mental status examination bring the psychiatrist to diagnostic conclusions, fitting the patient's syndrome to a disorder classified under *DSM-III.* This psychodynamic formulation represents the best notion of the development of the illness and its principal social, emotional, intrapsychic, and interpersonal components. Such a formulation suggests areas of deficit and also leads directly to a treatment plan.

The treatment plan encompasses whatever interventions are necessary to correct, if possible, the dysfunctions. It will consider the role of the significant others in the patient's life and how they may aid the recovery. It also should include the role of the therapist as well as the goals. The methods to reach these goals should also be identified.

Additional Reading
Kaplan, H. I., & Sacock, B. J. *Modern synopsis of comprehensive textbook of psychiatry III.* (3rd ed.). Baltimore: Williams & Wilkins, 1981.

T. G. Esau

Psychiatric Social Work. *See* Social Work.

Psychiatrist. A medical doctor who has received further specific training in the areas of mental health and disease. He has studied human thought, feeling, and behavior in its normal development and its aberrations. With training in both medicine and psychiatry, the psychiatrist stands ready to appreciate the emotional and physical connections within us in both health and disease.

The training for psychiatry includes a minimum of three years of premedical college, four years of medical school leading to an M.D., and four years of psychiatric residency. An approximation of a typical curriculum would include rotations through internal medicine and neurology during the first year or two. The early years usually concentrate on inpatient work with the more serious illnesses. The focus then shifts to outpatient treatment and later to special rotations, research, and pursuit of individual interests (administrative psychiatry, forensic psychiatry, community mental health centers, etc.).

Certification in psychiatry by the American Board of Psychiatry and Neurology is preferred but not required in all situations. Teaching appointments in medical schools require certification, but many clinical positions do not. Certification requires completion of an approved four-year residency training program, two years of experience, and passing a comprehensive written and oral exam. The oral exam consists of three separate hours. One hour involves examination of a psychiatric patient with an examiner present, followed by questions from several oral examiners. The other two hours involve viewing videotapes of psychiatric and neurological patients and then being questioned by examiners. About 40 to 50% of the U.S. psychiatrists are currently certified. Certification in child, administrative, and FORENSIC PSYCHIATRY is also currently available.

Child psychiatry is the most formal area of subspecialization. Other subspecialty areas are biological, geriatric, administrative, psychoanalysis, hospital, adolescent, and forensic psychiatry. Psychoanalysis involves further formal classroom training at a psychoanalytic institute, supervised analysis of one or two patients, and successful completion of one's own personal analysis by a training analyst.

One of the major current trends in psychiatry is the movement back toward general medicine, with increasing attention being paid to physical disease and mind-body relationships. Strong interest in biological and biochemical aspects of psychopathology is part of this movement. The discovery of endorphins and enkephalins and the apparent ability to consciously control their production in the brain have led to new insights into such areas

as acupuncture, the placebo effect, the importance of touching, and the healing value of the laying on of hands. Issues involved in forensic psychiatry, particularly the not guilty by reason of insanity defense, are also increasingly prominent in the field. The specifics of treatment and detention are receiving a great deal of attention. Finally, preventive psychiatry is an increasingly important area of work. Unfortunately, however, it is usually limited by lack of public interest and therefore lack of funding.

Indications for referral to psychiatrists include the suspicion of the presence of organic physical disease, the possible need for hospitalization, and the need for prescription of psychotropic medication. Some physical diseases involve psychological complaints. Depression, for example, may be the only early complaint of a patient with carcinoma of the head of the pancreas or with hypothyroidism. Depression may accompany a treatable dementia such as normal pressure hydrocephalus. Bizarre and impulsive behavior with unusual stereotyped thought patterns may be caused entirely by complex focal seizures. The psychiatrist will cooperate with other mental health professionals in the diagnosis and treatment of these various mind-body interfaces.

D. C. SCHUTZ

See AMERICAN PSYCHIATRIC ASSOCIATION.

Psychic Healing. One of the growing number of so-called paranormal phenomena that have recently come under organized scientific investigation. Falling outside of conventional medical models, psychic healing was once the sole province of the occult arts and the more esoteric branches of religion. Within the past century, however, researchers have, through controlled study and careful documentation, validated many of the healers' claims—despite enormous methodological obstacles and prejudices within both the scientific and religious communities. Departments of psychology and parapsychology at several major universities in the United States and abroad have taken part in this research, as have many independent foundations.

Psychic healers may be found in virtually all cultures, from the primitive to the scientifically sophisticated. In Great Britain, for example, the practice is so widespread that regulatory bodies have formed (such as the National Federation of Spiritual Healers), and the government has sanctioned "spiritual" healing in over 1,500 hospitals. In the United States, however, healers must generally operate within a religious context, where the recognized church function of "laying on of hands" circumvents laws prohibiting diagnosis and treatment by the non-medically trained.

Psychic healing is a form of mental healing, which can be traced back to prehistoric shamanism. Modern movements such as Mesmerism, Christian Science, spiritualistic healing, and the psychic surgery of the Philippines continue this ancient tradition. Some healings reported in the Bible, effected simply by prayer or touch, bear some formal similarities to psychic healings.

Well-known psychic healers of this century (cf. Krippner & Villoldo, 1976) include Edgar Cayce, Rolling Thunder, Olga and Ambrose Worrall, and Jose P. de Freitas—all of whom have submitted their practices to careful scientific study.

Many healers dislike the term *psychic* because of the vaudevillian images it conjures up. Terms such as spiritual, natural, mental, religious, paranormal, or parapsychological are often preferred. Psychic healing is generally distinguished from FAITH HEALING in that the locus of activity is different. Healing by faith may be seen to result from an attitude adopted by the one healed, whereas in psychic healing the one healed is considered the more or less passive recipient of something done to him or her by the healer.

The Practice of Psychic Healing. The field of psychic healing comprises a broad spectrum of theories and therapeutic techniques. If one observes merely the healers' external practices, one would conclude that there are virtually as many ways of doing psychic healing as there are healers themselves. However, most healers would agree that the essence of the process lies in the *being* of the healer and in the reality of a transcendent source rather than in the techniques. Whereas the surgeon's tool is the scalpel, the psychic healer's instrument is the self or spirit (conceived as the totality of one's being) in existential interaction both with the one being healed and with a power or Being beyond them both, in which both participate.

Viewed psychologically, psychic healing represents an ideal of human interrelationship. The moment of healing is the moment in which two selves become one in the sense of abandoning the egocentric pretense of separateness. In that moment there is a flow between the two that becomes rejuvenating for each.

Viewed phenomenologically, from the standpoint of the typical healer's experience the process may be described as follows: While healing, the healer goes into an altered state of consciousness that is characterized by an inner stillness in which he unselfconsciously centers on the task. The healer strives for inner balance and emotional calm, seeking freedom from emotional investment in the other. While healing, the healer experiences herself as being in vital and immediate relationship with some being or force beyond her ordinary self, from which or from whom she receives help and for which or for whom she is a channel or instrument. In this capacity the healer transmits something that flows toward the other and effects healing. The healer is not herself the source of the healing.

The transcendent reality for which the healer is a channel may be conceived as God, universal mind, electromagnetic force, one's own higher self, something else, or a combination of these, depending on the healer. From this transcendent reality the healer may receive pertinent information or power that enables healing to come about. The healer's emotional balance and attitudinal clarity are vital to contact with these transcendent sources.

In assessing the nature of the other's illness the healer may either ask questions verbally or scan the condition of the person by extrasensory means. This process (called psychic reading) may include sensing the other's feelings and experiencing his nonphysical, or energy, body. The healer receives relevant extrasensory information both spontaneously and in response to questions that he asks of himself. This extrasensory input comes in various modes depending on the healer and the situation. Interpretation of extrasensory information is usually based on the healer's own internal, experiential criteria. Extrasensory abilities are usually experienced intermittently rather than being totally at the healer's command.

During the phase of healing in which the healer is intervening, he focuses on and experiences an acceptance or love toward the other. In each instance the healer seeks to act in response to the other's need rather than according to the healer's own agenda. He may effect healing simply by being with the person in an unusually close or accepting way and just allowing to happen for the other whatever is to happen. Or he may actively seek to bring about or alter specific conditions in the other, using techniques that vary with the healer and the situation.

Many of these techniques have to do with

the transference of energy from the healer to the other. This energy often radiates from or through the healer's hands. During this process the healer may experience sensations relating to the flow of energy. Often he seeks to effect healing by actively visualizing some desired condition in the other's body or psyche, thereby bringing about change by the direct influence of thought. In working toward psychological healing the healer will often seek out the experiences in the other's past that are responsible for current maladies and work with the memories of these traumatic experiences to heal present disharmony. This process may revolve around verbal exchanges of information, extrasensory processing, or other techniques that vary with the healer and the context.

Healing may be effected with the healer either in the presence of, or absent from, the other. The healer experiences spatial distance as irrelevant to healing, and time seems also to have altered significance.

In psychic healing, then, the healer enters a reality in which he or she is continuous both with the other person and with a transcendent source that provides the effective power for creating wholeness and harmony in the other. The healer is an instrument or channel through which this transcendent power operates. The healer enters this reality by intending simply, but unequivocally, the good of the other.

Psychic healers view man's essential nature as contained not in the material body but in the "energy body," which is said to occupy the same space as the physical body. This energy body is detected visually by some healers as a colorful aura surrounding the physical body. The aura reflects the person's immediate physical and emotional state. In fact, aberrations in the flow or vibration level of this energy are believed to be the primary cause of physical and emotional maladies. Psychic healing is said to involve a flow of energy from the healer that raises the vibration of the other's energy to a level that is incompatible with disease.

Experimental Research. Much of the experimental research on healing centers around the hypothesized existence of these energies and the influence of thought upon them. One-to-one correlations have been established between the various colors that healers see in the aura and the specific frequencies of electrical activity measured on the surface of the skin (Ferguson, 1978). Other experiments have demonstrated, for example, the ability of some healers to alter the surface tension of water, to

influence plant growth, to decrease the time required to heal wounds in mice, to increase blood hemoglobin levels in humans—all of this simply by laying on of hands (Rindge, 1977). All these experiments have controlled for random error and yield statistical results well within accepted confidence levels.

Whatever energies are involved in psychic healing, they are apparently unaffected by spatial distance. Experiments with the well-known healer Olga Worrall have demonstrated her ability to increase the rate of plant growth (on one occasion by 830%) by simple visualization or prayer from 600 miles away. Worrall was also able to induce wave patterns in a cloud chamber from the same distance, again by visualization. In an extension of psychologist LeShan's (1974) work, Goodrich (1978) found that persons trained through meditation to enter a state of oneness with another were able to effect remote healing in medical patients. Most of these experiments clearly control for the often advanced alternative hypotheses of suggestion or placebo effect.

A Christian Response. Viewed phenomenologically, the ability to heal psychically is just another human capacity, on a par with sensation, locomotion, and thought. It is not, therefore, the paranormal phenomena themselves but rather the healer's philosophy that a Christian evaluation would address.

At the center of the gospel is an emphasis on the spiritual dimension of human beings as that which qualifies or defines them. Man is spirit. Psychic healers accept this premise wholeheartedly but at times seem to equate spirit with a quantifiable energy rather than with the existential qualities of freedom, responsibility, and transcendence. While psychic healing may involve some form of measurable energy, it would be, from a Christian viewpoint, a reductionistic error and a new, subtler determinism to attempt to confine the numinous aspects of man in this way.

Both Christianity and psychic healing view human beings as related to a transcendent source, from which comes the power for healing. However, whereas a particular healer may equate this source with the personal God of the Bible, she may also see it as, among other things, a "loving energy field" or even some aspect of her own self. While this may seem problematic theologically, from an experiential standpoint the process is the same for both Christian and psychic healer alike. What is essential is that one surrender to some higher power than one's own ego or conscious self.

Finally, both Christianity and psychic healing posit that love (in the sense of an absolutely unequivocal intent for the other's good) is the essence of the healer's gift and the sine qua non for healing. At its best the process of psychic healing involves the healer in a radical personal commitment to *be* love to the other. This is also the heart of a commitment to Christ. It is in this emphasis on love that Christian and psychic healer are most in agreement.

References

Ferguson, M. (Ed.). Electronic evidence of auras, chakras in UCLA study. *Brain-Mind Bulletin*, 1978, *3*(9), 1–2.

Goodrich, J. The psychic healing training and research project. In J. L. Fosshage & P. Olsen (Eds.), *Healing: Implications for psychotherapy*. New York: Human Sciences Press, 1978.

Krippner, S., & Villoldo, A. *The realms of healing*. Millbrae, Calif.: Celestial Arts, 1976.

LeShan, L. L. *The medium, the mystic, and the physicist*. New York: Viking, 1974.

Rindge, J. P. The use of non-human sensors. In G. W. Meek (Ed.), *Healers and the healing process*. Wheaton, Ill.: Theosophical Publishing House, 1977.

B. Van Dragt

See TRANSPERSONAL PSYCHOLOGY; PARAPSYCHOLOGY.

Psychoanalysis: Technique. Developed by Freud from the mid-1880s through the 1930s, psychoanalysis was the first truly psychological form of therapy for the treatment of mental and emotional maladjustments. It is considered the most in-depth approach to psychotherapy because of its frequency (four or five times weekly), its length (three to five years), and its focus on the reconstruction of early childhood experiences and mental functioning.

As a form of psychotherapy, psychoanalysis grows logically out of the psychoanalytic theory of personality development and psychopathology. This theory holds that maladjustments develop out of conflicts between biologically based drives such as sex and aggression, which arise from a group of processes known as the id, and the repressing forces of the personality, the ego defense mechanisms. Psychoanalysis is designed to identify these conflicts and overcome them. By becoming aware of previously hidden wishes and conflicts that were too threatening or anxiety provoking to be faced, patients are enabled to confront them more maturely, give up inappropriate defense mechanisms, and develop a balanced functioning between their instincts (id), their reality-judging functions (ego), and their moral standards (superego). Since conflicts between impulses and defenses were developed in the context of intimate relationships with parents and siblings, psychoanalysis places a strong emphasis on the healing nature of the therapeutic relationship.

According to psychoanalytic theory, anxiety-provoking wishes and feelings have been repressed because the ego was too weak to face them. Awareness of them would generate excessive anxiety because of the fear they would get out of control or because key people in the environment would react to them with punishment, rejection, or disapproval. Because the child's ego was too weak to cope with these psychic realities, the person had to rely excessively on defense mechanisms such as repression and projection. Although these defenses help avoid painful or frightening wishes and memories, they also use up a great deal of emotional energy and result in a denial or avoidance of some aspects of reality. Pathological symptoms are a kind of compromise between the repressed wish and the defenses in which the wish is consciously avoided but finds a substitute expression through the symptom. Repression of one's anger, for example, may enable the person to avoid the conscious awareness of being an angry person. But the repressed anger may show up in disguised form as self-hatred and depression. Until these previously avoided conflicts can be found and faced, the person cannot develop the ego strength to face reality, be honest with his or her emotions, and function efficiently and congruently.

Both the quality of the therapeutic relationship and a number of specific techniques are utilized to bring these previously repressed conflicts to the surface so they can be analyzed, understood, and resolved.

The Role of the Analyst. The psychoanalyst's role can be roughly divided into two parts. The first is the offering of a sensitive, caring relationship in which patients feel free to explore the painful psychic material that is at the root of their personality disturbance. This real relationship is the context for all psychoanalytic work, but it lies somewhat in the background as a necessary but not sufficient cause of effective analytic work. It includes the analyst's ability to hear and understand the patient's struggles without anxiety or condemnation as well as the ability to comprehend the meaning of previously repressed material. This role is that of deeply sensitive listener who hears both the conscious and unconscious mental processes of the patient.

The second part of the analyst's role consists of his or her technical procedures. These technical procedures are the analyst's actions or techniques. They comprise what analysts do as they listen empathically to their patients. These procedures center around encouraging the patient to free associate and interpreting the meaning of these associations. They also include the analyst's use of silence, dream interpretation, and the interpretation of resistances and transference.

Free Association. Since the psychoanalytic theory of pathology sees the roots of maladjustment in the conflict between the largely unconscious impulses and wishes of the id and the evaluative control functions of the ego, the techniques of psychoanalysis are aimed at resolving and reworking these conflicts. The basic rule of psychoanalysis is that the patient tells the analyst everything that comes to mind during the analytic hour. The purpose of this is to help patients go beyond their conscious, rational, ego-controlled thoughts in order to become aware of previously repressed wishes, thoughts, feelings, and experiences.

By saying everything that comes to mind, no matter how embarrassing, irrelevant, or painful it may seem, the psychoanalytic patient gives the analyst a full view of his or her psychological life. By listening carefully to the patient's free associations the analyst is able to sense painful areas, contradictions, or defenses patients are using to avoid facing aspects of their lives.

Resistance. Although patients seeking treatment consciously desire to change, psychoanalytic theory proposes that at an unconscious level they do not want to give up the defenses that hide painful or unacceptable feelings and wishes because they know of no other way of handling them. In psychoanalysis all the patient's efforts (both conscious and unconscious) to avoid these anxiety-provoking thoughts and feelings by continuing the defenses are called resistance. Resistance is simply the use of defense mechanisms during psychoanalytic treatment. Since it is the inappropriate use of defense mechanisms that keeps patients from facing the conflicts giving rise to their maladjustments, the analysis of resistances is one of the major therapeutic activities of the psychoanalyst. Common resistances include not talking, censoring one's thoughts, talking in a highly intellectual manner that avoids feelings, missing appointments, talking only of present concerns (rather than both the past and the present), and acting out one's hidden conflicts in pathological or defensive behaviors.

Psychoanalysts begin to help patients overcome their resistances and become aware of hidden conflicts by pointing out and demonstrating how the patient is resisting. They may observe, "It is interesting that each time we talk about your father you miss your next appointment," or, "When you mention your brother's death you seem to pass over it very quickly and change the subject." Once patients become aware they are resisting, the analyst helps them explore what memories, feelings, or wishes are being pushed from awareness and why. In each case it is some painful emotion such as fear, guilt, shame, or anger.

As patients become aware of what and why they are resisting, the analyst helps them explore the sources of these conflicts. If the patient consistently avoids any semblance of angry feelings in talking about experiences that normally prompt anger responses, the analyst encourages the patient to explore his family dynamics in order to learn why the patient is so fearful of experiencing angry feelings. By repeatedly analyzing these resistances and helping patients face upsetting emotions and memories, the analyst hopes to open the patient to finding better ways of coping. As this is done, the patient's ego grows progressively stronger and able to cope, and his id impulses are more maturely integrated into the total personality.

Interpretation. The psychoanalyst's primary therapeutic activity is interpretation. Interpretation consists of making previously unconscious mental processes conscious. This is done in conjunction with the analysis of resistances, since it is the resistances that keep these processes out of awareness during the analytic hour. Interpretations, however, go beyond analyzing resistances to explore in depth the meaning, cause, and dynamics of a psychological process or experience. In formulating interpretations that help patients understand their dynamics, analysts rely heavily on dreams and free associations to piece together a picture of the conflicts the patient has been avoiding.

For example, in the same or succeeding sessions a patient may discuss an aggressive colleague at work, a policeman he believes mistreated him, and a dream he had about his father. The analyst will see a pattern in which the patient is tending to view most of the significant men in his life as threatening to his masculinity. By asking the patient to give associations to these men, the reason for the fears will usually become apparent. In line with psychoanalytic theory, one hypothesis might be that the patient harbors competitive and resentful feelings toward male authority figures growing out of his childhood desire to replace his father as the object of his mother's love (the oedipus complex). By slowly uncovering resistances, making interpretations, and tying different bits of psychological experience together, analysts help patients gradually explore the roots of their current adjustment struggles and conflicts.

Transference. Another cornerstone of psychoanalytic technique is the process of transference. In transference patients experience (transfer) feelings or reactions toward a person in the present that are really a reliving of childhood reactions to other significant people. Although everyone transfers some reactions and feelings from childhood figures (such as parents and siblings) to adult social relations (such as spouses and employers), the psychoanalytic situation is set up to maximize this process so that the patient will relive and resolve earlier conflictual relationships. The frequency of sessions, the use of free association, the use of the couch (which prevents usual social interaction and encourages exploration of one's inner feelings), and the focus on dreams and past significant relationships are all designed to promote regression to earlier, more primitive psychological levels of functioning and transference. Within the transference patients experience their fears, guilt, sexual and aggressive wishes, and their defenses against these thoughts and feelings much as they did in childhood. This time, however, they experience them with a person (the analyst) who is not threatened and who can help them understand and accept their wishes and feelings and handle them in mature ways.

Psychoanalytic theory holds that as patients react to their analysts, earlier maladaptive relationships are brought into focus and can be understood and altered. Along with free association and interpretation, then, the transference relationship is one of the major procedures for uncovering repressed feelings and experiences.

The transference relationship is also a key to keeping the analysis from simply serving as an intellectual excursion into the past. By actively experiencing transferred feelings with the analyst the patient is able to struggle with difficult emotions on a firsthand basis. In this way the analyst in part becomes a substitute parent who is able to help patients cope with difficult wishes and feelings they felt they could not handle with their real parents.

Summary. Although some critics claim that psychoanalysis encourages people to act out their sexual and aggressive drives, this is not the case. The issue for analysts is being aware of one's wishes and drives so that one can face them and make mature, conscious choices that take into account one's wishes, the demands of reality, and one's own moral valuations.

During the last 40 years a wide variety of therapeutic alternatives to psychoanalysis have been developed. Most of these are of shorter duration, less expensive, and more focused on specific symptoms. Psychoanalysis itself has also been evolving as analysts place greater stress on the importance of the child's very earliest interpersonal relationships (first four years of life) and on the role of aggression in the development of maladjustment, and less emphasis on Freud's biological views of instincts. In spite of the variety of therapeutic approaches today, however, psychoanalysis continues to be one of the few depth therapies that attempt to make fundamental alterations in the structure of the patient's personality.

Additional Readings

Freud, S. *Therapy and technique.* New York: Collier Books, 1963. (Papers originally published between 1888 and 1937.)

Greenson, R. R. *The technique and practice of psychoanalysis.* New York: International Universities Press, 1967.

Menninger, K. *Theory of Psychoanalytic Technique.* New York: Harper & Row, 1958.

S. B. NARRAMORE

Psychoanalysis: Theory. *See* PSYCHOANALYTIC PSYCHOLOGY.

Psychoanalyst. Unlike most mental health practitioners who are identified by their particular disciplines (e.g., psychology, social work, psychiatry), psychoanalysts represent all the major mental health disciplines and have in common their commitment to the theory and practice of psychoanalysis. Psychoanalysts may operate from a variety of theoretical orientations (e.g., Freudian, Sullivanian, Kleinian), but all practice a very intensive form of therapy that generally involves seeing patients four or five times weekly for between three and five years.

The prerequisite for training in psychoanalysis is a degree in medicine, clinical psychology, clinical social work, or a related field. After being licensed to practice in one of the fields individuals desiring to practice psychoanalysis undergo a lengthy training program (typically four or more years) in a psychoanalytic institute. These institutes are run by local psychoanalytic associations rather than university medical schools or psychology departments, and the training is typically carried out on a part-time basis while students continue to practice in their respective professional fields. These psychoanalytic training programs consist of three components. The first is a set of courses in psychoanalytic theory and therapy. These cover the psychoanalytic theory of personality and psychopathology as well as the theory of psychoanalytic technique. The second part of the training consists of the control analyses. This involves receiving weekly individual supervision on at least three different psychoanalytic therapy cases over a period of years.

The third component of psychoanalytic training is the candidate's own personal psychoanalysis. This experience is considered the central and unique aspect of psychoanalytic training, since it is only by becoming aware of one's own conflicts and mental dynamics that one can be comfortable with and sensitive to the potentially confusing, frightening, or embarrassing thoughts and feelings one's psychoanalytic patients will be experiencing. The training analysis usually involves five sessions weekly for a minimum of three years.

After completing such a rigorous training program most psychoanalysts develop a full-time private practice of psychoanalysis or psychoanalytically oriented psychotherapy. Since psychoanalysis is very demanding work, most analysts also engage in some clinical supervision, teaching, or consultation for the diversity and balance these provide in their professional lives.

S. B. NARRAMORE

Psychoanalytic Family Therapy. The basic assumption underlying the psychoanalytic approach to family therapy is the reciprocal relationship between conflict among family members and conflict within the mind of any one member (Ackerman, 1966). The two levels constitute a circular feedback system; interpersonal conflict affects intrapsychic conflict, and vice versa.

According to Ackerman interpersonal conflict in the family group generally precedes the establishment of fixed patterns of intrapsychic conflict. Symptom formation is a late product of the processes of internalization of persistent and pathogenic forms of family conflict. Potentially, symptoms are reversible if the intrapsychic conflict can once more be externalized and placed into the field of family interaction where a new solution can be found. The psychoanalytic family therapist is, therefore, much more interested in historical family relationships than is the family therapist with a systems orientation. Current interactions are of interest only as they reexternalize issues that have become internalized in one or more family members.

At the beginning of the family's life cycle this approach stresses the unconscious factors in mate selection. Inevitably when two people marry they replicate in some way the relationship of their parents and re-create what is sometimes called the childhood emotional pattern. A mate is chosen who reduces one's anxiety and re-creates the warmth of the original parent-child relationship. The dynamics of romantic love allow for the denial of the more negative characteristics of the mate, which also mirror the pattern of the parents. In order to live with the tension of the partner's combined negative and positive characteristics, both spouses collude in the denial of these aspects and attempt to make the partner into exactly the kind of person who will meet one's innermost needs. When two partners are both healthy, well-adjusted individuals, these dynamics produce a healthy marriage. When the partners are poorly adjusted, the marriage will manifest greater difficulties, creating problems for the children born into the family.

In psychoanalytic family theory this process of inducing problems in the child as a result of marital distress is known as scapegoating, a concept borrowed directly from the biblical scapegoat, which carried the sins of the people Israel into the wilderness. As Framo describes this process (Boszormenyi-Nagy & Framo, 1965), it requires the existence of a group (the family) whose members feel threatened by some hint of evil (an undesirable characteristic or personality trait) and who agree to use some other person (a family member) to personify that evil, which can ultimately be eliminated by destroying the scapegoat (through a serious physical or emotional illness that takes him or her away from the family). In treatment the scapegoat is not held personally responsible for the symptoms thus induced by the family, and therapy will focus on finding a way to take the person out of the scapegoat role.

The scapegoating process, along with healthier processes that create the family's self-image, is often maintained by the formation of family myths. These involve patterns of mutually agreed upon, but distorted, roles for family members resulting from compromises between all family members so that each individual's self-identity and defenses are maintained through the myth. Collusion among family members allows the family to see itself as living up to its ideal image and avoiding other repudiated images. Children are recruited into the maintenance of family images first defined in the parents' unconscious marriage contract. When parents see in themselves characteristics that contradict the family myth, they may delegate a child or adolescent to resolve the issues for them, thus often reinforcing various kinds of undesirable behavior by which they themselves are unconsciously tempted. Such a child may then be expelled from the family in order to maintain its ideal image. Other children may be bound to the family, unable to leave because their loss would create an unbearable blank in the family's image.

The maintenance of the family myth inevitably leads to the creation of family secrets. Secrets may involve actual facts or events known by one family member and kept secret from others, such as a mother's abortion that is not shared with the children. They may also involve events or conditions known by all family members but simply not talked about, such as a father's alcoholism. Such secrets constitute a taboo. Other secrets involve shared or individual fantasies that are not talked about, such as incestuous feelings. Bringing such secrets into the open and discussing their impact on the family may be an important focus of family therapy.

Ghosts and skeletons in families are also emphasized in this approach. Skeletons are the facts that embarrass family members and may include such historical events as imprisonment, institutionalization in a mental hospital, defection from the military, or an illegitimate pregnancy. Because they constitute the family's darker side, skeletons often become secrets as well. Ghosts in the family are created when members of past generations continue to be psychologically present. Their presence is dysfunctional when unfinished business remains. Often ghosts result from unmourned deaths in the family. The mourning process is not an automatic one, and professional assistance may be needed to facilitate it. When the ghost is a living family member, family therapy may involve bringing this person into the therapeutic process.

Psychoanalytic family therapy is often indicated for serious, long-standing emotional problems that have resisted treatment from a structural, functional, or strategic perspective. It tends to involve long-term rather than short-term treatment and generally will involve several generations of family members.

References

Ackerman, N. W. *Treating the troubled family.* New York: Basic Books, 1966.

Boszormenyi-Nagy, I., & Framo, J. L. (Eds.), *Intensive family therapy: Theoretical and practical aspects.* New York: Harper & Row, 1965.

Additional Readings

Box, S., Copley, B., Magagna, J., Moustaki, E. (Eds.). *Psychotherapy with families: An analytic approach.* Boston: Routledge & Kegan Paul, 1981.

Skynner, A. C. R. *Systems of family and marital psychotherapy.* New York: Brunner/Mazel, 1976.

Stierlin, H. *Psychoanalysis and family therapy: Selected papers.* New York: Aronson, 1977.

H. VANDE KEMP

See FAMILY THERAPY: OVERVIEW.

Psychoanalytic Group Therapy. As a method of treating psychological disorders psychoanalysis focuses exclusively on the individual psyche. While Freud recognized the importance of social groups such as tribes, clans, and especially the family, his approach was to look at these groups primarily in terms of their effect on the psychological growth and development of individuals making up the groups. Thus, the notion of treating many persons simultaneously by group therapy was alien to the first psychoanalytic practitioners.

The extension of psychoanalytic personality theory and treatment procedures to group therapy began in the 1930s with the pioneering work of Trigant Burrows, Louis Wender, and Paul Schilder. Burrows referred to his group therapy as group analysis, Wender observed the phenomenon of transference in groups, and Schilder encouraged his group patients to say whatever came to their minds in an effort to model the technique of free association. Consolidators of the psychoanalytic group model included Samuel Slavson and Alexander Wolf, the former working with groups of children while the latter treated adults in group sessions.

While almost all types of group therapy utilize a number of psychoanalytic principles in their theory and technique, they differ significantly from psychoanalytic group therapy per se. Psychoanalytic group therapy, by definition, places primary emphasis on exploration of the latent, unconscious material of each group member. This does not mean that the observable behaviors of the group member are ignored or discounted as being unimportant. However, the psychoanalytic group therapist always attempts to move from the behaviors to the unconscious processes causing them.

This approach contrasts with nonanalytic groups, which tend to emphasize the meaning and significance of whatever is occurring in the group at the moment. Nonanalytic groups generally tend to focus on the here and now in the sessions rather than on the past as the prime determinant.

Basic Concepts. To understand how psychoanalytic group therapy works it will be helpful to review briefly the assumptions underlying individual psychoanalytic treatment. Psychoanalytic theory postulates that conflicts derived from experiences in certain stages of development result in quite specific forms of neurotic behavior in later years. The patient is unaware of these conflicts and resists their emergence into consciousness. This resistance precludes conscious recognition of the forbidden impulses, feelings, and thoughts that underlie the conflicts. The task of the psychoanalyst is to penetrate these defenses in order to foster awareness, and then resolution, of the unconscious conflicts. The technique of free association was developed to implement the goals of uncovering and resolving these conflicts.

This basic understanding of the origin and treatment of psychological disorders is applied to patients in a group setting in the following way. While members of a psychoanalytic group are not specifically told to free associate, they are asked to discuss whatever is on their minds at the moment, whether about themselves or other group members. This technique not only aids in unveiling unconscious material, it also helps to establish an attitude of openness and noncondemnation that will encourage deeper levels of self-disclosure from the group members. It further gives the members opportunity to become aware of their various resistances—e.g., being silent, seductive, hostile, or intellectualizing. While it is left up to the group therapist to interpret the meaning of the resistances and their relationship to childhood events, the group members assist the therapist by pointing out resistances in one another.

A special form of resistance occurring in group therapy involves a collusion among group members. In essence, two or more members team up unconsciously to divert the therapist and the group from looking at the teamed-up members' inner conflicts. Collusion may take many different forms, including romantic involvement, philosophical debating, and prolonged verbal conflicts. Collusion, as with any resistance, needs to be dealt with openly and forthrightly by the group and interpreted by the group therapist in a noncondemning manner.

Transference occurs when attitudes and behaviors toward significant figures in a person's past are projected onto the therapist. Psychoanalytic group therapy provides opportunity for transference not only between patient and therapist but also between patient and patient. Transference in the group provides a concrete example to patients of how their relationships with significant others in their past have colored their present thoughts, feelings, and relationships, especially those occurring in the group at the moment.

The therapist is not immune from the phenomenon of transference, since he or she will also react to patients at times as if they were persons from the past. This is called countertransference. Group therapy, due to the number of patients the therapist is working with, can compound the countertransference. While this can be especially stressful for the therapist, it can also strengthen him or her, provided there is a willingness and openness to deal with the countertransference feelings.

A one-time interpretation of a defense or uncovering of a conflict will almost never cause the patient to change permanently. Psychoanalytic theory asserts that a person's resistances must be pointed out numerous times before lasting change can occur. This accumulation of interpretations over time, and the cumulative effects of those interpretations, is called working through. Group therapy provides an ideal environment for working through, since the defenses and conflicts of the members are brought out repeatedly in each group session. For example, a person who intellectualizes as a primary defense will tend to intellectualize at every session, and as the group becomes comfortable with noncondemning confrontation, they will let the patient know that they see this defense in operation. After hearing this a number of times, and possibly from a number of different group members, the intellectualizing patient will begin to recognize and discard this defense.

Thus psychoanalytic group therapy, while adhering rather closely to Freud's individualistic theories of personality and treatment, offers advantages compared to individual analysis. The opportunities for the overt expression of unconscious material via transference, group free association, and working through are often more intense and more frequent than in individual psychoanalysis.

Christian Perspective. Psychoanalytic group therapy is open to the same criticisms from a Christian perspective as Freudian theory in general. The antireligious reductionism of doctrinaire Freudianism discounts the reality of spiritual experiences. The emphasis on the curative power of insight gained by interpretation ignores or discounts the emotional, behavioral, and spiritual components of change, all of which are recognized by Scripture. Insight without these components may produce no change at all. This is not to say, however, that psychoanalytic group therapy is without value. It can be a powerful tool in assisting persons to understand the effect their past has on their present, while helping them to alter destructive ways of dealing with themselves and others in the present.

Additional Readings

Abse, D. W. *Clinical notes on group-analytic psychotherapy.* Charlottesville: University Press of Virginia, 1974.

Slavson, S. R. *A textbook in analytic group psychotherapy.* New York: International Universities Press, 1964.

Wolf, A., & Schwartz, E. K. Psychoanalysis in groups. In H. Kaplan & B. Sadock (Eds.), *Comprehensive group psychotherapy.* Baltimore: Williams & Wilkins, 1971.

W. G. BIXLER

See GROUP PSYCHOTHERAPY.

Psychoanalytic Psychology. The branch of psychology founded by SIGMUND FREUD in the 1890s. It has gone through a series of alterations and refinements, both during Freud's lifetime and after.

During his early career Freud was heavily involved in research. He wrote a highly regarded monograph on aphasia and carried out some very careful histological studies on the eel. He also published, in 1884, a review of the medical uses of cocaine. Freud's medical and scientific training was in the thoroughly physicalistic tradition popular in German universities during the last half of the nineteenth century, which contended that all actions are the result of chemical and physical forces within the organism. Consequently all mental disorders were assumed to have an organic basis, such as brain lesions or inadequate blood circulation, and psychiatric therapy consisted of physical treatments such as drugs, altered diet, and electrical stimulation.

Although Freud was thoroughly trained in this tradition, his clinical work soon led him to look beyond strictly physical explanations of behavior to psychological ones. He discovered that many of the thoughts and feelings that influence personality functioning operate outside of conscious awareness, and he proposed a complex theory of psychology to take this into account. Because of its stress on inner personality processes, psychoanalysis is considered the first dynamic or depth psychology. The fact that psychological factors lie at the root of many personal maladjustments is almost universally accepted today, yet it was a radical departure from accepted psychiatric theory and practice in the last half of the nineteenth century. Therefore, Freud is seen as the father (or grandfather) of all later depth approaches to personality—even though many of those approaches reject some of the cornerstones of psychoanalytic theory. Whether or not one agrees with the specifics of psychoanalytic theory, there is no doubt that it has generated more study into the deeper dynamics of personality functioning than any other single school of psychology.

Although psychoanalysis is often thought of as a theory of psychopathology or, even more narrowly, as simply a technique of psychotherapy, it is actually a general psychology of human behavior. The essential features of the psychoanalytic theory of behavior are based on six basic assumptions: 1) unconscious mental processes exist; 2) all human behavior is motivated and purposeful; 3) past experiences influence current adjustments and reactions; 4) personality functioning is inherently conflictual and these conflicts can be understood on the basis of hypothetical mental structures such as id, ego, and superego; 5) psychological processes involve various quantities of energy, strength, or force; and 6) human behavior is influenced by interaction with the environment.

Over the course of the development of psychoanalysis these six basic assumptions have been formulated into six points of view or metapsychological assumptions. They are known respectively as the 1) topographical; 2) dynamic; 3) genetic; 4) structural; 5) economic; and 6) adaptive points of view. Psychoanalytic theory holds that to fully comprehend any human behavior we must understand it from each of these perspectives. These points of view function like sets of glasses or lenses that focus attention on different aspects of the same phenomenon in order to provide a complete picture.

The topographical point of view, for example, calls attention to the fact that the mental process in question has both conscious and unconscious aspects. The genetic view focuses on previous life experiences and patterns that have influenced the behavior. And the adaptive point of view looks at the environmental influences on behavior or mental processes. Since all other aspects of psychoanalytic theory are formulated in terms of these six assumptions or points of view, an understanding of them is central to a comprehensive view of psychoanalytic psychology.

The Topographical Point of View. During

Freud's early practice he treated a sizable number of hysterical personalities suffering from somatic symptoms. In looking into the onset and background of these symptoms he found that in each case the person had undergone some painful or traumatic experience that they had forgotten. He also found that when they recalled their experiences through hypnosis or catharsis, the symptoms often disappeared. Since all of Freud's first patients reported being sexually abused by their father, he concluded that the traumatic events that led to repression and maladjustment were sexual experiences. He soon began to question the possibility of such widespread sexual abuse of children by their parents, however, and suggested that the forgotten experiences were often not real but fantasized.

In time this concept evolved into his theory of drives, or motivation, and he concluded that the thoughts that prompted people to forget were sexual wishes growing out of a basic physiological drive. According to this view all people have strong sexual drives which strive for expression but which also create anxiety or guilt that causes them to be repressed. After the First World War, Freud broadened his theory of drives to include aggression as well as sexuality. He concluded that the destructiveness of war and much human behavior could not be explained unless some basic aggressive/destructive drive was postulated in addition to a sexual/loving one. Later analysts have further altered the psychoanalytic theory of motivation by including broader social goals and minimizing the concept of physical drives. Throughout the evolution of psychoanalytic theory, however, the concept of anxiety-producing wishes, experiences, and desires that are pushed from conscious awareness because of their unacceptability has remained constant.

Freud's observations on the role of unconscious thoughts in his neurotic patients was complemented by his study of dreams, hypnosis, slips of the tongue, and normal, momentary forgetting. He observed that in dreams, when normal censuring processes are relaxed, people often experience thoughts that are quite alien to their conscious wishes, thoughts, and feelings. He also realized that in posthypnotic suggestion people perform actions with no conscious awareness of why they are carrying them out. And in observing the everyday life of normal people he observed that many of us occasionally forget the name of a well-known acquaintance or accidentally slip and utter a word we had not intended to speak.

All these phenomena led Freud to conclude that there is a large area of mental life that operates outside conscious awareness. Some of this (e.g., our street address) is simply outside our immediate range of attention and can be easily recalled. Freud labeled these thoughts PRECONSCIOUS. Others can be recalled only with great effort, apparently because in some way the individual does not want to remember. These thoughts are labeled UNCONSCIOUS.

The Dynamic Point of View. At the same time Freud was developing his understanding of unconscious mental processes he was also formulating a dynamic view of personality. This viewpoint asserts that all human behavior is purposive and lawful. It is motivated, in other words, and directed toward certain goals. In the history of psychoanalysis various motivations have been proposed. As we have seen, Freud initially assumed it was the memory of traumatic sexual experiences that motivated neurotic individuals to repress these memories and caused neurotic problems. Later this portion of his theory was discarded, and Freud postulated the sexual drive as the prime motivator of behavior. In his final theory of motivation Freud recognized two primary drives, sexual and aggressive.

Although the sexual and aggressive drives have received the greatest emphasis in psychoanalytic theories of motivation, they are by no means the only ones considered. Adler, for example, stressed the drive for power or mastery in order to overcome feelings of inferiority. Jung, Horney, and Sullivan all criticized Freud's original overemphasis on the sexual sources of maladjustment and proposed broader personal and social motivations. In spite of their varying theories of motivation, however, all psychoanalytic theorists stress the goal-directed nature of human functioning.

The Genetic Point of View. This point of view asserts that neither normal nor pathological mental processes can be fully understood apart from the life history of the individual. Psychoanalysts assume that an individual's current manner of functioning is the result of the interaction of constitutional givens (such as the strength of drives) and the environment. The way that a person has learned to fulfill his basic drives within the context of the environment, especially the family and immediate social network, is the way he or she will attempt to satisfy these drives in adulthood.

The genetic viewpoint helps explain the reappearance of infantile behavior during adulthood. If people become partially fixated at one level of development they may later regress to that level of psychic functioning. Freud initially worked out his concepts of fixation and regression in terms of sexual development. He theorized that the sexual drive passes through three basic stages on the way to adult functioning. In the first, the oral phase (from birth until approximately 18 months), pleasure is largely associated with the mouth and activities of sucking and eating. In the next, the anal phase, Freud hypothesized that the locus of pleasure was especially linked to stimulation of the anal membranes and bowel functioning. Between 3 and 4 years of age the genitals were viewed as becoming the primary source of pleasure. Freud called this the phallic phase. (*See* PSYCHOSEXUAL DEVELOPMENT).

Since Freud was desirous of linking his psychological theories to existing scientific beliefs, he theorized that the sexual drive (libido) had a certain quantity of physical energy. If some of this energy is fixated at an early stage of psychosexual development (e.g., the oral), Freud concluded people do not have that energy available to move on to more mature developmental levels. Consequently under the impact of stress in later life they may return to the earlier stage. From this perspective persons suffering from depression, or from alcoholism and other addictions are presumed to be fixated at the oral level, where feeding and oral gratifications are prominent. Obsessive-compulsive personalities (obsessed with orderliness, cleanliness, and guilt) are viewed as fixated at the anal level, where issues of messiness and cleanliness are prominent. And hysterical personalities (who frequently demonstrate exaggerated femininity) are seen as fixated at the phallic level rather than moving on to the mature adult genital phase of sexuality.

The Structural Point of View. Freud spelled out the structural viewpoint of psychoanalysis in *The Ego and the Id*. This book marked the official beginning of ego psychology and opened psychoanalysis up to become a full-fledged general psychology rather than simply a way of viewing unconscious processes and psychological maladjustments. Although Freud had long talked of drives, defenses, and other mental processes included in his new conceptualization, he had never integrated these concepts in a comprehensive manner. In *The Ego and the Id* he described three sets of mental processes, systems, or structures. The first, the id, consists of the individual's drives, wishes, and impulses. These processes are the seat of motivation and are largely unconscious. Since they are uncon-

scious, they do not necessarily operate by the same logical processes that conscious ideas do. Consequently conflicting wishes, ideas, and feelings (e.g., love and hate) can coexist in the unconscious.

The ego consists of processes such as perception, memory, judgment, and motor control that are essential in relating to the world. The ego serves to reconcile the demands of the id with the demands of the environment in order to satisfy the drives as fully as possible while still attending to reality (including the reality of others' potential reactions to one's attempts at unbridled gratification). The development of the structural theory with its emphasis on the ego was essential if psychoanalysis was to ever become a general theory of psychology; the topographical and dynamic views were not sufficient to understand such functions as perception and memory, which are essential to a comprehensive understanding of human functioning.

In *The Ego and the Id*, the superego, comprising personality's moral functions, was considered a special structure gradually developing out of the ego. Roughly equivalent to the conscience, the superego contains both one's goals and aspirations (the ego ideal) and the self-corrective functions. It develops from the child's relationship with his parents and functions to approve or disapprove one's actions and to pass out praise (in the form of self-esteem) or punishment (in the form of guilt).

The Economic Point of View. Freud's clinical experience and his desire to build a theory of personality congruent with the materialistic science of his day led him to postulate the economic point of view. This assumes that there are quantitative factors involved in human behavior. To put it differently, Freud assumed that drives and affects and the individual's ways of handling them involved actual amounts (potentially quantifiable, at least in theory) of psychological energy. This concept and Freud's use of such terms as cathexis, which referred to the amount of energy attached to an idea, were based on the energy concepts of late-nineteenth-century physics.

Although the reality of such quantities of energy has often been questioned, most psychoanalysts feel the need for some type of hypothetical, quantifiable energy to explain human behavior. This hypothesis is used, for example, to account for the observation that some people's sexual and aggressive drives seem more powerful than those of others. It is also used to explain the phenomenon of resistance, in which a large amount of energy appears to be devoted to keeping ideas out of awareness during the process of psychotherapy. Psychoanalysts also use the concept of amounts of energy to explain the process of displacement, in which an amount of affect is changed (displaced) from one experience to another almost like a stream is diverted from its original bed.

The Adaptive Point of View. This final point of view stresses the fact that there is a reciprocal relationship between the individual and the environment and that personality development and functioning cannot be understood apart from this mutual adaptiveness. Although Freud repeatedly discussed this interaction, the adaptive point of view was not clearly formulated and articulated until Rapaport and Gill (1959) published "The Points of View and Assumptions of Metapsychology."

The Psychoanalytic Theory of Neurosis. The psychoanalytic theory of psychopathology views all psychoneurosis as growing out of conflicts between the id and the ego. If the individual's drives (for orthodox psychoanalysts, sex and aggression) are potentially too strong or threatening, the individual turns to various ego DEFENSE MECHANISMS such as repression to control the impulses and reduce the anxiety or guilt associated with them. These defense mechanisms are not fully successful, however, since they require a substantial expenditure of emotional energy and involve some denial, distortion, or avoidance of reality. Since the impulses keep struggling for expression, the ego must continue these defensive processes. The neurotic symptom is a sort of compromise in which the initial drive is at least partially repressed or is disguised sufficiently to be acceptable to the ego. In depression, for example, the unacceptable anger (id impulse) is repressed but reappears as self-hatred. In paranoia the anger is repressed and projected onto another person so that the paranoid person becomes the innocent victim of others' anger instead of an angry person. The superego can enter into this struggle on the side of either the id or the ego, although its most obvious manifestations in the neuroses is as an ally of the ego. In these cases the ego and superego team up to try to control the unacceptable id impulses.

In this formulation the problem can be traced to excessively powerful instincts, a weak ego, or a too harsh superego. To understand any individual neurotic it is necessary to know what the conflicts are between the id and the superego, why the ego cannot handle the drives, the defenses the ego uses in attempting

to cope with the drives, and how these processes ended up in the formation of the neurotic symptom or personality. Both constitutional and environmental factors are seen to be involved in this process, and neurotic problems are resolved when the ego becomes strong enough to manage the demands of the id and the three structures of the personality (id, ego, and superego) come into an appropriate balance. Health, in other words, involves a balance of fulfilling one's drives or needs in a nondestructive manner.

Psychotic pathologies are believed to develop in the same general way as the neuroses, but greater attention is given to basic ego defects arising out of experiences in the early years of infancy.

Psychoanalytic Psychology After Freud. In the years following Freud's death many modifications and developments have taken place in psychoanalytic thinking. The two major trends that encompass these are EGO PSYCHOLOGY and OBJECT RELATIONS THEORY. Although these two trends are intimately related and both flow from Freud's foundation, they have influenced psychoanalysis in slightly different ways. Psychoanalytic ego psychologists, such as Anna Freud, Heinz Hartmann, and Ernst Kris, placed increasing stress on the role of the ego in personality functioning and relatively less emphasis on id processes. Although drives and impulses are seen as no less important than they were in Freud's day, current psychoanalysts tend to see the health and ability of the ego to cope with internal and external threats as the critical factor in adjustment. They also suggest that the functions of the ego pass through normal developmental processes and that functions of the ego such as perception and memory cannot all be traced to the id and its conflicts with external reality. In focusing more on the ego these psychoanalysts also place a great deal of emphasis on the impact of early interpersonal relationships upon the development of the ego.

Object relations theory stresses the impact of interpersonal relationships on the development of the personality. Although Freud coined the phrase *object relation* and laid the groundwork for this emphasis, and while all analysts incorporate the concept of early interpersonal relationships into their theories, several British psychoanalysts (Melanie Klein, Harry Guntrip, and Donald Winnicott) have probed the importance of the dynamic relationship between infants and their primary provider in greater depth than other schools of psychoanalysis. Their research and writing suggest that the development of personality is strongly impacted by the infant's taking in (internalization) of its perceptions of its parents in the first year or two of life.

Evaluation. Although many Christians have dismissed psychoanalytic theory because of Freud's stress on sexuality and the belief that psychoanalysis promotes acting out of sinful impulses, a closer evaluation indicates that at least some aspects of psychoanalytic theory are congruent with scriptural teachings and with careful observation of human functioning. From a biblical perspective it seems that many aspects of the broad structure of psychoanalytic theory are consistent with a biblical view of human nature, while much of the specific content is questionable or in conflict.

Freud's stress on the existence of unconscious mental processes (the topographical view), for example, is supported by phenomena such as dreams and hypnosis, which demonstrate the activity of thoughts we are not consciously aware of. It is also consistent with scriptural passages that speak of the human personality's complexity and tendency to self-deceit (e.g., Jer. 17:9). Psychoanalysis' understanding of the role of defense mechanisms in warding off unacceptable wishes and feelings goes beyond scriptural descriptions of how we avoid facing painful reality but is consistent with that scripturally described process.

The psychoanalytic assumption that all behavior is purposeful and motivated is consistent with a biblical view of human nature that sees individuals as intelligent, self-determining, social persons created in the image of God. So is the genetic point of view, which asserts the continuity of childhood and adult experiences. Parents, for example, are instructed to train children properly so the parents can have assurance that their children will follow that way in adulthood (Prov. 22:6). The psychoanalytic belief that there is a reciprocal relationship between the individual and his or her environment (the adaptive point of view) is also consistent with scriptural teaching on the role of both personal and societal responsibility.

The structural division of personality into the id, ego, and superego and the economic viewpoint have no apparent biblical parallel. As hypothetical constructs, concepts such as ego, id, and superego can be seen as biblically neutral since they are simply shorthand ways of describing or conceptualizing certain personality processes. Their usefulness depends on the accuracy with which they allow us to describe the functioning of personality rather than on specific biblical witness to their accuracy. Freud's economic viewpoint, which postulates certain actual amounts of psychological energy, is another concept that needs to stand or fall on its utility rather than on an explicit scriptural teaching.

When we come to the specific content of Freud's theory, particularly his view of motivation, we encounter serious problems. Although Scripture has a great deal to say about human sexuality, it certainly does not give it the prominent motivational role that psychoanalysis does. In fact, the Bible rather clearly describes humanity's drive to be autonomous and godlike as the major motivating force behind human maladjustment. Similarly, Freud's theory of neurosis appears inadequate. Although the broad outline of conflicts that motivate defenses, which in turn produce neurotic symptoms, is widely accepted, most theorists question the central role Freud gave to the oedipus complex in this process. Broader social motivations and dynamics appear to be closer to both clinical observations and scriptural revelation.

Even given the compatibility of some of psychoanalytic theory with a Christian view of human nature, psychoanalysis leaves us with a truncated view of personality. Freud and his followers have provided a depth technique for exploring the dynamics of human personality. As such, psychoanalysis can provide a good deal of understanding of human functioning. However, it remains for Christians to thoroughly evaluate psychoanalytic theory in light of the biblical view of human nature, motivation, and growth. Even when that task is completed, psychoanalysis will not provide a full picture of human nature. Like all theories of personality, psychoanalysis gives only one perspective or way of looking at human personality. It is limited by the finitude of the theorist, the selection of methods of observation, and the complexities of the subject matter.

Reference
Rapaport, D., & Gill, M. The points of view and assumptions of metapsychology. *The International Journal of Psychoanalysis,* 1959, *40,* 153–162.

Additional Readings
Brenner, C. *An elementary textbook of psychoanalysis.* New York: International Universities Press, 1955.
Fine, R. *The development of Freud's thought: From the beginnings (1886–1900) through id psychology (1900–1914) to ego psychology (1914–1939).* New York: Aronson, 1973.
Freud, S. *New introductory lectures in psychoanalysis.* New York: Norton, 1933.

S. B. NARRAMORE

Psychoanalytic Psychotherapy. An intensive method of therapy based on psychoanalytic personality theory but differing somewhat from the technique of classical psychoanalysis. It is sometimes called psychoanalytically oriented psychotherapy or psychodynamic psychotherapy, although the latter term actually includes a number of insight-oriented therapies other than psychoanalytic psychotherapy (e.g., Gestalt and Adlerian therapy). Psychoanalytic psychotherapy was developed as a modification of psychoanalysis due to the inability of some patients to handle the intensive self-exploration of analysis and because of the desire to find a shorter, less expensive treatment that could be utilized with a greater variety of individuals.

Like psychoanalysis, psychoanalytic psychotherapy assumes that adult personality maladjustments grow out of conflicts between one's wishes or drives and forces that cause repression. It sees the roots of adult maladjustments in childhood experiences; stresses the role of sexual and aggressive drives; and conceptualizes maladjustments in terms of conflicts between the id, ego, and superego. It also shares its major therapeutic techniques with psychoanalysis, as well as its terminology of resistance, defense, transference, and interpretation.

While the understanding of personality development and psychopathology held by psychoanalysts and psychoanalytic psychotherapists is identical, the therapeutic goals and the course of therapy are slightly different. Traditional psychoanalysis is generally carried out on a four or five times a week basis for three to five years. The goal of this extensive therapy is a major restructuring of the total personality. By contrast, psychoanalytic psychotherapy involves between one and three sessions weekly for a period of one to three years. It is oriented more to eliminating symptoms and solving problems than to a radical restructuring of the personality.

In psychoanalysis patients are encouraged to follow the fundamental rule of free association and verbalize anything at all that comes to their minds during the analytic hour. Coupled with the analyst's nondirectiveness this promotes the exploration of every area of the patient's life, including those that at first seem irrelevant to the presenting problem. In contrast, psychoanalytic psychotherapy limits its focus more to issues surrounding the presenting problems and their development. In line with this more limited goal psychoanalytic psychotherapy does not rely as heavily on free association. While psychoanalytic psychotherapists do en-

courage patients to discuss everything that comes to mind, the psychotherapy is structured in a way that is frequently more focused and problem centered and does not result in true free association.

In psychoanalysis the therapist-patient relationship is the main focus of therapy. By encouraging the development of transference the psychoanalyst hopes to activate the main features of the patient's pathology within the patient's relationship to the analyst. In contrast, psychoanalytic psychotherapy does not focus as intensely on the transference, and the therapist endeavors to help the patient gain insight into conflicts, struggles, and problems without necessarily fully reliving them in the present relationship.

In both psychoanalysis and psychoanalytic psychotherapy the therapist's primary task is twofold: 1) to provide an atmosphere or relationship that encourages self-exploration; and 2) to help patients become aware of previously unconscious wishes, feelings, conflicts, and experiences through the technique of interpretation. In psychoanalysis interpretation is usually seen as the only significant therapeutic technique. Analysts listen carefully to patients' dreams and free associations in order to identify the patients' resistances and the warded-off wishes, feelings, and experiences. Any technique that would hinder the process of free association and the interpretation of resistance is viewed as countertherapeutic. By contrast, psychoanalytic psychotherapists may occasionally make careful use of advice or guidance, and they may even encourage certain neurotic defenses if these will further the patient's adaptation to the environment. Such techniques are considered inappropriate in psychoanalysis because they encourage dependency and may reinforce repression, whereas in psychoanalytic psychotherapy they are viewed as appropriate if they will help the patient achieve a higher level of functioning.

A final distinction between psychoanalysis and psychoanalytic psychotherapy is the depth of the patient's regression to primitive levels of thought and feelings. In psychoanalysis the reclining position, frequent sessions, use of free association, and relative anonymity and nondirectiveness of the analyst encourage patients to reexperience their emotional conflicts with the analyst. This regression to primitive or infantile levels of functioning is encouraged in order to understand the sources of adult maladjustments and rework them. In psychoanalytic psychotherapy, by contrast, the less frequent sessions, the shorter length of treatment, and the greater focus on symptoms and present conflicts mean that patients do not typically undergo such a deep regression. This reexperiencing of infantile feelings and reactions is not always viewed as crucial in the more problem-oriented approach of psychoanalytic psychotherapy.

Although it is generally agreed that psychoanalytic psychotherapy is significantly different from psychoanalysis, those differences are not clear-cut, and these two forms of therapy are best seen as different points on the same continuum. Both therapies stress the uncovering of repressed memories, wishes, and feelings; and both utilize transference, interpretation, and dream analysis. The difference is more in degree than kind. The more frequent the sessions, the greater the use of interpretation, the more the focus on transference and dream interpretation, and the deeper the patient's regression, the more the therapy can be considered psychoanalysis. The less frequent the sessions, the greater the focus on presenting and environmental problems, and the greater the therapist's reliance on techniques other than interpretation, the more appropriate the label *psychoanalytic psychotherapy* becomes.

Additional Readings

Fromm-Reichman, F. *Principles of intensive psychotherapy.* Chicago: University of Chicago Press, 1950.
Langs, R. *The technique of psychoanalytic psychotherapy* (2 vols.). New York: Aronson, 1973.

S. B. Narramore

See Psychoanalysis: Technique.

Psychobiology. Prior to 1960 the term referred to the many-sided approach to personality developed by psychiatrist Adolf Meyer, who used the term to emphasize the importance of dealing with mental as well as physical factors in human psychological problems. Meyer's holistic view recognized that there are multiple determinants of behavior. He believed that since mental illness was the result of the interaction of many factors, there should be an interdisciplinary approach to the subject that coordinated the findings of psychology, biology, and sociology (Meyer, 1950).

After 1960 the term reemerged in common usage and came to mean the broad science concerned with the biological bases of behavior. Not a formal discipline in and of itself, it is a collective field drawing together the research in many disciplines, including ethology, genetics, psychology, neurology, neurophysiology, biochemistry, endocrinology, pharmacology,

psychiatry, and anthropology. Psychobiology has developed rapidly during the last two decades because of the growing recognition of the interdependence of behavioral and biological processes.

Psychobiology seeks to analyze behavior in terms of the biological factors that might play a role. It seeks to discover which anatomical structures and pathways and which physiological processes might be involved in the mediation of specific behaviors. Psychobiology is related to but not identical with Physiological Psychology, which deals specifically with physiological mechanisms underlying behavior.

The field of psychobiology represents the culmination of a trend in thinking about human nature that can be traced back to Descartes. Philosophical and theological speculations prior to Descartes emphasized a dualism in human nature that stressed the effect of the mind on the body. Cartesian dualism, on the other hand, stressed a two-way interaction that helped place mind within the domain of biology, a viewpoint that later became a foundation of psychology.

Research in psychobiology includes studies in the hormonal control of behavior, developmental psychobiology, physiological determinants of instinctive behavior, comparative aspects of learning, determinants of perception, and drugs and behavior. Comparative animal research in all areas is also much more common than in psychology proper. A central thrust of psychobiological research has been to produce a better understanding of the relationship between the brain and the human person.

Psychobiological research exploring the biological foundations of the mind generally proceeds from assumptions that are materialistic and reductionistic. These assumptions state that mind is merely a product of brain activity. Psychobiologists thus seek to explain behavioral observations in terms of the neural substrates that are presumed to account for them. One of the most important principles of the psychobiology of the mind is that neural activity is the sole basis of mental activity and that psychological processes can be explained by neural ones (Uttal, 1978). Furthermore, the interconnectivity of neurons is viewed to be the proper level of investigation of psychobiology. This means, according to Uttal, that modern monistic psychobiology in its most fundamental premises is in profound logical and conceptual conflict with contemporary religious doctrine concerning human nature. He also points out that it leaves a most fundamental problem:

How does a unified mental state arise out of the action of huge numbers of individual neurons?

The Christian view of human beings does not suggest that the human mind is not related to brain states, but insists that the description of the human mind cannot be reduced to mere biology. MacKay (1974) argues that even the most complete description of the brain could not invalidate the Christian concepts of the mind and freedom.

Neurophysiological research itself does not clearly support the reductionistic, materialistic assumptions of psychobiology. As Uttal (1978) indicates, there is the unanswered question of when and how the electrical firing of collections of neurons turns into mental experience. As of yet there is no hint as to what properties of the sodium-potassium exchange that creates the electrical activity of neurons relate to one's experience of an emotion or a thought. Brain stimulation and recording experiments also have failed to reveal any portion of the brain that acts as a receiving area for combining elementary experiences into the holistic experience that composes the human mind. Brain stimulation experiments have also repeatedly failed to produce thinking, willing, or complex emotional experiences in human subjects.

Studies in the psychobiology of the mind have relied very heavily on the establishment of correlations between brain activity and the activity of the mind. But such correlations by themselves do not suggest that it is neural activity alone that gives rise to the experiences of mind.

In summary it can be said that the principles of psychobiology can serve to enrich the study of the human mind and behavior and their important connections to the physical structures of the brain. However, the more reductionistic and materialistic psychobiology becomes, the less likely it is that its themes and interpretations of data will be helpful in understanding the complexities of the human personality.

References

MacKay, D. M. *The clockwork image.* Downers Grove, Ill.: Inter-Varsity Press, 1974.
Meyer, A. *Collected Papers of Adolf Meyer* (E. E. Winters, Ed.). Baltimore: Johns Hopkins Press, 1950.
Uttal, W. R. *The psychobiology of mind.* New York: Halsted, 1978.

Additional Reading

Penfield, W. *The mystery of the mind.* Princeton, N.J.: Princeton University Press, 1975.

M. P. COSGROVE

Psychodrama. A form of psychotherapy based on the philosophy and theoretical principles of Jacob L. Moreno. A client, or "protagonist," acts out situations to creatively resolve conflicts in himself and with others. This is usually done in the context of a therapeutic or educational group. Psychodrama is an action-oriented approach that restores the individual's lost spontaneity, or ability to live creatively and wholeheartedly, through the use of dramatic interactions.

Historical Development. Moreno was born in Bucharest, Romania, in 1892. His early work in psychodrama was with children in the gardens of Vienna. He would assist them to act out their fantasies and problems. Moreno continued to develop his emerging theoretical system in work with Viennese prostitutes. It was in these brothels that the Moreno version of group psychotherapy was conceived. In 1921 he created the "theater of spontaneity," a totally new version of theater in which professional actors took on roles from newspaper accounts and enacted the stories.

In 1925 Moreno came to the United States. He founded a private psychiatric hospital at Beacon, New York, in 1936. Psychodrama was the primary therapeutic method. Within the next 11 years Moreno, although ridiculed by his peers, developed a unique group treatment that continues to flourish today. His ideas have permeated the encounter and human potential movements of the last 20 years.

Basic Instruments of Psychodrama. Moreno (1978) describes psychodrama as having five instruments. The stage is the first. Many therapeutic stages are circular in design, modeled after Moreno's circular, three-tiered stage with overhanging balcony and lights. The top level of the stage represents the highest level of involvement—the area wherein one places the agonies and ecstasies of life. Lower levels represent the steps of warming up—the periphery or external aspects of existence. These intricate designs are not necessary for a productive psychodrama but are helpful.

The second basic instrument is the protagonist, the individual who receives primary focus in the psychodrama. The protagonist re-creates situations from past, present, and future, portraying them with dramatic realism so that new behaviors may be learned and new cognitive patterns established. The protagonist acts as a representative of the group, often exploring a theme that the group has identified as meaningful to them.

A third instrument is the auxiliary ego. Auxiliary egos are representations of the protagonist's significant others. As the protagonist moves into action, he or she chooses group members to represent those individuals who are part of the scene being played. These roles are often parents, spouses, parts of the self, etc. The auxiliary becomes the other in the drama after having been given the necessary information to play the role (*see* ROLE REVERSAL TECHNIQUE).

Another type of auxiliary ego is the psychodramatic double. The double helps the protagonist to express thoughts and feelings that would otherwise remain suppressed. The double mimics the protagonist's bodily posture and mannerisms so that the highest level of identification may occur (*see* DOUBLE TECHNIQUE).

The group is considered a fourth instrument. Although psychodrama may be conducted individually in an office setting, it is generally applied as a group treatment. The group is strategically involved in the selection of the protagonist so that the issues to be explored are relevant to the lives of group members. The group members assist through becoming auxiliary egos and in their sharing and support following the psychodrama.

The process is guided by the fifth instrument, the director. The director assists the group in the selection of a protagonist, directs role reversals and scene setting, and acts as the overall coordinator of the drama. The director challenges the protagonist to achieve new insights and new behaviors—those that lead to healthier living. The whole process of the initial group warm-up activities, the enactments of the protagonist, and the verbal closure is guided by the director.

Therapeutic Process. The process of the psychodramatic session is threefold. The initial warm-up phase serves to lessen the social tensions and offers group members an opportunity to identify their feelings and needs. The warm-up is often an activity suggested by the director. Activities range from group interaction exercises to verbal sharing of concerns.

A group theme often becomes the criterion for the selection of the protagonist. The action phase then not only becomes a psychodramatic portrayal of an individual's private concern but represents the overall concern of the group. Common themes are returning to the community; handling anger, grief, marriage and family tension; and loss of self-esteem.

The protagonist, guided by the director, develops scenes that depict the conflict. Auxiliary egos are chosen to represent significant others in the scene, and role reversals are

conducted to determine the characters of the significant others. The action, whether past, present, or future, is dramatized in the here and now. Once maximum insight and catharsis occur, the intensity diminishes and sharing begins.

The group becomes the central focus of the sharing-integration phase. They share their common humanity with the protagonist. They relate the scenes portrayed on the stage to their own lives and to significant others. A group healing occurs, one relating to the initial group concern.

Theoretical Principles. Moreno's basic principles are sociometry, social atom, tele, roles, and spontaneity. *Sociometry* is the measurement of one's feelings of attraction, repulsion, and indifference to others on the basis of a specific criterion. Generally this is done in a therapeutic group or school classroom. A criterion could be "With what group members would you be willing to share a secret about yourself?" The sociogram is the basic measuring instrument. Haskell (1967) suggests several examples of sociometric tests.

Moreno used the concept of the *atom* to illustrate the relationship of the individual to significant others. It represents the smallest social unit where significant emotional relationships occur. Usually the social atom is represented as an illustration placing the individual at the center with lines reaching out like spokes to significant people. The content of the relationship—such as attraction, repulsion, or indifference—is then measured through sociometric techniques.

Tele refers to a feeling that is transmitted from one individual to another. Tele, however, is based on the assumption that one sees others clearly and without transference. Transference is a one-way projection of feelings toward another individual (such as the husband who unconsciously transfers feelings about his mother onto his wife). Tele assumes reciprocity. Both individuals have positive feelings such as mutual empathy. It is a two-way process of attaining and maintaining realistic relationships. Tele is the substance of significant relationships, the glue that cements the social atom and encourages it to expand.

Roles and *role playing* are important aspects of Moreno's thinking. A role is the characteristic function and contribution of the individual as well as the expected behavior and position defined by the group for the individual. Conflicts occur between the individual and societal demands, as can be seen in the conflicting roles of women in our culture. Role confusion is exhibited by adolescents who are developing and learning new roles. In these situations role training is a useful function of psychodrama. The individual explores role conflicts and develops new skills in these areas.

Spontaneity is a most important concept in psychodrama. Moreno considers spontaneity as self-initiating behavior, usually in response to some life situation. It requires novelty and adequacy. Without spontaneity the individual will display stereotypic robotlike behaviors. Pathological spontaneity occurs when the individual is being novel but demonstrates little competency or appropriateness in the situation. Such a response is psychosis.

The application of spontaneity to the psychodramatic enactment is very important. The protagonist is challenged to create novel roles and perceptions. Spontaneity for the passive individual could be the act of risking the expression of feelings or of developing more open and intimate relationships with others. For another who is extremely opinionated it may be a sincere attempt to listen to and respect the views of others. Spontaneity is seen by Moreno as basic to all forms of productive creative acts.

Applications. Psychodrama is applicable to three areas: therapy, training, and education. Most often group treatment lends itself well to this modality, especially in inpatient and partial hospitalization settings. Outpatient groups may also benefit. Another therapeutic use is known as psychodrama "a deux," or the application of psychodrama techniques to individual therapy.

Psychodrama is usually conducted as sociodrama when introduced into the educational system. This form is more familiarly known as role playing. It employs the use of stories and situations acted out for the affective and attitudinal learning of the students. Several other agencies use psychodrama techniques for training. The FBI trains its staff in hostage negotiation with psychodrama as do several police departments. Medical students treat trained auxiliary egos playing roles of patients whom these future doctors will be treating.

View of the Cosmos. Moreno believes that the God of the Hebrews and the Christ of the New Testament are no longer suitable supreme beings in our society. His new focus is on the "I-God," the infinitesimal part of the Universal Self that each person represents. "Every self is identical with the self of God. All have taken part in the creation of themselves and in creating others. Thus, we can become not only a part of the creation but a part of the creator

as well. The world becomes our world, the world of our choice, the world of our creation" (Moreno, 1941, p. xv).

Even amid speculation that Moreno was poetically describing a psychodramatic God, there was an unexpected reaction by others who condemned him as a megalomaniac. However, it seems that his intent was to encourage and invite each individual to search the fullest dimension of himself and others and to assume full responsibility for his own creating.

Moreno rates Christ as an extremely gifted psychodramatist. Christ is the Son of God only as we are all sons of a God. The Scriptures are viewed as a fallible record of events and not as a holy revelation of God.

It is important at this point to separate the invention from the inventor in this therapeutic modality. Psychodrama itself is neither Christian nor unchristian. It is an instrument, a psychotherapeutic scalpel which, in the hands of the Christian therapist, can assist in bringing about healing and integration for a client.

Many of the biblical guidelines for living are enhanced by psychodrama. Role reversal may produce a new understanding of one's relationship with another and therefore promote forgiving, healing, and loving. Role training assists the Christian in practicing more Christlike behaviors in simulated situations. Psychodrama as a therapeutic treatment or educational modality is compatible with a biblical Christian perspective.

References

Haskell, M. *An introduction to socioanalysis.* Long Beach: California Institute of Socioanalysis, 1967.

Additional Readings

Moreno, J. L. *Words of the father.* New York: Beacon House, 1941.
Moreno, J. L. *Who shall survive?* (3rd ed.). New York: Beacon House, 1978.
Moreno, J. L. *Psychodrama* (Vol. 1) (3rd ed.). New York: Beacon House, 1964.
Moreno, J. L., & Moreno, Z. T. *Psychodrama* (Vol. 3) (3rd ed.). New York: Beacon House, 1969.
Moreno, J. L. *The theatre of spontaneity* (2nd ed.). New York: Beacon House, 1973.
Starr, A. *Psychodrama: Rehearsal for living.* Chicago: Nelson, 1977.

J. H. VANDER MAY

Psychogenic Disorders. The concept of the psychogenic aspects of disease refers to those factors which create or influence physical symptoms but which have their origin in psychological needs or conflicts. No disease or disorder can be purely psychogenic; neither can any be purely somatogenic—i.e., without the effect of the psychological. All diseases vary in the proportions of each factor and thus can be imagined to fall along a continuum. The psychogenicity of a disorder suggests it serves some purpose of which the patient is usually unaware and is seldom even evident to those around.

During the eighteenth, nineteenth, and first half of the twentieth centuries medical treatment was basically directed toward the containment, reduction, and prevention of contagious diseases such as diptheria, smallpox, and tuberculosis. However, 65 to 75% of current hospital admissions are for disorders that are nonviral and are related to the psychology of the individual. It is now being realized that personality factors (e.g., coronary-prone personality) and behavioral life styles (e.g., smoking, exercise, stress) play a large role in many somatic complaints. The traditional medical dichotomy between those illnesses whose origin was in the body (somatogenic) and those of the mind (psychogenic) has largely disappeared. The mind and the body are now recognized as elements of a dynamically interacting system of health and disease (Engel, 1979). However, for practical purposes it is still useful to think in terms of the psychological causes of physical illness and of the value, reward, or purpose of the disorder.

Psychological events such as thoughts or feelings can induce physiological responses. For instance, if you see a snake crawling toward you on the floor, you will likely respond by feeling anxious, with an increase in heart rate, respiration, blood pressure, and muscle tone, even though the snake has done nothing to you. For some people even the thought of this is sufficient to evoke the reaction—a psychogenic response. Some psychogenic disorders occur in response to a previous learning event (e.g., a snake bite), while others serve some dynamic function. Some psychological problems may function in a way so as to gain something otherwise thought unavailable, such as attention or meaning. Others may serve to avoid something, such as responsibility or duty. Although the psychological factors may be clear to the clinician and even occasionally evident to others, they frequently are unknown to the patient. They are not an actual product of the person's mind, nor are they the conscious intention or manipulation of the individual.

In contrast to the negative perspective of some theorists who view psychogenic disorders as destructive, Hora (1977) and other existential therapists have stressed the constructive and important role of the illness. This approach views the disorder as a protective defense mechanism and as the best way the person currently knows to handle a difficulty in his life. Any more directly conscious expression, although eventually desirable, may be too stressful at the moment.

References

Engel, G. L. Resolving the conflict between medicine and psychiatry. *Residential Staff Physician*, 1979, *25*, 70–74.
Hora, T. *Existential meta-psychiatry.* New York: Seabury, 1977.

Additional Readings

Gottschalk, L. A. Psychosomatic medicine today: An overview. *Psychosomatics*, 1978, *19*(2), 89–93.
Henker, S. O. III. Conflicting definitions of the term psychosomatic. *Psychosomatics*, 1982, *23*(1), 10–11.
Reiser, M. F. Changing theoretical concepts in psychosomatic medicine. In S. Arieti (Ed.), *American handbook of psychiatry* (Vol. 4) (2nd ed.). New York: Basic Books, 1975.

G. MATHESON

See PSYCHOSOMATIC DISORDERS.

Psychogenic Pain Disorder. Pain experiences without any identifiable organic basis or any known physical cause. Most PAIN is a secondary phenomenon that occurs in response to a primary problem of structural or functional damage to the body. It is generally understood by both the patient and the physician to be the consequence of the injury or illness. "Psychogenic" is not intended to imply causation but rather to indicate the lack of positive physical findings. At the same time it provides a psychological way to describe or to give meaning to the pain. When psychogenic pain is seen as pain that is better understood in psychological terms rather than in terms of physical medicine, this respects the integrity of the pain experience and protects it from being viewed as just imagined or not real (Sternbach, 1974).

The most common understanding of psychogenic pain involves a conversion reaction mechanism in which stress that the individual is incapable of consciously acknowledging is dealt with by symbolic expression through body activities or sensations. Thus, thoughts, wishes, or fantasies can be dealt with unconsciously through the abnormal utilization of the body. Physiological manifestations through pain are generally the result of numerous factors originating in the individual's history of using bodily activities or sensations to achieve gratification or conflict resolution in relationships.

"Organ language" is an expression used to refer to the relationship between the described physical symptoms and the way a person refers to himself, his reactions, or his opinions. For example, psychogenic rheumatism can occur in people who "wouldn't stoop" to certain behavior, even when they meet "stiff" situations, as might a "spineless" person (Engel, 1975).

Engel (1959) has also identified the pain-prone patient syndrome, which involves repeated disability due to pain without any detectable physical cause. Characteristically the pain serves to punish and provide retribution for excessive guilt feelings in the person, who has often been raised in a family where pain was prominent as a sign of both guilt and parental caring. A condition of physical pain can therefore seem to alternate with "painful" social and environmental conditions; the more comfortable the life situation, the greater the pain, and vice versa (Pilling, Brannick, & Swenson, 1967).

Psychogenic pain can also be seen as a shared experience. If a child identifies with a parent, or a spouse with a spouse, then pain becomes a means of extending the identification even after the model is gone. The pain may serve to keep the important person "alive." Psychogenic pain may also serve as a form of interpersonal behavior, whether it is to solicit help, to maintain dependency, or to express passive-aggressive feelings toward an inconvenienced friend or family member.

In assessing psychogenic pain it is important to know that it may be experienced in any part of the body. To differentiate it from organic pain it is necessary to explore the person's history for factors suggesting pain as a means of dealing with psychodynamic tensions. Also, it is important to study the nature and description of the pain with respect to its frequency, intensity, location, radiation, and remedial factors, in that these frequently aid in distinguishing psychogenic from organic pain. For example, the vivid imagery in a description such as "like a hot poker up my back" suggests the pain may have a strong psychological involvement and meaning.

Therapeutically, psychogenic-pain sufferers are generally highly sensitive to implications that their pains are not real, imagined, or "in their heads." Consequently a clear acceptance of the pain as real is the initial requirement in treatment. Subsequently supportive or confrontational therapy may be conducted. For example, Schneider and Wulliemier (1979) have employed a physiotherapist both to acknowledge and physically treat the pain and to serve in a dynamic sense as a good mother figure. Additionally, a psychiatrist explores the psychological factors pertinent to the pain and serves as a bad father figure. This permits the working through of these transferred roles and a subsequent reduction in psychogenic symptoms over an extended period of time. Cohen (1979), among others has stressed the diversity in the expanding field of psychosomatic medicine, involving roles for several disciplines in the treatment of each patient. Frequently this interdisciplinary team involves a physician, who acknowledges and oversees the physical aspects; a psychotherapist, who confronts and explores the psychopathology of the patient; and a social worker, who addresses the social environment and the behavioral factors.

In summary, psychogenic pain is the physical expression through painful symptoms of psychological issues that cannot be addressed directly, emotionally, and consciously because of the individual's maladaptive character structures. Treatment is difficult because the interpretation of psychological causes often annoys the patient, who takes this as an insult or excuse to abandon treatment. Successful therapy needs to acknowledge the real pain as well as to explore the underlying psychological factors.

References

Cohen, S. I. Updating the model for psychotherapy of psychosomatic problems. *Psychotherapy in Psychosomatic Medicine*, 1979, *32*, 72–90.

Engel, G. L. "Psychogenic" pain and the pain-prone patient. *The American Journal of Medicine*, 1959, *26*, 899–918.

Engel, G. L. Psychological aspects of gastrointestinal disorders. Organic disorders in psychosomatic medicine. In M. F. Reiser, (Ed.), American handbook of psychiatry: Vol. 4. New York: Basic Books, 1975.

Pilling, L. F., Brannick, T. L., & Swenson, W. M. Psychological characteristics of psychiatric patients having pain as a presenting symptom. *The Canadian Medical Association Journal*, 1967, *97*, 387–394.

Schneider, P. B., & Wulliemier, F. The psychotherapy of the psychosomatic patient. *Psychotherapy in Psychosomatic Medicine*, 1979, *32*, 112–117.

Sternbach, R. A. *Pain patients. Traits and treatment.* New York: Academic Press, 1974.

G. MATHESON

See PSYCHOSOMATIC DISORDERS.

Psychohistory. Psychological studies of historical figures have existed since at least the nineteenth century, when the German psychiatrist Möbius was writing "pathographies." At the turn of the twentieth century, the fledgling Vienna Psychoanalytic Society was the scene of numerous psychological dissections of the famous dead. Freud himself produced one major psychobiographical work, *Leonardo da Vinci and a Memory of His Childhood* (1910/1975), and a psychological sketch of Dostoyevski. Freud's *Moses and Monotheism* (1938/1975) must be counted as largely psychohistorical as well. A psychobiography of Woodrow Wilson, attributed to Freud, seems rather to have been written by William Bullitt, with some collaboration with Freud. Early psychoanalysts such as Jones, Rank, and Abraham were soon publishing their own psychohistorical studies. To the present day psychohistory has remained overwhelmingly *psychoanalytic* history; with few exceptions, other psychological and psychiatric schools have had little impact on history writing.

It was not long before professional historians and social scientists perceived the potential usefulness of psychoanalysis for their disciplines. In 1930 Harold Laswell's *Psychopathology and Politics* appeared. Prominent anthropologists were beginning to use psychoanalytic insights in their writing of culture histories. In his 1958 Presidential Address before the American Historical Association, William Langer called familiarizing himself with psychoanalysis the historian's next assignment. Psychoanalytically informed studies of historical figures and movements by professional historians are by now legion. Psychoanalytic psychiatrists and psychologists, such as Erikson, Eissler, and Lifton, have continued to pursue such work.

Although there are variations in the mode in which psychoanalysis has been applied to history, many psychohistories have followed along the lines of Freud's *Leonardo* and *Moses and Monotheism* and, consequently, bear the methodological weaknesses of these two famous works. In *Leonardo*, Freud attempts to explain da Vinci's tension between art and science and his preference for certain artistic themes, as well as certain aspects of his character, with reference to his oedipus complex and latent homosexuality. Much of Freud's speculation is carried by the analysis of a putative childhood fantasy. In *Moses and Monotheism* three millennia of Jewish religious history are explained by the Jews' supposed murder of Moses and rejection of his doctrines, their subsequent collective repression of this event, and the eventual return of this recollection. This is an expression of Freud's penchant for explaining social (and sometimes individual) history with reference to a single, decisive archaic event—a *kairos*.

The difficulties with these works are obvious. In *Leonardo*, Freud had very little access to reliable historical data about his subject. Indeed, some of the information from which he constructed his hypothesis was actually erroneous. No account was taken of cultural or intellectual historical factors in the life of the artist. Large segments of his intellectual and

creative life were reductively explained as aspects of his psychopathology. And, most tellingly, da Vinci could not furnish Freud with any associations to his own fantasies or to the latter's interpretations. *Moses and Monotheism* harbors the same difficulties, with the added problematic assumption of a collective mind whose processes are identical to those in the individual psyche.

Erikson's *Young Man Luther* (1958), though in many respects wanting in scholarly and critical rigor, is a considerable advance on Freud's work. It elaborates the "great man in history" model in which the historical giant is seen not so much as imposing his idiosyncratic, psychopathologically determined will on his era as acknowledging needs and tensions in himself that are present in—but only dimly appreciated by—the members of society at large. By satisfying and resolving these needs and tensions in himself, the great individual thereby succeeds in satisfying and resolving them in others.

Lifton's (1975) "shared psychohistorical themes" is promising. He focuses upon themes, forms, and images that are shared among many individuals of a period or culture and attempts to correlate these patterns with specific types of experiences and preoccupations. Much of Lifton's work has focused on themes of death and survival, as exemplified in the survivors of overwhelming catastrophes such as Hiroshima and the Holocaust. A related theme is that of the individual's and society's attempt to attain some mode of immortality. His concept of Protean man as an individual characterized by a fluid identity and interminable experimentation and exploration (in reaction to his society's dislocation from the nourishing symbols of its past and in response to his constant bombardment with novel and evanescent cultural stimuli) is another fruit of the shared themes approach.

Evaluation and Summary. The contributions of psychoanalysis to history are substantial but have often been obscured by the speculative excesses of Freud and certain other psychohistorians. These include analyzing whole cultures and epochs as if they were personalities, making deep interpretations about the motives of dead persons notoriously resistant to furnishing their associations, ignoring all factors but the psychological ones, and abandoning the evidential and critical canons to which any good historian cleaves. Many scholars gratefully take such excesses, which any college sophomore could recognize, as sufficient excuse to be done with psychoanalysis once and for all. However, there is room for a middle way.

To begin with, one must appreciate that psychoanalysis is a *clinical* method, applicable to one situation alone—the ongoing interaction between therapist and patient in the consulting room. It is only here that one can listen to the train of associations; frame the questions, confrontations, and clarifications through which one garners so much of his information; observe the unfolding transference; and test one's clinical hypotheses against the patient's subsequent recollections and behavior. It is important to appreciate that when psychoanalysis is applied to history, what is transferred are insights about human nature originally arrived at by the psychoanalytic method, but not the method itself. Such insights applied to history cannot be treated with the same assurance as the clinically based propositions of psychoanalytic therapy.

If, however, the historian recognizes this, there is no reason why he cannot use psychoanalytic theory to draw limited inferences about the personalities of his subjects. Indeed, when he uses economics and social science in his work, it is generally their theory and insights that he is transplanting rather than their methods. The historian already has a rough and ready concept of individual motivation that can be considerably enriched by psychoanalytically informed systemization and appreciation of the role of unconscious motives, defensive processes, and intrapsychic conflicts in human affairs. However, psychoanalytically informed inferences can be used only with personages about whom one has a wealth of reliable information in the form of diaries, letters, reports of contemporaries, and perhaps even (as with Freud) accounts of their dreams. Their usage with whole cultures is much more problematic (Wallace, 1983). Psychodynamic factors must be placed within the context of all other factors. Because of this there is no justification for a subspecialty such as "psychohistory"; history is simply history, and will make use of any insights at its disposal—psychoanalytic ones included.

Greater than the aforementioned, however, is the role psychoanalysis can play in the historian's refining and monitoring of his best instrument—himself. To the extent that he becomes cognizant of his own historical conditioning, and the conscious and unconscious issues and affects deriving therefrom, then to that degree will he approach the unrealizable ideal of objectivity.

References

Erikson, E. *Young man Luther.* New York: Norton, 1958.

Freud, S. *Leonardo da Vinci and a memory of his childhood.* In J. Strachey (Ed. and trans.), *The standard edition of the complete psychological works of Sigmund Freud* (Vol. 11). London: Hogarth, 1975. (Originally Published, 1910.)

Freud, S. *Moses and monotheism.* In J. Strachey (Ed. and trans.), *The standard edition of the complete psychological works of Sigmund Freud* (Vol. 23). London: Hogarth, 1975. (Originally published, 1938.)

Lifton, R. K. (Ed.). *Explorations in psychohistory.* New York: Simon & Schuster, 1975.

Wallace, E. R. *Dynamic psychiatry in theory and practice.* Philadelphia: Lea & Febiger, 1983.

E. R. WALLACE IV

Psychoimagination Therapy. A therapy developed by J. E. Shorr in 1965 on the premise that the therapeutic use of imagery alone can serve as a modality for personality change (Shorr, 1972). The use of imagery as a clinical tool has a long history, being discussed and utilized by Freud, Jung, Leurner, and others. Shorr's approach espouses a broadly existential/phenomenological viewpoint blended with the interpersonal developmental theories of Laing and Sullivan.

Shorr suggests that a phenomenological approach to understanding human behavior is significantly enhanced by a knowledge of waking imagery. Imagination is viewed as the core of consciousness and the primary avenue of access to one's subjective inner world and experience. Imagery is used to circumvent the restraining influence of conscious censoring, thereby accessing more efficiently one's self-image, areas of conflict, and strategies for viewing and coping with the world. As an individual is allowed to project his own ego into imaginary situations, he can more safely and openly explore, differentiate, and integrate reality and fantasy, self and not-self, actuality and potentiality.

Emphasis in this therapeutic approach is on separating the individual's own view of self from the view of self ascribed to him by significant others. It is assumed that people need affirmation in order to grow. When they fail to receive this, false conceptions of self develop to compensate for the lack of affirmation of the true self. Exploration of thoughts, wishes, expectations, and feelings through imagery facilitates analysis of these false conceptions of self, and ideally the true self-identity is then helped to flourish.

Psychoimagination therapy is conducted in individual and group contexts. Over 2000 categories of imaginary situations have been developed by Shorr to reveal specific information about the client's personality, world view, self-definition, areas of conflict, and styles of defense. Although research on the approach is virtually nonexistent, Shorr argues that it is useful in general and neurotic populations, with certain obsessive-compulsive persons, and with some schizoid personalities.

Reference

Shorr, J. E. *Psycho-imagination therapy.* New York: Intercontinental Medical Book Corporation, 1972.

D. M. COOK

See IMAGERY, THERAPEUTIC USE OF.

Psycholinguistics. Psychologists interested in language have focused primarily on the issues of language development and the relationship between language and thought.

Developmentally, babies begin by making cooing and crying sounds, progress through babbling (consonant/vowel combinations), and typically utter their first word at about one year of age. By the end of the second year children are beginning to combine words into simple, two-word sentences. For the next year or so the child's speech seems to be telegraphic. It is as if the child has to pay for each word (much like a telegram), and thus only the essential words are spoken. There has been considerable controversy over the meaning behind these simple utterances. Some psychologists argue that infants understand and mean much more than they say (the "rich" interpretation), while others are convinced that infants say what they mean and no more (the "poor" interpretation). In any case, by using words the infant has demonstrated a significant cognitive advance, the ability to use symbols to represent objects or events.

Historically perhaps the most important controversy in psycholinguistics has revolved around the issue of *how* children develop language. Those psychologists with a behavioral or environmental orientation have tended to stress the importance of imitation and parental reinforcement, while others have emphasized inborn abilities in children for understanding and generating the rules that govern language. Obviously this represents a modern variation of the age-old nature/nurture controversy. An example of evidence for the environmental (nurture) point of view is the curious regularity with which "mama" or "dada" is a child's first word. Anyone who has observed parents interacting with their children would probably attribute this tendency to parental coaching. However, it must also be acknowledged that rules are important for language development (nature perspective). For example, a word that a child may use correctly through imitation (feet) will typically be misused once the rule for forming plurals (add *s*) is understood (foots). Therefore, at the present time both positions have substantial support, and both seem necessary for a comprehensive view of language development.

For some Christians, however, the most important issue in psycholinguistics has been the capacity for language in animals. Threatened by the evolutionary notion of the similarity between man and animal, these individuals have struggled to identify something that makes humanity unique, that gives a human being a special kind of dignity. Several possibilities have been suggested (e.g., tool use, humor, self-reflection), but one of the most popular candidates has been language use.

Most scientists would agree that in the natural state, language (in a narrow sense) is a uniquely human attribute. But the more complicated question is not the natural use of language but rather the capacity for language. Is it possible that given the right approach (e.g., sign language) apes and monkeys can learn to use language? Recent evidence suggests that the answer to that question may be at least a qualified yes. Therefore, if Christians are interested in establishing the dignity or uniqueness of man, they might be better advised to explore the biblical concept of being created in the image of God. This is particularly true since in the biblical narrative only mankind is honored by being created in God's image. A careful reading of Genesis 1 and 2 suggests that several things are implied by this honor: 1) people have the capacity for relationships with each other and God; 2) people are goal or task oriented; 3) people have a moral sense; and 4) people have rational capabilities.

R. L. BASSETT

See LANGUAGE DEVELOPMENT.

Psychological Birth. *See* MAHLER, MARGARET.

Psychological Factors Affecting Physical Condition. *See* PSYCHOSOMATIC DISORDERS.

Psychological Health. *See* HEALTHY PERSONALITY.

Psychological Measurement. A basic axiom in science is that numbers are only as sound as the measurement techniques from which they are derived. This is certainly the case in psychological measurement, where many of the variables assessed are not directly observed but are hypothetical. Because of this, much of psychological measurement is focused on a performance that is not necessarily equivalent to the psychological concept. For example, strength of motivation cannot be directly observed, so it is operationalized as, for example, the number of times an organism will cross an electrified grid to reach some goal. In general, psychological measurement consists of assessing a sample of behavior at one point or a series of points in time. The value of the assessment depends on how well the sample represents the entire behavior domain of interest.

Today psychological assessment in varied forms is used to describe, select, classify, compare, diagnose, and prognose. The settings are similarly varied and include education, industry, armed services, counseling centers, health care centers, and research settings.

Principles of Test Theory. Basic to measurement of any kind is test theory. Concepts such as reliability and validity provide information on the believability and use of all data collected. If an assessment process lacks either, the data are of little value.

Reliability. Reliability describes the extent to which measurements can be trusted to provide dependable information. Technically reliable assessment reflects true aspects of the trait measured, not chance or error conditions. A variety of empirical methods for estimating reliability exist; in each case, if some trait is being dependably measured, reliability will be high.

Stability reliability refers to the extent of agreement between two administrations of the same assessment technique separated in time. This method is often used with standardized tests purporting to measure a trait that remains relatively constant over time. Equivalence reliability refers to the extent of agreement among two or more forms of an assessment technique. This method is often used with standardized tests given repeatedly and where memory of earlier administrations is likely to be a factor. Also, more than one form may be used in group testing to discourage individuals from copying one another's answers. Internal consistency reliability refers to the extent of agreement among items making up an assessment. This method may be applied to a single administration of a single instrument, and so is often used with teacher-made or counselor-made measures.

A method used with interview data and behavioral observations is interrater reliability. This refers to the extent of agreement among data collected independently by different "judges" on the same client. If the judges are dependably identifying and recording the same traits, agreement will be high.

A final concept related to reliability is the standard error of measurement. This is a statistical measure of how much chance or error factors are a part of the data collected. The standard error of measurement provides some indication of the amount of discrepancy existing between the data obtained and true levels of the trait.

Validity. Validity describes the extent to which measurements meet the objectives for which they are designed. Reliability is necessary but not sufficient for validity. An assessment technique is not validated; rather, the use to which it is put is validated. That is, validity is dependent on context. For example, the Iowa Tests of Basic Skills may be valid measures of school achievement; however, when used in a different context—e.g., to measure temperament—they are invalid.

As with reliability, a variety of validity types exist. Content validity is reflected in an assessment technique that requires clients to perform on all behaviors and subject matter identified in the objectives. This validity is particularly relevant to standardized achievement measures and teacher-made tests.

Criterion-related validities refer to the extent to which measures predict or estimate some standard. In predictive validity the standard is in the future as, for example, in the relationship between the Scholastic Aptitude Test taken in high school and college grades. In concurrent validity the standard exists in the present, as in the ability of a projective interviewing technique to discriminate between clients with and without some psychopathology.

Construct validity is more difficult to demonstrate; however, it is extremely important to psychological measurement. Psychological variables such as intelligence, self-concept, personality, creativity, and aptitude are abstract rather than concrete; that is, they are constructs. Since these cannot be directly observed, a technique that attempts to measure such variables must develop an evidence-based case for its validity. This is done in a variety of ways, such as demonstrating parallels with other measures of the same construct; by not paralleling measures with which it is theoretically unrelated; by demonstrating age differentiation on constructs that change over the life span; by registering the effect of experimental variables (e.g., if the measure purports to assess depression, it should be sensitive to experimentally produced changes in depression), and so on. Construct validity is established on the strength of circumstantial evidence.

Norms. Although not as broadly relevant as reliability and validity, norms are useful in interpreting data by making available standards for comparison. They attempt to provide some uniform meaning from test to test and uniform units within a test. Common norm types include grade, age, percentile, and standard score norms. Of these four, only standard score norms provide unquestioned equality of units.

Norms are restricted to the population from which they are derived; thus, it is important to evaluate their applicability to particular clients. Also, comparison cross measures should be done with great caution, since composition of norming samples may vary, scale units may not be equivalent, and content may differ despite similar levels.

Methods of Data Collection. Psychological measurement is a process of information gathering and synthesizing; case studies, interviews, behavioral observations, and standardized tests represent some of the tools in this process. In general, tests and behavioral observations are most easily standardized, permit objective scoring, and result in quantifiable data; however, they do have a restricted range of content. Case studies and interviews can be structured to provide standardization, objectivity, and quantifiable data; however, they generally are more flexible to increase the variety of information collected. They also permit interaction, with the counselor following up information or requesting clarification. Comprehensive psychological assessment does not require either/or decisions among these techniques, but utilizes all as complements to each other.

Case studies. Case studies or histories provide the context in which data on current functioning are interpreted. Case studies include both biographical and autobiographical information; the former provides objective, factual data on the client's life, and the latter provides client perceptions and reactions to life events deemed salient. Data are collected through client interviews and other sources of information, such as friends, relatives, co-workers, and school and employment records. In analyzing case studies counselors are particularly alert for atypical types of data. These include nonnormative events, such as emigration during childhood, and unusual reactions to life events, such as amusement in discussing death of parents. Since data for case studies are often retrospective and originate from the client or people close to the client, bias and inaccuracy are likely. Therefore, independent verification whenever feasible is important.

Interview. The interview is a process of data collection through verbal communication. Information is not gleaned simply from the content of the interview. The process also provides valuable insights; the client's appearance, behavior, affect, quality of speaking, and so on, are important, particularly if they vary according to specific content being discussed.

Structured interviews may consist of an invariant sequence of questions addressed to all clients or a basic set of questions asked of all but with flexible order and additional questions raised depending on circumstances. Structured interviews tend to result in a greater amount of information and provide some comparability between clients and within a single client across sessions. On the other hand, they can be rather rigid and present an interrogationlike atmosphere. Unstructured interviews provide freedom to roam, with few if any constraints. These often promote a more natural atmosphere, but they also permit rambling and as a result gather less information. Another factor in the structure of interviews is the theoretical orientation of the counselor. Psychodynamic therapists, for example, may use free association techniques and attempt to interpret client responses, while Rogerian therapists, using nondirective techniques, may be more inclined to facilitate self-interpretations by the client.

Behavioral observation. Behavioral observation is more than "just looking"; it is deliberate, systematic, and guided by explicit objectives. There are informal, indirect, and formal methods. An example of informal methodology is the diary study, where a stream of behavior is described, often with much interpretation and value judgment. This is a weak source of data but a rich source of ideas for future, more controlled study. An example of indirect methodology is the retrospective report—e.g., reviewing one's childhood. It is indirect because it is based on memory rather than immediate observation. This method has been frequently used in developmental research and in case studies. It suffers many weaknesses, including distortion and selective memory.

Formal observational methods differ from informal and indirect methods in their level of control. This is accomplished by establishing ahead of time operational definitions (i.e., defining abstract concepts in concrete, measurable terms), recording codes, recording materials, and interrater reliability. Also, only observable behavior is recorded; broad categorical labels, such as altruism, are avoided, as are inferences and interpretation.

Two formal methods are time sampling and episode sampling. Time sampling is the systematic recording of previously selected and defined behavior during a number of randomly chosen time intervals. This provides a picture of typical behavior. Episode sampling is the systematic recording of preselected events, including preceding and consequent circumstances. This has been used, for example, to discover causes and consequences of a child's disruptive behavior in school.

A useful sequence in observational research and practice is to begin with informal or indirect observations, follow with time sampling for a systematic view of typical behavior, and then conduct episode sampling of particular events of interest.

Standardized tests. In general, psychological tests are intrusive, objective, and standardized measures of a sample of behavior. They are intrusive in that the client is aware of the assessment process and is actively fulfilling required tasks; they are objective in that scoring criteria are explicitly stated; and they are standardized in that there exists a uniformity of procedure in administration and scoring.

As with all psychological measurement the process of testing is secondary to defining objectives. Therefore, it is important to analyze the objectives for which tests are designed before making a selection. For example, some tests, such as the Stanford Achievement Tests, are designed to cover a specific content area. Others are designed to discriminate between clinical and nonclinical groups of individuals, as in the Minnesota Multiphasic Personality Inventory. Others are designed according to how well the test items measure specific traits, as in Cattell's Sixteen Personality Factor Questionnaire. And still others are written from theoretical models—e.g., the Edwards Personal Preference Schedule, which was designed from Murray's manifest need system.

Additional factors should be evaluated in selecting standardized tests. These include technical considerations, such as evidence for reliability and validity, and whether the types of reliability and validity reported correspond with one's intended use for the test. The applicability of norms and scales should also be evaluated. In addition, there are practical considerations, including cost, time limits, ease of administration, and availability of parallel forms.

A variety of available sources provide information about standardized tests, including the test manual itself, publishers' catalogs, and articles in professional journals. Undoubtedly the single most valuable resource today is Buros's *Mental Measurements Yearbooks*. These provide basic information on individual tests as well as comments from qualified reviewers.

Social Implications. Measurement permeates all of our society. Vast numbers of individuals participate in formal counseling where psychological assessment is utilized to clarify conditions from psychoses to marital compatibility. Industry screens job applicants with a variety of psychological assessments. Thousands of published standardized tests are available. Every individual participating in our public educational system experiences some type of psychological assessment. It is not surprising, then, that concerns are being raised about the role and influence of psychological assessment in our lives. The social issues are numerous and volatile, and only a few will be discussed here.

Invasion of privacy. Privacy is intimately related to self-determination. In the context of psychological measurement it relates to the right of the individual to decide what and how much will be disclosed of thoughts, feelings, and life experiences. Yet this raises a conflict, for effective measurement may require that the individual not be told how specific responses will be interpreted. One partial resolution to this dilemma is the concept of informed consent. Here the individual is informed about the purpose of the assessment, the type of data sought, and the use to which the data will be put; then voluntary consent or refusal is requested. However, the question consistently arises as to whether the client is truly informed, i.e., understands; this is particularly the case with minors and adults whose mental competence is in question.

Another issue here is confidentiality. Access to information collected through psychological assessment must be limited, but to whom is not always clear. Generally the client and counselor only should examine the data unless the client provides permission or anonymity is ensured and agreed upon. Again, this is less obvious in the case of minors, participants in institutional settings such as schools, or where the assessment reveals clear and immediate danger to the client.

Test bias. Test bias is a serious concern, although often misunderstood. Frequently bias is claimed when an identifiable group of people consistently perform poorly on a test; however, this is insufficient evidence for such an accusation. Only if these people will perform satisfactorily on the criterion predicted by the test, but are prohibited from doing so because of their low scores, is the test biased against them. On the other hand, if these people perform poorly on the test and poorly on the criterion, then the test has done its job; it has demonstrated predictive validity. A test measures a sample of behavior—i.e., what an individual does, not why the individual does it. Interpretation of the why and subsequent decisions are often where cultural biases are reflected. Also, a test can be used unfairly if it is administered to assess potential, particularly if decisions limiting the future are based on that assessment. A test samples current performance, and there is no reason to assume that future performance cannot be altered, given an altered environment.

Tests are culturally limited, however. They reflect the values, norms, perceptions, and communication styles of the designers and standardization samples. Thus, they may be invalid measures when administered to people of other cultures or subcultures.

Ethical standards. The extensive reliance on psychological assessment mandates that minimum qualifications be expected of users. Professionals who interpret and utilize data from psychological measures should be trained in test theory, should have basic knowledge of assessment areas (e.g., personality theory), and should be acquainted with the construction, assumptions, and uses of the assessment techniques under consideration. Also, professional organizations need to involve themselves in quality control of their members. A good example is the American Psychological Association, which requires its members to fulfill all the Ethical Principles of Psychologists, including Principle 8, Assessment Techniques: "In the development, publication, and utilization of psychological assessment techniques, psychologists make every effort to promote the welfare and best interests of the client. They guard against the misuse of assessment results. They respect the client's right to know the results, the interpretations made, and the bases for their conclusions and recommendations. Psychologists make every effort to maintain the security of tests and other assessment techniques within the limits of legal mandates. They strive to ensure the appropriate use of assessment techniques by others" (APA, 1981, p. 8).

Reference
American Psychological Association. *Ethical principles of psychologists.* Washington, D.C.: Author, 1981.

M. D. ROE

See PSYCHOLOGY, METHODS OF.

Psychological Roots of Religion.

The biblical and historical roots of religion have been studied for centuries, but only relatively recently have the psychological roots of religion been investigated. The sources of religious need in personality and the needs that are met by religion are two topics that developed out of this investigation. In many ways these two topics are like different sides of the same coin. They are inextricably connected, yet can be approached from different viewpoints. Most of the literature available on these topics is theoretical rather than empirical in nature, and therefore theories rather than experimental data will be presented.

Sources of Religious Need in Personality. One may appropriately ask, "Is there a religious need in personality?" One way to approach this question is to survey personality theories to see how they treat religion. Nearly all personality theories address religion as a normal or abnormal need and offer psychological explanations for it. Another approach is to consider the desire for religious experience within cultures. The desire for religious experience, which is both cross-generational and cross-cultural, yields evidence for a religious need in personality.

A theoretician's definition of religion and personality is foundational to his or her discussion of the source of religious need in personality. Five broad theoretical categories of religious needs in personality are outlined below, each having a particular view of religion and personality.

Innate or instinctual. The psychological view that religious needs are innate or instinctual has received little support. Although this position was commonly held at the turn of the century, few contemporary psychologists hold it at present. The position was challenged by James, who believed that religion was not an instinct but rather a complex mixture of a multitude of feelings, acts, attitudes, and values. James's (1961) view was readily accepted and soon eclipsed the "innate religion" view.

A result of personality development. Freud (1928) was probably the greatest proponent of the view that religious needs grow out of personality developmental processes. One of his basic assumptions was that religion is nothing other than psychological processes projected into the outer world. These processes were generated by personality development that occurred in four stages: oral, anal, phallic, and genital. The cornerstone of personality development is the resolution of the oedipus complex, which occurs in the phallic stage. Basically, the oedipus complex is a child's desire to kill the same sex parent so that he can fulfill his sexual fantasies with the opposite sex parent. The psychoanalytic cure for neuroses, of which religious desire was one, is to resolve the oedipus complex and the underlying libidinal conflict.

According to Freud religious practice was the culturally accepted way of expressing one's guilt over an unresolved oedipus complex. God was nothing more than an exalted father figure. Freud believed that religion was an illusion whose future was limited by the rise of modern-day science, which would disprove the myth of religion.

Erikson (1950) also has a developmental perspective on religious needs and personality development, but it is different from Freud's perspective. He believes that personality develops through eight stages that encompass the entire life cycle. Each stage presents a conflict to the individual, such as trust versus distrust or intimacy versus isolation. Personality is developed as an individual resolves these conflicts. According to Erikson religion has developed out of people's need to find reassurance and consolation in times of regression to an earlier stage of development. Thus, religious needs in personality grow out of one's need for reassurance in times of heightened conflict. Both Freud and Erikson view the source of religion as coming from a personality developmental process.

A result of moral development. Others have identified the source of religious needs to be the result of moral development. Kohlberg (1981) has postulated a process of six stages of moral development. The first stage is the obedience and punishment orientation. The motive behind a person's moral behavior in this stage is to avoid punishment and achieve gratification. The sixth stage is called universal ethical principles orientation and is characterized by moral behavior based on the highest values of human life. Kohlberg has demonstrated that people tend to move through these stages, but that most people become fixated at a particular stage. Very few ever attain stage six. He has also demonstrated that his theory is cross-cultural.

Moral stages are determined by the way a person resolves moral dilemmas and explains metaphysical phenomena. From this perspective religious needs are founded in one's moral development and are a systematic expression of one's moral developmental stage. A person's religious needs are contingent on his or her moral development, and the religious needs change in accordance with changes in moral development.

Existential phenomena. Religious needs can also be seen as coming from one's search for meaning, an encounter with the infinite, or an encounter with finitude. Frankl (1962) correlates religious needs with a person's desire to find meaning in a seemingly meaningless existence. A person seeking to make sense of nonsense in the metaphysical arena asks questions about the meaning of life, destiny, and values. A confrontation with these questions is seen as the source of religious need.

A person's encounters with the infinite or with his or her finitude are other existential sources of religion. As a person begins to explore the universe he quickly encounters its infinite nature, and some see this encounter with infinity as giving rise to religious thoughts. As soon as people encounter infinity, however, they are generally struck by their own finitude. Some, including Paul Tillich, believe that it is a person's encounter with finitude that leads him into religious thought.

Interpersonal phenomena. Several theorists hold that the source of religion is within the relational nature of man. Buber (1937) is one who takes this position, arguing that it is the relational aspect of human nature, the need to relate to an Other, that gives rise to religion. Religion, from this perspective, is found in the community that comes from the human desire to relate.

Needs That Are Met by Religion. Maslow (1962) formulated a hierarchical theory of human needs. Within this theory the six levels are physiological, safety, love and belonging, esteem, self-actualization, and transcendence needs. People cannot meet their higher needs until their lower needs are met. However, as soon as a person's lower needs are met, he strives to meet the higher ones.

Many of the needs met by religion can be viewed in terms of this theoretical model. Most religions offer some social welfare programs to help people meet their physiological needs for food and health. Religions also offer people love and a sense of belonging. Organized religions have long offered persons membership in a group; however, newer religions and cults now achieve this in various ways of peer pressure and harassment. Individuals find their need for esteem met in religion also. Most religious groups have parishioners from a range of socioeconomic classes, and individuals have the opportunity to relate to members of the same class as well as other classes. The ability to relate with others and utilize what psychologists call "social comparison" gives individuals a sense of self-esteem.

According to Maslow only a few people ever fulfill their needs for self-actualization and transcendence. Self-actualization is one's ability to fully realize his or her potential, particularly the ability to love and be loved. Transcendence is basically the spiritual search in life that goes beyond identity, individuality, and self-actualization. Most religions offer individuals opportunities for fulfillment in these areas. Of course, different religions vary in the degree to which they will tolerate divergent thinking, which is also part of this need.

Religion also offers fulfillment for other human needs. Intrapersonally it offers a person meaning in life, a sense of oneness with the universe, and a set of values. Interpersonally religion offers a person a sense of community with others and the fulfillment of relationship needs in areas such as authority, leadership, submission, servanthood, and altruism.

Integration and Conclusion. The response of the religious community to the behavioral sciences' explanation of the psychological roots of religion has covered the spectrum from ignorance, to acceptance, to outright rejection. Freud's reductionism, which views religion as the resolution of the oedipus complex, has usually been rejected as speculative. However, his perspective that unconscious forces play a part in religious behavior has been accepted by many Christians. Distorted views of God as a punitive or judgmental father have been traced to events in the early development of the person when he related to earthly parents who were harsh or judgmental. Freud's chief weakness was that he never considered the psychological sources of healthy religion that led the person to work and love well. In contrast, Erikson has proven helpful in the identification of life crises, which often accompany significant religious experiences such as conversion. However, Erikson also assumes that religion is a sign of regression in development and therefore represents immaturity. Thus, his theory of religious sources is not totally acceptable to most Christians.

The findings of Kohlberg have been embraced by a wide range of religious people as a biblically viable explanation of moral development. His theories are based on Piaget's concepts of cognitive development. Religious education has been the beneficiary of the correlation of moral development with cognitive developmental stages. For example, since it is not likely that a preadolescent will think abstractly, his need is for a concrete statement or experience of religion.

The existential and interpersonal statements of religious need probably are the most similar to those of the Bible. Encounters with one's finitude and with the infinite God are the heart of biblical expression, especially in the psalms. The great lack in existential psychology as it seeks to define religion is in relationship to the redemptive event of Christ. The Christian position is that one simply cannot establish a meaningful contact with God apart from Christ.

Many religious writers have identified with the human needs as defined by Maslow. The chief deficit of his theory, however, is its inherent self-centeredness. There is little focus on the human needs to give, to be a servant, or to generally promote the welfare of others, which are emphasized in Christianity. The self-actualized person and the sanctified person may appear the same behaviorally, but the motivation of the heart may differ.

Biblical data indicate that all people have a religious need (Rom. 1–3) and that this need is stimulated by both internal factors (e.g., conscience; Rom. 2:14–15) and external factors (e.g., general revelation; Rom. 1:20). Undoubtedly this religious need stems from the fact that all people are created in the image of God and therefore seek a relationship with the Creator (Gen. 1:27). Although we seek God as our Creator, he is the one who moved to restore a relationship with humanity through Jesus Christ (Rom. 3). Likewise he has instructed people individually and corporately (i.e., the church) to maintain relationships (1 John 4:7–21) and meet the needs of others (James 1:27).

Whether there is a one-to-one correspondence between these religious needs and those mentioned by psychological theories is open to question in many instances. More work needs to be done in defining the psychological base for religion. More work also needs to be done in defining a biblical theory of personality and human need. To date the emphasis has been on ontic qualities such as the heart, soul, mind, and body in the definition of the image of God in a person. The alternative that the image is relational and functional, defined in terms of how people give and receive love and engage in productive work may be a more fruitful source of exploration for a biblical psychology.

References

Buber, M. *I and thou.* New York: Scribners, 1937.

Erikson, E. H. *Childhood and society.* New York: Norton, 1950.

Frankl, V. E. *Man's search for meaning.* Boston: Beacon Press, 1962.

Freud, S. *The future of an illusion.* New York: Liveright, 1928.

James, W. *The varieties of religious experiences.* New York: Macmillan, 1961.

Kohlberg, L. *The philosophy of moral development.* San Francisco: Harper & Row, 1981.

Maslow, A. H. *Toward a psychology of being.* Princeton, N.J.: Van Nostrand, 1962.

Additional Readings

Fleck, J. R., & Carter, J. D. (Eds.). *Psychology and Christianity: Integrative readings.* Nashville: Abingdon, 1981.

Malony, H. N. (Ed.). *Current perspectives in the psychology of religion.* Grand Rapids: Eerdmans, 1977.

C. D. CAMPBELL and C. B. JOHNSON

See PSYCHOLOGY OF RELIGION

Psychological Types: Jung's View. Jung, Austrian analyst and one of Freud's principal students, developed a system of personality assessment in which he classified people into various types utilizing three polarities: extravert versus introvert, sensing versus intuitive, and thinking versus feeling (Jung, 1971). This system of personality types has been further developed by Isabelle Myers-Briggs, who added a fourth polarity, judging versus perceptive, and with her associates developed the Myers-Briggs Type Indicator, a psychological test designed to assess personality in terms of these four polarities (Myers, 1962). In this system a person's type is some combination of these four polarities—e.g., an extraverted-intuitive-feeling-judging type. In all there are 16 possible types in her system. Jung focused on only the 8 basic types associated with the first three polarities.

Extraversion versus introversion. Jung suggested that a person has as a basic orientation in life either an external, outward, and thus extraverted style or an internal, inward, and thus introverted style. Jung saw himself as an introvert along with most writers and other philosophers. He suggested, with reservation and without data, that one's inclination to be extraverted or introverted was inherited. An extravert is interested in and engages the visible world of reality; the introvert is interested in the universe within himself. The extravert is interested in breadth; the introvert in depth. The extravert usually has more relationships but these tend to be less intense; the introvert seeks intimacy from one or two people. The extravert is public and flexible; the introvert is private and more inflexible.

It is in this polarity that Jung has made the most valuable addition to understanding personality, for here he suggests that it is equally valuable and acceptable to be an introvert as an extravert, although society at large seems to value the latter. Myers suggests that only 25% of the population is introverted, the rest extraverted. The introvert enjoys and needs solitude and depth in relationships to be satisfied and productive in life; the extravert needs external stimulation and publicity. Thus, the extravert is more dependent on approval, the introvert inclined toward melancholy.

Sensing Versus Intuiting. What Jung called the irrational part of one's personality is the perceptive function, the part that gathers information. One can collect information primarily by using one's senses—i.e., by seeing and hearing. Likewise, one can collect information primarily by using intuition. An intuitive person uses his hunches and imagination to "observe" the world. It is as if he experiences a perfect mirror of the world inside, and he needs only to see more clearly his internal experience to properly understand the external world.

The sensing person is inclined to be concrete, fact oriented, practical, and realistic, while the intuitive person is abstract, fantasy oriented, creative, and imaginative. Sensing people understand the present in light of the past, while intuitives understand the present by speculating on the future. Intuitive persons think of possibilities and look for relationships between things or people; sensing people watch for facts and are more aware of the independent functions of individual elements in a system.

Thinking Versus Feeling. By far the most difficult function to understand is the so-called rational function, whereby one evaluates the information collected. While Jung believed the extraverted or introverted approach to life to be inherited, he believed both the perceptive and evaluative functions to be learned. One could collect information by means of thinking (a rational, intellectual, objective, and impersonal way) or by feeling (an internal, emotional, subjective, and personal way). Thus a person who is primarily a thinker is analytical, while one primarily a feeler is synthetical. A thinker takes apart to find truth; a feeler puts together to find truth. Justice is important to a thinker, mercy to a feeler; thus principles are foremost to the former, values to the latter. The thinker would do what is clearly right regardless of his feelings or those of others; the feeler would do what would least likely offend the feelings of anyone. Feeling in Jung's terminology tends to be an internal function because it is not definable in objective terms, while thinking, as an objective function, is more external.

It is important to note that this polarity is emotional and that, in a way, thinking and feeling are means of displaying the emotion that lies under all decisions. Thus feeling people are not more emotional; thinkers are not emotionless. Feelers show their emotions; thinkers keep their emotions private.

The Shadow. Jung believed that the conscious part of one's personality is the visible personality type (e.g., extraverted-intuitive-feeling), while the unconscious part is the complement, or what he called the shadow of one's personality. The shadow is primitive and thus less developed, and is also more volatile and uncontrolled. If unexplored, one's shadow can intrude into personality unexpectedly and harmfully, usually without compromise, as would typify an infantile expression. The purpose of life, in Jung's view, is to explore and develop one's shadow.

A person has all components of each of three Jungian polarities (or four Briggs polarities). When there is a very strong visible trait, the unconscious opposite trait is equally strong and activates itself in some kind of neurotic form. For example, a very sensing person in a threatening or unprotected moment may have exaggerated intuition and go with that intuition, defining it as a "sensible" observation.

The Combinations. Jung also described the general qualities of persons with each of the eight possible combinations of the three basic personality polarities.

The *extraverted-thinking* type is described as moral, rigid, objective, justice oriented, and truth oriented. He is less interested in religion than other types but is visibly altruistic. However, the unconscious part of this type may lead him to episodes of unexpected compromise because he is so exacting of himself, and he is secretly self-seeking. The end justifies the means. He is usually visibly positive and productive, unconsciously negative and even lazy.

The *extraverted-feeling* type Jung sees as primarily a female phenomenon. It is distinguished sometimes by an abhorrence of thinking, a certain absolutist or opinionated orientation, and an interest in being allowed to be free. This type is often generous, and in Briggs's terms is sometimes a vendor of good works. There is sometimes a lack of depth to commitments and relationships because they are made so easily. This type needs to see things to believe them and is overly dependent on the object sometimes to the exclusion of the

subject. Extraverted-feeling types are often hysterical when neurotic.

Jung indicates the *extraverted-sensing* type to be most interested in what is visibly real. Usually male, he is objective and practical, often to a fault. His aim is concrete enjoyment, and he is often loving and lovable, although deep love exchange is sometimes hard to maintain. He is physical in his orientation: he loves sexually, commits physically, and is often physically malaffected. On the negative side he is inclined to projections and criticism, as he sees only what is obvious.

The *extraverted-intuitive* type is easily committed to a cause or idea, but is not always consistent. He trusts his own intuitions at the risk of rational judgment. He is not always interested in others' welfare and can even exploit others unconsciously. He promotes new things and inspires courage. He often does not stay around long enough to reap the benefits of his work. His projections are even more severe than other extraverted types. In neurotic form he is compulsive.

The *introverted-thinking* type is by nature a philosopher, a thinker par excellence. Jung saw this type as valuing the so-called subject at the expense of the object. He may appear amiable, but he always seems distant, analytical, even superior. He is often calculating, and can be a formidable opponent because the genesis of his ideas is internal while his expression reflects thinking rather than feeling. He is usually stubborn, headstrong, and unamenable to influence. He is relatively uninterested in social interaction and, although concerned by his frequent social offenses, he seldom changes his demeanor. Introverted-thinking types are usually male and have a vague fear of women.

The *introverted-feeling* type is dominated by internality in that both introversion and feeling are internal functions. This type has had a sort of vision which he or she seeks to discover or create in visible reality. As still waters run deep, so this type has depth. Expressions of feelings are infrequent, perhaps because they are so deeply felt. Consequently these people are frequently misinterpreted as having no feeling. She (Jung's choice of pronoun) is often convinced of what other people think and is often unshakable in her opinion.

The first of the two introverted "irrational" types is *introverted-sensing*. This individual is guided by internal sensation, so that acquaintances often feel devalued in his presence. He is inclined toward fears and ambiguity, but he can also be especially responsible if he also possesses good judgment. Neurotic forms are compulsive.

The second is the *introverted-intuitive*. For him (usual gender) internal images are most important, and, in severe cases, revered. Thus he can be brilliant in perceiving symbols, possibilities, subjective experiences, and the indefinable. However, he is equally prone to visionary error. He professes but seldom debates. He rarely "believes"; rather, he "knows." Neurotic forms are subtle dependency and hypersensitivity.

Evaluation. Research on Jung's typology has been relatively sparse but generally supportive of his hypotheses. The majority of studies have employed the Myers-Briggs Type Indicator, which, as indicated earlier, includes one additional polarity and eight additional personality types. This test is, however, a very useful device for the measurement of the Jungian types in that it includes both attitudes and functions and has been well standardized.

Using the Myers-Briggs Type Indicator, Stricker and Ross (1963) showed that occupational interests among college students were related in many instances to the Jungian typology. Carlson (1980) has shown the kinds of significant differences in memories that introverted thinkers and extraverted feelers report, which are in accordance with the typology's hypotheses. Similarly Kilmann and Taylor (1974) obtained the predicted differences between introverts and extraverts with regard to the acceptance or rejection of a group learning experience. However, there is research that is inconsistent with Jung's view, and further research is needed.

Jung's system has stimulated interest in personality typology. When augmented by the Myers-Briggs additions, his work is a very useful tool in understanding differences among people. One weakness of his analysis is the absence of a concerted effort to deal with psychogenesis of types. Likewise, his focus is largely negative, following all the early analysts. He does not present much of the adaptive aspects of the various types, nor does he deal with interactions among types. Nevertheless, no other system of personality assessment is so incisive, useful, and provocative.

References

Carlson, R. Studies on Jungian typology: II. Representations of the personal world. *Journal of Personality and Social Psychology*, 1980, *38*, 801–810.
Jung, C. G. *Psychological types*. Princeton, N.J.: Princeton University Press, 1971.
Kilmann, R. H., & Taylor, V. A contingency approach to laboratory learning: Psychological types versus experiential norms. *Human Relations*, 1974, *27*, 891–909.
Myers, I. *The Myers-Briggs Type Indicator*. Princeton, N.J.: Educational Testing Service, 1962.
Stricker, L. J., & Ross, J. Intercorrelations and reliability of the Myers-Briggs Type Indicator scales. *Psychological Reports*, 1963, *12*, 287–293.

R. B. Johnson

See Introversion-Extraversion; Factor Theories of Personality.

Psychologist. Unlike the term *physician* or even *psychiatrist*, the word *psychologist* is laden with ambiguities. Just about everyone knows that a physician is someone who holds an accredited medical degree and is legally sanctioned to practice medicine. Many people also understand that a psychiatrist is a physician who specializes in the diagnosis and treatment of mental disorders. Few persons can tell you exactly what psychologist is.

The title *psychologist* has been used in two general senses. One refers to someone who studies psychological processes and the other refers to someone who ameliorates psychological difficulties. What adds to the confusion is that almost everyone is, in some sense, an expert on his or her own psychological processes, and, furthermore, the legal regulation of the practice of psychology has been lax. Only within the past couple of decades have the majority of states instituted licensing or certification statutes that control who can, and who cannot, represent himself or herself to the public as a psychologist.

Perhaps the best definition of a psychologist is someone who is eligible for full membership in the American Psychological Association. To achieve such eligibility one must earn a doctorate that is primarily psychological in nature from an accredited educational institution. Earning such a doctorate ordinarily implies that the candidate must complete a psychological dissertation that represents an original research contribution. While only about half the physicians in this country belong to the American Medical Association, nearly all legitimate psychologists hold membership in the American Psychological Association. Further, it should be noted that the Ph.D. is primarily a research degree. However, in the case of clinical and counseling psychologists a doctoral psychology program also includes substantial training and experience in applied areas. The same is true of some other areas of applied psychology (e.g., school psychology, industrial/organizational psychology), which also include internships within the doctoral program.

There are many different kinds of psychologists. Those most familiar to the general public are clinical psychologists, who ordinarily complete at least one full year of hospital internship work and a number of other preinternship clinical experiences. Their graduate training typically includes courses in such areas as psychopathology, clinical assessment, and psychotherapy. Many clinical psychologists have had considerably more training than this, and in some states it is necessary for the psychologist to complete an additional year of clinical training beyond the doctorate in order to be licensed for independent practice.

Most closely related to clinical psychologists are counseling psychologists. While there is much overlap in their actual training experiences, counseling psychologists are oriented somewhat more toward the normal while clinical psychologists are oriented somewhat more toward the abnormal.

The other kinds of psychologists described here ordinarily undertake little or no training in psychodiagnosis or psychotherapy and therefore should not be engaged in providing such services to the general public. There are, of course, some psychologists first trained in other than clinical areas who later become qualified as clinicians. The American Psychological Association, however, has fairly stringent criteria for such additional education to qualify someone as a clinician. Simply completing a clinical internship is ordinarily not sufficient.

Social psychologists study how people influence one another. They are especially concerned with how normal people interact. Many social psychologists work in academic settings, and some work in industry, in the military, or in consulting firms. Social psychologists are expert in such areas as attitude formation and change; how we form impressions of other people; factors that contribute to effective group performance; and the nature of altruism, aggression, bargaining, negotiation, competition, and cooperation. There is probably a close (but largely unexplored) connection between normal and abnormal behavior and therefore between what social and clinical psychologists study.

Social and personality psychologists are closely related. The close relationship between the two domains is reflected in the fact that of the 15 or so journals published by the American Psychological Association a single publication (*Journal of Personality and Social Psychology*) is devoted to both areas. Yet while many social psychologists have what might be termed a sociological or social theory orientation, nearly all personality psychologists are concerned with the functioning of the individual. Personality psychologists nevertheless study such socially relevant phenomena as the development of moral behavior, the nature of interpersonal anxiety, and the extent to which an individual's behavior is consistent in different situations. Personality psychologists also concern themselves with the nature-nurture (environment-heredity) controversy; the relationships among thinking, feeling, and acting; and sex role differences.

Developmental psychologists are concerned with how personality comes to be what it is. While developmental specialists have shown increasing interest in the extent to which people change or remain the same throughout their lifetimes, developmental psychologists have traditionally focused their research on children. Again there is overlap across specialties. For example, developmental psychologists, like personality psychologists, are concerned with how people acquire the values they hold.

Physiological psychologists are experts in determining the psychological effects of physiological conditions. There is a technical difference between physiological psychology and psychophysiology. The former refers to the mental and behavioral effects of physical phenomena (e.g., how brain tumors impair problem solving), and the latter refers to physical phenomena as reflections of psychological states (e.g., how electrical skin conductance reflects stress). In practice, however, the line between the two gets blurred. Physiological psychologists conduct research into the location and functions of various brain centers, the electrical activity of the brain, and other such topics as how color vision works and the effects on personality of various chemical substances. Neuropsychologists are typically clinical psychologists with extra specialization in the functioning of the nervous system, although some neuropsychologists are simply physiological psychologists.

Industrial/organizational psychologists often work for large companies, helping them to develop better work environments, construct personnel screening procedures, and trouble-shoot business problems of a psychological nature. Most industrial organizational psychologists are familiar with the complicated steps necessary to develop good aptitude and ability tests. Therefore they are often in charge of personnel testing programs.

Cognitive psychologists study how human beings think, usually with special attention to how people solve problems. Often they are especially interested in human intelligence and its measurement. Most cognitive psychologists—e.g., social, personality, developmental, and physiological psychologists—work in educational institutions, usually colleges and universities. However, some work for think tanks such as Rand Corporation.

Mathematical psychologists are knowledgeable about statistical methodologies and research methods. During the past 50 years highly sophisticated ways to analyze psychological data have emerged, and few research psychologists can hope to master all of these methods. Consequently some psychologists devote all their professional time to the study of mathematical methods and to the development of mathematical models. Such models usually take the form of equations for predicting some kind of behavioral outcome—e.g., performance in school or voting behavior. While some mathematical psychologists also have a substantive area of research (e.g., attitude research), many quantitative psychologists are concerned only with statistical methods.

Experimental psychologists can specialize in almost anything, but usually they conduct laboratory research to investigate such processes as sensation and perception. They are ordinarily expert in the methods of psychophysics, which have to do with ways in which sensations and perceptions are related to physical phenomena. Like most of the other kinds of psychologists mentioned, including cognitive and mathematical specialists, experimental psychologists ordinarily work in academic settings. Virtually all university psychologists, however, conduct some kind of research.

In some states psychologists are licensed only if they offer clinical services to the general public. In other states many kinds of psychologists are licensed—e.g., industrial psychologists who want to establish private consulting practices. In still other states the license granted to a psychologist is a generic one, and thus all psychologists who offer their services to the general public are given the same license, with exhortations not to practice beyond the limits of their training. Unfortunately, generic licensure is not always an effective way to regulate the conduct of psychological practice, and some psychologists continue to operate in areas beyond their competence.

The relationship between psychology and psychiatry has already been noted, and it may be useful to look at the roles of social workers and marriage counselors. While a Ph.D. ordinarily takes at least three years to earn, and in the case of a clinical or counseling psychologist four years or more, an individual can obtain a master's degree in social work within two years of continuous full-time study. There are many kinds of social workers. Only psychiatric social workers are trained to render psychotherapeutic services. Moreover, in many states a person may be employed as a social worker with only a bachelor's degree, but the job functionings of this person will entail little more than the dispensing of public assistance monies.

The practice of marriage counseling is poorly regulated in most states. Consequently, while many marriage therapists are well trained, many are not. Membership in the American Association of Marriage and Family Therapists is generally a good indication of competence in this specialty area.

Finally, there is a distinction between clinical counseling or psychotherapy and pastoral counseling. The functions of clinical and counseling psychologists are in many ways different from the functions of ministerial counselors.

Additional Readings

American Psychological Association. *Standards for providers of psychological services* (Rev. ed.). Washington, D.C.: Author, 1977.

American Psychological Association. *Psychology as a health care profession.* Washington, D.C.: Author, 1979.

American Psychological Association. *Careers in psychology.* Washington, D.C.: Author, 1980.

American Psychological Association. *Ethical principles of psychologists* (rev. ed.). Washington, D.C.: Author, 1981.

C. W. McLemore

Psychology, History of. In 1907 Herman Ebbinghaus penned the epigram, "Psychology has a long past but only a short history," a statement which in many respects remains true today. Psychology's past goes back at least 2,000 years into the early beginnings of philosophy. Its history goes back only to 1879, when Wilhelm Wundt founded the first psychology laboratory in Germany.

The Roots of Modern Psychology. Three disciplines played key roles in the growth and development of psychology: philosophy, physiology, and psychophysics. Most surveys of the history of psychology trace the philosophical beginnings at least as far back as Plato (ca. 427–347 B.C.) and Aristotle (384–323 B.C.). Plato's clear statement of the difference between mind and body gave philosophy and psychology one of their most enduring problems. His teaching that persons profoundly influence one another engendered the seeds of an environmentalism that reached its peak in the behaviorism school founded by John B. Watson. Aristotle wrote extensively on such "modern" psychological topics as memory, sleep, thinking, intelligence, motivation, emotion, growth, and development. His concept of the mind as a blank wax tablet (*tabula rasa*) upon which experience writes resulted in the doctrine that all knowledge comes from experience. Aristotle's three primary laws of association—similarity, contrast, and contiguity—provided the basis for the school of associationism.

René Descartes (1596–1650) freed philosophy from the bonds of theological and traditional dogmas and helped to establish the dominance of a new force—empiricism, the search for knowledge by the observation of nature itself. British empiricism and associationism, as represented in the works of Thomas Hobbes (1588–1679), John Locke (1632–1704), George Berkeley (1685–1753), David Hume (1711–1776), David Hartley (1705–1757), James Mill (1773–1836), and others, provided the basic subject matter for the newly emerging science of psychology. However, in order to move beyond theory toward a natural science of human nature, psychology needed to be able to attack the subject matter experimentally. The means for this attack came from the new field of experimental physiology.

Physiology developed into an experimental discipline during the early part of the nineteenth century. A critical discovery occurred in 1850. Hermann von Helmholtz (1821–1894), a German physicist and physiologist and one of the greatest scientists of the nineteenth century, measured the speed of the neural impulse. Others had said that such a measurement was impossible. The nerve impulse traveled too quickly to be measured. Maybe it was even instantaneous. Helmholtz calculated the speed to be a relatively slow 50–100 meters per second. His discovery suggested the possibility of isolating and measuring psychological events. Perhaps the mind could be measured and understood scientifically. Other physiological research studies (e.g., the localization of psychological functions in particular parts of the brain, the study of sensation and perception) provided additional impetus for the development of the new science of psychology.

The third root of modern psychology—psychophysics—developed out of the efforts of Gustav Fechner (1801–1887) to make his philosophy an exact science. Fechner sought to establish in a quantitative way the relationship between mind and body or between the psychological world and the physical world. In 1860 he published *Elements of Psychophysics*, which contained his calculations of the quantitative relationship between stimulus intensity and sensation. Early in the nineteenth century Immanuel Kant, the German philosopher, had maintained that psychology could not become a science because it was impossible to measure or experiment upon psychological phenomena and processes (Schultz, 1981). Fechner's work, combined with Helmholtz's, helped to dispel the pessimism of Kant.

The Founding of Modern Psychology. In 1879 Wilhelm Wundt (1832–1920) established the first formal psychological laboratory, in Leipzig, Germany. This marked the beginning of experimental psychology as an independent science. It took a man of great courage, with a solid background in experimental physiology and philosophy, to combine these two disciplines into a new science. Previously, in a handbook, *Principles of Physiological Psychology*, Wundt had outlined his goal of marking out a new domain of science. In 1881 he established a journal, *Philosophical Studies*, which was to be the official organ of his laboratory and the new science. With a handbook, a laboratory designed expressly for psychological research, and a scholarly journal, the new science of psychology was off to a good start.

Wundt's efforts attracted considerable attention. Students flocked to the Leipzig laboratory and to Wundt's lectures. At one time he had over 600 students in a class. Many of the students who came from the United States returned to found laboratories of their own. G. Stanley Hall, James McKeen Cattell, and Edward Bradford Titchener are just three of the many prominent pioneers of psychology who studied with Wundt.

Wundt believed that the subject matter of psychology was immediate experience. He wanted to analyze consciousness and experience into elemental components, in much the same way as the natural scientists were analyzing their subject matter. In a sense Wundt set out to produce a chemistry of the mind.

Since Wundt defined psychology as the science of experience, the method of psychology had to involve the observation of experience. Because experience is only observable by the person who has it, Wundt saw introspection or self-observation as his primary method. In order to maintain strict control he established explicit rules for the proper use of introspection in his laboratory. His trained observers acquired the necessary skills through a long period of apprenticeship and training. Observers in Wundt's reaction time experiments performed about 10,000 introspective observations before he considered them to be skilled enough to provide valid data (Boring, 1953).

Many critics give Wundt credit for founding psychology but charge him with leading it in the wrong direction. Introspection receives the brunt of much of the criticism. However, in recent years many of Wundt's later writings have received some long-overdue attention. Modern researchers are often surprised at the relevance of many of his ideas to current thinking. Wundt's three-factor theory of feeling, his view of schizophrenia, his theory of language, and his studies of apperception are being viewed with new interest.

The Early Schools of Psychology. Like other sciences in their early years psychology experienced a period when groups of psychologists became associated with the ideas and interests of particular leaders. These schools of psychology, as they are called, usually worked on similar problems and shared the same theoretical and methodological orientation. These schools often experienced a period of competition, growth, and ascendancy, followed by decline and replacement by a newer school.

Associationism. Associationism represents a principle of psychology more than it does a school of psychology. The principle derives from such philosophical questions as, How do we know? and Where do complex ideas come from? To these questions the British empiricist philosophers gave the following answers: We know by means of the senses. Complex ideas such as patriotism, which cannot be directly sensed, must come from the association of simpler ideas.

The associationistic movement received substantial support from the work of three men—Hermann Ebbinghaus, Ivan Pavlov, and Edward L. Thorndike.

Ebbinghaus (1850–1909) made his contribution only a few years after Wundt had declared that it was impossible to study the higher mental processes in an experimental way. Ebbinghaus examined the formation of associations by using nonsense syllables and showed that complex phenomena such as human learning and memory could be studied by carefully controlled research. Almost a century after publication many of his findings (e.g., his curve of forgetting) are still valid and cited by psychologists.

Pavlov (1849–1936), a Nobel Prize–winning physiologist, investigated the higher nervous centers of the brain using the technique of conditioning. In his research Pavlov shifted the emphasis from the association of ideas to the association of stimulus-response connections. His use of precise and objective measures created a trend in psychology toward greater objectivity in subject matter and methodology. Today the school of behaviorism most readily reflects the influence of Pavlov.

Thorndike (1874–1949) developed the best example of an associationistic system in psychology. To him psychology was the study of stimulus-response connections or associations. While Thorndike began his career studying learning in laboratory animals, he soon shifted his interest to human learning and became America's first educational psychologist.

Associationism survives today as a methodological tool, if not as a systematic position. Most psychologists view the association of variables as a fundamental task of science.

Structuralism. Wundt's founding of experimental psychology marked the beginning of the structuralism school. During the first two or three decades of psychology, structural psychology was *the* psychology. Structural psychologists proposed to analyze the structure of the human mind by means of introspection.

For Wundt the task of psychology was threefold: 1) to analyze conscious processes into basic elements; 2) to discover how these elements become connected; and 3) to determine the laws of connection.

Structuralism provided psychology with a strong scientific identity within the academic community. It also served as a ready target for the criticisms of the later schools—functionalism, behaviorism, and Gestalt psychology. These newer schools flourished as they organized their efforts against structuralism's strong orthodox position. Structuralism died of its own narrow dogmatism. Unfortunately it lacked the support that practical applications might have given. The contemporary role of structuralism is virtually nonexistent. Modern psychology accepts only the basic scientific attitude of structuralism.

Functionalism. Functionalism represents the first distinctly American school of psychology. It began in the psychology of William James (1842–1910) and shortly provided the bridge to Watson's behaviorism. The functionalists defined psychology as the study of the mind as it functions in adapting the organism to its environment. According to Woodworth and Sheehan (1964, p. 15), "a psychology that attempts to give an accurate and systematic answer to the question, 'What do men do?' and then goes on to the questions, 'How do they do it?' and 'Why do they do it?' is called a *functional psychology.*"

While James served as the pioneer of the functionalist movement, John Dewey (1859–1952), a respected philosopher, educator, and psychologist, wrote a paper in 1896 on the reflex arc, which marks the founding of functionalism. Other psychologists at the University of Chicago, especially James Angell (1869–1949) and Harvey Carr (1873–1954), molded and developed functionalism into a leading school of psychology.

By opposing the narrowness and restrictions of structuralism, functionalism performed an important service to American psychology. It expanded methodology beyond the technique of introspection by collecting data, using questionnaires, mental tests, physiological research, and objective descriptions of behavior. In addition functional psychologists pioneered in some of the most important areas of psychology: child psychology, animal and human learning, educational psychology, and psychopathology.

Functionalism no longer exists as a distinct school, even though psychology in the United States is largely functional in its orientation. Functionalism was such an overwhelming success that it was absorbed into contemporary psychology.

Behaviorism. At the age of 35 John B. Watson (1878–1958) led the revolt that produced the most influential and controversial school of American psychology. While the movement from structuralism to functionalism has been described as evolutionary, the movement to behaviorism was revolutionary. Watson declared the old order to be a failure. In a short time he succeeded in his efforts to destroy it.

Watson made the basic tenets of behaviorism simple and straightforward. He defined psychology as the scientific study of observable behavior. He wanted an objective science of behavior. Mentalistic concepts such as mind and consciousness, which had been carried over from philosophy, were to be discarded. The chief method of Watson's behaviorism was the conditioned reflex; however, he accepted and used other techniques for the observation of overt behavior. Introspection was relegated to the dust heap. An indication of Watson's rapid acceptance came with his election to the presidency of the American Psychological Association only two years after starting the revolt.

While Watson was the chief promoter and propagandist for behaviorism, four later psychologists expanded the horizons and developed subschools of behaviorism during the 1930s. Most of their influence has come through their theories of learning.

Edward Chace Tolman (1886–1959) rejected the strict stimulus-response theory of Watson in favor of a more eclectic viewpoint, often called purposive behaviorism. The molar aspects of behavior (i.e., the total response of the whole organism) rather than the elemental units studied by Watson received his attention. In this sense his theory combined the concepts of behaviorism and Gestalt psychology.

From his systematic study of learning Clark Leonard Hull (1884–1952) developed a complex hypothetico-deductive theory of behavior. Perhaps the most serious barrier to an understanding of Hull's theory is its intrinsic difficulty and complexity. Nevertheless, he exerted a great deal of influence on the study of learning and behavior.

Starting from a behavioristic orientation Edwin Ray Guthrie (1886–1959) influenced psychology through the formulation of an extremely simple learning theory. He promoted a theory of learning that depended on one principle: contiguity. All learning occurred because of the contiguity of a stimulus and a response in one trial. Repetition and reinforcement played no essential role in his system.

B. F. Skinner (1904–) ranks today as the most influential of the behaviorists. He developed a strictly descriptive form of behaviorism that is basically atheoretical. Intervening variables and physiological processes are not a part of his system, which is often called the empty-organism approach. Operant conditioning provides the focus of most of Skinner's work on learning and behavior. Among his most notable research studies are those dealing with schedules of reinforcement, verbal behavior, and behavior modification. Teaching machines and programmed learning represent two areas where his work has had a profound impact.

Of all the early schools of psychology in the United States behaviorism provoked the most criticism, attained the greatest popularity among psychologists, and exerted the most influence. It remains a powerful force in psychology today.

Gestalt psychology. As Watson started his revolt in the United States against structuralism and functionalism, a new movement in Germany revolted against Wundt. This movement, Gestalt psychology, eventually took on behaviorism as well. Basically it was a revolt against artifical analysis and elementism.

Max Wertheimer (1880–1943) founded Gestalt psychology, with assistance from Kurt Koffka (1886–1941) and Wolfgang Köhler (1887–1967). The perception of apparent movement provided Wertheimer with a chance to explain a phenomenon that the structuralists could not explain. His explanation was so simple and yet ingenious that it precipitated a new psychological school. According to Wertheimer apparent movement existed as a real phenomenon, irreducible to simpler sensations or elements of any kind.

The Gestalt psychologists defined psychology as the study of the immediate experience of the whole organism. While most of the traditional subject areas of psychology (e.g., learning, memory, personality) were studied, perception received the most attention. Most of the data for Gestalt psychology came from immediate, unanalyzed experience obtained through introspection. However, behavioral data were used, especially in studies of learning and problem solving.

The basic principle of Gestalt psychology developed out of a concern for the whole-part relationship. To the Gestaltists the whole is not just greater than the sum of its parts, nor is it any simple function of the parts. The whole is different from the sum of its parts. The whole dominates the parts, determines their characteristics, and constitutes the basic datum of psychology. Psychology, according to the Gestaltists, should study the molar aspects of behavior and experience.

The Gestalt school created an interest in problems that had been previously ignored. The Gestaltists initiated the study of insight and problem solving in animals and humans. They outlined the principles according to which our perceptions are organized. And they took a fresh look at conscious experience. Contemporary interest in cognitive psychology and phenomenology is traceable to the Gestalt movement.

Psychoanalysis. None of the other schools of psychology or their leaders (with the possible exception of behaviorism during the heyday of Watson) has enjoyed the popular appeal of psychoanalysis and Sigmund Freud (1856–1939). In fact, it is not unusual for lay persons to consider psychology and psychoanalysis synonymous terms. However, psychoanalysis as a school developed very differently from the other schools. It started outside of the university setting, expressed little interest in most of the traditional subject areas of psychology,

and focused almost entirely on the etiology, development, and treatment of abnormal behavior. While psychoanalysis has never been received enthusiastically by academic psychology, it has exerted considerable influence on psychology as well as many other disciplines.

The publication of *Studies in Hysteria* by Sigmund Freud and Josef Breuer in 1895 marks the beginning of the psychoanalytic school. Five years later Freud published *The Interpretation of Dreams*, which is now considered his most significant work. Shortly thereafter Freud's views began to attract attention. At first there was only a small and devoted coterie of followers. But gradually the following increased, and the movement became international in scope. In 1909 Freud accepted the invitation of G. Stanley Hall to speak at the twentieth anniversary celebration of Clark University. This was Freud's only visit to the United States. During the next decade the ranks of psychoanalysis were torn by disagreements and defections, but Freud's fame and influence continued to increase until his death.

Many of the basic ideas of psychoanalysis received initial exposure in *Studies in Hysteria*. Among these ideas were the importance of the unconscious in the development of the neuroses, the role of early traumatic sexual experiences, the importance of symbolism, and the relevance of transference. Freud's therapeutic techniques represent one of his most original contributions. After discarding hypnosis he developed the technique of free association, which consisted of instructing the patient to say whatever came to mind, without selection or rearrangement. Freud regarded dreams as "the royal road to the unconscious." By analyzing the symbolic content of dreams he believed he could gain greater access to the unconscious processes. Awareness of the unconscious forces, according to Freud, should enable the patient to free himself from those forces and lead a more rational and satisfying life.

Two early defectors from Freudian psychoanalysis, Carl Gustav Jung (1875–1961) and Alfred Adler (1870–1937), formulated their own theories. At one time Jung was the heir apparent of the psychoanalytic movement. In fact, Freud referred to him as the "crown prince." Jung's defection resulted from his disagreement on two major points. First, he redefined libido as a generalized life energy as opposed to Freud's sexual energy. He also believed that a person is not primarily determined by childhood experiences. He stressed the importance of future goals and aspirations as well as the past. Many of Jung's ideas are novel and thought provoking, such as his archetypes, which are a part of the collective unconscious. Basically Jung's theory, which he called analytical psychology, offers a much more optimistic view of human nature than Freud's deterministic view.

Adler's individual psychology developed out of his criticism of Freud's emphasis on sexual factors. In the theory Adler, like Jung, focused on the future rather than the past. Instead of dividing the personality into parts—such as id, ego, and superego—Adler stressed the unity of personality. He also emphasized the importance of social forces rather than biological forces in the shaping of human personality. According to Adler the basic goal or motivation underlying human behavior is a striving for superiority. For him the unconscious was much less important than the conscious in the determination of behavior. Contemporary psychoanalysis incorporates many of Adler's ideas, and he has had a significant influence on the development of humanistic psychology.

Karen Horney (1885–1952), Erich Fromm (1900–1980), and Harry Stack Sullivan (1892–1949) represent some of the more recent developers of psychoanalytic theory. Each of them has stressed the societal and interpersonal origins of neurotic behavior and made important contributions to the development of neo-Freudian psychoanalysis.

While psychoanalysis has been criticized for deficient methodology and a lack of scientific rigor, it remains an important force in modern psychology. Even Boring (1950), the historian of experimental psychology, calls Freud "the greatest originator of all, the agent of the *Zeitgeist* who accomplished the invasion of psychology by the principle of the unconscious process" (p. 743). Among the contributions of psychoanalysis to psychology several deserve mention: 1) it opened up new areas for research such as sex and the unconscious; 2) it suggested the importance of childhood and genetic factors in personality development; 3) it gave impetus to the study of motivation; and 4) it presented evidence for a number of defense mechanisms. Despite its appeal and acceptance by the general public, many academic psychologists consider psychoanalysis outside the mainstream of psychological thought.

The Postschool Era and Contemporary Developments. After the demise or assimilation of the earlier schools of psychology the later schools have demonstrated more staying power. There are still psychologists who identify their interests as Gestalt in orientation, and significant numbers of psychologists re-

gard themselves to be in the behavioristic or psychoanalytic tradition. However, many splinter groups have developed since the days of Watson and Freud.

Within behaviorism one of the most significant recent developments is referred to as the cognitive revolution. All behaviorists do not regard words such as *mind, consciousness,* and *feeling* as taboo. Increasingly since the early 1960s there has been a return to the study of consciousness. While behaviorism continues as a dominant force in American psychology, it is a different brand of behaviorism than that promoted by Watson and Skinner during the first 50 years of the school.

The fragmentation within psychoanalysis has been more extensive than the divisions within behaviorism. All behaviorists agree that some form of behavior should be the primary focus of study, but all psychoanalysts do not agree on the importance of the unconscious or the relevance of sex and aggression as motivators of behavior. Recent developments within psychoanalysis include ego psychology, object relations theory, and self psychology, each marked by some major departures from classical Freudian thought.

The closest approximation to a new school of psychology is the movement called humanistic psychology or the third force in psychology. Beginning in the early 1950s humanistic psychologists emphasized several themes: the importance of conscious experience as the primary phenomenon in the study of human beings; an emphasis on such human qualities as creativity, choice, and self-realization; a concern for the dignity and worth of man; an emphasis on meaningfulness in psychological research; and an interest in the development of individual human potential. Many of these themes can be found in the writings of earlier psychologists, but the humanistic psychologists have molded them into a movement. Existential psychology and phenomenological psychology share many of the same themes with humanistic psychology.

Several early trends in psychology continue to be important in modern psychology. Empiricism and quantification receive widespread support and emphasis. The search for the physiological correlates of behavior remains a powerful force. But perhaps the most dramatic trend is the trend toward professionalism.

Lightner Witmer founded the first psychological clinic in 1896 at the University of Pennsylvania, and in the 1930s almost all psychologists were still in academic positions.

Twenty years later the majority of psychologists could be found working outside the academic setting. The First and Second World Wars created a sudden need for professional psychologists to do psychological testing and to treat psychological problems. The community mental health movement, along with state hospitals and veterans hospitals, created additional positions for clinical psychologists. The demand for trained clinicians coming out of graduate school still seems to exceed the supply.

Industrial psychology represents another important growth area for professional psychology. Personnel psychology, human factors engineering, and consumer psychology are just three of the many areas of specialization. One of psychology's most pressing problems in the 1980s is the tension between the professional branch and the academic/scientific branch of psychology.

Conclusions. Modern twentieth-century psychology is a rapidly changing discipline. All aspects of human behavior provide subject matter for the study and application of psychology. The movement of psychology into such diverse fields as law, art, religion, and forensic medicine illustrates the breadth of the discipline. And in the process the discipline of psychology shows signs of becoming more open, tolerant, and human.

References

Boring, E. G. *A history of experimental psychology* (2nd ed.). New York: Appleton, 1950.
Boring, E. G. A history of introspection. *Psychological Bulletin*, 1953, 50, 169–189.
Schultz, D. *A history of modern psychology* (3rd ed.). New York: Academic Press, 1981.
Woodworth, R. S., & Sheehan, M. R. *Contemporary schools of psychology* (3rd ed.). New York: Ronald Press, 1964.

C. E. HENRY

Psychology, Methods of.

Since psychology is a science, the methods of psychology are the methods of science; however, the subject matter of a science determines the particular methods used. Because human behavior and mental processes are so varied, psychologists use many different methods. These have been developed to gain knowledge about the natural world, to study what Christians call natural, or general, revelation (Rom. 1:18–20). They are the most reliable means of learning about the created world, although they may lead to incorrect conclusions if not used properly.

In addition to this natural revelation God has given us his special revelation in Scripture. The study of the Bible leads us to a more complete knowledge of God and his creation. Since all truth is God's truth, these two revelations (natural and special) are complementary and not in conflict. When the two seem to be in conflict, it means that either the scientist has reached an incorrect conclusion or that the theologian has misinterpreted Scripture. Anyone who reads either science or theology knows that both errors occur.

Methods of Gathering Data. In general, psychologists develop hypotheses, gather data to test them, and evaluate the data to decide whether or not their hypotheses were correct. This process is the basis on which psychological theories are developed and tested. The nature of the hypotheses influences the ways data are gathered and evaluated.

The experimental method. When using the experimental method psychologists control the presence, absence, or intensity of factors thought to influence the behavior while keeping all other factors constant. As a result the experimenter can reach cause-effect conclusions, something he cannot do as well with other methods. The basic principle of this method is that one takes two groups of subjects and treats them both exactly the same, except in one way. Then, if the groups behave differently after the treatments, one concludes that the one different treatment caused the differences.

Although many scientists maintain that the experimental method is a creation of only the last 400 years, we find a good example of it recorded more than 2,500 years ago in the first chapter of the Book of Daniel. During their three years of education Daniel and his friends were to be fed rich food which they did not believe would be good for them. Daniel proposed that he and his friends eat only vegetables and water for 10 days, while the others ate the king's rich food. At the and of this time the teacher could compare how the two groups looked and decide which was the better diet. At the end of the 10 days those on vegetables and water looked healthier and better nourished, so they continued to eat such food.

In this experiment those eating the vegetables were the experimental group, and those eating the usual rich food were the control group. Both groups were treated exactly the same. Metaphorically speaking, they went to classes together, slept in the same dormitories, did the same physical work, and so forth. These variables are called the controlled variables or the constants. Diet was one factor that was different for the two groups. This variable, manipulated by the experimenter to see whether it causes a change, is called the independent variable. Finally, the appearance of the students was measured to see if there was any difference between the groups. This variable is called the dependent variable because the experimenter wants to find out whether or not it depends on the independent variable.

Since the appearance of the Hebrews was better than that of the others, the experimenter concluded that the diet of vegetables caused the difference. This is a logical conclusion, since that was the only way the groups were treated differently. Although modern experimenters would insist on some refinements to eliminate other possible causes, the basic idea of the experimental method is found in this incident in the Old Testament. It can lead to false conclusions if other variables change at the same time as the dependent one. For example, one investigator thought he had caused neurosis in rats by giving them an unsolvable conflict. Others showed that the odd behavior of the rats was caused by the high-pitched sound of his apparatus, not the conflict. Eliminating these confounding variables is a major task in designing an experiment.

The experimental method, preferred by many psychologists, sometimes cannot be used because it is impossible or unethical to manipulate the variables in question. Therefore, psychologists use a variety of other methods, descriptive methods that cannot show cause-effect relationships as easily, if at all.

Correlation methods. When using the simplest correlation methods psychologists take measurements of two variables and determine whether or not the two are related in any way—i.e., whether or not they are co-related. For example, a positive correlation shows up between scores on IQ tests and grades in school. Students who score high on such tests tend to make high grades. A negative correlation exists between sociability and suspiciousness, so that persons who are suspicious are generally less sociable.

The correlation methods usually provide an index to tell the degree of relationship. A correlation of $+1.00$ indicates a perfect positive relationship, one of -1.00 indicates a perfect negative relationship, and one of 0.00 indicates no relationship. Perfect relationships are seldom found in real life, but any degree of relationship is often helpful in predicting what persons will do. Although the relationships are not perfect, IQ scores can be used to predict how well an individual will do in school, high school grades to predict college grades, and so forth.

As with other descriptive methods, it is difficult to demonstrate cause-effect relationships with the correlation method. However, the method is very useful in many instances where psychologists cannot experiment. For example, there is a high correlation between the IQ of parents and that of their children. We do not know how much of this is caused by heredity and how much by environment. For obvious ethical reasons we cannot arbitrarily breed persons with given IQs, and then let some rear their own children while switching other parents and children. But we can use the correlation method and see what happens to the IQs of children who are reared by their natural parents and those reared by adoptive parents.

Observation methods. Another descriptive method is naturalistic observation, in which the scientist simply observes and records behavior in its natural setting without attempting to intervene. This is the most basic method of science, because all of science begins with the observations of the scientists. Although one cannot prove cause-effect relationships with this method, it is a valuable source of hypotheses about causes of behavior. For example, we know that many children drop out of Sunday school during their junior high years, and through observing the classes we may develop ideas about why they do.

If subjects know they are being observed, such knowledge may influence behavior. An observer, standing and writing on a clipboard, may result in a Sunday school class being much better or much worse than usual. This problem can be avoided by having the observer actually join the group—the method of the participant observer. Others in the group do not know that they are being observed, so their behavior is unchanged.

Written and oral methods. Some behaviors or attitudes are very difficult to observe, so psychologists can gather data through the use of questionnaires or surveys in which people are asked to report their behaviors or opinions on a variety of subjects. We are all familiar with the results of the U.S. Census, the Gallup poll, the Harris Poll, and surveys on everything from sexual behavior to religious attitudes. When such surveys are taken, it is essential that the sample be representative of the entire population from which it is drawn.

Another written method is the use of tests. Nearly everyone has taken an IQ test of one kind or another. Literally thousands of tests are available to measure achievement, aptitude, personality, values, interests, and so forth. Tests are essentially a kind of short-cut, a relatively small sample of behavior used to obtain a standardized measurement of a person.

The clinical interview is another descriptive method used to gather data. As an individual undergoes psychotherapy, the interview may be recorded and later analyzed as to the ideas discussed, the words used, the pauses taken, and so forth. Psychologists can use such an analysis to find marked changes taking place over the course of therapy.

Finally, clinical psychologists often write case histories. Case histories are essentially scientific biographies of individuals in which the psychologist reconstructs the important events over many years of their lives in an effort to see how various behavior patterns emerged. These case histories may be constructed from remembered events in the persons' lives or from personal documents and records.

All these methods of gathering data are valid means of learning about the created world, but they are used in different situations. In general the experimental method is most appropriate for studying those aspects of humans that are most similar to animals and for situations in which variables can be controlled and in which subjects are reacting rather than initiating. The other methods are most appropriate for studying those aspects of humans that are most similar to God and for situations in which variables cannot be controlled and in which subjects are active and initiating.

Methods of Evaluating Data. After data have been collected, they must be interpreted in some way. Usually verbal data, such as interviews and case studies, are simply summarized in a written report. However, if the data are in the form of numbers, statistics are usually used to summarize them and draw implications from them.

Descriptive statistics. Psychologists use some types of statistics for summarizing or describing large amounts of information. Sometimes the data are presented in a frequency distribution in which each score is represented. However, frequently the scores are summarized in just a few numbers. The most frequent types of such statistics are measures of central tendency and measures of variability.

Measures of central tendency, or averages, are used to represent the center of the frequency distribution. Although many measures exist, three appear most often: the mode is the score that occurs most frequently; the median is the middle score, with half the scores above it and half below; and the arithmetic mean is the sum of the scores divided by the number of scores (what most people call the average).

Measures of variability, or dispersion, describe how the scores are spread out around the measures of central tendency. The range is simply the difference between the highest and lowest scores. The variance and the standard deviation are more useful than the range. The variance is the average squared distance from the mean, and the standard deviation is the square root of the variance. About two-thirds of the scores fall within one standard deviation of the mean, and about 95% fall within two standard deviations.

Inferential statistics. Other types of statistics are used for drawing inferences, for making statements about an entire population when only a sample has been measured. In most national surveys about 1,500 people are chosen as representative of the whole population; then those making the survey state how 200 million people voted, what they think, what television shows they watch, and so forth. Statistics are also used to measure the size of the correlation, to tell whether or not there is a true correlation in the population, and to make predictions on the basis of the correlation.

Frequently psychologists conduct an experiment using several groups and want to know whether the differences between the groups are due to chance or if they indicate a real difference. By using standard techniques, such as the t-test or analysis of variance, they can find out how likely the differences are to have been caused by chance. If the probability of the results being produced by mere chance is less than 5%, the differences are said to be statistically significant. Some experimenters set this chance level at 1%, making an even more stringent criterion.

Ethical Principles. As psychologists have used these methods, a number of ethical problems have arisen. Although psychologists have wrestled with these problems and come to some conclusions, Christians should consider the problems again and see if they agree with the solutions.

Deception. The use of deception in psychological research and testing is a widely accepted practice. Psychologists argue that such deception is necessary in some types of research and that nothing is wrong with it as long as the subjects are told the truth before they leave the experiment. A similar situation is found in psychological testing. People do not know what they are revealing about themselves by their answers. As a result the public has become suspicious of psychologists and often tries to outwit them.

Invasion of privacy. This is probably not an issue when openly observing in a natural setting. However, it becomes an issue when one is observed through a one-way glass or from hiding, or while engaged in sexual activity, and so forth. It may also be an invasion of privacy to ask certain questions on tests or in an interview.

Harm to subjects. A basic principle is that psychologists should not do anything that will cause lasting harm to a research subject or patient. This is a valid principle, and we must be careful not to interpret it too loosely. If we imply to persons in an experiment that they are stupid, debriefing after the experiment may not remove the self-doubts that have been created. How is the subject to know if the experimenter was lying during the experiment or after it? A sexual question on a personality test may lead persons into temptation and sin rather than helping them. Therefore, psychologists must be careful to treat others with the respect and dignity due to individuals made in God's image.

Additional Readings

Agnew, N. M., & Pike, S. W. *The science game: An introduction to research in the behavioral sciences* (2nd ed.). Englewood Cliffs, N.J.: Prentice-Hall, 1978.
Collins, G. R. *The rebuilding of psychology: An integration of psychology and Christianity.* Wheaton, Ill.: Tyndale House, 1977.
Koteskey, R. L. *General psychology for Christian counselors.* Nashville: Abingdon, 1983.

R. L. KOTESKEY

See PSYCHOLOGICAL MEASUREMENT.

Psychology, Presuppositions of.

Presuppositions are assumptions about reality that have a major impact on all the sciences, including psychology. Presuppositions about the nature of the universe, cause and effect, human nature, and knowledge help guide science by giving it a framework from which to operate. Scientists, for example, may presuppose that the laws of matter operate similarly everywhere in the universe. By assuming some regularity in the universe they are able to investigate the problems in their sciences with more confidence in their theories and tools of investigation. Assumptions about the nature of human nature are likewise important for the psychologist in both research and clinical settings.

What the natural and social sciences have been slow to recognize is that presuppositions about reality and human nature affect the scientist's ability to be objective in the scientific process. Psychological research supports the notion that individuals resist interpretations of data that run counter to their expectations. This is certainly a possibility for psychology, which has many assumptions that run counter to the biblical picture of human nature.

Interest in the subjectivity of science was kindled by Kuhn's (1962) classic book, *The Structure of Scientific Revolutions.* It was Kuhn's contention that change in scientific ideas takes place as revolutions in whole paradigms, or sets of presuppositions about reality, because people's underlying beliefs about reality have to change before new contrasting ideas can be accepted. It has been suggested that in a scientific revolution people do not change their ideas. The scientists who hold the established views eventually die, and thus new ideas can become accepted.

Presuppositions in psychology serve as a framework within which research can be conducted and therapies can be developed. On the other hand, assumptions also affect the psychologist's objectivity and can become rigid dogmas in the face of conflicting data. The importance of psychologists being aware of their presuppositions cannot be overemphasized, because all psychologists have assumptions that undergird and influence their work whether they are aware of them or not. In addition, some of the subject matter of psychology is less accessible to experimental research and thus is more dependent on the psychologist's assumptions.

The presuppositions of psychologists can affect their work by limiting the subject matter they are willing to investigate, the methods of investigation, and the interpretations they place upon their data. Psychological research on the effects of a person's belief structure on his objectivity is substantial. Research areas such as cognitive dissonance, prejudice, and social aspects of perception illustrate the biasing potential of assumptions. The research process itself is also strongly affected by the psychologist's beliefs, as is illustrated by the phenomenon of experimenter expectancy (Barber, 1976) and the effect of subject beliefs on experimental results (Silverman, 1977).

The biasing effects of assumptions should not lead anyone to reject the search for truth as hopeless, but rather should challenge the psychologist to recognize the presuppositions of his field as well as the benefits of Christian assumptions in the study of human nature.

Basic Assumptions. The presuppositions that provide the framework within which most psychology is practiced are summarized below. It is important to note that these assumptions may be held as convenient to the methodology of science without necessarily believing that they specify truth about the nature of the way things really are. For example, a belief in determinism may actually be a belief in methodological determinism, which does not mean that a psychologist does not accept the concept of human freedom but that human behavior does seem to follow regular laws. Therefore, it may be useful to think of behavior as being determined.

Naturalism. This is an assumption at the core of secular science. It means that the universe can be explained completely by natural processes. This is a rejection of the idea of the God of the universe who ultimately provides the sustaining power of the universe and who can impact the universe in ways that according to our understanding go beyond natural law (e.g., miracles). For the psychologist naturalism means that the natural causes in the universe have to be the sole explanation for all that human beings are and can do.

Materialism. Related to naturalism is the psychologist's belief in materialism, which says that everything that exists in the universe is composed of matter-energy. This means that human nature in its entirety (behavior, thinking, feeling) is ultimately reducible to material explanations. It usually means that brain activity is equated with personhood.

Reductionism. This assumption means that explanations about human behavior and personhood can be reduced to or equated with explanations in terms of physical-chemical processes that accompany human activity. Mackay (1974) calls this type of thinking "nothing buttery," since reductionistic psychologists try to describe human nature as "nothing but" neuronal or chemical activity of some sort.

Determinism. Following directly from the assumptions of materialism and reductionism is the assumption of determinism, which says that all human behavior is completely caused by natural processes. This means that human beings do not personally decide their own actions, regardless of their feelings of freedom.

Evolution. This assumption attempts to provide an explanation for the uniqueness and complexity of human nature in a naturalistic order. Evolutionary theory would say that all of human nature has evolved from simpler organisms. This includes the idea that the complex human mind is a product of the evolution of the brain.

Empiricism. This assumption is both a method of knowing and a theory about human nature. Empiricism means that one can know only through the senses and with whatever scientific instrumentation expands the senses. Empiricism may be more radically stated as whatever cannot be shown to register as sensory data, such as God or mind, does not exist. Obviously empiricism can be a benefit to careful, scientific observation and control, but it also sets limits on what can be observed about human nature.

Empiricism may also be defined as a theory of human nature. The person in the empirical sense is a product of sensory input. The mind, according to empiricist John Locke, is a *tabula rasa*, a blank slate on which sensory experience writes. British empiricism of the 1800s contributed much to the behavioristic model in psychology, in which behavior alone is seen as acceptable data in psychology and the person is seen as a product of environmental factors.

Relativism. This is the assumption that there are no absolute standards of right or value to guide psychological research, counseling, or behavioral engineering. In a naturalistic universe all things related to morality and value become arbitrary and related to the individual person. Consequently there is much debate in psychology about the value and purpose of human life, values to guide counseling, and the moral structures by which society can be organized.

There are several counterassumptions in psychology that rebel against the rigid nature of the assumptions summarized above. Humanistic psychology, for example, assumes the freedom and personality of human nature. Transpersonal psychology emphasizes the immaterial essence of the universe and human nature; this assumption is labeled *pantheism* or *panpsychism.*

Biblical Presuppositions. Since beliefs are important to the development of psychology, Collins (1977) and Cosgrove (1979) suggest that Christian psychologists should build their psychology upon biblical presuppositions about reality and human nature. While the existence of God may not seem very pertinent to psychology, it should be clear that all of psychology's assumptions depend heavily on the natural basis for the origin and operation of the universe. For this reason Christians need to state very clearly their belief in the supernatural God of the universe. The assumption of a creator God gives psychology a source for the human person, a confidence in knowledge, additional revelation on human nature in the Bible, and a source of ethics and value. The immaterial essence of human nature gives a basis for human freedom and purpose and meaning in life. Christian beliefs about the fall of human nature and sanctification can expand the Christian's view of psychological problems and therapy. In general Christian assumptions support a needed balance in psychology. They can serve to correct psychology's limited view of human nature arising from its extreme positions on empiricism, materialism, determinism, and reductionism. At the same time Christian beliefs do not rule out the physical nature of the person, the laws of cause and effect, and the strong influences of nature and nurture on the human personality.

References

Barber, T. X. *Pitfalls in human research*. New York: Pergamon, 1976.
Collins, G. *The rebuilding of psychology*, Wheaton, Ill.: Tyndale House, 1977.
Cosgrove, M. P. *Psychology gone awry*. Grand Rapids: Zondervan, 1979.
Kuhn, T. *The structure of scientific revolutions*. Chicago: University of Chicago Press, 1962.
Mackay, D. *The clockwork image*. Downers Grove, Ill.: Inter-Varsity Press, 1974.
Silverman, I. *The human subject in the psychological laboratory*, New York: Pergamon, 1977.

M. P. Cosgrove

See Determinism and Free Will; Reductionism.

Psychology as Religion.

The similarity to religion of modern psychological theories of mental pathology and psychotherapy was noticed from the time these approaches emerged early in this century. Each theory was a kind of general psychological interpretation of the meaning of personal existence, complete with an explanation of what facilitates and what blocks the development of a healthy or ideal personality. Since all of these psychologies were based on secular philosophy and values, they were explicitly or implicitly hostile to religion, especially Christianity.

Initially these psychologies functioned as alternative world views or secular religions primarily in the lives of the psychotherapists, most of whom were drawn to modern psychology because they were already alienated from traditional Christianity or Judaism and were looking for an alternative understanding of life that could be interpreted as scientific and as compatible with the increasingly secular world. Even those who started training in psychology with a religious commitment often abandoned their faith or greatly reduced its importance. This replacement of religion by psychology was a common consequence of the immersion in a secular mental framework which assumed that religion and religious experience were psychological phenomena and that the supernatural did not truly exist. Religion was interpreted as an illusion at best, or as some kind of pathology at worst. This rejection of religion was largely a result of the acceptance of certain philosophic assumptions and values implicit in much of secular psychology. That psychology per se did not—and does not—logically or empirically require that one lose his religion is clear in the lives of such prominent psychologists as Stern (1981), Tournier (1957), Zilboorg (1962), and many others.

Psychology often came to serve the same religion-replacing function in the lives of the patients who entered therapy at a time of mental anguish actively looking for answers. It was a common occurrence for the patient to accept the theoretical framework of his therapist—to be "converted" to psychology. Such a change was facilitated by the frequency of the therapy sessions and by the reinforcing effect of any cures or benefits caused by, or attributed to, the therapist. Any negative experiences with religion that the patient might have had would also support the exchange of psychology for religion. Furthermore, in many respects the psychotherapist/patient interaction had something of the character of the religious relationship of master/disciple or confessor/penitent.

A fundamental way in which psychotherapy functions as a religion is that (at its best) it heals. The healing or cure aspect of psychotherapy is its primary justification, and one should not forget that healing, both psychological and physical, is a major concern of Christianity. It is probably no accident that the secular psychotherapies first developed in a period when healing was much neglected in the major Christian churches—especially those that ministered to the more educated and sophisticated.

Another important characteristic of psychology has been the serious involvement with religion and religious issues on the part of many psychological theorists and innovators. This was the case for the founders of psychotherapy, Freud and Jung, and Adler, who converted to a somewhat liberal Protestantism from a Jewish background. The following psychologists either started with a serious religious concern or clearly expressed such in their professional life (or both): William James, G. Stanley Hall, Carl Rogers, Erich Fromm, Rollo May, Karl Menninger, Gardner Murphy, Michael Murphy (Esalen founder), Elisabeth Kübler-Ross. Such examples strongly imply an affinity between the religious and the psychological mentality.

One interesting sociological feature of psychology has been its religious "denominational" character. Lasch (1976) has pointed out the presence of a "Catholic-Protestant" split in psychology. Freud and much of psychiatry stand for Catholicism—i.e., for orthodoxy and excommunication, doctrine, priestly mediation between the "sacred texts" and the patient, formality and distance between therapist and patient. Adler and his followers—the humanistic/self psychologists such as Rogers—created a psychological "Reformation." This involved taking psychology out of a special vocabulary and putting it into the vernacular. It also meant reducing the distinction between therapist and client, emphasizing empathy and emotion and the client's own interpretations. All of this resulted in a kind of psychological equivalent to the priesthood of all believers.

This "protestantized" version of psychology has tended to follow many of the paths taken by historical Protestantism: a gradual simplifying and watering down of theory (doctrine); increasing optimism about human nature among "mainline" psychologists; the splitting of the rest of "Protestant" psychology into various sects and movements. For example, encounter group psychology is much like revivalism (see Oden, 1972); Fromm's psychology is close to the social gospel; self-help psychology is an expression of positive-thinking Protestantism (e.g., Norman Vincent Peale); transpersonal psychology and related types are analogous to Mind Cure and aspects of Christian Science.

One psychologist not discussed by Lasch is Jung. A denominational interpretation nevertheless suggests itself. Jung is a mixture of "Catholic" psychoanalytic-psychiatric psychology and the "Protestant," less formal, counseling psychology. Hence, Jung should appeal to those who identify with aspects of both Catholicism and Protestantism, to those who seek Catholic intellectuality plus Protestant freedom of choice—a kind of "Episcopalian" psychological mentality. According to this rationale Jung should be popular with the especially educated and those with an interest in symbolism, ritual, and aesthetics. This seems, indeed, to be the case, as Jung is well received in Episcopal seminaries. Also the Jungian religious writers Morton Kelsey and John A. Sanford are both Episcopalians.

With the growth of psychotherapy and the increasing secularization of society, psycho-

logical ideas began to spread throughout the culture at large. Colleges and universities with their many psychology courses, plus such phenomena as newspaper advice columns, contributed greatly to the disseminating of psychology. An important consequence has been that today the public discourse (e.g., in the media) concerning people who are facing life crises—i.e., emotional, moral, and interpersonal problems—is almost entirely dominated by secular psychological theory. The older religious understanding of these issues is restricted to private life and, indeed, is no longer even understood by many secularized Westerners. There has been a triumph of the therapeutic over the theological (see Becker, 1975; Vitz, 1977; Lasch, 1978; Kilpatrick, 1983).

Specific Religious Characteristics of Modern Psychology. *Psychoanalysis: Freud.* The connections of Freud's thought and life with both Judaism and Christianity are deep and complex; only the most easily observed religious characteristics of psychoanalysis will be noted here.

Freud directly acknowledged the essential similarity between psychoanalytic therapy and religious counseling by describing psychoanalysis as "pastoral work in the best sense of the words" (1927/1959, p. 256). He thus recognized in psychoanalysis what is true of all secular psychotherapy and counseling; namely, that it is similar, and indeed a rival, to the long Christian tradition of confession and counseling.

In addition there were specific cultic characteristics of early psychoanalysis. Freud often functioned like the founder of a religion: he was surrounded by disciples who formed a kind of inner sanctum; the best and most loyal of these were given rings to designate their special status; a deep allegiance to Freud's ideas, especially the "dogma" of his sexual theories, was expected of any true follower. Freud likened himself to Moses and Jung (before the schism) to Joshua. Many of Freud's students broke from his ideas and were treated rather like heretics. The psychoanalytic establishment that emerged after Freud's death has often been compared to an orthodox religious organization that "excommunicated" deviants (see Roazen, 1975).

Freud was personally involved in religious issues all his life, and he wrote frequently on them (*Totem and Taboo*, 1913; *The Future of an Illusion*, 1927; *Moses and Monotheism*, 1938). In part this interest came from both religious and ethnic Jewish influence (see Klein, 1981; Ostow, 1982), but much of it came out of his complex hostility and attraction to Christianity (Zilboorg, 1962; Meng & Freud, 1963; Vitz, 1983, 1984).

Nonetheless, Freudian psychoanalysis never developed a positive synthesis to provide a clear meaning or answer to life. Instead, Freud always remained an analyst focused on the exploration of the unconscious. His attitude and that of psychoanalysis is pessimistic, stoical, and skeptical. He refused to provide a secular form of salvation since he saw religion in any form as an illusion to be rejected. Thus, Freudian theory, which is in important respects an antireligion, was never made into a positive alternative. Freud was very critical of those such as Jung or Adler who did make psychology into a kind of positive alternative to religion.

Analytical Psychology: Jung. Jung also was quite aware of the religious nature of psychotherapy, and the theological cast of much of his writing is apparent—e.g., in *Answer to Job* (1954), an extensive exercise in Scripture interpretation. Jung's explicit awareness of the religious issue is stated when he writes: "Patients force the psychotherapist into the role of priest, and expect and demand that he shall free them from distress. That is why we psychotherapists must occupy ourselves with problems which strictly speaking belong to the theologian," (Jung, 1933, p. 278).

Unlike Freud's, Jung's psychology provided positive, synthetic concepts that could serve as a conscious goal not only for therapy but for life as a whole. Jung responded far more to the patient's demand for a general relief from distress than did Freud. Jung's positive answer to religious needs is summarized by Jacobi, a prominent student of his: "Jungian psychotherapy is . . . a Heilsweg, in the twofold sense of the German word: a way of healing and a way of salvation. It has the power to cure. . . . In addition it knows the way and has the means to lead the individual to his "salvation," to the knowledge and fulfillment of his personality, which have always been the aim of spiritual striving. Jung's system of thought can be explained theoretically only up to a certain point; to understand it fully one must have experienced or better still, 'suffered' its living action in oneself. Apart from its medical aspect, Jungian psychotherapy is thus a system of education and spiritual guidance" (Jacobi 1973, p. 60). The process of Jungian movement on this path is, Jacobi continues, "both ethically and intellectually an extremely difficult task, which can be successfully performed only by the fortunate few, those elected and favored

by grace" (p. 127). The last stage on the Jungian path of individuation—salvation—is called self-realization. This goal of self-realization or actualization is at heart a gnostic one in which the commandment: "Know (and express) thyself" has replaced the Judeo-Christian: "Love God and others." (In certain respects all modern psychology of whatever theoretical persuasion, because of the emphasis on knowledge, can be interpreted as part of a vast gnostic heresy.)

Much Jungian psychology is not explicitly focused on individuation and self-realization but is concerned with interpreting the patient's dream symbolism. Here Jung's analysis is focused on the collective and personal unconscious of the patient and on archetypes, the anima (or animus), shadow, and other concepts. This suggests a different way in which psychology can function as religion. Jung acknowledges the patient's basic religious concerns, and Jungian psychology is directly applied to the "archetypal" expression of the patient's religious motives—e.g., in dreams about the wise old man (God archetype), dreams about rebirth, etc. Jung's discovery of the psychology of religious symbols is important, but there is with this a danger of substituting the psychological experience of one's religious nature for the religious salvation that comes through the transcendent God who acts in history (see Hostie, 1957). Those who make this mistake have truly treated psychology as religion.

Self or Humanistic Psychology: Rogers, Maslow, and Others. The clearest expression of psychology as religion is seen in the self psychologies. These place the self at the center of personality and make the growth or actualization of the self the primary goal both of life in general and of psychotherapy and counseling in particular. More specifically, self psychologies share all or most of the following characteristics:

1) An emphasis on the conscious self as an integrated, or at least potentially integrated, system. 2) An emphasis on the true self as entirely good, not characterized by any natural tendency to aggression or exploitation or to make self-indulgent or narcissistic choices. Such undesirable phenomena are attributed to the false self created by external factors such as family, traditional religion, society, or the economic system. 3) An emphasis on the true self as having almost unlimited capacity for change through freely made decisions. This process of choosing brings about self-actualization, the ideal way of being; self-

actualization is an ongoing process of change, not a finished state. 4) An emphasis on personality prior to self-actualization as primarily the result of learned social roles. That is, the false self is the product of social learning of an essentially arbitrary kind. 5) An emphasis on breaking with the past, especially with commitments to others, with tradition, with fixed moral codes. Morality is interpreted as personal, subjective, and relative. 6) An emphasis on getting in touch with and expressing emotions and feelings. This promotes a presumed greater awareness of the true self and greater self-acceptance and trust in one's instincts. 7) An emphasis on short-term counseling of relatively normal adults in contrast to theory focused on disturbed children or such problems as schizophrenia, manic-depressive symptoms, or alcoholism.

Examples of self psychology theories are those proposed by Rogers (1951, 1961), Maslow (1968), and Fromm (1947). The writings of May (1953) and the Gestalt psychology of Perls (1969) are also closely related. Such self psychology had much of its origin in Adler (1924), in Goldstein (1939), and in Jung's notion of self-realization. Most of the psychology that was immensely popular in the United States during the 1960s and 1970s was a form of self psychology. For example, transactional analysis (Berne, 1964) fits into this category. Movements such as Erhard Seminar Training (EST) combine self psychology with various other elements, usually from Eastern religions. Indeed, much of recent humanistic, self, and transpersonal psychology is indistinguishable from Eastern religion (see the *Journal of Transpersonal Psychology.*)

The general framework noted above served as an interpretation of the meaning of life that undermined or replaced Christianity in many cases. Some of the more specific claims of the self psychologists will make this clear. Rogers (1961) states that the goal of psychotherapy is to help the client become self-directing, self-confident, self-expressive, creative, and autonomous to such a degree that he experiences unconditional positive self-regard. The client is increasingly to experience himself as the only locus or source of values.

Fromm devotes many pages in his books to interpreting and reinterpreting parts of both the Old and New Testaments. The titles of some of his books illustrate his religious agenda—e.g., *The Dogma of Christ* (1963), *You Shall Be as Gods* (1966). Fromm (1947) explicitly states that his psychology would be untenable if the doctrine of original sin were true. He

believes that evil is in no way intrinsic to man's nature; self theory follows from this fundamental assumption, for obviously the self is to be perfectly trusted only if it is perfectly free of instrinsic evil. The Pelagian assumption of "I'm OK and you're OK" found throughout transactional analysis is a recent popular expression of this position (Berne, 1964; Harris, 1967).

Some of the popular American expressions of self theory have gone so far as to claim that the self is God; e.g., "You are the Supreme Being.... Reality is a reflection of your notions. Totally, Perfectly" (Frederick, 1974, pp. 171, 177; Schultz, 1979, reaches the same conclusion). Rogers's position in which the self is the sole locus of values comes close to the same thing. The influence, often indirect, of Sartre and other existential thinkers on the American self theorists has been substantial. Sartre states that once we've rejected God, "the Father," then "life has no meaning *a priori.* Before you come alive life is nothing; it's up to you to give it a meaning, and value is nothing else but the meaning that you choose (Sartre, 1947, p. 58).

Since Sartre (1957) also argues that man's goal is to become God, self psychology often can be interpreted as a commercialized American packaging of much of European existentialism.

The widespread acceptance of this self psychology (called selfism by Vitz, 1977) has been due in large part to works that popularized the original theories (e.g., transactional analysis). The strong public response has stemmed from various cultural and economic factors, and has had little to do with scientific knowledge. Contemporary upper-middle-class Americans—wealthy, increasingly secular, and with time on their hands—have been only too happy to find a rationale that encouraged them to develop an extremely self-centered way of living. Economic support for this kind of psychology came from the needs (and pleasures) of the consumer economy of the 1960s and 70s. Indeed, these self psychologies can be viewed as justifications and descriptions of the ideal consumer (Vitz, 1977). It was not surprising that many expressions and catchwords of self theory began showing up as advertising copy: Do it now! You're the boss! Honor thyself! Break tradition!

The relentless and single-minded search for and glorification of the self is a kind of psychological self-worship and is at direct cross-purposes with the Christian injunction to lose the self. Certainly Jesus Christ neither lived nor advocated a life that would qualify by today's standards as self-actualized. For the Christian the self is the problem, not the potential paradise. Understanding of this problem involves an awareness of sin, especially that of pride; correcting this condition requires the practices of such unself-actualized states as contrition, humility, obedience, and trust in God—attitudes either neglected or explicitly rejected by self theorists.

The problems posed by humanistic selfism are not new to Christianity. Indeed, they can be traced back to early conflicts with stoicism, Epicureanism, and other sophisticated Greco-Roman philosophical and ethical systems, especially gnosticism. Self-worship in the form of self-realization is in Jewish and Christian terms idolatry operating from the usual motive of unacknowledged egoism. Disguised self-love has long been recognized as the source of idolatry. "Idolatry is well understood in the Bible as differing from the pure worship of Israel's God in the fact of its personification and objectification of the human will in contrast with the superhuman transcendence of the true God. When an idol is worshipped, man is worshipping himself, his desires, his purposes, and his will. . . . As a consequence of this type of idolatry man was outrageously guilty of giving himself the status of God and of exalting his own will as of supreme worth" (Baab, 1949, pp. 105, 110).

One of the first psychologists to identify the way in which modern psychology with its emphasis on self-acceptance tended to undermine the idea of both sin and personal responsibility was Mowrer (1961). The problem remained neglected, however, until its analysis by Adams (1970) and Menninger (1973). Menninger notes the social and psychological benefits that follow from taking responsibility for one's actions, especially one's sinful behavior that has hurt others. The same point was made by Adams in his Christian critique of secular counseling theory and practice.

Some psychologists have justified self theory by pointing out the large number of people who suffer from low self-esteem and associated depression. However, these are often caused by biological factors—something that self theorists, because of their theoretical emphasis on social learning, usually fail to observe in patients. When biological factors are not involved, low self-esteem is itself often an inverted example of self-worship. At first this proposal might appear surprising, but the rationale is simple. Depression and low self-esteem are often the result of self-hatred or aggression

against the self that occur when one fails to meet one's own high standards of value and worth. Thus, optimistic pride and pessimistic depression both result from the self taking on the prerogative of creating the standards of self-worth and then judging how well one meets those standards (see Strong, 1977). In Christian terms, however, one's worth comes from God, not from one's self. A person is not to judge himself or herself as a success or failure; such judgments belong to God, and so to judge is to set oneself in God's place. Psychologically creating your own self-worth is like printing your own money; it leads to false prosperity— inflation followed by depression. It is not uncommon for self psychology sessions to give short-term elation only to be followed by depression. Kilpatrick (1983) accurately describes this creation of self-worth as wishful thinking.

Myers (1980) has collected much evidence from social and cognitive psychology demonstrating that the self is intrinsically biased in its own favor, thus documenting the natural human tendency to pride. He cites studies that show the following: 1) People are much more likely to accept responsibility for success than for failure. If I win, I accept credit, but if I lose, then it was bad luck, someone else's fault, etc. 2) Most people judge themselves as above average on most self-ratings. For example, 70% of the high school seniors taking the College Board rated themselves as above average leaders, only 2% as below average. In most marriages each person usually sees his or her positive contributions as greater than those of the spouse. In one survey 94% of college faculty reported themselves as better than their average colleagues. 3) People have a natural but unrealistic tendency to think their own judgment and beliefs are especially accurate. 4) Most people are very optimistic about their own future as compared to that of others. For example, most college students think things will work out much better for themselves than for the average student. 5) People tend to overestimate how morally they would act as compared with how they actually do act. For example, many more people say that they would help a stranger in need than actually do help when a real opportunity arises.

These and other studies led Myers to conclude that low self-esteem is not the great problem it is often claimed to be. Like other Christian critics Myers notes that Christianity is not essentially concerned with building high self-esteem but with admitting one's pride and then, with God's grace, forgetting or letting go of the self.

Bergin (1980) has cogently summarized the many value differences between a theistic and a humanistic or self-theory approach to psychotherapy. For example: humility and obedience are virtues (theistic) versus man is autonomous and supreme, and rejection of obedience as a virtue (humanistic). Love, affection, and self-transcendence are primary (theistic) versus personal needs and self-satisfaction are primary (humanistic). Commitment to marriage, emphasis on procreation and family life (theistic) versus open marriage, emphasis on recreational sex without long-term responsibility (humanistic). Forgiveness of others (theistic) versus self-acceptance and expression of accusatory feelings (humanistic). Bergin's comparisons clearly identify how self-oriented humanistic psychology has functioned as an alternative to religion and religious values. Other important treatments of the "religious" aspects of psychotherapy are the criticisms of Bobgan and Bobgan (1979) and the reflective analysis of McLemore (1982).

Yet another analysis of how self psychology functions as religion has been presented by Kilpatrick (1983), who focuses on the way in which the psychological categories of humanistic or self psychology function to replace religious categories. Slowly, and often quite subtly, God disappears from our thoughts and concerns, and preoccupation with the self comes to dominate. This self-preoccupation has several pathological consequences, especially destructive ones being the growth of subjectivism (see Frankl, 1967) and the loss of contact with reality. A person begins quickly to perceive others only, or primarily, in terms of his or her own self-needs. This leads to serious misperceptions of others as well as to an inability to view oneself objectively. Our desire for self-esteem gets in the way of objective self-awareness. Kilpatrick also points out how close self psychology is to such American traditions as the self-made man, and the frontier man who is constantly changing, moving on, always rejecting the notion of true commitment. Thus, self psychology, in spite of its opposition to tradition, is an example of one of America's oldest social attitudes.

In summary, the overriding religious character of much psychology is its tendency to replace God with the self. Intrinsic human pride and narcissism seem to have found one of their more effective expressions in modern psychology—a discipline that substitutes for the ancient, no longer appealing worship of the golden calf what might perhaps be called today's psychological worship of the golden self.

References

Adams, J. *Competent to counsel.* Philadelphia: Presbyterian and Reformed Publishing, 1970.

Adler, A. *The practice and theory of individual psychology.* New York: Harcourt, Brace, 1924.

Baab, O. J. *The theology of the Old Testament.* New York: Abingdon-Cokesbury, 1949.

Becker, E. *Escape from evil.* New York: Free Press, 1975.

Bergin, A. E. Psychotherapy and religious values. *Journal of Consulting and Clinical Psychology,* 1980, *48,* 95–105.

Berne, E. *Games people play.* New York: Grove, 1964.

Bobgan, M., & Bobgan, D. *The psychological way/the spiritual way.* Minneapolis: Bethany Fellowship, 1979.

Frankl, V. *Existential psychology.* New York: Washington Square Press, 1967.

Frederick, C. *est: Playing the game the new way.* New York: Delacorte, 1974.

Freud, S. Postscript to the question of lay analysis. In J. Strachey (Ed. & trans.), *The standard edition of the complete psychological works of Sigmund Freud* (Vol. 20). London: Hogarth, 1959. (Originally published, 1927.)

Fromm, E. *Man for himself.* New York: Rinehart, 1947.

Fromm, E. *The dogma of Christ.* New York: Holt, Rinehart, & Winston, 1963.

Fromm, E. *You shall be as gods.* New York: Holt, Rinehart, & Winston, 1966.

Goldstein, K. *The organism.* New York: American Book, 1939.

Harris, T. A. *I'm ok—you're ok.* New York: Avon, 1967.

Hostie, R. *Religion and the psychology of Jung.* New York: Sheed & Ward, 1957.

Jacobi, J. *The psychology of C. G. Jung* (8th ed.). New Haven: Yale University Press, 1973.

Jung, C. G. *Modern man in search of a soul.* New York: Harcourt, Brace, 1933.

Jung, C. G. *Answer to Job.* Cleveland: World Publishing, 1954.

Kilpatrick, W. K. *Psychological seduction.* Nashville: Thomas Nelson, 1983.

Klein, D. B. *Jewish origins of the psychoanalytic movement.* New York: Praeger, 1981.

Lasch, C. Sacrificing Freud. *New York Times Magazine Section,* February 22, 1976, pp. 11, 70–72.

Lasch, C. *The culture of narcissism.* New York: Norton, 1978.

Maslow, A. H. *Toward a psychology of being* (2nd ed.). Princeton, N.J.: Van Nostrand, 1968.

May, R. *Man's search for himself.* New York: Norton, 1953.

McLemore, C. *The scandal of psychotherapy.* Wheaton, Ill.: Tyndale House, 1982.

Meng, H., & Freud, E. (Eds.). *Psychoanalysis and faith: The letters of Sigmund Freud and Oskar Pfister,* New York: Basic Books, 1963.

Menninger, K. *Whatever happened to sin?* New York: Hawthorn, 1973.

Mowrer, O. H. *The crisis in psychiatry and religion.* Princeton, N.J.: Van Nostrand, 1961.

Myers, D. G. *The inflated self.* New York: Seabury, 1980.

Oden, T. C. *The intensive group experience: The new pietism.* Philadelphia: Westminster, 1972.

Ostow, M. (Ed.). *Judaism and psychoanalysis.* New York: Ktav Publishing, 1982.

Perls, F. S. *Gestalt therapy verbatim.* Lafayette, Calif.: Real People Press, 1969.

Roazen, P. *Freud and his followers.* New York: Knopf, 1975.

Rogers, C. R. *Client-centered therapy.* Boston: Houghton Mifflin, 1951.

Rogers, C. R. *On becoming a person.* Boston: Houghton Mifflin, 1961.

Sartre, J.-P. *Existentialism.* New York: Philosophical Library, 1947.

Sartre, J.-P. *Existentialism and human emotions.* New York: Philosophical Library, 1957.

Schultz, W. *Profound simplicity.* New York: Bantam, 1979.

Stern, E. M. *The other side of the couch.* New York: Pilgrim Press, 1981.

Strong, S. (Ed.). Christian counseling. *Counseling and Values,* 1977, *21,* 75–128.

Tournier, P. *The meaning of persons.* New York: Harper & Row, 1957.

Vitz, P. C. *Psychology as religion: The cult of self worship.* Grand Rapids: Eerdmans, 1977.

Vitz, P. C. Sigmund Freud's attraction to Christianity: Biographical evidence. *Psychoanalysis and Contemporary Thought,* 1983, *6,* 73–183.

Vitz, P. C. *Sigmund Freud's Christian unconscious.* New York: Guilford, 1984.

Zilboorg, G. *Psychoanalysis and religion.* New York: Farrar, Straus, & Cudahy, 1962.

P. C. Vitz

Psychology of Religion. The study of religion by psychologists. Although this definition may seem redundant, it serves as a way of distinguishing the psychology of religion from such concerns as religious psychology (*see* CHRISTIAN PSYCHOLOGY) and PSYCHOLOGY AS RELIGION. The psychology of religion refers to the psychological study of religious issues, just as there might be the psychological study of social or family or developmental issues. Therefore, the psychology of religion includes efforts to understand, predict, and control the thoughts, words, feelings, and actions of persons when they are acting religiously. And a fairly well accepted definition of acting religiously is that offered by James (1902/1961) in his Gifford Lectures: "Whatever men do in relation to that which they consider to be divine" (p. 42).

Psychological studies of religion have generally followed the distinction suggested by Berger (1974) in approaching religion either functionally or substantively. This distinction resembles somewhat the contrast made by James between roots and fruits. The functional approach to religion emphasizes the roots, or motivations, for religious behavior, while the substantive approach emphasizes the fruits, or the overt expressions, of such motivations. For example, Freud (1928) dealt entirely with the way religion served to assuage the neurotic individual's longing for a protective father figure (a functional approach), while Starbuck (1899) focused on the age and occasion of conversion (a substantive approach).

Although psychologists of religion have not shown a bias toward one approach or the other, at least two have expressed a preference for the substantive approach. James suggested that the fruits of religion were more important than the roots. He believed that it was more important to evaluate whether becoming religious resulted in greater mental health and personality integration than to study the motivations that led to religious behavior. His approach was an evaluation of the personal results of religion. James felt there could be good and bad religion, depending on its effects. It was better to study substantive (overt) religion than to study functional (covert) religion because such an approach avoided labeling someone religious who would deny the ascription. For example, to say that all people are religious because all people ask questions about the meaning of life seems inappropriate, since some people would satisfy that question by attending professional football games while others would attend church. Lemert suggested that there is a need to find a definition of religion that could be agreed upon by everyone. He proposed that only those behaviors which reflect belief in a transempirical reality and which are expressed by participation in a recognizable social group should be called religious. Thus, the church on the corner would be religious while the Rotary Club would not.

Historical Developments. *The early period.* American psychologists became leaders in the psychology of religion movement during the period 1880–1925. After that time religion became a taboo topic and was not revived as a legitimate area for investigation until the 1960s. The reasons for this demise and rebirth of interest are varied.

Although the movement was given its major impetus by the publication in 1902 of James's classic *The Varieties of Religious Experience,* the last decade of the nineteenth century had seen not only the first published study of conversion (Leuba, 1896) but also the first textbook (Starbuck, 1899). The concern with conversion was to be a dominant theme for study. James, more a theoretician than an empirical researcher, depended heavily on Starbuck's surveys for material in *The Varieties.*

The stability of the psychology of religion movement was due in no small part to the leadership of G. Stanley Hall. He had initially trained for the ministry but shifted to philosophy and psychology. His interest in religious issues remained strong, however, and as early as the 1880s he lectured to educators in Boston on the moral and religious training of children and adolescents. Although he is chiefly remembered for the encouragement and support he gave to others, Hall wrote *Adolescence* (1904) and *Jesus the Christ, in the Light of Psychology* (1917). Both dealt with the motivations and psychodynamic rationale for religious conversion, a phenomenon thought to be characteristic of the teen-age years.

Hall taught at, and subsequently became president of, Clark University. Here he gathered a group of students who engaged vigorously in a program of research in the psychology of religion. Out of this "Clark school" came many of the studies that made the psychology of religion a highly respected part of American psychology during the first two decades of this century. That Hall became the first president of the American Psychological Association no doubt added to the legitimacy which the movement acquired. Both the *American Journal of Psychology* and the *Psychological Bulletin* printed many articles on the psychology of religion, and beginning in 1904 the *Bulletin* carried an annual review of the literature in the field. One of Hall's most important contributions, however, was the establishment of a journal devoted to the psychology of religion, the *American Journal of Religious Psychology and Education*. It continued periodic publication under the title *Journal of Religious Psychology* until 1915. Perhaps the irregular appearance of the journal plus its demise were omens of a declining interest as early as the second decade of this century.

Among the students of Hall, J. H. Leuba was the most prolific. As contrasted with Starbuck, who offered no rationale for religion beyond the storm and stress of the adolescent quest for meaning and identity, Leuba offered a physiological reductionistic alternative. He followed Freud and others in explaining away the validity of supernatural objects of worship (i.e., gods) and suggested they were only physiological epiphenomena.

The tenor of much of this study during the first part of the century was strictly positivistic in that it explicitly saw itself as engaged in applying scientific rigor to "the most complex, the most inaccessible and, of all, the most sacred domain—that of religion" (Starbuck, 1899, p. 1). However, the majority of the researchers were not antagonistic toward religion and, to the contrary, were concerned to contribute to the progress of religion. It was this applied concern that some have thought was partially instrumental in the loss of respect that the field was later to have in the wider psychological community.

1920–1960. There is little doubt that the 1920s saw a rapid demise of interest in the field. The annual reviews of the field in the *Psychological Bulletin* were not published between 1928 and 1932. They ceased altogether after a single review in 1933. This decline persisted until the 1960s, during which the Society for the Scientific Study of Religion and the Christian Association for Psychological Studies were founded. Also the Catholic Psychological Association began meeting along with the American Psychological Association—an event that eventually led to the establishment of a division for the psychology of religion in the national association in the mid-1970s.

The reasons given for this hiatus of interest in the psychology of religion include: 1) an overly close alliance with theology and philosophy and with the goals of religious institutions; 2) the lack of an integrating theory around which to gather facts; 3) the overuse of the questionnaire as a method of data collection; 4) the rise of a behavioristic, positivistic world view that led to an avoidance of subjective introspection; 5) the emphasis on psychoanalytic interpretations which came to supersede empirical approaches; 6) the lack of an impact on general psychology. Although the movement had defined itself as empirical and positivistic, subsequent advances in social psychology, for example, did not incorporate interest in religion; thus the field became neglected in the viewpoint of mainline psychology. Many of the issues of the psychology of religion were taken over by religious-education and pastoral-counseling movements—both of which began in the late 1920s.

One of the major influences on this change of interest may have been the lack of belief in the importance of religion by psychologists. In contrast to sociologists, who understand religion to be one of the major institutions of society and a necessary field of study, many psychologists have been heavily influenced by scientism and consider religion to be a vestige of premodern times that is unhealthful and will be outgrown with the passing of the years. Therefore, those who study religion or are religious have been discounted by many general psychologists.

Current status. The contemporary revival of interest in the psychology of religion was due in no small part to a revival of interest in religion in the culture at large. The 1950s were the time of a religious revival in the United States. The first modern text in the field, Clark's *The Psychology of Religion: An Introduction to Religious Experience and Behavior* (1958), by its very title attests to a theme that has continued to occupy the interests of psychologists to the present; namely, the experience of being religious.

Another factor that has influenced the renewal of interest in the field has been the developing concern for the relation of religion and mental health. This was one of the concerns initiated by Freud's writings. It never fully disappeared from the scene, even though academic study of the psychology of religion did. Numerous writers in the field, beginning with Pfister and Boisen and continuing down to the present through Fromm, Menninger, and Ellis, have kept these issues alive.

Dittes (1968) noted several influences on the growth of the movement and commented on a lack of integrating theory for the field. His judgment was that this was a dangerous lack that might bring about another demise. Capps (1974) was more optimistic about the future. He felt that the new existentialist-humanist emphasis held much promise for a rediscovery of subjective introspection and individual experience. He further suggested that the greater willingness of psychologists of religion to deal with ontological questions, along with the opening up of the field to interdisciplinary study were encouraging developments.

Methods of Study. More than 20 different methods of study have been employed by psychologists of religion. Most of these involve self reports of one sort or another. Interviews, biographies, content analysis of diaries, and questionnaires have been used to investigate both functional dynamics and substantive behaviors. Although a number have investigated historical and cultural dimensions, psychologists of religion have typically focused on individual experience and behavior. Case studies were very common in some of the early work, and have again become a feature in recent investigations.

Much of the work has been correlational in format in that historical facts and verbal reports or answers have been related to certain types of religious behavior such as church attendance or devotional practice. Experimental studies in which the design involved the manipulation of an independent variable have been few. Several religious researchers have called for more of these types of investigations, but there is a continuing debate as to whether the phenomenon is of such a character to be amenable to experimental manipulation. As in numerous other areas of human behavior, religious behavior may be one of those areas which is destroyed when it is overcontrolled experimentally.

Some theorists are convinced that religion, at least in its substantive expressions, must remain a dependent and can never be treated as an independent variable. However, as Dittes (1968) noted, it is possible to treat such a religious behavior as church membership as either the dependent variable toward which one predicts on the basis of past cultural environments or as an independent variable on the basis of which one predicts future behavior such as opinions about nuclear war. Some may say that this is not true manipulation. However, it would be unethical to manipulate the social environment in order to see who would become religious, just as it would be unethical to withhold a known beneficial drug to see whether certain persons had natural immunity to a given illness.

Current Research. In the selected areas of interest discussed below, psychodynamics of religion and religious development are considered examples of a functional approach. Religious experience, religious orientation, and religious dimensions are substantive. These areas are presented as representative rather than exhaustive of the foci of psychology of religion.

Psychodynamics of religion. Without question the dominant force in psychodynamics has been psychoanalysis. Freud's writings reflect a persistent preoccupation with religious issues. They frequently include variations on his theme that religion is mass neurosis which, although preferable to individual neurosis, is based on a fixation at an immature level of development. He relates religious experience to a search for an exterior source of control for the unresolved ambivalence persons have toward parents to whom they ascribe unreasonable authority. Freud (1928) opined that religion should be superseded if not obliterated in order that mature development could progress.

From a more benign, less prejudgmental point of view, other authors have investigated the psychodynamics of religious experience. For example, Barkman (1968) suggested the possibility that verbal, emotional, social, and experiential personality types would be found more often in Reformed/Lutheran, Methodist, Anabaptist, and Catholic/Episcopalian religious groups because of the match between given types of religious expressions and these personality types. No validation of this has been attempted. Further, Benson and Spilka (1973) found that the more positive a person's self-esteem, the more likely he was to perceive God as loving, and vice versa, thus confirming a relationship between one's type of religious understanding and a predisposing personality dimension.

Religious development. In this area the research generally has affirmed religion and has had practical implications for religious education. Psychologists have been concerned with two issues: 1) How does religion relate to the developmental needs of persons from childhood through old age? 2) How does the content of religious beliefs change across the life span? Taking his cues from Piaget, Elkind (1970) proposed that the developing child's cognitive needs for conservation, representation, relations, and comprehension could be met through religion's offering of permanence in God, authority in Scripture, experience in worship, and meaning through providence respectively. Building on contemporary humanistic psychology, Clippinger (1973) proposed a model for personhood that includes a deep-seated religious need. Similar to Jung's religious dynamism, this need must be met or personality is truncated and inadequately developed. Thus religion is presented as meeting an innate and instinctive urge in persons.

Changes in religious belief is the other developmental issue that has been addressed. For example, Goldman (1964) studied the changes that occur in religious belief among English children and adolescents. He noted a shift from concrete, to literal, to symbolic understandings of religious ideas. Feldman (1979) did extensive survey research on changes in religious belief and practice during the college years and found, as was expected, a trend toward liberalization and secularization in this age group. More recently Fowler (1981), working within Kohlberg's theories of moral development, has proposed a theory of faith development that involves the relating of cognitive structures, innate needs for meaning, and the interpretation of religious symbols. His multistage model resembles Goldman in his basic thesis that maturation involves an increasing tolerance for others' beliefs and a tendency to interpret religious ideas symbolically (*see* FAITH).

Religious experience. The role that conversion played in the field at the turn of the century has been taken over by religious experience. With the increasing interest in altered states of consciousness and transpersonal psychology, religious experience has become a popular focus of attention. Clark (1968) has been the dominant voice in this area, having written about the mystical dimensions of religious experience for the past two decades. It has been his contention that modern society with its pragmatic, technological, rationalistic emphases militates against religious experience, which he, along with other theorists, considers a basic human proclivity. He has therefore advocated the use of triggers such as meditative practices and even psychedelic drugs to induce the experience. While not necessarily agreeing with his willingness to use pharmacological substances for this purpose, many other scholars agree with his analysis and encourage persons to indulge this dimension of their personalities. Among research-oriented psychologists Hood (1976) has been most active in investigating the correlates of intense mystical experience. He has related it to the type of church background, ego strength, nature experiences, and mental health.

Through the years the focal religious experience that has occupied the attention of psychologists of religion has been CONVERSION, and although other matters have assumed importance, there remains a persistent interest in this phenomenon as it applies to both Christianity and to newer religious movements in the United States. A recent publication (Johnson & Malony, 1982) summarizes the literature on Christian conversion, while an earlier volume (Needleman, 1978) attends to non-Christian movements.

Religious orientation. As originally conceived by Allport and Ross (1967), RELIGIOUS ORIENTATION has been the major theme in the psychology of religion for the last 15 years. Many investigations of this phenomenon have been undertaken. Originally conceived by Allport to explain the relationship between religiosity and prejudice, religion that is oriented intrinsically (toward inner, personal, private meaning) and religion that is extrinsically oriented (toward fellowship, pragmatic satisfaction, external value) have been contrasted in numerous studies. While Allport and his students found intrinsically oriented religion to be more idealistic and less related to ethnic prejudice, subsequent theorists have found less clear relationships between these orientations and other behaviors. Some have noted that the concepts behind the terms *intrinsic* and *extrinsic* are value loaded in favor of individualism—a characteristic not typically available to the average person. Others have concluded that the two orientations are not as clear conceptually as might be hoped. The research is ongoing and stimulating. Most recently an age-free form of the Extrinsic-Intrinsic Religious Orientation Scale has been designed to assess whether there is a tendency for persons to mature in one direction.

Religious dimensions. Finally, the last two decades have witnessed increasing attention paid to describing the several dimensions of religiousness. This line of research has attempted to develop taxonomies of how religious persons differ from one another. While it has been obvious that there are variations in beliefs among religious persons (e.g., fundamentalist, conservative, mainline, liberal), it has been less apparent that religious persons differ in religious knowledge, the importance of religion, openness to doubt, and participation. Among psychologists the most extensive research into these phenomena has been that of King and Hunt (1975). In a study involving a national sample they isolated a number of dimensions, including belief, devotional practices, church attendance, church activity, financial support, religious knowledge, rated importance of religion, intrinsic/extrinsic orientation, and attitude toward despair. Currently attempts are being made to see if this pattern can be replicated among racial and ethnic groups, since the original research was conducted among whites.

The religion of psychologists. One final aspect of research in psychology of religion should be noted; namely, studies of the religion of psychologists. Since all research in this century has indicated that psychologists are the least religious of all scientists, it has become of interest to see how, if at all, this pattern is changing in the present and what effect, if any, the religion of the psychologist has on the research that is done. In a recent study (Ragan, Malony, & Beit-Hallahmi, 1980) it was noted that while the previous pattern remains, an increasing number of psychologists are actively religious. And at least one theorist (Malony, 1972) has contended that only the religious psychologist knows the appropriate questions to ask of religion in psychological research.

References

Allport, G. W., & Ross, J. M. Personal religious orientation and prejudice. *Journal of Personality and Social Psychology*, 1967, *5*, 432–443.

Barkman, P. F. The relationship of personality modes to religious experience and behavior. *Journal of the American Scientific Affiliation*, 1968, *20*, 27–30.

Benson, P., & Spilka, B. God image as a function of self-esteem and locus of control. *Journal for the Scientific Study of Religion*, 1973, *12*, 297–310.

Berger, P. L. Some second thoughts on substantive versus functional definitions of religion. *Journal for the Scientific Study of Religion*, 1974, *13*, 125–133.

Capps, D. Contemporary psychology of religion: The task of theoretical reconstruction. *Social Research*, 1974, *41*, 362–383.

Clark, W. H. *The psychology of religion: An introduction to religious experience and behavior.* New York: Macmillan, 1958.

Clark, W. H. The psychology of religious experience. *Psychology Today*, 1968, *1*(9), 42–47; 68–69.

Clippinger, J. A. Toward a human psychology of personality. *Journal of Religion and Health*, 1973, *12*, 241–258.

Dittes, J. E. Psychology of religion. In N. Lindzey & E. Aronson (Eds.), *The handbook of social psychology* (2nd ed.). Reading, Mass.: Addison-Wesley, 1968.

Elkind, D. The origins of religion in the child. *Review of Religious Research*, 1970, *12*, 35–42.

Feldman, K. A. Change and stability of religious orientations during college. *Review of Religious Research*, 1969, *11*, 40–60.

Fowler, J. W. *Stages of faith.* San Francisco: Harper & Row, 1981.

Freud, S. *The future of an illusion.* New York: Liveright, 1928.

Goldman, R. *Religious thinking from childhood to adolescence.* New York: Seabury, 1964.

Hall, G. S. *Adolescence* (2 vols.). New York: Arno Press, 1904.

Hall, G. S. *Jesus, the Christ, in the light of psychology* (2 vols.). New York: Doubleday, 1917.

Hood, R. W. Conceptual criticisms of regressive explanations of mysticism. *Review of Religious Research*, 1976, *17*, 179–188.

James, W. *The varieties of religious experience.* New York: Modern Library, 1961. (Originally published, 1902.)

Johnson, C. B., Malony, H. N. *Christian conversion: Biblical and psychological perspectives.* Grand Rapids: Zondervan, 1982.

King, M. B. & Hunt, R. A. Measuring the religious variable: National replication. *Journal for the Scientific Study of Religion*, 1975, *14*, 13–22.

Lemert, C. C. Defining non-church religion. *Review of Religious Research*, 1975, *16*, 186–197.

Leuba, J. H. A study in the psychology of religious phenomena. *American Journal of Psychology*, 1896, *5*, 309–385.

Malony, H. N. The psychologist-Christian. *Journal of the American Scientific Affiliation*, 1972, *24*, 135–144.

Needleman, J. *Understanding the new religions.* New York: Seabury, 1978.

Ragan, C., Malony, H. N., & Beit-Hallahmi, B. Psychologists and religion: Professional factors and personal belief. *Review of Religious Research*, 1980, *21*, 208–217.

Starbuck, E. D. *Psychology of religion.* London: Walter Scott, 1899.

Additional Readings

Malony, H. N. (Ed.). *Current perspectives in the psychology of religion.* Grand Rapids: Eerdmans, 1977.

H. N. MALONY

Psycholytic Therapy. *See* PSYCHEDELIC THERAPY.

Psychopath. *See* ANTISOCIAL PERSONALITY DISORDER.

Psychopathology. *See* ABNORMAL PSYCHOLOGY.

Psychopathology in Primitive Cultures. This discussion must begin with three caveats. First, there is no one, uniform primitive culture; primitive, or preliterate, cultures differ from one another as much as from Western society. Second, primitive is by no means to be equated with primeval or simple; primitive cultures have histories as long as those of Western societies and social structures that are often more, not less, complicated than ours. Third, one must beware of interpreting primitive behaviors as psychopathological merely because they differ from Western norms.

This last, particularly ethnocentric bias is especially hazardous and all too common in many psychiatric examinations of primitive behaviors; it must to some extent be laid at the feet of Freud himself. Erwin Ackerknecht, physician, historian, and ethnologist, has trenchantly argued against psychopathological reductionism of primitive institutionalized behaviors: "When [primitive] religion is but 'organized schizophrenia,' then there is left no room or necessity for history, anthropology, sociology, etc. God's earth was, and is, but a gigantic state hospital and pathography becomes the unique and universal science" (1971, p. 61).

Such psychopathologizing has been particularly evident in studies conceptualizing shamans, sorcerers, and witches as so many cases of mental disorder. Rosen (1968), Jackson and Jackson (1970), Hoch (1974), Hippler (1976), and others have demonstrated that witches are more likely to be socially deviant than mentally ill and that witch doctors and seers, while often exceptional individuals, usually show no more psychopathology by the standards of their culture than their peers. Indeed, in their study of the Mescalero Apache, Boyer, Klopper, Brauer, and Kawai (1964) even proposed that shamans, if culturally deviant, are deviant in the direction of mental health. What all this points toward is a recognition of the cultural relativity of concepts such as normality and pathology. What is adjudged commonplace and adaptive in one culture may well be labeled pathological in another.

Specific Syndromes. In their excellent text Tseng and McDermott (1981) delineate five subtypes of culture-related specific psychiatric conditions: 1) those given a cultural interpretation and remedy (e.g., susto); 2) those resulting from specific culturally induced stressors (e.g., voodoo death and malgri); 3) those distinguished by well-defined psychiatric syndromes peculiar to the society (e.g., latah, amok); 4) those influenced on multiple levels by cultural factors (e.g., koro and windigo, or wiitiko); and 5) conditions possibly culture related (e.g., the diffuse hysterical and depersonalization symptoms of Puerto-Rican syndrome).

Susto occurs among Spanish-speaking persons in Latin America and the United States. Its symptoms of weakness, headache, diarrhea, fearfulness, anxiety, and tremulousness are precipitated by shocking or frightening experiences. The resultant syndrome is explained by the loss of one of several souls that are believed to reside in the body. Being culturally accepted, susto provides the sufferer with a valid reason to rest and recuperate and a socially ordained treatment—ritual recapture of the soul.

Malgri is a disorder manifesting anxiety and abdominal complaints found in many aboriginal Australian societies. It follows the breaking of a taboo and is believed to result from the invasion of the sufferer by the spirit he has offended. Voodoo death, or thanatomania, is psychological and physical wasting away in response to the belief that one has been victimized by malevolent magic.

Latah in Indonesia and imu among the Ainu of Japan are syndromes precipitated by startle reactions. The startled individual (usually a woman) may mimic the words or actions of the one who has startled her, may burst forth with obscenity and profanity, or may assume a guarded posture or strike out. Among Ainu women the most common occasion for such attacks seems to be seeing a snake. Some writers speculate that the symptoms of latah and imu serve to release otherwise repressed sensual and aggressive impulses. Amok, seen in southeastern Asia, is preceded by a period of brooding. Usually occurring in young males, it is precipitated by loss, rage, or shame and public insult. The individual seizes a dangerous weapon and indiscriminantly smites all in his path until he is himself killed or apprehended. If he survives, the episode is followed by amnesia and exhaustion.

Windigo, or wiitiko, psychosis afflicts Ojibwa Indians in the United States and Algonguin-speaking Indians in Canada. The sufferer believes himself afflicted with the cannibalistic windigo demon. It is often precipitated by an unsuccessful hunt. Preceded by withdrawal and morbid depression, the syndrome progresses to murderous and cannibalistic behavior. This psychosis occurs in an environment of severe cold and frequent famine and in a culture where males are pushed toward independence at an early age and base their self-esteem on their ability to secure game. Tseng and McDermott (1981) interpret windigo as a pathological adjustment of the modal Ojibwa personality to severe pressures.

Koro, or impotence panic, is encountered among the Chinese. It is a state of severe anxiety brought on by the conviction that one's penis is receding into his abdomen. Masturbation is a common precipitant, and it is related to the Chinese folk belief that semen (equated with life force) lost through masturbation is not replenished, as it is in normal intercourse. Epidemiologically, koro sufferers seem to come from households with physically or emotionally absent fathers and smothering mothers—classic aggravants of oedipal conflicts.

Interpretations. Theoretical interpretations of these and related syndromes vary widely. Many view them as nothing more than cultural variations of universal disorders such as schizophrenia and hysteria. Others see them as primary psychiatric syndromes in their own right. There is even disagreement over whether many of these syndromes are truly culture bound. Clearly, much empirical and epidemiological work remains to be done.

For many years it was believed that schizophrenia was relatively uncommon in primitive cultures. The evidence is equivocal, though it is becoming increasingly accepted that there are not significant differences in the prevalence of this psychosis in preliterate and Westernized societies. Moreover, the core symptoms are the same—hallucinations, delusions, thought disorder. Cultural factors seem to determine the content of delusions and hallucinations rather than affecting the underlying process of the disorder itself.

If certain primitive cultures appear to have indigenous syndromes, they also have their unique ways of treatment. While primitive psychopathology itself is far from elucidated, primitive psychotherapy is even less so (see Frank, 1973, and Torrey, 1972).

The investigation of preliterate psychopathology offers excellent opportunities to investigate the relationship between intrapsychic dynamics and social structure, and to understand the ways in which cultural institutions function variously as stressors and coping mechanisms. It also serves as a check to facile extrapolations from Western character and psychopathology to humanity in general.

References
Ackerknecht, E. H. *Medicine and ethnology.* Baltimore: Johns Hopkins University Press, 1971.
Boyer, L. B., Klopper, B., Brauer, F., & Kawai, H. Comparisons of shamans and pseudoshamans of the Apache of the Mescalero Indian Reservation. *Journal of Projective Techniques and Personality Assessment,* 1964, *28*(2), 173–180.
Frank, J. *Persuasion and healing* (Rev. ed.). Baltimore: Johns Hopkins University Press, 1973.
Hippler, A. C. Shamans, curers, and personality: Suggestions toward a theoretical model. In W. P. Lebra (Ed.), *Culture-bound syndromes, ethnopsychiatry, and alternate therapies.* Honolulu: University Press of Hawaii, 1976.
Hoch, E. M. Pir, faquir, and the psychotherapist. *Human Context,* 1974, *6*, 668–677.

Jackson, S., & Jackson, J. Primitive medicine and the historiography of psychiatry. In G. Mora & J. Brand (Eds.), *Psychiatry and its history: Methodological problems in research.* Springfield, Ill.: Thomas, 1970.
Rosen, G. *Madness in society.* Chicago: University of Chicago Press, 1968.
Torrey, E. F. *The mind game: Witch doctors and psychiatrists.* New York: Emerson Hall, 1972.
Tseng, W., & McDermott, J. F. *Culture, mind, and therapy: An introduction to cultural psychiatry.* New York: Brunner/Mazel, 1981.

Additional Readings
Kardiner, A. *The individual and his society.* New York: Columbia University Press, 1939.
Levine, R. *Culture, behavior, and personality,* Chicago: Aldine, 1973.

E. R. WALLACE IV

See CULTURE AND PSYCHOPATHOLOGY.

Psychopharmacology. The study of chemical substances that affect mental and behavioral activity. In 1952 chlorpromazine was first used on a trial basis with schizophrenics. Since then there has been a profound revolution in psychiatric treatment, affecting primarily patients with major psychiatric disturbances such as schizophrenia. The overall population of public mental hospitals has decreased dramatically since the first widespread use of phenothiazines in the mid-1950s. A great many patients who were institutionalized before the use of these drugs are now functioning well in the community.

Classes of Drugs. *Antipsychotics.* The antipsychotic drugs (also known as neuroleptics) are primarily indicated for the treatment of acute psychotic illness. This may be caused by schizophrenia or mania or simply a reaction to overwhelming stress. Psychosis is defined as the persistent misevaluation of perceptions, not attributable to a sensory defect or an afferent abnormality (abnormality in the nerve cells carrying messages to the brain), resulting in erroneous beliefs. There may also be actual misperceptions in the form of illusions or hallucinations, resulting in distortions or delusions that cannot be changed by rational argument or contradictory evidence.

The antipsychotic drugs have been used primarily to treat schizophrenia, both for acute exacerbations and for chronic maintenance therapy. They are also used for psychotic depressive reactions—i.e., a major depression with gross agitation, confusion, or delusions. Antipsychotics are often used in treating an acute manic state while patients are being started on lithium therapy. They do not actually end the manic episode, but they do slow the patient down and often can be discontinued after lithium treatment has been instituted.

They are primarily effective in reducing combativeness, tension, agitation, hyperactivity, hostility, negativism, acute delusional thinking, insomnia, anorexia, and poor self-care. They significantly reduce or eliminate hallucinations, ideas of reference, thought broadcasting, thought insertion, persecutory ideation, as well as various thought disorders including loosening of associations and racing or slowed thinking. The typical blocking and inability to focus attention found in schizophrenia are often helped greatly, as are the flattening of affect and the bizarre movements, such as posturing, waxy flexibility, grimacing, and inappropriate smiling. Symptoms such as absence of insight, poor judgment, chronic delusions, and personality idiosyncracies are much less responsive to antipsychotic medications.

Numerous antipsychotic medications have been studied extensively. To date no major differences in efficacy have been demonstrated in any of these drugs. The differences in the drugs relate primarily to the secondary effects of the medications, such as sedation. The predictors of a good response to antipsychotic drugs in acute situations have to do with individual patient issues. They may be related more to the severity of the illness than to the particular drug used, although this issue is currently under a great deal of study. Schizophrenic patients who are most responsive tend to be those who have a good prognosis—i.e., those who have a later age of onset, a higher level of functioning before their acute episode, a history of more than two years of continuous employment, rapid onset of symptoms, and less than two months of prior hospitalization. More chronic patients, with more personality deterioration, tend not to experience as much benefit from these medications, although major psychotic symptoms are usually reversible. The medications definitely shorten the length of hospitalization. With many patients having good support systems, using antipsychotic medications often eliminates the need for hospitalization.

There are at least 20 different antipsychotic drugs currently marketed in the United States, most of which are classified as phenothiazine medications. There are several other drugs that are nonphenothiazine antipsychotics, including haloperidol, butyrophenones, thioxanthenes, molindone, and loxapine. All the drugs are available in tablet or capsule form. Many of the agents are also available in liquid or injectable form for the acute situation where patients are either resistant to taking their medications or are not absorbing their medica-

tions well. In addition, there are some preparations that are injectable in slow-release forms, so that a person would need a shot perhaps on a weekly, biweekly, or even a monthly basis. These preparations are very useful for patients who have compliance problems.

The most common side effects of the antipsychotic drugs are sedation and extrapyramidal symptoms. Sedation can usually be eliminated with proper dosage and by taking all the dose at bedtime. There is some accommodation to sedation over time. The extrapyramidal symptoms include stiffness, muscle spasms, tremors, restlessness, blank stares, shuffling gait, and occasionally depression. These symptoms are treatable with anticholinergic medications used to treat Parkinson's disease.

The most troublesome side effect of the antipsychotics is tardive dyskinesia. This syndrome appears in patients who have been on large doses of medication for a long period of time, often many years, and is, unfortunately, often irreversible. (It has been noted in some patients to occur fairly soon after onset of treatment, but in these patients it is usually reversible.) Patients experience grimacing of their lips or protrusion of the tongue in often very disconcerting ways. In severe cases there may also be choreiform movements of the arms and trunk. The incidence of tardive dyskinesia may be as high as 30% in older patients, who are more likely than younger ones to develop the symptoms. This has resulted in efforts to keep the dose of antipsychotics as low as possible and to use those drugs chronically only when absolutely necessary.

Lithium. Lithium carbonate has been to the bipolar disorder patient what antipsychotic medications have been to the schizophrenic patient. Lithium is a basic element very closely associated with sodium. In fact lithium was first used as a sodium substitute. It has been in use in the United States since 1970 and in Europe since the 1950s as an effective treatment for bipolar disorder. Lithium carbonate is indicated for the treatment of the acute phase of mania, and will stabilize or break manic episodes with a 70 to 80% success rate in 10 to 14 days. It will also help to alleviate depressive episodes, although the improvement percentage is not quite so high. Perhaps even more importantly, lithium is very effective on a prophylactic basis in preventing manic and depressive episodes in patients with bipolar disorder. It is also used with many patients with recurrent unipolar depressions on a prophylactic basis. It is not effective in treating or preventing episodes of depression in patients with depressive characters or dysthymic disorder. The effectiveness of lithium is somewhat related to the severity of the illness. Patients who function well between episodes tend to have fewer relapses while taking lithium than patients with underlying or coexisting personality problems. Lithium is generally less effective with patients who tend to have a rapid cycling of their affective illness. There is also evidence that lithium may help some patients with atypical psychoses and patients with schizoaffective disorder.

The effectiveness of lithium carbonate depends on blood level, not dosage. The general therapeutic range is 0.6 to 1.2 meq./L. The drug tends to be ineffective at levels less than 0.6 meq./L., and when the level gets too high (1.5 meq./L.), toxic effects begin to appear. Within the therapeutic range, however, there are very few side effects. Occasionally patients develop a mild tremor. Some patients complain of nausea when they are first starting on this medication. Some experience increased thirst and urinary frequency. There may also be weight gain. As blood levels increase into the toxic range, many problems develop, including tremor, mental confusion, ataxia, nausea, vomiting, and diarrhea. At severely toxic ranges patients have convulsions and may go into coma or die. Because the toxic level is fairly close to the therapeutic level, lithium treatment is monitored by frequent blood level checks. On a maintenance basis these can be done monthly or bimonthly, but should generally be done more often when treatment is first started. Lithium levels should be checked as close as possible to 12 hours after the last dose of lithium. This enables a reasonable interpretation of the meaning of the blood level. There is some evidence that there may be long-term effects on the kidneys. There have been decreases in renal function noted in patients who have been on lithium on a long-term basis. However, these have not resulted in any major damage to kidney function to date. Nevertheless, patients should have kidney function studies on an annual basis. In addition, lithium has been shown to have effects on thyroid gland function in some patients.

Antidepressant drugs. Depression is probably the most common reason why patients seek psychiatric treatment or counseling. The major issue in antidepressant drug treatment is differential diagnosis. Depressed mood is not the only problem associated with depression. There is a continuum of severity of depressive illness, with an increasing number of symptoms appearing that affect major bodily func-

tions. This syndrome is known as endogenous depression and includes sleep and appetite disturbance, decreased energy, decreased interest, loss of pleasure, impaired concentration and attention, self-blame, hopelessness, preoccupation with death, loss of sexual interest, headaches and other somatic complaints, and often psychomotor agitation or retardation. The syndrome relates to altered neurobiological functioning in the central nervous system. Patients who have more of these symptoms are more likely to respond to antidepressant medication. Patients who have dysthymic disorder and characterologic depressions, with chronic low self-esteem, do not do as well on antidepressant medications, although some studies show that as many as 25% of these patients will benefit from antidepressant medications. The response rate for patients with true endogenous depression is about 70 to 75%. This fits in well with the hypothesis of a biological change in the functioning of the nervous system in a major depressive illness (see DEPRESSION: PHYSIOLOGICAL FACTORS).

Antidepressant medications normalize the biological changes in the brain associated with depression. As a result patients experience improved sleep, appetite, and energy level. Their concentration improves and they become more motivated. They are able to experience pleasure, and they regain interest in things. The medication does not change core neurotic conflicts or pathological interpersonal relationships. However, the medications do often facilitate participation in psychotherapy where previously a patient may have been so depressed that he was unable to act on the insights gained in therapy or was so confused that he was unable to participate in a meaningful way. After treatment with medications patients are often able to participate in therapy and institute significant changes in their lives.

Recent research has demonstrated that antidepressants may also be useful in the prevention of panic attack syndrome. They have also been effective in treating enuresis in children and some patients with chronic pain syndrome.

Improvement in depressive symptoms begins five to seven days after treatment is initiated in the newer agents, and 10 to 14 days in some of the earlier drugs. Maximal benefits may take three or four weeks. Patients are usually treated for three to four months at therapeutic dosage ranges, followed by a gradual tapering of the dose. Abrupt discontinuation of the medication often will cause a withdrawal syndrome with restless sleep, bizarre dreams, agitation, and nausea. Some patients have had seizures. Patients who have recurrent disabling depression may require long-term · maintenance treatment with the antidepressants or possibly with lithium carbonate. These are patients who often require hospitalization. There are no known long-term side effects of antidepressants.

There are eight tricyclic antidepressants currently marketed, with more on the way. These are usually the drugs of first choice for the treatment of endogenous depression. They are equally effective and vary primarily in the degree of sedation versus arousal. There are also variations in the degree of blockade of the neurotransmitters serotonin and norepinephrine, which may have treatment implications as the neurobiology of depression is further understood.

Monoamine oxidase inhibitors are used more frequently in Great Britain than in the United States. They are equally as effective as the other major class of antidepressant medications, the tricyclic antidepressants. However, there are significant dietary restrictions because of the risk of a sudden hypertensive episode caused by tyramine, a precursor of norepinephrine. As a result, patients are unable to eat foods with tyramine in them. Foods containing tyramine include beer, wine, pickled herring, cheese, chicken liver, yeast, coffee, broad bean pods, canned figs, and chocolate. Caffeine and antihistaminic drugs are also to be used with extreme caution.

In the United States the monoamine oxidase inhibitors tend to be used more with atypical depressions and are generally not a drug of choice for classical endogenous depressions. The three most commonly used monoamine oxidase inhibitors in the United States are isocrarboxazid (Marplan), phenelzine (Nardil), and tranylcypromine (Parnate). They are used most often with patients with anxious, phobic depressions, and they have often been very helpful with borderline personalities who manifest a great deal of dysphoric mood (sometimes known as hysteroid dysphoria).

In addition, there is a whole new generation of antidepressants on the horizon. These drugs have considerably less cardiotoxicity and will probably be much safer for older patients.

The antidepressants can be lethal. As little as a week's supply of medication may be enough to cause death. Care must be exercised with suicidal patients. They should be carefully monitored by a friend or family member. Hospitalization may be necessary. Peak response to the drugs may take as long as three to four weeks. Patients vary greatly in the amount of absorption and in the rates of metabolism of the drug, and some studies have shown as much as a fortyfold difference in blood levels between patients with the same dose of medication. Individual differences in susceptibility to side effects may mean that a given patient will need several trials before finding the right drug. Therapists should be patient and reassuring. It is very helpful to know and trust the psychiatrist who is prescribing the medication.

The antidepressants have a significant number of short-term side effects that can be quite a nuisance. Primary among these is sedation. All the antidepressants are sedating. For this reason the medication is most often prescribed to be taken at bedtime in a single daily dose. With proper dosage and with the right drug, it should be possible to get patients on a therapeutic dose of a medication without daytime sedation. In addition, many patients are troubled with dry mouth, and some have problems with constipation. There is also a tendency for blood pressure to be lowered, with resultant dizziness and lightheadedness. Other side effects are much less common, but patients should be encouraged to call their doctors to discuss any problems they feel may be caused by their medication.

Antianxiety drugs. The antianxiety drugs are by far the most popular drugs in our nation. Approximately two-thirds of the prescriptions for psychotropic drugs in 1970 were for antianxiety drugs or sedative hypnotic drugs. The vast majority of these prescriptions were not written by psychiatrists but rather by primary practice physicians. The antianxiety drugs have been quite lucrative for drug companies, and new medications are being introduced rapidly. There is considerable controversy about the use of these drugs, with a variety of viewpoints being expressed. Unfortunately these medications are often used as a substitute for problem solving, conflict resolution, or stress reduction techniques. The blame lies both with overly busy physicians and with patients who demand medication rather than dealing with their problems.

Antianxiety agents are legitimately prescribed for the relief of moderate to severe anxiety symptoms in acute stress situations; when usual therapeutic efforts are not successful at reducing severe symptoms; or when other anxiety control measures, such as relaxation or stress management techniques, do not sufficiently alleviate the anxiety. The usefulness of these agents in the chronic generalized anxiety states has not been fully assessed. Antianxiety drugs are often used as part of the treatment of depression when there is a significant degree of anxiety present. These drugs are also used in treating phobic conditions and panic disorder. There is some doubt that agoraphobia is effectively treated by these drugs because the learning that occurs while a person is on the drug appears not to generalize to a drug-free state. These drugs are also used for the management of acute alcohol withdrawal syndromes.

There is some abuse potential with antianxiety agents. The drugs have been shown to be physiologically addictive when used at high dosages for long periods of time, with a physiological withdrawal syndrome similar to alcohol withdrawal. This syndrome has received widespread publicity in the past few years. While it is a serious problem in some patients, it should be remembered that antianxiety medications are the most frequently prescribed drugs in the world. The incidence of abuse is quite small, well under ½ of 1%. A careful history should be obtained of the patient's use of alcohol or other sedatives prior to prescribing antianxiety agents. Addiction-prone personalities should not take these medications.

In addition to physiological dependence there is a psychological dependence syndrome in that people feel they need the medication in order to function. Occasionally this may come about because of a mild euphoric effect induced by the medication. More commonly it results because of the return of anxiety symptoms when the medication is stopped. In general, open-ended prescriptions for these medications should not be given. Patients on antianxiety agents should be followed carefully and should ideally be involved in some sort of ongoing psychotherapeutic treatment.

The barbiturates and meprobamate are the oldest antianxiety agents. They are still widely used, although many physicians consider them to be obsolete because of their high abuse potential. These drugs have a large amount of tolerance and also a low threshold of lethality, making them dangerous agents for patients who are at any risk for suicide. There are a large number of barbiturates available, differing primarily in their duration of action. They are widely used and abused as street drugs. Hydroxizine is used most often as a preoperative sedative. While it is not highly publicized, many patients achieve good control of anxiety with this medication.

The most frequently prescribed class of antianxiety agents are the benzodiazepines. This includes drugs such as Valium, Librium, Serax, Tranxene, Lorazepam, Xanax, and Centrax, all of which are marketed as antianxiety agents. They all have similar effects, differing primarily in their rapidity of absorption, onset of action, duration of action, and accumulation in body tissues. They are very safe drugs in general, with a low incidence of side effects and a very low lethality, making them difficult to use for suicide. The major side effect to be considered is sedation. Some patients also experience a paradoxical agitation with some of the medications. Other side effects are rare.

Practical Issues for Christian Therapists.
One major issue for a Christian counselor with a patient who is having fairly severe symptoms is whether or not to refer the patient for a medication evaluation. If the counselor is in a situation where a psychiatrist is employed or involved as a consultant, this evaluation can be done as part of an initial evaluation of the patient for treatment planning. Therapists should be acquainted with the symptoms of the major psychiatric syndromes, such as endogenous depression, mania, and schizophrenia. If these symptoms are noticed during evaluation or history gathering, patients should be evaluated by a psychiatrist. In addition, if the usual therapeutic approach to resolving depressive or anxiety symptoms does not result in improvement over a reasonable amount of time, a referral for a medication evaluation should be considered.

Many Christian counselors work in situations where they have an ongoing relationship with a Christian psychiatrist. The important concern is that the psychiatrist be competent in diagnostic assessment and expert in the use of psychotropic medications in conjunction with psychotherapy. He or she should be a person who is willing to communicate freely about patients with their therapist. Therapists should feel comfortable with the consulting psychiatrist as a professional and as a person irrespective of his Christian religious beliefs. A competent non-Christian psychopharmacologist might be more valuable than a Christian psychiatrist who is not knowledgeable about current psychotropic medications. The psychiatrist should be someone who is willing to discuss medications and their side effects with the patient and with the therapist. The psychiatrist also should be a good diagnostician. Proper treatment decisions require proper diagnostic assessment.

Resistance to medications. Many patients and therapists have problems with an illness model of psychological problems. It may conflict with the therapeutic ideology of the counselor, who may prefer to work with a growth-oriented model or a sin model. The therapist may feel that he or she has failed if the patient requires medication and therefore be reluctant to refer a patient for a drug evaluation. Similarly, patients may feel that Christians should not use medications, that somehow this is an admission of mental illness and that a Christian should not have mental illness. This might result in a fear of a poor testimony or present some threat to their faith. There is a very common fear among Christian people that a non-Christian psychiatrist would immediately attack their religious beliefs. While this may be true in some situations, the vast majority of psychiatrists are not interested in attacking other people's religious beliefs.

A basic approach that can be used in these situations is to realize that many mental illnesses are biological illnesses, particularly major mental illnesses such as schizophrenia, bipolar disorder, and major endogenous depression. A person with diabetes, arthritis, or an ulcer would not hesitate to seek medical care. While such patients might feel guilty about not being able to obtain healing by prayer, it is a rare patient who refuses medical care when he or she needs it. Furthermore, psychiatric evaluation might discover that the supposed emotional problem is actually a medical problem presenting with psychiatric symptoms.

Many patients also fear being overmedicated and unable to function as a result. These patients should be reminded that the goal of psychiatrists is not to sedate the patient but to work in an alliance for optimal drug therapy with the lowest dose of medication possible, the minimization of side effects, and the shortest possible duration of treatment.

Many therapists fear that medication will suppress symptoms and remove the patient's motivation for psychotherapy. This has been a subject of debate since the initiation of psychotropic drugs 30 years ago. To date there is no convincing evidence in the literature to support this fear. In fact, the opposite has been shown to be the case. Patients usually are better able to participate in therapy when they are optimally medicated. However, other issues may arise as a result of drug treatment that should be dealt with in therapy as any other issues would be. These have to do with feelings about having an illness and the effects of medication on the patient's ability to assume responsibility for thoughts, feelings, and behavior. Some patients are not sure if they are feeling better because they have done the work themselves or because their medication is working.

Conclusion. Psychotropic medication has tremendous potential to assist Christians having emotional difficulties. It is important to recognize the limitations of medication. These drugs are useful for the control of symptoms and the correction of certain biological problems in some patients. The drugs do not affect basic personality organization, character style, cognitive modes, or conscious and unconscious psychological conflicts. This material is all left for the therapist to work through with the patient.

Additional Readings
Baldessarini, R. J. *Chemotherapy in psychiatry*, Cambridge: Harvard University Press, 1977.
Lion, J. R. *The art of medicating psychiatric patients*. Baltimore: Williams & Wilkins, 1978.

R. J. SALINGER

Psychophysics. The attempt to study the relationship between the physical stimuli in our environment and the psychological sensations these stimuli produce. The two German scientists credited with founding psychophysics, Ernst Weber and Gustav Fechner, studied sensory thresholds. They, and many investigators who followed them, assumed that there was an absolute threshold for each sense, a stimulus value that marked a sharp cutoff between sensing and not sensing a stimulus. In the 1840s Weber began investigating the ability to perceive small differences between stimuli (difference thresholds). Using well-trained observers and very careful measurements, he found that the greater the magnitude of a stimulus, the greater the difference between it and another had to be for the first stimulus to be barely noticeable. He also discovered that the ratio of the noticeable difference to the magnitude of the stimulus was constant for each aspect of the stimulus he investigated (Weber's law). The ratios for various stimuli (e.g. brightness, loudness, weight) are known as Weber fractions and can be used to predict how much stimulus change is needed to be barely noticeable.

In 1860 Fechner published *Elements of Psychophysics*, which formalized psychophysical methods and also extended the relationship Weber had described. His revised equation, known as Fechner's law, states that sensation is a function of the logarithm of the stimulus magnitude multiplied by a constant (which can take on different values depending upon the sense and stimulus being investigated). Subsequent studies have shown that Weber's and Fechner's laws are fairly accurate except for extremely large or small stimulus values.

In the last 25 years investigators have questioned the assumption that there really are sharply defined sensory thresholds. Even Weber's observers varied in their ability to detect differences from trial to trial. He found it necessary to run many trials, defining threshold as the midpoint of a whole range of values (the interval of uncertainty), which could be detected in some trials but not in others. These fluctuations were thought to reflect random changes in testing conditions or in the observer, but not in the actual threshold.

Later experiments in which the stimulus was only presented in randomly selected trials have shown that people not only correctly discern when a stimulus is present or absent (hits), or occasionally miss stimuli (misses), but also report sensations in the absence of stimulation (false alarms). Furthermore, the percentage of hits and false alarms a person reports can vary depending upon his or her estimates of the probability that the stimulus will occur and with rewards or punishments for hits or false alarms.

These results led Tanner and Swets (1954) to propose signal detection theory to account for threshold phenomena. Threshold signals are always detected against a background of irrelevant "noise" in the brain and require the observer to make a decision as to whether something has occurred or not. The observer uses a criterion, a particular level of sensory activity, to make this decision. Only if the level of activity produced by background (or by the cumulative effects of background and the stimulus) exceeds the criterion will an observer report sensing the stimulus—producing a false alarm or a hit, respectively. The criterion can shift depending on a number of variables—such as the observer's expectancies, the rewards for hits, or penalties for false alarms—and must be taken into account in threshold experiments. A way to measure actual sensitivity apart from the fluctuations in the criterion has also been developed. (See Green & Swets, 1966; Gescheider, 1976).

References

Gescheider, G. A. *Psychophysics method and theory.* Hillsdale, N.J.: Lawrence Erlbaum Associates, 1976.

Green, D. M., & Swets, J. A. *Signal detection theory and psychophysics.* New York: Wiley, 1966.

Tanner, W. P., Jr., & Swets, J. A. A decision-making theory of visual detection. *Psychological Review,* 1954, *61,* 401–409.

E. L. Hillstrom

Psychosexual Development. The psychological development of an individual is intricately involved with the development of his or her sexuality. While psychosexual development occurs throughout life, it is probably predominant in the first six years of life and has seeds in the infant's earliest human contact. One's love relationship with parents will determine future loving relationships with the opposite sex. Adequately developed sexuality will also contribute to adult achievement, success, and capacity to accept failure.

Psychoanalytic authors, depending heavily and expanding upon Freud's ideas of infantile sexuality, dominate the literature on psychosexual development. Fenichel's (1945) remarkable summary work provides a review of the classical Freudian perspective. He begins with Freud and draws also upon Karl Abraham, Franz Alexander, Paul Federn, and Sandor Ferenczi. These authors suggest that there are various stages of psychosexual development during which certain aspects of sexuality and related psychology develop. Adequate parental love and proper adaptation lay the groundwork for good adult mental functioning, whereas inadequate adjustment during these periods is cause for FIXATIONS at one or more of these stages. Such psychosexual developmental fixations are at the root of the adult neurosis.

Freudian Developmental Stages. *Earliest infantile life (o–6 weeks).* During this phase the infant has an uncomplicated psychic apparatus and responds only with excitation or relaxation. The newborn has no real ego and is driven by instinctual forces, primarily the life-sustaining drive of hunger. The infant alternates between hunger/dissatisfaction and sleep/satisfaction. Freud (1936) suggests that birth causes a flooding with excitation, called birth trauma, and the manner in which the infant copes with the first excitation determines much of his later adjustment.

This first stage of life where the infant has no real sense of anything separate from himself is called primary narcissism. In the absence of boundaries between self and others (particularly the mother) the infant conceives of himself as omnipotent and is entirely self-serving. If he is hungry, he projects his feelings of omnipotence onto the outside world, and perhaps loses a sense of existence momentarily. Then when he is fed, he receives the omnipotence back.

While there may be some early sense of sexuality during this phase, sexual feelings are sufficiently merged with the hunger drive as to be indistinguishable. Even pleasure as such may not really exist.

Oral stage (1 week–18 months). The age span in this and all other stages is approximate. However, in the first year and a half of life the primary narcissism of earliest infancy is gradually replaced by the passive-receptive activity of eating. Increasingly the infant masters his own excitation and relaxation by means of his mouth. The mouth is used both to eat and to scream as a means of getting fed. This orality is so dominant that most of the infant's activities in his first year of life are mouth related.

Freud viewed these oral activities as also erotic. Infantile eroticism is not genital, as it is for later children and even more for adults; rather, it is a drive-related experience in which the infant seeks a reduction of libido (instinctual tension) by oral means. Some activities having infantile sexual overtones include thumb sucking, fondling of a comforter-blanket, and even screaming. It appears that eating is often simultaneously a hunger-satisfying and an erotic pleasurable experience for infants.

Abraham (1927) suggests that there are two substages of orality: a preambivalent phase, when the infant sucks and feeds for intrinsic pleasure, and the ambivalent phase, in which a sense of an external object feeding him has developed. In this second substage the infant both loves (feeds) and hates (bites) the feeding object. When the infant is feeding, he feels that he is not being fed a substance but that he is eating the mother in a kind of cannibalistic sense. This incorporation of the infant's first love object serves as the basis for later ways of relating to the world.

If one is fixated at the oral stage, whether by unknown personal factors or by inadequate parenting, he will retain in his psychological makeup evidence of orality and omnipotence. Earliest deprivations and fixations often result in schizophrenia or other psychotic disorders. Later fixations may lead to the development of a narcissistic or borderline personality disorder. Other oral fixations will show themselves in the symptoms of greed and unsatiable hunger in some form.

From a positive standpoint much adult sexuality relates to oral pleasure: kissing, sucking, and talking. However, drinking, smoking, and eating also retain a certain sexual quality in adult life, and oral deprivations in childhood are hypothesized to be involved in excesses in these areas.

Anal-sadistic stage (1–3 years). The overlap of time among the stages of psychosexual development indicates that one stage begins before its precursor has elapsed. In fact, all previous stages continue to have effect on all more advanced stages. The anal-sadistic stage is roughly the "terrible twos," during which time an infant struggles with limits and frequently responds with negativism.

In the oral phase of life the libidinal force of the ID, originates and predominates; in the second major phase of life the EGO develops. With the development of the ego the toddler begins to perceive a clearer distinction between himself and his environment. Kohut (1971) suggests that a "self" exists originally in the infant. However, most other psychodynamicists agree with Freud that the self develops in the anal stage as a consequence of the toddler encountering boundaries. It appears that the ego begins to define itself as separate by integrating the frequent limits set by parents and other environmental influences.

Freud labeled this second and third year of life "anal" because it is during this time of life that the infant finds pleasure of control in the sensations surrounding excretion. The "sadistic" part of this stage relates to what Freud and his followers suggest is the destructive tendencies of the child of this age. This destructive element can be seen in the gross motor activity and generally belligerent behavior of two-year-olds, but also, more internally, in the infant's desire to harm his environment (usually his mother) through defecation. Abraham (1927) suggests that this sadistic-destructive element predominates in the first half of the anal stage, whereas later the child learns the pleasure of retention. Abraham sees in this second subphase the seeds of love.

Two futher elements of the anal-sadistic stage are important. The first is that the infant, in feeling both destructive and pleasurable impulses, develops his first ambivalent feelings in life. AMBIVALENCE will be a part of his psychic experience hereafter. Second, these anal-sadistic and related feelings are highly libidinally charged and serve to eroticize the infant. Again, this stage of sexuality is not genitally localized but is localized in anal functions.

Neurotic results of fixations in the anal stage include the specifically anal neuroses (constipation, colitis, hemorrhoids) and related conditions such as obsessive-compulsive neurosis, hoarding, and germophobia. Fenichel (1945) also suggests that paranoia originates here, perhaps related to the failure of the infantile environment to provide adequate and gentle control.

The positive results of this phase contribute to both specifically sexual as well as general personality development. General characteristics include the development of personal value, ability to control impulses, self-restraint, and early forms of love. Sexuality is enhanced by the infant broadening his sense of erotic pleasure beyond the area of his mouth and developing other skin-related sensations of pleasure.

Phallic stage (3–7 years). This stage of life begins in some form near the end of the anal phase and continues until age 6 or 7 in normal development. It is the central component in the Freudian conception of personality development, for it is here that the ego at first has free reign and later is subjected to control by the development of the third major component of the psychic apparatus: the SUPEREGO.

This stage, often referred to as the genital phase, involves the localization of erotic pleasure in the genitals. Masturbation usually occurs and replaces previous sexual sublimations such as thumb sucking. In this stage the love object becomes more clearly sexual. Further, the self-love of the oral phase and the object-use of the anal now begin to be replaced by the rudiments of mutual love of self and object.

The dominant theme in boys during this time of life is what Freud called castration anxiety. The boy identifies his self with his penis, and his fear of punishment, harm, or annihilation results in the fear that he will lose his penis. Sometimes this fear is aggravated by adult comments and behavior, but largely the young boy seems to come by castration fear naturally because of his unduly high narcissistic self-evaluation.

In girls the complement to castration fear is penis envy. According to Freud girls feel cheated, wish they were "complete" genitally, and envy the visible genitals of boys. This envy generalizes to wishing they were boys, and can be the origin of female homosexuality.

Clearer distinctions are made between love and hate during this stage as one loves one parent more than the other. Tenderness develops as the result of striving to acquire and to admire external objects. Social feelings such as sympathy and antipathy develop and the child begins to imitate and idealize his parents and others.

For both girls and boys the climax of infantile sexuality is the oedipus complex, the love and erotic affection for the (opposite sex) parent. The complement of the love of one parent is the jealousy of the other and the "death wish" upon him or her. The oedipal

feelings remain latent for several years and are only slowly replaced by adult sexuality. Siblings or other adult figures may substitute for absent or emotionally unavailable parents.

The genital stage is completed with the onset of the superego. In the simplest sense this psychic entity is that which says no to the instinctual demands of the id, which has had pretty much free reign in the oral and anal stages. The coming of the superego resolves and finishes the oedipus complex and ends infantile innocence. This means that the infant becomes somewhat aware that he cannot have the heterogenital parent. Similarly, he cannot have all the unlimited sexual and other things he presumably wants.

Deprivations during the genital phase of infantile sexuality are primarily parents who are emotionally unavailable for oedipal feelings. Fixations at this stage lead to hysteria in some form and to the symptoms of seductiveness, dependency, passiveness, jealousy of same sex adults, and envy of the opposite sex. The positive results of this phase include the ability to love and experience genitally satisfying sexuality. Ideals, values, and the seeds of morality also germinate here.

Later stages. Freud had little to say about the period of life from 6 to 12 years, which he called latency, because he felt explicitly sexual development was dormant. At puberty the child reactivates old oedipal conflicts and begins to work them out in the form of early adult sexual experiences. Among others Sarnoff (1976) has suggested that latency is very important in psychosexual development. He argues that the latency child experiences humiliation, confusion, and early heterosexual development. Moral development also seems centralized here, as is the related cognitive development.

Puberty, or the onset of adultlike sexual feelings and capabilities, is clearly a watershed for adequate adult psychosexual development. However, puberty is not strictly a developmental stage, but rather a freeing and experimenting with previously established sexuality.

Critique and Evaluation. Although critics of Freud's theory of psychosexual development have come from both psychoanalytic and nonanalytic traditions, the most important critiques have come from the psychodynamic camp. It is said that Freud was remarkably correct in his overall analysis, given his limited access to thorough research. However, conclusions suggested by more recent research include the following: 1) there is more overlap between the stages of infantile development; 2) latency is a misnomer in that this period of life is actively sexual; 3) adolescence is an additional and important stage in psychosexual development; 4) object relationships are more central to ego development than Freud proposed; 5) the development of the self has a separate place beyond the more basic ego functions of the ego, id, and superego, and 6) some of Freud's basic conceptions of feminine psychology are inaccurate.

Bernstein and Warner (1981) summarize the evidence substantiating the overlap of the oral, anal, and phallic stages. Klein was perhaps the first to suggest that oedipal feelings develop in early infancy, not only in the genital stage. More recently Galenson and Roiphe (1976) have discovered that the genital stage may begin as early as 16 months, with observations of genital masturbation occurring even earlier.

Many contemporary psychoanalysts argue that the importance of object relationships in psychosexual development was deemphasized by Freud. Here again Klein (1975) was the first to propose an elaboration of the Freudian model, suggesting in 1921 that the infant first acquired object relationships with feces, then genitals, and finally the mother as he developed a capacity to love. Klein's conception has been challenged as too elaborate, but the importance of early and developing love objects in psychic development is of increasing significance to psychodynamicists.

Kohut (1971) has been the central figure in self psychology, although some of the pioneering work here was done by Jacobson (1964). These theorists suggest that the ego-id-superego formulation is insufficient to comprehend the human psyche. There is, they say, a more basic and yet more comprehensive and lasting entity. The self, they argue, develops very early in infancy parallel to the rest of the psychic apparatus. It is here that one finds the real essence of identity, self-value, and eventually the capacity to love. Kohut's work represents a critique of Freud's psychosexual theory in that it suggests that Freud's failure to see the centrality of self in development marks his theory as incomplete.

Criticism of Freud's psychology of women came first from two of Freud's female students, Karen Horney and Helene Deutsch. Horney (1926) described Freud's penis envy theory as an expression of male arrogance resulting from upbringing in a patriarchal society. Deutch (1944) posited that the mother did not favor the son, as Freud suggested, arguing that perhaps she favored her daughter because of easier identification.

Of major concern to these and other analysts is whether there exists a primary sex (male) and a secondary reaction to it (female), as Freud suggested, or whether each sex develops in parallel fashion. Stoller (1965) and Kleenan (1971) among others suggest the existence of a core gender identity in early infancy. Mixed gender identity is due to inadequate bonding with the mother, whereas adequate love from the mother will foster the separate but equal identities of male and female.

There is general agreement among all these writers that there is predominance of masochism, passivity, low self-esteem, and narcissism in women. When Freud found this phenomenon, he concluded it to be innate or reactionary in that the woman was incomplete. Others have suggested that it might come from cultural factors or from inadequate mothering of the female infant. Few analysts at this point would agree that the female is somehow biologically or psychically deficient. However, a clear understanding of female psychosexual development awaits further research.

References

Abraham, K. *Selected papers of Karl Abraham.* London: L. & V. Woolf, 1927.

Bernstein, A. E., & Warner, G. M. *An introduction to contemporary psychoanalysis.* New York: Aronson, 1981.

Deutch, H. *The psychology of women* (Vol. 1). New York: Grune & Stratton, 1944.

Fenichel, O. *The psychoanalytic theory of neurosis.* New York: Norton, 1945.

Freud, S. *The problem of anxiety.* New York: Norton, 1936.

Galenson, E., & Roiphe, H. Some suggested revisions concerning early female development. *Journal of the American Psychoanalytic Association,* 1976, *24,* 29–57.

Horney, K. The flight from womanhood: The masculinity-complex in women as viewed by men and by women. *International Journal of Psychoanalysis,* 1926, *7,* 324–339.

Jacobson, E. *The self and the object world.* New York: International Universities Press, 1964.

Kleenan, J. The establishment of core gender identity in normal girls. *Archives of Sexual Behavior,* 1971, *1,* 117–129.

Klein, M. *Love, guilt, and reparation.* New York: Delacorte, 1975.

Kohut, H. *The analysis of the self.* New York: International Universities Press, 1971.

Sarnoff, C. *Latency,* New York: Aronson, 1976.

Stoller, R. J. The sense of maleness. *Psychoanalytic Quarterly,* 1965, *34,* 207–218.

R. B. JOHNSON

See SEXUALITY.

Psychosexual Disorders. Disorders in this general diagnostic class all have sexual symptomatology based on a psychological etiology. Disorders of sexual functioning caused exclusively by organic factors are not therefore included. Three major subgroups of disorders exist within this class: GENDER IDENTITY disorders, PARAPHILIAS, and PSYCHOSEXUAL

DYSFUNCTIONS. In addition to these a miscellaneous subgroup includes ego-dystonic HOMOSEXUALITY. The general articles in each of these areas provide an overview of the subgroup and refer to the related articles on each specific psychosexual disorder.

Psychosexual Dysfunctions.

Dysfunctions of the sexual response cycle due to either too much or too little sexual appetite, or psychophysiological problems in the sexual response.

Sexual functioning is a prime example of the indivisibility of human functioning. It is evident that biological, psychological, and social factors all play major and often indistinguishable roles in the continued functioning or dysfunctioning of humans as sexual beings. Modern research confirms the obsolescence of single-causality thinking. Sexual functioning may be impaired by many different factors. Mental imagery produced by the brain, hormonal fluctuation, illness, drugs, aging, and relationship quality are just a few of the variables that affect sexual fulfillment.

Kaplan (1974) divides psychosexual dysfunctions into male and female groups. Male psychosexual dysfunctions are erectile dysfunction (impotence), premature ejaculation, and retarded ejaculation (Masters and Johnson's, 1970, term is ejaculatory incompetence). Female psychosexual dysfunctions are general sexual dysfunction (frigidity), orgastic dysfunction, and vaginismus.

INHIBITED SEXUAL DESIRE is believed to be the most prevalent of all the psychosexual dysfunctions in the American population. The persistent and pervasive inhibition of sexual desire is generally present due to unconscious psychological factors (the removal of which is tenaciously guarded against) and chronic life style stress.

INHIBITED SEXUAL EXCITEMENT involves impairment of the genital vasocongestive reaction. This psychophysiological lessening of genital blood supply results in diminished or absent penile erection and reduction of vaginal lubrication and swelling.

INHIBITED ORGASM in the male is termed retarded ejaculation or ejaculatory incompetence; in the female commonly used terms are orgastic dysfunction or anorgasmia. Orgasm for both sexes involves involuntary, .8 second muscle spasms.

No universally agreed-upon definition of premature EJACULATION exists. Some authorities, such as Kinsey, believe it is normal to ejaculate quickly after penile insertion and commencement of thrusting.

VAGINISMUS consists of involuntary spasms of the muscles at the entrance to the vagina, precluding entrance and occurring whenever any attempt is made to introduce any object into the vaginal opening. The contraction of the vaginal musculature is entirely involuntary.

DYSPAREUNIA is a medical term for painful sexual intercourse. Functional dyspareunia is used to refer to disorders that are without known organic/physical basis.

Prior to the pioneering research of Masters and Johnson (1966, 1970) clinical treatment of psychosexual dysfunctions, using traditional, psychodynamic methods, enjoyed limited success while being expensive and from one to two years in duration. Modern sex therapy methods enjoy a much higher success rate in 8 to 10 sessions.

References
Kaplan, H. S. *The new sex therapy: Active treatment of sexual dysfunctions.* New York: Brunner/Mazel, 1974.
Masters, W. H., & Johnson, V. E. *Human sexual response.* Boston: Little, Brown, 1966.
Masters, W. H., & Johnson, V. E. *Human sexual inadequacy.* Boston: Little, Brown, 1970.

J. R. DAVID

See SEXUAL RESPONSE PSYCHOLOGY; SEX THERAPY; SEXUALITY.

Psychosis. See PSYCHOTIC DISORDERS.

Psychosocial Development.

One of the most influential models of psychosocial development today is that of Erikson (1963), who provides an epigenetic conception of development in which the individual progresses through a hierarchy of stages across the life span. Each stage is characterized by a nuclear conflict that is present throughout life but comes to ascendancy at specific points in the life cycle. Positive resolution of each conflict relates to positive psychological health, prepares the individual for subsequent stages, and promotes effective involvement in an ever-widening social world.

Erikson's structure parallels Freud's psychosexual stages, but greater detail is given to adulthood. Freud's oral stage is associated with Erikson's nuclear conflict of basic trust versus basic mistrust; resolution of this conflict is based on the quality of the parent-child relationship. Freud's anal stage is associated with autonomy versus shame and doubt; here the child is dealing with self-control or foreign (i.e., parental) overcontrol. The phallic stage is associated with initiative versus guilt; the child plans and conquers, and then must deal with problems of guilt over goals contemplated and acts initiated. Latency is associated with industry versus inferiority, where the child focuses on winning recognition through production; formal education is a salient factor in this conflict.

Freud's genital stage is dissected by Erikson into four conflicts. The first, corresponding to self-concept issues of adolescence, is termed identity versus role confusion. The second, intimacy versus isolation, relates to fusing one's identity with another during young adulthood. The third, generativity versus stagnation, relates to productivity and social responsibilities of adulthood. The final conflict, ego integrity versus despair, is associated with late adulthood and focuses on life evaluation and attitude toward death.

Although Erikson's model is limited in application to Western societies, it contributes to psychology by viewing development from birth to old age, by moving from Freud's primarily sexual focus to societal and interpersonal influences, and by providing a framework for much fruitful research.

Reference

Erikson, E. H. *Childhood and society* (2nd ed.). New York: Norton, 1963.

M. D. ROE

See LIFE SPAN DEVELOPMENT.

Psychosomatic Disorders. Disorders whose etiology is believed to be at least in part related to emotional factors. Psychosomatic disorders have commonly been associated with those conditions that are a result of intense or chronic stress. When one is exposed to intense or prolonged situations that tax the psychological ability to adjust, a stressful condition is created. Numerous physiological reactions occur that help the individual cope with the unpredicted or unresolvable situation.

Gastrointestinal (peptic ulcers and ulcerative colitis) and cardiovascular disorders (including hypertension and migraine headache) have been most commonly thought of as being psychosomatic in orgin. However, since the mind and body interface on so many levels, it can be said that any condition that affects the mind (psyche) also has a bodily manifestation, and any condition that affects the body (soma) also has a psychological manifestation. Thus, psychosomatic disorders have become associated with a wide range of involuntary systems and organs. Other systems that may be affected are the respiratory, musculoskeletal, dermatologic, endocrine, genitourinary, and immunologic.

Over the last 20 years much has become known regarding a person's adaptation to his or her environment or life style. As a society becomes increasingly more industrialized, there is a commensurate increase in stress-related disorders. The frantic life some persons live may diminish their ability to adjust.

The term *stress* came from the field of physics. It pertains to an applied force or system or to forces that function to strain or compromise the integrity of a material or object. If an object is stressed enough, structural changes eventually occur. The behavioral sciences simply borrowed the word and its allied concepts applying them to overstimulation of human beings.

The human organism, unlike the object in physics, has a psychophysiologically mediating or corrective ability to sustain optimal functioning. Individuals have the ability to assess (cognitive appraisal) the perceived degree, intensity, and magnitude of the potentially stressful event. Along with this cognitive assessment is an arousal reaction that prepares the individual for some form of action to ameliorate or interrupt the stressful event. In order to prepare the body for action the sympathetic nervous system is activated. Some of the physiological responses stimulated by this activation are pupil dilation, inhibited peristalsis (process of digestion), sweating, increased heart rate and blood pressure, and a release of adrenalin by the adrenal medulla.

Selye (1956) first noted these sympathetic effects of stress and called them the general adaptation syndrome. This syndrome comprises three stages or levels of adjustment to stress (alarm phase, stage of resistance, and stage of exhaustion). Selye made the important observation that the hypophyseal-adrenocortical axis (the neuroendocrine process that regulates the release of epinephrine and norepinephrine) responds to excessive stress with the nonspecific response of this syndrome. Selye believed there is an optimal level of stress. Stress beyond this level results in the general adaptation syndrome. Each individual's ability to adjust is calibrated differently, being influenced by genetic and acquired physiological and behavioral factors.

Holmes and Rahe (1967) developed the Social Readjustment Rating Scale to help predict a psychosomatic disorder. This instrument is based on the premise that certain types of life experiences (43 in all) have more of an impact than others; for example, death of spouse is given a rating of 100 whereas getting married equals 50. They maintain that the chance of a change in health status for mild scores (150–199 points) is 37%, for moderate scores (200–299) is 50%, and for severe scores (above 300) is 75%. Though the instrument is empirically based, it fails to consider a multitude of factors that may influence an individual's adjustment, such as social support systems and personal-cognitive characteristics.

Other theories, though not necessarily supported empirically, have been developed to incorporate personality characteristics and psychological functioning. The following theories emphasize more of a psychological explanation than do the nonspecific stress theories of Selye and Holmes and Rahe.

Psychological explanations of psychosomatic illnesses attempt to account for why specific organ systems are affected while others are not. Dunbar (1943) postulated that certain personality profiles were prone to develop specific illnesses. She believed that particular personality characteristics would be predictive of specific physical illnesses such as diabetes. Except for the well-documented Type A personality there is little support for the theory. It has been found that individuals who exhibit Type A behavior (overly ambitious, competitive drive, aggressiveness, sense of time urgency) are at a higher risk to develop coronary heart disease.

Alexander (1950) believed that psychosomatic syndromes were caused by an interaction of both biologic and psychologic events. He formulated the specificity hypothesis, which states that a specific unconscious conflict in a constitutionally predisposed (organ weakness) individual would consistently present itself in a particular psychosomatic syndrome. He believed that peptic ulcer patients had a characteristic conflict over dependency needs. Asthma sufferers were afraid of losing their mothers. Patients with hypertension were viewed as having trouble handling hostile impulses. Neurodermatitis victims intensely craved physical closeness. To date, except for some slight evidence regarding individuals with peptic ulcers, there has been little support for Alexander's formulations.

Presently the most prominent theories that seek to account for psychosomatic disorders are multicausal and include such factors as genetic predisposition, stressful environmental situation, learned covert physiological responses, and faulty personal and family coping styles. The day of simple linear explanations for psychosomatic diseases is gone. The development of a psychosomatic disorder is now viewed as multidimensional. Treatment, therefore, involves breaking down the spectrum of possible causes and intervening where possible.

Since it is presently impossible to remove an individual's genetic vulnerability, intervention at this level is precluded. Generally treatment focuses on three aspects. The first is help the individual identify, minimize, or modify the presence of stressful situations. This may include education, psychotherapy, family therapy, and nutritional supplementation. Teaching the individual how to manage stress is the focus of the second phase. Here the person may be taught how to reduce his physiological reactivity or response to stress. This may be achieved by implementing one or more of the following therapeutic methods: medication, neuromuscular relaxation, biofeedback, controlled respiration, meditation, and hypnosis. Teaching the individual how to use stress to enhance living is the third phase. Typically this includes training in some form of strenuous exercise of recreation, such as jogging, swimming, or tennis. These three interventions either individually or collectively will promote physical and psychological adjustment to chronic stress conditions.

Future research in this area will seek to find those variables that are most predictive of a psychosomatic disorder. This is not a simple task by any means. Unidimensional theories were too simplistic; however, the multidimensional ones that have replaced them will be difficult to prove or, more importantly, to disprove.

References

Alexander, F. *Psychosomatic medicine: Its principles and applications.* New York: Norton, 1950.
Dunbar, H. F. *Psychosomatic diagnosis.* New York: Hoeber, 1943.
Holmes, T. H., & Rahe, R. H. The Social Readjustment Rating Scale. *Journal of Psychosomatic Research*, 1967, *11*, 213–218.
Selye, H. *The stress of life.* New York: McGraw-Hill, 1956.

K. R. KRACKE

Psychosynthesis. A therapeutic process developed by Italian psychiatrist Roberto Assagioli. Its goal is the harmonious integration of elements of the psyche under the direction of a personal center of consciousness or will. Psychosynthesis has affinities with humanistic and existential psychologies and with Jung's psychology, although it goes beyond these, especially in its emphasis on will and the direct experience of self.

Psychosynthesis attempts to deal with what it sees as an apparent duality between the personal self and the true self of which the personal self is usually unaware. The duality results from the dominance of subordinate aspects of personality, which obscure the true self that needs to be firmly established as a center of unity. The goal is first to develop a more integrated personality and second to develop a spiritual mode of living (Assagioli, 1973). According to Assagioli the lack of personal integration and the enslavement to inhibiting demands of subordinate aspects of personality can be overcome by the discovery of a higher level of the unconscious and a unifying transpersonal self to which one surrenders.

Assagioli (1965) distinguishes seven levels of the psyche. There are three levels of the unconscious: a lower unconscious composed of instincts, primitive drives toward self-preservation, complexes, deep dreams, and pathological manifestations; a middle unconscious composed of ordinary mental activities such as memory, ideas, and imagination accessible to consciousness; and a higher unconscious composed of higher drives that manifest themselves in aesthetic interest, intellectual curiosity, altruism, search for meaning, and similar intrinsically valuable pursuits. There are also three dimensions of consciousness: a field that includes whatever content is conscious at a given time; an organizing center within the field capable of exercising a directive will; and a higher transpersonal center, both related to the personal center and in touch with higher unconscious, which enables one to transcend ego concerns and bring into awareness an essential relatedness to the rest of reality. Surrounding and interacting with this multidimensional structure is the collective unconscious, by means of which there is a constant interchange with the general psychic environment.

Assagioli describes two forms of psychosynthesis. The first, personal psychosynthesis, which is relevant for the individual who seeks to reach the "normal state of the average man or woman," is directed toward eliminating repressions, inhibitions, inappropriate dependencies, and excessive self-centeredness. The goal of personal psychosynthesis is the reconstruction of the personality around a new authentic center. It involves a decision to formulate a plan of action or, for the more intuitive person, to be led by the spirit within. The means for attaining this goal include exploration of conscious and unconscious aspects of personality and the development of specific strengths and attitudes.

The second form of psychosynthesis, spiritual psychosynthesis, is relevant for individuals who have attained the ability to function normally without crippling inhibitions and conflicts. For these individuals the task is not the basic integration of personality but the proper assimilation of the inflowing superconscious energies from the higher levels of the unconscious, which lure them toward self-realization, and the integration of higher values and motives with preexisting aspects of the personality. For those who have attained a satisfactory degree of personal integration but fail to pursue a higher synthesis, normalcy itself may become a cause of neurosis. Further, spiritual psychosynthesis is illustrative of a general principle of interindividual and cosmic significance that affirms that individuals are not isolated but exist in intimate relation with all other individuals who are part of the spiritual superindividual reality.

Assagioli suggests a variety of techniques, exercises, and methods that therapists are to practice themelves before using them to help clients. The tools are such that eventually clients can use them independently as part of a lifelong development process. For personal psychosynthesis the therapist may use techniques of catharsis such as speaking, writing, and muscular discharge; exercises of disidentification and self-identification; exercises for training the will; and guiding imagery of ideal models or symbols to foster behavior more in keeping with an integrated personality. Techniques of spiritual psychosynthesis are directed toward releasing the energies of the spiritual self; they include the use of symbols to guide decisions, dialogue with an inner teacher or wise person, and exercises designed to develop intuition or specific states such as serenity.

Psychosynthesis appears to be compatible with some scriptural perspectives on the human personality, particularly in its emphasis on responsibility for one's decisions and behavior and on the capacity to develop the will to cooperate with higher spiritual principles. It tends, however, to give little attention to certain negative tendencies underlying human behavior and to concentrate heavily on individual development without giving much consideration to interpersonal dependence and responsibility.

References
Assagioli, R. *Psychosynthesis*. New York: Hobbs, Dorman, 1965.
Assagioli, R. *The act of will*. New York: Viking, 1973.
J. KOPAS

Psychotherapy. *See* COUNSELING AND PSYCHOTHERAPY: OVERVIEW; TRAINING IN COUNSELING

AND PSYCHOTHERAPY; GROUP PSYCHOTHERAPY; FAMILY THERAPY: OVERVIEW.

Psychotherapy, Eclecticism in. *See* ECLECTICISM IN PSYCHOTHERAPY.

Psychotherapy, Research in: Effectiveness of. Psychotherapy by trained professionals can be viewed as an industry with a therapeutic product. In an effort to monitor the industry and to provide the best services possible, the profession must continually upgrade its practices through sound research. Practitioners have the moral responsibility to protect consumers from potentially harmful therapy techniques and to ensure the most effective treatment will be appropriately used in the most cost-efficient manner. Possible researchers are faced with the monumental task of establishing an empirical base for this kind of psychotherapy practice.

In 1952 H. J. Eysenck revealed his controversial findings from a review of insurance company files that 72% of those diagnosed as psychoneurotic are improved in two years with or without professional psychological intervention. At the time a 60–70% success rate was being reported by most well-known psychology clinics (Eysenck, 1952). As a result the academic world responded with several decades of aggressive research to discover the causative components of psychotherapy and to ascertain its efficacy. The resulting research on psychotherapy outcome has thrown much doubt on Eysenck's original findings, resulting in the conclusion that psychotherapy has modestly positive effects (Bergin & Lambert, 1978). For example, Meltzoff and Kornreich (1970) conducted a review of 57 methodologically adequate and 44 methodologically questionable studies concerning the general effectiveness of psychotherapy and found that 84% of the adequate and 75% of the questionable studies reported overall positive results from psychotherapy. In a more recent review of 475 similar studies Smith, Glass, and Miller (1980) reported that the average client receiving therapy was better off than 80% of the people who do not. Although such generalized proclamations about the general effectiveness of psychotherapy are comforting to practitioners and academicians in the field, they do not reveal a great deal about specific processes of change in therapy, nor do their results indicate what can be done to improve psychotherapy.

A generic definition of psychotherapy implies an interpersonal process between two people, one needing help to improve personal functioning and the other offering assistance. From such a broad definition spring multiple questions. What kinds of problems are best handled by "trained" professionals? What is so special about trained professionals that qualifies them to help another person? Can't a friend, parent, minister, paraprofessional, stranger on the bus, or fortune teller perform the same function? Is the therapist's role that of a tutor, coaching a person through an intense period of psychological suffering, or is he a doctor, treating symptoms without much collaborative effort from the patient? What are the exact psychotherapeutic processes that are most likely to ensure improvement? Research may have shed light on such broad issues as the general effectiveness of psychotherapy, but before any assessment can be made of psychotherapy, one must arrive at some general consensus as to what constitutes "improvement" in personal functioning.

Improvement in Personal Functioning. This issue is of particular concern to the Christian counselor as well as to the believer seeking professional psychological help who may be faced with conflicting value systems within the therapeutic setting. For example, most would agree that murder is not the best way to resolve a death wish toward one's spouse, yet many would equivocate about whether it is improvement in personal functioning to help a homosexual learn to more effectively solicit dates from others of the same sex. There are many areas of potential conflict between traditional psychological values and those values espoused by revealed religion. For example, ministers often help sufferers overcome guilt feeling through the process of repentance and through encouraging closer adherence to gospel-based principles. On the other hand, a psychologist might prescribe that guilt is best overcome through relaxing repressive tendencies and abandoning a condemning value structure. Does real improvement in personal functioning mean giving up one's part in a "collective delusion" of a Supreme Morality or rather in putting one's life more in order by adhering more closely to religious codes of conduct? To the nonbeliever such questions may seem irrelevant, but to the believer they are all-important. At such points of discrepancy between counselor and client a decision concerning an appropriate referral needs to be made. Ultimately the responsibility for the decisions made on what constitutes improvement in each individual case lies with those participating in psychotherapy. Obviously there is a need for moral clarity. Though some may try to provide psychotherapy in a moral vacuum, many practitioners acknowledge that their values are inherent in their personal definitions of improvement. Such definitions are expressed in such language as "increased social adjustment," better "reality testing," or a decrease in the "presenting symptoms." The Christian counselor needs to be keenly aware of his or her own system of values and those of the client while striving to meet appropriate goals within a mutual definition of improved personal functioning.

In order to assess the effectiveness of psychotherapy it becomes necessary to devise means of measuring psychological functioning so that comparisons can be made between personal adjustment before and after treatment. The field of psychometrics—i.e., measuring and describing behavioral, mental, and emotional functioning—offers the researcher many psychodiagnostic tools: structured interviews, projective tests, behavioral tally sheets, self-report personality tests, objective rater systems, symptom checklists, etc. By the careful selection of psychometric measures dealing with the specific goals of psychotherapy, the researcher is able to draw at least tentative conclusions about the general effectiveness of the therapy provided. Criticism of research on psychotherapy outcome centers on the inadequacy of psychodiagnostic measures accurately to assess human functioning and on the misapplication of psychometrics in the course of such study (Lambert, 1983).

Most psychotherapy outcome studies have used traditional measures of change that focus to a great extent on either symptomatic relief or on subjective discomfort, without attending to the broader philosophical questions and implied values. The consumer of psychotherapy research should be aware that most researchers have attended to three major value sources: 1) the values of society at large in assessing the extent to which people perform social roles (e.g., work and school performance); 2) the values of the client, largely in the form of relief of subjective discomfort; 3) the values of professionals, or the extent to which people approach notions of ideal mental health (Strupp & Hadley, 1977). Religious values that differ from these perspectives are rarely represented in outcome studies.

Spontaneous Remission and Negative Effects. Having established a general definition of improvement in personal functioning and ways to measure it, the researcher must be aware of several variables that can cloud conclusions on the effectiveness of therapy.

Early researchers coined the term *spontaneous remission* to describe the phenomenon of patient improvement without professional psychological treatment. Close scrutiny shows that most people with emotional problems do not seek out mental health professionals for help, but instead turn to ministers, doctors, lawyers, friends, and family members (Bergin & Lambert, 1978). It is conceivable that these lay therapists may be more adept than trained professionals at forming therapeutic relationships, inducing insights, and giving needed counsel. Professionals could benefit from studying these natural therapeutic agents in the environment. Thus, what some researchers have thought to be individual characteristics of the client that lead to improvement are now believed to include certain elements of lay therapy that may be available to everyone: self-help materials; religious, legal, and medical personnel; family members and friends. The concept of spontaneous remission may also be used to describe the fact that in many studies using wait-list clients as treatment controls, these control-group clients often feel somewhat helped by the initial interview and assessment. Researchers using control groups to establish baseline differences between subjects who received therapy and those who did not receive therapy must therefore be extremely careful in defining no-therapy groups since "therapy" may be readily available in the natural environment or subtly within the confines of the study itself.

Another issue that blurs the validity of global ratings of the general effectiveness of psychotherapy is that although therapy is undertaken with the aim of improvement, research has shown that a percentage of patients are worse after treatment. This "deterioration effect" could be due to many different variables in psychotherapy: the therapist and the techniques he or she employs; the ill effects of diagnosing and labeling; the appearance of new symptoms; the unrealistic expectations on the part of the client; and the resulting guilt, failure, and disillusionment (Lambert, Bergin, & Collins, 1977). When it appears that certain techniques or therapist styles show consistently poor results, methods should be seriously scrutinized and perhaps abandoned entirely. Global studies of the effectiveness of psychotherapy often lump various techniques, methods, psychological orientations, and therapist styles together. Thus final conclusions about causal attribution are blurred by the various success rates of the different techniques, some of which may even have negative effects on clients. Those variables that seem to contribute the most to negative effects, aside from the traits clients bring with them to the relationship, include the level of therapist interpersonal skills such as warmth, empathy, and unconditional positive regard; the manner in which therapists terminate their relationship with clients (therapist rejection); and confrontive techniques, especially those that emphasize client weaknesses rather than strengths. A recent study (Sandell, 1981) indicated that poor results, if not negative effects, were the result of passive involvement by the therapist who did not help the client find and deal with a focal issue in therapy. In general, however, research on this topic suggests that most of the negative effects of therapy are related to the therapist as a person. This points up the need for careful selection and training of therapists as well as sound methods for restricting the practice of credentialed therapists.

Effects of Psychotherapeutical Methods. While there is empirical evidence that many therapies have beneficial effects, support for the superiority of one school of therapy over another is weak. Early reviews of this question (Bergin, 1971; Meltzoff & Kornreich, 1970; Luborsky, Singer, & Luborsky, 1975) concluded that no difference existed between the major schools. Most recent analysis (Bergin & Lambert, 1978; Smith, Glass, & Miller, 1980; Shapiro & Shapiro, 1982) using more reliable review techniques has drawn the same conclusion.

Shapiro and Shapiro (1982), for example, reviewed 143 outcome studies that compared two or more treatments and were listed in psychological abstracts between 1975 and 1979. In all there were 414 treated groups that were exposed to a variety of traditional methods such as dynamic, humanistic, behavioral, and cognitive methods. In general, mixed methods appeared to be most effective, with behavioral and cognitive methods following, and dynamic and humanistic methods showing the least effectiveness. Behavioral and cognitive methods had a definite superiority over verbal methods, yet differences between the outcomes of treatment methods were minimal. While individual therapy seemed to have better outcomes than group therapy, the difference in outcomes was not great. Surprisingly, length of therapy did not necessarily predict a positive outcome. Favorable results were reported when self-ratings and behavioral counts were analyzed, with unfavorable outcomes reported from hard nonpsychological data. The review suggests that therapy does have a moderate, relatively uniform, positive effect.

Client Variables. A great deal of psychotherapy research has centered on the client's contribution to the outcome of treatment. In fact some believe client variables are the most powerful determining force in positive and negative change (Bergin & Lambert, 1978). Those who seek treatment from professionals often feel demoralized, socially isolated, helpless, and overwhelmingly anxious and depressed. In addition to degree of pathology, which is clearly related to outcome, there are numerous other client variables that distinguish those who profit from therapy from those who do not.

Research focusing on patient demographic variables reveals that patients from lower socioeconomic backgrounds often want symptomatic relief and attribute their difficulties to physical problems rather than emotional ones. They also show a lack of desire for psychotherapy and its processes (Heitler, 1976). As a result, patients of lower socioeconomic status typically measured in income, level of education, and occupation, tend to be referred for inpatient and drug treatments, while those of higher socioeconomic status are more often accepted for individual outpatient, insight-oriented therapies. Education level also appears to correlate positively with length of stay in therapy. Lower socioeconomic status patients more often fail to keep initial appointments and drop out of treatment sooner than patients of higher educational levels and socioeconomic status (Garfield, 1978). Despite this trend there is no clear indication of a positive relationship between socioeconomic status and success or failure of psychotherapy for those lower-class patients who do remain in therapy until mutual agreement for termination is reached. Research on other demographic variables (such as race and sex) as predictors of continuation in and outcome of psychotherapy have been generally inconclusive or even contradictory (Lambert & Asay, 1984).

Many practitioners have suggested using a pretherapy role induction interview that prepares the patient by stating appropriate goals and expectations for therapy. The interview deals with the tendency toward premature termination among lower socioeconomic status patients. These brief interventions are intended to model ideal therapy behavior that facilitates productive psychotherapeutic processes among less psychologically sophisticated clients. The use of this procedure has resulted in substantial improvement in attendance rates among the socially disadvantaged (Lambert & Lambert, 1984). Other strategies include the use of alternative treatments and methods of changing the expectations of therapists for lower socioeconomic status patients.

Researchers have also studied the relationship of client personality variables (as measured by scores on traditional personality tests) to continuation in and outcome of psychotherapy. Certain personality variables such as associative ability, rigidity, wide interests, sensitivity to the environment, "feeling deeply," high energy level, and freedom from bodily concerns correlate with positive outcomes in psychotherapy. These variables when considered together may be labeled *ego strength*. Research has shown that client ego strength has a good prognostic value (Kernberg, 1973).

The nature of most psychotherapies requires active involvement of the patient; there is considerable agreement among therapists that a well-motivated client will have a greater chance of success. However, research on motivation is inconclusive, because the term is vague and various studies have used different definitions. In addition, the liquidity of this trait has made it difficult to study. Some patients may be highly motivated at the outset of therapy and then quickly lose their motivation. Despite these difficulties current research points out that patient involvement, defined as a positive manner of participating in therapy, is consistently a strong predictor of outcome and is relatively independent of therapist techniques and the level of relationship variables offered by the therapist (Gomes-Schwartz, 1978; Lothstein, 1978; Perry, Gelfand, & Marchovitch, 1979; Pomerleau, Adkins, & Pertschuk, 1978; Marziali, Marmar, & Krupnick, 1981).

Therapist Variables. Research exploring the relationship of therapist characteristics to therapeutic outcome is based on the assumption that such characteristics are fairly stable, constant for all clients, and manifested independently of the client. Much research has been undertaken to identify those therapist styles, behaviors, attributes, and attitudes (apart from specific intervention techniques) that enhance the client's chances for improvement. These variables are of great interest because it is possible to alter therapist attitude, behavior, and style through training or use them to select therapists for training.

Therapist demographic variables such as gender, age, race, and socioeconomic status, have shown no clear pattern in relationship to outcomes. Nor has extensive research on therapist personality variables yielded a clear

relationship to therapeutic outcome. It does appear that a better adjusted, more integrated, less anxious, and less defensive therapist will have better results in treatment. Therapists with emotional problems or neurotic needs may be hindered in offering effective treatment to clients (Lambert, Bergin, & Collins, 1977).

The role of training and experience in therapy outcome remains controversial. There is no evidence that trained and experienced therapists from one discipline (e.g., social work, psychiatry) are superior to another in obtaining positive results from treatment (Meltzoff & Kornreich, 1970). Durlack's (1979) review of empirical literature suggests that paraprofessionals can be as effective as professionals, especially when they are offering time-limited, highly structured treatments such as assertiveness training. On the other hand, they are not as likely to offer effective unstructured treatments (dynamic therapies, marital therapies, etc.) that require moment-to-moment decision making. There is evidence that carefully selected and rigorously trained noncredentialed therapists have an impact on clients that is every bit as potent as that of experienced credentialed therapists. However, the relative impact of professionals and paraprofessionals is hard to judge because they are not using the same procedures, since their role in mental health delivery is not the same.

In an effort to pinpoint the particular things that a therapist does during the therapy hour which lead to client improvement, many researchers have closely monitored the interpersonal processes of actual therapy sessions. It seems plausible that the most successful therapists are not successful because of their theoretical orientation or therapeutic techniques, but because of other variables. There are obviously successful therapists from all orientations, and their success may very well be due to common factors such as interpersonal styles, warmth, voice tone, gestures, etc.

The study of therapist-initiated process variables has necessitated the development of rating scales to code therapeutic interaction between therapists and clients. Such scales usually employ trained objective observers who rate speech content and the manner in which it was given. This coding is often done from audiotaped or videotaped segments chosen from a therapy session. Raters code interactions on specified scales such as genuineness, warmth, and empathy according to speech content, tone of voice, gestures, facial expression, and other nonverbal behavior. The relationship of process variables to outcome is correlational in nature and therefore cannot establish causality. Nevertheless, process studies have shed some light on the therapeutic exchange.

Process studies have yielded fairly consistent conclusions about what constitutes desirable therapist behavior. Active and positive participation by the therapist coincides with an improvement in outcome, while critical and judgmental therapist statements correlate with little improvement. Again the question of causality arises; it is plausible that good progress could lead to more positive and active therapist participation, while little improvement could lead to criticism by the therapist. Other process variables that correlate with positive outcome include fresh, vivid language; warm, empathic expressions; encouragements toward independence; and statements high in personal relevance to the client (e.g., statements about the client's defense mechanisms or anxiety source). Conversely, an artificial voice quality and stereotypic language correlate with a less favorable outcome (Rice, 1982).

Process studies have generally supported the Rogerian hypothesis that therapist behavior which communicates high levels of empathy, congruence, and unconditional positive regard leads to client improvement. Research regarding these conditions traditionally uses complex observer rating systems that focus on various components of therapist style such as communication patterns, speech content, and connotative meanings. It is assumed that a concerned, empathic, and genuine therapist will impart these feelings during therapy by the manner in which he or she participates. Research in this area has been plagued by differing definitions of what constitutes the minimal level of these facilitative conditions and by the obvious difficulties incurred in measuring therapeutic interactions. Impartial judges, using rating scales to score segments of the therapy while in process, have been able to achieve fairly consistent reliability, but their ratings do not always correlate adequately with the client's and therapist's ratings of the same segment. Although many studies have supported the original Rogerian hypothesis, other studies have been equivocal. Overall, therapist attitudes of the Rogerian variety have been shown to have a modest positive relationship to psychotherapy outcome (Lambert, DeJulio, & Stein, 1978). The importance of these factors is suggested even with behavioral and cognitive approaches (Lambert, 1983). However, because of the correlational nature of most process studies, causality is at best inferred and conclusions are viewed as tentative.

Client-Therapist Matching. Utilizing the concepts of client and therapist variables that influence outcome, researchers and practitioners have attempted to match clients and therapists on pertinent variables to form therapeutic dyads with the highest probability of positive outcome. The hypothesis is a simple one supported by common sense. People who tend to get along better because of complementary personality styles, similar interests, backgrounds, race, sex, social class, values, and expectations would naturally have an easier time forming a therapeutic or helping relationship. Although the idea seems basic enough, establishing empirical support has not been so simple.

Whitehorn and Botz (1954, 1960) pioneered a major thrust in matching client and therapist according to personality variables by categorizing therapists into two groups: A and B. Type A therapists are active during therapy, show high personal participation, and form trusting relationships with their clients. Type B therapists are passive, permissive, and demonstrate a marked use of interpretation and an instructional style during therapy. Through experimentation with the Strong Vocational Interest Blank, a 23-item scale was devised to categorize therapists according to these two types. It was found that Type A therapists typically reject manual and mechanical activities and show interest in leadership, while Type B therapists show interest in manual and mechanical professions. Traditionally Type A therapists are seen as being more effective in working with schizophrenics and Type B therapists in working with neurotics; however, the most recent review of empirical research shows that there is little support for the use of A-B scales to form client-therapist dyads for optimal outcome (Razin, 1977).

Of particular interest to the Christian counselor is the issue of congruence of client and therapist value systems and their influence on therapy outcome. This area of study is distinguished by its marked paucity of research. Of all the factors that could possibly influence therapy, values seem to be one of the most important; yet even though it is the backdrop against which all human interaction is displayed it has somehow been overlooked in research on variables influencing the outcome of psychotherapy. Amid bold declarations concerning client ego strength, the therapeutic relationship, necessary and sufficient conditions for improvement, and client and therapist variables, very little that is definite and useful has been said concerning the relative effects of value systems, or client-therapist congruence of values, on therapy outcome.

Although the commonsense notion of improving the results of psychotherapy through client-therapist matching is alluring, it has proven extremely difficult to support empirically. Research matching therapists and clients on demographic variables such as age, sex, socioeconomic status, and race, as well as therapists' personality variables and client diagnosis through the use of the A-B scales, has shown no clear relationship to outcome. It does appear that clients continue in therapy and report higher satisfaction when the client and therapist have similar expectations for therapy; as previously discussed, outcome can be improved by pretherapy training sessions with both therapists and clients to increase congruency of expectations. More research is needed to establish the relationship between the client and therapist and how this affects outcomes.

Conclusion. To date there are a few broad generalizations that can be made concerning research in psychotherapy and its outcomes. It appears that on the whole, participation in psychotherapy is better than having no therapy at all, and that above-average therapy can lead to excellent results. Research provides an empirical base for the traditional therapies: psychoanalysis, humanistic or person-centered, many of the behavioral procedures, and some of the cognitive therapies. All of these therapies have a broad range of usefulness in treating a variety of psychopathologies; however, research also indicates that certain disorders such as phobias, sexual dysfunctions, and compulsions are more successfully treated by more specially designed behavioral techniques. It seems obvious that the crisis-oriented and brief therapies are as successful as the more traditional long-term therapies, and may be more valued because they are more cost efficient.

Studies have shown that verbal therapies are worthwhile in improving personal functioning with a broad spectrum of disorders. The interpersonal factors that facilitate communication in therapy, such as warmth, interpersonal style, and personal influence, are important to therapy process and outcome. The techniques that a therapist uses give a rationale and practical approach to problem solving for the client who perhaps previously had been unable to grasp his particular source of difficulty or to conceive of an avenue for resolution. It appears that among the multiple variables affecting therapy outcome, client variables are most important (severity, onset, and duration of the presenting symptoms, support systems in the environment, personal ego strength, motivation for change, etc.). These are followed by the therapist variables (personal styles, attitudes, genuineness, etc.) and finally by the technique used during therapy.

One of the main problems concerning research in psychotherapy is the choice of measures used before and after therapy to determine change. There are many types of measures available to researchers—self-report measures, therapist evaluations, and trained detached observers to give ratings of behavioral scales. It is recommended that all these be used when evaluating therapy outcome. Comparison between these measures during the process of change may help reveal what exactly is happening as a result of therapy.

Most recent research avoids lumping therapies together by school or orientation since this does little to define what the therapist actually does during therapy. Instead, more recent studies name very detailed intervention procedures and their effects on very specific types of clients suffering from well-defined pathologies. This is a wise shift in emphasis, since most of the past global studies have left a heritage of vague generalizations that have no definite conclusions about change as a result of psychotherapy.

Researchers and practitioners involved in so human an endeavor as helping others through the practice of psychotherapy must continue to utilize all possible means to upgrade therapeutic services. Future studies will continue to add much to our growing knowledge of how best to help our fellow men and women through psychological intervention.

References

Bergin, A. E. The evaluation of therapeutic outcomes. In A. E. Bergin & S. L. Garfield (Eds.), *Handbook of psychotherapy and behavior change.* New York: Wiley, 1971.

Bergin, A. E., & Lambert, M. J. The evaluation of outcomes in psychotherapy. In S. L. Garfield & A. E. Bergin (Eds.), *Handbook of psychotherapy and behavior change: An empirical analysis* (2nd ed.). New York: Wiley, 1978.

Durlak, J. A. Comparative effectiveness of para-professional and professional helpers. *Psychological Bulletin,* 1979, *86,* 80–92.

Eysenck, H. J. The effects of psychotherapy: An evaluation. *Journal of Consulting Psychology,* 1952, *16,* 319–324.

Garfield, S. L. Research on client variables in psychotherapy. In S. L. Garfield & A. E. Bergin (Eds.), *Handbook of psychotherapy and behavior change: An empirical analysis,* (2nd ed.). New York: Wiley, 1978.

Gomes-Schwartz, B. Effective ingredients in psychotherapy: Prediction of outcome from process variables. *Journal of Consulting Clinical Psychology,* 1978, *46,* 1023–1035.

Heitler, J. B. Preparatory techniques in initiating expressive psychotherapy with lower-class, unsophisticated patients. *Psychological Bulletin,* 1976, *83,* 339–352.

Kernberg, D. F. Summary and conclusion of "psychotherapy and psychoanalysis: Final report of the Menninger Foundation's psychotherapy research project." *International Journal of Psychiatry,* 1973, *11,* 62–77.

Lambert, M. J. Introduction to assessment of psychotherapy outcome: Historical perspective and current issues. In M. J. Lambert, E. R. Christensen, & S. S. DeJulio (Eds.), *The assessment of psychotherapy outcome.* New York: Wiley, 1983.

Lambert, M. J., & Asay, T. P. Patient characteristics and their relationship to psychotherapy outcome. In M. Hersen, L. Michelson, & A. S. Bellack (Eds.), *Issues in psychotherapy research.* New York: Plenum, 1984.

Lambert, M. J., Bergin, A. E., & Collins, J. L. Therapist-induced deterioration in psychotherapy. In A. S. Gurman & A. M. Razin (Eds.), *Effective psychotherapy: A handbook of research.* New York: Pergamon, 1977.

Lambert, M. J., DeJulio, S. S., & Stein, D. M. Therapist interpersonal skills: Process, outcome, methodological considerations and recommendations for further research. *Psychological Bulletin,* 1978, *85,* 467–489.

Lambert, R. G., & Lambert, M. J. The effects of role preparation for psychotherapy on immigrant clients seeking mental health services in Hawaii. *The Journal of Community Psychology,* 1984, *12,* 263–275.

Lothstein. L. M. The group psychotherapy drop-out phenomenon revisited. *American Journal of Psychiatry,* 1978, *135*(12), 1492–1495.

Luborsky, L., Singer, B., & Luborsky, L. Comparative studies of psychotherapies. Is it true that "Everyone has won and all must have prizes?" *Archives of General Psychiatry,* 1975, *32,* 995–1001.

Marziali, E., Marmar, C., & Krupnick, J. Therapeutic alliance scales: Development and relationship to psychotherapy outcome. *American Journal of Psychiatry,* 1981, *138,* 361–364.

Meltzoff, J., & Kornreich, M. *Research in psychotherapy.* New York: Atherton, 1970.

Perry, C., Gelfand, R., & Marcovitch, P. The relevance of hypnotic susceptibility in the clinical context. *Journal of Abnormal Psychology,* 1979, *88,* 592–603.

Pomerleau, O., Adkins, D., & Pertschuk, M. Predictors of outcome and recidivism in smoking cessation treatment. *Addict Behavior,* 1978, *3,* 65–70.

Razin, A. M. S. A-B variable: Still promising after twenty years. In A. S. Gurman & A. M. Razin (Eds.), *Effective Psychotherapy. A handbook of research.* New York: Pergamon, 1977.

Rice, L. N. The relationship in client-centered therapy. In M. J. Lambert (Ed.), *Psychotherapy and patient relationships.* Homewood, Ill.: Dow Jones-Irwin, 1982.

Sandell, J. A. *An empirical study of negative factors in brief psychotherapy.* Nashville: Vanderbilt University Press, 1981.

Shapiro, D. A., & Shapiro, D. Meta-analysis of comparative therapy outcome studies: A replication and refinement. *Psychological Bulletin,* 1982, *92,* 581–604.

Smith, M. L., Glass, G. V., & Miller, T. I. *The benefits of psychotherapy.* Baltimore: Johns Hopkins University Press, 1980.

Strupp, H. H., & Hadley, S. W. A tripartite model of mental health and therapeutic outcomes: With special reference to negative effects in psychotherapy. *American Psychologist,* 1977, *32,* 187–196.

Whitehorn, J. C., & Botz, B. A. A study of psychotherapeutic relationships between physicians and schizophrenic patients. *American Journal of Psychiatry,* 1954, *111,* 321–331.

Whitehorn, J. C., & Botz, B. A. Further studies of the doctor as a crucial variable in the outcome of treatment of schizophrenic patients. *American Journal of Psychiatry,* 1960, *117,* 215–223.

M. J. LAMBERT, D. E. BARLEY, and E. L. WRIGHT

Psychotherapy with the Poor.
A Christian approaching the topic of psychotherapy with the poor is quickly overcome with the volume and weight of Scripture related to poverty. Four hundred thirty-one scriptural passages relate to the poor, with over 100 passages focusing on the Christian's duty to stand against the oppression of the poor.

In the Old Testament the theme of Israelite poverty and oppression during the Egyptian captivity is a core biblical model for defining the status of the poor and God's response to them (Exod. 3:5–6). The law given to the freed Hebrew nation makes the financial and practical aspects of God's plan for the poor even more explicit through the concept of the year of jubilee (Lev. 25). The Lord also saw the need to remind the oppressed not to become the oppressors. The psalms and proverbs are full of wisdom regarding the poor. This theme continues with even more emphasis in the prophets.

The New Testament is even more explicit in giving direction for the Christian treatment of the poor. Christ blesses the poor and warns the rich (Matt. 6:19–24; Luke 6:24). The Christian is to give to the poor in a nonpretentious manner (Matt. 6:1–4) and is to eschew the temptation of riches. The early church provided various forms of support for the poor, and the epistles contain frequent admonitions not to favor the rich (James 2) and to take great care not to further oppress the poor (James 5).

Psychologists, guided in practice by the American Psychological Association's *Ethical Principles of Psychologists,* find Paul's instructions mirrored in the standard suggesting that psychologists should contribute a portion of their services to work for which they receive little or no financial return (APA, 1981). Christian therapists are therefore under a double injunction, Christian and professional, to serve the poor and develop interventions that will assist God's plan of building up the poor.

Current Status of Research Literature. In 1972 the *Psychological Abstract Index* created two new categories, "Lower Class" and "Lower Income." Prior to the early 1970s the psychological, sociological, and anthropological literature was mainly descriptive of conditions facing the poor in America. The literature that spoke to the mental health needs of the poor was also descriptive (Hollingshead & Redlich, 1958). There were theoretical articles on treatment (Prince, 1969) and studies of personological variables (Karon, 1958) but little experimental data on mental health treatment for the poor. Lerner's (1972, 1974) five-year study is the major exception and is the most extensive of the experimental studies.

Throughout the literature on psychotherapy

with the poor there is a strong "etic" bias. This is a researcher-determined bias and is contrasted to an "emic," or subject-determined, bias. It is rare that the low-income subjects have much input in the design or interpretation of research conducted on the poor. This lack of emic research makes it necessary to accept with some caution academic conceptualizations of lower-income phenomena and related statements on psychotherapy with the poor.

Mental Health, Social Class, and Income Level. The landmark study on mental health, social class, and income level was *Social Class and Mental Illness* (Hollingshead & Redlich, 1958). This was followed by *A Decade Later: A Follow-up of Social Class and Mental Illness* (Myers & Bean, 1968). Among the more important conclusions of these studies are that the prevalence and type of psychiatric disorders and the kind of treatment administered were all significantly related to social class.

Over the 18 years represented by this research (1950–1968) the mental health bias has clearly been in favor of the higher income classes. This group reports a smaller proportion of mental problems, less severe pathology, and fewer occasions of organic or custodial treatment than the lower classes (Hollingshead & Redlich, 1958). Furthermore, the researchers discovered that patients from higher income classes had better community and family support systems and were more able to move on with their careers and personal lives following therapy than patients from the lower classes (Myers & Bean, 1968).

More recent data (Edwards, Greene, Abramowitz, & Davidson, 1979) indicate that the poor are benefiting from the community mental health centers system. These researchers were able to disconfirm three common hypotheses: that the poor would not seek psychotherapy, would receive less prestigious treatments from therapists with less training, and would benefit less from therapy than the more affluent. It remains to be seen how 1980 federal and state cutbacks to mental health systems will affect the favorable results reported by this study.

While the poor are apparently accepting and benefiting from help offered by the community mental health system, their mental illness problems remain greater both in terms of the severity of the disorder and the proportion of their class affected by at least a moderate-level mental disorder. Lerner (1972) argues that people from free, spacious, and growth-promoting environments do not tend to become psychotic. Rather, it is people from narrow, restrictive, and impoverished environ-

ments who are psychosis prone. Thus, psychotics are not usually social mutants arising by chance out of a healthy community but rather are faithful reflections of their family and societal contexts.

There is a good deal of support for the hypothesis that being poor encourages low self-concept and feelings of helplessness and depression (Carringer & Wilson, 1974). There is also evidence that all those who grow up in America face discontinuity that threaten their culturally established ideal self. These discontinuities seem to be greatest for the lower class (Getzels, 1974) and give rise to linguistic and problem-solving differences between higher and lower social classes. Getzels categorizes these differences as language and values-code differences. He posits an elaborated language code facilitating an achievement-values code for higher-income clients and a restricted language code facilitating a survival-values code for lower-income clients. Some of the language and values differences may promote mental illness, or these differences may lead to social isolation of the poor, which further feeds into the restrictive, pathology-promoting atmosphere described by Lerner.

Problems with the Lower-Income Client. One difficulty in treating poor people psychotherapeutically has been early termination rates. Stern, Moore, and Gross's (1975) study indicates that one of the significant predictors of early termination is discrepancy in social class. Siassi (1974) addresses this early dropout rate and the related problems involved in the frequently unequal status of client and therapist. He cites racial-class distrust as setting up a complex transference in which the patient behaves in a sadomasochistic way, giving himself up to the therapist but expecting the impossible in return. Issues of transference and countertransference are heightened by socioeconomic distance between client and therapist. Lerner's (1974) finding that incidence of disharmony in therapeutic goals was more highly correlated with early termination for lower-income clients than for higher-income clients supports Siassi's observation. Harmony of goals may be a rough measure of successfully resolved transference.

Other theorists argue that the lower-income person may be difficult to treat due to more basic class differences in linguistic and problem-solving approach (Getzels, 1974). Some studies have provided support for this hypothesis (Bernstein, 1964; Tallman & Miller, 1974). The nature of these linguistic differences needs further research. Treatment interventions based on attempts to bridge these differences have had good outcome rates (see Heitler, 1976; Kovacs, 1983).

One argument sometimes given as to why therapy with the poor will not work is the delay of gratification argument. According to Prince (1969) the poor are forced to live in a moment-to-moment situation and do not learn the value of delayed gratification. Several cognitive and social psychology experiments support the notion that lower-income individuals operate with immediate gratification reinforcement contingencies rather than delaying for greater reward (Bergin, 1974). The argument goes that since most insight or expressive therapy takes several months, since the results are slow to appear to the client, and since the poor operate on immediate gratification contingencies, these verbal therapies are not appropriate for lower-income individuals.

Lerner (1972) questions the assumption that there are no immediate partial gratifications for the client while therapy is in progress. If this were true, one wonders why anyone would continue therapy. She also points to various gambling practices in lower classes as good examples of accepted ways of taking a chance on delayed gratification. The odds may seem inappropriately unfavorable to a person in a higher class, but when one has little control over one's resources, such high risk taking seems more appropriate. Lerner reasons that it makes sense to put off a minor immediate reward in favor of a major later reward if one has enough control over one's life circumstances to ensure a reasonably stable and predictable future. That, however, is exactly what the poor lack (Lerner, 1972). Her findings demonstrated that lower-income clients are capable of remaining in therapy over longer periods of time (more than 20 weeks); and, if the client pushes for immediate results, this desire can be therapeutically used in negotiating stepwise goals.

Another related argument is that since the poor are lower in intelligence than middle- and higher-income groups, interactive therapies are not really feasible (Prince, 1969). White, Fichtenbaum, and Dollard (1964) found that lower-income people were more silent during their interview than higher-income clients. This finding has been taken as supportive of the argument. However, this conclusion has been disputed by a number of researchers who argue that while the poor may use language differently, they do not lack general verbal ability (Bonecutter, 1980; Labov, 1972). The poor are aware of using language differently and purposely reduce verbalizing with certain types of persons. The differences in verbal style are interpreted differently by different income groups. Middle- and upper-income groups may interpret linguistic difference as deficit or defiance (Wegner & Vallacher, 1977). Lower-income groups may interpret linguistic differences as deviant or not normal for plain folk.

There is also reason to question the conclusion that intelligence is lower for lower socioeconomic persons. It can be argued that there are no culture-free intelligence scales, and indeed there may be no such thing as a culture-free or generalized intelligence measure. A study of the relationship of income level and intelligence conducted by Jencks, Smith, Ackland, Bane, Cohen, Gintis, Heyns, and Michelson (1972) supports a definable difference hypothesis rather than the immutable deficit hypothesis. Socioeconomic language and problem-solving differences do exist but the meaning of these differences requires a value judgment and is not a scientific fact.

Some researchers cite the higher incidence of acting out among the poor as a difficulty in doing therapy with the low-income client. Prince (1969) feels that this is tied to their preference for concrete and authoritarian solutions. Minuchin, Chamberlain, and Graubard (1967) worked with lower-income adolescents who were identified in juvenile courts and in police records. Using a variety of behavioral and structured learning therapy scenarios (modeling, role play, homework, etc.) they were able to significantly reduce and even erase the acting-out behavior as measured by police and teacher records. The treatment approach was based on the notion that lower-income persons are rewarded for using language to manipulate persons (interpersonal manipulation) rather than using language to manipulate abstract ideas (symbolic manipulation). The favorable outcome of this treatment strategy supports the notion that in doing therapy with lower-income persons, the clinician should consider their greater likelihood of verbally or behaviorally manipulating persons rather than using language to symbolically discuss and solve problems.

The Lerner (1972) study offers a significant exception to the notion that the poor do best with concrete-authoritarian interventions (Prince, 1969). In fact, Lerner's research supports the notion that therapists who adopt more democratic, less authoritarian attitudes and styles with poor clients have a significantly higher positive outcome rate than do their more authoritarian, concrete, solution-giving counterparts.

Treating the Low-Income Client. If unequal

status and language style make meaningful interaction between therapist and lower-income client difficult, and if lower-income socioeconomic difficulties are associated with severe mental and emotional trauma, then would it not be wise to focus efforts on programs designed to raise the economic level of the poor rather than dealing with them individually in therapy? In a study of the Job Corps vocational rehabilitation program Odell (1974) found that sociological programs were significantly more effective than case work programs in helping delinquents get and keep jobs and experience improved self-image.

However, Edwards and Whitecraft (1974) found that the lower-income groups were significantly more unaware of social programs designed to help them than were higher-income groups. Richter (1974) demonstrated the effective use of student paraprofessionals as liaison workers between ghetto individuals and the vocational and counseling services designed to serve them. The need, therefore, is to bring available resources directly to the individual and translate them into his or her language. Both clinician and client may have to learn language and role style beyond their own socioeconomic level. Goldstein's (1973) studies investigating the teaching of middle-class language styles and roles to lower-income clients show the effectiveness of the language-and role-translation hypothesis.

The breadth and severity of the mental health problems among lower-income groups support the notion that a dual attack on their mental health difficulties is needed. The two areas of sociological-situational and psychological-developmental are necessarily connected for the client. Any effective program aimed at changing the depth and breadth of emotional and mental distress among the poor has to address changing the social conditions that facilitate the distress; it must also address the learned affective, cognitive, and linguistic styles that result from adapting to a low-income situation.

References

American Psychological Association. *Ethical principles of psychologists*. Washington, D.C.: Author, 1981.

Bergin, D. The reaction of frustration of middle class and lower class children. *Journal of Experimental Child Psychology*, 1974, *125*, 127–140.

Bernstein, B. Social class, speech systems, and psychotherapy. *British Journal of Sociology*, 1964, *15*, 54–64.

Bonecutter, B. Differences in symbolic and interpersonal language use across income level, sex and race (Doctoral dissertation, Illinois Institute of Technology, 1980). *Dissertation Abstracts International*, 1980.

Carringer, D., & Wilson, C. S. The effects of sex, socioeconomic class, race and kind of verbal reinforcement on the performance of black children. *Journal of Negro Education*, 1974, *43*, 212–220.

Edwards, A. M., & Whitecraft, C. J. Vocational service agencies and the disadvantaged. *Vocational Guidance Quarterly*, 1974, *23*, 49–53.

Edwards, D. W. Greene, L. R., Abramowitz, S. I., & Davidson, C. V. National health insurance, psychotherapy, and the poor. *American Psychologist*, 1979, *34*, 411–419.

Getzels, J. W. Socialization and education: A note on discontinuities. *Teachers College Record*, 1974, *76*, 218–225.

Goldstein, A. *Structured learning therapy: Toward a psychotherapy for the poor*. New York: Academic Press, 1973.

Heitler, J. Preparatory techniques in initiating expressive psychotherapy with lower-class, unsophisticated patients. *Psychological Bulletin*, 1976, *83*, 339–352.

Hollingshead, A. B., & Redlich, F. C. *Social class and mental illness*. New York: Wiley, 1958.

Jencks, G., Smith, M., Ackland, H., Bane, M., Cohen, D., Gintis, H., Heyns, B., & Michelson, S. *Inequality: A reassessment of the effect of family and schooling in America*. New York: Basic Books, 1972.

Karon, B. P. *The Negro personality*. New York: Springer Publishing, 1958.

Kovacs, A. L. (Ed.). Special issue on cultural and ethnic factors. *Psychotherapy: Theory Research and Practice*, 1983, *20*(2).

Labov, W. *Language in the inner city: Studies in the black english vernacular*. Philadelphia: University of Pennsylvania Press, 1972.

Lerner, B. *Therapy in the ghetto: Political impotence and personal disintegration*. Baltimore: Johns Hopkins University Press, 1972.

Lerner, B. Is psychotherapy relevant to the needs of the urban poor? In D. Evans & W. Claiborne (Eds.), *Mental health issues and the urban poor*. New York: Pergamon, 1974.

Minuchin, S., Chamberlain, P., & Graubard, P. A project to teach learning skills to disturbed, delinquent children. *American Journal of Orthopsychiatry*, 1967, *37*, 558–567.

Myers, J. K., & Bean, L. L. *A decade later: A follow-up of social class and mental illness*. New York: Wiley, 1968.

Odell, B. Accelerated entry into the opportunity structure: A socially-based treatment for delinquent youth. *Sociology and Social Research*, 1974, *58*, 312–317.

Prince, R. Psychotherapy and the chronically poor. In J. Finney (Ed.), *Cultural change, mental health and poverty*. Lexington: University of Kentucky Press, 1969.

Richter, H. Community development and psychotherapy in ghettoes. *Psychotherapy and Psychosomatics*, 1974, *24*, 269–280.

Siassi, I. Psychotherapy with women and men of lower classes. In V. Franks & V. Burtle (Eds.), *Women in therapy: New psychotherapy for a changing society*. New York: Brunner/Mazel, 1974.

Stern, S. L., Moore, S. F., & Gross, S. J. Confounding personality and social class in research on premature termination. *Journal of Consulting and Clinical Psychology*, 1975, *43*, 341–344.

Tallman, I., & Miller, G. Class differences in family problem solving: The effects of verbal ability, hierarchical structure, and role expectations. *Sociometry*, 1974, *37*, 13–37.

Wegner, D., & Vallacher, R. *Implicit psychology*. New York: Oxford University Press, 1977.

White, A. M., Fichtenbaum, L., & Dollard J. Evaluation of silence in initial interviews with psychiatric clinic patients. *Journal of Nervous and Mental Diseases*, 1964, *139*, 550–557.

Additional Reading

McGoldrick, M., Pearce, J. K., & Giordano, J. (Eds.). *Ethnicity and family therapy*. New York: Guilford Press, 1982.

B. E. BONECUTTER

Psychotic Disorders. It has been said that while a neurotic builds castles in the sky, a psychotic moves into them. This witticism contains a kernel of truth. Although most people have difficulties, they can at least distinguish reality from unreality. The cardinal characteristic of a psychotic disturbance is that the individual cannot adequately make this distinction in some important realm of life. The psychotic person, as it were, lives in a world of his or her own.

Some psychotic conditions are caused by organic impairments. Heavy alcohol intoxication, for example, can produce a psychotic state in which the intoxicated person experiences hallucinations. Many other physical abnormalities, from fevers to brain tumors, can produce organically based psychoses, some of which are reversible but many of which are permanent. The most commonly encountered psychotic disorders are Schizophrenia, Paranoia, Brief Reactive Psychosis, and Bipolar Disorder.

The majority of psychotic disorders confronting the average mental health practitioner are without a demonstrable organic basis. These functional psychoses generally take one of two forms, or show some combination of the two: affective or schizophrenic disorders. The major affective disorders involve serious mood deviations. Certain individuals, for example, become so depressed that they develop somatic delusions. One such delusion is that one is already dead; another is that one's intestines have turned to glass. Other individuals become extremely excited. During spells of elation they may run up huge charge bills, go without sleep for days on end, and perform many other actions that indicate their excitement to be beyond the bounds of normal joy and happiness.

The most commonly observed functional psychoses are the schizophrenias. These represent psychoses in which deviant affective states are not markedly visible, whereas cognitive aberrations are. In schizophrenia there is disharmony between thoughts, feelings, and actions (the person is either emotionally numb or inappropriate), but the most distinguishing feature is disordered thinking. More hospital beds are occupied by persons who have been diagnosed as schizophrenic than by persons with any other single malady. Of course, schizophrenics are not usually bedridden. It is just that seriously psychotic persons are typically unable to care adequately for themselves and thus require custodial attention.

To be diagnosed as manifesting a schizophrenic disorder the person must have serious delusions, hallucinations, or incoherence. There must also be evidence of deterioration from a previously higher level of functioning and the continuous presence of schizophreniform symptoms for at least six months.

Subtypes of schizophrenia include paranoid, catatonic, and undifferentiated. Paranoid schizophrenics typically manifest either persecutory delusions, grandiose delusions, delusional jealousy, or hallucinations with persecutory or grandiose content. Catatonic schizophrenics show either marked stupor, mutism, anatomical rigidity, chaotic excitement, or inappropriate if not bizarre posturing. Undifferentiated schizophrenics are those who do not meet the diagnostic criteria of another primary type but who nonetheless demonstrate delusions, hallucinations, incoherence, or grossly disorganized behavior.

DSM-III also allows for the diagnosis of persons who are paranoid but not schizophrenic. Such persons are classified either as showing paranoid disorder, paranoia (rare), shared paranoid disorder, or acute paranoid disorder.

Treatment of psychotic persons often requires hospitalization and almost always involves the administration of psychotropic drugs. Schizophrenic persons are usually given antipsychotic chemicals, while persons with major affective disorders are given antidepressants or antihallucinogens. Lithium has recently been discovered to be of significant help with the latter class of disorders as well.

C. W. McLemore

Psychotropic Medications. *See* Psychopharmacology.

Pubescence. As the child moves into sexual maturity and reproductive potency, pubescence is the physiological vestibule. Puberty is sometimes used to denote the actual arrival at reproductive capacity, with pubescence being used to denote a two-year transition during which physiological changes of a secondary nature are preparing for the primary transformations. The words derive from the Latin *pubertas* (the age of manhood) and *pubescere* (to grow hairy).

Pubescence will be regarded here as the span of months marked by the appearance of secondary sex characteristics and by the physiological maturing of the primary sex organs. In girls the observable phenomena include height growth spurt, breast buds, pubic hair, the first menstrual period, and axillary hair. In boys observable phenomena include height growth spurt, the enlargement of testicles and penis, pubic hair, voice change, the first ejaculation, facial hair, axillary hair, chest hair, and hair in ears.

In technological cultures pubescence corresponds with preadolescence or early adolescent years. But ADOLESCENCE is a complex of psychosocial factors that are enmeshed in the fabric of early sexual maturity. Pubescence, on the other hand, includes psychological dimensions but is primarily concerned with physiological phenomena. Except during the months between conception and age 15 months there is no other two-year period during which such major physiological changes occur in humans. In Stone Age cultures a rite of passage often follows closely on puberty to initiate the child into the adult world with its privileges and responsibilities.

While any of the physiological changes may be regarded as clues to emerging sexual maturity, McCandless (1970) found that adolescents themselves view first menstrual period and first ejaculation as major landmarks in their development. These landmarks indicate the onset of pubescence and are biologically triggered. It has not been established whether psychosocial factors may accelerate or delay their appearance, although in dairy breeding the constant presence of an adult male has been found to accelerate first estrus and consequent calving and first lactation. Average age for first menstruation for North American girls is now 12 years 2 months, down from 17 years 6 months in 1840 in Norway. Mean age of first ejaculation tends to run one year behind that of girls' first menstruation. The earlier pubescence has been thought to be a consequence of nutrition, heredity, better health, and even geographic location. Current attention is being given to light, both natural and synthetic, with focus on the production of melatonin in the pineal gland when the child is under conditions of total darkness. Melatonin circulates in the bloodstream and has a slowing effect on ovarian and testicular production and on the development of the primary sex organs in children. Light is being used to enhance fertility in animal husbandry and to regulate the waning cycles of menopausal women.

Among physiological changes at pubescence it is likely that hormonal brain chemistry is related to the dawning of reflective self-consciousness. Formal operational thought, essential for making complex moral choices, comes within reach at about the same time that concern for physical appearance drives the pubescent child to stand before the mirror asking the deep questions of life. These developments may be related to the last phases of meylinization of the nervous system with the high-speed transmitting sheath. The last nerves to be meylinized are the correlation fibers of the central cortex. The question remains open. Although Piaget anticipated it, he lacked today's physiological research resources to push the question (see COGNITIVE DEVELOPMENT).

Rites of passage at pubescence include religious rituals. In Christian tradition confirmation, first Communion, and baptism often are timed for pubescence. In other traditions there are special membership vows for those leaving childhood. Given the cortical, sexual, and psychosocial changes of the pubescence years, these remain significant agenda issues for those who guide in matters of evangelism, nurture, and development.

Reference
McCandless, B. R. *Adolescents: Behavior and development.* Hinsdale, Ill.: Dryden Press, 1970.

Additional Readings
Koteskey, R. L. Growing up too late, too soon. *Christianity Today,* 1981, 25(5), 24–28.
Wyshak, G. & Frisch, R. E. Delayed menarche and amenorrhea in ballet dancers. *The New England Journal of Medicine,* 1980, 303, 17–19.

D. M. Joy

See LIFE SPAN DEVELOPMENT.

Punishment. Behavioral consequences are classified as reinforcers and punishers. Reinforcers increase the frequency or likelihood of the responses that produce them, whereas punishers are stimuli or events that decrease response frequency or likelihood. A punisher may consist of an aversive stimulus, such as a painful electric shock, or it may be the removal of a positive reinforcer.

Punishment is one of the most common methods used to control behavior. Parents routinely spank their children for misbehavior; undesirable personal or social behavior often results in censure, snubbing, disapproval, or social banishment; and our legal system is based on punishment such as fines, incarceration, and removal from society.

Despite its prevalence punishment remains a controversial topic. Several arguments often are given against the willful use of punishment to control the behavior of others. These arguments normally concern the possible undesirable behavioral side effects that may accompany punishment. Such concern is justified; however, many of the unfavorable outcomes associated with punishment are due to the

Punishment

faulty application of punishment procedures rather than to any inherent shortcoming in the concept of punishment. In fact, much of human behavior is learned and closely regulated by natural aversive consequences without any serious ill effects.

One undesirable side effect is that severe punishment applied over a long period of time may have a general suppressive effect on behavior that is not being directly punished. Repeated harsh punishment, therefore, may not only eliminate troublesome behavior, but it also may stifle desirable behavior. This generalization effect of punishment is especially pronounced if the contingency between behavior and punishment is ambiguous and if punishment is applied to a wide range of responses in a variety of different settings.

Punishment also can result in chronic anxiety or other disruptive emotional states. The continual occurrence of potentially punishing stimuli (e.g., threats or stimuli that are associated with punishment) can result in persistent emotional conditioning. Such conditioning is more likely if punishment is applied inconsistently or unpredictably.

Sometimes patterns of behavior are punished even though they are not only permitted but expected at some later period of life (e.g., sexual curiosity). Consequently punishment may be effective in suppressing present behavior at the expense of later behavioral flexibility. In those situations where there is a genuine fear of suppressing behavior that may be required later in life, punishment should be replaced with a different behavioral control technique.

A frequent reaction to punishment is aggressive behavior. The person being punished may attack the punisher or displace aggressive reactions to an innocent third party. Negative modeling also may occur where the punished person models (imitates) the aggressive behavior of the person who applies the punishment.

Overall, most of the undesirable side effects of punishment can be eliminated or minimized by adhering to the following rules: 1) Undesirable behavior, and the conditions under which it will be punished, should be clearly defined. 2) Punishment should be consistently applied. 3) Each occurrence of the undesirable behavior should be punished. Occasional punishment may be ineffective and it may confuse desirable and undesirable patterns of behavior. 4) Punishment procedures should be selected that minimize the elicitation of emotional responses. 5) Punishment procedures should be combined with other behavioral control techniques (e.g., positive reinforcement); desirable

behavior should result in consequences that are clearly different than those for undesirable behavior. 6) The rejection or acceptance of punishment is directly related to the perceptions of the person being punished. Consequently the person being punished should be made to perceive that punitive sanctions are being applied for his benefit and not only for the convenience of the punisher.

Undesirable behavior also may be suppressed or eliminated through the removal of positive reinforcers. This method of punishment consists of depriving people of rewards and privileges that are normally available, such as loss of television viewing privileges, exclusion from social activities, monetary fines, etc. Although removal of positive reinforcement has not been as widely investigated as the application of aversive consequences, it has nonetheless been demonstrated to be an effective punisher. As in other forms of aversive control the amount of behavioral suppression produced through removal of reinforcement depends upon, among other things, the relative value of the reinforcer being removed and the relative magnitude of the opposing consequences. In contrast to the use of physical punishment, the removal of reinforcement seems to generate much weaker emotional effects, and it tends to foster an orientation toward those who control the desired positive reinforcers. If return of the reinforcer is made dependent upon performance of behavior other than the one being punished, rapid behavioral changes may result.

All other considerations aside, punishment of a response normally reduces its occurrence. Several characteristics can make a punishing stimulus more effective. 1) Aversive stimuli that have a sudden onset (e.g., a slap) are more effective than stimuli whose aversiveness grows gradually. 2) A punishing stimulus is more effective if it is delivered immediately after the response has been made rather than after some delay, unless the delay is bridged cognitively (e.g., through verbal instruction) or with a conditioned stimulus. 3) The suppressive properties of an aversive stimulus are related to its intensity; the greater the intensity, the greater the suppression. 4) Continual punishment of an undesirable behavior is more effective than intermittent or occasional punishment. 5) Punishment that is consistently applied is more effective than the haphazard or ambiguous application of aversive consequences.

There are several cases where punishment is ineffective in suppressing behavior regardless of how consistently it is applied. One case is when the punished response is the only way to obtain reinforcement. For example, if the performance of an undesirable behavior is the only way a child has of getting parental attention, then this behavior may persist despite the fact that it is punished. Another case is when the value of the reinforcement received by exhibiting the punished response exceeds the aversive properties of the punishing stimulus. In this case the value of the reinforcement is "worth" the punishment received. A third case where punishment is ineffective is when punishment itself become a stimulus signaling that positive reinforcement is forthcoming, or if the punishment signals a period of relief when further punishment will not be delivered. Under these conditions punishment may actually increase rather than suppress a response because punishment takes on the properties of a positive conditioned reinforcer. In fact, it has been argued that masochism may result from this discriminative function of punishment.

When aversive consequences follow a response, they generally suppress or eliminate that behavior. However, when punishment is discontinued, the punished response may reappear. Even if the punished response does not return, punishment alone does not normally bring about desired changes in behavior. Punishment does, however, make possible the occurrence of other behaviors. If these behaviors are strenghtened (e.g., through reinforcement), they may effectively replace the punished response. In fact, the degree to which other behavior is positively reinforced is one determinant of both the suppressive power of punishment and the extent to which punished responses are likely to return.

S. R. OSBORNE

See LEARNING; AVERSION THERAPY.

Pyromania. The compulsive urge to set fires, often accompanied by a desire to endanger the lives of others. The pyromaniac does not necessarily want to kill people with the fires he starts, and often expresses surprise and shock when this happens. The disturbance is most often classified as an obsessive-compulsive reaction or the manifestation of an antisocial or psychopathic personality. Characteristically the individual cannot explain or justify his behavior and usually claims he can't control it, or didn't know what he was doing.

Several theories have been proposed as to the motivation behind compulsive fire setting. These include the defiance of authority, an expression of hostility and aggression, and the attempt to resolve deep-seated sexual conflicts. The act may be directed at a specific person, family, or business, or it may be generalized anger directed at someone the pyromaniac does not even know. This hostility often originates in rejection and deprivation during childhood and reflects a fear of relationships and feelings of inadequacy. In cases involving unresolved sexual conflict the pyromaniac may feel forced to watch the fire he starts; he is sexually excited to the point of orgasm, but quickly feels guilt and may even attempt to help put out the fire he started.

D. L. SCHUURMAN

Qq

Quid Pro Quo. An agreement, usually unconscious, between two or more family members. Literally meaning "something for something," quid pro quos describe the intricate exchanges and understandings that define particular family relationships.

An example of a positive agreement is seen in the understanding that if the child behaves, he will be appropriately rewarded by the parent. Countless other quid pro quos—both healthy and unhealthy—govern how parent and child relate. Together they make up the relationship contract.

Negative quid pro quos abound in troubled marriages and families. For instance, a husband agrees to withhold comment on his wife's obesity while she tacitly accepts his chronic absence from the family. A major task in marriage and family therapy is to uncover dysfunctional quid pro quos and replace them with more adaptive exchanges.

J. A. LARSEN

See FAMILY THERAPY: OVERVIEW.

Rr

Rank, Otto (1884–1939). Recognized as one of the most important founders of psychoanalysis. Rank became a disciple and colleague of Freud at age 21, when he was introduced to Freud by Adler. At Freud's encouragement Rank did not study medicine but took a general curriculum at the University of Vienna and earned the Ph.D. in 1912 before continuing with extensive study in psychoanalysis. During his doctoral studies he served as secretary to the Vienna Psychoanalytic Society. By the time he had completed his doctoral studies, he had become a trusted member of Freud's inner circle and served as co-editor of *Imago* and *Internationale Zeitschrift fur Psychoanalyse.*

After his break with Jung and Adler, Freud solicited the loyalty of his closest associates, asking them to be his "praetorian guard." This Rank willingly did, and he spent a dozen productive years devoted to publications in the journals and beginning his own practice. But his own work ultimately led to a schism with Freud over his 1924 book, *The Trauma of Birth.* The idea of the birth trauma, the most famous of Rank's ideas, deviated from Freud's theory of the origins of anxiety by arguing that all anxiety originates from the child's separation from the mother. Ironically, Freud initially accepted the book as an important advance in psychoanalytic theory, but later viewed it as abandoning the sexual theory of anxiety with which Freud had become identified. As his relationship with Freud cooled, Rank experienced profound disorientation and anxiety himself, and he tried to patch up their relationship even as he began to disengage himself with a move to Paris in 1926. He finally moved to the United States, where his work won a sympathetic response from social workers; the

School of Social Work at the University of Pennsylvania was an influential center for dissemination of Rank's neopsychoanalytic views. He continued to write and to see clients until his death in 1939—less than a month after the death of his estranged mentor Freud.

Rank had a relatively small but faithful number of adherents until the 1970s, when he was "rediscovered" in connection with developments in ego psychology. He rejected biologically based drives and environmental events as determiners of behavior, arguing that "will" (his term for ego) was the cause of behavior. His view of neurosis employed a striking metaphor: the artist. In his 1932 book, *Art and Artist*, Rank argued that the creativity of the artist is like the conflict of the neurotic. Artists must contend with guilt because the novelty of their work is antisocial, breaking down the consensus of social reality. But where most people express their will through conformity to group views and artists must oppose the views of the group, the neurotic is a "failed artist" who is incapable of successful independence or opposition. The result is guilt, and the neurotic's maladjustment is traced through guilt to failure of the will.

In his 1936 book, *Will Therapy*, Rank sketched his view of therapy, which by now differed radically from Freud's. Eschewing the belief that neurosis was illness, Rank developed three ideas that profoundly affected future forms of therapy: the use of the analytic session as an occasion to explore the present feelings of the patient, the elucidation of rights of the patient, and the radical step of planning to terminate therapy rather than allowing it to continue indefinitely. In *Psychology and the Soul* (1931) Rank extended his theories to religion, viewing deity as a personification of will and the religious concern for the soul as the will to personal omnipotence.

L. S. SHAFFER

Rapaport, David (1911–1960). Born in Munkacs, Hungary, Rapaport was a leader in a politically radical Zionist youth movement. He studied mathematics and physics at the University of Budapest before his family joined their group's kibbutz in Palestine, where he worked as a surveyor. After two years they returned to Hungary, where he entered psychoanalysis for personal reasons and changed his field of study to psychology.

He received his Ph.D. from the Royal Hungarian University in 1938, then fled to the United States to escape the Nazis. After a brief stay in New York City he went to Osawatomie State Hospital in Kansas, where he began research on Metrazol shock therapy. In 1940 he moved to the Menninger Clinic at Topeka, where he soon became chief psychologist, director of psychology training, and director of research. Finding that administration was taking too much of his energy when he really wanted to do scholarly work, he moved to the Austin Riggs Center in Stockbridge, Massachussetts, in 1948. It was at Riggs that Rapaport made his most lasting contributions.

Rapaport's goal was to understand the nature of human thought, and he believed that psychoanalysis was the most fruitful approach to such an understanding. He believed that Freud's drive theory must be expanded by ego psychology into a general psychology. He thought that human thinking could be studied by a battery of diagnostic tests. Rapaport worked on systematizing psychological theory, especially its abstract level of theorizing, to explain its clinical theory. He was a theorist rather than a clinician and was not bound by the usual limits of psychoanalysis. Although he rejected behaviorism itself, he used concepts from Piaget's developmental psychology and from animal and human experimental psychology.

He wrote much, but is best known for three books. His *Diagnostic Psychological Testing* (1945), later revised and condensed by Holt, was a standard in the field for many years. In *Organization and Pathology of Thought* (1951) he presented his view of the psychoanalytic theory of thinking. Finally, he translated psychoanalysis into the idiom of contemporary psychology in *The Structure of Psychoanalytic Theory* (1959). His intricately and carefully reasoned writings must be carefully studied rather than simply read.

R. L. KOTESKEY

Rape. Sexual assault; a complex crime encompassing an entire range of sexual behaviors. Legal definitions vary from state to state, and the counselor should be informed of pertinent statutes. Interventions should focus on the victim's perceptions of the event and subsequent emotional and behavioral responses, bearing in mind that attempted assaults may be as damaging as those that legally are defined as completed acts.

Rape has in the past been principally interpreted as a sexual act on the part of the offender. It has subsequently been defined as an act of power or coercion involving violence. Continuing study indicates that the offender views the interaction as a means of both intimidation and sexual gratification.

The exact occurrence of rape is difficult to discern, since the report rate varies from one in four to one in nine. Annually there are over 55,000 rapes reported in the United States. Statistically about one woman in six will be subjected to an attempted rape during her lifetime, while one in 24 will become the victim of a completed rape. Though report rates are increasing, the phenomenon appears to be growing beyond that for which increased measurement can account.

Victims' response patterns closely mirror those for other crises, passing through a series of stages that have been labeled the *rape trauma syndrome*. In each stage certain tasks must be mastered for the victim's restoration. Counseling interventions also vary in each of the succeeding stages.

In the first stage, acute reaction, attention should be directed to a medical examination to determine possible venereal disease and pregnancy. Notification of family may also be appropriate. The counselor's role will be to provide support and information and to assist the victim in making decisions regarding making a police report.

This is followed by the period of outward adjustment, wherein problems encountered in the first stage bring various coping strategies into effect: denial, suppression, rationalization, etc. It is common for interest and conversation about the event to wane, and intervention is chiefly supportive as reactions run their course. If the counselor has not worked with family or close friends, it is wise to do so, paying attention to their anger, blame of victim, or sense that the victim is "ruined." If counselor intervention is initiated during this stage, the victim may resist reopening the situation, and the assistance may be limited to clarification of issues in the first stage and anticipation of those in the third.

The third stage, the integration stage, often begins with a sense of depression and a desire to talk with someone. This may be triggered by some event associated with the attack. Two central issues should be dealt with: the victim's self-perception (guilt, damaged, ruined) and her perceptions about the attacker (threat and security).

Personality styles have been found to relate to client-counselor interactions. Dependent persons utilize the counselor as an ally whose strength can be vicariously appropriated. Extraverts tend to be very open and free with their accounts of the victimization and do not require as intense a relationship with the counselor. Introverts will often avoid talking about the offense or subsequent responses with anyone.

Generally the counselor should attempt to establish a short-term rapport (unless extended therapy is indicated) and assist the victim in defining accurate perceptions of the event, effective coping strategies, and organization of a social support system. Social agencies are often available to provide specialized assistance.

Additional Readings

Burgess, A. W., & Holmstrom, L. L. *Rape: Victims of crisis.* Bowie, Md.: R. Brady, 1974.

Fox, S. S., & Scherl, D. J. Crisis intervention with victims of rape. *Social Work*, 1972, *17*(1), 37–42.

A. R. DENTON

See VICTIMS OF VIOLENT CRIMES.

Rational Disputation.

A treatment technique utilized in RATIONAL-EMOTIVE THERAPY and COGNITIVE-BEHAVIOR THERAPY. It is based on the theoretical rationale that 1) the manner in which an individual construes the world essentially determines his or her affect and behavior and 2) dysfunctional emotional reactions and behavior are mediated by distorted conceptualizations and the erroneous beliefs underlying these cognitions. The goal of rational disputation is the cessation of the client's maladaptive and faulty patterns of thinking and the development of adaptive and rational thought patterns. It endeavors to obtain this goal by evaluating the reasonableness of the client's specific misconceptions and underlying erroneous beliefs. Accordingly, the client is taught to 1) monitor his negative, self-defeating cognitions; 2) recognize the connections between cognition, affect, and behavior; 3) logically examine the evidence for and against his distorted cognitions; 4) substitute more reality-oriented interpretations for these faulty cognitions; and 5) learn to identify, dispute, and alter the underlying irrational beliefs that predispose him to distort his experiences (cf. Eph. 4:22–25; Rom. 12:2). Cognitive-behavior therapy differs from rational-emotive therapy in the implementation of this treatment technique in that the latter approach is more didactic. The use of rational disputation enables clients to recognize, test, and change their mistaken beliefs. They learn not simply to think more realistically and adaptively, but to think for themselves.

D. PECHEUR

Rational-Emotive Therapy.

A therapy developed in the 1950s by Albert Ellis, who became disenchanted with the convoluted theory of, and the passivity required in, classical psychoanalysis. Ellis claims that his basic premise can be traced to the Greek stoic Epictetus and is stated most clearly by Marcus Aurelius: "If thou art pained by any external thing, it is not this thing that disturbs thee, but thy own judgment about it. And it is in thy power to wipe out this judgment now."

Ellis has had an extremely productive career, and has done extensive work in the field of sexology. His major psychotherapeutic statement was *Reason and Emotion in Psychotherapy* (1962); since then his approach has been summarized in many different publications (e.g., Ellis & Harper, 1975). This approach has provided a broad and flexible framework for, and was a forerunner and part of, the cognitive-behavioral approach to psychotherapy that became very popular in the 1970s. It has had great impact on the whole field of psychotherapy and has produced many new applications and spin-offs (Wolfe & Brand 1977). Indeed, there can be a rational approach to any human problem, as its various proponents continue to demonstrate. Maultsby (1975), among others, has been an important popularizer by making this approach more concrete, specific, and behavioral. He has written several self-help books.

The Concept of Rationality. Rationality has a long history of meanings and definitions of which these present-day proponents, characterized by an ahistorical approach to behavior and philosophy, have little or no awareness. Ellis defines rationality in terms of four basic values: survival, maximizing pleasure (and avoiding all except internal, prosocial pain), being part of a social group, and attaining intimacy with a few of that group. Maultsby is more specific and sets up five criteria. Rational behavior and thinking: 1) is based on objective consensual reality; 2) is self-protective and life-enhancing; 3) enables goal achievement; 4) prevents significant conflict with others; and 5) prevents significant personal, emotional conflict. To be "rational" one must fulfill the first two criteria and at least one of the latter three.

The ABC Theory of Emotions. In connection with their definition of rationality, rational therapists have a theory of how emotions work (cf. Russell & Brandsma, 1974). The ABC theory is employed as a useful device to explain emotional response and distress. This theory postulates that all emotional responses are the result of cognitive processes, and the invariant sequence is: (A) perceptual processes—situational determinants; (B) cognitive processes—thinking, evaluating, self-talk; (C) physiological responses—feelings. It is implied in this sequence that thinking, or self-talk, is crucial in creating and maintaining emotional responses, and the important cognitive processes can be verbalized (with some effort) in simple declarative sentences. Thus, the talking to self that one does in evaluating complex stimuli is the root cause of emotional disorder. C responses can be produced by B alone. They can also become conditioned or habitualized to A stimuli with little or no intervening consciousness (B). The former is called a belief, and the latter an attitude or "thought shorthand." These processes can be either adaptive and efficient or disordered, depending on how well they match up with the criteria for rationality.

Rational Psychotherapy. Therapy leads clients to ask four basic questions: 1) What am I saying to myself? 2) Is it true? 3) What is the evidence for my belief? 4) What is the worst that could happen if . . . ? Clients are taught, often by written homework assignments

(Maultsby, 1971) or by persuasive argumentation, to separate As from Bs from Cs, facts from opinions, thoughts from feelings. An appropriate A section will pass the "camera check"; that is, all statements there can be verified by a camera with sound equipment. If they cannot pass the test, they belong in B. When all important beliefs have been identified and the person's feelings and behaviors are accounted for (B), patients are taught to identify their irrational ideas, their "sane" versus "insane" statements. Assuming a statement to be relevant to A, there are many kinds of irrational statements. The most common are positive and negative exaggeration, rationalization, catastrophizing, absolutistic statements, meaningless metaphors, lies, rhetorical questions, nonsequiturs, denial-minimizations, and overgeneralizations.

After these statements are identified and labeled, the client is taught to apply the logicoempirical method to his or her personal statements and hypotheses (as in the previous four questions and criteria for rationality). This is the D, or disputation, part of the ABC theory. Some proponents add an E section to specify a desired outcome in terms of feelings and behavior. Ellis has identified 12 major irrational ideas, but by far the four most common ones, with their rational alternatives, are those in Table R1. By argumentation and direct teaching the client is taught to challenge and replace his irrational thinking with rational alternatives. Then the client is given the homework assignment to visualize himself thinking and acting on the basis of his new cognitions and the desired outcomes. This is called rational-emotive imagery (REI) and is practiced several times each day, usually for specific problem situations. After this internal

Table R1

Irrational Idea	Rational Alternative
It upsets me.	Reality just is. I upset myself by how I think about it.
I have to . . .	I don't have to do anything. I will consider only my long-term best interests. "Musturbation" is self-abusive.
I should get what I want.	Everything is exactly as it should be. I may wish for, want, or desire what I want, but it is only *unfortunate* if I don't get it—not awful or a catastrophe!
My self-worth is defined by my behavior.	Behavior is only a small part of my total self. I can rate performances, in order to increase my efficiency, but it is illegitimate to even attempt to rate myself.

preparation behavioral techniques such as assertion training, role playing, and practicing are used to further imprint the new cognitions. Specific activities may be prescribed by the creative therapist to help the person test out experientially the irrationality of his position. Rational therapists differ in the extent to which they emphasize and apply various aspects of this process, but the above is a general outline of their approach.

Critical Perspective. The ability to think, abstract, and make sense out of reality is one of the greatest blessings that human beings have. Rational therapy is excellent in helping people to separate classes of problem behavior and to evaluate their own thinking, thus to be more responsible, make better choices, and stop whining. The thrust toward critical thinking and autonomous functioning is commendable. However, the strength of this approach is also its weakness. The implied view of persons is rather mechanical, overly cognitive, and exceedingly individualistic. Rational therapists translate everything into cognitions, including motivation, and assume that all cognitive processes can be easily verbalized and are available to awareness. They do not emphasize the interpersonal nature of the individual or his enmeshment in various systems (family, cultural, etc.).

The view of reality taken by most rational therapists is quite limited from a Christian perspective because they make the mistake of assuming that scientific methodology and principles define the universe. They often slip into scientism by transmuting legitimate methodological naturalism into illegitimate ontological naturalism; that is, they confuse a useful method with the nature of reality. Paradoxically the ones who most strenuously dispute the "religion" of Freud, Rogers, and any form of theism then proceed to set up their own religion based on empiricism and scientific method. It follows that ethics are always situational, since there are no absolutes except perhaps avoidance of social chaos and harm to others, and the attainment of one's personally defined goals—i.e., the values of rationality.

Rational therapists (with only a few notable exceptions) tend to have a negative orientation toward feelings. Their interest is not in integration of feelings but rather in controlling or eliminating them. On the whole, rational therapists do not emphasize listening carefully or empathic understanding. They are interested in words and semantics, not experiences or meanings. Thus they tend toward premature attacks on language, they do not hear or

understand deeper meanings, or see and understand nonverbal communication. This system is an excellent example of the advantages and pitfalls of a philosophy of science taken from the first half of the twentieth century. Christians would do well to use many of its insights to discipline their own thinking and behavior, but retain a critical posture toward several of the deficits in technique and, more importantly, its underlying assumptions and philosophical mistakes.

References

Ellis, A. *Reason and emotion in psychotherapy.* New York: Lyle Stewart, 1962.
Ellis, A., & Harper, R. A. *A new guide to rational living.* Englewood Cliffs, N.J.: Prentice-Hall, 1975.
Maultsby, M. C. *Help yourself to happiness through rational self counseling.* Boston: Malborough House, 1975.
Maultsby, M. C. Systematic, written homework in psychotherapy. *Psychotherapy: Theory, Research, and Practice,* 1971, *8,* 195–198.
Russell, P. L., & Brandsma, J. M. A theoretical and empirical integration of the rational-emotive and classical conditioning theories. *Journal of Consulting and Clinical Psychology,* 1974, *42,* 389–397.
Wolfe, J. L., & Brand, E. (Eds.). *Twenty years of rational therapy.* New York: Institute for Rational Living, 1977.

J. M. BRANDSMA

Rationalization. A person's attempt to justify, or present as reasonable, his maladaptive behavior. An unconsciously motivated ego DEFENSE MECHANISM, rationalization generally employs faulty logic or falsely ascribed lofty motives in an effort to avoid conscious awareness of the irrational, maladaptive nature of the defended behavior. This process serves two major roles: it reduces the pain and disappointment associated with failure to attain goals, and it works toward justifying particular behaviors. Several behaviors that together may indicate the use of rationalization are: 1) the attempt to find justification or defensible reasons for one's actions or attitudes; 2) anxiety or anger when those reasons are challenged; 3) inability to consciously perceive inconsistencies in reasoning or contradictory evidence.

R. LARKIN

Reaction Formation. The development of socially or personally acceptable attitudes and behaviors that are the opposite of repressed, unacceptable unconscious desires. This unconscious process provides reinforcement of the repression of those desires, helping to defend against their threatened intrusion into consciousness or overt expression.

Sustaining this double-level repression creates a serious drain on the individual's psychic energy. Yet it remains a fragile defense, under continual threat of a return of the repressed impulse to conscious awareness. Such a defensive structure often results in exaggerated fears and rigid belief systems that limit adaptability and promote severity in coping with the shortcomings of others. For example, this process may cover repressed hostility with an overwhelming show of kindness, unconscious desires for sexual promiscuity with celibacy or great moral restraint, or unconscious desires to commit some crime with strong demands that those particular criminals receive the severest punishment possible.

R. LARKIN

See DEFENSE MECHANISMS.

Reactive Attachment Disorder of Infancy.

The significant characteristic of reactive attachment disorder of infancy is extremely poor emotional and physical development, which commences before 8 months of age. Poor emotional development is indicated by a lack of age-appropriate signs of social responsiveness as well as apathy. Physically the infant fails to thrive. These symptoms are often seen in cases of emotional neglect either by the mother or due to an imposed institutionalization that leads to social isolation, leaving the infant unable to bond affectionally to others.

There are a number of signs that manifest the infant's lack of social responsivity. For example, by 2 months of age normal visual tracking of both eyes and faces may not be evident and the smiling response and visual reciprocity may be absent. At 4 to 5 months old the infant may fail to participate in playful games or to attempt vocal reciprocity, or may not show anticipatory reaching when approached to be picked up. Additionally, the infant may not reach naturally for the mother or be alert to the point of moving toward the caretaker's voice. At 7 to 8 months crawling, the establishment of visual or vocal communication with the caretaker, and beginning stages of imitation of the caretaker may still be lacking.

For diagnosis of this disorder the infant additionally needs to manifest a minimum of three of the following: a weak cry, excessive sleep, a lack of interest in the environment, hypomotility, poor muscle tone, or a weak rooting and grasping in response to feeding attempts. Also necessary for diagnosis is weight loss or failure to gain appropriate normal weight that cannot be explained by any physical disorder. Frequently a failure to gain weight is disproportionately greater than the failure to gain length; head circumference, however, is generally normal.

This diagnosis requires clear evidence that the infant lacks adequate care. This necessitates a home visit, observation of the mother and infant interaction during feeding and nonfeeding times, or reports by others of their observation of neglect. While child abuse may be observed, neglect is the more common problem. Pediatricians frequently hospitalize such infants immediately to assist with weight gain and to reverse the clinical picture by sufficient mothering. The reversal of symptoms is the ultimate confirmation of the diagnosis of reactive attachment disorder of infancy.

This disorder is clearly the result of situations that interfere with early emotional bonding between mother and infant. Such a mother may be preoccupied with her own emotional problems. She may be severely depressed and may well have been emotionally deprived during her own childhood. She probably feels emotionally isolated and likely lacks support systems. She may fear the infant's death and thus remove herself from the baby. Poor mothering skills or a lack of opportunities to learn about appropriate maternal behavior can contribute. There may also be feelings of indifference toward the infant, leading to maternal neglect. Colicky, lethargic, and difficult infants may frustrate the mother's ability to handle the situation and this may increase the chances of the disorder.

A factor other than maternal neglect that may contribute to this disorder is a lack of bodily contact during the first weeks of life. This can occur with extended periods in an incubator or other early separations from a caring adult.

Treatment of such infants generally requires hospitalization where the severity of the symptoms can be dealt with immediately. Severe cases can result in physical complications—e.g., starvation or dehydration—that could result in death before therapeutic assistance can be implemented. The safest setting, especially with physical complications, is the hospital. Here the infant's weight can be monitored, appropriate mothering and nourishment can be provided, and continual observation can be given until the infant is emotionally and physically responding appropriately.

Pediatricians, nurses, and hospital staff are required to notify the local child protective services or Department of Social Services in such incidences. Intervention takes place with an investigation of the home, including the mother-infant interactions, and inquiry among family, relatives, and neighbors who have observed the situation. If it is determined that the mother or others in the home cannot provide adequate care for the infant, foster care either with other family members or social agencies will be arranged temporarily. Frequently the mother will be referred for counseling to deal with her own needs and/or referred to a special mother-infant program specifically designed for cases of emotional neglect or child abuse. The mother or caretaker may be referred to a support group, such as Parents Anonymous, for parents having these difficulties. If mother and infant are separated, visits may be instituted where the two can be together under supervision; if the mother's capacity to care for the infant improves, the child may be reunited with her on a probationary basis. Generally social services remain involved in such cases until there is sufficient evidence of adequate mothering to warrant closing the case.

B. J. SHEPPERSON

See ATTACHMENT THEORY.

Reading Disabilities. In a broad sense all reading disabilities can be called dyslexia. Dyslexia literally means difficulty (*dys*) with the written word (*lexia*). Unfortunately the term *dyslexia* has come to describe a vast number of things. In an attempt to bring some clarity to the field the term *developmental dyslexia* is used to describe reading difficulties in an otherwise normal individual that are not attributable to lack of intelligence, emotional complications, educational deprivation, or neurological impairment.

In developmental dyslexia the child has significant difficulty in deciphering letters in a word and/or associating them with the sounds they represent. Frequently the child or adult may confuse or rotate letters and numbers that are similar; for example, *b* and *d*, *m* and *w*, *p* and *g*, *3* and *w*. Some individuals may have associated deficits in memory and in left-right orientation.

Many theories attempt to account for developmental dyslexia. Some have hypothesized visual and/or auditory perceptual deficits, others implicate a faulty short-term memory in assessing the relevant visual-aural information. Still others have emphasized deficient linguistic and temporal-spatial abilities. None as yet has proven conclusive.

In addition, deficits in reading may also arise from emotional factors or a lag or delay in the maturational skills needed to read.

Frequently emotional factors cause a child to be inept in developing or mastering the skills required to read. Four emotional factors commonly seen are lack of interest in academic endeavors, severe depression, low self-esteem, and low frustration tolerance. Each of these robs the child of the needed energy to give sustained attention to the frequently unsatisfying task of learning to read. However, these emotional characteristics may be secondary to either developmental dyslexia or delayed maturation in reading skills.

Some individuals have reading difficulties as a result of being at the low end of the bell-shaped curve of reading ability. For these individuals there is a maturation lag in acquiring reading skills. Typically these are known as slow readers. Such individuals do not usually show the many associated characteristics of developmental dyslexia. However, they find reading so frustrating that they are at risk of early school failure.

K. R. KRACKE

Reality Therapy. A reflection of the mid–twentieth-century reaction against psychoanalysis and the medical model of pathology and therapy. Glasser (1965) presented the theory and methodology, and continues to refine and expand the system.

In contrast to psychoanalysis, reality therapy emphasizes rationality and thinking over emotions, the present and future over the past, health and possibilities over illness. It projects the commonsense psychiatry of Adolf Meyer, and its emphasis on behavior reflects contemporary behavior therapy. When Glasser, late in his psychiatric residency, questioned established psychoanalytic premises, he found ready support from his teacher, G. L. Harrington (credited as a cofounder of reality therapy). Harrington had studied in the 1950's at the Menninger Clinic with Hellmuth Kaiser, who stressed the importance of interpersonal contact between the two parties in therapy (Barr, 1974). Glasser's thinking was supported by contemporary critics of prevailing psychiatric dogma, including psychologist O. H. Mowrer (who wrote the Foreword to *Reality Therapy*) and psychiatrist Thomas Szasz.

Like Szasz, Glasser rejects the concept of mental illness and the general use of psychiatric labels, seeing all functional pathology as irresponsible learned behavior. Reality therapy teaches clients to act responsibly to meet their human needs. The past is not scanned for reasons ("excuses") for the irresponsible behavior, but in the warm, supportive relationship plans are made to act in more responsible ways.

Glasser controls training in reality therapy through his Institute for Reality Therapy. His Educator Training Center similarly promotes the tenets of reality therapy in administration and teaching in elementary and secondary schools.

A View of Humanity. The basic concepts of reality therapy constitute a theory of human nature, both normal and disturbed. People behave in whatever ways they can to meet their needs. If their learning, situation, or resources are inadequate to meet their needs, they will be unfulfilled and miserable, and may be seen as disturbed or needing psychiatric care.

The essential human needs are the same in all cultures and situations. Physiological needs are rarely involved in psychopathology. Mental health professionals are concerned with two sets of basic needs: "the need to love and be loved and the need to feel that we are worthwhile to ourselves and to others" (Glasser, 1965, p. 9). The two-way need for love is both intrinsic and instrumental. People need at least one close relationship in order to meet their needs, including the need to feel worthwhile. Implicitly those who go to therapists do so because they lack other human involvements through which they can meet their needs. Glasser is not cynical when he says that paying a therapist is only "buying a friend."

Therapeutic assistance may also be needed when one loses an established object or source of love. Inability to love can be so painful and threatening to one's self-esteem that the person withdraws from efforts to relate and to meet socially dependent needs. The abilities to love and be loved are subject to a person's perception; a depressed or suicidal client may complain of unbearable loneliness, despite being surrounded by apparently devoted family and friends.

The ability to feel worthwhile to ourselves and to others resembles the common concept of self-esteem. In reality therapy it has distinctive bases. Although abundant love usually produces a sense of worth, unconditional love may not do so. "The child knows the difference between right and wrong behavior and is frustrated because receiving love for behavior that he knows is wrong does not allow him to feel worthwhile" (Glasser, 1965, p. 10). Morals and values are intricately related to self-esteem in reality therapy. Thus it is that disturbed behavior is identified as irrespon-

sible and based on inferior standards (not on an overly strong superego, as psychoanalysts may aver). Furthermore, responsible, mentally healthy behavior must not only meet one's own needs, but it also must not interfere with other people's meeting their own needs.

Reality therapy seems compatible with the biblical view of humanity in many ways. (Glasser professes Judaism, and he reports that Harrington is a Christian.) Glasser's emphasis on loving and needing involvement recalls Scripture, ranging from "it is not good for the man to be alone" (Gen. 2:18 NIV) to "the greatest of these is love" (1 Cor. 13:13). Self-worth is not so obviously a biblical doctrine, but we are made "a little lower than the heavenly beings" (Ps. 8:5), and God loved us so much "that he gave his one and only Son" (John 3:16). Of course, ethical standards and responsible behavior receive stronger biblical imperative. Reality therapy's most explicit moral bases are more humanistic than theocentric, but it rejects ethical neutrality and relativity, and views some behaviors as inherently wrong.

The Reality Therapist. Reality therapists represent many helping professions—e.g., social work, school administration, clinical psychology, guidance counseling, the ministry. Full-fledged reality therapists are certified by the Institute for Reality Therapy. Among 415 clinical and counseling psychologists in the American Psychological Association surveyed by Smith (1982), 1% identified with reality therapy.

If the reality therapist serves as a paid friend to the client, the friendship offers a tough love, with notable objectivity, firmness, and persuasiveness. The therapist assumes certain responsibilities for the involvement and makes them clear to the client, but he or she never assumes responsibility for the client's behaviors.

Reality therapy teaches clients (by model, exhortation, and practice) to meet their needs responsibly, respecting others' needs and rights. Techniques used to solve immediate problems are generalized to other situations so that clients become increasingly independent of therapy.

Sometimes the principles of reality therapy are oversimplified, suggesting that anybody can become a reality therapist. While the techniques can be succinctly stated, at several points the therapist's intuitive art and strength of personality are sorely tested. People who attempt to become reality therapists without careful training and supervision may be led astray by one or another idea taken out of context.

The Therapeutic Process. Glasser originally (1965, p. 21) identified three therapeutic procedures: involvement, rejecting unrealistic behavior, and teaching better ways to fulfill the client's needs. His training materials in the 1970s and a later essay (1980) identified the more familiar eight steps of reality therapy.

The first, make friends, includes the willingness to reveal one's own values and limitations and to become emotionally involved with one's clients—to be affected by their problems and suffer with them. Although Glasser downplays emotions, an emotional involvement requires the therapist to convey some empathy for the feelings clients express. The therapist must understand human behavior well enough to fathom the client's behavior and not be disgusted by it, however deviant. Each step of reality therapy is built on all preceding steps, and amateur attempts at reality therapy may fail most often by slighting the first step, through the therapist's inexperience or eagerness to change the client's behavior.

The second step asks the clients, "What are you doing?" This focuses on clients' behaviors, to persuade them that they choose to act as they do. Unlike rational-emotive therapy, reality therapy does not stress that clients also choose how they feel; it just ignores the debatable issue of emotions altogether. While the therapist may listen to feelings offered, the second step shifts the focus toward behavior, which is probably affecting the feelings anyway.

Step 3 follows by asking, "Is what you are doing helping you?" Clients evaluate their own behavior and come to recognize the ways it is unrealistic, irresponsible, or simply not meeting their major goals. The question departs significantly from Glasser's original second step—rejecting the unrealistic behavior. This earlier strategy invited misunderstanding in that the therapist more or less abruptly changed from unconditional friendship to critical rejection (Frazier & Laura, 1972). Almost surely Glasser rarely operated that way. Nonetheless, the therapist must make judgments, challenging a glib response like, "Sure; it makes me feel good to cuss out my teacher!" While making friends the therapist learns the client's needs and goals well enough to turn "Is it helping?" toward more fundamental or long-term goals.

Step 4 helps the client make a plan to do better. While clients should make substantial contributions to the plans made in therapy, the therapist may have to make suggestions, to proffer alternative plans, to modify plans to make them more realistic and readily attainable. However it is developed, the plan must be one the client will accept.

Step 5 gets a commitment to the plan. The commitment may be sealed with a handshake or in a written contract. The timetable usually involves having at least part of the plan completed by the next session, with scheduled evaluation points for the other parts.

The next two steps refer to the follow-up on the commitment. The sixth is to accept no excuses. If the commitment has not been kept, the therapist may say, "Yes, but you didn't do it, did you?" Then the commitment is renewed or the plan revised. Step 7 does not provide for punishment, but neither does the therapist interfere with natural consequences of the lapse. If an alcoholic client breaks a pledge of abstinence, the therapist would not upbraid or withhold therapy, but neither would he or she plead mercy from the client's spouse or judge.

Step 8 is never give up. The therapist's commitment involves sticking with therapy as long as the client is willing to work on the problems. If a plan fails, therapy picks up at the appropriate prior step and tries again. If a client resists even the mild, implicit confrontation of "Is it helping?" the therapist falls back to maintaining the friendship. So reality therapy may continuously recycle through the eight steps until clients themselves can accept and evaluate their behavior, assume responsibility for their plans, and make commitments to proper conduct.

Reality Therapy (1965) described applications in a residential treatment center for delinquent girls, a mental hospital chronic ward, public schools, and private practice. Glasser's next book, *Schools Without Failure* (1968), explicitly stressed the public school system, to which he devoted considerable attention. Besides California's Ventura School for Girls, where reality therapy was forged, other residential treatment programs for youths use reality therapy. Frazier and Laura (1972) described a church application, which failed because the minister did not follow the principles outlined above.

Evaluation. Two decades of development by a cohesive group of therapists from various backgrounds have honed reality therapy into a coherent and effective treatment for a wide variety of psychological problems. That cohesion could perpetuate blind spots. Conventionally trained therapists may charge that glossing over emotions fails to resolve underlying emotional problems. Techniques from rational-emotive therapy, when appropriate, could avert this criticism and still maintain the spirit of reality therapy. Then, nondirective therapists may challenge a therapy that even implicitly presumes to define reality for its clients.

It is not absolutely true, as often charged, that the principles of reality therapy are simple to understand and the therapeutic techniques easy to master. This therapy requires considerable insight into human behavior and artful applications to concrete personal situations. Still, reality therapy could be more widely adopted in pastoral counseling. Specific training in the therapy should not substitute for graduate education in psychology or clinical pastoral training, but reality therapy can be an effective tool for clerical counselors. Both the implied view of humankind and the therapeutic methods seem well suited to ministerial counseling roles.

Possibly the major limiting factor in widespread use of reality therapy, by ministers and other counselors, is its continued "ownership" by Glasser's organizations. While control over orthodoxy of the system has merit, if reality therapy were taught in other counselor-training programs, its apparent values could find wider application.

References

Barr, N. I. The responsible world of reality therapy. *Psychology Today*, 1974, 7(9), 64; 67–68.
Frazier, S. L., & Laura, R. S. Reality therapy: A critical examination. *Pastoral Psychology*, 1972, *23*, 39–49.
Glasser, W. *Reality therapy*. New York: Harper & Row, 1965.
Glasser, W. *Schools Without Failure*. New York: Harper & Row, 1968.
Glasser, W. Reality therapy. In N. Glasser (Ed.), *What are you doing?* New York: Harper & Row, 1980.
Smith, D. Trends in counseling and psychotherapy. *American Psychologist*, 1982, *37*, 802–809.

R. D. KAHOE

Reconstructive Psychotherapy.
Although there is no universally accepted classification of psychotherapies, reconstructive psychotherapy is generally distinguished from SUPPORTIVE PSYCHOTHERAPY and REEDUCATIVE PSYCHOTHERAPY by its depth of exploration and breadth of goals. Wolberg (1967) suggests that this general category of therapies has as its distinctive quality the goal of insight into unconscious levels of conflict. In this regard symptom relief is only part of the goal of a reconstructive therapy; the broader goal also includes a promotion of emotional development through insight.

Reconstructive psychotherapy is closely associated with psychoanalysis in that most of the therapies that would be generally classified as reconstructive have their origins in the psychoanalytic tradition. In addition to the classical psychoanalytic technique (*see* PSYCHOANALYSIS: TECHNIQUE), other therapies usually classified as reconstructive include PSYCHOANALYTIC PSYCHOTHERAPY, ADLERIAN PSYCHOTHERAPY, JUNGIAN ANALYSIS, the will therapy of OTTO RANK, and the dynamic-cultural therapies of KAREN HORNEY and HARRY STACK SULLIVAN.

Reference
Wolberg, L. *The technique of psychotherapy* (Vol. 1) (2nd ed.). New York: Grune & Stratton, 1967.

D. G. BENNER

Recreation, Therapeutic. *See* ACTIVITY THERAPY.

Reductionism.
A fundamental scientific theory, which states that one can explain a phenomenon of nature at one level of inquiry by showing how its mechanisms and processes arise out of a lower or more microscopic level. For example, the reductionism of science assumes that chemical reactions can be explained by appealing to the activity and properties of molecules and atoms, and ultimately to the physical forces holding atoms together. Reductionism in psychology assumes that all behavioral and mental phenomena can be explained in terms of the physical world. Physiological explanations seem to be the preferred level of explanation in psychology.

There are two forms of reductionism found in the natural sciences and psychology. Methodological reductionism in psychology refers to the decision to confine the language of psychology to expressions that are in principle reducible to a science such as physiological psychology. This is similar to methodological behaviorism, in which mental and psychological phenomena are not denied. In the interest of developing a scientific psychology, the language of private data is avoided in favor of behavioral language that is anchored in public observation. Metaphysical reductionism, on the other hand, asserts that for psychology are questions of theory are to be resolved by physiological explanations. This compares with metaphysical behaviorism, which assumes that all sentences in the mental language are really translatable into sentences of physical language.

Most psychology is built on the foundation of reductionism, with metaphysical reductionism being frequently held by psychology's leading scientists. This means that much of scientific psychology takes the position that human nature can be described and explained entirely by reference to neurophysiology or conditioned responses, and not to concepts such as mind or consciousness.

Metaphysical reductionism implies a belief in both materialism and determinism. This means that human beings have no immaterial essence but are entirely material, and that there are physical explanations for every aspect of personality and consciousness. Reductionism does not agree with the philosophical idea of emergentism, which teaches that the organization of parts into a compound structure results in the emergence of new properties that could not have been predicted even from a full knowledge of the parts and their interactions. In other words, reductionism believes that the whole of a person's behavior is nothing more than the sum of its parts.

There are abundant examples of reductionism in psychology from its founding until the present. Adopting the assumptions of materialism and empiricism from the natural sciences, psychology began as a field prone to reductive explanations. The psychophysics of Wundt, the founding father of psychology, suggested this kind of analysis. The term *Psychophysics* describes the relating of mind (psyche) to physical laws. Watson's school of behaviorism, which created the central philosophical foundation for psychology as it grew, encouraged the development of a unique reductive language in terms of conditioned reflexes.

One of the strongest proponents of a metaphysical reductionism in psychology today is B. F. Skinner, who believes that what have been labeled mental phenomena are really the result of physiological responses to environmental stimuli and can be totally explained by the contingencies of reinforcement in a person's environment. It is probably true that most psychologists invariably come to think of neurophysiology as the ultimate level of explanation for all mental and personal phenomena. Carlson (1980) in a popular physiological psychology textbook states, "Physiological psychologists believe that all natural phenomena (including human behavior) are subject to the laws of physics. Thus, the laws of behavior can be reduced to descriptions of physiological processes. No consideration has to be given to concepts such as free will" (p. 2).

Nowhere in science are the issues of reductionism and levels of explanation more debated than they are in psychology. The distance between psychology and any lower level of explanation is greater than between any other set of levels of explanation in science. Reducing genetics to biochemistry seems quite acceptable. But it is a much larger step to move from the human personality, with its thoughts, imaginations, and complex emotions, to the interaction of neurons in the brain.

It is precisely this metaphysical reductionism that is opposed to the Christian view of human nature. Neurophysiologist MacKay (1974) argues that even the most detailed description of the human brain will not exhaust the mystery of the person. MacKay calls the thinking of reductionism "nothing buttery" because of its tendency to say the person is "nothing but" an assemblage of functioning neurons. When the complexities of the human brain are explained in this way, they are actually just explained away. Explaining the human personality in terms of nothing-buttery allows the reductionist to deal with the complexities of human beings primarily by prior assumption. This is assuming there is nothing more to human nature than the physical; therefore, why look beyond physical explanations? The Christian has no problems with methodological reductionism, but feels that the assumptions of metaphysical reductionism clearly pass judgment on the makeup of human nature, when science should be open to investigating all levels of the human personality.

Another problem with reductionism is its decision on the proper level of inquiry. How does the reductionist decide where to base the description of human nature? Why is the organizational level of neurons a better level of description of a human being than the biochemistry of neural firing? To choose any level short of the subatomic world of physics seems to be practicing only a partial reductionism. But to explain human nature entirely in terms of quantum physics results in the loss of the subject matter entirely. It seems more reasonable to describe human nature on the levels of our ordinary experience—including spiritual, psychological, and physical levels. Descriptions at one level should never be considered complete nor be used to invalidate descriptions at other levels.

Neither neurophysiology nor Skinner's behaviorism should be considered sciences with sufficient maturity that one can immediately cancel all holistic explanations of human nature. Many schools of psychology have, in both theory and research, questioned the reductionism of behaviorism and neurophysiology. The ideas of Gestalt psychologists, rationalists such as Piaget and Chomsky, and cognitive behaviorists such as Tolman and Bandura, have rejected the reductionistic notion that detailed information about the physiological or behavioral components of a person produces a complete description of the person.

The limits of metaphysical reductionism do not rule out the advantages of a methodological reductionism to the Christian who is interested in a scientific psychology. In their work psychologists should use language as carefully and objectively as possible. Objective description of human behavior or neurophysiology may be a valuable starting point for psychology. Any psychological investigation that remains at these starting levels will be unable to deal with the complexities of the human personality. A reductionist's precise, objective investigation may be an appropriate place to start, but never an appropriate place to stop.

References

Carlson, N. R. *Physiology and behavior* (2nd ed.). Boston: Allyn & Bacon, 1980.

MacKay, D. M. *The clockwork image.* Downers Grove, Ill.: Inter-Varsity Press, 1974.

Additional Readings

Collins, G. R. *The rebuilding of psychology.* Wheaton, Ill.: Tyndale House, 1977.

Turner, M. B. *Psychology and the philosophy of science.* New York: Appleton-Century-Crofts, 1968.

M. P. Cosgrove

See PSYCHOLOGY, PRESUPPOSITIONS OF.

Reeducative Psychotherapy. The term Wolberg (1967) uses to describe a group of therapies falling between the two more usually recognized groups known as SUPPORTIVE PSYCHOTHERAPY and RECONSTRUCTIVE PSYCHOTHERAPY. Wolberg views the goal of reeducative approaches as interpersonal and behavioral education. Whereas supportive therapy aims for a restoration of equilibrium and reconstructive therapy aims for something closer to a reorganization of personality, reeducative therapy aims for symptom removal through direct attack. BEHAVIOR THERAPY, STRATEGIC THERAPY, REALITY THERAPY, DIRECT DECISION THERAPY, PERSONAL CONSTRUCTS THERAPY, and many of the sex and family therapies are examples of reeducative approaches.

Reference

Wolberg, L. *The technique of psychotherapy* (Vol. 1) (2nd ed.). New York: Grune & Stratton, 1967.

D. G. Benner

Reflection of Feeling. See EMPATHY.

Reframing Technique. The therapeutic technique of positively restating or paraphrasing what is perceived by an individual as negative. Used primarily in marriage and family therapy, this intervention helps to get clients out of blaming postures and into more functional interactions. Reframing aims to change the perception of one's own behavior or that of another.

For example, a distancing husband is criticized by his wife for not wanting to be close. The therapist reframes the husband's behavior as his way of trying to get the appropriate space he needs to feel comfortable in the marriage. Indirectly the therapist is stating that individuals differ with regard to their need for closeness and that these differences are normal. This understanding paves the way for a discussion of how the couple might achieve a workable compromise on this issue.

The terms *relabeling* and *positive connotation* are used interchangeably with reframing. The controlling behavior of a wife, for instance, is relabeled as her way of showing concern. When her motivation is given a positive connotation, the husband's attitude softens, and he can then proceed to propose alternative ways for her to express concern.

J. A. Larsen

See FAMILY THERAPY: OVERVIEW.

Regression. In psychoanalytic thought, regression is viewed as a DEFENSE MECHANISM, operating outside awareness, wherein an individual retreats to an earlier and therefore more primitive level of psychological development. It is closely connected to the concept of FIXATION in that the assumption is that the ego is weakened by unresolved past conflicts and the energy remaining with these conflicts. The individual, therefore, has a tendency to revert back to these points of fixation when faced with serious trauma or anxiety that cannot be managed by other means. Freud's metaphor for regression was an army that has left some of its troops behind at sites of earlier battles, and which in the face of a strong enemy (psychic conflict) retreats to previously established strongholds. Thus seen, the more serious the fixation, or the greater the number of points of fixation, the more prone the individual is to regression.

Although they are very closely related, regression may be viewed from the separate perspectives of the id, ego, or superego. From the perspective of the id regression is seen as a return to more primitive forms of instinctual expression. This is illustrated by the schizophrenic patient who might desire to be bottle fed or who may engage in very childlike expressions of aggression. From the perspective of the ego regression appears as the loss of one or more of the ego functions. The mute psychotic, for example, has lost the ego function of speech. From the perspective of the superego regression may be seen as involve the return to an earlier developmental level of morality. Thus, individuals in seriously regressed states sometimes show a return to a morality organized around exaggerated denial or reaction formation, both of these being typical of an earlier level of moral functioning. While regression may be seen as sometimes affecting one of these systems more than another, usually it is reflected in all three to one degree or another.

In classical psychoanalytic thought the psychopathologies are understood to result from a combination of fixation and regression. The diagnosis of regression requires the demonstration of more advanced levels of functioning being abandoned for more primitive levels. This is usually the case in the psychoses where impaired functioning has often been preceded by a period of much higher level functioning. The degree of the regression is assumed to be reflected in the severity of the psychopathology. Thus, schizophrenia is assumed to be associated with a regression to the very earliest level of development, the oral stage.

Abraham's (1953) classification of psychopathologies identified paranoia with a regression to the early part of the anal period, the compulsion neuroses with the late anal period, and hysteria with the phallic period. While these specific points of regression have been much debated, and alternatives presented and often more widely accepted (e.g., Kernberg, 1980), most psychoanalysts agree that the psychoses represent preoedipal points of fixation/regression, whereas the psychoneuroses represent fixation at an oedipal level, sometimes with the additional operation of regression, although more often without evidence of regression.

Some view regression as normal or even healthy under certain circumstances. For example, regressions seem to occur regularly during puberty and are probably necessary in order to assist the psychic organization of that stage. Similarly some degree of regression following a serious loss (e.g., the death of a loved one) is quite normal and, provided it does not last too long, probably assists in the mourning process. Sports and other play activities also contain an element of regression, frequently providing an outlet for controlled, socially acceptable aggression. Kris (1952) has described what he calls "regression in the service of the ego," wherein a controlled and partial regression allows for an enhancement of ego functions. This is particularly clear in

artistic activities but can also be seen to be operative in humor, imagination, aesthetic expression, and much of our intellectual activity. Arieti (1976) also has provided a very helpful discussion of regression in creativity. In all of these situations the ego of the individual is not overwhelmed, as is the case in psychosis. Rather, it is opened up to previously closed-off levels of the personality, and both the methods and contents of these more primitive levels then serve to enrich the ego.

It should be noted that this controlled regression in the service of the ego is precisely what happens in many psychotherapies (*see* REGRESSIVE THERAPY). In psychoanalysis, and to a lesser extent in psychoanalytic therapy, it is an indispensable component of the therapy process.

References

Abraham, K. *Selected papers on psycho-analysis.* New York: Basic Books, 1953.
Arieti, S. *Creativity.* New York: Basic Books, 1976.
Kernberg, O. *Internal world and external reality.* New York: Aronson, 1980.
Kris, E. *Psychoanalytic explorations on art.* New York: International Universities Press, 1952.

Additional Reading

Laughlin, M. C. *The ego and its defenses* (2nd ed.). New York: Aronson, 1979.

D. G. BENNER

Regressive Therapy. The utilization of a regressive process in a fashion that fosters human growth and development. Regressive therapy was first described by Cox and Esau (1974). Similar therapeutic approaches are known by other terms and are often associated with the psychoanalytic movement.

This approach to therapy is used with those persons who have healthy elements of ego functioning, but only at a regressed level. These elements are experienced as ego-syntonic despite terror, paranoia, or whatever pathological defenses have interfered. The purpose of the regressive therapeutic approach is to foster the exposure, experiencing, and sharing of these healthy elements in the context of as real a relationship as is available. The selection of the love object is made by the patient, preferably from natural family relationships. In the event no family member is available, because of death, mental illness, or incapacity to offer true love and caring, a surrogate object may be found in the therapist. This poses many problems, due to the limitations of a therapeutic relationship. Transference considerations may complicate such a process, as will the fact that the regressed patient seeks bonding to someone whom he experiences in a real, not just a fantasized, relationship.

In psychological and psychiatric literature regression is used in several ways. Some view it as a neurological phenomenon, brought about by various organic therapies such as electroconvulsive therapy and insulin coma therapy. Hypnotherapy is used for regressive purposes to enable the individual to retrieve previously unconscious affects and memories. Similarly, narcoanalysis allows the person to regress to earlier levels of consciousness for retrieval of significant affective experiences. In psychoanalytic psychotherapy regression is defined as a return to earlier levels of ego development. It is viewed as an ego-coping mechanism in response to severe anxiety-provoking experiences. In particular, the schizophrenic has been viewed as regressing into narcissism with a development of overt psychotic symptomatology. Regressive therapy views regression in a somewhat different manner than any of the above. This therapy uses regression in the service of the ego.

Regression in the service of the ego is a part of everyday life. Vacations, recreation, and other overt or symbolic activities and affects that awaken the child in us are beneficial regressions used to restore and renew at the emotional level. In transactional terms, if the child is sacrificed for the development of the adult and/or parent, an imbalance of pathological proportions develops. This results in a pattern of interpersonal and intrapsychic problems. In the emotionally disturbed individual there may be regressions in order to grow and develop one's personality. Regression in the transference relationship has been widely noted (see Searles, 1965).

Regressive therapy utilizes those regressive impulses that can aid the individual in identifying and experiencing a profound level of trust from which healthy psychotherapeutic object relatedness and growth may occur. The thesis of psychoanalytic treatment is that the patient is to be allowed to regress to deeper levels and then to grow. The development of a dependency transference allows for the exploration of this regression (see Balint, 1968). The regressive process in regressive therapy focuses more on regression within a real relationship and is applicable to psychiatric maladies not traditionally treated by a classic psychoanalytic method. Whereas the psychoanalytic approach tends to encourage fantasy concerning the therapist, diminishing the expression of real feelings in the treatment hour, regressive therapy seeks the genuine sharing of

real human expressions with the aim of bonding between the patient and love object. For obvious reasons it is best that such object be a family member if possible.

The goals of a regressive therapeutic process are the enhancement of those ego capacities which, although at a younger age of development, are more healthy than the current pathological functions. This is most startlingly demonstrated in schizophrenia, but the principle remains the same elsewhere. The development of trust between a love object and those regressed and healthy parts of the ego allows for working out and abandoning pathological defenses that are based on paranoia and mistrust.

The manner in which these goals are achieved is best understood in object relations theory. The cathexes in the afflicted individual are complex. In many schizophrenic patients—and in others as well—there are those fragments or segments of personality in which trust still is desired and intimacy is preferred. As in normal child growth and development trust is bonded in human relationships, especially parental ones. In a regressive therapeutic process the patient is given the opportunity to reexperience these hitherto covert but ego-syntonic desires in a new experience of trust. This has been done both in individual therapy, where the therapist becomes the object, and more commonly in a marital or family approach, where the original object is given opportunity to reestablish trust and thence promote a growth process in the family relationships.

For much of the past century parents have been viewed as the cause of psychiatric illness. Wiser observations point to the frequency with which both the parents and the child are victims of circumstances, pressures, and relationships that they did not consciously choose and that they may have a common desire to undo. Efforts are made, therefore, within regressive therapy to reexperience the events of the early childhood traumas together in a family context. This will often result in regressive desires and actions by the patient. Under no circumstances are these regressive behaviors forced or demanded. Rather, they are a natural outgrowth of the reexperience.

The regression may be only in certain aspects of life and around key events. It does not necessarily involve a total regression of all of life. The patient does not become a small child again, although there are certainly childish affects, desires, and relatedness that develop. The preferred therapeutic approach is for the patient to experience the regressive process in relationship to his natural environment, those relationships in which he grew and to which he still has a strong desire for bonding. When this is not possible and a strong regressive wish is evident in the psychotherapeutic process, a therapist may be such an object. There are, however, natural limits to this. The fantasy of the naïve could lead one into a major rescue effort without realizing that a therapist is a therapist, not a mother or father. If the therapist takes on the function of parent, he not only steps outside a role established by society but may hurt those to whom he belongs. On some occasions the therapist as object is sufficient for those patients who have less need of a full regressive approach and where only segments and specific issues are involved. Needless to say, this approach is most appropriate for the seasoned therapist who has at his command a wide range of psychotherapeutic techniques and experiences.

This method of treatment is based on interpersonal theory and calls upon an object relations theoretical framework. It views estrangement and the resulting desire for restitution of the relationship as the strongest need. The establishment and maintenance of bonding are synonymous with health. Subsequent differentiation is based on healthy bonding. This view is seen to be readily compatible with and supported by the biblical view of man as a lost creature. This is not the same, however, as saying that emotional problems are the result of conscious sin, or that restoration from serious psychopathology comes by a simplistic application of the principles of Christian living. It would suggest that a common core of psychopathology has to do with the loss and distortion of relationships.

References
Balint, M. *The basic fault: Therapeutic aspects of regression.* London: Tavistock Publications, 1968.
Cox, R. H., & Esau, T. G. *Regressive therapy.* New York: Brunner/Mazel, 1974.
Searles, H. F. *Collected papers on schizophrenia and related subjects.* New York: International Universities Press, 1965.

T. G. Esau

Rehearsal, Obsessional. A sort of dress rehearsal of an anticipated event that helps a person plan how to carry out a compulsive ritual in as socially inconspicuous manner as possible. Persons who have well-developed compulsions are usually able to carry out their compulsive rituals with ease in private settings. However, when a compulsive person is obligated to participate in a setting that makes the performance of the ritualistic behavior difficult, a serious dilemma occurs. Obsessional rehearsal is one solution.

For example, a person whose compulsive rituals include washing his or her hands seven times before picking up the eating utensils is faced with a serious dilemma when invited to sit at the head table at a large banquet. The compulsive person may choose to visit the banquet hall, locate the restroom closest to the head table, recruit a friend who could accompany him or her to the restroom, and ask the friend to open all necessary doors between the restroom and the banquet hall. By means of such planning, or obsessional rehearsal, the compulsive person is able to participate in what otherwise would be an impossible event. Obsessional rehearsal obviously adds a great deal of complexity and inconvenience to the already cluttered life of a compulsive.

J. R. Beck

Reinforcement. A substantial body of scientific evidence derived from operant conditioning research indicates that behavior is strongly influenced by its consequences. Consequences are classified according to the effect they have on behavior. Stimuli or events that increase the likelihood that a response will occur again are termed reinforcers, whereas stimuli or events that decrease the likelihood of response are termed punishers. Reinforcers are further distinguished according to whether their presentation or removal increases responding.

If the presentation of a reinforcer following a response increases the likelihood that the response will recur, then it is a *positive* reinforcer and the process is known as positive reinforcement. For example, giving a hungry animal a food pellet after a lever press response will increase the probability that the animal will press the lever again. In this case food serves as a positive reinforcer. Similarly, if parental praise increases the frequency with which a child makes his bed, then praise is a positive reinforcer for bed making.

If the removal of a stimulus or event increases the likelihood that the response will recur, then it is termed a *negative* reinforcer and the process is known as negative reinforcement. For example, if a response terminates or avoids a painful electric shock, then the response will be likely to occur again. In this case electric shock is a negative reinforcer. Escape and avoidance behaviors maintained by negative reinforcement are part of everyday life. People have ways of getting away when trapped in an unpleasant social situation, and they learn behaviors that enable them to avoid such unpleasant situations.

Types of Reinforcers and Their Results. Reinforcers also are classified as either primary or acquired. Primary reinforcers usually are related to the biological needs of the organism; acquired reinforcers are those resulting from the individual's experience with the environment. More specifically, a primary reinforcer is a stimulus or event that innately affects behavior without any prior experience. Positive primary reinforcers may be things that are vital to survival such as food and water, or they may be less obvious events such as sensory change or opportunities to explore a novel environment. Negative primary reinforcers may be such things as physically painful events, loud noises, bright lights and noxious odors.

A conditioned (secondary) reinforcer is a stimulus that, because it is consistently accompanied by a primary reinforcer, acquires reinforcing properties itself. For example, if an animal that has learned to press a lever to obtain food pellets is placed in a separate box and is fed pellets each time a buzzer is sounded, the buzzer will become a conditioned reinforcer and will sustain lever presses in the absence of food pellets. Similarly, stimuli that reliably accompany negative reinforcers acquire conditioned reinforcing properties, and their removal will reinforce behavior. For example, animals will perform a specified response to terminate a stimulus that is consistently followed by painful electric shock. However, conditioned reinforcers, both positive and negative, will lose their power if they are not accompanied by the primary reinforcer at least some of the time. By the proper use of conditioned reinforcement elaborate sequences of behavior can be trained and maintained with a single primary reinforcer that occurs at the end of the sequence.

A stimulus that has been associated with many types of primary as well as conditioned reinforcements may acquire the capacity to function as a generalized reinforcer. Money is an obvious illustration of a generalized reinforcer because it provides access to food, drink, shelter, entertainment, etc., and thereby becomes a reinforcer for a variety of activities. Social reinforcers also are thought to represent a special class of generalized reinforcers.

The concept of conditioned and generalized reinforcers helps bridge the gap between simple laboratory procedures and complex human and animal learning. The range of human behavior attributable directly to primary reinforcers is small. Moreover, the development of social reinforcers is particularly critical because human behavior is frequently strengthened, sustained, and modified by praise, approval, encouragement, positive attention, and affection.

Although there is little dispute about the validity of the principle of reinforcement, numerous alternative explanations have been proposed for the manner in which reinforcement produces its effect. Some early theories argued that reinforcers are events that ultimately satisfy some vital need of the organism; others argued that the sensations involved in performing these acts are themselves innately reinforcing. However, no single theory adequately accounts for the full range of activities and stimuli that can be used to reinforce behavior. Therefore, many psychologists have turned to defining reinforcers operationally in terms of their effect on behavior without attempting to identify why a particular event serves as a reinforcer.

Although it may not be possible to specify why a particular event is reinforcing, there are a number of factors that generally influence the effectiveness of a reinforcer. For example, the longer that rewards are delayed following responses, the less effective they tend to be unless the gap between response and reinforcement is bridged cognitively (e.g., through verbal instructions) or with a conditioned reinforcer. Primary positive reinforcers also are usually effective only if the organism has been deprived of them in the recent past; food is not likely to serve as reinforcer for an animal that is not hungry. Larger or higher quality reinforcers also are more effective than smaller or lower quality reinforcers. Schedules of reinforcement, which determine when appropriate responses will be reinforced, also are important. Schedules determine both the pattern of reinforced responding and how persistent responding will be if responses fail to produce reinforcement (extinction). Finally, the effectiveness of a given reinforcer is affected by the potency of other available reinforcers.

In addition to its ability to strengthen behavior, reinforcement can provide information concerning the appropriateness of behavior. New behavior can be shaped by selectively reinforcing bits of behavior that come successively closer to the desired behavior. Similarly, differential reinforcement can establish discriminations by reinforcing a response in the presence of one stimulus and withholding reinforcement in the presence of others.

Misunderstandings and Evaluation. The deliberate use of positive reinforcement to influence human behavior, especially in the form of tangible rewards, has given rise to ethical objections and concerns about the possible harmful effects that may result from such practices. A frequently expressed attitude is that desirable behavior should be intrinsically satisfying. One concern is that, if people are frequently rewarded, they will behave appropriately only when they are paid to do so. Some believe that reinforcing practices may interfere with the development of spontaneity, creativity, intrinsic motivational systems, and other highly valued self-determining personality characteristics. Others even consider the deliberate use of reinforcement as deceptive, manipulative, and an insult to the personal integrity of human beings. However, such negative attitudes often stem from basic misunderstandings and from the observed misapplication of reinforcement principles.

Much of the work on reinforcement principles has been conducted with animals in operant conditioning experiments. This has led to the erroneous belief that the use of reinforcement is somehow beneath human dignity. In addition, people tend to associate the use of reinforcement principles with behavioristic practitioners whose nonbiblical philosophies conflict with an acceptable Christian view of humans and human behavior. Finally, the use of reinforcement to bring about desirable behavior challenges beliefs that desirable behaviors (e.g., learning) are themselves inherently rewarding. Yet available evidence does not justify such beliefs; few behaviors are inherently rewarding for all people. Moreover, sometimes it is necessary to use external rewards to bring people into contact with the "natural rewards" associated with desirable behaviors.

The use of external rewards has lead to the false impression that the total province of reinforcement theory lies in the manipulation of behavior through materialistic reinforcement. However, abundant evidence suggests that reinforcement procedures, if thoughtfully and skillfully implemented, can produce enduring changes in social behavior and facilitate the acquisition of self-monitoring reinforcement systems. If rewards are repeatedly and explicitly associated with cues that signify competency or correctness, then these stimuli have informative value, and qualitative differences in performance may acquire secondary reinforcing properties. At this higher level of development cues that indicate the adequacy of one's performance may be as reinforcing as monetary incentives. Once informative response feedback becomes a source of personal satisfaction, then maintenance of behavior is less dependent on external or material incentives. The highest level of autonomy is achieved when behavior generates self-evaluative and self-reinforcing consequences; that is, when a person sets standards of achievement and creates self-rewarding or self-punishing consequences depending on the quality of his behavior relative to his self-imposed standards. Self-reinforcement may not only maintain behavior without external support, but it may override the influence of rewards that conflict with a person's own norms of acceptable behavior.

Reinforcement plays a vital role in the LEARNING process. Its thoughtful application is instrumental in helping shape desirable behavior. The application of reinforcement principles, often referred to as behavior modification, has been shown to be a fruitful approach to some behavior problems. Its successful application has been demonstrated in teaching, psychotherapy, industry, prisons, and institutions for the mentally retarded and emotionally disturbed. At the same time, if reinforcement procedures are improperly applied and the incentives inappropriate to the individual's development, then the use of reinforcement may be insulting as well as ineffective.

Additional Readings
Bandura, A. *Principles of behavior modification*. New York: Holt, Rinehart, & Winston, 1969.
Reynolds, G. S. *A primer of operant conditioning* (Rev. ed.). Glenview, Ill.: Scott, Foresman, 1975.

S. R. OSBORNE

Reinforcement, Schedule of. A behavior rule that specifies under what conditions a response will produce reinforcement. For example, a schedule of continuous reinforcements means that every appropriate response produces reinforcement. However, in most cases reinforcers do not occur on schedules of continuous reinforcement. Instead they are obtained on schedules of intermittent reinforcement.

Simple intermittent schedules can be classified into two types: ratio and interval. Ratio schedules prescribe that a certain number of responses must be made to produce reinforcement. Interval schedules prescribe that a given interval of time must elapse before response can be reinforced. Under ratio schedules the amount of time taken to make the required number of responses is irrelevant as long as the required number of responses are made. Alternatively, under the interval schedule the number of responses is irrelevant as long as the one response necessary for reinforcement occurs after the interval has elapsed.

Ratio and interval schedules are further classified into two types: fixed and variable. Under a variable schedule the number of responses or the amount of elapsed time required for one reinforcement varies from reinforcement to reinforcement in an irregular, but usually repeating, fashion. Under a fixed schedule the number of responses or the amount of elapsed time required for one reinforcement is always the same.

The value of a variable schedule is the average number of responses or time interval required for reinforcement. For example, a variable-ratio 70 (VR 70) schedule prescribes that, on the average, every 70th response produces reinforcement even though the exact number for any given reinforcement may vary from numbers much below 70 to numbers much larger. Similarly, a variable-interval schedule varies the amount of time that must elapse before a response can be reinforced. For example, a variable-interval one minute (VI 1-min) schedule prescribes that, on the average, after one minute has elapsed, a response produces reinforcement even though the exact interval of time may vary from times much longer than one minute to intervals much shorter.

The value of a fixed schedule is always the same. For example, a fixed-ratio 50 (FR 50) schedule prescribes that every 50th response produces reinforcement. Similarly, a fixed-interval one minute (FI 1-min) schedule prescribes that the first response that occurs after each one-minute interval produces reinforcement.

Each of these schedules of reinforcement produces a characteristic pattern of responding. Fixed-ratio schedules generate a rapid, continuous response rate following a pause after each reinforcement. Variable-ratio schedules also generate a fairly high, constant rate of responding. On fixed-interval schedules there is a pause after reinforcement; thereafter, responding increases gradually and then accelerates as time to reinforcement decreases. Variable-interval schedules maintain a constant, uninterrupted rate of responding. Overall, response rates are determined by the average interreinforcement interval; that is, shorter average intervals or response ratios maintain higher response rates.

When responses are no longer reinforced, they decrease in frequency and eventually cease. This extinction process is different for the various schedules of reinforcement. In general, the greater the difference between conditions prevailing during extinction and conditions when responses were reinforced, the more rapid the extinction. Behavior maintained by intermittent reinforcement is more resistant to extinction than behavior maintained by continuous reinforcement. A mother who occasionally reinforces her child's temper tantrums by comforting the child is building more persistent tantrums than the mother who always comforts an unhappy child.

There are many examples of schedules of reinforcement in everyday life. Behavior is reinforced on a fixed-ratio schedule when a factory pays a worker a certain amount each time a fixed number of items has been manufactured. Slot machines at gambling casinos pay off according to variable-ratio schedules of reinforcement. Bus drivers arrive at fixed intervals. An hour before a bus is due, no one looks to see if it is coming. But as the scheduled time nears, people tend to glance down the street more and more frequently. In contrast, dialing a telephone number after hearing a busy signal is an example of a variable-interval schedule.

Some psychologists study simple schedules of reinforcement because they believe that complex patterns of behavior are maintained by combinations and mixtures of simple schedules. Schedules of reinforcement also provide a convenient and stable set of procedures for laboratory investigations of LEARNING.

S. R. OSBORNE

Reinforcement, Self. The self-administration of positive reinforcers (rewarding events) or the self-removal of negative reinforcers (punishing events) contingent on a particular target behavior in the individual. In either case the intended purpose of self-reinforcement is to strengthen the target behavior. In contrast, self-punishment is defined as the self-removal of positive reinforcers or the self-administration of negative reinforcers.

To a great extent these concepts grew out of the research and theorizing of B. F. Skinner. His distinction between controlling and controlled responses was particularly important in stimulating research and writing on self-reinforcement. Controlling responses are the behaviors an individual uses to modify a target behavior in himself or in another person, whereas controlled responses are the changed behaviors. Human beings have the unique potential of being counselor and client, therapist and patient, experimenter and subject, or teacher and student within the same skin. This potential is based on the fact that persons can change themselves through the same operations they use to change others, and self-reinforcement is perhaps the most commonly used self-controlling operation.

Whereas positive self-reinforcement (the self-administration of rewards) is often used, negative self-reinforcement (the self-removal of punishers) has rarely been employed for clinical purposes. Positive self-reinforcement may involve the self-administration of tangible reinforcers such as candy or peanuts, token reinforcers such as points on a counter or checks on a sheet of paper, activity reinforcers such as taking a walk or reading a book, social reinforcers such as self-praise, and symbolic reinforcers such as self-evaluation or comparing one's own performance with a goal.

As normally practiced self-reinforcement consists of several operations: 1) presenting an immediate cue for the target behavior; 2) observing the target behavior when it occurs; 3) recording the occurrence of the target behavior or its by-products; 4) comparing one's own response with a performance objective or with a criterion for reinforcement; and 5) administering a positive reinforcer or removing a negative reinforcer. The common labels for these operations are self-cuing, self-observation, self-monitoring/self-recording, self-evaluation, and self-consequating, respectively.

The effects of self-reinforcement may be enhanced by self-administering an appropriate deprivation or satiation schedule, injesting certain drugs, noncontingently self-applying pleasant or aversive stimulation, providing oneself with choices, writing a performance contract, choosing back-up reinforcers before the intervention begins, or exposing oneself to a social model who is being reinforced for the same target behavior.

Self-reinforcement became an important treatment strategy during the 1970s. Because it developed out of basic research on LEARNING and social influence processes, it first appeared in the clinical procedures of psychotherapists who used behavioral and social learning approaches to treatment. Self-reinforcement has allowed patients and clients first to assist the professional therapist and then to take control of their own treatment.

Among the issues treated by self-reinforcement have been academic achievement and work output, alcoholism, angry outbursts, attentional deficits, dating and heterosexual relations, compulsions, devotional life and spiritual development, drug abuse, impulse control, phobias, physical exercise, smoking, social skills, speech problems, and using bad language.

P. W. CLEMENT

Reinforcement, Time out from. *See* TIME-OUT.

Relabeling Technique. *See* REFRAMING TECHNIQUE.

Relationship Enhancement Therapy. A didactic and behavioral therapy developed by Guerney (1977). Guerney and Vogelsong (1980) discuss the history of the development of the approach. In the early 1960s Guerney developed FILIAL THERAPY. Spurred on by the success obtained in training parents in new interactional skills for dealing with their troubled children, Guerney and his colleagues taught husbands and wives in distressed relationships Rogerian therapy skills for expression of feelings and responding to the expressions of others. Following empirical study of the effectiveness of the approach with couples, the therapeutic repertoire of methods was broadened and subsequently applied to other groups, including parents and their children, dating couples, and business and educational relationships.

The methods of relationship enhancement therapy essentially utilize the standard behavioral four-stage procedure of didactic presentation, modeling of relevant skills, practice of the modeled skills, and feedback. Daily practice and long-term maintenance of learned skills are emphasized. The core skills that are taught include how to be aware of and express one's feelings and desires in a relationship, how to understand the other's expressions and communicate that understanding empathically, how to facilitate or moderate the interactions of others to enhance their communication, how to resolve conflict, and how to maintain the change produced by these procedures.

Relationship enhancement therapy should be regarded as a therapeutic technique rather than as an approach to psychotherapy. As noted by Jacobson and Margolin (1979), therapists attempting to correct dysfunctional communication patterns between people have been moving steadily toward a general model of change that is essentially didactic and behavioral in nature. Relationship enhancement is one such package of behavior change technology, but it is not truly distinctive from other communication development packages. It has been shown to be useful in positively changing a couple's communication pattern but has not been shown to be superior to other similar methods. Finally, it should not be regarded as a total approach to marital (or other relationship) therapy, as it is increasingly clear that communication is one, but not the only, important area of need in a distressed relationship.

References

Guerney, B., Jr. *Relationship enhancement: Skill training programs for therapy, problem prevention, and enrichment.* San Francisco: Jossey-Bass, 1977.

Guerney, B., Jr., & Vogelsong, E. Relationship enhancement therapy. In R. Herink (Ed.), *The psychotherapy handbook.* New York: New American Library, 1980.

Jacobson, N., & Margolin, G. *Marital therapy.* New York: Brunner/Mazel, 1979.

S. L. JONES

Relaxation Training. A term commonly applied to a family of techniques that includes Jacobsonian progressive relaxation and its variants; autogenic training; alpha-wave, electromyography, and other forms of biofeedback targeted to relaxation; some forms of hypnotherapy; and meditation and yoga exercises more influenced by Eastern practices. Only Jacobsonian and related deep muscle relaxation procedures will be discussed here.

Jacobson, a physician, developed his technique of progressive relaxation for the treatment of anxious patients. Working from the Watsonian notion that emotions are peripheral in nature, Jacobson (1938) attempted to develop a procedure that would directly reduce the unpleasant experience of tension and anxiety. His procedures involved extensive exercises of tensing and relaxing all the muscle groups in the body.

Jacobson's work went largely unnoticed by mental health professionals until Joseph Wolpe began his pioneering work in developing systematic desensitization. Wolpe worked from the theory that to eliminate a conditioned anxiety response, the therapist must condition an antagonistic counter-response. Wolpe used the relaxation produced by Jacobson's exercises as the suitable antagonistic response. In the treatment of phobias, for example, Wolpe had the person learn progressive relaxation; then he slowly exposed the person imaginally to the feared stimulus while relaxed, so that relaxation rather than fear was increasingly associated with the phobic stimulus. In time it was shown that Wolpe's counterconditioning notions were untenable and that relaxation training was not essential to fear reduction. Nevertheless, many clients had received relaxation training with positive results, and the technique was increasingly being used as an integral part of many behavior therapy treatment approaches.

Wolpe condensed Jacobson's original procedures, and this shortened version is most commonly used today. Called Jacobsonian or progressive relaxation, the procedure in the initial stages calls for the client to progressively tense and relax major muscle groups (e.g., right hand, right forearm, right bicep, shoulders, etc.). It is thought that the tensing serves two major functions: highlighting the sensation of muscular tension, so that the person can better exercise conscious control to relax the musculature, and fatiguing the muscle, better allowing relaxation to occur. Each muscle group is tensed and relaxed separately, and the exercise closes with general bodily relaxation. In the early stages the exercises might take 30 to 40 minutes as each muscle group is tensed twice. As training progresses, the tensing is reduced to once and then eliminated, thus shortening the time required to complete the exercises (see Goldfried & Davison, 1976).

The most commonly used variants of the basic progressive relaxation procedure are: 1) differential relaxation, wherein similar procedures are used, but only certain body parts (as opposed to a whole body focus) are targeted for relaxation; 2) cue-controlled relaxation, where relaxation is paired with a cue word such as "calm," "relax," or "peace," so that subsequently concentrating on or saying that word may produce the experience of relaxation; and 3) variants of any of the above that use the standard procedures but present them in novel formats such as group settings or on audiotape, or combine the procedures with biofeedback, autosuggestion, or other techniques.

Progressive relaxation is still a part of standard systematic desensitization. In addition, it is a valuable part of many stress-management and anxiety-control treatment approaches, where it is used more as a self-management technique (i.e., a way to moderate the experience of anxiety and stress) than as a way of directly eradicating the problem. It has been shown to be a very helpful part of treatment for agoraphobia, social anxieties, alcohol abuse, and other problems. It is the treatment of choice for most forms of insomnia. It is a valuable component in the therapeutic management of chronic and acute pain. Lamaze childbirth procedures use a variant of relaxation procedures. Finally, it is widely used in the treatment of psychosomatic disorders such as migraine and tension headaches, essential hypertension, and a number of other disorders

(Taylor, 1982). Some suggest that it is just as effective as many forms of biofeedback.

The mode of action of relaxation training is unclear. Some evidence suggests that peripheral (muscular) relaxation induces a reduction in central nervous system sympathetic activity. Numerous studies have documented physical changes produced by relaxation which support this hypothesis, though the evidence is by no means totally consistent (Taylor, 1982). It should be noted that physical relaxation is not equivalent to meditation, and that there are many varieties of meditative practices. Care should be taken by the Christian that relaxation procedures used do not become infused with Eastern mystic practices.

References

Jacobson, E. *Progressive relaxation* (2nd ed.). Chicago: University of Chicago Press, 1938.
Goldfried, M., & Davison, G. *Clinical behavior therapy.* New York: Holt, Rinehart, & Winston, 1976.
Taylor, C. B. Adult medical disorders. In A. S. Bellack, M. Hersen, & A. E. Kazdin (Eds.), *International handbook of behavior modification and therapy.* New York: Plenum, 1982.

S. L. Jones

See Behavior Therapy.

Religion and Personality. The concepts of religion and personality have been closely associated in Western thought. The origin of the relationship is found in their etymologies. The Latin noun *persona* developed from the infinitive *per sonare*, which indicated the theatrical player projecting the voice through a mouth hole in the facial mask that designated a theatrical role. The English terms *person* and *personality* share *persona* as point of origin. From that context persona indicated a mask or façade suggestive of a social role. Persona was a social façade adopted in interpersonal contexts.

However, over time persona took on a second, contrary connotation. The surface designation did not correspond with the second usage which referred to the actor (and the accompanying thoughts, feelings, desires, etc.) behind the mask (Monte, 1980). The dual use of persona is an embodiment of the tension experienced when social roles and expectations lead the individual in directions that belie personal inclination, resulting in a disjointed or fragmented individual. Inner reality is divorced from outer requirements.

Religion is a binding force, uniting fragmented personality. The origin of *religion* lies in two Latin verbs. *Religio* denoted a binding or fastening together, and came to indicate a reverence and fear of deity. The reverence and fear manifested themselves in an apprehensiveness to fulfill a covenant obligation. *Religo* denoted a restraining or holding back. While the former points to the reverential aspects of religion, the latter points to the ethical-restraint role of religion's bridling of human motives and impulses. Hence, etymologically religion is seen as a force that reconnects human disjointedness and restrains errant impulses.

Psychological Analyses of Religion. The dimensions of reverence and restraint are incorporated into psychological analyses of religion. Freud's view is developed in *Totem and Taboo, Civilization and Its Discontents, The Future of an Illusion,* and *Moses and Monotheism.* For him, religion originates in the oedipus complex and its resolution. Respect and reverence for the father figure represent a displaced and sublimated hostility. Identification with the father figure occasions the introjection of values into the superego, the ethical-moral arm of personality.

The magnum opus of the psychological analyses of religious experience is James's *The Varieties of Religious Experience.* James's definition of religion as "the feelings, acts, and experiences of individual men in their solitude, so far as they apprehend themselves to stand in relation to whatever they may consider the divine" (James, 1902, pp. 32–33) emphasized the reverential, emotional, and sentimental dimensions of religion. Consistent with his pragmatic philosophy, he was more attuned to the fruits of religion than its roots. As well as giving life a sense of hallowedness and sacredness, the fruits of religion regulate individual action through ethical seriousness.

James's approach is reflected in the work of Allport (1937, 1950). The psychological impact of religion on the person is twofold, as the individual seeks to find his personal niche in creation and to develop a frame of reference for the meaning of life. The origin of one's religious quest lies in bodily needs, temperament and mental capacity, personal interests and values, the pursuit of rational explanations, and conformity to one's culture (Allport, 1950). Religion involves the whole individual.

Modern theories of personality may be secularized versions of older theological dogmas. Oates (1973) pointed out that recent holistic or self perspectives in personality parallel ancient Hebraic views of human nature. The Hebrews used *nephesh* to portray the unity or wholeness of the person when viewed from without. When wholeness was viewed from within, the term *leb* was used. These were translated *soul* and *heart*, respectively, in the Authorized Version.

Fromm (1955, 1973) suggested that the essence of human nature was to be found in five existential needs. According to him, personality originated in the needs for orientation and devotion, for rootedness, for relatedness and unity, for identity, and for excitation and stimulation. Religion provides a meaningful frame of reference and an object of devotion. It ties humans to the natural world, yet enables an individual to transcend the natural order. One's identity is contingent upon relationships with others of like orientation. Religious activities provide regular excitation and stimulation in the form of rituals, holidays, feasts, and celebrations.

Similar views are to be found in Buber's I-Thou relation and Maslow's hierarchy of needs. Allport (1950) suggested personality is operative in the formation of religious sentiments. Endogenous mechanisms of organic desire, temperament, psychogenic desires and spiritual values, and the pursuit of meaning are tempered by exogenous conformity pressure of culture. Thus, religion addresses the issues of individual identity as well as fostering a sense of community.

Religiousness and Personality. The relationship between religiousness and specific temperament or personality characteristics is complex (Sadler, 1970). Many theoretical predictions about religious individuals having different personalities stem from James (1902). James suggested individuals who were healthy experienced gradual conversions (were "once born"), but sudden converts ("twice born") individuals were sick of soul. In the latter case the experience of a divided self (ideal versus real self) is accentuated in evangelicalism, since it points to an incongruity of what *is* and what *ought to be*. Experienced as guilt and anxiety, the divided self motivates redemptive activities such as renunciation of the natural world. Thus, an individual needs to be twice born to change a divided self (natural and physical versus spiritual) into a unity (Oates, 1973). For these reasons it has been asserted and reported that sudden converts have more manifest anxiety than gradual converts or the unregenerate (Rokeach, 1960). Other research fails to confirm this idea (Sanua, 1969; Johnson & Malony, 1982), but in these studies there was no attempt to distinguish between state and trait anxiety.

The foregoing analysis localizes anxiety in human fallenness. However, state or trait anxiety may also involve human fraility and finiteness. In these cases anxiety may not be resolved by conversion or repentance for sin. Anxiety may involve uncertainty or fear over economic needs, human finiteness, and the existential dread of death. Growth in grace is upheld as a solution to the various sources of anxiety (Oates, 1955; Grounds, 1976).

Others (e.g., Ferm, 1959) have suggested that conversion leads to personality changes. Conversion as a radical process eventually changes behavior. If behavior is changed, then its underlying cause (i.e., personality) must have been transformed. If conversion is radical, it must alter the inner dimensions of human nature. Research into this area (Johnson & Malony, 1982) has failed to confirm such predictions, although it may be that traditional personality assessment instruments are insensitive to the nature of these personality changes.

While James did not do so, many theorists (e.g., Allport, Fromm, Freud) conceived of religiousness at two levels: the personal and the institutional. In the former the focus is on individual personality and how religion affects one's inner life. The institutional level is concerned with the external manifestations of religion, especially as group expectancies and conformity pressures influence the behavior of the individual. The question is then asked about the relative power of each level. Internal religion and institutional, external religion may countermand each other in the operation of personality.

In recent years social learning theorists (Rotter, 1966; Phares, 1973) have examined the situation-specific expectancy of the individual and its relation to belief and behavior. Individuals who expect to control their own outcomes, to dispense their own reinforcements, and to pursue self-control are described as having an internal locus of control. Individuals who expect to be influenced by the social situation, or chance, are termed external locus of control personalities. Rotter (1966) and others have developed assessment instruments to measure this internal-external dimension.

On the basis of the internal-external research one would predict that individuals who have intensely personal religious experiences would be internal in locus of control, while individuals whose religious experiences are of a more institutional, social nature would be external in expectancy and attribution. Such differences have indeed been found between various religions as well as within religious groups. Fundamentalist Protestants could be expected to have higher scores on an internal locus of control scale than liberal Protestants. Furnham (1982) found precisely those differences in clergy responding to an internal-external scale who were asked to describe their theological position, thus supporting other research literature.

Rokeach (1960, 1970, 1973) summarized his survey work as indicating that religious personalities were more authoritarian, more dogmatic, more closed-minded, and more ethnically prejudiced than less religious and nonreligious individuals. His interest in values and their relationship to religion grew out of participation in authoritarianism research (Adorno, Frenkel-Brunswik, Levinson, & Sanford 1950). His measure of religiousness was frequency of church attendance, which is more external.

Allport (1950) distinguished between intrinsic and extrinsic religious orientation, and linked these to personality differences. The extrinsic orientation to religion is pragmatic and self-serving, utilizing religion as means to personal ends. The intrinsic orientation embodies a basic trust of others and empathetic understanding of others. Allport contended that those of an intrinsic orientation were more open-minded and tolerant than the extrinsic. Rokeach agreed, but contended that most religious individuals had an extrinsic orientation to religion.

Allport and Ross (1967) found prejudice to be curvilinearly related to religiousness, not linearly as Rokeach suggested. They differentiated between four religious orientations: 1) intrinsic religious orientation, in which religious teachings are internalized to guide daily life; 2) extrinsic religious orientation, in which religion is used to advance personal ambition; 3) indiscriminately proreligious orientation, which uncritically endorses all religious ideas; and 4) antireligious orientation, which rejects all religious teachings. They found the intrinsically religious individual to be the least prejudiced, the extrinsically oriented more prejudiced, and the proreligious the most prejudiced. Antireligious persons were slightly more prejudiced than the intrinsically religious. These findings bear some similarity to the internal-external research.

Sanua (1969) reviewed the empirical literature on the relationship of religiousness to humanitarianism, social action, and mental health. While it could be argued that healthy religion ought to augment each of these, data do not unequivocally support the assertion. Internalized dogmas (especially ethical principles) are not always externalized in action.

What is taught in religious education may conflict with *how* it is taught.

For Christian psychologists and personality psychologists, personality's link to religion remains a riddle (Malony, 1977). The associations are complex and paradoxical. Religion has yet to fully actualize its potential in the ethical, healthy operation of personality.

References

Adorno, T. W., Frenkel-Brunswik, E., Levinson, D. J., & Sanford, R. N. *The authoritarian personality.* New York: Harper & Row, 1950.
Allport, G. W. *Personality: A psychological interpretation.* New York: Holt, 1937.
Allport, G. W. *The individual and his religion.* New York: Macmillan, 1950.
Allport, G. W., & Ross, J. M. Personal religious orientation and prejudice. *Journal of Personality and Social Psychology,* 1967, *5,* 432–443.
Ferm, R. *The psychology of Christian conversion.* Westwood, N.J.: Revell, 1959.
Fromm, E. *The sane society.* New York: Holt, Rinehart, & Winston, 1955.
Fromm, E. *Anatomy of human destructiveness.* New York: Holt, Rinehart, & Winston, 1973.
Furnham, A. F. Locus of control and theological beliefs. *Journal of Psychology and Theology,* 1982, *10,* 130–136.
Grounds, V. C. *Emotional problems and the gospel.* Grand Rapids: Zondervan, 1976.
James, W. *The varieties of religious experience.* New York: Longmans, Green, 1902.
Johnson, C. B., & Malony, H. N. *Christian conversion: Biblical and psychological perspectives.* Grand Rapids: Zondervan, 1982.
Malony, H. N. (Ed.). *Current perspectives in the psychology of religion.* Grand Rapids: Eerdmans, 1977.
Monte, C. *Beneath the mask* (2nd ed.). New York: Holt, Rinehart, & Winston, (1980).
Oates, W. E. *Anxiety in Christian experience.* Philadelphia: Westminster, 1955.
Oates, W. E. *The psychology of religion.* Waco, Tex.: Word Books, 1973.
Phares, E. J. *Locus of control in personality.* Morristown, N.J.: General Learning Press, 1973.
Rokeach, M. *The open and closed mind.* New York: Basic Books, 1960.
Rokeach, M. Faith, hope and bigotry. *Psychology Today,* 1970. *3*(11), 33–37; 58.
Rokeach, M. *The nature of human values.* New York: Free Press, 1973.
Rotter, J. B. Generalized expectancies for internal versus external control of reinforcement. *Psychological Monographs,* 1966, *80*(1), 1–28.
Sadler, W. A. *Personality and religion.* New York: Harper & Row, 1970.
Sanua, V. Religion, mental health, and personality: A review of empirical studies. *American Journal of Psychiatry,* 1969, *125,* 1203–1213.

R. L. TIMPE

See PSYCHOLOGY OF RELIGION.

Religious Concept Development. The investigation of the growth of religious understanding deals with the changes in meaning attributed to religion in the course of individual development. For the purpose of this article religion will be defined as one's thoughts in connection with God and his activities in the universe. A concept is an idea a person holds to, usually based on both knowledge and experience. One's concepts may change with exposure to new knowledge and experience.

In recent years a great deal of attention has been given to the role of cognition (intellect) as a central variable in all phases of development. Human thought is seen as an emerging, changing function that affects all aspects of personality functioning and growth. This means that the development of religious concepts presupposes cognitive development.

Present interest in cognitive development has been stimulated largely by the work of Piaget (1952). Piaget's work may be classified as an age-stage theory. His hypothesis was that a child's cognitive development proceeds through sequential stages that are progressively more mature and better defined. These stages are usually associated with particular ages. For Piaget cognitive development is accumulative. What is learned at one stage of development can be learned only if there have been the necessary prerequisite learnings during earlier stages. Piaget's four stages of intellectual development are the sensorimotor stage (birth to about 2 years), the preoperational stage (2 to 7 years), the concrete operations stage (7 to 11 years), and the formal operations stage (11 years and older). Most research in the development of religious concepts has focused on the last three stages. This emphasis does not imply, however, that religious conceptual development is totally nil during the first two years of life.

The most salient characteristics of the preoperational child's intellectual functioning are the use of newly acquired internal mental representations of external objects and the related language abilities. The internal object representations (symbols) allow for thinking. Preoperational thinking, however, is egocentric and inflexible. It is difficult for the child to understand that other people might think differently from himself or to distinguish between "real" and "pretend."

The concrete operations stage involves concrete thinking. The child now becomes less egocentric and comes to understand certain principles or relationships between ideas. However, thinking is rooted in concrete events and objects. The final step of cognitive development, formal operations, involves abstract thinking. The individual with these skills can entertain concepts with which he has had no experience. (See COGNITIVE DEVELOPMENT for a more complete discussion of characteristics of these stages.)

Overview of Research Findings. Although studies regarding the growth of religious understanding are not numerous by today's research standards, a number of investigations in this area have accumulated. General patterns of religious concept formation have been demonstrated. There appears to be a good fit between the Piagetian stages of cognitive development and the development of religious concepts and religious maturity.

Harms (1944) presented empirical evidence for age changes in the concept of God. Harms asked his subjects (ages 3–18) to draw how God looked when they pictured him in their mind, or to imagine the appearance of the highest being they thought to exist. Adolescents, who apparently objected to imagining God as such, were given the opportunity of drawing what to them represented religion or the highest ideal expressed in religion. Harms arrived at three broad classes of drawings that were related to age and reflected what he assumed to be universal stages of religious development. The three stages identified by Harms seem to correspond closely to the prelogical, egocentric thinking of Piaget's preoperational child; the concrete, logical thinking of the concrete operational child; and the abstract thinking of the formal operational child.

Deconchy (1965) employed a word-association procedure to study the development of ideas about God in 4,733 children ranging from 7 to 16 years of age. The task was to write five word associations to six inductor words, one of which was *God*. The associations to the inductor word *God* were grouped into 29 categories and along three age-related dimensions: attributivity, personalization, and interiorization.

The 7–10-year-old child thinks of God chiefly in terms of his attributes: 1) objective attributes such as greatness, omniscience, and omnipresence, 2) subjective attributes (qualities) such as goodness and justice; and 3) affective attributes such as strength and beauty. The theme of this age group seems to be God's transcendence. Deconchy called this stage attributivity. Personalization refers to the 11–14-year-old stage, when the child thinks of God as a person. The themes of fatherhood, redeemer, master, and sovereignty predominate. The final stage, interiorization, describes the 14–16-year-olds. These individuals think of God in terms of subjective abstract themes such as love, trust, doubt, and fear. The three stages mark the transition for the child from the God of his thoughts (attributivity) to the God of his life (interiorization).

Deconchy did not test younger children corresponding to Piaget's preoperational stage, and so was unable to identify a stage of religious development parallel to that stage. The stage of attributivity, with its emphasis on the attributes of God, would seem to parallel Piaget's concrete operational stage; the stage of interiorization, with its emphasis on subjective, abstract themes concerning God, appears to parallel formal operational thinking. The middle stage of personalization serves as a transition between the concrete stage of attributivity and the abstract stage of interiorization. The God themes of this middle stage are similar to both the affective attributes of attributivity and the internal qualities of interiorization.

Elkind (1961) defined religious identity in terms of spontaneous meanings children attach to their religious denomination. In three separate studies he investigated the growth of religious identity among Jewish (1961), Catholic (1962), and Congregational Protestant (1963) children. Elkind believed it was possible to distinguish three fairly distinct stages in the attainment of religious identity which held true of Jewish, Catholic, and Protestant children. He referred to these stages as global (5–7 years), concrete (7–9 years), and abstract (10–12 years). These three stages appear to parallel closely Piaget's preoperational, concrete operational, and formal operational stages.

Long, Elkind, and Spilka (1967) used an interview procedure in studying children's understanding of prayer. One hundred sixty boys and girls between the ages of 5 and 12 were interviewed. A set of semistructured questions was employed in order to explore developmental changes in the concept of prayer. The results suggested three major developmental stages in the child's understanding of the prayer concept. These stages were designated as global undifferentiated (5–7 years), concrete differentiated (7–9 years) and abstract differentiated (10–12 years). Again these three stages appear closely to parallel Piaget's preoperational, concrete operational, and formal operational stages.

Goldman (1964) studied religious thinking in 200 white Protestant children in England (10 boys and 10 girls at every age level from 6 through 16). He constructed a picture and story religious test, which consisted of three pictures (a family entering church, a boy or a girl at prayer, and a boy or girl looking at a mutilated Bible) and three Bible stories (Moses and the burning bush, the crossing of the Red Sea, and the temptation of Jesus). Each child was individually interviewed; and following the presentation of each picture or story, the child was asked a standardized set of questions about the material. From his analysis of these data Goldman then proceeded to identify three stages in the development of religious thinking that closely parallel the three Piagetian stages. Goldman labeled these stages preoperational intuitive thought (7/8 years mental age), concrete operational thought (7/8–13/14 years mental age), and formal (abstract) operational thought (13/14 years mental age).

All of these research findings clearly fit quite well into a three-stage Piagetian development. The progression is from the prelogical, global, egocentric, perception-bound thinking of Piaget's preoperational child; to the concrete, logical, reversible thinking of the concrete operational child, and finally to the abstract, theoretical, propositional thinking of the formal operational child.

The Teaching of Religious Concepts. Piaget believed that the intellectual content a child can interact with at any level of development depends upon his understanding of the world around him. Thus Piaget was concerned with specifying just what understandings the child has at each stage of development because these understandings limit the intellectual content that can be mastered at any level.

The pressing question for Christian education is whether or not Piaget's stages can be applied to the development of spiritual concepts in the life of the child. Christian educators Joy (1975) and Wakefield (1975) are two contemporary writers who have seen the relevance of Piaget's work for the development of mature biblical concepts in the home and church. While much biblical content is difficult and beyond the grasp of young children, these authors argue that Christian education curriculum should be built around the developmental stages identified in the above research.

Preoperational stage (2–7 years). Parents and educators must not expect too much of children at this age. The child does have difficulty in developing and relating biblical concepts. He utilizes percepts and images, but his thinking is fragmentary and discrete. He tries to understand biblical material, but his intellectual powers are not sufficiently developed to piece all the information together.

The biblical information that is given must be accurate and must be broken down to the preoperational child's level of comprehension.

However, even during this stage the child is building a world view. It is, therefore, an excellent time to create an awareness of God. Young children gain a preconceptual awareness of the nature of God by observing others who express the love of God through their behavior. The modeling behavior of both parents and Christian educators is crucial at this time.

Content is very important, but for the preoperational child the methodology of content presentation is also important. Teaching must not rely solely on verbal explanations. The Bible must be related to the firsthand experiences of the child. Deuteronomy 6:1–9 is instructive at this point. The teaching here is that childhood education is to be comprehensive in scope, making virtually all of life a school. It indicates that children are to be immersed in a total curriculum of experience and that God is to be related to the totality of experience.

Recognizing the above principles, Goldman (1965) recommends spiritual content that is related to the experience and spontaneous questions of children in this age group. The concept of God is to be simply and frequently expressed in connection with the everyday experiences of the child and his spontaneous questions. These expressions should emphasize the concepts of a God who loves and cares for us, and a God who has provided for us in this earthly home and who is always with us. In the home the aware parent can capitalize quite easily on this approach. In the church teachers may accomplish the same ends by establishing various learning centers in the classrooms that deal in simple fashion with the questions and needs of the child.

Beers (1975) is convinced that the preoperational child can learn certain theological concepts dealing with God, Jesus, the Bible, home and parents, and church and Sunday school. For example, he feels that the preoperational child can learn that God loves him, God provides sun and rain, God made the world, God made him, and that he should please and obey God. This approach is feasible if one remembers the cognitive characteristics of the preoperational child.

Memorization of specific scriptural content is also a viable possibility with this age group. Such themes as the child's behavior ("Love one another," John 4:7); creation ("God created the heaven and the earth," Gen. 1:1); the Lord's attitude to us ("He careth for you," 1 Peter 5:7); and our attitude to the Lord ("I will love thee, O Lord," Ps. 18:1) would be specific examples.

Again, these memorizations are to be related to the everyday experiences of the child.

Since children in this age group enjoy fantasy, play, and motoric involvement, the utilization of story playing offers a great opportunity to teach specific Bible content. When children can dramatize a story in simple form, they can more readily understand the story cognitively. The event becomes more real in story play. The drama does not need to be practiced but can be spontaneous. Possibilities for story playing are illustrated by the following: how Joshua conquered the land of Canaan (Josh. 9:1–11:23); the great ship that saved eight people (Gen. 6:1–9:17); and Palm Sunday (Matt. 21:1–11).

Concrete operational stage (7–11 years). In this stage the child is becoming more able to put facts together, to generalize and classify his experiences, and to reverse his thinking processes. Limitations, however, still accompany the advancement of this period. When a child is asked to use verbal propositions rather than objects, he must consider one statement at a time in reasoning the proposition through. His generalizing cannot go beyond particular situations or examples. His intellectual abilities are restricted to physical actions that he can internalize. His skill at grouping common relationships is a significant factor during this period.

When teaching content to the concrete operational child, one must remember that the child is concerned with concrete people, actions, and situations. Because this is true, factual information can be presented. Facts pertaining to the sources and people of the Christian faith would be appropriate at this time. Possible content might be drawn from the following: the life of Jesus; what is the Bible (Bible background facts); the story of a beautiful garden; creation (Gen. 1:1–3:24); the baby who was found in a river (Exod. 1:1–2:10); Gideon and his brave 300 (Judges 6:1–8:28); the shepherd boy's fight with the giant (1 Sam. 17:1–54); Daniel in the den of lions (Dan. 6); the manger at Bethlehem (Luke 2:1–20); the earliest missionaries (Acts 11:19–30; 13:1–14:28); Stephen with the shining face (Acts 6:1–8:3).

In teaching these concepts the emphasis is upon the children doing things, finding out, experimenting, and thinking creatively.

Formal operational stage (11 years and older). At this stage the individual develops the mental ability for mature conceptual thinking. There is present the capacity to think in abstract terms, utilizing the world of proposi-

997

tions. Problems can be approached in a systematic manner and solved by using logical procedures that are expressed in abstract form. In this stage the person is concerned with the theoretical, the remote, and the future.

It is important to link content in some way with the real life experiences and needs of individuals in this stage—e.g., the opposite sex, problems of science, life ambitions, happiness, the place of God in one's life. Biblical content must be correlated to issues of life.

Many biblical themes can be explored at this time: the inspiration of the Bible; parables; the attributes of God; Satan, his personality and power; the creation and fall of humankind; sin, its character and universality; the second coming of Christ; the study of any individual book of the Bible; the purpose of life as seen in the Scriptures; who I am according to the Bible; and the biblical concept of marriage.

Conclusion. The task of facilitating the development of mature spiritual concepts is obviously very complex. However, four factors appear to stand out. First, Bible-centered content must be present, but at the same time the methodology of presentation is crucial. Second, parents and educators must model the content they are attempting to teach. Third, that which is taught should be part of the child's real world in that the content is related to his present needs and experiences. Words are to be matched with experience and experience with words. Finally, scriptural material must be taught in a manner that is appropriate to the level of cognitive development of the child.

References

Beers, V. G. Teaching theological concepts to children. In R. B. Zuck & R. E. Clark (Eds.), *Childhood education in the church*. Chicago: Moody Press, 1975.

Deconchy, J. P. The idea of God: Its emergence between 7 and 16 years. In A. Godin (Ed.), *From religious experience to a religious attitude*. Chicago: Loyola University Press, 1965.

Elkind, D. The child's conception of his religious denomination I: The Jewish child. *Journal of Genetic Psychology*, 1961, *99*, 209–225.

Elkind, D. The child's conception of his religious denomination II: The Catholic child. *Journal of Genetic Psychology*, 1962, *101*, 185–195.

Elkind, D. The child's conception of his religious denomination III: The Protestant child. *Journal of Genetic Psychology*, 1963, *103*, 291–304.

Goldman, R. *Religious thinking from childhood to adolescence*. New York: Seabury, 1964.

Goldman, R. *Readiness for religion*. London: Routledge and K. Paul, 1965.

Harms, E. The development of religious experience in children. *American Journal of Sociology*, 1944, *50*, 112–122.

Joy, D. M. Why teach children. In R. B. Zuck & R. E. Clark (Eds.), *Childhood education in the church*. Chicago: Moody Press, 1975.

Long, D., Elkind, D., & Spilka, B. The child's conception of prayer. *Journal for the Scientific Study of Religion*, 1967, *6*, 101–109.

Piaget, J. *The origins of intelligence in children*. New York: International Universities Press, 1952.

Wakefield, N. Children and their theological concepts. In R. B. Zuck & R. E. Clark (Eds.), *Childhood education in the church*. Chicago: Moody Press, 1975.

S. N. BALLARD

See CHRISTIAN GROWTH.

Religious Defense Mechanisms. Freud postulated that we use DEFENSE MECHANISMS both normally and pathologically to cope with dysphoric emotions or affect, or to keep certain areas of conflict out of our awareness. Further, the development of personality characteristics was viewed in part as manifestations of the most frequently used ego defenses. Persons who are flexible and use a range of defense mechanisms are at an adaptive advantage, whereas those who use certain strategies excessively or inappropriately are at a disadvantage. In short, the development and use of ego defense mechanisms are normal adaptive processes, but specific ego defense mechanisms can be used adaptively or maladaptively.

It has often been charged that religiousness stems from a pathological state of mind or that it is pathological per se. Freud (1927/1953) argued that religion itself is a defense, a kind of universal obsessional neurosis, and a crutch for the neurotic. However, research has not generally supported this conclusion. Stark (1971) presents empirical evidence that the notion that there is a positive association between psychopathology and religious commitment is not simply false, but the opposite of the truth. Sanua (1969), in examining the evidence on the relationship between measures of religion, mental health, and personality, concluded that religion can function as a unifying and integrating force within personality, particularly through the incorporation of the underlying moral and ethical principles. The majority of religious persons, however, tend to internalize the divisive role of religion. His concern is that religious educators may be doing a better job of communicating the dogmatic, ritualistic, and separatist aspects of religion rather than its ethical and unifying aspects.

It appears, therefore, that religious attitudes can be used in either an adaptive or defensive manner. Underlying this possibility may be very different views of the impulses or natural instincts. If they are seen as basically evil and a threat to one's spiritual life, they will be repressed; if their potential for either good or evil is seen, a different set of defenses will be utilized. The individual who sees them as a threat has a tendency to feelings, to be primarily concerned with self-control, and to project sinfulness onto others. In contrast, the individual who recognizes their potential is more willing to admit unpleasant attitudes or impulses and less concerned with self-control than with relationships. The former may see God as repressive and be convinced that God holds all impulses as evil. Consequently the person is threatened by God, since his or her impulses continually arouse anxiety and fear.

The defense mechanisms themselves can likewise reflect adaptive or maladaptive uses, some of which appear to be characteristically religious. Denial, the refusal to believe or allow awareness of some unpleasant or threatening aspect of external reality, is a prime example. The reaction to death is often a glib, "The Lord giveth and the Lord taketh away," or "All things work together for good." The truth and beauty of these statements is lost when they are used to mask the deep pain of the loss of a loved one. Consequently the necessary grief work is not done, and the subsequent depression can be especially pronounced and intense.

Reaction formation, when a person develops attitudes and behaviors that are in direct opposition to underlying unconscious impulses, can often be used to hide the real urge or instinct by providing an opposing acceptable position. Some Christians, for example, place great exphasis on praising God for everything, including their losses and pain. Pruyser (1968) warns that inappropriate praise can sometimes backfire in anger and resentment toward God because it does not develop insight or understanding of the original feelings.

Rationalization, providing socially acceptable reasons for behavior that may be interpreted as questionable, can also be used in characteristic ways by Christians. One of Freud's major criticisms of religion was the hypocrisy he observed among Christians in Vienna, especially concerning the treatment of Jews. Rationalization serves as a very handy way of reducing the cognitive dissonance generated by the high standards for life held by Christians. An extravagant life style may be justified as essential for facilitating one's ministry. Or one may develop an elaborate system of excuses for not going to church rather than simply staying at home and feeling good about it.

In sublimation unacceptable behavior is modified to make it socially acceptable, especially to other Christians. The common conservative Christian notions of appropriate sex role behavior are a prime example. Sweet, submissive womanhood is preferred to responsible assertiveness in relationships. Not only might this be a personal liability in physical and emotional health, but it can also lead to a manipulative type of family control.

Finally, regression, the return to an earlier, more primitive level of functioning, can develop in uniquely religious patterns, particularly as it involves dependency. As Tournier (1964) has observed, although dependency on anything other than God is an obstacle to self-realization, it is possible to be too dependent on God. One can abdicate or evade responsibility for decisions or tasks that are thought to be unbearable. One can rely on faith to the exclusion of any good works. May (1953) feels Christians sometimes expect that they have a divine right to be taken care of.

In summary, excessive and/or inappropriate use of the defense mechanisms can retard emotional and spiritual development. Rather than honestly accepting ourselves and our motives, we choose to live a lie. Christians have the resource of God's unconditional love and acceptance, which ought to lead to forgiveness and confession. As Johnson (1945) has noted, the mature religious person is willing to take risks and is tolerant of doubt and frustration, yet is willing to devote himself to the task of discerning the ultimate meaning in life. Ideally this maturity would be reflected in our improved ability to love and accept each other, and in more flexible and diverse usage of the ego defense mechanisms.

References

Freud, S. *The future of an illusion.* New York: Liveright, 1953. (Originally published, 1927.)
Johnson, P. *Psychology of religion.* Nashville: Abingdon, 1945.
May, R. *Man's search for himself.* New York: Norton, 1953.
Pruyser, P. *A dynamic psychology of religion.* New York: Harper & Row, 1968.
Sanua, V. Religion, mental health, and personality: A review of empirical studies. *American Journal of Psychiatry,* 1969, *125*(9), 1203–1213.
Stark, R. Psychopathology and religious commitment. *Review of Religious Research,* 1971, *12*(3), 165–176.
Tournier, P. *The whole person in a broken world.* New York: Harper & Row, 1964.

R. E. Butman

See Christian Growth.

Religious Doubt. *See* Doubt.

Religious Health and Pathology. Religion can be the most potent health-inducing, health-maintaining force or the most insidious health-depleting, health-preventing influence in a person's life. An important difference between the manifestations of healthy and unhealthy religion appears to lie in the way individuals appropriate their religious beliefs (James, 1902). In a classic study Allport and Ross (1967) divided religious orientations into intrinsic and extrinsic. People who are intrinsically religious internalize their religious values, making them an integral part of their whole being and way of life. They are committed to transcending self-centeredness. Conversely, extrinsically oriented religious individuals employ their religion as means to achieve their own ends. They are more absorbed in self-interests, looking to secular sources for power. This description of intrinsic and extrinsic religious expressions makes it evident that the individual who is intrinsically religious expresses his or her faith in healthier ways. Although Allport and Ross did not associate these modes with any particular religion, their parallel to the biblical concept of living one's life to glorify either God or oneself makes them relevant to a discussion of healthy or unhealthy Christianity.

Healthy Christianity tends to be positively correlated with psychological health. This is an expected relationship in view of the fact that an individual's responses to life are determined by the hereditary and environmental circumstances that shape them. The resulting personality structure influences the way a person responds to religion. Likewise, the quality of a person's religion affects his or her response to life's circumstances. This interrelationship of mental and religious health implies that Christians who have had positive background experiences may be more prone to healthier religious attitudes and behaviors than those who have experienced deleterious circumstances. It could also be true that a non-Christian with healthy background experiences might be healthier psychologically than a Christian exposed to less favorable situations.

Several qualifying factors are involved in evaluating the quality of religious health. The first involves the cultural concepts on health. Since society's values reflect the influence of generations of sin, and since a consensus of the values is generally used as the criterion to evaluate psychological health, it is conceivable that the attributes of mental health will be viewed differently in certain aspects by Christians. This is particularly true in societies where Christian values are either decreasing in acceptance or else have not infiltrated the world view of the people. For Christians the concept of health would transcend the culture in whatever ways it conflicts with biblical norms.

Another consideration is that Christians, in their relationship to the Lord, have resources available to facilitate their growth in the direction of a more intrinsic religious orientation. This increases the possibility that their religion will enable them to overcome the less healthy effects of their background and thereby develop in more positive directions. Involved in their growth is the gradual awareness of the wholeness they actually possess through their commitment to Jesus Christ. This process of sanctification can lead them to a fuller realization of what it means to be all that God intended them to be.

A major consideration for the Christian is that religious health in its fullest sense has its roots in the restoration of the wholeness present in the creation. What constitutes health is within the nature of human beings, marred by the fall but restored and empowered through a relationship with Jesus Christ. Therefore, examples of the characteristics of healthy and unhealthy Christianity are discussed under selected rubrics of universal themes of human functioning that emanate from the very nature of man. Each is expressed as a set of polarities.

Several factors determine the point on the spectrum between the polarities that indicates maximum health. The first is the appropriate balance between the polarities. This vital equilibrium is present in individuals who accept and integrate into their total being the many aspects of their creatureliness. The second is that individuals necessarily fluctuate along the spectrum according to their need to adjust to the changing developmental and situational circumstances of life. For example, between the dependent-independent polarities a child or an invalid would be more dependent, whereas an adolescent would be moving toward the independent end. These differences that place individuals at different points along the spectrum demonstrate the broad possible range of health. A final necessary consideration is that at either extreme there is a precariously fine line between health and pathology. For example, along the self-sacrificing/self-accepting spectrum, self-sacrificing can enhance health or, carried too far and not balanced by self-appreciation, could become a masochistic tendency. This delicate balance is also an example of the constant tension Christians experience between their finiteness that glorifies God and their sinfulness that serves self.

Characteristics of Healthy Religion. The following five sets of polarities of human functioning suggest some insights about healthy and unhealthy religion.

Dependency-independency. Healthy religion fosters a harmonious balance between these two dimensions in a way that permits interdependency through developing and maintaining one's individual identity, and yet experiencing a sense of oneness with others. Overdependency can result in enmeshed relationships that deprive persons of growth in their own uniqueness. Differences tend to be seen as disloyalty. Guilt messages often are communicated to anyone either expressing something new or questioning aspects of the old. An exclusive attitude that results in isolation from other groups is apt to develop. Healthy realistic changes are hindered. Those who are dissatisfied find that to leave the group they must rebel or make a traumatic cut-off, neither of which permits healthy separation. On the other hand, too much independence inhibits mutual support, loyalty, and a sense of belonging and commitment.

A criterion to evaluate health in this area is the degree to which the dynamics of the religious group permits open channels to form that enable its members to develop their own potential, both within and outside the group, as well as mutually contribute to and benefit from strengths of the total membership.

Control-freedom. A synthesis of these two polarities encourages spontaneity, creativity, and self-direction tempered by inner discipline and external restraints. Healthy Christian communities provide the freedom from a nonjudgmental environment where their members sense an acceptance of the full range of emotions and ideas. There is therefore opportunity to try things on for fit and receive constructive feedback based on biblical principles. The paradoxical burden of each individual's freedom to depend wholly on God while accepting the responsibility of his own decisions is mitigated by group support.

Overstepping the freedom end results in lack of a sense of responsibility toward oneself and others. Accountability that permits helpful restraints tends to be lacking. Persons may feel leaderless and often powerless. On the other hand, overstepping the control end can lead to authoritarianism, legalism, and a constriction of affect, cognitions, or behaviors. Suppressed anger is often prevalent. A judgmental atmosphere develops, and a suspicious rather than a trusting attitude toward the world is more probable.

A criterion to check out health is the extent to which the structure of the group facilitates the possibility for its adherents to experience the quality of leadership and participation that results in a mutual openness, caring, and trust.

Self-denial—self-acceptance. An integration of these polarities results in adequate self-esteem. Recognition and acceptance of strengths and limitations are promoted by the religious community. The unconditional acceptance Christians have in Jesus Christ is stressed as the basis for self-worth. A distinction is made between true guilt, stemming from violation of scriptural moral principles, and false guilt, emanating from absolutized environmentally inculcated feelings. The latter feelings, often transformed into moral beliefs, are checked against Scripture and either relinquished or confessed. The forgiveness in Jesus Christ is presented not only as the source of release from sin but also as the channel through which even the consequences of failures when confessed are used for the growth of the individual and the glory of God.

A Christian fellowship that disproportionately stresses self-denial is often preoccupied with sin to the point of fostering masochism, sadism, workaholics, or self-deprecating individuals. Overstepping the opposite extreme leads to an inadequate sense of guilt and too much self-interest, often expressed in grandiosity, pride, and exaggerated demands for one's rights at the expense of others.

An indication of balance between the two extremes is the amount of energy available and used in a relaxed as opposed to an obsessive-compulsive way in order to minister to others. At the same time a personal satisfaction is evident whether at work or at play.

Stability-change. A healthy religious group, sensing the amount of change it can tolerate over a period of time, establishes an equilibrium between the amount of constancy it maintains and change it introduces. Periods of change that permit growth are alternated with times of stability wherein the group can assimilate and accommodate into its structure what is deemed worthy of internalization. The more settled periods also provide a rest from the ambiguities, risks, and anxieties that are normal accompaniments of change.

Extremes on the stability end result in a stagnation that hampers necessary adjustments to a changing society. The religious group is therefore hindered from exerting an influence on the direction and consequences of new developments. The seclusion that results from blocking new elements from entering the system smothers any sparks of renewal and regeneration. Apathy tends to develop from a lack of new challenges and stimulations. Too much change, however, can lead to a diminishing appreciation of the immutability of scriptural truths. Members may experience a decreasing sense of belonging. Adequately secure moorings that provide predictability are more easily undermined. Sufficient time for an in-depth evaluation of what to keep, modify, or change is less possible. Hyperactivity and confusion can result.

A key to a harmonious balance of change and stability is the degree to which a religious group tests its practices, old and new, against the realities of both society and Scripture. An additional test is the amount of order and calm confidence that reigns in contrast to disorganization, agitation, and anxiety.

Finiteness-transcendence. Christians find a consolidation of this aspect of their being through a relationship with the Godhead. The fact that human beings were created as finite creatures by a sovereign God implies that they need their limitations to fulfill fully their purpose of glorifying God. Nonetheless, infused in their nature is the need to reach out beyond themselves to a superior Being.

Religions based on anthropocentricism leave their followers susceptible to the paralysis of the despair that results from the inevitability of death. An inclination to hedonistic tendencies is more probable. The lack of ultimate significance could push persons to find meaning in less worthy directions—e.g., drugs, sexual aberrations, driven ambition, undue competitiveness, deification of man. Values become more relative. There is a failure to appropriate spiritual resources. Contrariwise, religious groups that minimize the finite aspects of humans and overemphasize the transcendent often are not as ready to realize their given opportunities and responsibilities. They are more apt to avoid taking responsibility, preferring to see the members of the Godhead as magicians who enable them to bypass the pain of growth toward maturity. Their concept of God, man, and the universe, therefore, is limited. Their excessive otherworldliness generally detracts from their influence on society.

Religious persons' wholesome acceptance of their finitude in the light of God's sovereign purpose for all of creation is evidenced by their reactions to life's events. They more realistically accept in themselves and others the normalcy of their humanness (e.g., hurt, downcast feelings in the face of a loss). Simultaneously they manifest in themselves, and encourage in others, an underlying hope and sense of purpose in all happenings.

The healthy Christian. Balance on any one of these polarities, or on any other additional single theme of human functioning, does not guarantee religious health. Rather, the dimensions of human beings created in God's image are so intricately interrelated that a harmonious integrated balance of all aspects of humanness is necessary. The promotion of such an ideal state of existence is possible only to the extent that the individuals constituting the religious group have experienced the restoration of the image of God in them through an acceptance of the redemptive work of Jesus Christ and the empowering of the Holy Spirit.

A word of caution is in order here. A personal relationship with God does not inevitably result in the realization of perfect harmony within oneself or with others. The apperception of God's healing is a lifelong process for the Christian that may not include a diminution of all the tangible effects of an imperfect world. However, Christian conversion does provide the inner strength, known by the intrinsically religious person, that infuses all life with meaning. There is the assurance that God's sovereignty works through the Christian's humanness. A religion imbued with this quality of transcendence of self-centeredness offers its members the necessary prerequisites to develop those characteristics that spell health.

References

Allport, G. W., & Ross. J. M. Personal religious orientation and prejudice. *Journal of Personality and Social Psychology*, 1967, *5*, 432–443.

James, W. *The varieties of religious experience.* New York: Longmans, Green, 1902.

Additional Readings

Oates, W. E. *When religion gets sick.* Philadelphia: Westminster, 1970.

Peck. M. S. *The road less traveled.* New York: Simon & Schuster, 1978.

Roberts, R. *Spirituality and human emotions.* Grand Rapids: Eerdmans, 1982.

F. J. WHITE

See RELIGION AND PERSONALITY; RELIGIOUS ORIENTATION.

Religious Issues in Therapy. *See* SPIRITUAL AND RELIGIOUS ISSUES IN THERAPY.

Religious Legalism. The term refers to a complex set of attitudes and beliefs organized around the conviction that certain laws must be obeyed in order to establish and maintain a relationship with God. These laws are usually considered divine in origin and therefore immutable. They may encompass any area of life, with no aspect of human activity considered too insignificant or private to warrant possible exemption from regulation.

A belief in a moral code is not, ipso facto, religious legalism. However, legalism results from such a belief when strict obedience to the code is conceived as being the sole or primary means of gaining and keeping the favor of the Deity. Legalism thrives on a distorted sense of obligation.

The theological roots of modern-day religious legalism may be traced to the intertestamental period, when a fundamental change occurred in the role of Old Testament law for the Jews. The concept of the covenant as the condition of membership in the people of God was replaced by that of obedience to the law. This obedience became the basis of God's verdict of pleasure or displeasure toward the individual. The sole mediator between God and man became the torah, and all relationships between God and man, Israel, or the world became subordinated to the torah. Most importantly, justification, righteousness, and life in the world to come were thought to be secured by obeying the law (Ladd, 1957).

This attitude was prevalent during the time of Christ and influenced the biblical precursors of twentieth-century legalism: Pharisaism, Judaizing theology, and gnosticism.

Pharisaism attempted to represent the true people of God by obeying the law, and in doing so hoped to prepare the way for the Messiah. The Pharisees observed all the legal prescriptions of Scripture in fine detail; they also held to the authority of the halakah, the body of legal descriptions that interpreted the law. The regulations increased in number and complexity to the point of pedantry. For example, because food could not be cooked on the sabbath, a debate arose between two groups as to whether water alone or both water and cooked food could be placed on a previously heated stove without committing a violation (Muller, 1976). The regulations became so difficult to obey that they proved a stumbling block to those who could not keep them all, and who thus felt they were outside the kingdom of God. Christ spoke to that tragic situation in his scathing denunciation of Pharisaical legalism (Matt. 23:4).

A variant of this form of legalism was introduced into the churches in Galatia, prompting Paul to write his famous letter on Christian liberty to the congregations in that province. The Judaizers, as they became known, infiltrated the churches, claiming that full salvation was impossible apart from observance of Jewish law and ritual. They were especially adamant that Gentile Christians be circumcised, since this was the symbol of membership in the New Israel. Paul's theological and emotional antipathy toward this form of legalism is quite evident in his sarcastic suggestion that those who argue for the necessity of circumcision should take the next logical step and castrate themselves (Gal. 5:12).

The Apostle also had to combat legalism in the form of incipient gnosticism at Colossae. This syncretistic heresy taught that the goal of life for gnostic adherents was to obtain true knowledge (gnosis), which would eventually allow them to leave the prison of the body and merge with the composite whole. Apparently a number of Colossian Christians were seeking heavenly visions as part of their rite of passage into a knowledge of the divine mysteries. They were informed that such visions could come about only by a rigorous discipline of asceticism and self-denial. Abstinence from food and drink, observance of initiatory and purifactory rites, and possibly a life of celibacy and mortification of the human body (Col. 2:21, 23) were all prescribed as part of the regimen necessary to obtain fullness of life (Martin, 1978).

While each of these ancient forerunners of present-day legalism differed from the other in certain respects, all three attempted to legislate certain behavior as the primary means of obtaining "salvation"—whether that was defined as hastening the advent of the Messiah, gaining membership in the New Israel, or seeking the eventual release of the soul from the confines of the body.

These forms of legalism did not die off; rather, they merely altered their appearance and continued to plague the church throughout the centuries. A study of church history would suggest that too often religious legalism has been the norm rather than the exception. American evangelicalism continues to wrestle with legalistic tendencies within its ranks, partly due to its Puritan roots and fundamentalist legacy. The Puritans, for example, at one time decreed that one could dress a baby on the sabbath but not kiss it; they also allowed that a man could comb his hair on that day but not shave his beard (Brinsmead, 1981b). Fundamentalism, while usually not as extreme, continues in a similar legalistic framework with its absolutizing prohibitions of many activities that do not have sufficient scriptural warrant.

An examination of the phenomenon of religious legalism reveals some striking similarities to OBSESSIVE-COMPULSIVE DISORDER (which includes characteristics of both obsessional neurosis and obsessional personality disorder, while recognizing that the former is usually more dysfunctional).

Religious legalism often infects the practitioner with a sense of moral superiority and a concomitant critical, condemning attitude toward those who do not conform to the same standards of conduct. This type of attitude is graphically illustrated in the biblical story of the Pharisee who stood in the temple thanking God that he was not like the terrible sinners around him. Christ warns that this type of self-exaltation can prevent a person from being justified before God (Luke 18:10–14). Similarly the obsessive-compulsive individual claims moral superiority and will often show an air of condescension to those around him. The manifestation of moral superiority most often hides feelings of inferiority and self-hatred that are then projected onto those who are deemed inferior. Just as the legalist must obey all the laws perfectly, so too the obsessive-compulsive person strives for perfection, avoiding tasks that might cause him to fail. Failure for the obsessional is equivalent to breaking the law for the legalist. Absolute perfection is the minimum acceptable standard for both.

Both types of persons have great difficulty with the gray areas of life. The legalist wishes to legislate every area of life and thus tends to concentrate on behavioral and religious minutiae. The obsessive-compulsive is characterized by aversion to ambiguity and a tendency to put all of life into neat, black-and-white categories.

Anxiety and fear are primary motivators for both the legalist and the obsessive-compulsive. The practitioner of legalism is driven to obedience by an overwhelming fear that God will punish or reject him if he does not obey perfectly. The person caught in obsessive-compulsiveness is driven to obey rules, obsessions, and compulsions by the unceasing threat of internal punishment meted out by the perfectionistic and hypercritical superego. Although the rules of conduct may differ for both types of person, they serve a similar function of assuring that catastrophe, whether spiritual or psychological, may be averted as long as the laws are obeyed or the compulsions followed.

Legalism is caused by biblical and doctrinal distortions and misunderstandings. Obsessive-compulsiveness can be traced in theory to a basic anxiety (Horney, 1950), defined as a feeling of profound insecurity, apprehensiveness, and helplessness in a world conceived as

potentially hostile. Thus, they are not the same phenomenon. However, the affinities between the two are such that they can exist hand-in-glove with each other. The intertwining of legalism and obsessive-compulsiveness creates a hybrid that is very resistant to alteration through counseling or psychotherapy.

Counseling of the legalist/obsessive-compulsive must be grounded in the therapeutic triad of empathy, genuineness, and unconditional acceptance on the part of the therapist. The importance of acceptance cannot be overstated. By accepting the client just as he or she is, the therapist models, although imperfectly, a loving, accepting Christ whose love is not contingent on one's being perfect, since he died for us while we were yet sinners (Rom. 5:8). At the same time this unconditional acceptance will help mitigate the destructiveness of the critical, perfectionistic superego.

An examination of the cognitive elements of the disorder will decrease their power over the person as he or she learns to look at the world, the self, and God in a new light. Individuals with this type of problem usually have very negative concepts of God stemming from doctrinal distortions and/or an equation of the heavenly Father with the person's punitive, rigid earthly father. Helping a person to gain insight into these aspects of the problem can prove both spiritually and emotionally liberating.

Lastly, the Reformation principle of *sola fide*, justification by faith alone apart from works or obedience to the law, can provide an antidote to the poison of legalism/obsessive-compulsiveness. Bruce (1977) notes that Paul's statement that Christ is the end of the law (Rom. 10:4) means that since Christ has come law has no place whatsoever in one's approach to God. "According to Paul," he adds, "the believer is *not* under the law as a rule of life—unless one thinks of the law of love, and that is a completely different kind of law, fulfilled not by obedience to a code but by the outworking of an inward power" (p. 192).

The New Testament does not make appeal for proper behavior on the basis of Old Testament rules. Christians' behavior throughout the New Testament is shaped and colored by what Christ has done. The law of Christ demands that believers forgive as they have been forgiven (Col. 3:13), accept one another as Christ has accepted them (Rom. 15:7), and place the same value on people that the blood of Christ places on them (Brinsmead, 1981a).

As Luther observed, no good work helps justify or save an unbeliever. Thus the person who wishes to do good works should begin not with the doing of works but with believing, which alone makes a person good; for nothing makes a person good except faith, or evil except unbelief.

Only faith in Christ can liberate the legalist/obsessive-compulsive from the twin tyrannies of the law and the superego. As he comes to experience the freedom and forgiveness in Jesus Christ, he begins to see that laws and compulsions are unnecessary and can be replaced by "works done out of spontaneous love in obedience to God" (Luther, 1943, p. 295).

References

Brinsmead, R. D. Jesus and the law. *Verdict*, 1981, *4*(4), 6–70. (a)

Brinsmead, R. D. Sabbatarianism re-examined. *Verdict*, 1981, *4*(6), 5–30. (b)

Bruce, F. F. *Paul, apostle of the heart set free*. Grand Rapids: Eerdmans, 1977.

Horney, K. *Neurosis and human growth*. New York: Norton, 1950.

Ladd, G. E. *A theology of the New Testament*. Grand Rapids: Eerdmans, 1974.

Luther, M. The freedom of a Christian. In M. Luther, *Three Treatises*. Philadelphia: Muhlenberg Press, 1943.

Martin. R. P. *New Testament foundations: A guide for Christian students* (Vol. 2). Grand Rapids: Eerdmans, 1978.

Muller, D. Pharisee. In C. Brown (Ed.), *Dictionary of New Testament theology* (Vol. 2). Grand Rapids: Eerdmans, 1976.

Additional Readings

Salzman. L. *Treatment of the obsessive personality*. New York: Aronson, 1980.

Shapiro, D. *Neurotic styles*. New York: Basic Books, 1965.

W. G. Bixler

Religious Need. *See* Psychological Roots of Religion.

Religious Orientation. The impact of motivational and sentimental factors on the individual's religious expression (Malony, 1977). Religious persons differ considerably in the depth, sentiments, and expressions of their religiousness. Religion may serve an instrumental function for those who *use* religion in the pursuit of personal ends or an integral function for those who *live* religion. These two function preferences illustrate varieties in religious orientations in which basic personality and temperamental processes influence religious behavior.

That an individual's religiousness has its foundation in a personality substratum has been a prominent theme among psychologists (e.g., Allport, 1937; Oates, 1973). Freud speculated that religion originated in the tribe's worship of a totem (an animal or plant that was normally taboo to the clan). The taboo was symbolic of a prohibition against incest within the clan, the source of which lay in sexual cathexes of the oedipus complex. Fear and guilt initiated a ban on incest and on marriage within the clan. In a seasonal act of sublimation the totem was sacrifically or ritualistically eaten as a symbolic substitution for the father's murder, the murder stemming from thwarted oedipal desires and hostility from the father's ban. Oedipal dynamics form the basis of organized religion; the doctrine of God is but a rearranged doctrine of the father (Freud, 1918).

Similar psychological accounts of the individual's religion are to be found in James's *Varieties of Religious Experience* and Erikson's *Young Man Luther*. Allport's (1950) fivefold account of origins includes organic needs, temperament and mental capacity, psychogenic interests and values, a desire for rational explanation, and response to surrounding culture. It seems apparent that an individual's religion grows out of personal needs and motives, especially those having some existential significance to the person (Oates, 1973).

The individual's religion is expressed in several ways (Smart, 1976). Ritual is the outer expression coordinated with an inner intention. The mythological dimension embodies the stories that are believed within the religion. The mythical and symbolic elements are formalized by theologians into doctrine. Inherent within religion lie the ethical prescriptions that govern the behavior of the individual. The social dimension represents those communal and organizational aspects supposed to be significant to the group of adherents. The ritualistic, mythological, doctrinal, ethical, and social aspects are external evidences of religion's existence. The experiential dimension comprises the subjective, internal, and invisible world in which the individual communes and worships. Variety in religious experience incorporates a confluence of diversity in content and variation in elemental strength.

Psychologists over the years have been intrigued with the interaction of sentimental and temperamental variables with religiousness. The literature on religious orientation owes much of its origin to the research finding that racial prejudice increases as religiousness increases. Further investigation revealed a more complex relationship in which racial prejudice was a curvilinear function of religiousness (Allport & Ross, 1967). When religiousness was measured by a self report of the frequency of church attendance (a standard measure of religiousness), individuals who reported attending church from once a month to once weekly were more prejudiced than individuals who did not attend at all. Those attending 11 times a month or more were less prejudiced than the nonattenders. It was this consistent finding that Allport and Ross sought to explain. They hypothesized that the motivation of different religious orientations was operating. The two poles of the religious orientation concept were the extrinsically oriented individual, whose religion serves self, and the intrinsically motivated person, whose self serves religion (Allport, 1960).

More specifically, Allport and Ross (1967) considered the motivation and uses each type makes of religion. "Persons with [extrinsic] orientation may find religion useful in a variety of ways—to provide security and solace, sociability and distraction, status and self-justification. The embraced creed is lightly held or else selectively shaped to fit more primary needs. . . . Persons with [intrinsic] orientation find their master motive in religion. Other needs, strong as they may be, are regarded as of less ultimate significance, and they are, so far as possible, brought into harmony with the religious beliefs and prescriptions" (p. 436).

Allport and Ross accounted for the relation between religiousness and prejudice by means of religious orientation. Extrinsically oriented individuals who attended church only occasionally were the highly prejudiced. The very frequent attenders were more likely to be intrinsic, and thus less racially prejudiced. To control for social desirability Allport and Ross used both intrinsic and extrinsic items with which the individual could disagree or agree on the religious orientation scale. In addition to consistently extrinsic and consistently intrinsic individuals, they found individuals who were indiscriminantly proreligious and others who were indiscriminantly antireligious. The indiscriminantly proreligious individuals were found to be highly prejudiced, more so than even the extrinsically oriented.

Hunt and King (1971) reviewed the empirical and conceptual literature on the intrinsic-extrinsic concept. Rather than being bipolarities on a unidimensional continuum, it was found to be a multidimensional construct, something that was anticipated by Allport and Ross (1967). Item analysis and factor analysis revealed two components in the extrinsic orientation: an instrumental one and a selfish one. Intrinsic religion was more personal and more relevant to all of life, and was associated with such religious practice components as church attendance and reading religious literature. Allport and Ross (1967) had intimated

that the extrinsic-intrinsic concept was, in fact, a complex of personality and cognitive variables; Hunt and King (1971) explicitly evaluated the construct as a pervasive personality and motivational process that could explain "secular" behavior as well as "religious" action. It is not surprising that extrinsic orientation correlated with aspects of authoritarianism (Adorno, Frenkel-Brunswick, Levinson, & Sanford, 1950), prejudice (Allport, 1954), closed-mindedness (Rokeach, 1960), and external locus of control.

What evolved to become a personality variable began for Allport (1950, 1954) as two types of religion. Interiorized religion became the intrinsic orientation; institutionalized religion became the extrinsic orientation. A related and parallel concept, suggested by Dittes (1971), is the church-sect typology. Two problems identified with each of these conceptual sets are conceptual sloppiness (i.e., imprecision of definition and theoretical mechanism) and value judgments (i.e., the purity of religion in the orientation and in the sect).

The church-sect distinction is usually credited to Troeltsch. The sect typified a primitive, pure state of religion initially independent of culture and society. But with growth and through time the culture imposed itself and compromised the purity of the sect. The church accommodated itself to culture, with increased insensitivity to social issues, by adopting the administrative structure and governance polity of secular institutions but with a greater eye toward social interaction and social norms. In doing so, the religious body moved from an intrinsic commitment to communal purity to an extrinsic association serving other than purely religious purposes.

In summary, the sociopsychological analysis of religious orientation posits the etiology of divergent religious life styles in underlying personality and motivational variations, and considers the style of one's religious expression to be founded on the personality substratum. When considered alongside sociological and cultural processes, the religious orientation approach explains varieties in religious expression such as asceticism, monasticism, and mysticism, as well as the once-born versus the twice-born typology of James (1902). The need for inner assurance and solace and the need for participation in external rituals arise from fundamental differences in human personality.

References

Adorno, T. W., Frenkel-Brunswik, E., Levinson, D. J., & Sanford, R. N. *The authoritarian personality.* New York: Harper & Row, 1950.

Allport. G. W. *Personality: A psychological interpretation.* New York: Holt, 1937.

Allport, G. W. *The individual and his religion.* New York: Macmillan, 1950.

Allport, G. W. *The nature of prejudice.* Reading, Mass.: Addison-Wesley, 1954.

Allport, G. W. *Personality and social encounter.* Boston: Beacon Press, 1960.

Allport, G. W., & Ross, J. M. Personal religious orientation and prejudice. *Journal of Personality and Social Psychology,* 1967, *5,* 432–443.

Dittes, J. E. Typing the typologies: Some parallels in the career of church-sect and extrinsic-intrinsic. *Journal for the Scientific Study of Religion,* 1971, *10,* 375–383.

Freud, S. *Totem and taboo,* New York: Moffat, Yard, 1918.

James, W. *The varieties of religious experience.* New York: Longmans, Green, 1902.

Hunt, R. A., & King, M. B. The intrinsic-extrinsic concept: A review and evaluation. *Journal for the Scientific Study of Religion,* 1971, *10,* 339–356.

Malony, H. N. (Ed.). *Current perspectives in the psychology of religion.* Grand Rapids: Eerdmans, 1977.

Oates, W. E. *The psychology of religion.* Waco, Tex.: Word Books, 1973.

Rokeach, M. *The open and closed mind.* New York: Basic Books, 1960.

Smart, N. *The religious experience of mankind* (2nd ed.). New York: Scribner's, 1976.

R. L. TIMPE

See PSYCHOLOGY OF RELIGION.

Religious Resources in Psychotherapy.

The process of psychotherapy involves the relationship between a mental health professional and a client who is seeking a solution to his or her problem. The therapist applies the findings of the behavioral sciences in a relationship characterized by genuineness, unconditional positive regard, and empathy. The goal is the solution of the person's problem in living. The extent to which religious resources (such as prayer, Scripture reading, laying on of hands, or use of devotional literature) are included in the therapeutic process is a matter of concern for Christian therapists who wish to be clinically responsible and yet make full use of all resources at their disposal.

A variety of theoretical perspectives inform Christians who practice psychotherapy. Like their non-Christian colleagues a majority seem to be identified with eclecticism, where the therapist selects techniques from different systems of psychotherapy and applies these to the client's problem. Very few Christian therapists articulate their reasons for the incorporation of religious resources in therapy. Furthermore, no theory of personality has been developed that incorporates a theology and psychology of prayer, the most commonly utilized resource. In most cases the prayer of the therapist or client is an extension of his or her way of life. Practice has outstripped theory building and testing.

Prayer and the use of the Bible seem to be the most commonly employed religious resources in psychotherapy. The principles involved in their utilization would seem to provide general guidance for the use of other resources.

Prayer. A broad definition of prayer includes the variety of human endeavors wherein people focus their attention on God. The process goes beyond simply talking with God to include other ways of experiencing the divine. In Christianity the experience is mediated through a personal relationship with Jesus Christ. To what extent, then, can this component of religious practice be included in psychotherapy?

Prayer is one dimension that can make the psychotherapeutic process uniquely Christian. The client has an opportunity to connect with the source of meaning in his life and recognize alternative sources of wisdom. A transcendent and supernatural element can be introduced in the therapy. However, there are certain theological and psychological dangers inherent in the use of prayer in therapy.

A theological danger is for the therapist or client to give prayer a value and place less than its biblical importance. This may be done by employing prayer as a psychological technique until a better strategy is found. Such a transitory view of the usefulness of prayer diminishes the biblical statement of its place in the life of the believer. Biblically prayer is not a technique but the way of life of the believer in relationship to God. At all times prayer is to be addressed to God and not to serve the function of two humans speaking to each other. The therapist must remain sensitive to the whole spectrum of the prayer experience, including confession, petition, intercession, and thanksgiving. The therapist models for the client his own ultimate dependence on God, even if he only says to the client, "I will be praying for you."

One of the psychological dangers that emerges when a client asks the therapist for prayer comes under the general category of avoidance. The client may be avoiding painful issues and may suggest prayer rather than further exploration and talk. If the therapist resists this avoidance, as would be correct, his theological orthodoxy may be called into question. This also must be seen as resistance. People seek to evade personal responsibility through an infantile desire that God make everything better. Such expectations require the therapeutic skill of confrontation in a context of acceptance.

Sometimes the therapist may resort to prayer with the client as an avoidance strategy. He may be experiencing the client's sexuality, feel threatened, and avoid the intimacy issue through prayer. Questions such as "How does the client want to *use* prayer?" "Am I as a therapist seeking to please the client with my prayers?" and "Is this prayer consistent with the client's need and theological tradition?" help the therapist avoid improper use of prayer and yet remain open to its appropriate use.

Notwithstanding the dangers, the use of prayer in therapy can mobilize the client's inner spiritual resources and provide help in dealing with problems. For example, prayer of thanksgiving and praise can change the focus of a person's life away from habitual complaints. Hope, essential to change in psychotherapy, can be generated through referring the client's life to God in prayer. The spoken prayer of the client can also be the reaffirmation of a covenantal relationship with God and others. The presence of the therapist stimulates accountability on the part of the client. With a prayer of confession the therapist can act in a priestly fashion and affirm the promise of divine forgiveness. Prayer can also open a person up to his potential and assist in the discovery of fulfillment once again. Such processes are central to psychotherapy.

The Scriptures. The use of the Bible also has dangers, challenges, and great potential. One problem with reading Bible passages to Christian clients is that they may be overfamiliar with the verses to the point of being unresponsive to their impact. The truth of the Bible may have minimal penetration in the day-to-day reality of their lives. To clients having problems with authority the Bible, a symbol of authority, evokes an unquestioning compliance or reflexive rebellion. The naïve therapist may seek either to browbeat the rebel or to shape the compliant person's behavior through proof texting. Such responses on the part of the therapist could well be a case of countertransference where his problems get in the way of effective therapy.

The Bible can also be misused through its simplistic application to human problems. One illustration of simplistic use of Scripture is when a therapist obtains behavioral change with the prescription of a particular verse. Such a change may be a transference cure— i.e., symptom removal through which the client seeks, consciously or unconsciously, to please the therapist. Such cures are superficial and not in the best interests of the client.

Another problem encountered by therapists who use the Bible in therapy is that they may have different interpretations of Scripture from those held by the client. For example, the therapist holds to an equalitarian view of the marriage relationship while his client has a hierarchical perspective. At this point the therapist needs to decide whether he will explicitly or implicitly subvert the client's values, terminate the therapeutic contract, or drastically sublimate personal values and work within the personal values of the client. In no instance, however, can there be a value-free therapy. Biblical interpretation will certainly influence the therapist's and client's therapeutic relationship.

The assets of the use of the Bible in therapy must not be minimized by its dangers. Like prayer it can refer the therapeutic endeavor to the divine dimension and help people realize their God-given potential. The Bible also gives direction and content to personal growth, and can lead a person to a deeper relationship with the divine Author. Such a journey can be facilitated through bibliotherapy. Here the client is encouraged to read portions of Scripture and apply them to life problems or challenges. For example, the unforgiving person may be referred to the parables of Jesus dealing with forgiveness. The feelings and thoughts generated by such an exercise may be fruitfully explored in subsequent sessions. In instances where the client is patently ignorant of the tenets of his faith, a referral may be made to a clergyman. Such concurrent treatment requires intelligent consultation, mutual trust, and the clarification of confidentiality issues.

The Question of Evangelism. One area of special concern in the use of prayer and Scripture in psychotherapy is evangelism. Should the therapist attempt to lead the client to Christ? One problem with such a question is that coming to Christ is viewed as a boundary that needs to be crossed. Evangelism is more than telling a person, "You are a sinner who needs to be saved." If conversion is also a process, evangelism may take place through the breaking down of the client's stereotypes of Christianity in the context of therapy. Here the client through the process of being respected, heard, and accepted by the therapist comes to see Christianity as something more than a list of don'ts. Psychotherapy can also be evangelistic when negative views of a punitive God are rectified. Such images of God may be a legacy of childhood development where the client related to an earthly father in a context of much hurt. Ideas of earthly father are here closely tied to heavenly father. In therapy the client may learn to develop new bonds of trust with the therapist. Such bonds, together with appropriate interpretation of the earthly/heavenly father connection, may lead to the possibility of new faith. Such a process is also evangelism.

Broader Questions. The debate over whether prayer and Scripture have a place in psychotherapy will continue unresolved until some central issues are dealt with by those involved in the integration of theology and psychology. Two of the most pressing of these are the need for a Christian theory of personality and the need for better understanding of the ingredients and process of change in therapy. The need for a personality theory consistent with the biblical record is crucial, not just to these questions but to the whole understanding of Christian psychotherapy. To date no such theory exists. In its absence Christians tend to approach prayer with eclecticism and pragmatism ("If it works, then pray"). This makes it an addendum rather than an integral part of therapy. Little thought may be given to the effects of an activity such as prayer on the total personality development of the client. Furthermore, without an overarching personality theory the therapist is hard pressed to explain why prayer sometimes does not work in the life of the client. Even when prayer seems efficacious, an eclectic approach can trade off short-term gains in psychotherapy for long-term benefits. Christian psychology is in search of a theory that will consistently integrate practices such as prayer and Scripture reading.

The process that produces change in psychotherapy also needs to be better understood. Research indicates both nonspecific and specific factors to be involved in the psychotherapeutic process. The nonspecific factors transcend theoretical approaches and emerge from a study of the relationship between the therapist and client. The ideal relationship is where the therapist and client relate well, the therapist sticks closely to the client's problems, and in an atmosphere of mutual trust and confidence the client feels free to say what he or she likes. In the context of such a relationship the therapist mobilizes powerful influencing forces that assist the patient toward the reversal of self-defeating patterns and toward growth. The nonspecific factors are not always curative in and of themselves. They are a necessary but not sufficient condition for a therapeutic reversal.

Specific factors can be viewed as the science of psychotherapy. They also transcend the theoretical perspective of the therapist and include the prescription of new responses to old and habitual maladaptive ways of responding; feedback to the client regarding his thinking, emotions, and behavior; and the generation of hope through a new perspective on the problem coupled with some possible solutions. The art of therapy is seen in the selection of these specific factors at the right moment. Means such as prayer and Scripture reading must be coupled with these specific and nonspecific factors so as not to violate both theological and psychological factors. For example, change for the growing Christian includes the development of a biblical mindset (Rom. 12:2). Such renewal requires a scriptural content, understanding of the psychology of cognition, appreciation for the developmental issues involved in an unbiblical mindset, and a therapeutic context that works with the Holy Spirit to reverse unhealthy cognitions and their outworking in behavior. Scripture and prayer in the hands of a sensitive therapist can be the agents of change and growth.

C. B. JOHNSON

See SPIRITUAL AND RELIGIOUS ISSUES IN THERAPY.

Remembering. *See* MEMORY.

Repetition Compulsion. The more or less irresistible impulse to repeat earlier experiences regardless of the pain they may produce. This principle is more fundamental than the pleasure principle and, in fact, seems incompatible with it. Freud described the repetition phenomenon but did not provide much of an explanation for it. Fairbairn (1954) views the behavior as an attempt to solve old conflicts and thereby attain healing of the ego splits that resulted from early childhood nonsatisfactory relationships. The goal in psychoanalysis or psychoanalytic psychotherapy is to replace repetition with remembering, thereby undoing the repetition compulsion.

Reference
Fairbairn, W. R. D. *An object relations theory of the personality.* New York: Basic Books, 1954.

D. G. BENNER

See PSYCHOANALYTIC PSYCHOLOGY; OBJECT RELATIONS THEORY.

Repression. The process by which anxiety-producing ideas or impulses are kept out of or removed from conscious awareness. It is recognized in a number of theoretical perspectives as the most basic of DEFENSE MECHANISMS and, ccording to Freud, provides the foundation on which most other defenses are constructed. Although the person is not consciously aware of repressed material or of the process of repression, this material continues to influence behavior.

When an idea or group of ideas associated with strong feeling, or affect, threatens to seriously lower self-esteem, conflict with deeply instilled values, or provoke anxiety, the ego seeks to remove this threat from consciousness. This process may involve repression of the idea with associated affect, the idea alone, or the affect alone. However, repressed material may gain conscious expression in various disguises. If the affect alone is repressed, the idea remaining in consciousness may be tied to an acceptable affect. When repression involves only the idea, the affect may become associated with an idea or object possessing no conscious connection to the threatening idea. Should both idea and affect be repressed, they may return to consciousness in some form of symbolic expression.

For example, an adult may have suffered a terrible act of child abuse in early years. If anger over this toward the abusing parent is fully repressed, leaving no conscious memory of the event or feelings surrounding it, it may seek conscious expression symbolically through anger toward some authority or parentlike figure not consciously associated with the parent. If affect alone is repressed, the person may recall the event with no conscious awareness of anger, even claiming instead feelings of love and forgiveness. The unexpressed anger may resurface, directed toward an unconscious parent substitute. If only the idea is repressed, conscious anger may again find an unconsciously chosen parent substitute as its object.

R. Larkin

Resistance in Psychotherapy. A client's efforts to obstruct the psychotherapeutic process and thwart the psychotherapist's efforts to help that client. All clients manifest resistance, although the degree to which they resist may vary from minimal to massive. Resistance is not a phenomenon limited to involuntary clients but is also characteristic of clients who come for therapy at their own initiative. Most psychotherapists believe that resistance is an important part of the psychotherapeutic process.

General Considerations. Why do clients resist the psychotherapy they have initiated? Why do they drag their feet in reaching psychotherapeutic goals that have been formulated specifically for their benefit? Cavanagh (1982) attributes client resistance to three factors. First, growth is painful. Clients may have to stop well-learned destructive behaviors such as making excuses, addictions, pretending, and being dependent. They may have to begin new and unfamiliar healthful behaviors such as becoming independent, assertive, responsible, and exerting self-control. Psychotherapy makes some healthful but difficult demands.

A second reason for resistance in psychotherapy is that maladaptive behavior meets a need or in some way gratifies the client. This is known as secondary gain. The client's symptoms may bring attention, disguise the real problem, provide an excuse for anger, or provide an unhealthy way of atoning for guilt through self-punishment. Third, persons may enter psychotherapy with the wrong motives or with limited commitment. They may go into psychotherapy in order to blame others, to get permission not to change, to validate a decision, to manipulate others, to satisfy others, to prove they are beyond help, or to defeat the counselor.

Cavanagh also lists some vivid examples of how clients resist. These include missing or being late to appointments, evading questions, intentionally boring the counselor, focusing on the therapist more than self, and trying to evoke certain responses such as shock or sympathy from the therapist. The client may claim to forget things, avoid sensitive content areas, dwell on irrelevant areas by repeatedly bringing up past experiences, or try to force the therapist into a no-win, paradoxical situation. All these common client behaviors may indicate resistance.

While Cavanagh provides a good overview of resistance, it should be noted that psychotherapists' perspectives on the specific nature and treatment of resistance vary according to their theoretical orientation. Anderson and Stewart (1983) have summarized psychoanalytic, behavioral, and family therapy approaches to resistance. These three approaches illustrate some of the similarities and differences in different therapists' perspectives on resistance.

Psychoanalytic Perspective. Psychoanalytically oriented therapists believe that resistance is largely unconscious and defensive. Since they also believe that most personality problems result from unresolved childhood conflicts, resistance is seen as an unconscious attempt on the part of the client to avoid disturbing those painful and frightening areas that have been sealed off in an attempt to minimize anxiety. As the transference relationship develops, the psychotherapist identifies and interprets the meaning of the client's resistances. As the client comes to understand and accept the psychotherapist's interpretations, he discovers what he has been avoiding and deals with it consciously in a more adaptive fashion. This is by no means a brief or easy process.

Resistance therefore is one of the primary concerns of psychoanalytically oriented psychotherapy. Resistance is considered to be inevitable, pervasive, and valuable. Anything that works against the progress of psychotherapy is considered to be resistance. The client's resistances guide the psychotherapeutic process because they reveal to the psychotherapist what the client is unconsciously hiding and what needs to be addressed. Working through resistance is the heart of psychoanalytic psychotherapy.

Behavioral Perspective. Behavior therapists' perspectives on resistance stand in bold contrast to psychoanalytic perspectives. Behavior therapists believe that resistance is an unnecessary annoyance that can be avoided by the therapist through a good relationship with the client, anticipation of flaws in the behavior change program, and giving careful instructions to the client. Instead of interpreting and working through resistance behavior therapists attempt to avoid it.

Behavior therapists do not acknowledge unconscious motivation or related concepts such as defensiveness. They believe that behavior is controlled primarily by environmental contingencies and associations the client has learned throughout life. Behavior therapists believe their role is an informative and technical role whereby they help clients learn new behaviors by identifying reinforcers, by counterconditioning, and by shaping. Behavior therapists focus on behaviors, not on presumed underlying causes, and they are not very concerned with early childhood experiences or conflicts.

Resistance is a concept that does not fit well within the behavioral theoretical framework. Even the term *resistance* is seldom found in behavioral literature. When clients do not cooperate, behavior therapists do not believe that it is due to unconscious defensiveness. Instead, they believe that resistance is due to a misunderstanding between therapists and client, or the client's failure to see the relevance of the behavior change program for his problem. Sometimes the therapist prescribes incre-

ments in the plan that are too large, and the client is unable to perform the prescribed behaviors. Most frequently clients resist because their misbehavior results in secondary gains.

Minimizing resistance is the responsibility of the behavior therapist. In addition to building good rapport the behavior therapist carefully explains both rationale and prescriptions in specific and concrete terms, prepares the client for anticipated difficulties, and rehearses prescribed tasks to ensure that the client understands them and can perform them. Behavior therapists minimize resistance due to secondary gains by teaching clients more effective behaviors for achieving their goals.

Family Therapy Perspective. The emergence of family therapy as a significant treatment modality has rekindled interest in resistance and added a new complexity to the concept. Family therapists are primarily concerned with the relationships among family members, the family's relationship to its social environment, and the family's rules governing those two relationships. Resistance is not viewed as the sole possession of an individual family member; rather, it is a force in the relationship that emanates from the family's rules and common assumptions. These rules are usually assumed or implied and may operate at an essentially unconscious level.

Family rules prescribing roles and relationships are very important to family functioning. They preserve the identity of the family and its members; they let members know where and how they fit in; they apportion the work of the family; and they provide guidance and organization for family members in times of stress and ambiguity. Family rules maintain balance, or homeostasis, within the family.

Families, however, face a series of developmental tasks that require change. Children are born and grow, income levels change, members age, parents die, members are added through birth or marriage, illnesses strike, and persons retire. While family rules help guide the family through these crises, the rules and structure must also change to accommodate some of these developments. Very often families break down and come for therapy when the rules are too resistant to change and the family cannot adapt to its environment or family members' needs. Family rules are very difficult to change because they are shared by several family members and are consensually validated. Family rules also span generations, having their roots in the parents' families of origin.

Families then come into therapy with rigid, maladaptive rules that have resulted in tensions between members and in the breakdown of at least one member, usually a child. The family usually wants the therapist to cure the symptomatic member but resists changes in the family rules and structure. The therapist resists treating only the symptomatic family member. Members' symptoms are seen as the result of family rules that are unhealthy or functionally autonomous, which means that at one point in development the rules were adaptive, but they became habitual and continued to operate long after they were helpful. The family therapist regards the family system as the client, not the individual.

Therefore, family therapists face a great deal of resistance in their work. The resistance is shared in varying degrees by all persons (including the therapist) in the therapeutic process and may be directed toward differing targets. Resistance may be adaptive or maladaptive, and the therapist's goal is to adjust and direct the resistance, not necessarily eliminate it. Family therapists must recognize resistance and use it therapeutically to restructure the family system.

Regardless of the therapist's theoretical orientation, resistance is always difficult for the therapist to handle because it seems like an attack against the therapist's person and competence. The therapist's tendency is to respond defensively. The best preparation for handling resistance therapeutically includes thorough professional preparation, self-confidence, and understanding that all therapists encounter resistance.

References

Anderson, C., & Stewart, S. *Mastering resistance.* New York: Guilford Press, 1983.
Cavanagh, M. E. *The counseling experience.* Monterey, Calif.: Brooks/Cole, 1982.

Additional Readings

Freud, S. *A general introduction to psychoanalysis* (Lecture 19). New York: Boni & Liveright, 1920.
Langs, R. *Resistances and interventions.* New York: Aronson, 1981.
Marshall, R. J. *Resistant interactions.* New York: Human Sciences Press, 1982.

C. D. DOLPH

Response Cost Contingency.
The withdrawal or loss of material reinforcers contingent upon the occurrence of an undesirable response.

There are two major forms of PUNISHMENT: 1) positive punishment, where an aversive consequence is presented to the organism after a response and results in the response becoming less likely to occur; and 2) negative punishment, where as a consequence of a response something is taken away from the organism, again resulting in the response becoming less probable. Response cost contingency is one of the most common forms of negative punishment (time-out being the other most common form).

An example of response cost contingency might go as follows. A teacher develops a token economy in a classroom for noncompliant children. Positive reinforcement in the form of tokens is given for appropriate behavior; these tokens can be redeemed for material rewards. When inappropriate behavior occurs, such as yelling or striking a peer, the teacher chooses not to ignore the behavior but to impose a response cost of loss of previously earned tokens. A child might have worked to earn 15 tokens earlier in the day, but incurs the loss of five tokens after yelling at the teacher. Response cost contingency is a technique widely used in token economies and behavior modification in general. It is used in more informal ways in child rearing (e.g., taking away a child's allowance or privileges as a result of disobedience) and in social policy (e.g., personal and corporate monetary fines for illegal behavior).

S. L. JONES

Response Generalization.
See GENERALIZATION.

Retirement.
Retirement, as we know it, is a product of twentieth-century industrialized society. Prior to this time workers did not systematically leave the work force solely because of age. Instead, diminished levels of activity or roles that demanded less physical involvement were taken on.

In his analysis of retirement Ward (1979) identified some of the reasons that retirement has become institutionalized. The first is population demographics; there are more older individuals. The increased productivity of workers and modernization of machinery has made for greater competition for available jobs. The net result has been that older workers are enticed from the work force to provide jobs for younger workers. Social Security and pension programs have made retirement a realistic alternative for many. Second, Ward suggests that a series of structural transformations in the economy are related to institutionalization of retirement. These include a general decline in agricultural employment, an increasing need for educational and technological skills (which many older adults lack), and an increase in white-collar jobs at the expense of blue-collar ones. Ward sees these transformations as directly increasing the ranks of the retired in several ways: 1) the skills of the older population are obsolete in the new technological society, making the older worker expendable; 2) there have been changes in personnel practices, especially mandatory retirement; 3) work may have lost its attractiveness, particularly if the work is boring or alienating; and 4) the fact that retirement itself has been legitimized contributes toward the trend of persons to retire. As a result, most adults expect to and eventually do retire.

Meaning of Retirement. Although there are several perspectives on the meaning of retirement, two appear most frequently in the literature. One view perceives retirement as trauma, resulting in an identity crisis of sorts. It is a time of transition when the primary role, at least in terms of time spent, is discontinued. This causes problems for several reasons: 1) Unlike many previous transition periods (e.g., marriage, birth of first child), the roles of the retiree, what he or she is supposed to do, are ill defined. 2) There are few role models to emulate. 3) Many writers believe that it is through the work role that society most directly and effectively interacts with each individual. Through the work role society knows who and what an individual is. Once that role is given up, society no longer knows how to respond to the retired person. 4) Once a person has given up the work role, he is ascribed a lesser status than he had while he was still working. Since he is no longer contributing to society, he is no longer important. 5) The significant drop in level of income frequently makes the retiree a virtual prisoner in his or her own home.

Conversely, another view conceptualizes retirement as life in a different form. The retiree is visualized as adapting to the role as he or she would to any other role change. In fact, previous role transitions are seen as preparing the person to make the switch from full-time worker to retiree easily. From this perspective the act of retiring is no more traumatic, the adjustment no more crucial, than any other significant life event. Retirement and the adjustment to it are seen as part of an individual. Life is a continuous process, and retirement and the adjustment to it are seen as an example of the continuity of life.

Research Literature. There is research data to support both these positions. In a number of surveys examining attitudes toward retire-

ment, retired individuals reported that they never were able to fill the gap left by leaving their job. They also reported that they felt useless. Additionally, retirees as a group tended to be less satisfied with their present life than when they were working, and less satisfied than their counterparts who were still working.

The belief that retirement results in a crisis also finds some support. Holstein (1981) interviewed 60 men who were retiring regarding their feelings about retirement. All but four of those men had experienced, or were experiencing, a crisis related to their retirement. Some were apparently making the transition smoothly, but at least half were struggling with issues related to identifying themselves and their role as a retiree.

The bulk of the research, however, shows that for most retirees the transition to retirement is neither overly stressful nor unpleasant (Atchley, 1976). The majority of retirees surveyed indicated that their identity, their feelings of self-worth, and their life satisfaction rested on more than one role. In fact, most reported that the recognition from family and friends and the satisfaction received from involvement in organizations such as churches and civic groups were significantly more important to self-worth and life satisfaction than was the work role. These persons indicated that the act of retiring was sometimes stressful, but that losses in the areas of family, friends, or health were far more devastating.

The idea that retirement is another of a lifelong series of transitions is also supported in the literature. Generally, research has found that retirement does not initiate an identity crisis, nor does it negatively affect other areas of life. Most retirees reported that instead of significant life-style changes, once retired they continue to engage in the same general activities as when they were working.

Surprisingly, although many retirees reported that they had increased the time spent in some activities (e.g., solitary or recreational), the freedom of the retired life and the relief from pressure of the job made the time engaged in selected activities more productive and enjoyable. Hence it was not more time but significantly greater quality time that was being spent in these activities.

Recently, in an effort to deal with this disparate data, researchers have examined adjustment styles in retirement. It has become clear that some individuals make a difficult adjustment to retirement. Conversely, for some the adjustment is easy and retirement satisfying. Kimmel and his colleagues (Walker, Kimmel, & Price, 1980) have sought to understand the relationship between personal characteristics and adjustment to retirement. In their research they identified a group of men who had made positive adjustments to retirement. These men had good health, adequate income, and continued to be active in various self-chosen activities. Kimmel found that their reasons for retirement were positive (e.g., spend more time with hobbies and family) and that they were more likely to have achieved occupationally what they had wanted to. The second group, however, had not made a positive adjustment to retirement. Typically they had not retired for positive, self-selected reasons; rather, retirement was due to health problems or because mandatory retirement age was reached. These men had inadequate retirement income, limited social support, and nothing to do. Occupationally they had not accomplished all that they had hoped. Somewhat surprisingly, these retirees had not really enjoyed their jobs, but working was better than being retired.

Further research has uncovered a relationship between types of careers and adjustment to retirement. Men who had unstable, discontinuous occupational careers (changed jobs frequently, switched career areas, or spent significant periods of time unemployed) were more likely to make a difficult transition to retirement. Men who had orderly careers were more likely to feel positive about their retirement.

These findings indicate that factors such as health, income, social support, and activity level play an important role in postretirement satisfaction. Generally the healthier the person, the more adequate the income, the more encompassing the support system (family, friends, church), and the more time spent in self-selected activities, the better the adjustment and the more satisfying the period of retirement.

Preparation for Retirement. For the family member, friend, pastor, or concerned professional these findings suggest that one important task is that of facilitating an easy transition to retirement. Anything that minimizes the abruptness of retirement should be encouraged. For example, the preretiree might be encouraged to participate in company or community sponsored financial or retirement planning programs. Some preretirees try out some of the roles or activities they intend to pursue. They practice their leisure activities, do volunteer work, or even dabble in a new job. This allows them to get a more accurate picture of what retirement will be like. This is important, as there will be more to one's retirement years than just fishing and golf.

It is sometimes said that the key to positive retirement is to remain active and keep busy. While this is generally true, research has found that keeping active, while important, is not as important as being involved in self-selected activities. There is a significant portion of the retired population who actually enjoy doing very little. They have worked hard and enjoy taking it easy. For many individuals, however, inactivity is death. There are numerous reports of busy individuals who discontinued activities upon retirement and then, as a result, had significant physical and emotional problems. However, individuals who select their own level of involvement fare better in the long run. They report more positive feelings about their retirement years. Interested helpers would do well to encourage the retiree to chose for himself or herself the nature, direction, and amount of activity the retirement years are to include.

References

Atchley, R. C. *The sociology of retirement.* New York: Halsted, 1976.
Holstein, K. A. *Ego identity versus diffusion preceding retirement.* Unpublished doctoral dissertation, Ohio State University, 1981.
Walker, J. W., Kimmel, D. C., & Price, K. F. Retirement style and retirement satisfaction: Retirees aren't all alike. *International Journal of Aging and Human Development,* 1980–1981, *12*(4), 267–281.
Ward, R. A. *The aging experience.* Philadelphia: Lippincott, 1979.

K. A. HOLSTEIN

See LIFE SPAN DEVELOPMENT.

Ritual. A pattern of repetitious behavior in an established routine, intended consciously or subconsciously for efficient achievement of personal fulfillment or anxiety reduction and for manipulative control with regard to some significant aspect of one's internal or external world. The objectives and the routine patterns designed to meet them may be physical, psychological, social, or spiritual. Indeed, they may include several of these facets of human experience simultaneously (Taylor & Thompson, 1972). Ritual is readily evident in at least three spheres of human function: worship, relationships, and work. In each of these areas ritual may be either pathological or healthy.

WORSHIP is the area of human behavior in which the role of ritual as been most obvious throughout human history (Westerhof & Willimon, 1980). This is probably due to the fact that humans universally experience relatively high levels of anxiety about spirituality, as we do about sexuality. Both are rooted in personality and character close to the center of our sense of identity. Both are forces driving toward relationship, which has its own inherent anxiety. Moreover, in religious and spiritual matters humans perceive themselves dealing with sacred, transcendent, divine relationship. Historically the sense of the sacred has carried with it an understandable sense of awesome encounter with the world of the unknown and eternal. Such encounter has usually produced a sense of anxiety or even dread. Only in the Judeo-Christian religion of unconditional grace is our encounter with God a source of relief, assurance, joy, and health.

The high anxiety function of religion has caused humans to experience a high level of need to conduct religious matters with great care. That carefulness tends to lead to the creation of closely controlled procedures for religious behavior: orthodox theology, rigid codes of ethical-moral conduct, and ritualization of the worship process (MacGregor, 1974). These controlled systems function as anxiety-reducing mechanisms in religions where the radical and redemptive nature of God's grace is not perceived or is not really trusted. As such ritualized religion becomes more and more tightly controlled for the purpose of managing the ever increasing religious anxiety, and the rituals tend to become increasingly compulsive and ultimately obsessive (Loder, 1966).

Ritual can also play a very constructive role in religion. It is helpful for Christians to adopt a generally agreed-upon perspective in theology, a functionally effective code of conduct, and a patterned worship process. Ritual in worship adds dignity and aesthetic quality to communal behavior and gives programmatic focus to the experiences of prayer, praise, and religious pronouncement.

Unfortunately there remains in all religion a tendency to cabalistic ritual in worship. Cabalistic worship is that in which the ritual has become an end in itself and has lost its rational connection between the procedure and the objective it was originally designed to achieve: personal fulfillment or anxiety reduction. Cabalistic ritual is always imbued with some significant degree of compulsivity. It is pathological in that it callouses both the soul and psyche by decreasing the sensitivity of the human spirit to the genuine meaning of worship. It has the same effect upon the psyche as a constant chafing has upon one's hand. It desensitizes that organ and creates a defensive

and protective callous at the place where the rub is. True worship always moves through ritual to encounter with God in his grandeur.

Ritual also plays an important role in the patterning of human relationships. Emerson thought that politeness was the ritual of society as prayers and praises are the ritual of the worshiping church. Since effective interpersonal relationships depend essentially upon trust, friendship requires that the agenda of mutual expectations be clearly and openly shared. The number and variety of individual differences, therefore, tend to enhance the desirability of predictable patterns and styles of interpersonal behavior. Thus the rituals of friendship arise and make the processes of friendship gratifying, comfortable, and edifying. Friendships, like personalities, can get sick. When they do, the rituals, or predictable behavior patterning, becomes compulsively oriented toward manipulative control by one or both of the persons in the relationship. The objective in that case is anxiety reduction by excessive dominance of one by the other. When that compulsivity is challenged or its goal achievement frustrated, it tends toward obsessiveness unless the wholesome objective of mutual fulfillment and gratification for all participants in the relationship can be brought back into focus.

It is clear that ritual also plays an important role in work behavior. Routines can enhance efficiency, particularly in our mass-production society. However, they can also sometimes obstruct job efficiency and must then be seen as pathological. Obsessive checking and rechecking of one's work exemplifies this.

The psychopathology most closely associated with pathological ritual is the OBSESSIVE-COMPULSIVE DISORDER. Obsessiveness and compulsivity are always fueled by insecurity and driven by the need for anxiety reduction through certainty or control. So an obsessive-compulsive personality may be manifested in the need to check and recheck a door lock or gas jet or in the repeated ritual of washing one's hands. Since these rituals enacted to achieve certainty and control do not result in significant change in the original insecurity, they tend to increase in intensity and in obsessional quality and move toward the pseudoomnipotent dynamics of magic. The rational link between the cause of the original insecurity and the function of the ritual is then no longer discernible. The process becomes a self-reinfecting exaggeration of the insecurity; that is, the insecurity fuels the obsessive ritual, which does not increase security by anxiety reduction. Fear therefore increases, and the intensity of the ritual is heightened to compensate for the increased anxiety.

Ritualistic behavior of this sort is clearly pathological whether it appears in work, worship, or relationships. The criteria for pathological ritual would seem to be the presence of any of the following conditions: 1) the relationship between the ritual and its objective is lost or nonfunctional; 2) the behavior obstructs the functioning of the life of the person or community; or 3) the enactment of the ritual increasingly fails in its objective of reducing anxiety and therefore escalates in frequency. In extreme cases only the self-limiting experiences of physical and psychic exhaustion or the limits of formal external constraint can control the infinite "wildfire" effect of the expansion of the self-defeating ritualistic behavior. (Salzman, 1980).

It is evident, therefore, that ritual may be constructive or destructive, depending on its nature and function. All wholesome idealism requires routines to lead humanity to civilization and aesthetic self-actualization. Efficiency in productivity requires precision and its inherent patterning. Communal life requires coordination, schedule, and ritualization if it is to achieve success, mutual trust, comfort, and gratification. Instruction in the faith requires the routines of catechesis in the symbology of theology and praxis if it is to achieve its growth-enhancing objectives. All of these tend to institutionalize themselves in constructive ritual. All are impaired by pathological ritual.

References

Loder, J. E. Religious pathology and Christian faith. Philadelphia: Westminster, 1966.
MacGregor, G. The rhythm of God. New York: Seabury, 1974.
Salzman, L. Treatment of the obsessive personality. New York: Aronson, 1980.
Taylor, J. C., & Thompson, G. R. Ritual, realism, and revolt. New York: Scribner's, 1972.
Westerhof, J. H., & Willimon, W. H. Liturgy and learning through the life cycle. New York: Seabury, 1980.

J. H. Ellens

Rogerian Personality Theory. See Self Theory.

Rogers, Carl Ransom (1902–). The founder of Person-Centered (client-centered) or nondirective, therapy. Rogers was born in Chicago, the middle child of a family of six in a fundamentalist Protestant home where the work ethic was revered. His family was loving but noncommunicative. During his youth he was a lonely child with few friends.

Early in his adult life he turned from Christianity to liberalistic humanism—largely, it seems, in reaction to the rather harsh religious convictions of his mother. She was a strong person who insisted on a separation between persons on the basis of religious differences. With equally strong convictions she held that, even at best, a person is never good enough. In contrast to this, Rogers's adult life has been characterized by what he himself calls "an obsession" with communication between people regardless of religious or other differences. He is also a champion of the belief in the inherent goodness of people.

In 1919 he entered the University of Wisconsin. Initially he studied agriculture, but in his sophomore year he switched to history in preparation for seminary training to become a "religious worker." Religious work was a program of the YMCA aimed at converting people to Protestantism through humanitarian services. In his junior year he took a six-month trip to China as one of the American student representatives to an international congress of the YMCA. During this trip he rapidly moved away from the childhood religion of his family. He experienced this change as a developmental liberation.

Upon graduation in 1924 he married and entered Union Theological Seminary in New York. In the freewheeling intellectual climate of that institution he thought himself right out of religious work. Humanitarian service had now become an end in itself for him. Accordingly, he left Union and enrolled in Teachers College, Columbia University, to study psychology.

At Teachers College, Rogers became acquainted with Dewey's pragmatism, and Dewey's influence on Rogers's thought has been considerable. For example, clinically Rogers was trained to become a dogmatic Freudian. For therapy this meant that the client would have to adapt himself to the methods and interpretations of the therapist if he were to obtain emotional healing. Dewey's experimentalism allowed Rogers to adopt an eclectic approach to therapy in which both the therapist's methods and the client's input contributed to the outcome of therapy. This meant that he could transform existing therapeutic dogmas into techniques, retaining those that proved effective in therapy while discarding those that did not.

For 12 years following his graduation from Teachers College, Rogers worked for the Society for the Prevention of Cruelty to Children in Rochester. There he collected a large number of effective therapeutic techniques, which ultimately were published in 1939 in his first book: *The Clinical Treatment of the Problem Child.*

Also during these years he came to a definitive position on his own nondirective approach to therapy. In doing so, he moved away from both the dogmatic Freudian and the eclectic pragmatistic approaches to therapy by insisting that the therapist should follow the lead of the client with regard to the direction, movement, and outcome of therapy. In subsequent years Rogers never wavered from this position.

From 1940 to 1944 Rogers taught at Ohio State University. During these years he wrote *Counseling and Psychotherapy* (1942), his first detailed description of nondirective therapy. The years from 1945 to 1957 were perhaps his most productive. During this time he taught at the University of Chicago and, with a sizable group of promising young therapists, did a great deal of important research in psychotherapy. He also completed his second major publication: *Client-Centered Therapy* (1951).

After a brief and personally disappointing stint at Wisconsin (1957–1963), Rogers moved to LaJolla, California, to become a resident fellow at the Western Behavioral Science Institute. Later (1970) he became affiliated with the Center for Studies of the Person, and remains there to date. Both these institutions were loosely organized around the promotion of research in human learning and growth.

During these years his interests moved from psychotherapy to group therapy and encounter groups, with a concomitant stress on the interpersonal rather than the intrapersonal. His interests also switched from the narrow confines of therapy to other areas of life such as education, family relations, industrial relations, and international relations. Some of his most thought-provoking publications date from these years: *On Becoming a Person* (1961), *Freedom to Learn* (1969), *Carl Rogers on Encounter Groups* (1970), *Carl Rogers on Personal Power* (1977), and *A Way of Being* (1980).

Additional Readings
Kirschenbaum, H. *On becoming Carl Rogers,* New York: Delacorte, 1979.
Van Belle, A. *Basic intent and therapeutic approach of Carl R. Rogers.* Toronto: Wedge Publishing Foundation, 1980.

H. A. VAN BELLE

See SELF THEORY.

Role Playing. The rehearsal or recapitulation of an event, real or imagined, with the goal of changing behavior, thinking, and/or feelings. As a therapeutic technique it is attributed to Moreno (1946), an Austrian psychiatrist who developed the American Society of Group Psychotherapy and Psychodrama and the journal *Group Psychotherapy.*

Role playing may be used by the counselor to serve several purposes: diagnosis, instruction and training, and as a catalyst for change in the client. On a diagnostic level the role-playing situation enables the counselor to better understand the client through watching him act out as a representation of real behavior. It may also serve to help demonstrate other alternatives and reactions, and therefore fulfill an instructional purpose. Participation in role-playing experiences also gives the counselee the opportunity to relive, reenact, or imagine situations that may be causing psychological pain, with the goal of changing patterns of thinking, feeling, or behaving. Observers or other participants also profit vicariously from the experience. One further benefit of role playing is the creation of a "comfort zone" whereby the client can play out a problem in a safe situation, gaining skills, experiencing emotions, and obtaining information.

Role playing may be used effectively with individuals in a one-to-one counseling setting, in groups, and even alone, as in practicing a speech or rehearsing possible responses to an upcoming situation. The person may role play himself in a particular situation (real or fictional), may switch roles, or may even observe others playing his role. The technique is generally applicable to most counseling situations and is particularly valuable with delinquents and criminals and for some marriage and relational problems. Because of the potential for change in behavioral, affective, and cognitive areas, role playing may be used as a tool with any therapeutic approach, as a main technique or in combination with others. As a therapeutic tool it may elicit strong, often deeply repressed emotions, and for that reason is potentially very dangerous under the direction of untrained persons.

Reference
Moreno, J. L: *Psychodrama* (Vol. 1). New York: Beacon House, 1946.

Additional Reading
Corsini, R. J. *Roleplaying in psychotherapy.* Chicago: Aldine, 1966.

D. L. SCHUURMAN

See PSYCHODRAMA.

Role Reversal Technique. A psychodramatic technique in which the client "becomes" a significant other or a part of himself. The client assumes the body posture, speech qualities, mannerisms, and any other qualities unique to the other. Not always is the significant other a person. The client may reverse roles with such objects such as a painting, an automobile, a pet, or a term paper.

The purposes of the role reversal are 1) to allow the client to experience the thoughts and feelings of the other; 2) to create an awareness of the consequences of the client's behaviors; 3) to assist an auxiliary ego to play the role of the other; 4) to assist the director in determining the content of the relationship; and 5) to assist the group in forming a picture of the client's conflict.

J. H. VANDER MAY

See PSYCHODRAMA.

Rolfing. See STRUCTURAL INTEGRATION.

Rorschach, Hermann (1884–1922). Swiss psychiatrist who developed the inkblot test that bears his name. Born in Zurich, he was nicknamed Kleck (inkblot) in school because he was interested in sketching and his father was an art teacher. He attended the universities of Neuchâtel, Zurich, Berlin, and Bern between 1904 and 1909 and received his M.D. from the University of Zurich in 1912. After a few months' work in Russia he returned to Switzerland to work in mental hospitals there. He advocated psychoanalysis and was elected vice-president of the Swiss Psychoanalytic Society in 1919.

While in medical school Rorschach did some studies on how people react to inkblots, but he never published the results and abandoned the area to concentrate on psychoanalysis. In 1917 he came across the dissertation of a Polish student who had used an inkblot test of eight cards to study fantasy in normal people and psychotics. After reading this dissertation, he devoted all his energy to the creation of an inkblot test and the development of its rationale.

In 1918 he began experimenting with 15 inkblots, using his patients as subjects. At the same time he began work on his book, *Psychodiagnostik*. The manuscript and the inkblots were sent to seven publishers, who all rejected it. He finally found one to publish it, but on the condition that only 10 rather than 15 cards be used. When the book appeared in 1921, the printer had reduced the cards in size, altered the colors, and introduced shading into the uniformly black areas on the cards.

Rorschach presented his test to the Swiss Psychiatric Society and the Swiss Psychoanalytic Society, but they showed little interest. The book was a complete failure. Most of the copies remained unsold in the basement of the publisher. When it was reviewed before the German Society of Experimental Psychology, William Stern denounced it as faulty, arbitrary, and showing no understanding of the human personality.

In spite of the initial poor reception of his ideas Rorschach's inkblot test has come to be a well-accepted and standard tool for clinical psychologists. It is the most commonly employed projective test in the United States and is second only to the Wechsler Adult Intelligence Scale in overall usage. This is a tribute to Hermann Rorschach, whose considerable creative abilities were unrecognized by his own generation.

R. L. KOTESKEY

Rorschach Inkblot Test. A projective measure of personality developed by Swiss psychiatrist Hermann Rorschach. The test consists of 10 reproductions of inkblots printed on cardboard. In his work in asylums and psychiatric clinics Rorschach observed that emotionally disturbed persons tended to perceive objects in their environment in a unique manner. To quantify these observations he began to record patient responses to nonspecific, accidental forms. Rorschach eventually developed a set of forms which he made by throwing ink on paper and folding the paper in half, thus allowing the ink to spread onto both halves. The designs were simple yet suggestive. Rorschach described his instrument as a psychiatric experiment (Rorschach, 1964).

Procedures of administering the test have been standardized. The cards are first shown one at a time to the subject. The examiner carefully records the associations made by the subject to the blots. The second phase of the test, the inquiry, consists of reviewing all responses to further clarify which feature of the card was the main determinant used by the subject in forming the percept. Some systems of the Rorschach advocate a third phase of the administration, testing the limits, in which the examiner attempts to discover whether or not the subject is able to visualize the most common or frequently given responses.

Scoring a Rorschach protocol is a complicated task requiring extensive experience and training (Goldfried, Stricker, & Weiner, 1971). Each response is scored for its location on the blot itself, the main characteristic of the blot used to determine the response (form, color, perceived movement, or shading), the content of the response (objects, humans, animals, landscapes, etc.), and the general quality of the response.

Over the years several schools of Rorschach interpretation have evolved. Beck, Hertz, Klopfer, Piotrowski, and Rapaport and Schafer have all developed interpretive and scoring systems. While there is a great deal of similarity, there are also sufficient differences to breed confusion among researchers. Recently Exner (1974) has developed a comprehensive synthesis of previous Rorschach systems.

Critics argue that the test is more subjective than objective and that the Rorschach is essentially an interview rather than psychological test (Zubin, Eron, & Schumer, 1965). Advocates, on the other hand, claim that insights into personality dynamics, defense mechanisms, and reality orientation can be gleaned from the Rorschach (Schafer, 1954). Published findings include general works on frequency of responses and specific works such

as the Rorschach responses of Nazi leaders (Miale & Selzer, 1975).

References

Exner, J. E. *The Rorschach: A comprehensive system* (Vol. 1). New York: Wiley, 1974.

Goldfried, M. R., Stricker, G., & Weiner, I. B. *Rorschach handbook of clinical and research applications.* Englewood Cliffs, N.J.: Prentice-Hall, 1971.

Miale, F. R., & Selzer, M. *The Nuremberg mind: The psychology of the Nazi leaders.* New York: Quadrangle Books, 1975.

Rorschach, H. *Psychodiagnostics* (6th ed.). Bern: Hans Huber, 1964.

Schafer, R. *Psychoanalytic interpretation in Rorschach testing: Theory and application.* New York: Grune & Stratton, 1954.

Zubin, J., Eron, L. D., & Schumer, F. *Experimental approach to projective techniques.* New York: Wiley, 1965.

J. R. BECK

See PERSONALITY ASSESSMENT; PSYCHOLOGICAL MEASUREMENT.

Rosenthal Effect. *See* SELF-FULFILLING PROPHECY.

Ss

Sadism. *See* SEXUAL SADISM.

Satyriasis. *See* EXCESSIVE SEXUAL DESIRE.

Schizoaffective Disorder. Clinicians diagnose schizoaffective disorder when both schizophrenia and a major mood disturbance are present together. Such combinations of symptoms have been observed since the early 1900s, but the label *schizoaffective* was not applied until about 1930. However this diagnosis has been controversial from the beginning, and the latest psychiatric diagnostic manual (*DSM-III*) suggests the category may not be needed at all. It was kept only for those occasions when clinicians cannot make a differential diagnosis between schizophrenia and one of the major affective disorders. Prior to the most recent controversy about 6% of all schizophrenias were considered schizoaffective type.

The major symptom of schizophrenia found in schizoaffective disorder is a mental content that disregards reality. The person's behavior and thinking have a decidedly bizarre, illogical, and disorganized quality, as compared to that found in the affective psychoses. The person might also experience delusions and/or hallucinations, the variety of which is partially determined by mood.

The affective disturbance of schizoaffective disorder can be either the manic or depressed type. If manic, then elation, excitement, hyperactivity, and excessive energy will predominate. Pressured speech and rapid thoughts frequently occur. Sometimes increased assertiveness and occasional hostility toward others is seen.

If depressed the person is seen as despondent, with feelings of helplessness and hope-lessness. Some report a sense of unreality, lack of feeling, or pervasive sense of dread. Delusions about sin and guilt are not unusual. Severe sleep and appetite disruptions are common. Suicidal ideation, if found, must be taken seriously.

The etiology of this disorder is not understood but is probably linked to causes of both schizophrenia and major mood disturbances. Research on these two disorders, though not conclusive, suggests a combination of genetic and/or biochemical factors together with stresses in early development.

Treatment usually requires a combination of hospitalization, chemotherapy, and psychotherapy. As with most disorders early detection and treatment increase the probability of control or amelioration. Hospitalization is frequently needed to reduce the stress the person faces in his home environment. Chemotherapy with antipsychotic medication is common practice. Mood-altering drugs or lithium may also help. If medications do not improve the condition, electroconvulsive treatment is occasionally used. Psychotherapy will initially be supportive and focus on developing a stable trusting relationship with someone who is objective. Later in psychotherapy the person can begin to test out unrealistic thinking.

M. R. NELSON

Schizoid Disorder of Childhood or Adolescence. This disorder characterizes a child whose capacity to form close social relationships has been impaired for a minimum of three months. While the disorder is rare, it is more common in boys than girls.

Children with this disorder function within a constricted framework. Warm, loving feelings are not experienced and intimate, one-to-one relationships are avoided. They have no close friends of their own peer-group age; furthermore, they express no interest in developing such interpersonal relationships. While their preference is to be alone, an attachment may be made to a parent, an adult, or a similarly isolated child.

These children usually appear aloof and distant, reserved, withdrawn, remaining on an emotionally flat level of affect. If pressure is asserted to become socially involved, they may stubbornly resist. Socially they tend to appear uncomfortable, awkward, not knowing what to do or say. They avoid and show no interest in activities involving other children. They prefer reclusiveness and often seem vague or self-absorbed. Daydreaming, a means of escape from others, is frequent. It is common for academic performance to be impaired as well.

For some children this tendency to withdraw and to avoid others seems to shift to an increase in socializing during the adolescent years. For others the withdrawal and detachment only become more fixed, leading to the adult schizoid personality disorder or schizophrenia.

It is likely that a child with this disorder does not experience a deep sense of belonging or of being fully accepted as a person. The lack of basic trust dominating the individual's being and style of relating probably stems from the early symbiotic mother-child relationship during infancy. Most likely it is influenced by the anxieties and fears experienced during and after the infancy period. Cameron (1963) suggests that even with close body contact during infancy these children never felt accepted; they have not had freedom in expressing their feelings, particularly normal aggression and rage. Ordinary feelings are protected so carefully from the outside world that it is as though they are locked in a steel drawer. It seems as though the threat of criticism or lack of acceptance is too great to risk the expression of genuine feelings.

Isolation is experienced by the child from early life. The message from the mother seems to be, "You need no one but me," yet an ambivalent message of love and rejection is communicated to the child. The child remains loyal to the parent, experiencing the double bind, but does not break the bond even later in childhood. To do so would threaten the security in the relationship with the mother upon whom the child is very dependent. Due to this dependency on the mother the child cannot express anger about the isolation and lack of freedom being experienced; this impedes the child's

progress toward independence and increased social relationships with other children.

In addition to viewing this disorder as a reflection of a dyadic symbiosis between mother and child it is important to consider also the broader system (the entire nuclear family as well as parts of the extended family). The intense need for detachment is most probably a reflection of grossly disturbed object relations within this critically important reference group. The disturbance in object relations can assume many forms. One of the most common consists of a poorly differentiated family group ruled by reactive emotional enmeshments in which the child is given no opportunity to differentiate a self from the corporate family identity. Any move to attach to others outside the family, express emotions different from those of the parents, or demonstrate spontaneity is viewed as a betrayal of the family and is punished covertly or overtly. Eventually the child learns not to break the implicit, unspoken family rules governing these behaviors; in essence he or she stops relating to others.

Treating a child or adolescent with schizoid disorder is very difficult. The defense structure of detachment and isolation along with a lack of trust in others make establishing a relationship with such a patient very difficult. It requires a great deal of patience and energy on the part of the therapist. This is particularly true when an individual psychotherapy model is used.

In a family therapy model the focus would be on all the members of the family, not only the identified patient. Here it is possible to investigate the family's means of communicating caring, affection, anger, and individuation. As the dynamics are explored, relationship bonds and the rules for living in this family become more apparent. In the information-gathering process a new way of communicating is being developed—i.e., the family's means of relating is made more explicit. Such modeling helps the identified patient to become aware of the appropriateness of talking about feelings in this safe environment, and it shows how people can share feelings without fragmenting themselves or their families.

References

Cameron, N. A. *Personality development and psychopathology.* Boston: Houghton Mifflin, 1963.

B. J. SHEPPERSON

Schizoid Personality Disorder. Individuals with this disorder fail to form social and intimate relationships effectively. They seem to lack warm feelings and are indifferent to the feelings, praise, or even the criticism of others. They show little desire to become socially involved, have few if any friends, and prefer being alone. They react to emotional situations with detachment and thus appear to be aloof. They often are humorless and dull. They rarely date or marry.

Until the appearance of *DSM-III* the term *schizoid* was used a great deal more broadly than it is at present. In the past it included almost all the patients who would now be classified as schizotypal personality disorder. These patients show thought, speech, and behavior patterns that are seen in schizophrenia but not the full manifestation of the psychosis. Many called schizoid in the past would now be considered avoidant or dependent personality disorders. Avoidant personalities do not relate well either, but show a yearning for relationship and extreme sensitivity to the feelings of others that are not seen in the schizoid. The dependent personalities are shy, less self-confident, and find it impossible to be alone.

Drawing these distinctions will help to clarify this group of disorders more precisely in the future. They all seem to be associated with disorders of very early object relations. The infant in his early interactions with another person requires a certain amount of response from that significant other. At one level the infant requires that his needs be met reasonably effectively and promptly. At a more complex level he needs appropriate feedback from his overtures of emotion, gesture, or play. At a still more complex level the child needs a response of gratitude for something of value given to the other. In the schizoid personality there is a failure or frustration of this reciprocal interaction, probably at the second or third level. Whether this is due to some defect in the perception of the child or the failure of the parent to provide adequate responses, or both, remains an unsolved question at the present.

In the meantime this reordering of categories has caused some difficulty in applying the results of previous research in the schizoid personality to these new groups. For example, some have had a strong impression that the schizoid personality is genetically linked with schizophrenia and even may be a premorbid manifestation of that disorder (Heston, 1970; Kallmann, 1946). When the schizotypal personality is left out of the research sample, this may not hold true.

Furthermore, the available evidence does not seem to indicate that the schizoid personality disorder naturally develops into schizophrenia. The long-term prognosis of these patients is good (Morris, Soroker, Burruss, 1954). As children they are often well-behaved, easily disciplined, and rarely aggressive. They seem to be little troubled by their social isolation and may actually be effectively involved in hobbies, intellectual activity, or even employment that does not require interacting with others.

Patients with a schizoid personality disorder usually seek therapy because they are depressed. But even when depression is severe, they are often referred by others who seem more aware of the sadness than does the patient. Patients rarely complain about their isolation, but occasionally a parent or mate will press them to be treated for this as well.

Treatment is usually difficult, since most therapists are accustomed to working within a warm and responsive relationship. Schizoid persons give little or no access to their inner life, either because it is not accessible to them or because they have little interest in it themselves. The therapeutic process is slow and laborious, and must be focused on the subtle interactions that occur during therapy. It is particularly important to emphasize those mirroring interchanges that reenact the ones which were deficient in infancy. These patients do respond to treatment and often get more benefit than seems possible.

Medication is usually of little benefit, and social support systems are difficult to develop. The support of a warm and loving church is particularly helpful, though the therapist or someone else must often actively encourage the fellowship to keep working with this person. Some are helped by more formal group therapy. The typical schizoid personality rarely stays involved without almost constant urging from others.

References

Heston, L. L. The genetics of schizophrenia and schizoid disease. *Science*, 1970, *167*, 249–256.

Kallmann, F. J. The genetic theory of schizophrenia: An analysis of 691 schizophrenic twin index families. *American Journal of Psychiatry*, 1946, *103*, 309–322.

Morris, D. P., Soroker, E., & Burruss, G. Follow-up studies of shy, withdrawn children. *American Journal of Orthopsychiatry*, 1954, *24*, 743–754.

C. M. BERRY

See PERSONALITY DISORDERS.

Schizophrenia. A clinical syndrome in which there is widespread disturbance of feeling, mood, and thought. The diagnosis is not made unless there is great intrapsychic pain, a breakdown of the ability to work effectively, and serious disordering of relationships. Since the appearance of *DSM-III* the diagnosis is still not made until the symptoms have persisted over at least six months.

The most intense form of schizophrenia occurs during the psychotic break, and this is its central clinical feature. These breaks, or complete disorganizations of the personality, typically occur in a young person, come on suddenly, and often have trivial provocation. Delusions and hallucinations are usually present, often occurring explosively. Since this "craziness" violates some innate human sense of order and coherence, such an event is terrifying, creating chaos in both the sufferer and those around. At the same time those who have had experience with schizophrenia recognize even in these psychotic responses something that is common to all persons, a disturbing caricature of elements that are fundamental to being human. Sullivan called schizophrenia a "human disease." This paradox of psychosis being both an alien and a familiar experience has made the schizophrenic the object of both reverence and hostility since early historical times.

Even though schizophrenia is frequently seen by health care professionals, and absorbs nearly one-half of the funds expended on mental health, it is not now generally thought of as a discrete disease. We have not arrived at any consensus within the profession as to either the cause or the nature of the condition, nor even exactly what is going on within the mind of the patient during this psychosis. There seem to be several patterns in which the condition develops and runs its course, and these may turn out to be different diseases. It also may still turn out to be something better considered as a single disease.

Since schizophrenia is such an ominous, destructive condition, the use of the term has been criticized by many as doing injury to the person so diagnosed. Yet there are so many afflicted, and so intensely so, that some term is needed to collect what information we do have about its nature and care. To avoid using a label enhances its mystery and creates more problems than it solves. Even with these reservations, the concept of an illness and the term *schizophrenia* are sufficiently useful to continue their use.

These diagnostic difficulties have made the vast research data somewhat confusing, but we do know that people fitting this description occur at a rate of about 8 to 10 per 1,000 rather consistently over different times and cultures. The pain, the economic loss, and the human burden these people place on any society have made schizophrenia always a matter of great public concern. In recent years the use of medication has radically changed the management of schizophrenia, but it continues to be our largest single public health problem.

The Syndrome. *Acute form.* When one becomes psychotic, there is a drastic change in how the world is perceived. These perceptual changes follow two courses. The most acute is the psychotic break. Here there is a marked change in affect, thought, and activity. The affect might be blunted, flat, or distinctly inappropriate. Almost universally there are intrusions of delusions into the thoughts and of hallucinations into the sensorium. The activity level frequently changes, and the person becomes either excited or withdrawn. Behavior then responds more or less appropriately to this disordered view of the world by becoming irrational, violent, withdrawn, or rigidly immobile.

Delusions are a central phenomenon of classical schizophrenia and at the same time its most puzzling feature. These are unquestioned convictions that seem to be implanted in the mind without valid evidence. By definition they are bizarre in that the content is patently absurd or at least has not reasonable basis in fact. They are experienced intensely, often with more assurance than even the strongest convictions of the normal mind. Because of this, one is not able to change them either by argument or evidence. They are often of a theological nature, even in people who usualy are not religious. Also, paranoid delusions of persecution are almost universal. With both, grandiosity is manifested by great self-confidence and often by the supreme assurance that the patient is the center of national, international, or even cosmic interest.

Delusions concerning changes in the nature of the body or its parts are not uncommon. A man might complain that his tissue is melting or turning to stone. There is often a change in how thoughts are experienced. For example, some schizophrenics become convinced that their thoughts are being broadcast at large against their will, or that others are inserting thoughts into their heads. A man once complained that "my brain is like a motor transmission that is broken down and the thoughts can't go through." These changes in the perception of mental function are rarely seen in any other condition, and when they do occur almost always indicate schizophrenia.

Hallucinations are distinct auditory sounds, usually human voices, that are experienced as coming from outside of the person hearing them. In schizophrenia they often are accusatory, make a running commentary on behavior or thoughts, or sometimes involve a conversation between several voices. They are usually disturbing but can be benign, even occasionally keeping an elderly person company.

The schizophrenic holds to his delusions and hallucinations doggedly, though paradoxically realizing that they are not "real." If one is asked, "Do you hear voices that are not there?" the answer is usually yes, though in other situations the person would be aware of the absurdity of such a question.

At first glance, because the thinking is so illogical, changes in thought or cognition seem to be at the center of schizophrenia; it seems to be a thought disorder. Almost always one can see ambivalence, or the easy acceptance of rationally opposite and mutually exclusive thoughts. An example of ambivalence is the awareness of both the reality and the unreality of the hallucinations. Opposite things are often equal, as in primary process thinking. Also, associations are said to be loose, or there is a lack of coherence in the way thoughts in sequence relate to each other; the thoughts seem to jump from one subject to another without logical connection. Most observers feel that these loose associations are actually rational, but that the patient does not express the connecting links. It is as though the schizophrenic assumes that the other person is mysteriously a party to his thoughts and stating associations is not necessary.

Speech is frequently disturbed in schizophrenia. Sometimes it is hurried, as though it were being pressured by rapid thoughts. Occasionally the opposite is true, and there is a marked poverty of both flow and content. On occasion words may flow out in a stream with no meaning whatsoever, or as what is called WORD SALAD.

Chronic form. A second manifestation of schizophrenia is the more chronic disorder, occurring before, between, and after these breaks. Here the wildness of the acute episode may not be seen, but the schizophrenic is rarely normal. Almost universally schizophrenics are awkward, socially inept, as though they are unable to tune into the social situation. Their shyness and insensitivity to the feelings of others make the adolescence of the schizophrenic very unhappy, since being able to feel and mold to the environment is of paramount importance in these years. Patients often try to conceal this deficit by stilted behavior or by assuming a stylized role within the group. Since schizophrenics rarely understand the nature of their problem, their lives are a series of repeated failures, resulting in a profound loss of self-esteem.

The schizophrenic also often has difficulty with employment. Many are simply unemployable, whatever effort is made to help them. They rarely are able to function at a level appropriate to their intelligence and skills. Their strangeness breeds lack of trust, and their insensitivity keeps them from working easily with others.

On occasion schizophrenics may seem to have minimal problems. Even here, on closer scrutiny, they are found to have odd ideas, involvement in superstitions and mental telepathy, or overvalued ideas of their own importance. They often are convinced that they have some sixth sense about other people and events, that they can feel others' feelings, or others can feel theirs. Many times there is a conviction in the observer that there is some eerie truth to these assumptions—the schizophrenic does seem to be clairvoyant.

Pathogenesis. What produces schizophrenia in a given individual? Even the most experienced experts can give no answer that is supported by common agreement. There are several schools of thought with rational explanations of the major phenomena, each with enthusiastic supporters. The great volume of research has served to elaborate these theories without clearly establishing one or another. A few of the more prominent of these are discussed here.

Psychoanalytic theories. Analysts usually begin with Freud's (1894/1962) fundamental insights into defense neuropsychoses. Freud believed that the particular symptoms of any mental abnormality can best be understood as a defensive response to intolerable psychic pain. The stress placed on the ego to mediate between powerful libidinal or aggressive drives and the more repressive social demands of the real world produces enough pain to demand relief. Psychosis or a complete mental breakdown is the last defensive maneuver available to the embattled ego.

Freud (1911/1958) applied these fundamental concepts to a paranoid breakdown. In response to stress Schreber, the patient, regressed to an earlier fixation around an unresolved homosexual attachment to his father. The threat of homosexuality in the face of its unbearable social disgrace produced a generalized withdrawal of libidinal energy from outside objects. This concentration of libido within the ego is the fundamental mechanism of the grandiosity of the paranoid. The delusions of persecution result from projections of this internal grandiosity and aggression onto the environment.

A great deal of analytic thought has enriched these fundamental insights since Freud's time. Klein (1949) laid the foundation of our contemporary understanding of object relations in her efforts to understand schizophrenia, seeing it as resulting from a failure of the mothering person to provide secure need satisfaction for the very young infant. The concept of a nurturing, or "good enough," maternal environment has been enlarged by Winnicott (1958), and the complex relationships of the primary objects of self and other by Mahler (1968).

Hartmann (1954) related the fundamental psychic conflict at the center of schizophrenia more to aggression than to libidinal forces. In Hartmann's view the outbursts of psychic energy of the psychotic break then secondarily disrupt perception, logical thought, and human relationships. These changing perceptual patterns determine the particular symptoms in an individual, but frustrated aggressive drives are at the base of all severe mental illness.

Menninger (Hall, 1959) added the social thinking of Adolph Meyer, seeing schizophrenia as a particularly violent reaction to pressure, with outside events more important than intrapsychic conflicts. This line of thought has had a powerful influence on the mental health field. One reason for this is the universal observation that schizophrenics do indeed suffer great stress in life, and a particularly stressful event often ushers in the psychotic breakdown. It is more difficult to conceptualize stress as the critical factor since many other individuals, subjected to the same or even worse conditions, do not develop schizophrenia.

Social theories. A second series of theoretical formulations regarding the etiology of schizophrenia emphasizes social influences. Sullivan (1953a, 1953b) identified profoundly disordered interpersonal relationships in these patients and saw this failure to establish intimacy as more damaging than more nebulous intrapsychic mechanisms. This emphasis has been the source of a good deal of work by such theorists as Fromm-Reichmann (1950) and Jacobson (1967).

More recently this line of thought has focused on the family, particularly the developing child's communications within the home. This thinking has gone in many directions, but the works of Lidz, Bateson, and Wynne have dominated the literature.

Ruth and Theodore Lidz (Lidz, Fleck, & Cornelison, 1965) studied mother-child interactions in schizophrenics and identified a tendency for these parents to foster a parasitic relationship in the child. In a study of the bonding in these homes two patterns emerged. In *marital skew* one partner so dominates the home that there is little or no opportunity for the individuation of others. In *marital schism* the parents are so divided that they receive no nurture from each other and lean too heavily on the children for their emotional needs. In either case the child tends to develop a severely pathological, defensive self-centeredness that prohibits normal psychological growth.

Bateson (Bateson, Jackson, Haley, & Weakland, 1956) studied another disorder he identified in the families of schizophrenics: the DOUBLE BIND. The term has become a very popular one, meaning almost any kind of conflicting statements. Technically the double bind describes a situation where a child is given a powerful negative injunction and at the same time an opposite command at a more abstract level. In the same process a third pressure is exerted to prevent escape. When this dilemma is repeatedly experienced in the home, this disordered thinking is reproduced within the child and forms the nidus of his or her own psychosis.

Wynne, Ryckoff, Day, and Hirsch (1958) describe a very common pattern seen in schizophrenic families in which there are powerful forces directed at the child to conform to role patterns that are defined by some system other than his own individuality. The establishment of real relationships, warmth, and support in such families is attempted by a pseudomutuality, or by role playing love and intimacy. The child in this home not only lacks nurture but also learns disordered patterns of communication. It is the threat of this complex, fragile system disintegrating under the real but unmet needs of the family that eventuates in the breakdown of schizophrenia.

Anyone with any experience dealing with the families of schizophrenics sees these patterns repeated again and again. Two difficulties arise when one attempts to make family disturbances the major factor in producing schizophrenia. For one thing, these same patterns are also very common in the families of patients suffering from other forms of serious psychopathology. Again, children who have grown up in homes completely dominated by a schizophrenic parent often not only survive intact but do well. One must then hypothesize that the disease will not occur without some defect in the capacity of the child to cope with such a difficult environment.

Biological theories. With the discovery of the major tranquilizers and their widespread use in schizophrenia beginning in the 1950s, biological influences have received a great deal of attention by theorists attempting to understand schizophrenia. These medications were found to influence the transmission of impulses from one neuron to another in the brain. This research into the neurotransmitters has gone in many directions, all fruitful in increasing the available data, yet none convincingly giving us a comprehensive unitary theory (Snyder, Banarjee, Yamamura, & Greenberg, 1974).

Since these brain amines can serve several different systems, changes in their activity could give a rational explanation of how so many different brain functions can change so rapidly in schizophrenia. However, the problem of understanding the psychopathology of something like schizophrenia on this basis is complicated by the observation that changes in these neurotransmitters can occur as a result of environmental events. Moreover, as yet there is not a clear answer to the question of what causes these chemical changes to take place spontaneously in the usual psychotic break. Whether this research will ever answer the greater question of the cause of schizophrenia or not, the use of these medications has radically improved our ability to care for the patient.

The fact that schizophrenia has a hereditary component also has encouraged many to seek a genetic explanation of the disease (Kety, 1976; Kendler, 1983). The incidence of the disorder in children of a schizophrenic parent seems to be about 8%. When both parents are schizophrenic, this rises to nearly 30%. In siblings the incidence is about 12% while in identical twins there is approximately a 50% chance of both having the illness.

Since siblings are ordinarily reared in similar environments, research has been undertaken in twins who were separated in infancy to distinguish the genetic from environmental influences. The incidence in twins reared by different families seems to be very similar to those in the same home. The fact that the father seems to have about the same genetic influence as the mother tends to rule out some unidentified intrauterine influence. Obviously these studies have been undertaken on small numbers of subjects and are difficult to make precise, but at the present they strongly suggest that there is a major genetic influence in the etiology of schizophrenia.

The fact that about half of identical twins do not both become schizophrenic is also of interest. Most commentators deduce from this that other influences must also be present before the disease will occur. Another way of explaining this would be that the syndrome can be produced in two ways; genetically and by some early brain injury such as a viral encephalitis. Should this hypothesis be confirmed, then the genetic form might be much more powerfully mediated by genes than can now be proven.

The Natural History of Schizophrenia. Schizophrenic breakdowns characteristically occur under stress. This is often a loss, especially of someone upon whom the patient has been dependent. In other cases pressure brought on the patient to do something that is impossible seems to cause a decompensation. The stresses of late adolescence to form a gratifying relationship with someone of the opposite sex or to get a job to support independence and self-esteem commonly seem instrumental in psychotic breaks.

The pressure to become independent, when it is impossible, usually brings conflict with the parents, either actual or fantasized. The grandiosity of the psychosis is ego restorative, in that it relieves the pain of the loss of self-esteem.

Another common crisis associated with the onset of schizophrenia originates in sexual problems. The psychotic break is often accompanied by a regression of the normal adolescent sexual development. The patient loses some of the sharp focus of sexuality around genital, gender-specific objects and finds sexual desire more diffused. When this occurs, the fear often strikes patients that they are becoming homosexual. Many times there is a soft childishness about them at this time that makes them attractive to people who are actually homosexual, encouraging sexual advances. The response of the patient is often violent, an event called homosexual panic.

In the acute form of schizophrenia these issues of self-esteem, conflict with parents over dependency, and homosexuality are almost universal. It is important to remember that they are only rarely significant after the acute attacks have subsided.

Even when the disorder is not ushered in by an acute break, its onset may be associated with stress, but here it is often around changes of the life cycle. Graduation from high school, marriage, childbirth, a promotion, menopause, and even the general deterioration of the older years involve the stress of change, and might explain why the onset occurs so frequently at these transition points of life.

The course any individual may follow once the syndrome develops is unpredictable. Approximately one quarter of those who experience an acute psychotic break will ultimately do well. This would include many who later are more precisely diagnosed as schizophreniform disorder and other psychoses. Of those who are indeed schizophrenic, the recovery rate will be less than 10%.

Approximately half of all true schizophrenics will have a chronic course in which the patient is severely limited and suffers distress over years. In the past such people have occupied the back wards of the old mental hospitals. These facilities grew and grew until they cared for thousands. One of the most optimistic hopes of the new care systems introduced in Great Britain and the United States during the 1960s was that these patients could live at home and get professional care in mental health centers close by.

The remaining patients will continue to suffer recurrent acute episodes or struggle with major limitation. Assisting this group to a more rewarding life offers our greatest challenge.

Management. Achieving the best possible management of the schizophrenic is a demanding task. The greatest single difficulty is the characteristic lack of insight; the patient lacks the capacity to understand that the major problem lies within himself. Schizophrenics almost universally project the blame for their failures and difficulties entirely on others and are often hostile to helpers. Over time, and with repeated failures, more insight does seem to develop, and then management must be broadened to include other things. If any of the following measures is inadequate, the overall program must be considered to be unstable.

Medication. Care at one time or another will almost always include medication. In general the positive symptoms, such as hallucinations, delusions, and severely disordered thinking, ususally respond well to proper medication. The negative symptoms, such as social ineptitude and most of the problems of the residual phase, are not much helped. In many instances medication given in lower doses over the life of the patient will reduce or control the recurrence of acute psychotic breaks. Since there are occasional adverse effects of long-term usage of the major tranquilizers used, the physician who is experienced in the use of these agents and knows the patient well will achieve the most benefit at the least risk.

Psychotherapy. This is universally considered important in the management of the schizophrenic. There is less agreement on what it is in the therapeutic relationship that helps, but everyone concedes that the patience of the therapist, as well as the capacity to maintain respect for the patient through a series of trials, is fundamental. Psychotherapists successfully treating schizophrenics invariably do respect the patient and the illness, and see in these unfortunate people something of real value. A steady attitude of love and hope is in itself therapeutic, since of all patients these are the most sensitive and responsive to the person and mindset of the therapist.

Once effective rapport has been established, there are two goals of psychotherapy. The first is supportive, which includes a wide range of schooling in essential living skills. It begins with the careful explanation to the family of what is wrong, what it means, and how they are involved in the process. Beyond this, supportive therapy rallies and trains a support system around the patient, even acting occasionally as an advocate in struggles with the larger community, especially those inevitable bureaucracies that tyrannize the life of the chronic schizophrenic. In no other patient is this kind of general support more important.

A second goal of psychotherapy is understanding. Until this understanding has been achieved, individual episodes are sealed over in the consciousness of the schizophrenic and nothing is learned. Again, the psychotherapy of these patients is difficult, but it will reduce recurrences and make life easier.

Community. Schizophrenics are ordinarily more sensitive than the normal person to the human need for community. They often perceive the family, the neighborhood, the ward, or any other group as a concrete and compelling unity, not the optional gathering the normal person sees. For this reason group therapy, milieu management, and establishment of a familylike situation is both difficult and imperative. An ideal context for treatment would be within a loving community where both the problems and the gifts of the patient are appreciated.

Employment. Insofar as the schizophrenic is sensitive to the reality of the community he feels a profound responsibility to contribute to its work. If he is unemployed, he feels guilty and loses confidence and prestige. Often getting the chronic schizophrenic into a steady job is a herculean task; but until this is accomplished, the overall management must be considered inadequate.

Marriage. The most difficult of all goals to achieve is an adequate marriage. At best the mate needs great patience and a determination to make the marriage and family work against many obstacles. The primary therapist needs either to support this person or see that it is done by others.

References

Bateson, G., Jackson, D. D., Haley, J., & Weakland, J. Toward a theory of schizophrenia. *Behavioral Science,* 1956, *1,* 251–264.

Freud, S. The neuro-psychoses of defence. In J. Strachey (Ed. and trans.), *The standard edition of the complete psychological works of Sigmund Freud* (Vol. 3). London: Hogarth, 1962. (Orginially published, 1894.)

Freud, S. Psycho-analytic notes on an autobiographical account of a case of paranoia (dementia paranoides). In J. Strachey (Ed. and trans.), *The standard edition of the complete psychological works of Sigmund Freud* (Vol. 12). London: Hogarth, 1958. (Originally published, 1911.)

Fromm-Reichmann, F. *Principles of intensive psychotherapy.* Chicago: University of Chicago Press, 1950.

Hall, B. H. (Ed.). *A psychiatrist's world: The selected papers of Karl Menninger, M.D.* New York: Viking, 1959.

Hartmann, H. Contribution to the metapsychology of schizophrenia. *Psychoanalytic Study of the Child,* 1954, *8,* 177–198.

Jacobson, E. Psychotic conflict and reality. New York: International Universities Press, 1967.

Kendler, K. S. Overview: A current perspective on twin studies of schizophrenia. *American Journal of Psychiatry,* 1983, *140,* 1413–1425.

Kety, S. S. Genetic aspects of schizophrenia. *Psychiatric Annals,* 1976, *6,* 11–32.

Klein, M. [The significance of early anxiety situations in the development of the ego.] In E. Jones (Ed.), *The psychoanalysis of children (3rd ed.).* London: Hogarth, 1949.

Lidz, T., Fleck, S., & Cornelison, A. R., *Schizophrenia and the family.* New York: International Universities Press, 1965.

Mahler, M. S. *On human symbiosis and the vicissitudes of individuation.* New York: International Universities Press, 1968.

Snyder, S. H., Banerjee, S. P., Yamamura, H. I., & Greenberg, D. Drugs, neurotransmitters, and schizophrenia. *Science,* 1974, *184,* 1243–1253.

Sullivan, H. S. *The interpersonal theory of psychiatry.* New York: Norton, 1953. (a)

Sullivan, H. S. *Conceptions of modern psychiatry* (2nd ed.). New York: Norton, 1953. (b)

Winnicott, D. W. The observation of infants in a set situation. In D. W. Winnicott, *Collected papers.* London: Tavistock, 1958.

Wynne, L. C., Ryckoff, I. M., Day, J., & Hirsch, S. I., Pseudo-mutuality in family relations of schizophrenics. *Psychiatry,* 1958, *21,* 205–220.

Additional Readings

Arieti, S. *Understanding and helping the schizophrenic.* New York: Basic Books, 1979.

Buss, A. H., & Buss, E. H. (Eds.), *Theories of schizophrenia.* New York: Atherton, 1969.

Gunderson, J. G., & Mosher, L. R. (Eds.), *Psychotherapy of schizophrenia.* New York: Aronson, 1975.

Kasanin, J. S. (Ed.), *Language and thought in schizophrenia.* New York: Norton, 1944.

C. M. BERRY

See PSYCHOTIC DISORDERS.

Schizophreniform Disorder.

A new diagnostic category in *DSM-III.* Diagnosis is made when an acute functional psychosis, indistinguishable from schizophrenia, occurs and remits within six months. The inclusion of this category encourages a distinction between brief, remitting psychoses and the longer lasting, more degenerative manifestations of schizophrenia.

This distinction was made early by Kraeplin (1919), who proposed a division of psychotic patients into two distinct categories: dementia praecox, currently called schizophrenia, and manic-depressive insanity. Dementia praecox followed an inevitably deteriorating course, while manic-depressives tended to recover. Later on, this dichotomy between the affective psychoses and schizophrenia was thought of more as a continuum, with patients falling along a bimodal curve, than as two distinct illnesses.

It soon became apparent that an important group of patients was found along the curve between these two. They tended to be young, with an acute onset, usually associated with an identifiable traumatic event. Affective features were common, and the course and prognosis much more favorable than schizophrenia. Since there was this vital difference in prognosis, a good deal of research has gone into understanding this illness and defining its differences from other functional psychoses (Tsuang, Dempsey, & Rauscher, 1976).

Kasanin (1933) designated this group as *schizoaffective,* and this has been the most commonly used term since then. This usage emphasizes the affective components that are seen many times in the acute symptom complex.

Other investigators emphasized the identifiable stress factors that characteristically were associated with the breakdown of this group but not necessarily with affective patients. They also tended to have a much more normal premorbid course than the schizophrenics. Langfeldt (1939) first used the term *schizophreniform psychosis* to describe these patients. Vaillant (1964) proposed the use of the term *remitting schizophrenia,* feeling that the affective symptoms and family history were not necessary features. Many other terms have been used since then, indicating the usefulness of defining the illness.

Since the *DSM-III* proposal, research has still not sharpened the boundaries of this category. Fogelson and his associates selected a group of patients in an outpatient clinic. In these patients the schizophreniform disorder did appear to be distinct from—though it was associated with—mania and depression in the personal and family histories (Fogelson, Cohen, & Pope, 1982). On the other hand, Coryell and Tsuang (1982) reviewed the group of patients considered schizophrenics who had been seen in the University of Iowa clinics between 1925 and 1950. They selected a list of those who would now be called schizophreniform and found that they resembled schizophrenics much more closely in both initial symptoms and family data.

Either way, the condition occurs frequently enough and is sufficiently distinct in its course and management that it has elicited a great deal of research attention. For the time being, delineating it simply by duration seems to be wise, though in the future we might hope that nuclear characteristics will be defined clearly enough to make these the basis of categorizing it.

In the meantime the best policy seems to be to reserve the term *schizophreniform disorder* for patients with an acute onset psychosis, who have demonstrated good premorbid functioning and who often appear to have affective features. The diagnosis of schizophrenia should be delayed until the course has extended over at least six months.

The acute episode is best managed as though the patient were schizophrenic, usually with major tranquilizers. When the onset is associated with depression, and particularly when there is a rapid remission of symptoms, the use of antidepressants in follow-up should be considered. In those patients who are manic at onset and who have a personal or family history of mania, lithium should be considered for the long-term management (Fogelson, et al., 1982).

References

Coryell, W., & Tsuang, M. T. DSM-III schizophreniform disorder. *Archives of General Psychiatry*, 1982, *39*, 66–69.

Forgelson, D. L., Cohen, B. M., & Pope, H. G., Jr. A study of DSM-III schizophreniform disorder. *American Journal of Psychiatry*, 1982, *139*, 1281–1285.

Kasanin, J. The acute schizoaffective psychoses. *American Journal of Psychiatry*, 1933, *13*, 97–126.

Kraeplin, E. *Dementia praecox and paraphrenia.* Edinburgh: E & S Livingstone, 1919.

Langfeldt, G. *The schizophreniform states.* Copenhagen: E. Munksgaard, 1939.

Tsuang, M. T., Dempsey, M., & Rauscher, F. A study of "atypical schizophrenia." *Archives of General Psychiatry*, 1976, *33*, 1157–1160.

Vaillant, G. E. Prospective prediction of schizophrenic remission. *Archives of General Psychiatry*, 1964, *11*, 509–518.

Additional Readings

Procci, W. R. Schizo-affective psychosis: Fact or fiction? *Archives of General Psychiatry*, 1976, *33*, 1167–1178.

Vaillant, G. An historical review of the remitting schizophrenias. *Journal of Nervous and Mental Diseases*, 1964, *138*, 48–56.

C. M. BERRY

Schizophrenogenic. *See* MOTHER, SCHIZOPHRENOGENIC.

Schizotypal Personality Disorder. A diagnosis used to describe those individuals whose general personality functioning is characterized by highly idiosyncratic perceptions, thought processes, behavior, and speech. Although their condition is not severe enough to warrant a diagnosis of schizophrenia, such persons will appear to be quite odd and unusual to those around them.

The symptoms associated with this disorder include at least four of the following: magical thinking (e.g., superstitiousness, clairvoyance, telepathy, bizarre fantasies or preoccupations); ideas of reference (the impression that the conversation or behavior of other persons has reference to oneself); social isolation or withdrawal; recurrent illusions (e.g., sensing the presence of a person or force not actually present, depersonalization); odd speech that is digressive, vague, overelaborate, circumstantial, or metaphorical; constricted or inappropriate affect that interferes with normal social interactions; paranoid ideation or marked suspiciousness; and undue social anxiety or hypersensitivity to real or imagined criticism (*DSM-III*). Associated features may include varying mixtures of anxiety, depression, and other dysphoric moods, as well as occasional transient psychotic symptoms during times of unusual stress. Schizotypal personalities may also hold rather eccentric convictions, such as bigotry, or fanatical religious beliefs.

Symptoms typically associated with the schizotypal disorder are usually of a chronic, long-term nature. These symptoms often first appear during adolescence. What may initially seem to be isolated, unrelated traits later become inflexible and rigid maladaptive patterns as the individual approaches early adulthood (Buss, 1966). Thus the unusual thinking and behavior are not the result of a reaction to a particular stressful event. Instead, this chronic maladaptive pattern markedly interferes with social and occupational functioning throughout most of the person's adult life (Gallatin, 1982). Such individuals rarely become truly schizophrenic, and most successfully avoid psychiatric hospitalization.

Differential diagnosis is a rather difficult task. A history of an active phase of schizophrenia with psychotic symptoms differentiates this disorder from schizophrenia, residual type. The oddities of behavior, thinking, perception, and speech distinguish it from schizoid and avoidant personality disorders, as well as depersonalization disorder. Frequently those diagnosed as borderline personality disorder also meet the criteria for schizotypal personality disorder, making it nearly impossible to differentiate between the two. In such cases both diagnoses are sometimes used simultaneously.

The precise etiology of this personality disorder remains unknown. Many theories abound, attributing this pattern of behavior to everything from genetic to environmental factors. Perhaps the origin of the disorder can best be thought of as being the result of an arrested or deviated development of the personality. This is eventually associated with a failure to establish an identity with constructive and socially useful adaptations, poor impulse control, and inappropriate or inadequate interpersonal skills (Kolb & Brodie, 1982). Whether this is the result of a genetic or teratogenic fetal insult or the lack of proper parenting and nurturance remains to be determined.

Treatment of such individuals is a very difficult undertaking. Their inability to form a working alliance with the therapist often frustrates attempts to conduct therapy in a more psychoanalytic or psychodynamic modality, with a few exceptions. Since they typically seek psychotherapy only during times of situational crisis or unusual stress, when their anxiety or depression becomes severe enough to cause noticeable distress, therapeutic approaches that are more short-term, behavioral, supportive, cognitive, directive, goal oriented, symptom focusing, and reality oriented will most likely have the greatest potential for success. The adjunctive use of medications is typically not very helpful, other than possibly to decrease the severity of troubling dysphoric moods during unusually stressful times. Antipsychotic medications have been ineffective in eliminating the bizarre characteristics of speech, behavior, thinking, and perceptions typically present. Such individuals are likely to terminate psychotherapy prematurely, usually as soon as the crisis that precipitated the contact is resolved. Only in rare cases will they remain beyond this point and undertake a more long-term, reconstructive form of psychotherapy. To result in more permanent personality changes, such treatment may last several years.

It should be noted that the use of the term *schizotypal personality* is of rather recent origin. Before *DSM-III* such individuals were typically diagnosed as simple schizophrenics or pseudoneurotic schizophrenics (Gallatin, 1982). The current nomenclature is perhaps more precise in that it draws attention to the chronic, nonpsychotic pattern that usually characterizes the entire adult life of such an individual.

References
Buss, A. H. *Psychopathology*. New York: Wiley, 1966.
Gallatin, J. E. *Abnormal psychology: Concepts, issues and trends*. New York: Macmillan, 1982.
Kolb, L. C., & Brodie, H. K. *Modern clinical psychiatry* (10th ed.). Philadelphia: Saunders, 1982.

J. D. Guy, Jr.

See Personality Disorders.

School Phobia. *See* Separation Anxiety Disorder of Childhood or Adolescence.

School Psychology. The beginnings of school psychology in America are usually associated with two events: the work of Lightner Witmer of the University of Pennsylvania and the establishment of a child study center in the Chicago Public Schools in 1899. As the result of his experience in diagnosing and treating children with learning difficulties Witmer recommended in 1896 to the American psychological Association that men be trained "to a new profession which will be exercised more particularly in connection with educational problems but for which the training of the psychologist will be prerequisite" (Magary, 1967, pp. 8–9). More than half a century later the Thayer Conference on School Psychology defined the school psychologist as "a psychologist with training and experience in education. He uses his special knowledge of assessment, learning, and interpersonal relationships to assist school personnel to enrich the experience and growth of all children, and to recognize and deal with exceptional children" (Cutts, 1955, p. 30).

In 1967 Division 16 of the American Psychological Association (School Psychology) established standards for the training of the school psychologist. Such training is to include the basic concepts of psychology through extensive theoretical and experimental study as well as training in clinical techniques. In order to apply this understanding in the school setting the school psychologist must also be well trained in education and experienced in work in the school setting (Magary, 1967). Although certification and university degree programs presently differ from state to state and from institution to institution, most require training and/or experience in both psychology and education. However, the balance between psychology and education differs considerably from program to program.

In the beginning school psychologists functioned primarily as testers and diagnosticians who presented their findings and recommendations to administrators, teachers, and parents. Increasingly, however, school psychologists have moved away from this role. Instead of working exclusively with problem children, the school psychologist now fosters sound mental health climates for all children through consultation with teachers and administrators. More time is spent working with small groups in diagnostic, remedial, and therapeutic activities than with individuals. Seriously disturbed children are referred to outside professionals or clinics rather than being treated in the school setting. School psychologists spend an increasing amount of time consulting with teachers and administrators, and in applying current findings of developmental, social, and physiological psychology to the school setting.

References

Cutts, N. E. (Ed.). *School psychologists at mid-century.* Washington, D.C.: American Psychological Association, 1955.

Magary, J. F. (Ed.). *School psychological services in theory and practice.* Englewood Cliffs, N.J.: Prentice-Hall, 1967.

O. C. SCANDRETTE

See EDUCATIONAL PSYCHOLOGY.

Schools of Psychology, Professional. *See* PROFESSIONAL SCHOOLS OF PSYCHOLOGY.

Scream Therapy. The early 1960s saw the birth of a number of schools of psychotherapy that elicit screaming. PRIMAL THERAPY was developed by Arthur Janov and quickly became the best known. Independently of Janov, another scream therapy called new identity process was developed by Casriel (1972). A few years later bio scream psychotherapy was developed by Saltzman (1980). The techniques and goals of these and other scream therapies are all quite similar. They share the foundational assumption that there is but one neurosis, an individual's response to unintegrated childhood pain. The technique of integration is screaming.

References

Casriel. D. *A scream away from happiness.* New York: Grosset & Dunlap, 1972.

Saltzman, N. Bio scream psychotherapy. In R. Herink (Ed.), *The psychotherapy handbook.* New York: New American Library, 1980.

D. G. BENNER

See PRIMAL THERAPY.

Screen Memory. In psychoanalytic terminology, a memory that is used as a shield to conceal another more important memory. Thus, for example, when a patient in psychoanalysis recalls playing in the bathroom at age 3 but does not remember the nature of the play, he is said to be providing a screen memory. The assumption is that the remainder of the memory is still unacceptable to consciousness, and the fragment is therefore offered as a substitute and a diversion.

Script Analysis. An attempt to facilitate understanding of the basic life theme underlying one's behavior. It is a technique of TRANSACTIONAL ANALYSIS, but goes beyond the analysis of single interpersonal interactions (transactions) or the analysis of a set of interactions (e.g., games) to an analysis of one's total life goal. Most persons are unaware of their script, and such understanding provides the freedom to redecide. This is based on the assumption that the decision for living out a given script was prematurely made by (not for) the individual in early childhood.

Steiner (1974) has given much attention to script analysis. He suggests that such analysis should begin by reflecting on the interactions the individual had with parents who either empowered or inhibited the individual through permissions or injunctions. This is called the script matrix. Next follows reflection on the decision whereby the person decided to live the life he is living. This involves reliving and reowning the process, coupled with giving up blame on one's parents.

Steiner mentions three basic scripts: depression—no love; madness—no mind; and addiction—no joy. Understanding these themes in one's life makes possible, but not probable, a change of life script to love, power, and happiness. Eric Berne, from whose ideas transactional analysis evolved, suggests that scripts are almost impossible to change.

Reference

Steiner, C. *Scripts people live.* New York: Grove Press, 1974.

H. N. MALONY

Sculpting. *See* FAMILY SCULPTURE TECHNIQUE; FAMILY CHOREOGRAPHY.

Secondary Gain. Freud formulated the idea that neurotic symptoms may provide secondary gains, or indirect opportunites for gratification. A symptom, though disturbing, may become valuable to the patient because of side benefits it affords after its development. Thus the woman complaining of recurring dizziness

may gain nurturing concern and attention while also avoiding adult responsibilities. The patient may have a resulting unconscious desire to keep the neurosis, a possibility that must be addressed in treatment.

See PRIMARY GAIN; RESISTANCE IN PSYCHOTHERAPY.

Secondary Process. Freud used this term to describe the mature ways of thinking that develop gradually and progressively during the first years of life. It is contrasted to PRIMARY PROCESS, which describes the primitive mental functioning characteristic of the young child whose ego is still immature. Secondary process thinking, according to psychoanalytic theory, is governed by the reality principle in that it is realistic, logical, and goal oriented. In contrast, primary process thinking is described as following the pleasure principle, which leads to immediate gratification of needs or drives. While secondary process thinking should characterize adult mental life, the presence of some primary process activity is not in itself necessarily pathological or suggestive of immaturity.

D. G. BENNER

See PSYCHOANALYTIC PSYCHOLOGY.

Secondary Reinforcer. In behavioral psychology, a stimulus that acquires reinforcing properties through association with primary reinforcers (e.g., food, water, air). A stimulus has become a secondary reinforcer (also called a conditioned reinforcer) when it increases the probability of behaviors preceding it. Thus, in animal studies a red light or a loud tone when paired with delivery of food may become a secondary reinforcer, and the animal will eventually perform specified behaviors when reinforced with presentation of the light or tone alone.

An example of a secondary reinforcer for humans is money. Money is not a primary reinforcer—i.e., it cannot by itself meet primary needs for food, water, or air. But people learn the association of money with acquisition of primary needs, and they will then work to be reinforced through the presentation of cash alone.

K. M. LATTEA

See LEARNING.

Self. The concept of the self is one of the most puzzling of all concepts. The self is in one respect the most familiar of all entities; I am constantly and pervasively aware of my self. Yet the self is also in some ways the most deeply mysterious of all the entities with which human beings deal.

One way of opening up the mystery of selfhood is to reflect on the way humans use the word *I*. When I say *I*, normally I am referring to a certain human person, Stephen Evans. However, the word *I* cannot be replaced by the name or other identifying label. For even if I became amnesiac, forgot my name, and no longer knew who I was, I would still in one sense know what I would be referring to by *I*. I would still be referring to *myself*, and it seems impossible for me to be mistaken about this. I am a self, a being who can not only say *I*, but can do so in this special manner. I can refer to myself as the self which I am conscious of being and which I cannot be mistaken in thinking myself to be, however mistaken my other beliefs about the self may be.

As many philosophers have argued (e.g., Bertocci, 1970), the concept of the self also seems essential to understanding human mental abilities, particularly cognitive functions. Knowing, particularly perceptual knowing, involves the unification of diverse elements. When a person hears a clock strike seven times and thereby comes to know that it is seven o'clock, the diverse experiences are in some way unified in her consciousness. An experience of succession is not the same as a succession of experiences. In order for a person to hear the seventh chime as the *seventh* chime, it would seem necessary for the person who hears the seventh chime to be the same person as the one who heard the first chime and to be aware of being the same person. In addition to the experience, then, it appears that there must exist a self that has these experiences, a self that persists over time (Castell, 1965).

The concept of a self that continues over time also seems essential for legal, moral, and religious practices. Unless the person who stands in the courtroom is in some sense the same person as the one who committed the crime, it would be unjust to punish the person. A person should not be convicted of doing what some other person did. Moral responsibility—praise and blame, reward and desert—similarly depend upon a continuing self. Morality may depend upon the self in a still stronger sense, for many believe it illogical to hold a person morally responsible for an act unless that act is freely performed by the person. Freedom of this sort is often regarded as a distinctive ability of the self.

The Christian faith requires the concept of the self for the same reasons as moral and legal practices, since God is viewed by Christians as the Judge of all the earth, who holds his creatures responsible for their actions and punishes them if they refuse to accept his mercy and forgiveness. Christianity also requires the self to make sense of life after death. Christians believe that after death believers will come to life again with new bodies and yet remain the same selves. Those Christians who do not deny the intermediate state between death and resurrection must also believe that people continue to exist as selves before the resurrection occurs.

The Rejection of the Self in Psychology. Despite the theoretical and practical significance of the concept of the self, and the fundamental importance of the concept for commonsense psychology and ordinary experience, the concept of the self has been for long periods practically abandoned by psychologists. Psychologists who disagree among themselves about almost everything else have agreed that the concept of the self was neither needed nor useful in psychology.

The banishment of the self is most evident in behaviorism, which regarded the self as a vestige of the medieval concept of soul (Watson, 1925). Skinner insists that "the free inner man who is held responsible for the behavior of the external biological organism is only a prescientific substitute for the kinds of causes which are discovered in the course of scientific analysis" (1953, p. 447). Those causes are believed by the behaviorist to lie outside the organism, not in a "self."

However, behaviorists are only the tip of the iceberg here. Trait psychologists appear to be studying a self of sorts, but a psychometrically observable set of tendencies is hardly a self in the traditional sense.

An attenuated self seems to survive as the ego in Freudian psychology, but the ego does not look much like a self in orthodox Freudian theory. Rather, it is a derivative of unconscious forces, part of a deterministic, warring, three-part system, which is described from an objective third-person standpoint.

Even thinkers who are sympathetic to the self ultimately shy away from the self as a substantial, continuing entity. James (1890), for example, ultimately concludes that psychology can find no use for the self as knowing entity, though he leaves open the possibility that for some other discipline it may be necessary to postulate a self as an entity. Over 60 years later Allport (1955) developed something that approximated the self in his concept of the "proprium." However, in the end he refused to say that the proprium was a true

substantial self. Although, like James, he leaves open the necessity to postulate a self for theological and philosophical purposes, such an entity is not necessary for psychology.

Reasons for Rejecting the Self. There have been various reasons for rejecting the self. First, the concept of the self as a substantial agent, an enduring entity that originates actions, seems inherently obscure and mysterious to many. It is very difficult to say what is the self which has experiences, apart from those experiences; very difficult to say what is the self which performs actions, apart from a description of those actions.

Second, the self seems tied to introspective methods in psychology. The self is what I am aware of (or fail to be aware of) when I reflect on my own mental states. As psychology moved away from such methods as proper for science, the concept of the self fell into disuse.

Third, the self has also been ignored because of a conviction that science requires objectivication. The self seems inherently subjective, something to be grasped and understood by participatory experience. Yet many psychologists believe that science requires objectivity, a third-person perspective, not a first-person perspective. This is why thinkers like Freud, who postulate something like a self, seem to denude it of its selflike qualities.

Fourth, the self has been thought to be a *homunculus*, an explanation of a person's behavior by postulating a little person inside the person, whose behavior is left unexplained. The self is then an evasion of the quest for psychological explanations, in which all behavior is attributed to the choice or the will of the agent.

Fifth, it has been thought by some that a psychology of the self will necessarily be individualistic and foster selfishness. Some Christians, especially, have seen a psychology of the self as an expression of human pride (Vitz, 1977).

Sixth, it has been charged that the concept of the self implies that humans have free will, and many psychologists see determinism as an essential presupposition of scientific psychology.

Finally, the use of the concept of the self has seemed to some to be implicitly dualistic, since the self as a self-conscious entity does not appear to be identical with its body. Dualism in turn is thought to be an unscientific, "religious" way of viewing human beings.

These reasons make psychologists' aversion to the self understandable. Yet many of the reasons appear shaky, especially from a Christian perspective. Some brief criticisms of each of the above points follow.

First, the fact that a self can be described only through its experiences and actions does not necessarily make it especially mysterious. Many entities (perhaps, ultimately, all entities) can be identified only by what they do. In any case, from a Christian perspective it seems plausible that there is something genuinely mysterious about selfhood. Must all mysteries be avoided?

Second, it also seems questionable as to whether introspection is an illegitimate method of gaining knowledge. Though introspection is certainly not infallible, it would seem to be a fact that we can and do learn things about ourselves by attending to our own stream of consciousness.

Third, the demand that the self be objectivized seems to be a question-begging assumption that the world consists entirely of things that can be understood completely in object terms, that no genuine subjects exist.

Fourth, to attribute an action to the choice of an agent is, admittedly, not to explain it. But the concept of the self is not necessarily a homunculus. The self is not a little person inside the person, but the person himself considered as a subject. Psychologists can still attempt to understand the choices of agents and explain how the choices are made, so employing a concept of self does not mean psychologists will have nothing to do.

Fifth, the concept of the self is not inherently individualistic, since it is possible to see a self as essentially related to others. Nor does a psychology of the self necessarily foster selfism or selfishness. From a Christian perspective the meaning of selfhood is found in self-denying love.

Sixth, it is not true that determinism is a necessary presupposition of psychology. Psychologists do not have to assume there are determining causes for all behavior in order to look for what determining causes there are. The actual "laws" that psychologists discover are invariably statistical, probabilistic, and culture based. Such empirical discoveries neither presuppose nor imply determinism. In any case it is possible to believe in the self and still embrace determinism. The issue of the self's existence should be separated from the question of its freedom.

Finally, it is by no means obvious that a psychology of the self must be dualistic, though it certainly will reject reductionistic materialism. A nonreductive monism or materialism may be adequate (Reichenbach, 1978).

However, Christian psychologists have in some cases rejected dualism too quickly, and a good case can be made for a biblical dualism (Cooper, 1982a, 1982b).

Theories of the Self. Besides telling us what a self is, a theory of the self should explain why human beings are selves, and how it is possible for them to be the same self over time while changing in various ways. Three major types of theories have emerged.

Materialistic theories. A simple account of the self is to identify it with the body. This helps to solve the problem of the relation of self to body. It also provides a solution for the problem of continuity in change, since the identity of the self can be explained in the same way as the continuing identity of any living physical object can be explained.

However, it is hard to see how the body can account for the uniquely subjective aspects of myself as an *I*. The bodily theory cannot be squared with our conviction that we transcend our bodies. It seems possible to us that a person could gain a new body and yet remain the same self. Even if this is in fact impossible, it is conceivable and intelligible; it happens constantly in fairy tales and science fiction. Out-of-body experiences are reported by near-death patients as well as Eastern mystics. If Christianity is true, having a new body is not just an abstract possibility but a future occurrence.

Certainly the human self is intimately related to the bodies and forms some kind of unity with it. But however close the union, it does not seem that it can be a strict identity.

Relational theories. A variety of thinkers have rejected materialism while attempting to avoid a substantial self. In general such theories see the self as a set or "bundle" of experiences (Hume, 1739/1888) or, more plausibly, as a relation between experiences.

One candidate for this relation is memory. Perhaps a self is a set of experiences that includes among its later members memory experiences of its earlier ones. Grice (1941) has developed a sophisticated version of this view, which goes back to Locke. However, it is hard to see how remembering one of my past actions *makes* me the same person as the one who acted; rather, it seems that it is the fact that I *am* the same person that makes it possible for me to remember the action.

Another candidate for the relation is qualitative similarity of traits. This view sees the self or identity of the person to consist in a set of traits or dispositions that might collectively be described as a personality or character. It is because a person exhibits a relatively stable personality that we regard him or her as the same person over time. Thus the problem of the identity of the self becomes the same as the psychological problem of identity, in which the person tries to discover his true personality or character. However, a person can change his or her personality drastically and still remain the same self. Saul becomes Paul and is in one sense a new person. But he must also in some sense be the same person, otherwise we could not say Paul was the man who formerly persecuted Christians. A person can change her identity in the psychological sense and still remain the same self. Also, a person or self must be seen as transcending her character or personality if she is to be regarded as in any way responsible for forming or altering that personality.

A third type of relational view might be termed the existentialist view. This view, a very difficult one to understand, holds that the self consists of activities but there is no substantial agent to perform those activities. Rather, the self is constituted by its own activities. Acts of consciousness occur, some of which are acts of knowing. When such acts take themselves as objects, what is thus taken is a self. Besides existentialists such as Sartre (1957), this view has recently been defended by Nozick (1981).

Agent theories. The traditional view is that the self is a continuing agent that has its experiences rather than simply being composed of them; that performs actions without consisting solely of those actions. Within this general framework, however, advocates of this view diverge sharply.

For example, advocates of the agent view disagree as to whether the self can be experienced. Some hold that all or at least many acts of consciousness include an awareness of the *I* that is conscious (Husserl, 1913/1962). Others agree that one can introspectively be aware of the self, but that this involves an apprehension of (very recent) past acts of the *I;* the act of apprehending cannot take itself as object (Campbell, 1957). Still others hold that the self cannot be apprehended in experience at all, but rather it is an explanatory hypothesis, a necessary postulate to account for the unity of experience.

Advocates of the traditional view also disagree about the nature of the self. Some follow Kant in viewing the true self as a timeless "noumenal" ego, whose true nature cannot be known. Bertocci (1970), on the other hand, views the self as completely temporal and empirically describable. Campbell (1957) adopts an intermediate position in which the self is viewed as a temporal entity whose nature is truly expressed in its empirical activities and character, but which is not completely reducible to those characteristics that are empirically describable. Campbell believes that in introspection, particularly in the situation of moral temptation, we are aware of the self as an entity that transcends its "personality," or characteristic patterns of desiring and acting, so that it is possible for a self to at least try to oppose its own "character."

The Return of the Self in Psychology. In psychology, after the initial banishment of the self, there seems to have been a slow, steady, and now massive return to the self, which is present in almost every tradition. This is perhaps most evident in third-force psychologies: humanistic psychology, existential psychology, and phenomenology. In these movements the person is clearly seen as a self-conscious, responsible being, who is not only driven by urges but moved by meanings and values.

The self has also made a strong comeback in psychoanalysis. Indeed, the history of one strand of the psychoanalytic movement is really the history of ego psychology. In his later work Freud himself began the process of seeing the ego as more than a weak derivative product, a process continued by Anna Freud and others, culminating in Erikson's vision of the self as a quest for identity. Perhaps closest of all to a true self is the British object-relations theory pioneered by Fairbairn and popularized by Guntrip (1971). In this view the ego is not merely an object in a system but a true self, which participates in the formation of the unconscious.

Within the behavioristic tradition the "cognitivization" of psychology has been remarkable, and it is obvious that a psychology that emphasizes cognition must make room for a cognizer. In place of the empty organism that contains only its learning history, psychologists such as Mischel and Bandura have developed social learning theories that recognize the importance of the "self-system" in understanding behavior. This cognitivization of psychology has even allowed for a rapprochement of sorts between Ellis's rational-emotive therapy and behavioral therapists.

Mention should also be made of Allport's pioneering book on the self, *Becoming* (1955). Before it was popular to do so, Allport attempted to rehabilitate a concept of the self with his notion of the "proprium," and in the process showed how psychology was still haunted by philosophical questions.

The Self and Christian Faith. Since the Christian believes that the ultimate reality is personal, and that ultimately the existence of a person lies behind the existence of everything else, Christians have a strong interest in preserving the person (Evans, 1977). Reductionistic accounts must therefore be resisted. The Christian psychologist will recognize that the human self is dependent on God and is not autonomous, and that the self is a part of the created order. The self is partially a product, and its activities are made possible by various impersonal processes. But there is a difference between explaining how selfhood is possible and explaining selfhood away. Psychology that is Christian must be a psychology that makes room for the concept of the self and related concepts, such as belief, desire, meaningful action, responsibility, and intention.

References

Allport, G. W. *Becoming*. New Haven: Yale University Press, 1955.

Bertocci, P. *The person God is*. New York: Humanities Press, 1970.

Campbell, C. A. *On selfhood and godhood*. New York: Macmillan, 1957.

Castell, A. *The self in philosophy*. New York: Macmillan, 1965.

Cooper, J. Dualism and the biblical view of human beings I. *The Reformed Journal*, 1982, *32*, 13–16. (a)

Cooper, J. Dualism and the biblical view of human beings II. *Reformed Journal*, 1982, *32*, 16–18. (b)

Evans, C. S. *Preserving the person*, Downers Grove, Ill.: Inter-Varsity Press, 1977.

Grice, H. P. Personal identity. *Mind*, 1941, *50*, 330–350.

Guntrip, H. *Psychoanalytic theory, therapy, and the self*. New York: Basic Books, 1971.

Hume, D. *A treatise of human nature*. Oxford: Clarendon Press, 1888. (Originally published, 1739.)

Husserl, E. *Ideas: General introduction to pure phenomenology*. New York: Collier, 1962. (Originally published, 1913.)

James, W. *Principles of psychology (Vol. 1)*. New York: Holt, 1890.

Nozick, R. *Philosophical explanations*. Cambridge: Harvard University Press, 1981.

Reichenbach, B. *Is man the phoenix?* Grand Rapids: Christian University Press, 1978.

Sartre, J. P. *The transcendence of the ego*. New York: Noonday Press, 1957.

Skinner, B. F. *Science and human behavior*. New York: Macmillan, 1953.

Vitz, P. C. *Psychology as religion: The cult of self-worship*. Grand Rapids: Eerdmans, 1977.

Watson, J. B. *Behaviorism*. New York: People's Institute Publishing, 1925.

C. S. EVANS

See CONSCIOUSNESS; MIND-BRAIN RELATIONSHIP; PERSONHOOD.

Self-Actualization. A major concept in organismic theories of personality. Organismic theories emphasize the unity, integrity, and organization of the organism as opposed to theories that segregate mind and body. Organismic theories begin with the assumption that the individual is an organized whole. One drive provides the motivation for all behaviors. Self-actualization operates as the sovereign motive for a plethora of individual actions. Specialized drives (e.g., aggressive, consummatory, and sexual impulses) are surface manifestations of the generalized drive of self-actualization. Self-actualization, operating as a comprehensive motive, accounts for the individual's striving to fulfill inherent potentialities.

Kurt Goldstein first developed self-actualization as a major theoretical construct. Influenced by Gestalt psychology, he believed the primary psychological organization operating in personality was the figure-ground relation. The figure was the principal, dominant, or consistent behavior of the organism that appeared against the backdrop (ground) of lesser behaviors and environmental processes.

Natural figures were those preferred by the organism and manifested in flexible, orderly responses to situations. Natural figures reflected the underlying potentials of the organism. Unnatural figures resulted when tasks were imposed upon the person by intense situations. As a consequence of unnatural figures the person's behavior may be rigid, inappropriate, and unadapting. For Goldstein physical and psychological health required natural figures.

New figures emerged as the fundamental tasks of life changed. Behind various figures was the drive to achieve one's innate potentialities. This striving for achievement of one's potential was termed self-actualization or self-realization. Self-actualization was a creative force within the organism, energizing it toward growth, completeness, and perfection. When a need existed, self-actualization induced the individual to replenish the deficiency or deprivation. Stability was achieved when energy was balanced throughout the organism.

Self-actualization was a universal phenomenon of nature that was expressed in various ways. The different expressions depended in part on the surrounding sociocultural milieu and the individual's potentialities. Goldstein maintained that the best method to define one's potentialities was to list one's preferences, especially as found in natural figures.

Although Goldstein favored organismic

variables within the individual as the cause of behavior, he did not conceive of the organism as immune from the environment. Self-actualization depended on the organism coming to terms with the environment. In doing so, opportunities to self-actualize would be possible as the individual avoided or conquered obstructions, threats, and pressures.

A second organismic theory of personality was proposed by Andras Angyal, who conceived of the organism and its environment as a unit called the biosphere. The biosphere and other systems normally evolved into differentiated yet interdependent systems. A general principle in nature, which Angyal called self-expansion, integrates these tendencies. A system such as personality would expand and differentiate so long as it did not endanger its unity. Although Angyal's terms were unique, the parallel to self-actualization is obvious.

Self-actualization is most closely associated with Maslow and Rogers. Maslow's (1970) holistic-organismic theory asserted that human behavior was motivated by basic needs (deficiency or D motives) and metaneeds (being or B motives). Basic needs were arranged in a hierarchical manner in which fundamental needs must be satisfied before higher needs could exert their influence. If an organism had a deficiency need, it acted to remove the deficit. Basic needs were dominant over the metaneeds and were ordered in this fashion: physiological needs, safety needs, belongingness and love needs, self-esteem, and self-actualization. Metaneeds were growth needs such as justice, truth, goodness, beauty, law and order, and perfection.

In an attempt to develop a healthy psychology Maslow made an extensive study of self-actualizers, including Lincoln, Jefferson, Whitman, Thoreau, Einstein, and Eleanor Roosevelt. Unique attributes of self-actualizers included a realistic orientation to life; acceptance of self, others, and nature; spontaneity; problem-centeredness instead of self-centeredness; and an air of detachment. Also noted were a need for periodic privacy, autonomy and independence, a fresh appreciation of people and things, profound mystical or religious experiences, identity with the human race, deep and intimate relationships with a few specially loved people, and democratic values and attitudes. Furthermore, self-actualizers distinguished between means and ends, had a philosophical sense of humor and a high degree of creativity, and resisted enculturation. Peak experiences seemed to be a focal point in self-actualizers (Maslow, 1964). Because basic needs were predominant self-actualization was expected only in mature adults.

Rogers's personality theory has much in common with that of Maslow. A major similarity is the commitment to an organismic perspective that asserts one master life force. However, Rogers expresses a very positive and optimistic view of human nature. Human nature is innately good; the individual becomes a free, independent, and purposive person when unencumbered by a restrictive environment. This Rousseaulike position reflects Rogers's therapeutic experience and religious orientation. Humans live up to their fullest potentialities when they are free to experience and free to satisfy their inner nature.

A central construct in Rogers's theory is the actualizing tendency, which manifests itself through self-maintenance, self-enhancement, self-actualization, and the organismic valuing process. As the only motivational construct the actualizing tendency is a biological force that motivates the individual to seek fulfillment of inborn tendencies. The actualizing tendency drives the person to become more fully human. For Rogers this is the essence of life. The actualizing tendency is "the inherent tendency of the organism to develop all its capacities in ways which serve to maintain or enhance the person" (Rogers, 1959, p. 196).

The motives advocated by other theorists are held as surface evidences of the underlying actualizing tendency, which serves the individual by reducing tensions in response to deficiency needs by means of basic organismic maintenance processes. From a psychological perspective the individual possesses a sense of personal identity (i.e., self-concept) and is devoted to maintenance of self-concept. This is termed *self-maintenance* by Rogers.

Other activities of the organism actually serve to increase tension for the purpose of enhancing the organism. Rather than maintaining an even distribution of energy (cf. homeostasis, tension reduction in Freud, and entropy in Jung), the individual actively concentrates energy upon an area of life. Self-enhancement is a similar process geared toward development of an area of self.

To Rogers self-actualization is a special case of the actualizing tendency applied to the portion of experience represented by the self-concept. To the extent that self-actualization is unified with the organismic valuing process, the individual is well adjusted.

Rogers addressed the question of how an organism selects certain experiences to maintain or enhance itself, while it avoids others not conducive to growth. The organismic valuing process, a special process within the actualizing tendency, serves to answer that question. Experiences are evaluated against a criterion. Experiences that are perceived as maintaining or enhancing the organism are valued and sought, while experiences that oppose maintenance or enhancement are devalued and avoided. The actualizing tendency assists the individual in becoming more adequate.

As Maslow studied self-actualized individuals, Rogers undertook a study of the fully functioning person. Individuals who are using their talents, realizing potentials, and moving toward a more complete knowledge and experience are described as fully functioning. Rogers (1961) listed the attributes of such an individual. The fully functioning individual is open to experience whereby the self is congruent with that experience and there is no need for defensiveness. Existential living describes the person who lives each moment to its fullest. In making decisions the fully functioning person relies on personal judgment and choice instead of social code or institutional convention. This concept of the good life also includes existential freedom, a subjective freedom in which one is free to live as one chooses and the individual accepts personal responsibility for actions. The optimally adjusted individual is also creative. In summary, the fully functioning individual is in tune with inborn potentialities, responds creatively and adaptively to changing environments, and is not a conformer or prisoner of society (cf. Maslow's self-actualizing personalities).

Some individuals point out similarities between the psychological concept of self-actualization and the theological doctrine of sanctification. Normally sanctification suggests the transformation of the person toward being more Christlike, becoming more the human God intends. Sanctification includes crises (cf. peak experiences with Wesleyan-Arminian entire sanctification) and process (cf. growth in grace). If God is the author of the actualizing tendency, it may well be that sanctification and self-actualization are essentially the same experience expressed in different terms.

References

Maslow, A. *Religions, values and peak experiences.* Columbus: Ohio State University Press, 1964.

Maslow, A. *Motivation and personality* (2nd ed.). New York: Harper & Row, 1970.

Rogers, C. R. A theory of therapy, personality and interpersonal relationships, as developed in the client-centered framework. In S. Koch (Ed.), *Psychology: A study of a science* (Vol. 3). New York: McGraw-Hill, 1959.

Rogers, C. R. *On becoming a person.* Boston: Houghton Mifflin, 1961.

R. L. TIMPE

See HUMANISTIC PSYCHOLOGY.

Self-Alienation. ALIENATION can be analyzed in terms of four ruptured relationships: between God and man, between man and man, within man himself, and between man and nature. Self-alienation, the disharmony and divisiveness within an individual, is readily apparent from the extent of human maladaptive behavior (e.g., neuroses, psychoses, alcoholism, drug addiction, acts of violence, and suicide).

There are many hypotheses offered to explain the divisiveness within human nature. Freud proposed a split between the conscious and the unconscious, wherein the larger part of human motivation in purported to lie beneath the surface of awareness. This accounts for the defense mechanisms that control human behavior and direct it in ways unknown to the individual. Other writers refer to the split between cerebral-intellectual and affective-emotional functions (Fromm, 1968), or the pitting of intellect against feeling, reason against passion, and head against heart (Roszak, 1969).

Personal meaninglessness in present times has been the theme of Frankl (1963) and his school of logotherapy. According to Frankl today's inner emptiness and meaninglessness are elements of an existential vacuum, leading to frustration and neurosis. May (1967) sees self-alienation in terms of a loss of personal significance, contending that contemporary man is hollow, lacking a center of personal strength and values. In a brilliant analysis of the effects of accelerative change on people Toffler (1970) discusses the impact of overloading on sensory, cognitive, and decisional levels of personal functioning.

The Judeo-Christian tradition places self-alienation consequent to the rebellion of original humankind, as described in the Book of Genesis. Adam and Eve, because of their pride and disobedience, were punished by banishment from the Garden of Eden, the state of perfect friendship with God. The resultant human condition, shared by all of Adam and Eve's descendants, is characterized by suffering, guilt, and death, as well as a darkened intelligence and weakened will (Hammes, 1978). Paul reflects on the internal devisiveness of human nature in his comment on the law of the spirit and the law of the flesh as being in conflict (Rom. 7:17–25).

References

Frankl, V. E. *Man's search for meaning.* Boston: Beacon Press, 1963.

Fromm, E. *The revolution of hope.* New York: Harper & Row, 1968.

Hammes, J.,A. *Human destiny: Exploring today's value systems.* Huntington, Ind.: Our Sunday Visitor, 1978.

May, R. *Psychology and the human dilemma.* Princeton, N.J.: Van Nostrand, 1967.

Roszak, T. *The making of a counter culture.* Garden City, N.Y.: Doubleday, 1969.

Toffler, A. *Future shock.* New York: Random House, 1970.

J. A. HAMMES

See EXISTENTIAL PSYCHOLOGY AND PSYCHOTHERAPY.

Self-Concept. The constellation of perceptions and attitudes that a person maintains with regard to himself. To speak of the self-concept in the singular is somewhat misleading, since there are many different "selves" or, more accurately, aspects of the self that are perceived and evaluated. One particular self-concept measure, the Tennessee Self-Concept Scale (Fitts, 1965), has identified eight different aspects of the self: identity self, judging self, behavioral self, physical self, moral-ethical self, personal self, family self, and social self. This is not necessarily an exhaustive list, nor is it the only way in which the various parts of the self can be conceptualized, but it serves to illustrate the complexity of this psychological construct.

An aspect of the self-concept that is of great interest to counselors and psychotherapists is the personal self, or what is more commonly known as SELF-ESTEEM. This is defined by Coopersmith (1967) as "the evaluation which the individual makes and customarily maintains with regard to himself: it expresses an attitude of approval or disapproval, and indicates the extent to which the individual believes himself to be capable, significant, successful, and worthy" (p. 5). Research studies have found that persons with low self-esteem are generally more influenced by pessimism and threat; are less capable of resisting pressures to conform; and are more burdened by fears, ambivalence, and self-doubt than persons with high self-esteem. In addition, individuals possessing high self-esteem tend to assume a more active role in social groups, to express their views more frequently, and are generally more creative than their low self-esteem counterparts (Coopersmith, 1967).

Other research studies have found a positive correlation between high self-esteem (characterized by self-acceptance) and the acceptance of others. That is, those who feel positively about themselves tend to feel the same way toward others, while those who dislike themselves tend to express the same rejecting attitude toward those around them. A similar study found that those who are self-accepting also perceive others as being accepting, whereas those disliking themselves tend to see others as having a similar rejecting attitude.

This latter finding ties in well with research examining the relationship between self-esteem and concept of God. These studies found that persons with low self-esteem tend to conceive of God as critical, rejecting, and distant, whereas those with high self-esteem tend to see God as more loving, personal, and close (Bixler, 1979). Since children often attribute to God the characteristics of their parents (Nelson, 1971), it would be logical to assume that an abused or neglected child would simultaneously develop a poor self-concept and a negative God concept.

The negative effects of a poor self-concept on interpersonal and intrapsychic functioning are thus well researched and documented. In addition, most counselors could cite numerous case examples attesting to the destructiveness inherent in the self-condemning attitudes of their clients. For these reasons many Christian therapists have championed the notion that self-esteem is an important and necessary part of the healthy personality and is therefore to be cultivated in therapy.

This viewpoint is not, however, without its critics. Vitz (1977), for example, argues that the emphasis on self-love and self-realization is antithetical to the biblical idea of love and is a product of secular humanism. He further states that secular psychology promotes self-worship while disparaging or ignoring traditional Christian virtues such as humility, obedience, and self-sacrifice.

When examined closely, the apparent conflict between these two perspectives may be more apparent than real. In fact, the warnings against sinful pride and the advocacy of Christian self-esteem may be seen as complementary rather than contradictory once the semantic and theological ambiguities are cleared up.

Those who are critical of the Christian self-esteem movement tend to emphasize the doctrine of total depravity, which holds that in every respect humans are inherently exploitative and self-seeking. To these critics the notion of Christian self-love is not only a contradiction in terms; it implies that self-centeredness is the solution rather than the problem. The major strength of this critique lies in its faithfulness to the biblical witness regarding the inherent sinfulness of the human race. Since most theologians define root-sin as pride or self-love, it would seem that this would eliminate any notion of Christian self-love. However, the force of this argument is mitigated by the fact that most advocates of Christian self-esteem actually mean self-acceptance when speaking of self-love.

Self-acceptance does not imply a denial of the doctrine of depravity; rather, it recognizes that something has been added to it. According to Hoekema (1975) this means that "since believers now belong to Christ's new creation, we are to see ourselves as new creatures in Christ, not just as depraved sinners. To be sure, apart from Christ, we are sinners, but we are no longer apart from Christ. In Christ we are now justified sinners, sinners who have the Holy Spirit dwelling within. Our way of looking at ourselves must not deny this newness, but affirm it" (p. 55).

Christians must, of course, continue to be wary of becoming prideful and self-centered, since the old nature continues to exist. In a very real sense the self-concept must remain in the eschatological tension between the already and the not yet. Christians are new creatures in Christ who still must be wary of selfishness. It is this need for wariness that prompts the warnings from the critics of Christian self-esteem.

However, a positive self-concept grounded in God's unconditional, electing love in Christ does not lead to selfishness. Rather, it relieves Christians of the burden of having to generate feelings of self-worth based on performance. Since they need not be slaves to ego-enhancing behavior, they can be free to be unselfish and to manifest virtues such as sacrifice, obedience, and humility. But without a healthy self-acceptance the practice of these virtues can easily become a neurotic striving to gain God's approval.

Christian self-esteem, rightly understood, does not lead to exploitative self-centeredness, but rather to an appreciation and acceptance of oneself and one's neighbor. This truth is beautifully expressed by Lewis (1961) in *The Screwtape Letters* when Screwtape writes: "The Enemy [God] wants him [man], in the end, to be so free from any bias in his own favor that he can rejoice in his own talents as frankly and gratefully as in his neighbor's talents. . . . He wants each man, in the long run, to be able to recognize all creatures (even himself) as glorious and excellent things. He wants to kill their animal self-love as soon as possible; but it is His long-term policy, I fear, to restore to them a new kind of self-love—a charity and gratitude for all selves, including their own; when

they have really learned to love their neighbors as themselves, they will be allowed to love themselves as their neighbors" (pp. 64–65).

References

Bixler, W. G. *Self-concept/God-concept congruency as a function of differential need for esteem and consistency.* Unpublished doctoral dissertation, Fuller Theological Seminary Graduate School of Psychology, 1979.

Coopersmith, S. *The antecedents of self-esteem.* San Francisco: W. H. Freeman, 1967.

Fitts, W. *Tennessee self-concept scale: Manual.* Nashville: Counselor Recordings and Tests, 1965.

Hoekema, A. *The Christian looks at himself.* Grand Rapids: Eerdmans, 1975.

Lewis, C. S. *The screwtape letters.* London: Centenary Press, 1942.

Nelson, M. The concept of God and feelings toward parents. *Journal of Individual Psychology,* 1971, *27*, 46–49.

Vitz, P. *Psychology as religion: The cult of self-worship.* Grand Rapids: Eerdmans, 1977.

W. G. BIXLER

Self-Concept Tests. The measurement of self-concept has been complicated by the problems of defining this construct. There are at least 30 measures of self-esteem and self-concept (Robinson & Shaver, 1973). Psychotherapists are especially concerned with the measurement of self-esteem, since improvements in this area are often thought to be the most important measure of effective psychotherapy (Prochaska, 1979). What is needed is systematic validation work so that we can more accurately and meaningfully measure these constructs.

Of the available measures the Tennessee Self-Concept Scale (Fitts, 1965) and the Piers-Harris Children's Self-Concept Scale (Piers, 1969) are the most highly recommended. The tests are psychometrically superior to the many other scales available. A third measure, the Janis-Field Feelings of Inadequacy Scale (Eagly, 1967) is widely used. Two scales that were especially developed for children but have also been widely used with adults are the Self-Esteem Scale (Rosenberg, 1965) and the Self-Esteem Inventory (Coopersmith, 1967).

Finally, three scales that attempt to measure the discrepancy between the real and idealized self are the Index of Adjustment and Values (Bills, Vance, & McLean, 1951), the Butler-Haigh Q-Sort (Butler & Haigh, 1954), and the Miskimins Self-Goal-Other Discrepancy Scale (Miskimins & Braucht, 1971).

Self-esteem has also been informally assessed from such self-report inventories as the Minnesota Multiphasic Personality Inventory, the Personality Research Form, the California Personality Inventory, and the Adjective Checklist, as well as the varied projective assessment measures. This approach is at best intuitive and highly dependent on the assessment skills of the examiner. It is not recommended from either a clinical or psychometric perspective, in light of the definitional confusion.

In summary, self-concept and self-esteem are closely related constructs. Both are plagued with ambiguities. The eight scales mentioned are widely considered to be the best of the many current scales specifically designed to measure them. Clinicians who use these measures must realize the limitations of present tests due to the sparse data available about the validity of these theoretical constructs.

References

Bills, R. E., Vance, E. L., & McLean, O. S. An index of adjustment and values. *Journal of Consulting Psychology,* 1951, *15,* 257–261.

Butler, J., & Haigh, G. Changes in the relation between self-concepts and ideal concepts consequent upon client-centered counseling. In C. R. Rogers & R. F. Dymond (Eds.), *Psychotherapy and personality change.* Chicago: University of Chicago Press, 1954.

Coopersmith, S. *The antecedents of self-esteem.* San Francisco: W. H. Freeman, 1967.

Eagly, A. H. Involvement as a determinant of response to favorable and unfavorable information. *Journal of Personality and Social Psychology,* 1967, *7,* 1–5. (Monograph) (Whole No. 643).

Fitts, W. *Tennessee self-concept scale: Manual.* Nashville: Counselor Recordings and Tests, 1965.

Miskimins, R. W., & Braucht, G. *Description of the self.* Fort Collins, Colo.: Rocky Mountain Behavioral Sciences Institute, 1971.

Piers, E. *Manual for the Piers-Harris children's self-concept scale.* Nashville: Counselor Recordings and Tests, 1969.

Prochaska, J. O. *Systems of psychotherapy: A transtheoretical approach.* Homewood, Ill.: Dorsey, 1979.

Robinson, J. P., & Shaver, P. R. *Measures of social psychological attitudes* (Rev. ed.). Ann Arbor, Mich.: Survey Research Center, 1973.

Rosenberg, M. *Society and the adolescent self-image.* Princeton, N.J.: Princeton University Press, 1965.

R. E. BUTMAN

See PSYCHOLOGICAL MEASUREMENT; PERSONALITY ASSESSMENT.

Self-Congruence. See CONGRUENCE.

Self-Consciousness.

This term has two major meanings, both of which are of interest to psychologists. First, self-consciousness refers to the awareness that humans have of their own selves: their behaviors, feelings, and thoughts. The term implies that this awareness extends to knowing; that these thoughts, feelings, and acts originate in the self rather than in some source outside the self. This characteristic—the ability to reflect on and be aware of one's self—is a major factor separating humans from the animal kingdom.

Second, self-consciousness is an ill-at-ease feeling experienced by a person who is uncomfortably aware of self in social situations. This is probably a feeling universally experienced at some time or another, since shyness is a common phenomenon. The self-conscious person will approach a gathering of people, strangers or friends, and experience a painful rush of feelings that everyone in the room is staring at him. Furthermore, the self-conscious person will also be convinced that everyone is evaluating him or her and that rejection is imminent. Although it may appear quiet and subdued on the outside, the self-conscious person's internal life is "a maze of thought highways cluttered with head-on collisions of sensations and noisy traffic jams of frustrated desires" (Zimbardo, 1977, p. 29).

Researchers vary in how they categorize self-consciousness. Some see it as central to the concept of SHYNESS. Buss (1980) describes self-consciousness as having two major manifestations: public (concern with the observable self and how others interact and react to it) and private (preoccupation with feelings, fantasies, and motives that are not seen by the public). The privately self-conscious person is concerned about the inadequacies and shortcomings of the self and thus is caught in a destructive mode of thinking. Buss feels that when public self-consciousness goes awry—i.e., when it becomes elaborate and extensive—social anxiety is the result. For Buss, social anxiety is embarrassment, shame, audience anxiety, and shyness. Hence self-consciousness is a precursor of, and an even larger concept than, shyness.

To other researchers, however, self-consciousness is simply a part of the larger framework of shyness. Crozier (1979b) views self-consciousness as a part of shyness and sees it as related to deficient or nonexistent assertiveness. Crozier conceptualizes shyness as an anxious feeling in social situations that makes a person want to withdraw from interaction with others. Shyness is accompanied by feelings of unhappiness, preoccupation with self, inhibition, and self-consciousness. Crozier defines situations that provoke self-consciousness as those that make or are seen to make large demands on one's competence or that increase or seem to increase the possibility of being criticized.

Most researchers agree that shyness (tension and inhibition around others) and sociability (the desire to be with others) are separate personality factors (Cheek & Buss, 1981). A consensus also seems to exist that self-consciousness, reticence, and low self-esteem fit together and are related to one another (Crozier, 1979a). Therapy for shyness and self-consciousness is most effective when it consists of methods designed to improve social skills rather than methods seeking to stimulate insight.

References

Buss, A. H. *Self-consciousness and social anxiety.* San Francisco: W. H. Freeman, 1980.
Cheek, J. M., & Buss, A. H. Shyness and sociability. *Journal of Personality and Social Psychology,* 1981, *41*(2), 330–339.
Crozier, W. R. Shyness as anxious self-preoccupation. *Psychological Reports,* 1979, *44*(3), 959–962. (a)
Crozier, W. R. Shyness as a dimension of personality. *British Journal of Social and Clinical Psychology,* 1979, *18*(1), 121–128. (b)
Zimbardo, P. G. *Shyness: What it is and what to do about it.* Reading, Mass.: Addison-Wesley, 1977.

J. R. Beck

Self-Control. In its most limited definition the term refers to an individual lowering the probability that he or she will engage in an undesirable behavior by manipulating a controlling reponse. A controlling response is a behavior that changes the likelihood that the target behavior will occur. The target behavior is the response the person is trying to modify. In its broader definition self-control is a label for all forms of self-change, self-management, self-modification, and self-regulation. Self-control may include the use of controlling responses to weaken, to strengthen, or to maintain a target behavior.

Human reflection on self-control has a very long history. The Greeks wrote about methods of self-control 4,000 years ago, and Paul encouraged temperance (a limited form of self-control) when writing to the early Christians (1 Cor. 9:24–27). In contrast to such early encouragements of self-control, a systematic exploration of how people can regulate their own behavior has a very short history.

Skinner (1953) played an important role in launching the contemporary research on self-regulation. He included a chapter on self-control in *Science and Human Behavior* (1953)—a chapter that had a catalytic impact on laboratory studies of self-control during the 1960s. Perhaps the most prolific such investigators during this period were F. H. Kanfer and his associates. Through an extensive series of laboratory studies they evaluated the effects of self-evaluation · and self-reinforcement. This basic research was soon followed by applied research on self-administered psychological treatments in children, adolescents, and adults. Not long after the publication of the first research articles on the clinical applications of self-control procedures the first book telling people how to control their own behav-

ior in a systematic, scientific fashion appeared (Watson & Tharp, 1972).

Two major developments promoted the wedding of experimental psychology and a personal self-control technology. First, behavior therapy, or behavior modification, began as a new movement within psychology and psychiatry during the late 1950s. In contrast to most forms of psychotherapy that had developed during the first half of the twentieth century, behavior therapy was presented as a describable, teachable, applied science rather than an elusive art. Increasing clarity in defining and describing treatment procedures facilitated teaching future therapists, and this new specificity stimulated early behavior therapists to instruct their patients to carry out some of the treatment procedures on themselves.

The second major development that accelerated the growth of self-control methods was biofeedback. In the 1960s laboratory scientists investigated the possibilities of instrumentally conditioning autonomic processes. Their work suggested that persons can learn to control responses that psychologists had traditionally assumed to be involuntary. For example, persons may be able to learn to raise or lower their own skin temperature or blood pressure on command.

The conceptual models underlying both behavior therapy and biofeedback supported the assumption that individuals control themselves through the same kinds of operations they use to influence other persons.

One procedure that may be used in self-control is the administration of setting events. Setting events are powerful factors that change a person's activity level or alter the individual's sensitivity to particular cues and consequences. The more common setting events are deprivation schedules, satiation schedules, psychotropic drugs, physical restraints, providing choices, pleasant stimulation, aversive stimulation, and providing a caring relationship.

Another self-control procedure is the use of cues (discriminative stimuli) and prods (unconditioned or conditioned stimuli). Whereas setting events alter the general state of the individual, cues and prods impact a relatively narrow band of behavior. Common self-regulation procedures based on cues or prods include choosing and defining a target behavior, presenting an immediate cue or prod for the target behavior, setting goals, setting peformance standards for consequating the target behavior, writing a performance contract, choosing reinforcers in advance, and providing a behavioral model.

A third self-management strategy is primary behavior. The individual holds a unique position as a behavior modifier; he can directly modify his own behavior by practicing a desired behavior, by engaging in a response that competes with an undesired behavior, or by withholding an undesired behavior. In contrast, there is no way one person can directly produce actions in another individual. Although counseling and psychotherapy have neglected the role of practice in changing human behavior, athletics and the performing arts have carefully attended to this aspect of the psychology of self-regulation.

Consequences and feedback are a fourth means of self-control. These interventions include self-observation, self-recording, comparing performance with a goal, and self-reinforcing or self-punishing.

All these various elements may be combined into self-administered treatment packages comparable to those administered by professional therapists in the past. The same kinds of strategies may be used to promote self-control in any person facing normal problems in living.

References
Skinner, B. F. *Science and human behavior.* New York: Macmillan, 1953.
Watson, D. L., & Tharp, R. G. *Self-directed behavior: Self-modification for personal adjustment.* Monterey, Calif.: Brooks/Cole, 1972.

P. W. CLEMENT

Self-Disclosure. The past two decades have seen an increasing emphasis in mental health circles on the importance of honesty and openness in human relationships. This emphasis has manifested itself in a number of ways: the crucial importance ascribed to authenticity by existential therapists; the stress placed by Rogers (1970) and his followers on the necessity for congruence on the part of therapists; Mowrer's (1961) emphasis on integrity; and the phenomenal growth of the encounter group movement. Jourard (1964), one of the strongest advocates of self-disclosure, set forth the proposition that self-disclosure promotes physical and mental health and satisfying human relationships. He hypothesized that the reason women tend to live longer than men is that women repress less (disclose more) than men. Not allowed by the culture to express their emotions openly, men repress more and as a result are more subject to degenerative psychosomatic illnesses. Research summarized by Jourard (1971) is supportive of this and other hypotheses he set forth earlier.

Self-disclosure appears to be a requisite for effective leadership. Studies of successful leaders by Krech, Crutchfield, and Ballachey (1962) suggest that a leader must be perceived as "one of us." Obviously a person who does not disclose, who hides behind a façade, who doesn't let people know who he is, cannot be perceived as "one of us."

Although there is considerable evidence that self-disclosure to friends or professionals can be beneficial to mental health, one should avoid telling everything to everybody. Everyone needs to retain some private areas in order to maintain identity and integrity (Miller, 1973). Research by Liberman, Yalom, and Miles (1973) has indicated that persons should not be pressured into revealing more than they wish to tell. They found that the only persons psychologically damaged in the encounter groups studied were in groups where the facilitator pressured participants to divulge more than they felt comfortable in revealing.

The contemporary emphasis on self-disclosure has had considerable impact on evangelical thinking. Miller (1973), Tournier (1967), and others have deplored the lack of openness found in many evangelical churches and have suggested that without openness there can be no true and meaningful Christian fellowship. Encounterlike groups have been suggested as means of opening honest channels of communication among church members. Leslie (1971) has written a manual for conducting such groups. Palmberg and Scandrette (1977) found considerable biblical support for self-disclosure.

Oden (1972) has pointed out that the encounter group is a demythologized and secularized form of a style of interpersonal interaction that characterized early Protestant pietism. According to Oden pietism emphasized here-and-now experience, intensive small group experience, honest confession, mutual pastoral care, and the operation of the Spirit at a level of nonverbal communication.

References
Jourard, S. M. *The transparent self.* Princeton, N.J.: Van Nostrand, 1964.
Jourard, S. M. *Self-disclosure: An experimental analysis of the transparent self.* New York: Wiley-Interscience, 1971.
Krech, D., Crutchfield, R. S., & Ballachey, E. L. *Individual in society.* New York: McGraw-Hill, 1962.
Leslie, R. C. *Sharing groups in the church.* Nashville: Abingdon, 1971.
Liberman, M. A., Yalom, I. D., & Miles, M. B. *Encounter groups: First facts.* New York: Basic Books, 1973.
Miller, K. *The becomers.* Waco, Tex.: Word Books, 1973.
Mowrer, O. H. *The crisis in psychiatry and religion.* Princeton, N.J.: Van Nostrand, 1961.
Oden, T. The new pietism. *Journal of Humanistic Psychology,* 1972, *12,* 24–41.
Palmberg, B. L., & Scandrette, O. C. Self-disclosure in

biblical perspective. *Journal of Psychology and Theology,* 1977, *5,* 209–219.

Rogers, C. R. *Carl Rogers on encounter groups.* New York: Harper & Row, 1970.

Tournier, P. *To understand each other.* Richmond: John Knox Press, 1967.

O. C. SCANDRETTE

Self-Disclosure, Therapist.

No clinician minimizes the value of appropriate self-disclosure. Rather, the controversy surrounds the question of what level and intensity of self-disclosure by the therapist best facilitates the helping process. Opinion varies considerably in the psychotherapeutic literature, especially between psychodynamically oriented and humanistically oriented theoreticians. Further, what may be an appropriate level and intensity in individual therapy may be inappropriate in a group setting, and vice versa. Researchers (e.g., Hammond, Hepworth, & Smith, 1977) have devoted considerable energy to exploring this issue and related matters in order to improve therapeutic communication.

Self-disclosure may be defined as giving another access to one's private life or to one's secret thoughts, feelings, and attitudes (McLemore, 1978). It is the antithesis of concealing one's own feelings and personality. For the therapist a high level of self-disclosure would be where he or she holds nothing back, even at the risk of embarrassment. Further, when negative feelings are shared, they would be used constructively, a process that Augsburger (1973) calls "care-fronting." Realizing how difficult it is for most persons to reveal their psychological problems, the therapist needs to recognize his own vulnerability. He must learn not to be afraid to experience fully his own personal conflicts in the therapeutic process; this is one of the most difficult tasks in doing psychotherapy and counseling.

As clients self-disclose, it is very likely that the therapist's own deep feelings of pain and joy, love and hate, hurt and tenderness will be touched. Recoiling from these reopened wounds the therapist may choose to deal with his fears and anxieties by not sharing. At times this may be appropriate. At other times these feelings may be the very substance that could facilitate the deepening of the therapeutic relationship and the healing of old wounds (see Copans & Singer, 1978). Learning to use personal experience in therapy and learning from therapy how to better conduct one's own life are parallel processes that go hand in hand. Copans and Singer argue that experiencing one's own wounds in therapy does not mean that one exposes them necessarily but that one is open to them. The process of learning to do this is gradual, and is facilitated by the therapist fully experiencing himself in therapy, not by rigorously removing himself from the process.

Self-disclosure by the therapist can have a number of positive benefits. Appropriate levels and intensity of sharing can build therapeutic rapport and trust. Further, they can serve as excellent models of interpersonal openness (Jourard, 1971; Jourard & Landsman, 1980). Third, they can demonstrate to clients that their problems are not necessarily unique and that previously unacceptable feelings, thoughts, and actions are OK. Finally, such appropriate self-disclosure often has a dyadic effect; that is, with appropriate rapport and trust persons tend to reciprocate self-disclosure unless it is too intense or unexpected. The therapist must be careful however, that self-disclosure does not impede the therapeutic process by diverting the focus of clients' awareness away from their own thoughts, actions, and feelings for prolonged periods of time. Further, such disclosure runs the risk of degenerating into listless sermons or personal stories that are irrelevant or intrusive.

Self-disclosure appropriately used might also be seen as a way of challenging clients (Egan, 1982). It is appropriate if it helps clients talk about themselves, if it helps them talk about their problems more concretely, if it helps them develop new frames of reference and perspectives, and if it helps them set realistic goals for themselves. Egan suggests that this is most likely to occur if self-sharing is selective and focused, is not a burden to the client, and is not used too often.

In short, self-disclosure in the therapeutic context is a risk. It spite of this, however, it is a skill that should be a part of the effective psychotherapist's repertory. The therapist should be willing and able to share himself deeply and in reasonable ways, but he should do so only if it is clear that it will facilitate the process of improving therapeutic communication.

References

Augsburger, D. *Caring enough to confront.* Scottdale, Pa.: Herald Press, 1973.

Copans, S., & Singer, T. *Who's the patient here? Portraits of the young psychotherapist.* New York: Oxford University Press, 1978.

Egan, G. *The skilled helper: Models, skills, and method for effective helping* (2nd ed.). Monterey, Calif.: Brooks/Cole, 1982.

Hammond, D., Hepworth, D., & Smith V. *Improving therapeutic communication.* San Francisco: Jossey-Bass, 1977.

Jourard, S. M. *The transparent self* (Rev. ed.). New York: Van Nostrand, Reinhold, 1971.

Jourard, S. M. & Landsman, T. *Healthy personality* (4th ed.). New York: Macmillan, 1980.

McLemore, C. *Clergyman's psychological handbook: Clinical information for pastoral counseling.* Grand Rapids: Eerdmans, 1978.

R. E. BUTMAN

Self-Esteem. One of the unique characteristics of human beings is their ability to describe and evaluate themselves. Self-esteem is the degree of positive or negative feeling that one has as a result of such assessment.

History of the Concept. The development and nature of the self has been of interest to modern psychology since James (1890) distinguished between self as knower (I) and self as known (Me). James further identified the material, social, and spiritual Me. For him the evaluations a person arrives at involve a comparison of aspirations, or "pretensions," with achievements.

Following James sociologists Cooley (1902) and Mead (1934) stressed the social origins and development of the self. Cooley introduced the notion of the looking-glass self, which is based on a person's perception of other people's perceptions of him. He felt, much like James, that people tend toward self-appreciation. Mead saw language as an essential part of self-description and assessment, and postulated the idea of a generalized self apart from more specific selves that function in particular situations.

From the early 1900s until the late 1940s comparatively little attention was paid to the study of the self-concept and self-esteem by academic psychology. This was largely due to the preoccupation of mainstream psychology with achieving an identity as a scientific discipline. In its effort to be objective and to model after the physical sciences, it tried to divorce itself from abstract, philosophical constructs and to focus on observable behavior.

Neopsychoanalytic theorists such as Adler, Horney, Fromm, and Sullivan, who emphasized the role of interpersonal relationships in the shaping of personality, touched on various aspects of self-conception and self-esteem. Adler's emphasis on the perception of defects as the dynamic behind striving for superiority is similar to contemporary conceptions of self-esteem. A basic component of Horney's (1950) theory was the need to value oneself and to be valued by others. Fromm (1939) saw self-love as critical to healthy interpersonal relationships. Sullivan (1953) described the self in wholly social terms and felt that the self-concept was learned through reflected appraisals of others made possible by the symbolic capacity of the human being.

With the emergence of humanistic psychology and its prominent theorists, Rogers, Maslow, and May, who have made self-processes the center of their theory and therapy, considerable theoretical and therapeutic work has focused on self-perception. This has included development of experimental investigation of issues related to the self, including self-esteem. The waning of more radical forms of behaviorism and its tentative marriage with rapidly developing cognitive psychology have also legitimated the study of self-referent constructs.

Coopersmith (1967), Rosenberg (1979), and Ziller (Ziller, Hagey, Smith, & Long, 1969) have developed the most explicit contemporary theories of self-esteem based on empirical studies. Coopersmith sees self-esteem as a personal evaluation of worth that has very strong feelings associated with it. He believes that self-esteem is determined by an interplay of a person's success, values, aspirations, and defenses. Rosenberg analyzes the self-concept in terms of attitudinal structures and sees self-esteem as a positive or negative orientation that is one of the most powerful human motives. Self-esteem is viewed as a function of reflected appraisals, social comparison processes, self-attribution, and psychological centrality. Ziller conceives of self-esteem as a buffer between the self and the social environment. His analysis is primarily in Gestalt, topological concepts.

Research in Self-Esteem. The importance of self-esteem is supported by a variety of empirical studies showing that it is associated with a wide variety of personal and interpersonal characteristics (Ellison, 1976). Self-esteem has been shown to be related to persuasibility and attitude change. Low self-esteem is associated with anxiety and neurotic behaviors, social inadequacy, and psychosomatic illnesses. Those with low self-esteem are more likely to be immaturely dependent, sensitive to criticism, approval oriented, and antisocial. They are more likely to feel unlovable, afraid of arguing with others, and too weak to overcome their deficits. Those with higher self-esteem are more active in group discussion, more intellectually curious, more likely to become leaders, less likely to conform, more satisfied with life, and more likely to have a positive relationship with God. They are less likely to be depressed, defensive in their relationships, and distrustful.

The most commonly accepted analysis of self-esteem regards it as the result of comparison between a person's perceived self, which is made up of the evaluations of other people and one's own evaluation based on self-observation, and the ideal self, which is a mixture of how one would like to be and feels he ought to be. The ideal self reflects values transmitted by the culture and emotionally significant other people. The level of positive self-esteem is a function of the degree of discrepancy between the ideal and perceived self. The greater the discrepancy, the lower the self-esteem.

Currently there is some debate as to whether there is one general, unified self-concept or whether there are many selves (Gergen, 1971) or dimensions of self-esteem. Although some recent literature suggests the existence of multiple components of the self, no personality theory has systematically identified what those components are and related them to self-esteem. There are a few scales—such as the Tennessee Self-Concept Scale (Fitts, 1965), which describes eight categories of reported self-concept—but these seem to be either empirically or theoretically limited.

Development of Self-Esteem. It is in the context of the parent-child relationship that feedback crucial for one's self-esteem begins. Acceptance of the child is basic to the development of positive self-esteem. Acceptance is communicated in various ways. For the infant and young child it is expressed through physical gentleness, time spent holding and talking, appropriateness and time lapse in meeting needs, and spontaneous play. For the older child it involves gentleness (not permissiveness) in discipline, time spent encouraging and affirming ideas and positive behavior, and use of language to express praise and affection. The impact of parental feedback in childhood is especially important because it occurs at a time when the child is developing basic conceptual categories where none existed before, and when the parent's input carries considerable weight because the child has comparatively little other feedback about himself and perceives his parents as omniscient.

Early parental evaluation is also given at the point of greatest language inability and received, therefore, in simplified emotional terms. As a result the child initially reads evaluations in "all or none" terms. With subsequent cognitive development and exposure to additional sources of input the person is able to be more selective and limited in his reception of evaluation, but a core feeling of good/bad self seems to be retained. In addition to information control the control of rewards and punishments allows the parent to communicate goodness and badness to the child. Finally, there is evidence to suggest that self-esteem is related to identification with one's parents, especially the mother. If a mother has low self-esteem, she is likely to foster a similar self-perception in her children by providing a negative model; by pushing the children so hard to make up for her inadequacies that they feel inferior because they can't meet her standards; or by being overly sensitive to their shortcomings because these might reflect on her inadequacies.

As the child develops, additional sources of feedback enter in. For the teen-ager peer evaluation is critical. For adults the assessment of marital partners, work supervisors, and peers is important. Various studies have indicated that those with higher self-esteem have higher goals and more successfully achieve them, though affirmation of the person apart from achievement seems important also.

Many of the key values that American society uses as the standards of worth are shaped by mass media and education and subsequently internalized and applied by parents, peers, authority figures, and spouses. These values center on what people do and how they compare with others. Failure to meet these criteria usually results in low self-worth. These values include appearance, achievement, affluence, assertion, and actualization. The more that one possesses or utilizes these qualities, the higher his self-esteem deserves to be, according to our society. As a result of the comparison base one's self-esteem is relatively vulnerable. Power, prestige, and personal rights are sought as ways to guard against negative self-evaluation.

Biblical Perspective. In contrast, biblical standards of self-esteem focus on what God thinks rather than what others think (1 Sam. 16:7). The biblical basis of self-esteem is grace, not works. Human beings do not have to achieve or possess anything to be worthwhile in God's eyes, though they have to be open to his love in order to experience affirmation.

The biblical building blocks of positive self-esteem are divine creation, redemption, confession, servanthood, and community. The act of divine creation contains several indications of the positive value God placed on his creation. First, he evaluated what he had made and said it was "very good" (Gen. 1:31). In addition, he assigned the major responsibility of administering his creation to Adam and Eve (Gen. 1:28). Significant responsibilities are not normally delegated unless the one charged is highly valued. God also cared for the man and woman by providing food for them (Gen. 1:29–30). Such provision is an act of love. Further, according to Psalm 139, God has special concern for each person he creates, and he gives each a special purpose in his plan (Rom. 12:3–6).

God did not stop treating human beings as worthwhile when sin entered the world. Instead he gave his most valuable possession as a sacrifice (Rom. 5:6–8) in order to redeem each person. Other passages (e.g., 1 Peter 2:9–10) specifically assert that he chose us, even while we were antagonistic toward him.

When Adam and Eve sinned, they immediately began blaming, denying, and hiding. These ego defense mechanisms were and are automatically invoked to protect the sense of self-esteem. None of them are effective, however. Unconfessed sin brings depression, disease, and guilt (Ps. 38). Instead of leaving persons without a way for the restoration both of spiritual communion and of self-worth, God provided confession as a means of cleansing, restoration, and renewed affirmation from God and others.

The key to positive self-esteem on a daily basis is to act with God's purposes and evaluation in mind. Such an orientation of servanthood (Col. 3:17, 23) frees a person from much of the anxiety and damage of social comparison and negative comments by others. Work and relationships are freed to be more caring and constructive, which in turn encourages reciprocated affirmation. The inner satisfaction of God's approval becomes a stable source of self-worth.

The biblical conception of community is as a place of affirmation where love reigns and destructive criticism is foreign (Col. 3:12–14), a place of equality where each person's contribution potential is recognized and affirmed (1 Cor. 12:14–27), and a place of counterculture where the prevailing cultural bases of unstable and competitive self-worth are replaced by biblical values (Eph. 4:11–17).

According to Scripture, positive self-esteem is not to be confused with the sin of pride. Pride involves an attitude of superiority over others and a spirit of independence from God. It is refusal to admit weakness and error, which amounts to an attempt to maintain the charade of perfection, or Godlikeness. More often than not arrogance is the sign of a person who really doesn't accept himself. The Bible warns against the improper elevation and overestimation of ourselves (Rom. 12:3; Gal. 6:3), while encouraging accuracy testing in order that we might take pride in ourselves (Gal. 6:4).

The other extreme from defensive pride is false humility. This is a belief that one is no good and has no ability to do anything, which usually has religious overtones. The belief is that to have a sense of positive self-esteem is to have pride, the sin which God abhors most (Prov. 6:16–17).

In contrast, true humility is compatible with healthy self-esteem. Appropriate self-worth involves the ability to see one's strengths and weaknesses, to admit and confess sins, but to still feel positive. True humility and positive self-esteem are based on accuracy rather than on feelings of superiority (pride) or feelings of inferiority (false humility). The greatest example of true humility and positive self-esteem is Jesus Christ (Phil. 2:3–8). Christ was clearly sinless and therefore truly humble, but also asserted who he was without apology. Scripture does not allow the conclusion that he was arrogant or that he belittled himself. Because of his worth, his servanthood and sacrifice have redemptive meaning. The Bible suggests that God's people are to have the same servant attitude as Christ, and implies that we are expected to properly love ourselves, as Christ did (Mark 12:31).

References

Cooley, C. H. *Human nature and the social order.* New York: Scribner's, 1902.
Coopersmith, S. *The antecedents of self-esteem.* San Francisco: W. H. Freeman, 1967.
Ellison, C. W. (Ed.), *Self esteem: A new look.* San Francisco: Harper & Row, 1982.
Fitts, W. *Tennessee self-concept scale: Manual.* Nashville: Counselor Recordings and Tests, 1965.
Fromm, E. Selfishness and self-love. *Psychiatry,* 1939, 2, 507–523.
Gergen, K. J. *The concept of self.* New York: Holt, Rinehart, & Winston, 1971.
Horney, K. *Neurosis and human growth: The struggle toward self-realization.* New York: Norton, 1950.
James, W. *Principles of psychology* (Vol. 1). New York: Holt, 1890.
Mead, G. H. *Mind, self, and society from the standpoint of a social behaviorist.* Chicago: University of Chicago Press, 1934.
Rosenberg, M. *Conceiving the self.* New York: Basic Books, 1979.
Sullivan, H. S. *The interpersonal theory of psychiatry.* New York: Norton, 1953.
Ziller, R. C., Hagey, J., Smith, M., & Long, B. H. Self-esteem: A self-social construct. *Journal of Consulting and Clinical Psychology,* 1969, 33, 84–95.

Additional Readings

Narramore, B. *You're someone special.* Grand Rapids: Zondervan, 1978.
Vitz, P. C. *Psychology as religion: The cult of self-worship.* Grand Rapids: Eerdmans, 1977.
Wagner, M. E. *The sensation of being somebody.* Grand Rapids: Zondervan, 1975.
Wells, L. E., & Marwell, G. *Self-esteem: Its conceptualization and measurement.* Beverly Hills, Calif.: Sage Publications, 1976.

C. W. ELLISON

See SELF-CONCEPT TESTS.

Self-Fulfilling Prophecy. A prediction or belief that serves to bring about its own fulfillment. The person believing it acts in such a way as to make the prophesied event more likely. It is sometimes called the Pygmalion effect after Ovid's and Shaw's account of people who shape others to be what the creators want them to be. It is also called the experimenter expectancy effect because researchers may unintentionally cause their experiments to come out as expected. The concept of the self-fulfilling prophecy was developed by Merton (1948), but it has been developed extensively by Rosenthal. In fact, it is sometimes called the Rosenthal effect.

The classic studies involve rats and schoolchildren. Rosenthal and Fode (1963) randomly divided 60 rats among 12 experimenters who were to teach their rats to run to the darker arm of a T-maze. Although all the rats were the same, six of the experimenters were told that they had "maze-bright" rats and the other six were told that they had "maze-dull" rats. From the beginning of the experiment the rats believed to be smart actually became better performers. They showed a daily improvement in their scores throughout the experiment, while those believed to be dumb improved only through the third day, then actually did worse. The "dull" rats refused to move from the starting position 29% of the time, while the "bright" ones refused only 11% of the time. The experimenters with the "bright" rats viewed their animals as brighter, more pleasant, and more likable, and were more relaxed with them. They described their own behavior as more pleasant, friendly, and enthusiastic, and handled their rats more often and more gently than the experimenters with the "dull" rats.

Rosenthal and Jacobson (1968) did a similar experiment in a real-life situation with teachers and schoolchildren. They gave all the children in a school an IQ test and told the teachers it was a test that would predict intellectual "blooming." They then randomly picked 20% of the students and told the teachers that these students would show a sudden spurt in intellectual growth. As with the rats, the only differences between the children were in the minds of the teachers. The children were tested eight months later, and it was found that the children randomly designated as bloomers increased in IQ scores by four more points than those not picked. Furthermore, the effect was greater in the lower grades than in the upper ones. The teachers may have paid greater attention to the bloomers, may have been more patient and more encouraging, and may have communicated that high standards were being set for them.

These experiments have been widely criticized, and literally hundreds of similar studies have been conducted. The effect is not always found, but it is found often enough for most people to believe it is real. Rosenthal (1976) reviewed all the studies he could locate, and 109 of the 311 studies found a statistically significant correlation. Thus, self-fulfilling prophecy is found only about one-third of the time, indicating that we do not understand the factors producing it well enough even to find the effect every time an experiment is run.

Rosenthal (1976) believes that four factors produce the effect. First, we tend to produce a warmer social-emotional climate for special people. Second, we give the special ones better feedback as to how they are doing. Third, we give them more material and more difficult material. Finally, we give the special ones more opportunities for responding.

Self-fulfilling prophecy is of concern not only in conducting experiments and in education, but in many other areas. People who believe they can only produce a little do so, while those who think they can do more actually do more. People taking surveys find the results they expect to find, influencing the responses. Hypnotists find that their success in hypnotizing a given person depends on whether or not they believe the person can be hypnotized. Psychotherapists have greater success if they believe the client can be helped.

The phenomenon of self-fulfilling prophecy has obvious implications for the church. Sunday school teachers who expect their children to misbehave may actually produce misbehavior. Pastors who expect trouble with their official board may elicit the trouble. Christian counselors who expect a patient to get worse may treat the patient in such a way that he or she actually does. Of course, if the Christian workers expect the best from people, they will be more likely to get it.

References

Merton, R. K. The self-fulfilling prophecy. *Antioch Review*, 1948, *8*, 193–210.
Rosenthal, R. *Experimenter effects in behavioral research* (Enl. ed.). New York: Irvington, 1976.
Rosenthal, R., & Fode, K. L. The effect of experimenter bias on the performance of the albino rat. *Behavioral Science*, 1963, *8*, 183–189.
Rosenthal, R., & Jacobson, L. *Pygmalion in the classroom*. New York: Holt, Rinehart, & Winston, 1968.

R. L. Koteskey

Self-Help Groups. *See* MUTUAL HELP GROUPS.

Self-Injurious Behavior. Any of a number of stereotyped or repetitive behaviors by which an individual causes damage to his or her body. It is perhaps the most dramatic and extreme from of chronic human psychopathology. Baumeister and Rollings (1976) have called it "the most distressing and bizarre of all behavioral aberrations that people exhibit. . . . There are probably few among us . . . who do not experience a quickened sense of anguish upon witnessing a child beat and brutalize himself" (pp. 1–2).

Any analysis of this behavioral excess raises three fundamental questions: Why do some people repeatedly inflict injury upon themselves? Why does such behavior persist in the face of severe consequences? What can be done to modify such behavior? Consideration of these matters raises other complex issues, and answers are still only partial.

Self-injurious behavior is a serious problem with the mentally retarded in many institutionalized settings. Because of the possibility that the individual might inflict severe damage upon himself, it is a problem that demands immediate attention on the part of the staff members. Such behavior forces people to respond. Like any other behavior it increases with the presence of reinforcing consequences, and the attention of well-meaning adults is often precisely such a reinforcer. There are varied forms of self-injurious behavior, the most common being headbanging, eye gouging, self-biting, self-scratching, tooth grinding, and rectal digging. These behaviors often occur in conjunction with other rhythmic stereotyped behaviors such as rocking, weaving, and finger flicking (Baumeister & Forehand, 1973). In certain cases the behavior appears to be part of the temporal pattern or topography of these stereotyped behaviors, whereas in other cases it appears to be under very specific stimulus control (Bachman, 1972). Some individuals will exhibit mild forms of self-injurious behavior that will be fairly stable and continuous, whereas others will show forms that occur in high-frequency bursts, resulting in serious tissue damage, only to cease once the injury has been inflicted. Shortly after the lesion heals, the individual will then exhibit another burst, and the cycle will be repeated, often for years.

There are five hypotheses about the etiology and/or maintenance of self-injurious behavior. The positive reinforcement hypothesis states that it is a learned operant, maintained by social reinforcement, which is delivered contingent upon the occurrence of the behavior. The negative reinforcement hypothesis suggests that at times it is maintained by the termination or avoidance of an aversive stimulus following the occurrence of a self-injurious act. The self-stimulation hypothesis contends that a certain amount of tactile, vestibular, and kinesthetic stimulation is necessary for the organism; and when it is not obtained, the organism will engage in activity that aims at increasing these levels of stimulation. The organic hypothesis states that self-injurious behavior is most often due to aberrant organic processes (e.g., brain damage, subseizures, metabolic or endocrine disorders). The final hypothesis, the psychodynamic, argues that the behavior is an infantile or fetal drive, a form of masochism, a rejection mechanism, displacement of anger or aggression, evidence of poor ego identity, or the search for body reality (Lester, 1972).

A review of research on treatment of self-injurious behavior (Butman, 1979) suggests that there are many effective means of suppressing it and replacing it with more adaptive behaviors. Of the treatments available, response contingent electrical shock, noxious odors, overcorrection, and certain types of reinforcement of other behavior strategies appear to produce the most durable changes in frequency and intensity. Certain legal, ethical, administrative, and procedural considerations make it incumbent upon researchers and clinicians to develop, refine, and evaluate other nonaversive alternatives to punishment for the treatment of this behavioral problem.

References

Bachman, J. A. Self-injurious behavior: A behavioral analysis. *Journal of Abnormal Psychology*, 1972, *80*, 211–224.

Baumeister, A. A., & Forehand, R. Stereotyped acts, In N. R. Ellis (Ed.), *International review of research in mental retardation* (Vol. 5). New York: Academic Press, 1973.

Baumeister, A. A., & Rollings, J. Self-injurious behavior. In N. R. Ellis (Ed.), *International review of research in mental retardation.* (Vol. 8). New York: Academic Press, 1976.

Butman, R. E. *The non-aversive treatment of self-injurious behavior in severely and profoundly retarded children.* Unpublished doctoral dissertation, Fuller Theological Seminary, 1979.

Lester, D. Self-mutilating behavior. *Psychological Bulletin*, 1972, *78*, 119–128.

R. E. BUTMAN

Self-Instruction. A type of cognitive-behavioral intervention associated with Meichenbaum (1977), who first used the technique with impulsive hyperactive children. The problem-solving deficits that Meichenbaum discovered through studies of these children were 1) they did not analyze their experience in cognitive mediational terms, and 2) they did not have rules formulated on the basis of this analysis to guide their actions. In developing a therapeutic intervention, therefore, Meichenbaum attempted to teach these children "(a) how to comprehend the task, (b) spontaneously produce mediators and strategies, and (c) use such mediators and strategies to guide, monitor, and control their performance" (1977, p. 31).

The treatment package that Meichenbaum and Goodman (1971) developed was called self-instructional training, and consisted of five steps: 1) the child observed the adult model performing the task as he talked out loud to himself; 2) the child performed the task under the direction of the adult's instruction; 3) the child performed the task using his own verbal instructions; 4) the child performed the task while whispering the instructions to himself; and 5) the child performed the task using covert instructions. This treatment package employs several intervention strategies common to many cognitive-behavioral interventions. During the first step the adult's instructions serve as a cognitive model for the child, an example of what his thoughts should be. The second step is a form of participant modeling, where the child and the adult model perform a task together. The actual self-instruction begins in step 3, where the child guides his performance with overt verbal instruction. Step 4 is a fading of the instructions, and step 5 moves the self-instruction from an overt to a covert level.

When research using this treatment approach was supportive of its usefulness with children, Meichenbaum returned to a group of patients who had been the subject of his doctoral dissertation, adult schizophrenics. In his dissertation study (Meichenbaum, 1969) a group of hospitalized schizophrenics received an operant training program to engage in "healthy talk" (relevant and coherent talk). While testing the schizophrenics Meichenbaum found that several spontaneously repeated the experimental instruction, "Give healthy talk; be coherent and relevant." A more elaborate self-instructional package for schizophrenics was then developed and tested by Meichenbaum and Cameron (1973), in which schizophrenic patients were taught to monitor and alter their own behavior and thinking. Meichenbaum and Cameron's results, replicated in a case study by Meyers, Mercatoris, and Sirota (1976), showed that such training significantly improved verbal and cognitive functioning among the schizophrenics.

More recently the use of self-instructional training has been expanded to treat a variety of adult as well as childhood disorders. For example, Genshaft and Hirt (1980) used self-instruction for the treatment of mathematics anxiety. Assertive deficits have also been treated with self-instructional training, either alone or in combination with behavioral rehearsal (Craighead, 1979). In addition, self-instructional methods have been incorporated into many coping-skill approaches.

While research evidence supports the usefulness of self-instruction, there are still several unanswered questions about this treatment approach. A primary concern is what self-instructions should be taught to clients—those that are specific to a certain task or those that are more general and conceptual? Also, the process by which self-instruction mediates behavior is poorly understood. Although Meichenbaum (1977) argues that thought is covert speech and that such covert speech regulates behavior, there is not agreement on this position. An additional question is how such Christian activities as prayer and Scripture memorization lend themselves to inclusion in such a treatment approach. However, in spite of these questions, self-instruction treatment approaches appear to have increasing acceptance as a way of modifying certain cognitive and behavioral responses.

References

Craighead, L. W. Self-instructional training for assertive-refusal behavior. *Behavior Therapy*, 1979, *10*, 529–542.

Genshaft, J. L., & Hirt, M. L. The effectiveness of self-instructional training to enhance math achievement in women. *Cognitive Therapy and Research*, 1980, *4*, 91–97.

Meichenbaum, D. The effects of instructions and reinforcement on thinking and language behavior of schizophrenics. *Behaviour Research and Therapy*, 1969, *7*, 101–114.

Meichenbaum, D. *Cognitive-behavior modification*. New York: Plenum, 1977.

Meichenbaum, D., & Cameron, R. Training schizophrenics to talk to themselves. *Behavior Therapy*, 1973, *4*, 515–534.

Meichenbaum, D., & Goodman, J. Training impulsive children to talk to themselves. *Journal of Abnormal Psychology*, 1971, *77*, 115–126.

Meyers, A., Mercatoris, M., & Sirota, A. Case Study: Use of covert self-instruction for the elimination of psychotic speech. *Journal of Consulting and Clinical Psychology*, 1976, *44*, 480–482.

E. M. Altmaier

See Cognitive-Behavior Therapy.

Self-Monitoring. The Behavior Therapy technique in which a client acts as observer and recorder of his own behavior, with the goal of producing useful data regarding the frequency and context of occurrence of specific behaviors. The technique is especially useful in gathering data on behaviors that are unobservable (e.g., thoughts or feelings) or when observation by another person would be inconvenient. Kanfer (1980) has suggested that in introducing self-monitoring to a client, it is useful to stress the importance of accurate record keeping, to clearly and concretely define the class of behaviors to be observed, to select convenient methods of record keeping, and to practice the technique in the session with the client.

Self-monitoring is primarily used as a technique for Behavioral Assessment. Its validity as an assessment technique has been challenged, in that clients can be quite inconsistent in the accuracy of their reports. However, it frequently generates useful information, and it is currently generally recommended to be used in conjunction with other assessment procedures. Self-monitoring is also an important component in behavior therapy procedures where client self-management is a critical aspect of treatment. Finally, self-monitoring may exert a therapeutic effect even when used in isolation, as when it reveals to clients an obvious need for change in a particular area (e.g., when a spouse's self-monitoring reveals that he rarely does anything positive for his spouse), or when it is incompatible with the problem behavior (e.g., when having a client monitor outbursts of rage interferes with getting angry).

Reference

Kanfer, F. Self-management methods. In F. Kanfer & A. Goldstein (Eds.), *Helping people change* (2nd ed.). New York: Pergamon, 1980.

S. L. Jones

Self-Perception Theory. The theory that we come to know our own attitudes and other internal states partially by inferring them from observations of our own behavior and its results. Designed by Bem as a radical behaviorist's alternative to cognitive dissonance theory, it is increasingly used to interpret socio-psychological phenomena.

Especially if our internal cues are weak, ambiguous, or uninterpretable, we evaluate our own attitudes and feelings as would an outside observer, who infers inner states based on an after-the-fact explanation of behavior within its environmental forces (Bem, 1972). Self-perception theory assumes that the best way to change attitudes and beliefs is to change behaviors. For example, when people start acting like Christians, they will infer that they really believe in Christianity, especially if they perceive no coercion to act this way.

Cognitive dissonance theory assumes that if we hold to two inconsistent cognitions, we will follow a psychological strain toward consistency by revising one or more of the conflictual behaviors or perceptions. Bem's (1967) replication of a number of the famous dissonance studies led him to consider self-perception theory as more parsimonious than dissonance theory. It appears that dissonance reduction operates when our actions are clearly discrepant from our attitudes, and that self-perception processes operate when our actions are compatible with our attitudes, although a step or two beyond them (Fazio, Zanna, & Cooper, 1977). Bem's 1972 refinement of his theory moved beyond behaviorism to an attribution interpretation. It is now used to explain the development of intrinsic motivation in achievement contexts, where it suggests that low external inducements are preferable to high inducements. This is one reason for not bribing youth through external rewards for such things as memorization of Scripture or for moral development. When such bribes are removed, intrinsic motivation for the desirable behaviors is much less than would be the case if high inducement rewards were not employed. The theory also interprets emotional misattribution, such as when naïve girls, who have previously been aroused by exciting games or even evangelistic services, may be seduced by their dates after the arousing event. Evangelists not only need to allow their hearers' emotions to mellow, but also to train them to understand how internal emotions are affected by social pressures and to develop communication skills that will develop godliness when they are aroused emotionally.

References

Bem, D. J. Self-perception: An alternative interpretation of cognitive dissonance phenomena. *Psychological Bulletin*, 1967, *74*, 183–200.

Bem, D. J. Self-perception theory. In L. Berkowitz (Ed.), *Advances in experimental social psychology* (Vol. 6). New York: Academic Press, 1972.

Fazio, R. H., Zanna, M. P., & Cooper, J. Dissonance and self-perception: An integrative view of each theory's proper domain of application. *Journal of Experimental Social Psychology*, 1977, *13*, 464–479.

R. W. Wilson

See Attribution Theory.

Self Psychology. The term is most closely associated with the work of psychoanalyst Heinz Kohut, who developed a theory of psychological development based on the construct of the self. Originating in infancy, the self integrates and adequately develops to produce healthy relationships in adult life; or, the self fragments and otherwise inadequately develops, producing the total range of adult psychopathologies. Kohut's work is presented in two volumes, *The Analysis of the Self* (1971) and *The Restoration of the Self* (1977).

Kohut asserted that the Freudian psychic apparatus (ego, id, superego) and the complexities surrounding this apparatus (castration fear, oedipus conflict, penis envy) are inadequate to describe the basic infantile psyche. The self is the center of the psychological universe. It comprises the total body of inner experiences of which the person is aware at any given time. It is not a part of the psyche, as are the ego, superego, and id. It might be said that the self is the sum of all these entities plus an unnamed integrating function.

Development of the Self. The development of a cohesive adult self has its beginnings in the second year of life, when the fragmentary cognitive precursors of the self are consolidated into a nucleus which Kohut called the infantile grandiose self. The child's natural tendencies at this stage are exhibitionism and idealization of omnipotently perceived caretakers. The absence of an experienced separation of self and others leads to the infant's grandiosity. The archaic representations of mother and self, experienced as one object, are called self-objects. If the caretakers are adequately nurturing, this structure enhances the development of the grandiose self. Under such conditions the self-object is further idealized, leading gradually to idealized parental image. These two components, the grandiose self and the idealized parental image, represent the two basic elements of the infant's self. The grandiose self is the seed from which grow adult self-confidence, assertiveness, and ambition, while the idealized parental image matures into admiration and love.

A central characteristic of the self is its bipolar nature. One pole of the self is ambitions; the other is ideals. Connecting the two poles are the talents and skills of the individual. A person is driven by his ambition and led by his ideals. Ambition is the mature form of childhood aggressivity, and leads to assertiveness. Ideals originate from childhood idealizing of parents and the subsequent inner and personal development of these ideals. Satisfying and productive life results from proper integration and cooperation of these parts of the bipolar self. Thus one learns to achieve and to nurture as well as to follow and be nurtured.

Kohut's stages of development of the self may be summarized as follows: 1) Narcissistic early infantile self-objects give way to 2) a developing sense of self along with control over self and the world. This is followed by 3) early love and hatred, with some of the earlier omnipotence of self and others having been abandoned, and 4) a mature loving based on proper distinction between self and others and realization of personal and others' limitations. More simply, "I am perfect" yields to "You are perfect" yields to "I am part of you and perfect" yields to "We are separate and perfect" yields to "We are separate and imperfect." Eventually, from the proper development of the grandiose self and the idealized parental image grows the nuclear self, or mature personality.

A later elaboration that Kohut (1977) made to this basic structure of the healthy (nuclear) self is that psychological health results from the integration of the "superficial" and the "deep." The superficial is that which is historical, factual, and predictable, while the deep is fantastic, creative, and unique. The former results primarily from a loving relationship with the father, the latter from similar contact with the mother. It is also implied that empathic mothering is the primary ingredient in moving infantile grandiosity to mature creativity. Good fathering moves the child's idealized parental image to proper admiration of others.

Psychopathology and Treatment. When the child does not receive adequate parenting, usually because of narcissistic and otherwise maladapted parents, the child remains fixated on archaic grandiose self and self-objects. Thus the self remains primitive and fails to develop adequately for satisfactory adult adjustment. Specifically, the person remains impaired in loving and valuing. The adult personality is also deprived of the energies invested in the maintaining of these early structures, and adult realistic activities are hampered by intrusions of these early narcissistic needs into daily life.

In psychotic disturbances delusional ideations result from very early grandiose self or self-object representations, and in narcissistic personality and behavior disorders the self is insufficiently developed to avoid undue fears and inappropriate grandiosity of the self. Kohut identifies the following symptoms as all due to early narcissistic injury (lack of love): sexual perversions, inhibitions in work and play, oversensitivity, undue rage, lack of humor and empathy, poor impulse control, feelings of emptiness and depression, and feeling not fully real. What has happened, Kohut suggests, is that defensive structures cover the low self-esteem, depression, feelings of rejection, and incessant hunger for approval. These defenses include the traditional mechanisms of defense but also include pseudovitality, undue romanticism, and hysterical features. Additionally, compensatory structures, essentially inadequate displacements, replace the desirable sublimations. Thus, the narcissistically injured person engages in neurotic behavior or delinquency in place of achievement and creativity, the natural results of properly integrated early narcissism.

Kohut's principal interest was in narcissistic disorders. These people, in his view, have had deficient experiences in two out of the three areas of the self (ambitions, ideals, and talents and skills). Such persons are vulnerable to narcissistic injuries, real or imagined, to which they respond with anxiety or fragmentation. They become easily hurt and defensive, and are unable to sustain a good self-esteem under disappointment or rejections. They may become lonely and feel empty or become unduly aggressive.

Whereas narcissistic personalities have achieved a cohesive self, however vulnerable, borderline patients have not achieved cohesiveness. Thus borderlines and lesser developed personalities such as schizoids, paranoids, and psychotics are not candidates for psychoanalysis. Neurotic persons can be dealt with primarily by attending to the fear of rejection and the inadequate self-supports.

Much of Kohut's work relates to the transference phenomenon occurring in analysis. If the therapist is empathic (loving) and distant without being disinterested, the patient projects his narcissistic injury on the therapist, allowing the basic analytic work to progress and resolve such injuries. The malfunctions associated with early damage are alleviated by the analyst allowing the patient freedom to be appropriately narcissistic. The therapist seeks to replace archaic self-object constructs with realistic appraisals of self and others. This is done by the therapist being empathic for the patient and concentrating on developing the person's ability to cope with disappointment. The therapist thus serves to encourage both poles of the self, ambitions and ideals, by serving first as the idealized parental image and then as a real person.

References
Kohut, H. *The analysis of the self.* New York: International Universities Press, 1971.
Kohut, H. *The restoration of the self.* New York: International Universities Press, 1977.

R. B. JOHNSON

Self-Punishment. A self-control procedure in which individuals present or remove a stimulus following their own behavior, thus weakening it. Examples include saying "Oh, that was dumb," slapping oneself on the hand, and administering an electric shock.

Self-punishment is especially helpful in situations where the undesirable behavior produces immediate reinforcement but also results in delayed aversive consequences. Examples include overeating, staying out too late, alcohol abuse, and going back to sleep in the morning after switching off the alarm. A portable shock apparatus has been developed that can be used to administer self-punishment. It has been used for a variety of undesirable behaviors, such as obsessive thoughts, homosexual fantasies, visiting "adult" bookstores, and dressing in clothes of the opposite sex.

A basic problem with self-punishment procedures is that their unpleasant nature results in little motivation to carry out the procedures. Only a person who is highly motivated to give up homosexual fantasies would consistently administer electric shock when these thoughts occur. Another disadvantage is that unlike self-reinforcement, the effectiveness of self-punishment is not well established.

Self-punishment is rarely used in a pure form. In those self-control procedures where self-punishment is used, it is generally used in conjunction with a self-reinforcement procedure. As with self-reinforcement, self-punishment carries connotations that are inconsistent with behavior theory unless it is clearly understood that the act of administering self-punishment is itself a learned response, which is maintained by the positively and negatively reinforcing consequences that the environment provides to support it.

R. K. BUFFORD

See PUNISHMENT; LEARNING.

Self-Reinforcement. *See* REINFORCEMENT, SELF.

Self Theory. Rogers developed his self theory well after he had formulated his PERSON CENTERED THERAPY. His view of personality grew out of his view of therapy, and the former can be understood only in the context of the latter.

In order to account for the personal changes which he observed clients going through in therapy, Rogers formulated his structural view of personality. Subsequently he formulated a statement on how personality evolves, which constitutes his theory of personality development. Finally, in answer to the question: What sort of person would emerge as the end product of a growth experience of the person-centered type? he formulated his normative, or ideal, view of personality.

Structural Perspective. Rogers's earliest (structural) theory of personality (Rogers, 1951) coincides with the time when his overall thinking was still structure bound rather than process oriented. He presented it in the form of 19 propositions.

The first seven propositions deal with the human organism and how it functions in its environment. According to Rogers, it functions as an organized whole, and as such it reacts to an experienced or perceived environment. It has only one motivating tendency—to actualize and enhance itself by fulfilling its experienced needs in a perceived world. This actualizing activity Rogers calls behavior.

The next five propositions deal with the development and function of the self. In accordance with the actualizing tendency the self differentiates out of the organism's total perceptual field. It becomes elaborated through the organism's interaction with its social environment, and it carries within itself values that are derived from both the organism and the social environment. The latter values are frequently perceived distortedly as coming from the organism rather than from the environment. Once the self has become established, it becomes that entity in relation to which all the experiences of a person become symbolized and perceived. The organism also tends to adopt only those ways of behaving that are consistent with this self-structure.

Propositions 13–16 deal with psychological maladjustment. Maladjustment occurs when certain organic experiences generate behaviors that are inconsistent with the self-structure. These may be significant experiences, and thus need to be related to the self. But because of their inconsistency with the self they are not taken up into the self-structure. The result of this is psychological tension. Experiences that are inconsistent with the self come to be perceived as a threat to the self, and in defense against this the self-concept tends to become more rigid, thereby shutting out an increasing number of significant experiences. Finally, propositions 17–19 describe how this trend can be reversed. Under certain conditions when there is no external threat to the self-structure, these inconsistent experiences may be allowed into awareness to be assimilated into a revised

self-structure. When this occurs, a person becomes more integrated within himself and thus also more accepting of others. Finally, he will replace his present value *system* with a more fluid organismic valuing *process* as a guide for his life.

Developmental Perspective. In his theory of the development of personality and the dynamics of behavior Rogers describes how the human infant develops into a full-fledged personality and how disintegrations and reintegrations can occur during this development. The characteristics of the human infant are essentially those of the human organism described above. For the infant, experience is reality. He reacts to his experience in an organized, total fashion and in accordance with his tendency to actualize himself. He values his experiences in terms of whether or not they enhance his organism. He behaves with adience toward those that do and with avoidance toward those that don't.

As the infant matures, certain experiences related to himself differentiate out of his total experiential world and become perceptually organized into a self-concept. Together with this newly developed awareness of his self the growing infant also develops a need to be regarded positively by significant others in his surroundings. This is a potent force in his life. Because of it the growing child is no longer exclusively oriented toward his own organismic valuing process but becomes at least partially oriented to the values of others.

These positive-regard satisfactions and frustrations can also come to be experienced by the child apart from the positive-regard transactions he may have with others around him. When this happens the child has, as it were, become his own significant social other. He has come to regard himself positively or negatively, independent of what others say about him. This Rogers calls self-regard.

Whenever significant others selectively value some aspects of the child as more worthy of positive regard than others, the child himself tends to become similarly selective in his self-regard. He then begins to avoid or seek out certain self-experiences solely in terms of whether or not they are worthy of self-regard. Whenever that occurs, the child is said to have acquired conditions of worth. If, however, the growing child were to experience only unconditional positive regard from others, then no conditions of worth would develop in him. His self-regard would thus also be unconditional, and his need for positive regard and self-regard would never be at variance with his organismic evaluation. For Rogers this would represent a fully functioning, psychologically well-adjusted individual.

However, this is not what actually happens in child development. More often than not development produces individuals who have conditions of worth. Because of their need for self-regard such individuals tend to perceive their experiences selectively, symbolizing those experiences that are consistent with their current self-concept and barring from awareness those experiences that are not. An incongruence thus arises between their selves and their experience. This tends to produce discrepancies in their behavior as well. Behaviors that enhance their self-concept will be at odds with behaviors that, while enhancing their total organism, are inconsistent with their self-concept.

If an individual has accumulated such a large degree of incongruence between his self and his experience that he can hardly keep it from coming to awareness, he becomes anxious. When his incongruence has increased to such proportions that he can no longer defend his self against it at all, his self disintegrates and his organism becomes disorganized. In such a state the organism may at one time behave in ways that are consistent with the self and at other times in ways that are not.

This "confused regnancy" in the individual's organism is the end result of the process of defense that started when the individuals obtained his first conditions of worth. The process can be reversed by decreasing the individual's conditions of worth and by increasing his unconditional self-regard. The conditional positive regard of others gave the individual his conditions of worth and caused him to be conditional in his self-regard. By the same reasoning others can remove these by making their positive regard toward him unconditional. This effectively eliminates the threat against which the individual defends his self-concept. With the threat removed, the process of defense can begin to reverse itself. The individual can symbolize more and more of his experiences into his awareness. He can revise and broaden his self-concept to include these new experiences, and as a result he can become more and more integrated. Thus, he experiences increased psychological adjustment and, like the infant, he once again uses his own organismic valuing process to regulate his behavior. The final result of this therapeutic process is that the individual becomes more and more of a fully functioning person.

Normative Perspective. The fully functioning person is the ultimate in actualization of the human organism. As a matter of fact, such a person does not exist. There are only persons moving in the direction of fully functioning, without ever reaching it. Thus the description of a fully functioning person is "pure form." It is an ideal or normative description of personality functioning (Rogers, 1969). Rogers's normative description coincides with that period in his development when his thinking had become fully dynamic and process oriented. It asks the questions: What is an optimal person?

Such a person is fully open to his experience. Every stimulus originating in the organism or the environment is freely relayed through the nervous system without distortion. There are no barriers to fully experiencing whatever is organismically present.

Second, such a person lives in an existential fashion. Each moment is new to him. No one can predict what he will do the next moment, since what he will do grows out of that moment. In such existential living the self and personality emerge from experience, rather than experience being twisted to fit a preconceived self-structure. This means that one becomes a participant in, and an observer of, the ongoing process of organismic experience rather than being in control over it.

Such living in the moment means an absence of rigidity, of tight organization, of the imposition of structure on experience. It means instead a maximum of adaptability, a discovery of structure *in* experience, a flowing, changing organization of self and personality, of which the most stable characteristics are openness to experience and the flexible resolution of one's existing needs in the existing environment.

Finally, such a person finds his organism a trustworthy means of arriving at the most satisfying behavior in each existential situation. He does what "feels right" in this immediate moment and generally finds this to be a competent and trustworthy guide for his behavior.

Rogers compares the organism of such a person to a giant computer. Because such a person is open to his experience, he has access to all the available data in the situation. Out of all these his organism comes up with the most economical avenue of need satisfaction in this existential situation. That is, it comes up with a way of behaving that feels right.

It is not infallible, however. Even the organism of a fully functioning person makes mistakes because at times some of the data will be missing. But this is not serious, since being open to his experience, the fully functioning person can quickly spot that error and quickly correct it. In fact, the computations of such a person will always be in a process of being corrected, because they will be continually checked against resulting behavior.

In summary, the fully functioning person who emerges from a theoretically optimal experience of personal growth is able to live fully in, and with, each and all of his feelings and reactions. He makes use of his organic equipment to sense as accurately as possible the existential situation within and without. He uses all of these data in awareness but recognizes that his total organism may be, and often is, wiser than his awareness. He allows his total organism in all its complexity to select from the multitude of possibilities that behavior which in this moment of time will be most generally and genuinely satisfying. He trusts his organism in its functioning, not because it is infallible, but because he can be fully open to the consequences of each of his actions and can correct those that prove to be less than satisfying.

He can experience all of his feelings, and is afraid of none. He is his own sifter of evidence but open to evidence from all sources. He is completely engaged in the process of being and becoming himself, and thus discovers that he is soundly and realistically social. He lives completely in this moment, but learns that this is the soundest living for all time. He is a fully functioning organism, and because of the awareness of himself that flows freely in and through his experiences he is a fully functioning person.

In Rogers's view of personality organismic processes take preeminence over self-processes. In this respect also he oriented himself more to Dewey's pragmatism than to existentialism or phenomenology. Thus, his theory of personality is not a self theory but an organismic theory. Growth rather than self-consistency is the basic intent of his view of personality.

Rogers believes in the inherent goodness (or positive directedness) of the individual person. He localizes the origin of evil (or negative directedness) in the environment—i.e., in the way significant others relate to the individual person. But he fails to explain how it is possible that inherently good persons become evil to each other when they relate to each other.

By identifying the problem of evil with a defect in one part of created human reality, Rogers fails to recognize that evil is sin—i.e., a matter of the human heart. He does not acknowledge that like redemption sin, and therefore evil, is total—i.e., that evil, like our deliverance from evil, affects the whole of created human reality. Because of his attitude he is driven to overvalue personality (our individual separateness) and to devalue communality (our membership in larger social wholes). Practically speaking, this means that Rogers's view of personality cannot account for the positive effect of socialization on the growth and development of personality.

References
Rogers, C. R. *Client-centered therapy.* Boston: Houghton Mifflin, 1951.
Rogers, C. R. *Freedom to learn.* Columbus, Ohio: C. E. Merrill, 1969.

H. A. VAN BELLE

Selye, Hans (1907–). Austrian physician best known to psychologists for his study of STRESS. Born in Vienna, he received his M.D. (1929) and Ph.D. (1931) from German University, Prague. He took a position at Johns Hopkins University in 1931; the following year he moved to McGill University in Montreal, where he remained from 1932 to 1945. In 1945 he moved to the University of Montreal, where he taught until his retirement in 1976.

According to Selye stress is the body's response to demands made on it. Selye refers to these demands as stressors. Stress, then, is a biological state manifested by a syndrome—i.e., a set of symptoms. On the basis of a long series of experiments with animals, he concluded that bodily stress reactions follow a three-state general adaptation syndrome. The three stages of this syndrome are an alarm reaction, a stage of resistance, and a stage of exhaustion.

In the alarm reaction the body mobilizes its resources to cope with added stress. The adrenal glands step up their output of adrenaline and noradrenaline. As these hormones enter the bloodstream, some bodily processes are speeded up and others are slowed, to concentrate bodily resources where they are needed. Common physiological responses during this stage are increased cardiac rate and output, increased blood pressure, increased respiratory rate, decreased blood supply to the visceral organs, increased blood supply to the vital organs (heart, brain, liver, peripheral muscles), and dilation of the pupils. These responses constitute a physiological "call to arms"—the fight, flight, or fright responses to the stressors.

If the stress persists, the individual enters a second stage, resistance. During this stage the person seems to develop a resistance to the particular stressor that provoked the alarm reaction. The symptoms that occurred during the first stage of stress disappear, even though the disturbing stimulation continues, and the physiological processes that had been disturbed during the alarm reaction appear to resume normal functioning.

If the stress still continues, the stage of exhaustion comes about. In this stage the body's resources are exhausted and the stress hormones are depleted. Unless a way of alleviating stress is found, a psychosomatic disease, organ failure, serious loss of health, or death may occur.

Two ideas appear to be central to Selye's theory. The first is that the body's response is the same regardless of the source of the stress. The second is that a continued pattern of these reactions ultimately results in physical breakdown.

Selye's major works are *The Physiology and Pathology of Exposure to Stress* (1950), *The Stress of Life* (1956), *Stress in Health and Disease* (1976), and *The Stress of My Life* (1977).

S. N. Ballard

Senile Psychosis. *See* Dementia.

Sensitive Period. Developing organisms, whether animals or human, encounter sensitive or critical periods when biological changes and environmental influences interact in such a way as to have a permanent effect. The earlier the period of influence, the more profound the consequences; damage to the fetus is greater in early pregnancy, and harm to the child is more severe during the first few years of life. If the expectant mother takes a drug such as Thalidomide or contracts a disease such as rubella (German measles) during the first three months of pregnancy, when the limb buds of the fetus are forming and the heart, eyes, ears, and other organs are taking shape, the damage to the child may be malformed arms and legs, an impaired heart, blindness, deafness, and in some cases retardation and even death. The fetus is less sensitive to these influences after the first trimester, although malnutrition of the mother, smoking, or excessive alcohol consumption may be harmful to the unborn at any time during the gestation period.

The human infant is more sensitive to becoming attached to the principal caretaker (usually the mother) during the first year of life than at any other time, and if neglected or mistreated during this time may become emotionally scarred (Bowlby, 1969). Studies of animals confirm the importance of early bonding; birds imprint on the first moving object within hours after hatching (Hess, 1973), and monkeys deprived of mothering are unable to relate to other monkeys and will engage in self-mutilation when under stress (Harlow, 1971). A dog or a cat growing up wild will not make a good pet even though given care when mature. The critical period for learning to love and for receiving love has passed.

Even as there are sensitive periods for physical development and for emotional attachment, so there also are sensitive periods for the acquisition of personality traits needed for optimal psychological functioning (Erikson, 1959). The first and most important component of a healthy personality is a sense of trust acquired by the baby during the first year, followed by a sense of autonomy in the toddler, initiative in the preschooler, industry at the elementary school age, identity at the high school level, intimacy in early adulthood, generativity in middle adulthood, and integrity in old age. Each component is sensitive to a particular time in the person's life and is dependent on the formation of the personality components preceding it.

Freud (1923/1961) believed that a sensitive or critical period exists for moral development. If a child has not acquired a superego or conscience before the age of 6, it will be either more difficult or impossible to develop a sensitivity to right and wrong at a later time. There is also evidence for an optimal time for toilet training (Sears, Maccoby, & Levin, 1957), language acquisition (Bloom, 1970), intellectual performance (Piaget, 1971), and classroom learning.

Parents and educators are understandably concerned when a child does not proceed at the optimal rate for learning a particular skill. There is now increasing interest in the consequences to the child who is pushed into activities for which he or she is not prepared. Growing up too fast too soon is the theme of Elkind's *The Hurried Child* (1981), which shows that damage may be as great for the child who is hurried as for the child who proceeds too slowly. Either way, the stage of growth has not been linked to its most sensitive period, resulting in less than optimal performance.

The Scriptures tell us to "train a child in the way he should go, and when he is old he will not turn from it" (Prov. 22:6). The sensitive period for training in appropriate behavior comes in childhood, and the effects of that training last for a lifetime.

References

Bloom, L. *Language development*. Cambridge: M.I.T. Press, 1970.

Bowlby, J. *Attachment and loss*. New York: Basic Books, 1969.

Elkind, D. *The hurried child*. Reading, Mass.: Addison-Wesley, 1981.

Erikson, E. H. *Identity and the life cycle*. New York: International Universities Press, 1959.

Freud, S. *The ego and the id*. In J. Strachey (Ed. and trans.), *The standard edition of the complete psychological works of Sigmund Freud* (Vol. 19). London: Hogarth, 1961. (Originally published, 1923.)

Harlow, H. F. *Learning to love*. San Francisco: Albion Publishing, 1971.

Hess, E. H. *Imprinting: Early experience and the developmental psychobiology of attachment*. New York: Van Nostrand, Reinhold, 1973.

Piaget, J. *Biology and knowledge*. Chicago: University of Chicago Press, 1971.

Sears, R. R., Maccoby, E. E., & Levin, H. *Patterns of child rearing*. Evanston, Ill.: Row, Peterson, 1957.

B. CLOUSE

See LIFE SPAN DEVELOPMENT; DEVELOPMENTAL PSYCHOLOGY.

Sensitivity Training Group. Often called a T-group, this is a psychoeducational technique in which a group of people meet together for the purpose of learning about group process, interpersonal relations, and themselves. Such groups are also sometimes called human relations groups or growth groups. Although they differ from ENCOUNTER GROUPS in their goal of understanding group dynamics, T-groups and encounter groups share much in common, and in many ways T-groups have been absorbed within encounter groups.

Sensory Deprivation. A technique that reduces or eliminates normal sensory input to our five senses, consequently producing cognitive and perceptual deficits, increased persuasibility, hallucinations, and altered brain activity. Studies of this phenomenon were stimulated by successful cases of brainwashing during the Korean War, when American soldiers were isolated for long periods of time in tiny underground cubicles that reduced movement and restricted light and sound except for propaganda messages.

Researchers at McGill University (Bexton, Heron, & Scott, 1954) simulated these conditions with volunteers who were paid $20 a day. They were to lie on a bed, their eyes covered with translucent goggles, their arms and legs covered with padded cardboard cylinders to reduce tactile stimulation, and their hearing restricted to the hum of a fan or a taped persuasive message about poltergeists that they could request to hear. Half of the subjects quit before 48 hours; those who remained had difficulty concentrating or performing complex tasks, experienced some perceptual and motor impairment, were more persuaded by the propaganda than were the controls, and experienced hallucinations. No one expected to find hallucinations.

Subsequent studies have confirmed these results, although variations in techniques have inevitably produced some inconsistencies. Researchers have used confinement to bed, confinement in an iron lung (a whole-body respirator previously used for polio victims), and submersion in water kept at body temperature to produce deprivation. Some researchers have used sensory deprivation, the complete elimination of sensory information (e.g., darkness or silence), and some have used perceptual deprivation, the elimination of patterned stimulation (e.g., uniform light or sound).

Deprivation of either type can produce some striking cognitive deficits. In spite of subjects' intentions to use the time for creative thinking, they almost always found themselves unable to concentrate during the experiment and were later unable to engage in study or other activities for some time afterward, especially after long (24 hours or more) periods of deprivation. Furthermore, duration of their deficit was proportional to the duration of their deprivation.

When subjects are reporting experiences during deprivation, their speech is often slurred and sentences may be poorly constructed. Simple learning and memory for previously learned material is intact, but problem solving is impaired (Zubek, 1969). Depth perception and susceptibility to certain illusions are mildly impaired, while acts requiring hand-eye coordination are more severely affected.

Hallucinations are of two types: Type A, which are characterized by formless or meaningless lights or sounds, and Type B, which are complex, organized, and meaningful. Voices, music, or complex animated scenes appear in Type B hallucinations. These hallucinations usually follow Type A experiences in sequence and are colorful, three-dimensional, and realistic. Subjects are not able to control their onset, content, or termination. They can be scanned with the eye but the movement in the scene sometimes causes eyestrain and even nausea. The hallucinations occur spontaneously; they are not disturbed by conversation or physical exercise but are disrupted by complex activities such as mental arithmetic.

Apparently hallucinations can be produced equally well by sensory or perceptual deprivation but are more frequent when the participant is lying down rather than sitting. The subject's sex, intelligence, personality, and prior expectations of having hallucinations do not affect the number of hallucinations experienced. Some investigators have wondered whether the hallucinations were really dreams recalled after awakening. However, neither the subjects' reports of their experiences nor their brain waves (EEGs) support this idea. Some hallucinations do occur when participants are drowsy, but most occur when the subjects are alert and awake. Hallucinations can occur after only half an hour of deprivation, and their frequency does not seem to increase as a function of time, at least after the first hour.

The hallucinations produced by sensory deprivation seem more like those produced by drugs such as LSD or mescaline than like psychotic experiences. The former are primarily visual, progressing from diffuse perceptions of light and geometric forms such as lattice work, cobwebs, and spirals to more organized and meaningful forms. These also produce diffuse and widespread distortions of the environmental setting. The experiences produced by drugs are usually more vivid, colorful, and consistent than those produced by sensory deprivation. By way of contrast, psychotic hallucinations are predominantly auditory (probably less than 5% are visual), appear full-blown, are usually superimposed on a normal environmental setting, and involve many more religious or supernatural figures than those produced by sensory deprivation and drugs.

Several attempts have been made to explain sensory deprivation hallucinations. For example, in the absence of external stimulation the brain may begin to interpret available retinal signals in peculiar ways, or perhaps the absence of external stimulation intensifies the normal imagery we all experience. Hallucinations in drowsy states may actually be hypnagogic (i.e., dreams in the waking state). Most investigators, however, would agree that at this point we still do not understand either the causes of these hallucinations or their underlying mechanisms.

References

Bexton, W. H., Heron, W., & Scott, T. H. Effects of decreased variation in the sensory environment. *Canadian Journal of Psychology*, 1954, 8, 70–76.

Zubek, J. P. (Ed.). *Sensory deprivation: Fifteen years of research*. New York: Appleton-Century-Crofts, 1969.

E. L. HILLSTROM

See CONSCIOUSNESS.

Sentence-Completion Tests. Verbal projective techniques widely used in both clinical practice and research. Generally stimulus words or sentence stems are given to the examinee which permit an almost unlimited variety of possible completions. Examples might be: Life is . . . ; The Bible . . . ; It is a terrible thing to be . . . ; God . . . ; It would be nice to forget . . . ; Fathers often . . . ; Most churches. . . . There are numerous published and unpublished forms of sentence-completion tests, the most widely used one being the Rotter Incomplete Sentences Blank. In all these forms sentence stems or stimulus words are formulated to elicit responses deemed relevant to the aspect of personality being assessed. The obvious advantage of this assessment technique, then, would be flexibility.

Sentence-completion tests are almost always used in conjunction with other personality assessment techniques to generate hypotheses reflecting certain attributes of individual persons. In this way the clinician or researcher can evaluate emotional, affective, or stylistic qualities of persons in as meaningful and reliable way as possible. This is indeed a challenge, since there is little agreement among personality theorists as to what personality is or what the term means. Unfortunately, the perspectives of theory, research, and testing have been relatively independent of one another, resulting in a great proliferation of tests and instruments to measure personality. Models that are truly integrative are urgently needed in clinical assessment to help the clinician or researcher more accurately and logically evaluate a person's cognitive and perceptual functions, how he feels and what his attitudes are.

In an effort to improve the psychometric qualities of the test for assessment purposes, the Rotter sentence test contains these instructions: "Complete these sentences to express your real feelings. Try to do every one. Be sure to make a complete sentence." The test is not timed. Each response is scored by the examiner on a seven-point scale according to the degree of adjustment or maladjustment indicated (guidelines and examples are given in the manual). This results in fairly objective scoring. One then sums the scores and gets a final score that is thought to be a total adjustment indicator. Rotter recommends that the test be used for screening purposes or that the response content be examined clinically for more specific diagnostic clues.

The test requires cooperation and accurate

self-report from the examinee. It is recommended that it be used in conjunction with one or more self-report or personality inventory (e.g., the Minnesota Multiphasic Personality Inventory, the Sixteen Personality Factor Questionnaire, the Edwards Personality Preference Schedule, the Mooney Problem Checklist) and one or more other projective technique (e.g., Children's Apperception Test, Thematic Apperception Test, or Rorschach). Many clinicians consider the test to be a good rapport builder in the initial stages of the assessment process and an opportunity to obtain information that might not be otherwise available to the examiner. The clinician must be careful about overgeneralizing from the sentence completion test. It is best to consider it as a behavioral sample that reflects a person's current life situation as well as enduring cognitive, perceptual, and emotional features of the individual.

An exciting recent development in a specialized application of the sentence completion technique is the Washington University Sentence Completion Test. It is based on Loevinger's (Loevinger, Wessler, & Redmore, 1970) construct of ego development, a seven-stage model of emotional growth. Each item is scored according to a specific level, and a composite score is obtained that is a rough measure of maturation.

References

Loevinger, J., Wessler, R., & Redmore, C. *Measuring ego development* (2 vols.). San Fransisco: Jossey-Bass, 1970.

R. E. BUTMAN

See PERSONALITY ASSESSMENT; PSYCHOLOGICAL MEASUREMENT.

Sentiment.
A word used by Allport (1950) to refer to interest, outlook, or system of beliefs. Sentiments spring from a person's course of development when stable units of personality begin to emerge. According to Allport personality emerges as a product of motivation and organization. This system of readiness or motivated organization prepares the person for adaptive behavior that may be manifested as a habit, trait, neurosis, or sentiment. It becomes sentiment when the behavior represents an organization of feeling and thought directed toward a definable object of value, such as one's mother, son, keepsake, neighborhood, or fatherland.

Sentiment may also involve more abstract ideas of value, either positive or negative, such as the nature of beauty or religion. Thus an atheist may have a negative sentiment with regard to all things considered religious, while a Christian would have a positive sentiment. Allport discussed extensively the nature of mature religious sentiment. He viewed this as disposition built through experience which is able to respond favorably and in certain habitual ways to conceptual objects and principles that the person regards as of the utmost importance as well as to what is regarded as permanent or central in the nature of things.

Reference

Allport, G. W. *The individual and his religion*, New York: Macmillan, 1950.

J. H. ROBERTSON

Separation. *See* LOSS AND SEPARATION.

Separation Anxiety Disorder of Childhood or Adolescence.
Painful anxiety brought on by the threat of or actual physical separation from a loved one, home, or other familiar environmental area. Separation anxiety, if not in excess in the first years of life, is normal. It is not normal when the separation leads to panic feelings far beyond normal expectancy for the child or adolescent's developmental age.

Children and adolescents with excessive separation difficulties often experience an overabundance of discomfort, refusing involvement in activities away from home. Commonly they refuse to be alone in their own rooms or beds and "shadow," or remain very close to, the parent. Fear exists whenever the perception is that personal and family safety seems threatened. Young children's fears tend to be generalized; older children's fears become more specific and attached to identifiable potential dangers. Adolescents with this disorder, particularly boys, tend to deny overconcern about their mother or any desires to be with her. Their behaviors manifest a hesitancy to leave home, reflecting anxiety about the separation.

Children with high separation difficulties are often seen as demanding, intrusive, and needing constant attention; alternately, some are described as unusually conscientious, conforming, and eager to please. Their interpersonal skills are fine as long as they do not experience any requests for separation. They may express not being loved or cared for and/or a desire to be dead. This disorder may begin as early as preschool age; paradoxically extreme cases tend to begin later, around the ages of 11–12. Generally the child has periods of increased anxiety, and then these decrease for a while. There are situations where the disorder persists for years. It can limit school attendance and a free, independent life style.

Etiological theories are varied. Some studies suggest that traumatic experiences (surgery, death) precede the initial anxiety attack. Others suggest that prior learning experiences in the family or hereditary characteristics make certain children more vulnerable to traumatic events. Many believe that it is an overprotective parent who contributes to the development of the anxiety. Children and their mothers (in a few cases fathers) have developed a mutually dependent relationship in which separation is quite distressing to both.

This excessive anxiety over being separated from parents can be viewed as the child's or adolescent's difficulty in maintaining a sense of personal security and safety; only in the presence of the parental figure or at home base does the child feel safe. Real life situations do occur where a child's security is threatened. Many times, however, children tune into the anxiety of the parents, whose fears, tensions, and anxieties are transmitted unconsciously to the child. The parents' anxiety is projected onto the child, who is unequipped developmentally to discriminate between one's own fears and those of others.

To meet the diagnostic criterion for separation anxiety disorder in *DSM-III* a child must evidence at least three of the following manifestations: 1) unrealistic worry about possible harm to major attachment figures and a fear of being left; 2) unrealistic worry that some harmful circumstance will separate the child from the attachment object— e.g., child will be lost, kidnapped, killed, or the victim of an accident; 3) persistent reticence or refusal to attend school in order to stay home or maintain contact with parents; 4) constant reluctance or refusal to go to sleep without being next to the parent or to sleep away from home; 5) persistent avoidance of being home alone and/or becoming emotionally upset when prohibited from following the parent around home; 6) repeated nightmares with separation themes; 7) complaints of physical symptoms on school days—e.g., stomachaches, headaches, nausea, vomiting; 8) excessive distress over anticipatory or actual separation from parents—e.g., temper tantrums, crying, pleading with parents not to leave (distress must be of panic proportions for children under 6 years); 9) social withdrawal, apathy, sadness, concentration problems with work or play when the parent is not present. This disturbance must have lasted a minimum of two weeks. In addition the disturbance must not be due to

other disorders such as pervasive developmental disorder or schizophrenia.

A knowledge of the separation-individuation theory and process is important in working with these patients. A child's need for mother and the behavior and moods this need elicits are frequently misunderstood. Inquiry into the excessive fear and anxiety yields the data necessary for intervention. For example, a nursery school girl having difficulty tolerating her mother's leaving said, "If you cut your finger at school there are no Band-aids." A trip to the medicine cabinet to see Band-aids, along with other simple interventions, served to convey that a teacher or counselor also could provide care and protection for her; a transition was being established between mother-help and others-help. In another instance a child internalized her mother's felt loss in leaving her at school when she went to work. Interventions such as talking about Mommy at work, child-level books written on the subject, and comments that the child was doing the same kinds of activity as mother was at work served to develop a greater conviction that the mother existed even when not present.

Interpretations of the sources of anxiety may be helpful for older children and adolescents in helping them understand the origin of the anxiety. Support from a counselor as well as clarification and some confrontation of separation issues may enable patients to improve. Such interventions are intended to increase awareness of one's capacity to handle more than one realized. With such support these dependent, needy aspects of one's personality can be strengthened.

Additional Reading
Edward, J., Ruskin, N., & Turrini, P. *Separation-individuation*. New York: Gardner Press, 1981.

B. J. SHEPPERSON

Separation-Individuation Process. *See* MAHLER, MARGARET.

Sex Differences. *See* WOMEN, PSYCHOLOGY OF.

Sex Identity. *See* GENDER IDENTITY.

Sex Therapy. Prior to the pioneering work of Masters and Johnson (1970) sexual problems were treated as symptoms of underlying psychological disturbance. Psychoanalysis was the treatment of choice, and the goal of such treatment was resolution of the underlying cause of the sexual problem. Masters and Johnson introduced a behavioral and relational approach to the treatment of sexual problems by asserting that such problems were best treated by involving both partners in the treatment program. Their approach embraces the belief that sexual problems are learned maladaptive responses. Therefore, the resolution of such problems lies in learning new sexual behavior patterns.

Kaplan (1974), building on Masters and Johnson's work, asserted that sexual problems cannot be separated from individual psychopathology and interpersonal relationships. Her treatment seeks to uncover and address underlying psychological problems and relationship conflicts, as well as help clients learn new, adaptive, sexual behaviors. Thus, Kaplan's approach combines psychoanalysis and the behavior therapies.

A variety of other treatment approaches incorporate components of the Masters and Johnson model. Worthy of note is the work of LoPiccolo and Lobitz (1972), who developed a therapy program to treat women with inhibited female orgasm. Their program encourages female clients to learn self-exploration and pleasuring strategies as a means of learning to experience orgasm.

Sexual Dysfunctions and Treatment Approaches. There are two major sexual dysfunctions in the male: INHIBITED SEXUAL EXCITEMENT (formerly called impotence) and problems associated with EJACULATION. There are three major sexual dysfunctions in the female: inhibited female sexual excitement (formerly called frigidity, orgasmic or orgastic dysfunction), VAGINISMUS (involuntary spasms of the muscles of the vagina), and DYSPAREUNIA (painful intercourse). INHIBITED SEXUAL DESIRE, a condition experienced by both men and women, is reported more frequently in women than in men. This condition refers to a generalized lack of interest in sex. INHIBITED SEXUAL DESIRE does not impair sexual functioning and is therefore not considered a sexual dysfunction. However, it may be as distressing as sexual dysfunctions.

The etiology of sexual dysfunctions is beyond the focus of this article. Additionally, the following discussion assumes that these sexual dysfunctions have a psychological rather than organic basis and that this basis has been determined by means of thorough medical evaluation.

Inhibited male sexual excitement. Inhibited sexual excitement in men is the inability to achieve and maintain an erection of sufficient magnitude and duration to engage in sexual intercourse. A distinction is made between primary inhibited sexual excitement (when erection in intercourse has never been successfully achieved and maintained) and secondary inhibited sexual excitement (when situational erectile dysfunction is being experienced).

The goals for treating primary inhibited sexual excitement were outlined by Masters and Johnson (1970) as follows: 1) remove the man's fears of failure; 2) teach the man to be an active participant in the love-making process; 3) reduce the partner's anxieties about the man's performance.

Kaplan (1974) identified a step-by-step plan for treatment of primary male inhibited sexual excitement. First, introduce nondemand pleasuring. The couple is to refrain from intercourse during this first phase, which can last one or two weeks, and is instructed to engage in nongenital pleasuring. Second, teach the squeeze technique (Semans, 1956). The couple is to engage in pleasuring, including genitals. When the man achieves a full erection, his partner squeezes the glans of his penis, at the frenulum, until he loses the erection. The couple is then to resume pleasuring, with genital stimulation. The process is repeated. Regaining the erection provides a basis for a positive expectancy that erection will return. Third, introduce thought management techniques. The couple is taught to use a variety of thought management techniques aimed at stopping any thoughts about losing the erection. Fourth, introduce intercourse. The couple engages in intercourse, and every possible distraction is removed. They are instructed to use the female superior (woman on top) position. There is no demand for orgasm the first few times. Kaplan and others have reported successful treatment outcome utilizing this approach.

The goal for treating secondary inhibited sexual excitement in men is to identify the psychological and relationship factors that may be inhibiting sexual arousal and excitement. The goals and procedures for treating primary inhibited sexual excitement may then be employed.

Ejaculatory problems. Masters and Johnson define premature ejaculation as occurring when the man cannot postpone ejaculation while the penis is in the vagina long enough to satisfy the woman at least 50% of the time. This definition is limited in its usefulness since it presumes that all women are satisfied via penile vaginal penetration. Kaplan offers a more useful definition of premature ejaculation: the absence of voluntary control over the ejaculation reflex after the man attains heightened sexual arousal.

The major goals for treatment of premature ejaculation are to enable the man to enjoy intercourse without performance anxiety and to enable the man to learn to delay ejaculation. This is accomplished by instructing the couple to abstain from intercourse and engage in sensate focus (mutual pleasuring). The woman is instructed to pleasure her partner, including his genitals. When the man becomes fully erect and aware that ejaculation is imminent, he signals his partner to stop pleasuring until the ejaculatory sensations subside. The woman resumes pleasuring and the process is repeated. This is continued until the man can postpone ejaculation.

Another technique, developed by Semans and utilized extensively by Masters and Johnson, calls for the couple to refrain from intercourse and engage in mutual pleasuring. The woman is encouraged to pleasure her partner using a variety of techniques. When the man's penis becomes fully erect and he becomes aware that ejaculation is about to occur, he signals his partner. She firmly squeezes his penis for several seconds with her thumb placed on the frenulum, just under the glans, until the erection subsides. Stimulation and the squeeze technique are repeated several times. When the man has gained sufficient control, intercourse is gradually introduced. The woman is asked to use the squeeze technique three to six times before attempting penile vaginal insertion. The couple is also taught the basilar squeeze technique so that intercourse need not be interrupted by dismounting to apply the Semans technique. The basilar squeeze technique calls for firm pressure to be applied at the base of the penis. This technique can be applied by the man or woman. The couple is instructed to use the female superior position. Once the penis has made entry into the vagina, the woman is instructed to remain still for at least 30 seconds. The man is to begin slow thrusting during the first several experiences with intercourse. As he is able to tolerate increased thrusting without ejaculation, he gains control over delaying ejaculation.

Retarded male ejaculation occurs with less frequency. Treatment is aimed at identifying the underlying psychological and relationship issues that may be mitigating factors. Then the man is led through a series of procedures beginning with 1) masturbating to ejaculation while alone, 2) masturbating to ejaculation in the presence of his partner, 3) partner mastur-

bation to ejaculation, and 4) partner masturbation nearly to ejaculation and rapid insertion into the vagina for ejaculation. Additionally, the sensate focus program may be initiated to decrease performance anxiety.

Semans reported a high rate of success treating ejaculatory problems using this technique. Masters and Johnson and Kaplan also have reported excellent results using these therapeutic procedures. In addition, psychotherapy, couple therapy, and group therapy are all utilized to treat male sexual problems.

Inhibited female sexual excitement. Inhibited sexual excitement in women is the inability to experience the pleasure of orgasm. The woman may experience sexual arousal, but she does not experience orgasm. Again a distinction is made between primary inhibited sexual excitement (orgasm has never been experienced) and secondary inhibited sexual excitement (situational orgasmic dysfunction is presently being experienced).

The goals of treatment are to 1) reduce the prohibition from experiencing sexual arousal and pleasure, 2) increase the woman's knowledge about her body's sexual functions, 3) increase the woman's ability to experience self- and partner-induced orgasmic pleasure.

LoPiccolo and Lobitz (1972) pointed to the importance of the woman's comfort with her own sexuality as a key to experiencing sexual excitement and orgasm. This, coupled with the woman's ability to experience orgasm through self-pleasuring, should often be accomplished prior to including the partner. Including the partner too early in the treatment process may increase the woman's anxiety and inhibition.

Masters and Johnson developed the sensate focus program to aid in the treatment of anorgasmia. The program assumes that the woman is able to experience orgasm through self-pleasuring. This treatment program begins with the request that the couple refrain from genital contact during the first stages of treatment. They are then instructed to take turns exploring each other's bodies on at least two occasions between sessions, but to avoid the breasts and genitals.

The purpose of the first stage of sensate focus is to teach the couple to give each other pleasure and to become aware of nongenital sensations. During the initial phase the couple is told to be as silent as possible, since words may detract the partners from sensations. In the next stage touching may include the breasts and genitals. The couple is encouraged to communicate to one another about what they find pleasurable. They should not try to experience orgasm and should not have intercourse.

At the final stage couples are instructed to continue the mutual pleasuring and at some point to assume the woman-on-top position. The couple is told that they may have intercourse in this position. They are asked to refrain from intercourse until arousal is at its peak. The woman is instructed to focus on the pleasure of the sensations and to experience orgasm whenever she is ready.

Masters and Johnson reported excellent treatment success of inhibited sexual excitement in women; in one study they reported success with 80% of the patients they treated.

The goal of treating secondary inhibited sexual excitement in women is to identify the psychological and relationship factors that may be inhibiting sexual arousal and excitement.

Vaginismus and dyspareunia. Masters and Johnson estimated that vaginismus accounts for less than 10% of female sexual dysfunction and that dyspareunia is experienced by 1 to 2% of adult women on more than an occasional basis. Vaginismus is more frequently a psychological rather than organic problem. Dyspareunia may be a function of organic difficulties at about the same frequency as psychological problems.

Relaxation exercises and the insertion of graduated plastic dilators are most commonly used by medical practitioners. If relationship issues have been addressed, the transition to painless intercourse is frequently accomplished.

Treatment of dyspareunia is most frequently performed by physicians, who seek to rule out an organic basis for the disorder. In the cases of psychogenic dyspareunia, gradual and gentle exposure to sexual activity has been effective.

Summary. Sex therapy has grown and developed during the past two decades. While incorporating the therapeutic strategies of Masters and Johnson, Kaplan, LoPiccolo and Lobitz, and others, many psychotherapists today have found it efficacious to concern themselves with apparently nonsexual issues while treating sexual problems. These include communication, problem-solving skills, and assertion. In so doing, they are experiencing success in treating those disorders that make human relationships less than enjoyable.

References

Kaplan, H. S. *The new sex therapy.* New York: Brunner/Mazel, 1974.
LoPiccolo, J., & Lobitz, W. C. The role of masturbation in the treatment of orgasmic dysfunction. *Archives of Sexual Behavior,* 1972, 2, 163–171.
Masters, W. H., & Johnson, V. E. *Human sexual inadequacy.* Boston: Little, Brown, 1970.
Semans, J. Premature ejaculation: A new approach. *Southern Medical Journal.* 1956, 49, 353–358.

R. R. FARRA

Sexual Deviations. *See* PARAPHILIAS.

Sexuality. This term has been used in a variety of ways. At the broadest possible level, the term *gender sexuality* in this article will refer to "the way of being in, and relating to, the world as a *male* or *female* person" (Kosnick, Carroll, Cunningham, Modras, & Schulte, 1977, p. 82). A second type of sexuality, here termed *erotic sexuality*, is that of passionate desire for the other; the longing for completion through interaction with another, which possibly but not necessarily includes emotional, intellectual, spiritual, or physical interaction with the other (Thielicke, 1964). Finally, when physical sexual action is the focus, the term *genital sexuality* will be used, even though the sexual expression may not involve the genitals at all. When experience at all of the above levels is the focus, the unqualified term *sexuality* will be used.

Theological Perspectives. *History of Christian thought.* The thinking of the early church in the West on the topic of sexuality was deeply influenced by hellenistic and gnostic thought forms (Bullough & Brundage, 1982; Kosnick et al., 1977). Departing from the historic Hebraic affirmation of body life and sexuality, many of the early church fathers (including Justin Martyr, Origen, Tertullian, Jerome, and Ambrose) viewed genital sexuality as at most acceptable only within marriage for procreation, while erotic passion was to be spurned at all costs. Virginity or chastity within an established marriage was viewed as a superior mode of life. Justin Martyr and others wrote approvingly of young people having themselves castrated for the kingdom; these acts were later declared self-mutilation and condemned by the church.

Augustine's writings were the central pillar of the thinking of the church until the Reformation. He argued that the conjugal act in marriage was in itself sinless since it led to procreation, but paradoxically suggested that the pleasure attached to that act was a consequence of original sin and that erotic desire was a product of man's lower, fleshly nature. Other writers later attempted to remove the stigma from sexuality (e.g., Thomas Aquinas), but Catholic thought until very recently continued to reflect Augustine's reasoning.

The Reformers, among their other amendments of Christian doctrine, rejected the Catholic doctrine of clerical celibacy and its implicit asceticism on scriptural grounds. Luther, Calvin, and others esteemed marriage and sexual union as the gifts of God; to both, sexuality was a natural part of human existence. Luther dealt with the topic in an especially frank and earthy manner. Subsequent Protestant thought on this theme tended to slip back and forth between a latent asceticism and the healthier balance achieved by the Reformers (Feucht, Coiner, Saver, & Hansen, 1961).

Biblical themes. Sexuality in all its forms was an intended part of the created order. Genesis 1:27 is viewed by most contemporary scholars as teaching that males and females were equally created in the image of God, and this gender differentiation and the institution of erotic and genital sexuality were hailed by God and man as very good. Genesis 2:24–25 persuasively refutes any notion that conjugal relations between husband and wife are in any way contrary to God's intended order.

The Old Testament also suggests that bodily existence, marriage, and sexual intercourse were all gifts of God. A major distinction between the Hebraic people and the pagan cultures about them was their refusal to overly spiritualize sex by attributing genital sexuality to God, or to degrade the gift of sexuality in general by attributing its origins to Satan or the fall. While genital sexuality in marriage was affirmed in the Old Testament, harsh condemnation was expressed for extramarital genital sexuality. At points in the Old Testament women were given a radical equality with men; in other places the Scriptures portray a patriarchal society that does not reflect the equality of the sexes indicated to have been God's intent before the fall.

To understand the treatment of sexuality in the New Testament one must first realize that the Scriptures do not attempt to give systematic attention to the topic in the same way in which they treat the great doctrines of human depravity and divine grace. Rather, the broad themes are briefly touched on in addressing specific problems of concern. Further, all New Testament writings are colored by the eschatology of the writers, who expected an imminent return of the Son of Glory. Most of Paul's writings that have been understood as antisexual (e.g., 1 Cor. 7) are better understood as being rooted in this view of eschatology. His positive, Hebraic affirmation of the place of sexuality in human existence is more clearly presented in Ephesians 5. Other New Testament passages do seem to portray a more negative view of sexuality (e.g., Rev. 14:4) but cannot be dealt with here.

Theological themes. In understanding our sexuality it is critical to affirm that human existence is inevitably an embodied, physical existence. The fact that sexuality in all its forms is intimately intertwined with physical processes cannot be used to denigrate that aspect of our being. "Thus does the 'biblical view' of man represent him as consisting of two principles, the cosmical and the holy, which unites the individual into a free and personal oneness of being" (McDonald, 1981, p. 78). While Scripture makes this differentiation, it never denigrates the physical at the expense of the immaterial, and it constantly emphasizes the unitive, integrated nature of our existence. It should be remembered that body life can be made spiritual or carnal; the term *flesh* (*sarx*) is in Scripture primarily an ethical term, and we can have a fleshly mind as well as a fleshly body.

Unlike classical reformed theologians such as Hodge and Berkhof, the neoorthodox theologian Barth viewed the gift of sexuality as fundamental to the image of God which humans reflect. Barth, and many since, have suggested that human sexuality reflects the differentiation of persons within the Godhead and God's intimately relational nature. "God created man in His own image, in correspondence with His own being and essence. . . . God is in relationship, and so too is the man created by Him" (Barth, cited in Small, 1974, pp. 131–132; see also Thielicke, 1964). Thus, our sexual natures reflect the nature of the Creator of the universe.

It must be remembered that all our experience of sexual life is conditioned by the fall. Brunner (1939) has suggested that as a result of the fall a "vast rent . . . runs right through human nature" (p. 348). In the area of sexuality, according to Brunner, this rent has two results: "a shame which cannot be overcome, and a longing which cannot be satisfied" (p. 348). That is, a sense of shame reminiscent of the shame of Adam and Eve over their nakedness and a lack of fulfillment of our desire to know the other (which results in an unsatisfied longing and personal isolation) are perpetually ours as a result of the fall. Further, Brunner points out that enmity between the sexes is the result of the fall. One result of this enmity is that in the agelong struggle between the sexes, in which males have largely been dominant, the original distinguishing characteristics of the sexes (aside from the obvious anatomical differences) have been blurred. We have little information about what God originally intended in differentiating male and female, as we have spent the eons since the creation re-creating ourselves in our own images.

Sexual ethics. Christian theology in dealing with human sexuality has mainly been preoccupied with the clear articulation of biblical moral standards. Recently more attention has been given to areas that have been called "borderline cases" (Thielicke, 1964, p. 199). In confronting the issues presented here, we are forced to struggle with the central principles underlying the ethics of God's revelation. To paraphrase Thielicke, in struggling with the ethics of homosexual orientation we grapple with the nature and purpose of gender differentiation; the problems of divorce, remarriage, and birth control lead us to struggle with the basic nature of marriage; and abortion and artificial insemination bring us face to face with the issue of the nature of life and parenthood.

Christian ethics is inherently deontological ethics. Sexual acts have meanings in and of themselves. Some sexual acts are clearly declared moral or immoral in the Scriptures. We might term these acts "objectively" moral or immoral. Other acts (e.g., petting, masturbation, sexual fantasy, fetishism) must be judged in regard to their morality by reference to the principles that are assumed to underlie God's clearer sexual absolutes. While several Christian writers have attempted to articulate these values, the criteria given by Kosnick et al. (1977, pp. 92–95.) are eloquently developed. It is argued that sexual acts are most likely to be wholesome and moral when they are self-liberating, other-enriching, honest, faithful, socially responsible, life-serving, and joyous.

Purposes of sexuality. Two of the major purposes of sexuality are the procreative and unitive functions (Kosnick et al., 1977, p. 86). Genesis 1:28 states clearly that procreation is a fundamental purpose of genital sexuality, and the Scriptures as a whole are so clear on this point that it needs no further elaboration.

Union is the other clear purpose of sex presented in Scripture. Genesis 2:24 suggests that becoming "one flesh" is foundational to marriage and that genital sexuality is in some way fundamental to this process. The exact meaning of "one flesh" is a topic of some debate. Some Scriptural passages suggest that becoming one flesh with another is in some sense an immediate and permanent result of sexual intercourse (e.g., 1 Cor. 6:16). Such a doctrine creates numerous philosophical and practical difficulties, including the question of the marital status of the person who has had intercourse with more than one person. Theologians generally conclude that becoming one flesh is used in several ways, the most important of which denotes a process of growth between married persons in which sexual intercourse is a necessary but not sufficient precondition. The end goal of the process is to be a unitary expression of fidelity, commitment, purpose, love, and ownership of the other (see Small, 1974).

Several biblical passages suggest a third purpose of sexuality, that of physical gratification and pleasure. Paul's discussion in 1 Corinthians 7 suggests that genital sexuality in marriage gratifies a passionate desire and that this function of marriage is not sinful. Proverbs 5:19 suggests that the exhilaration of physical love serves to enhance the stability of a marriage. This function is probably subservient to the larger purpose of union.

From a theological perspective a group of broader purposes of sexuality emerge. Kosnick et al. (1977) broadened the terms *procreative* and *unitive* to *creative* and *integrative* better to describe the broadest purposes of sexuality. They argue that our potential for "shared existence" (p. 85) with persons of the opposite sex calls us to the task of creative completion of our personhood, to the realization of our unfulfilled potentials. Sexuality reminds us experientially of our relational natures and thus beckons us toward integration with others, including a nongenital integration or fellowship with others beside our spouses. Thielicke (1964) similarly argues that eros opens up the person to the experience of greater levels of self-acceptance and growth. We might also argue that sexuality was divinely created to experientially teach us important truths about the Godhead and our relationship thereunto. As argued earlier, gender differentiation reflects God's differentiated personhood, and sexual union in marriage reflects the complementary truth of union across differentiation within the Godhead and between God and humankind. Sexuality as a part of marriage is obviously a part of the symbolic representation in that institution of the relationship between Christ and his church (Eph. 5:21–33). This symbolism was obvious in the Old Testament as well, where sexual passion was a prime metaphor for the relationship of Israel to her God, both in the positive, faithful sense (Song of Songs) and the negative, adulterous sense (e.g., Ezek. 23).

Biological Perspectives. Contemporary textbooks in human sexuality (e.g., Masters, Johnson, & Kolodny, 1982; McCary & McCary, 1982) provide excellent presentations of the issues briefly presented here and should be consulted for further detail.

Sexual anatomy. Genetic gender is fixed at the moment of conception. An embryo with a pair of XX sex-determining chromosomes is a genetic female; a genetic male possesses an XY pair of chromosomes. Some individuals are conceived with abnormal chromosomal arrangements that complicate the process of sexual differentiation.

Development of internal and external sexual anatomy is a function of hormonal levels in the developing fetus. The internal and external sexual anatomy of males and females is indistinguishable up until the sixth week or so after conception. Differentiation is practically complete around the twelfth week of development. Under the influence of androgens (male hormones) the internal and external sexual anatomy of a male begins to develop. In the absence of these hormones, or when the target tissues are unresponsive to the hormones, female anatomy develops. These processes occur regardless of the genetic sex of the fetus. That is, a genetic female under the influence of androgens will develop testes, penis, scrotum, etc., while a genetic male not exposed to androgens develops ovaries, uterus, vagina, etc. Such conditions are called pseudohermaphroditism. The true hermaphrodite, which is very rare, is the infant born with both true ovaries and testicular tissues and almost always with a uterus.

Sex hormones also influence the brain. The most well-documented gender differentiation is in the hypothalamus, which plays a major controlling function in the regulation of sex hormones. The hypothalamus in the female is patterned for cyclical hormone production, resulting after puberty in the ovulatory/menstrual cycle, while the male hypothalamus maintains a relatively constant level of sex hormone production. Other possible brain differences between females and males have been investigated, but none has been sufficiently established to be firmly reported. It cannot be firmly asserted that the culturally stereotypical differences in aggressiveness, emotionality, or sexual responsiveness are rooted in stable brain difficiencies.

The next major stage of sexual development occurs at puberty. Under the influence of suddenly escalating hormone levels, changes begin to occur in the genitals and in other secondary sex characteristics. For both males and females puberty results in enlargement of the external genitalia, growth of pubic and other body hair, and an overall growth spurt. Females begin to experience breast enlargement, menarche (first menstruation), ovulation, vaginal secretion (including nocturnal lubrication), and development of feminine body form due to changes in bone structure and muscle/fat ratios. Males experience voice deepening (due to growth of the larynx), growth of facial hair, increased potential for muscle growth, increased incidence of erection, and nocturnal emissions. Puberty normally occurs between ages 10 and 16 (one to two years later for boys than for girls), though earlier and later dates can occur. Neither pregnancy nor impregnation is possible before puberty.

Adulthood is a fairly stable period of sexuality from a biological perspective. Menopause is the cessation of ovulation and menstruation for women, a condition that can be accompanied by discomfort and distress. A very small percentage of males experience a similar lessening of hormone production with resulting distress called the male climacteric. Most people, male and female, experience a decrease in sexual desire with aging; but a cessation of desire or capacity for sexual response is no longer viewed as a normal aspect of aging.

The most important sex organs for the male are the penis, testicles, seminal vesicles, and prostate. The glans, or head of the penis, is richly ennervated and is highly sensitive to tactile stimulation. The testicles, seminal vesicles, and prostate all contribute to ejaculation. For some men the penile foreskin is surgically removed at birth (circumcision). Presence or absence of the foreskin does not seem to affect sexual response. The testes, along with the adrenal glands, produce the male sex hormones; the testes alone produce sperm.

The major female sexual organs are the labia majora and minora, clitoris, vagina, uterus, and ovaries. The clitoris and the outer one-third of the vagina and the labia minora are the most erotically sensitive areas of the female body. The clitoris, like the penis, has a glans, or head, which is richly ennervated and extremely sensitive to stimulation. The inner (deeper) two-thirds of the vagina seem to be less sensitive to stimulation. The ovaries produce the female sex hormones and the ova, which can be fertilized by sperm and implanted in the uterus for development and birth.

Sexual physiology. The degree to which sexual drive is a biologically rooted phenomenon is unclear. Research suggests that there is some correlation between intensity of sexual drive and testosterone levels in males (produced in the testicles and adrenal glands) and androgen levels in females (produced in the adrenal glands). This relationship of hormone levels and sex drive is a complex one, however, in that sex drive is also a function of a number of psychological factors as well. Low sexual desire is not necessarily a function of lowered hormone levels, and hypersexual desire is not necessarily a function of elevated hormone levels. Hormones do nothing to direct sexual desire; there are no firmly established sex hormone differences between heterosexuals and homosexuals. While sexual response is closely regulated by female hormone levels in most animals, it appears that there is no such relationship for human females.

Masters and Johnson's (1966) conceptualization of the phases of sexual response has been the most influential in this field. Based on empirical clinical research with volunteers, their conclusion is that males and females experience four stages of sexual response: excitement, plateau, orgasm, and resolution. The two basic changes in the body during sexual response are vasocongestion (concentration of blood in specific tissues) and muscular tension throughout the body, especially in the genital area.

The excitement stage results from effective sexual stimulation of any sort, physical or psychological. Males and females both begin to experience increased muscular tension, including the beginning of elevation of heart and respiration rates. Vasocongestion in the male results in erection of the penis. Erection is a hydraulic event resulting from engorgement of blood in the penis. Vasocongestion in females results in the beginning of swelling of the tissues in the genital area, including hardening (erection) of the clitoris and lubrication of the vagina, which results from seepage or "sweating" of the vaginal walls. Vaginal lubrication does not come from glands. Nipple erection from vasocogestion is typical in women and frequent in men. Testicular elevation begins for men in this stage.

The plateau stage continues and intensifies the same physiological reactions for both sexes. In women the labia swell and deepen their color, the vagina expands, the uterus moves within the abdomen to become more erect, the clitoris continues to engorge with blood and become more sensitve, and the breasts swell. A flush on the skin of the chest is common. In men erection becomes complete, as does elevation of the testicles. A small amount of fluid may pass from the penile opening before ejaculation; this fluid may contain live sperm. This is a major reason why interruption of coitus before ejaculation is not effective as a method of birth control. The length of the excitement and plateau stages varies widely.

Orgasm, frequently called climax or coming, is characterized for both sexes by a sharp peak of overall muscular tension, but especially rhythmic muscular contractions of the genital area (for women, the outer third of the vagina and the uterus; for men, the penis, urethra, and prostate). Males typically experience a sensation of "ejaculatory inevitability," which signals the beginning of orgasm but precedes ejaculation. After this point is reached, orgasm has begun and ejaculation is inevitable within seconds, even though stimulation ceases. For males, ejaculation and orgasm are usually parallel but differentiable events. Orgasm without ejaculation, and the reverse, are possible and have been documented.

There is some controversy about types of female orgasm. Freud believed that there were two types of orgasm, clitoral and vaginal. The clitoral orgasm was deemed less mature and more autistic, while the vaginal orgasm (produced in coitus only) was viewed as more mature. The research of Masters and Johnson (1966) and others has demonstrated to the satisfaction of most of the scientific world that there is only one type of orgasm, one which results from clitoral stimulation. They showed that the clitoris is stimulated indirectly during intercourse by penile thrusting, and that there is no physiological difference between orgasm during masturbation and orgasm during intercourse. These conclusions have not been universally accepted. For example, Singer and Singer (1978) differentiated between clitoral, uterine, and mixed orgasms. Their position, as well as those of classical Freudians and others who disagree with the conclusions of Masters and Johnson, are not now well accepted in the scientific community.

The final stage of sexual response is that of resolution. For males and females the resolution stage is most often characterized by a rapid return to the unaroused resting state. The changes of the excitement and plateau states reverse themselves rapidly. If the person has reached the late plateau stage but has not experienced orgasm, resolution takes a much longer time to occur, and this can result in a variety of uncomfortable lingering sensations. In this phase a major difference between females and males emerges. Females are biologically capable of being multiorgasmic through the continuation of sexual stimulation. Not all women desire such experience or find it pleasant, however. Males, on the other hand, experience a refractory period following orgasm during which continued sexual stimulation does not result in a return of erection and capacity for sexual response. This refractory period is typically brief in young men (seconds or minutes) and gradually lengthens in duration with age (extending to hours or even days in later years).

A number of researchers have criticized Masters and Johnson's conceptualization of sexual response cycles because of what is perceived as their physiological reductionism and ignoring of the prerequisites of sexual arousal—i.e., sexual desire.

Psychological Perspectives. *Sexual Development.* How do genetic males (or females) become psychological males (or females)? Perhaps the two predominant models of gender differentiation are the psychodynamic model and the biosocial model. The latter enjoys the greatest acceptance today.

There are actually a number of psychodynamic models; the classical one is that of Freud. Freud believed sex (libido) to be the primary drive of human existence. He believed that around ages 4–5 young children come to have strong sexual/affectional longings for the opposite sex parent. In both sexes this is not a well-focused genital sexual desire like that experienced in adolescence, but a more diffuse desire to possess all the attention and affection of the opposite sex parent. For both sexes this affection is accompanied by fear of the same sex parent, who is seen as a stronger, more competent competitor for the other parent's affection who might hurt the child in the rivalry. This fear leads, in normal development, to identification with the same sex parent (becoming like them, assuming their characteristics) as a way of vicariously having the special affection of the other parent. Gender identity develops through identification. This process can be complicated by disturbances in father-mother relationships, absence of either or both parents, and psychological disturbances of either or both parents.

The biosocial view of gender differentiation is primarily identified with John Money, who has conducted a great deal of research with cases of sexual deviancy, gender disturbance, and physical aberrations in sexual development (summarized in Masters et al., 1982). Money emphasizes the interaction of biological and learned or psychosocial factors in development. Biological factors, as discussed earlier, determine genital appearance of the newborn child. Genital appearance at birth influences the manner in which parents and others interact with the developing child, influencing the child to accept the socially defined role behaviors of male or female. Money and his colleagues believe there is a critical period for gender identity development; gender identity is usually set by age 3 and is largely impervious to change. Thus, children whose sex is misidentified at birth (e.g., the female misidentified as a male due to genital masculinization caused by high androgen levels during development) or children raised as the other sex due to parental psychological disturbance grow up with a relatively stable sense of themselves being of the other sex than they are physically.

Money believes that developments in childhood and adolescence, both physical development and the development of erotic feelings for the opposite sex, serve to further substantiate the person's gender identity. Behavioral psychologists have added speculations about development of sexual orientation to Money's formulation. They suggest that sexual desire is relatively unfocused in the child, and that each incremental experience of sexual arousal serves to "stamp in" a sexual orientation through conditioned association. Previous development of a firm gender identity can serve to channel this process. Thus, boys with a firm sense of gender identity know that they should expect sexual arousal to girls and generally seek such arousal in the forms of fantasy or experience. Arousal thus experienced further confirms gender identity and solidifies sexual orientation.

Sexual behavior. Sexual behavior occurs throughout the life cycle (see McCary & McCary, 1982, or Masters et. al., 1982, for summaries of relevant studies). Ultrasound studies have suggested that male infants experience erection within the womb. Erection in male babies and vaginal lubrication in females have been demonstrated soon after birth. Children seem to naturally experience stimulation of the genital area as pleasurable. Genital self-stimulation (masturbation) is common in young children. Orgasm is possible throughout the life cycle, even though maximal pleasure is not derived therefrom until after puberty. Prepubertal males do not ejaculate upon experience of orgasm. A variety of types of sex play continues throughout childhood for many children.

Genital sexual activity is common in adolescence. There is much disagreement among figures reported in the empirical literature from surveys of adolescent and adult sexual behavior. A major problem with this literature is the high rate of refusal to participate by teen-agers contacted for interviewing (or by the parents of adolescents contacted for their permission for their child to be interviewed). Early studies suggested a large disparity between the occurrence of male and female masturbation in adolescence, but this gap has been shrinking over the years. It can be said with some firmness that the large majority of adolescents have masturbated to orgasm at least once by age 18. The number who regularly practice masturbation is thought to be somewhat below the overall incidence.

Erotic dreams and nocturnal emissions (together commonly called wet dreams) are almost universal in boys during adolescence. Erection is common throughout the life cycle as a correlate to the rapid eye movement (REM) stage of sleep, the stage when dreaming is most likely. Wet dreams may represent a mechanism for the release of sexual tensions. It is less commonly known that the female correlate of erection, vaginal lubrication, occurs regularly in sleep during REM periods. While not as common as nocturnal emissions in males, orgasm during erotic dreams is not unusual for women; up to 50% report this occurrence by adulthood.

Figures on homosexual experience in adolescence are difficult to interpret, given the common sampling problems and the differences across studies in how homosexual experience is defined. Some studies have inquired about homosexual stimulation to orgasm, while others have used a much broader definition that might incorporate any sort of same sex sexual play, even in earliest childhood. The best summary of this data suggests that a substantial number of men, and to a lesser degree women, have fleeting homosexual experiences early in life. It appears that only about 2–3% of the male population and 1–2% of the females are exclusively homosexual in experience, with an additional 5–10% of each sex having at least one significant prolonged homosexual experience. Male homosexuals outnumber females two or three to one.

Intercourse before marriage is becoming more common and more accepted in American society. The consensus of a number of studies is that by age 16 close to 35% of males and 25% of females are nonvirgins; by age 19 about 70–80% of unmarried males and 60–70% of unmar-ried females are nonvirgins. These figures appear to represent a dramatic change in sexual behavior among females, who are becoming much more sexually active. These figures cannot be taken to indicate a complete swing toward promiscuity, however, as most adolescents do not report large numbers of sexual partners. Whereas in the 1950s many men reported first intercourse experience with a prostitute, most young men and women now report intercourse to occur in a caring relationship. Casual sex is perhaps only slightly more widespread today than in the past, but there is a much broader acceptance of sex with affection outside of marriage than was previously the case.

In adulthood most persons marry. The frequency of intercourse in marriage may have increased moderately over the past several decades. Frequency of coitus decreases steadily with age. In this, the sexual desires of the male seem to predominate, in that it is commonly reported that males' sexual desire peaks in late adolescence and the early 20s, declining thereafter. Females' sexual desire is reported to peak in he 30s and 40s. Adultery has become more common in the United States, with most recent studies suggesting that about 50% of males and 33% of females have had at least one extramarital experience of coitus. Those proportions are higher in younger groups. Some studies suggest that a fairly high percentage (up to one-half) of married couples experience moderate to strong dissatisfaction with their sexual relationship with their spouses.

Factors influencing sexual behavior. Research with adolescents and college students (Chilman, 1978) suggests that the following factors are associated with premarital coitus: increasing age, lower religiousness, greater permissiveness of peers, lessened influence of and communication with parents, higher self-esteem in boys but lower self-esteem in girls, lower academic achievement expectation, higher value of independence from family, permissiveness of parents, and basic sexual ideology or morality.

A number of factors that influence satisfaction with genital sexual experience have been identified in the clinical treatment literature. The factors that have been implicated in decreased sexual satisfaction include lack of information or actual misinformation about sexual response, deeply ingrained negative attitudes toward sex, anxiety due to fear of pregnancy or of intimacy, performance anxiety, fatigue or illness, and relationship disturbances. Many experts in the field who have advocated greater sexual enlightenment for our society are recognizing that the cost of sexual revolution has been greater emphasis on sexual performance relative to relational intimacy ·and subjective satisfaction. Some have suggested that the current trend emphasizing affection and relationship (but not necessarily marriage) before sex is a reaction against these trends. Possibly as another reaction to the cultural emphasis on sexual performance, sex therapists report an increasing number of persons seeking treatment for disorders of sexual desire. Increasingly people who find sex to be less important in life are viewed by themselves and others as abnormal.

Sexual dysfunctions must be differentiated from sexual deviations (or more commonly today, "variations"). Dysfunctions represent failures to perform adequately; deviations represent disorders in response to sexual objects. The most common sexual dysfunctions in women are disorders of arousal, orgasmic dysfunctions, vaginismus, and dyspareunia. Males experience disorders of arousal, erectile dysfunction, and premature or retarded ejaculation. (*See* SEX THERAPY.)

Sexuality and adjustment. What is the relationship between sexual functioning and personal adjustment? Views based on early dynamic formulations tended to link the two closely, so that sexual dysfunction was viewed as symptomatic of more deeply rooted personality disturbances; from these came the description of the sexually underresponsive woman as "frigid." Some writers pushed this view further to conclude that sexual response was the best index of adjustment.

In the early stages of the development of sex therapy as a speciality within mental health practice, the opposite ideology seemed to be pressed. Sexual functioning was viewed as a learned phenomenon without necessary linkages to other aspects of personality functioning. This conception was supported by the rapid successes in treatment of sexual dysfunction reported by Masters and Johnson and others.

The current view among many prominent sex therapists (see Leiblum & Pervin, 1980) is that neither of the above broad formulations is adequate. Rather, for some individuals sexual dysfunction represents a relatively simple problem amenable to brief intervention. For others the sexual disturbance is a problem for which more fundamental change is essential.

Integration. The interrelationships between the theological, biological, and psychological perspectives on sexuality are critical, but only

a sampling can be explored here. First, it should be stated that any definition of normality is conditioned by a priori assumptions regarding the nature of optimal human response and the purposes of that response. The implicit theory of most sex researchers and clinicians is that sexual functioning is, from an evolutionary perspective, intended for procreation, and has become endowed with tremendous pleasure-producing qualities as a spur to reproductive activity. Because species survival and pleasure are viewed as the highest human goods (with some emphasizing the primacy of individual hedonistic gratification and others the importance of subsuming individual pleasure to collective good), most writers in this field exhibit a broad acceptance of sexual behaviors. These writers would argue for a "scientific" basis for determination of normalcy based on empirical study of statistical frequency, pleasure derived, and harm/benefits produced by a particular behavior. Christians must recognize the implicit values behind such a scientific analysis and suggest alternatively that other purposes of sexuality must be considered in the determination of normalcy. Thus, despite the high statistical frequency, reported pleasure derived from, and lack of empirical evidence showing harm produced by premarital sex, Christians can assert that such actions are statistically frequent but not normal, in the sense that those actions violate the meaning and purpose for which the act of coitus was created by God. As noted earlier, however, Christians must struggle with empirical and clinical evidences in areas that might be called borderline (Thielicke, 1964), since these areas are not clearly dealt with in Scripture.

Our consideration of the purposes and nature of sexuality affects our definition of optimum sexuality. Optimum sexuality cannot be defined in terms of physical performance standards only, since such standards omit reference to the broader purposes of unity and reflection of spiritual truth that are important to sexual relationship. Optimum sexuality will be that which is most in accord with the purposes of sex; thus, optimum genital sexuality in marriage is appropriately open to procreation, is pleasurable, promoting of interpersonal union, and in its wholeness and holiness mirrors the nature of God and of Christ's relationship to his church. Such formulations of optimum sexuality are critical to judging the effectiveness of sex therapy in treatment of sexual dysfunctions, which to this point has been largely judged by the criteria of frequency and speed of orgasm. Such purely functional criteria can be seen from an integrated perspective to be important (to the purpose of pleasure) but limited. True enhancement of sexual life must have in focus a broader view of the meaning and purpose of sexuality.

References

Brunner, E. *Man in revolt*. London: Lutterworth, 1939.
Bullough, V., & Brundage, J. *Sexual practices and the medieval church*. Buffalo, N.Y.: Prometheus, 1982.
Chilman, C. *Adolescent sexuality in a changing American society*. Washington, D.C.: U.S. Government Printing Office, 1978.
Feucht, O., Coiner, H., Sauer, A., & Hansen, P. (Eds.). *Sex and the church*. St. Louis: Concordia, 1961.
Kosnick, A., Carroll, W., Cunningham, A., Modras, R., & Schulte, J. *Human sexuality: New directions in American Catholic thought*. New York: Paulist Press, 1977.
Leiblum, S., Pervin, L. (Eds.). *Principles and practice of sex therapy*. New York: Guilford, 1980.
Masters, W. H., & Johnson, V. E. *Human sexual response*. Boston: Little, Brown, 1966.
Masters, W. H., Johnson, V. E., & Kolodny, R. C. *Human sexuality*. Boston: Little, Brown, 1982.
McCary, J., & McCary, S. *McCary's human sexuality*. Belmont, Calif.: Wadsworth Publishing, 1982.
McDonald, H. D. *The Christian view of man*. Westchester, Ill.: Crossway, 1981.
Singer, J., & Singer, I. Types of female orgasm. In J. LoPiccolo & L. LoPiccolo (Eds.), *Handbook of sex therapy*. New York: Plenum, 1978.
Small, D. H. *Christian: Celebrate your sexuality*. Old Tappan, N.J.: Revell, 1974.
Thielicke, H. *The ethics of sex*. New York: Harper & Row, 1964.

S. L. Jones

See Sexual Response Psychology.

Sexual Masochism. Sexual excitement derived from personal suffering and pain. The term originated in the works of Leopold V. Sacher-Masoch, who wrote about fictional characters who received sexual pleasure from pain. Masochism has been broadened to include not only enduring pain for sexual excitement but also receiving gratification from self-denial and suffering in general.

Sexual masochists prefer, or indulge exclusively in, behavior such as being bound, beaten, spanked, stuck with pins, trampled, verbally abused, humiliated, or otherwise made to suffer in conjunction with the sexual act. Orgasm may be very difficult or impossible to achieve without such behavior.

The individual must actually take part in the behavior and not just fantasize it to be considered a sexual masochist. A sexual activity may not actually be harmful. However, the possibility of harm is frequently a part of the experience, and sometimes the risk taking is such that the activities may be even life-threatening. The central feature of masochism is not the pain or injury but submission to power. In the height of masochistic sexual excitement the pain itself is not experienced, but only the sensation of being overpowered.

In theory the masochist is less afraid of physical pain than of an imagined uncontrollable encounter. The pain and being overpowered are, in a sense, controllable, and therefore the lesser of two threats. The masochist's behavior circumvents the sexual inhibition that comes from an uncontrollable pain and rejection and thus allows sexual arousal to develop. The "powerful" woman (usually a prostitute) is the controllable substitute for a feared father figure.

The essential difference between masochism and sadism is that masochism stresses subjection to power. Sadists must subject the victim to pain or injury. Both the sadist and masochist engage in their sexual perversion as either a prerequisite or a replacement for coitus.

Sexual masochism is a learned behavior from childhood. The child may have received attention from hostile or destructive parents only when he was injured, ill, or failing in some way. So the child develops masochistic coping behavior that is coupled to sex as he matures sexually.

Treatment of sexual masochism is basically up to the therapist's discretion; there is little definitive data on effective psychological treatment modalities. Behavioral and insight-oriented treatments are the major exclusively psychological treatment methods. Behavioral therapy includes assertive training and desensitization. Insight-oriented therapy focuses on the restructuring of sexual attitudes through insight into the masochist's developmental process.

Chemotherapy is also utilized to help control extremely dangerous self-destructive behavior. Drugs are usually used in conjunction with other treatment procedures.

M. A. Campion

Sexual Response Psychology. The study of the human sexual response involves the investigation of the dynamic interaction of physiological and psychological factors. For example, sex hormone level will influence sexual interest and desire, while in a reciprocal manner acute or chronic stress may reduce hormonal levels and the accompanying sexual interest.

Physiological Factors. The interaction between the sex hormones and the brain plays a particularly important role in sexual behavior. The male sex hormone, androgen, has important effects on the sex centers and other parts of the brain, while the production of that substance is cerebrally controlled by the pituitary gland. Current understanding of the effects of androgen on adult sexual behavior suggests that it enhances the erotic drive of both men and women (Kaplan, 1974).

Men deprived of their source of testosterone by castration, or whose testosterone level is low due to any cause, gradually experience diminished sexual interest and inability to have penile erection. A more abrupt cessation of sexual interest and erection occurs upon medical prescription of antiandrogen medication.

Androgen, having known effect upon sex centers in the brain, is also a prerequisite for the sex drive in women. Testosterone increases the sex drive in women, especially when the androgen-estrogen ratio has been low. Women who are deprived of all sources of androgen due to surgery lose all sexual desire, cease having erotic dreams and fantasies, and are not aroused by previously effective sexual stimulation.

A person's psychological state influences the androgen level, which will vary markedly in response to sexual stimuli. For males, sexually stimulating experiences normally result in an increased blood testosterone level. Feelings of low self-esteem, depression, and anxiety, whether chronic or acute, routinely occur in association with a dramatically lowered androgen level. For females the effects of stress in reducing hormonal level are not so well understood, other than the fact that emotional crises may coexist with disturbances in the menstrual cycle in some women.

Sometimes it is easier to explain the absence of adequate sexual response than its presence. It is known that 80% or more of the difficulties in adequate sexual response are due to relatively common experiences. Kaplan (1974), reviewing available professional literature, found that physical factors accounted for less than 20% of sexual problems. Masters and Johnson (1970) and most professionals in the area of human sexuality have found that less than 15% of patients presenting themselves for treatment in regard to sexual functioning have serious psychiatric problems.

Psychological Factors. Six potential avenues for enhancing or impairing human sexual response are 1) the effect of past conditioning, 2) adequate information about anatomy and physiology, 3) myths and misconceptions, 4) quality of dyadic relationship, 5) past sexual experience, and 6) situational factors.

Past conditioning. The sexual atmosphere in the childhood home is a primary determinant of sexual responsiveness in adulthood. If parents model affection for each other and their children, subtle permission for sexuality results. If demonstrativeness, touching, and talking about sexual issues is tacitly forbidden, children may decide that sex is somehow dirty, ugly, or bad.

Adequate information about human anatomy and physiology. Inadequate information may result in feelings of awkwardness and confusion when contemplating or engaging in sexual behavior. Such negative feelings may impair or serve to end further engagement in sexual activity. Conversely, adequate knowledge should promote freedom to enjoy sexual activity.

Sexual myths and misconceptions. Often these misconceptions stem from information given by friends, relatives, or even experts. One common misconception is that males "know everything there is to know about sex," and are therefore responsible for the sexual satisfaction of their female partners. Thus, it is the man's duty to please his partner, and if she does not enjoy or receive satisfaction from the activity, it is his fault. Myths such as these are legion and cause untold pressures on both men and women. Accurate information allows individuals to make reasoned decisions about sexual behaviors, consistent with their personal values.

Communication and cooperation between spouses. Recent research indicates that dyadic communication about sexual issues is associated with greater frequency of intercourse and orgastic response but has no discernible impact on the presence of preexisting sexual dysfunction (Biggerstaff, David, & Lloyd, 1982). At the same time failure to express preferences for types, timing, etc., of sexual activity may eventually have harmful consequences. A lessening of motivation for cooperation could result from ineffective or absence of communication. A further complication may be the presence of hidden hostility and resentment toward the partner, based on objective reality or perceived injustice. Enhancing sexual responsiveness or resolving sexual nonresponsiveness is generally not possible without adequate communication and cooperation.

Past sexual experiences. The past experiences may have been uncomfortable, traumatic, disappointing, and may have produced guilt or anxiety. Since much of sexual behavior and appreciation of that behavior is a learned process, it is reasonable that early negative or positive experiences would condition persons for later pleasant or unpleasant experiences.

Situational factors. These could be psychological, environmental, or physical. A classic example is feeling rushed or being pressured to hurry up. Such pressure to perform may easily backfire and impede performance. Physical factors such as one's health status may impair sexual functioning. Certainly feelings of guilt, anger, frustration, or resentment may directly inhibit a person from having successful and enjoyable sexual activity. Masters and Johnson (1970) also mention "fear of performance" and "spectatoring," which also may affect sexual functioning. Fear of performance refers to a person being unable to perform sexually and then becoming extremely fearful and anxious during subsequent sexual encounters. Spectatoring refers to self-consciousness to the point of watching oneself and being unable to function adequately.

As with all aspects of human sexual functioning, a holistic, biopsychosocial approach is indicated. The psychology of sexual response unavoidably includes biological and social factors. It also highlights the simultaneous intensity and fragility of the sexual drive. The fragility of sexual functioning dictates a requirement to suspend moral judgments and instead endeavor to understand the complex, interacting forces.

References

Biggerstaff, E. D., David, J. R., & Lloyd, A. J. Female sexual dysfunction incidence rate in a military medical center. *Medical Bulletin*, 1982, *39*(3).

Kaplan, H. S. *The new sex therapy: Active treatment of sexual dysfunctions.* New York: Brunner/Mazel, 1974.

Masters, W. H., & Johnson, V. E. *Human sexual inadequacy.* Boston: Little, Brown, 1970.

J. R. DAVID

Sexual Sadism. Behavior that inflicts suffering on the victim in order to produce sexual excitement. The term *sadism* is derived from the Marquis de Sade, who according to accounts in his autobiographical writings inflicted great cruelty on his victims for sexual pleasure.

The sadistic act may follow coitus for more gratification, be involved with enhancing sexual desire, or used to produce orgasm without intercourse. Sadistic acts of violence can include sticking with needles, slashing with a razor, biting, beating, disembowelment, cutting off breasts, or defecating on the victim. The sadist may also derive sexual excitement from the odor or the taste of blood. The sadist derives little sexual satisfaction if the victim remains passive. There appears to be a need for power over the victim. The victim must be dominated, injured, or destroyed in order to achieve sexual fulfillment.

The sadist has a range of emotions during the sexual assaults, including anxiety, rage, vengeance, relief, and ecstasy that come from overpowering the victim. During the sadistic act the sadist appears to have little control over his behavior. Unless he is caught, he will continue to repeat the sadistic acts.

Sexual sadism covers a range of behavior. It is usually not considered pathological unless it brings marked physical harm to the victim. Much sadistic behavior goes unreported because the partners are cooperative and the sadistic acts are less life-threatening and violent.

The sexual sadistic behavior usually has its beginnings in adolescence and is found almost exclusively in males. During adolescence there are strong sexual emotions. If, by chance, they are paired with seeing someone receive physical pain such as being cut or beaten, then the adolescent may begin the conditioning process that results in sexual sadism. The sadist usually has a negative attitude toward sex and is feminine, undersexed, timid, and fearful of impotence. The sadistic behavior is designed to arouse strong emotion in the victim so that the sadist can peak his sexual mood to achieve orgasm.

Sexual sadism is rarely encountered in psychological or psychiatric practice today. Most clinical information of sadistic behavior is from accounts of prostitutes. The actual frequency of sexual sadistic behavior is not known.

Treatment may include insight-oriented psychotherapy, sex education, behavioral therapy, or chemotherapy. The use of drugs may produce sexual apathy that would diminish sexual arousal.

M. A. CAMPION

Shame. Generally defined as "an unpleasant emotional reaction by an individual to an actual or presumed negative judgment of himself by others resulting in self-depreciation vis-à-vis the group" (Ausubel, 1955, p. 382). Twentieth-century psychologists have not given the amount of consideration to shame as to other emotions, particularly anxiety, fear, and guilt.

Shame involves an objective act and a subjective feeling of the person. The objective act breaches a social convention and has as its consequence the subjective feeling of condemnation and derogation. Lynd (1958) notes that shame is experienced as "a wound to one's self-esteem, a painful feeling or sense of degradation excited by the consciousness of having done something unworthy of one's previous idea of one's own excellence" (p. 24). A sense of unworthiness or of being scorned originates in the breach of propriety. The individual engages in self-condemnation when modesty or another sentiment related to self-respect, especially in the eyes of another, has been violated.

Shame has its roots in Old English, where it meant to cover or hide an exposure. Covering up was a defense against being exposed, which wounded self-respect. Baldwin (1901) examined the historical development of shame and noted it involved two types of exposure. The more prominent occured in situations where the physical functions of elimination and sexuality were exposed. Freud and Ruth Benedict viewed shame as a defense against exhibitionism and voyeurism; shame was an assurance that privacy would be maintained. When an individual says, "I feel ashamed," the meaning may actually express, "I do not want to be seen."

A second type involves exposure in situations of an intellectual or moral nature. Baldwin maintained that in this form shame may reveal a simple weakness of the person (e.g., the presence of a physical handicap), a disappointment of social expectations (e.g., a bad judgment that led to embarrassment or exposure of ignorance or incompetence), or breach of social or moral prescription. Moral shame is a reaction to the negative moral evaluation of others and provides the major boundaries for acceptable behavior in "shame cultures."

A number of individuals have attempted to differentiate shame and guilt. It is commonly asserted that guilt is an internalized form of shame in which the individual judges himself, while shame is externalized in a group's judgment. Freud (1923/1961) maintained that shame is more external than guilt. Shame is based on disapproval from the outside, from other persons, while guilt (i.e., self-reproach) comes from criticism by self. Shame is a failure to live up to someone else's expectation, while guilt is the failure to live up to one's own expectation.

Alternate accounts have been offered by Piers and Singer (1971) and Alexander (1948). To Piers the essential difference is that guilt follows transgression of prohibitions, whereas failure to reach goals or ideals leads to shame. Alexander made a similar distinction. Guilt arises out of wrongdoing, whereas shame comes from inferiority. This distinction has been blurred in more recent writings. Ausubel (1955), writing of moral shame, says that it is

not necessary that the individual internalize and accept the values of the group, only that there be awareness of the group's value and a recognition that one's action has transgressed that value. If the individual had internalized and adopted the value and then acted contrary, guilt would accompany shame. In this latter case external sanctions are accompanied by internal ones.

Lynd (1958) summarized several attempts to explain the underlying mechanisms of shame. Experiences of shame develop from exposure, particularly unexpected exposure to sensitive and intimate aspects of oneself. While the exposure may be to others, it is also to oneself. The emotion is particularly strong when the exposure is unexpected and the individual is powerless to prevent it. Blushing and hiding one's face are immediate reactions to unexpected exposure.

Pain of unexpected exposure is particularly acute when one's action is inappropriate to the situation or incongruous with a positive self-image. Discrepancy of action and the prevailing social convention initiates shame in cultures where social convention is highly prescriptive and clearly defined.

Shame may have origins in threats to trust. When trust is threatened or destroyed, the person may question his adequacy or that of his world view. Trust makes an individual vulnerable, and exposure of that vulnerability is experienced as shame. Lynd observes, "Shame over sudden uncovering of incongruity mounts when what is exposed is inappropriate positive expectation, happy and confident commitment to a world that proves to be alien or nonexistent" (1958, p. 43).

References

Alexander, F. *Fundamentals of psychoanalysis.* New York: Norton, 1948.
Ausubel, D. P. Relationships between shame and guilt in the socializing process. *Psychological Review,* 1955, *62,* 378–390.
Baldwin, J. M. *Dictionary of philosophy and psychology* (Vol. 2). New York: Macmillan, 1901.
Freud, S. The ego and the id. In J. Strachey, Ed. and trans., *The standard edition of the complete psychological works of Sigmund Freud* (Vol. 19). London: Hogarth, 1961. (Originally published, 1923.)
Lynd, H. M. *On shame and the search for identity.* New York: Harcourt, Brace, 1958.
Piers, G., & Singer, M. *Shame and guilt.* New York: Norton, 1971.

R. L. TIMPE

Shaping. A technique in operant psychology whereby a new response is developed through differentially reinforcing ever closer approximations of the desired end behavior. An example would be teaching simple language to an autistic, withdrawn child—specifically, teaching the child to say "mama." In his current state the child occasionally emits cries, grunts, and other nonverbal sounds in no apparent pattern. The clinician would first determine what would serve as a reinforcer for the child by observing the sorts of activities the child engages in freely. Raisins are picked as the reinforcer since the child consumes them as often as possible.

Since the child has never uttered "mama," the response must be shaped. The clinician decides on a first approximation of the target behavior. Since speech is most likely to be appropriate when the child attends to the people about him, the first approximation picked is for the child to look in the direction of the clinician. When the child does look toward the clinician, he is immediately given a raisin; when he is looking away, no raisins are given. This pattern is called differential reinforcement of desired behavior.

After looking toward the clinician has become a frequent response, the clinician makes a closer approximation of the target necessary for reinforcement; looking at the clinician's face is the next chosen response. Again, this behavior is differentially reinforced. The process continues in this fashion through the painstaking gradual steps toward the desired end behavior. The following steps might be necessary: looking at the clinician's face, looking in her eyes, holding eye contact and making small lip movement, making any sound, making a sound at the loudness of normal speech, making a sound at least vaguely similar to "mm," closer approximations to "mm," approximations to "ma," articulating "ma," articulating "mama." Through this process the child might eventually be led to say "mama" in an appropriate manner. Other speech might be developed in a similar fashion. Prompting and modeling are other techniques that might be used to speed the learning process.

Shaping is used in developing specific desired patterns of animal behavior (a widely acclaimed example being that of the chicken playing a piano); in developing appropriate social behavior in the profoundly disturbed (the retarded, autistic, or psychotic); and, in less formal forms, in gradual skill development in normal persons.

S. L. JONES

See BEHAVIOR THERAPY; LEARNING.

Sheldon, William Herbert (1898–1977). American psychologist who worked out a rela-

tionship between physique and temperament. Born in Warwick, Rhode Island, he received an A.B. degree from Brown University in 1919 and an M.A. from the University of Colorado. He received a Ph.D. degree in psychology (1926) and an M.D. degree (1933) from the University of Chicago. Later he spent two years studying in Europe with Jung, Freud, and Kretschmer.

During his graduate work he taught at the University of Chicago, Northwestern University, and the University of Wisconsin. He became professor of psychology at the University of Chicago in 1936, went to Harvard in 1938, Columbia in 1947, and the University of Oregon in 1959, where he remained until his retirement in 1970. At the time of his death he was associated with the Biological Humanics Center in Cambridge, Massachusetts.

After carefully examining standardized photographs of thousands of naked men, Sheldon concluded that the variations of physique could be accounted for by three primary components: endomorphy, mesomorphy, and ectomorphy. Endomorphs have a predominance of soft roundness throughout their bodies with the digestive organs dominant. Mesomorphs show strength, hardness, and toughness with a predominance of bone and muscle. Ectomorphs are thin, flat-chested, and fragile. Sheldon saw these as extensions of the early layers of the embryo.

Correlated with the basic physiques are three basic temperaments. Endomorphs typically show viscerotonia, a general love of comfort, relaxation, sociability, people, food, and affection. Mesomorphs show somatotonia, a love of physical adventure, risk-taking, action, noise, courage, and aggression. Ectomorphs show cerebrotonia, a predominance of restraint, inhibition, and a desire for solitude and concealment. The correlations were quite high, with all of them at about $r = +.80$. Sheldon believed that both body build and temperament are primarily the result of heredity.

Most of Sheldon's writings represent attempts to identify and describe the major physiques and temperaments and then apply these to real life. His major works are *The Varieties of Human Physique* (1940), *The Varieties of Temperament* (1942), *Varieties of Delinquent Youth* (1949), and *Atlas of Men* (1954). He began work on similar atlases of women and children, but had greater difficulty in classifying them. Sheldon's emphasis on constitutional factors was not well received in an American psychology dominated by behaviorism. Furthermore, his studies were correlational, so he did not show the causal relationships between physique and temperament.

R. L. KOTESKEY

See CONSTITUTIONAL PERSONALITY THEORY.

Short-Term Anxiety-Provoking Psychotherapy. This brief, psychodynamically oriented psychotherapy was created by Sifneos (1972, 1979). In order for a client to be selected for inclusion in this therapy it must be clear that the individual 1) has been able to establish and maintain at least one significant extrafamilial relationship in the past; 2) has no recorded history of suicidal gestures or attempts; 3) has not been, nor currently is, diagnosed psychotic or borderline psychotic; 4) has sufficient ego strength to satisfactorily tolerate loss of important objects in the past without decompensating; and 5) has a well-defined complaint. If the client does not meet the above criteria, then he should be referred to an anxiety-suppressive brief therapy; such is primarily supportive and reeducative in nature, involving such tactics as environmental manipulation and reassurance along with the presentation of new information.

Sifneos has worked within the context of a university/medical complex in a major metropolitan area. Thus he has experienced little difficulty obtaining the highly select variety of clients appropriate to short-term anxiety-provoking psychotherapy.

Sifneos works from a traditional psychoanalytic framework. In his work he tends to focus primarily on oedipal issues, which he assumes to underlie most of his clients' complaints. Once these issues are worked through, along with the resistance that one typically encounters in dealing with them, it is time to terminate. It is integral to this method that the therapist not allow the client to dilute the therapeutic focus by free associating to other issues. When the client does begin to wander, it is the therapist's job to corral the subject and redirect the conversation to underlying oedipal material.

The major difference between short-term anxiety-provoking psychotherapy and traditional psychoanalysis is the activity level of the therapist. In a rather directive and active style the therapist first establishes a working therapeutic alliance with the client and then proceeds to clarify, interpret, and confront the various defenses the client uses to protect against the very real pain involved in facing oedipal material.

Sifneos's therapeutic style has been characterized as that of a benevolent senior lecturer (Mann & Goldman, 1982). He tends to channel the course of the therapy session much as if he were implementing a well-known, tried-and-true lesson plan he has been over many times. One particular area of predictability has to do with the typical stages through which a client passes.

The initial stage is characterized by a warm sense of optimism on the part of the client. Hopefulness that things will really be better abounds. This stage, which lasts anywhere from one to eight or ten sessions, melts into a middle phase of therapy that is much less emotionally buoyant. The warm glow of "everything will be okay" dissipates into a variety of colder, more conflictual feelings as the therapist's interpretations and confrontations begin to make an impact. This stage lasts anywhere from half a dozen sessions to 30 or more. The final phase of therapy is typically that of separation. Feelings that go with this stage are a mixture of the first two: the despair of being alone and responsible for oneself mixed with the optimism associated with experiencing one's own potency. This stage lasts from half a dozen sessions up to a dozen or more.

Sifneos does not put a specific time limit on the duration of psychotherapy. This practice is contrary to what other short-term psychodynamic theorists and therapists advise (e.g., Malan, 1976). He designs his treatment program based on the specific case. Using a predetermined termination date as a powerful metaphor for other inevitable separations in the client's life is a tactic that short-term anxiety-provoking psychotherapy does not utilize.

Critique. From Sifneos's writings it is difficult to learn how to use this approach. Much of the actual how-to technology is missing in comparison to other writers in the field (e.g., Davanloo, 1978). One can read many of the transcripts and be left to wonder about the principles involved and the timing for implementing them. This confusion is compounded further when anecdotes and illustrations seem to point primarily to the therapist rather than the therapy.

However, the approach does appear to be potentially quite valuable in helping a practitioner become more effective and efficient. The best prerequisite for using this technique is to have already engaged in a longer term psychodynamic therapy oneself. The other primary requirement would seem to be one's willingness to explore with an open mind new and potentially risky ways of being with a client. It is recommended that before one begins the approach that a competent supervisor in the area be available for consultation.

References

Davanloo, H. (Ed.). *Basic principles and techniques in short-term dynamic psychotherapy*. New York: Spectrum, 1978.

Malan, D. H. *The frontier of brief psychotherapy*. New York: Plenum, 976.

Mann, J., & Goldman, R. *A casebook in time-limited psychotherapy*. New York: McGraw-Hill, 1982.

Sifneos, P. E. *Short-term psychotherapy and emotional crisis*. Cambridge: Harvard University Press, 1972.

Sifneos, P. E. *Short-term dynamic psychotherapy: Evaluation and technique*. New York: Plenum, 1979.

V. L. SHEPPERSON

See SHORT-TERM THERAPIES.

Short-Term Dynamic Psychotherapy.

This article will describe the various patient selection criteria, assessment issues, and therapeutic approaches of D. H. Malan and Habib Davanloo. Other short-term dynamic approaches are described in SHORT-TERM ANXIETY PROVOKING PSYCHOTHERAPY and SHORT-TERM THERAPIES.

Malan's systematic treatment and research work in the area of brief dynamic therapy began with Michael Balint at the Tavistock Clinic in 1955 and continued through the 1970s (Malan, 1976a, 1976b). During the latter part of this time period Davanloo began exploring the limits of what was possible using this modality (Davanloo, 1978). His work built on Malan's foundational concepts and research; it has also gone beyond the frontiers that had been reached by Malan and his associates.

Both Malan and Davanloo have stretched the limits of patient selection criteria beyond limiting treatment solely to well-contained neurotics with circumscribed oedipal foci. They will also treat patients with more severe psychopathology: borderline, characterological, obsessional, phobic, and long-standing complex neuroses with less than clear, tidy limits to the disorder. Davanloo has also specified the following criteria: 1) at least one meaningful relationship in the past; 2) good ego strength that can withstand confrontation and moderate amounts of anxiety without psychotic decompensation; 3) an intellectual and emotional capability to focus and circumscribe a specific issue on which to work; and 4) a fair measure of insightfulness, flexibility, and motivation.

Initial assessment issues in the first several sessions for both of these theorists include the formulation of a situational conflict focus as well as the formulation of an underlying dynamic conflict focus. Typically one would expect the presenting problem to be a muted reflection of underlying nuclear issues stemming from early traumatic events and repetitive early family constellations of behavior. It is essential that the therapist be able to formulate a central focus (among the many possible for any one patient) that is both workable for the therapist and acceptable to the patient. While actively focusing on this central issue the therapist also evaluates the patient's ego strength, defensive structure, psychological-mindedness, intellecual functioning, motivation, insight, and responsiveness to interpretation; Davanloo also looks for early signs of transference and countertransference. Concurrent with this initial evaluation period Davanloo advocates that the therapist contract with the patient for a short period of trial therapy. This trial period essentially consists of using the basic therapeutic techniques to be used throughout therapy in order to assess more thoroughly the patient's capability to withstand the stress of this anxiety-arousing therapy.

Both Davanloo and Malan tend to use interpretation as their primary therapeutic technique; they also make full use of traditional tools of suggestion, abreaction, clarification, confrontation, and manipulation (allowing the client free choice to manipulate his own environment and learn from these experiences). Both therapists tend to be much more active in the sessions than a traditional longer term psychodynamic approach would dictate. Dependency of a passive variety is not encouraged; furthermore, one is encouraged to interpret both negative and symbiotic transference in order to prevent their development.

The most useful interpretations for Malan focus on making connections between the clients' reactions to the therapist and past reactions to parents (a transference-parent or T-P link). Davanloo's work represents a significant advance in this area. He posits two content triangles within which the therapist can make useful interpretations: the triangle of person and the triangle of conflict. The first involves interpersonal connections between the therapist, current significant others, and past significant others (T-C-P links); the second, intrapersonal connections between the client's impulses, defenses, and anxieties (I-D-A links). The degree to which a client can emotionally connect two or more points within and across these triangles is a good prognostic sign; the most useful connections tend to be T-C-P links where the client is able to connect all points of the person triangle (e.g., "The anger you are experiencing toward me right now seems very similar to how you described being furious with your boss this week; it also reminds me of the rage you went into as a child with your father when he ignored you").

Davanloo tends to be more confrontive in his technique than any other short-term dynamic therapist. Gentle but relentless questioning and confrontation of defenses against true feelings are the order of the day. Vagueness, avoidance, passivity, and minimizing of feelings are actively confronted. The anger and defensiveness that this confrontation arouses are then fair grist for the therapy mill; if one fails to interpret, clarify, and support these negative reactive feelings, therapy is likely to be unsuccessful. In a similar vein one is encouraged to relentlessly push for early transference feelings; it is deemed critical to interpret these feelings as well as a variety of other unconscious material (e.g., fantasies, dreams, and oblique meanings of words). When these techniques are used, treatment can be expected to last anywhere from 10 to 40 sessions.

The need for brief therapy in our current day and age is growing. For those therapists trained in traditional theoretical orientations this form of brief therapy is an ideal modality to explore further.

References

Davanloo, H. (Ed.), *Basic principles and techniques in short-term dynamic psychotherapy.* New York: Spectrum, 1978.

Malan, D. H. *The frontier of brief psychotherapy.* New York: Plenum, 1976. (a)

Malan, D. H. *Towards the validation of dynamic psychotherapy.* New York: Plenum, 1976. (b)

V. L. SHEPPERSON

Short-Term Therapies.

Today short-term therapy, or brief therapy, has gained a certain respectability. Traditionally this type of therapy has been viewed as a sort of stop-gap intervention that one resorts to if one does not have an adequate amount of time or expertise to do anything else. The current mainstream perspective has shifted. It is being recognized that significant intrapsychic and interpersonal change can be accomplished in a short period of time if one is willing to try something different.

Gurman (1981) adopts a perspective supportive of this new emphasis on briefer therapies. He maintains that a high percentage of all psychotherapy patients terminate treatment in less than 12 sessions, and thus the emphasis on briefer therapies is new only by design.

Brief therapies in general have a number of common ingredients. They tend to concentrate on just one or two salient issues or themes. They require the therapist to be relatively more active and directive than a traditional longer term therapist would be. The therapist has to be willing to assume more responsibility for what happens during each session without infringing on the client's autonomy or treating him like an infant.

The therapies requiring a short period of time have a significant number of differences from each other. These differences center around basic theoretical assumptions regarding the mechanism of change, criteria for patient selection, and therapeutic style and strategy. Approaches to these differences can be reasonably grouped into two major camps: brief individual therapies (psychodynamic and behavioral) and brief systems therapies.

Brief Psychodynamic Therapies. Theoretical assumptions. The basic curative element postulated by psychodynamic therapists practicing brief therapy is still insight. The client's insight into his own intrapsychic process is facilitated primarily by active clarification and interpretation of his resistance and transference, in roughly that chronological order. A highly focused beam of emotional energy is brought to bear on the defined issue at hand. This issue will typically vary across patients and therapists. Sifneos (1979), Wolberg (1965), Malan (1976), and to a lesser degree Davanloo (1978) tend to focus primarily on oedipal issues to the exclusion of what they view as themes of lesser importance. Particular attention is paid to evidence of oedipal struggles within the therapy relationship. Mann and Goldman (1982) take a distinctively different approach. They tend to pursue individuation-separation issues as a central theme. This pursuit is ensconced in a theoretical framework that is very time conscious: the very fact that one has so little time to work together is used as a powerful lever to push the client into the separation-individuation arena.

Criteria for patient selection. In general dynamic briefer therapists have relatively stringent requirements for allowing patients to work in a brief therapy format. Most of the theorists cited above will require all of the following qualities in a patient: resilient ego strength, a focused presenting problem, fair to good capacities for attention, relatively high motivation, a history of at least one past successful relational attachment, a better than average capability for insight, no prior suicide attempts, and no evidence of psychosis or borderline psychiatric conditions. Mann and

Goldman (1982) claim to have a much lower criterion; namely, good ego strength as demonstrated by the patient's ability to tolerate loss adequately in the past. If the above criteria are not met, the therapist will tend to switch therapeutic modalities from dynamic to supportive therapy. Sifneos refers to this as moving from short-term anxiety-provoking therapy to short-term anxiety-suppressive therapy.

Treatment strategy and techniques. Most brief dynamic theorists are stage oriented. The length of these stages is dependent on both therapist and client variables. The most important therapist variable is whether or not a predetermined termination date is part of the treatment plan (e.g., Mann sees all clients for only 12 sessions; the other theorists cited above vary their treatment length from 8 to 40 sessions, with 12 to 15 weekly sessions being modal). Although different descriptive terminologies are used to define treatment stages, the concepts are relatively similar. The initial stage is characterized by a bright, optimistic expectancy, the establishment of a supportive alliance, and the development of a positive transference. The therapist is actively assessing, defining, and clarifying the central issue with the client while establishing a trust base that will support the negative effect aroused later in treatment. This phase typically lasts from one to three sessions.

The second phase of therapy is initiated by a higher frequency of confrontive interpretations on the part of the therapist. The client's defenses and transferences are actively confronted in such a way as to arouse anxiety; the client may also be challenged to engage in a variety of different therapeutic activities (e.g., Wolberg, 1965). This is followed by a shift in the client's mood from buoyant expectancy of magical change to a potpourri of negative emotions. If the client does not leave treatment at this point, the prognosis for significant short-term change is enhanced. This stage lasts from 4 to 20 sessions, depending on the particular theorist's orientation and the severity of the client's disorder. The final stage of therapy finds the therapist pushing the client to integrate new ideas, feelings, and activities into his daily life. Most brief therapists will also work to help clients process their separation anxiety in a more healthy manner than they have been able to do in the past.

Brief Behavioral Therapy. *Theoretical assumptions.* Traditionally the subgroups within the behavioral school have emphasized the crucial importance of environmental factors in the change process. Classical and operant conditioning using a stimulus-response model was the accepted method of change. More recently cognitive behavior modification approaches have flourished. These approaches are more compatible with a social learning perspective in which cognitive mediating variables are accepted as causal in the change process. An excellent example of a broad-spectrum behavioral approach is the multimodal behavioral therapy of Lazarus (1976).

Criteria for patient selection. The primary benefit of brief behavior therapy is that one may tailor a particular behavioral approach to the level of intelligence, insight, judgment, and ego strength of each individual. The treatment door is wide open to the poor-functioning chronic schizophrenic as well as the bright, high-functioning neurotic (Wilson, 1981).

Treatment strategy and techniques. The initial step in this approach is to carry out a detailed behavioral assessment of a well-defined problem. The therapist then contracts with the client, either verbally or in writing, a specific agreement detailing the procedures they will follow, the number of sessions they will work together (most often 8–12 sessions to begin with for mild to moderately severe difficulties), and a contingency plan for dealing with any foreseeable difficulties. Typically if the patient appears to have more than one problem, the least difficult will be addressed first. Along with establishing the rewarding feeling of mastering one difficulty the behavioral brief therapist will often arrange for external positive reinforcements in order to enhance motivation. Thus, difficulties are addressed in a step-wise fashion, with the therapist functioning as a benevolent teacher-coach.

Brief Systems Therapies. *Theoretical assumptions.* Brief systems (marital and family) therapists assume that: 1) change can and will take place even without insight if the system is willing to follow the therapist's prescriptions; 2) change is cybernetic and follows principles of circular rather than linear causation (*see* FAMILY SYSTEMS THEORY); and 3) many problems in living that individuals bring to therapists are the result of a lack of coping skill rather than an excess of backlogged emotional garbage; that is, most psychological problems have pedestrian origins.

Criteria for patient selection. The systems therapist will typically include all of the significant individuals within the identified patient's current primary social grouping, whether they are related biologically or not. A central concern for most brief systems therapists, regardless of the nature or severity of the presenting problem, is to redefine the problem in such a way that the therapeutic system (therapist and family) can avoid getting enmeshed in nonproductive interpersonal clutter. Depending on the aptitude, interests, and resilience of the particular systems therapist an extremely broad range of difficulties can be treated using this modality.

Treatment strategy and techniques. The primary tool of the strategic brief therapist is directive rather than interpretation (Haley, 1976). Directives typically focus on how members within the system interact with one another and the sequence and structure of their interactional process.

Directives can be either compliance based or defiance based (Papp, 1980). When working with a cooperative system the therapist will frequently exercise his "expert authority" to involve as many members of the family as possible in an activity. This activity can be either within or between sessions. The therapist can direct this activity based on a straightforward or more indirect, metaphoric conceptualization of the problem. The effect of this intervention is to relabel or redefine a few strategic areas of the system's sequence of interaction; eventually this change in sequence will calcify into a structural change in the system. When the oppositional tendencies within the system are such that compliance-based directives are rendered impotent, the brief strategic therapist will move toward the use of defiance-based directives. This has become known as PARADOXICAL INTERVENTION, and the art of understanding and effecting such directives has received much attention in recent years.

Systems therapists are less stage oriented than are dynamic brief therapists. Some will tend to conceptualize intermediate phases in therapy that are viewed as necessary "halfway houses" to the desired restructure of the system (Haley, 1980).

The average length of treatment is usually between 12 and 20 sessions. The Milan group conducts what they have referred to as long brief therapy, typically they see a family for only 12 sessions, but each session is one month apart (Palazzoli-Selvini, Boscolo, Cecchin, and Prata, 1978). They contend that the system requires that amount of time to digest their carefully planned strategic interventions. This group is also distinctive in that they have used a "Greek chorus" concept in which an anonymous panel observes through a one-way mirror and sends in interventions which the cotherapist team can choose to be puzzled by, disagree with, passively acknowledge or actively applaud. This unique technique allows for a spatial representation of the ambivalence toward change present within most systems. The Greek chorus can push hard for transformation, while the cotherapists can express doubts and vote for homeostasis.

Summary. Some of the contrasts made between the major camps of brief therapy are in practice more theoretical than real, since many brief therapists are eclectic by disposition. For example, an individual might be seen alone, but treatment might flow from a systemic conceptualization of the client's problem, with both interpretations and directives being used as the therapist deems appropriate. The continued development of brief therapies is highly likely given the current economic and political climate. The use of these active, high-leverage treatment tactics is an area of conceptual and operational potency that the average clinician cannot afford to be without.

References

Davanloo, H. (Ed.). *Basic principles and techniques in short-term dynamic psychotherapy.* New York: Spectrum, 1978.

Gurman, A. Integrative marital therapy: Toward the development of an interpersonal approach. In S. H. Budman (Ed.), *Forms of brief therapy.* New York: Guilford, 1981.

Haley, J. *Problem solving therapy.* San Francisco: Jossey-Bass, 1976.

Haley, J. *Leaving home: The therapy of disturbed young people.* New York: McGraw-Hill, 1980.

Lazarus, A. A. *Multimodal behavior therapy.* New York: Springer Publications, 1976.

Malan, D. H. *The frontier of brief psychotherapy.* New York: Plenum, 1976.

Mann, J., & Goldman, R. *A casebook in time-limited psychotherapy.* New York: McGraw-Hill, 1982.

Palazzoli-Selvini, M., Boscolo, L., Cecchin, G., & Prata, G. *Paradox and counterparadox: A new model in the therapy of the family in schizophrenic transaction.* New York: Aronson, 1978.

Papp, P. The Greek chorus and other techniques of paradoxical therapy. *Family Process,* 1980, 19, 45–57.

Sifneos, P. E. *Short-term dynamic psychotherapy: Evaluation and technique.* New York: Plenum, 1979.

Wilson, G. T. Behavior therapy as a short-term therapeutic approach. In S. Budman (Ed.), *Forms of brief therapy.* New York: Guilford, 1981.

Wolberg, L. R. (Ed.), *Short-term psychotherapy.* New York: Grune & Stratton, 1965.

V. L. SHEPPERSON

Shyness. Being "afraid of people, especially people who for some reason are emotionally threatening: strangers because of their novelty or uncertainty, authorities who wield power, members of the opposite sex who represent potential intimate encounters" (Zimbardo, 1977, p. 12). It is a personal problem and social phenomenon that has received little attention from personality theorists and social researchers. Zimbardo's work is an exception.

Shyness has the effect of personal discomfort and inhibition of normal behavior patterns. It is particularly acute in interpersonal situations in which the person is the object of attention. Shyness is common and universal, in spite of the lack of attention given to it by psychologists. Zimbardo (1977) reports that more than 80% of one sample indicated feeling shy at some point in life, while 40% were still shy. Shyness is more prevalent in children than in the adults Zimbardo surveyed.

Shyness has a debilitating effect on interpersonal relationships. Other negative effects include awkwardness in social interaction, anxiety and self-doubt, and an inability to control bouts of shyness. On the positive side shyness carries favorable connotations of modesty, sophistication, and high class. Furthermore, shyness makes one appear selective, discreet, and introspective. It serves as a mask to prevent one from being noticed.

At the physiological level shyness is similar to other strong emotions. It causes sympathetic nervous system arousal; increased heart rate, blood pressure, and perspiration; and butterflies in the stomach. But there is one physical sign not normally involved in general arousal, one that shy people cannot hide: blushing. They tend to concentrate on these physical symptoms and may actually experience them before entering situations that bring on shyness (e.g., contact with strangers or the opposite sex, being the focal point of attention in a group, new social situations).

Blushing is accompanied by feelings of embarrassment. These feelings emanate from the chronic low self-esteem most shy persons experience. According to Zimbardo feelings of embarrassment are likely to occur when the individual believes that personal ineptness might be revealed, especially in a social context. Vulnerability may be covered by defensiveness or denial. Shyness is associated with a heightened sense of self-consciousness. Chronically shy people report engaging in self-analysis and introspection to an almost obsessive degree. Self-consciousness may be public, where the person is concerned about behaving badly, or it may be private, where the person is concerned with feeling badly. Zimbardo believes that public shyness carries a greater burden than private shyness: "The publicly shy cannot readily communicate their fears, uncertainties, good qualities, and desires to the appropriate others. Putting themselves in these nonreturnable self-containers, they don't get the help, advice, recognition and love everyone needs at one time or another" (1977, p. 31).

Theories on the origins of shyness vary considerably. Psychoanalytic theory views shyness as stemming from narcissistic preoccupation of the ego with itself. Psychoanalysts have found that quiet, unassuming, shy persons often have grandiose fantasies and hostilities. Traumatic social situations prevent direct venting of hostility and expression of dreamwork. Instead these are displaced into a morbid preoccupation with fantasies of grandiose forms. The irony is the extreme divergence between the modest nature of the outer life and the vivid form of the inner life. In the treatment of shy persons psychoanalysts have observed that as the shyness abates, underlying fears and hostilities are expressed more directly.

Some trait theorists assert that shyness is genetically transmitted. In his factor analytic personality theory R. B. Cattell postulated what he termed the H factor. Two traits comprise the H factor: H-(susceptibility to threat) and H+(boldness). H-individuals are shy because of a sensitive, easily aroused nervous system. This sensitivity contributes to shyness as the individual instinctively withdraws from conflict and threatening situations. Since the basic sensitivity of the nervous system is genetically inherited, there is little hope of change.

An alternate explanation comes from behaviorists. Shyness is conceived of as learned phobic reactions that originate in negative experiences with people, in not having learned proper social skills, and in being rewarded for inadequacy and incompetence. The attention of others is a social motivator for many persons; responses that are followed by attention are strengthened in form and frequency. If an individual acted shyly and received attention from others (especially if not acting shyly received no attention), then shy behavior could be conditioned.

Other views consider the labeling process and social programming. In the labeling view social psychologists suggest that individuals are labeled by self and others, based on particular events. Individuals attribute shyness to personal inadequacy and then are motivated to act in accord with the label. Individuals may be programmed to be shy by the passive nature of television viewing and by the socialization training of children by parents.

Reference
Zimbardo, P. G. *Shyness: What it is, what to do about it.* Reading, Mass.: Addison-Wesley, 1977.

R. L. TIMPE

Sibling Rivalry. Few concepts in the psychodynamics of family life have as universal acceptance within the popular domain as does sibling rivalry. Legendary, biblical, historical, literary, and everyday instances abound. It seems to be self-evident that human young will vie for the time and affection of their parents. The concept of sibling rivalry also has significant meaning and application in psychology.

Parents have always been hard pressed to find ways of being even-handed with their children, in the application of justice, in meting out rewards and praise. Moreover, few children, even twins, have identical needs and respond identically to given parental actions. Differences of age and sex as well as uniqueness of temperament practically ensure some sibling envy, jealousy, and rivalry. From an older child's side it is immaturity and nostalgia for earlier times that fan the flames of rivalry with a newborn or younger sibling. The senior child may express resentment and regret that he is being displaced by his baby brother or sister. He may regress in his habit training until he literally rivals the newborn in helplessness and apparent inaccessibility to reason. As transient phenomena, these manifestations may be simply puzzling, even amusing. If they persist, parents can be sorely distressed and the behavior may reflect psychopathology.

There appears to be a tendency for feelings of rivalry to recur at stress points, often throughout life. Grudges of middle-aged and elderly siblings testify to the tendency of some hard feelings to hang on. Another set of rivalries has to do with a pair of older siblings vying for the affection of the baby of the family. And the opposite, rivalry between two youngsters for the favoritism of an older sibling, is far from uncommon. Other situations involving rivalry are the normal competitive tussling for superiority in contests of skill, knowledge, strength, etc. For the most part these constitute desirable occasions for learning and growth. Good sportsmanship and fair play as well as flexibility of behavior and thought usually grow out of such experiences. Things tend to go wrong when parents intervene and fail to let the children work it out for themselves.

Movement beyond feelings of rivalry involves acceptance of a world less perfect, or less exclusively built around personal wishes and needs, than the child had hoped to experience. In accepting that he is not number one all the time, he renounces exclusivity. In affirming that he is worthy and can and will enjoy attention, achievement, and occasionally uniqueness, he renounces submission as a solution. Hence, in a combination of losing and winning, growth and perspective develop.

Creatively resolved rivalry leads to successful coping with difference, effective alternative expressions of excellence, training for competence, and acceptance of difference. Happily this outcome is commonly the rule. Failure to resolve rivalry may lead to residual and persistent envy, manipulation, scheming, plotting, grudges, alienation, revenge, sabotage, or even vendettas. Happily these situations are the exceptions.

Solidarity among children by ages 7–11 frequently replaces rivalry with teamwork, expressed in games, rules of fair play, sticking together, etc. Peer grouping effectively enforces such values as "never rat on a pal" and "never tell adults anything that will undermine a kid." If families are large enough, such groupings begin earlier and involve siblings, not just neighbor peers. A child from a successfully resolved sibling rivalry system is better equipped to enter and master peer rivalry demands, less apt to treat them as kin substitutes and use them for the working out of unfinished business from the family system.

Simply satisfying desires does not solve the problem of envy, nor does equalizing distribution neutralize jealousy. Parenting cannot totally preclude or eradicate rivalry. Wise, just, and loving parenting can, however, reduce its intensity and avoid fanning its flame.

Additional Readings
Bank, S. P., & Kahn, M.D. *The sibling bond.* New York: Basic Books, 1982.
Lamb, M. E. The development of sibling relationships in infancy: A short-term psychological study. *Child Development,* 1978, 49, 1189–1196.

E. A. LOOMIS, JR.

Sin, Psychological Consequences of. A biblical understanding of the psychological consequences of sin must begin with the fall and its disastrous effects for all of creation. The first three chapters of Genesis hold that all pain, suffering, and disorder stem, not from God's good intentions, but from the disobedience of Adam and Eve. In this sense it is right and proper to assert that all psychological disorder is the result of sin. However, this assertion must be qualified by the equally biblical notion that persons suffer psychologically not only because they are sinners and follow in Adam's train, but because they are victimized by a world infected by sin.

The third and fourth chapters of Genesis provide a vivid illustration of this. Adam and Eve commit the primal sin and are then made to suffer the consequences of their own actions as pain in childbirth and toiling by the sweat of one's brow. However, the next section of the narrative tells the story of the murder of Abel by his brother, Cain. The text makes it clear that Abel is killed because of his brother's jealous wrath and not because he had offended God. Abel is innocent of wrongdoing, and thus becomes the victim of the sin of his brother.

The Scriptures are replete with this dual understanding of the consequences of sin, consequences that stem from one's own evil and consequences brought about by the evil of others. A major biblical theme is God's recognition and condemnation of the victimizing capacity of sin. As Berkouwer (1971) notes, "Nowhere does the Scripture take an easy view of our sin on the false presumption that it is merely a sin against our fellowman. The anger of the Lord rests on that man who sheds an innocent man's blood. An unimaginable guilt may show its ugliness in human affairs: but just as unimaginable is the judgment against the man who spurns his neighbor and does injury to his fellowman who was made in the image of God" (p. 243). Injury to one's neighbor may take the form of actual physical abuse; however, the injury that can be inflicted on a person's mind and emotions is often more subtle and more damaging.

Another form of psychological damage can be attributed to the effects of the fall on the natural world. Paul alludes to this when he describes the entire creation as being subject to futility and enslaved to corruption so that it "groans and suffers" (Rom. 8:20–22). In essence the physical universe is injured and, in turn, can injure its inhabitants in such diverse ways as disease, flood, and famine. These distortions, or "injuries," of the physical creation are the result of sin, the first sin, and thus those who suffer psychological trauma due to these distortions may said to be suffering, albeit indirectly, the psychological consequences of sin.

That these physical distortions can cause psychological trauma is beyond dispute. A great number of diseases and physical maladies may seriously disrupt the psychological functioning of an afflicted person. For example, brain lesions or tumors may cause symptoms ranging from depression to hallucinations to gross sexual misconduct. Hypothyroidism (underactivity of the thyroid gland) may cause delusions, hallucinations, apathy, and slowness of thought. Involuntary crying or laughing may occur with the onset of multiple sclerosis, while hypoglycemia (low blood sugar) may precipitate full-blown anxiety attacks (Bockar, 1975). Also, there is a good deal of recent research suggesting that certain mental disorders such as schizophrenia and bipolar disorder may have genetic components.

Both natural and man-made disasters leave victims not only physically battered but psychologically paralyzed. The effects of a disaster such as an earthquake on victims can include hysterical reactions, phobic reactions, nightmares, anxiety, social withdrawal, and concentration loss, among other symptoms.

There is also the psychological victimization of persons by their fellow human beings. Paul's solemn warning to fathers to avoid provoking their children to anger "lest they become discouraged" (Col. 3:21) carries with it an implicit recognition that psychological damage can result from poor parenting.

The psychological damage to young children who have been physically or sexually abused is sometimes irreparable. Victims of rape and incest can develop depression, anxiety, dissociations, or other symptoms as a means of coping with the shame, frustration, fear, and rage associated with the traumatic experiences. These and other more subtle attacks on an individual's dignity and worth may precipitate emotional problems.

That extensive, and often permanent, psychological damage can be inflicted on persons by the sins of others cannot be denied. Thus, any counseling approach that wishes to take the concept of sin seriously must recognize that sin victimizes the innocent and that the psychological consequences of sin include the wounds and scars of the emotionally abused.

However, while affirming the biblical notion that sin victimizes, it must not be forgotten that the perpetrators of sin pay dearly, both spiritually and psychologically, for "missing the mark." To assume that sinning would have no psychological consequences would be to deny the holistic view of persons espoused by the Bible. "Scripture constantly makes it clear that sin is not something which corrupts relatively or partially, but a corruption which fully affects the radix, the root, of man's existence, and therefore man himself" (Berkouwer, 1962, p. 140).

The belief that persons suffer mental torment for their sins was until recently a belief firmly rooted in Western culture and reflected in the great literature—e.g., Shakespeare's

Lady MacBeth. It is ironic that what was one of the most important themes in Western literature is now denied by many behavioral scientists who are attempting to understand the nature of human personality and existence while ignoring the insights of a Shakespeare or Dostoevski.

It should be noted that not all psychologists deny the existence of sin or the consequences stemming from sinning. Menninger (1973) attempts to salvage the concept of sin from the dustbin of the current era. He documents how our society has chosen to ignore or destroy the notion of sin and the price that has been paid for doing so.

Sin and guilt cannot be separated biblically or psychologically; thus it is guilt that most profoundly affects the psyche of those who sin. This idea has had an ardent spokesman in Mowrer (1961; Mowrer & Veszelovszky, 1980), who holds that a certain degree of mental illness stems not from psychological guilt feelings but from real, actual guilt brought on by misdeeds—i.e., sin. While his terminology, which includes words such as guilt, confession, and expiation, is not as theologically precise as one might hope, Mowrer has attempted to shed light on the role of conscience and morals in mental disorder.

One of Mowrer's students, Smrtic (1979), describes a number of cases of persons with psychological symptoms such as anxiety, suspiciousness, mania, and suicidal gestures which he believes stem directly from wrong behavior and unconfessed sin. An exhaustive list of psychological symptoms related to actual sin in the life of individuals is not possible, due to the unique psychological makeup of each person. However, suffice it to say that feelings of meaninglessness, isolation, anxiety, and guilt may stem from the emptiness of being alienated from God by willful disobedience.

Neither Mowrer nor Smrtic would argue that unconfessed guilt is the cause of all psychological disturbance. However, they have provided a much-needed counterpoint to the idea that all mental disorder is the result of victimization and that none of it is caused by the disturbed person himself.

Thus, it is apparent that psychological disorders may be rooted in the sin of victimization, the sinfulness of the distorted creation, or the personal sin of the disturbed individual. The biblical doctrine of the spiritual, mental, and psychological unity of the person allows for the possibility that all three causative factors could be operating simultaneously in one individual. In this situation a variety of interventions would need to be utilized. For example, confession and prayer, psychotherapy, and medication might all be needed to help a person overcome the debilitating effects of depression.

A truly biblical approach to counseling and psychotherapy recognizes that while sin is the root cause, a loving response to a suffering person would involve spiritual, psychological, and medical forms of treatment in concert. As Tournier (1962) has so perceptibly noted, "Every psychological confession has religious significance, and every religious confession, whether ritual and sacramental or free, has its psychological effects. It is perhaps in this fact that we perceive most clearly the unity of the human being, and how impossible it is to dissociate the physical, psychological and religious aspects of his life" (p. 204).

References

Berkouwer, G. C. *Man: The image of God.* Grand Rapids: Eerdmans, 1962.

Berkouwer, G. C. *Sin.* Grand Rapids: Eerdmans, 1971.

Bockar, J. A. *Primer for the nonmedical psychotherapist.* New York: Spectrum, 1975.

Menninger, K. A. *Whatever became of sin?* New York: Hawthorn, 1973.

Mowrer, O. H. *The crisis in psychiatry and religion.* Princeton, N.J.: Van Nostrand, 1961.

Mowrer, O. H., & Veszelovszky, A.V. There indeed may be a "right way": Response to James D. Smrtic. *Psychotherapy: Theory, Research, and Practice,* 1980, *17,* 440–447.

Smrtic, J. D. Time to remove our theoretical blinders: Integrity therapy may be the right way. *Psychotherapy: Theory, Research, and Practice,* 1979, *16,* 185–189.

Tournier, P. *Guilt and grace.* New York: Harper & Row, 1962.

W. G. Bixler

Singleness. This term includes four groups of people, each with some similar issues but also unique problems and areas of concern: the never-married, the separated, the divorced, and the widowed. Their numbers are increasing rapidly, from 4 million in 1950 to an estimated 20 million in 1982. Social factors influence this greatly. It is now more acceptable for women to pursue their own interests, including attending college (in 1960 there were 1.2 million women in college as compared to 3.5 million in 1972), which tends to delay marriage. Singleness as a life style, though still carrying some social stigma, has become a more acceptable alternative, and freer sexual mores and less restrictive role constraints have had some influence on this.

A crucial element in the psychological health of the single person is his or her acceptance of the state of singleness, much as people can be happily or unhappily married. Whether the person is single by choice or not is a critical factor. One group of singles, such as the young or happily divorced, may plan to marry in the future but are contentedly single. There are those who have chosen singleness as a preferred life style (e.g., priests), the once-married who chose not to remarry, and those who simply do not want to marry. These groups face some issues that married people in our society do not face. However, they seem to handle them much better than those who are single not by choice—through death of a spouse, termination of a marriage, or the lack of opportunity to marry when they would like to.

There are advantages to being single. Frequently there is an increased mobility, freedom, and psychological and social autonomy. Singles often build sustaining friendships and support structures. They generally have more time to devote to career opportunities and other interests. Adams (1976) cites three factors that determine healthy singleness: economic independence, social and psychological autonomy, and the preference to remain single.

There are also disadvantages to being single, not all of which are experienced by every single. Some have an unfulfilled desire for children and a family of their own. Others report isolation, loneliness, insecurity, or lack of social status. Peer and social pressures to marry abound. Some social policies favor the married, and marriage legitimizes sexual experiences.

Between ages 30–34, 12% of men and 7% of women have never married. That percentage decreases to 7.9% and 5.2% respectively in the age group 35–39, and by age 65 only 4% of men and 6% of women have never married (Stein, 1976). More than 60% of all singles live in large cities, and that number is increasing. Cities offer more single-oriented attractions, and over the last decade families have been drawn to the suburbs. The median age of first marriage has risen for both men and women, from 20.3 in 1960 to 22.3 in 1983 for women, and from 22.8 to 24.8 for men.

Life as a single in a marriage-oriented society frequently produces significant pressures. Singles cope with these pressures through one of several strategies. Some choose the professional route, throwing all of their time and energy into their career. Others devote themselves to relationships. A segment opts for the individualistic route, stressing self-growth and development. Some take a supportive role in the lives of their friends, while others remain passive and isolated. Community activism is another available route. All of these strategies may of course be chosen by married persons but they generally do not have the same time and freedom to devote as singles.

Single old people who have never married tend to be lifelong isolates, but they are not especially lonely, presumably having gotten used to being alone (Gubrium, 1976). They tend to be more positive than divorced or widowed old people, and do not have to face the bereavement following a spouse's death that so affects most older people.

Men who are single tend to be less intimate in their friendships with other men than single women are in their friendships with other women. However, single women tend to be more isolated than single men. Isolation and lack of intimacy are often a result of a lack of support and care structures, combined with the stereotypes of society and role expectations.

Extensive analyses by Bernard (1972) reveal that single women tend to be happier than single men, who are more likely to show depression and phobic tendencies. Men who remain unmarried are not as successful as married men in terms of education, income, and occupation, but women who remain unmarried are higher achievers than married women. How much this relates to social pressures and role expectations and how much to other factors is unclear.

Problems that are brought to therapy by singles are often the same problems that married people may feel—loneliness, isolation, lack of support, insecurity. However, the single often has the added pressure of society's disapproval.

References

Adams, M. *Single blessedness*. New York: Basic Books, 1976.
Bernard, J. S. *The future of marriage*. New York: World, 1972.
Gubrium, J. F. Being single in old age. *International Journal of Aging and Human Development*. 1976, 6(1), 29–41.
Stein, P. J. *Single*. Englewood Cliffs, N.J.: Prentice-Hall, 1976.

Additional Readings

Cargan, L., & Melko, M. *Singles: Myths and realities*. Beverly Hills, Calif.: Sage Publications, 1982.
Simenauer, J., & Carroll, D. *Singles: The new Americans*. New York: Simon & Schuster, 1982.

D. L. SCHUURMAN

Single Parents. The single parent family is the fastest growing life style in America. In 1970, 11% of the children under 18 lived with one parent. By 1979 this figure had risen to 19.3%. Porter and Chatelain report that "according to U.S. Census Bureau statistics 45% of all children born today will spend at least one year living with one parent" (1981, p. 157). The only other family life style that is rapidly growing is the reconstituted family, often formed following life as a single parent family.

The single parent family is formed as a result of one of three events: divorce or separation, death of a parent, and birth (or adoption) of a child to an unmarried parent. Divorced parents constitute two-thirds of single parents, while never-married parents constitute one-fourth (Bilge & Kaufman, 1983). Of these one parent families 90% are headed by women, most of whom work. Seventy-three percent of divorced women work, while only 51% of married women work. Thus the majority of single parent families are headed by divorced, working women.

The single parent family experiences five specific areas of stress that differentiate it from the two parent family: lower income, more limited sense of power and control, diminished social support and involvement, reduced emotional support and physical assistance within the household, and often a traumatic event or series of events which began the new family life style.

The events that result in a single parent family are often stressful and unsettling, adding to the adjustment difficulties of the single parent. Where divorce has occurred, the tensions of the former marital relationship may linger on, creating special difficulties when decisions about the child require parental contact. Bitterness and resentment may remain, especially if the single parent did not want the divorce. The death of a parent is usually unexpected, since the age of the parents of minor children is generally between 25 and 40. Many never-married parents did not anticipate or make specific plans for becoming single parents. Thus, for most, single parenting is not a deliberate choice. It is often an unwelcome consequence, at best the better of two evils (conflicted marriage or single parenting). This may explain partially why most single parents report a more limited sense of power and control over their lives (Smith, 1980). They also report a sense of alienation, helplessness, and victimization.

The reduction of adult physical assistance and emotional support within the household further reinforces the sense of less power and control. One person cannot do what two did before. Some things won't get done. The parent may consequently feel increasing inadequacy and have no one within the family to turn to for emotional support.

Less time is available for social activities and participation in community life. The single parent often feels the responsibility of picking up the roles and activities of the other parent. Thus the parenting role becomes dominant, and personal desires and activities with other adults take second or third place.

Research has shown that 32% of single parent families, as compared to 51% of two parent families, know 20 or more neighbors (Smith, 1980). This may result from decreased time to spend with neighbors as well as the parent's response to the social stigma against one parent families that is often found in American culture.

Cross-cultural research has shown that single parent families are not unique to American society but exist in many cultures. Whether or not the single parent family becomes a personal and social problem depends on the availability of supportive social networks as well as the cultural attitudes toward it (Bilge & Kaufman, 1983). American society seems to provide few of these resources. Single parents often need to find and create their own support networks, another stressful responsibility.

Three types of social networks have been identified among single parents (McLanahan, Wedemeyer, & Adelberg, 1981). The family of origin provides some single parents almost all of their support, with division of labor occurring along the lines of traditional roles. This type of network provides direct services, such as home repairs, and emotional support, especially security and a sense of worth. It does not provide much opportunity for intimacy and social integration.

A second type of support structure is the extended network, composed usually of new female friends, especially other single mothers. This structure is often large, with various clusters of relationships. Different individuals are depended on for different kinds of support. These relationships are often less durable and less intense than the family of origin relationships. A large majority of the women who establish this kind of network are attempting to reestablish their independence and have high career aspirations. This network may not provide a great deal of security or sense of worth, but it does provide intimacy and opportunity for social integration.

A third type is the conjugal network, which includes the presence of a key male or spouse equivalent. Here two subtypes parallel the previous two networks depending on the parent's choice of focusing on mother role or career role.

All these networks provide varying degrees

and types of support to the single parent. The existence of such support networks is a critical variable in the functional character of the single parent family. Where these are present, both parent and children gain support and assistance.

The single parent family usually experiences financial stress. The income of families headed by women is about one-half of two parent families (Buehler & Hogan, 1980). A large number of wives and children experience downward economic mobility following divorce. Consequently many wives are forced to work in order to maintain a standard of living close to what they and the children have come to enjoy. This often reduces their time with the children, their involvement with other adults, and their ability to keep things at home as they once were.

Considerable concern is often voiced by Christians and by married individuals about the effect of single parenting on the children. While it is still clear that two parents are better than one, for both the parent's and the children's sake, research on the effects of single parenting has not shown that all other circumstances being equal, it is necessarily bad for the children. Rather, other variables are found to be more influential on negative outcomes for the children. Children who perceive greater conflict in their families (single or dual parent) were found to have lower self-concepts (Bilge & Kaufman, 1983). The presence of a socially supportive network was also found to be important for the healthy development of children (McLanahan, Wedemeyer, & Adelberg, 1981). Cross-cultural research seems to support the conclusion that the family structure (one parent versus two parents) is not the most significant variable in assessing the consequences to the children (Bilge & Kaufman, 1983).

Increasingly more fathers are obtaining custody of their children. At the same time, males within American culture have the least opportunity to develop good parenting skills, especially in the area of meeting the emotional needs of the children. Research has shown that the effect of fathers spending more time with their children and having the sole responsibility for child rearing is that their approach to discipline moves away from authoritarian methods toward the use of more nurturing methods (Smith & Smith, 1981). Clearly fathers, both single and married, do benefit from increased presence with their children, and could benefit from more extensive child-rearing training.

Single parents do have unique stresses and challenges, but given a supportive Christian network these parents can live a meaningful life for themselves and provide an effective, nurturing environment for their children.

References

Bilge, B., & Kaufman, G. Children of divorce and one-parent families: Cross cultural perspectives. *Family Relations,* 1983, *32*(1), 59–72.

Buehler, C. A., & Hogan, M. J. Managerial behavior and stress in families headed by divorced women: A proposed framework. *Family Relations,* 1980, *29*(4), 525–532.

McLanahan, S. S., Wedemeyer, N. V., & Adelberg, T. Network structure, social support and psychological well-being in the single parent family. *Journal of Marriage and the Family,* 1981, *43*(3), 601–612.

Porter, B. R., & Chatelain, R. S. Family life education for single parent families. *Family Relations,* 1981, *30*(4), 517–525.

Smith, M. J. The social consequences of single parenthood: A longitudinal perspective. *Family Relations,* 1980, *29*(1), 75–81.

Smith, R. M., & Smith, C. W. Child rearing and single parent fathers. *Family Relations,* 1981, *30*(3), 411–417.

A. D. COMPAAN

See CHILD CUSTODY.

Sixteen Personality Factor Questionnaire (16 PF).

An objective instrument designed to measure the basic dimensions of normal personality. The self-administering test exists in five forms that vary according to the particular testing situation. The basic form consists of 187 multiple-choice items that are answered by selecting one of three responses and are easily scored. Sixteen is the lower age limit for the test. The primary developer, R. B. Cattell, saw factor analysis as the best method for personality test construction and used that technique to develop this test.

Originally names for the 16 personality factors—e.g., "premsia" and "sizothymia"—were created so that the meaning of common words would not interfere with understanding. This labeling was a fine attempt at clarity. However, these terms became a liability because jargon-laden clinicians lost interest, prompting the test publisher to use recognized words such as warmth, conformity, and dominance.

The 16 PF takes approximately 50–60 minutes to complete. Questions have to do with behavior, interests, and preferences. Norms are available for high school students, college students, and general population groups. The instrument has the same advantages as most other objective personality questionnaires: good reliability, ease of administration and scoring, low cost, and standardization that allows for high research potential.

While the factor analytic construction of

this test promised "pure" factors without overlap, the scales are not as pure as was hoped. This, along with the highly technical development of the test, has caused it to fall a good deal short of the claims methodological purists made for it. The publisher, the Institute for Personality and Ability Testing, continues to produce many of the technical and clinical writings supporting the test, and a number of clinicians use it regularly. But it has disappointed its developers by not enjoying the widespread use it seemed destined to attain.

Assessing normal and mildly troubled people according to a wide range of traits will continue to be the strength of the Sixteen Personality Factor Questionnaire. As a part of a test battery or in vocational counseling the test complements other measures of nonpathological personality dimensions. Use in marital therapy may also hold some promise. Since some forms lack validity measures of test-taking attitudes, care should be used in evaluating the results without information on socially desirable response sets.

Now that computer scoring and interpretation is nearly routine in personality testing, the 16 PF has mated with a technology similar to the science that gave it birth. A primitive actuarial or probability-based interpretive system is available using computers to aid the clinician. The test will continue to be a good objective measure of normal personality traits. Even more likely is its continued use as a research tool helping psychologists uncover the dimensions and structure of personality. As the best factor-analytic personality questionnaire, Cattell's work will stand as a testimony to thoughtful psychological investigation.

Additional Readings

Cattell, R. B. *Personality and mood by questionnaire.* San Francisco: Jossey-Bass, 1973.

Cattell, R. B., Eber, H. W., & Tatsuoka, M. M. *Handbook for the Sixteen Personality Factor Questionnaire [16 PF].* Champaign, Ill.: Institute for Personality and Ability Testing, 1964.

Karson, S. E., & O'Dell, J. W. *Clinical use of the 16 PF.* Champaign, Ill.: Institute for Personality and Ability Testing, 1976.

Krug, S. E. *Interpreting 16 PF profile patterns.* Champaign, Ill.: Institute for Personality and Ability Testing, 1981.

D. SIMPSON

See PERSONALITY ASSESSMENT; PSYCHOLOGICAL MEASUREMENT; FACTOR THEORIES OF PERSONALITY.

Skinner, Burrhus Frederic (1904–).

The father of modern behavioral psychology. Son of a moderately prosperous lawyer, Skinner was born in Susquehanna, Pennsylvania, and grew up there in a middle-class Protestant family. He attended Hamilton College, completing his B.A. in 1926. Initially Skinner planned on a literary career, but he quickly gave this up, enrolling to study psychology at Harvard in 1927; here he completed hs M.A. in 1930 and Ph.D. in 1931.

Skinner became a national Research Council fellow (1931–1933) and then a junior fellow in the Society of Fellows (1933–1936) at Harvard; during this period he worked in the laboratory of experimental biologist W. J. Crozier. He taught at the University of Minnesota from 1930 to 1945, taking time out during 1942–1943 to conduct war research sponsored by General Mills, and for a Guggenheim fellowship in 1944–1945. Skinner became chairman of the Department of Psychology at Indiana University in 1945. He then went to Harvard as William James Lecturer in 1947, and joined the Department of Psychology there in 1948. He has remained at Harvard since then.

Skinner has played an important role in the development of behavioral research techniques and equipment; he developed the Skinner Box, the cumulative recorder, and the first teaching machines. Other distinctives include a dislike for formal theory and emphasis on single-subject research. Skinner argued that operant rather than respondent behavior is the primary form of animal and human behavior.

Among his many honors are the Warren Medal of the Society of Experimental Psychology in 1942; the Distinguished Scientific Contribution Award of the American Psychological Association in 1958; the Edward L. Thorndike Award in Education in 1966; the United States Air Force Hoyt-Vandenburg Trophy in 1967; the National Medal of Science in 1968; the Gold Medal of the American Psychological Foundation in 1971; the International Award of the Joseph P. Kennedy, Jr., Foundation for Mental Retardation in 1971; the Humanist of the Year Award of the American Humanist Society in 1972; the Creative Leadership Award for distinguished Contributions to Educational Research and Development, American Educational Research Association, in 1976; and the first annual award of the National Association for Retarded Citizens in 1978. Skinner has also received more than 20 honorary degrees.

The breadth of Skinner's intellectual interests is indicated by his many professional associations, which include, among others, fellow of the American Psychological Association; fellow of the Royal Society of Arts; and member of the National Academy of Sciences, the American Philosophical Society, the American Academy of Arts and Sciences, and the New York Academy of Sciences.

A prolific writer, Skinner has published numerous books dealing with a broad range of topics, from technical aspects of operant behavior to mental illness, education, politics, and social policy. His most influential works in psychology are *Science and Human Behavior* (1953), *Contingencies of Reinforcement* (1969), and *Beyond Freedom and Dignity* (1971). Skinner was influential in founding the *Journal of the Experimental Analysis of Behavior* and the Division of the Experimental Analysis of Behavior in the American Psychological Association.

Although Skinner has been tremendously influential and has received widespread acclaim, he is also a controversial figure who has frequently championed unpopular positions. Thus his critics are also numerous. Among the criticisms are charges that Skinner reduces men to robots or automatons; that he dehumanizes man, destroying freedom and personal responsibility; that he denies the existence of the mind; that he undermines the basis for morals through rejection of all but empirical bases for ethical decisions; that his emphasis on control of human behavior fosters totalitarianism; and that he confuses his personal philosophy with his science, resulting in scientism rather than science (Bufford, 1981; Cosgrove, 1982; Wheeler, 1973). Skinner is well aware of these criticisms, and has responded to them most extensively in "Answers for My Critics" (Skinner, 1973).

A signer of the Humanist Manifesto II, Skinner espouses materialistic humanism. In *Beyond Freedom and Dignity* he clearly articulates his anti-Christian philosophy. According to Skinner, man has no special moral sense; rather, environment has taught him to behave in certain ways. At times his humanistic views seem to shape his scientific conclusions (cf. Cosgrove, 1982). For example, he concludes that punishment has harmful effects and does not work, a view effectively challenged by Bufford (1982).

Because of Skinner's significant role in the development of modern behaviorism, many have come to view his religious perspectives as central to BEHAVIORAL PSYCHOLOGY. However, although Skinner's world view has shaped his research and theorizing, it is not an essential element of behavioral theory or therapy.

References

Bufford, R. K. *The human reflex: Behavioral psychology in biblical perspective.* San Francisco: Harper & Row, 1981.
Bufford, R. K. Behavioral views of punishment: A critique. *Journal of the American Scientific Affiliation,* 1982, *34,* 135–144.
Cosgrove, M. P. *B. F. Skinner's behaviorism.* Grand Rapids: Zondervan, 1982.
Skinner, B. F. Answers for my critics. In H. Wheeler (Ed.), *Beyond the punitive society.* San Francisco: W. H. Freeman, 1973.
Wheeler, H. (Ed.). *Beyond the punitive society.* San Francisco: W. H. Freeman, 1973.

R. K. BUFFORD

Sleep and Dreaming. Sleep is a strangely familiar state. It is familiar because we spend nearly one-third of our lives doing it; it is strange because its true function remains a mystery. Scientists are beginning to learn more about the sleep process and the physiological mechanisms that switch it on and off, but they still have few clues to the question of why we sleep.

Serious sleep research began in the 1930s but did not advance rapidly until scientists developed sophisticated electrophysiological recording equipment that could reliably measure the tiny electrical potentials produced by neural activity in the brain and by other parts of the body. These potentials are usually described by the frequency with which they increase and decrease. Frequencies are measured in Hertz (Hz) or cycles per second. For instance, brain waves, which are recorded on charts called electroencephalographs, or EEGs, are typically in the beta (13–40 Hz) or alpha (8–12 Hz) frequencies when we are awake but decrease to theta (4–8 Hz) or delta (1–4 Hz) when we sleep. Other electrophsiological measures useful in sleep research are recordings of eye movements and muscle potentials (electromyograms or EMGs).

One of the most surprising discoveries in sleep research utilizing these measures was that there are actually two types of sleep: REM sleep, associated with awake-type brain waves and rapid eye movements (REMs), and NREM sleep, associated with very slow, rolling eye movements and slow, synchronized brain wave activity (Cohen, 1980).

Another interesting discovery was that most people follow a definite pattern of REM and NREM sleep throughout the night. Before sleep onset our muscles relax and our brain wave pattern shifts from beta to primarily alpha waves. Sleep apparently begins abruptly. (Dement, 1972, demonstrated this by having a subject, with his eyes taped open, press a switch every 15 seconds when a bright light was flashed close to his face. Even in this unlikely condition sleep prevailed, and the subject suddenly stopped pressing the switch.) As sleep begins, we pass through four discernible stages of REM sleep. These stages are characterized by increasingly slower and higher amplitude brain waves; slow, rolling, and disconjugate eye movements; and decreased heart rate, breathing rate, and muscle tonus. In stages 3 and 4 high-voltage delta waves predominate in the EEG record and sleep is very sound. We generally spend 10 to 15 minutes in each of these stages.

About 90 minutes after sleep onset a number of physiological patterns abruptly change as we enter REM sleep. Brain waves suddenly switch from slow, high-amplitude delta waves to fast, low-amplitude beta waves. Our eyes begin darting to and fro rapidly under closed eyelids as if we were watching some event. Breathing rate, heart rate, and other autonomically controlled functions may rapidly accelerate or become quite variable. The onset of REM is generally associated with penile erection or increase in vaginal blood flow. Paradoxically, muscle tonus drops drastically, leaving voluntary muscles paralyzed except for brief twitchings in the hands and feet. The first REM session lasts about 10 minutes.

If we are awakened during REM sleep, we will probably realize we have been dreaming. Dreams reported during REM are typically narrative in form and tend to be more emotional or bizarre the longer we spend in REM before awakening. (Some people report that they never dream. When they are awakened during REM and are thus enabled to remember their dreams, they are surprised by their own vivid productions.)

During the remainder of the night sleep will alternate between REM and NREM about every 90 minutes. As the night progresses, the amount of time spent in stages 3 and 4 decreases and time in REM increases. In fact, toward morning REM sessions may turn into hour-long features.

The amount of time spent in REM and NREM seems to be controlled physiologically. Sleep onset is apparently initiated by neurons in the forebrain (preoptic area) and lower brain stem (midpontine region). REM phenomena (cortical desynchrony, eye movements, loss of muscle tonus) seem to be controlled by several structures in the pons. In addition, the allocation of sleep to nighttime and waking to daytime is probably synchronized by the suprachiasmatic nucleus of the hypothalamus. The physiological correlates of sleep have been easier to discover than the actual purpose of sleep.

Human sleep deprivation studies indicate that sleep is a very insistent drive but that loss of sleep produces surprisingly few physical or psychological consequences. Very prolonged sleep loss—5 to 10 days—consistently produces fine hand tremor, droopy eyelids, occasional double vision, lowered pain thresholds, and decreased alpha activity. The ability to do tasks that require sustained attention, effort, or concentration is moderately impaired. Behaviorally there may be evidence of confusion, disorientation, irritability, and brief visual or tactile hallucinations, but the personality remains intact. A few individuals (probably 5% or fewer) may show more disturbed psychotic-type behaviors, but these seem to be individuals with predeprivation adjustment problems (Webb, 1975).

Other studies have concentrated on selective deprivation of various sleep stages. Researchers have consistently found evidence for a physiological mechanism that tries to compensate for the loss of REM and stage 4 sleep. For instance, if subjects are awakened every time they start a REM episode, they have to be awakened more and more frequently to prevent REM as the night progresses. When sleeping undisturbed the next night, they produce much more REM than controls who had been awakened equally often during NREM sleep. Selective deprivation of stage 4 sleep also results in this "rebound" effect. Surprisingly, there is no known deleterious effect for either type of sleep deprivation.

People naturally differ quite a bit in the amount of sleep they need per day, especially with age. Newborns need 14–18 hours (50% in REM); 5-year-olds need 11 hours (25% in REM); and adults need seven or eight hours (25% in REM). People over 65, especially men, vary considerably in the amount and type of sleep they get. Total sleep time and nighttime awakenings increase, stage 4 sleep decreases by 15–30%, and stage 1 sleep doubles. Researchers believe that this alteration is probably due to a breakdown in the physiological control mechanism.

Most adults (90%) need seven to nine hours of sleep per day, but 7% report needing 6½ hours or less. Sleep researchers have also studied some exceptionally short sleepers— three middle-aged men who averaged three hours and a 70-year-old woman who needed only one hour of sleep per day. Several large-scale studies indicate that the amount of sleep needed by normal people is unrelated to physical or psychological health, sex, or intelligence. (Neurotic and psychotic depressives do have sleep disturbances; see SLEEP DISORDERS.)

Dreaming is another intriguing aspect of sleep that has been extensively studied. Hall (1966) and Snyder (1970) collected and studied

1,000 "home" and 650 "laboratory" dreams, respectively. They both found that only 1–5% of these were in exotic or unusual settings. About 95% of the dreams involved other persons, more than half of these known to the dreamer. Dreams did have dramatic themes, more frequently dealing with misfortune, failure, aggression, fear, and anger than with success, friendly encounters, or positive emotion. Few dreams were explicitly sexual (1–5%), perhaps a bit surprising given the physiological sexual arousal that accompanies REM episodes. The fantastic elements of dreaming seemed to come from loosened rules about how things should happen. Time does not flow inexorably forward; matter is not bound by gravity; one is not confined to one place at a time; and any improbable thing can happen.

At present the purpose of dreams seems as enigmatic as the purpose of sleep. There have been four basic explanations. Some groups of people (e.g., Eskimos of Hudson Bay, Pantani Malay people, and some parapsychologists and psychic researchers studying astral projection) believe that the soul leaves the body during sleep and that dreams are real experiences in a spiritual realm. So far there is no evidence to even try to evaluate this hypothesis.

A second very old but still current explanation is that dreams have a prophetic function. Books on turning dreams into useful knowledge of the future are probably more available today at our newsstands than they were to the Egyptians in 1350 B.C. when detailed instructions were inscribed on a recently discovered papyrus document. The Bible indicates that angels or the Holy Spirit have communicated prophetic information to persons in their dreams. In the Old Testament Joseph had a prophetic dream and interpreted another for Pharoah; in the New Testament, Joseph was warned to flee to Egypt with Mary and Jesus and was later told when to return. It is important to note that in all these cases the information was from a supernatural source and not just from the minds of men.

A more recent explanation is that dreams reflect the explicit or implicit life of the dreamer. Freud believed that dreams had manifest content, symbolic representation of unconscious and unfulfilled infantile sexual wishes. Dreams served to transform the latent content into a manifest content that was acceptable to the dreamer. Clinicians today are more likely to accept manifest content as a statement of an individual's immediate rather than infantile and general rather than purely sexual concerns. Dreams are seen more as an open, if symbolic, letter that we write to ourselves.

A fourth explanation is functional. Since dreaming occurs in REM sleep and REM sleep is physiologically controlled, dreaming must either directly or indirectly serve some physiological function—perhaps restoration or repair in the brain. Whatever this function may be, it is apparently not unique to humans, since all mammals also show REM-NREM cycles.

Even though they offer some insights, none of these explanations of dreaming, or of sleep, really answer the question of why we sleep and dream. The real answer may be hidden in the cloud of mystery surrounding our very nature.

References

Cohen, D. B. *Sleep and dreaming: Origins, nature and functions.* New York: Pergamon, 1980.

Dement, W. C. *Some must watch while some must sleep.* Stanford, Calif.: Stanford Alumni Association, 1972.

Hall, C. S., & Van de Castle, R. L. (Eds.), *The content analysis of dreams.* New York: Appleton-Century-Crofts, 1966.

Snyder, F. The phenomenology of dreaming. In L. Madow & L. H. Snow (Eds.), *The psychodynamic implications of the physiological study of dreams.* Springfield, Ill.: Thomas, 1970.

Webb, W. B. *Sleep, the gentle tyrant.* Englewood Cliffs, N.J.: Prentice-Hall, 1975.

E. L. HILLSTROM

See DREAMS, THERAPEUTIC USE OF.

Sleep Disorders. There are two types of sleep disorders: primary, which are disturbances in basic sleep processes, and insomnia, which is the inability to get sufficient sleep. The primary disorders include narcolepsy, sleep apnea, hypersomnia, nightmares, night terrors, sleepwalking, sleep talking, and nocturnal enuresis.

Primary Sleep Disorders. *Narcolepsy.* Individuals with narcolepsy experience sudden, brief, and compelling attacks of sleep that can last from 1 to 30 minutes and can occur one or more times a day (Hartman, 1973). These episodes occur spontaneously and are more likely when the narcoleptic is fatigued or has eaten a heavy meal. Attacks can also be precipitated by anger, fear, laughter, making love, or any event that generates strong emotions.

Three symptoms frequently accompanying narcoleptic attacks are cataplexy, hypnagogic hallucinations, and sleep paralysis (Webb, 1975). Cataplexy, present in about 70% of all episodes, is a sudden loss of muscle tonus and control. This may be partial, producing feelings of weakness, or virtually complete, causing the narcoleptic to collapse, totally unable to move. Hypnagogic hallucinations, present about 50% of the time, are unusual visual and auditory sensations, like dreams, that occur at the beginning of the narcoleptic episode. Sleep paralysis is a complete loss of muscle tonus that occasionally occurs during the transition from waking to sleep. In this disconcerting state the narcoleptic is conscious but temporarily unable to move.

Narcolepsy afflicts from two to five people out of every 1,000. Symptoms most frequently appear between the ages of 15 and 25, although they sometimes appear in children under 10 or in adults up to 40. Once symptoms surface, they remain a lifelong problem. Narcolepsy does have a genetic component, since 20 to 50% of diagnosed narcoleptics have relatives with the disorder.

Narcolepsy was once thought to be of psychogenic origin or perhaps related to epilepsy. Neither of these explanations is supported by research. The current hypothesis is that narcoleptic attacks are actually episodes of REM sleep that intrude into the waking state. Several observations support this belief. Electroencephalographic recordings of brain states during attacks are similar to those produced in REM sleep. Other characteristics of REM sleep—rapid eye movements (REM), dreaming, and loss of muscle tonus—have their counterparts in narcolepsy. The normal loss of muscle tonus in REM sleep, which probably protects us from acting out our dreams, may be responsible for the cataplexic phenomenon in narcoleptic episodes. Dreams, dimly sensed and soon forgotten in normal sleep, could produce frightening and bizarre hallucinations if they occur while the sleeper is still partly awake and conscious. Rapid eye movements also occur in both states. Another relevant observation is that narcoleptics can go directly from waking to REM sleep. Most sleepers do not experience REM until 90 minutes after sleep onset.

The actual cause of narcolepsy is not known, but it is probably due to a neurological dysfunction in brain-stem areas that initiate and control REM sleep. Even though narcolepsy cannot be cured, it can be treated. Patients suffering from cataplexy are sometimes helped by antidepressants, while other patients are benefited by stimulants. Daytime naps may also help alleviate symptoms.

Sleep Apnea. Some patients who come to sleep clinics are suffering from a condition called sleep apnea (Dement, 1972). These unfortunate individuals cannot sleep and breathe at the same time. Sleep onset apparently disables the brain respiratory control centers, stopping the movements of the diaphragm and intercostal muscles—and breathing—for 15 to 30 seconds. Blood levels of carbon dioxide increase, eventually forcing the respiratory muscles to function, but the lungs may still be unable to fill with air because the throat muscles have collapsed due to a loss of tonus. After 60 to 100 breathless seconds extreme levels of carbon dioxide awaken the sleeper, muscles regain tonus, and the patient gasps for breath.

Apparently some patients are able to adapt to this strange condition, literally awakening as often as 500 times a night, without any knowledge of their problem. These hypersomniacs complain that they sleep for long periods and take naps but never seem to feel rested. Other patients are awakened by the episodes but do not go back to sleep as easily. These patients suffer from insomnia. Sleep apnea is also responsible for some cases of sudden infant death syndrome, a mystifying condition in which healthy babies suddenly die in their sleep without apparent struggle. Premature babies are more vulnerable to apnea and sudden infant death than are full-term babies.

Several conditions are known to contribute to sleep apnea. One of these is an exaggerated loss of tonus in throat muscles during sleep, a problem that is made worse by extra weight on the neck in obese patients or by enlarged tonsils or adenoids which partially block the air passages. Another contributing condition, especially in babies, is a defective respiratory control center. Most people cannot voluntarily hold their breath until they die. If they try, blood levels of oxygen decrease and carbon dioxide increase, they lose consciousness, and the control center, stimulated by high levels of carbon dioxide, automatically initiates breathing. The control centers of babies with apnea do not always respond appropriately to increased carbon dioxide.

Apnea has been successfully treated in infants by implanting pacemakers in the diaphragm to stimulate breathing and by giving stimulants such as theophylline, a caffeinlike substance that stimulates the respiratory center. Adults may be given stimulants or encouraged to lose weight if they are obese. Some adults obtain relief when a small tube is surgically implanted in the neck. The tube extends from outside the neck to the trachea and allows the patient to breathe even if the throat becomes obstructed during sleep. (The tube opening can be closed during the day.)

Hypersomnia. Hypersomnia is a condition in which people sleep a long time at night and take long naps during the day but still are not satisfied or refreshed (Browman, Sampson, Krishnareddy, & Mitler, 1982). Besides being chronically sleepy, hypersomniacs may also appear to be lazy, slow, and insensitive to the world around them. They sleep 12 or more hours each day, in many cases spending much larger proportions of time in stage 3 and stage 4 sleep than do normal sleepers. They often awake with great difficulty, remaining disoriented and confused for up to an hour later.

Estimates of the frequency of hypersomnia run as high as 15%. In one large-scale study of 3,900 patients treated for sleep disorders, 51% were hypersomniacs. Of this group 43% suffered from sleep apnea, 25% from narcolepsy, and 9% from nonspecific neurological disorders of various kinds. Other miscellaneous causes were also present. Since hypersomnia has multiple causes, the appropriate treatment will vary from case to case.

Childhood Disorder. Another set of sleep disorders, which are much less severe and which occur most frequently in children, are nightmares, night terrors, and the parasomnias (sleepwalking, sleep talking, and nocturnal enuresis). Nightmares are frightening dreams that awaken the sleeper from REM sleep, whereas night terrors are abrupt awakenings from stage 4 sleep. Children experiencing night terrors may scream, sob, and awaken in a state of panic but be totally unable to recall a dream or to explain their fears. They usually do not remember the episode the next day. Night terrors occur most frequently in children from ages 3 to 5, whereas nightmares occur most frequently from ages 7 to 10. Both of these problems are usually outgrown and seldom need treatment. In a few instances nightmares and night terrors do persist into adulthood and may then be considered a sleep dysfunction. Adults with these problems can sometimes be treated with drugs that suppress REM or stage 4 sleep.

SOMNAMBULISM, or sleepwalking, is another sleep disturbance that occurs in stage 4 sleep. Today it is considered a transient disturbance in the sleep control mechanism. It is commonly outgrown and needs no special treatment.

Sleep talking usually occurs during stage 1 or just before entering sleep, although it has been found in REM sleep about 10% of the time. When it occurs in REM sleep, it is related to dreams. It is not usually considered a problem—at least for the sleep talker.

Nocturnal ENURESIS, or bedwetting, which is considered a clinical problem only in children who are 5 or older, is very common. In one large sample of subjects age 5 to 14, 29% reported a recent incident of bedwetting. The incidence was greatest for the 5- to 7-year-old group and then dropped sharply with age. Enuresis usually occurs during REM sleep and is more common among boys than girls.

Several variables may contribute to this problem: slower maturation, genetic predisposition, poor training habits, neurological or urological disorders, and possibly psychological problems. Treatments have included conditioning, controlling fluid intake at bedtime, medication, and psychotherapy. Successful treatment depends on proper diagnosis of the problem.

Most children with enuretic problems seem troubled and ashamed by them and really want to change. Parents should be advised not to overreact to the inconvenience or to exacerbate their children's guilt or shame. The great majority of children do outgrow this condition, although some may need professional help.

Insomnia. Insomnia, the inability to obtain a satisfactory amount of sleep, probably afflicts 14% of the general population fairly frequently. Many of its causes are environmental or situational, produced by the way we live. Some temporary insomnias are caused by specific situations that generate sorrow, fear, tension, or stress, and this emotional upheaval interferes with sleep. Other insomnias are the result of doing shift work, sleeping at different times on different days, thereby disrupting the body's natural circadian rhythms, which help to regulate sleep.

Some people act like insomniacs, complaining bitterly that they are not getting sufficient sleep, but find out that they actually are when tested in a sleep laboratory. A portion of these patients, the naturally short sleepers and the aged, think they need more sleep than they are getting. They can be helped to recognize that their sleep time is normal. Others in this catagory may be pseudoinsomniacs, who think they are not sleeping when in fact they are. Incredibly, some of these patients dream of being awake.

Another frequent source of insomnia is the overuse of sleeping pills. Chronic use is associated with a badly disturbed sleep pattern characterized by frequent awakenings. Almost all sleeping pills suppress REM sleep. When REM is suppressed, the brain mechanism responsible for producing REM works overtime to make up the deficit. When people start taking sleeping pills, the recommended dosage will work for one or two nights, but they will have to keep increasing the dosage every few nights to overcome the brain's increasing efforts to produce REM. If users then try to withdraw from the pills, they will experience excessive REM sleep accompanied by fragmented, disrupted sleep with vivid and horrifying dreams. The only way to break this cycle is by a gradual supervised withdrawal.

Other causes of insomnia are physical or psychopathological. Physical illnesses, such as kidney disease, and psychopathological conditions, such as psychoneurosis and bipolar disorder, can also cause insomnia. Still other causes such as apnea, probably have a neurological origin. A small percentage of the cases are endogenous, produced by a failure of the underlying sleep/waking mechanism itself.

References

Browman, C. P., Sampson, M. G., Krishnareddy, S. G., & Mitler, M. M. The drowsy crowd. *Psychology Today,* 1982, *16*(8), 35–38.
Dement, W. C. *Some must watch while some must sleep.* Stanford, Calif.: Stanford Alumni Association, 1972.
Hartman, E. L. *The function of sleep.* New Haven: Yale University Press, 1973.
Webb, W. B. *Sleep: The gentle tyrant.* Englewood Cliffs, N.J.: Prentice-Hall, 1975.

Additional Reading

Mendelson, W. B., Gillen, J. C., & Wyatt, R. J. *Human sleep and its disorders.* New York: Plenum, 1977.

E. L. Hillstrom

Sleepwalking. *See* Somnambulism.

Smoking. Tobacco smokers usually find it difficult to stop, even though smoking is a major health problem. Approximately 25% of the total U.S. population smokes. Smokers die more frequently than not smokers from heart disease, strokes, lung cancer, and other lung ailments. The risk of smokers having heart attacks is three times greater than for developing lung cancer. Although an ex-smoker can have the same lower nonsmoker's risk of developing lung cancer or heart attack after 5 to 10 years of not smoking, the damage from emphysema is irreversible.

One of the reasons people find it so difficult to stop smoking is that it affects physiological, psychological, and behavioral areas of one's life. The motives for smoking appear to be complex. The main reasons for continuing to smoke are thought to be: 1) smoking becomes a learned habit, and such habits are resistant to change; 2) smokers become addicted to the nicotine in cigarettes; and 3) smoking is highly pleasurable at the beginning, and the withdrawal symptoms associated with stopping are very disagreeable.

People learn to smoke usually through friends who pressure them. Although it is not pleasant at first, people learn to tolerate the discomfort with practice, and then begin to enjoy smoking with their friends. When smoking becomes pleasant, people start to smoke in other situations, and the habit spreads and becomes ingrained. Sometimes they smoke to cope with unpleasant feelings such as anger, tension, anxiety, or boredom.

Smoking may be difficult to stop because it provides such an immediate effect. The nicotine from an inhaled cigarette reaches the brain in seven seconds. If a person smokes a pack daily and takes 10 puffs on each cigarette, he will get more than 70,000 doses of nicotine per year. This is certainly a higher frequency of drug usage than that of an alcoholic or any other type of drug addict. There are few initial negative consequences of smoking. It takes health problems years to develop. Furthermore, smoking does not interfere with work performance; some people say smoking improves their work productivity. No other type of drug user can make this claim.

Recent research has shown that people who stop smoking are those who not only realize that smoking can truly be bad for their health, but they see themselves as personally susceptible to the serious consequences of continued smoking. Moderate smokers may know that smoking poses a serious threat to their health, but they do not see themselves as being personally vulnerable to health problems as a result of smoking.

There are several factors associated with heavy smoking, including age, sex, economic status, behavior of family and peers, school and athletic achievement, and psychological status. After leaving elementary school students are exposed to more older students and have greater opportunity to smoke and use other drugs. Young men used to smoke more than women, but this has changed. Young women now smoke as often as their male peers. The poor and uneducated are the heaviest smokers. Parents who smoke are more likely to have children who smoke. Since most people begin smoking with friends, possibly to appear more mature and independent, unassertive young people with low self-confidence or significant levels of anxiety are more susceptible to peer pressures to conform. Those who do well in school or athletics are less likely to smoke, as are those with a high sense of personal well-being.

Smoking

The habit of smoking can be prevented when young people are supervised and when there is a positive value to not smoking. It is beneficial when youths who are leaders help their friends avoid situations that might lead to smoking. Educating people so they can understand the consequences and resist pressures toward the use of tobacco is helpful. A person can best overcome influence from others if he is taught the expected arguments and ways to refute them ahead of time. This method is sometimes referred to as psychological innoculation. Assertiveness training can be an aid to resisting influence from others, as can learning to respond to the persuasive comment that "smokers are more independent" with the remark that "they aren't if they're addicted to cigarettes."

Other methods that make people more resistant to smoking are learning to cope with anxiety and increasing confidence and self-esteem. Anxiety can be reduced through a wide variety of physical and psychological practices, ranging from sports to relaxation techniques and meditation or prayer. A belief in God as the controller of the universe and a helper available to all can also reduce anxiety. Confidence and self-esteem usually increase when a person develops competence in skills or activities that others value or admire—such as athletic, academic, or work success. The rewards of these successes make the possible rewards of tobacco and other drugs less attractive.

Research has shown that not smoking is one of seven important health habits that are predictive of a long life. An effective method of quitting smoking has been presented by heart specialist Farquhar (1978). His method includes these steps: 1) Identify the problem. Find out the degree of health risk associated with your smoking patterns, keep track of how much you smoke, and examine your attitudes about stopping smoking. Develop counterarguments to attitudes that promote smoking and learn stress management techniques. 2) Build commitment to quitting smoking. Get friends and family to support your commitment. 3) Increase awareness of your smoking patterns. Keep a diary of when you smoke, where you are, what you're doing, and the intensity of your urge for each cigarette. 4) Build an action plan for quitting. Taper off your smoking. It is easier to stop if you smoke less than 15 cigarettes a day. Activate your social support and develop substitutes for smoking. Following this, make a contract with yourself to taper off and have a week, before you quit, when you smoke only four cigarettes daily. Then quit and use the supports and substitutes you have developed. 5) Evaluate your program. Check your records and the methods you are using. Rebuild your commitment to quitting. 6) Maintenance. Continue to use smoking suppression methods and relaxation skills to be comfortable as a nonsmoker.

Many smokers worry about gaining weight after they stop smoking, but the average weight gain for ex-smokers is actually only about three pounds, and that is rarely permanent. Another concern of smokers who consider quitting is withdrawal symptoms from the body's physical addiction to nicotine. Some people do experience increased irritability or lowered energy levels when they first stop smoking, but both disappear with time.

A person who is unsuccessful in the first or second attempt to stop smoking should not be deterred from the goal of becoming an ex-smoker. Continued efforts will bring success. Millions of people can attest to this. A former smoker saves several hundred dollars yearly by not buying cigarettes and by receiving preferential nonsmoker's insurance rates. Becoming an ex-smoker leads to an improved sense of well-being and a generally healthier, wealthier, and longer life.

Reference

Farquhar, J. W. *The American way of life need not be hazardous to your health.* New York: Norton, 1978.

M. A. NORFLEET

See HEALTH PSYCHOLOGY.

Social Comparison Theory. Festinger's (1954) theory of social comparison asserts that human beings tend toward self-evaluation. People want to know if their personal attributes such as feelings, beliefs, and abilities are appropriate or correct. Sometimes physical reality can provide the standard of evaluation (e.g., a belief concerning someone's height can be confirmed using a tape measure). However, such physical standards are not always available (it would be hard to find a yardstick for evaluating most attitudes). Under such conditions people rely on social reality; they compare themselves with others (social comparison). The theory further suggests that since similar others provide the most informative comparisons, these are the individuals most likely to serve as social reality, the standard of correctness or appropriateness.

This process of social comparison seems to play a role in many phenomena, including conformity. Certainly people often conform in an attempt to gain acceptance from others. But people also conform simply to be right. Imagine someone attending an event at a local theater. During the intermission he or she discovers that the signs indicating the men's and women's restrooms are missing. Faced with such a dilemma one's solution might be to observe the choices made by others and conform to the behavior of someone of the same sex. This same principle applies to following a driver who seems to know where he is going and avoiding an empty telephone booth when people are lined up at adjacent phones.

Social comparison provides further insight into why bystanders often do not help during emergencies. Generally emergencies are ambiguous, and thus before bystanders will intervene they must first determine that the situation is an actual emergency (Latané & Darley, 1970). Typically this involves maintaining an appearance of outward calm while observing the reactions of other bystanders. As a result, the bystanders may convince themselves that since everybody appears calm, the situation is a nonemergency and that nobody need intervene.

If social comparison is such a pervasive phenomenon (it also seems to play a role in such areas as affiliation, competition, group polarization, and the development of self-esteem), and it is not time or culture dependent, then it makes sense that God would have taken it into consideration when relating to his people throughout history. Such a perspective sheds light on certain passages of Scripture that can otherwise be problematic. For example, there is God's command that the Israelites should utterly destroy the nations inhabiting the promised land (Deut. 20:16–17). Certainly such a command represents a judgment upon the practices of those nations. But in addition such a command seems to have been designed to protect the integrity of the Israelites' faith (Deut. 20:18). Cohabitation with other nations would have led to social comparison along many dimensions, including beliefs. With alternative standards of correctness pagan notions could have crept into the Jewish faith. The seriousness of this threat was in fact confirmed when the Israelites did allow other nations to live in the promised land. This same principle seems to apply to marriage between Christians and non-Christians. The discrimination inherent in the command for Christians not to marry non-Christians (2 Cor. 6:14) becomes more understandable when its protective function is recognized.

Of course, a very significant issue in the discussion of social comparison and faith is the importance of the attribute being evaluated. It is possible that when a belief is particularly significant, the result may be an attempt by the believer to persuade rather than to compromise (Gordon, 1966). Such a possibility is intriguing and deserves further exploration.

References
Festinger, L. A theory of social comparison processes. *Human Relations*, 1954, 7, 117–140.
Gordon, B. F. Influence and social comparison as motives for affiliation. *Journal of Experimental Social Psychology*, 1966, Supplement 1, 55–65.
Latané, B., & Darley, J. M. *The unresponsive bystander: Why doesn't he help?* New York: Appleton-Century-Crofts, 1970.

R. L. Bassett

Social Influence Therapy. This therapy had its beginnings in the broad spectrum of theorists who believed that therapists function as influence agents. The work of Frank, Goldstein, Heller, and Sechrest on power, influence, and expectation effects in therapy served as the foundation for the integrative work of Gillis, who first recognized and articulated the tactical implications that therapist influence could have in therapy (Gillis, 1974).

Gillis's approach seeks to effect change by attempting to identify and analyze the many ways in which influence operates in therapy. Borrowing freely from other disciplines, especially social psychology, the approach is forthrightly manipulative in nature, using persuasive techniques and tactics derived primarily from the theories of attitude change, interpersonal attraction, cognitive dissonance theory, and placebo effects.

Therapy is considered to be a four-stage process: 1) enhancing the client's belief in and commitment to treatment; 2) establishment of the therapist's position of influence; 3) the use of this position to deliver the therapeutic attitude-changing message; and 4) provision of evidence that change is taking place. For example, research on cognitive dissonance reduction suggests that individuals value highly those things that they have worked hard to attain. Clients may thus be required to make some sacrifices in order to gain admission to therapy. Substantial fees or extensive test batteries may be used to accomplish this. Or the client may be required to read successful outcome case studies in order to enhance his belief in the value of therapy.

While social influence therapy does possess the rudiments of a system of therapy, it is best considered an alternative conceptual scheme with associated clinical techniques that can be applied to all systems of psychotherapy. Responsible use of therapist-controlled influence is desirable within a Christian frame of reference, where ethical guidelines and moral standards guide the influence in a manner that protects the client's integrity. Abuses of therapist influence are possible within this system, and the resulting compromise of client rights and countertherapeutic effects are certainly a reality.

Reference
Gillis, J. S. Social influence therapy. *Psychology Today*, December 1974, pp. 91–95.

D. M. Cook

Social Interest. Adler contended that human beings were essentially social, not merely sexual, beings. The central concept of his theory of personality is *Gemeinschaftsgefühl*, which has been translated as *social interest*. This translation leaves much to be desired. *Social* implies mores or collectivism. *Interest* implies something mild, cognitive, and ephemeral. Some of Adler's followers have contended that the ultimate concept is ineffable and cannot be reduced to words. Others have tried by offering humanistic identification or commitment to others. It involves feelings of brotherly love for other people in the present as well as a feeling of affinity for the whole human race past and future. The individual with social interest has integrated strivings for adjustment to reality, and these strivings enhance the strivings of others. A person motivated by social interest also has a commitment to understanding the psychic needs of other people and strives to become a significant other who can help fulfill those needs.

Brennan (1969) suggested that social interest involves both a phenomenological meaning and a transcendental meaning. The first involves the fact that I experience you as different (feeling), yet in a more fundamental way I experience our sameness as humans (social). The transcendental meaning refers to the fact that social interest cannot be understood through contemplation, but only through action and being with others. With social interest the transcendence is transcendence of one's own fictions that impinge upon the reality of the other.

According to Adlerians social interest also implies a rational and objective outlook. Individuals devoid of social interest become limited by idiosyncratic cognitive processes and private logic. These are fictions that protect against inferiority feelings at the expense of an accurate perception of reality. The participation in socially constructed reality is a commitment to learn what one's words and behavior mean to the other.

For Adler and his followers social interest is the essence of mental health. The individual is always unique but always involved with others. The healthy individual is one with a developing capacity to transcend his own limitations and relate to others. The healthy individual is characterized by mutual striving for achievement (Lichtenberg, 1963). Neurosis is characterized either by achievement without mutuality (i.e., self-centeredness) or by mutual strivings without achievement (e.g., passive dependency, suicide). The purpose of therapy based on INDIVIDUAL PSYCHOLOGY is to help the patient develop social interest.

References
Brennan, J. F. Autoeroticism or social feeling as basis of human development. *Journal of Individual Psychology*, 1969, *25*, 3–18.
Lichtenberg, P. Mutual achievement striving and social interest. *Journal of Individual Psychology*, 1963, *19*, 148–160.

T. L. Brink

Social Learning Theory. An approach to human behavior and personality that attempts to combine the principles of learning derived from behaviorism with the contributions of cognitive psychology. Like behaviorism it focuses on observable behaviors rather than postulating inner dynamics and drives not readily amenable to empirical investigation. Like phenomenological psychology, however, it views behavior from the perspective of the actor rather than the observer.

Rotter and Bandura have developed two separate formulations of social learning theory which, although somewhat different in their emphases, are complementary. Bandura emphasizes the social components of behavior, while Rotter focuses on psychological aspects.

Rotter's theory (Rotter, Chance, & Phares, 1972) views human behavior as being actively directed toward particular goals rather than passively controlled by environmental influences. Rotter postulates that the probability that an individual will engage in a particular pattern of behaviors depends on his expectancies concerning the outcomes to which those behaviors will lead and the value he places on those outcomes. For example, a college student is likely to spend time studying and writing term papers if she expects that these actions will lead to good grades and if she places high value on good grades. The subjective expectancies of outcomes and the values placed on them are a function of prior learning experiences of the individual in similar situations.

Psychopathology may occur as a result of difficulties encountered in any of the three major components of Rotter's formula (i.e., behavior potential, expectancies of reinforcement, and reinforcement values). For example, the individual may persist in behaviors that are inadequate for attaining certain desired reinforcements; he may have a very low expectancy of being able to attain desired outcomes (low freedom of movement); or he may place an excessively high need value on certain types of reinforcements. In addition, the person's minimal goal level, or the lowest outcome that he will accept as satisfactory, may be excessively high. As a result of such difficulties the individual is likely to engage in inappropriate (non-goal-oriented) behaviors that are commonly associated with anxiety, depression, and other forms of psychopathology.

The goal of psychotherapy, in Rotter's view, is to bring about a more gratifying level of functioning by revising expectancies to accord with the realities of the present situation, reducing minimal goal levels, learning to value alternate goals, and so on. Although behavior modification techniques may be used to alter behavior directly, the focus is placed on changing expectancies and values in order to indirectly change behavior.

Bandura's (1971) formulation of social learning theory may be viewed as a complement to Rotter's theory in that it explores the ways in which behaviors are learned and expectancies are developed. The most distinctive feature of Bandura's theory is the belief that most of our behavior is learned by observing other people and modeling our behavior after theirs. Bandura asserts that behavior is learned not only through the direct experience of reinforcement but also, and more importantly, through vicarious reinforcement (i.e., observation of reinforcements obtained by others) and self-reinforcement (via self-observation, self-evaluation, and feelings of pride, satisfaction, guilt, etc.).

Bandura emphasizes the importance of cognitive symbols in the process of personality development. Behaviors that are learned through observational attention are retained symbolically in the form of words and/or images in long-term memory until they are reproduced at a time when the individual is motivated to perform them.

Bandura espouses the principle of reciprocal determinism, by which he means that psychological processes are the product of a complex interaction of behavioral, cognitive, and environmental factors. While behavior is influenced by the environment, the environment is also partly a product of the person's own making, and a measure of control over one's own behavior is therefore possible.

Psychotherapeutic applications of Bandura's theory include the use of MODELING to reduce phobic reactions and self-directed behavior change therapy (Mahoney & Thoresen, 1974). In addition, social learning theory has had a major influence on current techniques of cognitive-behavior therapy. Social learning theory has received wide acceptance among contemporary psychologists because of its combination of behavioristic and cognitive approaches, its firm grounding in empirical research, and its numerous applications to psychotherapy.

From a biblical perspective social learning theory is generally compatible with the Christian view of persons, with its emphasis on the importance of both cognitive factors (the heart or mind) and overt behavior in human experience. Like Scripture, social learning theory sees a person as an active, rational agent, responsible for his own actions and able to change his own behaviors, yet ever subject to the influences of his social environment.

References

Bandura, A. *Social learning theory.* Morristown, N.J.: General Learning Press, 1971.

Mahoney, M., & Thoresen, C. *Self-control: Power to the person.* Monterey, Calif.: Brooks/Cole, 1974.

Rotter, J. B., Chance, J. E., & Phares, E. J. (Eds.). *Applications of a social learning theory of personality.* New York: Holt, Rinehart, & Winston, 1972.

R. A. MARTIN

See LEARNING.

Social Maturity Tests. A term used rather loosely to identify a small group of social psychological testing instruments used primarily in the assessment of the developmentally disabled. They are sometimes called social intelligence tests.

In general these tests attempt to measure the degree to which an individual has acquired the social behaviors that are usually expected of his age. It is important to note that it is not clear just what behaviors are subsumed under the concept of social maturity or social intelligence. In this sense social maturity testing is a somewhat vague assessment endeavor.

By far the most widely used of this category of tests is the Vineland Social Maturity Scale. Developed by E. A. Doll in the 1920s and 1930s during the zenith of intelligence testing, this scale was based on the idea that there are levels of development of social and personal competence that are normal for each chronological age. The result of testing is a so-called chronological age that attempts to indicate the individual's adequacy for daily living tasks. Useful with subjects from birth to 25 years, the scale is helpful in suggesting areas where further assessment or remedial training is needed.

A newer test similar to the Vineland is the Adaptive Behavior Scale developed in 1974 by the American Association of Mental Deficiency. In addition, the Social Maturity Scale of Webster, Stanford, and Freedman, developed in 1955, attempts to measure social maturity in terms of nonauthoritarianism. Together these tests represent the major contribution to a form of assessment that seeks to address a unique area at the interface of ability and personality testing.

D. M. Cook

See Psychological Measurement.

Social Modeling. *See* Modeling.

Social Network Intervention.
In terms of social anthropology social network is a construct of social relations. It involves an analysis of patterns of linkages between persons and the manner in which an individual is linked to the larger social structure. Three levels of analysis exist. The micro-level of analysis is linkage of the individual to intimates, family, extended kin, and close friends. The macro-level is community, social, and cultural organization, analyzed in terms of impersonal collectives. The mezzo-level is social network analysis: the personal linkages between persons (direct linkages) and through persons to others (indirect linkages).

The social network paradigm (Leinhardt, 1977) represents a conceptual schemata for mapping the mezzo-level of social linkages. Consider a Persian rug. A macro-level analysis considers the overall type of rug. A micro-level analysis involves the structure of any one square inch. A mezzo-level analysis traces how each color thread is tied to another thread to produce patterns. The threads are the content of social links; the knots are personal contacts.

Consider threads in terms of content (golf interest, political influence, dental skill). A dentist may be linked to persons in his life space who are dentists, politicians, or golfers, or some of each, or people with all three themes (direct linkages). The same dentist may have a political interest but know no politicians. Yet he may influence politicians via conversation with his golf partners who have political connections (indirect linkages). If the person has single theme links (he only knows dentists), the network will be sparse and simple in content and have few interconnections. If a person embodies many themes, he will link directly and completely to more persons. At the same time there will be more interconnections among the people in the network, thus indirectly linking him to many others (e.g., the dentist has golf friends who know his political friends).

A community, like a rug, is composed of many intersecting social themes that link different people directly and indirectly to each other. Thus a person does not have one social network. Rather, he participates in many different social networks, which indirectly interconnect. Social network analysis may focus on themes—e.g., rumor networks, political networks, community assistance networks. Or analysis may focus on persons—the connections an individual has to others (egocentric analysis). Social network analysis is applied in mental health to both theme analysis, such as family or assistance networks, and to individual analysis (Gottlieb, 1981).

From the standpoint of individual analysis a person is linked to approximately 1,500–2,000 persons—the finite limits of one's personal community. These persons can be arranged in zones. Zone 1 (personal) consists of family you live with or who are most important (1–10 persons). Zone 2 (intimate) consists of close intimates (2–20). Zone 3 (extended) consists of those with whom you regularly interact but who are not as important to you (50–100). Zone 4 (nominal) consists of persons you know or interact with casually (around 500 persons). Zone 5 (extended) consists of people linked indirectly to you via persons in the other zones (around 1,000 persons).

The first two zones, called the intimate psychosocial network (25 persons), form a relatively stable social system that mediates the relationships between the person and his social world (Pattison, Llamas, & Hurd, 1979). There are significant correlations between disturbances in this intimate social network and psychiatric disorders. It is important to note that social networks may be constructive and supportive, neutral, or destructive and pathogenic. Therefore a social network system should not be labeled a support system, because it may not operate as such.

The application of social network theory

and analysis has resulted in new mental health interventions (Pattison, 1981). First are thematic social network intervention: the construction of crisis information centers, the activation of mutual assistance programs, and the organization of informal community networks. The intent of such clinical programs is to activate latent and indirect social links into an active and direct linkage. The resulting social network can then assist persons in crisis, respond to emergencies, and provide sustaining emotional and material support.

A second intervention strategy is screening-planning-linking. Here the focus is on an individual in crisis who lacks good network resources. The network convener screens inactive, latent, or indirect links and convenes the personal network of the person to bring resources to his aid.

A third strategy is work with extended family, kin, and friend systems in which the social network is intact but dysfunctional. Here the network therapist, much as a family therapist, collates the network, identifies dysfunctional elements of the social system, and seeks to change the structure and function of the social network (Speck & Attneave, 1973).

A fourth strategy involves persons with pathological networks, such as drug and alcohol abusers, or inadequate networks such as chronic schizophrenics. Here the task of the network therapist is to recruit new members for the social network of the patient, constructing a new and more viable ongoing network.

The methods of social analysis can be applied to church and parish social systems (Pattison, 1977). The pastor can analyze the various social network themes that link parish members, as well as determine the social network resources available to an individual member. In turn, social network interventions can be employed to improve utilization of parish resources to meet the needs of the membership.

References

Gottlieb, B. (Ed.). *Social networks and social support in community mental health.* Beverly Hills. Calif.: Sage Publications, 1981.

Leinhardt, S. (Ed.). *Social networks: A developing paradigm.* New York: Academic Press, 1977.

Pattison, E. M. (Ed.). *Pastor and parish: A systems view.* Philadelphia: Fortress Press, 1977.

Pattison, E. M. (Ed.). *Clinical applications of social network theory.* New York: Human Sciences Press, 1981.

Pattison, E. M., Llamas, R., & Hurd, G. Social network mediation of anxiety. *Psychiatric Annals,* 1979, 9, 56–67.

Speck, R. V., & Attneave, C. L. *Family networks.* New York: Pantheon, 1973.

E. M. PATTISON

See FAMILY THERAPY OVERVIEW; FAMILY SYSTEMS THEORY.

Social Psychology. The scientific study of the personal and situational factors that influence an individual's social behavior.

The unit of study in social psychology is the person interacting with another individual, a person-other (P-O) unit. The other may be a specific individual or a generalized other. The other may actually be present, or the presence may be implied or inferred. In the latter case the influence of the other is mediated through the person's cognitions and social expectation.

The study of social behavior focuses on one of five levels. In each the identity of the person is paramount. The most basic level examines the person perceiving and interpreting the other's acts and dispositions (P→O). The person's implicit personality theory influences what impressions are formed of the other and what attributions are made. The person makes judgments about the causes of the other's behavior and evaluates his responsibility. Those judgments influence subsequent interactions between person and other.

The second level is also unilateral in perspective. The influence of the other on the person's social judgment process is the focus (P←O). Others affect the formation and development of one's attitudes and values. Developmentally the influence of the other is crucial in socialization of the person, especially in self-concept formation, sex typing, and sex role identification. These two levels also give attention to how the person strives for consistency of behavior and belief (e.g., cognitive consistency, cognitive dissonance, and balance theories).

The third level is bilateral and dyadic (P⇋O). The nature of dyadic relationships depends on the antecedents, maintainers, and consequences of interpersonal attraction (i.e., liking and loving). Attraction may be the basis of affiliation and altruism, of why persons become attached to others and under what circumstances they offer aid. Continuing the relationship depends on bargaining, social exchange, and cooperation. Competition and aggression alter the relationship substantively. When the norm of reciprocity fails or when costs outweigh benefits, interaction is terminated.

The final two levels examine groups and the individual's position within the group. In the fourth level the focus is on the person's influence upon group structure and process (O←P→O). The person's social power reflects his expertise, credibility, and leadership. The individual's persuasiveness determines the degree to which he can effect change in the group.

The final level examines group pressures on the person (O→P←O). The impact of the social and physical environment also operates to affect group behavior. Groups pressure members to comply with a uniformity of belief and attitude. The group's influence is measured by the person's conformity to group norms. When the group has authority and power, the change in the person's behavior is seen as obedience. Crowding and expectations about social distance and personal space also modify the person's social behavior.

Controversy exists about the proper location of social psychology in the academic hierarchy. Since the focus is on the person, some psychologists insist that it is a psychological speciality; sociologists respond that because the individual occupies a role and status within a group, social behavior lies within sociology. A few social psychologists hold it is neither psychology nor sociology but a separate discipline between the two, since the focus is on dyadic units instead of an individual or group per se.

Social psychologists generally ascribe to the scientific mode of investigation and use various experimental, field, and survey techniques. A minority have challenged its scientific status, pointing to the difficulty of replicating findings. The rationale is that social interaction occurs within a fixed sociocultural context that cannot be duplicated; social psychology is therefore a historical study rather than an experimental science.

A unique feature of social psychological experimentation is that interpersonal techniques investigate interpersonal behavior. The researcher is interested in interpersonal behavior (e.g., interpersonal attraction) but must use interpersonal relationships (i.e., roles of experimenter and subject with the inherent power and status differentials). Elaborate strategies for sorting the effects of the experimenter (e.g., Rosenthal effect, demand characteristics, etc.) from those under actual consideration have been proposed.

American interest in social psychology is nearly a century old. The first published study was Triplett's investigation in 1897 of social facilitation. The first textbooks in social psychology appeared in 1908 by William McDougall and Edward Ross. One of the first journals was the *Journal of Abnormal and Social Psychology*, which was founded in 1906. The major journal, *Journal of Personality and Social Psychology*, began in 1965 and serves as the official journal of Division 8 of the American Psychological Association. The division began operation in 1945. The individual esteemed by most social psychologists as its founder is Kurt Lewin. Lewin's applied and theoretical work in the 1930s and 1940s provided a great impetus to the systematic investigation of individual social behavior.

R. L. TIMPE

Social Work. A multifaceted profession historically related to the Judeo-Christian belief in meeting the financial needs of the poor. Beginning in the 1700s social work in America was basically a humanitarian effort by wealthy philanthropists who provided aid to persons unable to care for themselves. The misperception that social work today is confined solely to the administration of financial relief is still common.

Modern social work practice is conducted by trained professionals concerned with the interactions between people and their social environment that affect the ability of people to accomplish their life tasks, alleviate distress, and realize their aspirations. The function of the social worker is therefore to 1) enhance the problem-solving and coping capacities of people; 2) link people with systems that provide them with resources, services, and opportunities; 3) promote the effective and humane operation of these systems; 4) contribute to the development and improvement of social policy; 5) dispense material resources; and 6) serve as agents of social control (Pincus & Minohan, 1973).

The field of social work has three levels of practitioner skills. The beginning level is the B.S.W. (Bachelor of Social Work), which entails graduation from an accredited undergraduate school of social work. The most common and the most nationally recognized level of practice competency is the M.S.W. (Master of Social Work), which requires two years of graduate training. The Doctor of Social Work is generally reserved for those individuals involved in research in academic settings.

The core practice methods within social work include casework, group work, and community organization. These serve to prevent and to remedy individual and environmental dysfunction. Social casework, more commonly referred to today as CLINICAL SOCIAL WORK, is an area of specialization that focuses primarily on individual psychotherapy and family treatment. The theoretical orientation was originally influenced by the psychoanalytic movement in the early 1920s, but today draws from all major theories of personality development and treatment approaches. Common settings for casework include psychiatric hospitals, community mental health centers, probation and parole, family counseling agencies, schools, and private practice.

Social work educators have likened casework to restoring, reinforcing, and reshaping the psychosocial functioning of the individual and/or family that is having trouble in personal and social encounters. Social casework is viewed as an active form of psychotherapy that focuses on the study, diagnosis, and treatment of the social environment. In the final analysis the casework process is a problem-solving process designed to understand human behavior in light of environmental stresses and to bring appropriate material or psychological resources to bear on problem resolution (Perlman, 1977).

Group work is a way of serving individuals within and through small, face-to-face groups in order to bring about desired change. The group is viewed as a social system whose influences can be managed to develop client abilities, to modify self-images and perspectives, to resolve conflicts, and to inculcate new patterns of behavior (Vinter, 1965). Group work was traditionally practiced in national youth-serving agencies such as the YMCA and YWCA, settlement houses, and urban community centers. Today, however, group work is widely practiced in children's institutions, medical settings, rehabilitative centers, correctional centers, and facilities for both the mentally and physically disabled.

The third method of social practice, community organization, views the community as the identified client. Murphy (1954) defines this specialization as concerned chiefly with the work of the promotional and coordinating agencies aimed at raising money, seeking enactment of social legislation, or coordinating social welfare activities.

Regardless of which interventive method is utilized, the social work profession is built on scientific knowledge of human growth and behavior and ethical principles, the most crucial of which are the belief in the worth and dignity of every human being, utilization of a nonjudgmental attitude, and the protection of the right of each person to participate in all decisions concerning him.

Social work, like all helping professions, is confronted with many modern-day issues, problems, and trends that will greatly influence its future. Some of these issues include elimination of racism and poverty, development of workable and fair income-mainte-

nance programs, helping to develop a better distribution of health care, reducing crime and delinquency, and the preservation of individual liberties in a mass society (Ferguson, 1975). Within the profession itself critical issues that must be addressed include personnel training and deployment. The continual expansion of societal needs and pressures for service delivery will require constant reevaluation of tasks performed by both B.S.W. and M.S.W. social workers. Another issue that has met with widespread disagreement within the profession has been the emergence of private practice. Many individuals perceive the focus upon individual and family psychotherapy, as opposed to broader societal issues such as income maintenance, as a departure from the traditional role and function of social work. A final issue is the national focus of the National Association of Social Workers and the National Federation of Clinical Social Work for legal regulation of social work practice, thereby upgrading practice standards and protecting consumer rights.

Regardless of society's problems, the profession of social work will continue its fight to ensure individual integrity, family unity, and social justice for all individuals.

References

Ferguson, E. *Social work: An introduction* (3rd ed.). Philadelphia: Lippincott, 1975.
Murphy, C. *Community organization practice.* Boston: Houghton Mifflin, 1954.
Perlman, H. Social casework. In R. Morris (Ed.), *Encyclopedia of social work* (17th ed.). New York: National Association of Social Workers, 1977.
Pincus, H., & Minohan, A. *Social work practice: Model and method.* Itasca, Ill.: F. E. Peacock, 1973.
Vinter, R. Social group work. In *Encyclopedia of social work* (15th ed.). New York: National Association of Social Workers, 1965.

R. WELSH and P. PERRY

Sociobiology. "The systematic study of the biological basis of all social behavior" (Wilson, 1975, p. 4). Areas of study in this discipline include aggression, mating, parenthood, and social organization. Physiologically based characteristics, such as speed, coloring, and thickness of coat, ordinarily fall outside the domain of sociobiology.

In general, researchers in this area hold as a fundamental hypothesis that social behaviors are genetically inherited in the same way as physical features like coloring. Most sociobiologists are evolutionists and contend that a biological basis for social behavior exists because Darwin's theory of natural selection applies to behavioral patterns as well as physiological characteristics. Following Darwin's line of reasoning in *On the Origin of Species* they theorize that in the struggle for survival certain behaviors gave some animals an adaptive advantage over others, and that the proportion of animals exhibiting such behaviors then increased in succeeding generations. For example, an infant bird with a propensity to open its mouth will more likely be fed than one lacking this trait. If this trait is genetically induced, it will be passed on to more offspring in the next generation. After several generations infant birds who fail to open their mouths will have a diminished chance of survival (Scott, 1958).

Since Darwin many scientists have hypothesized that humans evolved from lower forms of life, hence it is not surprising that theories of animal sociobiology have been applied to humans. Some sociobiologists suggest that human conventions such as limited warfare, courtship and mating, taboos against adultery and incest, etc., are genetic in origin, having given a selective advantage to early manifesters of these behaviors.

It is important to note that evolution and the heritability of social behavior are distinct hypotheses, and that only heritability of social behavior is essential to the work of the sociobiologist. This position asserts that behavioral characteristics are passed on to succeeding generations through genes, while the theory of evolution postulates a mechanism by which such traits have emerged. Behavioral evolution presupposes the heritability of behavior, but the reverse is not logically required. For example, a biblical creationist might explain the heritability of aggressive behavior in terms of the fall. Such a person might hold that all aspects of creation, including the animal and human genetic pools, underwent various changes at the time of the fall and that such changes have since been passed along genetically. Although most sociobiologists are evolutionists, it is not a requirement, and those holding a nonevolutionary point of view of the origin of social behavior can play an active role in this area of study.

References
Scott, J. P. *Animal behavior.* Chicago: University of Chicago Press, 1958.
Wilson, E. O. *Sociobiology: A new synthesis,* Cambridge: Belknap Press, 1975.

Additional Reading
Micheal, R. *Sociobiology: Sense or nonsense.* Dordrecht: D. Reidel, 1979.

J. L. ROGERS

Sociometry. A branch of social psychology whose theory and basic techniques were formu-

lated by Moreno (1934). The journal *Sociometry* (since 1978 *The Social Psychology Quarterly*) began publication in 1936. The Sociometric Institute came into existence in 1942.

An early concern of sociometry was to evaluate the social climate of a group by determining the pattern of choice and rejection among group members. This was done by asking each member to indicate persons within or outside the group he would or would not like to associate with in a given activity. Findings were used to restructure groups and thereby improve social climate and increase productivity. This approach has been used in such diverse settings as college dormitories, classrooms, factories, penal institutions, and football teams. Most research studies have repeatedly shown that reciprocity of choice makes for greater satisfaction, more cohesiveness, and usually increased productivity.

Much sociometric research has been concerned with the relationship between frequency of choice and various demographic, sociological, and psychological variables. Factors studied include proximity, status, race, sex, age, intelligence, self-concept, self-disclosure, deviance, and scores on many personality inventories.

In the early years of sociometry research studies were usually action oriented, methodology was simple, and statistical treatment was rudimentary. Today, however, sociometric research is highly sophisticated, making much use of mathematical models, matrix algebra, factor analysis, analysis of variance, and regression analysis.

Less a distinct entity today than it was when formulated by Moreno, sociometry has been assimilated into the field of social psychology.

Reference
Moreno, J. L. *Who shall survive: A new approach to the problems of human interrelations.* Washington, D.C.: Nervous and Mental Disease Publishing Company, 1934.

Additional Reading
Moreno, J. L. *Sociometry and the science of man.* New York: Beacon House, 1956.

O. C. SCANDRETTE

Sociopath. *See* ANTISOCIAL PERSONALITY DISORDER.

Sodium Amytal Interview. *See* NARCOTHERAPY.

Soliloquy Technique. As used in PSYCHODRAMA this is an adaptation of the soliloquy in dramatic presentations. The protagonist temporarily discontinues action and dialogue with auxiliary egos portraying significant others and verbalizes the thoughts and feelings of the moment. Since it is spoken as if no one in the scene hears, the soliloquy spurs the protagonist to share genuine affect and reflect on his or her actions.

At the close of the soliloquy the director returns the protagonist to the previous action, where new insights are appplied. This technique is often used by a director to help the protagonist see more clearly his or her inner self.

J. H. VANDER MAY

Somatization Disorder. Until *DSM-III* employed the term *somatization disorder*, this clinical entity had been known as Briquet's syndrome or hysteria. The new term has confused rather than clarified the issues regarding its clinical presentation, diagnostic criteria, and prognostic indications.

Somatization disorder is predominantly seen in females, usually appearing before the age of 30. It is characterized by medically unexplainable recurrent or chronic ill health of multiple bodily systems. Typically the patient has made numerous visits to physicians and may have had an inordinate amount of hospitalizations and surgeries that have been fruitless.

Historically the disorder had its origin in antiquity, but not until Briquet's *Treatise on Hysteria* in 1859 was there any clear elucidation and quantification of data. After studying 430 patients with hysteria over a 10-year period, Briquet concluded that in women the age of onset was either prepubertal or before the age of 20. It is now believed that the incidence of this polysymptomatic disorder is 1 to 2% in the general population of women. The disorder seems to run in families; as high as 20% of first-degree female relatives suffer from the same disorder, whereas male relatives show an increased prevalence of sociopathy and alcoholism (Woerner & Guze, 1968). Also antisocial personality disorder seems to precede the onset of hysteria in a significant number of women.

Most of Briquet's patients manifested what he called "affective predominance," typified by being very fearful, afraid of being reprimanded, experiencing intense emotions for the slightest reason, crying easily, and being timid. These patterns of emotional response were consistent throughout childhood and into adulthood. In fact, even prior to clinical presentation one-third of Briquet's patients had poor health during childhood, such as migraine, abdominal pain, or disturbances of appetite. Approximately one-half of his total group had poor health either in childhood or the postpubertal to clinical onset period. Briquet found the patient's environment had a dramatic effect on the course of the disorder. Precipitating causes were largely related to acute or prolonged stress (e.g., loss of husband, marital or family conflicts). As stress theory would predict, those influences that calmed the nervous system improved the disorder, whereas those that excited the nervous system aggravated it.

The diagnostic criteria in *DSM-III* require a history of physical symptoms of several years' duration beginning before the age of 30 and complaints of at least 14 symptoms for women and 12 for men from a list of 37 symptoms. These symptoms are grouped into seven clusters: sickly symptoms, conversion or pseudoneurological symptoms, gastrointestinal symptoms, female reproductive symptoms, psychosexual symptoms, pain, and cardiopulmonary symptoms.

There are still diverse opinions regarding the etiology of the somatization disorder. Maany (1981) postulates that such a disorder may be a subtype of a masked depression. He suggests that the diverse somatic symptoms are simply depressive equivalents. Liskow, Clayton, Woodruff, Guze, and Cloniger (1977) maintain that a somatization disorder arises primarily from a hysterical personality core. However, others speculate that such a disorder has its origins in a still unknown pathophysiological process.

References

Liskow, B. I., Clayton, P., Woodruff, R., Guze, S. B., & Cloninger, R. Briquet's syndrome, hysterical personality, and the MMPI. *American Journal of Psychiatry*, 1977, *134*, 1137–1139.

Maany, I. Treatment of depression associated with Briquet's syndrome. *American Journal of Psychiatry*, 1981, *138*, 373–376.

Woerner, P. I., & Guze, S. B. A family and marital study of hysteria. *British Journal of Psychiatry*, 1968, *114*, 161–168.

K. R. KRACKE

Somatoform Disorders. In *DSM-III* five types of disorders that affect bodily function or perception have been classified as somatoform disorders. They are somatization disorder, conversion disorder, psychogenic pain disorder, hypochrondriasis, and atypical somatoform disorder. These disorders frequently occur with physical symptoms without apparent or gross organic dysfunction. They are viewed as psychological in origin, since they are not under voluntary control and are not the result of any pathophysiology. The somatoform disorders differ from psychosomatic disorders in that in this latter group an environmental event is associated with the onset or exacerbation of an actual physical condition.

In the past the somatization and conversion disorders were generally viewed as hysterical in nature. The SOMATIZATION DISORDER, characteristic of multiple and diverse symptomatology and history of ill health, can be conceived as a long-term hysterical disorder. A CONVERSION DISORDER can best be conceived as an acute hysterical condition where conflicting impulses are so intense they are immobilized by symbolic expression. PSYCHOGENIC PAIN DISORDER had not been given a diagnostic classification prior to *DSM-III*. The disorder is limited to localized pain without the presence of demonstrable organic etiology. However, this diagnosis can be made only after substantial psychological evidence for it has been found. HYPOCHONDRIASIS occurs when an individual's hypervigilance to physical cues or functioning culminates in either overinterpreting or misinterpreting sensations as evidence of an ongoing disease entity. Once diagnosed as a neurosis, it is now diagnosed as a somatoform disorder. Unfortunately the atypical somatoform disorder as defined by *DSM-III* is open to quite a bit of interpretation. This residual category allows for a somatoform diagnosis when the criteria for one of the other disorders has not been clearly met.

K. R. KRACKE

Somnambulism. Habitual sleepwalking. It is a fairly common phenomenon, occurring in approximately 10 to 15% of the population. As a SLEEP DISORDER it primarily affects males, is generally associated with childhood and early adolescence, and tends to run in families. It is often associated with other sleep disorders. Sleepwalking movements are generally rather simplistic or automatic, with more extended and complex behaviors being the exception rather than the rule. For instance, a person may get up, stand for a short time or take a few steps, and then return to bed. There are no reports of anyone ever being injured during a sleepwalking episode. Awakening a person during a sleepwalking episode is usually difficult; when it occurs, the person is typically disoriented and will have no dream recall or memory of the preceding events. Episodes of sleepwalking are usually sporadic, occurring perhaps only a few times in a person's life.

Sleepwalking has been interpreted as being a hysterical reaction, a dissociative reaction, or primarily an unconsciously motivated acting out of dreams. Scientific research indicates that sleepwalking occurs during slow-wave deep sleep (sleep stages 3 and 4) rather than during REM sleep, when dreaming takes place. Presently sleepwalking is interpreted more benignly and does not usually warrant professional intervention. In childhood, sleepwalking may be motivated by factors closer to the surface of consciousness rather than the unconscious. Discreet questioning will typically reveal such mental stressors as a worry about some aspect of home life or school. Childhood sleepwalking is usually developmental-phase specific and disappears with time. Chronic sleepwalking and sleepwalking in adulthood may be a manifestation of a personality disorder or may be indicative of more severe emotional distress.

D. S. McCULLOCH

Spearman, Charles Edward (1863–1945). British psychologist who pioneered in factor analysis in testing. Born in London, he served as an officer in the British Army from 1883 to 1897, when he decided that he wanted to study psychology. He received his Ph.D. degree in 1904 from the University of Leipzig, studying under Wundt, and did postdoctoral work with Kulpe at Würzburg and with Muller at Göttingen.

Spearman became reader (instructor) in experimental psychology at University College of the University of London in 1907. He was appointed professor of mind and logic in 1911 and professor of psychology in 1928, when the department of psychology was separated from the department of philosophy. He retired from the University of London in 1931 and held temporary teaching positions in the United States three times before his death.

In 1904, while still in Germany, Spearman published two papers that foreshadowed his most important contributions. Although he did not use the term *reliability coefficient* until 1907, one of his 1904 papers introduced the concept. He made many other contributions in the area of statistics and measurement. He developed a widely used rank-order correlation coefficient appropriate for use on data at the ordinal level of measurement. With one of his students, he proposed the Spearman-Brown prophecy formula as a method of estimating the reliability of a test when it is lengthened. These quantitative contributions have been lasting ones in psychology.

His second 1904 paper presented his two-factor theory of intelligence. He believed that all mental tasks involved both a general ability factor, g, and a specific ability factor, s. There is only one g, and it underlies every intellectual performance. However, there are as many s's as there are tasks, and they come into play only when doing one particular task. Thus one's performance is a combination of g and whatever s's are involved. This theory has been the subject of controversy for many years. Spearman later proposed possible group factors, such as verbal ability and spatial ability, and other general factors, such as perseveration, oscillation, and will.

Spearman did not write many books. His best-known ones are *The Principles of Cognition and the Nature of Intelligence* (1924), *The Abilities of Man* (1927), and *Psychology Down the Ages* (1937). This last is not a history of psychology but of selected problems that led up to his two-factor theory.

R. L. KOTESKEY

Speech Disorders. Speech and language are of primary importance for humans. Although we communicate in a number of ways, it is speech that is most important in providing interpersonal communication.

Speech develops rapidly in a youngster; most children say their first word at about 1 year of age. Within 6 to 12 months after the first birthday children are able to speak in simple sentences that contain mostly nouns and verbs. At 6 years of age children typically have vocabularies of around 10,000 words and are capable of rather complex sentence structure. By 7 or 8 most children possess adultlike speech, with articulation, syntax, and grammar similar to that of their role models—i.e., parents or guardians.

Speech is considered to be defective if it deviates far enough from what is considered normal that it calls attention to itself, interferes with communication, or causes the one speaking to become maladjusted (Van Riper, 1972). Regional dialects and foreign accents are not considered to be speech defects.

Disorders of Articulation. Articulation disorders are those in which the individual substitutes, omits, adds to, or distorts the sounds of speech. Lisping is an example of a substitution. Instead of "sister" a "th" sound is substituted, and the result is "thither." An omission is a failure to include all the syllables or all the vowel or consonant sounds. For example, "library" might be "libary"; "recognize" would be "reconize." Examples of additions would be "dinter" or "sumper" for "dinner" and "supper." "Chimbley" rather than "chimney" includes both an addition and a substitution. Distortions in speech approximate the correct sound but fail to correctly articulate the proper pronunciation. Rather than "fish" something like "fiss" would be the result.

Baby talk is also considered an articulation disorder. Instead of "water" the speaker says "wah-wah"; rather than "dinner" an older child might continue to use the more babyish "din-din." Articulation difficulties in many cases may be seen as improperly learning the correct sounds because the role models use speech incorrectly. Parents sometimes persist in using baby talk themselves around their youngster because it sounds cute. They may be surprised that their child finds it difficult to say "water" when the youngster consistently heard "wah-wah" during the formative time of speech acquisition.

Disorders of Voice. The human voice has elements of pitch, volume, and quality. A man's voice is usually lower in pitch than a woman's. If a man's voice is too high, it can cause distress because of ridicule. When a woman has a low voice, it usually does not result in embarrassment and may even be seen as a positive asset. Problems of pitch can have roots in hormonal imbalances, emotional difficulties, and physiological conditions such as long-term smoking, which can irritate the vocal cords.

Proper voice volume is necessary for good communication. If the voice is too weak, listeners may have a hard time understanding what is being said. Too loud a voice can be irritating. It can also be an indication of a hearing problem. Because of poor hearing the individual projects the voice at too loud a level, believing others hear as he or she does.

Quality of the voice might be described as pleasant, hoarse, raspy, etc. A chronically raspy or hoarse voice could be the result of injury or physiological problems of the vocal cords. Cancer operations sometimes necessitate removal of parts of the throat that produce speech. The speech therapist can often teach persons who have undergone throat operations to force air into the esophagus and release it in a controlled manner; speech is once again possible, but the quality will be very different. Also, an electronic sound generator held next to the throat while moving the mouth can replicate naturally made sounds, but again quality will be affected. It may be difficult for some people to make themselves initially understood by others who are not used to the unusual voice quality.

Stuttering. One of the most difficult speech problems is stuttering. Its origins are not completely understood, although the emotional element seems to be a key factor. It is untrue that tickling a baby will cause the child to be a stutterer. There are numerous other folktales about what causes stuttering—all unfounded. Stuttering consists of abnormal repetitions of speech sounds. It may also be seen as a hesitation before being able to say a word, and sometimes it is demonstrated by prolonging a syllable or part of speech. Occasionally there may be head movements or grimaces as the stutterer attempts to overcome a block in speech. The voice may even go up in pitch as one attempts to say the word. Very often there are certain sounds that give an individual stutterer greater difficulty. This person may learn to avoid words that have those sounds so stuttering can be diminished.

It is important to understand the difference between primary and secondary stuttering. Children between 2 and 4 will exhibit primary stuttering by repeating words and phrases; sometimes it will be quite severe (Van Riper, 1961). Children at this stage usually are oblivious to their speech dysfluency. Parents tend to become quite concerned that their youngster is going to be a stutterer, but in fact it is usually only a normal developmental condition of speech that comes and goes for several years. Many speech therapists believe that it is best not to point out this normal dysfluency to the child. Admonitions such as "Slow down when you talk" or "Think before you speak" only bring to the child's attention that something is wrong with the way he talks. If the child becomes self-conscious about how he speaks, it can lead to secondary stuttering, which is difficult to treat.

Children older than 7 or 8 as well as adults who stutter would be seen as having secondary stuttering. Secondary stuttering is true stuttering and usually requires long-term speech therapy. It is an interesting fact that most stutterers, even those with a severe problem, do not stutter when they sing. This could be due to the fact that different areas of the brain are responsible for singing and speaking. It would not mean that the area for speaking (Brocca's area) is in some way defective physiologically, but that it may have learned to handle speech improperly because of emotional factors.

More boys than girls are stutterers, and the reasons are not entirely clear. Boys may have more psychological pressure to "grow up" and "act like a man." This pressure may manifest itself in the form of stuttering.

Speech therapy for stutterers aids in disguising the stuttering. This is done by blending and flowing difficult words and sounds. It may be unrealistic to completely eliminate stuttering in many individuals. A major part of speech therapy for stutterers is improving self-concept. As there is improvement in one's self-confidence and as emotional factors are reduced, the stuttering itself may diminish.

Delayed Speech. Though there is wide variation in the age when children say their first words or speak in sentences, some children will not develop proper language and speech skills within what is considered a normal time period. When speech development is very slow, it can be an indication of a number of conditions. A hearing-impaired child will be unable to correctly mimic the sounds of speech. Thus, speech and language development will lag behind. For the deaf child or one who is profoundly hearing impaired, intelligent speech would be impossible were it not for the efforts of intensive speech therapy. A mentally retarded child will usually be slower in speech and language acquisition than a normal child. Generally the more retarded the individual, the slower will be the development of speech. In severely and profoundly retarded persons speech may not be possible at all.

Emotional problems may also interfere with language. An extreme example is the autistic child who, along with psychotic behavior, demonstrates peculiar speech or none at all. Less severe emotional problems can result in speech pattern difficulties.

Neurological Injury. Brain injury such as that sustained in a severe blow to the head can result in damage to the parts of the brain responsible for speech and language. Similarly, a stroke can affect speech if the areas of the brain responsible for language are involved.

Cerebral palsy is a condition resulting from neurological injury before or during the birth process. This happens because of pressure on the brain or lack of oxygen (anoxia), which causes brain cell damage. The result is a lack of muscular coordination. When it involves many of the voluntary muscles of the body, speech is affected because of inability to form words properly with the mouth and tongue. A majority of cerebral palsied children have speech difficulties. Depending on the nature and extent of the neurological condition as well as the age of the individual, speech therapy can do much to help acquire, relearn, and restore speech. Each situation is unique, and therefore therapy is different for each individual.

Aphasia. The absence of speech is aphasia. When it is the result of severe psychological trauma or injury to the brain areas in which speech is processed, it is referred to as acquired aphasia. When the individual has never spoken, it is called congenital aphasia. Expressive aphasia means that an individual cannot express a thought or use the correct words to communicate properly. If a person cannot understand spoken langauge, the individual has receptive aphasia.

Cleft Palate and Cleft Lip. Cleft palate is a birth defect that results in an incomplete roof in the mouth. It can involve either the soft palate, which is farther back in the mouth; the hard palate, which has bone that helps support the teeth; or both the hard and soft palates when the defect is extensive. The cleft is an opening directly from the mouth into the nostril. In some defects the cleft passes through the upper gum and teeth. A cleft of the lip is sometimes referred to as a harelip because it resembles the mouth of a hare or rabbit.

Modern surgical techniques can do a great deal to repair these birth defects. The trend in recent years has been to perform surgery before the child has had a chance to develop speech. This seems to aid in a more normal speech pattern than if repairs to the mouth are made well after the youngster has learned to talk. People with cleft palate have a characteristic nasal quality to their speech because of the escape of air from the mouth through the nose. A prosthesis, or artificial device, may be used that fits into the roof of the mouth, preventing air from passing into the nose and permitting more normal speech. Speech therapy can help correct the speech defects caused by the imperfect palate.

Dental Characteristics. When teeth are out of alignment or missing, it can result in speech problems. With proper dentistry and orthodontics this need not be a problem. However, when dental problems are not corrected, speech can be affected adversely. Generally, the longer one waits to correct problems that affect speech, the more ingrained will be the speech difficulty. It may take an adult rather lengthy speech therapy to correct defective speech patterns that have been established for years.

Speech Therapy. Speech therapists or speech pathologists are certified by the American Speech and Hearing Association, which sets the professional standards for certification requirements. Speech therapists typically have master's degrees or extensive clinical experience in the field of speech pathology. They are trained to diagnose speech problems and assist in remediating speech difficulties in children and adults. Speech therapists are employed in public and private schools, hospitals, rehabilitation clinics, and speech and hearing centers; some are in private practice. Therapists who work in public schools usually must be certified by the state department of education as well.

References
Van Riper, C. G. *Speech correction: Principles and methods* (5th ed.). Englewood Cliffs, N. J.: Prentice-Hall, 1972.
Van Riper, C. G. *Your child's speech problems*. New York: Harper & Row, 1961.

Additional Reading
Van Hattum, R. J. (Ed.). *Communication disorders*. New York: Macmillan, 1980.

N. SCHROER

See LANGUAGE DEVELOPMENT.

Spence, Kenneth Wartenbee (1907–1967). Neobehaviorist psychologist who sought to develop a general theory of behavior through an analysis of learning. Born in Chicago, Spence moved to Montreal, Canada, at 4 years of age and received his education at McGill University (B.A., 1929; M.A., 1930). He received his Ph.D. from Yale in 1933 under Yerkes. He then spent four years as a National Research Council fellow at the Yale Laboratories of Primate Biology in Orange Park, Florida, and one year teaching at the University of Virginia. In 1938 he went to the University of Iowa, and remained there until 1964, when he went to the University of Texas.

Spence arrived at Yale as a student the year after Clark Hull became a research professor there. From then on their thinking was intertwined. Hull said that Spence had contributed generously and effectively with suggestions and criticisms to his *Principles of Behavior*. After Hull's death Spence carried on with the same type of thinking, so much so that by 1959 Frank Logan called it the Hull-Spence Approach. Spence remained in Hull's shadow for his whole career.

Shortly after completing his doctorate Spence published an analysis of discrimination learning to explain transposition, a phenomenon that had been an embarrassment to behaviorists for many years. His theory of discrimination learning set the battle lines for years to come with psychologists who followed the lines of Gestalt psychology. He was primarily concerned with facts. Theory and methodology were justified in that they contributed to the gathering and ordering of facts. He placed an emphasis on fractional anticipatory goal responses, classically conditioned responses made as animals were responding in an experiment. For Spence motivation was complexly determined by several variables, and habit strength was a function of the number of stimulus-response pairings. Spence also served as an interpreter of the philosophy of science to psychologists.

Spence received many awards, including the American Psychological Association Distinguished Scientific Contribution Award in 1956, the first year it was given. He was the first psychologist invited to give the Silliman Lectures at Yale. The lectures were later published as *Behavior Theory and Conditioning* (1956) and show the relationship between his theorizing and his experimentation. He wrote many journal articles, some of which were gathered in *Behavior Theory and Learning* (1960).

R. L. KOTESKEY

Spiritual and Religious Issues in Therapy.

Increasingly the problems for which people seek help from psychotherapists involve spiritual and religious issues. These problems, caused or exacerbated by the increasing complexities of modern life, include life-span adjustment, conflicts, trauma, situational crises, problem-solving deficits, and interpersonal struggles, as well as existential issues in which counselees are searching for meaning to life and death, a sense of inner integration, a release from anxiety or despair, and greater fulfillment. As a result psychotherapists are being confronted with cries for help in areas that were formerly the domain of the clergy. The dilemma they face is how to handle the spiritual issues inherent in these problems in a way that assures their own as well as their clients' integrity.

Therapists can resolve this dilemma by attempting to maintain a neutral stance vis-à-vis the spiritual dimension of persons; ignoring the dimension; exhibiting a negativistic or, conversely, a patronizingly benevolent attitude; or recognizing the dimension as a crucial aspect of human life and seeking to find responsible ways to address it in therapy. For the Christian therapist who accepts God's revelation through the Holy Scriptures, only the last option is viable. Although the Bible does not present a systematic anthropology, it is clear in its teaching that human beings are created in the image of God and that it is impossible accurately to understand them apart from their intended relationship to the

Godhead. In fact, nowhere in Scripture is that relationship presented as an appendage to one's identity; it is the very essence of humanness (Berkouwer, 1962). The individual is portrayed as a whole being who cannot be divided into component parts. Although parts (e.g., body, soul, spirit) are referred to in Scripture, they overlap in meanings; they describe rather than compartmentalize persons. Therefore, ferreting out a person's spiritual dimension and treating it as a separate, more highly relevant (or irrelevant) category prevents a true understanding of personhood. Since "any view which abstracts man from this relation cannot penetrate the mystery of man" and "can make no more than a partial contribution to our understanding of man" (Berkouwer, 1962, p. 29), the Christian psychotherapist must take very seriously any issues that involve the client's relationship to the Creator.

Incorporating spiritual issues into the therapeutic process in a maximally beneficial way makes certain demands on the therapist. First, it is essential that the therapist possess a good level of clinical competence in order to deal sensitively with these therapeutic issues. Second, it is important that therapists identify and understand the beliefs and values inherent in their own world view and how these affect them personally. For Christians this includes a concerted effort to grapple in depth with the Word of God to arrive at an ever-growing, integrated, cognitive, and experiential understanding of the Scriptures. Christian therapists who develop the habit of contemplating the attributes of the Godhead and their meaning to themselves arrive at a third basic qualification, an understanding of self. Calvin observed most aptly that a person never attains true self-knowledge until he has first contemplated the face of God and then looked into himself. Therapists who meet these prerequisites are in a unique position to relate to clients and guide their growth in ways that are congruent with a scriptural understanding of God and his relationship to human beings created in his image. Moreover, when therapists develop an awareness of how every aspect of their world view governs their conduct, they should have a better understanding of their clinical functioning.

The compelling need for therapists to be aware of the ways their total being influences clients is highlighted by studies indicating that clients' changes in therapy are attributable more to personal characteristics of the therapist than to techniques (Bergin & Lambert, 1978). These studies are even more significant in light of a review of research done by Beutler (1979), which supports the hypothesis that clients tend to appropriate the attitudes, values, and beliefs of their therapists. Psychotherapists who are reputed to be Christians carry a particular responsibility in view of Halleck's (1976) observation that clients tend to seek help from therapists who share their belief and value system. If that is true, clients who seek out Christian therapists will expect the therapist's Christianity to affect the counseling process.

Principles for Dealing with Religious Issues. In dealing with religious issues the therapist who sees the importance of the above conditions would perceive the spiritual dimension of clients as part of their inherent nature and therefore accept the necessity of dealing with issues that arise from it. This implies the responsibility to examine thoroughly what a religiously expressed belief, affect, or behavior means to a client and how it translates itself in his total functioning. Glock (1962) suggests five dimensions—ideological (beliefs), experiential (feelings), intellectual (knowledge), ritualistic (practice), and consequential (effects)—that need examining in order to determine the significance of a religious issue for a person.

Pruyser (1978) stresses the necessity of making a religious assessment an integral part of the diagnostic evaluation. He proposes that clergy be trained to work with therapists, thereby mitigating the danger that therapists extend their interventions beyond their theological competency. An adequate assessment enables a therapist to be in continual touch with the spiritual disposition of his clients and to develop the acumen to recognize the nature and depth of healthy, neurotic, or even psychotic elements in religious stances. He would also learn to sense the times when addressing religious issues will be optimally effective. If religious issues are confronted too soon, some aspects of the client's faith might be undermined. Even when therapists sense the appropriate moment to deal with a religious issue, they must go gently, at the client's pace, uncovering the issue when it works naturally into the session but never imposing their own convictions.

In situations where supportive therapy is indicated in order to prevent or retard disintegration, a person may need to have his religious persuasion reinforced, regardless of how neurotic it may seem to the therapist. This judgment would be made in a similar manner to that involving a decision to reinforce existing defenses in order best to cope with life. In other cases the therapist may choose to be relatively inattentive to religious issues because they are not specifically a part of the problem being dealt with (although if a religious issue emanates from or contributes to the problem, it will be necessary to address it at the relevant time and in a beneficial manner).

In some cases spiritual issues may be appropriately and effectively dealt with in an explicit way in the process of therapy; at other times circumstances may dictate that they be more implicit in the therapeutic process. But whether these issues are dealt with explicitly or implicitly, therapists must always work within the parameter of respecting the client's freedom and responsibility to make personal decisions.

Unconditional acceptance—expressed by a person's responding comfortably and remaining fully present to an individual whose beliefs, values, or behavior are at variance with one's own—could be the significant factor that contributes to freeing the client in a way that will someday allow him to respond positively to the heavenly Father. In the meantime the therapist, as servant, is at the disposal of the client, thus fulfilling the biblical mandate to be willing to be an agent of caring even if not always of curing (see the parable of the good Samaritan, Luke 10:33–37), letting the ultimate outcome rest with the Creator. It appears that the proper view of the source of change includes the seeming paradox of accepting both God's sovereignty and the client's free choice.

Concerns in Handling Religious Issues. Christian therapists have both valid and invalid concerns about dealing with religious issues in therapy. One troubling area is the role of religious constructs. On the one hand, some therapists ascribe to the shibboleth that religious beliefs are inherently value laden and therefore subjective and not amenable to scientific investigation. Thus, dealing explicitly with them in the therapeutic process would jeopardize the therapist's neutrality by violating a frequently propagated supposition that counselors' values have no ethical place in the therapeutic process.

That objection has been refuted by philosophers (Kuhn, 1970) who have demonstrated that the objectivity of even a research hypothesis supposedly based purely on observed facts is tainted by the controlling beliefs behind its creator's world view. In the field of psychotherapy Bergin (1980) has argued for the impossibility of the therapist maintaining a neutral stance. Therapists have a responsbility, therefore, to recognize the subjective presuppositions of their own world views lest they fall prey to the influence of those presuppositions and thereby unwittingly be more subjective than those who have defined their position.

Paradoxically some therapists who themselves accept the tenets of Scripture as objective truth tend to resist their use in therapy for fear that they be employed as resistance to facing painful feelings. Strunk (1979) points out that "in the extreme form, the notion even denies the motivational power of a person's *Weltanschauung*, since a view of the universe requires an intellectual component" (p. 194). To perceive spiritual constructs merely as defensive strategies could actually increase resistance and eliminate their potency as a growth-inducing factor in an individual's life, since for many clients significant religious constructs are as indispensable to their self-concept as is an understanding of their feelings. Often a rational cognitive structure helps them identify values and understand affect and behavior (see Rokeach, 1973). Their beliefs could also be their most powerful coping mechanisms, enabling them to function in a relatively constructive manner in spite of nefarious influences in their lives.

A second source of concern lies in the concept of transference. Therapists are vulnerable to being perceived by the client as a parent figure. When God enters the picture, they become additionally subjected to possible distortions displaced from the client's relationship to God and projected onto the therapist. At these points the parent-God-therapist triad can develop into an undifferentiated system (Pattison, 1965). When this involves a true transference neurosis, it takes a skilled dynamically trained therapist to enable the client to work it through and arrive at a correctly differentiated concept of self, God, and therapist.

Pattison (1965) points out how transference can also lead to distortions in relation to God. Feelings generated consciously or unconsciously by a critical father are easily translated into doubt of God's unqualified acceptance. However, reactions can be used advantageously to facilitate development of a correct belief and a corresponding corrective experience vis-à-vis the Godhead as well as toward any present human relationships. To ignore these distortions would be to fail to lead the person to a healthier view of what is potentially the most vital, health-producing relationship possible—relationship with God himself.

Another potential danger is the therapist's countertransferential response to his or her own relationship to the Godhead. Any spiritual issue that is not resolved in a way that reduces reactivity increases the possibility of countertransference that is potentially detrimental to the therapeutic process. A related source of countertransference is the therapist's lack of appreciation of, or even disdain for, the beliefs and practices of particular religious groups. For example, a therapist may feel negative toward fundamentalism; specific denominational or nondenominational churches; or specific practices such as speaking in tongues, certain abstinences, set rituals, or stereotyped vocabulary. Unless the therapist can neutralize such potentially strong reactions, the client will sense the negative attitudes and these will interfere with therapeutic progress.

A further distortion that makes therapists hesitant to encourage the use of religious concepts is their frequent employment in the service of resistance. For example, Scripture passages may be taken out of context and proferred as a personal directive from God, as in the case of a person who resists looking at the obviously disastrous consequences of a decision because she is not to lean on her own understanding (Prov. 3:5) or the one who interprets "Honor your father and your mother" as legitimate reason not to individuate healthily from them.

Lovinger (1979) discusses several strategies similar to cognitive reframing to nondestructively counteract such resistances. First, he suggests what he calls joining the resistance. For example, in cases where patients are plagued by a lack of security he helps them appreciate the role of doubt in fortifying correct beliefs. Second, he advocates correcting false interpretations of Scripture by introducing alternate, more accurate, translations. This might include giving some instruction in a correct use of hermeneutics. For example, for the counselee who refuses to recognize anger, "Let not the sun go down upon your wrath" (Eph. 4:26) can be shown to indicate the necessity to work through hostile feelings rather than suppress or even repress them. Third, understanding the role of culture in applying certain texts can help an individual distinguish between unchanging biblical truth and cultural relatives that allow for various applications of a text according to culture and historical setting. For instance, standards of dress differ among Christians of different nations and epochs, but acceptance of the doctrine of the bodily resurrection of Jesus Christ does not.

Appropriation of Spiritual Resources. An understanding of valid principles as well as an awareness of the potential hazards in dealing with religious issues can encourage the therapist and, in turn, the client to appropriate the resources available to Christians. Nicholi's (1974) research among college students showed highly significant positive changes in self-esteem and meaning to life among new converts to Christianity. This suggests that therapists should take seriously the potential healing in a client's relationship brought about by appropriating spiritual resources. Similar research has been done with different problems and age groups (Horton, 1973).

In guiding a Christian client to appropriate the resources available to him or her the therapist must be aware of the particular attributes of the Godhead that can be the healing factor in the client's case. For example, clients who have had a weak, punitive, abusing, or absent parent may be more prone with the therapist's help to recognize and attempt to claim the deeper healing possible through gradually internalizing God as their own Abba, Father (Gal. 4:6)—i.e., experience him as their intimate "Daddy" yet perfect, omnipotent Father. Allison's (1968) research offers evidence that a late adolescent's relationship to the Lord as God, the Father, can mitigate an undue struggle to differentiate from parents.

Another member of the Godhead, the Holy Spirit, offers incalculable resources for healing. In his role as convictor he leads individuals to the recognition of and repentance for sins (John 16:8–9). As the encourager (John 14:26) he reminds them of the forgiveness offered through the redemptive work of Jesus Christ (1 John 1:9). This forgiveness can bring a client to a conscious realization of the healing effects of God's unconditional love. In the process the grace and mercy of Jesus Christ may become significant healing factors.

The therapist may find that he or she must depend upon Spirit-given discernment to guide clients to distinguish between actual scriptural truths and unhealthy internalized beliefs inculcated by their environment. This is particularly the case when it is necessary to separate true guilt from unwarranted guilt-producing injunctions from authority figures.

In his role as convictor, comforter, and guide, the Holy Spirit can be called upon to bring to the surface repressed memories that block healing. Although therapists differ in the strategies they follow in being open to the Holy Spirit working through them to facilitate the process, the aim is the same—i.e., to encourage the affective reliving of the actual events in order to arrive at a resolution of the emotional pain embedded in the memory. In the healing process the therapist needs to be comfortable with the possible expression of negative feelings that have been transferred to the Godhead. Alerting clients to instances where biblical characters were able to express such feelings can be helpful.

A further resource ordained by Scripture to promote healing is fellowship in the body of Christ (James 5:16). The group provides a source for authentic mutual caring, expressed through interaction and support. By encouraging the client to become a part of a local group—one as congruent as possible with the client's preferred style of fellowship—the therapist could also assist in the separation process in the terminal stage of therapy.

In utilizing any of these spiritual resources it is important that the therapist avoid becoming enmeshed in denominational differences—e.g., views of the manner in which the Holy Spirit works, what prayer format should be followed, or styles of worship that have no relevance to the issue at stake. Used appropriately, spiritual provisions can be an invaluable source of strength and a starting point for exploration of neurotic relationships. Then as insight into the neurotic aspects of human relationships develops, increased healing in those relationships can be a stabilizing factor, permitting an examination of the unhealthy elements that might have been transferred to the person's religion. Likewise, as the neurotic components in the individual's spiritual perspectives are resolved, the person has an even stronger base from which to explore more deeply rooted conflicts stemming from past relationships. In effect, it is a balancing process that fosters health in all relationships.

During the last stage of therapy an evaluation of the changes that have taken place in the client's spiritual perceptions is in order. This is particularly important in long-term therapy, where profound changes may have taken place in all relationships. It is possible that in spite of release from psychological pain, clients are confused about how their Christian faith fits into the healthier patterns of functioning. Their recognition of the part religious concepts played in their problems or of how much of their unhealthy functioning had been transferred to their relationship to the Godhead could create a confusion about the very relevance of faith. This problem is more apt to arise when the relationship with the Lord was not included as a vital part of the therapeutic process. Nonetheless there has probably been a metamorphosis in the client's beliefs, feelings, attitudes, and even religious behavior toward the Godhead in proportion to the degree of growth that has transpired.

For example, the client who enters therapy with a clinging, undifferentiated relationship with a parent figure probably relates to God in a parallel way, with magical expectations and behaviors following a symbiotic pattern. As she individuates from her parent, she may no longer be comfortable with former ways of relating to the Lord. Comfort with a new style of relating comes gradually. Christian therapists should be alert to such issues, which actually emanate from salutary changes, and draw them out in the session. The client may need help to learn a new repertoire of ways to affiliate with the Godhead. Intercession for others, thanksgiving, and worship may become gradually a more natural part of the relationship.

It is enriching to the client and glorifying to the Godhead when individuals terminate therapy as more fully integrated persons because healing has transpired and has begun to translate itself into every area of their lives as they relate to God, the world, and themselves.

References

Allison, M. Adaptive regression and intense religious experience. *Journal of Nervous and Mental Disorders*, 1968, *145*, 452–463.

Bergin, A. E. Psychotherapy and religious values. *Journal of Consulting and Clinical Psychology*, 1980, *48*, 95–105.

Bergin, A. E.; & Lambert, M. J. The evaluation of therapeutic outcomes. In S. L. Garfield & A. E. Bergin (Eds.), *Handbook of psychotherapy and behavioral change* (2nd ed.). New York: Wiley, 1978.

Berkouwer, G. C. *Man: The image of God*. Grand Rapids: Eerdmans, 1962.

Beutler, L. Values, beliefs, religion, and the persuasive influence of psychotherapy. *Psychotherapy: Theory, Research, and Practice*, 1979, *16*, 432–448.

Glock, C. Y. On the study of religious commitment. *Religious Education*, 1962, *42*, 98–110.

Halleck, S. L. Discussion of socially reinforced obsessing. *Journal of Cousulting and Clincal Psychology*, 1976, *45*, 146–147.

Horton, P. C. The mystical experience as a suicide preventive. *American Journal of Psychiatry*, 1973, *130*, 294–296.

Kuhn, T. S. *The structure of scientific revolutions* (2nd ed.). Chicago: University of Chicago Press, 1970.

Lovinger, R. J. Therapeutic strategies with religious resistances. *Psychotherapy: Theory, Research, and Practice*, 1979, *16*, 419–427.

Nicholi, A. M. A new dimension of the youth culture. *American Journal of Psychiatry*, 1974, *131*, 396–401.

Pattison, E. M. Transference and countertransference in pastoral care. *The Journal of Pastoral Care*, 1965, *6*, 193–202.

Pruyser, P. W. The seamy side of current religious beliefs. *Pastoral Psychology*. 1978, *26*, 150–167.

Rokeach, M. *The nature of human values*. New York: Free Press, 1973.

Strunk, O. J. The world view factor in psychotherapy. *Journal of Religion and Health*, 1979, *18*, 192–196.

F. J. WHITE

See RELIGIOUS RESOURCES IN PSYCHOTHERAPY; RELIGION AND PERSONALITY.

Spirituotherapy. A term referring to the work of Charles R. Solomon; though he advances no precise definition of the term, it is a registered trademark of Grace Fellowship International of Denver, Colorado. Grace Fellowship was founded in 1969 by Solomon, who holds a doctorate in education from the University of Northern Colorado. There are several branch offices in and outside the United States.

In his *Counseling with the Mind of Christ*, Solomon presents spirituotherapy as a counseling approach. He asserts that Christian counseling "endeavors, first of all, to lead a person to trust the Lord Jesus Christ as Savior and Lord and then to disciple him in spiritual growth" (p. 21); it also may be defined as witnessing.

The primary qualification for counselors is spiritual maturity, which includes belief in miracles and in the inerrancy of the Scriptures, and a life "where self has been dealt a deathblow." A Bible school education is highly recommended, whereas seminary training may be an asset or liability, "depending on the emphasis of the institution." Because, in Solomon's opinion, training is not yet available through a satisfactory wedding of theology and psychology, one must resort to home study, conferences, workshops, etc.

The process of spirituotherapy is cast in a simplified model of man. This model is presented to counselees through six elaborate charts. It stresses the conflict of the natural man with the spiritual man. Counseling deals with the obstacles to spiritual progress—e.g., unconfessed sin, lack of surrender, need for restitution, unforgiving spirit, fear, refusal to break sinful alliances, lack of faith, and refusal to suffer.

The initial hour is for creating trust and rapport; determining the counselee's stage of spiritual growth; understanding the presenting problem; gathering a personal history (35 questions are suggested); and exploring rejection in childhood as a uniquely powerful factor in emotional illness. It is very important that by the end of the initial session the counselee be given a general view of the answer to his problem and be helped to see "psychological *symptoms* as *spiritual* problems" (p. 66). A prayer commitment may be sought in the first hour, in which will is more important than feelings. Counselees are urged to read Scripture and devotional literature selected by Solomon, primarily from the victorious life movement.

Succeeding interviews are less structured. The diagrams disclose what teaching needs to be repeated; any commitment made in the first interview is assessed; focus is on the underlying problem rather than on the symptoms described as the presenting problem. Major goals are self-understanding and acceptance of one's "position in Christ," thus appropriating spiritual life and power. Solomon states that it is insufficient to use Scripture verses merely to gain victory over symptoms. They should be used to gain insight into the underlying problem, namely the self-life.

It may be unfair to evaluate spirituotherapy from the perspective of psychology. Solomon's writing is more for "soul-winning" by "personal workers" (see p. 58). He states that the approach is best used in local churches and is straighforward about the fact that familiarity with particular doctrine, language, and literature is necessary. His bibliography is almost exclusively devotional. There are many statements indicating a bias against psychology, medicine, and psychiatry. In fact, Solomon discredits experts in psychology as part of "this world's system" (p. 63); he admits, on the other hand, that there are extreme cases that should be referred to them, though these are a small minority and are not defined.

The influence of psychoanalysis is apparent. Insight is pursued, and there is repeated emphasis on rejection experiences of childhood as determinative of emotional problems (contradicting an otherwise radical reduction of all problems to spiritual). Also, human troubles as experienced in unemployment, marital stress, and depression are regarded as symptoms.

There is, in addition, a dualism between the created world and spirit. This derives more from Greek philosophy than from the Hebraic view of Old and New Testaments, in which the unity of the human person and race is affirmed as starkly as the solidarity of the people of God—all in the physical creation. From a Christian psychological perspective spirituotherapy appears too individual in emphasis. There is little recognition of the common grace of God in the healing helps of behavioral and clinical sciences. Also, grasping the cognitive content of spirituotherapy may well require literacy, intellectual ability, and reasonably good emotional health in addition to Christian commitment.

Reference
Solomon, C. R. *Counseling with the mind of Christ: The dynamics of spirituotherapy.* Old Tappan, N.J.: Revell, 1977.

Additional Readings
Solomon, C. R. *Handbook to happiness.* Denver: Grace Fellowship Press, 1971.
Solomon, C. R. *The ins and outs of rejection.* Denver: Heritage House, 1976.
Solomon, C. R. *The rejection syndrome.* Wheaton, Ill.: Tyndale House, 1982.

H. KLINGBERG, JR.

See CHRISTIAN COUNSELING AND PSYCHOTHERAPY.

Splitting. One of the most primitive ego DEFENSE MECHANISMS. The term is used in a variety of ways by different psychoanalytic theorists but generally describes a way of organizing external reality on the basis of whether the experiences are "pleasurable good" or "painful bad," these two types of experiences being split or kept apart in psychic life. It is thus a mechanism of defense frequently employed against ambivalent feelings toward a person or experience. Splitting is thought to be the predominant mechanism of defense in psychopathologies reflecting the earliest developmental arrest, such as schizophrenia or the borderline disorders.

D. G. BENNER

Sport Psychology. The branch of applied psychology that deals with athletes and athletic situations. Professional psychologists find this area to be a fertile arena for the study of motivation and human performance enhancement. The increased popularity of sports and the corresponding need for methods of enhancing human performance have created an increasing need for psychologists with expertise in this field.

Clinical psychologists originally entered the sports world to administer psychological tests and to counsel athletes who were not functioning at their expected level of performance. Presently sport psychologists serve as consultants to coaches and players by giving them information about behavioral techniques that should enhance every athlete's performance. Often along with medical doctors and ministers, licensed psychologists travel and live with professional athletes, teaching them game enhancement techniques such as the use of imagery, biofeedback, hypnosis, and relaxation techniques. They also counsel athletes in setting effective goals for themselves and dealing with personal problems.

As a branch of applied psychology sport psychology has its own organization, the North

American Society for Sports and Physical Activity, which publishes a journal and acts as a forum on this subject of growing interest.

D. S. McCulloch

Spouse Abuse. *See* Domestic Violence.

Squiggle Technique. *See* Winnicott, Donald Woods.

Stages of Family Development. *See* Family Life Cycle.

Stanford-Binet Intelligence Scale. One of the main psychological tests currently used in the assessment of intellectual development. It is also the test that gave birth to the well-known concept of intelligence quotient (IQ) as the ratio of mental age to chronological age.

In 1905 Alfred Binet was asked by the Minister of Public Instruction for the Paris schools to develop a test that would identify mentally retarded children. Binet and an associate, Theodore Simon, constructed a test of 30 items arranged in order of increasing difficulty. By 1908 a second scale had been developed. In 1911 a third revision, which included many more items and could be administered to a much broader age range, was published.

In the United States the first revision was completed by Lewis Terman at Stanford University in 1916. This translation resulted in such major changes that the test became known as the Stanford-Binet. In 1937 a second revision, which resulted in two equivalent forms (L and M) of the test, was completed. In 1960 a third revision, incorporating the best items from the two equivalent forms of 1937, was published as one test (L-M). In 1960 standard scores leading to a deviation IQ replaced the previously used ratio IQ. This major change makes it possible to compare scores across the age levels. The norms presently in use were published in 1972.

The Stanford-Binet is administered by a professional familiar with the testing instructions, materials, and scoring procedures. The test consists of a number of subtests grouped according to age level and takes approximately one hour to complete. For most age levels there are six different subtests. Some are verbal, such as a vocabulary test; the others are performance oriented, requiring the manipulation of objects such as block design. The successful completion or failure of a subtest determines the course of further testing.

In determing the level of intellectual development the basal age is first found. This is the age level at which all subtests are passed. From this point testing is continued upward until all subtests are failed. This is known as the ceiling age. The mental age is determined by adding to the basal age a certain number of months for each subtest successfully completed beyond the basal age.

Theoretically the highest mental age possible on the Stanford-Binet is 22 years and 10 months. According to the 1972 norms the average adult mental age is 16 years and 8 months. At approximately 14 years the mean mental age as determined by the Stanford-Binet begins to fall behind the chronological age. For this reason it is recommended that this test not be used as the only measure when assessing normal and superior adult populations. To calculate one's intelligence quotient (IQ) the determined mental age is divided by one's chronological age and then multiplied by 100.

W. W. Austin

See Intellectual Assessment; Psychological Measurement.

Starbuck, Edwin Diller (1866–1947). A pioneering figure in the Psychology of Religion. He was born at Bridgeport, Indiana, a rural Quaker community where religion was simply lived. That simple piety forged his character and influenced one of the country's longest careers in the psychology of religion and religious education.

Starbuck attended Quaker academies and earned an Indiana University A.B. in philosophy (1890), Harvard A.M. in psychology (1895), and Clark University Ph.D. in psychology with G. Stanley Hall (1897). Before going to Harvard, Starbuck taught Latin and mathematics in Indiana at Spiceland Academy and Vincennes University. After receiving his doctorate he taught education for seven years at Stanford University (1887–1904) and two years at Earlham College (1904–1906). The longest span of his career was in the State University of Iowa philosophy and psychology department (1906–1930). He spent his last years at the University of Southern California—eight years as professor emeritus of psychology.

Starbuck was one of the few people to make a full career of psychology of religion and related studies. At Indiana University the "new humanism" shook his Quaker piety, but his interest in religion flared the brighter. In December, 1892, his paper at the Indiana Teachers' Association outlined a science of psychology of religon. He chose Harvard for graduate study because it seemed most open to that pursuit.

By late 1893 Starbuck was circulating questionnaires on conversion, breaking habits, and religious development, seeking data on first-hand religious experience of individuals. After a year he began to notice consistencies in the conversion data—ages near puberty, similarity to habit breaking, and personality dissociation. He took his data and questionnaires to Clark and accumulated 1,265 cases of conversion, recorded on huge charts so that he could observe the commonalities. These questionnaire data formed the bases for *The Psychology of Religion* (1899), the first book-length study of the subject. Starbuck's psychology of religion was empirical, factual, but rarely reductionistic. He gave psychology of religion courses at Stanford as well as an educational psychology course that he believed to be the first university course in that field.

Starbuck taught his first course in character education in 1898. He took an extended sabbatical (1912–1914) to work on a massive religious education curriculum project with the Unitarian Church; church traditionalism frustrated completion of that project. He was soon challenged by the offer of a $20,000 prize by the Character Education Institution of Washington, D.C., for the best statement of character education. The committee Starbuck chaired won that prize in 1921 with a proposal that emphasized, not traditional indoctrination, but arousal of the child's creative interest and imagination—"a more natural approach in which the integrity of the child's personality was wholly respected" (1937, p. 243). The award and attendant public interest in character education led the State University of Iowa to establish the Institute of Character Research, which Starbuck headed 1923–1930. He took essentially the same work to Southern California.

Starbuck lived to see interest in empirical psychology of religion wane, until by 1930 only his and a few of his students' studies were visible in the United States. His autobiography (1937) cites his eleven books and other principal publications.

References
Starbuck, E. D. *The psychology of religion.* London: Walter Scott, 1899.
Starbuck, E. D. Religion's use of me. In V. Ferm (Ed.), *Religion in transition.* New York: Macmillan, 1937.
R. D. KAHOE

Status. This important concept in the description and analysis of group structure has sometimes been used to refer to position in a social system—e.g., father, lawyer, student. More generally, however, psychologists use the term to refer to the respect or prestige that is accorded a person who occupies a particular position.

An individual's status influences the way in which that person acts and also how other group members react to him or her. For example, status differences affect both the pattern and content of communication in groups. Not only do high-status persons speak more, but more communication tends to be directed toward them. Research on the interactions of psychiatrists, psychologists, and social workers has shown that even these individuals direct a disproportionate share of their remarks to those with greater status. In addition, high-status persons tend to confine most of their conversations to others of equal status.

Brown (1965) has described a universal norm concerning status effects on communication. Familiar address, such as that between intimate friends, characterizes messages directed toward those of lower status; while more formal address, like that occurring between strangers, characterizes messages directed toward one higher in status. Brown also observes that generally the person of higher status is the pacesetter in all steps toward greater intimacy.

While several studies have shown that high-status group members typically conform more to group norms than do low-status persons, the group may actually permit high-status members greater latitude in deviating from the majority position. On the basis of their past contribution to the group's goals, those of higher status may be given "idiosyncrasy credit," which permits greater nonconformity under certain circumstances. This seems particularly true when the success of the group may depend on granting the high-status person the necessary freedom to marshal resources for goal attainment. At the same time, the high-status person may be judged more harshly for his actions. For example, in one study of destructive obedience, subjects held the superior officer who gave the order more responsible than the soldier who executed it.

A person's status may also affect how other group members perceive his or her competence. Research investigating the effects of status on problem solving found that groups more readily accepted correct answers from high-status than from low-status members. Thus, the final product of a group may be influenced by the status of the member who has the best ideas.

Reference
Brown, R. W. *Social psychology*. New York: Free Press, 1965.
M. BOLT

See GROUP DYNAMICS.

Stealing. *See* KLEPTOMANIA.

Stereotype. A generalization about a group of people that distinguishes those people from others. Examples would include the belief that Americans are materialistic, that women are dependent, and that talkative persons are insecure. Stereotypes of ethnic groups have likely received the greatest amount of attention from psychologists.

A series of studies conducted at Princeton University demonstrates how researchers have attempted to measure stereotypes and also indicates the nature of their content. Katz and Braly (1933) presented students with a list of traits and asked them to indicate which ones were characteristic of 10 ethnic groups. Results suggested that Americans were perceived as industrious, intelligent, and materialistic; Jews were seen as shrewd, mercenary, and industrious; and Negroes were viewed as superstitious, lazy, and ignorant. Katz and Braly's procedure was replicated in the early 1950s and again in the late 1960s. Findings indicated considerable reduction in negative stereotyping for all the groups that were rated. Certain unfavorable traits were, however, still attributed to blacks. Whether this shift was real or simply reflected a greater unwillingness to report negative generalizations is unclear.

Psychologists have maintained that even though certain stereotypes may have a kernel of truth, they often produce a number of negative consequences. First, they result in an overestimation of differences between groups. Although the beliefs, values, and other characteristics of groups may be similar, stereotypes may result in those groups being viewed as vastly different. Second, stereotyping may result in an underestimation of the variations within groups. Individuals are prejudged on the basis of their category membership and a large number of distinguishable persons may be treated as equivalent. Third, stereotypes typically have not only descriptive but also evaluative content. They are ethnocentric judgments by which members of other groups are evaluated on the basis of local standards. As negative generalizations stereotypes may be used as a justification for hostility and oppres-

sion, thereby providing a major mechanism by which PREJUDICE is sustained.

Recent research suggests that stereotypes may be an inevitable consequence of normal perceptual and thought processes. The tendency to form categories and to make inferences on the basis of category membership reflects the need to simplify and find meaning in what would otherwise be a very complex world. It may be neither possible nor desirable for people to treat each entity they encounter as unique. Unless generalizations are made, they can neither anticipate the future nor adequately cope with the environment.

Once formed, stereotypes perpetuate themselves by influencing people's attention, interpretations, and memories. Individuals are more likely to notice instances that confirm rather than disconfirm their expectations. Moreover, the actions of others are likely to be interpreted in terms of stereotypes held of them. Research has also shown that memory is selective, and people best remember those facts that support their own beliefs.

Stereotypes may also be resistant to change because they constitute self-fulfilling prophecies, in which prior expectations confirm themselves. Stereotypes guide people's behavior, which in turn influences the responses of others in ways that are consistent with prior expectations. Individuals' beliefs about themselves are also influenced by the expectations and reactions of others to them.

Although stereotypes seem resistant to new information, they occasionally change in the light of disconfirming facts. In addition, researchers have found that once people become acquainted with a member of another group, they are often able to set aside their stereotypes and judge that person on the basis of his or her own merit.

Reference
Katz, D., & Braly, K. Racial stereotypes of one hundred college students. *Journal of Abnormal and Social Psychology*, 1933, *28*, 280–290.
M. BOLT

Stereotypy. Repetitive and rhythmic behaviors, often seen in institutions for the mentally retarded or severely emotionally disturbed. Common forms of stereotyped behavior include rocking, weaving, finger flicking, string or thread twirling, and excessive self-stimulation.

These repetitive acts are not unlike the circular reactions described by Piaget, in which a baby's action triggers a reaction, in the baby or in another, that in turn makes the baby repeat the action. Unlike these circular reactions stereotypy persists for years and seems to serve no apparent function. In fact, it frequently interferes with learning more adaptive and useful behaviors.

As Baumeister and Forehand (1973) have noted, stereotypy at times seems to be under specific stimulus control, whereas in other cases etiological and maintenance factors are not at all clear. Rates and intensities vary considerably throughout any given time frame, and the behavior is often associated with self-injurious behavior.

Several hypotheses have been proposed to explain these bizarre repetitive acts. One theory states that stereotypy is a learned behavior that is maintained by social reinforcement, which is delivered contingent upon the occurrence of the behavior. Others argue that it is used to avoid or terminate a more aversive stimulus (i.e., human contact for certain autistic children). A currently popular theory contends that stereotypy is an attempt by the organism to raise the level of tactile, vestibular, or kinesthetic stimulation necessary to maintain homeostasis. This seems plausible in institutionalized settings where only minimal human contact is the norm. In fact, research studies have demonstrated significant reductions in stereotypy by increasing the levels of stimulation in the environment through touch, music, movement, and vibratory massage (Lemke, 1974). Organic theories speculate that stereotypy is evidence of aberrant organic processes. Finally, psychodynamic theorists see stereotypy as an infantile or fetal drive, a search for body reality, or evidence of poor ego identity.

Interventions that focus on positive reinforcement for competing and incompatible behaviors, coupled with efforts to raise the levels of stimulation in the environment, seem to be the treatment of choice (Forehand & Baumeister, 1971). Gaining stimulus control over such repetitive behaviors is prerequisite to any meaningful program of behavior management and change.

References

Baumeister, A. A., & Forehand, R. Stereotyped acts. In N. Ellis (Ed.), *International review of research in mental retardation* (Vol. 5). New York: Academic Press, 1973.

Forehand, R., & Baumeister, A. A. Stereotyped rocking as a function of situation, IQ, and time. *Journal of Clinical Psychology*, 1971, *27*, 324–326.

Lemke, H. Self-abusive behavior in the mentally retarded. *American Journal of Occupational Therapy*, 1974, *28*, 94–98.

R. E. Butman

Stimulus Control. A concept usually associated with operant conditioning. Although operant conditioning emphasizes the role of consequences in shaping and maintaining actions, cues (discriminative stimuli) that precede the response that is reinforced also acquire controlling power. A stimulus controls a response whenever some dimension of responding (usually rate) varies as a function of whether that stimulus is present or absent.

For practical purposes if a person wishes to strengthen a behavior, the goal may be achieved by identifying a stimulus that is usually followed by the desired behavior and presenting that cue on the occasions when the behavior is desired. If a person wishes to weaken a behavior, the goal may be achieved by presenting a stimulus that is rarely followed by the undesired behavior, by removing cues that are usually followed by the undesired behavior, or by presenting a stimulus that is usually followed by a response that is incompatible with the undesired behavior.

An example of applying stimulus control procedures to weight reduction would be as follows: Jane was a 20-year-old college student who wished to lose 20 pounds. During an initial evaluation she and her psychologist identified the cues that were most commonly associated with her eating: the visual presence of almost any food, being in the kitchen for any reason, watching television, reading, talking to friends, the hours from 5:00 P.M. on Friday through bedtime on Sunday, inactivity, boredom, and nervousness. She and her therapist developed a plan which Jane initiated.

Jane agreed to eat only when seated at a table specifically designed for eating—e.g., the kitchen table at home or a dining table in the university cafeteria. Except for talking to persons who were eating with her, she would engage in no other activities while eating (no watching television while eating). She would take only one serving per sitting and would leave some of each serving uneaten in order to weaken the association between the mere presence of food and eating. After she had eaten solid foods, she recorded the time of day and would not eat again until at least three and a half hours had passed. Finally, she was to stay out of the kitchen unless she was preparing or eating a meal, and all foods were to be stored out of sight. No candy, cookies, crackers, nuts, or other munchies would be purchased or displayed in open dishes on the counter.

All of the above procedures were carried out by Jane, not the therapist. There were other elements in her total weight-control program, but the items listed are those that are appropriately classified as stimulus control procedures.

Stimulus control is particularly appropriate as an intervention for persons who clearly want to change their behavior. Even when a therapist is not sure of a client's motivation to change, stimulus control procedures should be tested before attempting more difficult, complex, or time-consuming interventions. When they fit a person's situation, stimulus control procedures are often the most efficient treatment available.

Verbal instructions are a very common form of stimulus control. From this perspective the Bible can be conceived as a complex of God-given stimuli which can control human behavior.

P. W. CLEMENT

See CONDITIONING, OPERANT; LEARNING.

Stimulus Generalization. *See* GENER-ALIZATION.

Strategic Therapy. A few major assumptions form the foundation for this type of therapy, which stems from the work of Erickson. First, it is a largely systemic therapy as it is practiced currently; that is, strategic practitioners think in terms of ongoing interactive sequences within a family system rather than individually rooted intrapsychic events. Another distinctive is that the practitioner rather than the client is assumed to be the primary source of change. A third hallmark is that strategic therapists think in terms of problem formation and problem resolution rather than in terms of helping the client to grow; consequently most strategic therapy is directive, brief therapy.

One of the most basic theoretical tenets of this approach is that clients come for help because they tend to mishandle everyday problems in living (Segal, 1981). When people ignore problems, take ineffective action on problems, or fail to realize that nothing can be done about a problem at the moment, they subsequently tend to try to solve their difficulties with "more of the same," or first-order change methods. The strategic therapist will often reframe the problems by applying second-order change tactics that redefine the meaning and nature of the difficulty.

A strategic style of intervention requires a facility for analogic or metaphoric thinking (see Rosen, 1982). For example, a strategic therapist would typically view a physical symptom as an indirect communicative tactic. Reframing a headache in analogic fashion might involve praising the patient for nobly

sacrificing his own well-being in the service of bearing his family's pain for them. Alternately the therapist might weave a metaphor that matches the situation initially and then tag a more constructive, resourceful end onto the story (Madanes, 1981). One primary result of such an approach is the introduction of more choice into any one family system. The encrusted, repetitive sequence of interpersonal transactions is interrupted and a new range of creative problem-solving options is introduced.

It is assumed within this approach that very little is learned without the client doing something. Insight is viewed as nothing more than an intermittent and benign epiphenomenon of problem resolution. The primary mechanism for learning therefore becomes the directive rather than the interpretation.

The skillful use of directives is an art in itself (Haley, 1976). The first step is to motivate the individual, couple, or family to follow the therapist's directive. This basic first step, common to all therapies, involves establishing rapport and trust. The second step involves giving one's directives in a precise and clear fashion. Should the first strategy for effecting change not work, then it behooves the therapist to look at the problem from a different perspective and try another directive. Typically such a progression begins with straightforward, compliance-based directives that depend on the family doing what they are told to do. Should the family sabotage such directives with a variety of passive ploys (for which they typically eschew responsibility), then the therapist should move to defiance-based directives, which rely on paradox. Paradox in this context is best understood as instructing the family to continue in their plight or get worse. Many frameworks for understanding why paradox works are extant; we do know, however, that it is an effective technique that works.

A final distinguishing quality of the strategic school is the use of positive connotation or reframing (Stanton, 1981). The behaviors of clients are invariably accepted as they are without labeling them resistant. Further, clients are praised for their symptomatic behavior in that it is often labeled as self-sacrificial or protective of other family members. For example, because the father does not want others in the family to have to endure his angry feelings, he sacrifices his physical health and develops an ulcer; because the child does not want his mother or father to have to deal with their own difficulties, he generates problem behaviors at school. Most clients are used to being misunderstood and blamed; when instead they are accepted in the midst of their symptoms, most feel they have been really understood, perhaps for the first time. Further, because these positive ascriptions do have kernels of systemic truth tucked away within them, the technique is effective.

References

Haley, J. *Problem-solving therapy: New strategies for effective family therapy.* San Francisco: Jossey-Bass, 1976.

Madanes, C. *Strategic family therapy.* San Francisco: Jossey-Bass, 1981.

Rosen, S. *My voice will go with you: The teaching tales of Milton H. Erickson, M.D.* New York: Norton, 1982.

Segal, L. Brief therapy II. In R. Corsini (Ed.), *Handbook of innovative psychotherapies,* New York: Wiley, 1981.

Stanton, M. Strategic approaches to family therapy. In A. S. Gurman & D. P. Kniskern (Eds.), *Handbook of family therapy.* New York: Brunner/Mazel, 1981.

V. L. Shepperson

See Short-Term Therapies; Paradoxical Intervention.

Stress. The inherent nature of a technological society is pregnant with stress-producing factors. The perpetual need for change compels people constantly to develop new coping mechanisms if they are to maintain an integrated cognitive psychosocial equilibrium. The problems it produces are evident in the recent proliferation of literature on stress. Yet there is a general lack of agreement on the definition of stress.

Selye (1950, 1956), the endocrinologist who introduced the concept of stress as a research topic, limited its meaning to nonspecific bodily responses to any demand. Physically it involves the hypertrophy of the adrenal cortex, atrophy of the thymus, and gastric ulceration. He called the entire physical process the general adaptation syndrome. With prolonged stress this includes three stages: 1) an alarm reaction consisting of an initial shock that lowers resistance and a countershock that triggers the defense mechanisms; 2) a stage of resistance in which the organism's capacity for response is increased; 3) an exhaustion stage in which the adaptive response breaks down. Selye conceived of a limited amount of "adaptation energy," which with repeated stress reactions depletes itself and causes aging (1950). He uses the term *stress* both negatively (distress) and positively (eustress).

The application of Selye's concepts to the psychological aspects of stress presents problems, since he used only physical stressors—e.g., surgical traumas, infections, heat, injury, and cold—in his research. In addition, he did not account for the differing environmental and internal stimulus conditions that produce specific patterns of response. Others (e.g., Rose, 1980) have since used nonphysical stressors such as unpredictability, fear, and unpleasantness, and have found that an endocrine response does occur but differs in degree and duration among individuals.

Although theoretical definitions of stress are provided by the psychoanalytic, developmental, sociological, ethnological, physiological, and neurobiological perspectives, Monat and Lazarus (1977), of the cognitive-behavioral school, present the most comprehensive definition. It includes as stressors "any event in which environmental demands, internal demands, or both, *tax* or *exceed* the adaptive resources of an individual, social system, or tissue system" (p. 3). They emphasize that any research must explicitly define the "antecedent conditions used to induce 'stress,' the response patterns measured as indices of 'stress,' and, finally, the intervening processes believed responsible for the nature of the responses" (p. 3). The demands that the duration, complexity, and frequency of stress place on the total person is an area in which further study is needed.

There are relatively strong data suggesting that stressful life events contribute to psychiatric disorders (Rutter, 1981). Six months following threatening events there is a sixfold increase in the rate of suicide, a two- to fivefold increase in the occurrence of depression, and a two- to threefold increase in the onset of schizophrenia. These traumatic events are more generally the common upsets such as marital difficulties, work problems, and a personal sense of rejection rather than such major disruptions as a death, critical illness, or a financial failure (although the stress of the latter could contribute to a psychiatric problem). The stressors that result in an affective disorder tend to center around the perception of a loss or a disturbed interpersonal relationship (Paykel, 1978).

There is also considerable evidence that the occurrence and severity of physical illnesses increase subsequent to stressful life changes. Holmes and Rahe (1967) define a stressful life change as any clustering of changes, pleasant or unpleasant, whose individual values add up to 150 or more life change units in a given period of time. This is measured by a self-administered questionnaire, known as the Social Readjustment Rating Scale, which they developed. An individual records the number of times the listed life changes occurred during the stipulated period. The points accorded to each item were determined by the authors' research on the severity and frequence of illness after particular changes occurred. The research dealt solely with life change and the onset of illness. Nonetheless, it does suggest implications for the relationship between the many changes people experience today and the effect on their organisms. Although there are methodological problems with the research, further studies have shown that the probability of illness increases when a person has undergone stressful life changes (Dohrenwend & Dohrenwend, 1974).

Many major threatening events are not followed by physical or psychological problems. In fact, some people experience seemingly harmful stressors in a positive growth-producing way. How individuals cope with potentially stress-producing situations is considered to be the key to these differences in stress reactions.

The role of the coping process in stress is not well understood. Lazarus (1975) divides it into two broad categories: direct actions, including problem-solving skills that aim to modify the actual stress, and palliative modes, which relieve the impact of the stress without changing the situation. Most individuals use a combination of both categories. How a person will cope with stress includes such variables as genetic background, sex, age, temperament, intelligence, and problem-solving skills. Vulnerability and protective factors act as catalysts to increase or decrease the effects of the stressors. In addition, the cognitive appraisal of the event is important, since the meaning an individual attributes to a life event as well as the sense of how to deal with it effectively play a significant role in the reaction to it (Rutter, 1981).

Cognitive-behavioral interventions seem to be the simplest yet most effective treatment orientation in dealing clinically with stress. The strategies used are cognitive restructuring, modeling, reeducation, and desensitization techniques. Biofeedback and relaxation training are also employed to change the stress response. Preventive group programs that give training in stress management are on the increase. The aim of these groups is to teach the participants to recognize their own responses to stress and learn to modify their internal and external environments in order to maintain their own appropriate balance between a maximally beneficial and minimally harmful level of stress. All techniques, whether aimed at cure or prevention, encourage individuals to transfer skills learned to actual life situations.

References

Dohrenwend, B. S., & Dohrenwend, B. P. (Eds.). *Stressful life events: Their nature and effects.* New York: Wiley, 1974.

Holmes, T. H., & Rahe, R. H. The social readjustment rating scale. *Journal of Psychosomatic Research*, 1967, *11*, 213–218.

Lazarus, R. S. A cognitively oriented psychologist looks at biofeedback. *American Psychologist*, 1975, *30*, 553–561.

Monat, A., & Lazarus, R. (Eds.), *Stress and coping, an anthology.* New York: Columbia University Press, 1977.

Paykel, E. S. Contribution of life events to causation of psychiatric illness. *Psychological Medicine*, 1978, *8*, 245–254.

Rose, R. M. D. Endocrine responses to stressful psychological events. *Psychiatric Clinics of North America*, 1980, *2*, 53–71.

Rutter, M. Stress, coping and development: Some issues and questions. *Journal of Child Psychology and Psychiatry and Allied Disciplines*, 1981, *4*, 323–356.

Selye, H. *The physiology and pathology of exposure to stress.* Montreal: Acta, 1950.

Selye, H. *The stress of life.* New York: McGraw-Hill, 1956.

F. J. WHITE

Stress Disorder. *See* POSTTRAUMATIC STRESS DISORDER.

Stress Inoculation. *See* COPING SKILLS THERAPIES.

Strong, Edward Kellogg, Jr. (1884–1963). Author of the STRONG-CAMPBELL INTEREST INVENTORY. He was born in Syracuse, New York, the son of a Presbyterian minister. He received his M.S. from the University of California at Berkeley in 1909 and his Ph.D. from Columbia University in 1911. After postdoctoral research at Columbia, military service, and teaching at Carnegie Institute of Technology, Strong went to Stanford University in 1923 and remained there for the rest of his career.

Although he was interested in advertising and marketing, Strong's major contribution was in the study of vocational interests. He published the Strong Vocational Interest Blank in 1927 and revised it in 1938. It has undergone several more revisions. The test does not predict success in an occupation; it only compares a person's interests with those of people in that occupation.

Strong was the author of *Vocational Interests of Men and Women* (1943), *Vocational Interests Eighteen Years after College* (1955), and many articles on vocational interest.

R. L. KOTESKEY

Strong-Campbell Interest Inventory. Widely acclaimed as the bellwether of career counseling and personnel selection, this test identifies an individual's interests and value patterns in order to provide an occupational orientation. Its authors, Edward K. Strong and David P. Campbell, asserted that these patterns, when compared to those in representative vocations, would predict job satisfaction, depending on how carefully they matched up. The test has been in use over half a century, has gone through several revisions, and has been the object of several thousand research investigations. Millions of copies of the measure have been sold, and it has launched and sustained many careers.

The test is a paper and pencil inventory that usually takes about 30 minutes to complete. It is machine scored and interpreted by any one of several computer services for a fee. The current form of the test is a merging of the earlier Strong Vocational Interest Blanks for men and women. The test consists of 325 items that are checked "like," "dislike," or "indifferent." These items are constructed on six occupational themes, and scores on these clusters indicate the examinee's orientation toward realistic, investigative, artistic, social, enterprising, and conventional values. The responses are then analyzed for overall interest trends, degree of consistency of 23 basic interest areas, and degree of similarity to persons in a wide range of vocational pursuits.

The test asks the examinee to respond to a listing of over 100 occupations, express interest in more than 50 behavioral activities and 39 amusements, and express preferences between 30 pairs of activities and 15 personal characteristics. Obviously such data can be valuable for course or career selection, employee counseling, personnel selection, research purposes, or for assessing the many factors that influence decision making.

Many believe the Strong-Campbell Interest Inventory to be the best vocational interest inventory available. It should not be interpreted in a rigid psychometric manner, but it should be used to generate hypotheses with regard to vocational issues. These should then be explored in depth both in the context of the counseling relationship and in the community. The test should never be used apart from more extensive psychological assessment that will help the person make the best possible decision with the data available. In addition, the Christian counselor ought to give careful thought to the perceived gifts and talents of the individual and the pressing needs of the community in making any recommendations about vocation, calling, or ministry. Multiple sources of feed-

back are likely to prove most helpful to the individual in making such difficult and important decisions. The Strong-Campbell Interest Inventory can be one useful source of such feedback.

R. E. BUTMAN

See VOCATIONAL COUNSELING; INTEREST MEASUREMENT.

Structural Analysis. The method used by TRANSACTIONAL ANALYSIS to understand what is happening within the individual.

First-order structural analysis initially involves reflection on the gestures, words, and postures of the individual to ascertain whether the person is acting from within the judgmental (parent), the rational (adult), or the uninhibited (child) part of his or her personality. These are termed ego states and refer to conscious or preconscious sets of attitudes and feelings. More refined analyses include assessing which part of the parent (nurturing or controlling) and of the child (adapted or free) are dominant at a given moment.

Second-order structural analysis involves exploring the inner drama resulting from the dynamic interaction among the ego states as they vie for power in the individual as well as reflecting on the parental and situational influences that have determined the special character of the ego states within the person.

These types of analyses are undertaken in transactional analysis therapy in efforts to increase insight and self-understanding toward the end that the client may make enlightened decisions to change.

H. N. MALONY

Structural Family Therapy. A body of theory and techniques dealing with the individual in his social context. Therapy based on this framework is directed toward changing the organization of the family. When the structure of the family group is transformed, the positions of members in that group are altered accordingly. As a result each individual's experiences change.

Structural family therapy is predicated on the fact that the individual is not an isolate. He or she is an acting and reacting member of social groups. To say that a person is influenced by his social context, which he also influences, may seem obvious. However, basing mental health techniques on this concept is a new approach.

The traditional techniques of mental health grew out of fascination with individual dynamics. This preoccupation dominated the field and led therapists to concentrate on exploring the intrapsychic. The resulting treatment techniques focused exclusively on the individual apart from his surroundings. An artificial boundary was drawn between the individual and his social context. The practice of intrapsychic psychotherapy maintained and reinforced the artificial boundary. Consequently, the individual came to be viewed as the site of pathology.

Structural family therapy was developed in the second half of the twentieth century by Salvador Minuchin and his co-workers. *Families of the Slums* (Minuchin, Montalvo, Guerney, Rosman, & Schumer, 1967) was the first attempt at a comprehensive exposition of structural family therapy. Minuchin and his colleagues were working with poverty-stricken underprivileged families grappling with day-to-day survival. There was a sense of urgency and necessity in approaching these families in a practical way that would alleviate stress. Therapies aimed toward understanding and insight rather than action seemed too far removed from the pressures of everyday problems of poor families. Minuchin and his co-workers developed a therapeutic approach that was founded on the immediacy of the present reality, was oriented toward solving problems, and, most importantly, viewed human problems within their social context. Other influences in structural family therapy are Haley's (1976) problem-solving approach and strategic techniques.

During the 1970s and 80s structural family therapists broadened their scope and began using their approach with middle-class psychosomatic families. Unlike most therapies, which had their roots in the middle class and were adapted to work with lower socioeconomic patients, structural family therapy was generated from work with the poor and subsequently expanded to other socioeconomic strata.

The theoretical underpinnings of structural family therapy rest on the belief that "the whole and the parts can be properly explained only in terms of the relations that exist between the parts" (Lane, 1970). Thus, focus is on the relationships that connect one part of the whole to another. Structuralism approaches all human phenomena with the intent of identifying the codes that regulate human relationships. Structure refers to the regulating codes manifested in the operational patterns through which people relate to one another in order to carry out func-

tions. The repertoire of structure that the family develops to carry out its ongoing functions takes on a character that is as unique to each family as the personality structure is to the individual.

The structural dimensions of transactions most often identified in structural family therapy are boundary, alignment, and power. According to Minuchin, "The boundaries of a subsystem are the rules defining who participates and how" (1974, p. 53). These rules dictate who is in and who is out of an operation. The clarity of boundaries within a family is a useful parameter for the evaluation of family functioning. Families can be conceived of as falling somewhere along a continuum whose poles are the two extremes of diffuse (enmeshed) and rigid (disengaged) boundaries. Most healthy families fall within the middle range of clearly defined boundaries.

Aponte speaks of alignment as the "joining or opposition of one member of a system to another in carrying out an operation" (1976, p. 434). Alignment statements, for example, would indicate whether the father agrees or disagrees with his wife's disciplinary action toward the children.

Power refers to the relative influence of each family member on the outcome of an activity. Power is not an absolute attribute but is relative to the operation. An indicator of power might be who speaks first or who becomes the gatekeeper of communication flow in the session.

The scope of the family therapist and the techniques he uses to pursue his goals are determined by his theoretical framework. Structural family therapy is a therapy of action. The focus of this therapy is to modify the present, not to explore or interpret the past. The therapist actively directs his own behavior and communications with the family so as to influence selected aspects of the family's transactions within or outside of the session. The therapist's task is to develop relational contexts that will allow, stimulate, and provoke change in transactional patterns associated with the problem.

References

Aponte, H. J. Underorganization in the poor family. In P. J. Guerin, (Ed.), *Family therapy: Theory and practice*. New York: Gardner, 1976.

Haley, J. *Problem-solving therapy*. San Francisco: Jossey-Bass, 1976.

Lane, M. *Introduction to structuralism*. New York: Basic Books, 1970.

Minuchin, S. *Families and family therapy*. Cambridge: Harvard University Press, 1974.

Minuchin, S., Montalvo, B., Guerney, B., Rosman, B., &

Schumer, F. *Families of the slums.* New York: Basic Books, 1967.

B. L. CARLTON

See FAMILY THERAPY: OVERVIEW.

Structural Integration. An approach to personality growth through working with the physical body and energy levels. It is also known as rolfing, after its creator, Ida Rolf. It is not strictly a technique or a psychotherapeutic process, yet psychological changes do occur through rolfing.

Rolf received the Ph.D. in biological chemistry from the College of Physicians and Surgeons of Columbia University. Building on homeopathy, yoga, and osteopathy, she began to develop a new approach to dealing with chronic situations in the body. Homeopathy is a branch or medicine that arouses the patient's own healing powers through increasing the symptoms, which leads to a healing crisis. In the early 1950s Rolf started teaching a 10-hour sequence of aligning the myofascial system. This came to be known as rolfing.

Rolfing, according to its followers, actually restructures the body. Based on the premise that individuality is shaped by experiences, environment, choices, goals, emotions, and intellect, rolfing suggests that just as our minds bear memories that have consequences on our emotional health, so do physical memories (injuries, anxieties, etc.) shape our physical bodies. These memories build up and result in posture problems, discomfort, depression, and susceptibility to illness and disease.

The goal of rolfing is to bring to the body a more resilient, higher energy system. It is an ongoing process. During the 10-hour cycle of work a rolfer uses physical pressure to stretch and guide the fascia to a place of easier movement. Fascia is the elastic tissue surrounding muscle in the body. It starts beneath the skin and positions muscles, bones, nerves, and organs. Also called the organ of structure, fascia makes up the shape of the individual and is abused through the normal process of living. Rolfing reverses this process, attempting to bring balance to the body.

In structural integration the concept of balance is the key factor in determining the serenity of the body. The basic belief of rolfing is that one can actually add structure to the body, causing a change in function that transcends the physical. A human being is basically an energy field in the larger energy of earth and gravity; greater awareness releases energy and frees it to be more available for individual functioning. Rolfing frees that energy. The results of this body work reach into the emotional, behavioral, and spiritual life of the individual, since chronic tension or strain eventually develops into emotional problems such as irritability or dependence. When the physical energy is released, it releases the whole system, intellectually and emotionally. Because of this, some emotional and physical pain is often experienced through the 10-hour cycle. Sometimes deeply repressed memories are released in intense emotional experiences, often relating the experience itself to a particular part of the body.

Rolf's work developed through the 1950s and was given increased exposure through Esalen in California, where she did some work with Perls and other contemporaries. In 1969 Esalen funded a research project to determine physiological effects of rolfing, including measurement of brain waves, blood, and urine, and psychological profiles. Testing was done before and after the 10-hour cycle, and significant changes were found in the clients (Rolf, 1971). In 1977 Rolf published a formal exposition of the nature of the human body complete with diagrams. The Rolf Institute in Boulder, Colorado, trains rolfers in the theory and practice of structural integration.

Reference
Rolf, I. P. *Rolfing.* Santa Monica, Calif.: Dennis-Landman, 1977.

D. L. SCHUURMAN

Structuralism. The school of psychology associated primarily with E. B. Titchener. It is also referred to as introspectionism and existentialism. Through its definition of psychology and its prescription of a methodology, structuralism was the force that led psychology away from mental philosophy into the realm of science. Ultimately it was a system whose deficiencies inspired the rise of behaviorism and functionalism as well as the psychologies of the Würzburg school and the Gestaltists.

The roots of structuralism lie in the experimental psychology of Wundt, who expressed the fundamental conviction that "psychology is the study of mental contents and that it is a science which approaches these contents chiefly through introspection and experimentation" (Heidbreder, 1933, p. 93). Wundt differentiated between physics and psychology as sciences based on immediate and mediate experience, respectively. Both were, however, sciences based on experience rather than metaphysics.

Titchener also defined psychology as the

science of mental life, distinguishing between mind and consciousness. Mind referred to the sum total of mental processes occurring in the lifetime of the individual (and thus could not be studied introspectively), and consciousness to the sum total of mental processes occurring now, at any given present time. Like Wundt, Titchener held that all science was based in experience. But physics (or natural science) differed from psychology in that physics studies aspects of the world, or experience, without reference to persons; psychology studies the world from the perspective of the person experiencing it. Thus, the subject matter of psychology became experience dependent on an experiencing person. Titchener further reduced the experiencing person to the nervous system, including the sense organs, thus adopting in theory Wundt's physiological psychology. This adoption created some conceptual problems in Titchener's system. The dependency he spoke of was not conceived as causality or any other direct relationship, since he subscribed to a psychophysical parallelism in which bodily processes and mental processes occur side by side, with no interaction between them.

The method of psychology was introspection, which Titchener contrasted with inspection, the observation of the physical world. Introspection, the observation of the contents of consciousness, must involve only description of mental contents, without interpretation or speculation or labeling of the stimulus. While ordinary habits and principles of common sense predispose persons to "see" objects and events, all the trained introspectionist was to report were the qualities of the stimulus. To do otherwise constituted the stimulus error, which involved seeing things rather than conscious contents.

In order to train introspectionists and to understand the mind Titchener had to specify the elements constituting the mind. He settled on three elementary processes: sensation, affection, and images. Sensations were the elements of perception, images the elements of ideas, and affections the elements of emotions. Each of these elements was also assigned attributes. Sensations and images were characterized by quality, intensity, duration, and clearness (which was also an essential characteristic of attention); affection was characterized by the first three, but lacked clearness. To these general attributes Titchener added particular attributes for some processes. The study of these attributes and processes constituted much of the experimental work completed by Titchener, his Cornell students, and his colleagues in the Society of Experimentalists. The study of mental processes also led Titchener to postulate what became known as the context theory of meaning, which held that a new mental process (or core) acquires its meaning from the constellation of mental processes within which it occurs.

Mental processes involved in the activity of the psychologist were analysis and synthesis (both descriptive) and causality (explanatory). These addressed, respectively, the questions of what (by reducing the material to its elements and describing these), how (by showing how the elements are arranged and combined), and why. Motivating the psychologist's activity was the search for understanding of the generalized human mind. In this goal Titchener opposed both an emphasis on individual differences (differential psychology) and the focus on applied psychology that became especially prevalent in America after World War I.

While structuralism may clearly be considered psychology's first paradigm (Kirsch, 1977), psychology soon underwent a fundamental revolution. The various schools that emerged were all, in one way or another, critical of structuralism. The Würzburg school challenged the analysis of thought in terms of images, sensations, and conscious contents, and modified the introspectionist method into a phenomenological one. The behaviorists questioned the mentalist emphasis. The Gestalt psychologists objected to the analysis of wholes into elements. The functionalists introduced the study of individual differences and the use of animals and children as subjects (even though they could not be trained in introspection). The psychoanalytic psychologists questioned the focus on consciousness and the disinterest in change.

Because its method was a rigid one, setting narrow limits on the scope of psychology, structuralism effectually died with its founder. However, it left behind the rich legacy of inspiration for the later experimental psychologies of the twentieth century.

References

Heidbreder, E. *Seven psychologies.* New York: Appleton-Century-Crofts, 1933.
Kirsch, I. Psychology's first paradigm. *Journal of the History of the Behavioral Sciences,* 1977, *13,* 317–325.

H. Vande Kemp

See Psychology, History of.

Stupor. A state in which the sensibilities are immobilized and the individual loses appreciation of his life and surroundings. In an organic sense it is synonymous with unconsciousness, as the person appears dazed and unresponsive. A benign stupor is associated with a disorder from which recovery may be expected. Malignant stupors, as in catatonic schizophrenia, carry little chance of recovery. A stupor may also occur as the result of severe panic reactions, as a response to a physical attack, or upon hearing bad news such as the loss of a job, friend, or relative. In most cases such stupors are temporary, although a prolonged immobility may lead to or indicate more serious problems.

D. L. Schuurman

Stuttering. *See* Speech Disorders.

Style of Life. One of the central concepts of Adler's system of Individual Psychology, along with inferiority feeling, social interest, and fictional goals. Adler's use of the term lacked precision, and at different times he described style of life in terms of personality structure, self, ego, unified coping system, and one's unique pattern of perceiving oneself and life's problems. The concept certainly overlaps the idea of fictional goals, but style of life is more general and includes one's characteristic behavior patterns as well as one's perception of goal.

Holism is a key aspect of the style of life. It is not a mere composite of separate characteristics, but the dominant whole that transcends the parts and whose impact is seen within each part. All behavior springs from the style of life. A person may appear to have contradictory ideas or competing goals, but this illusion is due to our failure to comprehend the underlying, unifying Gestalt.

Although the style of life embraces all aspects of an individual's personality, the Adlerian view is that the cognitive elements are central. The individual perceives external reality through the fictions and then selects an appropriate behavior. People are not driven by emotions. Emotions are produced in order to help individuals maintain a certain style of life.

Other characteristics of the style of life are uniqueness, creativity, and stability. Although every human being strives toward feelings of perfection and superiority, each person operates with different fictions, conceives of his goal differently, and comes out with a unique pattern of characteristics and habits, a style of life. Although both heredity and environment have some influence, they furnish only the building blocks from which the individual

fashions his style of life, the most creative and unique work of art. Although people can change their life styles, Adler believed that the period of early childhood was formative and that few people could change style of life without intensive psychotherapy.

Adler attributed all mental disorder to fundamental defects in the style of life. The entire clinical approach of individual psychology is geared to style of life: comprehending it, helping the patient to gain this insight, and then changing it.

The strongest critique of the style of life concept comes from empirical research on personality. There are too many cases where individuals have conflicting goals, where behavior is counterproductive, where interpersonal similarities outweigh the differences claimed by uniqueness, where behaviors change according to the situational demands or stage of the life cycle. The concept of a stable, unique, consistent, and unified style of life appears to be more of an ideal than an accurate generalization. Nevertheless, the concept may be a relevant approach in clinical work or spiritual counseling where the goal is to change the individual's fundamental orientation.

T. L. Brink

Sublimation. The process by which socially acceptable gratification of instinctual drives or desires is obtained through substitute activity. Though an unconscious process generally classed with the Defense Mechanisms, it does not involve repression or ego opposition to the instinctual drive. Rather, it is a healthy function of the normal ego, deflecting an unconscious and otherwise consciously unacceptable impulse into socially acceptable expression, substituting the aim and/or object of the impulse while permitting adequate discharge of mental energy associated with that impulse. Examples of this would include sublimation of aggressive impulses through becoming a soldier, a football player, or a business executive.

R. Larkin

Subliminal Perception. A process involving a response to stimulation that is too weak or too brief to be consciously reported. Subliminal perceptions result from stimuli that cause the sensory receptors to fire (sensory threshold) but are not strong enough to reach conscious awareness (perceptual threshold). They are perceptions, therefore, that are below (sub) the threshold (*limen*—Latin, threshold) of conscious awareness. A related term is subception, which is the reaction to an emotion-producing stimulus that is not perceived to the point of being reported but is detectable from a person's autonomic responses.

In experiments on subliminal perception weak stimuli of short duration are presented to subjects. The subjects report that they do not see the stimulus. However, if shock is paired with a subliminally presented stimulus, subjects will begin to show an emotional response to the presentation of the weak stimulus.

Subliminal perception is to be distinguished from discrimination without awareness. This phenomenon involves attending to only part of a stimulus field and not perceiving the unattended portions. This is not subliminal because subjects could sense the unattended things if they wanted to. In subliminal perception stimuli get into the brain, but are not strong enough to cause conscious awareness.

In experiments involving the subliminal presentation of "dirty words" or sexually explicit scenes to subjects, such stimuli can cause subjects to blush, turn away, or become excited without knowing what they have seen. In fact, subjects usually find it more difficult to recognize the dirty words than normal words of the same length. Psychologists who have run such studies have labeled this phenomenon perceptual defense. Where it might take a 100-millisecond flash to see the word *whale*, 200 milliseconds might be required to recognize the emotionally laden word *whore*. This specific result is known as perceptual censoring. There are also some subjects who are able to recognize the dirty words more easily than normal words, and this is appropriately called perceptual vigilance.

One question asked by psychologists concerning subliminal perception is how much can people be affected by the subliminal stimulation. In the past some individuals in advertising suggested that people can be motivated to buy products as a result of subliminally presented advertising. One experiment that initially created some alarm involved subliminally presenting "Eat Popcorn" and "Drink Coca-Cola" alternately on a motion picture screen every five seconds during a regular film in a New Jersey theater. The commercial firm that ran the study said that popcorn sales rose 57.5% and Coke sales 18.1%. Pertinent questions about experimental procedures were not answered by the experimenters, however, and such results have not been considered reliable.

Other research suggests that it is doubtful that subliminal cues could have a significant effect on people's attitudes or behaviors. It is felt that subliminal messages, which are weak stimuli, would not prove to be more effective than strong stimuli in changing attitudes.

M. P. Cosgrove

Substance-Use Disorders. The abuse of drugs is not a new phenomenon, but the extent of the abuse in the twentieth century is certainly unparalleled in human history. Drug abuse has become a major public health problem in the past 30 years. From 1962 to 1980 the percentage of Americans 18–25 years of age who have tried marijuana has increased from 4% to 68%. In the same span of years the percentage of 18–25-year-olds in America who have tried other drugs has increased from 3% to 33% (Wilford, 1981). In the 1950s American drug abuse consisted mainly of heroin usage by persons in large metropolitan areas. Thirty years later a wide variety of drugs is being used and misused by millions of Americans in all segments of society.

Illegal drug trade from parts of Asia and South America supplies many Western nations. Yet many parts of the globe have their own drug problems, including the misuse of medications, multiple drug use, and an increasing consumption of tobacco in spite of widespread publicity regarding its dangers (Cohen, 1981).

The emotional problems that result from the misuse of drugs are called substance-use disorders in *DSM-III*. A substance is defined as any chemical that modifies mood or behavior by affecting the central nervous system and whose use is subject to misuse. Such a definition obviously excludes the use of medications when they are used as prescribed. According to *DSM-III* other nonpathological usage of substances would include recreational use of marijuana (even though illegal). An arrest for drug usage does not automatically indicate the presence of a substance-use disorder.

Pathological use of substances may include legal drugs (such as caffeine) or illegal drugs (such as cocaine). A substance-use disorder is characterized by maladaptive behavior associated with the use of substances. These disorders are generally more prevalent among men than women. Such behavior falls into two major categories: abuse and dependence.

Abuse. A diagnosis of substance abuse is made when there is a pattern of pathological use of the substance lasting at least one month and constituting an impairment of functioning. Abuse of a substance may be continual and consistent, or it may occur in binges. Another way of defining substance abuse is usage that is viewed by surrounding subcultures as undesirable. For example, recreational use of alcohol in moderation is not considered substance abuse, nor is the restrained use of caffeine in beverages diagnosed as abuse.

A pathological pattern of substance use would be daylong intoxication, an inability to restrain or refrain from using the substance, or using the drug with full knowledge that such use is exacerbating a physical disorder. Impairment of function, a second criterion for diagnosing abuse, can include erratic or impulsive behavior, emotional inappropriateness, or criminal behavior.

Dependence. Substance dependence is a more serious form of substance abuse. The key factor in diagnosis is the presence of physiological dependence, evidenced either by tolerance or withdrawal. Tolerance of a drug occurs when more and more of the substance must be used to maintain the same effect (or a declining effect from using the same amount). Withdrawal is a physiological upset and craving when the drug intake is reduced or stopped. Usually a substance-specific syndrome will follow cessation or reduction, which can include anxiety, irritability, attention deficits, or agitation. Withdrawal can last from a few days to several weeks and can be mild (as in the case of tobacco) or severe (with alcohol or opioids). Substance dependence also includes social or occupational impairments or a pattern of pathological use, except with alcohol and cannabis, where dependence can be diagnosed even without the presence of impairments or pathological use patterns. Caffeine dependence is not considered a pathology in *DSM-III* because its use is not usually accompanied by impairments in functioning.

Major Disorders. The American Psychiatric Association divides the drugs of abuse into nine categories. Five of these substance groups are subject to both abuse and dependence: cannabis, opioids, amphetamines, alcohol, and barbituates. The use of three other substances can lead to abuse but not to physiological dependence: PCP, cocaine, and hallucinogens. The final drug, tobacco, can lead to physiological dependence, but a diagnosis of abuse is not made, since heavy use of tobacco is not usually accompanied by impairments in social or occupational functioning (*see* SMOKING). Alcohol and the problems associated with its use are discussed in a separate article (*see* ALCOHOL ABUSE AND DEPENDENCE).

Cannabis (MARIJUANA, hashish, THC) is a family of drugs derived from the cannabis plant. Its use is illegal in the United States but somewhat common. No known physiological dependence forms, but a moderate amount of psychological dependence can occur. Tolerance does form. The drug is taken orally or smoked. Cannabis euphoria includes a relaxation of inhibitions and some disoriented behavior.

The opioids (naturally occurring heroin, morphine, and synthetics such as methadone) are narcotics with high levels of physical and psychological dependence potential and with serious tolerance and withdrawal features. The drugs can be administered orally, smoked, or injected. Abuse and dependence of opioids usually go together. The annual death rate is high, often accompanied by violence or serious drug-induced health problems. Opioid users usually have a history of previous polydrug use (Schuckit, 1979).

Amphetamines (including "speed" and appetite suppressants) are stimulants that can be taken orally or injected. Their use can lead to increased alertness and insomnia. The barbituates (including the minor tranquilizers and some sedatives) are depressants that can give the effect of drunken behavior (slurred speech and disorientation). Both the amphetamines and barbituates can have legitimate medical uses under the supervision of a physician.

Cocaine usage has increased in the last quarter of the twentieth century. It is a narcotic and a stimulant, and can be either injected or sniffed. Freebase conversion allows the drug to be smoked. The hallucinogens are mostly used for brief periods of time and are best known for the illusions and hallucinations that occur following their use.

Tobacco dependence is physiologically and psychologically intense, probably due to the overlearned quality of the behavior, the ubiquitous presence of cues in the environment, and the unpleasant features of withdrawal.

Substance abuse often seems to occur in persons suffering from personality disorder, especially antisocial personality disorder. Certain features of the antisocial personality (chronic violation of societal rules and expectations, delinquency, truancy, running away behaviors) may predispose the person to drug abuse. The most powerful predictor of future drug abuse are signs of behavioral deviance in elementary school (Wilford, 1981). Some researchers have described a drug-dependent personality (not an official *DSM-III* classification) that includes low self-esteem, low capacity for affection, and low frustration tolerance.

Related Problems. Substance abusers frequently experience accompanying pathologies. For example, long-term use of cocaine can lead to paranoid ideation. The cost of obtaining illicit substances can lead to illegal actions and criminal behavior. If a drug abuser is trying to self-medicate for an anxiety or depressive disorder, the condition can worsen instead of improve due to incorrect administration. Drug abusers who experience extremely labile moods are also subject to violent outbursts. In addition to the accompanying pathologies, substance abusers can experience resulting psychopathologies such as the substance-induced organic mental disorders (intoxications, withdrawals, deliriums, hallucinosis, and amnestic disorders). Physical health often suffers and depression is frequently a resulting mood disturbance, as evidenced by high suicide rates among drug abusers.

Treatment. The traditional individual psychotherapeutic interventions have not been very successful with substance-abuse problems (Solomon & Keeley, 1982). Other methods such as psychosurgery, electroconvulsive therapy, hypnosis, and psychodrama have had unremarkable success. The most successful approaches are group approaches using homogeneous populations in residential treatment. Group rules, isolation of the abuser from previous drug-filled settings, high levels of motivation, and gradual return of privileges as behavior becomes better socialized seem to be the key factors in successful treatment (Glasscote, Sussex, Jaffe, Ball, & Brill, 1972). Teen Challenge is one such nationwide program, which also includes the spiritual dimension and a strong call to drug abusers to reform by being spiritually regenerated. Methadone maintenance is used with some success in helping heroin addicts ease off addiction, improve their physical health, and cease their illegal activities.

References

Cohen, S. *The substance abuse problems.* New York: Haworth Press, 1981.

Glasscote, R. M., Sussex, J. N., Jaffe, J. H., Ball, J., & Brill, L. *The treatment of drug abuse: Programs, problems, prospects.* Washington, D.C.: Joint Information Service, 1972.

Schuckit, M. A. *Drug and alcohol abuse: A clinical guide to diagnosis and treatment.* New York: Plenum, 1979.

Solomon, J., & Keeley, K. A. (Eds.). *Perspectives in alcohol and drug abuse: Similarities and differences.* Boston: Wright, 1982.

Wilford, B. B. *Drug abuse.* Chicago: American Medical Association, 1981.

J. R. BECK

Substitution. The process by which repressed impulses seek indirect discharge through substitute satisfactions in place of those originally desired. The psychic energy of the original instinct is displaced to any impulse connected by unconscious association with the repressed impulse. The substitute impulse, or derivative, then takes on increased intensity and perhaps altered emotional tone consistent with the original impulse. Most neurotic symptoms are such derivatives.

See DEFENSE MECHANISMS.

Suggestibility. Suggestion is a process of communication whereby individuals can be influenced by one or more persons to change their ideas, beliefs, attitudes, and/or behaviors without a critical response in return. Suggestibility reflects the individual degree of susceptibility to influence by suggestion. Although the correlative connection between suggestibility and personality is inconclusive, increased suggestibility can occur through the use of drugs and hypnosis. Other means of suggestion include social suggestion through an appeal to conformity, ceremonial ritual, and political and commercial propaganda. The place of suggestion in psychotherapy is of obvious importance and is usually studied within the framework of PLACEBO EFFECTS.

J. H. ROBERTSON

Suicide. The act of taking one's own life. It is an ancient practice that dates back to classical Greece and Rome. The Bible refers to five suicides, including the death of Judas Iscariot. The Japanese have long practiced hara-kiri, or death by suicide, in response to bringing dishonor on one's family. In our own culture the stock market crash of 1929 resulted in numerous suicides in the United States.

Suicide is a behavior that is a response to a problem. The problem may be internal or external, real or imaginary. For the victim suicide provides the sufficient solution to the problem. According to Baechler, "Suicide can be successful or *symbolic*, with all gradations in-between" (1975, p. 16). Suicide attempts can be serious, self-indulgent, or mere gestures. Suicide can be immediate (e.g., shooting) or long term (e.g., alcoholism). It can be deliberate or involuntary, intended or ventured, chosen or imposed (Baechler, 1975). Durkheim (1897/1951) classified suicides into three groups: egoistic (lack of social integration); altruistic (excessive identification such as a heroic self-sacrifice for others); and anomic (the response to loss or an economic disaster).

Labeling a person as suicidal or determining that a person has committed suicide is very difficult. In the 1950s Schneidman and Farberow established the Suicide Prevention Center in Los Angeles as a crisis intervention program for suicidal persons and a research center focusing on understanding suicidal behavior. The review of crisis calls, letters, social histories, and the suicidal events resulted in a very mixed description of the suicidal person. For instance, people who talk about suicide or even threaten suicide may or may not attempt suicide. Likewise, people who feel suicidal and have suicidal thoughts but reveal them to no one may or may not attempt suicide. The ability to predict suicidal attempts or even a successful suicide is quite difficult. Also, after a suicidal act there has been very little input concerning the person's behavior, thoughts, or feelings prior to the suicide attempt.

Social Patterns. According to the U.S. Census figures in 1978 there were 27,300 successful suicide attempts. Males exceeded females on a 3:1 ratio. The methods of suicide indicated that males tended to use more violent means such as firearms. However, since 1960 women have gradually been using more violent means for suicide. An important point is the lack of accurate documentation concerning suicides. For example, a person taking an overdose of medication may die of heart failure, asphyxiation, or other physical failure, and suicide will not be listed as cause of death. Farberow (1980) estimates that there are 50,000 direct suicidal deaths each year plus two million self-caused unintentional deaths.

It is similarly difficult to identify what is a suicide attempt. Hospital emergency rooms have a constant flow of patients who abuse medication and who could qualify for a suicide attempt but are discharged because their actions could not be supported as serious attempts. Also, family members may keep an attempt secret, or the individual may be alone and take an overdose but recover without medical intervention.

From what limited data is available it appears that white males are more likely to die by self-inflicted wounds than are blacks, except for the 25-to-34-year age range, where numbers for blacks and whites are similar. The same is true for females with the same age exception. Sociologically suicide is more prevalent among the affluent and homicide more common among the poor. One hypothesis suggests that affluent persons internalize anger, which results in self-inflicted injury, while the poor externalize their anger, resulting in homicide. Regardless of the sociological picture, Wekstein (1979) states, "In summary, self-destruction is not limited by status, profession, socioeconomic stratification, talent or sagacity. The more anguished are most likely

to be the vulnerable, while individuals who suffer from personality disorders or neurosis are statistically less likely to commit suicide. However, such a diagnosis does not make them immune" (pp. 92–93).

Psychodynamics. Using psychopathology as a guide, we often associate depression with suicide. This may be a prolonged depression where the person feels no hope, feels useless, rejected, and wants to end it all. Others may be reacting to the recent death of a spouse, parent, or child, and feel life is not worth pursuing without that person.

In some instances persons hear voices telling them to kill themselves. This psychotic condition may involve hearing voices only occasionally, or it may be a persistent obsession which a person feels unable to control. Such a person may feel compelled to carry out the commands of the voices to kill himself and will often use almost any means to do so. Such instruments as the broken edge of an ashtray or a window cord often suffice for a suicide attempt.

Others may be reacting to an unpleasant situation or are angry at someone and want to get even; they try to kill themselves as a gesture of revenge. This may be a hysterical response with total disregard for the consequences. Wrist slashing, drugs mixed with alcohol, or driving into a bridge abutment may be the impulsive means of dealing with the immediate crisis.

Severity of attempt is difficult to assess. Severity is usually assessed by the means the person utilizes, the way the attempt is made, and the result. A person taking 20 pills over an eight-hour period who merely falls asleep must be contrasted with the person who takes 20 pills within a five-minute period and dies.

Farberow has worked for decades on the issue of suicide. Recently he divided suicide attempts into two groups: indirect self-destructive behavior and direct self-destructive behavior (Farberow, 1980). Using patients with diabetes, Bureger's disease, and elderly chronically ill he divided them into these two groups on the basis of several variables. The direct self-destructive behavior group had eating and sleeping disorders, were easily fatigued and agitated, felt apathetic, and were losing weight. Cognitively they had serious difficulty concentrating, exhibited decreased mental productivity, had poor problem-solving skills, and lacked flexibility in thinking. Affectively they were depressed, angry, guilt oriented, anxious, and had dramatic mood swings. Occasionally they felt severe loss, worthlessness, powerlessness, and exhaustion; yet they desired to obtain surcease, to change others' behavior attitudes, and were invested in achievement, production, success, and recuperation. They had a low sense of futurity and reacted to stress on terms of short-term impact. Risk taking in this group was very high, and was expressed on an all-or-none basis. Lastly, coping skills were constriction, repression, and projection.

In contrast, the indirect self-destructive behavior group showed that physical symptoms were neglected, resulting in crises such as acidosis, gangrene, and malnutrition. There was no marked change in cognitive functioning, though reasoning was shallow and superficial. Affectively there appeared to be no outstanding characteristics. These persons often derived gratification from present experiences; were oriented toward self, not others; showed strong ability for denial and poor social adjustment; and had basically a low estimate of themselves with little involvement in achievement or production. The future held little promise for them. Rather, they were hedonistic and seemed to have little capacity for delay of reward. In essence they were fairly immature. The temporal aspect of their problem was related to long-term difficulties with health in their recent or precipitating conditions. These people sought excitement and stimulation, which resulted in focusing on the present. Their coping mechanisms were primarily denial, suppression, regression, and narcissism.

This research has provided a classification of direct and indirect suicide strategies and has brought important attention to indirect means. Presently much emphasis is being put on examining the possibility of indirect self-destructive behavior in relation to prolonged physical illness or psychological stress. Such areas as high-risk sports (Delk, 1980), gambling (Kusyszyn, 1980), and auto accidents (Selzer, 1980) are being studied for possible relationship to suicide. Though none of the research is conclusive, a number of the indirect self-destructive behavior criteria seem to apply to these groups, especially living for the present, pleasure seeking, and lack of clear denial of problems. Selzer (1980) investigated drunken drivers and found a clear denial of problems with alcohol. However, 68% of those arrested for drunken driving were alcoholics. McMurray (1970), using driver records six months prior to and following divorce, found that the number of accidents doubled in this group. Whether or not this is related to suicide is not clear. One-passenger fatal accidents may well be related to suicide as a result of intrapersonal stress. This line of thought also raises questions regarding high-risk occupations. Firemen and policemen may be involved in heroic acts that are in some way related to suicidal behavior.

Children have committed suicide on occasion, but the frequency is so small that it is difficult to get a clear picture of the psychodynamics involved. It appears to be related to stress, particularly within the family structure, as in serious cases of marital problems or the unexpected death of a parent or sibling.

Survivors. When a suicide occurs, the remaining family members usually have difficulty dealing with it. The pervasive feeling of guilt is often overwhelming. There are often questions such as "What could I have done to prevent it?" or "Why didn't I see it sooner?" A suicide is often followed by distorted communication, usually to protect children. Yet children are often very familiar with details of the suicide (Cain and Fast, 1972). Members of a suicide victim's family may also attempt suicide. A surviving spouse, for example, may feel that he or she cannot live without the deceased partner. In many instances psychotherapy with the surviving family members has resolved residual feelings effectively.

Prevention. Numerous communitites have established a hot line, crisis intervention, or contact program for handling suicidal persons. A patient, reassuring voice expressing concern may go a long way to stop a suicide attempt. Confrontation appears to be contraindicated. Helping a person look for alternatives to suicide, and possibly even accepting psychiatric hospitalization may be desirable. Intervention may involve a large number of contacts by phone with a person as well as being with him personally until the crisis situation is resolved. Encouraging regular involvement in a church, a community social program, and psychotherapy is advisable. Medications are usually indicated in helping the person to deal with depressed feelings. However, the medications need to be carefully supervised, as it is easy for the patient to stockpile them over months and even years. It is impossible to make a home suicide proof, but many things can be done to make it safer. Guns, for example, can be carefully locked, unloaded, and the ammunition locked away at a separate location. Cleaning solvents can be placed out of reach so that they are not tempting.

Involvement in psychotherapy often focuses on having the person define alternate ways of dealing with the crisis situation he is facing. It is important for the person to learn to express his feelings in a more effective way than in the past. This may also directly involve family members, co-workers, and possibly even employers in trying to resolve some of the stress factors related to the person's suicidal ideation or feelings. It is important to take suicidal conversations seriously even if the person is talking in jest.

References

Baechler, J. *Les suicides*. Paris: Calmann-L'evy, 1975.

Cain, C., & Fast, I. Children's disturbed reactions to parent suicide. In A. C. Caine (Ed.), *Survivors of suicide*. Springfield, Ill.: Thomas, 1972.

Delk, J. L. High-risk sports as indirect self-destructive behavior. In N. L. Farberow (Ed.), *The many faces of suicide*. New York: McGraw-Hill, 1980.

Durkheim, E. *Suicide*. Glencoe, Ill.: Free Press, 1951. (Originally published, 1897.)

Farberow, N. L. Indirect self-destructive behavior. In N. L. Farberow (Ed.), *The many faces of suicide*. New York: McGraw-Hill, 1980.

Kusyszyn, I. Gambling. In N. L. Farberow (Ed.), *The many faces of suicide*. New York: McGraw-Hill, 1980.

McMurray, L. Emotional stress on driving performance. *Behavior Research in Highway Safety*, 1970, *1*, 100–114.

Selzer, M. L. The accident process and drunken driving as indirect self-destructive activity. In N. L. Farberow (Ed.), *The many faces of suicide*. New York: McGraw-Hill, 1980.

Wekstein, L. *Handbook of suicidology*. New York: Brunner/Mazel, 1979.

T. M. JOHNSON

Sullivan, Harry Stack (1892–1949). American psychiatrist; the chief proponent of what is called the dynamic-cultural or interpersonal school of psychoanalysis. Along with Horney, Erikson, and Fromm he is generally seen as one of the major neo-Freudians. Sullivan deemphasized the orthodox psychoanalytic stress on biology in favor of the view that most psychological troubles are engendered by life experiences. He suggested that it takes people to make people sick, and it takes people to make people well. He saw human relationships as both the cause of, and the potential remedy for, psychological disturbance.

Born in Norwich, New York, Sullivan was graduated in 1917 from the Chicago College of Medicine and Surgery. However, he was significantly influenced by both philosophers and anthropologists, and the breadth of his thinking made these influences apparent. Sullivan, more than anyone else of his era, made an intensive and lifelong study of the ways in which individual people affect one another. He argued that nonorganic psychological problems are at root faulty ways of relating to others. The psychotherapist's job, therefore, is to correct the patient's self-defeating interpersonal styles and maneuvers. Sullivan's key clinical question routinely was: "What is this particular client trying to do to or with me, in this situation; how is he or she attempting to structure our time together?" While dynamically oriented therapists have stressed intrapsychic mental events and behaviorists have stressed overt actions, Sullivan advocated that both be carefully attended to, especially as they relate to past interpersonal experience.

Sullivan advocated the careful observation of exactly how the patient expresses himself or herself, how he or she gets along with other people outside of the consulting room, and what has gone on interpersonally in the past. He emphasized over and over that other people are the most important aspects of anyone's environment, and he even went so far as to say that without interpersonal relationships a human being is, in fact, hardly human at all. To Sullivan the very concept of personality had no meaning apart from a person's characteristic interpersonal relationships.

Sullivan believed that there was an essential continuity between psychological normality and abnormality. In this regard he was perhaps the earliest physician to reject the idea that psychological troubles are diseases. While recognizing that certain organic abnormalities, such as brain tumors, can radically alter behavior, he believed that most of the problems for which people consult therapists were essentially difficulties in living. Such difficulties centered upon the specific human challenge of achieving and maintaining intimate relationships with others.

Although a number of books by Sullivan are now available, most of these were put together from his clinical lecture notes, and in certain cases from his students' notes. Sullivan was primarily a teacher of psychotherapeutic method and only secondarily a writer. Nevertheless, some of his posthumous volumes have earned the status of psychiatric classics, including *The Psychiatric Interview* (1954), *Clinical Studies in Psychiatry* (1956), and *Schizophrenia as a Human Process* (1962). He was a highly influential teacher in one of the most prestigious psychiatric hospitals in the country, St. Elizabeth's in Washington. He was also pivotal in the establishment of Chestnut Lodge, in Rockville, Maryland, another major treatment center and training institute.

From a theological point of view there is a great deal to commend in Sullivan's thought. If we have been made in God's image, as Christians maintain, this seems to imply that we are intrinsically relational beings—that we have been *made* to relate to God and our fellows. It seems only fitting, therefore, that Christian psychologists pay special attention to the nature of relationships. While Sullivan himself may not have been especially religious, his overall orientation appears compatible with the Christian world view.

C. W. McLemore

See INTERPERSONAL PSYCHOLOGY.

Superego. One of three psychic structures postulated by Freud. In contrast to the id, which is seen as the seat of the individual's impulses and drives, and the ego, which includes the person's perceptual and judging functions, the superego is the source of morality and moral judgment. It functions as a kind of moral observer or watchman in the absence of parents and other socializing agents. It observes one's moral thoughts and actions, and passes out self-punishment in the form of guilt for misbehavior and self-esteem for good behavior.

Roughly equivalent to the conscience, the superego is believed by psychoanalysts to develop largely during the first six years of life in the context of intimate parent-child relationships. Although later psychoanalysts have enlarged and altered some aspects of Freud's theory, the general understanding of the superego closely follows that laid down by Freud. He believed the superego develops out of the ego under the impact of the child's oedipus complex, which he assumed to be a universal psychological experience.

During the oedipal period (roughly 4 to 6 years of age) the male child is theorized to develop a growing love for his mother, a resentment toward his father, and a desire to replace his father as the sole source of his mother's affections. Fearing punishment from his father because of his murderous and incestuous wishes, the child is forced to repress and renounce his unacceptable desires. In the process he sets up within his personality an inner mental picture or representation of his parents' judgments and prohibitions. These images merge with the child's earlier parental introjects to form the special part of the ego known as the superego. The superego, built up by taking in these parental standards and punishments, then begins to function in place of external parental control. Much like the ego observes and evaluates the individual's wishes in light of external reality, the superego observes and evaluates one's wishes and desires in light of internalized moral standards.

Freud hypothesized that as a result of this process, the forbidden impulses of love (toward the mother) and hatred (toward the father) are redirected by the superego toward the child's own personality. Now, instead of experiencing love and anger toward his parents, the child directs his love and anger at himself in the form of self-esteem and guilt, respectively. Self-esteem is now regulated by superego approval instead of the approval or disapproval of parents, and guilt over the violation of one's inner values replaces fear about the external consequences of one's behavior.

Although the main features of the superego are believed by psychoanalysts to be laid down in the first six years of life, the process of identifying with meaningful people and taking in both their standards and their corrective attitudes continues to shape one's superego throughout life, especially through the formative years of preadolescence and adolescence. Consciously chosen adult values also merge with internalized parental values to produce the unique form and content of the adult superego.

One interesting aspect of Freud's concept of the superego is his explanation of why the superego can be so harsh and punitive while in reality the parents may have been relatively loving and nonpunitive. Freud did not believe that the child's superego was simply an internalized version of parental prohibition. He believed that children project or attribute their own anger to their parents, so that when they take a mental picture of their parents into their superego, they take it not as the parents were in reality, but as the children have distorted them by their own anger. The strength of the superego's punishment, in other words, is not due simply to the parents' actual punitiveness but to the combined strength of the parents' punitiveness and the child's anger at the parents.

In therapy psychoanalytically oriented therapists attempt to help patients develop a superego that has realistic and necessary moral standards but is not punitive or overly restrictive. This is done by helping patients understand the early parent-child interactions that caused the superego to be either too lenient or too punitive, by assisting the patient in consciously selecting more appropriate or adult standards, and by modeling a responsible but accepting and nonpunitive approach to moral issues.

S. B. Narramore

See PSYCHOANALYTIC PSYCHOLOGY.

Superstition. Unreasoning fear or awe of something mysterious or imaginary; religious belief or practice founded on fear or ignorance.

The development of our modern concept of superstition and superstitious behavior has had a long history. From a Latin source meaning "to stand over," perhaps in awe or amazement, our English word derives from the Old French word meaning "to survive."

Prior to this century the religious emphasis in superstition was much more pronounced, some writers using religion and superstition interchangeably. With this in mind we might interpret the word *ignorance* in the definition above to include those beliefs founded on misunderstanding or misinterpretation. However, we should avoid the once common usage that considered all non-Christian belief systems as superstition. Current usage largely reflects the general sense of an irrational belief or behavior, perhaps reflecting the widespread deemphasis of religious thought and practice in contemporary American society. However, the origins of most common superstitions are still to be found in religious contexts.

A speculation as to the exact meaning of the Old French source word for superstition, "to survive," is that this word refers to old, pre-Christian beliefs or practices that survived into the Christian era. While philologically unlikely, this interpretation provides a number of useful insights into superstitions in the Anglo-American culture. While a number of such pagan survivals exist, not all are considered superstitions. Determination of why some beliefs of non-Christian origin are superstitions and others are not illustrates an important feature of superstition: the superstitious belief is out of its original context and has not become integrated into a new context.

Examples of pagan elements in Anglo-American culture that are not considered superstitions are the mistletoe and holly wreaths used as Christmas decorations. Initially these were central features of druidic rituals occurring around the winter solstice. Now they have been firmly incorporated into popular Christian practices and also greatly reduced in significance. Indeed, kissing under a sprig of mistletoe is but a faint echo of the salacious druidic fertility ritual from which this practice was derived. In contrast, the avoidance of black cats and the special significance given to the number 13, which originated in the amalgam of pagan and heretical Christian beliefs known as witchcraft, have not become integrated within alternate contexts. The relationship of these superstitious beliefs to their original context is for the most part severed, and it is at this point in time difficult to eliminate them from the popular mind. Thus, we find that superstitions are most often found expressed as isolated beliefs and actions that are removed from their original contexts or given greater emphasis and meaning than their current context can support.

There are important distinctions between MAGICAL THINKING, weakly organized or obscure belief systems, and superstition. Magical thinking is an attribute of most of us, and in general it is based on drawing false causal links between unconnected events. An example is the belief that thoughts or wishes can alter the course of material events. While there is an element of magical thinking to be found in superstition, the use of this concept in psychology refers particularly to exaggerated instances of the example given here. Weakly organized belief systems and belief systems employed by various subcultures (e.g., hexing, voodoo, or "root working") are not superstitions in the sense of our primary definition, although they are contexts for the origin of superstitions. The significance of these distinctions is found when evaluating superstition from a psychological and particularly a clinical viewpoint.

A particular problem encountered when superstitious beliefs complicate a clinical evaluation is that superstitiousness may be misinterpreted as psychopathology per se. Similarly, the presence of superstitious beliefs may lead to an overestimation of the severity of psychopathology when it is present. This is due to the confusion of superstition and magical thinking found even in the current diagnostic criteria of the American Psychiatric Association. Conversely, actual pathology might be misinterpreted by some as merely manifestations of superstition. This is often complicated when psychologically disturbed individuals use symbols common to superstitions to express their psychopathology.

In order to determine the true state of affairs in a given case we must first ask the question: Is the patient's behavior motivated by an expressible belief that relates his or her behavior causally to a desired outcome? This addresses the issue of magical thinking versus a belief in magic. If such a belief is in force, the possibility of psychopathology need not be ruled out, but accepting the superstitious belief as direct evidence of psychopathology must be avoided. The appropriateness of such a belief for the individual should be evaluated. Is the belief commonly held by other people from similar backgrounds or traditions? If this is the case, we must again exercise caution in interpretation of the patient's superstitious behavior vis-à-vis the possibility of psychopathology. In a situation where conflicting experience would seem to invalidate a superstitious belief, the psychologically healthy individual will abandon or modify that belief. The psychologically ill person will be more likely to reinterpret his experience in order to minimize the apparent conflict between belief and experience, or may even deny the validity of the experience.

Finally, the extent to which a belief interferes with an individual's daily life must be considered. The healthy individual is able to maintain normal activities regardless of his superstitious beliefs. The inability to do so, especially if there is a sudden onset of the superstitious behavior or avoidance of common activities, is highly suggestive of psychopathology, not superstition.

Additional Readings

Chrisman, N. J., & Maretzki, T. W. *Clinical applied anthropology.* Boston: D. Reidel, 1982.

Crapanzano, V., & Garrison, V. (Eds.). *Case studies in spirit possession.* New York: Wiley, 1977.

Kleinman, A. *Patients and healers in the context of culture.* Berkeley: University of California Press, 1980.

G. S. Hurd

See Psychopathology in Primitive Cultures.

Supportive Psychotherapy.

A type of psychological treatment that utilizes various techniques directed toward symptomatic improvement and reestablishment of a client's usual adaptive behaviors.

Distinctives and Objectives. Psychotherapy is a psychological treatment assisting people with emotional problems. The treatment may be one of three different kinds: supportive, reeducative, or reconstructive (Wolberg, 1977). The differences between these kinds of treatment center on their objectives and approaches. The many, varied schools of psychotherapy find their preference in one of these three kinds of treatment. An example of each is guidance (supportive), family therapy (reeducative), and psychoanalytic psychotherapy (reconstructive).

As suggested by its name, supportive therapy aims to *support* clients, strengthening their defenses and preventing them from getting worse during the healing process. This treatment works to bring a client to a place of emotional equilibrium as soon as possible; its intent is to bring about an improvement of the symptoms so that the client can resume a level of functioning close to his or her norm. Briefly, this therapy has three goals: 1) to strengthen existing defenses; 2) promote a level of func-

tioning in the individual adequate to meet the demands of his or her environment; and 3) to reduce or remove the detrimental external factors that prompt the stress. These somewhat modest goals are not intended to change personality structure, although sometimes constructive alterations occur on their own once restoration is made and the successful new adaptations have been achieved.

Supportive measures may be used in two ways: as a primary treatment or as an adjunct to reeducative or reconstructive psychotherapies. Wolberg (1977) suggests four reasons for using support: 1) as a temporary necessity for basically sound personality structures that are momentarily overwhelmed by transient pressures the person in unable to handle; 2) as a primary, extensive means of maintaining borderline and characterologically dependent clients in homeostasis; 3) to promote ego building, so that an individual can subsequently lend his or her efforts to more reconstructive psychotherapeutic work; and 4) as a temporary resting place during more intensive therapy when anxiety becomes too great for one to cope adequately.

Those who seem to benefit most from supportive psychotherapy are people who are experiencing an acute crisis and need temporary encouragement. Also, chronically disturbed individuals can function quite adequately when receiving ongoing support.

Supportive therapy is contraindicated in situations where authority issues are so predominant that the client becomes competitive and depreciating, and seeks control of the therapeutic process by aggressive or hostile means. This form of therapy is also contraindicated in situations where the client detaches and becomes helpless; in this instance supportive therapy only serves to encourage the pathologic dependency.

Therapeutic Approach and Techniques. Supportive therapy views the client as an individual capable of change. Furthermore, it is not assumed that insight is necessary for such change to occur. A more crucial curative ingredient is hopefulness; an individual will weather the necessary difficult times when he believes there is hope, even if that hope must be temporarily borrowed from the therapist. Therapeutic optimism is therefore an important qualification for the supportive therapist. He or she should also have, and be able to communicate, a concern for and nonjudgmental acceptance of the client. The therapist should also be flexible, as supportive therapeutic work typically draws on a broad range of techniques. The most important of these are described below.

Directive guidance. The giving of advice or guidance is a technique that must be carefully regulated to the needs of the client. Specific recommendations are suitable for anxious and disorganized individuals but not for those capable of making their own decisions. In general, advising a client in areas of life changes that may be irreversible should be avoided.

Nondirective guidance. This technique avoids some of the dangers of directive guidance yet still provides guidance. Here the therapist listens carefully and offers the client a summary of the problems he or she has described along with several approaches for resolution. The therapist assumes the person is capable of good judgment and places the responsibility for decisions on the client.

Environmental intervention. This technique consists of initiating stress-reducing changes in the environment when a client is unable to take action to improve his or her own life situation. Examples might be a phone call to an employer or to a medical facility for an appointment, or suggesting a change of housing or a vacation. This technique must be used carefully with those clients who easily become dependent.

Ventilation. Allowing a client to express previously suppressed emotions and thoughts often results in a noticeable reduction of emotional tension and the capability to think more clearly. This method should be used selectively. It should not be employed if tension escalates rapidly or disorganized thinking and behavior increase.

Reassurance. Encouragement can often be beneficial, particularly after the client has thoroughly expressed his or her feelings concerning a situation. General, pat statements, such as "Everything will be all right," are not supportive and usually shut down further communication.

Education. After the client's problems are determined, the therapist's participation can often have an educative component. The focus may be on providing the client with the information and experience for learning better ways to solve problems.

Diversion. This tactic redirects a client's thinking and/or behavior away from disturbing topics to less intense and more therapeutic ones. Diversion is used primarily with clients who become so absorbed in personal problems that they neglect other important areas of their lives. It is particularly useful

for those who are medically ill or experiencing chronic pain.

Other techniques. Other supportive measures include tension control such as self-relaxation, self-hypnosis, meditation, and biofeedback; milieu therapy, which includes environmental manipulation, home treatment, day treatment, occupational therapy, music therapy, dance therapy, and social therapy; pressure and coercion; persuasion; confession; chemotherapy; and inspirational self-help group therapies such as Alcoholics Anonymous or Parents United.

Biblical Evaluation. A basic theme of Scripture is growth and restoration. Central to life is the phenomenon of growth, the capacity to change, and the restorative process. The biblical message is that while pain, hurt, pathology, and sin exist, there is still hope for healing and wholeness.

Christ teaches us through his parables and discerning dialogues that people hear and respond at varying levels, depending on their circumstances and personal development. Children, adults, men, women, disciples, and Pharisees all heard the same message, but each responded quite differently. Depending on the situation, Jesus used a variety of approaches, such as guidance, instruction, encouragement, acceptance, and protection.

There is a similarity between some approaches of supportive psychotherapy and the approaches Jesus took. The directive approach is clear in such passages as "Go home to your people and report to them what great things the Lord has done for you, and how he had mercy on you" (Mark 5:19). Reassurance and encouragement are given as people hear a message of hope: "I am the way, and the truth, and the life" (John 14:6). Education is masterfully illustrated by, "He who has seen me has seen the Father" (John 14:9). "He that is without sin among you, let him be the first to throw a stone at her" (John 8:7) is a superb diversion tactic.

Supportive therapy therefore seems to be an important mode of psychological treatment, broadly compatible with Christ's own style of relating to people. Either as an adjunct or alternative to more reconstructive approaches, supportive techniques are clearly the treatment of choice in many situations.

Reference
Wolberg, L. R. *The technique of psychotherapy* (Vol. 1) (3rd ed.). New York: Grune & Stratton, 1977.

B.J. SHEPPERSON

Suppression. The conscious forcing of desires, thoughts, emotions, or impulses out of consciousness. This process of conscious inhibition differs from repression, which is an unconscious ego DEFENSE MECHANISM. It is possible, however, that material which the individual originally willfully removes from consciousness through suppression may eventually submit to unconscious repression, becoming unavailable to further conscious awareness, should it represent a sufficient threat to the ego. An example of suppression would be the person who is aware of feelings of strong hostility toward his boss, but chooses to force hostile thoughts and feelings from his awareness and focus on necessary businesslike cooperation.

R. LARKIN

Survivor Guilt. *See* POSTTRAUMATIC STRESS DISORDER.

Symbolic-Experiential Family Therapy. Carl Whitaker, the originator of symbolic-experiential family therapy, describes this approach as more of a philosophy than a theory. He also views family therapy as an art rather than a scientific procedure.

Symbolic-experiential family therapy requires two therapists who serve as guides in resolving the family's problems. Additional therapists may serve as consultants if a particular problem arises. For example, if the two main therapists are males and some family member feels that males are biased, a female therapist may serve as consultant for as many sessions as necessary. Or parents may object to their daughter dating a black male, and so a black therapist may be called as a consultant. The cotherapy model allows the family to learn from the therapist interaction and provides opportunity for the therapists to observe each other as well as the family process (Whitaker & Keith, 1981).

The focus of therapy is the here and now. The therapists teach the family that they can direct their own development in spite of the problems of the past. To facilitate this, family members need to respect generational differences and form healthy boundaries, learn how to participate in a family, and learn to individuate from the family. Each family member is encouraged to be flexible in his or her family roles. The therapists model this process by joining the family and separating from them throughout the sessions.

Whitaker is emphatic that all family members must participate in the sessions. If one family members does not show up, the session may be cancelled until the missing person

agrees to come. This procedure is explained in the initial setting up of an appointment. Not wanting to participate is a direct message about the ongoing family dynamics. Extended family members are invited to come as consultants to the family as often as they can. Participants may include former spouse, pastors, or others deeply concerned about the family. Just as a therapist can call in consultants, the family has the same right to assistance by calling family consultants (Napier & Whitaker, 1978).

The therapists attempt to increase interpersonal stress in the family in order to examine the relational dynamics and patterns of interaction. Such techniques as paradoxical intervention or "as if" situations are frequently utilized. For example, a suicidal mother may be asked, "How long do you think your family will mourn if you killed yourself?" The additional stress facilitates examining family members' thoughts and feelings during the session. Homework is not encouraged; in fact, family members are encouraged not to discuss the session between appointments. This is designed to keep the sessions emotionally charged.

Every family begins therapy with a family assessment. The stressors on the family are examined. Here the purpose is to become acquainted so that a relationship can develop. The early expression of empathy and concern for areas of family concern becomes the cornerstone for working together. Every family has its own distinct story, and the therapists need to know the story in order to assist them. During this assessment process interaction dynamics are observed and process hypotheses are formed so that the family dynamics can be examined and clarified during the course of therapy. If the family wishes to stop at some point, they are taking a risk and need to be encouraged to use their strengths. Keeping them in therapy would probably be for the therapists' needs and not for the family's. If they wish to return, they are welcome, and they may continue to develop at stages with intermittent breaks in therapy.

Whitaker is undoubtedly correct in not considering this a unique system of family therapy. It remains unresearched and largely untried by other than Whitaker and his associates.

References

Napier, A. Y., & Whitaker, C. A. *The family crucible.* New York: Harper & Row, 1978.
Whitaker, C. A., & Keith, V. Symbolic-experiential family therapy. In A. S. Gurman & D. P. Kniskern (Eds.),

Handbook of family therapy. New York: Brunner/Mazel, 1981.

Additional Readings
Whitaker, C. A. A family is a four dimensional relationship. In P. J. Guerin, Jr. (Ed.), *Family therapy.* New York: Gardner, 1976. (a)
Whitaker, C. A. Hindrance of theory in clinical work. In P. J. Guerin, Jr. (Ed.), *Family therapy.* New York: Gardner, 1976. (b)

T. M. Johnson

See Family Therapy: Overview.

Sympathy. A feeling of compassion for either a person or a group that is experiencing distress. It is also seen as a capacity for sharing the interests and concerns of another human being. Sympathy may arise even when there is no emotional attachment toward the person or group with whom one is sympathetic. Sympathy differs from Empathy in that the feelings of the sympathetic person remain essentially internal and knowledge of what caused the other person's feelings is not necessary. Sympathetic responses are feelings resulting from the observation of an emotion displayed by another. The sympathetic person becomes an imitator, although the sympathetic feeling need not be similar to the feeling of the other person.

Sympathy is regarded as a complex emotion because it presupposes that a person has the ability to perceive and understand the misfortunes of others as well as the ability to express this feeling to others. People vary widely in their sensitivity to others. The emotional climate of the home is considered the greatest influence in the development of sympathetic feelings. If the parents are considerate of other people's feelings and are able to express them in a positive way, the children are more likely to adopt similar attitudes.

J. H. Robertson

Symptom Prescription. *See* Paradoxical Intervention.

Syncope. The temporary loss of consciousness as a result of a failure in the supply of blood to the brain, as in fainting. It is sometimes a hysterical or conversion symptom, but may also occur in psychosomatic disorders when emotional stress interferes with the circulation of blood to the brain.

Syndrome. A group or pattern of symptoms that occur concurrently and are indicative of a recognizable disease or condition. This term is similar to, but less specific than, *disease* or *disorder.*

Systematic Desensitization. A therapeutic procedure based on the framework of learning theory. Wolpe (1958) is generally credited for its development. The specific goal of treatment is to substitute relaxation responses for debilitating anxiety or fear responses in specific triggering situations. The approach assumes that anxiety and fear symptoms are learned or conditioned and therefore can be deconditioned. Therefore, systematic desensitization, together with most Behavior Therapy, has developed directly from the application of laboratory research in the behavioral sciences.

The history of desensitization dates to a model experiment by Jones (1924). She eliminated a young boy's fear responses to small animals by gradually exposing the boy to the feared animal, in this case a rabbit. The child sat in a high chair eating while the animal was introduced into the room a considerable distance away. Over a series of trials the rabbit was moved closer and closer to the boy, each time with the boy in his chair eating. After many such sessions the boy was eventually able to hold the rabbit on his lap with no evidence of fear.

No one applied the results of Jones's research until Wolpe and his colleagues became interested in treating anxiety symptoms. From their work they formulated a four-step procedure that is generally still followed today.

First, the therapist obtains a detailed account from the client of those situations triggering anxiety. From this information the therapist constructs one or more anxiety hierarchies. This is a list of situations ranked by the client from least to most anxiety-arousing. An example of a hierarchy used to treat a phobia about leaving the house might include the following, beginning with the situation arousing the least anxiety and ending with the one arousing the most: 1) going to the door of the house; 2) opening the front door of the house; 3) going out on the porch; 4) going down the steps; 5) walking out to the front walk; 6) going to the edge of the property; 7) walking to the end of the block; 8) walking down the second block.

Second, the therapist trains the client to relax. Wolpe favored Jacobson's (1938) progressive relaxation procedure for this purpose. The therapist systematically directs the client alternately to contract, then relax, each individual muscle group in his body. Through this excercise the client becomes progressively more relaxed and comfortable.

Third, the desensitization process begins. While the client relaxes in the comfortable state, the therapist has him vividly imagine each scene in the hierarchy. The presentation is done over several trials, each trial beginning with the least anxiety-producing event and continuing through the hierarchy until the client first notices muscle tension and/or anxiety. At that time the client signals the therapist, usually by lifting an index finger. The therapist then helps the client restore the relaxed state by visualizing a peaceful scene. When the client again relaxes and signals the therapist, a second trial on the hierarchy starts. Trials continue until the person can visualize going through each step of the hierarchy without feeling anxiety or muscle tension. At that point the hierarchy is considered deconditioned, and supposedly anxiety has been eliminated as a response to those visualized situations.

During the fourth step the client acts out the hierarchy behaviorally. A person deconditioned on the above hierarchy will actually go out of the house and walk down the block. If successfully desensitized, the person will experience a decrease in anxiety.

Compared to more dynamically oriented therapies the desensitization procedure is relatively brief. However, its effectiveness has been well documented both experimentally and therapeutically. Its value lies in the treatment of phobias and anxiety evoked by specific situations. This value is also the major limitation, as most anxiety conditions are not so easily connected to specific situations.

Some therapists claim the approach is naïve, meaning that only symptoms are treated, while personality, the quality of the relationship, transference, and other important aspects of therapy are ignored. These are the major deficiencies in the approach. Some dynamically oriented theorists warn that symptom substitution might occur or that the disorder could become more severe. Neither has generally been found.

Finally, the approach in its extreme treats persons as mechanistic and reactive. No emphasis is placed on a relation to God as central to understanding human beings. However, this criticism is not aimed at the method as much as toward the philosophical reasoning underlying most behavioristic views of persons.

References
Jacobson, E. *Progressive relaxation* (2nd ed.). Chicago: University of Chicago Press, 1938.
Jones, M. C. The elimination of children's fears. *Journal of Experimental Psychology*, 1924, 7, 382–390.
Wolpe, J. *Psychotherapy by reciprocal inhibition*. Stanford, Calif.: Stanford University Press, 1958.

M. R. NELSON

Tt

Talion Law. An unconscious belief in punishment in kind, as in the saying, "An eye for an eye, and a tooth for a tooth." It carries with it the fear that all the injury one intends or actually does will be punished by an infliction of the same injury. This fear of retribution, called talion dread, is a significant neurotic symptom, and may be tied to real or imagined desires to injure another.

TAT. *See* THEMATIC APPERCEPTION TEST.

Telephone Therapy. Currently the primary use of the telephone in therapy is found in crisis "hot lines," which are available in most urban areas. These centers are staffed by paraprofessional workers with various levels of training; most are given very little initial instruction in crisis intervention and only a modicum of continuing education (Burns & Dixon, 1974). Due to the intrinsically stressing nature of this work and the lack of adequate preparatory or in-service training, turnover and burn-out rates for this type of telephone therapy are high (Greenstone & Leviton, 1979).

The telephone can be used in other therapy modalities besides crisis intervention. Relationship-based therapies of all varieties can be done over the phone. This type of ongoing telephone therapy generally is the result of a person having begun work with a therapist in one location and then relocating in another area where a compatible therapist is not available. Almost always some initial or intermittent contact on a face-to-face basis is required, both for therapeutic maintainence of rapport and the safe release of repressed, and often intense, emotions, which are difficult to express on a sustained basis over the telephone.

While working with a client in this sort of on-going therapy the therapist should be acutely aware of several variables. The first has to do with the physical setting of the client on the other end of the line. It is good, particularly for visually oriented therapists, to inquire regarding the client's physical milieu. One can ask the client to close his or her eyes while talking with you, imagine you with them in the room, and then describe in detail what they see. Subsequently it behooves the therapist to place himself in that physical niche using whatever imagery is at his command. This is necessary if one is striving to establish adequate levels of identification and empathy with the client.

The second variable requiring the therapist's awareness pertains to the use of language. In the absence of kinesthetic or visual stimuli one is required to extract every last ounce of meaning from the auditory information available. One should therefore endeavor to pace with or match the client's use of language. This use of NEUROLINGUISTIC PROGRAMMING techniques is critical for the maintenance of rapport and empathy.

The final awareness needed by a telephone therapist pertains to the use of face-to-face "booster" sessions of intense therapeutic work as needed. If the therapist feels out of touch or puzzled with the course of treatment, he or she should ask that the client use an audiovisual telephone apparatus (particularly as this tool becomes more available) or request a face-to-face interview. The need for such adjunctive methods will obviously depend on the client, the therapist, and the quality and nature of their relationship.

References

Burns, J. L., & Dixon, M. C. Crisis theory, active learning and the training of telephone crisis volunteers. *Journal of Community Psychology*, 1974, *2*, 120–125.

Greenstone, J. L., & Leviton, S. C. *The crisis intervener's handbook* (Vol. 2). Dallas: Crisis Management Workshops, 1979.

V. L. Shepperson

Television Viewing, Effects of. Forty years ago television was virtually unknown. Today it is a resident in 98% of homes in the United States and is rapidly spreading throughout the world. It is estimated that in a typical year over 700 commercial stations in the United States broadcast 4.7 million hours of programming. The typical TV is on over six hours per day. The average American who lives to age 75 may spend the equivalent of 57 working years watching television. Researchers have found that actual viewing time increases during preschool years, dips slightly upon entrance to school, increases steadily from age 8 to early adolescence, and then levels off in later teen years. This same pattern has been found in Europe, Canada, and Australia. The typical American child will spend about 15,000 hours watching television between the ages of 5 and 18, which is approximately 30% more time than is spent in school.

In light of the pervasive and captivating character of television, it is important to ask what people are viewing and what effects the medium and content of television have upon people.

The Nature of Television Programming. In order to understand the program content of television, it must be understood that most television is a commercial enterprise in the United States. American television continues to be dominated by three major networks (CBS, ABC, NBC), although the rapid rise of cable television during the 1970s has stimulated the increase of competitive, specialized alternative cable networks. The nature of television programming is that the networks provide those programs that will draw the most viewers so that revenues from advertisers can be maximized. Program content is determined primarily on the basis of the Nielsen ratings. That is, the percentage of homes with televisions that are tuned to a program and how a program is faring in comparison with other programs being shown at the same time will determine the life of a program. Network executives attempt to assess viewer desires and schedule those programs that will be highly competitive, thus highly lucrative. The networks spend over a billion dollars per year just for prime-time programming. In 1980 the networks and stations received revenues of almost 9 billion dollars and profits through advertising of 1.6 billion dollars.

The most profitable programs are those shown during prime time and for children. Because children and adults alike are most apt to view programs that attract and keep their attention, and therefore give advertisers a chance to gain access, the kind of programs which are developed tend to be those with action, controversy, simplicity, and standardization. The focus is on entertainment rather than education because 80% of viewers watch television mainly for purposes of relaxation, not instruction. Over 20 million (40% of) regular viewers walked away from their sets recently during a prime-time presidential press conference.

As a result of the profit-making foundation of television, children are exposed to between 400,000 and 675,000 commercials by the time they reach 18. In addition they will watch as many as 20,000 violent TV deaths, or roughly one per hour, as part of the high action, attention-grabbing program formula.

Major Research Findings. What are the effects of watching television in general? Of exposure to commercials, violence, and other types of material? These questions have stimulated approximately 3,000 predominantly English-language publications since 1955. Over 60% of the publications have appeared since 1975.

Television potentially has both negative and positive effects. However, most of the research that has been done to date has focused on the possible harmful effects of TV on children and youth. These effects may be grouped into three categories: interpersonal relationships, values and thought processes, and health.

Effect on relationship. Researchers have found that television owners report spending up to 15% more time watching TV than on conversation and other social activities. Further, it was discovered that 60% of families altered their sleeping patterns and 55% changed their mealtimes when television was introduced into their homes. Among activities found to decrease in a study done in Europe and the United States were sleep, conversation, household care, a variety of leisure activities, and out-of-home social gatherings. It has been estimated that 78% of Americans with children use the TV, at least occasionally, as an electronic babysitter. The pattern seems to be one which decreases the amount of social interaction both inside and outside the home.

The implications of such a pattern are significant. With regard to children the lessening of interaction between parents and between parents and children may result in deficits of the social skills and intimacy modeling necessary for them to develop healthy peer relations. Also, their own future marital and parental functioning may be influenced. Television may draw people away from the kind of close interaction necessary to establish and maintain intimacy. Although no causal relationships have been confirmed, one other possible side effect is the alienation of minimally interactive marital partners and the encouragement of divorces in response.

Related to the alienating effects is the tendency of TV programs to portray quick-fix solutions to complicated problems. Television tends to present an oversimplified, action-oriented world in which little time is given to dialogue and thoughtful problem solving. As children and youth view TV relationships and solutions, they are given an orientation that is incompatible with the realities of everyday life. This may promote a tendency to give up efforts to solve interpersonal problems through discourse and negotiation in exchange for solutions of violence or escape.

A considerable number of studies have examined the relationship between viewing TV violence and subsequent antisocial and aggressive behavior. Up to 80% of prime-time shows include beatings, shootings, or stabbings at the rate of five violent acts per hour. Saturday cartoons are worse. They average as many as 25 violent incidents per hour. Most of the research has been conducted in the United States, and it is possible that there may be variations from culture to culture. Three major theories have been developed in relation to this issue: social learning theory, instigation theory, and the catharsis hypothesis.

Social learning theory hypothesizes that watching televised violence increases subsequent aggression as a function of social modeling and vicarious consequences. Instigation theories suggest that viewing violence stimulates generalized emotional arousal, which in turn may instigate actual aggression. The catharsis hypothesis predicts that viewing violence will decrease actual aggression by diverting and draining aggressive impulses through the visualized fantasy. With the exception of a handful of studies, the catharsis theory has not been supported. In spite of some confusion that resulted from the politically influenced report of the U.S. surgeon general in 1972, the findings of both correlational and experimental studies are highly consistent. There is a definite relationship between viewing televised violence and aggressive behavior. The relationship is mediated by a variety of factors such as age, sex, socioeconomic status, aggressive personality orientation, and other social-familial variables. Nevertheless, it is clear that televised violence strongly promotes antisocial behavior in a small percentage of children and has a small but significant effect on a large proportion.

There is some evidence that viewing violence may also lead to a kind of desensitization whereby those who watch repeated acts of violence become less concerned about victims of violence and suffering in real life. They may be less likely to provide assistance to such victims in emergency situations. Research indicates that the alpha waves of subjects viewing exciting shows are like those of people quietly sitting in the dark, suggesting that TV may cause people to be inattentive and detached.

Effects on values and thought processes. During the 1970s TV programming began to air more explicit sexual material with greater frequency. Incidents of all types of sexual behavior shown, with the exception of displaying actual physical intercourse, have increased, though most television sex is still talk and innuendo. To date there have not been any studies on how children are affected. Such research is significantly limited by moral and ethical concerns, as it should be. Adolescents between 12 and 16 years old have been found to have a high degree of comprehension of sexual innuendos aired on prime-time programs.

Apart from explicit sexuality it is conceivable that TV's portrayal of relationships affects viewer values in several ways. It is likely that relationships are seen as more hedonistic and romantic than they actually are by those who watch TV a great deal. Furthermore, there is considerable concern that TV promotes sex role and racial stereotyping through the frequency and ways in which minority people and women are presented.

Several analyses of sex role portrayals have revealed that there are far more males than females presented; that males are usually employed in prestigious positions, while women are given nonwork roles focusing on romance and family; and that females on children's programs are seen as generally passive, punished for high levels of effort. Youth is emphasized as more important in women than men. The range of occupational options open to women on TV is much more restricted than for men. In the 1977 U.S. Commission on Civil Rights report almost 90% of TV characters were found to be white. With regard to minority representation, nonblack minorities are typically shown unfavorably, often as villains and victims of violence. Blacks are the most frequently shown minority people. They are more likely to be cast in minor roles, and although they are often placed in positive roles as good people, they are seldom found in leadership positions without a white coleader.

Television has been shown to affect values and thinking in other ways. In studies assessing the impact of television on people with no prior television exposure, TV has been shown to be associated with the deterioration of reading skills and verbal fluency. Commercial viewing for preadolescent boys has been found to be related to field dependence and impulsivity. Other studies show some evidence of negative effects of TV viewing on school grades. Some have suggested that the fast pace, loud noise, and changing images of TV programs lead to lessened attention span and greater difficulty in the traditional learning format of the typical school classroom, while others have argued that TV disrupts the imaginative and reflective thinking of children. Current research does not allow a definitive position on these speculations.

The type and frequency of programming may also affect moral and religious values of viewers. By and large television programs do not reflect traditional religious and moral values, unless these are being presented as out of date and old-fashioned. The spiritual dimension of life is essentially ignored, with the exception of occasional specials and early Sunday morning programming. The morality that is presented on prime-time programs is largely relativistic morality, except for the broad themes that such things as murder and cruelty are wrong. Nevertheless, the presentation of various acts of violence and immorality, while not explicitly condoned, tends to glamorize such behavior. The absence of positive religious programming promotes a view in which religion is irrelevant.

The heavy emphasis on advertising in commercial television is likely to lead to a materialistic or consumption-oriented value system. Indeed, the way in which products are presented even for children, encourages the development of a self-concept that is based on what one has or how one looks in comparison to others. Some research shows that children exposed to commercials are more likely to choose their friends on the basis of advertised toys that their friends possess, or to choose playing with an advertised toy over playing with friends. Television

advertising has been shown to promote observable parent-child conflicts and negativistic attitudes toward parents.

Research on the relationship between television viewing and emotions indicates that heavy prime-time viewers see the world as more dangerous than lighter viewers. They are less likely to trust people in general and more likely to overestimate their own chances of being the victims of violence. This is not surprising given the fact that TV criminals are 100 times more likely to murder someone than real-life criminals.

Effects on health. The last concern of researchers has to do with the possible effects of TV advertising on health. The primary focus has been on the promotion of poor nutritional habits through the heavy advertising of between-meal snacks that are loaded with sugar. Research indicates that children under 8 appear not to distinguish between commercials and programs, and that children under 7 are unable to understand the intention of TV advertisements. On the other hand, by age 11 most regular TV viewers have become almost cynical about commercials; they watch them less and differentiate them from programs. Under intense industry pressure the Federal Trade Commission in 1981 declined a regulatory role in relation to children's advertising.

Positive effects. In recent years attention has begun to shift to the positive effects of television and to equipping children with critical viewing skills as a means of defending themselves from the negative influences of TV. Among the possible positive effects of TV viewing that have some research support are early intellectual growth and vocabulary expansion; exposure to varied people, roles, and nonimmediate experiences (documentaries and reports from other parts of the world); relaxation; the modeling effects of prosocial behaviors displayed on TV; and the provision of a common base of information and understanding for the diverse people of American society.

Additional Readings

Bandura, A. What TV violence can do to your child. In O. N. Larsen (Ed.), *Violence and the Mass Media.* New York: Harper & Row, 1968.

Comstock, G., Chaffee, S., Katzman, N., McCombs, M., & Roberts, D. *Television and human behavior.* Columbia University Press, 1978.

Feshbach, S., & Singer, R. D. *Television and aggression: An experimental field study.* San Francisco: Jossey-Bass, 1971.

Liebert, R. M., Sprafkin, J. N., & Davidson, E. S. *The early window* (2nd ed.). New York: Pergamon, 1982.

Murray, J. P. *Television and youth.* Boys Town, Neb.: Boys Town Center for the Study of Youth Development, 1980.

Surgeon General's Scientific Advisory Committee on Television and Social Behavior. *Television and growing up: The impact of televised violence.* Washington, D.C.: United States Government Printing Office, 1972.

Tannenbaum, P. H., & Zillmann, D. Emotional arousal in the facilitation of aggression through communication. In L. Berkowitz (Ed.), *Advances in experimental social psychology* (Vol. 8). New York: Academic Press, 1975.

United States Federal Communications Commission. *Television programming for children: A report of the Children's Television Task Force* (Vol. 1). Washington, D.C.: Federal Communications Commission, Children's Television Task Force, 1979.

C. W. ELLISON

Temperament. Theorists in the area of personality development have generally espoused one of two contrasting views about the nature of human development. Psychoanalytic theorists such as Freud and Erikson have viewed personality development as a series of ordered, biologically determined stages. At each stage the individual must resolve a developmental crisis. If the individual fails to do so, personality development is stifled. Other researchers, such as Bandura and Mischel, have described personality development as a continuous process of interaction with the environment. According to these theorists the environment slowly and methodically acts to mold and shape individual personality.

While both viewpoints contain some truth, research over the past two decades indicates that there is at least one more factor affecting personality development: temperament. Psychologists and psychiatrists interested in temperament point out that children are not merely passive recipients of their environment. Rather, children actively mold and shape their environment at the same time their environment is molding and shaping them. To truly understand personality development, according to these researchers, we need to understand how a child *transacts* with his environment. Allport has defined temperament as "the characteristic phenomena of an individual's nature, including his susceptibility to emotional stimulation, his customary strength and speed of response, the quality of his prevailing mood, and all the peculiarities of fluctuation and intensity of mood, these being regarded as dependent on constitutional make-up, and therefore largely hereditary in origin" (1961, p. 34).

Allport's definition suggests four temperaments: emotionality, activity, sociability, and impulsivity. These have been integrated into a theory of temperament by Plomin and several of his colleagues (Buss & Plomin, 1975; Horn, Plomin, & Rosenman, 1976; Rowe & Plomin, 1977). Plomin has conducted considerable re-

search in an effort to prove that these temperaments 1) are present in each individual from infancy to adulthood; 2) are largely genetically transmitted, so that children will inherit some of the temperamental characteristics of each parent; and 3) are fairly stable throughout an individual's life span, meaning that active children should tend to become active adults and shy children should tend to become shy adults.

Research by Plonin and others seems to indicate that activity level is moderately stable throughout an individual's life span, and family and twin studies suggest that activity level is largely inherited from parents. Research on sociability indicates that extraversion in general and sociability toward strangers in particular seem to match the characteristics of a temperament as prescribed by Allport. Evidence on the stability and heritability of emotionality and impulsivity is somewhat less favorable to Plomin's theory, though Zuckerman, Buchsbaum, and Murphy (1980) have demonstrated that sensation seeking is a stable personality trait that appears to be inherited from one's parents. Sensation seeking as defined by Zuckerman et al. includes many of the elements of Plomin's hypothesized impulsivity temperament.

While Plomin's research has concentrated on the inheritance of temperaments and on the stability of temperament throughout an individual's life span, a group of five researchers in New York has been more interested in investigating how temperament influences a child's interactions with her environment and how these interactions shape personality development as the child grows and matures. From in-depth observation of a relatively small number of children and detailed interviews with their parents these investigators have identified nine temperaments: activity level, rhythmicity, approach-withdrawal, adaptability, intensity of reaction, threshold of responsiveness, quality of mood, distractability, and attention span and persistence (Thomas, Chess, Birch, Hertzig, & Korn, 1963). Further analysis of the data suggested that most children could be classified into one of three temperamental types. The easy child tends to display a positive mood, low intensity responses, and an approach orientation toward novel stimuli. This child generally adapts readily to new situations and tends to follow regular daily schedules. In contrast, the difficult child's temperamental pattern is almost the antithesis of the easy child's. The difficult child tends to display a negative mood, high intensity responses, a withdrawal orientation toward novel stimuli, and so on. Finally, the slow-to-warm-up child is characterized by a somewhat negative mood and a withdrawal orientation similar to the difficult child's, but a low activity level and relatively low intensity reactions similar to the easy child's.

Thomas and his colleagues have studied these temperaments and temperamental types in an effort to explain why children, even children reared in the same family, can develop radically different personalities in response to fairly similar environments. The final results of this study have yet to be published. The results may shed light on the complex interactions between temperament and environment, and further our understanding of important psychological stages in the child's life.

References
Allport, G. W. *Pattern and growth in personality.* New York: Holt, Rinehart, & Winston, 1961.
Buss, A. H., & Plomin, R. *A temperament theory of personality.* New York: Wiley, 1975.
Horn, J. M., Plomin, R., & Rosenman, R. Heritability of personality traits in adult male twins. *Behavior Genetics,* 1976, *6*, 17–30.
Rowe, D. C., & Plomin, R. Temperament in early childhood. *Journal of Personality Assessment,* 1977, *41*, 150–156.
Thomas, A., Chess, S., Birch, H. G., Hertzig, M., & Korn, S. *Behavioral individuality in early childhood.* New York: New York University Press, 1963.
Zuckerman, M., Buchsbaum, M. S., & Murphy, D. L. Sensation-seeking and its biological correlates. *Psychological Bulletin,* 1980, *88*, 187–214.

J. J. McHenry

See Personality; Heredity and Environment in Human Development.

Temper Tantrum. An excessive and inappropriate emotional outburst, such behavior can be seen throughout the life span but is most common during the preschool and early school years. In its most extreme form the behavior can be quite manipulative and coercive in that it demands a response. The important decision is whether or not to intervene, and if so, exactly how.

In its milder form the temper tantrum can be ignored, which will lead to what behaviorists call extinction. Competing and/or incompatible behaviors should be reinforced so that a large alternative behavioral repertoire is available. Positive reinforcement for good behavior is far more effective in the long run than punishment for inappropriate behavior. Attention by well-meaning adults can serve to reinforce and maintain such emotional outbursts.

With children temper tantrums usually follow the consequences of breaking rules. All rules should be clearly explained in advance. The reasons behind the rules and the consequences of breaking them should be fully clarified. Temper tantrums at times appear to be ways of testing the limits.

If extinction and reinforcing incompatible or competing behaviors prove unsatisfactory, alternative forms of discipline should be used. Assertive, direct commands may prove to be effective (Canter & Canter, 1976), as may a timeout procedure (Patterson, 1971). Threats or verbal attacks on the child should be avoided. The parent or teacher should also consider that the inappropriate behavior may be modeled on a regular basis for the child by peers or adults.

If the temper tantrums are frequent, the possibility of a problem in some aspect of the home or school situation should be considered. The rules may be vague or too difficult; the commands may not be direct or sufficiently clear; the child may not be getting enough attention for appropriate behavior; the child may be sick or tired; or the parents may be under significant stress. Spanking as an intervention strategy is recommended by some as a last resort, given careful guidelines (Narramore, 1979).

As with all behavior or emotional disorders, the clinician must be sensitive to the total picture. The personalities of the teachers and parents, the school or home environment, the needs and abilities of the child, and the community environment may all influence a given incident. Whatever intervention is selected, one must be careful to implement it with sensitivity.

References
Canter, L, & Canter, M. *Assertive discipline: A take charge approach for today's educator.* Seal Beach, Calif.: Canter & Associates, 1976.
Narramore, B. *Parenting with love and limits.* Grand Rapids: Zondervan, 1979.
Patterson, G. R. *Families.* Champaign, Ill.: Research Press, 1971.

R. E. Butman

Tension. Defined technically as a reaction or force produced by muscular contraction, tension also refers to a particular emotional state very similar to anxiety—with feelings of tightness or tautness, apprehension, increased alertness, inability to relax, and restlessness—or to mental strain.

There are many possible causes of tension. It may be due to some types of medical or organic disease (Jacobson, 1970), or to such biological factors as insufficient sleep, inadequate nutrition, and effects of drugs or medications. However, tension is more commonly the result of psychological and religious stress or distress (Collins, 1977). Such stress may include personal or family conflicts, sexual incompatibility, divorce and separation, business or academic pressures, life changes, boredom, traumatic experiences, religious guilt due to sin, or even false guilt. More fundamentally tension is often due to maladaptive ways of thinking (e.g., expecting perfection from oneself and others, dwelling only on the negative, jumping to premature and often wrong conclusions, catastrophizing or magnifying the problem). Such thinking can lead to maladaptive behaviors (e.g., overworking, avoiding work), which in turn may cause more tension.

Intense prolonged states of tension can have deleterious effects, similar to those produced by excessive stress or distress. Such effects may include states of fatigue, exhaustion, and insomnia; various types of nervousness and emotional maladjustment, particularly anxiety states; addiction to alcohol or drugs; increased susceptibility to high blood pressure, hardening of the arteries, heart attack, and stroke; headaches, ulcers, and a number of other physical disorders; and spiritual problems such as guilt, loss of faith, spiritual dryness, and bitterness. Tension can therefore produce negative physical, psychological, and spiritual effects. However, it can also draw our attention to significant problems in our lives that may have caused the tension in the first place, and motivate us to deal with such problems or seek help for them. Tension is a danger signal that may lead to further growth and blessing if we respond appropriately.

There are a number of ways of overcoming excessive or prolonged tension. Spiritually the use of prayer with thanksgiving (Phil. 4:6–7) and meditation on God's Word or Christian meditation (see Ray, 1977) are powerful means. Fellowship with a group of believers involving intimate and open sharing, confession, and prayer is also important (cf. James 5:16). Psychologically a number of tension-reducing strategies aimed toward relaxation are available, including progressive relaxation (the alternate tensing and relaxing of different muscle groups), passive meditation, pleasant imagery, self-hypnosis, and autosuggestion (see Woolfolk & Richardson, 1978). Listening to soothing or uplifting music can also be helpful. Other psychological methods for coping with tension include stress-inoculation strategies (Meichenbaum, 1977), rational self-talk and other forms of cognitive restructuring, biofeedback, time management skills (including time

for rest, recreation, and vacation), and realistic goal setting (see Collins, 1977; Woolfolk & Richardson, 1978). From a Christian perspective cognitive restructuring or changing one's maladaptive thinking will require learning to think more biblically and truthfully (Phil. 4:8), using the Scriptures as the foundation (see Backus & Chapian, 1980). The use of passive meditation and self-hypnosis for relaxation has been questioned by Collins (1977) as perhaps being of dubious value, particularly for Christians. He points out that such techniques for escaping from stress or tension may dull our thinking, open our minds to harmful influences, desensitize the conscience, and promise happiness without dealing with the issue of sin.

Physically tension can be reduced by regular exercise, proper nutrition, and sufficient sleep. A physician should be consulted if organic or medical disease is suspected. Where necessary, medication can aid in reducing tension states. A professional counselor or psychotherapist may also be needed if tension continues to be experienced over a period of time with obvious deleterious effects.

References

Backus, W., & Chapian, M. *Telling yourself the truth.* Minneapolis: Bethany Fellowship, 1980.
Collins, G. R. *You can profit from stress.* Santa Ana, Calif.: Vision House, 1977.
Jacobson, E. *Modern treatment of tense patients.* Springfield, Ill.: Thomas, 1970.
Meichenbaum, D. *Cognitive-behavior modification: An integrative approach.* New York: Plenum, 1977.
Ray, D. *The art of Christian meditation.* Wheaton, Ill.: Tyndale House, 1977.
Woolfolk, R., & Richardson, F. *Stress, sanity, and survival.* New York: Monarch, 1978.

S. Y. Tan

See Relaxation Training.

Terman, Lewis Madison (1877–1956). American psychologist best known for his work in intelligence testing. Born in Indiana, he grew up on a farm and entered Central Normal College in Danville in 1892. By the age of 21 he had three degrees from that institution. He became a high school principal, but wanted to teach psychology and needed a degree from a recognized school. He entered Indiana University in 1901 and earned his A.B. and M.A. degrees within two years. He completed his Ph.D. at Clark University in 1905 in spite of ill health.

Because of a pulmonary hemorrhage he was advised to move to a warm climate. He served as principal of a high school in San Bernardino, California, for one year before beginning to teach at Los Angeles State Normal School. In 1910 he moved to Stanford University, where he remained until he retired in 1942. He remained active in research until his death.

Next to Binet, Terman's name is most frequently associated with the testing movement. Terman spent more time on the Binet test and became more of a specialist on it than Binet himself. Others had translated Binet's test, but Terman extensively revised it and standardized it on American children. Although he called it the Stanford Revision of the Binet-Simon Scale of Intelligence, it was essentially a brand-new scale that bore only superficial resemblance to Binet's test. The scale, standardization information, and directions for administration were published in his *Measurement of Intelligence* (1916), which immediately became the standard work on intelligence testing. Terman multiplied Stern's mental quotient by 100 to remove the decimal point and renamed it the intelligence quotient, or IQ. The Stanford-Binet was revised in 1937, 1960, and 1972, and is widely used today.

Recognizing the need to identify intellectually gifted children, Terman began a comprehensive, long-term study of them in 1921. The subjects were 1,528 California children with IQs bove 140. Initial results showed that these children were alert, eager, social, interested, and interesting. He followed them until his death 35 years later and found that they were healthier and more stable than average and kept their high ability into adulthood. These findings were reported in *Genetic Studies of Genius* (5 vols., 1926–1959). Terman was general editor of the series and principal author of all except one volume. He also attempted to estimate the IQs of 300 major historical figures, many of whom compared as children with those in his study.

R. L. KOTESKEY

See INTELLECTUAL ASSESSMENT.

T-Group. *See* SENSITIVITY TRAINING GROUP.

Thematic Apperception Test (TAT). A projective test used as a means to uncover and understand both the conscious and unconscious processes of an individual. The test was developed in 1934 by Henry A. Murray. The third revision, published in 1943, is widely used today for diagnostic purposes in PERSONALITY ASSESSMENT and treatment planning.

The Thematic Apperception Test may be administered to any person over the age of 4. The test consists of 31 cards, 30 of which have a black-and-white picture. The remaining card is totally blank. Usually only between 10 and 20 cards are administered, depending on the sex and age of the individual being tested and the purposes for which the test is given. During administration the individual is shown one picture at a time and is asked to construct a story that tells what is presently happening, what led up to the event, what the people are thinking and feeling, and what will occur in the future. Hence the name "thematic," referring to the themes elicited, and "apperceptive" for the perceptual-interpretive processes involved in constructing a story to the picture.

The underlying rationale for the test is that the spontaneous stories given in response to these pictures, many of which depict ambiguous human situations, require the individual to draw on his past experiences and current needs and sentiments. The aim of the test is to confront the subject with a variety of pictured situations that will elicit indications about which of these situations are personally important or associated with conflict. Both conscious and unconscious processes are assumed to be influential in the individual's imaginative creations and affect both the content and manner in which the story is told.

The Thematic Apperception Test is administered and interpreted by a psychologist who is familiar with the test materials, procedures, and norms. Findings from the interpretation are given after a careful synthesis and integration of all the test material and are reported as inferential statements. Frequently the Thematic Apperception Test is adminstered with other psychological tests, particularly the projective Rorschach test. These two projective measures together provide the professional with complementary and relatively comprehensive data concerning the individual's personality functioning.

W. W. AUSTIN

Theme-Centered Interactional Groups. Model of group work that has as its most essential characteristic the setting of an explicit theme or focus for the group interaction. This theme is announced by the group leader at the beginning of each session. The goal is then to optimize, not maximize, the degree of theme-centeredness, bringing it into balance with the interactional and less task-centered aspects of the group experience. Because of this balancing of content and process, it has been suggested that the model is useful not just in group psychotherapy but also in group processes as diverse as the classroom, committee or other task group, or growth group. Another reason for its usefulness in such different types of groups is that it is primarily a model of group process and only secondarily a set of techniques for group leadership.

The theme-centered interactional approach was developed by Ruth Cohn, a European psychoanalyst and group psychotherapist. Trained at the Zurich Psychoanalytic Institute, she emigrated to the United States in 1941. It was in the context of her group supervision of psychotherapists that she developed the theme-centered approach. In fact, for a number of years the approach was primarily seen as a model of supervision of therapists. A common theme would be countertransference, and Cohn would seek to help therapists better understand the ways in which it operated both by discussing the concept theoretically and by examining its operation in the present experience of the group members. Later she became interested in applying the model to other types of groups, and its ties with psychotherapy supervision came to be a thing of the past.

Although Cohn did not see her model as strictly a psychoanalytic one, she did bring to it a number of psychoanalytic concepts and values. The most important of these is the precedence given in psychoanalysis to resistance. She stressed that resistances against the theme should always be given precedence over anything else, particularly over a rigid pursuit of the theme. Thus any personal or collective distractions should be responded to: not analyzed, but rather expressed. This also reflects the psychoanalytic principle of free association in that group members are encouraged to express whatever thoughts they have, without censoring or regard for slavish focus on the theme.

The approach also reflects the influence of the sensitivity group movement. While Cohn adopted some of the techniques of this tradition, she rejected its anti-intellectual bias. She argued that sensitivity is not enough. By this she meant that people not only need to sense and come to self-awareness, but they also need to think. As a result of this, theme-centered interactional groups retain something of the flavor of sensitivity groups but additionally encourage thinking and rational discussion.

The most important of the philosophical concepts underlying the theme-centered approach are the related concepts of autonomy and interdependence. Cohn argued that sensitivity groups overemphasized autonomy at the expense of interdependence. Consequently the theme-centered approach elevates these two concepts to positions of equal emphasis, making it a task of the group leader to attempt a balance between the autonomy of group members and their interdependence. Other dimensions of group experience that the approach also sees as important to be kept in balance are emotional expression versus cognitive expression, focus on content versus process, focus on intrapsychic experience versus interpersonal experience, and focus on the past versus the present.

Because there has been very little research done on the theme-centered interactional approach, it is difficult to speak with any confidence about its effectiveness. One study (Sheehan, 1977) demonstrated significant positive changes in both self-esteem and self-evaluation during theme-centered growth groups. However, much more research is necessary.

Although the model seems to have important implications for GROUP PSYCHOTHERAPY, its greatest application seems to be as an approach to personal and professional growth. In 1966 Cohn founded her first training institute in the method and called it the Workshop Institute for Living-Learning. Since then branches have been established in a number of cities and countries in Europe and North America. These institutes offer groups for professionals as well as the general public and also provide consultation to community groups interested in the method.

Reference

Sheehan, M. C. The effects of theme-centered growth groups on the self-concept, self-esteem, and interpersonal openness of adults (Doctoral dissertation, Columbia University Teachers College, 1977). *Dissertation Abstracts International*, 1978, *38*, 5656-b. (University Microfilms No. 78-04,468)

Additional Readings

Shafer, J. B. P., & Galinsky, M. D. *Models of group therapy and sensitivity training.* Englewood Cliffs, N.J.: Prentice-Hall, 1974.

Cohn, R. C. Style and spirit of the theme-centered interactional method. In C. J. Sager & H. S. Kaplan (Eds.), *Progress in group and family therapy.* New York: Brunner/Mazel, 1972.

D. G. BENNER

Therapeutic Community. A constant concern throughout history has been the development of effective and responsible ways of relating to members of our society who, for whatever reason, deviate from the norms. We have passed through many reforms as definitions of deviance and society's response to it have evolved. Therapeutic community stands as one example of a more humanitarian approach to mental illness that began in the late nineteenth century and gained momentum in the twentieth century.

Therapeutic community involves the self-conscious creation of a social organization within which the total resources of both patients and staff, as well as the total environment, will be used to their optimum potential to further treatment. The total organization is seen as a vital force in determining therapeutic outcome. Patients are involved in leadership and treatment. All relationships, whether patient-staff, patient-patient, or staff-staff, are seen as potentially therapeutic and examined to maximize this potential. The emotional climate and the physical environment are created to facilitate treatment.

Origins and Development. The therapeutic community approach evolved in the historical context of psychiatry's pursuit of more humanitarian treatment of those suffering from mental illness. The humanitarian approach looked on mental illness as sickness and the sufferers as persons in need of care, comfort, and cleanliness in their surroundings. Other important influences were interpersonal psychology and psychiatry, milieu therapy, group therapeutic techniques, social psychiatry, and administrative therapy (Almond, 1974).

During the 1940s much research and analysis brought into perspective the psychiatric hospital as a small society, the dynamics of which could either facilitate or inhibit treatment. It was recognized that the institution was a hybrid form of society that disregarded family needs; the benefits and needs of relationships between the opposite sex and various age groups were ignored. Instead it created subcultures in which the patient insulated himself from staff and treatment personnel, who in turn insulated themselves from the controlling bureaucracy. These decision makers were removed from the patient to such an extent as to be almost unaware of his needs.

Social and administrative therapies focused on the organizational, administrative, and sociocultural processes in terms of their role in treatment. Sullivan's emphasis on communication, the role of culture, the significance of the intensity and meaning of behavior, the role of the environment in determining the functional use of behavior, the definition of the role of the psychiatrist as a participant-observer, and the training of staff in interpersonal skills contributed to this new approach to mental illness (Sullivan, 1953, 1956).

Milieu therapy, with its focus on the physical environment and social structure, developed at the same time as the therapeutic community approach. It essentially involved paying attention to and using the environment of the patient toward therapeutic goals. This concept was eventually expanded to include the role of all persons relating to the patient as significant in the treatment process.

Prior to 1935 psychopathology was usually understood in terms of intrapsychic conflict, even though social adjustment was the criterion most often used for measuring improvement. A new interest in the social relationships of patients led to the concept of group treatment techniques. Thus, the treatment of individuals through the medium of the group developed and made a significant contribution to the therapeutic community approach.

The merging of psychiatric and sociological concepts of mental illness in social psychiatry led to a serious study of potentialities for treatment inherent within community relationships. This included staff-patient, patient-patient, and patient-administrator relationships. Interpersonal relations and environmental influences were considered important factors in etiology, diagnosis, and treatment (Greenblatt, York, & Brown, 1955; Freeman, 1965).

The term *administrative therapy* was used by some to describe an approach developed at this time that emphasized open doors, increased liberty and self-determination, a meaningful work program with appropriate incentives, and useful and healthy use of leisure time (Clark, 1964; Taylor, 1958). Those using this term distinguish between administrative therapy and therapeutic community. The lines of separation between the approaches are, however, sketchy.

From this brief historical sketch it can be seen how influential the various therapeutic developments of the day were in the evolution of the therapeutic community concept of treatment. This was a period of major advance in the treatment of mental illness, and therapeutic community was one dimension of that development.

Almond (1974) identifies the beginnings of therapeutic community in the work of Maxwell Jones at Belmont Hospital in England during the years 1947–1959. However, while Jones is definitely the individual most clearly identified with the development of therapeutic community, others were also involved in similar activities.

Bion and Rickman (Taylor, 1958) introduced and developed new principles of treatment at the Northfield Military Hospital Training Wing in 1943 to bring unruly soldiers under control. They used group methods and a reduction of the traditional authoritarian structure to create a feeling of belonging and a social environment. They felt this gave the men a sense of responsibility and enabled them to deal with their own problems and antisocial behavior. In 1946 Bion's methods were further developed in the second Northfield experiment. An open-door policy, more parole, improved nurse-patient relationships, gainful employment, and a general focus on interpersonal relationships was also being introduced in several other hospitals at the same time. As early as 1938 Bierer introduced therapeutic social clubs at Runwell Mental Hospital for inpatients.

Maxwell Jones served at the Effort Syndrome Unit, Mill Hill, from 1939 to 1945. Several principles developed in this unit were later refined and modified to form the therapeutic community model. The authoritarian hierarchy was broken to permit free communications among all staff and patients, nurses were actively involved in treatment, and patients were educated concerning their symptomatology. Additionally, sociodrama and role playing as therapeutic techniques were practiced, treatment was defined as all-pervasive in the patient's total experience, and problem solving through group discussion rather than appeal to authority was introduced. Many of these concepts were poorly developed and very much in an experimental stage.

From 1945 to 1947 Jones developed the Ex-Prisoner-of-War Unit, Dartford, Kent. Repatriated prisoners of war were the patients. The experimental nature of this unit allowed for the development of the principles introduced at Mill Hill, and an extensive work therapy program was an added feature. The use of psychodrama and group therapy was greatly developed. From 1947 to 1959 Jones was associated with the Neurosis Unit, Belmont Hospital. During these years the concept of therapeutic community matured and was articulated and refined through scholarly interaction. From 1959 to 1962 Jones served in several capacities in the United States, which served to make his work more widely known. He returned to Scotland in 1963, and there developed a therapeutic community at Melrose (Dingleton Hospital) that embodied the principles of therapeutic community.

Sullivan's early emphasis on the part played by the hospital environment and the role of nurses is a precursor to the use of the therapeutic community model in the United States and Canada. One of the best-known therapeutic community programs in the United States was the Yale–New Haven Community Hospital, which opened in January, 1960. Under the medical direction of Thomas Detre this unit, known as Tompkins I, developed clearly as a therapeutic community. The consultation work carried on by Jones in North America during the 1960s and 1970s also assisted in the adoption of the principles of therapeutic community in numerous other psychiatric hospitals.

Principles of Therapeutic Community. Since the concepts of therapeutic community developed over a period of time, a description of its principles must specify the period being described. Because the most careful studies of therapeutic community were conducted on its application by Jones at Dingleton Hospital from 1963 onward, and because this program was the basis of many of Jones's own observations (Jones, 1966, 1968b), it is the basis of the following discussion.

The total community as treatment agent. Jones felt that the major distinctive of therapeutic community is the way in which an institution's total resources are self-consciously pooled to facilitate treatment (Jones, 1959). Administrators, clinicians, support staff, and patients were all viewed as a part of the total treatment team. All would also be involved in community meetings where the question of their positive or negative influence on treatment was discussed. These groups were designed to enhance the sensitivity of staff to their role in treatment.

This approach led to a redefining of the roles of those normally defined as treatment staff (i.e., psychiatrists, psychologists, and social workers) so as to permit the inclusion of nurses, administrators, maintenance staff, and recreational staff in the treatment team. This was accomplished through the blurring of role distinctions and the inclusion of all relevant staff in patient assessment and treatment groups. One of the ways this blurring was accomplished was through the discouragement of dress distinction perpetuated through uniforms or typical attire for various professional groups.

Perhaps the best example of this principle is the treatment role established for nurses. Jones began involving nurses in discussion groups with patients and as participants in sociodrama. They soon were referred to as social therapists and were recognized as important culture carriers. Because of their intensive involvement with patients they were accepted as key contributors to diagnosis and treatment discussions.

The role of the patient evolved from essentially a passive role to one in which the patient was urged to assume all the responsibility he or she was capable of assuming for his or her own progress toward health and the improvement of fellow patients. Some emphasis on patients' learning to understand their problems began early. The patient was then expected to participate in discussion groups to help others to understand their problems. Patients were given opportunity and encouraged to provide meaningful feedback to fellow patients concerning their behavior and its effects. The patient's role was defined as that of a collaborator in treatment and later as that of a culture carrier in relation to the orientation of new patients.

It is obvious that to accomplish such a redefinition of role for nurses and patients a corresponding change of role for psychologists, social workers, and doctors was needed. The flattening of the traditional hierarchical structure and the facilitation of open communication was essential.

The creation of community. The concept of culture and the role it plays in therapy are crucial. Jones defined culture as "a cluster of socially determined attitudes and behavior patterns grouped and elaborated around structurally defined roles and relationships" (1952, p. 66). The culture was created with the intent of maximizing the resocialization of patients. In this context he spoke of doctors as social engineers. The staff and patients who had been in the institution for some time were described as culture carriers whose responsibility was to transmit the culture of the institution to new members. A treatment goal was to help the patient to adapt to the culture of the program and to learn to find new and satisfying roles in such a social context. The assumption was that he would then become more effective in adapting in the community after discharge. Psychopathology was expressed in relationships and could be dealt with through education, confrontation, and modeling by staff and patients.

An underlying principle was that of permissiveness. A pervasive attitude of permissiveness facilitated the patient's expression of symptomatology, which was dealt with through a supportive teaching of new behavior as the unacceptable behavior was confronted. The culture of the society was described in terms of permissiveness, understanding, helpfulness, mutual responsibility, inquiry, expression of feeling, democratic-equalitarian organization, and the facing of tensions, conflicts, or role confusion that arise (Rapoport, 1959). The redefinition of the patient in this culture gave him a strong sense of belonging and facilitated

his identification with the culture and his motivation toward treatment.

The principle of open communication, which negated the traditional concept of lines of communication, was recognized early and developed to play an increasingly important role. The goal was to develop the freest communication possible between patients and staff. It was discovered that this eliminated much distortion that often occurred if communication was limited to formalized channels. Nonverbal communication was studied, and acting out was viewed as communication. The giving and receiving of feedback was encouraged. The question of confidentiality or privileged communication was dealt with by extending the circumference of confidentiality to include the total community, and the sharing of the most intimate material in the group became the norm (Jones, 1953).

Permissiveness coupled with open communication and the broader concept of confidentiality made it possible to deal with unacceptable deviations from the cultural norms in a group context. This reduced manipulation and the playing of one staff against another. In the context of an accepting group a person was encouraged and, if necessary, required to look at his behavior and its implications. Through group discussion the patient was helped to discuss his deviant behavior and to recognize its outcome for self and others (Jones, 1968a). This was spoken of as social learning.

All of this had implications for the role of leadership and the exercise of authority in the community. The hierarchical structure of the organization was flattened. Authority was dispersed through the community on a horizontal plane, with staff and patients assuming authority commensurate with their function. Authority was experienced as residing in the official leader only at times of crisis when it was necessary that he function decisively. Otherwise, Jones described his function as leadership from behind or as a catalyst. This concept of latent leadership permitted the development of leadership skills and functions among staff and patients.

Programs and techniques in theory. A summary of approaches used in therapeutic community philosophy included learning theory, psychodrama, work therapy, and a problem-solving orientation, in addition to the more traditional use of drug therapy, psychoanalytic techniques, and group therapy. These more specific approaches were used in the context of a community designed for treatment.

General learning theory and the Gestalt

theory of learning were used to explain the social learning approach practiced. The focus was on understanding and unlearning habitual patterns of behavior found to be ineffectual and the learning of new, more adequate and satisfying ways of coping. Acknowledging and revising the emotional responses to behaviors was central, and for this reason there was a strong emphasis on the expression of feelings (Jones, 1968b).

Psychodrama was used to facilitate the expression and identification of feelings. Buried dynamics of behavior were explored through projective techniques. Work therapy was developed into a very useful approach with helpful outcomes in patient self-worth and constructive use of time. With the emphasis on treatment being the function of all staff, the personnel in the work therapy program took on real significance. Work therapy was also developed to contribute to a sense of community as well as training skills.

Decision making by consensus was one of the more radical focuses of therapeutic community. Any unilateral decision was seen as contradictory to its basic philosophy. A genuine attempt at reaching unanimity required providing rationale for decisions to patients and staff, which often involved sharing of information not traditionally available to either patients or frontline staff. However, the communication of respect and significance to members of the community proved to be of great benefit, especially to patients. The mutual education and learning that grew out of this approach was deemed to justify the large amount of time consumed in the process.

Out of this grew an approach to problem solving that became clearly defined. The approach was to solve community problems, which often involved a person's personal problems, by group discussion rather than through appeal to authority. Third party intervention was not accepted as a way of resolving interpersonal or personal issues. Turning the community problem into what is referred to as a living-learning situation, the process involved bringing together all involved parties in the presence of a group facilitator and the airing of all feelings, interpretations, expectations, and accusations. The facilitator sought to create a social learning experience for participants as they moved toward resolution and reconciliation. The timing of these encounters and the skill of the therapists was crucial. The confrontation was sought as close to the experience as possible unless the situation was such as to suggest

delay would be more effective. These concepts were applied to staff as well as to patients.

Another process developed was the "postmortem meeting," which followed many activities and was intended to maximize the learning potential in each experience. The modeling provided by the more expert staff for other staff and patients in these activities was very helpful and educative.

Current Status. Since Jones's early work therapeutic communities have proliferated. Many applications of the concept, however, bear little resemblance to the original communities developed by Jones. Therapeutic community approaches have continued to be utilized in psychiatric hospitals and have also been adopted in a number of nonhospital drug treatment programs. Residential programs such as Synanon and Daytop Village are therapeutic community programs. Freudenberger (1972) has described an application of therapeutic community principles within a psychoanalytic private practice, and a number of other nonresidential applications have been described (e.g., Siroka & Siroka, 1971). While therapeutic community is certainly not a major contemporary treatment modality or approach, it has played an important role in shaping much current mental health philosophy.

References

Almond, R. *The healing community.* New York: Aronson, 1974.
Clark, D. H. *Administrative therapy.* Philadelphia: Lippincott, 1964.
Freeman, H. L. (Ed.). *Psychiatric hospital care.* London: Bailliere, Tindall, & Cassell, 1965.
Freudenberger, H. J. The therapeutic community in private practice. *Psychoanalytic Review*, 1972, *59*, 375–388.
Greenblatt, M., York, R. H., & Brown, E. L. *From custodial to therapeutic care in mental hospitals.* New York: Russell Sage Foundation, 1955.
Jones, M. *Social psychiatry.* London: Tavistock Publications, 1952.
Jones, M. *Therapeutic community.* New York: Basic Books, 1953.
Jones, M. Towards a clarification of the "therapeutic community" concept. *British Journal of Medical Psychology*, 1959, *32*, 200–205.
Jones, M. Therapeutic community practice. *American Journal of Psychiatry*, 1966, *122*, 1275–1279.
Jones, M. *Beyond therapeutic community.* New Haven: Yale University Press, 1968. (a)
Jones, M. *Social psychiatry in practice.* Hammondsworth: Penguin, 1968. (b)
Rapoport, R. N. *Community as doctor.* Springfield, Ill.: Thomas, 1960.
Siroka, R. W., & Siroka, E. K. Psychodrama and the therapeutic community. In L. Plank, G. B. Gottsegen, & M. G. Gottsegen (Eds.), *Confrontation.* New York: Macmillan, 1971.
Sullivan, H. S. *The interpersonal theory of psychiatry.* H. S. Perry & M. L. Gawel (Eds.). New York: Norton, 1953.
Sullivan, H. S. *Clinical studies in psychiatry.* H. S. Perry,

M. L. Gawel, & M. Gibbon (Eds.). New York: Norton, 1956.

Taylor, F. K. A history of group and administrative therapy in Great Britain. *British Journal of Medical Psychology*, 1958, *31*, 153–173.

G. C. TAYLOR

Therapeutic Double Bind. Developed by Erickson, this concept refers to the therapeutic tactic of placing the client in a situation facing two choices where either choice would be acceptable to the therapist and supportive of the therapy process. The therapist frames these choices in such a way as to place the client in a quandary, a benign DOUBLE BIND. These quandaries block or disrupt the client's habitual attitudes and responses and force change.

As an example, Erickson might say something like the following to a young child experiencing difficulty leaving his mother and going to school: "I think you will find that as you get older, leaving your mother will come quite easily. In fact, I think you will notice that it will happen soon. I wonder if you would like that good feeling of being able to go to school by yourself to come within one month or two." The obvious role of suggestion in this example shows the important role the therapeutic double bind plays in Erickson's approach to hypnosis, which is where this technique has been most perfected.

Additional Reading
Erickson, M. H., Rossi, E. L., & Rossi, S. I. *Hypnotic realities.* New York: Irvington Publishers, 1976.

D. G. BENNER

See HYPNOTHERAPY, INDIRECT.

Therapist-Induced Psychopathology. *See* IATROGENIC PSYCHOPATHOLOGY.

Thinking. Thinking encompasses a wide range of internal, symbolic processes, such as problem solving, reasoning, and hypothesis testing. Most psychologists assume that such processes influence behavior, although not necessarily in any simple or direct way. Thinking is contrasted with learning, which refers to influences of past experiences on one's abilities or performances. While there is considerable interest in how thinking develops, thinking per se is concerned with internal, symbolic operations upon experience. For example, words (one type of symbol) may denote particular objects or events, classes of these, or abstract concepts (Rock of Gibralter, tree, justice, etc.). In thinking, hypothetical or imaginary manipulations of the things denoted can occur. "The future statesman chopped down the cherry tree" is a verbal substitute for a possible event that need not have occurred.

Major Models of Thinking. Psychology has seen several distinct and important approaches to thinking. One was Watson's (1930) attempt to reduce thinking to internal speech, or "talking to oneself." Watson reasoned that speech that has become internal (i.e., thought) can be explained like any other simple motor behavior. His attempt to do so was crucial in extending the concept of classical conditioning from observable behavior to higher thought processes. Thus, spoken words can become substitutes for the situations to which they refer. For example, the conjunction of the word *fire* with fire makes the word capable of eliciting subtle responses like those fire itself presumably elicits, much as a bell, after being paired with meat powder, made Pavlov's dog salivate. However, what Watson needed to demonstrate, but could not, was that thought as subvocal speech produces traces of muscular movements like those accompanying speech, such as contractions of the larynx. Despite his failure and inconclusive results subsequently, the approach had a chastening influence on facile, subjective accounts of private events. Watsonian and other versions of behaviorism continue to have influence, particularly in modern attempts to find objective ways to measure these processes.

The Gestalt approach radically challenged the behaviorist approach in several ways. First, the thinker was conceived actively to discover the order and meaning that wait to be apprehended; one is not a passive pawn of experiences. Second, thinking requires the capacity to find patterns and relationships; it cannot be reduced to piecemeal accumulation of simple abilities to make more complex ones. For example, the discovery of a pattern in a string of digits to be recalled differs from rote memorization of the numbers serially; yet the exercise of this ability can improve retention. Finally, Gestaltists frankly recognized that thinking involves mental processes that cannot be explained in terms of motor behavior.

While the Gestalt approach introduced provocative ideas to deal with complex processes, it was too vague as a theory to be tested directly. Another weakness was its inability to explain how the crucial abilities to discover order and meaning arise during development.

The cognitive-developmental approach of Piaget and others addressed the problem of thinking in a developmental perspective. Perhaps their greatest contribution was to demonstrate qualitative changes in thinking processes emerging beween the ages of around 5 to 7 in Western society. These changes are summarized by the idea of conservation of number, volume, weight, mass, etc. Conservation of number, for example, is shown by a child's stating that the number of coins has not changed when they are spread out rather than bunched together. Similarly, other kinds of conservation show that the child no longer judges some quantity to have changed when one noncrucial dimension—e.g., spaces between the coins—changes. Piaget's explanation of these changes relies heavily on an analogy between thinking and biological processes found in the adaptation between the organism and its environment. To the extent this analogy has weaknesses, the theory itself has limitations, although its influence and importance cannot be overestimated. There are also alternative explanations of the same phenomena, particularly in Bruner's (1973) theory.

As the cognitive-developmental approach of Piaget was influenced by biological concepts, the information-processing approach was strongly influenced by developments in computer technology. The analogy of human thinking to the computer is based on the assumption that humans are processors of information. This assumption underlies numerous attempts to simulate human thinking processes using carefully constructed computer programs while comparing their performance on actual thinking tasks with human subjects. The logic of computer simulation is that if the performances of people and programs are very similar, the assumptions built into the programs concerning how people think must be accurate. There is a flaw in this logic in that the end result of human thinking and computer simulated "thinking" can be the same without the underlying processes being identical. Additionally, the analogy between human and machine information processing is imperfect and limiting. Nonetheless, it cannot be denied that this approach has stimulated a great deal of research that sheds light on thinking processes, particularly problem solving (Newell & Simon, 1972).

While this discussion has focused on only a few of the major approaches to thinking, it illustrates the diversity among current approaches. This diversity stems largely from the complexity of thinking and its close relationship to other topics in psychology. Thus it can be viewed profitably from different angles. Most current investigations of thinking are carried out by experimental psychologists, who are also often concerned with related topics such as memory, learning, and perception. However, thinking is also studied in other branches of psychology, including developmental (as noted earlier), social, personality, and testing.

Types of Thinking. A brief discussion of some types of thinking that figure prominently in current investigations will serve to show the complexity and fruitfulness of this field.

One type of thinking is illustrated by simple concept learning. The most common setup for concept learning experiments has the experimenter presenting stimuli serially to subjects and signaling each as either an instance or noninstance of a concept (example: red circle—yes, red square—yes, green square—no; answer: redness). Ingenious variations on this simple paradigm have shown that subjects' concept learning occurs through testing hypotheses over the learning trials. This work was important in revising theories that regarded concept learning as no different from simple motor learning.

Another type of thinking relates to the distinction between rote and meaningful learning. Rote learning deals with mechanically applying previously learned rules to new tasks, as in using mathematical formulas. Meaningful learning involves acquiring new ideas and the ability to use them appropriately through relating them to one's older relevant concepts. For example, children might gain a meaningful understanding of the concept of probability by relating it to what they already know from their own experience regarding the likelihood of rain on a given day. Closely related to this type of thinking is the study of how meaningful concepts and information are organized in memory, how people search their memories, store new concepts, and the like.

PROBLEM SOLVING is a topic that has been investigated extensively. Another topic is deductive reasoning, two examples of which are classical syllogisms ("All men are mortal; Socrates is a man; therefore, Socrates is mortal") and algebra story problems. Studies contrasting formal reasoning and optimal strategies for solving problems with human performance are revealing in much the same way that rational models of economic behavior are useful in showing how people deviate from this ideal behavior.

Another type of thinking that is less well understood is creative thinking. In contrast with practical techniques to stimulate creative thinking, which have been used widely for years, information from rigorous studies of creative thinking is difficult to find. However, interesting suggestions have come from Arieti (1976), Rothenberg (1971), and others.

In traditional Christian theology rationality is understood to be one aspect of the image of God in which humanity was created. A person's thinking is an expression of one's heart, or core (Prov. 23:7). Although concepts, reasoning, problem solving, and the like are concerned with the essence of thinking, the biblical framework suggests an expanded appreciation for thinking in relation to the purposes of the Creator. A modest beginning that is compatible with this view is found in Polanyi's (1958) theory of personal knowledge. According to Polanyi even scientific thinking is rooted fundamentally in tacit powers for apprehending reality, and in the passion to exercise them, with which human beings are endowed.

References

Arieti, S. *Creativity: The magic synthesis.* New York: Basic Books, 1976.

Bruner, J. S. *Beyond the information given.* New York: Norton, 1973.

Newell, A., & Simon, H. A. *Human problem solving.* Englewood Cliffs, N.J.: Prentice-Hall, 1972.

Polanyi, M. *Personal knowledge.* Chicago: University of Chicago Press, 1958.

Rothenberg, A. The process of Janusian thinking in creativity. *Archives of General Psychiatry,* New York: 1971, *24,* 195–205.

Watson, J. B. *Behaviorism* (Rev. ed.). New York: Norton, 1930.

D. R. RIDLEY

Thorndike, Edward Lee (1874–1949). Pioneer in learning theory. Born in Williamsburg, Massachusetts, where his father was a lawyer and later a clergyman, he graduated from Wesleyan University in 1895 and went to Harvard to study under William James. He earned another bachelor's degree at Harvard in 1896 and a master's degree in 1897. He transferred to Columbia, where he was awarded the Ph.D. in 1898. After one year of teaching at Western Reserve, he returned to Columbia in 1899 and remained there until his retirement in 1939.

Thorndike is sometimes called the founder of animal psychology because of his early work with chicks learning mazes and cats discovering how to get out of locked cages. However, shortly after his appointment to Columbia his major interests shifted to human learning and education. He developed psychological tests and a theory of intelligence. He studied individual differences, sex differences, fatigue, interests, attitudes, and vocabulary. As the most influential educational psychologist of his time he wrote leading college textbooks as well as texts for children.

His major contribution was in the area of learning. Thorndike created connectionism, an experimental approach to associationism. The older philosophical associationism was concerned with connections between ideas, but Thorndike was concerned with connections between stimuli and responses. Although he called this trial-and-accidental-success learning, it has more frequently been called trial-and-error learning. He formulated three laws to account for this learning. The law of readiness referred to the circumstance under which the learner would be satisfied or annoyed, a physiological matter determined by maturation. The law of exercise referred to the strengthening of connections through use of practice or their weakening through disuse. The law of effect stated that responses became "stamped in" or "stamped out" because of their consequences, a "satisfying state of affairs" or an "annoying state of affairs." He later modified the laws of exercise and effect, but remained a connectionist all his life.

Thorndike wrote 507 articles and books, a record equaled by few others. His doctoral dissertation, *Animal Intelligence,* was one of his most important works. It was published in 1898 and republished with other related studies in 1911. The first edition of *Educational Psychology* appeared in 1903 and *Introduction to the Theory of Mental and Social Measurements* in 1904. Thorndike has had a profound influence on modern learning theory. His emphasis on stimulus-response bonds and reinforcement are core concepts in most neo-behavioristic theories.

R. L. KOTESKEY

Thought Stopping. A behavioral technique used to help persons troubled by recurring uncontrolled thoughts and worries. Examples include obsessive rumination about cleanliness that persists even after careful washing, excessive fear of riding in automobiles or planes, and extreme fearfulness about being robbed or assaulted.

The basic technique involves four steps. First, the individual is asked to describe recent experiences in which the troublesome thoughts occurred. As he begins to describe the troublesome thoughts, the therapist suddenly and emphatically says "stop." This process is repeated several times. Second, the person is asked to imagine himself in the unpleasant situation and to signal when he begins thinking obsessive thoughts. Again there are several repetitions of the procedure. When this step is complete, the therapist has developed control over the unwanted thoughts by means of the "stop" commands.

Third, the client is taught to say "stop" aloud to his own thoughts. Typically the client initially makes a feeble and unconvincing effort, and must be encouraged to be emphatic. Finally the person is told to think "stop" in response to the troublesome thoughts.

The individual gradually experiences difficulty in thinking the troublesome thoughts and must be encouraged to make a conscious effort to produce them to facilitate the therapy process. This process permits additional exposure to the "stop" command and helps the person learn to produce and eliminate the thought at will. This is especially important where the troubling thoughts are exaggerated forms of normal concerns, such as checking to see that the doors are locked.

Technically thought stopping is a form of AVERSION THERAPY that uses contingent punishment. Procedural variations include use of electric shock in place of the word "stop," use of similar procedure to stop unwanted visual images, and use of thought stopping together with covert assertion. Although research on thought stopping is fairly limited, preliminary results are promising.

R. K. BUFFORD

See BEHAVIOR THERAPY; COGNITIVE-BEHAVIOR THERAPY.

Thumb Sucking. The earliest form of habitual manipulation of the body and usually also the earliest form of self-stimulation. It is extremely common during the first two years of life and should be viewed with concern only if it persists after ages 6 or 7. However, even then it is rarely sufficient reason for a psychological referral if it appears alone and is not part of a constellation of other behaviors and feelings that in aggregate constitute a problem.

Sucking the thumb appears to serve two possible purposes. First, it may be viewed as an expression of a basic sucking impulse designed to ensure survival. Although it may begin as a reflex, a second purpose or meaning is added when the child begins to use thumb sucking to produce comfort or body pleasuring. Freud viewed the behavior as gratification of oral sexuality. Thus viewed, it is essential if the child's psychosexual development is to proceed beyond the oral stage toward more mature levels.

Whether or not thumb sucking is sexual, it is without question an absorbing and deeply satisfying behavior for the child. It has been suggested that parental anxiety over their children's thumb sucking not only is usually unnecessary but may also reflect parents' unconscious or conscious connection between thumb sucking and masturbatory activity. Thus their own early conflicts and concerns over masturbation may be reactivated when they observe their children's thumb sucking.

Attempts to eliminate thumb sucking through mechanical restraints or noxious substances are rarely effective and often counterproductive. Usually the behavior will be outgrown and can be ignored. However, if it persists, behavior modification techniques are often helpful.

D. G. BENNER

Thurstone, Louis Leon (1887–1955). American psychologist best known for his work in measuring intelligence. Born in Chicago, he studied electrical engineering and received his M.E. from Cornell in 1912. For a year he served as an assistant to Thomas Edison and for a brief time taught mathematics. His growing interest in learning, especially the mathematical relationship between practice and improvement, led to graduate study at the University of Chicago, where he received his Ph.D. in 1917.

He taught psychology at the Carnegie Institute of Technology from 1915 to 1923, spent a year in government research in Washington, then returned to teach at the University of Chicago. He remained at Chicago from 1924 until 1952, when he moved to the University of North Carolina.

Thurstone's lifelong interest in applying mathematics to psychology led to his contributions in the area of measurement. He attacked the concept of mental age, noting that it cannot be applied to adults because scores do not continue to increase with increasing age. He suggested using the individual's percentile rank in a given age group, but other psychologists thought that this would confuse teachers, so little was done. Of course, this is essentially the way adult IQs are determined today.

He also did not think of intelligence as consisting of a single general factor. He introduced the technique of factor analysis into intelligence testing and concluded that measuring intelligence involved measuring several different primary abilities, such as verbal comprehension, word fluency, number manipulation, space visualization, associative memory, perceptual speed, and logical reasoning. His works on intelligence include *The Nature of Intelligence* (1924), *The Measurement of Intelligence* (1925), *The Vectors of the Mind*

(1935), *Primary Mental Abilities* (1938), and *Multiple-Factor Analysis* (1947).

Thurstone's theoretical and experimental work in multiple factor analysis was initiated in 1929, although he had derived his original equation while he was still at Carnegie. In addition to applying it to intelligence, he applied it to other areas, such as perception. He is known for work on simple structure and other contributions to the development of multiple factor analysis. He also contributed to the construction of modern scaling techniques and their use in attitude measurement in *Measurement of Attitudes* (1929). His attitude scales were used to assess attitudes toward war, other races, communism, capital punishment, and so forth. Thurstone was among the founders of the Psychometric Society and its journal, *Psychometrika*.

R. L. KOTESKEY

See INTELLIGENCE; INTELLECTUAL ASSESSMENT.

Tic Disorder. Tics are repetitive involuntary stereotyped movements. An individual will admit that he or she has the urge to make them, can consciously suppress them for a time, is aware of mounting tension with such suppression, and experiences a sense of relief after their execution.

Tics appear most commonly about the face and are usually manifested as blinking, grinning, smirking, lip licking, or nose and forehead wrinkling. They may also involve any portion of the body.

In the past tics were thought to have a hysterical component. However, tics occasionally appear in individuals who demonstrate obsessional and compulsive traits. A tic, regardless whether the origin is psychogenic or the result of brain injury or physiological malfunction, may be exacerbated by stress. Tics disappear during sleep and diminish when the individual is preoccupied.

Most tics are viewed as a behavior that was learned or had its origin in a past traumatic experience or stressful situation. Thus, the tic can be considered a truncated movement of withdrawal or aggression that may have been the only possible response. Children are more susceptible to tic disorders due to their less mature inhibitory controls.

DSM-III makes the most definitive classification of tics (stereotyped movement disorders). They are broken down into either transient tic disorder, chronic motor tic disorder, Tourette's disorder, or atypical tic disorder. TOURETTE'S DISORDER (Gilles de la Tourette's syndrome) is characterized by complicated and widespread tics, most notably vocal tics that may be manifested by grunting noises or obscene and abusive language.

Though it is generally assumed that there is a psychogenic origin in transient and chronic motor tics, no evidence has substantiated a psychogenic basis for Tourette's syndrome. Most studies seem to implicate a genetic-familial predisposition or central nervous system pathology etiology. Tourette, who discovered the condition, believed that the disorder was inherited, since two of his nine patients had affected relatives. Other research has shown that approximately 30% of patients with Tourette's and other tics have positive family history of such a disorder.

While psychoanalytic treatment for transient and chronic motor tic disorders has been unsuccessful, most other tic disorders are being rather successfully treated through behavioral techniques. Typically this form of treatment involves the use of an extinction program known as negative practice, or mass practice, wherein the individual is persuaded to repeat the undesired tic voluntarily until the point of exhaustion. Since negative practice is a tedious and time-consuming method, it has been combined with a form of anxiety-relief conditioning. Here the patient is administered an unpleasant stimulus while the tic is being repeated, and the unpleasant stimulus is terminated simultaneously with cessation of the tic. Negative practice and anxiety-relief conditioning used together have been found to be more successful than either one alone.

K. R. KRACKE

Time-out. This behavioral technique, literally time out from positive reinforcement, involves removal of a person from the opportunity to obtain positive reinforcement. It is the most popular form of negative PUNISHMENT and is readily implemented in any behavior modification program. An example of a time-out procedure would be a teacher who places a misbehaving child in the hall until the child "quiets down." While in the hall the child misses the opportunity to earn reinforcement (the attention of peers and the general stimulation of the classroom), and the disruptive behavior should decrease. In order for time-out to be effective, the situation from which the individual is withdrawn must be enjoyable or reinforcing.

D. G. BENNER

See BEHAVIOR THERAPY.

Titchener, Edward Bradford (1867–1927). Founder of STRUCTURALISM. He was born in

Chichester, England, and attended Malvern College and Oxford, where he studied philosophy and the classics and later became a research assistant in physiology. He then went to Leipzig, where he studied for two years, receiving his doctorate in 1892. Although he actually saw little of Wundt, Wundt made a lifelong impression on him.

Titchener would have liked to remain in England but the British were not ready for pioneering work in psychology. After a year as extension lecturer in biology at Oxford, he went to Cornell University in the United States. He remained at Cornell the rest of his life, teaching psychology, directing the laboratory, and directing more than 50 doctoral dissertations. He was a dogmatic individual who refused to change as American psychology did. Although elected a charter member of the American Psychological Association in 1892, he resigned a year later. He even refused to attend meetings when the convention was held in Ithaca. In 1904 he founded his own group, the Experimentalists, and dominated the meetings.

Titchener's psychology was an extension of Wundt's structuralism. Psychology was defined as the study of conscious experience. There were three basic classes of the elements of consciousness. Sensations (sights, sounds, tastes, etc.) were the elements of perceptions, and Titchener claimed there were 42,415 possible ones. Images were the elements of ideas, and affective states were the elements of emotion. Each basic element could have the attributes of quality, intensity, duration, and clearness, and sometimes extensity.

Titchener also explored the problems of attention, the arrangement of conscious elements. Like Wundt he accepted the principle of association. His context theory of meaning held that one mental process was the meaning of another. The context of related processes gave meaning to the core of sensation and mages. Like Wundt, Titchener used introspection as his method of observation.

Titchener wrote 216 articles and notes and a dozen books. He also attempted to translate Wundt's *Principles of Physiological Psychology* several times, but Wundt always had a new edition out before Titchener could get the previous one translated. His most important books are *An Outline of Psychology* (1896), *The Primer of Psychology* (1898), a four-volume *Experimental Psychology* (1901–1905), and *Textbook of Psychology* (1910). Most of his books were introductory and experimental texts, but were significant in outlining his position.

R. L. KOTESKEY

Toilet Training. The process of acquiring control over bowels and bladder elimination presents a special challenge to many children and parents. If attempted too early or in an overly harsh or critical manner, it can be the occasion of a fierce battle of wills and can lead to a variety of maladaptive behaviors in the child. However, if approached with skill and understanding, it can be a satisfying experience for both parent and child.

Several approaches to toilet training have been developed in recent years. The best known and most widely used is that developed by Azrin and Foxx and described in their book *Toilet Training in Less Than a Day* (1974). Based on research done in toilet training profoundly retarded individuals, this highly effective approach eliminates the major frustrations that can accompany toilet training. This article will describe Azrin and Foxx's procedure.

Before beginning training, parents should determine that the child can perform the following tasks: 1) imitate a simple action that is modeled by a parent; 2) identify the major parts of the body by pointing to them; and 3) follow simple instructions, such as "Sit down," "Follow me," "Give me your cup." A child who is at least 20 months old and who can perform these tasks should be ready to be trained.

The parent who will do the training should plan to spend up to a full day and to ensure that he or she and the child will not be disturbed by external distractions. In advance of the training the trainer must identify all the specific skills the child will need to master, such as going to the potty chair, grasping and lowering pants, sitting down, urinating, wiping, pulling up pants, removing pot, carrying pot to toilet, emptying contents into toilet, flushing, and replacing pot.

The trainer uses a doll to model all these actions. As the doll carries out each task, the parent praises the doll's successes. When the parent finishes the modeling session, he or she asks the child to play the role of the trainer and to walk the doll through the same sequence of actions again. Next the parent models the desired behaviors without using the doll. Then the parent asks the child to play the role of trainer and to model for the parent the specified skills.

To cause a frequent need for urination the trainer gives the child something to drink about once every five minutes. These drinks are used along with food and treats as reinforcers for successful performance of skills by the child. These tangible reinforcers are accompanied by extensive praise, applause, hugs, and kisses. The program must include a large variety of reinforcers, immediate reinforcement following a success, and frequent reinforcement. The parent checks the child's pants about once every five minutes. If the pants are dry, the parent reinforces the child. If the pants are wet, the parent first reprimands the child and then ignores him for five minutes. Following this time-out the trainer requires the child to come from different locations in the house to the bathroom and to engage in the prescribed sequence of toileting behaviors.

The trainer uses verbal prompts extensively. In early stages of training the parent can manually guide the child through desired actions until the child performs them in response to an oral request. Throughout training the parent states how pleased significant other persons will be when they hear of the child's successes. These persons include the absent parent, siblings, grandparents and other relatives, and characters from story books and television.

During the course of training verbal prompts and frequent reinforcements are gradually stopped. By the end of the training session prompts are eliminated and reinforcement is only delivered for urinating in the potty chair. During subsequent days no reminders to urinate are given; however, the parent does check the child's pants before meals, naps, and bedtime. Dry pants produce praise. Wet pants lead to a reprimand and instructions to change his or her pants and to practice the actions of going to the bathroom.

The average length of the training session is four hours, with a range of one-half to 14 hours. Younger children take longer to train than older children, but almost all children who pass the readiness tests given above can be successfully trained.

Reference

Azrin, N. H., & Foxx, R. M. *Toilet training in less than a day.* New York: Simon & Schuster, 1974.

P. W. CLEMENT

Token Economy. A system of psychological treatment or intervention, based on the principles of operant conditioning, in which tokens serve as the immediate consequences for the treated behaviors. Technically these tokens are known as tangible conditioned reinforcers. They may consist of items such as points, poker chips, check marks, marbles, paper punches on a card, entries in a "bank book," or literal tokens. Such items are linked to back-up consequences, which may be either reinforcing or punishing, in that the tokens are exchanged for these back-ups. Token economies usually emphasize the use of positive back-up reinforcers, which involve consequences such as money, food, access to activites, or other privileges. Less frequently tokens may be linked to punishing consequences. The most common punishing consequences are response costs such as fines.

The conceptual model underlying the token economy assumes that abnormal behaviors are influenced by the same variables that affect normal behaviors. The behaviors that get people into trouble in families, schools, or communities are actions. Actions are greatly modified by their consequences. Whereas certain environmental changes may produce reflexive responses, actions may produce changes in the actor's environment. Such changes are called consequences. B. F. Skinner and developers of the token economy have emphasized the use of positive consequences. When a token, such as a check mark on a card, can later be exchanged for a positive consequence, the token becomes an immediate positive reinforcer.

For example, John, a 33-year-old chronic schizophrenic, attended a day treatment program at a local church. One of John's problems was that he usually failed to make eye contact and appropriate social greetings when first encountering another person. He set a personal goal to increase the frequency of greeting other persons within the day treatment program. He carried a small card in his shirt pocket. Whenever a staff member observed John making a social greeting, the staff member punched John's card with a distinctive paper punch. Each hole constituted a token. Each day John could go to the program's reinforcer cafeteria and purchase such items as snacks, beverages, and toiletries. Each item had a cash value. Each punch on John's card was worth a specified amount.

Long before psychology became an identified discipline, various cultures had developed complex token economies. Their tokens became known as money. In most cases money had no inherent value. It derived its value from what it could purchase; thus, money became the most pervasive tangible conditioned reinforcer.

In *Walden Two*, Skinner provided a grand design for an entire community that ran on a token economy based on the principles of operant conditioning. Skinner described an ideal community based on a science of behavior. One of the distinctive features of this fictitious community was that it ran without punishment. Skinner argued against aversive and coercive techniques to control people's behavior. In reference to social influences he wrote, "I insist that Jesus, who was apparently the first to discover the power of refusing to punish, must have hit upon the principle by accident. He certainly had none of the experimental evidence which is available to us today" (1948, p. 261).

Within contemporary psychology the token economy developed as part of the behavior modification movement. During the 1950s a limited number of psychologists began applying the concepts and procedures of operant conditioning to problems in living. They demonstrated that the approaches Skinner had developed in working with rats and pigeons could be applied to people. Over time clinical researchers demonstrated that operant procedures could alleviate various forms of serious psychological disturbances (Ayllon & Azrin, 1968; Kazdin, 1977).

Obviously the token economy simply involves paying people to do what is socially desirable. In contrast to the protests of some critics who argue that people should do what they are supposed to do without having to be paid, the Bible seems to give directions that are consistent with the token economy. For example, Jesus declared, "A worker should be given his pay" (Luke 10:7).

In the clinical example given earlier, offering social greetings was John's "work" in the day treatment program. Engaging in cooperative social play is the work of children in treatment for aggressive acts toward others. Performing academic assignments is the work of learning disabled students in special classrooms. Putting on and buttoning their own pants is the work of retarded children in state hospitals. In each such case the Bible and contemporary psychological technology seem to be in harmony.

References

Ayllon, T., & Azrin, N. H. *The token economy: A motivational system for therapy and rehabilitation.* New York: Appleton-Century-Crofts, 1968.

Kazdin, A. E. *The token economy: A review and evaluation.* New York: Plenum, 1977.

Skinner, B. F. *Walden two.* New York: Macmillan, 1948.

P. W. CLEMENT

See APPLIED BEHAVIOR ANALYSIS; BEHAVIOR THERAPY.

Tolman, Edward Chace (1886–1959).

American behavioral psychologist. Born in West Newton, Massachusetts, he was the son of a prosperous factory owner. At his father's urging he earned a bachelor's degree in electrochemistry in 1911 from the Massachusetts Institute of Technology. However, rather than entering the family business he entered Harvard to study philosophy and psychology. He received his M.A. in 1912 and his Ph.D. in 1915.

After serving as a psychology instructor at Northwestern University from 1915 to 1918, Tolman moved to the University of California at Berkeley, where he remained, with two brief interruptions, until his retirement in 1954. During World War II he served in the Office of Strategic Services. When he refused to sign a loyalty oath in California, he taught at Harvard and the University of Chicago (1950–1953). He led the successful fight against the oath and was reinstated by an order of the California Supreme Court.

Although he was trained in the structuralist tradition, during graduate school he spent a month in Germany with Koffka and was introduced to behaviorism. He developed a system he called purposive behaviorism, a cross between behaviorism and Gestalt psychology. He believed that all behavior was goal directed. He introduced the concept of intervening variables so that psychology would have a way of making statements about inner states and processes that cannot be observed.

Tolman's cognitive theory of learning was the major alternative to Hull's theory of learning between 1930 and 1950. He postulated that repeated performance of a task builds up sign-Gestalts, learned relationships between cues in the environment and the organism's expectations. If a rat or person is put in a maze, expectancies are formed at each choice point. If the rat gets to the food, his expectancies are confirmed. Soon a pattern of sign-Gestalts, a cognitive map, is established. The organism gets to know something about its environment. Although Tolman never developed a fully integrated system, his experiments challenged Hull's theory.

Several times he revised his system in articles, frequently renaming concepts, but he remained a purposive behaviorist. His success at achieving an integration of Gestalt psychology and behaviorism is shown in the fact that some historians today classify him as a behaviorist, and others as a Gestalt psychologist. He did his own thinking instead of fitting into an existing system. Tolman's major work was *Purposive Behavior in Animals and Men* (1932).

R. L. KOTESKEY

Tooth Grinding. *See* Bruxism.

Touch in Psychotherapy. *See* Physical Contact in Psychotherapy.

Tourette's Disorder. A complex of tics that begin in childhood. Tics are sudden, spasmodic, involuntary motor movements. In Tourette's disorder the severe, chronic tics usually involve the upper body, often including the face, shoulders, and arms. Multiple vocal tics make up an essential part of the clinical picture. Frequently the vocal tics begin as a semiaudible throat clearing, but they often progress to barklike sounds, intelligible words, and coprolalia (an involuntary utterance of obscene words). The intensity of these symptoms varies across days, weeks, or months, but the clinical signs should be present for more than one year before the diagnosis is made. The symptoms initially appear when the child is between 2 and 15 years of age. Although the tics are viewed as involuntary, the child usually has the ability to suppress them voluntarily for brief periods of time lasting up to several hours.

Tourette's disorder is also known as Gilles de la Tourette's syndrome and *maladie des tics*. This syndrome may last the patient's lifetime.

Mental health experts do not agree on the etiology of this disorder. Some writers have sugggested hereditary factors, based on the observation that some patients' parents have had histories of simple tics or other motoric problems. Others have argued that organic brain disease underlies Tourette's disorder, but available autopsy reports have failed to identify an organic basis. Investigators have used the electroencephalograph to study this disorder, but such reasearch has not helped to pinpoint the cause. Hypotheses also exist regarding a possible psychological etiology, but none has gained general acceptance.

In the absence of any consensus on etiology, clinical investigators have focused on finding effective treatments. Although earlier writers on Tourette's disorder described a progressive, psychologically degenerative syndrome that would end in mental incompetence, recent clinical studies have provided a more positive picture.

Haloperidol has become the most commonly used drug in the pharmacological treatment of Tourette's disorder. While the effectiveness of this drug in treating this particular disorder has not been confirmed through controlled studies, many clinical trials have demonstrated its positive impact. Trifluoproma-zine and thioridazine are two other antipsychotic drugs that have also been reported as useful in providing symptomatic relief.

Controlled studies on the effectiveness of psychological treatments for Tourette's disorder are also lacking. Some case histories have been published in which psychodynamic therapies are claimed to have been helpful, but since the mid-1960s an increasing number of single-subject studies on the behavioral treatment of this disorder have been published. Taken together their findings suggest that all of the following procedures may be helpful: 1) operant conditioning carried out by parents in the home and teachers in the school with a focus on strengthening behaviors that are incompatible with the tics; 2) massed, or negative, practice of the most socially offensive tics; 3) group contingencies designed to focus the attention of classmates and peers on appropriate behaviors in the patient and to help them ignore the tics; 4) self-monitoring and self-reinforcement; 5) relaxation training; and 6) aversive conditioning.

P. W. Clement

Tournier, Paul (1898–). Swiss physician who, perhaps more than any other writer, has shown how biblical and psychological insights can be integrated to promote physical, emotional, and spiritual health. Furthermore, he is probably the most widely read writer in the world on psychology from a biblical perspective. Originally written in French, Tournier's books have been translated into many languages and have been instrumental in helping evangelical Christians overcome the prejudice which they have had against psychology. Written in a well-reasoned but popular style, Tournier's books have dealt with such diverse topics as neurosis, loneliness, guilt, marriage, human development, love, interpersonal relationships, and retirement.

Born in Geneva, Paul was the second child of Calvinist pastor Louis Tournier and his second wife, Elizabeth. His father died when Paul was 3 months old, and his mother died six years later. Paul and his sister were taken into the home of Jacques Ormond, their mother's brother. Because Mrs. Ormond had both physical and emotional problems, the home proved to be an unsatisfactory environment for the two orphans. Except for mathematics Paul was a poor student and was ridiculed by his classmates.

During his teen years Tournier was befriended by his Greek teacher, Jules Dubois, who realized how much his shy pupil needed companionship. Dubois invited Tournier to his home, engaged him in lengthy discussions, and made him feel that his ideas were worthwhile. This gave Tournier confidence that he could hold his own in intellectual discussion and encouraged him to mix socially with others. As a result, he quickly became a student leader at the University of Geneva and was eventually elected president of a countrywide student organization.

Although Tournier had earlier been an indifferent student, he did very well as a medical student at the University of Geneva. After graduating he went to Paris for a year's internship, then took a four-year internship at the Geneva Polyclinic. In 1928 he entered private medical practice in Geneva and continued in it until his retirement. Although he has treated many patients with emotional and psychological problems and is often referred to as a psychiatrist, he has had no formal training in psychiatry and has never referred to himself as anything other than a general practitioner.

Influence of the Oxford Group. Prior to 1932 Tournier was an idealist and a staunch defender of the Christian faith. He had studied Calvin's writings carefully and was impressed by the logical coherence of his theological system. Intellectual acceptance and defense of Calvinistic theology did not, however, give Tournier a vibrant living faith. It was not until his encounter with the Oxford Group in 1932, at the age of 34, that Tournier's faith became the vital core of his life.

He first became aware of the Oxford Group as the result of a striking transformation that occurred in a former patient who had been in contact with the group. The remarkable change in this woman prompted Tournier to investigate the movement. His first contact was disappointing. Expecting to receive an exposition of principles and methods, he heard only anecdotes of how lives of members had been changed. The group stressed absolute surrender to God and guidance of the Holy Spirit through meditation and sharing in group fellowship. However, in a later personal encounter with a member of the group, Tournier was impressed with the man's candor in sharing the experiences of his life. Through this encounter Tournier was encouraged both to meditate and to share his feelings with others. As he did so, he became increasingly aware of God as a forgiving, healing, and guiding presence in his life. Tournier became an active member of the Oxford Group and continued his association with them for 14 years (1932–1946). However, when the movement changed

its name to Moral Rearmament and its emphasis to labor-management relations and international affairs, he felt impelled to resign.

In 1946 Tournier took part in the first Evangelical Academy at Bad Boll, Germany. This meeting was the outgrowth of a conviction of a young German theologian that theologians and doctors should meet to work out a new approach to healing founded on the gospel. This meeting was decisive for Tournier because it both supported and helped give direction to his task of treating the whole person. The following year Tournier and other doctors interested in treating the whole person met at the Chateau de Bossey near Geneva. Annual meetings of what has come to be called the Bossey Group continue to this day. Two of Tournier's books, *A Doctor's Casebook in the Light of the Bible* and *Guilt and Grace*, are drawn from studies originally presented to the Bossey Group.

Tournier's Psychology. Much to the chagrin of some of his readers Tournier has never attempted to present his psychological thinking in a systematic way. In fact, he denies that his work represents a theory or psychological position, preferring to view his writings as those of a doctor shaing some of his insights and experiences. That there is a consistent, even if not comprehensive, psychology within his writings is made clear in Collins's *The Christian Psychology of Paul Tournier* (1973). The following discussion is based in large part on Collins's analysis.

Tournier believes that human life is too complicated to be fitted into any theoretical framework. Human beings simultaneously belong to two worlds—the natural world and the supernatural world. Each person has a body, a psyche (the part that experiences emotions), and a mind. Each of these entities can influence the other, and all can be studied scientifically. However, a human being is also a spiritual being, and the supernatural world cannot be studied by the scientific method. According to Tournier, the spiritual part of a person can be apprehended only by "spiritual communion" between the doctor and the patient.

In his books Tournier makes frequent references to Freudian and Jungian concepts. Few of the concepts cited are rejected completely; some are accepted without reservation. In many cases, however, Tournier either limits the universality of the concepts or expands them by giving them a spiritual dimension. Karpeles and Scandrette (1980) suggest that while both Freud and Jung obviously influenced Tournier in major ways, of the two he is probably closest to Jung. This is evidenced by his shared emphasis with Jung on the purposive, spiritual nature of persons as well as his employment of phenomenological methods in therapy.

Tournier believes that there are innate individual differences in temperament and that people are profoundly affected by environmental events. Collins identifies the four most crucial factors in Tournier's model of human development to be love, suffering, identification, and adaptation. Tournier divides the life span into three epochs: childhood, adulthood, and old age. He stresses the importance of a stable home where children are loved and disciplined. Although he has relatively little to say about adolescence, he sees this as a period in which youth free themselves from childhood involvements and achieve emancipation from parental standards and beliefs. It is a time when young people choose values, friends, a life partner, and a vocation. Adulthood is seen as a period of self-directing activity. Tournier believes that 40 is not too soon to think about old age and plan for retirement.

Tournier recognizes five observable causes of behavior: instincts and innate tendencies, unconscious forces, conscious choices, social influence, and the conflict between the urge to assert and actualize the self and the urge to serve others. He sees humans as having many of the basic instincts of animals but believes that the impulse of adventure and security are peculiar to humans. Tournier accepts the psychoanalytic view that dreams reveal a great deal about the unconscious influences on behavior. He also accepts the validity of the psychoanalytic defense mechanisms. Although he agrees that the unconscious has a strong influence on behavior, he believes in the primacy of choice, for "to live is to choose." A severe conflict between conscious choice and unconscious impulses can lead to neurosis. Social influences can instill prejudice, distort thinking, predispose to disease, and lead to immorality. Tournier believes that two societal myths—progress and evolution—have adversely affected individual behavior. He does not believe that the urge to actualize the self and the urge to serve others are irreconcilable. In fact, these two impulses may be complementary, since a person must accept himself before he can move to loving service to others.

Although Tournier does not espouse any particular theory of learning, he believes that children should be taught values, responsibility, and how to make decisions. He believes that traditional education has tended to emphasize memorization of facts, to discourage curiosity, and to foster competition. Tournier seems to have been little influenced by behaviorism and seldom mentions the theories of Skinner and other behaviorists.

Although Tournier has little to say about thinking, he does distinguish between intuitive thinking, which is based on feelings, and logical thinking. Intuitive thinking is more often seen in children, primitive people, and creative individuals.

Tournier's writings make frequent reference to the emotions—particularly to fear, love, jealousy, anxiety, guilt, loneliness, and inferiority. He stresses the importance of acknowledging and accepting one's emotions. When one is faced with a strong emotion, there are three possible ways to react. First, the emotion may be repressed. This frequently leads to neurotic symptoms, including psychosomatic illness. Second, one may give free reign to the emotion. This typically causes the emotion to increase in intensity. Third, one can put himself into the hands of God, committing the emotion to him.

Obviously strongly influenced by phenomenological psychology, Tournier believes that perception influences how we see the world, how we see others, and even how we see ourselves.

Although some have criticized him for bringing God into his theories, Tournier believes that human beings cannot be completely understood by scientifically observable phenomena; they can be understood only in the context of the supernatural. Tournier's attempts to show how the psychological and the supernatural interact are sometimes unclear and confusing, due in large part to the difficulty of harmonizing biblical and psychological language.

Tournier's view on instinctive behavior seems rather outmoded. Today there is virtual consensus that, except for a few physiological drives, there are no human instincts. Even if instincts exist, their presence really explains nothing about human behavior. As Collins points out, postulating the "adventure" instinct appears to raise more questions than it answers.

Personality, according to Tournier, consists of two parts: the person and the personage. The personage is that part of the personality that we reveal to the world. The person, the more authentic self, is usually obscured by the personage. Although the person and the personage are distinct from each other, they are indissolubly connected because one influences the other. Although the personage tends to mold the person, the person influences and partially reveals itself through the personage. When the person and the personage are not in harmony, the individual is confused and may develop neurotic symptoms. Tournier's concept of the relationship between the person and the personage is an original and fruitful idea. Although clearly related to the Jungian concept of persons, Tournier's ideas at this point are better developed and may represent his most important theoretical contribution.

Tournier's Therapy. According to Tournier there are four characteristics that appear in almost all neurotics: anxiety; sterility, or non-productivity; self-defeating behavior; and inner conflict. Neuroses can be due to physical, psychological, or spiritual causes, alone or in combination. One's ability to cope with psychological pressure may be lowered by physical disability or disease. Parental rejection or overprotection of children can trigger problems in later life. If repressed, negative feelings about the self can give rise to neurosis.

The essence of therapy for Tournier is dialogue. Therapists must be skillful in their application of techniques, but even more important is that they must be deeply interested in people. Since Tournier believes that all healing ultimately is from God rather than the therapist, he states that both believers and unbelievers may be successful therapists. However, he also states the importance of having the spiritual concern of a man or woman of God if a person is to help others.

Although he believes that the therapist should usually be nondirective, Tournier does not hesitate to make interpretations if he feels that this would be helpful. Sometimes he feels it is helpful to the client for the therapist to talk about his own problems and struggles. Intellectual discussions should be avoided. The therapist should not criticize, judge, or condemn the client. Most important of all is the personality of the therapist. He or she must be patient, sincerely concerned, willing to listen. He should express confidence, love, and acceptance.

Collins's (1973) analysis of Tournier's case histories leads him to conclude that four basic goals seem to underlie his therapy: 1) to help the person break out of vicious circles that hinder maturity; 2) to expand consciousness—i.e., to make the unconscious conscious; 3) to help the person accept that which cannot be changed; and 4) to bring the person into contact with Christ for what Tournier calls

soul healing. In order to meet these goals Tournier (1957) suggests three basic techniques: catharsis, transference monitoring and interpretation, and philosophical dialogue. Philosophical dialogue involves the consideration of theological issues for which technical psychotherapy has no answers.

The following stages appear to be typical in Tournier's therapy (Collins, 1973). 1) In order to ensure the spiritual communion which Tournier feels is vital to successful dialogue, he prepares for his interviews by prayer and meditation. 2) When the patient arrives, Tournier listens carefully and tries to understand. 3) As therapy proceeds, Tournier gives acceptance and support. 4) As the patient feels more at ease in the relationship, Tournier helps the patient understand himself. 5) When the patient discovers things about himself that he doesn't like, Tournier relates some of his own problems and struggles. 6) Finally, through dialogue, Tournier and the patient work together toward the appropriate goal.

Theological Belief. Tournier's theological beliefs have been influenced by his boyhood religious instruction, by Calvin's writings, and by the writings of three modern theologians—Brunner, Barth, and Buber. Last, but not least, has been his careful study of the Bible. For Tournier the only reliable source for theological thinking is the Bible. The Bible is not only a book of history; it tells what God is like and what he expects of human beings. Although Tournier believes the Bible to be authoritative, he believes also that God speaks to us through nature, through history, through dreams, and through thoughts that come to us during prayer and meditation. If messages from these extrabiblical sources clearly contradict the Bible, however, they should be rejected.

Tournier accepts the biblical account of salvation. It is through Jesus Christ, who lived on earth as a man, died on the cross to atone for the sins of mankind, and rose from the grave, that salvation and eternal life are available. Unlike most evangelicals, however, he believes that Christ's death assured salvation to *all* men. The difference between the Christian and the nonbeliever is that the Christian knows and rejoices in his salvation. According to Tournier the purpose of evangelism and missions is to proclaim that salvation is assured to all people. This point of view is implied in many of his writings. The most explicit statement of his universalist position, however, is contained in a letter to a theology student writing a thesis on his universalism (Musick, 1978). In this letter he states: "That you say as a theologian that I am a universalist is evident in the sense that I believe that Jesus was sent into the world to save the sinners that we all are.... I believe that this great plan of salvation is universal, concerns not only all men but the universality of the world, and that Jesus on the cross has accomplished this salvation.... This plan of God therefore seems to be collective, global, universal" (p. 81).

Tournier endorses the ecumenical movement because he believes that the prejudice and self-righteousness of denominationalism have done much harm. The greatest weakness of the church in Tournier's opinion is the tendency to be legalistic, moralistic, and ritualistic. Because we live in a broken world, Tournier feels strongly that the church must be concerned with social problems. However, he also states that there is a danger of becoming so preoccupied with social concerns that the church may neglect to proclaim Christ.

Major Contributions. Tournier's greatest contribution has been his integration of psychology and Christianity. He has shown that much of psychological theory is compatible with Scripture and has consequently helped break down the prejudice that conservative Christians have had against psychology. Tournier has even shown that some of the theories of controversial figures such as Freud are not in conflict with biblical truth. Although he has not resolved all of the conflicts between psychology and religion, he is convinced that if both are correctly interpreted, there will be no conflict between psychological findings and Scripture. He has also shown that Christians as well as non-Christians can benefit from psychological counseling and other aspects of applied psychology.

Another major contribution is Tournier's emphasis on the importance of involvement with other people. Because he felt that his own life had been transformed when, under the influence of the Oxford Group, he began to relate intimately with others, Tournier has stressed the importance of close relationships. This would seem to be an important emphasis in an age of urban depersonalization when people have many acquaintances but few, if any, intimate friends. Some writers have suggested that many people who are seeing psychotherapists would not need to do so if they had an intimate friend with whom to relate.

A third major contribution is Tournier's practical guides to living. In his books he has given helpful guidelines on such diverse problems as improving marital relations, handling guilt, overcoming loneliness, understanding other people, dealing with sexual impulses, growing old, finding God's will, and living a better Christian life.

References

Collins, G. R. *The Christian psychology of Paul Tournier.* Grand Rapids: Baker, 1973.

Karpeles, M., & Scandrette, O. Paul Tournier's reaction to Freud and Jung. *Christian Association for Psychological Studies Bulletin,* 1980, 6(3), 19–30.

Musick, D. D. *Paul Tournier's universalism.* Unpublished master's thesis, Wheaton College Graduate School, 1978.

Tournier, P. *The meaning of persons.* New York: Harper & Row, 1957.

Additional Reading

Peaston, M. *Personal living: An introduction to Paul Tournier.* New York: Harper & Row, 1972.

O. C. SCANDRETTE

Training in Counseling and Psychotherapy.

The training of counselors and psychotherapists occurs within several disciplines (e.g., social work, nursing, psychology, psychiatry, psychoanalysis, family therapy). While discipline and context have differed, there has nonetheless been a remarkable degree of consistency in training emphases across disciplines. Many of these emphases have had their roots in psychological theory and research.

Training in Core Conditions. Perhaps the strongest influence on the process of training has been the work of Carl Rogers and his associates. Beginning in the 1960s the person-centered orientation to counseling has influenced the training of practitioners by its emphasis on the "necessary and sufficient" therapeutic attitudes of empathic understanding, unconditional positive regard (warmth), and congruence (genuineness). Rogers (1957) described a method for training in these attitudes whereby the student listened to audiotaped interviews, role played with other students, observed interviews, conducted interviews, participated in group therapy, and received personal therapy.

Rogers's emphasis on the training of facilitative attitudes in the therapist was somewhat altered by Truax and Carkhuff (1967) with their development of human relations training. Their program contains a more structured didactic component, whereby therapeutic conditions are translated into observable therapist responses and behaviors. Their training program has had the most lasting influence on the training of counselors. Most currently popular training programs for beginning counselors (e.g., Egan, 1982) build on the use of core conditions taught in a structured didactic-experiential manner. Kurts and Marshall

(1982) note that even training programs not formally identified as training in these core dimensions still tend to emphasize therapist response skills (e.g., empathy, respect, reflection of feelings, immediacy) that have their roots in the person-centered approach.

Given the relative dominance of this approach, one would assume that its effectiveness in training therapists who then achieve positive outcomes with their clients has been satisfactorily demonstrated. Unfortunately this is not the case. While we know that some therapy is more effective than no therapy at all (Smith, Glass, & Miller, 1980), reviews of outcome literature suggest that the most powerful predictors of successful therapy outcome are client characteristics. After client variables, therapist characteristics, including quality of relationship, are the next most important influence. Further, the available research (e.g., Lambert, DeJulio, & Stein, 1978) suggests that empathy, warmth, and genuineness have only a modest relationship to eventual outcome.

In spite of the lack of strong evidence for the effectiveness of person-centered approaches there is a continuing use of teaching relationship skills to counselors and therapists. Also, because training in core conditions has such demonstrable effects on counselor behavior, these training programs have been well developed and systematically researched. The question of the effectiveness of these skills in counseling interactions, however, is not yet resolved.

Video Equipment in Teaching and Supervision. With the development of video recording and audio cassette recorders, new methods of training and supervision using this equipment were also developed. For example, the widespread use of audiotaping allows supervisors and counselors to process interviews more thoroughly than via material presented by the counselor-trainee from memory. Several "bug-in-the-ear" devices aid supervision by allowing the supervisor to speak directly to the counselor-trainee during interviews. However, it is in the training area that technological advances have had the most impact. Two currently popular training approaches are microcounseling and interpersonal process recall.

Microcounseling. Microcounseling (Ivey, 1971) was originally conceived as an adaptation of a microtraining model applied to teaching. It emphasizes breaking complex skills down into small behavioral subunits that can be described, modeled, practiced, observed, and corrected through the use of video-

tape feedback. Ivey and his colleagues use this approach to teach three basic counseling skills: attentiveness, accurate reflection of feeling, and summarization of feelings. Other skills for which microcounseling training methods have been used are giving direction, expressing feelings, self-disclosure, interpretation, and immediacy.

The training model (Ivey & Authier, 1978) consists of four steps. The first is a baseline interview, in which the trainee interviews a volunteer client on videotape. The second is training, in which the trainee reads materials describing the skill, observes video models performing the skill, views the baseline interview with a supervisor, and compares his or her performance to the modeled examples. The third step is reinterview, in which the trainee conducts a second videotaped interview, emphasizing the target skill. The fourth is review, in which the trainee reviews the videotaped second session with a supervisor.

Microcounseling's significance is that it clearly defines desired interviewing behaviors and uses videotape models and review to train counselors in the target skills. Research (see Matarazzo, 1978) has generally been supportive of the effectiveness of this approach in teaching basic skills to beginning counselors.

Interpersonal process recall. This is a structured method of video replay for counselors developed by Kagan and his associates (Kagan, 1980). The four assumptions behind the use of this approach as a training method are 1) that people are their own best source of knowledge about themselves; 2) that we all have implicit theories about human behavior; 3) that verbally labeling interpersonal and intrapersonal processes provides order and structure; and 4) that counselors must understand human interactions in order to be effective.

Based on these assumptions, interpersonal process recall has developed into a structured training sequence where the counselor views videotapes of his or her interview with a supervisor who functions as an inquirer to guide the recall session. While the counselor-trainee chooses where in the tape to stop to make observations, the inquirer's role is to facilitate the discussion with effective questioning. Questions such as, "Do you recall what you were feeling?" "What thoughts were you having about the client?" "What did you want from her there?" and "What did you want to happen after that?" guide the discussion to the feelings, thoughts, expectations, and associations of the counselor.

Interpersonal process recall has been evaluated in several contexts (see McQuellon, 1982). It appears to be an effective method of training, and is also beneficial when used with clients to accelerate their progress in therapy. In particular, it influences trainees to better recognize and respond to affect and to demonstrate greater use of empathy in counseling interviews.

Supervision. Supervision is a key element of the training process. However, the term *supervision* has been used to describe a wide range of activities. Loganbill, Hardy, and Delworth (1982) define supervision as "an intensive, interpersonally-focused, one-to-one relationship in which one person is designated to facilitate the development of therapeutic competence in the other person" (p. 4). Within this definition they see four major supervisory functions: monitoring client welfare, enhancing growth of competence within stages, promoting transition between stages, and evaluating trainee progress.

Their model is based on developmental theory. It argues that trainees move through three stages (stagnation, confusion, and integration) across eight issues: competence, emotional awareness, autonomy, theoretical identity, respect for individual differences, purpose and direction, personal motivation, and professional ethics. An additional assumption is that development occurs throughout the therapist's lifetime; consequently, Loganbill et al. believe that these issues are faced on several different occasions throughout a counselor's or therapist's development.

Within supervision itself there are several intervention strategies that can be used. First, a supervisor may work to provide support to the trainee. This support includes qualities of the relationship that reduce anxiety and foster an atmosphere of trust and confidence. A second intervention is the use of confrontations. Confrontations serve to highlight discrepancies between the trainee's feelings, attitudes, and counseling behaviors. Third, supervision functions to help the counselor learn skills of conceptualization; these skills allow the counselor to better understand both the client and the nature of the therapeutic process. A supervisor may also function in a prescriptive manner—identifying needed treatment plans for the counselor, giving the counselor examples of ways to phrase certain ideas, and so on. Finally, supervisors may provide skills training.

Overall during supervision there needs to be an emphasis on the supervisor understanding the dynamics of the client and the trainee, particularly as these are in conflict (Mueller & Kell, 1971). And as Stoltenberg (1981) has noted, counselors vary in their level of development, from dependence through autonomy, which necessitates careful assessment of the abilities and needs of the supervised counselor or therapist.

Issues in Training. In the complex task of training counselors and therapists there are several relevant issues. For example, should therapists be required to have personal therapy? Is it better to train within a single theoretical orientation or across several?

Perhaps the most important issue is how to select students for therapy training. There seems to be a shared belief that certain types of persons are better therapists; thus, selection programs have attempted to measure personality variables such as warmth, perceptiveness, and so on, and correlate them with success as a therapist. However, the research evidence to date does not indicate that any particular characteristic is associated with successful training outcome. As Matarazzo (1978) noted, since counseling is a human interaction endeavor, we would be safe in assuming that therapists who are flexible and open-minded would do better. However, research showing that therapists can induce deterioration as well as improvement in their clients has meant that selection remains a concern. Yet there are no definable, measurable selection criteria currently shown to be clearly associated with therapeutic success.

In spite of the lack of research support for certain personality variables in predicting success, it seems clear that psychological disturbance in the trainee will hinder his or her response to training. Thus, many training programs may encourage or require therapy experience. For example, a survey of clinical psychology programs approved by the American Psychological Association (Wampler & Strupp, 1976) found that 67% of the responding programs actively encourage therapy for their students, while an additional 4% require it. Since maturity and personal understanding may be achieved through several routes, most training programs endorse therapy as an adjunct to training when it is needed by the trainee rather than as an across-the-board requirement.

Future issues in training will probably arise in three areas. First, although several methods for teaching basic skills are available to trainers, there is less agreement on what skills to teach, how to measure their acquisition, and whether their use results in improved client welfare. Second, the training of more advanced skills must be explored. While supervision is a key aspect of imparting advanced therapy methods, there should be more specification of what skills are needed and how best to help trainees acquire them. Finally, the integration of therapy training with overall professional training must be clarified. The balance of theory and practice and the timing of therapy training are important issues in the training of psychologists; they are relevant for other helping professions as well.

References

Egan, G. *The skilled helper*. Monterey, Calif.: Brooks/Cole, 1982.

Ivey, A. E. *Microcounseling: Innovations in interviewing training*. Springfield, Ill.: Thomas, 1971.

Ivey, A. E., & Authier, J. *Microcounseling: Innovations in interviewing, counseling, psychotherapy, and psychoeducation*. Springfield, Ill.: Thomas, 1978.

Kagan, N. Influencing human interactions: Eighteen years with IPR. In A. K. Hess (Ed.), *Psychotherapy supervision: Theory, research, and practice*. New York: Wiley, 1980.

Kurtz, P. D., & Marshall, E. K. Evolution of interpersonal skills training. In E. K. Marshall, P. D. Kurtz, et al. (Eds.), *Interpersonal helping skills*. San Francisco: Jossey-Bass, 1982.

Lambert, M. J., DeJulio, S. S., & Stein, D. M. Therapist interpersonal skills: Process, outcome, methodological considerations, and recommendations for future research. *Psychological Bulletin*, 1978, *85*, 467–489.

Loganbill, C., Hardy, E., & Delworth, U. Supervision: A conceptual model. *The Counseling Psychologist*, 1982, *10*(1), 3–42.

Matarazzo, R. Research on the teaching and learning of psychotherapeutic skills. In S. L. Garfield & A. E. Bergin (Eds.), *Handbook of psychotherapy and behavior change* (2nd ed.). New York: Wiley, 1978.

McQuellon, R. P. Interpersonal process recall. In E. K. Marshall, P. D. Kurtz, et al. (Eds.), *Interpersonal helping skills*. San Francisco: Jossey-Bass, 1982.

Mueller, W. J., & Kell, B. L. *Coping with conflict: Supervising counselors and psychotherapists*. New York: Appleton-Century-Crofts, 1971.

Rogers, C. R. The necessary and sufficient conditions of therapeutic personality change. *Journal of Consulting Psychology*, 1957, *21*, 95–103.

Smith, M. L., Glass, G. V., & Miller, T. I. *The benefits of psychotherapy*. Baltimore: Johns Hopkins Press, 1980.

Stoltenberg, C. Approaching supervision from a developmental perspective: The counselor complexity model. *Journal of Counseling Psychology*, 1981, *28*, 59–65.

Truax, C. B., & Carkhuff, R. R. *Toward effective counseling and psychotherapy: Training and practice*. Chicago: Aldine, 1967.

Wampler, L. D., & Strupp, H. H. Personal therapy for students in clinical psychology: A matter of faith? *Professional Psychology*, 1976, *7*, 195–201.

E. M. Altmaier

See Counseling and Psychotherapy: Overview; Psychotherapy, Research in, Effectiveness of.

Trait. As used by psychologists and biologists, the term refers to any relatively enduring characteristic that may be used to describe a group or individual. The existence of a trait is inferred from repeated observations across a diverse range of circumstances. Some biologists reserve the term for genetic characteristics as opposed to ecological or environmental-induced ones (cf. dominant or recessive traits).

If the trait is one present in all members of a specific group, then it is a common trait. But if the trait reflects only one individual's consistency, it is termed a unique trait. The trait description may refer to behavioral or manifest consistency in diverse situations or may infer causation through underlying constructs. In the former case the trait is a surface trait, while in the latter case it is a source trait. As behavioral indicators surface traits are readily observed, but source traits are the inferred, underlying structures. In Allport's analysis traits are constructs that give rise to equivalent actions in response to diverse stimuli or to equivalent stimuli yielding related but distinct responses. Traits render stimuli and responses functionally equivalent. Thus, there may be multiple indicators of a trait.

Based on multiple observations a trait description is an abstraction of the common elements in those observations into a pattern and a generalization of the pattern to other situations or individuals. A trait's relative strength is a probability statement of likely action.

Controversy exists as to whether traits are real characteristics of actors or the inferential products of observers. As an advocate of the first position Allport conceived of traits as neuropsychic structures, while many personality and social psychologists view traits as attributions made by observers about persons. In the first case traits are used as causal explanation for latent consistency in behavior, a consistency modified only slightly by environmental demand. In the latter position traits are labels used by observers as descriptions of apparent consistency in behavior. The attribution of a label may initiate a filtering process that selectively ignores disconfirming evidence.

While traits are ascribed to human intellect, most trait theories are concerned with emotional, social, or personality domains. The most prominent trait concepts (as causal structures) are found in the works of Allport and R. B. Cattell.

Some theorists equate traits and types. However, a majority seem to follow the direction of Eysenck, who places them on a continuum of specificity-generality. Specific responses are organized into a habitual response, sets of habitual responses in a trait, and sets of traits into a type. As traits order diverse behaviors, types order traits.

R. L. TIMPE

See TEMPERAMENT; PERSONALITY; TYPE.

Tranquilizer. Any of a number of drugs used to reduce anxiety, tension, or agitation. Technically the term refers to a group of phrenotropic compounds whose effects are primarily exerted at a subcortical level. This results in no interference with consciousness, in contrast to hypnotic and sedative drugs, which also have a calming effect. Common usage of the term distinguishes between minor tranquilizers (such as Valium, Miltown, and Librium), which are antianxiety agents, and major tranquilizers (such as chlorpromazine or Thorazine), which are antipsychotic agents. Minor tranquilizers are used principally in the treatment of anxiety, while major tranquilizers are used principally in the treatment of schizophrenia.

D. G. BENNER

See PSYCHOPHARMACOLOGY.

Transactional Analysis. A theory of personality, a view of psychopathology, a mode of psychotherapy, and a philosophy of life. In each of these the primary data for consideration are observable ways in which persons interact with each other. These interpersonal interactions are called transactions, and it is the belief of this approach that an analysis of these transactions is the prime means for understanding and changing persons.

As a theory of personality transactional analysis assumes that those behaviors, attitudes, and styles that charaterize persons are habits they have developed in efforts to obtain "strokes" from other persons with whom they interact. "Stimulus hunger" is seen as the basic motivation of life. This term refers to the innate desire to interact with the world, and most of all the desire to interact with other people. Personality is therefore a style of interacting with others from whom one seeks recognition, status, and intimacy. Personality does not result, as Freud suggested, from an individual need for pleasure but from a social need for others. In this regard transactional analysis is more like ego psychology than psychoanalysis.

As a view of psychopathology transactional analysis assumes that persons are born innocent and trusting. They yearn for intimacy, and they reach out confidently to others. Over time

two events commonly occur. People become stereotyped and they become defensive. They give up on experiencing intimacy—that for which persons have a need—and settle for the types of interpersonal relationships (or transactions) that lead to isolation and negative self-images. These types of transactions are called games, and they always end in bad feelings for both persons involved. Games are those types of interactions that always result in negative endings and reinforce a person's bad feelings.

As a mode of psychotherapy transactional analysis assumes that if persons become aware of the self-defeating, intimacy-destroying, isolation-producing ways in which they are interacting with others, and they decide to change these into more fulfilling manners of relating, they can. Transactional analysis affirms the capacity of people to recognize and analyze and alter their behavior. As contrasted with psychoanalysis, which is pessimistic about persons' abilities to become aware of their dynamics because of its presumption that psychopathology is determined by the unconscious, transactional analysis is optimistic about the ability of persons to gain such insight because it presumes that the origins of these problems is in conscious and subconscious ego states that are available for introspection.

As a philosophy of life transactional analysis affirms the potential and possibility of intimacy in human relationships. It is prescriptive, not just descriptive, of what human life ought to be, and it has ideal states toward which it feels society ought to be committed. For example, in Steiner's *Scripts People Live* (1974) a significant section is devoted to a critique of the type of society that promotes isolation and competition. Transactional analysis is optimistic and realistic at the same time. It is idealistic in terms of what human life was meant to be, and it works with persons and with institutions to make them more humane in the sense that they better induce intimacy among people.

Background. While transactional analysis includes a number of contemporary theorists (e.g., Harris, Steiner, Jongeward, James), it evolved from the ideas of one man, Eric Berne. Berne was a psychiatrist who practiced most of his life in the San Francisco area. He had gone through several years of training to be a psychoanalyst prior to being told he would not be approved in 1956. It has often been assumed that because of this disappointing experience Berne decided to create his own theory in contrast to psychoanalysis. This is only partially true; Berne had begun much earlier to state his opinions about the need for a shorter form of treatment than psychoanalysis and for a view of personality that emphasized the ego rather than the id. These ideas germinated during his experience of growing up in the home of a father who was a physician to the poor in Toronto. While a United States army psychiatrist, he published five papers on clinical intuition.

In the late 1950s Berne began to conduct weekly seminars for professionals in his San Francisco office. This led to the publication of *Transactional Analysis in Psychotherapy* (1961), which is said to be the formal beginning of the movement. Many of the recent leaders of the International Transactional Analysis Association and writers in the *Transactional Analysis Journal* were participants in Berne's weekly seminars. There they became stimulated by his "social psychiatry" (a label often ascribed to transactional analysis) and went on to make significant theoretical contributions of their own.

In his seminars Berne placed great emphasis on simple language. He discounted fancy verbiage and cautioned professionals not to use incomprehensible technical jargon. He was interested in finding easy-to-understand terms that patients could fathom and could use in their own effort to get well. He reportedly said after listening patiently to an elaborate case presentation replete with jargon, "That is all well and good. All I know is the patient is not getting cured" (reported in Steiner, 1974, p. 14). In spite of the fact that some professionals criticized transactional analysis for its use of colloquial, folksy, undignified terms such as "games," "trading stamps," and "fairy tales," Berne was unapologetic in his insistence that theory should be sharable and usable.

Basic Concepts. Among these terms were the ones used by Berne to denote ego states. It was his conviction that behavior was a function of the role persons perceived themselves to be playing in transactions with other persons. These perceived roles are determined by the state of mind, or ego state, of the person at a given time. Although he recognized that people's mental states were complex and unique, Berne suggested that they could be grouped under three major types: the "parent," the "adult," and the "child" ego states.

Parent ego states are those in which a person experiences directive, nurturing, criti-cal, prescriptive, and/or protective inclinations. Transactional analysis distinguishes between critical and nurturing parent ego states and suggests that these attitudes and feelings are usually derivatives of people's experiences with their own parents.

Child ego states are those in which a person experiences impulsive, accommodating, fearful, enthusiastic, pleasureful, intuitive, hurtful, and/or gleeful inclinations. Transactional analysis distinguishes between the free and adapted child ego states and suggests that these feelings, too, are derivatives of peoples' experiences with others from whom they have learned these childlike attitudes. Further, transactional analysis sees the child ego state as the repository of natural, innate energy and self-affirmation. The "little professor" component of the child ego state is that unlearned wisdom with which children are endowed and upon which persons can draw for unlearned wisdom.

Adult ego states are those in which a person experiences pragmatic, rational, realistic, functional inclinations leading toward problem solving and cooperation. Transactional analysis perceives the adult ego state as energized by the child ego state and influenced by the parent ego state. It suggests that the adult should dominate life and that problems ensue when persons interact with each other on the basis of the prejudgments of the parent or the impulsiveness of the child. However, the hyperrationality characteristic of those who have blocked off their parent or their child ego states presents an equal problem. The optimal state of affairs is one in which there is a free-flowing relationship between the three ego states with the adult dominating.

Relationship to Psychoanalysis. This model of psychic structure illustrates transactional analysis's similarity to as well as its difference from psychoanalysis. Both theories contend that inner personality structure is important, although their terms for the components differ and their presumptions about levels of consciousness are dissimilar. The terms *id, ego,* and *super-ego* seem similar to *parent, adult,* and *child.* Psychoanalysis assumes that the id is unconscious and that the ego and superego operate in unconscious, preconscious, and conscious states. Transactional analysis, in contrast, contends that they are all conscious ego states.

Furthermore, whereas psychoanalysis concludes that the ego and superego are structures that evolve from the id, transactional analysis feels that the parent and adult ego states coexist with the child from an early time in a person's life. From this point of view the ego (of which the parent, adult, and child ego states are parts) exists as a psychic structure along with the id almost from the very beginning of life.

Moreover, these ego states exist in the conscious or preconscious mind and are available to the person for reflection. This is a critical difference from psychoanalysis, which believes that much of the personality is unconscious and available to awareness only through such procedures as free association and dream analysis. Transactional analysis is very hopeful about people's attempts to understand themselves. In this sense the psychoanalytic model of personality as an iceberg of which only a small part can be seen above the water is turned upside down by transactional analysis. Personality is like an inverted iceberg where most of the ice is above the water and can be seen.

Both psychoanalysis and transactional analysis assume that personality structure develops through life experiences. However, whereas psychoanalysis contends that memories become distorted and repressed, transactional analysis is convinced that past memories have been stored in the mind just exactly as they happened and can be recalled. The mind is like a phonographic and photographic recorder that stores experiences and later expresses itself through the several ego states to which the person has access through introspection.

The final difference between psychoanalysis and transactional analysis regards the nature of neurotic behavior. Both are learning theories that emphasize habits. Both emphasize the uncanny tendency of persons to repeat behavior that is self-destructive and unproductive. Pathology for both is continuing to give old answers to present problems. Two emphases are distinctive in transactional analysis, however.

First, transactional analysis is larger in structure and in concept than psychoanalysis. Freud was primarily concerned with the tendency to repeat behavior that held down the repressed anxiety associated with anger and sex. Transactional analysis agrees with this, but in addition is concerned with total life goals and the person's orientation to the world. Thus, it talks of life positions that underlie the living out of life scripts which extend across a lifetime.

The second distinctive of transactional analysis is the nature of the motivation that underlies the repetition compulsion which characterizes psychopathology. The psychoanalytic understanding is grounded in the fear of a negative consequence—i.e., a repressed impulse getting out of control. In contrast, transactional analysis sees repeated unproductive behavior (i.e., games) as based on the avoidance of a positive consequence. Human behavior, as noted, is the result of the instinctive urge to relate to others. Optimal relating involves intimacy—free, spontaneous, trustful, energized transactions. However, intimate relationships are unpredictable, risky, and therefore frightening. Persons are attracted to intimacy and afraid of it at the same time. Because of the exhilaration it evokes, they long for it; but because of its lack of sureness, they settle for less than intimacy and construct games to guarantee it will not occur. They do not trust themselves to be intimate. This is quite different from the psychoanalytic point of view.

The Therapy Process. The transactional analyst works on a threefold model: analysis, experience, decision. The first step is structural analysis, in which clients are led into an analysis of the dominant ego states that characterize their interactions with others. Then they explore the genesis of these relative emphases in relationships with parents and in other significant experiences. They then attempt to analyze the transactions they are having with important persons to assess patterns and to ascertain the nature of games that may be present. Through depth reflection the person is led into intuitions about life scripts and basic life positions.

In the experience part of therapy the client is led through re-creations of important events and significant interactions. Reexperiencing is encouraged because it is assumed that insight by itself is not healing. Insight provides the basis for change, but change comes through reexperiencing and redecision. Many procedures are utilized to facilitate such experiencing. The transactional analyst is an active therapist and engages in intentional interventions to evoke the involvement of the client emotionally as well as cognitively.

Ultimately the transactional analyst is convinced that change comes by redecision. The therapist assumes the role of the nurturing parent and encourages the client in thinking that life can change. Although premature decision, which is not based in emotional reexperience, is abortive, in the final analysis change will never occur unless individuals determine to courageously try to be different. Transactional analysts believe that people can take control of their lives and that healing can occur provided such decisions are grounded in depth insight.

Evaluation. There are a number of underlying assumptions in transactional analysis that Christian counselors would do well to consider. Examples of such assumptions are that persons are born with a trusting, open, intimacy-seeking attitude (the I'M OK, You're OK life position) but lose it in the process of living and that healing means a rediscovery and resertion of that basic attitude toward life. Christians would agree with this and would call it being created in the image of God. Yet Christians would not agree that other life positions (I'M OK, You're Not OK; I'm Not OK, You're OK; I'm Not OK, You're Not OK) are only misperceptions. They too are real. The issue for the Christian is not wrong attitudes or incorrect perceptions, but sin. In fact, the Christian assumes that the most correct statement of reality is I'm Not OK, You're Not OK. As the Bible states, "All have sinned and come short of the glory of God" (Rom. 3:23). Transactional analysis does not have a serious enough doctrine of the human condition from the Christian point of view.

Another issue has to do with what happens when persons affirm their OK-ness. It is not simply a change of attitude or the making of a new decision, as transactional analysis would contend, but a recognition that sin is present and only God can make it right. No effort or insight can return persons to the I'm OK, You're OK position. The Christian gospel says that God in Christ has done this for us (cf. Rom. 8). He has forgiven our sin and restored us to a position of OK-ness. Thus, the Christian corrective to transactional analysis is I'm Not OK, You're Not OK, but That's OK. This is redemption as well as healing.

Transactional analysis makes very sound assumptions that can be used by Christian counselors if they keep in mind that it is based on humanistic presuppositions which need supplementing by the affirmations of the Christian faith.

References
Berne, E. *Transactional analysis in psychotherapy.* New York: Grove Press, 1961.
Steiner, C. *Scripts people live.* New York: Grove Press, 1974.
H. N. MALONY

See SCRIPT ANALYSIS.

Transcendental Meditation. *See* MEDITATION.

Transference.
The term means literally to convey information or content from one person, place, or situation to another. The psychological usage expresses a special type of relationship with another person. The usual pattern is for a person in the present to be experienced as though he or she were a person in the past. Thus transference, at least from a psychoanalytic point of view, is basically a repetition of an old object relationship in which attitudes and feelings, either positive or negative, pertaining to a former relationship have been shifted onto a new person in the present. Another way of describing this is to say that a mode of perceiving and responding to the world that was developed in and appropriate to childhood is inappropriately transferred into the adult context (Peck, 1978).

Although when broadly defined, transference can be seen to occur in all relationships to some degree, its role in therapy has been the focus of most attention. Here the patient displaces or transfers specific affective or cognitive contents that pertain to another person in an earlier developmental relationship onto the therapist.

Therapeutic Perspectives. Transference phenomena have long been a primary concern of psychoanalysts and psychoanalytic psychotherapists. Freudian theory asserts that the patient transfers to the therapist the attributes or images of significant persons from the past, usually the parents, and thus repeats the experiences of childhood in the process of psychotherapy (Freud, 1949). Furthermore, transference is assumed to be primarily unconscious and to take place in therapy without the patient having awareness of the distortion. Some therapists (Alexander, 1956) label the transference situation as irrational, due to the belief that the present responses made sense only in the past environment and are now repeated in the therapeutic context. Yet transference is the sine qua non of dynamic psychotherapy in that it gives the opportunity to deal with unresolved conflicts of the past.

While other theoretical orientations recognize the existence of transference phenomena, none of them place such emphasis on the importance of transference or locate the emotionalized experiences so completely in the past. Jung (1968) understood transference to be a special case of projection, a psychological mechanism that carries over subjective contents from both the personal unconscious (shadow) and the collective unconscious (archetypes) to the object of the therapist. He maintained that transference is never voluntary and intentional; it takes place spontaneously and without provocation. The handling of transference may be a part of Jungian psychotherapy, but it is not essential.

Adlerian theory (Ansbacher & Ansbacher, 1964) presents transference as a special kind of social feelings in the development of social interest. The feelings that the patient has toward the therapist are to be accepted as valuable and genuine but need not be analyzed and interpreted as in psychoanalysis. Effective psychotherapy does not depend on working through a transference neurosis. Rather, the emotional exchanges between patient and therapist serve as a model for the patient's further growth in attaining a wholesome sense of social interest.

Adherents to transactional analysis consider transference to be the patient's attempt to substitute the therapist for the parent (Berne, 1961). This substitutionary tendency is easily observed in the transactions between patient and therapist. The transference situation happens when the therapist sends an adult-to-adult stimulus message but receives a child-to-parent response. This crossed transaction corresponds to the Freudian concept of transference. Very little attention is given to transference in transactional analysis; instead, more concern is shown for learning how to make better contact with one's own ego states and to transact effectively and appropriately with other people.

Therapies that reflect existential, phenomenological, and perceptual perspectives tend to see the transference situation as real feelings in a here-and-now relationship (May, Angel, & Ellenberger, 1958). Boss (1963) has asserted that the patient does not transfer feelings that he or she had for a parent to the therapist; instead, the patient presents to the therapist life data that never developed beyond a limited and restricted form of infantile experience. So the phenomena are to be understood in terms of perception and relatedness to the world rather than a displacement of detachable feelings from one person to another. Perls (1973), too, observed that transference in therapy relates more to what has been missing in an individual's life than what has been experienced previously. Specifically, transference stems from personal deficits instead of forgotten emotionalized childhood experiences. The person has introjected parts of the environment in an attempt to shortcut the growth process of self-realization. These introjections and deficits become unfinished Gestalts and must be completed in therapy.

One of the most practical approaches to understanding and dealing with transference comes from the behavioral orientation (Dollard & Miller, 1950). The behavioral view holds that transference is a special form of generalized learning. The therapist's presence provides a social situation much like those in which the patient has previously been punished or rewarded by significant other persons. The stimuli of the therapist provoke the same responses from the patient that were learned in earlier interactions with significant human figures. Either a negative or positve transference response will be provoked depending on the specific therapist stimulus effect. The behavior therapist helps the client to resolve the transference situation by teaching him to discriminate between different sets of stimuli and then to learn how to respond appropriately.

Summary. Therapeutic approaches to transference range from scrutinizing all of the patient's reactions to the therapist for transference information, to viewing transference as nonessential and irrelevant to pscyhotherapy (Leites, 1979). The phenomena that characterize transference exist in virtually all object relationships and so are certainly present in the therapeutic context. The most plausible position to take on this aspect of human behavior appears to be an integration of the existential and behavioral perspectives. Transference is then seen as involving genuine here-and-now feelings for the therapist that are generalized by the person from previous learning conditions. It is also reasonable to suppose that some of the dynamics of this generalization of past experiences lie somewhat out of the person's awareness.

References

Alexander, F. *Psychoanalysis and psychotherapy.* New York: Norton, 1956.

Ansbacher, H. L., & Ansbacher, R. R. (Eds.). *The individual psychology of Alfred Adler.* New York: Harper & Row, 1964.

Berne, E. *Transactional analysis.* New York: Grove Press, 1961.

Boss, M. *Psychoanalysis and deseinanalysis.* New York: Basic Books, 1963.

Dollard, J., & Miller, N. E. *Personality and psychotherapy.* New York: McGraw-Hill, 1950.

Freud, S. *An outline of psychoanalysis.* New York: Norton, 1949.

Jung, C. G. *Analytical psychology: Its theory and practice.* New York: Pantheon, 1968.

Leites, N. *Interpreting transference.* New York: Norton, 1979.

May, R., Angel, E., & Ellenberger, H. F. *Existence: A new dimension in psychiatry and psychology.* New York: Basic Books, 1958.

Peck, M. S. *The road less traveled.* New York: Simon & Schuster, 1978.

Perls, F. *The Gestalt approach and eyewitness to therapy.* Ben Lomond, Calif.: Science & Behavior Books, 1973.

D. SMITH

See PSYCHOANALYTIC PSYCHOLOGY.

Transference Cure. *See* FLIGHT INTO HEALTH.

Transference Neurosis. An artificial neurosis appearing in psychoanalysis wherein the early oedipal situation is re-created in the transference relationship to the analyst. In this regressed·state the patient relives the original infantile conflicts. Psychoanalysis usually has as its goal the creation and resolution of the transference neurosis. In contrast, psychoanalytic psychotherapy attempts to keep the transference from developing to this point.

See PSYCHOANALYSIS: TECHNIQUE.

Transfer of Learning. The influence that LEARNING in one situation has upon learning or behaving in other situations. The importance of transfer is evident in the assumption of most educational programs that whatever is learned in specific tasks will be retained and used appropriately outside of instructional settings.

It is often difficult to demonstrate whether learning in specific situations results in better performance on subsequent tasks. One problem is that, while a distinct task (e.g., learning to play handball) may facilitate subsequent learning (e.g., playing tennis), this improved performance may not simply be due to the transfer of specfic learned skills but also to what is called learning to learn. In such a situation of general or nonspecific transfer learning skills are acquired through previous experience with a variety of learning situations. For example, practicing driving several types of automobiles may facilitate learning to drive a particular type of automobile. In this example the increased facility may be attributed to experience with the particular feature of one type of automobile, experience with general features shared by more than one type, or both.

The number of ways in which instances of transfer can differ reveals the complexity of these phenomena. First, transfer can be either positive or negative. Postive transfer occurs when prior learning facilitates or increases the learning in a subsequent task, as in the example of learning to drive. Negative transfer describes the case in which prior learning impedes or inhibits learning in a new task. A common example occurs whenever learning the sound system of one language (e.g., English) impedes learning the sound system of another, dissimilar language (e.g., Chinese).

Second, transfer can be either lateral or vertical. Lateral transfer is the influence of learning a task on learning other tasks at a similar level of complexity. Vertical transfer is the influence of learning a task on learning more complex tasks requiring a higher level of

ability. This is particularly important for learning in any area in which tasks can be organized into a hierarchical order according to complexity, with the learning of the simplest tasks tranferring to learning at higher levels.

Third, transfer can occur in many areas of learning, including the broad, distinct domains of cognitive, affective, and psychomotor learning.

Thus, it is not surprising that there are currently no all-inclusive theories to explain transfer phenomena. Rather, the emphasis is on theories that explain only certain kinds of transfer. This modern approach is a radical departure from the assumption, widely held until the early twentieth century, that academic training in a few formal disciplines can positively affect all subsequent learning by training "faculties" of the mind. As FACULTY PSYCHOLOGY declined and behaviorally oriented research on learning took its place, the earlier assumption was abandoned.

A key generalization in academic learning is that the major concepts and principles of a subject provide more positive transfer than does specific information. One application to Bible study is that emphasizing important themes and concepts throughout Scripture, rather than specific details, will facilitate students' study of unfamiliar books and passages.

D. R. RIDLEY

Transient Situational Disturbances. *See* ADJUSTMENT DISORDERS.

Transpersonal Psychology. This psychology posits a transcendent, nonmaterial reality that goes beyond the realm of individual personality and underlies and binds together all phenomena. Its language and concepts differ markedly from both conventional science and mainstream Christianity. Some scholars refer to the field, which has few unanimous premises, as spiritual psychology; others, the science of consciousness. Transpersonal psychology has been called the fourth force in psychology, after psychoanalysis, behaviorism, and humanistic psychology.

Philosophical Background. The underpinnings of transpersonal psychology are similar to those of Eastern (principally Indian) philosophy and the mystical traditions of Christianity and other world faiths. God is seen largely as immanent rather than as transcendent. Most theorists agree that 1) individuals can directly experience the underlying transcendent reality, which is related to the spiritual dimension of human life; and that 2) such experience involves expansion of consciousness beyond ordinary conceptual thinking and ego awareness. Some transpersonal psychologists allege that traditional religions have lost sight of such self-transcendence (the heart of spirituality) by falling into legalism and dogmatism.

Transpersonal psychologists avoid reductionistic methods of investigation. They see individuals, their behavior, and their experience as complex entities that are not to be reduced to lower levels of analysis. Occasional investigations employ conventional scientific methods based on logical positivism; however, greater use is made of Gestalt, phenomenological, and existential methods. The major method is an experiential empiricism that relies on presumably self-validating experiences.

Transpersonal psychologists view the human person as more than a complicated machine, a higher animal, or even ordinary waking human consciousness. They often think of people in terms of levels or states of consciousness. Self-transcendence, the ultimate human goal, is considered a dissolving of ego boundaries to experience a transformation or expansion of consciousness. Mystical awareness, or insight, is the most notable state of expanded consciousness. Before a healthy self-transcending expansion of consciousness can occur, the person must establish a solid ego awareness or self-identity. Without such sense of self, loosening of ego boundaries may be identified with psychosis. Self-transcendence optimally is sought only in the context of social, moral, and ethical considerations. Transpersonal psychology encourages the pursuit of total health: body, emotions, mind, intellect, and spirit.

History. Transpersonal psychology grew out of humanistic psychology during the 1960s. Its leaders thought humanism failed to go far enough in its vision for human existence. Sutich (1976), who was almost completely paralyzed from youth, considered mystical experiences to cast doubt on basic humanistic understandings. Maslow's (1968, 1971) concepts of being-language and the values of being led him to a similar position. Maslow observed that the values of being (such as love, truth, justice, beauty), inherent in any truly transcendent experience, are those characteristics by which religious people define God. Miles Vich, now editor of *The Journal of Transpersonal Psychology*, and Grof (1979), known for work on LSD-induced states of awareness, also worked with Sutich in founding transpersonal psychology.

Inspired by Julian Huxley's transhumanism, Sutich first called the movement transhumanistic psychology. However, he and Maslow agreed on the term *transpersonal psychology*, and the journal bearing that title was launched in 1969. The Association for Transpersonal Psychology was formed in 1971, with Alyce Green of the Menninger Foundation as its first president. The association managed the journal and provided a forum for scholars, who were gradually attracted to the movement. The first national and international transpersonal conferences were held in 1973 and have been regular events since then. In 1979 a Transpersonal Psychology Interest Group was formed within the American Psychological Association, and has had annual meetings thereafter.

Many regional and local transpersonal organizations have sprung up. Schools specializing in transpersonal psychology include the California Institute of Transpersonal Psychology, headed by Robert Frager. Transpersonal programs typically require students to be engaged in their own spiritual quests (see Fadiman & Frager, 1976), with programs comprehensive enough to include physical discipline ("body work," such as hatha yoga or tai chi), emotional training, meditation, and other spiritual disciplines, as well as intellectual study.

Academic Study. Transpersonal psychologists are interested in a variety of topics involving spiritual well-being and alteration of consciousness. Topics related to individuals include nonego states of awareness, the role of various ego states in human development, transcendent experience, relationships between healthy and unhealthy transcendence of ego boundaries (mysticism and psychosis), personal transformation, creativity, full health, development of human potential, spiritual growth, and the achievement of liberation (samadhi, self-realization). Studies regarding society include building new relationships between science and the humanities, the transformation of society toward spiritual values, societal health, group or shared consciousness, the organic unity of all persons (related to such ideas as the mystical body of Christ or the body of the Buddha), and the application of transpersonal concepts to social structures: business, science, education, human services, and religion.

The study of altered states of consciousness includes dreams, imagery, hypnosis, autogenic states, meditation, mysticism, extrasensory perception, precognition (prophecy), out-of-body experiences, and drug-altered states of consciousness. While some transpersonal psychologists consider various parapsychological phenomena in their domain, others do not. Additional areas of study include spiritual disciplines, ways to achieve control over altered states, and the integration of Eastern and Western views of the person.

Several transpersonal scholars have attempted classifications or "maps" of consciousness. Normal waking consciousness is considered only the most familiar form, with the psychoanalytic preconscious and unconscious relatively close to the ordinary personal consciousness. Increasingly remote are ontogenetic consciousness (concerned with issues of personal finitude, birth, death, and suffering); transpersonal consciousness (the realm of deep dreamless sleep, Zen satori, influence of good and evil spirits, and some religious ecstasy); and transcendent consciousness (mystical experience with a content—e.g., an idea of God). Beyond that lie layers of deepening mystical experience. As a composite this "map" represents the view of no single transpersonal psychologist, but illustrates some interests in the field.

Some earlier psychologies are considered relevant to transpersonal psychology, including Jung's ideas about collective unconscious and similar notions in James's writings. Other backgrounds include psychosynthesis (Assagioli, 1965), Frankl's logotherapy, Gestalt therapy, and various existential and phenomenological theories. The works of spiritual guides and mystics (Progoff, 1980) and interpreters of Indian philosophy (e.g., Trungpa, 1973) figure prominently. Some of the most important current work is being done by Grof (1979), Ring (1980), Tart (1975a, 1975b), Walsh (Walsh & Vaughan, 1980), and Wilber (1981).

Transpersonal Therapy. Transpersonal therapists typically work at whatever level is needed to produce the integration needed by the client. Most refer to counsel those with some interest in and capacity for spiritual work. Starting with the client's existential realities, life situation, and unique constellation of assets and liabilities, the therapist fosters a healthy integration of all the person's functions. Such integration typically is viewed as a spiritual task in itself.

Transpersonal therapies deal most explicitly with spiritual pathologies. Typical problems include spiritual pride, prejudices, fanaticism, dogmatism, legalistic mentality, unproductive guilt, excessive introspection, blindness to value, hedonism, general ego-centeredness or self-preoccupation, fascination with the occult

or cultism, overvaluing of paranormal powers, spiritual shortcuts or consolations, avoidance of genuine and manifest life tasks for artificial ones, spiritual materialism, impatience for growth, difficulty in "letting go," excessive rationality, and fixation on lower level needs (pleasure, "highs," power, good feelings, esteem of others).

Transpersonal therapists draw methods from logotherapy, psychosynthesis, Jungian analysis, Gestalt and existential therapies; music, dance, and art therapies; LSD-assisted therapy; and various spiritual disciplines. Popular techniques include meditation, relaxation, centering exercises, focusing, breathing practices, physical disciplines or "body work," guided imagery, autogenic training, hypnosis, sensory deprivation, biofeedback, dream logs and dreamwork, inner dialogues, music, art, and sports (Boorstein, 1980; Reynolds, 1980; Vaughan, 1979; Welwood, 1979).

Critique. Christians may be suspicious of transpersonal psychology's bases in non-Christian, Eastern religions. In principle, Eastern meditative techniques and other disciplines are separable from the belief system in which they originated, but they may lead gradually into non-Christian world views. Actually meditation and mystical experiences are inherent in the history and practice of Christianity. While they are found more in the Eastern Orthodox and Catholic traditions than in the Protestant, they are congruent with evangelical Christianity (e.g., Brandt, 1979). Transpersonal psychology is not anti-Christian, but it is open to sundry religious and spiritual traditions.

Transpersonal psychology suggests a welcome corrective to a rigidly materialistic science. However, the basic premises of the two approaches are so different that rapprochement would seem remote. Few people trained in traditional science can give credence to the nonmaterial as a scientific entity, even if they profess a personal religious faith. Nonetheless, some theoretical physicists suggest various forces or energies that might qualify as "underlying transcendent realities." The earnest psychological or religious practitioner can exercise reserve about radical departures from traditional concepts of reality, while remaining open to the claims of competing constructions.

References

Assagioli, R. *Psychosynthesis.* New York: Nobbs, Dorman, 1965.
Boorstein, S. (Ed.), *Transpersonal psychotherapy.* Palo Alto, Calif.: Science & Behavior Books, 1980.
Brandt, P. *Two-way prayer.* Waco, Tex.: Word Books, 1979.
Fadiman, J., & Frager, R. *Personality and personal growth.* New York: Harper & Row, 1976.

Grof, S. *The principles of LSD psychotherapy*. New York: Hunter House, 1979.

Maslow, A. H. *Toward a psychology of being* (2nd ed.). Princeton, N.J.: Van Nostrand, 1968.

Maslow, A. H. *The farther reaches of human nature*. New York: Viking 1971.

Progoff, I. *The practice of process meditation*. New York: Dialogue House Library, 1980.

Reynolds, D. K. *The quiet therapies*. Honolulu: University Press of Hawaii, 1980.

Ring, K. *Life at death: A scientific investigation of the near-death experience*. New York: Coward, McCann & Geoghenan, 1980.

Sutich, A. J. *The founding of humanistic and transpersonal psychology: A personal account*. Unpublished doctoral dissertation, Humanistic Psychology Institute, 1976.

Tart, C. T. *States of consciousness*. New York: Dutton, 1975. (a)

Tart, C. T. (Ed.). *Transpersonal psychologies*. New York: Harper & Row, 1975. (b)

Trungpa, C. *Cutting through spiritual materialism*. Berkeley, Calif.: Shambhala, 1973.

Vaughan, F. *Awakening intuition*. Garden City, N.Y.: Anchor/Doubleday, 1979.

Walsh, R. N., & Vaughan, F. (Eds.). *Beyond ego: Transpersonal dimensions in psychology*. New York: St. Martin's Press, 1980.

Welwood, J. (Ed.). *The meeting of the ways: Explorations in East-West psychology*. New York: Schocken, 1979.

Wilbur, K. *Up from Eden*. Garden City, N.Y.: Anchor/Doubleday, 1981.

M. J. MEADOW AND R. D. KAHOE

Transsexualism. A rare condition in which the late adolescent or adult individual consciously identifies as a member of the opposite sex. The diagnosis of transsexualism is made for individuals whose disturbance is not associated with another mental disorder such as schizophrenia, and in the absence of any physical intersex or genetic abnormality, when these criteria are fullfilled: 1) a strong desire to live as a member of the opposite sex and to have one's own genitals removed; 2) pronounced discomfort with one's anatomic sex to the point of feeling that one's sexual anatomy is inappropriate; and 3) a continuous and persisting sexual identity disturbance (not stress related) for a minimum of two years. The male transsexual reports a persistent feeling that "I am a woman trapped in a man's body."

The cross-gender identity is so profound that these individuals adopt a name of the other sex, choose to participate in culturally stereotyped activities associated with the other sex, and take on the behavior and mannerisms typically associated with the other sex. Far more than simply feeling inadequate to fulfill social expectations associated with their natural gender role, transsexual individuals chronically dress in clothes of the other sex, consider their own genitals as repugnant, and repeatedly request surgical or hormonal sex reassignment from physicians. In some cases male transsexuals attempt and succeed in mutilation or amputation of their genitals.

Clinically this condition is associated with a moderate to severe coexisting personality disturbance and is correlated with anxiety, severe depression, suicidal ideation, and suicide attempt. Social and occupational maladjustments are also commonly correlated with transsexualism.

Diagnostically individuals with this disorder are subclassified according to their sexual orientation and sexual history. Asexual transsexuals report never having experienced strong sexual feelings and often have little history of sexual activity. Homosexual transsexuals have predominant sexual arousal patterns and sexual object choice activity with members of the same anatomic sex preceding the full onset of the transsexual syndrome; however, these persons do not perceive the sexual behavior as homosexual because of their identification as being really a member of the other sex. Heterosexual transsexuals report a history of sexual behavior predominantly with one or more members of the opposite anatomic sex.

Disturbed parent-child relationships are almost always associated with transsexualism, together with a history of childhood effeminacy in boys or excessive childhood masculinity in the case of a girl. The major theories of etiology and pathogenesis for male transsexualism describe the family dynamics of an overly close relationship between the boy and the mother coupled with a passive, physically absent father. Data suggest that while mothers of male homosexuals are likely to be domineering and overprotective toward their sons, the mothers of transsexuals are likely to be also particularly competitive with their sons during childhood and early adolescence and are more likely to encourage "blissful closeness" with their sons—i.e., to identify closely with the male child (Stoller, 1975). As children female transsexuals are reportedly very active, to the point of displaying excessive physical aggression, particularly toward boys. There are tomboy preferences for male playmates and masculine attire. Their avoidance of feminine sex-typed activities differs from a more normal tomboy phase in that it exends well after the onset of puberty.

Transsexual adults typically evidence GENDER IDENTITY DISORDER in childhood, and the full transsexual syndrome for asexual and homosexual transsexuals occurs by late adolescence or early adulthood in most cases. Heterosexual transsexualism may have a later age onset.

The preferred treatment strategy is early identification and prevention by early intervention—in childhood or adolescence, if possible. One to two decades ago many clinicians considered psychological treatment of transsexualism to be impossible and therefore recommended hormonal and surgical sex-reassignment procedures (Green & Money, 1969). However, numerous legal, ethical, psychological, and surgical problems accompany attempted sex-reassignment procedures. Emerging follow-up data now suggest that such medical sex-reassignment procedures are not necessarily an ameliorative treatment, because many cases appear to be as poorly, or even more poorly, adjusted after such procedures than before the intervention (e.g., Meyer & Reter, 1979). At the same time, extensive behavior therapy techniques have been demonstrated to be effective in reversing a cross-gender identity in a number of late adolescent and early adulthood cases of transsexualism (e.g., Barlow, Abel, & Blanchard, 1979; Barlow, Reynolds, & Agras, 1973). A clinical psychologist and psychiatrist specializing in sexual problems have published one documented case of an adult male transsexual who experienced a change to a normal gender identity following a conversion and faith healing experience (Barlow, Abel, & Blanchard, 1977). Behavior therapy techniques for children with gender identity disorder have proven effective in reversing the cross-gender identity disturbance, and also hold promise as a preventative early intervention treatment strategy for emerging transsexualism (Rekers, 1978, 1982).

An ethical and theological understanding of transsexualism should consider the scriptural emphasis on biological, social, and moral distinctions based on sex. Human beings were created in the image of God as male and female (Gen. 1:27). The institution of heterosexual marriage was divinely created (Gen. 2:20–24); the husband and wife were both naked and were intended by God to feel no shame about their physical sexual anatomy (Gen. 2:25) and their sexual intercourse in marriage (Heb. 13:4). All sexual relationships outside of heterosexual marriage are immoral, sinful, and contrary to the created purpose of the body (e.g., Deut. 5:18; 1 Cor. 6:12–7:9).

Specific biblical commands are uniquely and differentially given to males (e.g., Eph. 5:25–6:4; Titus 2:2, 6–7) and to females (e.g., Eph. 5:22–24; 1 Tim. 2:9–12; 5:14). Among these differential normative teachings for males and females are specific references to clothing. Deuteronomy 22:5 states, "A woman must not wear men's clothing, nor a man wear women's clothing, for the Lord your God detests anyone who does this." Although the transsexual's urge or temptation to cross dress is not specifically mentioned here, the behavioral act of cross dressing itself is categorically prohibited by God. For the homosexual transsexual all homosexual acts are sinful (Leviticus 18:22; Romans 1:24–28). Many biblical passages prohibit all overt sexual behaviors between two members of the same anatomic sex, making no exception for individuals who psychologically perceive the relationship in some other context, even though cases of transsexualism have been recognized from antiquity (cf. Green & Money, 1969). First Corinthians 6:9–10 specifically designates the effeminate male and homosexuals as unrighteous.

In the biblical context the therapeutic goal of promoting cross-gender identification through psychotherapy or sex-reassignment medical procedures would be contrary to God's creative purpose for the individual. Psychological interventions would more appropriately pursue the goal of assisting the individual to achieve the identity, behavior, physical appearance, and clothing that properly corresponds to the person's sexual anatomic status.

References

Barlow, D. H., Abel, G. G., & Blanchard, E. B. Gender identity change in transsexuals: An exorcism. *Archives of Sexual Behavior*, 1977, *6*, 387–395.

Barlow, D. H., Abel, G. G., & Blanchard, E. B. Gender identity change in transsexuals. *Archives of General Psychiatry*, 1979, *36*, 1001–1007.

Barlow, D. H., Reynolds, E. J., & Agras, W. S. Gender identity change in a transsexual. *Archives of General Psychiatry*, 1973, *28*, 569–576.

Green, R., & Money, J. (Eds.). *Transsexualism and sex reassignment*. Baltimore: Johns Hopkins University Press, 1969.

Meyer, J. K. & Reter, D. J. Sex reassignment: Follow-up. *Archives of General Psychiatry*, 1979, *36*, 1010–1015.

Rekers, G. A. Sexual problems: Behavior modification. In B. B. Wolman (Ed.), *Handbook of treatment of mental disorders in childhood and adolescents*. Englewood Cliffs, N.J.: Prentice-Hall, 1978.

Rekers, G. A. *Shaping your child's sexual identity*. Grand Rapids: Baker, 1982.

Stoller, R. J. *Sex and gender: The transsexual experiment* (Vol. 2). New York: Aronson, 1975.

G. A. REKERS

See SEXUALITY; GENDER IDENTITY.

Transvestism. This psychosexual disorder occurs in adult and postpubescent adolescent males. The distinguishing characteristic is wearing feminine clothing, which is associated with sexual arousal at least in an initial phase of the condition. Intense frustration is reported when this cross dressing is interfered with, and many transvestites report a tension release or anxiety reduction during episodes of cross dressing. Most (about 89%) transvestites are heterosexual. Although 64% are married and most appear unremarkably masculine in their everyday life, their episodes of cross dressing are often accompanied by elaborate use of feminine cosmetics and wigs; shaving of legs and underarms; and feminine or exaggeratedly caricatured feminine gestures, mannerisms, postures, and gait (Bentler & Prince, 1970).

The clinical picture of transvestic phenomena ranges from wearing women's panties under the usual male clothing throughout the day in some cases, to episodic solitary wearing of lingerie or a few female clothing articles in one-third of the cases, to elaborate cross dressing in the privacy of the home in most cases, to extensive involvement in a transvestic subculture including episodic appearances in public while fully cross dressed in a minority of cases. Some cross dressed men appear indistinguishable from women if seen in public, while others have a much lesser degree of convincing female appearance depending on the extensiveness of cross dressing, makeup, shaving practices, and body mannerism skill. Forty-two percent have told no one about their cross dressing (Prince & Bentler, 1972).

The diagnostic criteria include: 1) repeated and persistent cross dressing by a male with a predominantly heterosexual orientation; 2) the association of cross dressing with sexual excitement, at least in early phases of the disorder; and 3) report of intense frustration with the interference of cross dressing.

Further, the differential diagnosis of transvestism excludes those cases meeting the criteria for TRANSSEXUALISM where there is a persistent wish to live as the other sex and to be rid of one's own sexual organs. In transsexualism there is rarely any sexual excitement associated with the cross dressing. The transvestite male has a male sexual identity; however, in rare cases transvestism can progress into transsexualism (Wise & Meyer, 1980).

Female impersonation differs from transvestism in that the act of cross dressing does not result in sexual arousal and the interference with cross dressing does not result in intense frustration. Some male homosexuals occasionally cross dress while cruising heterosexual bars or social clubs as a means of seeking male partners on whom they perform fellatio or manual masturbation, with the heterosexual male partner being unaware of the masquerade. In rare cases the homosexual male is also diagnosed as a transvestite if the cross dressing causes sexual arousal. Transvestism is distinguished from cases of cross dressing for purpose of relief of tension or "gender discomfort" without any history of sexual excitement associated with the cross dressing; these are potential cases of atypical gender identity disorder rather than transvestism. Approximately 15% of transvestites report sadomasochistic interests.

While 20% of the wives of transvestites are unaware of their husbands' cross dressing, many transvestites seek to involve their wives by cross dressing during sexual intercourse or seeking assistance in makeup or feminine clothing selection from their wives. While 23% of the wives are accepting of the transvestism, many others are distressed by the cross dressing and insist on psychological treatment or on separation or divorce.

The etiology of transvestism typically involves childhood or early adolescent cross dressing experience (54% report cross dressing before age 10), typically at home or in private (Stoller, 1968). Cases of partial cross dressing typically progress to total cross dressing. A favorite feminine clothing article may be used with masturbation and become an erotic stimulus in itself. Some transvestites experience progressive disappearance of the sexual arousal by feminine clothing, while the cross dressing continues to be an anxiety-reducing condition. Survey data have not supported the hypothesis that broken homes, poor father image, and dominant mothers are etiological factors (Prince & Bentler, 1972). Four percent of transvestites report the childhood experience of humiliation from being forced to cross dress in girl's clothing. Some transvestites have been previously diagnosed with GENDER IDENTITY DISORDER OF CHILDHOOD (Zuger, 1978).

In a study of 504 cases of transvestism, 23% reported being Roman Catholic, 12% conservative Protestant, 45% liberal Protestant, 4% Jewish, and 13% agnostic or atheist (Prince & Bentler, 1972). Transvestites report themselves to be less conservative religiously than transsexuals. However, the Bible teaches that the behavioral act of cross dressing is prohibited by God: "A woman must not wear men's clothing, nor a man wear women's clothing, for the Lord your God detests anyone who does this" (Deut. 22:5). In 1 Corinthians 6:9, the list of types of wicked individuals who will not inherit the kingdom of God includes the Greek term *malakoi*, which refers to soft, effeminate males, with the emphasis on clothing, which thereby implies transvestism. A biblically based theology of man affirms the creation of human beings in the image of God as male and female (Gen. 1:27) in which the sexual distinction is so significant to God that a blurring of the sexual differentiation by cross dressing is specifically prohibited.

Because God created sexual attraction and sexual arousal for the marriage relationship, cross dressing for sexual pleasure is an unfortunate perversion of the created purpose of sexual expression. The empirical data also indicate that cross dressing contributes to marital conflict in a large proportion of married transvestites, and 36% of divorced transvestites reported that cross dressing was a cause of the divorce (Prince & Bentler, 1972). Therefore, both biblical revelation and empirical findings indicate that cross dressing for sexual arousal (transvestism) interferes with a normal sexual relationship in marriage.

In this moral and theological context the ethically proper response to the condition of transvestism would include repentance of the sexual sin and a restoration of a proper marital relationship. Marriage counseling, psychotherapy, and behavior therapy have all been found helpful for cases of marital conflict and transvestism. Specifically, aversion therapy techniques have been reported to be successful in treating adult transvestism in a number of studies that reported substantial reduction or elimination of the urge to cross dress (Rekers, 1978). Periodic follow-up "booster" treatments have been found to be necessary for generalization and maintenance of behavioral treatment effects. However, only 9% of a large sample of transvestites reported they had undertaken serious treatment (Prince & Bentler, 1972). The preferred clinical intervention would be early identification in childhood or adolescence, coupled with early behavioral treatment intervention prior to adulthood, to prevent the full syndrome of transvestism. Behavioral treatment studies (Rekers, 1978, 1982) have demonstrated this approach to be effective.

References

Bentler, P. M., & Prince, C. V. Psychiatric symptomatology in transvestites. *Journal of Clinical Psychology*, 1970, *26*, 434-435.

Prince, C. V., & Bentler, P. M. Survey of 504 cases of transvestism. *Psychological Reports*, 1972, *31*, 903-917.

Rekers, G. A. Sexual problems: Behavior modification. In B. B. Wolman (Ed.), *Handbook of treatment of mental disorders in childhood and adolescence*. Englewood Cliffs, N.J.: Prentice-Hall, 1978.

Rekers, G. A. *Shaping your child's sexual identity*. Grand Rapids: Baker, 1982.

Stoller, R. J. *Sex and gender: On the development of masculinity and femininity*. New York: Science House, 1968.

Wise, T. N., & Meyer, J. K. The border area between transvestism and gender dysphoria: Transvestitic applicants for sex reassignment. *Archives of Sexual Behavior*, 1980, *9*, 327-342.

Zuger, B. Effeminate behavior present in boys from childhood: Ten additional years of follow-up. *Comprehensive Psychiatry*, 1978, *19*, 363-369.

G. A. REKERS

See SEXUALITY.

Traumatic Neurosis. *See* POSTTRAUMATIC STRESS DISORDER.

Triadic-Based Family Therapy.

The focus on an interpersonal triangle within the family cuts across most of the traditional schools of family therapy; this is true regardless of whether the theoretical orientation is psychoanalytic, structural, strategic, problem-solving, experiential, or communicational. Historically family therapy grew from an initial focus on dyads (e.g., the mother-child dyad as exemplified in the schizophrenogenic mother notion of Fromm-Reichman, 1948). Since that time a major shift has taken place, and many individuals have focused on triads as opposed to individuals, dyads, or larger units of study. Ravich (1967) notes that there is a vast difference between a two-person and a three-person system.

Triadic-based family therapy is primarily identified with the work of Zuk (1969, 1971). Haley (1976, 1980) and Bowen (1966) have also made important contributions.

Theoretical Considerations. One of the best known claims for the importance of triadic family therapy was made by Bowen: "The basic building block of any emotional system is the triangle. When emotional tension in a two person system exceeds a certain level it triangles in a third person, permitting the tension to shift around within the triangle. Any two in the original triangle can add a new member. An emotional system is composed of a series of interlocking triangles. It is a clinical fact that the original two person tension system will resolve itself automatically when contained within a three person system, one of whom remains emotionally detached" (1966, p. 368). Haley (1967) has elaborated on this theoretical foundation by describing three primary characteristics of the "perverse" triangle: 1) The members are not peers; one is in a different generation from the other two. 2) In the process of interaction one person forms a coalition with the single person from the other generation against the remaining third party. This coalition is not an alliance in which the two operate independently of the third; rather, it is a process of dual action against the third person. 3) The emotional coalition between the two persons is denied frequently, especially when the parties are queried regarding a specific act. This pattern is seen most frequently in a clinical situation when a family appears with a symptomatic child connected to one overinvolved parent and one emotionally detached parent. This particular pattern of family interaction has been intrapersonalized and institutionalized by psychoanalytic theory as the oedipal conflict.

When the typical family is broken down into triads, a staggering complexity of units for study is generated; in the average American family of two parents, two children, and two sets of grandparents, this group of eight people generates 56 possible triangles. Any one person in the family is involved in 21 different triangles concurrently, each of which has the potential for an intergenerational coalition of a perverse nature. Within this network no two individuals are in the same position relative to the overall context. These triangles are intimately related. Adaptive behavior within one triangle may have maladaptive repercussions in another triangle. When all triangles are amicable, no problems appear; but when one individual is the nexus for two triangles that are in conflict, tension is generated within that individual. If the tension exceeds a certain critical level, it may manifest itself in symptomatic behavior. This behavior is seen in this theoretical framework as both a cry for help and protection from the anxiety generated by the triadic conflict.

Treatment Considerations. High levels of therapist activity within this primarily brief treatment modality are almost always required for effective treatment. The primary role of the triadic therapist is to serve as a flexible mediator, challenger, positive reframer of transactions, and shifting coalition partner within the extant family triangles (Haley, 1976; Zuk, 1971). The goal is to shift the balance of pathogenic relating among family members so that newer, more constructive family hierarchies (composed of interlocking series of triangles) become possible. It is assumed that once the structure of the family is rearranged, communication patterns will be forced to change and individual symptomatic behavior will improve (Haley, 1980). Change comes about when families begin behaving differently, whether or not insight into their own interaction process occurs.

It is inevitable that the family will involve the therapist in their covert triangulations. It is therefore critical that the therapist take cognizance of his or her coalition status at any one point in time. An excellent method for maintaining coalition neutrality has been proposed by Palazzoli-Selvini, Boscolo, Cecchin, and Prata (1980). In this method the therapist, in front of the whole family, systematically queries each family member in turn regarding specific aspects of the relationship between any other two family members (e.g., "Johnny, can you tell me what Mommie and Suzie fight the most about?"). This method serves to make implicit family triangulations explicit and to keep the net coalition valence of the therapist neutral at the end of such a circular interview.

This intervention style and way of thinking about families constitutes a growing edge within the field. It is highly likely that the focus on triads, combined with innovative therapeutic methods, will provide a cutting edge for continued growth and development within the mainstream of systems therapy.

References

Bowen, M. The use of family theory in clinical practice. *Comprehensive Psychiatry*, 1966, 7, 345–374.
Fromm-Reichman, F. Notes on the development of treatment of schizophrenics by psychoanalytic psychotherapy. *Psychiatry*, 1948, 11, 263–273.
Haley, J. Toward a theory of pathological systems. In G. Zuk & I. Boszormenyi-Nagy (Eds.), *Family therapy and disturbed families*. Palo Alto, Calif.: Science & Behavior Books, 1967.
Haley, J. *Problem solving therapy*. San Francisco: Jossey-Bass, 1976.
Haley, J. *Leaving home*. New York: McGraw-Hill, 1980.
Palazzoli-Selvini, M., Boscolo, L., Cecchin, G., & Prata, G. Hypothesizing, circularity, neutrality: Three guidelines for the conductor of the session. *Family Process*, 1980, 19, 3–12.
Ravich, R. Psychotherapy for the whole family. *American Journal of Psychotherapy*, 1967, 21, 132–134.
Zuk, G. H. Triadic-based family therapy. *International Journal of Psychiatry*, 1969, 8, 539–548.
Zuk, G. H. *Family therapy*. New York: Behavior Publications, 1971.

V. L. Shepperson

See Family Therapy: Overview.

Triangle. In the context of family therapy a triangle consists of three people stuck in repetitious, maladaptive patterns of interaction. Troubled families frequently contain a central triangle made up of the mother, father, and a problem child. This threesome becomes the primary focus of family therapy, which seeks to alleviate stress by transforming dysfunctional triangular interactions into adaptive transactions among the three.

Triangles create problems because they involve a breach of family or generational boundaries. For example, when unresolved conflict in marriage prompts spouse A to draw an outsider in for support, a triangle is formed. The support helps spouse A to feel better, but it siphons off energy from the marriage. Furthermore, spouse B resents the outsider, whose support hardens spouse A's position and deepens the marital polarization. Hence, triangles not only feed on tension, they also produce conflict.

J. A. LARSEN

See FAMILY SYSTEMS THEORY; FAMILY SYSTEMS THERAPY; TRIADIC-BASED FAMILY THERAPY.

Trust. An act of dependency upon another person for the fulfillment of biological, psychological, social, or spiritual needs that cannot be met independently. It is subjective confidence in the intentions and ability of another to promote and/or guard one's well-being that leads a person to risk possible harm or loss. Trust, then, involves both perceptual and behavioral dimensions. Perceiving another person as trustworthy does not constitute trust, nor does simply engaging in a risk-taking behavior without some positive expectancy about the response. Perceiving someone as trustworthy *and* placing oneself in a position of vulnerability due to the possibility of betrayal is trust. Trust may involve the vulnerability of one's self-concept and emotional well-being, relationships, possessions, social and economic position, or physical being.

Trust is not usually an all-or-none phenomenon. There are degrees of trust, which can be assessed by the level of positive expectancy about someone's trustworthiness together with the magnitude of damage involved if betrayal occurs. A process of observation and testing typically occurs before significant outcomes are entrusted. As confidence increases, subjective assessment of the risk involved tends to decrease and greater (objective) acts of trust occur. Interpersonal attraction and reciprocated acts of disclosure appear to facilitate the development of trust.

It seems that people differ in their general tendency to trust people. Some persons are so trusting they are called gullible. Others are so suspicious that they are paranoid. Erikson (1963) suggests that this basic orientation is due to the adequacy with which basic needs of the infant were met during the helplessness of the first year of life. Two scales widely used to assess such a generalized trust orientation are the Philosophy of Human Nature Scale (Wrightsman, 1974) and the Interpersonal Trust Scale (Rotter, 1967).

Acts of trusting vary considerably. They may involve the safekeeping of property, acceptance of a persuasive communication, seeking help for problems, selection of a physician, or sharing of confidential information. The diversity of trust acts may be categorized into three general types of trust: persuasive, functional, and personal. Persuasive trust involves a belief in the validity of a message and the integrity of a messenger so that an idea is accepted or a product is bought. Acceptance of the appeals of politicians, evangelists, and vacuum cleaner salespeople requires this kind of trust. Functional trust is confidence in the capacity and expertise of the one being trusted to competently fulfill a function, such as flying an airplane or doing surgery. Personal trust is the expectancy that another will accept voluntarily disclosed intimate information, treat it with value, and act in one's best interest. This is the trust of intimate friends. More than one kind of trust may be expressed toward another person. Trust of one type may facilitate the other types in certain situations.

The act of entrusting specific outcomes to a specific person at a given point in time involves a complex mixture of one's history of trust encounters in general and in similar situations; the level and kind of felt need; information about the other person's sincerity, capability, integrity, and intentions based on direct and indirect observation; the kind of relationship that exists; the kind and degree of trust required; and the situational context.

The phenomenon of trust has been studied by psychologists from the perspectives of laboratory experimentation in bargaining and negotiation (Deutsch, 1962), developmental theory (Erikson, 1963), encounter group therapy (Schutz, 1967), self-disclosure theory and research (Cozby, 1973), and measurement (Rotter, 1967; Wrightsman, 1974).

One of the most basic concepts in the Bible is that of faith. Faith is a perspective that affects both perception and practice. It involves a sense of confidence about the truth of biblical statements regarding the existence and nature of phenomena beyond immediate sensory experience, including God, and about the ultimate spiritual consequences of various decisions and behaviors. The Hebraic and early Christian understanding of faith merged belief and behavior in a manner that is synonymous with trust. Without actions that express belief, belief is not regarded as faith (James 2:14–26).

The Bible can be understood as a record of the qualities of God that encourage perception of him as absolutely trustworthy (1 John 4:9). The illustrations of his capabilities (Eph. 3:20), integrity (1 Peter 1:17), and love (1 John 4:9) revealed in historical accounts of his relationships with specific people are intended to enable all people to believe and entrust the direction and decisions of their lives to him. The incarnation of Christ further demonstrated the desire of God to act for the benefit of humanity through his redemptive act of self-sacrifice (Rom. 5:8).

In addition, the Scriptures repeatedly demonstrate the positive consequences of actually trusting God (Ps. 22:4–5; Rev. 21:3–7) and the negative results of failing to do so (1 Kings 21:21–25; Rev. 20:15) as means of motivating people throughout history to act on their biblically based perceptions of his character.

References

Cozby, P. C. Self-disclosure: A literature review. *Psychological Bulletin*, 1973, *79*, 73–91.

Deutsch, M. Cooperation and trust: Some notes. In M. R. Jones (Ed.), *Nebraska symposium on motivation* (Vol. 10). Lincoln: University of Nebraska Press, 1962.

Erikson, E. H. *Childhood and society* (2nd ed.). New York: Norton, 1963.

Rotter, J. B. A new scale for the measurement of interpersonal trust. *Journal of Personality*, 1967, *35*, 651–665.

Schutz, W. E. *Joy*. New York: Grove Press, 1967.

Wrightsman, L. S. *Assumptions about human nature: A social-psychological approach*. Monterey, Calif.: Brooks/Cole, 1974.

C. W. Ellison

Twin Studies. *See* Heredity and Environment in Human Development.

Type. Generally, an ideal specimen or exemplar for defining a category. In practice it refers to an individual who possesses most of the defining qualities.

Prominent use of types is found in personality typologies. A type theory of personality is one in which classification categories are defined and usually tied to underlying biological processes. Different personality types are explained by biological differences.

The oldest typology is that developed by Hippocrates, systematized by Galens, and formalized by Kant. Four temperaments were described. The *sanguine* type was even dispositioned, warmhearted, optimistic, and energetic. The *choleric* was quick to action, assertive, and prone to hostility and anger. Depression, sadness, and anxiety characterized the *melancholic*. The *phlegmatic* type was listless and lethargic. These temperament types, it was hypothesized, resulted from the predominance of one of four body humors: blood, yellow bile, black bile, or phlegm, respectively.

Modern typologies are either psychological or physical. Jung's (1960) analytical psychology postulated two psychological or attitude types. It presumed a neurological basis, but this was never fully described. The *introverted* type was hesitant, reflective, withdrawn, and lived in an inner, subjective world. The *extraverted* type focused on the external, objective world and consequently was action oriented, sociable, outgoing, and adaptable to situations. Attitude types were supplemented by four ego functions (i.e., functional types) of sensing, intuiting, thinking, and feeling. The former two were irrational functions, while the latter were rational. Attitude types combined with functional types to yield eight personality types (introverted sensing, extraverted sensing, introverted intuiting, etc.).

Eysenck (1967) explained the attitude types by reference to the arousal level of the ascending reticular activating system (ARAS). Extraverts (including sanguine and choleric types) are low in ARAS arousal, while introverts (phlegmatic and melancholic types) exhibit high ARAS arousal. Emotional stability characterizes the sanguine and phlegmatic types, while choleric and melancholic types are emotionally labile (i.e., high in neuroticism). ARAS arousal reflects a variant level of visceral brain arousal, which is low in normals but high in neurotics. Thus, Eysenck used the extraversion-introversion and emotional stability–neuroticism dimensions as axes for a Cartesian coordinate system to explain the classical temperaments. The sanguine was a normal extravert, the choleric was a neurotic extravert, the melancholic was a neurotic introvert, and the phlegmatic was a normal introvert.

Body typologies associate temperament with physique. Kretschmer (1925) developed a body typology postulating two normal temperament types: the schizoid and cycloid. The schizoid type was unsociable, quiet, and serious, while the cycloid was sociable, good natured, humorous, and impulsive (cf. Jung's introversion and extraversion). Under psychotic attack schizoids became schizophrenic, while cycloids were manic depressives. He noted that schizophrenics were either tall and thin or athletic, and manic depressives were typically pyknic.

This physical typology was modified by Sheldon (1954) to link three temperament types with physique (i.e., somatotype). The somatotype of mesomorphy (highly developed skeleton and musculature) yielded a temperament type of somatotonia, denoting a craving for activity and power, aggressiveness, ruthlessness, and risk taking. Endomorphy (massive viscera) was linked to viscerotonia, the love of comfort, gluttony, sociability, and affection. Ectomorphy (lanky, nonmuscular, thin physique) corresponds to cerebrotonia, evidenced by excessive restraint, social inhibition, and intelligence.

References

Eysenck, H. J. *The biological basis of personality.* Springfield, Ill.: Thomas, 1967.

Jung, C. G. A psychological theory of types. In H. Read, M. Fordham, & G. Adler (Eds.), *Collected Works* (Vol. 8), New York: Pantheon Books, 1960.

Kretschmer, E. *Physique and character.* New York: Harcourt, 1925.

Sheldon, W. H. *Atlas of men: A guide for somatotyping the adult male at all ages.* New York: Harper, 1954.

R. L. TIMPE

See PSYCHOLOGICAL TYPES: JUNG'S VIEW; FACTOR THEORIES OF PERSONALITY.

Uu

Ulcers. Open sores that can occur inside the body or on its outer surface. The term is commonly used to refer to a peptic ulcer, which is an ulcer in the upper gastrointestinal tract. The two major forms of peptic ulcer are chronic duodenal ulcers, which occur in the part of the small intestine leading out of the stomach and gastric ulcers, which occur in the upper part of the stomach. *Peptic* refers to the fact that these ulcers are caused partially by digestive juices, one of which is acid-pepsin.

Ulcers occur in approximately 10% of the population. They are much more common in men than women. Duodenal ulcers occur four times more often than gastric ulcers. The highest incidence of gastric ulcers is from age 60 to 70, whereas it is highest for duodenal ulcers when a person is in the 50s.

The primary symptom of an ulcer is stomach pain that is often relieved by eating or by taking antacids. Some people with gastric ulcers lose weight because they develop an aversion to food; eating increases their discomfort. Ulcers may cause internal bleeding, which is passed as black, tarry stools or as red blood when bleeding is massive. Many people with ulcers have no symptoms.

Treatment focuses on relieving pain and helping the ulcer heal. The most widely accepted treatment is the administration of cimetidine, which inhibits acid secretion. It is also common to give antacids, which are effective and less expensive but may require more frequent dosage. Ulcer patients are instructed not to take aspirin and not to drink alcohol, since these substances irritate the stomach lining. In addition, drinks containing caffeine, such as coffee and tea, are omitted from the diet because these drinks stimulate the secretion of gastric acid. Peptic ulcers usually heal within one to three months with active medical treatment. Surgery is indicated when there are complications such as nonresponsiveness to medications, obstruction, or when the ulcer perforates and allows stomach acids to pass directly into the abdomen.

People who develop ulcers are often described as hard-driving, successful individuals who have strong needs to please and to receive attention from others. They are also characterized as stressed, tense, and conflicted between needs for dependence and independence. Ulcer sufferers seem to have an overreactive digestive system in response to chronic stress. A person who is prone to gastric upset can take preventive action by avoiding aspirin, caffeine, and alcohol; and by learning better relaxation and communication skills in order to cope with stress and to meet personal needs more effectively.

M. A. NORFLEET

See PSYCHOSOMATIC DISORDERS.

Unconditional Positive Regard. A term popularized by Rogers. It is central to his theory of personality development and his PERSON-CENTERED THERAPY. The idea is not new with Rogers, but was utilized more profoundly by him than others.

The roots of this idea may be seen in the Judeo-Christian concepts of the dignity of human persons as image bearers of God and of the unconditional quality of God's unmerited grace toward unworthy humans. Rogers's perspective was therefore shaped by his early upbringing in the Christian faith.

The Judeo-Christian notion of the dignity of humanness gives rise to concepts of human freedom and the inherent value of persons. Combined with the idea of imaging God, it implies a growth-oriented destiny, inherent in humanness, requiring freedom for self-actualization of all the potentials for human personality development with which God has endowed us. God's grace, moreover, guarantees a context of proximate and ultimate freedom within which humans may freely experiment and grow, confident that God's grace is always greater than all our sin.

The unconditional positive regard of one human for another—e.g., a parent for a child or a therapist for a patient—frees the other to accept the challenge of his or her own potentials for growth and/or healing. Rogers, in adopting this perspective on personality formation and therapy, reflects the unconditional grace model of redemption as biblically expressed.

Influences on the Rogerian formulation of this concept can be traced from the positive thinking movement through Dewey to Rogers. However, a crucial difference must be noted between Dewey and Rogers. Dewey romantically assumed the inherent goodness of humans, expecting permissiveness to enable the flourishing of positive native characteristics in human personality development. Rogers is not that kind of romantic. He recognizes the native human potential for pathology and evil, and values the function of discipline, constraint, and guidance for personality development. His emphasis on unconditional positive regard for inciting growth and healing expresses his conviction that it is in that context of affirmation that humans flourish. Unconditional positive regard is an affirmation of a human person in his or her brokenness and distortions, as well as in his or her strengths and growth options. With that affirmation a person will be more receptive to the externally imposed disciplines that produce self-discipline and the positive growth options that will replace self-destructive ones.

J. H. Ellens

See Self Theory; Humanistic Psychology.

Unconscious. Thoughts, feelings, and other mental processes that are not currently in conscious awareness are considered unconscious. Three of the most obvious examples of unconscious processes are forgetting the name of a friend, slips of the tongue, and posthypnotic suggestion. In forgetting a friend's name we are aware that we know it but just cannot bring it to consciousness. In slips of the tongue we "accidentally" say one word when we consciously

intend to say another. We may say *loathe* instead of *love*, *hell* instead of *hail*, or *sex* instead of *six*.

A person under hypnosis may be given the suggestion to take off his watch, open the window, or unbutton his jacket at a specified time after coming out of hypnosis. He is also told that he will not remember the command. When the time comes, for no reason he is aware of he suddenly takes off his watch, unbuttons his jacket, or walks over and opens the window. Just as in accidental forgetting and slips of the tongue, mental processes that impact the person's actions are going on outside of conscious awareness.

Some people speak of the unconscious as if it were a concrete psychological entity or a location where unwanted thoughts and feelings are dispatched—a kind of psychological basement. More accurately, unconscious simply refers to the current status of a thought or feelings. Either we are aware of it or we are not. The level of awareness varies along a continuum from complete awareness to total unawareness.

Although sensitive poets, artists, and thinkers had long been aware of the reality and power of unconscious psychological processes, Freud was the first to systematically explore the nature and function of unconsciousness. He identified three levels of awareness. In addition to the conscious level he postulated preconscious and unconscious levels. Preconscious thoughts or feelings, while not being in immediate awareness, can be called to attention with relatively little effort. One's age, phone number, or address are good examples. Most of the time we are not consciously thinking about these things, but at any moment they can be recalled by simply turning our attention to them. Since there is a finite number of thoughts that can occupy our conscious minds at any one time, most thoughts have to be out of awareness. But by turning our attention to them we can immediately bring many of these thoughts and feelings to mind. These readily available thoughts are called preconscious.

Unconscious thoughts are much less accessible to awareness. They typically become accessible only with much effort because they are purposely (although unconsciously) banned from awareness. The individual wants to avoid remembering because the repressed experience would be too painful. For example, people involved in a tragic accident who lose their sight (hysterical blindness) or those who cannot remember any of their life before age 8 or 10 are probably pushing unpleasant experiences and feelings from awareness. These thoughts and feelings may be very difficult to remember. In fact, one of the major goals of insight-oriented therapy is to help people overcome their repressions in order to face previously avoided painful memories, feelings, thoughts, or wishes.

Since preconscious thoughts are out of awareness simply because we are attending to other things, they are considered descriptively unconscious. Unconscious thoughts, however, are considered dynamically unconscious because they are actively kept from awareness in order to avoid the anxiety, guilt, or pain associated with them. It is the dynamic interaction of anxiety or guilt-producing thoughts or memories with defense mechanisms such as repression that results in truly unconscious (as opposed to preconscious) thoughts. This dynamic nature of unconscious thoughts also explains how they can continue to impact personality adjustment long after they are forgotten. If an individual has to expend a considerable amount of emotional energy keeping unconscious thoughts from awareness, this defensive process limits and impoverishes the personality and can be a key factor in causing personality maladjustment.

Unconscious thoughts also operate differently from conscious ones and are not necessarily rational. In dreams, for example, two or more people or ideas may be merged into one (condensation), and mutually contradictory or exclusive ideas (such as a dead person talking) may coexist.

Although few psychologists accept all of Freud's theorizing, his views on the presence of unconscious thoughts, wishes, and feelings are now nearly universally accepted. So too is the belief that these unconscious thoughts have meaning and influence our conscious choices and decisions. However, theorists still debate the content of the unconscious, and most would not agree with Freud's belief that the most important of these repressed thoughts are sexual in nature.

S. B. NARRAMORE

See PSYCHOANALYTIC PSYCHOLOGY; COLLECTIVE UNCONSCIOUS.

Underachiever. A person who fails to produce or perform at the level for which he is qualified and capable. Although this may be in any area of life, it usually refers to academic performance, thus is most pronounced in childhood and adolescence. It is not usually considered a diagnostic entity; rather, it is a symptomatic end point of a number of conditions.

The most common etiological conditions that may contribute to underachievement include unequal ego development (i.e., verbal skills are much more advanced or retarded than motor skills); negative conditioning (i.e., greater rewards are given for not achieving than for achieving); overevaluation of a child's ability; unrecognized minor perceptual motor problems; illness in the child or family; separation anxiety; and crisis in the family. Mild degrees of underachievement are widely prevalent, estimated to be between 10 and 20%. Prevalence of more serious underachievement is difficult to judge. Underachievement is twice as common in boys as in girls.

The classical picture of the family of the underachieving child describes the father as being inadequate, weak, and passive, with a history of poor school and work performance and lacking intellectual interests. The mother is described as being dissatisfied, unhappy in marriage, more competent and intellectual than the father, and having high ambitions for the child's achievement. It is not uncommon to find an underachiever in a family whose other members are adequate or outstanding achievers.

The clinical picture of underachieving children includes listlessness, apathy, and low self-esteem. They are loners or associate with younger individuals or peers who are on the periphery. Most of them experience chronic friction with their total environment and may be observed to be depressed or hostile. Neurotic underachievers may present a façade of industriousness, compliance, and reaction formation that assists in protecting them from their hostility.

Psychological testing can often assist in the diagnosis of underachievement. The Wechsler Intelligence Scale for Children frequently reveals a pattern of verbal subscales being superior to performance subscales, gaps in information, patchy knowledge, and weak arithmetic, concentration, and coding skills. The Rorschach will often reveal obsessive-compulsive features with despondent tendencies, and passive resistance and withdrawal into fantasies. The Minnesota Multiphasic Personality Inventory will often show obsessive-compulsive features with resistances on an unconscious level.

In a diagnostic interview such a child appears bright, verbal, and socially sophisticated. He or she tends to blame the school and parents for any problems. Low self-esteem will be manifested, as will helplessness, dependency, anger, and an absence of experienced pleasure. In judging a child to be an underachiever one must rule out the following: a normal average child who has been overestimated; a child who has an undetected developmental disorder; and a child with a psychiatric disorder such as depression or a personality disorder.

Treatment consists of identification of the problem, evaluation of etiological factors, and a collaborative approach to active intervention.

Since chronic maladaptive patterns are readily established, the earlier the identification and intervention, the better the prognosis. Pastors are often in an excellent position to assist in early identification, since they often know the entire family and work with children and adolescents in smaller groups than is possible in the schools.

Once the problem has been identified, it is important to have a comprehensive evaluation, including the social history, psychological tests, and psychiatric interview. Specialized procedures may be necessary depending on the outcome. Active treatment involves working with the child, the parents, and the school in a collaborative mode. The type of individual therapy will depend on the basic etiology. It could be traditional psychotherapy, behavioral therapy, tutorial therapy, or a combination of these. Since underachievers often avoid stress or unpleasant experiences, it is often difficult to engage them in therapy.

It is important to help parents gain insight into the dynamics of the problem, especially their role in the origin or perpetuation of the problem. They often need much support because of the secondary problems. The school usually needs guidance in providing a consistent and constructive approach to an underachieving child. The therapist must always remain aware of the child's school performance. The church can be of assistance in providing support to the parents. However, it is even more important for church leaders to provide role models with whom the child can relate warmly, and to assist the child in establishing appropriate short- and long-range goals.

Additional Readings

Ekstein, R., & Motto, R. *From learning for love to love of learning.* New York: Brunner/Mazel, 1969.
Harris, I. *Emotional blocks to learning.* New York: Free Press, 1961.
Holt, J. *How children fail.* New York: Pitman, 1964.

F. WESTENDORP

Undoing. An ego DEFENSE MECHANISM consisting of the performance of some activity perceived as the opposite of that against which the ego is seeking defense. This unconscious process is designed to undo, atone for, or otherwise annul an objectionable thought, behavior, or impulse. The undoing activity may be actually or only "magically" an opposite. Undoing frequently includes unconsciously motivated expiatory acts, apologizing or repenting, countercompulsions, self-inflicted punishment or penance, and some compulsive ceremonials. Undoing is often seen in the obsessive-compulsive psychoneurosis. An example would be the compulsion to repeatedly wash one's hands in an unconscious attempt to undo and defend against the guilt and conflict associated with habitual masturbation.

R. LARKIN

Utilization Technique. More a philosophy of treatment than a specific technique. It is an approach that requires the therapist to flexibly meet the client in his internal model of the world rather than asking the client to be made over in the image of the therapist. Erickson has been given much of the credit for pioneering this approach. Although the term has historically been used particularly with hypnotherapy, it is in fact applicable to most other types of change procedures.

In order to apply this approach the counselor must first carefully observe the client's speech, demeanor, and manner of self-preservation, as would any astute clinician. The second step involves building on one's observational base through a process of sequential questions: Through which sensory channel(s) does this person primarily process information? What idiosyncratic values and beliefs about himself does this person hold? What unique storehouse of memories does this individual possess? What repertoire of skills and gifts are accessible to this person? Once these determinations have been made intuitively or logically, the clinician then moves to the final stage of tailoring his technique to utilize the characteristics of the person. On any particular occasion this might mean utilizing a behavioral, Gestalt, hypnotic, rational-emotive, dynamic, or systemic approach. It is true that this utilization approach is demanding. However, it is also probably what each therapist would want for himself or herself if roles were reversed.

V. L. SHEPPERSON

See HYPNOTHERAPY, INDIRECT.

Vv

Vaginismus. Involuntary spasms of the muscles at the entrance to the vagina, precluding entrance and occurring whenever an attempt is made to introduce any object into the vaginal opening. A key element in understanding and treating vaginismus is accepting the fact that the contraction of the vaginal musculature is entirely involuntary.

Vaginismus is a precise clinical entity different from a straightforward fear of intercourse. Many women suffering from vaginismus are sexually responsive and orgastic as long as intercourse is not attempted.

As one might easily imagine, vaginismus is an acutely vexing situation for the wife and husband. The wife invariably wants to overcome the "snapping shut" of the vaginal opening (which is beyond her conscious control) while simultaneously being frightened of the cure. The husband's response will vary along a continuum between being angry and blaming his wife or being frustrated and blaming himself.

The preferred first step in treatment is to have a sensitive physician conduct a vaginal examination of the wife in the presence of her husband. This is the only sure way to know that the condition is vaginismus and not the result of a physical obstruction or phobic avoidance of intercourse. Both husband and wife are generally relieved to know that the condition is not willful or physically based.

Vaginismus is not necessarily associated with mental disturbance in the wife or marital discord in the couple. Often a detailed social history will reveal no apparent basis for the dysfunction. This is understandable, since the adverse stimulus that has become associated with intercourse or simple vaginal insertion, whether real or fantasized, may not lie within the wife's conscious awareness. Some events that may contribute to the onset of vaginismus include pelvic disease, traumatic pelvic examination, rape at an early age, fear of men and ignorance about sex—in short, any experience evoking pain or fear and readily associated with coitus.

Treatment of vaginismus through various techniques of modern SEX THERAPY has proven 100% effective in those cases where the woman completes the prescribed regimen (Kaplan, 1974). While exact procedures will vary with orientation of the sex therapist, treatment may be divided into three major steps. The first, already mentioned, is a physical examination to definitively establish that vaginismus is present. This may be done by the couple alone in the privacy of their home or conducted by a physician with the husband present.

The next step is to address the wife's phobic avoidance of vaginal entry. This may be done through simple reassurance, hypnosis, relaxation medication, or systematic desensitization.

The third step is the gradual insertion of progressively larger objects into the vaginal opening. Whether the wife or the husband inserts the objects and what actual objects are used should be dictated by the unique circumstances of the case. Obviously a great deal of care and sensitivity must be shown by the husband and therapist in effecting this deconditioning process. The wife must be supported to embrace or fully experience the uneasy feelings that will accompany insertion of the progressively larger objects.

As in most psychotherapy the time of greatest anxiety and resistance occurs when it is no longer possible to avoid the actual decision to relinquish the symptom. When the wife realizes that resolution is her responsibility, in that she must insert or agree to have inserted an object into her vagina, some degree of avoidance or resistance, panic or anxiety, is bound to occur. The skill, power, and training of the therapist are crucial at this time.

Regardless of the type of object inserted into the vagina, whether it be plastic or glass catheters or the wife's or husband's finger(s), the sizing of the objects and the care with which they are inserted should be sufficiently nonthreatening so as to ensure success. The same is true for the initial insertion of the husband's penis in that it should be gradual, without thrusting, and withdrawn upon the wife's request.

While the incidence of vaginismus is relatively rare, it is a common cause of unconsummated marriages. Modern sex therapy treatment as outlined here is eminently successful and preferable to surgical treatment or forcibly attained vaginal entry. Traditional psychotherapy without the concrete steps mentioned here is unlikely to be successful.

Reference
Kaplan, H. S. *The new sex therapy: Active treatment of sexual dysfunctions.* New York: Brunner/Mazel, 1974.
J. R. DAVID

Values and Psychotherapy. Freud defined psychotherapy as a technical procedure applied to mental disorders. Like surgery it was intended to be an objective procedure that did not involve the personality or beliefs of the practitioner in a direct way. Since the time of Freud it has been standard procedure for therapists to avoid disclosing their own values and to avoid shaping the values of the client. Such an objective, professional attitude is admirable, and it has been a standard for training and practice for many years.

Unfortunately it has been impossible to maintain such an objective approach to therapeutic counseling. As it turns out, the nature of client psychological difficulties and the interaction between therapist and client required to overcome these difficulties necessarily involve values. This insight has been slow in coming. It has been stimulated in part by developments in the humanistic therapies, such as those espoused by Rogers, Fromm, May and others. These therapists have recognized that many of the difficulties that we call psychological are in fact difficulties of moral choice and life style. Because of this, such therapists gradually became more open about their values and the ways in which values might operate in the psychotherapy process. Certainly their definitions of good mental health or of the personalities that were expected to result from good therapy have been highly value laden.

In contrast to the humanistic therapists who employ the relationship between therapist and client as one of the means of mediating therapeutic change, behavior therapists have resisted this trend. Although they object to the theories and techniques of Freud, they agree with the Freudian perspective in the sense that they consider therapy to be the application of technical procedures involving values to a minimal extent. The revival of the concept of psychotherapy as a kind of technology by behavior therapists is somewhat ironic in that it places them on the same side of the fence as their archrival, psychoanalysis.

However, modern scholarship and research indicate that behavior therapy is no less value laden than psychoanalysis or humanistic psychotherapies. There is a growing consensus in the mental health disciplines that psychotherapy is a value-oriented procedure and that one cannot avoid making value choices in the process of attempting to help a troubled client.

The notion that values are an inevitable and pervasive part of psychotherapy is supported by a number of scholarly papers and research articles that examine both the process and the outcome of treatment. Strupp, Hadley, and Gomes-Schwartz (1977) have argued that there are at least three different value systems at play in every therapeutic enterprise: the values of the client, the values of the practitioner, and values in the community at large. They point out that our ways of defining mental health are all based on cultural choices as to what is good functioning and what is a good life style. While the standards by which these choices are made are often implicit, a careful examination of the mental health literature shows the value themes threaded throughout. For example: "If following psychotherapy, a patient manifests increased self-assertion coupled with abrasiveness, is this good or a poor therapy outcome? . . . If . . . a patient obtains a divorce, is this to be regarded as a desirable or an undesirable change? A patient may turn from homosexuality to heterosexuality, or he may become more accepting of either; an ambitious, striving person may abandon previously valued goals and become more placid. . . . How are such changes to be evaluated?" (Strupp et al., 1977, pp. 92–93). In addition: "In increasing number, patients enter psychotherapy not for the cure of traditional 'symptoms' but (at least ostensibly) for the purpose of finding meaning in their lives, for actualizing themselves, or for maximizing their potential" (Strupp et al., 1977, p. 93).

The amazing thing about this type of literature is that it shows that psychological procedures are intricately interwoven with secularized moral systems (London, 1964; Lowe, 1976). As this literature has developed, it has become more and more evident not only that values are involved in psychotherapy, but that the values of the community of professional therapists have a certain slant or bias. Standards for good living are thus being established by the mental health disciplines as they increasingly influence the attitudes, beliefs, and values of both clients and public. Therapists therefore are becoming secular moralists who are promoting changes in life styles and in the values of the culture or community while at the same time appearing to apply a technical method to psychological disturbances as though these applications were objective and value free (Bergin, 1980a).

The impossibility of a value-free therapy can be illustrated by the work of Rogers, who personally values the freedom of the individual and attempts to help his clients choose their own values in a free and permissive atmosphere. Despite Rogers's admirable devotion to the client's freedom from coercion by the therapist or others, two separate studies done a decade apart (Murray, 1956; Truax, 1966) showed that Rogers systematically rewarded and punished verbal behavior that he did and did not approve of in his clients. His values influenced the format of the therapy sessions as well as their outcomes. If a person who intends to be nondirective cannot be, then it is unlikley that others can be objective and value free in their very human interactions with their clients (Bergin, 1971).

Another way of documenting the influence of values on the mental health enterprise is to consider the way in which change in mental health is judged by practitioners and researchers. These judgments are based on rating scales or measures of personality, behavior, and attitudes. It has been shown that even in the modern technical behavior therapies, as well as other therapies, value choices are being made in the selection of these criteria of measurement (Bergin, 1963, 1980b; Kitchener, 1980).

Types of Values in Psychotherapy. Almost every conceivable type of value is endorsed by one psychotherapist or another. However, there are certain trends that reflect the humanistic and mechanistic backgrounds of most psychotherapists. This is seen most vividly in the tendency of therapists to endorse a relativistic approach to values, or what is frequently referred to as situation ethics. From the viewpoint of Christian psychologists or religious clients, many of the values commonly endorsed by therapists may be considered counterproductive or even immoral. There is also an antireligious and antitraditional morality trend among a fairly large minority of therapists. One of the common complaints among more conservative, religious people is the lack of harmony they often experience between their values and those of their counselor or therapist.

It is a fact that the values of mental health professionals differ on the average from those of the public at large, and especially the more religious public. These contrasts have been documented at general levels, such as in the great differences between professionals and the public who endorse traditional beliefs in God, the reality of the spiritual, the efficacy of prayer, and belief in the divinity of Christ. The contrasts also exist with respect to specific values such as those pertaining to sex, authority, family life, etc. (Bergin, 1980b).

The existence of this contrast has opened the way for a rather full debate and consideration of how values may be dealt with in psychotherapy in the most fruitful way. Some professionals argue that their values are superior to those of the public at large and that their values are mentally healthy (Ellis, 1980). However, there is no evidence that this position is valid. The tendency for professional therapists to assume that their values are superior and that they are healthy and enlightening for the average person has been challenged. It has also been pointed out that the assumption by mental health professionals that their values have some inherent psychological validity puts therapists in the role of secular priests, who act as though they have the right to promote their personal and subjective views through what is supposed to be an objective and professional practice (Bergin, 1980c). The debate over these matters has led to the question of whether specific value orientations should be used to develop specific therapies.

Development of Value-Oriented Therapies. One of the controversial developments in psychotherapy is the attempt to organize therapy goals and processes in terms of specific values. While this is an attempt to do overtly what is often done covertly under the guise of professional clinical work, it is still an unpopular approach. It has been promoted, however, by people from opposite ends of the value spectrum. For example, Ellis (1980) argues that positive therapeutic change is inevitably a value modification process, and he attempts to implement what he considers to be mentally healthy values by means of his cognitive and behavioral interventions. Some of his valued outcomes, such as greater rationality and self-control, are endorsed by many therapists of various persuasions; but many of his objectives, such as "sex without guilt," are the exact opposite of what orthodox religious people value, as these values are derived from interpretations of Scripture. A number of attempts have been made to frame therapeutic procedures within the context of a traditional, spiritual perspective. Some of these are overtly and explicitly Christian in orientation. Others endorse moral values similar to those of orthodox Christians, but omit references to theology or Scripture. Still others concern themselves with a more eclectic approach to values in the therapeutic setting (Cf. Collins, 1981).

As different groups emerge who espouse value orientations consistent with their particular religion or subculture, the problem arises that a kind of therapeutic denominationalism may result. To the extent that values are an essential part of the therapeutic enterprise, perhaps this is inevitable; but it can go too far and cause schisms that prevent cooperative use of new discoveries regarding effective treatment.

The enlightened approach seems to be to take one's values and place them in the midst of the therapeutic marketplace for competitive evaluation and testing. Some Christian psychologists are carefully examining in a research context the effectiveness of merging spiritual imagery and values with some of the traditional therapeutic techniques (Propst, 1980). This approach holds promise in that it merges the spiritual or philosophical approach that is basic to values with the empirical approach that is basic to the psychological and psychiatric sciences.

Values Common to the Therapies. One of the consequences of encouraging openness about values has been that more agreement may be emerging from the different vantage points than would have been expected. An informal survey (Bergin, 1983a) has revealed a possible consensus regarding a number of values that affect the life style and morality of clients in psychotherapy. While this consensus is nowhere near 100%, the amount of agreement on some subjects pertinent to psychological functioning has been surprising. For instance, there seems to be a great deal of agreement regarding the advantages of marital fidelity, even though some highly visible

writers and therapists do not seem to value this particular behavior. It may be that the majority favoring fidelity is not a large majority; but its existence is surprising in light of what we often read in professional textbooks and in the media accounts of professional opinions. But it remains to be shown by careful empirical study just what the consequences of infidelity are. Although there is a massive amount of evidence in the clinical and research literature, it has never been systematized. The sources and consequences of many other values are now being addressed in light of the growing interest in the effects of value dimensions upon life styles and mental health. The question is, "Are there mentally healthy values or life styles?" Scripture implies that this is likely to be so; but such a belief does not yet have a persuasive position within the the the professional milieu (Bergin, 1983b).

Another consequence of the growing openness regarding values is that clients increasingly have the option of selecting a therapist according to his or her orientation. One no longer simply chooses between a psychoanalyst or behavior therapist, but between an analyst or behaviorist who does or does not have spiritual convictions and biblically based moral values. Therapies especially relevant to specific groups or subcultures thus seem to be emerging gradually.

Some Dangers. While religious therapists have a strong interest in explicit value discussions and emphases, their enthusiasm for this aspect of life and of therapeutic change can lead to problems if it is emphasized too strongly. Obviously it would be unethical to trample on the values of patients or clients with whom we disagree. It would also be unwise practice to focus largely on value issues when other issues may be at the nucleus of the disorder. Thus, an emphasis on technical expertise, the ability to diagnose accurately the causes of a problem, and the capacity to sympathetically guide a person through a difficult change process should be the primary concerns. It is vital for the therapist interested in the role of values in psychotherapy to be open but not coercive, to be a competent professional and not a missionary for his particular system of belief while at the same time being honest enough to recognize his own value commitments and the ways in which they may be health promoting. Mature professionals will recognize that their own beliefs and values can introduce biases in their thinking and perceptions, and that immersion in value discussions can sometimes be an escape into cognitive intellectualizing and an avoidance of the hard work of effecting personality reconstruction. As value-oriented discussion becomes more common, it is likely that good practice will require referral also to become more common, since value clashes will be antitherapeutic.

While the dilemmas involved are very real, exciting new developments in the psychotherapeutic arena are promised. Many difficulties in past approaches were caused by a failure to discern some of the real value issues that may underlie what look like simply psychological matters. It is instructive to realize that psychotherapy is but one example of the dilemma common to all applied psychologies; namely, that any attempt to apply a technique requires a decision as to the goals or outcomes the technique is attempting to obtain. Any time we select goals we are implementing values; therefore, all applied psychologies are inevitably value laden.

References

Bergin, A. E. The effects of psychotherapy: Negative results revisited. *Journal of Counseling Psychology*, 1963, *10*, 244–250.

Bergin, A. E. Carl Rogers' contribution to a fully functioning psychology. In A. Maher & L. Pearson (Eds.), *Creative developments in psychotherapy* (Vol. 1). Cleveland: Western Reserve University Press, 1971.

Bergin, A. E. Psychotherapy and religious values. *Journal of Consulting and Clinical Psychology*, 1980, *48*, 95–105. (a)

Bergin, A. E. Behavior therapy and ethical relativism: Time for clarity. *Journal of Consulting and Clinical Psychology*, 1980, *48*, 11–13. (b)

Bergin, A. E. Religious and humanistic values: A reply to Ellis and Walls. *Journal of Consulting and Clinical Psychology*, 1980, *48*, 642–645. (c)

Bergin, A. E. Proposed values for guiding and evaluating psychotherapy. In A. P. Gomez & F. B. Currea (Eds.), *Psicoterapias 1983*. Bogota: Universidad de los Andes 1983. (a)

Bergin, A. E. Religiosity and mental health: A critical reevaluation and meta-analysis. *Professional Psychology*, 1983, *14*, 170–184. (b)

Collins, G. R. *Psychology and theology: Prospects for integration*. Nashville: Abingdon, 1981.

Ellis, A. Psychotherapy and atheistic values: A response to A. E. Bergin's "Psychotherapy and religious values." *Journal of Consulting and Clinical Psychology*, 1980, *48*, 635–639.

Kitchener, R. F. Ethical relativism and behavior therapy. *Journal of Consulting and Clinical Psychology*, 1980, *48*, 1–7.

London, P. *The modes and morals of psychotherapy*. New York: Holt, Rinehart, & Winston, 1964.

Lowe, C. M. *Value orientations in counseling and psychotherapy: The meanings of mental health* (2nd ed.). Cranston, R. I.: Carroll Press, 1976.

Murray, E. J. A content-analysis method for studying psychotherapy. *Psychological Monographs*, 1956, *70* (13, Whole No. 420).

Propst, L. R. The comparative efficacy of religious and nonreligious imagery for the treatment of mild depression in religious individuals. *Cognitive Therapy and Research*, 1980, *4*, 167–178.

Strupp, H. H., Hadley, S. W., & Gomes-Schwartz, B. *Psychotherapy for better or worse: An analysis of the problem of negative effects*. New York: Aronson, 1977.

Truax, C. B. Reinforcement and non-reinforcement in Rogerian psychotherapy. *Journal of Abnormal Psychology*, 1966, *71*, 1–9.

A. E. Bergin

Values Assessment. Numerous scales have been developed for the purpose of values assessment. Some are broad in scope and provide a comprehensive picture of one's interests, attitudes, and values, while others are more specific and inquire into only one or two areas. Two of the most widely used measures are the Allport-Vernon-Lindzey Study of Values and the Strong-Campbell Interest Inventory.

The Study of Values was developed by G. W. Allport, P. E. Vernon, and G. Lindzey in 1951. The inventory is designed to assess the relative strength of one's values and interests in six areas: theoretical, economic, aesthetic, social, political, and religious. The items were originally formulated on the basis of the theoretical framework of Spranger (1928), a German philosopher. The final item selection used in the measure was based on the internal consistency within the six areas assessed.

The Study of Values is one of the simpler psychological tests to take, score, and interpret. Items are grouped into either two or four statements representing different values. The individual is forced to choose between the alternative statements with little, if any, indication as to which value is being assessed. The forced choice format reveals the relative strength of the values in that if the individual scores high in any one value, some other values must therefore be lowered. Norms are available for high school and college students and for several occupational groups.

The Strong-Campbell Interest Inventory provides information about one's basic interests and the various vocational fields that best suit these interests. This inventory is the 1974 edition of the Strong Vocational Interest Blank and reflects the culmination of years of research by E. K. Strong and D. P. Campbell on the original inventory constructed by Strong in 1927. Two major changes include the introduction of a theoretical framework to aid in the interpretation process and the combining of the men's and women's forms, with the elimination of sex-oriented items, into a single test booklet.

Through years of research Strong and Campbell found that one's basic interests are fairly well established by early adulthood and do not radically change for most people throughout the remainder of life. The inventory consists of 325 items that assess six general occupational themes (e.g., investigative, artistic); 23 basic interest scales (e.g., science, public speaking); and 124 occupational scales (e.g., banker, priest). In five sections of the inventory one marks "like," "dislike," or "indifferent" to indicate his or her preferences having to do with occupations, school subjects, activities, amusement, and day-to-day contact with various types of people. In the two remaining sections one marks "yes," "no," or "?" to self-descriptive statements and his preferences between paired items. The inventory is scored by computer at designated agencies. Results are expressed in numerical scores with reference to the whole sample taking the test. Also, interpretive phrases such as "high," "moderately low," "average" are used to help the individual better understand how he or she scored in comparison with others.

Reference
Spranger, E. *Types of Men.* Halle: Niemeyer, 1928.

W. W. AUSTIN

See PSYCHOLOGICAL MEASUREMENT.

Values Clarification.

Values Clarification. An approach to moral and values education developed by Louis Raths and his associates in the mid-1960s. It was based on some of the conceptual ideas of Dewey and Rogers. Raths wanted to develop an approach to moral education that would help people deal positively with the many value-loaded issues of our complex society. It seemed that an approach to moral education was needed that would be an alternative to either indoctrinative moralizing or complete neglect of value areas of life.

Values and Valuing. The educational approach of values clarification is based on specific understandings of values and the valuing process. Values are defined as guidelines emerging from life experiences that guide behavior in future experiences. It is believed that a person's values emerge from that person's experiences and that it is therefore inappropriate to expect one person to have or adopt the same set of values as another person. Thus, it seems inappropriate to base moral and values education on transmitting or imposing an external set of values. The values clarification solution is to build an educational approach upon the nature of the process by which values emerge, rather than upon the content of a set of prescribed values. The valuing process is the way by which one comes to hold some particular values. It is believed that a person

does not truly value something unless the value emerged through this process.

Criteria for Values. Seven specific criteria for a value are based on the following elements.

Choosing freely. It is believed that if a person has been tricked or forced into believing something or acting in a certain way, it could not be said that the person values that idea or action. Choosing freely also implies some intellectual understanding.

Choosing among alternatives. Unless a person is allowed to choose from among alternatives, it seems inadequate to say that a free choice has truly been made.

Choosing after thoughtful consideration of the consequences of each alternative. The key word of this criterion is *consequences.* The goodness or badness of an alternative is based on pragmatic consequences. If one alternative is truly better than another, it ought to be evident to people doing the choosing.

Prizing and cherishing. A value is not merely any choice, but something that a person is positive about. A person may at times choose the lesser of two evils, but it would be wrong to say that the choice was a real guiding value.

Affirming. One should be willing to publicly affirm or to be publicly associated with a value statement or action.

Acting upon choices. If one really values something, having chosen it after thoughtful consideration of its consequences, then one ought to be willing to live with the consequences by acting upon the value.

Repeating. Most people can get up enough courage to try something once. Such acting does not represent a true value unless the action is repeated consistently, in each situation that calls for the value.

Value Education. Such an understanding of the valuing process suggests a new purpose and methodology for value education. The purpose of moral and value education is not to impose a set of external values, but to respect individual freedom by helping people become more aware of the values that actually do guide their behavior. The new methodology is based on the necessity for a person to understand alternative values. It is also based on the idea that values are not merely verbal propositional statements to be learned and repeated, but are freely chosen and consistently acted upon guidelines for behavior. Thus, values cannot adequately be understood as content of instruction but as conclusions from life.

The educational process of clarification involves reflective examination of life and its value-rich situations. Personal values are examined in light of the criteria of the valuing process. A value that does not satisfy the criteria is judged not to be a personal value. The role of the teacher becomes that of a nondirective facilitator who merely helps a student clarify the values that are alrady there.

The activities a teacher uses in values clarification primarily involve asking questions and other nondirective strategies. The most popular strategies include what are known as clarifying responses and a values continuum. Clarifying responses are questions asked by the teacher to get the learner to do some personal reflection upon a particular value and how well it fits the criteria of the valuing process. The values continuum strategy involves identifying the two extreme choices of a particular value issue and then asking students to place themselves somewhere on the continuum. Students are then asked to discuss among themselves how each one has made the decision and how one's decision compares with the criteria of the valuing process. In all cases it is inappropriate for the teacher or other students to impose a set of values or right answers on a student.

Values clarification has become a very popular educational pproach in K-12 schools, in nonformal education, and in Christian ministry settings. Its popularity seems to rest on three factors. First, it is a very simple instructional tool to use. It requires little expertise on the part of the instructor, especially in the area of moral philosophy and social ethics. Second, it is unoffensive and safe since it does not require a specific right answer to issues of moral and social values. This factor has been especially attractive to public education in the pluralistic American society. Third, there is usually a positive feeling of accomplishment when it is used. Educators feel as though they have done something important, students feel affirmed in their own values and identity, and there is usually a better atmosphere of warmth and trust developed in the learning environment.

Because the primary focus of values clarification is on the nature of the valuing process itself and on avoiding indoctrination, proponents of values clarification have always been hesitant to suggest that any one set of values is more right than another set. They claim to be able to offer a value-free approach to moral education.

Criticisms and Evaluation. Because of the value-free orientation of values clarification its conceptual foundation has been strongly criticized by being ethically relativistic. It tends to send the message that it is acceptable to believe whatever one wants to as long as it was self-chosen from alternatives, is prized, and is consistently acted upon.

A second major criticism of the values clarification conceptual foundation is that it makes no distinction between personal preferences and tastes, social and cultural values, and ethical and moral values. The values clarification technique helps people feel good about their own identity and personal tastes, but it is then indiscriminately used when approaching moral issues. Some critics believe that because values clarification does not make a distinction between personal preferences and moral values, it should not be used with reference to moral issues.

Criticisms of the educational procedures of values clarification rest on three points. First, it appears to be too conceptually abstract and too verbal to be appropriately used with preteen-agers. Since preteen-agers usually respect adult opinions and actions as authoritative, it may be that a teacher using values clarification instructional techniques is in fact imposing a set of values—including the value that all things are equally acceptable and that there is no right and wrong. Second, it is claimed that the values clarification group instructional technique ignores the very strong power of peer influence upon learners. It is suggested that in any kind of group discussion the opinion leaders of the group will have more influence on the values of others than is assumed by the clarification process. Values clarification technique, it is said, ignores the sociological interaction of a learning experience and focuses only on individualistic psychological factors.

Third, the outcomes of the values clarification educational process seem to be identified with such phrases as "it works," "warmth," "trust," "feeling good about oneself." These are very similar to the general outcomes associated with nondirective therapy, upon which many of the values clarification educational ideas are based. Therefore, it may be that the success of values clarification is not attributable to its concepts of value, ethics, or education, but to its therapeutic power.

Since its introduction in the mid-1960s values clarification's major spokespersons have been Sidney B. Simon and Howard Kirschenbaum. Simon has written several practical manuals and conducted many seminars and in-service training sessions for teachers. Kirschenbaum has kept alive the conceptual thinking about values clarification through his involvement with the National Humanistic Education Center. He has offered a revision of the previously stated seven criteria and the valuing process. He has suggested that the valuing process includes five dimensions: thinking, feeling, choosing, communicating, and acting. He does not suggest this as a new orientation for values clarification but as a more comprehensive analysis of the valuing process upon which the instructional techniques are based.

Additional Readings
Kirschenbaum, H., & Simon, S. B. (Eds.). *Readings in values clarification.* Minneapolis: Winston Press, 1973.
Raths, L. E., Harmin, M., & Simon, S. B. *Values and teaching: Working with values in the classroom.* Columbus: Merrill, 1966.
Simon, S. B., Howe, L., & Kirschenbaum, H. *Values clarification: A handbook of practical strategies for teachers and students.* New York: Hart Publishing, 1972.

R. B. McKean

Verbigeration. Also known as cataphasia, this is the monotonous or morbid repetition of sentences, words, or phrases, usually without any apparent meaning. It is common in schizophrenic reactions, where a patient will utter the same reply to any line of questioning.

Vertigo. A psychophysiologic reaction to internal stress or conflict in which an individual feels that he or the world around him is spinning. Vertigo is sometimes caused by conditions in the inner ear or other organic disease, but may also be a psychosomatic reaction. In the latter case vertigo may serve as a defense against unacceptable impulses or as an escape from a threatening situation.

Victims of Violent Crimes. These persons are usually distinguished from victims of domestic violence, property crimes, and harm suffered from natural or accidental injury. Victims of violent crimes are those who have innocently suffered psychological and/or physical harm resulting from some illegal activity. For example, robbery, rape, homicide, and assault are proscribed behaviors for which laws provide penalties. There are also property crimes that may cause psychological stress but that are not considered to be violent. Burglary may occur when no victim is present, but it can generate a crisis as disruptive as robbery.

A determination of who is the victim can often be technical and should be considered carefully when an agency or member of a helping profession decides to provide assistance. Too narrow a definition may leave persons with serious psychological, physical, or social needs without service.

The Victim and Services. Historically the victim has held a role outside the criminal justice and social service systems. The criminal justice system has traditionally been unconcerned with the problems and needs of such persons. To a considerable extent the victim still has no formal status within the criminal proceedings and, as a result, has no specific rights or access to goods and services. After the contact with law enforcement personnel, the victim becomes a witness for the prosecution whose sole benefits are limited to those of witnesses. For those who do not perform such a role, much of the process is limited to restitution (which has historically been uncollected) or to civil proceedings against persons who for the most part are judgment-proof. Social service systems also have traditionally not viewed victims as a special group with special needs.

Consideration of the victim has grown in recent decades. Interpretation of crime statistics through victim surveys and methods of compensating victims began during the 1960s in the United States. Services for victims began in early 1974, with greater development occurring in the last half of that decade. Numerous compensation programs were initiated, and research is increasingly being focused on the "forgotten person" within the system.

The criminal justice system, however, still functions to a great extent either in opposition to or secondary to the interests of the victim.

Victim Perceptions and Crisis Intervention. It has sometimes been assumed that different types of victimization require different types of intervention. While it is true, for example, that the intervention with a sexual assault victim may be procedurally different from that of a purse snatching, the crisis intervention process is functionally identical. Knudten, Meade, Knudten, and Doerner (1976) found great similarity in both the needs and responses of victims of varying crimes in a sample population of 2,000 persons. Research by Denton (1979) confirmed that finding.

Perceptions or assessments of situations are assumed to strongly influence emotional responses to such situations. It has been noted that victims of crime may perceive the incident as threat, loss, or challenge, depending on the degree of stress involved (Golan, 1978). High stress situations tend to produce a perception of threat and an emotional response of anxiety. Somewhat less stress in a situation is associated with a perception of loss and emotions of depression. Low stress situations are perceived as challenge and are accompanied by anxiety plus resolve.

Therapeutic intervention will depend largely on which of the perceptions the victim uses to define the situation. Victims generally define the events as threat, regardless of crime type, with some secondary loss perceptions (Denton, 1979). These perceptions represent the initial interpretation of the experience and are subject to change over time. Some change occurs among those who initially define the experience as a low-stress event (challenge or no-impact) and who in time come to view the event as a high-stress experience. Such changes are important to therapeutic interventions.

The counselor should focus the intervention on establishing a rapport sufficient to offer support and allow assessment of and assistance with 1) the victim's perceptions of the event, 2) the victim's ability and methods of coping with what for most is a short-term crisis, and 3) organization of the client's support system.

Awareness of the victim's perceptions of the event allows the intervenor to determine and assist in managing feelings of anxiety and depression. High-stress responses should direct the intervenor to build on an accurate understanding of the experience and utilize the victim's situational supports (family, friends, clergy). Victims with challenge perceptions more often require brief support and specific information about subsequent prevention, replacement of lost items, claims and documents, etc.

It is important to help manage the immediate social context. In many instances close friends and relatives are upset and may themselves require assistance. It should be noted that such disturbed relationships can be as serious a threat to the victim as the initial event.

The role of the client's faith should not be neglected. Religious commitment has been found to be an important variable in predictive studies, and as such can be a legitimate and powerful tool in the therapeutic process. Clergy and other religious associates can lend considerable situational support. The role of faith and forgiveness can provide necessary release from attitudes that hinder the healing process.

Information about and assistance with the criminal justice process is often necessary. Questions about what will happen, where, and when are anxiety producing. Support, particularly if the offense produced a formal crisis, may be critical. The normal healing process can begin within hours and is usually resolved within 24 hours to four weeks. Often this process is well under way when painful experiences must be recalled and relived. Many victims find the court experience more difficult than the original victimization.

The counselor should develop resources within the community to provide immediate access to and obtainment of specific social needs. This may best be facilitated by a local victim assistance program, rape crisis center, or crisis intervention agency. The intervenor should also make provision for cases for whom the brief nature of crisis intervention is not sufficient. Other short-term therapy or psychotherapy may be indicated. Information should be collected concerning available state compensation for various fiscal losses associated with medical costs or lost work resulting from the crime.

Research has consistently isolated one centrally important service activity upon which all intervenors should capitalize. In the words of the responders, "Someone cared about me."

References

Denton, R. *What they think/what they do: A study of the perceptions and service utilization of victims of violent crime.* Unpublished dissertation, School of Applied Social Sciences, Case Western Reserve University, 1979.

Golan, N. *Treatment in crisis situations.* New York: Free Press, 1978.

Knudten, R. D., Meade, A., Knudten, M., & Doerner, W. *Victims and witnesses: Their experiences with crime and the criminal justice system.* Washington, D.C.: National Institute of Law Enforcement and Criminal Justice, U.S. Department of Justice, 1976.

Additional Reading

Viano, E., & Drapkin, I. *Victimology: A new focus* (5 vols.). Lexington, Mass.: Lexington Books, 1974–75.

A. R. DENTON

Video Feedback in Therapy. The use of videotape techniques in therapeutic treatment has developed rapidly since the acceptance of this equipment in psychological healing. Berger (1970), a psychiatrist, was a pioneer in the innovative applications of video for many settings, including training and treatment.

Video feedback may take several forms. A particular session may be taped and instantly replayed to the client, the tape may be played back at a later time, or certain sections of it may be used. As a tool in a total plan of treatment, its adaptability for particular counselors and clients is nearly unlimited and should be geared to the needs of the client. Creative counselors can find many innovative uses for videotape, both for their own diagnostic role and for increasing awareness and encouraging change in their clients.

A rationale for the use of video feedback in therapy is based on the belief that what people report that they do and think, as in a typical counseling session, is not necessarily what they actually do. Video feedback allows the client to obtain a clearer picture of himself. An increase in self-awareness and the understanding of one's impact on others and others on self often lead to change. Emotional and intellectual insights gained from observing oneself in relationship to others can lead to change in image, attitude, self-concept, reactions, and behavior. Videotape provides an undistorted reproduction of the situation in which the meaning and nuances can be open to interpretation but the actions cannot. Both verbal and nonverbal communication are important indicators of self, and incongruencies can be readily pointed out and recognized with the use of video playback. One is able to see and experience oneself more objectively through this tool than is usually possible through other methods.

As a diagnostic tool and also a springboard for the therapeutic process video can be a powerful therapeutic resource. Initial anxiety and self-criticism is natural, and often is followed gradually by awareness of the need for change and avenues for making that happen. With groups video feedback can take many forms, including playback without sound to facilitate concentration on nonverbal signs, taping the group's reaction to an earlier tape, and instant replay requested by any member of the group. With the premise that self-image is based on how one perceives self, and how one perceives others perceive him, video feedback is a tool that facilitates bringing this process to awareness. Consensual validation has a powerful effect on an individual. It is particularly beneficial for confronting denial, discrepancies between affect and content, and verbal and nonverbal differences. Feedback can focus on a specific action or behavior that is reinforced through what the person or group can actually see for themselves. The group process is therefore enhanced through feedback, self-image exposure, confrontation, and testing out of new behaviors. Video feedback is also effectively used in family therapy in similar situations and for similar reasons.

The use of video equipment in therapy raises ethical issues of privacy and confidentiality. However, these issues are not insurmountable and do not substantially differ from those involved in therapy that does not employ such techniques. Video feedback will not make an inadequate or ill-trained therapist a good therapist. It is a tool, which, used properly and in the right hands, can be a powerful force in the therapeutic process. Beyond the traditional uses video feedback has been used effectively with delinquents and drug addicts, multiple personalities, terminal patients, and following suicide attempts (showing the survivor the steps he went through in the reviving process), as well as for sexual dysfunction problems.

Reference
Berger, M. (Ed.). *Videotape techniques in psychiatric training and treatment*, New York: Brunner/Mazel, 1970.
D. L. SCHUURMAN

Vineland Social Maturity Scale. *See* SOCIAL MATURITY TESTS.

Vocational Counseling. Historically vocational counseling has been organized around the premise that "social progress must be engineered more by the improvement of man as learner, worker, and citizen than by the improvement of man's physical technology" (Wrenn, 1964, p. xi). Although there is no general agreement on the precise origin of the vocational counseling movement (some would attribute it to Frank Parsons at the turn of the twentieth century), it emerged historically as an integral part of the ideological, industrial, urban transformation of America.

The human and the technological have become almost a unity in today's world, but the vocational counseling movement has through the years developed more sophisticated theories and applications regarding the human side of the equation. Together theory and application represent vocational development and vocational counseling, each dependent on the other.

Theories of vocational development are the base upon which vocational counseling rests. Initially vocational theories focused on occupations and, through descriptions of the characteristics of people successfully employed in them, merely matched people and positions. Then in the 1950s more dynamic theories of careers emerged that dealt with how people choose, enter, and progress in their vocations, which were conceived of in a broader sense than just "a job." Instead of studying occupations as static entities, whereby prediction of success in an occupation is treated as though the position and the characteristics of the person filling it would remain the same throughout the person's lifetime, theorists began to look at the whole sequence (the career) of work experiences occurring during the course of a person's life (Super, 1969).

With the new emphasis on career as a sequence of changing personal characteristics and work experiences, theorists began to make use of the concept of life stages. Eli Ginzberg, Robert Havighurst, Anne Roe, Donald Super, and David Tiedeman made major contributions to the understanding of the lifelong process of decision making and the relationship of needs, values, interests, coping abilites, and self-concept to career decision making. In addition, Super and Crites have worked extensively on the concept of vocational maturity, noting the difference between the ability to plan and the ability to deal with realistic preferences.

It should be obvious that the applied side of the movement, vocational counseling, is much more involved than just matching a person to a specific job. Crites (1974) has reviewed the major approaches and contrasted them along the dimensions of diagnosis, process, outcomes, interview techniques, test interpretation, and use of occupational information. Diagnosis is the hallmark of the trait-and-factor approach, the first of five that Crites reviews. He caricatures it as "three interviews and a cloud of dust," or assigning a battery of tests (interview 1), interpreting the test results (interview 2), briefing the client on the use of the occupational information file (interview 3), and sending the client on his or her way (cloud of dust) without having tried or changed a thing.

According to Crites the trait-and-factor approach does have enough assets to find expression in one form or another in most of the other approaches. The person-centered approach, while highlighting the importance of the client's participation throughout the entire decision-making process, has a hard time introducing information into the interview process. The psychodynamic approach broadens the process by including internal motivational factors, but at times it can be excessive. With its greater emphasis on maturational than motivational factors the developmental approach, which is founded on Super's theory of vocational development, is favored by Crites as the most comprehensive and coherent of the various vocational counseling approaches. Finally, rather than focusing on the antecedents of vocational behavior, the behavioral approach focuses on the conditioning of vocational behavior by its consequences. This has the advantage of emphasizing the actual behaviors involved in the decision-making process.

A recent development has been to move away from the one-on-one interview to a group-oriented approach. This has helped to correct some of the sex bias and lack of information regarding career opportunities for women that can go undetected in the interview approach. Career decisions can be made anywhere, but learning God's will is going to occur more freely in the company of fellow believers. It is important that we seek first the kingdom of God as our calling, and within the context of the body of believers begin to select those work activities that bring honor and glory to the Lord and further his kingdom (Farnsworth & Lawhead, 1981). It is likely that by praying, studying the Bible, and utilizing whatever professional resources are available as a group of Christians committed to one another, each person will be more likely to relate the occupation he or she chooses to the needs of others. The Christian's career is not a personal possession, but service to others.

References

Crites, J. O. Career counseling: A review of major approaches. *The Counseling Psychologist.* 1974, *4*(3), 3–23.
Farnsworth, K. E., & Lawhead, W. H. *Life planning: A Christian approach to careers* (Rev. ed.). Downers Grove, Ill.: Inter-Varsity Press, 1981.
Super, D. E. Vocational development theory: Persons, positions, and processes. *The Counseling Psychologist,* 1969, *1*(1), 2–9.
Wrenn, C. G. Preface. In H. Borow (Ed.), *Man in a world at work.* Boston: Houghton Mifflin, 1964.

K. E. FARNSWORTH

See STRONG-CAMPBELL INTEREST INVENTORY.

Volition. *See* WILL.

Voyeurism. The act of achieving sexual pleasure by furtively watching others disrobing or in a state of nudity. The voyeur, or Peeping Tom, is generally a young male who obtains sexual gratification by looking at the genitals of another or by observing sexual acts. To be able to see others in one of these states the voyeur will often peer in windows at night. While watching, or "peeping," the individual may engage in masturbatory play, sometimes to orgasm.

This desire to see, by stealth, is so intense that it surpasses in importance the normal sexual act. The voyeur is not interested in making contact with the person of his sexual desires. His primary interest is to achieve orgasmic expression by viewing others. If he is apprehended, it is for loitering and prowling. Rarely does he become a more serious sexual deviant.

Viewing others in various stages of undress

occurs on a continuum from secretly looking at girlie magazines or advertisements of female underclothing to going to "peep shows" or to bars where nude dancing is provided. These more legitimate forms of peeping are harmless to others. On the other extreme of the continuum is the socially isolated person who prowls around the neighborhood looking for the opportunity to see something. He will often sneak around backyards and come right up to the bedroom windows, peering through cracks in the curtains. While he is harmless, the threats imagined by the one watched are often traumatic.

This pattern of behavior may develop when the normal curiosity of youth is coupled with shyness, inadequate relations with the other sex, or experiences that titillate the curiosity, such as peep shows or magazines. Viewing the body of an attractive female is quite stimulating sexually for most males. The privacy and mystery that generally surround sexual activities tend to increase curiosity about them. Peeping satisfies some of the curiosity and to some extent meets the voyeur's sexual needs without the trauma of actually approaching a female, and thus without the failure and lowered self-status that such an approach might bring. The suspense and danger associated with peeping may actually intensify the emotional excitement and sexual stimulation.

Liberalization of laws concerning "adult" movies and magazines have probably removed much of the secrecy from sexual behavior. They provide an alternative source of gratification for would-be peepers. However the voyeur's need to spy on sexual behavior of unsuspecting couples is still met only in the actual peeping.

L. N. FERGUSON

Ww

Watson, John Broadus (1878–1958). Father of American BEHAVIORAL PSYCHOLOGY. Born and raised in Greenville, South Carolina, he received an M.A. from Furman University, then went to the University of Chicago, where he received his Ph.D. in 1903 and remained as an instructor. In 1908 Watson left Chicago for Johns Hopkins. Forced to resign from Johns Hopkins in 1920 due to adverse publicity about his divorce, he subsequently entered the advertising business.

While in Chicago, Watson began studying the relationship between animal and human behavior and helped found an animal laboratory. This work was continued at Johns Hopkins. The first published statement of his behaviorist views was in an article entitled "Psychology as the Behaviorist Views It" (1913). Watson's most important books include *Behavior, an Introduction to Comparative Psychology* (1914), *Psychology from the Standpoint of a Behaviorist* (1919), and a semipopular book, *Behaviorism* (1925).

Waston led the revolt against introspection, the study of conscious experience, which then dominated American psychology. He noted that introspection was not suited to the study of animals. An avowed materialist, he objected to concepts such as mind, consciousness, volition, and emotion, stating that psychology should be the science of directly observable behavior. Watson advocated direct observations of behavior and adopted the conditioned reflex method of Russian physiologist Ivan Pavlov.

A strong environmentalist, Watson believed that the conditioned reflex was the basic learning mechanism. His conditioned reflex method has come to be known as classical conditioning or respondent conditioning.

B. F. Skinner's research indicates that most behavior is operant rather than reflexive in nature, and that the conditioned reflex plays a much more minor role than Watson believed. Also, genetic and other biological factors clearly play a much larger role than Watson recognized. However, strict materialism and emphasis on the study of observable behavior continue to characterize modern behaviorism, and Watson's role as the founder of American behaviorism remains secure.

R. K. BUFFORD

Weber, Ernst Heinrich (1795–1878). German physiologist who laid the groundwork for experimental psychology. The son of a theology professor, he was born in Wittenberg. He completed his early studies at Wittenberg and was awarded the doctorate in 1815 at Leipzig, where he spent his entire career, teaching anatomy and physiology from 1817 until his retirement in 1871.

Weber made contributions to all areas of physiology. His publications include research on the physiology of the circulatory system, the ear, the eye, the liver, and especially the skin. He published a Latin monograph, *On Touch* (1834), and an article in Wagner's *Handbook of Physiology* (1846) in which he further elaborated his findings on the skin senses. Although both are now considered classics, his findings attracted little attention until the publication of *The Sense of Touch and the Common Sensibility* (1851).

In *On Touch* he announced his discovery of what came to be known as Weber's law. This was a statement of the first really quantitative law in psychology. Weber set out to determine the smallest difference between two weights that could just be discriminated, the just noticeable difference. He found this to be not a given value, but a constant ratio. For example, if the ratio is 1:40, a weight of 41 grams is reported as being just noticeably different from one of 40 grams, and one of 123 grams as just noticeably different from one of 120 grams. Weber conducted experiments on other senses and found other ratios, but generally found the ratio was a constant within any sense. Although he did not realize it at first, this was the beginning of psychophysics, later developed by Eachner.

Weber also determined the accuracy of the two-point threshold, the distance between two points needed before subjects report feeling two distinct sensations. If the distance is less than this threshold, subjects report feeling only one point; if more, they report two points. He found that the two-point threshold differed in various parts of the body, that it was very small for the fingertips and large for the back. This was the first systematic, experimental demonstration of the threshold, a concept widely used in psychology even today.

He also contributed articles on the improvement of medical education, emphasizing the need to adopt scientific methods. He urged the application of scientific findings and was a cofounder of the German Polytechnic Society.

R. L. Koteskey

Wechsler Intelligence Tests. Psychologist David Wechsler has developed several scales for the measurement of intelligence. At present three tests are widely used by professionals. Each test consists of a number of subtests with standardized questions and tasks for a particular age group. The results lead to an understanding of one's major mental abilities and a full-scale deviation IQ score. The deviation IQ is a relative measure of one's performance in comparison to others in the same age group.

The Wechsler Adult Intelligence Scale–Revised (WAIS–R) was published in 1982. Preceding this most recent revision were the Wechsler-Bellevue Intelligence Scale Form I, published in 1939, and the Wechsler Adult Intelligence Scale (WAIS), published in 1955. The WAIS–R is administered by a professional familiar with the testing procedures, materials, and scoring systems. It may be given to any individual over the age of 16. The actual test consists of 11 subtests, six verbal and five performance. The verbal subtests require the individual to verbally express his or her answer to questions in several categories: information, digit span, vocabulary, arithmetic, comprehension, and similarities.

The five performance tests, some of which require the manipulation of objects, include picture completion, picture arrangement, block design, object assembly, and digit symbol. Norms for the various age groups have been developed. The test results in a determination of one's verbal IQ, performance IQ, and full-scale IQ. Since scaled scores rather than raw scores are used in the determination of IQ, the scores reflect one's performance in comparison to others of the same age group.

The Wechsler Intelligence Scale for Children–Revised (WISC–R) was published in 1974. The original Wechsler Intelligence Scale for children (WISC) was published in 1949. The WISC–R is administered to children between the ages of 6 years and 16. The test consists of 12 subtests, six verbal and six performance. However, all subtests are not always administered. The various subtests in the WISC–R are intended to assess the child's performance under fixed conditions and in as many areas as possible. The six verbal tests include information, similarities, arithmetic, vocabulary, comprehension, and digit span. The six performance tests include picture completion, picture arrangement, block design, object assembly, coding, and mazes. Norms for every four-month interval within the age span between 6 and 16 have been determined. The test results are given as a verbal IQ, performance IQ, and full-scale IQ and allow for comparison within one's age group.

The Wechsler Preschool and Primary Scale of Intelligence (WPPSI) was published in 1963. It is administered to children between the ages of 4 and 6. It consists of 11 subtests, six verbal and five performance. The test results are a verbal, performance, and full-scale IQ.

The Wechsler Scales require from 60 to 90 minutes to administer. Usually the test is given in its entirety during a single session. Due to the nature of the testing procedures and materials the test must be administered individually and under good testing conditions.

W. W. Austin

See Intellectual Assessment.

Wertheimer, Max (1880–1943). One of the three originators of Gestalt psychology. Born in Prague, Czechoslovakia, where his father directed a commercial school, he studied law at the university there. He later shifted to the study of philosophy and psychology, finally going to Würzburg, where he received a Ph.D. degree in 1904.

Little is known about Wertheimer's activities between 1904 and 1910, but he spent time in Prague, Vienna, and Berlin. In the summer of 1910, while on a train from Vienna to the Rhineland for a vacation, Wertheimer conceived a new way to deal with apparent movement. He got off the train at Frankfurt, bought a toy stroboscope, and began testing his hypothesis in his hotel room. He contacted an old friend at the University of Frankfurt who offered him a tachistoscope and introduced him to two new assistants at the Psychological Institute. These assistants, Köhler and Koffka, had completed their degrees within the last two years and they became Wertheimer's first two subjects. From that time on their lives and work were intricately interwoven in Gestalt psychology.

Wertheimer lectured at Frankfurt until 1916, when he went to the University of Berlin. During World War I he conducted research of military value on listening devices. In 1929 he was granted a professorship at Frankfurt, but he stayed only until 1933, when he was among the first group of refugee scholars to arrive in New York. He joined the New School for Social Research in 1934 and remained there until his death.

Wertheimer's work on apparent movement, the phi phenomenon, led to the emphasis on the "whole" of experience rather than on the elementism of the structuralists. This emphasis on the whole is illustrated in his principles of organization describing how our perception if naturally organized. Objects near each other tend to be grouped together, as do objects that are similar. If certain parts of our perceptual organization are left out, we tend to complete it, to make the Gestalt complete.

Wertheimer's other major contribution is reflected in the title of his only book in English, *Productive Thinking* (1945). All of the cognitive processes are redefined in terms of the conception of Gestalt. His essential argument is that recentering takes place in problem solving so that new forms of figure-ground organization occur. Wertheimer was the least published of the Gestalt leaders, but his articles were pivotal.

R. L. Koteskey

Wholistic Health and Therapy. *See* HOLISTIC HEALTH AND THERAPY.

Will. Although we know by experience that we have the ability to commence or cease behavior, and in so doing manifest the presence of a volitional component in our personality, the interest of psychologists in this subject has been minimal. This is rather surprising, since

Wundt and James, two of the key historical figures in psychology, contributed much to an understanding of the will. James, for example, argued that self-initiated behaviors are the consequence of mental images of the act that is to be performed. When we conceptualize a certain idea, and when that moves us into an action we are capable of performing, "will" has been demonstrated. In contrast, a wish involves a similar process, but we are incapable of engaging in the conceptualized behavior. Wundt, an avowed determinist, posited that the problems of psychology were problems of volition, a position that led to his voluntarism movement.

As the discipline of psychology developed at the turn of the century, concern with volition waned, and an antimentalistic approach came in vogue. Global concepts such as will, intention, and self-control were replaced by more scientifically credible terms such as drive, motive, conscious, and unconscious. Implicit in this movement was a deterministic model, which was epitomized in both the psychoanalytic and behavioristic traditions and which facilitated a rejection of the self-determined, self-directed man. This change in orientation is understood best in the context of the philosophical and scientific heritage of the field. Danziger (1979), for example, has argued that although Wundt is known for his structuralistic scientific approach to psychology, there is evidence to suggest that he never intended it to be other than a branch of philosophy. In essence the tension surrounding volition is in reality a conflict between scientific respectability and philosophical integrity. Irwin (1942), referring to this issue, concludes that psychologists have avoided volition because of the importance of experimental methods, so that "problems have been determined by methods rather than methods by problems" (p. 115).

In 1968 a symposium at the American Psychological Association meetings entitled "Whatever Happened to the Will in American Psychology?" raised an important historical question and stimulated a renewed interest in volition (e.g., Gilbert, 1970; Kimble & Perlmuter, 1970), as did a conference in England on the philosophy of psychology in 1971 (Brown, 1974). However, the content and methodology of North American psychology is still not greatly concerned with the subject.

The Will in Psychology. One might best understand the current status of volition viewing it from five theoretical viewpoints: behavioristic, developmental, experimental, psychoanalytic, and humanistic psychology.

In *Beyond Freedom and Dignity* (1971) Skinner posits that a belief in an autonomous man who is responsible for self-directed action is fallacious and comes from a lack of understanding of the real cause of human behavior: the environment. This "empty box" view of human beings precludes any investigation of volition. In contrast both Erikson and Piaget stress the importance of volition in the development of the child.

Erikson, in outlining the autonomy versus shame and doubt stage of ages 2 to 3 claims that an inevitable clash of wills occurs between parents and children. Ideally a firmly supportive atmosphere for the child will create a control of the will without a loss of self-esteem. In a slightly different vein Piaget conceptualizes the development of will as being based on self-identity and disequilibrium in moral conflicts. When a child leaves the early egocentric stages for growth, the expenditure of energy in decision making is based on the will reestablishing the priority of various values. As a result the child, faced with the conflict of watching television or doing homework, exercises the will and determines an appropriate course of action based on the internalized value system.

Westcott (1983) has suggested that will may be researched as an experience in and of itself, rather than as an objective quantifiable entity. Although a body of experimental research looking at the issues of volition, control, and freedom does exist (Brehm & Brehm, 1981), he argues that an understanding of the phenomenology of volition is most appropriate. Rather than laboratory work, what is needed is dialectic and semantic investigation in terms of how people describe will when they are confronted with choices. Westcott perceives his sample not as subjects but as respondents or coinvestigators.

Freud's first published case, Frau Emmy von N., raised the issue of will versus counterwill. He suggested that when we want to do something, a counterwill responds. In times of stress and fatigue we find ourselves following the defeating messages and go against our will. Similarly Shapiro (1981) argues that although those with rigid personalities describe a weakness of will in decision making, the reality is that they have underlying unrecognized wishes and intentions. Jung followed a similar line of argument in claiming that will is part of consciousness and is influenced by unconscious instincts. Rank, the neo-Freudian, saw the central problem of life as being the exercise of the will. The neurotic, in fleeing from responsibility, experiences defeat and a lack of

will to independence. The therapeutic process is a reinforcing of the fact that in order to grow and develop, the patient needs to choose responsibly even to the extent of challenging the analyst and setting a time for termination.

Humanistic psychology, represented by May, Maslow, and others, reacted to the deterministic influence of psychoanalysis and behaviorism, claiming it undermined personal responsibility. A person always has the capacity to choose and experience freedom, and the will has the power to affect any environmental influence.

The Will in Theology. Although the biblical concept of heart is often stereotyped as the seat of the emotions, this only captures one component of its function. In actuality the heart is all that is within, including the cognitive, emotional, and volitional. Paul's appeal to "believe in your heart" (Rom. 10:9) is a holistic emphasis that touches all of who we are. Subsumed under this is the issue of choosing or willing. Similarly when Jesus, referring to the Jews, said, "You refuse to come to me" (John 5:40), he also stressed the fact that "You do not have the love of God in your hearts" (5:42). In other words, a lack of cognitive and emotional understanding produced a constraint of the will to choose correctly.

The Christian who understands "Rejoice in the Lord always" (Phil. 4:4) recognizes that this injunction is an appeal to the will, since it is a command; but the intent of the verse goes beyond the will into the cognitive and emotional. It is not just a blind choice but a full appreciation and experience of the Lord and who he is. A careful reading of other New Testament commands shows that they also are an appeal to the whole person.

As to its origin, volition is usually seen by Christians as being part of the image of God in humans (Berkhof, 1939). As such it mirrors one of the characteristics of God. Although mankind's ability to choose in the right direction was marred by the fall, it did not deny one's capacity to choose.

Recognizing will as part of the image of God, much current popular Christian psychology has been influenced by the cognitive behavior modification tradition, in which freedom to choose one's thoughts and emotions is stressed. Rychlak (1979), in commenting on the popular psychologies, has suggested that one reason why the self-help movement works is because of its stress on the power to choose and overcome one's circumstances. The potential problem for the Christian counselor, however, is that an excessive preoccupation with this approach will implicitly deny the holistic emphasis contained in the biblical concept of heart.

In sum, Christians in articulating their own position on the will need to remain loyal to the interrelatedness of all the components of the whole person.

References

Berkof, L. *Systematic theology*. Grand Rapids: Eerdmans, 1939.

Brehm, S., & Brehm, J. *Psychological reactance: A theory of freedom and control*. New York: Academic Press, 1981.

Brown, S. C. (Ed.). *Philosophy of psychology*. New York: Barnes & Noble, 1974.

Danziger, K. The social origins of modern psychology. In A. R. Buss (Ed.), *Psychology in social context*. New York: Irvington Publishers, 1979.

Gilbert, A. Whatever happened to the will in American psychology? *Journal of the History of the Behavioral Sciences*, 1970, 6, 52–58.

Irwin, F. W. The concept of volition in experimental psychology. In F. Clarke & M. Nahm (Eds.), *Philosophical essays in honor of Edgar Arthur Singer, Jr*. Philadelphia: University of Pennsylvania Press, 1942.

Kimble, G., & Perlmuter, L. The problem of volition. *Psychological Review*, 1970, 77, 361–384.

Rychlak, J. F. *Discovering free will and personal responsibility*. New York: Oxford University Press, 1979.

Shapiro, D. *Autonomy and rigid character*. New York: Basic Books, 1981.

Skinner, B. F. *Beyond freedom and dignity*. New York: Knopf, 1971.

Westcott, M. R. Volition is a nag. Paper presented at Research Conference in Honor of Richard L. Solomon, University of Pennsylvania, 1983.

R. WILSON

See DETERMINISM AND Free WILL.

Will Therapy. A form of treatment associated with OTTO RANK who assumed that the central element in neuroses was the birth trauma. He believed this trauma to lead to two basic desires: the desire to return to the womb and the desire to reenact separation and achieve a more satisfactory degree of independence. In will therapy patients are encouraged to assert themselves and strengthen their will, thereby moving toward independence.

Winnicott, Donald Woods (1896–1971). British pediatrician and psychoanalyst. In recent years his work has become increasingly popular among psychoanalysts and child psychiatrists throughout the world.

Winnicott differed from the pioneers in the field of psychoanalysis in two ways. First, he took the theory of emotional development back into earliest infancy, even before birth. Thus, a large part of his work was devoted to the verbal exploration of what is preverbal in the history of the individual. The second difference was the way in which he presented his ideas and theories. He described himself as being nonintellectual. His thinking was shaped by his training in psychoanalysis, but his unique contribution to the general theory of psychoanalysis arose out of his clinical experience and observations.

Winnicott is best known for his therapeutic work with children. He did not always use psychoanalysis on the child, but rather selected his mode of therapy according to the child's need. If he did choose to use psychoanalysis, the technique most often employed was the squiggle game—the drawing technique which he developed. This technique involves an impulsive line drawn by the therapist, which the child has to turn into something; then the child makes a squiggle which the therapist has to turn into something. After each squiggle is completed, the child free associates to it as a stimulus.

Winnicott did not attach any magical quality to the squiggle game, but saw it as one way of getting into contact with the child so as to help the psychotherapeutic consultation come alive for both child and analyst. In this way the child's experiences as presented in the interview and the interaction between child and therapist help make the interpretation by the therapist more meaningful to the child.

Getting the parent involved in their child's treatment was important to Winnicott, and the squiggle game facilitated this. He would use the child's drawings in consultations with the parents to help them recognize themes and conflicts. In this way the parents could best support the child in the changes resulting from therapy.

Additional Readings

Davis, M., & Wallbridge, D. *Boundary and space: An introduction to the work of D. W. Winnicott*. New York: Brunner/Mazel, 1981.

Winnicott, D. W. *Therapeutic consultations in child psychiatry*. New York: Basic Books, 1971. (a)

Winnicott, D. W. *Playing and reality*. New York: Basic Books, 1971. (b)

B. JOSCELYNE

Women, Psychology of. Since the earliest history of psychology most psychologists have been male. Similarly most of the attention has been focused on the male gender. The female gender was not studied in great detail, possibly because females were almost considered to be a different species. The small amount of work on the female psyche was often filled with myth and stereotypes. However, very recently this began to change. The female of the species is now receiving more attention as an object of study.

Partly this was the result of societal

changes. The old notions of women's behavior began to crumble with changes in society in the last 20 years. Expectations for women and their behavior were not met, and behavioral scientists began to wonder if they should perhaps look again at this phenomenon of woman. Thus, it is not that disciplines such as psychology of women came about because of the women's movement, but rather phenomena such as renewed interest in the psychology of women as well as the women's movement itself came about because of changes that occurred in society (Williams, 1977).

Topics subsumed under the general heading of psychology of women cover a wide range and impinge on social psychology, developmental psychology, and physiological psychology. Areas within the realm of social psychology include such concerns as sex differences in social interactions and behavior, as well as the study of theories of the emergence of those sex differences. Areas subsumed under developmental psychology include such issues as sex role development and the discussion of various unique stresses that women encounter at various stages of the life cycle. Finally physiological psychology studies the effects of biological changes (e.g., menopause) on behavior.

History. The study of the psychology of women as a separate discipline within psychology began around the turn of the century. Prior to that time there was much myth and romanticization surrounding both woman and her role. At that time there existed the notion of woman as a different order of being. A major feature of her difference was her relative lack of characteristics valued in males, such as originality, creativity, and educability. Around 1900 there developed in the United States a school of psychology known as functionalism, whose defining feature was its incorporation of evolutionary theory into the subject matter of psychology. This marriage of evolutionary theory and psychology was seen in the study of female behavior in terms of female brain size. For example, societal observations at that time showed females to be generally less involved in intellectual pursuits of any type. There were very few women enrolled in universities or serving as leaders in business and industry. Evolutionary theory provided an explanation for this lack of intellectual pursuits among women: namely, since women had a smaller brain size, they were obviously lower on the evolutionary scale than men and thus less intelligent. This explained their absence in achievement related areas. Thus a societal observation was explained by reference to

some innate biological female trait. Likewise the concept of maternal instinct, which maintained that woman's nurturing behavior is an innate biological determinant shared with other female animals, was readily incorporated into the early doctrines of psychology.

The notion of the innateness of behavior and instincts, a common theme in early psychology, held sway in the study of female psychology until the mid-1920s, when the behaviorists began to successfully challenge the entire concept of instinct in humans, holding that most human behavior is learned. While a naïve approach to evolution provided an explanation of innateness for a phenomenon that was obviously largely the product of societal norms (women's participation in society), the tendency to ascribe innateness to socially conditioned behaviors in women is still a widespread phenomenon.

The study of women as "a different order of being" continued into the era of psychoanalysis. Freud's view of women was conditioned by his own personal experiences within the strongly patriarchal milieu of central Europe. He confessed to a great ignorance of that mysterious creature, the female. Several times he stated that he confined his descriptions to the male child because the corresponding process in the little girl was unknown. He also described the sexual life of adult women "as a dark continent for psychology."

It was not until female psychoanalysts began to enter the discipline in the 1940s that women ceased to be called a different order of being. Early writers such as Helene Deutsch began to suggest that the psychology and experience of women could be made intelligible. Her work and that of subsequent psychoanalysts, however, remained largely trait oriented, rather than state oriented. (By "trait" is meant the existence of some enduring personality characteristic which is responsible for the individual's behavior and which is not easily modifiable by the environment. "State" refers to a less stable disposition of the individual that is often a product of the situation in which the individual finds himself or herself.) In the early 1950s, female psychology began to move slowly away from a trait orientation, largely through the impetus of such writers as Karen Horney and Margaret Mead.

Current Research. Today a substantial amount of trait-type research still exists in the study of the psychology of women, especially as it relates to sex differences. A cursory examination of the *Psychology of Women Quarterly* (the major journal of the area) typically shows that about one-third to one-half of the articles are concerned with sex differences. However, in the last few years this approach to research has been questioned by leaders in the field. For example, Unger (1981) warned against interpreting sex differences as being totally due to the gender and traits of the different sexes. She suggested that sex-related differences found in the laboratory may be due to the particular research methodology that is used. She also suggested that sex and gender should not be treated as individual difference variables. Rather, they should be viewed from a social cognition framework.

The role of social cognitions has become a big issue in social psychology. It also has important implications for the study of sex differences. The notion of social cognition suggests that assumptions about one's own sex-related characteristics and those of others interact with social context and situational factors to produce what are frequently termed *sex-different behaviors*. The ideas or thoughts that one has in mind lead one to act in a certain way (sex-different behaviors). Furthermore these ideas for behavior frequently come from cues from the social context and situation factors. One often looks at others to pick up cues as to how one should behave in a new setting. Indeed, research in the area has indicated that sex-characteristic behaviors may be actively induced in individuals by others who interact with them (Snyder, Tanke, & Bercheid, 1977). It is probable that the elusiveness of sex differences in research may be partially attributed to the different research methodologies used in the different studies. Some research methodologies may subtly suggest to women that they should behave with more feminine behavior, while others may not. For example, it has been found that sex-of-subject effects are found more frequently in the field as opposed to laboratory studies. Numerous explanations have been advanced for this finding, including the idea that individuals involved in an everyday ongoing situation may be influenced by more concern for societal norms.

One main issue in current research is the determination of these social cognitions that influence male and female behavior. For example, one fairly consistent finding is that observers in a laboratory perceive situations as a more important determiner of the behavior of males, whereas dispositional explanations are seen as more important for understanding females. This difference of perception occurs even though the situational constraints are kept equal for both males and females. The prevalence of this cognition suggests that there is still a stronger tendency to evaluate females in terms of biologically related enduring traits.

The impetus for the switch to a social cognition approach to psychology of women came not only from the general area of social psychology but also from research within the area of psychology of women itself. The earliest work in this area came from some of the cross-cultural work of Mead, who began to suggest that not all women in all cultures behave similarly. In her now classic book, *Sex and Temperament in Three Primitive Societies* (1935), she found the behaviors and temperaments of men and women to vary drastically across societies. For example, in one tribe both men and women exhibited "maternal" nurturant behavior and were equally concerned with the care of children. Aggression by anyone was met with serious disapproval. In still another society both sexes were ruthless, aggressive, and strongly sexual, with little or no interest in the maternal nurturing aspects of personality. Finally, in a third tribe, the roles and characteristics of men and women were the reverse of those considered appropriate in our society. The women took charge of all important business and domestic affairs. The little girls were the more active of the two sexes, were curious, exploratory, and free. The men spent most of their time carving, painting, and gossiping, and the small boys were much less active than the small girls. These findings led Mead to begin to develop her ideas about the cultural standardization of temperament and the role of social conditioning that selected certain characteristics to reinforce and neglected or punished others. All cultures distinguished roles based on sex; however, the behavior considered appropriate for each sex varied with the culture.

The early work by Mead and others began to stimulate a closer look at how behaviors considered sexually appropriate in our society were conditioned. There was also a thrust to determine if indeed there was a differential conditioning process going on in the sexes. This has led to an examination of the interaction processes between parents and infants and children. Do parents or other adult figures react differently to male and female children? There is a growing body of literature to suggest that they do. For example, research into the interactions between teachers and children in a nursery school found differential responses to the children at that age. Teachers were much more likely to send boys off to work by themselves or to reinforce girls for passivity and boys for aggression. Boys were usually encouraged more often to do a task themselves, whereas the teacher was willing to do the task for the little girl. Such differential interactions, of course, may have a large impact on later adult experiences of confidence and independence (Serbin & O'Leary, 1975).

Methodological problems. Despite problems and distortions in the past history of the psychology of women and sex differences, the latter area is still an important area of study. The question of what types of gender-related differences really do exist, whether from nature or nurture, is important. However, this area is beset with many difficulties. Not only is there the issue of social cognitions and their impact on the actual behavior of the individual in a research setting, but there are also some blatant research biases. Grady (1981) summarized the most important of these methodological problems.

There is a paucity of actual research dealing with females. Most research still uses males. There is also a tendency to use different laboratory procedures for males and females. Research involving the latter is more likely to involve simply questionnaires and is less likely to include aggression, largely because of the discomfort of the male experimenters. Furthermore, questionnaires administered often have biased response categories. For example, in several studies the behavior of a woman could only be described as passive, aggressive, or deviant. If a woman happened to take an active role with regard to the issue in question, she was limited in her responses. Most research related to sex differences is atheoretical. If sex differences are found, there is usually an inadequate interpretation of the results. The finding of a sex difference is usually considered to be an explanation in itself, and there is usually little effort made to examine further the reasons why the sex difference existed. Thus, sex or gender is often treated as an explanation in research rather than as a starting point for scientific inquiry.

An additional problem with atheoretical research is that negative findings are usually not published, while positive ones are reported in the literature. The implications become clearer when one understands the differences between theoretical and atheoretical research in sex differences. In the latter the researcher says in his or her introduction that he or she is merely doing an investigation to determine whether or not there is a sex difference with respect to a certain behavior. She is usually doing the research because she predicts that there will be a difference. If there are no significant sex differences, the experimenter's hypothesis was not confirmed, and since there are no significant statistics, the research is not likely to be published. Theoretical research is essentially testing the difference between two theories. An experimenter is interested in determining which theory of behavior is valid. If one theory is valid, the experimenter would predict no sex differences with respect to a specific situation. However, if another theory is valid, one would predict sex differences in a specific situation. Either way there are valid, potentially reportable findings. But with atheoretical research at present, only studies that have found significant sex differences usually get published.

The final problem in the area of sex differences relates to the social cognition phenomenon. There is the tendency in research to assume that differences found between females and males are due to gender, when they may in fact be due to a differential response on the part of the environment to the man and the woman.

Sex differences. While there are methodological difficulties in the study of sex differences, this is still an important area for research. Several questions have been extensively studied. One issue is the evaluation of self and others with respect to performance in some area. Deaux (1976) concluded that the performance of other men and women is evaluated in a manner consistent with one's expectations and stereotypes as to the types of behaviors in which men and women would be expected to excel.

For example, in one piece of research identical professional scientific articles were distributed to different judges who were asked to evaluate their quality. Some articles were given a bogus female author, while others were given a bogus male author. Judges consistently rated articles supposedly done by male authors as superior. Apparently the judges (both male and female) had expectations that males would write better articles.

This same phenomenon was present for a number of traditionally male tasks. If women were portrayed as actually succeeding at a traditional male task, such as gaining admission to medical schools, their success was attributed not to their skills or intelligence but rather to some accidental environmental factor or luck, whereas men's success in the same task was usually attributed to their native intelligence or skill. When judges were asked to account for the success of both men and women in traditional female skills, such as nurturing children or cooking a meal, however, men's success was more likely to be attributed to luck. Thus it appears that individuals' actual perceptions of the performance of men and women are somewhat distorted by their expectations of how well men and women should do at certain tasks. Social cognitions play an important role in this phenomenon.

This phenomenon also exists with reference to self-evaluations. Research has found that when men and women evaluated their own behaviors, they followed the societal pattern of expectations. For example, in a traditional male activity in which the experimenter could control whether success was due to skill or luck, females were more likely to attribute their success to luck regardless of the actual reality of the situation. Thus, in accordance with the social cognition hypothesis, it appears that men's and women's evaluations and ultimately their performances (in which confidence is always a factor) are influenced to some extent by societal expectations.

Sex differences have also been examined in such areas as aggression and altruism, and strategies of interaction. The behavior of altruism—i.e., whether a man or woman is more likely to help someone in difficulty—was found to vary with circumstances and thus expectations. For example, in a social psychological experiment in which men and women felt someone needed help, men were more likely to help if the help required was of a masculine type, whereas women were more likely to help if the help required was of a feminine type. It was also found that both sexes were more likely to help someone of the opposite sex than someone of the same sex. Research in the area of strategies of interaction has found a similar pattern. Early studies of compliance had suggested that women were more likely than men to comply. However, some recent work in this area has found different results. The results of one recent study were remarkably clear. On feminine topics men showed more conformity than women, and on masculine topics women conformed more than men. When the topics were neutral, there were no differences in the conformity of men and women.

One final area of sex differences is the study of aggression. The statement that men are more aggressive than women is one of the few generalizations that has held up under the analysis of careful investigation. Despite these findings it is clear that women, unfortunately, can be as aggressive as men on some occasions.

An examination of the crime rates are enlightening; while the absolute numbers for men are greater, there have always been women who commit violent crimes. Furthermore, in the decade from 1960 to 1970 the number of women arrested for crimes increased 74% (compared to 25% for men), and the increase in violent crimes by women was nearly as high (69%). Because we can assume that biology has not altered in that time period, we must conclude that women are either learning to be more aggressive or are becoming more willing to display aggressive behavior. There probably is a biological component that may predispose men to aggression. However, this biological factor, if it does exist, only creates a greater readiness to learn aggressive behaviors. The individual, whether male or female, must still acquire the relevant behaviors and then choose to act in an aggressive manner. Some evidence suggests that women do quite well in the learning stage but simply hold back in the performance.

Despite the possibility of biological differences Scripture seems to imply some choice in the matter of acting violently, not only in the Ten Commandments, but also in the overall injunction to love one's enemies and to do good to those that hate you. There does not seem to be a separate set of rules for males and females in this regard.

Summary. An examination of the literature in the area of sex differences and the psychology of women suggests that societal standards, expectations, and stereotypes play a large role. Indeed, Mead's work suggests that customs and human standards are a crucial factor in this area. Certainly maleness and femaleness in North America have been well defined by the culture at large. Paul, however, states that Christians are no longer to conform to the standards or expectations of this world: "Let God transform you inwardly by a complete change of your mind" (Rom. 12:2). It is societal standards, not Scripture, that have dictated that men are to be dominant and women are not and men are to excel at more things than women.

The notions of dominance and power, however, even though very much a part of our society and social cognitions, are foreign to Christ. Jesus says to his disciples: "You know that in the world the recognized rulers [those whom we expect to be in charge and to have more power and to be better at things] lord it over their subjects and their great men make them feel the weight of authority. This is not the way it is to be among you. [Don't have the same expectations.] Whoever wants to be great must be your servant and whoever wants to be first must be the willing slave of all. For even the Son of Man did not come to be served but to serve and to give up his life as a ransom for many" (Mark 10:42–45, NEB)

The Scriptures assert that expectations for behavior are very different in the body of Christ. The social cognitions of the world are not the social cognitions of the church.

References

Deaux, K. *The behavior of men and women.* Monterey, Calif.: Brooks/Cole, 1976.

Grady, K. Sex bias in research design. *Psychology of Women Quarterly,* 1981, 5, 628–636.

Mead, M. *Sex and temperament in three primitive societies.* New York: Morro, 1935.

Serbin, L. A., & O'Leary, K. D. How nursery schools teach girls to shut up. *Psychology Today,* 1975, 9(7), 56–58, 102–103.

Snyder, M., Tanke, E. D., & Bercheid, E. Social perception and interpersonal behavior: On the self-fulfilling nature of social stereotypes. *Journal of Personality and Social Psychology,* 1977, 35, 656–666.

Unger, R. K. Sex as a social reality: Field and laboratory research. *Psychology of Women Quarterly,* 1981, 5, 645–653.

Williams, J. H. *Psychology of women: Behavior in a biosocial context.* New York: Norton, 1977.

L. R. Propst

Woodworth, Robert Sessions (1869–1962). American experimental psychologist. After receiving his A.B. degree from Amherst College in 1891, Sessions taught high school science and college mathematics before studying psychology and philosophy at Harvard (M.A. 1897). After receiving his Ph.D. from Columbia in 1899, he taught physiology in New York City hospitals for three years and studied under Sherrington in Liverpool. In 1903 he returned to Columbia, where he remained until his first retirement in 1945. He continued teaching there until his second retirement in 1958 at 89 years of age. In 1956 he received the first Gold Medal Award of the American Psychological Foundation for his work as an integrator and organizer of psychology.

Woodworth did not belong to any school of psychology, such as behaviorism or functionalism, and expressed his dislike for the constraints imposed by such schools. He came as near to being a truly general experimental psychologist as anyone ever did. He became a rallying point for the middle-of-the-road position in psychology.

According to Woodworth psychology must begin by investigating the nature of the stimulus and the response. Then it must consider the organism as interpolated between the stimulus and the response. Rather than an S-R psychology, Woodworth wanted an S-O-R psychology. Psychology must study both consciousness and behavior. Observation, experimentation, and introspection were all valid methods for psychology. As early as 1897 Woodworth spoke of developing a "motivology." He wanted a dynamic psychology, one concerned with the interpretations of the causal factors in change, concerned with motivation. His primary concern was with the driving forces that activate a person, with determining why people feel and act as they do.

Woodworth's list of publications is long, and his work has influenced many generations of students. His revision of Ladd's *Physiological Psychology* (1911) became a standard handbook for more than 20 years. *Dynamic Psychology* (1918) was a plea for a functional psychology which included the topic of motivation. His clear and simple introductory text, *Psychology* (1921), went through five editions by 1947 and outsold all other texts for 25 years. *Contemporary Schools of Psychology* (1931) was revised in 1948 and again in 1964. His *Experimental Psychology* (1938) was revised in 1954 and is a classic in the area. His last work, *Dynamics of Behavior,* was published when he was 89.

R. L. Koteskey

Word Salad. A jumbled collection of words, expressed either vocally or in writing, that have no meaningful connection. It is caused by severe psychotic decompensation in certain thought disorders. In thought disorders looseness in associative or logical reasoning varies from occasional minor lapses in rational thought, termed cognitive slippage, to more disorderly reasoning, confusion, and finally to incoherence. Word salad falls near the extreme of incoherence. Such difficulty represents serious disorganization in personality. It is found in some cases of acute schizophrenia, particularly hebephrenic schizophrenia. Autistic involvement and neologisms, or made-up words, usually add to the confusion of word salads.

The person expressing the word salad has little or no recognition of the incomprehensibility of his verbal exchange. Careful listening will sometimes allow the content to become intelligible, but only if other information about the speaker and his or her context is considered. Trying to communicate with the person in this state is futile. To reduce this symptom treatment for the psychotic condition with chemotherapy is necessary. As the intensity of the condition clears, the person will usually be able to communicate more reasonably.

M. R. NELSON

Workaholism. The mythology of the American work ethic is both astounding and frightening. As the twentieth century draws to a close, the citizens of our land contemplate a rich history of folk heroes such as John D. Rockefeller, John Henry, and Paul Bunyan. However, they also seem to be redefining their own lives in terms of pleasure, self-worth, time off, and comfortable work environments. In fact, there seems to have been a national change of attitude about the unimportance of work. However, to the nearly seven million workaholics, work will never go out of style.

The best definition of a workaholic is a person who is compulsively addicted to his or her job. Such persons work for work's sake and tend not to make a major impact. It is routine to work 60- to 70-hour weeks, showing up on holidays or weekends. For the workaholic there is no viable alternative to work, no other activity that uses energy, demands attention, and provides regular social interaction around some visible outcome. Most workaholics (nearly 70%) are not only happy at work but also with the rest of their lives (Machlowitz, 1980). Indeed their lives are given credibility by the social approval and attention (from grateful managers) they receive.

There are three major questions for mental health professionals about those persons who are workaholics. 1) Is the compulsive addiction to work a neurotic, anxiety-coping strategy? 2) Does work become a substitute for family and friends, if not all interpersonal relations? 3) Do the taxing, long hours invested in work lead to burnout and subsequent stress-related illnesses?

At the present there is no psychopathology directly attributed to being a workaholic (Macklowitz, 1980). This may in part be due to the work habits of many psychiatrists and psychologists. Those professionals who do view the workaholic as pathological suggest a diagnosis of either obsessive-compulsive neurosis or adjustment reaction to adult life. It is suggested that because of a lack of reliable studies, a range of behavioral and psychological dysfunction may presently be labeled as workaholism.

Certain attitudes traditionally viewed as dysfunctional—such as poor self-image, rigidity, omniscience, and disturbed interpersonal relationships—do characterize these people. Pines (1980) discusses research indicating that stress and high-pressure work demands may not be the critical factors; rather, the critical factor may be the manner in which the individual copes. The person who takes an active role in his work and family and believes he is making an impact is usually healthy. The person who is pessimistic and believes he has little control over his life is a much more significant health risk. These persons are more prone to burnout. It is suggested that counselors be cautious in attributing psychopathology to the workaholic until further, more definitive research is completed.

The disturbed family life of the workaholic does appear to be a well-documented fact. It appears that the workaholic places his family at a lower priority than his attempts to gratify his work strivings. This neglect, if not abuse, of the family and its members is of great concern to therapists. Many workaholics avoid the demands of family and domestic duties under the guise of providing a better life style for their loved ones. Hence a whole entourage of therapists, maids, daycare workers, nannies, repairmen, gymnastic instructors, etc., may be employed to compensate for the absent parent. It appears that where the family is concerned, the workaholic believes in substituting his away-from-home work for the interpersonal contact, love, warmth, and nurturance his spouse and children need. The effect is disastrous.

Certainly the biblical admonitions concerning the family (specifically Deut. 4:9–10) cannot be fulfilled with an absent parent. Further, the lack of a loving, nurturing father or mother dispels the child's ability to love or feel loved by God or by other persons (Matt. 19:19). The importance of early childhood stimulation and nurturance as well as the functioning of a healthy family unit are important vital ingredients to maturity (Lewis, 1979).

Perhaps the most documented dysfunctions related to work addiction are the stress-related physiological illnesses. The demanding schedules and intensity of work causes acute anxiety and stress, leading to cardiac conditions, nervous disorders, organ failures, and high blood pressure. Freidman and Rosenman (1974) have identified the Type A and Type B personality. The hallmarks of Type A are excessive competitive drive and intense time urgency. Type A persons are as much as seven times more likely to develop coronary heart disease or other illnesses as their Type B counterparts. To deal with this, many companies now have physical fitness directors. Learning to relax properly and maintaining a regular program of physical exercise, however, are only Band-aids for the workaholic.

The cure for the workaholic must involve the insight that work is his number one life priority and that this has some destructive consequences for himself and probably for others. Sometimes a workaholic can be made aware that he is not making the contribution he wants and is drowning in details and demands. Certainly the workaholic who has trusted Christ must consider how the lordship of work relates to God's intended Lordship of Christ. Pursuing the reasoning of priority and clarifying who he is really serving has produced significant change in Christian workaholics. Ecclesiastes 2:17–26 and Luke 12:13–21 are but two of the biblical passages pertaining to the workaholic.

Finally, it should not be assumed that the addiction to work is always outside the home. In Luke 10:38–42 Jesus visits the home of Mary and Martha. Mary chose to enjoy Jesus. In contrast, the workaholic Martha was disturbed by all the preparation. She chose to work, to prepare a dinner. She became emotionally upset and distracted. Frustration over getting everything just right so overwhelmed her that she complained directly to Jesus about Mary. Mary had chosen rightly the simple life of listening to Jesus. Not only had Martha chosen not to listen to Jesus because of her busyness, but she caused anger and bitterness to enter her relationship with her sister. Modern-day workaholics therefore should take all the more precautions against becoming distracted and losing eternal benefits for themselves and their families.

References

Freidman, M., & Rosenman, R. H. *Type-A behavior and your heart.* New York: Knopf, 1974.

Lewis, J. M. *How's your family?* New York: Brunner/Mazel, 1979.

Machlowitz, M. *Workaholics, living with them, working with them.* Reading, Mass.: Addison-Wesley, 1980.

Pines, M. Psychological hardiness. *Psychology Today,* 1980, *14*(7), 34–44, 98.

F. B. WICHERN

See STRESS; HEALTH PSYCHOLOGY.

Work and Play. From earliest times work and its complement, play, have been objects of human reflection. God had scarcely created the world before man got his first work assignment, to till and keep the Garden of Eden (Gen. 2:15). But the first account of work predates even this, for God himself worked at creation and then rested at its completion (Gen. 2:2). These first references to work are positive. God freely chose and heartily approved of his own work (Gen. 1:31), and Adam's tasks were perfectly suited to the marvelous life of Eden.

It did not take long for this picture to change. The next chapter recounts the fall of man and God's ensuing judgment. The ground was cursed, and man faced "toil . . . thorns and thistles . . . sweat" (Gen. 3:17–19). This is the base for the tradition that work is a curse, a penalty for sin. This view has enjoyed strong and extensive support, yet the earlier images of work as a desirable thing will not go away.

For those who see work as a curse, play is delicious shirking or an attempt to recoup one's powers for fresh work. The person who majors in play is a fool or a scoundrel. And he might be charged with impiety because he has so little regard for the force of the fall.

To say work is not, of course, to say that it serves no good purpose. If "an idle mind is the devil's workshop," then man needs someone to keep him busy at some worthwhile task, such as survival. As he struggles to make ends meet, he comes face to face with his own finitude, insecurity, and even wretchedness. In this condition he is disposed to seek and depend on God. He may even come to see his toil as a form of expiation or purgative for evil thoughts and deeds.

The "work-as-curse" people stress the indignity rather than the dignity of work. Without awkward and back-breaking tasks man has room for vanity and indolence. The idle rich are too smooth and self-pleased. They need blisters and grime to bring them around, to acquaint or reacquaint them with their mortality and insufficiency.

Medieval monasticism did little to dignify ordinary work. The line between sacred and secular or profane activity was clear enough. One has only to glance at a typical monastery schedule to see that prayer and other worship was central. Rising at two in the morning, the typical eighth-century Benedictine attended his first service at two-thirty. Again and again he was recalled to worship until late-afternoon vespers signaled day's end. This was the sanctified life. All the others—the merchants, farmers, and craftsmen—went through their own dismal routines. They did not enjoy the high and peaceful callings of their more spiritual brothers. Within the monasteries, when work was to be done, simple, repetitive, manual labor was popular since it freed the mind for communion with God.

Martin Luther's disdain for this framework of thought is legendary. In his commentary on Genesis 13:13 he writes that mundane tasks have "no appearance of sanctity; and yet these very works in connection with the household are more desirable than all the works of all the monks and nuns" (1960, p. 349). His theological populism was infectious, and Christendom's view of work has never been the same. Luther contended that a man could be called by God to a station in the workaday world just as surely as to the traditional ministry.

As a spokesman for the dignity of ordinary work Luther was not alone. John Calvin developed this theme, and it is an integral part of Reformed thinking today. Reference to Genesis 1:28 recurs in the literature. This "cultural mandate" generates the conviction that God's children are to bring all of creation under his blessed sovereignty. The fisherman has his part no less than the pastor. Colossians 1:15–20, with its reference to the reconciliation of all things on earth to Christ, underscores and renews the Genesis mandate.

Max Weber's classic, *The Protestant Ethic and the Spirit of Capitalism* (1930), ties the thought of Luther and Calvin to the subsequent economic life of Europe. His work demonstrates the impact of theology on culture, and it stands over against the Marxist view that man is, at base, economically motivated.

Two centuries after Calvin's death the Industrial Revolution in England stimulated a fresh look at the nature of work. While there were important gains in productivity and economic vitality, the impact on men was often frightful. The predatory style of some enthusiastic capitalists left little room for worker dignity and welfare. Farmers and craftsmen laid aside their tools and trooped to the mills, where many suffered from the depersonalizing grind of factory work.

Victorian writers Thomas Carlyle and John Ruskin pinned a good deal of blame on laissez-faire economics and called for a rediscovery of the joys and honor of craftsmanship. Mass production by machine was, in their estimation, a life-denying institution.

Ruskin and Carlyle were, of course, upstaged by their fellow Victorian, Karl Marx. His forceful picture of oppression, with accompanying theory, prescription, and prophecy, has mustered forces of social change for the better part of a century. And at the center of this movement is a view of what human work should and should not be. A considerable body of current literature on alienation is one of his legacies, and his solution joins a host of utopian visions, including those of Plato, Campanella, More, Skinner, and millenarians.

If the nineteenth century was preoccupied with work the twentieth has become fixed on leisure. In our time philosophers and theologians have given us a fresh understanding of

and respect for play. Drawing on sources as old as Aristotle and as stolid as Kant, they have psychologized the definitions of work and play. Whereas work was once understood in terms of physical compulsion, it is now tied to a sense of compulsion. The definition is more attitudinal than circumstantial.

On this model a person may be at play while he struggles to meet a business deadline. It's all in his perspective. If he wholeheartedly gives himself over to his task, relatively oblivious to payoffs or penalties, he is playing. On the other hand, he may be working even if he is in the middle of a volleyball game. His frantic search for fun or his uneasy attempts to gain peer approval can make volleyball work.

De Grazia (1962) in particular links work and play with time consciousness. The man at leisure and play is so preoccupied with the matter at hand that he loses his sense of time. Indeed, the expression "leisure time" is contradictory. On the other hand, the man at work is a clock-watcher; he is so dissatisfied with his present task that he constantly looks beyond it to a later, liberating moment. His time drags.

There has been something of a Counter-Reformation in this connection. Catholic and secular thinkers alike have found fault with the Calvinistic attention to rectitude and service in every moment of life. Novak (1976) shows why play, the realm of ends rather than means, is so central to human well-being. Cox (1969) reaffirms the Catholic regard for celebration. Alongside homo faber (man the worker) and homo sapiens (man the knower), Cox stands homo festives (man the celebrator) and homo fantasia (man the dreamer and mythmaker). De Grazia (1962) is naturally close to Catholic sentiment, since he relies so heavily on Aquinas's favorite philosopher, Aristotle.

The controversy boils down to this: Does man work in order to play, or play in order to work afresh? The Calvinist is concerned that all of life become a stewardly act unto God. Play for him is essentially renewal for Christian service. The more Catholic tradition gives the contemplative and celebrative life primacy, for this is our heavenly destiny. So play comes in our finest and not our furtive hours.

Each tradition counters the excesses of the other. And whether work or play is ultimate, the penultimate does not suffer dishonor, since the literature is so strongly supportive of both.

Humanistic psychologist Jourard (1974) synthesizes the traditions in his account of the whole, healthy person. He stresses the value of work and provides guidelines for vocational satisfaction. But his counsel extends to leisure as well. The person who neglects either aspect faces turmoil and dissolution.

Virtually all Christian psychologists, theologians, and philosophers now argue that the proper Christian life, even with its suffering, should bear the marks of play. God, they reason, would have us whole, absorbed in life, and at peace. Crippling and dreary alienation is understood not as the price of Christian discipleship, but as the mark of sub-Christian living.

References

Cox, H. *The feast of fools.* Cambridge: Harvard University Press, 1969.

de Grazia, S. *Of time, work, and leisure.* New York: Twentieth Century Fund, 1962.

Jourard, S. *Healthy personality: An approach from the viewpoint of humanistic psychology.* New York: Macmillan, 1974.

Luther, M. Lectures on Genesis. In J. Pelikan (Ed.), *Luther's Works* (vol. 2). St. Louis: Concordia, 1960.

Novak, M. *The joy of sports.* New York: Basic Books, 1976.

Weber, M. *The Protestant ethic and the spirit of capitalism.* New York: Scribners, 1930.

Additional Readings

Gerber, E., & Morgan, W. *Sport and the body: A philosophical symposium.* Philadelphia: Lea and Febiger, 1979.

Huizinga, J. *Homo ludens: A study of the play-element in culture.* New York: Roy Publishers, 1950.

Ryken, L. Puritan work ethic: The dignity of life's labors. *Christianity Today,* October 19, 1979, pp. 14–19.

M. COPPENGER

Work Motivation. When people become involved in working toward a goal, motivation is almost always a matter of concern. Lay persons and professionals alike recognize that performance in virtually any setting depends on more than just ability. A professional baseball player with enormous talent may become an average performer if a long-term, guaranteed, multimillion-dollar contract undermines his willingness to work hard, i.e., his motivation. Psychologists have symbolized the joint impact of ability and motivation on performance in a simple formula: Performance = Ability × Motivation. Notice that the relationship is multiplicative. If either ability or motivation is missing, performance reduces to zero.

In work organizations motivational problems are particularly important, since organizational effectiveness and even survival usually depend on high levels of worker performance. Whereas ability problems can be handled effectively by raising hiring standards or developing training programs, motivational problems are often regarded as the intangibles in the performance equation. Pep talks and pay raises are often seen as the only solutions to motivational problems. While there are no instant remedies for such difficulties, organizational psychology can offer a number of theoretical perspectives and research findings that can help managers and workers better understand specific problem situations and identify potentially successful solutions.

Motivation can be broken down into two aspects: arousal and choice. Arousal has to do with the question of what gets us moving in the first place. For example, why should a person come to work at all; or once there, why should he or she put forth any effort? The role of choice in motivations is also crucial. Once we get moving, how do we choose a direction in which to go? Many motivational problems are of this type. For example, the highly capable job candidate must be motivated to choose our organization. Several people in our office may need to be motivated to choose work over socializing during the day. Theories and research on work motivation can be seen as dealing primarily with either the arousal or choice aspects of motivation. Both theory and research can identify some common principles for enhancing worker motivation.

Arousal Theories. Arousal theories of motivation identify the various needs and values capable of moving people to action. These theories typically focus on one particular need or classfication of many needs.

Two important need theories of motivation have been proposed by White (1959) and McClelland (1961). White's theory of effectance motivation suggests that people have a need to master their environment—i.e., to see themselves as competent. A scholar's pursuit of learning for its own sake is a good example. To the extent that competence is important to an individual, jobs that are challenging and offer variety will be most motivating.

In a related vein McClelland maintains that people differ in their need for achievement, the desire to perform challenging tasks and do them well. Persons high in the need for achievement have been shown to prefer moderately difficult tasks and immediate feedback on their work, and are less concerned with extrinsic rewards for work (e.g., pay) than with rewards that come from the work itself. Interestingly, need for achievement across different organizations and countries has been found to be positively correlated with economic growth. Even more important McClelland has shown that people can increase their need for achievement through training, with subsequent positive effects on business growth.

Maslow's (1954) need hierarchy and Alderfer's (1972) ERG theory are closely related attempts to classify human needs. Maslow postulates a prepotent hierarchy of five basic needs: physiological, safety, love, esteem, and actualization. Through factor analysis Alderfer reduced this list to three: existence, relatedness, and growth. Alderfer also differs with Maslow on the question of prepotency. He believes that higher order growth needs may take priority over existence or relatedness needs, regardless of whether the latter have been satisfied. Scholars, missionaries, and political revolutionaries are among those whose work motivation often seems to bypass physical comforts and friends for the sake of a higher cause.

Another theorist who places considerable emphasis on the power of higher order needs to enhance motivation is Herzberg (1966). His classification scheme divides potential work rewards into two types: hygienes and motivators. Hygienes, such as good pay, competent supervision, and pleasant working conditions, help prevent workers from becoming dissatisfied and thus demotivated. Motivators, such as achievement, recognition, and advancement opportunities, can increase worker job satisfaction and therefore motivation. The critical point in Herzberg's theory is that attempts to increase worker motivation must not only attend to the lower order needs or hygienes, but must also provide workers with opportunities to fulfill their higher order needs. While research support for Herzberg's theory has been inconsistent, his emphasis on the importance of higher order needs in motivating modern workers is well taken.

Choice Theories. There are essentially four major choice theories of motivation: Skinner's operant conditioning approach, expectancy theory, goal-setting theory, and equity theory. These all represent perspectives on how individuals decide upon ways of directing their energies.

Skinner's operant conditioning approach is an attempt to bypass the whole question of needs and conscious choices. To discover what moves persons we should simply observe their behavior, its consequences, and the situations in which it occurs. If we observe a person working harder in a high-paying job than in a low-paying job, we assume that high pay is positively reinforcing—i.e., motivating—for that individual. Without going further into the intricacies of the conditioning approach, we should note some of its rather straightforward, motivation-enhancing principles. First, what is reinforcing for one person may not be for another. Thus, motivational programs should

be individualized as much as is practical. Second, nonreinforcement extinguishes behaviors. The moral here is that desirable worker behavior—e.g., punctuality—cannot be ignored without undesirable consequences. Third, punishment is an effective way of stopping undesirable behavior but has some very negative side effects such as hostility and passivity. Fourth, Skinner's emphasis on environmental determinism should remind us that a poor performer may not be suffering from poor motivation but rather may be encountering obstacles in the work situation—e.g., an outdated copying machine.

In contrast to Skinner's view expectancy theory emphasizes the cognitive aspects of choices. When a worker chooses to work hard on a particular task, expectancy theory claims that he has expectations about the chances that a particular level of effort will lead to a particular level of performance. Similarly he has an expectation that that level of performance will result in certain job rewards—e.g., pay increase, promotion. Workers choose, then, to work hard at the tasks they perceive to lead to outcomes they value. Several important motivational principles follow. First, performance expectations of supervisors must be realistic to the worker. If not, the worker's expectation that he can actually reach the desired level of performance is reduced, and his motivation to work goes down. Second, explicit linkages between performance and valued rewards must be made if motivation is to be maximized. Salary systems that tie pay increases to such nonperformance factors as seniority are clear examples of a violation of this principle.

Goal-setting theory was first proposed by Locke (1968). It has three basic tenets: 1) Hard goals are better than easy goals as long as they are accepted. 2) Worker participation in goal setting increases commitment to and acceptance of goals. 3) The more specific and well-defined the goal, the greater its impact on motivation. Although a very simple theory, goal-setting has been found to have powerful and reliable effects on worker motivation in both laboratory research and in actual organizational settings. It should not be overlooked in any program directed at increasing worker motivation.

Equity theory is similar to expectancy theory in its cognitive emphasis. However, its focus is on the motivational impact of worker perceptions of equity. Essentially the theory maintains that workers evaluate their own job inputs (e.g., time and energy spent) and outcomes (e.g., salary, status) relative to those of other relevant comparison persons (e.g., co-workers). To the extent that others, for example, are seen as receiving more money for less work, the individual will feel underbenefited, and his motivation and performance will decrease. This theory draws attention to worker perceptions of the relative fairness of the distribution of benefits and reponsibilities within an organization.

In conclusion, there is no monolithic theory or work motivation in organizational psychology, nor is one likely to be seen in the near future. Each of the available theories, however, offers particular insights that may be uniquely appropriate for handling specific motivational problems.

References
Alderfer, C. P. *Existence, relatedness, and growth: Human needs in organizational settings.* New York: Free Press, 1972.
Herzberg, F. *Work and the nature of man.* Cleveland: World, 1966.
Locke, E. A., Toward a theory of task motivation and incentives. Organizational Behavior and Human Performance, 1968, *3,* 157–189.
Maslow, A. H. *Motivation and personality.* New York: Harper, 1954.
McClelland, D. *The achieving society.* Princeton, N.J.: Van Nostrand, 1961.
White, R. W. Motivation reconsidered: The concept of competence. *Psychological Reports,* 1959, *66,* 297–333.

D. D. McKenna

Worship. An Anglo-Saxon term implying esteem, gratitude, and praise for someone who has demonstrated worthiness for such respect and adoration. It is derived from the Old English *worthship,* referring to the worthiness of the object of worship. The Latin word most used in reference to worship in the medieval church was *leiturgia,* from which we get *liturgy.* Liturgy is a strategy or pattern for action toward a chosen goal. The pattern or strategy is derived from the goal to be achieved. Thus, in liturgy form comes from the nature and shape of the content of the action. This is true in worship and in daily work. We may refer to the liturgy of work or of worship, but standard usage today is confined mainly to worship.

Christian worship is not mainly a program for teaching Christian truth, nor an emotional pep rally where one can get one's spiritual batteries charged. Worship is the celebration of the historical facts that God was uniquely in Jesus of Nazareth, reconciling the world to himself, and that God has always and continues to maintain and shepherd his creation in gracious providence and eternal love.

The celebration of worship arises from the individual and communal delight and relief of knowing those two historical facts. Worship is, therefore, the celebration of gratitude and hope. It is the act and experience of taking profound and grateful account of God's nature and behavior: he is for us, not against us. He is not a threat but our consolation. The psychological principle undergirding worship's redemptive value is that people who can be grateful can be healthy and people who cannot be grateful cannot be healthy. The purpose of worship is to enhance spiritual wholeness, emotional health, and creatively holy life, while expressing gratitude to God. Experiencing and celebrating the joy and relief of God's grace in forgiveness and providence produces the fulfillment of that purpose.

History. Christian worship is normally communal, an act and experience of persons in congregation. The Judeo-Christian worship tradition began in an individualistic pattern. The patriarchs from Adam to Jacob often worshiped alone. That pattern persisted during the era of the Judges, though communal worship had been developed. Israel worshiped as a nation during Moses' leadership. Shiloh was a place of national communal worship during the early years in Canaan and was prominent in Israel's life by the era of Samuel. After a struggle with persisting individualism and tribalism in worship, Israel came to a unified communal worship when David brought the ark of the covenant to Jerusalem. This communal liturgical experience gave rise to the psalms of David, sung in Israel's worship. Communal worship came to full bloom with the building of Solomon's temple.

The believing community was split by Jeroboam between worship at Dan and Beersheba, and after the exile between Samaria and Jerusalem. However, when Israel honored its communal worship ideal, assembling as congregation at the temple in Jerusalem, its life as a nation and as a worshiping community centered in the liturgy of the great day of atonement. After the exile this focus was sturdily maintained, while the rise of synagogues came into vogue in local communities. These were centers of religious instruction, not worship centers as such.

The history of the Christian movement and its worship is equally meaningful. Early Christians seem to have gathered rather spontaneously for worship (Acts 2). They worshiped with emphasis upon communal celebration, in a free-form style, though they continued to practice the Israelite rituals and met in the synagogues. By the second century there was no uniform universal Christian liturgy, but numerous strong liturgical movements. Professional clergy, sacraments, catechetical programs, and preaching lectionaries were already everywhere in use. The church as an insitution was forming.

In the third century Hippolytus standardized the liturgy mainly on the form current in Justin's time. A considerable variety in forms of worship throughout the churches of Europe, Asia, and Africa persisted, nonetheless, until the official promulgation of the first Roman rite in the seventh century. The liturgies of the Eastern churches tended to be less stereotyped and even more celebrational than those of the Western, or Roman, Church. After Gregory the liturgies of the West have varied little from the first Roman rite, except those of the Reformation churches. The Roman Catholic church has simplified some elements for local convenience.

The liturgies of the Reformation churches were shaped by a radical reaction to the formalism of the Roman rite. This reaction took two directions. The mainstream of Anglican Catholicism under Henry VIII flows into contemporary Episcopal and Methodist usage and endeavors to preserve as much of the historic liturgy of Christendom as is theologically and practically possible in the present age in local usage. The mainstream of Reformed liturgy flows into contemporary Presbyterian, Reformed, Baptist, Congregational, and most fundamentalist and evangelical usage. It endeavors to dispense with as much of the Roman rite as it can without losing distinctive Christian character and gospel-centered meaning. Lutheranism preserves some of both these mainstreams, adhering in significant degree to the cardinal elements of the Roman form while endeavoring to inspire it with the biblical and evangelical spontaneity and vitality sought by the Reformers.

Unfortunately large deficits persist in Protestant liturgies. In their attempt to avoid the formalism into which the Roman rite had fallen by the sixteenth century, they have tended to become mere contexts for preaching. That would have been appropriate to the teaching sessions of the early church's synagogues but not to worship in the third-century churches or in the liturgy of Gregory the Great. Protestantism has so significantly lost its sense of worship and liturgy as celebration that its people go "to sermon," not to worship. That is an excess deriving from the Reformation emphasis on the centrality of the Word at the expense of the sacraments. The result is a devaluing of the essential function of worship:

the mediation to needy persons of the consolation of the gospel of grace, through the symbolic acts, elements, and sequences of the liturgy, for the psychological and spiritual healing of the congregation as individuals and as community.

Function and Structure. The function of worship is psychological and spiritual healing through the celebration of God's grace. Liturgy therefore must have the function of enacting the process of celebrating that grace. The psychospiritual dynamics of celebration involve symbolic elements such as bread and wine, the centrality of the pulpit, Bible, and the shape of the sanctuary; symbolic sequences such as opening greetings followed by God's law, congregational penitence, God's absolution, and eucharistic celebration of the gift of grace; psychospiritual growth in insight, anxiety reduction, relief from guilt, joy in God's peace, and comfort in Christian fellowship; and the reshaping of the worshipers' discipleship as they move from the sanctuary to renew the world.

The structure of liturgy should come from the demands of that function, as it did in the Old Testament temple rites and in the first Roman rite. The worshiper moves, in properly redemptive worship, from the world of work to the sanctuary, through the encounter with God to confession of sin, absolution, celebration of that absolution in the Eucharist, expressions and gifts of gratitude, sermonic guidance for the life of grace in the world of work, and finally the benediction. The psychospiritual process recapitulates our personal conversion processes. We move from the world to God. Then we move through the psychospiritual stages of greeting, guilt, grace, gratitude, and guidance. Then we move back to the world as renewed persons, renewing God's world. That is the healing and redeeming process worship is intended to be, was in Scripture, and endeavored to be in the historic Christian church.

Protestantism, particularly its American products in fundamentalism and evangelicalism, uniformly lacks this psychospiritual understanding of true worship. The focus on didactic sermons as the center of worship has turned Protestant worship into an essentially cognitive process, largely oriented on the left hemisphere of the brain. But worship should be more of a right hemisphere celebration, a response of the heart as celebration of God's unconditional, radical, and universal grace.

Additional Readings

Allinder, W. *Responses . . . to alterations in worship services . . . designed to enhance the use of the right hemisphere of the brain in worship.* Unpublished DMin Project, Drew University Theological School, 1983.

Ellens, J. H. *Psychology in worship.* New York: Harper & Row, 1983.

Springer, S. P., & Deutsch, G. *Left brain, right brain.* San Francisco: W. H. Freeman, 1981.

J. H. ELLENS

See RITUAL.

Wundt, Wilhelm (1832–1920). Commonly considered the founder of psychology. The son of a Lutheran pastor, he was born in the village of Neckarau (near Heidelberg), Germany. His early education was from a young vicar whom Wundt liked better than his parents. When the vicar was transferred to another village, Wundt went to live with him until he was ready for the university at 19. To earn a living and study science while doing it, Wundt decided to become a physician, studying at Tübingen, Heidelberg, and Berlin. He received his doctorate from Heidelberg in 1855.

He taught physiology at Heidelberg from 1857 to 1874. During these years his conception of psychology as an independent and experimental science began to emerge. After one year at Zurich, Wundt began the most important phase of his career, his years at Leipzig. He was appointed professor of philosophy in 1875 and worked there continuously for 45 years until his death.

Although there is much controversy over the exact date, some time soon after arriving at Leipzig, Wundt established a psychological laboratory, offered courses in experimental psychology, and began a journal (*Philosophical Studies*) to publish research originating in his laboratory. In 1879 one of his students published the first research with Wundt from the new laboratory. In 1979 the American Psychological Association had a celebration to recognize the century of psychology's existence.

Wundt was the founder of what is now called structuralism. The subject matter of psychology was immediate experience, which was studied using the method of introspection. Experience was to be broken down into its elements of sensations and feelings. Wundt's doctrine of apperception then accounted for unified conscious experience. Most of the research at his laboratory involved sensation, reaction time, attention, and feelings.

His most important work, perhaps the most important work in the history of psychology, is his *Principles of Physiological Psychology*, published in two parts in 1873 and 1874. This appeared in six editions over the next 37 years, establishing psychology as a laboratory sci-

ence with its own problems and methods. Although structuralism died, Wundt's system was most important in the development of psychology. Functionalism, behaviorism, and Gestalt psychology emerged as direct criticisms of it. Wundt *was* psychology for nearly 20 years.

R. L. KOTESKEY

See PSYCHOLOGY, HISTORY OF.

Würzburg School. In Germany the Würzburg School helped to set up a clearer differentiation between act and content psychologies, parallelling the opposition between functionalism and structuralism in the United States. It also stressed purposiveness and wholeness, opposing the elementistic and atomistic approaches of structuralism and associationism. Chronologically the members of the Würzburg School are Oswald Külpe (who founded the laboratory in 1894), A. Mayer, J. Orth, Karl Marbe, H. J. Watt, Narziss Ach, August Messer, and Karl Bühler.

These psychologists employed the method of systematic experimental introspection, which involved the performance of a complex task such as judging or remembering, followed by a retrospective report of the subject's experiences during the original task. The whole experience was methodically described, time period by time period.

The contributions of Mayer and Orth demonstrated that a subject's responses depend on unanalyzable and indescribable conscious attitudes (*Bewusstseinslage*) having an affective tone, depending on internal as well as external stimuli. Marbe added such states as doubt, hesitation, and confidence, which were thought to be neither sensations, images, nor feelings. In his studies of judgments Marbe often found that subjects did not know how the judgments were made, thus shedding doubt on the theory that judgment involves the mental retention of the image of one object while comparing it with the impression of a second.

The research of Watt and Ach contributed the observation that a mental set or determining tendency (*Einstellung*) was often brought about by the task (*Aufgabe*) itself, so that the conscious work was done as soon as the instructions were comprehended. A good example of this is involved in the reading of music: the exact notes played are determined initially by the key signature and do not require a conscious judgment for each note read.

Messer and Bühler did most to develop the doctrine of imageless thought, the view that the actual thought processes, though they can be examined by introspection, are not sensory or imaginal in character. Thoughts are elements devoid of sensory quality or intensity, but possessing clearness, assurance, and vividness. The controversy over the existence of thoughts apart from images continues to the present day.

H. VANDE KEMP

Yy

Yerkes, Robert Mearns (1876–1956). A pioneer in the development of comparative psychology. He was born in Breadysville, Pennsylvania, and studied at Ursinus College, intending to go into medicine. He went to Harvard in 1897 and became interested first in zoology, then in philosophy and psychology. At Harvard he earned another A.B. in 1898, an M.A. in 1899, and a Ph.D. in 1902.

Yerke taught at Harvard from 1902 to 1917. During this time he collaborated with J. B. Watson, who was making a comparative study of vision in animals. Although Yerkes was not a behaviorist, Watson was impressed with his work with animals. Also, Yerkes had just translated some of Pavlov's papers that reported the discovery of the conditioned reflex.

When the United States entered World War I, in April, 1917, Yerkes was asked to organize American psychologists to assist the military. As chairman of the General Committee on Psychology he directed work on such topics as the effects of high altitude, morale, and gas masks. However, he is most widely known for his work in developing intelligence tests to be used to classify recruits, to eliminate the unfit, and to identify the superior.

The development of these intelligence tests, the Army Alpha for literates and the Beta for illiterates, was an amazing feat. By July 7, 1917, his committee had developed a plan to test the entire military, prepared 10 forms of the group tests and 5 forms of the individual tests, written an examiner's guide, and validated their tests on 400 subjects. By October 1, 1917, testing was in progress to further evaluate the tests so that they could be revised. The revision was completed by April, 1918, and by the end of 1918 tests had been given to 1,726,000 men.

After his military work during World War I and a brief stay at the University of Minnesota, he spent the years from 1924 to 1944 as research professor at Yale.

Yerkes's other major contribution was the development of comparative psychology. He studied crabs, turtles, frogs, rats, mice, worms, crows, doves, pigs, monkeys, apes, and humans. His first book was *The Dancing Mouse* (1907) and his last was *Chimpanzees: A Laboratory Colony* (1943). Probably his most significant work was *The Great Apes* (1929). In 1929 he realized a long-time ambition by establishing the Yale Laboratories of Primate Biology in Orange Park, Florida. It was renamed the Yerkes Laboratories of Primate Biology when he retired from active administration in 1941.

R. L. KOTESKEY

Zz

Zaraleya Psychoenergetic Technique. A method of gaining greater consciousness and awareness and of increasing self-actualization. It was devoleped by Zaraleya (1980), and is used within the setting of humanistic psychotherapy. The goal is for individuals to learn to control their psychic energy, with the end result of making it work positively toward self-growth.

The technique involves monitoring the flow of psychic energy within and between people by having the participants keep a journal record of the process of the psychotherapy. This record is kept on four charts representing four hypothesized consecutive phases of psychic energy flow—transcendence, interactivity, synergy, and transformation. The participants use this information to locate their place within each phase of psychotherapy, and thus are able to focus their energy in a constructive direction.

Reference
Zaraleya. Zaraleya psychoenergetic technique. In R. Herink (Ed.), *The psychotherapy handbook.* New York: New American Library, 1980.

J. H. ROBERTSON

Zeigarnik Effect. A series of experiments conducted by Bluma Zeigarnik revealed that people tend to remember uncompleted tasks better than completed ones. This effect is thought to be due to the persistence of drive inherent in tasks left uncompleted, in that an intention to perform a task may create a sense of psychic tension that persists until the task is completed. In the initial experiments subjects were interrupted while performing a number of tasks. Unfinished tasks were subsequently recalled more frequently than finished ones. The intention to reach a set goal is said to

correspond to a tension within the system of a person. The tension is released once the goal is reached.

This tendency is not necessarily unhealthy, but may be carried to neurotic extremes if an individual becomes totally preoccupied with what he has left unfinished and fails to derive any sense of accomplishment from completion of goals. The theory corresponds to Freud's basic assumptions about the persistence of unfulfilled wishes, and suggests that MEMORY is not just a matter of association bonds but rather involves motivation and emotion as well.

D. L. SCHUURMAN

Zoophilia. The achievement of sexual pleasure or arousal through the use of animals. The range of behavior may be from sexual excitement in connection with stroking and fondling of animals to actual sexual intercourse. Kinsey's work showed about 1% of the males studied had been involved in one fashion or another with animals. The usual choices of animals were dogs, chickens, horses, or cows. The behavior is more frequent among males.

This behavior is most common in the preadolescent years and in rural areas. It is often associated with the upper educational level and may occur as a result of sexual isolation from females. Zoophilia is rare among adults, but may be seen in persons with lower intellectual abilities or where the influence of alcohol is involved.

Cases have been reported where sadistic attacks are made on animals in conjunction with sexual involvement. In many areas it is a crime to have sexual relations with an animal. The Levitical law states that "lying" with any animal is punishable by death, for both males and females (Lev. 18:23; 20:15–16).

Treatment would involve teaching responsible behavior control and increasing social skills.

L. N. FERGUSON

Z-Process Attachment Therapy. A system of human bonding that is applied to psychological disorders that are viewed primarily as attachment disturbances, or disturbances of human bonding. Originally known as rage reduction, it was developed by Zaslow (1981).

According to Zaslow the face is considered the essential focal area of social interaction and human bonding. Thus, human attachment is formed primarily through face-to-face orienting reactions, and major resistances to human attachment center on the face. Z-process attachment therapy seeks to free the individual by facilitating attachment and growth and by reducing psychological resistances. This is accomplished under the full control of the therapist by activating arousal to a peak of full rage. The rage is maximized with face-to-face and eye-to-eye contact with the therapist while the client's body is securely held by a group of other persons. When the rage is resolved, resistances collapse and the energy once channeled into unresolved anger can now be freed for productive integrative growth.

The basic method of this approach to therapy is a holding session, with conditions varying according to age levels. A young child requires one adult holder, an older child may require two to four, and adolescents and adults may require six to twelve holders. The amount of time for each therapy session will vary from 10 minutes for infants to five hours with adults. The approach has been described by Zaslow as applicable to a variety of psychological disorders. Like many other newer therapies, however, it remains unresearched and therefore as yet unproven.

Reference

Zaslow, R. W. Z-process attachment therapy. In R. J. Corsini (Ed.), *Handbook of innovative psychotherapies.* New York: Wiley, 1981

J. H. ROBERTSON